Collins

SCRABBLE™
BRAND Crossword Game
DICTIONARY

D1637906

Published by Collins
An imprint of HarperCollins Publishers
Westerhill Road
Bishopbriggs
Glasgow G64 2QT

Third Edition 2016

10 9 8 7 6 5 4 3 2 1

© HarperCollins Publishers 2008, 2012, 2013, 2016

ISBN 978-0-00-758912-8

www.harpercollins.co.uk/scrabble

Typeset by Sharon McTeir, Creative Publishing Services

Printed in Great Britain by Clays Ltd, St Ives plc

If you would like to comment on any aspect of this book, please contact us at the given address or online.
E-mail: puzzles@harpercollins.co.uk
 facebook.com/collinsdictionary
 @collinsdict

EDITORS

Ian Brookes
Andrew Holmes
Mary O'Neill
Elspeth Summers

COMPUTING SUPPORT
Thomas Widmann

FOR THE PUBLISHER
Gerry Breslin
Kerry Ferguson

Contents

Abbreviations

adj	adjective
adv	adverb
conj	conjunction
det	determiner
interj	interjection
n	noun
pl	plural
prep	preposition
pron	pronoun
vb	verb

Introduction

The *Collins Scrabble Dictionary* is the ideal reference book for people who play Scrabble for enjoyment, in a social or family setting. This dictionary doesn't include every word eligible for Scrabble, but does contain the most commonly used of the 276,000-plus words in *Collins Official Scrabble Words 2015*, the definitive Scrabble wordlist. The concise definitions in the *Scrabble Dictionary* allow players to check the meaning of words, as well as to use the book for settling arguments during games.

The *Collins Scrabble Dictionary* contains words of up to 8 letters in length. However, references to longer words playable in Scrabble are included. These longer words output in bold, and are introduced by a chevron symbol (>). Because this dictionary is designed for family play, it does not include offensive terms. Such words are, on the other hand, included in the *Collins Official Scrabble Words 2015*, the complete wordlist for tournaments and club competitions, along with words of 9–15 letters.

How the Wordlist is Arranged

Words are listed in alphabetical order, although some inflected forms are included in the base form entry to save space. These appear in bold, after the base form. If the inflected form is created by the simple addition of a letter or letters, then only these letters are shown, for example:

ABET, -S, -TED, -TING

If there is some other spelling change, then the whole inflected form is shown:

ABATE, -D, -S, ABATING

Similarly, word forms derived from the base form are included at the end of the base form entry if this does not affect the alphabetical sequence, for example:

ABATE, -D, -S, ABATING *vb*
make or become less strong
ABATER -S

Inflected and derived forms have a separate entry in the alphabetical list if another word interrupts the alphabetical sequence:

AGER, -S *n* something that ages
AGERATUM *n* tropical American plant with thick clusters of purplish-blue flowers
AGES ▸ age

AGNATE, -S *adj* related through a common male ancestor ▷ *n* descendant by male links from a common male ancestor
AGNATHAN *n* type of jawless eel-like aquatic vertebrate
AGNATIC ▸ agnate

A black triangle symbol (▶) is used to refer readers to another related entry in the dictionary. Inflected and derived forms which are separate from their base form are referred back to the main entry in this way.

Two-letter Words

A sound knowledge of the 124 two-letter words is crucial to success in Scrabble, not least because they are so useful in enabling 'tagging plays', as explained below in the Forming Words section. For this reason, these are supplied in a separate list on pages xiii–xvi as well as being included in the body of the text.

Special Scrabble Words

To help family players learn and use some of the most useful words in the game, the *Collins Scrabble Dictionary* includes a number of special panel entries, drawing attention to more than 200 words of particular interest or utility. For the most part these are words which are less likely to form part of a novice player's natural vocabulary, and the emphasis is on particularly useful three-letter words, on high probability seven-letter bonus words, on words that are especially useful when you have either too many vowels on your rack or too many consonants, and on selected shorter words that use the high-value consonants **J**, **K**, **Q**, **X** and **Z**. But just for fun we have also featured a few of the unusual and exciting words of the kind that Scrabble players dream about. Realistically, you may well never get the chance to play words like **ZOOTAXY**, **TZADDIQ** and **QUETZAL**. But imagine the thrill (and the score!) if you did...

There are also paragraphs at the start of every letter section which offer advice on useful words beginning with that letter.

The *Collins Scrabble Dictionary* is designed to be useful to new players and Scrabble veterans alike – we hope you enjoy using it!

Forming Words

The key to successful Scrabble is constant awareness of the opportunities for forming words on the board. The obvious way to play a new word is to place it so that it intersects with a word already on the board through a common letter:

			D_2		
			O_1		
	L_1	U_1	C_3	K_5	
			T_1		
			O_1		
			R_1		

The common letter is known as a floater, in this case the floater being **C**. Skilful players are occasionally able to play through two or more floaters, whether the floating letters are adjacent or (even more difficult!) separated. A good deal of Scrabble skill revolves around using floaters, and on denying the use of floaters to your opponent.

Other methods of forming words, however, create more than one new word in the process, giving a higher score. The two main ways of doing this are 'hooking' and 'tagging'.

Hooking

Hooking involves 'hanging' one word on another – the word already on the board acts as a 'hook' on which the other word can be hung – changing the first word in the process. When you form a word by hooking, you add a letter to the beginning or end of a word on the board, transforming it into a longer word as you do so:

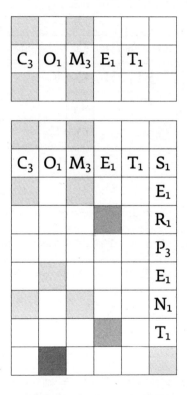

In this example, you get the points for **COMETS** as well as for **SERPENTS**. Plurals ending in **S** provide some of the most obvious – and useful – end-hooks. But there are plenty of other end-hooks as well. There are also lots of useful front-hooks.

Consider the following example:

If you happened to have **C**, **E**, **F**, **I**, **K** and **L** among the letters on your rack, you could play the following, taking full advantage of the valuable **X** played by your opponent:

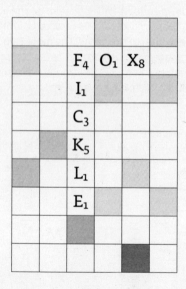

Here you get the 13 points for **FOX** as well as those for **FICKLE**. So you can see that hooking is generally a much more profitable method of word-formation than simply playing a word through one that is already on the board.

Obviously, not all words provide hooks. Some words cannot form other words by having a letter added to either their front or their back; these are known as 'blockers', as they prevent other players from adding words by hooking.

Tagging

Playing a word parallel to one already on the board, so that one or more tiles are in contact, is known as tagging. Tagging is more difficult than hooking because you need to form one additional word for each tile in contact with the word on the board. In most circumstances, these will be two-letter words, which is why these words are so vital to the game. The more two-letter words you know, the greater your opportunities for fitting words onto the board through tagging – and of running up some impressive scores! Very skilful players have even been known to make 7-letter parallel plays!

For example, consider the following situation (your opponent has started the game with **SHAM** and you have **E,E,H,I,S,T** and **X** on your rack):

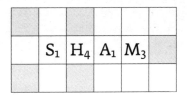

You could play **HEXES** so that it also forms **SH**, **HE**, **AX** and **ME** (all valid two-letter words), thus adding the scores for these three words to the points you make from **HEXES**:

	S_1	H_4	A_1	M_3	
	H_4	E_1	X_8	E_1	S_1

A particular advantage of tagging is that it allows you to benefit from valuable tiles twice in one go, as in the example above where **X** is used in both **HEXES** and **AX**.

Other Word-forming Techniques

There are other ways of forming new words from letters already on the board. For example, it is sometimes possible to 'infill' between existing letters, or to extend existing words at the front or back by adding more than one letter. Thus, if your opponent opens with **COVER**, placing the **C** on the double-letter square, you may be able to prefix it with **DIS** making **DISCOVER** and earning a triple-word score. But hooking and tagging are by far the most common techniques.

Two-letter Words

Where many inexperienced Scrabble players go wrong is that they think the longer a word is, the better it is to know, as it's likely to score more. In fact, the key to a good Scrabble vocabulary is a good knowledge of short words.

The reason for that is you can use the short words to 'hook' the word you want to play on the board, allowing you to play parallel to another word, rather than always going through it crosswise. That way you will usually make more than one word each shot, gaining you a higher score.

8 POINTS = BAD PLAY   **25 POINTS = GOOD PLAY**

Notice how by using the same letters from your rack, you have scored seventeen more points. But notice also that little word **FA** which enabled you to fit the play in. And there we have the first, essential thing you have to know to improve your game: **all the allowable two-letter words**. Yes, all of them.

There are 124 of these to learn, but to make the list more manageable, you can divide them into three groups:

1. The ones you already know.

2. The ones you already know, but may not have realized were words.

3. The ones you probably don't know.

There are thirty-seven two-letter words which most people would know and which would appear in most dictionaries:

AH	AM	AN	AS	AT	AX	AY	BE	BY	DO	EH
GO	HA	HE	HI	HO	IF	IN	IS	IT	LA	LO
MA	ME	MY	NO	OF	OH	ON	OR	OX	PA	SO
TO	UP	US	WE							

So straight away you only have eighty-seven new ones to learn. But it's not even as bad as that, because now we move on to the second group: the ones you know, but don't know you know.

These include:

Contractions

AD (advertisement)	**PO** (chamberpot)
MO (moment)	**RE** (regarding)
OP (operation)	**TA** (thank you)

Interjections and exclamations

AW	ER	HM	MM	OI	OW	OY
SH	ST	UH	UM	UR	YA	YO

Letters of the alphabet

AR	EF	EL	EM	EN	ES	EX

Then add in **ID** (a psychiatric term), **PI** (a Greek letter and mathematical term) and **YE** (the old form of **YOU**), and that's another thirty taken care of with no trouble at all.

Fifty-six to go. These are the ones you probably don't know, so let's set them out where you can get the measure of them:

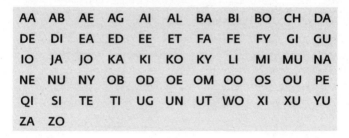

AA	AB	AE	AG	AI	AL	BA	BI	BO	CH	DA
DE	DI	EA	ED	EE	ET	FA	FE	FY	GI	GU
IO	JA	JO	KA	KI	KO	KY	LI	MI	MU	NA
NE	NU	NY	OB	OD	OE	OM	OO	OS	OU	PE
QI	SI	TE	TI	UG	UN	UT	WO	XI	XU	YU
ZA	ZO

If all this looks a bit gobbledygookish, you may be surprised to know that even some of these are more familiar to you than you might realize. An **AB** is an abdominal muscle, as in toning up your abs and your pecs. **MU**, **NU** and **XI** are Greek letters. **OM** is what Buddhists chant as part of their prayers.

Having said that, it can't be denied that some of the definitions are genuinely obscure. To go from start to finish, **AA** is a word from Hawaiian, meaning a rough volcanic rock. And a **ZO** is a Himalayan cross-breed of a yak and a cow, also spelt **ZHO**, **DZO**, **DZHO** or **DSO**.

Now, where else but in Scrabble can you go from Hawaii to the Himalayas in one step? Have a look at the two-letter words every so often. Once you're happy with the first two groups (i.e. the common ones, the contractions, the interjections, the letters, plus **ID**, **PI** and **YE**), have a real go at mastering the unusual ones. They really are the essential first step to improving your game.

Aa

A forms a two-letter word when followed by any one of **A, B, D, E, G, H, I, L, M, N, R, S, T, W, X** and **Y** - 16 letters out of 26 - so it's a really useful tile. There are also a number of short high-scoring words beginning with **A**. **Axe** (10 points) and **adze** (14 points) are good examples, but don't forget their US variants, **ax** (9 points) and **adz** (13 points). Also remember their plurals and the verb form **axed** (12 points). **Aye** (6) and **ay** (5) are handy for tight corners.

AA, -S *n* volcanic rock

AAH, -ED, -ING, -S *vb* exclaim in pleasure

AAL, -S *n* Asian shrub or tree

> An **aal** is an East Indian shrub, useful for getting rid of annoying multiples of A.

AALII *n* bushy shrub

> An **aalii** is a tropical tree, great for getting rid of surplus As and Is.

AALS ▸ aal

AARDVARK *n* S African anteater with long ears and snout

AARDWOLF *n* nocturnal mammal

AARGH *same as* ▸ **argh**

AARRGH *same as* ▸ **argh**

AARRGHH *same as* ▸ **argh**

AARTI, -S *n* Hindu ceremony

AAS ▸ aa

AASVOGEL *n* South African bird of prey

AB, -S *n* abdominal muscle

ABA, -S *n* type of Syrian cloth

ABAC, -S *n* mathematical diagram

ABACA, -S *n* species of banana

ABACI ▸ abacus

ABACK *adv* towards the back; backwards

ABACS ▸ abac

ABACTOR, -S *n* cattle thief

ABACUS, ABACI, -ES *n* mathematical instrument

ABAFT *adv* by the rear of (a ship) ▷ *adj* closer to the stern

ABAKA, -S *n* abaca

ABALONE, -S *n* edible sea creature

ABAMP, -S *same as* ▸ **abampere**

ABAMPERE *n* cgs unit of current

ABAMPS ▸ abamp

ABAND, -ED, -ING, -S *vb* abandon

ABANDON, -S *vb* desert or leave ▷ *n* lack of inhibition

ABANDS ▸ aband

ABAPICAL *adj* away from or opposite the apex

ABAS ▸ aba

ABASE, -D, -S, ABASING *vb* humiliate or degrade (oneself)

ABASEDLY

ABASER -S

ABASH, -ES, -ING *vb* cause to feel ill at ease

ABASHED *adj* embarrassed and ashamed

ABASHES ▸ abash

ABASHING ▸ abash

ABASIA, -S *n* disorder affecting ability to walk

ABASING ▸ abase

ABASK *adv* in pleasant warmth

ABATABLE ▸ abate

ABATE, -D, -S, ABATING *vb* make or become less strong

ABATER -S

ABATIS, -ES *n* rampart of felled trees

ABATOR, -S *n* person who effects an abatement

ABATTIS *same as* ▸ **abatis**

ABATTOIR *n* where animals are killed for food

ABATTU *adj* dejected

ABATURE, -S *n* trail left by hunted stag

ABAXIAL *adj* facing away from the axis

ABAXILE *adj* away from the axis

ABAYA, -S *n* Arab outer garment

ABB, -S *n* yarn used in weaving

ABBA, -S *n* Coptic bishop

ABBACY, ABBACIES *n* office of abbot or abbess

ABBAS ▸ abba

ABBATIAL *adj* relating to abbot, abbess, or abbey

ABBE, -S *n* French abbot

ABBED *adj* displaying strong abdominal muscles

ABBES ▸ abbe

ABBESS, -ES *n* nun in charge of a convent

ABBEY, -S *n* dwelling place of monks or nuns

ABBOT, -S *n* head of an abbey of monks

ABBOTCY

ABBS ▸ abb

ABCEE, -S *n* alphabet

ABDABS *n* highly nervous state

ABDICANT ▸ abdicate

ABDICATE *vb* give up a responsibility

ABDOMEN, -S, ABDOMINA *n* part of the body

ABDUCE, -D, -S, ABDUCING *vb* abduct

ABDUCENS *n as in* **abducens nerve** cranial nerve

ABDUCENT *adj* (of a muscle) abducting

ABDUCES ▸ abduce

ABDUCING ▸ abduce

ABDUCT, -ED, -S *vb* carry off, kidnap

ABDUCTEE

ABDUCTOR

ABEAM *adj* at right angles to a ship

ABEAR, -ING, -S, ABORE, ABORNING *vb* bear or behave

ABED *adv* in bed

ABEGGING *adj* in the act of begging

ABEIGH *adv* aloof

ABELE, -S *n* white poplar tree

ABELIA, -S n garden plant with pink or white flowers

ABELIAN

ABELMOSK n tropical plant

ABER, -S n estuary

ABERRANT adj showing aberration ▷ n person whose behaviour is aberrant

ABERRATE vb deviate from what is normal

ABERS ► aber

ABESSIVE n grammatical case indicating absence

ABET, -S, -TED, -TING vb help in wrongdoing

ABETMENT

ABETTAL -S

ABETTER, -S ► abet

ABETTING ► abet

ABETTOR, -S ► abet

ABEYANCE n state of being suspended

ABEYANCY n abeyance

ABEYANT ► abeyance

ABFARAD, -S n unit of capacitance

ABHENRY, -S n unit of inductance

ABHOR, -RED, -S vb detest utterly

ABHORRER

ABID ► abide

ABIDANCE ► abide

ABIDE, ABID, ABIDDEN, -D, -S vb endure, put up with

ABIDER -S

ABIDING, -S adj lasting ▷ n action of one who abides

ABIES n fir tree

ABIETIC adj as in abietic acid yellowish powder

ABIGAIL, -S n maid for a lady

ABILITY n competence, power

ABIOSIS, ABIOSES n absence of life

ABIOTIC

ABITUR, -S n German examination

ABJECT, -ED, -S adj utterly miserable ▷ vb throw down

ABJECTLY

ABJOINT, -S vb cut off

ABJURE, -D, -S, ABJURING vb deny or renounce on oath

ABJURER -S

ABLATE, -D, -S, ABLATING vb remove by ablation

ABLATION n removal of an organ

ABLATIVE n case of nouns ▷ adj relating to the ablative case

ABLATOR, -S n heat shield of a space craft

ABLAUT, -S n vowel gradation

ABLAZE adj burning fiercely ▷ adv on fire

ABLE, -R, -S, -ST, ABLING adj capable, competent ▷ vb enable

ABLED adj having physical powers

ABLEGATE n papal envoy

ABLEISM, -S n discrimination against disabled people

ABLEIST -S

ABLER ► able

ABLES ► able

ABLEST ► able

ABLET, -S n freshwater fish

ABLING ► able

ABLINGS adv possibly

ABLINS adv Scots word meaning perhaps

ABLOOM adj in flower

ABLOW adj blooming

ABLUENT, -S n substance used for cleansing

ABLUSH adj blushing

ABLUTED adj washed thoroughly

ABLUTION n ritual washing of a priest's hands

ABLY adv competently or skilfully

ABMHO, -S n unit of electrical conductance

ABNEGATE vb deny to oneself

ABNORMAL adj not normal or usual ▷ n abnormal person or thing

ABOARD adv onto a vehicle ▷ adj onto a vehicle

ABODE, -D, -S, ABODING n home, dwelling ▷ vb forebode

ABOHM, -S n unit of resistance

ABOIDEAU n dyke with sluicegate

ABOIL adj boiling

ABOITEAU same as ► aboideau

ABOLISH vb do away with

ABOLLA, -E, -S n Roman cloak

ABOMA, -S n South American snake

ABOMASA ► abomasum

ABOMASAL ► abomasum

ABOMASI ► abomasus

ABOMASUM, ABOMASA n compartment of a stomach

ABOMASUS, ABOMASI n abomasum

ABOON Scots word for ► above

ABORAL adj away from the mouth

ABORALLY

ABORD, -ED, -ING, -S vb accost

ABORE ► abear

ABORIGEN n aborigine

ABORIGIN n aborigine

ABORNE adj Shakespearean form of auburn

ABORNING ► abear

ABORT, -ED, -ING, -S vb terminate ▷ n termination or failure

ABORTEE, -S n woman having an abortion

ABORTER, -S ► abort

ABORTING ► abort

ABORTION n operation to end a pregnancy

ABORTIVE adj unsuccessful

ABORTS ► abort

ABORTUS n aborted fetus

ABOUGHT ► aby

ABOULIA, -S same as ► abulia

ABOULIC

ABOUND, -ED, -S vb be plentiful

ABOUT adv nearly, approximately

ABOUTS prep about

ABOVE, -S adv higher (than) ▷ n something that is above

ABRACHIA n condition of having no arms

ABRADANT ► abrade

ABRADE, -D, -S, ABRADING vb wear down by friction

ABRADER -S

ABRAID, -ED, -S vb awake

ABRAM adj auburn

ABRASAX same as ► abraxas

ABRASION n scraped area on the skin

ABRASIVE adj harsh and unpleasant ▷ n substance for cleaning

ABRAXAS n ancient charm composed of Greek letters

ABRAY, -ED, -ING, -S vb awake

ABRAZO, -S n embrace

ABREACT, -S vb alleviate through abreaction

ABREAST adj side by side

ABREGE, -S n abridgment

ABRI, -S n shelter or place of refuge, esp in wartime

ABRICOCK n apricot

ABRIDGE, -D, -S vb shorten by using fewer words

ABRIDGER

ABRIM adj full to the brim

ABRIN, -S n poisonous compound

ABRIS ► abri

ABROACH adj (of a cask, barrel, etc) tapped

ABROAD, -S adv in a foreign country ▷ adj in general circulation ▷ n foreign place

ABROGATE vb cancel (a law or agreement) formally

ABROOKE, -D, -S vb bear or tolerate

ABROSIA, -S n condition involving refusal to eat

ABRUPT, -ER, -S adj sudden, unexpected ▷ n abyss
ABRUPTLY

ABS ► ab

ABSCESS n inflamed swelling ▷ vb form a swelling

ABSCIND, -S vb cut off

ABSCISE, -D, -S vb separate or be separated by abscission

ABSCISIC adj as in **abscisic acid** type of acid

ABSCISIN n plant hormone

ABSCISS same as ► **abscissa**

ABSCISSA n cutting off

ABSCISSE same as ► **abscissa**

ABSCOND, -S vb leave secretly

ABSEIL, -ED, -S vb go down by a rope ▷ n instance of abseiling

ABSEILER n person who abseils

ABSEILS ► abseil

ABSENCE, -S n being away

ABSENT, -ED, -S adj not present ▷ vb stay away

ABSENTEE n person who is not present

ABSENTER ► absent

ABSENTLY adv in an absent-minded manner

ABSENTS ► absent

ABSEY, -S n alphabet

ABSINTH same as ► **absinthe**

ABSINTHE n liqueur

ABSINTHS ► absinth

ABSIT, -S n leave from college

ABSOLUTE adj complete, perfect ▷ n something absolute

ABSOLVE, -D, -S vb declare to be free from sin

ABSOLVER

ABSONANT adj unnatural and unreasonable

ABSORB, -S vb soak up (a liquid)

ABSORBED adj engrossed

ABSORBER n thing that absorbs

ABSORBS ► absorb

ABSTAIN, -S vb choose not to do something

ABSTERGE vb cleanse

ABSTRACT adj existing as an idea ▷ n summary ▷ vb summarize

ABSTRICT vb release

ABSTRUSE adj not easy to understand

ABSURD, -ER, -S adj incongruous or ridiculous ▷ n conception of the world
ABSURDLY

ABTHANE, -S n ancient Scottish church territory

ABUBBLE adj bubbling

ABULIA, -S n pathological inability to take decisions
ABULIC

ABUNA, -S n male head of Ethiopian family

ABUNDANT adj plentiful

ABUNE Scots word for ► **above**

ABURST adj bursting

ABUSABLE ► abuse

ABUSAGE, -S n wrong use

ABUSE, -D, -S, ABUSING vb use wrongly ▷ n prolonged ill-treatment

ABUSER -S

ABUSION, -S n wrong use or deception

ABUSIVE adj rude or insulting

ABUT, -S, -TED, -TING vb be next to or touching

ABUTILON n shrub

ABUTMENT n construction supporting the end of a bridge

ABUTS ► abut

ABUTTAL, -S same as ► **abutment**

ABUTTED ► abut

ABUTTER, -S n owner of adjoining property

ABUTTING ► abut

ABUZZ adj noisy, busy with activity etc

ABVOLT, -S n unit of potential difference in the electromagnetic system

ABWATT, -S n unit of power

ABY, ABOUGHT, -ING, -S vb pay the penalty for

> Remember this word can be expanded to **baby** and **gaby** and also to **abye** and **abys**.

ABYE, -ING, -S same as ► **aby**

ABYING ► aby

ABYS ► aby

ABYSM, -S archaic word for ► **abyss**

ABYSMAL adj extremely bad, awful

ABYSMS ► abysm

ABYSS, -ES n very deep hole or chasm

ABYSSAL adj of the ocean depths

ABYSSES ► abyss

ACACIA, -S n tree or shrub

ACADEME, -S n place of learning

ACADEMIA n academic world

ACADEMIC adj of a university ▷ n lecturer at a university

ACADEMY n society for arts or sciences

ACAI, -S n berry

ACAJOU, -S n type of mahogany

ACALEPH, -S n invertebrate

ACALEPHE n acaleph

ACALEPHS ► acaleph

ACANTH, -S n acanthus

ACANTHA, -E, -S n thorn or prickle

ACANTHI ► acanthus

ACANTHIN n organic chemical

ACANTHS ► acanth

ACANTHUS, ACANTHI n prickly plant

ACAPNIA, -S n lack of carbon dioxide

ACARBOSE n diabetes medicine

ACARI ► acarus

ACARIAN ► acarus

ACARID, -S n small arachnid ▷ adj of these arachnids

ACARIDAN same as ► **acarid**

ACARIDS ► acarid

ACARINE, -S n acarid

ACAROID adj resembling a mite

ACARPOUS adj producing no fruit

ACARUS, ACARI n type of mite

ACATER, -S n buyer of provisions

ACATES n provisions

ACATOUR, -S n buyer of provisions

ACAUDAL adj having no tail

ACAUDATE same as ► **acaudal**

ACAULINE adj having no stem

ACAULOSE same as ► **acauline**

ACAULOUS adj having a short stem

ACCA, -S n academic

ACCABLE adj dejected or beaten

ACCAS ► acca

ACCEDE, -D, -S, ACCEDING vb consent or agree (to)

ACCEDER -S

ACCEND, -ED, -S vb set alight

ACCENT, -ED, -S n style of pronunciation ▷ vb place emphasis on

ACCENTOR n songbird

ACCENTS ► accent

ACCEPT, -S vb receive willingly

ACCEPTED adj generally approved

ACCEPTEE n person who has been accepted

ACCEPTER ► accept

ACCEPTOR *n* person signing a bill of exchange
ACCEPTS ► accept
ACCESS, -ED, -ES *n* right to approach ► *vb* obtain data
ACCIDENT *n* mishap, often causing injury
ACCIDIA, -S *same as* ► accidie
ACCIDIE, -S *n* spiritual sloth
ACCINGE, -D, -S *vb* put a belt around
ACCITE, -D, -S, ACCITING *vb* summon
ACCLAIM, -S *vb* applaud, praise ► *n* enthusiastic approval
ACCLOY, -ED, -S *vb* choke or clog
ACCOAST, -S *vb* accost
ACCOIED ► accoy
ACCOIL, -S *n* welcome ► *vb* gather together
ACCOLADE *n* award ► *vb* give an award
ACCOMPT, -S *vb* account
ACCORAGE *vb* encourage
ACCORD, -ED, -S *n* agreement, harmony ► *vb* fit in with
ACCORDER
ACCOST, -ED, -S *vb* approach and speak to ► *n* greeting
ACCOUNT, -S *n* report, description ► *vb* judge to be
ACCOURT, -S *vb* entertain
ACCOUTER *same as* ► accoutre
ACCOUTRE *vb* provide with equipment
ACCOY, ACCOIED, -ED, -ING, -S *vb* soothe
ACCOYLD *vb* past tense of accoil
ACCOYS ► accoy
ACCREDIT *vb* give official recognition to
ACCRETE, -D, -S *vb* grow together
ACCREW, -ED, -S *vb* accrue
ACCRUAL, -S *n* act of accruing
ACCRUE, -D, -S, ACCRUING *vb* increase gradually
ACCURACY *n* representation of truth
ACCURATE *adj* exact, correct
ACCURSE, -S *vb* curse
ACCURSED *adj* under a curse
ACCURSES ► accurse
ACCURST *same as* ► accursed
ACCUSAL, -S *n* accusation
ACCUSANT *n* person who accuses
ACCUSE, -S *vb* charge with wrongdoing

ACCUSED *n* person accused of a crime
ACCUSER, -S ► accuse
ACCUSES ► accuse
ACCUSING ► accuse
ACCUSTOM *vb* make used to
ACE, -D, -S, ACING *n* playing card with one symbol on it ► *adj* excellent ► *vb* serve an ace in racquet sports
ACEDIA, -S *same as* ► accidie
ACELDAMA *n* place with ill feeling
ACENTRIC *adj* without a centre ► *n* acentric chromosome or fragment
ACEQUIA, -S *n* irrigation ditch
ACER, -S *n* type of tree
ACERATE *same as* ► aerated
ACERATED *adj* having sharp points
ACERB, -ER, -EST *adj* bitter
ACERBATE *vb* embitter or exasperate
ACERBER ► acerb
ACERBEST ► acerb
ACERBIC *adj* harsh or bitter
ACERBITY *n* bitter speech or temper
ACEROLA, -S *n* cherry-like fruit
ACEROSE *adj* shaped like a needle
ACEROUS *same as* ► acerose
ACERS ► acer
ACERVATE *adj* growing in heaps or clusters
ACERVULI > acervulus
ACES ► ace
ACESCENT *adj* slightly sour or turning sour ► *n* something that is turning sour
ACETA ► acetum
ACETAL, -S *n* colourless liquid
ACETAMID *same as* > acetamide
ACETATE, -S *n* salt or ester of acetic acid
ACETATED *adj* combined with acetic acid
ACETATES ► acetate
ACETIC *adj* of or involving vinegar
ACETIFY *vb* become vinegar
ACETIN, -S *n* type of acetate
ACETONE, -S *n* colourless liquid used as a solvent
ACETONIC
ACETOSE *same as* ► acetous
ACETOUS *adj* containing acetic acid
ACETOXYL *n* medicine used to treat acne
ACETUM, ACETA *n* solution that has dilute acetic acid as solvent

ACETYL, -S *n* the monovalent group CH_3CO-
ACETYLIC
ACH *interj* Scots expression of surprise
ACHAENIA > achaenium
ACHAGE, -S *n* pain
ACHAR, -S *n* spicy pickle made from mango
ACHARNE *adj* furiously violent
ACHARS ► achar
ACHARYA, -S *n* religious teacher and spiritual guide
ACHATES *same as* ► acates
ACHE, -D, -S *n* dull continuous pain ► *vb* be in or cause continuous dull pain
ACHENE, -S *n* type of fruit
ACHENIA ► achenium
ACHENIAL ► achene
ACHENIUM, ACHENIA *n* achene
ACHES ► ache
ACHIER ► achy
ACHIEST ► achy
ACHIEVE, -D, -S *vb* gain by hard work or ability
ACHIEVER
ACHILLEA *n* type of plant with white, yellow, or purple flowers, often grown in gardens
ACHINESS ► achy
ACHING, -S ► ache
ACHINGLY ► ache
ACHINGS ► aching
ACHIOTE, -S *n* annatto
ACHIRAL *adj* of a tuber producing arrowroot
ACHKAN, -S *n* man's coat in India
ACHOLIA, -S *n* bile condition
ACHOO, -S *interj, n* (sound of) a sneeze
ACHROMAT *n* lens designed to bring light of two wavelengths to the same focal point
ACHROMIC *adj* colourless
ACHY, ACHIER, ACHIEST *adj* affected by a continuous dull pain
ACICULA, -E, -S *n* needle-shaped part
ACICULAR
ACICULUM *n* bristle that supports the appendages of some polychaetes
ACID, -ER, -EST, -S *n* corrosive compound that combines with a base to form a salt ► *adj* containing acid
ACIDEMIA *n* abnormally high level of acid in blood
ACIDER ► acid
ACIDEST ► acid

ACIDIC adj containing acid
ACIDIER ► acidy
ACIDIEST ► acidy
ACIDIFY vb convert into acid
ACIDITY n quality of being acid
ACIDLY ► acid
ACIDNESS ► acid
ACIDOSIS, ACIDOSES n abnormal increase in the acidity of the blood and bodily fluids
ACIDOTIC
ACIDS ► acid
ACIDURIA n abnormally high level of acid in urine
ACIDY, ACIDIER, ACIDIEST adj resembling or containing acid
ACIERAGE n iron-plating of metal
ACIERATE vb change (iron) into steel
ACIFORM adj shaped like a needle
ACINAR adj of small sacs
ACING ► ace
ACINI ► acinus
ACINIC ► acinus
ACINOSE ► acinus
ACINOUS ► acinus
ACINUS, ACINI n parts of a gland
ACKEE, -S n tropical tree
ACKER, -S same as ► **acca**
ACKNOW, ACKNEW, -N, -S vb recognize
ACKNOWNE adj aware
ACKNOWS ► acknow
ACLINIC adj unbending
ACMATIC adj highest or ultimate
ACME, -S n highest point of achievement or excellence
ACMIC same as ► **acmatic**
ACMITE n chemical with pyramid-shaped crystals
ACNE, -S n pimply skin disease
ACNED adj marked by acne
ACNES ► acne
ACNODAL ► acnode
ACNODE, -S n mathematical term
ACOCK adv cocked
ACOELOUS adj not having a stomach
ACOEMETI n order of monks
ACOLD adj feeling cold
ACOLYTE, -S n follower or attendant
ACOLYTH, -S n acolyte
ACONITE, -S n poisonous plant with hoodlike flowers
ACONITIC
ACONITUM same as ► **aconite**

ACORN, -S n nut of the oak tree
ACORNED adj covered with acorns
ACORNS ► acorn
ACOSMISM n belief that no world exists outside the mind
ACOSMIST
ACOUCHI, -S n South American rodent with a white-tipped tail
ACOUCHY same as ► **acouchi**
ACOUSTIC adj of sound and hearing
ACQUAINT vb make familiar, inform
ACQUEST, -S n something acquired
ACQUIGHT vb acquit
ACQUIRAL ► acquire
ACQUIRE, -D, -S vb gain, get
ACQUIREE n one who acquires
ACQUIRER ► acquire
ACQUIRES ► acquire
ACQUIS n as in **acquis communautaire** European Union laws
ACQUIST, -S n acquisition
ACQUIT, -S vb pronounce (someone) innocent
ACQUITE, -S vb acquit
ACQUITS ► acquit
ACRASIA, -S n lack of willpower
ACRASIN, -S n chemical
ACRATIC ► acrasia
ACRAWL adv crawling
ACRE, -S n measure of land, 4840 square yards (4046.86 square metres)
ACREAGE, -S n land area in acres ⊳ adj of or relating to a large allotment of land, esp in a rural area
ACRED adj having acres of land
ACRES ► acre
ACRID, -ER, -EST adj pungent, bitter
ACRIDIN, -S n acridine
ACRIDINE n colourless crystalline solid
ACRIDINS ► acridin
ACRIDITY ► acrid
ACRIDLY ► acrid
ACRIMONY n bitterness and resentment felt about something
ACRO, -S n event where acrobatic skiing moves are performed to music
ACROBAT, -S n person skilled in gymnastic feats requiring agility and balance

ACRODONT adj (of reptile teeth) fused at the base to the jawbones ⊳ n acrodont reptile
ACROGEN, -S n flowerless plant
ACROLECT n most correct form of language
ACROLEIN n colourless or yellowish flammable poisonous pungent liquid
ACROLITH n wooden sculpture with the head, hands, and feet in stone
ACROMIA ► acromion
ACROMIAL ► acromion
ACROMION, ACROMIA n outermost edge of the spine of the shoulder blade
ACRONIC adj acronical
ACRONYM, -S n word formed from the initial letters of other words, such as NASA
ACROS ► acro
ACROSOME n structure in reproductive cell
ACROSS adv from side to side(of)
ACROSTIC n lines of writing in which the first or last letters of each line spell a word or saying
ACROTER, -S n plinth
ACROTIC adj of a surface
ACROTISM n absence of pulse
ACRYLATE n chemical compound in plastics and resins
ACRYLIC, -S adj (synthetic fibre, paint, etc) made from acrylic acid ⊳ n man-made fibre used for clothes and blankets
ACRYLYL, -S n type of monovalent group
ACT, -ED, -S n thing done ⊳ vb do something
ACTA n minutes of meeting
ACTABLE ► act
ACTANT, -S n grammatical term
ACTED ► act
ACTIN, -S n protein
ACTINAL adj part of a jellyfish
ACTING, -S n art of an actor ⊳ adj temporarily performing the duties of
ACTINIA, -E, -S n type of sea anemone
ACTINIAN n sea anemone
ACTINIAS ► actinia
ACTINIC adj (of radiation) producing a photochemical effect
ACTINIDE n member of the actinide series

ACTINISM ▸ actinic
ACTINIUM, -S n radioactive chemical element
ACTINOID adj having a radiate form, as a sea anemone or starfish ▸ n member of the actinide series
ACTINON, -S same as ▸ actinide
ACTINS ▸ actin
ACTION, -ED, -S n process of doing something ▸ vb put into effect
ACTIONER n film with a fast-moving plot, usually containing scenes of violence
ACTIONS ▸ action
ACTIVATE vb make active
ACTIVE, -S adj moving, working ▸ n active form of a verb
ACTIVELY
ACTIVISE same as ▸ activize
ACTIVISM n taking direct or militant action to achieve a political or social end
ACTIVIST
ACTIVITY n state of being active
ACTIVIZE vb make active
ACTON, -S n jacket
ACTOR, -S n person who acts in a play, film, etc
ACTORISH
ACTORLY adj of or relating to an actor
ACTORS ▸ actor
ACTRESS n woman who acts in a play, film, broadcast, etc
ACTRESSY adj exaggerated and affected in manner
ACTS ▸ act
ACTUAL adj existing in reality
ACTUALLY adv really, indeed
ACTUALS pl n commercial commodities that can be bought and used
ACTUARY n statistician who calculates insurance risks
ACTUATE, -D, -S vb start up (a device)
ACTUATOR
ACTURE, -S n action
ACUATE, -D, -S, ACUATING adj sharply pointed ▸ vb sharpen
ACUITY, ACUITIES n keenness of vision or thought
ACULEATE adj cutting ▸ n insect, such as a bee, with a sting
ACULEUS, ACULEI n prickle or spine, such as the thorn of a rose
ACUMEN, -S n ability to make good judgments

ACUPOINT n points on the body stimulated with acupuncture or acupressure
ACUSHLA, -S n Irish endearment
ACUTANCE n physical rather than subjective measure of the sharpness of a photographic image
ACUTE, -R, -S, -ST adj severe ▸ n accent over a letter to indicate the quality or length of its sound, as over e in café
ACUTELY
ACYCLIC adj not cyclic
ACYL, -S n member of the monovalent group of atoms RCO-
ACYLATE, -D, -S vb add acyl group to
ACYLOIN, -S n organic chemical compound
ACYLS ▸ acyl
AD, -S n advertisement
ADAGE, -S n wise saying, proverb
ADAGIAL
ADAGIO, -S adv (to be played) slowly and gracefully ▸ n movement or piece to be performed slowly
ADAMANCE n being adamant
ADAMANCY n being adamant
ADAMANT, -S adj unshakable in determination or purpose ▸ n any extremely hard or apparently unbreakable substance
ADAMSITE n yellow poisonous crystalline solid that readily sublimes
ADAPT, -ED, -ING, -S vb alter for new use or new conditions
ADAPTER, -S same as ▸ adaptor
ADAPTING ▸ adapt
ADAPTION n adaptation
ADAPTIVE ▸ adapt
ADAPTOR, -S n device for connecting several electrical appliances to a single socket
ADAPTS ▸ adapt
ADAW, -ED, -ING, -S vb subdue
ADAXIAL adj facing the axis
ADAYS adv always
ADBOT, -S n spyware that collects information about a person to display targeted adverts
ADD, -ED, -S vb combine (numbers or quantities)
ADDABLE
ADDAX, -ES n antelope
ADDEBTED adj indebted
ADDED ▸ add

ADDEDLY ▸ add
ADDEEM, -ED, -S vb adjudge
ADDEND, -S n any of a set of numbers that is to be added
ADDENDA ▸ addendum
ADDENDS ▸ addend
ADDENDUM, ADDENDA n addition
ADDER, -S n small poisonous snake
ADDIBLE adj addable
ADDICT, -ED, -S n person who is unable to stop doing or taking something ▸ vb cause (someone or oneself) to become dependent (on something)
ADDIES ▸ addy
ADDING, -S n act or instance of addition ▸ adj of, for, or relating to addition
ADDIO, -S interj farewell ▸ n cry of addio
ADDITION n adding
ADDITIVE n something added, esp to a foodstuff, to improve it or prevent deterioration ▸ adj characterized or produced by addition
ADDITORY adj adding to something
ADDLE, -D, -S, ADDLING vb become muddled ▸ adj indicating a muddled state
ADDOOM, -ED, -S vb adjudge
ADDORSED adj back to back
ADDRESS, ADDREST n place where a person lives ▸ vb mark the destination, as on an envelope
ADDS ▸ add
ADDUCE, -D, -S, ADDUCING vb mention something as evidence or proof
ADDUCENT
ADDUCER -S
ADDUCT, -ED, -S vb movement of a muscle ▸ n compound
ADDUCTOR n muscle that adducts
ADDUCTS ▸ adduct
ADDY, ADDIES n e-mail address
ADEEM, -ED, -ING, -S vb cancel
ADELGID, -S n type of small sap-feeding insect
ADENINE, -S n chemical
ADENITIS n inflammation of a gland or lymph node
ADENOID adj of or resembling a gland
ADENOIDS pl n tissue at the back of the throat
ADENOMA, -S n tumour occurring in glandular tissue

ADENOSIS, ADENOSES n disease of glands

ADENYL, -S n enzyme

ADENYLIC adj as in **adenylic acid** nucleotide consisting of adenine, ribose or deoxyribose, and a phosphate group

ADENYLS ▸ adenyl

ADEPT, -ER, -EST, -S n very skilful (person) ▷ adj proficient in something requiring skill

ADEPTLY

ADEQUACY ▸ adequate

ADEQUATE adj sufficient, enough

ADERMIN, -S n vitamin

ADESPOTA n anonymous writings

ADESSIVE n grammatical case denoting place

ADHAN, -S n call to prayer

ADHARMA, -S n wickedness

ADHERE, -D, -S, ADHERING vb stick (to)

ADHEREND n something attached by adhesive

ADHERENT n devotee, follower ▷ adj sticking or attached

ADHERER, -S ▸ adhere

ADHERES ▸ adhere

ADHERING ▸ adhere

ADHESION n sticking (to)

ADHESIVE n substance used to stick things together ▷ adj able to stick to things

ADHIBIT, -S vb administer or apply

ADIEU, -S, -X n goodbye

> Very useful when you want to say goodbye to a surplus of vowels. And remember its plural can be either **adieus** or **adieux**.

ADIOS, -ES sentence substitute Spanish for goodbye ▷ n goodbye

ADIPIC adj as in **adipic acid** crystalline solid used in the preparation of nylon

ADIPOSE adj of or containing fat ▷ n animal fat

ADIPOSIS, ADIPOSES n obesity

ADIPOUS adj made of fat

ADIPSIA, -S n complete lack of thirst

ADIT, -S n shaft into a mine, for access or drainage

ADJACENT adj near or next (to) ▷ n side lying between a specified angle and a right angle in a right-angled triangle

ADJIGO, -S n SW Australian yam plant with edible tubers

ADJOIN, -ED, -S vb be next to

ADJOINT, -S n type of mathematical matrix

ADJOURN, -S vb close (a court) at the end of a session

ADJUDGE, -D, -S vb declare (to be)

ADJUNCT, -S n something incidental added to something else

ADJURE, -D, -S, ADJURING vb command (to do)

ADJURER -S

ADJUROR, -S ▸ adjure

ADJUST, -ED, -S vb adapt to new conditions

ADJUSTER

ADJUSTOR

ADJUTAGE n nozzle

ADJUTANT n army officer in charge of routine administration

ADJUVANT adj aiding or assisting ▷ n something that aids or assists

ADLAND, -S n advertising industry and the people who work in it

ADMAN, ADMEN n man who works in advertising

ADMASS, -ES n mass advertising

ADMEN ▸ adman

ADMIN, -S n administration

ADMIRAL, -S n highest naval rank

ADMIRE, -D, -S vb regard with esteem and approval

ADMIRER -S

ADMIRING ▸ admire

ADMIT, -S, -TED vb confess, acknowledge

ADMITTEE n one who admits

ADMITTER ▸ admit

ADMIX, -ED, -ES, -ING, -T vb mix or blend

ADMONISH vb reprove sternly

ADNATE adj growing closely attached to an adjacent part or organ

ADNATION

ADNEXA pl n organs adjoining the uterus

ADNEXAL

ADNOUN, -S n adjective used as a noun

ADO, -S n fuss, trouble

ADOBE, -S n sun-dried brick

ADOBO, -S n Philippine dish

ADONIS n beautiful young man

ADONISE, -D, -S vb adorn

ADONIZE, -D, -S vb adorn

ADOORS adv at the door

ADOPT, -ING, -S vb take (someone else's child) as one's own

ADOPTED adj having been adopted

ADOPTEE, -S n one who has been adopted

ADOPTER, -S n person who adopts

ADOPTING ▸ adopt

ADOPTION ▸ adopt

ADOPTIVE adj related by adoption

ADOPTS ▸ adopt

ADORABLE adj very attractive

ADORABLY

ADORE, -D, -S vb love intensely

ADORER -S

ADORING ▸ adore

ADORN, -ED, -ING, -S vb decorate, embellish

ADORNER -S

ADOS ▸ ado

ADOWN adv down

ADOZE adv asleep

ADPRESS vb press together

ADRAD adj afraid

ADRATE, -S n price or tariff that businesses pay to advertise

ADREAD, -ED, -S vb dread

ADRED adj filled with dread

ADRENAL, -S adj near the kidneys ▷ n adrenal gland

ADRIFT adv drifting

ADROIT, -ER adj quick and skilful

ADROITLY

ADRY adj dry

ADS ▸ ad

ADSCRIPT n serf

ADSORB, -ED, -S vb condense to form a thin film

ADSORBER

ADSPEAK, -S n kind of language or jargon used in advertising or in advertisements

ADSUKI, -S same as ▸ **adzuki**

ADSUM sentence substitute I am present

ADUKI, -S same as ▸ **adzuki**

ADULARIA n white or colourless glassy variety of orthoclase

ADULATE, -D, -S vb flatter or praise obsequiously

ADULATOR

ADULT, -S adj fully grown, mature ▷ n adult person or animal

ADULTLY

ADUMBRAL adj shadowy

ADUNC adj hooked

ADUNCATE adj hooked

A

ADUNCITY n quality of being hooked

ADUNCOUS adj hooked

ADUST, -ED, -ING, -S vb dry up or darken by heat

ADVANCE, -S vb go or bring forward ▷ n forward movement ▷ adj done or happening before an event

ADVANCED adj at a late stage in development

ADVANCER ► advance

ADVANCES ► advance

ADVECT, -ED, -S vb move horizontally in air

ADVENE, -D, -S, ADVENING vb add as extra

ADVENT, -S n arrival

ADVERB, -S n word that adds information about a verb, adjective, or other adverb

ADVERSE, -R adj unfavourable

ADVERT, -ED, -S n advertisement ▷ vb draw attention (to)

ADVEW, -ED, -ING, -S vb look at

ADVICE, -S n recommendation as to what to do

ADVISE, -S vb offer advice to

ADVISED adj considered, thought-out

ADVISEE, -S n person receiving advice

ADVISER, -S n person who offers advice, eg on careers to students or school pupils

ADVISES ► advise

ADVISING ► advise

ADVISOR, -S same as ► adviser

ADVISORY adj giving advice ▷ n statement giving advice or a warning

ADVOCAAT n liqueur with a raw egg base

ADVOCACY n active support of a cause or course of action

ADVOCATE vb propose or recommend ▷ n person who publicly supports a cause

ADVOWSON n right of presentation to a vacant benefice

ADWARD, -ED, -S vb award

ADWARE, -S n computer software

ADWOMAN, ADWOMEN n woman working in advertising

ADYNAMIA n loss of vital power or strength, esp as the result of illness

ADYNAMIC

ADYTUM, ADYTA n sacred place in ancient temples

ADZ same as ► adze

This is the American spelling of **adze**, and is one of the essential short words to know for using the Z.

ADZE, -D, -S, ADZING n woodworking tool ▷ vb use an adze

ADZUKI, -S n type of plant

AE determiner one

AECIA ► aecium

AECIAL ► aecium

AECIDIA ► aecidium

AECIDIAL ► aecidium

AECIDIUM, AECIDIA same as ► aecium

AECIUM, AECIA n area of some fungi

AEDES n type of mosquito which transmits yellow fever and dengue

AEDICULE n door or a window framed by columns and a pediment

AEDILE, -S n magistrate of ancient Rome

AEDINE adj of a species of mosquito

AEFALD adj single

AEFAULD adj single

AEGIRINE n green mineral

AEGIRITE n green mineral

AEGIS, -ES n sponsorship, protection

AEGLOGUE n eclogue

AEGROTAT n certificate allowing a candidate to pass an examination missed through illness

AEMULE, -D, -S, AEMULING vb emulate

AENEOUS adj brass-coloured or greenish-gold

AENEUS, -ES n aquarium fish

AEOLIAN adj of or relating to the wind

AEON, -S n immeasurably long period of time

This little word gets played when you have too many vowels. And it has a partner **eoan**, meaning of the dawn: but beware, unlike **aeon**, it does not take a plural S.

AEONIAN adj everlasting

AEONIC ► aeon

AEONS ► aeon

AEQUORIN n type of protein

This word for a kind of protein secreted by jellyfish is one of the most frequently played 8-letter words using

the Q: it's not easy to spot but can give a good score for a difficult-looking rack!

AERADIO, -S n radio system for pilots

AERATE, -D, -S, AERATING vb put gas into (a liquid), as when making a fizzy drink

AERATION

AERATOR -S

AERIAL, -S adj in, from, or operating in the air ▷ n metal pole, wire, etc, for receiving or transmitting radio or TV signals

AERIALLY

AERIE, -S a variant spelling (esp US) of ► eyrie

This word for an eagle's nest is a great one for dealing with a surplus of vowels. And it has several variants: **aery, aiery, ayrie, eyrie** and **eyry**.

AERIED adj in a very high place

AERIER ► aery

AERIES ► aerie

AERIEST ► aery

AERIFIED ► aerify

AERIFIES ► aerify

AERIFORM adj having the form of air

AERIFY, AERIFIED, AERIFIES vb change or cause to change into a gas

AERILY ► aery

AERO, -S n aerodynamic vehicle or component

AEROBAT, -S n person who does stunt flying

AEROBE, -S n organism that requires oxygen to survive

AEROBIA ► aerobium

AEROBIC adj designed for or relating to aerobics

AEROBICS n exercises designed to increase the amount of oxygen in the blood

AEROBIUM, AEROBIA same as ► aerobe

AEROBOMB n bomb dropped from aircraft

AEROBOT, -S n unmanned aircraft used esp in space exploration

AEROBUS n monorail suspended by an overhead cable

AERODART n metal arrow dropped from an aircraft as a weapon

AERODUCT n air duct

AERODYNE n aircraft that derives its lift from aerodynamic forces

AEROFOIL n part of an aircraft, such as the wing, designed to give lift

AEROGEL, -S n colloid

AEROGRAM n airmail letter on a single sheet of paper that seals to form an envelope

AEROLITE n stony meteorite consisting of silicate minerals

> An **aerolite** is another name for a meteorite, and is important because the chance to play this 8-letter bonus word comes up very frequently.

AEROLITH n meteorite

AEROLOGY n study of the atmosphere, particularly its upper layers

AERONAUT n person who flies in a lighter-than-air craft, esp the pilot or navigator

AERONOMY n science of the earth's upper atmosphere

AEROS ► aero

AEROSAT, -S n communications satellite

AEROSOL, -S n pressurized can from which a substance can be dispensed as a fine spray

AEROSTAT n lighter-than-air craft, such as a balloon

AEROTONE n bath incorporating air jets for massage

AERUGO, -S (esp of old bronze) another name for > **verdigris**

AERY, AERIER, AERIEST adj lofty, insubstantial, or visionary

AESC, -ES n rune

AESCULIN n chemical in horse-chestnut bark

AESIR pl n Norse gods

AESTHETE n person who has or affects an extravagant love of art

AESTIVAL adj of or occurring in summer

AETATIS adj at the age of

AETHER, -S same as ► **ether**

AETHERIC

AFALD adj single

AFAR, -S adv at, from, or to a great distance ▷ n great distance

AFARA, -S n African tree

AFARS ► afar

AFAWLD adj single

AFEAR, -ING, -S vb frighten

AFEARD an archaic or dialect word for ► **afraid**

AFEARED same as ► **afeard**

AFEARING ► afear

AFEARS ► afear

AFEBRILE adj without fever

AFF adv off

AFFABLE adj friendly and easy to talk to

AFFABLY

AFFAIR n event or happening

AFFAIRE, -S n love affair

AFFAIRS pl n personal or business interests

AFFEAR, -D, -ED, -S vb frighten

AFFEARE, -S vb frighten

AFFEARED ► affear

AFFEARES ► affeare

AFFEARS ► affear

AFFECT, -S vb act on, influence ▷ n emotion associated with an idea or set of ideas

AFFECTED adj displaying affectation

AFFECTER ► affect

AFFECTS ► affect

AFFEER, -ED, -S vb assess

AFFERENT adj directing inwards to a body part, esp the brain or spinal cord ▷ n nerve that conveys impulses towards an organ of the body

AFFIANCE vb bind (a person or oneself) in a promise of marriage ▷ n solemn pledge, esp a marriage contract

AFFIANT, -S n person who makes an affidavit

AFFICHE, -S n poster

AFFIED ► affy

AFFIES ► affy

AFFINAL adj affine

AFFINE, -S adj involving transformations which preserve collinearity ▷ n relation by marriage

AFFINED adj closely related

AFFINELY ► affine

AFFINES ► affine

AFFINITY n close connection or liking

AFFIRM, -ED, -S vb declare to be true

AFFIRMER

AFFIX, -ED, -ES, -ING vb attach or fasten ▷ n word or syllable added to a word to change its meaning

AFFIXAL

AFFIXER -S

AFFIXIAL ► affix

AFFIXING ► affix

AFFLATED adj inspired

AFFLATUS n supposed divine inspiration, esp in poetry

AFFLICT, -S vb give pain or grief to

AFFLUENT adj having plenty of money ▷ n tributary stream

AFFLUX, -ES n flowing towards a point

AFFOGATO n dessert made by pouring espresso over ice cream

AFFOORD, -S vb consent

AFFORCE, -D, -S vb strengthen

AFFORD, -ED, -S vb have enough money to buy

AFFOREST vb plant trees on

AFFRAP, -S vb strike

AFFRAY, -ED, -S n noisy fight, brawl ▷ vb frighten

AFFRAYER

AFFRET, -S n furious attack

AFFRIGHT vb frighten ▷ n sudden terror

AFFRONT, -S n insult ▷ vb hurt someone's pride or dignity

AFFRONTE adj facing

AFFRONTS ► affront

AFFUSION n baptizing of a person by pouring water onto his or her head

AFFY, AFFIED, AFFIES, -DE, -ING vb trust

AFGHAN, -S n type of blanket

AFGHANI, -S n monetary unit of Afghanistan

AFGHANS ► afghan

AFIELD adv away from one's usual surroundings or home

AFIRE adj on fire

AFLAJ ► falaj

AFLAME adj burning

AFLOAT adj floating ▷ adv floating

AFLUTTER adv in or into a nervous or excited state

AFOCAL adj relating to a method for transferring an image without bringing it into focus

AFOOT adj happening, in operation ▷ adv happening

AFORE adv before

AFOUL adj in or into a state of difficulty, confusion, or conflict (with)

AFRAID adj frightened

AFREET, -S n powerful evil demon or giant monster

AFRESH adv again, anew

AFRIT, -S same as ► **afreet**

AFRO, -S n bush-like frizzy hairstyle

AFRONT adv in front

AFROS ► afro

A

AFT *adv* at or towards the rear of a ship or aircraft ▷ *adj* at or towards the rear of a ship or aircraft

AFTER *adv* at a later time

AFTEREYE *vb* gaze at someone or something that has passed

AFTERS *n* sweet course of a meal

AFTERSUN *n* moisturizing lotion applied to the skin to soothe sunburn and avoid peeling

AFTERTAX *adj* after tax has been paid

AFTMOST *adj* furthest towards rear

AFTOSA, -S *n* foot-and-mouth disease

AG, -S *n* agriculture

AGA, -S *n* title of respect

AGACANT *adj* irritating

AGACANTE *adj* irritating

AGACERIE *n* coquetry

AGAIN *adv* once more

AGAINST *prep* in opposition or contrast to

AGALLOCH *another name for* ▷ **eaglewood**

AGALWOOD *n* eaglewood

AGAMA, -S *n* small lizard

AGAMETE, -S *n* reproductive cell

AGAMI, -S *n* South American bird

AGAMIC *adj* asexual

AGAMID, -S *same as* ▷ **agama**

AGAMIS ▷ **agami**

AGAMOID, -S *n* lizard of the agamid family

AGAMONT, -S *another name for* ▷ **schizont**

AGAMOUS *adj* without sex

AGAPE, AGAPAE, AGAPAI, -S *adj* (of the mouth) wide open ▷ *n* love feast among the early Christians

AGAPEIC

AGAR, -S *n* jelly-like substance obtained from seaweed and used as a thickener in food

AGARIC, -S *n* type of fungus

AGAROSE, -S *n* gel used in chemistry

AGARS ▷ **agar**

AGARWOOD *n* aromatic wood of an Asian tree

AGAS ▷ **aga**

AGAST, -ED, -ING, -S *adj* aghast ▷ *vb* terrify or be terrified

AGATE, -S *n* semiprecious form of quartz with striped colouring ▷ *adv* on the way

AGATISE, -D, -S *same as* ▷ **agatize**

AGATIZE, -D, -S *vb* turn into agate

AGATOID *adj* like agate

AGAVE, -S *n* tropical plant

AGAZE *adj* gazing at something

AGAZED *adj* amazed

AGE, -S *n* length of time a person or thing has existed ▷ *vb* make or grow old

AGED *adj* old

AGEDLY

AGEDNESS

AGEE *adj* awry, crooked, or ajar ▷ *adv* awry

AGEING, -S *n* fact or process of growing old ▷ *adj* becoming or appearing older

AGEISM, -S *n* discrimination against people on the grounds of age

AGEIST -S

AGELAST, -S *n* someone who never laughs

AGELESS *adj* apparently never growing old

AGELONG *adj* lasting for a very long time

AGEMATE, -S *n* person the same age as another person

AGEN *archaic form of* ▷ **again**

AGENCY, AGENCIES *n* organization providing a service

AGENDA, -S *n* list of things to be dealt with, esp at a meeting

AGENDUM, -S *same as* ▷ **agenda**

AGENE, -S *n* chemical used to whiten flour

AGENESES ▷ **agenesis**

AGENESIA *n* imperfect development

AGENESIS, AGENESES *n* (of an animal or plant) imperfect development

AGENETIC

AGENISE, -D, -S *same as* ▷ **agenize**

AGENIZE, -D, -S *vb* whiten using agene

AGENT, -ED, -S *n* person acting on behalf of another ▷ *vb* act as an agent

AGENTIAL

AGENTING

AGENTIVE *adj* grammatical case of indicating the agent of a verb ▷ *n* agentive case

AGENTRY *n* acting as agent

AGENTS ▷ **agent**

AGER, -S *n* something that ages

AGERATUM *n* tropical American plant with thick clusters of purplish-blue flowers

AGERS ▷ **ager**

AGES ▷ **age**

AGEUSIA, -S *n* lack of the sense of taste

AGGADA, -S, AGGADOT, AGGADOTH *n* explanation in Jewish literature

AGGADAH, -S *same as* ▷ **aggada**

AGGADAS ▷ **aggada**

AGGADIC *adj* of aggada

AGGADOT ▷ **aggada**

AGGADOTH ▷ **aggada**

AGGER *n* rampart

AGGERS *adj* aggressive

AGGIE, -S *n* American agricultural student

AGGRACE, -D, -S, AGRASTE *vb* add grace to

AGGRADE, -D, -S *vb* build up by the deposition of sediment

AGGRATE, -D, -S *vb* gratify

AGGRESS *vb* attack first or begin a quarrel

AGGRI *adj* of African beads

AGGRIEVE *vb* grieve

AGGRO, -S *n* aggressive behaviour

AGGRY *adj* of African beads

AGHA, -S *same as* ▷ **aga**

AGHAST *adj* overcome with amazement or horror

AGILA, -S *n* eaglewood

AGILE, -R, -ST *adj* nimble, quick-moving

AGILELY

AGILITY

AGIN *prep* against, opposed to

AGING, -S *same as* ▷ **ageing**

AGINNER, -S *n* someone who is against something

AGIO, -S *n* difference between the nominal and actual values of a currency

AGIOTAGE *n* business of exchanging currencies

AGISM, -S *same as* ▷ **ageism**

AGIST, -ED, -ING, -S *vb* care for and feed (cattle or horses) for payment

AGISTER, -S *n* person who grazes cattle for money

AGISTING ▷ **agist**

AGISTOR, -S *n* person who grazes cattle for money

AGISTS ▷ **agist**

AGITA, -S *n* acid indigestion

AGITABLE ▷ **agitate**

AGITANS *adj as in* **paralysis agitans** Parkinson's disease

AGITAS ▷ **agita**

AGITATE, -D, -S *vb* disturb or excite

AGITATO *adv* (to be performed) in an agitated manner

AGITATOR *n* person who agitates for or against a cause, etc

AGITPOP, -S *n* use of pop music to promote political propaganda

AGITPROP *n* political agitation and propaganda

AGLARE *adj* glaring

AGLEAM *adj* glowing

AGLEE *same as* ▶ **agley**

AGLET, -S *n* metal tag

AGLEY *adj* awry

AGLIMMER *adj* glimmering

AGLITTER *adj* sparkling, glittering

AGLOO, -S *same as* ▶ **aglu**

AGLOSSAL ▶ **aglossia**

AGLOSSIA *n* congenital absence of the tongue

AGLOW *adj* glowing

AGLU, -S *n* breathing hole made in ice by a seal

AGLY *Scots word for* ▶ **wrong**

AGLYCON, -S *n* chemical compound

AGLYCONE *same as* ▶ **aglycon**

AGLYCONS ▶ **aglycon**

AGMA, -S *n* symbol used to represent a velar nasal consonant

AGMINATE *adj* gathered or clustered together

AGNAIL, -S *another name for* ▶ **hangnail**

AGNAME, -S *n* name additional to first name and surname

AGNAMED *adj* having an agname

AGNAMES ▶ **agname**

AGNATE, -S *adj* related through a common male ancestor ▷ *n* descendant by male links from a common male ancestor

AGNATHAN *n* type of jawless eel-like aquatic vertebrate

AGNATIC ▶ **agnate**

AGNATION ▶ **agnate**

AGNISE, -D, -S, AGNISING *vb* acknowledge

AGNIZE, -D, -S, AGNIZING *vb* acknowledge

AGNOMEN, -S, AGNOMINA *n* name used by ancient Romans

AGNOSIA, -S *n* loss of power to recognize familiar objects

AGNOSIC

AGNOSTIC *n* person who believes that it is impossible

to know whether God exists ▷ *adj* of agnostics

AGO *adv* in the past

AGOG *adj* eager or curious

AGOGE, -S *n* ancient Greek tempo

AGOGIC, -S *n* musical accent

AGOING *adj* moving

AGON, -ES, -S *n* ancient Greek festival

AGONAL *adj* of agony

AGONE *an archaic word for* ▶ **ago**

AGONES ▶ **agon**

AGONIC *adj* forming no angle

AGONIES ▶ **agony**

AGONISE, -D, -S *same as* ▶ **agonize**

AGONISM, -S *n* struggle between opposing forces

AGONIST, -S *n* any muscle that is opposed in action by another muscle

AGONIZE, -D, -S *vb* worry greatly

AGONS ▶ **agon**

AGONY, AGONIES *n* extreme physical or mental pain

AGOOD *adv* seriously or earnestly

AGORA, -E, -S *n* place of assembly in ancient Greece

AGOROT *pl n* Israeli coins

AGOROTH *same as* ▶ **agorot**

AGOUTA, -S *n* Haitian rodent

AGOUTI, -ES, -S *n* rodent

AGOUTY *n* agouti

AGRAFE, -S *same as* ▶ **agraffe**

AGRAFFE, -S *n* loop and hook fastening

AGRAPHA ▶ **agraphon**

AGRAPHIA *n* loss of the ability to write, resulting from a brain lesion

AGRAPHIC

AGRAPHON, AGRAPHA *n* saying of Jesus not in Gospels

AGRARIAN *adj* of land or agriculture ▷ *n* person who favours the redistribution of landed property

AGRASTE ▶ **aggrace**

AGRAVIC *adj* of zero gravity

AGREE, -ING, -S *vb* be of the same opinion

AGREED *adj* determined by common consent

AGREEING ▶ **agree**

AGREES ▶ **agree**

AGREGE, -S *n* winner in examination for university teaching post

AGREMENS *n* amenities

AGREMENT *n* diplomatic approval of a country

AGRESTAL *adj* (of uncultivated plants such as weeds) growing on cultivated land

AGRESTIC *adj* rural

AGRIA, -S *n* appearance of pustules

AGRIMONY *n* yellow-flowered plant with bitter-tasting fruits

AGRIN, -S *adv* grinning ▷ *n* type of protein

AGRISE, -D, -S, AGRISING *vb* fill with fear

AGRIZE, -D, -S, AGRIZING *vb* fill with fear

AGRO, -S *n* student of agriculture

AGROLOGY *n* scientific study of soils and their potential productivity

AGRONOMY *n* science of soil management and crop production

AGROS ▶ **agro**

AGROUND *adv* onto the bottom of shallow water ▷ *adj* on the ground or bottom, as in shallow water

AGRYPNIA *n* inability to sleep

AGRYZE, -D, -S, AGRYZING *vb* fill with fear

AGS ▶ **ag**

AGUACATE *n* avocado

AGUE, -S *n* periodic fever with shivering

AGUED *adj* suffering from fever

AGUELIKE ▶ **ague**

AGUES ▶ **ague**

AGUEWEED *n* N American plant with clusters of pale blue-violet or white flowers

AGUISE, -D, -S, AGUISING *vb* dress

AGUISH ▶ **ague**

AGUISHLY ▶ **ague**

AGUISING ▶ **aguise**

AGUIZE, -D, -S, AGUIZING *vb* dress

AGUNA, AGUNOT, AGUNOTH *n* (in Jewish law) woman whose husband will not grant her a divorce

AGUNAH *same as* ▶ **aguna**

AGUNOT ▶ **aguna**

AGUNOTH ▶ **aguna**

AGUTI, -S *n* agouti

AH, -ED, -ING, -S *interj* exclamation expressing surprise, joy etc ▷ *vb* say ah

AHA *interj* exclamation

AHCHOO *interj* sound made by someone sneezing

AHEAD *adv* in front

AHEAP *adv* in a heap

AHED ▶ **ah**

A

AHEIGHT adv at height

AHEM interj clearing of the throat in order to attract attention

AHEMERAL adj not constituting a full 24-hour day

AHENT adv behind

AHI, -S n yellowfin tuna

> A very useful one to catch!

AHIGH adv at height

AHIMSA, -S n the law of reverence for every form of life

AHIND adv behind

AHING ► ah

AHINT adv behind

AHIS ► ahi

AHOLD adv holding

AHORSE adv on horseback

AHOY interj hail used to call a ship

AHS ► ah

AHULL adv with sails furled

AHUNGRY adj very hungry

AHURU, -S n type of small pink cod of SW Pacific waters

AI, -S n shaggy-coated slow-moving animal of South America

AIA, -S n female servant in E Asia

AIBLINS Scots word for ► perhaps

AID, -ED, -ING, -S n (give) assistance or support ▷ vb help financially or in other ways

AIDA, -S n cotton fabric with a natural mesh

AIDANCE, -S n help

AIDANT, -S adj helping ▷ n helper

AIDAS ► aida

AIDE, -S n assistant

AIDED ► aid

AIDER, -S ► aid

AIDES ► aide

AIDFUL adj helpful

AIDING ► aid

AIDLESS adj without help

AIDMAN, AIDMEN n military medical assistant

AIDOI adj of the genitals

AIDOS Greek word for ► shame

AIDS ► aid

AIERY, AIERIES n eyrie

AIGA, -S n Māori word for family

AIGHT adv all right

AIGLET, -S same as ► aglet

AIGRET, -S same as ► aigrette

AIGRETTE n long plume worn on hats or as a headdress, esp one of long egret feathers

AIGUILLE n rock mass or mountain peak shaped like a needle

AIKIDO, -S n Japanese self-defence

AIKONA interj South African expression meaning no

AIL, -ED, -S vb trouble, afflict

AILANTO, -S n Asian tree

AILED ► ail

AILERON, -S n movable flap on an aircraft wing which controls rolling

AILETTE, -S n shoulder armour

AILING adj sickly

AILMENT, -S n illness

AILS ► ail

AIM, -ED, -ING, -S vb point (a weapon or missile) or direct (a blow or remark) at a target ▷ n aiming

AIMER -S

AIMFUL adj with purpose or intention

AIMFULLY

AIMING ► aim

AIMLESS adj having no purpose

AIMS ► aim

AIN, -S variant of ► ayin

AINE adj French word for elder (male)

> Though it doesn't score much, it is useful to remember when you have too many vowels. And it can be extended to **ainee**, the feminine form.

AINEE n French word for elder (female)

AINGA, -S n Māori word for village

AINS ► ain

AINSELL, -S n Scots word meaning own self

AIOLI, -S n garlic mayonnaise

AIR, -ED n mixture of gases forming the earth's atmosphere ▷ vb make known publicly

AIRBAG, -S n safety device in a car

AIRBALL, -S n missed shot that fails to touch the rim of the basket

AIRBASE, -S n centre from which military aircraft operate

AIRBOARD n inflatable body board

AIRBOAT, -S n boat

AIRBORNE adj carried by air

AIRBOUND adj heading into the air

AIRBRICK n brick with holes in it, put into the wall of a building for ventilation

AIRBRUSH n atomizer that sprays paint by compressed air ▷ vb paint using an airbrush

AIRBURST n explosion of a bomb, shell, etc, in the air ▷ vb (of a bomb, shell, etc) to explode in the air

AIRBUS, -ES n commercial passenger aircraft

AIRCHECK n recording of a radio broadcast

AIRCOACH n bus travelling to and from an airport

AIRCON, -S n air conditioner

AIRCRAFT n any machine that flies, such as an aeroplane

AIRCREW, -S n crew of an aircraft

AIRDATE, -S n date of a programme broadcast

AIRDRAWN adj imaginary

AIRDROME same as > aerodrome

AIRDROP, -S n delivery of supplies by parachute ▷ vb deliver (supplies, etc) by an airdrop

AIRED ► air

AIRER, -S n device on which clothes are hung to dry

AIRFARE, -S n money for an aircraft ticket

AIRFIELD n place where aircraft can land and take off

AIRFLOW, -S n flow of air past a moving object

AIRFOIL, -S same as ► aerofoil

AIRFRAME n body of an aircraft, excluding its engines

AIRGAP, -S n gap between parts in an electrical machine

AIRGLOW, -S n faint light in the night sky

AIRGRAPH n photographic reduction of a letter for sending airmail

AIRGUN, -S n gun fired by compressed air

AIRHEAD, -S n stupid person

AIRHOLE, -S n hole that allows the passage of air

AIRIER ► airy

AIRIEST ► airy

AIRILY adv in a light-hearted and casual manner

AIRINESS n quality or condition of being fresh, light, or breezy

AIRING, -S n exposure to air for drying or ventilation

AIRLESS adj stuffy

AIRLIFT, -S n transport of troops or cargo by aircraft when other routes are blocked ▷ vb transport by airlift

AIRLIKE ▸ air

AIRLINE, -S n company providing scheduled flights for passengers and cargo

AIRLINER n large passenger aircraft

AIRLINES ▸ airline

AIRLOCK, -S n air bubble blocking the flow of liquid in a pipe

AIRMAIL, -S n system of sending mail by aircraft ▷ adj of, used for, or concerned with airmail ▷ vb send by airmail

AIRMAN, AIRMEN n member of an air force

AIRN, -ED, -ING, -S Scots word for ▸ iron

AIRPARK, -S n car park at airport

AIRPLANE same as > aeroplane

AIRPLAY, -S n broadcast performances of a record on radio

AIRPORT, -S n airfield for civilian aircraft, with facilities for aircraft maintenance and passengers

AIRPOST, -S n system of delivering mail by air

AIRPOWER n strength of a nation's air force

AIRPROOF vb make something airtight

AIRPROX n near collision involving aircraft

AIRS pl n manners put on to impress people

AIRSCAPE n picture or view of sky

AIRSCREW n aircraft propeller

AIRSHAFT n shaft for ventilation

AIRSHED, -S n air over a particular geographical area

AIRSHIP, -S n lighter-than-air self-propelled aircraft

AIRSHOT, -S n shot that misses the ball completely

AIRSHOW, -S n occasion when an air base is open to the public

AIRSICK adj nauseated from travelling in an aircraft

AIRSIDE, -S n part of an airport nearest the aircraft

AIRSOME adj cold

AIRSPACE n atmosphere above a country, regarded as its territory

AIRSPEED n speed of an aircraft relative to the air in which it moves

AIRSTOP, -S n helicopter landing-place

AIRSTRIP n cleared area where aircraft can take off and land

AIRT, -ED, -ING, -S n point of the compass ▷ vb direct

AIRTH, -ED, -ING, -S same as ▸ airt

AIRTIGHT adj sealed so that air cannot enter

AIRTIME, -S n time period on radio and TV

AIRTING ▸ airt

AIRTRAM, -S n cable car

AIRTS ▸ airt

AIRVAC, -S n evacuation by air ambulance

AIRWARD adj into air

AIRWARDS adv into air

AIRWAVE, -S n radio wave used in radio and television broadcasting

AIRWAY, -S n air route used regularly by aircraft

AIRWISE adv towards the air

AIRWOMAN, AIRWOMEN ▸ airman

AIRY, AIRIER, AIRIEST adj well-ventilated

AIS ▸ ai

AISLE, -S n passageway separating seating areas, rows of shelves, etc

AISLED

AISLEWAY n aisle

AISLING, -S Irish word for ▸ dream

AIT, -S n islet, esp in a river

AITCH, -ES n letter h or the sound represented by it

AITS ▸ ait

AITU, -S n half-human half-divine being

This demigod is often played to dispose of an excess of vowels.

AIVER, -S n working horse

AIYEE interj expressing alarm

AIZLE, -S n Scots word for hot ashes

AJAR adv (of a door) partly open ▷ adj not in harmony

AJEE same as ▸ agee

This Scots word meaning ajar is often useful for disposing of the J. It has an alternative spelling **agee**.

AJI, -S n type of spicy pepper

AJIVA, -S n Jainist term for non-living thing

AJOWAN, -S n plant related to caraway

AJUGA, -S n garden plant

AJUTAGE, -S n nozzle

AJWAN, -S n plant related to caraway

AKA, -S n type of New Zealand vine

One of the key short words when it comes to using the K.

AKARYOTE n cell without a nucleus

AKAS ▸ aka

AKATEA, -S n New Zealand vine with white flowers

AKE, -D, -S, AKING vb old spelling of ache

AKEAKE, -S n New Zealand tree

AKEBIA, -S n E Asian climbing plant

AKED ▸ ake

AKEDAH, -S n binding of Isaac in Bible

AKEE, -S same as ▸ ackee

AKELA, -S n adult leader of a pack of Cub Scouts

AKENE, -S same as ▸ achene

AKENIAL ▸ achene

AKES ▸ ake

AKHARA, -S n (in India) gymnasium

AKIMBO adj as in **with arms akimbo** with hands on hips and elbows projecting outwards

AKIN adj related by blood

AKINESES ▸ akinesis

AKINESIA n loss of power to move

AKINESIS, AKINESES same as ▸ akinesia

AKINETIC ▸ akinesia

AKING ▸ ake

AKIRAHO, -S n small New Zealand shrub with white flowers

AKITA, -S n large dog

AKKAS slang word for ▸ money

AKRASIA, -S n weakness of will

AKRATIC

AKVAVIT, -S same as ▸ aquavit

AL, -S same as ▸ aal

ALA, -E n winglike structure

ALAAP, -S n part of raga in Indian music

ALACHLOR n type of herbicide

ALACK archaic or poetic word for ▸ alas

ALACRITY n speed, eagerness

A

ALAE ▸ ala

ALAIMENT *old spelling of* ▸ allayment

ALALIA, -S *n* complete inability to speak

ALAMEDA, -S *n* public walk lined with trees

ALAMO, -S *n* poplar tree

ALAMODE, -S *n* soft light silk used for shawls and dresses, esp in the 19th century

ALAMORT *adj* exhausted and downcast

ALAMOS ▸ alamo

ALAN, -S *n* member of ancient European nomadic people

ALAND, -S *vb* come onto land

ALANE *Scots word for* ▸ **alone**

ALANG, -S *n* type of grass in Malaysia

ALANIN, -S *n* alanine

ALANINE, -S *n* chemical

ALANINS ▸ alanin

ALANNAH, -S *interj* term of endearment ▸ *n* cry of alannah

ALANS ▸ alan

ALANT, -S *n* flowering plant used in herbal medicine

ALANYL, -S *n* chemical found in proteins

ALAP, -S *n* Indian vocal music without words

ALAPA, -S *n* part of raga in Indian music

ALAPS ▸ alap

ALAR *adj* relating to, resembling, or having wings or alae

ALARM, -ED, -S *n* sudden fear caused by awareness of danger ▸ *vb* fill with fear **ALARMING**

ALARMISM ▸ alarmist

ALARMIST *n* person who alarms others needlessly ▸ *adj* causing needless alarm

ALARMS ▸ alarm

ALARUM, -ED, -S *n* alarm, esp a call to arms ▸ *vb* raise the alarm

ALARY *adj* of, relating to, or shaped like wings

ALAS *adv* unfortunately, regrettably

ALASKA, -S *n* dessert made of cake and ice cream

ALASTOR, -S *n* avenging demon

ALASTRIM *n* form of smallpox

ALATE, -S *adj* having wings or winglike extensions ▸ *n* winged insect

ALATED *adj* having wings

ALATES ▸ alate

ALATION, -S *n* state of having wings

ALAY, -ED, -ING, -S *vb* allay

ALB, -S *n* long white robe worn by a Christian priest

ALBA, -S *n* song of lament

ALBACORE *n* tuna found in warm seas, eaten for food

ALBAS ▸ alba

ALBATA, -S *n* variety of German silver consisting of nickel, copper, and zinc

ALBE *old word for* ▸ **albeit**

ALBEDO, -ES, -S *n* ratio of the intensity of light

ALBEE *archaic form of* ▸ **albeit**

ALBEIT *conj* even though

ALBERGO, ALBERGHI *n* Italian word for inn

ALBERT, -S *n* watch chain

ALBICORE *n* species of tuna

ALBINAL ▸ albino

ALBINESS *n* female albino

ALBINIC ▸ albino

ALBINISM ▸ albino

ALBINO, -S *n* person or animal with white skin and hair and pink eyes

ALBITE, -S *n* type of mineral **ALBITIC**

ALBITISE *same as* ▸ **albitize**

ALBITIZE *vb* turn into albite

ALBIZIA, -S *n* mimosa

ALBIZZIA *n* mimosa

ALBS ▸ alb

ALBUGO, -S *n* opacity of the cornea

ALBUM, -S *n* book with blank pages for keeping photographs or stamps in

ALBUMEN, -S *same as* ▸ **albumin**

ALBUMIN, -S *n* protein found in blood plasma, egg white, milk, and muscle

ALBUMOSE *the US name for* ▸ **proteose**

ALBUMS ▸ album

ALBURNUM *former name for* ▸ **sapwood**

ALCADE, -S *same as* ▸ **alcalde**

ALCAHEST *same as* ▸ **alkahest**

ALCAIC, -S *n* verse consisting of strophes with four tetrametric lines

ALCAIDE, -S *n* commander of a fortress or castle

ALCALDE, -S *n* (in Spain and Spanish America) the mayor or chief magistrate in a town

ALCATRAS *n* pelican

ALCAYDE, -S *n* alcaide

ALCAZAR, -S *n* Moorish palace or fortress

ALCHEMIC ▸ alchemy

ALCHEMY *n* medieval form of chemistry

ALCHERA, -S *n* mythical Golden Age

ALCHYMY *old spelling of* ▸ **alchemy**

ALCID, -S *n* bird of the auk family

ALCIDINE *adj* relating to a family of sea birds including the auks, guillemots, and puffins

ALCIDS ▸ alcid

ALCO, -S *same as* ▸ **alko**

ALCOHOL, -S *n* colourless flammable liquid present in intoxicating drinks

ALCOLOCK *n* breath-alcohol ignition-interlock device

ALCOOL, -S *n* form of pure grain spirit distilled in Quebec

ALCOPOP, -S *n* alcoholic drink that tastes like a soft drink

ALCORZA, -S *n* Spanish sweet

ALCOS ▸ alco

ALCOVE, -S *n* recess in the wall of a room

ALCOVED *adj* with or in an alcove

ALCOVES ▸ alcove

ALDEA, -S *n* Spanish village

ALDEHYDE *n* one of a group of chemical compounds derived from alcohol by oxidation

ALDER, -S *n* tree related to the birch

ALDERFLY *n* insect with large broad-based hind wings, which produces aquatic larvae

ALDERMAN, ALDERMEN *n* formerly, senior member of a local council

ALDERN *adj* made of alder wood

ALDERS ▸ alder

ALDICARB *n* crystalline compound used as a pesticide

ALDOL, -S *n* colourless or yellowish oily liquid

ALDOLASE *n* enzyme present in the body

ALDOLS ▸ aldol

ALDOSE, -S *n* type of sugar

ALDOXIME *n* oxime formed by reaction between hydroxylamine and an aldehyde

ALDRIN, -S *n* brown to white poisonous crystalline solid

ALE, -S *n* kind of beer

ALEATORY *adj* dependent on chance

A

ALEBENCH n bench at alehouse

ALEC, -S same as ▶ **aleck**

ALECK, -S n irritatingly oversmart person

ALECOST, -S another name for ▶ **costmary**

ALECS ▶ **alec**

ALEE adj on or towards the lee

ALEF, -S n first letter of Hebrew alphabet

ALEFT adv at or to left

ALEGAR, -S n malt vinegar

ALEGGE, -D, -S, ALEGGING vb alleviate

ALEHOUSE n public house

ALEMBIC, -S n anything that distils

ALENCON, -S n elaborate lace worked on a hexagonal mesh

ALENGTH adv at length

ALEPH, -S n first letter in the Hebrew alphabet

ALEPINE, -S n type of cloth

ALERCE, -S n wood of the sandarac tree

ALERION, -S n eagle in heraldry

ALERT, -ED, -ER, -EST, -ING, -S adj watchful, attentive ▷ n warning of danger ▷ vb warn of danger

ALERTLY

ALES ▶ **ale**

ALETHIC adj of philosophical concepts

ALEURON, -S n outer layer of seeds

ALEURONE same as ▶ **aleuron**

ALEURONS ▶ **aleuron**

ALEVIN, -S n young fish, esp a young salmon or trout

ALEW, -S n cry to call hunting hounds

ALEWIFE, ALEWIVES n North American fish

ALEWS ▶ **alew**

ALEXIA, -S n disorder of the central nervous system

ALEXIC

ALEXIN, -S n protein in blood serum

ALEXINE, -S same as ▶ **alexin**

ALEXINIC ▶ **alexin**

ALEXINS ▶ **alexin**

ALEYE, -D, -S, ALEYING vb allay

ALF, -S n uncultivated Australian

ALFA, -S n type of grass

ALFAKI, -S same as ▶ **alfaqui**

ALFALFA, -S n kind of plant used to feed livestock

ALFAQUI, -S n expert in Muslim law

ALFAQUIN same as ▶ **alfaqui**

ALFAQUIS ▶ **alfaqui**

ALFAS ▶ **alfa**

ALFEREZ n Spanish standard-bearer

ALFORJA, -S n saddlebag made of leather or canvas

ALFREDO adj cooked with a cheese and egg sauce

ALFRESCO adj in the open air ▷ adv in the open air

ALFS ▶ **alf**

ALGA, -E, -S n multicellular organism

ALGAL

ALGAROBA same as > **algarroba**

ALGAS ▶ **alga**

ALGATE adv anyway

ALGATES adv anyway

ALGEBRA, -S n branch of mathematics using symbols to represent quantities

ALGERINE n soft striped woollen cloth

ALGESES ▶ **algesis**

ALGESIA, -S n capacity to feel pain

ALGESIC

ALGESIS, ALGESES n feeling of pain

ALGETIC ▶ **algesia**

ALGICIDE n any substance that kills algae

ALGID adj chilly or cold

ALGIDITY

ALGIN, -S n seaweed solution

ALGINATE n salt or ester of alginic acid

ALGINIC adj as in **alginic acid** powdery substance extracted from kelp

ALGINS ▶ **algin**

ALGOID adj resembling or relating to algae

ALGOLOGY n branch of biology concerned with the study of algae

ALGOR, -S n chill

ALGORISM n Arabic or decimal system of counting

ALGORS ▶ **algor**

ALGUACIL n Spanish law officer

ALGUAZIL n Spanish law officer

ALGUM, -S n type of wood mentioned in Bible

ALIAS, -ED, -ES adv also known as ▷ n false name ▷ vb give or assume an alias

ALIASING n error in a vision or sound signal

ALIBI, -ED, -ES, -ING, -S n plea of being somewhere else when a crime was committed ▷ vb provide someone with an alibi

ALIBLE adj nourishing

ALICANT, -S n wine from Alicante in Spain

ALIDAD, -S same as ▶ **alidade**

ALIDADE, -S n surveying instrument

ALIDADS ▶ **alidad**

ALIEN, -ED, -ING, -S adj foreign ▷ n foreigner ▷ vb transfer (property, etc) to another

ALIENAGE

ALIENATE vb cause to become hostile

ALIENED ▶ **alien**

ALIENEE, -S n person to whom a transfer of property is made

ALIENER, -S ▶ **alien**

ALIENING ▶ **alien**

ALIENISM n study and treatment of mental illness

ALIENIST n psychiatrist who specializes in the legal aspects of mental illness

ALIENLY ▶ **alien**

ALIENOR, -S n person who transfers property to another

ALIENS ▶ **alien**

ALIF, -S n first letter of Arabic alphabet

ALIFORM adj wing-shaped

ALIFS ▶ **alif**

ALIGARTA n alligator

ALIGHT, -ED, -S vb step out of (a vehicle) ▷ adj on fire ▷ adv on fire

ALIGN, -ED, -ING, -S vb bring (a person or group) into agreement with the policy of another

ALIGNER, -S

ALIKE adj like, similar ▷ adv in the same way

ALIMENT, -S n something that nourishes the body ▷ vb support or sustain

ALIMONY n allowance paid under a court order to a separated or divorced spouse

ALINE, -D, -S, ALINING a rare spelling of ▶ **align**

ALINER -S

ALIPED, -S n bat-like creature ▷ adj having digits connected by a membrane

ALIQUANT adj denoting or belonging to a number that is not an exact divisor of a given number

ALIQUOT, -S adj of or denoting an exact divisor of a number ▷ n exact divisor

ALISMA, -S n marsh plant

ALISON, -S same as ▶ **alyssum**

A

ALIST adj leaning over

ALIT rare past tense and past participle of ▸ **alight**

ALIUNDE adj from a source under consideration

ALIVE adj living, in existence

ALIYA, -S same as ▸ **aliyah**

ALIYAH, -S, ALIYOT, ALIYOTH n immigration to the Holy Land

ALIYAS ▸ **aliya**

ALIYOS n remission of sin in Jewish faith

ALIYOT ▸ **aliyah**

ALIYOTH ▸ **aliyah**

ALIZARI, -S n madder from Middle East

ALIZARIN n brownish-yellow powder or orange-red crystalline solid

ALIZARIS ▸ **alizari**

ALKAHEST n hypothetical universal solvent sought by alchemists

ALKALI, -ES, -S n substance which combines with acid and neutralizes it to form a salt

ALKALIC adj geographical term

ALKALIES ▸ **alkali**

ALKALIFY vb make or become alkaline

ALKALIN adj alkaline

ALKALINE adj having the properties of or containing an alkali

ALKALIS ▸ **alkali**

ALKALISE same as ▸ **alkalize**

ALKALIZE vb make alkaline

ALKALOID n any of a group of organic compounds containing nitrogen

ALKANE, -S n saturated hydrocarbon

ALKANET, -S n European plant whose roots yield a red dye

ALKANNIN same as ▸ **alkanet**

ALKENE, -S n unsaturated hydrocarbon

ALKIE same as ▸ **alky**

ALKIES ▸ **alky**

ALKINE, -S n alkyne

ALKO, -S n slang word for alcoholic

ALKOXIDE n chemical compound containing oxygen

ALKOXY adj of a type of chemical compound containing oxygen

ALKY, ALKIES n slang word for alcoholic

ALKYD, -S n synthetic resin

ALKYL, -S n the monovalent group CnH2n+1

ALKYLATE vb add alkyl group to a compound

ALKYLIC ▸ **alkyl**

ALKYLS ▸ **alkyl**

ALKYNE, -S n any unsaturated aliphatic hydrocarbon

ALL, -S adj whole quantity or number (of) ▷ adv wholly, entirely ▷ n entire being, effort, or property

ALLANITE n rare black or brown mineral

ALLATIVE n word in grammatical case denoting movement towards

ALLAY, -ED, -S vb reduce (fear or anger)

ALLAYER -S

ALLAYING ▸ **allay**

ALLAYS ▸ **allay**

ALLEDGE, -D, -S vb allege

ALLEE, -S n avenue

ALLEGE, -S, ALLEGING vb state without proof

ALLEGED adj stated but not proved

ALLEGER, -S ▸ **allege**

ALLEGES ▸ **allege**

ALLEGGE, -D, -S vb alleviate

ALLEGING ▸ **allege**

ALLEGORY n story with an underlying meaning as well as the literal one

ALLEGRO, -S adv (to be played) in a brisk lively manner ▷ n piece or passage to be performed in a brisk lively manner

ALLEL, -S n form of gene

ALLELE, -S n variant form of a gene

ALLELIC

ALLELISM

ALLELS ▸ **allel**

ALLELUIA n song of praise to God

ALLERGEN n substance capable of causing an allergic reaction

ALLERGIC adj having or caused by an allergy ▷ n person suffering from an allergy

ALLERGIN n allergen

ALLERGY n extreme sensitivity to a substance, which causes the body to react to it

ALLERION n eagle in heraldry

ALLEY, -S n narrow street or path

ALLEYCAT n homeless cat that roams in back streets

ALLEYED adj having alleys

ALLEYS ▸ **alley**

ALLEYWAY n narrow passage with buildings or walls on both sides

ALLHEAL, -S n plant with reputed healing powers

ALLIABLE adj able to form an alliance

ALLIAK, -S n Inuit sledge

ALLIANCE n state of being allied

ALLICE, -S n species of fish

ALLICIN, -S n chemical found in garlic

ALLIED adj joined, as by treaty, agreement, or marriage

ALLIES ▸ **ally**

ALLIGATE vb join together

ALLIS, -ES n species of fish

ALLIUM, -S n type of plant

ALLNESS n being all

ALLNIGHT adj lasting all night

ALLOBAR, -S n form of element

ALLOCATE vb assign to someone or for a particular purpose

ALLOD, -S same as ▸ **allodium**

ALLODIA ▸ **allodium**

ALLODIAL adj (of land) held as an allodium

ALLODIUM, ALLODIA n lands held free from rent or services due to an overlord

ALLODS ▸ **allod**

ALLOGAMY n cross-fertilization in flowering plants

ALLOMONE n chemical substance secreted by certain animals

ALLONGE, -D, -S n paper extension to bill of exchange ▷ vb (in fencing) lunge

ALLONS interj French word meaning let's go

ALLONYM, -S n name assumed by a person

ALLOPATH n person who practises or is skilled in allopathy

ALLOSAUR n any large carnivorous bipedal dinosaur common in North America in late Jurassic times

ALLOT, -S, -TED vb assign as a share or for a particular purpose

ALLOTTEE n person to whom something is allotted

ALLOTTER n person who allots

ALLOTYPE n type of specimen that differs from the original type

ALLOTYPY n existence of allotypes

ALLOVER, -S n fabric completely covered with a pattern

ALLOW, -ED, -ING, -S vb permit

ALLOXAN, -S n chemical found in uric acid

ALLOY, -ED, -ING, -S n mixture of two or more metals ▷ vb mix (metals)

ALLOZYME n different form of an enzyme

ALLS ► all

ALLSEED, -S n type of plant

ALLSORTS pl n assorted sweets

ALLSPICE n spice made from the berries of a tropical American tree

ALLUDE, -D, -S, ALLUDING vb refer indirectly to

ALLURE, -D, -S n attractiveness ▷ vb entice or attract

ALLURER -S

ALLURING adj extremely attractive

ALLUSION n indirect reference

ALLUSIVE adj containing or full of allusions

ALLUVIA ► alluvium

ALLUVIAL adj of or relating to alluvium ▷ n soil consisting of alluvium

ALLUVION n wash of the sea or of a river

ALLUVIUM, ALLUVIA n fertile soil deposited by flowing water

ALLY, ALLIES, -ING vb unite or be united, esp formally, as by treaty, confederation, or marriage ▷ n country, person, or group allied with another

ALLYL, -S n containing the monovalent group CH2:CHCH2−

ALLYLIC

ALLYOU pron all of you

ALMA, -S same as ► almah

ALMAGEST n medieval treatise concerning alchemy or astrology

ALMAH, -S n Egyptian dancing girl

ALMAIN, -S n German dance

ALMANAC, -S n yearly calendar with detailed information on anniversaries, phases of the moon, etc

ALMANACK same as ► almanac

ALMANACS ► almanac

ALMAS ► alma

ALME, -S same as ► almeh

ALMEH, -S n Egyptian dancing girl

ALMEMAR, -S n area in a synagogue

ALMERY, ALMERIES n cupboard for church vessels

ALMES ► alme

ALMIGHTY adj all-powerful ▷ adv extremely

ALMIRAH, -S n cupboard

ALMNER, -S n almoner

ALMOND, -S n edible oval-shaped nut which grows on a small tree

ALMONDY adj containing or resembling almond

ALMONER, -S n formerly, a hospital social worker

ALMONRY n house of an almoner, usually the place where alms were given

ALMOST adv very nearly

ALMOUS Scots word for ► alms

ALMS pl n gifts to the poor

ALMSMAN, ALMSMEN n person who gives or receives alms

ALMUCE, -S n fur-lined hood or cape

ALMUD, -S n Spanish unit of measure

ALMUDE, -S same as ► almud

ALMUDS ► almud

ALMUG, -S n type of wood mentioned in Bible

ALNAGE, -S n measurement in ells

ALNAGER, -S n inspector of cloth

ALNAGES ► alnage

ALNICO, -S n alloy including iron, nickel, and cobalt

ALOCASIA n type of tropical plant

ALOD, -S n feudal estate with no superior

ALODIA ► alodium

ALODIAL ► alodium

ALODIUM, ALODIA, -S same as ► allodium

ALODS ► alod

ALOE n plant with fleshy spiny leaves

ALOED adj containing aloes

ALOES another name for > eaglewood

ALOETIC, -S ► aloe

ALOFT adv in the air ▷ adj in or into a high or higher place

ALOGIA, -S n inability to speak

ALOGICAL adj without logic

ALOHA, -S a Hawaiian word for ► hello

ALOIN, -S n crystalline compound

ALONE adv without anyone or anything else

ALONELY

ALONG adv forward

ALONGST adv along

ALOO, -S n (in Indian cookery) potato

ALOOF adj distant or haughty in manner

ALOOFLY

ALOOS ► aloo

ALOPECIA n loss of hair

ALOPECIC

ALOUD adv in an audible voice ▷ adj in a normal voice

ALOW adj in or into the lower rigging of a vessel, near the deck

ALOWE Scots word for ► ablaze

ALP, -S n high mountain

ALPACA, -S n Peruvian llama

ALPACCA, -S same as ► alpaca

ALPEEN, -S n Irish cudgel

ALPHA, -S n first letter in the Greek alphabet

ALPHABET n set of letters used in writing a language

ALPHAS ► alpha

ALPHORN, -S n wind instrument

ALPHOSIS n absence of skin pigmentation, as in albinism

ALPHYL, -S n univalent radical

ALPINE, -S adj of high mountains ▷ n mountain plant

ALPINELY

ALPINISM ► alpinist

ALPINIST n mountain climber

ALPS ► alp

ALREADY adv before the present time

ALRIGHT adj all right

ALS ► al

ALSIKE, -S n clover native to Europe and Asia

ALSO adv in addition, too

ALSOON same as ► alsoone

ALSOONE adv as soon

ALT, -S n octave directly above the treble staff

ALTAR, -S n table used for Communion in Christian churches

ALTARAGE n donations placed on altar for priest

ALTARS ► altar

ALTER, -ED, -ING, -S vb make or become different

ALTERANT n alternative

ALTERED ▸ alter
ALTERER, -S ▸ alter
ALTERING ▸ alter
ALTERITY n quality of being different
ALTERN adj alternate
ALTERNAT n practice of deciding precedence by lot
ALTERNE, -S n neighbouring but different plant group
ALTERS ▸ alter
ALTESSE, -S n French word for highness
ALTEZA, -S n Spanish word for highness
ALTEZZA, -S n Italian word for highness
ALTHAEA, -S n type of plant
ALTHEA, -S same as ▸ **althaea**
ALTHO conj short form of although
ALTHORN, -S n valved brass musical instrument
ALTHOUGH conj despite the fact that; even though
ALTITUDE n height above sea level
ALTO, -S n (singer with) the highest adult male voice ▷ adj denoting an instrument, singer, or voice with this range
ALTOIST, -S n person who plays the alto saxophone
ALTOS ▸ alto
ALTRICES pl n altricial birds
ALTRUISM n unselfish concern for the welfare of others
ALTRUIST
ALTS ▸ alt
ALU, -S same as ▸ **aloo**
ALUDEL, -S n pear-shaped vessel
ALULA, -E, -S n tuft of feathers
ALULAR
ALUM, -S n double sulphate of aluminium and potassium
ALUMIN, -S same as ▸ **alumina**
ALUMINA, -S n aluminium oxide
ALUMINE, -S n French word for alumina
ALUMINIC adj of aluminium
ALUMINS ▸ alumin
ALUMINUM same as ▸ **aluminium**
ALUMISH adj like alum
ALUMIUM, -S old name for ▸ **aluminium**
ALUMNA, -E n female graduate of a school, college, etc
ALUMNUS, ALUMNI n graduate of a college

ALUMROOT n North American plant
ALUMS ▸ alum
ALUNITE, -S n white, grey, or reddish mineral
ALURE, -S n area behind battlements
ALUS ▸ alu
ALVAR, -S n area of exposed limestone
ALVEARY n beehive
ALVEATED adj with vaults like beehive
ALVEOLAR adj articulated with the alveoli ▷ n alveolar consonant
ALVEOLE, -S n alveolus
ALVEOLUS, ALVEOLI n sockets in which the roots of teeth are embedded
ALVINE adj of or relating to the intestines or belly
ALWAY same as ▸ **always**
ALWAYS adv at all times
ALYSSUM, -S n garden plant with small yellow or white flowers
AM vb form of the present tense of be
AMA, -S n vessel for water
AMABILE adj sweet
AMADAVAT same as ▸ **avadavat**
AMADODA pl n grown men
AMADOU, -S n spongy substance made from fungi
AMAH, -S n (in the East, formerly) a nurse or maidservant
AMAIN adv with great strength, speed, or haste
AMAKOSI ▸ inkhosi
AMALGAM, -S n blend or combination
AMANDINE n protein found in almonds
AMANDLA, -S n political slogan calling for power to the Black population
AMANITA, -S n type of fungus
AMANITIN n poison from amanita
AMARACUS n marjoram
AMARANT, -S n amaranth
AMARANTH n imaginary flower that never fades
AMARANTS ▸ amarant
AMARELLE n variety of sour cherry that has pale red fruit and colourless juice
AMARETTO, AMARETTI n Italian liqueur with a flavour of almonds
AMARNA adj pertaining to the reign of the Pharaoh Akhenaton

AMARONE, -S n strong dry red Italian wine
AMAS ▸ ama
AMASS, -ED, -ES, -ING vb collect or accumulate
AMASSER -S
AMATE, -D, -S, AMATING vb match
AMATEUR, -S n person who engages in a sport or activity as a pastime rather than as a profession ▷ adj not professional
AMATING ▸ amate
AMATIVE a rare word for ▸ **amorous**
AMATOL, -S n explosive mixture
AMATORY adj relating to love
AMAUT, -S n hooded coat worn by Inuit women
AMAUTI, -S same as ▸ **amaut**
AMAUTIK, -S same as ▸ **amaut**
AMAUTIS ▸ amauti
AMAUTS ▸ amaut
AMAZE, -D, -S vb surprise greatly, astound
AMAZEDLY
AMAZING adj causing wonder or astonishment
AMAZON, -S n any tall, strong, or aggressive woman
AMBACH, -ES same as ▸ **ambatch**
AMBAGE, -S n ambiguity
AMBAN, -S n Chinese official
AMBARI, -S same as ▸ **ambary**
AMBARIES ▸ ambary
AMBARIS ▸ ambari
AMBARY, AMBARIES n tropical Asian plant that yields a fibre similar to jute
AMBASSY n embassy
AMBATCH n tree or shrub
AMBEER, -S n saliva coloured by tobacco juice
AMBER, -S n clear yellow fossil resin ▷ adj brownish-yellow
AMBERED adj fixed in amber
AMBERINA n type of glassware
AMBERITE n powder like amber
AMBEROID n synthetic amber
AMBEROUS adj like amber
AMBERS ▸ amber
AMBERY adj like amber
AMBIANCE same as ▸ **ambience**
AMBIENCE n atmosphere of a place
AMBIENT, -S adj surrounding ▷ n ambient music

AMBIT, -S n limits or boundary

AMBITION n desire for success

AMBITS ► ambit

AMBITTY adj crystalline and brittle

AMBIVERT n person who is intermediate between an extrovert and an introvert

AMBLE, -D, -S vb walk at a leisurely pace ▷ n leisurely walk or pace

AMBLER -S

AMBLING, -S n walking at a leisurely pace

AMBO, -NES, -S n early Christian pulpit

AMBOINA, -S same as ► amboyna

AMBONES ► ambo

AMBOS ► ambo

AMBOYNA, -S n mottled curly-grained wood

AMBRIES ► ambry

AMBROID, -S same as ► amberoid

AMBROSIA n anything delightful to taste or smell

AMBRY, AMBRIES n cupboard in the wall of a church

AMBSACE, -S n double ace, the lowest throw at dice

AMBULANT adj moving about from place to place

AMBULATE vb wander about or move from one place to another

AMBUSH, -ED, -ES n act of waiting in a concealed position to make a surprise attack ▷ vb attack from a concealed position

AMBUSHER

AME, -S n soul

AMEARST old form of ► amerce

AMEBA, -E, -S same as ► amoeba

AMEBAN

AMEBEAN same as ► amoebean

AMEBIC ► ameba

AMEBOID same as ► amoeboid

AMEER, -S n (formerly) the ruler of Afghanistan

AMEERATE n country ruled by an ameer

AMEERS ► ameer

AMEIOSIS, AMEIOSES n absence of pairing of chromosomes during meiosis

AMELCORN n variety of wheat

AMELIA, -S n congenital absence of arms or legs

AMEN, -ED, -ING, -S n term used at the end of a prayer or religious statement ▷ vb say amen

AMENABLE adj likely or willing to cooperate

AMENABLY

AMENAGE, -D, -S vb tame

AMEND, -ED, -ING vb make small changes

AMENDE, -S n public apology

AMENDED ► amend

AMENDER, -S ► amend

AMENDES ► amende

AMENDING ► amend

AMENDS n recompense for injury, insult, etc

AMENE adj pleasant

AMENED ► amen

AMENING ► amen

AMENITY n useful or enjoyable feature

AMENS ► amen

AMENT, -S n catkin

AMENTA ► amentum

AMENTAL ► amentum

AMENTIA, -S n old word for congenital mental disability

AMENTS ► ament

AMENTUM, AMENTA same as ► ament

AMERCE, -D, -S, AMERCING vb punish by a fine

AMERCER -S

AMES ► ame

AMESACE, -S same as ► ambsace

AMETHYST n bluish-violet variety of quartz used as a gemstone ▷ adj purple or violet

AMI n male friend

AMIA, -S n species of fish

AMIABLE adj friendly, pleasant-natured

AMIABLY

AMIANTUS n amianthus

AMIAS ► amia

AMICABLE adj friendly

AMICABLY

AMICE, -S n item of clothing

AMICUS, AMICI n Latin for friend

AMID prep in the middle of, among ▷ n amide

AMIDASE, -S n enzyme

AMIDE, -S n any organic compound containing the group –CONH2

AMIDIC

AMIDIN, -S n form of starch

AMIDINE, -S n crystalline compound

AMIDINS ► amidin

AMIDMOST adv in the middle

AMIDO adj containing amide

AMIDOGEN n chemical compound derived from ammonia

AMIDOL, -S n chemical used in developing photographs

AMIDONE, -S n pain-killing drug

AMIDS same as ► amid

AMIDSHIP adj in the middle of a ship

AMIDST same as ► amid

AMIE, -S n female friend

AMIGA, -S n Spanish female friend

AMIGO, -S n friend

AMILDAR, -S n manager in India

AMIN, -S same as ► amine

AMINE, -S n chemical

AMINIC

AMINITY n amenity

AMINO, -S n as in **amino acid** type of organic compound which is an essential component of proteins

AMINS ► amin

AMIR, -S n (formerly) the ruler of Afghanistan

AMIRATE -S

AMIS, -ES archaic form of ► amice

AMISS, -ES adv wrongly, badly ▷ adj wrong, faulty ▷ n evil deed

AMISSING adj missing

AMITIES ► amity

AMITOSIS, AMITOSES n unusual form of cell division

AMITOTIC

AMITROLE n pesticide

AMITY, AMITIES n friendship

AMLA, -S n species of Indian tree

AMMAN, -S same as ► amtman

AMMETER, -S n instrument for measuring electric current

AMMINE, -S n chemical compound

AMMINO adj containing ammonia molecules

AMMIRAL, -S old word for ► admiral

AMMO, -S n ammunition

AMMOCETE n ammocoete

AMMOLITE n fossilized ammonite shell

AMMON, -S n Asian wild sheep

AMMONAL, -S n explosive

AMMONATE same as ► ammine

AMMONIA, -S n strong-smelling alkaline gas containing hydrogen and nitrogen

A

AMMONIAC n strong-smelling gum resin obtained from the stems of a N Asian plant

AMMONIAS ► ammonia

AMMONIC adj of ammonia

AMMONIFY vb treat or impregnate with ammonia or a compound of ammonia

AMMONITE n fossilized spiral shell of an extinct sea creature

AMMONIUM n type of monovalent chemical group

AMMONO adj using ammonia

AMMONOID n type of fossil

AMMONS ► ammon

AMMOS ► ammo

AMNESIA, -S n loss of memory

AMNESIAC

AMNESIC -S

AMNESTIC adj relating to amnesia

AMNESTY n general pardon for offences against a government ▷ vb overlook or forget (an offence)

AMNIA ► amnion

AMNIC adj relating to amnion

AMNIO, -S n amniocentesis

AMNION, AMNIA, -S n innermost of two membranes enclosing an embryo

AMNIONIC

AMNIOS ► amnio

AMNIOTE, -S n group of animals

AMNIOTIC adj of or relating to the amnion

AMOEBA, -E, -S n microscopic single-celled animal able to change its shape

AMOEBAN

AMOEBEAN same as > amoebaean

AMOEBIC ► amoeba

AMOEBOID adj of, related to, or resembling amoebae

AMOK, -S n frenzied state

AMOKURA, -S n type of sea bird

AMOLE, -S n American plant

AMOMUM, -S n plant of ginger family

AMONG prep in the midst of

AMONGST same as ► among

AMOOVE, -D, -S, AMOOVING vb stir someone's emotions

AMORAL adj without moral standards

AMORALLY

AMORANCE n condition of being in love

AMORANT

AMORCE, -S n small percussion cap

AMORET, -S n sweetheart

AMORETTO, AMORETTI n (esp in painting) a small chubby naked boy representing a cupid

AMORINO, AMORINI same as ► amoretto

AMORISM, -S ► amorist

AMORIST, -S n lover or a writer about love

AMOROSO, -S adv (to be played) lovingly ▷ n sherry

AMOROUS adj feeling, showing, or relating to love

AMORT adj in low spirits

AMORTISE same as ► amortize

AMORTIZE vb pay off (a debt) gradually by periodic transfers to a sinking fund

AMOSITE, -S n form of asbestos

AMOTION, -S n act of removing

AMOUNT, -ED, -S n extent or quantity ▷ vb be equal or add up to

AMOUR, -S n love affair

AMOVE, -D, -S, AMOVING vb stir someone's emotions

AMOWT, -S same as ► amaut

AMP, -ED, -ING, -S n ampere ▷ vb excite or become excited

AMPASSY n ampersand

AMPED ► amp

AMPERAGE n strength of an electric current measured in amperes

AMPERE, -S n basic unit of electric current

AMPHIBIA n class of amphibians

AMPHIOXI > amphioxus

AMPHIPOD n type of marine or freshwater crustacean with a flat body

AMPHORA, -E, -S n two-handled ancient Greek or Roman jar

AMPHORAL

AMPHORIC adj resembling the sound of blowing into a bottle

AMPING ► amp

AMPLE, -R, -ST adj more than sufficient

AMPLEXUS n mating in amphibians

AMPLIFY vb increase the strength of (a current or sound signal)

AMPLY adv fully or generously

AMPOULE, -S n small sealed glass vessel

AMPS ► amp

AMPUL, -S n ampoule

AMPULE, -S same as ► ampoule

AMPULLA, -E n dilated end part of certain tubes in the body

AMPULLAR

AMPULS ► ampul

AMPUTATE vb cut off (a limb or part of a limb) for medical reasons

AMPUTEE, -S n person who has had a limb amputated

AMREETA, -S same as ► amrita

AMRIT, -S n liquid used in the Amrit Ceremony

AMRITA, -S n ambrosia of the gods that bestows immortality

AMRITS ► amrit

AMTMAN, -S n magistrate in parts of Europe

AMTRAC, -S n amphibious tracked vehicle

AMTRACK, -S same as ► amtrac

AMTRACS ► amtrac

AMTRAK, -S same as ► amtrac

AMU, -S n unit of mass

AMUCK, -S same as ► amok

AMULET, -S n something carried or worn as a protection against evil

AMULETIC

AMUS ► amu

AMUSABLE adj capable of being amused

AMUSE, -D, -S vb cause to laugh or smile

AMUSEDLY

AMUSER -S

AMUSETTE n type of light cannon

AMUSIA, -S n inability to recognize musical tones

AMUSIC

AMUSING adj mildly entertaining

AMUSIVE adj deceptive

AMYGDAL, -S n almond

AMYGDALA n almond-shaped part, such as a tonsil or a lobe of the cerebellum

AMYGDALE n small hole in volcanic rock filled with minerals

AMYGDALS ► amygdal

AMYGDULE same as ► amygdale

AMYL, -S n chemical compound

AMYLASE, -S n enzyme

AMYLENE, -S *another name (no longer in technical usage) for* ▸ **pentene**

AMYLIC *adj* of or derived from amyl

AMYLOGEN *n* soluble part of starch

AMYLOID, -S *n* complex protein ▸ *adj* starchlike

AMYLOSE, -S *n* type of chemical

AMYLS ▸ **amyl**

AMYLUM, -S *another name for* ▸ **starch**

AMYTAL, -S *n as in* **sodium amytal** type of sedative

AN *adj* form of a used before vowels ▸ *n* additional condition

ANA, -S *adv* in equal quantities ▸ *n* collection of reminiscences

ANABAENA *n* type of freshwater alga

ANABAS *n* type of fish

ANABASIS, ANABASES *n* military expedition to the interior of a country

ANABATIC *adj* (of air currents) rising upwards, esp up slopes

ANABLEPS *n* type of tropical freshwater fish with eyes adapted for seeing both in air and water

ANABOLIC *adj* of or relating to anabolism

ANACONDA *n* large S American snake

ANADEM, -S *n* garland for the head

ANAEMIA, -S *n* deficiency in the number of red blood cells

ANAEMIC *adj* having anaemia

ANAEROBE *n* organism that does not require oxygen

ANAGLYPH *n* type of stereoscopic picture

ANAGOGE, -S *n* allegorical interpretation
ANAGOGIC

ANAGOGY *same as* ▸ **anagoge**

ANAGRAM, -S *n* word or phrase made by rearranging the letters of another word or phrase

ANAL *adj* of the anus

ANALCIME *same as* ▸ **analcite**

ANALCITE *n* white, grey, or colourless zeolite mineral

ANALECTA *same as* ▸ **analects**

ANALECTS *pl n* selected literary passages from one or more works

ANALEMMA *n* scale shaped like a figure of eight

ANALGIA, -S *same as* ▸ **analgesia**

ANALLY ▸ **anal**

ANALOG, -S *same as* ▸ **analogue**

ANALOGA ▸ **analogon**

ANALOGIC ▸ **analogy**

ANALOGON, ANALOGA *n* analogue

ANALOGS ▸ **analog**

ANALOGUE *n* something that is similar in some respects to something else ▸ *adj* displaying information by means of a dial

ANALOGY *n* similarity in some respects

ANALYSE, -D *vb* make an analysis of (something)
ANALYSER

ANALYSIS, ANALYSES *n* separation of a whole into its parts for study and interpretation

ANALYST, -S *n* person skilled in analysis

ANALYTE, -S *n* substance that is being analysed

ANALYTIC *adj* relating to analysis ▸ *n* analytical logic

ANALYZE, -D, -S *same as* ▸ **analyse**
ANALYZER

ANAN *interj* expression of failure to understand

ANANA *n* pineapple

> More than two As on your rack is bad news, but there are a number of short words that use three As, of which this word is one.

ANANAS, -ES *n* plant related to the pineapple

ANANDA, -S *n* Buddhist principle of extreme happiness

ANANKE, -S *n* unalterable necessity

ANAPAEST *n* metrical foot of three syllables, the first two short, the last long

ANAPEST, -S *same as* ▸ **anapaest**

ANAPHASE *n* third stage of mitosis

ANAPHOR, -S *n* word referring back to a previous word

ANAPHORA *n* use of a word that has the same reference as a word used previously

ANAPHORS ▸ **anaphor**

ANARCH, -S *n* instigator or personification of anarchy

ANARCHAL ▸ **anarchy**

ANARCHIC ▸ **anarchy**

ANARCHS ▸ **anarch**

ANARCHY *n* lawlessness and disorder

ANAS ▸ **ana**

ANASARCA *n* accumulation of fluid within subcutaneous connective tissue

ANATA, -S *n* Buddhist belief

ANATASE, -S *n* rare blue or black mineral

ANATEXIS, ANATEXES *n* partial melting of rocks

ANATHEMA *n* detested person or thing

ANATMAN, -S *same as* ▸ **anata**

ANATOMIC ▸ **anatomy**

ANATOMY *n* science of the structure of the body

ANATOXIN *n* bacterial toxin used in inoculation

ANATROPY *n* plant ovule inverted by a bending of the stalk

ANATTA, -S *n* annatto

ANATTO, -S *same as* ▸ **annatto**

ANAXIAL *adj* asymmetrical

ANBURY, ANBURIES *n* soft spongy tumour occurring in horses and oxen

ANCE *dialect form of* ▸ **once**

ANCESTOR *n* person from whom one is descended

ANCESTRY *n* lineage or descent

ANCHO, -S *n* chili pepper

ANCHOR, -ED *n* heavy hooked device to fasten a ship to the sea bottom ▸ *vb* fasten with or as if with an anchor

ANCHORET *n* anchorite

ANCHORS *pl n* brakes of a motor vehicle

ANCHOS ▸ **ancho**

ANCHOVY *n* small strong-tasting fish

ANCHUSA, -S *n* Eurasian plant

ANCHUSIN *same as* ▸ **alkanet**

ANCIENT, -S *adj* dating from very long ago ▸ *n* member of a civilized nation in the ancient world, esp a Greek, Roman, or Hebrew

ANCILE, ANCILIA *n* mythical Roman shield

ANCILLA, -E, -S *n* Latin word for servant

ANCLE, -S *old spelling of* ▸ **ankle**

ANCOME, -S *n* inflammation

ANCON *n* projecting bracket

ANCONAL

ANCONE, -S *same as* ▸ **ancon**

ANCONEAL ▸ ancon
ANCONES ▸ ancone
ANCONOID ▸ ancon
ANCORA adv Italian for encore
ANCRESS n female anchorite
AND, -S n additional matter or problem
ANDANTE, -S adv (to be played) moderately slowly ▷ n passage or piece to be performed moderately slowly
ANDESINE n feldspar mineral of the plagioclase series
ANDESITE n fine-grained tan or grey volcanic rock
ANDESYTE n andesite
ANDIRON, -S n iron stand for supporting logs in a fireplace
ANDRO, -S n type of hormone
ANDROGEN n type of steroid
ANDROID, -S n robot resembling a human ▷ adj resembling a human being
ANDROS ▸ andro
ANDS ▸ and
ANDVILE, -S old form of ▸ anvil
ANE, -S Scots word for ▸ one
ANEAR, -ED, -ING, -S adv nearly ▷ vb approach
ANEATH Scots word for ▸ beneath
ANECDOTA pl n unpublished writings
ANECDOTE n short amusing account of an incident
ANECHOIC adj having a low degree of reverberation of sound
ANELACE, -S same as ▸ anlace
ANELE, -D, -S, ANELING vb anoint, esp to give extreme unction to
ANELLI pl n pasta shaped like small rings
ANEMIA, -S n anaemia
ANEMIC same as ▸ anaemic
ANEMONE, -S n plant with white, purple, or red flowers
ANEMOSIS, ANEMOSES n cracking in timber caused by wind affecting growing tree
ANENST dialect word for ▸ against
ANENT prep lying against
ANERGIA, -S n anergy
ANERGIC ▸ anergy
ANERGY, ANERGIES n lack of energy
ANERLY Scots word for ▸ only
ANEROID, -S adj not containing a liquid ▷ n barometer that does not contain liquid

ANES ▸ ane
ANESTRA ▸ anestrum
ANESTRI ▸ anestrus
ANESTRUM, ANESTRA n anestrus
ANESTRUS, ANESTRI same as ▸ anoestrus
ANETHOL, -S n substance derived from oil of anise
ANETHOLE n white water-soluble crystalline substance with a liquorice-like odour
ANETHOLS ▸ anethol
ANETIC adj medically soothing
ANEURIN, -S a less common name for ▸ thiamine
ANEURISM same as ▸ aneurysm
ANEURYSM n permanent swelling of a blood vessel
ANEW adv once more
ANGA, -S n part in Indian music
ANGAKOK, -S n Inuit shaman
ANGARIA, -S n species of shellfish
ANGARY, ANGARIES n right to use the property of a neutral state during a war
ANGAS ▸ anga
ANGEKKOK n Inuit shaman
ANGEKOK, -S n Inuit shaman
ANGEL, -ED, -ING, -S n spiritual being believed to be an attendant or messenger of God ▷ vb provide financial support for
ANGELIC adj very kind, pure, or beautiful
ANGELICA n aromatic plant
ANGELING ▸ angel
ANGELS ▸ angel
ANGELUS n series of prayers
ANGER, -ED, -ING, -S n fierce displeasure or extreme annoyance ▷ vb make (someone) angry
ANGERLY adv old form of angrily
ANGERS ▸ anger
ANGICO, -S n South American tree
ANGINA, -S n heart disorder causing sudden severe chest pains
ANGINAL
ANGINOSE
ANGINOUS
ANGIOMA, -S n tumour consisting of a mass of blood vessels or lymphatic vessels
ANGKLUNG n Asian musical instrument
ANGLE, -D, -S n space between or shape formed

by two lines or surfaces that meet ▷ vb bend or place (something) at an angle
ANGLEDUG n earthworm
ANGLEPOD n American wild flower
ANGLER, -S n person who fishes with a hook and line
ANGLES ▸ angle
ANGLICE adv in English
ANGLIFY same as ▸ anglicize
ANGLING, -S n art or sport of fishing with a hook and line
ANGLIST, -S same as ▸ anglicist
ANGLO, -S n White inhabitant of the US not of Latin extraction
ANGOLA same as ▸ angora
ANGORA, -S n variety of goat, cat, or rabbit with long silky hair
ANGRIER ▸ angry
ANGRIES ▸ angry
ANGRIEST ▸ angry
ANGRILY ▸ angry
ANGRY, ANGRIER, ANGRIES, ANGRIEST adj full of anger ▷ n angry person
ANGST, -S n feeling of anxiety
ANGSTIER ▸ angsty
ANGSTROM n unit of length used to measure wavelengths
ANGSTS ▸ angst
ANGSTY, ANGSTIER adj displaying angst
ANGUINE adj of, relating to, or similar to a snake
ANGUIPED adj having snakes for legs ▷ n mythological Persian creature with snakes for legs
ANGUISH n great mental pain ▷ vb afflict or be afflicted with anguish
ANGULAR adj (of a person) lean and bony
ANGULATE adj having angles or an angular shape ▷ vb make or become angular
ANGULOSE same as ▸ angulous
ANGULOUS adj having angles
ANHEDRAL n downward inclination of an aircraft wing in relation to the lateral axis
ANHINGA, -S n type of bird
ANI, -S n tropical bird
ANICCA, -S n Buddhism belief
ANICONIC adj (of images of deities, symbols, etc) not portrayed in a human or animal form
ANICUT, -S n dam in India
ANIGH adv near

ANIGHT *adv* at night
ANIL, -S *n* West Indian shrub
ANILE *adj* of or like a feeble old woman
ANILIN, -S *n* aniline
ANILINE, -S *n* colourless oily liquid
ANILINS ▸ anilin
ANILITY ▸ anile
ANILS ▸ anil
ANIMA, -S *n* feminine principle as present in the male unconscious
ANIMACY *n* state of being animate
ANIMAL, -S *n* living creature capable of voluntary motion, esp one other than a human being ▸ *adj* of animals
ANIMALIC
ANIMALLY *adv* physically
ANIMALS ▸ animal
ANIMAS ▸ anima
ANIMATE, -S *vb* give life to ▸ *adj* having life
ANIMATED *adj* interesting and lively
ANIMATER *same as* ▸ **animator**
ANIMATES ▸ animate
ANIMATI ▸ animato
ANIMATIC *n* animated film sequence
ANIMATO, ANIMATI, -S *n* piece of music performed in a lively manner
ANIMATOR *n* person who makes animated cartoons
ANIMATOS ▸ animato
ANIME, -S *n* type of Japanese animation
ANIMI ▸ animus
ANIMISM, -S *n* belief that natural objects possess souls
ANIMIST -S
ANIMUS, ANIMI, -ES *n* hatred, animosity
ANION, -S *n* ion with negative charge
ANIONIC
ANIRIDIA *n* absence of the iris, due to a congenital condition or an injury
ANIRIDIC
ANIS ▸ ani
ANISE, -S *n* plant with liquorice-flavoured seeds
ANISEED, -S *n* liquorice-flavoured seeds of the anise plant
ANISES ▸ anise
ANISETTE *n* liquorice-flavoured liqueur made from aniseed
ANISIC ▸ anise

ANISOLE, -S *n* colourless pleasant-smelling liquid used as a solvent
ANKER, -S *n* old liquid measure for wine
ANKERITE *n* greyish to brown mineral that resembles dolomite
ANKERS ▸ anker
ANKH, -S *n* ancient Egyptian symbol
ANKLE, -D, -S, ANKLING *n* joint between the foot and leg ▸ *vb* move
ANKLET, -S *n* ornamental chain worn round the ankle
ANKLING ▸ ankle
ANKLONG, -S *n* Asian musical instrument
ANKLUNG, -S *n* Asian musical instrument
ANKUS, -ES *n* stick used, esp in India, for goading elephants
ANKUSH, -ES *n* Indian weapon
ANKYLOSE *vb* (of bones in a joint, etc) to fuse or stiffen by ankylosis
ANLACE, -S *n* medieval short dagger with a broad tapering blade
ANLAGE, -N, -S *n* organ or part in the earliest stage of development
ANLAS, -ES *same as* ▸ **anlace**
ANN, -S *n* old Scots word for a widow's pension
ANNA, -S *n* former Indian coin worth one sixteenth of a rupee
ANNAL, -S *n* recorded events of one year
ANNALISE *vb* record in annals
ANNALIST ▸ annal
ANNALIZE *vb* record in annals
ANNALS ▸ annal
ANNAS ▸ anna
ANNAT, -S *n* old Scots word for a widow's pension
ANNATES *pl n* money paid to the Pope
ANNATS ▸ annat
ANNATTA, -S *n* annatto
ANNATTO, -S *n* tropical tree
ANNEAL, -ED, -S *vb* toughen by heating and slow cooling ▸ *n* act of annealing
ANNEALER
ANNELID, -S *n* type of worm with a segmented body
ANNEX, -ED, -ING *vb* seize (territory)
ANNEXE, -S *n* extension to a building
ANNEXED ▸ annex
ANNEXES ▸ annexe
ANNEXING ▸ annex

ANNEXION *n* old form of annexation
ANNEXURE *n* something that is added
ANNICUT, -S *n* dam in India
ANNO *adv* Latin for in the year
ANNONA, -S *n* American tree or shrub
ANNOTATE *vb* add notes to (a written work)
ANNOUNCE *vb* make known publicly
ANNOY, -ED, -S *vb* irritate or displease
ANNOYER -S
ANNOYING *adj* causing irritation or displeasure
ANNOYS ▸ annoy
ANNS ▸ ann
ANNUAL, -S *adj* happening once a year ▸ *n* plant that completes its life cycle in a year
ANNUALLY
ANNUITY *n* fixed sum paid every year
ANNUL, -LED, -S *vb* declare (something, esp a marriage) invalid
ANNULAR, -S *adj* ring-shaped ▸ *n* ring finger
ANNULATE *adj* having, composed of, or marked with rings ▸ *n* annelid
ANNULET, -S *n* moulding in the form of a ring
ANNULI ▸ annulus
ANNULLED ▸ annul
ANNULOSE *adj* having a body formed of a series of rings
ANNULS ▸ annul
ANNULUS, ANNULI *n* area between two concentric circles
ANOA, -S *n* type of small cattle
ANOBIID, -S *n* any type of beetle
ANODAL ▸ anode
ANODALLY ▸ anode
ANODE, -S *n* positive electrode in a battery, valve, etc
ANODIC
ANODISE, -D, -S *same as* ▸ **anodize**
ANODISER *same as* ▸ **anodizer**
ANODISES ▸ anodise
ANODIZE, -D, -S *vb* coat (metal) with a protective oxide film by electrolysis
ANODIZER *n* something that anodizes
ANODIZES ▸ anodize
ANODYNE, -S *n* something that relieves pain or distress**

A

▷ *adj* relieving pain or distress
ANODYNIC
ANOESIS, ANOESES *n* feeling without understanding
ANOESTRA > anoestrus
ANOESTRI > anoestrus

This is the plural of **anoestrus**, a period of sexual inactivity between periods of oestrus. It is one of the most frequently played of all 8-letter bonuses, and the same combination of letters yields no fewer than six other words: **arsonite, notaries, notarise, rosinate** and **senorita**. It is well worth becoming acquainted with commonly occurring multiple-choice letter combinations like this, as it gives your game great flexibility.

ANOETIC > anoesis
ANOINT, -ED, -S *vb* smear with oil as a sign of consecration
ANOINTER
ANOLE, -S *n* type of lizard
ANOLYTE, -S *n* part of electrolyte around anode
ANOMALY *n* something that deviates from the normal, irregularity
ANOMIC > anomie
ANOMIE, -S *n* lack of social or moral standards
ANOMY *same as* ▶ **anomie**
ANON *adv* in a short time, soon
ANONYM, -S *n* anonymous person or publication
ANONYMA, -S *n* main vessel in the arterial network
ANONYMS ▶ anonym
ANOOPSIA *n* squint in which the eye turns upwards
ANOPIA, -S *n* inability to see
ANOPSIA, -S *n* squint in which the eye turns upwards
ANORAK, -S *n* light waterproof hooded jacket
ANORETIC *n* anorectic
ANOREXIA *n* psychological disorder characterized by fear of becoming fat and refusal to eat
ANOREXIC
ANOREXY *old name for* ▶ **anorexia**
ANORTHIC *another word for* > **triclinic**
ANOSMIA, -S *n* loss of the sense of smell
ANOSMIC

ANOTHER *adj* one more
ANOUGH *adj* enough
ANOUROUS *adj* having no tail
ANOVULAR *adj* without ovulation
ANOW *adj* old form of enough
ANOXEMIA *same as* > **anoxaemia**
ANOXEMIC
ANOXIA, -S *n* lack or absence of oxygen
ANOXIC
ANS *pl n* as in **ifs and ans** things that might have happened, but which did not
ANSA, -E *n* either end of Saturn's rings
ANSATE *adj* having a handle or handle-like part
ANSATED *adj* ansate
ANSERINE *adj* of or resembling a goose ▷ *n* chemical compound
ANSEROUS *same as* ▶ **anserine**
ANSWER, -ED, -S *n* reply to a question, request, letter, etc ▷ *vb* give an answer (to)
ANSWERER
ANT, -S *n* small insect living in highly-organized colonies
ANTA, -E, -S *n* pilaster
ANTACID, -S *n* substance that counteracts acidity ▷ *adj* having the properties of this substance
ANTAE ▶ anta
ANTALGIC *n* pain-relieving drug
ANTAR, -S *old word for* ▶ **cave**
ANTARA, -S *n* South American panpipes
ANTARS ▶ antar
ANTAS ▶ anta
ANTBEAR, -S *n* aardvark
ANTBIRD, -S *n* South American bird
ANTE, -D, -ED, -ING, -S *n* player's stake in poker ▷ *vb* place (one's stake) in poker
ANTECEDE *vb* go before, as in time, order, etc
ANTED ▶ ante
ANTEDATE *vb* precede in time ▷ *n* earlier date
ANTEED ▶ ante
ANTEFIX, -A *n* carved ornament
ANTEING ▶ ante
ANTELOPE *n* deerlike mammal with long legs and horns

ANTENATI *pl n* people born before certain date
ANTENNA, -E, -S *n* insect's feeler
ANTENNAL
ANTEPAST *n* appetizer
ANTERIOR *adj* the front
ANTEROOM *n* small room leading into a larger one, often used as a waiting room
ANTES ▶ ante
ANTETYPE *n* earlier form
ANTEVERT *vb* displace (an organ or part) by tilting it forward
ANTHELIA > anthelion
ANTHELIX *n* prominent curved fold of cartilage just inside the outer rim of the external ear
ANTHEM, -ED, -S *n* song of loyalty, esp to a country ▷ *vb* provide with an anthem
ANTHEMIA > anthemion
ANTHEMIC ▶ anthem
ANTHEMIS *n* genus of herbs of Mediterranean and SW Asia
ANTHEMS ▶ anthem
ANTHER, -S *n* part of a flower's stamen containing pollen
ANTHERAL
ANTHERID *n* antheridium
ANTHERS ▶ anther
ANTHESIS, ANTHESES *n* time when a flower begins reproductive cycle
ANTHILL, -S *n* mound near an ants' nest
ANTHODIA > anthodium
ANTHOID *adj* resembling a flower
ANTHRAX *n* dangerous disease of cattle and sheep, communicable to humans
ANTHRO, -S *n* short for anthropology
ANTI, -S *adj* opposed (to) ▷ *n* opponent of a party, policy, or attitude
ANTIACNE *adj* inhibiting the development of acne
ANTIAIR *adj* countering attack by aircraft or missile
ANTIAR, -S *another name for* ▶ **upas**
ANTIARIN *n* poison derived from antiar
ANTIARS ▶ antiar
ANTIATOM *n* atom composed of antiparticles
ANTIBIAS *adj* countering bias
ANTIBODY *n* protein produced in the blood, which destroys bacteria
ANTIBOSS *adj* acting against bosses

ANTIBUG adj acting against computer bugs

ANTIC n actor in a ludicrous or grotesque part ▷ adj fantastic

ANTICAL adj position of plant parts

ANTICAR n opposed to cars

ANTICISE same as ▸ **anticize**

ANTICITY adj opposed to cities

ANTICIZE vb play absurdly

ANTICK, -ED, -S vb perform antics

ANTICKE, -S archaic form of ▸ **antique**

ANTICKED ▸ **antick**

ANTICKES ▸ **anticke**

ANTICKS ▸ **antick**

ANTICLY adv grotesquely

ANTICOLD adj preventing or fighting the common cold

ANTICOUS adj on the part of a flower furthest from the stem

ANTICS pl n absurd acts or postures

ANTICULT n organization that is opposed to religious cults

ANTIDORA > **antidoron**

ANTIDOTE n substance that counteracts a poison ▷ vb counteract with an antidote

ANTIDRUG adj intended to discourage illegal drug use

ANTIDUNE n type of sand hill or inclined bedding plane

ANTIENT, -S old spelling of ▸ **ancient**

ANTIFAT adj acting to remove or prevent fat

ANTIFLU adj acting against influenza

ANTIFOAM adj allowing gas to escape rather than form foam

ANTIFOG adj preventing the buildup of moisture on a surface

ANTIFUR adj opposed to the wearing of fur garments

ANTIGANG adj designed to restrict the activities of criminal gangs

ANTIGAY adj hostile to homosexuals

ANTIGEN, -S n substance causing the blood to produce antibodies

ANTIGENE n antigen

ANTIGENS ▸ **antigen**

ANTIGUN adj opposed to the possession of guns

ANTIHERO n central character in a book, film, etc, who lacks the traditional heroic virtues

ANTIJAM adj preventing jamming

ANTIKING n rival to an established king

ANTILEAK adj preventing leaks

ANTILEFT adj opposed to the left wing in politics

ANTILIFE adj opposed to living in harmony with the natural order

ANTILOCK adj designed to prevent overbraking

ANTILOG, -S n number whose logarithm to a given base is a given number

ANTILOGY n contradiction in terms

ANTIMALE adj opposed to men

ANTIMAN adj opposed to men

ANTIMASK n interlude in a masque

ANTIMERE n body part or organ that mirrors a similar structure on the other side

ANTIMINE adj designed to counteract landmines

ANTIMONY n brittle silvery-white metallic element

ANTIMUON n antiparticle of a muon

ANTING, -S n rubbing of ants by birds on their feathers

ANTINODE n point of amplitude of displacement of opposite value to a node

ANTINOME n opposite

ANTINOMY n contradiction between two laws or principles that are reasonable in themselves

ANTINUKE same as > **antinuker**

ANTIPHON n hymn sung in alternate parts by two groups of singers

ANTIPILL adj (of a material) not forming pills

ANTIPODE n exact or direct opposite

ANTIPOLE n opposite pole

ANTIPOPE n pope set up in opposition to the one chosen by church laws

ANTIPYIC n drug acting against suppuration

ANTIQUE, -D, -S n object of an earlier period, valued for its beauty, workmanship, or age ▷ adj made in an earlier period ▷ vb give an antique appearance to

ANTIQUER n collector of antiques

ANTIQUES ▸ **antique**

ANTIQUEY adj having the appearance of an antique

ANTIRED adj of a particular colour of antiquark

ANTIRIOT adj designed for the control of crowds

ANTIROCK adj designed to prevent a vehicle from rocking

ANTIROLL adj designed to prevent a vehicle from tilting

ANTIRUST adj (of a product or procedure) effective against rust ▷ n substance or device that prevents rust

ANTIS ▸ **anti**

ANTISAG adj preventing sagging

ANTISERA > **antiserum**

ANTISHIP adj designed for attacking ships

ANTISKID adj intended to prevent skidding

ANTISLIP adj acting to prevent slipping

ANTISMOG adj reducing smog

ANTISNOB n person opposed to snobbery

ANTISPAM adj intended to prevent spam

ANTISTAT n substance preventing static electricity

ANTITANK adj (of weapons) designed to destroy military tanks

ANTITAX adj opposed to taxation

ANTITHET n example of antithesis

ANTITYPE n something foreshadowed by a type or symbol

ANTIWAR adj opposed to war

ANTIWEAR adj preventing wear

ANTIWEED adj killing or preventing weeds

ANTLER, -S n branched horn of a male deer

ANTLERED adj having antlers

ANTLERS ▸ **antler**

ANTLIA, -E n butterfly proboscis

ANTLIATE adj relating to antlia

ANTLIKE adj of or like an ant or ants

ANTLION, -S n type of insect resembling a dragonfly

ANTONYM, -S n word that means the opposite of another

ANTONYMY n use of antonyms

A

ANTPITTA n S American bird whose diet consists mainly of ants

ANTRA ► antrum

ANTRAL ► antrum

ANTRE, -S n cavern or cave

ANTRORSE adj directed or pointing upwards or forwards

ANTRUM, ANTRA, -S n natural cavity, esp in a bone

ANTS ► ant

ANTSY, ANTSIER, ANTSIEST adj restless, nervous, and impatient

ANURA pl n order of animals that comprises frogs and toads

ANURAL adj without a tail

ANURAN, -S n type of amphibian

ANURESIS, ANURESES n inability to urinate

ANURETIC

ANURIA, -S n result of a kidney disorder

ANURIC

ANUROUS adj lacking a tail

ANUS, -ES n opening at the end of the alimentary canal, through which faeces are discharged

ANVIL, -ED, -ING, -LED, -S n heavy iron block on which metals are hammered into particular shapes ▷ vb forge on an anvil

ANVILTOP n type of stormcloud formation

ANXIETY n state of being anxious

ANXIOUS adj worried and tense

ANY adj one or some, no matter which ▷ adv at all

ANYBODY n any person at random

ANYHOW adv anyway

ANYMORE adv at present

ANYON, -S n (in mathematics) projective representation of a Lie group

ANYONE, -S pron any person ▷ n any person at random

ANYONS ► anyon

ANYPLACE adv in, at, or to any unspecified place

ANYROAD a northern English dialect word for ► anyway

ANYTHING pron any object, event, or action whatever ▷ n any thing at random

ANYTIME adv at any time

ANYWAY adv at any rate, nevertheless

ANYWAYS nonstandard word for ► anyway

ANYWHEN adv at any time

ANYWHERE adv in, at, or to any place

ANYWISE adv in any way or manner

ANZIANI pl n Italian word for councillors

AORIST, -S n tense of the verb in classical Greek

AORISTIC

AORTA, -E, -S n main artery of the body, carrying oxygen-rich blood from the heart

AORTAL

AORTIC

AORTITIS n inflammation of the aorta

AOUDAD, -S n wild mountain sheep

APACE adv swiftly

APACHE, -S n Parisian gangster or ruffian

APADANA, -S n ancient Persian palace hall

APAGE interj Greek word meaning go away

APAGOGE, -S n reduction to absurdity

APAGOGIC

APAID ► apay

APANAGE, -S same as ► appanage

APANAGED adj having apanage

APANAGES ► apanage

APAREJO, -S n kind of packsaddle made of stuffed leather cushions

APART adv to pieces or in pieces

APATETIC adj of or relating to coloration that disguises and protects an animal

APATHY, APATHIES n lack of interest or enthusiasm

APATITE, -S n pale green to purple mineral, found in igneous rocks

APAY, APAID, -D, -ING, -S vb old word meaning satisfy

APE, -D, -S, APING n tailless monkey such as the chimpanzee or gorilla ▷ vb imitate

APEAK adj in a vertical or almost vertical position

APED ► ape

APEDOM, -S n state of being an ape

APEEK adv nautical word meaning vertically

APEHOOD, -S n state of being ape

APELIKE ► ape

APEMAN, APEMEN n primate thought to have been the forerunner of humans

APEPSIA, -S n digestive disorder

APEPSY, APEPSIES n apepsia

APER, -S n person who apes

APERCU, -S n outline

APERIENT adj having a mild laxative effect ▷ n mild laxative

APERIES ► apery

APERITIF n alcoholic drink taken before a meal

APERS ► aper

APERT adj open

APERTURE n opening or hole

APERY, APERIES n imitative behaviour

APES ► ape

APETALY > apetalous

APEX, -ES n highest point

APGAR n as in **apgar score** system for determining the condition of an infant at birth

APHAGIA, -S n refusal or inability to swallow

APHAKIA, -S n absence of the lens of an eye

APHANITE n type of fine-grained rock, such as a basalt

APHASIA, -S n disorder of the central nervous system

APHASIAC

APHASIC -S

APHELIA ► aphelion

APHELIAN ► aphelion

APHELION, APHELIA n point of a planet's orbit that is farthest from the sun

APHESIS, APHESES n gradual disappearance of an unstressed vowel at the beginning of a word

APHETIC

APHETISE vb lose a vowel at the beginning of a word

APHETIZE vb lose a vowel at the beginning of a word

APHICIDE n substance for killing aphids

APHID, -S n small insect which sucks the sap from plants

APHIDES ► aphis

APHIDIAN ► aphid

APHIDS ► aphid

APHIS, APHIDES n type of aphid such as the blackfly

APHOLATE n type of pesticide

APHONIA, -S n loss of the voice caused by damage to the vocal tract

APHONIC -S adj affected with aphonia ▷ n person affected with aphonia

APHONIES ► aphony

APHONOUS ▶ aphonia

APHONY, APHONIES same as ▶ **aphonia**

APHORISE same as ▶ **aphorize**

APHORISM n short clever saying expressing a general truth

APHORIST

APHORIZE vb write or speak in aphorisms

APHOTIC adj characterized by or growing in the absence of light

APHTHA, -E n small ulceration

APHTHOUS

APHYLLY > aphyllous

APIAN adj of, relating to, or resembling bees

APIARIAN adj of or relating to the breeding and care of bees ▷ n apiarist

APIARIES ▶ apiary

APIARIST n beekeeper

APIARY, APIARIES n place where bees are kept

APICAL, -S adj of, at, or being an apex ▷ n sound made with the tip of the tongue

APICALLY

APICES plural of ▶ **apex**

APICIAN adj of fine or dainty food

APICULUS, APICULI n short sharp point

APIECE adv each

APIEZON adj as in **apiezon oil** oil left by distillation

APIMANIA n extreme enthusiasm for bees

APING ▶ ape

APIOL, -S n substance derived from parsley seeds

APIOLOGY n study of bees

APIOLS ▶ apiol

APISH adj stupid or foolish

APISHLY

APISM, -S n behaviour like an ape

APLANAT, -S n aplanatic lens

APLASIA, -S n congenital absence of an organ

APLASTIC adj relating to or characterized by aplasia

APLENTY adv in plenty

APLITE, -S n type of igneous rock

APLITIC

APLOMB, -S n calm self-possession

APLUSTRE n stern ornament on an ancient Greek ship

APNEA, -S same as ▶ **apnoea**

APNEAL

APNEIC

APNEUSIS, APNEUSES n gasping inhalation followed by short exhalation

APNOEA, -S n temporary inability to breathe

APNOEAL

APNOEIC

APO, -S n type of protein

APOAPSIS, APOAPSES n point in an orbit furthest from the object orbited

APOCARP, -S n apocarpous gynoecium or fruit

APOCARPY n presence of many carpels

APOCOPE, -S n omission of the final sound or sounds of a word

APOCOPIC

APOCRINE adj denoting a type of glandular secretion

APOD, -S n animal without feet

APODAL adj (of snakes, eels, etc) without feet

APODE, -S n animal without feet

APODOSIS, APODOSES n consequent of a conditional statement

APODOUS same as ▶ **apodal**

APODS ▶ apod

APOGAEIC ▶ apogee

APOGAMIC ▶ apogamy

APOGAMY n type of reproduction in some ferns

APOGEAL ▶ apogee

APOGEAN ▶ apogee

APOGEE, -S n point of moon's orbit

APOGEIC

APOGRAPH n exact copy

APOLLO, -S n strikingly handsome youth

APOLOG, -S same as ▶ **apologue**

APOLOGAL ▶ apologue

APOLOGIA n formal written defence of a cause

APOLOGS ▶ apolog

APOLOGUE n allegory or moral fable

APOLOGY n expression of regret for wrongdoing

APOLUNE, -S n point in a lunar orbit

APOMICT, -S n organism, esp a plant, produced by apomixis

APOMIXIS, APOMIXES n type of asexual reproduction

APOOP adv on the poop deck

APOPHONY n change in the quality of vowels

APOPHYGE n outward curve at each end of the shaft of a column, adjoining the base or capital

APOPLAST n nonprotoplasmic component of a plant

APOPLEX vb afflict with apoplexy

APOPLEXY n stroke

APORETIC ▶ aporia

APORIA, -S n doubt, real or professed, about what to do or say

APORT adj on or towards the port side

APOS ▶ apo

APOSITIA n unwillingness to eat

APOSITIC

APOSPORY n development of the gametophyte from the sporophyte without the formation of spores

APOSTACY same as ▶ **apostasy**

APOSTASY n abandonment of one's religious faith or other belief

APOSTATE n person who has abandoned his or her religion, political party, or cause ▷ adj guilty of apostasy

APOSTIL, -S n marginal note

APOSTLE, -S n one of the twelve disciples chosen by Christ to preach his gospel

APOTHECE n obsolete word for shop

APOTHEGM n short cryptic remark containing some general or generally accepted truth; maxim

APOTHEM, -S n geometrical term

APOZEM, -S n medicine dissolved in water

APP, -S n application program

APPAID ▶ appay

APPAIR, -ED, -S vb old form of impair

APPAL, -S vb dismay, terrify

APPALL, -ED, -S same as ▶ **appal**

APPALS ▶ appal

APPALTO, APPALTI n Italian word for contact

APPANAGE n land granted by a king for the support of a younger son

APPARAT, -S n Communist Party organization

APPAREL, -S n clothing ▷ vb clothe, adorn, etc

APPARENT adj readily seen, obvious ▷ n heir apparent

A

APPAY, APPAID, -D, -ING, -S old word for ▶ **satisfy**

APPEACH old word for ▶ **accuse**

APPEAL, -ED, -S vb make an earnest request ▷ n earnest request

APPEALER

APPEAR, -ED, -S vb become visible or present

APPEARER

APPEASE, -D, -S vb pacify (a person) by yielding to his or her demands

APPEASER

APPEL, -S n stamp of the foot, used to warn of one's intent to attack

APPELLEE n person who is accused or appealed against

APPELLOR n person initiating a law case

APPELS ▶ **appel**

APPEND, -ED, -S vb join on, add

APPENDIX n separate additional material at the end of a book

APPENDS ▶ **append**

APPERIL, -S old word for ▶ **peril**

APPERILL old word for ▶ **peril**

APPERILS ▶ **apperil**

APPESTAT n part of the brain that regulates hunger and satiety

APPETENT adj eager

APPETISE vb stimulate the appetite

APPETITE n desire for food or drink

APPETIZE vb stimulate the appetite

APPLAUD, -S vb show approval of by clapping one's hands

APPLAUSE n approval shown by clapping one's hands

APPLE, -S n round firm fleshy fruit that grows on trees

APPLET, -S n computing program

APPLEY, APPLIEST adj resembling or tasting like an apple

APPLIED adj (of a skill, science, etc) put to practical use

APPLIER, -S ▶ **apply**

APPLIES ▶ **apply**

APPLIEST ▶ **appley**

APPLIQUE n decoration or trimming of one material sewn or otherwise fixed onto another ▷ vb sew or fix (a decoration) on as an appliqué

APPLY, APPLIES, -ING vb make a formal request

APPOINT, -S vb assign to a job or position

APPORT, -S n production of objects at a seance

APPOSE, -D, -S, APPOSING vb place side by side or near to each other

APPOSER -S

APPOSITE adj suitable, apt

APPRAISE vb estimate the value or quality of

APPRESS vb press together

APPRISE, -D, -S vb make aware (of)

APPRISER

APPRIZE, -D, -S same as ▶ **apprise**

APPRIZER

APPRO, -S n approval

APPROACH vb come near or nearer (to) ▷ n approaching or means of approaching

APPROOF, -S old word for ▶ **trial**

APPROS ▶ **appro**

APPROVAL n consent

APPROVE, -D, -S vb consider good or right

APPROVER

APPS ▶ **app**

APPUI, -S n support

APPUIED ▶ **appuy**

APPUIS ▶ **appui**

APPULSE, -S n close approach of two celestial bodies

APPUY, APPUIED, -ED, -ING, -S vb support

APRACTIC ▶ **apraxia**

APRAXIA, -S n disorder of the central nervous system

APRAXIC

APRES prep French word for after

APRICATE vb bask in sun

APRICOCK old word for ▶ **apricot**

APRICOT, -S n yellowish-orange juicy fruit like a small peach ▷ adj yellowish-orange

APRON, -ED, -ING, -S n garment worn over the front of the body to protect the clothes ▷ vb equip with an apron

APRONFUL n amount held in an apron

APRONING ▶ **apron**

APRONS ▶ **apron**

APROPOS adv appropriate(ly)

APROTIC adj (of solvents) neither accepting nor donating hydrogen ions

APSARAS n Hindu water sprite

APSE, -S n arched or domed recess, esp in a church

APSIDAL ▶ **apsis**

APSIS, APSIDES n points in the elliptical orbit of a planet or satellite

APSO, -S n Tibetan terrier

APT, -ED, -ER, -EST, -ING, -S adj having a specified tendency ▷ vb be fitting

APTAMER, -S n artificially-created DNA or RNA molecule

APTED ▶ **apt**

APTER ▶ **apt**

APTERAL adj (esp of a classical temple) not having columns at the sides

APTERIA ▶ **apterium**

APTERISM ▶ **apterous**

APTERIUM, APTERIA n bare patch on the skin of a bird

APTEROUS adj (of insects) without wings, as silverfish and springtails

APTERYX n kiwi (the bird)

APTEST ▶ **apt**

APTING ▶ **apt**

APTITUDE n natural ability

APTLY ▶ **apt**

APTNESS ▶ **apt**

APTOTE, -S n noun without inflections

APTOTIC

APTS ▶ **apt**

APYRASE, -S n enzyme

APYRETIC ▶ **apyrexia**

APYREXIA n absence of fever

AQUA, -E, -S n water

This Latin word for water, together with its plural **aquae** or **aquas**, comes up over and over again.

AQUACADE same as ▶ **aquashow**

AQUAE ▶ **aqua**

AQUAFARM vb cultivate fish or shellfish

AQUAFER, -S n aquifer

AQUAFIT, -S n type of aerobic exercise done in water

AQUALUNG n mouthpiece attached to air cylinders, worn for underwater swimming

AQUANAUT n person who lives and works underwater

AQUARIA ▶ **aquarium**

AQUARIAL ▶ **aquarium**

AQUARIAN n person who keeps an aquarium

AQUARIST n curator of an aquarium

AQUARIUM, AQUARIA n tank in which fish and other underwater creatures are kept

AQUAS ▶ aqua

AQUASHOW n exhibition of swimming and diving, often accompanied by music

AQUATIC adj living in or near water ▷ n marine or freshwater animal or plant

AQUATICS pl n water sports

AQUATINT n print like a watercolour, produced by etching copper ▷ vb etch (a block, etc) in aquatint

AQUATONE n fitness exercise in water

AQUAVIT, -S n grain- or potato-based spirit

AQUEDUCT n structure carrying water across a valley or river

AQUEOUS adj of, like, or containing water

AQUIFER, -S n deposit of rock containing water used to supply wells

AQUILINE adj (of a nose) curved like an eagle's beak

AQUILON, -S n name for the north wind

AQUIVER adv quivering

AR, -S n letter R

ARAARA, -S another name for ▶ trevally

ARABA, -S n Asian carriage

This is one of the short words that can help you deal with a surplus of As.

ARABESK, -S same as > arabesque

ARABIC adj as in **gum arabic** gum exuded by certain acacia trees

ARABICA, -S n high-quality coffee bean

ARABIN, -S n essence of gum arabic

ARABIS n type of plant

ARABISE, -D, -S vb make or become Arab

ARABIZE, -D, -S vb make or become Arab

ARABLE, -S adj suitable for growing crops on ▷ n arable land or farming

ARACEOUS same as ▶ aroid

ARACHIS n Brazilian plant

ARACHNID n eight-legged invertebrate, such as a spider, scorpion, tick, or mite

ARAISE, -D, -S, ARAISING vb old form of raise

ARAK, -S same as ▶ arrack

ARALIA, -S n type of plant

ARAME, -S n Japanese edible seaweed

ARAMID, -S n synthetic fibre

ARANEID, -S n member of the spider family

ARANEOUS adj like a spider's web

ARAPAIMA n very large primitive freshwater teleost fish that occurs in tropical S America

ARAPONGA n South American bird with a bell-like call

ARAPUNGA n South American bird with a bell-like call

ARAR, -S n African tree

ARAROBA, -S n Brazilian leguminous tree

ARARS ▶ arar

ARAYSE, -D, -S, ARAYSING vb old form of raise

ARB, -S short for > **arbitrage**

ARBA, -S n Asian carriage

ARBALEST n large medieval crossbow, usually cocked by mechanical means

ARBALIST same as ▶ arbalest

ARBAS ▶ arba

ARBELEST n arbalest

ARBITER, -S n person empowered to judge in a dispute

ARBITRAL adj of or relating to arbitration

ARBLAST, -S n arbalest

ARBOR, -ES, -S n revolving shaft or axle in a machine

ARBOREAL adj of or living in trees

ARBORED adj having arbors

ARBORES ▶ arbor

ARBORET, -S n old name for an area planted with shrubs

ARBORETA > arboretum

ARBORETS ▶ arboret

ARBORIO, -S n as in **arborio rice** variety of round-grain rice used for making risotto

ARBORISE same as ▶ arborize

ARBORIST n specialist in the cultivation of trees

ARBORIZE vb give or take on a treelike branched appearance

ARBOROUS adj of trees

ARBORS ▶ arbor

ARBOUR, -S n glade sheltered by trees

ARBOURED adj having arbours

ARBOURS ▶ arbour

ARBS ▶ arb

ARBUSCLE n small tree

ARBUTE, -S old name for ▶ arbutus

ARBUTEAN ▶ arbutus

ARBUTES ▶ arbute

ARBUTUS n evergreen shrub with strawberry-like berries

ARC, -ED, -KED, -S n part of a circle or other curve ▷ vb form an arc

ARCADE, -D, -S n covered passageway lined with shops ▷ vb provide with an arcade

ARCADIA, -S n traditional idealized rural setting

ARCADIAN n person who leads a rural life

ARCADIAS ▶ arcadia

ARCADING ▶ arcade

ARCANA, -S n either of the two divisions of a pack of tarot cards

ARCANE adj mysterious and secret

ARCANELY

ARCANIST n person with secret knowledge

ARCANUM, -S n profound secret or mystery known only to initiates

ARCATURE n small-scale arcade

ARCED ▶ arc

ARCH, -ES, -EST n curved structure supporting a bridge or roof ▷ vb (cause to) form an arch ▷ adj superior, knowing

ARCHAEA n order of prokaryotic microorganisms

ARCHAEAL same as ▶ archaean

ARCHAEAN, ARCHEAN n type of microorganism

ARCHAEI ▶ archaeus

ARCHAEON same as ▶ archaean

ARCHAEUS, ARCHAEI n spirit believed to inhabit a living thing

ARCHAIC adj ancient

ARCHAISE same as ▶ archaize

ARCHAISM n archaic word or phrase

ARCHAIST

ARCHAIZE vb give an archaic appearance or character to, as by the use of archaisms

ARCHDUKE n duke of specially high rank

ARCHEAN same as ▶ archaean

ARCHED adj provided with or spanned by an arch or arches

ARCHEI ▶ archeus

A

ARCHER, -S *n* person who shoots with a bow and arrow

ARCHERY *n* art or sport of shooting with a bow and arrow

ARCHES ► **arch**

ARCHEST ► **arch**

ARCHEUS, ARCHEI *n* spirit believed to inhabit a living thing

ARCHFOE, -S *n* chief enemy

ARCHI ► **arco**

ARCHIL, -S *a variant spelling of* ► **orchil**

ARCHINE, -S *n* Russian unit of length equal to about 71 cm

ARCHING, -S ► **arch**

ARCHIVAL ► **archive**

ARCHIVE, -D, -S *n* collection of records or documents ▷ *vb* store (documents, data, etc) in an archive or other repository

ARCHLET, -S *n* small arch

ARCHLUTE *n* old bass lute

ARCHLY ► **arch**

ARCHNESS ► **arch**

ARCHON, -S *n* (in ancient Athens) one of the nine chief magistrates

ARCHWAY, -S *n* passageway under an arch

ARCHWISE *adv* like an arch

ARCIFORM *adj* shaped like an arch

ARCING, -S ► **arc**

ARCKED ► **arc**

ARCKING, -S ► **arc**

ARCMIN, -S *n* 1/60 of a degree of an angle

ARCO, ARCHI, -S *adv* musical direction meaning with bow ▷ *n* bow of a stringed instrument

ARCOLOGY *n* architecture blending buildings with the natural environment

ARCOS ► **arco**

ARCS ► **arc**

ARCSEC, -S *n* 1/3600 of a degree of an angle

ARCSINE, -S *n* trigonometrical function

ARCTIC, -S *adj* very cold ▷ *n* high waterproof overshoe with buckles

ARCTIID, -S *n* type of moth

ARCTOID *adj* like a bear

ARCUATE *adj* shaped or bent like an arc or bow

ARCUATED *same as* ► **arcuate**

ARCUS, -ES *n* circle around the cornea of the eye

ARD, -S *n* primitive plough

ARDEB, -S *n* unit of dry measure

ARDENCY ► **ardent**

ARDENT *adj* passionate

ARDENTLY

ARDOR, -S *same as* ► **ardour**

ARDOUR, -S *n* passion

ARDRI, -S *n* Irish high king

ARDRIGH, -S *n* Irish high king

ARDRIS ► **ardri**

ARDS ► **ard**

ARDUOUS *adj* hard to accomplish, strenuous

ARE, -S *n* unit of measure, 100 square metres ▷ *vb* form of the present tense of be

AREA, -E, -S *n* part or region

AREACH, -ED, -ES, ARRAUGHT *vb* old form of reach

AREAD, -ING, -S, ARED, AREDD *vb* old word meaning declare

AREAE ► **area**

AREAL ► **area**

AREALLY ► **area**

AREAR, -S *n* old form of arrear

AREAS ► **area**

AREAWAY, -S *n* passageway

ARECA, -S *n* type of palm tree

ARED ► **aread**

AREDD ► **aread**

AREDE, -S, AREDING *vb* old word meaning declare

AREFY, AREFIED, AREFIES, -ING *vb* dry up

AREG *a plural of* ► **erg**

AREIC *adj* relating to area

ARENA, -S *n* seated enclosure for sports events

ARENE, -S *n* aromatic hydrocarbon

ARENITE, -S *n* any arenaceous rock

ARENITIC

ARENOSE *adj* sandy

ARENOUS *adj* sandy

AREOLA, -E, -S *n* small circular area

AREOLAR

AREOLATE

AREOLE, -S *n* space outlined on a surface

AREOLOGY *n* study of the planet Mars

AREPA, -S *n* Colombian cornmeal cake

ARERE *adv* old word meaning backwards

ARES ► **are**

ARET, -S *vb* old word meaning entrust

ARETE, -S *n* sharp ridge separating two glacial valleys

ARETHUSA *n* N American orchid

ARETS ► **aret**

ARETT, -ED, -ING, -S *vb* old word meaning entrust

AREW *adv* old word meaning in a row

ARF, -S *n* barking sound

ARGAL, -S *same as* ► **argali**

ARGALA, -S *n* Indian stork

ARGALI, -S *n* wild sheep

ARGALS ► **argal**

ARGAN, -S *n* Moroccan tree

ARGAND, -S *n* lamp with a hollow circular wick

ARGANS ► **argan**

ARGEMONE *n* prickly poppy

ARGENT, -S *n* silver

ARGENTAL *adj* of or containing silver

ARGENTIC *adj* of or containing silver in the divalent or trivalent state

ARGENTS ► **argent**

ARGENTUM *an obsolete name for* ► **silver**

ARGH *interj* cry of pain

ARGHAN, -S *n* agave plant

ARGIL, -S *n* clay, esp potters' clay

ARGINASE *n* type of enzyme

ARGININE *n* essential amino acid

ARGLE, -D, -S, ARGLING *vb* quarrel

ARGOL, -S *n* chemical compound

ARGON, -S *n* inert gas found in the air

ARGONAUT *n* paper nautilus

ARGONON, -S *n* inert gas

ARGONS ► **argon**

ARGOSY, ARGOSIES *n* large merchant ship

ARGOT, -S *n* slang or jargon

ARGOTIC

ARGUABLE *adj* capable of being disputed

ARGUABLY *adv* it can be argued that

ARGUE, -D, -S, ARGUING *vb* try to prove by giving reasons

ARGUER -S

ARGUFIED ► **argufy**

ARGUFIER ► **argufy**

ARGUFY, ARGUFIED, ARGUFIES *vb* argue or quarrel, esp over something trivial

ARGUING ► **argue**

ARGULUS, ARGULI *n* parasite on fish

ARGUMENT *n* quarrel

ARGUS, -ES *n* any of various brown butterflies

ARGUTE *adj* shrill or keen

ARGUTELY

ARGYLE, **-S** *adj* with a diamond-shaped pattern ▷ *n* sock with this pattern

ARGYLL, **-S** *n* sock with diamond pattern

ARGYRIA, **-S** *n* staining of skin by exposure to silver

ARGYRITE *n* mineral containing silver sulphide

ARHAT, **-S** *n* Buddhist who has achieved enlightenment

ARIA, **-S** *n* elaborate song for solo voice, esp one from an opera

ARIARY, **ARIARIES** *n* currency of Madagascar

ARIAS ▶ **aria**

ARID, **-ER**, **-EST** *adj* parched, dry
  ARIDITY
  ARIDLY
  ARIDNESS

ARIEL, **-S** *n* type of Arabian gazelle

ARIETTA, **-S** *n* short aria

ARIETTE, **-S** *same as* ▶ **arietta**

ARIGHT *adv* rightly

ARIKI, **-S** *n* first-born male or female in a notable family

ARIL, **-S** *n* appendage on certain seeds

ARILED *adj* having an aril

ARILLARY *adj* having an aril

ARILLATE ▷ **arillated**

ARILLI ▶ **arillus**

ARILLODE *n* structure in certain seeds

ARILLOID *adj* of or like an aril

ARILLUS, **ARILLI** *n* aril

ARILS ▶ **aril**

ARIOSE *adj* songlike

ARIOSO, **ARIOSI**, **-S** *n* recitative with the lyrical quality of an aria

ARIOT *adv* riotously

ARIPPLE *adv* in ripples

ARISE, **-N**, **-S**, **ARISING**, **AROSE** *vb* come about

ARISH, **-ES** *n* field that has been mown

ARISING ▶ **arise**

ARISTA, **-E**, **-S** *n* stiff bristle
  ARISTATE

ARISTO, **-S** *n* aristocrat

ARK, **-ED**, **-ING**, **-S** *n* boat built by Noah, which survived the Flood ▷ *vb* place in an ark

ARKITE *n* passenger in ark

ARKOSE, **-S** *n* type of sandstone
  ARKOSIC

ARKS ▶ **ark**

ARLE, **-D**, **-S**, **ARLING** *vb* make downpayment

ARM, **-S** *n* limbs from the shoulder to the wrist ▷ *vb* supply with weapons

ARMADA, **-S** *n* large number of warships

ARMAGNAC *n* dry brown brandy

ARMAMENT *n* military weapons

ARMATURE *n* revolving structure in an electric motor or generator

ARMBAND, **-S** *n* band worn on the arm

ARMCHAIR *n* upholstered chair with side supports for the arms ▷ *adj* taking no active part

ARMED *adj* equipped with or supported by arms, armour, etc

ARMER, **-S** ▶ **arm**

ARMERIA, **-S** *n* generic name for the plant thrift

ARMERS ▶ **armer**

ARMET, **-S** *n* close-fitting medieval visored helmet with a neck guard

ARMFUL, **-S**, **ARMSFUL** *n* as much as can be held in the arms

ARMGAUNT *adj* word in Shakespeare of uncertain meaning

ARMGUARD *n* covering to protect the arm

ARMHOLE, **-S** *n* opening in a garment through which the arm passes

ARMIES ▶ **army**

ARMIGER, **-S** *n* person entitled to bear heraldic arms

ARMIGERO *n* armiger

ARMIGERS ▶ **armiger**

ARMIL, **-S** *n* bracelet

ARMILLA, **-E**, **-S** *n* bracelet

ARMILS ▶ **armil**

ARMING, **-S** *n* act of taking arms or providing with arms

ARMLESS ▶ **arm**

ARMLET, **-S** *n* band worn round the arm

ARMLIKE ▶ **arm**

ARMLOAD, **-S** *n* amount carried in the arms

ARMLOCK, **-S** *vb* grip someone's arms

ARMOIRE, **-S** *n* large cabinet

ARMONICA *n* glass harmonica

ARMOR, **-ING**, **-S** *same as* ▶ **armour**

ARMORED *same as* ▶ **armoured**

ARMORER, **-S** *same as* ▶ **armourer**

ARMORIAL *adj* of or relating to heraldry or heraldic arms ▷ *n* book of coats of arms

ARMORIES ▶ **armory**

ARMORING ▶ **armor**

ARMORIST *n* heraldry expert

ARMORS ▶ **armor**

ARMORY, **ARMORIES** *same as* ▶ **armoury**

ARMOUR, **-S** *n* metal clothing formerly worn to protect the body in battle ▷ *vb* equip or cover with armour

ARMOURED *adj* having a protective covering

ARMOURER *n* maker, repairer, or keeper of arms or armour

ARMOURS ▶ **armour**

ARMOURY *n* place where weapons are stored

ARMOZEEN *n* material used for clerical gowns

ARMOZINE *n* material used for clerical gowns

ARMPIT, **-S** *n* hollow under the arm at the shoulder

ARMREST, **-S** *n* part of a chair or sofa that supports the arm

ARMS ▶ **arm**

ARMSFUL ▶ **armful**

ARMURE, **-S** *n* silk or wool fabric with a small cobbled pattern

ARMY, **ARMIES** *n* military land forces of a nation

ARMYWORM *n* caterpillar of a widely distributed noctuid moth

ARNA, **-S** *n* Indian water buffalo

ARNATTO, **-S** *n* annatto

ARNICA, **-S** *n* temperate or arctic plant

ARNOTTO, **-S** *n* annatto

ARNUT, **-S** *n* plant with edible tubers

AROBA, **-S** *n* Asian carriage

AROHA, **-S** *n* love, compassion, or affection

AROID, **-S** *n* type of plant

AROINT, **-ED**, **-S** *vb* drive away

AROLLA, **-S** *n* European pine tree

AROMA, **-S** *n* pleasant smell

AROMATIC *adj* having a distinctive pleasant smell ▷ *n* something, such as a plant or drug, that gives off a fragrant smell

AROSE ▶ **arise**

AROUND *adv* on all sides (of)

AROUSAL, **-S** ▶ **arouse**

AROUSE, **-D**, **-S**, **AROUSING** *vb* stimulate, make active

AROUSER, **-S**

A

AROW adv in a row

AROYNT, -ED, -S vb old word meaning to drive away

ARPA, -S n website concerned with structure of the internet

ARPEGGIO n notes of a chord played or sung in quick succession

ARPEN, -S n old French measure of land

ARPENT, -S n former French unit of length

ARQUEBUS n portable long-barrelled gun dating from the 15th century

ARRACK, -S n alcoholic drink distilled from grain or rice

ARRAH interj Irish exclamation

ARRAIGN, -S vb bring (a prisoner) before a court to answer a charge

ARRANGE, -D, -S vb plan **ARRANGER**

ARRANT adj utter, downright **ARRANTLY**

ARRAS, -ES n tapestry wall-hanging

ARRASED adj having an arras

ARRASENE n material used in embroidery

ARRASES ▸ arras

ARRAUGHT ▸ areach

ARRAY, -ED, -ING, -S n impressive display or collection ▷ vb arrange in order

ARRAYAL -S

ARRAYER, -S n ▸ array

ARRAYING ▸ array

ARRAYS ▸ array

ARREAR n singular of arrears

ARREARS pl n money owed

ARRECT adj pricked up

ARREEDE, -S vb old word meaning declare

ARREST, -ED, -S vb take (a person) into custody ▷ n act of taking a person into custody

ARRESTEE n arrested person

ARRESTER n person who arrests

ARRESTOR n person or thing that arrests

ARRESTS ▸ arrest

ARRET, -S n judicial decision

ARRHIZAL adj without roots

ARRIAGE, -S n Scottish feudal service

ARRIBA interj exclamation of pleasure or approval

ARRIDE, -D, -S, ARRIDING vb old word meaning gratify

ARRIERE adj French word meaning old-fashioned

ARRIERO, -S n Spanish word for mule driver

ARRIS, -ES n sharp edge at the meeting of two surfaces

ARRISH, -ES n corn stubble

ARRIVAL, -S n arriving

ARRIVE, -D, -S, ARRIVING vb reach a place or destination

ARRIVER -S

ARROBA, -S n unit of weight in Spanish-speaking countries

ARROCES ▸ arroz

ARROGANT adj proud and overbearing

ARROGATE vb claim or seize without justification

ARROW, -ING, -S n pointed shaft shot from a bow

ARROWED adj having an arrow pattern

ARROWING ▸ arrow

ARROWS ▸ arrow

ARROWY adj like an arrow

ARROYO, -S n usually dry stream bed

ARROZ, ARROCES, -ES n Spanish word for rice, used in name of various dishes

ARS ▸ ar

ARSENAL, -S n place where arms and ammunition are made or stored

ARSENATE n salt or ester of arsenic acid

ARSENIC, -S n toxic grey element ▷ adj of or containing arsenic

ARSENIDE n compound in which arsenic is the most electronegative element

ARSENITE n salt or ester of arsenous acid

ARSENO adj containing arsenic

ARSENOUS same as > arsenious

ARSES ▸ arsis

ARSHEEN, -S n old measure of length in Russia

ARSHIN, -S n old measure of length in Russia

ARSHINE, -S n old measure of length in Russia

ARSHINS ▸ arshin

ARSINE, -S n colourless poisonous gas

ARSINO adj containing arsine

ARSIS, ARSES n long or stressed syllable in a metrical foot

ARSON, -S n crime of intentionally setting property on fire

ARSONIST

ARSONITE n person committing arson

ARSONOUS adj of arson

ARSONS ▸ arson

ART, -S n creation of works of beauty, esp paintings or sculpture

ARTAL a plural of ▸ **rotl**

ARTEFACT n something made by human beings

ARTEL, -S n cooperative union

ARTERIAL adj of an artery ▷ n major road

ARTERY, ARTERIES n one of the tubes carrying blood from the heart

ARTESIAN adj as in **artesian well** sunken well receiving water from a higher altitude

ARTFUL adj cunning, wily **ARTFULLY**

ARTHOUSE n cinema which shows artistic films

ARTI, -S n ritual performed in homes and temples

ARTIC, -S n articulated vehicle

ARTICLE, -D, -S n written piece in a magazine or newspaper ▷ vb bind by a written contract

ARTICS ▸ artic

ARTIER ▸ arty

ARTIES ▸ arty

ARTIEST ▸ arty

ARTIFACT same as ▸ **artefact**

ARTIFICE n clever trick

ARTIGI, -S n kind of hooded coat worn in Canada

ARTILY ▸ arty

ARTINESS ▸ arty

ARTIS ▸ arti

ARTISAN, -S n skilled worker, craftsman

ARTIST, -S n person who produces works of art, esp paintings or sculpture

ARTISTE, -S n professional entertainer such as a singer or dancer

ARTISTIC adj of or characteristic of art or artists

ARTISTRY n artistic skill

ARTISTS ▸ artist

ARTLESS adj free from deceit or cunning

ARTMAKER n person who creates art

ARTS ▸ art

ARTSIE n arts student

ARTSIER ▸ artsy

ARTSIES ▸ artsy

ARTSIEST ▸ artsy

ARTSMAN, ARTSMEN old word for > **craftsman**

ARTSY, ARTSIER, ARTSIES, ARTSIEST adj interested in the arts ▷ n person interested in the arts

ARTWORK, -S n all the photographs and illustrations in a publication

ARTY, ARTIER, ARTIES, ARTIEST adj having an affected interest in art ▷ n person interested in art

ARUGOLA, -S n salad plant

ARUGULA, -S another name for ▶ **rocket**

ARUHE, -S n edible root of a fern

ARUM, -S n type of plant

ARUSPEX variant spelling of ▶ **haruspex**

ARVAL adj of ploughed land

ARVEE, -S n short for recreational vehicle (RV)

ARVICOLE n water rat

ARVO, -S n afternoon

ARY dialect form of ▶ **any**

ARYL, -S n an aromatic group

ARYTHMIA n any variation

ARYTHMIC

AS, -AR adv used to indicate amount or extent in comparisons ▷ n ancient Roman unit of weight

ASANA, -S n any of various postures in yoga

ASAR ▶ **as**

ASARUM, -S n dried strong-scented root

ASBESTIC ▶ **asbestos**

ASBESTOS n fibrous mineral which does not burn

ASBESTUS n asbestos

ASCARED adj afraid

ASCARID, -S n type of parasitic nematode

ASCARIS n ascarid

ASCAUNT adv old word meaning slantwise

ASCEND, -ED, -S vb go or move up

ASCENDER n part of some lower-case letters that extends above the body of the letter

ASCENDS ▶ **ascend**

ASCENT, -S n ascending

ASCESIS, ASCESES n exercise of self-discipline

ASCETIC, -S adj (person) abstaining from worldly pleasures and comforts ▷ n person who abstains from worldly comforts and pleasures

ASCI ▶ **ascus**

ASCIAN, -S n person living in the tropics

ASCIDIA ▶ **ascidium**

ASCIDIAN n type of minute marine invertebrate, such as the sea squirt

ASCIDIUM, ASCIDIA n part of a plant that is shaped like a pitcher

ASCITES n accumulation of serous fluid in the peritoneal cavity

ASCITIC

ASCOCARP n (in some ascomycetous fungi) a globular structure containing the asci

ASCON, -S n type of sponge having an oval shape and a thin body wall

ASCONCE adv old form of askance

ASCONOID adj like an ascon

ASCONS ▶ **ascon**

ASCORBIC adj as in **ascorbic acid** vitamin present in citrus fruits, tomatoes, and green vegetables

ASCOT, -S n type of cravat

ASCRIBE, -D, -S vb attribute, as to a particular origin

ASCUS, ASCI n saclike structure in fungi

ASDIC, -S an early form of ▶ **sonar**

ASEA adv towards the sea

ASEISMIC adj denoting a region free of earthquakes

ASEITY, ASEITIES n existence derived from itself, having no other source

ASEPSIS, ASEPSES n aseptic condition

ASEPTATE adj not divided into cells or sections by septa

ASEPTIC, -S adj free from harmful bacteria ▷ n aseptic substance

ASEXUAL adj without biological sex

ASH, -ED, -ES, -ING n powdery substance left when something is burnt ▷ vb reduce to ashes

ASHAKE adv shaking

ASHAME, -S, ASHAMING vb make ashamed

ASHAMED adj feeling shame

ASHAMES ▶ **ashame**

ASHAMING ▶ **ashame**

ASHCAKE, -S n cornmeal bread

ASHCAN, -S n large metal dustbin

ASHED ▶ **ash**

ASHEN adj pale with shock

ASHERY, ASHERIES n place where ashes are made

ASHES ▶ **ash**

ASHET, -S n shallow oval dish or large plate

ASHFALL, -S n dropping of ash from a volcano

ASHIER ▶ **ashy**

ASHIEST ▶ **ashy**

ASHINE adv old word meaning shining

ASHINESS ▶ **ashy**

ASHING ▶ **ash**

ASHIVER adv shivering

ASHKEY, -S n winged fruit of the ash

ASHLAR, -ED, -S n block of hewn stone ▷ vb build with ashlars

ASHLER, -ED, -S same as ▶ **ashlar**

ASHLESS ▶ **ash**

ASHMAN, ASHMEN n man who shovels ashes

ASHORE adv towards or on land ▷ adj on land, having come from the water

ASHPAN, -S n pan or tray to catch ashes

ASHPLANT n walking stick made from an ash sapling

ASHRAF ▶ **sherif**

ASHRAM, -S n religious retreat where a Hindu holy man lives

ASHRAMA, -S n stage in Hindu spiritual life

ASHRAMS ▶ **ashram**

ASHTANGA n type of yoga

ASHTRAY, -S n receptacle for tobacco ash and cigarette butts

ASHY, ASHIER, ASHIEST adj pale greyish

ASIAGO, -S n type of cheese

ASIDE, -S adv one side ▷ n remark not meant to be heard by everyone present

ASININICO, -S n old Spanish word for fool

ASININE adj stupid, idiotic

ASK, -ED, -S vb say (something) in a form that requires an answer

ASKANCE, -D, -S adv with an oblique glance ▷ vb turn aside

ASKANT, -ED, -S same as ▶ **askance**

ASKARI, -S n (in East Africa) a soldier or policeman

ASKED ▶ **ask**

ASKER, -S ▶ **ask**

ASKESIS, ASKESES n practice of self-discipline

ASKEW adj one side, crooked

ASKING, -S ▶ **ask**

A

ASKLENT Scots word for
▶ aslant

ASKOS, ASKOI n ancient
Greek vase

ASKS ▶ ask

ASLAKE, -D, -S, ASLAKING
vb slake

ASLANT adv at a slant (to),
slanting (across)

ASLEEP adj sleeping

ASLOPE adj sloping

ASLOSH adj awash

ASMEAR adj smeared

ASOCIAL, -S n person who
avoids social contact

ASP, -S n small poisonous
snake

ASPARKLE adv sparkling

ASPARTIC adj as in **aspartic
acid** nonessential amino
acid that is a component of
proteins

ASPECT, -ED, -S n feature or
element ▷ vb look at

ASPEN, -S n kind of poplar tree
▷ adj trembling

ASPER, -S n former Turkish
monetary unit

ASPERATE adj (of plant parts)
having a rough surface due to
a covering of short stiff hairs
▷ vb make rough

ASPERGE, -D, -S vb sprinkle
ASPERGER

ASPERITY n roughness of
temper

ASPEROUS same as
▶ asperate

ASPERS ▶ asper

ASPERSE, -D, -S vb spread
false rumours about
ASPERSER
ASPERSOR

ASPHALT, -S n black hard
tarlike substance used for
road surfaces etc ▷ vb cover
with asphalt

ASPHERIC adj not spherical
▷ n lens that is not
completely spherical

ASPHODEL n plant with
clusters of yellow or white
flowers

ASPHYXIA n suffocation

ASPHYXY same as ▶ asphyxia

ASPIC, -S n savoury jelly used
to coat meat, eggs, fish, etc

ASPICK, -S old word for ▶ asp

ASPICS ▶ aspic

ASPIDIUM, ASPIDIA n variety
of fern

ASPINE, -S old word for
▶ aspen

ASPIRANT n person who
aspires ▷ adj aspiring or
striving

ASPIRATA n rough stop

ASPIRATE vb pronounce
with an h sound ▷ n h sound
▷ adj (of a stop) pronounced
with a forceful and audible
expulsion of breath

ASPIRE, -D, -S vb yearn (for),
hope (to do or be)
ASPIRER -S

ASPIRIN, -S n drug used to
relieve pain and fever

ASPIRING ▶ aspire

ASPIRINS ▶ aspirin

ASPIS, -ES n horned viper

ASPISH adj like an asp

ASPORT, -ED, -S vb old word
meaning take away

ASPOUT adv spouting

ASPRAWL adv sprawling

ASPREAD adv spreading

ASPRO, -S n associate
professor at an academic
institution

ASPROUT adv sprouting

ASPS ▶ asp

ASQUAT adv squatting

ASQUINT adj with a glance
from the corner of the eye

ASRAMA, -S n stage in Hindu
spiritual life

ASS, -ES n donkey

ASSAGAI, -S same as
▶ assegai

ASSAI, -S adv (usually
preceded by a musical
direction) very ▷ n Brazilian
palm tree

ASSAIL, -ED, -S vb attack
violently
ASSAILER

ASSAIS ▶ assai

ASSAM, -S n (in Malaysia)
tamarind as used in cooking

ASSART, -ED, -S vb clear
ground for cultivation

ASSASSIN n person who
murders a prominent person

ASSAULT, -S n violent attack
▷ vb attack violently

ASSAY, -ED, -S n analysis of a
substance ▷ vb make such
an analysis
ASSAYER -S

ASSAYING ▶ assay

ASSAYS ▶ assay

ASSEGAAI same as ▶ assegai

ASSEGAI, -S n slender spear
used in S Africa ▷ vb spear
with an assegai

ASSEMBLE vb collect or
congregate

ASSEMBLY n assembled group

ASSENT, -ED, -S n agreement
or consent ▷ vb agree or
consent

ASSENTER n person
supporting another's
nomination

ASSENTOR n voter legally
required to endorse the
nomination of a candidate

ASSENTS ▶ assent

ASSERT, -ED, -S vb declare
forcefully
ASSERTER
ASSERTOR

ASSES ▶ ass

ASSESS, -ED, -ES vb judge the
worth or importance of

ASSESSOR n person who
values property for taxation
or insurance purposes

ASSET, -S n valuable or useful
person or thing

ASSEVER, -S vb old form of
asseverate

ASSEZ adv (as part of a musical
direction) fairly

ASSIEGE, -D, -S vb old form of
besiege

ASSIENTO n former slave
trade treaty between Britain
and Spain

ASSIGN, -ED, -S vb appoint
(someone) to a job or task
▷ n person to whom property
is assigned

ASSIGNAT n paper money
issued in France by the
Constituent Assembly in 1789

ASSIGNED ▶ assign

ASSIGNEE n person to whom
some right, interest, or
property is transferred

ASSIGNER ▶ assign

ASSIGNOR n person who
transfers or assigns property

ASSIGNS ▶ assign

ASSIST, -ED, -S vb give help or
support ▷ n pass by a player
which enables another player
to score a goal
ASSISTER
ASSISTOR

ASSIZE, -D, -S, ASSIZING
n sitting of a legislative
assembly

ASSIZER, -S n weights and
measures official

ASSIZES ▶ assize

ASSIZING ▶ assize

ASSLIKE ▶ ass

ASSOIL, -ED, -S vb absolve

ASSONANT > assonance

ASSONATE vb show
assonance

ASSORT, -S vb arrange or
distribute equally

ASSORTED adj consisting of
various types mixed together

ASSORTER ▶ assort

ASSORTS ▸ assort
ASSOT, -S, -TED vb old word meaning make infatuated
ASSOTT vb besot
ASSOTTED ▸ assot
ASSUAGE, -D, -S vb relieve (pain, grief, thirst, etc)
ASSUAGER
ASSUME, -S vb take to be true without proof
ASSUMED adj false
ASSUMER, -S ▸ assume
ASSUMES ▸ assume
ASSUMING adj expecting too much ▷ n action of one who assumes
ASSURE, -S, ASSURING vb promise or guarantee
ASSURED, -S adj confident ▷ n beneficiary under a life assurance policy
ASSURER, -S ▸ assure
ASSURES ▸ assure
ASSURING ▸ assure
ASSUROR, -S ▸ assure
ASSWAGE, -D, -S old spelling of ▸ assuage
ASTABLE adj not stable
ASTANGA, -S same as ▸ ashtanga
ASTARE adv staring
ASTART, -ED, -S old word for ▸ start
ASTASIA, -S n inability to stand
ASTATIC adj not static
ASTATIDE n binary compound of astatine with a more electropositive element
ASTATINE n radioactive nonmetallic element
ASTATKI, -S n fuel derived from petroleum
ASTEISM, -S n use of irony
ASTELIC ▸ astely
ASTELY, ASTELIES n lack of central cylinder in plants
ASTER, -S n plant with daisy-like flowers
ASTERIA, -S n gemstone with starlike light effect
ASTERID, -S n variety of flowering plant
ASTERISK n star-shaped symbol (*) used in printing or writing to indicate a footnote, etc ▷ vb mark with an asterisk
ASTERISM n three asterisks arranged in a triangle to draw attention to the text that follows
ASTERN adv at or towards the stern of a ship ▷ adj at or towards the stern of a ship

ASTERNAL adj not connected or joined to the sternum
ASTEROID n any of the small planets that orbit the sun between Mars and Jupiter ▷ adj of, relating to, or belonging to the class Asteroidea

> Be especially aware of this word because its combination of common letters makes it one of the most often played 8-letter bonus words.

ASTERS ▸ aster
ASTERT, -ED, -S vb start
ASTHANGA n type of yoga
ASTHENIA n abnormal loss of strength
ASTHENIC adj of, relating to, or having asthenia ▷ n person having long limbs and a small trunk
ASTHENY same as ▸ asthenia
ASTHMA, -S n illness causing difficulty in breathing
ASTHORE, -S n Irish endearment
ASTIGMIA n defect of a lens resulting in the formation of distorted images
ASTILBE, -S n type of plant
ASTIR adj out of bed
ASTOMOUS adj having no mouth
ASTONE, -D, -S, ASTONING same as ▸ astonish
ASTONIED adj stunned
ASTONIES ▸ astony
ASTONING ▸ astone
ASTONISH vb surprise greatly
ASTONY, ASTONIES same as ▸ astonish
ASTOOP adv stooping
ASTOUND, -S vb overwhelm with amazement
ASTRAGAL n small convex moulding, usually with a semicircular cross section
ASTRAL, -S adj of stars ▷ n oil lamp
ASTRALLY
ASTRAND adv on shore
ASTRAY adv off the right path
ASTRICT, -S vb bind, confine, or constrict
ASTRIDE adv with a leg on either side (of) ▷ adj with a leg on either side
ASTRINGE vb cause contraction
ASTROID, -S n hypocycloid having four cusps
ASTRUT adv old word meaning in a protruding way

ASTUCITY n quality of being astute
ASTUN, -NED, -S vb old form of astonish
ASTUTE, -R, -ST adj perceptive or shrewd
ASTUTELY
ASTYLAR adj without columns or pilasters
ASUDDEN adv old form of suddenly
ASUNDER adv into parts or pieces ▷ adj into parts or pieces
ASURA, -S n demon in Hindu mythology
ASWARM adj filled, esp with moving things
ASWAY adv swaying
ASWIM adv floating
ASWING adv swinging
ASWIRL adv swirling
ASWOON adv swooning
ASYLA ▸ asylum
ASYLEE, -S n person who is granted asylum
ASYLUM, ASYLA, -S n refuge or sanctuary
ASYNDETA ▸ asyndeton
ASYNERGY same as > asynergia
ASYSTOLE n absence of heartbeat
AT, -S n Laotian monetary unit worth one hundredth of a kip
ATAATA, -S n grazing marine gastropod
ATABAL, -S n N African drum
ATABEG, -S n Turkish ruler
ATABEK, -S n Turkish ruler
ATABRIN, -S n drug formerly used for treating malaria
ATABRINE same as ▸ atabrin
ATABRINS ▸ atabrin
ATACTIC adj attribute of a polymer
ATAGHAN, -S a variant of ▸ yataghan
ATALAYA, -S n watchtower in Spain
ATAMAN, -S n elected leader of the Cossacks
ATAMASCO n N American lily
ATAP, -S n palm tree of S Asia
ATARAXIA, -S n calmness or peace of mind
ATARAXIC same as > ataractic
ATARAXY same as ▸ ataraxia
ATAVIC ▸ atavism
ATAVISM, -S n recurrence of a trait present in distant ancestors
ATAVIST -S

ATAXIA, -S n lack of muscular coordination
ATAXIC -S
ATAXY, ATAXIES same as ▶ ataxia
ATCHIEVE same as ▶ achieve
ATE ▶ eat
ATEBRIN, -S n drug formerly used to treat malaria
ATECHNIC adj without technical ability ▷ n person with no technical ability
ATELIC adj of action without end
ATELIER, -S n workshop, artist's studio
ATEMOYA, -S n tropical fruit tree
ATENOLOL n type of beta-blocker
ATES n shop selling confectionery
ATHAME, -S n witch's ceremonial knife
ATHANASY n absence of death
ATHANOR, -S n alchemist's furnace
ATHEISE, -D, -S vb speak atheistically
ATHEISM, -S n belief that there is no God
ATHEIST -S
ATHEIZE, -D, -S vb speak atheistically
ATHELING n (in Anglo-Saxon England) a prince of any of the royal dynasties
ATHENEUM same as ▷ athenaeum
ATHEOUS adj without a belief in god
ATHERINE n small fish
ATHEROMA n fatty deposit on or within an artery
ATHETISE vb reject as not genuine
ATHETIZE vb reject as not genuine
ATHETOID ▷ athetosis
ATHIRST adj having an eager desire
ATHLETA, -S same as ▶ athlete
ATHLETE, -S n person trained in or good at athletics
ATHLETIC adj physically fit or strong
ATHODYD, -S another name for ▶ ramjet
ATHRILL adv feeling thrills
ATHROB adv throbbing
ATHWART adv transversely
ATIGI, -S n type of parka worn by the Inuit in Canada

ATILT adj in a tilted or inclined position
ATIMY, ATIMIES n loss of honour
ATINGLE adv tingling
ATISHOO, -S n sound of a sneeze
ATLAS, ATLANTES, -ES n book of maps
ATLATL, -S n Native American throwing stick
ATMA, -S same as ▶ atman
ATMAN, -S n personal soul or self
ATMAS ▶ atma
ATMOLOGY n study of aqueous vapour
ATMOLYSE vb separate gases by filtering
ATMOLYZE vb separate gases by filtering
ATMOS, -ES n (short for) atmosphere
ATOC, -S n skunk
ATOCIA, -S n inability to have children
ATOCS ▶ atoc
ATOK, -S n skunk
ATOKAL adj having no children
ATOKE, -S n part of a worm
ATOKOUS adj having no children
ATOKS ▶ atok
ATOLL, -S n ring-shaped coral reef enclosing a lagoon
ATOM, -S n smallest unit of matter which can take part in a chemical reaction
ATOMIC adj of or using atomic bombs or atomic energy
ATOMICAL
ATOMICS n science of atoms
ATOMIES ▶ atomy
ATOMISE, -D, -S same as ▶ atomize
ATOMISER same as ▶ atomizer
ATOMISES ▶ atomise
ATOMISM, -S n ancient philosophical theory
ATOMIST -S
ATOMIZE, -D, -S vb reduce to atoms or small particles
ATOMIZER n device for discharging a liquid in a fine spray
ATOMIZES ▶ atomize
ATOMS ▶ atom
ATOMY, ATOMIES n atom or minute particle
ATONABLE ▶ atone
ATONAL adj (of music) not written in an established key
ATONALLY

ATONE, -D, -S, ATONING vb make amends (for sin or wrongdoing)
ATONER -S
ATONIA, -S n lack of normal muscle tone
ATONIC, -S adj carrying no stress ▷ n unaccented or unstressed syllable
ATONIES ▶ atony

The plural of **atony**, this is another of the most frequently played 7-letter bonus words that it is essential to know.

ATONING ▶ atone
ATONY, ATONIES n lack of normal tone or tension, as in muscles
ATOP adv on top
ATOPIC adj of or relating to hypersensitivity to certain allergens
ATOPY, ATOPIES n tendency to be hypersensitive to certain allergens
ATRAMENT n old word meaning black liquid
ATRAZINE n white crystalline compound
ATREMBLE adv trembling
ATRESIA, -S n absence of or unnatural narrowing of a body channel
ATRESIC
ATRETIC
ATRIA ▶ atrium
ATRIAL ▶ atrium
ATRIP adj (of an anchor) no longer caught on the bottom
ATRIUM, ATRIA, -S n upper chamber of either half of the heart
ATROCITY n wickedness
ATROPHIA n wasting disease
ATROPHIC ▶ atrophy
ATROPHY n wasting away of an organ or part ▷ vb (cause to) waste away
ATROPIA, -S n atropine
ATROPIN, -S same as ▶ atropine
ATROPINE n poisonous alkaloid obtained from deadly nightshade
ATROPINS ▶ atropin
ATROPISM n condition caused by using belladonna
ATROPOUS adj growing straight
ATS ▶ at
ATT n old Siamese coin
ATTABOY, -S sentence substitute expression of approval or exhortation

ATTACH, -ES vb join, fasten, or connect

ATTACHE n specialist attached to a diplomatic mission

ATTACHED adj fond of

ATTACHER ▸ attach

ATTACHES ▸ attach

ATTACK, -ED, -S vb launch a physical assault (against) ⊳ n act of attacking

ATTACKER

ATTAGIRL humorous feminine version of ▸ attaboy

ATTAIN, -ED, -S vb achieve or accomplish (a task or aim)

ATTAINER

ATTAINT, -S vb pass judgment of death ⊳ n dishonour

ATTAP, -S n palm tree of South Asia

ATTAR, -S n fragrant oil made from roses

ATTASK, -ED, -S, -T old word for > criticize

ATTEMPER vb modify by blending

ATTEMPT, -S vb try, make an effort ⊳ n effort or endeavour

ATTEND, -ED, -S vb be present at

ATTENDEE n person who is present at a specified event

ATTENDER ▸ attend

ATTENDS ▸ attend

ATTENT, -S old word for > attention

ATTENTAT n attempt

ATTENTS ▸ attent

ATTERCOP n spider

ATTEST, -S vb affirm the truth of, be proof of

ATTESTED adj (of cattle) certified to be free from a disease, such as tuberculosis

ATTESTER ▸ attest

ATTESTOR ▸ attest

ATTESTS ▸ attest

ATTIC, -S n space or room within the roof of a house

ATTICISE same as ▸ atticize

ATTICISM n elegant, simple, and clear expression

ATTICIST

ATTICIZE vb conform or adapt to the norms of Attica

ATTICS ▸ attic

ATTIRE, -D, -S n fine or formal clothes ⊳ vb dress, esp in fine elegant clothes

ATTIRING

ATTITUDE n way of thinking and behaving

ATTONCE adv old word for at once

ATTONE, -D, -S, ATTONING vb old word meaning appease

ATTORN, -ED, -S vb acknowledge a new owner of land as one's landlord

ATTORNEY n person legally appointed to act for another

ATTORNS ▸ attorn

ATTRACT, -S vb arouse the interest or admiration of

ATTRAP, -S vb adorn

ATTRIST, -S vb old word meaning to sadden

ATTRIT, -S vb wear down or dispose of gradually

ATTRITE, -D, -S vb wear down

ATTRITS ▸ attrit

ATTUENT adj carrying out attuition

ATTUITE, -D, -S vb perceive by attuition

ATTUNE, -D, -S, ATTUNING vb adjust or accustom (a person or thing)

ATUA, -S n spirit or demon

ATWAIN adv old word meaning into two parts

ATWEEL Scots word for ▸ well

ATWEEN an archaic or Scots word for ▸ between

ATWITTER adv twittering

ATWIXT old word for ▸ between

ATYPIC adj not typical

ATYPICAL adj not typical

AUA, -S n yellow-eye mullet

This Māori word for a kind of mullet is very often played to balance a rack by getting rid of a surplus of vowels.

AUBADE, -S n song or poem greeting the dawn

AUBERGE, -S n inn or tavern

AUBRETIA same as > aubrietia

AUBRIETA same as > aubrietia

AUBURN, -S adj (of hair) reddish-brown ⊳ n moderate reddish-brown colour

AUCEPS, -ES n old word meaning person who catches hawks

AUCTION, -S n public sale in which articles are sold to the highest bidder ⊳ vb sell by auction

AUCUBA, -S n Japanese laurel

AUDACITY > audacious

AUDAD, -S n wild African sheep

AUDIAL adj of sound

AUDIBLE, -D, -S adj loud enough to be heard ⊳ n audible change of tactics

in American football ⊳ vb call an audible

AUDIBLY

AUDIENCE n group of spectators or listeners

AUDIENT, -S n person who hears

AUDILE, -S n person with a faculty for auditory imagery ⊳ adj of or relating to such a person

AUDING, -S n practice of listening to try to understand

AUDIO, -S adj of sound or hearing ⊳ n sound

AUDIT, -ED, -S n official examination of business accounts ⊳ vb examine (business accounts) officially

AUDITEE, -S n one who is audited

AUDITING n act of auditing

AUDITION n test of a performer's ability for a particular role or job ⊳ vb test or be tested in an audition

AUDITIVE n person who learns primarily by listening

AUDITOR, -S n person qualified to audit accounts

AUDITORY adj of or relating to hearing

AUDITS ▸ audit

AUE interj Māori exclamation

Another Māori exclamation, so useful for getting rid of surplus vowels. But, unlike **aua**, it does not take an S.

AUF, -S old word for ▸ oaf

AUFGABE, -S n word used in psychology to mean task

AUFS ▸ auf

AUGEND, -S n number to which a number is added

AUGER, -S n tool for boring holes

AUGH interj expressing frustration

AUGHT, -S adv in any least part ⊳ n less common word for nought

AUGITE, -S n black or greenish-black mineral

AUGITIC

AUGMENT, -S vb increase or enlarge ⊳ n vowel prefix forming a past tense

AUGUR, -ED, -ING, -S vb be a sign of (future events) ⊳ n religious official who interpreted omens

AUGURAL

AUGURER, -S old word for ▸ augur

AUGURIES ▸ augury

A

AUGURING ► augur

AUGURS ► augur

AUGURY, AUGURIES *n* foretelling of the future

AUGUST, -ER, -S *adj* dignified and imposing ▷ *n* auguste

AUGUSTE, -S *n* type of circus clown

AUGUSTER ► august

AUGUSTES ► auguste

AUGUSTLY ► august

AUGUSTS ► august

AUK, -S *n* sea bird with short wings

AUKLET, -S *n* type of small auk

AUKS ► auk

AULA, -S *n* hall

AULARIAN *n* Oxford University student belonging to hall

AULAS ► aula

AULD, -ER, -EST *a Scots word for* **► old**

AULIC *adj* relating to a royal court

AULNAGE, -S *n* measurement in ells

AULNAGER *n* inspector of cloth

AULNAGES ► aulnage

AULOS, AULOI *n* ancient Greek pipe

AUMAIL, -ED, -S *old word for* **► enamel**

AUMBRY, AUMBRIES *same as* **► ambry**

AUMIL, -S *n* manager in India

AUNE, -S *n* old French measure of length

AUNT, -S *n* father's or mother's sister

AUNTER, -S *old word for* > **adventure**

AUNTHOOD ► aunt

AUNTIE, -S *n* aunt

AUNTLIER ► auntly

AUNTLIKE ► aunt

AUNTLY, AUNTLIER *adj* of or like an aunt

AUNTS ► aunt

AUNTY *same as* **► auntie**

AURA, -E, -S *n* distinctive air or quality of a person or thing

AURAL *adj* of or using the ears or hearing

AURALITY

AURALLY

AURAR *plural of* **► eyrir**

AURAS ► aura

AURATE, -S *n* salt of auric acid

AURATED *adj* combined with auric acid

AURATES ► aurate

AUREATE *adj* covered with gold, gilded

AUREI ► aureus

AUREITY *n* attributes of gold

AURELIA, -S *n* large jellyfish

AURELIAN *n* person who studies butterflies and moths

AURELIAS ► aurelia

AUREOLA, -E, -S *same as* **► aureole**

AUREOLE, -D, -S *n* halo ▷ *vb* encircle

AURES ► auris

AUREUS, AUREI *n* gold coin of the Roman Empire

AURIC *adj* of or containing gold in the trivalent state

AURICLE, -S *n* upper chamber of the heart

AURICLED

AURICULA *n* alpine primrose with leaves shaped like a bear's ear

AURIFIED ► aurify

AURIFIES ► aurify

AURIFORM *adj* shaped like an ear

AURIFY, AURIFIED, AURIFIES *vb* turn into gold

AURIS, AURES *n* medical word for ear

AURIST, -S *a former name for* > **audiologist**

AUROCHS *n* recently extinct European wild ox

AURORA, -E, -S *n* bands of light seen in the sky

AURORAL

AUROREAN *adj* of dawn

AUROUS *adj* of or containing gold, esp in the monovalent state

AURUM, -S *n* gold

AUSFORM, -S *vb* temper steel

AUSPEX *same as* **► augur**

AUSPICE, -S *n* patronage or guidance

AUSTERE, -R *adj* stern or severe

AUSTRAL, -S *adj* southern ▷ *n* former monetary unit of Argentina

AUSUBO, -S *n* tropical tree

AUTACOID *n* any natural internal secretion, esp one that exerts an effect similar to a drug

AUTARCH, -S *n* absolute ruler

AUTARCHY *n* absolute power or autocracy

AUTARKIC ► autarky

AUTARKY *n* policy of economic self-sufficiency

AUTECISM > autecious

AUTEUR, -S *n* director

AUTHOR, -ED, -S *n* writer of a book etc ▷ *vb* write or originate

AUTISM, -S *n* disorder characterized by lack of response to people and limited ability to communicate

AUTIST, -S *n* autistic person

AUTISTIC ► autism

AUTISTS ► autist

AUTO, -ED, -ING, -S *n* automobile ▷ *vb* travel in an automobile

AUTOBAHN *n* German motorway

AUTOBANK *n* automated teller machine

AUTOBODY *n* body of a motor vehicle

AUTOBUS *n* motor bus

AUTOCADE *another name for* > **motorcade**

AUTOCAR, -S *n* motor car

AUTOCARP *n* fruit produced through self-fertilization

AUTOCARS ► autocar

AUTOCOID *n* hormone

AUTOCRAT *n* ruler with absolute authority

AUTOCUE, -S *n* electronic television prompting device

AUTODIAL *vb* dial a telephone number automatically

AUTODYNE *adj* using the same elements and valves as oscillator and detector ▷ *n* autodyne circuit

AUTOED ► auto

AUTOGAMY *n* self-fertilization in flowering plants

AUTOGENY *n* hypothetical process by which living organisms first arose on earth from nonliving matter

AUTOGIRO *n* self-propelled aircraft resembling a helicopter but with an unpowered rotor

AUTOGYRO *same as* **► autogiro**

AUTOHARP *n* zither-like musical instrument

AUTOING ► auto

AUTOLOAD *vb* load automatically

AUTOLOGY *n* study of oneself

AUTOLYSE *vb* undergo or cause to undergo autolysis

AUTOLYZE *same as* **► autolyse**

AUTOMAN, AUTOMEN *n* car manufacturer

AUTOMAT, -S *n* vending machine

AUTOMATA > automaton

AUTOMATE *vb* make (a manufacturing process) automatic
AUTOMATS ► **automat**
AUTOMEN ► **automan**
AUTONOMY *n* self-government
AUTONYM, -S *n* writing published under the real name of an author
AUTOPEN, -S *n* mechanical device used to produce imitation signatures
AUTOPSIA *n* autopsy
AUTOPSIC ► **autopsy**
AUTOPSY *n* examination of a body to determine the cause of death
AUTOPTIC
AUTOPUT, -S *n* motorway in the former Yugoslavia
AUTOS ► **auto**
AUTOSAVE *n* computer facility for automatically saving data ▷ *vb* save (computer data) automatically
AUTOSOME *n* type of chromosome
AUTOTEST *n* motor race in which standard cars are driven round a circuit
AUTOTOMY *n* casting off by an animal of a part of its body, to facilitate escape when attacked
AUTOTUNE *n* software that changes a recording of a vocal track
AUTOTYPE *n* photographic process for producing prints in black and white, using a carbon pigment ▷ *vb* process using autotype
AUTOTYPY
AUTOVAC, -S *n* vacuum pump in a car petrol tank
AUTUMN, -S *n* season between summer and winter
AUTUMNAL *adj* of, occurring in, or characteristic of autumn
AUTUMNS ► **autumn**
AUTUMNY *adj* like autumn
AUTUNITE *n* yellowish fluorescent radioactive mineral
AUXESIS, AUXESES *n* increase in cell size without division
AUXETIC, -S *n* something that promotes growth
AUXILIAR *old word for* > **auxiliary**
AUXIN, -S *n* plant hormone that promotes growth
AUXINIC

AUXOCYTE *n* any cell undergoing meiosis
AVA, -S *adv* at all ▷ *n* Polynesian shrub
AVADAVAT *n* Asian weaverbird with usu red plumage, often kept as a cagebird
AVAIL, -ED, -ING, -S *vb* be of use or advantage (to) ▷ *n* use or advantage
AVAILE, -S *old word for* ► **lower**
AVAILED ► **avail**
AVAILES ► **availe**
AVAILFUL *old word for* > **useful**
AVAILING ► **avail**
AVAILS ► **avail**
AVAL *adj* of a grandparent
AVALE, -D, -S, AVALING *old word for* ► **lower**
AVANT *prep* before
AVANTI *interj* forward!
AVANTIST *n* proponent of the avant-garde
AVARICE, -S *n* greed for wealth
AVAS ► **ava**
AVAST *sentence substitute* stop! cease!
AVATAR, -S *n* appearance of a god in animal or human form
AVAUNT, -ED, -S *sentence substitute* go away! depart! ▷ *vb* go away; depart
AVE, -S *n* expression of welcome or farewell
AVEL, -S *a variant of* ► **ovel**
AVELLAN *adj* of hazelnuts
AVELLANE *same as* ► **avellan**
AVELS ► **avel**
AVENGE, -D, -S, AVENGING *vb* take revenge in retaliation for (harm done) or on behalf of (a person harmed)
AVENGER -S
AVENIR, -S *n* future
AVENS, -ES *n* any of several temperate or arctic rosaceous plants
AVENTAIL *n* front flap of a helmet
AVENTRE, -D, -S *old word for* ► **thrust**
AVENTURE *old form of* > **adventure**
AVENUE, -S *n* wide street
AVER, -RED, -RING, -S *vb* state to be true
AVERAGE, -D, -S *n* typical or normal amount or quality ▷ *adj* usual or typical ▷ *vb* calculate the average of
AVERAGER *n* average adjuster
AVERAGES ► **average**

AVERMENT ► **aver**
AVERRED ► **aver**
AVERRING ► **aver**
AVERS ► **aver**
AVERSE *adj* disinclined or unwilling
AVERSELY
AVERSION *n* strong dislike
AVERSIVE *n* tool or technique intended to repel animals etc
AVERT, -ED, -ING, -S *vb* turn away
AVERTER -S
AVES ► **ave**
AVGAS, -ES, -SES *n* aviation fuel
AVIAN, -S *adj* of or like a bird ▷ *n* bird
AVIANISE *same as* ► **avianize**
AVIANIZE *vb* modify microorganisms in a chicken embryo
AVIANS ► **avian**
AVIARIES ► **aviary**
AVIARIST *n* person who keeps an aviary
AVIARY, AVIARIES *n* large cage or enclosure for birds
AVIATE, -D, -S, AVIATING *vb* pilot or fly in an aircraft
AVIATIC *adj* pertaining to aviation
AVIATING ► **aviate**
AVIATION *n* art of flying aircraft
AVIATOR, -S *n* pilot of an aircraft
AVIATRIX
AVICULAR *adj* of small birds
AVID, -ER, -EST *adj* keen or enthusiastic
AVIDIN, -S *n* protein found in egg-white
AVIDITY *n* quality or state of being avid
AVIDLY ► **avid**
AVIDNESS ► **avid**
AVIETTE, -S *n* aeroplane driven by human strength
AVIFAUNA *n* all the birds in a particular region
AVIFORM *adj* like a bird
AVIGATOR *another word for* ► **aviator**
AVINE *adj* of birds
AVION, -S *n* aeroplane
AVIONIC ► **avionics**
AVIONICS *n* science and technology of electronics applied to aeronautics and astronautics
AVIONS ► **avion**
AVISE, -D, -S, AVISING *old word for* ► **advise**
AVISO, -S *n* boat carrying messages

AVITAL adj of a grandfather

AVIZE, -D, -S, AVIZING old word for ▸ **advise**

AVO, -S n Macao currency unit

AVOCADO, -S n pear-shaped tropical fruit with a leathery green skin and yellowish-green flesh

AVOCET, -S n long-legged wading bird

AVODIRE, -S n African tree

AVOID, -ED, -ING, -S vb prevent from happening

AVOIDANT adj (of behaviour) demonstrating a tendency to avoid intimacy or interaction with others

AVOIDED ▸ **avoid**

AVOIDER, -S ▸ **avoid**

AVOIDING ▸ **avoid**

AVOIDS ▸ **avoid**

AVOISION n nonpayment of tax

AVOS ▸ **avo**

AVOSET, -S n avocet

AVOUCH, -ED, -ES vb vouch for

AVOUCHER

AVOURE, -S old word for ▸ **avowal**

AVOUTRER old word for > **adulterer**

AVOW, -ING, -S vb state or affirm

AVOWABLE

AVOWABLY

AVOWAL -S

AVOWED ▸ **avow**

AVOWEDLY ▸ **avow**

AVOWER, -S ▸ **avow**

AVOWING ▸ **avow**

AVOWRY, AVOWRIES old word for ▸ **avowal**

AVOWS ▸ **avow**

AVOYER, -S n former Swiss magistrate

AVRUGA, -S n herring roe

AVULSE, -D, -S, AVULSING vb take away by force

AVULSION n forcible tearing away of a bodily structure or part

AVYZE, -D, -S, AVYZING old word for ▸ **advise**

AW variant of ▸ **all**

AWA adv away

AWAIT, -ED, -ING, -S vb wait for

AWAITER -S

AWAKE, -D, -S, AWOKE, AWOKEN vb emerge or rouse from sleep ▸ adj not sleeping

AWAKEN, -ED, -S vb awake

AWAKENER

AWAKES ▸ **awake**

AWAKING, -S ▸ **awake**

AWANTING adj missing

AWARD, -ED, -ING, -S vb give (something, such as a prize) formally ▷ n something awarded, such as a prize

AWARDEE -S

AWARDER, -S ▸ **award**

AWARDING ▸ **award**

AWARDS ▸ **award**

AWARE, -R, -ST adj having knowledge, informed

AWARN, -ED, -ING, -S vb old form of warn

AWASH adv washed over by water ▷ adj washed over by water

AWATCH adv watching

AWATO, -S n New Zealand caterpillar

AWAVE adv in waves

AWAY, -S adv from a place ▷ adj not present ▷ n game played or won at an opponent's ground

AWAYDAY, -S n day trip taken for pleasure

AWAYES old word for ▸ **away**

AWAYNESS ▸ **away**

AWAYS ▸ **away**

AWDL, -S n traditional Welsh poem

AWE, -D, -ING, -S, AWING n wonder and respect mixed with dread ▷ vb fill with awe

AWEARIED old word for ▸ **weary**

AWEARY old form of ▸ **weary**

AWEATHER adj towards the weather

AWED ▸ **awe**

AWEE adv for a short time

AWEEL interj Scots word meaning well

AWEIGH adj (of an anchor) no longer hooked onto the bottom

AWEING ▸ **awe**

AWELESS ▸ **awe**

AWES ▸ **awe**

AWESOME adj inspiring awe

AWETO, -S n New Zealand caterpillar

AWFUL, -LER adj very bad or unpleasant ▷ adv very

AWFULLY adv in an unpleasant way

AWFY adv (Scots) awfully, extremely

AWHAPE, -D, -S, AWHAPING old word for ▸ **amaze**

AWHATO, -S n New Zealand caterpillar

AWHEEL adv on wheels

AWHEELS same as ▸ **awheel**

AWHETO, -S n New Zealand caterpillar

AWHILE adv for a brief time

AWHIRL adv whirling

AWING ▸ **awe**

AWK, -S n type of programming language

This provides a useful high-scoring outlet for what can be the awkward letters W and K.

AWKWARD adj clumsy or ungainly

AWL, -S n pointed tool for piercing wood, leather, etc

AWLBIRD, -S n woodpecker

AWLESS ▸ **awe**

AWLS ▸ **awl**

AWLWORT, -S n type of aquatic plant

AWMOUS Scots word for ▸ **alms**

AWMRIE, -S n cupboard for church vessels

AWMRY n cupboard for church vessels

AWN, -S n bristles on grasses

AWNED

AWNER, -S n machine for removing awns

AWNIER ▸ **awny**

AWNIEST ▸ **awny**

AWNING, -S n canvas roof supported by a frame to give protection against the weather

AWNINGED adj sheltered with awning

AWNINGS ▸ **awning**

AWNLESS ▸ **awn**

AWNS ▸ **awn**

AWNY, AWNIER, AWNIEST adj having awns

AWOKE ▸ **awake**

AWOKEN ▸ **awake**

AWOL, -S n person who is absent without leave

AWORK adv old word meaning at work

AWRACK adv in wrecked condition

AWRONG adv old word meaning wrongly

AWRY adj with a twist to one side, askew

AWSOME adj old form of awesome

AX same as ▸ **axe**

AXAL adj of an axis

AXE, -D, AXING n tool with a sharp blade for felling trees or chopping wood ▷ vb dismiss (employees), restrict (expenditure), or terminate (a project)

AXEBIRD, -S n nightjar

AXED ▸ **axe**

A

AXEL, -S n ice-skating movement

AXELIKE adj like an axe in form

AXELS ▸ axel

AXEMAN, AXEMEN n man who wields an axe, esp to cut down trees

AXENIC adj (of a biological culture) free from other microorganisms

AXES ▸ axis

AXIAL adj forming or of an axis

AXIALITY

AXIALLY

AXIL, -S n angle where the stalk of a leaf joins a stem

AXILE adj of, relating to, or attached to the axis

AXILEMMA same as ▸ axolemma

AXILLA, -E, -S n area under a bird's wing

AXILLAR, -S same as ▸ axillary

AXILLARY adj of, relating to, or near the armpit ▷ n one of the feathers growing from the axilla of a bird's wing

AXILLAS ▸ axilla

AXILS ▸ axil

AXING ▸ ax

AXINITE, -S n crystalline substance

AXIOLOGY n theory of values, moral or aesthetic

AXIOM, -S n generally accepted principle

AXION, -S n type of hypothetical elementary particle

AXIS, AXES, -ES n imaginary line round which a body can rotate

AXISED adj having an axis

AXISES ▸ axis

AXITE, -S n type of gunpowder

AXLE, -S n shaft on which a wheel or pair of wheels turns

AXLED adj having an axle

AXLES ▸ axle

AXLETREE n bar fixed across the underpart of a wagon or carriage

AXLIKE ▸ ax

AXMAN, AXMEN same as ▸ axeman

AXOID, -S n type of curve

AXOLEMMA n membrane that encloses the axon of a nerve cell

AXOLOTL, -S n aquatic salamander of central America

AXON, -S n threadlike extension of a nerve cell

AXONAL

AXONE, -S same as ▸ axon

AXONEMAL ▸ axoneme

AXONEME, -S n part of cell consisting of proteins

AXONES ▸ axone

AXONIC ▸ axon

AXONS ▸ axon

AXOPLASM n part of cell

AXSEED, -S n crown vetch

AY, -S adv ever ▷ n expression of agreement

AYAH, -S n Indian or Malay maidservant or nursemaid in former British Empire

AYAYA, -S n type of Inuit singing

AYE, -S n affirmative vote or voter ▷ adv always

AYELP adv yelping

AYENBITE old word for ▸ remorse

AYES ▸ aye

AYGRE old word for ▸ eager

AYIN, -S n 16th letter in the Hebrew alphabet

AYONT adv beyond

AYRE, -S old word for ▸ air

AYRIE, -S old word for ▸ eyrie

AYS ▸ ay

AYU, -S n small Japanese fish

> This comes up quite often, being an extension of both **ay** and **yu**, showing how important it is to know those little 'hook' words.

AYURVEDA n ancient medical treatise on the art of healing and prolonging life

AYUS ▸ ayu

AYWORD, -S n old word meaning byword

AZALEA, -S n garden shrub grown for its showy flowers

AZAN, -S n call to prayer

AZERTY n European version of keyboard

AZIDE, -S n type of chemical compound

AZIDO adj containing an azide

AZIMUTH, -S n arc of the sky between the zenith and the horizon

AZINE, -S n organic compound

AZIONE, -S n musical drama

AZLON, -S n fibre made from protein

AZO adj of the divalent group -N:N-

> **Azo** is a chemical term you will want to play often, but it does not take an S. It takes an N to form **azon**.

AZOIC adj without life

AZOLE, -S n organic compound

AZOLLA, -S n tropical water fern

AZON, -S n type of drawing paper

AZONAL adj not divided into zones

AZONIC adj not confined to a zone

AZONS ▸ azon

AZOTE, -D, -S an obsolete name for ▸ nitrogen

AZOTEMIA same as > azotaemia

AZOTEMIC > azotaemia

AZOTES ▸ azote

AZOTH, -S n panacea postulated by Paracelsus

AZOTIC adj of, containing, or concerned with nitrogen

AZOTISE, -D, -S same as ▸ azotize

AZOTIZE, -D, -S vb combine or treat with nitrogen or a nitrogen compound

AZOTOUS adj containing nitrogen

AZOTURIA n presence of excess nitrogen in urine

AZUKI, -S same as ▸ adzuki

AZULEJO, -S n Spanish porcelain tile

> An **azulejo** is a kind of brightly coloured tile, beautiful in its combination of the J and Z.

AZURE, -S n (of) the colour of a clear blue sky ▷ adj deep blue

AZUREAN adj azure

AZURES ▸ azure

AZURIES ▸ azury

AZURINE, -S n blue dye

AZURITE, -S n azure-blue mineral associated with copper deposits

AZURN old word for ▸ azure

AZURY, AZURIES adj bluish ▷ n bluish colour

AZYGIES ▸ azygy

AZYGOS, -ES n biological structure not in a pair

AZYGOUS adj developing or occurring singly

AZYGY, AZYGIES n state of not being joined in a pair

AZYM, -S n unleavened bread

AZYME, -S same as ▸ azym

AZYMITE, -S n member of a church using unleavened bread in the Eucharist

AZYMOUS adj unleavened

AZYMS ▸ azym

Bb

B forms a two-letter word before every vowel except **U** - and with **Y** as well. With a **B** in your rack, you can play lots of short words that will give you relatively high scores. The best of these are **box** (12 points), **bez** (14 points) and **biz** (14 points), but don't forget **bay** (8), **by** (7), **bow** (8), **boy** (8), **buy** (8) and **bye** (8).

BA, -S *n* symbol for the soul in Ancient Egyptian religion
BAA, -ED *vb* the characteristic bleating sound of a sheep ▷ *n* cry made by a sheep
BAAING -S
BAAL, -IM, -S *n* any false god or idol
BAALEBOS *n* master of the house
BAALIM ▶ baal
BAALISM, -S ▶ baal
BAALS ▶ baal
BAAS, -ES *South African word for* **▶ boss**
BAASKAAP *same as* **▶ baaskap**
BAASKAP, -S *n* (in South Africa) control by Whites of non-Whites
BAASSKAP *same as* **▶ baaskap**
BABA, -S *n* small cake of leavened dough
BABACO, -S *n* greenish-yellow egg-shaped fruit
BABACU, -S *n* type of Brazilian palm tree
BABALAS *adj* South African word for drunk
BABAS ▶ baba
BABASSU, -S *n* Brazilian palm tree with hard edible nuts
BABBELAS *same as* **▶ babalas**
BABBITRY *same as* **▶ babbitt**
BABBITT, -S *vb* line (a bearing) or face (a surface) with a similar soft alloy
BABBLE, -D, -S *vb* talk excitedly or foolishly ▷ *n* muddled or foolish speech
BABBLER, -S *n* person who babbles
BABBLES ▶ babble
BABBLIER ▶ babbly
BABBLING ▶ babble
BABBLY, BABBLIER ▶ babble

BABE, -S *n* baby
BABEL, -S *n* confused mixture of noises or voices
BABELDOM
BABELISH
BABELISM
BABES ▶ babe
BABESIA, -S *n* parasite causing infection in cattle
BABICHE, -S *n* thongs or lacings of rawhide
BABIED ▶ baby
BABIER ▶ baby
BABIES ▶ baby
BABIEST ▶ baby
BABIRUSA *n* Indonesian wild pig with an almost hairless skin and huge curved canine teeth
BABKA, -S *n* cake
BABLAH, -S *n* type of acacia
BABOO *same as* **▶ babu**
BABOOL, -S *n* type of acacia
BABOON, -S *n* large monkey with a pointed face and a long tail
BABOOS ▶ baboo
BABOOSH *same as* **▶ babouche**
BABOUCHE *n* Middle-Eastern slipper
BABU, -S *n* title or form of address used in India
BABUCHE, -S *same as* **▶ babouche**
BABUDOM, -S ▶ babu
BABUISM, -S ▶ babu
BABUL, -S *n* N African and Indian tree with small yellow flowers
BABUS ▶ babu
BABUSHKA *n* headscarf tied under the chin, worn by Russian peasant women
BABY, BABIED, BABIER, BABIES, BABIEST, -ING *n* very young child or animal

▷ *adj* comparatively small of its type ▷ *vb* treat as a baby
BABYCINO *same as*
> **babyccino**
BABYDOLL, -S *n* woman's short nightdress
BABYFOOD *n* puréed food for babies
BABYHOOD ▶ baby
BABYING ▶ baby
BABYISH ▶ baby
BABYLIKE *adj* like a baby
BABYSIT, BABYSAT, -S *vb* look after a child in its parents' absence
BAC, -S *n* baccalaureate
BACALAO, -S *n* dried salt cod
BACALHAU *same as*
▶ **bacalao**
BACCA, -E, -S *n* berry
BACCALA, -S *same as*
▶ **bacalao**
BACCARA, -S *same as*
▶ **baccarat**
BACCARAT *n* card game involving gambling
BACCARE *same as* **▶ backare**
BACCAS ▶ bacca
BACCATE, -D *adj* like a berry in form, texture, etc
BACCHANT *n* priest or votary of Bacchus
BACCHIAC ▶ bacchius
BACCHIAN *same as*
▶ **bacchic**
BACCHIC *adj* riotously jovial
BACCHIUS, BACCHII *n* metrical foot of one short syllable followed by two long ones
BACCIES ▶ baccy
BACCO, -ES, -S *n* tobacco
BACCY, BACCIES *n* tobacco
BACH, -ED, -ES, -ING, -S *same as* **▶ batch**
BACHA, -S *n* Indian English word for young child

B

BACHATA, -S n type of dance music originating in the Dominican Republic

BACHCHA, -S n Indian English word for young child

BACHED ▸ bach

BACHELOR n unmarried man

BACHES ▸ bach

BACHING ▸ bach

BACHS ▸ bach

BACILLAR same as > **bacillary**

BACILLUS, BACILLI n rod-shaped bacterium

BACK, -S n rear part of the human body, from the neck to the pelvis ▷ vb (cause to) move backwards ▷ adj situated behind ▷ adv at, to, or towards the rear

BACKACHE n ache or pain in one's back

BACKARE interj instruction to keep one's distance; back off

BACKBAND n back support

BACKBAR, -S n area behind a bar where bottles are stored

BACKBEAT n beat in music not usually accented

BACKBEND n gymnastic exercise in which the trunk is bent backwards until the hands touch the floor

BACKBITE, BACKBIT vb talk spitefully about an absent person

BACKBOND n legal document

BACKBONE n spinal column

BACKBURN vb clear an area of bush by creating a fire ▷ n act or result of backburning

BACKCAST n backward casting of fishing rod ▷ vb cast a fishing rod backwards

BACKCHAT n impudent replies

BACKCOMB vb comb (the hair) towards the roots to give more bulk to a hairstyle

BACKDATE vb make (a document) effective from a date earlier than its completion

BACKDOOR adj secret, underhand, or obtained through influence

BACKDOWN n abandonment of an earlier claim

BACKDROP vb provide a backdrop to (something)

BACKED adj having a back or backing

BACKER, -S n person who gives financial support

BACKET, -S n shallow box

BACKFALL n fall onto the back

BACKFAT, -S n layer of fat in animals between the skin and muscle

BACKFILE n archives of a newspaper or magazine

BACKFILL vb refill an excavated trench, esp (in archaeology) at the end of an investigation ▷ n soil used to do this

BACKFIRE vb (of a plan) fail to have the desired effect ▷ n (in an engine) explosion of unburnt gases in the exhaust system

BACKFIT, -S vb overhaul nuclear power plant

BACKFLIP, -S n backwards somersault

BACKFLOW n reverse flow

BACKHAND n stroke played with the back of the hand facing the direction of the stroke ▷ adv with a backhand stroke ▷ vb play (a shot) backhand

BACKHAUL vb transmit data

BACKHOE, -D, -S n digger ▷ vb dig with a backhoe

BACKIE, -S n ride on the back of someone's bicycle

BACKING, -S n support

BACKLAND n undeveloped land behind a property

BACKLASH n sudden and adverse reaction ▷ vb create a sudden and adverse reaction

BACKLESS adj (of a dress) low-cut at the back

BACKLIFT n backward movement of bat

BACKLINE n defensive players in a sports team as a unit

BACKLIST n publisher's previously published books that are still available ▷ vb put on a backlist

BACKLIT adj illuminated from behind

BACKLOAD n load for lorry on return journey ▷ vb load a lorry for a return journey

BACKLOG, -S n accumulation of things to be dealt with

BACKLOT, -S n area outside a film or television studio used for outdoor filming

BACKMOST adj furthest back

BACKOUT, -S n instance of withdrawing (from an agreement, etc)

BACKPACK n large pack carried on the back ▷ vb go hiking with a backpack

BACKREST n support for the back of something

BACKROOM n place where research or planning is done, esp secret research in wartime

BACKRUSH n seaward return of wave

BACKS ▸ back

BACKSAW, -S n small handsaw

BACKSEAT n seat at the back, esp of a vehicle

BACKSET, -S n reversal ▷ vb attack from the rear

BACKSEY, -S n sirloin

BACKSIDE n buttocks

BACKSLAP vb demonstrate effusive joviality

BACKSLID > backslide

BACKSPIN n backward spin given to a ball to reduce its speed at impact

BACKSTAB vb attack deceitfully

BACKSTAY n stay leading aft from the upper part of a mast to the deck or stern

BACKSTOP n screen or fence to prevent balls leaving the playing area ▷ vb provide with backing or support

BACKTALK n argumentative discourse

BACKUP, -S n support or reinforcement

BACKVELD n (in South Africa) remote sparsely populated area

BACKWARD same as > **backwards**

BACKWASH n water washed backwards by the motion of a boat ▷ vb remove oil from (combed wool)

BACKWIND vb direct airflow into the back of a sail

BACKWOOD > backwoods

BACKWORD n act or an instance of failing to keep a promise or commitment

BACKWORK n work carried out under the ground

BACKWRAP n back support

BACKYARD n yard at the back of a house, etc

BACLAVA, -S same as ▸ **baklava**

BACLOFEN n drug used to treat stroke victims

BACON, -S n salted or smoked pig meat

BACONER, -S n pig that weighs between 83 and 101 kg, from which bacon is cut

BACONS ▸ bacon

B

BACRONYM same as
> **backronym**

BACS ► **bac**

BACTERIA pl n large group of microorganisms
BACTERIC

BACTERIN n vaccine prepared from bacteria

BACULA ► **baculum**

BACULINE adj relating to flogging

BACULITE n fossil

BACULUM, BACULA, -S n bony support in the penis of certain mammals

BAD, -DER, -DEST, -S adj not good ▷ n unfortunate or unpleasant events collectively ▷ adv badly

BADDER ► **bad**

BADDEST ► **bad**

BADDIE, -S n bad character in a story, film, etc, esp an opponent of the hero

BADDISH ► **bad**

BADDY same as ► **baddie**

BADE ► **bid**

BADGE, -D, -S, BADGING n emblem worn to show membership, rank, etc ▷ vb put a badge on

BADGER, -ED, -S n nocturnal burrowing mammal ▷ vb pester or harass
BADGERLY

BADGES ► **badge**

BADGING ► **badge**

BADINAGE n playful and witty conversation ▷ vb engage in badinage

BADIOUS adj chestnut; brownish-red

BADLAND ► **badlands**

BADLANDS pl n any deeply eroded barren area

BADLY adv poorly

BADMAN, BADMEN n hired gunman, outlaw, or criminal

BADMASH n evil-doer ▷ adj naughty or bad

BADMEN ► **badman**

BADMOUTH vb speak unfavourably about (someone or something)

BADNESS ► **bad**

BADS ► **bad**

BADWARE, -S n software designed to harm a computer system

BAEL, -S n type of spiny Indian tree

BAETYL, -S n magical meteoric stone

BAFF, -ED, -ING, -S vb strike ground with golf club

BAFFIES pl n slippers

BAFFING ► **baff**

BAFFLE, -D, -S vb perplex or puzzle ▷ n device to limit or regulate the flow of fluid, light, or sound
BAFFLER -S

BAFFLING adj impossible to understand

BAFFS ► **baff**

BAFFY n obsolete golf club

BAFT, -S n coarse fabric

BAG, -GED, -S n flexible container with an opening at one end ▷ vb put into a bag

BAGARRE, -S n brawl

BAGASS same as ► **bagasse**

BAGASSE, -S n pulp of sugar cane or similar plants

BAGEL, -ED, -ING, -LED, -S n hard ring-shaped bread roll ▷ vb win a tennis set by six games to love

BAGFUL, -S, BAGSFUL n amount (of something) that can be held in a bag

BAGGAGE, -S n suitcases packed for a journey

BAGGED ► **bag**

BAGGER, -S n person who packs groceries

BAGGIE, -S n plastic bag

BAGGIER ► **baggy**

BAGGIES ► **baggie**

BAGGIEST ► **baggy**

BAGGILY ► **baggy**

BAGGING, -S ► **bag**

BAGGIT, -S n unspawned salmon

BAGGY, BAGGIER, BAGGIEST adj hanging loosely

BAGH, -S n (in India and Pakistan) a garden

BAGHOUSE n dust-filtering chamber

BAGHS ► **bagh**

BAGIE, -S n turnip

BAGLESS adj (esp of a vacuum cleaner) not containing a bag

BAGLIKE ► **bag**

BAGMAN, BAGMEN n travelling salesman

BAGNETTE variant of ► **baguette**

BAGNIO, -S n bathing-house

BAGPIPE, -D vb play the bagpipes

BAGPIPER ► **bagpipes**

BAGPIPES pl n musical wind instrument with reed pipes and an inflatable bag

BAGS ► **bag**

BAGSFUL ► **bagful**

BAGUET, -S same as ► **baguette**

BAGUETTE n narrow French stick loaf

BAGUIO, -S n hurricane

BAGWASH n laundry that washes clothes without drying or pressing them

BAGWIG, -S n 18th-century wig with hair pushed back into a bag

BAGWORM, -S n type of moth

BAH interj expression of contempt or disgust

BAHADA, -S same as ► **bajada**

BAHADUR, -S n title formerly conferred by the British on distinguished Indians

BAHOOKIE n Scottish informal word for the buttocks

BAHT, -S n standard monetary unit of Thailand, divided into 100 satang

BAHU, -S n (in India) daughter-in-law

BAHUT, -S n decorative cabinet

BAIDAR, -S same as ► **baidarka**

BAIDARKA n narrow hunting boat

BAIDARS ► **baidar**

BAIL, -ED, -ING, -S n money deposited with a court as security for a person's reappearance ▷ vb pay bail for (a person)

BAILABLE adj eligible for release on bail

BAILBOND n document guaranteeing a prisoner released on bail will attend court

BAILED ► **bail**

BAILEE, -S n person to whom the possession of goods is transferred under a bailment

BAILER, -S ► **bail**

BAILEY, -S n outermost wall or court of a castle

BAILIE, -S n (in Scotland) a municipal magistrate

BAILIFF, -S n sheriff's officer who serves writs and summonses

BAILING ► **bail**

BAILLI, -S n magistrate

BAILLIE, -S variant of ► **bailie**

BAILLIS ► **bailli**

BAILMENT n contractual delivery of goods in trust to a person for a specific purpose

BAILOR, -S n owner of goods entrusted to another under a bailment

BAILOUT, -S n instance of helping (a person,

organization, etc) out of a predicament

BAILS ▶ bail

BAILSMAN, BAILSMEN n one standing bail for another

BAININ, -S n Irish collarless jacket made of white wool

BAINITE, -S n mixture of iron and iron carbide found in incompletely hardened steels

BAIRN, -S n child
BAIRNISH
BAIRNLY

BAISA, -S n small unit of currency in Oman

BAIT, -ED, -S n piece of food on a hook or in a trap to attract fish or animals ▷ vb put a piece of food on or in (a hook or trap)
BAITER -S

BAITFISH n small fish used as bait

BAITH adj both

BAITING, -S ▶ bait

BAITS ▶ bait

BAIZA, -S n Omani unit of currency

BAIZE, -D, -S, BAIZING n woollen fabric used to cover billiard and card tables ▷ vb line or cover with such fabric

BAJADA, -S n sloping surface formed from rock deposits

BAJAN, -S n freshman at Aberdeen University

BAJRA, -S n Indian millet

BAJREE, -S variant of ▶ bajra

BAJRI, -S variant of ▶ bajra

BAJU, -S n Malay jacket

BAKE, -D, -N, -S vb cook by dry heat as in an oven ▷ n party at which the main dish is baked

BAKELITE n tradename for a class of resin

BAKEMEAT n pie

BAKEN ▶ bake

BAKEOFF, -S n baking competition

BAKER, -S n person whose business is to make or sell bread, cakes, etc

BAKERIES ▶ bakery

BAKERS ▶ baker

BAKERY, BAKERIES n place where bread, cakes, etc are baked or sold

BAKES ▶ bake

BAKESHOP n bakery

BAKEWARE n dishes for baking

BAKGAT adj fine, excellent, marvellous

BAKING, -S n process of cooking bread, cakes, etc

▷ adj (esp of weather) very hot and dry

BAKKIE, -S n small truck

BAKLAVA, -S n rich pastry of Middle Eastern origin

BAKLAWA, -S same as ▶ baklava

BAKSHISH same as > **baksheesh**

BAL, -S n balmoral

BALADIN, -S n dancer

BALADINE n female dancer

BALADINS ▶ baladin

BALAFON, -S n type of W African xylophone

BALANCE, -S n stability of mind or body ▷ vb weigh in a balance

BALANCED adj having weight equally distributed

BALANCER n person or thing that balances

BALANCES ▶ balance

BALAS, -ES n red variety of spinel, used as a gemstone

BALATA, -S n tropical American tree yielding a latex-like sap

BALAYAGE vb highlight hair by painting dye onto sections

BALBOA, -S n standard currency unit of Panama

BALCONET n small balcony

BALCONY n platform on the outside of a building with a rail along the outer edge

BALD, -ED, -ER, -EST, -S adj having little or no hair on the scalp ▷ vb make bald

BALDHEAD n person without dreadlocks

BALDIE, -S same as ▶ baldy

BALDIER ▶ baldy

BALDIES ▶ baldie

BALDIEST ▶ baldy

BALDING adj becoming bald

BALDISH ▶ bald

BALDLY ▶ bald

BALDNESS ▶ bald

BALDPATE n type of duck

BALDRIC, -S n wide silk sash or leather belt worn across the body

BALDRICK same as ▶ baldric

BALDRICS ▶ baldric

BALDS ▶ bald

BALDY, BALDIER, BALDIEST adj bald ▷ n bald person

BALE, -D, -S same as ▶ bail

BALEEN, -S n whalebone

BALEFIRE n bonfire

BALEFUL adj vindictive or menacing

BALER, -S ▶ bail

BALES ▶ bale

BALING, -S n act of baling

BALISAUR n badger-like animal

BALISE, -S n electronic beacon used on a railway

BALISTA, -E, -S same as ▶ ballista

BALK, -ED, -S, BAULKERS vb stop short, esp suddenly or unexpectedly ▷ n roughly squared heavy timber beam

BALKER -S

BALKIER ▶ balky

BALKIEST ▶ balky

BALKILY ▶ balky

BALKING, -S ▶ balk

BALKLINE n line delimiting the balk area on a snooker table

BALKS ▶ balk

BALKY, BALKIER, BALKIEST adj inclined to stop abruptly and unexpectedly

BALL, -ED, -S n round or nearly round object, esp one used in games ▷ vb form into a ball

BALLAD, -ED, -S n narrative poem or song ▷ vb sing or write a ballad

BALLADE, -S n verse form

BALLADED ▶ ballad

BALLADES ▶ ballade

BALLADIC ▶ ballad

BALLADIN same as ▶ **baladin**

BALLADRY n ballad poetry or songs

BALLADS ▶ ballad

BALLAN, -S n species of fish

BALLANT, -S vb write a ballad

BALLAST, -S n substance used to stabilize a ship when it is not carrying cargo ▷ vb give stability to

BALLAT, -ED, -S vb write a ballad

BALLBOY, -S n boy who retrieves balls during a tennis, football, etc, match

BALLCLAY n clay suitable for ceramics

BALLCOCK n device for regulating the flow of a liquid into a tank

BALLED ▶ ball

BALLER, -S n ball-game player

BALLET, -ED, -S n classical style of expressive dancing based on conventional steps ▷ vb sing ballads
BALLETIC

BALLGAME n any game played with a ball

BALLGIRL n girl who retrieves balls during a tennis, football, etc, match

BALLGOWN n long formal dress

BALLHAWK n skilled basketball player ▷ vb act as a ballhawk

BALLIES ▶ bally

BALLING, -S ▶ ball

BALLISTA n ancient catapult for hurling stones, etc

BALLIUM, -S same as ▶ bailey

BALLON, -S n light, graceful quality

BALLONET n air or gas compartment in a nonrigid airship

BALLONNE n bouncing step

BALLONS ▶ ballon

BALLOON, -S n inflatable rubber bag used as a plaything or decoration ▷ vb fly in a balloon

BALLOT, -ED, -S n method of voting ▷ vb vote or ask for a vote from

BALLOTEE

BALLOTER

BALLOW, -S n heavy club

BALLPARK n stadium used for baseball games

BALLPEEN adj as in **ballpeen hammer** type of hammer

BALLROOM n large hall for dancing

BALLS ▶ ball

BALLUTE, -S n inflatable balloon parachute

BALLY, BALLIES another word for ▶ ballyhoo

BALLYARD n baseball ground

BALLYHOO n exaggerated fuss ▷ vb advertise or publicize by sensational or blatant methods

BALLYRAG same as ▶ bullyrag

BALM, -ED, -ING, -S n aromatic substance used for healing and soothing ▷ vb apply balm to

BALMIER ▶ balmy

BALMIEST ▶ balmy

BALMILY ▶ balmy

BALMING ▶ balm

BALMLIKE ▶ balm

BALMORAL n laced walking shoe

BALMS ▶ balm

BALMY, BALMIER, BALMIEST adj (of weather) mild and pleasant

BALNEAL adj of or relating to baths or bathing

BALNEARY same as ▶ balneal

BALONEY, -S n foolish talk; nonsense

BALOO, -S n bear

BALS ▶ bal

BALSA, -S n very light wood from a tropical American tree

BALSAM, -ED, -S n type of fragrant balm ▷ vb embalm

BALSAMIC

BALSAMY

BALSAS ▶ balsa

BALTI, -S n spicy Indian dish served in a metal dish

BALTIC adj very cold

BALTIS ▶ balti

BALU, -S same as ▶ baloo

BALUN, -S n electrical device

BALUS ▶ balu

BALUSTER n set of posts supporting a rail ▷ adj (of a shape) swelling at the base and rising in a concave curve to a narrow stem or neck

BAM, -MED, -MING, -S vb cheat

BAMBI, -S n born-again middle-aged biker

BAMBINO, BAMBINI, -S n young child, esp an Italian one

BAMBIS ▶ bambi

BAMBOO, -S n tall treelike tropical grass with hollow stems

BAMMED ▶ bam

BAMMER, -S ▶ bam

BAMMING ▶ bam

BAMPOT, -S n fool

BAMS ▶ bam

BAN, -I, -NED vb prohibit or forbid officially ▷ n unit of currency in Romania and Moldova

BANAK, -S n type of Central American tree

BANAL, -ER, -EST adj ordinary and unoriginal

BANALISE

BANALITY

BANALIZE

BANALLY

BANANA n yellow crescent-shaped fruit

BANANAS adj crazy

BANAUSIC adj merely mechanical

BANC, -S n as in **in banc** sitting as a full court

BANCO, -S n call made in gambling games

BANCS ▶ banc

BAND, -ED, -S n group of musicians playing together ▷ vb unite

BANDA, -S n African thatched hut

BANDAGE, -D, -S n piece of material used to cover a wound or wrap an injured limb ▷ vb cover with a bandage

BANDAGER

BANDAID adj (of a solution or remedy) temporary

BANDANA, -S same as ▶ bandanna

BANDANNA n large brightly coloured handkerchief or neckerchief

BANDAR, -S n species of monkey

BANDARI, -S n Indian English word for female monkey

BANDARS ▶ bandar

BANDAS ▶ banda

BANDBOX n lightweight usually cylindrical box for hats

BANDEAU, -S, -X n narrow ribbon worn round the head

BANDED ▶ band

BANDEIRA n 17th-century Portuguese slave-hunting expedition in Brazil

BANDELET n moulding round top of column

BANDER, -S ▶ band

BANDEROL same as > banderole

BANDERS ▶ bander

BANDFISH n Mediterranean fish with an elongated body

BANDH, -S n (in India) a general strike

BANDIED ▶ bandy

BANDIER ▶ bandy

BANDIES ▶ bandy

BANDIEST ▶ bandy

BANDING, -S n practice of grouping schoolchildren according to ability

BANDIT, -S, -TI n robber, esp a member of an armed gang

BANDITO, -S n Mexican bandit

BANDITRY ▶ bandit

BANDITS ▶ bandit

BANDITTI ▶ bandit

BANDMATE n fellow member of band

BANDOG, -S n ferocious dog

BANDOOK, -S same as ▶ bundook

BANDORA, -S same as ▶ bandore

BANDORE, -S n 16th-century musical instrument

BANDPASS n range of frequencies transmitted through a bandpass filter

BANDROL, -S same as > banderole

B

BANDS ► band
BANDSAW, -S n power saw with continuous blade
BANDSMAN, BANDSMEN n player in a musical band
BANDSTER n binder of wheat sheaves
BANDURA, -S n type of lute
BANDY, BANDIED, BANDIER, BANDIES, BANDIEST adj having legs curved outwards at the knees ▷ vb exchange (words) in a heated manner **BANDYING**
BANDYMAN, BANDYMEN n carriage or cart
BANE, -D, -S, BANING n person or thing that causes misery or distress ▷ vb cause harm or distress to (someone)
BANEFUL adj destructive, poisonous, or fatal
BANES ► bane
BANG, -ED, -ING, -S vb make a short explosive noise
BANGALAY n Australian tree valued for its hard red wood
BANGALOW n Australian palm tree native to New South Wales and Queensland
BANGED ► bang
BANGER, -S n old decrepit car
BANGING ► bang
BANGKOK, -S n type of straw hat
BANGLE, -D, -S n bracelet worn round the arm or the ankle
BANGS ► bang
BANGSTER n ruffian
BANGTAIL n horse's tail cut straight across but not through the bone
BANI ► ban
BANIA, -S same as ► **banyan**
BANIAN, -S same as ► **banyan**
BANIAS ► bania
BANING ► bane
BANISH, -ED, -ES vb send (someone) into exile **BANISHER**
BANISTER same as > **bannister**
BANJAX, -ED, -ES vb ruin; destroy

Meaning to ruin or confound, this is a great word to remember, with its high-scoring combination of J and X.

BANJO, -ES, -S n guitar-like musical instrument with a circular body
BANJOIST

BANK, -ED, -S n institution offering services such as the safekeeping and lending of money ▷ vb deposit (cash or cheques) in a bank
BANKABLE adj likely to ensure financial success
BANKBOOK n record of deposits, withdrawals, and interest held by depositors at certain banks
BANKCARD n card guaranteeing payment of cheque
BANKED ► bank
BANKER, -S n manager or owner of a bank
BANKERLY
BANKET, -S n gold-bearing conglomerate found in South Africa
BANKING, -S ► bank
BANKIT, -S same as > **banquette**
BANKNOTE n piece of paper money
BANKROLL n roll of currency notes ▷ vb provide the capital for
BANKRUPT n person declared by a court to be unable to pay his or her debts ▷ adj financially ruined ▷ vb make bankrupt
BANKS ► bank
BANKSIA, -S n Australian evergreen tree or shrub
BANKSIDE n riverside
BANKSMAN, BANKSMEN n crane driver's helper
BANKSTER n banker whose illegal practices have been exposed
BANLIEUE n suburb of a city
BANNABLE ► ban
BANNED ► ban
BANNER, -ED, -S n long strip of cloth displaying a slogan, advertisement, etc ▷ vb (of a newspaper headline) to display (a story) prominently ▷ adj outstandingly successful
BANNERET n small banner
BANNEROL same as > **banderole**
BANNERS ► banner
BANNET, -S n bonnet
BANNING, -S n act of banning
BANNOCK, -S n round flat cake made from oatmeal or barley
BANNS pl n public declaration, esp in a church, of an intended marriage

BANOFFEE n filling for a pie, consisting of toffee and banana
BANOFFI, -S same as ► **banoffee**
BANQUET, -S n elaborate formal dinner ▷ vb hold or take part in a banquet
BANS same as ► **banns**
BANSELA, -S same as ► **bonsela**
BANSHEE, -S n (in Irish folklore) female spirit whose wailing warns of a coming death
BANSHIE, -S same as ► **banshee**
BANT, -ED, -S n string ▷ vb tie with string
BANTAM, -S n small breed of chicken
BANTED ► bant
BANTENG, -S n wild ox
BANTER, -ED, -S vb tease jokingly ▷ n teasing or joking conversation
BANTERER
BANTIES ► banty
BANTING, -S ► bant
BANTLING n young child
BANTS ► bant
BANTY, BANTIES n bantam
BANXRING n tree-shrew
BANYA, -S n traditional Russian steam bath
BANYAN, -S n Indian tree
BANYAS ► banya
BANZAI, -S interj patriotic cheer, battle cry, or salutation
BAOBAB, -S n African tree with a thick trunk and angular branches
BAP, -S n large soft bread roll
BAPTISE, -D, -S same as ► **baptize**
BAPTISER
BAPTISIA n species of wild flower
BAPTISM, -S n Christian religious ceremony
BAPTIST, -S n one who baptizes
BAPTIZE, -D, -S vb perform baptism on
BAPTIZER
BAPU, -S n spiritual father
BAR, -RED, -S n rigid usually straight length of metal, wood, etc, longer than it is wide or thick ▷ vb fasten or secure with a bar
BARACAN, -S same as ► **barracan**

B

BARATHEA n fabric made of silk and wool or cotton and rayon, used esp for coats

BARAZA, **-S** n place where public meetings are held

BARB, **-ED**, **-ING**, **-S** n cutting remark ▷ vb provide with a barb or barbs

BARBAL adj of a beard

BARBARIC adj cruel or brutal

BARBASCO n S American plant

BARBATE, **-D** adj having tufts of long hairs

BARBE, **-S** n Waldensian missionary

BARBECUE n grill on which food is cooked over hot charcoal, usu outdoors ▷ vb cook (food) on a barbecue

BARBED ► barb

BARBEL, **-S** n long thin growth that hangs from the jaws of certain fishes, such as the carp

BARBELL, **-S** n long metal rod to which heavy discs are attached at each end for weightlifting

BARBELS ► barbel

BARBEQUE same as ► barbecue

BARBER, **-ED**, **-S** n person who cuts men's hair and shaves beards ▷ vb cut the hair of

BARBERRY n shrub with orange or red berries

BARBERS ► barber

BARBES ► barbe

BARBET, **-S** n type of small tropical bird

BARBETTE n earthen platform inside a parapet

BARBICAN n walled defence to protect a gate or drawbridge of a fortification

BARBICEL n minute hook on the barbule of a feather

BARBIE, **-S** short for ► barbecue

BARBING ► barb

BARBITAL same as > barbitone

BARBLESS ► barb

BARBOLA, **-S** n creation of small models of flowers, etc from plastic paste

BARBOT, **-S** same as ► burbot

BARBOTTE same as ► burbot

BARBS ► barb

BARBULE, **-S** n very small barb

BARBUT, **-S** n open-faced helmet

BARBWIRE n barbed wire

BARBY same as ► barbecue

BARCA, **-S** n boat

BARCHAN, **-S** n crescent-shaped shifting sand dune

BARCHANE same as ► barchan

BARCHANS ► barchan

BARCODE, **-S** n machine-readable code printed on goods

BARCODED adj having a barcode

BARCODES ► barcode

BARD, **-ING**, **-S** n poet ▷ vb place a piece of pork fat on

BARDE, **-D**, **-S** same as ► bard

BARDIC ► bard

BARDIE, **-S** n type of Australian grub

BARDIER ► bardy

BARDIES ► bardy

BARDIEST ► bardy

BARDING ► bard

BARDISM, **-S** ► bard

BARDLING n inferior poet

BARDO, **-S** n (in Tibetan Buddhism) the state of the soul between its death and its rebirth

BARDS ► bard

BARDSHIP ► bard

BARDY, **BARDIER**, **BARDIEST** ► bard

BARE, **-D**, **-R**, **-S**, **-ST**, **BARING** adj unclothed, naked ▷ vb uncover

BAREBACK adv (of horse-riding) without a saddle ▷ vb ride bareback

BAREBOAT n boat chartered without crew, provisions, etc

BAREBONE n computer casing containing bare essentials

BARED ► bare

BAREFIT same as ► barefoot

BAREFOOT adv with the feet uncovered

BAREGE, **-S** n light silky gauze fabric made of wool ▷ adj made of such a fabric

BAREGINE n curative ingredient in thermal waters

BAREHAND vb handle with bare hands

BAREHEAD adv with head uncovered

BARELAND adj as in **bareland croft** refers to a croft with no croft house

BARELY adv only just

BARENESS ► bare

BARER ► bare

BARES ► bare

BARESARK another word for ► berserk

BAREST ► bare

BARF, **-ED**, **-ING**, **-S** vb vomit ▷ n act of vomiting

BARFI, **-S** n type of Indian dessert

BARFING ► barf

BARFIS ► barfi

BARFLY, **BARFLIES** n person who frequents bars

BARFS ► barf

BARFUL adj presenting difficulties

BARGAIN, **-S** n agreement establishing what each party will give, receive, or perform in a transaction ▷ vb negotiate the terms of an agreement

BARGE, **-D**, **-S**, **BARGING** n flat-bottomed boat used to transport freight ▷ vb push violently

BARGEE, **-S** n person in charge of a barge

BARGEESE ► bargoose

BARGELLO n zigzag tapestry stitch

BARGEMAN, **BARGEMEN** same as ► bargee

BARGES ► barge

BARGEST, **-S** same as ► barghest

BARGHEST n mythical goblin in the shape of a dog

BARGING ► barge

BARGOON, **-S** Canadian word for ► bargain

BARGOOSE, **BARGEESE** n type of goose; sheldrake

BARGUEST same as ► barghest

BARHOP, **-S** vb visit several bars in succession

BARIC adj of or containing barium

BARILLA, **-S** n impure mixture of sodium carbonate and sodium sulphate

BARING ► bare

BARISH adj quite thinly covered

BARISTA, **-S** n person who makes and sells coffee in a coffee bar

BARITE, **-S** n colourless or white mineral

BARITONE n (singer with) the second lowest adult male voice ▷ adj relating to or denoting a baritone

BARIUM, **-S** n soft white metallic element

BARK, **-ED**, **-S** vb (of a dog) make its typical loud abrupt cry

BARKAN, **-S** same as ► barchan

BARKED ▸ bark

BARKEEP, -S n barkeeper

BARKEN, -ED, -S vb become dry with a bark-like outer layer

BARKER, -S n person at a fairground who calls loudly to passers-by in order to attract customers

BARKHAN, -S same as ▸ barchan

BARKIER ▸ barky

BARKIEST ▸ barky

BARKING adj mad

BARKLESS ▸ bark

BARKS ▸ bark

BARKY, BARKIER, BARKIEST adj having the texture or appearance of bark

BARLEDUC n French preserve made of currants

BARLESS ▸ bar

BARLEY n tall grasslike plant cultivated for grain ▷ sentence substitute cry for truce or respite from the rules of a game

BARLOW, -S n type of strong knife

BARM, -S n yeasty froth on fermenting malt liquors

BARMAID, -S n woman who serves in a pub

BARMAN, BARMEN same as ▹ bartender

BARMIE same as ▸ barmy

BARMIER ▸ barmy

BARMIEST ▸ barmy

BARMILY ▸ barmy

BARMKIN, -S n protective wall around castle

BARMPOT, -S n foolish or deranged person

BARMS ▸ barm

BARMY, BARMIER, BARMIEST adj insane

BARN, -ED, -ING, -S n large building on a farm used for storing grain ▷ vb keep in a barn

BARNACLE n shellfish that lives attached to rocks, ship bottoms, etc

BARNED ▸ barn

BARNET, -S n hair

BARNEY, -ED, -S n noisy fight or argument ▷ vb argue or quarrel

BARNIER ▸ barny

BARNIEST ▸ barny

BARNING ▸ barn

BARNLIKE ▸ barn

BARNS ▸ barn

BARNWOOD n aged and weathered boards, esp those salvaged from dismantled barns

BARNY, BARNIER, BARNIEST adj reminiscent of a barn

BARNYARD n yard adjoining a barn

BAROCCO, -S same as ▸ baroque

BAROCK, -S same as ▸ baroque

BAROGRAM n record of atmospheric pressure traced by a barograph or similar instrument

BAROLO, -S n red Italian wine

BAROMETZ n fern whose woolly rhizomes resemble a lamb

BARON, -S n member of the lowest rank of nobility

BARONAGE n barons collectively

BARONESS n woman holding the rank of baron

BARONET, -S n commoner who holds the lowest hereditary British title

BARONG, -S n broad-bladed cleaver-like knife used in the Philippines

BARONIAL adj of, relating to, or befitting a baron or barons

BARONIES ▸ barony

BARONNE, -S n baroness

BARONS ▸ baron

BARONY, BARONIES n domain or rank of a baron

BAROQUE, -S n style of art, architecture, or music ▷ adj ornate in style

BAROSAUR n large dinosaur

BAROSTAT n device for maintaining constant pressure, such as one used in an aircraft cabin

BAROUCHE n type of horse-drawn carriage

BARP, -S n hillock or bank of stones

BARQUE, -S n sailing ship, esp one with three masts

BARRA, -S n barramundi

BARRABLE ▸ bar

BARRACAN n thick, strong fabric

BARRACE, -S n record of teams entering a sports contest

BARRACK vb criticize loudly or shout against (a team or speaker)

BARRACKS pl n building used to accommodate military personnel

BARRAGE, -D, -S n continuous delivery of questions, complaints, etc ▷ vb attack or confront with a barrage

BARRANCA n ravine or precipice

BARRANCO same as ▸ barranca

BARRAS ▸ barra

BARRAT, -ED, -S n fraudulent dealings ▷ vb quarrel

BARRATER same as ▸ barrator

BARRATOR n person guilty of barratry

BARRATRY n (formerly) the vexatious stirring up of quarrels or bringing of lawsuits

BARRATS ▸ barrat

BARRE, -ED, -ING, -S n rail at hip height used for ballet practice ▷ vb execute guitar chords by laying the index finger over some or all of the strings ▷ adv by using the barre

BARRED ▸ bar

BARREED ▸ barre

BARREING ▸ barre

BARREL, -ED, -S n cylindrical container with rounded sides and flat ends ▷ vb put in a barrel

BARREN, -ER adj (of a woman or female animal) incapable of producing offspring

BARRENLY

BARRENS pl n (in North America) a stretch of land that is sparsely vegetated

BARRES ▸ barre

BARRET, -S n small flat cap resembling a biretta

BARRETOR n quarrelsome person

BARRETRY same as ▸ barratry

BARRETS ▸ barret

BARRETTE n clasp or pin for holding women's hair in place

BARRICO, -S n small container for liquids

BARRIE adj very good

BARRIER, -S n anything that prevents access, progress, or union ▷ vb create or form a barrier

BARRIES ▸ barry

BARRING, -S ▸ bar

BARRIO, -S n Spanish-speaking quarter in a town or city, esp in the US

BARRIQUE n wine barrel made of oak

BARRO adj embarrassing

B

BARROOM, -S n room or building where alcoholic drinks are served over a counter

BARROW, -S n wheelbarrow

BARRULET n narrow band across heraldic shield

BARRY, BARRIES n mistake or blunder

BARS ▸ bar

BARSTOOL n high stool in bar

BARTEND, -S vb serve drinks from a bar

BARTER, -ED, -S vb trade (goods) in exchange for other goods ▷ n trade by the exchange of goods
BARTERER

BARTISAN same as ▸ **bartizan**

BARTIZAN n small turret projecting from a wall, parapet, or tower

BARTON, -S n farmyard

BARTSIA, -S n type of semiparasitic plant

BARWARE, -S n glasses, etc used in a bar

BARWOOD, -S n red wood from small African tree

BARYE, -S n unit of pressure

BARYON, -S n elementary particle that has a mass greater than or equal to that of the proton

BARYONIC adj of or relating to a baryon

BARYONS ▸ baryon

BARYTA, -S same as ▸ **barite**

BARYTE, -S same as ▸ **baryta**

BARYTIC ▸ baryta

BARYTON, -S n bass viol with sympathetic strings as well as its six main strings

BARYTONE adj having the last syllable unaccented ▷ n word in which the last syllable is unaccented

BARYTONS ▸ baryton

BAS ▸ ba

BASAL adj of, at, or constituting a base
BASALLY

BASALT, -S n dark volcanic rock

BASALTES n unglazed black stoneware

BASALTIC ▸ basalt

BASALTS ▸ basalt

BASAN, -S n sheepskin tanned in bark

BASANITE n black basaltic rock

BASANS ▸ basan

BASANT, -S n Pakistani spring festival

BASCINET same as ▸ **basinet**

BASCULE, -S n drawbridge that operates by a counterbalanced weight

BASE, -D, -R, -ST, BASING n bottom or supporting part of anything ▷ vb use as a basis (for) ▷ adj dishonourable or immoral

BASEBALL n type of team ball game

BASEBAND n transmission technique using a narrow range of frequencies

BASEBORN adj born of humble parents

BASED ▸ base

BASEEJ pl n Iranian volunteer militia

BASELARD n short sword

BASELESS adj not based on fact

BASELINE n value or starting point on an imaginary scale with which other things are compared

BASELOAD n constant part of an electrical power supply

BASELY ▸ base

BASEMAN, BASEMEN n fielder positioned near a base

BASEMENT n partly or wholly underground storey of a building

BASEN Spenserian spelling of ▸ **basin**

BASENESS ▸ base

BASENJI, -S n small breed of dog

BASEPATH n diamond-shaped path between bases on a baseball field

BASER ▸ base

BASES ▸ basis

BASEST ▸ base

BASH, -ED, -ES vb hit violently or forcefully ▷ n heavy blow

BASHAW, -S n important or pompous person

BASHED ▸ bash

BASHER, -S ▸ bash

BASHES ▸ bash

BASHFUL adj shy or modest

BASHING, -S ▸ bash

BASHLESS adj not ashamed

BASHLIK, -S n Caucasian hood

BASHLYK, -S same as ▸ **bashlik**

BASHMENT same as > **dancehall**

BASHO n grand tournament in sumo wrestling

BASHTAG, -S n (on Twitter) hashtag used for abusive comments

BASIC, -S adj of or forming a base or basis ▷ n fundamental principle, fact, etc

BASICITY n state of being a base

BASICS ▸ basic

BASIDIA ▸ basidium

BASIDIAL ▸ basidium

BASIDIUM, BASIDIA n spore-forming structure in fungi

BASIFIED ▸ basify

BASIFIER ▸ basify

BASIFY, BASIFIED, BASIFIES vb make basic

BASIJ same as ▸ **baseej**

BASIL, -S n aromatic herb used in cooking

BASILAR adj of or situated at a base

BASILARY same as ▸ **basilar**

BASILECT n debased dialect

BASILIC ▸ basilica

BASILICA n rectangular church with a rounded end and two aisles

BASILISK n legendary serpent said to kill by its breath or glance

BASILS ▸ basil

BASIN, -S n round open container
BASINAL
BASINED

BASINET, -S n close-fitting medieval helmet of light steel usually with a visor

BASINFUL n amount a basin will hold

BASING ▸ base

BASINS ▸ basin

BASION, -S n (in anatomy) midpoint on the forward border of the foramen magnum

BASIS, BASES n fundamental principles etc from which something is started or developed

BASK, -ED, -ING, -S vb lie in or be exposed to something, esp pleasant warmth

BASKET, -S n container made of interwoven strips of wood or cane

BASKETRY n art or practice of making baskets

BASKETS ▸ basket

BASKING ▸ bask

BASKS ▸ bask

BASMATI, -S n variety of long-grain rice with slender aromatic grains

BASNET, -S same as ▸ **basinet**

B

BASOCHE, -S *n* society of medieval French lawyers who performed comic plays

BASON, -S *same as* ▶ **basin**

BASOPHIL *adj* (of cells or cell contents) easily stained by basic dyes ▷ *n* basophil cell, esp a leucocyte

BASQUE, -D, -S *n* tight-fitting bodice for women

BASQUINE *n* tight-fitting bodice

BASS, -ED, -ES, -EST, -ING *n* (singer with) the lowest adult male voice ▷ *adj* relating to or denoting a bass ▷ *vb* speak or sing in a low pitch

BASSE *same as* ▶ **bass**

BASSED ▶ **bass**

BASSER *n* someone who plays bass guitar or double bass

BASSES ▶ **bass**

BASSEST ▶ **bass**

BASSET, -ED, -S *n* breed of hound ▷ *vb* (of rock) protrude through earth's surface

BASSETT, -S *same as* ▶ **basset**

BASSI ▶ **basso**

BASSIER ▶ **bassy**

BASSIEST ▶ **bassy**

BASSINET *n* wickerwork or wooden cradle or pram, usually hooded

BASSING ▶ **bass**

BASSIST, -S *n* player of a double bass, esp in a jazz band

BASSLINE *n* (in jazz, rock, and pop music) part played by the bass guitar

BASSLY ▶ **bass**

BASSNESS ▶ **bass**

BASSO, BASSI, -S *n* singer with a bass voice

BASSOON, -S *n* low-pitched woodwind instrument

BASSOS ▶ **basso**

BASSWOOD *n* N American linden tree

BASSY, BASSIER, BASSIEST *adj* manifesting strong bass tones

BAST, -S *n* fibrous material used for making rope, matting, etc

BASTA *interj* enough; stop

BASTE, -D, -S *vb* moisten (meat) during cooking with hot fat

BASTER -S

BASTI, -S *n* (in India) a slum inhabited by poor people

BASTIDE, -S *n* small isolated house in France

BASTILE, -S *same as* ▶ **bastille**

BASTILLE *n* prison

BASTING, -S *n* loose temporary stitches

BASTION, -S *n* projecting part of a fortification

BASTIS ▶ **basti**

BASTLE, -S *n* fortified house

BASTO, -S *n* ace of clubs in certain card games

BASTS ▶ **bast**

BASUCO, -S *n* illegal cocaine-based drug

BAT, -S, -TED *n* any of various types of club used to hit the ball in certain sports ▷ *vb* strike with or as if with a bat

BATABLE

BATARD, -S *n* canoe made of birchbark

BATATA, -S *n* sweet potato

BATAVIA, -S *n* variety of lettuce with smooth pale green leaves

BATBOY, -S *n* boy who works at baseball games

BATCH, -ED, -ES *n* group of people or things dealt with at the same time ▷ *vb* group (items) for efficient processing

BATCHER -S

BATCHING ▶ **batch**

BATE, -D, -S, BATING *vb* (of hawks) to jump violently from a perch to the falconer's fist

BATEAU, -X *n* light flat-bottomed boat used on rivers in Canada and the northern US

BATED ▶ **bate**

BATELESS ▶ **bate**

BATELEUR *n* African bird of prey with a short tail and long wings

BATEMENT *n* reduction

BATES ▶ **bate**

BATFISH *n* type of angler fish with a flattened scaleless body

BATFOWL, -S *vb* catch birds by temporarily blinding them with light

BATGIRL, -S *n* girl who works at baseball games

BATH, -S *n* large container in which to wash the body ▷ *vb* wash in a bath

BATHCUBE *n* cube of soluble scented material for use in a bath

BATHE, -D, -S *vb* swim in open water for pleasure

BATHER

BATHERS *pl n* swimming costume

BATHES ▶ **bathe**

BATHETIC *adj* containing or displaying bathos

BATHING, -S *n* act of bathing

BATHLESS ▶ **bath**

BATHMAT, -S *n* mat to stand on after a bath

BATHMIC ▶ **bathmism**

BATHMISM *n* growth-force

BATHORSE *n* officer's packhorse

BATHOS, -ES *n* sudden change from a serious subject to a trivial one

BATHROBE *n* loose-fitting garment for wear before or after a bath or swimming

BATHROOM *n* room with a bath, sink, and usu a toilet

BATHS ▶ **bath**

BATHTUB, -S *n* bath, esp one not permanently fixed

BATHYAL *adj* relating to an ocean depth of between 200 and 2000 metres

BATIK, -ED, -ING, -S *n* process of printing fabric using wax to cover areas not to be dyed ▷ *vb* treat material with this process

BATING ▶ **bate**

BATISTE, -S *n* fine plain-weave cotton fabric: used esp for shirts and dresses

BATLER, -S *n* flat piece of wood for beating clothes, etc before washing

BATLET, -S *same as* ▶ **batler**

BATLIKE ▶ **bat**

BATMAN, BATMEN *n* officer's servant in the armed forces

BATOLOGY *n* study of brambles

BATON, -ED, -ING, -S *n* thin stick used by the conductor of an orchestra ▷ *vb* carry or wave a baton

BATOON, -ED, -S *same as* ▶ **baton**

BATS ▶ **bat**

BATSMAN, BATSMEN *n* person who bats or specializes in batting

BATSWING *adj* in the form of the wing of a bat

BATT, -S *same as* ▶ **bat**

BATTA, -S *n* soldier's allowance

BATTALIA *n* arrangement of army prepared for battle

BATTAS ▶ **batta**

B

BATTEAU, -X same as
▶ **bateau**
BATTED ▶ **bat**
BATTEL, -ED, -S vb make
fertile
BATTELER
BATTEN, -ED, -S n strip of
wood fixed to something,
esp to hold it in place ▷ vb
strengthen or fasten with
battens
BATTENER
BATTER, -S vb hit repeatedly
▷ n mixture of flour, eggs,
and milk, used in cooking
BATTERED adj subjected to
persistent physical violence
BATTERER n person who
batters someone
BATTERIE n movement in
ballet involving the legs
beating together
BATTERO, -S n heavy club
BATTERS ▶ **batter**
BATTERY n device that
produces electricity in a
torch, radio, etc ▷ adj kept in
series of cages for intensive
rearing
BATTIER ▶ **batty**
BATTIES ▶ **batty**
BATTIEST ▶ **batty**
BATTIK, -S same as ▶ **batik**
BATTILL, -S vb fatten an
animal
BATTILY adv in an eccentric or
crazy manner
BATTING, -S ▶ **bat**
BATTLE, -D, -S, BATTLING n
fight between large armed
forces ▷ vb struggle
BATTLEAX same as
> **battleaxe**
BATTLED ▶ **battle**
BATTLER, -S ▶ **battle**
BATTLES ▶ **battle**
BATTLING ▶ **battle**
BATTS ▶ **batt**
BATTU adj (in ballet) involving
a beating movement
BATTUE, -S n beating of
woodland or cover to force
game to flee in the direction
of hunters
BATTUTA, -S n (in music) a
beat
BATTUTO, -S n (in Italian
cookery) selection of
chopped herbs
**BATTY, BATTIER, BATTIES,
BATTIEST** adj eccentric or
crazy ▷ n bottom; bum
BATWING adj shaped like the
wings of a bat, as a black tie,
collar, etc

BATWOMAN, BATWOMEN n
female servant in any of the
armed forces
BAUBEE, -S same as
▶ **bawbee**
BAUBLE, -S, BAUBLING n
trinket of little value
BAUCHLE, -D, -S vb shuffle
along
BAUD, -S n unit used to
measure the speed of
transmission of electronic
data
BAUDEKIN old variant of
> **baldachin**
BAUDRIC, -S same as
▶ **baldric**
BAUDRICK same as ▶ **baldric**
BAUDRICS ▶ **baudric**
BAUDRONS n name for a cat
BAUDS ▶ **baud**
BAUERA, -S n small
evergreen Australian shrub
BAUHINIA n type of climbing
or shrubby plant
BAUK, -ED, -ING, -S same as
▶ **balk**
BAULK, -ED, -ING, -S same
as ▶ **balk**
BAULKER, -S
BAULKIER ▶ **baulky**
BAULKILY ▶ **baulky**
BAULKING ▶ **baulk**
BAULKS ▶ **baulk**
BAULKY, BAULKIER same as
▶ **balky**
BAUR, -S n humorous
anecdote; joke
BAUSOND adj (of animal)
dappled with white spots
BAUXITE, -S n claylike
substance that is the chief
source of aluminium
BAUXITIC
BAVAROIS n cold dessert
consisting of a rich custard
set with gelatine
BAVIN, -ED, -ING, -S n bundle
of brushwood or firewood
▷ vb bind (brushwood or
firewood) into bavins
BAWBEE, -S n former Scottish
silver coin
BAWBLE, -S same as
▶ **bauble**
BAWCOCK, -S n fine fellow
BAWDKIN, -S same as
> **baldachin**
BAWDRIC, -S n heavy belt to
support sword
BAWK, -S n type of Atlantic
seabird
BAWL, -ED, -S vb shout or
weep noisily ▷ n loud shout
or cry
BAWLER -S

BAWLEY, -S n small fishing
boat
BAWLING, -S ▶ **bawl**
BAWLS ▶ **bawl**
BAWN, -S n fortified enclosure
BAWNEEN, -S same as
▶ **bainin**
BAWNS ▶ **bawn**
BAWR, -S same as ▶ **baur**
BAWSUNT adj black and
white in colour
BAWTIE, -S n name for a dog
BAWTY same as ▶ **bawtie**
BAXTER, -S old variant of
▶ **baker**
BAY, -ED, -ING, -S n wide
semicircular indentation of a
shoreline ▷ vb howl in deep
tones
BAYADEER same as
▶ **bayadere**
BAYADERE n dancing girl,
esp one serving in a Hindu
temple ▷ adj (of fabric, etc)
having horizontal stripes
BAYAMO, -S n Cuban strong
wind
BAYARD, -S n bay horse
BAYBERRY n
tropical American tree that
yields an oil used in making
bay rum
BAYE, -S vb bathe
BAYED ▶ **bay**
BAYES ▶ **baye**
BAYFRONT n shoreline of
a bay
BAYING ▶ **bay**
BAYLE, -S n barrier
BAYMAN, BAYMEN n
fisherman
BAYNODDY n person who
fishes in a bay
BAYONET, -S n sharp blade
that can be fixed to the end
of a rifle ▷ vb stab with a
bayonet
BAYOU, -S n (in the southern
US) a sluggish marshy
tributary of a lake or river
BAYS ▶ **bay**
BAYSIDE, -S n shore of a bay
BAYT, -ED, -ING, -S same as
▶ **bate**
BAYWOOD, -S n light soft
wood of a tropical American
mahogany tree
BAYYAN, -S n Islamic
declaration
BAZAAR, -S n sale in aid of
charity
BAZAR, -S same as ▶ **bazaar**
BAZAZZ, -ES same as
▶ **pizzazz**
BAZOO, -S a US slang word for
▶ **mouth**

BAZOOKA, -S n portable rocket launcher that fires an armour-piercing projectile

BAZOOS ► bazoo

BAZOUKI, -S same as ► **bouzouki**

BAZZ, -ED, -ES, -ING vb throw (an object)

BAZZAZZ same as ► **pizzazz**

BAZZED ► bazz

BAZZES ► bazz

BAZZING ► bazz

BDELLIUM n African or W Asian tree that yields a gum resin

BE vb exist or live

BEACH, -ED, -ES, -ING n area of sand or pebbles on a shore ▷ vb run or haul (a boat) onto a beach

BEACHBOY n male lifeguard on beach

BEACHED ► beach

BEACHES ► beach

BEACHIER ► beachy

BEACHING ► beach

BEACHY, BEACHIER adj with gentle sandy slopes

BEACON, -ED, -S n fire or light on a hill or tower, used as a warning ▷ vb guide or warn

BEAD, -ED, -S n small piece of plastic, wood, etc, pierced for threading ▷ vb decorate with beads

BEADER, -S n person making things with beads

BEADIER ► beady

BEADIEST ► beady

BEADILY ► beady

BEADING, -S n strip of moulding used for edging furniture

BEADLE, -S n (formerly) a minor parish official who acted as an usher

BEADLIKE ► bead

BEADMAN, BEADMEN same as ► **beadsman**

BEADROLL n list of persons for whom prayers are to be offered

BEADS ► bead

BEADSMAN, BEADSMEN n person who prays for another's soul, esp one paid or fed for doing so

BEADWORK same as ► **beading**

BEADY, BEADIER, BEADIEST adj small, round, and glittering

BEAGLE, -D, -S n small hound with short legs and drooping ears ▷ vb hunt with beagles, normally on foot

BEAGLER, -S n person who hunts with beagles

BEAGLES ► beagle

BEAGLING ► beagle

BEAK, -S n projecting horny jaws of a bird

BEAKED

BEAKER, -S n large drinking cup

BEAKIER ► beaky

BEAKIEST ► beaky

BEAKLESS ► beak

BEAKLIKE ► beak

BEAKS ► beak

BEAKY, BEAKIER, BEAKIEST ► beak

BEAL, -S n infected sore

BEALING, -S n infected sore

BEALS ► beal

BEAM, -ED, -S n broad smile ▷ vb smile broadly

BEAMER, -S n full-pitched ball bowled at the batsman's head

BEAMIER ► beamy

BEAMIEST ► beamy

BEAMILY ► beam

BEAMING, -S ► beam

BEAMISH adj smiling

BEAMLESS ► beam

BEAMLET, -S n small beam

BEAMLIKE ► beam

BEAMS ► beam

BEAMY, BEAMIER, BEAMIEST ► beam

BEAN, -ED, -ING, -S n seed or pod of various plants, eaten as a vegetable or used to make coffee etc ▷ vb strike on the head

BEANBAG, -S n small cloth bag filled with dried beans and thrown in games

BEANBALL n baseball intended to hit batter's head

BEANED ► bean

BEANERY n cheap restaurant

BEANIE, -S n close-fitting woollen hat

BEANING ► bean

BEANLIKE ► bean

BEANO, -S n celebration or party

BEANPOLE n pole used to support bean plants

BEANS ► bean

BEANY same as ► **beanie**

BEAR, -ED, -S, BORNE vb support or hold up (something) ▷ vb lower the price of (a security) ▷ n type of omnivorous mammal

BEARABLE adj endurable

BEARABLY

BEARBINE n type of bindweed

BEARCAT, -S n lesser panda

BEARD, -ED, -ING, -S n hair growing on the lower parts of a man's face ▷ vb oppose boldly

BEARDIE, -S n another name for bearded loach

BEARDIER ► beardy

BEARDIES ► beardie

BEARDING ► beard

BEARDS ► beard

BEARDY, BEARDIER adj having a beard

BEARE, -S same as ► **bear**

BEARED ► bear

BEARER, -S n person who carries, presents, or upholds something

BEARES ► beare

BEARHUG, -S n wrestling hold in which the arms are locked tightly round an opponent's chest and arms ▷ vb hold an opponent in a bearhug

BEARING, -S ► bear

BEARISH adj like a bear

BEARLIKE ► bear

BEARPAW, -S n paw of a bear

BEARS ► bear

BEARSKIN n tall fur helmet worn by some British soldiers

BEARWARD n bear keeper

BEARWOOD another name for ► **cascara**

BEAST, -ED, -ING, -S n large wild animal ▷ vb torture someone using excessive physical exercise

BEASTIE, -S n small animal

BEASTILY same as > **bestially**

BEASTING ► beast

BEASTLY adj unpleasant or disagreeable ▷ adv extremely

BEASTS ► beast

BEAT, -EN, -S vb strike with a series of violent blows ▷ n stroke or blow ▷ adj totally exhausted

BEATABLE

BEATBOX n drum machine simulated by a human voice ▷ vb simulate a drum machine with a human voice

BEATEN ► beat

BEATER, -S n device used for beating

BEATH, -ED, -ING, -S vb dry; heat

BEATIER ► beaty

BEATIEST ► beaty

BEATIFIC adj displaying great happiness

BEATIFY vb take first step towards making (a dead person) a saint

BEATING, -S ► beat

BEATLESS ► beat

BEATNIK, -S n young person in the late 1950s who rebelled against conventional attitudes etc

BEATS ► beat

BEATY, BEATIER, BEATIEST adj (of music) having a strong rhythm

BEAU, -S, -X n boyfriend or admirer

BEAUCOUP n large amount

BEAUFET, -S same as ► buffet

BEAUFFET same as ► buffet

BEAUFIN, -S same as ► biffin

BEAUISH adj vain and showy

BEAUS ► beau

BEAUT, -ER, -EST, -S n person or thing that is outstanding or distinctive ▷ adj good or excellent ▷ interj exclamation of joy or pleasure

BEAUTIED ► beauty

BEAUTIES ► beauty

BEAUTIFY vb make beautiful

BEAUTS ► beaut

BEAUTY, BEAUTIED, BEAUTIES n combination of all the qualities of a person or thing that delight the senses and mind ▷ interj expression of approval or agreement ▷ vb make beautiful

BEAUX ► beau

BEAUXITE same as ► bauxite

BEAVER, -ED, -S n amphibious rodent with a big flat tail ▷ vb work steadily or assiduously

BEAVERY n place for keeping beavers

BEBEERU, -S n tropical American tree

BEBLOOD, -S vb stain with blood

BEBOP, -PED, -S same as ► bop

BEBOPPER

BEBUNG, -S n vibrato effect on clavichord

BECALL, -ED, -S vb use insulting words about someone

BECALM, -S vb make calm

BECALMED adj (of a sailing ship) motionless through lack of wind

BECALMS ► becalm

BECAME ► become

BECAP, -PED, -S vb put cap on

BECARPET vb lay carpet on

BECASSE, -S n woodcock

BECAUSE conj on account of the fact that; on account of being; since

BECHALK, -S vb mark with chalk

BECHAMEL n thick white sauce flavoured with onion and seasoning

BECHANCE vb happen (to)

BECHARM, -S vb delight

BECK, -ED, -ING, -S n stream ▷ vb attract someone's attention by nodding or gesturing

BECKE, -S same as ► beak

BECKED ► beck

BECKES ► becke

BECKET, -S n clevis forming part of one end of a sheave

BECKING ► beck

BECKON, -ED, -S vb summon with a gesture ▷ n summoning gesture

BECKONER

BECKS ► beck

BECLAMOR vb clamour excessively

BECLASP, -S vb embrace

BECLOAK, -S vb dress in cloak

BECLOG, -S vb put clogs on

BECLOTHE vb put clothes on

BECLOUD, -S vb cover or obscure with a cloud

BECLOWN, -S vb clown around

BECOME, BECAME, -S vb come to be

BECOMING adj attractive or pleasing ▷ n any process of change

BECOWARD vb make cowardly

BECRAWL, -S vb crawl all over

BECRIME, -D, -S vb make someone guilty of a crime

BECROWD, -S vb crowd with something

BECRUST, -S vb cover with crust

BECUDGEL vb arm with cudgel

BECURL, -ED, -S vb curl

BECURSE, -D, -S, BECURST vb curse

BED, -DED, -S n piece of furniture on which to sleep ▷ vb plant in a bed

BEDABBLE vb dabble; moisten

BEDAD interj by God (oath)

BEDAGGLE vb soil by trailing through dirt

BEDAMN, -ED, -S vb damn

BEDARKEN vb make dark

BEDASH, -ED, -ES vb sprinkle with liquid

BEDAUB, -ED, -S vb smear with something sticky or dirty

BEDAWIN, -S same as ► bedouin

BEDAZE, -D, -S, BEDAZING vb daze

BEDAZZLE vb dazzle or confuse, as with brilliance

BEDBATH, -S n washing of a sick person in bed

BEDBOARD n base of bed

BEDBUG, -S n small blood-sucking wingless insect that infests dirty houses

BEDCHAIR n adjustable chair to support invalid in bed

BEDCOVER n cover for bed

BEDDED ► bed

BEDDER, -S n (at some universities) a college servant employed to keep students' rooms in order

BEDDING, -S ► bed

BEDE, -S n prayer

BEDEAFEN vb deafen

BEDECK, -ED, -S vb cover with decorations

BEDEGUAR n growth found on rosebushes

BEDEL, -S archaic spelling of ► beadle

BEDELL, -S same as ► beadle

BEDELS ► bedel

BEDEMAN, BEDEMEN same as ► beadsman

BEDERAL, -S same as ► bedral

BEDES ► bede

BEDESMAN, BEDESMEN same as ► beadsman

BEDEVIL, -S vb harass, confuse, or torment

BEDEW, -ED, -ING, -S vb wet or cover with or as if with drops of dew

BEDFAST an archaic word for > bedridden

BEDFRAME n framework of bed

BEDGOWN, -S n night dress

BEDHEAD, -S n untidy state of hair, esp caused by sleeping

BEDIAPER vb put a nappy on

BEDIDE ► bedye

BEDIGHT, -S vb array or adorn ▷ adj adorned or bedecked

BEDIM, -MED, -S vb make dim or obscure

BEDIMPLE vb form dimples in

BEDIMS ► bedim

BEDIRTY vb make dirty

BEDIZEN, -S vb dress or decorate gaudily or tastelessly

BEDLAM, -S n noisy confused situation

BEDLAMER n young harp seal

BEDLAMP, -S n bedside light

B

BEDLAMS ► bedlam

BEDLESS ► bed

BEDLIKE adj like a bed

BEDLINER n lining for the bed of a truck

BEDMAKER n person who makes beds

BEDMATE, -S n person who shares a bed

BEDOTTED adj scattered; strewn

BEDOUIN, -S n member of any of the nomadic tribes of Arabs

BEDPAN, -S n shallow bowl used as a toilet by bedridden people

BEDPLATE n heavy metal platform or frame to which an engine or machine is attached

BEDPOST, -S n vertical support on a bedstead

BEDQUILT n padded bed cover

BEDRAIL, -S n rail along the side of a bed connecting the headboard with the footboard

BEDRAL, -S n minor church official

BEDRAPE, -D, -S vb adorn

BEDRENCH vb drench

BEDREST, -S n rest in bed, eg to recover from illness

BEDRID same as ► bedridden

BEDRITES ► bedrite

BEDRIVEL vb drivel around

BEDROCK, -S n solid rock beneath the surface soil

BEDROLL, -S n portable roll of bedding

BEDROOM, -S n room used for sleeping

BEDROP, -S, -T vb drop on

BEDRUG, -S vb drug excessively

BEDS ► bed

BEDSHEET n sheet for bed

BEDSIDE, -S n area beside a bed ▷ adj placed at or near the side of the bed

BEDSIT, -S n furnished sitting room with a bed

BEDSKIRT n drapery round the edge of a bed

BEDSOCK, -S n sock worn in bed

BEDSONIA n bacterium causing diseases such as trachoma

BEDSORE, -S n ulcer on the skin, caused by a lengthy period of lying in bed due to illness

BEDSTAND n bedside table

BEDSTEAD n framework of a bed

BEDSTRAW n plant with small white or yellow flowers

BEDTICK, -S n case containing stuffing in mattress

BEDTIME, -S n time when one usually goes to bed

BEDU adj relating to beduins

BEDUCK, -ED, -S vb duck under water

BEDUIN, -S variant of ► bedouin

BEDUMB, -ED, -S vb make dumb

BEDUNCE, -D, -S vb cause to look or feel foolish

BEDUNG, -ED, -S vb spread with dung

BEDUST, -ED, -S vb cover with dust

BEDWARD adj towards bed

BEDWARDS adv towards bed

BEDWARF, -S vb hamper growth of

BEDYE, BEDYDE, -D, -ING, -S vb dye

BEE, -S n insect that makes wax and honey

BEEBEE, -S n air rifle

BEEBREAD n mixture of pollen and nectar prepared by worker bees and fed to the larvae

BEECH, -ES n tree with a smooth greyish bark

BEECHEN

BEECHIER ► beechy

BEECHNUT n small brown triangular edible nut of the beech tree

BEECHY, BEECHIER ► beech

BEEDI, -ES n Indian cigarette

BEEDIE same as ► beedi

BEEDIES ► beedi

BEEF, -ED, -ING, -S, BEEVES n flesh of a cow, bull, or ox ▷ vb complain

BEEFALO, -S n cross between cow and buffalo

BEEFCAKE n muscular man as displayed in photographs

BEEFED ► beef

BEEFIER ► beefy

BEEFIEST ► beefy

BEEFILY ► beefy

BEEFING ► beef

BEEFLESS ► beef

BEEFS ► beef

BEEFWOOD n any of various trees that produce very hard wood

BEEFY, BEEFIER, BEEFIEST adj like beef

BEEGAH, -S same as ► bigha

BEEHIVE, -S n structure in which bees live

BEEHIVED adj (esp of a hairstyle) shaped like a beehive

BEEHIVES ► beehive

BEELIKE ► bee

BEELINE, -D, -S n most direct route between two places ▷ vb make a beeline for (something)

BEEN vb past participle of be

BEENAH, -S n understanding; insight

BEENTO, -S n person who has resided in Britain ▷ adj of, relating to, or characteristic of such a person

BEEP, -ED, -ING, -S n high-pitched sound, like that of a car horn ▷ vb (cause to) make this noise

BEEPER -S

BEER, -S n alcoholic drink brewed from malt and hops

BEERAGE, -S n brewing industry

BEERFEST n beer festival

BEERHALL n large public room where beer is consumed

BEERIER ► beery

BEERIEST ► beery

BEERILY ► beery

BEERMAT, -S n small mat put under a glass of beer

BEERNUT, -S n coated peanut eaten as a snack

BEERS ► beer

BEERSIES pl n (NZ) beers

BEERY, BEERIER, BEERIEST adj smelling or tasting of beer

BEES ► bee

BEESOME same as ► bisson

BEESTING adj as in **beesting lips** of lips, pouting

BEESTUNG adj as in **beestung lips** of lips, pouting

BEESWAX n wax secreted by bees, used in polishes etc ▷ vb polish with such wax

BEESWING n light filmy crust that forms in port wine

BEET, -ED, -ING, -S n plant with an edible root and leaves ▷ vb improve or make better

BEETFLY n type of fly which is a common pest of beets and mangel-wurzels

BEETING ► beet

BEETLE, -D, -S n insect with a hard wing cover on its back ▷ vb scuttle or scurry

BEETLER, -S n one who operates a beetling machine

B

BEETLES ▸ beetle
BEETLING ▸ beetle
BEETROOT n type of beet plant with a dark red root
BEETS ▸ beet
BEEVES ▸ beef
BEEYARD, -S n place where bees are kept
BEEZER, -S n person or chap ▷ adj excellent
BEFALL, -EN, -S, BEFELL vb happen to (someone)
BEFANA, -S n Italian gift-bearing good fairy
BEFELD archaic past participle of ▸ **befall**
BEFELL ▸ befall
BEFFANA, -S same as ▸ **befana**
BEFINGER vb mark by handling
BEFINNED adj with fins
BEFIT, -S, -TED vb be appropriate or suitable for
BEFLAG, -S vb decorate with flags
BEFLEA, -ED, -S vb infect with fleas
BEFLECK, -S vb fleck
BEFLOWER vb decorate with flowers
BEFLUM, -S vb fool; deceive
BEFOAM, -ED, -S vb cover with foam
BEFOG, -GED, -S vb surround with fog
BEFOOL, -ED, -S vb make a fool of
BEFORE adv indicating something earlier in time, in front of, or preferred to ▷ prep preceding in space or time
BEFOUL, -ED, -S vb make dirty or foul
BEFOULER
BEFRET, -S vb fret about something
BEFRIEND vb become friends with
BEFRINGE vb decorate with fringe
BEFUDDLE vb confuse, muddle, or perplex
BEG, -GED, -S vb solicit (money, food, etc), esp in the street
BEGAD interj emphatic exclamation
BEGALL, -ED, -S vb make sore by rubbing
BEGAN ▸ begin
BEGAR, -S n compulsory labour
BEGAT archaic past tense of ▸ **beget**

BEGAZE, -D, -S, BEGAZING vb gaze about or around
BEGEM, -MED, -S vb decorate with gems
BEGET, -S, BEGOT, BEGOTTEN vb cause or create
BEGETTER
BEGGAR, -ED, -S n person who begs, esp one who lives by begging ▷ vb be beyond the resources of
BEGGARLY adj meanly inadequate
BEGGARS ▸ beggar
BEGGARY n extreme poverty or need
BEGGED ▸ beg
BEGGING, -S ▸ beg
BEGHARD, -S n member of a 13th century Christian brotherhood
BEGIFT, -ED, -S vb give gift or gifts to
BEGILD, -ED, -S, BEGILT vb gild
BEGIN, BEGAN, -S, BEGUN vb start
BEGINNE, -S same as ▸ **beginning**
BEGINNER n person who has just started learning to do something
BEGINNES ▸ beginne
BEGINS ▸ begin
BEGIRD, -ED, -S, BEGIRT vb surround
BEGIRDLE vb surround with girdle
BEGIRDS ▸ begird
BEGIRT ▸ begird
BEGLAD, -S vb make glad
BEGLAMOR same as ▸ **beglamour**
BEGLOOM, -S vb make gloomy
BEGNAW, -ED, -S vb gnaw at
BEGO, -ES, -ING, -NE, BEWENT vb harass; beset
BEGONIA, -S n tropical plant with waxy flowers
BEGORAH same as ▸ **begorra**
BEGORED adj smeared with gore
BEGORRA interj emphatic exclamation, regarded as a characteristic utterance of Irishmen
BEGORRAH same as ▸ **begorra**
BEGOT ▸ beget
BEGOTTEN ▸ beget
BEGRIM, -S same as ▸ **begrime**
BEGRIME, -D, -S vb make dirty
BEGRIMS ▸ begrim
BEGROAN, -S vb groan at

BEGRUDGE vb envy (someone) the possession of something
BEGS ▸ beg
BEGUILE, -D, -S vb cheat or mislead
BEGUILER
BEGUIN, -S another name for ▸ **beghard**
BEGUINE, -S n S American dance
BEGUINS ▸ beguin
BEGULF, -ED, -S vb overwhelm
BEGUM, -S n Muslim woman of high rank
BEGUN ▸ begin
BEGUNK, -ED, -S vb delude; trick
BEHALF, BEHALVES n interest, part, benefit, or respect
BEHAPPEN vb befall
BEHATTED adj wearing a hat
BEHAVE, -D, -S, BEHAVING vb act or function in a particular way
BEHAVER, -S
BEHAVIOR same as ▸ **behaviour**
BEHEAD, -ED, -S vb remove the head from
BEHEADAL
BEHEADER
BEHELD ▸ behold
BEHEMOTH n huge person or thing
BEHEST, -S n order or earnest request
BEHIGHT, -S vb entrust
BEHIND, -S adv indicating position to the rear, lateness, responsibility, etc ▷ n buttocks ▷ prep in or to a position further back than ▷ adj in a position further back
BEHOLD, BEHELD, -S vb look (at)
BEHOLDEN adj indebted or obliged
BEHOLDER ▸ behold
BEHOLDS ▸ behold
BEHOOF, -S n advantage or profit
BEHOOVE, -D, -S same as ▸ **behove**
BEHOTE, -S, BEHOTING same as ▸ **behight**
BEHOVE, -D, -S, BEHOVING vb be necessary or fitting for
BEHOVELY adj useful
BEHOVES ▸ behove
BEHOVING ▸ behove
BEHOWL, -ED, -S vb howl at

B

BEIGE, -R, -S, -ST *adj* pale brown ▷ *n* very light brown
BEIGEL, -S *same as* ▸ **bagel**
BEIGER ▸ **beige**
BEIGES ▸ **beige**
BEIGEST ▸ **beige**
BEIGIER ▸ **beigy**
BEIGIEST ▸ **beigy**
BEIGNE, -S *variant of* ▸ **beignet**
BEIGNET, -S *n* square deep-fried pastry served hot and sprinkled with icing sugar
BEIGY, BEIGIER, BEIGIEST ▸ **beige**
BEIN, -ED, -ING, -S *adj* financially comfortable ▷ *vb* fill
BEING, -S ▸ **be**
BEINING ▸ **bein**
BEINKED *adj* daubed with ink
BEINNESS ▸ **bein**
BEINS ▸ **bein**
BEJADE, -D, -S, BEJADING *vb* jade; tire
BEJANT, -S *same as* ▸ **bajan**
BEJESUIT *vb* convert to Jesuitism
BEJEWEL, -S *vb* decorate with or as if with jewels
BEJUMBLE *vb* jumble up
BEKAH, -S *n* half shekel
BEKISS, -ED, -ES *vb* smother with kisses
BEKNAVE, -D, -S *vb* treat as a knave
BEKNIGHT *vb* esteem
BEKNOT, -S *vb* tie a knot or knots in
BEKNOWN *adj* known about
BEL, -S *n* unit for comparing two power levels or measuring the intensity of a sound
BELABOR, -S *same as* ▸ **belabour**
BELABOUR *vb* attack verbally or physically
BELACE, -D, -S, BELACING *vb* decorate with lace
BELADY, BELADIED, BELADIES *vb* call a lady
BELAH, -S *n* Australian tree which yields a useful timber
BELAMIES ▸ **belamy**
BELAMOUR *n* beloved person
BELAMY, BELAMIES *n* close friend
BELAR, -S *same as* ▸ **belah**
BELATE, -D, -S, BELATING *vb* cause to be late
BELATED *adj* late or too late
BELATES ▸ **belate**
BELATING ▸ **belate**
BELAUD, -ED, -S *vb* praise highly

BELAY, -ED, -ING, -S *vb* secure a line to a pin or cleat ▷ *n* attachment (of a climber) to a mountain
BELAYER -S
BELCH, -ED, -ES, -ING *vb* expel wind from the stomach noisily through the mouth ▷ *n* act of belching
BELCHER -S
BELDAM, -S *n* old woman, esp an ugly or malicious one
BELDAME, -S *same as* ▸ **beldam**
BELDAMS ▸ **beldam**
BELEAP, -ED, -S, -T *vb* leap over
BELEE, -D, -ING, -S *vb* put on sheltered side
BELFRIED *adj* with a belfry
BELFRY, BELFRIES *n* part of a tower where bells are hung
BELGA, -S *n* former Belgian monetary unit worth five francs
BELGARD, -S *n* kind gaze
BELGAS ▸ **belga**
BELIE, -D, -S, BELYING *vb* show to be untrue
BELIEF, -S *n* faith or confidence
BELIER, -S ▸ **belie**
BELIES ▸ **belie**
BELIEVE, -D, -S *vb* accept as true or real
BELIEVER
BELIKE *adv* perhaps
BELIQUOR *vb* cause to be drunk
BELITTLE *vb* treat as having little value or importance
BELIVE *adv* speedily
BELL, -ED, -S *n* hollow cup-shaped instrument that emits a ringing sound when struck ▷ *vb* utter (such a sound)
BELLBIND *n* bindweed-type climber
BELLBIRD *n* Australasian bird with bell-like call
BELLBOY, -S *n* man or boy employed to carry luggage and answer calls for service
BELLBUOY *n* buoy with a bell
BELLCAST *adj* relating to a style of roof with a bell shape
BELLCOTE *n* small roofed structure for bell
BELLE, -S *n* beautiful woman, esp the most attractive woman at a function
BELLED ▸ **bell**
BELLEEK, -S *n* kind of thin fragile porcelain with a lustrous glaze

BELLES ▸ **belle**
BELLETER *n* person who makes bells
BELLHOP, -S *same as* ▸ **bellboy**
BELLIED ▸ **belly**
BELLIES ▸ **belly**
BELLING, -S ▸ **bell**
BELLINI, -S *n* Prosecco and peach cocktail
BELLMAN, BELLMEN *n* man who rings a bell, esp (formerly) a town crier
BELLOCK, -S *vb* shout
BELLOW, -ED *vb* make a low deep cry like that of a bull ▷ *n* loud deep roar
BELLOWER
BELLOWS *pl n* instrument for pumping a stream of air into something
BELLPULL *n* handle, rope, or cord pulled to operate a doorbell or servant's bell
BELLS ▸ **bell**
BELLWORT *n* N American plant with slender bell-shaped yellow flowers
BELLY, BELLIED, BELLIES *n* part of the body of a vertebrate which contains the intestines ▷ *vb* (cause to) swell out
BELLYFUL *n* more than one can tolerate
BELLYING ▸ **belly**
BELON, -S *n* type of oyster
BELONG, -ED, -S *vb* be the property of
BELONGER *n* native-born Caribbean
BELONGS ▸ **belong**
BELONS ▸ **belon**
BELOVE, -S, BELOVING *vb* love
BELOVED, -S *adj* dearly loved ▷ *n* person dearly loved
BELOVES ▸ **belove**
BELOVING ▸ **belove**
BELOW *adv* at or to a position lower than, under ▷ *prep* at or to a position lower than
BELOWS *same as* ▸ **bellows**
BELS ▸ **bel**
BELT, -ED, -S *n* band of cloth, leather, etc, worn usu around the waist ▷ *vb* fasten with a belt
BELTER, -S *n* outstanding person or event
BELTING, -S *n* material used to make a belt or belts ▷ *adj* excellent
BELTLESS ▸ **belt**

B

BELTLINE n line separating car's windows from main body

BELTMAN, BELTMEN n (formerly) a member of a beach life-saving team

BELTS ► belt

BELTWAY, -S n people and institutions located in the area bounded by the Washington Beltway

BELUGA, -S n large white sturgeon

BELYING ► belie

BEMA, -S, -TA n speaker's platform in the assembly in ancient Athens

BEMAD, -DED, -S vb cause to become mad

BEMADAM, -S vb call a person madam

BEMADDED ► bemad

BEMADDEN vb cause to become mad

BEMADS ► bemad

BEMAS ► bema

BEMATA ► bema

BEMAUL, -ED, -S vb maul

BEMAZED adj amazed

BEMBEX, -ES n type of wasp

BEMBIX, -ES same as ► bembex

BEMEAN, -ED, -S, -T a less common word for ► demean

BEMEDAL, -S vb decorate with medals

BEMETE, -D, -S, BEMETING vb measure

BEMINGLE vb mingle

BEMIRE, -D, -S, BEMIRING vb soil with or as if with mire

BEMIST, -ED, -S vb cloud with mist

BEMIX, -ED, -ES, -ING, -T vb mix thoroughly

BEMOAN, -ED, -S vb express sorrow or dissatisfaction about

BEMOANER

BEMOCK, -ED, -S vb mock

BEMOIL, -ED, -S vb soil with mud

BEMOUTH, -S vb endow with a mouth

BEMUD, -DED, -S vb cover with mud

BEMUDDLE vb confound

BEMUDS ► bemud

BEMUFFLE vb muffle up

BEMURMUR vb murmur at

BEMUSE, -S vb confuse

BEMUSED adj puzzled or confused

BEMUSES ► bemuse

BEMUSING ► bemuse

BEMUZZLE vb put muzzle on

BEN, -S n mountain peak ▷ adv in ▷ adj inner

BENADRYL n tradename of an antihistamine drug used in sleeping tablets

BENAME, -D, -S, BENAMING an archaic word for ► name

BENCH, -ED, -ES, -ING n long seat ▷ vb put a person on a bench

BENCHER, -S n member of the governing body of one of the Inns of Court

BENCHES ► bench

BENCHIER ► benchy

BENCHING ► bench

BENCHTOP adj for use at bench ▷ n flat surface area

BENCHY, BENCHIER adj (of a hillside) hollowed out in benches

BEND, -ED, -S vb (cause to) form a curve ▷ n curved part

BENDABLE

BENDAY, -ED, -S vb (printing) reproduce using Benday technique

BENDED ► bend

BENDEE, -S same as ► bendy

BENDER, -S n makeshift shelter

BENDIER ► bendy

BENDIEST ► bendy

BENDING, -S ► bend

BENDLET, -S n narrow diagonal stripe on heraldic shield

BENDS ► bend

BENDWAYS same as ► bendwise

BENDWISE adv diagonally

BENDY, BENDIER, BENDIEST, -S adj flexible or pliable ▷ n okra

BENE, -S n blessing

BENEATH prep below ▷ adv below

BENEDICK n recently-married man

BENEDICT n newly married man

BENEFACT vb be benefactor to

BENEFIC adj rare word for beneficent

BENEFICE n church office providing its holder with an income ▷ vb provide with a benefice

BENEFIT, -S n something that improves or promotes ▷ vb do or receive good

BENEMPT a past participle of ► name

BENES ► bene

BENET, -S, -TED vb trap (something) in a net

BENGA, -S n type of Kenyan popular music featuring guitars

BENI, -S n sesame plant

BENIGHT, -S vb shroud in darkness

BENIGN, -ER adj showing kindliness

BENIGNLY

BENIS ► beni

BENISEED n sesame

BENISON, -S n blessing, esp a spoken one

BENITIER n basin for holy water

BENJAMIN same as ► benzoin

BENNE n another name for ► sesame

BENNET, -S n Eurasian and N African plant with yellow flowers

BENNI, -S n sesame

BENNIES ► benny

BENNIS ► benni

BENNY, BENNIES n US word for a man's overcoat

BENOMYL, -S n fungicide

BENS ► ben

BENT, -S adj not straight ▷ n personal inclination, propensity, or aptitude

BENTHAL ► benthos

BENTHIC ► benthos

BENTHOAL ► benthos

BENTHON, -S same as ► benthos

BENTHOS n animals and plants living at the bottom of a sea or lake

BENTIER ► benty

BENTIEST ► benty

BENTO, -S n thin lightweight box used in Japanese cuisine

BENTS ► bent

BENTWOOD n wood bent in moulds, used mainly for furniture ▷ adj made from such wood

BENTY, BENTIER, BENTIEST adj covered with bentgrass

BENUMB, -ED, -S vb make numb or powerless

BENZAL, -S n transparent crystalline substance

BENZENE, -S n flammable poisonous liquid used as a solvent, insecticide, etc

BENZIDIN same as > benzidine

BENZIL, -S n yellow compound radical

BENZIN, -S same as ► benzine

B

BENZINE, -S n volatile liquid used as a solvent

BENZINS ▸ benzin

BENZOATE n any salt or ester of benzoic acid

BENZOIC adj of, containing, or derived from benzoic acid or benzoin

BENZOIN, -S n gum resin used in ointments, perfume, etc

BENZOL, -S n crude form of benzene

BENZOLE, -S same as ▸ **benzol**

BENZOLS ▸ benzol

BENZOYL, -S n the monovalent group C_6H_5CO-

BENZYL, -S n molecular fragment of certain alcohols and solvents **BENZYLIC**

BEPAINT, -S vb dye; paint

BEPAT, -S, -TED vb pat

BEPEARL, -S vb decorate with pearls

BEPELT, -ED, -S vb pelt energetically

BEPEPPER vb shower with small missiles

BEPESTER vb pester persistently

BEPIMPLE vb form pimples on

BEPITY, BEPITIED, BEPITIES vb feel great pity for

BEPLUMED adj decorated with feathers

BEPOMMEL vb beat vigorously

BEPOWDER vb cover with powder

BEPRAISE vb praise highly

BEPROSE, -D, -S vb (of poetry) reduce to prose

BEPUFF, -ED, -S vb puff up

BEQUEATH vb dispose of (property) as in a will

BEQUEST, -S n legal gift of money or property by someone who has died

BERAKE, -D, -S, BERAKING vb rake thoroughly

BERASCAL vb accuse of being rascal

BERATE, -D, -S, BERATING vb scold harshly

BERAY, -ED, -ING, -S vb soil; defile

BERBER, -S same as ▸ **berbere**

BERBERE, -S n hot-tasting Ethiopian paste

BERBERIN same as > **berberine**

BERBERIS n shrub with red berries

BERBERS ▸ berber

BERBICE n as in **berbice chair** large armchair with long arms that can be folded inwards to act as leg rests

BERCEAU, -X n arched trellis for climbing plants

BERCEUSE n lullaby

BERE, -S n barley

BEREAVE, -N, -S vb deprive (of) something or someone valued, esp through death

BEREAVED adj having recently lost a close friend or relative through death

BEREAVEN ▸ bereave

BEREAVER ▸ bereave

BEREAVES ▸ bereave

BEREFT adj deprived

BERES ▸ bere

BERET, -S n round flat close-fitting brimless cap

BERETTA, -S n type of pistol

BERG, -S n iceberg

BERGALL, -S n fish of the wrasse family

BERGAMA, -S n type of Turkish rug

BERGAMOT n small Asian tree, the fruit of which yields an oil used in perfumery

BERGEN, -S n large rucksack with a capacity of over 50 litres

BERGENIA n evergreen ground-covering plant

BERGERE, -S n type of French armchair

BERGFALL n avalanche

BERGHAAN same as ▸ **bergmehl**

BERGMEHL n light powdery variety of calcite

BERGS ▸ berg

BERGYLT, -S n large northern marine food fish

BERHYME, -D, -S vb mention in poetry

BERIBERI n disease caused by dietary deficiency of thiamine

BERIMBAU n Brazilian single-stringed bowed instrument, used to accompany capoeira

BERIME, -D, -S, BERIMING same as ▸ **berhyme**

BERINGED adj wearing a ring or rings

BERK, -S n stupid person

BERKO adj berserk

BERKS ▸ berk

BERLEY, -ED, -S n bait scattered on water to attract fish ▷ vb scatter (bait) on water

BERLIN, -S n fine wool yarn used for tapestry work, etc

BERLINE, -S same as ▸ **berlin**

BERLINS ▸ berlin

BERM, -ED, -ING, -S n narrow grass strip between the road and the footpath in a residential area ▷ vb create a berm

BERME, -S same as ▸ **berm**

BERMED ▸ berm

BERMES ▸ berme

BERMING ▸ berm

BERMS ▸ berm

BERMUDAS pl n close-fitting shorts that come down to the knees

BERNICLE n barnacle goose

BEROB, -BED, -S vb rob

BEROBED adj wearing a robe

BEROBS ▸ berob

BEROUGED adj wearing rouge

BERRET, -S same as ▸ **beret**

BERRETTA same as ▸ **biretta**

BERRIED ▸ berry

BERRIES ▸ berry

BERRIGAN n Australian tree with hanging branches

BERRY, BERRIED, BERRIES n small soft stoneless fruit ▷ vb bear or produce berries **BERRYING**

BERSEEM, -S n Mediterranean clover grown as a forage crop and to improve the soil

BERSERK, -S adj frenziedly violent or destructive ▷ n fearsome Norse warrior

BERTH, -ED, -S n bunk in a ship or train ▷ vb dock (a ship)

BERTHA, -S n wide deep capelike collar, often of lace, usually to cover up a low neckline

BERTHAGE n place for mooring boats

BERTHAS ▸ bertha

BERTHE, -S n type of lace collar

BERTHED ▸ berth

BERTHES ▸ berthe

BERTHING n act of berthing

BERTHS ▸ berth

BERYL, -S n hard transparent mineral **BERYLINE**

BERYLLIA n beryllium oxide

BERYLS ▸ beryl

BES, -ES variant of ▸ **beth**

BESAINT, -S vb give saint status to

BESANG ▸ besing

BESAT ▸ besit

BESAW ▸ besee

BESCORCH vb scorch badly

B

BESCOUR, -S vb scour thoroughly

BESCRAWL vb cover with scrawls

BESCREEN vb conceal with screen

BESEE, BESAW, -ING, -N, -S vb provide for; mind

BESEECH, BESOUGHT vb ask earnestly

BESEEING ▸ besee

BESEEKE, -S archaic form of ▸ beseech

BESEEM, -ED, -S vb be suitable for

BESEEMLY adj becoming; suitable

BESEEMS ▸ beseem

BESEEN ▸ besee

BESEES ▸ besee

BESES ▸ bes

BESET, -S vb trouble or harass constantly

BESETTER

BESHADOW vb darken with shadow

BESHAME, -D, -S vb cause to feel shame

BESHINE, -S, BESHONE vb illuminate

BESHIVER vb shatter

BESHONE ▸ beshine

BESHOUT, -S vb shout about

BESHREW, -S vb wish evil on

BESHROUD vb cover with a shroud

BESIDE prep at, by, or to the side of

BESIDES prep in addition ▷ adv in addition

BESIEGE, -D, -S vb surround with military forces

BESIEGER

BESIGH, -ED, -S vb sigh for

BESING, BESANG, -S, BESUNG vb sing about joyfully

BESIT, BESAT, -S vb suit; fit

BESLAVE, -D, -S vb treat as slave

BESLAVER vb fawn over

BESLAVES ▸ beslave

BESLIME, -D, -S vb cover with slime

BESMEAR, -S vb smear over

BESMILE, -D, -S vb smile on

BESMIRCH vb tarnish (someone's name or reputation)

BESMOKE, -D, -S vb blacken with smoke

BESMOOTH vb smooth

BESMUDGE vb blacken

BESMUT, -S vb blacken with smut

BESMUTCH same as ▸ besmirch

BESMUTS ▸ besmut

BESNOW, -ED, -S vb cover with snow

BESOGNIO n worthless person

BESOIN, -S n need

BESOM, -ED, -ING, -S n broom made of twigs ▷ vb sweep with a besom

BESONIAN same as ▸ bezonian

BESOOTHE vb soothe

BESORT, -ED, -S vb fit

BESOT, -S vb make stupid or muddled

BESOTTED adj infatuated

BESOUGHT ▸ beseech

BESOULED adj having a soul

BESPAKE ▸ bespeak

BESPAT ▸ bespit

BESPATE ▸ bespit

BESPEAK, BESPAKE, -S, BESPOKEN vb indicate or suggest

BESPEED, BESPED, -S vb get on with (doing something)

BESPICE, -D, -S vb flavour with spices

BESPIT, BESPAT, BESPATE, -S vb cover with spittle

BESPOKE adj (esp of a suit) made to the customer's specifications

BESPOKEN ▸ bespeak

BESPORT, -S vb amuse oneself

BESPOT, -S vb mark with spots

BESPOUSE vb marry

BESPOUT, -S vb speak pretentiously

BESPREAD vb cover (a surface) with something

BESPRENT adj sprinkled over

BEST, -ED, -ING, -S adj most excellent of a particular group etc ▷ adv in a manner surpassing all others ▷ n utmost effort ▷ vb defeat

BESTAD Spenserian form of ▸ bestead

BESTADDE Spenserian form of ▸ bestead

BESTAIN, -S vb stain

BESTAR, -S vb decorate with stars

BESTEAD, -S vb serve; assist ▷ adj beset (by)

BESTED ▸ best

BESTI, -S Indian English word for ▸ shame

BESTIAL, -S adj brutal or savage

BESTIARY n medieval collection of descriptions of animals

BESTICK, -S, BESTUCK vb cover with sharp points

BESTIE, -S n best friend

BESTILL, -S vb cause to be still

BESTING ▸ best

BESTIR, -S vb cause (oneself) to become active

BESTIS ▸ besti

BESTORM, -S vb assault

BESTOW, -ED, -S vb present (a gift) or confer (an honour)

BESTOWAL

BESTOWER

BESTREAK vb streak

BESTREW, -N, -S vb scatter or lie scattered over (a surface)

BESTRIDE, BESTRID, BESTRODE vb have or put a leg on either side of

BESTROW, -N, -S same as ▸ bestrew

BESTS ▸ best

BESTUCK ▸ bestick

BESTUD, -S vb set with, or as with studs

BESUITED adj wearing a suit

BESUNG ▸ besing

BESWARM, -S vb swarm over

BET, -S, -TED n wager between two parties predicting different outcomes of an event ▷ vb predict

BETA, -S n second letter in the Greek alphabet, a consonant, transliterated as b

BETACISM vb type of speech impediment

BETAINE, -S n sweet-tasting alkaloid that occurs in the sugar beet

BETAKE, -N, -S, BETAKING, BETOOK vb as in betake oneself go

BETAS ▸ beta

BETATRON n type of particle accelerator for producing high-energy beams of electrons

BETATTER vb make ragged

BETAXED adj burdened with taxes

BETCHA interj bet you

BETE, -D, -S, BETING same as ▸ beet

BETEEM, -ED, -S vb accord

BETEEME, -S same as ▸ beteem

BETEEMED ▸ beteem

BETEEMES ▸ beteeme

BETEEMS ▸ beteem

BETEL, -S n Asian climbing plant, the leaves and nuts of which can be chewed

BETELNUT n seed of the betel palm

BETELS ▶ betel
BETES ▶ bete
BETH, -S n second letter of the Hebrew alphabet, transliterated as b
BETHANK, -S vb thank
BETHEL, -S n seaman's chapel
BETHESDA n church building of certain Christian denominations
BETHINK, -S vb cause (oneself) to consider or meditate
BETHORN, -S vb cover with thorns
BETHRALL vb make slave of
BETHS ▶ beth
BETHUMB, -S vb (of books) wear by handling
BETHUMP, -S vb thump hard
BETHWACK vb strike hard with flat object
BETIDE, BETID, -D, -S, BETIDING, BETIGHT vb happen (to)
BETIME, -D, -S, BETIMING vb befall
BETING ▶ bete
BETISE, -S n folly or lack of perception
BETITLE, -D, -S vb give title to
BETOIL, -ED, -S vb tire through hard work
BETOKEN, -S vb indicate or signify
BETON, -S n concrete
BETONIES ▶ betony
BETONS ▶ beton
BETONY, BETONIES n North American plant
BETOOK ▶ betake
BETOSS, -ED, -ES vb toss about
BETRAY, -ED, -S vb hand over or expose (one's nation, friend, etc) treacherously to an enemy
BETRAYAL
BETRAYER
BETREAD, -S, BETROD vb tread over
BETRIM, -S vb decorate
BETROD ▶ betread
BETROTH, -S vb promise to marry or to give in marriage
BETS ▶ bet
BETTA, -S n fighting fish
BETTED ▶ bet
BETTER, -ED, -S adj more excellent than others ▷ adv in a more excellent manner ▷ pl n one's superiors ▷ vb improve upon
BETTIES ▶ betty
BETTING, -S ▶ bet

BETTONG, -S n short-nosed rat kangaroo
BETTOR, -S n person who bets
BETTY, BETTIES n type of short crowbar
BETWEEN adv indicating position in the middle, alternatives, etc ▷ prep at a point intermediate to two other points in space, time, etc
BETWIXT adv between
BEUNCLED adj having many uncles
BEURRE, -S n butter
BEVATRON n proton synchrotron at the University of California
BEVEL, -ED, -ING, -LED, -S n slanting edge ▷ vb slope
BEVELER -S
BEVELLER ▶ bevel
BEVELS ▶ bevel
BEVER, -ED, -ING, -S n snack ▷ vb have a snack
BEVERAGE n drink
BEVERED ▶ bever
BEVERING ▶ bever
BEVERS ▶ bever
BEVIES ▶ bevy
BEVOMIT, -S vb vomit over
BEVOR, -S n armour protecting lower part of face
BEVUE, -S n careless error
BEVVY, BEVVIED, BEVVIES, -ING n alcoholic drink ▷ vb drink alcohol
BEVY, BEVIES n flock or group
BEWAIL, -ED, -S vb express great sorrow over
BEWAILER
BEWARE, -D, -S, BEWARING vb be on one's guard (against)
BEWEARY vb cause to be weary
BEWEEP, -S, BEWEPT vb express grief through weeping
BEWENT ▶ bego
BEWEPT ▶ beweep
BEWET, -S, -TED vb make wet
BEWIG, -GED, -S vb adorn with a wig
BEWILDER vb confuse utterly
BEWINGED adj having wings
BEWITCH vb attract and fascinate
BEWORM, -ED, -S vb fill with worms
BEWORRY vb beset with worry
BEWRAP, -S, -T vb wrap up
BEWRAY, -ED, -S an obsolete word for ▶ betray
BEWRAYER

BEY, -S n title in the Ottoman Empire

A **bey** was an official in the Ottoman empire. If someone plays this remember that you can of course put an O in front of it to make **obey**.

BEYLIC, -S n province ruled over by a bey
BEYLIK, -S same as ▶ beylic
BEYOND, -S prep at or to a point on the other side of ▷ adv at or to the far side of something ▷ n unknown, esp life after death
BEYS ▶ bey
BEZ, -ES n part of deer's horn

This word for the tine of a deer's horn is one of the essential short words for using the Z.

BEZANT, -S n medieval Byzantine gold coin
BEZAZZ, -ES another word for ▶ pizzazz
BEZEL, -S n sloping edge of a cutting tool
BEZES ▶ bez
BEZIL, -S archaic word for >alcoholic
BEZIQUE, -S n card game for two or more players

This card game played with two decks of cards combines the Q and Z and would make a wonderful bonus word.

BEZOAR, -S n hard mass, such as a stone or hairball, in the stomach and intestines of animals
BEZONIAN n knave or rascal
BEZZANT, -S same as ▶ bezant
BEZZAZZ same as ▶ bezazz
BEZZIE, -S n best friend
BEZZLE, -D, -S, BEZZLING vb waste (money)
BEZZY same as ▶ bezzie
BHAGEE, -S same as ▶ bhaji
BHAI, -S n Indian form of address for a man
BHAJAN, -S n singing of devotional songs and hymns
BHAJEE, -S same as ▶ bhaji
BHAJI, -A, -S n Indian deep-fried savoury of chopped vegetables in spiced batter
BHAKTA, -S n Hindu term for devotee of God
BHAKTI, -S n loving devotion to God leading to nirvana

B

BHANG, -S *n* preparation of Indian hemp

BHANGRA, -S *n* Punjabi folk music combined with elements of Western pop music

BHANGS ▶ bhang

BHARAL, -S *n* wild Himalayan sheep

BHAT *n* currency of Thailand

BHAVAN, -S *n* (in India) a large house or building

BHAWAN, -S *same as* ▶ **bhavan**

BHEESTIE *same as* ▶ **bhishti**

BHEESTY *same as* ▶ **bhishti**

BHEL, -S *same as* ▶ **bael**

BHELPURI *n* Indian dish of puffed rice and vegetables

BHELS ▶ bhel

BHIKHU, -S *n* fully ordained Buddhist monk

BHINDI, -S *same as* ▶ **bindhi**

BHISHTI, -S *n* (formerly in India) a water-carrier

BHISTEE, -S *same as* ▶ **bhishti**

BHISTI, -S *same as* ▶ **bhishti**

BHISTIE, -S *same as* ▶ **bhishti**

BHISTIS ▶ bhisti

BHOONA, -S *same as* ▶ **bhuna**

BHOOT, -S *same as* ▶ **bhut**

BHUNA, -S *n* Indian sauce

BHUT, -S *n* Hindu term for type of ghost

BI *short for* ▶ **bisexual**

BIACETYL *n* liquid with strong odour

BIALI, -S *same as* ▶ **bialy**

BIALIES ▶ bialy

BIALIS ▶ biali

BIALY, BIALIES, -S *n* type of bagel

BIANNUAL *adj* occurring twice a year ▷ *n* something that happens biannually

BIAS, -ES *n* mental tendency, esp prejudice ▷ *vb* cause to have a bias ▷ *adj* slanting obliquely ▷ *adv* obliquely

BIASED

BIASEDLY

BIASING, -S

BIASNESS ▶ bias

BIASSED *same as* ▶ **biased**

BIASSES *same as* ▶ **biases**

BIASSING *same as* ▶ **biasing**

BIATHLON *n* contest combining skiing with rifle shooting

BIAXAL *same as* ▶ **biaxial**

BIAXIAL *adj* (esp of a crystal) having two axes

BIB, -BED, -S *same as* ▶ **bibcock**

BIBASIC *adj* with two bases

BIBATION *n* drinking to excess

BIBB, -S *n* wooden support on a mast for the trestletrees

BIBBED ▶ bib

BIBBER, -S *n* drinker

BIBBERY *n* drinking to excess

BIBBING, -S *n* act of bibbing

BIBBLE, -S *n* pebble

BIBBS ▶ bibb

BIBCOCK, -S *n* tap with a nozzle bent downwards

BIBE, -S *n* (in Newfoundland folklore) spirit whose wailing warns of a coming death

BIBELOT, -S *n* attractive or curious trinket

BIBES ▶ bibe

BIBFUL, -S *n as in* **spill a bibful** divulge secrets

BIBLE, -S *n* any book containing the sacred writings of a religion

BIBLESS ▶ bib

BIBLICAL *adj* of, occurring in, or referring to the Bible

BIBLIKE ▶ bib

BIBLIST, -S *same as* > **biblicist**

BIBS ▶ bib

BIBULOUS *adj* addicted to alcohol

BICARB, -S *n* bicarbonate of soda

BICAUDAL *adj* having two tails

BICCY, BICCIES *n* biscuit

BICE, -S *n* medium blue colour

BICEP *same as* ▶ **biceps**

BICEPS, -ES *n* muscle with two origins, esp the muscle that flexes the forearm

BICES ▶ bice

BICHIR, -S *n* African freshwater fish with an elongated body

BICHORD *adj* having two strings for each note

BICHROME *adj* having two colours

BICKER, -ED, -S *vb* argue over petty matters ▷ *n* petty squabble

BICKERER

BICKIE, -S *short for* ▶ **biscuit**

BICOLOR, -S *same as* ▶ **bicolour**

BICOLOUR *adj* two-coloured

BICONVEX *adj* (of a lens) having convex faces on both sides

BICORN, -S *adj* having two horns or hornlike parts

BICORNE, -S *same as* ▶ **bicorn**

BICORNS ▶ bicorn

BICRON, -S *n* billionth part of a metre

BICUSPID *adj* having two points ▷ *n* bicuspid tooth

BICYCLE, -D, -S *n* vehicle with two wheels, one behind the other, pedalled by the rider ▷ *vb* ride a bicycle

BICYCLER

BICYCLIC *adj* of, forming, or formed by two circles, cycles, etc

BID, BADE, -DEN, -S *vb* offer (an amount) in attempting to buy something ▷ *n* offer of a specified amount, as at an auction

BIDARKA, -S *same as* ▶ **baidarka**

BIDARKEE, -S *same as* ▶ **bidarka**

BIDDABLE *adj* obedient

BIDDABLY

BIDDEN ▶ bid

BIDDER, -S ▶ bid

BIDDIES ▶ biddy

BIDDING, -S ▶ bid

BIDDY, BIDDIES *n* woman, esp an old gossipy one

BIDE, -D, -S *vb* stay or continue

BIDENT, -S *n* instrument with two prongs

BIDENTAL *n* sacred place where lightning has struck

BIDENTS ▶ bident

BIDER, -S ▶ bide

BIDES ▶ bide

BIDET, -S *n* low basin for washing the genital area

BIDI, -S *same as* ▶ **beedi**

BIDING, -S ▶ bide

BIDIS ▶ bidi

BIDON, -S *n* oil drum

BIDS ▶ bid

BIELD, -ED, -ING, -S *n* shelter ▷ *vb* shelter or take shelter

BIELDIER ▶ bieldy

BIELDING ▶ bield

BIELDS ▶ bield

BIELDY, BIELDIER *adj* sheltered

BIEN *adv* well

BIENNALE *n* event occurring every two years

BIENNIA ▶ biennium

BIENNIAL *adj* occurring every two years ▷ *n* plant that completes its life cycle in two years

BIENNIUM, BIENNIA *n* period of two years

BIER, -S *n* stand on which a body or coffin rests before burial

BIFACE, -S *n* prehistoric stone tool

BIFACIAL *adj* having two faces or surfaces

BIFF, -ED, -ING, -S n blow with the fist ▷ vb give (someone) such a blow

BIFFER, -S n someone, such as a sportsperson, who has a reputation for hitting hard

BIFFIES ► biffy

BIFFIN, -S n variety of red cooking apple

BIFFING ► biff

BIFFINS ► biffin

BIFFO, -S n fighting or aggressive behaviour ▷ adj aggressive

BIFFS ► biff

BIFFY, BIFFIES n outdoor toilet

BIFID adj divided into two by a cleft in the middle

BIFIDA ► bifid

BIFIDITY ► bifid

BIFIDLY ► bifid

BIFIDUM, BIFIDA, -S n type of bacterium

BIFIDUS n bacteria of the human digestive system

BIFILAR adj having two parallel threads, as in the suspension of certain measuring instruments

BIFLEX adj bent or flexed in two places

BIFOCAL adj having two different focuses

BIFOCALS pl n spectacles with lenses permitting near and distant vision

BIFOLD, -S n something folded in two places

BIFORATE adj having two openings, pores, or perforations

BIFORKED adj two-pronged

BIFORM adj having or combining the characteristics of two forms, as a centaur

BIFORMED same as ► biform

BIFTAH, -S same as ► bifter

BIFTER, -S n cigarette

BIG, -GED, -GER, -GEST, -S adj of considerable size, height, number, or capacity ▷ adv on a grand scale ▷ vb build

BIGA, -E n chariot drawn by two horses

BIGAMIES ► bigamy

BIGAMIST ► bigamy

BIGAMOUS ► bigamy

BIGAMY, BIGAMIES n crime of marrying a person while still legally married to someone else

BIGARADE n Seville orange

BIGAROON same as > bigarreau

BIGEMINY n heart complaint

BIGENER, -S n hybrid between individuals of different genera

BIGEYE, -S n type of red marine fish

BIGFOOT, BIGFEET, -S n yeti ▷ vb throw one's weight around

BIGG, -S n type of barley

BIGGED ► big

BIGGER ► big

BIGGEST ► big

BIGGETY same as ► biggity

BIGGIE, -S n something big or important

BIGGIN, -S n plain close-fitting cap

BIGGING, -S ► big

BIGGINS ► biggin

BIGGISH ► big

BIGGITY adj conceited

BIGGON, -S same as ► biggin

BIGGS ► bigg

BIGGY same as ► biggie

BIGHA, -S n in India, unit for measuring land

BIGHEAD, -S n conceited person

BIGHORN, -S n large wild mountain sheep

BIGHT, -ED, -ING, -S n long curved shoreline ▷ vb fasten or bind with a bight

BIGLY ► big

BIGMOUTH n noisy, indiscreet, or boastful person

BIGNESS ► big

BIGNONIA n tropical American climbing shrub

BIGOS, -ES n Polish stew

BIGOT, -S n person who is intolerant, esp regarding religion or race

BIGOTED

BIGOTRY n attitudes, behaviour, or way of thinking of a bigot

BIGOTS ► bigot

BIGS ► big

BIGSTICK adj of or relating to irresistible military strength

BIGTIME adj important

BIGUINE, -S same as ► beguine

BIGWIG, -S n important person

BIHOURLY adj occurring every two hours

BIJOU, -S, -X adj (of a house) small but elegant ▷ n something small and delicately worked

A **bijou** is a French word for a jewel, and it is indeed a jewel to play, getting rid of awkward letters for a good score. And remember that the plural can be **bijous** or **bijoux**.

BIJUGATE adj (of compound leaves) having two pairs of leaflets

BIJUGOUS same as ► bijugate

BIJURAL adj relating to two coexisting legal systems

BIJWONER same as ► bywoner

BIKE, -D, -S same as ► bicycle

BIKER, -S n person who rides a motorcycle

BIKES ► bike

BIKEWAY, -S n cycle lane

BIKIE, -S n member of a motorcycle gang

BIKING, -S ► bike

BIKINI, -S n woman's brief two-piece swimming costume

BIKINIED

BIKKIE, -S slang word for ► biscuit

BILABIAL adj of, relating to, or denoting a speech sound articulated using both lips ▷ n bilabial speech sound

BILANDER n small two-masted cargo ship

BILAYER, -S n part of cell membrane

BILBERRY n bluish-black edible berry

BILBIES ► bilby

BILBO, -ES, -S n (formerly) a sword with a marked temper and elasticity

BILBOA, -S same as ► bilbo

BILBOES ► bilbo

BILBOS ► bilbo

BILBY, BILBIES n Australian marsupial with long pointed ears and grey fur

BILE, -D, -S, BILING n bitter yellow fluid secreted by the liver ▷ vb boil

BILEVEL, -S n hairstyle with two different lengths

BILGE, -D, -S, BILGING n nonsense ▷ vb (of a vessel) to take in water at the bilge

BILGIER ► bilgy

BILGIEST ► bilgy

BILGING ► bilge

BILGY, BILGIER, BILGIEST ► bilge

BILIAN, -S n type of tree used for its wood

BILIARY adj of bile, the ducts that convey bile, or the gall

B

bladder ▷ *n* disease found in dogs

BILIMBI, -S *n* type of fruit-bearing tree

BILINEAR *adj* of or referring to two lines

BILING ► bile

BILIOUS *adj* sick, nauseous

BILK, -ED, -ING, -S *vb* cheat, esp by not paying ▷ *n* swindle or cheat

BILKER -S

BILL, -ED, -S *n* money owed for goods or services supplied ▷ *vb* send or present an account for payment to (a person)

BILLABLE *adj* that can be charged to a client

BILLBOOK *n* business record of bills received, paid, etc

BILLBUG, -S *n* type of weevil

BILLED ► bill

BILLER, -S *n* stem of a plant

BILLET, -ED, -S *vb* assign a lodging to (a soldier) ▷ *n* accommodation for a soldier in civil lodgings

BILLETEE

BILLETER

BILLFISH *n* type of fish with elongated jaws, such as the spearfish and marlin

BILLFOLD *n* small folding case, usually of leather, for holding paper money, documents, etc

BILLHEAD *n* printed form for making out bills

BILLHOOK *n* tool with a hooked blade, used for chopping etc

BILLIARD *n* (modifier) of or relating to billiards

BILLIE *same as* ► **billy**

BILLIES, BILLIES ► billies

BILLING, -S *n* prominence given in programmes, advertisements, etc, to performers or acts

BILLION, -S *n* one thousand million ▷ *determiner* amounting to a billion

BILLMAN, BILLMEN *n* person who uses a billhook

BILLON, -S *n* alloy consisting of gold or silver and a base metal

BILLOW, -ED, -S *n* large sea wave ▷ *vb* rise up or swell out

BILLOWY *adj* full of or forming billows

BILLS ► bill

BILLY *n* metal can or pot for cooking on a camp fire

BILLYBOY *n* type of river barge

BILLYCAN *same as* ► **billy**

BILLYO *as in* **like billyo** phrase used to emphasize or intensify something

BILLYOH *same as* ► **billyo**

BILOBAR *same as* ► **bilobate**

BILOBATE *adj* divided into or having two lobes

BILOBED *same as* ► **bilobate**

BILSTED, -S *n* American gum tree

BILTONG, -S *n* strips of dried meat

BIMA, -S *same as* ► **bema**

BIMAH, -S *same as* ► **bema**

BIMANAL *same as* ► **bimanous**

BIMANOUS *adj* having two hands as opposed to four feet

BIMANUAL *adj* using or requiring both hands

BIMAS ► bima

BIMBASHI *n* Turkish military official

BIMBETTE *n* particularly unintelligent bimbo

BIMBLE *n* *as in* **bimble box** type of dense Australian tree

BIMBO, -ES, -S *n* attractive but empty-headed young person

BIMENSAL *adj* occurring every two months

BIMESTER *n* period of two months

BIMETAL, -S *n* material made from two sheets of metal

BIMETHYL *another word for* ► **ethane**

BIMINI, -S *n* type of awning for a yacht

BIMODAL *adj* having two modes

BIMORPH, -S *n* assembly of piezoelectric crystals

BIN, -NED, -NING, -S *n* container for rubbish or for storing grain, coal, etc ▷ *vb* put in a rubbish bin

BINAL *adj* twofold

BINARIES ► binary

BINARISM *n* state of being binary

BINARY, BINARIES *adj* composed of, relating to, or involving two ▷ *n* something composed of two parts or things

BINATE *adj* occurring in two parts or in pairs

BINATELY

BINAURAL *adj* relating to, having, or hearing with both ears

BIND, -S *vb* make secure with or as if with a rope ▷ *n* annoying situation

BINDABLE

BINDER, -S *n* firm cover for holding loose sheets of paper together

BINDERY *n* bookbindery

BINDHI, -S *same as* ► **bindi**

BINDI, -S *n* decorative dot worn in the middle of the forehead, esp by Hindu women

BINDING, -S ► bind

BINDIS ► bindi

BINDLE, -S *n* small packet

BINDS ► bind

BINDWEED *n* plant that twines around a support

BINE, -S *n* climbing or twining stem of various plants

BINER, -S *n* clip used by climbers

BINES ► bine

BING, -S *n* heap or pile, esp of spoil from a mine

BINGE, -D, -S *n* bout of excessive indulgence ▷ *vb* indulge in a binge

BINGEING *n* act of indulging in a binge

BINGER, -S ► binge

BINGES ► binge

BINGIES ► bingy

BINGING, -S *n* act of indulging in a binge

BINGLE, -D, -S, BINGLING *n* minor crash or upset, as in a car or on a surfboard ▷ *vb* layer (hair)

BINGO, -ED, -ES, -ING, -S *n* gambling game ▷ *sentence substitute* cry by the winner of a game of bingo ▷ *vb* (in Scrabble) play all seven of one's tiles in a single turn

BINGS ► bing

BINGY, BINGIES *Australian slang for* ► **stomach**

BINIOU, -S *n* small high-pitched Breton bagpipe

BINIT, -S *n* (computing) early form of bit

BINK, -S *n* ledge

BINMAN, BINMEN *another name for* ► **dustman**

BINNACLE *n* box holding a ship's compass

BINNED ► bin

BINNING ► bin

BINOCLE, -S *n* binocular-style telescope

BINOCS > binocular

BINOMIAL *adj* consisting of two terms ▷ *n* mathematical expression consisting of two terms, such as $3x + 2y$

BINS ▸ bin

BIO, -S short for > **biography**

BIOASSAY n method of determining the effect of a change to substance ▷ vb subject to a bioassay

BIOBANK, -S n large store of human samples for medical research

BIOBLAST same as ▸ **bioplast**

BIOCHIP, -S n small glass or silicon plate containing an array of biochemical molecules or structures

BIOCIDAL ▸ biocide

BIOCIDE, -S n substance used to destroy living things

BIOCLEAN adj free from harmful bacteria

BIOCYCLE n cycling of chemicals through the biosphere

BIODATA n information regarding an individual's education and work history

BIODOT, -S n temperature-sensitive device stuck to the skin in order to monitor stress

BIOETHIC > bioethics

BIOFACT, -S n item of biological information

BIOFILM, -S n thin layer of living organisms

BIOFUEL, -S n gaseous, liquid, or solid substance of biological origin used as a fuel ▷ vb fuel (a vehicle, etc) using biofuel

BIOG, -S short form of > **biography**

BIOGAS, -ES n gaseous fuel produced by the fermentation of organic waste

BIOGEN, -S n hypothetical protein

BIOGENIC adj originating from a living organism

BIOGENS ▸ biogen

BIOGENY n principle that a living organism must originate from a parent form similar to itself

BIOGRAPH vb write biography of

BIOGS ▸ biog

BIOHERM, -S n mound of material laid down by sedentary marine organisms

BIOLOGIC adj of or relating to biology ▷ n drug that

is derived from a living organism

BIOLOGY n study of living organisms

BIOLYSIS, BIOLYSES n death and dissolution of a living organism

BIOLYTIC

BIOMASS n total number of living organisms in a given area

BIOME, -S n major ecological community

BIOMETER n device for measuring natural radiation

BIOMETRY n analysis of biological data

BIOMORPH n form or pattern resembling living thing

BIONIC adj having a part of the body that is operated electronically

BIONICS n study of biological functions to create electronic versions

BIONOMIC > bionomics

BIONOMY n laws of life

BIONT, -S n living thing

BIONTIC

BIOPHOR, -S n hypothetical material particle

BIOPHORE same as ▸ **biophor**

BIOPHORS ▸ biophor

BIOPIC, -S n film based on the life of a famous person

BIOPLASM n living matter

BIOPLAST n very small unit of bioplasm

BIOPLAY, -S n play based on the life of a famous person

BIOPSIC ▸ biopsy

BIOPSY, BIOPSIED, BIOPSIES n examination of tissue from a living body ▷ vb perform a biopsy on

BIOPTIC

BIOS ▸ bio

BIOSCOPE n kind of early film projector

BIOSCOPY n examination of a body to determine whether it is alive

BIOSOLID n residue from treated sewage

BIOTA, -S n plant and animal life of a particular region or period

BIOTECH, -S n biotechnology

BIOTIC, -S adj of or relating to living organisms ▷ n living organism

BIOTICAL same as ▸ **biotic**

BIOTICS ▸ biotic

BIOTIN, -S n vitamin of the B complex, abundant in egg yolk and liver

BIOTITE, -S n black or dark green mineral of the mica group

BIOTITIC

BIOTOPE, -S n small area that supports its own distinctive community

BIOTOXIN n toxic substance produced by a living organism

BIOTRON, -S n climate-control chamber

BIOTROPH n parasitic organism, esp a fungus

BIOTYPE, -S n group of genetically identical plants within a species, produced by apomixis

BIOTYPIC

BIOVULAR adj (of twins) from two separate eggs

BIOWASTE n organic or biodegradable waste

BIPACK, -S n obsolete filming process

BIPAROUS adj producing offspring in pairs

BIPARTED adj divided into two parts

BIPARTY adj involving two parties

BIPED, -S n animal with two feet ▷ adj having two feet

BIPEDAL adj having two feet

BIPEDS ▸ biped

BIPHASIC adj having two phases

BIPHENYL n white or colourless crystalline solid used as a heat-transfer agent

BIPLANE, -S n aeroplane with two sets of wings, one above the other

BIPOD, -S n two-legged support or stand

BIPOLAR adj having two poles

BIPRISM, -S n prism having a highly obtuse angle to facilitate beam splitting

BIRACIAL adj for, representing, or including members of two races, esp White and Black

BIRADIAL adj showing both bilateral and radial symmetry, as certain sea anemones

BIRAMOSE same as ▸ **biramous**

BIRAMOUS adj divided into two parts, as the appendages of crustaceans

B

BIRCH, -ED, -ES n tree with thin peeling bark ▷ vb flog with a birch
BIRCHEN
BIRCHING n act of birching
BIRCHIR, -S same as ▶ bichir
BIRD, -ED, -S n creature with feathers and wings, most types of which can fly ▷ vb hunt for birds
BIRDBATH n small basin or trough for birds to bathe in, usually in a garden
BIRDCAGE n wire or wicker cage in which captive birds are kept
BIRDCALL n characteristic call or song of a bird
BIRDDOG, -S n dog used or trained to retrieve game birds
BIRDED ▶ bird
BIRDER, -S n birdwatcher
BIRDFARM n place where birds are kept
BIRDFEED n food for birds
BIRDIE, -D, -S n score of one stroke under par for a hole ▷ vb play (a hole) in one stroke under par
BIRDING, -S ▶ bird
BIRDLIFE n birds collectively
BIRDLIKE ▶ bird
BIRDLIME n sticky substance smeared on twigs to catch small birds ▷ vb smear (twigs) with birdlime to catch (small birds)
BIRDMAN, BIRDMEN n man concerned with birds, such as a fowler or ornithologist
BIRDS ▶ bird
BIRDSEED n mixture of various kinds of seeds for feeding cage birds
BIRDSEYE n type of primrose
BIRDSHOT n small pellets designed for shooting birds
BIRDSONG n musical call of a bird or birds
BIRDWING n type of butterfly
BIREME, -S n ancient galley having two banks of oars
BIRETTA, -S n stiff square cap worn by the Catholic clergy
BIRIANI, -S same as ▶ biryani
BIRIYANI same as ▶ biriani
BIRK, -S n birch tree ▷ adj consisting or made of birch
BIRKEN adj relating to the birch tree
BIRKIE, -R, -S, -ST n spirited or lively person ▷ adj lively
BIRKS ▶ birk
BIRL, -ED, -S same as ▶ burl
BIRLE, -S same as ▶ burl
BIRLED ▶ birl

BIRLER, -S ▶ birl
BIRLES ▶ birle
BIRLING, -S ▶ birl
BIRLINN, -S n small Scottish book
BIRLS ▶ birl
BIRO, -S n tradename of a kind of ballpoint pen
BIRR, -ED, -ING, -S vb make or cause to make a whirring sound ▷ n whirring sound
BIRRETTA same as ▶ biretta
BIRRING ▶ birr
BIRROTCH n Ethiopian monetary unit
BIRRS ▶ birr
BIRSE, -D, -S, BIRSING n bristle ▷ vb bruise
BIRSIER ▶ birsy
BIRSIEST ▶ birsy
BIRSING ▶ birse
BIRSLE, -D, -S, BIRSLING vb roast
BIRSY, BIRSIER, BIRSIEST adj bristly
BIRTH, -ED, -S n process of bearing young ▷ vb give birth to
BIRTHDAY n anniversary of the day of one's birth
BIRTHDOM n birthright
BIRTHED ▶ birth
BIRTHER, -S n person who believes Barack Obama was not born in the USA
BIRTHING ▶ birth
BIRTHS ▶ birth
BIRYANI, -S n Indian rice-based dish
BIS adv twice ▷ sentence substitute encore! again!
BISCACHA same as ▶ viscacha
BISCOTTO, BISCOTTI n small Italian biscuit
BISCUIT, -S n small flat dry sweet or plain cake ▷ adj pale brown
BISCUITY adj reminiscent of biscuit
BISE, -S n cold dry northerly wind
BISECT, -ED, -S vb divide into two equal parts
BISECTOR n straight line or plane that bisects an angle
BISECTS ▶ bisect
BISERIAL adj in two rows
BISES ▶ bise
BISEXUAL adj sexually attracted to both men and women ▷ n bisexual person
BISH, -ES n mistake
BISHOP, -ED, -S n clergyman who governs a diocese ▷ vb make a bishop

BISK, -S a less common spelling of ▶ bisque
BISMAR, -S n type of weighing scale
BISMARCK n type of pastry
BISMARS ▶ bismar
BISMUTH, -S n pinkish-white metallic element
BISNAGA, -S n type of cactus
BISOM, -S same as ▶ besom
BISON, -S same as ▶ buffalo
BISQUE, -S n thick rich soup made from shellfish
BISSON, -ED, -S adj blind ▷ vb cause to be blind
BIST a form of the second person singular of ▶ be
BISTABLE adj (of an electronic system) having two stable states ▷ n bistable system
BISTATE adj involving two states
BISTER, -S same as ▶ bistre
BISTERED
BISTORT, -S n Eurasian plant with a spike of small pink flowers
BISTOURY n long surgical knife with a narrow blade
BISTRE, -S n water-soluble pigment
BISTRED
BISTRO, -S n small restaurant
BISTROIC
BIT, -S n small piece, portion, or quantity
BITABLE ▶ bite
BITCH, -ED, -ES n female dog, fox, or wolf ▷ vb complain or grumble
BITCHEN same as ▶ bitching
BITCHERY n spiteful talk
BITCHES ▶ bitch
BITCHIER ▶ bitchy
BITCHILY ▶ bitchy
BITCHING adj wonderful or excellent
BITCHY, BITCHIER adj spiteful or malicious
BITCOIN, -S n type of digital currency
BITE, -S, BITTEN vb grip, tear, or puncture the skin, as with the teeth or jaws ▷ n act of biting
BITEABLE
BITER-S ▶ bite
BITESIZE adj small enough to put in the mouth whole
BITEWING n dental x-ray film
BITING, -S ▶ bite
BITINGLY ▶ bite
BITINGS ▶ biting
BITLESS adj without a bit
BITMAP, -S n picture created by colour or shading on

a visual display unit ▷ *vb* create a bitmap of

BITO, -S *n* African and Asian tree

BITONAL *adj* consisting of black and white tones

BITOS ► bito

BITOU *n as in* **bitou bush** type of sprawling woody shrub

BITS ► bit

BITSER, -S *n* mongrel dog

BITSIER ► bitsy

BITSIEST ► bitsy

BITSTOCK *n* handle or stock of a tool into which a drilling bit is fixed

BITSY, BITSIER, BITSIEST *adj* very small

BITT, -ED, -S *n* strong post on the deck of a ship for securing lines ▷ *vb* secure (a line) by means of a bitt

BITTACLE *same as* ► **binnacle**

BITTE *interj* you're welcome

BITTED ► bitt

BITTEN ► bite

BITTER, -ED, -ER *adj* having a sharp unpleasant taste ▷ *n* beer with a slightly bitter taste ▷ *adv* very ▷ *vb* make or become bitter

BITTERLY

BITTERN, -S *n* wading marsh bird with a booming call

BITTERS *pl n* bitter-tasting spirits flavoured with plant extracts

BITTIE, -S *n* small piece

BITTIER ► bitty

BITTIES ► bittie

BITTIEST ► bitty

BITTILY *adv* in a disjointed way

BITTING, -S ► bitt

BITTOCK, -S *n* small amount

BITTOR, -S *n* bittern

BITTOUR, -S *same as* ► **bittor**

BITTS ► bitt

BITTUR, -S *same as* ► **bittor**

BITTY, BITTIER, BITTIEST *adj* lacking unity, disjointed

BITUMED *adj* covered with bitumen

BITUMEN, -S *n* black sticky substance obtained from tar or petrol

BITWISE *adj* relating to an operator in a programming language that manipulates bits

BIUNIQUE *adj* relating to a one-to-one correspondence

BIVALENT *adj* associated together in pairs ▷ *n* structure consisting of two homologous chromosomes

BIVALVE, -S *adj* (of a marine mollusc) with two hinged segments to its shell ▷ *n* sea creature with a shell consisting of two hinged valves

BIVALVED

BIVIA ► bivium

BIVINYL, -S *another word for* ► **butadiene**

BIVIOUS *adj* offering a choice of two different ways

BIVIUM, BIVIA *n* parting of ways

BIVOUAC, -S *n* temporary camp in the open air ▷ *vb* camp in a bivouac

BIVVY, BIVVIED, BIVVIES, -ING *n* small tent or shelter ▷ *vb* camp in a bivouac

BIWEEKLY *adv* every two weeks ▷ *n* periodical published every two weeks

BIYEARLY *adv* every two years

BIZ, -ZES *n* business

BIZARRE, -S *adj* odd or unusual ▷ *n* bizarre thing

BIZARRO, -S *n* bizarre person

BIZAZZ, -ES *same as* ► **pizazz**

BIZCACHA *same as* ► **viscacha**

BIZE, -S *n* dry, cold wind in France

BIZNAGA, -S *same as* ► **bisnaga**

BIZONAL ► bizone

BIZONE, -S *n* place comprising two zones

BIZZES ► biz

BIZZIES ► bizzy

BIZZO, -S *n* empty and irrelevant talk or ideas

BIZZY, BIZZIES *n* policeman

BLAB, -BED, -S *vb* reveal (secrets) indiscreetly

BLABBER, -S *vb* talk without thinking ▷ *n* person who blabs

BLABBIER ► blabby

BLABBING ► blab

BLABBY, BLABBIER *adj* talking too much; indiscreet

BLABS ► blab

BLACK, -ED, -ER, -EST, -S *adj* of the darkest colour, like coal ▷ *n* darkest colour ▷ *vb* make black

BLACKBOY *n* grass tree

BLACKCAP *n* brownish-grey warbler, the male of which has a black crown

BLACKED ► black

BLACKEN, -S *vb* make or become black

BLACKER ► black

BLACKEST ► black

BLACKFIN *n* type of tuna

BLACKFLY *n* type of black aphid that infests beans, sugar beet, and other plants

BLACKGUM *n* US tree

BLACKING *n* preparation for giving a black finish to shoes, metals, etc

BLACKISH ► black

BLACKLEG *n* person who continues to work during a strike ▷ *vb* refuse to join a strike

BLACKLY ► black

BLACKOUT *n* extinguishing of all light as a precaution against an air attack

BLACKS ► black

BLACKTOP *n* bituminous mixture used for paving

BLAD, -DED, -DING, -S *same as* ► **blaud**

BLADDER, -S *n* sac in the body where urine is held

BLADDERY

BLADDING ► blad

BLADE, -S *n* cutting edge of a weapon or tool

BLADED

BLADER, -S *n* person skating with in-line skates

BLADES ► blade

BLADIER ► blady

BLADIEST ► blady

BLADING, -S *n* act or instance of skating with in-line skates

BLADS ► blad

BLADY, BLADIER, BLADIEST *adj as in* **blady grass** coarse leafy Australasian grass

BLAE, -R, -ST *adj* bluish-grey

BLAES *n* hardened clay or shale

BLAEST ► blae

BLAFF, -ED, -ING, -S *n* West Indian stew ▷ *vb* make a barking noise

BLAG, -GED, -S *vb* obtain by wheedling or cadging ▷ *n* robbery, esp with violence

BLAGGER, -S

BLAGGING ► blag

BLAGS ► blag

BLAGUE, -S *n* pretentious but empty talk

BLAGUER, -S

BLAGUEUR *n* bluffer

BLAH, -ED, -ER, -EST, -ING, -S *n* worthless or silly talk ▷ *adj* uninteresting ▷ *vb* talk nonsense or boringly

BLAIN, -S *n* blister, blotch, or sore on the skin

BLAISE *same as* ► **blaes**

BLAIZE *same as* ► **blaes**

B

BLAM, -MED, -MING, -S n representation of the sound of a bullet being fired ▷ vb make the noise of a bullet being fired

BLAMABLE ▶ blame

BLAMABLY ▶ blame

BLAME, -S, BLAMING vb consider (someone) responsible ▷ n responsibility for something that is wrong

BLAMED euphemistic word for ▶ damned

BLAMEFUL adj deserving blame

BLAMER, -S ▶ blame

BLAMES ▶ blame

BLAMING ▶ blame

BLAMMED ▶ blam

BLAMMING ▶ blam

BLAMS ▶ blam

BLANCH, -ED, -ES vb become white or pale

BLANCHER

BLANCO, -ED, -S n whitening substance ▷ vb whiten (something) with blanco

BLAND, -ED, -ER, -EST, -ING, -S adj dull and uninteresting ▷ n bland thing ▷ vb as in **bland out** become bland

BLANDISH vb persuade by mild flattery

BLANDLY ▶ bland

BLANDS ▶ bland

BLANK, -ED, -ER, -EST, -S adj not written on ▷ n empty space ▷ vb cross out, blot, or obscure

BLANKET, -S n large thick cloth used as covering for a bed ▷ adj applying to a wide group of people, situations, conditions, etc ▷ vb cover as with a blanket

BLANKETY n euphemism for any taboo word

BLANKIE, -S n child's security blanket

BLANKING ▶ blank

BLANKLY ▶ blank

BLANKS ▶ blank

BLANKY same as ▶ blankie

BLANQUET n variety of pear

BLARE, -D, -S, BLARING vb sound loudly and harshly ▷ n loud harsh noise

BLARNEY, -S n flattering talk ▷ vb cajole with flattery

BLART, -ED, -ING, -S vb sound loudly and harshly

BLASE adj indifferent or bored through familiarity

BLASH, -ED, -ES, -ING n splash ▷ vb splash (something) with liquid

BLASHIER ▶ blashy

BLASHING ▶ blash

BLASHY, BLASHIER adj windy and rainy

BLAST, -S n explosion ▷ vb blow up (a rock etc) with explosives ▷ interj expression of annoyance

BLASTED adv extreme or extremely ▷ adj blighted or withered

BLASTEMA n mass of animal cells that will regenerate a lost organ or tissue

BLASTER, -S ▶ blast

BLASTIE, -S n ugly creature

BLASTIER ▶ blasty

BLASTIES ▶ blastie

BLASTING n distortion of sound caused by overloading certain components of a radio system

BLASTOFF n launching of a rocket

BLASTOID n extinct echinoderm found in fossil form

BLASTOMA n tumour composed of embryonic tissue that has not yet developed a specialized function

BLASTS ▶ blast

BLASTULA n early form of an animal embryo

BLASTY, BLASTIER adj gusty

BLAT, -S, -TED, -TING vb cry out or bleat like a sheep

BLATANCY ▶ blatant

BLATANT adj glaringly obvious

BLATE, -D, -R, -S, -ST, BLATING adj shy; ill at ease ▷ vb babble (something)

BLATHER, -S vb speak foolishly ▷ n foolish talk

BLATING ▶ blate

BLATS ▶ blat

BLATT, -S n newspaper

BLATTANT same as ▶ blatant

BLATTED ▶ blat

BLATTER, -S n, vb prattle

BLATTING ▶ blat

BLATTS ▶ blatt

BLAUBOK, -S n South African antelope

BLAUD, -ED, -ING, -S vb slap

BLAW, -ED, -ING, -N, -S vb blow

BLAWORT, -S n harebell

BLAWS ▶ blaw

BLAY, -S n small river fish

BLAZAR, -S n type of active galaxy

BLAZE, -D, BLAZING n strong fire or flame ▷ vb burn or shine brightly

BLAZER, -S n lightweight jacket, often in the colours of a school etc

BLAZERED

BLAZES pl n hell

BLAZING ▶ blaze

BLAZON, -ED, -S vb proclaim publicly ▷ n coat of arms

BLAZONER

BLAZONRY n art or process of describing heraldic arms in proper form

BLAZONS ▶ blazon

BLEACH, -ED, -ES vb make or become white or colourless ▷ n bleaching agent

BLEACHER

BLEAK, -ER, -EST, -S adj exposed and barren ▷ n type of fish found in slow-flowing rivers

BLEAKISH

BLEAKLY

BLEAKY same as ▶ bleak

BLEAR, -ED, -ER, -EST, -ING, -S vb make (eyes or sight) dim with or as if with tears ▷ adj bleary

BLEARIER ▶ bleary

BLEARILY ▶ bleary

BLEARING ▶ blear

BLEARS ▶ blear

BLEARY, BLEARIER adj with eyes dimmed, as by tears or tiredness

BLEAT, -ED, -S vb (of a sheep, goat, or calf) utter its plaintive cry ▷ n cry of sheep, goats, and calves

BLEATER -S

BLEATING ▶ bleat

BLEATS ▶ bleat

BLEB, -S n fluid-filled blister on the skin

BLEBBIER ▶ blebby

BLEBBING n formation of bleb

BLEBBY, BLEBBIER ▶ bleb

BLEBS ▶ bleb

BLECH interj expressing disgust

BLED ▶ bleed

BLEE, -S n complexion; hue

BLEED, BLED, -S vb lose or emit blood

BLEEDER, -S n despicable person

BLEEDING ▶ bleed

BLEEDS ▶ bleed

BLEEP, -ED, -ING, -S n high-pitched signal or beep ▷ vb make such a noise

B

BLEEPER, -S *n* small portable radio receiver that makes a bleeping signal
BLEEPING ▸ bleep
BLEEPS ▸ bleep
BLEES ▸ blee
BLELLUM, -S *n* babbler; blusterer
BLEMISH *n* defect or stain ▷ *vb* spoil or tarnish
BLENCH, -ED, -ES *vb* shy away, as in fear
BLENCHER
BLEND, -ED, -S *vb* mix or mingle (components or ingredients) ▷ *n* mixture
BLENDE, -S *n* mineral consisting mainly of zinc sulphide
BLENDED ▸ blend
BLENDER, -S *n* electrical appliance for puréeing vegetables etc
BLENDES ▸ blende
BLENDING ▸ blend
BLENDS ▸ blend
BLENNY, BLENNIES *n* small fish with a tapering scaleless body
BLENT *a past participle of* ▸ **blend**
BLERT, -S *n* foolish person
BLESBOK, -S *n* S African antelope
BLESBUCK *same as* ▸ **blesbok**
BLESS, -ES, BLEST *vb* make holy by means of a religious rite
BLESSED
BLESSER -S
BLESSING ▸ bless
BLEST ▸ bless
BLET, -S, -TED, -TING *n* state of decay in certain fruits, due to overripening ▷ *vb* go soft
BLETHER, -S *same as* ▸ **blather**
BLETS ▸ blet
BLETTED ▸ blet
BLETTING ▸ blet
BLEUATRE *adj* blueish
BLEW ▸ blow
BLEWART, -S *same as* ▸ **blawort**
BLEWITS *n* type of edible fungus with a pale brown cap and a bluish stalk
BLEY, -S *same as* ▸ **blay**
BLIGHT, -ED, -S *n* person or thing that spoils or prevents growth ▷ *vb* cause to suffer a blight
BLIGHTER *n* irritating person
BLIGHTS ▸ blight
BLIGHTY *n* home country; home leave

BLIKSEM *interj* South African expression of surprise
BLIMBING *same as* ▸ **bilimbi**
BLIMEY *interj* exclamation of surprise or annoyance
BLIMP, -ED, -ING, -S *n* small airship ▷ *vb* swell out
BLIMPERY *n* complacent or reactionary behaviour
BLIMPING ▸ blimp
BLIMPISH *adj* complacent and reactionary
BLIMPS ▸ blimp
BLIMY *same as* ▸ **blimey**
BLIN, -NED, -NING, -S *Scots word for* ▸ **blind**
BLIND, -ED, -EST, -S *adj* unable to see ▷ *vb* deprive of sight ▷ *n* covering for a window
BLINDAGE *n* (esp formerly) a protective screen or structure, as over a trench
BLINDED ▸ blind
BLINDER, -S *n* outstanding performance
BLINDEST ▸ blind
BLINDGUT *same as* ▸ **caecum**
BLINDING *n* sand or grit spread over a road surface to fill up cracks ▷ *adj* making one blind or as if blind
BLINDLY ▸ blind
BLINDS ▸ blind
BLING, -ED, -ER, -EST, -S *adj* flashy ▷ *n* ostentatious jewellery ▷ *vb* make ostentatious or flashy
BLINGIER ▸ blingy
BLINGING *adj* flashy and expensive
BLINGS ▸ bling
BLINGY, BLINGIER *same as* ▸ **bling**
BLINI *pl n* Russian pancakes made of buckwheat flour and yeast
BLINIS *same as* ▸ **blini**
BLINK, -ED, -S *vb* close and immediately reopen (the eyes) ▷ *n* act of blinking
BLINKARD *n* something that twinkles
BLINKED ▸ blink
BLINKER *vb* provide (a horse) with blinkers ▷ *n* flashing light for sending messages
BLINKERS *same as* ▸ **blind**
BLINKING *adv* extreme or extremely
BLINKS ▸ blink
BLINNED ▸ blin
BLINNING ▸ blin
BLINS ▸ blin

BLINTZ *n* thin pancake folded over a filling usually of apple, cream cheese, or meat
BLINTZE, -S *same as* ▸ **blintz**
BLINY *same as* ▸ **blini**
BLIP, -PED, -PING, -S *n* spot of light on a radar screen indicating the position of an object ▷ *vb* produce such a noise
BLIPVERT *n* very short television advertisement
BLISS, -ED, -ES, -ING *n* perfect happiness ▷ *vb* make or become perfectly happy
BLISSFUL *adj* serenely joyful or glad
BLISSING ▸ bliss
BLIST *archaic form of* ▸ **blessed**
BLISTER, -S *n* small bubble on the skin ▷ *vb* (cause to) have blisters
BLISTERY
BLIT, -S, -TED, -TING *vb* move (a block of data) in a computer's memory
BLITE, -S *n* type of herb
BLITHE, -ST *adj* casual and indifferent
BLITHELY
BLITHER, -S *same as* ▸ **blether**
BLITHEST ▸ blithe
BLITS ▸ blit
BLITTED ▸ blit
BLITTER, -S *n* circuit that transfers large amounts of data within a computer's memory
BLITTING ▸ blit
BLITZ, -ED, -ES, -ING *n* violent and sustained attack by aircraft ▷ *vb* attack suddenly and intensively
BLITZER -S
BLIVE *same as* ▸ **belive**
BLIZZARD *n* blinding storm of wind and snow ▷ *vb* (of weather) be stormy with wind and snow
BLOAT, -ING, -S *vb* cause to swell, as with liquid or air ▷ *n* abnormal distention of the abdomen in cattle, sheep, etc
BLOATED *adj* swollen, as with a liquid, air, or wind
BLOATER, -S *n* salted smoked herring
BLOATING ▸ bloat
BLOATS ▸ bloat
BLOB, -BED, -BING, -S *n* soft mass or drop ▷ *vb* put blobs, as of ink or paint, on
BLOBBIER
BLOBBY

B

BLOC, -S n people or countries combined by a common interest

BLOCK, -ED, -S n large solid piece of wood, stone, etc ▷ vb obstruct or impede by introducing an obstacle

BLOCKADE n sealing off of a place to prevent the passage of goods ▷ vb impose a blockade on

BLOCKAGE n act of blocking or state of being blocked

BLOCKED ► block

BLOCKER, -S n person or thing that blocks

BLOCKIE, -S n owner of a small property, esp a farm

BLOCKIER ► blocky

BLOCKIES ► blockie

BLOCKING n interruption of anode current in a valve

BLOCKISH adj lacking vivacity or imagination

BLOCKS ► block

BLOCKY, BLOCKIER adj like a block, esp in shape and solidity

BLOCS ► bloc

BLOG, -GED, -S n journal written on-line and accessible to users of the internet ▷ vb write a blog

BLOGGER -S

BLOGGING ► blog

BLOGPOST n single posting made as part of a blog

BLOGRING n group of blogs joined in a ring

BLOGROLL n list of blogs

BLOGS ► blog

BLOKART, -S n single-seat three-wheeled vehicle propelled by the wind

BLOKE, -S n man

BLOKEDOM n state of being a bloke

BLOKEISH adj denoting or exhibiting the characteristics believed typical of an ordinary man

BLOKES ► bloke

BLOKEY, BLOKIER, BLOKIEST same as ► blokeish

BLOKISH same as ► blokeish

BLONCKET adj blue-grey

BLOND, -S adj (of men's hair) of a light colour ▷ n person, esp a man, having light-coloured hair and skin

BLONDE, -R, -S, -ST n fair-haired (person) ▷ adj (of hair) fair

BLONDINE vb dye hair blonde

BLONDING n act or an instance of dyeing hair blonde

BLONDISH ► blond

BLONDS ► blond

BLOOD, -S n red fluid that flows around the body ▷ vb initiate (a person) to war or hunting

BLOODED adj (of horses, cattle, etc) of good breeding

BLOODFIN n silvery red-finned S American freshwater fish, popular in aquariums

BLOODIED ► bloody

BLOODIER ► bloody

BLOODIES ► bloody

BLOODILY ► bloody

BLOODING ► blood

BLOODRED adj having a deep red colour

BLOODS ► blood

BLOODY, BLOODIED, BLOODIER, BLOODIES adj covered with blood ▷ adv extreme or extremely ▷ vb stain with blood

BLOOEY adj out of order; faulty

BLOOIE same as ► blooey

BLOOK, -S n book published on a blog

BLOOM, -S n blossom on a flowering plant ▷ vb (of flowers) open

BLOOMED adj (of a lens) coated to reduce light lost by reflection

BLOOMER, -S n stupid mistake

BLOOMERS pl n woman's baggy underwear

BLOOMERY n place in which malleable iron is produced directly from iron ore

BLOOMIER ► bloomy

BLOOMING n act of blooming

BLOOMS ► bloom

BLOOMY, BLOOMIER adj having a fine whitish coating on the surface

BLOOP, -ED, -ING, -S vb (baseball) hit a ball into air beyond infield

BLOOPER, -S n stupid mistake

BLOOPIER ► bloopy

BLOOPING ► bloop

BLOOPS ► bloop

BLOOPY, BLOOPIER adj (in baseball) relating to a ball hit into the air beyond the infield

BLOOSME, -D, -S archaic form of ► blossom

BLORE, -S n strong blast of wind

BLOSSOM, -S n flowers of a plant ▷ vb (of plants) flower

BLOSSOMY

BLOT, -S, -TED n spot or stain ▷ vb cause a blemish in or on

BLOTCH, -ED, -ES n discoloured area or stain ▷ vb become or cause to become marked by such discoloration

BLOTCHY adj covered in or marked by blotches

BLOTLESS ► blot

BLOTS ► blot

BLOTTED ► blot

BLOTTER, -S n sheet of blotting paper

BLOTTIER ► blotty

BLOTTING n blot analysis

BLOTTO adj extremely drunk

BLOTTY, BLOTTIER adj covered in blots

BLOUBOK, -S same as ► blaubok

BLOUSE, -D, -S, BLOUSING n woman's shirtlike garment ▷ vb hang or cause to hang in full loose folds

BLOUSIER ► blousy

BLOUSILY ► blousy

BLOUSING ► blouse

BLOUSON, -S n short loose jacket with a tight waist

BLOUSY, BLOUSIER adj loose; blouse-like

BLOVIATE vb discourse at length

BLOW, BLEW, -ED, -N, -S vb (of air, the wind, etc) move ▷ vb hard hit

BLOWBACK n gases escaping to the rear

BLOWBALL n dandelion seed head

BLOWBY, -S n leakage of gas past the piston of an engine at maximum pressure

BLOWDART n dart from a blowpipe

BLOWDOWN n accidental burst of a cooling pipe in a nuclear reactor

BLOWED ► blow

BLOWER, -S n mechanical device, such as a fan, that blows

BLOWFISH a popular name for ► puffer

BLOWFLY n fly that lays its eggs in meat

BLOWGUN, -S same as ► blowpipe

BLOWHARD n boastful person ▷ adj blustering or boastful

BLOWHOLE n nostril of a whale

BLOWIE, -S n bluebottle

BLOWIER ► blowy

BLOWIES ► blowie

BLOWIEST ► blowy

BLOWING, -S n moving of air

BLOWKART n land vehicle with a sail

BLOWLAMP another name for > **blowtorch**

BLOWN ► blow

BLOWOFF, -S n discharge of a surplus fluid

BLOWOUT, -S n sudden loss of air in a tyre

BLOWPIPE n long tube from which darts etc are shot by blowing

BLOWS ► blow

BLOWSE, -S n large, red-faced woman

BLOWSED same as ► **blowsy**

BLOWSES ► blowse

BLOWSIER ► blowsy

BLOWSILY ► blowsy

BLOWSY, BLOWSIER adj fat, untidy, and red-faced

BLOWTUBE n tube for blowing air or oxygen into a flame to intensify its heat

BLOWUP, -S n fit of temper

BLOWY, BLOWIER, BLOWIEST adj windy

BLOWZE, -S variant of ► **blowse**

BLOWZED same as ► **blowsy**

BLOWZES ► blowze

BLOWZIER ► blowzy

BLOWZILY ► blowzy

BLOWZY, BLOWZIER same as ► **blowsy**

BLUB, -BED, -BING, -S a slang word for ► **blubber**

BLUBBER, -S vb sob without restraint ▷ adj swollen or fleshy ▷ n fat of whales, seals, etc

BLUBBERY adj of, containing, or like blubber

BLUBBING ► blub

BLUBS ► blub

BLUCHER, -S n high shoe with laces over the tongue

BLUDE, -S Scots form of ► **blood**

BLUDGE, -D, -S, BLUDGING vb evade work ▷ n easy task

BLUDGEON n short thick club ▷ vb hit with a bludgeon

BLUDGER, -S n person who scrounges

BLUDGES ► bludge

BLUDGING ► bludge

BLUDIE, -R, -ST Scots form of ► **bloody**

BLUDY same as ► **bludie**

BLUE, -D, -R, -ST n colour of a clear unclouded sky ▷ adj of the colour blue ▷ vb make or become blue

BLUEBACK n type of salmon

BLUEBALL n type of European herb

BLUEBEAT n type of West Indian pop music of the 1960s

BLUEBELL n flower with blue bell-shaped flowers

BLUEBILL another name for ► **scaup**

BLUEBIRD n North American songbird with a blue plumage

BLUEBOOK n (in Britain) a government publication, usually the report of a commission

BLUEBUCK same as ► **blaubok**

BLUEBUSH n blue-grey herbaceous Australian shrub

BLUECAP, -S another name for ► **bluetit**

BLUECOAT n person who wears blue uniform

BLUED ► blue

BLUEFIN, -S another name for ► **tunny**

BLUEFISH n type of bluish marine food and game fish

BLUEGILL n common N American sunfish, an important freshwater food and game fish

BLUEGOWN n in past, pauper, recipient of blue gown on king's birthday

BLUEGUM, -S n widely cultivated Australian tree

BLUEHEAD n type of fish

BLUEING, -S ► blue

BLUEISH same as ► **bluish**

BLUEJACK n type of oak tree

BLUEJAY, -S n N American jay

BLUELINE n blue-toned photographic proof

BLUELY ► blue

BLUENESS ► blue

BLUENOSE n puritanical or prudish person

BLUER ► blue

BLUES pl n type of music

BLUESIER ► bluesy

BLUESMAN, BLUESMEN n blues musician

BLUEST ► blue

BLUESTEM n type of tall grass

BLUESY, BLUESIER ► blues

BLUET, -S n N American plant with small four-petalled blue flowers

BLUETICK n fast-running dog

BLUETIT, -S n small European bird

BLUETS ► bluet

BLUETTE, -S n short, brilliant piece of music

BLUEWEED n Eurasian weed with blue flowers and pink buds

BLUEWING n type of duck

BLUEWOOD n type of Mexican shrub

BLUEY, -S, BLUIER, BLUIEST adj bluish ▷ n informal Australian word meaning blanket

BLUFF, -ED, -EST, -ING, -S vb pretend to be confident in order to influence (someone) ▷ n act of bluffing ▷ adj good-naturedly frank and hearty

BLUFFER -S

BLUFFLY ► bluff

BLUFFS ► bluff

BLUGGY, BLUGGIER same as ► **bloody**

BLUID, -S Scots word for ► **blood**

BLUIDIER ► bluidy

BLUIDS ► bluid

BLUIDY, BLUIDIER ► bluid

BLUIER ► bluey

BLUIEST ► bluey

BLUING, -S ► blue

BLUISH adj slightly blue

BLUME, -D, -S, BLUMING Scots word for ► **bloom**

BLUNDER, -S n clumsy mistake ▷ vb make a blunder

BLUNGE, -D, -S, BLUNGING vb mix clay with water

BLUNGER, -S n large vat in which the contents are mixed by rotating arms

BLUNGES ► blunge

BLUNGING ► blunge

BLUNK, -ED, -ING, -S vb ruin; botch

BLUNKER -S

BLUNT, -ED, -ER, -EST, -ING, -S adj not having a sharp edge or point ▷ vb make less sharp

BLUNTISH

BLUNTLY

BLUR, -RED, -RING, -S vb make or become vague or less distinct ▷ n something vague, hazy, or indistinct

BLURB, -ED, -ING, -S n promotional description, as on the jacket of a book ▷ vb describe or recommend in a blurb

BLURBIST n writer of blurbs

BLURBS ► blurb

BLURRED ► blur
BLURRIER ► blurry
BLURRILY ► blur
BLURRING ► blur
BLURRY, BLURRIER ► blur
BLURS ► blur
BLURT, -ED, -S vb utter suddenly and involuntarily
BLURTER -S
BLURTING ► blurt
BLURTS ► blurt
BLUSH, -ED, -ES vb become red in the face, esp from embarrassment or shame ▷ n reddening of the face
BLUSHER, -S n cosmetic for giving the cheeks a rosy colour
BLUSHES ► blush
BLUSHET, -S n modest young woman
BLUSHFUL ► blush
BLUSHING ► blush
BLUSTER, -S vb speak loudly or in a bullying way ▷ n empty threats or protests
BLUSTERY adj (of wind) noisy or gusty
BLYPE, -S n piece of skin peeled off after sunburn
BO n interj exclamation uttered to startle or surprise someone ▷ n fellow, buddy
BOA, -S n large nonvenomous snake
BOAB, -S short for ► baobab
BOAK, -ED, -ING, -S same as ► boke
BOAR, -S n uncastrated male pig
BOARD, -ED, -S n long flat piece of sawn timber ▷ vb go aboard (a train, aeroplane, etc)
BOARDER, -S n person who pays rent for accommodation in someone else's home
BOARDING n act of embarking on an aircraft, train, ship, etc
BOARDMAN, BOARDMEN n man who carries a sandwich board
BOARDS ► board
BOARFISH n type of spiny-finned marine fish with a compressed body, a long snout, and large eyes
BOARISH adj coarse, cruel, or sensual
BOARS ► boar
BOART, -S same as ► bort
BOAS ► boa
BOAST, -S vb speak too proudly about one's talents etc ▷ n bragging statement

BOASTED same as ► boast
BOASTER, -S ► boast
BOASTFUL adj tending to boast
BOASTING ► boast
BOASTS ► boast
BOAT, -ED, -S n small vehicle for travelling across water ▷ vb travel in a boat
BOATABLE adj able to be carried by boat
BOATBILL n nocturnal tropical American wading bird with a broad flattened bill
BOATED ► boat
BOATEL, -S n waterside hotel catering for boating people
BOATER, -S n flat straw hat
BOATFUL, -S ► boat
BOATHOOK n hooked pole used for fending off other vessels or obstacles
BOATIE, -S n boating enthusiast
BOATING, -S n rowing, sailing, or cruising in boats as a form of recreation
BOATLIFT n evacuation by boat
BOATLIKE ► boat
BOATLOAD n amount of cargo or number of people held by a boat or ship
BOATMAN, BOATMEN n man who works on, hires out, or repairs boats
BOATNECK n wide open neck on garment
BOATPORT n enclosure for boats
BOATS ► boat
BOATSMAN, BOATSMEN same as ► boatman
BOATTAIL n type of blackbird
BOATYARD n place where boats are kept, repaired, etc
BOB, -BED, -BING, -S vb move or cause to move up and down repeatedly ▷ n short abrupt movement, as of the head
BOBA, -S n type of Chinese tea
BOBAC, -S same as ► bobak
BOBAK, -S n type of marmot
BOBAS ► boba
BOBBED ► bob
BOBBER, -S n type of float for fishing
BOBBERY n mixed pack of hunting dogs ▷ adj noisy or excitable
BOBBIES ► bobby
BOBBIN, -S n reel on which thread is wound

BOBBINET n netted fabric of hexagonal mesh, made on a lace machine
BOBBING ► bob
BOBBINS ► bobbin
BOBBISH adj cheery
BOBBLE, -D, -S, BOBBLING n small ball of material, usu for decoration ▷ vb (of a ball) to bounce erratically because of an uneven playing surface
BOBBLIER ► bobbly
BOBBLING ► bobble
BOBBLY, BOBBLIER adj (of fabric) covered in small balls; worn
BOBBY, BOBBIES n policeman
BOBBYSOX pl n bobbysocks
BOBCAT, -S n N American feline
BOBECHE, -S n candle drip-catcher
BOBFLOAT n small buoyant float, usually consisting of a quill stuck through a piece of cork
BOBLET, -S n two-man bobsleigh
BOBO, -S n rich person who holds bohemian values
BOBOL, -LED, -S n type of fraud ▷ vb commit a bobol
BOBOLINK n American songbird
BOBOLLED ► bobol
BOBOLS ► bobol
BOBOS ► bobo
BOBOTIE, -S n dish of curried mince
BOBOWLER n large moth
BOBS ► bob
BOBSKATE n child's skate with two parallel blades
BOBSLED, -S same as > bobsleigh
BOBSTAY, -S n stay between a bowsprit and the stem of a vessel
BOBTAIL, -S n docked tail ▷ adj having the tail cut short ▷ vb dock the tail of
BOBWHEEL n poetic device
BOBWHITE n brown N American quail
BOBWIG, -S n type of short wig
BOCACCIO n edible American fish
BOCAGE, -S n wooded countryside characteristic of northern France
BOCCA, -S n mouth
BOCCE, -S same as ► boccie
BOCCI, -S same as ► boccie
BOCCIA, -S same as ► boccie

B

BOCCIE, -S n Italian version of bowls

BOCCIS ► bocci

BOCK, -ED, -ING, -S a variant spelling of ► **boke**

BOCKEDY adj (of a structure, piece of furniture, etc) unsteady

BOCKING ► bock

BOCKS ► bock

BOD, -S n person

BODACH, -S n old man

BODDLE, -S same as ► **bodle**

BODE, -D, -S vb portend or presage

BODEFUL adj portentous

BODEGA, -S n shop in a Spanish-speaking country that sells wine

BODEMENT ► bode

BODES ► bode

BODGE, -D, -S, BODGING vb make a mess of

BODGER, -S adj worthless or second-rate

BODGES ► bodge

BODGIE, -R, -S, -ST n unruly or uncouth young man, esp in the 1950s ▷ adj inferior

BODGING ► bodge

BODHI n as in **bodhi tree** holy tree of Buddhists

BODHRAN, -S n shallow one-sided drum popular in Irish and Scottish folk music

BODICE, -S n upper part of a dress

BODIED ► body

BODIES ► body

BODIKIN, -S n little body

BODILESS adj having no body or substance

BODILY adj relating to the body ▷ adv by taking hold of the body

BODING, -S ► bode

BODINGLY ► bode

BODINGS ► boding

BODKIN, -S n blunt large-eyed needle

BODLE, -S n small obsolete Scottish coin

BODRAG, -S n enemy attack

BODS ► bod

BODY, BODIED, BODIES, -ING n entire physical structure of an animal or human ▷ vb give form to

BODYLINE n (in cricket) fast bowling aimed at the batsman's body

BODYMAN, BODYMEN n person who repairs car bodies

BODYSIDE n side of a body of a vehicle

BODYSUIT n one-piece undergarment for a baby

BODYSURF vb ride a wave by lying on it without a surfboard

BODYWASH n liquid soap for use in the shower or bath

BODYWORK n outer shell of a motor vehicle

BOEHMITE n type of grey, red, or brown mineral

BOEP, -S n South African word for a big belly

BOERBUL, -S n crossbred mastiff used esp as a watchdog

BOERBULL same as ► **boerbul**

BOERBULS ► boerbul

BOERTJIE South African word for ► **friend**

BOET, -S n brother

BOEUF, -S n as in **boeuf bourguignon** type of beef casserole

BOFF, -ED, -ING, -S n boffin ▷ vb hit

BOFFIN, -S n scientist or expert

BOFFING ► boff

BOFFINS ► boffin

BOFFINY adj like a boffin

BOFFO, -S n boffin

BOFFOLA, -S n great success

BOFFOS ► boffo

BOFFS ► boff

BOG, -GED, -GING, -S n wet spongy ground ▷ vb mire or delay

BOGAN, -S n youth who dresses and behaves rebelliously

BOGART, -ED, -S vb monopolize or keep to oneself selfishly

BOGBEAN, -S same as ► **buckbean**

BOGEY, -ED, -ING, -S n evil or mischievous spirit ▷ vb play (a hole) in one stroke over par

BOGEYISM n demonization

BOGEYMAN, BOGEYMEN n frightening person, real or imaginary, used as a threat, esp to children

BOGEYS ► bogey

BOGGARD, -S same as ► **boggart**

BOGGART, -S n ghost or poltergeist

BOGGED ► bog

BOGGER, -S n lavatory

BOGGIER ► boggy

BOGGIEST ► boggy

BOGGING ► bog

BOGGISH ► bog

BOGGLE, -D, -S, BOGGLING vb be surprised, confused, or alarmed

BOGGLER -S

BOGGY, BOGGIER, BOGGIEST ► **bog**

BOGHEAD adj relating to variety of coal from which paraffin can be derived

BOGHOLE, -S n natural hole of wet spongy ground

BOGIE, -D, -ING, -S same as ► **bogey**

BOGLAND, -S n area of wetland

BOGLE, -D, -S, BOGLING n rhythmic dance performed to ragga music ▷ vb perform such a dance

BOGMAN, BOGMEN n body of a person found preserved in a peat bog

BOGOAK, -S n oak or other wood found preserved in peat bogs; bogwood

BOGONG, -S n large nocturnal Australian moth

BOGS ► bog

BOGUE, -S n type of Mediterranean fish

BOGUS adj not genuine

BOGUSLY

BOGWOOD, -S same as ► **bogoak**

BOGY same as ► **bogey**

BOGYISM, -S same as ► **bogeyism**

BOGYMAN, BOGYMEN same as ► **bogeyman**

BOH, -S same as ► **bo**

BOHEA, -S n black Chinese tea

BOHEMIA, -S n area frequented by unconventional (esp creative) people

BOHEMIAN adj unconventional in lifestyle or appearance ▷ n person, esp an artist or writer, who lives an unconventional life

BOHEMIAS ► bohemia

BOHO, -S short for ► **bohemian**

BOHRIUM, -S n element artificially produced in minute quantities

BOHS ► boh

BOIL, -ED, -S vb change from a liquid to a vapour so quickly that bubbles are formed ▷ n state or action of boiling

BOILABLE

BOILER, -S n piece of equipment which provides hot water

B

BOILERY n place where water is boiled to extract salt

BOILING, -S adj very hot ▷ n sweet

BOILOFF, -S n quantity of liquified gases lost in evaporation

BOILOVER n surprising result in a sporting event, esp in a horse race

BOILS ▶ boil

BOING, -ED, -ING, -S vb rebound making a noise

BOINK, -ED, -ING, -S same as ▶ boing

BOISERIE n finely crafted wood-carving

BOITE, -S n artist's portfolio

BOK, -S n S African antelope

> This useful K word, meaning an antelope, that can take quite a number of front extensions, forming words like **blesbok, bontbok, reitbok, rhebok**, and even, if you are lucky, **jambok** or **sjambok**.

BOKE, -D, -S, BOKING vb retch or vomit ▷ n retch

BOKKEN, -S n wooden practice sword in kendo

BOKO, -S slang word for ▶ nose

BOKS ▶ bok

BOLA n missile used by gauchos and Indians of South America

BOLAR adj relating to clay

BOLAS, -ES same as ▶ bola

BOLD, -ED, -ER, -EST, -ING, -S adj confident and fearless ▷ n boldface ▷ vb be or make bold

BOLDEN, -ED, -S vb make bold

BOLDER ▶ bold

BOLDEST ▶ bold

BOLDFACE n weight of type characterized by thick heavy lines ▷ vb print in boldface

BOLDING ▶ bold

BOLDLY ▶ bold

BOLDNESS ▶ bold

BOLDS ▶ bold

BOLE, -S n tree trunk

BOLERO, -S n (music for) traditional Spanish dance

BOLES ▶ bole

BOLETE, -S same as ▶ boletus

BOLETUS, BOLETI n type of fungus

BOLIDE, -S n large exceptionally bright meteor that often explodes

BOLINE, -S n (in Wicca) a knife

BOLIVAR, -S n standard monetary unit of Venezuela, equal to 100 céntimos

BOLIVIA, -S n type of woollen fabric

BOLL, -ED, -EN, -ING, -S n rounded seed capsule of cotton, flax, etc ▷ vb form into a boll

BOLLARD, -S n short thick post used to prevent the passage of motor vehicles

BOLLED ▶ boll

BOLLEN ▶ boll

BOLLING ▶ boll

BOLLS ▶ boll

BOLLWORM n any of various moth caterpillars that feed on and destroy cotton bolls

BOLO, -S n large single-edged knife, originating in the Philippines

BOLOGNA, -S n type of sausage

BOLONEY, -S a variant spelling of ▶ baloney

BOLOS ▶ bolo

BOLSHIE, -R, -S adj difficult or rebellious ▷ n any political radical

BOLSHY same as ▶ bolshie

BOLSON, -S n desert valley surrounded by mountains, with a shallow lake at the centre

BOLSTER, -S vb support or strengthen ▷ n long narrow pillow

BOLT, -ED, -S, BOULTERS n sliding metal bar for fastening a door etc ▷ vb run away suddenly

BOLTER -S

BOLTHEAD n glass receptacle used in chemistry

BOLTHOLE n place of escape from danger

BOLTING, -S ▶ bolt

BOLTLESS ▶ bolt

BOLTLIKE ▶ bolt

BOLTONIA n N American plant with daisy-like flowers with white, violet, or pinkish rays

BOLTROPE n rope sewn to the foot or luff of a sail to strengthen it

BOLTS ▶ bolt

BOLUS, -ES same as ▶ bole

BOMA, -S n enclosure set up to protect a camp, herd of animals, etc

BOMB, -ED, -S n container fitted with explosive material ▷ vb attack with bombs

BOMBABLE

BOMBARD, -S vb attack with heavy gunfire or bombs ▷ n ancient type of cannon that threw stone balls

BOMBARDE n alto wind instrument similar to the oboe

BOMBARDS ▶ bombard

BOMBAST, -S n pompous language ▷ vb speak pompous language

BOMBAX, -ES n type of S American tree

BOMBE, -S n dessert of ice cream lined or filled with custard, cake crumbs, etc ▷ adj (of furniture) having a projecting swollen shape

BOMBED ▶ bomb

BOMBER, -S n aircraft that drops bombs

BOMBES ▶ bombe

BOMBESIN n hormone found in brain

BOMBING, -S ▶ bomb

BOMBLET, -S n small bomb

BOMBLOAD n quantity of bombs carried at one time

BOMBO, -S same as ▶ bumbo

BOMBORA, -S n submerged reef

BOMBOS ▶ bombo

BOMBS ▶ bomb

BOMBSITE n area where the buildings have been destroyed by bombs

BOMBYCID n type of moth of the silkworm family

BOMBYX, -ES n type of moth

BOMMIE, -S n outcrop of coral reef

BON adj good

BONA pl n goods

BONACI, -S n type of fish

BONAMANO, BONAMANI n gratuity

BONAMIA, -S n parasite

BONANZA, -S n sudden good luck or wealth

BONASSUS same as ▶ bonasus

BONASUS n European bison

BONBON, -S n sweet

BONCE, -S n head

BOND, -S n something that binds, fastens or holds together ▷ vb bind

BONDABLE

BONDAGE, -S n slavery

BONDAGER

BONDED adj consisting of, secured by, or operating under a bond or bonds

BONDER, -S same as > bondstone

B

BONDING, -S n process by which individuals become emotionally attached to one another

BONDLESS ▶ bond

BONDMAID n unmarried female serf or slave

BONDMAN, BONDMEN same as ▶ bondsman

BONDS ▶ bond

BONDSMAN, BONDSMEN n person bound by bond to act as surety for another

BONDUC, -S n type of North American tree

BONE, -D, -S n any of the hard parts in the body that form the skeleton ▷ vb remove the bones from (meat for cooking etc)

BONEBED, -S n site where dinosaur fossils are found

BONED ▶ bone

BONEFISH n type of silvery marine game fish occurring in warm shallow waters

BONEHEAD n stupid or obstinate person

BONELESS ▶ bone

BONEMEAL n product of dried and ground animal or bones, used as a fertilizer or in stock feeds

BONER, -S n blunder

BONES ▶ bone

BONESET, -S n N American plant with flat clusters of small white flowers

BONEY, -ER, -EST same as ▶ bony

BONEYARD an informal name for a ▶ cemetery

BONEYER ▶ boney

BONEYEST ▶ boney

BONFIRE, -S n large outdoor fire

BONG, -ED, -ING, -S n deep reverberating sound, as of a large bell ▷ vb make a deep reverberating sound

BONGO, -ES, -S n small drum played with the fingers

BONGOIST n bongo player

BONGOS ▶ bongo

BONGRACE n shade for face

BONGS ▶ bong

BONHAM, -S n piglet

BONHOMIE n cheerful friendliness

BONIATO, -S n sweet potato

BONIBELL same as > bonnibell

BONIE same as ▶ bonny

BONIER ▶ bony

BONIEST ▶ bony

BONIFACE n pub landlord

BONINESS ▶ bony

BONING, -S ▶ bone

BONISM, -S n doctrine that the world is good, although not the best of all possible worlds

BONIST -S

BONITO, -ES, -S n small tuna-like marine food fish

BONJOUR interj hello

BONK, -ED, -S vb hit

BONKERS adj crazy

BONKING, -S ▶ bonk

BONKS ▶ bonk

BONNE, -S n housemaid or female servant

BONNET, -ED, -S n metal cover over a vehicle's engine ▷ vb place a bonnet on

BONNIE same as ▶ bonny

BONNIER ▶ bonny

BONNIES ▶ bonny

BONNIEST ▶ bonny

BONNILY ▶ bonny

BONNOCK, -S n thick oatmeal cake

BONNY, BONNIER, BONNIES, BONNIEST adj beautiful ▷ adv agreeably or well ▷ n beautiful person

BONOBO, -S n type of anthropoid ape of central W Africa

BONSAI n ornamental miniature tree or shrub

BONSELA, -S n small gift of money

BONSELLA same as ▶ bonsela

BONSOIR interj good evening

BONSPELL same as ▶ bonspiel

BONSPIEL n curling match

BONTBOK, -S n antelope found in S Africa

BONTEBOK n S African antelope

BONUS, -ED, -ES, -SED, -SES n something given, paid, or received above what is due or expected ▷ vb (in Scrabble) play all seven of one's tiles in a single turn

BONUSING n (in Scrabble) act of playing all seven of one's tiles in a single turn

BONUSSED ▶ bonus

BONUSSES ▶ bonus

BONXIE, -S n great skua

BONY, BONIER, BONIEST adj having many bones

BONZA same as ▶ bonzer

BONZE, -S n Chinese or Japanese Buddhist priest or monk

BONZER adj excellent

BONZES ▶ bonze

BOO, -ED, -S interj shout of disapproval ▷ vb shout 'boo' to show disapproval

BOOAI, -S same as ▶ boohai

BOOAY, -S same as ▶ boohai

BOOB, -ED, -ING, -S n foolish mistake ▷ vb make a foolish mistake ▷ adj of poor quality, similar to that provided in prison

BOOBHEAD n repeat offender in a prison

BOOBIE same as ▶ booby

BOOBIES ▶ booby

BOOBING ▶ boob

BOOBIRD, -S n person who boos

BOOBISH adj doltish

BOOBOO, -S n blunder

BOOBOOK, -S n small spotted Australian brown owl

BOOBOOS ▶ booboo

BOOBS ▶ boob

BOOBY, BOOBIES n foolish person

BOOBYISH

BOOBYISM

BOOCOO, -S same as ▶ beaucoup

BOODIE n type of kangaroo

BOODIED ▶ boody

BOODIES ▶ boody

BOODLE, -D, -S, BOODLING n money or valuables, counterfeit, or used as a bribe ▷ vb give or receive money corruptly or illegally

BOODLER -S

BOODY, BOODIED, BOODIES, -ING vb sulk

BOOED ▶ boo

BOOFHEAD n stupid person

BOOFY, BOOFIER, BOOFIEST adj muscular and strong but stupid

BOOGALOO n type of dance performed to rock and roll music ▷ vb dance a boogaloo

BOOGER, -S n dried mucus from the nose

BOOGEY, -ED, -S same as ▶ boogie

BOOGIE, -D, -S vb dance to fast pop music ▷ n session of dancing to pop music

BOOGY, -ING same as ▶ boogie

BOOGYMAN, BOOGYMEN same as ▶ bogeyman

BOOH, -ED, -ING, -S same as ▶ boo

BOOHAI, -S n as in up the boohai thoroughly lost

BOOHED ▶ booh

B

BOOHING ▶ booh

BOOHOO, -ED, -S vb sob or pretend to sob noisily ▷ n distressed or pretended sobbing

BOOHS ▶ booh

BOOING, -S n act of booing

BOOJUM, -S n American tree

BOOK, -ED, -S n number of pages bound together between covers ▷ vb reserve (a place, passage, etc) in advance

BOOKABLE

BOOKBAG, -S n bag for books

BOOKCASE n piece of furniture containing shelves for books

BOOKED ▶ book

BOOKEND, -S n one of a pair of supports for holding books upright ▷ vb occur or be located on either side (of something)

BOOKER, -S ▶ book

BOOKFUL, -S ▶ book

BOOKIE, -S short for > **bookmaker**

BOOKIER ▶ booky

BOOKIES ▶ bookie

BOOKIEST ▶ booky

BOOKING, -S n reservation, as of a table or seat

BOOKISH adj fond of reading

BOOKLAND n common land given to private owner

BOOKLESS ▶ book

BOOKLET, -S n thin book with paper covers

BOOKLICE > booklouse

BOOKLORE n knowledge or beliefs gleaned from books

BOOKMAN, BOOKMEN n learned person

BOOKMARK n address for a website stored on a computer so that the user can easily return to the site ▷ vb identify and store (a website) so that one can return to it quickly and easily

BOOKMEN ▶ bookman

BOOKOO, -S same as ▶ **boocoo**

BOOKRACK n rack for holding books

BOOKREST n stand for supporting open book

BOOKS ▶ book

BOOKSHOP n shop where books are sold

BOOKSIE same as ▶ **booksy**

BOOKSY, BOOKSIER adj inclined to be bookish or literary

BOOKWORK n academic study

BOOKWORM n person devoted to reading

BOOKY, BOOKIER, BOOKIEST adj bookish

BOOL, -ED, -ING, -S n bowling ball ▷ vb play bowls

BOOM, -ED, -S vb make a loud deep echoing sound ▷ n loud deep echoing sound

BOOMBOX n portable stereo system

BOOMBURB n large suburb that is growing quickly

BOOMED ▶ boom

BOOMER, -S n large male kangaroo

BOOMIER ▶ boomy

BOOMIEST ▶ boomy

BOOMING, -S ▶ boom

BOOMKIN, -S n short boom projecting from the deck of a ship

BOOMLET, -S n small boom in business, birth rate, etc

BOOMS ▶ boom

BOOMTOWN n town that is enjoying sudden prosperity or has grown rapidly

BOOMY, BOOMIER, BOOMIEST adj characterized by heavy bass sound

BOON, -S n something extremely useful, helpful, or beneficial

BOONDOCK adj of or relating to the boondocks

BOONER, -S n young working-class person from Canberra

BOONGARY n tree kangaroo of NE Queensland, Australia

BOONIES short form of > **boondocks**

BOONLESS ▶ boon

BOONS ▶ boon

BOOR, -S n rude or insensitive person

BOORD, -S obsolete spelling of ▶ **board**

BOORDE, -S obsolete spelling of ▶ **board**

BOORDS ▶ boord

BOORISH adj ill-mannered, clumsy, or insensitive

BOORKA, -S same as ▶ **burka**

BOORS ▶ boor

BOORTREE same as ▶ **bourtree**

BOOS ▶ boo

BOOSE, -D, -S, BOOSING same as ▶ **booze**

BOOST, -ED, -ING, -S n encouragement or help ▷ vb improve

BOOSTER, -S n small additional injection of a vaccine

BOOSTING ▶ boost

BOOSTS ▶ boost

BOOT, -ING, -S n outer covering for the foot that extends above the ankle ▷ vb kick

BOOTABLE

BOOTCUT adj (of trousers) slightly flared at the bottom of the legs

BOOTED adj wearing boots

BOOTEE, -S n baby's soft shoe

BOOTERY n shop where boots and shoes are sold

BOOTH, -S n small partly enclosed cubicle

BOOTHOSE n stocking worn with boots

BOOTHS ▶ booth

BOOTIE n Royal Marine

BOOTIES ▶ booty

BOOTIKIN n small boot

BOOTING ▶ boot

BOOTJACK n device that grips the heel of a boot to enable the foot to be withdrawn easily

BOOTLACE n strong lace for fastening a boot

BOOTLAST n foot shape placed in boots or shoes to keep their shape

BOOTLEG, -S adj produced, distributed, or sold illicitly ▷ vb make, carry, or sell (illicit goods) ▷ n something made or sold illicitly

BOOTLESS adj of little or no use

BOOTLICK vb seek favour by servile or ingratiating behaviour

BOOTS ▶ boot

BOOTY, BOOTIES n valuable articles obtained as plunder

BOOZE, -D, -S n (consume) alcoholic drink ▷ vb drink alcohol, esp in excess

BOOZER, -S n person who is fond of drinking

BOOZES ▶ booze

BOOZEY same as ▶ **boozy**

BOOZIER ▶ boozy

BOOZIEST ▶ boozy

BOOZILY ▶ boozy

BOOZING, -S ▶ booze

BOOZY, BOOZIER, BOOZIEST adj inclined to or involving excessive drinking of alcohol

BOP, **-PED**, **-PING**, **-S** *vb* dance to pop music ▷ *n* form of jazz with complex rhythms and harmonies

BOPEEP, **-S** *n* quick look; peek

BOPPED ▶ bop

BOPPER, **-S** ▶ bop

BOPPIER ▶ boppy

BOPPIEST ▶ boppy

BOPPING ▶ bop

BOPPISH *same as* ▶ boppy

BOPPY, **BOPPIER**, **BOPPIEST** *adj* resembling or suggesting bebop

BOPS ▶ bop

BOR, **-S** *n* neighbour

BORA, **-S** *n* Aboriginal ceremony

BORACES ▶ borax

BORACHIO *n* pig's skin wine carrier

BORACIC *same as* ▶ boric

BORACITE *n* white mineral that forms salt deposits of magnesium borate

BORAGE, **-S** *n* Mediterranean plant with star-shaped blue flowers

BORAK, **-S** *n* rubbish

BORAL, **-S** *n* type of fine powder

BORANE, **-S** *n* any compound of boron and hydrogen

BORAS ▶ bora

BORATE, **-D**, **-S**, **BORATING** *n* salt or ester of boric acid ▷ *vb* treat with borax, boric acid, or borate

BORAX, **BORACES**, **-ES** *n* soluble white mineral occurring in alkaline soils and salt deposits

BORAZON, **-S** *n* extremely hard form of boron nitride

BORD, **-S** *obsolete spelling of* ▶ board

BORDAR, **-S** *n* smallholder who held cottage in return for menial work

BORDE, **-S** *obsolete spelling of* ▶ board

BORDEAUX *adj* any of several wines produced around Bordeaux

BORDER, **-ED**, **-S** *n* dividing line between political or geographical regions ▷ *vb* provide with a border

BORDERER *n* person who lives in a border area, esp the border between England and Scotland

BORDERS ▶ border

BORDES ▶ borde

BORDS ▶ bord

BORDURE, **-S** *n* outer edge of a shield, esp when decorated distinctively

BORE, **-D**, **-S** *vb* make (someone) weary by being dull

BOREAL *adj* of or relating to the north or the north wind

BOREALIS *adj as in* **aurora borealis** lights seen around the North Pole

BOREAS, **-ES** *n* name for the north wind

BORECOLE *another name for* ▶ kale

BORED ▶ bore

BOREDOM, **-S** *n* state of being bored

BOREE, **-S** *same as* ▶ myall

BOREEN, **-S** *n* country lane or narrow road

BOREES ▶ boree

BOREHOLE *n* hole driven into the ground to obtain geological information, release water, etc

BOREL, **-S** *adj* unlearned ▷ *n* boring tool

BORER, **-S** *n* machine or hand tool for boring holes

BORES ▶ bore

BORESOME *adj* boring

BORGO, **-S** *n* small attractive medieval village

BORIC *adj* of or containing boron

BORIDE, **-S** *n* compound in which boron is the most electronegative element

BORING, **-S** *n* act or process of making or enlarging a hole ▷ *adj* dull

BORINGLY

BORK, **-ED**, **-S** *vb* dismiss from a job unfairly

BORKING, **-S** *n* act of incorrectly configuring a device

BORKS ▶ bork

BORLOTTI *pl n as in* **borlotti bean** variety of kidney bean

BORM, **-ED**, **-ING**, **-S** *vb* smear with paint, oil, etc

BORN *adj* possessing certain qualities from birth

BORNA *n as in* **borna disease** viral disease found in mammals, esp horses

BORNE ▶ bear

BORNEOL, **-S** *n* white solid terpene alcohol

BORNITE, **-S** *n* type of mineral

BORNITIC

BORNYL, **-S** *n as in* **bornyl alcohol** white solid alcohol from a Malaysian tree

BORON, **-S** *n* element used in hardening steel

BORONIA, **-S** *n* Australian aromatic flowering shrub

BORONIC ▶ boron

BORONS ▶ boron

BOROUGH, **-S** *n* town or district with its own council

BORREL *adj* ignorant

BORRELIA *n* type of bacterium

BORRELL *same as* ▶ borrel

BORROW, **-ED**, **-S** *vb* obtain (something) temporarily

BORROWER

BORS ▶ bor

BORSCH, **-ES** *same as* ▶ borscht

BORSCHT, **-S** *n* Russian soup based on beetroot

BORSHCH *same as* ▶ borscht

BORSHT, **-S** *same as* ▶ borscht

BORSIC, **-S** *n* composite material used in aviation

BORSTAL, **-S** *n* (formerly in Britain) prison for young criminals

BORSTALL *same as* ▶ borstal

BORSTALS ▶ borstal

BORT, **-S** *n* inferior grade of diamond used for cutting and drilling

BORTIER ▶ borty

BORTIEST ▶ borty

BORTS ▶ bort

BORTSCH *same as* ▶ borscht

BORTY, **BORTIER**, **BORTIEST** ▶ bort

BORTZ, **-ES** *same as* ▶ bort

BORZOI, **-S** *n* tall dog with a long silky coat

BOS ▶ bo

BOSBOK, **-S** *same as* ▶ bushbuck

BOSCAGE, **-S** *n* mass of trees and shrubs

BOSCHBOK *same as* ▶ bushbuck

BOSH, **-ES** *n* empty talk, nonsense

BOSHBOK, **-S** *same as* ▶ bushbuck

BOSHES ▶ bosh

BOSHTA *same as* ▶ boshter

BOSHTER *adj* excellent

BOSHVARK *same as* > boschvark

BOSIE, **-S** *n* (in cricket) another term for googly

BOSK, **-S** *n* small wood of bushes and small trees

BOSKAGE, **-S** *same as* ▶ boscage

BOSKER *adj* excellent

B

BOSKET, -S n clump of small trees or bushes
BOSKIER ► bosky
BOSKIEST ► bosky
BOSKS ► bosk
BOSKY, BOSKIER, BOSKIEST adj containing or consisting of bushes or thickets
BOSOM, -ED, -ING, -S n chest of a person ▷ adj very dear ▷ vb embrace
BOSOMIER ► bosomy
BOSOMING ► bosom
BOSOMS ► bosom
BOSOMY, BOSOMIER adj (of a woman) having large breasts
BOSON, -S n type of elementary particle
BOSONIC
BOSQUE, -S same as ► bosk
BOSQUET, -S same as ► basket
BOSS, -ED, -ER, -ES, -EST n raised knob or stud ▷ vb employ, supervise, or be in charge of ▷ adj excellent
BOSSBOY, -S n Black African foreman of a gang of workers
BOSSDOM, -S n bosses collectively
BOSSED ► boss
BOSSER ► boss
BOSSES ► boss
BOSSEST ► boss
BOSSET, -S n either of the rudimentary antlers found in young deer
BOSSIER ► bossy
BOSSIES ► bossy
BOSSIEST ► bossy
BOSSILY ► bossy
BOSSING, -S n act of shaping malleable metal
BOSSISM, -S n domination of political organizations by bosses
BOSSY, BOSSIER, BOSSIES, BOSSIEST same as ► boss
BOSTANGI n imperial Turkish guard
BOSTHOON n boor
BOSTON, -S n card game for four, played with two packs
BOSTRYX n phenomenon in which flowers develop on one side only
BOSUN, -S same as > boatswain
BOT, -TED, -TING vb scrounge
BOTA, -S n leather container
BOTANIC, -S same as > botanical
BOTANICA n botany
BOTANICS ► botanic
BOTANIES ► botany

BOTANISE same as ► botanize
BOTANIST ► botany
BOTANIZE vb collect or study plants
BOTANY, BOTANIES n study of plants
BOTARGO, -S n relish consisting of the roe of mullet or tuna, salted and pressed into rolls
BOTAS ► bota
BOTCH, -ED, -ES vb spoil through clumsiness ▷ n badly done piece of work or repair
BOTCHER -S
BOTCHERY n instance of botching
BOTCHES ► botch
BOTCHIER ► botchy
BOTCHILY ► botchy
BOTCHING ► botch
BOTCHY, BOTCHIER adj clumsily done or made
BOTE, -S n compensation given for injury or damage to property
BOTEL, -S same as ► boatel
BOTES ► bote
BOTFLY, BOTFLIES n type of stout-bodied hairy fly
BOTH pron two considered together ▷ adj two considered together ▷ determiner two
BOTHAN, -S n unlicensed drinking house
BOTHER, -ED, -S vb take the time or trouble ▷ n trouble, fuss, or difficulty ▷ interj exclamation of slight annoyance
BOTHIE same as ► bothy
BOTHIES ► bothy
BOTHOLE, -S n hole made by the larva of the botfly
BOTHRIUM, BOTHRIA n groove-shaped sucker on tapeworm
BOTHY, BOTHIES n hut used for temporary shelter
BOTHYMAN, BOTHYMEN n man who lives in bothy
BOTNET, -S n network of infected computers
BOTONE adj having lobes at the ends
BOTONEE same as ► botone
BOTONNEE same as ► botone
BOTOXED adj indicating someone who has had Botox treatment
BOTRYOID adj shaped like a bunch of grapes

BOTRYOSE same as ► botryoid
BOTRYTIS n type of fungus which causes plant diseases
BOTS n digestive disease of horses and some other animals
BOTT, -S same as ► bot
BOTTARGA same as ► botargo
BOTTE, -S n thrust or hit
BOTTED ► bot
BOTTEGA, -S n workshop; studio
BOTTES ► botte
BOTTIES ► botty
BOTTINE, -S n light boot for women or children
BOTTING ► bot
BOTTLE, -D, -S n container for holding liquids ▷ vb put in a bottle
BOTTLER, -S n exceptional person or thing
BOTTLES ► bottle
BOTTLING ► bottle
BOTTOM, -ED, -S n lowest, deepest, or farthest removed part of a thing ▷ adj lowest or last ▷ vb provide with a bottom
BOTTOMER n pit worker
BOTTOMRY n loan in which a ship's owner pledges the ship as security
BOTTOMS ► bottom
BOTTONY same as ► botone
BOTTS ► bott
BOTTY, BOTTIES n diminutive for bottom
BOTULIN, -S n potent toxin which causes botulism
BOTULISM n severe food poisoning
BOUBOU, -S n long flowing garment
BOUCHE, -S n notch cut in top corner of shield
BOUCHEE, -S n small pastry case filled with a savoury mixture
BOUCHES ► bouche
BOUCLE, -S n looped yarn giving a knobbly effect ▷ adj of or designating such a yarn or fabric
BOUCLEE, -S n support for a cue in billiards using the hand
BOUCLES ► boucle
BOUDERIE n sulkiness
BOUDIN, -S n French version of a black pudding
BOUDOIR, -S n woman's bedroom or private sitting room

BOUFFANT adj (of a hairstyle) having extra height through backcombing ▷ n bouffant hair style

BOUFFE, -S n type of light or satirical opera common in France during the 19th century

BOUGE, -D, -S, BOUGING vb move

BOUGET, -S n budget

BOUGH, -S n large branch of a tree

BOUGHED

BOUGHPOT n container for displaying boughs

BOUGHS ▶ bough

BOUGHT, -S n curve

BOUGHTEN archaic past participle of ▶ buy

BOUGHTS ▶ bought

BOUGIE, -S n medical instrument

BOUGING ▶ bouge

BOUILLI, -S n stew

BOUILLON n thin clear broth or stock

BOUK, -S n bulk; volume

BOULDER, -S n large rounded rock ▷ vb convert into boulders

BOULDERY

BOULE same as ▶ boulle

BOULES n game popular in France

BOULLE, -S adj relating to a type of marquetry much used on French furniture from the 17th century ▷ n something ornamented with such marquetry

BOULT, -ED, -S same as ▶ bolt

BOULTER

BOULTERS ▶ bolt

BOULTING ▶ boult

BOULTS ▶ boult

BOUN, -ED, -ING, -S vb prepare to go out

BOUNCE, -D, -S vb (of a ball etc) rebound from an impact ▷ n act of rebounding

BOUNCER, -S n person employed at a disco etc to remove unwanted people

BOUNCES ▶ bounce

BOUNCIER ▶ bouncy

BOUNCILY ▶ bouncy

BOUNCING adj vigorous and robust

BOUNCY, BOUNCIER adj lively, exuberant, or self-confident

BOUND, -ING vb jump suddenly ▷ n sudden jump ▷ adj certain

BOUNDARY n dividing line that indicates the farthest limit

BOUNDED adj (of a set) having a bound

BOUNDEN adj morally obligatory

BOUNDER, -S n morally reprehensible person

BOUNDING ▶ bound

BOUNDS pl n limit

BOUNED ▶ boun

BOUNING ▶ boun

BOUNS ▶ boun

BOUNTIED ▶ bounty

BOUNTIES ▶ bounty

BOUNTREE another name for ▶ bourtree

BOUNTY, BOUNTIES n generosity

BOUQUET, -S n bunch of flowers

BOURBON, -S n whiskey made from maize

BOURD, -ED, -ING, -S n prank ▷ vb jest or joke

BOURDER, -S n prankster

BOURDING ▶ bourd

BOURDON, -S n 16-foot organ stop of the stopped diapason type

BOURDS ▶ bourd

BOURG, -S n French market town, esp one beside a castle

BOURGEON same as ▶ burgeon

BOURGS ▶ bourg

BOURKHA, -S same as ▶ burka

BOURLAW, -S same as ▶ byrlaw

BOURN, -S n (in S Britain) stream

BOURNE, -S same as ▶ bourn

BOURNS ▶ bourn

BOURREE, -S n traditional French dance in fast duple time

BOURRIDE n Mediterranean fish soup

BOURSE, -S n stock exchange of continental Europe, esp Paris

BOURSIER n stock-exchange worker

BOURSIN, -S n tradename of a smooth white creamy cheese, often flavoured with garlic

BOURTREE n elder tree

BOUSE, -D, -S, BOUSING vb raise or haul with a tackle

BOUSIER ▶ bousy

BOUSIEST ▶ bousy

BOUSING ▶ bouse

BOUSOUKI same as ▶ bouzouki

BOUSY, BOUSIER, BOUSIEST adj drunken; boozy

BOUT, -S n period of activity or illness

BOUTADE, -S n outburst

BOUTIQUE n small clothes shop

BOUTON, -S n knob-shaped contact between nerve fibres

BOUTONNE adj reserved or inhibited

BOUTONS ▶ bouton

BOUTS ▶ bout

BOUVIER, -S n large powerful dog

BOUZOUKI n Greek stringed musical instrument

BOVATE, -S n obsolete measure of land

BOVID, -S n type of ruminant

BOVINE, -S n domesticated bovine mammal

BOVINELY

BOVINITY

BOVVER, -S n rowdiness, esp caused by gangs of teenage youths

BOW, -S vb lower (one's head) or bend (one's knee or body) as a sign of respect or shame ▷ n movement made when bowing

BOWAT, -S n lamp

BOWBENT adj bent; bow-like

BOWED adj lowered, bent forward, or curved

BOWEL, -ED, -ING, -LED, -S n intestine, esp the large intestine ▷ vb remove the bowels

BOWER, -ED, -ING, -S n shady leafy shelter ▷ vb surround as with a bower

BOWERIES ▶ bowery

BOWERING ▶ bower

BOWERS ▶ bower

BOWERY, BOWERIES n farm

BOWES poetic plural form of ▶ bough

BOWET, -S same as ▶ bowat

BOWFIN, -S n N American freshwater fish

BOWFRONT adj having a front that curves outwards

BOWGET, -S n obsolete variant of ▶ budget

BOWHEAD, -S n type of large-mouthed arctic whale

BOWHUNT, -S vb hunt using a bow and arrows

BOWIE n as in bowie knife type of hunting knife

B

B

BOWING, -S *n* musical technique
BOWINGLY
BOWKNOT, -S *n* decorative knot usually having two loops and two loose ends
BOWL, -ED *n* round container with an open top ▷ *vb* roll smoothly along the ground
BOWLDER, -S *same as* ▶ **boulder**
BOWLED ▶ **bowl**
BOWLEG, -S *n* leg curving outwards like a bow between the ankle and the thigh
BOWLER, -S *n* player who sends (a ball) towards the batsman
BOWLESS ▶ **bow**
BOWLFUL, -S *same as* ▶ **bowl**
BOWLIKE ▶ **bow**
BOWLINE, -S *n* line used to keep the sail taut against the wind
BOWLING, -S *n* game in which bowls are rolled at a group of pins
BOWLLIKE ▶ **bowl**
BOWLS *n* game involving biased wooden bowls and a small bowl (the jack)
BOWMAN, BOWMEN *n* archer
BOWNE, -D, -S, BOWNING *same as* ▶ **boun**
BOWPOT, -S *same as* ▶ **boughpot**
BOWR, -S *n* muscle
BOWS ▶ **bow**
BOWSAW, -S *n* saw with a thin blade in a bow-shaped frame
BOWSE, -D, -S, BOWSING *same as* ▶ **bouse**
BOWSER, -S *n* tanker containing fuel for aircraft, military vehicles, etc
BOWSES ▶ **bowse**
BOWSEY, -S *same as* ▶ **bowsie**
BOWSHOT, -S *n* distance an arrow travels from the bow
BOWSIE, -S *n* low-class, mean or obstreperous person
BOWSING ▶ **bowse**
BOWSMAN, BOWSMEN *n* man who hunts using a bow and arrows
BOWSPRIT *n* spar projecting from the bow of a sailing ship
BOWWOOD, -S *n* tree of the mulberry family, native to south-central US
BOWWOW, -ED, -S *n* imitation of the bark of a dog ▷ *vb* make a noise like a dog

BOWYANG, -S *n* band worn round trouser leg below knee
BOWYER, -S *n* person who makes or sells archery bows
BOX, -ED, -ES *n* container with a firm flat base and sides ▷ *vb* put into a box
BOXBALL, -S *n* street ball game
BOXBERRY *n* fruit of the partridgeberry or wintergreen
BOXBOARD *n* tough paperboard made from wood and wastepaper pulp: used for making boxes, etc
BOXCAR, -S *n* closed railway freight van
BOXED ▶ **box**
BOXEN *adj* made of boxwood
BOXER, -S *n* person who participates in the sport of boxing
BOXES ▶ **box**
BOXFISH *another name for* > **trunkfish**
BOXFUL, -S *same as* ▶ **box**
BOXHAUL, -S *vb* method for bringing a square-rigged ship onto a new tack
BOXIER ▶ **boxy**
BOXIEST ▶ **boxy**
BOXILY ▶ **boxy**
BOXINESS ▶ **boxy**
BOXING, -S *n* sport of fighting with the fists
BOXLA, -S *n* type of lacrosse played indoors
BOXLIKE ▶ **box**
BOXPLOT, -S *n* (in statistics) type of graph
BOXROOM, -S *n* small room in which boxes, cases, etc may be stored
BOXTHORN *n* matrimony vine
BOXTY, BOXTIES *n* type of Irish potato pancake
BOXWOOD, -S *n* hard yellow wood of the box tree, used to make tool handles, etc
BOXY, BOXIER, BOXIEST *adj* squarish or chunky
BOY, -ED, -ING, -S *n* male child ▷ *vb* act the part of a boy in a play
BOYAR, -S *n* member of an old order of Russian nobility
BOYARD, -S *same as* ▶ **boyar**
BOYARISM ▶ **boyar**
BOYARS ▶ **boyar**
BOYAU, -X *n* connecting trench
BOYCHICK *same as* ▶ **boychik**
BOYCHIK, -S *n* young boy**

BOYCOTT, -S *vb* refuse to deal with (an organization or country) ▷ *n* instance of boycotting
BOYED ▶ **boy**
BOYF, -S *n* boyfriend
BOYG, -S *n* troll-like mythical creature
BOYHOOD, -S *n* state or time of being a boy
BOYING ▶ **boy**
BOYISH *adj* of or like a boy in looks, behaviour, or character
BOYISHLY
BOYKIE, -S *n* chap or fellow
BOYLA, -S *n* Australian Aboriginal word for magician
BOYO, -S *n* boy or young man: often used in direct address
BOYS ▶ **boy**
BOYSY, BOYSIER, BOYSIEST *adj* suited to or typical of boys or young men
BOZO, -S *n* man, esp a stupid one
BOZZETTO, BOZZETTI *n* small sketch of planned work
BRA *same as* > **brassiere**
BRAAI, -ED, -ING, -S *vb* grill or roast (meat) over open coals
BRAATA *n* small portion added to a purchase to encourage the customer to return
BRAATAS *same as* ▶ **braata**
BRABBLE, -D, -S *rare word for* ▶ **squabble**
BRABBLER
BRACCATE *adj* (of birds) having feathered legs
BRACCIO, BRACCIA *n* former unit of measurement; length of man's arm
BRACE, -D *n* object fastened to something to straighten or support it ▷ *vb* steady or prepare (oneself) for something unpleasant
BRACELET *n* ornamental chain or band for the wrist
BRACER, -S *n* person or thing that braces
BRACERO, -S *n* Mexican World War II labourer
BRACERS ▶ **bracer**
BRACES *pl n* pair of straps worn over the shoulders for holding up the trousers
BRACH, -ES, -S *n* female dog
BRACHAH, -S, BRACHOT *n* blessing
BRACHES ▶ **brach**
BRACHET, -S *same as* ▶ **brach**

BRACHIA ▸ brachium

BRACHIAL adj of or relating to the arm or to an armlike part or structure ▷ n brachial part or structure

BRACHIUM, BRACHIA n arm, esp the upper part

BRACHOT ▸ brachah

BRACHS ▸ brach

BRACING, -S adj refreshing and invigorating ▷ n system of braces used to strengthen or support

BRACIOLA, BRACIOLE n Italian meat roulade

BRACK, -S same as ▸ barmbrack

BRACKEN, -S n large fern

BRACKET, -S n pair of characters used to enclose a section of writing ▷ vb put in brackets

BRACKISH adj (of water) slightly salty

BRACKS ▸ brack

BRACONID n type of fly with parasitic larva

BRACT, -S n leaf at the base of a flower

BRACTEAL

BRACTED

BRACTLET variant of ▸ bracteole

BRACTS ▸ bract

BRAD, -DED, -DING, -S n small tapered nail with a small head

BRADAWL, -S n small boring tool

BRADDED ▸ brad

BRADDING ▸ brad

BRADOON, -S same as ▸ bridoon

BRADS ▸ brad

BRAE, -S n hill or slope

BRAEHEID n summit of a hill or slope

BRAES ▸ brae

BRAG, -GED, -GEST, -S vb speak arrogantly and boastfully ▷ n boastful talk or behaviour ▷ adj boastful

BRAGGART n person who boasts loudly ▷ adj boastful

BRAGGED ▸ brag

BRAGGER, -S ▸ brag

BRAGGEST ▸ brag

BRAGGIER ▸ braggy

BRAGGING ▸ brag

BRAGGY, BRAGGIER adj boastful

BRAGLY ▸ brag

BRAGS ▸ brag

BRAHMA, -S n breed of domestic fowl

BRAHMAN, -S n member of highest Hindu caste

BRAHMANI n woman of the highest Hindu caste

BRAHMANS ▸ brahman

BRAHMAS ▸ brahma

BRAHMIN, -S same as ▸ brahman

BRAID, -EST, -S vb interweave (hair, thread, etc) ▷ n length of hair etc that has been braided ▷ adj broad ▷ adv broadly

BRAIDE adj given to deceit

BRAIDED adj flowing in several shallow interconnected channels

BRAIDER, -S ▸ braid

BRAIDEST ▸ braid

BRAIDING n braids collectively

BRAIDS ▸ braid

BRAIL, -ED, -ING, -S n one of several lines fastened to a fore-and-aft sail to aid in furling it ▷ vb furl (a fore-and-aft sail) using brails

BRAILLE, -D, -S n system of writing for the blind ▷ vb print or write using this method

BRAILLER n device for producing text in braille

BRAILLES ▸ braille

BRAILS ▸ brail

BRAIN, -ED, -ING, -S n soft mass of nervous tissue in the head ▷ vb hit (someone) hard on the head

BRAINBOX n skull

BRAINED ▸ brain

BRAINIAC n highly intelligent person

BRAINIER ▸ brainy

BRAINILY ▸ brainy

BRAINING ▸ brain

BRAINISH adj impulsive

BRAINPAN n skull

BRAINS ▸ brain

BRAINY, BRAINIER adj clever

BRAIRD, -ED, -S vb appear as shoots

BRAISE, -D, -S, BRAISING vb cook slowly in a covered pan with a little liquid

BRAIZE, -S n sea bream

BRAK, -S n crossbred dog ▷ adj (of water) slightly salty

BRAKE, -D, -S n device for slowing a vehicle ▷ vb apply a brake

BRAKEAGE

BRAKEMAN, BRAKEMEN n crew member of a goods or passenger train

BRAKES ▸ brake

BRAKIER ▸ braky

BRAKIEST ▸ braky

BRAKING, -S n act of braking

BRAKS ▸ brak

BRAKY, BRAKIER, BRAKIEST adj brambly

BRALESS ▸ bra

BRAMBLE, -D, -S n Scots word for blackberry ▷ vb pick blackberries

BRAMBLY

BRAME, -S n powerful feeling of emotion

BRAN, -NED, -NING, -S n husks of cereal grain ▷ vb clean with water in which bran has been boiled

BRANCARD n couch on shafts, carried between two horses

BRANCH, -ED, -ES n secondary stem of a tree ▷ vb (of stems, roots, etc) divide, then develop in different directions

BRANCHER n young bird learning to fly

BRANCHES ▸ branch

BRANCHIA n gill in aquatic animals

BRANCHY ▸ branch

BRAND, -S n particular product ▷ vb mark with a brand

BRANDADE n French puréed fish dish

BRANDED adj identifiable as being the product of a particular company

BRANDER, -S ▸ brand

BRANDIED ▸ brandy

BRANDIES ▸ brandy

BRANDING ▸ brand

BRANDISE n three-legged metal stand for cooking pots

BRANDISH vb wave (a weapon etc) in a threatening way ▷ n threatening or defiant flourish

BRANDS ▸ brand

BRANDY, BRANDIED, BRANDIES n alcoholic spirit distilled from wine ▷ vb give brandy to

BRANE, -S n hypothetical component of string theory

BRANGLE, -D, -S vb quarrel noisily

BRANK, -ED, -ING vb walk with swaggering gait

BRANKIER ▸ branky

BRANKING ▸ brank

BRANKS pl n (formerly) iron bridle used to restrain scolding women

B

BRANKY, BRANKIER *adj* ostentatious

BRANLE, -S *n* old French country dance performed in a linked circle

BRANNED ► **bran**

BRANNER, -S *n* person or machine that treats metal with bran

BRANNIER ► **branny**

BRANNING ► **bran**

BRANNY, BRANNIER *adj* having the appearance or texture of bran

BRANS ► **bran**

BRANSLE, -S *another word for* ► **brantle**

BRANT, -S *n* type of small goose

BRANTAIL *n* singing bird with red tail

BRANTLE, -S *n* French country dance

BRANTS ► **brant**

BRAP *interj* exclamation used to imitate a burst of gunfire

BRAS, -ES *archaic form of* ► **brass**

BRASCO, -S *n* lavatory

BRASERO, -S *n* metal grid for burning coals

BRASES ► **bras**

BRASH, -ED, -ER, -ES, -EST, -ING *adj* offensively loud, showy, or self-confident ▷ *n* loose rubbish, such as broken rock, hedge clippings, etc ▷ *vb* assault

BRASHIER ► **brashy**

BRASHING ► **brash**

BRASHLY ► **brash**

BRASHY, BRASHIER *adj* loosely fragmented

BRASIER, -S *same as* ► **brazier**

BRASIL, -S *same as* ► **brazil**

BRASILIN *same as* ► **brazilin**

BRASILS ► **brasil**

BRASS, -ED, -ES, -ING *n* alloy of copper and zinc ▷ *vb* make irritated or annoyed

BRASSAGE *n* amount charged by government for making coins

BRASSARD *n* identifying armband or badge

BRASSART *same as* ► **brassard**

BRASSED ► **brass**

BRASSES ► **brass**

BRASSET, -S *same as* ► **brassart**

BRASSICA *n* any plant of the cabbage and turnip family

BRASSIE, -S *n* former name for a golf club

BRASSIER ► **brassy**

BRASSIES ► **brassie**

BRASSILY ► **brassy**

BRASSING ► **brass**

BRASSISH ► **brass**

BRASSY, BRASSIER *vb* showy and vulgar

BRAST, -ING, -S *same as* ► **burst**

BRAT, -S *n* unruly child

BRATCHET *n* hunting dog

BRATLING *n* small badly-behaved child

BRATPACK *n* group of precocious and successful young actors, writers, etc

BRATS ► **brat**

BRATTICE *n* partition of wood or treated cloth used to control ventilation in a mine ▷ *vb* fit with a brattice

BRATTIER ► **bratty**

BRATTISH *same as* ► **brattice**

BRATTLE, -D, -S *vb* make a rattling sound

BRATTY, BRATTIER ► **brat**

BRAUNCH *old variant of* ► **branch**

BRAUNITE *n* brown or black mineral

BRAVA, -S *n* professional assassin

BRAVADO, -S *n* showy display of self-confidence ▷ *vb* behave with bravado

BRAVAS ► **brava**

BRAVE, -D, -S, -ST, BRAVING *adj* having or showing courage, resolution, and daring ▷ *n* Native American warrior ▷ *vb* confront with resolution or courage

BRAVELY

BRAVER -S

BRAVERY ► **brave**

BRAVES ► **brave**

BRAVEST ► **brave**

BRAVI ► **bravo**

BRAVING ► **brave**

BRAVO, BRAVI, -ED, -ES, -ING, -S *interj* well done! ▷ *n* cry of 'bravo' ▷ *vb* cry or shout 'bravo'

BRAVURA, -S, BRAVURE *n* display of boldness or daring

BRAW, -ER, -EST *adj* fine or excellent, esp in appearance or dress

BRAWL, -ED, -S *n* noisy fight ▷ *vb* fight noisily

BRAWLER -S

BRAWLIE, -R *adj* in good health

BRAWLING ► **brawl**

BRAWLS ► **brawl**

BRAWLY ► **braw**

BRAWN, -S *n* physical strength

BRAWNED

BRAWNIER ► **brawny**

BRAWNILY ► **brawny**

BRAWNS ► **brawn**

BRAWNY, BRAWNIER *adj* muscular and strong

BRAWS *pl n* fine apparel

BRAXY, BRAXIES *n* acute and usually fatal bacterial disease of sheep

BRAY, -ED, -ING, -S *vb* (of a donkey) utter its loud harsh sound ▷ *n* donkey's loud harsh sound

BRAYER -S

BRAZA, -S *n* Spanish unit of measurement

BRAZE, -D, -S, BRAZING *vb* join (two metal surfaces) with brass ▷ *n* high-melting solder or alloy used in brazing

BRAZEN, -ED, -S *adj* shameless and bold ▷ *vb* face and overcome boldly or shamelessly

BRAZENLY

BRAZENRY *adj* audacity

BRAZENS ► **brazen**

BRAZER, -S ► **braze**

BRAZES ► **braze**

BRAZIER, -S *n* portable container for burning charcoal or coal

BRAZIERY

BRAZIL, -S *n* red wood used for cabinetwork

BRAZILIN *n* pale yellow soluble crystalline solid

BRAZILS ► **brazil**

BRAZING ► **braze**

BREACH, -ED, -ES *n* breaking of a promise, obligation, etc ▷ *vb* break (a promise, law, etc)

BREACHER

BREAD, -ED, -ING, -S *n* food made by baking a mixture of flour and water or milk ▷ *vb* cover (food) with breadcrumbs before cooking

BREADBIN *n* container for bread

BREADBOX *n* airtight container for bread, cakes, etc

BREADED ► **bread**

BREADIER ► **bready**

BREADING ► **bread**

BREADNUT *n* type of Central American and Caribbean tree

BREADS ► **bread**

BREADTH, -S *n* extent of something from side to side

BREADY, BREADIER adj having the appearance or texture of bread

BREAK, -S, BROKEN vb separate into pieces ▷ n act of breaking

BREAKAGE n act or result of breaking

BREAKER, -S n large wave

BREAKING ► break

BREAKOFF n act or an instance of breaking off or stopping

BREAKOUT n escape, esp from prison or confinement

BREAKS ► break

BREAKUP, -S n separation or disintegration

BREAM, -ED, -ING, -S n Eurasian freshwater fish ▷ vb clean debris (from the bottom of a vessel)

BREARE, -S same as ► brier

BREASKIT same as ► brisket

BREAST, -ED, -S n either of the milk-secreting glands on a woman's chest ▷ vb reach the summit of

BREATH, -S n taking in and letting out of air during breathing

BREATHE, -S vb take in oxygen and give out carbon dioxide

BREATHED adj denoting a speech sound in which the vocal cords do not vibrate

BREATHER n short rest

BREATHES ► breathe

BREATHS ► breath

BREATHY adj (of the speaking voice) accompanied by an audible emission of breath

BRECCIA, -S n type of rock
BRECCIAL

BRECHAM, -S n straw horse-collar

BRECHAN, -S same as ► brecham

BRED, -S n person who lives in a small remote place

BREDE, -D, -S, BREDING archaic spelling of ► braid

BREDIE, -S n meat and vegetable stew

BREDING ► brede

BREDREN, -S same as ► brethren

BREDRIN, -S same as ► brethren

BREDS ► bred

BREE, -S n broth, stock, or juice

BREECH, -ED n lower part ▷ vb fit (a gun) with a breech

BREECHES pl n trousers extending to just below the knee

BREED, -S vb produce new or improved strains of (domestic animals or plants) ▷ n group of animals etc within a species that have certain clearly defined characteristics

BREEDER, -S n person who breeds plants or animals

BREEDING ► breed

BREEDS ► breed

BREEKS pl n trousers

BREEM same as ► breme

BREENGE, -D, -S vb lunge forward ▷ n violent movement

BREER, -ED, -ING, -S another word for ► braird

BREES ► bree

BREESE, -S same as ► breeze

BREEST, -S same as ► breast

BREEZE, -D, -S, BREEZING n gentle wind ▷ vb move quickly or casually

BREEZIER ► breezy

BREEZILY ► breezy

BREEZING ► breeze

BREEZY, BREEZIER adj windy

BREGMA, -S, -TA, -TE n point on the top of the skull

BREHON, -S n (formerly) judge in Ireland

BREI, -ING, -S vb speak with a uvular r, esp in Afrikaans

BREID, -S n bread

BREIING ► brei

BREINGE, -D, -S same as ► breenge

BREIS ► brei

BREIST, -S Scot word for ► breast

BREKKIE same as ► brekky

BREKKY, BREKKIES slang word for > breakfast

BRELOQUE n charm attached to watch chain

BREME adj well-known

BREN, -NING, -S n type of machine gun ▷ vb burn

BRENNE, -S vb burn

BRENNING ► bren

BRENS ► bren

BRENT, -ER, -EST, -S n type of goose ▷ adj steep

BRER, -S n brother: usually prefixed to a name

BRERE, -S same as ► brier

BRERS ► brer

BRESAOLA n (in Italian cookery) air-dried, salted beef

BRETESSE another word for ► brattice

BRETHREN ► brother

BRETON, -S n hat with an upturned brim and a rounded crown

BRETTICE same as ► brattice

BREVE, -S n accent placed over a vowel to indicate shortness

BREVET, -ED, -S n document entitling a commissioned officer to hold temporarily a higher military rank ▷ vb promote by brevet
BREVETCY

BREVETE adj patented

BREVETED ► brevet

BREVETS ► brevet

BREVIARY n book of prayers to be recited daily by a Roman Catholic priest

BREVIATE n summary

BREVIER, -S n (formerly) size of printer's type approximately equal to 8 point

BREVIS, -ES same as ► brewis

BREVITY n shortness

BREW, -ED, -S vb make (beer etc) by steeping, boiling, and fermentation ▷ n beverage produced by brewing

BREWAGE, -S n product of brewing

BREWED ► brew

BREWER, -S ► brew

BREWERY n place where beer, etc is brewed

BREWING, -S n quantity of a beverage brewed at one time

BREWIS, -ES n bread soaked in broth, gravy, etc

BREWPUB, -S n pub that incorporates a brewery on its premises

BREWS ► brew

BREWSKI, -S n beer

BREWSTER n person, particularly a woman, who brews

BREY, -ED, -ING, -S same as ► brei

BRIAR, -S n S European shrub with a hard woody root (briarroot)

BRIARD, -S n medium-sized dog

BRIARED ► briar

BRIARIER ► briary

BRIARS ► briar

BRIARY, BRIARIER adj resembling or containing briar

BRIBABLE ► bribe

BRIBE, -D, -S, BRIBING vb offer or give something to someone to gain favour,

B

influence, etc ▷ n something given or offered as a bribe

BRIBEE, -S n one who is bribed

BRIBER, -S ▶ bribe

BRIBERY n process of giving or taking bribes

BRIBES ▶ bribe

BRIBING ▶ bribe

BRICHT, -ER Scot word for ▶ bright

BRICK, -ED, -S n (rectangular block of) baked clay used in building ▷ vb build, enclose, or fill with bricks

BRICKBAT n blunt criticism

BRICKED ▶ brick

BRICKEN adj made of brick

BRICKIE, -S n bricklayer

BRICKIER ▶ bricky

BRICKIES ▶ brickie

BRICKING ▶ brick

BRICKLE, -S variant of ▶ brittle

BRICKS ▶ brick

BRICKY, BRICKIER vb resembling brick

BRICOLE, -S n billiards shot

BRIDAL, -S adj of a bride or a wedding ▷ n wedding or wedding feast

BRIDALLY

BRIDE, -D, -S, BRIDING n woman who has just been or is about to be married ▷ vb act as a bride

BRIDEMAN, BRIDEMEN n bridegroom's attendant

BRIDES ▶ bride

BRIDGE, -D, -S n structure for crossing a river etc ▷ vb build a bridge over (something)

BRIDGING n timber struts fixed between floor or roof joists

BRIDIE, -S n semicircular pie containing meat and onions

BRIDING ▶ bride

BRIDLE, -D, -S, BRIDLING n headgear for controlling a horse ▷ vb show anger or indignation

BRIDLER -S

BRIDOON, -S n horse's bit; small snaffle used in double bridles

BRIE, -S same as ▶ bree

BRIEF, -ED, -EST adj short in duration ▷ n condensed statement or written synopsis ▷ vb give information and instructions to (a person)

BRIEFER -S

BRIEFING n meeting for giving out detailed information or instructions

BRIEFLY ▶ brief

BRIEFS pl n men's or women's underpants without legs

BRIER, -S same as ▶ briar

BRIERED

BRIERIER ▶ briery

BRIERS ▶ brier

BRIERY, BRIERIER ▶ brier

BRIES ▶ brie

BRIG, -S n two-masted square-rigged ship

BRIGADE, -D, -S n army unit smaller than a division ▷ vb organize into a brigade

BRIGALOW n type of acacia tree

BRIGAND, -S n bandit

BRIGHT, -ER adj emitting or reflecting much light ▷ adv brightly

BRIGHTEN vb make or become bright or brighter

BRIGHTER ▶ bright

BRIGHTLY ▶ bright

BRIGHTS pl n high beam of the headlights of a motor vehicle

BRIGS ▶ brig

BRIGUE, -D, -S vb solicit

BRIGUING

BRIK, -S n Tunisian pastry

BRIKI, -S same as ▶ cezve

BRIKS ▶ brik

BRILL, -ER, -EST, -S n type of European flatfish popular as a food fish ▷ adj brilliant

BRILLO, -S n tradename for a type of scouring pad impregnated with a detergent

BRILLS ▶ brill

BRIM, -MED, -MING, -S n upper rim of a vessel ▷ vb fill or be full to the brim

BRIMFUL adj completely filled with

BRIMFULL same as ▶ brimful

BRIMING, -S n phosphorescence of sea

BRIMLESS ▶ brim

BRIMMED ▶ brim

BRIMMER, -S n vessel, such as a glass or bowl, filled to the brim

BRIMMING ▶ brim

BRIMS ▶ brim

BRIN, -S n thread of silk from silkworm

BRINDED adj streaky or patchy

BRINDISI n song sung in celebration

BRINDLE, -S n brindled animal

BRINDLED adj brown or grey streaked with a darker colour

BRINDLES ▶ brindle

BRINE, -D, -S, BRINING n salt water ▷ vb soak in or treat with brine

BRINER -S

BRING, -S, BROUGHT, BRUNG vb carry, convey, or take to a designated place or person

BRINGER -S

BRINGING ▶ bring

BRINGS ▶ bring

BRINIER ▶ briny

BRINIES ▶ briny

BRINIEST ▶ briny

BRINING ▶ brine

BRINISH ▶ brine

BRINJAL, -S n dark purple tropical fruit, cooked and eaten as a vegetable

BRINK, -S n edge of a steep place

BRINKMAN, BRINKMEN n one who goes in for brinkmanship

BRINKS ▶ brink

BRINNY, BRINNIES n stone, esp when thrown

BRINS ▶ brin

BRINY, BRINIER, BRINIES, BRINIEST adj very salty ▷ n sea

BRIO, -S n liveliness

BRIOCHE, -S n soft roll or loaf made from a very light yeast dough, sometimes mixed with currants

BRIONY, BRIONIES same as ▶ bryony

BRIOS ▶ brio

BRIQUET, -S same as ▷ briquette

BRIS, -ES, -SES n ritual circumcision of male babies

BRISANCE n shattering effect or power of an explosion or explosive

BRISANT

BRISE n type of jump

BRISES ▶ bris

BRISK, -ED, -ER, -EST, -ING, -S adj lively and quick ▷ vb enliven

BRISKEN, -S vb make or become more lively or brisk

BRISKER ▶ brisk

BRISKEST ▶ brisk

BRISKET, -S n beef from the breast of a cow

BRISKIER ▶ brisky

BRISKING ▶ brisk

BRISKISH ▶ brisk

BRISKLY ▶ brisk

BRISKS ▶ brisk

BRISKY, BRISKIER another word for ▶ brisk

BRISLING same as ▶ sprat

BRISS same as ▶ bris

B

BRISSES ► bris

BRISTLE, -D, -S *n* short stiff hair ⊳ *vb* (cause to) stand up like bristles
BRISTLY

BRISTOL *n as in* **bristol board** type of heavy cardboard

BRISURE, -S *n* mark of cadency in heraldry

BRIT, -S *n* young of a herring, sprat, or similar fish

BRITCHES *same as*
► breeches

BRITH, -S *same as* **► bris**

BRITS ► brit

BRITSKA, -S *same as*
► britzka

BRITT, -S *n* young herring or sprat

BRITTLE, -D, -R, -S *adj* hard but easily broken ⊳ *vb* make brittle ⊳ *n* crunchy sweet made with treacle and nuts
BRITTLY

BRITTS ► britt

BRITZKA, -S *n* long horse-drawn carriage

BRITZSKA *same as* **► britzka**

BRIZE, -S *same as* **► breeze**

BRO, -S *n* family member

BROACH, -ED, -ES *vb* introduce (a topic) for discussion ⊳ *n* spit for roasting meat
BROACHER

BROAD, -ER, -EST, -S *adj* having great breadth or width ⊳ *n* broad part of something

BROADAX *same as*
► broadaxe

BROADAXE *n* broad-bladed axe

BROADEN, -S *vb* make or become broad or broader

BROADER ► broad

BROADEST ► broad

BROADISH ► broad

BROADLY ► broad

BROADS ► broad

BROADWAY *n* wide road

BROAST, -ED, -S *vb* cook by broiling and roasting

BROCADE, -D, -S *n* rich fabric woven with a raised design ⊳ *vb* weave with such a design

BROCAGE, -S *another word for*
> brokerage

BROCARD, -S *n* basic principle of civil law

BROCATEL *n* heavy upholstery brocade

BROCCOLI *n* type of cabbage with greenish flower heads

BROCH, -S *n* (in Scotland) a circular dry-stone tower large enough to serve as a fortified home

BROCHAN, -S *n* type of thin porridge

BROCHE, -D, -S, BROCHING *adj* woven with a raised design, as brocade

BROCHO, -S *same as*
► brachah

BROCHS ► broch

BROCHURE *n* booklet that contains information about a product or service

BROCK, -S *n* badger

BROCKAGE *same as*
> brokerage

BROCKED *adj* having different colours

BROCKET, -S *n* small tropical American deer with small unbranched antlers

BROCKIT *same as* **► brocked**

BROCKRAM *another word for*
► breccia

BROCKS ► brock

BROCOLI, -S *same as*
► broccoli

BROD, -DED, -DING, -S *vb* prod

BRODDLE, -D, -S *vb* poke or pierce (something)

BRODEKIN *another word for*
► buskin

BRODKIN, -S *same as*
► brodekin

BRODS ► brod

BROEKIES *pl n* underpants

BROG, -GED, -GING, -S *n* bradawl

BROGAN, -S *n* heavy laced, usually ankle-high, work boot

BROGGED ► brog

BROGGING ► brog

BROGH, -S *same as* **► broch**

BROGS ► brog

BROGUE, -S *n* gentle accent
BROGUERY
BROGUISH

BROIDER, -S *archaic word for*
> embroider

BROIDERY *n* old form of embroidery

BROIL, -ED, -ING, -S *vb* cook by direct heat under a grill ⊳ *n* process of broiling

BROILER, -S *n* young tender chicken for roasting

BROILING ► broil

BROILS ► broil

BROKAGE *another word for*
> brokerage

BROKE, -D, -S *vb* negotiate or deal

BROKEN ► break

BROKENLY ► break

BROKER, -ED, -S *n* agent who buys or sells goods, securities, etc ⊳ *vb* act as a broker (in)

BROKERY *n* work done by a broker

BROKES ► broke

BROKING, -S ► broke

BROLGA, -S *n* large grey Australian crane with a trumpeting call

BROLLY, BROLLIES *n* umbrella

BROMAL, -S *n* synthetic liquid formerly used medicinally

BROMANCE *n* close friendship between two men

BROMATE, -D, -S *same as*
> brominate

BROME, -S *n* type of grass

BROMELIA *n* type of plant

BROMELIN *n* protein-digesting enzyme found in pineapple

BROMES ► brome

BROMIC *adj* of or containing bromine in the trivalent or pentavalent state

BROMID, -S *same as*
► bromide

BROMIDE, -S *n* chemical compound used in medicine and photography

BROMIDIC *adj* ordinary

BROMIDS ► bromid

BROMIN, -S *same as*
► bromine

BROMINE, -S *n* dark red liquid element that gives off a pungent vapour

BROMINS ► bromin

BROMISE, -D, -S *same as*
► bromize

BROMISM, -S *n* bromine poisoning

BROMIZE, -D, -S *vb* treat with bromine

BROMMER, -S *n* S African word for bluebottle

BROMO, -S *n* something that contains bromide

BRONC, -S *same as* **► bronco**

BRONCHI ► bronchus

BRONCHIA *pl n* bronchial tubes

BRONCHO, -S *same as*
► bronco

BRONCHUS, BRONCHI *n* either of the two branches of the windpipe

BRONCO, -S *n* (in the US) wild or partially tamed pony

BRONCS ► bronc

BROND, -S *n* old form of brand

B

BRONZE, -D, -S n alloy of copper and tin ▷ adj made of, or coloured like, bronze ▷ vb (esp of the skin) make or become brown

BRONZEN adj made of or the colour of bronze

BRONZER, -S n cosmetic applied to the skin to simulate a sun tan

BRONZES ▶ bronze

BRONZIER ▶ bronzy

BRONZIFY vb cause to become colour of bronze

BRONZING n blue pigment

BRONZITE n type of orthopyroxene often having a metallic or pearly sheen

BRONZY, BRONZIER ▶ bronze

BROO, -S n brow of hill

BROOCH, -ED, -ES n ornament with a pin, worn fastened to clothes ▷ vb decorate with a brooch

BROOD, -ED, -S n number of birds produced at one hatching ▷ vb (of a bird) sit on or hatch eggs

BROODER, -S n structure used for rearing young chickens or other fowl

BROODIER ▶ broody

BROODILY ▶ broody

BROODING ▶ brood

BROODS ▶ brood

BROODY, BROODIER adj moody and sullen

BROOK, -ED, -ING, -S n small stream ▷ vb bear or tolerate

BROOKIE, -S n brook trout

BROOKING ▶ brook

BROOKITE n reddish-brown to black mineral

BROOKLET n small brook

BROOKS ▶ brook

BROOL, -S n low roar

BROOM, -ED, -ING, -S n long-handled sweeping brush ▷ vb sweep with a broom

BROOMIER ▶ broomy

BROOMING ▶ broom

BROOMS ▶ broom

BROOMY, BROOMIER adj covered with growth of broom

BROOS ▶ broo

BROOSE, -S n race at country wedding

BROS ▶ bro

BROSE, -S n oatmeal or pease porridge, sometimes with butter or fat added

BROSY, BROSIER, BROSIEST adj smeared with porridge

BROTH, -S n soup, usu containing vegetables

BROTHA, -S n informal term for an African-American man

BROTHER, BRETHREN, -S n boy or man with the same parents as another person ▷ interj exclamation of amazement, disgust, surprise, disappointment, etc ▷ vb treat someone like a brother

BROTHIER ▶ brothy

BROTHS ▶ broth

BROTHY, BROTHIER adj having appearance or texture of broth

BROUGH, -S same as **▶ broch**

BROUGHAM n horse-drawn closed carriage with a raised open driver's seat in front

BROUGHS ▶ brough

BROUGHT ▶ bring

BROUGHTA same as **▶ braata**

BROUHAHA n loud confused noise

BROUZE, -S same as **▶ broose**

BROW, -S n part of the face (from the eyes to the hairline)

BROWBAND n strap of a horse's bridle that goes across the forehead

BROWBEAT vb frighten (someone) with threats

BROWBONE n bone of the brow

BROWED adj having a brow

BROWLESS ▶ brow

BROWN, -ED, -EST, -S n colour of earth or wood ▷ adj (of bread) made from wheatmeal or wholemeal flour ▷ vb make or become brown

BROWNER, -S n brown object

BROWNEST ▶ brown

BROWNIE, -S n small square nutty chocolate cake

BROWNIER ▶ browny

BROWNIES ▶ brownie

BROWNING n substance used to darken gravies

BROWNISH ▶ brown

BROWNOUT n dimming or reduction in the use of electric lights in a city

BROWNS ▶ brown

BROWNY, BROWNIER ▶ brown

BROWS ▶ brow

BROWSE, -D, -S vb look through in a casual manner ▷ n instance of browsing

BROWSER, -S n software package that enables a user to read hypertext, esp on the Internet

BROWSES ▶ browse

BROWSIER ▶ browsy

BROWSING ▶ browse

BROWST, -S n brewing (of ale, tea)

BROWSY, BROWSIER ▶ browse

BRR same as **▶ brrr**

> This is useful if your consonant-heavy rack is giving you the shivers. And if you are even colder, **brrr** is available.

BRRR interj used to suggest shivering

BRU, -S South African word for **▶ friend**

BRUCELLA n type of bacterium

BRUCHID, -S n type of beetle

BRUCIN, -S same as **▶ brucine**

BRUCINE, -S n bitter poisonous alkaloid resembling strychnine

BRUCINS ▶ brucin

BRUCITE, -S n white translucent mineral

BRUCKLE adj brittle

BRUGH, -S n large house

BRUHAHA, -S same as **▶ brouhaha**

BRUILZIE same as **▶ brulzie**

BRUIN, -S n name for a bear, used in children's tales, fables, etc

BRUISE, -D, -S n discoloured area on the skin caused by an injury ▷ vb cause a bruise on

BRUISER, -S n strong tough person

BRUISES ▶ bruise

BRUISING adj causing bruises, as by a blow ▷ n bruise or bruises

BRUIT, -ED, -ING, -S vb report ▷ n abnormal sound heard within the body

BRUITER -S

BRULE, -S n archaic short word for a person of mixed Canadian Indian and White ancestry

BRULOT, -S n coffee-based alcoholic drink, served flaming

BRULYIE, -S same as **▶ brulzie**

BRULZIE, -S n noisy dispute

BRUMAL adj of, characteristic of, or relating to winter

BRUMBY, BRUMBIES n wild horse

BRUME, -S n heavy mist or fog

BRUMMER, -S *same as*
▶ **brommer**
BRUMOUS ▶ **brume**
BRUNCH, -ED, -ES *n* breakfast and lunch combined ▷ *vb* eat brunch
BRUNCHER
BRUNET, -S *n* boy or man with dark brown hair
BRUNETTE *n* girl or woman with dark brown hair
BRUNG ▶ **bring**
BRUNIZEM *n* prairie soil
BRUNT, -ED, -ING, -S *n* main force or shock of a blow, attack, etc ▷ *vb* suffer the main force or shock of a blow, attack, etc
BRUS ▶ **bru**
BRUSH, -ES *n* device made of bristles, wires, etc ▷ *vb* clean, scrub, or paint with a brush
BRUSHED *adj* treated with a brushing process
BRUSHER, -S ▶ **brush**
BRUSHES ▶ **brush**
BRUSHIER ▶ **brushy**
BRUSHING ▶ **brush**
BRUSHOFF *n* abrupt dismissal or rejection
BRUSHUP, -S *n* the act or an instance of tidying one's appearance
BRUSHY, BRUSHIER *adj* like a brush
BRUSK, -ER, -EST *same as*
▶ **brusque**
BRUSQUE, -R *adj* blunt or curt in manner or speech
BRUSSELS *adj as in* **brussels sprout** small cabbage-like vegetable
BRUSSEN *adj* bold
BRUST, -ING, -S *same as*
▶ **burst**
BRUT, -S *adj* (of champagne or sparkling wine) very dry ▷ *n* very dry champagne
BRUTAL *adj* cruel and vicious
BRUTALLY
BRUTE, -D, -S, -ST *n* brutal person ▷ *adj* wholly instinctive or physical, like an animal
BRUTELY
BRUTER, -S *n* diamond cutter
BRUTES ▶ **brute**
BRUTEST ▶ **brute**
BRUTIFY *less common word for* ▶ **brutalize**
BRUTING, -S *n* diamond cutting
BRUTISH *adj* of or like an animal

BRUTISM, -S *n* stupidity; vulgarity
BRUTS ▶ **brut**
BRUX, -ED, -ES, -ING *vb* grind one's teeth
BRUXISM, -S *n* habit of grinding the teeth, esp unconsciously
BRYOLOGY *n* branch of botany concerned with the study of bryophytes
BRYONY, BRYONIES *n* wild climbing hedge plant
BRYOZOAN *n* type of aquatic invertebrate which forms colonies of polyps
BUAT, -S *same as* ▶ **bowat**
BUAZE, -S *n* fibrous African plant
BUB, -S *n* youngster
BUBA, -S *another name for*
▶ **yaws**
BUBAL, -S *n* any of various antelopes
BUBALE, -S *n* large antelope
BUBALINE *adj* (of antelopes) related to or resembling the bubal
BUBALIS *same as* ▶ **bubal**
BUBALS ▶ **bubal**
BUBAS ▶ **buba**
BUBBA, -S *n* ordinary American person
BUBBE, -S *n* Yiddish word for grandmother
BUBBIE *same as* ▶ **bubbe**
BUBBLE, -D, -S, BUBBLING *n* ball of air in a liquid or solid ▷ *vb* form bubbles
BUBBLER, -S *n* drinking fountain
BUBBLES ▶ **bubble**
BUBBLIER ▶ **bubbly**
BUBBLIES ▶ **bubbly**
BUBBLING ▶ **bubble**
BUBBLY, BUBBLIER, BUBBLIES *adj* excited and lively ▷ *n* champagne
BUBINGA, -S *n* reddish-brown wood from African tree
BUBKES *n* very small amount
BUBKIS *n* nothing
BUBO, -ES *n* inflammation and swelling of a lymph node, esp in the armpit or groin
BUBOED
BUBONIC
BUBS ▶ **bub**
BUBU, -S *same as* ▶ **boubou**
BUBUKLE, -S *n* red spot on skin
BUBUS ▶ **bubu**
BUCARDO, -S *n* type of Spanish mountain goat, recently extinct

BUCATINI *pl n* pasta in the shape of long tubes
BUCCAL *adj* of or relating to the cheek
BUCCALLY
BUCCINA, -S *n* curved Roman horn
BUCELLAS *n* type of Portuguese white wine
BUCHU, -S *n* S African shrub whose leaves are used as an antiseptic and diuretic
BUCK, -ED, -S *n* male of the goat, hare, kangaroo, rabbit, and reindeer ▷ *vb* (of a horse etc) jump with legs stiff and back arched
BUCKAROO *n* cowboy
BUCKAYRO *same as*
▶ **buckaroo**
BUCKBEAN *n* type of marsh plant with white or pink flowers
BUCKED ▶ **buck**
BUCKEEN, -S *n* (in Ireland) poor young man who aspires to the habits and dress of the wealthy
BUCKER, -S ▶ **buck**
BUCKEROO *same as*
▶ **buckaroo**
BUCKERS ▶ **bucker**
BUCKET, -ED, -S *n* open-topped roughly cylindrical container ▷ *vb* rain heavily
BUCKEYE, -S *n* N American tree with erect clusters of white or red flowers and prickly fruits
BUCKHORN *n* horn from a buck, used for knife handles, etc
BUCKIE, -S *n* whelk or its shell
BUCKING, -S ▶ **buck**
BUCKISH ▶ **buck**
BUCKLE, -D, -S *n* clasp for fastening a belt or strap ▷ *vb* fasten or be fastened with a buckle
BUCKLER, -S *n* small round shield worn on the forearm ▷ *vb* defend
BUCKLES ▶ **buckle**
BUCKLING *another name for* ▶ **bloater**
BUCKO, -ES, -S *n* lively young fellow: often a term of address
BUCKRAKE *n* large rake attached to tractor
BUCKRAM, -S *n* cotton or linen cloth stiffened with size, etc ▷ *vb* stiffen with buckram
BUCKS ▶ **buck**

B

B

BUCKSAW, -S n woodcutting saw

BUCKSHEE adj free

BUCKSHOT n large lead pellets used for shooting game

BUCKSKIN n skin of a male deer ▷ adj greyish-yellow

BUCKSOM same as ▶ buxom

BUCKS -S

BUCKTAIL n in fishing, fly with appearance of minnow

BUCKU, -S same as ▶ buchu

BUCOLIC, -S adj of the countryside or country life ▷ n pastoral poem

BUD, -DED, -S n swelling on a plant that develops into a leaf or flower ▷ vb produce buds

BUDDER -S

BUDDHA, -S n person who has achieved a state of perfect enlightenment

BUDDIED ▶ buddy

BUDDIER ▶ buddy

BUDDIES ▶ buddy

BUDDIEST ▶ buddy

BUDDING, -S ▶ bud

BUDDLE, -D, -S, BUDDLING n sloping trough in which ore is washed ▷ vb wash (ore) in a buddle

BUDDLEIA n shrub with long spikes of purple flowers

BUDDLES ▶ buddle

BUDDLING ▶ buddle

BUDDY, BUDDIED, BUDDIER, BUDDIES, BUDDIEST, -ING n friend ▷ vb act as a friend to ▷ adj friendly

BUDGE, -D, -S, BUDGING vb move slightly ▷ n lambskin dressed for the fur to be worn on the outer side

BUDGER -S

BUDGEREE adj good

BUDGERO, -S same as ▶ budgerow

BUDGEROW n barge used on the Ganges

BUDGERS ▶ budger

BUDGES ▶ budge

BUDGET, -ED, -S n financial plan for a period of time ▷ vb plan the expenditure of (money or time) ▷ adj cheap

BUDGETER

BUDGIE, -S n short form of budgerigar

BUDGING ▶ budge

BUDLESS ▶ bud

BUDLIKE ▶ bud

BUDMASH same as ▶ badmash

BUDO, -S n combat and spirit in martial arts

BUDS ▶ bud

BUDWOOD, -S n branch with buds that is used for grafting

BUDWORM, -S n pest that eats tree leaves and buds

BUFF, -ED, -EST, -S n soft flexible undyed leather ▷ adj dull yellowish-brown ▷ vb clean or polish with soft material

BUFFA ▶ buffo

BUFFABLE ▶ buff

BUFFALO, -S n member of the cattle tribe ▷ vb confuse

BUFFE ▶ buffo

BUFFED ▶ buff

BUFFEL adj as in **buffel grass** grass used for pasture in Africa, India, and Australia

BUFFER, -ED, -S vb protect from shock

BUFFEST ▶ buff

BUFFET, -ED, -S n counter where drinks and snacks are served ▷ vb knock against or about

BUFFETER

BUFFI ▶ buffo

BUFFIER ▶ buffy

BUFFIEST ▶ buffy

BUFFING, -S ▶ buff

BUFFO, BUFFE, BUFFI, -S n (in Italian opera of the 18th century) comic part, esp one for a bass

BUFFOON, -S n clown or fool

BUFFOS ▶ buffo

BUFFS ▶ buff

BUFFY, BUFFIER, BUFFIEST adj having appearance or texture of buff

BUFO, -S n type of toad

BUG, -GED, -S n insect ▷ vb irritate

BUGABOO, -S n imaginary source of fear

BUGBANE, -S n European plant whose flowers are reputed to repel insects

BUGBEAR, -S n thing that causes obsessive anxiety

BUGEYE, -S n oyster-dredging boat

BUGGAN, -S n evil spirit

BUGGANE, -S same as ▶ buggan

BUGGANS ▶ buggan

BUGGED ▶ bug

BUGGIER ▶ buggy

BUGGIES ▶ buggy

BUGGIEST ▶ buggy

BUGGIN, -S same as ▶ buggan

BUGGING, -S ▶ bug

BUGGINS ▶ buggin

BUGGY, BUGGIER, BUGGIES, BUGGIEST n light horse-drawn carriage ▷ adj infested with bugs

BUGLE, -D, -S, BUGLING n instrument like a small trumpet ▷ vb play or sound (on) a bugle

BUGLER -S

BUGLET, -S n small bugle

BUGLING ▶ bugle

BUGLOSS n hairy Eurasian plant with clusters of blue flowers

BUGONG, -S same as ▶ bogong

BUGOUT, -S n act of running away

BUGS ▶ bug

BUGSEED, -S n form of tumbleweed

BUGSHA, -S same as ▶ buqsha

BUGWORT, -S another name for ▶ bugbane

BUHL, -S same as ▶ boulle

BUHLWORK n woodwork with decorative inlay

BUHR, -S same as ▶ burr

BUHUND, -S n type of Norwegian dog

BUIBUI, -S n black cloth worn as a shawl by Muslim women

BUIK, -S same as ▶ book

BUILD, -ED, -S, BUILT vb make, construct, or form by joining parts or materials ▷ n shape of the body

BUILDER, -S n person who constructs houses and other buildings

BUILDING ▶ build

BUILDOUT n expansion, development, or growth

BUILDS ▶ build

BUILDUP, -S n gradual approach to a climax or critical point

BUILT ▶ build

BUIRDLY adj well-built

BUIST, -ED, -ING, -S vb brand sheep with identification mark

BUKE, -S same as ▶ book

BUKKAKE, -S n Japanese noodle dish

BUKSHEE, -S n person in charge of paying wages

BUKSHI, -S same as ▶ bukshee

BULB, -ED, -ING, -S n onion-shaped root which grows into a flower or plant ▷ vb form into the shape of a bulb

BULBAR adj of or relating to a bulb, esp the medulla oblongata

BULBED ▶ bulb

BULBEL, -S same as ► bulbil

BULBIL, -S n small bulblike organ growing on plants such as the onion and tiger lily

BULBING ► bulb

BULBLET, -S n small bulb at base of main bulb

BULBOUS adj round and fat

BULBS ► bulb

BULBUL, -S n songbird of tropical Africa and Asia

BULGAR, -S same as ► bulgur

BULGE, -D, -S n swelling on a normally flat surface ▷ vb swell outwards

BULGER -S

BULGHUR, -S same as ► bulgur

BULGIER ► bulgy

BULGIEST ► bulgy

BULGINE, -S same as ► bullgine

BULGING ► bulge

BULGUR, -S n kind of dried cracked wheat

BULGY, BULGIER, BULGIEST ► bulge

BULIMIA, -S n eating disorder

BULIMIAC

BULIMIC -S

BULIMIES ► bulimy

BULIMUS n terrestrial mollusc

BULIMY, BULIMIES ► bulimia

BULK, -ED, -S n volume, size, or magnitude of something ▷ vb cohere or cause to cohere in a mass

BULKAGE -S

BULKER, -S n ship that carries bulk cargo

BULKHEAD n partition in a ship or aeroplane

BULKIER ► bulky

BULKIEST ► bulky

BULKILY ► bulky

BULKING, -S n expansion of excavated material to a greater volume

BULKS ► bulk

BULKY, BULKIER, BULKIEST adj very large and massive, esp so as to be unwieldy

BULL, -ED, -S n male bovine animal ▷ vb raise the price of (a security)

BULLA, -E n leaden seal affixed to a papal bull

BULLACE, -S n small Eurasian tree of which the damson is the cultivated form

BULLAE ► bulla

BULLARY n boilery for preparing salt

BULLATE adj puckered or blistered in appearance

BULLBARS pl n large protective metal grille on the front of some vehicles

BULLBAT, -S another name for > nighthawk

BULLCOOK n casual or odd job worker in a camp

BULLDOG, -S n thickset dog with a broad head and a muscular body

BULLDOZE vb demolish or flatten with a bulldozer

BULLDUST n fine dust

BULLED ► bull

BULLER, -ED, -S vb make bubbling sound

BULLET, -ED, -S n small piece of metal fired from a gun ▷ vb move extremely quickly

BULLETIN n short official report or announcement ▷ vb make known by bulletin

BULLETS ► bullet

BULLEY, -S n fishing boat with two masts

BULLFROG n large American frog with a deep croak

BULLGINE n steam locomotive

BULLHEAD n type of small northern mainly marine fish

BULLHORN n portable loudspeaker having a built-in amplifier and microphone

BULLIED ► bully

BULLIER ► bully

BULLIES ► bully

BULLIEST ► bully

BULLING, -S ► bull

BULLION, -S n gold or silver in the form of bars

BULLISH adj like a bull

BULLNECK n enlarged neck

BULLNOSE n rounded exterior angle, as where two walls meet

BULLOCK, -S n young bull ▷ vb work hard and long

BULLOCKY n driver of a team of bullocks

BULLOSA adj as in **epidermolysis bullosa** type of genetic skin disorder

BULLOUS adj blistered

BULLPEN, -S n large cell where prisoners are confined together temporarily

BULLPOUT n type of fish

BULLRING n arena for staging bullfights

BULLRUSH same as ► bulrush

BULLS ► bull

BULLSEYE n central disc of a target

BULLSHOT n cocktail of vodka and beef stock

BULLWEED n knapweed

BULLWHIP n long tapering heavy whip, esp one of plaited rawhide ▷ vb whip with a bullwhip

BULLY, BULLIED, BULLIER, BULLIES, BULLIEST, -ING n person who hurts, persecutes, or intimidates weaker people ▷ vb hurt, intimidate, or persecute (a weaker or smaller person) ▷ adj dashing

BULLYBOY n ruffian or tough, esp a hired one

BULLYING ► bully

BULLYISM ► bully

BULLYRAG vb bully, esp by means of cruel practical jokes

BULNBULN another name for ► lyrebird

BULRUSH n tall stiff reed

BULRUSHY

BULSE, -S n purse or bag for diamonds

BULWADDY same as > bullwaddy

BULWARK, -S n wall used as a fortification ▷ vb defend or fortify with or as if with a bulwark

BUM, -MED, -MEST, -MING, -S n loafer or idler ▷ vb get by begging ▷ adj of poor quality

BUMALO same as ► bummalo

BUMALOTI same as > bummaloti

BUMBAG, -S n small bag attached to a belt and worn round the waist

BUMBAZE, -D, -S vb confuse; bewilder

BUMBLE, -D, -S vb speak, do, or move in a clumsy way ▷ n blunder or botch

BUMBLER -S

BUMBLING ► bumble

BUMBO, -S n African tree

BUMBOAT, -S n any small boat used for ferrying goods to a ship at anchor or at a mooring

BUMBOS ► bumbo

BUMELIA, -S n thorny shrub

BUMF, -S n official documents or forms

BUMFLUFF n soft and fluffy growth of hair on the chin of an adolescent

BUMFS ► bumf

BUMKIN, -S same as ► bumpkin

BUMMALO, -S n Bombay duck

BUMMAREE n dealer at Billingsgate fish market

BUMMED ▸ bum

BUMMEL n stroll

BUMMELS ▸ stroll

BUMMER, -S n unpleasant or disappointing experience

BUMMEST ▸ bum

BUMMING ▸ bum

BUMMLE, -D, -S, BUMMLING Scots variant of ▸ **bumble**

BUMMOCK, -S n submerged mass of ice projecting downwards

BUMP, -ED, -S vb knock or strike with a jolt ▹ n dull thud from an impact or collision

BUMPER, -ED, -S n bar on the front and back of a vehicle ▹ adj unusually large or abundant ▹ vb toast with a full drinking glass

BUMPH, -S same as ▸ **bumf**

BUMPIER ▸ bumpy

BUMPIEST ▸ bumpy

BUMPILY ▸ bumpy

BUMPING, -S ▸ bump

BUMPKIN, -S n awkward simple country person

BUMPS ▸ bump

BUMPY, BUMPIER, BUMPIEST adj having an uneven surface

BUMS ▸ bum

BUMSTER adj (of trousers) cut very low at the hips

BUMSTERS pl n trousers cut very low at the hips

BUMWAD, -S n type of sketching paper

BUN, -S n small sweet bread roll or cake

BUNA, -S n synthetic rubber

BUNBURY vb make up a story to avoid an unwanted engagement

BUNCE, -D, -S, BUNCING n windfall; boom ▹ vb charge someone too much money

BUNCH, -ED n number of things growing, fastened, or grouped together ▹ vb group or be grouped together in a bunch

BUNCHER, -S n person who groups things together

BUNCHES pl n hair tied into two sections

BUNCHIER ▸ bunchy

BUNCHILY ▸ bunchy

BUNCHING ▸ bunch

BUNCHY, BUNCHIER adj composed of or resembling bunches

BUNCING ▸ bunce

BUNCO, -ED, -ES, -ING, -S n swindle, esp one by confidence tricksters ▹ vb swindle

BUNCOMBE same as ▸ **bunkum**

BUNCOS ▸ bunco

BUND, -E, -ED, -ING, -S n (in Germany) confederation ▹ vb form into an embankment

BUNDH, -S same as ▸ **bandh**

BUNDIED ▸ bundy

BUNDIES ▸ bundy

BUNDING ▸ bund

BUNDIST, -S ▸ bund

BUNDLE, -D, -S n number of things gathered loosely together ▹ vb cause to go roughly or unceremoniously

BUNDLER -S

BUNDLING ▸ bundle

BUNDOOK, -S n rifle

BUNDS ▸ bund

BUNDT, -S n type of sweet cake

BUNDU, -S n largely uninhabited wild region far from towns

BUNDWALL n concrete or earth wall surrounding a storage tank

BUNDY, BUNDIED, BUNDIES, -ING n time clock at work ▹ vb register arrival or departure from work on a time clock

BUNFIGHT n tea party

BUNG, -ED, -ING, -S n stopper for a cask etc ▹ vb close with a bung

BUNGALOW n one-storey house

BUNGED ▸ bung

BUNGEE, -S n strong elastic cable

BUNGER, -S n firework

BUNGEY, -S same as ▸ **bungee**

BUNGHOLE n hole in a cask or barrel through which liquid can be drained

BUNGIE, -S same as ▸ **bungee**

BUNGING ▸ bung

BUNGLE, -D, -S vb spoil through incompetence ▹ n blunder or muddle

BUNGLER -S

BUNGLING ▸ bungle

BUNGS ▸ bung

BUNGWALL n Australian fern with an edible rhizome

BUNGY same as ▸ **bungee**

BUNHEAD, -S n ballerina

BUNIA, -S same as ▸ **bunnia**

BUNION, -S n inflamed swelling on the big toe

BUNJE, -S same as ▸ **bungee**

BUNJEE, -S same as ▸ **bungee**

BUNJES ▸ bunje

BUNJIE, -S same as ▸ **bungee**

BUNJY same as ▸ **bungee**

BUNK, -ED, -ING, -S n narrow shelflike bed ▹ vb prepare to sleep

BUNKER, -ED, -S n sand-filled hollow forming an obstacle on a golf course ▹ vb drive (the ball) into a bunker

BUNKIE, -S n short for bunkhouse

BUNKING ▸ bunk

BUNKMATE n person who sleeps in the same quarters as another

BUNKO, -ED, -ING, -S same as ▸ **bunco**

BUNKS ▸ bunk

BUNKUM, -S n nonsense

BUNN, -S same as ▸ **bun**

BUNNET, -S same as ▸ **bonnet**

BUNNIA, -S n Hindu shopkeeper

BUNNIES ▸ bunny

BUNNS ▸ bunn

BUNNY, BUNNIES n child's word for a rabbit

BUNODONT adj (of the teeth of certain mammals) having cusps that are separate and rounded

BUNRAKU, -S n Japanese puppet theatre

BUNS ▸ bun

BUNSEN, -S n as in **bunsen burner** gas burner used in scientific labs

BUNT, -ED, -S vb (of an animal) butt (something) with the head or horns ▹ n act or an instance of bunting

BUNTAL, -S n straw obtained from leaves of the talipot palm

BUNTED ▸ bunt

BUNTER, -S n batter who deliberately taps ball lightly

BUNTIER ▸ bunty

BUNTIEST ▸ bunty

BUNTING, -S n decorative flags

BUNTLINE n one of several lines fastened to the foot of a square sail

BUNTS ▸ bunt

BUNTY, BUNTIER, BUNTIEST ▸ bunt

BUNYA, -S n tall dome-shaped Australian coniferous tree

B

BUNYIP, -S n legendary monster said to live in swamps and lakes

BUOY, -ED, -ING, -S n floating marker anchored in the sea ▷ vb prevent from sinking

BUOYAGE, -S n system of buoys

BUOYANCE same as ► buoyancy

BUOYANCY n ability to float in a liquid or to rise in a fluid

BUOYANT adj able to float

BUOYED ► buoy

BUOYING ► buoy

BUOYS ► buoy

BUPKES same as ► bubkes

BUPKIS same as ► bubkis

BUPKUS same as ► bubkes

BUPLEVER n type of plant

BUPPIE, -S n affluent young Black person

BUPPY variant of ► buppie

BUQSHA, -S n former Yemeni coin

BUR, -S same as ► burr

BURA, -S same as ► buran

BURAN, -S n blizzard, with the wind blowing from the north and reaching gale force

BURAS ► bura

BURB, -S n suburb

BURBLE, -D, -S vb make a bubbling sound ▷ n bubbling or gurgling sound

BURBLER -S

BURBLIER ► burbly

BURBLING ► burble

BURBLY, BURBLIER adj burbling

BURBOT, -S n freshwater fish of the cod family that has barbels around its mouth

BURBS ► burb

BURD, -S Scots form of ► bird

BURDASH n fringed sash worn over coat

BURDEN, -ED, -S n heavy load ▷ vb put a burden on

BURDENER

BURDIE, -S Scots form of ► birdie

BURDIZZO n surgical instrument

BURDOCK, -S n weed with prickly burrs

BURDS ► burd

BUREAU, -S, -X n office that provides a service

BURET, -S same as ► burette

BURETTE, -S n glass tube for dispensing known volumes of fluids

BURFI, -S same as ► barfi

BURG, -S n fortified town

BURGAGE, -S n type of tenure of land or tenement in a town or city

BURGANET same as ► burgonet

BURGEE, -S n triangular or swallow-tailed flag flown from the mast of a merchant ship

BURGEON, -S vb develop or grow rapidly ▷ n bud of a plant

BURGER, -S n hamburger

BURGESS n (in England) citizen or freeman of a borough

BURGH, -S n Scottish borough **BURGHAL**

BURGHER, -S n citizen

BURGHS ► burgh

BURGHUL, -S same as ► bulgur

BURGLAR, -S n person who enters a building to commit a crime, esp theft ▷ vb burgle

BURGLARY n crime of entering a building as a trespasser to commit theft or another offence

BURGLE, -D, -S, BURGLING vb break into (a house, shop, etc)

BURGONET n light 16th-century helmet, usually made of steel, with hinged cheekpieces

BURGOO, -S n porridge

BURGOUT, -S same as ► burgoo

BURGRAVE n military governor of a German town or castle, esp in the 12th and 13th centuries

BURGS ► burg

BURGUNDY adj dark-purplish red

BURHEL, -S same as ► bharal

BURIAL, -S n burying of a dead body

BURIED ► bury

BURIER, -S n person or thing that buries

BURIES ► bury

BURIN, -S n steel chisel used for engraving metal, wood, or marble

BURINIST

BURITI, -S n type of palm tree

BURK, -S same as ► berk

BURKA, -S same as ► burqa

BURKE, -D, -S, BURKING vb suppress or silence

BURKER -S

BURKHA, -S n all-enveloping garment worn by some Muslim women

BURKING ► burke

BURKINI, -S n swimming costume covering the whole body apart from the face, hands, and feet

BURKITE, -S ► burke

BURKS ► burk

BURL, -ED, -ING, -S n small knot or lump in wool ▷ vb remove the burls from (cloth)

BURLAP, -S n coarse fabric woven from jute, hemp, or the like

BURLED ► burl

BURLER, -S ► burl

BURLESK, -S same as > burlesque

BURLETTA n type of comic opera

BURLEY, -ED, -S same as ► berley

BURLIER ► burly

BURLIEST ► burly

BURLILY ► burly

BURLING ► burl

BURLS ► burl

BURLY, BURLIER, BURLIEST adj (of a person) broad and strong

BURN, -ED, -S, -T vb be or set on fire ▷ n injury or mark caused by fire or exposure to heat

BURNABLE

BURNER, -S n part of a stove or lamp that produces the flame

BURNET, -S n type of rose

BURNIE, -S n sideburn

BURNING, -S ► burn

BURNISH vb make smooth and shiny by rubbing ▷ n shiny finish

BURNOOSE same as ► burnous

BURNOUS n long circular cloak with a hood, worn esp by Arabs

BURNOUSE same as ► burnous

BURNOUT, -S n failure of a mechanical device from excessive heating

BURNS ► burn

BURNSIDE n land along side of burn

BURNT ► burn

BUROO, -S n informal Scottish or Irish name for an unemployment benefit office

BURP, -ED, -ING, -S n belch ▷ vb belch

BURPEE, -S n type of physical exercise movement

BURPING ► burp

BURPS ► burp

B

BURQA, -S *n* garment worn by some Muslim women in public

This Arab garment illustrates the fact that Q doesn't always have to be followed by U. It has several variants including **burka** and **burkha**.

BURR, -ED, -ING, -S *n* small rotary file ▷ *vb* form a rough edge on (a workpiece)

BURRAMYS *n* very rare Australian mountain pigmy possum

BURRATA, -S *n* type of Italian cheese

BURRED ► burr

BURREL, -S *same as* ► **bharal**

BURRELL, -S *variant of* ► **bharal**

BURRELS ► burrel

BURRER, -S *n* person who removes burrs

BURRFISH *n* type of fish with sharp spines

BURRHEL, -S *same as* ► **bharal**

BURRIER ► burry

BURRIEST ► burry

BURRING ► burr

BURRITO, -S *n* tortilla folded over a filling of minced beef, chicken, cheese, or beans

BURRO, -S *n* donkey, esp one used as a pack animal

BURROW, -ED, -S *n* hole dug in the ground by a rabbit etc ▷ *vb* dig holes in the ground

BURROWER

BURRS ► burr

BURRY, BURRIER, BURRIEST *adj* full of or covered in burs

BURS ► bur

BURSA, -E, -S *n* small fluid-filled sac that reduces friction between movable parts of the body

BURSAL

BURSAR, -S *n* treasurer of a school, college, or university

BURSARY *n* scholarship

BURSAS ► bursa

BURSATE ► bursa

BURSE, -S *n* flat case used at Mass as a container for the corporal

BURSEED, -S *n* type of plant

BURSERA *adj* of a type of gum tree

BURSES ► burse

BURSICON *n* hormone produced by the insect brain

BURSITIS *n* inflammation of a bursa, esp one in the shoulder joint

BURST, -ED, -EN, -ING, -S *vb* break or cause to break open or apart suddenly and noisily ▷ *n* sudden breaking open or apart ▷ *adj* broken apart

BURSTER -S

BURSTIER ► bursty

BURSTING ► burst

BURSTONE *same as* > **buhrstone**

BURSTS ► burst

BURSTY, BURSTIER *adj* occurring or happening in sudden bursts; irregular

BURTHEN, -S *archaic word for* ► **burden**

BURTON, -S *n* type of hoisting tackle

BURWEED, -S *n* any of various plants that bear burs, such as the burdock

BURY, BURIED, BURIES, -ING *vb* place in a grave

BUS, -ED, -ES, -SED, -SES *n* large motor vehicle for carrying passengers between stops ▷ *vb* travel by bus

BUSBAR, -S *n* electrical conductor

BUSBIES ► busby

BUSBOY, -S *n* waiter's assistant

BUSBY, BUSBIES *n* tall fur hat worn by some soldiers

BUSED ► bus

BUSERA, -S *n* Ugandan alcoholic drink made from millet

BUSES ► bus

BUSGIRL, -S *n* waiter's assistant

BUSH, -ES *n* dense woody plant, smaller than a tree ▷ *vb* fit a bush to (a casing or bearing)

BUSHBABY *n* small African tree-living mammal with large eyes

BUSHBUCK *n* small nocturnal spiral-horned antelope of Africa

BUSHED *adj* extremely tired

BUSHEL, -ED, -S *n* obsolete unit of measure equal to 8 gallons ▷ *vb* alter or mend (a garment)

BUSHELER

BUSHER, -S ► bush

BUSHES ► bush

BUSHFIRE *n* uncontrolled fire in the bush

BUSHFLY *n* small black Australian fly

BUSHGOAT *n* S African antelope

BUSHIDO, -S *n* feudal code of the Japanese samurai

BUSHIE *same as* ► **bushy**

BUSHIER ► bushy

BUSHIES ► bushy

BUSHIEST ► bushy

BUSHILY ► bushy

BUSHING, -S *same as* ► **bush**

BUSHLAND *n* land characterized by natural vegetation

BUSHLESS ► bush

BUSHLIKE ► bush

BUSHLOT, -S *n* small wooded area of land

BUSHMAN, BUSHMEN *n* person who lives or travels in the bush

BUSHMEAT *n* meat taken from any animal native to African forests

BUSHMEN ► bushman

BUSHPIG, -S *n* wild brown or black forest pig of tropical Africa and Madagascar

BUSHTIT, -S *n* small grey active North American songbird

BUSHVELD *n* bushy countryside

BUSHWA, -S *n* nonsense

BUSHWAH, -S *same as* ► **bushwa**

BUSHWALK *vb* hike through bushland

BUSHWAS ► bushwa

BUSHY, BUSHIER, BUSHIES, BUSHIEST *adj* (of hair) thick and shaggy ▷ *n* person who lives in the bush

BUSIED ► busy

BUSIER ► busy

BUSIES ► busy

BUSIEST ► busy

BUSILY *adv* in a busy manner

BUSINESS *n* purchase and sale of goods and services

BUSING, -S ► bus

BUSK, -ED, -S *vb* act as a busker ▷ *n* strip of whalebone, wood, steel, etc, inserted into the front of a corset

BUSKER -S

BUSKET, -S *n* bouquet

BUSKIN, -S *n* (formerly) sandal-like covering

BUSKINED *adj* relating to tragedy

BUSKING, -S ► busk

BUSKINS ► buskin

BUSKS ► busk

BUSKY *same as* ► **bosky**

BUSLOAD, -S *n* number of people bus carries**

BUSMAN, BUSMEN *n* person who drives a bus

BUSS *archaic or dialect word for* ► **kiss**

BUSSED ► **bus**

BUSSES ► **bus**

BUSSING, -S ► **bus**

BUSSU, -S *n* type of palm tree

BUST, -ED, -S *n* chest of a human being ▷ *adj* broken ▷ *vb* burst or break

BUSTARD, -S *n* type of bird

BUSTED ► **bust**

BUSTEE, -S *same as* ► **basti**

BUSTER, -S *n* person or thing destroying something as specified

BUSTI, -S *same as* ► **basti**

BUSTIC, -S *n* type of small American tree

BUSTIER, -S *n* close-fitting strapless women's top

BUSTIEST ► **busty**

BUSTING, -S ► **bust**

BUSTIS ► **busti**

BUSTLE, -D, -S *vb* hurry with a show of activity or energy ▷ *n* energetic and noisy activity

BUSTLER -S

BUSTLINE *n* shape or size of woman's bust

BUSTLING ► **bustle**

BUSTS ► **bust**

BUSTY, BUSTIEST *adj* (of a woman) having a prominent bust

BUSULFAN *n* drug used to treat cancer

BUSUUTI, -S *n* garment worn by Ugandan women

BUSY, BUSIED, BUSIER, BUSIES, BUSIEST, -ING *adj* actively employed ▷ *vb* keep (someone, esp oneself) busy

BUSYBODY *n* meddlesome or nosy person

BUSYING ► **busy**

BUSYNESS ► **busy**

BUSYWORK *n* unproductive work

BUT, -S *prep* except ▷ *adv* only ▷ *n* outer room of a two-roomed cottage: usually the kitchen

BUTANE, -S *n* gas used for fuel

BUTANOIC *adj as in* **butanoic acid** kind of acid

BUTANOL, -S *n* colourless substance

BUTANONE *n* colourless soluble flammable liquid used mainly as a solvent for resins

BUTCH, -ES, -EST *adj* markedly or aggressively

masculine ▷ *n* strong, rugged man

BUTCHER, -S *n* person who slaughters animals or sells their meat ▷ *vb* kill and prepare (animals) for meat

BUTCHERY *n* senseless slaughter

BUTCHES ► **butch**

BUTCHEST ► **butch**

BUTCHING *n* dialect word for butchering

BUTE, -S *n* drug used illegally to dope horses

BUTENE, -S *n* pungent colourless gas

BUTEO, -S *n* type of American hawk

BUTES ► **bute**

BUTLE, -D, -S, BUTLING *vb* act as butler

BUTLER, -ED, -S *n* chief male servant ▷ *vb* act as a butler

BUTLERY *n* butler's room

BUTLES ► **butle**

BUTLING ► **butle**

BUTMENT, -S *same as* ► **abutment**

BUTOH, -S *n* style of contemporary Japanese dance

BUTS ► **but**

BUTSUDAN *n* (in Buddhism) small household altar

BUTT, -ED, -ING, -S *n* thicker or blunt end of something, such as the end of the stock of a rifle ▷ *vb* strike or push with the head or horns

BUTTALS *n* abuttal

BUTTE, -S *n* isolated steep flat-topped hill

BUTTED ► **butt**

BUTTER, -ED, -S *n* edible fatty yellow solid made from cream ▷ *vb* put butter on

BUTTERY *n* (in some universities) room in which food and drink are sold to students ▷ *adj* containing, like, or coated with butter

BUTTES ► **butte**

BUTTIES ► **butty**

BUTTING ► **butt**

BUTTLE, -D, -S, BUTTLING *vb* act as butler

BUTTOCK, -S *n* either of the two fleshy masses that form the human rump ▷ *vb* perform a kind of wrestling manoeuvre on a person

BUTTON, -ED *n* small disc or knob sewn to clothing ▷ *vb* fasten with buttons

BUTTONER

BUTTONS *n* page boy

BUTTONY ► **button**

BUTTRESS *n* structure to support a wall ▷ *vb* support with, or as if with, a buttress

BUTTS ► **butt**

BUTTY, BUTTIES *n* sandwich

BUTTYMAN, BUTTYMEN *n* coalmine worker

BUTUT, -S *n* Gambian monetary unit worth one hundredth of a dalasi

BUTYL, -S *n* substituent group of a certain carbon compound

BUTYLATE *vb* introduce butyl into (compound)

BUTYLENE *same as* ► **butene**

BUTYLS ► **butyl**

BUTYRAL, -S *n* type of resin

BUTYRATE *n* any salt or ester of butyric acid

BUTYRIC *adj as in* **butyric acid** type of acid

BUTYRIN, -S *n* colourless liquid found in butter

BUTYROUS *adj* butyraceous

BUTYRYL, -S *n* radical of butyric acid

BUVETTE, -S *n* roadside café

BUXOM, -ER, -EST *adj* (of a woman) healthily plump

BUXOMLY

BUY, -S *vb* acquire by paying money for ▷ *n* thing acquired through payment

BUYABLE -S

BUYBACK, -S *n* repurchase by a company of some or all of its shares from an early investor

BUYER, -S *n* customer

BUYING, -S *n as in* **panic buying** the buying up of large quantities of something feared to be scarce

BUYOFF, -S *n* purchase

BUYOUT, -S *n* purchase of a company

BUYS ► **buy**

BUZKASHI *n* team sport played in Afghanistan

BUZUKI, -A, -S *same as* ► **bouzouki**

BUZZ, -ED, -ES *n* rapidly vibrating humming sound ▷ *vb* make a humming sound

BUZZARD, -S *n* bird of prey of the hawk family

BUZZBAIT *n* fishing lure with small blades that stir the water

BUZZCUT, -S *n* very short haircut

BUZZED ► **buzz**

B

BUZZER, -S *n* electronic device that produces a buzzing sound as a signal

BUZZES ► buzz

BUZZIER ► buzzy

BUZZIEST ► buzzy

BUZZING, -S ► buzz

BUZZKILL *n* someone or something that spoils the enjoyment of others

BUZZSAW, -S *n* power-operated circular saw

BUZZWIG, -S *n* bushy wig

BUZZWORD *n* vogue word in a certain community or among a particular group

BUZZY, BUZZIER, BUZZIEST *adj* making a buzzing sound

BWANA, -S *n* (in E Africa) master, often used as a respectful form of address

BWAZI, -S *same as* **► buaze**

BY, -S *prep* indicating agent, nearness, movement past, etc ▷ *adv* near ▷ *n* pass to the next round

BYCATCH *n* unwanted fish and sea animals caught along with the desired kind

BYCOKET, -S *n* former Italian high-crowned hat

BYDE, -D, -S, BYDING *same as* **► bide**

BYE, -S *n* situation where a player or team wins a round by having no opponent ▷ *interj* goodbye ▷ *sentence substitute* goodbye

BYELAW, -S *n* rule made by a local authority

BYES ► bye

BYGONE, -S *adj* past ▷ *n* article from a former time

BYKE, -D, -S, BYKING *n* wasp's nest ▷ *vb* swarm

BYLANDER *same as* **► bilander**

BYLANE, -S *n* side lane or alley off a road

BYLAW, -S *n* rule made by a local authority

BYLINE, -D, -S, BYLINING *n* line under the title of a newspaper or magazine article giving the author's name ▷ *vb* give a byline to **BYLINER -S**

BYLIVE *same as* **► belive**

BYNAME, -S *n* nickname

BYNEMPT *archaic past participle of* **► bename**

BYPASS, -ED, -ES, BYPAST *n* main road built to avoid a city ▷ *vb* go round or avoid

BYPATH, -S *n* little-used path or track, esp in the country

BYPLACE, -S *n* private place

BYPLAY, -S *n* secondary action or talking carried on apart while the main action proceeds

BYRE, -S *n* shelter for cows

BYREMAN, BYREMEN *n* man who works in byre

BYRES ► byre

BYRL, -ED, -ING, -S *same as* **► birl**

BYRLADY *interj* short for By Our Lady

BYRLAKIN *interj* By Our Ladykin

BYRLAW, -S *same as* **► bylaw**

BYRLED ► byrl

BYRLING ► byrl

BYRLS ► byrl

BYRNIE, -S *n* archaic word for coat of mail

BYROAD, -S *n* secondary or side road

BYROOM, -S *n* private room

BYS ► by

BYSSAL *adj* of mollusc's byssus

BYSSI ► byssus

BYSSINE *adj* made from flax

BYSSOID *adj* consisting of fine fibres

BYSSUS, BYSSI, -ES *n* mass of threads that attaches an animal to a hard surface

BYSTREET *n* obscure or secondary street

BYTALK, -S *n* trivial conversation

BYTE, -S *n* group of bits processed as one unit of data

BYWAY, -S *n* minor road

BYWONER, -S *n* poor tenant-farmer

BYWORD, -S *n* person or thing regarded as a perfect example of something

BYWORK, -S *n* work done outside usual working hours

BYZANT, -S *same as* **► bezant**

Cc

C can be a tricky letter to use, especially as it only forms a single two-letter word **ch**. But if you remember this, you won't waste time racking your brains for two-letter words. There are, however, plenty of good three-letter words beginning with **C**. **Cox** scores 12 points, while **caw, cow** and **coy** are each worth 8 and **caz, coz** and **cuz** are worth 14. It's also a good idea to remember the short words starting with **C** that don't contain any vowels: **cly** and **cwm** as well as **ch**.

CAA, -ED, -ING, -S a Scot word for ► call

CAATINGA n Brazilian semi-arid scrub forest

CAB, -BED, -BING, -S n taxi ▷ vb take a taxi

CABA same as ► cabas

CABAL, -LED, -S n small group of political plotters ▷ vb form a cabal

CABALA, -S a variant spelling of ► kabbalah

CABALISM

CABALIST

CABALLED ► cabal

CABALLER ► cabal

CABALS ► cabal

CABANA, -S n tent used as a dressing room by the sea

CABARET, -S n dancing and singing show in a nightclub

CABAS n reticule

CABBAGE, -D, -S n vegetable with a large head of green leaves ▷ vb steal

CABBAGEY

CABBAGY

CABBALA, -S a variant spelling of ► kabbalah

CABBALAH same as ► cabala

CABBALAS ► cabbala

CABBED ► cab

CABBIE, -S n taxi driver

CABBING ► cab

CABBY same as ► cabbie

CABER, -S n tree trunk tossed in competition at Highland games

CABERNET n type of grape, or the red wine made from it

CABERS ► caber

CABESTRO n halter made from horsehair

CABEZON, -S n large fish

CABEZONE same as ► cabezon

CABEZONS ► cabezon

CABILDO, -S n Spanish municipal council

CABIN, -ED, -ING, -S n compartment in a ship or aircraft ▷ vb confine in a small space

CABINET, -S n piece of furniture with drawers or shelves

CABINING ► cabin

CABINS ► cabin

CABLE, -D, -S n strong thick rope; a wire or bundle of wires that conduct electricity ▷ vb (esp formerly) send (someone) a message by cable

CABLER, -S n cable broadcasting company

CABLES ► cable

CABLET, -S n small cable

CABLEWAY n transport system involving cars, buckets, etc, suspended on cables

CABLING, -S ► cable

CABMAN, CABMEN n driver of a cab

CABOB, -BED, -S vb roast on a skewer

CABOC, -S n type of Scottish cheese

CABOCEER n indigenous African appointed to deal with European slave traders

CABOCHED adj in heraldry, with the face exposed, but neck concealed

CABOCHON n smooth domed gem, polished but unfaceted

CABOCS ► caboc

CABOMBA, -S n type of aquatic plant

CABOODLE n lot, bunch, or group

CABOOSE, -S n guard's van on a train

CABOSHED same as ► caboched

CABOTAGE n coastal navigation or shipping, esp within the borders of one country

CABOVER, -S n truck or lorry in which the cab is over the engine

CABRE adj heraldic term designating an animal rearing

CABRESTA variant of ► cabestro

CABRESTO variant of ► cabestro

CABRETTA n soft leather obtained from the skins of certain South American or African sheep

CABRIE, -S n pronghorn antelope

CABRILLA n type of food fish occurring in warm seas around Florida and the Caribbean

CABRIO, -S short for > cabriolet

CABRIOLE n type of furniture leg featuring a tapering curve

CABRIOS ► cabrio

CABRIT, -S n pronghorn antelope

CABS ► cab

CABSTAND n taxi-rank

CACAFOGO same as > cacafuego

CACAO, -S same as ► cocoa

C

CACHACA, -S n white Brazilian rum made from sugar cane
CACHALOT n sperm whale
CACHE, -D, -S, CACHING n hidden store of weapons or treasure ▷ vb store in a cache
CACHEPOT n ornamental container for a flowerpot
CACHES ▶ cache
CACHET, -ED, -S n prestige, distinction ▷ vb apply a commemorative design to an envelope, as a first-day cover
CACHEXIA n generally weakened condition of body or mind
CACHEXIC
CACHEXY same as
▶ cachexia
CACHING ▶ cache
CACHOLOT same as
▶ cachalot
CACHOU, -S same as
▶ catechu
CACHUCHA n graceful Spanish solo dance in triple time
CACIQUE, -S n Native American chief in a Spanish-speaking region
CACK, -ED, -ING, -S n nonsense ▷ vb defecate
CACKIER ▶ cacky
CACKIEST ▶ cacky
CACKING ▶ cack
CACKLE, -D, -S, CACKLING vb laugh shrilly ▷ n cackling noise
CACKLER -S
CACKS ▶ cack
CACKY, CACKIER, CACKIEST adj dirty or worthless
CACODOXY n heterodoxy
CACODYL, -S n oily poisonous liquid with a strong garlic smell
CACOEPY n bad or mistaken pronunciation
CACOLET, -S n seat fitted to the back of a mule
CACOLOGY n bad choice of words
CACOMIXL n carnivorous mammal
CACONYM, -S n erroneous name
CACONYMY
CACOON, -S n large seed of the sword-bean
CACTI ▶ cactus
CACTOID adj resembling a cactus
CACTUS, CACTI, -ES n fleshy desert plant with spines but no leaves

CACUMEN, -S, CACUMINA n apex
CAD, -S n dishonourable man
CADAGA, -S n eucalyptus tree
CADAGI, -S same as ▶ cadaga
CADASTER n register of ownership, boundaries, and value of property
CADASTRE same as
▶ cadaster
CADAVER, -S n corpse
CADDICE, -S same as ▶ caddis
CADDIE, -D, -S, CADDYING n person who carries a golfer's clubs ▷ vb act as a caddie
CADDIS, -ES n type of coarse woollen yarn, braid, or fabric
CADDISED adj trimmed with a type of ribbon
CADDISES ▶ caddis
CADDISH ▶ cad
CADDY same as ▶ caddie
CADDYING ▶ caddie
CADDYSS same as ▶ caddis
CADE, -S n juniper tree ▷ adj (of a young animal) left by its mother and reared by humans
CADEAU, -X n present
CADEE, -S old form of ▶ cadet
CADELLE, -S n type of beetle that feeds on flour, grain, and other stored foods
CADENCE, -D, -S n rise and fall in the pitch of the voice ▷ vb modulate musically
CADENCY same as ▶ cadence
CADENT adj having cadence
CADENZA, -S n complex solo passage in a piece of music
CADES ▶ cade
CADET, -S n young person training for the armed forces or police
CADGE, -D, -S, CADGING vb get (something) by taking advantage of someone's generosity
CADGER, -S n person who cadges
CADGES ▶ cadge
CADGIER ▶ cadgy
CADGIEST ▶ cadgy
CADGING ▶ cadge
CADGY, CADGIER, CADGIEST adj cheerful
CADI, -S n judge in a Muslim community
CADIE, -S n messenger
CADIS ▶ cadi
CADMIC ▶ cadmium
CADMIUM, -S n bluish-white metallic element used in alloys
CADRANS n instrument used in gem cutting

CADRE, -S n group of people trained to form the core of a political or military unit
CADS ▶ cad
CADUAC, -S n windfall
CADUCEAN ▶ caduceus
CADUCEUS, CADUCEI n mythical staff carried by Hermes (Mercury)
CADUCITY n perishableness
CADUCOUS adj (of parts of a plant or animal) shed during the life of the organism
CAECA ▶ caecum
CAECAL ▶ caecum
CAECALLY ▶ caecum
CAECITIS n inflammation of the caecum
CAECUM, CAECA n pouch at the beginning of the large intestine
CAEOMA, -S n aecium in some rust fungi that has no surrounding membrane
CAERULE same as ▶ cerule
CAESAR, -S n any emperor, autocrat, dictator, or other powerful ruler
CAESE interj Shakespearean interjection
CAESIOUS adj having a waxy bluish-grey coating
CAESIUM, -S n silvery-white metallic element used in photocells
CAESTUS same as ▶ cestus
CAESURA, -E, -S n pause in a line of verse
CAESURAL
CAESURIC
CAF, -S n short for cafeteria
CAFARD, -S n feeling of severe depression
CAFE, -S n small or inexpensive restaurant serving light refreshments
CAFF, -S n café
CAFFEIN, -S same as
▶ caffeine
CAFFEINE n stimulant found in tea and coffee
CAFFEINS ▶ caffein
CAFFEISM n addiction to caffeine
CAFFILA, -S n caravan train
CAFFS ▶ caff
CAFILA, -S same as ▶ caffila
CAFS ▶ caf
CAFTAN, -S same as ▶ kaftan
CAFTANED adj wearing caftan
CAFTANS ▶ caftan
CAG, -S same as ▶ cagoule
CAGANER, -S n figure of a squatting defecating person
CAGE, -D, -S, CAGING n enclosure of bars or wires, for

keeping animals or birds ▷ *vb* confine in a cage
CAGEFUL, -S *n* amount which fills a cage to capacity
CAGELIKE ▶ **cage**
CAGELING, -S *n* bird kept in a cage
CAGER, -S *n* basketball player
CAGES ▶ **cage**
CAGEWORK *n* something constructed as if from the bars of a cage
CAGEY, CAGIER, CAGIEST *adj* reluctant to go into details
CAGILY
CAGINESS ▶ **cagy**
CAGING ▶ **cage**
CAGMAG, -S *adj* done shoddily ▷ *vb* chat idly
CAGOT, -S *n* member of a class of French outcasts
CAGOUL, -S *same as* ▶ **cagoule**
CAGOULE, -S *n* lightweight hooded waterproof jacket
CAGOULS ▶ **cagoul**
CAGS ▶ **cag**
CAGY *same as* ▶ **cagey**
CAGYNESS
CAHIER, -S *n* notebook
CAHOOT, -S *n* partnership
CAHOUN, -S *n* type of S American palm tree
CAHOW, -S *n* Bermuda petrel
CAID, -S *n* Moroccan district administrator
CAILLACH *same as* >**cailleach**
CAILLE, -S *n* quail
CAIMAC, -S *same as* ▶ **caimacam**
CAIMACAM *n* Turkish governor of a sanjak
CAIMACS ▶ **caimac**
CAIMAN, -S *same as* ▶ **cayman**
CAIN, -S *n* (in Scotland and Ireland) payment in kind
CAIQUE, -S *n* long narrow light rowing skiff used on the Bosporus
CAIRD, -S *n* travelling tinker
CAIRN, -S *n* mound of stones erected as a memorial or marker
CAIRNED *adj* marked by a cairn
CAIRNIER ▶ **cairny**
CAIRNS ▶ **cairn**
CAIRNY, CAIRNIER *adj* covered with cairns
CAISSON, -S *same as* >**cofferdam**
CAITIFF, -S *n* cowardly or base person ▷ *adj* cowardly
CAITIVE, -S *n* captive

CAJAPUT, -S *same as* ▶ **cajuput**
CAJEPUT, -S *same as* ▶ **cajuput**
CAJOLE, -D, -S, CAJOLING *vb* persuade by flattery
CAJOLER -S
CAJOLERY ▶ **cajole**
CAJOLES ▶ **cajole**
CAJOLING ▶ **cajole**
CAJON, -ES *n* Peruvian wooden box used as a drum
CAJUN *n* music of the Cajun people
CAJUPUT, -S *n* small tree or shrub
CAKE, -D, -S *n* sweet food baked from a mixture of flour, eggs, etc ▷ *vb* form into a hardened mass or crust
CAKEAGE, -S *n* charge in a restaurant for serving cake brought in from outside
CAKEBOX *n* box for a cake
CAKED ▶ **cake**
CAKEHOLE *n* slang word for mouth
CAKES ▶ **cake**
CAKEWALK *n* dance based on a march with the prize of a cake for the best performers ▷ *vb* perform the cakewalk
CAKEY ▶ **cake**
CAKIER ▶ **caky**
CAKIEST ▶ **caky**
CAKINESS ▶ **cake**
CAKING, -S ▶ **cake**
CAKY, CAKIER, CAKIEST ▶ **cake**
CAL *adj* short for calorie
CALABASH *n* type of large round gourd
CALABAZA *n* variety of squash
CALADIUM *n* type of tropical plant
CALALOO, -S *same as* ▶ **calalu**
CALALU, -S *n* edible leaves of various plants
CALAMAR, -S *n* any member of the squid family
CALAMARI *n* squid cooked for eating, esp cut into rings and fried in batter
CALAMARS ▶ **calamar**
CALAMARY *variant of* ▶ **calamari**
CALAMATA *same as* ▶ **kalamata**
CALAMI ▶ **calamus**
CALAMINE *n* pink powder consisting chiefly of zinc oxide, used in skin lotions and ointments ▷ *vb* apply calamine

CALAMINT *n* aromatic Eurasian plant with clusters of purple or pink flowers
CALAMITE *n* type of extinct treelike plant related to the horsetails
CALAMITY *n* disaster
CALAMUS, CALAMI *n* tropical Asian palm
CALANDO *adv* (to be performed) with gradually decreasing tone and speed
CALANTHE *n* type of orchid
CALASH, -ES *n* horse-drawn carriage with low wheels and a folding top
CALATHEA *n* S American plant often grown as a greenhouse or house plant for its variegated leaves
CALATHI ▶ **calathus**
CALATHOS *same as* ▶ **calathus**
CALATHUS, CALATHI *n* vase-shaped basket represented in ancient Greek art, used as a symbol of fruitfulness
CALCANEA >**calcaneum**
CALCANEI >**calcaneus**
CALCAR, -IA, -S *n* spur or spurlike process
CALCEATE *vb* to shoe
CALCED *adj* wearing shoes
CALCES ▶ **calx**
CALCIC *adj* of, containing, or concerned with lime or calcium
CALCIFIC *adj* forming or causing to form lime or chalk
CALCIFY *vb* harden by the depositing of calcium salts
CALCINE, -D, -S *vb* oxidize (a substance) by heating
CALCITE, -S *n* colourless or white form of calcium carbonate
CALCITIC
CALCIUM, -S *n* silvery-white metallic element
CALCRETE *another name for* ▶ **caliche**
CALCSPAR *another name for* ▶ **calcite**
CALCTUFA *another name for* ▶ **tufa**
CALCTUFF *another name for* ▶ **tufa**
CALCULAR *adj* relating to calculus
CALCULUS, CALCULI *n* branch of mathematics dealing with infinitesimal changes to a variable number or quantity
CALDARIA >**caldarium**

C

CALDERA, -S n large basin-shaped crater at the top of a volcano

CALDRON, -S same as ▸ cauldron

CALECHE, -S a variant of ▸ calash

CALEFY, CALEFIED, CALEFIES vb make warm

CALENDAL ▸ calends

CALENDAR n chart showing a year divided up into months, weeks, and days ▸ vb enter in a calendar

CALENDER n machine in which paper or cloth is smoothed by passing it between rollers ▸ vb smooth in such a machine

CALENDRY n place where calendering is carried out

CALENDS pl n first day of each month in the ancient Roman calendar

CALESA, -S n horse-drawn buggy

CALF, -S, CALVES n young cow, bull, elephant, whale, or seal

CALFHOOD n state of being a calf

CALFLESS ▸ calf

CALFLICK another word for ▸ cowlick

CALFLIKE ▸ calf

CALFS ▸ calf

CALFSKIN n fine leather made from the skin of a calf

CALIBER, -S same as ▸ calibre

CALIBRE, -S n person's ability or worth

CALIBRED

CALICES ▸ calix

CALICHE, -S n bed of sand or clay in arid regions

CALICLE, -S same as ▸ calycle

CALICO, -ES, -S n white cotton fabric

CALID adj warm

CALIDITY

CALIF, -S same as ▸ caliph

CALIFATE same as >caliphate

CALIFONT n gas water heater

CALIFS ▸ calif

CALIGO, -ES, -S n speck on the cornea causing poor vision

CALIMA, -S n Saharan dust-storm

CALIPASH n greenish glutinous edible part of the turtle

CALIPEE, -S n edible part of the turtle found next to the lower shell

CALIPER, -S same as ▸ calliper

CALIPH, -S n Muslim ruler

CALIPHAL

CALISAYA n bark of a type of tropical tree from which quinine is extracted

CALIVER, -S n type of musket

CALIX, CALICES, -ES n cup

CALK, -ED, -S same as ▸ caulk

CALKER -S

CALKIN, -S same as ▸ calk

CALKING, -S ▸ calk

CALKINS ▸ calkin

CALKS ▸ calk

CALL, -ED, -S vb name ▸ n cry, shout

CALLA, -S n S African plant with a white funnel-shaped spathe enclosing a yellow spadix

CALLABLE adj (of a security) subject to redemption before maturity

CALLAIS n type of green stone

CALLALOO n leafy green vegetable

CALLALOU n crabmeat soup

CALLAN, -S same as ▸ callant

CALLANT, -S n youth

CALLAS ▸ calla

CALLBACK n telephone call made in response to an earlier call

CALLBOY, -S n person who notifies actors when it is time to go on stage

CALLED ▸ call

CALLEE, -S n computer function being used

CALLER, -S n person or thing that calls, esp a person who makes a brief visit ▸ adj (of food, esp fish) fresh

CALLET, -S n scold

CALLID adj cunning

CALLING, -S n vocation, profession

CALLIOPE n steam organ

CALLIPEE same as ▸ calipee

CALLIPER n metal splint for supporting the leg ▸ vb measure the dimensions of (an object) with callipers

CALLOP, -S n edible Australian freshwater fish

CALLOSE, -S n carbohydrate found in plants

CALLOUS adj showing no concern for other people's feelings ▸ vb make or become callous

CALLOUT, -S n inset text within a printed article

CALLOW, -ER, -S adj young and inexperienced ▸ n someone young and inexperienced

CALLOWLY adj in a manner suggesting immaturity or inexperience

CALLOWS ▸ callow

CALLS ▸ call

CALLTIME n time available for making calls on a mobile phone

CALLUNA, -S n type of heather

CALLUS, -ED, -ES n area of thick hardened skin ▸ vb produce or cause to produce a callus

CALM, -ED, -ER, -EST, -S adj not agitated or excited ▸ n peaceful state ▸ vb make or become calm

CALMANT, -S n sedative

CALMED ▸ calm

CALMER ▸ calm

CALMEST ▸ calm

CALMIER ▸ calmy

CALMIEST ▸ calmy

CALMING, -S ▸ calm

CALMLY ▸ calm

CALMNESS ▸ calm

CALMS ▸ calm

CALMY, CALMIER, CALMIEST adj tranquil

CALO, -S n military servant

CALOMEL, -S n colourless tasteless powder

CALORIC, -S adj of heat or calories ▸ n hypothetical fluid formerly postulated as the embodiment of heat

CALORIE, -S n unit of measurement for the energy value of food

CALORISE same as ▸ calorize

CALORIST n believer in caloric theory

CALORIZE vb coat (a ferrous metal) by spraying with aluminium powder and then heating

CALORY same as ▸ calorie

CALOS ▸ calo

CALOTTE, -S n skullcap worn by Roman Catholic clergy

CALOTYPE n early photographic process

CALOYER, -S n monk of the Greek Orthodox Church, esp of the Basilian Order

CALP, -S n type of limestone

CALPA, -S n Hindu unit of time

CALPAC, -S n large black brimless hat

CALPACK, -S same as ▸ calpac

CALPACS ▸ calpac

CALPAIN, -S n type of enzyme

CALPAS ▸ calpa

CALPS ▶ calp
CALQUE, -D, -S, CALQUING
same as ▶ **caulk**
CALTHA, -S *n* marsh marigold
CALTHROP *same as* ▶ **caltrop**
CALTRAP, -S *same as*
▶ **caltrop**
CALTROP, -S *n* floating Asian plant
CALUMBA, -S *n*
Mozambiquan root used for medicinal purposes
CALUMET, -S *n* peace pipe
CALUMNY *n* false or malicious statement ▷ *vb* make a false or malicious statement about (a person)
CALUTRON *n* device used for the separation of isotopes
CALVADOS *n* type of apple brandy
CALVARIA *n* top part of the skull of vertebrates
CALVARY *n* representation of Christ's crucifixion
CALVE, -D, CALVING *vb* give birth to a calf
CALVER, -ED, -S *vb* prepare fish for cooking
CALVES ▶ calf
CALVING ▶ calve
CALX, CALCES, -ES *n* powdery metallic oxide formed when an ore or mineral is roasted
CALYCATE ▶ calyx
CALYCEAL *adj* resembling a calyx
CALYCES ▶ calyx
CALYCINE *adj* relating to, belonging to, or resembling a calyx
CALYCLE, -S *n* cup-shaped structure, as in the coral skeleton
CALYCLED
CALYCOID *adj* resembling a calyx
CALYCULE *n* bracts surrounding the base of the calyx
CALYCULI > calyculus
CALYPSO, -S *n* West Indian song with improvised topical lyrics
CALYPTER *n* alula
CALYPTRA *n* membranous hood covering the spore-bearing capsule of mosses and liverworts
CALYX, CALYCES, -ES *n* outer leaves that protect a flower bud
CALZONE, -S, CALZONI *n* folded pizza filled with cheese, tomatoes, etc

CAM, -MED, -MING, -S *n* device that converts a circular motion to a to-and-fro motion ▷ *vb* furnish (a machine) with a cam
CAMA *n* hybrid offspring of a camel and a llama
CAMAIEU, -X *n* cameo
CAMAIL, -S *n* covering of chain mail
CAMAILED
CAMAN, -S *n* wooden stick used to hit the ball in shinty
CAMARON, -S *n* shrimp
CAMAS, -ES *same as*
▶ **camass**
CAMASH, -ES *same as*
▶ **camass**
CAMASS, -ES *n* type of North American plant
CAMBER, -ED, -S *n* slight upward curve to the centre of a surface ▷ *vb* form or be formed when a surface that curves upwards to its centre
CAMBIA ▶ cambium
CAMBIAL ▶ cambium
CAMBISM, -S ▶ cambist
CAMBIST, -S *n* dealer or expert in foreign exchange
CAMBIUM, CAMBIA, -S *n* meristem that increases the girth of stems and roots
CAMBOGE, -S *n* type of gum resin
CAMBOGIA *another name for* ▶ **gamboge**
CAMBOOSE *n* cabin built as living quarters for a gang of lumbermen
CAMBREL, -S *a variant of* ▶ **gambrel**
CAMBRIC, -S *n* fine white linen fabric
CAMCORD, -S *vb* film with a camcorder
CAME ▶ come
CAMEL, -S *n* humped mammal
CAMELEER *n* camel-driver
CAMELEON *same as*
> **chameleon**
CAMELIA, -S *same as*
▶ **camellia**
CAMELID, -S *adj* of or relating to camels ▷ *n* any animal of the camel family
CAMELINE *n* material made from camel hair
CAMELISH ▶ camel
CAMELLIA *n* evergreen ornamental shrub with white, pink, or red flowers
CAMELOID *n* member of the camel family

CAMELOT, -S *n* supposedly idyllic period or age
CAMELRY *n* troops mounted on camels
CAMELS ▶ camel
CAMEO, -ED, -ING, -S *n* brooch or ring with a profile head carved in relief ▷ *vb* appear in a brief role
CAMERA, -E, -S *n* apparatus used for taking still or moving images
CAMERAL *adj* of or relating to a judicial or legislative chamber
CAMERAS ▶ camera
CAMES *same as* ▶ **canvas**
CAMESE, -S *same as* ▶ **camise**
CAMI *n* camisole
CAMION, -S *n* lorry, or, esp formerly, a large dray
CAMIS *n* light robe
CAMISA, -S *n* smock
CAMISADE *same as*
▶ **camisado**
CAMISADO *n* (formerly) an attack made under cover of darkness
CAMISAS ▶ camisa
CAMISE, -S *n* loose light shirt, smock, or tunic originally worn in the Middle Ages
CAMISIA, -S *n* surplice
CAMISOLE *n* woman's bodice-like garment
CAMLET, -S *n* tough waterproof cloth
CAMMED ▶ cam
CAMMIE, -S *n* webcam award
CAMMING ▶ cam
CAMO, -S *n* short for camouflage
CAMOGIE, -S *n* form of hurling played by women
CAMOMILE *n* aromatic plant, used to make herbal tea
CAMOODI, -S *a Caribbean name for* ▶ **anaconda**
CAMORRA, -S *n* secret criminal group
CAMOS ▶ camo
CAMOTE, -S *n* type of sweet potato
CAMP, -ED, -EST, -S *vb* stay in a camp ▷ *adj* consciously artificial ▷ *n* (place for) temporary lodgings consisting of tents, huts, or cabins
CAMPAGNA, CAMPAGNE *same as* > **champaign**
CAMPAIGN *n* series of coordinated activities designed to achieve a goal ▷ *vb* take part in a campaign

CAMPANA, -S n bell or bell shape

CAMPED ► camp

CAMPER, -S n person who lives or temporarily stays in a tent, cabin, etc

CAMPERY n campness

CAMPEST ► camp

CAMPFIRE n outdoor fire in a camp

CAMPHANE n one of the terpene hydrocarbons

CAMPHENE n colourless crystalline insoluble terpene

CAMPHINE n type of solvent

CAMPHIRE an archaic name for ► henna

CAMPHOL, -S another word for ► borneol

CAMPHONE n combined mobile phone and digital camera

CAMPHOR, -S n aromatic crystalline substance

CAMPI ► campo

CAMPIER ► campy

CAMPIEST ► campy

CAMPILY ► campy

CAMPING, -S ► camp

CAMPION, -S n red, pink, or white wild flower

CAMPLE, -D, -S, CAMPLING vb argue

CAMPLY ► camp

CAMPNESS ► camp

CAMPO, CAMPI, -S n level or undulating savanna country

CAMPONG, -S n in Malaysia, a village

CAMPOREE n local meeting or assembly of Scouts

CAMPOS ► campo

CAMPOUT, -S n camping trip

CAMPS ► camp

CAMPSITE n area on which holiday makers may pitch a tent

CAMPUS, -ED, -ES n grounds of a university or college ▷ vb restrict a student to campus, as a punishment

CAMPY, CAMPIER, CAMPIEST adj consciously artificial

CAMS ► cam

CAMSHAFT n part of an engine consisting of a rod to which cams are fixed

CAMSHO adj crooked

CAMSHOCH same as ► camsho

CAMSTANE same as ► camstone

CAMSTONE n limestone used for whitening stone doorsteps

CAMUS, -ES n type of loose robe

CAMWOOD, -S n W African leguminous tree

CAN, -S, COULD vb be able to ▷ vb put (food etc) into a can ▷ n metal container for food or liquids

CANADA, -S n canada goose

CANAIGRE n southern US dock, the root of which yields a substance used in tanning

CANAILLE n masses or rabble

CANAKIN, -S same as ► cannikin

CANAL, -ED, -ING, -LED, -S n artificial waterway ▷ vb dig a canal through

CANALISE same as ► canalize

CANALIZE vb give direction to

CANALLED ► canal

CANALLER n canal boat worker

CANALS ► canal

CANAPE, -S n small piece of bread or toast with a savoury topping

CANARD, -S n false report

CANARY, CANARIED, CANARIES n small yellow songbird often kept as a pet ▷ vb perform a dance called the canary

CANASTA, -S n card game like rummy, played with two packs

CANASTER n coarsely broken dried tobacco leaves

CANBANK, -S n container for receiving cans for recycling

CANCAN, -S n lively high-kicking dance performed by a female group

CANCEL, -ED, -S vb stop (something that has been arranged) from taking place ▷ n new leaf or section of a book replacing a defective one

CANCELER

CANCELLI pl n any lattice-like structures

CANCELS ► cancel

CANCER, -S n serious disease resulting from a malignant growth or tumour

CANCERED adj affected by cancer

CANCERS ► cancer

CANCHA, -S n toasted maize

CANCRINE adj crab-like

CANCROID adj resembling a cancerous growth ▷ n skin cancer, esp one of only moderate malignancy

CANDELA, -S n unit of luminous intensity

CANDENT adj emitting light as a result of being heated to a high temperature

CANDID, -ER, -S adj honest and straightforward ▷ n unposed photograph

CANDIDA, -S n yeastlike parasitic fungus which causes thrush

CANDIDAL

CANDIDER ► candid

CANDIDLY ► candid

CANDIDS ► candid

CANDIE n South Indian unit of weight

CANDIED adj coated with sugar

CANDIES ► candy

CANDIRU, -S n parasitic freshwater catfish of the Amazon region

CANDLE, -D, -S, CANDLING n stick of wax enclosing a wick, burned to produce light ▷ vb test by holding up to a candle

CANDLER -S

CANDOCK, -S n type of water lily, or horsetail

CANDOR, -S same as ► candour

CANDOUR, -S n honesty and straightforwardness

CANDY, CANDIES, -ING n sweet or sweets ▷ vb make sweet

CANDYMAN, CANDYMEN n itinerant seller of toffee

CANE, -D, -S n stem of the bamboo or similar plant ▷ vb beat with a cane

CANEGRUB n Australian grub that feeds on sugarcane

CANEH, -S n Hebrew unit of length

CANELLA, -S n fragrant cinnamon-like inner bark of a W Indian tree, used as a spice and in medicine

CANEPHOR n sculpted figure carrying a basket on its head

CANER, -S ► cane

CANES ► cane

CANEWARE n type of unglazed stoneware

CANFIELD n gambling game adapted from a type of patience

CANFUL, -S, CANSFUL n amount a can will hold

CANG, -S same as ► cangue

CANGLE, -D, -S, CANGLING vb wrangle

CANGS ► cang

CANGUE, -S n (formerly in China) a wooden collar worn as a punishment

CANID, -S n animal of the dog family

CANIER ▸ cany

CANIEST ▸ cany

CANIKIN, -S same as ▸ **cannikin**

CANINE, -S adj of or like a dog ▷ n sharp pointed tooth between the incisors and the molars

CANING, -S n beating with a cane as a punishment

CANINITY ▸ canine

CANISTEL n Caribbean fruit

CANISTER n metal container ▷ vb put into canisters

CANITIES n grey hair

CANKER, -ED, -S n ulceration, ulcerous disease ▷ vb infect or become infected with or as if with canker

CANKERY adj like a canker

CANKLE, -S n thickened ankle on an overweight person

CANN, -S vb direct a ship's steering

CANNA, -S n type of tropical plant

CANNABIC ▸ cannabis

CANNABIN n greenish-black poisonous resin obtained from the Indian hemp plant

CANNABIS n Asian plant with tough fibres

CANNACH, -S n cotton grass

CANNAE vb can not

CANNAS ▸ canna

CANNED ▸ can

CANNEL, -S n type of dull coal

CANNELON n type of meat loaf

CANNELS ▸ cannel

CANNER, -S n person or organization whose job is to can foods

CANNERY n factory where food is canned

CANNIBAL n person who eats human flesh

CANNIE same as ▸ **canny**

CANNIER ▸ canny

CANNIEST ▸ canny

CANNIKIN n small can, esp one used as a drinking vessel

CANNILY ▸ canny

CANNING, -S ▸ can

CANNOLI, -S n Sicilian pudding of pasta shells filled with sweetened ricotta

CANNON, -ED, -S n gun of large calibre ▷ vb collide (with)

CANNONRY n volley of artillery fire

CANNONS ▸ cannon

CANNOT vb can not

CANNS ▸ cann

CANNULA, -E, -S n narrow tube for insertion into a bodily cavity

CANNULAR adj shaped like a cannula

CANNULAS ▸ cannula

CANNY, CANNIER, CANNIEST adj shrewd, cautious ▷ adv quite

CANOE, -D, -S n light narrow open boat propelled by a paddle or paddles ▷ vb use a canoe

CANOEING

CANOEIST

CANOEMAN, CANOEMEN n man who canoes

CANOER, -S ▸ canoe

CANOES ▸ canoe

CANOLA, -S n cooking oil extracted from a variety of rapeseed

CANON, -S n priest serving in a cathedral

CANONESS n woman belonging to any one of several religious orders

CANONIC same as > **canonical**

CANONISE same as ▸ **canonize**

CANONIST n specialist in canon law

CANONIZE vb declare (a person) officially to be a saint

CANONRY n office, benefice, or status of a canon

CANONS ▸ canon

CANOODLE vb kiss and cuddle

CANOPIC adj of ancient Egyptian vase

CANOPY, CANOPIED, CANOPIES n covering above a bed, door, etc ▷ vb cover with or as if with a canopy

CANOROUS adj tuneful

CANS ▸ can

CANSFUL ▸ canful

CANSO, -S n love song

CANST vb form of 'can' used with the pronoun thou or its relative form

CANSTICK n candlestick

CANT, -ED, -EST, -S n insincere talk ▷ vb use cant ▷ adj oblique

CANTAL, -S n French cheese

CANTALA, -S n tropical American plant, the agave

CANTALS ▸ cantal

CANTAR, -S variant form of ▸ **kantar**

CANTATA, -S n musical work consisting of arias, duets, and choruses

CANTATE, -S n 98th psalm sung as a nonmetrical hymn

CANTDOG, -S same as ▸ **canthook**

CANTED ▸ cant

CANTEEN, -ED, -S vb move at gait between trot and gallop

CANTER, -ED, -S n restaurant attached to a workplace or school

CANTEST ▸ cant

CANTHAL ▸ canthus

CANTHARI > cantharus

CANTHI ▸ canthus

CANTHIC adj relating to the canthus

CANTHOOK n wooden pole with a hook used for handling logs

CANTHUS, CANTHI n inner or outer corner or angle of the eye

CANTIC ▸ cant

CANTICLE n short hymn with words from the Bible

CANTICO, -S vb dance as part of an act of worship

CANTICOY same as ▸ **cantico**

CANTICUM n canticle

CANTIER ▸ canty

CANTIEST ▸ canty

CANTILY ▸ canty

CANTINA, -S n bar or wine shop, esp in a Spanish-speaking country

CANTING, -S ▸ cant

CANTION n song

CANTLE, -D, -S, CANTLING n back part of a saddle that slopes upwards ▷ vb set up, or stand, on high

CANTLET, -S n piece

CANTLING ▸ cantle

CANTO, -S same as ▸ **cantus**

CANTON, -ED, -S n political division of a country, esp Switzerland ▷ vb divide into cantons

CANTONAL

CANTOR, -S n man employed to lead services in a synagogue

CANTORIS adj (in antiphonal music) to be sung by the cantorial side of a choir

CANTORS ▸ cantor

CANTOS ▸ canto

CANTRAIP n witch's spell or charm

CANTRAP, -S same as ▸ **cantraip**

CANTRED, -S n district comprising a hundred villages

CANTREF, -S same as ► cantred

CANTRIP, -S n magic spell ▷ adj (of an effect) produced by black magic

CANTS ► cant

CANTUS, -ES n medieval form of church singing

CANTY, CANTIER, CANTIEST adj lively

CANULA, -E, -S same as ► cannula

CANULAR adj shaped like a cannula

CANULAS ► canula

CANULATE same as > cannulate

CANVAS, -ED, -ES n heavy coarse cloth ▷ vb cover with, or be applied to, canvas **CANVASER**

CANVASS vb try to get votes or support (from) ▷ n canvassing

CANY, CANIER, CANIEST adj cane-like

CANYON, -S n deep narrow valley

CANZONA, -S n type of 16th- or 17th-century contrapuntal music

CANZONE, -S, CANZONI n Provençal or Italian lyric, often in praise of love or beauty

CANZONET n short, cheery, or lively Italian song

CANZONI ► canzone

CAP, -PED, -S n soft close-fitting covering for the head ▷ vb cover or top with something

CAPA, -S n type of Spanish cloak

CAPABLE, -R adj having the ability (for)

CAPABLY

CAPACITY n ability to contain, absorb, or hold ▷ adj of the maximum amount or number possible

CAPAS ► capa

CAPE, -D, -S, CAPING n short cloak ▷ vb cut and remove the hide of an animal

CAPEESH same as ► capisce

CAPELAN, -S another word for ► capelin

CAPELET, -S n small cape

CAPELIN, -S n type of small marine food fish

CAPELINE n cap-shaped bandage to cover the head or an amputation stump

CAPELINS ► capelin

CAPELLET n wen-like swelling on a horse

CAPER, -ED, -ING n high-spirited prank ▷ vb skip about

CAPERER -S

CAPERS pl n pickled flower buds of a Mediterranean shrub used in sauces

CAPES ► cape

CAPESKIN n soft leather obtained from the skins of a type of lamb or sheep having hairlike wool ▷ adj made of this leather

CAPEWORK n use of the cape by the matador in bullfighting

CAPEX, -ES n capital expenditure

CAPFUL, -S n quantity held by a (usually bottle) cap

CAPH, -S n letter of the Hebrew alphabet

CAPI ► capo

CAPIAS, -ES n (formerly) a writ directing the arrest of a named person

CAPING ► cape

CAPISCE interj expression meaning do you understand?

CAPITA ► caput

CAPITAL, -S n chief city of a country ▷ adj involving or punishable by death

CAPITAN, -S another name for ► hogfish

CAPITANO, CAPITANI n chief; captain

CAPITANS ► capitan

CAPITATE n largest of the bones of the human wrist

CAPITAYN n captain

CAPITOL, -S n (in America) building housing the state legislature

CAPITULA > capitulum

CAPIZ, -ES n bivalve shell of a mollusc

CAPLE, -S n horse

CAPLESS ► cap

CAPLET, -S n medicinal tablet, usually oval in shape, coated in a soluble substance

CAPLIN, -S same as ► capelin

CAPMAKER ► cap

CAPO, CAPI, -S n device used to raise the pitch of a stringed instrument

CAPOEIRA n Brazilian combination of martial art and dance

CAPON, -S n cock fowl fattened for eating

CAPONATA n Sicilian antipasto relish

CAPONIER n covered passageway built across a ditch as a military defence

CAPONISE same as ► caponize

CAPONIZE vb make (a cock) into a capon

CAPONS ► capon

CAPORAL, -S n strong coarse dark tobacco

CAPOS ► capo

CAPOT, -S, -TED n winning of all the tricks by one player ▷ vb score a capot (against)

CAPOTE, -S n long cloak or soldier's coat, usually with a hood

CAPOTS ► capot

CAPOTTED ► capot

CAPOUCH same as ► capuche

CAPPED ► cap

CAPPER, -S ► cap

CAPPING, -S ► cap

CAPRATE, -S n any salt of capric acid

CAPRESE, -S n salad of mozzarella, basil, and tomatoes

CAPRI adj as in **capri pants** women's tight-fitting trousers

CAPRIC adj (of a type of acid) smelling of goats

CAPRICCI > capriccio

CAPRICE, -S same as > capriccio

CAPRID, -S n any member of the goat family

CAPRIFIG n wild variety of fig of S Europe and SW Asia

CAPRIFY vb induce figs to ripen

CAPRINE adj of or resembling a goat

CAPRIOLE n upward but not forward leap made by a horse ▷ vb perform a capriole

CAPRIS ► capri

CAPROATE n any salt of caproic acid

CAPROCK, -S n layer of rock that overlies a salt dome

CAPROIC adj as in **caproic acid** oily acid found in milk

CAPRYLIC variant of ► capric

CAPS ► cap

CAPSICIN n liquid or resin extracted from capsicum

CAPSICUM n kind of pepper used as a vegetable or as a spice

CAPSID, -S n outer protein coat of a mature virus **CAPSIDAL**

CAPSIZAL ▸ capsize

CAPSIZE, -D, -S vb (of a boat) overturn accidentally

CAPSOMER n one of the units making up a viral capsid

CAPSTAN, -S n rotating cylinder round which a ship's rope is wound

CAPSTONE n one of a set of slabs on the top of a wall, building, etc

CAPSULAR adj relating to a capsule

CAPSULE, -D, -S n soluble gelatine case containing a dose of medicine ▷ adj very concise ▷ vb contain within a capsule

CAPTAIN, -S n commander of a ship or civil aircraft ▷ vb be captain of

CAPTAN, -S n type of fungicide

CAPTCHA, -S n test in which the user of a website has to decipher a distorted image

CAPTION, -S n title or explanation accompanying an illustration ▷ vb provide with a caption

CAPTIOUS adj tending to make trivial criticisms

CAPTIVE, -D, -S n person kept in confinement ▷ adj kept in confinement ▷ vb take prisoner

CAPTOR, -S n person who captures a person or animal

CAPTURE, -D, -S vb take by force ▷ n capturing **CAPTURER**

CAPUCCIO n hood

CAPUCHE, -S n large hood or cowl, esp that worn by Capuchin friars

CAPUCHED adj hooded

CAPUCHES ▸ capuche

CAPUCHIN n S American monkey with thick hair on the top of its head

CAPUERA, -S variant of ▸ capoeira

CAPUL, -S same as ▸ caple

CAPUT, CAPITA n main or most prominent part of an organ or structure

CAPYBARA n very large S American rodent

CAR, -S n motor vehicle designed to carry a small number of people

CARABAO, -S n water buffalo

CARABID, -S n type of beetle

CARABIN, -S same as ▸ carbine

CARABINE same as ▸ carbine

CARABINS ▸ carabin

CARACAL, -S n lynx with reddish fur, which inhabits deserts of N Africa and S Asia

CARACARA n carrion-eating bird of S North, Central, and S America

CARACK, -S same as ▸ carrack

CARACOL, -S same as ▸ caracole

CARACOLE n half turn to the right or left ▷ vb execute a half turn to the right or left

CARACOLS ▸ caracol

CARACT, -S n sign or symbol

CARACUL, -S n fur from the skins of newly born lambs of the karakul sheep

CARAFE, -S n glass bottle

CARAGANA n pea tree

CARAGEEN same as > carrageen

CARAMBA interj Spanish interjection similar to 'wow!'

CARAMEL, -S n chewy sweet made from sugar and milk ▷ vb turn into caramel

CARANGID n type of marine fish

CARANNA, -S n gumlike substance

CARAP, -S n crabwood

CARAPACE n hard upper shell of tortoises and crustaceans

CARAPAX n carapace

CARAPS ▸ carap

CARASSOW same as ▸ curassow

CARAT, -S n unit of weight of precious stones

CARATE, -S n tropical disease

CARATS ▸ carat

CARAUNA, -S same as ▸ caranna

CARAVAN, -S n large enclosed vehicle for living in ▷ vb travel or have a holiday in a caravan

CARAVEL, -S n two- or three-masted sailing ship

CARAWAY, -S n plant whose seeds are used as a spice

CARB, -S n carbohydrate

CARBAMIC adj as in **carbamic acid** hypothetical compound known only in carbamate salts

CARBAMYL n radical from carbamic acid

CARBARN, -S n streetcar depot

CARBARYL n organic compound of the carbamate group

CARBEEN, -S n Australian eucalyptus tree

CARBENE, -S n neutral divalent free radical, such as methylene: CH_2

CARBIDE, -S n compound of carbon with a metal

CARBIES ▸ carby

CARBINE, -S n light automatic rifle

CARBINOL same as ▸ methanol

CARBO, -S n carbohydrate

CARBOLIC adj as in **carbolic acid** phenol, when it is used as a disinfectant

CARBON, -S n nonmetallic element

CARBONIC adj containing carbon

CARBONS ▸ carbon

CARBONYL n the divalent group =CO

CARBORA, -S n former name for the koala

CARBORNE adj travelling by car

CARBOS ▸ carbo

CARBOXYL adj as in **carboxyl group** functional group in organic acids

CARBOY, -S n large bottle with a protective casing **CARBOYED**

CARBS ▸ carb

CARBURET vb combine or mix (a gas) with carbon or carbon compounds ▷ vb combine with carbon

CARBY, CARBIES n short for carburettor

CARCAJOU a North American name for > wolverine

CARCAKE, -S n (formerly, in Scotland) a cake traditionally made for Shrove Tuesday

CARCANET n jewelled collar or necklace

CARCASE, -D, -S same as ▸ carcass

CARCASS n dead body of an animal ▷ vb make a carcass of

CARCEL, -S n French unit of light

CARCERAL adj relating to prison

CARD, -ED, -S n piece of thick stiff paper or cardboard ▷ vb comb out fibres of wool or cotton before spinning

CARDAMOM n spice obtained from the seeds of a tropical plant

CARDAMON same as ▶ cardamom

CARDAMUM same as ▶ cardamom

CARDAN n as in **cardan joint** type of universal joint

CARDCASE n small case for holding business cards

CARDECU, -S n old French coin (a quarter of a crown)

CARDECUE same as ▶ cardecu

CARDECUS ▶ cardecu

CARDED ▶ card

CARDER, -S ▶ card

CARDI, -S n cardigan

CARDIA, -E, -S n lower oesophageal sphincter

CARDIAC, -S adj of the heart ▷ n person with a heart disorder

CARDIAE ▶ cardia

CARDIAS ▶ cardia

CARDIE, -S short for ▶ cardigan

CARDIGAN n knitted jacket

CARDINAL n high-ranking clergyman of the RC Church ▷ adj fundamentally important

CARDING, -S ▶ card

CARDIO, -S adj exercising heart ▷ n cardiovascular exercise

CARDIOID n heart-shaped curve

CARDIOS ▶ cardio

CARDIS ▶ cardi

CARDITIC ▶ carditis

CARDITIS n inflammation of the heart

CARDON, -S n variety of cactus

CARDOON, -S n thistle-like S European plant

CARDS ▶ card

CARDUUS n thistle

CARDY same as ▶ cardie

CARE, -D, -S vb be concerned ▷ n careful attention, caution

CAREEN, -ED, -S vb tilt over to one side

CAREENER

CAREER, -ED, -S n series of jobs that a person has through their life ▷ vb rush in an uncontrolled way ▷ adj having chosen to dedicate his or her life to a particular occupation

CAREERER

CAREFREE adj without worry or responsibility

CAREFUL adj cautious in attitude or action

CARELESS adj done or acting with insufficient attention

CARELINE n telephone service set up by a company or other organization

CAREME, -S n period of Lent

CARER, -S n person who looks after someone who is ill or old, often a relative

CARES ▶ care

CARESS, -ED, -ES n gentle affectionate touch or embrace ▷ vb touch gently and affectionately

CARESSER

CARET, -S n proofreading symbol

CARETAKE, CARETOOK vb work as a caretaker

CARETS ▶ caret

CAREWARE n computer software licensed in exchange for a donation to charity

CAREWORN adj showing signs of worry

CAREX, CARICES n any member of the sedge family

CARFARE, -S n fare that a passenger is charged for a ride on a bus, etc

CARFAX, -ES n place where principal roads or streets intersect

CARFOX, -ES same as ▶ carfax

CARFUL, -S n maximum number of people a car will hold

CARGEESE ▶ cargoose

CARGO, -ED, -ES, -ING, -S n goods carried by a ship, aircraft, etc ▷ vb load

CARGOOSE, CARGEESE n crested grebe

CARGOS ▶ cargo

CARHOP, -S n waiter or waitress at a drive-in restaurant ▷ vb work as a carhop

CARIACOU n type of deer

CARIAMA, -S another word for ▶ seriema

CARIBE, -S n piranha

CARIBOO, -S same as ▶ caribou

CARIBOU, -S n large N American reindeer

CARICES ▶ carex

CARIED adj (of teeth) decayed

CARIERE, -S obsolete word for ▶ career

CARIES n tooth decay

CARILLON n set of bells played by keyboard or mechanically ▷ vb play a carillon

CARINA, -E, -S n keel-like part or ridge

CARINAL adj keel-like

CARINAS ▶ carina

CARINATE adj having a keel or ridge

CARING, -S adj feeling or showing care and compassion for other people ▷ n practice or profession of providing social or medical care

CARINGLY

CARIOCA, -S n Brazilian dance similar to the samba

CARIOLE, -S n small open two-wheeled horse-drawn vehicle

CARIOSE same as ▶ carious

CARIOUS adj (of teeth or bone) affected with caries

CARITAS n divine love; charity

CARJACK, -S vb attack (a car driver) to rob them or to steal the car ▷ vb steal a car, by force, from a person who is present

CARJACOU variation of ▶ cariacou

CARK, -ED, -ING, -S vb break down

CARL, -S another word for ▶ churl

CARLE, -S same as ▶ carl

CARLESS ▶ car

CARLIN, -S same as ▶ carling

CARLINE, -S same as ▶ carling

CARLING, -S n fore-and-aft beam in a vessel

CARLINS ▶ carlin

CARLISH adj churlish

CARLOAD, -S n amount that can be carried by a car

CARLOCK, -S n type of Russian isinglass

CARLOT, -S n boor

CARLS ▶ carl

CARMAKER n car manufacturing company

CARMAN, CARMEN n man who drives a car or cart

CARMINE, -S adj vivid red ▷ n vivid red colour, sometimes with a purplish tinge

CARN, -S n cairn

CARNAGE, -S n extensive slaughter of people

CARNAL, -S adj of a physical or sensual nature ▷ vb act in a carnal manner

CARNALLY

CARNAUBA n Brazilian fan palm tree

CARNEOUS adj fleshy

CARNET, -S n type of customs licence

CARNEY, -ED, -S same as ▶ carny

CARNIE same as ▶ carny

CARNIED ▶ carny

CARNIER ▶ carny

CARNIES ▶ carny

CARNIEST ▶ carny

CARNIFEX n executioner

CARNIFY vb be altered so as to resemble skeletal muscle

CARNIVAL n festive period with processions, music, and dancing in the street

CARNOSE adj fleshy

CARNS ▶ carn

CARNY, CARNIED, CARNIER, CARNIES, CARNIEST, -ING vb coax or cajole or act in a wheedling manner ▷ n person who works in a carnival ▷ adj sly

CARNYX, -ES n bronze Celtic war trumpet

CAROACH same as ▶ caroche

CAROB, -S n pod of a Mediterranean tree, used as a chocolate substitute

CAROCH same as ▶ caroche

CAROCHE, -S n stately ceremonial carriage used in the 16th and 17th centuries

CAROL, -ED, -LED, -S n joyful Christmas hymn ▷ vb sing carols

CAROLER -S

CAROLI ▶ carolus

CAROLING ▶ carol

CAROLLED ▶ carol

CAROLLER ▶ carol

CAROLS ▶ carol

CAROLUS, CAROLI n any of several coins struck in the reign of a king called Charles

CAROM, -ED, -ING, -S n shot in which the cue ball is caused to contact one object ball after another ▷ vb carambole

CAROMEL, -S vb turn into caramel

CAROMING ▶ carom

CAROMS ▶ carom

CARON, -S n inverted circumflex

CAROTENE n orange-red hydrocarbons found in many plants

CAROTID, -S n either of the two arteries supplying blood to the head ▷ adj of either of these arteries

CAROTIN, -S same as ▶ carotene

CAROUSAL n merry drinking party

CAROUSE, -D, -S vb have a merry drinking party

CAROUSEL n revolving conveyor belt for luggage or photographic slides

CAROUSER ▶ carouse

CAROUSES ▶ carouse

CARP, -ED, -S n large freshwater fish ▷ vb complain, find fault

CARPAL, -IA, -S n wrist bone

CARPALE same as ▶ carpal

CARPALIA ▶ carpal

CARPALS ▶ carpal

CARPED ▶ carp

CARPEL, -S n female reproductive organ of a flowering plant

CARPER, -S ▶ carp

CARPET, -ED, -S n heavy fabric for covering floors ▷ vb cover with a carpet

CARPHONE n (formerly) phone designed for use in a car

CARPI ▶ carpus

CARPING, -S adj tending to make petty complaints ▷ n petty complaint

CARPOOL, -S vb share the use of a single car to travel to work or school

CARPORT, -S n shelter for a car, consisting of a roof supported by posts

CARPS ▶ carp

CARPUS, CARPI n set of eight bones of the wrist

CARR, -S n area of bog or fen in which scrub has become established

CARRACK, -S n galleon used as a merchantman

CARRACT, -S same as ▶ carrack

CARRAT, -S same as ▶ carat

CARRAWAY same as ▶ caraway

CARRECT, -S same as ▶ carrack

CARREL, -S n small individual study room or private desk

CARRELL, -S same as ▶ carrel

CARRELS ▶ carrel

CARRIAGE n one of the sections of a train for passengers

CARRICK n as in carrick bend type of knot

CARRIED ▶ carry

CARRIER, -S n person or thing that carries something

CARRIES ▶ carry

CARRIOLE same as ▶ cariole

CARRION, -S n dead and rotting flesh

CARRITCH n catechism

CARROCH variant of ▶ caroche

CARROM, -ED, -S same as ▶ carom

CARRON n as in carron oil ointment of limewater and linseed oil

CARROT, -S n long tapering orange root vegetable

CARROTIN n carotene

CARROTS ▶ carrot

CARROTY adj (of hair) reddish-orange

CARRS ▶ carr

CARRY, CARRIED, CARRIES, -ING vb take from one place to another

CARRYALL n light four-wheeled horse-drawn carriage usually designed to carry four passengers

CARRYCOT n light portable bed for a baby, with handles and a hood

CARRYING ▶ carry

CARRYON, -S n fuss or commotion

CARRYOUT n hot cooked food bought in a shop for consumption elsewhere

CARS ▶ car

CARSE, -S n riverside area of flat fertile alluvium

CARSEY, -S slang word for ▶ toilet

CARSHARE same as ▶ carpool

CARSICK adj nauseated from riding in a car

CARSPIEL n curling match which has a car as a prize

CART, -ED, -ING, -S n open two-wheeled horse-drawn vehicle ▷ vb carry, usu with some effort

CARTA, -S n charter

CARTABLE ▶ cart

CARTAGE, -S n process or cost of carting

CARTAS ▶ carta

CARTE, -S n fencing position

CARTED ▶ cart

CARTEL, -S n association of competing firms formed to fix prices

CARTER, -S ▶ cart

CARTES ▶ carte

CARTFUL, -S n amount a cart can hold

CARTING ▶ cart

CARTLOAD n amount a cart can hold

CARTON, -ED, -S n container made of cardboard or waxed paper ▷ vb enclose (goods) in a carton

CARTOON, -S n humorous or satirical drawing ▷ vb depict in a cartoon

CARTOONY adj of or like a cartoon

CARTOP adj designed to be transported on top of a vehicle

CARTOUCH same as ▷ cartouche

CARTROAD n road for carts to drive on

CARTS ► cart

CARTWAY, -S n way by which carts travel

CARUCAGE n tax due on a carucate

CARUCATE n area of land an oxen team could plough in a year

CARUNCLE n fleshy outgrowth on the heads of certain birds, such as a cock's comb

CARVE, -D, -S vb cut to form an object

CARVEL, -S same as ► caravel

CARVEN an archaic or literary past participle of ► carve

CARVER, -S n carving knife

CARVERY n restaurant where customers pay a set price for unrestricted helpings

CARVES ► carve

CARVIES ► carvy

CARVING, -S n figure or design produced by carving stone or wood

CARVY, CARVIES n caraway seed

CARWASH n drive-through structure containing automated equipment for washing cars

CARYATIC ► caryatid

CARYATID n supporting column in the shape of a female figure

CARYOTIN variant of ► karyotin

CASA, -S n house

CASABA, -S n kind of winter muskmelon

CASAS ► casa

CASAVA, -S same as ► cassava

CASBAH, -S n citadel of a N African city

CASCABEL n knoblike protrusion on a type of cannon

CASCABLE same as ► cascabel

CASCADE, -D, -S n waterfall ▷ vb flow or fall in a cascade

CASCARA, -S n bark of a N American shrub, used as a laxative

CASCHROM n wooden hand-plough

CASCO, -S n Argentinian homestead

CASE, -D, -S n instance, example ▷ vb inspect (a building) with the intention of burgling it

CASEASE, -S n proteolytic enzyme

CASEATE, -D, -S vb undergo caseation

CASEBOOK n book in which records of legal or medical cases are kept

CASED ► case

CASEFY, CASEFIED, CASEFIES vb make or become similar to cheese

CASEIC adj relating to cheese

CASEIN, -S n phosphoprotein forming the basis of cheese

CASELAW, -S n law established by previous cases

CASELOAD n number of cases that a worker deals with at any one time

CASEMAN, CASEMEN n in printing, a person who sets and corrects type

CASEMATE n armoured compartment in a ship or fortification in which guns are mounted

CASEMEN ► caseman

CASEMENT n window that is hinged on one side

CASEMIX n mix or type of patients treated by a hospital or medical unit

CASEOSE, -S n peptide produced by the peptic digestion of casein

CASEOUS adj of or like cheese

CASERN, -S n (formerly) a billet or accommodation for soldiers in a town

CASERNE, -S same as ► casern

CASERNS ► casern

CASES ► case

CASETTE, -S variant of ► cassette

CASEVAC, -S vb evacuate (a casualty) from a combat zone, usu by air

CASEWORK n social work based on close study

CASEWORM n caddis worm

CASH, -ED, -ES, -ING n banknotes and coins ▷ adj of, for, or paid in cash ▷ vb obtain cash for

CASHABLE

CASHAW, -S n winter squash

CASHBACK n discount offered in return for immediate payment

CASHBOOK n journal in which cash receipts and payments are recorded

CASHBOX n box for holding cash

CASHED ► cash

CASHES ► cash

CASHEW, -S n edible kidney-shaped nut

CASHIER, -S n person responsible for handling cash in a bank, shop, etc ▷ vb dismiss with dishonour from the armed forces

CASHING ► cash

CASHLESS adj using credit cards or electronic money transfers instead of coins or banknotes

CASHMERE n fine soft wool obtained from goats

CASHOO, -S n catechu

CASIMERE same as ► cassimere

CASIMIRE variant of ► cassimere

CASING, -S n protective case, covering

CASINO, CASINI, -S n public building or room where gambling games are played

CASITA, -S n small house

CASK, -ED, -ING, -S n large barrel ▷ vb put into a cask

CASKET, -ED, -S n small box for valuables ▷ vb put into a casket

CASKIER ► casky

CASKIEST ► casky

CASKING ► cask

CASKS ► cask

CASKY, CASKIER, CASKIEST adj (of wine) having a musty smell due to resting too long in the cask

CASPASE, -S n type of enzyme

CASQUE, -S n helmet or a helmet-like process or structure

CASQUED

CASSABA, -S same as ► casaba

CASSATA, -S n ice cream usually containing nuts and candied fruit

CASSAVA, -S n starch obtained from the roots of

a tropical American plant, used to make tapioca

CASSENA, -S same as ► cassina

CASSENE, -S same as ► cassina

CASSETTE n (formerly) plastic container for magnetic tape

CASSIA, -S n tropical plant whose pods yield a mild laxative

CASSIE, -S n type of thorny shrub

CASSINA, -S n American tree

CASSINE, -S same as ► cassina

CASSINO, -S n card game for two to four players

CASSIOPE n type of evergreen shrub

CASSIS, -ES n blackcurrant cordial

CASSOCK, -S n long tunic, usu black, worn by priests

CASSONE, -S n highly-decorated Italian dowry chest

CASSPIR, -S n armoured military vehicle

CAST, -S n actors in a play or film collectively ▷ vb select (an actor) to play a part in a play or film

CASTABLE adj able to be cast

CASTANET > castanets

CASTAWAY n shipwrecked person ▷ adj shipwrecked or put adrift ▷ vb cause (a ship, person, etc) to be shipwrecked or abandoned

CASTE, -S n any of the hereditary classes into which Hindu society is divided

CASTED adj having a caste

CASTEISM n belief in, and adherence to, the caste system

CASTELLA > castellum

CASTER, -S n person or thing that casts

CASTERED adj having casters

CASTERS ► caster

CASTES ► caste

CASTING, -S ► cast

CASTLE, -S n large fortified building ▷ vb (in chess) make a move involving king and rook

CASTLED adj like a castle in construction

CASTLES ► castle

CASTLING n (in chess) act of castling

CASTOCK, -S n kale stalk

CASTOFF, -S n person or thing that has been discarded or abandoned

CASTOR, -S same as ► caster

CASTORY n dye derived from beaver pelts

CASTRAL adj relating to camps

CASTRATE vb remove the testicles of

CASTRATO, CASTRATI n male singer who retains a soprano or alto voice

CASTS ► cast

CASUAL, -S adj careless, nonchalant ▷ n occasional worker

CASUALLY

CASUALTY n person killed or injured in an accident or war

CASUIST, -S n person who attempts to resolve moral dilemmas

CASUS n event

CAT, -S, -TED, -TING n small domesticated furry mammal ▷ vb flog with a cat-'o-nine-tails

CATACOMB n underground burial place

CATALASE n enzyme that catalyses the decomposition of hydrogen peroxide

CATALO, -ES, -S same as ► cattalo

CATALOG, -S same as > catalogue

CATALOS ► catalo

CATALPA, -S n tree of N America and Asia with bell-shaped whitish flowers

CATALYSE vb speed up (a chemical reaction) by a catalyst

CATALYST n substance that speeds up a chemical reaction without itself changing

CATALYZE same as ► catalyse

CATAPAN, -S n governor in the Byzantine Empire

CATAPHOR n word that refers to or stands for another word used later

CATAPULT n Y-shaped device with a loop of elastic, used by children for firing stones ▷ vb shoot forwards or upwards violently

CATARACT n eye disease in which the lens becomes opaque

CATARRH, -S n excessive mucus in the nose and throat, during or following a cold

CATASTA, -S n platform on which slaves were presented for sale

CATATONY another word for > catatonia

CATAWBA, -S n type of red North American grape

CATBIRD, -S n North American songbird

CATBOAT, -S n sailing vessel

CATBRIAR same as ► catbrier

CATBRIER n greenbrier

CATCALL, -S n derisive whistle or cry ▷ vb utter such a call (at)

CATCH, -ES, CAUGHT vb seize, capture ▷ n device for fastening a door, window, etc

CATCHALL n something designed to cover a variety of situations

CATCHCRY n well-known much-used phrase, perhaps associated with a particular group

CATCHED rarely used past tense of ► catch

CATCHEN archaic form of ► catch

CATCHER, -S n person or thing that catches, esp in a game or sport

CATCHES ► catch

CATCHFLY n type of plant with sticky calyxes and stems on which insects are trapped

CATCHIER ► catchy

CATCHILY adv in a pleasant or catchy way

CATCHING ► catch

CATCHT same as ► catched

CATCHUP, -S a variant spelling (esp US) of ► ketchup

CATCHY, CATCHIER adj (of a tune) pleasant and easily remembered

CATCLAW, -S n type of shrub; black bead

CATCON, -S n catalytic converter

CATE n delicacy

CATECHIN n soluble yellow solid substance found in mahogany wood

CATECHOL n colourless crystalline phenol found in resins and lignins

CATECHU, -S n astringent resinous substance

CATEGORY n class, group

CATELOG, -S obsolete word for > catalogue

CATENA, -E, -S n connected series, esp of patristic comments on the Bible

CATENANE n type of chemical compound

CATENARY n curve assumed by a heavy uniform flexible cord hanging freely from two points ▷ adj of, resembling, relating to, or constructed using a catenary or suspended chain

CATENAS ► catena

CATENATE vb arrange or be arranged in a series of chains or rings

CATENOID n geometrical surface generated by rotating a catenary about its axis

CATER, -ED, -S vb provide what is needed or wanted, esp food or services

CATERAN, -S n (formerly) a member of a band of brigands in the Scottish highlands

CATERED ► cater

CATERER, -S n person whose job is to provide food for social events

CATERESS n female caterer

CATERING n supplying of food for a social event

CATERS ► cater

CATES pl n choice dainty food

CATFACE, -S n deformity of the surface of a tree trunk, caused by fire or disease

CATFALL, -S n line used as a tackle for hoisting an anchor to the cathead

CATFIGHT n fight between two women

CATFISH n fish with whisker-like barbels round the mouth

CATFLAP, -S n small flap in a door to let a cat go through

CATFOOD, -S n food for cats

CATGUT, -S n strong cord used to string musical instruments and sports rackets

CATHEAD, -S n fitting at the bow of a vessel for securing the anchor when raised

CATHECT, -S vb invest mental or emotional energy in

CATHEDRA n bishop's throne

CATHETER n tube inserted into a body cavity to drain fluid

CATHETUS n straight line or radius perpendicular to another line or radius

CATHEXIS, CATHEXES n concentration of psychic energy on a single goal

CATHISMA n short hymn used as a response

CATHODAL ► cathode

CATHODE, -S n negative electrode, by which electrons leave a circuit

CATHODIC

CATHOLE, -S n hole in a ship through which ropes are passed

CATHOLIC adj (of tastes or interests) covering a wide range ▷ n member of the Roman Catholic Church

CATHOOD, -S n state of being a cat

CATION, -S n positively charged ion

CATIONIC

CATJANG, -S n tropical shrub

CATKIN, -S n drooping flower spike of certain trees

CATLIKE ► cat

CATLIN, -S same as ► catling

CATLING, -S n long double-edged surgical knife for amputations

CATLINS ► catlin

CATMINT, -S n Eurasian plant with scented leaves that attract cats

CATNAP, -S vb doze ▷ n short sleep or doze

CATNAPER

CATNEP, -S same as ► catmint

CATNIP, -S same as ► catmint

CATOLYTE n part of the electrolyte that surrounds the cathode in an electrolytic cell

CATS ► cat

CATSKIN, -S n skin and/or fur of a cat

CATSPAW, -S n person used by another as a tool

CATSUIT, -S n one-piece usually close-fitting trouser suit

CATSUP, -S a variant (esp US) of ► ketchup

CATTABU, -S n cross between common cattle and zebu

CATTAIL, -S n reed mace

CATTALO, -S n hardy breed of cattle

CATTED ► cat

CATTERY n place where cats are bred or looked after

CATTIE same as ► catty

CATTIER ► catty

CATTIES ► catty

CATTIEST ► catty

CATTILY ► catty

CATTING ► cat

CATTISH ► cat

CATTLE pl n domesticated cows and bulls

CATTLEYA n tropical American orchid cultivated for its purplish-pink or white showy flowers

CATTY, CATTIER, CATTIES, CATTIEST adj spiteful ▷ n unit of weight, used esp in China

CATWALK, -S n narrow pathway or platform

CATWORKS n machinery on a drilling platform

CATWORM, -S n type of carnivorous worm

CAUCUS, -ED, -ES n local committee or faction of a political party ▷ vb hold a caucus

CAUDA, -E n tail of an animal

CAUDAD adv towards the tail or posterior part

CAUDAE ► cauda

CAUDAL adj at or near an animal's tail

CAUDALLY

CAUDATE, -S adj having a tail or a tail-like appendage ▷ n lizard-like amphibian

CAUDATED same as ► caudate

CAUDATES ► caudate

CAUDEX, -ES, CAUDICES n thickened persistent stem base of some herbaceous perennial plants

CAUDICLE n stalk to which an orchid's pollen masses are attached

CAUDILLO n (in Spanish-speaking countries) a military or political leader

CAUDLE, -D, -S, CAUDLING n hot spiced wine drink made with gruel, formerly used medicinally ▷ vb make such a drink

CAUDRON, -S Spenserian spelling of ► cauldron

CAUF, CAUVES n cage for holding live fish in the water

CAUGHT ► catch

CAUK, -S n type of barite

CAUKER, -S n one who caulks

CAUKS ► cauk

CAUL, -S n membrane sometimes covering a child's head at birth

CAULD, -ER, -EST, -S a Scot word for ► cold

CAULDRON n large pot used for boiling

CAULDS ► cauld

CAULES ► caulis

CAULICLE n small stalk or stem

CAULINE adj relating to or growing from a plant stem

CAULIS, CAULES n main stem of a plant

CAULK, -ED, -S vb fill in (cracks) with paste etc

CAULKER -S

CAULKING ▸ caulk

CAULKS ▸ caulk

CAULOME, -S n plant's stem structure, considered as a whole

CAULS ▸ caul

CAUM, -ED, -ING, -S same as ▸ cam

CAUP, -S n type of quaich

CAURI, -S n former coin of Guinea

CAUSA, -E n reason or cause

CAUSABLE ▸ cause

CAUSAE ▸ causa

CAUSAL, -S adj of or being a cause ▸ n something that suggests a cause

CAUSALLY

CAUSE, -D, -S, CAUSING n something that produces a particular effect ▸ vb be the cause of

CAUSEN old infinitive of ▸ cause

CAUSER, -S ▸ cause

CAUSERIE n informal talk or conversational piece of writing

CAUSERS ▸ causer

CAUSES ▸ cause

CAUSEWAY n raised path or road across water or marshland

CAUSEY, -S n cobbled street ▸ vb cobble

CAUSEYED

CAUSING ▸ cause

CAUSTIC, -S adj capable of burning by chemical action ▸ n caustic substance

CAUTEL, -S n craftiness

CAUTER, -S n cauterizing instrument

CAUTERY n coagulation of blood or destruction of body tissue by cauterizing

CAUTION, -S n care, esp in the face of danger ▸ vb warn, advise

CAUTIOUS adj showing caution

CAUVES ▸ cauf

CAVA, -S n Spanish sparkling wine

CAVALERO n cavalier

CAVALIER adj showing haughty disregard ▸ n gallant gentleman

CAVALLA, -S n type of tropical fish

CAVALLY same as ▸ cavalla

CAVALRY n part of the army

CAVAS ▸ cava

CAVASS, -ES n Turkish armed police officer

CAVATINA, CAVATINE n solo song resembling a simple aria

CAVE, -D, -S n hollow in the side of a hill or cliff ▸ vb hollow out

CAVEAT, -ED, -S n warning ▸ vb introduce a caveat

CAVEATOR n person who enters a caveat

CAVEATS ▸ caveat

CAVED ▸ cave

CAVEFISH n small N American freshwater fish

CAVEL, -S n drawing of lots among miners for an easy and profitable place at the coalface

CAVELIKE adj resembling a cave

CAVELS ▸ cavel

CAVEMAN, CAVEMEN n prehistoric cave dweller

CAVER ▸ cave

CAVERN, -ED, -S n large cave ▸ vb shut in or as if in a cavern

CAVERS ▸ caving

CAVES ▸ cave

CAVESSON n kind of hard noseband, used (esp formerly) in breaking a horse in

CAVETTO, CAVETTI, -S n concave moulding, shaped to a quarter circle in cross section

CAVIAR, -S n salted sturgeon roe, regarded as a delicacy

CAVIARE, -S same as ▸ caviar

CAVIARIE same as ▸ caviar

CAVIARS ▸ caviar

CAVICORN adj (of sheep, goats, etc) having hollow horns as distinct from the solid antlers of deer ▸ n sheep, goat, etc with hollow horns

CAVIE n hen coop

CAVIER, -S same as ▸ caviar

CAVIES ▸ cavy

CAVIL, -ED, -ING, -LED, -S vb make petty objections ▸ n petty objection

CAVILER, -S

CAVILLER ▸ cavil

CAVILS ▸ cavil

CAVING, CAVERS, -S n sport of exploring caves

CAVITARY adj containing cavities

CAVITATE vb form cavities or bubbles

CAVITIED ▸ cavity

CAVITY, CAVITIES n hollow space

CAVORT, -ED, -S vb skip about

CAVORTER

CAVY, CAVIES n type of small rodent

CAW, -ED, -S n cry of a crow, rook, or raven ▸ vb make this cry

CAWING -S

CAWK, -S same as ▸ cauk

CAWKER, -S n metal projection on a horse's shoe to prevent slipping

CAWKS ▸ cawk

CAWS ▸ caw

CAXON, -S n type of wig

CAY, -S n low island or bank composed of sand and coral fragments

CAYENNE, -S n very hot condiment

CAYENNED adj seasoned with cayenne

CAYENNES ▸ cayenne

CAYMAN, -S n S American reptile similar to an alligator

CAYS ▸ cay

CAYUSE, -S n small pony used by Native Americans

CAZ short for ▸ casual

> **Caz** is slang for casual, and is one of the essential short words for using the Z.

CAZH adj casual

CAZIQUE, -S same as ▸ cacique

> This word means a Native American chief, and its plural **caziques** was once played as a 9-timer (that is, a word spanning two triple-word squares) earning the highest score for a single word ever officially recorded in a game of Scrabble, 392 points.

CEAS same as ▸ caese

CEASE, -D, -S vb bring or come to an end

CEASING -S

CEAZE, -D, -S, CEAZING obsolete spelling of ▸ seize

CEBID, -S n any member of the Cebidae family of New World monkeys

CEBOID, -S same as ▸ cebid

CECA ▸ cecum

CECAL ▸ cecum

CECALLY ▸ cecum

CECILS pl n fried meatballs

CECITIES ▸ cecity

CECITIS n inflammation of the c(a)ecum

CECITY, CECITIES n rare word for blindness

CECROPIA n large North American moth

CECROPIN n antimicrobial peptide originally derived from the cecropia moth

CECUM, CECA same as ▸ **caecum**

CEDAR, -S n evergreen coniferous tree ▷ adj made of the wood of a cedar tree

CEDARED adj covered with cedars

CEDARN adj relating to cedar

CEDARS ▸ cedar

CEDARY adj like cedar

CEDE, -D, -S, CEDING vb surrender (territory or legal rights)

CEDER -S

CEDI, -S n standard monetary unit of Ghana, divided into 100 pesewas

CEDILLA, -S n character placed under a c in some languages

CEDING ▸ cede

CEDIS ▸ cedi

CEDRATE, -S n citron

CEDRINE adj relating to cedar

CEDULA, -S n form of identification in Spanish-speaking countries

CEE, -S n third letter of the alphabet

CEIBA, -S n type of tropical tree

CEIL, -ED, -S vb line (a ceiling) with plaster, boarding, etc

CEILER -S

CEILI, -S variant spelling of ▸ **ceilidh**

CEILIDH, -S n social gathering for singing and dancing

CEILING, -S n inner upper surface of a room ▷ vb make a ceiling

CEILIS ▸ ceili

CEILS ▸ ceil

CEINTURE n belt

CEL, -S short for ▸ **celluloid**

CELADON, -S n type of porcelain having a greyish-green glaze: mainly Chinese

CELEB, -S n celebrity

CELERIAC n variety of celery with a large turnip-like root

CELERIES ▸ celery

CELERITY n swiftness

CELERY, CELERIES n vegetable with long green crisp edible stalks

CELESTA, -S n instrument like a small piano

CELESTE, -S same as ▸ **celesta**

CELIAC, -S same as ▸ **coeliac**

CELIBACY ▸ celibate

CELIBATE adj unmarried, esp because of a religious vow ▷ n celibate person

CELL, -S n smallest unit of an organism that is able to function independently

CELLA, -E n inner room of a classical temple

CELLAR, -ED, -S n underground room for storage ▷ vb store in a cellar

CELLARER n monastic official responsible for food, drink, etc

CELLARET n case, cabinet, or sideboard with compartments for holding wine bottles

CELLARS ▸ cellar

CELLED adj cellular

CELLI ▸ cello

CELLING, -S n formation of cells

CELLIST, -S ▸ cello

CELLMATE n person with whom a prisoner shares a prison cell

CELLO, CELLI, -S n large low-pitched instrument of the violin family

CELLOSE, -S n disaccharide obtained by the hydrolysis of cellulose by cellulase

CELLS ▸ cell

CELLULAR adj of or consisting of cells ▷ n cellular phone

CELLULE, -S n very small cell

CELOM, -ATA, -S same as ▸ **coelom**

CELOMIC

CELOSIA, -S same as > **cockscomb**

CELOTEX n tradename for a type of insulation board

CELS ▸ cel

CELT, -S n stone or metal axelike instrument with a bevelled edge

CEMBALO, CEMBALI, -S n harpsichord

CEMBRA, -S n Swiss pine

CEMENT, -ED, -S n powder mixed with water and sand to make mortar or concrete ▷ vb join, bind, or cover with cement

CEMENTA ▸ cementum

CEMENTED ▸ cement

CEMENTER ▸ cement

CEMENTS ▸ cement

CEMENTUM, CEMENTA n thin bonelike tissue that covers the dentine in the root of a tooth

CEMETERY n place where dead people are buried

CEMITARE obsolete spelling of ▸ **scimitar**

CENACLE, -S n supper room, esp one on an upper floor

CENDRE adj ash-blond

CENOBITE same as > **coenobite**

CENOTAPH n monument honouring soldiers who died in a war

CENOTE, -S n natural well formed by the collapse of an overlying limestone crust

CENOZOIC adj of or relating to the most recent geological era

CENS n type of annual property rent

CENSE, -D, -S, CENSING vb burn incense near or before (an altar, shrine, etc)

CENSER, -S n container for burning incense

CENSES ▸ cense

CENSING ▸ cense

CENSOR, -ED, -S n person authorized to prohibit anything considered obscene or objectionable ▷ vb ban or cut parts of (a film, book, etc)

CENSUAL ▸ census

CENSURE, -D, -S n severe disapproval ▷ vb criticize severely

CENSURER

CENSUS, -ED, -ES n official count of a population ▷ vb conduct a census

CENT, -S n hundredth part of a monetary unit such as the dollar or euro

CENTAGE, -S n rate per hundred

CENTAI ▸ centas

CENTAL, -S n unit of weight equal to 100 pounds (45.3 kilograms)

CENTARE, -S same as ▸ **centiare**

CENTAS, CENTAI n monetary unit of Lithuania

CENTAUR, -S n mythical creature

CENTAURY n plant with purplish-pink flowers

CENTAVO, -S n monetary unit in Portugal and many Latin American countries

CENTER, -ED, -S same as
▷ **centre**

CENTESIS, CENTESES n
surgical puncturing of part
of the body with a hollow
needle, to extract fluid

CENTIARE n unit of area equal
to one square metre

CENTILE, -S n (in statistics)
another word for percentile

CENTIME, -S n monetary unit
worth one hundredth of a
franc

CENTIMO, -S n monetary
unit of Costa Rica, Paraguay,
Peru, and Venezuela

CENTINEL obsolete variant of
▷ **sentinel**

CENTNER, -S n unit of weight
equivalent to 100 pounds
(45.3 kilograms)

CENTO, -NES, -S n piece
of writing composed of
quotations from other
authors

CENTOIST n one who
composes centos

CENTONEL obsolete variant of
▷ **sentinel**

CENTONES ▷ **cento**

CENTOS ▷ **cento**

CENTRA ▷ **centrum**

CENTRAL, -S adj of, at, or
forming the centre ▷ n
workplace serving as a
telecommunications facility

CENTRE, -S n middle point or
part ▷ vb put in the centre of
something

CENTRED adj mentally and
emotionally confident,
focused, and well-balanced

CENTRES ▷ **centre**

CENTRIC adj being central or
having a centre

CENTRIES ▷ **centry**

CENTRING n temporary
structure used to support an
arch during construction

CENTRISM ▷ **centrist**

CENTRIST n person favouring
political moderation

CENTRODE n locus produced
by plotting the course of two
bodies in relative motion

CENTROID n centre of mass of
an object of uniform density,
esp of a geometric figure

CENTRUM, CENTRA, -S
n main part or body of a
vertebra

CENTRY, CENTRIES obsolete
variant of ▷ **sentry**

CENTS ▷ **cent**

CENTU n Lithuanian money
unit

CENTUM, -S adj denoting or
belonging to certain Indo-
European languages ▷ n
hundred

CENTUPLE n one hundredfold

CENTURY n period of 100
years

CEORL, -S n freeman of the
lowest class in Anglo-Saxon
England

CEORLISH

CEP, -S another name for
▷ **porcino**

CEPAGE, -S n grape variety or
type of wine

CEPE, -S another spelling of
▷ **cep**

CEPHALAD adv towards the
head or anterior part

CEPHALIC adj of or relating
to the head ▷ n remedy for
pains in the head

CEPHALIN n phospholipid,
similar to lecithin, that
occurs in the nerve tissue
and brain

CEPHEID, -S n type of variable
star with a regular cycle of
variations in luminosity

CEPS ▷ **cep**

CERAMAL, -S same as
▷ **cermet**

CERAMIC n hard brittle
material ▷ adj made of
ceramic

CERAMICS n art of producing
ceramic objects

CERAMIDE n class of
compounds used as
moisturizers

CERAMIST ▷ **ceramics**

CERASIN, -S n meta-arabinic
acid

CERASTES n type of
venomous snake, esp the
horned viper

CERATE, -S n hard ointment or
medicated paste

CERATED adj (of certain birds,
such as the falcon) having
a cere

CERATES ▷ **cerate**

CERATIN, -S same as
▷ **keratin**

CERATOID adj having the
shape or texture of animal
horn

CERCAL adj of or relating to
a tail

CERCARIA n one of the larval
forms of trematode worms

CERCI ▷ **cercus**

CERCIS, -ES n type of tree or
shrub

CERCLAGE n treatment of
a malfunctioning cervix by

means of a suture in early
pregnancy

CERCOPID n froghopper or
spittlebug

CERCUS, CERCI n one of a
pair of sensory appendages
on some insects and other
arthropods

CERE, -D, -S, CERING n soft
waxy swelling at the base of
the upper beak of a parrot
▷ vb wrap in a cerecloth

CEREAL, -S n grass plant with
edible grain, such as oat or
wheat

CEREBRA ▷ **cerebrum**

CEREBRAL same as
> **cacuminal**

CEREBRIC ▷ **cerebrum**

CEREBRUM, CEREBRA n main
part of the brain

CERED ▷ **cere**

CEREMENT n any burial
clothes

CEREMONY n formal act or
ritual

CEREOUS adj waxlike

CERES ▷ **cere**

CERESIN, -S n white wax
extracted from ozocerite

CERESINE same as ▷ **ceresin**

CERESINS ▷ **ceresin**

CEREUS, -ES n type of
tropical American cactus

CERGE n large altar candle

CERIA, -S n ceric oxide

CERIC adj of or containing
cerium in the tetravalent
state

CERING ▷ **cere**

CERIPH, -S same as ▷ **serif**

CERISE, -S adj cherry-red ▷ n
moderate to dark red colour

CERITE, -S n hydrous silicate
of cerium

CERIUM, -S n steel-grey
metallic element

CERMET, -S n material
consisting of a metal matrix
with ceramic particles
disseminated through it

CERNE, -D, -S, CERNING
obsolete variant of ▷ **encircle**

CERNUOUS adj (of some
flowers or buds) drooping

CERO, -S n type of large food
fish

CEROON, -S n hide-covered
bale

CEROS ▷ **cero**

CEROTIC adj as in **cerotic acid**
white insoluble odourless
wax

CEROTYPE n process for
preparing a printing plate

C

CEROUS adj of or containing cerium in the trivalent state

CERRADO, -S n vast area of tropical savanna in Brazil

CERRIAL adj relating to the cerris

CERRIS, -ES n Turkey oak

CERT, -S n certainty

CERTAIN adj positive and confident

CERTES adv with certainty

CERTIE n as in **by my certie** assuredly

CERTIFY vb confirm, attest to

CERTS ▶ cert

CERTY n as in **by my certy** assuredly

CERULE adj sky-blue

CERULEAN n deep blue colour

CERULEIN n type of dyestuff

CERUMEN, -S n wax secreted by glands in the external ear

CERUSE, -S n white lead

CERUSITE same as > cerussite

CERVELAS n French garlicky pork sausage

CERVELAT n smoked sausage made from pork and beef

CERVEZA, -S n Spanish word for beer

CERVICAL adj of or relating to the neck or cervix

CERVICES ▶ cervix

CERVICUM n flexible region between the prothorax and head in insects

CERVID, -S n type of ruminant mammal characterized by the presence of antlers

CERVINE adj resembling or relating to a deer

CERVIX, CERVICES, -ES n narrow entrance of the womb

CESAREAN variant of > caesarean

CESARIAN US variant of > caesarean

CESIOUS same as ▶ caesious

CESIUM, -S same as ▶ caesium

CESS, -ED, -ES, -ING n any of several special taxes, such as a land tax in Scotland ▷ vb tax or assess for taxation

CESSE obsolete variant of ▶ cease

CESSED ▶ cess

CESSER, -S n coming to an end of a term interest or annuity

CESSES ▶ cess

CESSING ▶ cess

CESSION, -S n ceding

CESSPIT, -S same as ▶ cesspool

CESSPOOL n covered tank or pit for collecting and storing sewage or waste water

CESTA, -S n in jai alai, the basket used to throw and catch the pelota

CESTI ▶ cestus

CESTODE, -S n type of parasitic flatworm such as the tapeworms

CESTOI ▶ cestos

CESTOID, -S adj (esp of tapeworms and similar animals) ribbon-like in form ▷ n ribbon-like worm

CESTOS, CESTOI, -ES same as ▶ cestus

CESTUI, -S n legal term to designate a person

CESTUS, CESTI, -ES n girdle of Aphrodite

CESURA, -E, -S a variant spelling of ▶ caesura **CESURAL**

CESURE, -S same as ▶ caesura

CETACEAN n fish-shaped sea mammal such as a whale or dolphin ▷ adj relating to these mammals

CETANE, -S n colourless liquid hydrocarbon, used as a solvent

CETE, -S n group of badgers

CETERACH n scale-fern

CETES ▶ cete

CETOLOGY n branch of zoology concerned with the study of whales (cetaceans)

CETYL, -S n univalent alcohol radical

CETYWALL n valerian

CEVICHE, -S n Peruvian seafood dish

CEZVE, -S n small metal pot for brewing coffee

CH pron obsolete form of I

CHA, -S n tea

CHABLIS n dry white French wine

CHABOUK, -S n type of whip

CHABUK, -S same as ▶ chabouk

CHACE, -D, -S, CHACING obsolete variant of ▶ chase

CHACHKA, -S n cheap trinket

CHACING ▶ chace

CHACK, -ED, -ING, -S vb bite

CHACMA, -S n type of baboon with coarse greyish hair, occurring in S and E Africa

CHACO, -ES same as ▶ shako

CHACONNE n musical form consisting of a set of variations on a repeated melodic bass line

CHACOS ▶ chaco

CHAD, -S n small pieces removed during the punching of holes in punch cards, printer paper, etc

CHADAR, -S same as ▶ chuddar

CHADARIM ▶ cheder

CHADARS ▶ chadar

CHADDAR, -S same as ▶ chuddar

CHADDOR, -S same as ▶ chuddar

CHADLESS adj (of a keypunch) not producing chads

CHADO, -S n Japanese tea ceremony

CHADOR, -S same as ▶ chuddar

CHADOS ▶ chado

CHADRI n shroud which covers the body from head to foot

CHADS ▶ chad

CHAEBOL, -S n large, usually family-owned, business group in South Korea

CHAETA, -E n the chitinous bristles on the body of annelids **CHAETAL**

CHAFE, -D, -S, CHAFING vb make sore or worn by rubbing

CHAFER, -S n large beetle

CHAFES ▶ chafe

CHAFF, -ED, -S n grain husks ▷ vb tease good-naturedly

CHAFFER, -S vb haggle

CHAFFERY n bargaining

CHAFFIER ▶ chaffy

CHAFFING ▶ chaff

CHAFFRON same as ▶ chamfron

CHAFFS ▶ chaff

CHAFFY, CHAFFIER ▶ chaff

CHAFING ▶ chafe

CHAFT, -S n jaw

CHAGAN, -S n Mongolian royal or imperial title

CHAGRIN, -S n annoyance and disappointment ▷ vb embarrass and annoy

CHAI, -S n tea, esp as made in India with added spices

CHAIN, -ED, -ING, -S n flexible length of connected metal links ▷ vb restrict or fasten with or as if with a chain

CHAINE, -S adj (of a dance turn) producing a full rotation for every two steps taken ▷ vb produce a full rotation for every two steps taken

CHAINED ▸ chain

CHAINER, -S *n* person who chains

CHAINES ▸ chaine

CHAINING ▸ chain

CHAINLET *n* small chain

CHAINMAN, CHAINMEN *n* person who does the chaining in a survey

CHAINS ▸ chain

CHAINSAW *n* motor-driven saw with teeth linked in a continuous chain ▷ *vb* operate a chainsaw

CHAIR, -ED, -ING, -S *n* seat with a back, for one person ▷ *vb* preside over (a meeting)

CHAIRMAN, CHAIRMEN *n* person in charge of a company's board of directors or a meeting ▷ *vb* act as chairman of

CHAIRS ▸ chair

CHAIS ▸ chai

CHAISE, -S *n* light horse-drawn carriage

CHAKRA, -S *n* (in yoga) any of the seven major energy centres in the body

CHAL, -S *n* in Romany, person or fellow

CHALAH, -S, CHALOT, CHALOTH *same as* ▸ challah

CHALAN, -ED, -S *vb* (in India) to cause an accused person to appear before a magistrate ▷ *n* invoice, pass, or voucher

CHALAZA, -E, -S *n* one of a pair of spiral threads holding the yolk of a bird's egg in position

CHALAZAL

CHALAZIA ▸ chalazion

CHALCID, -S *n* type of tiny insect

CHALDER, -S *n* former Scottish dry measure

CHALDRON *n* unit of capacity equal to 36 bushels

CHALEH, -S *same as* ▸ challah

CHALET, -S *n* kind of Swiss wooden house with a steeply sloping roof

CHALICE, -S *n* large goblet

CHALICED *adj* (of plants) having cup-shaped flowers

CHALICES ▸ chalice

CHALK, -ED, -ING, -S *n* soft white rock consisting of calcium carbonate ▷ *vb* draw or mark with chalk

CHALKIER ▸ chalky

CHALKING ▸ chalk

CHALKPIT *n* quarry for chalk

CHALKS ▸ chalk

CHALKY, CHALKIER ▸ chalk

CHALLA, -S *same as* ▸ challah

CHALLAH, -S, CHALLOT, CHALLOTH *n* type of bread

CHALLAN, -S *same as* ▸ chalan

CHALLAS ▸ challa

CHALLIE, -S *same as* ▸ challis

CHALLIS *n* lightweight plain-weave fabric

CHALLOT ▸ challah

CHALLOTH ▸ challah

CHALLY *same as* ▸ challis

CHALONE, -S *n* any internal secretion that inhibits a physiological process or function

CHALONIC

CHALOT ▸ chalah

CHALOTH ▸ chalah

CHALS ▸ chal

CHALUPA, -S *n* Mexican dish

CHALUTZ *n* member of an organization of immigrants to Israeli agricultural settlements

CHAM, -S *an archaic word for* ▸ khan

CHAMADE, -S *n* (formerly) a signal by drum or trumpet inviting an enemy to a parley

CHAMBER *n* hall used for formal meetings ▷ *vb* act lasciviously

CHAMBERS *pl n* judge's room for hearing private cases not taken in open court

CHAMBRAY *n* smooth light fabric of cotton, linen, etc, with white weft and a coloured warp

CHAMBRE *adj* (of wine) at room temperature

CHAMELOT *same as* ▸ camlet

CHAMETZ *n* leavened food which may not be eaten during Passover

CHAMFER, -S *same as* ▸ chase

CHAMFRON *n* piece of armour for a horse's head

CHAMISA, -S *n* American shrub

CHAMISAL *n* place overgrown with chamiso

CHAMISAS ▸ chamisa

CHAMISE, -S *same as* ▸ chamiso

CHAMISO, -S *n* four-wing saltbush

CHAMLET, -S *same as* ▸ camlet

CHAMMY, CHAMMIED, CHAMMIES *same as* ▸ chamois

CHAMOIS *n* small mountain antelope or a piece of leather from its skin, used for polishing ▷ *vb* polish with a chamois

CHAMOIX *same as* ▸ chamois

CHAMP, -ED, -ING, -S *vb* chew noisily

CHAMPAC, -S *n* type of tree

CHAMPACA *same as* ▸ champac

CHAMPACS ▸ champac

CHAMPAK, -S *same as* ▸ champac

CHAMPART *n* granting of land to a person for a portion of the crops

CHAMPED ▸ champ

CHAMPER ▸ champ

CHAMPERS *n* champagne

CHAMPIER ▸ champy

CHAMPING ▸ champ

CHAMPION *n* overall winner of a competition ▷ *vb* support ▷ *adj* excellent ▷ *adv* very well

CHAMPS ▸ champ

CHAMPY, CHAMPIER *adj* (of earth) churned up (by cattle, for example)

CHAMS ▸ cham

CHANA, -S *n* (in Indian cookery) chickpeas

CHANCE, -D, -S, CHANCING *n* likelihood, probability ▷ *vb* risk, hazard

CHANCEL, -S *n* part of a church containing the altar and choir

CHANCER, -S *n* unscrupulous or dishonest opportunist

CHANCERY *n* Lord Chancellor's court, now a division of the High Court of Justice

CHANCES ▸ chance

CHANCEY *same as* ▸ chancy

CHANCIER ▸ chancy

CHANCILY ▸ chancy

CHANCING ▸ chance

CHANCRE, -S *n* small hard growth which is the first sign of syphilis

CHANCY, CHANCIER *adj* uncertain, risky

CHANDLER *n* dealer, esp in ships' supplies

CHANFRON *same as* ▸ chamfron

CHANG, -S *n* loud discordant noise

C

CHANGA interj in Indian English, an expression of approval or agreement

CHANGE, -D, -S, CHANGING n becoming different ▷ vb make or become different

CHANGER -S

CHANGEUP n type of baseball pitch

CHANGING ▶ change

CHANGS ▶ chang

CHANK, -S n shell of several types of sea conch, used to make bracelets

CHANNEL, -S n band of broadcasting frequencies ▷ vb direct or convey through a channel

CHANNER, -S n gravel

CHANOYO, -S a variant of ▶ chado

CHANOYU, -S same as ▶ chado

CHANSON, -S n song

CHANT, -ED, -ING, -S vb utter or sing (a slogan or psalm) ▷ n rhythmic or repetitious slogan

CHANTAGE n blackmail

CHANTED ▶ chant

CHANTER, -S n (on bagpipes) pipe on which the melody is played

CHANTEY, -S the usual US spelling for ▶ shanty

CHANTIE n chamber pot

CHANTIES ▶ chanty

CHANTING ▶ chant

CHANTOR, -S same as ▶ chanter

CHANTRY n endowment for the singing of Masses for the founder

CHANTS ▶ chant

CHANTY, CHANTIES same as ▶ shanty

CHAO n Vietnamese rice porridge

CHAOLOGY n study of chaos theory

CHAORDIC adj combining elements of chaos and order

CHAOS, -ES n complete disorder or confusion

CHAOTIC

CHAP, -PED, -PING, -S n man or boy ▷ vb make or become raw and cracked, esp by exposure to cold

CHAPATI, -S n (in Indian cookery) flat thin unleavened bread

CHAPATTI same as ▶ chapati

CHAPBOOK n book of popular ballads, stories, etc, formerly sold by chapmen or pedlars

CHAPE, -S n metal tip or trimming for a scabbard

CHAPEAU, -S, -X n hat

CHAPEL, -S n place of worship with its own altar, within a church

CHAPELRY n district legally assigned to and served by an Anglican chapel

CHAPELS ▶ chapel

CHAPERON n older or married woman who supervises a young unmarried woman ▷ vb act as a chaperon to

CHAPES ▶ chape

CHAPESS n woman

CHAPITER same as ▶ capital

CHAPKA, -S same as ▶ czapka

CHAPLAIN n clergyman attached to a chapel, military body, or institution

CHAPLESS adj lacking a lower jaw

CHAPLET, -S n garland for the head ▷ vb create a garland

CHAPMAN, CHAPMEN n travelling pedlar

CHAPPAL, -S n one of a pair of sandals, usually of leather, worn in India

CHAPPATI same as ▶ chapati

CHAPPED ▶ chap

CHAPPESS same as ▶ chapess

CHAPPIE, -S n man or boy

CHAPPIER ▶ chappy

CHAPPIES ▶ chappie

CHAPPING ▶ chap

CHAPPY, CHAPPIER adj (of skin) chapped

CHAPS ▶ chap

CHAPT adj chapped

CHAPTER, -S n division of a book ▷ vb divide into chapters

CHAPTREL n capital of a pillar supporting an arch

CHAQUETA n South American cowboy jacket

CHAR, -RED, -RING, -S vb blacken by partial burning ▷ n charwoman

CHARA n type of green freshwater algae

CHARACID same as ▶ characin

CHARACIN n type of small carnivorous freshwater fish of Central and S America and Africa

CHARACT, -S n distinctive mark

CHARADE n absurd pretence

CHARADES n game in which teams act out each syllable of a word or phrase

CHARANGA n type of orchestra used in performing traditional Cuban music

CHARANGO n Andean ten-stringed mandolin

CHARCOAL n black substance formed by partially burning wood ▷ adj very dark grey ▷ vb write, draw, or blacken with charcoal

CHARD, -S n variety of beet

CHARE, -D, -S, CHARING same as ▶ char

CHARET, -S obsolete variant of ▶ chariot

CHARETTE n public brainstorming session

CHARGE, -D, -S vb ask as a price ▷ n price charged

CHARGER, -S n device for charging an accumulator

CHARGES ▶ charge

CHARGING n act of charging

CHARIDEE n jocular spelling of charity, as pronounced in a mid-Atlantic accent

CHARIER ▶ chary

CHARIEST ▶ chary

CHARILY adv cautiously

CHARING ▶ chare

CHARIOT, -S n two-wheeled horse-drawn vehicle ▷ vb ride in a chariot

CHARISM, -S same as ▶ charisma

CHARISMA n person's power to attract or influence people

CHARISMS ▶ charism

CHARITY n organization that gives help, such as money or food, to those in need

CHARK, -ED, -ING, -S vb char

CHARKA, -S same as ▶ charkha

CHARKED ▶ chark

CHARKHA, -S n (in India) a spinning wheel, esp for cotton

CHARKING ▶ chark

CHARKS ▶ chark

CHARLADY same as ▶ charwoman

CHARLEY, -S n as in **charley horse** muscle stiffness after strenuous exercise

CHARLIE, -S n fool

CHARLIER n as in **charlier shoe** special light horseshoe

CHARLIES ▶ charlie

CHARLOCK n weed with hairy leaves and yellow flowers

CHARM, -S n attractive quality ▷ vb attract, delight

C

CHARMED adj delighted or fascinated

CHARMER, -S n attractive person

CHARMFUL adj highly charming or enchanting

CHARMING adj attractive

CHARMS ▸ charm

CHARNECO n type of sweet wine

CHARNEL, -S adj ghastly ▷ n ghastly thing

CHAROSET n dish eaten at Passover

CHARPAI, -S same as ▸ charpoy

CHARPIE, -S n lint pieces used to make surgical dressings

CHARPOY, -S n type of bedstead

CHARQUI, -S n meat, esp beef, cut into strips and dried

CHARQUID

CHARR, -S same as ▸ char

CHARRED ▸ char

CHARRIER ▸ charry

CHARRING ▸ char

CHARRO, -S n Mexican cowboy

CHARRS ▸ charr

CHARRY, CHARRIER adj of or relating to charcoal

CHARS ▸ char

CHART, -ED, -ING, -S n graph, table, or diagram showing information ▷ vb plot the course of

CHARTA, -S n charter

CHARTED ▸ chart

CHARTER, -S n document granting or demanding certain rights ▷ vb hire by charter

CHARTING ▸ chart

CHARTISM n historical reform movement in Britain

CHARTIST n supporter of chartism

CHARTS ▸ chart

CHARY, CHARIER, CHARIEST adj wary, careful

CHAS ▸ cha

CHASE, -D, -S vb run after quickly in order to catch or drive away ▷ n chasing, pursuit

CHASER -S

CHASING, -S ▸ chase

CHASM, -S n deep crack in the earth ▷ vb create a chasm

CHASMAL

CHASMED

CHASMIC

CHASMIER ▸ chasmy

CHASMS ▸ chasm

CHASMY, CHASMIER adj full of chasms

CHASSE, -D, -ED, -S n one of a series of gliding steps in ballet ▷ vb perform either of these steps

CHASSEUR n member of a unit specially trained and equipped for swift deployment ▷ adj designating or cooked in a sauce consisting of white wine and mushrooms

CHASSIS n frame, wheels, and mechanical parts of a vehicle

CHASTE, -R, -ST adj pure and modest

CHASTELY

CHASTEN, -S vb subdue by criticism

CHASTER ▸ chaste

CHASTEST ▸ chaste

CHASTISE vb scold severely

CHASTITY n state of being chaste

CHASUBLE n long sleeveless robe worn by a priest when celebrating Mass

CHAT, -S, -TED, -TING n informal conversation ▷ vb have an informal conversation

CHATBOT, -S n computer program that simulates conversation with human users over the internet

CHATCHKA variant of > tchotchke

CHATCHKE same as > tchotchke

CHATEAU, -S, -X n French castle

CHATLINE n telephone service enabling callers to join in general conversation with each other

CHATON, -S n in jewellery, a stone with a reflective metal foil backing

CHATROOM n site on the Internet where users have group discussions by e-mail

CHATS ▸ chat

CHATTA, -S n umbrella

CHATTED ▸ chat

CHATTEL, -S n item of movable personal property

CHATTER, -S vb speak quickly and continuously about unimportant things ▷ n idle talk

CHATTERY

CHATTI, -S n (in India) earthenware pot

CHATTIER ▸ chatty

CHATTIES ▸ chatty

CHATTILY ▸ chatty

CHATTING ▸ chat

CHATTIS ▸ chatti

CHATTY, CHATTIER, CHATTIES adj (of a person) fond of friendly, informal conversation ▷ n (in India) earthenware pot

CHAUFE, -D, -S, CHAUFING obsolete variant of ▸ chafe

CHAUFER, -S same as ▸ chauffer

CHAUFES ▸ chaufe

CHAUFF, -ED, -S obsolete variant of ▸ chafe

CHAUFFER n small portable heater or stove

CHAUFFS ▸ chauff

CHAUFING ▸ chaufe

CHAUMER, -S n chamber

CHAUNCE, -D, -S archaic variant of ▸ chance

CHAUNGE, -S archaic variant of ▸ change

CHAUNT, -ED, -S a less common variant of ▸ chant

CHAUNTER

CHAUNTRY same as ▸ chantry

CHAUNTS ▸ chaunt

CHAUSSES n tight-fitting medieval garment covering the feet and legs, usually made of chain mail

CHAUVIN, -S n chauvinist

CHAV, -S n insulting word for a young working-class person who wears casual sports clothes

CHAVE vb old dialect term for "I have"

CHAVETTE n insulting word for a young working-class woman who wears casual sports clothes

CHAVISH ▸ chav

CHAVS ▸ chav

CHAVVY, CHAVVIER adj relating to or like a chav

CHAW, -ED, -ING, -S vb chew (tobacco), esp without swallowing it ▷ n something chewed, esp a plug of tobacco

CHAWDRON n entrails

CHAWED ▸ chaw

CHAWER, -S ▸ chaw

CHAWING ▸ chaw

CHAWK, -S n jackdaw

CHAWS ▸ chaw

CHAY, -S n plant of the madder family

CHAYA, -S same as ▸ chay

CHAYOTE, -S n tropical climbing plant

CHAYROOT n root of the chay plant

CHAYS ► chay

CHAZAN, -IM, -S same as ► cantor

CHAZZAN, -S variant of ► chazan

CHAZZEN, -S same as ► chazzan

CHE pron dialectal form meaning "I"

CHEAP, -ED, -ER, -EST, -ING, -S adj costing relatively little ▷ adv at very little cost ▷ n bargain ▷ vb take the cheapest option

CHEAPEN, -S vb lower the reputation of

CHEAPER ► cheap

CHEAPEST ► cheap

CHEAPIE, -S n something inexpensive

CHEAPING ► cheap

CHEAPISH ► cheap

CHEAPLY ► cheap

CHEAPO, -S n very cheap and possibly shoddy thing

CHEAPS ► cheap

CHEAPY same as ► cheapie

CHEAT, -ED, -S vb act dishonestly to gain profit or advantage ▷ n person who cheats

CHEATER -S

CHEATERY n cheating

CHEATING ► cheat

CHEATS ► cheat

CHEBEC, -S n type of boat

CHECHAKO same as > cheechako

CHECHIA, -S n Berber skullcap

CHECK, -ED, -S vb examine or investigate ▷ n control designed to ensure accuracy

CHECKBOX n small clickable box on a computer screen

CHECKED ► check

CHECKER same as ► chequer

CHECKERS n game for two players using a checkerboard and small pieces

CHECKIER ► checky

CHECKING n act of checking

CHECKOFF n paying of an employee's union dues straight from their salary

CHECKOUT n counter in a supermarket, where customers pay

CHECKROW n row of plants, esp corn ▷ vb plant in checkrows

CHECKS ► check

CHECKSUM n digit attached to the end of a message to verify data

CHECKUP, -S n thorough medical examination

CHECKY, CHECKIER adj having a pattern of alternating tinctures or furs

CHEDARIM same as ► chadarim

CHEDDAR, -S n type of smooth hard yellow or whitish cheese

CHEDDARY

CHEDDITE n type of explosive

CHEDER, CHADARIM, -S n Jewish religious education

CHEDITE, -S same as ► cheddite

CHEEK, -ED, -ING, -S n either side of the face below the eye ▷ vb speak impudently to

CHEEKFUL n quantity that can be held in a cheek

CHEEKIER ► cheeky

CHEEKILY ► cheeky

CHEEKING ► cheek

CHEEKS ► cheek

CHEEKY, CHEEKIER adj impudent, disrespectful

CHEEP, -ED, -ING, -S n young bird's high-pitched cry ▷ vb utter a cheep

CHEEPER -S

CHEER, -ED vb applaud or encourage with shouts ▷ n shout of applause or encouragement

CHEERER -S

CHEERFUL adj having a happy disposition

CHEERIER ► cheery

CHEERILY ► cheery

CHEERING n act of cheering

CHEERIO, -S interj goodbye ▷ n small red cocktail sausage ▷ sentence substitute farewell greeting

CHEERLED > cheerlead

CHEERLY adv cheerful or cheerfully

CHEERO, -S same as ► cheerio

CHEERS interj drinking toast ▷ sentence substitute drinking toast

CHEERY, CHEERIER adj cheerful

CHEESE, -D, -S, CHEESING n food made from coagulated milk curd ▷ vb stop

CHEESIER ► cheesy

CHEESILY ► cheesy

CHEESING ► cheese

CHEESY, CHEESIER adj like cheese

CHEETAH, -S n large fast-running spotted African wild cat

CHEEWINK same as ► chewink

CHEF, -ED, -FED, -FING, -ING, -S n cook in a restaurant ▷ vb work as a chef

CHEFDOM, -S n state or condition of being a chef

CHEFED ► chef

CHEFFED ► chef

CHEFFIER ► cheffy

CHEFFING ► chef

CHEFFY, CHEFFIER adj relating to or characteristic of chefs

CHEFING ► chef

CHEFS ► chef

CHEGOE, -S same as ► chigger

CHEKA, -S n secret police set up in Russia in 1917

CHEKIST, -S n member of the cheka

CHELA, -E, -S n disciple of a religious teacher

CHELATE, -D, -S n coordination compound ▷ adj of or possessing chelae ▷ vb form a chelate

CHELATOR

CHELIPED n (on a arthropod) either of two legs which each carry a claw

CHELLUP, -S n noise

CHELOID, -S a variant spelling of ► keloid

CHELONE, -S n hardy N American plant

CHELP, -ED, -ING, -S vb (esp of women or children) to chatter or speak out of turn

CHEM, -S n chemistry

CHEMIC, -S vb bleach ▷ n chemist

CHEMICAL n substance used in or resulting from a reaction involving changes to atoms or molecules ▷ adj of chemistry or chemicals

CHEMICS ► chemic

CHEMISE, -S n woman's loose-fitting slip

CHEMISM, -S n chemical action

CHEMIST, -S n shop selling medicines and cosmetics

CHEMMY, CHEMMIES n gambling card game

CHEMO, -S n short form of chemotherapy

CHEMS ► chem

CHEMURGY n branch of chemistry

CHENAR, -S n oriental plane tree

CHENET, -S another word for ► genip

CHENILLE n (fabric of) thick tufty yarn

CHENIX, -ES n ancient measure, slightly more than a quart

CHENOPOD n plant of the beetroot family

CHEQUE, -S n written order to one's bank to pay money from one's account

CHEQUER n piece used in Chinese chequers ▷ vb make irregular in colour or character

CHEQUERS n game of draughts

CHEQUES ► cheque

CHEQUIER ► chequy

CHEQUING adj as in **chequing account** (in Canada) account against which cheques can be drawn

CHEQUY, CHEQUIER same as ► **checky**

CHER adj dear or expensive

CHERE feminine variant of ► **cher**

CHERISH vb cling to (an idea or feeling)

CHEROOT, -S n cigar with both ends cut flat

CHERRY, CHERRIED, CHERRIER, CHERRIES, n small red or black fruit with a stone ▷ adj deep red ▷ vb cheer

CHERT, -S n microcrystalline form of silica

CHERTIER ► cherty

CHERTS ► chert

CHERTY, CHERTIER ► chert

CHERUB, -IM, -S n angel, often represented as a winged child

CHERUBIC

CHERUBIN n cherub ▷ adj cherubic

CHERUBS ► cherub

CHERUP, -ED, -S same as ► **chirrup**

CHERVIL, -S n aniseed-flavoured herb

CHESHIRE n breed of American pig

CHESIL, -S n gravel or shingle

CHESNUT, -S rare variant of ► **chestnut**

CHESS, -ES n board game for two players

CHESSEL, -S n mould used in cheese-making

CHESSES ► chess

CHESSMAN, CHESSMEN n piece used in chess

CHEST, -ED, -ING, -S n front of the body, from neck to waist

▷ vb hit with the chest, as with a ball in football

CHESTFUL n amount a chest will hold

CHESTIER ► chesty

CHESTILY ► chesty

CHESTING ► chest

CHESTNUT, n reddish-brown edible nut ▷ adj (of hair or a horse) reddish-brown

CHESTS ► chest

CHESTY, CHESTIER adj symptomatic of chest disease

CHETAH, -S same as ► **cheetah**

CHETH, -S same as ► **heth**

CHETNIK, -S n member of a Serbian nationalist paramilitary group

CHETRUM, -S n monetary unit in Bhutan

CHEVAL n as in **cheval glass** full-length mirror that can swivel

CHEVALET n bridge of a stringed musical instrument

CHEVEN, -S n chub

CHEVEREL n kid or goatskin leather

CHEVERIL same as ► **cheverel**

CHEVERON same as ► **chevron**

CHEVERYE same as ► **chiefery**

CHEVET, -S n semicircular or polygonal east end of a church

CHEVIED ► chevy

CHEVIES ► chevy

CHEVILLE n peg of a stringed musical instrument

CHEVIN, -S same as ► **cheven**

CHEVIOT, -S n type of British sheep reared for its wool

CHEVRE, -S n any cheese made from goats' milk

CHEVRET, -S n type of goats' cheese

CHEVRON, -S n V-shaped pattern ▷ vb make a chevron

CHEVRONY adj in heraldry, bearing chevrons

CHEVY, CHEVIED, CHEVIES, -ING same as ► **chivy**

CHEW, -ED, -ING, -S vb grind (food) between the teeth ▷ n act of chewing

CHEWABLE

CHEWER -S

CHEWET, -S n type of meat pie

CHEWIE n chewing gum

CHEWIER ► chewy

CHEWIES ► chewy

CHEWIEST ► chewy

CHEWING ► chew

CHEWINK, -S n towhee

CHEWS ► chew

CHEWY, CHEWIER, CHEWIES, CHEWIEST adj requiring a lot of chewing ▷ n dog's rubber toy

CHEZ prep at the home of

CHI, -S n 22nd letter of the Greek alphabet

> Chi is a letter of the Greek alphabet. It can also be spelt **khi**.

CHIA, -S n plant of the mint family

CHIACK, -ED, -S vb tease or banter ▷ n good-humoured banter

CHIANTI, -S n dry red Italian wine

CHIAO n Chinese coin equal to one tenth of one yuan

CHIAS ► chia

CHIASM, -S same as ► **chiasma**

CHIASMA, -S n biological term

CHIASMAL

CHIASMI ► chiasmus

CHIASMIC ► chiasma

CHIASMS ► chiasm

CHIASMUS, CHIASMI n reversal of the order of words in the second of two parallel phrases

CHIASTIC

CHIAUS, -ED, -ES same as ► **chouse**

CHIB, -BED, -BING, -S vb in Scots English, stab or slash with a sharp weapon ▷ n sharp weapon

CHIBOL, -S n spring onion

CHIBOUK, -S n Turkish tobacco pipe with an extremely long stem

CHIBS ► chib

CHIC, -ER, -EST, -S adj stylish, elegant ▷ n stylishness, elegance

CHICA, -S n Spanish young girl

CHICANA, -S n female chicano

CHICANE, -D, -S n obstacle in a motor-racing circuit ▷ vb deceive or trick by chicanery

CHICANER

CHICANO, -S n American citizen of Mexican origin

CHICAS ► chica

CHICCORY a variant spelling of ► **chicory**

CHICER ► chic

CHICEST ► chic

CHICH, -ES another word for ► **chickpea**

CHICHA, -S n Andean drink made from fermented maize

CHICHES ▶ chich
CHICHI, -ER, -S adj affectedly pretty or stylish ▷ n quality of being affectedly pretty or stylish
CHICK, -S n baby bird
CHICKEE, -S n open-sided, thatched building on stilts
CHICKEN, -S n domestic fowl ▷ adj cowardly ▷ vb lose one's nerve
CHICKORY same as ▶ chicory
CHICKPEA n edible yellow pealike seed
CHICKS ▶ chick
CHICLE, -S n gumlike substance obtained from the sapodilla
CHICLY ▶ chic
CHICNESS ▶ chic
CHICO, -S n spiny chenopodiaceous shrub
CHICON, -S same as ▶ chicory
CHICORY n plant whose leaves are used in salads
CHICOS ▶ chico
CHICOT, -S n dead tree
CHICS ▶ chic
CHIDE, CHID, CHIDDEN, -D, -S, CHODE vb rebuke, scold
CHIDER -S
CHIDING, -S ▶ chide
CHIEF, -ER, -EST, -S n head of a group of people ▷ adj most important
CHIEFDOM n any tribal social group led by a chief
CHIEFER ▶ chief
CHIEFERY n lands belonging to a chief
CHIEFESS n female chief
CHIEFEST ▶ chief
CHIEFLY adv especially ▷ adj of or relating to a chief or chieftain
CHIEFRY same as ▶ chiefery
CHIEFS ▶ chief
CHIEL, -S n young man
CHIELD, -S same as ▶ chiel
CHIELS ▶ chiel
CHIFFON, -S n fine see-through fabric ▷ adj made of chiffon
CHIFFONY
CHIGETAI n variety of the Asiatic wild ass of Mongolia
CHIGGER, -S n parasitic larva of various mites
CHIGNON, -S n knot of hair pinned up at the back of the head ▷ vb make a chignon
CHIGOE, -S same as ▶ chigger
CHIGRE, -S same as ▶ chigger
CHIK, -S n slatted blind

CHIKARA, -S n Indian seven-stringed musical instrument
CHIKHOR, -S same as ▶ chukar
CHIKOR, -S same as ▶ chukar
CHIKS ▶ chik
CHILD, -ED, -ING, -REN, -S n young human being, boy or girl ▷ vb give birth
CHILDBED n condition of giving birth to a child
CHILDE, -S n young man of noble birth
CHILDED ▶ child
CHILDER dialect variant of ▶ children
CHILDES ▶ childe
CHILDING ▶ child
CHILDISH adj immature, silly
CHILDLY ▶ child
CHILDREN ▶ child
CHILDS ▶ child
CHILE, -S a variant spelling of ▶ chilli
CHILI, -ES, -S same as ▶ chilli
CHILIAD, -S n group of one thousand
CHILIASM n belief in the Second Coming of Christ
CHILIAST
CHILIDOG n hot dog served with chilli sauce
CHILIES ▶ chili
CHILIS ▶ chili
CHILL, -ED, -EST, -S n feverish cold ▷ vb make (something) cool or cold ▷ adj unpleasantly cold
CHILLADA n spicy Mexican dish made of fried vegetables and pulses
CHILLAX vb take rest or recreation, as from work
CHILLED ▶ chill
CHILLER, -S n cooling or refrigerating device
CHILLEST ▶ chill
CHILLI, -ES n small red or green hot-tasting capsicum pod, used in cooking
CHILLIER ▶ chilly
CHILLIES ▶ chilli
CHILLILY ▶ chilly
CHILLING ▶ chill
CHILLIS ▶ chilli
CHILLS ▶ chill
CHILLUM, -S n short pipe used for smoking
CHILLY, CHILLIER adj moderately cold
CHILOPOD n type of arthropod of the class which includes the centipedes
CHIMAERA same as ▶ chimera

CHIMAR, -S same as ▶ chimere
CHIMB, -S same as ▶ chime
CHIMBLEY same as ▶ chimney
CHIMBLY same as ▶ chimney
CHIMBS ▶ chimb
CHIME, -D, -S, CHIMING n musical ringing sound of a bell or clock ▷ vb make a musical ringing sound
CHIMENEA n freestanding outdoor fireplace
CHIMER, -S ▶ chime
CHIMERA, -S n unrealistic hope or idea
CHIMERE, -S n gown worn by bishops
CHIMERIC same as ▶ chimera
CHIMERID n fish of the genus Chimaera
CHIMERS ▶ chimer
CHIMES ▶ chime
CHIMINEA n free-standing outdoor fireplace with a rounded body
CHIMING ▶ chime
CHIMLA, -S same as ▶ chimney
CHIMLEY, -S same as ▶ chimney
CHIMNEY, -S n hollow vertical structure for carrying away smoke from a fire ▷ vb climb two vertical, parallel, chimney-like rock faces
CHIMO interj Inuit greeting and toast
CHIMP, -S n chimpanzee
CHIN, -NED, -NING, -S n part of the face below the mouth ▷ vb hit someone in the chin
CHINA, -S n fine earthenware or porcelain
CHINAMAN, CHINAMEN n type of ball bowled in cricket
CHINAMPA n in Mesoamerican agriculture, an artificially created island used for growing crops
CHINAR, -S same as ▶ chenar
CHINAS ▶ china
CHINBONE n front part of the mandible which forms the chin
CHINCH, -ED, -ES n (S US) bedbug ▷ vb be frugal or miserly
CHINCHY adj tightfisted
CHINDIT, -S n Allied soldier fighting behind the Japanese lines in Burma during World War II
CHINE, -D, -S, CHINING same as ▶ chime

CHINESE adj of or relating to China

CHING, -S n high-pitched ring or chime

CHINING ▸ chine

CHINK, -ED, -ING, -S n small narrow opening ▷ vb make a light ringing sound

CHINKARA n Indian gazelle

CHINKED ▸ chink

CHINKIER ▸ chinky

CHINKING ▸ chink

CHINKS ▸ chink

CHINKY, CHINKIER ▸ chink

CHINLESS adj having a receding chin

CHINNED ▸ chin

CHINNING ▸ chin

CHINO n durable cotton twill cloth

CHINOIS n conical sieve

CHINONE, -S n benzoquinone

CHINOOK, -S n wind found in the Rocky Mountains

CHINOS pl n trousers made of a kind of hard-wearing cotton

CHINS ▸ chin

CHINSE, -D, -S, CHINSING vb fill the seams of a boat

CHINTS, -ES obsolete variant of ▸ chintz

CHINTZ, -ES n printed cotton fabric with a glazed finish

CHINTZY adj of or covered with chintz

CHINWAG, -S n chat

CHIP, -PED, -S n strip of potato, fried in deep fat ▷ vb break small pieces from

CHIPMUCK another word for ▸ chipmunk

CHIPMUNK n small squirrel-like N American rodent with a striped back

CHIPOTLE n dried chilli pepper

CHIPPED ▸ chip

CHIPPER, -S vb chirp or chatter

CHIPPIE same as ▸ chippy

CHIPPIER ▸ chippy

CHIPPIES ▸ chippy

CHIPPING ▸ chip

CHIPPY, CHIPPIER, CHIPPIES n fish-and-chip shop ▷ adj resentful or oversensitive about being perceived as inferior

CHIPS ▸ chip

CHIPSET, -S n highly integrated circuit on the motherboard of a computer

CHIRAGRA n gout occurring in the hands

CHIRAL > chirality

CHIRK, -ED, -ER, -EST, -ING, -S vb creak, like a door ▷ adj spritely; high-spirited

CHIRL, -ED, -ING, -S vb warble

CHIRM, -ED, -ING, -S n chirping of birds ▷ vb (esp of a bird) to chirp

CHIRO, -S n informal name for chiropractor

CHIRP, -ED, -S vb (of a bird or insect) make a short high-pitched sound ▷ n chirping sound

CHIRPER -S

CHIRPIER ▸ chirpy

CHIRPILY ▸ chirpy

CHIRPING n act of chirping

CHIRPS ▸ chirp

CHIRPY, CHIRPIER adj lively and cheerful

CHIRR, -ED, -ING, -S vb (esp of certain insects, such as crickets) to make a shrill trilled sound ▷ n sound of chirring

CHIRRE, -S same as ▸ chirr

CHIRRED ▸ chirr

CHIRREN pl n dialect form of children

CHIRRES ▸ chirre

CHIRRING ▸ chirr

CHIRRS ▸ chirr

CHIRRUP, -S vb (of some birds) to chirp repeatedly ▷ n chirruping sound

CHIRRUPY

CHIRT, -ED, -ING, -S vb squirt

CHIRU, -S n Tibetan antelope

CHIS ▸ chi

CHISEL, -S n metal tool with a sharp end for shaping wood or stone ▷ vb carve or form with a chisel

CHISELED same as > chiselled

CHISELER ▸ chisel

CHISELS ▸ chisel

CHIT, -S, -TED, -TING n short official note, such as a receipt ▷ vb sprout

CHITAL, -S n type of deer

CHITCHAT n chat, gossip ▷ vb gossip

CHITIN, -S n outer layer of the bodies of arthropods

CHITLIN, -S n pig intestine cooked and served as a dish

CHITLING > chitlings

CHITLINS ▸ chitlin

CHITON, -S n (in ancient Greece and Rome) a loose woollen tunic

CHITOSAN n polysaccharide derived from chitin

CHITS ▸ chit

CHITTED ▸ chit

CHITTER, -S vb twitter or chirp

CHITTIER ▸ chitty

CHITTIES ▸ chitty

CHITTING ▸ chit

CHITTY, CHITTIER, CHITTIES adj childish ▷ vb sprout

CHIV, -S, -VED, -VING n knife ▷ vb stab (someone)

CHIVALRY n courteous behaviour, esp by men towards women

CHIVAREE n charivari ▷ vb perform a chivaree

CHIVARI same as > charivari

CHIVE, -D, CHIVING n small Eurasian plant ▷ vb file or cut off

CHIVES same as ▸ chive

CHIVIED ▸ chivy

CHIVIES ▸ chivy

CHIVING ▸ chive

CHIVS ▸ chiv

CHIVVED ▸ chiv

CHIVVIED ▸ chivvy

CHIVVIES ▸ chivvy

CHIVVING ▸ chiv

CHIVVY, CHIVVIED, CHIVVIES same as ▸ chivy

CHIVY, CHIVIED, CHIVIES, -ING vb harass or nag ▷ n hunt

CHIZ, -ZED, -ZES, -ZING n cheat ▷ vb cheat

CHIZZ same as ▸ chiz

CHIZZED ▸ chiz

CHIZZES ▸ chiz

CHIZZING ▸ chiz

CHLAMYS n woollen cloak worn by ancient Greek soldiers

CHLOASMA n patches of darker colour on a person's skin

CHLORAL, -S n colourless oily liquid with a pungent odour

CHLORATE n type of chemical salt

CHLORDAN same as > chlordane

CHLORIC adj of or containing chlorine in the pentavalent state

CHLORID, -S n type of chlorine compound

CHLORIDE n compound of chlorine and another substance

CHLORIDS ▸ chlorid

CHLORIN, -S same as ▸ chlorine

CHLORINE n strong-smelling greenish-yellow gaseous element, used to disinfect water

CHLORINS ▸ chlorin

CHLORITE n any of a group of green soft secondary minerals

CHLOROUS adj of or containing chlorine in the trivalent state

CHOANA, -E n posterior nasal aperture

CHOBDAR, -S n in India and Nepal, king's macebearer or attendant

CHOC, -S short form of > chocolate

CHOCCY, CHOCCIER, CHOCCIES n chocolate ▷ adj made of (a person) by strangling or smothering of, or resembling chocolate

CHOCHO, -S same as ▶ chayote

CHOCK, -ED, -ING, -S n block or wedge used to prevent a heavy object from moving ▷ vb secure by a chock ▷ adv as closely or tightly as possible

CHOCKER adj full up

CHOCKFUL adj filled to capacity

CHOCKING ▶ chock

CHOCKO, -S same as ▶ choco

CHOCKS ▶ chock

CHOCO, -S n member of the Australian army

CHOCS ▶ choc

CHOCTAW, -S n movement in ice-skating

CHODE ▶ chide

CHOENIX same as ▶ chenix

CHOG, -S n core of a piece of fruit

CHOICE, -R, -S, -ST n choosing ▷ adj of high quality **CHOICELY**

CHOIL, -S n end of a knife blade next to the handle

CHOIR, -ED, -ING, -S n organized group of singers, esp in church ▷ vb sing in chorus

CHOIRBOY n boy who sings in a church choir

CHOIRED ▶ choir

CHOIRING ▶ choir

CHOIRMAN, CHOIRMEN n man who sings in a choir

CHOIRS ▶ choir

CHOKE, -S, CHOKING vb hinder or stop the breathing of (a person) by strangling or smothering ▷ n device found in a petrol engine

CHOKED adj disappointed or angry

CHOKER, -S n tight-fitting necklace

CHOKES ▶ choke

CHOKEY, -S, CHOKIER, CHOKIEST n slang word for prison ▷ adj involving, caused by, or causing choking

CHOKIDAR n in India, a gatekeeper

CHOKIER ▶ chokey

CHOKIES ▶ choky

CHOKIEST ▶ chokey

CHOKING ▶ choke

CHOKO, -S n pear-shaped fruit of a tropical American vine, eaten as a vegetable

CHOKRA, -S n in India, a boy or young man

CHOKRI, -S n in India, a girl or young woman

CHOKY, CHOKIES same as ▶ chokey

CHOLA, -S n Hispanic girl

CHOLATE, -S n salt of cholic acid

CHOLEMIA same as > cholaemia

CHOLENT, -S n meal prepared on Friday and left to cook until eaten for Sabbath lunch

CHOLER, -S n bad temper

CHOLERA, -S n serious infectious disease

CHOLERIC adj bad-tempered

CHOLERS ▶ choler

CHOLI, -S n short-sleeved bodice, as worn by Indian women

CHOLIAMB n imperfect iambic trimeter, with a spondee as the last foot

CHOLIC adj as in cholic acid crystalline acid found in bile

CHOLINE, -S n colourless viscous soluble alkaline substance present in animal tissues

CHOLIS ▶ choli

CHOLLA, -S n type of spiny cactus

CHOLLERS pl n jowls or cheeks

CHOLO, -S n chicano gangster

CHOLTRY n caravanserai

CHOMETZ same as ▶ chametz

CHOMMIE, -S n (in informal South African English) friend

CHOMP, -ED, -ING, -S vb chew noisily ▷ n act or sound of chewing in this manner

CHOMPER -S

CHON, -S n North and South Korean monetary unit

CHONDRAL adj of or relating to cartilage

CHONDRE, -S another word for > chondrule

CHONDRI ▶ chondrus

CHONDRIN n resilient translucent bluish-white substance that forms the matrix of cartilage

CHONDRUS, CHONDRI n cartilage

CHONS ▶ chon

CHOOF, -ED, -ING, -S vb go away

CHOOK, -ED, -ING, -S n hen or chicken ▷ vb make the sound of a hen of chicken

CHOOKIE, -S same as ▶ chook

CHOOKING ▶ chook

CHOOKS ▶ chook

CHOOM, -S n Englishman

CHOON, -S n slang term for music that one likes

CHOOSE, -S, CHOOSING, CHOSEN vb select from a number of alternatives

CHOOSER -S

CHOOSEY same as ▶ choosy

CHOOSIER ▶ choosy

CHOOSILY adv in a fussy or choosy way

CHOOSING ▶ choose

CHOOSY, CHOOSIER adj fussy, hard to please

CHOP, -PED, -S vb cut with a blow from an axe or knife ▷ n cutting or sharp blow

CHOPIN, -S same as ▶ chopine

CHOPINE, -S n sandal-like shoe popular in the 18th century

CHOPINS ▶ chopin

CHOPPED ▶ chop

CHOPPER, -S n helicopter ▷ vb travel by helicopter

CHOPPIER ▶ choppy

CHOPPILY ▶ choppy

CHOPPING ▶ chop

CHOPPY, CHOPPIER adj (of the sea) fairly rough

CHOPS ▶ chop

CHORAGI ▶ choragus

CHORAGIC ▶ choragus

CHORAGUS, CHORAGI n leader of a chorus

CHORAL, -S adj of a choir

CHORALE, -S n slow stately hymn tune

CHORALLY ▶ choral

CHORALS ▶ choral

CHORD, -S n straight line joining two points on a curve ▷ vb provide (a melodic line) with chords

CHORDA, -E n in anatomy, a cord

CHORDAL ▶ chord

CHORDATE n type of animal which includes the vertebrates

CHORDED ▶ chord

CHORDING n distribution of chords throughout a piece of harmony

CHORDS ▶ chord

CHORE, -D, -S, CHORING n routine task ▷ vb carry out chores

CHOREA, -S n disorder of the nervous system
CHOREAL

CHOREBOY n boy who does chores

CHORED ▶ chore

CHOREE, -S n trochee

CHOREGI ▶ choregus

CHOREGIC ▶ choregus

CHOREGUS, CHOREGI n in ancient Greece, the producer and financier of a dramatist's works

CHOREIC ▶ chorea

CHOREMAN, CHOREMEN n handyman

CHOREOID adj resembling chorea

CHORES ▶ chore

CHOREUS same as ▶ choree

CHORIA ▶ chorion

CHORIAL ▶ chorion

CHORIAMB n metrical foot used in classical verse

CHORIC adj in the manner of a chorus

CHORINE, -S n chorus girl

CHORING ▶ chore

CHORIOID same as ▶ choroid

CHORION, CHORIA, -S n outer membrane forming a sac around an embryo

CHORISIS, CHORISES n multiplication of leaves etc by branching or splitting
CHORISM -S

CHORIST, -S n choir member

CHORIZO, -S n kind of highly seasoned pork sausage of Spain or Mexico

CHOROID, -S adj resembling the chorion, esp in being vascular ▷ n vascular membrane of the eyeball

CHORRIE, -S n dilapidated old car

CHORTEN, -S n Buddhist shrine

CHORTLE, -D, -S vb chuckle in amusement ▷ n amused chuckle
CHORTLER

CHORUS, -ED, -ES n large choir ▷ vb sing or say together

CHOSE, -S n item of property

CHOSEN ▶ choose

CHOSES ▶ chose

CHOTA adj (in British Empire Indian usage) small

CHOTT, -S a variant spelling of ▶ shott

CHOU, -X n type of cabbage

CHOUGH, -S n large black Eurasian and N African bird of the crow family

CHOULTRY same as ▶ choltry

CHOUNTER same as ▶ chunter

CHOUSE, -D, -S, CHOUSING vb cheat

CHOUSER -S

CHOUSH, -ES n Turkish messenger

CHOUSING ▶ chouse

CHOUT, -S n blackmail

CHOUX ▶ chou

CHOW, -ED, -ING, -S n thick-coated dog with a curled tail, orig. from China ▷ vb eat

CHOWCHOW same as ▶ chow

CHOWDER, -S n thick soup containing clams or fish ▷ vb make a chowder of

CHOWDOWN n act of eating a lot of food

CHOWED ▶ chow

CHOWING ▶ chow

CHOWK, -S n marketplace or market area

CHOWRI, -ES, -S n fly-whisk

CHOWRY same as ▶ chowri

CHOWS ▶ chow

CHOWSE, -D, -S, CHOWSING same as ▶ chouse

CHOWTIME n mealtime

CHRESARD n amount of water present in the soil that is available to plants

CHRISM, -S n consecrated oil used for anointing in some churches

CHRISMA ▶ chrismon

CHRISMAL n chrism container

CHRISMON, CHRISMA n monogram and symbol of Christ's name

CHRISMS ▶ chrism

CHRISOM, -S same as ▶ chrism

CHRISTEN vb baptize

CHRISTIE same as ▶ christy

CHRISTOM same as ▶ chrisom

CHRISTY n skiing turn for stopping or changing direction quickly

CHROMA, -S n attribute of a colour

CHROMATE n any salt or ester of chromic acid

CHROME, -D, -S n anything plated with chromium ▷ vb

plate with chromium ▷ adj of or having the appearance of chrome

CHROMEL, -S n nickel-based alloy

CHROMENE n chemical compound

CHROMES ▶ chrome

CHROMIC adj of or containing chromium in the trivalent state

CHROMIDE n any member of the cichlid family of fish

CHROMIER ▶ chromy

CHROMING ▶ chrome

CHROMISE same as ▶ chromize

CHROMITE n brownish-black mineral which is the only commercial source of chromium

CHROMIUM n grey metallic element used in steel alloys and for electroplating

CHROMIZE vb chrome-plate

CHROMO, -S n picture produced by lithography

CHROMOLY n type of steel alloy

CHROMOS ▶ chromo

CHROMOUS adj of or containing chromium in the divalent state

CHROMY, CHROMIER ▶ chrome

CHROMYL, -S n the divalent radical CrO_2

CHRONAXY same as > chronaxie

CHRONIC, -S adj (of an illness) lasting a long time ▷ n chronically-ill patient

CHRONON, -S n unit of time

CHTHONIC same as > chthonian

CHUB, -S n European freshwater fish of the carp family

CHUBASCO n in Mexico, a hurricane

CHUBBIER ▶ chubby

CHUBBILY ▶ chubby

CHUBBY, CHUBBIER adj plump and round

CHUBS ▶ chub

CHUCK, -ED, -ING, -S vb throw ▷ n cut of beef from the neck to the shoulder

CHUCKER, -S n person who throws something

CHUCKIE, -S n small stone

CHUCKING ▶ chuck

CHUCKLE, -D, -S vb laugh softly ▷ n soft laugh
CHUCKLER

CHUCKS ▶ chuck

C

CHUCKY same as ► chuckie

CHUDDAH, -S same as ► chuddar

CHUDDAR, -S n large shawl or veil

CHUDDER, -S same as ► chuddar

CHUDDIES pl n underpants

CHUDDY n chewing gum

CHUFA, -S n type of sedge

CHUFF, -ER, -EST, -ING, -S vb (of a steam engine) move while making a puffing sound ▷ n puffing sound of or as if of a steam engine ▷ adj boorish

CHUFFED adj very pleased

CHUFFER ► chuff

CHUFFEST ► chuff

CHUFFIER ► chuffy

CHUFFING ► chuff

CHUFFS ► chuff

CHUFFY, CHUFFIER adj boorish and surly

CHUG, -GED, -GING, -S n short dull sound like the noise of an engine ▷ vb operate or move with this sound

CHUGALUG vb gulp down a drink in one go

CHUGGED ► chug

CHUGGER, -S ► chug

CHUGGING ► chug

CHUGS ► chug

CHUKAR, -S n common Indian partridge

CHUKKA, -S n period of play in polo

CHUKKAR, -S same as ► chukka

CHUKKAS ► chukka

CHUKKER, -S same as ► chukka

CHUKOR, -S same as ► chukar

CHUM, -MED, -MING, -S n close friend ▷ vb be or become an intimate friend (of)

CHUMASH n printed book containing one of the Five Books of Moses

CHUMLEY, -S same as ► chimney

CHUMMAGE n formerly, fee paid by a prisoner for sole occupancy of a cell

CHUMMED ► chum

CHUMMIER ► chummy

CHUMMIES ► chummy

CHUMMILY ► chummy

CHUMMING ► chum

CHUMMY, CHUMMIER, CHUMMIES adj friendly ▷ n chum

CHUMP, -ED, -S n stupid person ▷ vb chew noisily

CHUMPING n collecting wood for bonfires on Guy Fawkes Day

CHUMPS ► chump

CHUMS ► chum

CHUMSHIP n friendship

CHUNDER, -S vb vomit ▷ n vomit

CHUNK, -ED, -S n thick solid piece ▷ vb break up into chunks

CHUNKIER ► chunky

CHUNKILY ► chunky

CHUNKING n mnemonic technique involving grouping together of a number of items

CHUNKS ► chunk

CHUNKY, CHUNKIER adj (of a person) broad and heavy

CHUNNEL, -S n rail tunnel linking England and France

CHUNNER, -S same as ► chunter

CHUNTER, -S vb mutter or grumble incessantly in a meaningless fashion

CHUPATI, -S same as ► chupatti

CHUPATTI variant spelling of ► chapati

CHUPATTY same as ► chupatti

CHUPPA, -S variant of ► chuppah

CHUPPAH, -S, CHUPPOT, CHUPPOTH n canopy under which a marriage is performed

CHUPPAS ► chuppa

CHUPPOT ► chuppah

CHUPPOTH ► chuppah

CHUR interj expression of agreement

CHURCH, -ED, -ES n building for public Christian worship ▷ vb bring someone to church for special ceremonies

CHURCHLY adj appropriate to, associated with, or suggestive of church life and customs

CHURCHY adj like a church, church service, etc

CHURIDAR n as in **churidar pyjamas** long tight-fitting trousers, worn by Indian men and women

CHURINGA n sacred amulet of the native Australians

CHURL, -S n surly ill-bred person

CHURLISH adj surly and rude

CHURLS ► churl

CHURN, -ED, -S n machine in which cream is shaken to make butter ▷ vb stir (cream) vigorously to make butter

CHURNER -S

CHURNING n quantity of butter churned at any one time

CHURNS ► churn

CHURR, -ED, -ING, -S same as ► chirr

CHURRO, -S n Spanish dough stick snack

CHURRS ► churr

CHURRUS n hemp resin

CHUSE, -D, -S, CHUSING obsolete variant of ► choose

CHUT, -S interj expression of surprise or annoyance ▷ n such an expression

CHUTE, -D, -S, CHUTING n steep slope down which things may be slid ▷ vb descend by a chute

CHUTIST -S

CHUTNEE, -S same as ► chutney

CHUTNEY, -S n pickle made from fruit, vinegar, spices, and sugar

CHUTS ► chut

CHUTZPA, -S same as ► chutzpah

CHUTZPAH n unashamed self-confidence

CHUTZPAS ► chutzpa

CHYACK, -ED, -S same as ► chiack

CHYLDE archaic word for ► child

CHYLE, -S n milky fluid formed in the small intestine during digestion

CHYLIFY vb be turned into chyle

CHYLOUS ► chyle

CHYLURIA n presence of chyle in urine

CHYME, -S n partially digested food that leaves the stomach

CHYMIC, -S same as ► chemic

CHYMIFY vb form into chyme

CHYMIST, -S same as ► chemist

CHYMOSIN another name for ► rennin

CHYMOUS ► chyme

CHYND adj chined

CHYPRE, -S n perfume made from sandalwood

CHYTRID, -S n variety of fungus

CIABATTA, CIABATTE n type of bread made with olive oil

CIAO an informal word for ► **hello**

CIBATION n feeding

CIBOL, -S same as ► **chibol**

CIBORIUM, CIBORIA n goblet-shaped lidded vessel used to hold consecrated wafers in Holy Communion

CIBOULE, -S same as ► **chibol**

CICADA, -E, -S n large insect that makes a high-pitched drone

CICALA, -S, CICALE same as ► **cicada**

CICATRIX n scar

CICELY, CICELIES n type of plant

CICERO, -S n measure for type that is somewhat larger than the pica

CICERONE, CICERONI n person who guides and informs sightseers ▷ vb act as a cicerone

CICEROS ► **cicero**

CICHLID, -S n type of tropical freshwater fish popular in aquariums

CICHLOID

CICINNUS n scorpioid cyme

CICLATON n rich material of silk and gold

CICOREE, -S same as ► **chicory**

CICUTA, -S n spotted hemlock

CICUTINE same as ► **coniine**

CID, -S n leader

CIDARIS n sea urchin

CIDE, -D, -S, CIDING Shakespearean variant of ► **decide**

CIDER, -S n alcoholic drink made from fermented apple juice

CIDERKIN n weak type of cider

CIDERS ► **cider**

CIDERY ► **cider**

CIDES ► **cide**

CIDING ► **cide**

CIDS ► **cid**

CIEL, -ED, -S same as ► **ceil**

CIELING -S

CIERGE, -S same as ► **cerge**

CIG, -S same as ► **cigarette**

CIGAR, -S n roll of cured tobacco leaves for smoking

CIGARET, -S same as > **cigarette**

CIGARS ► **cigar**

CIGGIE, -S same as > **cigarette**

CIGGY same as > **cigarette**

CIGS ► **cig**

CILANTRO same as > **coriander**

CILIA ► **cilium**

CILIARY adj of or relating to cilia

CILIATE, -S n type of protozoan

CILIATED

CILICE, -S n haircloth fabric or garment

CILIUM, CILIA n short thread projecting from a cell that causes movement

CILL, -S a variant spelling (used in the building industry) for ► **sill**

CIMAR, -S same as ► **cymar**

CIMBALOM n type of dulcimer, esp of Hungary

CIMELIA pl n (especially, ecclesiastical) treasures

CIMEX, CIMICES n type of heteropterous insect, esp the bedbug

CIMIER, -S n crest of a helmet

CIMINITE n type of igneous rock

CIMOLITE n clayey, whitish mineral

CINCH, -ED, -ES n easy task ▷ vb fasten a girth around (a horse)

CINCHING

CINCHONA same as ► **calisaya**

CINCT adj encircled

CINCTURE n something, such as a belt or girdle, that goes around another thing ▷ vb encircle

CINDER, -ED, -S n piece of material that will not burn, left after burning coal ▷ vb burn to cinders

CINDERY

CINE, -S n as in cine camera camera able to film moving pictures

CINEAST, -S same as ► **cineaste**

CINEASTE n enthusiast for films

CINEASTS ► **cineast**

CINEMA, -S n place for showing films

CINEOL, -S n colourless oily liquid with a camphor-like odour and a spicy taste

CINEOLE, -S same as ► **cineol**

CINEOLS ► **cineol**

CINEPLEX n (tradename for) a large cinema complex

CINERARY adj of (someone's) ashes

CINEREA, -S n grey matter of the brain and nervous system

CINEREAL adj ashy

CINEREAS ► **cinerea**

CINERIN, -S n either of two organic compounds used as insecticides

CINES ► **cine**

CINGULA ► **cingulum**

CINGULAR adj ring-shaped

CINGULUM, CINGULA n girdle-like part of certain structures

CINNABAR n heavy red mineral containing mercury

CINNAMIC ► **cinnamon**

CINNAMON n spice obtained from the bark of an Asian tree

CINNAMYL n univalent radical of cinnamic compounds

CINQ, -S n number five

CINQUAIN n stanza of five lines

CINQUE, -S n number five in cards, dice, etc

CION, -S same as ► **scion**

CIOPPINO n Italian rich fish stew

CIPAILLE n type of pie traditional in Quebec

CIPHER, -ED, -S n system of secret writing ▷ vb put (a message) into secret writing

CIPHERER

CIPHONY n ciphered telephony

CIPOLIN, -S n Italian marble with alternating white and green streaks

CIPPUS, CIPPI n pillar bearing an inscription

CIRCA prep approximately, about

CIRCAR, -S n in India, part of a province

CIRCITER prep around, about

CIRCLE, -D, -S n perfectly round geometric figure, line, or shape ▷ vb move in a circle (round)

CIRCLER -S

CIRCLET, -S n circular ornament worn on the head

CIRCLING ► **circle**

CIRCLIP, -S n type of fastener

CIRCS pl n circumstances

CIRCUIT, -S n complete route or course, esp a circular one ▷ vb make or travel in a circuit around (something)

CIRCUITY n (of speech, reasoning, etc) a roundabout or devious quality

CIRCULAR adj in the shape of a circle ▷ n letter for general distribution

CIRCUS, -ES n travelling company of acrobats, clowns, performing animals, etc

CIRCUSSY

CIRCUSY

C

CIRE, -S adj (of fabric) treated with a heat or wax process to make it smooth ▷ n such a surface on a fabric

CIRL, -S n bird belonging to the bunting family

CIRQUE, -S n steep-sided semicircular hollow found in mountainous areas

CIRRATE adj bearing or resembling cirri

CIRRI ► cirrus

CIRRIPED same as > **cirripede**

CIRROSE same as ► **cirrate**

CIRROUS same as ► **cirrate**

CIRRUS, CIRRI, -ES n high wispy cloud

CIRSOID adj resembling a varix

CIS adj having two groups of atoms on the same side of a double bond

CISCO, -ES, -S n whitefish, esp the lake herring of cold deep lakes of North America

CISELEUR n person who is expert in ciselure

CISELURE n art or process of chasing metal

CISLUNAR adj of or relating to the space between the earth and the moon

CISSIER ► cissy

CISSIES ► cissy

CISSIEST ► cissy

CISSING, -S n appearance of pinholes, craters, etc, in paintwork

CISSOID, -S n type of geometric curve

CISSUS, -ES n type of climbing plant

CISSY, CISSIER, CISSIES, CISSIEST same as ► **sissy**

CIST, -S n wooden box for holding ritual objects used in ancient Rome and Greece

CISTED

CISTERN, -S n water tank, esp one that holds water for flushing a toilet

CISTERNA n sac or partially closed space containing body fluid, esp lymph or cerebrospinal fluid

CISTERNS ► cistern

CISTIC adj cist-like

CISTRON, -S n section of a chromosome that encodes a single polypeptide chain

CISTS ► cist

CISTUS, -ES n type of plant

CISTVAEN n pre-Christian stone coffin or burial chamber

CIT, -S n pejorative term for a town dweller

CITABLE ► cite

CITADEL, -S n fortress in a city

CITAL, -S n court summons

CITATION n commendation for bravery

CITATOR, -S n legal publication

CITATORY ► citation

CITE, -D, -S, CITING vb quote, refer to

CITEABLE

CITER -S

CITESS, -ES n female cit

CITHARA, -S n ancient stringed musical instrument

CITHER, -S same as ► **cittern**

CITHERN, -S same as ► **cittern**

CITHERS ► cither

CITHREN, -S same as ► **cithara**

CITIED adj having cities

CITIES ► city

CITIFY, CITIFIED, CITIFIES vb cause to conform to or adopt the customs, habits, or dress of city people

CITING ► cite

CITIZEN, -S n native or naturalized member of a state or nation

CITO adv swiftly

CITOLA, -S n type of medieval stringed instrument

CITOLE, -S a rare word for ► **cittern**

CITRAL, -S n volatile liquid with a lemon-like odour

CITRANGE n type of acidic and aromatic orange

CITRATE, -S n any salt or ester of citric acid

CITRATED adj treated with a citrate

CITRATES ► citrate

CITREOUS adj of a greenish-yellow colour

CITRIC adj of or derived from citrus fruits or citric acid

CITRIN, -S n vitamin P

CITRINE, -S n brownish-yellow variety of quartz: a gemstone

CITRININ n type of mycotoxin

CITRINS ► citrin

CITRON, -S n lemon-like fruit of a small Asian tree

CITROUS same as ► **citrus**

CITRUS, -ES n type of tropical or subtropical tree or shrub

CITRUSSY adj having or resembling the taste or colour of a citrus fruit

CITRUSY same as ► **citrussy**

CITS ► cit

CITTERN, -S n medieval stringed instrument

CITY, CITIES n large or important town

CITYFY, CITYFIED, CITYFIES same as ► **citify**

CITYWARD adv towards a city

CITYWIDE adj occurring throughout a city

CIVE, -S same as ► **chive**

CIVET, -S n spotted catlike African mammal

CIVIC adj of a city or citizens

CIVICISM n principle of civil government

CIVICS n study of the rights and responsibilities of citizenship

CIVIE, -S same as ► **civvy**

CIVIL adj relating to the citizens of a state

CIVILIAN adj not belonging to the armed forces ▷ n person who is not a member of the armed forces or police

CIVILISE same as ► **civilize**

CIVILIST n civilian

CIVILITY n polite or courteous behaviour

CIVILIZE vb refine or educate (a person)

CIVILLY ► civil

CIVILS n civil engineering

CIVISM, -S n good citizenship

CIVVY, CIVVIES n civilian

CIZERS archaic spelling of ► **scissors**

CLABBER, -S vb cover with mud

CLACH, -ED, -ES, -ING, -S n stone ▷ vb kill by stoning

CLACHAN, -S n small village

CLACHED ► clach

CLACHES ► clach

CLACHING ► clach

CLACHS ► clach

CLACK, -ED, -ING, -S n sound made by two hard objects striking each other ▷ vb make this sound

CLACKBOX n casing enclosing a clack

CLACKED ► clack

CLACKER, -S n object that makes a clacking sound

CLACKING ► clack

CLACKS ► clack

CLAD, -S vb bond a metal to (another metal), esp to form a protective coat

CLADDAGH n Irish ring

CLADDED adj covered with cladding

CLADDER, -S ► clad

CLADDIE, -S another name for ► korari

CLADDING ► clad

CLADE, -S n group of organisms sharing a common ancestor

CLADISM, -S ► cladist

CLADIST, -S n proponent of cladistics

CLADODE, -S n stem resembling and functioning as a leaf

CLADS ► clad

CLAES Scots word for ► clothes

CLAFOUTI same as > clafoutis

CLAG, -GED, -GING, -S n sticky mud ▷ vb stick, as mud

CLAGGIER ► claggy

CLAGGING ► clag

CLAGGY, CLAGGIER adj stickily clinging, as mud

CLAGS ► clag

CLAIM, -S, -ING, -S vb assert as a fact ▷ n assertion that something is true

CLAIMANT n person who makes a claim

CLAIMED ► claim

CLAIMER, -S ► claim

CLAIMING ► claim

CLAIMS ► claim

CLAM, -MED, -MING, -S n edible shellfish with a hinged shell ▷ vb gather clams

CLAMANCY n urgency

CLAMANT adj noisy

CLAMBAKE n picnic, often by the sea, at which clams, etc, are baked

CLAMBE old variant of ► climb

CLAMBER, -S vb climb awkwardly ▷ n climb performed in this manner

CLAME, -S archaic variant of ► claim

CLAMLIKE ► clam

CLAMMED ► clam

CLAMMER, -S n person who gathers clams

CLAMMIER ► clammy

CLAMMILY ► clammy

CLAMMING ► clam

CLAMMY, CLAMMIER adj unpleasantly moist and sticky

CLAMOR, -ED, -S same as ► clamour

CLAMORER

CLAMOUR, -S n loud protest ▷ vb make a loud noise or outcry

CLAMP, -ED, -S n tool with movable jaws for holding

things together tightly ▷ vb fasten with a clamp

CLAMPER, -S n spiked metal frame fastened to the sole of a shoe ▷ vb tread heavily

CLAMPING n act of clamping

CLAMPS ► clamp

CLAMS ► clam

CLAMWORM the US name for the ► ragworm

CLAN, -S n group of families with a common ancestor

CLANG, -ED, -S vb make a loud ringing metallic sound ▷ n ringing metallic sound

CLANGBOX n device fitted to a jet-engine to change the direction of thrust

CLANGED ► clang

CLANGER, -S n obvious mistake

CLANGING ► clang

CLANGOR, -S same as ► clangour

CLANGOUR n loud continuous clanging sound ▷ vb make or produce a loud resonant noise

CLANGS ► clang

CLANK, -ED, -S n harsh metallic sound ▷ vb make such a sound

CLANKIER ► clanky

CLANKING ► clank

CLANKS ► clank

CLANKY, CLANKIER adj making clanking sounds

CLANNISH adj (of a group) tending to exclude outsiders

CLANS ► clan

CLANSHIP n association of families under the leadership of a chieftain

CLANSMAN, CLANSMEN n man belonging to a clan

CLAP, -PED, -S, -T vb applaud by hitting the palms of one's hands sharply together ▷ n act or sound of clapping

CLAPDISH same as > clackdish

CLAPNET, -S n net that can be closed instantly by pulling a string

CLAPPED ► clap

CLAPPER, -S n piece of metal inside a bell ▷ vb make a sound like a clapper

CLAPPING ► clap

CLAPS ► clap

CLAPT ► clap

CLAPTRAP n foolish or pretentious talk

CLAQUE, -S n group of people hired to applaud

CLAQUER, -S same as ► claqueur

CLAQUES ► claque

CLAQUEUR n member of a claque

CLARAIN, -S n one of the four major lithotypes of banded coal

CLARENCE n closed four-wheeled horse-drawn carriage, having a glass front

CLARET, -ED, -S n dry red wine from Bordeaux ▷ adj purplish-red ▷ vb drink claret

CLARIES ► clary

CLARIFY vb make (a matter) clear and unambiguous

CLARINET n keyed woodwind instrument with a single reed

CLARINO, CLARINI, -S adj relating to a high passage for the trumpet in 18th-century music ▷ n high register of the trumpet

CLARION, -S n obsolete high-pitched trumpet ▷ adj clear and ringing ▷ vb proclaim loudly

CLARITY n clearness

CLARKIA, -S n N American plant cultivated for its red, purple, or pink flowers

CLARO, -ES, -S n mild light-coloured cigar

CLARSACH n Celtic harp of Scotland and Ireland

CLART, -ED, -ING vb to dirty

CLARTIER ► clarty

CLARTING ► clart

CLARTS pl n lumps of mud, esp on shoes

CLARTY, CLARTIER adj dirty, esp covered in mud

CLARY, CLARIES n European plant with aromatic leaves and blue flowers

CLASH, -ED, -ES vb come into conflict ▷ n fight, argument

CLASHER -S

CLASHING ► clash

CLASP, -ED, -S n device for fastening things ▷ vb grasp or embrace firmly

CLASPER -S

CLASPING ► clasp

CLASPS ► clasp

CLASPT old inflection of ► clasp

CLASS, -ED n group of people sharing a similar social position ▷ vb place in a class

CLASSER -S

CLASSES ► classis

CLASSIC, -S adj being a typical example of something ▷ n

C

author, artist, or work of art of recognized excellence

CLASSICO adj (of Italian wines) coming from the centre of a specific wine-growing region

CLASSICS ▶ classic

CLASSIER ▶ classy

CLASSIFY vb divide into groups with similar characteristics

CLASSILY ▶ classy

CLASSING ▶ class

CLASSIS, CLASSES n governing body of elders or pastors

CLASSISM n belief that people from certain social or economic classes are superior to others **CLASSIST**

CLASSMAN, CLASSMEN n graduate of Oxford University with a classed honours degree

CLASSON, -S n elementary atomic particle

CLASSY, CLASSIER adj stylish and elegant

CLAST, -S n fragment of a clastic rock

CLASTIC, -S adj composed of fragments ▷ n clast

CLASTS ▶ clast

CLAT, -S, -TED, -TING n irksome or troublesome task ▷ vb scrape

CLATCH, -ED, -ES vb move making a squelching sound

CLATS ▶ clat

CLATTED ▶ clat

CLATTER, -S n (make) a rattling noise ▷ vb make a rattling noise, as when hard objects hit each other **CLATTERY**

CLATTING ▶ clat

CLAUCHT, -S vb seize by force

CLAUGHT, -S same as ▶ claucht

CLAUSAL ▶ clause

CLAUSE, -S n section of a legal document

CLAUSTRA > claustrum

CLAUSULA n type of cadence in polyphony

CLAUT, -ED, -ING, -S same as ▶ clat

CLAVATE adj shaped like a club with the thicker end uppermost

CLAVATED same as ▶ clavate

CLAVE, -S n one of a pair of hardwood sticks struck together to make a hollow sound

CLAVECIN n harpsichord

CLAVER, -ED, -S vb talk idly ▷ n idle talk

CLAVES ▶ clave

CLAVI ▶ clavus

CLAVICLE n bone connecting the shoulder blade to the breastbone

CLAVIE, -S n tar-barrel traditionally set alight in Moray in Scotland on Hogmanay

CLAVIER, -S n any keyboard instrument

CLAVIES ▶ clavie

CLAVIGER n key- or club-bearer

CLAVIS n key

CLAVUS, CLAVI n corn on the toe

CLAW, -ED, -ING, -S n sharp hooked nail of a bird or beast ▷ vb tear with claws or nails

CLAWBACK n recovery of a sum of money

CLAWED ▶ claw

CLAWER, -S ▶ claw

CLAWING ▶ claw

CLAWLESS ▶ claw

CLAWLIKE adj resembling a claw or claws

CLAWS ▶ claw

CLAXON, -S same as ▶ klaxon

CLAY, -ED, -ING, -S n fine-grained earth used to make bricks and pottery ▷ vb cover or mix with clay

CLAYBANK n dull brownish-orange colour

CLAYED ▶ clay

CLAYEY, CLAYIER, CLAYIEST ▶ clay

CLAYING ▶ clay

CLAYISH ▶ clay

CLAYLIKE ▶ clay

CLAYMORE n large two-edged sword formerly used by Scottish Highlanders

CLAYPAN, -S n layer of stiff impervious clay situated just below the surface of the ground

CLAYS ▶ clay

CLAYWARE n pottery

CLEAN, -ED, -EST, -S adj free from dirt or impurities ▷ vb make (something) free from dirt ▷ adv completely

CLEANER, -S n person or thing that removes dirt

CLEANEST ▶ clean

CLEANING n act of cleaning something

CLEANISH adj quite clean

CLEANLY adv easily or smoothly ▷ adj habitually clean or neat

CLEANOUT n act or instance of cleaning (something) out

CLEANS ▶ clean

CLEANSE, -D, -S vb make clean

CLEANSER n cleansing agent, such as a detergent

CLEANSES ▶ cleanse

CLEANUP, -S n process of cleaning up or eliminating something

CLEAR, -ED, -EST, -S adj free from doubt or confusion ▷ adv in a clear or distinct manner ▷ vb make or become clear

CLEARAGE n clearance

CLEARCUT n act of felling all trees in area

CLEARED ▶ clear

CLEARER, -S ▶ clear

CLEAREST ▶ clear

CLEARING n treeless area in a wood

CLEARLY adv in a clear, distinct, or obvious manner

CLEAROUT n act or instance of removing (things or material)

CLEARS ▶ clear

CLEARWAY n stretch of road on which motorists may stop in an emergency

CLEAT, -ED, -ING, -S n wedge ▷ vb supply or support with a cleat or cleats

CLEAVAGE n division or split

CLEAVE, -D, -S, CLOVEN vb split apart ▷ n split

CLEAVER n butcher's heavy knife with a square blade

CLEAVERS n plant with small white flowers and sticky fruits

CLEAVES ▶ cleave

CLEAVING ▶ cleave

CLECHE adj (in heraldry) voided so that only a narrow border is visible

CLECK, -ED, -S vb (of birds) to hatch ▷ n piece of gossip

CLECKIER ▶ clecky

CLECKING ▶ cleck

CLECKS ▶ cleck

CLECKY, CLECKIER ▶ cleck

CLEEK, -ED, -ING, -IT, -S n large hook, such as one used to land fish ▷ vb seize

CLEEP, -ED, -ING, -S same as ▶ clepe

CLEEVE, -S n cliff

CLEF, -S n symbol at the beginning of a stave to show the pitch

CLEFT, -ED, -ING, -S vb split ▷ n opening

CLEG, -S another name for a ► horsefly

CLEIDOIC adj as in **cleidoic egg** egg of birds and insects

CLEIK, -S same as ► cleek

CLEM, -MED, -MING, -S vb be hungry or cause to be hungry

CLEMATIS n climbing plant with large colourful flowers

CLEMENCY n kind or lenient treatment

CLEMENT adj (of weather) mild

CLEMMED ► clem

CLEMMING ► clem

CLEMS ► clem

CLENCH, -ED, -ES vb close or squeeze (one's teeth or fist) tightly ▷ n firm grasp or grip

CLENCHER

CLEOME, -S n type of herbaceous or shrubby plant

CLEPE, -D, -S, CLEPING, CLEPT vb call by the name of

CLERGY, CLERGIES n priests and ministers as a group

CLERIC, -S n member of the clergy

CLERICAL adj of clerks or office work

CLERICS ► cleric

CLERID, -S n beetle that preys on other insects

CLERIHEW n form of comic or satiric verse

CLERISY n learned or educated people

CLERK, -ED, -ING, -S n employee who keeps records, files, and accounts ▷ vb work as a clerk

CLERKDOM

CLERKESS n female office clerk

CLERKING ► clerk

CLERKISH ► clerk

CLERKLY adj of or like a clerk ▷ adv in the manner of a clerk

CLERKS ► clerk

CLERUCH, -S n settler in a cleruchy

CLERUCHY n type of colony of ancient Athens

CLEUCH, -S same as ► clough

CLEUGH, -S same as ► clough

CLEVE, -S same as ► cleeve

CLEVEITE n crystalline variety of the mineral uraninite

CLEVER, -ER adj intelligent, quick at learning

CLEVERLY

CLEVES ► cleve

CLEVIS, -ES n type of fastening used in agriculture

CLEW, -ED, -ING, -S n ball of thread, yarn, or twine ▷ vb coil or roll into a ball

CLICHE, -S n expression or idea that is no longer effective because of overuse ▷ vb use a cliché (in speech or writing)

CLICHED

CLICHEED

CLICK, -ED, -S n short sharp sound ▷ vb make this sound

CLICKER -S

CLICKET, -S vb make a click

CLICKING ► click

CLICKS ► click

CLIED ► cly

CLIENT, -S n person who uses the services of a professional person or company

CLIENTAL

CLIES ► cly

CLIFF, -S n steep rock face, esp along the sea shore ▷ vb scale a cliff

CLIFFED

CLIFFIER ► cliffy

CLIFFS ► cliff

CLIFFTOP n top of a cliff

CLIFFY, CLIFFIER ► cliff

CLIFT, -S same as ► cliff

CLIFTED

CLIFTIER ► clifty

CLIFTS ► clift

CLIFTY, CLIFTIER ► clift

CLIMATAL ► climate

CLIMATE, -D, -S n typical weather conditions of an area ▷ vb acclimatize

CLIMATIC

CLIMAX, -ED, -ES n most intense point of an experience, series of events, or story ▷ vb reach a climax

CLIMB, -ED, -S vb go up, ascend ▷ n climbing

CLIMBER, -S n person or thing that climbs

CLIMBING ► climb

CLIMBS ► climb

CLIME, -S n place or its climate

CLINAL ► cline

CLINALLY ► cline

CLINAMEN n bias

CLINCH, -ED, -ES vb settle (an argument or agreement) decisively ▷ n movement in which one competitor holds on to the other to avoid punches

CLINCHER n something decisive

CLINCHES ► clinch

CLINE, -S n variation within a species

CLING, -ED, -ING, -S, CLUNG vb hold tightly or stick closely

▷ n tendency of cotton fibres in a sample to stick to each other

CLINGER -S

CLINGIER ► clingy

CLINGING ► cling

CLINGS ► cling

CLINGY, CLINGIER ► cling

CLINIC, -S n building where outpatients receive medical treatment or advice

CLINICAL adj of a clinic

CLINICS ► clinic

CLINIQUE same as ► clinic

CLINK, -ED, -ING, -S n light sharp metallic sound ▷ vb make a light sharp metallic sound

CLINKER, -S n fused coal left over in a fire or furnace ▷ vb form clinker during burning

CLINKING ► clink

CLINKS ► clink

CLINT, -S n section of a limestone pavement separated from others by fissures

CLIP, -PED, -S vb cut with shears or scissors ▷ n short extract of a film

CLIPART, -S n large collection of simple drawings stored in a computer

CLIPE, -D, -S, CLIPING same as ► clype

CLIPPED ► clip

CLIPPER n fast commercial sailing ship

CLIPPERS pl n tool for clipping

CLIPPIE, -S n bus conductress

CLIPPING ► clip

CLIPS ► clip

CLIPT old inflection of ► clip

CLIQUE, -D, -S, CLIQUING n small exclusive group ▷ vb form a clique

CLIQUEY, CLIQUIER adj exclusive, confined to a small group

CLIQUING ► clique

CLIQUISH ► clique

CLIQUISM ► clique

CLIQUY same as ► cliquey

CLITELLA > clitellum

CLITHRAL same as > cleithral

CLITIC, -S adj (of a word) incapable of being stressed ▷ n clitic word

CLITORAL ► clitoris

CLITORIC ► clitoris

CLITORIS n small sensitive organ at the front of the vulva

CLITTER, -S vb stridulate

CLIVERS same as ► cleavers

CLIVIA, -S n plant belonging to the Amaryllid family

CLOACA, -E, -S n body cavity in most animals
CLOACAL
CLOAK, -ED, -ING, -S n loose sleeveless outer garment ▷ vb cover or conceal
CLOAM, -S adj made of clay or earthenware ▷ n clay or earthenware pots, dishes, etc, collectively
CLOBBER, -S vb hit ▷ n belongings, esp clothes
CLOCHARD n tramp
CLOCHE, -S n cover to protect young plants
CLOCK, -ED, -S n instrument for showing the time ▷ vb record (time) with a stopwatch
CLOCKER -S
CLOCKING ▸ clock
CLOCKS ▸ clock
CLOD, -DED, -DING, -S n lump of earth ▷ vb pelt with clods
CLODDIER ▸ cloddy
CLODDING ▸ clod
CLODDISH ▸ clod
CLODDY, CLODDIER ▸ clod
CLODLY ▸ clod
CLODPATE n dull or stupid person
CLODPOLE same as ▸ clodpate
CLODPOLL same as ▸ clodpate
CLODS ▸ clod
CLOFF, -S n cleft of a tree
CLOG, -GED, -S vb obstruct ▷ n wooden or wooden-soled shoe
CLOGGER, -S n clogmaker
CLOGGIER ▸ cloggy
CLOGGILY ▸ clog
CLOGGING ▸ clog
CLOGGY, CLOGGIER ▸ clog
CLOGS ▸ clog
CLOISON, -S n partition
CLOISTER n covered pillared arcade, usu in a monastery ▷ vb confine or seclude in or as if in a monastery
CLOKE, -D, -S, CLOKING same as ▸ cloak
CLOMB a past tense and past participle of ▸ climb
CLOMP, -ED, -ING, -S same as ▸ clump
CLON, -S same as ▸ clone
CLONAL ▸ clone
CLONALLY ▸ clone
CLONE, -D, -S n animal or plant produced artificially from the cells of another animal or plant ▷ vb produce as a clone
CLONER -S

CLONIC ▸ clonus
CLONING, -S ▸ clone
CLONISM, -S n series of clonic spasms
CLONK, -ED, -ING, -S vb make a loud dull thud ▷ n loud thud
CLONKIER ▸ clonky
CLONKING ▸ clonk
CLONKS ▸ clonk
CLONKY, CLONKIER same as ▸ clunky
CLONS ▸ clon
CLONUS, -ES n type of convulsion
CLOOP, -S n sound made when a cork is drawn from a bottle
CLOOT, -S n hoof
CLOOTIE adj as in clootie dumpling kind of dumpling
CLOOTS ▸ cloot
CLOP, -PED, -PING, -S vb make a sound as of a horse's hooves ▷ n sound of this nature
CLOQUE, -S n fabric with an embossed surface
CLOSABLE ▸ close
CLOSE, -D, -S, -ST vb shut ▷ n end, conclusion ▷ adj near ▷ adv closely, tightly
CLOSELY
CLOSEOUT n termination of an account on which the margin is exhausted
CLOSER, -S ▸ close
CLOSES ▸ close
CLOSEST ▸ close
CLOSET, -ED, -S n cupboard ▷ adj private, secret ▷ vb shut (oneself) away in private
CLOSEUP, -S n photo taken close to subject
CLOSING, -S ▸ close
CLOSURE, -D, -S n closing ▷ vb (in a deliberative body) to end (debate) by closure
CLOT, -S, -TED n soft thick lump formed from liquid ▷ vb form soft thick lumps
CLOTBUR, -S n burdock
CLOTE, -S n burdock
CLOTH, -S n (piece of) woven fabric
CLOTHE, -D vb put clothes on
CLOTHES n garments
CLOTHIER n maker or seller of clothes or cloth
CLOTHING ▸ clothe
CLOTHS ▸ cloth
CLOTPOLL same as ▸ clodpoll
CLOTS ▸ clot
CLOTTED ▸ clot
CLOTTER, -S vb to clot
CLOTTIER ▸ clotty
CLOTTING ▸ clot

CLOTTISH ▸ clot
CLOTTY, CLOTTIER adj full of clots
CLOTURE, -D, -S n closure in the US Senate ▷ vb end (debate) in the US Senate by cloture
CLOU, -S n crux; focus
CLOUD, -ED, -S n mass of condensed water vapour floating in the sky ▷ vb become cloudy
CLOUDAGE n mass of clouds
CLOUDED ▸ cloud
CLOUDIER ▸ cloudy
CLOUDILY ▸ cloudy
CLOUDING ▸ cloud
CLOUDLET n small cloud
CLOUDS ▸ cloud
CLOUDY, CLOUDIER adj having a lot of clouds
CLOUGH, -S n gorge or narrow ravine
CLOUR, -ED, -ING, -S vb to thump or dent
CLOUS ▸ clou
CLOUT, -ED, -ING, -S n hard blow ▷ vb hit hard
CLOUTER -S
CLOVE, -S n tropical evergreen myrtaceous tree
CLOVEN ▸ cleave
CLOVER, -S n plant with three-lobed leaves
CLOVERED adj covered with clover
CLOVERS ▸ clover
CLOVERY ▸ clover
CLOVES ▸ clove
CLOVIS n as in clovis point flint projectile dating from the 10th millennium BC
CLOW, -ED, -ING, -S n clove ▷ vb rake with a clow
CLOWDER, -S n collective term for a group of cats
CLOWED ▸ clow
CLOWING ▸ clow
CLOWN, -ED, -S n comic entertainer in a circus ▷ vb behave foolishly
CLOWNERY
CLOWNING
CLOWNISH
CLOWS ▸ clow
CLOY, -ED, -S vb cause weariness through an excess of something initially pleasurable
CLOYE, -S vb to claw
CLOYED ▸ cloy
CLOYES ▸ cloye
CLOYING adj sickeningly sweet
CLOYLESS adj not cloying
CLOYMENT n satiety

CLOYS ► cloy
CLOYSOME adj cloying
CLOZE, -S n as in **cloze test** test of the ability to understand text
CLUB, -BED, -S n association of people with common interests ▷ vb hit with a club
CLUBABLE same as > clubbable
CLUBBED ► club
CLUBBER, -S n person who regularly frequents nightclubs
CLUBBIER ► clubby
CLUBBILY ► clubby
CLUBBING ► club
CLUBBISH adj clubby
CLUBBISM n advantage gained through membership of a club or clubs
CLUBBIST
CLUBBY, CLUBBIER adj sociable, esp effusively so
CLUBFACE n face of golf club
CLUBFOOT, CLUBFEET n congenital deformity of the foot
CLUBHAND n congenital deformity of the hand
CLUBHAUL vb force (a sailing vessel) onto a new tack, esp in an emergency
CLUBHEAD n head of golf club
CLUBLAND n area of London which contains most of the famous clubs
CLUBMAN, CLUBMEN n man who is an enthusiastic member of a club or clubs
CLUBMATE n friend or contemporary in the same club
CLUBMEN ► clubman
CLUBMOSS n type of green moss-like plant
CLUBROOM n room in which a club meets
CLUBROOT n disease of cabbages
CLUBRUSH n any rush of the genus Scirpus
CLUBS ► club
CLUCK, -ED, -ING, -S n low clicking noise made by a hen ▷ vb make this noise
CLUCKER, -S n chicken
CLUCKIER ► clucky
CLUCKING ► clucky
CLUCKS ► cluck
CLUCKY, CLUCKIER adj wishing to have a baby
CLUDGIE, -S n toilet
CLUE, -D, -ING, -S, CLUING n something that helps to solve a mystery or puzzle

▷ vb help solve a mystery or puzzle
CLUELESS adj stupid
CLUES ► clue
CLUEY, CLUIER, CLUIEST adj (Australian) well-informed and adroit
CLUING ► clue
CLUMBER, -S n type of thickset spaniel
CLUMP, -ED, -ING, -S n small group of things or people ▷ vb walk heavily
CLUMPER -S
CLUMPET, -S n large chunk of floating ice
CLUMPIER ► clumpy
CLUMPING ► clump
CLUMPISH ► clump
CLUMPS ► clump
CLUMPY, CLUMPIER ► clump
CLUMSIER ► clumsy
CLUMSILY ► clumsy
CLUMSY, CLUMSIER adj lacking skill or physical coordination
CLUNCH, -ES n hardened clay
CLUNG ► cling
CLUNK, -ED, -ING, -S n dull metallic sound ▷ vb make such a sound
CLUNKER, -S n dilapidated old car or other machine
CLUNKIER ► clunky
CLUNKING ► clunk
CLUNKS ► clunk
CLUNKY, CLUNKIER adj making a clunking noise
CLUPEID, -S n type of fish
CLUPEOID n type of soft-finned fish
CLUSIA, -S n tree of the tropical American genus Clusia
CLUSTER, -S n small close group ▷ vb gather in clusters
CLUSTERY
CLUTCH, -ED, -ES vb grasp tightly ▷ n mechanical device
CLUTCHY adj (of a person) tending to cling
CLUTTER, -S vb scatter objects about (a place) untidily ▷ n untidy mess
CLUTTERY adj full of clutter
CLY, CLIED, CLIES, -ING vb steal or seize

> A little word meaning to seize or steal, this can be useful when you are short of vowels.

CLYPE, -D, -S, CLYPING vb tell tales ▷ n person who tells tales

CLYPEAL ► clypeus
CLYPEATE ► clypeus
CLYPED ► clype
CLYPEI ► clypeus
CLYPES ► clype
CLYPEUS, CLYPEI n cuticular plate on the head of some insects
CLYPING ► clype
CLYSTER, -S a former name for an ► enema
CNEMIAL ► cnemis
CNEMIS, CNEMIDES n shin or tibia
CNIDA, -E n nematocyst
COACH, -ED, -ES n long-distance bus ▷ vb train, teach
COACHDOG n Dalmatian dog
COACHED ► coach
COACHEE, -S n person who receives training from a coach
COACHER, -S ► coach
COACHES ► coach
COACHIER ► coachy
COACHIES ► coachy
COACHING ► coach
COACHMAN, COACHMEN n driver of a horse-drawn coach or carriage
COACHY, COACHIER, COACHIES n coachman ▷ adj resembling or pertaining to a coach
COACT, -ED, -ING, -S vb act together
COACTION n any relationship between organisms within a community
COACTIVE
COACTOR, -S ► coact
COACTS ► coact
COADIES ► coady
COADMIRE vb admire together
COADMIT, -S vb admit together
COADY, COADIES n sauce made from molasses
COAEVAL, -S n contemporary
COAGENCY n joint agency
COAGENT -S
COAGULUM, COAGULA n any coagulated mass
COAITA, -S n spider monkey
COAL, -ED, -ING, -S n black rock consisting mainly of carbon, used as fuel ▷ vb take in, or turn into coal
COALA, -S same as ► koala
COALBALL n in coal, nodule containing petrified plant or animal remains
COALBIN, -S n bin for holding coal

COALBOX n box for holding coal

COALDUST n dust from coal

COALED ► coal

COALER, -S n ship, train, etc, used to carry or supply coal

COALESCE vb come together, merge

COALFACE n exposed seam of coal in a mine

COALFISH n type of dark-coloured food fish occurring in northern seas

COALHOLE n small coal cellar

COALIER ► coaly

COALIEST ► coaly

COALIFY vb turn into coal

COALING ► coal

COALISE, -D, -S vb form a coalition

COALIZE, -D, -S same as ► coalise

COALLESS adj without coal

COALMAN, COALMEN n man who delivers coal

COALMINE n mine from which coal is extracted

COALPIT, -S n pit from which coal is extracted

COALS ► coal

COALSACK n dark nebula near the constellation Cygnus

COALSHED n shed in which coal is stored

COALY, COALIER, COALIEST ► coal

COALYARD n yard in which coal is stored

COAMING, -S n raised frame round a ship's hatchway for keeping out water

COANCHOR vb co-present a TV programme

COANNEX vb annex with something else

COAPPEAR vb appear jointly

COAPT, -ED, -ING, -S vb secure

COARB, -S n spiritual successor

COARSE, -R, -ST adj rough in texture

COARSELY

COARSEN, -S vb make or become coarse

COARSER ► coarse

COARSEST ► coarse

COARSISH ► coarse

COASSIST vb assist jointly

COASSUME vb assume jointly

COAST, -ED, -S n place where the land meets the sea ▷ vb move by momentum, without the use of power

COASTAL

COASTER, -S n small mat placed under a glass

COASTING ► coast

COASTS ► coast

COAT, -S n outer garment with long sleeves ▷ vb cover with a layer

COATE, -S same as ► quote

COATED adj covered with an outer layer, film, etc

COATEE, -S n short coat, esp for a baby

COATER, -S n machine that applies a coating to something

COATES ► coate

COATI, -S n type of omnivorous mammal

COATING, -S n covering layer

COATIS ► coati

COATLESS adj without a coat

COATRACK n rack for hanging coats on

COATROOM n cloakroom

COATS ► coat

COATTAIL n long tapering tail at the back of a man's tailored coat

COATTEND vb attend jointly

COATTEST vb attest jointly

COAUTHOR n person who shares the writing of a book, article, etc, with another ▷ vb be the joint author of (a book, article, etc)

COAX, -ED, -ES vb persuade gently

COAXAL same as ► coaxial

COAXED ► coax

COAXER, -S ► coax

COAXES ► coax

COAXIAL adj (of a cable) transmitting by means of two concentric conductors separated by an insulator

COAXING, -S n act of coaxing

COB, -BED, -BING, -S n stalk of an ear of maize ▷ vb beat

COBAEA, -S n tropical climbing shrub

COBALT, -S n brittle silvery-white metallic element

COBALTIC adj of or containing cobalt, esp in the trivalent state

COBALTS ► cobalt

COBB, -S same as ► cob

COBBED ► cob

COBBER, -S n friend

COBBIER ► cobby

COBBIEST ► cobby

COBBING ► cob

COBBLE, -D, -S n cobblestone ▷ vb pave (a road) with cobblestones

COBBLER, -S n shoe mender

COBBLERY n shoemaking or shoemending

COBBLES ► cobble

COBBLING ► cobble

COBBS ► cobb

COBBY, COBBIER, COBBIEST adj short and stocky

COBIA, -S n large dark-striped game fish

COBLE, -S n small single-masted flat-bottomed fishing boat

COBLOAF n round loaf of bread

COBNUT, -S another name for ► hazelnut

COBRA, -S n venomous hooded snake of Asia and Africa

COBRIC

COBS ► cob

COBURG, -S n rounded loaf with a cross cut on the top

COBWEB, -S n spider's web

COBWEBBY

COBZA, -S n Romanian lute

COCA, -S n S American shrub

COCAIN, -S same as ► cocaine

COCAINE, -S n drug used illegally as a narcotic and as an anaesthetic

COCAINS ► cocain

COCAS ► coca

COCCAL ► coccus

COCCI ► coccus

COCCIC ► coccus

COCCID, -S n type of homopterous insect

COCCIDIA > coccidium

COCCIDS ► coccid

COCCO, -S n taro

COCCOID, -S ► coccus

COCCOS ► cocco

COCCOUS ► coccus

COCCUS, COCCI n any spherical or nearly spherical bacterium

COCCYX, COCCYGES, -ES n bone at the base of the spinal column

COCH, -ES obsolete variant of ► coach

COCHAIR, -S vb chair jointly

COCHES ► coch

COCHIN, -S n large breed of domestic fowl

COCHLEA, -E, -S n spiral tube in the internal ear

COCHLEAR adj of or relating to the cochlea ▷ n spoonful

COCHLEAS ► cochlea

COCINERA n in Mexico, a female cook

COCK, -ED, -ING, -S n male bird, esp of domestic fowl ▷ vb draw back (the hammer of a gun) to firing position

COCKADE, -S *n* feather or rosette worn on a hat as a badge
COCKADED
COCKAPOO *n* cross between a cocker spaniel and a poodle
COCKATOO *n* crested parrot of Australia or the East Indies
COCKBILL *vb* tilt up one end of
COCKBIRD *n* male bird
COCKBOAT *n* any small boat
COCKCROW *n* daybreak
COCKED ► cock
COCKER, -ED, -S *n* devotee of cockfighting ▷ *vb* pamper or spoil by indulgence
COCKEREL *n* young domestic cock
COCKERS ► cocker
COCKET, -S *n* document issued by a customs officer
COCKEYE, -S *n* eye affected with strabismus or one that squints
COCKEYED *adj* crooked, askew
COCKEYES ► cockeye
COCKIER ► cocky
COCKIES ► cocky
COCKIEST ► cocky
COCKILY ► cocky
COCKING ► cock
COCKISH *adj* wanton
COCKLE, -D, -S, COCKLING *n* edible shellfish ▷ *vb* fish for cockles
COCKLER, -S *n* person employed to gather cockles
COCKLES ► cockle
COCKLIKE *adj* resembling a cock
COCKLING ► cockle
COCKLOFT *n* small loft, garret, or attic
COCKNEY, -S *n* native of London, esp its East End ▷ *adj* characteristic of cockneys or their dialect
COCKNIFY *same as* **> cockneyfy**
COCKPIT, -S *n* pilot's compartment in an aircraft
COCKS ► cock
COCKSHOT *another name for* **► cockshy**
COCKSHUT *n* dusk
COCKSHY *n* target aimed at in throwing games
COCKSIER ► cocksy
COCKSPUR *n* spur on the leg of a cock
COCKSURE *adj* overconfident, arrogant
COCKSY, COCKSIER *adj* cocky
COCKTAIL *n* mixed alcoholic drink

COCKUP, -S *n* something done badly ▷ *vb* ruin or spoil
COCKY, COCKIER, COCKIES, COCKIEST *adj* conceited and overconfident ▷ *n* farmer whose farm is regarded as small or of little account
COCO, -S *n* coconut palm
COCOA, -S *n* powder made from the seed of the cacao tree
COCOANUT *same as* **► coconut**
COCOAS ► cocoa
COCOBOLA *n* type of rosewood
COCOBOLO *same as* **► cocobola**
COCOMAT, -S *n* mat made from coconut fibre
COCONUT, -S *n* large hard fruit of a type of palm tree
COCOON, -ED, -S *n* silky protective covering of a silkworm ▷ *vb* wrap up tightly for protection
COCOONER *n* person who retreats to a secure family environment
COCOONS ► cocoon
COCOPAN, -S *n* (in South Africa) a small wagon running on narrow-gauge railway lines used in mines
COCOPLUM *n* tropical shrub or its fruit
COCOS ► coco
COCOTTE, -S *n* small fireproof dish in which individual portions of food are cooked
COCOYAM, -S *n* food plant of West Africa with edible underground stem
COCREATE *vb* create jointly
COCTILE *adj* made by exposing to heat
COCTION, -S *n* boiling
COD, -DED, -DING, -S *n* large food fish of the North Atlantic ▷ *adj* having the character of an imitation or parody ▷ *vb* make fun of
CODA, -S *n* final part of a musical composition
CODABLE *adj* capable of being coded
CODAS ► coda
CODDED ► cod
CODDER, -S *n* cod fisherman or his boat
CODDING ► cod
CODDLE, -D, -S, CODDLING *vb* pamper, overprotect ▷ *n* stew made from ham and bacon scraps
CODDLER -S

CODE, -D, -S *n* system by which messages can be communicated secretly or briefly ▷ *vb* put into code
CODEBOOK *n* book containing the means to decipher a code
CODEBTOR *n* fellow debtor
CODEC, -S *n* set of electrical equipment
CODED ► code
CODEIA, -S *n* codeine
CODEIN, -S *same as* **► codeine**
CODEINA, -S *obsolete variant of* **► codeine**
CODEINE, -S *n* drug used as a painkiller
CODEINS ► codein
CODELESS *adj* lacking a code
CODEN, -S *n* identification code assigned to a publication
CODENAME *same as* **► codeword**
CODENS ► coden
CODER, -S *n* person or thing that codes
CODERIVE *vb* derive jointly
CODERS ► coder
CODES ► code
CODESIGN *vb* design jointly
CODETTA, -S *n* short coda
CODEWORD *n* (esp in military use) a word used to identify a classified plan, operation, etc
CODEX, -ES, CODICES *n* volume of manuscripts of an ancient text
CODFISH *n* cod
CODGER, -S *n* old man
CODICES ► codex
CODICIL, -S *n* addition to a will
CODIFIED ► codify
CODIFIER ► codify
CODIFY, CODIFIED, CODIFIES *vb* organize (rules or procedures) systematically
CODILLA, -S *n* coarse tow of hemp and flax
CODILLE, -S *n* in the card game ombre, term indicating that the game is won
CODING, -S ► code
CODIRECT *vb* direct jointly
CODIST, -S *n* codifier
CODLIN, -S *same as* **► codling**
CODLING, -S *n* young cod
CODLINS ► codlin
CODOLOGY *n* art or practice of bluffing or deception
CODOMAIN *n* set of values that a function is allowed to take
CODON, -S *n* part of a DNA molecule

C

CODPIECE n bag covering the male genitals, attached to the breeches

CODRIVE, -N, -S, CODROVE vb take alternate turns driving a car with another person

CODRIVER n one of two drivers who take turns to drive a car

CODRIVES ▸ codrive

CODROVE ▸ codrive

CODS ▸ cod

COED, -S adj educating boys and girls together ▷ n school or college that educates boys and girls together

COEDIT, -ED, -S vb edit (a book, newspaper, etc) jointly **COEDITOR**

COEDS ▸ coed

COEFFECT n secondary effect

COEHORN, -S n type of small artillery mortar

COELIAC, -S adj of or relating to the abdomen ▷ n person who has coeliac disease

COELOM, -S n body cavity of many multicellular animals

COELOME, -S same as ▸ coelom

COELOMIC ▸ coelom

COELOMS ▸ coelom

COEMBODY vb embody jointly

COEMPLOY vb employ together

COEMPT, -ED, -S vb buy up something in its entirety

COENACLE same as ▸ cenacle

COENACT, -S vb enact jointly

COENAMOR vb enamour jointly

COENDURE vb endure together

COENOBIA > coenobium

COENURE, -S variant form of ▸ coenurus

COENURUS, COENURI n encysted larval form of a type of tapeworm with many encapsulated heads

COENZYME n type of nonprotein organic molecule

COEQUAL, -S n equal ▷ adj of the same size, rank, etc

COEQUATE vb equate together

COERCE, -D, -S, COERCING vb compel, force **COERCER -S**

COERCION n act or power of coercing

COERCIVE ▸ coerce

COERECT, -S vb erect together

COESITE, -S n polymorph of silicon dioxide

COEVAL, -S n contemporary ▷ adj contemporary **COEVALLY**

COEVOLVE vb evolve together

COEXERT, -S vb exert together

COEXIST, -S vb exist together, esp peacefully despite differences

COEXTEND vb extend or cause to extend equally in space or time

COFACTOR n type of nonprotein substance

COFF, -ED, -ING, -S, COFT vb buy

COFFEE, -S n drink made from the roasted and ground seeds of a tropical shrub ▷ adj medium-brown

COFFER, -ED, -S n chest, esp for storing valuables ▷ vb store

COFFIN, -ED, -S n box in which a corpse is buried or cremated ▷ vb place in or as in a coffin

COFFING ▸ coff

COFFINS ▸ coffin

COFFLE, -D, -S, COFFLING n (esp formerly) line of slaves, beasts, etc, fastened together ▷ vb fasten together in a coffle

COFFRET, -S n small coffer

COFFS ▸ coff

COFIRING n combustion of two different types of fuel at the same time

COFOUND, -S vb found jointly

COFT ▸ coff

COG, -GED, -S n one of the teeth on the rim of a gearwheel ▷ vb roll (cast-steel ingots) to convert them into blooms

COGENCE, -S ▸ cogent

COGENCY ▸ cogent

COGENER, -S n congener

COGENT adj forcefully convincing **COGENTLY**

COGGED ▸ cog

COGGER, -S n deceiver

COGGIE, -S n quaich or drinking cup

COGGING, -S ▸ cog

COGGLE, -D, -S, COGGLING vb wobble or rock

COGGLIER ▸ coggly

COGGLING ▸ coggle

COGGLY, COGGLIER ▸ coggle

COGIE, -S same as ▸ coggie

COGITATE vb think deeply about

COGITO, -S n philosophical theory

COGNAC, -S n French brandy

COGNATE, -S adj derived from a common original form ▷ n cognate word or language

COGNISE, -D, -S same as ▸ cognize **COGNISER**

COGNIZE, -D, -S vb perceive, become aware of, or know **COGNIZER**

COGNOMEN n nickname

COGNOSCE vb in Scots law, to give judgment upon

COGNOVIT n in law, a defendant's confession that the case against him or her is just

COGON, -S n type of coarse tropical grass used for thatching

COGS ▸ cog

COGUE, -S n wooden pail or drinking vessel

COGWAY, -S n rack railway

COGWHEEL same as > gearwheel

COHAB, -S n cohabitor

COHABIT, -S vb live together as spouses without being married

COHABS ▸ cohab

COHEAD, -ED, -S vb head jointly

COHEIR, -S n person who inherits jointly with others

COHEN, -S same as ▸ kohen

COHERE, -D, -S, COHERING vb hold or stick together

COHERENT adj logical and consistent

COHERER, -S n electrical component

COHERES ▸ cohere

COHERING ▸ cohere

COHESION n sticking together

COHESIVE adj sticking together to form a whole

COHIBIT, -S vb restrain

COHO, -ES, -S n type of Pacific salmon

COHOBATE vb redistil (a distillate), esp by allowing it to mingle with the remaining matter

COHOE same as ▸ coho

COHOES ▸ coho

COHOG, -S n quahog, an edible clam

COHOLDER n joint holder

COHORN, -S same as ▸ coehorn

COHORT, -S n band of associates

COHOS ► coho
COHOSH, -ES n type of North American plant
COHOST, -ED, -S vb host jointly
COHUNE, -S n tropical feather palm
COIF, -FED, -FING, -ING, -S vb arrange the hair of ▷ n close-fitting cap worn in the Middle Ages
COIFED adj wearing a coif
COIFFE, -S vb coiffure
COIFFED ► coif
COIFFES ► coiffe
COIFFEUR n hairdresser
COIFFING ► coif
COIFFURE n hairstyle ▷ vb dress or arrange (the hair)
COIFING ► coif
COIFS ► coif
COIGN, -ED, -ING, -S vb wedge ▷ n quoin
COIGNE, -S same as ► coign
COIGNED ► coign
COIGNES ► coigne
COIGNING ► coign
COIGNS ► coign
COIL, -ED, -ING, -S vb wind in loops ▷ n something coiled
COILER -S
COIN, -ED, -S n piece of metal money ▷ vb invent (a word or phrase)
COINABLE
COINAGE, -S n coins collectively
COINCIDE vb happen at the same time
COINED ► coin
COINER, -S ► coin
COINFECT vb infect at same time as other infection
COINFER, -S vb infer jointly
COINHERE vb inhere together
COINING, -S ► coin
COINMATE n fellow inmate
COINOP adj (of a machine) operated by putting a coin in a slot
COINS ► coin
COINSURE vb insure jointly
COINTER, -S vb inter together
COINVENT vb invent jointly
COIR, -S n coconut fibre, used for matting
COISTREL n knave
COISTRIL same as ► coistrel
COIT, -S n buttocks
COJOIN, -ED, -S vb conjoin
COKE, -D n solid fuel left after gas has been distilled from coal ▷ vb become or convert into coke
COKELIKE

COKERNUT same as ► coconut
COKES, -ES n fool
COKIER ► coky
COKIEST ► coky
COKING, -S n act of coking
COKY, COKIER, COKIEST adj like coke
COL, -S n high mountain pass
COLA, -S n dark brown fizzy soft drink
COLANDER n perforated bowl for straining or rinsing foods
COLAS ► cola
COLBY, COLBIES, -S n type of mild-tasting cheese
COLCHICA > colchicum
COLD, -ER, -EST, -S adj lacking heat ▷ n lack of heat
COLDCOCK vb knock to the ground
COLDER ► cold
COLDEST ► cold
COLDIE, -S n cold can or bottle of beer
COLDISH ► cold
COLDLY ► cold
COLDNESS ► cold
COLDS ► cold
COLE, -S same as ► cabbage
COLEAD, -S, COLED vb lead together
COLEADER
COLES ► cole
COLESEED n seeds or plants of the cole
COLESLAW n salad dish of shredded raw cabbage in a dressing
COLESSEE n joint lessee
COLESSOR n joint lessor
COLETIT, -S n coal tit
COLEUS, -ES n Old World plant
COLEWORT same as ► cabbage
COLEY, -S same as ► coalfish
COLIBRI, -S n hummingbird
COLIC, -S n severe pains in the stomach and bowels
COLICIN, -S n bactericidal protein
COLICINE n antibacterial protein
COLICINS ► colicin
COLICKY adj relating to or suffering from colic
COLICS ► colic
COLIES ► coly
COLIFORM n type of bacteria of the intestinal tract
COLIN, -S n quail
COLINEAR same as > collinear
COLINS ► colin
COLISEUM n large building, such as a stadium or theatre,

used for entertainments, sports, etc
COLISTIN n polymyxin antibiotic
COLITIC ► colitis
COLITIS n inflammation of the colon
COLL, -ED, -S vb embrace
COLLAGE, -D, -S n type of art form ▷ vb make a collage
COLLAGEN n protein found in cartilage and bone that yields gelatine when boiled
COLLAGES ► collage
COLLAPSE vb fall down suddenly ▷ n collapsing
COLLAR, -ED, -S n part of a garment round the neck ▷ vb seize, arrest
COLLARD, -S n variety of the cabbage with a crown of edible leaves
COLLARED ► collar
COLLARET n small collar
COLLARS ► collar
COLLATE, -D, -S vb gather together, examine, and put in order
COLLATOR n person or machine that collates texts or manuscripts
COLLECT, -S vb gather together ▷ n short prayer
COLLED ► coll
COLLEEN, -S n girl
COLLEGE, -S n place of higher education
COLLEGER n member of a college
COLLEGES ► college
COLLEGIA > collegium
COLLET, -ED, -S n (in a jewellery setting) a band or coronet-shaped claw that holds an individual stone ▷ vb mount in a collet
COLLIDE, -D, -S vb crash together violently
COLLIDER n particle accelerator in which beams of particles are made to collide
COLLIDES ► collide
COLLIE n silky-haired sheepdog
COLLIED ► colly
COLLIER, -S n coal miner
COLLIERY n coal mine
COLLIES ► colly
COLLING, -S n embrace
COLLINS n type of cocktail
COLLOGUE vb confer confidentially
COLLOID, -S n suspension of particles in a solution ▷ adj relating to the gluelike

C

material found in certain degenerating tissues

COLLOP, -S n small slice of meat

COLLOQUE vb converse

COLLOQUY n conversation or conference

COLLS ▸ coll

COLLUDE, -D, -S vb act in collusion
COLLUDER

COLLUVIA > colluvium

COLLY, COLLIED, COLLIES, -ING n soot or grime, such as coal dust ▷ vb begrime

COLLYRIA > collyrium

COLOBI > colobus

COLOBID ▸ colobus

COLOBOMA n structural defect of the eye, esp in the choroid, retina, or iris

COLOBUS, COLOBI n type of Old World monkey

COLOCATE vb locate together

COLOG, -S n logarithm of the reciprocal of a number

COLOGNE, -S n mild perfume
COLOGNED

COLOGS ▸ colog

COLON, -S n punctuation mark (:)

COLONE, -S variant of ▸ colon

COLONEL, -S n senior commissioned army or air-force officer

COLONES ▸ colone

COLONI ▸ colonus

COLONIAL n inhabitant of a colony ▷ adj of or inhabiting a colony or colonies

COLONIC, -S adj of or relating to the colon ▷ n irrigation of the colon

COLONIES ▸ colony

COLONISE same as ▸ colonize

COLONIST n settler in a colony

COLONIZE vb make into a colony

COLONS ▸ colon

COLONUS, COLONI n ancient Roman farmer

COLONY, COLONIES n people who settle in a new country but remain ruled by their homeland

COLOPHON n publisher's symbol on a book

COLOR, -S same as ▸ colour

COLORADO adj (of a cigar) of middling colour and strength

COLORANT n any substance that imparts colour, such as a pigment, dye, or ink

COLORED US spelling of ▸ coloured

COLORER, -S ▸ color

COLORFUL ▸ color

COLORING ▸ colour

COLORISE same as > colourize

COLORISM ▸ color

COLORIST ▸ color

COLORIZE same as > colourize

COLORMAN, COLORMEN same as ▸ colourman

COLORS ▸ color

COLORWAY variant of > colourway

COLORY same as ▸ coloury

COLOSSAL adj very large

COLOSSUS, COLOSSI n huge statue

COLOTOMY n colonic incision

COLOUR, -S n appearance of things as a result of reflecting light ▷ vb apply colour to

COLOURED adj having colour

COLOURER ▸ colour

COLOURS ▸ colour

COLOURY adj possessing colour

COLPITIS another name for > vaginitis

COLS ▸ col

COLT, -ED, -ING, -S n young male horse ▷ vb to fool

COLTAN, -S n metallic ore

COLTED ▸ colt

COLTER, -S same as ▸ coulter

COLTHOOD n state of being a colt

COLTING ▸ colt

COLTISH adj inexperienced

COLTS ▸ colt

COLTWOOD n plant mentioned in Spenser's Faerie Queene

COLUBRID n type of snake such as the grass snake and whip snakes

COLUGO, -S n flying lemur

COLUMBIC another word for ▸ niobic

COLUMEL, -S n in botany, the central column in a capsule

COLUMN, -S n pillar ▷ vb create a column
COLUMNAL
COLUMNAR

COLUMNEA n flowering plant

COLUMNED ▸ column

COLUMNS ▸ column

COLURE, -S n either of two great circles on the celestial sphere

COLY, COLIES n S African arboreal bird

COLZA, -S n Eurasian plant with bright yellow flowers

COMA, -E, -S n state of deep unconsciousness

COMADE ▸ comake

COMAE ▸ coma

COMAKE, COMADE, -S, COMAKING vb make together

COMAKER -S

COMAL ▸ coma

COMANAGE vb manage jointly

COMARB, -S same as ▸ coarb

COMART, -S n covenant

COMAS ▸ coma

COMATE, -S adj having tufts of hair ▷ n companion

COMATIC ▸ coma

COMATIK, -S variant of ▸ komatik

COMATOSE adj in a coma

COMATULA same as > comatulid

COMB, -ED, -ING, -S n toothed implement for arranging the hair ▷ vb use a comb on

COMBAT, -ED, -S vb fight, struggle ▷ n fight or struggle
COMBATER

COMBE, -S same as ▸ comb

COMBED ▸ comb

COMBER, -S n long curling wave

COMBES ▸ combe

COMBI, -S n combination boiler

COMBIER ▸ comby

COMBIES ▸ comby

COMBIEST ▸ comby

COMBINE, -S vb join together ▷ n association of people or firms for a common purpose

COMBINED n competitive event consisting of two skiing competitions

COMBINER ▸ combine

COMBINES ▸ combine

COMBING ▸ comb

COMBINGS pl n loose hair or fibres removed by combing, esp from animals

COMBIS ▸ combi

COMBLE, -S n apex; zenith

COMBLESS adj without a comb

COMBLIKE adj resembling a comb

COMBO, -S n small group of jazz musicians

COMBOVER n hairstyle in which thinning hair is combed over the scalp

COMBS ▸ comb

COMBUST, -S adj invisible due to proximity to the sun ▷ vb burn

COMBWISE *adv* in the manner of a comb

COMBY, COMBIER, COMBIES, COMBIEST *adj* comb-like ▷ *n* combination boiler

COME, CAME, -S, -TH *vb* move towards a place, arrive

COMEBACK *n* return to a former position ▷ *vb* return, esp to the memory

COMEDDLE *vb* mix

COMEDIAN *n* entertainer who tells jokes

COMEDIC *adj* of or relating to comedy

COMEDIES ▶ comedy

COMEDIST *n* writer of comedies

COMEDO, -S *the technical name for* ▷ **blackhead**

COMEDOWN *n* decline in status ▷ *vb* come to a place regarded as lower

COMEDY, COMEDIES *n* humorous play, film, or programme

COMELIER ▶ comely

COMELILY ▶ comely

COMELY, COMELIER *adj* nice-looking

COMEMBER *n* fellow member

COMEOVER *n* person who has come from Britain to the Isle of Man to settle

COMER, -S *n* person who comes

COMES ▶ come

COMET, -S *n* heavenly body with a long luminous tail

COMETARY

COMETH ▶ come

COMETHER *n* coaxing; allure

COMETIC ▶ comet

COMETS ▶ comet

COMFIER ▶ comfy

COMFIEST ▶ comfy

COMFILY *adv* in a manner suggestive of or promoting comfort

COMFIT, -S *n* sugar-coated sweet

COMFORT, -S *n* physical ease or wellbeing ▷ *vb* soothe, console

COMFREY, -S *n* tall plant with bell-shaped flowers

COMFY, COMFIER, COMFIEST *adj* comfortable

COMIC, -S *adj* humorous, funny ▷ *n* comedian

COMICAL *adj* amusing

COMICE, -S *n* kind of pear

COMICS ▶ comic

COMING, -S ▶ come

COMINGLE *same as* > commingle

COMINGS ▶ coming

COMIQUE, -S *n* comic actor

COMITAL *adj* relating to a count or earl

COMITIA, -S *n* ancient Roman assembly

COMITIAL

COMITY, COMITIES *n* friendly politeness, esp between different countries

COMIX *n* comic books in general

COMM *n as in* **comm badge** small wearable badge-shaped radio transmitter and receiver

COMMA, -S, -TA *n* punctuation mark (,)

COMMAND, -S *vb* order ▷ *n* authoritative instruction that something must be done

COMMANDO *n* (member of) a military unit trained for swift raids in enemy territory

COMMANDS ▶ command

COMMAS ▶ comma

COMMATA ▶ comma

COMMENCE *vb* begin

COMMEND, -S *vb* praise

COMMENT, -S *n* remark ▷ *vb* make a comment

COMMER, -S *same as* ▶ comer

COMMERCE *n* buying and selling, trade ▷ *vb* to trade

COMMERE, -S *n* female compere

COMMERGE *vb* merge together

COMMERS ▶ commer

COMMIE, -S *adj* communist

COMMIS *n* apprentice waiter or chef ▷ *adj* (of a waiter or chef) apprentice

COMMISH *n* commissioner

COMMIT, -S *vb* perform (a crime or error)

COMMIX, -ED, -ES, -T *a rare word for* ▶ mix

COMMO, -S *short for* > communist

COMMODE, -S *n* seat with a hinged flap concealing a chamber pot

COMMODO *same as* ▶ comodo

COMMON, -ED *adj* occurring often ▷ *n* area of grassy land belonging to a community ▷ *vb* sit at table with strangers

COMMONER *n* person who does not belong to the nobility

COMMONEY *n* playing marble of a common sort

COMMONLY *adv* usually

COMMONS *n* people not of noble birth viewed as forming a political order

COMMOS ▶ commo

COMMOT, -S *n* in medieval Wales, a division of land

COMMOTE, -S *same as* ▶ commot

COMMOTS ▶ commot

COMMOVE, -D, -S *vb* disturb

COMMS *pl n* communications

COMMUNAL *adj* shared

COMMUNE, -D, -S *n* group of people who live together and share everything ▷ *vb* feel very close (to)

COMMUNER

COMMUTE, -D, -S *vb* travel daily to and from work ▷ *n* journey made by commuting

COMMUTER *n* person who commutes to and from work

COMMUTES ▶ commute

COMMY *same as* ▶ commie

COMODO *adv* (to be performed) at a convenient relaxed speed

COMORBID *adj* (of illness) happening at same time as other illness

COMOSE *another word for* ▶ comate

COMOUS *adj* hairy

COMP, -ED, -S *n* person who sets and corrects type ▷ *vb* set or correct type

COMPACT, -S *adj* closely packed ▷ *n* small flat case containing a mirror and face powder ▷ *vb* pack closely together

COMPADRE *n* masculine friend

COMPAGE *obsolete form of* ▶ compages

COMPAGES *n* structure or framework

COMPAND, -S *vb* (of a transmitter signal) to compress before, and expand after, transmission

COMPANY *n* business organization ▷ *vb* associate or keep company with someone

COMPARE, -D, -S *vb* examine (things) and point out the resemblances or differences

COMPARER

COMPART, -S *vb* divide into parts

COMPAS *n* rhythm in flamenco

COMPASS n instrument for showing direction ▷ vb encircle or surround

COMPAST adj rounded

COMPEAR, -S vb in Scots law, to appear in court

COMPED ▶ comp

COMPEER, -S n person of equal rank, status, or ability ▷ vb to equal

COMPEL, -S vb force (to be or do)

COMPEND, -S n compendium

COMPER, -S n person who regularly enters competitions

COMPERE, -D, -S n person who presents a stage, radio, or television show ▷ vb be the compere of

COMPERS ▶ comper

COMPESCE vb curb

COMPETE, -D, -S vb try to win or achieve (a prize, profit, etc)

COMPILE, -D, -S vb collect and arrange (information), esp to make a book

COMPILER n person who compiles information

COMPILES ▶ compile

COMPING, -S n act of comping

COMPITAL adj pertaining to crossroads

COMPLAIN vb express resentment or displeasure

COMPLEAT an archaic spelling of ▶ complete

COMPLECT vb interweave or entwine

COMPLETE adj thorough, absolute ▷ vb finish

COMPLEX, -ED, -ES adj made up of parts ▷ n whole made up of parts ▷ vb form a complex

COMPLICE n associate or accomplice

COMPLIED ▶ comply

COMPLIER ▶ comply

COMPLIES ▶ comply

COMPLIN, -S same as ▶ compline

COMPLINE n last service of the day in the Roman Catholic Church

COMPLINS ▶ complin

COMPLISH vb accomplish

COMPLOT, -S n plot or conspiracy ▷ vb plot together

COMPLY, COMPLIED, COMPLIES vb act in accordance (with)

COMPO, -S n mixture of materials, such as mortar, plaster, etc ▷ adj intended to last for several days

COMPONE same as ▶ compony

COMPONY adj made up of alternating metal and colour, colour and fur, or fur and metal

COMPORT, -S vb behave (oneself) in a specified way

COMPOS ▶ compo

COMPOSE, -S vb put together

COMPOSED adj calm

COMPOSER n person who writes music

COMPOSES ▶ compose

COMPOST, -S n decayed plants used as a fertilizer ▷ vb make (vegetable matter) into compost

COMPOT, -S same as ▶ compote

COMPOTE, -S n fruit stewed with sugar

COMPOTS ▶ compot

COMPOUND adj (thing, esp chemical) made up of two or more combined parts or elements ▷ vb combine or make by combining ▷ n fenced enclosure containing buildings

COMPRESS vb squeeze together ▷ n pad applied to stop bleeding or cool inflammation

COMPRINT vb print jointly

COMPRISE vb be made up of or make up

COMPRIZE same as ▶ comprise

COMPS ▶ comp

COMPT, -ED, -ING, -S obsolete variant of ▶ count

COMPTER, -S n formerly, a prison

COMPTING ▶ compt

COMPTS ▶ compt

COMPULSE vb compel

COMPUTE, -D, -S vb calculate, esp using a computer ▷ n calculation

COMPUTER n electronic machine that stores and processes data

COMPUTES ▶ compute

COMRADE, -S n fellow member of a union or socialist political party

COMS pl n one-piece woollen undergarment with long sleeves and legs

COMSAT, -S n communications satellite

COMSYMP, -S n disparaging term for a person sympathetic to communism

COMTE, -S n European nobleman

COMUS, -ES n wild party

CON, -NED, -S vb deceive, swindle ▷ n convict ▷ prep with

CONACRE, -D, -S n farming land let for a season or for eleven months ▷ vb let conacre

CONARIA ▶ conarium

CONARIAL ▶ conarium

CONARIUM, CONARIA n pineal gland

CONATION n psychological element that tends towards activity or change

CONATIVE adj aspect of some verbs indicating the effort of the agent in performing the verb

CONATUS n effort or striving of natural impulse

CONCAUSE n shared cause

CONCAVE, -D, -S adj curving inwards ▷ vb make concave

CONCEAL, -S vb cover and hide

CONCEDE, -D, -S vb admit to be true

CONCEDER

CONCEDO interj I allow; I concede (a point)

CONCEIT, -S n too high an opinion of oneself ▷ vb like or be able to bear (something, such as food or drink)

CONCEITY adj full of conceit

CONCEIVE vb imagine, think

CONCENT, -S n concord, as of sounds, voices, etc

CONCEPT, -S n abstract or general idea

CONCEPTI > conceptus

CONCEPTS ▶ concept

CONCERN, -S n anxiety, worry ▷ vb worry (someone)

CONCERT, -S n musical entertainment

CONCERTO, CONCERTI n large-scale composition for a solo instrument and orchestra

CONCERTS ▶ concert

CONCETTO, CONCETTI n conceit, ingenious thought

CONCH, -S same as ▶ concha

CONCHA, -E, -S n any bodily organ or part resembling a shell in shape

CONCHAL

CONCHATE adj shell-shaped

CONCHE, -D, -S, CONCHING vb (in chocolate-making) to use a conche

CONCHIE, -S n conscientious objector

CONCHING ▶ **conche**

CONCHO, -S n American metal ornament

CONCHOID n type of plane curve

CONCHOS ▶ **concho**

CONCHS ▶ **conch**

CONCHY same as ▶ **conchie**

CONCISE, -D, -R, -S adj brief and to the point ▷ vb mutilate

CONCLAVE n secret meeting

CONCLUDE vb decide by reasoning

CONCOCT, -S vb make up (a story or plan)

CONCOLOR adj of a single colour

CONCORD, -S n state of peaceful agreement, harmony ▷ vb agree

CONCOURS n contest

CONCRETE n mixture of cement, sand, stone, and water, used in building ▷ vb cover with concrete ▷ adj made of concrete

CONCREW, -S vb grow together

CONCUPY n concupiscence

CONCUR, -S vb agree

CONCUSS vb injure (the brain) by a fall or blow

COND old inflection of ▶ **con**

CONDEMN, -S vb express disapproval of

CONDENSE vb make shorter

CONDER, -S n person who directs the steering of a vessel

CONDIE, -S n culvert; tunnel

CONDIGN adj (esp of a punishment) fitting

CONDO, -ES, -S n condominium

CONDOLE, -D, -S vb express sympathy with someone in grief, pain, etc
CONDOLER

CONDONE, -D, -S vb overlook or forgive (wrongdoing)
CONDONER

CONDOR, -ES, -S n large vulture of S America

CONDOS ▶ **condo**

CONDUCE, -D, -S vb lead or contribute (to a result)
CONDUCER

CONDUCT, -S n management of an activity ▷ vb carry out (a task)

CONDUCTI > **conductus**

CONDUCTS ▶ **conduct**

CONDUIT, -S n channel or tube for fluid or cables

CONDYLAR ▶ **condyle**

CONDYLE, -S n rounded projection on the articulating end of a bone

CONE, -D, -S, CONING n object with a circular base, tapering to a point ▷ vb shape like a cone or part of a cone

CONELRAD n US defence and information system for use in the event of air attack

CONENOSE n bloodsucking bug of the genus Triatoma

CONEPATE same as ▶ **conepatl**

CONEPATL n skunk

CONES ▶ **cone**

CONEY, -S same as ▶ **cony**

CONF, -S n online forum

CONFAB, -S n conversation ▷ vb converse

CONFECT, -S vb prepare by combining ingredients

CONFER, -S vb discuss together

CONFEREE n person who takes part in a conference

CONFERS ▶ **confer**

CONFERVA n type of threadlike green alga typically occurring in fresh water

CONFESS vb admit (a fault or crime)

CONFEST adj admitted

CONFETTI n small pieces of coloured paper thrown at weddings

CONFETTO n sweetmeat

CONFIDE, -D, -S vb tell someone (a secret)
CONFIDER

CONFINE, -S vb keep within bounds ▷ n limit

CONFINED adj enclosed or restricted

CONFINER ▶ **confine**

CONFINES ▶ **confine**

CONFIRM, -S vb prove to be true

CONFIT, -S n preserve

CONFIX, -ED, -ES vb fasten

CONFLATE vb combine or blend into a whole

CONFLICT n disagreement ▷ vb be incompatible

CONFLUX n merging or following together, especially of rivers

CONFOCAL adj having a common focus or common foci

CONFORM, -S vb comply with accepted standards or customs

CONFOUND vb astound, bewilder

CONFRERE n colleague

CONFRONT vb come face to face with

CONFS ▶ **conf**

CONFUSE, -S vb mix up

CONFUSED adj lacking a clear understanding of something

CONFUSES ▶ **confuse**

CONFUTE, -D, -S vb prove wrong
CONFUTER

CONGA, -S, -ED, -ING, -S n dance performed by a number of people in single file ▷ vb dance the conga

CONGE, -D, -ING, -S n permission to depart or dismissal, esp when formal ▷ vb take one's leave

CONGEAL, -S vb (of a liquid) become thick and sticky

CONGED ▶ **conge**

CONGEE, -D, -S same as ▶ **conge**

CONGEING ▶ **conge**

CONGENER n member of a class, group, or other category, esp any animal of a specified genus

CONGENIC adj (of inbred animal cells) genetically identical except for a single gene locus

CONGER, -S n large sea eel

CONGES ▶ **conge**

CONGEST, -S vb crowd or become crowded to excess

CONGIARY n Roman emperor's gift to the people or soldiers

CONGIUS, CONGII n unit of liquid measure equal to 1 imperial gallon

CONGLOBE vb gather into a globe or ball

CONGO, -ES, -S same as ▶ **congou**

CONGOU, -S n kind of black tea from China

CONGRATS sentence substitute congratulations

CONGREE, -D, -S vb agree

CONGREET vb (of two or more people) to greet one another

CONGRESS n formal meeting for discussion

CONGRUE, -D, -S vb agree

CONI ▶ **conus**

CONIA, -S same as ▶ **coniine**

CONIC adj having the shape of a cone

CONICAL adj cone-shaped

CONICINE same as ▸ coniine

CONICITY ▸ conical

CONICS n branch of geometry

CONIDIA ▸ conidium

CONIDIAL ▸ conidium

CONIDIAN ▸ conidium

CONIDIUM, CONIDIA n asexual spore formed at the tip of a specialized filament in certain types of fungi

CONIES ▸ cony

CONIFER, -S n cone-bearing tree, such as the fir or pine

CONIFORM adj cone-shaped

CONIINE, -S n colourless poisonous soluble liquid alkaloid found in hemlock

CONIMA, -S n gum resin from the conium hemlock tree

CONIN, -S same as ▸ coniine

CONINE, -S same as ▸ coniine

CONING ▸ cone

CONINS ▸ conin

CONIOSIS, CONIOSES n any disease or condition caused by dust inhalation

CONIUM, -S n N temperate umbelliferous plant, esp hemlock

CONJECT, -S vb conjecture

CONJEE, -D, -S vb prepare as, or in, a conjee (a gruel of boiled rice and water)

CONJOIN, -S vb join or become joined

CONJOINT adj united, joint, or associated

CONJUGAL adj of marriage

CONJUNCT adj joined ▷ n one of the propositions or formulas in a conjunction

CONJUNTO n style of Mexican music

CONJURE, -D, -S vb perform tricks that appear to be magic

CONJURER same as ▸ conjuror

CONJURES ▸ conjure

CONJUROR n person who performs magic tricks for people's entertainment

CONJURY n magic

CONK, -ED, -ING, -S n nose ▷ vb strike (someone) on the head or nose

CONKER n nut of the horse chestnut

CONKERS n game played with conkers tied on strings

CONKIER ▸ conky

CONKIEST ▸ conky

CONKING ▸ conk

CONKOUT, -S n time when a machine stops working

CONKS ▸ conk

CONKY, CONKIER, CONKIEST adj affected by the timber disease, conk

CONMAN, CONMEN n person who uses confidence tricks to swindle or defraud

CONN, -S same as ▸ con

CONNATE adj existing in a person or thing from birth

CONNE, -S same as ▸ con

CONNECT, -S vb join together

CONNED ▸ con

CONNER, -S same as ▸ conder

CONNES ▸ conne

CONNIE, -S n tram or bus conductor

CONNING, -S ▸ con

CONNIVE, -D, -S vb allow (wrongdoing) by ignoring it

CONNIVER

CONNOR, -S n type of saltwater fish

CONNOTE, -D, -S vb imply or suggest

CONNS ▸ conn

CONODONT n toothlike fossil derived from an eel-like animal

CONOID, -S n geometric surface ▷ adj conical, cone-shaped

CONOIDAL same as ▸ conoid

CONOIDIC ▸ conoid

CONOIDS ▸ conoid

CONQUER, -S vb defeat

CONQUEST n conquering

CONQUIAN same as ▸ cooncan

CONS ▸ con

CONSEIL, -S n advice

CONSENT, -S n agreement, permission ▷ vb permit, agree to

CONSERVE vb protect from harm, decay, or loss ▷ n jam containing large pieces of fruit

CONSIDER vb regard as

CONSIGN, -S vb put somewhere

CONSIST, -S vb be composed (of)

CONSOL n consolidated annuity, a British government bond

CONSOLE, -D, -S vb comfort in distress ▷ n panel of controls for electronic equipment

CONSOLER

CONSOLS pl n irredeemable British government securities

CONSOMME n thin clear meat soup

CONSORT, -S vb keep company (with) ▷ n spouse of a monarch

CONSPIRE vb plan a crime together in secret

CONSPUE, -D, -S vb spit on with contempt

CONSTANT adj continuous ▷ n unvarying quantity

CONSTATE vb affirm

CONSTER, -S obsolete variant of ▸ construe

CONSTRUE vb interpret ▷ n something that is construed, such as a piece of translation

CONSUL, -S n official representing a state in a foreign country

CONSULAR n anyone of consular rank

CONSULS ▸ consul

CONSULT, -S vb go to for advice or information

CONSULTA n official planning meeting

CONSULTS ▸ consult

CONSUME, -D, -S vb eat or drink

CONSUMER n person who buys goods or uses services

CONSUMES ▸ consume

CONSUMPT n quantity used up; consumption

CONTACT, -S n communicating ▷ vb get in touch with ▷ interj (formerly) call made by the pilot to indicate the engine is ready for starting

CONTAGIA > contagium

CONTAIN, -S vb hold or be capable of holding

CONTANGO n postponement of payment for and delivery of stock ▷ vb arrange such a postponement of payment

CONTE, -S n tale or short story, esp of adventure

CONTECK, -S n contention

CONTEMN, -S vb regard with contempt

CONTEMPO adj contemporary

CONTEMPT n dislike and disregard

CONTEND, -S vb deal with

CONTENT, -S n meaning or substance of a piece of writing ▷ adj satisfied with things as they are ▷ vb make (someone) content

CONTES ▸ conte

CONTESSA n Italian countess

CONTEST, -S n competition or struggle ▷ vb dispute, object to

CONTEXT, -S n circumstances of an event or fact

CONTINUA > **continuum**

CONTINUE vb (cause to) remain in a condition or place

CONTINUO n continuous bass part, usu played on a keyboard instrument

CONTLINE n space between the bilges of stowed casks

CONTO, -S n former Portuguese monetary unit worth 1000 escudos

CONTORNO, CONTORNI n in Italy, side dish of salad or vegetables

CONTORT, -S vb twist out of shape

CONTOS > **conto**

CONTOUR, -S n outline ▷ vb shape so as to form or follow the contour of something

CONTRA, -S n counter-argument

CONTRACT n (document setting out) a formal agreement ▷ vb make a formal agreement (to do something)

CONTRAIL n aeroplane's vapour trail

CONTRAIR adj contrary

CONTRARY n complete opposite ▷ adj opposed, completely different ▷ adv in opposition

CONTRAS > **contra**

CONTRAST n obvious difference ▷ vb compare in order to show differences

CONTRAT, -S old form of ▷ **contract**

CONTRATE adj (of gears) having teeth set at a right angle to the axis

CONTRATS > **contrat**

CONTRIST vb make sad

CONTRITE adj sorry and apologetic

CONTRIVE vb make happen

CONTROL, -S n power to direct something ▷ vb have power over

CONTROLE adj officially registered

CONTROLS > **control**

CONTROUL obsolete variant of ▷ **control**

CONTUND, -S vb pummel

CONTUSE, -D, -S vb injure (the body) without breaking the skin

CONURBAN adj relating to an urban region

CONURBIA n conurbations considered collectively

CONURE, -S n small American parrot

CONUS, CONI n any of several cone-shaped structures

CONVECT, -S vb circulate hot air by convection

CONVENE, -D, -S vb gather or summon for a formal meeting

CONVENER n person who calls a meeting

CONVENES > **convene**

CONVENOR same as ▷ **convener**

CONVENT, -S n building where nuns live ▷ vb summon

CONVERGE vb meet or join

CONVERSE vb have a conversation ▷ n opposite or contrary ▷ adj reversed or opposite

CONVERSO n medieval Spanish Jew converting to Catholicism

CONVERT, -S vb change in form, character, or function ▷ n person who has converted to a different belief or religion

CONVEX, -ED, -ES adj curving outwards ▷ vb make convex

CONVEXLY

CONVEY, -ED, -S vb communicate (information)

CONVEYAL n act or means of conveying

CONVEYED > **convey**

CONVEYER same as ▷ **conveyor**

CONVEYOR n person or thing that conveys

CONVEYS > **convey**

CONVICT, -S vb declare guilty ▷ n person serving a prison sentence ▷ adj convicted

CONVINCE vb persuade by argument or evidence

CONVIVE, -D, -S vb feast together

CONVO, -S n conversation

CONVOKE, -D, -S vb call together

CONVOKER

CONVOLVE vb wind or roll together

CONVOS > **convo**

CONVOY, -ED, -S n group of vehicles or ships travelling together ▷ vb escort while in transit

CONVULSE vb (of part of the body) undergo violent spasms

CONWOMAN, CONWOMEN n woman who uses confidence tricks to swindle or defraud

CONY, CONIES n rabbit

COO, -ED, -S vb (of a dove or pigeon) make a soft murmuring sound ▷ n sound of cooing ▷ interj exclamation of surprise, awe, etc

COOCOO old spelling of ▷ **cuckoo**

COOED > **coo**

COOEE, -D, -ING, -S interj call to attract attention ▷ vb utter this call ▷ n calling distance

COOER, -S > **coo**

COOEY, -ED, -ING, -S same as ▷ **cooee**

COOF, -S n simpleton

COOING, -S > **coo**

COOINGLY > **coo**

COOINGS > **cooing**

COOK, -ED, -S vb prepare (food) by heating ▷ n person who cooks food

COOKABLE adj able to be cooked ▷ n something that can be cooked

COOKBOOK n book containing recipes and instructions for cooking

COOKED > **cook**

COOKER, -S n apparatus for cooking heated by gas or electricity

COOKERY n art of cooking

COOKEY, -S same as ▷ **cookie**

COOKIE, -S n biscuit

COOKING, -S > **cook**

COOKLESS adj devoid of a cook

COOKMAID n maid who assists a cook

COOKOFF, -S n cookery competition

COOKOUT, -S n party where a meal is cooked and eaten out of doors

COOKROOM n room in which food is cooked

COOKS > **cook**

COOKSHOP n shop that sells cookery equipment

COOKTOP, -S n flat unit for cooking in saucepans or the top part of a stove

COOKWARE n cooking utensils

COOKY same as ▷ **cookie**

COOL, -ED, -EST, -S adj moderately cold ▷ vb make or become cool ▷ n coolness

COOLABAH n Australian tree that grows along rivers,

with smooth bark and long narrow leaves

COOLAMON n shallow dish of wood or bark, used for carrying water

COOLANT, -S n fluid used to cool machinery while it is working

COOLDOWN n gentle stretching exercises after strenuous activity

COOLED ▸ cool

COOLER, -S n container for making or keeping things cool

COOLEST ▸ cool

COOLIBAH same as ▸ **coolabah**

COOLIBAR same as ▸ **coolabah**

COOLIE, -S n unskilled Oriental labourer

COOLING, -S as in **regenerative cooling** method of cooling rocket combustion chambers

COOLISH ▸ cool

COOLIST, -S n person who does not believe in global warming

COOLLY ▸ cool

COOLNESS ▸ cool

COOLS ▸ cool

COOLTH, -S n coolness

COOLY same as ▸ **coolie**

COOM, -ED, -ING, -S n waste material ▷ vb blacken

COOMB, -S same as ▸ **comb**

COOMBE, -S same as ▸ **comb**

COOMBS ▸ coomb

COOMED ▸ coom

COOMIER ▸ coomy

COOMIEST ▸ coomy

COOMING ▸ coom

COOMS ▸ coom

COOMY, COOMIER, COOMIEST adj grimy

COON, -S n raccoon

COONCAN, -S n card game for two players, similar to rummy

COONDOG, -S n dog trained to hunt raccoons

COONS ▸ coon

COONSKIN n pelt of a raccoon

COONTIE, -S n evergreen plant of S Florida

COONTY same as ▸ **coontie**

COOP, -ED, -ING, -S n cage or pen for poultry ▷ vb confine in a restricted area

COOPER, -ED, -S n person who makes or repairs barrels ▷ vb make or mend (barrels, casks, etc)

COOPERY same as > **cooperage**

COOPING ▸ coop

COOPS ▸ coop

COOPT, -ED, -ING, -S vb add (someone) to a group by the agreement of the existing members

COOPTION

COORIE, -D, -S same as ▸ **courie**

COOS ▸ coo

COOSEN, -ED, -S same as ▸ **cozen**

COOSER, -S n stallion

COOSIN, -ED, -S same as ▸ **cozen**

COOST Scots form of ▸ **cast**

COOT, -S n small black water bird

COOTCH, -ED, -ES n hiding place ▷ vb hide

COOTER, -S n type of freshwater turtle

COOTIE, -S n body louse

COOTIKIN n gaiter

COOTS ▸ coot

COP, -PED, -PING, -S same as ▸ **copper**

COPAIBA, -S n resin obtained from certain tropical trees

COPAIVA, -S same as ▸ **copaiba**

COPAL, -S n resin used in varnishes

COPALM, -S n aromatic resin

COPALS ▸ copal

COPARENT n fellow parent

COPASTOR n fellow pastor

COPATRON n fellow patron

COPAY, -S n amount payable for treatment by person with medical insurance

COPE, -D, -S vb deal successfully (with) ▷ n large ceremonial cloak worn by some Christian priests

COPECK, -S same as ▸ **kopeck**

COPED ▸ cope

COPEMATE n partner

COPEN, -S n shade of blue

COPEPOD, -S n type of minute crustacean

COPER, -ED, -ING, -S n horse-dealer ▷ vb smuggle liquor to deep-sea fishermen

COPES ▸ cope

COPIABLE n able to be copied

COPIED ▸ copy

COPIER, -S n machine that copies

COPIES ▸ copy

COPIHUE, -S n Chilean bellflower

COPILOT, -S n second pilot of an aircraft ▷ vb act as a copilot

COPING, -S n sloping top row of a wall

COPIOUS adj abundant, plentiful

COPITA, -S n tulip-shaped sherry glass

COPLANAR adj lying in the same plane

COPLOT, -S vb plot together

COPOUT, -S n act of avoiding responsibility

COPPED ▸ cop

COPPER, -ED, -S n soft reddish-brown metal ▷ adj reddish-brown ▷ vb coat or cover with copper

COPPERAH same as ▸ **copra**

COPPERAS n ferrous sulphate

COPPERED ▸ copper

COPPERS ▸ copper

COPPERY ▸ copper

COPPICE, -S n small group of trees growing close together ▷ vb trim back (trees or bushes) to form a coppice

COPPICED

COPPIES ▸ coppy

COPPIN, -S n ball of thread

COPPING ▸ cop

COPPINS ▸ coppin

COPPLE, -S n hill rising to a point

COPPRA, -S same as ▸ **copra**

COPPY, COPPIES n small wooden stool

COPRA, -S n dried oil-yielding kernel of the coconut

COPRAH, -S same as ▸ **copra**

COPRAS ▸ copra

COPREMIA same as > **copraemia**

COPREMIC same as > **copraemic**

COPRINCE n fellow prince

COPROSMA n Australasian shrub sometimes planted for ornament

COPS ▸ cop

COPSE, -D, -S, COPSING same as ▸ **coppice**

COPSHOP, -S n police station

COPSIER ▸ copsy

COPSIEST ▸ copsy

COPSING ▸ copse

COPSY, COPSIER, COPSIEST adj having copses

COPTER, -S n helicopter

COPULA, -E, -S n verb used to link the subject and complement of a sentence

COPULAR

COPURIFY vb purify together

COPY, COPIED, COPIES *n* thing made to look exactly like another ▷ *vb* make a copy of

COPYABLE

COPYBOOK *n* book of specimens for imitation

COPYBOY, -S *n* formerly, in journalism, boy who carried copy and ran errands

COPYCAT, -S *n* person who imitates or copies someone ▷ *vb* imitate with great attention to detail

COPYDESK *n* desk where newspaper copy is edited

COPYEDIT *vb* prepare text for printing by styling, correcting, etc

COPYGIRL *n* female copyboy

COPYHOLD *n* tenure less than freehold of land in England evidenced by a copy of the Court roll

COPYING, -S *n* act of copying

COPYISM, -S *n* slavish copying

COPYIST, -S *n* person who makes written copies

COPYLEFT *n* permission to use something free of charge ▷ *vb* use copyright law to make (work, esp software) free to use

COPYREAD *vb* subedit

COQUET, -S *vb* behave flirtatiously

COQUETRY *n* flirtation

COQUETS ▸ coquet

COQUETTE *n* woman who flirts

COQUI, -S *n* type of tree-dwelling frog

COQUILLA *n* type of South American nut

COQUILLE *n* any dish, esp seafood, served in a scallop shell

COQUINA, -S *n* soft limestone

COQUIS ▸ coqui

COQUITO, -S *n* Chilean palm tree yielding edible nuts and a syrup

COR, -S *interj* exclamation of surprise, amazement, or admiration ▷ *n* Hebrew measure of dry weight

CORACLE, -S *n* small round boat of wicker covered with skins

CORACOID *n* paired ventral bone of the pectoral girdle in vertebrates

CORAGGIO *interj* exhortation to hold one's nerve

CORAL, -S *n* hard substance formed from the skeletons of

very small sea animals ▷ *adj* orange-pink

CORALLUM, CORALLA *n* skeleton of any zoophyte

CORALS ▸ coral

CORAM *prep* before, in the presence of

CORAMINE *n* type of stimulant

CORANACH *same as* ▸ **coronach**

CORANTO, -S *same as* ▸ **courante**

CORBAN, -S *n* gift to God

CORBE, -S *obsolete variant of* ▸ **corbel**

CORBEAU, -S *n* blackish green colour

CORBEIL, -S *n* carved ornament in the form of a basket of fruit, flowers, etc

CORBEL, -ED, -S *n* stone or timber support sticking out of a wall ▷ *vb* lay (a stone or brick) so that it forms a corbel

CORBES ▸ corbe

CORBIE, -S *n* raven or crow

CORBINA, -S *n* type of North American whiting

CORBY *same as* ▸ **corbie**

CORCASS *n* in Ireland, marshland

CORD *n* thin rope or thick string ▷ *adj* (of fabric) ribbed ▷ *vb* bind or furnish with a cord or cords

CORDAGE, -S *n* lines and rigging of a vessel

CORDATE *adj* heart-shaped

CORDED *adj* tied or fastened with cord

CORDELLE *vb* to tow

CORDER, -S ▸ cord

CORDIAL, -S *adj* warm and friendly ▷ *n* drink with a fruit base

CORDINER *n* shoemaker

CORDING, -S ▸ cord

CORDITE, -S *n* explosive used in guns and bombs

CORDLESS *adj* powered by an internal battery rather than a power cable

CORDLIKE ▸ cord

CORDOBA, -S *n* standard monetary unit of Nicaragua

CORDON, -ED, -S *n* chain of police, soldiers, etc, guarding an area ▷ *vb* put or form a cordon (around)

CORDOVAN *n* fine leather made principally from horsehide

CORDS *pl n* trousers made of corduroy

CORDUROY *n* cotton fabric with a velvety ribbed surface

CORDWAIN *an archaic name for* ▸ **cordovan**

CORDWOOD *n* wood that has been cut into lengths of four feet so that it can be stacked in cords

CORE, -D, -S, CORING *n* central part of certain fruits, containing the seeds ▷ *vb* remove the core from

COREDEEM *vb* redeem together

COREGENT *n* joint regent

COREIGN, -S *vb* reign jointly

CORELATE *same as* > **correlate**

CORELESS ▸ core

CORELLA, -S *n* white Australian cockatoo

COREMIUM, COREMIA *n* spore-producing organ of certain fungi

CORER, -S ▸ core

CORES ▸ core

CORF, CORVES *n* wagon or basket used formerly in mines

CORGI, -S *n* short-legged sturdy dog

CORIA ▸ corium

CORIES ▸ cory

CORING ▸ core

CORIOUS *adj* leathery

CORIUM, CORIA, -S *n* deep inner layer of the skin

CORIVAL, -S *same as* ▸ **corrival**

CORIXID, -S *n* type of water bug

CORK, -S *n* thick light bark of a Mediterranean oak ▷ *vb* seal with a cork ▷ *adj* made of cork

CORKAGE, -S *n* restaurant's charge for serving wine bought elsewhere

CORKED *adj* (of wine) spoiled through having a decayed cork

CORKER, -S *n* splendid or outstanding person or thing

CORKIER ▸ corky

CORKIEST ▸ corky

CORKING *adj* excellent

CORKIR, -S *n* lichen from which red or purple dye is made

CORKLIKE ▸ cork

CORKS ▸ cork

CORKTREE *n* type of evergreen oak tree

CORKWING *n* type of greenish or bluish European fish

C

CORKWOOD n type of small tree of the southeastern US, with very lightweight porous wood

CORKY, CORKIER, CORKIEST same as ► **corked**

CORM, -S n bulblike underground stem of certain plants

CORMEL, -S n new small corm arising from the base of a fully developed one

CORMIDIA > **cormidium**

CORMLET, -S n small corm

CORMLIKE adj resembling a corm

CORMOID adj like a corm

CORMOUS ► **corm**

CORMS ► **corm**

CORMUS, -ES n corm

CORN, -ING, -S n cereal plant such as wheat or oats ▷ vb feed (animals) with corn, esp oats

CORNACRE same as ► **conacre**

CORNAGE, -S n rent fixed according to the number of horned cattle pastured

CORNBALL n person given to mawkish or unsophisticated behaviour

CORNCAKE n kind of cornmeal flatbread

CORNCOB, -S n core of an ear of maize, to which the kernels are attached

CORNCRIB n ventilated building for the storage of unhusked maize

CORNEA, -E, -S n transparent membrane covering the eyeball
CORNEAL

CORNED adj preserved in salt or brine

CORNEL, -S n type of plant such as the dogwood and dwarf cornel

CORNEOUS adj horny

CORNER, -ED, -S n area or angle where two converging lines or surfaces meet ▷ vb force into a difficult or inescapable position

CORNET, -S n former cavalry officer

CORNETCY n commission or rank of a cornet

CORNETS ► **cornet**

CORNETT, -S n musical instrument

CORNETTO, CORNETTI same as ► **cornett**

CORNETTS ► **cornett**

CORNFED adj fed on corn

CORNFLAG n gladiolus

CORNFLY n small fly

CORNHUSK n outer protective covering of an ear of maize

CORNI ► **corno**

CORNICE, -D, -S n decorative moulding round the top of a wall ▷ vb furnish or decorate with or as if with a cornice

CORNICHE n coastal road, esp one built into the face of a cliff

CORNICLE n wax-secreting organ on an aphid's abdomen

CORNIER ► **corny**

CORNIEST ► **corny**

CORNIFIC adj producing horns

CORNIFY vb turn soft tissue hard

CORNILY ► **corny**

CORNING ► **corn**

CORNIST, -S n horn-player

CORNLAND n land suitable for growing corn or grain

CORNLOFT n loft for storing corn

CORNMEAL n meal made from maize

CORNMILL n flour mill

CORNMOTH n moth whose larvae feed on grain

CORNO, CORNI n French horn

CORNPIPE n musical instrument made from a stalk of corn etc

CORNPONE n American corn bread

CORNRENT n rent for land that is paid in corn

CORNROW, -S n hairstyle in which the hair is plaited in close parallel rows ▷ vb style the hair in a cornrow

CORNS ► **corn**

CORNSILK n threads on an ear of maize

CORNU, -A n part or structure resembling a horn or having a hornlike pattern
CORNUAL

CORNUS, -ES n any member of the genus Cornus, such as dogwood

CORNUTE, -S adj having or resembling cornua ▷ vb make a cuckold of

CORNUTED same as ► **cornute**

CORNUTES ► **cornute**

CORNUTO, -S n cuckold

CORNWORM n cornmoth larva

CORNY, CORNIER, CORNIEST adj unoriginal or oversentimental

COROCORE same as ► **corocoro**

COROCORO n South Asian vessel fitted with outriggers

CORODY, CORODIES n feudal law

COROLLA, -S n petals of a flower collectively

CORONA, -E, -S n ring of light round the moon or sun

CORONACH n dirge or lamentation for the dead

CORONAE ► **corona**

CORONAL, -S n circlet for the head ▷ adj of or relating to a corona or coronal

CORONARY adj of the arteries surrounding the heart ▷ n coronary thrombosis

CORONAS ► **corona**

CORONATE vb to crown

CORONEL, -S n iron head of a tilting spear

CORONER, -S n official responsible for the investigation of deaths

CORONET, -S n small crown

CORONIAL adj relating to a coroner

CORONIS n symbol used in Greek writing

CORONIUM n highly-ionized iron and nickel seen as a green line in the solar coronal spectrum

CORONOID adj crown-shaped

COROTATE vb rotate together

COROZO, -S n tropical American palm whose seeds yield a useful oil

CORPORA ► **corpus**

CORPORAL n noncommissioned officer in an army ▷ adj of the body

CORPORAS n communion cloth

CORPS n military unit with a specific function

CORPSE, -D, -S n dead body ▷ vb laugh or cause to laugh involuntarily or inopportunely while on stage

CORPSMAN, CORPSMEN n medical orderly or stretcher-bearer

CORPUS, CORPORA, -ES n collection of writings, esp by a single author

CORRADE, -D, -S vb erode by the abrasive action of rock particles

CORRAL, -S n enclosure for cattle or horses ▷ vb put in a corral

CORREA, -S n Australian evergreen shrub with large showy tubular flowers

CORRECT, -S adj free from error, true ▷ vb put right

CORRETTO n espresso containing alcohol

CORRIDA, -S the Spanish word for ▷ **bullfight**

CORRIDOR n passage in a building or train

CORRIE, -S same as ▷ **cirque**

CORRIVAL a rare word for ▷ **rival**

CORRODE, -D, -S vb eat or be eaten away by chemical action or rust

CORRODER

CORRODY same as ▷ **corody**

CORRUPT, -S adj open to or involving bribery ▷ vb make corrupt

CORS ▷ **cor**

CORSAC, -S n type of fox of central Asia

CORSAGE, -S n small bouquet worn on the bodice of a dress

CORSAIR, -S n pirate

CORSE, -S n corpse

CORSELET n one-piece undergarment combining a corset and bra

CORSES ▷ **corse**

CORSET, -ED, -S n women's undergarment ▷ vb dress or enclose in, or as in, a corset

CORSETRY n making of or dealing in corsets

CORSETS ▷ **corset**

CORSEY, -S n pavement or pathway

CORSITE, -S n type of rock

CORSIVE, -S n corrodent

CORSLET, -S same as ▷ **corselet**

CORSNED, -S n ordeal to discover innocence or guilt

CORSO, -S n promenade

CORTEGE, -S n funeral procession

CORTEX, -ES, CORTICES n outer layer of the brain or other internal organ

CORTICAL

CORTILE, CORTILI n open, internal courtyard

CORTIN, -S n adrenal cortex extract

CORTINA, -S n weblike part of certain mushrooms

CORTINS ▷ **cortin**

CORTISOL n principal glucocorticoid secreted by the adrenal cortex

CORULER, -S n joint ruler

CORUNDUM n hard mineral used as an abrasive

CORVEE, -S n day's unpaid labour owed by a feudal vassal to his lord

CORVES ▷ **corf**

CORVET, -ED, -S same as ▷ **curvet**

CORVETTE n lightly armed escort warship ▷ vb participate in social activities with fellow Corvette car enthusiasts

CORVID, -S n any member of the crow family

CORVINA, -S same as ▷ **corbina**

CORVINE adj of, relating to, or resembling a crow

CORVUS, -ES n type of ancient hook

CORY, CORIES n catfish belonging to the South American Corydoras genus

CORYBANT n wild attendant of the goddess Cybele

CORYLUS n hazel genus

CORYMB, -S n flat-topped flower cluster

CORYMBED

CORYPHE, -S n coryphaeus

CORYPHEE n leading dancer of a corps de ballet

CORYPHES ▷ **coryphe**

CORYZA, -S n acute inflammation in the nose

CORYZAL

COS same as ▷ **cosine**

COSCRIPT vb script jointly

COSE, -D, -S, COSING vb get cosy

COSEC, -S same as ▷ **cosecant**

COSECANT n ratio of the hypotenuse to the opposite side in a right-angled triangle

COSECH, -S n hyperbolic cosecant

COSECS ▷ **cosec**

COSED ▷ **cose**

COSES ▷ **cose**

COSET, -S n mathematical set

COSEY, -S n tea cosy

COSH, -ED, -ES, -ING n heavy blunt weapon ▷ vb hit with a cosh

COSHER, -ED, -S vb pamper or coddle

COSHERER

COSHERY n Irish chief's right to lodge at his tenants' houses

COSHES ▷ **cosh**

COSHING ▷ **cosh**

COSIE same as ▷ **cosy**

COSIED ▷ **cosy**

COSIER, -S n cobbler

COSIES ▷ **cosy**

COSIEST ▷ **cosy**

COSIGN, -ED, -S vb sign jointly

COSIGNER

COSILY ▷ **cosy**

COSINE, -S n trigonometric function

COSINESS ▷ **cosy**

COSING ▷ **cose**

COSMEA, -S n plant of the genus Cosmos

COSMESIS, COSMESES n aesthetic covering on a prosthesis to make it look more natural

COSMETIC n preparation used to improve the appearance of a person's skin ▷ adj improving the appearance only

COSMIC adj of the whole universe

COSMICAL same as ▷ **cosmic**

COSMID, -S n segment of DNA

COSMIN, -S same as ▷ **cosmine**

COSMINE, -S n substance resembling dentine

COSMINS ▷ **cosmin**

COSMISM, -S n Russian cultural and philosophical movement

COSMIST -S

COSMOID adj having two inner bony layers and a cosmine outer layer

COSMOS, -ES n universe

COSPLAY, -S n recreational activity in which people interact while dressed as fictional characters

COSS, -ES another name for ▷ **kos**

COSSACK, -S n Slavonic warrior-peasant

COSSES ▷ **coss**

COSSET, -ED, -S vb pamper ▷ n any pet animal, esp a lamb

COSSIE, -S n informal name for a swimming costume

COST, -ED, -S n amount of money, time, labour, etc, required for something ▷ vb have as its cost

COSTA, -E n riblike part, such as the midrib of a plant leaf

COSTAL, -S n strengthening rib of an insect's wing

COSTALLY

COSTAR, -S n actor who shares the billing with another ▷ vb share the billing with another actor

COSTARD, -S n English variety of apple tree

COSTARS ▸ costar

COSTATE adj having ribs

COSTATED same as ▸ costate

COSTE, -S vb draw near

COSTEAN, -S vb mine for lodes

COSTED ▸ cost

COSTER, -S n person who sells fruit, vegetables etc from a barrow

COSTES ▸ coste

COSTING, -S as in **marginal costing** method of cost accounting

COSTIVE adj having or causing constipation

COSTLESS ▸ cost

COSTLY, COSTLIER adj expensive

COSTMARY n herbaceous Asian plant

COSTREL, -S n flask, usually of earthenware or leather

COSTS ▸ cost

COSTUME, -D, -S n style of dress of a particular place or time, or for a particular activity ▷ vb provide with a costume

COSTUMER same as ▸ costumier

COSTUMES ▸ costume

COSTUMEY adj (stage) costume-like; unrealistic

COSTUS, -ES n Himalayan herb with an aromatic root

COSY, COSIED, COSIES, COSIEST, -ING adj warm and snug ▷ n cover for keeping things warm ▷ vb make oneself snug and warm

COT, -S, -TED, -TING n baby's bed with high sides ▷ vb entangle or become entangled

COTAN, -S same as > cotangent

COTE, -D, -S, COTING same as ▸ cot

COTEAU, -S, -X n hillside

COTED ▸ cote

COTELINE n kind of muslin

COTENANT n person who holds property jointly or in common with others

COTERIE, -S n exclusive group, clique

COTES ▸ cote

COTH, -S n hyperbolic cotangent

COTHURN, -S same as > cothurnus

COTHURNI ▸ cothurnus

COTHURNS ▸ cothurn

COTIDAL adj (of a line on a tidal chart) joining points at which high tide occurs simultaneously

COTILLON same as > cotillion

COTING ▸ cote

COTINGA, -S n tropical bird

COTININE n substance used to indicate presence of nicotine

COTISE, -D, -S, COTISING same as ▸ cottise

COTLAND, -S n grounds that belong to a cotter

COTQUEAN n coarse woman

COTS ▸ cot

COTT, -S same as ▸ cot

COTTA, -E, -S n short form of surplice

COTTABUS n ancient Greek game involving throwing wine into a vessel

COTTAE ▸ cotta

COTTAGE, -S n small house in the country

COTTAGER n person who lives in a cottage

COTTAGES ▸ cottage

COTTAGEY adj resembling a cottage

COTTAR, -S same as ▸ cotter

COTTAS ▸ cotta

COTTED ▸ cot

COTTER, -ED, -S n pin or wedge used to secure machine parts ▷ vb secure (two parts) with a cotter

COTTID, -S n type of fish typically with a large head, tapering body, and spiny fins

COTTIER, -S same as ▸ cotter

COTTING ▸ cot

COTTISE, -D, -S n type of heraldic decoration ▷ vb (in heraldry) decorate with a cottise

COTTOID adj resembling a fish of the genus Cottus

COTTON, -ED, -S n white downy fibre covering the seeds of a tropical plant ▷ vb take a liking

COTTONY

COTTOWN, -S Scots variant of ▸ cotton

COTTS ▸ cott

COTTUS, -ES n type of fish with four yellowish knobs on its head

COTURNIX n variety of quail

COTWAL, -S n Indian police officer

COTYLE, COTYLAE, -S n cuplike cavity

COTYLOID adj shaped like a cup ▷ n small bone forming part of the acetabular cavity in some mammals

COTYPE, -S n type specimen in biological study

COUCAL, -S n type of ground-living bird of Africa, S Asia, and Australia, with long strong legs

COUCH, -ED, -ES n piece of upholstered furniture for seating more than one person ▷ vb express in a particular way

COUCHANT adj in a lying position

COUCHE adj in heraldry (of a shield), tilted

COUCHED ▸ couch

COUCHEE, -S n reception held late at night

COUCHER, -S ▸ couch

COUCHES ▸ couch

COUCHING n method of embroidery

COUDE, -S adj relating to the construction of a reflecting telescope ▷ n type of reflecting telescope

COUGAN, -S n drunk and rowdy person

COUGAR, -S n puma

COUGH, -ED, -ING, -S vb expel air from the lungs abruptly and noisily ▷ n act or sound of coughing

COUGHER, -S

COUGUAR, -S same as ▸ cougar

COULD ▸ can

COULDEST same as ▸ couldst

COULDST vb form of 'could' used with the pronoun thou or its relative form

COULEE, -S n flow of molten lava

COULIS n thin purée of vegetables or fruit

COULISSE n timber grooved to take a sliding panel

COULOIR, -S n deep gully on a mountain side, esp in the French Alps

COULOMB, -S n SI unit of electric charge

COULTER, -S n blade at the front of a ploughshare

COUMARIC ▸ coumarin

COUMARIN n white vanilla-scented crystalline ester

COUMAROU n tonka bean tree, or its seed

COUNCIL, -S n group meeting for discussion or consultation ▷ adj of or by a council

COUNSEL, -S n advice or guidance ▷ vb give guidance to

COUNT, -ED, -ING, -S vb say numbers in order ▷ n counting

COUNTER, -S n long flat surface in a bank or shop ▷ vb oppose, retaliate against ▷ adv in the opposite direction

COUNTESS n woman holding the rank of count or earl

COUNTIAN n dweller in a given county

COUNTIES ▶ county

COUNTING ▶ count

COUNTROL obsolete variant of ▶ control

COUNTRY n nation

COUNTS ▶ count

COUNTY, COUNTIES n (in some countries) division of a country ▷ adj upper-class

COUP, -ED, -ING, -S n successful action ▷ vb turn or fall over

COUPE, -S n sports car with two doors and a sloping fixed roof

COUPED ▶ coup

COUPEE, -S n dance movement

COUPER, -S n dealer

COUPES ▶ coupe

COUPING ▶ coup

COUPLE, -D, -S n two people who are married or romantically involved ▷ vb connect, associate

COUPLER, -S n mechanical device

COUPLES ▶ couple

COUPLET, -S n two consecutive lines of verse

COUPLING n device for connecting things, such as railway carriages

COUPON, -S n piece of paper entitling the holder to a discount or gift

COUPS ▶ coup

COUPURE, -S n entrenchment made by besieged forces behind a breach

COUR, -ING, -S obsolete variant of ▶ cover

COURAGE, -S n ability to face danger or pain without fear

COURANT, -S n courante ▷ adj (of an animal) running

COURANTE n old dance in quick triple time

COURANTO same as ▶ courante

COURANTS ▶ courant

COURB, -ED, -ING, -S vb to bend

COURD obsolete variant of ▶ covered

COURE, -D, -S obsolete variant of ▶ cover

COURIE, -D, -S vb nestle or snuggle

COURIER, -S n person employed to look after holiday-makers ▷ vb send (a parcel, letter, etc) by courier

COURIES ▶ courie

COURING ▶ cour

COURLAN, -S another name for ▶ limpkin

COURS ▶ cour

COURSE, -D n series of lessons or medical treatment ▷ vb (of liquid) run swiftly

COURSER, -S n swift horse

COURSES another word for ▶ menses

COURSING n hunting with hounds trained to hunt game by sight

COURT, -ED, -ING, -S n body which decides legal cases ▷ vb try to gain the love of

COURTER, -S n suitor

COURTESY n politeness, good manners

COURTIER n attendant at a royal court

COURTING ▶ court

COURTLET n small court

COURTLY adj ceremoniously polite

COURTS ▶ court

COUSCOUS n type of semolina used in North African cookery

COUSIN, -S n child of one's uncle or aunt

COUSINLY

COUSINRY n collective term for cousins

COUSINS ▶ cousin

COUTA, -S n traditional Australian sailing boat

COUTEAU, -X n large two-edged knife used formerly as a weapon

COUTER, -S n armour designed to protect the elbow

COUTH, -ER, -EST, -S adj refined ▷ n refinement

COUTHIE, -R adj sociable

COUTHS ▶ couth

COUTHY same as ▶ couthie

COUTIL, -S n type of tightly-woven twill cloth

COUTILLE same as ▶ coutil

COUTILS ▶ coutil

COUTURE, -S n high-fashion designing and dressmaking ▷ adj relating to high fashion design and dress-making

COUVADE, -S n custom in certain cultures relating to childbirth

COUVERT, -S another word for ▶ cover

COUZIN, -S n South African word for a friend

COVALENT ▶ covalency

COVARY, COVARIED, COVARIES vb vary together maintaining a certain mathematical relationship

COVE, -D, -S n small bay or inlet ▷ vb form an architectural cove in

COVELET, -S n small cove

COVEN, -S n meeting of witches

COVENANT n contract ▷ vb agree by a covenant

COVENS ▶ coven

COVENT, -S same as ▶ convent

COVER, -ED, -S vb place something over, to protect or conceal ▷ n anything that covers

COVERAGE n amount or extent covered

COVERALL n thing that covers something entirely

COVERED ▶ cover

COVERER, -S ▶ cover

COVERING another word for ▶ cover

COVERLET n bed cover

COVERLID same as ▶ coverlet

COVERS ▶ cover

COVERSED adj as in **coversed sine** obsolete function in trigonometry

COVERT, -S adj concealed, secret ▷ n thicket giving shelter to game birds or animals

COVERTLY

COVERUP, -S n concealment of a mistake, crime, etc

COVES ▶ cove

COVET, -ED, -ING, -S vb long to possess (what belongs to someone else)

COVETER -S

COVETISE n covetousness

COVETOUS adj jealously longing to possess something

COVETS ▶ covet

COVEY, -S n small flock of grouse or partridge

COVIN, -S *n* conspiracy between two or more persons

COVINE, -S *n* conspiracy between people to injure someone else

COVING, -S *same as* ► **cove**

COVINOUS *adj* deceitful

COVINS ► **covin**

COVYNE, -S *same as* ► **covin**

COW, -ED, -ING, -S *n* mature female of certain mammals ▷ *vb* intimidate, subdue

COWAGE, -S *n* tropical climbing plant

COWAL, -S *n* shallow lake or swampy depression supporting vegetation

COWAN, -S *n* drystone waller

COWARD, -ED, -S *n* person who lacks courage ▷ *vb* show (someone) up to be a coward

COWARDLY *adj* of or characteristic of a coward

COWARDRY *n* cowardice

COWARDS ► **coward**

COWBANE, -S *n* poisonous marsh plant

COWBELL, -S *n* bell hung around a cow's neck

COWBERRY *n* evergreen shrub of N temperate and arctic regions

COWBIND, -S *n* any of various bryony plants, esp the white bryony

COWBIRD, -S *n* American oriole with a dark plumage and short bill

COWBOY, -ED, -S *n* (in the US) ranch worker who herds and tends cattle ▷ *vb* work or behave as a cowboy

COWED ► **cow**

COWEDLY ► **cow**

COWER, -ED, -ING, -S *vb* cringe in fear

COWFISH *n* type of trunkfish with hornlike spines over the eyes

COWFLAP, -S *n* cow dung

COWFLOP, -S *n* foxglove

COWGIRL, -S *n* female cowboy

COWGRASS, -S *n* red clover

COWHAGE, -S *same as* ► **cowage**

COWHAND, -S *same as* ► **cowboy**

COWHEARD *same as* ► **cowherd**

COWHEEL, -S *n* heel of a cow, used as cooking ingredient

COWHERB, -S *n* European plant with clusters of pink flowers

COWHERD, -S *n* person employed to tend cattle

COWHIDE, -D, -S *n* hide of a cow ▷ *vb* lash with a cowhide whip

COWHOUSE *n* byre

COWIER ► **cowy**

COWIEST ► **cowy**

COWING ► **cow**

COWINNER *n* joint winner

COWISH, -ES *adj* cowardly ▷ *n* N American plant with an edible root

COWITCH *another name for* ► **cowage**

COWK, -ED, -ING, -S *vb* retch or feel nauseated

COWL, -S *same as* ► **cowling**

COWLED *adj* wearing a cowl

COWLICK, -S *n* tuft of hair over the forehead

COWLIKE *adj* like a cow

COWLING, -S *n* cover on an engine

COWLS ► **cowl**

COWMAN, COWMEN *n* man who owns cattle

COWORKER *n* fellow worker

COWP, -ED, -ING, -S *same as* ► **coup**

COWPAT, -S *n* pool of cow dung

COWPEA, -S *n* type of tropical climbing plant

COWPED ► **cowp**

COWPIE, -S *n* cowpat

COWPING ► **cowp**

COWPLOP, -S *n* cow dung

COWPOKE, -S *n* cowboy

COWPOX, -ES *n* disease of cows

COWPS ► **cowp**

COWPUNK, -S *n* music that combines country music and punk

COWRIE, -S *n* brightly-marked sea shell

COWRITE, -S, COWROTE *vb* write jointly

COWRITER

COWRY *same as* ► **cowrie**

COWS ► **cow**

COWSHED, -S *n* byre

COWSKIN, -S *same as* ► **cowhide**

COWSLIP, -S *n* small yellow wild European flower

COWTOWN, -S *n* rural town in a cattle-raising area

COWTREE, -S *n* South American tree that produces latex

COWY, COWIER, COWIEST *adj* cowlike

COX, -ED, -ES, -ING *n* coxswain ▷ *vb* act as cox of (a boat)

COXA, -E *n* technical name for the hipbone or hip joint

COXAL

COXALGIA *n* pain in the hip joint

COXALGIC

COXALGY *same as* ► **coxalgia**

COXCOMB, -S *same as* > **cockscomb**

COXED ► **cox**

COXES ► **cox**

COXIB, -S *n* anti-inflammatory drug

COXIER ► **coxy**

COXIEST ► **coxy**

COXINESS ► **coxy**

COXING ► **cox**

COXITIS *n* inflammation of the hip joint

COXLESS ► **cox**

COXSWAIN *n* person who steers a rowing boat

COXY, COXIER, COXIEST *adj* cocky

COY, -ED, -ER, -EST, -ING, -S *adj* affectedly shy or modest ▷ *vb* caress

COYAU, -S *n* type of steep roof

COYDOG, -S *n* cross between a coyote and a dog

COYED ► **coy**

COYER ► **coy**

COYEST ► **coy**

COYING ► **coy**

COYISH ► **coy**

COYISHLY ► **coy**

COYLY ► **coy**

COYNESS ► **coy**

COYOTE, -S *n* prairie wolf of N America

COYPOU, -S *same as* ► **coypu**

COYPU, -S *n* beaver-like aquatic rodent

COYS ► **coy**

COYSTREL *same as* ► **coistrel**

COYSTRIL *same as* ► **coistrel**

COZ, -ZES *archaic word for* ► **cousin**

> **Coz** is an old word for **cousin**, and a good one to know for using the Z.

COZE, -D, -S, COZING *vb* to chat

COZEN, -ED, -ING, -S *vb* cheat, trick

COZENAGE

COZENER -S

COZES ► **coze**

COZEY, -S *n* tea cosy

COZIE *same as* ► **cozey**

COZIED ► **cozy**

COZIER, -S *n* cobbler

COZIES ► **cozy**

COZIEST ► **cozy**

COZILY ► **cozy**

COZINESS ► **cozy**

COZING ▸ coze

COZY, COZIED, COZIES, COZIEST, -ING same as
▸ cosy

COZZES ▸ coz

COZZIE, -S n swimming costume

CRAAL, -ED, -ING, -S vb enclose in a craal (or kraal)

CRAB, -BED, -BING, -S n edible shellfish with ten legs, the first pair modified into pincers

CRABBER, -S n crab fisherman

CRABBIER ▸ crabby

CRABBILY ▸ crabby

CRABBING ▸ crab

CRABBIT adj Scots word meaning bad-tempered

CRABBY, CRABBIER adj bad-tempered

CRABLIKE adj resembling a crab

CRABMEAT n edible flesh of a crab

CRABS ▸ crab

CRABWISE adv (of motion) sideways

CRABWOOD n- tropical American tree

CRACHACH pl n (in Wales) elitists

CRACK, -S vb break or split partially ▸ n sudden sharp noise ▸ adj first-rate, excellent

CRACKED adj damaged by cracking ▸ n sharp noise

CRACKER n thin dry biscuit

CRACKERS adj insane

CRACKET, -S n low stool, often one with three legs

CRACKIE n small mongrel dog

CRACKIER ▸ cracky

CRACKIES ▸ cracky

CRACKING adj very fast

CRACKJAW adj difficult to pronounce ▸ n word or phrase that is difficult to pronounce

CRACKLE, -D, -S vb make small crackling popping noises ▸ n crackling sound

CRACKLY adj making a cracking sound

CRACKNEL n type of hard plain biscuit

CRACKPOT adj eccentric ▸ n eccentric person

CRACKS ▸ crack

CRACKUP, -S n collapse

CRACKY, CRACKIER, CRACKIES adj full of cracks ▸ n something that is full of cracks

CRACOWE, -S n medieval shoe with a sharply pointed toe

CRADLE, -D, -S n baby's bed on rockers ▸ vb hold gently as if in a cradle

CRADLER -S

CRADLING n framework of iron or wood, esp as used in the construction of a ceiling

CRAFT, -ED, -ING, -S n occupation requiring skill with the hands ▸ vb make skilfully

CRAFTER, -S n person doing craftwork

CRAFTIER ▸ crafty

CRAFTILY ▸ crafty

CRAFTING ▸ craft

CRAFTS ▸ craft

CRAFTY, CRAFTIER adj skilled in deception

CRAG, -S n steep rugged rock

CRAGFAST adj stranded on a crag

CRAGGED same as ▸ craggy

CRAGGER, -S n member of a carbon reduction action group

CRAGGIER ▸ craggy

CRAGGILY ▸ craggy

CRAGGY, CRAGGIER adj having many crags

CRAGS ▸ crag

CRAGSMAN, CRAGSMEN n rock climber

CRAIC, -S n Irish word meaning fun

CRAIG, -S a Scot word for
▸ crag

CRAKE, -D, -S, CRAKING n bird of the rail family, such as the corncrake ▸ vb to boast

CRAM, -MED, -S vb force into too small a space ▸ n act or condition of cramming

CRAMBE, -S n any plant of the genus Crambe

CRAMBO, -ES, -S n word game

CRAME, -S n merchant's booth or stall

CRAMESY same as
▸ cramoisy

CRAMFULL adj very full

CRAMMED ▸ cram

CRAMMER, -S n person or school that prepares pupils for an examination

CRAMMING n act of cramming

CRAMOISY adj of a crimson colour ▸ n crimson cloth

CRAMP, -ING, -S n painful muscular contraction ▸ vb affect with a cramp

CRAMPED adj closed in

CRAMPER, -S n spiked metal plate used as a brace for the feet in throwing the stone

CRAMPET, -S n cramp iron

CRAMPIER ▸ crampy

CRAMPING ▸ cramp

CRAMPIT, -S same as
▸ crampet

CRAMPON, -S n spiked plate strapped to a boot for climbing on ice ▸ vb climb using crampons

CRAMPOON same as
▸ crampon

CRAMPS ▸ cramp

CRAMPY, CRAMPIER adj affected with cramp

CRAMS ▸ cram

CRAN, -S n unit of capacity used for measuring fresh herring, equal to 37.5 gallons

CRANAGE, -S n use of a crane

CRANCH, -ED, -ES vb to crunch

CRANE, -D, -S, CRANING n machine for lifting and moving heavy weights ▸ vb stretch (one's neck) to see something

CRANEFLY n fly with long legs, slender wings, and a narrow body

CRANES ▸ crane

CRANIA ▸ cranium

CRANIAL adj of or relating to the skull

CRANIATE adj having a skull or cranium ▸ n vertebrate

CRANING ▸ crane

CRANIUM, CRANIA, -S n skull

CRANK, -ED, -ER, -EST, -ING, -S n arm projecting at right angles from a shaft ▸ vb turn with a crank ▸ adj (of a sailing vessel) easily keeled over by the wind

CRANKIER ▸ cranky

CRANKILY ▸ cranky

CRANKING ▸ crank

CRANKISH adj somewhat eccentric or bad-tempered

CRANKLE, -D, -S vb bend or wind

CRANKLY adj vigorously

CRANKOUS adj fretful

CRANKPIN n short cylindrical pin in a crankshaft, to which the connecting rod is attached

CRANKS ▸ crank

CRANKY, CRANKIER same as
▸ crankish

CRANNIED ▸ cranny

CRANNIES ▸ cranny

CRANNOG, -S n ancient Celtic lake or bog dwelling

CRANNOGE same as
▸ crannog

CRANNOGS ▸ crannog

CRANNY, CRANNIED, CRANNIES n narrow

opening ▷ *vb* become full of crannies

CRANS ▶ **cran**

CRANTS, -ES *n* garland carried in front of a maiden's bier

CRAP *n* rubbish, nonsense

CRAPAUD, -S *n* frog or toad

CRAPE, -D, -S, CRAPING *same as* ▶ **crepe**

CRAPIER ▶ **crapy**

CRAPIEST ▶ **crapy**

CRAPING ▶ **crape**

CRAPLE, -S *same as* ▶ **grapple**

CRAPOLA, -S *n* rubbish

CRAPPIE, -S *n* N American freshwater fish)

CRAPPIER ▶ **crappy**

CRAPPIES ▶ **crappie**

CRAPPY, CRAPPIER *adj* worthless, lousy

CRAPS *pl n* game using two dice

CRAPY, CRAPIER, CRAPIEST ▶ **crape**

CRARE, -S *n* type of trading vessel

CRASES ▶ **crasis**

CRASH, -ED, -ES *n* collision involving a vehicle or vehicles ▷ *vb* (cause to) collide violently with a vehicle, a stationary object, or the ground ▷ *adj* requiring or using great effort in order to achieve results quickly

CRASHER -S

CRASHING *adj* extreme

CRASHPAD *n* place to sleep or live temporarily

CRASIS, CRASES *n* fusion or contraction of two adjacent vowels into one

CRASS, -ER, -EST *adj* stupid and insensitive

CRASSLY

CRATCH, -ES *n* rack for holding fodder for cattle, etc

CRATE, -D, -S, CRATING *n* large wooden container for packing goods ▷ *vb* put in a crate

CRATEFUL

CRATER, -ED, -S *n* bowl-shaped opening at the top of a volcano ▷ *vb* make or form craters

CRATES ▶ **crate**

CRATHUR, -S *same as* ▶ **cratur**

CRATING ▶ **crate**

CRATON, -S *n* stable part of the earth's continental crust

CRATONIC

CRATUR, -S *n* whisky or whiskey

CRAUNCH *same as* ▶ **crunch**

CRAUNCHY

CRAVAT, -S *n* man's scarf worn like a tie ▷ *vb* wear a cravat

CRAVATE, -S *same as* ▶ **cravat**

CRAVATS ▶ **cravat**

CRAVE, -D, -S *vb* desire intensely

CRAVEN, -ED, -S *adj* cowardly ▷ *n* coward ▷ *vb* make cowardly

CRAVENLY

CRAVER, -S ▶ **crave**

CRAVES ▶ **crave**

CRAVING, -S *n* intense desire or longing

CRAW, -S *n* pouchlike part of a bird's oesophagus

CRAWDAD, -S *n* crayfish

CRAWFISH *same as* ▶ **crayfish**

CRAWL, -ED, -S *vb* move on one's hands and knees ▷ *n* crawling motion or pace

CRAWLER, -S *n* servile flatterer

CRAWLIER ▶ **crawly**

CRAWLING *n* defect in freshly applied paint or varnish characterized by bare patches and ridging

CRAWLS ▶ **crawl**

CRAWLWAY *n* in a mine, low passageway that can only be negotiated by crawling

CRAWLY, CRAWLIER *adj* feeling like creatures are crawling on one's skin

CRAWS ▶ **craw**

CRAY, -S *n* crayfish

CRAYER, -S *same as* ▶ **crare**

CRAYFISH *n* edible shellfish like a lobster

CRAYON, -ED, -S *n* stick or pencil of coloured wax or clay ▷ *vb* draw or colour with a crayon

CRAYONER

CRAYS ▶ **cray**

CRAYTHUR *variant of* ▶ **cratur**

CRAZE, -S *n* short-lived fashion or enthusiasm ▷ *vb* make mad

CRAZED *adj* wild and uncontrolled

CRAZES ▶ **craze**

CRAZIER ▶ **crazy**

CRAZIES ▶ **crazy**

CRAZIEST ▶ **crazy**

CRAZILY ▶ **crazy**

CRAZING, -S *n* act of crazing

CRAZY, CRAZIER, CRAZIES, CRAZIEST *adj* ridiculous ▷ *n* crazy person

CREACH, -S *same as* ▶ **creagh**

CREAGH, -S *n* foray

CREAK, -ED, -ING, -S *n* (make) a harsh squeaking sound ▷ *vb* make or move with a harsh squeaking sound

CREAKIER ▶ **creaky**

CREAKILY ▶ **creak**

CREAKING ▶ **creak**

CREAKS ▶ **creak**

CREAKY, CREAKIER ▶ **creak**

CREAM, -ED, -ING, -S *n* fatty part of milk ▷ *vb* beat to a creamy consistency

CREAMER, -S *n* powdered milk substitute for use in coffee

CREAMERY *n* place where dairy products are made or sold

CREAMIER ▶ **creamy**

CREAMILY ▶ **creamy**

CREAMING ▶ **cream**

CREAMS ▶ **cream**

CREAMY, CREAMIER *adj* resembling cream in colour, taste, or consistency

CREANCE, -S *n* long light cord used in falconry

CREANT *adj* formative

CREASE, -D, -S, CREASING *n* line made by folding or pressing ▷ *vb* crush or line

CREASER -S

CREASIER ▶ **creasy**

CREASING ▶ **crease**

CREASOTE *same as* ▶ **creosote**

CREASY, CREASIER ▶ **crease**

CREATE, -D, -S, CREATING *vb* make, cause to exist

CREATIC *adj* relating to flesh or meat

CREATIN, -S *same as* ▶ **creatine**

CREATINE *n* metabolite involved in biochemical reactions

CREATING ▶ **create**

CREATINS ▶ **creatin**

CREATION *n* creating or being created

CREATIVE *adj* imaginative or inventive ▷ *n* person who is creative professionally

CREATOR, -S *n* person who creates

CREATRIX

CREATURE *n* animal, person, or other being

CRECHE, -S *n* place where small children are looked after

CRED, -S *n* short for credibility

CREDAL ▶ **creed**

CREDENCE *n* belief in the truth or accuracy of a statement

CREDENDA > **credendum**

CREDENT adj believing or believable

CREDENZA n type of small sideboard

CREDIBLE adj believable **CREDIBLY**

CREDIT, -ED n system of allowing customers to receive goods and pay later ▷ vb enter as a credit in an account

CREDITOR n person to whom money is owed

CREDITS pl n list of people responsible for the production of a film, programme, or record

CREDO, -S n creed

CREDS ▶ cred

CREE, -ING, -S vb soften grain by boiling or soaking

CREED, -S n statement or system of (Christian) beliefs or principles **CREEDAL**

CREEING ▶ cree

CREEK, -S n narrow inlet or bay

CREEKIER ▶ creeky

CREEKS ▶ creek

CREEKY, CREEKIER adj abounding in creeks

CREEL, -ED, -ING, -S n wicker basket used by anglers ▷ vb to fish using creels

CREEP, -ED, -ING, -S, CREPT vb move quietly and cautiously ▷ n creeping movement

CREEPAGE n imperceptible movement

CREEPED ▶ creep

CREEPER, -S n creeping plant ▷ vb train a plant to creep

CREEPIE, -S n low stool

CREEPIER ▶ creepy

CREEPIES ▶ creepie

CREEPILY ▶ creepy

CREEPING ▶ creep

CREEPS ▶ creep

CREEPY, CREEPIER adj causing a feeling of fear or disgust

CREES ▶ cree

CREESE, -D, -S, CREESING same as ▶ kris

CREESH, -ED, -ES vb lubricate

CREESHY adj greasy

CREESING ▶ creese

CREM, -S n crematorium

CREMAINS pl n cremated remains of a body

CREMANT adj (of wine) moderately sparkling

CREMATE, -D, -S vb burn (a corpse) to ash

CREMATOR n furnace for cremating corpses

CREME, -S n cream

CREMINI, -S n variety of mushroom

CREMONA, -S same as ▶ cromorna

CREMOR, -S n cream

CREMOSIN adj crimson

CREMS ▶ crem

CREMSIN same as ▶ cremosin

CRENA, -S n cleft or notch

CRENATE adj having a scalloped margin, as certain leaves

CRENATED same as ▶ crenate

CRENEL, -ED, -S n opening formed in the top of a wall having slanting sides ▷ vb crenellate

CRENELLE same as ▶ crenel

CRENELS ▶ crenel

CRENSHAW n variety of melon

CREODONT n type of extinct Tertiary mammal, the ancestor of modern carnivores

CREOLE, -S n language developed from a mixture of languages ▷ adj of or relating to a creole

CREOLIAN n Creole

CREOLISE vb (of a pidgin language) to become the native language of a speech community

CREOLIST n student of creole languages

CREOLIZE same as ▶ creolise

CREOSOL, -S n insoluble oily liquid

CREOSOTE n dark oily liquid made from coal tar and used for preserving wood ▷ vb treat with creosote

CREPANCE n injury to a horse's hind leg caused by being struck by the shoe of the other hind foot

CREPE, -D, -S, CREPING n fabric or rubber with a crinkled texture ▷ vb cover or drape with crepe ▷ vb to crimp or frizz

CREPERIE n eating establishment that specializes in pancakes

CREPES ▶ crepe

CREPEY same as ▶ crepy

CREPIER ▶ crepy

CREPIEST ▶ crepy

CREPING ▶ crepe

CREPITUS n crackling chest sound heard in pneumonia and other lung diseases

CREPON, -S n thin material made of fine wool and/or silk

CREPS pl n slang term for training shoes

CREPT ▶ creep

CREPY, CREPIER, CREPIEST adj (esp of the skin) having a dry wrinkled appearance like crepe

CRESCENT n (curved shape of) the moon as seen in its first or last quarter ▷ adj crescent-shaped

CRESCIVE adj increasing

CRESOL, -S n aromatic compound

CRESS, -ES n plant with strong-tasting leaves, used in salads

CRESSET, -S n metal basket mounted on a pole

CRESSY, CRESSIER ▶ cress

CREST, -S n top of a mountain, hill, or wave ▷ vb come to or be at the top of

CRESTA adj as in **cresta run** high-speed tobogganing down a steep narrow passage

CRESTAL, -S ▶ crystal

CRESTED ▶ crest

CRESTING same as ▶ crest

CRESTON, -S n hogback

CRESTS ▶ crest

CRESYL, -S n tolyl

CRESYLIC adj of, concerned with, or containing creosote or cresol

CRESYLS ▶ cresyl

CRETIC, -S n metrical foot

CRETIN, -S n insulting term for a stupid person

CRETISM, -S n lying

CRETONNE n heavy printed cotton fabric used in furnishings

CRETONS pl n spread made from pork fat and onions

CREUTZER n former copper and silver coin of Germany or Austria

CREVALLE n any fish of the family Carangidae

CREVASSE n deep open crack in a glacier ▷ vb make a break or fissure in (a dyke, wall, etc)

CREVETTE n shrimp

CREVICE, -S n narrow crack or gap in rock **CREVICED**

CREW, -ED, -ING, -S n people who work on a ship or aircraft ▷ vb serve as a crew member (on)

CREWCUT, -S n very short haircut

CREWE, -S n type of pot

CREWED ► crew
CREWEL, -S n fine worsted yarn used in embroidery ▷ vb embroider in crewel
CREWES ► crewe
CREWING ► crew
CREWLESS adj lacking a crew
CREWMAN, CREWMEN n member of a ship's crew
CREWMATE n colleague on the crew of a boat or ship
CREWMEN ► crewman
CREWNECK n plain round neckline in sweaters
CREWS ► crew
CRIA, -S n baby llama, alpaca, or vicuna
CRIANT adj garish
CRIAS ► cria
CRIB, -BED, -BING, -S n piece of writing stolen from elsewhere ▷ vb copy (someone's work) dishonestly
CRIBBAGE n card game for two to four players
CRIBBED ► crib
CRIBBER, -S ► crib
CRIBBING ► crib
CRIBBLE, -D, -S vb to sift
CRIBELLA > cribellum
CRIBLE adj dotted
CRIBRATE adj sievelike
CRIBROSE adj pierced with holes
CRIBROUS same as ► cribrose
CRIBS ► crib
CRIBWORK same as ► crib
CRICETID n any member of the family Cricetidae, such as the hamster and vole
CRICK, -ED, -ING, -S n muscle spasm or cramp in the back or neck ▷ vb cause a crick in
CRICKET, -S n outdoor sport ▷ vb play cricket
CRICKEY same as ► crikey
CRICKING ► crick
CRICKS ► crick
CRICKY same as ► crikey
CRICOID, -S adj of or relating to part of the larynx ▷ n this cartilage
CRIED ► cry
CRIER, -S n (formerly) official who made public announcements
CRIES ► cry
CRIKEY interj expression of surprise
CRIM, -S short for ► criminal
CRIME, -D, -S, CRIMING n unlawful act ▷ vb charge with a crime
CRIMEFUL adj criminal
CRIMEN, CRIMINA n crime
CRIMES ► crime

CRIMINA ► crimen
CRIMINAL n person guilty of a crime ▷ adj of crime
CRIMINE interj expression of surprise
CRIMING ► crime
CRIMINI same as ► crimine
CRIMINIS as in **particeps criminis** accomplice in crime
CRIMINY interj cry of surprise
CRIMMER, -S a variant spelling of ► krimmer
CRIMP, -ED, -ING, -S vb fold or press into ridges ▷ n act or result of crimping
CRIMPER -S
CRIMPIER ► crimpy
CRIMPING ► crimp
CRIMPLE, -D, -S vb crumple, wrinkle, or curl
CRIMPS ► crimp
CRIMPY, CRIMPIER ► crimp
CRIMS ► crim
CRIMSON, -S adj deep purplish-red ▷ n deep or vivid red colour ▷ vb make or become crimson
CRINAL adj relating to the hair
CRINATE adj having hair
CRINATED same as ► crinate
CRINE, -D, -S, CRINING vb to shrivel
CRINGE, -D, -S, CRINGING vb flinch in fear ▷ n act of cringing
CRINGER -S
CRINGLE, -S n eye at the edge of a sail
CRINING ► crine
CRINITE, -S adj covered with soft hairs or tufts ▷ n sedimentary rock
CRINKLE, -D, -S n wrinkle, crease, or fold ▷ vb become slightly creased or folded
CRINKLY adj wrinkled ▷ n old person
CRINOID, -S n type of primitive echinoderm
CRINOSE adj hairy
CRINUM, -S n type of mostly tropical plant
CRIOLLO, -S n native or inhabitant of Latin America of European descent ▷ adj of, relating to, or characteristic of a criollo or criollos
CRIOS, -ES n multicoloured woven woollen belt
CRIPE variant of ► cripes
CRIPES interj expression of surprise
CRIPPLE, -D, -S vb make lame or disabled
CRIPPLER
CRIS variant of ► kris
CRISE n crisis

CRISES ► crisis
CRISIC adj relating to a crisis
CRISIS, CRISES n crucial stage, turning point
CRISP, -EST, -ING, -S adj fresh and firm ▷ n very thin slice of potato fried till crunchy ▷ vb make or become crisp
CRISPATE adj having a curled or waved appearance
CRISPED same as ► crispate
CRISPEN, -S vb make crisp
CRISPER, -S n compartment in a refrigerator
CRISPEST ► crisp
CRISPIER ► crispy
CRISPIES pl n as in **rice crispies** puffed grains of rice, eaten esp as breakfast cereal
CRISPILY ► crispy
CRISPIN, -S n cobbler
CRISPING ► crisp
CRISPINS ► crispin
CRISPLY ► crisp
CRISPS ► crisp
CRISPY, CRISPIER adj hard and crunchy
CRISSA ► crissum
CRISSAL ► crissum
CRISSUM, CRISSA n area or feathers surrounding the cloaca of a bird
CRISTA, -E n structure resembling a ridge or crest
CRISTATE adj having a crest
CRIT, -S abbreviation of > criticism
CRITERIA > criterion
CRITH, -S n unit of weight for gases
CRITIC, -S n professional judge of any of the arts
CRITICAL adj very important or dangerous
CRITICS ► critic
CRITIQUE n critical essay ▷ vb review critically
CRITS ► crit
CRITTER, -S a dialect word for ► creature
CRITTUR, -S same as ► critter
CRIVENS interj expression of surprise
CRIVVENS same as ► crivens
CROAK, -ED, -ING, -S vb (of a frog or crow) give a low hoarse cry ▷ n low hoarse sound
CROAKER, -S n animal, bird, etc, that croaks
CROAKIER ► croaky
CROAKILY ► croak
CROAKING ► croak
CROAKS ► croak
CROAKY, CROAKIER ► croak
CROC, -S short for ► crocodile**

CROCEATE adj saffron-coloured

CROCEIN, -S n any one of a group of red or orange acid azo dyes

CROCEINE same as ► **crocein**

CROCEINS ► **crocein**

CROCEOUS adj saffron-coloured

CROCHE, -S n knob at the top of a deer's horn

CROCHET, -S vb make by looping and intertwining yarn with a hooked needle ▷ n work made in this way

CROCI ► **crocus**

CROCINE adj relating to the crocus

CROCK, -ING, -S n earthenware pot or jar ▷ vb become or cause to become weak or disabled

CROCKED adj injured

CROCKERY n dishes

CROCKET, -S n carved ornament in the form of a curled leaf or cusp

CROCKING ► **crock**

CROCKPOT n tradename for a brand of slow cooker

CROCKS ► **crock**

CROCOITE n rare orange secondary mineral

CROCS ► **croc**

CROCUS, CROCI, -ES n flowering plant

CROFT, -ED, -S n small farm worked by one family in Scotland ▷ vb farm land as a croft

CROFTER, -S n owner or tenant of a small farm, esp in Scotland or northern England

CROFTING n system or occupation of working land in crofts

CROFTS ► **croft**

CROG, -GED, -GING, -S vb ride on a bicycle as a passenger

CROGGIES ► **croggy**

CROGGING ► **crog**

CROGGY, CROGGIES n ride on a bicycle as a passenger

CROGS ► **crog**

CROJIK, -S n triangular sail

CROMACK, -S same as ► **crummock**

CROMB, -ED, -ING, -S same as ► **crome**

CROMBEC, -S n African Old World warbler with colourful plumage

CROMBED ► **cromb**

CROMBING ► **cromb**

CROMBS ► **cromb**

CROME, -D, -S, CROMING n hook ▷ vb use a crome

CROMLECH n circle of prehistoric standing stones

CROMORNA n one of the reed stops in an organ

CROMORNE variant of ► **cromorna**

CRON, -S n computer application that schedules tasks chronologically

CRONE, -S n witchlike old woman

CRONET, -S n hair which grows over the top of a horse's hoof

CRONIES ► **crony**

CRONISH ► **crone**

CRONK, -ER, -EST adj unfit

CRONS ► **cron**

CRONY, CRONIES n close friend

CRONYISM n appointing friends to high-level posts

CROODLE, -D, -S vb nestle close

CROOK, -ER, -EST, -ING, -S n dishonest person ▷ vb bend or curve

CROOKED adj bent or twisted

CROOKER ► **crook**

CROOKERY n illegal or dishonest activity

CROOKEST ► **crook**

CROOKING ► **crook**

CROOKS ► **crook**

CROOL, -ED, -ING, -S vb spoil

CROON, -ED, -ING, -S vb sing, hum, or speak in a soft low tone ▷ n soft low singing or humming

CROONER -S

CROONIER ► **croony**

CROONING ► **croon**

CROONS ► **croon**

CROONY, CROONIER adj singing like a crooner

CROOVE, -S n animal enclosure

CROP, -PED, -PING, -S n cultivated plant ▷ vb cut very short

CROPFUL, -S n quantity that can be held in the craw

CROPFULL adj satiated ▷ n amount that a crop can take

CROPFULS ► **cropful**

CROPLAND n land on which crops are grown

CROPLESS adj without crops

CROPPED ► **crop**

CROPPER, -S n person who cultivates or harvests a crop

CROPPIE same as ► **croppy**

CROPPIES ► **croppy**

CROPPING ► **crop**

CROPPY, CROPPIES n rebel in the Irish rising of 1798

CROPS ► **crop**

CROPSICK adj sick from excessive food or drink

CROQUET, -S n game played on a lawn in which balls are hit through hoops ▷ vb drive away a ball by hitting one's own when the two are in contact

CROQUIS n rough sketch

CRORE, -S n (in Indian English) ten million

CROSIER, -S n staff carried by bishops as a symbol of pastoral office ▷ vb bear or carry such a staff

CROSS, -ED, -ES, -EST, CROST vb move or go across (something) ▷ n structure, symbol, or mark of two intersecting lines ▷ adj angry, annoyed

CROSSARM n in mining, horizontal bar on which a drill is mounted

CROSSBAR n horizontal bar across goalposts or on a bicycle ▷ vb provide with crossbars

CROSSBIT > **crossbite**

CROSSBOW n weapon consisting of a bow fixed across a wooden stock

CROSSCUT vb cut across ▷ adj cut across ▷ n transverse cut or course

CROSSE n light staff used in playing lacrosse

CROSSED ► **cross**

CROSSER, -S ► **cross**

CROSSES ► **cross**

CROSSEST ► **cross**

CROSSING n place where a street may be crossed safely

CROSSISH ► **cross**

CROSSLET n cross having a smaller cross near the end of each arm

CROSSLY ► **cross**

CROSSPLY adj having layers of fabric with cords running diagonally

CROSSTIE n railway sleeper

CROSSWAY same as > **crossroad**

CROST ► **cross**

CROSTATA n type of fruit tart

CROSTINO, CROSTINI n piece of toasted bread served with a savoury topping

CROTAL, -S n any of various lichens used in dyeing wool

CROTALA ► **crotalum**

CROTALE, -S n type of small cymbal

CROTALS ▸ crotal

CROTALUM, CROTALA n ancient castanet-like percussion instrument

CROTCH, -ES n part of the body between the tops of the legs

CROTCHED

CROTCHET n musical note half the length of a minim

CROTON, -S n type of shrub or tree, the seeds of which yield croton oil

CROTONIC adj as in **crotonic acid** type of colourless acid

CROTONS ▸ croton

CROTTLE, -S same as **▸ crotal**

CROUCH, -ED, -ES vb bend low with the legs and body close ▷ n this position

CROUP, -ED, -ING, -S n throat disease of children, with a cough ▷ vb have croup

CROUPADE n leap by a horse, pulling the hind legs towards the belly

CROUPE, -S same as **▸ croup**

CROUPED ▸ croup

CROUPER, -S obsolete variant of **▸ crupper**

CROUPES ▸ croupe

CROUPIER n person who collects bets and pays out winnings at a gambling table in a casino

CROUPILY ▸ croup

CROUPING ▸ croup

CROUPON, -S n type of highly-polished flexible leather

CROUPOUS ▸ croup

CROUPS ▸ croup

CROUPY ▸ croup

CROUSE adj lively, confident, or saucy

CROUSELY

CROUT, -S n sauerkraut

CROUTE, -S n small round of toasted bread on which a savoury mixture is served

CROUTON, -S n small piece of fried or toasted bread served in soup

CROUTS ▸ crout

CROW, -ED, -S n large black bird with a harsh call ▷ vb (of a cock) make a shrill squawking sound

CROWBAIT n worn-out horse

CROWBAR, -S n iron bar used as a lever ▷ vb use a crowbar to lever (something)

CROWBOOT n type of Inuit boot made of fur and leather

CROWD, -ED, -ING, -S n large group of people or things

▷ vb gather together in large numbers

CROWDER -S

CROWDIE, -S n porridge of meal and water

CROWDING ▸ crowd

CROWDS ▸ crowd

CROWDY same as **▸ crowdie**

CROWEA, -S n Australian shrub with pink flowers

CROWED ▸ crow

CROWER, -S ▸ crow

CROWFOOT, CROWFEET n type of plant

CROWING, -S n act of crowing

CROWN, -ED, -S n monarch's headdress of gold and jewels ▷ vb put a crown on the head of (someone) to proclaim him or her monarch

CROWNER, -S n promotional label

CROWNET, -S n coronet

CROWNING n coronation

CROWNLET n small crown

CROWNS ▸ crown

CROWS ▸ crow

CROWSTEP n set of steps to the top of a gable on a building

CROZE, -S n recess cut at the end of a barrel or cask to receive the head

CROZER, -S n machine which cuts grooves in cask staves

CROZES ▸ croze

CROZIER, -S same as **▸ crosier**

CROZZLED adj blackened or burnt at the edges

CRU n (in France) a vineyard, group of vineyards, or wine-producing region

CRUBEEN, -S n pig's trotter

CRUCES ▸ crux

CRUCIAL adj very important

CRUCIAN, -S n European fish

CRUCIATE adj shaped or arranged like a cross ▷ n cruciate ligament

CRUCIBLE n pot in which metals are melted

CRUCIFER n type of plant with four petals arranged like a cross

CRUCIFIX n model of Christ on the Cross

CRUCIFY vb put to death by fastening to a cross

CRUCK, -S n wooden timber supporting the end of certain roofs

CRUD, -DED, -DING, -S n sticky or encrusted substance ▷ interj expression of disgust, disappointment,

etc ▷ vb cover with a sticky or encrusted substance

CRUDDIER ▸ cruddy

CRUDDING ▸ crud

CRUDDLE, -D, -S vb curdle

CRUDDY, CRUDDIER adj dirty or unpleasant

CRUDE, -R, -S, -ST adj rough and simple ▷ n crude oil

CRUDELY

CRUDIER ▸ crudy

CRUDIEST ▸ crudy

CRUDITES pl n selection of raw vegetables often served with a variety of dips before a meal

CRUDITY ▸ crude

CRUDO, -S n sliced raw seafood

CRUDS ▸ crud

CRUDY, CRUDIER, CRUDIEST adj raw

CRUE, -S obsolete variant of **▸ crew**

CRUEL, -ER, -EST, -LER adj delighting in others' pain

CRUELLS same as **▸ cruels**

CRUELLY ▸ cruel

CRUELS n disease of cattle and sheep

CRUELTY n deliberate infliction of pain or suffering

CRUES ▸ crue

CRUET, -S n small container for salt, pepper, etc, at table

CRUFT, -S n redundant technical hardware

CRUISE, -D, -S, CRUISING n sea trip for pleasure ▷ vb sail from place to place for pleasure

CRUISER, -S n fast warship

CRUISES ▸ cruise

CRUISEY same as **▸ cruisy**

CRUISIE, -S same as **▸ cruizie**

CRUISIER ▸ cruisy

CRUISIES ▸ cruisie

CRUISING ▸ cruise

CRUISY, CRUISIER adj relaxed or easy-going

CRUIVE, -S n animal enclosure

CRUIZIE, -S n oil lamp

CRULLER, -S n light sweet ring-shaped cake, fried in deep fat

CRUMB, -ED, -ING n small fragment of bread or other dry food ▷ vb prepare or cover (food) with breadcrumbs ▷ adj (esp of pie crusts) made with a mixture of biscuit crumbs, sugar, etc

CRUMBER -S

CRUMBIER ▸ crumby

CRUMBING ▸ crumb

CRUMBLE, -D, -S vb break into fragments ▷ n pudding of

stewed fruit with a crumbly topping

CRUMBLY adj easily crumbled or crumbling

CRUMBS interj expression of dismay or surprise

CRUMBUM, -S n rogue

CRUMBY, CRUMBIER adj full of crumbs

CRUMEN, -S n deer's larmier or tear-pit

CRUMENAL n purse

CRUMENS ► crumen

CRUMHORN n medieval woodwind instrument of bass pitch

CRUMMACK same as ► **crummock**

CRUMMIE n cow with a crumpled horn

CRUMMIER ► crummy

CRUMMIES ► crummy

CRUMMILY adv in a manner suggestive of or indicating poor quality

CRUMMOCK n stick with a crooked head

CRUMMY, CRUMMIER, CRUMMIES adj of poor quality ▷ n lorry that carries loggers to work from their camp

CRUMP, -ED, -ER, -EST, -ING, -S vb thud or explode with a loud dull sound ▷ n crunching, thudding, or exploding noise ▷ adj crooked

CRUMPET, -S n round soft yeast cake, eaten buttered

CRUMPIER ► crumpy

CRUMPING ► crump

CRUMPLE, -D, -S vb crush, crease ▷ n untidy crease or wrinkle

CRUMPLY

CRUMPS ► crump

CRUMPY, CRUMPIER adj crisp

CRUNCH, -ED, -ES vb bite or chew with a noisy crushing sound ▷ n crunching sound

CRUNCHER

CRUNCHY

CRUNK, -S n form of hip-hop music originating in the Southern US

CRUNKED adj excited or intoxicated

CRUNKLE, -D, -S Scots variant of ► **crinkle**

CRUNKS ► crunk

CRUNODAL ► crunode

CRUNODE, -S n mathematical term

CRUOR, -ES, -S n blood clot

CRUPPER, -S n strap that passes from the back of a saddle under a horse's tail

CRURA ► crus

CRURAL adj of or relating to the leg or thigh

CRUS, CRURA n leg, esp from the knee to the foot

CRUSADE, -D, -S n medieval Christian war to recover the Holy Land from the Muslims ▷ vb take part in a crusade

CRUSADER

CRUSADO, -S n former gold or silver coin of Portugal

CRUSE, -S n small earthenware jug or pot

CRUSET, -S n goldsmith's crucible

CRUSH, -ED, -ES, -ING vb compress so as to injure, break, or crumple ▷ n dense crowd

CRUSHER -S

CRUSIAN, -S variant of ► **crucian**

CRUSIE, -S same as ► **cruizie**

CRUSILY adj (in heraldry) strewn with crosses

CRUST, -ED, -ING, -S n hard outer part of something, esp bread ▷ vb cover with or form a crust

CRUSTA, -E, -S n hard outer layer

CRUSTAL adj of or relating to the earth's crust

CRUSTAS ► crusta

CRUSTATE adj covered with a crust

CRUSTED ► crust

CRUSTIER ► crusty

CRUSTIES ► crusty

CRUSTILY ► crusty

CRUSTING ► crust

CRUSTOSE adj having a crustlike appearance

CRUSTS ► crust

CRUSTY, CRUSTIER, CRUSTIES adj having a crust ▷ n dirty type of punk or hippy whose lifestyle involves travelling and squatting

CRUSY same as ► **cruizie**

CRUTCH, -ED, -ES n long sticklike support with a rest for the armpit ▷ vb support or sustain (a person or thing) as with a crutch

CRUVE, -S same as ► **cruive**

CRUX, CRUCES, -ES n crucial or decisive point

CRUZADO, -S same as ► **crusado**

CRUZEIRO n former monetary unit of Brazil, replaced by the cruzeiro real

CRUZIE, -S same as ► **cruizie**

CRWTH, -S n ancient stringed instrument of Celtic origin

> This old Celtic musical instrument makes a fine tune when your rack is all consonants.

CRY, CRIED, CRIES vb shed tears ▷ n fit of weeping

CRYBABY n person, esp a child, who cries too readily

CRYER, -S same as ► **crier**

CRYING, -S ► cry

CRYINGLY ► cry

CRYINGS ► crying

CRYOBANK n place for storing genetic material at low temperature

CRYOGEN, -S n substance used to produce low temperatures

CRYOGENY n cryogenic science

CRYOLITE n white or colourless mineral

CRYONIC adj relating to or involving cryonics

CRYONICS n practice of freezing a human corpse in the hope of restoring it to life in the future

CRYOSTAT n apparatus for maintaining a constant low temperature

CRYOTRON n switch working at the temperature of liquid helium

CRYPT, -S n vault under a church, esp one used as a burial place

CRYPTAL

CRYPTIC adj obscure in meaning, secret

CRYPTO, -S n person who is a secret member of an organization or sect

CRYPTON, -S n krypton

CRYPTOS ► crypto

CRYPTS ► crypt

CRYSTAL, -S n symmetrically shaped solid formed naturally ▷ adj bright and clear

CSARDAS n type of Hungarian folk dance

CTENE, -S n locomotor organ found in ctenophores (or comb jellies)

CTENIDIA > ctenidium

CTENOID adj toothed like a comb, as the scales of perches

CUATRO, -S n four-stringed guitar

CUB, -BED, -S n young wild animal such as a bear or fox

C

▷ adj young or inexperienced ▷ vb give birth to cubs

CUBAGE, -S same as ▶ **cubature**

CUBANE, -S n rare octahedral hydrocarbon

CUBATURE n determination of the cubic contents of something

CUBBED ▶ cub

CUBBIER ▶ cubby

CUBBIES ▶ cubby

CUBBIEST ▶ cubby

CUBBING, -S ▶ cub

CUBBISH ▶ cub

CUBBY, CUBBIER, CUBBIES, CUBBIEST n cubbyhole ▷ adj short and plump

CUBE, -D, -S, CUBING n object with six equal square sides ▷ vb cut into cubes

CUBEB, -S n SE Asian woody climbing plant with brownish berries

CUBED ▶ cube

CUBER, -S ▶ cube

CUBES ▶ cube

CUBHOOD, -S n state of being a cub

CUBIC, -S adj having three dimensions ▷ n cubic equation

CUBICA, -S n fine shalloon-like fabric

CUBICAL adj of or related to volume

CUBICAS ▶ cubica

CUBICITY n property of being cubelike

CUBICLE, -S n enclosed part of a large room, screened for privacy

CUBICLY ▶ cubic

CUBICS ▶ cubic

CUBICULA > **cubiculum**

CUBIFORM adj having the shape of a cube

CUBING ▶ cube

CUBISM, -S n style of art in which objects are represented by geometrical shapes

CUBIST -S

CUBISTIC

CUBIT, -S n old measure of length based on the length of the forearm

CUBITAL adj of or relating to the forearm

CUBITI ▶ cubitus

CUBITS ▶ cubit

CUBITUS, CUBITI n elbow

CUBLESS adj having no cubs

CUBOID, -S adj shaped like a cube ▷ n geometric solid whose six faces are rectangles

CUBOIDAL same as ▶ **cuboid**

CUBOIDS ▶ cuboid

CUBS ▶ cub

CUCKING adj as in cucking stool stool in which suspected witches were tested

CUCKOO, -ED, -S n migratory bird ▷ adj insane or foolish ▷ interj imitation or representation of the call of a cuckoo ▷ vb repeat over and over

CUCUMBER n long green-skinned fleshy fruit used in salads

CUCURBIT n type of tropical or subtropical creeping plant

CUD, -S n partially digested food chewed by a ruminant

CUDBEAR, -S another name for ▶ **orchil**

CUDDEN, -S n young coalfish

CUDDIE same as ▶ **cuddy**

CUDDIES ▶ cuddy

CUDDIN, -S same as ▶ **cudden**

CUDDLE, -D, -S, CUDDLING n hug ▷ vb hold close

CUDDLER -S

CUDDLIER ▶ cuddly

CUDDLING ▶ cuddle

CUDDLY, CUDDLIER ▶ cuddle

CUDDY, CUDDIES n small cabin in a boat

CUDGEL, -ED, -S n short thick stick used as a weapon ▷ vb use a cudgel

CUDGELER

CUDGERIE n type of large tropical tree with light-coloured wood

CUDS ▶ cud

CUDWEED, -S n type of temperate plant

CUE, -D, -S, CUING n signal to an actor or musician to begin speaking or playing ▷ vb give a cue to

CUEING, -S same as ▶ **cue**

CUEIST, -S n snooker or billiards player

CUES ▶ cue

CUESTA, -S n long low ridge with a steep scarp slope and a gentle back slope

CUFF, -ED, -ING, -S n end of a sleeve ▷ vb hit with an open hand

CUFFABLE adj able to be folded down at the ankle

CUFFED ▶ cuff

CUFFIN, -S n man

CUFFING ▶ cuff

CUFFINS ▶ cuffin

CUFFLE, -D, -S, CUFFLING vb scuffle

CUFFLESS adj having no cuff(s)

CUFFLING ▶ cuffle

CUFFLINK n detachable fastener for shirt cuff

CUFFO adv free of charge

CUFFS ▶ cuff

CUIF, -S same as ▶ **coof**

CUING ▶ cue

CUIRASS n piece of armour, of leather or metal covering the chest and back ▷ vb equip with a cuirass

CUISH, -ES same as ▶ **cuisse**

CUISINE, -S n style of cooking

CUISSE, -S n piece of armour for the thigh

CUISSER, -S same as ▶ **cooser**

CUISSES ▶ cuisse

CUIT, -S n ankle

CUITER, -ED, -S vb pamper

CUITIKIN n gaiter

CUITS ▶ cuit

CUITTLE, -D, -S vb wheedle

CUKE, -S n cucumber

CULCH, -ES n the basis of an oyster bed

CULCHIE, -R, -S n rough or unsophisticated country-dweller from outside Dublin ▷ adj rough or unsophisticated

CULET, -S n flat face at the bottom of a gem

CULEX, -ES, CULICES n type of mosquito

CULICID, -S n type of dipterous insect

CULICINE n any member of the genus Culex containing mosquitoes

CULINARY adj of kitchens or cookery

CULL, -ED, -S vb choose, gather ▷ n culling

CULLAY, -S n soapbark tree

CULLED ▶ cull

CULLER, -S n person employed to cull animals

CULLET, -S n waste glass for melting down to be reused

CULLIED ▶ cully

CULLIES ▶ cully

CULLING, -S ▶ cull

CULLION, -ES n rascal

CULLIS, -ES same as ▶ **coulisse**

CULLS ▶ cull

CULLY, CULLIED, CULLIES, -ING n pal ▷ vb to trick

CULLYISM n state of being a dupe

CULM, -ED, -ING, -S n coal-mine waste ▷ vb form a culm or grass stem

CULMEN, CULMINA n summit

CULMING ▶ culm

CULMS ▶ culm

CULOTTE ▶ culottes

CULOTTES pl n women's knee-length trousers cut to look like a skirt

CULPA, -E n act of neglect

CULPABLE adj deserving blame

CULPABLY

CULPAE ▶ culpa

CULPRIT, -S n person guilty of an offence or misdeed

CULSHIE, -R, -S n rough or unsophisticated country-dweller from outside Dublin ▷ adj rough or unsophisticated

CULT, -S n specific system of worship ▷ adj very popular among a limited group of people

CULTCH, -ES same as ▶ culch

CULTER, -S same as ▶ coulter

CULTI ▶ cultus

CULTIC adj of or relating to a religious cult

CULTIER ▶ culty

CULTIEST ▶ culty

CULTIGEN n cultivated species of plant that did not come from a wild type

CULTISH adj intended to appeal to a small group of fashionable people

CULTISM, -S ▶ cult

CULTIST, -S ▶ cult

CULTIVAR n cultivated plant produced from a natural species

CULTLIKE adj resembling a cult

CULTRATE adj shaped like a knife blade

CULTS ▶ cult

CULTURAL adj of or relating to artistic or social pursuits

CULTURE, -S n ideas, customs, and art of a particular society ▷ vb grow (bacteria) for study

CULTURED adj showing good taste or manners

CULTURES ▶ culture

CULTUS, CULTI, -ES another word for ▶ cult

CULTY, CULTIER, CULTIEST same as ▶ cultish

CULVER, -S an archaic or poetic name for ▶ pigeon

CULVERIN n long-range medium to heavy cannon used during the 15th, 16th, and 17th centuries

CULVERS ▶ culver

CULVERT, -S n drain under a road or railway ▷ vb direct water through a culvert

CUM prep with

CUMACEAN n type of small marine crustacean

CUMARIC ▶ cumarin

CUMARIN, -S same as ▶ coumarin

CUMARONE variant spelling of ▶ coumarone

CUMBENT adj lying down

CUMBER, -ED, -S vb obstruct or hinder ▷ n hindrance or burden

CUMBERER

CUMBIA, -S n Colombian style of music

CUMBROUS adj awkward because of size, weight, or height

CUMBUNGI n type of tall Australian marsh plant

CUMEC, -S n unit of volumetric rate of flow

CUMIN, -S n sweet-smelling seeds of a Mediterranean plant, used in cooking

CUMMER, -S n gossip

CUMMIN, -S same as ▶ cumin

CUMQUAT, -S same as ▶ kumquat

CUMSHAW, -S n (used, esp formerly, by beggars in Chinese ports) a present or tip

CUMULATE vb accumulate ▷ adj heaped up

CUMULET, -S n variety of domestic fancy pigeon

CUMULI ▶ cumulus

CUMULOSE adj full of heaps

CUMULOUS adj resembling or consisting of cumulus clouds

CUMULUS, CUMULI n thick white or dark grey cloud

CUNABULA n cradle

CUNDY, CUNDIES n sewer

CUNEAL same as ▶ cuneiform

CUNEATE adj wedge-shaped: cuneate leaves are attached at the narrow end

CUNEATED same as ▶ cuneate

CUNEATIC adj cuneiform

CUNEI ▶ cuneus

CUNETTE, -S n small trench dug in the main ditch of a fortification

CUNEUS, CUNEI n small wedge-shaped area of the cerebral cortex

CUNIFORM same as ▶ cuneiform

CUNIT, -S n one hundred cubic feet

CUNJEVOI n plant of tropical Asia and Australia

CUNNER, -S n fish of the wrasse family

CUNNING, -S adj clever at deceiving ▷ n cleverness at deceiving

CUP, -PED, -S n small bowl-shaped drinking container with a handle ▷ vb form (one's hands) into the shape of a cup

CUPBOARD n piece of furniture or alcove with a door, for storage ▷ vb store in a cupboard

CUPCAKE, -S n small cake baked in a cup-shaped foil or paper case

CUPEL, -ED, -ING, -LED, -S n refractory pot in which gold or silver is refined ▷ vb refine (gold or silver) by means of cupellation

CUPELER -S

CUPELLER ▶ cupel

CUPELS ▶ cupel

CUPFUL, -S, CUPSFUL n amount a cup will hold

CUPGALL, -S n gall found on oakleaves

CUPHEAD, -S n type of bolt or rivet with a cup-shaped head

CUPID, -S n figure representing the Roman god of love

CUPIDITY n greed for money or possessions

CUPIDS ▶ cupid

CUPLIKE ▶ cup

CUPMAN, CUPMEN n drinking companion

CUPOLA, -ED, -S n domed roof or ceiling ▷ vb provide with a cupola

CUPOLAR

CUPPA, -S n cup of tea

CUPPED ▶ cup

CUPPER, -S same as ▶ cuppa

CUPPIER ▶ cuppy

CUPPIEST ▶ cuppy

CUPPING, -S ▶ cup

CUPPY, CUPPIER, CUPPIEST adj cup-shaped

CUPREOUS adj of copper

CUPRIC adj of or containing copper in the divalent state

CUPRITE, -S n red secondary mineral

CUPROUS adj of or containing copper in the monovalent state

CUPRUM, -S an obsolete name for ▶ copper

CUPS ▶ cup

CUPSFUL ▶ cupful

CUPULA, -E n dome-shaped structure

CUPULAR same as ▶ cupulate

CUPULATE adj shaped like a small cup

CUPULE, -S n cup-shaped part or structure

CUR, -S n mongrel dog

CURABLE adj capable of being cured

CURABLY

CURACAO, -S n orange-flavoured liqueur

CURACIES ► curacy

CURACOA, -S same as ► curacao

CURACY, CURACIES n work or position of a curate

CURAGH, -S same as ► currach

CURARA, -S same as ► curare

CURARE, -S n poisonous resin of a S American tree

CURARI, -S same as ► curare

CURARINE n alkaloid extracted from curare, used as a muscle relaxant in surgery

CURARIS ► curari

CURARISE same as ► curarize

CURARIZE vb paralyse or treat with curare

CURASSOW n gallinaceous ground-nesting bird

CURAT, -S n cuirass

CURATE, -D, -S, CURATING n clergyman who assists a parish priest ▷ vb be in charge of (an art exhibition or museum)

CURATION n work of a curator

CURATIVE n something able to cure ▷ adj able to cure

CURATOR, -S n person in charge of a museum or art gallery

CURATORY

CURATRIX n female curator

CURATS ► curat

CURB, -ED, -S n something that restrains ▷ vb control, restrain

CURBABLE adj capable of being restrained

CURBED ► curb

CURBER, -S ► curb

CURBING, -S the US spelling of ► kerbing

CURBLESS adj having no restraint

CURBS ► curb

CURBSIDE n pavement

CURCH, -ES n woman's plain cap or kerchief

CURCHEF, -S same as ► curch

CURCHES ► curch

CURCULIO n type of American weevil

CURCUMA, -S n type of tropical Asian tuberous plant

CURCUMIN n yellow dye derived from turmeric

CURD, -ED, -ING, -S n coagulated milk, used to make cheese ▷ vb turn into or become curd

CURDIER ► curdy

CURDIEST ► curdy

CURDING ► curd

CURDLE, -D, -S, CURDLING vb turn into curd, coagulate

CURDLER -S

CURDS ► curd

CURDY, CURDIER, CURDIEST ► curd

CURE, -D, -S vb get rid of (an illness or problem) ▷ n (treatment causing) curing of an illness or person

CURELESS

CURER, -S

CURET, -S same as ► curette

CURETTE, -D, -S n surgical instrument for scraping tissue from body cavities ▷ vb scrape with a curette

CURF, -S n type of limestone

CURFEW, -S n law ordering people to stay inside after a specific time

CURFS ► curf

CURIA, -E, -S n papal court and government of the Roman Catholic Church

CURIAL

CURIE, -S n standard unit of radioactivity

CURIET, -S n cuirass

CURING, -S n act of curing

CURIO, -S n rare or unusual object valued as a collector's item

CURIOSA pl n curiosities

CURIOUS adj eager to learn or know

CURITE, -S n oxide of uranium and lead

CURIUM, -S n radioactive element artificially produced from plutonium

CURL, -ED, -S n curved piece of hair ▷ vb make (hair) into curls or (of hair) grow in curls

CURLER, -S n pin or small tube for curling hair

CURLEW, -S n long-billed wading bird

CURLI pl n curled hairlike processes on the surface of the E. coli bacterium

CURLICUE n ornamental curl or twist ▷ vb curl or twist elaborately, as in curlicues

CURLIER ► curly

CURLIES pl n as in **have by the short and curlies** have completely in one's power

CURLIEST ► curly

CURLILY ► curly

CURLING, -S n game like bowls, played with heavy stones on ice

CURLS ► curl

CURLY, CURLIER, CURLIEST adj tending to curl

CURLYCUE same as ► curlicue

CURN, -S n grain (of corn etc)

CURNEY same as ► curny

CURNIER ► curny

CURNIEST ► curny

CURNS ► curn

CURNY, CURNIER, CURNIEST adj granular

CURPEL, -S same as ► crupper

CURR, -ED, -ING, -S, vb to purr

CURRACH, -S a Scot or Irish name for ► coracle

CURRAGH, -S same as ► currach

CURRAN, -S n black bun

CURRANT, -S n small dried grape

CURRANTY

CURRED ► curr

CURRENCY n money in use in a particular country

CURRENT, -S adj of the immediate present ▷ n flow of water or air in one direction

CURRICLE n two-wheeled open carriage drawn by two horses side by side

CURRIE same as ► curry

CURRIED ► curry

CURRIER, -S n person who curries leather

CURRIERY n trade, work, or place of occupation of a currier

CURRIES ► curry

CURRING ► curr

CURRISH adj of or like a cur

CURRS ► curr

CURRY, CURRIED, CURRIES, -ING n Indian dish of meat or vegetables in a hot spicy sauce ▷ vb prepare (food) with curry powder

CURS ► cur

CURSAL ► cursus

CURSE, -S vb swear (at) ▷ n swearword

CURSED -ER

CURSEDLY ► curse

CURSER, -S ► curse

CURSES ► curse

CURSI ► cursus

CURSILLO n short religious retreat

CURSING, -S ► curse

CURSITOR n clerk in the Court of Chancery

CURSIVE, -S n handwriting done with joined letters ▷ adj of handwriting or print in which letters are joined in a flowing style

CURSOR, -ES, -S n movable point of light that shows a specific position on a visual display unit

CURSORY adj quick and superficial

CURST same as ► cursed

CURSUS, CURSI n Neolithic parallel earthworks

CURT, -ER, -EST adj brief and rather rude

CURTAIL, -S vb cut short

CURTAIN n piece of cloth hung at a window or opening as a screen ▷ vb provide with curtains

CURTAINS pl n death or ruin

CURTAL, -S adj cut short ▷ n animal whose tail has been docked

CURTALAX same as > curtalaxe

CURTALS ► curtal

CURTANA, -S n unpointed sword displayed at a coronation as an emblem of mercy

CURTATE adj shortened

CURTAXE, -S same as > curtalaxe

CURTER ► curt

CURTEST ► curt

CURTESY n widower's life interest in his wife's estate

CURTLY ► curt

CURTNESS ► curt

CURTSEY, -S same as ► curtsy

CURTSY, CURTSIED, CURTSIES n woman's gesture of respect ▷ vb make a curtsy

CURULE adj (in ancient Rome) of the highest rank, esp one entitled to use a curule chair

CURVATE adj curved

CURVATED same as ► curvate

CURVE, -D, -S, CURVING n continuously bending line with no straight parts ▷ vb form or move in a curve

CURVEDLY

CURVET, -ED, -S n horse's low leap with all four feet off the ground ▷ vb make such a leap

CURVEY same as ► curvy

CURVIER ► curvy

CURVIEST ► curvy

CURVING ► curve

CURVITAL adj relating to curvature

CURVITY n curvedness

CURVY, CURVIER, CURVIEST ► curve

CUSCUS, -ES n large Australian nocturnal possum

CUSEC, -S n unit of flow equal to 1 cubic foot per second

CUSH, -ES n cushion

CUSHAT, -S n wood pigeon

CUSHAW, -S same as ► cashaw

CUSHES ► cush

CUSHIE, -S same as ► cushat

CUSHIER ► cushy

CUSHIES ► cushie

CUSHIEST ► cushy

CUSHILY ► cushy

CUSHION, -S n bag filled with soft material, to make a seat more comfortable ▷ vb lessen the effects of

CUSHIONY

CUSHTY interj exclamation of pleasure, agreement, approval, etc

CUSHY, CUSHIER, CUSHIEST adj easy

CUSK, -S n type of food fish of northern coastal waters, with a single long dorsal fin

CUSP, -S n pointed end, esp on a tooth

CUSPAL

CUSPATE adj having a cusp or cusps

CUSPATED same as ► cuspate

CUSPED same as ► cuspate

CUSPID, -S n tooth having one point

CUSPIDAL same as > cuspidate

CUSPIDES ► cuspis

CUSPIDOR another word (esp US) for ► spittoon

CUSPIDS ► cuspid

CUSPIER ► cuspy

CUSPIEST ► cuspy

CUSPIS, CUSPIDES n in anatomy, tapering structure

CUSPS ► cusp

CUSPY, CUSPIER, CUSPIEST adj (of a computer program) well-designed and user-friendly

CUSS, -ES, -ING n curse, oath ▷ vb swear (at)

CUSSED adj obstinate

CUSSEDLY

CUSSER, -S same as ► cooser

CUSSES ► cuss

CUSSING ► cuss

CUSSO, -S n tree of the rose family

CUSSWORD n swearword

CUSTARD, -S n sweet yellow sauce made from milk and eggs

CUSTARDY

CUSTOCK, -S same as ► castock

CUSTODE, -S n custodian

CUSTODY n protective care

CUSTOM n long-established activity or action ▷ adj made to the specifications of an individual customer

CUSTOMED adj accustomed

CUSTOMER n person who buys goods or services

CUSTOMS n duty charged on imports or exports

CUSTOS n superior in the Franciscan religious order

CUSTREL, -S n knave

CUSTUMAL another word for > customary

CUSUM, -S n analysis technique used in statistics

CUT, -S vb open up, penetrate, wound, or divide with a sharp instrument

CUTAWAY, -S adj (of a drawing or model) having part of the outside omitted to reveal the inside ▷ n man's coat cut diagonally from the front waist to the back of the knees

CUTBACK, -S n decrease or reduction ▷ vb shorten by cutting

CUTBANK, -S n steep banking at a bend in a river

CUTBLOCK, -S n area where logging is permitted

CUTCH, -ES same as ► catechu

CUTCHA adj crude

CUTCHERY same as > cutcherry

CUTCHES ► cutch

CUTDOWN, -S n decrease

CUTE, -R, -ST adj appealing or attractive

CUTELY

CUTENESS

CUTES ► cutis

CUTESIE same as ► cutesy

CUTESIER ► cutesy

CUTEST ► cute

CUTESY, CUTESIER adj affectedly cute or coy

CUTEY, -S same as ► cutie

CUTGLASS adj (of an accent) upper-class

CUTGRASS n any grass of the genus Leersia

CUTICLE, -S n skin at the base of a fingernail or toenail

CUTICULA n cuticle

CUTIE, -S n person regarded as appealing or attractive, esp a girl or woman

CUTIKIN, -S same as ▸ **cuitikin**

CUTIN, -S n waxy waterproof substance

CUTINISE same as ▸ **cutinize**

CUTINIZE vb become or cause to become covered or impregnated with cutin

CUTINS ▸ **cutin**

CUTIS, CUTES, -ES a technical name for the ▸ **skin**

CUTLAS, -ES same as ▸ **cutlass**

CUTLASS n curved one-edged sword formerly used by sailors

CUTLER, -S n maker of cutlery

CUTLERY n knives, forks, and spoons

CUTLET, -S n small piece of meat like a chop

CUTLETTE n flat croquette of minced meat

CUTLINE, -S n caption

CUTOFF, -S n limit or termination

CUTOUT, -S n something that has been cut out from something else

CUTOVER, -S n transitional period in IT system changeover

CUTPURSE n pickpocket

CUTS ▸ **cut**

CUTSCENE n non-interactive scene in a computer game

CUTTABLE adj capable of being cut

CUTTAGE, -S n propagation by using parts taken from growing plants

CUTTER, -S n person or tool that cuts

CUTTIER ▸ **cutty**

CUTTIES ▸ **cutty**

CUTTIEST ▸ **cutty**

CUTTING, -S ▸ **cut**

CUTTLE, -D, -S, CUTTLING vb to whisper

CUTTO, -ES n large knife

CUTTOE same as ▸ **cutto**

CUTTOES ▸ **cutto**

CUTTY, CUTTIER, CUTTIES, CUTTIEST adj short or cut short ▷ n something cut short

CUTUP, -S n joker or prankster

CUTWATER n forward part of the stem of a vessel, which cuts through the water

CUTWORK, -S n type of openwork embroidery

CUTWORM, -S n caterpillar of various types of moth

CUVEE, -S n individual batch or blend of wine

CUVETTE, -S n shallow dish or vessel for holding liquid

CUZ, -ES, -ZES n cousin

> **Cuz** is another word for **cousin**, great for using the Z.

CUZZIE, -S n close friend or family member

CWM, -S same as ▸ **cirque**

> **Cwm** is a Welsh word meaning a valley, a useful one to remember because it doesn't contain any vowels.

CWTCH, -ED, -ES, -ING vb be snuggled up

> This delightful Welsh word meaning to cuddle is not likely to come up, but it might just help you out of a tight spot one day when your rack is all consonants.

CYAN, -S n highly saturated green-blue ▷ adj of this colour

CYANAMID same as > **cyanamide**

CYANATE, -S n any salt or ester of cyanic acid

CYANIC adj as in **cyanic acid** colourless poisonous volatile liquid acid

CYANID, -S same as ▸ **cyanide**

CYANIDE, -D, -S n extremely poisonous chemical compound ▷ vb treat with cyanide

CYANIDS ▸ **cyanid**

CYANIN, -S same as ▸ **cyanine**

CYANINE, -S n blue dye used in photography

CYANINS ▸ **cyanin**

CYANISE, -D, -S vb turn into cyanide

CYANITE, -S a variant spelling of ▸ **kyanite**

CYANITIC

CYANIZE, -D, -S same as ▸ **cyanise**

CYANO adj containing cyanogen

CYANOGEN n poisonous colourless flammable gas

CYANOSE same as ▸ **cyanosis**

CYANOSED adj affected by cyanosis

CYANOSIS, CYANOSES n blueness of the skin, caused by a deficiency of oxygen in the blood

CYANOTIC

CYANS ▸ **cyan**

CYANURET n cyanide

CYATHI ▸ **cyathus**

CYATHIUM, CYATHIA n inflorescence of the type found on the poinsettia

CYATHUS, CYATHI n ancient measure of wine

CYBER adj involving computers

CYBERPET n electronic toy that simulates the activities of a pet

CYBERWAR n information warfare

CYBORG, -S n (in science fiction) a living being enhanced by computer implants

CYBRID, -S n cytoplasmic hybrid

CYCAD, -S n type of tropical or subtropical plant

CYCAS, -ES n palm tree of the genus Cycas

CYCASIN, -S n glucoside, toxic to mammals, occurring in cycads

CYCLAMEN n plant with red, pink, or white flowers ▷ adj of a dark reddish-purple colour

CYCLASE, -S n enzyme which acts as a catalyst in the formation of a cyclic compound

CYCLE, -D, -S vb ride a bicycle ▷ n bicycle

CYCLECAR n any light car with an engine capacity of 1100cc or less

CYCLED ▸ **cycle**

CYCLER, -S same as ▸ **cyclist**

CYCLERY n business dealing in bicycles and bicycle accessories

CYCLES ▸ **cycle**

CYCLEWAY n path or way designed, and reserved for, cyclists

CYCLIC adj recurring or revolving in cycles

CYCLICAL n short-term trend, of which reversal is expected ▷ adj cyclic

CYCLICLY ▸ **cyclic**

CYCLIN, -S n type of protein

CYCLING, -S ▸ **cycle**

CYCLINS ▸ **cyclin**

CYCLISE, -D, -S same as ▸ **cyclize**

CYCLIST, -S n person who rides a bicycle

CYCLITOL n alicyclic compound

CYCLIZE, -D, -S vb be cyclical

CYCLO, -S n type of rickshaw

CYCLOID, -S adj resembling a circle ▷ n mathematical curve

CYCLONAL ▸ cyclone

CYCLONE, -S n violent wind moving round a central area

CYCLONIC

CYCLOPES ▸ cyclops

CYCLOPIC ▸ cyclops

CYCLOPS, CYCLOPES n type of copepod characterized by having one eye

CYCLOS ▸ cyclo

CYCLOSIS, CYCLOSES n circulation of cytoplasm or cell organelles, such as food vacuoles in some protozoans

CYCLUS, -ES n cycle

CYDER, -S same as ▸ **cider**

CYESIS, CYESES the technical name for > **pregnancy**

CYGNET, -S n young swan

CYLICES ▸ cylix

CYLIKES ▸ cylix

CYLINDER n solid or hollow body with straight sides and circular ends

CYLIX, CYLICES, CYLIKES a variant of ▸ **kylix**

CYMA, -E, -S n moulding with a double curve, part concave and part convex

CYMAR, -S n woman's short fur-trimmed jacket, popular in the 17th and 18th centuries

CYMAS ▸ cyma

CYMATIA ▸ cymatium

CYMATICS n therapy involving sound waves directed at the body

CYMATIUM, CYMATIA n top moulding of a classical cornice or entablature

CYMBAL, -S n percussion instrument

CYMBALER

CYMBALO, -S another name for ▸ **dulcimer**

CYMBALOM same as ▸ **cimbalom**

CYMBALOS ▸ cymbalo

CYMBALS ▸ cymbal

CYMBIDIA > cymbidium

CYMBLING same as ▸ **cymling**

CYME, -S n type of flower cluster

CYMENE, -S n colourless insoluble liquid

CYMES ▸ cyme

CYMLIN, -S same as ▸ **cymling**

CYMLING, -S n pattypan squash

CYMLINS ▸ cymlin

CYMOGENE n mixture of volatile flammable hydrocarbons

CYMOID adj resembling a cyme or cyma

CYMOL, -S same as ▸ **cymene**

CYMOSE adj having the characteristics of a cyme

CYMOSELY

CYMOUS adj relating to a cyme

CYNANCHE n any disease characterized by inflammation and swelling of the throat

CYNIC, -S n person who believes that people always act selfishly ▷ adj of or relating to Sirius, the Dog Star

CYNICAL adj believing that people always act selfishly

CYNICISM n attitude or beliefs of a cynic

CYNICS ▸ cynic

CYNODONT n carnivorous mammal-like reptile

CYNOSURE n centre of attention

CYPHER, -ED, -S same as ▸ **cipher**

CYPRES, -ES n legal doctrine

CYPRESS n evergreen tree with dark green leaves

CYPRIAN, -S n licentious or profligate person

CYPRID, -S n cypris

CYPRIDES ▸ cypris

CYPRIDS ▸ cyprid

CYPRINE, -S adj relating to carp ▷ n type of silicate mineral

CYPRINID n type of mainly freshwater fish, usu with toothless jaws

CYPRIS, CYPRIDES n member of the genus Cypris (small bivalve freshwater crustaceans)

CYPRUS, -ES same as ▸ **cypress**

CYPSELA, -E n dry one-seeded fruit of the daisy and related plants

CYST, -S n (abnormal) sac in the body containing fluid or soft matter

CYSTEIN, -S same as ▸ **cysteine**

CYSTEINE n sulphur-containing amino acid

CYSTEINS ▸ cystein

CYSTIC adj of, relating to, or resembling a cyst

CYSTID, -S n cystidean

CYSTINE, -S n sulphur-containing amino acid

CYSTITIS n inflammation of the bladder

CYSTOID, -S adj resembling a cyst or bladder ▷ n tissue mass that resembles a cyst but lacks an outer membrane

CYSTS ▸ cyst

CYTASE, -S n cellulose-dissolving enzyme

CYTASTER another word for ▸ **aster**

CYTE, -S n biological cell

CYTIDINE n nucleoside formed by the condensation of cytosine and ribose

CYTISI ▸ cytisus

CYTISINE n poisonous alkaloid found in laburnum seeds

CYTISUS, CYTISI n any plant of the broom genus, Cytisus

CYTODE, -S n mass of protoplasm without a nucleus

CYTOGENY n origin and development of plant cells

CYTOID adj resembling a cell

CYTOKINE n type of protein that carries signals to neighbouring cells

CYTOLOGY n study of plant and animal cells

CYTON, -S n main part of a neuron

CYTOSINE n white crystalline pyrimidine occurring in nucleic acids

CYTOSOL, -S n solution in a biological cell

CYTOSOME n body of a cell excluding its nucleus

CZAPKA, -S n leather and felt peaked military helmet of Polish origin

CZAR, -S same as ▸ **tsar**

CZARDAS n Hungarian national dance of alternating slow and fast sections

CZARDOM, -S ▸ czar

CZAREVNA a variant spelling (esp US) of ▸ **tsarevna**

CZARINA, -S variant spelling (esp US) of ▸ **tsarina**

CZARISM, -S a variant spelling (esp US) of ▸ **tsarism**

CZARIST, -S n supporter of the czar

CZARITSA n Russian empress

CZARITZA same as ▸ **czarina**

CZARS ▸ czar

Dd

D forms a two-letter word before every vowel except **U**. There are plenty of good three-letter words beginning with **D**, particularly those with a **Y** or **W**: **day, dye** and **dew** are worth 7 points each, for example. And don't forget **dex** and **dux** for 11 points each and the invaluable **dzo** for 13 points.

DA, -S *n* Burmese knife

DAAL, -S *n* (in Indian cookery) split pulses

DAB, -BED, -BING, -S *vb* pat lightly ▷ *n* small amount of something soft or moist

DABBA, -S *n* in Indian cookery, round metal box used to transport hot food

DABBED ▶ dab

DABBER, -S *n* pad used by printers for applying ink by hand

DABBING ▶ dab

DABBITY *n* temporary tattoo

DABBLE, -D, -S, DABBLING *vb* be involved in something superficially

DABBLER ▶ dab

DABCHICK *n* type of small grebe

DABS ▶ dab

DABSTER, -S *n* incompetent or amateurish worker

DACE, -S *n* small European freshwater fish

DACHA, -S *n* country cottage in Russia

DACITE, -S *n* volcanic rock

DACK, -ED, -ING, -S *vb* remove the trousers from (someone) by force

DACKER, -ED, -S *vb* walk slowly

DACKING ▶ dack

DACKS ▶ dack

DACOIT, -S *n* (in India and Myanmar) a member of a gang of armed robbers

DACOITY *n* (in India and Myanmar) robbery by an armed gang

DACRON, -S *n* US tradename for a synthetic polyester fibre or fabric

DACTYL, -S *n* metrical foot of three syllables, one long followed by two short

DACTYLAR *adj* poetry term

DACTYLI ▶ dactylus

DACTYLIC *same as* ▶ **dactyl**

DACTYLS ▶ dactyl

DACTYLUS, DACTYLI *n* tip of a squid's tentacular club

DAD, -DED, -DING, -S *n* father ▷ *vb* act or treat as a father

DADA, -S *n* nihilistic artistic movement of the early 20th century

DADAISM, -S *same as* ▶ **dada**

DADAIST, -S ▶ dada

DADAS ▶ dada

DADDED ▶ dad

DADDIES ▶ daddy

DADDING ▶ dad

DADDLE, -D, -S, DADDLING *vb* walk unsteadily

DADDOCK, -S *n* core of a dead tree

DADDY, DADDIES *n* father

DADGUM *mild form of* ▶ **damned**

DADO, -ED, -ES, -ING, -S *n* lower part of an interior wall decorated differently from the upper part ▷ *vb* provide with a dado

DADS ▶ dad

DAE, -ING, -S *a Scot word for* ▶ **do**

DAEDAL *adj* skilful or intricate

DAEDALIC *same as* > **daedalian**

DAEING ▶ dae

DAEMON, -ES, -S *same as* ▶ **demon**

DAEMONIC

DAES ▶ dae

DAFF, -ED, -S *vb* frolic

DAFFIER ▶ daffy

DAFFIES ▶ daffy

DAFFIEST ▶ daffy

DAFFILY ▶ daffy

DAFFING, -S ▶ daff

DAFFS ▶ daff

DAFFY, DAFFIER, DAFFIES, DAFFIEST *adj* daft ▷ *n* daffodil

DAFFODIL *n* yellow trumpet-shaped flower that blooms in spring ▷ *adj* brilliant yellow

DAFT, -ER, -EST *adj* foolish or crazy

DAFTAR, -S *Indian word for* ▶ **office**

DAFTER ▶ daft

DAFTEST ▶ daft

DAFTIE, -S *n* foolish person

DAFTLY ▶ daft

DAFTNESS ▶ daft

DAG, -GED, -S *n* character ▷ *vb* cut daglocks from sheep

DAGABA, -S *n* shrine for Buddhist relics

DAGGED ▶ dag

DAGGER, -ED, -S *n* short weapon with pointed blade ▷ *vb* stab with a dagger

DAGGIER ▶ daggy

DAGGIEST ▶ daggy

DAGGING, -S ▶ dag

DAGGLE, -D, -S, DAGGLING *vb* trail through water

DAGGY, DAGGIER, DAGGIEST *adj* amusing

DAGLOCK, -S *n* dung-caked lock of wool around the hindquarters of a sheep

DAGOBA, -S *n* dome-shaped Buddhist shrine

DAGS ▶ dag

DAGWOOD, -S *n* European shrub

DAH, -S *n* long sound used in Morse codes

DAHABEAH *n* houseboat used on the Nile

DAHABIAH *same as* ▶ **dahabeah**

DAHABIEH *n* Egyptian houseboat

DAHABIYA n Egyptian houseboat

DAHL, -S same as ▶ **dhal**

DAHLIA, -S n brightly coloured garden flower

DAHLS ▶ **dahl**

DAHOON, -S n evergreen shrub

DAHS ▶ **dah**

DAIDLE, -D, -S, DAIDLING vb waddle about

DAIDZEIN n type of protein

DAIKER, -ED, -S vb walk slowly

DAIKO, -S n Japanese drum

DAIKON, -S another name for ▶ **mooli**

DAIKOS ▶ **daiko**

DAILY, DAILIES adj occurring every day or every weekday ▷ adv every day ▷ n daily newspaper

DAIMEN adj occasional

DAIMIO, -S same as ▶ **daimyo**

DAIMOKU, -S n Nichiren Buddhist chant

DAIMON, -S same as ▶ **demon**

DAIMONES pl n disembodied souls

DAIMONIC ▶ **daimon**

DAIMONS ▶ **daimon**

DAIMYO, -S n magnate in Japan from the 11th to the 19th century

DAINE, -D, -S, DAINING vb condescend

DAINT, -S adj dainty ▷ n dainty

DAINTIER ▶ **dainty**

DAINTIES ▶ **dainty**

DAINTILY ▶ **dainty**

DAINTS ▶ **daint**

DAINTY, DAINTIER, DAINTIES adj delicate or elegant ▷ n small cake or sweet

DAIQUIRI n iced drink containing rum, lime juice, and sugar

DAIRY, DAIRIES n place for the processing or sale of milk and its products ▷ adj of milk or its products

DAIRYING n business of producing, processing, and selling dairy products

DAIRYMAN, DAIRYMEN n man employed to look after cows

DAIS, -ES n raised platform in a hall, used by a speaker

DAISHIKI n upper garment

DAISIED ▶ **daisy**

DAISY, DAISIES n small wild flower with a yellow centre and white petals

DAK n system of mail delivery or passenger transport

A **dak** is an old mail or transport system, often useful for disposing of the K.

DAKER, -ED, -ING, -S vb walk slowly

DAKERHEN n European bird

DAKERING ▶ **daker**

DAKERS ▶ **daker**

DAKOIT, -S same as ▶ **dacoit**

DAKOITI, -S same as ▶ **dakoit**

DAKOITS ▶ **dakoit**

DAKOITY n armed robbery

DAKS an informal name for ▶ **trousers**

DAL, -S same as ▶ **decalitre**

DALAPON, -S n herbicide

DALASI, -S n standard monetary unit of The Gambia, divided into 100 bututs

DALE n (esp in N England) valley

DALED, -S same as ▶ **daleth**

DALEDH, -S n letter of Hebrew alphabet

DALEDS ▶ **daled**

DALES ▶ **dale**

DALESMAN, DALESMEN n person living in a dale, esp in the dales of N England

DALETH, -S n fourth letter of the Hebrew alphabet

DALGYTE, -S another name for ▶ **bilby**

DALI, -S n type of tree

DALLES, DALLE pl n stretch of a river between high rock walls, with rapids and dangerous currents

DALLIED ▶ **dally**

DALLIER, -S ▶ **dally**

DALLIES ▶ **dally**

DALLOP, -S n semisolid lump

DALLY, DALLIED, DALLIES, -ING vb waste time

DALMAHOY n bushy wig

DALMATIC n wide-sleeved tunic-like vestment open at the sides, worn by deacons and bishops

DALS ▶ **dal**

DALT, -S n foster child

DALTON, -S n atomic mass unit

DALTONIC > **daltonism**

DALTONS ▶ **dalton**

DALTS ▶ **dalt**

DAM, -MED, -MING, -S n barrier built across a river to create a lake ▷ vb build a dam across (a river)

DAMAGE, -D vb harm, spoil ▷ n harm to a person or thing

DAMAGER -S

DAMAGES pl n money awarded as compensation for injury or loss

DAMAGING ▶ **damage**

DAMAN, -S n the Syrian rock hyrax

DAMAR, -S same as ▶ **dammar**

DAMASK, -ED, -S n fabric with a pattern woven into it, used for tablecloths etc ▷ vb ornament (metal) by etching or inlaying, usually with gold or silver

DAMASKIN vb decorate metal

DAMASKS ▶ **damask**

DAMASSIN n patterned damask

DAMBOARD n draughtboard

DAMBROD, -S n draughtboard

DAME, -S n woman

DAMEWORT n sweet-scented perennial plant with mauve or white flowers

DAMFOOL, -S adj foolish ▷ n foolish person

DAMIANA, -S n herbal medicine

DAMMAR, -S n any of various resins obtained from SE Asian trees

DAMME interj exclamation of surprise

DAMMED ▶ **dam**

DAMMER, -S same as ▶ **dammar**

DAMMING ▶ **dam**

DAMMIT interj exclamation of surprise

DAMN, -ING, -S interj exclamation of annoyance ▷ adj extreme(ly) ▷ vb condemn as bad or worthless

DAMNABLE adj annoying

DAMNABLY adv in a detestable manner

DAMNDEST n utmost

DAMNED, -ER adj condemned to hell ▷ adv extreme or extremely

DAMNER, -S n person who damns

DAMNEST, -S same as > **damnedest**

DAMNIFY vb cause loss or damage to (a person)

DAMNING ▶ **damn**

DAMNS ▶ **damn**

DAMOISEL same as ▶ **damsel**

DAMOSEL, -S same as ▶ **damsel**

DAMOZEL, -S *n* young girl or unmarried woman

DAMP, -ED, -EST, -S *adj* slightly wet ▷ *n* slight wetness, moisture ▷ *vb* make damp

DAMPEN, -ED, -S *vb* reduce the intensity of
DAMPENER

DAMPER, -S *n* movable plate to regulate the draught in a fire

DAMPEST ▶ damp

DAMPIER ▶ dampy

DAMPIEST ▶ dampy

DAMPING, -S *n* moistening or wetting

DAMPISH ▶ damp

DAMPLY ▶ damp

DAMPNESS ▶ damp

DAMPS ▶ damp

DAMPY, DAMPIER, DAMPIEST *adj* damp

DAMS ▶ dam

DAMSEL, -S *n* young woman

DAMSON, -S *n* small blue-black plumlike fruit

DAN, -S *n* in judo, any of the 10 black-belt grades of proficiency

DANAZOL, -S *n* synthetic male hormone

DANCE, -D, -S *vb* move the feet and body rhythmically in time to music ▷ *n* series of steps and movements in time to music
DANCER -S

DANCETTE *another name for* ▶ **chevron**

DANCETTY *adj* having a zigzag pattern

DANCEY, DANCIER, DANCIEST *adj* of, relating to, or resembling dance music

DANCICAL *n* type of dance show set to pop music

DANCIER ▶ dancey

DANCIEST ▶ dancey

DANCING, -S ▶ dance

DANCY *adj* (of music) appropriate for dancing

DANDER, -ED, -S *n* stroll ▷ *vb* stroll

DANDIER ▶ dandy

DANDIES ▶ dandy

DANDIEST ▶ dandy

DANDIFY *vb* dress like or cause to resemble a dandy

DANDILY ▶ dandy

DANDLE, -D, -S, DANDLING *vb* move (a child) up and down on one's knee
DANDLER -S

DANDRIFF *same as* ▶ **dandruff**

DANDRUFF *n* loose scales of dry dead skin shed from the scalp

DANDY, DANDIER, DANDIES, DANDIEST *n* man who is overconcerned with the elegance of his appearance ▷ *adj* very good
DANDYISH
DANDYISM

DANEGELD *n* tax levied in Anglo-Saxon England to provide protection from Viking invaders

DANEGELT *same as* ▶ **danegeld**

DANELAGH *same as* ▶ **danelaw**

DANELAW, -S *n* Danish law in parts of Anglo-Saxon England

DANEWEED *n* dwarf elder

DANEWORT *n* dwarf elder

DANG, -ED, -ING, -S *a euphemistic word for* ▶ **damn**

DANGER, -ED, -S *n* state of being vulnerable to injury, loss, or evil ▷ *vb* in archaic usage, endanger

DANGING ▶ dang

DANGLE, -D, -S, DANGLING *vb* hang loosely ▷ *n* act of dangling or something that dangles
DANGLER -S

DANGLIER ▶ dangly

DANGLING ▶ dangle

DANGLY, DANGLIER ▶ dangle

DANGS ▶ dang

DANIO, -S *n* type of tropical freshwater fish

DANISH, -ES *n* sweet pastry

DANK, -ER, -EST, -S *adj* unpleasantly damp and chilly ▷ *n* unpleasant damp and chilliness
DANKISH
DANKLY
DANKNESS

DANNY, DANNIES *n* hand (used esp when addressing children)

DANS ▶ dan

DANSAK, -S *n* type of Indian dish

DANSEUR, -S *n* male ballet dancer

DANSEUSE *n* female ballet dancer

DANT, -ED, -ING, -S *vb* intimidate

DANTON, -ED, -S *same as* ▶ **daunton**

DANTS ▶ dant

DAP, -PED, -PING, -S *vb* engage in type of fly fishing

DAPHNE, -S *n* ornamental Eurasian shrub

DAPHNIA, -S *n* type of water flea

DAPHNID, -S *n* water flea

DAPPED ▶ dap

DAPPER, -ER, -S *adj* (of a man) neat in appearance ▷ *n* fisherman or -woman who uses a bobbing bait
DAPPERLY

DAPPING ▶ dap

DAPPLE, -D, -S, DAPPLING *vb* mark or become marked with spots or patches of a different colour ▷ *n* mottled or spotted markings ▷ *adj* marked with dapples or spots

DAPS ▶ dap

DAPSONE, -S *n* antimicrobial drug

DAQUIRI, -S *n* rum cocktail

DARAF, -S *n* unit of elastance equal to a reciprocal farad

DARB, -S *n* something excellent

DARBAR, -S *n* hall in Sikh temple

DARBIES *pl n* handcuffs

DARBS ▶ darb

DARCY, DARCIES, -S *n* unit expressing the permeability coefficient of rock

DARE, -D, -S *vb* be courageous enough to try (to do something) ▷ *n* challenge to do something risky

DAREFUL *adj* daring

DARER, -S ▶ dare

DARES ▶ dare

DARESAY *vb* venture to say

DARG, -S *n* day's work

DARGA, -S *n* Muslim shrine

DARGAH, -S *n* tomb of a Muslim saint

DARGAS ▶ darga

DARGLE, -S *n* wooded hollow

DARGS ▶ darg

DARI, -S *n* variety of sorghum

DARIC, -S *n* gold coin of ancient Persia

DARING, -S *adj* willing to take risks ▷ *n* courage to do dangerous things
DARINGLY

DARIOLE, -S *n* small cup-shaped mould

DARIS ▶ dari

DARK, -ED, -ER, -EST, -ING, -S *adj* having little or no light ▷ *n* absence of light ▷ *vb* in archaic usage, darken

DARKEN, -ED, -S vb make or become dark or darker **DARKENER**

DARKER ▶ dark

DARKEST ▶ dark

DARKING ▶ dark

DARKISH ▶ dark

DARKLE, -D, -S vb grow dark

DARKLIER ▶ darkly

DARKLING adj in the dark or night

DARKLY, DARKLIER ▶ dark

DARKMANS n slang term for night-time

DARKNESS ▶ dark

DARKNET, -S n covert communication network on the Internet

DARKROOM n darkened room for processing photographic film

DARKS ▶ dark

DARKSOME adj dark or darkish

DARLING, -S n much-loved person ▷ adj much-loved

DARN, -S vb mend (a garment) with a series of interwoven stitches ▷ n patch of darned work

DARNDEST n utmost

DARNED, -ER adj damned

DARNEL, -S n weed that grows in grain fields

DARNER, -S ▶ darn

DARNEST, -S same as ▶ darndest

DARNING, -S ▶ darn

DARNS ▶ darn

DAROGHA, -S n in India, manager

DARRAIGN same as ▶ deraign

DARRAIN, -S vb clear of guilt

DARRAINE vb clear of guilt

DARRAINS ▶ darrain

DARRAYN, -S vb clear of guilt

DARRE, -D, -S, DARRING vb archaic spelling of dare

DARSHAN, -S n Hindu blessing

DART, -ED n small narrow pointed missile ▷ vb move or direct quickly and suddenly

DARTER, -S n type of aquatic bird

DARTING ▶ dart

DARTITIS n nervous twitching while playing darts

DARTLE, -D, -S, DARTLING vb move swiftly

DARTRE, -S n skin disease

DARTROUS adj having a skin disease

DARTS n game in which darts are thrown at a dartboard

DARZI, -S n tailor in India

DAS ▶ da

DASH, -ED, -ES vb move quickly ▷ n sudden quick movement

DASHEEN, -S another name for ▶ taro

DASHEKI, -S n upper garment

DASHER, -S n one of the boards surrounding an ice-hockey rink

DASHES ▶ dash

DASHI, -S n clear stock made from dried fish and kelp

DASHIER ▶ dashy

DASHIEST ▶ dashy

DASHIKI, -S n large loose-fitting buttonless upper garment

DASHING adj stylish and attractive

DASHIS ▶ dashi

DASHPOT, -S n device for damping vibrations

DASHY, DASHIER, DASHIEST adj showy

DASSIE, -S n type of hoofed rodent-like animal

DASTARD, -S n contemptible sneaking coward

DASTARDY n cowardice

DASYPOD, -S n armadillo

DASYURE, -S n small marsupial of Australia, New Guinea, and adjacent islands

DATA n information consisting of observations, measurements, or facts

DATABANK n store of a large amount of information

DATABASE n store of information in a form that can be easily handled by a computer ▷ vb put data into a database

DATABLE ▶ date

DATABUS n computing term

DATACARD n smart card

DATAFLOW n as in **dataflow architecture** means of arranging computer data processing

DATAGRAM n (in computing) self-contained unit of data transmitted in a packet-switched network

DATAL, -S adj slow-witted ▷ n day labour

DATALLER n worker paid by the day

DATALS ▶ datal

DATARIA, -S n Roman Catholic office

DATARY, DATARIES n head of the dataria

DATCHA, -S same as ▶ dacha

DATE, -S n specified day of the month ▷ vb mark with the date

DATEABLE

DATEBOOK n list of forthcoming events

DATED adj old-fashioned

DATEDLY

DATELESS ▶ date

DATELINE n information about the place and time an article was written

DATER, -S n person who dates

DATES ▶ date

DATING, -S n any of several techniques for establishing the age of objects

DATIVAL ▶ dative

DATIVE, -S adj denoting a grammatical case ▷ n grammatical case

DATIVELY

DATO, -S n chief of any of certain Muslim tribes in the Philippine Islands

DATOLITE n colourless mineral

DATOS ▶ dato

DATTO, -S n Datsun car

DATUM, -S n single piece of information in the form of a fact or statistic

DATURA, -S n type of plant

DATURIC

DATURINE n poisonous alkaloid

DAUB, -ED, -S vb smear or spread quickly or clumsily ▷ n crude or badly done painting

DAUBE, -S n braised meat stew

DAUBED ▶ daub

DAUBER, -S ▶ daub

DAUBERY n act or an instance of daubing

DAUBES ▶ daube

DAUBIER ▶ dauby

DAUBIEST ▶ dauby

DAUBING, -S ▶ daub

DAUBRY, DAUBRIES n unskilful painting

DAUBS ▶ daub

DAUBY, DAUBIER, DAUBIEST ▶ daub

DAUD, -ED, -ING, -S n lump or chunk of something ▷ vb (in dialect) whack

DAUGHTER n female child ▷ adj denoting a cell, chromosome, etc produced by the division of one of its own kind

DAULT, -S n foster child

DAUNDER, -S vb stroll

DAUNER, -ED, -S vb stroll

D

DAUNT, -ED, -S vb intimidate
DAUNTER -S

DAUNTING adj intimidating or worrying

DAUNTON, -S vb dishearten

DAUNTS ▶ daunt

DAUPHIN, -S n (formerly) eldest son of the king of France

DAUPHINE n wife of a dauphin

DAUPHINS ▶ dauphin

DAUR, -ED, -ING, -S a Scot word for ▶ dare

DAUT, -ED, -ING, -S vb fondle

DAUTIE, -S n darling

DAUTING ▶ daut

DAUTS ▶ daut

DAVEN, -ED, -ING, -S vb pray

DAVIDIA, -S n Chinese shrub

DAVIES ▶ davy

DAVIT, -S n crane, usu one of a pair, at a ship's side, for lowering and hoisting a lifeboat

DAVY, DAVIES n miner's safety lamp

DAW, -ED, -EN, -ING, -S n archaic, dialect, or poetic name for a jackdaw ▷ vb old word for dawn

> This is another name for a **jackdaw**. It is worth remembering that not only does this little word take D, K, N, S and T at the back, to make **dawd, dawk, dawn, daws** and **dawt**, but you can put an A on the front of it to make **adaw**.

DAWAH, -S n practice of educating non-Muslims about the message of Islam

DAWBAKE, -S n foolish or slow-witted person

DAWBRY, DAWBRIES n unskilful painting

DAWCOCK, -S n male jackdaw

DAWD, -ED, -ING, -S vb thump

DAWDLE, -D, -S, DAWDLING vb walk slowly, lag behind

DAWDLER -S

DAWDS ▶ dawd

DAWED ▶ daw

DAWEN ▶ daw

DAWING ▶ daw

DAWISH ▶ daw

DAWK, -S same as ▶ dak

DAWN, -ED, -S n daybreak ▷ vb begin to grow light

DAWNER, -ED, -S vb stroll

DAWNEY adj (of a person) dull or slow

DAWNING, -S ▶ dawn

DAWNLIKE ▶ dawn

DAWNS ▶ dawn

DAWS ▶ daw

DAWT, -ED, -ING, -S vb fondle

DAWTIE, -S n darling

DAWTING ▶ dawt

DAWTS ▶ dawt

DAY n period of 24 hours

DAYAN, -IM, -S n senior rabbi, esp one who sits in a religious court

DAYBED, -S n narrow bed for day use

DAYBOAT, -S n small sailing boat with no sleeping accommodation

DAYBOOK, -S n book in which transactions are recorded as they occur

DAYBOY, -S n boy who attends a boarding school but returns home each evening

DAYBREAK n time in the morning when light first appears

DAYCARE, -S n care provided during the working day for people who might be at risk if left on their own

DAYCH, -ED, -ES, -ING vb thatch

DAYDREAM n pleasant fantasy indulged in while awake ▷ vb indulge in idle fantasy

DAYFLY, DAYFLIES another name for ▶ mayfly

DAYGIRL, -S n girl who attends a boarding school but returns home each evening

DAYGLO n fluorescent colours

DAYGLOW, -S n fluorescent colours

DAYLIGHT n light from the sun

DAYLILY n any of various plants having lily-like flowers

DAYLIT ▶ daylight

DAYLONG adv lasting the entire day

DAYMARE, -S n bad dream during the day

DAYMARK, -S n navigation aid

DAYNT, -S adj dainty ▷ n thing or condition that is extravagant or best

DAYPACK, -S n small rucksack

DAYROOM, -S n communal living room in a residential institution

DAYS adv during the day, esp regularly

DAYSACK, -S n rucksack

DAYSAIL, -S vb take day trip on a sailing boat or yacht

DAYSHELL n thistle

DAYSIDE, -S n side of a planet nearest the sun

DAYSMAN, DAYSMEN n umpire

DAYSTAR, -S a poetic word for ▶ sun

DAYTALE, -S n day labour

DAYTALER n worker paid by the day

DAYTALES ▶ daytale

DAYTIME, -S n time from sunrise to sunset

DAYWEAR, -S n clothes for everyday or informal wear

DAYWORK, -S n daytime work

DAZE, -D, -S, DAZING vb stun, by a blow or shock ▷ n state of confusion or shock

DAZEDLY

DAZER -S

DAZZLE, -D, -S, DAZZLING vb impress greatly ▷ n bright light that dazzles

DAZZLER -S

DE prep of or from

DEACON, -ED, -S n ordained minister ranking immediately below a priest ▷ vb make a deacon of

DEACONRY n office or status of a deacon

DEACONS ▶ deacon

DEAD, -ED, -EST, -ING, -S adj no longer alive ▷ n period during which coldness or darkness is most intense ▷ adv extremely ▷ vb in archaic usage, die or kill

DEADBEAT n lazy useless person

DEADBOLT n bolt operated without a spring

DEADBOY, -S same as ▶ deadman

DEADED ▶ dead

DEADEN, -ED, -S vb make less intense

DEADENER

DEADER, -S ▶ dead

DEADEST ▶ dead

DEADEYE, -S n either of two disclike blocks used to tighten a shroud on a boat

DEADFALL n type of trap using a heavy weight to crush prey

DEADHEAD n person who does not pay on a bus, at a game, etc ▷ vb cut off withered flowers from (a plant)

DEADING ▶ dead

DEADLIER ▶ deadly

DEADLIFT vb weightlifting term

DEADLINE n time limit ▷ vb put a time limit on an action, decision, etc

DEADLOCK n point in a dispute at which no agreement can be reached ▷ vb bring or come to a deadlock

DEADLY, DEADLIER adj likely to cause death ▷ adv extremely

DEADMAN, DEADMEN n item used in construction

DEADNESS ► dead

DEADPAN, -S adv showing no emotion or expression ▷ adj deliberately emotionless ▷ n deadpan expression or manner

DEADS ► dead

DEADWOOD n dead trees or branches

DEAERATE vb remove air from

DEAF, -ER, -EST adj unable to hear

DEAFEN, -ED, -S vb make deaf, esp temporarily

DEAFER ► deaf

DEAFEST ► deaf

DEAFISH ► deaf

DEAFLY ► deaf

DEAFNESS ► deaf

DEAIR, -ED, -ING, -S vb remove air from

DEAL, -ING, -S, -T n agreement or transaction ▷ vb inflict (a blow) on ▷ adj of fir or pine

DEALATE, -S adj (of insects) having lost their wings after mating ▷ n insect that has shed its wings

DEALATED same as ► dealate

DEALATES ► dealate

DEALBATE adj bleached

DEALER, -S n person whose business involves buying and selling

DEALFISH n long thin fish

DEALIGN, -S vb fall out of agreement with (a political party)

DEALING ► deal

DEALINGS pl n transactions or business relations

DEALS ► deal

DEALT ► deal

DEAN, -ED, -ING, -S n chief administrative official of a college or university faculty ▷ vb punish (a student) by sending them to the dean

DEANER, -S n shilling

DEANERY n office or residence of a dean

DEANING ► dean

DEANS ► dean

DEANSHIP ► dean

DEAR, -ER, -S n someone regarded with affection ▷ adj much-loved

DEARE, -D, -S, DEARING vb harm

DEARER ► dear

DEARES ► deare

DEAREST, -S n term of affection

DEARIE same as ► deary

DEARIES ► deary

DEARING ► deare

DEARLING n darling

DEARLY adv very much

DEARN, -ED, -ING, -S vb hide

DEARNESS ► dear

DEARNFUL adj secret

DEARNING ► dearn

DEARNLY ► dearn

DEARNS ► dearn

DEARS ► dear

DEARTH, -S n inadequate amount, scarcity

DEARY, DEARIES n term of affection: now often sarcastic or facetious

DEASH, -ED, -ES, -ING vb remove ash from

DEASIL, -S adv in the direction of the apparent course of the sun ▷ n motion in this direction

DEASIUL, -S n motion towards the sun

DEASOIL, -S n motion towards the sun

DEATH, -S n permanent end of life in a person or animal

DEATHBED n bed where a person is about to die or has just died

DEATHCUP n poisonous fungus

DEATHFUL adj murderous

DEATHIER ► deathy

DEATHLY adv like death ▷ adj resembling death

DEATHS ► death

DEATHY, DEATHIER ► death

DEAVE, -D, -S, DEAVING vb deafen

DEAW, -ED, -ING, -S n archaic spelling of dew ▷ vb cover with dew

DEAWIE

DEAWY

DEB, -S n debutante

DEBACLE, -S n disastrous failure

DEBAG, -GED, -S vb remove the trousers from (someone) by force

DEBAR, -RED, -S vb prevent, bar

DEBARK, -ED, -S vb remove the bark from (a tree)

DEBARKER

DEBARRED ► debar

DEBARS ► debar

DEBASE, -D, -S, DEBASING vb lower in value, quality, or character

DEBASER -S

DEBATE, -D, -S n discussion ▷ vb discuss formally

DEBATER -S

DEBATING n act of debating

DEBAUCH vb make (someone) bad or corrupt ▷ n instance or period of extreme dissipation

DEBBY, DEBBIER, DEBBIES, DEBBIEST n debutante ▷ adj of, or resembling a debutante

DEBE, -S n tin

DEBEAK, -ED, -S vb remove part of the beak of poultry

DEBEARD, -S vb remove beard from mussel

DEBEL, -LED, -S vb beat in war

DEBES ► debe

DEBILE adj lacking strength

DEBILITY n weakness, infirmity

DEBIT, -ED, -ING, -S n sum owing entered on the left side of an account ▷ vb charge (an account) with a debt

DEBITOR, -S n person in debt

DEBITS ► debit

DEBONAIR adj (of a man) charming and refined

DEBONE, -D, -S, DEBONING vb remove bones from

DEBONER -S

DEBOSH, -ED, -ES vb debauch

DEBOSS, -ED, -ES vb carve a design into

DEBOUCH vb move out from a narrow place to a wider one ▷ n outlet or passage, as for the exit of troops

DEBOUCHE same as ► debouch

DEBRIDE, -D, -S vb remove dead tissue from

DEBRIEF, -S vb receive a report from (a soldier, diplomat, etc) after an event

DEBRIS n fragments of something destroyed

DEBRUISE vb (in heraldry) overlay or partly cover

DEBS ► deb

DEBT, -S *n* something owed, esp money

DEBTED *adj* in debt

DEBTEE, -S *n* person owed a debt

DEBTLESS ▸ debt

DEBTOR, -S *n* person who owes money

DEBTS ▸ debt

DEBUD, -DED, -S *same as* ▸ **disbud**

DEBUG, -GED, -S *vb* find and remove defects in (a computer program) ▸ *n* something that locates and removes defects in a device, system, etc
DEBUGGER

DEBUNK, -ED, -S *vb* expose the falseness of
DEBUNKER

DEBUR, -S *vb* remove burs from (a piece of machined metal)

DEBURR, -ED, -S *vb* remove burrs from (a workpiece)

DEBURS ▸ debur

DEBUS, -ED, -ES, -ING, -SED, -SES *vb* unload (goods) or (esp of troops) to alight from a motor vehicle

DEBUT, -ED, -ING, -S *n* first public appearance of a performer ▸ *vb* make a debut

DEBUTANT *n* person making a first appearance in a particular capacity

DEBUTED ▸ debut

DEBUTING ▸ debut

DEBUTS ▸ debut

DEBYE, -S *n* unit of electric dipole moment

DECAD, -S *n* ten years

DECADAL ▸ decade

DECADE, -S *n* period of ten years

DECADENT *adj* characterized by decay or decline, as in being self-indulgent or morally corrupt ▸ *n* decadent person

DECADES ▸ decade

DECADS ▸ decad

DECAF, -S *n* decaffeinated coffee ▸ *adj* decaffeinated

DECAFF, -S *n* decaffeinated coffee

DECAFS ▸ decaf

DECAGON, -S *n* geometric figure with ten faces

DECAGRAM *n* ten grams

DECAL, -ED, -ING, -LED, -S *vb* transfer (a design) by decalcomania

DECALOG, -S *same as* ▸ **decalogue**

DECALS ▸ decal

DECAMP, -ED, -S *vb* depart secretly or suddenly

DECAN, -S *n* one of three divisions of a sign of the zodiac

DECANAL *adj* of or relating to a dean or deanery

DECANE, -S *n* liquid alkane hydrocarbon

DECANI *adj* to be sung by the decanal side of a choir

DECANOIC *adj* as in **decanoic acid** white crystalline insoluble carboxylic acid

DECANS ▸ decan

DECANT, -ED, -S *vb* pour (a liquid) from one container to another

DECANTER *n* stoppered bottle for wine or spirits

DECANTS ▸ decant

DECAPOD, -S *n* creature, such as a crab, with five pairs of walking limbs ▸ *adj* of, relating to, or belonging to these creatures

DECARB, -ED, -S *vb* decoke

DECARE, -S *n* ten ares or 1000 square metres

DECAY, -ED, -ING, -S *vb* become weaker or more corrupt ▸ *n* process of decaying
DECAYER -S

DECCIE, -S *n* decoration

DECEASE, -S *n* death

DECEASED *adj* dead ▸ *n* dead person

DECEASES ▸ decease

DECEDENT *n* deceased person

DECEIT, -S *n* behaviour intended to deceive

DECEIVE, -D, -S *vb* mislead by lying
DECEIVER

DECEMVIR *n* member of a board of ten magistrates in Ancient Rome

DECENARY *adj* of or relating to a tithing

DECENCY *n* conformity to the prevailing standards of what is right

DECENNIA > decennium

DECENT *adj* (of a person) polite and morally acceptable

DECENTER *vb* put out of centre

DECENTLY ▸ decent

DECENTRE *vb* put out of centre

DECERN, -ED, -S *vb* decree or adjudge

DECIARE, -S *n* one tenth of an are or 10 square metres

DECIBEL, -S *n* unit for measuring the intensity of sound

DECIDE, -S, DECIDING *vb* (cause to) reach a decision

DECIDED *adj* unmistakable

DECIDER, -S *n* thing that determines who wins a match or championship

DECIDES ▸ decide

DECIDING ▸ decide

DECIDUA, -E, -S *n* membrane lining the uterus of some mammals during pregnancy
DECIDUAL

DECIGRAM *n* tenth of a gram

DECILE, -S *n* one of nine values of a variable divided into ten equal groups

DECIMAL, -S *n* fraction written in the form of a dot followed by one or more numbers ▸ *adj* relating to or using powers of ten

DECIMATE *vb* destroy or kill a large proportion of

DECIME, -S *n* former French coin

DECIPHER *vb* work out the meaning of (something illegible or in code)

DECISION *n* judgment, conclusion, or resolution

DECISIVE *adj* having a definite influence

DECISORY *adj* deciding

DECK, -S *n* area of a ship that forms a floor ▸ *vb* dress or decorate

DECKED *adj* having a wooden deck or platform

DECKEL, -S *same as* ▸ **deckle**

DECKER, -S ▸ deck

DECKHAND *n* seaman assigned various duties on the deck of a ship

DECKING, -S *n* wooden platform in a garden

DECKLE, -D, -S *n* frame used to contain pulp on the mould in the making of handmade paper

DECKLESS *adj* without a deck

DECKO, -ED, -ING, -S *n* look ▸ *vb* have a look

DECKS ▸ deck

DECLAIM, -S *vb* speak loudly and dramatically

DECLARE, -D, -S *vb* state firmly and forcefully

DECLARER *n* person who declares

DECLARES ▸ declare

DECLASS vb lower in social status or position

DECLASSE adj having lost social standing or status

DECLAW, -ED, -S vb remove claws from

DECLINAL adj bending down ▷ n action of politely refusing or declining

DECLINE, -D, -S vb become smaller, weaker, or less important ▷ n gradual weakening or loss

DECLINER

DECLUTCH vb disengage the clutch of a motor vehicle

DECO, -S adj as in **art deco** style of art, jewellery, design, etc

DECOCT, -ED, -S vb extract the essence from (a substance) by boiling

DECODE, -D, -S vb convert from code into ordinary language

DECODER -S

DECODING n act of decoding

DECOKE, -D, -S, DECOKING n decarbonize

DECOLOR, -S vb bleach

DECOLOUR vb deprive of colour, as by bleaching

DECOMMIT vb withdraw from a commitment or agreed course of action

DECOR, -S n style in which a room or house is decorated

DECORATE vb make more attractive by adding something ornamental

DECOROUS adj polite, calm, and sensible in behaviour

DECORS ▸ decor

DECORUM, -S n polite and socially correct behaviour

DECOS ▸ deco

DECOUPLE vb separate two joined entities or subsystems

DECOY, -ED, -ING, -S n person or thing used to lure someone into danger ▷ vb lure away by means of a trick

DECOYER -S

DECREASE vb make or become less ▷ n lessening, reduction

DECREE, -D, -S n law made by someone in authority ▷ vb order by decree

DECREER -S

DECREET, -S n final judgment or sentence of a court

DECREPIT adj weakened or worn out by age or long use

DECRETAL n papal decree ▷ adj of or relating to a decretal or a decree

DECREW, -ED, -S vb archaic word for decrease

DECRIAL, -S ▸ decry

DECRIED ▸ decry

DECRIER, -S ▸ decry

DECRIES ▸ decry

DECROWN, -S vb depose

DECRY, DECRIED, DECRIES, -ING vb express disapproval of

DECRYPT, -S vb decode (a message)

DECTET, -S n ten musicians

DECUBITI ▸ decubitus

DECUMAN, -S n large wave

DECUPLE, -D, -S vb increase by ten times ▷ n amount ten times as large as a given reference ▷ adj increasing tenfold

DECURIA, -S n group of ten

DECURIES ▸ decury

DECURION n local councillor

DECURVE, -S vb curve downwards

DECURVED adj bent or curved downwards

DECURVES ▸ decurve

DECURY, DECURIES n (in ancient Rome) a body of ten men

DEDAL same as ▸ daedal

DEDALIAN adj of Daedalus

DEDANS n open gallery at the server's end of the court

DEDENDUM, DEDENDA n radial distance between the pitch circle and root of a gear tooth

DEDICANT n person who dedicates

DEDICATE vb commit (oneself or one's time) wholly to a special purpose or cause

DEDIMUS n legal term

DEDUCE, -D, -S, DEDUCING vb reach (a conclusion) by reasoning from evidence

DEDUCT, -ED, -S vb subtract

DEE, -ING, -S a Scot word for ▸ die

DEED, -ED, -ER, -EST, -ING, -S n something that is done ▷ vb convey or transfer (property) by deed ▷ adj Scots form of dead

DEEDFUL adj full of exploits

DEEDIER ▸ deedy

DEEDIEST ▸ deedy

DEEDILY ▸ deedy

DEEDING ▸ deed

DEEDLESS adj without exploits

DEEDS ▸ deed

DEEDY, DEEDIER, DEEDIEST adj hard-working

DEEING ▸ dee

DEEJAY, -ED, -S n disc jockey ▷ vb work or act as a disc jockey

DEEK interj look at!

DEELY adj as in **deely boppers** hairband with two bobbing antennae-like attachments

DEEM, -ED, -ING, -S, DEMPT vb consider, judge

DEEMSTER n title of one of the two justices in the Isle of Man

DEEN, -S n din

DEEP, -ER, -EST, -S adj extending to or situated far down, inwards, backwards, or sideways ▷ n any deep place on land or under water

DEEPEN, -ED, -S vb make or become deeper or more intense

DEEPENER

DEEPER ▸ deep

DEEPEST ▸ deep

DEEPFELT adj sincere

DEEPIE, -S n 3D film

DEEPLY ▸ deep

DEEPMOST adj deepest

DEEPNESS ▸ deep

DEEPS ▸ deep

DEER, -S n large wild animal, the male of which has antlers

DEERE, -S adj serious ▷ n deer

DEERFLY n insect related to the horsefly

DEERHORN n horn of a deer

DEERLET, -S n ruminant mammal

DEERLIKE adj like a deer

DEERS ▸ deer

DEERSKIN n hide of a deer

DEERWEED n forage plant

DEERYARD n gathering place for deer

DEES ▸ dee

DEET, -S n insect-repellent

DEEV, -S n mythical monster

DEEVE, -D, -S, DEEVING vb deafen

DEEVS ▸ deev

DEEWAN, -S n chief of a village in India

DEF, -FER, -FEST adj very good

DEFACE, -D, -S, DEFACING vb deliberately spoil the appearance of

DEFACER -S

DEFAME, -D, -S, DEFAMING vb attack the good reputation of

DEFAMER -S

D

DEFANG, -ED, -S vb remove the fangs of

DEFAST adj defaced

DEFASTE adj defaced

DEFAT, -S, -TED vb remove fat from

DEFAULT, -S n failure to do something ▷ vb fail to fulfil an obligation

DEFEAT, -ED, -S vb win a victory over ▷ n defeating

DEFEATER

DEFECATE vb discharge waste from the body

DEFECT, -ED, -S n imperfection, blemish ▷ vb desert one's cause or country to join the opposing forces

DEFECTOR

DEFENCE, -D, -S n resistance against attack ▷ vb provide with defence

DEFEND, -ED, -S vb protect from harm or danger

DEFENDER

DEFENSE, -D, -S same as ▷ defence

DEFER, -S vb delay (something) until a future time

DEFERENT adj conveying outwards, down, or away ▷ n type of circle in the Ptolemaic system

DEFERRAL same as > deferment

DEFERRED adj withheld over a certain period

DEFERRER ▶ defer

DEFERS ▶ defer

DEFFER ▶ def

DEFFEST ▶ def

DEFFLY archaic form of ▶ deftly

DEFFO interj definitely: an expression of agreement or consent

DEFI, -S n challenge

DEFIANCE n open resistance or disobedience

DEFIANT adj marked by resistance or bold opposition, as to authority

DEFICIT, -S n amount by which a sum of money is too small

DEFIED ▶ defy

DEFIER, -S ▶ defy

DEFIES ▶ defy

DEFILADE n protection provided by obstacles against enemy crossfire from the rear, or observation ▷ vb provide protection for by defilade

DEFILE, -D, -S, DEFILING vb treat (something sacred or important) without respect ▷ n narrow valley or pass

DEFILER -S

DEFINE, -D, -S, DEFINING vb state precisely the meaning of

DEFINER -S

DEFINITE adj firm, clear, and precise ▷ n something that is firm, clear, and precise

DEFIS ▶ defi

DEFLATE, -D, -S vb (cause to) collapse through the release of air

DEFLATER

DEFLATOR

DEFLEA, -ED, -S vb remove fleas from

DEFLECT, -S vb (cause to) turn aside from a course

DEFLEX, -ES vb turn downwards

DEFLUENT adj running downwards

DEFO interj (slang) definitely

DEFOAM, -ED, -S vb remove foam from

DEFOAMER

DEFOCUS vb put out of focus

DEFOG, -GED, -S vb clear of vapour

DEFOGGER

DEFORCE, -D, -S vb withhold (property, esp land) wrongfully or by force from the rightful owner

DEFORCER

DEFOREST vb clear of trees

DEFORM, -S vb put out of shape or spoil the appearance of

DEFORMED adj disfigured or misshapen

DEFORMER ▶ deform

DEFORMS ▶ deform

DEFOUL, -ED, -S vb defile

DEFRAG, -S vb defragment

DEFRAUD, -S vb cheat out of money, property, etc

DEFRAY, -ED, -S vb provide money for (costs or expenses)

DEFRAYAL

DEFRAYER

DEFREEZE, DEFROZE, DEFROZEN vb defrost

DEFRIEND vb remove (a person) from the list of one's friends on a social networking website

DEFROCK, -S vb deprive (a priest) of priestly status

DEFROST, -S vb make or become free of ice

DEFROZE ▶ defreeze

DEFROZEN ▶ defreeze

DEFT, -ER, -EST adj quick and skilful in movement

DEFTLY

DEFTNESS

DEFUEL, -ED, -S vb remove fuel from

DEFUNCT, -S adj no longer existing or operative ▷ n deceased person

DEFUND, -ED, -S vb stop funds to

DEFUSE, -D, -S, DEFUSING vb remove the fuse of (an explosive device)

DEFUSER -S

DEFUZE, -D, -S, DEFUZING same as ▶ defuse

DEFY, DEFIED, DEFIES, -ING vb resist openly and boldly

DEG, -GED, -GING, -S vb water (a plant, etc)

DEGAGE adj unconstrained in manner

DEGAME, -S n tree of South and Central America

DEGAMI, -S same as ▶ degame

DEGAS, -ES, -SED, -SES vb remove gas from (a container, vacuum tube, liquid, adsorbent, etc)

DEGASSER

DEGAUSS n demagnetize

DEGENDER vb remove reference to gender from

DEGERM, -ED, -S vb remove germs from

DEGGED ▶ deg

DEGGING ▶ deg

DEGLAZE, -D, -S vb dilute meat sediments in (a pan) in order to make a sauce or gravy

DEGOUT, -ED, -S n disgust ▷ vb cover (something) with gouts or drops of something

DEGRADE, -D, -S vb reduce to dishonour or disgrace

DEGRADER

DEGRAS n emulsion used for dressing hides

DEGREASE vb remove grease from

DEGREE, -S n stage in a scale of relative amount or intensity

DEGREED adj having a degree

DEGREES ▶ degree

DEGS ▶ deg

DEGU, -S n small S American rodent

DEGUM, -MED, -S vb remove gum from

DEGUS ▶ degu

DEGUST, -ED, -S *vb* taste, esp with care or relish

DEHAIR, -ED, -S *vb* remove hair

DEHISCE, -D, -S *vb* (of the seed capsules of some plants) to burst open spontaneously

DEHORN, -ED, -S *vb* remove or prevent the growth of the horns of (cattle, sheep, or goats)
DEHORNER

DEHORS *prep* apart from

DEHORT, -ED, -S *vb* dissuade
DEHORTER

DEI ▸ deus

DEICE, -D, -S, DEICING *vb* free or be freed of ice
DEICER -S

DEICIDAL ▸ deicide

DEICIDE, -S *n* act of killing a god

DEICING ▸ deice

DEICTIC, -S *adj* proving by direct argument ▸ *n* term whose reference depends on the context

DEID, -ER, -EST, -S *a Scot word for* ▸ **dead**

DEIF, -ER, -EST *a Scot word for* ▸ **deaf**

DEIFIC *adj* making divine or exalting to the position of a god

DEIFICAL *adj* divine

DEIFIED ▸ deify

DEIFIER, -S ▸ deify

DEIFIES ▸ deify

DEIFORM *adj* having the form or appearance of a god

DEIFY, DEIFIED, DEIFIES, -ING *vb* treat or worship as a god

DEIGN, -ED, -ING, -S *vb* agree (to do something), but as if doing someone a favour

DEIL, -S *a Scot word for* ▸ **devil**

DEINDEX *vb* cause to become no longer index-linked

DEIONISE *same as* ▸ **deionize**

DEIONIZE *vb* remove ions from (water, etc), esp by ion exchange

DEISEAL, -S *n* clockwise motion

DEISHEAL *n* clockwise motion

DEISM, -S *n* belief in God but not in divine revelation
DEIST -S
DEISTIC

DEITY, DEITIES *n* god or goddess

DEIXIS, DEIXES, -ES *n* use or reference of a deictic word

DEJECT, -S *vb* have a depressing effect on ▸ *adj* downcast

DEJECTA *pl n* waste products excreted from the body

DEJECTED *adj* unhappy

DEJECTS ▸ deject

DEJEUNE, -S *n* lunch

DEJEUNER *n* lunch

DEJEUNES ▸ dejeune

DEKAGRAM *n* ten grams

DEKALOGY *n* series of ten related works

DEKARE, -S *n* unit of measurement equal to ten ares

DEKE, -D, -ING, -S, DEKING *vb* movement used in ice hockey or box lacrosse ▸ *n* such a shot or movement

DEKKO, -ED, -ING, -S *n* look ▸ *vb* have a look

DEL, -S *n* differential operator

DELAINE, -S *n* sheer wool or wool and cotton fabric

DELAPSE, -D, -S *vb* be inherited

DELATE, -D, -S, DELATING *vb* (formerly) to bring a charge against
DELATION
DELATOR -S

DELAY, -ED, -ING, -S *vb* put off to a later time ▸ *n* act of delaying
DELAYER -S

DELE, -D, -ING, -S *n* sign indicating that typeset matter is to be deleted ▸ *vb* mark (matter to be deleted) with a dele

DELEAD, -ED, -S *vb* remove lead from

DELEAVE, -D, -S *vb* separate copies

DELEBLE *adj* able to be deleted

DELED ▸ dele

DELEGACY *n* elected standing committee at some British universities

DELEGATE *n* person chosen to represent others, esp at a meeting ▸ *vb* entrust (duties or powers) to someone

DELEING ▸ dele

DELENDA *pl n* items for deleting

DELES ▸ dele

DELETE, -D, -S, DELETING *vb* remove (something written or printed)

DELETION *n* act of deleting or fact of being deleted

DELETIVE ▸ delete

DELETORY ▸ delete

DELF, -S *n* kind of earthenware

DELFT, -S *n* tin-glazed earthenware, typically having blue designs on white

DELI, -S *n* delicatessen

DELIBATE *vb* taste

DELIBLE *adj* able to be deleted

DELICACY *n* being delicate

DELICATE *adj* fine or subtle in quality or workmanship ▸ *n* delicacy

DELICE, -S *n* delicacy

DELICT, -S *n* wrongful act for which the person injured has the right to a civil remedy

DELIGHT, -S *n* (source of) great pleasure ▸ *vb* please greatly

DELIME, -D, -S, DELIMING *vb* remove lime from

DELIMIT, -S *vb* mark or lay down the limits of

DELINK, -ED, -S *vb* remove or break a link

DELIRIUM, DELIRIA *n* state of excitement and mental confusion, often with hallucinations

DELIS ▸ deli

DELISH *adj* delicious

DELIST, -ED, -S *vb* remove from a list

DELIVER, -S *vb* carry (goods etc) to a destination

DELIVERY *n* delivering

DELL, -S *n* small wooded hollow

DELLIER ▸ delly

DELLIES ▸ delly

DELLIEST ▸ delly

DELLS ▸ dell

DELLY, DELLIER, DELLIES, DELLIEST *n* delicatessen ▸ *adj* full of dells

DELO, -S *an informal word for* ▸ **delegate**

DELOPE, -D, -S, DELOPING *vb* shoot into the air

DELOS ▸ delo

DELOUSE, -D, -S *vb* rid (a person or animal) of lice
DELOUSER

DELPH, -S *n* kind of earthenware

DELPHIC *adj* obscure or ambiguous

DELPHIN, -S *n* fatty substance from dolphin oil

DELPHS ▸ delph

DELS ▸ del

DELT, -S *n* deltoid muscle

DELTA, -S *n* fourth letter in the Greek alphabet
DELTAIC
DELTIC

DELTOID, -S n muscle acting to raise the arm ▷ adj shaped like a Greek capital delta

DELTS ▸ delt

DELUBRUM n shrine

DELUDE, -D, -S, DELUDING vb deceive

DELUDER -S

DELUGE, -D, -S, DELUGING n great flood ▷ vb flood

DELUSION n mistaken idea or belief

DELUSIVE

DELUSORY

DELUSTER same as ▸ delustre

DELUSTRE vb remove the lustre from

DELUXE adj rich, elegant, superior, or sumptuous

DELVE, -D, -S, DELVING vb research deeply (for information)

DELVER -S

DEMAGOG, -S same as > demagogue

DEMAGOGY n demagoguery

DEMAIN, -S n demesne

DEMAINE, -S n demesne

DEMAINS ▸ demain

DEMAN, -NED, -S vb reduce the workforce of (a plant, industry, etc)

DEMAND, -ED, -S vb request forcefully ▷ n forceful request

DEMANDER

DEMANNED ▸ deman

DEMANS ▸ deman

DEMARCHE n move, step, or manoeuvre, esp in diplomatic affairs

DEMARK, -ED, -S vb demarcate

DEMARKET vb discourage consumers from buying

DEMARKS ▸ demark

DEMAST, -ED, -S vb remove the mast from

DEMAYNE, -S n demesne

DEME, -S n (in preclassical Greece) the territory inhabited by a tribe

DEMEAN, -ED, -S vb lower (oneself) in dignity, status, or character

DEMEANE n demesne

DEMEANED ▸ demean

DEMEANES n demesne

DEMEANOR same as > demeanour

DEMEANS ▸ demean

DEMENT, -S vb deteriorate mentally, esp because of old age

DEMENTED adj mad

DEMENTI, -S n denial

DEMENTIA n state of serious mental deterioration

DEMENTIS ▸ dementi

DEMENTS ▸ dement

DEMERARA n brown crystallized cane sugar from the Caribbean and nearby countries

DEMERGE, -D, -S vb separate a company from another

DEMERGER n separation of two or more companies which have previously been merged

DEMERGES ▸ demerge

DEMERIT, -S n fault, disadvantage ▷ vb deserve

DEMERSAL adj living or occurring on the bottom of a sea or a lake

DEMERSE, -D, -S vb immerse

DEMES ▸ deme

DEMESNE, -S n land surrounding a house

DEMETON, -S n insecticide

DEMIC adj of population

DEMIES ▸ demy

DEMIGOD, -S n being who is part mortal, part god

DEMIJOHN n large bottle with a short neck, often encased in wicker

DEMILUNE n outwork in front of a fort, shaped like a crescent moon

DEMINER, -S n person who removes mines

DEMINING n act of removing mines

DEMISE, -D, -S, DEMISING n eventual failure (of something successful) ▷ vb transfer for a limited period

DEMISS adj humble

DEMISSLY

DEMIST, -ED, -S vb remove condensation from (a windscreen)

DEMISTER n device in a motor vehicle to free the windscreen of condensation

DEMISTS ▸ demist

DEMIT, -S, -TED vb resign (an office, position, etc)

DEMIURGE n (in the philosophy of Plato) the creator of the universe

DEMIVEG n person who eats poultry and fish, but no red meat ▷ adj denoting a person who eats poultry and fish, but no red meat

DEMIVOLT n half turn on the hind legs

DEMO, -ED, -ING n demonstration, organized expression of public opinion ▷ vb demonstrate

DEMOB, -BED, -S vb demobilize

DEMOCRAT n advocate of democracy

DEMODE adj out of fashion

DEMODED adj out of fashion

DEMOED ▸ demo

DEMOI ▸ demos

DEMOING ▸ demo

DEMOLISH vb knock down or destroy (a building)

DEMOLOGY n demography

DEMON, -S n evil spirit

DEMONESS n female demon

DEMONIAC adj appearing to be possessed by a devil ▷ n person possessed by an evil spirit or demon

DEMONIAN adj of a demon

DEMONIC adj evil

DEMONISE same as ▸ demonize

DEMONISM n study of demons

DEMONIST

DEMONIZE vb make into a demon

DEMONRY ▸ demon

DEMONS ▸ demon

DEMOS, DEMOI, -ES n people of a nation regarded as a political unit

DEMOTE, -D, -S, DEMOTING vb reduce in status or rank

DEMOTIC, -S adj of the common people ▷ n demotic script of ancient Egypt

DEMOTING ▸ demote

DEMOTION ▸ demote

DEMOTIST ▸ demotic

DEMOUNT, -S vb remove (a motor, gun, etc) from its mounting or setting

DEMPSTER same as ▸ deemster

DEMPT ▸ deem

DEMUR, -RED, -S vb raise objections or show reluctance ▷ n act of demurring

DEMURE, -D, -R, -S, -ST, DEMURING adj quiet, reserved, and rather shy ▷ vb archaic for look demure ▷ n archaic look for demure look

DEMURELY

DEMURRAL n act of demurring

DEMURRED ▸ demur

DEMURRER n any objection raised

DEMURS ► demur

DEMY, DEMIES n size of printing paper, 17½ by 22½ inches (444.5 × 571.5 mm)

DEMYSHIP n scholarship at Oxford University

DEN, -NED, -NING, -S n home of a wild animal ▷ vb live in or as if in a den

DENAR, -I, -S n standard monetary unit of Macedonia, divided into 100 deni

DENARIES ► denary

DENARIUS, DENARII n ancient Roman silver coin, often called a penny in translation

DENARS ► denar

DENARY, DENARIES same as ► denarius

DENATURE vb change the nature of

DENAY, -ED, -ING, -S vb deny

DENAZIFY vb free or declare (people, institutions, etc) freed from Nazi influence or ideology

DENCH adj excellent

DENDRITE n threadlike extension of a nerve cell

DENDROID adj freely branching ▷ n something that branches freely

DENDRON, -S same as ► dendrite

DENE, -S n narrow wooded valley

DENET, -S, -TED vb remove from the former Net Book Agreement

DENGUE, -S n viral disease transmitted by mosquitoes

DENI, -S n monetary unit of the FYROM

DENIABLE adj able to be denied

DENIABLY

DENIAL, -S n statement that something is not true

DENIED ► deny

DENIER, -S n unit of weight used to measure the fineness of nylon or silk

DENIES ► deny

DENIM n hard-wearing cotton fabric, usu blue

DENIMED adj wearing denim

DENIMS pl n jeans or overalls made of denim

DENIS ► deni

DENIZEN, -S n inhabitant ▷ vb make a denizen

DENNED ► den

DENNET, -S n carriage for one horse

DENNING ► den

DENOTATE vb denote

DENOTE, -D, -S, DENOTING vb be a sign of

DENOTIVE

DENOUNCE vb speak vehemently against

DENS ► den

DENSE, -R, -ST adj closely packed

DENSELY

DENSIFY vb make or become dense

DENSITY n degree to which something is filled or occupied

DENT, -ED, -ING, -S n hollow in the surface of something, made by hitting it ▷ vb make a dent in

DENTAL, -S adj of teeth or dentistry ▷ n dental consonant

DENTALIA > dentalium

DENTALLY ► dental

DENTALS ► dental

DENTARIA n botanical term

DENTARY n lower jawbone with teeth

DENTATE adj having teeth or teethlike notches

DENTATED adj having teeth

DENTED ► dent

DENTEL, -S n architectural term

DENTELLE n bookbinding term

DENTELS ► dentel

DENTEX, -ES n large predatory fish

DENTICLE n small tooth or toothlike part, such as any of the placoid scales of sharks

DENTIL, -S n architectural ornament

DENTILED

DENTIN, -S same as ► dentine

DENTINAL ► dentine

DENTINE, -S n hard dense tissue forming the bulk of a tooth

DENTING ► dent

DENTINS ► dentin

DENTIST, -S n person qualified to practise dentistry

DENTOID adj resembling a tooth

DENTS ► dent

DENTURAL ► denture

DENTURE, -S n false tooth

DENUDATE adj denuded ▷ vb denude

DENUDE, -D, -S, DENUDING vb remove the covering or protection from

DENUDER -S

DENY, DENIED, DENIES, -ING vb declare to be untrue

DEODAND, -S n thing forfeited to charity because it has caused a death

DEODAR, -S n Himalayan cedar with drooping branches

DEODARA, -S same as ► deodar

DEODARS ► deodar

DEODATE, -S n offering to God

DEONTIC, -S adj of or relating to such ethical concepts as obligation and permissibility

DEORBIT, -S vb go out of orbit

DEOXY adj having less oxygen than a specified related compound

DEP, -S n small shop where newspapers, sweets, soft drinks, etc are sold

DEPAINT, -S vb depict

DEPART, -S vb leave

DEPARTED adj dead ▷ n dead person

DEPARTEE ► depart

DEPARTER ► depart

DEPARTS ► depart

DEPECHE, -D, -S n message ▷ vb dispatch; rid oneself of

DEPEINCT vb paint

DEPEND, -ED, -S vb put trust (in)

DEPEOPLE vb reduce population

DEPERM, -ED, -S vb demagnetize

DEPICT, -ED, -S vb produce a picture of

DEPICTER

DEPICTOR

DEPILATE vb remove the hair from

DEPLANE, -D, -S vb disembark from an aeroplane

DEPLETE, -D, -S vb use up

DEPLETER

DEPLORE, -D, -S vb condemn strongly

DEPLORER

DEPLOY, -ED, -S vb get (troops or resources) ready for immediate action

DEPLOYER

DEPLUME, -D, -S vb deprive of feathers

DEPOLISH vb remove the polish from

DEPONE, -D, -S, DEPONING vb declare (something) under oath

DEPONENT n person who makes a statement on oath ▷ adj having a passive form but active meaning

DEPONES ► depone

DEPONING ► depone

DEPORT, -ED, -S vb remove forcibly from a country

DEPORTEE n person deported or awaiting deportation

DEPORTER ► deport

DEPORTS ► deport

DEPOSAL, -S n deposition; giving of testimony under oath

DEPOSE, -D, -S, DEPOSING vb remove from an office or position of power
DEPOSER -S

DEPOSIT, -S vb put down ▷ n sum of money paid into a bank account

DEPOT, -S n building where goods or vehicles are kept when not in use ▷ adj (of a drug) designed for gradual release

DEPRAVE, -S vb make morally bad

DEPRAVED adj morally bad

DEPRAVER ► deprave

DEPRAVES ► deprave

DEPRENYL n drug combating effects of ageing

DEPRESS vb make sad

DEPRIVAL ► deprive

DEPRIVE, -S vb prevent from (having or enjoying)

DEPRIVED adj lacking adequate living conditions, education, etc

DEPRIVER ► deprive

DEPRIVES ► deprive

DEPS ► dep

DEPSIDE, -S n organic chemical compound

DEPTH, -S n distance downwards, backwards, or inwards

DEPURANT adj purifying

DEPURATE vb cleanse or purify or to be cleansed or purified

DEPUTE, -D, -S, DEPUTING vb appoint (someone) to act on one's behalf ▷ n deputy

DEPUTIES ► deputy

DEPUTING ► depute

DEPUTISE same as
► deputize

DEPUTIZE vb act as deputy

DEPUTY, DEPUTIES n person appointed to act on behalf of another

DEQUEUE, -D, -S vb remove (an item) from a queue of computing tasks

DERACINE adj uprooted from their usual environment ▷ n person who has been uprooted from their usual environment

DERAIGN, -S vb contest (a claim, suit, etc)

DERAIL, -ED, -S vb cause (a train) to go off the rails ▷ n device to make locomotives leave the rails to avoid a collision or accident

DERAILER same as ► derail

DERAILS ► derail

DERANGE, -D, -S vb disturb the order or arrangement of
DERANGER

DERAT, -S, -TED vb remove rats from

DERATE, -D, -S vb assess the value of some types of property at a lower rate than others for local taxation
DERATING

DERATION vb end rationing of (food, petrol, etc)

DERATS ► derat

DERATTED ► derat

DERAY, -ED, -ING, -S vb go mad

DERBY, DERBIES n bowler hat

DERE, -D, -S, DERING vb injure

DERECHO, -S n long, fast-moving line of severe storms

DERED ► dere

DERELICT adj unused and falling into ruins ▷ n social outcast, vagrant

DERES ► dere

DERHAM, -S same as
► dirham

DERIDE, -D, -S, DERIDING vb treat with contempt or ridicule
DERIDER -S

DERIG, -GED, -S vb remove equipment, eg from stage set

DERING ► dere

DERINGER same as
> derringer

DERISION n act of deriding

DERISIVE adj mocking, scornful

DERISORY adj too small or inadequate to be considered seriously

DERIVATE n derivative ▷ vb derive (something)

DERIVE, -D, -S, DERIVING vb take or develop (from)
DERIVER -S

DERM, -S same as ► derma

DERMA, -S n beef or fowl intestine used as a casing for certain dishes, esp kishke

DERMAL adj of or relating to the skin

DERMAS ► derma

DERMATIC adj of skin

DERMIC ► dermis

DERMIS, -ES another name for
► corium

DERMOID, -S adj of or resembling skin ▷ n congenital cystic tumour whose walls are lined with epithelium

DERMS ► derm

DERN, -ED, -ING, -S n concealment ▷ vb keep hidden

DERNFUL adj sorrowful

DERNIER adj last

DERNING ► dern

DERNLY adv sorrowfully

DERNS ► dern

DERO, -S n tramp or derelict

DEROGATE vb detract from
▷ adj debased or degraded

DEROS ► dero

DERRICK, -S n simple crane
▷ vb raise or lower the jib of (a crane)

DERRIERE n backside

DERRIES ► derry

DERRIS, -ES n E Indian woody climbing plant

DERRO, -S n vagrant

DERRY, DERRIES n derelict house, esp one used by tramps

DERTH, -S same as ► dearth

DERV, -S n diesel oil, when used for road transport

DERVISH n member of a Muslim religious order noted for a frenzied whirling dance

DERVS ► derv

DESALT, -ED, -S vb desalinate
DESALTER

DESAND, -ED, -S vb remove sand from

DESCALE, -D, -S vb remove a hard coating from inside (a kettle or pipe)

DESCALER n something that removes limescale

DESCALES ► descale

DESCANT, -S n tune played or sung above a basic melody ▷ adj denoting the highest member in a family of musical instruments ▷ vb compose or perform a descant (for a piece of music)

DESCEND, -S vb move down (a slope etc)

DESCENT, -S n descending

DESCHOOL vb educate by means other than a school

DESCRIBE vb give an account of (something or someone) in words

DESCRIED ► descry

DESCRIER ► descry

DESCRIES ▸ descry
DESCRIVE vb describe
DESCRY, DESCRIED, DESCRIES vb catch sight of
DESEED, -ED, -S vb remove the seeds from (eg a fruit)
DESEEDER n person who deseeds
DESEEDS ▸ deseed
DESELECT vb refuse to select (an MP) for re-election
DESERT, -ED, -S n region with little or no vegetation because of low rainfall ▷ vb abandon (a person or place) without intending to return
DESERTER
DESERTIC adj (of soil) developing in hot climates
DESERTS ▸ desert
DESERVE, -D, -S vb be entitled to or worthy of
DESERVER
DESEX, -ED, -ES, -ING vb desexualize
DESHI, -S same as ▸ desi
DESI, -S adj (in Indian English) indigenous or local ▷ n (in Indian English) indigenous or local person
DESIGN, -ED, -S vb work out the structure or form of (something), by making a sketch or plans ▷ n preliminary drawing
DESIGNEE n person designated to do something
DESIGNER n person who draws up original sketches or plans from which things are made ▷ adj designed by a well-known designer
DESIGNS ▸ design
DESILVER vb remove silver from
DESINE, -D, -S, DESINING same as ▸ design
DESINENT > desinence
DESINES ▸ desine
DESINING ▸ desine
DESIRE, -D, -S, DESIRING vb want very much ▷ n wish, longing
DESIRER -S
DESIROUS adj having a desire for
DESIS ▸ desi
DESIST, -ED, -S vb stop (doing something)
DESK, -S n piece of furniture with a writing surface and drawers
DESKFAST n breakfast eaten at one's desk at work
DESKILL, -S vb mechanize or computerize (a job) thereby

reducing the skill required to do it
DESKING, -S n desks and related furnishings in a given space, eg an office
DESKMAN, DESKMEN n police officer in charge in police station
DESKNOTE n small computer
DESKS ▸ desk
DESKTOP, -S adj (of a computer) small enough to use at a desk ▷ n computer small enough to use at a desk
DESMAN, -S n either of two molelike amphibious mammals
DESMID, -S n type of mainly unicellular freshwater green alga
DESMINE, -S n type of mineral
DESMOID, -S adj resembling a tendon or ligament ▷ n very firm tumour of connective tissue
DESNOOD, -S vb remove the snood of a turkey poult to reduce the risk of cannibalism
DESOLATE adj uninhabited and bleak ▷ vb deprive of inhabitants
DESORB, -ED, -S vb change from an adsorbed state to a gaseous or liquid state
DESORBER n something that desorbs
DESORBS ▸ desorb
DESOXY same as ▸ deoxy
DESPAIR, -S n total loss of hope ▷ vb lose hope
DESPATCH same as ▸ dispatch
DESPIGHT obsolete form of ▸ despite
DESPISAL ▸ despise
DESPISE, -D, -S vb regard with contempt
DESPISER
DESPITE, -D, -S prep in spite of ▷ n contempt ▷ vb show contempt for
DESPOIL, -S vb plunder
DESPOND, -S vb lose heart or hope
DESPOT, -S n person in power who acts unfairly or cruelly
DESPOTAT n despot's domain
DESPOTIC ▸ despot
DESPOTS ▸ despot
DESSE, -S n desk
DESSERT, -S n sweet course served at the end of a meal
DESSES ▸ desse
DESTAIN, -S vb remove stain from

DESTINE, -S vb set apart or appoint
DESTINED adj certain to be or to do something
DESTINES ▸ destine
DESTINY n future marked out for a person or thing
DESTOCK, -S vb reduce the amount of stock
DESTREAM vb take (pupils) out of classes that are organized by ability
DESTRESS vb make or become less stressed
DESTRIER an archaic word for ▸ warhorse
DESTROY, -S vb ruin, demolish
DESTRUCT vb destroy intentionally for safety ▷ n act of destructing ▷ adj capable of self-destruction
DESUGAR, -S vb remove sugar from
DESULFUR same as > desulphur
DESYATIN n Russian unit of area
DESYNE, -D, -S, DESYNING same as ▸ design
DETACH, -ES vb disengage and separate
DETACHED adj (of a house) not joined to another house
DETACHER ▸ detach
DETACHES ▸ detach
DETAIL, -S n individual piece of information ▷ vb list fully
DETAILED adj having many details
DETAILER ▸ detail
DETAILS ▸ detail
DETAIN, -ED, -S vb delay (someone)
DETAINEE
DETAINER n wrongful withholding of the property of another person
DETAINS ▸ detain
DETANGLE vb remove tangles from (esp hair)
DETASSEL vb remove top part of corn plant
DETECT, -ED, -S vb notice
DETECTER
DETECTOR n instrument used to find something
DETECTS ▸ detect
DETENT, -S n mechanism to check movement in one direction only
DETENTE, -S n easing of tension between nations
DETENTS ▸ detent
DETENU, -S n prisoner

DETENUE, -S n female prisoner

DETENUS ► detenu

DETER, -RED, -S vb discourage (someone) from doing something by instilling fear or doubt

DETERGE, -D, -S vb wash or wipe away

DETERGER n detergent

DETERGES ► deterge

DETERRED ► deter

DETERRER ► deter

DETERS ► deter

DETEST, -ED, -S vb dislike intensely
DETESTER

DETHATCH vb remove dead grass from lawn

DETHRONE vb remove from a throne or position of power

DETICK, -ED, -S vb remove ticks from
DETICKER

DETINUE, -S n action brought by a plaintiff to recover goods wrongfully detained

DETONATE vb explode

DETORT, -ED, -S vb twist or distort

DETOUR, -ED, -S n route that is not the most direct one ▷ vb deviate or cause to deviate from a direct route or course of action

DETOX, -ED, -ES, -ING n treatment to rid the body of poisonous substances ▷ vb undergo treatment to rid the body of poisonous substances

DETOXIFY vb remove poison from

DETOXING ► detox

DETRACT, -S vb make (something) seem less good

DETRAIN, -S vb leave or cause to leave a railway train, as passengers, etc

DETRAQUE n insane person

DETRITAL ► detritus

DETRITUS n loose mass of stones and silt worn away from rocks

DETRUDE, -D, -S vb force down or thrust away or out

DETRUSOR n muscle in the wall of the bladder

DETUNE, -D, -S, DETUNING vb change pitch of (stringed instrument)

DEUCE, -S, DEUCING vb score deuce in tennis ▷ n score of forty all

DEUCED adj damned
DEUCEDLY

DEUCES ► deuce

DEUCING ► deuce

DEUDDARN n two-tiered Welsh dresser

DEUS, DEI, DI n god

DEUTERIC adj (of mineral) formed by metasomatic changes

DEUTERON n nucleus of a deuterium atom, consisting of one proton and one neutron

DEUTON, -S old form of ► deuteron

DEUTZIA, -S n shrub with clusters of pink or white flowers

DEV, -S same as ► deva

> **Dev** is a Sanskrit word for a good spirit; related words are **deev** and **deva**

DEVA, -S n (in Hinduism and Buddhism) divine being or god

DEVALL, -ED, -S vb stop

DEVALUE, -D, -S vb reduce the exchange value of (a currency)

DEVAS ► deva

DEVEIN, -ED, -S vb remove vein from

DEVEL, -ED, -ING, -LED, -S same as ► devvel

DEVELOP, -S vb grow or bring to a later, more elaborate, or more advanced stage

DEVELOPE old form of ► develop

DEVELOPS ► develop

DEVELS ► devel

DEVERBAL n word deriving from verb

DEVEST, -ED, -S variant spelling of ► divest

DEVI, -S n Hindu goddess

DEVIANCE n act or state of being deviant

DEVIANCY same as ► deviance

DEVIANT, -S adj (person) deviating from what is considered acceptable behaviour ▷ n person whose behaviour deviates from what is considered to be acceptable

DEVIATE, -D, -S vb differ from others in belief or thought
DEVIATOR

DEVICE, -S n machine or tool used for a specific purpose

DEVIL, -ED, -ING, -LED, -S n evil spirit ▷ vb prepare (food) with a highly flavoured spiced mixture

DEVILDOM n domain of evil spirits

DEVILED ► devil

DEVILESS n female devil

DEVILET, -S n young devil

DEVILING ► devil

DEVILISH adj cruel or unpleasant ▷ adv extremely

DEVILISM n doctrine of devil

DEVILKIN n small devil

DEVILLED ► devil

DEVILRY n mischievousness

DEVILS ► devil

DEVILTRY same as ► devilry

DEVIOUS adj insincere and dishonest

DEVIS ► devi

DEVISAL, -S n act of inventing, contriving, or devising

DEVISE, -D, -S, DEVISING vb work out (something) in one's mind ▷ n disposition of property by will

DEVISEE, -S n person to whom property, esp realty, is devised by will

DEVISER, -S ► devise

DEVISES ► devise

DEVISING ► devise

DEVISOR, -S n person who devises property, esp realty, by will

DEVLING, -S n young devil

DEVO, -S n short for devolution

DEVOICE, -D, -S vb make (a voiced speech sound) voiceless

DEVOID adj completely lacking (in)

DEVOIR, -S n duty

DEVOLVE, -D, -S vb pass to a successor or substitute

DEVON, -S n bland processed meat in sausage form, eaten cold in slices

DEVONIAN adj denoting the fourth period of the Palaeozoic era

DEVONS ► devon

DEVORE, -S n velvet fabric with a raised pattern

DEVOS ► devo

DEVOT, -S n devotee

DEVOTE, -S, DEVOTING vb apply or dedicate to a particular purpose

DEVOTED adj showing loyalty or devotion

DEVOTEE, -S n person who is very enthusiastic about something

DEVOTES ► devote

DEVOTING ► devote

DEVOTION n strong affection for or loyalty to someone or something

DEVOTS ▶ devot

DEVOUR, -ED, -S vb eat greedily

DEVOURER

DEVOUT, -ER adj deeply religious

DEVOUTLY

DEVS ▶ dev

DEVVEL, -S vb strike with blow

DEW, -ED, -ING, -S n drops of water that form on the ground at night from vapour in the air ▷ vb moisten with or as with dew

DEWAN, -S n (formerly in India) the chief or finance minister of a state ruled by an Indian prince

DEWANI, -S n post of dewan

DEWANNY same as ▶ dewani

DEWANS ▶ dewan

DEWAR, -S n as in **dewar flask** type of vacuum flask

DEWATER, -S vb remove water from

DEWAX, -ED, -ES, -ING vb remove wax from

DEWBERRY n type of bramble with blue-black fruits

DEWCLAW, -S n nonfunctional claw on a dog's leg

DEWDROP, -S n drop of dew

DEWED ▶ dew

DEWFALL, -S n formation of dew

DEWFULL obsolete form of ▶ due

DEWIER ▶ dewy

DEWIEST ▶ dewy

DEWILY ▶ dewy

DEWINESS ▶ dewy

DEWING ▶ dew

DEWITT, -ED, -S vb kill, esp hang unlawfully

DEWLAP, -S n loose fold of skin hanging under the throat in dogs, cattle, etc

DEWLAPT

DEWLESS ▶ dew

DEWOOL, -ED, -S vb remove wool from

DEWORM, -ED, -S vb rid of worms

DEWORMER

DEWPOINT n temperature at which water droplets form in the air

DEWS ▶ dew

DEWY, DEWIER, DEWIEST adj moist with or as with dew

DEX, -ES n dextroamphetamine

Short for dextroamphetamine, a stimulant drug, this is another of the key words to know for using the X. It can be extended to **dexy** or **dexie**.

DEXIE, -S n pill containing dextroamphetamine

DEXTER, -S adj of or on the right side of a shield, etc, from the bearer's point of view ▷ n small breed of beef cattle

DEXTRAL, -S n right-handed person

DEXTRAN, -S n polysaccharide compound

DEXTRIN, -S n sticky substance obtained from starch

DEXTRINE same as ▶ dextrin

DEXTRINS ▶ dextrin

DEXTRO adj dextrorotatory or rotating to the right

DEXTROSE n glucose occurring in fruit, honey, and the blood of animals

DEXTROUS same as > dexterous

DEXY same as ▶ dexie

DEY, -S n title given to commanders or governors of the Janissaries of Algiers

DEZINC, -ED, -S vb remove zinc from

DHAK, -S n tropical Asian tree

DHAL, -S n curry made from lentils or beans

DHAMMA, -S variant of ▶ dharma

DHANSAK, -S n any of a variety of Indian dishes

DHARMA, -S n moral law or behaviour

DHARMIC

DHARNA, -S n (in India) a method of obtaining justice

DHIKR, -S n Sufi religious ceremony

DHIMMI, -S n non-Muslim living in a state governed by sharia law

DHOBI, -S n (in India, Malaya, East Africa, etc, esp formerly) a washerman

DHOL, -S n type of Indian drum

DHOLAK, -S n type of two-headed drum

DHOLE, -S n fierce canine mammal

DHOLL, -S same as ▶ dhal

DHOLS ▶ dhol

DHOOLY, DHOOLIES same as ▶ doolie

DHOORA, -S same as ▶ durra

DHOOTI, -S same as ▶ dhoti

DHOOTIE, -S same as ▶ dhoti

DHOOTIS ▶ dhooti

DHOTI, -S n long loincloth worn by men in India

DHOURRA, -S same as ▶ durra

DHOW, -S n Arab sailing ship

DHURNA, -S same as ▶ dharna

DHURRA, -S same as ▶ durra

DHURRIE, -S same as ▶ durrie

DHUTI, -S same as ▶ dhoti

DHYANA, -S n type of Hindu meditation

DI ▶ deus

DIABASE, -S n altered dolerite

DIABASIC

DIABETES n disorder in which an abnormal amount of urine containing an excess of sugar is excreted

DIABETIC n person who has diabetes ▷ adj of or having diabetes

DIABLE, -S n type of sauce

DIABLERY same as > diablerie

DIABLES ▶ diable

DIABOLIC adj of the Devil

DIABOLO, -S n game using a spinning top and a cord fastened to two sticks

DIACETYL n aromatic compound

DIACID, -S n lead plaster

DIACIDIC adj capable of neutralizing two protons with one molecule

DIACIDS ▶ diacid

DIACONAL adj of or associated with a deacon or the diaconate

DIACT, -S same as ▶ diactine

DIACTINE adj two-rayed ▷ n two-rayed sponge spicule

DIACTS ▶ diact

DIADEM, -ED, -S n crown ▷ vb adorn or crown with or as with a diadem

DIADOCHI pl n six generals who fought for control of the Alexandrian Empire

DIADOCHY n replacement of one element in a crystal by another

DIADROM, -S n complete course of pendulum

DIADEM n figure cut into stone

DIAGNOSE vb determine by diagnosis

D

DIAGONAL adj from corner to corner ▷ n diagonal line

DIAGRAM, -S n sketch showing the form or workings of something ▷ vb show in or as if in a diagram

DIAGRAPH n device for enlarging or reducing maps, plans, etc

DIAGRID, -S n diagonal structure network

DIAL, -ED, -LED, -S n face of a clock or watch ▷ vb operate the dial or buttons on a telephone in order to contact (a number)

DIALECT, -S n form of a language spoken in a particular area

DIALED ▶ dial

DIALER, -S ▶ dial

DIALING, -S ▶ dial

DIALIST, -S n dial-maker

DIALLAGE n green or brownish-black variety of the mineral augite

DIALLED ▶ dial

DIALLEL, -S n interbreeding among a group of parents ▷ adj (of lines) not parallel, meeting, or intersecting

DIALLER, -S ▶ dial

DIALLING, -S ▶ dial

DIALLIST same as ▶ dialist

DIALOG, -ED, -S same as ▶ dialogue

DIALOGER

DIALOGIC ▶ dialogue

DIALOGS ▶ dialog

DIALOGUE n conversation between two people, esp in a book, film, or play ▷ vb put into the form of a dialogue

DIALS ▶ dial

DIALYSE, -D vb separate by dialysis

DIALYSER n machine that performs dialysis

DIALYSIS, DIALYSES n filtering of blood through a membrane to remove waste products

DIALYTIC

DIALYZE, -D, -S same as ▶ dialyse

DIALYZER same as ▶ dialyser

DIALYZES ▶ dialyze

DIAMANTE adj decorated with artificial jewels or sequins ▷ n fabric so covered

DIAMETER n (length of) a straight line through the centre of a circle or sphere

DIAMIDE, -S n compound containing two amido groups

DIAMIN, -S same as ▶ diamine

DIAMINE, -S n any chemical compound containing two amino groups in its molecules

DIAMINS ▶ diamin

DIAMOND, -S n exceptionally hard precious stone ▷ adj (of an anniversary) the sixtieth ▷ vb stud or decorate with diamonds

DIAMYL adj with two amyl groups

DIANDRY n practice of having two husbands

DIANE adj as in **steak diane** kind of steak

DIANODAL adj going through a node

DIANOIA, -S n perception and experience regarded as lower modes of knowledge

DIANTHUS n type of widely cultivated Eurasian plant

DIAPASE, -S same as ▶ diapason

DIAPASON n either of two stops found throughout the range of a pipe organ

DIAPAUSE vb undergo diapause ▷ n period of suspended development and growth

DIAPENTE n (in classical Greece) the interval of a perfect fifth

DIAPER, -ED, -S n nappy ▷ vb decorate with a geometric pattern

DIAPHONE n set of all realizations of a given phoneme in a language

DIAPHONY n style of two-part polyphonic singing

DIAPIR, -S n type of geologic formation

DIAPIRIC

DIAPSID, -S n reptile with two holes in rear of skull

DIARCH adj (of a vascular bundle) having two strands of xylem

DIARCHAL ▶ diarchy

DIARCHIC ▶ diarchy

DIARCHY n government by two states, individuals, etc

DIARIAL ▶ diary

DIARIAN ▶ diary

DIARIES ▶ diary

DIARISE, -D, -S same as ▶ diarize

DIARIST, -S n person who writes a diary

DIARIZE, -D, -S vb record in diary

DIARRHEA same as > diarrhoea

DIARY, DIARIES n (book for) a record of daily events, appointments, or observations

DIASCIA, -S n S African plant, usu with pink flowers

DIASCOPE n optical projector used to display transparencies

DIASPORA n dispersion or spreading of a people

DIASPORE n white, yellowish, or grey mineral

DIASTASE n enzyme that converts starch into sugar

DIASTEM, -S same as ▶ diastema

DIASTEMA n abnormal space, fissure, or cleft in a bodily organ or part

DIASTEMS ▶ diastem

DIASTER, -S n stage in cell division

DIASTOLE n dilation of the chambers of the heart

DIASTRAL ▶ diaster

DIASTYLE adj having columns about three diameters apart ▷ n diastyle building

DIATOM, -S n microscopic unicellular alga

DIATOMIC adj containing two atoms

DIATOMS ▶ diatom

DIATONIC adj of a regular major or minor scale

DIATREME n volcanic vent produced by an eruption of gas

DIATRETA > diatretum

DIATRIBE n bitter critical attack

DIATRON, -S n circuit that uses diodes

DIAXON, -S n bipolar cell

DIAZEPAM n minor tranquillizer used to treat epilepsy

DIAZIN, -S same as ▶ diazine

DIAZINE, -S n organic compound

DIAZINON n type of insecticide

DIAZINS ▶ diazin

DIAZO, -ES adj relating to a method for reproducing documents ▷ n document produced by this method

DIAZOLE, -S n type of organic compound

DIAZOS ▶ diazo

DIB, -BED, -BING, -S vb fish by allowing the bait to bob and dip on the surface

DIBASIC *adj* (of an acid) containing two acidic hydrogen atoms

DIBBED ▸ dib

DIBBER, -S *same as* ▸ dibble

DIBBING ▸ dib

DIBBLE, -D, -S, DIBBLING *n* small gardening tool ▷ *vb* make a hole in (the ground) with a dibble

DIBBLER -S

DIBBS *n* money

DIBBUK, -IM, -S *variant spelling of* ▸ dybbuk

DIBS ▸ dib

DIBUTYL *adj* with two butyl groups

DICACITY *n* playful teasing

DICAMBA, -S *n* type of weedkiller

DICAST, -S *n* juror in ancient Athens

DICASTIC

DICE, -D, -S *n* small cube with numbered spots ▷ *vb* cut (food) into small cubes

DICENTRA *n* Asian or N American ornamental plant

DICER, -S ▸ dice

DICES ▸ dice

DICEY, DICIER, DICIEST *adj* dangerous or risky

DICH *interj* archaic expression meaning "may it do"

DICHASIA ▸ dichasium

DICHORD, -S *n* two-stringed musical instrument

DICHOTIC *adj* relating to or involving the stimulation of each ear simultaneously by different sounds

DICHROIC *adj* having or consisting of only two colours

DICHT, -ED, -ING, -S *vb* wipe

DICIER ▸ dicey

DICIEST ▸ dicey

DICING, -S ▸ dice

DICK, -S *n* fellow

DICKENS *n* euphemism for devil

DICKER, -ED, -S *vb* trade (goods) by bargaining ▷ *n* petty bargain or barter

DICKERER *n* person who dickers

DICKERS ▸ dicker

DICKEY, -S *same as* ▸ dicky

DICKIE *same as* ▸ dicky

DICKIER ▸ dicky

DICKIES ▸ dicky

DICKIEST ▸ dicky

DICKS ▸ dick

DICKTY, DICKTIER *same as* ▸ dicty

DICKY, DICKIER, DICKIES, DICKIEST *n* false shirt front ▷ *adj* shaky or weak

DICLINY > diclinous

DICOT, -S *n* type of flowering plant

DICOTYL, -S *n* type of flowering plant

DICROTAL *same as* ▸ dicrotic

DICROTIC *adj* having or relating to a double pulse for each heartbeat

DICT, -ED, -ING, -S *vb* dictate

DICTA ▸ dictum

DICTATE, -D, -S *vb* say aloud for someone else to write down ▷ *n* authoritative command

DICTATOR *n* ruler who has complete power

DICTED ▸ dict

DICTIER ▸ dicty

DICTIEST ▸ dicty

DICTING ▸ dict

DICTION, -S *n* manner of pronouncing words and sounds

DICTS ▸ dict

DICTUM, DICTA, -S *n* formal statement

DICTY, DICTIER, DICTIEST *adj* conceited; snobbish

DICYCLIC *adj* having the perianth arranged in two whorls

DICYCLY

DID ▸ do

DIDACT, -S *n* instructive person

DIDACTIC *adj* intended to instruct

DIDACTS ▸ didact

DIDACTYL *adj* having only two toes on each foot ▷ *n* animal with only two toes on each foot

DIDAKAI, -S *same as* ▸ didicoy

DIDAKEI, -S *same as* ▸ didicoy

DIDAPPER *n* small grebe

DIDDER, -ED, -S *vb* shake with fear

DIDDICOY *same as* ▸ didicoy

DIDDIER ▸ diddy

DIDDIES ▸ diddy

DIDDIEST ▸ diddy

DIDDLE, -D, -S, DIDDLING *vb* swindle

DIDDLER -S

DIDDLEY, -S *n* worthless amount

DIDDLIES ▸ diddly

DIDDLING ▸ diddle

DIDDLY, DIDDLIES *n* worthless amount

DIDDUMS *interj* expression of sympathy, esp to a child

DIDDY, DIDDIER, DIDDIES, DIDDIEST *n* Scots word for a foolish person ▷ *adj* foolish

DIDICOI, -S *same as* ▸ didicoy

DIDICOY, -S *n* (in Britain) a person who lives like a Gypsy but is not a true Romany

DIDIE *same as* ▸ didy

DIDIES ▸ didy

DIDO, -ES, -S *n* antic

DIDRACHM *n* two-drachma piece

DIDST *form of the past tense of* ▸ do

DIDY, DIDIES *n* (US) child's word for nappy

DIDYMIUM *n* metallic mixture once thought to be an element

DIDYMOUS *adj* in pairs or in two parts

DIDYNAMY *n* (of stamens) being in two unequal pairs

DIE, -D, -ING, -S *vb* cease all biological activity permanently ▷ *n* shaped block used to cut or form metal

DIEB, -S *n* N African jackal

DIEBACK, -S *n* disease of trees and shrubs ▷ *vb* (of plants) to suffer from dieback

DIEBS ▸ dieb

DIECIOUS *same as* > dioecious

DIED ▸ die

DIEDRAL, -S *same as* ▸ dihedral

DIEDRE, -S *n* large shallow groove or corner in a rock face

DIEGESIS, DIEGESES *n* utterance of fact

DIEGETIC *adj* relating to a factual narrative

DIEHARD, -S *n* person who resists change

DIEING ▸ die

DIEL, -S *n* 24-hour period ▷ *adj* of or lasting for any 24-hour period

DIELDRIN *n* highly toxic insecticide

DIELS ▸ diel

DIELYTRA *n* genus of herbaceous plants

DIEMAKER *n* one who makes dies

DIENE, -S *n* type of hydrocarbon

DIEOFF, -S *n* process of dying in large numbers

DIERESIS, DIERESES same as
> **diaeresis**

DIERETIC

DIES ► die

DIESEL, -ED, -S vb drive diesel-fuelled vehicle ▷ n diesel engine

DIESIS, DIESES n (in ancient Greek theory) any interval smaller than a whole tone

DIESTER, -S n synthetic lubricant

DIESTOCK n device holding the dies used to cut an external screw thread

DIESTRUM another word for
> **dioestrus**

DIESTRUS same as
> **dioestrus**

DIET, -ED, -S n food that a person or animal regularly eats ▷ vb follow a special diet so as to lose weight ▷ adj (of food) suitable for a weight-reduction diet

DIETARY adj of or relating to a diet ▷ n regulated diet

DIETED ► diet

DIETER, -S ► diet

DIETETIC adj prepared for special dietary requirements

DIETHER, -S n chemical compound

DIETHYL, -S adj as in **diethyl ether** ether

DIETINE, -S n low-ranking diet

DIETING, -S ► diet

DIETIST n another word for
> **dietitian**

DIETS ► diet

DIF, -S same as ► **diff**

DIFF, -S n (slang) difference

DIFFER, -ED, -S vb be unlike

DIFFORM adj irregular in form

DIFFRACT vb cause to undergo diffraction

DIFFS ► diff

DIFFUSE, -D, -S vb spread over a wide area ▷ adj widely spread

DIFFUSER n person or thing that diffuses

DIFFUSES ► diffuse

DIFFUSOR same as
► **diffuser**

DIFS ► dif

DIG, -GING, -S vb cut into, break up, and turn over or remove (earth), esp with a spade ▷ n digging

DIGAMIES ► digamy

DIGAMIST ► digamy

DIGAMMA, -S n letter of the Greek alphabet

DIGAMOUS ► digamy

DIGAMY, DIGAMIES n second marriage

DIGERATI pl n people who earn large amounts of money through internet-related business

DIGEST, -ED, -S vb subject to a process of digestion ▷ n shortened version of a book, report, or article

DIGESTER n apparatus or vessel, such as an autoclave, in which digestion is carried out

DIGESTIF n something, esp a drink, taken as an aid to digestion, either before or after a meal

DIGESTOR same as
► **digester**

DIGESTS ► digest

DIGGABLE adj that can be dug

DIGGED a past tense of ► **dig**

DIGGER, -S n machine used for digging

DIGGING ► dig

DIGGINGS pl n material that has been dug out

DIGHT, -ED, -ING, -S vb adorn or equip, as for battle

DIGICAM, -S n digital camera

DIGIPACK n (esp formerly) type of packaging for a CD or DVD

DIGIT, -S n finger or toe

DIGITAL, -S adj displaying information as numbers ▷ n one of the keys on the manuals of an organ or piano, etc

DIGITATE adj (of leaves) having leaflets in the form of a spread hand

DIGITISE same as ► **digitize**

DIGITIZE vb transcribe (data) into a digital form for processing by a computer

DIGITRON n type of tube for displaying information

DIGITS ► digit

DIGITULE n any small finger-like process

DIGLOT, -S n bilingual book

DIGLYPH, -S n ornament in Doric frieze with two grooves

DIGNIFY vb add distinction to

DIGNITY n serious, calm, and controlled behaviour or manner

DIGONAL adj of or relating to a symmetry operation

DIGOXIN, -S n glycoside extracted from the leaves of the woolly foxglove

DIGRAPH, -S n two letters used to represent a single sound

DIGRESS vb depart from the main subject in speech or writing

DIGS ► dig

DIGYNIAN adj relating to plant class Digynia

DIGYNOUS another word for
► **digynian**

DIHEDRA ► dihedron

DIHEDRAL adj having or formed by two intersecting planes ▷ n figure formed by two intersecting planes

DIHEDRON, DIHEDRA n figure formed by two intersecting planes

DIHYBRID n offspring of two individuals that differ with respect to two pairs of genes

DIHYDRIC adj (of an alcohol) containing two hydroxyl groups per molecule

DIKA, -S n wild mango

DIKAST, -S same as ► **dicast**

DIKDIK, -S n small African antelope

DIKE, -D, -S, DIKING same as
► **dyke**

DIKER, -S n builder of dikes

DIKES ► dike

DIKETONE n as in **diphenylene diketone** compound used in dye manufacture, aka anthraquinone

DIKING ► dike

DIKKOP, -S n type of brownish shore bird with a large head and eyes

DIKTAT, -S n dictatorial decree

DILATANT adj tending to dilate ▷ n something, such as a catheter, that causes dilation

DILATATE same as ► **dilate**

DILATE, -D, -S, DILATING vb make or become wider or larger

DILATER, -S same as
► **dilator**

DILATES ► dilate

DILATING ► dilate

DILATION ► dilate

DILATIVE ► dilate

DILATOR, -S n something that dilates an object

DILATORY adj tending or intended to waste time

DILEMMA, -S n situation offering a choice between two undesirable alternatives

DILEMMIC

DILIGENT adj careful and persevering in carrying out duties

DILL, -ED, -S vb flavour with dill ▷ n sweet-smelling herb

DILLI, -S n dilly bag; small bag, esp one made of plaited grass and used for carrying food

DILLIER ▸ dilly

DILLIES ▸ dilly

DILLIEST ▸ dilly

DILLING, -S ▸ dill

DILLIS ▸ dilli

DILLS ▸ dill

DILLWEED n dill plant or its foliage

DILLY, DILLIER, DILLIES, DILLIEST adj foolish ▷ n person or thing that is remarkable

DILSCOOP n type of shot in cricket in which the ball goes over the wicketkeeper's head

DILUENT, -S adj causing dilution or serving to dilute ▷ n substance used for or causing dilution

DILUTE, -D, -S, DILUTING vb make (a liquid) less concentrated, esp by adding water ▷ adj (of a liquid) thin and watery

DILUTEE -S

DILUTER, -S ▸ dilute

DILUTES ▸ dilute

DILUTING ▸ dilute

DILUTION n act of diluting or state of being diluted

DILUTIVE adj having effect of decreasing earnings per share

DILUTOR, -S n thing intended to have a diluting effect

DILUVIA ▸ diluvium

DILUVIAL adj of a flood, esp the great Flood described in the Old Testament

DILUVIAN same as ▸ **diluvial**

DILUVION same as ▸ **diluvium**

DILUVIUM, DILUVIA n glacial drift

DIM, -MED, -MEST, -S adj badly lit ▷ vb make or become dim

DIMBLE, -S n wooded hollow; dingle

DIMBO, -ES, -S n unintelligent person

DIME, -S n coin of the US and Canada, worth ten cents

DIMER, -S n type of molecule

DIMERIC adj of a dimer

DIMERISE same as ▸ **dimerize**

DIMERISM ▸ dimerous

DIMERIZE vb react or cause to react to form a dimer

DIMEROUS adj consisting of or divided into two segments, as the tarsi of some insects

DIMERS ▸ dimer

DIMES ▸ dime

DIMETER, -S n type of verse

DIMETHYL n ethane

DIMETRIC adj of, relating to, or shaped like a quadrilateral

DIMINISH vb make or become smaller, fewer, or less

DIMITY, DIMITIES n light strong cotton fabric with woven stripes or squares

DIMLY ▸ dim

DIMMABLE adj that can be dimmed

DIMMED ▸ dim

DIMMER, -S ▸ dim

DIMMEST ▸ dim

DIMMING, -S n as in **global dimming** decrease in the amount of sunlight reaching the earth

DIMMISH ▸ dim

DIMNESS ▸ dim

DIMORPH, -S n either of two forms of a substance that exhibits dimorphism

DIMOUT, -S n reduction of lighting

DIMP, -S n in Northern English dialect, a cigarette butt

DIMPLE, -D, -S, DIMPLING n small natural dent, esp in the cheeks or chin ▷ vb produce dimples by smiling

DIMPLIER ▸ dimply

DIMPLING ▸ dimple

DIMPLY, DIMPLIER ▸ dimple

DIMPS ▸ dimp

DIMPSY, DIMPSIES n twilight

DIMS ▸ dim

DIMWIT, -S n stupid person

DIMYARY adj with two adductor muscles

DIN, -NED, -NING, -S n loud unpleasant confused noise ▷ vb instil (something) into someone by constant repetition

DINAR, -S n monetary unit

DINARCHY same as ▸ **diarchy**

DINARS ▸ dinar

DINDLE, -D, -S, DINDLING another word for ▸ **dinnle**

DINE, -D, -S vb eat dinner

DINER, -S n person eating a meal

DINERIC adj of or concerned with the interface between immiscible liquids

DINERO, -S n money

DINERS ▸ diner

DINES ▸ dine

DINETTE, -S n alcove or small area for use as a dining room

DINFUL adj noisy

DING, -S n small dent in a vehicle ▷ vb ring or cause to ring, esp with tedious repetition

DINGBAT, -S n any unnamed object

DINGDONG n sound of a bell or bells ▷ vb make such a sound

DINGE, -D, DINGING n dent ▷ vb make a dent in (something)

DINGER, -S n (in baseball) home run

DINGES, -ES n jocular word for something whose name is unknown or forgotten

DINGEY, -S same as ▸ **dinghy**

DINGHY, DINGHIES n small boat, powered by sails, oars, or a motor ▷ vb ignore or avoid a person or event

DINGIED ▸ dingy

DINGIER ▸ dingy

DINGIES ▸ dingy

DINGIEST ▸ dingy

DINGILY ▸ dingy

DINGING ▸ dinge

DINGLE, -S n small wooded hollow or valley

DINGO, -ED, -ES, -ING, -S n Australian wild dog ▷ vb act in a cowardly manner

DINGS ▸ ding

DINGUS, -ES same as ▸ **dinges**

DINGY, DINGIED, DINGIER, DINGIES, DINGIEST, -ING adj lacking light ▷ vb ignore or avoid a person or event

DINIC, -S n remedy for vertigo

DINING, -S n act of dining

DINITRO adj containing two nitro groups

DINK, -ED, -ER, -EST, -ING, -S adj neat or neatly dressed ▷ vb carry (a second person) on a horse, bicycle, etc ▷ n ball struck delicately

DINKEY, -S n small locomotive

DINKIE, -S n affluent married childless person ▷ adj designed for or appealing to dinkies

DINKIER ▸ dinky

DINKIES ▸ dinkie

DINKIEST ▸ dinky

DINKING ▸ dink

DINKLY, DINKLIER adj neat

DINKS ▸ dink

D

DINKUM, -S *n* truth or genuineness

DINKY, DINKIER, DINKIEST *adj* small and neat

DINMONT, -S *n* neutered sheep

DINNA *vb* a Scots word for do not

DINNAE *vb* (Scots) do not

DINNED ► din

DINNER, -ED, -S *vb* dine ▷ *n* main meal of the day

DINNING ► din

DINNLE, -D, -S, DINNLING *vb* shake

DINO, -S *n* dinosaur

DINOSAUR *n* type of extinct prehistoric reptile, many of which were of gigantic size

DINS ► din

DINT, -ED, -ING, -S variant of ► dent

DINTLESS

DIOBOL, -S *n* ancient Greek coin

DIOBOLON same as ► diobol

DIOBOLS ► diobol

DIOCESAN *adj* of or relating to a diocese ▷ *n* bishop of a diocese

DIOCESE, -S *n* district over which a bishop has control

DIODE, -S *n* semiconductor device

DIOECIES ► dioecy

DIOECISM > dioecious

DIOECY, DIOECIES *n* state of being dioecious

DIOICOUS same as > dioecious

DIOL, -S *n* any of a class of alcohols that have two hydroxyl groups in each molecule

DIOLEFIN *n* type of polymer

DIOLS ► diol

DIOPSIDE *n* colourless or pale-green pyroxene mineral

DIOPTASE *n* green glassy mineral

DIOPTER, -S same as ► dioptre

DIOPTRAL ► dioptre

DIOPTRE, -S *n* unit for measuring the refractive power of a lens

DIOPTRIC *adj* of or concerned with dioptrics

DIORAMA, -S *n* miniature three-dimensional scene

DIORAMIC

DIORISM, -S *n* definition; clarity

DIORITE, -S *n* dark coarse-grained igneous plutonic rock

DIORITIC

DIOTA, -S *n* type of ancient vase

DIOXAN, -S *n* colourless insoluble toxic liquid

DIOXANE, -S same as ► dioxan

DIOXANS ► dioxan

DIOXID, -S same as ► dioxide

DIOXIDE, -S *n* oxide containing two oxygen atoms per molecule

DIOXIDS ► dioxid

DIOXIN, -S *n* poisonous chemical by-product of certain weedkillers

DIP, -PED, -S, -T *vb* plunge quickly or briefly into a liquid ▷ *n* dipping

DIPCHICK same as ► dabchick

DIPHASE *adj* of, having, or concerned with two phases

DIPHASIC same as ► diphase

DIPHENYL another name for ► biphenyl

DIPHONE, -S *n* combination of two speech sounds

DIPLEGIA *n* paralysis of corresponding parts on both sides of the body

DIPLEGIC

DIPLEX *adj* permitting simultaneous transmission in both directions

DIPLEXER *n* device that enables the simultaneous transmission of more than one signal

DIPLOE, -S *n* spongy bone separating the two layers of compact bone of the skull

DIPLOGEN *n* heavy hydrogen

DIPLOIC *adj* relating to diploe

DIPLOID, -S *adj* denoting a cell or organism with pairs of homologous chromosomes ▷ *n* diploid cell or organism

DIPLOIDY

DIPLOMA, -S *vb* bestow diploma on ▷ *n* qualification awarded by a college on successful completion of a course

DIPLOMAT *n* official engaged in diplomacy

DIPLON, -S another name for ► deuteron

DIPLONT, -S *n* animal or plant that has the diploid number of chromosomes in its somatic cells

DIPLOPIA *n* visual defect in which a single object is seen in duplicate

DIPLOPIC

DIPLOPOD *n* type of arthropod such as the millipede

DIPLOSIS, DIPLOSES *n* doubling of the haploid number of chromosomes

DIPLOZOA *n* type of parasitic worm

DIPNET, -S *vb* fish using fishing net on pole

DIPNOAN, -S *n* lungfish

DIPNOOUS *adj* having lungs and gills

DIPODIC ► dipody

DIPODY, DIPODIES *n* metrical unit consisting of two feet

DIPOLAR ► dipole

DIPOLE, -S *n* two equal but opposite electric charges or magnetic poles separated by a small distance

DIPPABLE ► dip

DIPPED ► dip

DIPPER, -S *n* ladle used for dipping

DIPPIER ► dippy

DIPPIEST ► dippy

DIPPING, -S ► dip

DIPPY, DIPPIER, DIPPIEST *adj* odd, eccentric, or crazy

DIPROTIC *adj* having two hydrogen atoms

DIPS ► dip

DIPSAS, DIPSADES *n* type of snake

DIPSO, -S *n* dipsomaniac or alcoholic

DIPSTICK *n* notched rod dipped into a container to measure the level of a liquid

DIPT ► dip

DIPTERA, -S *n* order of insects with two wings

DIPTERAL *adj* having a double row of columns

DIPTERAN *n* dipterous insect ▷ *adj* having two wings or winglike parts

DIPTERAS ► diptera

DIPTEROI ► dipteros

DIPTERON same as ► dipteran

DIPTEROS, DIPTEROI *n* Greek building with double columns

DIPTYCA, -S same as ► diptych

DIPTYCH, -S *n* painting on two hinged panels

DIQUARK, -S *n* particle in physics

DIQUAT, -S *n* type of herbicide

DIRAM, -S *n* money unit of Tajikistan

DIRDAM, **-S** *same as* ▸ **dirdum**

DIRDUM, **-S** *n* tumult

DIRE, **-R**, **-ST** *adj* disastrous, urgent, or terrible

DIRECT, **-ED**, **-ER**, **-S** *adj* (of a route) shortest, straight ▷ *adv* in a direct manner ▷ *vb* lead and organize

DIRECTLY *adv* in a direct manner

DIRECTOR *n* person or thing that directs or controls

DIRECTS ▸ **direct**

DIREFUL *same as* ▸ **dire**

DIRELY ▸ **dire**

DIREMPT, **-S** *vb* separate with force

DIRENESS ▸ **dire**

DIRER ▸ **dire**

DIREST ▸ **dire**

DIRGE, **-S** *n* slow sad song of mourning

DIRGEFUL

DIRHAM, **-S** *n* standard monetary unit of Morocco

DIRHEM, **-S** *same as* ▸ **dirham**

DIRIGE, **-S** *n* dirge

DIRIGENT *adj* directing

DIRIGES ▸ **dirige**

DIRIGISM *same as* > **dirigisme**

DIRIMENT *adj* (of an impediment to marriage in canon law) totally invalidating

DIRK, **-ED**, **-ING**, **-S** *n* dagger, formerly worn by Scottish Highlanders ▷ *vb* stab with a dirk

DIRKE, **-S** *variant of* ▸ **dirk**

DIRKED ▸ **dirk**

DIRKES ▸ **dirke**

DIRKING ▸ **dirk**

DIRKS ▸ **dirk**

DIRL, **-ED**, **-ING**, **-S** *vb* tingle; vibrate

DIRNDL, **-S** *n* full gathered skirt

DIRT, **-ED**, **-ING**, **-S** *vb* soil ▷ *n* unclean substance, filth

DIRTBAG, **-S** *n* filthy person

DIRTBALL *n* insulting word for a contemptible person

DIRTED ▸ **dirt**

DIRTIED ▸ **dirty**

DIRTIER ▸ **dirty**

DIRTIES ▸ **dirty**

DIRTIEST ▸ **dirty**

DIRTILY ▸ **dirty**

DIRTING ▸ **dirt**

DIRTS ▸ **dirt**

DIRTY, **DIRTIED**, **DIRTIER**, **DIRTIES**, **DIRTIEST**, **-ING** *adj*

covered or marked with dirt ▷ *vb* make dirty

DIS *same as* ▸ **diss**

DISA, **-S** *n* type of orchid

DISABLE, **-S** *vb* make ineffective, unfit, or incapable

DISABLED *adj* lacking a physical power, such as the ability to walk

DISABLER ▸ **disable**

DISABLES ▸ **disable**

DISABUSE *vb* rid (someone) of a mistaken idea

DISADORN *vb* deprive of ornamentation

DISAGREE *vb* argue or have different opinions

DISALLOW *vb* reject as untrue or invalid

DISALLY *vb* separate

DISANNEX *vb* disunite

DISANNUL *vb* cancel

DISAPPLY *vb* make (law) invalid

DISARM, **-ED**, **-S** *vb* deprive of weapons

DISARMER

DISARRAY *n* confusion and lack of discipline ▷ *vb* throw into confusion

DISAS ▸ **disa**

DISASTER *n* occurrence that causes great distress or destruction

DISAVOW, **-S** *vb* deny connection with or responsibility for

DISBAND, **-S** *vb* (cause to) cease to function as a group

DISBAR, **-S** *vb* deprive (a barrister) of the right to practise

DISBARK, **-S** *same as* > **disembark**

DISBARS ▸ **disbar**

DISBENCH *vb* remove from bench

DISBOSOM *vb* disclose

DISBOUND *adj* unbound

DISBOWEL *vb* disembowel

DISBUD, **-S** *vb* remove superfluous buds from (a plant, esp a fruit tree)

DISBURSE *vb* pay out

DISC, **-ED**, **-ING**, **-S** *n* flat circular object ▷ *vb* work (land) with a disc harrow

DISCAGE, **-D**, **-S** *vb* release from cage

DISCAL *adj* relating to or resembling a disc

DISCANDY *vb* melt; dissolve

DISCANT, **-S** *same as* ▸ **descant**

DISCARD, **-S** *vb* get rid of (something or someone) as useless or undesirable ▷ *n* person or thing that has been cast aside

DISCASE, **-D**, **-S** *vb* remove case from

DISCED ▸ **disc**

DISCEPT, **-S** *vb* discuss

DISCERN, **-S** *vb* see or be aware of (something) clearly

DISCERP, **-S** *vb* divide

DISCI ▸ **discus**

DISCIDE, **-D**, **-S** *vb* split

DISCINCT *adj* loosely dressed, without belt

DISCING ▸ **disc**

DISCIPLE *vb* teach ▷ *n* follower of the doctrines of a teacher, esp Jesus Christ

DISCLAIM *vb* deny (responsibility for or knowledge of something)

DISCLESS *adj* having no disc

DISCLIKE ▸ **disc**

DISCLOSE, **DISCLOST** *vb* make known

DISCO, **-ED**, **-ES**, **-ING**, **-S** *vb* go to a disco ▷ *n* nightclub where people dance to amplified pop records

DISCOER **-S**

DISCOID, **-S** *adj* like a disc ▷ *n* dislike object

DISCOING ▸ **disco**

DISCOLOR *same as* > **discolour**

DISCORD, **-S** *n* lack of agreement or harmony between people ▷ *vb* disagree

DISCOS ▸ **disco**

DISCOUNT *vb* take no account of something ▷ *n* deduction from the full price of something

DISCOURE *vb* discover

DISCOVER *vb* be the first to find or to find out about

DISCREET *adj* careful to avoid embarrassment, esp by keeping confidences secret

DISCRETE *adj* separate, distinct

DISCROWN *vb* deprive of a crown

DISCS ▸ **disc**

DISCURE, **-D**, **-S** *old form of* ▸ **discover**

DISCUS, **DISCI**, **-ES** *n* object thrown in sports competitions

DISCUSS *vb* consider (something) by talking it over

DISDAIN, -S n feeling of superiority and dislike ▷ vb refuse with disdain

DISEASE, -S vb make uneasy ▷ n illness, sickness

DISEASED adj having or affected with disease

DISEASES ▶ disease

DISEDGE, -D, -S vb render blunt

DISENDOW vb take away an endowment from

DISENROL vb remove from register

DISEUR, -S same as ▶ diseuse

DISEUSE, -S n (esp formerly) an actress who presents dramatic recitals

DISFAME, -D, -S n discredit ▷ vb throw into disrepute or remove fame (from)

DISFAVOR same as ▶ disfavour

DISFLESH vb reduce flesh of

DISFORM, -S vb change form of

DISFROCK another word for ▶ unfrock

DISGAVEL vb deprive of quality of gavelkind

DISGEST, -S vb digest

DISGORGE vb empty out, discharge

DISGOWN, -S vb remove gown from

DISGRACE n condition of shame, loss of reputation, or dishonour ▷ vb bring shame upon (oneself or others)

DISGRADE vb degrade

DISGUISE vb change the appearance to conceal the identity ▷ n mask, costume, or manner that disguises

DISGUST, -S n great loathing or distaste ▷ vb sicken, fill with loathing

DISH, -ES n shallow container used for holding or serving food ▷ vb put into a dish

DISHABIT vb dislodge

DISHABLE obsolete form of ▶ disable

DISHDASH same as ▷ dishdasha

DISHED adj shaped like a dish

DISHELM, -S vb remove helmet from

DISHERIT vb disinherit

DISHES ▶ dish

DISHEVEL vb disarrange (the hair or clothes) of (someone)

DISHFUL, -S n the amount that a dish is able to hold

DISHIER ▶ dishy

DISHIEST ▶ dishy

DISHING, -S ▶ dish

DISHLIKE ▶ dish

DISHMOP, -S n mop for cleaning dishes

DISHOARD vb put previously withheld (money) into circulation

DISHOME, -D, -S vb deprive of home

DISHONOR same as ▷ dishonour

DISHORN, -S vb remove horns from

DISHORSE vb dismount

DISHOUSE vb deprive of home

DISHPAN, -S n large pan for washing dishes, pots, etc

DISHRAG, -S n dishcloth

DISHWARE n tableware

DISHY, DISHIER, DISHIEST adj good-looking

DISINTER vb dig up

DISINURE vb render unaccustomed

DISJECT, -S vb break apart

DISJOIN, -S vb disconnect or become disconnected

DISJOINT vb take apart or come apart at the joints ▷ adj (of two sets) having no members in common

DISJUNCT adj not united or joined ▷ n one of the propositions or formulas in a disjunction

DISJUNE, -D, -S n breakfast ▷ vb breakfast

DISK, -ED, -ING, -S same as ▶ disc

DISKER, -S n person who breaks up earth with a type of farm implement

DISKETTE n floppy disk

DISKING ▶ disk

DISKLESS ▶ disk

DISKLIKE ▶ disk

DISKS ▶ disk

DISLEAF, -S vb remove leaf or leaves from

DISLEAL archaic form of ▶ disloyal

DISLEAVE variant of ▶ disleaf

DISLIKE, -D, -S vb consider unpleasant or disagreeable ▷ n feeling of not liking something or someone

DISLIKEN vb render dissimilar to

DISLIKER ▶ dislike

DISLIKES ▶ dislike

DISLIMB, -S vb remove limbs from

DISLIMN, -S vb efface

DISLINK, -S vb disunite

DISLOAD, -S vb unload

DISLODGE vb remove (something) from a previously fixed position

DISLOIGN vb put at a distance

DISLOYAL adj not loyal, deserting one's allegiance

DISMAL, -ER adj gloomy and depressing

DISMALLY

DISMALS pl n gloomy state of mind

DISMAN, -S vb remove men from

DISMASK, -S vb remove mask from

DISMAST, -S vb break off the mast or masts of (a sailing vessel)

DISMAY, -ED, -S vb fill with alarm or depression ▷ n alarm mixed with sadness

DISMAYD adj word used by Spenser meaning misshapen

DISMAYED ▶ dismay

DISMAYL vb remove a coat of mail from

DISMAYS ▶ dismay

DISME, -S old form of ▶ dime

DISMISS vb remove (an employee) from a job ▷ sentence substitute order to end an activity or give permission to disperse

DISMODED adj no longer fashionable

DISMOUNT vb get off a horse or bicycle ▷ n act of dismounting

DISNEST, -S vb remove from nest

DISOBEY, -S vb neglect or refuse to obey

DISODIUM n compound containing two sodium atoms

DISOMIC adj having an extra chromosome in the haploid state

DISOMY DISOMIES

DISORBED adj thrown out of orbit

DISORDER n state of untidiness and disorganization ▷ vb upset the order of

DISOWN, -ED, -S vb deny any connection with (someone)

DISOWNER

DISPACE, -D, -S vb move or travel about

DISPARK, -S vb release

DISPART, -S vb separate

DISPATCH vb send off to a destination or to perform a task ▷ n official communication or report, sent in haste

DISPATHY obsolete spelling of ▸ **dyspathy**

DISPEACE n absence of peace

DISPEL, -S vb destroy or remove

DISPENCE same as ▸ **dispense**

DISPEND, -S vb spend

DISPENSE vb distribute in portions

DISPERSE vb scatter over a wide area ▷ adj of or consisting of the particles in a colloid or suspension

DISPIRIT vb make downhearted

DISPLACE vb move from the usual location

DISPLANT vb displace

DISPLAY, -S vb make visible or noticeable ▷ n displaying

DISPLE, -D, -S, DISPLING vb punish

DISPLODE obsolete word for ▸ **explode**

DISPLUME vb remove feathers from

DISPONE, -D, -S vb transfer ownership

DISPONEE vb person whom something is disponed to

DISPONER ▸ **dispone**

DISPONES ▸ **dispone**

DISPONGE same as ▸ **dispunge**

DISPORT, -S vb indulge (oneself) in pleasure ▷ n amusement

DISPOSAL n getting rid of something

DISPOSE, -S vb place in a certain order

DISPOSED adj willing or eager

DISPOSER ▸ **dispose**

DISPOSES ▸ **dispose**

DISPOST, -S vb remove from post

DISPRAD old form of ▸ **dispread**

DISPREAD vb spread out

DISPRED, -S old spelling of ▸ **dispread**

DISPRIZE vb scorn

DISPROOF n facts that disprove something

DISPROVE vb show (an assertion or claim) to be incorrect

DISPUNGE vb expunge

DISPURSE another word for ▸ **disburse**

DISPUTE, -D, -S n disagreement, argument ▷ vb argue about (something)

DISPUTER

DISQUIET n feeling of anxiety ▷ vb make (someone) anxious ▷ adj uneasy or anxious

DISRANK, -S vb demote

DISRATE, -D, -S vb punish (an officer) by lowering in rank

DISROBE, -D, -S vb undress **DISROBER**

DISROOT, -S vb uproot

DISRUPT, -S vb interrupt the progress of

DISS, -ED, -ES, -ING vb treat (a person) with contempt

DISSAVE, -D, -S vb spend savings

DISSAVER n person who dissaves

DISSAVES ▸ **dissave**

DISSEAT, -S vb unseat

DISSECT, -S vb cut something open to examine it

DISSED ▸ **diss**

DISSEISE vb deprive of seisin

DISSEIZE same as ▸ **disseise**

DISSENT, -S vb disagree ▷ n disagreement

DISSERT, -S n give or make a dissertation; dissertate

DISSERVE vb do a disservice to

DISSES ▸ **diss**

DISSEVER vb break off or become broken off

DISSIGHT n eyesore

DISSING ▸ **diss**

DISSOLVE vb (cause to) become liquid ▷ n scene filmed or televised by dissolving

DISSUADE vb deter (someone) by persuasion from doing something

DISTAFF, -S, DISTAVES n rod on which wool etc is wound for spinning

DISTAIN, -S vb stain; tarnish

DISTAL adj (of a bone, limb, etc) situated farthest from the point of attachment **DISTALLY**

DISTANCE n space between two points

DISTANT adj far apart

DISTASTE n dislike, disgust

DISTAVES ▸ **distaff**

DISTEND, -S vb (of part of the body) swell

DISTENT, -S adj bloated; swollen ▷ n breadth; distension

DISTHENE n bluish-green mineral

DISTICH, -S n unit of two verse lines

DISTIL, -S vb subject to or obtain by distillation

DISTILL, -S same as ▸ **distil**

DISTILS ▸ **distil**

DISTINCT adj not the same

DISTOME, -S n parasitic flatworm

DISTORT, -S vb misrepresent (the truth or facts)

DISTRACT vb draw the attention of (a person) away from something

DISTRAIL n trail made by aircraft flying through cloud

DISTRAIN, -S vb seize (personal property) to enforce payment of a debt

DISTRAIT adj absent-minded or preoccupied

DISTRESS n extreme unhappiness ▷ vb upset badly

DISTRICT n area of land regarded as an administrative or geographical unit ▷ vb divide into districts

DISTRIX n splitting of the ends of hairs

DISTRUST vb regard as untrustworthy ▷ n feeling of suspicion or doubt

DISTUNE, -D, -S vb cause to be out of tune

DISTURB, -S vb intrude on

DISTYLE, -S n temple with two columns

DISULFID same as > **disulfide**

DISUNION ▸ **disunite**

DISUNITE vb cause disagreement among

DISUNITY n dissension or disagreement

DISUSAGE n disuse

DISUSE, -S, DISUSING vb stop using ▷ n state of being no longer used

DISUSED adj no longer used

DISUSES ▸ **disuse**

DISUSING ▸ **disuse**

DISVALUE vb belittle

DISVOUCH vb dissociate oneself from

DISYOKE, -D, -S vb unyoke

DIT, -S, -TED, -TING, -TIT vb stop something happening ▷ n short sound used in the spoken representation of telegraphic codes

DITA, -S n tropical shrub

DITAL, -S n key for raising pitch of lute string

DITAS ▸ **dita**

DITCH, -ED, -ES, -ING n narrow channel dug in the earth for drainage or

irrigation ▷ vb abandon
DITCHER -S
DITE, -D, -S, DITING vb set down in writing
DITHECAL adj having two thecae
DITHEISM n belief in two equal gods
DITHEIST
DITHER, -ED, -S vb be uncertain or indecisive ▷ n state of indecision or agitation
DITHERER
DITHERY
DITHIOL, -S n chemical compound
DITING ▸ dite
DITOKOUS adj producing two eggs
DITONE, -S n interval of two tones
DITS ▸ dit
DITSY, DITSIER, DITSIEST same as ▸ ditzy
DITT, -S same as ▸ dit
DITTANY n aromatic plant
DITTAY, -S n accusation; charge
DITTED ▸ dit
DITTIED ▸ ditty
DITTIES ▸ ditty
DITTING ▸ dit
DITTIT ▸ dit
DITTO, -ED, -ING, -S n same ▷ adv in the same way ▷ sentence substitute used to avoid repeating or to confirm agreement with an immediately preceding sentence ▷ vb copy
DITTS ▸ ditt
DITTY, DITTIED, DITTIES, -ING vb set to music ▷ n short simple poem or song
DITZ, -ES n silly scatterbrained person
DITZY, DITZIER, DITZIEST adj silly and scatterbrained
DIURESIS, DIURESES n excretion of an unusually large quantity of urine
DIURETIC n drug that increases the flow of urine ▷ adj acting to increase the flow of urine
DIURNAL, -S adj happening during the day or daily ▷ n service book containing all the canonical hours except matins
DIURON, -S n type of herbicide
DIV, -S n dividend
DIVA, -S n distinguished female singer

DIVAGATE vb digress or wander
DIVALENT n element that can unite with two atoms ▷ adj having two valencies or a valency of two
DIVAN, -S n low backless bed
DIVAS ▸ diva
DIVE, -D, -S vb plunge headfirst into water ▷ n diving
DIVEBOMB vb bomb while making steep dives
DIVED ▸ dive
DIVER n person who works or explores underwater
DIVERGE, -D, -S vb separate and go in different directions
DIVERS adj various ▷ determiner various
DIVERSE, -D, -S vb turn away ▷ adj having variety, assorted
DIVERSLY ▸ divers
DIVERT, -ED, -S vb change the direction of
DIVERTER
DIVES ▸ dive
DIVEST, -ED, -S vb strip (of clothes)
DIVI, -ED, -S alternative spelling of ▸ divvy
DIVIDANT adj distinct
DIVIDE, -S, DIVIDING vb separate into parts ▷ n division, split
DIVIDED adj split
DIVIDEND n sum of money representing part of the profit made, paid by a company to its shareholders
DIVIDER n screen used to divide a room into separate areas
DIVIDERS pl n compasses with two pointed arms, used for measuring or dividing lines
DIVIDES ▸ divide
DIVIDING ▸ divide
DIVIDIVI n tropical tree
DIVIDUAL adj divisible
DIVIED ▸ divi
DIVINE, -D, -S, -ST, DIVINING adj of God or a god ▷ vb discover (something) by intuition or guessing ▷ n priest who is learned in theology
DIVINELY
DIVINER -S
DIVING, -S ▸ dive
DIVINIFY vb give divine status to
DIVINING ▸ divine
DIVINISE same as ▸ divinize
DIVINITY n study of religion
DIVINIZE vb make divine

DIVIS ▸ divi
DIVISIM adv separately
DIVISION n dividing, sharing out
DIVISIVE adj tending to cause disagreement
DIVISOR, -S n number to be divided into another number
DIVNA vb do not
DIVO, -S n male diva
DIVORCE, -D, -S n legal ending of a marriage ▷ vb legally end one's marriage (to)
DIVORCEE n person who is divorced
DIVORCER ▸ divorce
DIVORCES ▸ divorce
DIVOS ▸ divo
DIVOT, -S n small piece of turf
DIVS ▸ div
DIVULGE, -D, -S vb make known, disclose
DIVULGER
DIVULSE, -D, -S vb tear apart
DIVVY, DIVVIED, DIVVIER, DIVVIES, DIVVIEST, -ING vb divide and share ▷ adj dialect word for stupid
DIVYING alternative present participle of ▸ divvy
DIWAN, -S same as ▸ dewan
DIXI interj I have spoken
DIXIE, -S n large metal pot for cooking, brewing tea, etc
DIXIT, -S n statement
DIXY same as ▸ dixie
DIYA, -S n small oil lamp, usu made from clay
DIZAIN, -S n ten-line poem
DIZEN, -ED, -ING, -S archaic word for ▸ bedizen
DIZYGOUS another word for ▷ dizygotic
DIZZARD, -S n dunce
DIZZIED ▸ dizzy
DIZZIER ▸ dizzy
DIZZIES ▸ dizzy
DIZZIEST ▸ dizzy
DIZZILY ▸ dizzy
DIZZY, DIZZIED, DIZZIER, DIZZIES, DIZZIEST, -ING adj having or causing a whirling sensation ▷ vb make dizzy
DJEBEL, -S n a variant spelling of ▸ jebel
DJELLABA n kind of loose cloak with a hood, worn by men esp in North Africa and the Middle East
DJEMBE, -S n W African drum
DJIBBA, -S same as ▸ jubbah
DJIBBAH, -S same as ▸ jubbah
DJIBBAS ▸ djibba
DJIN, -S same as ▸ jinn
DJINNI, DJINN same as ▸ jinni**

DJINNS ► djinn
DJINNY same as ► jinni
DJINS ► djin
DO, DID, -EN, -ES, -EST, -ETH, -ING, -NE, -S vb perform or complete (a deed or action) ▷ n party, celebration
DOAB, -S n alluvial land between two converging rivers
DOABLE adj capable of being done
DOABS ► doab
DOAT, -ED, -S same as ► dote
DOATER -S
DOATING, -S ► doat
DOATS ► doat
DOB, -BED, -BING, -S vb as in **dob in** inform against or report
DOBBER, -S n informant or traitor
DOBBIE same as ► dobby
DOBBIES ► dobby
DOBBIN, -S n name for a horse
DOBBING ► dob
DOBBINS ► dobbin
DOBBY, DOBBIES n attachment to a loom, used in weaving small figures
DOBCHICK same as ► dabchick
DOBE, -S same as ► adobe
DOBHASH n interpreter
DOBLA, -S n medieval Spanish gold coin, probably worth 20 maravedis
DOBLON, -ES, -S a variant spelling of ► doubloon
DOBRA, -S n standard monetary unit of São Tomé e Principe
DOBRO, -S n type of acoustic guitar
DOBS ► dob
DOBSON, -S n larva of dobsonfly
DOBY same as ► dobie
DOC, -S same as ► doctor
DOCENT, -S n voluntary worker who acts as a guide
DOCETIC adj believing that the humanity of Christ was apparent and not real
DOCHMIAC ► dochmius
DOCHMIUS, DOCHMII n five-syllable foot
DOCHT ► dow
DOCIBLE adj easily tamed
DOCILE, -R, -ST adj (of a person or animal) easily controlled
DOCILELY
DOCILITY
DOCIMASY n close examination

DOCK, -ED, -S n enclosed area of water where ships are loaded, unloaded, or repaired ▷ vb bring or be brought into dock
DOCKAGE, -S n charge levied upon a vessel for using a dock
DOCKED ► dock
DOCKEN, -S n something of no value or importance
DOCKER, -S n person employed to load and unload ships
DOCKET, -ED, -S n label on a delivery, stating contents, delivery instructions, etc ▷ vb fix a docket to (a package or other delivery)
DOCKHAND n dock labourer
DOCKING, -S ► dock
DOCKISE, -D, -S same as ► dockize
DOCKIZE, -D, -S vb convert into docks
DOCKLAND n area around the docks
DOCKS ► dock
DOCKSIDE n area next to dock
DOCKYARD n place where ships are built or repaired
DOCO, -S n (slang) documentary
DOCQUET, -S same as ► docket
DOCS ► doc
DOCTOR, -ED, -S n person licensed to practise medicine ▷ vb alter in order to deceive
DOCTORAL
DOCTORLY
DOCTRESS same as > doctoress
DOCTRINE n body of teachings of a religious, political, or philosophical group
DOCU, -S n documentary film
DOCUMENT n piece of paper providing an official record of something ▷ vb record or report (something) in detail
DOCUS ► docu
DOCUSOAP n reality television programme in the style of a documentary
DOD, -DED, -DING, -S vb clip
DODDARD, -S adj archaic word for missing branches; rotten ▷ n tree missing its top branches through rot
DODDED ► dod
DODDER, -ED, -S n move unsteadily ▷ n type of rootless parasitic plant
DODDERER
DODDERY

DODDIER ► doddy
DODDIES ► doddy
DODDIEST ► doddy
DODDING ► dod
DODDLE, -S n something easily accomplished
DODDY, DODDIER, DODDIES, DODDIEST n bad mood ▷ adj sulky
DODGE, -D, -S vb avoid (a blow, being seen, etc) by moving suddenly ▷ n cunning or deceitful trick
DODGEM, -S n bumper car
DODGER, -S n person who evades a responsibility or duty
DODGERY n deception
DODGES ► dodge
DODGIER ► dodgy
DODGIEST ► dodgy
DODGING, -S ► dodge
DODGY, DODGIER, DODGIEST adj dangerous, risky
DODKIN, -S n coin of little value
DODMAN, -S n snail
DODO, -ES, -S n large flightless extinct bird
DODOISM -S
DODS ► dod
DOE n female deer, hare, or rabbit
DOEK, -S n square of cloth worn on the head by women
DOEN ► do
DOER, -S n active or energetic person
DOES ► do
DOESKIN, -S n skin of a deer, lamb, or sheep
DOEST ► do
DOETH ► do
DOF informal South African word for ► stupid
DOFF, -ED, -ING, -S vb take off or lift (one's hat) in polite greeting
DOFFER -S
DOG, -S n domesticated four-legged mammal ▷ vb follow (someone) closely
DOGATE, -S n office of doge
DOGBANE, -S n N American plant
DOGBERRY n any of certain plants that have berry-like fruits
DOGBOLT, -S n bolt on cannon
DOGCART, -S n light horse-drawn two-wheeled cart
DOGDOM, -S n world of dogs

D

DOGE, -S n (formerly) chief magistrate of Venice or Genoa

DOGEAR, -ED, -S vb fold down the corner of (a page) ▷ n folded-down corner of a page

DOGEATE, -S n office of doge

DOGEDOM, -S n domain of doge

DOGES ▸ doge

DOGESHIP ▸ doge

DOGEY, -S same as ▸ dogie

DOGFACE, -S n WW2 US soldier

DOGFIGHT vb fight in confused way ▷ n close-quarters combat between fighter aircraft

DOGFISH n small shark

DOGFOOD, -S n food for a dog

DOGFOX, -ES n male fox

DOGGED, -ER adj stubbornly determined

DOGGEDLY

DOGGER, -S n Dutch fishing vessel with two masts

DOGGEREL n poorly written poetry, usu comic

DOGGERS ▸ dogger

DOGGERY n surly behaviour

DOGGESS n female dog

DOGGIE same as ▸ doggy

DOGGIER ▸ doggy

DOGGIES ▸ doggy

DOGGIEST ▸ doggy

DOGGING, -S ▸ dog

DOGGISH adj of or like a dog

DOGGO adv in hiding and keeping quiet

DOGGONE, -D, -R, -S interj exclamation of annoyance, disappointment, etc ▷ vb damn ▷ adj damnedest

DOGGREL, -S same as ▸ doggerel

DOGGY, DOGGIER, DOGGIES, DOGGIEST n child's word for a dog ▷ adj of or like a dog

DOGHOLE, -S n squalid dwelling place

DOGHOUSE n kennel

DOGIE, -S n motherless calf

DOGLEG, -S n sharp bend ▷ vb go off at an angle ▷ adj of or with the shape of a dogleg

DOGLIKE ▸ dog

DOGMA, -S, -TA n doctrine or system of doctrines proclaimed by authority as true

DOGMAN, DOGMEN n person who directs a crane whilst riding on an object being lifted by it

DOGMAS ▸ dogma

DOGMATA ▸ dogma

DOGMATIC adj habitually stating one's opinions forcefully or arrogantly

DOGMEN ▸ dogman

DOGNAP, -ED, -S vb carry off and hold (a dog), usually for ransom

DOGNAPER

DOGPILE, -S n pile of bodies formed by people jumping on top of each other

DOGREL, -S n doggerel

DOGS ▸ dog

DOGSBODY n person who carries out boring tasks for others ▷ vb act as a dogsbody

DOGSHIP, -S n condition of being a dog

DOGSHOW, -S n competition in which dogs are judged

DOGSKIN, -S n leather from dog's skin

DOGSLED, -S n sleigh drawn by dogs

DOGSLEEP n feigned sleep

DOGTAIL n type of grass

DOGTAIL, -S same as ▸ dogstail

DOGTOOTH, DOGTEETH n medieval carved ornament

DOGTOWN, -S n community of prairie dogs

DOGTROT, -S n gently paced trot

DOGVANE, -S n light windvane mounted on the side of a vessel

DOGWATCH n either of two watches aboard ship, from four to six pm or from six to eight pm

DOGWOOD, -S n type of tree or shrub

DOGY same as ▸ dogie

DOH, -S n in tonic sol-fa, first degree of any major scale ▷ interj exclamation of annoyance when something goes wrong

This is one of the very useful short words denoting a note of the musical scale.

DOHYO, -S n sumo wrestling ring

DOILED same as ▸ doilt

DOILIED adj having a doily

DOILIES ▸ doily

DOILT, -ER, -EST adj foolish

DOILY, DOILIES n decorative lacy paper mat, laid on a plate

DOING ▸ do

DOINGS pl n deeds or actions

DOIT, -S n former small copper coin of the Netherlands

DOITED adj foolish or childish, as from senility

DOITIT same as ▸ doited

DOITKIN, -S same as ▸ doit

DOITS ▸ doit

DOJO, -S n room or hall for the practice of martial arts

DOL, -S n unit of pain intensity, as measured by dolorimetry

DOLCE, -S, DOLCI n dessert ▷ adv (to be performed) gently and sweetly

DOLCETTO n variety of grape

DOLCI ▸ dolce

DOLDRUMS pl n depressed state of mind

DOLE, -D, -S, DOLING n money received from the state while unemployed ▷ vb distribute in small quantities

DOLEFUL adj dreary, unhappy

DOLENT adj sad

DOLENTE adv (to be performed) in a sorrowful manner

DOLERITE n dark igneous rock such as augite

DOLES ▸ dole

DOLESOME same as ▸ doleful

DOLIA ▸ dolium

DOLICHOS n tropical vine

DOLINA, -S same as ▸ doline

DOLINE, -S n depression of the ground surface formed in limestone regions

DOLING ▸ dole

DOLIUM, DOLIA n genus of molluscs

DOLL, -ED, -ING, -S n small model of a human being, used as a toy ▷ vb as in **doll up** dress up

DOLLAR, -S n standard monetary unit of many countries

DOLLARED adj flagged with a dollar sign

DOLLARS ▸ dollar

DOLLDOM, -S ▸ doll

DOLLED ▸ doll

DOLLHOOD ▸ doll

DOLLIED ▸ dolly

DOLLIER, -S n person who operates a dolly

DOLLIES ▸ dolly

DOLLING ▸ doll

DOLLISH ▸ doll

DOLLOP, -ED, -S n lump (of food) ▷ vb serve out (food)

DOLLS ▸ doll

DOLLY, DOLLIED, DOLLIES, -ING adj attractive and unintelligent ▷ n wheeled support for a camera ▷ vb wheel a camera on a dolly

DOLMA, -DES, -S *n* vine leaf stuffed with a filling of meat and rice

DOLMAN, -S *n* long Turkish outer robe

DOLMAS ▶ dolma

DOLMEN, -S *n* prehistoric monument

DOLMENIC

DOLOMITE *n* mineral consisting of calcium magnesium carbonate

DOLOR, -S *same as* ▶ **dolour**

DOLOROSO *adv* (to be performed) in a sorrowful manner

DOLOROUS *adj* sad, mournful

DOLORS ▶ dolor

DOLOS, -SE *n* knucklebone of a sheep, buck, etc, used esp by diviners

DOLOUR, -S *n* grief or sorrow

DOLPHIN, -S *n* sea mammal of the whale family

DOLS ▶ dol

DOLT, -S *n* stupid person

DOLTISH

DOM, -S *n* title given to various monks and to certain of the canons regular

DOMAIN, -S *n* field of knowledge or activity

DOMAINAL

DOMAINE, -S *n* French estate

DOMAINS ▶ domain

DOMAL *adj* of a house

DOMANIAL ▶ domain

DOMATIUM, DOMATIA *n* plant cavity inhabited by commensal insects or mites or, occasionally, microorganisms

DOME, -D, -S, DOMING *n* rounded roof built on a circular base ▷ *vb* cover with or as if with a dome

DOMELIKE

DOMESDAY *same as* ▶ **doomsday**

DOMESTIC *adj* of one's own country or a specific country ▷ *n* person whose job is to do housework in someone else's house

DOMETT, -S *n* wool and cotton cloth

DOMIC *adj* dome-shaped

DOMICAL ▶ dome

DOMICIL, -S *same as* ▶ **domicile**

DOMICILE *n* place where one lives ▷ *vb* establish or be established in a dwelling place

DOMICILS ▶ domicil

DOMIER ▶ domy

DOMIEST ▶ domy

DOMINANT *adj* having authority or influence ▷ *n* dominant allele or character

DOMINATE *vb* control or govern

DOMINE, -S *n* clergyman

DOMINEE, -S *n* minister of the Dutch Reformed Church

DOMINEER *vb* act with arrogance or tyranny

DOMINEES ▶ dominee

DOMINES ▶ domine

DOMING ▶ dome

DOMINICK, -S *n* breed of chicken

DOMINIE, -S *n* minister or clergyman: also used as a term of address

DOMINION *same as* ▶ **dominium**

DOMINIUM *n* ownership or right to possession of property, esp realty

DOMINO, -S *n* small rectangular block marked with dots, used in dominoes

DOMINOES *n* game in which dominoes with matching halves are laid together

DOMINOS ▶ domino

DOMOIC *adj as in* **domoic acid** kind of amino acid

DOMS ▶ dom

DOMY, DOMIER, DOMIEST *adj* having a dome or domes

DON, -NED, -NING, -S *vb* put on (clothing) ▷ *n* member of the teaching staff at a university or college

DONA, -S *n* Spanish lady

DONAH, -S *n* woman

DONAIR, -S *same as* ▶ **doner**

DONARY, DONARIES *n* thing given for holy use

DONAS ▶ dona

DONATARY *n* recipient

DONATE, -D, -S, DONATING *vb* give, esp to a charity or organization

DONATION *n* donating

DONATISM *n* doctrine and beliefs relating to an early Christian sect

DONATIVE *n* gift or donation ▷ *adj* of or like a donation

DONATOR, -S ▶ donate

DONATORY *n* recipient

DONDER, -ED, -S *vb* beat (someone) up ▷ *n* wretch

DONE ▶ do

DONEE, -S *n* person who receives a gift

DONEGAL, -S *n* type of tweed

DONENESS *n* extent to which something is cooked

DONER *n as in* **doner kebab** grilled meat and salad served in pitta bread with chilli sauce

DONG, -ED, -ING, -S *n* deep reverberating sound of a large bell ▷ *vb* (of a bell) to make a deep reverberating sound

DONGA, -S *n* steep-sided gully created by soil erosion

DONGED ▶ dong

DONGING ▶ dong

DONGLE, -S *n* electronic device

DONGOLA, -S *n* leather tanned using a particular method

DONGS ▶ dong

DONING, -S *n* act of giving blood

DONJON, -S *n* heavily fortified central tower of a castle

DONKEY, -S *n* long-eared member of the horse family

DONKO, -S *n* tearoom or cafeteria in a factory, wharf area, etc

DONNA, -S *n* Italian lady

DONNARD *same as* ▶ **donnert**

DONNART *same as* ▶ **donnert**

DONNAS ▶ donna

DONNAT, -S *n* lazy person

DONNE, -S *same as* ▶ **donnee**

DONNED ▶ don

DONNEE, -S *n* subject or theme

DONNERD *adj* stupid

DONNERED *same as* ▶ **donnert**

DONNERT *adj* stunned

DONNES ▶ donne

DONNIES ▶ donny

DONNIKER *same as* > **donnicker**

DONNING ▶ don

DONNISH *adj* serious and academic

DONNISM, -S *n* loftiness

DONNOT, -S *n* lazy person

DONNY, DONNIES *same as* ▶ **danny**

DONOR, -S *n* person who gives blood or organs for medical use

DONS ▶ don

DONSHIP, -S *n* state or condition of being a don

DONSIE, -R, -ST *adj* rather unwell

DONSY *same as* ▶ **donsie**

DONUT, -S, -TED *same as* ▶ **doughnut**

DONZEL, -S *n* man of high birth

DOO, -S *a Scot word for* ▶ **dove**

DOOB, -S *n* type of Indian grass

DOOBIE, -S *same as* ► doob

DOOBREY, -S *n* thingumabob

DOOBRIE, -S *same as* ► doobrey

DOOBRY *n* thing whose name is unknown or forgotten

DOOBS ► doob

DOOCE, -D, -S, DOOCING *vb* dismiss (an employee) because of comments they have posted on the Internet

DOOCOT, -S *n* dovecote

DOODAD, -S *same as* ► doodah

DOODAH, -S *n* unnamed thing

DOODIES ► doody

DOODLE, -D, -S, DOODLING *vb* scribble or draw aimlessly ▷ *n* shape or picture drawn aimlessly

DOODLER -S

DOODOO, -S *n* excrement

DOODY, DOODIES *same as* ► doodoo

DOOFER, -S *n* thingamajig

DOOFUS, -ES *n* slow-witted or stupid person

DOOK, -ED, -ING, -S *n* wooden plug driven into a wall to hold a nail, screw, etc ▷ *vb* dip or plunge

DOOKET, -S *n* dovecote

DOOKING ► dook

DOOKS ► dook

DOOL, -S *n* boundary marker

DOOLALLY *adj* out of one's mind

DOOLAN, -S *n* Roman Catholic

DOOLE, -S *same as* ► dool

DOOLEE, -S *same as* ► doolie

DOOLES ► doole

DOOLIE, -S *n* enclosed couch on poles for carrying passengers

DOOLS ► dool

DOOLY *same as* ► doolie

DOOM, -ED, -ING, -S *n* death or a terrible fate ▷ *vb* destine or condemn to death or a terrible fate

DOOMFUL

DOOMIER ► doomy

DOOMIEST ► doomy

DOOMILY ► doomy

DOOMING ► doom

DOOMS ► doom

DOOMSDAY *n* day on which the Last Judgment will occur

DOOMSMAN, DOOMSMEN *n* pessimist

DOOMSTER *n* person habitually given to predictions of impending disaster or doom

DOOMY, DOOMIER, DOOMIEST *adj* despondent or pessimistic

DOON *same as* ► down

DOONA, -S *n* large quilt used as a bed cover

DOOR, -S *n* hinged or sliding panel for closing the entrance to a building, room, etc

DOORBELL *n* device for visitors to announce presence at a door

DOORCASE *same as* > doorframe

DOORED *adj* having a door

DOORJAMB *n* vertical post forming one side of a door frame

DOORKNOB *n* knob for opening and closing a door

DOORLESS ► door

DOORMAN, DOORMEN *n* man employed to be on duty at the entrance to a large public building

DOORMAT, -S *n* mat for wiping dirt from shoes before going indoors

DOORMEN ► doorman

DOORN, -S *n* thorn

DOORNAIL *n as in* **dead as a doornail** dead beyond any doubt

DOORNS ► doorn

DOORPOST *same as* ► doorjamb

DOORS ► door

DOORSILL *n* horizontal member of wood, stone, etc, forming the bottom of a doorframe

DOORSMAN, DOORSMEN *n* doorkeeper

DOORSTEP *n* step in front of a door

DOORSTOP *n* object which prevents a door from closing or striking a wall

DOORWAY, -S *n* opening into a building or room

DOORYARD *n* yard in front of the front or back door of a house

DOOS ► doo

DOOSRA, -S *n* delivery in cricket

DOOWOP, -S *n* style of singing in harmony

DOOZER, -S *same as* ► doozy

DOOZIE, -S *same as* ► doozy

DOOZY *n* something excellent

DOP, -PED, -S *n* small drink ▷ *vb* fail to reach the required standard in (an examination, course, etc)

DOPA, -S *n* precursor to dopamine

DOPAMINE *n* chemical found in the brain that acts as a neurotransmitter

DOPANT, -S *n* element or compound used to dope a semiconductor

DOPAS ► dopa

DOPATTA, -S *n* headscarf

DOPE, -D, -S, -ST *n* additive used to improve the properties of something ▷ *vb* apply a dopant ▷ *adj* excellent

DOPER, -S *n* person who administers dope

DOPES ► dope

DOPEST ► dope

DOPESTER *n* person who makes predictions, esp in sport or politics

DOPEY, DOPIER, DOPIEST *adj* half-asleep, drowsy

DOPIAZA, -S *n* Indian meat or fish dish cooked in onion sauce

DOPIER ► dopey

DOPIEST ► dopey

DOPILY ► dopey

DOPINESS ► dopey

DOPING, -S ► dope

DOPPED ► dop

DOPPER, -S *n* member of an Afrikaner church which practises a strict Calvinism

DOPPIE, -S *n* cartridge case

DOPPING, -S ► dop

DOPPIO, -S *n* double measure, esp of espresso coffee

DOPS ► dop

DOPY *same as* ► dopey

DOR, -RED, -RING, -S *n* European dung beetle ▷ *vb* mock

DORAD, -S *n* South American river fish

DORADO, -S *n* large marine percoid fish

DORADS ► dorad

DORB, -S *same as* ► dorba

DORBA, -S *n* stupid, inept, or clumsy person

DORBS ► dorb

DORBUG, -S *n* type of beetle

DORE, -S *n* walleye fish

DOREE, -S *n* type of fish

DORES ► dore

DORHAWK, -S *n* nightjar

DORIC *adj* rustic

DORIDOID *n* shell-less mollusc

DORIES ► dory

DORIS *n* woman

DORISE, -D, -S, DORISING *same as* ► dorize

DORIZE, -D, -S, DORIZING *vb* become Doric

DORK, -S *n* stupid person

DORKIER ► **dorky**
DORKIEST ► **dorky**
DORKISH *adj* stupid or contemptible
DORKS ► **dork**
DORKY, DORKIER, DORKIEST ► **dork**
DORLACH, -S *n* quiver of arrows
DORM, -S *same as* > **dormitory**
DORMANCY ► **dormant**
DORMANT, -S *n* supporting beam ▷ *adj* temporarily quiet, inactive, or not being used
DORMER, -S *n* window that sticks out from a sloping roof
DORMERED *adj* having dormer windows
DORMERS ► **dormer**
DORMICE ► **dormouse**
DORMIE *adj* (in golf) leading by as many holes as there are left
DORMIENT *adj* dormant
DORMIN, -S *n* hormone found in plants
DORMOUSE, DORMICE *n* small mouselike rodent with a furry tail
DORMS ► **dorm**
DORMY *same as* ► **dormie**
DORNECK, -S *same as* ► **dornick**
DORNICK, -S *n* heavy damask cloth
DORNOCK, -S *n* type of coarse fabric
DORP, -S *n* small town
DORPER, -S *n* breed of sheep
DORPS ► **dorp**
DORR, -S *same as* ► **dor**
DORRED ► **dor**
DORRING ► **dor**
DORRS ► **dorr**
DORS ► **dor**
DORSA ► **dorsum**
DORSAD *adj* towards the back or dorsal aspect
DORSAL, -S *adj* of or on the back ▷ *n* dorsal fin
DORSALLY
DORSE, -S *n* type of small fish
DORSEL, -S *another word for* ► **dossal**
DORSER, -S *n* hanging tapestry
DORSES ► **dorse**
DORSUM, DORSA *n* the back
DORT, -ED, -ING, -S *vb* sulk
DORTER, -S *n* dormitory
DORTIER ► **dorty**
DORTIEST ► **dorty**
DORTING ► **dort**
DORTOUR, -S *same as* ► **dorter**

DORTS ► **dort**
DORTY, DORTIER, DORTIEST *adj* haughty, or sullen
DORY, DORIES *n* spiny-finned edible sea fish
DORYMAN, DORYMEN *n* person who fishes from a small boat called a dory
DOS ► **do**
DOSA, -I, -S *n* Indian pancake made from rice flour
DOSAGE, -S *same as* ► **dose**
DOSAI ► **dosa**
DOSAS ► **dosa**
DOSE, -D, -S, DOSING *n* specific quantity of a medicine taken at one time ▷ *vb* give a dose to
DOSEH, -S *n* former Egyptian religious ceremony
DOSER, -S ► **dose**
DOSES ► **dose**
DOSH, -ES *n* money
DOSHA, -S *n* (in Hinduism) any of the three energies believed to be in the body
DOSHES ► **dosh**
DOSING ► **dose**
DOSOLOGY *same as* > **dosiology**
DOSS, -ED, -ES, -ING *vb* sleep, esp in a dosshouse ▷ *n* bed, esp in a dosshouse
DOSSAL, -S *n* ornamental hanging used in churches
DOSSED ► **doss**
DOSSEL, -S *same as* ► **dossal**
DOSSER, -S *n* bag or basket for carrying objects on the back
DOSSERET *n* stone above column supporting an arch
DOSSERS ► **dosser**
DOSSES ► **doss**
DOSSIER, -S *n* collection of documents about a subject or person
DOSSIL, -S *n* lint for dressing wound
DOSSING ► **doss**
DOST *a singular form of the present tense (indicative mood) of* ► **do**
DOT, -S, -TED, -TING *n* small round mark ▷ *vb* mark with a dot
DOTAGE, -S *n* weakness as a result of old age
DOTAL ► **dot**
DOTANT, -S *another word for* ► **dotard**
DOTARD, -S *n* person who is feeble-minded through old age
DOTARDLY
DOTATION *n* act of giving a dowry

DOTCOM, -S *n* company that does most of its business on the Internet
DOTE, -D, -S *vb* love to an excessive or foolish degree
DOTER -S
DOTH *a singular form of the present tense of* ► **do**
DOTIER ► **doty**
DOTIEST ► **doty**
DOTING, -S ► **dote**
DOTINGLY ► **dote**
DOTINGS ► **doting**
DOTISH *adj* foolish
DOTS ► **dot**
DOTTED ► **dot**
DOTTEL, -S *same as* ► **dottle**
DOTTER, -S ► **dot**
DOTTEREL *n* rare kind of plover
DOTTERS ► **dotter**
DOTTIER ► **dotty**
DOTTIEST ► **dotty**
DOTTILY ► **dotty**
DOTTING ► **dot**
DOTTLE, -R, -S, -ST *n* tobacco left in a pipe after smoking ▷ *adj* relating to dottle
DOTTLED *adj* foolish
DOTTLER ► **dottle**
DOTTLES ► **dottle**
DOTTLEST ► **dottle**
DOTTREL, -S *same as* ► **dotterel**
DOTTY, DOTTIER, DOTTIEST *adj* rather eccentric
DOTY, DOTIER, DOTIEST *adj* (of wood) rotten
DOUANE, -S *n* customs house
DOUANIER *n* customs officer

> This is a French word for a customs official; it's not easy to see in play, but its combination of common letters makes it one of the 8-letter bonus words that comes up most often.

DOUAR, -S *same as* ► **duar**
DOUBLE, -D, DOUBLING *adj* as much again in number, amount, size, etc ▷ *adv* twice over ▷ *n* twice the number, amount, size, etc ▷ *vb* make or become twice as much or as many
DOUBLER -S
DOUBLES *n* game between two pairs of players
DOUBLET, -S *n* man's close-fitting jacket, with or without sleeves
DOUBLING ► **double**
DOUBLOON *n* former Spanish gold coin
DOUBLURE *n* decorative lining of vellum or leather,

etc, on the inside of a book cover

DOUBLY adv in a greater degree, quantity, or measure

DOUBT, -ED, -ING, -S n uncertainty about the truth, facts, or existence of something ▷ vb question the truth of

DOUBTER -S

DOUBTFUL adj unlikely ▷ n person who is undecided or uncertain about an issue

DOUBTING ▸ doubt

DOUBTS ▸ doubt

DOUC, -S n Old World monkey

DOUCE, -R, -ST adj quiet

DOUCELY

DOUCET, -S n former flute-like instrument

DOUCEUR, -S n gratuity, tip, or bribe

DOUCHE, -D, -S n stream of water onto or into the body ▷ vb cleanse or treat by means of a douche

DOUCHING n act of douching

DOUCINE, -S n type of moulding for cornice

DOUCS ▸ douc

DOUGH, -S n thick mixture used for making bread etc

DOUGHBOY n infantryman, esp in World War I

DOUGHIER ▸ doughy

DOUGHNUT n small cake of sweetened dough fried in deep fat ▷ vb surround a speaker to give the impression that Parliament is crowded

DOUGHS ▸ dough

DOUGHT ▸ dow

DOUGHTY adj brave and determined

DOUGHY, DOUGHIER adj resembling dough in consistency, colour, etc

DOUK, -ED, -ING, -S same as ▸ dook

DOULA, -S n woman who supports families during pregnancy and childbirth

DOULEIA, -S same as ▸ dulia

This word refers to the inferior veneration accorded to saints and angels, as distinct from **latria**, the veneration accorded to God alone, and is another of the few 7-letter words that use all five vowels. It's surprising how often you want to do this!

DOUM, -S n as in **doum palm** variety of palm tree

DOUMA, -S same as ▸ duma

DOUMS ▸ doum

DOUN same as ▸ down

DOUP, -S n bottom

DOUPIONI n type of fabric

DOUPS ▸ doup

DOUR, -ER, -EST adj sullen and unfriendly

DOURA, -S same as ▸ durra

DOURAH, -S same as ▸ durra

DOURAS ▸ doura

DOURER ▸ dour

DOUREST ▸ dour

DOURINE, -S n infectious venereal disease of horses

DOURLY ▸ dour

DOURNESS ▸ dour

DOUSE, -D, -S, DOUSING vb drench with water or other liquid ▷ n immersion

DOUSER -S

DOUT, -ED, -ING, -S vb extinguish

DOUTER -S

DOUX adj sweet

DOUZEPER n distinguished person

DOVE, -D, -S, DOVING vb be semi-conscious ▷ n bird with a heavy body, small head, and short legs

DOVECOT, -S same as ▸ dovecote

DOVECOTE n structure for housing pigeons

DOVECOTS ▸ dovecot

DOVED ▸ dove

DOVEISH adj dovelike

DOVEKEY, -S same as ▸ dovekie

DOVEKIE, -S n small short-billed auk

DOVELET, -S n small dove

DOVELIKE ▸ dove

DOVEN, -ED, -ING, -S vb pray

DOVER, -ED, -ING, -S vb doze ▷ n doze

DOVES ▸ dove

DOVETAIL n joint containing wedge-shaped tenons ▷ vb fit together neatly

DOVIE, -R, -ST Scots word for ▸ stupid

DOVING ▸ dove

DOVISH ▸ dove

DOW, DOCHT, DOUGHT, -ED, -ING, -S vb archaic word meaning be of worth

DOWABLE adj capable of being endowed

DOWAGER, -S n widow possessing property or a title obtained from her husband

DOWAR, -S same as ▸ duar

DOWD, -S n woman who wears unfashionable clothes

DOWDIER ▸ dowdy

DOWDIES ▸ dowdy

DOWDIEST ▸ dowdy

DOWDILY ▸ dowdy

DOWDS ▸ dowd

DOWDY, DOWDIER, DOWDIES, DOWDIEST adj dull and old-fashioned ▷ n dowdy woman

DOWDYISH

DOWDYISM

DOWED ▸ dow

DOWEL, -ED, -LED, -S n wooden or metal peg used as a fastener ▷ vb join pieces of wood using dowels

DOWELING n joining of two pieces of wood using dowels

DOWELLED ▸ dowel

DOWELS ▸ dowel

DOWER, -ED, -ING, -S n life interest in a part of her husband's estate allotted to a widow by law ▷ vb endow

DOWERIES ▸ dowery

DOWERING ▸ dower

DOWERS ▸ dower

DOWERY, DOWERIES same as ▸ dowry

DOWF adj dull; listless

DOWFNESS

DOWIE, -R, -ST adj dull and dreary

DOWING ▸ dow

DOWL, -S n fluff

DOWLAS, -ES n coarse fabric

DOWLE, -S same as ▸ dowl

DOWLIER ▸ dowly

DOWLIEST ▸ dowly

DOWLNE, -S obsolete form of ▸ down

DOWLNEY

DOWLS ▸ dowl

DOWLY, DOWLIER, DOWLIEST adj dull

DOWN, -ED, -ING, -S adv indicating movement to or position in a lower place ▷ adj depressed, unhappy ▷ vb drink quickly ▷ n soft fine feathers

DOWNA obsolete Scots form of ▸ cannot

DOWNBEAT adj gloomy ▷ n first beat of a bar

DOWNBOW, -S n (in music) a downward stroke of the bow across the strings

DOWNCAST adj sad, dejected ▷ n ventilation shaft

DOWNCOME same as ▸ downcomer

DOWNCRY vb denigrate or disparage

DOWNED ▸ down

DOWNER, -S n depressing experience

DOWNFALL n sudden loss of success or power

DOWNFLOW n something that flows down

DOWNHAUL n line for hauling down a sail or for increasing the tension at its luff

DOWNHILL adj going or sloping down ▷ adv towards the bottom of a hill ▷ n downward slope

DOWNHOLE adj (in the oil industry) denoting any piece of equipment that is used in the well itself

DOWNIER ► downy

DOWNIES ► downy

DOWNIEST ► downy

DOWNILY adv in a manner resembling or indicating a layer of soft fine feathers or hairs

DOWNING ► down

DOWNLAND same as ► downs

DOWNLESS ► down

DOWNLIKE ► down

DOWNLINK n satellite transmission channel

DOWNLOAD vb transfer data from one computer to another ▷ n file transferred in such a way

DOWNLOW, -S n as in **on the downlow** not widely known

DOWNMOST adj lowest

DOWNPIPE n pipe for carrying rainwater from a roof gutter to the ground or to a drain

DOWNPLAY vb play down

DOWNPOUR n heavy fall of rain

DOWNRATE vb reduce in value or importance

DOWNRUSH n instance of rushing down

DOWNS pl n low grassy hills, esp in S England

DOWNSIDE n disadvantageous aspect of a situation

DOWNSIZE vb reduce the number of people employed by (a company)

DOWNSPIN n sudden downturn

DOWNTICK n small decrease

DOWNTIME n time during which a computer or other machine is not working

DOWNTOWN n central or lower part of a city, esp the main commercial area ▷ adv towards, to, or into this area ▷ adj of, relating to, or situated in the downtown area

DOWNTROD adj downtrodden

DOWNTURN n drop in the success of an economy or a business

DOWNWARD same as > **downwards**

DOWNWARP n wide depression in the earth's surface

DOWNWASH n downward deflection of an airflow, esp one caused by an aircraft wing

DOWNWIND adj in the same direction towards which the wind is blowing

DOWNY, DOWNIER, DOWNIES, DOWNIEST adj covered with soft fine hair or feathers ▷ n as in **the downy** bed

DOWNZONE vb reduce density of housing in area

DOWP, -S same as ► doup

DOWRY, DOWRIES n property brought by a woman to her husband at marriage

DOWS ► dow

DOWSABEL n sweetheart

DOWSE, -D, -S same as ► douse

DOWSER -S

DOWSET, -S same as ► doucet

DOWSING, -S n act of dowsing

DOWT, -S n cigarette butt

DOXAPRAM n drug used to stimulate the respiration

DOXASTIC adj of or relating to belief ▷ n branch of logic that studies the concept of belief

DOXIE same as ► doxy

DOXIES ► doxy

DOXOLOGY n short hymn of praise to God

DOXY, DOXIES n opinion or doctrine, esp concerning religious matters

DOY, -S n beloved person: used esp as an endearment

DOYEN, -S n senior member of a group, profession, or society

DOYENNE -S

DOYLEY, -S same as ► doily

DOYLY, DOYLIES same as ► doily

DOYS ► doy

DOZE, -S vb sleep lightly or briefly ▷ n short sleep

DOZED adj (of timber or rubber) rotten or decayed

DOZEN, -ED, -ING, -S n set of twelve vb stun

DOZENTH -S

DOZER, -S ► doze

DOZES ► doze

DOZIER ► dozy

DOZIEST ► dozy

DOZILY ► dozy

DOZINESS ► dozy

DOZING, -S ► doze

DOZY, DOZIER, DOZIEST adj feeling sleepy

DRAB, -BER, -BEST, -S adj dull and dreary ▷ n light olive-brown colour

DRABBET, -S n yellowish-brown fabric of coarse linen

DRABBIER ► drabby

DRABBISH adj slightly drab

DRABBLE, -D, -S vb make or become wet or dirty

DRABBLER n part fixed to bottom of sail

DRABBLES ► drabble

DRABBY, DRABBIER adj slightly drab

DRABETTE n type of rough linen fabric

DRABLER, -S same as ► drabbler

DRABLY ► drab

DRABNESS ► drab

DRABS ► drab

DRAC same as ► drack

DRACAENA n type of tropical plant often cultivated as a house plant for its decorative foliage

DRACENA, -S same as ► dracaena

DRACHM, -S same as ► dram

DRACHMA, -E, -I, -S n former monetary unit of Greece

DRACHMS ► drachm

DRACK adj (esp of a woman) unattractive

DRACO n as in **draco lizard** flying lizard

DRACONE, -S n large container towed by a ship

DRACONIC same as > **draconian**

DRAD archaic past of ► dread

DRAFF, -S n residue of husks used as a food for cattle

DRAFFIER ► draffy

DRAFFISH adj worthless

DRAFFS ► draff

DRAFFY, DRAFFIER ► draff

DRAFT, -ED, -ING, -S same as ► draught

DRAFTEE, -S n conscript

DRAFTER, -S ► draft

DRAFTIER ► drafty

DRAFTILY ► drafty

DRAFTING ► draft

DRAFTS ► draft

DRAFTY, DRAFTIER same as ► draughty

D

DRAG, -GED, -GING, -S vb pull with force, esp along the ground ▷ n person or thing that slows up progress

DRAGEE, -S n sweet made of a nut, fruit, etc, coated with a hard sugar icing

DRAGGED ▸ drag

DRAGGER, -S ▸ drag

DRAGGIER ▸ draggy

DRAGGING ▸ drag

DRAGGLE, -D, -S vb make or become wet or dirty by trailing on the ground

DRAGGY, DRAGGIER adj slow or boring

DRAGLINE same as ▸ dragrope

DRAGNET, -S n net used to scour the bottom of a pond or river

DRAGOMAN, DRAGOMEN n (in some Middle Eastern countries) professional interpreter or guide

DRAGON, -S n mythical fire-breathing monster like a huge lizard

DRAGONET n type of small spiny-finned fish with a flat head and a slender brightly coloured body

DRAGONNE adj dragonlike

DRAGONS ▸ dragon

DRAGOON, -S n heavily armed cavalryman ▷ vb coerce, force

DRAGROPE n rope used to drag military equipment, esp artillery

DRAGS ▸ drag

DRAGSMAN, DRAGSMEN n carriage driver

DRAGSTER n car specially built or modified for drag racing

DRAGWAY, -S n race course for drag racing

DRAIL, -ED, -ING, -S n weighted hook used in trolling ▷ vb fish with a drail

DRAIN, -ED, -ING, -S n pipe or channel that carries off water or sewage ▷ vb draw off or remove liquid from

DRAINAGE n system of drains

DRAINED ▸ drain

DRAINER, -S n person or thing that drains

DRAINING ▸ drain

DRAINS ▸ drain

DRAISENE same as ▸ draisine

DRAISINE n light rail vehicle

DRAKE, -S n male duck

DRAM, -MED, -MING, -S n small amount of a strong alcoholic drink, esp whisky ▷ vb drink a dram

DRAMA, -S n serious play for theatre, television, or radio

DRAMADY same as ▸ dramedy

DRAMAS ▸ drama

DRAMATIC adj of or like drama

DRAMEDY n television or film drama in which there are important elements of comedy

DRAMMACH n oatmeal mixed with cold water

DRAMMED ▸ dram

DRAMMING ▸ dram

DRAMMOCK same as ▸ drammach

DRAMS ▸ dram

DRAMSHOP n bar

DRANGWAY n narrow lane

DRANK ▸ drink

DRANT, -ED, -ING, -S vb drone

DRAP, -PED, -PING, -S a Scot word for ▸ drop

DRAPABLE ▸ drape

DRAPE, -D, DRAPING vb cover with material, usu in folds ▷ n piece of cloth hung at a window or opening as a screen

DRAPER, -S n person who sells fabrics and sewing materials

DRAPERY n fabric or clothing arranged and draped

DRAPES pl n material hung at an opening or window to shut light or to provide privacy

DRAPET, -S n cloth

DRAPEY, DRAPIEST adj hanging in loose folds

DRAPIER, -S n draper

DRAPIEST ▸ drapey

DRAPING ▸ drape

DRAPPED ▸ drap

DRAPPIE, -S n little drop

DRAPPING ▸ drap

DRAPPY n drop (of liquid)

DRAPS ▸ drap

DRASTIC, -S n strong purgative ▷ adj strong and severe

DRAT, -S, -TING interj exclamation of annoyance ▷ vb curse

DRATTED adj wretched

DRATTING ▸ drat

DRAUGHT vb make preliminary plan ▷ n current of cold air, esp in an enclosed space ▷ adj (of an animal) used for pulling heavy loads

DRAUGHTS n game for two players using a draughtboard and 12 draughtsmen each

DRAUGHTY adj exposed to draughts of air

DRAUNT, -ED, -S same as ▸ drant

DRAVE archaic past of ▸ drive

DRAW, -N, -S, DREW vb sketch (a figure, picture, etc) with a pencil or pen ▷ n attraction

DRAWABLE ▷

DRAWBACK n disadvantage ▷ vb move backwards

DRAWBAR, -S n strong metal bar on a tractor, locomotive, etc

DRAWBORE n hole bored through tenon

DRAWCORD n cord for drawing tight eg round a hood

DRAWDOWN n decrease

DRAWEE, -S n person or organization on which payment is drawn

DRAWER n sliding box-shaped part of a piece of furniture, used for storage

DRAWERS pl n undergarment worn on the lower part of the body

DRAWING, -S ▸ draw

DRAWL, -ED, -S vb speak slowly, with long vowel sounds ▷ n drawling manner of speech

DRAWLER -S

DRAWLIER ▸ drawly

DRAWLING ▸ drawl

DRAWLS ▸ drawl

DRAWLY, DRAWLIER ▸ drawl

DRAWN ▸ draw

DRAWS ▸ draw

DRAWTUBE n type of tube used in a telescope

DRAY, -ED, -ING, -S vb pull using cart ▷ n low cart used for carrying heavy loads

DRAYAGE, -S n act of transporting something a short distance

DRAYED ▸ dray

DRAYING ▸ dray

DRAYMAN, DRAYMEN n driver of a dray

DRAYS ▸ dray

DREAD, -ED, -EST, -ING, -S vb anticipate with apprehension or fear ▷ n great fear ▷ adj awesome

DREADER -S

DREADFUL n cheap, often lurid or sensational book or magazine ▷ adj very disagreeable or shocking

DREADING ▸ dread

DREADLY ▸ dread

DREADS ▸ dread

DREAM, -ED, -S, -T n imagined events experienced while asleep ▷ vb see imaginary pictures in the mind while asleep ▷ adj ideal
DREAMER, -S n person who dreams habitually
DREAMERY n dream world
DREAMFUL ▶ dream
DREAMIER ▶ dreamy
DREAMILY ▶ dreamy
DREAMING ▶ dream
DREAMS ▶ dream
DREAMT ▶ dream
DREAMY, DREAMIER adj vague or impractical
DREAR, -ER, -EST, -S same as ▶ dreary
DREARE, -S obsolete form of ▶ drear
DREARER ▶ drear
DREARES ▶ dreare
DREAREST ▶ drear
DREARIER ▶ dreary
DREARIES ▶ dreary
DREARILY ▶ dreary
DREARING n sorrow
DREARS ▶ drear
DREARY, DREARIER, DREARIES adj dull, boring ▷ n dreary thing or person
DRECK, -S n rubbish
DRECKIER ▶ drecky
DRECKISH adj like rubbish
DRECKS ▶ dreck
DRECKY, DRECKIER ▶ dreck
DREDGE, -D, -S, DREDGING vb clear or search (a river bed or harbour) by removing silt or mud
DREDGER, -S n machine used to remove mud from a river bed or harbour
DREDGES ▶ dredge
DREDGING ▶ dredge
DREE, -D, -ING, -R, -S, -ST vb endure ▷ adj dreary
DREG n small quantity
DREGGIER ▶ dreggy
DREGGISH adj foul
DREGGY, DREGGIER adj like or full of dregs
DREGS pl n solid particles that settle at the bottom of some liquids
DREICH, -ER adj dreary
DREIDEL, -S n spinning top
DREIDL, -S same as ▶ dreidel
DREIGH, -ER same as ▶ dreich
DREK, -S same as ▶ dreck
DREKKIER ▶ drekky
DREKKISH same as ▶ dreckish
DREKKY, DREKKIER ▶ drek
DREKS ▶ drek
DRENCH, -ED, -ES, DRENT vb make completely wet ▷ n act

or an instance of drenching
DRENCHER
DREPANID n type of moth of the superfamily which comprises the hook-tip moths
DRERE, -S obsolete form of ▶ drear
DRESS, -ED, -ES, DREST n one-piece garment for a woman or girl ▷ vb put clothes on ▷ adj suitable for a formal occasion
DRESSAGE n training of a horse to perform manoeuvres in response to the rider's body signals
DRESSED ▶ dress
DRESSER, -S n piece of furniture with shelves and with cupboards
DRESSES ▶ dress
DRESSIER ▶ dressy
DRESSILY ▶ dressy
DRESSING n sauce for salad
DRESSY, DRESSIER adj (of clothes) elegant
DREST ▶ dress
DREVILL, -S n offensive person
DREW ▶ draw
DREY, -S n squirrel's nest
DRIB, -BED, -BING, -S vb flow in drops
DRIBBER -S
DRIBBLE, -D, -S vb (allow to) flow in drops ▷ n small quantity of liquid falling in drops
DRIBBLER
DRIBBLET same as ▶ driblet
DRIBBLY ▶ dribble
DRIBLET, -S n small amount
DRIBS ▶ drib
DRICE, -S n pellets of frozen carbon dioxide
DRICKSIE same as ▶ druxy
DRIED ▶ dry
DRIEGH adj tedious
DRIER, -S ▶ dry
DRIES ▶ dry
DRIEST ▶ dry
DRIFT, -ED, -S vb be carried along by currents of air or water ▷ n something piled up by the wind or current
DRIFTAGE n act of drifting
DRIFTED ▶ drift
DRIFTER, -S n person who moves aimlessly from place to place or job to job
DRIFTIER ▶ drifty
DRIFTING n act of drifting
DRIFTNET n fishing net that drifts with the tide
DRIFTPIN same as ▶ drift
DRIFTS ▶ drift
DRIFTY, DRIFTIER ▶ drift

DRILL, -ED, -S n tool or machine for boring holes ▷ vb bore a hole in (something) with or as if with a drill
DRILLER -S
DRILLING n type of hard-wearing cloth
DRILLS ▶ drill
DRILY adv in a dry manner
DRINK, DRANK, -ING, -S vb swallow (a liquid) ▷ n (portion of) a liquid suitable for drinking
DRINKER, -S n person who drinks
DRINKING ▶ drink
DRINKS ▶ drink
DRIP, -PED, -PING, -S, -T vb (let) fall in drops ▷ n falling of drops of liquid
DRIPLESS
DRIPPER -S
DRIPPIER ▶ drippy
DRIPPILY ▶ drippy
DRIPPING ▶ drip
DRIPPY, DRIPPIER adj mawkish, insipid, or inane
DRIPS ▶ drip
DRIPT ▶ drip
DRISHEEN n pudding made of sheep's intestines filled with meal and sheep's blood
DRIVABLE ▶ drive
DRIVE, -N, -S vb guide the movement of (a vehicle) ▷ n journey by car, van, etc
DRIVEL, -ED, -S n foolish talk ▷ vb speak foolishly
DRIVELER
DRIVEN ▶ drive
DRIVER, -S n person who drives a vehicle
DRIVES ▶ drive
DRIVEWAY n path for vehicles connecting a building to a public road
DRIVING, -S ▶ drive
DRIZZLE, -D, -S n very light rain ▷ vb rain lightly
DRIZZLY
DROGER, -S n W Indian boat
DROGHER, -S same as ▶ droger
DROGUE, -S n any funnel-like device used as a sea anchor
DROGUET, -S n woollen fabric
DROICH, -S n dwarf
DROICHY adj dwarfish
DROID, -S same as ▶ android
DROIL, -ED, -ING, -S vb carry out boring menial work
DROIT, -S n legal or moral right or claim
DROKE, -S n small group of trees

DROLE, -R, -S, -ST adj amusing ▷ n scoundrel

DROLL, -ED, -ER, -EST, -ING, -S vb speak wittily ▷ adj quaintly amusing

DROLLERY n humour

DROLLEST ▸ droll

DROLLING ▸ droll

DROLLISH adj somewhat droll

DROLLS ▸ droll

DROLLY ▸ droll

DROME, -S same as
> **aerodrome**

DROMIC adj relating to running track

DROMICAL same as ▸ dromic

DROMOI ▸ dromos

DROMON, -S same as
▸ **dromond**

DROMOND, -S n sailing vessel of the 12th to 15th centuries

DROMONS ▸ dromon

DROMOS, DROMOI n Greek passageway

DRONE, -D, -S, DRONING n male bee ▷ vb make a monotonous low dull sound

DRONER -S

DRONGO, -ES, -S n tropical songbird

DRONIER ▸ drony

DRONIEST ▸ drony

DRONING ▸ drone

DRONISH ▸ drone

DRONKLAP n South African word for a drunkard

DRONY, DRONIER, DRONIEST adj monotonous

DROOB, -S n pathetic person

DROOG, -S n ruffian

DROOGISH

DROOK, -ED, -ING, -S same as
▸ **drouk**

DROOKIT same as ▸ droukit

DROOKS ▸ drook

DROOL, -ED, -ING, -S vb show excessive enthusiasm (for)

DROOLIER ▸ drooly

DROOLING ▸ drool

DROOLS ▸ drool

DROOLY, DROOLIER adj tending to drool

DROOME, -S obsolete form of
▸ **drum**

DROOP, -ED, -S vb hang downwards loosely ▷ n act or state of drooping

DROOPIER ▸ droopy

DROOPILY ▸ droopy

DROOPING ▸ droop

DROOPS ▸ droop

DROOPY, DROOPIER adj hanging or sagging downwards

DROP, -PED, -PING, -S, -T vb (allow to) fall vertically

▷ n small quantity of liquid forming a round shape

DROPFLY n (angling) artificial fly

DROPHEAD adj as in
drophead coupe two-door car with a folding roof and sloping back

DROPKICK n kick in which a ball is dropped and then kicked

DROPLET, -S n very small drop of liquid

DROPLOCK adj as in **droplock loan** type of bank loan ▷ n type of bank loan

DROPOUT, -S n person who rejects conventional society

DROPPED ▸ drop

DROPPER, -S n small tube with a rubber part at one end

DROPPING ▸ drop

DROPPLE, -S n trickle

DROPS ▸ drop

DROPSEED n type of grass

DROPSHOT n type of tennis shot

DROPSIED ▸ dropsy

DROPSY, DROPSIES n illness in which watery fluid collects in the body

DROPT ▸ drop

DROPTOP, -S n convertible car

DROPWISE adv in form of a drop

DROPWORT n Eurasian plant with cream-coloured flowers, related to the rose

DROSERA, -S n insectivorous plant

DROSHKY n four-wheeled carriage, formerly used in Russia

DROSKY, DROSKIES same as
▸ **droshky**

DROSS, -ES n scum formed on the surfaces of molten metals

DROSSY DROSSIER

DROSTDY, -S n office of landdrost

DROUGHT, -S n prolonged shortage of rainfall

DROUGHTY

DROUK, -ED, -ING, -S vb drench

DROUKIT adj drenched

DROUKS ▸ drouk

DROUTH, -S same as
▸ **drought**

DROUTHY adj thirsty or dry

DROVE, -D, -S vb drive livestock ▷ n moving crowd

DROVER, -S n person who drives sheep or cattle

DROVES ▸ drove

DROVING, -S ▸ drove

DROW, -S n sea fog

DROWN, -ED, -ING, -S vb die or kill by immersion in liquid

DROWND, -ED, -S dialect form of ▸ drown

DROWNED ▸ drown

DROWNER, -S ▸ drown

DROWNING ▸ drown

DROWNS ▸ drown

DROWS ▸ drow

DROWSE, -D, -S, DROWSING vb be sleepy, dull, or sluggish ▷ n state of being drowsy

DROWSIER ▸ drowsy

DROWSILY ▸ drowsy

DROWSING ▸ drowse

DROWSY, DROWSIER adj feeling sleepy

DRUB, -BED, -BING, -S vb beat as with a stick ▷ n blow, as from a stick

DRUBBER -S

DRUCKEN adj drunken

DRUDGE, -D, -S, DRUDGING n person who works hard at uninteresting tasks ▷ vb work at such tasks

DRUDGER -S

DRUDGERY n uninteresting work that must be done

DRUDGES ▸ drudge

DRUDGING ▸ drudge

DRUDGISM ▸ drudge

DRUG, -GED, -GING, -S n substance used in the treatment or prevention of disease ▷ vb give a drug to (a person or animal) to cause sleepiness or unconsciousness

DRUGGER, -S n druggist

DRUGGET, -S n coarse fabric used as a protective floor-covering, etc

DRUGGIER ▸ druggy

DRUGGING ▸ drug

DRUGGIST n pharmacist

DRUGGY, DRUGGIER ▸ drug

DRUGLESS adj having no drugs

DRUGS ▸ drug

DRUID, -S n member of an ancient order of priests in the pre-Christian era

DRUIDESS

DRUIDIC

DRUIDISM

DRUIDRY

DRUM, -MED, -S n percussion instrument ▷ vb play (music) on a drum

DRUMBEAT n sound made by beating a drum

DRUMBLE, -D, -S vb be inactive

DRUMFIRE n heavy, rapid, and continuous gunfire, the

sound of which resembles rapid drumbeats
DRUMFISH n one of several types of fish that make a drumming sound
DRUMHEAD n part of a drum that is struck
DRUMLIER ▶ drumly
DRUMLIKE ▶ drum
DRUMLIN, -S n streamlined mound of glacial drift
DRUMLY, DRUMLIER adj dismal; dreary
DRUMMED ▶ drum
DRUMMER, -S n person who plays a drum or drums
DRUMMIES ▶ drummy
DRUMMING n act of drumming
DRUMMOCK same as
▶ drammock
DRUMMY, DRUMMIES n (in South Africa) drum majorette
DRUMROLL n continued repeated sound of drum
DRUMS ▶ drum
DRUNK, -ER, -EST, -S adj intoxicated with alcoholic drink ▷ n drunk person
DRUNKARD n person who frequently gets drunk
DRUNKEN adj drunk or frequently drunk
DRUNKER ▶ drunk
DRUNKEST ▶ drunk
DRUNKISH adj rather drunk
DRUNKS ▶ drunk
DRUPE, -S n fleshy fruit with a stone, such as the peach or cherry
DRUPEL, -S same as
▶ drupelet
DRUPELET n small drupe, usually one of a number forming a compound fruit
DRUPELS ▶ drupel
DRUPES ▶ drupe
DRUSE, -S n aggregate of small crystals within a cavity
DRUSEN pl n small deposits of material on the retina
DRUSES ▶ druse
DRUSY, DRUSIER, DRUSIEST adj made of tiny crystals
DRUTHER n preference
DRUTHERS n preference
DRUXY, DRUXIER, DRUXIEST adj (of wood) having decayed white spots
DRY, DRIED, DRIES, DRIEST, -EST, -S adj lacking moisture ▷ vb make or become dry
DRYABLE
DRYAD, -ES, -S n wood nymph
DRYADIC

DRYAS n alpine plant with white flowers
DRYBEAT, -S vb beat severely
DRYER, -S ▶ dry
DRYEST ▶ dry
DRYING, -S ▶ dry
DRYISH adj fairly dry
DRYLAND, -S n arid area
DRYLOT, -S n livestock enclosure
DRYLY same as ▶ **drily**
DRYMOUTH n condition of insufficient saliva
DRYNESS ▶ dry
DRYPOINT n copper engraving technique using a hard steel needle
DRYS ▶ dry
DRYSTONE adj (of a wall) made without mortar
DRYSUIT, -S n waterproof rubber suit for wearing in esp cold water
DRYWALL, -S n wall built without mortar ▷ vb build a wall without mortar
DRYWELL, -S n type of sewage disposal system
DSO, -S same as ▶ **zho**

A **dso** is a kind of Himalayan ox; the other forms are **dzo**, **zho**, **dzho** and **zo** and it's worth remembering all of them.

DSOBO, -S same as ▶ **zobo**
DSOMO, -S same as ▶ **zhomo**
DSOS ▶ dso
DUAD, -S a rare word for
▶ pair
DUAL, -LED, -LING, -S adj having two parts, functions, or aspects ▷ n dual number ▷ vb make (a road) into a dual carriageway
DUALIN, -S n explosive substance
DUALISE, -D, -S same as
▶ dualize
DUALISM, -S n state of having two distinct parts
DUALIST -S
DUALITY n state or quality of being two or in two parts
DUALIZE, -D, -S vb cause to have two parts
DUALLED ▶ dual
DUALLIE, -S n pickup truck with dual rear tyres
DUALLING ▶ dual
DUALLY ▶ dual
DUALS ▶ dual
DUAN, -S n poem
DUAR, -S n Arab camp
DUARCHY same as ▶ **diarchy**
DUARS ▶ duar

DUATHLON n athletic contest in which each athlete competes in running and cycling events
DUB, -BED, -S vb give (a person or place) a name or nickname ▷ n style of reggae record production
DUBBER -S
DUBBIN, -ED, -S n thick grease applied to leather to soften and waterproof it ▷ vb apply dubbin to
DUBBING, -S ▶ dub
DUBBINS ▶ dubbin
DUBBO, -S adj stupid ▷ n stupid person
DUBIETY n state of being doubtful
DUBIOUS adj feeling or causing doubt
DUBITATE vb doubt
DUBNIUM, -S n chemical element
DUBONNET n dark purplish-red colour
DUBS ▶ dub
DUBSTEP, -S n genre of electronic music
DUCAL adj of a duke
DUCALLY
DUCAT, -S n former European gold or silver coin
DUCATOON n former silver coin
DUCATS ▶ ducat
DUCDAME interj Shakespearean nonsense word
DUCE, -S, DUCI n leader
DUCHESS n woman who holds the rank of duke ▷ vb overwhelm with flattering attention
DUCHESSE n type of satin
DUCHY, DUCHIES n territory of a duke or duchess
DUCI ▶ duce
DUCK, -ED, -S n water bird ▷ vb move (the head or body) quickly downwards
DUCKBILL n duckbilled platypus
DUCKED ▶ duck
DUCKER, -S ▶ duck
DUCKFOOT adj as in **duckfoot quote** chevron-shaped quotation mark
DUCKIE same as ▶ **ducky**
DUCKIER ▶ ducky
DUCKIES ▶ ducky
DUCKIEST ▶ ducky
DUCKING, -S ▶ duck
DUCKISH n twilight
DUCKLING n baby duck
DUCKMOLE another word for
▶ duckbill

DUCKPIN, -S n short bowling pin

DUCKS ▸ duck

DUCKTAIL n Teddy boy's hairstyle

DUCKWALK vb walk in a squatting posture

DUCKWEED n type of small stemless aquatic plant

DUCKY, DUCKIER, DUCKIES, DUCKIEST n darling or dear ▷ adj delightful

DUCT, -ED, -S vb convey via a duct ▷ n tube, pipe, or channel through which liquid or gas is conveyed

DUCTAL

DUCTILE adj (of a metal) able to be shaped into sheets or wires

DUCTING, -S ▸ duct

DUCTLESS ▸ duct

DUCTS ▸ duct

DUCTULE, -S n small duct

DUCTWORK n system of ducts

DUD, -S n ineffectual person or thing ▷ adj bad or useless

DUDDER, -ED, -S n door-to-door salesman ▷ vb tremble or shudder

DUDDERY n place where old clothes are sold

DUDDIE, -R, -S, -ST adj ragged ▷ n friend or a chum

DUDDY same as ▸ **duddie**

DUDE, -D, -S, DUDING vb dress fashionably ▷ n man

DUDEEN, -S n clay pipe with a short stem

DUDENESS n state of being a dude

DUDES ▸ dude

DUDETTE, -S n woman who behaves like a dude

DUDGEON, -S n anger or resentment

DUDHEEN, -S n type of pipe

DUDING ▸ dude

DUDISH ▸ dude

DUDISHLY ▸ dude

DUDISM, -S n being a dude

DUDS ▸ dud

DUE, -D, DUING vb supply with ▷ adj expected or scheduled to be present or arrive ▷ n something that is owed or required ▷ adv directly or exactly

DUECENTO n thirteenth century (in Italian art)

DUED ▸ due

DUEFUL adj proper

DUEL, -ED, -LED, -S n formal fight with deadly weapons between two people

▷ vb fight in a duel

DUELER -S

DUELING, -S ▸ duel

DUELIST, -S ▸ duel

DUELLED ▸ duel

DUELLER, -S ▸ duel

DUELLI ▸ duello

DUELLING ▸ duel

DUELLIST ▸ duel

DUELLO, DUELLI, -S n art of duelling

DUELS ▸ duel

DUELSOME adj given to duelling

DUENDE, -S n Spanish goblin

DUENESS ▸ due

DUENNA, -S n (esp in Spain) elderly woman acting as chaperone to a young woman

DUES pl n membership fees

DUET, -ED, -ING, -S, -TED, -TING n piece of music for two performers ▷ vb perform a duet

DUETT, -S same as ▸ **duet**

DUETTED ▸ duet

DUETTI ▸ duetto

DUETTING ▸ duet

DUETTINO n simple duet

DUETTIST ▸ duet

DUETTO, DUETTI, -S same as ▸ **duet**

DUETTS ▸ duett

DUFF, -ED, -EST, -S adj broken or useless ▷ vb change the appearance of or give a false appearance to (old or stolen goods) ▷ n mishit golf shot

DUFFEL, -S n heavy woollen cloth with a thick nap

DUFFER, -S n dull or incompetent person

DUFFEST ▸ duff

DUFFING, -S ▸ duff

DUFFLE, -S same as ▸ **duffel**

DUFFS ▸ duff

DUFUS, -ES same as ▸ **doofus**

DUG, -S Scottish word for ▸ **dog**

DUGITE, -S n medium-sized Australian venomous snake

DUGONG, -S n whalelike mammal of tropical waters

DUGOUT, -S n (at a sports ground) covered bench where managers and substitutes sit

DUGS ▸ dug

DUH interj ironic response to a question or statement

This word provides a useful front hook to **uh**.

DUHKHA, -S same as ▸ **dukkha**

DUI ▸ duo

DUIKER, -S n small African antelope

DUING ▸ due

DUIT, -S n former Dutch coin

DUKA, -S n shop

DUKE, -D, DUKING vb fight with fists ▷ n nobleman of the highest rank

DUKEDOM, -S n title, rank, or position of a duke

DUKELING n low-ranking duke

DUKERY, DUKERIES n duke's domain

DUKES pl n fists

DUKESHIP ▸ duke

DUKING ▸ duke

DUKKA, -S n mix of ground roast nuts and spices

DUKKAH, -S same as ▸ **dukka**

DUKKAS ▸ dukka

DUKKHA, -S n Buddhist belief that all things are suffering

DULCE, -S n sweet food or drink

DULCET, -S adj (of a sound) soothing or pleasant ▷ n soft organ stop

DULCETLY

DULCIAN, -S n precursor to the bassoon

DULCIANA n sweet-toned organ stop, controlling metal pipes of narrow scale

DULCIANS ▸ dulcian

DULCIFY vb make pleasant or agreeable

DULCIMER n tuned percussion instrument

DULCINEA n man's sweetheart

DULCITE, -S n sweet substance

DULCITOL another word for ▸ **dulcite**

DULCOSE, -S another word for ▸ **dulcite**

DULE, -S n suffering; misery

DULIA, -S n veneration accorded to saints

DULL, -ED, -ER, -EST, -ING, -S adj not interesting ▷ vb make or become dull

DULLARD, -S n dull or stupid person

DULLED ▸ dull

DULLER ▸ dull

DULLEST ▸ dull

DULLIER ▸ dully

DULLIEST ▸ dully

DULLING ▸ dull

DULLISH ▸ dull

DULLNESS ▸ dull

DULLS ▸ dull

DULLY, DULLIER, DULLIEST ▸ dull

DULNESS ► dull

DULOSIS, DULOSES *n* behaviour where one species of ant forces members of another to work for them **DULOTIC**

DULSE, -S *n* seaweed with large red edible fronds

DULY *adv* in a proper manner

DUM *adj* steamed

DUMA, -S *n* elective legislative assembly established by Tsar Nicholas II

DUMAIST, -S *n* member of duma

DUMAS ► duma

DUMB, -ED, -ER, -EST, -ING, -S *vb* silence ▷ *adj* lacking the power to speak

DUMBBELL *n* short bar with a heavy red ball or disc at each end, used for physical exercise

DUMBCANE *n* West Indian aroid plant

DUMBED ► dumb

DUMBER ► dumb

DUMBEST ► dumb

DUMBHEAD *n* dunce

DUMBING ► dumb

DUMBLY ► dumb

DUMBNESS ► dumb

DUMBO, -S *n* slow-witted unintelligent person

DUMBS ► dumb

DUMBSHOW *n* actions performed without words in a play

DUMBSIZE *vb* reduce the number in a workforce to the point it becomes ineffective

DUMDUM, -S *n* soft-nosed bullet

DUMELA *sentence substitute* hello

DUMFOUND *same as* **> dumbfound**

DUMKA, -S, DUMKY *n* Slavonic lyrical song

DUMMERER *n* person who pretends to be dumb

DUMMIED ► dummy

DUMMIER ► dummy

DUMMIES ► dummy

DUMMIEST ► dummy

DUMMKOPF *n* stupid person

DUMMY, DUMMIED, DUMMIER, DUMMIES, DUMMIEST, -ING *adj* sham ▷ *n* figure representing the human form ▷ *adj* imitation, substitute ▷ *vb* prepare a dummy of (a proposed book, page, etc)

DUMOSE *adj* bushlike **DUMOSITY**

DUMOUS *same as* **► dumose**

DUMP, -ED *vb* drop or let fall in a careless manner ▷ *n* place where waste materials are left

DUMPBIN, -S *n* unit in a bookshop displaying a particular publisher's books

DUMPCART *n* cart for dumping without handling

DUMPED ► dump

DUMPEE, -S *n* person dumped from a relationship

DUMPER, -S ► dump

DUMPIER ► dumpy

DUMPIES ► dumpy

DUMPIEST ► dumpy

DUMPILY ► dumpy

DUMPING, -S ► dump

DUMPISH *same as* **► dumpy**

DUMPLE, -D, -S *vb* form into dumpling shape

DUMPLING *n* small ball of dough cooked and served with stew

DUMPS *pl n* state of melancholy or depression

DUMPSITE *n* location of dump

DUMPSTER *n* refuse skip

DUMPY, DUMPIER, DUMPIES, DUMPIEST, -ING *n* dumpy person ▷ *adj* short and plump

DUN, -NED, -NER, -NEST, -NING, -S *adj* brownish-grey ▷ *vb* demand payment from (a debtor) ▷ *n* demand for payment

DUNAM, -S *n* unit of area measurement

DUNCE, -S *n* person who is stupid or slow to learn

DUNCEDOM

DUNCERY *n* duncelike behaviour

DUNCES ► dunce

DUNCH, -ED, -ES, -ING *vb* push against gently

DUNCICAL *adj* duncelike

DUNCISH *adj* duncelike

DUNDER, -S *n* cane juice lees

DUNE, -S *n* mound or ridge of drifted sand

DUNELAND *n* land characterized by dunes

DUNELIKE ► dune

DUNES ► dune

DUNG, -ED, -ING, -S *n* faeces from animals such as cattle ▷ *vb* cover (ground) with manure

DUNGAREE *n* coarse cotton fabric used chiefly for work clothes, etc

DUNGED ► dung

DUNGEON, -S *vb* hold captive in dungeon ▷ *n* underground prison cell

DUNGER, -S *n* old decrepit car

DUNGHEAP *n* pile of dung

DUNGHILL *n* heap of dung

DUNGIER ► dungy

DUNGIEST ► dungy

DUNGING ► dung

DUNGMERE *n* cesspool

DUNGS ► dung

DUNGY, DUNGIER, DUNGIEST ► dung

DUNITE, -S *n* ultrabasic igneous rock **DUNITIC**

DUNK, -ED, -S *vb* dip (a biscuit or bread) in a drink or soup before eating it **DUNKER -S**

DUNKING, -S *n* act of dunking

DUNKS ► dunk

DUNLIN, -S *n* small sandpiper

DUNNAGE, -S *n* loose material used for packing cargo

DUNNAKIN *n* lavatory

DUNNART, -S *n* type of insectivorous marsupial

DUNNED ► dun

DUNNER ► dun

DUNNESS ► dun

DUNNEST ► dun

DUNNIER ► dunny

DUNNIES ► dunny

DUNNIEST ► dunny

DUNNING ► dun

DUNNINGS

DUNNISH ► dun

DUNNITE, -S *n* explosive containing ammonium picrate

DUNNO *vb* slang for don't know

DUNNOCK, -S *n* hedge sparrow

DUNNY, DUNNIER, DUNNIES, DUNNIEST *n* in Australia, toilet ▷ *adj* like or relating to a dunny

DUNS ► dun

DUNSH, -ED, -ES, -ING *same as* **► dunch**

DUNT, -ED, -ING, -S *n* blow ▷ *vb* strike or hit

DUO, DUI, -S *same as* **► duet**

DUODENA ► duodenum

DUODENAL ► duodenum

DUODENUM, DUODENA *n* first part of the small intestine, just below the stomach

DUOLOG, -S *same as* **► duologue**

DUOLOGUE *n* (in drama) conversation between only two speakers

DUOMO, DUOMI, -S *n* cathedral in Italy

DUOPOLY *n* situation when control of a commodity is

D

vested in two producers or suppliers

DUOPSONY n two rival buyers controlling sellers

DUOS ▶ duo

DUOTONE, -S n process for producing halftone illustrations

DUP, -PED, -PING, -S vb open

DUPABLE ▶ dupe

DUPATTA, -S n scarf worn in India

DUPE, -D, -S vb deceive or cheat ▷ n person who is easily deceived

DUPER -S

DUPERIES ▶ dupery

DUPERS ▶ duper

DUPERY, DUPERIES ▶ dupe

DUPES ▶ dupe

DUPING, -S n act of duping

DUPION, -S n silk fabric made from the threads of double cocoons

DUPLE adj having two beats in a bar

DUPLET, -S n pair of electrons shared between two atoms in a covalent bond

DUPLEX, -ED, -ES vb duplicate ▷ n apartment on two floors ▷ adj having two parts

DUPLEXER n telecommunications system

DUPLEXES ▶ duplex

DUPLY, DUPLIED, DUPLIES, -ING vb give a second reply

DUPONDII > dupondius

DUPPED ▶ dup

DUPPIES ▶ duppy

DUPPING ▶ dup

DUPPY, DUPPIES n spirit or ghost

DUPS ▶ dup

DURA, -S same as ▶ durra

DURABLE adj long-lasting

DURABLES pl n goods that require infrequent replacement

DURABLY ▶ durable

DURAL, -S n alloy of aluminium and copper

DURAMEN, -S another name for > **heartwood**

DURANCE, -S n imprisonment

DURANT, -S n tough, leathery cloth

DURAS ▶ dura

DURATION n length of time that something lasts

DURATIVE adj denoting an aspect of verbs that includes the imperfective and the progressive ▷ n durative aspect of a verb

DURBAR, -S n (formerly) the court of a native ruler or a governor in India

DURDUM, -S same as ▶ dirdum

DURE, -D, -S vb endure

DUREFUL adj lasting

DURES ▶ dure

DURESS, -ES n compulsion by use of force or threats

DURESSE same as ▶ duress

DURESSES ▶ duress

DURGAH, -S same as ▶ dargah

DURGAN, -S n dwarf

DURGY, DURGIER, DURGIEST adj dwarflike

DURIAN, -S n SE Asian tree whose very large oval fruits have a hard spiny rind and an evil smell

DURING prep throughout or within the limit of (a period of time)

DURION, -S same as ▶ durian

DURMAST, -S n large Eurasian oak tree with lobed leaves

DURN, -ING, -S same as ▶ darn

DURNDEST same as > **darnedest**

DURNED, -ER ▶ durn

DURNING ▶ durn

DURNS ▶ durn

DURO, -S n silver peso of Spain or Spanish America

DUROC, -S n breed of pig

DUROS ▶ duro

DUROY, -S n coarse woollen fabric

DURR, -S same as ▶ durra

DURRA, -S n Old World variety of sorghum

DURRIE n cotton carpet made in India, often in rectangular pieces fringed at the ends

DURRIES ▶ durry

DURRS ▶ durr

DURRY, DURRIES n cigarette

DURST a past tense of ▶ dare

DURUKULI n S American monkey

DURUM, -S n variety of wheat

DURZI, -S n Indian tailor

DUSH, -ED, -ES, -ING vb strike hard

DUSK, -ED, -ER, -EST, -ING, -S n time just before nightfall, when it is almost dark ▷ adj shady ▷ vb make or become dark

DUSKEN, -ED, -S vb grow dark

DUSKER ▶ dusk

DUSKEST ▶ dusk

DUSKIER ▶ dusky

DUSKIEST ▶ dusky

DUSKILY ▶ dusky

DUSKING ▶ dusk

DUSKISH ▶ dusk

DUSKLY ▶ dusk

DUSKNESS ▶ dusk

DUSKS ▶ dusk

DUSKY, DUSKIER, DUSKIEST adj dark in colour

DUST, -ED, -S n small dry particles of earth, sand, or dirt ▷ vb remove dust from (furniture) by wiping

DUSTBALL n ball of dust

DUSTBIN, -S n large container for household rubbish

DUSTCART n truck for collecting household rubbish

DUSTCOAT n light, loose-fitting long coat

DUSTED ▶ dust

DUSTER, -S n cloth used for dusting

DUSTHEAP n accumulation of refuse

DUSTIER ▶ dusty

DUSTIEST ▶ dusty

DUSTILY ▶ dusty

DUSTING, -S ▶ dust

DUSTLESS ▶ dust

DUSTLIKE ▶ dust

DUSTMAN, DUSTMEN n man whose job is to collect household rubbish

DUSTOFF, -S n casualty evacuation helicopter

DUSTPAN, -S n short-handled shovel

DUSTRAG, -S n cloth for dusting

DUSTS ▶ dust

DUSTUP, -S n quarrel, fight, or argument

DUSTY, DUSTIER, DUSTIEST adj covered with dust

DUTCH, -ES n wife

DUTCHMAN, DUTCHMEN n piece of wood, metal, etc, used to repair or patch faulty workmanship

DUTEOUS adj dutiful or obedient

DUTIABLE adj (of goods) requiring payment of duty

DUTIED adj liable for duty

DUTIES ▶ duty

DUTIFUL adj doing what is expected

DUTY, DUTIES n work or a task performed as part of one's job

DUUMVIR, -I, -S n one of two coequal magistrates or officers

DUVET, -S same as ▶ doona

DUVETINE same as ▶ duvetyn

DUVETS ▶ duvet

DUVETYN, -S *n* soft napped velvety fabric of cotton, silk, wool, or rayon
DUVETYNE *same as* ▶ **duvetyn**
DUVETYNS ▶ **duvetyn**
DUX, -ES *n* (in Scottish and certain other schools) the top pupil in a class or school

A **dux** is a leader, and is often useful for disposing of the X.

DUXELLES *n* paste of mushrooms and onions
DUXES ▶ **dux**
DUYKER, -S *same as* ▶ **duiker**
DVANDVA, -S *n* class of compound words
DVORNIK, -S *n* Russian doorkeeper
DWAAL, -S *n* state of absent-mindedness
DWALE, -S *n* deadly nightshade
DWALM, -ED, -ING, -S *vb* faint
DWAM, -MED, -MING, -S *n* stupor or daydream ▷ *vb* faint or fall ill
DWANG, -S *n* short piece of wood inserted in a timber-framed wall
DWARF, -ED, -ER, -EST, -ING, -S, DWARVES *adj* undersized ▷ *n* person who is smaller than average ▷ *vb* cause (someone or something) to seem small by being much larger
DWARFISH
DWARFISM *n* condition of being a dwarf
DWARFS ▶ **dwarf**
DWARVES ▶ **dwarf**
DWAUM, -ED, -ING, -S *same as* ▶ **dwam**
DWEEB, -S *n* stupid or uninteresting person
DWEEBIER ▶ **dweeby**
DWEEBISH ▶ **dweeby**
DWEEBS ▶ **dweeb**
DWEEBY, DWEEBIER *adj* like or typical of a dweeb
DWELL, -ED, -ING, -S, DWELT *vb* live, reside ▷ *n* regular pause in the operation of a machine
DWELLER -S
DWILE, -S *n* floor cloth
DWINDLE, -D, -S *vb* grow less in size, strength, or number
DWINE, -D, -S, DWINING *vb* languish
DYABLE ▶ **dye**
DYAD, -S *n* operator that is the unspecified product of two vectors

DYADIC, -S *adj* of or relating to a dyad ▷ *n* sum of a particular number of dyads
DYADS ▶ **dyad**
DYARCHAL ▶ **dyarchy**
DYARCHIC ▶ **dyarchy**
DYARCHY *same as* ▶ **diarchy**
DYBBUK, -S *n* (in Jewish folklore) the body of a person possessed by the soul of a dead sinner
DYE, -D, -S *n* colouring substance ▷ *vb* colour (hair or fabric) by applying a dye
DYEABLE
DYEING -S
DYELINE, -S *same as* ▶ **diazo**
DYER, -S ▶ **dye**
DYES ▶ **dye**
DYESTER, -S *n* dyer
DYESTUFF *n* substance that can be used as a dye or from which a dye can be obtained
DYEWEED, -S *n* plant that produces dye
DYEWOOD, -S *n* any wood from which dyes and pigments can be obtained
DYEWORKS *n* place where dye is made
DYING, -S ▶ **die**
DYINGLY ▶ **die**
DYINGS ▶ **dying**
DYKE, -D, -S, DYKING *n* wall built to prevent flooding ▷ *vb* protect with a dyke
DYNAMIC *adj* full of energy, ambition, and new ideas ▷ *n* energetic or driving force
DYNAMICS *n* branch of mechanics concerned with motions of bodies
DYNAMISE *same as* ▶ **dynamize**
DYNAMISM *n* great energy and enthusiasm
DYNAMIST
DYNAMITE *n* explosive made of nitroglycerine ▷ *vb* blow (something) up with dynamite
DYNAMIZE *vb* cause to be dynamic
DYNAMO, -S *n* device for converting mechanical energy into electrical energy
DYNAST, -S *n* hereditary ruler
DYNASTIC ▶ **dynasty**
DYNASTS ▶ **dynast**
DYNASTY *n* sequence of hereditary rulers
DYNATRON *n as in* **dynatron oscillator** type of oscillator
DYNE, -S *n* cgs unit of force
DYNEIN, -S *n* class of proteins
DYNEL, -S *n* trade name for synthetic fibre

DYNES ▶ **dyne**
DYNODE, -S *n* electrical component
DYSCHROA *n* discolouration of skin
DYSGENIC *adj* referring to the degeneration of a race or strain
DYSLALIA *n* defective speech characteristic of those affected by aphasia
DYSLEXIA *n* disorder causing impaired ability to read
DYSLEXIC
DYSLOGY *n* uncomplimentary remarks
DYSMELIA *n* condition of missing or stunted limbs
DYSMELIC
DYSODIL, -S *n* yellow or green mineral
DYSODILE *same as* ▶ **dysodil**
DYSODILS ▶ **dysodil**
DYSODYLE *same as* ▶ **dysodil**
DYSPATHY *n* dislike
DYSPEPSY *same as* > **dyspepsia**
DYSPHAGY *same as* > **dysphagia**
DYSPNEA, -S *same as* ▶ **dyspnoea**
DYSPNEAL
DYSPNEIC
DYSPNOEA *n* difficulty in breathing or in catching the breath
DYSPNOIC
DYSTAXIA *n* lack of muscular coordination resulting in shaky limb movements and unsteady gait
DYSTAXIC *adj* relating to or affected by dystaxia
DYSTOCIA *n* abnormal, slow, or difficult childbirth
DYSTONIA *n* neurological disorder
DYSTONIC
DYSTOPIA *n* imaginary place where everything is as bad as it can be
DYSURIA, -S *n* difficult or painful urination
DYSURIC
DYSURY, DYSURIES *same as* ▶ **dysuria**
DYTISCID *n* type of carnivorous aquatic beetle with large flattened back legs used for swimming
DYVOUR, -S *n* debtor
DYVOURY *n* bankruptcy
DZEREN, -S *n* Chinese yellow antelope
DZHO, -S *same as* ▶ **zho**
DZO, -S *a variant spelling* of ▶ **zo**

D

Ee

E is the most common tile in the game and, while it is only worth one point, as the most frequent letter in English it is extremely useful, especially when it comes to forming bonus words scoring an extra 50 points. Many words contain two or more **E**s, so, unlike many tiles, it does no harm to have two **E**s on your rack and even three can be manageable. Keep in mind three-letter words formed by an **E** on either side of a consonant, like **eye**, **ewe** and **eve** (6 points each), and **eke** (7). **E** can also be handy for getting rid of double consonants: think of words like **egg** or **ebb** (each 5 points). **E** also combines well with **K**: as well as **eke**, we have **elk** and **eek** (both 7), and **ewk** (10). If you have an **X** on your rack, **E** offers you all kinds of options: just think of all the words that begin with **ex-**, like **exhaust** (17), which will give you a 50-point bonus if you use all of your tiles to form it. And don't forget **ex** itself, a nice little word that earns you 9 points, and also the very useful **exo** for 10 points. Just as important are **jee** for 10 points, **zee** for 12 points and **zed** for 13 points.

EA, **-S** *n* river
EACH *pron* every (one) taken separately ▷ *determiner* every (one) of two or more considered individually ▷ *adv* for, to, or from each one
EADISH, **-ES** *n* aftermath
EAGER, **-ER**, **-EST**, **-S** *adj* showing or feeling great desire, keen ▷ *n* eagre
EAGERLY
EAGLE, **-D**, **-S**, **EAGLING** *n* bird of prey ▷ *vb* in golf, score two strokes under par for a hole
EAGLET, **-S** *n* young eagle
EAGLING ▶ **eagle**
EAGRE, **-S** *n* tidal bore, esp of the Humber or Severn estuaries
EALE, **-D**, **-S**, **EALING** *n* beast in Roman legend ▷ *vb* to ail
EAN, **-ED**, **-ING**, **-S** *vb* give birth
EANLING, **-S** *n* newborn lamb
EANS ▶ **ean**
EAR, **-S** *n* organ of hearing, esp the external part of it ▷ *vb* (of cereal plants) to develop such parts
EARACHE, **-S** *n* pain in the ear
EARBALL, **-S** *n* device used in acupressure
EARBASH *vb* talk incessantly
EARBOB, **-S** *n* earring
EARBUD, **-S** *n* small earphone
EARCON, **-S** *n* sound representing object or event
EARD, **-ED**, **-ING**, **-S** *vb* bury

EARDROP *n* pendant earring
EARDROPS *pl n* liquid medication for inserting into the external ear
EARDRUM, **-S** *n* part of the ear which enables one to hear sounds
EARDS ▶ **eard**
EARED *adj* having an ear or ears
EARFLAP, **-S** *n* either of two pieces of fabric or fur attached to a cap
EARFUL, **-S** *n* scolding or telling-off
EARHOLE, **-S** *n* the external opening of the ear
EARING, **-S** *n* line fastened to a corner of a sail for reefing
EARL, **-S** *n* British nobleman ranking next below a marquess
EARLAP, **-S** *same as* ▶ **earflap**
EARLDOM, **-S** *n* rank, title, or dignity of an earl or countess
EARLESS ▶ **ear**
EARLIER ▶ **early**
EARLIES ▶ **early**
EARLIEST ▶ **early**
EARLIKE ▶ **ear**
EARLOBE, **-S** *n* fleshy lower part of the outer ear
EARLOCK, **-S** *n* curl of hair close to ear
EARLS ▶ **earl**

EARLSHIP *n* title or position of earl
EARLY, **EARLIER**, **EARLIES**, **EARLIEST** *adv* before the expected or usual time ▷ *adj* occurring or arriving before the correct or expected time ▷ *n* something which is early
EARMARK, **-S** *vb* set (something) aside for a specific purpose ▷ *n* distinguishing mark
EARMUFF, **-S** *n* item of clothing for keeping the ears warm
EARN, **-ED**, **-ING**, **-S** *vb* obtain by work or merit
EARNER **-S**
EARNEST, **-S** *adj* serious and sincere ▷ *n* part payment given in advance
EARNING ▶ **earn**
EARNINGS *pl n* money earned
EARNS ▶ **earn**
EARPHONE *n* receiver for a radio etc, held to or put in the ear
EARPICK, **-S** *n* instrument for removing ear wax
EARPIECE *n* earphone in a telephone receiver
EARPLUG, **-S** *n* piece of soft material placed in the ear to keep out water or noise
EARRING, **-S** *n* ornament for the lobe of the ear
EARS ▶ **ear**

EARSHOT, -S n hearing range

EARST adv first; previously

EARSTONE n calcium carbonate crystal in the ear

EARTH, -ED, -ING, -S n planet that we live on ▷ vb connect (a circuit) to earth

EARTHEN adj made of baked clay or earth

EARTHIER ► earthy

EARTHILY ► earthy

EARTHING ► earth

EARTHLY adj conceivable or possible ▷ n chance

EARTHMAN, EARTHMEN n (esp in science fiction) an inhabitant or native of the earth

EARTHNUT n perennial umbelliferous plant of Europe and Asia, with edible dark brown tubers

EARTHPEA n peanut; groundnut

EARTHS ► earth

EARTHSET n setting of the earth below the lunar horizon

EARTHWAX n ozocerite

EARTHY, EARTHIER adj coarse or crude

EARWAX, -ES nontechnical name for ► cerumen

EARWIG, -S n small insect with a pincer-like tail ▷ vb eavesdrop **EARWIGGY**

EARWORM, -S n irritatingly catchy tune

EAS ► ea

EASE, -D, -S n freedom from difficulty, discomfort, or worry ▷ vb give bodily or mental ease to

EASEFUL adj characterized by or bringing ease

EASEL, -S n frame to support an artist's canvas or a blackboard

EASELED adj mounted on easel

EASELESS ► ease

EASELS ► easel

EASEMENT n right of a landowner to make limited use of a neighbour's land

EASER, -S ► ease

EASES ► ease

EASIED ► easy

EASIER ► easy

EASIES ► easy

EASIEST ► easy

EASILY adv without difficulty

EASINESS n quality or condition of being easy to accomplish, do, obtain, etc

EASING, -S n as in **quantitative easing** increasing the supply of money to stimulate the economy

EASLE, -S n hot ash

EASSEL adv easterly

EASSIL adv easterly

EAST, -ED, -S n (direction towards) the part of the horizon where the sun rises ▷ adj in the east ▷ adv in, to, or towards the east ▷ vb move or turn east

EASTER, -S n most important festival of the Christian Church

EASTERLY adj of or in the east ▷ adv towards the east ▷ n wind from the east

EASTERN adj situated in or towards the east

EASTERS ► easter

EASTING, -S n net distance eastwards made by a vessel moving towards the east

EASTLAND adj, n (of or relating to) land in east

EASTLIN adj easterly

EASTLING adj easterly

EASTLINS adv eastward

EASTMOST adj furthest east

EASTS ► east

EASTWARD same as > eastwards

EASY, EASIED, EASIER, EASIES, EASIEST, -ING adj not needing much work or effort ▷ vb stop rowing

EAT, ATE, -EN, -S vb take (food) into the mouth and swallow it

EATABLE adj fit or suitable for eating

EATABLES pl n food

EATAGE, -S n grazing rights

EATCHE, -S n adze

EATEN ► eat

EATER, -S ► eat

EATERIE same as ► eatery

EATERIES ► eatery

EATERS ► eater

EATERY, EATERIES n restaurant or eating house

EATH adj easy

EATHE same as ► eath

EATHLY ► eath

EATING, -S ► eat

EATS ► eat

EAU, -S, -X same as ► ea

EAVE, -S n overhanging edge of a roof

EAVED adj having eaves

EAVES ► eave

EBAUCHE, -S n rough sketch

EBAYER, -S n any person who uses eBay

EBAYING, -S n buying or selling using eBay

EBB, -ED, -ING, -S vb (of tide water) flow back ▷ n flowing back of the tide

EBBET, -S n type of newt

EBBING ► ebb

EBBLESS ► ebb

EBBS ► ebb

EBENEZER n chapel

EBENISTE n cabinetmaker

EBIONISE same as ► ebionize

EBIONISM n doctrine that the poor shall be saved

EBIONIZE vb preach ebionism

EBON, -S poetic word for ► ebony

EBONICS n dialect used by African-Americans

EBONIES ► ebony

EBONISE, -D, -S same as ► ebonize

EBONIST, -S n carver of ebony

EBONITE, -S another name for > vulcanite

EBONIZE, -D, -S vb stain or otherwise finish in imitation of ebony

EBONS ► ebon

EBONY, EBONIES n hard black wood ▷ adj deep black

EBOOK, -S n book in electronic form

EBRIATE adj drunk

EBRIATED same as ► ebriate

EBRIETY n drunkenness

EBRIOSE adj drunk

EBURNEAN adj made of ivory

ECAD, -S n organism whose form has been affected by its environment

ECARTE, -S n card game for two, played with 32 cards and king high

ECAUDATE adj tailless

ECBOLE, -S n digression

ECBOLIC, -S adj inducing labour ▷ n drug or agent that induces labour

ECCE interj behold

ECCLESIA n (in formal Church usage) a congregation

ECCO interj look there

ECCRINE adj of or denoting glands that secrete externally

ECCRISIS, ECCRISES n excrement

ECCRITIC n purgative

ECDEMIC adj not indigenous or endemic

ECDYSES ► ecdysis

ECDYSIAL ► ecdysis

ECDYSIS, ECDYSES n shedding of the cuticle in

E

E

arthropods or the outer epidermal layer in reptiles

ECDYSON, -S *same as* ▶ **ecdysone**

ECDYSONE *n* hormone secreted by the prothoracic gland of insects

ECDYSONS ▶ **ecdyson**

ECESIC ▶ **ecesis**

ECESIS, -ES *n* establishment of a plant in a new environment

ECH *same as* ▶ **eche**

ECHAPPE, -S *n* leap in ballet

ECHARD, -S *n* water that is present in the soil but cannot be utilized by plants

ECHE, -D, -S, ECHING *vb* eke out

ECHELLE, -S *n* ladder; scale

ECHELON, -S *n* level of power or responsibility ▷ *vb* assemble in echelon

ECHES ▶ **eche**

ECHIDNA, -E, -S *n* Australian spiny egg-laying mammal

ECHINATE *adj* covered with spines, bristles, or bristle-like outgrowths

ECHING ▶ **eche**

ECHINI ▶ **echinus**

ECHINOID *n* type of echinoderm of the class which includes the sea urchins and sand dollars

ECHINUS, ECHINI *n* ovolo moulding between the shaft and the abacus of a Doric column

ECHIUM, -S *n* type of Eurasian and African plant

ECHIURAN *n* spoonworm

ECHO, -ED, -ES, -ING, -S *n* repetition of sounds by reflection of sound waves off a surface ▷ *vb* repeat or be repeated as an echo

ECHOER -S

ECHOEY, ECHOIER, ECHOIEST *adj* producing echoes

ECHOGRAM *n* record made by echography

ECHOIC *adj* characteristic of or resembling an echo

ECHOIER ▶ **echoey**

ECHOIEST ▶ **echoey**

ECHOING ▶ **echo**

ECHOISE, -D, -S *same as* ▶ **echoize**

ECHOISM, -S *n* onomatopoeia as a source of word formation

ECHOIST -S

ECHOIZE, -D, -S *vb* repeat like echo

ECHOLESS ▶ **echo**

ECHOS ▶ **echo**

ECHT *adj* real

ECLAIR, -S *n* finger-shaped pastry filled with cream and covered with chocolate

ECLAMPSY *same as* > **eclampsia**

ECLAT, -S *n* brilliant success

ECLECTIC *adj* selecting from various styles, ideas, or sources ▷ *n* person who takes an eclectic approach

ECLIPSE, -D *n* temporary obscuring of one star or planet by another ▷ *vb* surpass or outclass

ECLIPSER

ECLIPSIS, ECLIPSES *same as* ▶ **ellipsis**

ECLIPTIC *n* apparent path of the sun ▷ *adj* of or relating to an eclipse

ECLOGITE *n* rare coarse-grained basic rock

ECLOGUE, -S *n* pastoral or idyllic poem, usually in the form of a conversation or soliloquy

ECLOSE, -D, -S, ECLOSING *vb* emerge

ECLOSION *n* emergence of an insect larva from the egg or an adult from the pupal case

ECO, -S *n* ecology activist

ECOCIDAL ▶ **ecocide**

ECOCIDE, -S *n* total destruction of an area of the natural environment

ECOD *same as* ▶ **egad**

ECOFREAK *n* environmentalist

ECOGIFT, -S *n* donation of land for environmental purposes

ECOLODGE *n* eco-friendly tourist accommodation

ECOLOGIC ▶ **ecology**

ECOLOGY *n* study of the links between living things and their environment

ECOMAP, -S *n* diagram showing the links between an individual and their community

ECONOBOX *n* fuel efficient utility vehicle

ECONOMIC *adj* of economics

ECONOMY *n* system of interrelationship of money, industry, and employment in a country ▷ *adj* denoting a class of air travel that is cheaper than first-class

ECONUT, -S *n* environmentalist

ECORCHE, -S *n* anatomical figure without the skin

ECOS ▶ **eco**

ECOSTATE *adj* with no ribs or nerves

ECOTAGE, -S *n* sabotage for ecological motives

ECOTONAL ▶ **ecotone**

ECOTONE, -S *n* zone between two major ecological communities

ECOTOPIA *n* ecologically ideal area or society

ECOTOUR, -S *n* holiday taking care not to damage environment ▷ *vb* take an ecotour

ECOTOXIC *adj* harmful to animals, plants or the environment

ECOTYPE, -S *n* organisms within a species that have adapted to a particular environment

ECOTYPIC

ECOZONE, -S *n* large area with an ecosystem

ECRASEUR *n* surgical device consisting of a heavy wire loop

ECRU, -S *adj* pale creamy-brown ▷ *n* greyish-yellow to a light greyish colour

ECSTASIS, ECSTASES *same as* ▶ **ecstasy**

ECSTASY *n* state of intense delight

ECSTATIC *adj* in a trancelike state of great rapture or delight ▷ *n* person who has periods of intense trancelike joy

ECTASES ▶ **ectasis**

ECTASIA, -S *n* distension or dilation of a duct, vessel, or hollow viscus

ECTASIS, ECTASES *same as* ▶ **ectasia**

ECTATIC ▶ **ectasia**

ECTHYMA, -S *n* local inflammation of the skin

ECTODERM *n* outer germ layer of an animal embryo

ECTOGENE *n* type of gene

ECTOGENY *n* (of bacteria, etc) development outside the host

ECTOMERE *n* any of the blastomeres that later develop into ectoderm

ECTOPIA, -S *n* congenital displacement of an organ or part

ECTOPIC

ECTOPY, ECTOPIES *same as* ▶ **ectopia**

ECTOSARC n ectoplasm of an amoeba or any other protozoan
ECTOZOA ▶ ectozoon
ECTOZOAN same as ▶ ectozoon
ECTOZOIC ▶ ectozoon
ECTOZOON, ECTOZOA n parasitic organism that lives on the outside of its host
ECTROPIC ▶ ectropion
ECTYPAL ▶ ectype
ECTYPE, -S n copy as distinguished from a prototype
ECU, -S n any of various former French gold or silver coins
ECUELLE, -S n covered soup bowl with handles
ECUMENE, -S n inhabited area of the world
ECUMENIC adj tending to promote unity among Churches
ECURIE, -S n team of motor-racing cars
ECUS ▶ ecu
ECZEMA, -S n skin disease causing intense itching
ED, -S n editor
EDACIOUS adj devoted to eating
EDACITY
EDAMAME, -S n immature soybeans boiled in the pod
EDAPHIC adj of or relating to the physical and chemical conditions of the soil
EDDIED ▶ eddy
EDDIES ▶ eddy
EDDISH, -ES n pasture grass
EDDO, -ES same as ▶ taro
EDDY, EDDIED, EDDIES, -ING n circular movement of air, water, etc ▷ vb move with a circular motion
EDEMA, -S, -TA same as ▶ oedema
EDENIC adj delightful, like the Garden of Eden
EDENTAL adj having few or no teeth
EDENTATE n mammal with few or no teeth, such as an armadillo or a sloth ▷ adj denoting such a mammal
EDGE, -D, -S n border or line where something ends or begins ▷ vb provide an edge or border for
EDGEBONE n aitchbone
EDGED ▶ edge
EDGELESS ▶ edge
EDGER, -S ▶ edge
EDGES ▶ edge

EDGEWAYS adv with the edge forwards or uppermost
EDGEWISE same as ▶ edgeways
EDGIER ▶ edgy
EDGIEST ▶ edgy
EDGILY ▶ edgy
EDGINESS ▶ edgy
EDGING, -S n anything placed along an edge to finish it ▷ adj relating to or used for making an edge
EDGY, EDGIER, EDGIEST adj nervous or irritable
EDH, -S n character of the runic alphabet
EDIBLE adj fit to be eaten
EDIBLES pl n articles fit to eat
EDICT, -S n order issued by an authority
EDICTAL
EDIFICE, -S n large building
EDIFIED ▶ edify
EDIFIER, -S ▶ edify
EDIFY, EDIFIED, EDIFIES vb improve morally by instruction
EDIFYING
EDILE, -S variant spelling of ▶ aedile
EDIT, -ED, -S vb prepare (a book, film, etc) for publication or broadcast ▷ n act of editing
EDITABLE
EDITING -S
EDITION, -S n number of copies of a new publication printed at one time ▷ vb produce multiple copies of (an original work of art)
EDITOR, -S n person who edits
EDITRESS n female editor
EDITRIX n female editor
EDITS ▶ edit
EDS ▶ ed
EDUCABLE adj capable of being trained or educated ▷ n person with learning difficulties who is capable of being educated
EDUCATE, -S vb teach
EDUCATED adj having an education, esp a good one
EDUCATES ▶ educate
EDUCATOR n person who educates
EDUCE, -D, -S, EDUCING vb evolve or develop
EDUCIBLE
EDUCT, -S n substance separated from a mixture without chemical change
EDUCTION n something educed
EDUCTIVE ▶ educe

EDUCTOR, -S ▶ educe
EDUCTS ▶ educt
EE, -N Scots word for ▶ eye
EECH, -ED, -ES, -ING same as ▶ eche
EEEW interj exclamation of disgust
EEJIT, -S Scots and Irish word for ▶ idiot
EEK interj indicating shock or fright
EEL, -S n snakelike fish
EELFARE, -S n young eel
EELGRASS n type of submerged marine plant with grasslike leaves
EELIER ▶ eely
EELIEST ▶ eely
EELLIKE adj resembling an eel
EELPOUT, -S n marine eel-like blennioid fish
EELS ▶ eel
EELWORM, -S n any of various nematode worms
EELWRACK n grasslike plant growing in seawater
EELY, EELIER, EELIEST ▶ eel
EEN ▶ ee
EENSY, EENSIER, EENSIEST adj very small
EERIE, -R, -ST adj uncannily frightening or disturbing
EERILY
EERINESS
EERY same as ▶ eerie
EEVEN, -S n evening
EEVN, -S n evening
EEVNING, -S n evening
EEVNS ▶ eevn
EEW interj exclamation of disgust
EF, -S n the letter F
EFF, -ED, -S vb use bad language
EFFABLE adj capable of being expressed in words
EFFACE, -D, -S, EFFACING vb remove by rubbing
EFFACER -S
EFFECT, -ED n change or result caused by someone or something ▷ vb cause to happen, accomplish
EFFECTER
EFFECTOR n nerve ending that terminates in a muscle or gland
EFFECTS pl n personal belongings
EFFED ▶ eff
EFFEIR, -ED, -S vb suit
EFFENDI, -S n (in the Ottoman Empire) a title of respect
EFFERE, -D, -S, EFFERING same as ▶ effeir

EFFERENT adj carrying or conducting outwards ▷ n type of nerve

EFFERES ► effere

EFFERING ► effere

EFFETE adj powerless, feeble **EFFETELY**

EFFICACY n quality of being successful in producing an intended result

EFFIERCE vb archaic word meaning make fierce

EFFIGIAL ► effigy

EFFIGY, EFFIGIES n image or likeness of a person

EFFING, -S ► eff

EFFLUENT n liquid discharged as waste ▷ adj flowing out or forth

EFFLUVIA > effluvium

EFFLUX, -ES same as > effluence

EFFORCE, -D, -S vb force

EFFORT, -S n physical or mental exertion

EFFRAIDE archaic form of ► afraid

EFFRAY, -S archaic form of ► affray

EFFS ► eff

EFFULGE, -D, -S vb radiate

EFFUSE, -D, -S, EFFUSING vb pour or flow out ▷ adj (esp of an inflorescence) spreading out loosely

EFFUSION n unrestrained outburst

EFFUSIVE adj openly emotional, demonstrative

EFS ► ef

EFT, -S n dialect or archaic name for a newt ▷ adv again

EFTEST adj nearest at hand

EFTS ► eft

EFTSOONS, EFTSOON adv soon afterwards

EGAD, -S n mild oath or expression of surprise

EGAL adj equal

EGALITE, -S n equality

EGALITY n equality

EGALLY ► egal

EGENCE, -S n need

EGENCY, EGENCIES same as ► egence

EGER, -S same as ► eagre

EGEST, -ED, -ING, -S vb excrete (waste material)

EGESTA pl n anything egested, as waste material from the body

EGESTED ► egest

EGESTING ► egest

EGESTION ► egest

EGESTIVE ► egest

EGESTS ► egest

EGG, -ED, -ING, -S n object laid by birds and other creatures, containing a developing embryo ▷ vb urge or incite, esp to daring or foolish acts

EGGAR, -S same as ► egger

EGGCORN, -S n misspelling caused by the mishearing of a word

EGGCUP, -S n cup for holding a boiled egg

EGGED ► egg

EGGER, -S n moth with brown body and wings

EGGERIES ► eggery

EGGERS ► egger

EGGERY, EGGERIES n place where eggs are laid

EGGFRUIT n fruit of eggplant

EGGHEAD, -S n intellectual person

EGGIER ► eggy

EGGIEST ► eggy

EGGING ► egg

EGGLER, -S n egg dealer: sometimes itinerant

EGGLESS ► egg

EGGMASS n intelligentsia

EGGNOG, -S n drink made of raw eggs, milk, sugar, spice, and brandy or rum

EGGPLANT n dark purple tropical fruit, cooked and eaten as a vegetable

EGGS ► egg

EGGSHELL n hard covering round the egg of a bird or animal ▷ adj (of paint) having a very slight sheen

EGGWASH n beaten egg for brushing on pastry

EGGWHISK same as > eggbeater

EGGY, EGGIER, EGGIEST adj soaked in or tasting of egg

EGIS, -ES rare spelling of ► aegis

EGLATERE archaic name for > eglantine

EGLOMISE n gilding

EGMA, -S mispronunciation of ► enigma

EGO, -S n conscious mind of an individual

EGOISM, -S n excessive concern for one's own interests

EGOIST, -S n person who is preoccupied with his own interests

EGOISTIC

EGOITY, EGOITIES n essence of the ego

EGOLESS adj without an ego

EGOMANIA n obsessive concern with one's own needs and desires

EGOS ► ego

EGOSURF, -S vb search for one's own name on the internet

EGOTISE, -D, -S same as ► egotize

EGOTISM, -S n concern only for one's own interests and feelings

EGOTIST, -S n conceited boastful person

EGOTIZE, -D, -S vb talk or write in self-important way

EGRESS, -ED, -ES same as ► emersion

EGRET, -S n lesser white heron

EGYPTIAN n type of typeface

EH, -ED, -ING, -S interj exclamation of surprise or inquiry ▷ vb say 'eh'

EIDE ► eidos

EIDENT adj diligent

EIDER, -S n Arctic duck

EIDETIC, -S adj (of images) exceptionally vivid, allowing detailed recall of something ▷ n person with eidetic ability

EIDOLA ► eidolon

EIDOLIC ► eidolon

EIDOLON, EIDOLA, -S n unsubstantial image

EIDOS, EIDE n intellectual character of a culture or a social group

EIGHT, -S n one more than seven ▷ adj amounting to eight

EIGHTEEN n eight and ten ▷ adj amounting to eighteen ▷ determiner amounting to eighteen

EIGHTH, -S n number eight in a series ▷ adj coming after the seventh and before the ninth ▷ adv after the seventh person, position, event, etc

EIGHTHLY same as ► eighth

EIGHTHS ► eighth

EIGHTIES ► eighty

EIGHTS ► eight

EIGHTVO, -S another word for ► octavo

EIGHTY, EIGHTIES n eight times ten ▷ adj amounting to eighty ▷ determiner amounting to eighty

EIGNE adj firstborn

EIK, -ED, -ING, -S variant form of ► eke

EIKON, -ES, -S variant spelling of ► icon

EIKS ► eik

EILD, -S n old age

EILDING, -S n fuel

EILDS ► eild

EINA interj exclamation of pain

EINE pl n eyes

EINKORN, -S n variety of wheat of Greece and SW Asia

EINSTEIN n scientific genius

EIRACK, -S n young hen

EIRENIC variant spelling of ► irenic

EIRENICS n theology concerned with unity among churches

EISEL, -S n vinegar

EISELL, -S same as ► eisel

EISELS ► eisel

EISH interj South African exclamation

EISWEIN, -S n wine made from grapes frozen on the vine

EITHER pron one or the other (of two) ▷ adv likewise ▷ determiner one or the other (of two)

EJECT, -ED, -ING, -S vb force out, expel

EJECTA pl n matter thrown out by a volcano or during a meteorite impact

EJECTED ► eject

EJECTING ► eject

EJECTION ► eject

EJECTIVE adj relating to or causing ejection ▷ n ejective consonant

EJECTOR, -S n person or thing that ejects

EJECTS ► eject

EJIDO, -S n communal farmland in Mexico

EKE, -D, -S, EKING vb increase, enlarge, or lengthen

EKISTIC ► ekistics

EKISTICS n science or study of human settlements

EKKA, -S n type of one-horse carriage

EKLOGITE same as ► eclogite

EKPWELE, -S n former monetary unit of Equatorial Guinea

EKTEXINE n in pollen and spores, the outer of the two layers that make up the exine

EKUELE same as ► ekpwele

EL, -S n American elevated railway

ELAIN, -S same as ► triolein

ELAN, -S n style and vigour

ELANCE, -D, -S, ELANCING vb throw a lance

ELAND, -S n large antelope of southern Africa

ELANET, -S n bird of prey

ELANS ► elan

ELAPHINE adj of or like a red deer

ELAPID, -S n mostly tropical type of venomous snake

ELAPINE adj of or like an elapid

ELAPSE, -D, -S, ELAPSING vb (of time) pass by

ELASTANE n synthetic fibre that is able to return to its original shape after being stretched

ELASTASE n enzyme that digests elastin

ELASTIC, -S adj resuming normal shape after distortion ▷ n tape or fabric containing interwoven strands of flexible rubber

ELASTIN, -S n fibrous scleroprotein

ELATE, -S, ELATING vb fill with high spirits, exhilaration, pride or optimism

ELATED adj extremely happy and excited

ELATEDLY

ELATER, -S n elaterid beetle

ELATERID n type of beetle of the family which constitutes the click beetles

ELATERIN n white crystalline substance found in elaterium, used as a purgative

ELATERS ► elater

ELATES ► elate

ELATING ► elate

ELATION, -S n feeling of great happiness and excitement

ELATIVE, -S adj denoting a grammatical case in Finnish and other languages ▷ n elative case

ELBOW, -ED, -S n joint between the upper arm and the forearm ▷ vb shove or strike with the elbow

ELBOWING n act of elbowing

ELBOWS ► elbow

ELCHEE, -S n ambassador

ELCHI, -S same as ► elchee

ELD, -S n old age

ELDER, -S adj older ▷ n older person

ELDERLY adj (fairly) old

ELDERS ► elder

ELDEST, -S adj, n oldest (child)

ELDIN, -S n fuel

ELDING, -S same as ► eldin

ELDINS ► eldin

ELDORADO n place of great riches or fabulous opportunity

ELDRESS n woman elder

ELDRICH same as ► eldritch

ELDRITCH adj weird, uncanny

ELDS ► eld

ELECT, -ED, -ING, -S vb choose by voting ▷ adj appointed but not yet in office

ELECTEE, -S n someone who is elected

ELECTING ► elect

ELECTION n choosing of representatives by voting

ELECTIVE adj chosen by election ▷ n optional course or hospital placement undertaken by a medical student

ELECTOR, -S n someone who has the right to vote in an election

ELECTRET n permanently polarized dielectric material

ELECTRIC adj produced by, transmitting, or powered by electricity ▷ n electric train, car, etc

ELECTRO, -S vb (in printing) make a metallic copy of a page

ELECTRON n elementary particle in all atoms that has a negative electrical charge

ELECTROS ► electro

ELECTRUM n alloy of gold (55–88 per cent) and silver used for jewellery and ornaments

ELECTS ► elect

ELEGANCE n dignified grace in appearance, movement, or behaviour

ELEGANCY same as ► elegance

ELEGANT adj pleasing or graceful in dress, style, or design

ELEGIAC, -S adj mournful or plaintive ▷ n elegiac couplet or stanza

ELEGIAST n writer of elegies

ELEGIES ► elegy

ELEGISE, -D, -S same as ► elegize

ELEGIST, -S ► elegize

ELEGIT, -S n writ delivering debtor's property to plaintiff

ELEGIZE, -D, -S vb compose an elegy or elegies (in memory of)

ELEGY, ELEGIES n mournful poem, esp a lament for the dead

ELEMENT, -S n component part

ELEMI, -S n fragrant resin obtained from various tropical trees

ELENCH, -S n refutation in logic

ELENCHI ▸ elenchus

ELENCHIC ▸ elenchus

ELENCHS ▸ elench

ELENCHUS, ELENCHI *n* refutation of an argument by proving the contrary of its conclusion

ELENCTIC *adj* refuting an argument by proving the falsehood of its conclusion

ELEPHANT *n* huge four-footed thick-skinned animal with ivory tusks and a long trunk

ELEVATE, -S *vb* raise in rank or status

ELEVATED *adj* higher than normal ▷ *n* railway that runs on an elevated structure

ELEVATES ▸ elevate

ELEVATOR *n* lift for carrying people

ELEVEN, -S *n* one more than ten ▷ *adj* amounting to eleven ▷ *determiner* amounting to eleven

ELEVENTH *n* (of) number eleven in a series ▷ *adj* coming after the tenth in numbering or counting order, position, time, etc

ELEVON, -S *n* aircraft control surface usually fitted to tailless or delta-wing aircraft

ELF, -ED, -ING, -S, ELVES *n* (in folklore) small mischievous fairy ▷ *vb* entangle (esp hair)

ELFHOOD -S

ELFIN, -S *adj* small and delicate ▷ *n* young elf

ELFING ▸ elf

ELFINS ▸ elfin

ELFISH *adj* of, relating to, or like an elf or elves ▷ *n* supposed language of elves

ELFISHLY

ELFLAND, -S *another name for* ▸ **fairyland**

ELFLIKE ▸ elf

ELFLOCK, -S *n* lock of hair

ELFS ▸ elf

ELHI *adj* informal word for or relating to elementary high school

ELIAD, -S *n* glance

ELICHE, -S *n* pasta in the form of spirals

ELICIT, -ED, -S *vb* bring about (a response or reaction)

ELICITOR

ELIDE, -D, -S, ELIDING *vb* omit (a vowel or syllable) from a spoken word

ELIDIBLE

ELIGIBLE *adj* meeting the requirements or qualifications needed ▷ *n*

eligible person or thing

ELIGIBLY

ELINT, -S *n* electronic intelligence

ELISION, -S *n* omission of a syllable or vowel from a spoken word

ELITE, -S *n* most powerful, rich, or gifted members of a group ▷ *adj* of, relating to, or suitable for an elite

ELITISM, -S *n* belief that society should be ruled by a small group of superior people

ELITIST -S

ELIXIR, -S *n* legendary liquid

ELK, -S *n* large deer of N Europe and Asia

ELKHORN *n* as in **elkhorn fern** fern with a large leaf like an elk's horn

ELKHOUND *n* powerful breed of dog

ELKS ▸ elk

ELL, -S *n* obsolete unit of length

ELLAGIC *adj* of an acid derived from gallnuts

ELLIPSE *n* oval shape

ELLIPSIS, ELLIPSES *n* omission of letters or words in a sentence

ELLIPTIC *adj* relating to or having the shape of an ellipse

ELLOPS, -ES *same as* ▸ **elops**

ELLS ▸ ell

ELLWAND, -S *n* stick for measuring lengths

ELM, -S *n* tree with serrated leaves

ELMEN *adj* of or relating to elm trees

ELMIER ▸ elmy

ELMIEST ▸ elmy

ELMS ▸ elm

ELMWOOD, -S *n* wood from an elm tree

ELMY, ELMIER, ELMIEST *adj* of or relating to elm trees

ELOCUTE, -D, -S *vb* speak as if practising elocution

ELODEA, -S *n* type of American plant

ELOGE, -S *same as* ▸ **eulogy**

ELOGIES ▸ elogy

ELOGIST, -S ▸ elogy

ELOGIUM, -S *same as* ▸ **eulogy**

ELOGY, ELOGIES *same as* ▸ **eulogy**

ELOIGN, -ED, -S *vb* remove (oneself, one's property, etc) to a distant place

ELOIGNER

ELOIN, -ED, -ING, -S *same as* ▸ **eloign**

ELOINER -S

ELONGATE *vb* make or become longer ▷ *adj* long and narrow

ELOPE, -D, -S, ELOPING *vb* (of two people) run away secretly to get married

ELOPER -S

ELOPS, -ES *n* type of fish

ELOQUENT *adj* (of speech or writing) fluent and persuasive

ELPEE, -S *n* LP, long-playing record

ELS ▸ el

ELSE *adv* in addition or more

ELSEWISE *adv* otherwise

ELSHIN, -S *n* cobbler's awl

ELSIN, -S *variant of* ▸ **elshin**

ELT, -S *n* young female pig

ELTCHI, -S *variant of* ▸ **elchee**

ELTS ▸ elt

ELUANT, -S *same as* ▸ **eluent**

ELUATE, -S *n* solution of adsorbed material obtained during the process of elution

ELUDE, -D, -S, ELUDING *vb* escape from by cleverness or quickness

ELUDER -S

ELUDIBLE *adj* able to be eluded

ELUDING ▸ elude

ELUENT, -S *n* solvent used for eluting

ELUSION, -S ▸ elude

ELUSIVE *adj* difficult to catch or remember

ELUSORY *adj* avoiding the issue

ELUTE, -D, -S, ELUTING *vb* wash out (a substance) by the action of a solvent

ELUTION -S

ELUTOR, -S ▸ elute

ELUVIA ▸ eluvium

ELUVIAL ▸ eluvium

ELUVIATE *vb* remove material suspended in water in a layer of soil by the action of rainfall

ELUVIUM, ELUVIA, -S *n* mass of sand, silt, etc

ELVAN, -S *n* type of rock

ELVANITE *variant of* ▸ **elvan**

ELVANS ▸ elvan

ELVEN *adj* like an elf

ELVER, -S *n* young eel

ELVES ▸ elf

ELVISH *same as* ▸ **elfish**

ELVISHLY

ELYSIAN *adj* delightful, blissful

ELYTRA ▸ elytron

ELYTRAL ▸ elytron

ELYTROID ► elytron
ELYTRON, ELYTRA *n* either of the horny front wings of beetles and some other insects
ELYTROUS
ELYTRUM *same as* ► elytron
EM, -S *n* square of a body of any size of type, used as a unit of measurement
EMACIATE *vb* become or cause to become abnormally thin
EMACS, -EN *n* powerful computer program
EMAIL, -ED, -S *n* electronic mail ▷ *vb* send a message by electronic mail
EMAILER -S
EMAILING ► email
EMAILS ► email
EMANANT ► emanate
EMANATE, -D, -S *vb* issue, proceed from a source
EMANATOR
EMBACE, -S, EMBACING *variant of* ► embase
EMBAIL, -ED, -S *vb* enclose in a circle
EMBALE, -D, -S, EMBALING *vb* bind
EMBALL, -ED, -S *vb* enclose in a circle
EMBALM, -ED, -S *vb* preserve (a corpse) from decay by the use of chemicals etc
EMBALMER
EMBANK, -ED, -S *vb* protect, enclose, or confine with an embankment
EMBANKER
EMBAR, -RED, -S *vb* close in with bars
EMBARGO *n* order by a government prohibiting trade with a country ▷ *vb* put an embargo on
EMBARK, -ED, -S *vb* board a ship or aircraft
EMBARRAS *n* embarrassment
EMBARRED ► embar
EMBARS ► embar
EMBASE, -D, -S, EMBASING, EMBASTE *vb* degrade or debase
EMBASSY *n* offices or official residence of an ambassador
EMBASTE ► embase
EMBATHE, -D, -S *vb* bathe with water
EMBATTLE *vb* deploy (troops) for battle
EMBAY, -ED, -ING, -S *vb* form into a bay
EMBAYLD *archaic past form of* ► embail

EMBAYS ► embay
EMBED, -DED, -S *vb* fix firmly in something solid ▷ *n* journalist accompanying an active military unit
EMBER, -S *n* glowing piece of wood or coal in a dying fire
EMBEZZLE *vb* steal money that has been entrusted to one
EMBITTER *vb* make (a person) resentful or bitter
EMBLAZE, -D, -S *vb* cause to light up
EMBLAZER
EMBLAZON *vb* decorate with bright colours
EMBLEM, -ED, -S *n* object or design that symbolizes a quality, type, or group ▷ *vb* represent or signify
EMBLEMA *n* mosaic decoration
EMBLEMED ► emblem
EMBLEMS ► emblem
EMBLIC, -S *n* type of Indian tree
EMBLOOM, -S *vb* adorn with blooms
EMBODIED ► embody
EMBODIER ► embody
EMBODY, EMBODIED, EMBODIES *vb* be an example or expression of
EMBOG, -GED, -S *vb* sink down into a bog
EMBOGUE, -D, -S *vb* go out through a narrow channel or passage
EMBOIL, -ED, -S *vb* enrage or be enraged
EMBOLDEN *vb* encourage (someone)
EMBOLI ► embolus
EMBOLIC *adj* of or relating to an embolus or embolism
EMBOLIES ► emboly
EMBOLISE *same as* ► embolize
EMBOLISM *n* blocking of a blood vessel by a blood clot or air bubble
EMBOLIZE *vb* cause embolism in (a blood vessel)
EMBOLUS, EMBOLI *n* material that blocks a blood vessel
EMBOLY, EMBOLIES *n* infolding of an outer layer of cells so as to form a pocket in the surface
EMBORDER *vb* edge or border
EMBOSK, -ED, -S *vb* hide or cover
EMBOSOM, -S *vb* enclose or envelop, esp protectively

EMBOSS, -ES, EMBOST *vb* create a decoration that stands out on (a surface)
EMBOSSED *adj* (of a design or pattern) standing out from a surface
EMBOSSER ► emboss
EMBOSSES ► emboss
EMBOST ► emboss
EMBOUND, -S *vb* surround or encircle
EMBOW, -ED, -ING, -S *vb* design or create (a structure) in the form of an arch or vault
EMBOWEL, -S *vb* bury or embed deeply
EMBOWER, -S *vb* enclose in or as in a bower
EMBOWING ► embow
EMBOWS ► embow
EMBOX, -ED, -ES, -ING *vb* put in a box
EMBRACE, -D, -S *vb* clasp in the arms, hug ▷ *n* act of embracing
EMBRACER
EMBRAID, -S *vb* braid or interweave
EMBRASOR *n* one who embraces
EMBRAVE, -D, -S *vb* adorn or decorate
EMBREAD, -S *vb* braid
EMBROIL, -S *vb* involve (a person) in problems
EMBROWN, -S *vb* make or become brown
EMBRUE, -D, -S, EMBRUING *variant spelling of* ► imbrue
EMBRUTE, -D, -S *variant of* ► imbrute
EMBRYO, -S *n* unborn creature in the early stages of development
EMBRYOID
EMBRYON, -S *variant of* ► embryo
EMBRYOS ► embryo
EMBUS, -ED, -ES, -ING, -SED, -SES *vb* cause (troops) to board a transport vehicle
EMBUSIED ► embusy
EMBUSIES ► embusy
EMBUSING ► embus
EMBUSQUE *n* man who avoids military conscription by obtaining a government job
EMBUSSED ► embus
EMBUSSES ► embus
EMBUSY, EMBUSIED, EMBUSIES *vb* keep occupied
EMCEE, -D, -ING, -S *n* master of ceremonies ▷ *vb* act as master of ceremonies (for or at)

E

EMDASH, -ES n long dash in punctuation

EME, -S n uncle

EMEER, -S variant of ▶ emir

EMEERATE variant of ▶ emirate

EMEERS ▶ emeer

EMEND, -ED, -ING, -S vb remove errors from

EMENDALS pl n funds put aside for repairs

EMENDATE vb make corrections

EMENDED ▶ emend

EMENDER, -S ▶ emend

EMENDING ▶ emend

EMENDS ▶ emend

EMERALD, -S n bright green precious stone ▷ adj bright green

EMERAUDE archaic variant of ▶ emerald

EMERG, -S n part of a hospital dealing with emergencies

EMERGE, -D, -S vb come into view

EMERGENT adj coming into being or notice ▷ n aquatic plant with stem and leaves above the water

EMERGES ▶ emerge

EMERGING ▶ emerge

EMERGS ▶ emerg

EMERIED ▶ emery

EMERIES ▶ emery

EMERITA, -E, -S adj retired, but retaining an honorary title ▷ n woman who is retired, but retains an honorary title

EMERITUS, EMERITI adj retired, but retaining an honorary title ▷ n man who is retired, but retains an honorary title

EMEROD, -S n haemorrhoid

EMEROID, -S variant of ▶ emerod

EMERSE same as ▶ emersed

EMERSED adj protruding above the surface of the water

EMERSION n act or an instance of emerging

EMERY, EMERIED, EMERIES, -ING n hard mineral used for smoothing and polishing ▷ vb apply emery to

EMES ▶ eme

EMESIS, EMESES, -ES technical name for ▶ vomiting

EMETIC, -S n substance that causes vomiting ▷ adj causing vomiting

EMETICAL same as ▶ emetic

EMETICS ▶ emetic

EMETIN, -S same as ▶ emetine

EMETINE, -S n white bitter poisonous alkaloid

EMETINS ▶ emetin

EMEU, -S variant of ▶ emu

EMEUTE, -S n uprising or rebellion

EMIC, -S adj of or relating to a significant linguistic unit ▷ n emic viewpoint or approach

EMICANT ▶ emicate

EMICATE, -S vb twinkle

EMICS ▶ emic

EMICTION n passing of urine **EMICTORY**

EMIGRANT n person who leaves one place or country, esp a native country, to settle in another

EMIGRATE vb go and settle in another country

EMIGRE, -S n someone who has left his or her native country for political reasons

EMINENCE n position of superiority or fame

EMINENCY same as ▶ eminence

EMINENT adj distinguished, well-known

EMIR, -S n Muslim ruler

EMIRATE, -S n emir's country

EMIRS ▶ emir

EMISSARY n agent sent on a mission by a government ▷ adj (of veins) draining blood from sinuses in the dura mater to veins outside the skull

EMISSILE adj able to be emitted

EMISSION n act of giving out heat, light, a smell, etc **EMISSIVE**

EMIT, -S, -TED, -TING vb give out

EMITTER, -S n person or thing that emits

EMITTING ▶ emit

EMLETS pl n as in **blood-drop emlets** Chilean plant

EMMA, -S n former communications code for the letter A

EMMARBLE vb decorate with marble

EMMAS ▶ emma

EMMER, -S n variety of wheat

EMMESH, -ED, -ES variant of ▶ enmesh

EMMET, -S n tourist or holiday-maker

EMMEW, -ED, -ING, -S vb restrict

EMMOVE, -D, -S, EMMOVING vb cause emotion in

EMMY, -S n award for outstanding television performances and productions

EMO, -S n type of music

EMOCORE, -S n punk rock with lyrics that deal with emotional subjects

EMODIN, -S n type of chemical compound

EMOJI, -S n digital icon used in electronic communication

EMONG variant of ▶ among

EMONGES variant of ▶ among

EMONGEST variant of ▶ amongst

EMONGST variant of ▶ amongst

EMOS ▶ emo

EMOTE, -D, -S, EMOTING vb display exaggerated emotion, as if acting **EMOTER, -S**

EMOTICON n any of several combinations of symbols used in email and texting

EMOTING ▶ emote

EMOTION, -S n strong feeling

EMOTIVE adj tending to arouse emotion

EMOVE, -D, -S, EMOVING vb cause to feel emotion

EMPACKET vb wrap up

EMPAIRE, -D, -S variant of ▶ impair

EMPALE, -D, -S, EMPALING less common spelling of ▶ impale **EMPALER -S**

EMPANADA n Spanish meat-filled pastry

EMPANEL, -S vb enter on a list (names of persons to be summoned for jury service)

EMPARE, -D, -S, EMPARING archaic variant of ▶ impair

EMPARL, -ED, -S variant of ▶ imparl

EMPART, -ED, -S variant of ▶ impart

EMPATHIC adj of or relating to empathy

EMPATHY n ability to understand someone else's feelings

EMPATRON vb treat in the manner of a patron

EMPAYRE, -D, -S archaic variant of ▶ impair

EMPEACH variant of ▶ impeach

EMPEOPLE vb bring people into

EMPERCE, -D, -S *archaic variant of* ▸ **empierce**

EMPERIES ▸ **empery**

EMPERISE *variant of* ▸ **emperize**

EMPERISH *vb* damage or harm

EMPERIZE *vb* act like an emperor

EMPEROR, -S *n* ruler of an empire

EMPERY, EMPERIES *n* dominion or power

EMPHASIS, EMPHASES *n* special importance or significance

EMPHATIC *adj* showing emphasis ▷ *n* emphatic consonant, as used in Arabic

EMPIERCE *vb* pierce or cut

EMPIGHT, -S *adj* attached or positioned ▷ *vb* attach or position

EMPIRE, -S *n* group of territories under the rule of one state or person

EMPIRIC, -S *n* person who relies on empirical methods

EMPLACE, -D, -S *vb* put in place or position

EMPLANE, -D, -S *vb* board or put on board an aeroplane

EMPLEACH *variant of* ▸ **impleach**

EMPLONGE *variant of* ▸ **implunge**

EMPLOY, -ED, -S *vb* engage or make use of the services of (a person) in return for money ▷ *n* state of being employed

EMPLOYE, -S *same as* ▸ **employee**

EMPLOYED ▸ **employ**

EMPLOYEE *n* person who is hired to work for someone in return for payment

EMPLOYER *n* person or organization that employs someone

EMPLOYES ▸ **employe**

EMPLOYS ▸ **employ**

EMPLUME, -D, -S *vb* put a plume on

EMPOISON *vb* embitter or corrupt

EMPOLDER *variant spelling of* ▸ **impolder**

EMPORIUM, EMPORIA *n* large general shop

EMPOWER, -S *vb* enable, authorize

EMPRESS *n* woman who rules an empire

EMPRESSE *adj* keen; zealous

EMPRISE, -S *n* chivalrous or daring enterprise

EMPRIZE, -S *variant of* ▸ **emprise**

EMPT, -ED, -ING, -S *vb* empty

EMPTIED ▸ **empty**

EMPTIER, -S ▸ **empty**

EMPTIES ▸ **empty**

EMPTIEST ▸ **empty**

EMPTILY ▸ **empty**

EMPTING ▸ **empt**

EMPTINGS *variant of* ▸ **emptins**

EMPTINS *pl n* liquid leavening agent made from potatoes

EMPTION, -S *n* process of buying something

EMPTS ▸ **empt**

EMPTY, EMPTIED, EMPTIES, EMPTIEST *adj* containing nothing ▷ *vb* make or become empty ▷ *n* empty container, esp a bottle

EMPTYING

EMPTYSIS, EMPTYSES *n* act of spitting up blood

EMPURPLE *vb* make or become purple

EMPUSA, -S *n* goblin in Greek mythology

EMPUSE, -S *variant of* ▸ **empusa**

EMPYEMA, -S *n* collection of pus in a body cavity

EMPYEMIC

EMPYESIS, EMPYESES *n* pus-filled boil on the skin

EMPYREAL *variant of* ▸ **empyrean**

EMPYREAN *n* heavens or sky ▷ *adj* of or relating to the sky or the heavens

EMS ▸ **em**

EMU, -S *n* large Australian flightless bird with long legs

EMULATE, -D, -S *vb* attempt to equal or surpass by imitating

EMULATOR

EMULE, -D, -S, EMULING *variant of* ▸ **emulate**

EMULGE, -D, -S, EMULGING *vb* remove liquid from

EMULGENT

EMULING ▸ **emule**

EMULOUS *adj* desiring or aiming to equal or surpass another

EMULSIFY *vb* (of two liquids) join together

EMULSIN, -S *n* enzyme that is found in almonds

EMULSION *n* light-sensitive coating on photographic film ▷ *vb* paint with emulsion paint

EMULSIVE

EMULSOID *n* sol with a liquid disperse phase

EMULSOR, -S *n* device that emulsifies

EMUNGE, -D, -S, EMUNGING *vb* clean or clear out

EMURE, -D, -S, EMURING *variant of* ▸ **immure**

EMUS ▸ **emu**

EMYD, -S *n* freshwater tortoise or terrapin

EMYDE, -S *same as* ▸ **emyd**

EMYDS ▸ **emyd**

EMYS *n* freshwater tortoise or terrapin

EN *n* unit of measurement, half the width of an em

ENABLE, -D, -S, ENABLING *vb* provide (a person) with the means (to do something)

ENABLER -S

ENACT, -ED, -ING, -S *vb* establish by law

ENACTION

ENACTIVE

ENACTOR -S

ENACTORY ▸ **enact**

ENACTS ▸ **enact**

ENACTURE ▸ **enact**

ENALLAGE *n* act of using one grammatical form in the place of another

ENAMEL, -ED, -S *n* glasslike coating applied to metal etc to preserve the surface ▷ *vb* cover with enamel

ENAMELER

ENAMINE, -S *n* type of unsaturated compound

ENAMOR, -S *same as* ▸ **enamour**

ENAMORED *same as* > **enamoured**

ENAMORS ▸ **enamor**

ENAMOUR, -S *vb* inspire with love

ENARCH, -ED, -ES *variant of* ▸ **inarch**

ENARGITE *n* sulphide of copper and arsenic

ENARM, -ED, -ING, -S *vb* provide with arms

ENATE, -S *adj* growing out or outwards ▷ *n* relative on the mother's side

ENATIC *adj* related on one's mother's side

ENATION, -S ▸ **enate**

ENAUNTER *conj* in case that

ENCAENIA *n* festival of dedication or commemoration

ENCAGE, -D, -S, ENCAGING *vb* confine in or as in a cage

ENCALM, -ED, -S *vb* becalm, settle

E

ENCAMP, **-ED**, **-S** *vb* set up in a camp

ENCARPUS *n* decoration of fruit or flowers on a frieze

ENCASE, **-D**, **-S**, **ENCASING** *vb* enclose or cover completely

ENCASH, **-ED**, **-ES** *vb* exchange (a cheque) for cash

ENCASING ▸ **encase**

ENCASTRE *adj* (of a beam) fixed at the ends

ENCAVE, **-D**, **-S**, **ENCAVING** *variant of* ▸ **incave**

ENCEINTE *n* boundary wall enclosing a defended area

ENCHAFE, **-D**, **-S** *vb* heat up

ENCHAIN, **-S** *vb* bind with chains

ENCHANT, **-S** *vb* delight and fascinate

ENCHARGE *vb* give into the custody of

ENCHARM, **-S** *vb* enchant

ENCHASE, **-D**, **-S** *less common word for* ▸ **chase**
ENCHASER

ENCHEER, **-S** *vb* cheer up

ENCHORIC *same as* > **enchorial**

ENCIERRO *n* Spanish bull run

ENCINA, **-S** *n* type of oak
ENCINAL

ENCIPHER *vb* convert (a message, document, etc) from plain text into code or cipher

ENCIRCLE *vb* form a circle around

ENCLASP, **-S** *vb* clasp

ENCLAVE, **-D**, **-S** *n* part of a country entirely surrounded by another ▷ *vb* hold in an enclave

ENCLISIS, **ENCLISES** *n* state of being enclitic

ENCLITIC *adj* relating to a monosyllabic word treated as a suffix ▷ *n* enclitic word or linguistic form

ENCLOSE, **-D**, **-S** *vb* surround completely
ENCLOSER

ENCLOTHE *vb* clothe

ENCLOUD, **-S** *vb* hide with clouds

ENCODE, **-D**, **-S** *vb* convert (a message) into code
ENCODER -S

ENCODING *n* act of encoding

ENCOLOUR *vb* give a colour to

ENCOLURE *n* mane of a horse

ENCOMIA ▸ **encomium**

ENCOMION *variant of* ▸ **encomium**

ENCOMIUM, **ENCOMIA** *n* formal expression of praise

ENCORE, **-D**, **-S**, **ENCORING** *interj* again, once more ▷ *n* extra performance due to enthusiastic demand ▷ *vb* demand an extra or repeated performance

ENCRADLE *vb* put in a cradle

ENCRATY *n* control of one's desires, actions, etc

ENCREASE *variant form of* ▸ **increase**

ENCRINAL > **encrinite**

ENCRINIC > **encrinite**

ENCROACH *vb* intrude gradually on a person's rights or land

ENCRUST, **-S** *vb* cover with a layer of something

ENCRYPT, **-S** *vb* put (a message) into code

ENCUMBER *vb* hinder or impede

ENCYCLIC *n* letter sent by the Pope to all bishops

ENCYST, **-S** *vb* enclose or become enclosed by a cyst, thick membrane, or shell
ENCYSTED

END, **-ED**, **-S** *n* furthest point or part ▷ *vb* bring or come to a finish

ENDAMAGE *vb* cause injury to

ENDAMEBA *same as* > **endamoeba**

ENDANGER *vb* put in danger

ENDARCH *adj* having the first-formed xylem internal to that formed later

ENDARCHY *n* state of being endarch

ENDART, **-ED**, **-S** *variant of* ▸ **indart**

ENDASH, **-ES** *n* short dash in punctuation

ENDBRAIN *n* part of the brain

ENDCAP, **-S** *n* display placed at the end of a shop aisle

ENDEAR, **-ED**, **-S** *vb* cause to be liked

ENDEAVOR *same as* > **endeavour**

ENDED ▸ **end**

ENDEIXIS, **ENDEIXES** *n* sign or mark

ENDEMIAL *same as* ▸ **endemic**

ENDEMIC, **-S** *adj* present within a particular area or group of people ▷ *n* endemic disease or plant
ENDEMISM

ENDER, **-S** ▸ **end**

ENDERMIC *adj* (of a medicine) acting by absorption through the skin

ENDERON, **-S** *variant of* ▸ **andiron**

ENDERS ▸ **ender**

ENDEW, **-ED**, **-ING**, **-S** *variant of* ▸ **endue**

ENDEXINE *n* inner layer of an exine

ENDGAME, **-S** *n* closing stage of a game of chess

ENDGATE, **-S** *n* tailboard of a vehicle

ENDING, **-S** *n* last part or conclusion of something

ENDIRON, **-S** *variant of* ▸ **andiron**

ENDITE, **-D**, **-S**, **ENDITING** *variant of* ▸ **indict**

ENDIVE, **-S** *n* curly-leaved plant used in salads

ENDLANG *variant of* ▸ **endlong**

ENDLEAF, **-S** *n* endpaper in a book

ENDLESS *adj* having no end

ENDLONG *adv* lengthways or on end

ENDMOST *adj* nearest the end

ENDNOTE, **-S** *n* note at the end of a section of writing

ENDOCARP *n* inner layer of a fruit

ENDOCAST *n* cast made of the inside of a cranial cavity to show the size and shape of a brain

ENDODERM *n* inner germ layer of an animal embryo

ENDODYNE *same as* ▸ **autodyne**

ENDOGAMY *n* marriage within one's own tribe or similar unit

ENDOGEN, **-S** *n* plant that increases in size by internal growth

ENDOGENY *n* development by internal growth

ENDOPOD, **-S** *n* inner branch of a two-branched crustacean

ENDORSE, **-D**, **-S** *vb* give approval to

ENDORSEE *n* person in whose favour a negotiable instrument is endorsed

ENDORSER ▸ **endorse**

ENDORSES ▸ **endorse**

ENDORSOR ▸ **endorse**

ENDOSARC *same as* > **endoplasm**

ENDOSMOS *same as* > **endosmose**

ENDOSOME *n* sac within a biological cell

ENDOSS, **-ED**, **-ES** *vb* endorse

ENDOSTEA > **endosteum**

ENDOW, -ED, -ING, -S vb provide permanent income for

ENDOWER -S

ENDOZOA ► endozoon

ENDOZOIC adj (of a plant) living within an animal

ENDOZOON, ENDOZOA variant of ► **entozoon**

ENDPAPER n either of two leaves pasted to the inside of the cover of a book

ENDPLATE n any usually flat platelike structure at the end of something

ENDPLAY n technique in card games ▷ vb force (an opponent) to make a particular lead near the end of a hand

ENDPOINT n point at which anything is complete

ENDRIN, -S n type of insecticide

ENDS ► end

ENDSHIP, -S n small village

ENDUE, -D, -S, ENDUING vb invest or provide, as with some quality or trait

ENDURE, -D, -S vb bear (hardship) patiently

ENDURER -S

ENDURING adj long-lasting

ENDURO, -S n long-distance race for vehicles

ENDWAYS adv having the end forwards or upwards ▷ adj vertical or upright

ENDWISE same as ► **endways**

ENDYSIS, ENDYSES n formation of new layers of integument after ecdysis

ENDZONE, -S n (in American football) area at either end of the playing field

ENE, -S variant of ► **even**

ENEMA, -S, -TA n medicine that helps to empty the bowels

ENEMY, ENEMIES n hostile person or nation, opponent ▷ adj of or belonging to an enemy

ENERGIC ► energy

ENERGID, -S n nucleus and cytoplasm in a syncytium

ENERGIES ► energy

ENERGISE same as ► **energize**

ENERGIZE vb give vigour to

ENERGY, ENERGIES n capacity for intense activity

ENERVATE vb deprive of strength or vitality ▷ adj deprived of strength or vitality

ENERVE, -D, -S, ENERVING vb enervate

ENES ► ene

ENEW, -ED, -ING, -S vb force a bird into water

ENFACE, -D, -S, ENFACING vb write, print, or stamp (something) on the face of (a document)

ENFANT, -S n French child

ENFEEBLE vb weaken

ENFELON, -S vb infuriate

ENFEOFF, -S vb invest (a person) with possession of a freehold estate in land

ENFESTED adj made bitter

ENFETTER vb fetter

ENFEVER, -S vb make feverish

ENFIERCE vb make ferocious

ENFILADE n burst of gunfire sweeping from end to end along a line of troops ▷ vb attack with an enfilade

ENFILED adj passed through

ENFIRE, -D, -S, ENFIRING vb set alight

ENFIX, -ED, -ES, -ING variant of ► **infix**

ENFLAME, -D, -S variant of ► **inflame**

ENFLESH vb make flesh

ENFLOWER vb put flowers on

ENFOLD, -ED, -S vb cover by wrapping something around

ENFOLDER

ENFORCE, -D, -S vb impose obedience (to a law etc)

ENFORCER

ENFOREST vb make into a forest

ENFORM, -ED, -S variant of ► **inform**

ENFRAME, -D, -S vb put inside a frame

ENFREE, -D, -S vb release, make free

ENFREEZE, ENFROZE, ENFROZEN vb freeze

ENFROSEN archaic past participle of ► **enfreeze**

ENFROZE ► enfreeze

ENFROZEN ► enfreeze

ENG, -S another name for ► **agma**

ENGAGE, -S vb take part, participate ▷ adj (of an artist) morally or politically committed to some ideology

ENGAGED adj pledged to be married

ENGAGEE adj (of a female artist) morally or politically committed to some ideology

ENGAGER, -S ► engage

ENGAGES ► engage

ENGAGING adj charming

ENGAOL, -ED, -S vb put into gaol

ENGENDER vb produce, cause to occur

ENGILD, -ED, -S, ENGILT vb cover with or as if with gold

ENGINE, -D, -S, ENGINING n any machine which converts energy into mechanical work ▷ vb put an engine in

ENGINEER n person trained in any branch of engineering ▷ vb plan in a clever manner

ENGINER, -S ► engine

ENGINERY n collection or assembly of engines

ENGINES ► engine

ENGINING ► engine

ENGINOUS adj ingenious or clever

ENGIRD, -ED, -S, ENGIRT vb surround

ENGIRDLE variant of ► **engird**

ENGIRDS ► engird

ENGIRT ► engird

ENGLISH vb put spin on a billiard ball

ENGLOBE, -D, -S vb surround as if in a globe

ENGLOOM, -S vb make dull or dismal

ENGLUT, -S vb devour ravenously

ENGOBE, -S n liquid put on pottery before glazing

ENGORE, -D, -S, ENGORING vb pierce or wound

ENGORGE, -D, -S vb clog with blood

ENGORING ► engore

ENGOULED adj (in heraldry) with ends coming from the mouths of animals

ENGRACE, -D, -S vb give grace to

ENGRAFF, -S variant of ► **engraft**

ENGRAFT, -S vb graft (a shoot, bud, etc) onto a stock

ENGRAIL, -S vb decorate or mark with small carved notches

ENGRAIN, -S variant spelling of ► **ingrain**

ENGRAM, -S n physical basis of an individual memory in the brain

ENGRAMMA variant of ► **engram**

ENGRAMME variant of ► **engram**

ENGRAMS ► engram

ENGRASP, -S vb grasp or seize

ENGRAVE, -D, -N, -S vb carve (a design) onto a hard surface

ENGRAVER

E

E

ENGRIEVE vb grieve

ENGROOVE vb put a groove in

ENGROSS vb occupy the attention of (a person) completely

ENGS ► eng

ENGUARD, -S vb protect or defend

ENGULF, -ED, -S vb cover or surround completely

ENGULPH, -S variant of ► engulf

ENHALO, -ED, -ES, -S vb surround with or as if with a halo

ENHANCE, -D, -S vb increase in quality, value, or attractiveness
ENHANCER

ENHEARSE variant of ► inhearse

ENHUNGER vb cause to be hungry

ENHYDROS n piece of chalcedony that contains water

ENIAC, -S n early type of computer built in the 1940s

ENIGMA, -S, -TA n puzzling thing or person

ENISLE, -D, -S, ENISLING vb put on or make into an island

ENJAMB, -ED, -S vb (of a line of verse) run over into the next line

ENJOIN, -ED, -S vb order (someone) to do something
ENJOINER

ENJOY, -ED, -ING, -S vb take joy in
ENJOYER -S

ENKERNEL vb put inside a kernel

ENKINDLE vb set on fire

ENLACE, -D, -S, ENLACING vb bind or encircle with or as with laces

ENLARD, -ED, -S vb put lard on

ENLARGE, -D, -S vb make or grow larger

ENLARGEN variant of ► enlarge

ENLARGER n optical instrument for making enlarged photographs

ENLARGES ► enlarge

ENLEVE adj having been abducted

ENLIGHT, -S, ENLIT vb light up

ENLINK, -ED, -S vb link together

ENLIST, -ED, -S vb enter the armed forces
ENLISTEE
ENLISTER

ENLIT ► enlight

ENLIVEN, -S vb make lively or cheerful

ENLOCK, -ED, -S vb lock or secure

ENLUMINE vb illuminate

ENMESH, -ED, -ES vb catch or involve in or as if in a net or snare

ENMEW, -ED, -ING, -S variant of ► emmew

ENMITY, ENMITIES n ill will, hatred

ENMOSSED adj having a covering of moss

ENMOVE, -D, -S, ENMOVING variant of ► emmove

ENNAGE, -S n number of ens in printed matter

ENNEAD, -S n group or series of nine
ENNEADIC

ENNEAGON another name for ► nonagon

ENNOBLE, -D, -S vb make noble, elevate
ENNOBLER

ENNOG, -S n back alley

ENNUI, -ED, -S, ENNUYED, ENNUYING n boredom, dissatisfaction ▷ vb bore

ENNUYE adj bored

ENNUYED ► ennui

ENNUYEE same as ► ennuye

ENNUYING ► ennui

ENODAL adj having no nodes

ENOKI, -S variant of > enokitake

ENOL, -S n type of organic compound

ENOLASE, -S n type of enzyme

ENOLIC ► enol

ENOLOGY usual US spelling of ► oenology

ENOLS ► enol

ENOMOTY n division of the Spartan army in ancient Greece

ENOPHILE n lover of wine

ENORM variant of ► enormous

ENORMITY n great wickedness

ENORMOUS adj very big, vast

ENOSIS, ENOSES, -ES n union of Greece and Cyprus

ENOUGH, -S adj as much or as many as necessary ▷ n sufficient quantity ▷ adv sufficiently

ENOUNCE, -D, -S vb enunciate

ENOW, -S archaic word for ► enough

ENPLANE, -D, -S vb board an aircraft

ENPRINT, -S n standard photographic print

ENQUEUE, -D, -S vb add (an item) to a queue of computing tasks

ENQUIRE, -D, -S same as ► inquire
ENQUIRER
ENQUIRY

ENRACE, -D, -S, ENRACING vb bring in a race of people

ENRAGE, -D, -S, ENRAGING vb make extremely angry

ENRANGE, -D, -S vb arrange, organize

ENRANK, -ED, -S vb put in a row

ENRAPT > enrapture

ENRAUNGE archaic variant of ► enrange

ENRAVISH vb enchant

ENRHEUM, -S vb pass a cold on to

ENRICH, -ED, -ES vb improve in quality
ENRICHER

ENRIDGED adj ridged

ENRING, -ED, -S vb put a ring round

ENRIVEN adj ripped

ENROBE, -D, -S, ENROBING vb dress in or as if in a robe
ENROBER -S

ENROL, -S vb (cause to) become a member

ENROLL, -ED, -S same as ► enrol

ENROLLEE ► enrol

ENROLLER ► enrol

ENROLLS ► enroll

ENROLS ► enrol

ENROOT, -ED, -S vb establish (plants) by fixing their roots in the earth

ENROUGH, -S vb roughen

ENROUND, -S vb encircle

ENS, ENTIA n being or existence in the most general abstract sense

ENSAMPLE n example ▷ vb make an example

ENSATE adj shaped like a sword

ENSCONCE vb settle firmly or comfortably

ENSCROLL variant of ► inscroll

ENSEAL, -ED, -S vb seal up

ENSEAM, -ED, -S vb put a seam on

ENSEAR, -ED, -S vb dry

ENSEMBLE n all the parts of something taken together ▷ adv all together or at once ▷ adj (of a film or play) involving several separate but often interrelated story lines

ENSERF, -ED, -S vb enslave

ENSEW, -ED, -ING, -S variant of ▸ ensue

ENSHEATH variant of > insheathe

ENSHELL, -S variant of ▸ inshell

ENSHIELD vb protect

ENSHRINE vb cherish or treasure

ENSHROUD vb cover or hide as with a shroud

ENSIFORM adj shaped like a sword blade

ENSIGN, -ED, -S n military officer ▷ vb mark with a sign **ENSIGNCY**

ENSILAGE n process of ensiling green fodder ▷ vb make into silage

ENSILE, -D, -S, ENSILING vb store and preserve (green fodder) in an enclosed pit or silo

ENSKY, ENSKIED, ENSKIES, -ED, -ING vb put in the sky

ENSLAVE, -D, -S vb make a slave of (someone) **ENSLAVER**

ENSNARE, -D, -S vb catch in or as if in a snare **ENSNARER**

ENSNARL, -S vb become tangled in

ENSORCEL vb enchant

ENSOUL, -ED, -S vb endow with a soul

ENSPHERE vb enclose in or as if in a sphere

ENSTAMP, -S vb imprint with a stamp

ENSTEEP, -S vb soak in water

ENSTYLE, -D, -S vb give a name to

ENSUE, -D, -S vb come next, result

ENSUING adj following subsequently or in order

ENSUITE, -S n bathroom attached to another room

ENSURE, -D, -S, ENSURING vb make certain or sure **ENSURER -S**

ENSWATHE vb bind or wrap

ENSWEEP, -S, ENSWEPT vb sweep across

ENTAIL, -ED, -S vb bring about or impose inevitably ▷ n restriction imposed by entailing an estate **ENTAILER**

ENTAME, -D, -S, ENTAMING vb make tame

ENTAMEBA same as > entamoeba

ENTAMED ▸ entame

ENTAMES ▸ entame

ENTAMING ▸ entame

ENTANGLE vb catch or involve in or as if in a tangle

ENTASES ▸ entasis

ENTASIA, -S same as ▸ entasis

ENTASIS, ENTASES n slightly convex curve given to the shaft of a structure

ENTASTIC adj (of a disease) characterized by spasms

ENTAYLE, -D, -S variant of ▸ entail

ENTELLUS n langur of S Asia

ENTENDER vb make more tender

ENTENTE, -S n friendly understanding between nations

ENTER, -ED, -S vb come or go in

ENTERA ▸ enteron

ENTERAL same as ▸ enteric

ENTERATE adj with an intestine separate from the outer wall of the body

ENTERED ▸ enter

ENTERER, -S ▸ enter

ENTERIC, -S adj intestinal ▷ n infectious disease of the intestines

ENTERING ▸ enter

ENTERON, ENTERA, -S n alimentary canal

ENTERS ▸ enter

ENTETE adj obsessed

ENTETEE variant of ▸ entete

ENTHALPY n property of a thermodynamic system

ENTHETIC adj (esp of infectious diseases) introduced into the body from without

ENTHRAL, -S vb hold the attention of

ENTHRALL same as ▸ enthral

ENTHRALS ▸ enthral

ENTHRONE vb place (someone) on a throne

ENTHUSE, -D, -S vb (cause to) show enthusiasm

ENTIA ▸ ens

This means entities, and because of the common letters it uses it is one of the most frequently played 5-letter words, at least towards the end of the game.

ENTICE, -D, -S vb attract by exciting hope or desire, tempt **ENTICER -S**

ENTICING ▸ entice

ENTIRE, -S adj including every detail, part, or aspect of something ▷ n state of being entire

ENTIRELY adv without reservation or exception

ENTIRES ▸ entire

ENTIRETY n state of being entire or whole

ENTITIES ▸ entity

ENTITLE, -D, -S vb give a right to

ENTITY, ENTITIES n separate distinct thing

ENTODERM same as ▸ endoderm

ENTOIL, -ED, -S archaic word for ▸ ensnare

ENTOMB, -ED, -S vb place (a corpse) in a tomb

ENTOMIC adj denoting or relating to insects

ENTOPIC adj situated in its normal place or position

ENTOPTIC adj (of visual sensation) resulting from structures within the eye itself

ENTOTIC adj of or relating to the inner ear

ENTOZOA ▸ entozoon

ENTOZOAL ▸ entozoon

ENTOZOAN same as ▸ entozoon

ENTOZOIC adj of or relating to an entozoon

ENTOZOON, ENTOZOA n internal parasite

ENTRAIL vb twist or entangle

ENTRAILS pl n intestines

ENTRAIN, -S vb board or put aboard a train

ENTRALL variant of ▸ entrails

ENTRANCE n way into a place ▷ vb delight ▷ adj necessary in order to enter something

ENTRANT, -S n person who enters a university, contest, etc

ENTRAP, -S vb trick into difficulty etc

ENTREAT, -S vb ask earnestly

ENTREATY n earnest request

ENTREE, -S n dish served before a main course

ENTREMES variant of > entremets

ENTRENCH vb establish firmly

ENTREPOT n warehouse for commercial goods

E

E

ENTRESOL *another name for*
▶ **mezzanine**
ENTREZ *interj* enter
ENTRIES ▶ **entry**
ENTRISM, -S *variant of*
▶ **entryism**
ENTRIST -S
ENTROLD *adj* word used
by Spenser meaning
surrounded
ENTROPIC ▶ **entropy**
ENTROPY *n* lack of
organization
ENTRUST, -S *vb* put into the
care or protection of
ENTRY, ENTRIES *n* entrance
▷ *adj* necessary in order to
enter something
ENTRYISM *n* joining a political
party to change its principles
ENTRYIST
ENTRYWAY *n* entrance
passage
ENTS *pl n* (college)
entertainments
ENTWINE, -D, -S *vb* twist
together or around
ENTWIST, -S *vb* twist together
or around
ENUF *common intentional
literary misspelling of*
▶ **enough**
ENURE, -D, -S, ENURING
variant spelling of ▶ **inure**
ENURESIS, ENURESES *n*
involuntary discharge of
urine, esp during sleep
ENURETIC
ENURING ▶ **enure**
ENURN *same as* ▶ **inurn**
ENURNED *same as* ▶ **inurned**
ENURNING *same as*
▶ **inurning**
ENURNS *same as* ▶ **inurns**
ENVASSAL *vb* make a vassal of
ENVAULT, -S *vb* enclose in a
vault; entomb
ENVEIGLE *same as* ▶ **inveigle**
ENVELOP, -S *vb* wrap up,
enclose
ENVELOPE *n* folded gummed
paper cover for a letter
ENVELOPS ▶ **envelop**
ENVENOM, -S *vb* fill or
impregnate with venom
ENVIABLE *adj* arousing envy,
fortunate
ENVIABLY
ENVIED ▶ **envy**
ENVIER, -S ▶ **envy**
ENVIES ▶ **envy**
ENVIOUS *adj* full of envy
ENVIRO, -S *n*
environmentalist
ENVIRON *vb* encircle or
surround

ENVIRONS *pl n* surrounding
area, esp of a town
ENVIROS ▶ **enviro**
ENVISAGE *vb* conceive of as a
possibility
ENVISION *vb* conceive of as a
possibility, esp in the future
ENVOI, -S *same as* ▶ **envoy**
ENVOY, -S *n* messenger
ENVY, ENVIED, ENVIES *n*
feeling of discontent aroused
by another's good fortune
▷ *vb* grudge (another's good
fortune, success, or qualities)
ENVYING -S
ENWALL, -ED, -S *vb* wall in
ENWALLOW *vb* sink or plunge
ENWALLS ▶ **enwall**
ENWHEEL, -S *archaic word for*
▶ **encircle**
ENWIND, -S, ENWOUND *vb*
wind or coil around
ENWOMB, -ED, -S *vb* enclose
in or as if in a womb
ENWOUND ▶ **enwind**
ENWRAP, -S *vb* wrap or
cover up
ENWREATH *vb* surround or
encircle with or as with a
wreath or wreaths
ENZIAN, -S *n* gentian violet
ENZONE, -D, -S, ENZONING *vb*
enclose in a zone
ENZOOTIC *adj* (of diseases)
affecting animals within a
limited region ▷ *n* enzootic
disease
ENZYM, -S *same as*
▶ **enzyme**
ENZYME, -S *n* complex protein
that acts as a catalyst
ENZYMIC
ENZYMS ▶ **enzym**
EOAN *adj* of or relating to the
dawn
EOBIONT, -S *n* hypothetical
chemical precursor of a
living cell
EOCENE *adj* of, denoting, or
formed in the second epoch
of the Tertiary period
EOHIPPUS *n* extinct dog-sized
ancestor of the horse
EOLIAN *adj* of or relating to
the wind

6-letter words tend to be
among the least known and
least used, because they
leave you at the mercy of the
tile bag without scoring
that extra 50 points you
would get for using all 7
letters. This word, meaning
relating to the wind, often
comes in useful for dumping
a surplus of vowels. Its

alternative spelling **aeolian**
is even better for this, and
what's more will get you a
bonus!

EOLIENNE *n* type of fine cloth
EOLIPILE *variant of*
▶ **aeolipile**
EOLITH, -S *n* stone used as
a primitive tool in Eolithic
times
EOLITHIC
EOLOPILE *variant of*
▶ **aeolipile**
EON, -S *n* two or more eras
EONIAN *adj* of or relating to
an eon
EONISM, -S *n* adoption of
female dress and behaviour
by a male
EONS ▶ **eon**
EORL, -S *n* Anglo-Saxon
nobleman
EOSIN, -S *n* red crystalline
water-insoluble derivative of
fluorescein
EOSINE, -S *same as* ▶ **eosin**
EOSINIC ▶ **eosin**
EOSINS ▶ **eosin**
EOTHEN *adv* from the East
EPACRID, -S *n* type of heath-
like plant
EPACRIS *n* genus of the
epacrids
EPACT, -S *n* difference in time
between the solar year and
the lunar year
EPAGOGE, -S *n* inductive
reasoning
EPAGOGIC
EPANODOS *n* return to main
theme after a digression
EPARCH, -S *n* bishop or
metropolitan in charge of an
eparchy
EPARCHY *n* diocese of the
Eastern Christian Church
EPATANT *adj* startling or
shocking
EPATER, -ED, -S *vb* shock
conventional people
EPAULE, -S *n* shoulder of a
fortification
EPAULET, -S *same as*
▶ **epaulette**
EPAXIAL *adj* above the axis
EPAZOTE, -S *n* type of herb
EPEE, -S *n* straight-bladed
sword used in fencing
EPEEIST, -S *n* one who uses or
specializes in using an epee
EPEES ▶ **epee**
EPEIRA, -S *same as* ▶ **epeirid**
EPEIRIC *adj* in, of, or relating
to a continent
EPEIRID, -S *n* type of spider

EPENDYMA n membrane lining the ventricles of the brain and the central canal of the spinal cord

EPERDU adj distracted

EPERDUE adj distracted

EPERGNE, -S n ornamental centrepiece for a table

EPHA, -S same as ► **ephah**

EPHAH, -S n Hebrew unit of dry measure

EPHAS ► **epha**

EPHEBE, -S, EPHEBI n (in ancient Greece) youth about to enter full citizenship **EPHEBIC**

EPHEBOS, EPHEBOI same as ► **ephebe**

EPHEBUS same as ► **ephebe**

EPHEDRA, -S n gymnosperm shrub

EPHEDRIN same as > **ephedrine**

EPHELIS n freckle

EPHEMERA n something transitory or short-lived

EPHOD, -S n embroidered vestment worn by priests

EPHOR, -I, -S n one of a board of senior magistrates in several ancient Greek states **EPHORAL** **EPHORATE**

EPIBLAST n outermost layer of an embryo, which becomes the ectoderm at gastrulation

EPIBLEM, -S n outermost cell layer of a root

EPIBOLIC ► **epiboly**

EPIBOLY n process that occurs during gastrulation in vertebrates

EPIC, -S n long poem, book, or film about heroic events or actions ▷ adj very impressive or ambitious **EPICAL** **EPICALLY**

EPICALYX n small sepal-like bracts in some flowers

EPICARP, -S n outermost layer of the pericarp of fruits

EPICEDE, -S same as > **epicedium**

EPICEDIA > **epicedium**

EPICENE, -S adj having the characteristics of both sexes; hermaphroditic ▷ n epicene person or creature

EPICIER, -S n grocer

EPICISM, -S n style or trope characteristic of epics

EPICIST, -S n writer of epics

EPICLIKE adj resembling or reminiscent of an epic

EPICOTYL n part of an embryo plant stem above the cotyledons but beneath the terminal bud

EPICS ► **epic**

EPICURE, -S n person who enjoys good food and drink

EPICYCLE n (in the Ptolemaic system) a small circle, around which a planet was thought to revolve

EPIDEMIC n widespread occurrence of a disease ▷ adj (esp of a disease) affecting many people in an area

EPIDERM, -S same as > **epidermis**

EPIDOTE, -S n green mineral **EPIDOTIC**

EPIDURAL n spinal anaesthetic injected to relieve pain during childbirth ▷ adj on or over the outermost membrane covering the brain and spinal cord

EPIFAUNA n animals that live on the surface of the seabed

EPIFOCAL adj situated or occurring at an epicentre

EPIGAEAL same as ► **epigeal**

EPIGAEAN same as ► **epigeal**

EPIGAMIC adj denoting an animal feature that attracts the opposite sex

EPIGEAL adj of or relating to a form of seed germination

EPIGEAN same as ► **epigeal**

EPIGEIC same as ► **epigeal**

EPIGENE adj formed or taking place at or near the surface of the earth

EPIGENIC adj pertaining to the theory of the gradual development of the embryo

EPIGEOUS same as ► **epigeal**

EPIGON, -S same as ► **epigone**

EPIGONE, -S, EPIGONI n inferior follower or imitator **EPIGONIC**

EPIGONS ► **epigon**

EPIGONUS same as ► **epigone**

EPIGRAM, -S n short witty remark or poem

EPIGRAPH n quotation at the start of a book

EPIGYNY > **epigynous**

EPILATE, -D, -S vb remove hair from

EPILATOR n electrical appliance for plucking unwanted hair

EPILEPSY n disorder of the nervous system causing loss of consciousness and sometimes convulsions

EPILOG, -S same as ► **epilogue**

EPILOGIC ► **epilogue**

EPILOGS ► **epilog**

EPILOGUE n short speech or poem at the end of a literary work, esp a play

EPIMER, -S n isomer

EPIMERE, -S n dorsal part of the mesoderm of a vertebrate embryo

EPIMERIC > **epimerism**

EPIMERS ► **epimer**

EPIMYSIA > **epimysium**

EPINAOS, EPINAOI n rear vestibule

EPINASTY n increased growth of the upper surface of a plant part

EPINOSIC adj unhealthy

EPIPHANY n moment of great or sudden revelation

EPIPHYTE n plant that grows on another plant but is not parasitic on it

EPIPLOIC ► **epiploon**

EPIPLOON n greater omentum

EPIPOLIC > **epipolism**

EPISCIA, -S n creeping plant

EPISCOPE n optical device that projects an enlarged image

EPISCOPY n area overseen

EPISEMON n emblem

EPISODAL same as ► **episodic**

EPISODE, -S n incident in a series of incidents

EPISODIC adj occurring at irregular intervals

EPISOMAL adj of or like an episome

EPISOME, -S n unit of genetic material (DNA) in bacteria that can be replicated

EPISPERM n protective outer layer of certain seeds

EPISPORE n outer layer of certain spores

EPISTASY same as > **epistasis**

EPISTLE, -D, -S n letter, esp of an apostle ▷ vb preface

EPISTLER n writer of an epistle or epistles

EPISTLES ► **epistle**

EPISTOME n area between the mouth and antennae of crustaceans

EPISTYLE n lowest part of an entablature that bears on the columns

EPITAPH, -S n commemorative inscription

on a tomb ▷ vb compose an epitaph

EPITASIS, EPITASES n (in classical drama) part of a play in which the main action develops

EPITAXES ► epitaxis

EPITAXIC ► epitaxy

EPITAXIS, EPITAXES same as ► epitaxy

EPITAXY n growth of a thin layer on the surface of a crystal

EPITHECA n outer and older layer of the cell wall of a diatom

EPITHEM, -A, -S n external topical application

EPITHET, -S n descriptive word or name ▷ vb name

EPITOME, -S n typical example **EPITOMIC**

EPITONIC adj undergoing too great a strain

EPITOPE, -S n site on an antigen at which a specific antibody becomes attached

EPITRITE n metrical foot with three long syllables and one short one

EPIZOA ► epizoon

EPIZOAN, -S same as ► epizoon

EPIZOIC adj (of an animal or plant) growing or living on the exterior of a living animal **EPIZOISM**

EPIZOITE n organism that lives on an animal but is not parasitic on it

EPIZOON, EPIZOA n animal that lives on the body of another animal

EPIZOOTY n animal disease

EPOCH, -S n period of notable events

EPOCHA, -S same as ► epoch

EPOCHAL ► epoch

EPOCHAS ► epocha

EPOCHS ► epoch

EPODE, -S n part of a lyric ode that follows the strophe and the antistrophe **EPODIC**

EPONYM, -S n name derived from the name of a real or mythical person **EPONYMIC**

EPONYMY n derivation of names of places, etc, from those of persons

EPOPEE, -S n epic poem

EPOPOEIA same as ► epopee

EPOPT, -S n one initiated into mysteries

EPOS, -ES n body of poetry in which the tradition of a people is conveyed

EPOXIDE, -S n chemical compound

EPOXY, EPOXIED, EPOXIES, -ED, -ING adj of or containing a specific type of chemical compound ▷ n epoxy resin ▷ vb glue with epoxy resin

EPRIS adj enamoured

EPRISE feminine form of ► epris

EPSILON, -S n fifth letter of the Greek alphabet

EPSOMITE n sulphate of magnesium

EPUISE adj exhausted

EPUISEE feminine form of ► epuise

EPULARY adj of or relating to feasting

EPULIS, EPULIDES, -ES n swelling of the gum

EPULOTIC n scarring

EPURATE, -D, -S vb purify

EPYLLION, EPYLLIA n miniature epic

EQUABLE adj even-tempered **EQUABLY**

EQUAL, -ED, -ING, -LED, -S adj identical in size, quantity, degree, etc ▷ n person or thing equal to another ▷ vb be equal to

EQUALI pl n pieces for a group of instruments of the same kind

EQUALING ► equal

EQUALISE same as ► equalize

EQUALITY n state of being equal

EQUALIZE vb make or become equal

EQUALLED ► equal

EQUALLY ► equal

EQUALS ► equal

EQUANT, -S n circle in which a planet was formerly believed to move

EQUATE, -D, -S, EQUATING vb make or regard as equivalent

EQUATION n mathematical statement that two expressions are equal

A rack that contains Q and a jumble of vowels can look unpromising, but if you mentally affix the U to the Q and then look for likely letter strings you will soon arrive at ATION, from where it is only a short step to this useful 8-letter word, one of the most frequently

played bonuses containing Q.

EQUATIVE adj (in grammar) denoting the equivalence or identity of two terms

EQUATOR, -S n imaginary circle round the earth

EQUERRY n attendant to a member of a royal family

EQUES n (in ancient Rome) horseman

EQUID, -S n any animal of the horse family

EQUINAL same as ► equine

EQUINE, -S adj of or like a horse ▷ n any animal of the horse family

EQUINELY

EQUINIA, -S n glanders

EQUINITY n horse-like nature

EQUINOX n time of year when day and night are of equal length

EQUIP, -PED, -S vb provide with supplies, components, etc

EQUIPAGE n horse-drawn carriage, esp one elegantly equipped and attended by liveried footmen ▷ vb equip

EQUIPE, -S n (esp in motor racing) team

EQUIPPED ► equip

EQUIPPER ► equip

EQUIPS ► equip

EQUISETA > equisetum

EQUITANT adj having the base folded around the stem

EQUITES pl n cavalry

EQUITY, EQUITIES n fairness

EQUIVOKE same as > equivoque

ER interj sound made when hesitating in speech

ERA, -S n period of time considered as distinctive

ERADIATE less common word for ► radiate

ERAS ► era

ERASABLE ► erase

ERASE, -D, -S, ERASING vb destroy all traces of

ERASER, -S n object for erasing something written

ERASES ► erase

ERASING ► erase

ERASION, -S n act of erasing

This means the act of erasing: not an exciting word, but its combination of common letters makes it one of the most frequently played 7-letter bonus words.

ERASURE, -S n erasing

ERATHEM, -S n stratum of rocks representing a specific geological era

ERBIA, -S n oxide of erbium

ERBIUM, -S n metallic element of the lanthanide series

ERE, -D, -S, ERING prep before ▷ vb plough

ERECT, -ED, -ING, -S vb build ▷ adj upright

ERECTER, -S same as ▶ erector

ERECTILE adj capable of becoming erect

ERECTING ▶ erect

ERECTION n act of erecting or the state of being erected

ERECTIVE adj tending to erect

ERECTLY ▶ erect

ERECTOR, -S n any muscle that raises a part or makes it erect

ERECTS ▶ erect

ERED ▶ ere

ERELONG adv before long

EREMIC adj of or relating to deserts

EREMITAL ▶ eremite

EREMITE, -S n Christian hermit

EREMITIC

EREMURUS, EREMURI n type of herb

ERENOW adv long before the present

EREPSIN, -S n mixture of proteolytic enzymes secreted by the small intestine

ERES ▶ ere

ERETHIC ▶ erethism

ERETHISM n abnormally high degree of irritability or sensitivity in any part of the body

EREV, -S n day before

EREWHILE adv short time ago

ERF, ERVEN n plot of land marked off for building purposes

ERG, -S same as > **ergometer**

ERGASTIC adj consisting of the non-living by-products of protoplasmic activity

ERGATE, -S n worker ant

ERGATIVE adj denoting a verb that takes the same noun as either direct object or subject ▷ n ergative verb

ERGATOID ▶ ergate

ERGO, -S same as > **ergometer**

ERGODIC adj of or relating to the probability that any state will recur

ERGOGRAM n tracing produced by an ergograph

ERGON, -S n work

ERGOS ▶ ergo

ERGOT, -S n fungal disease of cereal

ERGOTIC

ERGOTISE same as ▶ ergotize

ERGOTISM n ergot poisoning

ERGOTIZE vb inflict ergotism upon

ERGOTS ▶ ergot

ERGS ▶ erg

ERHU, -S n Chinese two-stringed violin

ERIACH, -S same as ▶ eric

ERIC, -S n (in old Irish law) fine paid by a murderer to the family of his or her victim

ERICA, -S n genus of plants including heathers

ERICK, -S same as ▶ eric

ERICOID adj (of leaves) small and tough, resembling those of heather

ERICS ▶ eric

ERIGERON n type of plant

ERING ▶ ere

ERINGO, -ES, -S same as ▶ eryngo

ERINITE, -S n arsenate of copper

ERINUS, -ES n type of plant

ERIONITE n common form of zeolite

ERISTIC, -S adj of, relating, or given to controversy or logical disputation ▷ n person who engages in logical disputes

ERK, -S n aircraftman or naval rating

ERLANG, -S n unit of traffic intensity in a telephone system

ERLKING, -S n malevolent spirit who carries off children

ERM interj expression of hesitation

ERMELIN, -S n ermine

ERMINE, -S n stoat in northern regions

ERMINED adj clad in the fur of the ermine

ERMINES ▶ ermine

ERN, -ED, -ING, -S archaic variant of ▶ earn

ERNE, -S n fish-eating (European) sea eagle

ERNED ▶ ern

ERNES ▶ erne

ERNING ▶ ern

ERNS ▶ ern

ERODABLE ▶ erode

ERODE, -D, -S, ERODING vb wear away

ERODENT -S

ERODIBLE ▶ erode

ERODING ▶ erode

ERODIUM, -S n type of geranium

EROGENIC same as > **erogenous**

EROS, -ES n love

EROSE adj jagged or uneven, as though gnawed or bitten

EROSELY

EROSES ▶ eros

EROSIBLE adj able to be eroded

EROSION, -S n wearing away of rocks or soil

EROSIVE

EROTEMA, -S n rhetorical question

EROTEME, -S same as ▶ erotema

EROTESIS, EROTESES same as ▶ erotema

EROTETIC adj pertaining to a rhetorical question

ERR, -ED, -S vb make a mistake

ERRABLE adj capable of making a mistake

ERRANCY n state or an instance of erring or a tendency to err

ERRAND, -S n short trip to do something for someone

ERRANT, -S adj behaving in a manner considered to be unacceptable ▷ n knight-errant

ERRANTLY

ERRANTRY n way of life of a knight errant

ERRANTS ▶ errant

ERRATA ▶ erratum

ERRATIC, -S adj irregular or unpredictable ▷ n rock that has been transported by glacial action

ERRATUM, ERRATA n error in writing or printing

ERRED ▶ err

ERRHINE, -S adj causing nasal secretion ▷ n errhine drug or agent

ERRING, -S ▶ err

ERRINGLY ▶ err

ERRINGS ▶ erring

ERROR, -S n mistake, inaccuracy, or misjudgment

ERRORIST n one who makes errors

ERRORS ▶ error

ERRS ▶ err

ERS, -ES same as ▶ ervil

ERSATZ, -ES *adj* made in imitation ▷ *n* ersatz substance or article

ERSES ▸ ers

ERST *adv* long ago

ERUCIC *adj* as in **erucic acid** crystalline fatty acid

ERUCT, -ED, -ING, -S *vb* belch

ERUCTATE *same as* ▸ **eruct**

ERUCTED ▸ eruct

ERUCTING ▸ eruct

ERUCTS ▸ eruct

ERUDITE, -S *adj* having great academic knowledge ▷ *n* erudite person

ERUGO, -S *n* verdigris

ERUMPENT *adj* bursting out or developing as though bursting through

ERUPT, -ED, -ING, -S *vb* eject (steam, water, or volcanic material) violently

ERUPTION

ERUPTIVE *adj* erupting or tending to erupt ▷ *n* type of volcanic rock

ERUPTS ▸ erupt

ERUV, -IM, -IN, -S *n* area within which certain activities forbidden to be done on the Sabbath are permitted

ERVEN ▸ erf

ERVIL, -S *n* type of vetch

ERYNGIUM *n* type of temperate and subtropical plant

ERYNGO, -ES, -S *n* type of plant with toothed or lobed leaves

ERYTHEMA *n* patchy inflammation of the skin

ERYTHRON *n* red blood cells and their related tissues

ES, -ES *n* letter S

ESCALADE *n* assault by the use of ladders, esp on a fortification ▷ *vb* gain access to (a place) by the use of ladders

ESCALADO *n* escalade

ESCALATE *vb* increase in extent or intensity

ESCALIER *n* staircase

ESCALLOP *another word for* ▸ **scallop**

ESCALOP, -S *another word for* ▸ **scallop**

ESCALOPE *n* thin slice of meat, esp veal

ESCALOPS ▸ escalop

ESCAPADE *n* mischievous adventure

ESCAPADO *n* escaped criminal

ESCAPE, -D, -S, ESCAPING *vb* get free (of) ▷ *n* act of escaping

ESCAPEE, -S *n* person who has escaped

ESCAPER, -S ▸ escape

ESCAPES ▸ escape

ESCAPING ▸ escape

ESCAPISM *n* taking refuge in fantasy to avoid unpleasant reality

ESCAPIST

ESCAR, -S *same as* ▸ **esker**

ESCARGOT *n* variety of edible snail, usually eaten with a sauce made of melted butter and garlic

ESCAROLE *n* variety of endive with broad leaves, used in salads

ESCARP, -ED, -S *n* inner side of the ditch separating besiegers and besieged ▷ *vb* make into a slope

ESCARS ▸ escar

ESCHALOT *another name for a* ▸ **shallot**

ESCHAR, -S *n* dry scab or slough

ESCHEAT, -S *n* possessions that become state property in the absence of an heir ▷ *vb* attain such property

ESCHEW, -ED, -S *vb* abstain from, avoid

ESCHEWAL

ESCHEWER

ESCOLAR, -S *n* slender spiny-finned fish

ESCORT, -ED, -S *n* people following another person for protection or as an honour ▷ *vb* act as an escort to

ESCOT, -ED, -ING, -S, -TED *vb* maintain

ESCRIBE, -D, -S *vb* make a mathematical drawing

ESCROC, -S *n* conman

ESCROL, -S *same as* ▸ **escroll**

ESCROLL, -S *n* scroll

ESCROLS ▸ escrol

ESCROW, -ED, -S *n* item delivered to a third party pending fulfilment of a condition ▷ *vb* place (money, a document, etc) in escrow

ESCUAGE, -S *(in medieval Europe) another word for* ▸ **scutage**

ESCUDO, -S *n* former monetary unit of Portugal

ESCULENT *adj* edible ▷ *n* any edible substance

ESERINE, -S *n* crystalline alkaloid

ESES ▸ es

ESILE, -S *n* vinegar

ESKAR, -S *same as* ▸ **esker**

ESKER, -S *n* long ridge of gravel, sand, etc

ESKY, ESKIES *n* portable insulated container

ESLOIN, -ED, -S *same as* ▸ **eloign**

ESLOYNE, -D, -S *same as* ▸ **eloign**

ESNE, -S *n* household slave

ESNECY, ESNECIES *n* inheritance law

ESNES ▸ esne

ESOPHAGI > esophagus

ESOTERIC *adj* understood by only a small number of people with special knowledge

ESOTERY

ESPADA, -S *n* sword

ESPALIER *n* shrub or fruit tree trained to grow flat ▷ *vb* train (a plant) on an espalier

ESPANOL *n* Spanish person

ESPARTO, -S *n* grass of S Europe and N Africa

ESPECIAL *adj* special

ESPIAL, -S *n* act or fact of being seen or discovered

ESPIED ▸ espy

ESPIEGLE *adj* playful

ESPIER, -S ▸ espy

ESPIES ▸ espy

ESPOIR, -S *n* category of wrestler

ESPOUSAL *n* adoption or support

ESPOUSE, -D, -S *vb* adopt or give support to (a cause etc)

ESPOUSER

ESPRESSO *n* strong coffee made by forcing steam or boiling water through ground coffee beans

ESPRIT, -S *n* spirit, liveliness, or wit

ESPUMOSO *n* sparkling wine

ESPY, ESPIED, ESPIES, -ING *vb* catch sight of

ESQUIRE, -D, -S *n* courtesy title placed after a man's name ▷ *vb* escort

ESQUISSE *n* sketch

ESS, -ES *n* letter S

ESSAY, -ED, -ING, -S *n* short literary composition ▷ *vb* attempt

ESSAYER -S

ESSAYISH ▸ essay

ESSAYIST *n* person who writes essays

ESSAYS ▸ essay

ESSE *n* existence**

ESSENCE, -S n most important feature of a thing which determines its identity

ESSES ▸ ess

ESSIVE, -S n grammatical case

ESSOIN, -ED, -S n excuse ▷ vb excuse for not appearing in court

ESSOINER

ESSONITE variant spelling of > hessonite

ESSOYNE, -S same as ▸ essoin

EST, -S n treatment intended to help people towards psychological growth

ESTACADE n defensive arrangement of stakes

ESTANCIA n (in Spanish America) a large estate or cattle ranch

ESTATE, -D, -S, ESTATING n landed property ▷ vb provide with an estate

ESTEEM, -ED, -S n high regard ▷ vb think highly of

ESTER, -S n chemical compound

ESTERASE n any of a group of enzymes that hydrolyse esters

ESTERIFY vb change or cause to change into an ester

ESTERS ▸ ester

ESTHESES ▸ esthesis

ESTHESIA US spelling of > aesthesia

ESTHESIS, ESTHESES n esthesia

ESTHETE, -S US spelling of ▸ aesthete

ESTHETIC

ESTIMATE vb calculate roughly ▷ n approximate calculation

ESTIVAL usual US spelling of ▸ aestival

ESTIVATE usual US spelling of > aestivate

ESTOC, -S n short stabbing sword

ESTOILE, -S n heraldic star with wavy points

ESTOP, -PED, -S vb preclude by estoppel

ESTOPPEL n rule precluding a person from denying the truth of a statement of facts

ESTOPS ▸ estop

ESTOVER same as ▸ estovers

ESTOVERS pl n right allowed by law to tenants of land to cut timber, esp for fuel and repairs

ESTRADE, -S n dais or raised platform

ESTRAGON another name for ▸ tarragon

ESTRAL US spelling of ▸ oestral

ESTRANGE vb separate and live apart from (one's spouse)

ESTRAY, -ED, -S n stray domestic animal of unknown ownership ▷ vb stray

ESTREAT, -S n true copy of or extract from a court record ▷ vb send an extract of the court record

ESTREPE, -D, -S vb lay waste

ESTRICH n ostrich

ESTRIDGE n ostrich

ESTRIN, -S US spelling of ▸ oestrin

ESTRIOL, -S usual US spelling of ▸ oestriol

ESTRO, -S n poetic inspiration

ESTROGEN usual US spelling of > oestrogen

ESTRONE, -S usual US spelling of ▸ oestrone

ESTROS ▸ estro

ESTROUS ▸ estrus

ESTRUAL ▸ estrus

ESTRUM, -S usual US spelling of ▸ oestrum

ESTRUS, -ES usual US spelling of ▸ oestrus

ESTS ▸ est

ESTUARY n mouth of a river

ESURIENT adj greedy

ET dialect past tense of ▸ eat

ETA, -S n seventh letter in the Greek alphabet

ETACISM, -S n pronunciation of eta as a long vowel sound

ETAERIO, -S n aggregate fruit

> This strange-looking word is a type of fruit, and because it uses the commonest letters it is, along with **otarine**, the most frequently played of all bonus words.

ETAGE, -S n floor in a multi-storey building

ETAGERE, -S n stand with open shelves for displaying ornaments, etc

ETAGES ▸ etage

ETALAGE, -S n display

ETALON, -S n device used in spectroscopy

ETAMIN, -S same as ▸ etamine

ETAMINE, -S n cotton or worsted fabric of loose weave

ETAMINS ▸ etamin

ETAPE, -S n public storehouse

ETAS ▸ eta

ETAT, -S n state

ETATISM, -S same as ▸ etatisme

ETATISME n authoritarian control by the state

ETATISMS ▸ etatisme

ETATIST ▸ etatisme

ETATISTE ▸ etatisme

ETATS ▸ etat

ETCETERA n number of other items

ETCH, -ED, -ES vb wear away or cut the surface of (metal, glass, etc) with acid

ETCHANT, -S n any acid or corrosive used for etching

ETCHED ▸ etch

ETCHER, -S ▸ etch

ETCHES ▸ etch

ETCHING, -S n picture printed from an etched metal plate

ETEN, -S n giant

ETERNAL, -S adj without beginning or end ▷ n eternal thing

ETERNE archaic or poetic word for ▸ eternal

ETERNISE same as ▸ eternize

ETERNITY n infinite time

ETERNIZE vb make eternal

ETESIAN, -S adj (of NW winds) recurring annually in the summer in the E Mediterranean ▷ n etesian wind

ETH, -S same as ▸ edh

ETHAL, -S n cetyl alcohol

ETHANAL, -S n colourless volatile pungent liquid

ETHANE, -S n odourless flammable gas

ETHANOIC adj as in **ethanoic acid** acetic acid

ETHANOL, -S same as ▸ alcohol

ETHANOYL n substance consisting of or containing the monovalent group CH_3CO-

ETHE adj easy

ETHENE, -S same as ▸ ethylene

ETHEPHON n synthetic plant-growth regulator

ETHER, -S n colourless anaesthetic

ETHERCAP n spider

ETHEREAL adj extremely delicate

ETHERIAL same as ▸ ethereal

ETHERIC ▸ ether

ETHERIFY vb change (a compound, such as an alcohol) into an ether

ETHERION n gas formerly believed to exist in air

ETHERISE same as ► etherize

ETHERISH ► ether

ETHERISM n addiction to ether

ETHERIST

ETHERIZE vb subject (a person) to the anaesthetic influence of ether fumes

ETHERS ► ether

ETHIC n moral principle

ETHICAL, -S adj of or based on a system of moral beliefs ▷ n drug available only by prescription

ETHICIAN ► ethics

ETHICISE same as ► ethicize

ETHICISM ► ethics

ETHICIST ► ethics

ETHICIZE vb make or consider as ethical

ETHICS n code of behaviour

ETHINYL, -S same as ► ethynyl

ETHION, -S n type of pesticide

ETHIOPS n dark-coloured chemical compound

ETHMOID, -S adj denoting or relating to a specific bone of the skull ▷ n ethmoid bone

ETHNARCH n ruler of a people or province, as in parts of the Roman and Byzantine Empires

ETHNE ► ethnos

ETHNIC, -S adj relating to a people or group that shares a culture, religion, or language ▷ n member of an ethnic group, esp a minority group

ETHNICAL same as ► ethnic

ETHNICS ► ethnic

ETHNONYM n name of ethnic group

ETHNOS, ETHNE, -ES n ethnic group

ETHOGRAM n description of animal's behaviour

ETHOLOGY n study of the behaviour of animals in their normal environment

ETHONONE another name for ► ketene

ETHOS, -ES n distinctive spirit and attitudes of a people, culture, etc

ETHOXIDE n any of a class of saltlike compounds

ETHOXY, ETHOXIES same as ► ethoxyl

ETHOXYL, -S n univalent radical

ETHS ► eth

ETHYL, -S adj type of chemical hydrocarbon group

ETHYLATE same as ► ethoxide

ETHYLENE n poisonous gas used as an anaesthetic and as fuel

ETHYLIC ► ethyl

ETHYLS ► ethyl

ETHYNE, -S another name for ► acetylene

ETHYNYL, -S n univalent radical

ETIC, -S adj relating to linguistic terms analysed without regard to structural function ▷ n etic approach or viewpoint

ETIOLATE vb become pale and weak

ETIOLIN, -S n yellow pigment

ETIOLOGY n study of the causes of diseases

ETNA, -S n container used to heat liquids

ETOILE, -S n star

ETOUFFEE n spicy Cajun stew

ETOURDI adj foolish

ETOURDIE feminine form of ► etourdi

ETRANGER n foreigner

ETRENNE, -S n New Year's gift

ETRIER, -S n short portable ladder or set of webbing loops

ETTERCAP n spider

ETTIN, -S n giant

ETTLE, -D, -S, ETTLING vb intend

ETUDE, -S n short musical composition for a solo instrument

ETUI, -S n small usually ornamented case

ETWEE, -S same as ► etui

E is a very desirable letter, but sometimes you can have too much of even this good thing. This word for a needle-case, a variant of **etui**, can help you dispose of a few of them.

ETYMA ► etymon

ETYMIC ► etymon

ETYMON, ETYMA, -S n earliest form of a word or morpheme from which another is derived

ETYPIC n unable to conform to type

ETYPICAL same as ► etypic

EUCAIN, -S same as ► eucaine

EUCAINE, -S n crystalline optically active substance

EUCAINS ► eucain

EUCALYPT n myrtaceous tree

EUCARYON same as ► eukaryote

EUCARYOT same as ► eukaryote

EUCHARIS n S American plant cultivated for its large white fragrant flowers

EUCHRE, -D, -S, EUCHRING n US and Canadian card game ▷ vb prevent (a player) from making his contracted tricks

EUCLASE, -S n brittle green gem

EUCRITE, -S n type of stony meteorite

EUCRITIC

EUCYCLIC adj (of plants) having the same number of leaves in each whorl

EUDAEMON same as ► eudemon

EUDAIMON same as ► eudaemon

This word for a benevolent spirit is difficult to spot in play, but is one of those high-probability 8-letter bonus words using many vowels that are well worth special attention. It has variant spellings **eudaemon** and **eudemon**.

EUDEMON, -S n benevolent spirit or demon

EUGARIE, -S another name for ► pipi

EUGE interj well done!

EUGENIA, -S n plant of the clove family

EUGENIC ► eugenics

EUGENICS n study of methods of improving the human race

EUGENISM

EUGENIST

EUGENOL, -S n oily liquid used in perfumery

EUGH, -S archaic form of ► yew

EUGHEN archaic form of ► yew

EUGHS ► eugh

EUGLENA, -S n type of freshwater unicellular organism

EUGLENID same as ► euglena

EUK, -ED, -ING, -S vb itch

EUKARYON same as > eukaryote

EUKARYOT same as > eukaryote

EUKED ► euk

EUKING ► euk

EUKS ► euk

EULACHAN *same as* ▸ **eulachon**

EULACHON *n* salmonoid food fish

EULOGIA, -E, -S *n* blessed bread

This is one of the few 7-letter words using all the vowels. What's more, it can take a plural in E as well as S, giving **eulogiae**, which can be great for getting you out of vowel trouble.

EULOGIES ▸ **eulogy**

EULOGISE *same as* ▸ **eulogize**

EULOGIST ▸ **eulogize**

EULOGIUM *same as* ▸ **eulogy**

EULOGIZE *vb* praise (a person or thing) highly in speech or writing

EULOGY, EULOGIES *n* speech or writing in praise of a person

EUMERISM *n* collection of similar parts

EUMONG, -S *same as* ▸ **eumung**

EUMUNG, -S *n* any of various Australian acacias

EUNUCH, -S *n* castrated man

EUOI *n* cry of Bacchic frenzy

This is a cry expressing Bacchic frenzy, and is forever coming in useful to dispose of a surplus of vowels. It has the less commonly played but still useful variants **evoe**, **evhoe** and **evohe**.

EUONYMIN *n* extract derived from the bark of the euonymus

EUONYMUS *n* type of N temperate tree or shrub

EUOUAE, -S *n* musical term

This word is remarkable in that it contains no consonants. You will be surprised at how often you will be glad to play it!

EUPAD, -S *n* antiseptic powder

EUPATRID *n* (in ancient Greece) hereditary noble or landowner

EUPEPSIA *n* good digestion

EUPEPSY *same as* ▸ **eupepsia**

EUPEPTIC ▸ **eupepsia**

EUPHENIC *adj* of or pertaining to biological improvement

EUPHOBIA *n* fear of good news

EUPHON, -S *n* glass harmonica

EUPHONIA *same as* ▸ **euphony**

EUPHONIC *adj* denoting or relating to euphony

EUPHONS ▸ **euphon**

EUPHONY *n* pleasing sound

EUPHORIA *n* sense of elation

EUPHORIC

EUPHORY *same as* ▸ **euphoria**

EUPHOTIC *adj* denoting the part of a sea or lake with enough light to enable photosynthesis

EUPHRASY *same as* > **eyebright**

EUPHROE, -S *n* wooden block through which the lines of a crowfoot are rove

EUPHUISE *same as* ▸ **euphuize**

EUPHUISM *n* artificial prose style of the Elizabethan period

EUPHUIST

EUPHUIZE *vb* write in euphuism

EUPLOID, -S *adj* having chromosomes in an exact multiple of the haploid number ▷ *n* euploid cell or individual

EUPLOIDY

EUPNEA, -S *same as* ▸ **eupnoea**

EUPNEIC ▸ **eupnoea**

EUPNOEA, -S *n* normal relaxed breathing

EUPNOEIC

EUREKA, -S *n* exclamation of triumph at finding something

EURIPUS, EURIPI *n* strait or channel with a strong current or tide

EURO, -S *n* unit of the single currency of the European Union

EUROBOND *n* bond issued in a eurocurrency

EUROCRAT *n* member, esp a senior member, of the administration of the European Union

EUROKIES ▸ **euroky**

EUROKOUS ▸ **euroky**

EUROKY, EUROKIES *n* ability of an organism to live under different conditions

EUROLAND *n* area containing the countries using the euro

EURONOTE *n* form of euro-commercial paper consisting

of short-term negotiable bearer notes

EUROPIUM *n* silvery-white element of the lanthanide series

EUROPOP, -S *n* type of pop music by European artists

EUROS ▸ **euro**

EUROZONE *n* area containing the countries using the euro

EURYBATH *n* organism that can live at different depths underwater

EURYOKY *same as* ▸ **euroky**

EURYTHMY *n* dancing style in which the rhythm of music is expressed through body movements

EUSOCIAL *adj* using division of labour

EUSOL, -S *n* solution of eupad in water

EUSTACY ▸ **eustatic**

EUSTASY ▸ **eustatic**

EUSTATIC *adj* denoting worldwide changes in sea level

EUSTELE, -S *n* central cylinder of a seed plant

EUSTYLE, -S *n* building with columns optimally spaced

EUTAXIA, -S *n* condition of being easily melted

EUTAXIES ▸ **eutaxy**

EUTAXITE *n* banded volcanic rock

EUTAXY, EUTAXIES *n* good order

EUTECTIC *adj* having the lowest freezing point possible for the mixture ▷ *n* eutectic mixture

EUTEXIA, -S *same as* ▸ **eutaxia**

EUTHYMIA *n* pleasant state of mind

EUTROPHY > **eutrophic**

EUTROPIC ▸ **eutropy**

EUTROPY *n* chemical structure

EUXENITE *n* rare brownish-black mineral

EVACUANT *adj* serving to promote excretion ▷ *n* evacuant agent

EVACUATE *vb* send (someone) away from a place of danger

EVACUEE, -S *n* person evacuated from a place of danger

EVADABLE ▸ **evade**

EVADE, -D, -S, EVADING *vb* get away from or avoid

EVADER -S

EVADIBLE ▸ **evade**

EVADING ▸ **evade**

EVALUATE vb find or judge the value of

EVANESCE vb fade gradually from sight

EVANGEL, -S n gospel of Christianity

EVANGELY n gospel

EVANISH poetic word for ▸ **vanish**

EVASIBLE ▸ **evasion**

EVASION, -S n act of evading something by cunning or illegal means

EVASIVE adj not straightforward

EVE, -S n evening or day before some special event

EVECTION n irregularity in the moon's motion caused by perturbations of the sun and planets

EVEJAR, -S n nightjar

EVEN, -ED, -EST adj flat or smooth ▷ adv equally ▷ vb make even ▷ n eve
EVENER -S

EVENFALL n early evening

EVENING n end of the day or early part of the night ▷ adj of or in the evening

EVENINGS adv in the evening, esp regularly

EVENLY ▸ **even**

EVENNESS ▸ **even**

EVENS adv (of a bet) winning the same as the amount staked if successful

EVENSONG n evening prayer

EVENT, -ED, -S n anything that takes place ▷ vb take part in or ride (a horse) in eventing

EVENTER, -S ▸ **eventing**

EVENTFUL adj full of exciting incidents

EVENTIDE n evening

EVENTING n riding competitions, usu involving cross-country, jumping, and dressage

EVENTIVE adj relating to an event

EVENTS ▸ **event**

EVENTUAL adj ultimate

EVER adv at any time

EVERMORE adv for all time to come

EVERNET, -S n hypothetical form of internet

EVERSION ▸ **evert**

EVERT, -ED, -ING, -S vb turn (some body part) outwards or inside out

EVERTOR, -S n any muscle that turns a part outwards

EVERTS ▸ **evert**

EVERY adj each without exception

EVERYDAY adj usual or ordinary ▷ n ordinary day

EVERYMAN; EVERYMEN n ordinary person; common man

EVERYONE pron every person

EVERYWAY adv in every way

EVES ▸ **eve**

EVET, -S n eft

EVHOE interj cry of Bacchic frenzy

EVICT, -ED, -ING, -S vb legally expel (someone) from his or her home
EVICTEE -S

EVICTION ▸ **evict**

EVICTOR, -S ▸ **evict**

EVICTS ▸ **evict**

EVIDENCE n ground for belief ▷ vb demonstrate, prove

EVIDENT, -S adj easily seen or understood ▷ n item of evidence

EVIL, -ER, -EST, -LER, -LEST, -S n wickedness ▷ adj harmful ▷ adv in an evil manner

EVILDOER n wicked person

EVILER ▸ **evil**

EVILEST ▸ **evil**

EVILLER ▸ **evil**

EVILLEST ▸ **evil**

EVILLY ▸ **evil**

EVILNESS ▸ **evil**

EVILS ▸ **evil**

EVINCE, -D, -S, EVINCING vb make evident
EVINCIVE

EVIRATE, -D, -S vb deprive of strength or vigour

EVITABLE adj able to be avoided

EVITATE, -D, -S archaic word for ▸ **avoid**

EVITE, -D, -S, EVITING archaic word for ▸ **avoid**

EVO, -S informal word for ▸ **evening**

EVOCABLE ▸ **evoke**

EVOCATE, -D, -S vb evoke

EVOCATOR n person or thing that evokes

EVOE interj cry of Bacchic frenzy

EVOHE interj cry of Bacchic frenzy

EVOKE, -D, -S, EVOKING vb call or summon up (a memory, feeling, etc)

EVOKER -S

EVOLUE, -S n colonial term for an African educated according to European principles

EVOLUTE, -D, -S n geometric curve ▷ adj having the margins rolled outwards ▷ vb evolve

EVOLVE, -D, -S, EVOLVING vb develop gradually

EVOLVENT adj evolving ▷ n involute curve

EVOLVER, -S ▸ **evolve**

EVOLVES ▸ **evolve**

EVOLVING ▸ **evolve**

EVONYMUS same as ▸ **euonymus**

EVOS ▸ **evo**

EVOVAE, -S n mnemonic used in sacred music

EVULGATE vb make public

EVULSE, -D, -S, EVULSING vb extract by force

EVULSION n act of extracting by force

EVZONE, -S n soldier in an elite Greek infantry regiment

EWE, -S n female sheep

EWER, -S n large jug with a wide mouth

EWES ▸ **ewe**

EWEST Scots word for ▸ **near**

EWFTES Spenserian plural of ▸ **eft**

EWGHEN archaic form of ▸ **yew**

EWHOW interj expression of pity or regret

EWK, -ED, -ING, -S vb itch

Ewk is a dialect word for **itch**. It's a handy little word and a good one to remember in case you end up with both K and W, and remember that it's a verb, so you can have **ewks, ewked** and **ewking**. It's also worth knowing its variants **euk, yeuk, youk, yuck** and **yuke**!

EWT, -S archaic form of ▸ **newt**

EX, -ED, -ES, -ING prep not including ▷ n former spouse, significant other, etc ▷ vb cross out or delete

EXABYTE, -S n very large unit of computer memory

EXACT, -ED, -EST, -S adj correct and complete in every detail ▷ vb demand (payment or obedience)

EXACTA, -S n horse-racing bet

EXACTED ▸ **exact**

EXACTER, -S ▸ **exact**

EXACTEST ▸ **exact**

EXACTING adj making rigorous or excessive demands

EXACTION n act of obtaining or demanding money as a right

EXACTLY adv precisely, in every respect ▷ interj just so! precisely!

EXACTOR, -S ▸ exact

EXACTS ▸ exact

EXACUM, -S n type of tropical plant

EXAHERTZ n very large unit of frequency

EXALT, -ING, -S vb praise highly

EXALTED adj high or elevated in rank, position, dignity, etc

EXALTER, -S ▸ exalt

EXALTING ▸ exalt

EXALTS ▸ exalt

EXAM, -S n examination

EXAMEN, -S n examination of conscience

EXAMINE, -D, -S vb look at closely

EXAMINEE n person who sits an exam

EXAMINER ▸ examine

EXAMINES ▸ examine

EXAMPLAR archaic form of ▸ exemplar

EXAMPLE, -D, -S n specimen typical of its group

EXAMS ▸ exam

EXANTHEM same as > exanthema

EXAPTED adj biologically adapted

EXAPTIVE adj involving biological adaptation

EXARATE adj (of the pupa of some insects) having legs, wings, antennae, etc, free and movable

EXARCH, -S n head of certain autonomous Orthodox Christian Churches ▷ adj (of a xylem strand) having the first-formed xylem external to that formed later

EXARCHAL

EXARCHY same as > exarchate

EXCAMB, -ED, -S vb exchange

EXCAVATE vb unearth buried objects from (a piece of land) methodically to learn about the past

EXCEED, -ED, -S vb be greater than

EXCEEDER

EXCEL, -LED, -S vb be superior to

EXCEPT, -ED, -S prep other than, not including ▷ vb leave out; omit; exclude

EXCEPTOR

EXCERPT, -S n passage taken from a book, speech, etc ▷ vb take a passage from a book, speech, etc

EXCERPTA > excerptum

EXCERPTS ▸ excerpt

EXCESS, -ED, -ES n state or act of exceeding the permitted limits ▷ vb make (a position) redundant

EXCHANGE vb give or receive (something) in return for something else ▷ n act of exchanging

EXCHEAT, -S same as ▸ escheat

EXCIDE, -D, -S, EXCIDING vb cut out

EXCIMER, -S n excited dimer which would remain dissociated in the ground state

EXCIPLE, -S n part of a lichen

EXCISE, -D, -S, EXCISING n tax on goods produced for the home market ▷ vb cut out or away

EXCISION

EXCITANT adj able to excite or stimulate ▷ n something able to excite

EXCITE, -S vb arouse to strong emotion

EXCITED adj emotionally aroused, esp to pleasure or agitation

EXCITER, -S n person or thing that excites

EXCITES ▸ excite

EXCITING adj causing excitement

EXCITON, -S n excited electron bound to the hole produced by its excitation

EXCITOR, -S n type of nerve

EXCLAIM, -S vb speak suddenly, cry out

EXCLAVE, -S n territory owned by a country, but surrounded by another

EXCLUDE, -D, -S vb keep out, leave out

EXCLUDEE

EXCLUDER

EXCRETA n excrement

EXCRETAL

EXCRETE, -D, -S vb discharge (waste matter) from the body

EXCRETER

EXCUBANT adj keeping guard

EXCUDIT sentence substitute (named person) made this

EXCURSE, -D, -S vb wander

EXCURSUS n incidental digression from the main topic

EXCUSAL, -S ▸ excuse

EXCUSE, -D, -S, EXCUSING n explanation offered to justify (a fault etc) ▷ vb put forward a reason or justification for (a fault etc)

EXCUSER -S

EXCUSIVE adj excusing

EXEAT, -S n leave of absence from school or some other institution

EXEC, -S n executive

EXECRATE vb feel and express loathing and hatred of (someone or something)

EXECS ▸ exec

EXECUTE, -D, -S vb put (a condemned person) to death

EXECUTER

EXECUTOR n person appointed to perform the instructions of a will

EXECUTRY n condition of being an executor

EXED ▸ ex

EXEDRA, -E, -S n building, room, portico, or apse containing a continuous bench

EXEEM, -ED, -ING, -S same as ▸ exeme

EXEGESIS, EXEGESES n explanation of a text, esp of the Bible

EXEGETE, -S n person who practises exegesis

EXEGETIC adj of or relating to exegesis

EXEME, -D, -S, EXEMING vb set free

EXEMPLA ▸ exemplum

EXEMPLAR n person or thing to be copied, model

EXEMPLE, -S same as ▸ example

EXEMPLUM, EXEMPLA n anecdote that supports a moral point

EXEMPT, -ED, -S adj not subject to an obligation etc ▷ vb release from an obligation etc ▷ n person who is exempt from an obligation, tax, etc

EXEQUIAL ▸ exequy

EXEQUY, EXEQUIES n funeral rite

> Meaning a funeral rite, this word combines X and Q. Even better is its plural **exequies**, which would earn an extra 50 points for using all your tiles.

E

E

EXERCISE n activity to train the body or mind ▷ vb make use of

EXERGIES ► exergy

EXERGUAL ► exergue

EXERGUE, -S n space on the reverse of a coin or medal

EXERGY, EXERGIES n maximum amount of useful work obtainable from a system

EXERT, -ED, -ING, -S vb use (influence, authority, etc) forcefully or effectively

EXERTION

EXERTIVE

EXES ► ex

EXEUNT vb (they) go out

EXFIL, -ED, -S vb exfiltrate

EXHALANT adj emitting a vapour or liquid ▷ n organ or vessel that emits a vapour or liquid

EXHALE, -D, -S, EXHALING vb breathe out

EXHALENT same as ► exhalant

EXHALES ► exhale

EXHALING ► exhale

EXHAUST, -S vb tire out ▷ n gases ejected from an engine as waste products

EXHEDRA, -E same as ► exedra

EXHIBIT, -S vb display to the public ▷ n object exhibited to the public

EXHORT, -ED, -S vb urge earnestly

EXHORTER

EXHUMATE same as ► exhume

EXHUME, -D, -S, EXHUMING vb dig up (something buried, esp a corpse)

EXHUMER -S

EXIES n hysterics

EXIGEANT adj exacting

EXIGENCE same as ► exigency

EXIGENCY n urgent demand or need

EXIGENT, -S adj urgent ▷ n emergency

EXIGIBLE adj liable to be exacted or required

EXIGUITY ► exiguous

EXIGUOUS adj scanty or meagre

EXILABLE ► exile

EXILE, -D, -S, EXILING n prolonged, usu enforced, absence from one's country ▷ vb expel from one's country

EXILER -S

EXILIAN ► exile

EXILIC ► exile

EXILING ► exile

EXILITY n poverty or meagreness

EXIMIOUS adj select and distinguished

EXINE, -S n outermost coat of a pollen grain or a spore

EXING ► ex

EXIST, -ED, -S vb have being or reality

EXISTENT adj in existence ▷ n person or a thing that exists

EXISTING ► exist

EXISTS ► exist

EXIT, -ED, -ING, -S n way out ▷ vb go out

EXITANCE n measure of the ability of a surface to emit radiation

EXITED ► exit

EXITING ► exit

EXITLESS ► exit

EXITS ► exit

EXO informal word for > excellent

> **Exo** is an informal Australian way of saying excellent. This is a great little word as it allows you to combine X with two of the most common tiles in the game, E and O.

EXOCARP, -S same as ► epicarp

EXOCRINE adj relating to a gland, such as the sweat gland, that secretes externally through a duct ▷ n exocrine gland

EXOCYTIC adj outside biological cell

EXODE, -S n exodus

EXODERM, -S same as ► ectoderm

EXODES ► exode

EXODIC ► exode

EXODIST, -S ► exodus

EXODOS, EXODOI n processional song performed at the end of a play

EXODUS, -ES n departure of a large number of people

EXOERGIC adj (of a nuclear reaction) occurring with evolution of energy

EXOGAMIC ► exogamy

EXOGAMY n act of marrying a person from another tribe, clan, etc

EXOGEN, -S n type of plant

EXOGENIC adj formed or occurring on the earth's surface

EXOGENS ► exogen

EXOMION, -S same as ► exomis

EXOMIS, -ES n sleeveless jacket

EXON, -S n one of the officers who command the Yeomen of the Guard

EXONIC

EXONUMIA n objects of interest to numismatists that are not coins, such as medals and tokens

EXONYM, -S n name given to a place by foreigners

EXOPHAGY n (among cannibals) custom of eating only members of other tribes

EXOPLASM another name for > ectoplasm

EXOPOD, -S same as > exopodite

EXORABLE adj able to be persuaded or moved by pleading

EXORCISE same as ► exorcize

EXORCISM ► exorcize

EXORCIST ► exorcize

EXORCIZE vb expel (evil spirits) by prayers and religious rites

EXORDIA ► exordium

EXORDIAL ► exordium

EXORDIUM, EXORDIA n introductory part or beginning, esp of an oration or discourse

EXOSMIC > exosmosis

EXOSMOSE same as > exosmosis

EXOSPORE n outer layer of the spores of some algae and fungi

EXOTERIC adj intelligible to or intended for more than a select or initiated minority

EXOTIC, -S adj having a strange allure or beauty ▷ n non-native plant

EXOTICA pl n (collection of) exotic objects

EXOTICS ► exotic

EXOTISM, -S n something exotic

EXOTOXIC ► exotoxin

EXOTOXIN n toxin produced by a microorganism and secreted into the surrounding medium

EXPAND, -S vb make or become larger

EXPANDED adj (of printer's type) wider than usual for a particular height

EXPANDER n device for exercising and developing the muscles of the body

EXPANDOR same as ► expander

EXPANDS ► expand

EXPANSE, -S n uninterrupted wide area

EXPAT, -S n short for expatriate

EXPECT, -ED, -S vb regard as probable

EXPECTER n person who expects

EXPECTS ► expect

EXPEDITE vb hasten the progress of ▷ adj unimpeded or prompt

EXPEL, -LED, -S vb drive out with force

EXPELLEE

EXPELLER

EXPEND, -ED, -S vb spend, use up

EXPENDER

EXPENSE, -D, -S n cost ▷ vb treat as an expense

EXPERT, -ED, -S n person with extensive skill or knowledge in a particular field ▷ adj skilful or knowledgeable ▷ vb experience

EXPERTLY

EXPIABLE adj capable of being expiated or atoned for

EXPIATE, -D, -S vb make amends for

EXPIATOR

EXPIRANT n one who expires

EXPIRE, -D, -S, EXPIRING vb finish or run out

EXPIRER -S

EXPIRIES ► expiry

EXPIRING ► expire

EXPIRY, EXPIRIES n end, esp of a contract period

EXPLAIN, -S vb make clear and intelligible

EXPLANT, -S vb transfer (living tissue) from its natural site to a new site or to a culture medium ▷ n piece of tissue treated in this way

EXPLICIT adj precisely and clearly expressed ▷ n word used to indicate the end of a book

EXPLODE, -D, -S vb burst with great violence, blow up

EXPLODER

EXPLOIT, -S vb take advantage of for one's own purposes ▷ n notable feat or deed

EXPLORE, -D, -S vb investigate

EXPLORER

EXPO, -S n exposition, large public exhibition

EXPONENT n person who advocates an idea, cause, etc ▷ adj offering a declaration, explanation, or interpretation

EXPORT, -ED, -S n selling or shipping of goods to a foreign country ▷ vb sell or ship (goods) to a foreign country

EXPORTER

EXPOS ► expo

EXPOSAL, -S ► expose

EXPOSE, -S, EXPOSING vb uncover or reveal ▷ n bringing of a crime, scandal, etc to public notice

EXPOSED adj not concealed

EXPOSER, -S ► expose

EXPOSES ► expose

EXPOSING ► expose

EXPOSIT, -S vb state

EXPOSOME n collection of environmental factors which can affect a person's health

EXPOSURE n exposing

EXPOUND, -S vb explain in detail

EXPRESS vb put into words ▷ adj explicitly stated ▷ n fast train or bus stopping at only a few stations ▷ adv by express delivery

EXPRESSO variant of ► espresso

EXPUGN, -ED, -S vb storm

EXPULSE, -D, -S vb expel

EXPUNCT, -S vb expunge

EXPUNGE, -D, -S vb delete, erase, blot out

EXPUNGER

EXPURGE, -D, -S vb purge

EXSCIND, -S vb cut off or out

EXSECANT n trigonometric function

EXSECT, -ED, -S vb cut out

EXSERT, -ED, -S vb thrust out ▷ adj protruded or stretched out from (something)

EXTANT adj still existing

EXTASY, EXTASIES same as ► ecstasy

EXTATIC same as ► ecstatic

EXTEND, -ED, -S vb draw out or be drawn out, stretch

EXTENDER n person or thing that extends

EXTENDS ► extend

EXTENSE adj extensive ▷ n extension; expanse

EXTENSOR n muscle that extends a part of the body

EXTENT, -S n range over which something extends, area

EXTERIOR n part or surface on the outside ▷ adj of, on, or coming from the outside

EXTERN, -S n person with an official connection to an institution but not residing in it

EXTERNAL adj of, situated on, or coming from the outside ▷ n external circumstance or aspect, esp one that is superficial or inessential

EXTERNAT n day school

EXTERNE, -S same as ► extern

EXTERNS ► extern

EXTINCT, -S adj having died out ▷ vb extinguish

EXTINE, -S same as ► exine

EXTIRP, -ED, -S vb extirpate

EXTOL, -S vb praise highly

EXTOLD archaic past participle of ► extol

EXTOLL, -ED, -S same as ► extol

EXTOLLER ► extol

EXTOLLS ► extoll

EXTOLS ► extol

EXTORT, -ED, -S vb get (something) by force or threats

EXTORTER

EXTRA, -S adj more than is usual, expected or needed ▷ n additional person or thing ▷ adv unusually or exceptionally

EXTRACT, -S vb pull out by force ▷ n something extracted, such as a passage from a book etc

EXTRADOS n outer curve or surface of an arch or vault

EXTRAIT, -S n extract

EXTRANET n intranet modified to allow outside access

EXTRAS ► extra

EXTREAT, -S n extraction ▷ vb extract or eliminate (something)

EXTREMA ► extremum

EXTREMAL n clause in a recursive definition

EXTREME, -R, -S adj of a high or the highest degree or intensity ▷ n either of the two limits of a scale or range

EXTREMUM, EXTREMA n extreme point

EXTROPY n supposition that human life will expand

E

throughout the universe via technology

EXTRORSE adj turned or opening outwards or away from the axis

EXTRUDE, -D, -S vb squeeze or force out
EXTRUDER

EXTUBATE vb remove tube from hollow organ

EXUDATE, -S same as
> **exudation**

EXUDE, -D, -S, EXUDING vb (of a liquid or smell) seep or flow out slowly and steadily

EXUL, -LED, -LING, -S vb exile; banish

EXULT, -ED, -ING, -S vb be joyful or jubilant

EXULTANT adj elated or jubilant, esp because of triumph or success

EXULTED ▶ exult

EXULTING ▶ exult

EXULTS ▶ exult

EXURB, -S n residential area beyond suburbs

EXURBAN ▶ exurbia

EXURBIA, -S n region outside the suburbs of a city

EXURBS ▶ exurb

EXUVIA, -E n cast-off exoskeleton of animal
EXUVIAL

EXUVIATE vb shed (a skin or similar outer covering)

EXUVIUM n cast-off exoskeleton of animal

EYALET, -S n province of Ottoman Empire

EYAS, -ES n nestling hawk or falcon

EYASS, -ES same as
▶ **eyas**

EYE, -D, -ING, -S, EYING n organ of sight ▷ vb look at carefully or warily

EYEABLE adj pleasant to look at

EYEBALL, -S n ball-shaped part of the eye ▷ vb eye

EYEBANK, -S n place in which corneas are stored

EYEBAR, -S n bar with flattened ends with holes for connecting pins

EYEBATH, -S n small cup for applying medication to the eye

EYEBEAM, -S n glance

EYEBLACK another name for
▶ **mascara**

EYEBLINK n very small amount of time

EYEBOLT, -S n type of threaded bolt

EYEBROW, -S n line of hair on the bony ridge above the eye ▷ vb equip with artificial eyebrows

EYECUP, -S same as
▶ **eyebath**

EYED ▶ eye

EYEDNESS ▶ eye

EYEDROPS n medicine applied to the eyes in drops

EYEFOLD, -S n fold of skin above eye

EYEFUL, -S n view

EYEGLASS n lens for aiding defective vision

EYEHOLE, -S n hole through which something is passed

EYEHOOK, -S n hook attached to a ring at the extremity of a rope or chain

EYEING ▶ eye

EYELASH n short hair that grows out from the eyelid

EYELESS ▶ eye

EYELET, -ED, -S n small hole for a lace or cord to be passed through ▷ vb supply with an eyelet or eyelets

EYELEVEL adj level with a person's eyes

EYELIAD, -S same as
▶ **oeillade**

EYELID, -S n fold of skin that covers the eye when it is closed

EYELIFT, -S n cosmetic surgery for eyes

EYELIKE ▶ eye

EYELINER n cosmetic used to outline the eyes

EYEN pl n eyes

EYEPATCH n material worn over an injured eye

EYEPIECE n lens in a microscope, telescope, etc, into which the person using it looks

EYEPOINT n position of a lens at which the sharpest image is obtained

EYER, -S n someone who eyes

EYES ▶ eye

EYESHADE n opaque or tinted translucent visor

EYESHINE n reflection of light from animal eye at night

EYESHOT, -S n range of vision

EYESIGHT n ability to see

EYESOME adj attractive

EYESORE, -S n ugly object

EYESPOT, -S n small area of pigment

EYESTALK n movable stalk bearing a compound eye at its tip

EYESTONE n device for removing foreign body from eye

EYETOOTH, EYETEETH n either of the two canine teeth in the upper jaw

EYEWASH n nonsense

EYEWATER n lotion for the eyes

EYEWEAR, -S n spectacles; glasses

EYEWINK, -S n wink of the eye; instant

EYING ▶ eye

EYLIAD, -S same as
▶ **oeillade**

EYNE poetic plural of ▶ eye

EYOT, -S n island

EYRA, -S n reddish-brown variety of the jaguarondi

EYRE, -S n obsolete circuit court

EYRIE, -S n nest of an eagle

EYRIR n Icelandic monetary unit

EYRY same as ▶ eyrie

EZINE, -S n magazine available only in electronic form

Ff

F is a useful letter in Scrabble: it begins three two-letter words (**fa**, **fe** and **fy**). There are also quite a few words that combine **F** with **X** or **Z**, allowing high scores, particularly if you can hit a bonus square with them. **Fax**, **fix** and **fox** are good examples (13 points each), and don't forget **fez** and **fiz** (15 points each). **Fay**, **fey**, **fly**, **foy** and **fry** can also be useful (9 each).

FA, -S *same as* ► **fah**

FAA, -ING, -N, -S *Scot word for* ► **fall**

FAB, -BER, -BEST, -S *adj* excellent ▷ *n* fabrication

FABBY, FABBIER, FABBIEST *same as* ► **fab**

FABLE, -S *n* story with a moral ▷ *vb* relate or tell (fables)

FABLED *adj* made famous in legend

FABLER, -S ► **fable**

FABLES ► **fable**

FABLET, -S *n* large smartphone able to perform many of the functions of a tablet computer

FABLIAU, -X *n* comic usually ribald verse tale

FABLING, -S ► **fable**

FABRIC, -S *n* knitted or woven cloth ▷ *vb* build

FABRIQUE *n* (in Quebec) group of laypersons who hold church property in trust for the parish

FABS ► **fab**

FABULAR *adj* relating to fables

FABULATE *vb* make up fables

FABULISE *vb* make up fables

FABULISM *n* literary technique of placing fantastical elements in mundane settings

FABULIST *n* person who invents or recounts fables

FABULIZE *vb* make up fables

FABULOUS *adj* excellent

FABURDEN *n* early form of counterpoint

FACADE, -S *n* front of a building

FACE, -D, -S *n* front of the head ▷ *vb* look or turn towards

FACEABLE

FACEBAR, -S *n* wrestling hold

FACEBOOK *vb* search for (someone) on the Facebook website

FACED ► **face**

FACEDOWN *vb* confront and force (someone or something) to back down

FACELESS *adj* impersonal, anonymous

FACELIFT *n* cosmetic surgery for the face

FACEMAIL *n* computer-generated face that delivers messages on screen

FACEMAN, FACEMEN *n* miner who works at the coalface

FACEMASK *n* protective mask for the face

FACEMEN ► **faceman**

FACEOFF, -S *n* when opposing skaters compete for the puck at the start of an ice hockey game

FACER, -S *n* difficulty or problem

FACES ► **face**

FACET, -ED, -S, -TED *n* aspect ▷ *vb* cut facets in (a gemstone)

FACETE *adj* witty and humorous

FACETED ► **facet**

FACETELY ► **facete**

FACETIAE *pl n* humorous or witty sayings

FACETIME *vb* talk with (someone) via the FaceTime application

FACETING *n* act of faceting

FACETS ► **facet**

FACETTED ► **facet**

FACEUP *adj* with the face or surface exposed

FACIA, -E, -S *same as* ► **fascia**

FACIAL, -S *adj* of or relating to the face ▷ *n* beauty treatment for the face

FACIALLY

FACIAS ► **facia**

FACIEND, -S *n* multiplicand

FACIES *n* general form and appearance

FACILE *adj* (of a remark, argument, etc) superficial

FACILELY

FACILITY *n* skill

FACING, -S *n* lining or covering for decoration or reinforcement

FACONNE, -S *adj* denoting a fabric with the design woven in ▷ *n* such a fabric

FACT, -S *n* event or thing known to have happened or existed

FACTA ► **factum**

FACTFUL ► **fact**

FACTICE, -S *n* soft rubbery material

FACTION, -S *n* (dissenting) minority group within a larger body

FACTIOUS *adj* of or producing factions

FACTIS, -ES *variant of* ► **factice**

FACTIVE *adj* giving rise to the presupposition that a sentence is true

FACTOID, -S *n* piece of unreliable information believed to be true

FACTOR, -ED, -S *n* element contributing to a result ▷ *vb* engage in the business of a factor

FACTORY *n* building where goods are manufactured

FACTOTUM *n* person employed to do all sorts of work

FACTS ► **fact**

F

FACTUAL adj concerning facts rather than opinions or theories

FACTUM, FACTA, -S n something done, deed

FACTURE, -S n construction

FACULA, -E n any of the bright areas on the sun's surface **FACULAR**

FACULTY n physical or mental ability

FAD, -S n short-lived fashion

FADABLE ▸ fade

FADAISE, -S n silly remark

FADDIER ▸ faddy

FADDIEST ▸ faddy

FADDISH ▸ fad

FADDISM, -S ▸ fad

FADDIST, -S ▸ fad

FADDLE, -D, -S, FADDLING vb mess around, toy with

FADDY, FADDIER, FADDIEST adj unreasonably fussy, particularly about food

FADE, -D, -S vb (cause to) lose brightness, colour, or strength ▷ n act or an instance of fading

FADEAWAY n fading to the point of disappearance

FADED ▸ fade

FADEDLY ▸ fade

FADEIN, -S n gradual appearance of image on film

FADELESS adj not subject to fading

FADEOUT, -S n gradual disappearance of image on film

FADER, -S ▸ fade

FADES ▸ fade

FADEUR, -S n blandness, insipidness

FADGE, -D, -S, FADGING vb agree ▷ n package of wool in a wool-bale

FADIER ▸ fady

FADIEST ▸ fady

FADING, -S n variation in strength of received radio signals

FADLIKE ▸ fad

FADO, -S n type of melancholy Portuguese folk song

FADS ▸ fad

FADY, FADIER, FADIEST adj faded

FAE Scot word for ▸ from

FAECAL adj of, relating to, or consisting of faeces

FAECES pl n waste matter discharged from the body

FAENA, -S n matador's final actions before the kill

FAERIE, -S n land of fairies

FAERY same as ▸ faerie

FAFF, -ED, -ING, -S vb dither or fuss

FAFFIER ▸ faffy

FAFFIEST ▸ faffy

FAFFING ▸ faff

FAFFS ▸ faff

FAFFY, FAFFIER, FAFFIEST adj awkward and time-consuming to do or use

FAG, -GED, -S n tiresome work ▷ vb work hard

FAGGING -S

FAGGOT, -ED, -S n ball of chopped liver, herbs, and bread ▷ vb collect into a bundle or bundles **FAGGOTY**

FAGGY ▸ fag

FAGIN, -S n criminal

FAGOT, -ED, -S same as ▸ faggot

FAGOTER -S

FAGOTING same as >**faggoting**

FAGOTS ▸ fagot

FAGOTTO, FAGOTTI, -S n bassoon

FAGS ▸ fag

FAH, -S n (in tonic sol-fa) fourth degree of any major scale

FAHLBAND n thin bed of schistose rock impregnated with metallic sulphides

FAHLERZ n copper ore

FAHLORE, -S n copper ore

FAHS ▸ fah

FAIBLE, -S variant of ▸ foible

FAIENCE, -S n tin-glazed earthenware

FAIK, -ED, -ING, -S vb grasp

FAIKES n sandy rock

FAIKING ▸ faik

FAIKS ▸ faik

FAIL, -ED, -S vb be unsuccessful ▷ n instance of not passing an exam or test

FAILING, -S n weak point ▷ prep in the absence of

FAILLE, -S n soft light ribbed fabric of silk, rayon, or taffeta

FAILOVER n automatic transfer to a backup computer system in the event of a primary system failure

FAILS ▸ fail

FAILURE, -S n act or instance of failing

FAIN, -ED, -ER, -EST, -ING, -S adv gladly ▷ adj willing or eager ▷ vb desire

FAINE, -S variant of ▸ fain

FAINEANT n lazy person ▷ adj indolent

FAINED ▸ fain

FAINER ▸ fain

FAINES ▸ faine

FAINEST ▸ fain

FAINING ▸ fain

FAINITES interj cry for truce or respite from the rules of a game

FAINLY ▸ fain

FAINNE, -S n badge worn by advocates of the Irish language

FAINNESS ▸ fain

FAINS ▸ fain

FAINT, -ED, -EST, -ING, -S adj lacking clarity, brightness, or volume ▷ vb lose consciousness temporarily ▷ n temporary loss of consciousness **FAINTER -S**

FAINTIER ▸ fainty

FAINTING ▸ faint

FAINTISH ▸ faint

FAINTLY ▸ faint

FAINTS ▸ faint

FAINTY, FAINTIER ▸ faint

FAIR, -ED, -ER, -EST, -S adj unbiased and reasonable ▷ adv fairly ▷ n travelling entertainment ▷ vb join together to form a smooth shape

FAIRGOER n person attending fair

FAIRIER ▸ fairy

FAIRIES ▸ fairy

FAIRIEST ▸ fairy

FAIRILY ▸ fairy

FAIRING, -S n structure fitted round part of a vehicle to reduce drag

FAIRISH adj moderately good, well, etc

FAIRLEAD n block or ring through which a line is rove

FAIRLY adv moderately

FAIRNESS ▸ fair

FAIRS ▸ fair

FAIRWAY, -S n area between the tee and the green

FAIRY, FAIRIER, FAIRIES, FAIRIEST n imaginary small creature ▷ adj of or relating to a fairy or fairies **FAIRYDOM** **FAIRYISM**

FAITH, -S n strong belief, esp without proof

FAITHED adj having faith or a faith

FAITHER, -S Scot word for ▸ father

FAITHFUL adj loyal

FAITHING n practising a faith

FAITHS ▸ faith

FAITOR, -S n traitor, impostor

FAITOUR, -S n impostor

FAIX interj have faith

FAJITAS, FAJITA pl n Mexican dish

FAKE, -D, -S, FAKING vb cause something not genuine to appear so by fraud ▷ n person, thing, or act that is not genuine ▷ adj not genuine

FAKEER, -S same as ► **fakir**

FAKEMENT n something false, counterfeit

FAKER, -S ► **fake**

FAKERIES ► **fakery**

FAKERS ► **faker**

FAKERY, FAKERIES ► **fake**

FAKES ► **fake**

FAKEY, -S, FAKIER, FAKIEST adj, adv (of a skateboarding manoeuvre) travelling backwards ▷ n skateboarding position in which the skateboarder faces backwards

FAKIE, -S same as ► **fakey**

FAKIER ► **fakey**

FAKIES ► **fakie**

FAKIEST ► **fakey**

FAKING ► **fake**

FAKIR, -S n Muslim who spurns worldly possessions

FAKIRISM

FALAFEL, -S n ball or cake made from chickpeas

FALAJ, AFLAJ n kind of irrigation channel in ancient Oman

FALBALA, -S n gathered flounce, frill, or ruffle

FALCADE, -S n movement of a horse

FALCATE adj shaped like a sickle

FALCATED same as ► **falcate**

FALCES ► **falx**

FALCHION n short and slightly curved medieval sword broader towards the point

FALCON, -S n small bird of prey

FALCONER n person who breeds or trains hawks or who follows the sport of falconry

FALCONET n type of small falcon

FALCONRY n art of training falcons

FALCONS ► **falcon**

FALCULA, -E, -S n sharp curved claw, esp of a bird

FALDAGE, -S n feudal right

FALDERAL n showy but worthless trifle ▷ vb sing nonsense words

FALDEROL same as ► **falderal**

FALDETTA n Maltese woman's garment with a stiffened hood

FALL, -EN, -S vb drop through the force of gravity ▷ n falling

FALLACY n false belief

FALLAL, -S n showy ornament, trinket, or article of dress

FALLAWAY n friendship that has been withdrawn

FALLBACK n something that recedes or retreats

FALLEN ► **fall**

FALLER, -S n any device that falls or operates machinery by falling

FALLFISH n large N American freshwater fish resembling the chub

FALLIBLE adj (of a person) liable to make mistakes

FALLIBLY

FALLING, -S ► **fall**

FALLOFF, -S n decline or drop

FALLOUT, -S n radioactive particles spread as a result of a nuclear explosion ▷ vb disagree and quarrel ▷ sentence substitute order to leave a parade or disciplinary formation

FALLOW, -ED, -ER, -S adj (of land) ploughed but left unseeded to regain fertility ▷ n land treated in this way ▷ vb leave (land) unseeded after ploughing and harrowing it

FALLS ► **fall**

FALSE, -D, -R, -S, -ST, FALSING adj not true or correct ▷ adv in a false or dishonest manner ▷ vb falsify

FALSELY

FALSERS n colloquial term for false teeth

FALSES ► **false**

FALSEST ► **false**

FALSETTO n voice pitched higher than one's natural range

FALSIE, -S n pad used to enlarge breast shape

FALSIFY vb alter fraudulently

FALSING ► **false**

FALSISH ► **false**

FALSISM, -S ► **false**

FALSITY n state of being false

FALTBOAT n collapsible boat made of waterproof material stretched over a light framework

FALTER, -ED, -S vb be hesitant, weak, or unsure ▷ n uncertainty or hesitancy in speech or action

FALTERER

FALX, FALCES n sickle-shaped anatomical structure

FAME, -D, -S, FAMING n state of being widely recognized ▷ vb make known or famous

FAMELESS

FAMILIAL adj of or relating to the family

FAMILIAR adj well-known ▷ n demon supposed to attend a witch

FAMILIES ► **family**

FAMILISM n beliefs of a mystical Christian religious sect

FAMILIST adj relating to familism

FAMILLE, -S n type of Chinese porcelain

FAMILY, FAMILIES n group of parents and their children ▷ adj suitable for parents and children together

FAMINE, -S n severe shortage of food

FAMING ► **fame**

FAMISH, -ES vb be or make very hungry or weak

FAMISHED adj very hungry

FAMISHES ► **famish**

FAMOUS, -ED, -ES adj very well-known ▷ vb make famous

FAMOUSLY adv excellently

FAMULUS, FAMULI n (formerly) the attendant of a sorcerer or scholar

FAN, -NED, -S n object used to create a current of air ▷ vb blow or cool with a fan

FANAL, -S n lighthouse

FANATIC, -S n person who is excessively enthusiastic about something ▷ adj excessively enthusiastic

FANBASE, -S n body of admirers

FANBOY, -S n obsessive fan of a subject or hobby

FANCIED adj imaginary

FANCIER, -S n person interested in plants or animals

FANCIES ► **fancy**

FANCIEST ► **fancy**

FANCIFUL adj not based on fact

F

FANCIFY vb make more beautiful

FANCILY ► fancy

FANCY, FANCIES, FANCIEST, -ING adj elaborate, not plain ▷ n sudden irrational liking or desire ▷ vb suppose; imagine

FAND, -ED, -ING, -S vb try

FANDANGO n lively Spanish dance

FANDED ► fand

FANDING ► fand

FANDOM, -S n collectively, the fans of a sport, pastime or person

FANDS ► fand

FANE, -S n temple or shrine

FANEGA, -S n Spanish unit of measurement

FANEGADA n Spanish unit of land area

FANEGAS ► fanega

FANES ► fane

FANFARE, -D, -S n tune played on brass instruments ▷ vb perform a fanfare

FANFARON n braggart

FANFIC, -S n fiction based on work by other authors

FANFOLD, -S vb fold (paper) like a fan

FANG, -ED, -ING, -S n snake's tooth which injects poison ▷ vb seize

FANGA, -S same as ► fanega

FANGED ► fang

FANGING ► fang

FANGIRL, -S n enthusiastic female devotee of something

FANGLE, -D, -S, FANGLING vb fashion

FANGLESS ► fang

FANGLIKE ► fang

FANGLING ► fangle

FANGO, -S n mud from thermal springs in Italy

FANGS ► fang

FANION, -S n small flag used by surveyors

FANJET, -S same as ► turbofan

FANK, -ED, -ING, -S n sheep pen ▷ vb put sheep in a pen

FANKLE, -D, -S, FANKLING vb entangle ▷ n tangle

FANKS ► fank

FANLIGHT n semicircular window over a door or window

FANLIKE ► fan

FANNED ► fan

FANNEL, -S n ecclesiastical vestment

FANNELL, -S variant of ► fannel

FANNELS ► fannel

FANNER, -S ► fan

FANNING, -S ► fan

FANO, -S same as ► fanon

FANON, -S n collar-shaped vestment

FANOS ► fano

FANS ► fan

FANSITE, -S n website aimed at fans of a celebrity, film, etc

FANSUB, -S n fan-produced subtitling of films

FANTAD, -S n nervous, agitated state

FANTAIL, -S n small New Zealand bird with a tail like a fan

FANTASIA n musical composition of an improvised nature

FANTASIE same as ► fantasy

FANTASM, -S archaic spelling of ► phantasm

FANTAST, -S n dreamer or visionary

FANTASY n far-fetched notion ▷ adj of a type of competition ▷ vb fantasize

FANTEEG, -S n nervous, agitated state

FANTIGUE variant of ► fanteeg

FANTOD, -S n crotchety or faddish behaviour

FANTOM, -S archaic spelling of ► phantom

FANTOOSH adj pretentious

FANUM, -S n temple

FANWISE adj like a fan

FANWORT, -S n aquatic plant

FANZINE, -S n magazine produced by fans

FAP adj drunk

FAQIR, -S same as ► fakir

Meaning a Hindu ascetic, this is one of those invaluable words allowing you to play the Q without a U. It can also be spelt **fakeer, fakir** and **faquir**.

FAQUIR, -S variant of ► faqir

FAR, -RED, -RING, -S, -THER, -THEST adv at, to, or from a great distance ▷ adj remote in space or time ▷ vb go far

FARAD, -S n unit of electrical capacitance

FARADAIC same as ► faradic

FARADAY, -S n quantity of electricity

FARADIC adj of an intermittent asymmetric alternating current

FARADISE same as ► faradize

FARADISM n therapeutic use of faradic currents

FARADIZE vb treat (an organ or part) with faradic currents

FARADS ► farad

FARAND adj pleasant or attractive in manner or appearance

FARAWAY adj very distant

FARAWAYS same as ► faraway

FARCE, -D, -S n boisterous comedy ▷ vb enliven (a speech, etc) with jokes

FARCER, -S same as ► farceur

FARCES ► farce

FARCEUR, -S n writer of or performer in farces

FARCEUSE n female farceur

FARCI adj (of food) stuffed

FARCICAL adj ludicrous

FARCIE same as ► farci

FARCIED adj afflicted with farcy

FARCIES ► farcy

FARCIFY vb turn into a farce

FARCIN, -S n equine disease

FARCING, -S ► farce

FARCINS ► farcin

FARCY, FARCIES n form of glanders, a bacterial disease of horses

FARD, -ED, -S n paint for the face, esp white paint ▷ vb paint (the face) with fard

FARDAGE, -S n material laid beneath or between cargo

FARDED ► fard

FARDEL, -S n bundle or burden

FARDEN, -S n farthing

FARDING, -S ► fard

FARDS ► fard

FARE, -D, -S, FARING n charge for a passenger's journey ▷ vb get on (as specified)

FAREBOX n box where money for bus fares is put

FARED ► fare

FARER, -S ► fare

FARES ► fare

FAREWELL interj goodbye ▷ n act of saying goodbye and leaving ▷ vb say goodbye ▷ adj parting or closing

FARFAL, -S same as ► felafel

FARFALLE n pasta in bow shapes

FARFALS ► farfal

FARFEL, -S same as ► felafel

FARFET adj far-fetched

FARINA, -S n flour or meal made from any kind of cereal grain

FARING ► fare

FARINHA, -S n cassava meal

FARINOSE adj similar to or yielding farina

FARL, -S n thin cake of oatmeal, often triangular in shape

FARLE, -S same as ▸ **farl**

FARLS ▸ **farl**

FARM, -S n area of land for growing crops or rearing livestock ▷ vb cultivate (land)

FARMABLE

FARMED adj (of fish or game) reared on a farm

FARMER, -S n person who owns or runs a farm

FARMERY n farm buildings

FARMHAND n person who is hired to work on a farm

FARMING, -S n business or skill of agriculture

FARMLAND n land that is used for or suitable for farming

FARMOST adj most distant

FARMS ▸ **farm**

FARMWIFE n woman who works on a farm

FARMWORK n tasks carried out on a farm

FARMYARD n small area of land enclosed by or around the farm buildings

FARNESOL n type of alcohol

FARNESS ▸ **far**

FARO, -S n gambling game

FAROLITO n votive candle

FAROS ▸ **faro**

FAROUCHE adj sullen or shy

FARRAGO, -S n jumbled mixture of things

FARRAND variant of ▸ **farand**

FARRANT variant of ▸ **farand**

FARRED ▸ **far**

FARREN, -S n allotted ground

FARRIER, -S n person who shoes horses

FARRIERY n art, work, or establishment of a farrier

FARRING ▸ **far**

FARROW, -ED, -S n litter of piglets ▷ vb (of a sow) give birth ▷ adj (of a cow) not calving in a given year

FARRUCA, -S n flamenco dance performed by men

FARS ▸ **far**

FARSE, -D, -S, FARSING vb insert into

FARSIDE, -S n part of the Moon facing away from the Earth

FARSING ▸ **farse**

FART, -ED, -ING, -S n emission of gas from the anus ▷ vb emit gas from the anus

FARTHEL, -S same as ▸ **farl**

FARTHER ▸ **far**

FARTHEST ▸ **far**

FARTHING n former British coin equivalent to a quarter of a penny

FARTING ▸ **fart**

FARTLEK, -S n in sport, another name for interval training

FARTS ▸ **fart**

FAS ▸ **fa**

FASCES pl n (in ancient Rome) a bundle of rods containing an axe

FASCI ▸ **fascio**

FASCIA, -E, -S n outer surface of a dashboard

FASCIAL

FASCIATE adj (of stems and branches) abnormally flattened due to coalescence

FASCICLE same as ▸ **fascicule**

FASCINE, -S n bundle of long sticks used in construction

FASCIO, FASCI n political group

FASCIOLA n band

FASCIOLE n band

FASCISM, -S n right-wing totalitarian political system

FASCISMO, FASCISMI Italian word for ▸ **fascism**

FASCISMS ▸ **fascism**

FASCIST, -S n adherent or practitioner of fascism ▷ adj characteristic of or relating to fascism

FASCISTA, FASCISTI Italian word for ▸ **fascist**

FASCISTS ▸ **fascist**

FASCITIS same as > **fasciitis**

FASH, -ED, -ES, -ING n worry ▷ vb trouble

FASHERY n difficulty, trouble

FASHES ▸ **fash**

FASHING ▸ **fash**

FASHION, -S n style popular at a particular time ▷ vb form or make into a particular shape

FASHIONY adj of or relating to fashion

FASHIOUS adj troublesome

FAST, -ED, -EST, -S adj (capable of) acting or moving quickly ▷ adv quickly ▷ vb go without food, esp for religious reasons ▷ n period of fasting

FASTBACK n car having a back that forms one continuous slope from roof to rear

FASTBALL n ball pitched at the pitcher's top speed

FASTED ▸ **fast**

FASTEN, -ED, -S vb make or become firmly fixed or joined

FASTENER

FASTER, -S ▸ **fast**

FASTEST ▸ **fast**

FASTI pl n in ancient Rome, business days

FASTIE, -S n deceitful act

FASTING, -S ▸ **fast**

FASTISH ▸ **fast**

FASTLY ▸ **fast**

FASTNESS n fortress, safe place

FASTS ▸ **fast**

FASTUOUS adj arrogant

FAT, -S, -TED, -TER, -TEST, -TING adj having excess flesh on the body ▷ n extra flesh on the body ▷ vb fatten

FATAL adj causing death or ruin

FATALISM n belief that all events are predetermined

FATALIST

FATALITY n death caused by an accident or disaster

FATALLY adv resulting in death or disaster

FATBACK, -S n fat from the upper part of a side of pork

FATBIRD, -S n nocturnal bird

FATE, -S, FATING n power supposed to predetermine events ▷ vb predetermine

FATED adj destined

FATEFUL adj having important, usu disastrous, consequences

FATES ▸ **fate**

FATHEAD, -S n stupid person

FATHER, -ED, -S n male parent ▷ vb be the father of (offspring)

FATHERLY adj kind or protective, like a father

FATHERS ▸ **father**

FATHOM, -ED, -S n unit of length ▷ vb understand

FATHOMER

FATIDIC adj prophetic

FATIGATE vb fatigue

FATIGUE, -D, -S n extreme physical or mental tiredness ▷ vb tire out

FATING ▸ **fate**

FATLESS ▸ **fat**

FATLIKE ▸ **fat**

FATLING, -S n young farm animal fattened for killing

FATLY ▸ **fat**

FATNESS ▸ **fat**

FATS ▸ **fat**

FATSIA, -S n type of shrub

FATSO, -ES, -S *n* disparaging term for a fat person

FATSTOCK *n* livestock fattened and ready for market

FATTED ► **fat**

FATTEN, -ED, -S *vb* (cause to) become fat
FATTENER

FATTER ► **fat**

FATTEST ► **fat**

FATTIER ► **fatty**

FATTIES ► **fatty**

FATTIEST ► **fatty**

FATTILY ► **fatty**

FATTING ► **fat**

FATTISH ► **fat**

FATTISM, -S *n* discrimination on the basis of weight
FATTIST -S

FATTRELS *n* ends of ribbon

FATTY, FATTIER, FATTIES, FATTIEST *adj* containing fat ▷ *n* insulting word for a fat person

FATUITY *n* foolish thoughtlessness

FATUOUS *adj* foolish

FATWA, -ING, -S *n* religious decree issued by a Muslim leader ▷ *vb* issue a fatwa

FATWAH, -ED, -S *same as* ► **fatwa**

FATWAING ► **fatwa**

FATWAS ► **fatwa**

FATWOOD, -S *n* wood used for kindling

FAUBOURG *n* suburb or quarter, esp of a French city

FAUCAL, -S *adj* of or relating to the fauces

FAUCES *n* area of the mouth

FAUCET, -S *n* tap

FAUCETRY *n* art or practice of making faucets

FAUCETS ► **faucet**

FAUCHION *n* short sword

FAUCHON, -S *variant of* ► **fauchion**

FAUCIAL *same as* ► **faucal**

FAUGH *interj* exclamation of disgust, scorn, etc

FAULD, -S *n* piece of armour

FAULT, -ED, -ING, -S *n* responsibility for something wrong ▷ *vb* criticize or blame
FAULTFUL

FAULTIER ► **faulty**

FAULTILY ► **faulty**

FAULTING ► **fault**

FAULTS ► **fault**

FAULTY, FAULTIER *adj* badly designed or not working properly

FAUN, -S *n* (in Roman legend) mythological creature

FAUNA, -E, -S *n* animals of a given place or time

FAUNAL

FAUNALLY

FAUNIST -S

FAUNLIKE ► **faun**

FAUNS ► **faun**

FAUNULA, -E *n* fauna of a small single environment

FAUNULE, -S *same as* ► **faunula**

FAUR, -ER, -EST *Scot word for* ► **far**

FAURD *adj* favoured

FAURER ► **faur**

FAUREST ► **faur**

FAUSTIAN *adj* of or relating to Faust, esp reminiscent of his bargain with the devil

FAUT, -ED, -ING, -S *Scot word for* ► **fault**

FAUTEUIL *n* armchair, the sides of which are not upholstered

FAUTING ► **faut**

FAUTOR, -S *n* patron

FAUTS ► **faut**

FAUVE, -S *adj* of the style of the Fauve art movement ▷ *n* member of the Fauve art movement

FAUVETTE *n* singing bird, warbler

FAUVISM, -S ► **fauve**

FAUVIST, -S *n* artist following the Fauve style of painting

FAUX *adj* false

FAVA, -S *n* type of bean

FAVE, -R, -S, -ST *short for* >**favourite**

FAVEL, -S *adj* (of a horse) dun-coloured ▷ *n* fallow-coloured horse

FAVELA, -S *n* (in Brazil) a shanty or shantytown

FAVELL *variant of* ► **favel**

FAVELLA, -S *n* group of spores

FAVELS ► **favel**

FAVER ► **fave**

FAVES ► **fave**

FAVEST ► **fave**

FAVICON, -S *n* icon displayed before a website's URL

FAVISM, -S *n* type of anaemia

FAVONIAN *adj* of or relating to the west wind

FAVOR, -ED, -ING, -S *same as* ► **favour**

FAVORER, -S ► **favour**

FAVORING ► **favor**

FAVORITE *same as* >**favourite**

FAVORS ► **favor**

FAVOSE *same as* >**faveolate**

FAVOUR, -ED, -S *n* approving attitude ▷ *vb* prefer
FAVOURER

FAVOUS *adj* resembling honeycomb

FAVRILE, -S *n* type of iridescent glass

FAVUS, -ES *n* infectious fungal skin disease

FAW, -S *n* gypsy

A **faw** is a gypsy, a good word for taking advantage of a nearby bonus square.

FAWN, -ED, -S *n* young deer ▷ *adj* light yellowish-brown ▷ *vb* seek attention from (someone) by insincere flattery
FAWNER -S

FAWNIER ► **fawny**

FAWNIEST ► **fawny**

FAWNING, -S ► **fawn**

FAWNLIKE ► **fawn**

FAWNS ► **fawn**

FAWNY, FAWNIER, FAWNIEST *adj* of a fawn colour

FAWS ► **faw**

FAX, -ED, -ES, -ING *n* electronic system ▷ *vb* send (a document) by this system

FAXABLE *adj* able to be faxed

FAXED ► **fax**

FAXES ► **fax**

FAXING ► **fax**

FAY, -ED, -ER, -EST, -ING, -S *n* fairy or sprite ▷ *adj* of or resembling a fay ▷ *vb* fit or be fitted closely or tightly

A **fay** is a fairy, but it can also be a verb meaning to fit directly. It has a variant **fey**. Both are useful high-scoring short words.

FAYALITE *n* rare brown or black mineral

FAYED ► **fay**

FAYENCE, -S *variant of* ► **faience**

FAYER ► **fay**

FAYEST ► **fay**

FAYING ► **fay**

FAYNE, -D, -S, FAYNING *archaic spelling of* ► **feign**

FAYRE, -S *pseudo-archaic spelling of* ► **fair**

FAYS ► **fay**

FAZE, -S, FAZING *vb* disconcert or fluster

FAZED *adj* worried or disconcerted

FAZENDA, -S *n* large estate or ranch

FAZES ► **faze**

FAZING ► **faze**

FE, -S n variant of Hebrew letter *pe*, transliterated as *f*

FEAGUE, -D, -S, FEAGUING vb whip or beat

FEAL, -ED, -S vb conceal

FEALTY, FEALTIES n (in feudal society) subordinate's loyalty

FEAR, -ED, -ING, -S n distress or alarm caused by impending danger or pain ▷ vb be afraid of (something or someone)

FEARE, -S n companion

FEARED ▶ fear

FEARER, -S ▶ fear

FEARES ▶ feare

FEARFUL adj feeling fear

FEARING ▶ fear

FEARLESS ▶ fear

FEARS ▶ fear

FEARSOME adj terrifying

FEART adj (Scots) afraid

FEASANCE n performance of an act

FEASE, -D, -S, FEASING vb perform an act

FEASIBLE adj able to be done, possible

FEASIBLY

FEASING ▶ fease

FEAST, -ED, -ING, -S n lavish meal ▷ vb eat a feast

FEASTER -S

FEASTFUL adj festive

FEASTING ▶ feast

FEASTS ▶ feast

FEAT, -ED, -ER, -EST, -ING, -S n remarkable, skilful, or daring action ▷ adj neat ▷ vb make neat

FEATEOUS adj neat

FEATER ▶ feat

FEATEST ▶ feat

FEATHER, -S n one of the barbed shafts forming the plumage of birds ▷ vb fit or cover with feathers

FEATHERY

FEATING ▶ feat

FEATLY, FEATLIER ▶ feat

FEATOUS variant of ▶ feateous

FEATS ▶ feat

FEATUOUS variant of ▶ feateous

FEATURE, -S n part of the face, such as the eyes ▷ vb have as a feature or be a feature in

FEATURED adj having features as specified

FEATURES ▶ feature

FEAZE, -D, -S, FEAZING same as ▶ feeze

FEBLESSE n feebleness

FEBRIFIC adj causing or having a fever

FEBRILE adj very active and nervous

FECAL same as ▶ faecal

FECES same as ▶ faeces

FECHT, -ING, -S Scot word for ▶ fight

FECHTER -S

FECIAL, -S adj heraldic

FECIT vb (he or she) made it

FECKLESS adj ineffectual or irresponsible

FECKLY adv dialect word meaning mostly

FECULA, -E, -S n type of starch

FECULENT adj filthy, scummy, muddy, or foul

FECUND adj fertile

FED, -S n FBI agent

FEDARIE, -S n accomplice

FEDAYEE, -N n (in Arab states) a commando

FEDELINI n type of pasta

FEDERACY n alliance

FEDERAL, -S adj of a system of governance ▷ n supporter of federal union or federation

FEDERARY variant of ▶ fedarie

FEDERATE vb unite in a federation ▷ adj federal

FEDEX, -ED, -ES, -ING vb send by FedEx

FEDORA, -S n man's soft hat with a brim

FEDS ▶ fed

FEE, -ING, -S n charge paid to be allowed to do something ▷ vb pay a fee to

FEEB, -S n contemptible person

FEEBLE, -D, -R, -S, -ST, FEEBLING adj lacking physical or mental power ▷ vb make feeble

FEEBLISH

FEEBLY

FEEBS ▶ feeb

FEED, -ING, -INGS, -S vb give food to ▷ n act of feeding

FEEDABLE

FEEDBACK n information received in response to something done

FEEDBAG, -S n any bag in which feed for livestock is sacked

FEEDBOX n trough, manger

FEEDER, -S n baby's bib

FEEDHOLE n small hole through which cable etc is inserted

FEEDING ▶ feed

FEEDINGS ▶ feed

FEEDLOT, -S n area where livestock are fattened rapidly

FEEDPIPE n pipe through which something is supplied to a machine or system

FEEDS ▶ feed

FEEDYARD n place where cattle are kept and fed

FEEING ▶ fee

FEEL, -S vb have a physical or emotional sensation of ▷ n act of feeling

FEELBAD adj inducing depression

FEELER, -S n organ of touch in some animals

FEELESS ▶ fee

FEELGOOD adj causing or characterized by a feeling of self-satisfaction

FEELING, -S ▶ feel

FEELS ▶ feel

FEEN, -S n in Irish dialect, an informal word for 'man'

FEER, -ED, -S vb make a furrow

FEERIE, -S n fairyland

FEERIN, -S n furrow

FEERING, -S ▶ feer

FEERINS ▶ feerin

FEERS ▶ feer

FEES ▶ fee

FEESE, -D, -S, FEESING vb perturb

FEET ▶ foot

FEETLESS ▶ foot

FEEZE, -D, -S, FEEZING vb beat ▷ n rush

FEG, -S same as ▶ fig

FEGARY, FEGARIES variant of ▶ vagary

FEGS ▶ feg

FEH, -S same as ▶ fe

FEHM, -E n medieval German court

FEHMIC

FEHS ▶ feh

FEIGN, -ED, -ING, -S vb pretend

FEIGNER -S

FEIJOA, -S n evergreen myrtaceous shrub of S America

FEIJOADA n Brazilian stew of black beans, meat and vegetables

FEIJOAS ▶ feijoa

FEINT, -ED, -ER, -EST, -ING n sham attack meant to distract an opponent ▷ vb make a feint ▷ adj printing term meaning ruled with faint lines

FEINTS pl n leavings of the second distillation of Scotch malt whisky

FEIRIE, -R, -ST *adj* nimble

FEIS *n* Irish music and dance festival

FEIST, -S *n* small aggressive dog

FEISTIER ► feisty

FEISTILY ► feisty

FEISTS ► feist

FEISTY, FEISTIER *adj* showing courage or spirit

FELAFEL, -S *same as* ► falafel

FELDGRAU *n* ordinary German soldier (from uniform colour)

FELDSHER *n* (in Russia) a medical doctor's assistant

FELDSPAR *n* hard mineral that is the main constituent of igneous rocks

FELICIA, -S *n* type of African herb

FELICITY *n* happiness

FELID, -S *n* any animal belonging to the cat family

FELINE, -S *adj* of cats ▷ *n* member of the cat family

FELINELY

FELINITY

FELL, -ED, -EST, -S *vb* cut or knock down ▷ *adj* cruel or deadly

FELLA, -S *nonstandard variant of* ► fellow

FELLABLE ► fell

FELLAH, -IN, -S *n* peasant in Arab countries

FELLAS ► fella

FELLED ► fell

FELLER, -S *n* person or thing that fells

FELLEST ► fell

FELLIES ► felly

FELLING, -S ► fell

FELLNESS ► fell

FELLOE, -S *n* (segment of) the rim of a wheel

FELLOW, -ED, -S *n* man or boy ▷ *adj* in the same group or condition ▷ *vb* join as a companion

FELLOWLY *adj* friendly, companionable

FELLOWS ► fellow

FELLS ► fell

FELLY, FELLIES *same as* ► felloe

FELON, -S *n* (formerly) person guilty of a felony ▷ *adj* evil

FELONIES ► felony

FELONOUS *adj* wicked

FELONRY *n* felons collectively

FELONS ► felon

FELONY, FELONIES *n* serious crime

FELSIC *adj* relating to igneous rock

FELSITE, -S *n* any fine-grained igneous rock

FELSITIC

FELSPAR, -S *same as* ► feldspar

FELSTONE *same as* ► felsite

FELT, -ED, -S *n* matted fabric ▷ *vb* become matted

FELTER, -ED, -S *vb* mat together

FELTIER ► felty

FELTIEST ► felty

FELTING, -S *n* felted material

FELTLIKE ► felt

FELTS ► felt

FELTY, FELTIER, FELTIEST ► felt

FELUCCA, -S *n* narrow lateen-rigged vessel

FELWORT, -S *n* type of plant

FEM, -S *n* type of igneous rock

FEMALE, -S *adj* of the sex which bears offspring ▷ *n* female person or animal

FEMALITY

FEME, -S *n* woman or wife

FEMERALL *n* ventilator or smoke outlet on a roof

FEMERELL *n* ventilator or smoke outlet in a roof

FEMES ► feme

FEMETARY *variant of* ► fumitory

FEMICIDE *n* killing of a woman or girl

FEMINACY *n* feminine character

FEMINAL *adj* feminine, female

FEMINAZI *n* militant feminist

FEMININE, -S *n* women collectively

FEMININE *adj* having qualities traditionally regarded as suitable for, or typical of, women ▷ *n* short for feminine noun

FEMINISE *same as* ► feminize

FEMINISM *n* advocacy of equal rights for women

FEMINIST *n* person who advocates equal rights for women ▷ *adj* of, relating to, or advocating feminism

FEMINITY ► feminal

FEMINIZE *vb* make or become feminine

FEMITER, -S *variant of* ► fumitory

FEMME, -S *n* woman or wife

FEMMY, FEMMIER, FEMMIEST *adj* markedly or exaggeratedly feminine

FEMORA ► femur

FEMORAL *adj* of the thigh

FEMS ► fem

FEMUR, FEMORA, -S *n* thighbone

FEN, -S *n* low-lying flat marshy land

FENAGLE, -D, -S *variant of* ► finagle

FENCE, -D, -S *n* barrier of posts linked by wire or wood ▷ *vb* enclose with or as if with a fence

FENCER, -S *n* person who fights with a sword

FENCEROW *n* uncultivated land flanking a fence

FENCERS ► fencer

FENCES ► fence

FENCIBLE *n* person who undertook military service in defence of their homeland only

FENCING, -S *n* sport of fighting with swords

FEND, -ED, -ING, -S *vb* give support (to someone, esp oneself) ▷ *n* shift or effort

FENDER, -S *n* low metal frame in front of a fireplace

FENDERED *adj* having a fender

FENDERS ► fender

FENDIER ► fendy

FENDIEST ► fendy

FENDING ► fend

FENDS ► fend

FENDY, FENDIER, FENDIEST *adj* thrifty

FENESTRA *n* small opening in or between bones

FENI, -S *n* Goan alcoholic drink

FENING, -S *n* small currency unit of Bosnia-Herzegovina

FENIS ► feni

FENITAR, -S *variant of* ► fumitory

FENKS *n* whale blubber

FENLAND, -S ► fen

FENMAN, FENMEN ► fen

FENNEC, -S *n* type of nocturnal desert fox

FENNEL, -S *n* fragrant plant

FENNIER ► fenny

FENNIES ► fenny

FENNIEST ► fenny

FENNING *same as* ► fening

FENNISH ► fen

FENNY, FENNIER, FENNIES, FENNIEST *adj* boggy or marshy ▷ *n* feni

FENS ► fen

FENT, -S *n* piece of waste fabric

FENTANYL *n* narcotic drug used in medicine to relieve pain

FENTHION *n* type of pesticide

FENTS ► fent

FENURON, -S n type of herbicide

FEOD, -S same as ► **feud**

FEODAL

FEODARY

FEOFF, -ED, -ING, -S same as ► **fief**

FEOFFEE, -S n (in feudal society) a vassal granted a fief by his lord

FEOFFER, -S ► **feoff**

FEOFFING ► **feoff**

FEOFFOR, -S ► **feoff**

FEOFFS ► **feoff**

FER same as ► **far**

FERACITY > **feracious**

FERAL, -S adj wild ▷ n person who displays such tendencies and appearance

FERBAM, -S n powder used as a fungicide

FERE, -R, -S, -ST n companion ▷ adj fierce

FERETORY n shrine, usually portable, for a saint's relics

FERIA, -E, -S n weekday on which no feast occurs

FERIAL adj of or relating to a feria

FERIAS ► **feria**

FERINE same as ► **feral**

FERITY, FERITIES ► **feral**

FERLIE same as ► **ferly**

FERLY, FERLIED, FERLIER, FERLIES, FERLIEST, -ING adj wonderful ▷ n wonder ▷ vb wonder

FERM, -S variant of ► **farm**

FERMATA, -S, FERMATE another word for ► **pause**

FERMENT, -S n any agent that causes fermentation ▷ vb (cause to) undergo fermentation

FERMI, -S n unit of length

FERMION, -S n type of particle

FERMIS ► **fermi**

FERMIUM, -S n chemical element

FERMS ► **ferm**

FERN, -S n flowerless plant with fine fronds

FERNALLY n seedless plant that is not a true fern

FERNBIRD n small brown and white New Zealand swamp bird with a fernlike tail

FERNERY n place where ferns are grown

FERNIER ► **ferny**

FERNIEST ► **ferny**

FERNING, -S n production of a fern-like pattern

FERNINST same as ► **fornenst**

FERNLESS ► **fern**

FERNLIKE ► **fern**

FERNS ► **fern**

FERNSHAW n fern thicket

FERNY, FERNIER, FERNIEST ► **fern**

FEROCITY > **ferocious**

FERRATE, -S n type of salt

FERREL, -ED, -S variant of ► **ferrule**

FERREOUS adj containing or resembling iron

FERRET, -ED, -S n tamed polecat ▷ vb hunt with ferrets

FERRETER

FERRETY

FERRIAGE n transportation by ferry

FERRIC adj of or containing iron

FERRIED ► **ferry**

FERRIES ► **ferry**

FERRITE, -S n type of ceramic compound

FERRITIC

FERRITIN n type of protein

FERROUS adj of or containing iron in the divalent state

FERRUGO, -S n disease affecting plants

FERRULE, -D, -S n metal cap to strengthen the end of a stick ▷ vb equip (a stick, etc) with a ferrule

FERRUM, -S Latin word for ► **iron**

FERRY, FERRIED, FERRIES, -ING n boat for transporting people and vehicles ▷ vb carry by ferry

FERRYMAN, FERRYMEN n someone who provides a ferry service

FERTILE, -R adj capable of producing young, crops, or vegetation

FERULA, -E, -S n large Mediterranean plant

FERULE, -D, -S, FERULING same as ► **ferrule**

FERVENCY another word for ► **fervour**

FERVENT adj intensely passionate and sincere

FERVID, -ER same as ► **fervent**

FERVIDLY

FERVOR, -S same as ► **fervour**

FERVOUR, -S n intensity of feeling

FES ► **fe**

FESCUE, -S n pasture and lawn grass with stiff narrow leaves

FESS, -ED, -ING vb confess

FESSE, -S n horizontal band across a shield

FESSED ► **fess**

FESSES ► **fesse**

FESSING ► **fess**

FESSWISE adv in heraldry, with a horizontal band across the shield

FEST, -S n event at which the emphasis is on a particular activity

FESTA, -S n festival

FESTAL, -S adj festive ▷ n festivity

FESTALLY

FESTAS ► **festa**

FESTER, -ED, -S vb grow worse and increasingly hostile ▷ n small ulcer or sore containing pus

FESTIER ► **festy**

FESTIEST ► **festy**

FESTIVAL n organized series of special events or performances

FESTIVE adj of or like a celebration

FESTOON, -S vb hang decorations in loops ▷ n decorative chain

FESTS ► **fest**

FESTY, FESTIER, FESTIEST adj dirty

FET, -S, -TED, -TING vb fetch

FETA, -S n white salty Greek cheese

FETAL adj of, relating to, or resembling a fetus

FETAS ► **feta**

FETATION n state of pregnancy

FETCH, -ED, -ES vb go after and bring back ▷ n ghost or apparition of a living person

FETCHER, -S n person or animal that fetches

FETCHES ► **fetch**

FETCHING adj attractive

FETE, -D, -S, FETING n gala, bazaar, etc, usu held outdoors ▷ vb honour or entertain regally

FETERITA n type of sorghum

FETES ► **fete**

FETIAL, -ES, -S n ancient Roman herald ▷ adj of or relating to the fetiales

FETIALIS n priest in ancient Rome

FETIALS ► **fetial**

FETICH, -ES same as ► **fetish**

FETICHE variant of ► **fetish**

FETICHES ► **fetish**

FETICIDE n destruction of a fetus in the uterus

F

FETID, -ER, -EST *adj* stinking
FETIDITY
FETIDLY
FETING ▸ fete
FETISH, -ES *n* irrational devotion (to an object, activity, etc)
FETLOCK, -S *n* projection behind and above a horse's hoof
FETOLOGY *n* branch of medicine concerned with the fetus in the uterus
FETOR, -S *n* offensive stale or putrid odour
FETS ▸ fet
FETT, -S *variant of* ▸ **fet**
FETTA, -S *variant of* ▸ **feta**
FETTED ▸ fet
FETTER, -ED, -S *n* chain or shackle for the foot ▹ *vb* restrict
FETTERER
FETTING ▸ fet
FETTLE, -D, -S *same as* ▸ **fettling**
FETTLER, -S *n* person employed to maintain railway tracks
FETTLES ▸ fettle
FETTLING *n* refractory material used to line the hearth of puddling furnaces
FETTS ▸ fett
FETUS, -ES *n* embryo of a mammal in the later stages of development
FETWA, -S *variant of* ▸ **fatwa**
FEU, -ED, -ING, -S *n* (in Scotland) type of rent ▹ *vb* grant land to a person who pays a feu
FEUAR, -S *n* tenant of a feu
FEUD, -ED, -S *n* long bitter hostility between two people or groups ▹ *vb* carry on a feud
FEUDAL *adj* of or like feudalism
FEUDALLY
FEUDARY *n* holder of land through feudal right
FEUDED ▸ feud
FEUDING, -S ▸ feud
FEUDIST, -S *n* person who takes part in a feud or quarrel
FEUDS ▸ feud
FEUED ▸ feu
FEUING ▸ feu
FEUS ▸ feu
FEUTRE, -D, -S, FEUTRING *vb* place in a resting position
FEVER, -ING, -S *n* (illness causing) high body temperature ▹ *vb* affect

with or as if with fever
FEVERED
FEVERFEW *n* bushy European plant with white flower heads, formerly used medicinally
FEVERING ▸ fever
FEVERISH *adj* suffering from fever
FEVEROUS *same as* ▸ **feverish**
FEVERS ▸ fever
FEW, -ER, -EST, -S *adj* not many ▹ *n as in* **the few** small number of people considered as a class
FEWMET, -S *variant of* ▸ **fumet**
FEWNESS ▸ few
FEWS ▸ few
FEWTER, -ED, -S *variant of* ▸ **feutre**
FEWTRILS *n* trifles, trivia
FEY, -ED, -ER, -EST, -ING, -S *adj* whimsically strange ▹ *vb* clean out
FEYLY
FEYNESS
FEZ, -ES, -ZES *n* brimless tasselled cap, orig. from Turkey
FEZZED *adj* wearing a fez
FEZZES ▸ fez
FEZZY ▸ fez
FIACRE, -S *n* small four-wheeled horse-drawn carriage
FIANCE, -S *n* man engaged to be married
FIANCEE, -S *n* woman who is engaged to be married
FIANCES ▸ fiance
FIAR *n* property owner
FIARS *n* legally fixed price of corn
FIASCO, FIASCHI, -ES, -S *n* ridiculous or humiliating failure
FIAT, -ED, -ING, -S *n* arbitrary order ▹ *vb* issue a fiat
FIAUNT, -S *n* fiat
FIB, -BED, -BING, -S *n* trivial lie ▹ *vb* tell a lie
FIBBER -S
FIBBERY ▸ fib
FIBBING ▸ fib
FIBER, -S *same as* ▸ **fibre**
FIBERED ▸ fibre
FIBERISE *same as* ▸ **fiberize**
FIBERIZE *vb* break into fibres
FIBERS ▸ fiber
FIBRANNE *n* synthetic fabric
FIBRATE, -S *n* drug used to lower fat levels in the body

FIBRE, -S *n* thread that can be spun into yarn
FIBRED
FIBRIL, -S *n* small fibre
FIBRILAR
FIBRILLA *same as* ▸ **fibril**
FIBRILS ▸ fibril
FIBRIN, -S *n* white insoluble elastic protein
FIBRO, -S *n* mixture of cement and asbestos fibre
FIBROID, -S *adj* (of structures or tissues) containing or resembling fibres ▹ *n* benign tumour composed of fibrous connective tissue
FIBROIN, -S *n* tough elastic protein
FIBROMA, -S *n* type of benign tumour
FIBROS ▸ fibro
FIBROSE, -D, -S *vb* become fibrous
FIBROSIS *n* formation of an abnormal amount of fibrous tissue
FIBROTIC
FIBROUS *adj* consisting of, containing, or resembling fibres
FIBS ▸ fib
FIBSTER, -S *n* fibber
FIBULA, -E, -S *n* slender outer bone of the lower leg
FIBULAR
FICAIN, -S *n* cysteine proteinase isolated from the latex of figs
FICE, -S *n* small aggressive dog
FICHE, -S *n* film for storing publications in miniature
FICHU, -S *n* woman's shawl or scarf
FICIN, -S *n* enzyme
FICKLE, -D, -R, -S, -ST, FICKLING *adj* changeable, inconstant ▹ *vb* puzzle
FICKLY
FICO, -ES, -S *n* worthless trifle
FICTILE *adj* moulded or capable of being moulded from clay
FICTION, -S *n* literary works of the imagination
FICTIVE *adj* of, relating to, or able to create fiction
FICTOR, -S *n* sculptor
FICUS, -ES *n* type of plant
FID, -S *n* spike for separating strands of rope in splicing
FIDDIOUS *vb* treat someone as Coriolanus, in the eponymous play, dealt with Aufidius
FIDDLE, -D, -S *n* violin ▹ *vb* play the violin

FIDDLER, -S *n* person who plays the fiddle

FIDDLES ► fiddle

FIDDLEY, -S *n* area of a vessel

FIDDLIER ► fiddly

FIDDLING *adj* trivial ▷ *n* act of fiddling

FIDDLY, -ED, **FIDDLIER** *adj* awkward to do or use

FIDEISM, -S *n* theological doctrine

FIDEIST -S

FIDELITY *n* faithfulness

FIDES *n* faith or trust

FIDGE, -D, -S, FIDGING *obsolete word for* ► **fidget**

FIDGET, -ED, -S *vb* move about restlessly ▷ *n* person who fidgets

FIDGETER

FIDGETY

FIDGING ► fidge

FIDIBUS *n* spill for lighting a candle or pipe

FIDO, -S *n* generic term for a dog

FIDS ► fid

FIDUCIAL *adj* used as a standard of reference or measurement

FIE, -ST *same as* ► **fey**

FIEF, -S *n* land granted by a lord in return for war service

FIEFDOM, -S *n* (in Feudal Europe) the property owned by a lord

FIEFS ► fief

FIELD, -ED, -ING, -S *n* piece of land used for pasture or growing crops ▷ *vb* stop, catch, or return (the ball) as a fielder

FIELDER, -S *n* (in certain sports) player whose task is to field the ball

FIELDING ► field

FIELDS ► field

FIEND, -S *n* evil spirit

FIENDISH *adj* of or like a fiend

FIENDS ► fiend

FIENT, -S *n* fiend

FIER, -S *same as* ► **fere**

FIERCE, -R, -ST *adj* wild or aggressive

FIERCELY

FIERE, -S *same as* ► **fere**

FIERIER ► fiery

FIERIEST ► fiery

FIERILY ► fiery

FIERS ► fier

FIERY, FIERIER, FIERIEST *adj* consisting of or like fire

FIEST ► fie

FIESTA, -S *n* religious festival, carnival

FIFE, -D, -S, FIFING *n* small high-pitched flute ▷ *vb* play (music) on a fife

FIFER -S

FIFTEEN, -S *n* five and ten ▷ *adj* amounting to fifteen ▷ *determiner* amounting to fifteen

FIFTH, -S *n* (of) number five in a series ▷ *adj* of or being number five in a series ▷ *adv* after the fourth person, position, event, etc

FIFTHLY *same as* ► **fifth**

FIFTHS ► fifth

FIFTIES ► fifty

FIFTIETH *adj* being the number of fifty in order ▷ *n* one of 50 equal or parts

FIFTY, FIFTIES *n* five times ten ▷ *adj* amounting to fifty ▷ *determiner* amounting to fifty

FIFTYISH

FIG, -GED, -GING, -S *n* soft pear-shaped fruit ▷ *vb* dress (up) or rig (out)

FIGEATER *n* large beetle

FIGGED ► fig

FIGGERY *n* adornment, ornament

FIGGING ► fig

FIGHT, -ING, -S, FOUGHT, FOUGHTEN *vb* struggle (against) in battle or physical combat ▷ *n* aggressive conflict between two (groups of) people

FIGHTER, -S *n* boxer

FIGHTING ► fight

FIGHTS ► fight

FIGJAM, -S *n* very conceited person

FIGMENT, -S *n* fantastic notion, invention, or fabrication

FIGO, -S *variant of* ► **fico**

FIGS ► fig

FIGTREE, -S *n* tree that produces figs

FIGULINE *adj* of or resembling clay ▷ *n* article made of clay

FIGURAL *adj* composed of or relating to human or animal figures

FIGURANT *n* ballet dancer who does group work but no solo roles

FIGURATE *adj* exhibiting or produced by figuration

FIGURE, -S, FIGURING *n* numerical symbol ▷ *vb* calculate (sums or amounts)

FIGURED *adj* decorated with a design

FIGURER, -S ► figure

FIGURES ► figure

FIGURINE *n* statuette

FIGURING ► figure

FIGURIST *n* user of numbers

FIGWORT, -S *n* N temperate plant

FIKE, -D, -S, FIKING *vb* fidget

FIKERY, FIKERIES *n* fuss

FIKES ► fike

FIKIER ► fiky

FIKIEST ► fiky

FIKING ► fike

FIKISH *adj* fussy

FIKY, FIKIER, FIKIEST *adj* fussy

FIL *same as* ► **fils**

FILA ► filum

FILABEG, -S *variant of* ► **filibeg**

FILACER, -S *n* formerly, English legal officer

FILAGREE *same as* ► **filigree**

FILAMENT *n* fine wire in a light bulb that gives out light

FILANDER *n* species of kangaroo

FILAR *adj* of thread

FILAREE, -S *n* type of storksbill, a weed

FILARIA, -E *n* type of parasitic nematode worm

FILARIAL

FILARIAN

FILARIID *adj* of or relating to a family of threadlike roundworms

FILASSE, -S *n* vegetable fibre such as jute

FILATORY *n* machine for making threads

FILATURE *n* act or process of spinning silk, etc, into threads

FILAZER, -S *variant of* ► **filacer**

FILBERD, -S *variant of* ► **filbert**

FILBERT, -S *n* hazelnut

FILCH, -ED, -ES, -ING *vb* steal (small amounts)

FILCHER -S

FILE, -D, -S, FILING *n* box or folder used to keep documents in order ▷ *vb* place (a document) in a file

FILEABLE

FILECARD *n* type of brush with sharp steel bristles, used for cleaning the teeth of a file

FILED ► file

FILEFISH *n* tropical fish with a narrow body

FILEMOT, -S *n* type of brown colour

FILENAME *n* codified name of a file a computer system

F

FILER, -S ► file

FILES ► file

FILET, -ED, -ING, -S variant of ► fillet

FILFOT, -S variant of ► fylfot

FILIAL adj of or befitting a son or daughter

FILIALLY

FILIATE, -D, -S vb fix judicially the paternity of (a child)

FILIBEG, -S n kilt worn by Scottish Highlanders

FILICIDE n act of killing one's own son or daughter

FILIFORM adj having the form of a thread

FILIGREE n delicate ornamental work of gold or silver wire ▷ adj made of filigree ▷ vb decorate with or as if with filigree

FILII ► filius

> This plural of **filius**, a Latin word for son, is the only 5-letter word that lets you get rid of three Is!

FILING ► file

FILINGS pl n shavings removed from a file

FILIOQUE n theological term found in the Nicene Creed

FILISTER same as ► fillister

FILIUS, FILII n son

FILK, -S n parodic type of folk music with science fiction lyrics

FILL, -ED, -S vb make or become full

FILLABLE

FILLE, -S n girl

FILLED ► fill

FILLER, -S n substance that fills a gap or increases bulk

FILLES ► fille

FILLET, -ED, -S n boneless piece of meat or fish ▷ vb remove the bones from

FILLETER n person who fillets

FILLETS ► fillet

FILLIBEG same as ► filibeg

FILLIES ► filly

FILLING, -S n substance that fills a gap or cavity ▷ adj (of food) substantial and satisfying

FILLIP, -ED, -S n something that adds stimulation or enjoyment ▷ vb stimulate or excite

FILLO, -S variant of ► filo

FILLS ► fill

FILLY, FILLIES n young female horse

FILM, -ED, -ING, -S n projected images creating the illusion of movement ▷ vb photograph with a movie or video camera ▷ adj connected with films or the cinema

FILMABLE

FILMCARD n cinema loyalty card

FILMDOM, -S n cinema industry

FILMED ► film

FILMER, -S n film-maker

FILMFEST n film festival

FILMGOER n person who goes regularly to the cinema

FILMI, -S adj of or relating to Indian films

FILMIC adj of or suggestive of films or the cinema

FILMIER ► filmy

FILMIEST ► filmy

FILMILY ► filmy

FILMING ► film

FILMIS ► filmi

FILMISH ► film

FILMLAND n cinema industry

FILMLESS ► film

FILMLIKE ► film

FILMS ► film

FILMSET, -S vb set (type matter) by filmsetting

FILMY, FILMIER, FILMIEST adj very thin, delicate

FILO, -S n type of flaky Greek pastry in very thin sheets

FILOSE adj resembling a thread or threadlike process

FILS n monetary unit of Bahrain, Iraq, Jordan, and Kuwait

FILTER, -ED, -S n device permitting fluid to pass but retaining solids ▷ vb remove impurities from (a substance) with a filter

FILTERER

FILTH, -S n disgusting dirt

FILTHIER ► filthy

FILTHILY ► filthy

FILTHS ► filth

FILTHY, FILTHIER adj characterized by or full of filth ▷ adv extremely

FILTRATE n filtered gas or liquid ▷ vb remove impurities with a filter

FILTRE adj as in **cafe filtre** a strong black filtered coffee

FILUM, FILA n any threadlike structure or part

FIMBLE, -S n male plant of the hemp

FIMBRIA, -E n fringe or fringelike margin or border

FIMBRIAL

FIN, -NED, -NING, -S n any of the appendages of some aquatic animals ▷ vb provide with fins

FINABLE adj liable to a fine

FINAGLE, -D, -S vb get or achieve by craftiness or trickery

FINAGLER

FINAL adj at the end ▷ n deciding contest

FINALE, -S n concluding part of a performance

FINALIS n musical finishing note

FINALISE same as ► finalize

FINALISM n doctrine that final causes determine the course of all events

FINALIST n competitor in a final

FINALITY n condition or quality of being final or settled

FINALIZE vb put into final form

FINALLY adv after a long delay

FINALS pl n deciding part of a competition

FINANCE, -D, -S vb provide or obtain funds for ▷ n system of money, credit, and investment

FINBACK, -S another name for ► rorqual

FINCA, -S n Spanish villa

FINCH, -ES n small songbird with a short strong beak

FINCHED adj with streaks or spots on the back

FINCHES ► finch

FIND, -S vb discover by chance ▷ n person or thing found, esp when valuable

FINDABLE

FINDER, -S n small telescope fitted to a larger one

FINDING, -S ► find

FINDRAM, -S variant of ► finnan

FINDS ► find

FINE, -D, -S adj very good ▷ n payment imposed as a penalty ▷ vb impose a fine on

FINEABLE same as ► finable

FINED ► fine

FINEER, -ED, -S variant of ► veneer

FINEISH ► fine

FINELESS ► fine

FINELY adv into small pieces

FINENESS n state or quality of being fine

FINER, -S ► fine

FINERIES ► finery

FINERS ► finer

FINERY, FINERIES n showy clothing

FINES ▸ fine

FINESPUN adj spun or drawn out to a fine thread

FINESSE, -D, -S n delicate skill ▷ vb bring about with finesse **FINESSER**

FINEST, -S n (in the US) police of a particular city

FINFISH n fish with fins, as opposed to shellfish

FINFOOT, -S n type of aquatic bird

FINGAN, -S variant of ▸ finjan

FINGER, -S n one of the four long jointed parts of the hand ▷ vb touch or handle with the fingers

FINGERED adj marked or dirtied by handling

FINGERER ▸ finger

FINGERS ▸ finger

FINI, -S n end; finish

FINIAL, -S n ornament at the apex of a gable or spire

FINIALED adj having a finial or finials

FINIALS ▸ finial

FINICAL another word for ▸ finicky

FINICKIN variant of ▸ finicky

FINICKY adj excessively particular, fussy

FINIKIN variant of ▸ finicky

FINIKING variant of ▸ finicky

FINING, -S n process of removing bubbles from molten glass

FINIS, -ES ▸ fini

FINISH, -ES vb bring to an end, stop ▷ n end, last part

FINISHED adj perfected

FINISHER n craftsman who carries out the final tasks in a manufacturing process

FINISHES ▸ finish

FINITE, -S adj having limits in space, time, or size ▷ n verb limited by person, number, tense or mood

FINITELY

FINITISM n mathematical philosophy which rejects infinite quantities

FINITIST n one who believes in or advocates finitism

FINITO adj finished

FINITUDE ▸ finite

FINJAN, -S n small, handleless coffee cup

FINK, -ED, -ING, -S n strikebreaker ▷ vb inform (on someone), as to the police

FINLESS ▸ fin

FINLIKE ▸ fin

FINLIT, -S n understanding of the concepts associated with finance

FINMARK, -S n monetary unit of Finland

FINNAC, -S variant of ▸ finnock

FINNACK, -S variant of ▸ finnock

FINNACS ▸ finnac

FINNAN, -S n smoked haddock

FINNED ▸ fin

FINNER, -S another name for ▸ rorqual

FINNESKO n reindeer-skin boot

FINNICKY variant of ▸ finicky

FINNIER ▸ finny

FINNIEST ▸ finny

FINNING ▸ fin

FINNMARK n Finnish monetary unit

FINNOCK, -S n young sea trout on its first return to fresh water

FINNSKO variant of ▸ finnesko

FINNY, FINNIER, FINNIEST adj relating to or containing many fishes

FINO, -S n very dry sherry

FINOCHIO same as > finocchio

FINOS ▸ fino

FINS ▸ fin

FINSKO variant of ▸ finnesko

FIORD, -S same as ▸ fjord

FIORIN, -S n type of temperate perennial grass

FIPPENCE n fivepence

FIPPLE, -S n wooden plug forming a flue in the end of a pipe

FIQH, -S n Islamic jurisprudence

FIQUE, -S n hemp

FIR, -S n pyramid-shaped tree

FIRE, -D, -S n state of combustion producing heat, flames, and smoke ▷ vb operate (a weapon) so that a bullet or missile is released **FIREABLE**

FIREARM, -S n rifle, pistol, or shotgun

FIREBACK n ornamental iron slab against the back wall of a hearth

FIREBALL n ball of fire at the centre of an explosion

FIREBASE n artillery base from which heavy fire is directed at the enemy

FIREBIRD n any of various songbirds having a bright red plumage, esp the Baltimore oriole

FIREBOAT n motor vessel with fire-fighting apparatus

FIREBOMB n bomb that is designed to cause fires ▷ vb detonate such a bomb

FIREBOX n furnace chamber of a boiler in a steam locomotive

FIREBRAT n type of small primitive wingless insect

FIREBUG, -S n person who deliberately sets fire to property

FIREBUSH n as in **Chilean firebush** South American shrub with scarlet flowers

FIRECLAY n heat-resistant clay used in the making of firebricks, furnace linings, etc

FIRED ▸ fire

FIREDAMP n explosive gas, composed mainly of methane, formed in mines

FIREDOG, -S n either of two metal stands supporting logs in a fire

FIREFANG vb become overheated through decomposition

FIREFLY n beetle that glows in the dark

FIREHALL n US and Canadian word for fire station

FIREHOSE n hose used to extinguish fires

FIRELESS ▸ fire

FIRELIT adj lit by firelight

FIRELOCK n obsolete type of gunlock with a priming mechanism ignited by sparks

FIREMAN, FIREMEN n man who puts out fires and rescues people

FIREMARK n plaque indicating that a building is insured

FIREMEN ▸ fireman

FIREPAN, -S n metal container for a fire in a room

FIREPINK n wildflower belonging to the pink family

FIREPIT, -S n hole dug in the ground for a fire

FIREPLUG n US and New Zealand name for a fire hydrant

FIREPOT, -S n Chinese fondue-like cooking pot

FIRER, -S ▸ fire

F

FIREREEL n fire engine
FIREROOM n stokehold
FIRERS ▸ firer
FIRES ▸ fire
FIRESHIP n vessel set alight and directed among enemy warships
FIRESIDE n hearth
FIRETRAP n building that would burn easily or one without fire escapes
FIREWALL n appliance that prevents unauthorized access to a computer network from the internet ▷ vb protect (a computer system) or block (unwanted access) with a firewall
FIREWEED n first vegetation growing in burnt-over areas
FIREWOOD n wood for burning
FIREWORK n device ignited to produce colourful sparks and explosions
FIREWORM n cranberry worm
FIRIE, -S n in Australian English, informal word for a firefighter
FIRING, -S n discharge of a firearm
FIRK, -ED, -ING, -S vb beat
FIRKIN, -S n small wooden barrel or similar container
FIRKING ▸ firk
FIRKINS ▸ firkin
FIRKS ▸ firk
FIRLOT, -S n unit of measurement for grain
FIRM, -ED, -EST, -ING, -S adj not soft or yielding ▷ adv in an unyielding manner ▷ vb make or become firm ▷ n business company
FIRMAN, -S n edict of an Oriental sovereign
FIRMED ▸ firm
FIRMER, -S ▸ firm
FIRMEST ▸ firm
FIRMING ▸ firm
FIRMLESS adj unstable
FIRMLY ▸ firm
FIRMNESS ▸ firm
FIRMS ▸ firm
FIRMWARE n fixed form of software programmed into a read-only memory
FIRN, -S another name for ▸ neve
FIRRIER ▸ firry
FIRRIEST ▸ firry
FIRRING, -S n wooden battens used in building construction

FIRRY, FIRRIER, FIRRIEST adj of, relating to, or made from fir trees
FIRS ▸ fir
FIRST adj earliest in time or order ▷ n person or thing coming before all others ▷ adv before anything else
FIRSTLY adv coming before other points, questions, etc
FIRSTS pl n saleable goods of the highest quality
FIRTH, -S n narrow inlet of the sea, esp in Scotland
FIRWOOD, -S n wood of the fir tree
FISC, -S n state or royal treasury
FISCAL, -S adj of government finances, esp taxes ▷ n (in some countries) a public prosecutor
FISCALLY
FISCS ▸ fisc
FISGIG, -S variant of ▸ fishgig
FISH, -ED, -ES n cold-blooded vertebrate with gills, that lives in water ▷ vb try to catch fish
FISHABLE
FISHBALL n fried ball of flaked fish and mashed potato
FISHBOAT n boat used for fishing
FISHBOLT n bolt used for fastening a fishplate to a rail
FISHBONE n bone of a fish
FISHBOWL n goldfish bowl
FISHCAKE n mixture of flaked fish and mashed potatoes formed into a flat circular shape
FISHED ▸ fish
FISHER, -S n fisherman
FISHERY n area of the sea used for fishing
FISHES ▸ fish
FISHEYE, -S n type of lens
FISHFUL adj teeming with fish
FISHGIG, -S n pole with barbed prongs for impaling fish
FISHHOOK n sharp hook used in angling, esp one with a barb
FISHIER ▸ fishy
FISHIEST ▸ fishy
FISHIFY vb change into fish
FISHILY ▸ fishy
FISHING, -S n job or pastime of catching fish
FISHKILL n mass killing of fish by pollution
FISHLESS ▸ fish
FISHLIKE ▸ fish

FISHLINE n line used on a fishing-rod
FISHMEAL n ground dried fish used as feed for farm animals or as a fertilizer
FISHNET, -S n open mesh fabric resembling netting
FISHPOLE n boom arm for a microphone
FISHPOND ▸ fish
FISHSKIN n skin of a fish
FISHTAIL n nozzle placed over a Bunsen burner to produce a fanlike flame ▷ vb slow an aeroplane by swerving the tail
FISHWAY, -S n fish ladder
FISHWIFE n coarse scolding woman
FISHWORM n worm used as fishing bait
FISHY, FISHIER, FISHIEST adj of or like fish
FISK, -ED, -ING, -S vb frisk
FISNOMIE n physiognomy
FISSATE ▸ fissile
FISSILE adj capable of undergoing nuclear fission
FISSION, -S n splitting
FISSIPED adj having toes separated from one another ▷ n fissiped animal
FISSIVE ▸ fissile
FISSLE, -D, -S, FISSLING vb rustle
FISSURAL ▸ fissure
FISSURE, -D, -S n long narrow cleft or crack ▷ vb crack or split apart
FIST, -ED, -S n clenched hand ▷ vb hit with the fist
FISTFUL, -S n quantity that can be held in a fist or hand
FISTIANA n world of boxing
FISTIC adj of or relating to fisticuffs or boxing
FISTICAL
FISTIER ▸ fisty
FISTIEST ▸ fisty
FISTING, -S n act of fisting
FISTMELE n measurement of the height of the string of a braced bow
FISTNOTE n note in printed text preceded by the fist symbol
FISTS ▸ fist
FISTULA, -E, -S n long narrow ulcer
FISTULAR same as ▸ fistulous
FISTULAS ▸ fistula
FISTY, FISTIER, FISTIEST ▸ fist
FIT, -S, -TED, -TEST, -TING, -TINGS vb be appropriate

or suitable for ▷ *adj*
appropriate ▷ *n* way in
which something fits

FITCH, -ES *n* fur of the polecat
or ferret

FITCHE *adj* pointed

FITCHEE *variant of* ▶ **fitche**

FITCHES ▶ **fitch**

FITCHET, -S *same as* ▶ **fitch**

FITCHEW, -S *archaic name for*
▶ **polecat**

FITCHY *variant of* ▶ **fitche**

FITFUL *adj* occurring in
irregular spells
FITFULLY

FITLY, FITLIER, FITLIEST *adv*
in a proper manner or place
or at a proper time

FITMENT, -S *n* accessory
attached to a machine

FITNA, -S *n* state of trouble
or chaos

FITNESS *n* state of being fit

FITS ▶ **fit**

FITT, -S *n* song

FITTABLE ▶ **fit**

FITTE, -S *variant of* ▶ **fitt**

FITTED ▶ **fit**

FITTER, -S ▶ **fit**

FITTES ▶ **fitte**

FITTEST ▶ **fit**

FITTING ▶ **fit**

FITTINGS ▶ **fit**

FITTS ▶ **fitt**

FIVE *n* one more than four
▷ *adj* amounting to five
▷ *determiner* amounting
to five

FIVEFOLD *adj* having five
times as many or as much
▷ *adv* by five times as many
or as much

FIVEPIN ▶ **fivepins**

FIVEPINS *n* bowling game
played esp in Canada

FIVER, -S *n* five-pound note

FIVES *n* ball game resembling
squash

FIX, -ES *vb* make or become
firm, stable, or secure ▷ *n*
difficult situation
FIXABLE

FIXATE, -D, -S, FIXATING *vb*
become or cause to become
fixed

FIXATIF, -S *variant of*
▶ **fixative**

FIXATING ▶ **fixate**

FIXATION *n* obsessive interest
in something

FIXATIVE *n* liquid used to
preserve or hold things
in place ▷ *adj* serving or
tending to fix

FIXATURE *n* something that
holds an object in place

FIXED *adj* attached or placed
so as to be immovable
FIXEDLY

FIXER, -S *n* solution used to
make a photographic image
permanent

FIXES ▶ **fix**

FIXING *n* means of attaching
one thing to another

FIXINGS *pl n* apparatus or
equipment

FIXIT, -S *n* solution to a
complex problem ▷ *adj* that
fixes things

FIXITIES ▶ **fixity**

FIXITS ▶ **fixit**

FIXITY, FIXITIES *n* state of
being fixed

FIXIVE ▶ **fix**

FIXT *adj* fixed

FIXTURE, -S *n* permanently
fitted piece of household
equipment

FIXURE, -S *n* firmness

FIZ *variant of* ▶ **fizz**

FIZGIG, -S *vb* inform on
someone to the police

FIZZ, -ED, -ES, -ING, -INGS *vb*
make a hissing or bubbling
noise ▷ *n* hissing or bubbling
noise

FIZZEN, -S *variant of* ▶ **foison**

FIZZER, -S *n* anything that
fizzes

FIZZES ▶ **fizz**

FIZZGIG, -S *variant of*
▶ **fishgig**

FIZZIER ▶ **fizzy**

FIZZIEST ▶ **fizzy**

FIZZILY *adv* in a fizzy manner

FIZZING ▶ **fizz**

FIZZINGS ▶ **fizz**

FIZZLE, -D, -S, FIZZLING *vb*
make a weak hissing or
bubbling sound ▷ *n* hissing
or bubbling sound

FIZZY, FIZZIER, FIZZIEST
▶ **fizz**

FJELD, -S *n* high rocky plateau

FJORD, -S *n* long narrow inlet
of the sea between cliffs
FJORDIC

FLAB, -S *n* unsightly body fat

FLABBIER ▶ **flabby**

FLABBILY ▶ **flabby**

FLABBY, FLABBIER *adj* having
flabby flesh

FLABELLA > **flabellum**

FLABS ▶ **flab**

FLACCID *adj* soft and limp

FLACK, -ED, -ING, -S *vb* flutter

FLACKER, -S *vb* flutter like
a bird

FLACKERY ▶ **flack**

FLACKET, -S *n* flagon ▷ *vb*
flap or flutter about

FLACKING ▶ **flack**

FLACKS ▶ **flack**

FLACON, -S *n* small stoppered
bottle or flask

FLAFF, -ED, -ING, -S *vb* flap

FLAFFER, -S *vb* flutter

FLAFFING ▶ **flaff**

FLAFFS ▶ **flaff**

FLAG, -GED, -GING, -S *n* piece
of cloth attached to a pole
as an emblem or signal ▷ *vb*
mark with a flag or sticker

FLAGELLA > **flagellum**

FLAGGED ▶ **flag**

FLAGGER, -S ▶ **flag**

FLAGGIER ▶ **flaggy**

FLAGGING ▶ **flag**

FLAGGY, FLAGGIER *adj*
drooping

FLAGLESS ▶ **flag**

FLAGMAN, FLAGMEN *n*
person who has charge of
a flag

FLAGON, -S *n* wide bottle

FLAGPOLE *n* pole for a flag

FLAGRANT *adj* openly
outrageous

FLAGS ▶ **flag**

FLAGSHIP *n* admiral's ship

FLAIL, -ED, -ING, -S *vb* wave
about wildly ▷ *n* tool
formerly used for threshing
grain by hand

FLAIR, -S *n* natural ability

FLAK, -S *n* anti-aircraft fire

FLAKE, -D, -S, FLAKING *n*
small thin piece, esp chipped
off something ▷ *vb* peel off
in flakes

FLAKER -S

FLAKEY *same as* ▶ **flaky**

FLAKIER ▶ **flaky**

FLAKIES *n* dandruff

FLAKIEST ▶ **flaky**

FLAKILY ▶ **flaky**

FLAKING ▶ **flake**

FLAKS ▶ **flak**

FLAKY, FLAKIER, FLAKIEST
adj made or made of flakes

FLAM, -MED, -MING, -S *n*
falsehood, deception, or
sham ▷ *vb* cheat or deceive

FLAMBE, -S *vb* cook or serve
(food) in flaming brandy
▷ *adj* (of food) served in
flaming brandy

FLAMBEAU *n* burning torch,
as used in night processions

FLAMBEE, -D, -S *same as*
▶ **flambe**

FLAMBES ▶ **flambe**

FLAME, -D, -S *n* luminous
burning gas coming from
burning material ▷ *vb* burn
brightly
FLAMELET

F

FLAMEN, -S, FLAMINES n (in ancient Rome) type of priest

FLAMENCO n rhythmical Spanish dance accompanied by a guitar and vocalist

FLAMENS ▸ **flamen**

FLAMEOUT n failure of an aircraft jet engine in flight due to extinction of the flame ▷ vb (of a jet engine) to fail in flight or to cause (a jet engine) to fail in flight

FLAMER, -S ▸ **flame**

FLAMES ▸ **flame**

FLAMFEW, -S n fantastic trifle

FLAMIER ▸ **flamy**

FLAMIEST ▸ **flamy**

FLAMINES ▸ **flamen**

FLAMING adj burning with flames ▷ adv extremely

FLAMINGO n large pink wading bird with a long neck and legs

FLAMM, -S variant of ▸ **flam**

FLAMMED ▸ **flam**

FLAMMING ▸ **flam**

FLAMMS ▸ **flamm**

FLAMMULE n small flame

FLAMS ▸ **flam**

FLAMY, FLAMIER, FLAMIEST ▸ **flame**

FLAN, -S n open sweet or savoury tart

FLANCARD n armour covering a horse's flank

FLANCH, -ED, -ES variant of ▸ **flaunch**

FLANE, -D, FLANING vb walk idly, saunter

FLANERIE n aimless strolling or lounging

FLANES n arrows

FLANEUR, -S n idler or loafer

FLANGE, -S n projecting rim or collar ▷ vb attach or provide (a component) with a flange

FLANGED

FLANGER -S

FLANGING n act of flanging

FLANING ▸ **flane**

FLANK, -ED, -ING, -S n part of the side between the hips and ribs ▷ vb be at or move along the side of

FLANKEN, -S n cut of beef

FLANKER, -S n one of a detachment of soldiers guarding the flanks

FLANKING ▸ **flank**

FLANKS ▸ **flank**

FLANNEL, -S n small piece of cloth for washing the face ▷ vb talk evasively

FLANNEN, -S adj made of flannel

FLANNIE, -S same as ▸ **flanny**

FLANNY n shirt made of flannel

FLANS ▸ **flan**

FLAP, -PED, -PING, -S vb move back and forwards or up and down ▷ n action or sound of flapping

FLAPERON n control flap on aircraft wing

FLAPJACK n chewy biscuit made with oats

FLAPLESS ▸ **flap**

FLAPPED ▸ **flap**

FLAPPER, -S n (in the 1920s) an unconventional young woman

FLAPPIER ▸ **flappy**

FLAPPING ▸ **flap**

FLAPPY, FLAPPIER adj loose

FLAPS ▸ **flap**

FLARE, -D, FLARING vb blaze with a sudden unsteady flame ▷ n sudden unsteady flame

FLARES pl n trousers with legs that widen below the knee

FLAREUP, -S n outbreak of something

FLARIER ▸ **flary**

FLARIEST ▸ **flary**

FLARING ▸ **flare**

FLARY, FLARIER, FLARIEST adj flare-like

FLASER, -S n type of sedimentary structure in rock

FLASH, -ED, -ES, -EST n sudden burst of light or flame ▷ adj vulgarly showy ▷ vb emit or reflect light suddenly or intermittently

FLASHER -S

FLASHGUN n type of electronic flash for a camera

FLASHIER ▸ **flashy**

FLASHILY ▸ **flashy**

FLASHING n watertight material used to cover joins in a roof

FLASHY, FLASHIER adj showy in a vulgar way

FLASK, -S n flat bottle

FLASKET, -S n long shallow basket

FLASKS ▸ **flask**

FLAT, -S, -TED, -TEST, -TING adj level and horizontal ▷ adv in or into a flat position ▷ n flat surface ▷ vb live in a flat

FLATBACK n flat-backed ornament, designed for viewing from front

FLATBED, -S n type of printing machine

FLATBOAT n flat-bottomed boat for transporting goods on a canal

FLATCAP, -S n Elizabethan man's hat

FLATCAR, -S n flatbed

FLATETTE n very small flat

FLATFEET ▸ **flatfoot**

FLATFISH n sea fish, such as the sole, which has a flat body

FLATFOOT, FLATFEET n flattening of the instep arch

FLATFORM n thick, level sole on a shoe

FLATHEAD n common Australian flatfish

FLATIRON n (formerly) an iron for pressing clothes that was heated by being placed on a stove

FLATLAND n land notable for its levelness

FLATLET, -S n small flat

FLATLINE vb flat line on medical equipment monitoring one's vital signs

FLATLING adv in a flat or prostrate position ▷ adj with the flat side, as of a sword

FLATLONG adv prostrate

FLATLY ▸ **flat**

FLATMATE n person with whom one shares a flat

FLATNESS ▸ **flat**

FLATPACK n pieces packed into a flat box for home assembly

FLATPICK vb play (a guitar, etc) by plucking individual strings with a plectrum

FLATS ▸ **flat**

FLATTED ▸ **flat**

FLATTEN, -S vb make or become flat or flatter

FLATTER, -S vb praise insincerely

FLATTERY n excessive or insincere praise

FLATTEST ▸ **flat**

FLATTIE, -S n flat tyre

FLATTING ▸ **flat**

FLATTISH adj somewhat flat

FLATTOP, -S n informal name for an aircraft carrier

FLATTY n flat shoe

FLATUOUS ▸ **flatus**

FLATUS, -ES n gas generated in the alimentary canal

FLATWARE n cutlery

FLATWASH n laundry that can be ironed mechanically

FLATWAYS adv with the flat or broad side down or in contact with another surface

FLATWISE same as ▸ **flatways**

FLATWORK n laundry that can be ironed mechanically

FLATWORM n worm, such as a tapeworm, with a flattened body

FLAUGHT, -S vb flutter

FLAUNCH n cement or mortar slope to throw off water ▷ vb cause to slope in this manner

FLAUNE, -S variant of ▶ **flam**

FLAUNT, -ED, -S vb display (oneself or one's possessions) arrogantly ▷ n act of flaunting
FLAUNTER

FLAUNTY adj characterized by or inclined to ostentatious display

FLAUTA, -S n tortilla rolled around a filling

FLAUTIST n flute player

FLAVA, -S n individual style

FLAVANOL n type of flavonoid

FLAVAS ▶ flava

FLAVIN, -S n heterocyclic ketone

FLAVINE, -S same as ▶ **flavin**

FLAVINS ▶ flavin

FLAVONE, -S n crystalline compound occurring in plants

FLAVONOL n flavonoid said to offer protection against heart disease

FLAVOR, -ED, -S same as ▶ **flavour**
FLAVORER

FLAVORY adj flavoursome

FLAVOUR, -S n distinctive taste ▷ vb give flavour to

FLAVOURY adj flavoursome

FLAW, -ED, -ING, -S n imperfection or blemish ▷ vb make or become blemished, defective, or imperfect

FLAWIER ▶ flawy

FLAWIEST ▶ flawy

FLAWING ▶ flaw

FLAWLESS ▶ flaw

FLAWN, -S variant of ▶ **flam**

FLAWS ▶ flaw

FLAWY, FLAWIER, FLAWIEST ▶ flaw

FLAX, -ES n plant grown for its stem fibres and seeds

FLAXEN adj (of hair) pale yellow

FLAXES ▶ flax

FLAXIER ▶ flaxy

FLAXIEST ▶ flaxy

FLAXSEED n seed of the flax plant, which yields linseed oil

FLAXY, FLAXIER, FLAXIEST same as ▶ **flaxen**

FLAY, -ED, -ING, -S same as ▶ **fley**
FLAYER -S

FLAYSOME adj frightening

FLEA, -S n small bloodsucking insect

FLEABAG, -S n dirty or unkempt person, esp a woman

FLEABANE n as in **Canadian fleabane** small plant thought to ward off fleas

FLEABITE n bite of a flea

FLEADH, -S n festival of Irish music, dancing, and culture

FLEAM, -S n lancet used for letting blood

FLEAPIT, -S n shabby cinema or theatre

FLEAS ▶ flea

FLEASOME adj having fleas

FLEAWORT n type of plant

FLECHE, -S n slender spire

FLECK, -ED, -ING, -S n small mark, streak, or speck ▷ vb speckle

FLECKER, -S same as ▶ **fleck**

FLECKIER ▶ flecky

FLECKING ▶ fleck

FLECKS ▶ fleck

FLECKY, FLECKIER ▶ fleck

FLECTION n act of bending or the state of being bent

FLED ▶ flee

FLEDGE, -D, -S, FLEDGING vb feed and care for (a young bird) until it is able to fly

FLEDGIER ▶ fledgy

FLEDGING ▶ fledge

FLEDGY, FLEDGIER adj feathery or feathered

FLEE, FLED, -ING, -S vb run away (from)

FLEECE, -D, -S, FLEECING n sheep's coat of wool ▷ vb defraud or overcharge
FLEECER -S

FLEECH, -ED, -ES vb flatter

FLEECIE, -S n person who collects fleeces for baling

FLEECIER ▶ fleecy

FLEECIES ▶ fleecie

FLEECILY ▶ fleecy

FLEECING ▶ fleece

FLEECY, FLEECIER adj made of or like fleece ▷ n person who collects fleeces after shearing and prepares them for baling

FLEEING ▶ flee

FLEER, -ED, -ING, -S vb grin or laugh at ▷ n derisory glance or grin
FLEERER -S

FLEES ▶ flee

FLEET, -ED, -EST, -S n number of warships organized as a unit ▷ adj swift in movement ▷ vb move rapidly
FLEETER

FLEETING adj rapid and soon passing

FLEETLY ▶ fleet

FLEETS ▶ fleet

FLEG, -GED, -GING, -S vb scare

FLEHMEN, -S vb (of mammal) grimace

FLEISHIG same as ▶ **fleishik**

FLEISHIK adj containing or derived from meat or meat products

FLEME, -D, -S, FLEMIT vb drive out

FLEMING n inhabitant of Flanders or a Flemish-speaking Belgian

FLEMISH vb stow (a rope) in a Flemish coil

FLEMIT ▶ fleme

FLENCH, -ED, -ES same as ▶ **flense**
FLENCHER

FLENSE, -D, -S, FLENSING vb strip (a whale, seal, etc) of (its blubber or skin)
FLENSER -S

FLESH, -ED, -ES, -ING n soft part of a human or animal body

FLESHER, -S n person or machine that fleshes hides or skins

FLESHES ▶ flesh

FLESHIER ▶ fleshy

FLESHILY ▶ fleshy

FLESHING ▶ flesh

FLESHLY adj fleshy; fat

FLESHPOT n pot in which meat is cooked

FLESHY, FLESHIER adj plump

FLETCH, -ED, -ES same as ▶ **fledge**

FLETCHER n person who makes arrows

FLETCHES ▶ fletch

FLETTON, -S n type of brick

FLEUR, -S n flower emblem used in heraldry

FLEURET, -S same as > **fleurette**

FLEURON, -S n decorative piece of pastry

FLEURS ▶ fleur

FLEURY same as ▶ **flory**

FLEW ▶ fly

FLEWED adj having large flews

FLEWS pl n upper lip of a bloodhound or similar dog

FLEX, -ED, -ES, -ING n flexible insulated electric cable ▷ vb bend

FLEXAGON n hexagon made from a single pliable strip of triangles

FLEXED ▶ flex

FLEXES ► flex

FLEXIBLE adj easily bent
FLEXIBLY

FLEXILE same as **► flexible**

FLEXING ► flex

FLEXION, -S n act of bending a joint or limb

FLEXO n, adj, adv flexography

FLEXOR, -S n type of muscle

FLEXOS ► flexo

FLEXTIME same as **> flexitime**

FLEXUOSE same as **► flexuous**

FLEXUOUS adj full of bends or curves

FLEXURAL ► flexure

FLEXURE, -S n act of flexing or the state of being flexed

FLEXWING n collapsible fabric wing used in hang gliding

FLEY, -ING, -S vb be afraid or cause to be afraid

FLIBBERT n small piece or bit

FLIC, -S n French police officer

FLICHTER vb flutter

FLICK, -ED, -ING, -S vb touch or move in a quick movement ▷ n tap or quick stroke

FLICKER, -S vb shine unsteadily or intermittently ▷ n unsteady brief light
FLICKERY

FLICKING ► flick

FLICKS ► flick

FLICS ► flic

FLIED ► fly

FLIER, -S ► fly

FLIES ► fly

FLIEST ► fly

FLIGHT, -ED, -S n journey by air ▷ vb cause (a ball, dart, etc) to float slowly or deceptively towards its target

FLIGHTY adj frivolous and fickle

FLIM, -S n five-pound note

FLIMFLAM n nonsense ▷ vb deceive

FLIMP, -ED, -ING, -S vb steal

FLIMS ► flim

FLIMSIER ► flimsy

FLIMSIES ► flimsy

FLIMSILY ► flimsy

FLIMSY, FLIMSIER, FLIMSIES adj not strong or substantial ▷ n thin paper used for making carbon copies

FLINCH, -ED, -ES same as **► flense**
FLINCHER

FLINDER, -S n fragment ▷ vb scamper about flutteringly

FLING, -ING, -S, FLUNG vb throw, send, or move forcefully or hurriedly ▷ n spell of self-indulgent enjoyment

FLINGER -S

FLINKITE n anhydrous phosphate

FLINT, -ED, -ING, -S n hard grey stone ▷ vb fit or provide with a flint

FLINTIER ► flinty

FLINTIFY vb turn to flint

FLINTILY ► flinty

FLINTING ► flint

FLINTS ► flint

FLINTY, FLINTIER adj cruel

FLIP, -PED, -PEST, -S vb throw (something small or light) carelessly ▷ n snap or tap ▷ adj flippant

FLIPBOOK n book of drawings made to seem animated by flipping pages

FLIPFLOP n rubber sandal

FLIPPANT adj treating serious things lightly

FLIPPED ► flip

FLIPPER, -S n limb of a sea animal adapted for swimming

FLIPPEST ► flip

FLIPPIER ► flippy

FLIPPING n act or instance of flipping

FLIPPY, FLIPPIER adj (of clothes) moving to and fro as the wearer walks

FLIPS ► flip

FLIPSIDE n reverse or opposite side

FLIR, -S n forward looking infrared radar

FLIRT, -ED, -ING, -S vb behave as if physically attracted to someone ▷ n person who flirts

FLIRTER -S

FLIRTIER ► flirty

FLIRTING ► flirt

FLIRTISH ► flirt

FLIRTS ► flirt

FLIRTY, FLIRTIER ► flirt

FLISK, -ED, -ING, -S vb skip

FLISKIER ► flisky

FLISKING ► flisk

FLISKS ► flisk

FLISKY, FLISKIER ► flisk

FLIT, -S, -TED, -TING vb move lightly and rapidly ▷ n act of flitting

FLITCH, -ED, -ES n side of pork salted and cured ▷ vb cut (a tree trunk) into flitches

FLITE, -D, -S, FLITING vb scold or rail at ▷ n dispute or scolding

FLITS ► flit

FLITT, -S adj fleet ▷ vb to flit

FLITTED ► flit

FLITTER, -S ► flit

FLITTERN n bark of young oak tree

FLITTERS ► flitter

FLITTING ► flit

FLITTS ► flitt

FLIVVER, -S n old, cheap, or battered car

FLIX, -ED, -ES, -ING n fur ▷ vb have fur

FLIXWEED n plant of the mustard family

FLOAT, -ED vb rest on the surface of a liquid ▷ n object used to help someone or something float

FLOATAGE same as **► flotage**

FLOATANT n substance used in fly-fishing, to help dry flies to float

FLOATCUT adj as in **floatcut file** file with rows of parallel teeth

FLOATED ► float

FLOATEL, -S same as **► flotel**

FLOATER, -S n person or thing that floats

FLOATIER ► floaty

FLOATING adj moving about, changing

FLOATS pl n footlights

FLOATY, FLOATIER adj filmy and light

FLOB, -BED, -BING, -S vb spit

FLOC, -S same as **► flock**
FLOCCED

FLOCCI ► floccus

FLOCCING ► floc

FLOCCOSE adj consisting of or covered with woolly tufts or hairs

FLOCCULE n small aggregate of flocculent material

FLOCCULI > flocculus

FLOCCUS, FLOCCI n downy or woolly covering ▷ adj (of a cloud) having the appearance of woolly tufts

FLOCK, -ED, -ING, -S n number of animals of one kind together ▷ vb gather in a crowd ▷ adj (of wallpaper) with a velvety raised pattern

FLOCKIER ► flocky

FLOCKING ► flock

FLOCKS ► flock

FLOCKY, FLOCKIER ► flock

FLOCS ► floc

FLOE, -S n sheet of floating ice

FLOG, -GED, -S vb beat with a whip or stick
FLOGGER -S
FLOGGING ► flog
FLOGS ► flog
FLOKATI, -S n Greek hand-woven shaggy woollen rug
FLONG, -S n material used for making moulds in stereotyping
FLOOD, -ED, -S n overflow of water onto a normally dry area ▷ vb cover or become covered with water
FLOODER -S
FLOODING n submerging of land under water
FLOODLIT adj illuminated with a floodlight
FLOODS ► flood
FLOODWAY n conduit for floodwater
FLOOEY adj awry
FLOOIE same as ► flooey
FLOOR, -ED, -ING, -S n lower surface of a room ▷ vb knock down
FLOORAGE n area of floor
FLOORED ► floor
FLOORER, -S n coup de grâce
FLOORING ► floor
FLOORPAN n bottom part of a motor vehicle's interior
FLOORS ► floor
FLOP, -PED, -PING, -S vb bend, fall, or collapse loosely or carelessly ▷ n failure
FLOPOVER n TV visual effect of page being turned
FLOPPED ► flop
FLOPPER, -S ► flop
FLOPPIER ► floppy
FLOPPIES ► floppy
FLOPPILY ► floppy
FLOPPING ► flop
FLOPPY, FLOPPIER, FLOPPIES adj hanging downwards, loose ▷ n floppy disk
FLOPS ► flop
FLOR, -S n type of yeast
FLORA, -E, -S n plants of a given place or time
FLORAL, -S adj consisting of or decorated with flowers ▷ n class of perfume
FLORALLY
FLORAS ► flora
FLOREAT, FLOREANT vb may (a person, institution, etc) flourish
FLORENCE n type of fennel
FLORET, -S n part of a composite flower head
FLORID, -ER adj with a red or flushed complexion
FLORIDLY

FLORIER ► flory
FLORIEST ► flory
FLORIGEN n hypothetical plant hormone
FLORIN, -S n former British and Australian coin
FLORIST, -S n seller of flowers
FLORS ► flor
FLORUIT, -S prep (he or she) flourished in ▷ n such a period in a person's life
FLORULA, -E n flora of a small single environment
FLORULE, -S same as ► florula
FLORY, FLORIER, FLORIEST adj containing a fleur-de-lys
FLOSCULE n floret
FLOSH, -ES n hopper-shaped box
FLOSS, -ED, -ES, -ING n fine silky fibres ▷ vb clean (between the teeth) with dental floss
FLOSSER -S
FLOSSIE variant of ► flossy
FLOSSIER ► flossy
FLOSSILY ► flossy
FLOSSING ► floss
FLOSSY, FLOSSIER adj consisting of or resembling floss
FLOTA, -S n formerly, Spanish commercial fleet
FLOTAGE, -S n act or state of floating
FLOTANT adj in heraldry, flying in the air
FLOTAS ► flota
FLOTE, -D, -S, FLOTING n aquatic perennial grass ▷ vb skim (eg milk)
FLOTEL, -S n (in the oil industry) a rig or boat used as accommodation
FLOTES ► flote
FLOTILLA n small fleet or fleet of small ships
FLOTING ► flote
FLOTSAM, -S n floating wreckage
FLOUNCE, -D, -S vb go with emphatic movements ▷ n flouncing movement
FLOUNCY
FLOUNDER vb move with difficulty, as in mud ▷ n edible flatfish
FLOUR, -ED, -ING, -S n powder made by grinding grain, esp wheat ▷ vb sprinkle with flour
FLOURIER ► floury
FLOURING ► flour

FLOURISH vb be active, successful, or widespread ▷ n dramatic waving motion
FLOURS ► flour
FLOURY, FLOURIER ► flour
FLOUSE, -D, -S, FLOUSING vb splash
FLOUSH, -ED, -ES variant of ► flouse
FLOUSING ► flouse
FLOUT, -ED, -ING, -S vb deliberately disobey (a rule, law, etc)
FLOUTER -S
FLOW, -ED, -ING, -S vb (of liquid) move in a stream ▷ n act, rate, or manner of flowing
FLOWABLE adj capable of flowing
FLOWAGE, -S n act of overflowing or the state of having overflowed
FLOWED ► flow
FLOWER, -S n part of a plant that produces seeds ▷ vb produce flowers, bloom
FLOWERED adj decorated with a floral design
FLOWERER n plant that flowers at a specified time or in a specified way
FLOWERET another name for ► floret
FLOWERS ► flower
FLOWERY adj decorated with a floral design
FLOWING ► flow
FLOWN ► fly
FLOWS ► flow
FLOX adj as in flox silk type of silk
FLU, -S n any of various viral infections
FLUATE, -S n fluoride
FLUB, -BED, -BING, -S vb bungle
FLUBBER -S
FLUBDUB, -S n bunkum
FLUBS ► flub
FLUE, -S n passage or pipe for smoke or hot air
FLUED adj having a flue
FLUELLEN n type of plant
FLUELLIN same as ► fluellen
FLUENCE, -S ► fluency
FLUENCY n quality of being fluent
FLUENT, -S adj able to speak or write with ease ▷ n variable quantity in fluxions
FLUENTLY
FLUERIC adj of or relating to fluidics
FLUERICS pl n fluidics
FLUES ► flue

F

FLUEWORK n collectively, organ stops

FLUEY, FLUIER, FLUIEST adj involved in, caused by, or like influenza

FLUFF, -ED, -ING, -S n soft fibres ▷ vb make or become soft and puffy

FLUFFER, -S n person employed on a railway to clear the tracks

FLUFFIER ▸ fluffy

FLUFFILY ▸ fluffy

FLUFFING ▸ fluff

FLUFFS ▸ fluff

FLUFFY, FLUFFIER adj of, resembling, or covered with fluff

FLUGEL, -S n grand piano or harpsichord

FLUID, -S n substance able to flow and change its shape ▷ adj able to flow or change shape easily

FLUIDAL

FLUIDIC ▸ fluidics

FLUIDICS n study and use of the flow of fluids in tubes

FLUIDIFY vb make fluid

FLUIDISE same as ▸ fluidize

FLUIDITY n state of being fluid

FLUIDIZE vb make fluid

FLUIDLY ▸ fluid

FLUIDRAM n British imperial measure

FLUIDS ▸ fluid

FLUIER ▸ fluey

FLUIEST ▸ fluey

FLUISH ▸ flu

FLUKE, -D, -S, FLUKING n accidental stroke of luck ▷ vb gain, make, or hit by a fluke

FLUKEY same as ▸ fluky

FLUKIER ▸ fluky

FLUKIEST ▸ fluky

FLUKILY ▸ fluky

FLUKING ▸ fluke

FLUKY, FLUKIER, FLUKIEST adj done or gained by an accident

FLUME, -D, -S, FLUMING n narrow sloping channel for water ▷ vb transport (logs) in a flume

FLUMMERY n silly or trivial talk

FLUMMOX vb puzzle or confuse

FLUMP, -ED, -ING, -S vb move or fall heavily

FLUNG ▸ fling

FLUNK, -ED, -ING, -S vb fail ▷ n low grade below the pass standard

FLUNKER -S

FLUNKEY, -S same as ▸ flunky

FLUNKIE same as ▸ flunky

FLUNKIES ▸ flunky

FLUNKING ▸ flunk

FLUNKS ▸ flunk

FLUNKY, FLUNKIES n servile person

FLUOR, -S same as > fluorspar

FLUORENE n white insoluble crystalline solid

FLUORIC adj of, concerned with, or produced from fluorine or fluorspar

FLUORID same as ▸ fluoride

FLUORIDE n compound containing fluorine

FLUORIDS same as ▸ fluorid

FLUORIN, -S same as ▸ fluorine

FLUORINE n toxic yellow gas: most reactive of all the elements

FLUORINS ▸ fluorin

FLUORITE same as > fluorspar

FLUORS ▸ fluor

FLURR, -ED, -ING, -S vb scatter

FLURRIED ▸ flurry

FLURRIES ▸ flurry

FLURRING ▸ flurr

FLURRS ▸ flurr

FLURRY, FLURRIED, FLURRIES n sudden commotion ▷ vb confuse

FLUS ▸ flu

FLUSH, -ED, -ES, -EST vb blush or cause to blush ▷ n blush ▷ adj level with the surrounding surface ▷ adv so as to be level

FLUSHER -S

FLUSHIER ▸ flushy

FLUSHING n extra feeding given to ewes before mating to increase the lambing percentage

FLUSHY, FLUSHIER adj ruddy

FLUSTER, -S vb make nervous or upset ▷ n nervous or upset state

FLUSTERY

FLUTE, -S n wind instrument ▷ vb utter in a high-pitched tone

FLUTED adj having decorative grooves

FLUTER, -S n craftsman who makes flutes or fluting

FLUTES ▸ flute

FLUTEY, -ER adj resembling a flute in sound

FLUTIER ▸ fluty

FLUTIEST ▸ fluty

FLUTINA, -S n type of accordion

FLUTING, -S n design of decorative grooves

FLUTIST, -S same as ▸ flautist

FLUTTER, -S vb wave rapidly ▷ n flapping movement

FLUTTERY adj flapping rapidly

FLUTY, FLUTIER, FLUTIEST ▸ flute

FLUVIAL adj of rivers

FLUX, -ED, -ES, -ING n constant change or instability ▷ vb make or become fluid

FLUXGATE n type of magnetometer

FLUXING ▸ flux

FLUXION, -S n rate of change of a function

FLUXIVE ▸ flux

FLUYT, -S n Dutch sailing ship

FLY, FLEW, FLIED, FLIES, FLIEST, FLOWN, -EST vb move through the air on wings or in an aircraft ▷ n fastening at the front of trousers ▷ adj sharp and cunning

FLYABLE

FLYAWAY, -S adj (of hair) very fine and soft ▷ n person who is frivolous or flighty

FLYBACK, -S n item of electrical equipment

FLYBANE, -S n type of campion

FLYBELT, -S n strip of tsetse-infested land

FLYBLOW, FLYBLEW, -S vb contaminate ▷ n egg or young larva of a blowfly

FLYBLOWN adj covered with blowfly eggs

FLYBLOWS ▸ flyblow

FLYBOAT, -S n any small swift boat

FLYBOOK, -S n small case or wallet for storing artificial flies

FLYBOY, -S n air force pilot

FLYBY, -S n flight past a particular position or target

FLYER, -S ▸ fly

FLYEST ▸ fly

FLYHAND, -S n device on a printing press

FLYING, -S ▸ fly

FLYLEAF n blank leaf at the beginning or end of a book

FLYLESS ▸ fly

FLYLINE, -S n type of line used in fly fishing

FLYMAKER n person who makes fishing flies

FLYMAN, FLYMEN *n* stagehand

FLYOFF, -S *n* all water transferred from the earth to the atmosphere

FLYOVER, -S *n* road passing over another by a bridge

FLYPAPER *n* paper with a sticky poisonous coating, used to kill flies

FLYPAST, -S *n* ceremonial flight of aircraft over a given area

FLYPE, -D, -S, FLYPING *vb* fold back

FLYPITCH *n* area for unlicensed stalls at markets

FLYSCH, -ES *n* type of marine sedimentary facies

FLYSHEET *n* part of tent

FLYSPECK *n* small speck of the excrement of a fly ▷ *vb* mark with flyspecks

FLYSPRAY *n* insecticide sprayed from an aerosol

FLYTE, -D, -S *same as* ▶ **flite**

FLYTIER, -S *n* person who makes their own fishing flies

FLYTING, -S ▶ **flyte**

FLYTRAP, -S *n* any of various insectivorous plants

FLYWAY, -S *n* usual route used by birds when migrating

FLYWHEEL *n* heavy wheel regulating the speed of a machine

FOAL, -ED, -S *n* young of a horse or related animal ▷ *vb* give birth to a foal

FOALFOOT *n* coltsfoot

FOALING, -S *n* act of flanging

FOALS ▶ **foal**

FOAM, -ED, -S *n* mass of small bubbles on a liquid ▷ *vb* produce foam

FOAMABLE

FOAMER, -S *n* (possibly obsessive) enthusiast

FOAMIER ▶ **foamy**

FOAMIEST ▶ **foamy**

FOAMILY ▶ **foamy**

FOAMING, -S ▶ **foam**

FOAMLESS ▶ **foam**

FOAMLIKE ▶ **foam**

FOAMS ▶ **foam**

FOAMY, FOAMIER, FOAMIEST *adj* of, resembling, consisting of, or covered with foam

FOB, -BED, -BING, -S *n* short watch chain ▷ *vb* cheat

FOCACCIA *n* flat Italian bread made with olive oil and yeast

FOCAL *adj* of or at a focus

FOCALISE *same as* ▶ **focalize**

FOCALIZE *less common word for* ▶ **focalize**

FOCALLY ▶ **focal**

FOCUS, FOCI, -ED, -ES, -ING, -SED, -SES *n* point at which light or sound waves converge ▷ *vb* bring or come into focus

FOCUSER -S

FODDER, -ED, -S *n* feed for livestock ▷ *vb* supply (livestock) with fodder

FODDERER

FODGEL *adj* buxom

FOE, -S *n* enemy, opponent

FOEDARIE *variant of* ▶ **fedarie**

FOEFIE *adj as in* **foefie slide** rope along which a person may traverse

FOEHN, -S *same as* ▶ **fohn**

FOEMAN, FOEMEN *n* enemy in war

FOEN *same as* ▶ **foe**

FOES ▶ **foe**

FOETAL *same as* ▶ **fetal**

FOETID, -ER *same as* ▶ **fetid**

FOETIDLY

FOETOR, -S *same as* ▶ **fetor**

FOETUS, -ES *same as* ▶ **fetus**

FOG, -GED, -S *n* mass of condensed water vapour in the lower air ▷ *vb* cover with steam

FOGASH, -ES *n* type of Hungarian pike perch

FOGBOUND *adj* prevented from operating by fog

FOGBOW, -S *n* faint arc of light sometimes seen in a fog bank

FOGDOG, -S *n* spot sometimes seen in fog near the horizon

FOGEY, -S *n* old-fashioned person

FOGEYDOM

FOGEYISH

FOGEYISM

FOGFRUIT *n* wildflower of the verbena family

FOGGAGE, -S *n* grass grown for winter grazing

FOGGED ▶ **foggy**

FOGGER, -S *n* device that generates a fog

FOGGIER ▶ **foggy**

FOGGIEST ▶ **foggy**

FOGGILY ▶ **fog**

FOGGING, -S *n* act of fogging

FOGGY, FOGGIER, FOGGIEST ▶ **fog**

FOGHORN, -S *n* large horn sounded to warn ships in fog

FOGIE, -S *variant of* ▶ **fogey**

FOGLE, -S *n* silk handkerchief

FOGLESS ▶ **fog**

FOGLIGHT *n* motor-vehicle light used in fog

FOGMAN, FOGMEN *n* person in charge of railway fog-signals

FOGOU, -S *n* subterranean building found in Cornwall

FOGRAM, -S *n* fogey

FOGS ▶ **fog**

FOGY *same as* ▶ **fogey**

FOGYDOM -S

FOGYISH ▶ **fogy**

FOGYISM, -S ▶ **fogy**

FOH *interj* expression of disgust

FOHN, -S *n* type of warm dry wind

FOIBLE, -S *n* minor weakness or slight peculiarity

FOID, -S *n* rock-forming mineral similar to feldspar

FOIL, -ED, -S *vb* ruin (someone's plan) ▷ *n* metal in a thin sheet, esp for wrapping food

FOILABLE

FOILING, -S

FOILIST, -S *n* person who fences with a foil

FOILS ▶ **foil**

FOILSMAN, FOILSMEN *n* person who uses or specializes in using a foil

FOIN, -ED, -ING, -S *n* thrust or lunge with a weapon ▷ *vb* thrust with a weapon

FOISON, -S *n* plentiful supply or yield

FOIST, -ED, -ING, -S *vb* force or impose on

FOISTER -S

FOLACIN, -S *n* folic acid

FOLATE, -S *n* folic acid

FOLD, -ED, -ING, -S *vb* bend so that one part covers another ▷ *n* folded piece or part

FOLDABLE

FOLDAWAY *adj* (of a bed) able to be folded and put away when not in use

FOLDBACK *n* (in multitrack recording) a process for returning a signal to a performer instantly

FOLDBOAT *another name for* ▶ **faltboat**

FOLDED ▶ **fold**

FOLDER, -S *n* piece of folded cardboard for holding loose papers

FOLDEROL *same as* ▶ **falderal**

FOLDERS ▶ **folder**

FOLDING, -S ▶ **fold**

FOLDOUT, -S *another name for* ▸ **gatefold**

FOLDS ▸ **fold**

FOLDUP, -S *n* something that folds up

FOLEY, -S *n* footsteps editor

FOLIA ▸ **folium**

FOLIAGE, -S *n* leaves

FOLIAGED *adj* having foliage

FOLIAGES ▸ **foliage**

FOLIAR *adj* of or relating to a leaf or leaves

FOLIATE, -S *adj* relating to, possessing, or resembling leaves ▷ *vb* ornament with foliage or with leaf forms such as foils

FOLIATED *adj* ornamented with or made up of foliage or foils

FOLIATES ▸ **foliate**

FOLIC *adj as in* **folic acid** any of a group of vitamins of the B complex

FOLIE, -S *n* madness

FOLIO, -ED, -ING, -S *n* sheet of paper folded in half to make two leaves of a book ▷ *adj* of or made in the largest book size ▷ *vb* number the leaves of (a book) consecutively

FOLIOLE, -S *n* part of a compound leaf

FOLIOS ▸ **folio**

FOLIOSE *adj* (of a tree) leaf-bearing

FOLIOUS *adj* foliose

FOLIUM, FOLIA, -S *n* plane geometrical curve

FOLK, -S *n* people in general ▷ *adj* traditional to the common people of a country

FOLKIE, -R, -S, -ST *n* devotee of folk music ▷ *adj* of or relating to folk music

FOLKISH ▸ **folk**

FOLKLAND *n* former type of land tenure

FOLKLIFE *n* traditional customs, arts, crafts, and other forms of cultural expression of a people

FOLKLIKE ▸ **folk**

FOLKLORE *n* traditional beliefs and stories of a people

FOLKMOOT *n* (in early medieval England) an assembly of the people of a district, town, or shire

FOLKMOT, -S *same as* ▸ **folkmoot**

FOLKMOTE *same as* ▸ **folkmoot**

FOLKMOTS ▸ **folkmot**

FOLKS ▸ **folk**

FOLKSIER ▸ **folksy**

FOLKSILY ▸ **folksy**

FOLKSONG *n* traditional song

FOLKSY, FOLKSIER *adj* simple and unpretentious

FOLKTALE *n* tale or legend from an oral tradition

FOLKWAY *singular form of* ▸ **folkways**

FOLKWAYS *pl n* traditional and customary ways of living

FOLKY *same as* ▸ **folkie**

FOLLES ▸ **follis**

FOLLICLE *n* small cavity in the body, esp one from which a hair grows

FOLLIED ▸ **folly**

FOLLIES ▸ **folly**

FOLLIS, FOLLES *n* Roman coin

FOLLOW, -ED, -S *vb* go or come after

FOLLOWER *n* disciple or supporter

FOLLOWS ▸ **follow**

FOLLOWUP *n* further action

FOLLY, FOLLIED, FOLLIES, -ING *n* foolishness ▷ *vb* behave foolishly

FOMENT, -ED, -S *vb* encourage or stir up (trouble)

FOMENTER

FOMES *n* any material that may harbour pathogens

FOMITE -S

FON, -NED, -NING, -S *vb* compel

FOND, -ED, -ER, -EST, -ING, -S *adj* tender, loving ▷ *n* background of a design, as in lace ▷ *vb* dote

FONDA, -S *n* Spanish hotel

FONDANT, -S *n* (sweet made from) flavoured paste of sugar and water ▷ *adj* (of a colour) soft

FONDAS ▸ **fonda**

FONDED ▸ **fond**

FONDER ▸ **fond**

FONDEST ▸ **fond**

FONDING ▸ **fond**

FONDLE, -D, -S, FONDLING *vb* caress

FONDLER -S

FONDLY ▸ **fond**

FONDNESS ▸ **fond**

FONDS ▸ **fond**

FONDU, -S *n* ballet movement

FONDUE, -D, -S, FONDUING *n* Swiss dish ▷ *vb* cook and serve (food) as a fondue

FONDUS ▸ **fondu**

FONE *variant of* ▸ **foe**

FONLY *adv* foolishly

FONNED ▸ **fon**

FONNING ▸ **fon**

FONS ▸ **fon**

FONT, -S *n* bowl in a church for baptismal water

FONTAL

FONTANEL *n* soft membranous gap in an infant's skull

FONTANGE *n* type of tall headdress

FONTINA, -S *n* mild Italian cheese

FONTLET, -S ▸ **font**

FONTS ▸ **font**

FOO, -S *n* temporary computer variable or file

FOOBAR *same as* ▸ **fubar**

FOOD, -S *n* what one eats; solid nourishment

FOODBANK *n* charity which distributes food to the needy

FOODERY *n* restaurant

FOODFUL *adj* supplying abundant food

FOODIE, -S *n* gourmet

FOODISM, -S *n* enthusiasm for and interest in good food

FOODLAND *n* land on which food is produced

FOODLESS ▸ **food**

FOODOIR, -S *n* book or blog that combines a personal memoir with recipes

FOODS ▸ **food**

FOODSHED *n* the area through which food is transported from farm to consumer

FOODWAYS *pl n* customs and traditions relating to food and its preparation

FOODY *same as* ▸ **foodie**

FOOFARAW *n* vulgar ornamentation

FOOL, -ED, -S *n* person lacking sense or judgment ▷ *vb* deceive (someone)

FOOLERY *n* foolish behaviour

FOOLFISH *n* orange filefish or winter flounder

FOOLING, -S ▸ **fool**

FOOLISH *adj* unwise, silly, or absurd

FOOLS ▸ **fool**

FOOLSCAP *n* size of paper, 34.3 x 43.2 centimetres

FOOS ▸ **foo**

FOOSBALL *n* US and Canadian name for table football

FOOT, FEET, -ED *n* part of the leg below the ankle ▷ *vb* kick

FOOTAGE, -S *n* amount of film used

FOOTBAG, -S *n* type of sport

FOOTBALL *n* game played by two teams kicking a ball in an attempt to score goals

FOOTBAR, -S *n* any bar used by the foot

FOOTBATH *n* vessel for bathing the feet

FOOTBED, -S *n* insole in a boot or shoe

FOOTBOY, -S *n* boy servant

FOOTED ▶ foot

FOOTER, -ED, -S *n* person who goes on foot ▷ *vb* potter

FOOTFALL *n* sound of a footstep

FOOTGEAR *another name for* ▶ **footwear**

FOOTHILL *n* lower slope of a mountain or a relatively low hill at the foot of a mountain

FOOTHOLD *n* secure position from which progress may be made

FOOTIE, -S *same as* ▶ **footy**

FOOTIER ▶ footy

FOOTIES ▶ footie

FOOTIEST ▶ footy

FOOTING, -S *n* basis or foundation

FOOTLE, -D, -S *vb* loiter aimlessly ▷ *n* foolishness

FOOTLER -S

FOOTLESS ▶ foot

FOOTLIKE ▶ foot

FOOTLING *adj* trivial ▷ *n* trifle

FOOTLONG *n* type of extra-long frankfurter

FOOTMAN, FOOTMEN *n* male servant in uniform

FOOTMARK *n* mark or trace of mud, wetness, etc, left by a person's foot on a surface

FOOTMEN ▶ footman

FOOTMUFF *n* muff used to keep the feet warm

FOOTNOTE *n* note printed at the foot of a page ▷ *vb* supply (a page, book, etc) with footnotes

FOOTPACE *n* normal or walking pace

FOOTPAD, -S *n* highwayman, on foot rather than horseback

FOOTPAGE *n* errand-boy

FOOTPATH *n* narrow path for walkers only

FOOTPOST *n* post delivered on foot

FOOTPUMP *n* pump operated with the foot

FOOTRA, -S *variant of* ▶ **foutra**

FOOTRACE *n* race run on foot

FOOTRAS ▶ footra

FOOTREST *n* something that provides a support for the feet, such as a low stool, rail, etc

FOOTROPE *n* part of a boltrope to which the foot of a sail is stitched

FOOTRULE *n* rigid measure, one foot in length

FOOTS *pl n* sediment that accumulates at the bottom of a vessel

FOOTSAL, -S *n* type of indoor football with five players on each side

FOOTSIE, -S *n* flirtation involving the touching together of feet

FOOTSLOG *vb* march

FOOTSORE *adj* having sore or tired feet, esp from much walking

FOOTSTEP *n* step in walking

FOOTSY *variant of* ▶ **footsie**

FOOTWALL *n* rocks on the lower side of an inclined fault plane or mineral vein

FOOTWAY, -S *n* way or path for pedestrians

FOOTWEAR *n* anything worn to cover the feet

FOOTWELL *n* part of a car in which the foot pedals are located

FOOTWORK *n* skilful use of the feet, as in sport or dancing

FOOTWORN *adj* footsore

FOOTY, FOOTIER, FOOTIEST *n* football ▷ *adj* mean

FOOZLE, -D, -S, FOOZLING *vb* bungle (a shot) ▷ *n* bungled shot

FOOZLER -S

FOP, -PED, -PING, -S *n* man excessively concerned with fashion ▷ *vb* act like a fop

FOPLING, -S *n* vain affected dandy

FOPPED ▶ fop

FOPPERY *n* clothes, affectations, etc, of or befitting a fop

FOPPING ▶ fop

FOPPISH ▶ fop

FOPS ▶ fop

FOR *prep* indicating benefit, receipt, timespan, distance, etc

FORA ▶ forum

FORAGE, -D, -S, FORAGING *vb* search about (for) ▷ *n* food for cattle or horses

FORAGER -S

FORAM, -S *n* marine protozoan

FORAMEN, -S, FORAMINA *n* natural hole

FORAMS ▶ foram

FORANE *adj as in* **vicar forane** type of Roman Catholic priest

FORAY, -ED, -ING, -S *n* brief raid or attack ▷ *vb* raid or ravage (a town, district, etc)

FORAYER -S

FORB, -S *n* any herbaceous plant that is not a grass

FORBAD ▶ forbid

FORBADE ▶ forbid

FORBEAR, FORBARE, -S, FORBORNE *vb* cease or refrain (from doing something)

FORBID, FORBAD, FORBADE, -S *vb* prohibit, refuse to allow

FORBIDAL

FORBODE, -D, -S *vb* obsolete word meaning forbid ▷ *n* obsolete word meaning forbidding

FORBORE *past tense of* ▶ **forbear**

FORBORNE ▶ forbear

FORBS ▶ forb

FORBY *adv* besides

FORBYE *same as* ▶ **forby**

FORCAT, -S *n* convict or galley slave

FORCE, -S, FORCING *n* strength or power ▷ *vb* compel, make (someone) do something

FORCED *adj* compulsory

FORCEDLY

FORCEFUL *adj* emphatic and confident

FORCEOUT *n* play in baseball in which a runner is forced to run to next base and is put out

FORCEPS, FORCIPES *pl n* surgical pincers

FORCER, -S ▶ force

FORCES ▶ force

FORCIBLE *adj* involving physical force or violence

FORCIBLY

FORCING ▶ force

FORCIPES ▶ forceps

FORD, -ED, -ING, -S *n* shallow place where a river may be crossed ▷ *vb* cross (a river) at a ford

FORDABLE

FORDID ▶ fordo

FORDING ▶ ford

FORDLESS ▶ ford

FORDO, FORDID, -ES, -ING, -NE *vb* destroy

FORDONNE *vb as in* **from fordonne** fordone

FORDS ▶ ford

FORE, -S *adj* in, at, or towards the front ▷ *n* front part

F

▷ *interj* golfer's shouted warning

FOREARM, -S *n* arm from the wrist to the elbow ▷ *vb* prepare beforehand

FOREBAY, -S *n* reservoir or canal

FOREBEAR *n* ancestor

FOREBITT *n* post at a ship's foremast for securing cables

FOREBODE *vb* warn of or indicate (an event, result, etc) in advance

FOREBODY *n* part of a ship forward of the foremast

FOREBOOM *n* boom of a foremast

FOREBY *variant of* ► **forby**

FOREBYE *variant of* ► **forby**

FORECAR, -S *n* vehicle attached to a motorcycle

FORECAST *vb* predict (weather, events, etc) ▷ *n* prediction

FOREDATE *vb* antedate

FOREDECK *n* deck between the bridge and the forecastle

FOREDO, FOREDID, -ES, -NE *same as* ► **fordo**

FOREDOOM *vb* doom or condemn beforehand

FOREFACE *n* muzzle of an animal

FOREFEEL, FOREFELT *vb* have a premonition of

FOREFEET ► **forefoot**

FOREFELT ► **forefeel**

FOREFEND *same as* ► **forfend**

FOREFOOT, FOREFEET *n* either of the front feet of an animal

FOREGO, -ES *same as* ► **forgo**

FOREGOER

FOREGONE *adj* gone or completed

FOREGUT, -S *n* anterior part of the digestive tract of vertebrates

FOREHAND *n* stroke played with the palm of the hand facing forward ▷ *adj* (of a stroke) made with the wrist facing the direction of play ▷ *adv* with a forehand stroke ▷ *vb* play (a shot) forehand

FOREHEAD *n* part of the face above the eyebrows

FOREHENT *vb* seize in advance

FOREHOCK *n* foreleg cut of bacon or pork

FOREHOOF *n* front hoof

FOREIGN *adj* not of, or in, one's own country

FOREKING *n* previous king

FOREKNOW, FOREKNEW *vb* know in advance

FOREL, -S *n* type of parchment

FORELADY *n* forewoman of a jury

FORELAID ► **forelay**

FORELAIN ► **forelie**

FORELAND *n* headland, cape, or coastal promontory

FORELAY, FORELAID, -S *archaic word for* ► **ambush**

FORELEG, -S *n* either of the front legs of an animal

FORELEND, FORELENT *vb* give up

FORELIE, FORELAIN, -S *vb* lie in front of

FORELIFT *vb* lift up in front

FORELIMB *n* front or anterior limb

FORELOCK *n* lock of hair over the forehead ▷ *vb* secure (a bolt) by means of a forelock

FORELS ► **forel**

FOREMAN, FOREMEN *n* person in charge of a group of workers

FOREMAST *n* mast nearest the bow of a ship

FOREMEAN *vb* intend in advance

FOREMEN ► **foreman**

FOREMILK *n* first milk drawn from a cow's udder prior to milking

FOREMOST *adv* first in time, place, or importance ▷ *adj* first in time, place, or importance

FORENAME *n* first name

FORENOON *n* morning

FORENSIC *adj* used in or connected with courts of law

FOREPART *n* first or front part in place, order, or time

FOREPAST *adj* bygone

FOREPAW, -S *n* either of the front feet of a land mammal

FOREPEAK *n* interior part of a vessel that is furthest forward

FOREPLAN *vb* plan in advance

FORERAN ► **forerun**

FORERANK *n* first rank

FOREREAD *vb* foretell

FORERUN, FORERAN, -S *vb* serve as a herald for

FORES ► **fore**

FORESAID *less common word for* > **aforesaid**

FORESAIL *n* main sail on the foremast of a ship

FORESAW ► **foresee**

FORESAY, -S *vb* foretell

FORESEE, FORESAW, -N, -S *vb* see or know beforehand

FORESEER

FORESHEW *variant of* ► **foreshow**

FORESHIP *n* fore part of a ship

FORESHOW *vb* indicate in advance

FORESIDE *n* front or upper side or part

FORESKIN *n* fold of skin covering the tip of the penis

FORESLOW *variant of* ► **forslow**

FOREST, -ED, -S *n* large area with a thick growth of trees ▷ *vb* create a forest (in)

FORESTAL

FORESTAY *n* adjustable stay used on ships

FORESTED ► **forest**

FORESTER *n* person skilled in forestry

FORESTRY *n* science of planting and caring for trees

FORESTS ► **forest**

FORETELL, FORETOLD *vb* tell or indicate beforehand

FORETIME *n* time already gone

FORETOLD ► **foretell**

FORETOP, -S *n* platform at the top of the foremast

FOREVER, -S *adv* without end ▷ *n* very long time

FOREWARD *n* vanguard ▷ *vb* guard (something) in front

FOREWARN *vb* warn beforehand

FOREWENT *past tense of* ► **forego**

FOREWIND *n* favourable wind

FOREWING *n* either wing of the anterior pair of an insect's two pairs of wings

FOREWORD *n* introduction to a book

FOREWORN *same as* ► **forworn**

FOREX, -ES *n* foreign exchange

FOREYARD *n* yard for supporting the foresail of a square-rigger

FORFAIR, -S *vb* perish

FORFAIRN *adj* worn out

FORFAIRS ► **forfair**

FORFAULT *variant of* ► **forfeit**

FORFEIT, -S *n* thing lost or given up as a penalty for a fault or mistake ▷ *vb* lose as a forfeit ▷ *adj* lost as a forfeit

FORFEND, -S *vb* protect or secure

FORFEX, -ES n pair of pincers, esp the paired terminal appendages of an earwig

FORGAT past tense of ▸ **forget**

FORGAVE ▸ **forgive**

FORGE, -D, -S n place where metal is worked, smithy ▷ vb make a fraudulent imitation of (something)
FORGEMAN FORGEMEN

FORGER, -S ▸ **forge**

FORGERY n illegal copy of something

FORGES ▸ **forge**

FORGET, -S vb fail to remember

FORGING, -S n process of producing a metal component by hammering

FORGIVE, FORGAVE, -N, -S vb cease to blame or hold resentment against, pardon
FORGIVER

FORGO, -ES, -ING, -NE vb do without or give up
FORGOER -S

FORGOT past tense of ▸ **forget**

FORHAILE vb distress

FORHENT, -S variant of ▸ **forehent**

FORHOO, -ED, -S vb forsake

FORHOOIE variant of ▸ **forhoo**

FORHOOS ▸ **forhoo**

FORHOW, -ED, -S variant of ▸ **forhoo**

FORINSEC adj foreign

FORINT, -S n standard monetary unit of Hungary

FORJUDGE vb deprive of a right by the judgment of a court

FORK, -ING, -S, -SFUL n tool for eating food ▷ vb pick up, dig, etc with a fork

FORKBALL n method of pitching in baseball

FORKED adj having a fork or forklike parts
FORKEDLY

FORKER, -S ▸ **fork**

FORKFUL, -S ▸ **fork**

FORKHEAD n forked head of a rod

FORKIER ▸ **forky**

FORKIEST ▸ **forky**

FORKING ▸ **fork**

FORKLESS ▸ **fork**

FORKLIFT n vehicle for loading goods on wooden pallets

FORKLIKE ▸ **fork**

FORKS ▸ **fork**

FORKSFUL ▸ **fork**

FORKTAIL n bird belonging to the flycatcher family

FORKY, FORKIER, FORKIEST adj forked

FORLANA, -S n Venetian dance

FORLEND, -S, FORLENT variant of ▸ **forelend**

FORLESE, -S, FORLORE vb lose, forsake

FORLORN, -S adj lonely and unhappy ▷ n forsaken person

FORM, -ED, -S n shape or appearance ▷ vb give a (particular) shape to or take a (particular) shape
FORMABLE
FORMABLY

FORMAL, -S adj of or characterized by conventions of behaviour ▷ n woman's evening gown

FORMALIN n solution of formaldehyde in water

FORMALLY ▸ **formal**

FORMALS ▸ **formal**

FORMANT, -S n any of several frequency ranges

FORMAT, -ED, -S n size and shape of a publication ▷ vb arrange in a format

FORMATE, -S n type of salt or ester of formic acid ▷ vb fly aircraft in formation

FORMATED ▸ **format**

FORMATES ▸ **formate**

FORMATS ▸ **format**

FORME, -S n type matter assembled and ready for printing

FORMED ▸ **form**

FORMEE, -S n type of heraldic cross

FORMER, -S adj of an earlier time, previous ▷ n person or thing that forms or shapes

FORMERLY adv in the past

FORMERS ▸ **former**

FORMES ▸ **forme**

FORMFUL adj imaginative

FORMIATE variant of ▸ **formate**

FORMIC adj of, relating to, or derived from ants

FORMICA, -S n tradename for any of various laminated plastic sheets

FORMING, -S ▸ **form**

FORMLESS adj without a definite shape or form

FORMOL, -S same as ▸ **formalin**

FORMS ▸ **form**

FORMULA, -E, -S n written form of a scientific or mathematical rule

FORMULAR adj of or relating to formulas ▷ n model or set form

FORMULAS ▸ **formula**

FORMWORK n arrangement of wooden boards to shape concrete

FORMYL, -S n the monovalent group CHO-

FORNENST prep situated against or facing towards

FORNENT variant of ▸ **fornenst**

FORNICAL ▸ **fornix**

FORNIX, FORNICES n any archlike structure

FORPET, -S n quarter of a peck (measure)

FORPINE, -D, -S vb waste away

FORPIT, -S variant of ▸ **forpet**

FORRAD, -ER, -S adv forward ▷ n forward

FORRAY, -ED, -S archaic variant of ▸ **foray**

FORREN adj foreign

FORRIT adv forward(s)

FORSAID variant of ▸ **forsay**

FORSAKE, -S vb withdraw support or friendship from

FORSAKEN adj completely deserted or helpless

FORSAKER ▸ **forsake**

FORSAKES ▸ **forsake**

FORSAY, FORSAID, -S vb renounce

FORSLACK vb be neglectful

FORSLOE, -D, -S variant of ▸ **forslow**

FORSLOW, -S vb hinder

FORSOOK past tense of ▸ **forsake**

FORSOOTH adv indeed

FORSPEAK, FORSPOKE vb bewitch

FORSPEND, FORSPENT vb exhaust

FORSPOKE ▸ **forspeak**

FORSWATT adj sweat-covered

FORSWEAR, FORSWORE vb renounce or reject

FORSWINK vb exhaust through toil

FORSWORE ▸ **forswear**

FORSWORN past participle of ▸ **forswear**

FORSWUNK adj overworked

FORT, -ING, -S n fortified building or place ▷ vb fortify

FORTE n thing at which a person excels ▷ adv loudly

F

FORTED ► fort
FORTES ► fortis
FORTH adv forwards, out, or away ▷ prep out of
FORTHINK vb regret
FORTHY adv therefore
FORTIES ► forty
FORTIETH adj being the number of forty in order ▷ n one of 40 equal parts
FORTIFY vb make (a place) defensible, as by building walls
FORTING ► fort
FORTIS, FORTES adj (of a consonant) articulated with considerable muscular tension ▷ n type of consonantal pronunciation
FORTLET, -S ► fort
FORTRESS n large fort or fortified town ▷ vb protect with or as if with a fortress
FORTS ► fort
FORTUITY n chance or accidental occurrence
FORTUNE, -D, -S n luck, esp when favourable ▷ vb befall
FORTY, FORTIES n four times ten ▷ adj amounting to forty ▷ determiner amounting to forty
FORTYISH
FORUM, FORA, -S n meeting or medium for open discussion or debate
FORWARD same as ► forwards
FORWARDS adv towards or at a place further ahead in space or time
FORWARN, -S archaic word for ► forbid
FORWASTE vb lay waste
FORWEARY vb exhaust
FORWENT past tense of ► forgo
FORWHY adv for what reason
FORWORN adj weary
FORZA, FORZE n force
FORZANDO, FORZANDI another word for > sforzando
FORZATO, FORZATI, -S variant of ► forzando
FORZE ► forza
FOSS same as ► fosse
FOSSA, -E, -S n anatomical depression, trench, or hollow area
FOSSATE adj having cavities or depressions
FOSSE, -S n ditch or moat, esp one dug as a fortification
FOSSED adj having a ditch or moat
FOSSES ► fosse

FOSSETTE n small depression or fossa, as in a bone
FOSSICK, -S n search, esp for gold or precious stones
FOSSIL, -S n hardened remains of an animal or plant preserved in rock ▷ adj of, like, or being a fossil
FOSSOR, -S n grave digger
FOSSULA, -E n small fossa
FOSTER, -ED, -S vb promote the growth or development of ▷ adj of or involved in fostering a child
FOSTERER
FOSTRESS n female fosterer
FOTHER, -ED, -S vb stop a leak in a ship's hull
FOU, -ER, -EST, -S adj full ▷ n bushel
FOUAT, -S n succulent pink-flowered plant
FOUD, -S n sheriff in Orkney and Shetland
FOUDRIE, -S n foud's district or office
FOUDS ► foud
FOUER ► fou
FOUEST ► fou
FOUET, -S n archaic word for a whip
FOUETTE, -S n step in ballet
FOUGADE, -S n booby-trapped pit or type of mine
FOUGASSE n type of bread made with olive oil
FOUGHT ► fight
FOUGHTEN ► fight
FOUGHTY adj musty
FOUL, -ED, -ER, -EST, -S adj loathsome or offensive ▷ n violation of the rules ▷ vb make dirty or polluted
FOULARD, -S n soft light fabric
FOULDER, -S vb flash like lightning
FOULE, -S n type of woollen cloth
FOULED ► foul
FOULER ► foul
FOULES ► foule
FOULEST ► foul
FOULIE, -S n bad mood
FOULING, -S ► foul
FOULLY ► foul
FOULMART n polecat
FOULNESS n state or quality of being foul
FOULS ► foul
FOUMART, -S former name for the ► polecat
FOUND, -ED, -ING, -S vb set up or establish (an institution, etc)

FOUNDER, -S vb break down or fail ▷ n person who establishes an institution, etc
FOUNDING ► found
FOUNDRY n place where metal is melted and cast
FOUNDS ► found
FOUNT, -S same as ► font
FOUNTAIN n jet of water
FOUNTFUL adj full of springs
FOUNTS ► fount
FOUR, -S n one more than three ▷ adj amounting to four ▷ determiner amounting to four
FOURBALL n type of golf match for two pairs
FOURCHEE n type of heraldic cross
FOUREYED adj wearing spectacles
FOURFOLD adj having four times as many or as much ▷ adv by four times as many or as much
FOURGON, -S n long covered wagon
FOURPLAY n supply of television, internet, landline and mobile phone services by one provider
FOURPLEX n building that contains four separate dwellings
FOURS ► four
FOURSES n snack eaten at four o'clock
FOURSOME n group of four people
FOURTEEN n four and ten ▷ adj amounting to fourteen ▷ determiner amounting to fourteen
FOURTH, -S n (of) number four in a series ▷ adj of or being number four in a series ▷ adv after the third person, position, event, etc
FOURTHLY
FOUS ► fou
FOUSSA, -S n Madagascan civet-like animal
FOUSTY, FOUSTIER archaic variant of ► fusty
FOUTER, -ED, -S same as ► footer
FOUTH, -S n abundance
FOUTRA, -S n fig; expression of contempt
FOUTRE, -D, -S, FOUTRING vb footer
FOVEA, -E, -S n any small pit in the surface of a bodily organ or part
FOVEAL
FOVEATE
FOVEATED

FOVEOLA, -E, -S n small fovea

FOVEOLAR

FOVEOLE, -S same as
► foveola

FOVEOLET same as
► foveola

FOWL, -ED, -S n domestic
cock or hen ▷ vb hunt or
snare wild birds

FOWLER, -S ► fowling

FOWLING, -S n shooting or
trapping of birds for sport or
as a livelihood

FOWLPOX n viral infection of
poultry and other birds

FOWLS ► fowl

FOWTH, -S variant of ► fouth

FOX, -ED, -ES n reddish-brown
bushy-tailed animal of the
dog family ▷ vb perplex or
deceive

FOXBERRY n lingonberry

FOXED ► fox

FOXES ► fox

FOXFIRE, -S n glow emitted
by certain fungi

FOXFISH n type of shark

FOXGLOVE n tall plant with
purple or white flowers

FOXHOLE, -S n small pit dug
for protection

FOXHOUND n dog bred for
hunting foxes

FOXHUNT, -S n hunting of
foxes with hounds ▷ vb hunt
foxes with hounds

FOXIE, -S n fox terrier

FOXIER ► foxy

FOXIES ► foxie

FOXIEST ► foxy

FOXILY ► foxy

FOXINESS ► foxy

FOXING, -S n piece of leather
used on part of the upper of
a shoe

FOXLIKE ► fox

FOXSHARK n thresher shark

FOXSHIP, -S n cunning

FOXSKIN, -S adj made from
the skin of a fox ▷ n skin
of a fox

FOXTAIL, -S n type of grass

FOXTROT, -S n ballroom
dance with slow and quick
steps ▷ vb perform this
dance

FOXY, FOXIER, FOXIEST
adj of or like a fox, esp in
craftiness

FOY, -S n loyalty

This unusual word for
loyalty can be a good scorer.

FOYBOAT, -S n small rowing
boat

FOYER, -S n entrance hall in a
theatre, cinema, or hotel

FOYLE, -D, -S, FOYLING
variant of ► foil

FOYNE, -D, -S, FOYNING
variant of ► foin

FOYS ► foy

FOZIER ► fozy

FOZIEST ► fozy

FOZINESS ► fozy

FOZY, FOZIER, FOZIEST adj
spongy

FRA, -S n brother: a title
given to an Italian monk
or friar

FRAB, -BED, -BING, -S vb nag

FRABBIT adj peevish

FRABJOUS adj splendid

FRABS ► frab

FRACAS, -ES n noisy quarrel

FRACK, -ED, -S adj bold ▷ vb
release oil or gas from rock by
fracking

FRACKER, -S n individual or
company which engages in
fracking

FRACKING n method of
releasing oil or gas from
rock

FRACKS ► frack

FRACT, -ED, -ING, -S vb break

FRACTAL, -S n
mathematically repeating
structure ▷ adj of, relating
to, or involving such a
process

FRACTED ► fract

FRACTI ► fractus

FRACTING ► fract

FRACTION n numerical
quantity that is not a whole
number ▷ vb divide

FRACTS ► fract

FRACTUR, -S variant of
► fraktur

FRACTURE n breaking, esp of
a bone ▷ vb break

FRACTURS ► fractur

FRACTUS, FRACTI n ragged-
shaped cloud formation

FRAE Scot word for ► from

FRAENUM, FRAENA, -S n fold
of membrane or skin that
supports an organ

FRAG, -GED, -S vb kill or
wound (a fellow soldier or
superior officer) deliberately

FRAGGING

FRAGILE, -R adj easily broken
or damaged

FRAGMENT n piece broken off
▷ vb break into pieces

FRAGOR, -S n sudden sound

FRAGRANT adj sweet-
smelling

FRAGS ► frag

FRAIL, -ER, -EST, -S adj
physically weak ▷ n rush

basket for figs or raisins

FRAILISH

FRAILLY

FRAILTEE variant of ► frailty

FRAILTY n physical or moral
weakness

FRAIM, -S n stranger

FRAISE, -D, -S, FRAISING n
neck ruff worn during the
16th century ▷ vb provide a
rampart with a palisade

FRAKTUR, -S n style of
typeface

FRAMABLE ► frame

FRAME, -D, -S n structure
giving shape or support ▷ vb
put together, construct

FRAMER, -S

FRAMING, -S n frame,
framework, or system of
frames

FRAMPAL same as
► frampold

FRAMPLER n quarrelsome
person

FRAMPOLD adj peevish

FRANC, -S n monetary unit

FRANCISE same as
► francize

FRANCIUM n radioactive
metallic element

FRANCIZE vb make French

FRANCO adj post-free

FRANCS ► franc

FRANION, -S n lover,
paramour

FRANK, -ED, -EST, -ING, -S adj
honest and straightforward
in speech or attitude ▷ n
official mark on a letter
permitting delivery ▷ vb put
such a mark on (a letter)

FRANKER, -S

FRANKLIN n (in 14th- and
15th-century England) a
landholder of free but not
noble birth

FRANKLY adv in truth

FRANKS ► frank

FRANKUM, -S n spruce resin

FRANTIC adj distracted with
rage, grief, joy, etc

FRANZY, FRANZIER adj
irritable

FRAP, -PED, -PING, -S vb lash
down or together

FRAPE, -D, -S, FRAPING adj
tightly bound ▷ vb alter
information on a person's
social networking profile

FRAPEAGE n act of altering
information on a person's
social networking profile

FRAPED ► frape

FRAPES ► frape

FRAPING ► frape

FRAPPANT adj striking, vivid

FRAPPE, -E, -S adj (of drinks) chilled ▷ n type of drink

FRAPPED ▶ frap

FRAPPEE ▶ frappe

FRAPPES ▶ frappe

FRAPPING ▶ frap

FRAPS ▶ frap

FRAS ▶ fra

FRASCATI n dry or semisweet white wine from the Lazio region of Italy

FRASS, -ES n refuse left by insects and insect larvae

FRAT, -S n member of a fraternity

FRATCH, -ES n quarrel

FRATCHY adj quarrelsome

FRATE, FRATI n friar

FRATER, -S n mendicant friar or a lay brother in a monastery or priory

FRATERY

FRATI ▶ frate

FRATRY, FRATRIES ▶ frater

FRATS ▶ frat

FRAU, -S n married German woman

FRAUD, -S n (criminal) deception, swindle

FRAUDFUL

FRAUGHAN n small shrub

FRAUGHT, -S adj tense or anxious ▷ vb archaic word for load ▷ n archaic word for freight

FRAULEIN n unmarried German woman

FRAUS ▶ frau

FRAUTAGE n cargo

FRAWZEY, -S n celebration

FRAY, -ED, -S n noisy quarrel or conflict ▷ vb make or become ragged at the edge

FRAYING -S

FRAZIL, -S n small pieces of ice that form in turbulently moving water

FRAZZLE, -D, -S n exhausted state ▷ vb tire out

FREAK, -ED, -ING, -S n abnormal person or thing ▷ adj abnormal ▷ vb streak with colour

FREAKERY n as in **control freakery** obsessive need to be in control of events

FREAKFUL variant of ▶ freakish

FREAKIER ▶ freaky

FREAKILY ▶ freaky

FREAKING ▶ freak

FREAKISH adj of, related to, or characteristic of a freak

FREAKOUT n heightened emotional state

FREAKS ▶ freak

FREAKY, FREAKIER adj weird, peculiar

FRECKLE, -S n small brown spot on the skin ▷ vb mark or become marked with freckles

FRECKLED

FRECKLY

FREDAINE n escapade

FREE, -D, -ING, -S, -ST adj able to act at will, not compelled or restrained ▷ vb release, liberate

FREEBEE, -S variant of ▶ freebie

FREEBIE, -S n something provided without charge ▷ adj without charge

FREEBOOT vb act as a freebooter

FREEBORN adj not born in slavery

FREED ▶ free

FREEDMAN, FREEDMEN n man freed from slavery

FREEDOM, -S n being free

FREEFALL adj as in **freefall parachuting** parachuting in which the jumper manoeuvres in free fall before opening the parachute

FREEFORM n irregular flowing shape, often used in industrial or fabric design ▷ adj freely flowing, spontaneous

FREEGAN, -S n person who avoids buying consumer goods

FREEHAND adj drawn without guiding instruments

FREEHOLD n tenure of land for life without restrictions ▷ adj of or held by freehold

FREEING ▶ free

FREELOAD vb act as a freeloader

FREELY ▶ free

FREEMAN, FREEMEN n person who has been given the freedom of a city

FREENESS ▶ free

FREER, -S n liberator

FREERIDE n extreme form of skiing, snowboarding, or mountain biking

FREERS ▶ freer

FREES ▶ free

FREESIA, -S n plant with fragrant tubular flowers

FREEST ▶ free

FREET, -S n omen or superstition

FREETIER ▶ freety

FREETS ▶ freet

FREETY, FREETIER adj superstitious

FREEWARE n computer software that may be distributed and used without payment

FREEWAY, -S n motorway

FREEWILL n apparent human ability to make choices that are not externally determined

FREEZE, -S, FREEZING, FROZE, FROZEN vb turn from liquid to solid by the reduction of temperature ▷ n period of very cold weather

FREEZER, -S n insulated cabinet for cold-storage of perishable foods

FREEZES ▶ freeze

FREEZING ▶ freeze

FREIGHT, -S n commercial transport of goods ▷ vb send by freight

FREIT, -S variant of ▶ freet

FREITIER ▶ freity

FREITS ▶ freit

FREITY, FREITIER adj superstitious

FREMD, -S adj, n alien or strange (person or thing)

FREMIT, -S same as ▶ fremd

FREMITUS n vibration felt by a hand placed on the body

FRENA ▶ frenum

FRENCH, -ED, -ES vb cut (food) into thin strips

FRENEMY n supposed friend who behaves in a treacherous manner

FRENETIC adj uncontrolled, excited ▷ n madman

FRENNE, -S variant of ▶ fremd

FRENULA ▶ frenulum

FRENULAR ▶ frenulum

FRENULUM, FRENULA n group of bristles on the hind wing of some moths

FRENUM, FRENA, -S same as ▶ fraenum

FRENZIED adj filled with or as if with frenzy

FRENZIES ▶ frenzy

FRENZILY ▶ frenzy

FRENZY, FRENZIES n wild excitement or agitation ▷ vb make frantic

FREON, -S n tradename for an aerosol refrigerant

FREQUENT adj happening often ▷ vb visit habitually

FRERE, -S n friar

FRESCADE n shady place or cool walk

FRESCO, -ED, -ES, -S n watercolour painting done on wet plaster ▷ vb paint a fresco

FRESCOER

FRESH, -ED, -ES, -EST, -ING adj newly made, acquired, etc ▷ adv recently ▷ vb freshen

FRESHEN, -S vb make or become fresh or fresher

FRESHER, -S n first-year student

FRESHES ► fresh

FRESHEST ► fresh

FRESHET, -S n sudden overflowing of a river

FRESHIE, -S n new Indian immigrant to the UK

FRESHING ► fresh

FRESHISH ► fresh

FRESHLY ► fresh

FRESHMAN, FRESHMEN same as ► fresh

FRESNEL, -S n unit of frequency equivalent to 1012 hertz

FRET, -S, -TED, -TING vb be worried ▷ n worried state

FRETFUL adj irritable

FRETLESS ► fret

FRETS ► fret

FRETSAW, -S n fine saw with a narrow blade, used for fretwork

FRETSOME adj vexing

FRETTED ► fret

FRETTER, -S ► fret

FRETTIER ► fretty

FRETTING ► fret

FRETTY, FRETTIER adj decorated with frets

FRETWORK n decorative carving in wood

FRIABLE adj easily crumbled

FRIAND, -S n small almond cake

FRIANDE, -S variant of ► friand

FRIANDS ► friand

FRIAR, -S n member of a male Roman Catholic religious order

FRIARIES ► friary

FRIARLY ► friar

FRIARS ► friar

FRIARY, FRIARIES n house of friars

FRIB, -S n piece of wool removed from a fleece during classing

FRIBBLE, -D, -S vb fritter away ▷ n wasteful or frivolous person or action ▷ adj frivolous

FRIBBLER

FRIBS ► frib

FRICADEL variant of > **frikkadel**

FRICANDO n larded and braised veal fillet

FRICHT, -ED, -S vb frighten

FRICOT, -S n Acadian stew of potatoes, meat or fish

FRICTION n resistance met with by a body moving over another

FRIDGE, -D, -S, FRIDGING n apparatus in which food and drinks are kept cool ▷ vb archaic word for chafe

FRIED ► fry

FRIEND, -ED, -S n person whom one knows well and likes ▷ vb befriend

FRIENDLY adj showing or expressing liking ▷ n match played for its own sake and not as part of a competition

FRIENDS ► friend

FRIER, -S same as ► fryer

FRIES ► fry

FRIEZE, -D, -S, FRIEZING n ornamental band on a wall ▷ vb give a nap to (cloth)

FRIG, -ES, -GED, -GING, -S vb behave foolishly or aimlessly ▷ n fridge

FRIGATE, -S n medium-sized fast warship

FRIGES ► frig

FRIGGED ► frig

FRIGGER, -S ► frig

FRIGGING ► frig

FRIGHT, -ED, -S n sudden fear or alarm

FRIGHTEN vb scare or terrify

FRIGHTS ► fright

FRIGID, -ER adj formal or stiff in temperament

FRIGIDLY

FRIGOT, -S variant of ► **frigate**

FRIGS ► frig

FRIJOL, -ES n variety of bean

FRIJOLE variant of ► **frijol**

FRIJOLES ► frijol

FRILL, -ED, -ING, -S n gathered strip of fabric attached at one edge ▷ vb adorn or fit with a frill or frills

FRILLER -S

FRILLERY n fabric or clothing arranged in frills

FRILLIER ► frilly

FRILLIES pl n flimsy women's underwear

FRILLING ► frill

FRILLS ► frill

FRILLY, FRILLIER adj with a frill or frills

FRINGE, -D, -S n hair cut short and hanging over the forehead ▷ vb decorate with a fringe ▷ adj (of theatre) unofficial or unconventional

FRINGIER ► fringy

FRINGING n act of fringing

FRINGY, FRINGIER adj having a fringe

FRIPON, -S n rogue

FRIPPER, -S n dealer in old clothes

FRIPPERY n useless ornamentation

FRIPPET, -S n frivolous or flamboyant young woman

FRIS, -ES same as ► **friska**

FRISBEE, -S n tradename of a light plastic disc for throwing in a game

FRISE n fabric with a long normally uncut nap used for upholstery and rugs

FRISEE, -S n endive

FRISES ► fris

FRISETTE n curly or frizzed fringe, often an artificial hairpiece, worn by women on the forehead

FRISEUR, -S n hairdresser

FRISK, -ED, -ING, -S vb move or leap playfully ▷ n playful movement

FRISKA, -S n (in Hungarian music) the fast movement of a piece

FRISKED ► frisk

FRISKER, -S ► frisk

FRISKET, -S n part of a hand printing press

FRISKFUL ► frisk

FRISKIER ► frisky

FRISKILY ► frisky

FRISKING ► frisk

FRISKS ► frisk

FRISKY, FRISKIER adj lively or high-spirited

FRISSON, -S n shiver of fear or excitement

FRIST, -ED, -ING, -S archaic word for ► **postpone**

FRISURE, -S n styling the hair into curls

FRIT, -S, -TED, -TING n basic materials for making glass, glazes for pottery, etc ▷ vb fuse (materials) in making frit

FRITES pl n chipped potatoes

FRITFLY n type of small black fly

FRITH, -S same as ► **firth**

FRITS ► frit

FRITT, -S same as ► **frit**

FRITTATA n flat thick Italian omelette

FRITTED ► frit

FRITTER, -S n piece of food fried in batter ▷ vb waste or squander

FRITTING ▶ frit

FRITTS ▶ fritt

FRITURE n archaic word for ▶ fritter

FRITZ, -ED, -ING n as in **on the fritz** in a state of disrepair ▷ vb (of an appliance, etc) become broken or start malfunctioning

FRIULANO n type of Italian cheese

FRIVOL, -ED, -S vb behave frivolously

FRIVOLER

FRIZ variant of ▶ frizz

FRIZADO, -S n fine frieze-like fabric

FRIZE, -D, -S, FRIZING n coarse woollen fabric ▷ vb freeze

FRIZER, -S n person who gives nap to cloth

FRIZES ▶ frize

FRIZETTE same as ▶ frisette

FRIZING ▶ frize

FRIZZ, -ED, -ES, -ING vb form (hair) into stiff wiry curls ▷ n hair that has been frizzed

FRIZZER -S

FRIZZIER ▶ frizzy

FRIZZIES n condition of having frizzy hair

FRIZZILY ▶ frizzy

FRIZZING ▶ frizz

FRIZZLE, -D, -S vb cook or heat until crisp and shrivelled ▷ n tight curl

FRIZZLER

FRIZZLY

FRIZZY, FRIZZIER adj (of the hair) in tight crisp wiry curls

FRO, -S adv away ▷ n afro

FROCK, -ED, -S n dress ▷ vb invest (a person) with the office or status of a cleric

FROCKING n coarse material suitable for making frocks or work clothes

FROCKS ▶ frock

FROE, -S n cutting tool

FROG, -S n type of amphibian

FROGBIT, -S n floating aquatic Eurasian plant

FROGEYE, -S n plant disease

FROGEYED adj affected by frogeye

FROGEYES ▶ frogeye

FROGFISH n type of angler fish

FROGGED adj decorated with frogging

FROGGERY n place where frogs are kept

FROGGIER ▶ froggy

FROGGING n decorative fastening of looped braid on a coat

FROGGY, FROGGIER adj like a frog

FROGLET, -S n young frog

FROGLIKE ▶ frog

FROGLING n young frog

FROGMAN, FROGMEN n swimmer with equipment for working under water

FROGS ▶ frog

FROIDEUR n coldness

FROING, -S n as in **toing and froing** going back and forth

FROISE, -S n kind of pancake

FROLIC, -S vb run and play in a lively way ▷ n lively and merry behaviour ▷ adj full of merriment or fun

FROLICKY adj frolicsome

FROLICS ▶ frolic

FROM prep indicating the point of departure, source, etc

FROMAGE, -S n as in **fromage frais** low-fat soft cheese

FROMENTY same as ▶ frumenty

FROND, -S n long leaf or leaflike part of a fern, palm, or seaweed

FRONDAGE n fronds collectively

FRONDED adj having fronds

FRONDENT adj leafy

FRONDEUR n 17th-century French rebel

FRONDOSE adj leafy or like a leaf

FRONDOUS adj leafy or like a leaf

FRONDS ▶ frond

FRONS, FRONTES n plate on the head of some insects

FRONT, -ED, -EST, -ING, -S n fore part ▷ adj of or at the front ▷ vb face (onto)

FRONTAGE n facade of a building

FRONTAL, -S adj of, at, or in the front ▷ n decorative hanging for the front of an altar

FRONTED ▶ front

FRONTER, -S n front side

FRONTES ▶ frons

FRONTEST ▶ front

FRONTIER n area of a country bordering on another

FRONTING ▶ front

FRONTLET n small decorative loop worn on a woman's forehead

FRONTMAN, FRONTMEN n nominal leader who lacks real power or authority

FRONTON, -S n wall against which pelota or jai alai is played

FRONTOON variant of ▶ fronton

FRONTS ▶ front

FRORE adj very cold or frosty

FROREN variant of ▶ frore

FRORN variant of ▶ frore

FRORNE variant of ▶ frore

FRORY adj frozen

FROS ▶ fro

FROSH, -ES n freshman

FROST, -S n white frozen dew or mist ▷ vb become covered with frost

FROSTBIT > frostbite

FROSTED, -S adj (of glass) having a rough surface to make it opaque ▷ n type of ice cream dish

FROSTIER ▶ frosty

FROSTILY ▶ frosty

FROSTING n sugar icing

FROSTNIP n milder form of frostbite

FROSTS ▶ frost

FROSTY, FROSTIER adj characterized or covered by frost

FROTH, -ED, -S n mass of small bubbles ▷ vb foam

FROTHER -S

FROTHERY n anything insubstantial, like froth

FROTHIER ▶ frothy

FROTHILY ▶ froth

FROTHING n act of frothing

FROTHS ▶ froth

FROTHY, FROTHIER ▶ froth

FROTTAGE n act or process of taking a rubbing from a rough surface for a work of art

FROUFROU n swishing sound, as made by a long silk dress

FROUGHY adj rancid

FROUNCE, -D, -S vb wrinkle

FROUZY, FROUZIER same as ▶ frowzy

FROW, -S same as ▶ froe

FROWARD adj obstinate

FROWARDS same as ▶ froward

FROWIE, -R, -ST variant of ▶ froughy

FROWN, -ED, -ING, -S vb wrinkle one's brows in worry, anger, or thought ▷ n frowning expression

FROWNER -S

FROWS ▶ frow

FROWSIER ► frowsy

FROWST, -ED, -S n hot and stale atmosphere ▷ vb abandon oneself to such an atmosphere

FROWSTER

FROWSTY adj stale or musty

FROWSY, FROWSIER same as ► **frowzy**

FROWY variant of ► **froughy**

FROWZIER ► frowzy

FROWZILY ► frowzy

FROWZY, FROWZIER adj dirty or unkempt

FROZE ► freeze

FROZEN ► freeze

FROZENLY ► freeze

FRUCTAN, -S n type of polymer of fructose

FRUCTED adj fruit-bearing

FRUCTIFY vb (cause to) bear fruit

FRUCTIVE adj fruitful

FRUCTOSE n crystalline sugar occurring in many fruits

FRUG, -GED, -GING, -S vb perform the frug, a 1960s dance

FRUGAL adj thrifty, sparing

FRUGALLY

FRUGGED ► frug

FRUGGING ► frug

FRUGS ► frug

FRUICT, -S obsolete variant of ► **fruit**

FRUIT, -ED, -ING, -S n part of a plant containing seeds ▷ vb bear fruit

FRUITAGE n process, state, or season of producing fruit

FRUITED ► fruit

FRUITER, -S n fruit grower

FRUITERY n fruitage

FRUITFUL adj useful or productive

FRUITIER ► fruity

FRUITILY ► fruity

FRUITING ► fruit

FRUITION n fulfilment of something worked for or desired

FRUITIVE adj enjoying

FRUITLET n small fruit

FRUITS ► fruit

FRUITY, FRUITIER adj of or like fruit

FRUMENTY n kind of porridge made from hulled wheat boiled with milk, sweetened, and spiced

FRUMP, -ED, -ING, -S n dowdy woman ▷ vb mock or taunt

FRUMPIER ► frumpy

FRUMPILY ► frumpy

FRUMPING ► frump

FRUMPISH same as ► **frumpy**

FRUMPLE, -D, -S vb wrinkle or crumple

FRUMPS ► frump

FRUMPY, FRUMPIER adj (of a woman, clothes, etc) dowdy or unattractive

FRUSH, -ED, -ES, -ING vb break into pieces

FRUST, -S n fragment

FRUSTA ► frustum

FRUSTS ► frust

FRUSTULE n hard siliceous cell wall of a diatom

FRUSTUM, FRUSTA, -S n part of a solid

FRUTEX, FRUTICES n shrub

FRUTIFY vb malapropism for notify

FRY, FRIED, FRIES vb cook or be cooked in fat or oil ▷ n dish of fried food

FRYABLE

FRYBREAD n Native American fried bread

FRYER, -S n person or thing that fries

FRYING, -S ► fry

FRYPAN, -S n long-handled shallow pan used for frying

FUB, -BED, -BING, -S vb cheat

FUBAR adj irreparably damaged or bungled

FUBBED ► fub

FUBBERY n cheating

FUBBIER ► fubby

FUBBIEST ► fubby

FUBBING ► fub

FUBBY, FUBBIER, FUBBIEST adj chubby

FUBS ► fub

FUBSY, FUBSIER, FUBSIEST adj short and stout

FUCHSIA, -S n ornamental shrub

FUCHSIN, -S n greenish crystalline substance

FUCHSINE same as ► **fuchsin**

FUCHSINS ► fuchsin

FUCHSITE n form of mica

FUCI ► fucus

FUCOID, -S n type of seaweed

FUCOIDAL n type of seaweed

FUCOIDS ► fucoid

FUCOSE, -S n aldose

FUCOUS same as ► **fucoidal**

FUCUS, FUCI, -ES n type of seaweed

FUCUSED adj archaic word meaning made up with cosmetics

FUCUSES ► fucus

FUD, -S n rabbit's tail

FUDDIER ► fuddy

FUDDIES ► fuddy

FUDDIEST ► fuddy

FUDDLE, -D, -S, FUDDLING vb cause to be intoxicated or confused ▷ n confused state

FUDDLER -S

FUDDY, FUDDIER, FUDDIES, FUDDIEST n old-fashioned person ▷ adj old-fashioned

FUDGE, -D, -S, FUDGING n soft caramel-like sweet ▷ vb make (an issue) less clear deliberately ▷ interj mild exclamation of annoyance

FUDGIER ► fudgy

FUDGIEST ► fudgy

FUDGING ► fudge

FUDGY, FUDGIER, FUDGIEST adj resembling or containing fudge

FUDS ► fud

FUEHRER, -S n leader: applied esp to Adolf Hitler

FUEL, -ED, -ING, -LED, -LING, -S n substance burned or treated to produce heat or power ▷ vb provide with fuel

FUELER -S

FUELLER, -S ► fuel

FUELLING ► fuel

FUELS ► fuel

FUELWOOD n any wood used as a fuel

FUERO, -S n Spanish code of laws

FUFF, -ED, -ING, -S vb puff

FUFFIER ► fuffy

FUFFIEST ► fuffy

FUFFING ► fuff

FUFFS ► fuff

FUFFY, FUFFIER, FUFFIEST adj puffy

FUG, -GED, -GING, -S n hot stale atmosphere ▷ vb sit in a fug

FUGACITY n property of a gas that expresses its tendency to escape or expand

FUGAL adj of, relating to, or in the style of a fugue

FUGALLY

FUGATO, -S adj in the manner or style of a fugue ▷ n movement, section, or piece in this style

FUGGED ► fug

FUGGIER ► fuggy

FUGGIEST ► fuggy

FUGGILY ► fug

FUGGING ► fug

FUGGY, FUGGIER, FUGGIEST ► **fug**

FUGHETTA n short fugue

FUGIE, -S n runaway

FUGIO, -S n former US copper coin

FUGITIVE n person who flees, esp from arrest or pursuit ▷ adj fleeing

FUGLE, -D, -S, FUGLING vb act as a fugleman

FUGLEMAN, FUGLEMEN n (formerly) a soldier used as an example for those learning drill

FUGLES ▶ fugle

FUGLING ▶ fugle

FUGS ▶ fug

FUGU, -S n puffer fish

U is not normally a desirable letter to have on your rack unless you happen to have the Q, and two Us can be trouble. This Japanese fish can help you out.

FUGUE, -D, -S, FUGUING n type of musical composition ▷ vb be in a dreamlike, altered state of consciousness

FUGUIST, -S n composer of fugues

FUGUS ▶ fugu

FUHRER, -S same as ▶ fuehrer

FUJI, -S n type of African music

FULCRA ▶ fulcrum

FULCRATE ▶ fulcrum

FULCRUM, FULCRA, -S n pivot about which a lever turns

FULFIL, -S vb achieve (a desire or promise)

FULFILL, -S same as ▶ fulfil

FULFILS ▶ fulfil

FULGENCY ▶ fulgent

FULGENT adj shining brilliantly

FULGID same as ▶ fulgent

FULGOR, -S n brilliance

FULGOUR, -S variant of ▶ fulgor

FULGURAL > fulgurate

FULHAM, -S n loaded die

FULL, -ED, -EST, -ING, -S adj containing as much or as many as possible ▷ adv completely ▷ vb clean, shrink, and press cloth

FULLAGE, -S n price charged for fulling cloth

FULLAM, -S variant of ▶ fulham

FULLAN, -S variant of ▶ fulham

FULLBACK n defensive player

FULLED ▶ full

FULLER, -ED, -S n person who fulls cloth for a living ▷ vb forge (a groove) or caulk (a riveted joint) with a fuller

FULLERY n place where fulling is carried out

FULLEST ▶ full

FULLFACE n in printing, a letter that takes up full body size

FULLING ▶ full

FULLISH ▶ full

FULLNESS ▶ full

FULLS ▶ full

FULLY adv greatest degree or extent

FULMAR, -S n Arctic sea bird

FULMINE, -D, -S vb fulminate

FULMINIC adj as in **fulminic acid**, unstable volatile acid

FULNESS ▶ full

FULSOME, -R adj distastefully excessive or insincere

FULVID variant of ▶ fulvous

FULVOUS adj of a dull brownish-yellow colour

FUM, -S n phoenix, in Chinese mythology

FUMADO, -ES, -S n salted, smoked fish

FUMAGE, -S n hearth money

FUMARASE n enzyme

FUMARATE n salt of fumaric acid

FUMARIC adj as in **fumaric acid** colourless crystalline acid

FUMAROLE n vent in or near a volcano from which hot gases, esp steam, are emitted

FUMATORY n chamber where insects and fungi are destroyed by fumigation

FUMBLE, -D, -S, FUMBLING vb handle awkwardly ▷ n act of fumbling

FUMBLER -S

FUME, -S, FUMING vb be very angry

FUMED adj (of wood) having been exposed to ammonia fumes

FUMELESS ▶ fume

FUMELIKE ▶ fume

FUMER, -S ▶ fume

FUMEROLE variant of ▶ fumarole

FUMERS ▶ fumer

FUMES ▶ fume

FUMET, -S n liquor from cooking fish, meat, or game

FUMETTE, -S variant of ▶ fumet

FUMETTO, FUMETTI, -S n speech balloon in a comic or cartoon

FUMIER ▶ fumy

FUMIEST ▶ fumy

FUMIGANT n substance used for fumigating

FUMIGATE vb disinfect with fumes

FUMING ▶ fume

FUMINGLY ▶ fume

FUMITORY n chiefly European plant with spurred flowers, formerly used medicinally

FUMOSITY ▶ fume

FUMOUS ▶ fume

FUMS ▶ fum

FUMULUS, FUMULI n smokelike cloud

FUMY, FUMIER, FUMIEST ▶ fume

FUN, -NED, -NER, -NEST, -NING, -S n enjoyment or amusement ▷ vb trick ▷ adj providing amusement or entertainment

FUNBOARD n type of surfboard

FUNCKIA, -S n type of plant resembling the lily

FUNCTION n purpose something exists for ▷ vb operate or work

FUNCTOR, -S n performer of a function

FUND, -ED n stock of money for a special purpose ▷ vb provide money to

FUNDABLE

FUNDER -S

FUNDI, -S n expert or boffin

FUNDIC ▶ fundus

FUNDIE, -S n fundamentalist Christian

FUNDING, -S ▶ fund

FUNDIS ▶ fundi

FUNDLESS ▶ fund

FUNDS pl n money that is readily available

FUNDUS n base of an organ

FUNDY n fundamentalist

FUNEBRAL variant of > funebrial

FUNEBRE adj funereal or mournful

FUNERAL, -S n ceremony of burying or cremating a dead person

FUNERARY adj of or for a funeral

FUNEREAL adj gloomy or sombre

FUNEST adj lamentable

FUNFAIR, -S n entertainment with machines to ride on and stalls

FUNFEST, -S n enjoyable time

FUNG, -S same as ▶ funk

FUNGAL, -S adj of, derived from, or caused by a fungus

or fungi ▷ *n* fungus or fungal infection

FUNGI ▶ fungus

FUNGIBLE *n* goods replaceable by similar goods of equal quantity or weight ▷ *adj* having the quality of fungibles

FUNGIC ▶ fungus

FUNGO, -ED, -ES, -ING, -S *n* in baseball, act of tossing and hitting the ball ▷ *vb* toss and hit a ball

FUNGOID, -S *adj* resembling a fungus

FUNGOING ▶ fungo

FUNGOS ▶ fungo

FUNGOUS *adj* appearing and spreading quickly like a fungus

FUNGS ▶ fung

FUNGUS, FUNGI, -ES *n* plant such as a mushroom or mould

FUNHOUSE *n* amusing place at fairground

FUNICLE, -S *n* stalk that attaches an ovule to the wall of the ovary

FUNICULI ▷ funiculus

FUNK, -ED, -ING, -S *n* style of dance music with a strong beat ▷ *vb* avoid (doing something) through fear

FUNKER -S

FUNKHOLE *n* dugout

FUNKIA, -S *n* hosta

FUNKIER ▶ funky

FUNKIEST ▶ funky

FUNKILY ▶ funky

FUNKING ▶ funk

FUNKS ▶ funk

FUNKSTER *n* performer or fan of funk music

FUNKY, FUNKIER, FUNKIEST *adj* (of music) having a strong beat

FUNNED ▶ fun

FUNNEL, -ED, -S *n* cone-shaped tube ▷ *vb* (cause to) move through or as if through a funnel

FUNNER ▶ fun

FUNNEST ▶ fun

FUNNIER ▶ funny

FUNNIES *pl n* comic strips in a newspaper

FUNNIEST ▶ funny

FUNNILY ▶ funny

FUNNING ▶ fun

FUNNY, FUNNIER, FUNNIEST *adj* comical, humorous ▷ *n* joke or witticism

FUNNYMAN, FUNNYMEN *n* comedian

FUNPLEX *n* large amusement centre

FUNS ▶ fun

FUNSTER, -S *n* funnyman

FUR, -S *n* soft hair of a mammal ▷ *vb* cover or become covered with fur

FURACITY > furacious

FURAL, -S *n* furfural

FURAN, -S *n* colourless flammable toxic liquid heterocyclic compound

FURANE, -S *variant of* ▶ furan

FURANOSE *n* simple sugar containing a furan ring

FURANS ▶ furan

FURBALL, -S *n* ball of fur regurgitated by an animal

FURBELOW *n* flounce, ruffle, or other ornamental trim ▷ *vb* put a furbelow on (a garment)

FURBISH *vb* smarten up

FURCA, -E *n* any forklike structure, esp in insects

FURCAL

FURCATE, -D, -S *vb* divide into two parts ▷ *adj* forked, branching

FURCRAEA *n* plant belonging to the Agave family

FURCULA, -E *n* any forklike part or organ

FURCULAR

FURCULUM *same as* ▶ furcula

FURDER *same as* ▶ further

FUREUR, -S *n* rage or anger

FURFAIR, -S *variant of* ▶ furfur

FURFUR, -ES, -S *n* scurf or scaling of the skin

FURFURAL *n* colourless liquid used as a solvent

FURFURAN *same as* ▶ furan

FURFURES ▶ furfur

FURFUROL *variant of* ▶ furfural

FURFURS ▶ furfur

FURIBUND *adj* furious

FURIES ▶ fury

FURIOSO, -S *adv* in a frantically rushing manner ▷ *n* passage or piece to be performed in this way

FURIOUS *adj* very angry

FURKID, -S *n* companion animal

FURL, -ED, -ING, -S *vb* roll up and fasten (a sail, umbrella, or flag) ▷ *n* act or an instance of furling

FURLABLE

FURLANA, -S *variant of* ▶ forlana

FURLED ▶ furl

FURLER, -S ▶ furl

FURLESS ▶ fur

FURLING ▶ furl

FURLONG, -S *n* unit of length

FURLOUGH *n* leave of absence ▷ *vb* grant a furlough to

FURLS ▶ furl

FURMENTY *same as* ▶ frumenty

FURMETY *same as* ▶ frumenty

FURMITY *same as* ▶ frumenty

FURNACE, -D, -S *n* enclosed chamber containing a very hot fire ▷ *vb* burn in a furnace

FURNISH *vb* provide with furniture

FUROL, -S *variant of* ▶ furfural

FUROLE, -S *variant of* ▶ furfural

FUROLS ▶ furol

FUROR, -S *same as* ▶ furore

FURORE, -S *n* very excited or angry reaction

FURORS ▶ furor

FURPHY, FURPHIES *n* rumour or fictitious story

FURPIECE *n* item of clothing made of or decorated with fur

FURR, -S *vb* furrow

FURRED *same as* ▶ furry

FURRIER, -S *n* dealer in furs

FURRIERY *n* occupation of a furrier

FURRIES ▶ furry

FURRIEST ▶ furry

FURRILY ▶ furry

FURRINER *n* dialect rendering of foreigner

FURRING, -S ▶ fur

FURROW, -ED, -S *n* trench made by a plough ▷ *vb* make or become wrinkled

FURROWER

FURROWY

FURRS ▶ furr

FURRY, FURRIES, FURRIEST *adj* like or covered with fur or something furlike ▷ *n* child's fur-covered toy animal

FURS ▶ fur

FURTH *adv* out

FURTHER, -S *adv* in addition ▷ *adj* more distant ▷ *vb* promote

FURTHEST *adv* to the greatest degree ▷ *adj* most distant

FURTIVE *adj* sly and secretive

FURUNCLE *technical name for* ▶ boil

FURY, FURIES *n* wild anger

F

F

FURZE, -S n gorse

FURZY, FURZIER, FURZIEST ▶ **furze**

FUSAIN, -S n fine charcoal pencil

FUSARIUM, FUSARIA n type of fungus

FUSAROL, -S variant of ▶ **fusarole**

FUSAROLE n type of architectural moulding

FUSAROLS ▶ **fusarol**

FUSBALL, -S same as ▶ **foosball**

FUSC adj dark or dark-brown

FUSCOUS adj of a brownish-grey colour

FUSE, -D, -S, FUSING n cord containing an explosive for detonating a bomb ▷ vb (cause to) fail as a result of a blown fuse

FUSEE, -S n (in early clocks and watches) a spirally grooved spindle

FUSEL, -S n mixture of amyl alcohols, propanol, and butanol

FUSELAGE n body of an aircraft

FUSELESS ▶ **fuse**

FUSELIKE ▶ **fuse**

FUSELS ▶ **fusel**

FUSES ▶ **fuse**

FUSHION, -S n spirit

FUSIBLE adj capable of being melted

FUSIBLY

FUSIDIC adj as in **fusidic acid** kind of acid

FUSIFORM adj elongated and tapering at both ends

FUSIL, -S n light flintlock musket

FUSILE adj easily melted

FUSILEER same as ▶ **fusilier**

FUSILIER n soldier of certain regiments

FUSILLI, -S n spiral-shaped pasta

FUSILS ▶ **fusil**

FUSING ▶ **fuse**

FUSION, -S n melting ▷ adj of a style of cooking

FUSIONAL

FUSK, -ED, -ING, -S vb obtain data from (a website) by using a fusker

FUSKER, -S n piece of hacking software

FUSKING ▶ **fusk**

FUSKS ▶ **fusk**

FUSS, -ED, -ES, -ING n needless activity or worry ▷ vb make a fuss

FUSSBALL same as ▶ **foosball**

FUSSED ▶ **fuss**

FUSSER, -S ▶ **fuss**

FUSSES ▶ **fuss**

FUSSIER ▶ **fussy**

FUSSIEST ▶ **fussy**

FUSSILY ▶ **fussy**

FUSSING ▶ **fuss**

FUSSPOT, -S n person who is difficult to please and complains often

FUSSY, FUSSIER, FUSSIEST adj inclined to fuss

FUST, -ED, -ING, -S vb become mouldy

FUSTET, -S n wood of the Venetian sumach shrub

FUSTIAN, -S n (formerly) a hard-wearing fabric of cotton mixed with flax or wool ▷ adj cheap

FUSTIC, -S n large tropical American tree

FUSTIER ▶ **fusty**

FUSTIEST ▶ **fusty**

FUSTILY ▶ **fusty**

FUSTING ▶ **fust**

FUSTOC, -S variant of ▶ **fustic**

FUSTS ▶ **fust**

FUSTY, FUSTIER, FUSTIEST adj stale-smelling

FUSUMA n Japanese sliding door

FUTCHEL, -S n timber support in a carriage

FUTHARC, -S same as ▶ **futhark**

FUTHARK, -S n phonetic alphabet consisting of runes

FUTHORC, -S same as ▶ **futhark**

FUTHORK, -S same as ▶ **futhark**

FUTILE, -R, -ST adj unsuccessful or useless

FUTILELY

FUTILITY n lack of effectiveness or success

FUTON, -S n Japanese-style bed

FUTSAL, -S n form of association football

FUTTOCK, -S n one of the ribs in the frame of a wooden vessel

FUTURAL adj relating to the future

FUTURE n time to come ▷ adj yet to come or be ▷ v ▶ **fuse**

FUTURES pl n type of commodity trading

FUTURISM n early 20th-century artistic movement

FUTURIST

FUTURITY n future

FUTZ, -ED, -ES, -ING vb fritter time away

FUZE, -D, -S, FUZING same as ▶ **fuse**

FUZELESS adj without a fuze

FUZES ▶ **fuze**

FUZIL, -S variant of ▶ **fusil**

FUZING ▶ **fuze**

FUZZ, -ED, -ES, -ING n mass of fine or curly hairs or fibres ▷ vb make or become fuzzy

FUZZBALL n ball of fuzz

FUZZBOX n device that distorts sound

FUZZED ▶ **fuzz**

FUZZES ▶ **fuzz**

FUZZIER ▶ **fuzzy**

FUZZIEST ▶ **fuzzy**

FUZZILY ▶ **fuzzy**

FUZZING ▶ **fuzz**

FUZZLE, -D, -S, FUZZLING vb make drunk

FUZZTONE n device distorting electric guitar sound

FUZZY, FUZZIER, FUZZIEST adj of, like, or covered with fuzz

FY interj exclamation of disapproval

FYCE, -S variant of ▶ **fice**

FYKE, -D, -S, FYKING n fish trap ▷ vb catch fish in this manner

FYLE, -S variant of ▶ **file**

FYLFOT, -S rare word for ▶ **swastika**

FYNBOS, -ES n area of low-growing, evergreen vegetation

FYRD, -S n militia of an Anglo-Saxon shire

FYTTE, -S n song

Gg

Only three two-letter words begin with **G** (**gi**, **go** and **gu**). Knowing these will save you worrying about other possibilities. There are quite a few short words beginning with **G** that use **Y**, which can prove very useful. These include **gay, gey** and **guy** (7 points each), as well as **gym** and **gyp** (9 points each). And don't forget the very useful **gox** for 11 points.

GAB, -BED, -BING, -S *vb* talk or chatter ▷ *n* mechanical device

GABBA, -S *n* type of electronic dance music

GABBARD, -S *same as* ▸ **gabbart**

GABBART, -S *n* Scottish sailing barge

GABBAS ▸ **gabba**

GABBED ▸ **gab**

GABBER, -S ▸ **gab**

GABBIER ▸ **gabby**

GABBIEST ▸ **gabby**

GABBING ▸ **gab**

GABBLE, -D, -S, GABBLING *vb* speak rapidly and indistinctly ▷ *n* rapid indistinct speech

GABBLER -S

GABBRO, -S *n* dark basic plutonic igneous rock

GABBROIC

GABBROID *adj* gabbro-like

GABBROS ▸ **gabbro**

GABBY, GABBIER, GABBIEST *adj* talkative

GABELLE, -S *n* salt tax levied until 1790

GABELLED

GABELLER *n* person who collects the gabelle

GABELLES ▸ **gabelle**

GABFEST, -S *n* prolonged gossiping or conversation

GABIES ▸ **gaby**

GABION, -S *n* cylindrical metal container filled with stones

GABIONED

GABLE, -S *n* triangular upper part of a wall between sloping roofs

GABLED

GABLET, -S *n* small gable

GABLING ▸ **gable**

GABNASH *n* chatter

GABOON, -S *n* dark wood

GABS ▸ **gab**

GABY, GABIES *n* simpleton

GACH, -ED, -ES, -ING *vb* behave boastfully

GACHER, -S *n* person who gaches

GACHES ▸ **gach**

GACHING ▸ **gach**

GAD, -DED, -DING, -S *vb* go about in search of pleasure ▷ *n* carefree adventure

GADABOUT *n* pleasure-seeker

GADARENE *adj* headlong

GADDED ▸ **gad**

GADDER, -S ▸ **gad**

GADDI, -S *n* cushion on an Indian prince's throne

GADDING ▸ **gad**

GADDIS ▸ **gaddi**

GADE, -S *same as* ▸ **gad**

GADFLY, GADFLIES *n* fly that bites cattle

GADGE, -S *n* man

GADGET, -S *n* small mechanical device or appliance

GADGETRY *n* gadgets

GADGETS ▸ **gadget**

GADGETY ▸ **gadget**

GADGIE, -S *n* fellow

GADI, -S *n* Indian throne

GADID, -S *n* type of marine fish

GADIS ▸ **gadi**

GADJE, -S *same as* ▸ **gadgie**

GADJO, -S *same as* ▸ **gorgio**

GADLING, -S *n* vagabond

GADMAN, GADMEN *n* person who drives horses at the plough

GADOID, -S *adj* of the cod family of marine fishes ▷ *n* gadoid fish

GADROON, -S *n* type of decorative moulding

GADS ▸ **gad**

GADSMAN, GADSMEN *n* person who uses a gad when driving animals

GADSO *n* archaic expression of surprise

GADWALL, -S *n* type of duck related to the mallard

GADZOOKS *interj* mild oath

GAE, -D, -ING, -N, -S *Scot word for* ▸ **go**

GAFF, -ED, -S *n* stick with an iron hook for landing large fish ▷ *vb* hook or land (a fish) with a gaff

GAFFE, -S *n* social blunder

GAFFED ▸ **gaff**

GAFFER, -S *n* foreman or boss

GAFFES ▸ **gaffe**

GAFFING, -S ▸ **gaff**

GAFFS ▸ **gaff**

GAFFSAIL *n* quadrilateral fore-and-aft sail on a sailing vessel

GAG, -GED, -GING, -S *vb* choke or retch ▷ *n* cloth etc put into or tied across the mouth

GAGA *adj* senile

GAGAKU, -S *n* type of traditional Japanese music

GAGE, -D, -S, GAGING *vb* gauge ▷ *n* (formerly) an object thrown down as a challenge to fight

GAGEABLE

GAGEABLY

GAGER, -S *same as* ▸ **gauger**

GAGES ▸ **gage**

GAGGED ▸ **gag**

GAGGER, -S *n* person or thing that gags

GAGGERY *n* practice of telling jokes

GAGGING ▸ **gag**

GAGGLE, -D, -S, GAGGLING *n* disorderly crowd ▷ *vb* (of geese) to cackle

GAGING ▸ **gage**

GAGMAN, GAGMEN n person who writes gags for a comedian

GAGS ► gag

GAGSTER, -S n standup comedian

GAHNITE, -S n dark green mineral

GAID, -S same as **► gad**

GAIETY, GAIETIES n cheerfulness

GAIJIN n (in Japan) a foreigner

GAILLARD same as **► galliard**

GAILY adv merrily

GAIN, -ED, -EST, -ING vb acquire or obtain ▷ n profit or advantage ▷ adj straight or near

GAINABLE

GAINER, -S n person or thing that gains

GAINEST ► gain

GAINFUL adj useful or profitable

GAINING ► gain

GAININGS pl n profits or earnings

GAINLESS ► gain

GAINLY, GAINLIER adj graceful or well-formed ▷ adv conveniently or suitably

GAINS pl n profits or winnings

GAINSAY, GAINSAID, -S vb deny or contradict

GAINST short for **► against**

GAIR, -S n strip of green grass on a hillside

GAIRFOWL same as **► garefowl**

GAIRS ► gair

GAIT, -ED, -ING, -S n manner of walking ▷ vb teach (a horse) a particular gait

GAITA, -S n type of bagpipe

GAITED ► gait

GAITER, -S n cloth or leather covering for the lower leg

GAITERED adj wearing gaiters

GAITERS ► gaiter

GAITING ► gait

GAITS ► gait

GAITT, -S Scots word for **► gate**

GAJO, -S same as **► gorgio**

GAL, -S n girl

GALA, -S n festival

GALABEA, -S same as **► djellaba**

GALABEAH same as **► djellaba**

GALABEAS ► galabea

GALABIA, -S same as **► djellaba**

GALABIAH same as **► djellaba**

GALABIAS ► galabia

GALABIEH same as **► djellaba**

GALABIYA same as **► djellaba**

GALACTIC adj of the Galaxy or other galaxies

GALAGE, -S same as **► galosh**

GALAGO, -S another name for **► bushbaby**

GALAH, -S n Australian cockatoo

GALANGA, -S same as **> galingale**

GALANGAL same as **> galingale**

GALANGAS ► galanga

GALANT n 18th-century style of music

GALANTY n as in **galanty show** pantomime shadow play

GALAPAGO n tortoise

GALAS ► gala

GALATEA, -S n strong twill-weave cotton fabric

GALAVANT same as **> gallivant**

GALAX, -ES n coltsfoot

GALAXY, GALAXIES n system of stars

GALBANUM n bitter aromatic gum resin

GALE, -D, -S, GALING n strong wind ▷ vb be very stormy

GALEA, -E, -S n part or organ shaped like a helmet

GALEATE

GALEATED

GALED ► gale

GALENA, -S n soft bluish-grey mineral

GALENIC

GALENITE same as **► galena**

GALENOID adj pertaining to galena

GALERE, -S n group of people having a common interest

GALES ► gale

GALETTE, -S n type of savoury pancake

GALILEE, -S n type of porch or chapel

GALING ► gale

GALIOT, -S n small swift galley

GALIPOT, -S n resin obtained from several species of pine

GALIVANT same as **> gallivant**

GALL, -ED, -S n impudence ▷ vb annoy

GALLABEA same as **► djellaba**

GALLABIA same as **► djellaba**

GALLANT, -S adj brave and noble ▷ n man who tried to impress with fashionable clothes or daring acts ▷ vb court or flirt (with)

GALLATE, -S n salt of gallic acid

GALLEASS n three-masted lateen-rigged galley

GALLED ► gall

GALLEIN, -S n type of dyestuff

GALLEON, -S n large three-masted sailing ship

GALLERIA n central court through several storeys of a shopping centre

GALLERY n room or building for displaying works of art ▷ vb tunnel; form an underground gallery

GALLET, -ED, -S vb use mixture to support a roof-slate

GALLETA, -S n low-growing, coarse grass

GALLETED ► gallet

GALLETS ► gallet

GALLEY, -S n kitchen of a ship or aircraft

GALLFLY n any of several small insects

GALLIARD n spirited dance in triple time for two persons, popular in the 16th and 17th centuries ▷ adj lively

GALLIASS same as **► galleass**

GALLIC adj of or containing gallium in the trivalent state

GALLICA, -S n variety of rose

GALLICAN adj favouring restriction of papal control of the French church

GALLICAS ► gallica

GALLIED ► gally

GALLIER ► gally

GALLIES ► gally

GALLIEST ► gally

GALLING adj annoying or bitterly humiliating

GALLIOT, -S same as **► galiot**

GALLIPOT same as **► galipot**

GALLISE, -D, -S vb use method to increase the quantity of wine produced

GALLIUM, -S n soft grey metallic element

GALLIVAT n Oriental armed vessel

GALLIZE, -D, -S same as **► gallise**

GALLNUT, -S n type of plant gall that resembles a nut

GALLOCK adj left-handed

GALLON, -S n liquid measure of eight pints, equal to 4.55 litres

GALLOON, -S n narrow band of cord, gold braid, etc

GALLOOT, -S same as ► galoot

GALLOP, -ED, -S n horse's fastest pace ▷ vb go or ride at a gallop

GALLOPER

GALLOUS adj of or containing gallium in the divalent state

GALLOW same as ► gallow

GALLOWAY n breed of hornless beef cattle

GALLOWED ► gallow

GALLOWS n wooden structure used for hanging criminals

GALLS ► gall

GALLUMPH same as ► galumph

GALLUS, -ES adj bold ▷ n suspender for trousers

GALLUSED adj held up by galluses

GALLUSES ► gallus

GALLY, GALLIED, GALLIER, GALLIES, GALLIEST, -ING vb frighten ▷ adj (of land) damp or barren

GALOCHE, -D, -S same as ► galosh

GALOOT, -S n clumsy or uncouth person

GALOP, -ED, -ING, -PED, -S n 19th-century dance in quick duple time ▷ vb dance a galop

GALOPADE same as ► galop

GALOPED ► galop

GALOPIN, -S n boy who ran errands for a cook

GALOPING ► galop

GALOPINS ► galopin

GALOPPED ► galop

GALOPS ► galop

GALORE, -S adv in abundance ▷ adj in abundance ▷ n abundance

GALOSH, -ED, -ES n waterproof overshoe ▷ vb cover with galoshes

GALOSHE same as ► galosh

GALOSHED ► galosh

GALOSHES ► galosh

GALOWSES Shakespearean plural for ► gallows

GALS ► gal

GALTONIA n type of bulbous plant with waxy white flowers and a fragrant scent

GALUMPH, -S vb leap or move about clumsily

GALUT, -S same as ► galuth

GALUTH, -S n exile of Jews from Palestine

GALUTS ► galut

GALVANIC adj of or producing an electric current generated by chemical means

GALVO, -S n instrument for measuring electric current

GALYAC, -S same as ► galyak

GALYAK, -S n smooth glossy fur

GAM, -MED, -MING, -S n school of whales ▷ vb (of whales) form a school

GAMA, -S n tall perennial grass

GAMASH, -ES n type of gaiter

GAMAY, -S n red grape variety

GAMB, -S n in heraldry, the whole foreleg of a beast

GAMBA, -S n second-largest member of the viol family

GAMBADE, -S same as ► gambado

GAMBADO, -S n leap or gambol; caper ▷ vb perform a gambado

GAMBAS ► gamba

GAMBE, -S same as ► gamb

GAMBESON n garment worn under mail in the Middle Ages

GAMBET, -S n tattler

GAMBETTA n redshank

GAMBIA, -S same as ► gambier

GAMBIER, -S n astringent resinous substance

GAMBIR, -S same as ► gambier

GAMBIST, -S n person who plays the (viola da) gamba

GAMBIT, -ED, -S n opening move intended to secure an advantage ▷ vb sacrifice a chess piece to gain a better position

GAMBLE, -D, -S vb play games of chance to win money ▷ n risky undertaking

GAMBLER -S

GAMBLING ► gamble

GAMBO, -ES, -S n farm cart

GAMBOGE, -S n gum resin

GAMBOGIC

GAMBOL, -ED, -S vb jump about playfully, frolic ▷ n frolic

GAMBOS ► gambo

GAMBREL, -S n hock of a horse or similar animal

GAMBROON n type of linen cloth

GAMBS ► gamb

GAMBUSIA n small fish that feeds on mosquito larvae

GAME, -D, -S, -ST n amusement or pastime ▷ vb play games ▷ adj brave

GAMEBAG, -S n bag for carrying hunted game birds

GAMEBOOK n book containing a range of possible strategies for a game

GAMECOCK n cock bred and trained for fighting

GAMED ► game

GAMEFISH n fish caught for sport

GAMEFOWL n cock bred for cockfighting

GAMELAN, -S n type of percussion orchestra

GAMELIKE ► game

GAMELY adv in a brave or sporting manner

GAMENESS n courage or bravery

GAMEPLAY n plot of a computer or video game or the way that it is played

GAMER, -S n person who plays computer games

GAMES ► game

GAMESIER ► gamesy

GAMESMAN, GAMESMEN n one who practises gamesmanship

GAMESOME adj full of merriment

GAMEST ► game

GAMESTER n someone who plays games

GAMESY, GAMESIER adj sporty

GAMETAL ► gamete

GAMETE, -S n reproductive cell

GAMETIC

GAMEY, GAMIER, GAMIEST adj having the smell or flavour of game

GAMGEE n as in gamgee tissue type of wound-dressing

GAMIC adj (esp of reproduction) requiring the fusion of gametes

GAMIER ► gamey

GAMIEST ► gamey

GAMIFY, GAMIFIED, GAMIFIES vb add gamelike elements to a task to encourage participation

GAMILY ► gamey

GAMIN, -S n street urchin

GAMINE, -S n slim boyish young woman

GAMINESS ► gamey

GAMING, -S n playing games

GAMINS ► gamin

GAMMA, -S n third letter of the Greek alphabet

GAMMADIA > gammadion

GAMMAS ► gamma

GAMMATIA > gammation

GAMME, -S n musical scale

GAMMED ► gam

GAMMER, -S n dialect word for an old woman

GAMMES ► gamme

GAMMIER ► gammy

GAMMIEST ► gammy

GAMMING ► gam

GAMMOCK, -S vb clown around

GAMMON, -ED, -S n cured or smoked ham ▷ vb score a double victory in backgammon over

GAMMONER

GAMMY, GAMMIER, GAMMIEST adj (of the leg) lame

GAMODEME n isolated breeding population

GAMONE, -S n chemical used by gametes

GAMP, -S n umbrella

GAMPISH adj bulging

GAMPS ► gamp

GAMS ► gam

GAMUT, -S n whole range or scale (of music, emotions, etc)

GAMY same as ► **gamey GAMYNESS**

GAN, -NED, -NING, -S vb go

GANACHE, -S n rich icing or filling

GANCH, -ED, -ES, -ING vb impale

GANDER, -ED, -S n male goose ▷ vb look

GANDY adj as in **gandy dancer** railway track maintenance worker

GANE ► go

GANEF, -S n unscrupulous opportunist

GANEV, -S same as ► **ganef**

GANG, -ED, -S n (criminal) group ▷ vb become or act as a gang

GANGBO, -S n order restricting the activities of a gang member

GANGED ► gang

GANGER, -S n foreman of a gang of labourers

GANGING, -S ► gang

GANGLAND n criminal underworld

GANGLE, -D, -S vb move awkwardly

GANGLIA ► ganglion

GANGLIAL ► ganglion

GANGLIAR ► ganglion

GANGLIER ► gangly

GANGLING adj lanky and awkward

GANGLION, GANGLIA n group of nerve cells

GANGLY, GANGLIER same as ► **gangling**

GANGPLOW n plough designed to produce parallel furrows

GANGREL, -S n wandering beggar

GANGRENE n decay of body tissue as a result of disease or injury ▷ vb become or cause to become affected with gangrene

GANGS ► gang

GANGSMAN, GANGSMEN n foreman

GANGSTA, -S n member of a street gang

GANGSTER n member of a criminal gang

GANGUE, -S n valueless material in an ore

GANGWAY, -S same as > **gangplank**

GANISTER n type of sedimentary rock

GANNED ► gan

GANNET, -S n large sea bird

GANNETRY n gannets' breeding-place

GANNETS ► gannet

GANNING ► gan

GANOF, -S same as ► **ganef**

GANOID, -S adj of the scales of certain fishes ▷ n ganoid fish

GANOIN, -S n the outer layer of fish scales

GANOINE, -S same as ► **ganoin**

GANOINS ► ganoin

GANS ► gan

GANSEY, -S n jersey or pullover

GANT, -ED, -ING, -S vb yawn

GANTLET, -S n section of a railway where two tracks overlap ▷ vb make railway tracks form a gantlet

GANTLINE n line rove through a sheave for hoisting men or gear

GANTLOPE same as ► **gauntlet**

GANTRY, GANTRIES n structure supporting something

GANTS ► gant

GANYMEDE n potboy

GANZFELD n type of experiment used in parapsychology

GAOL, -ED, -ING, -S same as ► **jail**

GAOLBIRD n person who is or has been confined to gaol, esp repeatedly

GAOLED ► gaol

GAOLER, -S ► gaol

GAOLING ► gaol

GAOLLESS adj without a gaol

GAOLS ► gaol

GAP, -PED, -S n break or opening

GAPE, -D vb stare in wonder ▷ n act of gaping

GAPER, -S n person or thing that gapes

GAPES n disease of young domestic fowl

GAPESEED n person who stares, mouth agape, at something

GAPEWORM n type of parasitic worm that lives in the trachea of birds

GAPIER ► gapy

GAPIEST ► gapy

GAPING, -S adj wide open ▷ n state of having a gaping mouth

GAPINGLY

GAPLESS ► gap

GAPO, -S n forest near a river, flooded in the rainy season

GAPOSIS n gap between closed fastenings on a garment

GAPPED ► gap

GAPPER, -S n person taking a year out of education

GAPPIER ► gappy

GAPPIEST ► gappy

GAPPING, -S n the act of taking a gap year

GAPPY, GAPPIER, GAPPIEST ► **gap**

GAPS ► gap

GAPY, GAPIER, GAPIEST ► **gape**

GAR, -RED, -RING, -S same as ► **garpike**

GARAGE, -D, -S n building used to house cars ▷ vb put or keep a car in a garage

GARAGEY adj (of music) in a garage style

GARAGING n accommodation for housing a motor vehicle

GARAGIST n person who runs a garage

GARB, -ED, -ING, -S n clothes ▷ vb clothe

GARBAGE, -S n rubbish

GARBAGEY

GARBAGY

GARBANZO another name for ► **chickpea**

GARBE, -S n in heraldry, a wheat-sheaf

GARBED ▶ garb

GARBES ▶ garbe

GARBING ▶ garb

GARBLE, -S, GARBLING vb jumble (a story, quotation, etc), esp unintentionally ▷ n act of garbling

GARBLED adj (of a story etc) jumbled and confused

GARBLER, -S ▶ garble

GARBLES ▶ garble

GARBLESS ▶ garb

GARBLING ▶ garb

GARBO, -S n dustman

GARBOARD n bottommost plank of a vessel's hull

GARBOIL, -S n confusion or disturbance

GARBOS ▶ garbo

GARBS ▶ garb

GARBURE, -S n thick soup from Bearn in France

GARCINIA n tropical tree

GARCON, -S n waiter

GARDA, -I n member of the Irish police force

GARDANT, -S same as ▶ **guardant**

GARDEN, -ED, -S n piece of land for growing flowers, fruit, or vegetables ▷ vb cultivate a garden

GARDENER n person who works in or takes care of a garden as an occupation or pastime

GARDENIA n large fragrant white waxy flower

GARDENS ▶ garden

GARDYLOO n act of throwing slops from a window

GARE, -S n filth ▷ adj greedy; covetous

GAREFOWL n great auk

GARES ▶ gare

GARFISH same as ▶ **garpike**

GARGANEY n small Eurasian duck, closely related to the mallard

GARGET, -S n inflammation of the mammary gland

GARGETY

GARGLE, -D, -S, GARGLING vb wash the throat ▷ n liquid used for gargling

GARGLER -S

GARGOYLE n waterspout carved in the form of a grotesque face, esp on a church ▷ vb provide with gargoyles

GARI, -S n thinly sliced pickled ginger

GARIAL, -S same as ▶ **gavial**

GARIGUE, -S n open shrubby vegetation of dry Mediterranean regions

GARIS ▶ gari

GARISH, -ED, -ES adj crudely bright or colourful ▷ vb heal
GARISHLY

GARJAN, -S same as ▶ **gurjun**

GARLAND, -S n wreath of flowers worn or hung as a decoration ▷ vb decorate with garlands

GARLIC, -S n pungent bulb of a plant of the onion family

GARLICKY adj containing or resembling the taste or odour of garlic

GARLICS ▶ garlic

GARMENT, -S n article of clothing ▷ vb cover or clothe

GARMS pl n clothing

GARNER, -ED, -S vb collect or store ▷ n place for storage or safekeeping

GARNET, -S n red semiprecious stone

GARNI adj garnished

GARNISH vb decorate (food) ▷ n decoration for food

GAROTE, -D, -S, GAROTING same as ▶ **garrotte**

GAROTTE, -D, -S same as ▶ **garrotte**

GAROTTER

GAROUPA, -S in Chinese and SE Asian cookery, another name for ▶ **groper**

GARPIKE, -S n primitive freshwater bony fish

GARRAN, -S same as ▶ **garron**

GARRE, -S vb compel

GARRED ▶ gar

GARRES ▶ garre

GARRET, -S n attic in a house

GARRETED adj living in a garret

GARRETS ▶ garret

GARRIGUE same as ▶ **garigue**

GARRING ▶ gar

GARRISON n troops stationed in a town or fort ▷ vb station troops in

GARRON, -S n small sturdy pony

GARROT, -S n goldeneye duck

GARROTE, -D, -S same as ▶ **garrotte**

GAROTTER

GARROTS ▶ garrot

GARROTTE n Spanish method of execution by strangling ▷ vb kill by this method

GARRYA, -S n catkin-bearing evergreen shrub

GARS ▶ gar

GART vb compel

GARTER, -ED, -S n band used to hold up a sock or stocking ▷ vb secure with a garter

GARTH, -S n courtyard surrounded by a cloister

GARUDA, -S n Hindu god

GARUM, -S n fermented fish sauce

GARVEY, -S n small flat-bottomed yacht

GARVIE, -S n sprat

GARVOCK, -S n sprat

GAS, -ES, -SED, -SES n airlike substance that is not liquid or solid ▷ vb poison or render unconscious with gas

GASAHOL, -S n mixture of petrol and alcohol used as fuel

GASALIER same as ▶ **gasolier**

GASBAG, -S n person who talks too much ▷ vb talk in a voluble way

GASCON, -S n boaster

GASEITY n state of being gaseous

GASELIER same as ▶ **gasolier**

GASEOUS adj of or like gas

GASES ▶ gas

GASFIELD n area in which natural gas is found underground

GASH, -ED, -ER, -ES, -EST, -ING vb make a long deep cut in ▷ n long deep cut ▷ adj witty

GASHFUL adj full of gashes

GASHING ▶ gash

GASHLY, GASHLIER adv wittily ▷ adj hideous; ghastly

GASHOUSE n gasworks

GASIFIED ▶ gasify

GASIFIER ▶ gasify

GASIFIES ▶ gasify

GASIFORM adj in a gaseous form

GASIFY, GASIFIED, GASIFIES vb change into a gas

GASKET, -S n type of seal

GASKETED adj having a gasket

GASKETS ▶ gasket

GASKIN, -S n lower part of a horse's thigh

GASKING, -S same as ▶ **gasket**

GASKINS ▶ gaskin

GASLESS ▶ gas

GASLIGHT n lamp in which light is produced by burning gas

GASLIT adj lit by gas

GASMAN, GASMEN n man employed by a gas company

GASOGENE n siphon bottle

GASOHOL, -S n mixture of petrol and alcohol used as fuel

GASOLENE same as ▸ **gasoline**

GASOLIER n branched hanging fitting for gaslights

GASOLINE n petrol

GASP, -ED, -S vb draw in breath sharply or with difficulty ▸ n convulsive intake of breath

GASPER, -S n person who gasps

GASPIER ▸ **gaspy**

GASPIEST ▸ **gaspy**

GASPING, -S ▸ **gasp**

GASPS ▸ **gasp**

GASPY, GASPIER, GASPIEST ▸ **gasp**

GASSED ▸ **gas**

GASSER, -S n drilling or well that yields natural gas

GASSES ▸ **gas**

GASSIER ▸ **gassy**

GASSIEST ▸ **gassy**

GASSILY ▸ **gassy**

GASSING, -S ▸ **gas**

GASSY, GASSIER, GASSIEST adj filled with gas

GAST, -ED, -ING, -S vb frighten

GASTER, -ED, -S vb frighten

GASTFULL adj dismal

GASTHAUS n guest house

GASTIGHT adj not allowing gas to enter or escape

GASTING ▸ **gast**

GASTNESS n dread

GASTRAEA n hypothetical primeval form posited by Haeckel

GASTRAL adj relating to the stomach

GASTREA, -S same as ▸ **gastraea**

GASTRIC adj of the stomach

GASTRIN, -S n polypeptide hormone

GASTRULA n saclike animal embryo

GASTS ▸ **gast**

GASWORKS n plant where coal gas is made

GAT, -S n pistol or revolver

GATCH, -ED, -ES, -ING vb behave boastfully

GATCHER, -S n person who gatches

GATCHES ▸ **gatch**

GATCHING ▸ **gatch**

GATE, -D, -S, -ING, GATINGS n movable barrier, usu hinged, in a wall or fence ▸ vb provide with a gate or gates

GATEAU, -S, -X n rich elaborate cake

GATED ▸ **gate**

GATEFOLD n oversize page in a book or magazine that is folded in

GATELEG, -S n table having hinged legs that swing out

GATELESS ▸ **gate**

GATELIKE ▸ **gate**

GATEMAN, GATEMEN n gatekeeper

GATEPOST n post on which a gate is hung

GATER, -S variant of ▸ **gator**

GATES ▸ **gate**

GATEWAY, -S n entrance with a gate

GATH, -S n (in Indian music) second section of a raga

GATHER, -ED, -S vb assemble ▸ n act of gathering

GATHERER n

GATHS ▸ **gath**

GATING ▸ **gate**

GATINGS ▸ **gate**

GATLING n as in **gatling gun** kind of machine-gun

GATOR, -S shortened form of ▸ **alligator**

GATS ▸ **gat**

GATVOL adj in South African English, fed up

GAU, -S n district set up by the Nazi Party

GAUCH vb behave boastfully

GAUCHE, -D, -S, -ST, GAUCHING adj socially awkward ▸ vb make gauche

GAUCHELY

GAUCHER, -S n gauche person

GAUCHES ▸ **gauche**

GAUCHEST ▸ **gauche**

GAUCHING ▸ **gauche**

GAUCHO, -S n S American cowboy

GAUCIE variant of ▸ **gaucy**

GAUCY, GAUCIER, GAUCIEST adj plump or jolly

GAUD, -ED, -ING, -S n article of cheap finery ▸ vb decorate gaudily

GAUDERY n cheap finery or display

GAUDGIE, -S same as ▸ **gadgie**

GAUDIER ▸ **gaudy**

GAUDIES ▸ **gaudy**

GAUDIEST ▸ **gaudy**

GAUDILY ▸ **gaudy**

GAUDING ▸ **gaud**

GAUDS ▸ **gaud**

GAUDY, GAUDIER, GAUDIES, GAUDIEST adj vulgarly bright or colourful ▸ n

festival held at some schools and colleges

GAUFER, -S n wafer

GAUFFER, -S same as ▸ **goffer**

GAUFRE, -S same as ▸ **gaufer**

GAUGE, -D, -S vb estimate or judge ▸ n measuring instrument ▸ adj of a pressure measurement

GAUGER, -S n person or thing that gauges

GAUGES ▸ **gauge**

GAUGING, -S ▸ **gauge**

GAUJE, -S same as ▸ **gadgie**

GAULT, -S n stiff compact clay or thick heavy clayey soil

GAULTER, -S n person who digs gault

GAULTS ▸ **gault**

GAUM, -ED, -ING, -S vb understand

GAUMIER ▸ **gaumy**

GAUMIEST ▸ **gaumy**

GAUMING ▸ **gaum**

GAUMLESS variant spelling of ▸ **gormless**

GAUMS ▸ **gaum**

GAUMY, GAUMIER, GAUMIEST adj clogged

GAUN ▸ **go**

GAUNCH, -ED, -ES same as ▸ **ganch**

GAUNT, -ED, -ER, -EST, -ING, -S adj lean and haggard ▸ vb yawn

GAUNTLET n heavy glove with a long cuff ▸ vb run (or cause to run) the gauntlet

GAUNTLY ▸ **gaunt**

GAUNTREE same as ▸ **gantry**

GAUNTRY same as ▸ **gantry**

GAUNTS ▸ **gaunt**

GAUP, -ED, -ING, -S same as ▸ **gawp**

GAUPER, -S

GAUPUS, -ES same as ▸ **gawpus**

GAUR, -S n large wild member of the cattle tribe

GAUS ▸ **gau**

GAUSS, -ES n cgs unit of magnetic flux density

GAUSSIAN adj denoting the mathematical principles of K F Gauss

GAUZE, -S n transparent loosely-woven fabric

GAUZIER ▸ **gauzy**

GAUZIEST ▸ **gauzy**

GAUZILY ▸ **gauzy**

GAUZY, GAUZIER, GAUZIEST adj resembling gauze

GAVAGE, -S n forced feeding by means of a tube

GAVE ▸ **give**

GAVEL, -ED, -ING, -LED, -S *n* small hammer banged on a table ▷ *vb* use a gavel to restore order

GAVELMAN, GAVELMEN *n* gavelkind tenant

GAVELOCK *n* iron crowbar

GAVELS ▸ **gavel**

GAVIAL, -S *n as in* **false gavial** small crocodile

GAVOT, -S *same as* ▸ **gavotte**

GAVOTTE, -D, -S *n* old formal dance ▷ *vb* dance a gavotte

GAW, -S *n as in* **weather gaw** partial rainbow

GAWCY, GAWCIER, GAWCIEST *same as* ▸ **gaucy**

GAWD, -S *same as* ▸ **gaud**

GAWK, -ED, -ING, -S *vb* stare stupidly ▷ *n* clumsy awkward person

GAWKER -S

GAWKIER ▸ **gawky**

GAWKIES ▸ **gawky**

GAWKIEST ▸ **gawky**

GAWKILY ▸ **gawky**

GAWKING ▸ **gawk**

GAWKISH *same as* ▸ **gawky**

GAWKS ▸ **gawk**

GAWKY, GAWKIER, GAWKIES, GAWKIEST *adj* clumsy or awkward ▷ *n* clumsy or awkward person

GAWMOGE, -S *n* clownish person

GAWP, -ED, -ING, -S *vb* stare stupidly

GAWPER -S

GAWPUS, -ES *n* silly person

GAWS ▸ **gaw**

GAWSIE, -R, -ST *same as* ▸ **gaucy**

GAWSY *same as* ▸ **gaucy**

GAY, -ER, -EST, -S *adj* carefree and merry ▷ *n* homosexual person

GAYAL, -S *n* type of ox

GAYDAR, -S *n* supposed ability to recognize if another person is homosexual

GAYER ▸ **gay**

GAYEST ▸ **gay**

GAYETY, GAYETIES *same as* ▸ **gaiety**

GAYLY ▸ **gay**

GAYNESS ▸ **gay**

GAYS ▸ **gay**

GAYSOME *adj* full of merriment

GAYWINGS *n* flowering wintergreen

GAZABO, -ES, -S *n* fellow or companion

GAZAL, -S *same as* ▸ **ghazal**

GAZANG, -ED, -S *vb* inconvenience a buyer by declining to sell a house just before the purchase is completed

GAZANIA, -S *n* S African plant

GAZAR, -S *n* type of silk cloth

GAZE, -D, -S *vb* look fixedly ▷ *n* fixed look

GAZEBO, -ES, -S *n* summerhouse with a good view

GAZED ▸ **gaze**

GAZEFUL *adj* gazing

GAZELLE, -S *n* small graceful antelope

GAZEMENT *n* view

GAZER, -S ▸ **gaze**

GAZES ▸ **gaze**

GAZETTE, -D, -S *n* official publication containing announcements ▷ *vb* announce or report (facts or an event) in a gazette

GAZIER ▸ **gazy**

GAZIEST ▸ **gazy**

GAZING, -S ▸ **gaze**

GAZOGENE *same as* ▸ **gasogene**

GAZON, -S *n* sod used to cover a parapet in a fortification

GAZOO, -S *n* kazoo

GAZOOKA, -S *same as* ▸ **gazoo**

GAZOON, -S *same as* ▸ **gazon**

GAZOOS ▸ **gazoo**

GAZPACHO *n* Spanish soup made from tomatoes, peppers, etc, and served cold

GAZUMP, -ED, -S *vb* raise the price of a property after verbally agreeing it with (a prospective buyer) ▷ *n* act or an instance of gazumping

GAZUMPER

GAZUNDER *vb* reduce an offer on a property immediately before purchase ▷ *n* act or instance of gazundering

GAZY, GAZIER, GAZIEST *adj* prone to gazing

GEAL, -ED, -ING, -S *vb* congeal

GEALOUS *Spenserian spelling of* ▸ **jealous**

GEALOUSY *Spenserian spelling of* ▸ **jealousy**

GEALS ▸ **geal**

GEAN, -S *n* white-flowered tree

GEAR, -ED, -S *n* set of toothed wheels used to change direction or speed ▷ *vb* prepare or organize for something

GEARBOX *n* case enclosing a set of gears in a motor vehicle

GEARCASE *n* protective casing for gears

GEARE, -S *Spenserian spelling of* ▸ **jeer**

GEARED ▸ **gear**

GEARES ▸ **geare**

GEARHEAD *n* part in engine gear system

GEARING, -S *n* system of gears designed to transmit motion

GEARLESS ▸ **gear**

GEARS ▸ **gear**

GEASON *adj* wonderful

GEAT, -S *n* in casting, the channel which leads to a mould

GEBUR, -S *n* tenant farmer

GECK, -ED, -ING, -S *vb* beguile

GECKO, -ES, -S *n* small tropical lizard

GECKS ▸ **geck**

GED, -S *Scots word for* ▸ **pike**

GEDACT, -S *n* flutelike stopped metal diapason organ pipe

GEDDIT *interj* exclamation meaning *do you understand it?*

GEDECKT, -S *same as* ▸ **gedact**

GEDS ▸ **ged**

GEE, -D, -ING, -S *interj* mild exclamation of surprise, admiration, etc ▷ *vb* move (an animal, esp a horse) ahead

GEEBUNG, -S *n* Australian tree or shrub

GEED ▸ **gee**

GEEGAW, -S *same as* ▸ **gewgaw**

GEEING ▸ **gee**

GEEK, -S *n* boring, unattractive person

GEEKDOM -S

GEEKED *adj* highly excited

GEEKERY *n* preoccupation with, or great knowledge about, a specialized subject

GEEKIER ▸ **geeky**

GEEKIEST ▸ **geeky**

GEEKISH *adj* of or like a geek

GEEKISM, -S *n* preoccupation with subjects generally considered unfashionable or boring

GEEKS ▸ **geek**

GEEKY, GEEKIER, GEEKIEST *adj* of or like a geek

GEELBEK, -S *n* edible marine fish

GEEP, -S *n* cross between a goat and a sheep

GEEPOUND *another name for* ▸ **slug**

GEEPS ▸ **geep**

GEES ▸ **gee**

G

G

GEESE ▸ goose

GEEST, -S n area of heathland in N Germany and adjacent areas

GEEZ interj expression of surprise

GEEZAH, -S variant spelling of ▸ geezer

GEEZER, -S n man

GEFILTE adj as in **gefilte fish** dish of fish stuffed with various ingredients

GEFUFFLE same as > kerfuffle

GEFULLTE adj as in **gefullte fish** dish of fish stuffed with various ingredients

GEGGIE, -S Scottish, esp Glaswegian, slang word for the ▸ mouth

GEISHA, -S n (in Japan) professional female companion for men

GEIST, -S n spirit

GEIT, -ED, -ING, -S n border on clothing ▷ vb put a border on (an article of clothing)

GEL, -LED, -LING, -S n jelly-like substance ▷ vb form a gel

GELABLE adj capable of forming a gel

GELADA, -S n NE African baboon

GELANDE adj as in **gelande jump** jump made in downhill skiing

GELANT, -S same as ▸ gellant

GELASTIC adj relating to laughter

GELATE, -D, -S, GELATING vb form a gel

GELATI, -S n layered dessert

GELATIN, -S same as ▸ gelatine

GELATINE n substance made by boiling animal bones

GELATING ▸ gelate

GELATINS ▸ gelatin

GELATION n act or process of freezing a liquid

GELATIS ▸ gelati

GELATO, -S n Italian frozen dessert, similar to ice cream

GELCAP, -S n medicine enclosed in gelatine

GELCOAT, -S n thin layer of gel or resin applied to the surface

GELD, -ED, -S vb emasculate; weaken ▷ n tax on land in Anglo-Saxon and Norman England

GELDER, -S

GELDING, -S ▸ geld

GELDS ▸ geld

GELEE, -S n jelly

GELID, -ER, -EST adj very cold, icy, or frosty

GELIDITY

GELIDLY

GELLANT, -S n compound that forms a solid structure

GELLED ▸ gel

GELLIES ▸ gelly

GELLING ▸ gel

GELLY, GELLIES same as > gelignite

GELOSY, GELOSIES Spenserian spelling of ▸ jealousy

GELS ▸ gel

GELSEMIA > gelsemium

GELT, -S n money

GEM, -MED, -MING, -S n precious stone or jewel ▷ vb set or ornament with gems

GEMATRIA n numerology of the Hebrew language and alphabet

GEMCLIP, -S n paperclip

GEMEL, -S n in heraldry, parallel bars

GEMFISH n Australian food fish with a delicate flavour

GEMINAL adj occurring in pairs

GEMINATE adj combined in pairs ▷ vb arrange or be arranged in pairs

GEMINI n expression of surprise

GEMINIES ▸ geminy

GEMINOUS adj in pairs

GEMINY, GEMINIES n pair

GEMLIKE ▸ gem

GEMMA, -E n reproductive structure in liverworts, mosses, etc

GEMMAN, GEMMEN dialect form of > gentleman

GEMMATE, -D, -S adj (of some plants and animals) having gemmae ▷ vb produce or reproduce by gemmae

GEMMED ▸ gem

GEMMEN ▸ gemman

GEMMEOUS adj gem-like

GEMMERY n gems collectively

GEMMIER ▸ gemmy

GEMMIEST ▸ gemmy

GEMMILY ▸ gemmy

GEMMING ▸ gem

GEMMULE, -S n result of asexual reproduction by sponges

GEMMY, GEMMIER, GEMMIEST ▸ gem

GEMOLOGY n branch of mineralogy that is concerned with gems and gemstones

GEMONY same as ▸ jiminy

GEMOT, -S n (in Anglo-Saxon England) a legal or administrative assembly

GEMOTE, -S same as ▸ gemot

GEMOTS ▸ gemot

GEMS ▸ gem

GEMSBOK, -S same as ▸ oryx

GEMSBUCK same as ▸ oryx

GEMSHORN n type of medieval flute

GEMSTONE n precious or semiprecious stone, esp one which has been cut and polished

GEN, -NED, -NING n information ▷ vb gain information

GENA, -S n cheek

GENAL

GENAPPE, -S n smooth worsted yarn used for braid, etc

GENAS ▸ gena

GENDARME n member of the French police force

GENDER, -ED, -S n state of being male or female ▷ vb assign a gender to

GENE, -S n part of a cell

GENERA ▸ genus

GENERAL, -S adj common or widespread ▷ n very senior army officer ▷ vb act as a general

GENERALE singular form of > generalia

GENERALS ▸ general

GENERANT n something that generates

GENERATE vb produce or bring into being

GENERIC, -S adj of a class, group, or genus ▷ n drug, food product, etc that does not have a trademark

GENEROUS adj free in giving

GENES ▸ gene

GENESIS, GENESES n beginning or origin

GENET, -S n type of agile catlike mammal

GENETIC adj of genes or genetics

GENETICS n study of heredity and variation in organisms

GENETRIX n female progenitor

GENETS ▸ genet

GENETTE, -S same as ▸ genet

GENEVA, -S n gin

GENIAL adj cheerful and friendly

GENIALLY

GENIC adj of or relating to a gene or genes

GENIE, -S n (in fairy tales) magical wish-granting servant

GENII ▸ genius

GENIP, -S same as ▸ **genipap**

GENIPAP, -S n evergreen Caribbean tree

GENIPAPO n tropical American tree

GENIPAPS ▸ genipap

GENIPS ▸ genip

GENISTA, -S n any member of the broom family

GENITAL adj of the reproductive organs

GENITALS pl n external reproductive organs

GENITIVE n grammatical case indicating possession ▷ adj denoting such a grammatical case

GENITOR, -S n biological father

GENITRIX same as ▸ **genetrix**

GENITURE n birth

GENIUS, GENII, -ES n (person with) an exceptional ability

GENIZAH, -S, GENIZOT, GENIZOTH n repository for sacred objects which may not be destroyed

GENLOCK, -S n generator locking device ▷ vb activate a genlock

GENNAKER n type of sail for boats

GENNED ▸ gen

GENNEL, -S same as ▸ **ginnel**

GENNET, -S n female donkey or ass

GENNIES ▸ genny

GENNING ▸ gen

GENNY, GENNIES same as ▸ **genoa**

GENOA, -S n large triangular jib sail

GENOCIDE n murder of a race of people

GENOGRAM n expanded family tree

GENOISE, -S n rich sponge cake

GENOM, -S same as ▸ **genome**

GENOME, -S n all genetic material within an organism

GENOMIC

GENOMICS n branch of molecular genetics concerned with the study of genomes

GENOMS ▸ genom

GENOTYPE n genetic constitution of an organism

GENRE, -S n style of literary, musical, or artistic work

GENRO, -S n group of Japanese statesmen

GENS, GENTES n (in ancient Rome) a group of aristocratic families

GENSENG, -S same as ▸ **ginseng**

GENT n gentleman

GENTEEL adj affectedly proper and polite

GENTES ▸ gens

GENTIAN, -S n mountain plant with deep blue flowers

GENTIER ▸ genty

GENTIEST ▸ genty

GENTIL adj gentle

GENTILE, -S n non-Jewish person ▷ adj used to designate a place or the inhabitants of a place

GENTILIC adj tribal

GENTLE, -D, -R, -S, -ST, GENTLING adj mild or kindly ▷ vb tame or subdue (a horse) ▷ n maggot, esp when used as bait in fishing

GENTLY

GENTOO, -S n grey-backed penguin

GENTRICE n high birth

GENTRIES ▸ gentry

GENTRIFY vb cause a neighbourhood to appeal to the middle classes

GENTRY, GENTRIES n term for people just below the nobility in social rank

GENTS n men's public toilet

GENTY, GENTIER, GENTIEST adj neat

GENU, -A n any knee-like bend in a structure or part

GENUINE adj not fake, authentic

GENUS, GENERA, -ES n group of animals or plants

GEO, -S n (esp in Shetland) a small fjord or gully

GEOCACHE vb search for hidden containers using GPS as a recreational activity

GEOCARPY n ripening of fruits below ground, as occurs in the peanut

GEOCODE, -D, -S vb assign geographical coordinates to a physical location using a digital code

GEODATA n information about geographical location held in a digital format

GEODE, -S n cavity within a rock mass or nodule

GEODESIC adj of the geometry of curved surfaces ▷ n shortest line between two points on a curve

GEODESY n study of the shape and size of the earth

GEODETIC same as ▸ **geodesic**

GEODIC ▸ geode

GEODUCK, -S n king clam

GEOFACT, -S n rock shaped by natural forces

GEOGENY same as ▸ **geogony**

GEOGNOST ▸ geognosy

GEOGNOSY n early form of geology

GEOGONIC ▸ geogony

GEOGONY n science of the earth's formation

GEOID, -S n hypothetical surface

GEOIDAL

GEOLATRY n worship of the earth

GEOLOGER ▸ geology

GEOLOGIC ▸ geology

GEOLOGY n study of the earth

GEOMANCY n prophecy made from casting down a handful of earth

GEOMANT, -S n geomancer

GEOMETER n person who is practised in or who studies geometry

GEOMETRY n branch of mathematics dealing with points, lines, curves, and surfaces

GEOMYOID adj relating to burrowing rodents of the genus Geomys

GEOPHAGY n practice of eating earth, clay, chalk, etc, found in some primitive tribes

GEOPHONE n device for recording seismic movement

GEOPHYTE n perennial plant that propagates by means of buds below the soil surface

GEOPONIC adj of or relating to agriculture, esp as a science

GEOPROBE n probing device used for sampling soil

GEORGIC, -S adj agricultural ▷ n poem about rural or agricultural life

GEOS ▸ geo

GEOTAG, -S n geographical co-ordinates digitally applied to data ▷ vb apply a geotag to data

GEOTAXIS, GEOTAXES n movement of an organism

G

G

in response to the stimulus of gravity

GEOTHERM n line or surface within or on the earth connecting points of equal temperature

GER, -S n portable Mongolian dwelling

GERAH, -S n ancient Hebrew unit of weight

GERANIAL n cis- isomer of citral

GERANIOL n type of alcohol with an odour of roses

GERANIUM n cultivated plant with red, pink, or white flowers

GERARDIA n any plant of the genus Gerardia

GERBE, -S same as ► garbe

GERBERA, -S n type of plant

GERBES ► gerbe

GERBIL, -S n burrowing desert rodent of Asia and Africa

GERBILLE same as ► gerbil

GERBILS ► gerbil

GERE, -S Spenserian spelling of ► gear

GERENT, -S n person who rules or manages

GERENUK, -S n slender antelope

GERES ► gere

GERLE, -S Spenserian spelling of ► girl

GERM, -ED, -ING, -S n microbe, esp one causing disease ▷ vb sprout

GERMAIN, -S same as ► germen

GERMAINE same as ► germen

GERMAINS ► germain

GERMAN, -S n type of dance ▷ adj having the same parents as oneself

GERMANE adj relevant

GERMANIC adj of or containing germanium in the tetravalent state

GERMANS ► german

GERMED ► germ

GERMEN, -S, **GERMINA** n cells that gives rise to the germ cells

GERMFREE ► germ

GERMIER ► germy

GERMIEST ► germy

GERMIN, -S same as ► germen

GERMINA ► germen

GERMINAL adj of or in the earliest stage of development

GERMING ► germ

GERMINS ► germin

GERMLIKE ► germ

GERMS ► germ

GERMY, **GERMIER**, **GERMIEST** adj full of germs

GERNE, -D, -S, **GERNING** vb grin

GERONIMO interj shout given by US paratroopers as they jump into battle

GERONTIC adj of or relating to the senescence of an organism

GEROPIGA n grape syrup used to sweeten inferior port wines

GERS ► ger

GERT adv in dialect, great or very big

GERTCHA interj get out of here!

GERUND, -S n noun formed from a verb

GESNERIA n S American plant grown for its brightl flowers

GESSE, -D, -S, **GESSING** Spenserian spelling of ► guess

GESSO, -ES n plaster used for painting or in sculpture ▷ vb apply gesso to

GESSOED

GEST, -S n notable deed or exploit

GESTALT, -S n perceptual pattern or structure

GESTANT adj laden

GESTAPO, -S n any secret state police organization

GESTATE, -D, -S vb carry (young) in the uterus during pregnancy

GESTE, -S same as ► gest

GESTIC adj consisting of gestures

GESTICAL

GESTS ► gest

GESTURAL ► gesture

GESTURE, -D, -S n movement to convey meaning ▷ vb gesticulate

GESTURER

GET, -S, **GOT** vb obtain or receive

GETA, -S n type of Japanese wooden sandal

GETABLE ► get

GETAS ► geta

GETAWAY, -S n used in escape

GETOUT, -S n excuse to get out of doing something

GETS ► get

GETTABLE ► get

GETTER, -ED, -S n person or thing that gets ▷ vb remove (a gas) by the action of a getter

GETTING, -S ► get

GETUP, -S n outfit

GEUM, -S n type of herbaceous plant

GEWGAW, -S n showy but valueless trinket ▷ adj showy and valueless

GEWGAWED adj decorated gaudily

GEWGAWS ► gewgaw

GEY, -ER, -EST adv extremely ▷ adj gallant

GEYAN adv somewhat

GEYER ► gey

GEYEST ► gey

GEYSER, -ED, -S n spring that discharges steam and hot water ▷ vb erupt like a geyser

GHARIAL, -S same as ► gavial

GHARRI, -S same as. ► gharry

GHARRIES ► gharry

GHARRIS ► gharri

GHARRY, **GHARRIES** n (in India) horse-drawn vehicle

GHAST, -ED, -ING, -S vb terrify

GHASTFUL adj dismal

GHASTING ► ghast

GHASTLY adj unpleasant ▷ adv unhealthily

GHASTS ► ghast

GHAT, -S n (in India) steps leading down to a river

GHAUT, -S n small cleft in a hill

GHAZAL, -S n Arabic love poem

GHAZEL, -S same as ► ghazal

GHAZI, -ES, -S n Muslim fighter against infidels

GHEE, -S n (in Indian cookery) clarified butter

GHERAO, -ED, -ES, -S n form of industrial action in India ▷ vb trap an employer in his or her office, to indicate the workforce's discontent

GHERKIN, -S n small pickled cucumber

GHESSE, -D, -S, **GHESSING**, **GHEST** Spenserian spelling of ► guess

GHETTO, -ED, -ES, -S n slum area inhabited by a deprived minority ▷ vb ghettoize

GHI, -S same as ► ghee

GHIBLI, -S n fiercely hot wind of North Africa

GHILGAI, -S same as ► gilgai

GHILLIE, -D, -S n type of tongueless shoe ▷ vb act as a g(h)illie

GHIS ► ghi

GHOST, -ED, -ING, -S n disembodied spirit of a dead person ▷ vb ghostwrite

GHOSTIER ▸ ghosty
GHOSTING ▸ ghost
GHOSTLY adj frightening in appearance or effect
GHOSTS ▸ ghost
GHOSTY, GHOSTIER adj pertaining to ghosts
GHOUL, -S n person with morbid interests
GHOULIE, -S n goblin
GHOULISH adj of or relating to ghouls
GHOULS ▸ ghoul
GHRELIN, -S n hormone that stimulates appetite
GHUBAR adj as in **ghubar numeral** type of numeral
GHYLL, -S same as ▸ **gill**
GI, -S n white suit worn in martial arts
GIAMBEUX n jambeaux; leg armour
GIANT, -S n mythical being of superhuman size ▷ adj huge
GIANTESS same as ▸ **giant**
GIANTISM same as > **gigantism**
GIANTLY adj giantlike
GIANTRY n collective term for giants
GIANTS ▸ giant
GIARDIA, -S n species of parasite
GIB, -BED, -BING, -S n metal wedge, pad, or thrust bearing ▷ vb fasten or supply with a gib
GIBBER, -ED, -S vb speak or utter rapidly and unintelligibly ▷ n boulder
GIBBET, -ED, -S n gallows for displaying executed criminals ▷ vb put to death by hanging on a gibbet
GIBBING ▸ gib
GIBBON, -S n agile tree-dwelling ape of S Asia
GIBBOSE same as ▸ **gibbous**
GIBBOUS adj (of the moon) between half and fully illuminated
GIBBSITE n mineral consisting of hydrated aluminium oxide
GIBE, -D, -S, GIBING vb make jeering or scoffing remarks (at) ▷ n derisive or provoking remark
GIBEL, -S n Prussian carp
GIBER, -S ▸ gibe
GIBES ▸ gibe
GIBING ▸ gibe
GIBINGLY ▸ gibe
GIBLET ▸ giblets
GIBLETS pl n gizzard, liver, heart, and neck of a fowl
GIBLI, -S same as ▸ **ghibli**

GIBS ▸ gib
GIBSON, -S n martini garnished with onion
GIBUS, -ES n collapsible top hat
GID, -S n disease of sheep
GIDDAP interj exclamation used to make a horse go faster
GIDDAY interj expression of greeting
GIDDIED ▸ giddy
GIDDIER ▸ giddy
GIDDIES ▸ giddy
GIDDIEST ▸ giddy
GIDDILY ▸ giddy
GIDDUP same as ▸ **giddyup**
GIDDYING ▸ giddy
GIDDY, GIDDIED, GIDDIER, GIDDIES, GIDDIEST, -ING adj having or causing a feeling of dizziness ▷ vb make giddy
GIDDYAP same as ▸ **giddyup**
GIDDYUP interj exclamation used to make a horse go faster
GIDGEE, -S n small acacia tree
GIDJEE, -S same as ▸ **gidgee**
GIDS ▸ gid
GIE, -D, -ING, -N, -S Scot word for ▸ **give**
GIF, -S n file held in GIF format
GIFT, -S n present ▷ vb make a present of
GIFTABLE adj suitable as gift ▷ n something suitable as gift
GIFTED adj talented
GIFTEDLY
GIFTEE, -S n person given a gift
GIFTING, -S n act of gifting
GIFTLESS ▸ gift
GIFTS ▸ gift
GIFTSHOP n shop selling articles suitable for gifts
GIFTWARE n anything that may be given as a present
GIFTWRAP vb wrap (a gift) in decorative wrapping paper
GIG, -GED, -GING, -S n single performance by pop or jazz musicians ▷ vb play a gig or gigs
GIGA, -S, GIGHE same as ▸ **gigue**
GIGABIT, -S n unit of information in computing
GIGABYTE n one thousand and twenty-four megabytes
GIGAFLOP n measure of computer processing speed
GIGANTIC adj enormous
GIGAS ▸ giga
GIGATON, -S n unit of explosive force

GIGAWATT n unit of power equal to 1 billion watts
GIGGED ▸ gig
GIGGING ▸ gig
GIGGIT, -ED, -S vb move quickly
GIGGLE, -D, -S vb laugh nervously or foolishly ▷ n such a laugh
GIGGLER -S
GIGGLIER ▸ giggly
GIGGLING ▸ giggle
GIGGLY, GIGGLIER ▸ giggle
GIGHE ▸ giga
GIGLET, -S n flighty girl
GIGLOT, -S same as ▸ **giglet**
GIGMAN, GIGMEN n one who places great importance on respectability
GIGOT, -S n leg of lamb or mutton
GIGS ▸ gig
GIGUE, -S n piece of music incorporated into the classical suite
GILA, -S n large venomous brightly coloured lizard
GILBERT, -S n unit of magnetomotive force
GILCUP, -S same as ▸ **giltcup**
GILD, -ED, -S vb put a thin layer of gold on
GILDEN adj gilded
GILDER, -S ▸ gild
GILDHALL same as > **guildhall**
GILDING, -S ▸ gild
GILDS ▸ gild
GILDSMAN, GILDSMEN ▸ gild
GILET, -S n waist- or hip-length garment
GILGAI, -S n natural water hole
GILGIE, -S n type of freshwater crayfish
GILL, -ING n radiating structure beneath the cap of a mushroom ▷ vb catch (fish) or (of fish) to be caught in a gill net
GILLAROO n type of brown trout
GILLED ▸ gill
GILLER, -S ▸ gill
GILLET, -S n mare
GILLIE, -D n (in Scotland) attendant for hunting or fishing ▷ vb act as a gillie
GILLIES ▸ gilly
GILLING ▸ gill
GILLION, -S n (no longer in technical use) one thousand million
GILLNET, -S n net designed to catch fish by the gills ▷ vb fish using a gillnet**

GILLS pl n breathing organs in fish and other water creatures

GILLY, GILLIES, -ING vb act as a gillie

GILLYVOR n type of carnation

GILPEY, -S n mischievous, frolicsome boy or girl

GILPY, GILPIES same as ▸ gilpey

GILT, -S n young sow

GILTCUP, -S n buttercup

GILTHEAD n type of fish

GILTS ▸ gilt

GILTWOOD adj made of wood and gilded

GIMBAL, -ED vb support on gimbals

GIMBALS pl n set of pivoted rings

GIMCRACK adj showy but cheap ▸ n cheap showy trifle or gadget

GIMEL, -S n third letter of the Hebrew alphabet

GIMLET, -ED, -S n small tool ▸ adj penetrating or piercing ▸ vb make holes in (wood) using a gimlet

GIMMAL, -S n ring composed of interlocking rings ▸ vb provide with gimmals

GIMME, -S interj give me! ▸ n term used in shot putt

GIMMER, -S n year-old ewe

GIMMES ▸ gimme

GIMMICK, -S n something designed to attract attention ▸ vb make gimmicky **GIMMICKY**

GIMMIE, -S n very short putt in golf

GIMMOR, -S n mechanical device

GIMP, -ED, -ING, -S n tapelike trimming of silk, wool, or cotton, often stiffened with wire ▸ vb slang term for limp

GIMPIER ▸ gimpy

GIMPIEST ▸ gimpy

GIMPING ▸ gimp

GIMPS ▸ gimp

GIMPY, GIMPIER, GIMPIEST same as ▸ gammy

GIN, -NED, -S n spirit flavoured with juniper berries ▸ vb free (cotton) of seeds with an engine

GINCH, -ES same as ▸ gitch

GING, -S n child's catapult

GINGAL, -S n type of musket mounted on a swivel

GINGALL, -S same as ▸ gingal

GINGALS ▸ gingal

GINGE, -S n person with ginger hair

GINGELEY same as ▸ gingili

GINGELI, -S same as ▸ gingili

GINGELLI same as ▸ gingili

GINGELLY same as ▸ gingili

GINGELY same as ▸ gingili

GINGER, -ED, -S n root of a tropical plant, used as a spice ▸ adj light reddish-brown ▸ vb add the spice ginger to (a dish)

GINGERLY adv cautiously ▸ adj cautious

GINGERS ▸ ginger

GINGERY adj like or tasting of ginger

GINGES ▸ ginge

GINGHAM, -S n cotton cloth, usu checked or striped

GINGILI, -S n oil obtained from sesame seeds

GINGILLI same as ▸ gingili

GINGIVA, -E same as ▸ gum **GINGIVAL**

GINKGO, -ES, -S same as ▸ ginkgo

GINGLE, -S same as ▸ jingle

GINGLYMI ▸ ginglymus

GINGS ▸ ging

GINHOUSE n building where cotton is ginned

GINK, -S n man or boy

GINKGO, -ES, -S n ornamental Chinese tree

GINKS ▸ gink

GINN same as ▸ jinn

GINNED ▸ gin

GINNEL, -S n narrow passageway between buildings

GINNER, -S ▸ gin

GINNERY another word for ▸ ginhouse

GINNIER ▸ ginny

GINNIEST ▸ ginny

GINNING, -S ▸ gin

GINNY, GINNIER, GINNIEST adj relating to the spirit gin

GINS ▸ gin

GINSENG, -S n (root of) a plant

GINSHOP, -S n tavern

GIO, -S same as ▸ geo

GIOCOSO adv (of music) to be expressed joyfully or playfully

GIOS ▸ gio

GIP, -PED, -PING, -S same as ▸ gyp

GIPON, -S another word for ▸ jupon

GIPPED ▸ gip

GIPPER, -S ▸ gip

GIPPIES ▸ gippy

GIPPING ▸ gip

GIPPY, GIPPIES n starling

GIPS ▸ gip

GIPSEN, -S obsolete word for ▸ gypsy

GIPSY, GIPSIED, GIPSIES, -ING n member of a nomadic people ▸ vb live like a gypsy **GIPSYDOM GIPSYISH**

GIPSYISM n gipsy custom

GIRAFFE, -S n African ruminant mammal

GIRAFFID adj giraffe-like ▸ n member of the Giraffidae family

GIRASOL, -S n type of opal

GIRASOLE same as ▸ girasol

GIRASOLS ▸ girasol

GIRD, -ED, -S vb put a belt round ▸ n blow or stroke

GIRDER, -S n large metal beam

GIRDING, -S ▸ gird

GIRDLE, -D, -S, GIRDLING n woman's elastic corset ▸ vb surround or encircle

GIRDLER, -S n person or thing that girdles

GIRDLES ▸ girdle

GIRDLING ▸ girdle

GIRDS ▸ gird

GIRKIN, -S same as ▸ gherkin

GIRL, -S n female child

GIRLHOOD n state or time of being a girl

GIRLIE, -S adj suited to young women ▸ n little girl

GIRLIER ▸ girly

GIRLIES ▸ girlie

GIRLIEST ▸ girly

GIRLISH adj of or like a girl in looks, behaviour, innocence, etc

GIRLOND, -S obsolete word for ▸ garland

GIRLS ▸ girl

GIRLY, GIRLIER, GIRLIEST same as ▸ girlie

GIRN, -ED, -ING, -S vb snarl

GIRNEL, -S n large chest for storing meal

GIRNER, -S ▸ girn

GIRNIE, -R, -ST adj peevish

GIRNING ▸ girn

GIRNS ▸ girn

GIRO, -S n system of transferring money

GIROLLE, -S n chanterelle mushroom

GIRON, -S n part of a heraldic shield **GIRONIC**

GIRONNY adj divided into segments from the fesse point

GIRONS ▸ giron

GIROS ▸ giro

GIROSOL, -S same as ▸ girasol

GIRR, -S same as ▸ gird

GIRSH, -ES n currency unit of Saudi Arabia

GIRT, -ED, -ING, -S vb gird; bind

GIRTH, -ED, -ING, -S n measurement round something ▷ vb fasten a girth on (a horse)

GIRTING ▸ girt

GIRTLINE n gantline

GIRTS ▸ girt

GIS ▸ gi

GISARME, -S n long-shafted battle-axe

GISMO, -S same as ▸ gizmo

GIST, -S n substance or main point of a matter

GIT, -S, -TED, -TING vb dialect version of get

GITANA, -S n female gypsy

GITANO, -S n male gypsy

GITCH, -ES n underwear

GITE, -S n self-catering holiday cottage for let in France

GITS ▸ git

GITTED ▸ git

GITTERN, -S n obsolete medieval instrument ▷ vb play the gittern

GITTIN n Jewish divorce

GITTING ▸ git

GIUST, -ED, -ING, -S same as ▸ joust

GIUSTO adv as observed strictly

GIUSTS ▸ giust

GIVABLE ▸ give

GIVE, GAVE, -S vb present (something) to another person ▷ n resilience or elasticity

GIVEABLE

GIVEAWAY n something that reveals hidden feelings or intentions ▷ adj very cheap or free

GIVEBACK n reduction in wages in return for some other benefit, in time of recession

GIVED same as ▸ gyved

GIVEN, -S n assumed fact

GIVER, -S ▸ give

GIVES ▸ give

GIVING, -S ▸ give

GIZMO, -S n device

GIZZ, -ES n wig

GIZZARD, -S n part of a bird's stomach

GIZZEN, -ED, -S vb (of wood) to warp

GIZZES ▸ gizz

GJETOST, -S n type of Norwegian cheese

GJU, -S n type of violin used in Shetland

This unusual word for a Shetland fiddle is great for disposing of awkward letters for a good score.

GLABELLA n elevation of the frontal bone above the nose

GLABRATE same as ▸ glabrous

GLABROUS adj without hair or a similar growth

GLACE, -D, -ED, -ING, -S adj preserved in a thick sugary syrup ▷ vb ice or candy (cakes, fruits, etc)

GLACIAL, -S adj of ice or glaciers ▷ n ice age

GLACIATE vb cover or become covered with glaciers or masses of ice

GLACIER, -S n slow-moving mass of ice

GLACIS, -ES n slight incline

GLAD, -DED, -DER, -DEST, -DING, -S adj pleased and happy ▷ vb become glad ▷ n gladiolus

GLADDEN, -S vb make glad

GLADDER ▸ glad

GLADDEST ▸ glad

GLADDIE, -S n gladiolus

GLADDING ▸ glad

GLADDON, -S n stinking iris

GLADE, -S n open space in a forest

GLADFUL adj full of gladness

GLADIATE adj shaped like a sword

GLADIER ▸ glady

GLADIEST ▸ glady

GLADIOLA same as > gladiolus

GLADIOLE same as > gladiolus

GLADIOLI > gladiolus

GLADIUS n short sword used by Roman legionaries

GLADLY, GLADLIER ▸ glad

GLADNESS ▸ glad

GLADS ▸ glad

GLADSOME adj joyous or cheerful

GLADWRAP n in New Zealand English, thin film for wrapping food ▷ vb cover with gladwrap

GLADY, GLADIER, GLADIEST ▸ glade

GLAIK, -S n prank

GLAIKET same as ▸ glaikit

GLAIKIT adj foolish

GLAIKS ▸ glaik

GLAIR, -ED, -ING, -S n white of egg ▷ vb apply glair to (something)

GLAIRE, -S same as ▸ glair

GLAIRED ▸ glair

GLAIRES ▸ glaire

GLAIRIER ▸ glairy

GLAIRIN, -S n viscous mineral deposit

GLAIRING ▸ glair

GLAIRINS ▸ glairin

GLAIRS ▸ glair

GLAIRY, GLAIRIER ▸ glair

GLAIVE, -S archaic word for ▸ sword

GLAIVED adj armed with a sword

GLAIVES ▸ glaive

GLAM, -MED, -MER, -MEST, -MING, -S n magical illusion ▷ vb make oneself look glamorous ▷ adj glamorous

GLAMMER ▸ glammy

GLAMMING ▸ glam

GLAMMY, GLAMMIER adj glamorous

GLAMOR, -ED, -S same as ▸ glamour

GLAMOUR, -S n alluring charm or fascination ▷ vb bewitch

GLAMPING n camping with luxurious physical comforts

GLAMS ▸ glam

GLANCE, -D, -S, GLANCING vb look rapidly or briefly ▷ n brief look

GLANCER, -S n log or pole used to protect trees from damage

GLANCES ▸ glance

GLANCING ▸ glance

GLAND, -S n organ that produces and secretes substances

GLANDERS n highly infectious bacterial disease of horses, sometimes transmitted to man

GLANDES ▸ glans

GLANDS ▸ gland

GLANDULE n small gland

GLANS, GLANDES n any small rounded body or glandlike mass

GLARE, -D, -S vb stare angrily ▷ n angry stare ▷ adj smooth and glassy

GLAREAL adj (of a plant) growing in cultivated land

GLARED ▸ glare

GLAREOUS adj resembling the white of an egg

GLARES ▸ glare

GLARIER ▸ glary

GLARIEST ▸ glary

GLARING adj conspicuous

GLARY, GLARIER, GLARIEST ▸ glare

GLAIRES ▸ glaire

GLAIRIER ▸ glairy

GLAIRIN, -S n viscous mineral deposit

GLAIRING ▸ glair

GLAIRINS ▸ glairin

GLAIRS ▸ glair

GLAIRY, GLAIRIER ▸ glair

G

GLASNOST n policy of openness and accountability, esp, formerly, in the USSR

GLASS, -ED, -ING n hard brittle substance ▷ vb cover with, enclose in, or fit with glass

GLASSEN adj glassy

GLASSES pl n pair of lenses for correcting faulty vision

GLASSFUL n amount held by a full glass

GLASSIE same as ▸ **glassy**

GLASSIER ▸ **glassy**

GLASSIES ▸ **glassy**

GLASSIFY vb turn into glass

GLASSILY ▸ **glassy**

GLASSINE n glazed translucent paper used for book jackets

GLASSING ▸ **glass**

GLASSMAN, GLASSMEN n man whose work is making or selling glassware

GLASSY, GLASSIER, GLASSIES adj like glass ▷ n glass marble

GLAUCOMA n eye disease

GLAUCOUS adj covered with a bluish waxy or powdery bloom

GLAUM, -ED, -ING, -S vb snatch

GLAUR, -S n mud or mire

GLAURIER ▸ **glaury**

GLAURS ▸ **glaur**

GLAURY, GLAURIER ▸ **glaur**

GLAZE, -D, -S vb fit or cover with glass ▷ n transparent coating

GLAZEN adj glazed

GLAZER, -S ▸ **glaze**

GLAZES ▸ **glaze**

GLAZIER, -S n person who fits windows with glass

GLAZIERY

GLAZIEST ▸ **glazy**

GLAZILY ▸ **glaze**

GLAZING, -S n surface of a glazed object

GLAZY, GLAZIEST ▸ **glaze**

GLEAM, -ED, -S n small beam or glow of light ▷ vb emit a gleam

GLEAMER, -S n mirror used to cheat in card games

GLEAMIER ▸ **gleamy**

GLEAMING ▸ **gleam**

GLEAMS ▸ **gleam**

GLEAMY, GLEAMIER ▸ **gleam**

GLEAN, -ED, -ING, -S vb gather (facts etc) bit by bit

GLEANER -S

GLEAVE, -S same as ▸ **sword**

GLEBA, -E n mass of spores

GLEBE, -S n land granted to a member of the clergy

GLEBIER ▸ **gleby**

GLEBIEST ▸ **gleby**

GLEBOUS adj gleby

GLEBY, GLEBIER, GLEBIEST adj relating to a glebe

GLED, -S n kite

GLEDE, -S same as ▸ **gled**

GLEDGE, -D, -S, GLEDGING vb glance sideways

GLEDS ▸ **gled**

GLEE, -ING, -S n triumph and delight ▷ vb be full of glee

GLEED, -S n burning ember or hot coal

GLEEFUL adj merry or joyful

GLEEING ▸ **glee**

GLEEK, -ED, -ING, -S vb jeer

GLEEMAN, GLEEMEN n minstrel

GLEENIE -S n guinea fowl

GLEES ▸ **glee**

GLEESOME adj full of glee

GLEG, -GER, -GEST adj quick

GLEGLY

GLEGNESS

GLEI, -S same as ▸ **gley**

GLEN, -S n deep narrow valley, esp in Scotland

GLENLIKE

GLENOID, -S adj resembling or having a shallow cavity ▷ n shallow cavity

GLENS ▸ **glen**

GLENT, -ED, -ING, -S same as ▸ **glint**

GLEY, -ED, -S n bluish-grey compact sticky soil ▷ vb squint

GLEYING -S

GLIA, -S n web of tissue that supports nerve cells

GLIADIN, -S n protein of cereals with a high proline content

GLIADINE same as ▸ **gliadin**

GLIADINS ▸ **gliadin**

GLIAL ▸ **glia**

GLIAS ▸ **glia**

GLIB, -BED, -BER, -BEST, -BING, -S adj fluent but insincere or superficial ▷ vb render glib, smooth, or slippery

GLIBBERY adj slippery

GLIBBEST ▸ **glib**

GLIBBING ▸ **glib**

GLIBLY ▸ **glib**

GLIBNESS ▸ **glib**

GLIBS ▸ **glib**

GLID, -DER, -DEST adj moving smoothly and easily

GLIDDERY adj slippery

GLIDDEST ▸ **glid**

GLIDE, -D, -S, GLODE vb move easily and smoothly ▷ n smooth easy movement

GLIDER, -S n flying phalanger

GLIDES ▸ **glide**

GLIDING, -S n sport of flying gliders

GLIFF, -ING, -S n slap

GLIFT, -S n moment

GLIKE, -S same as ▸ **gleek**

GLIM, -S n light or lamp

GLIME, -D, -S, GLIMING vb glance sideways

GLIMMER, -S vb shine faintly, flicker ▷ n faint gleam

GLIMMERY

GLIMPSE, -D, -S n brief or incomplete view ▷ vb catch a glimpse of

GLIMPSER

GLIMS ▸ **glim**

GLINT, -ED, -ING, -S vb gleam brightly ▷ n bright gleam

GLINTIER ▸ **glinty**

GLINTING ▸ **glint**

GLINTS ▸ **glint**

GLINTY, GLINTIER ▸ **glint**

GLIOMA, -S, -TA n tumour of the brain and spinal cord

GLIOSIS, GLIOSES n process leading to scarring in the nervous system

GLISK, -S n glimpse

GLISSADE n gliding step in ballet ▷ vb perform a glissade

GLISSE, -S n type of dance step

GLISTEN, -S vb gleam by reflecting light ▷ n gleam or gloss

GLISTER, -S archaic word for ▸ **glitter**

GLIT, -S n slimy matter

GLITCH, -ES n small problem that stops something from working

GLITCHY

GLITS ▸ **glit**

GLITTER, -S vb shine with bright flashes ▷ n sparkle or brilliance

GLITTERY

GLITZ, -ED, -ES, -ING n ostentatious showiness ▷ vb make something more attractive

GLITZIER ▸ **glitzy**

GLITZILY ▸ **glitzy**

GLITZING ▸ **glitz**

GLITZY, GLITZIER adj showily attractive

GLOAM, -S n dusk

GLOAMING n twilight

GLOAMS ▸ **gloam**

GLOAT, -ED, -S vb regard one's own good fortune with pleasure ▷ n act of gloating

GLOATER -S

GLOATING n act of gloating

GLOATS ▸ gloat

GLOB, -S n rounded mass of thick fluid

GLOBAL adj worldwide

GLOBALLY

GLOBATE adj shaped like a globe

GLOBATED same as ▸ **globate**

GLOBBY, GLOBBIER adj thick and lumpy

GLOBE, -D, -S, GLOBING n sphere with a map of the earth on it ▷ vb form or cause to form into a globe

GLOBI ▸ globus

GLOBIER ▸ globy

GLOBIEST ▸ globy

GLOBIN, -S n protein component

GLOBING ▸ globe

GLOBINS ▸ globin

GLOBOID, -S adj shaped approximately like a globe ▷ n globoid body

GLOBOSE adj spherical or approximately spherical ▷ n globose object

GLOBOUS same as ▸ **globose**

GLOBS ▸ glob

GLOBULAR adj shaped like a globe or globule ▷ n globular star cluster

GLOBULE, -S n small round drop

GLOBULET n small globule

GLOBULIN n simple protein found in living tissue

GLOBUS, GLOBI n any spherelike structure

GLOBY, GLOBIER, GLOBIEST adj round

GLOCHID, -S n barbed spine on a plant

GLODE ▸ glide

GLOGG, -S n hot alcoholic mixed drink

GLOIRE, -S n glory

GLOM, -MED, -MING, -S vb attach oneself to or associate oneself with

GLOMERA ▸ glomus

GLOMMED ▸ glom

GLOMMING ▸ glom

GLOMS ▸ glom

GLOMUS, GLOMERA n small anastomosis in an artery or vein

GLONOIN, -S n nitroglycerin

GLOOM, -ED, -ING, -S n melancholy or depression ▷ vb look sullen or depressed

GLOOMFUL

GLOOMIER ▸ gloomy

GLOOMILY ▸ gloomy

GLOOMING ▸ gloom

GLOOMS ▸ gloom

GLOOMY, GLOOMIER adj despairing or sad

GLOOP, -ED, -ING, -S vb cover with a viscous substance

GLOOPIER ▸ gloopy

GLOOPING ▸ gloop

GLOOPS ▸ gloop

GLOOPY, GLOOPIER ▸ gloop

GLOP, -PED, -PING, -S vb cover with a viscous substance

GLOPPIER ▸ gloppy

GLOPPING ▸ glop

GLOPPY, GLOPPIER ▸ glop

GLOPS ▸ glop

GLORIA, -S n silk, wool, cotton, or nylon fabric

GLORIED ▸ glory

GLORIES ▸ glory

GLORIFY vb make (something) seem more worthy than it is

GLORIOLE another name for a ▸ **halo**

GLORIOSA n bulbous African tropical plant

GLORIOUS adj brilliantly beautiful

GLORY, GLORIED, GLORIES, -ING n praise or honour ▷ vb triumph or exalt

GLOSS, -ED, -ES, -ING n surface shine or lustre ▷ vb make glossy

GLOSSA, -E, -S n paired tonguelike lobe in the labium of an insect

GLOSSAL

GLOSSARY n list of special or technical words with definitions

GLOSSAS ▸ glossa

GLOSSED ▸ gloss

GLOSSEME n smallest meaningful unit of a language, such as stress, form, etc

GLOSSER, -S ▸ gloss

GLOSSES ▸ gloss

GLOSSIER ▸ glossy

GLOSSIES ▸ glossy

GLOSSILY ▸ glossy

GLOSSINA n tsetse fly

GLOSSING ▸ gloss

GLOSSIST same as > **glossator**

GLOSSY, GLOSSIER, GLOSSIES adj smooth and shiny ▷ n expensively produced magazine

GLOST, -S n lead glaze used for pottery

GLOTTAL adj of the glottis

GLOTTIC adj of or relating to the tongue or the glottis

GLOTTIS n vocal cords and the space between them

GLOUT, -ED, -ING, -S vb look sullen

GLOVE, -S n covering for the hand

GLOVEBOX n small compartment in a car for miscellaneous articles

GLOVED ▸ glove

GLOVER, -S n person who makes or sells gloves

GLOVES ▸ glove

GLOVING, -S ▸ glove

GLOW, -ED, -S vb emit light and heat without flames ▷ n glowing light

GLOWER, -ED, -S n scowl ▷ vb stare angrily

GLOWFLY n firefly

GLOWING adj full of praise

GLOWLAMP n small light consisting of two or more electrodes in an inert gas

GLOWS ▸ glow

GLOWWORM n European beetle which produces a greenish light

GLOXINIA n tropical plant with large bell-shaped flowers

GLOZE, -D, -S vb explain away ▷ n flattery or deceit

GLOZING -S

GLUCAGON n hormone that releases glucose into the blood

GLUCAN, -S n any polysaccharide consisting of a polymer of glucose

GLUCINA, -S n oxide of glucinum

GLUCINIC > glucinium

GLUCINUM same as > **glucinium**

GLUCONIC adj as in **gluconic acid** acid that occurs naturally in fruit

GLUCOSE, -S n kind of sugar found in fruit

GLUCOSIC

GLUE, -D, -ING, -S, GLUING n natural or synthetic sticky substance ▷ vb fasten with glue

GLUEBALL n hypothetical composite subatomic particle

GLUED ▸ glue

GLUEING ▸ glue

GLUEISH same as ▸ **gluish**

GLUELIKE ▸ glue

GLUEPOT, -S n container for holding glue

GLUER, -S ▸ glue

GLUES ▸ glue

G

GLUEY, GLUIER, GLUIEST
► glue
GLUG, -GED, -GING, -S n word
representing a gurgling
sound ▷ vb drink noisily,
taking big gulps
GLUHWEIN n mulled wine
GLUIER ► gluey
GLUIEST ► gluey
GLUILY ► glue
GLUINESS ► glue
GLUING ► glue
GLUISH adj having the
properties of glue
GLUM, -MER, -MEST adj
sullen or gloomy
GLUME, -S n one of a pair of
dry membranous bracts in
grasses
GLUMELLA n palea
GLUMES ► glume
GLUMLY ► glum
GLUMMER ► glum
GLUMMEST ► glum
GLUMNESS ► glum
GLUMPIER ► glumpy
GLUMPILY ► glumpy
GLUMPISH ► glumpy
GLUMPS n state of sulking
GLUMPY, GLUMPIER adj
sullen
GLUMS n gloomy feelings
GLUNCH, -ED, -ES vb look
sullen
GLUON, -S n hypothetical
particle
GLURGE, -S n stories
supposed to be true but often
fabricated
GLUT, -S, -TED, -TING n
excessive supply ▷ vb
oversupply
GLUTAEAL ► glutaeus
GLUTAEUS, GLUTAEI same as
► gluteus
GLUTAMIC adj as in **glutamic
acid** nonessential amino acid
that plays a part in nitrogen
metabolism
GLUTCH, -ED, -ES vb swallow
GLUTE, -S same as ► gluteus
GLUTEAL ► gluteus
GLUTEI ► gluteus
GLUTELIN n water-insoluble
plant protein found in cereals
GLUTEN, -S n protein found in
cereal grain
GLUTENIN n type of protein
GLUTENS ► gluten
GLUTES ► glute
GLUTEUS, GLUTEI n any of the
three muscles of the buttock
GLUTS ► glut
GLUTTED ► glut
GLUTTING ► glut
GLUTTON, -S n greedy person

GLUTTONY n practice of
eating too much
GLYCAN, -S n polysaccharide
GLYCEMIA US spelling of
> glycaemia
GLYCEMIC
GLYCERIA n manna grass
GLYCERIC adj of, containing,
or derived from glycerol
GLYCERIN same as
► glycerol
GLYCEROL n colourless
odourless syrupy liquid
GLYCERYL n (something)
derived from glycerol
GLYCIN, -S same as ► glycine
GLYCINE, -S n nonessential
amino acid
GLYCINS ► glycin
GLYCOGEN n starchlike
carbohydrate stored in the
liver and muscles of humans
and animals
GLYCOL, -S n another name
(not in technical usage) for
a diol
GLYCOLIC
GLYCONIC n verse consisting
of a spondee, choriamb and
pyrrhic
GLYCOSE, -S n any of various
monosaccharides
GLYCOSYL n glucose-derived
radical
GLYCYL, -S n radical of glycine
GLYPH, -S n carved channel
or groove
GLYPHIC
GLYPTAL, -S n alkyd resin
GLYPTIC adj of or relating to
engraving or carving
GLYPTICS n art of engraving
precious stones
GNAMMA variant of
► namma
GNAR, -RED, -RING, -S same
as ► gnarl
GNARL, -ING, -S n any knotty
protuberance or swelling
on a tree ▷ vb knot or cause
to knot
GNARLED adj rough, twisted,
and knobbly
GNARLIER ► gnarly
GNARLING ► gnarl
GNARLS ► gnarl
GNARLY, GNARLIER adj good
GNARR, -S same as ► gnarl
GNARRED ► gnar
GNARRING ► gnar
GNARRS ► gnarr
GNARS ► gnar
GNASH, -ED, -ES, -ING vb
grind (the teeth) together
▷ n act of gnashing the
teeth

GNASHER n tooth
GNASHERS pl n teeth, esp
false ones
GNASHES ► gnash
GNASHING ► gnash
GNAT, -S n small biting two-
winged fly
GNATHAL same as ► gnathic
GNATHIC adj of or relating to
the jaw
GNATHION n lowest point
of the midline of the lower
jaw: a reference point in
craniometry
GNATHITE n appendage of an
arthropod that is specialized
for grasping or chewing
GNATLIKE ► gnat
GNATLING n small gnat
GNATS ► gnat
GNATTY, GNATTIER adj
infested with gnats
GNATWREN n small bird of
the gnatcatcher family
GNAW, -ED, -N, -S vb bite or
chew steadily ▷ n act or an
instance of gnawing
GNAWABLE
GNAWER -S
GNAWING, -S ► gnaw
GNAWN ► gnaw
GNAWS ► gnaw
GNEISS, -ES n coarse-grained
metamorphic rock
GNEISSIC
GNOCCHI n dumplings
GNOME, GNOMAE, -S n
imaginary creature like a
little old man
GNOMIC adj of pithy sayings
GNOMICAL same as
► gnomic
GNOMISH ► gnome
GNOMIST, -S n writer of pithy
sayings
GNOMON, -S n stationary
arm on a sundial
GNOMONIC
GNOSIS, GNOSES n
supposedly revealed
knowledge of spiritual
truths
GNOSTIC, -S adj of, relating to,
or possessing knowledge ▷ n
one who knows
GNOW, -S n Australian wild
bird
GNU, -S n ox-like S African
antelope
GO, GANE, GAUN, -ES, -NE, -S
vb move to or from a place
▷ n attempt
GOA, -S n Tibetan gazelle
GOAD, -ED, -ING, -S vb
provoke (someone) to
take some kind of action,

usu in anger ▷ *n* spur or provocation

GOADLIKE

GOADSMAN, GOADSMEN *n* person who uses a goad

GOADSTER *n* goadsman

GOAF, -S *n* waste left in old mine workings

GOAL, -ED, -ING, -S *n* posts through which the ball or puck has to move to score to ▷ *vb* in rugby, to convert a try into a goal

GOALBALL *n* game played with a ball that emits sound

GOALED ▸ **goal**

GOALIE, -S *n* goalkeeper

GOALING ▸ **goal**

GOALLESS ▸ **goal**

GOALPOST *n* one of the two posts marking the limit of a goal

GOALS ▸ **goal**

GOALWARD *adv* towards a goal

GOANNA, -S *n* large Australian lizard

GOARY *variant spelling of* ▸ **gory**

GOAS ▸ **goa**

GOAT, -S *n* sure-footed ruminant animal with horns

GOATEE, -S *n* pointed tuft-like beard

GOATEED

GOATFISH *n* red mullet

GOATHERD *n* person who looks after a herd of goats

GOATIER ▸ **goaty**

This means more like a goat: it may seem a silly sort of word but because it uses such common letters it has the chance to play it as a bonus comes up very frequently.

GOATIES ▸ **goaty**

GOATIEST ▸ **goaty**

GOATISH *adj* of, like, or relating to a goat

GOATLIKE ▸ **goat**

GOATLING *n* young goat

GOATS ▸ **goat**

GOATSE, -S *n* deliberately offensive image placed maliciously into a website

GOATSKIN *n* leather made from the skin of a goat

GOATWEED *n* plant of the genus Capraria

GOATY, GOATIER, GOATIES, GOATIEST *n* pointed tuft-like beard ▷ *adj* resembling a goat

GOB, -BED, -BING, -S *n* lump of a soft substance ▷ *vb* spit

GOBAN, -S *n* board on which go is played

GOBANG, -S *n* Japanese board-game

GOBANS ▸ **goban**

GOBAR *adj as in* **gobar numeral** kind of numeral

GOBBED ▸ **gob**

GOBBET, -S *n* lump, esp of food

GOBBI ▸ **gobbo**

GOBBIER ▸ **gobby**

GOBBIEST ▸ **gobby**

GOBBING ▸ **gob**

GOBBLE, -D, -S, GOBBLING *vb* eat hastily and greedily ▷ *n* rapid gurgling cry of the male turkey ▷ *interj* imitation of this sound

GOBBLER, -S *n* turkey

GOBBLES ▸ **gobble**

GOBBLING ▸ **gobble**

GOBBO, GOBBI *n* hunchback

GOBBY, GOBBIER, GOBBIEST *adj* loudmouthed and offensive

GOBI, -S *n* (in Indian cookery) cauliflower

GOBIES ▸ **goby**

GOBIID, -S *n* member of the genus Gobius

GOBIOID, -S *n* type of spiny-finned fish

GOBIS ▸ **gobi**

GOBLET, -S *n* drinking cup without handles

GOBLIN, -S *n* (in folklore) small malevolent creature

GOBO, -ES, -S *n* shield placed around a microphone

GOBONEE *same as* ▸ **gobony**

GOBONY *adj* in heraldry, composed of a row of small, alternately-coloured, squares

GOBOS ▸ **gobo**

GOBS ▸ **gob**

GOBURRA, -S *n* kookaburra

GOBY, GOBIES *n* small spiny-finned fish

GOD, -DED, -DING, -S *n* spirit or being worshipped as having supernatural power ▷ *vb* deify

GODCHILD *n* child for whom a person stands as godparent

GODDED ▸ **god**

GODDEN, -S *n* evening greeting

GODDESS *n* female divinity

GODDING ▸ **god**

GODET, -S *n* triangular piece of material inserted into a garment

GODETIA, -S *n* plant with showy flowers

GODETS ▸ **godet**

GODHEAD, -S *n* essential nature and condition of being a god

GODHOOD, -S *n* state of being divine

GODLESS *adj* wicked or unprincipled

GODLIER ▸ **godly**

GODLIEST ▸ **godly**

GODLIKE *adj* resembling or befitting a god or God

GODLILY ▸ **godly**

GODLING, -S *n* little god

GODLY, GODLIER, GODLIEST *adj* devout or pious

GODOWN, -S *n* (in East Asia and India) warehouse

GODROON, -S *same as* ▸ **gadroon**

GODS ▸ **god**

GODSEND, -S *n* something unexpected but welcome

GODSHIP, -S *n* divinity

GODSO *same as* ▸ **gadso**

GODSON, -S *n* male godchild

GODSPEED *n* expression of one's good wishes for a person's success and safety

GODWARD *adv* towards God

GODWARDS *same as* ▸ **godward**

GODWIT, -S *n* shore bird with long legs and an upturned bill

GOE *same as* ▸ **go**

GOEL, -S *n* in Jewish law, blood-avenger

GOER, -S *n* person who attends something regularly

GOES ▸ **go**

GOEST *vb* archaic 2nd person sing present of go

GOETH *vb* archaic 3rd person sing present of go

GOETHITE *n* black, brown, or yellow mineral

GOETIC ▸ **goety**

GOETY, GOETIES *n* witchcraft

GOEY, GOIER, GOIEST *adj* go-ahead

GOFER, -S *n* employee or assistant performing menial tasks

GOFF, -ED, -ING, -S *obsolete variant of* ▸ **golf**

GOFFER, -ED, -S *vb* press pleats into (a frill) ▷ *n* ornamental frill made by pressing pleats

GOFFING ▸ **goff**

GOFFS ▸ **goff**

GOGGA, -S *n* any small insect

GOGGLE, -D, -S, GOGGLING *vb* (of the eyes) bulge ▷ *n* fixed or bulging stare

GOGGLER, -S *n* big-eyed scad

G

GOGGLES ▸ goggle
GOGGLIER ▸ goggly
GOGGLING ▸ goggle
GOGGLY, GOGGLIER
▸ **goggle**
GOGLET, -S n long-necked water-cooling vessel
GOGO, -S n disco
GOHONZON n (in Nichiren Buddhism) paper scroll to which devotional chanting is directed
GOIER ▸ goey
GOIEST ▸ goey
GOING, -S ▸ go
GOITER, -S same as ▸ **goitre**
GOITERED
GOITRE, -S n swelling of the thyroid gland in the neck
GOITRED
GOITROUS
GOJI, -S same as > **wolfberry**
GOLCONDA n source of wealth or riches, esp a mine
GOLD, -ER, -EST, -S n yellow precious metal ▷ adj made of gold
GOLDARN, -S euphemistic variant of ▸ **goddamn**
GOLDBUG, -S n American beetle with a bright metallic lustre
GOLDEN, -ED, -ER, -S adj made of gold ▷ vb gild
GOLDENLY
GOLDER ▸ gold
GOLDEST ▸ gold
GOLDEYE, -S n N American fish
GOLDFISH n orange fish kept in ponds or aquariums
GOLDIER ▸ goldy
GOLDIES ▸ goldy
GOLDIEST ▸ goldy
GOLDISH ▸ gold
GOLDLESS ▸ gold
GOLDS ▸ gold
GOLDSIZE n adhesive used to fix gold leaf to a surface
GOLDTAIL n as in **goldtail moth** European moth with white wings and a soft white furry body with a yellow tail tuft
GOLDTONE adj gold-coloured ▷ n photographic image printed on a glass-plate with a painted golden backing
GOLDURN, -S variant of ▸ **goddamn**
GOLDWORK n gold objects collectively
GOLDY, GOLDIER, GOLDIES, GOLDIEST adj gold-like ▷ n goldfinch

GOLE, -S obsolete spelling of ▸ **goal**
GOLEM, -S n (in Jewish legend) artificially created human
GOLES ▸ gole
GOLF, -ED, -S n outdoor sport ▷ vb play golf
GOLFER, -S n person who plays golf
GOLFIANA pl n golfing collectibles
GOLFING, -S ▸ golf
GOLFS ▸ golf
GOLGOTHA n place of burial
GOLIARD, -S n one of a number of wandering scholars
GOLIARDY
GOLIAS, -ED, -ES vb behave outrageously
GOLIATH, -S n giant
GOLLAN, -S n yellow flower
GOLLAND, -S same as ▸ **gollan**
GOLLANS ▸ gollan
GOLLAR, -ED, -S same as ▸ **goller**
GOLLER, -ED, -S vb roar
GOLLIED ▸ golly
GOLLIES ▸ golly
GOLLOP, -ED, -S vb eat or drink (something) quickly or greedily
GOLLOPER
GOLLY, GOLLIED, GOLLIES, -ING interj exclamation of mild surprise ▷ vb spit
GOLOSH, -ED, -ES same as ▸ **galosh**
GOLOSHE same as ▸ **galosh**
GOLOSHED ▸ golosh
GOLOSHES ▸ golosh
GOLP, -S same as ▸ **golpe**
GOLPE, -S n in heraldry, a purple circle
GOLPS ▸ golp
GOMBEEN, -S n usury
GOMBO, -S same as ▸ **gumbo**
GOMBRO, -S same as ▸ **gumbo**
GOMBROON n Persian and Chinese pottery and porcelain wares
GOMBROS ▸ gombro
GOMER, -S n unwanted hospital patient
GOMERAL, -S same as ▸ **gomeril**
GOMEREL, -S same as ▸ **gomeril**
GOMERIL, -S n Scots word for a slow-witted person
GOMERS ▸ gomer
GOMOKU, -S another word for ▸ **gobang**

GOLE, -S obsolete spelling of ▸ **goal**
GOMPA, -S n Tibetan monastery
GOMUTI, -S n E Indian feather palm
GOMUTO, -S same as ▸ **gomuti**
GON, -S n geometrical grade
GONAD, -S n organ producing reproductive cells
GONADAL
GONADIAL
GONADIC
GONCH, -ES same as ▸ **gitch**
GONDELAY same as ▸ **gondola**
GONDOLA, -S n long narrow boat used in Venice
GONE ▸ go
GONEF, -S same as ▸ **ganef**
GONENESS n faintness from hunger
GONER, -S n person or thing beyond help or recovery
GONFALON n banner hanging from a crossbar
GONFANON same as ▸ **gonfalon**
GONG, -ED, -ING, -S n rimmed metal disc ▷ vb sound a gong
GONGLIKE
GONGSTER n person who strikes a gong
GONGYO, -S n Buddhist ceremony
GONIA ▸ gonion
GONIDIA ▸ gonidium
GONIDIAL ▸ gonidium
GONIDIC ▸ gonidium
GONIDIUM, GONIDIA n green algal cell in the thallus of a lichen
GONIF, -S same as ▸ **ganef**
GONIFF, -S same as ▸ **ganef**
GONIFS ▸ gonif
GONION, GONIA n point or apex of the angle of the lower jaw
GONIUM n immature reproductive cell
GONK, -S n stuffed toy, often used as a mascot
GONNA vb going to
GONOCYTE n any cell which may potentially undergo meiosis
GONODUCT n duct leading from a gonad to the exterior, through which gametes pass
GONOF, -S same as ▸ **ganef**
GONOPH, -S same as ▸ **ganef**
GONOPOD, -S n either of the reproductive organs of insects
GONOPORE n external pore in insects, earthworms, etc,

through which the gametes are extruded

GONOSOME n individuals, collectively, in a colonial animal that are involved with reproduction

GONS ▸ gon

GONYS, -ES n lower outline of a bird's bill

GONZO, -S adj wild or crazy ▷ n wild or crazy person

GOO, -S n sticky substance

GOOBER, -S another name for ▸ peanut

GOOBY, GOOBIES n spittle

GOOD, -S adj giving pleasure ▷ n benefit

GOODBY, -S same as ▸ goodbye

GOODBYE, -S n expression used on parting ▷ interj expression used on parting ▷ sentence substitute farewell

GOODBYS ▸ goodby

GOODIE same as ▸ goody

GOODIER ▸ goody

GOODIES ▸ goody

GOODIEST ▸ goody

GOODISH ▸ good

GOODLY, GOODLIER adj considerable

GOODMAN, GOODMEN n husband

GOODNESS n quality of being good ▷ interj exclamation of surprise

GOODS ▸ good

GOODSIRE n grandfather

GOODTIME adj wildly seeking pleasure

GOODWIFE n mistress of a household

GOODWILL n kindly feeling

GOODY, GOODIER, GOODIES, GOODIEST n hero in a book or film ▷ interj child's exclamation of pleasure ▷ adj smug and sanctimonious

GOODYEAR n euphemistic term for the Devil

GOOEY, GOOIER, GOOIEST adj sticky and soft

GOOF, -ED, -ING, -S n mistake ▷ vb make a mistake

GOOFBALL n barbiturate sleeping pill

GOOFED ▸ goof

GOOFIER ▸ goofy

GOOFIEST ▸ goofy

GOOFILY ▸ goofy

GOOFING ▸ goof

GOOFS ▸ goof

GOOFUS, -ES n slow-witted or stupid person

GOOFY, GOOFIER, GOOFIEST adj silly or ridiculous

GOOG, -S n egg

GOOGLE, -D, -S, GOOGLING vb search on the internet using a search engine

GOOGLIES ▸ googly

GOOGLING ▸ google

GOOGLY, GOOGLIES n ball that spins unexpectedly on the bounce

GOOGOL, -S n number shown as one followed by 100 zeros

GOOGS ▸ goog

GOOIER ▸ gooey

GOOIEST ▸ gooey

GOOILY ▸ gooey

GOOINESS n quality of being gooey

GOOKY, GOOKIER, GOOKIEST adj sticky and messy

GOOL, -S n corn marigold

GOOLD, -S Scots word for ▸ gold

GOOLS ▸ gool

GOOMBAH, -S n patron or mentor

GOOMBAY, -S n Bahamian soft drink

GOON, -S n person hired to commit violent acts

GOONDA, -S n (in India) habitual criminal

GOONERY n behaviour typical of goons

GOONEY, -S n albatross

GOONIE, -S Scots word for a ▸ gown

GOONIER ▸ goony

GOONIES ▸ goonie

GOONIEST ▸ goony

GOONS ▸ goon

GOONY, GOONIER, GOONIEST ▸ goon

GOOP, -S n rude or ill-mannered person

GOOPED adj as in **gooped up** sticky with goop

GOOPIER ▸ goopy

GOOPIEST ▸ goopy

GOOPS ▸ goop

GOOPY, GOOPIER, GOOPIEST ▸ goop

GOOR, -S same as ▸ gur

GOORAL, -S same as ▸ goral

GOORIE, -S same as ▸ kuri

GOOROO, -S same as ▸ guru

GOORS ▸ goor

GOORY same as ▸ goor

GOOS ▸ goo

GOOSE, GEESE, -D, -S, GOOSING n web-footed bird like a large duck ▷ vb prod (someone) playfully in the bottom

GOOSEGOB n gooseberry

GOOSEGOG n gooseberry

GOOSERY n place for keeping geese

GOOSES ▸ goose

GOOSEY, -S same as ▸ goosy

GOOSIER ▸ goosy

GOOSIES ▸ goosy

GOOSIEST ▸ goosy

GOOSING ▸ goose

GOOSY, GOOSIER, GOOSIES, GOOSIEST adj of or like a goose ▷ n goose

GOPAK, -S n Russian peasant dance

GOPHER, -ED, -S n American burrowing rodent ▷ vb burrow

GOPIK, -S n money unit of Azerbaijan

GOPURA, -S n gateway tower of an Indian temple

GOPURAM, -S same as ▸ gopura

GOPURAS ▸ gopura

GOR, -S interj God! ▷ n seagull

GORA, -S n (in Indian English) White or fair-skinned male

GORAL, -S n small S Asian goat antelope

GORAMY, GORAMIES same as ▸ gourami

GORAS ▸ gora

GORBELLY n large belly

GORBLIMY same as > gorblimey

GORCOCK, -S n male of the red grouse

GORCROW, -S n carrion crow

GORDITA, -S n small thick tortilla

GORE, -D, -S, GORING n blood from a wound ▷ vb pierce with horns

GOREFEST n film featuring excessive depictions of bloodshed

GORES ▸ gore

GORGE, -D, -S, GORGING n deep narrow valley ▷ vb eat greedily

GORGEDLY

GORGEOUS adj strikingly beautiful or attractive

GORGER, -S ▸ gorge

GORGERIN another name for ▸ necking

GORGERS ▸ gorger

GORGES ▸ gorge

GORGET, -S n collar-like piece of armour

GORGETED

GORGIA, -S n improvised sung passage

GORGING ▸ gorge

G

GORGIO, -S n word used by gypsies for a non-gypsy

GORGON, -S n terrifying or repulsive woman

GORHEN, -S n female red grouse

GORI, -S n (in Indian English) White or fair-skinned female

GORIER ▸ gory

GORIEST ▸ gory

GORILLA, -S n largest of the apes, found in Africa

GORILY ▸ gory

GORINESS ▸ gory

GORING, -S ▸ gore

GORIS ▸ gori

GORM, -ED, -ING, -S n foolish person ▷ vb understand

GORMAND, -S same as ▸ gourmand

GORMED ▸ gorm

GORMIER ▸ gormy

GORMIEST ▸ gormy

GORMING ▸ gorm

GORMLESS adj stupid

GORMS ▸ gorm

GORMY, GORMIER, GORMIEST adj gormless

GORP, -ED, -ING, -S same as ▸ gawp

GORS ▸ gor

GORSE, -S n prickly yellow-flowered shrub

GORSEDD, -S n meeting held daily before an eisteddfod

GORSES ▸ gorse

GORSIER ▸ gorsy

GORSIEST ▸ gorsy

GORSOON, -S n young boy

GORSY, GORSIER, GORSIEST ▸ gorse

GORY, GORIER, GORIEST adj horrific or bloodthirsty

GOS ▸ go

GOSH interj exclamation of mild surprise or wonder

GOSHAWK, -S n large hawk

GOSHT, -S n Indian meat dish

GOSLET, -S n pygmy goose

GOSLING, -S n young goose

GOSPEL, -S n any of the first four books of the New Testament ▷ adj denoting a kind of religious music ▷ vb teach the gospel

GOSPELER same as > gospeller

GOSPELLY ▸ gospel

GOSPELS ▸ gospel

GOSPODA ▸ gospodin

GOSPODAR n hospodar

GOSPODIN, GOSPODA n Russian title of address, often indicating respect

GOSPORT, -S n aeroplane communication device

GOSS, -ED, -ING vb spit

GOSSAMER n very fine fabric

GOSSAN, -S n oxidized portion of a mineral vein in rock

GOSSE, -S variant of ▸ gorse

GOSSED ▸ goss

GOSSES ▸ gosse

GOSSIB, -S n gossip

GOSSING ▸ goss

GOSSIP, -ED, -S n idle talk, esp about other people ▷ vb engage in gossip

GOSSIPER

GOSSIPRY n idle talk

GOSSIPS ▸ gossip

GOSSIPY ▸ gossip

GOSSOON, -S n boy, esp a servant boy

GOSSYPOL n toxic crystalline pigment that is a constituent of cottonseed oil

GOSTER, -ED, -S vb laugh uncontrollably

GOT ▸ get

GOTCH, -ES same as ▸ gitch

GOTCHA, -S adj as in **gotcha lizard** Australian name for a crocodile

GOTCHES ▸ gotch

GOTCHIES pl n underwear

GOTH, -S n aficionado of Goth music and fashion

GOTHIC, -S adj of or relating to a literary style ▷ n family of heavy script typefaces

GOTHIER ▸ gothy

GOTHIEST ▸ gothy

GOTHITE, -S same as ▸ goethite

GOTHS ▸ goth

GOTHY, GOTHIER, GOTHIEST adj characteristic of Gothic clothing or music

GOTTA vb got to

GOTTEN past participle of ▸ get

GOUACHE, -S n (painting using) watercolours mixed with glue

GOUGE, -D, -S, GOUGING vb scoop or force out ▷ n hole or groove

GOUGER, -S n person or tool that gouges

GOUGERE, -S n choux pastry flavoured with cheese

GOUGERS ▸ gouger

GOUGES ▸ gouge

GOUGING ▸ gouge

GOUJEERS same as ▸ goodyear

GOUJON, -S n small strip of food

GOUK, -S same as ▸ gowk

GOULASH n rich stew seasoned with paprika

GOURA, -S n large, crested ground pigeon found in New Guinea

GOURAMI, -S n large SE Asian labyrinth fish

GOURAS ▸ goura

GOURD, -S n fleshy fruit of a climbing plant

GOURDE, -S n standard monetary unit of Haiti

GOURDFUL n as much as a gourd will hold

GOURDIER ▸ gourdy

GOURDS ▸ gourd

GOURDY, GOURDIER adj (of horses) swollen-legged

GOURMAND n person who is very keen on food and drink

GOURMET, -S n connoisseur of food and drink

GOUSTY, GOUSTIER adj dismal

GOUT, -S n drop or splash (of something)

GOUTFLY n fly whose larvae infect crops

GOUTIER ▸ gouty

GOUTIEST ▸ gouty

GOUTILY ▸ gouty

GOUTS ▸ gout

GOUTTE, -S n heraldic device

GOUTWEED n Eurasian plant with white flowers and creeping underground stems

GOUTWORT n bishop's weed

GOUTY, GOUTIER, GOUTIEST adj afflicted with the disease gout

GOV, -S n boss

GOVERN, -ED, -S vb rule, direct, or control ▷ n ability to be governed

GOVERNOR n official governing a province or state

GOVERNS ▸ govern

GOVS ▸ gov

GOWAN, -S n any of various flowers growing in fields

GOWANED

GOWANY

GOWD, -ER, -EST, -S Scots word for ▸ gold

GOWF, -ED, -ING, -S vb strike

GOWFER, -S

GOWK, -S n stupid person

GOWL, -ED, -ING, -S n substance in the corner of the eyes after sleep ▷ vb howl

GOWLAN, -S same as ▸ gollan

GOWLAND, -S same as ▸ gollan

GOWLANS ▸ gowlan

GOWLED ▸ gowl

GOWLING ▶ gowl

GOWLS ▶ gowl

GOWN, -ED, -ING, -S *n* woman's long formal dress ▷ *vb* supply with or dress in a gown

GOWNBOY, -S *n* foundationer schoolboy who wears a gown

GOWNED ▶ gown

GOWNING ▶ gown

GOWNMAN, GOWNMEN *n* professional person who wears a gown

GOWNS ▶ gown

GOWNSMAN, GOWNSMEN *same as* ▶ **gownman**

GOWPEN, -S *n* pair of cupped hands

GOX, -ES *n* gaseous oxygen

> **Gox** is gaseous oxygen, especially useful if you can use it to hit a bonus square.

GOYLE, -S *n* ravine

GOZZAN, -S *same as* ▶ **gossan**

GRAAL, -S *n* holy grail

GRAB, -BED, -BING, -S *vb* grasp suddenly, snatch ▷ *n* sudden snatch

GRABBER -S

GRABBIER ▶ grabby

GRABBING ▶ grab

GRABBLE, -D, -S *vb* scratch or feel about with the hands

GRABBLER

GRABBY, GRABBIER *adj* greedy or selfish

GRABEN, -S *n* elongated trough of land

GRABS ▶ grab

GRACE, -D, -S, GRACING, GRASTE *n* beauty and elegance ▷ *vb* honour

GRACEFUL *adj* having beauty of movement, style, or form

GRACES ▶ grace

GRACILE *adj* gracefully thin or slender

GRACILIS, GRACILES *n* thin muscle on the inner thigh

GRACING ▶ grace

GRACIOSO *n* clown in Spanish comedy

GRACIOUS *adj* kind and courteous ▷ *interj* expression of mild surprise or wonder

GRACKLE, -S *n* American songbird with a dark iridescent plumage

GRAD, -S *n* graduate

GRADABLE *adj* capable of being graded ▷ *n* word of this kind

GRADATE, -D, -S *vb* change or cause to change imperceptibly

GRADATIM *adv* step by step

GRADDAN, -S *vb* dress corn

GRADE, -D, -S, GRADING *n* place on a scale of quality, rank, or size ▷ *vb* arrange in grades

GRADELY *adj* fine

GRADER, -S *n* person or thing that grades

GRADES ▶ grade

GRADIENT *n* (degree of) slope ▷ *adj* sloping uniformly

GRADIN, -S *n* ledge above or behind an altar

GRADINE, -S *same as* ▶ **gradin**

GRADING, -S ▶ grade

GRADINO, GRADINI *n* step above an altar

GRADINS ▶ gradin

GRADS ▶ grad

GRADUAL, -S *adj* occurring or moving in small stages ▷ *n* antiphon or group of several antiphons

GRADUAND *n* person who is about to graduate

GRADUATE *vb* receive a degree or diploma ▷ *n* holder of a degree

GRADUS, -ES *n* book of études or other musical exercises

GRAECISE *same as* ▶ **graecize**

GRAECIZE *vb* make or become like the ancient Greeks

GRAFF, -ED, -ING, -S *same as* ▶ **graft**

GRAFFITI *pl n* words or drawings scribbled or sprayed on walls etc

GRAFFITO *n* instance of graffiti

GRAFFS ▶ graff

GRAFT, -ED, -S *n* surgical transplant of skin or tissue ▷ *vb* transplant (living tissue) surgically

GRAFTAGE *n* in horticulture, the art of grafting

GRAFTED ▶ graft

GRAFTER, -S ▶ graft

GRAFTING ▶ graft

GRAFTS ▶ graft

GRAHAM, -S *n* cracker made of graham flour

GRAIL, -S *n* any desired ambition or goal

GRAILE, -S *same as* ▶ **grail**

GRAILS ▶ grail

GRAIN, -ED, -S *n* seedlike fruit of a cereal plant ▷ *vb* paint in imitation of the grain of wood or leather

GRAINAGE *n* duty paid on grain

GRAINE, -S *n* eggs of the silkworm

GRAINED ▶ grain

GRAINER, -S ▶ grain

GRAINES ▶ graine

GRAINIER ▶ grainy

GRAINING *n* pattern or texture of the grain of wood, leather, etc

GRAINS ▶ grain

GRAINY, GRAINIER *adj* resembling, full of, or composed of grain

GRAIP, -S *n* long-handled gardening fork

GRAITH, -ED, -S *vb* clothe

GRAITHLY

GRAKLE, -S *same as* ▶ **grackle**

GRALLOCH *n* entrails of a deer ▷ *vb* disembowel (a deer killed in a hunt)

GRAM, -MES, -S *n* metric unit of mass

GRAMA, -S *n* type of grass

GRAMARY *same as* ▶ **gramarye**

GRAMARYE *n* magic, necromancy, or occult learning

GRAMAS ▶ grama

GRAMASH *n* type of gaiter

GRAME, -S *n* sorrow

GRAMERCY *interj* many thanks

GRAMES ▶ grame

GRAMMA, -S *n* pasture grass of the South American plains

GRAMMAGE *n* weight of paper expressed as grams per square metre

GRAMMAR, -S *n* branch of linguistics

GRAMMAS ▶ gramma

GRAMME *same as* ▶ **grame**

GRAMMES ▶ gram

GRAMOCHE *same as* ▶ **gramash**

GRAMP, -S *n* grandfather

GRAMPA, -S *variant of* ▶ **grandpa**

GRAMPIES ▶ grampy

GRAMPS ▶ gramp

GRAMPUS *n* dolphin-like mammal

GRAMPY, GRAMPIES *n* grandfather

GRAMS ▶ gram

GRAN, -S *n* grandmother

GRANA ▶ granum

GRANARY *n* storehouse for grain

GRAND, -ER, -EST, -S adj large or impressive, imposing ▷ n thousand pounds or dollars
GRANDAD, -S n grandfather
GRANDAM, -S n archaic word for grandmother
GRANDAME same as ▶ grandam
GRANDAMS ▶ grandam
GRANDDAD same as ▶ grandad
GRANDDAM same as ▶ grandam
GRANDE feminine form of ▶ grand
GRANDEE, -S n Spanish nobleman of the highest rank
GRANDER ▶ grand
GRANDEST ▶ grand
GRANDEUR n magnificence
GRANDKID n grandchild
GRANDLY ▶ grand
GRANDMA, -S n grandmother
GRANDPA, -S n grandfather
GRANDS ▶ grand
GRANDSIR same as > grandsire
GRANDSON n male grandchild
GRANFER, -S n grandfather
GRANGE, -S n country house with farm buildings
GRANGER, -S n keeper or member of a grange
GRANGES ▶ grange
GRANITA, -S n Italian iced drink
GRANITE, -S n very hard igneous rock
GRANITIC
GRANNAM, -S n old woman
GRANNIE same as ▶ granny
GRANNIED ▶ granny
GRANNIES ▶ granny
GRANNOM, -S n type of caddis fly esteemed as a bait by anglers
GRANNY, GRANNIED, GRANNIES n grandmother ▷ vb defeat without conceding a single point
GRANOLA, -S n muesli-like breakfast cereal
GRANS ▶ gran
GRANT, -ED, -ING, -S vb consent to fulfil (a request) ▷ n money provided by a government for a specific purpose
GRANTEE, -S n person to whom a grant is made
GRANTER, -S ▶ grant
GRANTING ▶ grant
GRANTOR, -S n person who makes a grant
GRANTS ▶ grant

GRANULAR adj of or like grains
GRANULE, -S n small grain
GRANUM, GRANA n membrane layers in a chloroplast
GRAPE, -D, GRAPING n small juicy green or purple berry ▷ vb grope
GRAPERY n building where grapes are grown
GRAPES n abnormal growth on the fetlock of a horse
GRAPEY, GRAPIER, GRAPIEST ▶ grape
GRAPH, -ED, -ING, -S n type of graph ▷ vb draw or represent in a graph
GRAPHEME n smallest meaningful contrastive unit in a writing system
GRAPHENE n layer of graphite one atom thick
GRAPHIC adj vividly descriptive
GRAPHICS pl n diagrams, graphs, etc, esp as used on a television programme or computer screen
GRAPHING ▶ graph
GRAPHITE n soft black form of carbon, used in pencil leads
GRAPHIUM n stylus (for writing)
GRAPHS ▶ graph
GRAPIER ▶ grapey
GRAPIEST ▶ grapey
GRAPING ▶ grape
GRAPLE, -S same as ▶ grapple
GRAPLIN, -S same as ▶ grapnel
GRAPLINE same as ▶ grapnel
GRAPLINS ▶ graplin
GRAPNEL, -S n device with several hooks
GRAPPA, -S n type of spirit
GRAPPLE, -D, -S vb try to cope with (something difficult) ▷ n grapnel
GRAPPLER
GRAPY ▶ grape
GRASP, -ED, -S vb grip something firmly ▷ n grip or clasp
GRASPER -S
GRASPING adj greedy or avaricious
GRASPS ▶ grasp
GRASS, -ED, -ES, -ING n common type of plant ▷ vb cover with grass
GRASSER, -S n police informant
GRASSES ▶ grass
GRASSIER ▶ grassy

GRASSILY ▶ grassy
GRASSING ▶ grass
GRASSUM, -S n in Scots law, sum paid when taking a lease
GRASSY, GRASSIER adj covered with, containing, or resembling grass
GRASTE archaic past participle of ▶ grace
GRAT ▶ greet
GRATE, -D, -S vb rub into small bits on a rough surface ▷ n framework of metal bars for holding fuel in a fireplace
GRATEFUL adj feeling or showing gratitude
GRATER, -S n tool with a sharp surface for grating food
GRATES ▶ grate
GRATIFY vb satisfy or please ▷ adj giving one satisfaction or pleasure
GRATIN, -S n crust of browned breadcrumbs
GRATINE adj cooked au gratin
GRATINEE vb cook au gratin
GRATING, -S adj harsh or rasping ▷ n framework of metal bars covering an opening
GRATINS ▶ gratin
GRATIS adj free, for nothing
GRATTOIR n scraper made of flint
GRATUITY n money given for services rendered, tip
GRAUNCH vb crush or destroy
GRAUPEL, -S n soft hail or snow pellets
GRAV, -S n unit of acceleration
GRAVAMEN n that part of an accusation weighing most heavily against an accused
GRAVE, -D, -N, -S, -ST n hole for burying a corpse ▷ adj causing concern ▷ vb cut, carve, sculpt, or engrave ▷ adv to be performed in a solemn manner
GRAVEL, -ED, -S n mixture of small stones and coarse sand ▷ vb cover with gravel
GRAVELLY adj covered with gravel
GRAVELS ▶ gravel
GRAVELY ▶ grave
GRAVEN ▶ grave
GRAVER, -S n any of various tools
GRAVES ▶ grave
GRAVEST ▶ grave
GRAVID adj pregnant
GRAVIDA, -E, -S n pregnant woman
GRAVIDLY ▶ gravid

GRAVIES ► gravy
GRAVING, -S ► grave
GRAVIS adj as in **myasthenia gravis** chronic muscle-weakening disease
GRAVITAS n seriousness or solemnity
GRAVITON n postulated quantum of gravitational energy
GRAVITY n force of attraction
GRAVLAKS same as ► gravlax
GRAVLAX n dry-cured salmon
GRAVS ► grav
GRAVURE, -S n method of intaglio printing
GRAVY, GRAVIES n juices from meat in cooking
GRAY, -ED, -ER, -EST, -ING, -S same as ► grey
GRAYBACK same as ► greyback
GRAYED ► gray
GRAYER ► gray
GRAYEST ► gray
GRAYFISH n dogfish
GRAYFLY n trumpet fly
GRAYHEAD n one with grey hair
GRAYHEN, -S n female of the black grouse
GRAYING ► gray
GRAYISH ► gray
GRAYLAG, -S same as ► greylag
GRAYLE, -S n holy grail
GRAYLING n fish of the salmon family
GRAYLIST vb hold (someone) in suspicion, without actually excluding him or her from a particular activity
GRAYLY ► gray
GRAYMAIL n tactic to avoid prosecution in an espionage case
GRAYNESS ► grey
GRAYOUT, -S n impairment of vision due to lack of oxygen
GRAYS ► gray
GRAZABLE ► graze
GRAZE, -D, -S vb feed on grass ▷ n slight scratch or scrape
GRAZER -S
GRAZIER, -S n person who feeds cattle for market
GRAZING, -S n land on which grass for livestock is grown
GRAZIOSO adv (of music) to be played gracefully
GREASE, -D, -S, GREASING n soft melted animal fat ▷ vb apply grease to
GREASER, -S n mechanic, esp of motor vehicles

GREASES ► grease
GREASIER ► greasy
GREASIES ► greasy
GREASILY ► greasy
GREASING ► grease
GREASY, GREASIER, GREASIES adj covered with or containing grease ▷ n shearer
GREAT, -ER, -S adj large in size or number ▷ n distinguished person
GREATEN, -S vb make or become great
GREATER ► great
GREATEST n most outstanding individual in a given field
GREATLY ► great
GREATS ► great
GREAVE, GREAVING n piece of armour for the shin ▷ vb grieve
GREAVED
GREAVES pl n residue left after the rendering of tallow
GREAVING ► greave
GREBE, -S n diving water bird
GREBO, -S same as ► greebo
GRECE, -S n flight of steps
GRECIAN, -S same as ► grece
GRECISE, -D, -S same as ► graecize
GRECIZE, -D, -S same as ► graecize
GRECQUE, -S n ornament of Greek origin
GREE, -ING, -S n superiority or victory ▷ vb come or cause to come to agreement or harmony
GREEBO, -ES n unkempt or dirty-looking young man
GREECE, -S same as ► grece
GREED, -S n excessive desire for food, wealth, etc
GREEDIER ► greedy
GREEDILY ► greedy
GREEDS ► greed
GREEDY, GREEDIER adj having an excessive desire for something
GREEGREE same as ► grigri
GREEING ► gree
GREEK, -ED, -ING vb represent text as grey lines on a computer screen
GREEN, -ED, -EST, -S adj of a colour between blue and yellow ▷ n colour between blue and yellow ▷ vb make or become green
GREENBUG n common name for Schizaphis graminum
GREENED ► green

GREENER, -S n recent immigrant
GREENERY n vegetation
GREENEST ► green
GREENEYE n small slender fish with pale green eyes
GREENFLY n green aphid, a common garden pest
GREENIE n conservationist
GREENIER ► greeny
GREENIES ► greenie
GREENING n process of making or becoming more aware of environmental considerations
GREENISH ► green
GREENLET n type of insectivorous songbird
GREENLIT adj given permission to proceed
GREENLY ► green
GREENS ► green
GREENTH, -S n greenness
GREENWAY n linear open space, with pedestrian and cycle paths
GREENY, GREENIER ► green
GREES ► gree
GREESE, -S, GREESING same as ► grece
GREET, GRAT, -ED, -S, GRUTTEN vb meet with expressions of welcome ▷ n weeping
GREETE, -S same as ► greet
GREETED ► greet
GREETER, -S n person who greets people
GREETES ► greete
GREETING n act or words of welcoming on meeting
GREETS ► greet
GREFFIER n registrar
GREGALE, -S n northeasterly wind occurring in the Mediterranean
GREGATIM adv in flocks or crowds
GREGE, -D, -S, GREGING vb make heavy
GREGO, -S n short, thick jacket
GREIGE, -S adj (of a fabric or material) not yet dyed ▷ n unbleached or undyed cloth or yarn
GREIN, -ED, -ING, -S vb desire fervently
GREISEN, -S n light-coloured metamorphic rock
GREISLY same as ► grisly
GREMIAL, -S n type of cloth used in Mass
GREMLIN, -S n imaginary being
GREMMIE, -S n young surfer

GREMMY same as
▶ **gremmie**

GREN, -NED, -NING, -S same as ▶ **grin**

GRENACHE n variety of grape

GRENADE, -S n small bomb

GRENNED ▶ gren

GRENNING ▶ gren

GRENS ▶ gren

GRESE, -S same as ▶ **grece**

GRESSING same as ▶ **grece**

GREVE, -S same as ▶ **greave**

GREW, -ED, -ING, -S vb shudder

GREWSOME archaic or US spelling of ▶ **gruesome**

GREX, -ES n group of plants

GREY, -ED, -ER, -EST, -S adj of a colour between black and white ▷ n grey colour ▷ vb become or make grey

GREYBACK n any of various animals having a grey back, such as the grey whale and the hooded crow

GREYED ▶ grey

GREYER ▶ grey

GREYEST ▶ grey

GREYHEAD n one having grey hair

GREYHEN, -S n female of the black grouse

GREYING, -S ▶ grey

GREYISH ▶ grey

GREYLAG, -S n large grey goose

GREYLIST vb hold (someone) in suspicion, without actually excluding him or her from a particular activity

GREYLY ▶ grey

GREYNESS ▶ grey

GREYS ▶ grey

GRIBBLE, -S n type of small marine crustacean

GRICE, -D, -S vb collect objects concerned with railways ▷ n object collected or place visited by a railway enthusiast

GRICER -S

GRICING, -S ▶ grice

GRID, -DED, -DING, -S n network of horizontal and vertical lines, bars, etc ▷ vb form a grid pattern

GRIDDER, -S n American football player

GRIDDING ▶ grid

GRIDDLE, -D, -S n flat iron plate for cooking ▷ vb cook (food) on a griddle

GRIDE, -D, -S, GRIDING vb grate or scrape harshly ▷ n harsh or piercing sound

GRIDELIN n greyish violet colour

GRIDES ▶ gride

GRIDING ▶ gride

GRIDIRON n frame of metal bars for grilling food ▷ vb cover with parallel lines

GRIDLOCK n situation where traffic is not moving ▷ vb (of traffic) to obstruct (an area)

GRIDS ▶ grid

GRIECE, -D, -S same as ▶ **grece**

GRIEF, -S n deep sadness

GRIEFER, -S n online gamer who spoils the game for others on purpose

GRIEFFUL adj stricken with grief

GRIEFS ▶ grief

GRIESIE same as ▶ **grisy**

GRIESLY same as ▶ **grisy**

GRIESY same as ▶ **grisy**

GRIEVANT n any person with a grievance

GRIEVE, -D, -S vb (cause to) feel grief ▷ n farm manager or overseer

GRIEVER -S

GRIEVING ▶ grieve

GRIEVOUS adj very severe or painful

GRIFF, -S n information

GRIFFE, -S n carved ornament at the base of a column

GRIFFIN, -S n mythical monster

GRIFFON, -S same as ▶ **griffin**

GRIFFS ▶ griff

GRIFT, -ED, -ING, -S vb swindle

GRIFTER -S

GRIG, -GED, -GING, -S n lively person ▷ vb fish for grigs

GRIGRI, -S n African talisman, amulet, or charm

GRIGS ▶ grig

GRIKE, -S n fissure in rock

GRILL, -ING, -S n device on a cooker ▷ vb cook under a grill

GRILLADE n grilled food

GRILLAGE n arrangement of beams and crossbeams used as a foundation on soft ground

GRILLE, -S n grating over an opening

GRILLED adj cooked on a grill or gridiron

GRILLER, -S ▶ grill

GRILLERY n place where food is grilled

GRILLES ▶ grille

GRILLING ▶ grill

GRILLION n extremely large but unspecified number, quantity, or amount ▷ determiner amounting to a grillion

GRILLS ▶ grill

GRILSE, -S n salmon on its first return from the sea to fresh water

GRIM, -MER, -MEST adj stern

GRIMACE, -D, -S n ugly or distorted facial expression ▷ vb make a grimace

GRIMACER

GRIME, -D, -S, GRIMING n ingrained dirt ▷ vb make very dirty

GRIMIER ▶ grimy

GRIMIEST ▶ grimy

GRIMILY ▶ grime

GRIMING ▶ grime

GRIMLY ▶ grim

GRIMMER ▶ grim

GRIMMEST ▶ grim

GRIMNESS ▶ grim

GRIMOIRE n textbook of sorcery and magic

GRIMY, GRIMIER, GRIMIEST ▶ grime

GRIN, -NED, -S vb smile broadly, showing the teeth ▷ n broad smile

GRINCH, -ES n person whose attitude has a depressing effect

GRIND, -ING, -S vb crush or rub to a powder ▷ n hard work

GRINDED obsolete past participle of ▶ **grind**

GRINDER, -S n device for grinding substances

GRINDERY n place in which tools and cutlery are sharpened

GRINDING ▶ grind

GRINDS ▶ grind

GRINNED ▶ grin

GRINNER, -S ▶ grin

GRINNING ▶ grin

GRINS ▶ grin

GRIOT, -S n (in W Africa) member of a caste recording tribal history

GRIP, -PED, -PING, -S n firm hold or grasp ▷ vb grasp or hold tightly

GRIPE, -D, -S vb complain persistently ▷ n complaint

GRIPER -S

GRIPEY, GRIPIER, GRIPIEST adj causing gripes

GRIPING, -S n act of griping

GRIPLE same as ▶ **gripple**

GRIPMAN, GRIPMEN n cable-car operator

GRIPPE, -S former name for
> **influenza**
GRIPPED ► **grip**
GRIPPER, -S ► **grip**
GRIPPES ► **grippe**
GRIPPIER ► **grippy**
GRIPPING ► **grip**
GRIPPLE, -S adj greedy ▷ n
hook
GRIPPY, GRIPPIER adj having
grip
GRIPS ► **grip**
GRIPSACK n travel bag
GRIPT archaic variant of
► **gripped**
GRIPTAPE n rough tape
for sticking to a surface to
provide a greater grip
GRIPY same as ► **gripey**
GRIS same as ► **grece**
GRISE, -D, -S, GRISING vb
shudder
GRISELY same as ► **grisly**
GRISEOUS adj streaked or
mixed with grey
GRISES ► **grise**
GRISETTE n (esp formerly) a
French working-class girl,
esp a pretty or flirtatious one
GRISGRIS same as ► **grigri**
GRISING ► **grise**
GRISKIN, -S n lean part of a
loin of pork
GRISLED another word for
► **grizzled**
GRISLY, GRISLIER, GRISLIES
adj horrifying or ghastly ▷ n
large American bear
GRISON, -S n type of mammal
GRISSINI pl n thin crisp
breadsticks
GRISSINO n Italian breadstick
GRIST, -S n grain for grinding
GRISTER, -S n device for
grinding grain
GRISTLE, -S n tough stringy
animal tissue found in meat
GRISTLY
GRISTS ► **grist**
GRISY adj grim
GRIT, -S, -TED, -TEST n rough
particles of sand ▷ vb spread
grit on (an icy road etc) ▷ adj
great
GRITH, -S n security or peace
guaranteed for a period of
time
GRITLESS ► **grit**
GRITS ► **grit**
GRITTED ► **grit**
GRITTER, -S n vehicle that
spreads grit on the roads
GRITTEST ► **grit**
GRITTIER ► **gritty**
GRITTILY ► **gritty**

GRITTING n spreading grit on
road surfaces
GRITTY, GRITTIER adj
courageous and tough
GRIVET, -S n E African
monkey
GRIZ n grizzly bear
GRIZE, -S same as ► **grece**
GRIZZLE, -S vb whine or
complain ▷ n grey colour
GRIZZLED adj grey-haired
GRIZZLER ► **grizzle**
GRIZZLES ► **grizzle**
GRIZZLY n large American
bear ▷ adj somewhat grey
GROAN, -ED, -S n deep sound
of grief or pain ▷ vb utter
a groan
GROANER, -S n person or
thing that groans
GROANFUL adj sad
GROANING ► **groan**
GROANS ► **groan**
GROAT n fourpenny piece
GROATS pl n hulled and
crushed grain of various
cereals
GROCER, -S n shopkeeper
selling foodstuffs
GROCERY n business or
premises of a grocer
GROCKED same as ► **grokked**
GROCKING same as
► **grokking**
GROCKLE, -S n tourist in SW
England
GRODY, GRODIER, GRODIEST
adj unpleasant
GROG, -GED, -GING, -S n
spirit, usu rum, and water
▷ vb drink grog
GROGGERY n grogshop
GROGGIER ► **groggy**
GROGGILY ► **groggy**
GROGGING ► **grog**
GROGGY, GROGGIER adj
faint, shaky, or dizzy
GROGRAM, -S n coarse fabric
GROGS ► **grog**
GROGSHOP n drinking place,
esp one of disreputable
character
GROIN, -ED, -ING, -S n place
where the legs join the
abdomen ▷ vb provide or
construct with groins
GROK, -KED, -KING, -S vb
understand completely and
intuitively
GROKED same as ► **grokked**
GROKING same as ► **grokking**
GROKKED ► **grok**
GROKKING ► **grok**
GROKS ► **grok**
GROMA, -S n Roman
surveying instrument

GROMET, -S same as
► **grommet**
GROMMET, -S n ring or eyelet
GROMWELL n hairy flowering
plant
GRONE, -D, -S, GRONING
obsolete word for ► **groan**
GROOF, -S n face, or front of
the body
GROOLY, GROOLIER adj
gruesome
GROOM, -ED, -S n person who
looks after horses ▷ vb make
or keep one's clothes and
appearance neat and tidy
GROOMER -S
GROOMING ► **groom**
GROOMS ► **groom**
GROOVE, -D, -S, GROOVING
n long narrow channel in a
surface
GROOVER, -S n device that
makes grooves
GROOVES ► **groove**
GROOVIER ► **groovy**
GROOVILY ► **groovy**
GROOVING ► **groove**
GROOVY, GROOVIER adj
attractive or exciting
GROPE, -D, -S, GROPING
vb feel about or search
uncertainly ▷ n instance of
groping
GROPER, -S n type of large fish
of warm and tropical seas
GROPES ► **grope**
GROPING ► **grope**
GROSBEAK n finch with a
large powerful bill
GROSCHEN n former Austrian
monetary unit worth one
hundredth of a schilling
GROSER, -S n gooseberry
GROSERT, -S another word for
► **groser**
GROSET, -S another word for
► **groser**
GROSS, -ED, -ES, -EST, -ING
adj flagrant ▷ n twelve
dozen ▷ vb make as total
revenue before deductions
▷ interj exclamation
indicating disgust
GROSSART another word for
► **groser**
GROSSED ► **gross**
GROSSER, -S ► **gross**
GROSSES ► **gross**
GROSSEST ► **gross**
GROSSING ► **gross**
GROSSLY ► **gross**
GROSZ, -E, -Y n Polish
monetary unit
GROT, -S n rubbish
GROTTIER ► **grotty**

G

GROTTO, -ES, -S *n* small picturesque cave
GROTTOED *adj* having a grotto
GROTTOES ▸ grotto
GROTTOS ▸ grotto
GROTTY, GROTTIER *adj* nasty or in bad condition
GROUCH, -ED, -ES *vb* grumble or complain ▷ *n* person who is always complaining
GROUCHY *adj* bad-tempered
GROUF, -S *same as* ▸ **groof**
GROUGH, -S *n* natural channel or fissure in a peat moor
GROUND, -S *n* surface of the earth ▷ *adj* on or of the ground ▷ *vb* base or establish
GROUNDED *adj* sensible and down-to-earth
GROUNDEN *obsolete variant of* ▸ **ground**
GROUNDER *n* (in baseball) ball that travels along the ground
GROUNDS ▸ ground
GROUP, -ED, -S *n* number of people or things regarded as a unit ▷ *vb* place or form into a group
GROUPAGE *n* gathering people or objects into a group or groups
GROUPED ▸ group
GROUPER, -S *n* large edible sea fish
GROUPIE, -S *n* ardent fan of a celebrity or of a sport or activity
GROUPING *n* set of people or organizations who act or work together to achieve a shared aim
GROUPIST *n* follower of a group
GROUPLET *n* small group
GROUPOID *n* magma
GROUPS ▸ group
GROUPY *same as* ▸ **groupie**
GROUSE, -D, -S, -ST, GROUSING *n* stocky game bird ▷ *vb* grumble or complain ▷ *adj* fine or excellent ▷ *adj* excellent
GROUSER -S
GROUT, -ED, -ING *n* thin mortar ▷ *vb* fill up with grout
GROUTER -S
GROUTIER ▸ grouty
GROUTING ▸ grout
GROUTS *pl n* sediment or grounds
GROUTY, GROUTIER *adj* sullen or surly

GROVE, -S *n* small group of trees
GROVED
GROVEL, -ED, -S *vb* behave humbly in order to win a superior's favour
GROVELER
GROVES ▸ grove
GROVET, -S *n* wrestling hold
GROVY, GROVIER, GROVIEST *adj* like a grove
GROW, -N, -S *vb* develop physically
GROWABLE *adj* able to be cultivated
GROWER, -S *n* person who grows plants
GROWING, -S ▸ grow
GROWL, -ED, -ING, -S *vb* make a low rumbling sound ▷ *n* growling sound
GROWLER, -S *n* person, animal, or thing that growls
GROWLERY *n* place to retreat to, alone, when ill-humoured
GROWLIER ▸ growly
GROWLING ▸ growl
GROWLS ▸ growl
GROWLY, GROWLIER ▸ growl
GROWN ▸ grow
GROWNUP, -S *n* adult
GROWS ▸ grow
GROWTH, -S *n* growing ▷ *adj* of or relating to growth
GROWTHY *adj* rapid-growing
GROYNE, -S *n* wall built out from the shore to control erosion
GROZING *adj as in* **grozing iron** iron for smoothing joints between lead pipes
GRR *interj* expressing anger or annoyance
GRRL, -S *n as in* **riot grrl** young woman who enjoys feminist punk rock

This slang term for a girl who likes loud rock music can come in useful when you are short of vowels. And it can also be spelt **grrrl**.

GRRRL, -S *n as in* **riot grrrl** young woman who enjoys feminist punk rock.
GRUB, -BED, -BING, -S *n* legless insect larva ▷ *vb* search carefully for something
GRUBBER, -S *n* person who grubs
GRUBBIER ▸ grubby
GRUBBILY ▸ grubby
GRUBBING ▸ grub
GRUBBLE, -D, -S *same as* ▸ **grabble**

GRUBBY, GRUBBIER *adj* dirty
GRUBS ▸ grub
GRUBWORM *another word for* ▸ **grub**
GRUDGE, -D, -S *vb* be unwilling to give or allow ▷ *n* resentment ▷ *adj* planned or carried out in order to settle a grudge
GRUDGER -S
GRUDGING ▸ grudge
GRUE, -D, -ING, -S, GRUING *n* shiver or shudder ▷ *vb* shiver or shudder
GRUEL, -ED, -LED, -S *n* thin porridge ▷ *vb* subject to exhausting experiences
GRUELER -S
GRUELING *same as* > **gruelling**
GRUELLED ▸ gruel
GRUELLER ▸ gruel
GRUELS ▸ gruel
GRUES ▸ grue
GRUESOME *adj* causing horror and disgust
GRUFE, -S *same as* ▸ **groof**
GRUFF, -ED, -ER, -EST, -ING, -S *adj* rough or surly in manner or voice ▷ *vb* talk gruffly
GRUFFER ▸ gruffy
GRUFFILY ▸ gruffy
GRUFFING ▸ gruff
GRUFFISH ▸ gruff
GRUFFLY ▸ gruff
GRUFFS ▸ gruff
GRUFFY, GRUFFIER *adj* gruff
GRUFTED *adj* dirty
GRUGRU, -S *n* tropical American palm
GRUIFORM *adj* relating to an order of birds, including cranes and bustards
GRUING ▸ grue
GRUM, -MER, -MEST *adj* surly
GRUMBLE, -D, -S *vb* complain ▷ *n* complaint
GRUMBLER
GRUMBLY
GRUME, -S *n* clot
GRUMLY ▸ grum
GRUMMER ▸ grum
GRUMMEST ▸ grum
GRUMMET, -S *same as* ▸ **grommet**
GRUMNESS ▸ grum
GRUMOSE *same as* ▸ **grumous**
GRUMOUS *adj* (esp of plant parts) consisting of granular tissue
GRUMP, -ED, -ING, -S *n* surly or bad-tempered person ▷ *vb* complain or grumble
GRUMPH, -ED, -S *vb* grunt
GRUMPHIE *n* pig
GRUMPHS ▸ grumph

GRUMPHY *same as* ► **grumphie**
GRUMPIER ► **grumpy**
GRUMPIES ► **grumpy**
GRUMPILY ► **grumpy**
GRUMPING ► **grump**
GRUMPISH *same as* ► **grumpy**
GRUMPS ► **grump**
GRUMPY, GRUMPIER, GRUMPIES *adj* bad-tempered ▷ *n* bad-tempered person
GRUND *n as in* **grund mail** payment for right of burial
GRUNDIES *pl n* men's underpants
GRUNGE, -S *n* style of rock music with a fuzzy guitar sound
GRUNGER, -S *n* fan of grunge music
GRUNGES ► **grunge**
GRUNGEY *adj* messy or dirty
GRUNGY, GRUNGIER *adj* squalid or seedy
GRUNION, -S *n* Californian marine fish that spawns on beaches
GRUNT, -ED, -ING, -S *vb* make a low short gruff sound, like a pig ▷ *n* pig's sound
GRUNTER, -S *n* person or animal that grunts, esp a pig
GRUNTING ► **grunt**
GRUNTLE, -D, -S *vb* grunt or groan
GRUNTS ► **grunt**
GRUSHIE *adj* healthy and strong
GRUTCH, -ED, -ES *vb* grudge
GRUTTEN ► **greet**
GRUYERE, -S *n* hard flat whole-milk cheese with holes
GRYCE, -S *same as* ► **grice**
GRYDE, -D, -S, GRYDING *same as* ► **gride**
GRYESY *adj* grey
GRYFON, -S *same as* ► **griffin**
GRYKE, -S *same as* ► **grike**
GRYPE, -S *same as* ► **gripe**
GRYPHON, -S *same as* ► **griffin**
GRYPT *archaic form of* ► **gripped**
GRYSBOK, -S *n* small antelope
GRYSELY *same as* ► **grisly**
GRYSIE *same as* ► **grisy**
GU, -S *same as* ► **gju**
GUACHARO *another name for* ► **oilbird**
GUACO, -S *n* any of several plants used as an antidote to snakebite
GUAIAC, -S *same as* ► **guaiacum**

GUAIACOL *n* yellowish creosote-like liquid
GUAIACS ► **guaiac**
GUAIACUM *n* tropical American evergreen tree
GUAIOCUM *same as* ► **guaiacum**
GUAN, -S *n* type of bird of Central and S America
GUANA, -S *another word for* ► **iguana**
GUANACO, -S *n* S American animal related to the llama
GUANAS ► **guana**
GUANASE, -S *n* type of enzyme
GUANAY, -S *n* type of cormorant
GUANGO, -S *n* rain tree
GUANIDIN *same as* > **guanidine**
GUANIN, -S *same as* ► **guanine**
GUANINE, -S *n* white almost insoluble compound
GUANINS ► **guanin**
GUANO, -S *n* dried sea-bird manure
GUANS ► **guan**
GUANXI, -S *n* Chinese social concept
GUANYLIC *adj as in* **guanylic acid** nucleotide consisting of guanine, ribose or deoxyribose, and a phosphate group
GUAR, -S *n* Indian plant
GUARACHA *same as* ► **huarache**
GUARACHE *same as* ► **huarache**
GUARACHI *same as* ► **huarache**
GUARANA, -S *n* type of shrub native to Venezuela
GUARANI, -S *n* standard monetary unit of Paraguay
GUARANTY *n* pledge of responsibility for fulfilling another person's obligations in case of default
GUARD, -ING, -S *vb* watch over to protect or to prevent escape ▷ *n* person or group that guards
GUARDAGE *n* state of being in the care of a guardian
GUARDANT *adj* (of a beast) shown full face ▷ *n* guardian
GUARDDOG *n* dog trained to protect premises
GUARDED *adj* cautious or noncommittal
GUARDEE, -S *n* guardsman
GUARDER, -S ► **guard**

GUARDIAN *n* keeper or protector ▷ *adj* protecting or safeguarding
GUARDING ► **guard**
GUARDS ► **guard**
GUARISH *vb* heal
GUARS ► **guar**
GUAVA, -S *n* yellow-skinned tropical American fruit
GUAYULE, -S *n* bushy shrub of the southwestern US
GUB, -BED, -BING, -S *n* Scots word for mouth ▷ *vb* hit or defeat
GUBBAH, -S *same as* ► **gub**
GUBBED ► **gub**
GUBBING ► **gub**
GUBBINS *n* object of little or no value
GUBS ► **gub**
GUCK, -S *n* slimy matter
GUCKIER ► **gucky**
GUCKIEST ► **gucky**
GUCKS ► **guck**
GUCKY, GUCKIER, GUCKIEST *adj* slimy and mucky
GUDDLE, -D, -S, GUDDLING *vb* catch (fish) with the hands ▷ *n* muddle
GUDE *Scots word for* ► **good**
GUDEMAN, GUDEMEN *n* male householder
GUDES *n* goods
GUDESIRE *n* grandfather
GUDEWIFE *n* female householder
GUDGEON, -S *n* small freshwater fish ▷ *vb* trick or cheat
GUE, -S *same as* ► **gju**
GUELDER *adj as in* **guelder rose** kind of shrub
GUENON, -S *n* slender Old World monkey
GUERDON, -S *n* reward or payment ▷ *vb* give a guerdon to
GUEREZA, -S *n* handsome colobus monkey
GUERIDON *n* small ornately-carved table
GUERILLA *same as* > **guerrilla**
GUERITE, -S *n* turret used by a sentry
GUERNSEY *n* seaman's knitted woollen sweater
GUES ► **gue**
GUESS, -ED, -ES, -ING *vb* estimate or draw a conclusion without proper knowledge ▷ *n* estimate or conclusion reached by guessing
GUESSER -S
GUEST, -ED, -ING, -S *n* person entertained at another's

GUESTEN expense ▷ *vb* appear as a visiting player or performer

GUESTEN, -S *vb* stay as a guest in someone's house

GUESTING ▶ guest

GUESTS ▶ guest

GUFF, -S *n* nonsense

GUFFAW, -ED, -S *n* crude noisy laugh ▷ *vb* laugh in this way

GUFFIE, -S *Scots word for* ▶ **pig**

GUFFS ▶ guff

GUGA, -S *n* gannet chick

GUGGLE, -D, -S, GUGGLING *vb* drink making a gurgling sound

GUGLET, -S *same as* ▶ **goglet**

GUICHET, -S *n* grating, hatch, or small opening in a wall

GUID *Scot word for* ▶ **good**

GUIDABLE ▶ guide

GUIDAGE, -S *n* guidance

GUIDANCE *n* leadership, instruction, or advice

GUIDE, -D, -S *n* person who conducts tour expeditions ▷ *vb* act as a guide for

GUIDER -S

GUIDEWAY *n* track controlling the motion of something

GUIDING, -S ▶ guide

GUIDON, -S *n* small pennant

GUIDS *pl n* possessions

GUILD, -S *n* organization or club

GUILDER, -S *n* former monetary unit of the Netherlands

GUILDRY *n* in Scotland, corporation of merchants

GUILDS ▶ guild

GUILE, -D, -S, GUILING *n* cunning or deceit ▷ *vb* deceive

GUILEFUL

GUILER, -S *n* deceiver

GUILES ▶ guile

GUILING ▶ guile

GUILT, -ED, -ING, -S *n* fact or state of having done wrong ▷ *vb* make (a person) feel guilty

GUILTIER ▶ guilty

GUILTILY ▶ guilty

GUILTING ▶ guilt

GUILTS ▶ guilt

GUILTY, GUILTIER *adj* responsible for an offence or misdeed

GUIMBARD *n* Jew's harp

GUIMP, -S *same as* ▶ **guimpe**

GUIMPE, -D, -S, GUIMPING *n* short blouse worn under a pinafore dress ▷ *vb* make with gimp

GUIMPS ▶ guimp

GUINEA, -S *n* former British monetary unit

GUINEP, -S *n* type of tropical American tree

GUIPURE, -S *n* heavy lace

GUIRO, -S *n* percussion instrument made from a hollow gourd

GUISARD, -S *n* guiser

GUISE, -D, -S *n* false appearance ▷ *vb* disguise or be disguised in fancy dress

GUISER, -S *n* mummer, esp at Christmas or Halloween revels

GUISES ▶ guise

GUISING, -S ▶ guise

GUITAR, -S *n* stringed instrument

GUITGUIT *n* bird belonging to the family Coerebidae

GUIZER, -S *same as* ▶ **guiser**

GUL, -S *n* design used in oriental carpets

GULA, -S *n* gluttony

GULAG, -S *n* forced-labour camp

GULAR, -S *adj* of or situated in the throat or oesophagus ▷ *n* throat or oesophagus

GULAS ▶ gula

GULCH, -ED, -ES, -ING *n* deep narrow valley ▷ *vb* swallow fast

GULDEN, -S *same as* ▶ **guilder**

GULE *Scots word for* ▶ **marigold**

GULES *n* red in heraldry

GULET, -S *n* wooden Turkish sailing boat

GULF, -ED, -ING, -S *n* large deep bay ▷ *vb* swallow up

GULFIER ▶ gulfy

GULFIEST ▶ gulfy

GULFING ▶ gulf

GULFLIKE ▶ gulf

GULFS ▶ gulf

GULFWEED *n* type of brown seaweed

GULFY, GULFIER, GULFIEST ▶ **gulf**

GULL, -ED, -ING, -S *n* long-winged sea bird ▷ *vb* cheat or deceive

GULLABLE *same as* ▶ **gullible**

GULLABLY

GULLED ▶ gull

GULLER, -S *n* deceiver

GULLERY *n* breeding-place for gulls

GULLET, -S *n* muscular tube from the mouth to the stomach

GULLEY, -ED, -S *same as* ▶ **gully**

GULLIBLE *adj* easily tricked

GULLIBLY

GULLIED ▶ gully

GULLIES ▶ gully

GULLING ▶ gull

GULLISH *adj* stupid

GULLS ▶ gull

GULLWING *adj* (of vehicle door) opening upwards

GULLY, GULLIED, GULLIES, -ING *n* channel cut by running water ▷ *vb* make (channels) in (the ground, sand, etc)

GULOSITY *n* greed or gluttony

GULP, -ED, -ING, -S *vb* swallow hastily ▷ *n* gulping

GULPER -S

GULPH, -S *archaic word for* ▶ **gulf**

GULPIER ▶ gulpy

GULPIEST ▶ gulpy

GULPING ▶ gulp

GULPS ▶ gulp

GULPY, GULPIER, GULPIEST ▶ **gulp**

GULS ▶ gul

GULY *adj* relating to gules

GUM, -MED, -S *n* firm flesh in which the teeth are set ▷ *vb* stick with gum

GUMBALL, -S *n* round piece of chewing gum

GUMBO, -S *n* mucilaginous pods of okra

GUMBOIL, -S *n* abscess on the gum

GUMBOOT *n* rubber boot

GUMBOOTS *pl n* Wellington boots

GUMBOS ▶ gumbo

GUMBOTIL *n* sticky clay formed by the weathering of glacial drift

GUMDROP, -S *n* hard jelly-like sweet

GUMLANDS *pl n* infertile land where kauri once grew

GUMLESS ▶ gum

GUMLIKE ▶ gum

GUMLINE, -S *n* line where gums meet teeth

GUMMA, -S, -TA *n* rubbery tumour

GUMMED ▶ gum

GUMMER, -S *n* punch-cutting tool

GUMMI, -S *n* gelatin-based flavoured sweet

GUMMIER ▶ gummy

GUMMIES ▶ gummy

GUMMIEST ▶ gummy

GUMMILY ▶ gummy

GUMMING, -S ▶ gum

GUMMIS ▶ gummi

GUMMITE, -S n orange or yellowish amorphous secondary mineral

GUMMOSE, -S same as ▶ gummous

GUMMOSIS n abnormal production of gum in trees

GUMMOUS adj resembling or consisting of gum

GUMMY, GUMMIER, GUMMIES, GUMMIEST adj toothless ▷ n type of small crustacean-eating shark

GUMNUT, -S n hardened seed container of the gumtree

GUMP, -ED, -ING, -S vb guddle

GUMPHION n funeral banner

GUMPING ▶ gump

GUMPS ▶ gump

GUMPTION n resourcefulness

GUMS ▶ gum

GUMSHOE, -D, -S n waterproof overshoe ▷ vb act stealthily

GUMTREE, -S n any of various trees that yield gum

GUMWEED, -S n any of several yellow-flowered plants

GUMWOOD, -S same as ▶ gumtree

GUN, -NED, -NEN, -S n weapon with a tube from which missiles are fired ▷ vb cause (an engine) to run at high speed

GUNBOAT, -S n small warship

GUNDIES ▶ gundy

GUNDOG, -S n dog trained to work with a hunter or gamekeeper

GUNDY, GUNDIES n toffee

GUNFIGHT n fight between persons using firearms ▷ vb fight with guns

GUNFIRE, -S n repeated firing of guns

GUNFLINT n piece of flint in a flintlock's hammer used to strike the spark that ignites the charge

GUNG adj as in **gung ho** extremely or excessively enthusiastic about something

GUNGE, -D, -S, GUNGING n sticky unpleasant substance ▷ vb block or encrust with gunge

GUNGIER ▶ gungy

GUNGIEST ▶ gungy

GUNGING ▶ gunge

GUNGY, GUNGIER, GUNGIEST ▶ gunge

GUNHOUSE n on a warship, an armoured rotatable enclosure for guns

GUNITE, -S n mortar sprayed in a very dense concrete layer

GUNK, -ED, -ING, -S n slimy or filthy substance ▷ vb cover with gunk

GUNKHOLE vb make a series of short boat excursions

GUNKIER ▶ gunky

GUNKIEST ▶ gunky

GUNKING ▶ gunk

GUNKS ▶ gunk

GUNKY, GUNKIER, GUNKIEST ▶ gunk

GUNLAYER n person who aims a ship's gun

GUNLESS ▶ gun

GUNLOCK, -S n mechanism in some firearms

GUNMAKER n person who makes guns

GUNMAN, GUNMEN n armed criminal

GUNMETAL n alloy of copper, tin, and zinc ▷ adj dark grey

GUNNAGE, -S n number of guns carried by a warship

GUNNED ▶ gun

GUNNEL, -S same as ▶ gunwale

GUNNEN ▶ gun

GUNNER, -S n artillery soldier

GUNNERA, -S n type of herbaceous plant

GUNNERS ▶ gunner

GUNNERY n use or science of large guns

GUNNIES ▶ gunny

GUNNING, -S ▶ gun

GUNNY, GUNNIES n strong coarse fabric used for sacks

GUNNYBAG same as > gunnysack

GUNPAPER n cellulose nitrate explosive made by treating paper with nitric acid

GUNPLAY, -S n use of firearms, as by criminals

GUNPOINT n muzzle of a gun

GUNPORT, -S n porthole or other opening for a gun

GUNROOM, -S n the mess allocated to junior officers

GUNS ▶ gun

GUNSEL, -S n criminal who carries a gun

GUNSHIP, -S n ship or helicopter armed with heavy guns

GUNSHOT, -S n shot or range of a gun

GUNSIGHT n device on a gun which helps the user to aim

GUNSMITH n person who manufactures or repairs firearms, esp portable guns

GUNSTICK n ramrod

GUNSTOCK n wooden handle to which the barrel of a rifle is attached

GUNSTONE n cannonball

GUNTER, -S n type of gaffing

GUNWALE, -S n top of a ship's side

GUNYAH, -S n hut or shelter in the bush

GUP, -S n gossip

GUPPY, GUPPIES n small colourful aquarium fish

GUPS ▶ gup

GUQIN, -S n type of Chinese zither

GUR, -S n unrefined cane sugar

GURAMI, -S same as ▶ gourami

GURDIES ▶ gurdy

GURDWARA n Sikh place of worship

GURDY, GURDIES n winch on a fishing boat

GURGE, -D, -S, GURGING vb swallow up

GURGLE, -D, -S n bubbling noise ▷ vb (of water) to make low bubbling noises when flowing

GURGLET, -S same as ▶ goglet

GURGLIER ▶ gurgly

GURGLING ▶ gurgle

GURGLY, GURGLIER adj making gurgling sounds

GURGOYLE same as ▶ gargoyle

GURJUN, -S n S or SE Asian tree that yields a resin

GURL, -ED, -ING, -S vb snarl

GURLET, -S n type of pickaxe

GURLIER ▶ gurly

GURLIEST ▶ gurly

GURLING ▶ gurl

GURLS ▶ gurl

GURLY, GURLIER, GURLIEST adj stormy

GURN, -ED, -ING, -S variant spelling of ▶ girn

GURNARD, -S n spiny armour-headed sea fish

GURNED ▶ gurn

GURNET, -S same as ▶ gurnard

GURNEY, -S n wheeled stretcher for transporting hospital patients

GURNING ▶ gurn

GURNS ▶ gurn

GURRAH, -S n type of coarse muslin

GURRIER, -S n low-class tough ill-mannered person

GURRY, GURRIES n dog-fight

GURS ▶ gur

GURSH, -ES n unit of currency in Saudi Arabia

GURU, -S n Hindu or Sikh religious teacher or leader

GURUDOM, -S n state of being a guru

GURUISM, -S ► guru

GURUS ► guru

GURUSHIP, -S ► guru

GUS ► gu

GUSH, -ED, -ES, -ING vb flow out suddenly and profusely ▷ n sudden copious flow

GUSHER, -S n spurting oil well

GUSHES ► gush

GUSHIER ► gushy

GUSHIEST ► gushy

GUSHILY ► gushy

GUSHING ► gush

GUSHY, GUSHIER, GUSHIEST adj displaying excessive sentimentality

GUSLA, -S n Balkan single-stringed musical instrument

GUSLAR, -S n player of the gusla

GUSLAS ► gusla

GUSLE, -S same as ► gusla

GUSLI, -S n Russian harp-like musical instrument

GUSSET, -S n piece of material sewn into a garment to strengthen it ▷ vb put a gusset in (a garment)

GUSSETED

GUSSIE n young pig

GUSSY, GUSSIED, GUSSIES, -ING vb dress elaborately

GUST, -ED, -ING, -S n sudden blast of wind ▷ vb blow in gusts

GUSTABLE n anything that can be tasted

GUSTED ► gust

GUSTFUL adj tasty

GUSTIE adj tasty

GUSTIER ► gusty

GUSTIEST ► gusty

GUSTILY ► gusty

GUSTING ► gust

GUSTLESS adj tasteless

GUSTO, -ES, -S n enjoyment or zest

GUSTS ► gust

GUSTY, GUSTIER, GUSTIEST adj windy and blustery

GUT, -TED, -TING n intestine ▷ vb remove the guts from ▷ adj basic or instinctive

GUTCHER, -S n grandfather

GUTFUL, -S n bellyful

GUTLESS adj cowardly

GUTLIKE ► gut

GUTROT, -S n upset stomach

GUTS, -ED, -ES, -ING vb devour greedily

GUTSER, -S n as in **come a gutser** fall heavily to the ground

GUTSES ► guts

GUTSFUL, -S n bellyful

GUTSIER ► gutsy

GUTSIEST ► gutsy

GUTSILY ► gutsy

GUTSING ► guts

GUTSY, GUTSIER, GUTSIEST adj courageous

GUTTA, -E, -S n small drop-like ornament

GUTTATE, -S adj covered with small drops or drop-like markings ▷ vb exude droplets of liquid

GUTTATED same as ► guttate

GUTTATES ► guttate

GUTTED ► gut

GUTTER, -ED, -S n shallow channel for carrying away water ▷ vb (of a candle) burn unsteadily

GUTTERY

GUTTIER ► gutty

GUTTIES ► gutty

GUTTIEST ► gutty

GUTTING ► gut

GUTTLE, -D, -S, GUTTLING vb eat greedily

GUTTLER -S

GUTTURAL adj (of a sound) produced at the back of the throat ▷ n guttural consonant

GUTTY, GUTTIER, GUTTIES, GUTTIEST n urchin or delinquent ▷ adj courageous

GUTZER, -S n bad fall

GUV, -S informal name for ► governor

GUY, -ED, -ING, -S n man or boy ▷ vb make fun of

GUYLE, -D, -S, GUYLING same as ► guile

GUYLER -S

GUYLINE, -S n guy rope

GUYLINER n eyeliner worn by men

GUYLINES ► guyline

GUYLING ► guyle

GUYOT, -S n flat-topped submarine mountain

GUYS ► guy

GUYSE, -S same as ► guise

GUZZLE, -D, -S, GUZZLING vb eat or drink greedily

GUZZLER, -S n person or thing that guzzles

GUZZLES ► guzzle

GUZZLING ► guzzle

GWEDUC, -S same as ► geoduck

GWEDUCK, -S same as ► geoduck

GWEDUCS ► gweduc

GWINE dialect form of ► going

GWINIAD, -S n powan

GWYNIAD, -S n type of freshwater white fish

GYAL, -S same as ► gayal

GYBE, -D, -S, GYBING vb (of a sail) swing suddenly from one side to the other ▷ n instance of gybing

GYELD, -S n guild

GYLDEN adj golden

GYM, -S n gymnasium

GYMBAL, -S same as ► gimbal

GYMKHANA n horse-riding competition

GYMMAL, -S same as ► gimmal

GYMNASIA > gymnasium

GYMNASIC > gymnasium

GYMNAST, -S n expert in gymnastics

GYMNIC adj gymnastic

GYMP, -ED, -ING, -S same as ► gimp

GYMPIE, -S n tall tree with stinging hairs on its leaves

GYMPING ► gymp

GYMPS ► gymp

GYMS ► gym

GYMSLIP, -S n tunic or pinafore formerly worn by schoolgirls

GYMSUIT, -S n costume worn for gymnastics

GYNAE, -S adj gynaecological ▷ n gynaecology

GYNAECEA > gynaeceum

GYNAECIA > gynaecium

GYNAES ► gynae

GYNANDRY n hermaphroditism

GYNARCHY n government by women

GYNECIA ► gynecium

GYNECIC adj relating to the female sex

GYNECIUM, GYNECIA same as > **gynoecium**

GYNECOID same as > **gynaecoid**

GYNIATRY n gynaecology: medicine concerned with diseases in women

GYNIE, -S n gynaecology

GYNNEY, -S n guinea hen

GYNNY, GYNNIES same as ► gynney

GYNO, -S n gynaecologist

GYNOECIA > gynoecium

GYNOS ► gyno

GYNY n gynaecology

GYOZA, **-S** n Japanese fried dumpling

GYP, **-PED**, **-PING**, **-S** vb swindle, cheat, or defraud ▷ n act of cheating

This little word, meaning to swindle, can be useful when you are short of vowels.

GYPLURE, **-S** n synthetic version of a gypsy moth pheromone

GYPO, **-S** n small-scale independent logger

GYPPED ▸ gyp

GYPPER, **-S** ▸ gyp

GYPPIE same as ▸ **gippy**

GYPPIES ▸ gyppy

GYPPING ▸ gyp

GYPPY, **GYPPIES** same as ▸ **gippy**

GYPS ▸ gyp

GYPSEIAN adj relating to gypsies

GYPSEOUS ▸ gypsum

GYPSIED ▸ gypsy

GYPSIES ▸ gypsy

GYPSTER, **-S** n swindler

GYPSUM, **-S** n chalklike mineral

GYPSY, **GYPSIED**, **GYPSIES**, **-ING** n member of a nomadic people ▷ vb live like a gypsy

GYPSYDOM

GYPSYISH

GYPSYISM n state of being a gypsy

GYRAL adj having a circular, spiral, or rotating motion

GYRALLY

GYRANT adj gyrating

GYRASE, **-S** n topoisomerase enzyme

GYRATE, **-D**, **-S**, **GYRATING** vb rotate or spiral about a point or axis ▷ adj curved or coiled into a circle

GYRATION n act or process of gyrating

GYRATOR, **-S** n electronic circuit that inverts the impedance

GYRATORY ▸ gyrate

GYRE, **-D**, **-S**, **GYRING** n circular or spiral movement or path ▷ vb whirl

GYRENE, **-S** n nickname for a member of the US Marine Corps

GYRES ▸ gyre

GYRI ▸ gyrus

GYRING ▸ gyre

GYRO, **-S** n gyrocompass

GYROCAR, **-S** n two-wheeled car

GYRODYNE n aircraft with rotor

GYROIDAL adj spiral

GYROLITE n silicate

GYRON, **-S** same as ▸ giron

GYRONIC

GYRONNY same as ▸ gironny

GYRONS ▸ gyron

GYROS ▸ gyro

GYROSE adj marked with sinuous lines

GYROSTAT same as > gyroscope

GYROUS adj gyrose

GYRUS, **GYRI**, **-ES** n convolution

GYTE, **-S** n spoilt child

GYTRASH n spirit that haunts lonely roads

GYTTJA, **-S** n sediment on lake bottom

GYVE, **-D**, **-S**, **GYVING** vb shackle or fetter ▷ n fetters

G

Hh

H forms a two-letter word in front of every vowel except **U** (and you can make **uh** with **U**), making it a versatile tile when you want to form words in more than one direction. It also goes with **M** to make **hm**. As **H** is worth 4 points on its own, you can earn some very high scores by doing this: even **ha, he, hi** and **ho** will give 5 points each. There are lots of good short words beginning with **H**, like **haw, hew, how, hay, hey** and **hoy** (9 each), while **hyp** can be useful if you are short of vowels. More high-scoring words with **H** include **haj, hex** and **hox** for 13 points each, and never forget the invaluable **zho** for 15 points.

HA *interj* exclamation of triumph, surprise, or scorn

HAAF, -S *n* fishing ground off the Shetland and Orkney Islands

HAAR, -S *n* cold sea mist or fog off the North Sea

HABANERA *n* slow Cuban dance in duple time

HABANERO *n* variety of chilli pepper

HABDABS *n* highly nervous state

HABDALAH *n* prayer at end of Jewish sabbath

HABENDUM *n* part of a deed defining the limits of ownership

HABILE *adj* skilful

HABIT, -ING, -S *n* established way of behaving ▷ *vb* clothe

HABITAN, -S *same as* ▶ **habitant**

HABITANT *n* person who lives in a place

HABITAT, -S *n* natural home of an animal or plant

HABITED *adj* dressed in a habit

HABITING ▶ **habit**

HABITS ▶ **habit**

HABITUAL *adj* done regularly and repeatedly ▷ *n* person with a habit

HABITUDE *n* habit or tendency

HABITUE, -S *n* frequent visitor to a place

HABITUS *n* general physical state

HABLE *old form of* ▶ **able**

HABOOB, -S *n* sandstorm

HABU, -S *n* large venomous snake

HACEK, -S *n* pronunciation symbol in Slavonic language

HACHIS *n* hash

HACHURE, -D, -S *n* shading drawn on a map to indicate steepness of a hill ▷ *vb* mark or show by hachures

HACIENDA *n* ranch or large estate in Latin America

HACK, -ED, -S *vb* cut or chop violently ▷ *n* (inferior) writer or journalist ▷ *adj* unoriginal or of a low standard

HACKABLE

HACKBOLT *n* shearwater

HACKBUT, -S *another word for* ▶ **arquebus**

HACKED ▶ **hack**

HACKEE, -S *n* chipmunk

HACKER, -S *n* computer enthusiast

HACKERY *n* journalism

HACKETTE *n* informal, derogatory term for female journalist

HACKIE, -S *n* US word meaning cab driver

HACKING, -S ▶ **hack**

HACKLE, -D, HACKLING *same as* ▶ **heckle**

HACKLER -S

HACKLES *pl n* hairs which rise in response to emotion

HACKLET, -S *n* kittiwake

HACKLIER ▶ **hackly**

HACKLING ▶ **hackle**

HACKLY, HACKLIER *adj* rough or jagged

HACKMAN, HACKMEN *n* taxi driver

HACKNEY, -S *n* taxi ▷ *vb* make commonplace and banal by too frequent use

HACKS ▶ **hack**

HACKSAW, -N, -S *n* small saw for cutting metal ▷ *vb* cut with a hacksaw

HACKWORK *n* dull repetitive work

HAD, -DEN, -DING, -S *vb* Scots form of hold

HADAL *adj* denoting very deep zones of the oceans

HADARIM ▶ **heder**

HADAWAY *sentence substitute* exclamation urging the hearer to refrain from delay

HADDEN ▶ **had**

HADDEST *same as* ▶ **hadst**

HADDIE, -S *n* finnan haddock

HADDING ▶ **had**

HADDOCK, -S *n* edible sea fish of N Atlantic

HADE, -D, -S, HADING *n* angle made to the vertical by the plane of a fault or vein ▷ *vb* incline from the vertical

HADEDAH, -S *n* large grey-green S African ibis

HADES ▶ **hade**

HADING ▶ **hade**

HADITH, -S *n* body of legend about Mohammed and his followers

HADJ, -ES *same as* ▶ **hajj**

HADJEE, -S *same as* ▶ **hadji**

HADJES ▶ **hadj**

HADJI, -S *same as* ▶ **hajji**

HADROME, -S *n* part of xylem

HADRON, -S *n* type of elementary particle

HADRONIC

HADS ▶ **had**

HADST singular form of the past tense (indicative mood) of ▶ **have**

HAE, -D, -ING, -N, -S Scot variant of ▶ **have**

HAEM, -S n red organic pigment containing ferrous iron

HAEMAL adj of the blood

HAEMATAL same as ▶ **haemal**

HAEMATIC n agent that stimulates the production of red blood cells

HAEMATIN n dark bluish or brownish pigment

HAEMIC same as ▶ **haematic**

HAEMIN, -S n haematin chloride

HAEMOID same as > **haematoid**

HAEMONY n plant mentioned in Milton's poetry

HAEMS ▶ **haem**

HAEN ▶ **hae**

HAEREDES ▶ **haeres**

HAEREMAI interj Māori expression of welcome ▷ n act of saying 'haeremai'

HAERES, HAEREDES same as ▶ **heres**

HAES ▶ **hae**

HAET, -S n whit

HAFF, -S n lagoon

HAFFET, -S n side of head

HAFFIT, -S same as ▶ **haffet**

HAFFLIN, -S same as ▶ **halfling**

HAFFS ▶ **haff**

HAFIZ, -ES n title for a person who knows the Koran by heart

HAFNIUM, -S n metallic element found in zirconium ores

HAFT, -ED, -ING, -S n handle of an axe, knife, or dagger ▷ vb provide with a haft

HAFTARA, -S same as ▶ **haftarah**

HAFTARAH, HAFTAROS, HAFTAROT n short reading from the Prophets

HAFTARAS ▶ **haftara**

HAFTAROS ▶ **haftarah**

HAFTAROT ▶ **haftarah**

HAFTED ▶ **haft**

HAFTER, -S ▶ **haft**

HAFTING ▶ **haft**

HAFTORAH, HAFTOROS, HAFTOROT same as ▶ **haftarah**

HAFTS ▶ **haft**

HAG, -GED, -GING, -S n ugly old woman ▷ vb hack

HAGADIC same as ▶ **haggadic**

HAGADIST same as > **haggadist**

HAGBERRY same as ▶ **hackberry**

HAGBOLT, -S same as ▶ **hackbolt**

HAGBORN adj born of a witch

HAGBUSH same as ▶ **arquebus**

HAGBUT, -S same as ▶ **arquebus**

HAGDEN, -S same as ▶ **hackbolt**

HAGDON, -S same as ▶ **hackbolt**

HAGDOWN, -S same as ▶ **hackbolt**

HAGFISH n any of various primitive eel-like vertebrates

HAGG, -S n boggy place

HAGGADA, -S same as ▶ **haggadah**

HAGGADAH, HAGGADOT n book containing the order of service of the traditional Jewish Passover meal

HAGGADAS ▶ **haggada**

HAGGADIC ▶ **haggadah**

HAGGADOT ▶ **haggadah**

HAGGARD, -S adj looking tired and ill ▷ n hawk that has reached maturity before being caught

HAGGED ▶ **hag**

HAGGING ▶ **hag**

HAGGIS, -ES n Scottish dish

HAGGISH ▶ **hag**

HAGGLE, -D, -S vb bargain or wrangle over a price

HAGGLER, -S

HAGGLING n act of haggling

HAGGS ▶ **hagg**

HAGLET, -S same as ▶ **hacklet**

HAGLIKE ▶ **hag**

HAGRIDE, -S, HAGRODE vb torment or obsess

HAGRIDER

HAGS ▶ **hag**

HAH, -S same as ▶ **ha**

HAHA, -S n wall or other boundary marker that is set in a ditch

HAHNIUM, -S n transuranic element

HAHS ▶ **hah**

HAICK, -S same as ▶ **haik**

HAIDUK, -S n rural brigand

HAIK, -A, -S n Arab's outer garment

HAIKAI same as ▶ **haiku**

HAIKS ▶ **haik**

HAIKU, -S n Japanese verse form in 17 syllables

HAIL, -ED, -ING, -S n (shower of) small pellets of ice ▷ vb fall as or like hail ▷ sentence substitute exclamation of greeting

HAILER -S

HAILIER ▶ **haily**

HAILIEST ▶ **haily**

HAILING ▶ **hail**

HAILS ▶ **hail**

HAILSHOT n small scattering shot

HAILY, HAILIER, HAILIEST ▶ **hail**

HAIMISH same as ▶ **heimish**

HAIN, -ED, -S vb Scots word meaning save

HAINCH, -ED, -ES Scots form of ▶ **haunch**

HAINED ▶ **hain**

HAINING, -S ▶ **hain**

HAINS ▶ **hain**

HAINT, -S same as ▶ **haunt**

HAIQUE, -S same as ▶ **haik**

HAIR, -ING, -S n threadlike growth on the skin ▷ vb provide with hair

HAIRBALL n mass of hair that forms in the stomach of animals

HAIRBAND n band worn around head to control hair

HAIRBELL same as ▶ **harebell**

HAIRCAP, -S n type of moss

HAIRCUT, -S n act or an instance of cutting the hair

HAIRDO, -S n hairstyle

HAIRED adj with hair

HAIRGRIP n small bent clasp used to fasten the hair

HAIRIER ▶ **hairy**

HAIRIEST ▶ **hairy**

HAIRIF, -S another name for ▶ **cleavers**

HAIRILY adv in a hairy manner

HAIRING ▶ **hair**

HAIRLESS adj having little or no hair ▷ n as in **Mexican hairless** small breed of hairless dog

HAIRLIKE ▶ **hair**

HAIRLINE n edge of hair at the top of the forehead ▷ adj very fine or narrow

HAIRLOCK n lock of hair

HAIRNET, -S n any of several kinds of light netting worn over the hair

HAIRPIN, -S n U-shaped wire used to hold the hair in place

HAIRS ▶ **hair**

HAIRST, -ED, -S Scots form of ▶ **harvest**

HAIRTAIL n spiny-finned fish

HAIRWING n fishing lure tied with hair

HAIRWORK n thing made from hair

HAIRWORM n any of various hairlike nematode worms

HAIRY, HAIRIER, HAIRIEST adj covered with hair

HAITH interj Scots oath

HAJ, -ES same as ► **hadj**

A **haj** is a Muslim pilgrimage to Mecca, and one of the key words to remember for using the J. It can also be spelt **hadj** or **hajj**, and one who makes a haj is called a **hadjee, hadji, haji** or **hajji**.

HAJI, -S same as ► **hajji**

HAJJ, -ES n pilgrimage a Muslim makes to Mecca

HAJJAH, -S n Muslim woman who has made a pilgrimage to Mecca

HAJJES ► **hajj**

HAJJI, -S n Muslim who has made a pilgrimage to Mecca

HAKA, -S n ceremonial Māori dance with chanting

HAKAM, -S n text written by a rabbi

HAKARI, -S n Māori ritual feast

HAKAS ► **haka**

HAKE, -S n edible sea fish of N hemisphere

HAKEA, -S n Australian tree or shrub with hard woody fruit

HAKEEM, -S same as ► **hakim**

HAKES ► **hake**

HAKIM, -S n Muslim judge, ruler, or administrator

HAKU, -S in New Zealand English, same as ► **kingfish**

HALACHA, -S, HALACHOT n Jewish religious law

HALACHIC

HALAKAH, -S same as ► **halacha**

HALAKHA, -S, HALAKHOT, HALAKOTH same as ► **halacha**

HALAKHAH same as ► **halacha**

HALAKHAS ► **halakha**

HALAKHIC ► **halakhah**

HALAKHOT ► **halakha**

HALAKIC ► **halakha**

HALAKIST ► **halakha**

HALAKOTH ► **halakha**

HALAL, -LED, -S n meat from animals slaughtered according to Muslim law ▷ adj of or relating to such meat ▷ vb kill (animals) in this way

HALALA, -S n money unit in Saudi Arabia

HALALAH, -S same as ► **halala**

HALALAS ► **halala**

HALALLED ► **halal**

HALALS ► **halal**

HALATION n bright ring surrounding a light source

HALAVAH, -S same as ► **halvah**

HALAZONE n type of disinfectant

HALBERD, -S n spear with an axe blade

HALBERT, -S same as ► **halberd**

HALCYON, -S adj peaceful and happy ▷ n mythological bird

HALE, -D, -S, -ST, HALING adj healthy, robust ▷ vb pull or drag

HALENESS

HALER, -S, -U same as ► **heller**

HALES ► **hale**

HALEST ► **hale**

HALF, -S n either of two equal parts ▷ adj denoting one of two equal parts ▷ adv to the extent of half

HALFA, -S n African grass

HALFBACK n player positioned immediately behind the forwards

HALFBEAK n type of fish with a short upper jaw and a protruding lower jaw

HALFEN same as ► **half**

HALFLIFE n time taken for half of the atoms in a radioactive material to undergo decay

HALFLIN, -S same as ► **halfling**

HALFLING n person only half-grown

HALFLINS ► **halflin**

HALFNESS ► **half**

HALFPACE n landing on staircase

HALFPIPE n U-shaped object used in skateboarding stunts

HALFS ► **half**

HALFTIME n rest period between the two halves of a game

HALFTONE n illustration showing lights and shadows by means of very small dots ▷ adj relating to, used in, or made by halftone

HALFWAY adj at or to half the distance

HALFWIT, -S n foolish or stupid person

HALIBUT, -S n large edible flatfish of N Atlantic

HALICORE n dugong

HALID, -S same as ► **halide**

HALIDE, -S n binary compound

HALIDOM, -S n holy place or thing

HALIDOME same as ► **halidom**

HALIDOMS ► **halidom**

HALIDS ► **halid**

HALIER, -OV, -S n former currency unit of Slovakia

HALIMOT, -S n court held by lord

HALIMOTE same as ► **halimot**

HALIMOTS ► **halimot**

HALING ► **hale**

HALIOTIS, HALIOTES n type of shellfish

HALITE, -S n colourless or white mineral

HALITOUS ► **halitus**

HALITUS n vapour

HALL, -S n entrance passage

HALLAH, -S, HALLOT variant spelling of ► **challah**

HALLAL, -S same as ► **halal**

HALLALI, -S n bugle call

HALLALOO same as ► **halloo**

HALLALS ► **hallal**

HALLAN, -S n partition in cottage

HALLEL, -S n (in Judaism) section of the liturgy

HALLIAN, -S same as ► **hallion**

HALLIARD same as ► **halyard**

HALLING, -S n Norwegian country dance

HALLION, -S n lout

HALLMARK n typical feature ▷ vb stamp with a hallmark

HALLO, -ED, -ES, -ING, -S same as ► **halloo**

HALLOA, -ED, -S same as ► **halloo**

HALLOED ► **hallo**

HALLOES ► **hallo**

HALLOING ► **hallo**

HALLOO, -ED, -S interj shout used to call hounds at a hunt ▷ sentence substitute shout to attract attention, esp to call hounds at a hunt ▷ n shout of "halloo" ▷ vb shout (something) to (someone)

HALLOS ► **hallo**

HALLOT ► **hallah**

HALLOTH same as ► **challah**

HALLOUMI n salty white sheep's cheese from Greece

or Turkey, usually eaten grilled

HALLOW, **-S** vb consecrate or set apart as being holy

HALLOWED adj regarded as holy

HALLOWER ► hallow

HALLOWS ► hallow

HALLS ► hall

HALLUCAL ► hallux

HALLUX, HALLUCES n first digit on the hind foot of an animal

HALLWAY, **-S** n entrance area

HALLYON, **-S** same as ► hallion

HALM, **-S** same as ► haulm

HALMA, **-S** n board game

HALMS ► halm

HALO, **-ED**, **-ES**, **-ING**, **-S** n ring of light round the head of a sacred figure ▷ vb surround with a halo

HALOGEN, **-S** n any of a group of nonmetallic elements

HALOID, **-S** adj resembling or derived from a halogen ▷ n compound containing halogen atoms in its molecules

HALOING ► halo

HALOLIKE ► halo

HALON, **-S** n any of a class of chemical compounds

HALOS ► halo

HALOSERE n plant community that originates and develops in conditions of high salinity

HALOUMI, **-S** same as ► halloumi

HALSE, **-D**, **-S**, **HALSING** vb embrace

HALSER **-S**

HALT, **-ED**, **-S** vb come or bring to a stop ▷ n temporary stop ▷ adj lame

HALTER, **-ED**, **-S** n strap round a horse's head with a rope to lead it with ▷ vb put a halter on (a horse)

HALTERE, **-S** n one of a pair of modified hind wings in dipterous insects

HALTERED ► halter

HALTERES ► haltere

HALTERS ► halter

HALTING, **-S** ► halt

HALTLESS ► halt

HALTS ► halt

HALUTZ, **-IM** variant spelling of ► chalutz

HALVA, **-S** same as ► halvah

HALVAH, **-S** n E Mediterranean, Middle

Eastern, or Indian sweetmeat

HALVAS, **-S** same as ► halva

HALVE, **-D**, **-S** vb divide in half

HALVER **-S**

HALVING, **-S** n act of halving

HALWA, **-S** n type of sweet Indian dish

HALYARD, **-S** n rope for raising a ship's sail or flag

HAM, **-MED**, **-MING**, **-S** n smoked or salted meat from a pig's thigh ▷ vb overact

HAMADA, **-S** n rocky plateau in desert

HAMAL, **-S** n (in Middle Eastern countries) a porter or servant

HAMARTIA n flaw in character which leads to the downfall of the protagonist in a tragedy

HAMATE, **-S** adj hook-shaped ▷ n small bone in the wrist

HAMATSA, **-S** n Native Canadian dance

HAMAUL, **-S** same as ► hamal

HAMBLE, **-D**, **-S**, **HAMBLING** vb mutilate

HAMBONE, **-D**, **-S** vb strike body to provide percussion

HAMBURG, **-S** same as > hamburger

HAME, **-D**, **-S**, **HAMING** n Scots word for home ▷ vb to home

HAMEWITH adv Scots word meaning homewards

HAMFAT, **-S** n mediocre performer

HAMING ► hame

HAMLET, **-S** n small village

HAMMADA, **-S** same as ► hamada

HAMMAL, **-S** same as ► hamal

HAMMAM, **-S** n bathing establishment

HAMMED ► ham

HAMMER, **-ED**, **-S** n tool ▷ vb hit (as if) with a hammer

HAMMERER

HAMMIER ► hammy

HAMMIEST ► hammy

HAMMILY ► hammy

HAMMING ► ham

HAMMOCK, **-S** same as ► hummock

HAMMY, HAMMIER, HAMMIEST adj (of an actor) overacting or tending to overact

HAMOSE adj shaped like a hook

HAMOUS same as ► hamose

HAMPER, **-ED**, **-S** vb make it difficult for (someone or something) to move or progress ▷ n large basket with a lid

HAMPERER

HAMPSTER same as ► hamster

HAMS ► ham

HAMSTER, **-S** n small rodent with a short tail and cheek pouches

HAMULAR ► hamulus

HAMULATE ► hamulus

HAMULI ► hamulus

HAMULOSE ► hamulus

HAMULOUS ► hamulus

HAMULUS, HAMULI n biological attribute

HAMZA, **-S** n sign used in Arabic to represent the glottal stop

HAMZAH, **-S** same as ► hamza

HAMZAS ► hamza

HAN archaic inflected form of ► have

HANAP, **-S** n medieval drinking cup

HANAPER, **-S** n small wickerwork basket

HANAPS ► hanap

HANCE, **-S** same as ► haunch

HANCH, **-ED**, **-ES**, **-ING** vb try to bite

HAND, **-ED**, **-ING**, **-S** n part of the body at the end of the arm ▷ vb pass, give

HANDAX, **-E**, **-ES** n small axe held in one hand

HANDBAG n woman's small bag

HANDBAGS pl n incident in which people threaten to fight

HANDBALL n game in which two teams try to throw a ball into their opponent's goal ▷ vb pass (the ball) with a blow of the fist

HANDBELL n bell rung by hand, esp one of a tuned set used in musical performance

HANDBILL n small printed notice

HANDBOOK n small reference or instruction book

HANDCAR, **-S** n small railway vehicle

HANDCART n simple cart pushed or pulled by hand, used for transporting goods

HANDCLAP n act of clapping hands

HANDCUFF n one of a linked pair of metal rings for locking

H

round wrists ▷ *vb* put handcuffs on

HANDED ► **hand**

HANDER, -S ► **hand**

HANDFAST *n* agreement, esp of marriage, confirmed by a handshake ▷ *vb* betroth or marry (two persons or another person) by joining the hands

HANDFEED, HANDFED *vb* feed (a person or an animal) by hand

HANDFUL, -S, HANDSFUL *n* amount that can be held in the hand

HANDGRIP *n* covering on the handle of a racket or club

HANDGUN, -S *n* firearm such as a pistol

HANDHELD *adj* held in position by the hand ▷ *n* computer that can be held in the hand

HANDHOLD *n* object, crevice, etc, that can be used as a grip or support, as in climbing

HANDICAP *n* physical or mental disability ▷ *vb* make it difficult for (someone) to do something

HANDIER ► **handy**

HANDIEST ► **handy**

HANDILY *adv* in a handy way or manner

HANDING ► **hand**

HANDISM, -S *n* discrimination against left- or right-handed people

HANDJAR, -S *n* Persian dagger

HANDKNIT *adj, n* (garment) knitted by hand

HANDLE, -D, -S *n* part of an object that is held so that it can be used ▷ *vb* hold, feel, or move with the hands

HANDLER, -S *n* person who controls an animal

HANDLES ► **handle**

HANDLESS ► **hand**

HANDLIKE ► **hand**

HANDLINE *n* hand-operated fishing line

HANDLING *n* act or an instance of picking up, turning over, or touching something

HANDLIST *n* rough list

HANDLOOM *n* weaving device operated by hand

HANDMADE *adj* made by hand, not by machine

HANDMAID *n* person or thing that serves as a useful but subordinate purpose

HANDOFF, -S *n* (in rugby) act of warding off an opposing player

HANDOUT, -S *n* clothing, food, or money given to a needy person

HANDOVER *n* transfer or surrender

HANDPASS *vb* pass the ball by striking it with the hand

HANDPICK *vb* choose or select with great care, as for a special job or purpose

HANDPLAY *n* fighting with fists

HANDRAIL *n* rail alongside a stairway, to provide support

HANDROLL *n* large dried-seaweed cone filled with cold rice and other ingredients

HANDS ► **hand**

HANDSAW, -S *n* any saw for use in one hand only

HANDSEL, -S *n* gift for good luck ▷ *vb* give a handsel to (a person)

HANDSET, -S *n* telephone mouth- and earpiece in a single unit

HANDSEWN *adj* sewn by hand

HANDSFUL ► **handful**

HANDSOME *adj* (esp of a man) good-looking ▷ *n* term of endearment for a beloved person

HANDWORK *n* work done by hand rather than by machine

HANDWRIT > **handwrite**

HANDY, HANDIER, HANDIEST *adj* convenient, useful

HANDYMAN, HANDYMEN *n* man who is good at making or repairing things

HANEPOOT *n* variety of muscat grape

HANG, -ED, -S, HUNG *vb* attach or be attached at the top with the lower part free

HANGABLE *adj* suitable for hanging

HANGAR, -ED, -S *n* large shed for storing aircraft ▷ *vb* put in a hangar

HANGBIRD *n* any bird, esp the Baltimore oriole, that builds a hanging nest

HANGDOG, -S *adj* guilty, ashamed ▷ *n* furtive or sneaky person

HANGED ► **hang**

HANGER, -S *n* curved piece of wood, wire, etc with a hook

HANGFIRE *n* failure to fire

HANGI, -S *n* Māori oven

HANGING, -S ► **hang**

HANGIS ► **hangi**

HANGMAN, HANGMEN *n* man who executes people by hanging

HANGNAIL *n* piece of skin partly torn away from the base or side of a fingernail

HANGNEST *same as* ► **hangbird**

HANGOUT, -S *n* place where one lives or that one frequently visits

HANGOVER *n* headache and nausea as a result of drinking too much alcohol

HANGRY, HANGRIER *adj* irritable as a result of feeling hungry

HANGS ► **hang**

HANGTAG, -S *n* attached label

HANGUL *n* Korean language

HANGUP, -S *n* emotional or psychological or problem

HANIWA *n* Japanese funeral offering

HANJAR, -S *same as* ► **handjar**

HANK, -ED, -ING, -S *n* coil, esp of yarn ▷ *vb* attach (a sail) to a stay by hanks

HANKER, -ED, -S *vb* desire intensely

HANKERER

HANKIE *same as* ► **hanky**

HANKIES ► **hanky**

HANKING ► **hank**

HANKS ► **hank**

HANKY, HANKIES *n* handkerchief

HANSA, -S *same as* ► **hanse**

HANSE, -S *n* medieval guild of merchants

HANSEL, -ED, -S *same as* ► **handsel**

HANSES ► **hanse**

HANSOM, -S *n* two-wheeled one-horse carriage

HANT, -ED, -ING, -S *same as* ► **haunt**

HANTLE, -S *n* good deal

HANTS ► **hant**

HANUKIAH *n* candelabrum having nine branches that is lit during the festival of Hanukkah

HANUMAN, -S *n* type of monkey

HAO, -S *n* monetary unit of Vietnam

HAOMA, -S *n* type of ritual drink

HAOS ► **hao**

HAP, -PED, -PING, -S *n* luck ▷ *vb* cover up

HAPAX, -ES *n* word that appears once in a work of literature

HAPHTARA *same as*
► **haftarah**

HAPKIDO, -S *n* Korean martial art

HAPLESS *adj* unlucky

HAPLITE, -S *n variant of*
HAPLITIC

HAPLOID, -S *adj* denoting a cell or organism with unpaired chromosomes ▷ *n* haploid cell or organism
HAPLOIDY

HAPLONT, -S *n* organism with a haploid number of chromosomes

HAPLOPIA *n* normal single vision

HAPLOSIS, HAPLOSES *n* production of a haploid number of chromosomes during meiosis

HAPLY *archaic word for*
► **perhaps**

HAPPED ► **hap**

HAPPEN, -ED, -S *vb* take place, occur

HAPPI, -S *n* type of loose Japanese coat

HAPPIED ► **happy**

HAPPIER ► **happy**

HAPPIES ► **happy**

HAPPIEST ► **happy**

HAPPILY ► **happy**

HAPPING ► **hap**

HAPPIS ► **happi**

HAPPOSHU *n* beer-like Japanese drink

HAPPY, HAPPIED, HAPPIER, HAPPIES, HAPPIEST, -ING *adj* feeling or causing joy ▷ *vb* make happy

HAPS ► **hap**

HAPTEN, -S *n* incomplete antigen

HAPTENE, -S *same as*
► **hapten**
HAPTENIC

HAPTENS ► **hapten**

HAPTERON *n* organ of attachment in some aquatic plants

HAPTIC *adj* relating to or based on the sense of touch

HAPTICAL *same as* ► **haptic**

HAPTICS *n* science of sense of touch

HAPU, -S *n* subtribe

HAPUKA, -S *another name for*
► **groper**

HAPUKU, -S *same as*
► **hapuka**

HAPUS ► **hapu**

HAQUETON *same as*
> **hacqueton**

HARAAM *same as* ► **haram**

HARAKEKE *in New Zealand English, another name for*
► **flax**

HARAM, -S *n* anything that is forbidden by Islamic law

HARAMBEE *n* work chant used on the E African coast ▷ *interj* cry of harambee

HARAMS ► **haram**

HARANGUE *vb* address angrily or forcefully ▷ *n* angry or forceful speech

HARASS, -ES *vb* annoy or trouble constantly
HARASSED
HARASSER

HARBOR, -ED, -S *same as*
► **harbour**
HARBORER

HARBOUR, -S *n* sheltered port ▷ *vb* maintain secretly in the mind

HARD, -ER, -EST *adj* firm, solid, or rigid ▷ *adv* with great energy or effort

HARDASS *n* tough person

HARDBACK *n* book with a stiff cover ▷ *adj* of or denoting a hardback

HARDBAG, -S *n* rigid container on a motorcycle

HARDBAKE *n* almond toffee

HARDBALL *n as in* **play hardball** act in a ruthless or uncompromising way

HARDBEAM *same as*
► **hornbeam**

HARDBODY *n* attractive person with a muscular physique

HARDBOOT *n* type of skiing boot

HARDCASE *n* tough person ▷ *adj* relating to a container that has a rigid structure

HARDCORE *n* style of rock music with short fast songs and little melody

HARDEDGE *n* style of painting in which vividly coloured subjects are clearly delineated ▷ *adj* of, relating to, or denoting this style of painting

HARDEN, -S *vb* make or become hard ▷ *n* rough fabric made from hards

HARDENED *adj* toughened by experience

HARDENER *n* person or thing that hardens

HARDENS ► **harden**

HARDER ► **hard**

HARDEST ► **hard**

HARDFACE *n* uncompromising person

HARDHACK *n* woody plant

HARDHAT, -S *n* hat made of a hard material for protection ▷ *adj* typical of construction workers

HARDHEAD *same as*
> **hardheads**

HARDIER ► **hardy**

HARDIES ► **hardy**

HARDIEST ► **hardy**

HARDILY *adv* in a hardy manner

HARDISH ► **hard**

HARDLINE *adj* uncompromising

HARDLY *adv* scarcely or not at all

HARDMAN, HARDMEN *n* tough, ruthless, or violent man

HARDNESS *n* quality or condition of being hard

HARDNOSE *n* tough person

HARDOKE, -S *n* burdock

HARDPACK *n* rigid backpack

HARDPAN, -S *n* hard impervious layer of clay below the soil

HARDROCK *adj* concerned with extracting minerals other than coal ▷ *n* tough uncompromising man

HARDS *pl n* coarse fibres and other refuse from flax and hemp

HARDSET *adj* in difficulties

HARDSHIP *n* suffering

HARDTACK *n* kind of hard saltless biscuit, formerly eaten by sailors

HARDTAIL *n* mountain bike with no rear suspension

HARDTOP, -S *n* car equipped with a metal or plastic roof

HARDWARE *n* metal tools or implements

HARDWIRE *vb* instal permanently in computer

HARDWOOD *n* wood of a broad-leaved tree such as oak or ash

HARDY, HARDIER, HARDIES, HARDIEST *adj* able to stand difficult conditions ▷ *n* any blacksmith's tool made with a square shank

HARE, -D, -S, HARING *n* animal like a large rabbit, with longer ears and legs ▷ *vb* run (away) quickly

HAREBELL *n* blue bell-shaped flower

HARED ► **hare**

HARELD, -S *n* long-tailed duck

HARELIKE ► **hare**

H

HARELIP, -S n slight split in the upper lip

HARES ► hare

HAREWOOD n sycamore wood that has been stained for use in furniture making

HARIANA, -S n Indian breed of cattle

HARICOT, -S n variety of French bean

HARIGALS same as > harigalds

HARIJAN, -S n member of an Indian caste

HARING ► hare

HARIRA, -S n Moroccan soup

HARISH adj like hare

HARISSA, -S n hot paste

HARK, -ED, -ING, -S vb listen

HARKEN, -ED, -S same as ► hearken

HARKENER

HARKING ► hark

HARKS ► hark

HARL, -ED, -S same as ► herl

HARLING -S

HARM, -ED, -ING, -S vb injure physically, mentally, or morally ▷ n physical, mental, or moral injury

HARMALA, -S n African plant

HARMALIN n chemical derived from harmala

HARMAN, -S n constable

HARMED ► harm

HARMEL, -S same as ► harmala

HARMER, -S ► harm

HARMFUL adj causing or tending to cause harm

HARMIN, -S same as ► harmalin

HARMINE, -S same as ► harmalin

HARMING ► harm

HARMINS ► harmin

HARMLESS adj safe to use, touch, or be near

HARMONIC adj of harmony ▷ n overtone of a musical note produced when that note is played

HARMONY n peaceful agreement and cooperation

HARMOST, -S n Spartan governor

HARMOSTY n office of a harmost

HARMS ► harm

HARN, -S n coarse linen

HARNESS n arrangement of straps for attaching a horse to a cart or plough ▷ vb put a harness on

HARNS ► harn

HARO, -S interj cry meaning alas

HAROSET, -S n Jewish dish eaten at Passover

HAROSETH same as ► haroset

HAROSETS ► haroset

HARP, -ED, -ING, -S n large triangular stringed instrument ▷ vb play the harp

HARPER -S

HARPIES ► harpy

HARPIN n type of protein

HARPING ► harp

HARPINGS pl n wooden members used for strengthening the bow of a vessel

HARPINS same as ► harpings

HARPIST, -S ► harp

HARPOON, -S n barbed spear attached to a rope for hunting whales ▷ vb spear with a harpoon

HARPS ► harp

HARPY, HARPIES n nasty or bad-tempered woman

HARRIDAN n nagging or vicious woman

HARRIED ► harry

HARRIER, -S n cross-country runner

HARRIES ► harry

HARROW, -ED, -S n implement used to break up lumps of soil ▷ vb draw a harrow over

HARROWER

HARRUMPH vb clear or make the noise of clearing the throat

HARRY, HARRIED, HARRIES, -ING vb keep asking (someone) to do something

HARSH, -ED, -ER, -ES, -EST, -ING adj severe and difficult to cope with ▷ vb ruin or end a state of elation

HARSHEN, -S vb make harsh

HARSHER ► harsh

HARSHES ► harsh

HARSHEST ► harsh

HARSHING ► harsh

HARSHLY ► harsh

HARSLET, -S same as ► haslet

HART, -S n adult male deer

HARTAL, -S n (in India) closing shops or suspending work

HARTBEES same as > hartbeest

HARTELY archaic spelling of ► heartily

HARTEN, -ED, -S same as ► hearten

HARTS ► hart

HARUMPH, -S same as ► harrumph

HARUSPEX n priest in ancient Rome

HARVEST, -S n (season for) the gathering of crops ▷ vb gather (a ripened crop)

HAS ► have

HASH, -ED, -ES, -ING n dish of diced cooked meat and vegetables reheated ▷ vb chop into small pieces

HASHEESH same as ► hashish

HASHES ► hash

HASHIER ► hashy

HASHIEST ► hashy

HASHING, -S ► hash

HASHISH n illegal drug made from the cannabis plant

HASHMARK n character (#)

HASHTAG, -S n word or phrase used to denote the topic of a Twitter post

HASHY, HASHIER, HASHIEST ► hash

HASK, -S n archaic name for a basket for transporting fish

HASLET, -S n loaf of cooked minced pig's offal, eaten cold

HASP, -ED, -ING, -S n type of fastening ▷ vb secure (a door, window, etc) with a hasp

HASS, -ES n as in white hass oatmeal pudding made with sheep's gullet

HASSAR, -S n South American catfish

HASSEL, -S variant of ► hassle

HASSES ► hass

HASSIUM, -S n chemical element

HASSLE, -D, -S, HASSLING n trouble, bother ▷ vb bother or annoy

HASSOCK, -S n cushion for kneeling on in church

HASSOCKY

HAST singular form of the present tense (indicative mood) of ► have

HASTA Spanish for ► until

HASTATE adj shaped like a spear

HASTATED same as ► hastate

HASTE, -D, -S n (excessive) quickness ▷ vb hasten

HASTEFUL

HASTEN, -ED, -S *vb* (cause to) hurry
HASTENER
HASTES ► haste
HASTIER ► hasty
HASTIEST ► hasty
HASTILY ► hasty
HASTING, -S ► haste
HASTY, HASTIER, HASTIEST *adj* (too) quick
HAT, -S, -TED *n* covering for the head, often with a brim ▷ *vb* supply (a person) with a hat or put a hat on (someone)
HATABLE ► hate
HATBAND, -S *n* band or ribbon around a hat
HATBOX, -ES *n* box or case for a hat or hats
HATBRUSH *n* brush for hats
HATCH, -ED, -ES *vb* (cause to) emerge from an egg ▷ *n* hinged door covering an opening in a floor or wall
HATCHECK *n* cloakroom
HATCHED ► hatch
HATCHEL, -S *same as* ► **heckle**
HATCHER, -S ► hatch
HATCHERY *n* place where eggs are hatched under artificial conditions
HATCHES ► hatch
HATCHET, -S *n* small axe
HATCHETY *adj* like a hatchet
HATCHING ► hatch
HATCHWAY *n* opening in the deck of a ship
HATE, -D, -S, HATING *vb* dislike intensely ▷ *n* intense dislike
HATEABLE
HATEFUL *adj* causing or deserving hate
HATELESS ► hate
HATER, -S ► hate
HATERENT *same as* ► **hatred**
HATERS ► hater
HATES ► hate
HATFUL, -S, HATSFUL *n* amount a hat will hold
HATGUARD *n* string to keep a hat from blowing off
HATH *form of the present tense (indicative mood) of* ► **have**
HATHA *n as in* **hatha yoga** form of yoga
HATING ► hate
HATLESS ► hat
HATLIKE ► hat
HATMAKER *n* maker of hats
HATPEG, -S *n* peg to hang hat on

HATPIN, -S *n* pin used to secure a woman's hat to her hair
HATRACK, -S *n* rack for hanging hats on
HATRED, -S *n* intense dislike
HATS ► hat
HATSFUL ► hatful
HATSTAND *n* frame or pole equipped with hooks or arms for hanging up hats, coats, etc
HATTED ► hat
HATTER, -ED, -S *n* person who makes and sells hats ▷ *vb* annoy
HATTERIA *n* species of reptile
HATTERS ► hatter
HATTING, -S ► hat
HATTOCK, -S *n* small hat
HAUBERK, -S *n* long sleeveless coat of mail
HAUBOIS *same as* ► **hautboy**
HAUD, -ING, -S, HUDDEN *Scot word for* ► **hold**
HAUF, -S *Scot word for* ► **half**
HAUGH, -S *n* low-lying often alluvial riverside meadow
HAUGHT *same as* ► **haughty**
HAUGHTY *adj* proud, arrogant
HAUL, -ED, -S *vb* pull or drag with effort ▷ *n* hauling
HAULAGE, -S *n* (charge for) transporting goods
HAULBACK *n* (in lumbering) line used to bring a cable back
HAULD, -S *Scots word for* ► **hold**
HAULED ► haul
HAULER, -S *same as* ► **haulier**
HAULIER, -S *n* firm or person that transports goods by road
HAULING, -S *n* act of hauling
HAULM, -S *n* stalks of beans, peas, or potatoes collectively
HAULMIER ► haulmy
HAULMS ► haulm
HAULMY, HAULMIER *adj* having haulms
HAULOUT, -S *n* act of hauling a boat out of water
HAULS ► haul
HAULST *same as* ► **halse**
HAULT *same as* ► **haughty**
HAULYARD *same as* ► **halyard**
HAUN, -S *n* Scot word for hand
HAUNCH, -ED, -ES *n* human hip or fleshy hindquarter of an animal ▷ *vb* cause (an animal) to come down on its haunches

HAUNS ► haun
HAUNT, -S *vb* visit in the form of a ghost ▷ *n* place visited frequently
HAUNTED *adj* frequented by ghosts
HAUNTER, -S ► haunt
HAUNTING *adj* memorably beautiful or sad
HAUNTS ► haunt
HAURIANT *adj* rising
HAURIENT *same as* ► **hauriant**
HAUSE, -D, -S, HAUSING *same as* ► **halse**
HAUSEN, -S *n* variety of sturgeon
HAUSES ► hause
HAUSFRAU *n* German housewife
HAUSING ► hause
HAUT, -ER, -EST *same as* ► **haughty**
HAUTBOIS *same as* ► **hautboy**
HAUTBOY, -S *n* type of strawberry
HAUTE *adj* French word meaning high
HAUTER ► haut
HAUTEST ► haut
HAUTEUR, -S *n* haughtiness
HAUYNE, -S *n* blue mineral containing calcium
HAVARTI, -S *n* Danish cheese
HAVDALAH *n* ceremony at the end of the Sabbath
HAVDOLOH *same as* ► **havdalah**
HAVE, HAS, -S *vb* possess, hold
HAVELOCK *n* cap flap covering the back of the neck
HAVEN, -ED, -ING, -S *n* place of safety ▷ *vb* secure or shelter in or as if in a haven
HAVEOUR, -S *same as* ► **havior**
HAVER, -ED, -ING, -S *vb* talk nonsense ▷ *n* nonsense
HAVEREL, -S *n* fool
HAVERING ► haver
HAVERS ► haver
HAVES ► have
HAVILDAR *n* noncommissioned officer in the Indian army, equivalent in rank to sergeant
HAVING, -S ► have
HAVIOR, -S *same as* ► **haviour**
HAVIOUR, -S *n* possession
HAVOC, -KED, -S *n* disorder and confusion ▷ *vb* lay waste
HAVOCKER

HAW, -ED, -ING, -S n hawthorn berry ▷ vb make an inarticulate utterance

HAWALA, -S n Middle Eastern system of money transfer

HAWBUCK, -S n bumpkin

HAWEATER n resident of Manitoulin Island, Ontario

HAWED ► haw

HAWFINCH n European finch with a stout bill and brown plumage with black-and-white wings

HAWING ► haw

HAWK, -ED, -S n bird of prey ▷ vb offer (goods) for sale in the street or door-to-door

HAWKBELL n bell fitted to a hawk's leg

HAWKBILL same as > hawksbill

HAWKBIT, -S n any of three perennial plants

HAWKED ► hawk

HAWKER, -S n travelling salesman

HAWKEY, -S same as ► hockey

HAWKEYED adj having extremely keen sight

HAWKEYS ► hawkey

HAWKIE, -S n cow with white stripe on face

HAWKING, -S another name for ► falconry

HAWKISH adj favouring the use of force rather than diplomacy

HAWKIT adj having a white streak

HAWKLIKE ► hawk

HAWKMOTH n narrow-winged moth

HAWKNOSE n hooked nose

HAWKS ► hawk

HAWKSHAW n private detective

HAWKWEED n hairy plant with clusters of dandelion-like flowers

HAWM, -ED, -ING, -S vb be idle and relaxed

HAWS ► haw

HAWSE, -D, -S, HAWSING vb of boats: pitch violently when at anchor

HAWSER, -S n large rope used on a ship

HAWSES ► hawse

HAWSING ► hawse

HAWTHORN n thorny shrub or tree

HAY, -ED, -S n grass cut and dried as fodder ▷ vb cut, dry, and store (grass, clover, etc) as fodder

HAYBAND, -S n rope made by twisting hay together

HAYBOX, -ES n airtight box used to keep partially cooked food warm

HAYCOCK, -S n pile of hay left until dry enough to move

HAYED ► hay

HAYER, -S n person who makes hay

HAYEY, HAYIER, HAYIEST ► hay

HAYFIELD n field of hay

HAYFORK, -S n long-handled fork

HAYIER ► hayey

HAYIEST ► hayey

HAYING, -S ► hay

HAYLAGE, -S n type of hay for animal fodder

HAYLE, -S n welfare

HAYLOFT, -S n loft for storing hay

HAYMAKER n person who helps to cut, turn, toss, spread, or carry hay

HAYMOW, -S n part of a barn where hay is stored

HAYRACK, -S n rack for holding hay for feeding to animals

HAYRAKE, -S n large rake used to collect hay

HAYRICK, -S same as ► haystack

HAYRIDE, -S n pleasure trip in hay wagon

HAYS ► hay

HAYSEED, -S n seeds or fragments of grass or straw

HAYSEL, -S n season for making hay

HAYSTACK n large pile of stored hay

HAYWARD, -S n parish officer in charge of enclosures and fences

HAYWIRE, -S adj (of things) not functioning properly ▷ n wire for binding hay

HAZAN, -IM, -S same as ► cantor

HAZARD, -ED, -S n something that could be dangerous ▷ vb put in danger

HAZARDER

HAZARDRY n taking of risks

HAZARDS ► hazard

HAZE, -D, -S n mist, often caused by heat ▷ vb make or become hazy

HAZEL, -S n small tree producing edible nuts ▷ adj (of eyes) greenish-brown

HAZELHEN n type of grouse

HAZELLY ► hazel

HAZELNUT n nut of a hazel shrub, which has a smooth shiny hard shell

HAZELS ► hazel

HAZER, -S ► haze

HAZES ► haze

HAZIER ► hazy

HAZIEST ► hazy

HAZILY ► hazy

HAZINESS ► hazy

HAZING, -S ► haze

HAZMAT, -S n hazardous material

HAZY, HAZIER, HAZIEST adj not clear, misty

HAZZAN, -IM, -S same as ► cantor

HE, -S pron male person or animal ▷ n male person or animal ▷ interj expression of amusement or derision

HEAD n upper or front part of the body ▷ adj chief, principal ▷ vb be at the top or front of

HEADACHE n continuous pain in the head

HEADACHY adj suffering from, caused by, or likely to cause a headache

HEADAGE, -S n payment to farmer based on animals owned

HEADBAND n ribbon or band worn around the head

HEADBANG vb nod one's head violently to the beat of loud rock music

HEADCASE n insane person

HEADED adj having a head or heads

HEADEND, -S n facility from which cable television is transmitted

HEADER, -S n striking a ball with the head

HEADFAST n mooring rope at the bows of a ship

HEADFISH same as ► sunfish

HEADFUL, -S n amount head will hold

HEADGATE n gate used to control the flow of water at the upper end of a lock or conduit

HEADGEAR n hats collectively

HEADHUNT vb recruit employee from another company

HEADIER ► heady

HEADIEST ► heady

HEADILY ► heady

HEADING, -S same as ► head

HEADLAMP same as > headlight

HEADLAND n area of land jutting out into the sea
HEADLESS adj without a head
HEADLIKE ► head
HEADLINE n title at the top of a newspaper article, esp on the front page
HEADLOCK n wrestling hold
HEADLONG adj with the head first ▷ adv with the head foremost
HEADMAN, HEADMEN n chief or leader
HEADMARK n characteristic
HEADMEN ► headman
HEADMOST less common word for ► **foremost**
HEADNOTE n note at book chapter head
HEADPIN, -S another word for ► **kingpin**
HEADPOND n artificial pond behind a dam
HEADRACE n channel that carries water to a water wheel, turbine, etc
HEADRAIL n end of the table from which play is started, nearest the baulkline
HEADREST n support for the head, as on a dentist's chair or car seat
HEADRIG, -S n edge of ploughed field
HEADRING n African head decoration
HEADROOM n space above person's head in a vehicle
HEADROPE n rope round an animal's head
HEADS adv with the side of a coin with a head on it uppermost
HEADSAIL n any sail set forward of the foremast
HEADSET, -S n pair of headphones
HEADSHIP n position or state of being a leader, esp the head teacher of a school
HEADSHOT n photo of person's head
HEADSMAN, HEADSMEN n (formerly) an executioner who beheaded condemned persons
HEADSTAY n rope from mast to bow on ship
HEADWALL n steep slope at the head of a glacial cirque
HEADWARD same as > **headwards**
HEADWAY, -S same as ► **headroom**

HEADWIND n wind blowing against the course of an aircraft or ship
HEADWORD n key word placed at the beginning of a line, paragraph, etc, as in a dictionary entry
HEADWORK n intellectual labour
HEADY, HEADIER, HEADIEST adj intoxicating or exciting
HEAL, -ED, -S vb make or become well
HEALABLE
HEALD, -ED, -ING, -S same as ► **heddle**
HEALED ► heal
HEALEE, -S n person who is being healed
HEALING, -S ► heal
HEALS ► heal
HEALSOME Scots word for > **wholesome**
HEALTH, -S n normal (good) condition of someone's body ▷ interj exclamation wishing someone good health as part of a toast
HEALTHY adj having good health
HEAME old form of ► **home**
HEAP, -ED, -S n pile of things one on top of another ▷ vb gather into a pile
HEAPER -S
HEAPIER ► heapy
HEAPIEST ► heapy
HEAPING adj (of a spoonful) heaped
HEAPS ► heap
HEAPY, HEAPIER, HEAPIEST adj having many heaps
HEAR, -S vb perceive (a sound) by ear
HEARABLE
HEARD, -S same as ► **herd**
HEARE, -S old form of ► **hair**
HEARER, -S ► hear
HEARES ► heare
HEARIE old form of ► **hairy**
HEARING, -S ► hear
HEARKEN, -S vb listen
HEARS ► hear
HEARSAY, -S n gossip, rumour
HEARSE, -D, -S, HEARSING n funeral car used to carry a coffin ▷ vb put in hearse
HEARSIER ► hearsy
HEARSING ► hearse
HEARSY, HEARSIER adj like a hearse
HEART, -ED, -ING n organ that pumps blood round the

body ▷ vb (of vegetables) form a heart
HEARTEN, -S vb encourage, make cheerful
HEARTH, -S n floor of a fireplace
HEARTIER ► hearty
HEARTIES ► hearty
HEARTILY adv thoroughly or vigorously
HEARTING ► heart
HEARTLET n little heart
HEARTLY adv vigorously
HEARTPEA same as > **heartseed**
HEARTS n card game
HEARTY, HEARTIER, HEARTIES adj substantial, nourishing ▷ n comrade, esp a sailor
HEAST, -S same as ► **hest**
HEASTE, -S same as ► **hest**
HEASTS ► heast
HEAT, -S vb make or become hot ▷ n state of being hot
HEATABLE
HEATED adj angry and excited
HEATEDLY
HEATER, -S n device for supplying heat
HEATH, -S n area of open uncultivated land
HEATHEN, -S n person who does not believe in an established religion ▷ adj of or relating to heathen peoples
HEATHER, -S n low-growing plant ▷ adj of a heather colour
HEATHERY
HEATHIER ► heathy
HEATHS ► heath
HEATHY, HEATHIER ► heath
HEATING, -S n device or system for supplying heat
HEATLESS ► heat
HEATS ► heat
HEATSPOT n spot on skin produced by heat
HEATWAVE n prolonged period of unusually hot weather
HEAUME n large helmet reaching the shoulders
HEAVE, -D, -S, HOVEN vb lift with effort ▷ n heaving
HEAVEN, -S n place believed to be the home of God
HEAVENLY adj of or like heaven
HEAVENS ► heaven
HEAVER, -S ► heave
HEAVES ► heave
HEAVIER ► heavy
HEAVIES ► heavy

H

HEAVIEST ▶ heavy
HEAVILY ▶ heavy
HEAVING, -S ▶ heave
HEAVY, HEAVIER, HEAVIES, HEAVIEST adj of great weight ▷ n person hired to threaten violence
HEAVYISH n rather heavy
HEAVYSET adj stockily built
HEBDOMAD n number seven or a group of seven
HEBE, -S n any of various flowering shrubs
HEBEN n old form of ▶ ebony
HEBENON, -S n source of poison
HEBENS ▶ heben
HEBES ▶ hebe
HEBETANT adj causing dullness
HEBETATE adj (of plant parts) having a blunt or soft point ▷ vb make or become blunted
HEBETIC adj of or relating to puberty
HEBETUDE n mental dullness or lethargy
HEBONA, -S same as ▶ hebenon
HEBRAISE same as ▶ hebraize
HEBRAIZE vb become or cause to become Hebrew or Hebraic
HECATOMB n sacrifice of 100 oxen
HECH interj expression of surprise
HECHT, -ING, -S same as ▶ hight
HECK, -S interj mild exclamation of surprise, irritation, etc ▷ n frame for obstructing the passage of fish in a river
HECKLE, -D, -S, HECKLING vb interrupt with comments, questions, or taunts ▷ n instrument for combing flax or hemp
HECKLER -S
HECKS ▶ heck
HECKUVA adj heck of a
HECTARE, -S n one hundred ares
HECTIC, -S adj rushed or busy ▷ n hectic fever or flush
HECTICAL same as ▶ hectic
HECTICLY ▶ hectic
HECTICS ▶ hectic
HECTOR, -ED, -S vb bully ▷ n blustering bully
HECTORER
HECTORLY

HEDARIM same as ▶ hadarim
HEDDLE, -D, -S, HEDDLING n frame on a loom ▷ vb pass thread through a heddle
HEDER, HADARIM, -S variant spelling of ▶ cheder
HEDERA, -S n ivy
HEDERAL
HEDERS ▶ heder
HEDGE, -D, -S n row of bushes forming a barrier or boundary ▷ vb be evasive or noncommittal
HEDGEHOG n small mammal with a protective covering of spines
HEDGEHOP vb (of an aircraft) to fly close to the ground, as in crop spraying
HEDGEPIG same as ▶ hedgehog
HEDGER, -S ▶ hedge
HEDGEROW n bushes forming a hedge
HEDGERS ▶ hedger
HEDGES ▶ hedge
HEDGIER ▶ hedgy
HEDGIEST ▶ hedgy
HEDGING, -S ▶ hedge
HEDGY, HEDGIER, HEDGIEST ▶ hedge
HEDONIC ▶ hedonism
HEDONICS n branch of psychology concerned with the study of pleasant and unpleasant sensations
HEDONISM n doctrine that pleasure is the most important thing in life
HEDONIST
HEED, -ED, -ING, -S n careful attention ▷ vb pay careful attention to
HEEDER -S
HEEDFUL ▶ heed
HEEDIER ▶ heedy
HEEDIEST ▶ heedy
HEEDING ▶ heed
HEEDLESS adj taking no notice
HEEDS ▶ heed
HEEDY, HEEDIER, HEEDIEST adj heedful; attentive
HEEHAW, -ED, -S interj representation of the braying sound of a donkey ▷ vb make braying sound
HEEL, -ED, -S n back part of the foot ▷ vb repair the heel of (a shoe)
HEELBALL n mixture of beeswax and lampblack used by shoemakers
HEELBAR, -S n small shop where shoes are repaired

HEELED ▶ heel
HEELER, -S n dog that herds cattle by biting at their heels
HEELING, -S ▶ heel
HEELLESS ▶ heel
HEELPOST n post for carrying the hinges of a door or gate
HEELS ▶ heel
HEELTAP, -S n layer of leather, etc, in the heel of a shoe
HEEZE, -D, -S, HEEZING Scots word for ▶ hoist
HEEZIE, -S n act of lifting
HEEZING ▶ heeze
HEFT, -ED, -ING, -S vb assess the weight of (something) by lifting ▷ n weight
HEFTE same as ▶ heave
HEFTED ▶ heft
HEFTER, -S ▶ heft
HEFTIER ▶ hefty
HEFTIEST ▶ hefty
HEFTILY ▶ hefty
HEFTING ▶ heft
HEFTS ▶ heft
HEFTY, HEFTIER, HEFTIEST adj large, heavy, or strong
HEGARI, -S n African sorghum
HEGEMON, -S n person in authority
HEGEMONY n political domination
HEGIRA, -S n emigration escape or flight
HEGUMEN, -S n head of a monastery of the Eastern Church
HEGUMENE n head of Greek nunnery
HEGUMENS ▶ hegumen
HEGUMENY n office of hegumen
HEH, -S interj exclamation of surprise or inquiry
HEID, -S Scot word for ▶ head
HEIFER, -S n young cow
HEIGH same as ▶ hey
HEIGHT, -S n distance from base to top
HEIGHTEN vb make or become higher or more intense
HEIGHTH, -S obsolete form of ▶ height
HEIGHTS ▶ height
HEIL, -ED, -ING, -S vb give a German greeting
HEIMISH adj comfortable
HEINIE, -S n buttocks
HEINOUS adj evil and shocking
HEIR, -ED, -ING, -S n person entitled to inherit property or rank ▷ vb inherit
HEIRDOM, -S n succession by right of blood

HEIRED ► heir
HEIRESS n woman who inherits or expects to inherit great wealth
HEIRING ► heir
HEIRLESS ► heir
HEIRLOOM n object that has belonged to a family for generations
HEIRS ► heir
HEIRSHIP n state or condition of being an heir
HEISHI n Native American shell jewellery
HEIST, -ED, -ING, -S n robbery ▷ vb steal or burgle
HEISTER -S
HEITIKI, -S n Māori neck ornament of greenstone
HEJAB, -S same as ► hijab
HEJIRA, -S same as ► hegira
HEJRA, -S same as ► hegira
HEKETARA n small shrub that has flowers with white petals and yellow centres
HEKTARE, -S same as ► hectare
HELCOID adj having ulcers
HELD ► hold
HELE, -D, -S, HELING vb as in **hele in** insert (cuttings, etc) into soil
HELENIUM n plant with daisy-like yellow or variegated flowers
HELES ► hele
HELIAC same as ► heliacal
HELIACAL adj as in **heliacal rising** rising of a celestial object at approximately the same time as the rising of the sun
HELIAST, -S n ancient Greek juror
HELIBUS n helicopter carrying passengers
HELICAL adj spiral
HELICASE n enzyme vital to all living organisms
HELICES ► helix
HELICITY n projection of the spin of an elementary particle on the direction of propagation
HELICOID adj shaped like a spiral ▷ n any surface resembling that of a screw thread
HELICON, -S n bass tuba
HELICOPT vb transport using a helicopter
HELIDECK n landing deck for helicopters on ships, oil platforms, etc
HELILIFT vb transport by helicopter

HELIMAN, HELIMEN n helicopter pilot
HELING ► hele
HELIO, -S n instrument for sending messages in Morse code
HELIODOR n clear yellow form of beryl used as a gemstone
HELIOS ► helio
HELIOSIS, HELIOSES n bad effect of overexposure to the sun
HELIPAD, -S n place for helicopters to land and take off
HELIPORT n airport for helicopters
HELISKI, -S vb ski down a mountain after ascending it by helicopter
HELISTOP n landing place for helicopter
HELITACK n use of helicopters to extinguish a forest fire
HELIUM, -S n very light colourless odourless gas
HELIX, HELICES, -ES n spiral
HELL, -ED, -ING, -S n believed to be where wicked people go when they die ▷ vb act wildly
HELLBENT adj intent
HELLBOX n (in printing) container for broken type
HELLCAT, -S n spiteful fierce-tempered woman
HELLED ► hell
HELLER, -S n monetary unit of the Czech Republic and Slovakia
HELLERI, -S n Central American fish
HELLERS ► heller
HELLERY n wild or mischievous behaviour
HELLFIRE n torment of hell, imagined as eternal fire
HELLHOLE n unpleasant or evil place
HELLICAT n evil creature
HELLIER, -S n slater
HELLING ► hell
HELLION, -S n rough or rowdy person, esp a child
HELLISH adj very unpleasant ▷ adv (intensifier) extremely
HELLKITE n bird of prey from hell
HELLO, -ED, -ES, -ING, -S interj expression of greeting or surprise ▷ n act of saying 'hello' ▷ sentence substitute expression of greeting ▷ vb say hello
HELLOVA same as ► helluva

HELLS ► hell
HELLUVA adj extremely good
HELLWARD adj towards hell
HELM, -ED, -ING, -S n tiller or wheel for steering a ship ▷ vb direct or steer
HELMER, -S n film director
HELMET, -S n hard hat worn for protection
HELMETED
HELMING ► helm
HELMINTH n any parasitic worm, esp a nematode or fluke
HELMLESS ► helm
HELMS ► helm
HELMSMAN, HELMSMEN n person at the helm who steers the ship
HELO, -S n helicopter
HELOT, -S n serf or slave
HELOTAGE same as ► helotism
HELOTISM n condition or quality of being a helot
HELOTRY n serfdom or slavery
HELOTS ► helot
HELP, -ED, -S vb make something easier, better, or quicker for (someone) ▷ n assistance or support
HELPABLE
HELPDESK n place where advice is given by telephone
HELPED ► help
HELPER, -S ► help
HELPFUL adj giving help
HELPING, -S n single portion of food
HELPLESS adj weak or incapable
HELPLINE n telephone line set aside for callers to contact an organization for help with a problem
HELPMATE n companion and helper, esp a spouse
HELPMEET less common word for ► helpmate
HELPS ► help
HELVE, -D, -S, HELVING n handle of a hand tool such as an axe or pick ▷ vb fit a helve to (a tool)
HEM, -MED, -MING, -S n bottom edge of a garment ▷ vb provide with a hem
HEMAGOG, -S same as > hemagogue
HEMAL same as ► haemal
HEMATAL same as ► hemal
HEMATEIN same as > haematein
HEMATIC, -S same as ► haematic

H

HEMATIN, -S *same as*
► **haematin**

HEMATINE *n* red dye

HEMATINS ► **hematin**

HEMATITE *n* red, grey, or black
mineral

HEMATOID *same as*
> **haematoid**

HEMATOMA *same as*
> **haematoma**

HEME, -S *same as* ► **haem**

HEMIC *same as* ► **haematic**

HEMIN, -S *same as* ► **haemin**

HEMINA, -S *n* old liquid
measure

HEMINS ► **hemin**

HEMIOLA, -S *n* rhythmic
device

HEMIOLIA *same as*
► **hemiola**

HEMIOLIC ► **hemiola**

HEMIONE, -S *same as*
► **hemionus**

HEMIONUS *n* Asian wild ass

HEMIOPIA *n* defective vision
seeing only halves of things
HEMIOPIC

HEMIPOD, -S *same as*
► **hemipode**

HEMIPODE *n* button quail

HEMIPODS ► **hemipod**

HEMIPTER *n* insect with
beaklike mouthparts

HEMLINE, -S *n* level to which
the hem of a skirt hangs

HEMLOCK, -S *n* poisonous
plant

HEMMED ► **hem**

HEMMER, -S *n* attachment
on a sewing machine for
hemming

HEMMING ► **hem**

HEMOCOEL *same as*
> **haemocoel**

HEMOCYTE *same as*
> **haemocyte**

HEMOID *same as*
> **haematoid**

HEMOLYSE *vb* break down
so that haemoglobulin is
released

HEMOLYZE *vb* undergo or
make undergo hemolysis

HEMOSTAT *same as*
> **haemostat**

HEMP, -S *n* Asian plant with
tough fibres
HEMPEN

HEMPIE *variant of* ► **hempy**

HEMPIER ► **hempy**

HEMPIES ► **hempy**

HEMPIEST ► **hempy**

HEMPLIKE ► **hemp**

HEMPS ► **hemp**

HEMPSEED *n* seed of hemp

HEMPWEED *n* climbing weed

**HEMPY, HEMPIER, HEMPIES,
HEMPIEST** *adj* of or like
hemp ▷ *n* rogue

HEMS ► **hem**

HEN, -NED, -NING, -S *n* female
domestic fowl ▷ *vb* lose
one's courage

HENBANE, -S *n* poisonous
plant with sticky hairy leaves

HENBIT, -S *n* European plant
with small dark red flowers

HENCE *adv* from this time
▷ *interj* begone! away!

HENCHMAN, HENCHMEN
n person employed by
someone powerful to carry
out orders

HENCOOP, -S *n* cage for
poultry

HEND, -ED, -ING, -S *vb* seize

HENEQUEN *n* agave plant
native to Yucatán

HENEQUIN *same as*
► **henequen**

HENGE, -S *n* monument
from the Neolithic and
Bronze Ages

HENHOUSE *n* coop for hens

HENIQUEN *same as*
► **henequen**

HENIQUIN *same as*
► **heniquen**

HENLEY, -S *n* type of sweater

HENLIKE ► **hen**

HENNA, -ED, -ING, -S *n*
reddish dye made from a
shrub or tree ▷ *vb* dye (the
hair) with henna

HENNED ► **hen**

HENNER, -S *n* challenge

HENNERY *n* place or farm for
keeping poultry

HENNIER ► **henny**

HENNIES ► **henny**

HENNIEST ► **henny**

HENNIN, -S *n* former women's
hat

HENNING ► **hen**

HENNINS ► **hennin**

HENNISH ► **hen**

**HENNY, HENNIER, HENNIES,
HENNIEST** *adj* like a hen ▷ *n*
cock that looks like a hen

HENOTIC *adj* acting to
reconcile

HENPECK, -S *vb* (of a woman)
to harass or torment (a man)

HENRY, HENRIES, -S *n* unit of
electrical inductance

HENS ► **hen**

HENT, -ED, -ING, -S *vb* seize
▷ *n* anything that has been
grasped, esp by the mind

HEP, -PER, -PEST, -S *same
as* ► **hip**

HEPAR, -S *n* compound
containing sulphur

HEPARIN, -S *n* polysaccharide
present in most body tissues

HEPARS ► **hepar**

HEPATIC, -S *adj* of the liver ▷ *n*
any of various drugs for use in
treating diseases of the liver

HEPATICA *n* woodland plant
with white, mauve, or pink
flowers

HEPATICS ► **hepatic**

HEPATISE *same as*
► **hepatize**

HEPATITE *n* mineral
containing sulphur

HEPATIZE *vb* turn into liver

HEPATOMA *n* cancer of liver

HEPCAT, -S *n* person who
is hep

HEPPER ► **hep**

HEPPEST ► **hep**

HEPS ► **hep**

HEPSTER, -S *same as*
► **hipster**

HEPT *archaic spelling of*
► **heaped**

HEPTAD, -S *n* group or series
of seven

HEPTAGON *n* geometric
figure with seven sides

HEPTANE, -S *n* alkane found in
petroleum

HEPTARCH > **heptarchy**

HEPTOSE, -S *n* any
monosaccharide with seven
carbon atoms per molecule

HER *pron* refers to anything
personified as feminine
▷ *adj* belonging to her
▷ *determiner* of, belonging to,
or associated with her

HERALD, -ED, -S *n* person
who announces important
news ▷ *vb* signal the
approach of

HERALDIC *adj* of or relating to
heraldry

HERALDRY *n* study of coats of
arms and family trees

HERALDS ► **herald**

HERB, -S *n* plant used for
flavouring in cookery, and in
medicine

HERBAGE, -S *n* herbaceous
plants collectively

HERBAGED *adj* with grass
growing on it

HERBAGES ► **herbage**

HERBAL, -S *adj* of or relating
to herbs, usually culinary or
medicinal herbs ▷ *n* book
describing and listing the
properties of plants

HERBAR, -S *same as*
► **herbary**

HERBARIA > **herbarium**
HERBARS ► **herbar**
HERBARY n herb garden
HERBED adj flavoured with herbs
HERBELET same as ► **herblet**
HERBIER ► **herby**
HERBIEST ► **herby**
HERBIST, -S same as > **herbalist**
HERBLESS ► **herb**
HERBLET, -S n little herb
HERBLIKE ► **herb**
HERBOSE same as ► **herbous**
HERBOUS adj with abundance of herbs
HERBS ► **herb**
HERBY, HERBIER, HERBIEST adj abounding in herbs
HERCULES n as in **hercules beetle** very large tropical American beetle
HERD, -ED, -S n group of animals feeding and living together ▷ vb collect into a herd
HERDBOY, -S n boy who looks after herd
HERDED ► **herd**
HERDEN, -S n type of coarse cloth
HERDER, -S same as ► **herdsman**
HERDESS n female herder
HERDIC, -S n small horse-drawn carriage
HERDING, -S n act of herding
HERDLIKE ► **herd**
HERDMAN, HERDMEN same as ► **herdsman**
HERDS ► **herd**
HERDSMAN, HERDSMEN n man who looks after a herd of animals
HERDWICK n hardy breed of sheep
HERE, -S adv in, at, or to this place or point ▷ n this place
HEREAT adv because of this
HEREAWAY same as > **hereabout**
HEREBY adv by means of or as a result of this
HEREDES ► **heres**
HEREDITY n passing on of characteristics from one generation to another
HEREFROM adv from here
HEREIN adv in this place, matter, or document
HEREINTO adv into this place, circumstance, etc
HERENESS n state of being here
HEREOF adv of or concerning this

HEREON archaic word for ► **hereupon**
HERES, HEREDES ► **here**
HERESY, HERESIES n opinion contrary to accepted opinion or belief
HERETIC, -S n person who holds unorthodox opinions
HERETO adv this place, matter, or document
HERETRIX n in Scots law, female inheritor
HEREUNTO archaic word for ► **hereto**
HEREUPON adv following immediately after this
HEREWITH adv with this
HERIED ► **hery**
HERIES ► **hery**
HERIOT, -S n (in medieval England) a death duty paid to the lord
HERISSE adj with bristles
HERISSON n spiked beam used as fortification
HERITAGE n something inherited
HERITOR, -S n person who inherits
HERITRIX
HERL, -S n barb or barbs of a feather
HERLING, -S n Scots word for a type of fish
HERLS ► **herl**
HERM, -S n (in ancient Greece) a stone head of Hermes
HERMA, -E, -I same as ► **herm**
HERMAEAN adj type of statue
HERMAI ► **herma**
HERMETIC adj sealed so as to be airtight
HERMIT, -S n person living in solitude, esp for religious reasons
HERMITIC
HERMITRY n life as hermit
HERMITS ► **hermit**
HERMS ► **herm**
HERN, -S archaic or dialect word for ► **heron**
HERNIA, -E, -S n medical problem
HERNIAL
HERNIATE n form hernia
HERNS ► **hern**
HERNSHAW same as > **heronshaw**
HERO, -ES, -S n principal character in a film, book, etc
HEROIC adj courageous
HEROICAL same as ► **heroic**
HEROICLY ► **heroic**
HEROICS pl n extravagant behaviour

HEROIN, -S n highly addictive illegal drug derived from morphine
HEROINE, -S n principal female character in a novel, play, etc
HEROINS ► **heroin**
HEROISE, -D, -S same as ► **heroize**
HEROISM, -S n great courage and bravery
HEROIZE, -D, -S vb make into hero
HERON, -S n long-legged wading bird
HERONRY n colony of breeding herons
HERONS ► **heron**
HERONSEW same as > **heronshaw**

H

HEROON, -S n temple or monument dedicated to hero
HEROS ► **hero**
HEROSHIP ► **hero**
HERPES, -ES n any of several inflammatory skin diseases
HERPETIC adj of or relating to herpes ▷ n person suffering from herpes
HERPTILE adj denoting, relating to, or characterizing both reptiles and amphibians
HERRIED ► **herry**
HERRIES ► **herry**
HERRING, -S n important food fish of northern seas
HERRY, HERRIED, HERRIES, -ING vb harry
HERS pron something belonging to her
HERSALL, -S n rehearsal
HERSE, -S n harrow
HERSED adj arranged like a harrow
HERSELF pron feminine singular reflexive form
HERSES ► **herse**
HERSHIP, -S n act of plundering
HERSTORY n history from a female point of view or as it relates to women
HERTZ, -ES n unit of frequency
HERY, HERIED, HERIES, -ING vb praise
HERYE, -D, -S same as ► **hery**
HERYING ► **hery**
HES ► **he**
HESITANT adj undecided or wavering
HESITATE vb be slow or uncertain in doing something
HESP, -ED, -ING, -S same as ► **hasp**

HESPERID n species of butterfly

HESPING ► hesp

HESPS ► hesp

HESSIAN, -S n coarse jute fabric

HESSITE, -S n black or grey metallic mineral

HEST, -S archaic word for ► **behest**

HET adj Scots word for ► **hot**

HETAIRIA n society

HETE, -S, HETING same as ► **hight**

HETH, -S n eighth letter of the Hebrew alphabet

HETHER same as ► **hither**

HETHS ► heth

HETING ► hete

HETMAN, -S, HETMEN another word for ► **ataman**

HEUCH, -S Scots word for ► **crag**

HEUCHERA n N American plant with heart-shaped leaves and mostly red flowers

HEUCHS ► heuch

HEUGH, -S same as ► **heuch**

HEUREKA, -S same as ► **eureka**

HEURETIC same as > **heuristic**

HEURISM, -S n use of logic

HEVEA, -S n rubber-producing South American tree

HEW, -ED, -N, -S vb cut with an axe

HEWABLE

HEWER -S

HEWGH interj sound made to imitate the flight of an arrow

HEWING, -S ► hew

HEWN ► hew

HEWS ► hew

HEX, -ED, -ES adj of or relating to hexadecimal notation ▷ n evil spell ▷ vb bewitch

> This word meaning to bewitch is a really useful one for using the X.

HEXACT, -S n part of a sponge with six rays

HEXAD, -S n group or series of six

HEXADE, -S same as ► **hexad**

HEXADIC ► hexad

HEXADS ► hexad

HEXAFOIL n pattern with six lobes

HEXAGLOT n book written in six languages

HEXAGON, -S n geometrical figure with six sides

HEXAGRAM n star formed by extending the sides of a regular hexagon to meet at six points

HEXAMINE n fuel for camping stoves

HEXANE, -S n liquid alkane existing in five isomeric forms

HEXANOIC adj as in **hexanoic acid** insoluble oily carboxylic acid found in coconut and palm oils and in milk

HEXAPLA, -S n edition of the Old Testament

HEXAPLAR

HEXAPOD, -S n six-footed arthropod

HEXAPODY n verse measure consisting of six metrical feet

HEXARCH adj (of a plant) with six veins

HEXARCHY n alliance of six states

HEXED ► hex

HEXENE, -S same as ► **hexylene**

HEXER, -S ► hex

HEXEREI, -S n witchcraft

HEXERS ► hexer

HEXES ► hex

HEXING, -S ► hex

HEXONE, -S n colourless insoluble liquid ketone

HEXOSAN, -S n form of polysaccharide

HEXOSE, -S n monosaccharide, such as glucose

HEXYL, -S adj of or consisting of a specific group of atoms

HEXYLENE n chemical compound similar to ethylene

HEXYLIC ► hexyl

HEXYLS ► hexyl

HEY, -ED, -ING, -S interj expression of surprise or for catching attention ▷ vb perform a country dance

HEYDAY, -S n time of greatest success, prime

HEYDEY, -S variant of ► **heyday**

HEYDUCK, -S same as ► **haiduk**

HEYED ► hey

HEYING ► hey

HEYS ► hey

HI interj hello

HIANT adj gaping

HIATAL ► hiatus

HIATUS, -ES n pause or interruption in continuity

HIBACHI, -S n portable brazier for heating and cooking food

HIBERNAL adj of or occurring in winter

HIBISCUS n tropical plant with large brightly coloured flowers

HIC interj representation of the sound of a hiccup

HICATEE, -S same as ► **hiccatee**

HICCATEE n tortoise of West Indies

HICCOUGH same as ► **hiccup**

HICCUP, -ED, -S n spasm of the breathing organs ▷ vb make a hiccup

HICCUPY

HICK, -ER, -EST, -S n unsophisticated country person ▷ adj unsophisticated

HICKEY, -S n object or gadget

HICKIE, -S same as ► **hickey**

HICKISH ► hick

HICKORY n N American nut-bearing tree

HICKS ► hick

HICKWALL n green woodpecker

HICKYMAL n titmouse

HID ► hide

HIDABLE ► hide

HIDAGE, -S n former tax on land

HIDALGA, -S n Spanish noblewoman

HIDALGO, -S n member of the lower nobility in Spain

HIDDEN ► hide

HIDDENLY ► hide

HIDDER, -S n young ram

HIDE, HID, HIDDEN, -D, -S vb put (oneself or an object) somewhere difficult to see or find ▷ n place of concealment, esp for a bird-watcher

HIDEAWAY n private place

HIDED ► hide

HIDELESS ► hide

HIDEOUS adj ugly, revolting

HIDEOUT, -S n hiding place

HIDER, -S ► hide

HIDES ► hide

HIDING, -S ► hide

HIDLING n hiding place

HIDLINGS adv in secret

HIDLINS same as ► **hidlings**

HIDROSIS, HIDROSES n any skin disease affecting the sweat glands

HIDROTIC

HIE, -D, -ING, -S, HYING vb hurry

HIELAMAN n Australian Aboriginal shield

HIELAND adj characteristic of Highlanders

HIEMAL less common word for ▸ **hibernal**

HIEMS n winter

HIERARCH n person in a position of high-priestly authority

HIERATIC adj of or relating to priests ▸ n hieratic script of ancient Egypt

HIERURGY n performance of religious drama or music

HIES ▸ **hie**

HIGGLE, -D, -S, HIGGLING less common word for ▸ **haggle**

HIGGLER -S

HIGH, -ED, -EST, -ING, -S adj being a relatively great distance from top to bottom; tall ▸ adv at or to a height ▸ n high place or level ▸ vb hie

HIGHBALL n tall drink of whisky with soda water or ginger ale and ice ▸ vb move at great speed

HIGHBORN adj of noble or aristocratic birth

HIGHBOY, -S n tall chest of drawers in two sections

HIGHBRED adj of noble breeding

HIGHBROW n intellectual and serious person ▸ adj concerned with serious, intellectual subjects

HIGHBUSH adj (of bush) growing tall ▸ n tall-growing bush

HIGHED ▸ **high**

HIGHER, -ED, -S n advanced level of the Scottish Certificate of Education ▸ vb raise up

HIGHEST ▸ **high**

HIGHING ▸ **high**

HIGHISH ▸ **high**

HIGHJACK same as ▸ **hijack**

HIGHLAND n relatively high ground

HIGHLIFE n African music genre

HIGHLY adv extremely

HIGHMAN, HIGHMEN n dice weighted to make it fall in particular way

HIGHMOST adj highest

HIGHNESS n condition of being high or lofty

HIGHRISE n tall building

HIGHROAD n main road

HIGHS ▸ **high**

HIGHSPOT n highlight

HIGHT, -ED, -S, HOTE, HOTEN vb archaic word for name or call

HIGHTAIL vb go or move in a great hurry

HIGHTED ▸ **hight**

HIGHTH, -S old form of ▸ **height**

HIGHTING n oath

HIGHTOP, -S n top of ship's mast

HIGHTS ▸ **hight**

HIGHVELD n high-altitude grassland region of E South Africa

HIGHWAY, -S n main road

HIJAB, -S n covering for the head and face

HIJACK, -ED, -S vb seize control of (an aircraft or other vehicle) while travelling ▸ n instance of hijacking

HIJACKER

HIJINKS n lively enjoyment

HIJRA, -S same as ▸ **hijrah**

HIJRAH, -S same as ▸ **hegira**

HIJRAS ▸ **hijra**

HIKE, -D, -S, HIKING n long walk in the country, esp for pleasure ▸ vb go for a long walk

HIKER -S

HIKOI, -ED, -ING, -S n walk or march, esp a Māori protest march ▸ vb take part in such a march

HILA ▸ **hilum**

HILAR ▸ **hilus**

HILARITY n mirth and merriment

HILCH, -ED, -ES, -ING vb hobble

HILD same as ▸ **hold**

HILDING, -S n coward

HILI ▸ **hilus**

HILL, -ED, -ING, -S n raised part of the earth's surface ▸ vb form into a hill or mound

HILLER -S

HILLFOLK n people living in the hills

HILLFORT n fortified hilltop

HILLIER ▸ **hilly**

HILLIEST ▸ **hilly**

HILLING, -S ▸ **hill**

HILLMEN same as ▸ **hillfolk**

HILLO, -ED, -ES, -ING, -S same as ▸ **hello**

HILLOA, -ED, -S same as ▸ **halloa**

HILLOCK, -S n small hill

HILLOCKY

HILLOED ▸ **hillo**

HILLOES ▸ **hillo**

HILLOING ▸ **hillo**

HILLOS ▸ **hillo**

HILLS ▸ **hill**

HILLSIDE n side of a hill

HILLTOP, -S n top of hill

HILLY, HILLIER, HILLIEST ▸ **hill**

HILT, -ED, -ING, -S n handle of a sword or knife ▸ vb supply with a hilt

HILTLESS

HILUM, HILA n scar on a seed

HILUS, HILI rare word for ▸ **hilum**

HIM, -S pron refers to a male person or animal ▸ n male person

HIMATION, HIMATIA n (in ancient Greece) a cloak draped around the body

HIMBO, -S n slang, usually derogatory term for an attractive but empty-headed man

HIMS ▸ **him**

HIMSELF pron masculine singular reflexive form

HIN, -S n Hebrew unit of capacity

HINAHINA same as ▸ **mahoe**

HINAU, -S n New Zealand tree

HIND, -MOST, -S adj situated at the back ▸ n female deer

HINDCAST vb test (a mathematical model)

HINDER, -ED, -S vb get in the way of ▸ adj situated at the back

HINDERER

HINDFOOT, HINDFEET n back foot

HINDGUT, -S n part of the vertebrate digestive tract

HINDHEAD n back of head

HINDLEG, -S n back leg

HINDMILK n breast milk produced after the first part of feeding

HINDMOST ▸ **hind**

HINDS ▸ **hind**

HINDWARD adj at back

HINDWING n back wing

HING, -S n asafoetida

HINGE, -D, -S, HINGING n device for holding two parts so one can swing freely ▸ vb depend (on)

HINGER, -S n tool for making hinges

HINGES ▸ **hinge**

HINGING ▸ **hinge**

HINGS ▸ **hing**

HINKY, HINKIER, HINKIEST adj strange

HINNIE n sweetheart

HINNY, HINNIED, HINNIES, -ING n offspring of a male horse and a female donkey ▸ vb whinny

HINS ▸ **hin**

H

HINT, -ED, -S n indirect suggestion ▷ vb suggest indirectly
HINTER -S
HINTING, -S ▸ hint
HINTS ▸ hint
HIOI, -S n New Zealand plant of the mint family
HIP, -PER, -PEST, -S, -T n either side of the body between the pelvis and the thigh ▷ adj aware of or following the latest trends ▷ interj exclamation used to introduce cheers
HIPBONE, -S n either of the bones that form the sides of the pelvis
HIPLESS ▸ hip
HIPLIKE ▸ hip
HIPLINE, -S n widest part of a person's hips
HIPLY ▸ hip
HIPNESS ▸ hip
HIPPARCH n (in ancient Greece) a cavalry commander
HIPPED adj having a hip or hips
HIPPEN, -S n baby's nappy
HIPPER ▸ hip
HIPPEST ▸ hip
HIPPIC adj of horses
HIPPIE same as ▸ **hippy**
HIPPIER ▸ hippy
HIPPIES ▸ hippy
HIPPIEST ▸ hippy
HIPPIN, -S same as ▸ **hippen**
HIPPING, -S same as ▸ **hippen**
HIPPINS ▸ hippin
HIPPISH adj in low spirits
HIPPO, -S n hippopotamus
HIPPURIC adj as in **hippuric acid** crystalline solid excreted in the urine of mammals
HIPPUS, -ES n spasm of eye
HIPPY, HIPPIER, HIPPIES, HIPPIEST n person whose behaviour implies a rejection of values ▷ adj having large hips
HIPPYDOM
HIPPYISH adj pertaining to or like a hippy
HIPS ▸ hip
HIPSHOT adj having a dislocated hip
HIPSTER n enthusiast of modern jazz
HIPSTERS pl n trousers cut so that the top encircles the hips
HIPT ▸ hip
HIRABLE ▸ hire
HIRAGANA n Japanese system of writing
HIRAGE, -S n fee for hiring

HIRCINE adj of or like a goat, esp in smell
HIRE, -D, -S vb pay to have temporary use of ▷ n hiring
HIREABLE
HIREAGE, -S same as ▸ **hirage**
HIRED ▸ hire
HIREE, -S n hired person
HIRELING n derogatory term for a person who works only for wages
HIRER, -S ▸ hire
HIRES ▸ hire
HIRING, -S ▸ hire
HIRLING, -S n Scots word for a type of fish
HIRPLE, -D, -S, HIRPLING vb limp ▷ n limping gait
HIRRIENT n trilled sound
HIRSEL, -ED, -S vb sort into groups
HIRSLE, -D, -S, HIRSLING vb wriggle or fidget
HIRSTIE adj dry
HIRSUTE adj hairy
HIRUDIN, -S n anticoagulant
HIS adj belonging to him
HISH, -ED, -ES, -ING same as ▸ **hiss**
HISN dialect form of ▸ **his**
HISPID adj covered with stiff hairs or bristles
HISS, -ED, -ES n sound like that of a long s (as an expression of contempt) ▷ vb utter a hiss ▷ interj exclamation of derision or disapproval
HISSELF dialect form of ▸ **himself**
HISSER, -S ▸ hiss
HISSES ▸ hiss
HISSIER ▸ hissy
HISSIES ▸ hissy
HISSIEST ▸ hissy
HISSING, -S ▸ hiss
HISSY, HISSIER, HISSIES, HISSIEST n temper tantrum ▷ adj sound similar to a hiss
HIST, -ED, -ING, -S interj exclamation used to attract attention ▷ vb make hist sound
HISTAMIN variant of > **histamine**
HISTED ▸ hist
HISTIDIN variant of > **histidine**
HISTIE same as ▸ **hirstie**
HISTING ▸ hist
HISTIOID same as ▸ **histoid**
HISTOGEN n obsolete botanical term
HISTOID adj (esp of a tumour)
HISTONE, -S n any of a group of proteins present in cell nuclei

HISTORIC adj famous or significant in history
HISTORY n (record or account of) past events
HISTRIO, -S n actor
HISTRION same as ▸ **histrio**
HISTRIOS ▸ histrio
HISTS ▸ hist
HIT, -S, -TING vb strike, touch forcefully ▷ n hitting
HITCH, -ED, -ES, -ING n minor problem ▷ vb obtain (a lift) by hitchhiking
HITCHER -S
HITCHIER ▸ hitchy
HITCHILY ▸ hitch
HITCHING ▸ hitch
HITCHY, HITCHIER ▸ hitch
HITHE, -S n small harbour
HITHER, -ED, -S adv or towards this place ▷ vb come
HITHERTO adv until this time
HITHES ▸ hithe
HITLESS ▸ hit
HITMAKER n successful performer or producer of popular music
HITMAN, HITMEN n professional killer
HITS ▸ hit
HITTABLE ▸ hit
HITTER, -S n boxer who has a hard punch rather than skill or finesse
HITTING ▸ hit
HIVE, -D, HIVING n structure in which social bees live and rear their young ▷ vb cause (bees) to collect or (of bees) to collect inside a hive
HIVELESS
HIVELIKE
HIVER, -S n person who keeps beehives
HIVES n allergic reaction
HIVEWARD adj towards hive
HIVING ▸ hive
HIYA sentence substitute informal term of greeting
HIZEN, -S n type of Japanese porcelain
HIZZ, -ED, -ES, -ING same as ▸ **hiss**
HIZZONER n nickname for mayor
HM interj sound made to express hesitation or doubt
HMM same as ▸ **hm**

This variant of **hm**, like its shorter form, can be useful when you have a shortage of vowels.

HMMM interj expressing thoughtful consideration

HO, -ING, -S interj imitation or representation of the sound of a deep laugh ▷ n cry of 'ho' ▷ vb halt

HOA, -ED, -ING, -S same as ▸ ho

HOACTZIN same as ▸ hoatzin

HOAED ▸ hoa

HOAGIE, -S n sandwich made with long bread roll

HOAGY same as ▸ hoagie

HOAING ▸ hoa

HOAR, -ED, -ING, -S adj covered with hoarfrost ▷ vb make hoary

HOARD, -ED, -S n store hidden away for future use ▷ vb save or store

HOARDER -S

HOARDING n large board for displaying advertisements

HOARDS ▸ hoard

HOARED ▸ hoar

HOARHEAD n person with white hair

HOARIER ▸ hoary

HOARIEST ▸ hoary

HOARILY ▸ hoary

HOARING ▸ hoar

HOARS ▸ hoar

HOARSE, -R, -ST adj (of a voice) rough and unclear

HOARSELY

HOARSEN, -S vb make or become hoarse

HOARSER ▸ hoarse

HOARSEST ▸ hoarse

HOARY, HOARIER, HOARIEST adj grey or white(-haired)

HOAS ▸ hoa

HOAST, -ED, -ING, -S n cough ▷ vb cough

HOASTMAN, HOASTMEN n shipper of coal

HOASTS ▸ hoast

HOATZIN, -S n South American bird

HOAX, -ED, -ES, -ING n deception or trick ▷ vb deceive or play a trick upon

HOAXER -S

HOB, -BED, -BING, -S n flat top part of a cooker ▷ vb cut or form with a hob

HOBBER, -S n machine used in making gears

HOBBIES ▸ hobby

HOBBING ▸ hob

HOBBISH adj like a clown

HOBBIT, -S n one of an imaginary race of half-size people

HOBBITRY

HOBBLE, -D, -S, HOBBLING vb walk lamely ▷ n strap, rope,

etc, used to hobble a horse

HOBBLER -S

HOBBY, HOBBIES n activity pursued in one's spare time

HOBBYISM

HOBBYIST

HOBDAY, -S vb alleviate a breathing problem in certain horses

HOBDAYED

HOBJOB, -S vb do odd jobs

HOBLIKE ▸ hob

HOBNAIL, -S n short nail with a large head for protecting soles ▷ vb provide with hobnails

HOBNOB, -S vb be on friendly terms (with)

HOBNOBBY

HOBO, -ED, -ES, -ING, -S n tramp or vagrant ▷ vb live as hobo

HOBODOM -S

HOBOISM, -S ▸ hobo

HOBOS ▸ hobo

HOBS ▸ hob

HOC adj Latin for this

HOCK, -ED, -ING, -S n joint in the leg of an animal corresponding to a human ankle ▷ vb pawn

HOCKER -S

HOCKEY, -S n team sport

HOCKING ▸ hock

HOCKLE, -D, -S, HOCKLING vb spit

HOCKS ▸ hock

HOCKSHOP n pawnshop

HOCUS, -ED, -ES, -ING, -SED, -SES vb take in

HOD, -DED, -DING, -S n open wooden box attached to a pole ▷ vb bob up and down

HODAD, -S n person who pretends to be a surfer

HODADDY same as ▸ hodad

HODADS ▸ hodad

HODDED ▸ hod

HODDEN, -S n coarse homespun cloth

HODDIN, -S same as ▸ hodden

HODDING ▸ hod

HODDINS ▸ hoddin

HODDLE, -D, -S, HODDLING vb waddle

HODJA, -S n respectful Turkish form of address

HODMAN, HODMEN n hod carrier

HODS ▸ hod

HOE, -D, -ING, -S n long-handled tool used for loosening soil or weeding ▷ vb scrape or weed with a hoe

HOECAKE, -S n maize cake

HOED ▸ hoe

HOEDOWN, -S n boisterous square dance

HOEING ▸ hoe

HOELIKE ▸ hoe

HOER, -S ▸ hoe

HOES ▸ hoe

HOG, -GED, -S n castrated male pig ▷ vb take more than one's share of

HOGAN, -S n wooden dwelling covered with earth

HOGBACK, -S n narrow ridge of steeply inclined rock strata

HOGEN, -S n strong alcoholic drink

HOGFISH n type of fish

HOGG, -S same as ▸ hog

HOGGED ▸ hog

HOGGER, -S ▸ hog

HOGGEREL n year-old sheep

HOGGERS ▸ hogger

HOGGERY n hogs collectively

HOGGET, -S n young unsheared sheep

HOGGIN, -S n finely sifted gravel

HOGGING, -S same as ▸ hoggin

HOGGINS ▸ hoggin

HOGGISH adj selfish, gluttonous, or dirty

HOGGS ▸ hogg

HOGH, -S n ridge of land

HOGHOOD, -S n condition of being hog

HOGHS ▸ hogh

HOGLIKE ▸ hog

HOGMANAY n New Year's Eve

HOGMANE, -S n short stiff mane

HOGMENAY variant of ▸ hogmanay

HOGNOSE, -S n as in **hognose snake** puff adder

HOGNOSED adj as in **hognosed skunk** any of several American skunks having a broad snoutlike nose

HOGNOSES ▸ hognose

HOGNUT, -S another name for ▸ pignut

HOGS ▸ hog

HOGSHEAD n large cask

HOGTIE, -D, -S, HOGTYING vb tie together the legs or the arms and legs of

HOGWARD, -S n person looking after hogs

HOGWASH n nonsense

HOGWEED, -S n any of several umbelliferous plants

HOH, -ED, -ING, -S same as ▸ ho

HOHA adj bored or annoyed

HOHED ▶ hoh

HOHING ▶ hoh

HOHS ▶ hoh

HOI, -ED, -ING, -S same as ▶ hoy

HOICK, -ED, -ING vb raise abruptly and sharply

HOICKS, -ED, -ES interj cry used to encourage hounds to hunt ▷ vb shout hoicks

HOIDEN, -ED, -S same as ▶ hoyden

HOIED ▶ hoi

HOIING ▶ hoi

HOIK, -ED, -ING, -S same as ▶ hoick

HOING ▶ ho

HOIS ▶ hoi

HOISE, -D, -S, HOISING same as ▶ hoist

HOISIN, -S n Chinese sweet spicy sauce

HOISING ▶ hoise

HOISINS ▶ hoisin

HOIST, -ED, -ING, -S vb raise or lift up ▷ n device for lifting things

HOISTER -S

HOISTMAN, HOISTMEN n person operating a hoist

HOISTS ▶ hoist

HOISTWAY n shaft for a hoist

HOKA, -S n red cod

HOKE, -D, -S, HOKING vb overplay (a part, etc)

HOKEY, HOKIER, HOKIEST adj corny

HOKI, -S n fish of New Zealand waters

HOKIER ▶ hokey

HOKIEST ▶ hokey

HOKILY ▶ hokey

HOKINESS ▶ hokey

HOKING ▶ hoke

HOKIS ▶ hoki

HOKKU same as ▶ haiku

HOKONUI, -S n illicit whisky

HOKUM, -S n rubbish, nonsense

HOKYPOKY n trickery

HOLARCHY n system composed of interacting holons

HOLARD, -S n amount of water contained in soil

HOLD, HELD, -S vb keep or support in or with the hands or arms ▷ n act or way of holding

HOLDABLE

HOLDALL, -S n large strong travelling bag

HOLDBACK n part of a horse harness

HOLDDOWN n control function in a computer

HOLDEN past participle of ▶ hold

HOLDER, -S n person or thing that holds

HOLDFAST n act of gripping strongly

HOLDING, -S ▶ hold

HOLDOUT, -S n (in US English) someone or thing that refuses to change

HOLDOVER n official who continues in office after his or her term has expired

HOLDS ▶ hold

HOLDUP, -S n robbery, esp an armed one

HOLE, -D, -S n area hollowed out in a solid ▷ vb make holes in

HOLELESS

HOLESOM same as ▶ holesome

HOLESOME same as > wholesome

HOLEY, -ER, -EST adj full of holes

HOLIBUT, -S same as ▶ halibut

HOLIDAY, -S n time spent away from home for rest or recreation ▷ vb spend a holiday

HOLIER ▶ holy

HOLIES ▶ holy

HOLIEST ▶ holy

HOLILY adv in a holy, devout, or sacred manner

HOLINESS n state of being holy

HOLING, -S ▶ hole

HOLISM, -S n view that a whole is greater than the sum of its parts

HOLIST -S

HOLISTIC adj considering the complete person, physically and mentally

HOLISTS ▶ holist

HOLK, -ED, -ING, -S vb dig

HOLLA, -ED, -ING, -S same as ▶ hollo

HOLLAND, -S n coarse linen cloth, used esp for furnishing

HOLLAS ▶ holla

HOLLER, -ED, -S n shout, yell ▷ vb shout or yell

HOLLIDAM same as ▶ halidom

HOLLIES ▶ holly

HOLLO, -ED, -ES, -ING, -S interj cry for attention, or of encouragement ▷ vb shout

HOLLOA, -ED, -S same as ▶ hollo

HOLLOED ▶ hollo

HOLLOES ▶ hollo

HOLLOING ▶ hollo

HOLLOO, -ED, -S same as ▶ halloo

HOLLOS ▶ hollo

HOLLOW, -ED, -ER, -S adj having a hole or space inside ▷ n cavity or space ▷ vb form a hollow in

HOLLOWLY

HOLLY, HOLLIES n evergreen tree with prickly leaves and red berries

HOLM, -S n island in a river, lake, or estuary

HOLME, -S same as ▶ holm

HOLMIA, -S n oxide of holmium

HOLMIC adj of or containing holmium

HOLMIUM, -S n silver-white metallic element

HOLMS ▶ holm

HOLO, -S n short for hologram

HOLOCENE adj of the most recent epoch of the Quaternary period

HOLOGAMY n condition of having gametes like ordinary cells

HOLOGRAM n three-dimensional photographic image

HOLOGYNY n inheritance of genetic traits through females only

HOLON, -S n autonomous self-reliant unit, esp in manufacturing

HOLONIC

HOLOPTIC adj with eyes meeting at the front

HOLOS ▶ holo

HOLOTYPE n original specimen from which a description of a new species is made

HOLOZOIC adj (of animals) obtaining nourishment by feeding on plants or other animals

HOLP past tense of ▶ help

HOLPEN past participle of ▶ help

HOLS pl n holidays

HOLSTEIN n breed of cattle

HOLSTER, -S n leather case for a pistol, hung from a belt ▷ vb return (a pistol) to its holster

HOLT, -S n otter's lair

HOLUBTSI pl n cabbage rolls

HOLY, HOLIER, HOLIES, HOLIEST adj of God or a god ▷ n sacred place

HOLYDAM, -S same as
► **halidom**
HOLYDAME same as
► **halidom**
HOLYDAMS ► holydam
HOLYDAY, -S n day on which a
religious festival is observed
HOLYTIDE n time for special
religious observance
HOM, -S n sacred plant of the
Parsees and ancient Persians
HOMA, -S same as ► **hom**
HOMAGE, -D, -S, HOMAGING
n show of respect or
honour towards someone
or something ▷ vb render
homage to
HOMAGER -S
HOMALOID n geometrical
plane
HOMAS ► homa
HOMBRE, -S slang word for
► **man**
HOMBURG, -S n man's soft
felt hat
HOME, -D, -S n place where
one lives ▷ adj of one's
home, birthplace, or native
country ▷ adv to or at home
▷ vb direct towards (a point
or target)
HOMEBIRD n person who is
reluctant to leave their home
HOMEBOY n person whose
life and interests are centred
on the home
HOMEBOY, -S n close friend
HOMEBRED adj raised or bred
at home ▷ n animal bred
at home
HOMEBREW n home-made
beer
HOMED ► home
HOMEFELT adj felt personally
HOMEGIRL ► homeboy
HOMELAND n country from
which a person's ancestors
came
HOMELESS adj having
nowhere to live ▷ pl n people
who have nowhere to live
HOMELIER ► homely
HOMELIKE ► home
HOMELILY ► homely
HOMELY, HOMELIER adj
simple, ordinary, and
comfortable
HOMELYN, -S n species of ray
HOMEMADE adj made at
home
HOMEOBOX adj of genes that
regulate cell development
HOMEOSIS, HOMEOSES n
process of one part coming
to resemble another
HOMEOTIC

HOMEPAGE n main page of
website
HOMEPORT n port where
vessel is registered
HOMER, -ED, -ING, -S n
homing pigeon ▷ vb score a
home run in baseball
HOMERIC adj grand or heroic
HOMERING ► homer
HOMEROOM n common
room at school
HOMERS ► homer
HOMES ► home
HOMESICK adj sad because
missing one's home and
family
HOMESITE n site for building
house
HOMESPUN adj (of
philosophies or opinions)
plain and unsophisticated
▷ n cloth made at home or
made of yarn spun at home
HOMESTAY n period spent
living as a guest in someone's
home
HOMETOWN n town where
one lives or was born
HOMEWARD adj going home
▷ adv towards home
HOMEWARE n crockery,
furniture, and furnishings
with which a house, room,
etc, is furnished
HOMEWORK n school work
done at home
HOMEY, -S same as ► **homy**
HOMICIDE n killing of a
human being
HOMIE, -S short for
► **homeboy**
HOMIER ► homy
HOMIES ► homie
HOMIEST ► homy
HOMILIES ► homily
HOMILIST ► homily
HOMILY, HOMILIES n speech
telling people how they
should behave
HOMINES ► homo
HOMINESS ► homy
HOMING, -S adj relating to
the ability to return home
after travelling ▷ n ability to
return home after travelling
HOMINIAN same as
► **hominid**
HOMINID, -S n man or any
extinct forerunner of man
▷ adj of or belonging to this
family
HOMINIES ► hominy
HOMININ, -S n member of a
zoological family
HOMININE adj characteristic
of humans

HOMININS ► hominin
HOMINISE same as
► **hominize**
HOMINIZE vb make suitable
for humans
HOMINOID n manlike animal
▷ adj of or like man
HOMINY, HOMINIES n
coarsely ground maize
HOMME, -S French word for
► **man**
HOMMOCK, -S same as
► **hummock**
HOMMOS, -ES same as
► **hummus**
HOMO, HOMINES, -S n
homogenized milk
HOMODONT adj (of most
nonmammalian vertebrates)
having teeth that are all of
the same type
HOMODYNE adj of
strengthened radio waves
HOMOGAMY n simultaneous
maturation of all the anthers
and stigmas of a flower
HOMOGENY n similarity in
structure of individuals or
parts because of common
ancestry
HOMOGONY n condition in a
plant of having stamens and
styles of the same length in
all the flowers
HOMOLOG, -S same as
> **homologue**
HOMOLOGY n condition of
being homologous
HOMONYM, -S n word that is
spelt the same as another
HOMONYMY n the quality of
being pronounced or spelt in
the same way
HOMOS ► homo
HOMOTONY > homotonic
HOMOTYPE n something
with same structure as
something else
HOMOTYPY
HOMS ► hom
HOMUNCLE n homunculus
HOMY, HOMIER, HOMIEST
adj like a home
HON, -S short for ► **honey**
HONAN, -S n silk fabric of
rough weave
HONCHO, -ED, -ES, -S n
person in charge ▷ vb
supervise or be in charge of
HOND, -S old form of ► **hand**
HONDA, -S n loop used to
make a lasso
HONDLE, -D, -S, HONDLING vb
negotiate on price
HONDS ► hond

H

H

HONE, -D, -S, HONING vb sharpen ▷ n fine whetstone used for sharpening edged tools and knives

HONER -S

HONEST, -ER adj truthful and moral

HONESTLY adv in an honest manner ▷ interj expression of disgust, surprise, etc

HONESTY n quality of being honest

HONEWORT n European plant that has clusters of small white flowers

HONEY, -ED, -ING, -S n edible substance made by bees; term of endearment ▷ vb sweeten with or as if with honey

HONEYBEE n bee widely domesticated as a source of honey and beeswax

HONEYBUN n term of endearment

HONEYDEW n sugary substance produced by aphids and similar insects

HONEYED ▸ honey

HONEYFUL adj full of honey

HONEYING ▸ honey

HONEYPOT n container for honey

HONEYS ▸ honey

HONG, -ING, -S n (in China) a factory, warehouse, etc ▷ vb archaic form of hang

HONGI, -ED, -ES, -ING, -S n Māori greeting in which people touch noses ▷ vb touch noses

HONGING ▸ hong

HONGIS ▸ hongi

HONGS ▸ hong

HONIED same as ▸ honey

HONIEDLY ▸ honey

HONING ▸ hone

HONK, -ED, -ING, -S n sound made by a car horn ▷ vb (cause to) make this sound

HONKER, -S n person or thing that honks

HONKING ▸ honk

HONKS ▸ honk

HONOR, -ED, -ING same as ▸ honour

HONORAND n person being honoured

HONORARY adj held or given only as an honour

HONORED ▸ honor

HONOREE, -S same as ▸ honorand

HONORER, -S ▸ honour

HONORING ▸ honor

HONORS same as ▸ honours

HONOUR, -ED, -S n sense of honesty and fairness ▷ vb give praise and attention to

HONOUREE n person who is honoured

HONOURER ▸ honour

HONOURS ▸ honour

HONS ▸ hon

HOO interj expression of joy, excitement, etc

HOOCH, -ES n alcoholic drink, esp illicitly distilled spirits

HOOCHIE, -S n immoral woman

HOOD, -ING, -S n head covering, often attached to a coat or jacket ▷ vb cover with or as if with a hood

HOODED adj (of a garment) having a hood

HOODIA, -S n any of several southern African succulent plants

HOODIE, -S n hooded sweatshirt

HOODIER ▸ hoody

HOODIES ▸ hoodie

HOODIEST ▸ hoody

HOODING ▸ hood

HOODLESS ▸ hood

HOODLIKE ▸ hood

HOODLUM, -S n violent criminal, gangster

HOODMAN, HOODMEN n blindfolded person in blindman's buff

HOODMOLD n moulding over door or window

HOODOO, -ED, -S n (cause of) bad luck ▷ vb bring bad luck to

HOODS ▸ hood

HOODWINK vb trick, deceive

HOODY, HOODIER, HOODIEST ▸ hood

HOOEY, -S n nonsense ▷ interj nonsense

HOOF, -ING, -S, HOOVES n horny covering of the foot of a horse, deer, etc ▷ vb kick or trample with the hooves

HOOFBEAT n sound made by hoof on the ground

HOOFED adj having a hoof or hoofs

HOOFER, -S n professional dancer

HOOFING ▸ hoof

HOOFLESS ▸ hoof

HOOFLIKE ▸ hoof

HOOFROT, -S n disease of hoof

HOOFS ▸ hoof

HOOK, -S n curved object used to hang, hold, or pull something ▷ vb fasten or catch (as if) with a hook

HOOKA, -S same as ▸ hookah

HOOKAH, -S n oriental pipe

HOOKAS ▸ hooka

HOOKED adj bent like a hook

HOOKER, -S n person or thing that hooks

HOOKEY, -S same as ▸ hooky

HOOKIER ▸ hooky

HOOKIES ▸ hooky

HOOKIEST ▸ hooky

HOOKING, -S n act of hooking

HOOKLESS ▸ hook

HOOKLET, -S n little hook

HOOKLIKE ▸ hook

HOOKNOSE n nose with a pronounced outward and downward curve

HOOKS ▸ hook

HOOKUP, -S n contact of an aircraft with the hose of a tanker aircraft

HOOKWORM n blood-sucking worm with hooked mouthparts

HOOKY, HOOKIER, HOOKIES, HOOKIEST n truancy, usually from school ▷ adj hooklike

HOOLEY, -S n lively party

HOOLICAN same as > hoolachan

HOOLIE, -S same as ▸ hooley

HOOLIER ▸ hooly

HOOLIES ▸ hoolie

HOOLIEST ▸ hooly

HOOLIGAN n rowdy young person

HOOLOCK, -S n Indian gibbon

HOOLY, HOOLIER, HOOLIEST adj careful or gentle

HOON, -ED, -ING, -S n loutish youth who drives irresponsibly ▷ vb drive irresponsibly

HOOP, -ED, -ING, -S n rigid circular band ▷ vb surround with or as if with a hoop

HOOPER, -S rare word for ▸ cooper

HOOPING ▸ hoop

HOOPLA, -S n fairground game

HOOPLESS ▸ hoop

HOOPLIKE ▸ hoop

HOOPOE, -S n bird with a pinkish-brown plumage

HOOPOO, -S same as ▸ hoopoe

HOOPS ▸ hoop

HOOPSTER n basketball player

HOOR, -S n unpleasant or difficult thing

HOORAH, -ED, -S same as ▸ hurrah

HOORAY, -ED, -S same as ▸ hurrah

HOORD, -S same as ▸ hoard

HOOROO same as ▶ **hurrah**

HOORS ▶ **hoor**

HOOSEGOW slang word for ▶ **jail**

HOOSGOW, -S same as ▶ **jail**

HOOSH, -ED, -ES, -ING vb shoo away

HOOT, -ED, -ING n sound of a car horn ▷ vb sound (a car horn) ▷ interj exclamation of impatience or dissatisfaction

HOOTCH, -ES same as ▶ **hooch**

HOOTED ▶ **hoot**

HOOTER, -S n device that hoots

HOOTIER ▶ **hooty**

HOOTIEST ▶ **hooty**

HOOTING ▶ **hoot**

HOOTS same as ▶ **hoot**

HOOTY, HOOTIER, HOOTIEST ▶ **hoot**

HOOVE, -D, HOOVING same as ▶ **heave**

HOOVEN

HOOVER, -ED, -S vb vacuum-clean (a carpet, furniture, etc)

HOOVES ▶ **hoof**

HOOVING ▶ **hoove**

HOP, -PED, -S vb jump on one foot ▷ n instance of hopping

HOPAK, -S n type of Ukrainian dance

HOPBIND, -S n stalk of the hop

HOPBINE, -S same as ▶ **hopbind**

HOPDOG, -S n species of caterpillar

HOPE, -D, -S, HOPING vb want (something) to happen or be true ▷ n expectation of something desired

HOPEFUL, -S adj having, expressing, or inspiring hope ▷ n person considered to be on the brink of success

HOPELESS adj having or offering no hope

HOPER, -S ▶ **hope**

HOPES ▶ **hope**

HOPFIELD n field where hops are grown

HOPING ▶ **hope**

HOPINGLY ▶ **hope**

HOPLITE, -S n (in ancient Greece) a heavily armed infantryman

HOPLITIC

HOPPED ▶ **hop**

HOPPER, -S n container for storing substances

HOPPIER ▶ **hoppy**

HOPPIEST ▶ **hoppy**

HOPPING, -S ▶ **hop**

HOPPLE, -D, -S, HOPPLING same as ▶ **hobble**

HOPPLER -S

HOPPUS adj as in **hoppus foot** unit of volume for round timber

HOPPY, HOPPIER, HOPPIEST adj tasting of hops

HOPS ▶ **hop**

HOPSACK, -S n roughly woven fabric

HOPTOAD, -S n toad

HORA, -S n traditional Israeli or Romanian circle dance

HORAH, -S same as ▶ **hora**

HORAL less common word for ▶ **hourly**

HORARY adj relating to the hours

HORAS ▶ **hora**

HORDE, -D, -S, HORDING n large crowd ▷ vb form, move in, or live in a horde

HORDEIN, -S n simple protein, rich in proline, that occurs in barley

HORDEOLA > **hordeolum**

HORDES ▶ **horde**

HORDING ▶ **horde**

HORDOCK, -S same as ▶ **hardoke**

HORE same as ▶ **hoar**

HORIZON, -S n apparent line that divides the earth and the sky

HORK, -ED, -ING, -S vb spit

HORKEY, -S same as ▶ **hockey**

HORKING ▶ **hork**

HORKS ▶ **hork**

HORLICKS n as in **make a horlicks** make a mistake or a mess

HORME, -S n (in Jungian psychology) fundamental vital energy

HORMESES ▶ **hormes**

HORMESIS n beneficial effect of exposure to a very small amount of a toxic substance

HORMETIC adj relating to hormesis

HORMIC ▶ **horme**

HORMONAL ▶ **hormone**

HORMONE, -S n substance secreted by certain glands

HORMONIC

HORN, -S n one of a pair of bony growths ▷ vb provide with a horn or horns

HORNBEAK n garfish

HORNBEAM n tree with smooth grey bark

HORNBILL n bird with a bony growth on its large beak

HORNBOOK n page of religious text with flattened cow horn over it

HORNBUG, -S n stag beetle

HORNED adj having a horn, horns, or hornlike parts

HORNER, -S n dealer in horn

HORNET, -S n large wasp with a severe sting

HORNFELS n hard fine-grained metamorphic rock

HORNFUL, -S n amount a horn will hold

HORNGELD n feudal rent based on number of cattle

HORNIER ▶ **horny**

HORNIEST ▶ **horny**

HORNILY ▶ **horny**

HORNING, -S ▶ **horn**

HORNISH adj like horn

HORNIST, -S n horn player

HORNITO, -S n small vent in volcano

HORNLESS ▶ **horn**

HORNLET, -S n small horn

HORNLIKE ▶ **horn**

HORNPIPE n (music for) a solo dance, traditionally performed by sailors

HORNPOUT n catfish

HORNS ▶ **horn**

HORNTAIL n wasplike insect

HORNWORK n bastion in fortifications

HORNWORM n caterpillar of hawk moth

HORNWORT n aquatic plant

HORNY, HORNIER, HORNIEST adj of or like horn

HOROEKA, -S n New Zealand tree

HOROKAKA n low-growing New Zealand plant with fleshy leaves and pink or white flowers

HOROLOGE rare word for > **timepiece**

HOROLOGY n art of making clocks and watches or of measuring time

HOROPITO n New Zealand plant

HOROPTER n locus of points in space that have the same disparity as fixation

HORRENT adj bristling

HORRIBLE adj disagreeable, unpleasant ▷ n horrible thing

HORRIBLY adv in a horrible manner

HORRID, -ER adj disagreeable, unpleasant

HORRIDLY

HORRIFIC adj causing horror

HORRIFY vb cause to feel horror or shock

HORROR n (thing or person causing) terror or hatred ▷ adj having a frightening subject

H

H

HORRORS pl n fit of depression or anxiety ▷ interj expression of dismay, sometimes facetious

HORS adv as in **hors d'oeuvre** appetizer

HORSE, -D, -S n large animal with hooves, a mane, and a tail ▷ vb provide with a horse

HORSEBOX n trailer used for transporting horses

HORSECAR n streetcar drawn by horses

HORSED ► horse

HORSEFLY n large bloodsucking fly

HORSEMAN, HORSEMEN n person skilled in riding

HORSEPOX n viral infection of horses

HORSES ► horse

HORSEWAY n road for horses

HORSEY, HORSIER, HORSIEST adj very keen on horses

HORSIE, -S n child's word for a horse

HORSIER ► horsey

HORSIES ► horsie

HORSIEST ► horsey

HORSILY ► horsey

HORSING, -S ► horse

HORST, -S n ridge of land

HORSTE, -S variant of ► horst

HORSTS ► horst

HORSY same as ► horsey

HOS ► ho

HOSANNA, -S interj exclamation of praise to God ▷ n act of crying "hosanna" ▷ vb cry hosanna

HOSANNAH same as ► hosanna

HOSANNAS ► hosanna

HOSE, -D, -N, -S, HOSING n flexible pipe for conveying liquid ▷ vb water with a hose

HOSEL, -S n socket in head of golf club

HOSELIKE ► hose

HOSELS ► hosel

HOSEMAN, HOSEMEN n fireman in charge of hose

HOSEN ► hose

HOSEPIPE n

HOSER, -S n person who swindles or deceives others

HOSES ► hose

HOSEY, -ED, -ING, -S vb claim possession

HOSIER, -S n person who sells stockings, etc

HOSIERY n stockings, socks, and tights collectively

HOSING ► hose

HOSPICE, -S n nursing home for the terminally ill

HOSPITAL n place where people who are ill are looked after and treated

HOSPITIA > hospitium

HOSPODAR n (formerly) the governor or prince of Moldavia or Wallachia under Ottoman rule

HOSS, -ES n horse

HOST, -ED, -S n person who entertains guests ▷ vb be the host of

HOSTA, -S n ornamental plant

HOSTAGE, -S n person who is illegally held prisoner

HOSTAS ► hosta

HOSTED ► host

HOSTEL, -ED, -S n building providing accommodation ▷ vb stay in hostels

HOSTELER same as > hosteller

HOSTELRY n inn, pub

HOSTELS ► hostel

HOSTESS n woman who receives and entertains guests ▷ vb act as hostess

HOSTIE, -S n informal Australian word for an air hostess

HOSTILE, -S adj unfriendly ▷ n hostile person

HOSTING, -S ► host

HOSTLER, -S another name (esp Brit) for ► ostler

HOSTLESS adj lacking a host

HOSTLY ► host

HOSTRY, HOSTRIES n lodging

HOSTS ► host

HOT, -S, -TED, -TEST adj having a high temperature ▷ vb make or become hot

HOTBED, -S n any place encouraging a particular activity

HOTBLOOD n type of horse

HOTBOX, -ES n container maintained at a high temperature to heat its contents

HOTCAKE, -S n pancake

HOTCH, -ED, -ES, -ING vb jog

HOTCHPOT n collecting of property so that it may be redistributed in equal shares

HOTDOG, -S vb perform a series of manoeuvres in skiing, etc

HOTE ► hight

HOTEL, -S n establishment providing lodging and meals

HOTELDOM n hotel business

HOTELIER n owner or manager of a hotel

HOTELING n office practice in which desk space is booked

in advance by an employee as required

HOTELMAN, HOTELMEN n hotel owner

HOTELS ► hotel

HOTEN ► hight

HOTFOOT, -S adv quickly and eagerly ▷ vb move quickly

HOTHEAD, -S n excitable or fiery person

HOTHOUSE n greenhouse

HOTLINE, -S n direct telephone link for emergency use

HOTLINER n person running a phone-in radio programme

HOTLINES ► hotline

HOTLINK, -S n area on website connecting to another site

HOTLY ► hot

HOTNESS ► hot

HOTPLATE n heated metal surface on an electric cooker

HOTPOT, -S n casserole topped with potatoes

HOTPRESS vb subject (paper, cloth, etc) to heat and pressure

HOTROD, -S n car with a modified engine for increased power

HOTS ► hot

HOTSHOT, -S n important person or expert, esp when showy

HOTSPOT, -S n place where wireless broadband is provided

HOTSPUR, -S n impetuous or fiery person

HOTTED ► hot

HOTTER, -ED, -S vb simmer

HOTTEST ► hot

HOTTIE, -S n attractive person

HOTTING, -S n stealing fast cars to put on a show of skilful driving

HOTTISH adj fairly hot

HOTTY same as ► hottie

HOUDAH, -S same as ► howdah

HOUDAN, -S n breed of light domestic fowl

HOUF, -ED, -ING, -S same as ► howf

HOUFF, -ED, -ING, -S same as ► howf

HOUFING ► houf

HOUFS ► houf

HOUGH, -ED, -ING, -S n in Scotland, a cut of meat corresponding to shin ▷ vb hamstring (cattle, horses, etc)

HOUHERE, -S n small evergreen New Zealand tree

HOUMMOS same as
➤ **hummus**
HOUMOUS same as
➤ **hummus**
HOUMOUS, -ES same as
➤ **hummus**
HOUND, -ED, -ING, -S n
hunting dog ▷ vb pursue
relentlessly
HOUNDER -S
HOUNGAN, -S n voodoo priest
HOUR n twenty-fourth part of
a day, sixty minutes
HOURI, -S n any of the
nymphs of paradise
HOURLIES ➤ **hourly**
HOURLONG adj lasting an
hour
HOURLY, HOURLIES adv
(happening) every hour ▷ adj
of, occurring, or done once
every hour ▷ n something
that is done by the hour
HOURS pl n indefinite time
HOUSE, -D, -S n building
used as a home ▷ vb give
accommodation to
HOUSEBOY n male domestic
servant
HOUSED ➤ **house**
HOUSEFLY n common fly
often found in houses
HOUSEFUL n full amount
or number that can be
accommodated in a
particular house
HOUSEL, -ED, -S vb give the
Eucharist to (someone)
HOUSEMAN, HOUSEMEN n
junior hospital doctor
HOUSER, -S ➤ **house**
HOUSES ➤ **house**
HOUSESIT, HOUSESAT vb
live in and look after a house
during the absence of its
owner or owners
HOUSETOP n rooftop
**HOUSEY, HOUSIER,
HOUSIEST** adj of or like
house music
HOUSING, -S n (providing of)
houses
HOUSLING adj of sacrament
▷ n growing of the climbing
stem of the hop into a dense
mass
HOUT, -ED, -S same as ➤ **hoot**
HOUTING, -S n type of fish
HOUTS ➤ **hout**
HOVE, -D, -S, HOVING vb swell
HOVEA, -S n Australian plant
with purple flowers
HOVED ➤ **hove**
HOVEL, -ED, -ING, -LED, -S
n small dirty house or hut
▷ vb shelter or be sheltered
in a hovel

HOVELLER n man working
on boat
HOVELS ➤ **hovel**
HOVEN ➤ **heave**
HOVER, -ED, -ING, -S vb (of a
bird etc) remain suspended in
one place in the air ▷ n act of
hovering
HOVERER -S
HOVERFLY n hovering wasp-
like fly
HOVERING ➤ **hover**
HOVERS ➤ **hover**
HOVES ➤ **hove**
HOVING ➤ **hove**
HOW, -S adv in what way, by
what means ▷ n the way
a thing is done ▷ sentence
substitute supposed
Native American greeting
HOWBE same as
➤ **howbeit**
HOWBEIT adv in archaic
usage, however
HOWDAH, -S n canopied seat
on an elephant's back
HOWDIE n midwife
**HOWDY, HOWDIED,
HOWDIES, -ING** vb greet
someone
HOWE, -S n depression in the
earth's surface
HOWEVER adv nevertheless
HOWF, -ED, -ING, -S n haunt,
esp a public house ▷ vb visit a
place frequently
HOWFF, -ED, -ING, -S vb visit a
place frequently
HOWFING ➤ **howf**
HOWFS ➤ **howf**
HOWITZER n large gun firing
shells at a steep angle
HOWK, -ED, -ING, -S vb dig
(out or up)
HOWKER -S
HOWL, -ED, -S n loud wailing
cry ▷ vb utter a howl
HOWLBACK same as
> **howlround**
HOWLED ➤ **howl**
HOWLER, -S n stupid mistake
HOWLET, -S another word
for ➤ **owl**
HOWLING, -S adj great ▷ n act
of wailing
HOWLS ➤ **howl**
HOWRE, -S same as ➤ **hour**
HOWS ➤ **how**
HOWSO same as
> **howsoever**
HOWZAT interj cry in cricket
appealing for dismissal of
batsman
HOWZIT informal word for
➤ **hello**
HOX, -ED, -ES, -ING vb
hamstring

This is a word found in
Shakespeare's plays, and it
means to cut a horse's
hamstring. It's one of the
many short words with X
that can get you a high
score.

HOY, -ED, -ING, -S interj cry
used to attract someone's
attention ▷ n freight barge
▷ vb drive animal with cry
HOYA, -S n any of various
E Asian or Australian plants
HOYDEN, -ED, -S n wild or
boisterous girl ▷ vb behave
like a hoyden
HOYED ➤ **hoy**
HOYING ➤ **hoy**
HOYLE, -S n archer's mark
used as a target
HOYS ➤ **hoy**
HRYVNA, -S n standard
monetary unit of Ukraine
HRYVNIA, -S n money unit of
Ukraine
HRYVNYA, -S same as
➤ **hryvna**
HUANACO, -S same as
➤ **guanaco**
HUAQUERO n
Central American tomb
robber
HUARACHE n Mexican sandal
HUARACHO same as
➤ **huarache**
HUB, -S n centre of a wheel,
through which the axle
passes
HUBBIES ➤ **hubby**
HUBBLY, HUBBLIER adj
having an irregular surface
HUBBUB, -S n confused noise
of many voices
HUBBUBOO same as
➤ **hubbub**
HUBBUBS ➤ **hubbub**
HUBBY, HUBBIES n husband
HUBCAP, -S n metal disc that
protects the hub of a wheel
HUBLESS adj without a hub
HUBRIS, -ES n pride,
arrogance
HUBS ➤ **hub**
HUCK, -ED, -ING, -S same as
> **huckaback**
HUCKERY adj ugly
HUCKING ➤ **huck**
HUCKLE, -D, -S, HUCKLING n
hip or haunch ▷ vb force out
or arrest roughly
HUCKS ➤ **huck**
HUCKSTER n person using
aggressive methods of selling
▷ vb peddle
HUDDEN ➤ **haud**
HUDDLE, -D, -S, HUDDLING vb
hunch (oneself) through cold

H

or fear ▷ *n* small group

HUDDLER -S

HUDDUP *interj* get up

HUDNA, -S *n* truce or ceasefire for a fixed duration

HUDUD, -S *n* set of laws and punishments in the Koran

HUE, -S *n* colour, shade

HUED *adj* having a hue or colour as specified

HUELESS ► hue

HUER, -S *n* pilchard fisherman

HUES ► hue

HUFF, -ED, -S *n* passing mood of anger or resentment ▷ *vb* blow or puff heavily

HUFFER, -S ► huffing

HUFFIER ► huffy

HUFFIEST ► huffy

HUFFILY ► huff

HUFFING, -S *n* practice of inhaling fumes for intoxicating effects

HUFFISH ► huff

HUFFKIN, -S *n* type of muffin

HUFFS ► huff

HUFFY, HUFFIER, HUFFIEST ► huff

HUG, -GED, -GING, -S *vb* clasp tightly in the arms, usu with affection ▷ *n* tight or fond embrace

HUGE, -R, -ST *adj* very big

HUGELY *adv* very much

HUGENESS ► huge

HUGEOUS *same as* ► huge

HUGER ► huge

HUGEST ► huge

HUGGABLE ► hug

HUGGED ► hug

HUGGER, -S ► hug

HUGGIER ► huggy

HUGGIEST ► huggy

HUGGING ► hug

HUGGY, HUGGIER, HUGGIEST *adj* sensitive and caring

HUGS ► hug

HUGY *same as* ► huge

HUH *interj* exclamation of derision or inquiry

HUHU, -S *n* type of hairy New Zealand beetle

HUI, -S *n* meeting of Māori people

HUIA, -S *n* extinct bird of New Zealand

HUIC *interj* in hunting, a call to hounds

HUIPIL, -ES, -S *n* Mayan woman's blouse

HUIS ► hui

HUISACHE *n* American tree

HUISSIER *n* doorkeeper

HUITAIN, -S *n* verse of eighteen lines

HULA, -S *n* swaying Hawaiian dance

HULE, -S *same as* ► ule

HULK, -ED, -S *n* body of an abandoned ship ▷ *vb* move clumsily

HULKIER ► hulky

HULKIEST ► hulky

HULKING *adj* bulky, unwieldy

HULKS ► hulk

HULKY, HULKIER, HULKIEST *same as* ► hulking

HULL, -ED, -ING, -S *n* main body of a boat ▷ *vb* remove the hulls from

HULLER -S

HULLIER ► hully

HULLIEST ► hully

HULLING ► hull

HULLO, -ED, -ES, -ING, -S *same as* ► hello

HULLOA, -ED, -S *same as* ► halloa

HULLOED ► hullo

HULLOES ► hullo

HULLOING ► hullo

HULLOO, -ED, -S *same as* ► halloo

HULLOS ► hullo

HULLS ► hull

HULLY, HULLIER, HULLIEST *adj* having husks

HUM, -MED, -S *vb* make a low continuous vibrating sound ▷ *n* humming sound

HUMA, -S *n* mythical bird

HUMAN, -S *adj* of or typical of people ▷ *n* human being

HUMANE, -R, -ST *adj* kind or merciful

HUMANELY

HUMANISE *same as* ► humanize

HUMANISM *n* belief in human effort rather than religion

HUMANIST

HUMANITY *n* human race

HUMANIZE *vb* make human or humane

HUMANLY *adv* by human powers or means

HUMANOID *adj* resembling a human being in appearance ▷ *n* (in science fiction) a robot or creature resembling a human being

HUMANS ► human

HUMAS ► huma

HUMATE, -S *n* decomposed plants used as fertilizer

HUMBLE, -D, -S, -ST *adj* conscious of one's failings ▷ *vb* cause to feel humble, humiliate

HUMBLER -S

HUMBLING ► humble

HUMBLY ► humble

HUMBUG, -S *n* hard striped peppermint sweet ▷ *vb* cheat or deceive (someone)

HUMBUZZ *n* type of beetle

HUMDRUM, -S *adj* ordinary, dull ▷ *n* monotonous routine, task, or person

HUMECT, -ED, -S *vb* make moist

HUMEFY, HUMEFIED, HUMEFIES *same as* ► humify

HUMERAL, -S *adj* of or relating to the humerus ▷ *n* silk shawl worn by a priest at High Mass; humeral veil

HUMERUS, HUMERI *n* bone from the shoulder to the elbow

HUMF, -ED, -ING, -S *same as* ► humph

HUMHUM, -S *n* Indian cotton cloth

HUMIC *adj* of, derived from, or resembling humus

HUMICOLE *n* any plant that thrives on humus

HUMID, -ER, -EST *adj* damp and hot

HUMIDEX *n* system of measuring discomfort

HUMIDIFY *vb* make the air in (a room) more humid or damp

HUMIDITY *n* dampness

HUMIDLY ► humid

HUMIDOR, -S *n* humid place for storing cigars, tobacco, etc

HUMIFY, HUMIFIED, HUMIFIES *vb* convert or be converted into humus

HUMILITY *n* quality of being humble

HUMINT, -S *n* human intelligence

HUMITE, -S *n* mineral containing magnesium

HUMITURE *n* measure of both humidity and temperature

HUMLIE, -S *n* hornless cow

HUMMABLE ► hum

HUMMAUM, -S *same as* ► hammam

HUMMED ► hum

HUMMEL, -S *adj* (of cattle) hornless ▷ *vb* remove horns from

HUMMER, -S ► hum

HUMMING, -S ► hum

HUMMLE *adj* as in hummle bonnet type of Scottish cap

HUMMOCK, -S *n* very small hill ▷ *vb* form into a hummock or hummocks

HUMMOCKY

HUMMUM, -S same as
▸ **hammam**

HUMMUS, -ES n creamy dip

HUMOGEN, -S n type of
fertilizer

HUMOR, -ED, -ING, -S same as
▸ **humour**

HUMORAL adj denoting
or relating to a type of
immunity

HUMORED ▸ **humor**

HUMORESK n humorous
musical composition

HUMORFUL ▸ **humor**

HUMORING ▸ **humor**

HUMORIST n writer or
entertainer who uses
humour in his or her work

HUMOROUS adj amusing, esp
in a witty or clever way

HUMORS ▸ **humor**

HUMOUR, -ED, -S n ability to
say or perceive things that
are amusing ▷ vb be kind and
indulgent to

HUMOUS, -ES same as
▸ **humus**

HUMP, -ED, -ING, -S n raised
piece of ground ▷ vb carry
or heave

HUMPBACK same as
> **hunchback**

HUMPED ▸ **hump**

HUMPEN, -S n old German
drinking glass

HUMPER, -S ▸ **hump**

HUMPH, -ED, -ING, -S interj
exclamation of annoyance
or scepticism ▷ vb exclaim
humph

HUMPIER ▸ **humpy**

HUMPIES ▸ **humpy**

HUMPIEST ▸ **humpy**

HUMPING ▸ **hump**

HUMPLESS ▸ **hump**

HUMPLIKE ▸ **hump**

HUMPS ▸ **hump**

HUMPTY, HUMPTIES n low
padded seat

**HUMPY, HUMPIER, HUMPIES,
HUMPIEST** adj full of humps
▷ n primitive hut

HUMS ▸ **hum**

HUMSTRUM n medieval
musical instrument

HUMUS, -ES n decomposing
matter in the soil

HUMUSY

HUMVEE, -S n military vehicle

HUN, -S n member of any of
several nomadic peoples

HUNCH, -ED, -ES, -ING n
feeling or suspicion not based
on facts ▷ vb draw (one's
shoulders) up or together

HUNDRED, -S n ten times
ten ▷ adj amounting to a
hundred

HUNG ▸ **hang**

HUNGAN, -S same as
▸ **houngan**

HUNGER, -ED, -S n discomfort
or weakness from lack of
food ▷ vb want very much

HUNGERLY adj hungry

HUNGERS ▸ **hunger**

HUNGOVER adj suffering from
hangover

HUNGRIER ▸ **hungry**

HUNGRILY ▸ **hungry**

HUNGRY, HUNGRIER adj
desiring food

HUNH same as ▸ **huh**

HUNK n large piece

HUNKER, -ED vb squat

HUNKERS pl n haunches

HUNKIER ▸ **hunky**

HUNKIEST ▸ **hunky**

HUNKS, -ES n grumpy old
person

HUNKY, HUNKIER, HUNKIEST
adj excellent

HUNNISH ▸ **hun**

HUNS ▸ **hun**

HUNT, -S vb seek out and kill
(wild animals) for food or
sport ▷ n hunting

HUNTABLE

HUNTAWAY n sheepdog
trained to drive sheep by
barking

HUNTED adj harassed and
worn

HUNTEDLY ▸ **hunt**

HUNTER, -S n person or
animal that hunts wild
animals

HUNTING, -S n pursuit and
killing or capture of wild
animals

HUNTRESS same as ▸ **hunter**

HUNTS ▸ **hunt**

HUNTSMAN, HUNTSMEN
n man who hunts wild
animals, esp foxes

HUP, -PED, -PING, -S vb cry
hup to get a horse to move

HUPIRO, -S n in New
Zealand English, same as
> **stinkwood**

HUPPAH, -S, HUPPOT variant
spelling of ▸ **chuppah**

HUPPED ▸ **hup**

HUPPING ▸ **hup**

HUPPOT ▸ **huppah**

HUPPOTH same as ▸ **huppot**

HUPS ▸ **hup**

HURCHEON same as ▸ **urchin**

HURDEN, -S same as
▸ **harden**

HURDIES pl n buttocks or
haunches

HURDLE, -D, -S, HURDLING n
light barrier for jumping over
in some races ▷ vb jump over
(something)

HURDLER -S

HURDS same as ▸ **hards**

HURL, -ED, -S vb throw or
utter forcefully ▷ n act or an
instance of hurling

HURLBAT, -S same as
▸ **whirlbat**

HURLED ▸ **hurl**

HURLER, -S ▸ **hurl**

HURLEY, -S n another word
for the game of hurling

HURLIES ▸ **hurly**

HURLING, -S n Irish game like
hockey

HURLS ▸ **hurl**

HURLY, HURLIES n wheeled
barrow

HURRA, -ED, -ING, -S same as
▸ **hurrah**

HURRAH, -ED, -S interj
exclamation of joy or
applause ▷ n cheer of joy or
victory ▷ vb shout "hurrah"

HURRAING ▸ **hurra**

HURRAS ▸ **hurra**

HURRAY, -ED, -S same as
▸ **hurrah**

HURRIED adj done quickly or
too quickly

HURRIER, -S ▸ **hurry**

HURRY, HURRIES vb (cause
to) move or act very quickly
▷ n doing something or the
need to do something quickly

HURRYING

HURST, -S n wood

HURT, -ING, -S vb cause
physical or mental pain to
▷ n physical or mental pain
▷ adj injured or pained

HURTER -S

HURTFUL adj unkind

HURTING ▸ **hurt**

HURTLE, -D, -S, HURTLING vb
move quickly or violently

HURTLESS adj uninjured

HURTLING ▸ **hurtle**

HURTS ▸ **hurt**

HUSBAND, -S n man to whom
one is married ▷ vb use
economically

HUSH, -ES, -ING vb make or be
silent ▷ n stillness or silence
▷ interj plea or demand for
silence

HUSHABY interj used in
quietening a baby or child
to sleep ▷ n lullaby ▷ vb
quieten to sleep

HUSHABYE same as
▸ **hushaby**

HUSHED ▸ **hush**

HUSHEDLY ▸ **hush**

H

HUSHER, -ED, -S same as
► **usher**
HUSHES ► **hush**
HUSHFUL adj quiet
HUSHIER ► **hushy**
HUSHIEST ► **hushy**
HUSHING, -S ► **hush**
HUSHY, HUSHIER, HUSHIEST
adj secret
HUSK, -ED, -S n outer covering
of certain seeds and fruits
▷ vb remove the husk from
HUSKER -S
HUSKIER ► **husky**
HUSKIES ► **husky**
HUSKIEST ► **husky**
HUSKILY ► **husky**
HUSKING, -S ► **husk**
HUSKLIKE ► **husk**
HUSKS ► **husk**
HUSKY, HUSKIER, HUSKIES,
HUSKIEST adj slightly hoarse
▷ n Arctic sledge dog with
thick hair and a curled tail
HUSO, -S n sturgeon
HUSS, -ES n flesh of the
European dogfish
HUSSAR, -S n lightly armed
cavalry soldier
HUSSES ► **huss**
HUSSIF, -S n sewing kit
HUSTINGS pl n political
campaigns and speeches
before an election
HUSTLE, -D, -S, HUSTLING vb
push about, jostle ▷ n lively
activity or bustle
HUSTLER -S
HUSWIFE, -S, HUSWIVES
same as ► **housewife**
HUT, -S, -TED n small house,
shelter, or shed ▷ vb equip
with huts
HUTCH, -ED, -ES, -ING n cage
for pet rabbits etc ▷ vb store
or keep in or as if in a hutch
HUTCHIE, -S n temporary
shelter
HUTCHING ► **hutch**
HUTIA, -S n rodent of West
Indies
HUTLIKE ► **hut**
HUTMENT, -S n number or
group of huts
HUTS ► **hut**
HUTTED ► **hut**
HUTTING, -S ► **hut**
HUTZPA, -S same as
► **hutzpah**
HUTZPAH, -S variant spelling
of ► **chutzpah**
HUTZPAS ► **hutzpa**
HUZOOR, -S n person of rank
in India
HUZZA, -ED, -ING, -S same as
► **huzzah**

HUZZAH, -ED, -S archaic word
for ► **hurrah**
HUZZAING ► **huzza**
HUZZAS ► **huzza**
HWAN another name for
► **won**
HWYL, -S n emotional fervour,
as in the recitation of poetry

This Welsh word can come
in very useful for dealing
with a consonant-heavy
rack.

HYACINE, -S same as
► **hyacinth**
HYACINTH n sweet-smelling
spring flower that grows
from a bulb
HYAENA, -S same as ► **hyena**
HYAENIC
HYALIN, -S n glassy
translucent substance
HYALINE, -S adj clear and
translucent, with no fibres
or granules ▷ n glassy
transparent surface
HYALINS ► **hyalin**
HYALITE, -S n clear and
colourless variety of opal in
globular form
HYALOGEN n insoluble
substance in body structures
HYALOID, -S adj clear and
transparent ▷ n delicate
transparent membrane
HYBRID, -S n offspring of two
plants or animals of different
species ▷ adj of mixed origin
HYBRIS, -ES same as ► **hubris**
HYDATID, -S n cyst containing
tapeworm larvae
HYDATOID adj watery
HYDRA, -E, -S n mythical
many-headed water serpent
HYDRACID n acid, such as
hydrochloric acid, that does
not contain oxygen
HYDRAE ► **hydra**
HYDRAGOG n drug that
removes water
HYDRANT, -S n outlet from
a water main with a nozzle
for a hose
HYDRANTH n polyp in
a colony of hydrozoan
coelenterates
HYDRANTS ► **hydrant**
HYDRAS ► **hydra**
HYDRASE, -S n enzyme that
removes water
HYDRATE, -S n chemical
compound of water with
another substance ▷ vb treat
or impregnate with water
HYDRATED adj (of a
compound) chemically
bonded to water molecules

HYDRATES ► **hydrate**
HYDRATOR ► **hydrate**
HYDREMIA same as
> **hydraemia**
HYDRIA, -E n (in ancient
Greece and Rome) a large
water jar
HYDRIC adj of or containing
hydrogen
HYDRID, -S same as
► **hydroid**
HYDRIDE, -S n compound
of hydrogen with another
element
HYDRIDS ► **hydrid**
HYDRILLA n aquatic plant
used as an oxygenator in
aquaria and pools
HYDRO, -S n hotel offering
facilities for hydropathy ▷ adj
short for hydroelectric
HYDROGEL n gel in which the
liquid constituent is water
HYDROGEN n light flammable
colourless gas that combines
with oxygen to form water
HYDROID, -S adj of an order
of colonial hydrozoan
coelenterates ▷ n hydroid
colony or individual
HYDROMA, -S same as
► **hygroma**
HYDROMEL n another word
for 'mead' (the drink)
HYDRONIC adj using hot
water in heating system
HYDROPIC ► **hydropsy**
HYDROPS n anaemia in a
fetus
HYDROPSY same as ► **dropsy**
HYDROS ► **hydro**
HYDROSKI n hydrofoil used
on some seaplanes to provide
extra lift when taking off
HYDROSOL n sol that has
water as its liquid phase
HYDROUS adj containing
water
HYDROXY adj of a type of
chemical compound
HYDROXYL n the monovalent
group −OH or the ion OH−
HYDROZOA > **hydrozoon**
HYDYNE, -S n type of rocket
fuel
HYE, -D, -ING, -S same as ► **hie**
HYEN, -S same as ► **hyena**
HYENA, -S n scavenging
doglike mammal of Africa
and S Asia
HYENIC
HYENINE adj of hyenas
HYENOID adj of or like hyenas
HYENS ► **hyen**
HYES ► **hye**
HYETAL adj of or relating to
rain, rainfall, or rainy regions

HYGEIST, -S same as
> **hygienist**
HYGIEIST same as > **hygienist**
HYGIENE, -S n principles of
health and cleanliness
HYGIENIC adj promoting
health or cleanliness
HYGROMA, -S n swelling soft
tissue that occurs over a joint
HYING ▸ **hie**
HYKE, -S same as ▸ **haik**
HYLA, -S n type of
tropical American tree frog
HYLDING, -S same as
▸ **hilding**
HYLE, -S n wood
HYLEG, -S n dominant planet
when someone is born
HYLES ▸ **hyle**
HYLIC adj solid
HYLICISM n materialism
HYLICIST
HYLISM, -S same as
▸ **hylicism**
HYLIST -S
HYLOBATE n gibbon
HYLOIST, -S n materialist
HYLOZOIC > **hylozoism**
HYMEN, -S n membrane
partly covering a girl's vaginal
opening
HYMENAL
HYMENEAL adj of or relating
to marriage ▷ n wedding
song or poem
HYMENEAN n wedding song
HYMENIA ▸ **hymenium**
HYMENIAL ▸ **hymenium**
HYMENIUM, HYMENIA n (in
some fungi) a layer of cell-
producing spores
HYMENS ▸ **hymen**
HYMN, -ED, -ING, -S n
Christian song of praise sung
to God or a saint ▷ vb express
(praises, thanks, etc) by
singing hymns
HYMNAL, -S n book of hymns
▷ adj of, relating to, or
characteristic of hymns
HYMNARY same as ▸ **hymnal**
HYMNBOOK n book
containing the words and
music of hymns
HYMNED ▸ **hymn**
HYMNIC ▸ **hymn**
HYMNING ▸ **hymn**
HYMNIST, -S n person who
composes hymns
HYMNLESS ▸ **hymn**
HYMNLIKE ▸ **hymn**
HYMNODY n composition or
singing of hymns
HYMNS ▸ **hymn**

HYNDE, -S same as ▸ **hind**
HYOID, -S adj of or relating
to the hyoid bone ▷ n
horseshoe-shaped bone
HYOIDAL adj of or relating to
the hyoid bone
HYOIDEAN same as
▸ **hyoidal**
HYOIDS ▸ **hyoid**
HYOSCINE n colourless
viscous liquid alkaloid
HYP, -PED, -PING, -S n short
for hypotenuse ▷ vb offend
HYPALGIA n reduced ability to
feel pain
HYPATE, -S n string of lyre
HYPE, -D, -S n intensive
or exaggerated publicity
or sales promotion ▷ vb
promote (a product) using
intensive or exaggerated
publicity
HYPER -S
HYPERGOL n type of fuel
HYPERNYM n superordinate
HYPERON, -S n any baryon
that is not a nucleon
HYPEROPE n person with
hyperopia
HYPERS ▸ **hyper**
HYPES ▸ **hype**
HYPESTER n person who gives
a product intense publicity
HYPHA, -E n any of the
filaments in the mycelium of
a fungus
HYPHAL
HYPHEMIA n bleeding inside
eye
HYPHEN, -ED, -S n
punctuation mark (-) ▷ vb
hyphenate
HYPHENIC
HYPHY, HYPHIES n type of
hip-hop music
HYPING, -S ▸ **hype**
HYPNIC, -S n sleeping drug
HYPNOID adj of or relating to
a state resembling sleep
HYPNONE, -S n sleeping drug
HYPNOSIS, HYPNOSES n
artificially induced state of
relaxation
HYPNOTEE n person being
hypnotized
HYPNOTIC adj of or (as if)
producing hypnosis ▷ n drug
that induces sleep
HYPNUM, -S n species of
moss
HYPO, -ED, -ING, -S vb inject
with a hypodermic syringe
HYPOACID adj abnormally
acidic

HYPOBOLE n act of
anticipating objection
HYPOCIST n type of juice
HYPODERM n layer of thick-
walled tissue in some plants
HYPOED ▸ **hypo**
HYPOGAEA > **hypogaeum**
HYPOGEA ▸ **hypogeum**
HYPOGEAL adj occurring or
living below the surface of
the ground
HYPOGEAN ▸ **hypogeum**
HYPOGENE adj formed,
taking place, or originating
beneath the surface of the
earth
HYPOGEUM, HYPOGEA n
underground vault, esp one
used for burials
HYPOGYNY adj having the
gynoecium above the other
floral parts
HYPOID, -S adj as in **hypoid
gear** type of gear ▷ n hypoid
gear
HYPOING ▸ **hypo**
HYPONEA, -S same as
▸ **hypopnea**
HYPONOIA n underlying
meaning
HYPONYM, -S n word whose
meaning is included as part
of another
HYPONYMY
HYPOPNEA same as
> **hypopnoea**
HYPOPYON n pus in eye
HYPOS ▸ **hypo**
HYPOTHEC n charge on
property in favour of a
creditor
HYPOXIA, -S n deficiency in
oxygen delivery
HYPOXIC
HYPPED ▸ **hyp**
HYPPING ▸ **hyp**
HYPS ▸ **hyp**
HYPURAL adj below the tail
HYRACES ▸ **hyrax**
HYRACOID n hyrax
HYRAX, HYRACES, -ES n type
of hoofed rodent-like animal
of Africa and Asia
HYSON, -S n Chinese green
tea
HYSSOP, -S n sweet-smelling
herb used in folk medicine
HYSTERIA n state of
uncontrolled excitement,
anger, or panic
HYSTERIC adj of or suggesting
hysteria
HYTE adj insane
HYTHE, -S same as ▸ **hithe**

H

I i

The letter **I** can prove a difficult tile to use effectively in Scrabble. It's one of the most common tiles in the game, so you often end up with two or more on your rack, but it can be hard to get rid of. Where I does come in very useful, though, is in the number of everyday short words that can be formed from it, which are very helpful when you need to form short words in addition to the main word that you want to play. These words include **in**, **is**, **it** (2 points each), **id** (3) and **if** (5). Other handy words are **icy** (8), **ivy** (9) and **imp** (7). Don't forget the three-letter words that use **K**: **ilk**, **ink** and **irk** (7 each), while **iwi** for 6 points can be very useful in getting rid of a surplus of Is.

IAMB, -S n metrical foot of two syllables

IAMBI ► iambus

IAMBIC, -S adj written in a type of metrical unit ▷ n iambic foot, line, or stanza

IAMBIST, -S n one who writes iambs

IAMBS ► iamb

IAMBUS, IAMBI, -ES same as ► iamb

IANTHINE adj violet

IATRIC adj relating to medicine or physicians

IATRICAL same as ► iatric

IBADAH, IBADAT n following of Islamic beliefs and practices

IBERIS, -ES n plant with white or purple flowers

IBEX, -ES, IBICES n wild goat

IBIDEM adv in the same place

IBIS, -ES n large wading bird with long legs

IBOGAINE n dopamine blocker

IBRIK, -S same as ► cezve

ICE, -S, n water in the solid state, formed by freezing liquid water ▷ vb form or cause to form ice

ICEBALL, -S n ball of ice

ICEBERG, -S n large floating mass of ice

ICEBLINK n yellowish-white reflected glare in the sky over an ice field

ICEBOAT, -S n boat that breaks up bodies of ice in water ▷ vb pilot an iceboat

ICEBOUND adj covered or made immobile by ice

ICEBOX, -ES n refrigerator

ICECAP, -S n mass of ice permanently covering an area

ICED adj covered with icing

ICEFALL, -S n part of a glacier

ICEFIELD n very large flat expanse of ice floating in the sea; large ice floe

ICEFISH vb fish through a hole in the ice on a lake

ICEHOUSE n building for storing ice

ICEKHANA n motor race on a frozen lake

ICELESS ► ice

ICELIKE ► ice

ICEMAKER n device for making ice

ICEMAN, ICEMEN n person who sells or delivers ice

ICEPACK, -S n bag or folded cloth containing ice

ICER, -S n person who ices cakes

ICES ► ice

ICESCAPE n landscape covered in ice

ICESTONE n cryolite

ICEWINE, -S n dessert wine made from grapes that have frozen before being harvested

ICEWORM, -S n small worm found in glaciers

ICH, -ED, -ES, -ING, -S archaic form of ► eke

> A Shakespearean spelling of **eke**, this is a useful little word worth remembering because of its unusual combination of letters and relatively high score.

ICHABOD interj the glory has departed

ICHED ► ich

ICHES ► ich

ICHING ► ich

ICHNITE, -S n trace fossil

ICHOR, -S n fluid said to flow in the veins of the gods

ICHOROUS

ICHS ► ich

ICHTHIC same as ► ichthyic

ICHTHYIC adj of, relating to, or characteristic of fishes

ICHTHYS n early Christian emblem

ICICLE, -S n tapering spike of ice

ICICLED adj covered with icicles

ICICLES ► icicle

ICIER ► icy

ICIEST ► icy

ICILY adv in an icy or reserved manner

ICINESS n condition of being icy or very cold

ICING, -S n mixture used to decorate cakes

ICK, -S interj expression of disgust

> An interjection expressing disgust, this is one of the highest-scoring three-letter words beginning with I. It does not take an S, but it does take a Y to make **icky**.

ICKER, -S n ear of corn

ICKIER ► icky

ICKIEST ► icky

ICKILY ► icky

ICKINESS ► icky

ICKLE, -R, -ST *ironically childish word for* ▶ **little**

ICKS ▶ **ick**

ICKY, ICKIER, ICKIEST *adj* sticky

ICON, -ES, -S *n* picture of Christ or another religious figure

ICONIC *adj* relating to the character of an icon

ICONICAL *same as* ▶ **iconic**

ICONIFY *vb* render as an icon

ICONISE, -D, -S *same as* ▶ **iconize**

ICONIZE, -D, -S *vb* render as an icon

ICONS ▶ **icon**

ICTAL ▶ **ictus**

ICTERIC, -S ▶ **icterus**

ICTERID, -S *n* bird of the oriole family
ICTERINE

ICTERUS *n* yellowing of plant leaves

ICTIC ▶ **ictus**

ICTUS, -ES *n* metrical or rhythmic stress in verse feet

ICY, ICIER, ICIEST *adj* very cold

ID, -S *n* mind's instinctive unconscious energies

IDANT, -S *n* chromosome

IDE *n* silver orfe fish

IDEA, -S *n* plan or thought formed in the mind
IDEAED

IDEAL, -S *adj* most suitable ▷ *n* conception of something that is perfect

IDEALESS ▶ **idea**

IDEALISE *same as* ▶ **idealize**

IDEALISM *n* tendency to seek perfection in everything
IDEALIST

IDEALITY ▶ **ideal**

IDEALIZE *vb* regard or portray as perfect or nearly perfect

IDEALLY ▶ **ideal**

IDEOLOGY *corruption of* ▶ **ideology**

IDEALS ▶ **ideal**

IDEAS ▶ **idea**

IDEATA ▶ **ideatum**

IDEATE, -D, -S, IDEATING *vb* form or have an idea of
IDEATION
IDEATIVE

IDEATUM, IDEATA *n* objective reality

IDEE, -S *n* idea

IDEM *adj* same

IDENT, -S *n* short visual image that works as a logo

IDENTIC *adj* having the same intention regarding another power

IDENTIFY *vb* prove or recognize as being a certain person or thing

IDENTITY *n* state of being a specified person or thing

IDENTS ▶ **ident**

IDEOGRAM *n* symbol that directly represents a concept or thing

IDEOLOGY *n* body of ideas and beliefs of a group, nation, etc

IDES *n* specific date of each month in the Roman calendar

IDIOCY, IDIOCIES *n* utter stupidity

IDIOGRAM *another name for* > **karyogram**

IDIOLECT *n* variety or form of a language used by an individual

IDIOM, -S *n* group of words with special meaning

IDIOT, -S *n* foolish or stupid person

IDIOTCY *same as* ▶ **idiocy**

IDIOTIC *adj* of or resembling an idiot

IDIOTISH *same as* ▶ **idiotic**

IDIOTISM *archaic word for* ▶ **idiocy**

IDIOTS ▶ **idiot**

IDIOTYPE *n* unique part of antibody

IDLE, -D, -S, -ST, IDLING *adj* not doing anything ▷ *vb* spend (time) doing very little
IDLEHOOD
IDLENESS

IDLER, -S *n* person who idles

IDLES ▶ **idle**

IDLESSE, -S ▶ **idle**

IDLEST ▶ **idle**

IDLING ▶ **idle**

IDLY ▶ **idle**

IDOCRASE *n* green, brown, or yellow mineral

IDOL, -S *n* object of excessive devotion

IDOLA ▶ **idolum**

IDOLATER ▶ **idolatry**

IDOLATOR *n* one who worships idols

IDOLATRY *n* worship of idols

IDOLISE, -D, -S *same as* ▶ **idolize**
IDOLISER

IDOLISM, -S ▶ **idol**

IDOLIST, -S ▶ **idolize**

IDOLIZE, -D, -S *vb* love or admire excessively
IDOLIZER

IDOLON *n* mental picture

IDOLS ▶ **idol**

IDOLUM, IDOLA *n* mental picture

IDONEITY ▶ **idoneous**

IDONEOUS *adj* appropriate

IDS ▶ **id**

IDYL, -S *same as* ▶ **idyll**

IDYLIST, -S *same as* ▶ **idyllist**

IDYLL, -S *n* scene or time of great peace and happiness

IDYLLIAN *same as* ▶ **idyllic**

IDYLLIC *adj* of or relating to an idyll

IDYLLIST *n* writer of idylls

IDYLLS ▶ **idyll**

IDYLS ▶ **idyl**

IF, -S *n* uncertainty or doubt

IFF *conj* in logic, a shortened form of if and only if

> This word is one of the highest-scoring three-letter words beginning with I, and of course provides a useful extension to **if**.

IFFIER ▶ **iffy**

IFFIEST ▶ **iffy**

IFFILY *adv* in an iffy manner

IFFINESS, -S ▶ **iffy**

IFFY, IFFIER, IFFIEST *adj* doubtful, uncertain

IFS ▶ **if**

IFTAR, -S *n* meal eaten by Muslims

IGAD *same as* ▶ **egad**

IGAPO, -S *n* flooded forest

IGARAPE, -S *n* canoe route

IGG, -ED, -ING, -S *vb* antagonize

IGLOO, -S *n* Inuit house

IGLU, -S *same as* ▶ **igloo**

IGNARO, -ES, -S *n* ignoramus

IGNATIA, -S *n* dried seed

IGNEOUS *adj* (of rock) formed as molten rock cools

IGNIFY, IGNIFIED, IGNIFIES *vb* turn into fire

IGNITE, -D, -S, IGNITING *vb* catch fire or set fire to

IGNITER, -S *n* person or thing that ignites

IGNITES ▶ **ignite**

IGNITING ▶ **ignite**

IGNITION *n* system that ignites the fuel-and-air mixture to start an engine

IGNITOR, -S *same as* ▶ **igniter**

IGNITRON *n* mercury-arc rectifier controlled by a subsidiary electrode

IGNOBLE, -R *adj* dishonourable
IGNOBLY

IGNOMIES ▶ **ignomy**

IGNOMINY *n* humiliating disgrace

IGNOMY, IGNOMIES *Shakespearean variant of* ▸ **ignominy**

IGNORAMI > **ignoramus**

IGNORANT *adj* lacking knowledge ▷ *n* ignorant person

IGNORE, -D, -S, IGNORING *vb* refuse to notice, disregard deliberately ▷ *n* disregard

IGNORER -S

IGUANA, -S *n* large tropical American lizard

IGUANIAN

IGUANID, -S *same as* ▸ **iguana**

IHRAM, -S *n* white robes worn by Muslim pilgrims to Mecca

IJTIHAD, -S *n* effort of deriving a legal ruling from the Koran

IKAN, -S *n* (in Malaysia) fish

IKAT, -S *n* method of creating patterns in fabric

IKEBANA, -S *n* Japanese art of flower arrangement

IKON, -S *same as* ▸ **icon**

ILEA ▸ **ileum**

This is the plural of **ileum**, part of the small intestine, and is often useful as a rack-balancing play when you have too many vowels.

ILEAC *adj* of or relating to the ileum

ILEAL *same as* ▸ **ileac**

ILEITIS *n* inflammation of the ileum

ILEUM, ILEA *n* lowest part of the small intestine

ILEUS, -ES *n* obstruction of the intestine

ILEX, -ES, ILICES *n* any of a genus of trees or shrubs that includes holly

ILIA ▸ **ilium**

ILIAC *adj* of or relating to the ilium

ILIACUS *n* iliac

ILIAD, -S *n* epic poem

ILIAL ▸ **ilium**

ILICES ▸ **ilex**

ILIUM, ILIA *n* part of the hipbone

ILK, -S *n* type ▷ *determiner* each

ILKA *same as* ▸ **ilk**

ILKADAY, -S *n* every day

ILKS ▸ **ilk**

ILL, -ER, -EST, -S *adj* not in good health ▷ *n* evil, harm ▷ *adv* badly

ILLAPSE, -D, -S *vb* slide in

ILLATION *rare word for* > **inference**

ILLATIVE *adj* of or relating to illation ▷ *n* illative case

ILLEGAL, -S *adj* against the law ▷ *n* person who entered or attempted to enter a country illegally

ILLER ▸ **ill**

ILLEST ▸ **ill**

ILLIAD, -S *n* wink

ILLICIT *adj* illegal

ILLINIUM *n* type of radioactive element

ILLIPE, -S *n* Asian tree

ILLIQUID *adj* (of an asset) not easily convertible into cash

ILLISION *n* act of striking against

ILLITE, -S *n* clay mineral of the mica group

ILLITIC

ILLNESS *n* disease or indisposition

ILLOGIC, -S *n* reasoning characterized by lack of logic

ILLS ▸ **ill**

ILLTH, -S *n* condition of poverty or misery

ILLUDE, -D, -S, ILLUDING *vb* trick or deceive

ILLUME, -D, -S, ILLUMING *vb* illuminate

ILLUMINE *vb* throw light in or into

ILLUMING ▸ **illume**

ILLUPI, -S *same as* ▸ **illipe**

ILLUSION *n* deceptive appearance or belief

ILLUSIVE *same as* ▸ **illusory**

ILLUSORY *adj* seeming to be true, but actually false

ILLUVIA ▸ **illuvium**

ILLUVIAL ▸ **illuvium**

ILLUVIUM, ILLUVIA *n* material washed down from one soil layer to a lower one

ILLY *adv* badly

ILMENITE *n* black mineral found in igneous rocks as layered deposits and in veins

IMAGE, -D, -S *n* mental picture of someone or something ▷ *vb* picture in the mind

IMAGER, -S *n* device that produces images

IMAGERY *n* images collectively, esp in the arts

IMAGES ▸ **image**

IMAGINAL *adj* of, relating to, or resembling an imago

IMAGINE *vb* form a mental image of ▷ *sentence substitute* exclamation of surprise

IMAGINER

IMAGINES ▸ **imago**

IMAGING, -S ▸ **image**

IMAGISM, -S *n* poetic movement

IMAGIST -S

IMAGO, IMAGINES, -ES, -S *n* mature adult insect

IMAM, -S *n* leader of prayers in a mosque

IMAMATE, -S *n* region or territory governed by an imam

IMAMS ▸ **imam**

IMARET, -S *n* (in Turkey) a hospice for pilgrims or travellers

IMARI, -S *n* Japanese porcelain

IMAUM, -S *same as* ▸ **imam**

IMBALM, -ED, -S *same as* ▸ **embalm**

IMBALMER

IMBAR, -RED, -S *vb* bar in

IMBARK, -ED, -S *vb* cover in bark

IMBARRED ▸ **imbar**

IMBARS ▸ **imbar**

IMBASE, -D, -S, IMBASING *vb* degrade

IMBATHE, -D, -S *vb* bathe

IMBECILE *n* stupid person ▷ *adj* stupid or senseless

IMBED, -DED, -S *same as* ▸ **embed**

IMBIBE, -D, -S, IMBIBING *vb* drink (alcoholic drinks)

IMBIBER -S

IMBITTER *same as* ▸ **embitter**

IMBIZO, -S *n* meeting in S Africa

IMBLAZE, -D, -S *vb* depict heraldically

IMBODY, IMBODIED, IMBODIES *same as* ▸ **embody**

IMBOLDEN *same as* ▸ **embolden**

IMBORDER *vb* enclose in a border

IMBOSK, -ED, -S *vb* conceal

IMBOSOM, -S *vb* hold in one's heart

IMBOSS, -ED, -ES *same as* ▸ **emboss**

IMBOWER, -S *vb* enclose in a bower

IMBRAST *Spenserian past participle of* ▸ **embrace**

IMBREX, IMBRICES *n* curved tile

IMBROWN, -S *vb* make brown

IMBRUE, -D, -S, IMBRUING *vb* stain, esp with blood

IMBRUTE, -D, -S *vb* reduce to a bestial state**

IMBUE, -D, -S, IMBUING *vb* fill or inspire with (ideals or principles)
IMBURSE, -D, -S *vb* pay
IMID, -S *n* immunomodulatory drug
IMIDE, -S *n* any of a class of organic compounds
IMIDIC
IMIDO
IMIDS ► imid
IMINE, -S *n* any of a class of organic compounds
IMINO
IMITABLE ► imitate
IMITANCY *n* tendency to imitate
IMITANT, -S *same as* **> imitation**
IMITATE, -D, -S *vb* take as a model
IMITATOR
IMMANE *adj* monstrous
IMMANELY
IMMANENT *adj* present within and throughout something
IMMANITY ► immane
IMMANTLE *vb* cover with a mantle
IMMASK, -ED, -S *vb* disguise
IMMATURE *n* young animal ▷ *adj* not fully developed
IMMENSE, -R *adj* extremely large
IMMERGE, -D, -S *archaic word for* **► immerse**
IMMERSE, -S *vb* involve deeply, engross
IMMERSED *adj* sunk or submerged
IMMERSER ► immerse
IMMERSES ► immerse
IMMESH, -ED, -ES *variant of* **► enmesh**
IMMEW, -ED, -ING, -S *vb* confine
IMMIES ► immy
IMMINENT *adj* about to happen
IMMINGLE *vb* blend or mix together
IMMINUTE *adj* reduced
IMMIT, -S, -TED *vb* insert
IMMIX, -ED, -ES, -ING *vb* mix in
IMMOBILE *adj* not moving
IMMODEST *adj* behaving in an indecent or improper manner
IMMOLATE *vb* kill as a sacrifice
IMMOMENT *adj* of no value
IMMORAL *adj* morally wrong, corrupt
IMMORTAL *adj* living forever ▷ *n* person whose fame will last for all time

IMMOTILE *adj* not capable of moving spontaneously and independently
IMMUNE, -S *adj* protected against a specific disease ▷ *n* immune person or animal
IMMUNISE *same as* **► immunize**
IMMUNITY *n* ability to resist disease
IMMUNIZE *vb* make immune to a disease
IMMURE, -D, -S, IMMURING *vb* imprison
IMMY, IMMIES *n* image-orthicon camera
IMP, -ED, -S *n* (in folklore) creature with magical powers ▷ *vb* method of repairing the wing of a hawk or falcon
IMPACT, -ED, -S *n* strong effect ▷ *vb* have a strong effect on
IMPACTER
IMPACTOR
IMPAINT, -S *vb* paint
IMPAIR, -ED, -S *vb* weaken or damage
IMPAIRER
IMPALA, -S *n* southern African antelope
IMPALE, -D, -S, IMPALING *vb* pierce with a sharp object
IMPALER -S
IMPANATE *adj* embodied in bread
IMPANEL, -S *variant spelling (esp US) of* **► empanel**
IMPANNEL *same as* **► impanel**
IMPARITY *less common word for* **> disparity**
IMPARK, -ED, -S *vb* make into a park
IMPARL, -ED, -S *vb* parley
IMPART, -ED, -S *vb* communicate (information)
IMPARTER
IMPASSE, -S *n* situation in which progress is impossible
IMPASTE, -D, -S *vb* apply paint thickly to
IMPASTO, -S *n* technique of applying paint thickly ▷ *vb* apply impasto
IMPAVE, -D, -S, IMPAVING *vb* set in a pavement
IMPAVID *adj* fearless
IMPAVING ► impave
IMPAWN, -ED, -S *vb* pawn
IMPEACH *vb* charge with a serious crime against the state
IMPEARL, -S *vb* adorn with pearls

IMPED ► imp
IMPEDE, -D, -S, IMPEDING *vb* hinder in action or progress
IMPEDER -S
IMPEDOR, -S *n* component that offers impedance
IMPEL, -LED, -S *vb* push or force (someone) to do something
IMPELLER *n* vaned rotating disc of a centrifugal pump, compressor, etc
IMPELLOR *same as* **► impeller**
IMPELS ► impel
IMPEND, -ED, -S *vb* be about to happen
IMPERIA ► imperium
IMPERIAL *adj* of or like an empire or emperor ▷ *n* wine bottle holding the equivalent of eight normal bottles
IMPERIL, -S *vb* put in danger
IMPERIUM, IMPERIA *n* supreme power of Roman consuls and emperors
IMPETIGO *n* contagious skin disease
IMPETUS *n* incentive, impulse
IMPHEE, -S *n* African sugar cane
IMPI, -ES, -S *n* group of Zulu warriors
IMPIETY *n* lack of respect or religious reverence
IMPING, -S ► imp
IMPINGE, -D, -S *vb* affect or restrict
IMPINGER
IMPINGS ► imping
IMPIOUS *adj* showing a lack of respect or reverence
IMPIS ► impi
IMPISH *adj* mischievous
IMPISHLY
IMPLANT, -S *n* something put into someone's body ▷ *vb* put (something) into someone's body
IMPLATE, -D, -S *vb* sheathe
IMPLEACH *vb* intertwine
IMPLEAD, -S *vb* sue or prosecute
IMPLED
IMPLEDGE *vb* pledge
IMPLETE, -D, -S *vb* fill
IMPLEX, -ES *n* part of an arthropod
IMPLICIT *adj* expressed indirectly
IMPLIED *adj* hinted at or suggested
IMPLIES ► imply
IMPLODE, -D, -S *vb* collapse inwards**

IMPLORE, -D, -S vb beg earnestly
IMPLORER
IMPLUNGE vb submerge
IMPLUVIA ▷ impluvium
IMPLY, IMPLIES, -ING vb indicate by hinting, suggest
IMPOCKET vb put in a pocket
IMPOLDER vb make into a polder
IMPOLICY n act or an instance of being injudicious or impolitic
IMPOLITE adj showing bad manners
IMPONE, -D, -S, IMPONING vb impose
IMPONENT n person who imposes a duty, etc
IMPONES ▷ impone
IMPONING ▷ impone
IMPOROUS adj not porous
IMPORT, -ED, -S vb bring in (goods) from another country ▷ n something imported
IMPORTER
IMPOSE, -D, -S vb force the acceptance of
IMPOSER -S
IMPOSEX n acquisition by female organisms of male characteristics
IMPOSING adj grand, impressive
IMPOST, -ED, -S n tax, esp a customs duty ▷ vb classify (imported goods) according to the duty payable on them
IMPOSTER
IMPOSTOR n person who cheats or swindles by pretending to be someone else
IMPOSTS ▷ impost
IMPOT, -S n slang term for the act of imposing
IMPOTENT adj powerless ▷ n one who is impotent
IMPOTS ▷ impot
IMPOUND, -S vb take legal possession of, confiscate
IMPOWER, -S less common spelling of ▶ empower
IMPREGN, -S vb impregnate
IMPRESA, -S n heraldic device
IMPRESE, -S same as ▶ impresa
IMPRESS vb affect strongly, usu favourably ▷ n impressing
IMPRESSE n heraldic device
IMPREST, -S n fund of cash used to pay incidental expenses
IMPRIMIS adv in the first place

IMPRINT, -S n mark made by printing or stamping ▷ vb produce (a mark) by printing or stamping
IMPRISON vb put in prison
IMPRO, -S n short for improvisation
IMPROPER adj indecent
IMPROS ▷ impro
IMPROV, -S n improvisational comedy
IMPROVE, -D, -S vb make or become better
IMPROVER
IMPROVS ▷ improv
IMPS ▷ imp
IMPUDENT adj cheeky, disrespectful
IMPUGN, -ED, -S vb challenge the truth or validity of
IMPUGNER
IMPULSE, -D, -S vb give an impulse to ▷ n sudden urge to do something
IMPUNITY n exemption or immunity from punishment or recrimination
IMPURE, -R, -ST adj having dirty or unwanted substances mixed in
IMPURELY
IMPURITY n impure element or thing
IMPURPLE vb colour purple
IMPUTE, -D, -S, IMPUTING vb attribute responsibility to
IMPUTER -S
IMSHI interj go away!
IMSHY same as ▶ imshi
IN, -S prep indicating position inside, state or situation, etc ▷ adv indicating position inside, entry into, etc ▷ adj fashionable ▷ n way of approaching or befriending a person ▷ vb take in
INACTION n act of doing nothing
INACTIVE adj idle
INANE, -R, -S, -ST adj senseless, silly ▷ n something that is inane
INANELY
INANGA, -S n common type of New Zealand grass tree
INANITY n lack of intelligence or imagination
INAPT adj not apt or fitting
INAPTLY
INARABLE adj not arable
INARCH, -ED, -ES vb graft (a plant)
INARM, -ED, -ING, -S vb embrace

INASMUCH conj as in **inasmuch as**, in view of the fact that
INAURATE adj gilded ▷ vb cover in gold
INBEING, -S n existence in something else
INBENT adj bent inwards
INBOARD adj (of a boat's engine) inside the hull ▷ adv within the sides of or towards the centre of a vessel or aircraft
INBOARDS same as ▶ inboard
INBORN adj existing from birth, natural
INBOUND, -S vb pass into the playing area from outside it ▷ adv coming in
INBOX, -ES n folder which stores in-coming email messages
INBREAK, -S n breaking in
INBRED, -S n inbred person or animal ▷ adj produced as a result of inbreeding
INBREED, -S vb breed from closely related individuals
INBRING, -S vb bring in
INBUILT adj present from the start
INBURST, -S n irruption ▷ vb burst in
INBY adv into the house or an inner room ▷ adj located near or nearest to the house
INBYE adv near the house
INCAGE, -D, -S, INCAGING vb confine in or as in a cage
INCANT, -ED, -S vb chant (a spell)
INCASE, -D, -S, INCASING variant spelling of ▶ encase
INCAVE, -D, -S, INCAVING vb hide
INCAVI ▷ incavo
INCAVING ▷ incave
INCAVO, INCAVI n incised part of a carving
INCEDE, -D, -S, INCEDING vb advance
INCENSE, -D, -S vb make very angry ▷ n substance that gives off a perfume when burned
INCENSER n incense burner
INCENSES ▷ incense
INCENSOR n incense burner
INCENT, -ED, -S vb provide incentive
INCENTER same as ▶ incentre
INCENTRE n centre of an inscribed circle
INCENTS ▷ incent

INCEPT, -ED, -S vb (of organisms) to ingest (food) ▷ n rudimentary organ
INCEPTOR

INCH, -ED, -ES, -ING n unit of length ▷ vb move slowly and gradually

INCHASE, -D, -S same as ▸ enchase

INCHED ▸ inch

INCHER, -S n something measuring given amount of inches

INCHES ▸ inch

INCHING ▸ inch

INCHMEAL adv gradually

INCHOATE adj just begun and not yet properly developed ▷ vb begin

INCHPIN, -S n cervine sweetbread

INCHTAPE n measuring tape marked out in inches

INCHWORM n larva of a type of moth

INCIDENT n something that happens ▷ adj related (to) or dependent (on)

INCIPIT, -S n Latin introductory phrase

INCISAL adj relating to the cutting edge of incisors and cuspids

INCISE, -D, -S, INCISING vb cut into with a sharp tool

INCISION n cut, esp one made during a surgical operation

INCISIVE adj direct and forceful

INCISOR, -S n front tooth, used for biting into food
INCISORY

INCISURE n incision or notch in an organ or part

INCITANT n something that incites

INCITE, -D, -S, INCITING vb stir up, provoke
INCITER -S

INCIVIL archaic form of ▸ uncivil

INCIVISM n neglect of a citizen's duties

INCLASP, -S vb clasp

INCLE, -S same as ▸ inkle

INCLINE, -S vb lean, slope ▷ n slope

INCLINED adj having a disposition

INCLINER ▸ incline

INCLINES ▸ incline

INCLIP, -S vb embrace

INCLOSE, -D, -S less common spelling of ▸ enclose
INCLOSER

INCLUDE, -S vb have as part of the whole

INCLUDED adj (of the stamens or pistils of a flower) not protruding beyond the corolla

INCLUDES ▸ include

INCOG, -S n incognito

INCOME, -S n amount of money earned

INCOMER, -S n person who comes to a place in which they were not born

INCOMES ▸ income

INCOMING adj coming in ▷ n act of coming in

INCONIE adj fine or delicate

INCONNU, -S n whitefish of Arctic waters

INCONNUE n unknown woman

INCONNUS ▸ inconnu

INCONY adj fine or delicate

INCORPSE vb incorporate

INCREASE vb make or become greater in size, number, etc ▷ n rise in number, size, etc

INCREATE adj (esp of gods) never having been created

INCROSS n variation produced by inbreeding ▷ vb produce by inbreeding

INCRUST, -S same as ▸ encrust

INCUBATE vb (of a bird) hatch (eggs) by sitting on them

INCUBI ▸ incubus

INCUBOUS adj having overlapping leaves

INCUBUS, INCUBI n (in folklore) type of demon

INCUDAL ▸ incus

INCUDATE ▸ incus

INCUDES ▸ incus

INCULT adj (of land) uncultivated

INCUMBER less common spelling of ▸ encumber

INCUR, -RED, -S vb cause (something unpleasant) to happen

INCURVE, -D, -S vb curve or cause to curve inwards

INCUS, INCUDES n bone in the ear of mammals

INCUSE, -D, -S, INCUSING n design stamped or hammered onto a coin ▷ vb impress (a design) in a coin ▷ adj stamped or hammered onto a coin

INCUT, -S adj cut or etched in ▷ n indent in rock used as a foothold

INDABA, -S n (among South Africans) a meeting to discuss a serious topic

INDAGATE vb investigate

INDAMIN, -S same as ▸ indamine

INDAMINE n organic base used in the production of the dye safranine

INDAMINS ▸ indamin

INDART, -ED, -S vb dart in

INDEBTED adj owing gratitude for help or favours

INDECENT adj morally offensive

INDEED adv really, certainly ▷ interj expression of indignation or surprise

INDEEDY interj indeed

INDENE, -S n colourless liquid hydrocarbon

INDENT, -ED, -S vb make a dent in
INDENTER
INDENTOR

INDEVOUT adj not devout

INDEW, -ED, -ING, -S same as ▸ indue

INDEX, -ED, -ES, -ING n alphabetical list of subjects dealt with in a book ▷ vb provide (a book) with an index
INDEXAL
INDEXER -S

INDIA, -S n code word for the letter I

INDICAN, -S n compound secreted in the urine

INDICANT n something that indicates

INDICATE vb be a sign or symptom of

INDICES plural of ▸ index

INDICIA ▸ indicium

INDICIAL ▸ indicium

INDICIUM, INDICIA n notice

INDICT, -ED, -S vb formally charge with a crime
INDICTEE
INDICTER
INDICTOR

INDIE, -S adj (of rock music) released by an independent record label ▷ n independent record company

INDIGEN, -S same as ▸ indigene

INDIGENE n indigenous person, animal, or thing

INDIGENS ▸ indigen

INDIGENT adj extremely poor ▷ n impoverished person

INDIGEST n undigested mass ▷ vb suffer indigestion

INDIGN adj undeserving
INDIGNLY
INDIGO, -ES, -S adj deep violet-blue ▷ n dye of this colour
INDIGOID adj of, concerned with, or resembling indigo or its blue colour ▷ n any of a number of synthetic dyes or pigments related in chemical structure to indigo
INDIGOS ► indigo
INDIRECT adj done or caused by someone or something else
INDITE, -D, -S, INDITING vb write
INDITER -S
INDIUM, -S n soft silvery-white metallic element
INDOCILE adj difficult to discipline or instruct
INDOL, -S same as ► **indole**
INDOLE, -S n crystalline heterocyclic compound
INDOLENT adj lazy
INDOLES ► indole
INDOLS ► indol
INDOOR adj inside a building
INDOORS adj inside or into a building
INDORSE, -D, -S variant spelling of ► **endorse**
INDORSEE n the person to whom a note or bill is indorsed
INDORSER ► indorse
INDORSES ► indorse
INDORSOR ► indorse
INDOW, -ED, -ING, -S archaic variant of ► **endow**
INDOXYL, -S n water-soluble crystalline compound
INDRAFT, -S same as > **indraught**
INDRAWN adj drawn or pulled in
INDRENCH vb submerge
INDRI same as ► **indris**
INDRIS, -ES n large lemuroid primate
INDUCE, -D, -S, INDUCING vb persuade or influence
INDUCER -S
INDUCIAE n time limit for a defendant to appear in court
INDUCING ► induce
INDUCT, -ED, -S vb formally install (someone) in office
INDUCTEE n military conscript
INDUCTOR n device designed to create inductance in an electrical circuit
INDUCTS ► induct

INDUE, -D, -S, INDUING variant spelling of ► **endue**
INDULGE, -D, -S vb allow oneself pleasure
INDULGER
INDULIN, -S same as ► **induline**
INDULINE n any of a class of blue dyes obtained from aniline and aminoazobenzene
INDULINS ► indulin
INDULT, -S n type of faculty granted by the Holy See
INDUNA, -S n (in South Africa) a Black African overseer
INDURATE vb make or become hard or callous ▷ adj hardened, callous, or unfeeling
INDUSIA ► indusium
INDUSIAL ► indusium
INDUSIUM, INDUSIA n outgrowth on the undersurface of fern leaves
INDUSTRY n manufacture of goods
INDUVIAE pl n withered leaves
INDUVIAL
INDWELL, -S, INDWELT vb (of a spirit, principle, etc) to inhabit
INEARTH, -S poetic word for ► **bury**
INEDIBLE adj not fit to be eaten
INEDIBLY
INEDITA pl n unpublished writings
INEDITED adj not edited
INEPT, -ER, -EST adj clumsy, lacking skill
INEPTLY
INEQUITY n injustice or unfairness
INERM adj without thorns
INERMOUS same as ► **inerm**
INERRANT same as > **inerrable**
INERT, -ER, -EST, -S n inert thing ▷ adj without the power of motion or resistance
INERTIA, -E, -S n feeling of unwillingness to do anything
INERTIAL

This is not the easiest of words to see in play, but its combination of common letters makes it one of the most frequently played of 7-letter bonuses, while its plurals, which can be **inertiae** or **inertias**, are among the 8-letter bonus

words that come up most often.

INERTLY ► inert
INERTS ► inert
INESSIVE n grammatical case in Finnish
INEXACT adj not exact or accurate
INEXPERT n unskilled person ▷ adj lacking skill
INFALL, -S vb move towards (something) under the influence of gravity
INFAME, -D, -S, INFAMING vb defame
INFAMIES ► infamy
INFAMING ► infame
INFAMISE same as ► **infamize**
INFAMIZE vb make infamous
INFAMOUS adj well-known for something bad
INFAMY, INFAMIES n state of being infamous
INFANCY n early childhood
INFANT, -S n very young child ▷ adj of, relating to, or designed for young children
INFANTA, -S n (formerly) daughter of a king of Spain or Portugal
INFANTE, -S n (formerly) any son of a king of Spain or Portugal, except the heir to the throne
INFANTRY n soldiers who fight on foot
INFANTS ► infant
INFARCT, -S n localized area of dead tissue ▷ vb obstruct the blood supply to part of a body
INFARE, -S vb enter
INFAUNA, -E, -S n animals that live in ocean and river beds
INFAUNAL
INFAUST adj unlucky
INFECT, -ED, -S vb affect with a disease ▷ adj contaminated or polluted with or as if with a disease
INFECTER
INFECTOR
INFECUND less common word for > **infertile**
INFEED, -S n action of supplying a machine with a material
INFEFT, -ED, -S vb give possession of heritable property
INFELT adj heartfelt
INFEOFF, -S same as ► **enfeoff**

INFER, -RED, -S *vb* work out from evidence
INFERE *adv* together
INFERIAE *pl n* offerings made to the spirits of the dead
INFERIOR *adj* lower in quality, position, or status ▷ *n* person of lower position or status
INFERNAL *adj* of hell
INFERNO, -S *n* intense raging fire
INFERRED ▶ **infer**
INFERRER ▶ **infer**
INFERS ▶ **infer**
INFEST, -ED, -S *vb* inhabit or overrun in unpleasantly large numbers
INFESTER
INFICETE *adj* not witty
INFIDEL, -S *n* person with no religion ▷ *adj* of unbelievers or unbelief
INFIELD, -S *n* area of the field near the pitch
INFIGHT, -S, INFOUGHT *vb* box at close quarters
INFILL, -ED, -S *vb* fill in ▷ *n* act of filling or closing gaps in something
INFIMUM, INFIMA, -S *n* greatest lower bound
INFINITE *adj* without any limit or end ▷ *n* something without any limit or end
INFINITY *n* endless space, time, or number
INFIRM, -ED, -ER, -S *vb* make infirm ▷ *adj* physically or mentally weak
INFIRMLY
INFIX, -ED, -ES, -ING *vb* fix firmly in ▷ *n* affix inserted into the middle of a word
INFIXION
INFLAME, -D, -S *vb* make angry or excited
INFLAMER
INFLATE, -D, -S *vb* expand by filling with air or gas
INFLATER
INFLATOR
INFLATUS *n* act of breathing in
INFLECT, -S *vb* change (the voice) in tone or pitch
INFLEXED *adj* curved or bent inwards and downwards towards the axis
INFLICT, -S *vb* impose (something unpleasant) on
INFLIGHT *adj* provided during flight in an aircraft
INFLOW, -S *n* something, such as liquid or gas, that flows in ▷ *vb* flow in

INFLUENT *adj* flowing in ▷ *n* something flowing in, esp a tributary
INFLUX, -ES *n* arrival or entry of many people or things
INFO, -S *n* information
INFOBAHN *same as* ▶ **internet**
INFOLD, -ED, -S *variant spelling of* ▶ **enfold**
INFOLDER
INFORCE, -D, -S *same as* ▶ **enforce**
INFORM, -ED, -S *vb* tell ▷ *adj* without shape
INFORMAL *adj* relaxed and friendly
INFORMED ▶ **inform**
INFORMER *n* person who informs to the police
INFORMS ▶ **inform**
INFOS ▶ **info**
INFOTECH *n* information technology
INFOUGHT ▶ **infight**
INFRA *adv* (esp in textual annotation) below
INFRACT, -S *vb* violate or break (a law, an agreement, etc)
INFRARED *adj* of or using rays below the red end of the visible spectrum ▷ *n* infrared part of the spectrum
INFRINGE *vb* break (a law or agreement)
INFRUGAL *adj* wasteful
INFULA *same as* ▶ **infulae**
INFULAE *pl n* two ribbons hanging from a bishop's mitre
INFUSE, -D, -S, INFUSING *vb* fill (with an emotion or quality)
INFUSER, -S *n* any device used to make an infusion
INFUSES ▶ **infuse**
INFUSING ▶ **infuse**
INFUSION *n* infusing
INFUSIVE
INFUSORY *adj* containing infusoria ▷ *n* infusorian, a tiny water-dwelling mammal
ING, -S *n* meadow near a river
INGAN, -S *Scots word for* ▶ **onion**
INGATE, -S *n* entrance
INGATHER *vb* gather together or in (a harvest)
INGENER, -S *Shakespearean form of* ▶ **engineer**
INGENIUM *n* genius
INGENU, -S *n* artless or inexperienced boy or young man

INGENUE, -S *n* inexperienced girl or young woman
INGENUS ▶ **ingenu**
INGEST, -ED, -S *vb* take (food or liquid) into the body
INGESTA *pl n* nourishment taken through the mouth
INGESTED ▶ **ingest**
INGESTS ▶ **ingest**
INGINE, -S *n* genius
INGLE, -S *n* fire in a room or a fireplace
INGLOBE, -D, -S *vb* shape as a sphere
INGO, -ES *n* revelation
INGOING, -S *same as* ▶ **ingo**
INGOT, -ED, -ING, -S *n* oblong block of cast metal ▷ *vb* shape (metal) into ingots
INGRAFT, -S *variant spelling of* ▶ **engraft**
INGRAIN, -S *vb* impress deeply on the mind or nature ▷ *adj* (of carpets) made of fibre that is dyed before being spun ▷ *n* carpet made from ingrained yarn
INGRAM, -S *adj* ignorant ▷ *n* ignorant person
INGRATE, -S *n* ungrateful person ▷ *adj* ungrateful
INGRESS *n* entrance
INGROOVE *vb* cut a groove into
INGROSS *archaic form of* ▶ **engross**
INGROUND *adj* sunk into ground ▷ *vb* fix (something) in the ground or in a foundation
INGROUP, -S *n* highly cohesive and relatively closed social group
INGROWN *adj* grown abnormally into the flesh
INGROWTH *n* act of growing inwards
INGRUM, -S *adj* ignorant ▷ *n* ignorant person
INGS ▶ **ing**
INGUINAL *adj* of or relating to the groin
INGULF, -ED, -S *variant spelling of* ▶ **engulf**
INGULPH, -S *archaic form of* ▶ **engulf**
INHABIT, -S *vb* live in
INHALANT *n* medical preparation inhaled to help breathing problems ▷ *adj* inhaled for its soothing or therapeutic effect
INHALE, -D, -S, INHALING *vb* breathe in (air, smoke, etc)
INHALER, -S *n* container for an inhalant**

INHALES ▸ inhale

INHALING ▸ inhale

INHAUL, -S n line for hauling in a sail

INHAULER same as ▸ **inhaul**

INHAULS ▸ inhaul

INHAUST, -S vb drink in

INHEARSE vb bury

INHERCE, -D, -S same as ▸ **inhearse**

INHERE, -D, -S, INHERING vb be an inseparable part (of)

INHERENT adj existing as an inseparable part

INHERES ▸ inhere

INHERING ▸ inhere

INHERIT, -S vb receive (money etc) from someone who has died

INHESION less common word for ▸ **inherence**

INHIBIN, -S n peptide hormone

INHIBIT, -S vb restrain (an impulse or desire)

INHOLDER n inhabitant

INHOOP, -ED, -S vb confine

INHUMAN adj cruel or brutal

INHUMANE same as ▸ **inhuman**

INHUMATE vb bury

INHUME, -D, -S, INHUMING vb inter

INHUMER -S

INIA ▸ inion

INIMICAL adj unfavourable or hostile

INION, INIA, -S n most prominent point at the back of the head

INIQUITY n injustice or wickedness

INISLE, -D, -S, INISLING vb put on or make into an island

INITIAL, -S adj first, at the beginning ▷ n first letter, esp of a person's name ▷ vb sign with one's initials

INITIATE vb begin or set going ▷ n recently initiated person ▷ adj initiated

INJECT, -ED, -S vb put (a fluid) into the body with a syringe

INJECTOR

INJELLY vb place in jelly

INJERA, -S n white Ethiopian flatbread, similar to a crepe

INJOINT, -S vb join

INJUNCT, -S vb issue a legal injunction against (a person)

INJURE, -D, -S, INJURING vb hurt physically or mentally

INJURER -S

INJURIES ▸ injury

INJURING ▸ injure

INJURY, INJURIES n physical hurt

INK, -ED, -ING, -S n coloured liquid used for writing or printing ▷ vb mark in ink (something already marked in pencil)

INKBERRY n North American holly tree

INKBLOT, -S n abstract patch of ink

INKED ▸ ink

INKER, -S ▸ ink

INKHORN, -S n (formerly) a small portable container for ink

INKHOSI, AMAKOSI, -S n Zulu clan chief

INKIER ▸ inky

INKIEST ▸ inky

INKINESS ▸ inky

INKING ▸ ink

INKJET, -S adj of a method of printing ▷ n inkjet printer

INKLE, -D, -S n kind of linen tape used for trimmings ▷ vb hint

INKLESS ▸ ink

INKLIKE ▸ ink

INKLING, -S n slight idea or suspicion

INKOSI, -S same as ▸ **inkhosi**

INKPAD, -S n pad used for rubber-stamping or fingerprinting

INKPOT, -S n ink-bottle

INKS ▸ ink

INKSPOT, -S n ink stain

INKSTAIN n stain made by ink

INKSTAND n stand or tray for holding writing tools and containers for ink

INKSTONE n stone used in making ink

INKWELL, -S n small container for ink

INKWOOD, -S n type of tree

INKY, INKIER, INKIEST adj dark or black

INLACE, -D, -S, INLACING variant spelling of ▸ **enlace**

INLAID ▸ inlay

INLAND, -S adv in or towards the interior of a country ▷ adj of or in the interior of a country or region ▷ n interior of a country or region

INLANDER

INLAY, INLAID, -ING, -S n inlaid substance or pattern ▷ vb decorate by inserting wooden pieces

INLAYER -S

INLET, -S n water extending from the sea into the land ▷ vb insert or inlay

INLIER, -S n outcrop of rocks surrounded by younger rocks

INLOCK, -ED, -S vb lock up

INLY adv inwardly

INLYING adj situated within or inside

INMATE, -S n person living in an institution such as a prison

INMESH, -ED, -ES variant spelling of ▸ **enmesh**

INMOST adj innermost

INN, -ED, -S n pub or small hotel, esp in the country ▷ vb stay at an inn

INNAGE, -S n type of measurement

INNARDS pl n internal organs

INNATE adj being part of someone's nature, inborn

INNATELY

INNATIVE adj native

INNED ▸ inn

INNER, -S adj happening or located inside ▷ n red innermost ring on a target

INNERLY

INNERVE, -D, -S vb supply with nervous energy

INNING, -S n division of baseball match

INNIT interj isn't it

INNLESS adj without inns

INNOCENT adj not guilty of a crime ▷ n innocent person, esp a child

INNOVATE vb introduce new ideas or methods

INNS ▸ inn

INNUENDO n indirect reference to something rude or unpleasant

INNYARD, -S n courtyard of an inn

INOCULUM, INOCULA n substance used in giving an inoculation

INORB, -ED, -ING, -S vb enclose in or as if in an orb

INORNATE adj simple

INOSINE, -S n type of molecule making up cell

INOSITE, -S same as ▸ **inositol**

INOSITOL n cyclic alcohol

INOTROPE n drug for controlling muscular contractions

INPHASE adj in the same phase

INPOUR, -ED, -S vb pour in

INPUT, -S, -TED n resources put into a project etc ▷ vb enter (data) in a computer

INPUTTER

INQILAB, -S n (in India, Pakistan, etc) revolution
INQUERE, -D, -S Spenserian form of ▸ **inquire**
INQUEST, -S n official inquiry into a sudden death
INQUIET, -S vb disturb
INQUIRE, -D, -S vb seek information or ask (about)
INQUIRER
INQUIRY n question
INRO n Japanese seal-box
INROAD, -S n invasion or hostile attack
INRUN, -S n slope down which ski jumpers ski
INRUSH, -ES n sudden and overwhelming inward flow
INS ▸ in
INSANE, -R, -ST adj mentally ill
INSANELY
INSANIE, -S n insanity
INSANITY n state of being insane
INSCAPE, -S n essential inner nature of a person, etc
INSCIENT adj ignorant
INSCONCE vb fortify
INSCRIBE vb write or carve words on
INSCROLL vb write on a scroll
INSCULP, -S vb engrave
INSCULPT adj engraved
INSEAM, -ED, -S vb contain
INSECT, -S n small animal with six legs
INSECTAN
INSECURE adj anxious, not confident
INSEEM, -ED, -S vb cover with grease
INSERT, -S vb put inside or include ▷ n something inserted
INSERTED adj (of a muscle) attached to the bone that it moves
INSERTER ▸ insert
INSERTS ▸ insert
INSET, -S, -TED n small picture inserted within a larger one ▷ vb place in or within ▷ adj decorated with something inserted
INSETTER
INSHEATH vb sheathe
INSHELL, -S vb retreat, as into a shell
INSHIP, -S vb travel or send by ship
INSHORE adj close to the shore ▷ adv towards the shore
INSHRINE variant spelling of ▸ **enshrine**

INSIDE, -S prep in or to the interior of ▷ adj on or of the inside ▷ adv on, in, or to the inside, indoors ▷ n inner side, surface, or part
INSIDER, -S n someone who has privileged knowledge
INSIDES ▸ inside
INSIGHT, -S n deep understanding
INSIGNE same as ▸ **insignia**
INSIGNIA n badge or emblem of honour or office
INSINEW, -S vb connect or strengthen, as with sinews
INSIPID adj lacking interest, spirit, or flavour
INSIST, -ED, -S vb demand or state firmly
INSISTER
INSNARE, -D, -S less common spelling of ▸ **ensnare**
INSNARER
INSOFAR adv to the extent
INSOLATE vb expose to sunlight, as for bleaching
INSOLE, -S n inner sole of a shoe or boot
INSOLENT n insolent person ▷ adj rude and disrespectful
INSOLES ▸ insole
INSOMNIA n inability to sleep
INSOMUCH adv such an extent
INSOOTH adv indeed
INSOUL, -ED, -S variant of ▸ **ensoul**
INSOURCE vb subcontract work to a company under the same general ownership
INSPAN, -S vb harness (animals) to (a vehicle)
INSPECT, -S vb check closely or officially
INSPHERE variant spelling of ▸ **ensphere**
INSPIRE, -S vb fill with enthusiasm, stimulate
INSPIRED adj brilliantly creative
INSPIRER ▸ inspire
INSPIRES ▸ inspire
INSPIRIT vb fill with vigour
INSTABLE less common word for ▸ **unstable**
INSTAL, -S same as ▸ **install**
INSTALL, -S vb put in and prepare (equipment) for use
INSTALS ▸ instal
INSTANCE n particular example ▷ vb mention as an example
INSTANCY n quality of being urgent or imminent
INSTANT, -S n very brief time ▷ adj happening at once

INSTAR, -S vb decorate with stars ▷ n stage in the development of an insect
INSTATE, -D, -S vb place in a position or office
INSTEAD adv as a replacement or substitute
INSTEP, -S n part of the foot
INSTIL, -S vb introduce (an idea etc) gradually into someone's mind
INSTILL, -S same as ▸ **instil**
INSTILS ▸ instil
INSTINCT n inborn tendency to behave in a certain way ▷ adj animated or impelled (by)
INSTRESS vb create or sustain
INSTROKE n inward stroke
INSTRUCT vb order to do something
INSUCKEN adj of a sucken
INSULA, -E n pyramid-shaped area of the brain
INSULANT n insulation
INSULAR, -S adj not open to new ideas, narrow-minded ▷ n islander
INSULATE vb reduce the transfer of electricity, heat, or sound by lining with nonconducting material
INSULIN, -S n hormone produced in the pancreas
INSULSE adj stupid
INSULT, -ED, -S vb behave rudely to, offend ▷ n insulting remark or action
INSULTER
INSURANT n holder of an insurance policy
INSURE, -S, INSURING vb protect by insurance
INSURED, -S adj covered by insurance ▷ n those covered by an insurance policy
INSURER, -S n person or company that sells insurance
INSURES ▸ insure
INSURING ▸ insure
INSWATHE vb bind or wrap
INSWEPT adj narrowed towards the front
INSWING, -S n movement of a bowled ball
INTACT adj not changed or damaged in any way
INTACTLY
INTAGLIO, INTAGLI n (gem carved with) an engraved design
INTAKE, -S n amount or number taken in
INTARSIA n mosaic of inlaid wood

INTEGER, -S n positive or negative whole number or zero

INTEGRAL adj being an essential part of a whole ▷ n sum of a large number of very small quantities

INTEGRIN n protein that acts as a signal receptor between cells

INTEL, -S n US military intelligence

INTEND, -S vb propose or plan (to do something)

INTENDED adj planned or future ▷ n person whom one is to marry

INTENDER ▸ intend

INTENDS ▸ intend

INTENSE, -R adj of great strength or degree

INTENT, -S n intention ▷ adj paying close attention

INTENTLY

INTER, -RED, -S vb bury (a dead body)

INTERACT vb act on or in close relation with each other

INTERAGE adj between different ages

INTERBED vb lie between strata of different minerals

INTERCOM n internal communication system with loudspeakers

INTERCUT another word for ▸ crosscut

INTERESS vb interest

INTEREST n desire to know or hear more about something ▷ vb arouse the interest of

INTERIM, -S adj temporary, provisional, or intervening ▷ n intervening time ▷ adv meantime

INTERIOR n inside ▷ adj inside, inner

INTERLAP less common word for ▸ overlap

INTERLAY vb insert (layers) between ▷ n material, such as paper, placed between a printing plate and its base

INTERMAT n patch of seabed devoid of vegetation

INTERMIT vb suspend (activity) or (of activity) to be suspended temporarily or at intervals

INTERMIX vb mix together

INTERN, -ED, -S vb imprison, esp during a war ▷ n trainee doctor in a hospital

INTERNAL adj of or on the inside ▷ n medical examination of the inside of the body

INTERNE, -S same as ▸ intern

INTERNED ▸ intern

INTERNEE n person who is interned

INTERNES ▸ interne

INTERNET n worldwide computer network

INTERNS ▸ intern

INTERRED ▸ inter

INTERREX n person who governs during an interregnum

INTERROW adj occurring between rows

INTERS ▸ inter

INTERSEX n condition of having characteristics intermediate between those of a male and a female

INTERTIE n short roofing timber

INTERVAL n time between two particular moments or events

INTERWAR adj of or happening in the period between World War I and World War II

INTERWEB same as ▸ internet

INTHRAL, -S archaic form of ▸ enthral

INTHRALL archaic form of ▸ enthral

INTHRALS ▸ inthral

INTHRONE archaic form of ▸ enthrone

INTI, -S n former monetary unit of Peru

INTIFADA n Palestinian uprising against Israel in the West Bank and Gaza Strip

INTIL Scot form of ▸ into

INTIMA, -E, -S n innermost layer of an organ or part

INTIMACY n close or warm friendship

INTIMAE ▸ intima

INTIMAL ▸ intima

INTIMAS ▸ intima

INTIMATE adj having a close personal relationship ▷ n close friend ▷ vb hint at or suggest

INTIME adj intimate

INTIMISM n school of impressionist painting

INTIMIST

INTIMITY n intimacy

INTINE, -S n inner wall of a pollen grain or a spore

INTIRE archaic form of ▸ entire

INTIS ▸ inti

INTITLE, -D, -S archaic form of ▸ entitle

INTITULE vb (in Britain) to entitle (an act of parliament)

INTO prep indicating motion towards the centre, result of a change, etc

INTOED adj having inward-turning toes

INTOMB, -ED, -S same as ▸ entomb

INTONACO n wet plaster surface on which frescoes are painted

INTONATE vb pronounce with a rise and fall of the voice

INTONE, -D, -S, INTONING vb speak or recite in an unvarying tone of voice

INTONER -S

INTORT, -ED, -S vb twist inward

INTOWN adj infield

INTRA prep within

INTRADA, -S n prelude

INTRADAY adj occurring within one day

INTRADOS n inner curve or surface of an arch or vault

INTRANET n internal network that makes use of Internet technology

INTRANT, -S n one who enters

INTREAT, -S archaic spelling of ▸ entreat

INTRENCH less common spelling of ▸ entrench

INTREPID adj fearless, bold

INTRIGUE vb make interested or curious ▷ n secret plotting

INTRINCE adj intricate

INTRO, -S n introduction

INTROFY vb increase the wetting properties

INTROIT, -S n short prayer said or sung

INTROLD variant of ▸ entrold

INTROMIT vb enter or insert or allow to enter or be inserted

INTRON, -S n stretch of DNA

INTRONIC adj of or like an intron

INTRONS ▸ intron

INTRORSE adj turned inwards or towards the axis

INTROS ▸ intro

INTRUDE, -D, -S vb come in or join in without being invited

INTRUDER n person who enters a place without permission

INTRUDES ▸ intrude

INTRUST, -S same as ▸ entrust

INTUBATE *vb* insert a tube or cannula into (a hollow organ)

INTUIT, -ED, -S *vb* know or discover by intuition

INTURN, -S *n* inward turn

INTURNED *adj* turned inward

INTURNS ▸ inturn

INTUSE, -S *n* contusion

INTWINE, -D, -S *less common spelling of* **▸ entwine**

INTWIST, -S *vb* twist together

INUKSHUK *n* stone used by Inuit people to mark a location

INUKSUK, INUKSUIT, -S *same as* **▸ inukshuk**

INULA, -S *n* plant of the elecampane genus

INULASE, -S *n* enzyme

INULIN, -S *n* fructose polysaccharide

INUNDANT ▸ inundate

INUNDATE *vb* flood

INURBANE *adj* not urbane

INURE, -D, -S, INURING *vb* cause to accept or become hardened to

INURN, -ED, -ING, -S *vb* place (esp cremated ashes) in an urn

INUST *adj* burnt in

INUSTION

INUTILE *adj* useless

INVADE, -D, -S, INVADING *vb* enter (a country) by military force

INVADER -S

INVALID, -S *n* disabled or chronically ill person ▷ *vb* dismiss from active service because of illness or injury ▷ *adj* having no legal force

INVAR, -S *n* alloy made from iron and nickel

INVASION *n* invading

INVASIVE *adj* of or relating to an invasion, intrusion, etc

INVEAGLE *archaic form of* **▸ inveigle**

INVECKED *same as* **▸ invected**

INVECTED *adj* bordered with small convex curves

INVEIGH, -S *vb* criticize strongly

INVEIGLE *vb* coax by cunning or trickery

INVENIT *sentence substitute* (he or she) designed it

INVENT, -ED, -S *vb* think up or create (something new)

INVENTER *same as* **▸ inventor**

INVENTOR *n* person who invents, esp as a profession

INVENTS ▸ invent

INVERITY *n* untruth

INVERSE, -D, -S *vb* make something opposite or contrary in effect ▷ *adj* reversed in effect, sequence, direction, etc ▷ *n* exact opposite

INVERT, -ED, -S *vb* turn upside down or inside out

INVERTER *n* any device for converting a direct current into an alternating current

INVERTIN *same as* **▸ invertase**

INVERTOR *same as* **▸ inverter**

INVERTS ▸ invert

INVEST, -ED, -S *vb* spend (money, time, etc) with the expectation of profit

INVESTOR

INVEXED *adj* concave

INVIABLE *adj* not viable, esp financially

INVIABLY

INVIOUS *adj* without paths or roads

INVIRILE *adj* unmanly

INVISCID *adj* not viscid

INVITAL *adj* not vital

INVITE, -D, -S *vb* request the company of ▷ *n* invitation

INVITEE, -S *n* one who is invited

INVITER, -S ▸ invite

INVITES ▸ invite

INVITING *adj* tempting, attractive ▷ *n* old word for invitation

INVOCATE *archaic word for* **▸ invoke**

INVOICE, -D, -S *n* bill for goods or services ▷ *vb* present (a customer) with an invoice

INVOKE, -D, -S, INVOKING *vb* put (a law or penalty) into operation

INVOKER -S

INVOLUTE *adj* complex, intricate, or involved ▷ *n* curve described by the free end of a thread as it is wound around another curve ▷ *vb* become involute

INVOLVE, -D, -S *vb* include as a necessary part

INVOLVER

INWALL, -ED, -S *vb* surround with a wall

INWARD *adj* directed towards the middle ▷ *adv* towards the inside or middle ▷ *n* inward part

INWARDLY *adv* within the private thoughts or feelings

INWARDS *adv* towards the inside or middle of something

INWEAVE, -D, -S, INWOVE, INWOVEN *vb* weave together

INWICK, -ED, -S *vb* perform a type of curling stroke

INWIND, -S, INWOUND *vb* wind or coil around

INWIT, -S *n* conscience

INWITH *adv* within

INWITS ▸ inwit

INWORK, -ED, -S *vb* work in

INWORN *adj* worn in

INWOUND ▸ inwind

INWOVE ▸ inweave

INWOVEN ▸ inweave

INWRAP, -S *less common spelling of* **▸ enwrap**

INYALA, -S *n* antelope

IO, -S *interj* exclamation of triumph ▷ *n* cry of "io"

IODATE, -D, -S, IODATING *same as* **▸ iodize**

IODATION

IODIC *adj* of or containing iodine

IODID, -S *same as* **▸ iodide**

IODIDE, -S *n* chemical compound

IODIDS ▸ iodid

IODIN, -S *same as* **▸ iodine**

IODINATE *vb* cause to combine with iodine

IODINE, -S *n* bluish-black element

IODINS ▸ iodin

IODISE, -D, -S, IODISING *same as* **▸ iodize**

IODISER -S

IODISM, -S *n* poisoning caused by iodine or its compounds

IODIZE, -D, -S, IODIZING *vb* treat with iodine

IODIZER -S

IODOFORM *n* yellow crystalline insoluble volatile solid

IODOPHOR *n* substance in which iodine is combined with an agent that renders it soluble

IODOPSIN *n* violet light-sensitive pigment in the retina

IODOUS *adj* of or containing iodine

IODURET, -S *n* iodide

IODYRITE *n* silver iodide

IOLITE, -S *n* grey or violet-blue dichroic mineral

ION, -S *n* electrically charged atom

IONIC *adj* of or in the form of ions

IONICITY n ionic character

IONICS pl n study of ions

IONISE, -D, -S, IONISING same as ► **ionize**

IONISER, -S same as ► **ionizer**

IONISES ► **ionise**

IONISING ► **ionise**

IONIUM, -S n naturally occurring radioisotope of thorium

IONIZE, -D, -S, IONIZING vb change into ions

IONIZER, -S n person or thing that ionizes

IONIZES ► **ionize**

IONIZING ► **ionize**

IONOGEN, -S n compound that exists as ions when dissolved

IONOMER, -S n type of thermoplastic

IONONE, -S n yellowish liquid mixture

IONS ► **ion**

IOPANOIC adj as in **iopanoic acid** type of acid containing iodine

IOS ► **io**

IOTA, -S n ninth letter in the Greek alphabet

This word for a Greek letter is another of those that come in handy when you are trying to rid your rack of too many vowels.

IOTACISM n pronunciation tendency in Modern Greek

IOTAS ► **iota**

IPECAC, -S n type of S American shrub

IPOMOEA, -S n convolvulaceous plant

IPPON, -S n winning point awarded in a judo or karate competition

IRACUND adj easily angered

IRADE, -S n written edict of a Muslim ruler

IRATE, -R, -ST adj very angry

IRATELY

IRE, -D, -S, IRING vb anger ▷ n anger

IREFUL

IREFULLY

IRELESS

IRENIC adj tending to conciliate or promote peace

IRENICAL same as ► **irenic**

IRENICON variant spelling of > eirenicon

IRENICS n branch of theology

IRES ► **ire**

IRID, -S n type of iris

IRIDAL

IRIDEAL

IRIDES ► **iris**

IRIDIAL ► **irid**

IRIDIAN ► **irid**

IRIDIC adj of or containing iridium

IRIDISE, -D, -S vb make iridescent

IRIDIUM, -S n very hard corrosion-resistant metal

IRIDIZE, -D, -S vb make iridescent

IRIDS ► **irid**

IRING ► **ire**

IRIS, IRIDES, -ED, -ES, -ING n part of the eye ▷ vb display iridescence

IRISATE, -D, -S vb make iridescent

IRISCOPE n instrument that displays the prismatic colours

IRISED ► **iris**

IRISES ► **iris**

IRISING ► **iris**

IRITIC ► **iritis**

IRITIS, -ES n inflammation of the iris of the eye

Since a plague of Is tends to afflict every Scrabble player's rack at regular intervals, it is well worth knowing words like this one, which use several of the wretched letter!

IRK, -ED, -ING, -S vb irritate, annoy

IRKSOME adj irritating, annoying

IROKO, -S n tropical African hardwood tree

IRON, -ED, -S n strong silvery-white metallic element ▷ adj made of iron ▷ vb smooth (clothes or fabric) with an iron

IRONBARK n Australian eucalyptus with hard rough bark

IRONCLAD adj covered or protected with iron ▷ n large wooden 19th-century warship with armoured plating

IRONE, -S n fragrant liquid

You may surprise your opponent by adding an E to **iron** if you know this word for a kind of aromatic oil.

IRONED ► **iron**

IRONER, -S ► **iron**

IRONES ► **irone**

IRONIC adj using irony

IRONICAL same as ► **ironic**

IRONIER ► **irony**

IRONIES ► **irony**

IRONIEST ► **irony**

IRONING, -S n clothes to be ironed

IRONISE, -D, -S same as ► **ironize**

IRONIST, -S ► **ironize**

IRONIZE, -D, -S vb use or indulge in irony

IRONLESS ► **iron**

IRONLIKE ► **iron**

IRONMAN, IRONMEN n very strong man

IRONNESS ► **iron**

IRONS ► **iron**

IRONSIDE n person with great stamina or resistance

IRONWARE n domestic articles made of iron

IRONWEED n plant with purplish leaves

IRONWOOD n any of various trees, such as hornbeam, with exceptionally hard wood

IRONWORK n work done in iron, esp decorative work

IRONY, IRONIER, IRONIES, IRONIEST n grammatical device ▷ adj of, resembling, or containing iron

IRREAL adj unreal

IRRIGATE vb supply (land) with water by artificial channels or pipes

IRRISION n mockery

IRRISORY adj mocking

IRRITANT adj causing irritation ▷ n something that annoys or irritates

IRRITATE vb annoy, anger

IRRUPT, -ED, -S vb enter forcibly or suddenly

IS vb form of the present tense of be

ISABEL, -S n brown yellow colour

ISABELLA same as ► **isabel**

ISABELS ► **isabel**

ISAGOGE, -S n academic introduction

ISAGOGIC > isagogics

ISARITHM n line on a map connecting places with the same population density

ISATIN, -S n yellowish-red crystalline compound

ISATINE, -S same as ► **isatin**

ISATINIC ► **isatin**

ISATINS ► **isatin**

ISBA, -S n log hut

ISCHEMIA same as > ischaemia

ISCHEMIC > ischaemia

ISCHIA ► **ischium**

ISCHIAL ► **ischium**

ISCHIUM, ISCHIA *n* part of the hipbone
ISCHURIA *n* retention of urine
ISH, -ES *n* issue

> An **ish** is a word for an issue in Scots law. If you have I, S and H on your rack, remember that as well as adding **ish** to the ends of many words, you can also play those letters as a word in its own right.

ISIT *sentence substitute* expression used in response to a statement
ISLAND, -ED, -S *n* piece of land surrounded by water ▷ *vb* cause to become an island
ISLANDER *n* person who lives on an island
ISLANDS ► island
ISLE, -D, -S, ISLING *vb* make an isle of ▷ *n* island
ISLELESS *adj* without islands
ISLEMAN, ISLEMEN *n* islander
ISLES ► isle
ISLESMAN, ISLESMEN *same as* ► isleman
ISLET, -S *n* small island
ISLETED *adj* having islets
ISLETS ► islet
ISLING ► isle
ISM, -S *n* doctrine, system, or practice

> While **ism** can be added to the ends of many words as a suffix, it's worth remembering as a word in its own right.

ISMATIC *adj* following fashionable doctrines
ISMS ► ism
ISNA *vb* is not
ISNAE *same as* ► isna
ISO, -S *n* short segment of film that can be replayed easily
ISOAMYL, -S *n as in* **isoamyl acetate** colourless volatile compound
ISOBAR, -S *n* line showing equal pressure
ISOBARE, -S *same as* ► isobar
ISOBARIC *adj* having equal atmospheric pressure
ISOBARS ► isobar
ISOBASE, -S *n* line connecting points of equal land upheaval
ISOBATH, -S *n* line showing equal depth of water
ISOBRONT *n* line connecting points of simultaneous storm development
ISOBUTYL *n as in* **methyl isobutyl ketone** colourless insoluble liquid ketone used

as a solvent for organic compounds
ISOCHASM *n* line connecting points of equal aurorae frequency
ISOCHEIM *n* line on a map connecting places with the same mean winter temperature
ISOCHIME *same as* ► isocheim
ISOCHOR, -S *n* line showing equal pressure and temperature
ISOCHORE *same as* ► isochor
ISOCHORS ► isochor
ISOCHRON *n* line on an isotope ratio diagram
ISOCLINE *same as* > isoclinal
ISOCRACY *n* form of government in which all people have equal powers
ISOCRYME *n* line connecting points of equal winter temperature
ISODICON, ISODICA *n* short anthem
ISODOMON, ISODOMA *n* masonry formed of uniform blocks, with courses are of equal height
ISODOMUM *same as* ► isodomon
ISODONT, -S *n* animal in which the teeth are of similar size
ISODOSE, -S *n* dose of radiation applied in radiotherapy
ISOETES *n* quillwort
ISOFORM, -S *n* protein similar in function but not form to another
ISOGAMIC *same as* ► isogamy
ISOGAMY *n* fusion of similar gametes
ISOGENIC *same as* > isogenous
ISOGENY > isogenous
ISOGLOSS *n* line drawn on a linguistic map
ISOGON, -S *n* equiangular polygon
ISOGONAL *same as* ► isogonic
ISOGONE, -S *same as* ► isogonic
ISOGONIC *adj* having, making, or involving equal angles ▷ *n* imaginary line connecting points on the earth's surface having equal magnetic declination
ISOGONS ► isogon
ISOGONY ► isogonic

ISOGRAFT *vb* grafting tissue from a donor genetically identical to the recipient
ISOGRAM, -S *same as* ► isopleth
ISOGRAPH *n* line connecting points of the same linguistic usage
ISOGRIV, -S *n* line showing equal angular bearing
ISOHEL, -S *n* line showing equal sunshine
ISOHYET, -S *n* line showing equal rainfall
ISOKONT, -S *same as* > isokontan
ISOLABLE ► isolate
ISOLATE, -D, -S *vb* place apart or alone ▷ *n* isolated person or group
ISOLATOR
ISOLEAD, -S *n* line on a ballistic graph
ISOLEX, -ES *n* line on map showing where a particular word is used
ISOLINE, -S *same as* ► isopleth
ISOLOG > isologous
ISOLOGS > isologous
ISOLOGUE > isologous
ISOMER, -S *n* compound that has the same molecular formula as another
ISOMERE, -S *same as* ► isomer
ISOMERIC ► isomer
ISOMERS ► isomer
ISOMETRY *n* distance-preserving injective map between metric spaces
ISOMORPH *n* substance or organism that exhibits isomorphism
ISONOME, -S *n* line on a map showing equal abundance of a species
ISONOMIC ► isonomy
ISONOMY *n* equality before the law of the citizens of a state
ISOPACH, -S *n* line showing equal thickness
ISOPHONE *n* isogloss marking off an area in which a particular feature of pronunciation is found
ISOPHOTE *n* line on a diagram of a celestial object joining points of equal brightness
ISOPLETH *n* line on a map connecting places with the same amount of some geographical phenomenon

ISOPOD, -S *n* type of crustacean ▷ *adj* of this type of crustacean
ISOPODAN
ISOPRENE *n* colourless volatile liquid with a penetrating odour
ISOS ► **iso**
ISOSPIN, -S *n* number used to classify elementary particles
ISOSPORY *n* condition of having spores of only one kind
ISOSTACY *n* state of balance in earth's crust
ISOSTASY *same as* ► **isostacy**
ISOTACH, -S *n* line showing equal wind speed
ISOTHERE *n* line on a map linking places with the same mean summer temperature
ISOTHERM *n* line on a map connecting points of equal temperature
ISOTONE, -S *n* atom with same number of neutrons as another
ISOTONIC *adj* (of two or more muscles) having equal tension
ISOTOPE, -S *n* atom with same atomic number as another
ISOTOPIC
ISOTOPY
ISOTRON, -S *n* device for separating small quantities of isotopes
ISOTROPY > **isotropic**
ISOTYPE, -S *n* pictorial presentation of statistical information
ISOTYPIC
ISOZYME, -S *n* variant of an enzyme
ISOZYMIC
ISSEI, -S *n* first-generation Japanese immigrant
ISSUABLE *adj* capable of issuing or being issued
ISSUABLY
ISSUANCE *n* act of issuing

ISSUANT *adj* emerging or issuing
ISSUE, -D, -S, ISSUING *n* topic of interest or discussion ▷ *vb* make (a statement etc) publicly
ISSUER -S
ISTANA, -S *n* (in Malaysia) a royal palace
ISTHMI ► **isthmus**
ISTHMIAN *n* inhabitant of an isthmus ▷ *adj* relating to or situated in an isthmus
ISTHMIC ► **isthmus**
ISTHMOID ► **isthmus**
ISTHMUS, ISTHMI *n* narrow strip of land connecting two areas of land
ISTLE, -S *n* fibre obtained from various agave and yucca trees
IT *pron* refers to a nonhuman, animal, plant, or inanimate object ▷ *n* player whose turn it is to catch the others in children's games
ITA, -S *n* type of palm
ITACISM, -S *n* pronunciation of the Greek letter eta
ITACONIC *adj as in* **itaconic acid**, white colourless crystalline carboxylic acid
ITALIC, -S *adj* (of printing type) sloping to the right ▷ *n* style of printing type
ITAS ► **ita**
ITCH, -ED, -ES *n* skin irritation causing a desire to scratch ▷ *vb* have an itch
ITCHIER ► **itchy**
ITCHIEST ► **itchy**
ITCHILY ► **itch**
ITCHING, -S ► **itch**
ITCHWEED *n* white hellebore
ITCHY, ITCHIER, ITCHIEST ► **itch**
ITEM, -ED, -ING, -S *n* single thing in a list or collection ▷ *adv* likewise ▷ *vb* itemize
ITEMISE, -D, -S *same as* ► **itemize**
ITEMISER

ITEMIZE, -D, -R, -S *vb* make a list of
ITEMIZER
ITEMS ► **item**
ITERANCE ► **iterate**
ITERANT ► **iterate**
ITERATE, -D, -S *vb* repeat
ITERUM *adv* again
ITHER *Scot word for* ► **other**
ITS *pron* belonging to it ▷ *adj* of or belonging to it
ITSELF *pron* reflexive form of *it*
IURE *adv* by law
IVIED *adj* covered with ivy
IVIES ► **ivy**
IVORIED ► **ivory**
IVORIES *pl n* keys of a piano
IVORIST, -S *n* worker in ivory
IVORY *n* bony substance forming the tusks of elephants ▷ *adj* yellowish-white
IVRESSE, -S *n* drunkenness
IVY, IVIES *n* evergreen climbing plant
IVYLEAF *adj as in* **ivyleaf geranium** type of geranium plant
IVYLIKE ► **ivy**
IWI *n* Māori tribe

> This Māori word for a tribe is a great one for getting rid of an awkward combination of letters.

IWIS *archaic word for* > **certainly**
IXIA, -S *n* southern African plant
IXNAY *interj* nix
IXODID, -S *n* hard-bodied tick
IXORA, -S *n* flowering shrub
IXTLE, -S *same as* ► **istle**
IZAR, -S *n* long garment worn by Muslim women
IZARD, -S *n* type of goat-antelope
IZARS ► **izar**
IZVESTIA *n* news
IZZARD, -S *n* letter Z
IZZAT, -S *n* honour or prestige

Jj

J, being worth 8 points on its own, is a good tile for scoring well with, especially as it combines well with **Z** to make **jiz** and with **X** to make great words like **jeux**, **jinx** and **jynx**. However, **J** is a difficult letter when it comes to making bonus words scoring that extra 50 points, so you will normally want to play it off fairly quickly. There are two two-letter words that begin with **J**: **ja** and **jo**. As **J** has such a high value, look out for double- and triple-letter squares when playing these. There are plenty of good three-letter words starting with **J**: **jab** (12 points), **jak** (14), **jam** (12), **jar** (10), **jaw** (13), **jay** (13), **jet** (10), **jib** (12), **jig** (11), **job** (12), **jog** (11), **jot** (10), **joy** (13), **jug** (11) and **jut** (10).

JA interj yes ▷ sentence substitute yes

JAB, -BED, -BING, -S vb poke sharply ▷ n quick punch or poke

JABBER, -ED, -S vb talk rapidly or incoherently ▷ n rapid or incoherent talk
JABBERER

JABBING ▶ jab

JABBLE, -D, -S, JABBLING vb ripple

JABERS interj Irish exclamation

JABIRU, -S n large white-and-black Australian stork

JABOT, -S n frill or ruffle on the front of a blouse or shirt

JABS ▶ jab

JACAL, -ES, -S n Mexican daub hut

JACAMAR, -S n tropical American bird with an iridescent plumage

JACANA, -S n long-legged long-toed bird

JACARE, -S another name for ▶ cayman

JACCHUS n small monkey

JACENT adj lying

JACINTH, -S another name for ▶ hyacinth

JACINTHE n hyacinth

JACINTHS ▶ jacinth

JACK, -ED n device for raising a motor vehicle or other heavy object ▷ vb lift or push (an object) with a jack

JACKAL, -S n doglike wild animal of Africa and Asia ▷ vb behave like a jackal

JACKAROO same as ▶ jackeroo

JACKASS n fool

JACKBOOT n high military boot ▷ vb oppress

JACKDAW, -S n Eurasian bird of the crow family

JACKED ▶ jack

JACKEEN, -S n slick self-assertive lower-class Dubliner

JACKER, -S n labourer

JACKEROO n young male management trainee on a sheep or cattle station ▷ vb work as a jackeroo

JACKERS ▶ jacker

JACKET, -S n short coat ▷ vb put a jacket on (someone or something)
JACKETED

JACKFISH n small pike fish

JACKING, -S ▶ jack

JACKLEG, -S n unskilled worker

JACKLING n particular way of winning the ball in rugby

JACKMAN, JACKMEN n retainer

JACKPOT, -S n largest prize that may be won in a game ▷ vb accumulate stake money in a prize fund

JACKROLL vb gang-rape

JACKS n type of game

JACKSTAY n object to which a sail edge is fastened along a yard

JACOBIN, -S n variety of fancy pigeon

JACOBUS n English gold coin

JACONET, -S n light cotton fabric

JACQUARD n fabric in which the design is incorporated into the weave

JACULATE vb hurl

JACUZZI, -S n type of bath or pool

JADE, -S, JADING n semiprecious stone ▷ adj bluish-green ▷ vb exhaust or make exhausted from work or use

JADED adj tired and unenthusiastic
JADEDLY

JADEITE, -S n usually green or white mineral

JADELIKE ▶ jade

JADERY, JADERIES n shrewishness

JADES ▶ jade

JADING ▶ jade

JADISH ▶ jade

JADISHLY ▶ jade

JADITIC ▶ jade

JAEGER, -S n German or Austrian marksman

JAFFA, -S n (in cricket) well-bowled ball

JAG, -GING, -S n period of uncontrolled indulgence in an activity ▷ vb cut unevenly

JAGA, -ED, -ING, -S n guard ▷ vb guard or watch

JAGER, -S same as ▶ jaeger

JAGG, -S same as ▶ jag

JAGGARY same as ▶ jaggery

JAGGED, -ER ▶ jag

JAGGEDLY ▶ jag

JAGGER, -S n pedlar

JAGGERY n coarse brown sugar

JAGGHERY same as ▸ **jaggery**

JAGGIER ▸ **jaggy**

JAGGIES ▸ **jaggy**

JAGGIEST ▸ **jaggy**

JAGGING ▸ **jag**

JAGGS ▸ **jagg**

JAGGY, JAGGIER, JAGGIES, JAGGIEST adj prickly ▷ n jagged computer image

JAGHIR, -S n Indian regional governance

JAGHIRE, -S n Indian regional governance

JAGHIRS ▸ **jaghir**

JAGIR, -S n Indian regional governance

JAGLESS ▸ **jag**

JAGRA, -S n Hindu festival

JAGS ▸ **jag**

JAGUAR, -S n large S American spotted cat

JAI interj victory (to)

JAIL, -ED, -ING, -S n prison ▷ vb send to prison

JAILABLE

JAILBIRD n person who has often been in prison

JAILED ▸ **jail**

JAILER, -S n person in charge of a jail

JAILING ▸ **jail**

JAILLESS ▸ **jail**

JAILOR, -S same as ▸ **jailer**

JAILS ▸ **jail**

JAK, -S same as ▸ **jack**

JAKE adj slang word meaning all right

JAKES, -ES n toilet; lavatory

JAKEY, -S n sometimes derogatory Scots word for a homeless alcoholic

JAKFRUIT same as ▸ **jackfruit**

JAKS ▸ **jak**

JALABIB ▸ **jilbab**

JALAP, -S n Mexican convolvulaceous plant

JALAPENO n very hot type of green chilli pepper, used esp in Mexican cookery

JALAPIC ▸ **jalap**

JALAPIN, -S n purgative resin

JALAPS ▸ **jalap**

JALEBI, -S n type of Asian sweet fried snack

JALFREZI adj (in Indian cookery) stir-fried with green peppers, onions, and green chillies ▷ n curry made with green peppers, onions, and green chillies

JALLEBI, -S same as ▸ **jalebi**

JALOP, -S same as ▸ **jalap**

JALOPIES ▸ **jalopy**

JALOPPY same as ▸ **jalopy**

JALOPS ▸ **jalop**

JALOPY, JALOPIES n old car

JALOUSE, -D, -S vb suspect

JALOUSIE n window blind or shutter constructed from angled slats of wood, plastic, etc

JAM, -MED, -S vb pack tightly into a place ▷ n fruit preserve or hold-up of traffic

JAMAAT, -S n Islamic council

JAMADAR, -S n Indian army officer

JAMB, -ED, -ING, -S n side post of a door or window frame ▷ vb climb up a crack in rock

JAMBART, -S same as ▸ **greave**

JAMBE, -S same as ▸ **jamb**

JAMBEAU, -S, -X, JAMBEUX another word for ▸ **greave**

JAMBED ▸ **jamb**

JAMBEE, -S n light cane

JAMBER, -S same as ▸ **greave**

JAMBES ▸ **jambe**

JAMBEUX ▸ **jambeau**

JAMBIER, -S n greave

JAMBING ▸ **jamb**

JAMBIYA, -S n curved dagger

JAMBIYAH same as ▸ **jambiya**

JAMBIYAS ▸ **jambiya**

JAMBO sentence substitute E African salutation

JAMBOK, -S same as ▸ **sjambok**

JAMBOLAN n Asian tree

JAMBONE, -S n type of play in the card game euchre

JAMBOOL, -S same as ▸ **jambolan**

JAMBOREE n large gathering or celebration

JAMBS ▸ **jamb**

JAMBU, -S same as ▸ **jambolan**

JAMBUL, -S same as ▸ **jambolan**

JAMBUS ▸ **jambu**

JAMDANI, -S n patterned muslin

JAMES, -ES n jemmy

JAMJAR, -S n container for preserves

JAMLIKE ▸ **jam**

JAMMABLE ▸ **jam**

JAMMED ▸ **jam**

JAMMER, -S ▸ **jam**

JAMMIER ▸ **jammy**

JAMMIES informal word for ▸ **pyjamas**

JAMMIEST ▸ **jammy**

JAMMING ▸ **jam**

JAMMY, JAMMIER, JAMMIEST adj lucky

JAMON n as in **jamon serrano** cured ham from Spain

JAMPAN, -S n type of sedan chair used in India

JAMPANEE n jampan bearer

JAMPANI, -S same as ▸ **jampanee**

JAMPANS ▸ **jampan**

JAMPOT, -S n container for preserves

JAMS ▸ **jam**

JANE, -S n girl or woman

JANGLE, -D, -S, JANGLING vb (cause to) make a harsh ringing noise ▷ n harsh ringing noise

JANGLER -S

JANGLIER ▸ **jangly**

JANGLING ▸ **jangle**

JANGLY, JANGLIER adj making a jangling sound

JANIFORM adj with two faces

JANISARY same as ▸ **janissary**

JANITOR, -S n caretaker of a school or other building

JANITRIX

JANIZAR, -S same as ▸ **janissary**

This is an old word for a Turkish soldier, combining J and Z. If your opponent plays it, remember that you can add not only an S to it to form the plural, but also a Y, making the variant spelling **janizary**.

JANIZARY same as ▸ **janissary**

JANKER, -S n device for transporting logs

JANN, -S n lesser jinn

JANNEY, -ED, -S vb act as a disguised reveller at Christmas

JANNIED ▸ **janny**

JANNIES ▸ **janny**

JANNOCK, -S same as ▸ **jonnock**

JANNS ▸ **jann**

JANNY, JANNIED, JANNIES, -ING n janitor ▷ vb work as a janitor

JANSKY, -S n unit of flux density

JANTEE archaic version of ▸ **jaunty**

JANTY, JANTIER, JANTIES, JANTIEST n petty officer ▷ adj (in archaic usage) jaunty

JAP, -PED, -PING, -S vb splash

JAPAN, -NED, -S n very hard varnish, usu black ▷ vb cover with this varnish ▷ adj relating to or varnished with japan

JAPANISE same as ► **japanize**

JAPANIZE vb make Japanese

JAPANNED ► **japan**

JAPANNER ► **japan**

JAPANS ► **japan**

JAPE, -D, -S, JAPING, JAPINGS n joke or prank ▷ vb joke or jest (about)

JAPER -S

JAPERIES ► **japery**

JAPERS ► **japer**

JAPERY, JAPERIES ► **jape**

JAPES ► **jape**

JAPING ► **jape**

JAPINGLY ► **jape**

JAPINGS ► **jape**

JAPONICA n shrub with red flowers

JAPPED ► **jap**

JAPPING ► **jap**

JAPS ► **jap**

JAR, -RED, -S n wide-mouthed container ▷ vb have a disturbing or unpleasant effect

JARARACA n South American snake

JARARAKA same as ► **jararaca**

JARFUL, -S, JARSFUL same as ► **jar**

JARGON, -ED, -S n specialized technical language ▷ vb use or speak in jargon

JARGONEL n pear

JARGONS ► **jargon**

JARGONY ► **jargon**

JARGOON, -S same as ► **jargon**

JARHEAD, -S n US Marine

JARINA, -S n South American palm tree

JARK, -S n seal or pass

JARKMAN, JARKMEN n forger of passes or licences

JARKS ► **jark**

JARL, -S n Scandinavian chieftain or noble

JARLDOM -S

JAROOL, -S n Indian tree

JAROSITE n yellow to brown mineral

JAROVISE same as ► **jarovize**

JAROVIZE vb vernalize

JARP, -ED, -ING, -S vb strike or smash

JARRAH, -S n Australian eucalypt yielding valuable timber

JARRED ► **jar**

JARRING, -S ► **jar**

JARS ► **jar**

JARSFUL ► **jarful**

JARTA, -S n heart

JARUL, -S variant of ► **jarool**

JARVEY, -S n hackney coachman

JARVIE, -S same as ► **jarvey**

JASEY, -S n wig

JASIES ► **jasy**

JASMIN, -S same as ► **jasmine**

JASMINE, -S n shrub with sweet-smelling yellow or white flowers

JASMINS ► **jasmin**

JASP, -S another word for ► **jasper**

JASPE, -S adj resembling jasper ▷ n subtly striped woven fabric

JASPER, -S n variety of quartz

JASPERY

JASPES ► **jaspe**

JASPIS, -ES archaic word for ► **jasper**

JASPS ► **jasp**

JASS, -ES obsolete variant of ► **jazz**

JASSID, -S n leafhopper

JASY, JASIES n wig

JATAKA, -S n text describing the birth of Buddha

JATO, -S n jet-assisted takeoff

JATROPHA n poisonous shrub of C America used primarily as a biofuel

JAUK, -ED, -ING, -S vb dawdle

JAUNCE, -D, -S, JAUNCING vb prance

JAUNDICE n disease marked by yellowness of the skin ▷ vb distort (the judgment, etc) adversely

JAUNSE, -D, -S, JAUNSING same as ► **jaunce**

JAUNT, -ED, -ING, -S n short journey for pleasure ▷ vb make such a journey

JAUNTEE old spelling of ► **jaunty**

JAUNTIE old spelling of ► **jaunty**

JAUNTIER ► **jaunty**

JAUNTIES ► **jaunty**

JAUNTILY ► **jaunty**

JAUNTING ► **jaunt**

JAUNTS ► **jaunt**

JAUNTY, JAUNTIER, JAUNTIES adj sprightly and cheerful ▷ n master-at-arms on a naval ship

JAUP, -ED, -ING, -S same as ► **jarp**

JAVA, -S n coffee or a variety of it

JAVEL, -S adj as in **javel water** bleach or disinfectant

JAVELIN, -S n light spear thrown in sports

competitions ▷ vb spear with a javelin

JAVELINA n collared peccary

JAVELINS ► **javelin**

JAVELS ► **javel**

JAW, -ED, -S n one of the bones in which the teeth are set ▷ vb talk lengthily

JAWAN, -S n (in India) a soldier

JAWARI, -S n variety of sorghum

JAWBONE, -D, -S n lower jaw of a person or animal ▷ vb try to persuade by virtue of one's high office or position

JAWBONER

JAWBOX, -ES n metal sink

> This Scots word for a sink combines the J and X, and of course its plural **jawboxes**, earning an extra 50 points, would be even better.

JAWED ► **jaw**

JAWFALL, -S n depression

JAWHOLE, -S n cesspit

JAWING, -S ► **jaw**

JAWLESS ► **jaw**

JAWLIKE ► **jaw**

JAWLINE, -S n outline of the jaw

JAWS ► **jaw**

JAY, -S n type of bird

JAYBIRD, -S ► **jay**

JAYCEE, -S n member of a Junior Chamber of Commerce

JAYGEE, -S n lieutenant junior grade in the US army

JAYS ► **jay**

JAYVEE, -S n junior varsity sports team

JAYWALK, -S vb cross or walk in a street recklessly or illegally

JAZERANT n coat of metal plates sewn onto cloth

JAZY, JAZIES n wig

> This means a wig and is a wonderfully useful little word, combining J and Z for a high score.

JAZZ, -ED, -ES, -ING n kind of music ▷ vb play or dance to jazz music

JAZZBO, -S n jazz musician or fan

JAZZED ► **jazz**

JAZZER, -S ► **jazz**

JAZZES ► **jazz**

JAZZIER ► **jazzy**

JAZZIEST ► **jazzy**

JAZZILY ► **jazzy**

JAZZING ► **jazz**

JAZZLIKE ► **jazz**

JAZZMAN ► **jazz**

JAZZMEN ► jazz

JAZZY, JAZZIER, JAZZIEST adj flashy or showy

JEALOUS adj fearful of losing (something) to a rival

JEALOUSE vb be jealous of

JEALOUSY n state of or an instance of feeling jealous

JEAN n tough twill-weave cotton fabric

JEANED adj wearing jeans

JEANETTE n light jean cloth

JEANS pl n casual denim trousers

JEAT, -S n jet

JEBEL, -S n hill or mountain in an Arab country

JEDI, -S n person claiming to live according to the Jedi philosophy

JEE, -D, -ING, -S variant of ► gee

JEEL, -ED, -ING, -S vb make into jelly

JEELIE same as ► jeely

JEELIED ► jeely

JEELIES ► jeely

JEELING ► jeel

JEELS ► jeel

JEELY, JEELIED, JEELIES, -ING n jelly ▷ vb make into jelly

JEEP, -ED, -ING, -S n small military four-wheel drive road vehicle ▷ vb travel in a jeep

JEEPERS interj mild exclamation of surprise

JEEPING ► jeep

JEEPNEY, -S n Filipino bus converted from a jeep

JEEPS ► jeep

JEER, -ED, -S vb scoff or deride ▷ n cry of derision

JEERER -S

JEERING, -S ► jeer

JEERS ► jeer

JEES ► jee

JEESLY same as ► jeezly

JEEZ interj expression of surprise or irritation

JEEZE same as ► jeez

JEEZELY same as ► jeezly

JEEZLY adj used as an intensifier

JEFE, -S n (in Spanish-speaking countries) a military or political leader

JEFF, -ED, -ING, -S vb downsize or close down (an organization)

JEGGINGS pl n women's leggings designed to look like tight denim jeans

JEHAD, -S same as ► jihad

JEHADEEN same as ► jihadeen

JEHADI, -S same as ► jihadi

JEHADISM same as ► jihadism

JEHADIST

JEHADS ► jehad

JEHU, -S n fast driver

JEJUNA ► jejunum

JEJUNAL ► jejunum

JEJUNE adj simple or naive

JEJUNELY

JEJUNITY

JEJUNUM, JEJUNA, -S n part of the small intestine

JELAB, -S same as ► jellaba

JELL, -ED, -ING, -S vb form into a jelly-like substance

JELLABA, -S n loose robe with a hood

JELLABAH same as ► jellaba

JELLABAS ► jellaba

JELLED ► jell

JELLIED ► jelly

JELLIES ► jelly

JELLIFY vb make into or become jelly

JELLING ► jell

JELLO, -S n (in US English) type of dessert

JELLS ► jell

JELLY, JELLIED, JELLIES, -ING n fruit-flavoured clear dessert set with gelatine ▷ vb jellify

JELUTONG n Malaysian tree

JEMADAR, -S n native officer serving as a mercenary in India

JEMBE, -S n hoe

JEMIDAR, -S same as ► jemadar

JEMIMA, -S n boot with elastic sides

JEMMY, JEMMIED, JEMMIER, JEMMIES, JEMMIEST, -ING n short steel crowbar used by burglars ▷ vb prise (something) open with a jemmy ▷ adj neat

JENNET, -S n female donkey or ass

JENNY, JENNIES same as ► jennet

JEOFAIL, -S n oversight in legal pleading

JEON, -S n Korean pancake

JEOPARD, -S vb put in jeopardy

JEOPARDY n danger ▷ vb put in jeopardy

JERBIL, -S variant spelling of ► gerbil

JERBOA, -S n small mouselike rodent with long hind legs

JEREED, -S same as ► jerid

JEREMIAD n long mournful complaint

JEREPIGO n sweet fortified wine similar to port

JERID, -S n wooden javelin

JERK, -ED, -S vb move or throw abruptly ▷ n sharp or abruptly stopped movement

JERKER -S

JERKIER ► jerky

JERKIES ► jerky

JERKIEST ► jerky

JERKILY ► jerky

JERKIN, -S n sleeveless jacket

JERKING, -S ► jerk

JERKINS ► jerkin

JERKS ► jerk

JERKY, JERKIER, JERKIES, JERKIEST adj characterized by jerks ▷ n type of cured meat

JEROBOAM n wine bottle holding the equivalent of four normal bottles

JERQUE, -D, -S, JERQUING vb search for contraband

JERQUER -S

To **jerque** is to search a vessel for stolen goods, and if you have the right additional letters to make **jerqued, jerquer, jerques** or **jerquing**, using all your letters, you would get a really great score.

JERREED, -S variant spelling of ► jerid

JERRICAN n five-gallon fuel can

JERRID, -S n blunt javelin

JERRY, JERRIES short for ► jeroboam

JERRYCAN n flat-sided can used for storing or transporting liquids, esp motor fuel

JERSEY, -S n knitted jumper

JERSEYED

JESS, -ED, -ES, -ING n short leather strap used in falconry ▷ vb put jesses on (a hawk or falcon)

JESSAMY n fop

JESSANT adj emerging

JESSE same as ► jess

JESSED ► jess

JESSES ► jess

JESSING ► jess

JEST, -ED, -S vb joke ▷ n something done or said for amusement

JESTBOOK n book of amusing stories

JESTED ► jest

JESTEE, -S n person about whom a joke is made

JESTER, -S n professional clown at court

JESTFUL ▶ jest
JESTING, -S ▶ jest
JESTS ▶ jest
JESUS n French paper size
JET, -S, -TED, -TING n aircraft driven by jet propulsion ▷ vb fly by jet aircraft
JETBEAD, -S n ornamental shrub
JETE, -S n dance step
JETFOIL, -S n type of hydrofoil that is propelled by water jets
JETLAG, -S n tiredness caused by crossing timezones in jet flight
JETLIKE ▶ jet
JETLINER n commercial airliner powered by jet engines
JETON, -S n gambling chip
JETPACK, -S n wearable harness with jets, used for transport
JETPORT, -S n airport for jet planes
JETS ▶ jet
JETSAM, -S n goods thrown overboard to lighten a ship
JETSOM, -S same as ▶ jetsam
JETSON, -S archaic form of ▶ jetsam
JETTED ▶ jet
JETTIED ▶ jetty
JETTIER ▶ jetty
JETTIES ▶ jetty
JETTIEST ▶ jetty
JETTING ▶ jet
JETTISON vb abandon
JETTON, -S n counter or token
JETTY, JETTIED, JETTIER, JETTIES, JETTIEST, -ING n small pier ▷ adj of or resembling jet, esp in colour or polish ▷ vb equip with a cantilevered floor
JETWAY, -S n tradename of device used in airports
JEU, -X n game

> **Jeu** is the French word for game or play. The plural form, **jeux**, is a great little word, using both J and X, particularly if you can play it on a double- or triple-word square.

JEUNE adj young
JEUX ▶ jeu
JEWEL, -ED, -ING, -LED, -S n precious or semiprecious stone ▷ vb fit or decorate with a jewel or jewels
JEWELER, -S same as ▶ jeweller
JEWELING ▶ jewel
JEWELLED ▶ jewel
JEWELLER n dealer in jewels

JEWELRY same as ▶ jewellery
JEWELS ▶ jewel
JEWFISH n freshwater catfish
JEWIE, -S n jewfish
JEZAIL, -S n Afghan musket

> A **jezail** is a kind of Afghan musket, and if you have an S to go with it, earning the extra 50 points, so much the better.

JEZEBEL, -S n shameless or scheming woman
JHALA, -S n Indian musical style
JHATKA, -S n slaughter of animals for food according to Sikh law
JIAO, -S n Chinese currency unit
JIB, -S same as ▶ jibe
JIBB, -ED, -S same as ▶ jibe
JIBBA, -S n long, loose coat worn by Muslim men
JIBBAH, -S same as ▶ jubbah
JIBBAS ▶ jibba
JIBBED ▶ jibb
JIBBER, -ED, -S variant of ▶ gibber
JIBBING, -S ▶ jibb
JIBBONS pl n spring onions
JIBBOOM, -S n spar forming an extension of the bowsprit
JIBBS ▶ jibb
JIBE, -D, -S, JIBING vb taunt or jeer ▷ n insulting or taunting remark
JIBER -S
JIBINGLY ▶ jibe
JIBS ▶ jib
JICAMA, -S n pale brown turnip
JIFF, -S same as ▶ jiffy
JIFFIES ▶ jiffy
JIFFS ▶ jiff
JIFFY, JIFFIES n very short period of time
JIG, -GED, -S n type of lively dance ▷ vb dance a jig
JIGGER, -ED, -S n small whisky glass ▷ vb interfere or alter
JIGGIER ▶ jiggy
JIGGIEST ▶ jiggy
JIGGING, -S ▶ jig
JIGGISH ▶ jig
JIGGLE, -D, -S, JIGGLING vb move up and down with short jerky movements ▷ n short jerky motion
JIGGLIER ▶ jiggly
JIGGLING ▶ jiggle
JIGGLY, JIGGLIER ▶ jiggle
JIGGY, JIGGIER, JIGGIEST adj resembling a jig
JIGLIKE ▶ jig
JIGOT, -S same as ▶ gigot
JIGS ▶ jig

JIGSAW, -ED, -N, -S n type of game ▷ vb cut with a jigsaw
JIHAD, -S n Islamic holy war against unbelievers
JIHADEEN pl n jihadists
JIHADI, -S n person who takes part in a jihad
JIHADISM n Islamic fundamentalist movement that favours jihads
JIHADIST
JIHADS ▶ jihad
JILBAB, JALABIB, -S n long robe worn by Muslim women
JILGIE n freshwater crayfish
JILL, -S variant spelling of ▶ gill
JILLAROO n female jackeroo
JILLET, -S n flighty or capricious woman
JILLION, -S n extremely large number or amount
JILLS ▶ jill
JILT, -ED, -ING, -S vb leave or reject (one's lover) ▷ n woman who jilts a lover
JILTER -S
JIMCRACK same as ▶ gimcrack
JIMINY interj expression of surprise
JIMJAMS, JIMJAM pl n state of nervous tension, excitement, or anxiety
JIMMIE same as ▶ jimmy
JIMMIED ▶ jimmy
JIMMIES ▶ jimmy
JIMMINY interj expression of surprise
JIMMY, JIMMIED, JIMMIES, -ING same as ▶ jemmy
JIMP, -ER, -EST adj handsome
JIMPIER ▶ jimpy
JIMPIEST ▶ jimpy
JIMPLY adv neatly
JIMPNESS ▶ jimp
JIMPSON same as ▶ jimson
JIMPY, JIMPIER, JIMPIEST adj neat and tidy
JIMSON, -S n as in **jimson weed** type of poisonous plant
JIN, -S n Chinese unit of weight
JINGAL, -S n swivel-mounted gun
JINGALL, -S same as ▶ jingal
JINGALS ▶ jingal
JINGBANG n entirety of something
JINGKO, -ES same as ▶ gingko
JINGLE, -D, -S, JINGLING n catchy verse or song used in an advert ▷ vb (cause to) make a gentle ringing sound
JINGLER -S

JINGLET, -S n sleigh-bell clapper

JINGLIER ► jingly

JINGLING ► jingle

JINGLY, JINGLIER ► jingle

JINGO, -ES n loud and bellicose patriot; chauvinism

JINGOISH

JINGOISM n aggressive nationalism

JINGOIST

JINJILI, -S n type of sesame

JINK, -ED, -ING, -S vb move quickly or jerkily in order to dodge someone ▷ n jinking movement

JINKER, -ED, -S n vehicle for transporting timber ▷ vb carry or transport in a jinker

JINKING ► jink

JINKS ► jink

JINN ► jinni

JINNE interj South African exclamation

JINNEE same as **► jinni**

JINNI, JINN, -S, JINNS n spirit in Muslim mythology

JINS ► jin

JINX, -ED, -ES, -ING n person or thing bringing bad luck ▷ vb be or put a jinx on

JIPIJAPA n plant whose leaves are used for making panama hats

JIPYAPA, -S same as **► jipijapa**

JIRBLE, -D, -S, JIRBLING vb pour carelessly

JIRD, -S n gerbil

JIRGA, -S n Afghan council

JIRKINET n bodice

JIRRE same as **► jinne**

JITNEY, -S n small cheap bus

JITTER, -ED, -S vb be anxious or nervous

JITTERY adj nervous

JIUJITSU variant spelling of **► jujitsu**

JIUJUTSU same as **► jujitsu**

JIVE, -D, -S, -ST, JIVING n lively dance of the 1940s and '50s ▷ vb dance the jive ▷ adj pertaining to or indicative of jive

JIVEASS adj misleading or phoney ▷ n person who loves fun and excitement

JIVED ► jive

JIVER, -S ► jive

JIVES ► jive

JIVEST ► jive

JIVEY, JIVIER, JIVIEST adj jazzy; lively

JIVING ► jive

JIVY same as **► jivey**

JIZ n wig

When you find yourself with J and Z but nothing else that looks promising, there may well be an I on the board around which you can form **jiz**, which means a wig.

JIZZ, -ES n term for the characteristics that identify a particular species of bird or plant

JNANA, -S n type of yoga

JO n Scots word for sweetheart

JOANNA, -S n piano

JOANNES same as **► johannes**

JOB, -BED, -S n occupation or paid employment ▷ vb work at casual jobs

JOBATION n scolding

JOBBED ► job

JOBBER, -S n person who jobs

JOBBERY n practice of making private profit out of a public office

JOBBIE, -S n referring to a thing usually specified in the preceding part of a sentence

JOBBING, -S adj doing individual jobs for payment ▷ n act of seeking work

JOBE, -D, -S, JOBING vb scold

JOBLESS pl n as in **the jobless** unemployed people ▷ adj unemployed

JOBNAME, -S n title of position

JOBS ► job

JOBSHARE n arrangement in which two people divide the duties for one job between them

JOCK, -S n athlete

JOCKDOM, -S n world of male athletes

JOCKETTE n female athlete

JOCKEY, -ED, -S n person who rides horses in races ▷ vb ride (a horse) in a race

JOCKIER ► jocky

JOCKIEST ► jocky

JOCKISH adj macho

JOCKNEY, -S n the Scots dialect influenced by cockney speech patterns

JOCKO, -S n chimpanzee

JOCKS ► jock

JOCKY, JOCKIER, JOCKIEST adj indicating or appropriate to a male athlete

JOCO, -S adj relaxed ▷ n joke

JOCOSE adj playful or humorous

JOCOSELY

JOCOSITY

JOCULAR adj fond of joking

JOCUND adj merry or cheerful

JOCUNDLY

JODEL, -LED, -S same as **► yodel**

JODHPUR n as in **jodhpur boots** ankle-length leather riding boots

JODHPURS pl n riding breeches

JOE, -S same as **► jo**

JOEY, -S n young kangaroo

JOG, -GED, -S vb run at a gentle pace, esp for exercise ▷ n slow run

JOGGER, -S n person who runs at a jog for exercise

JOGGING, -S ► jog

JOGGLE, -D, -S, JOGGLING vb shake or move jerkily ▷ n act of joggling

JOGGLER -S

JOGPANTS pl n trousers worn for jogging

JOGS ► jog

JOGTROT, -S n easy bouncy gait ▷ vb move at a jogtrot

JOHANNES n Portuguese gold coin minted in the early 18th century

JOHN, -S n toilet

JOHNBOAT n small flat-bottomed boat

JOHNNIE same as **► johnny**

JOHNNY, JOHNNIES n chap

JOHNS ► john

JOIN, -ED, -S vb become a member (of) ▷ n place where two things are joined

JOINABLE

JOINDER, -S n act of joining, esp in legal contexts

JOINED ► join

JOINER, -S n maker of finished woodwork

JOINERY n joiner's work

JOINING, -S ► join

JOINS ► join

JOINT, -S adj shared by two or more ▷ n place where bones meet but can move ▷ vb divide meat into joints

JOINTED adj having a joint or joints

JOINTER, -S n tool for pointing mortar joints

JOINTING ► joint

JOINTLY ► joint

JOINTS ► joint

JOINTURE n provision made by a husband for his wife after his death

JOIST, -ED, -ING, -S n horizontal beam ▷ vb construct (a floor, roof, etc) with joists

JOJOBA, -S n shrub of SW North America

JOKE, -D, -S n thing said or done to cause laughter ▷ vb make jokes

JOKER, -S n person who jokes

JOKES ▶ joke

JOKESOME ▶ joke

JOKESTER n person who makes jokes

JOKEY, JOKIER, JOKIEST adj intended as a joke

JOKILY ▶ joke

JOKINESS ▶ joke

JOKING, -S n act of joking

JOKINGLY ▶ joke

JOKINGS ▶ joking

JOKOL Shetland word for ▶ yes

JOKY same as ▶ jokey

JOL, -LED, -LING, -S n party ▷ vb have a good time

JOLE, -D, -S, JOLING vb knock

JOLL, -S variant of ▶ jole

JOLLED ▶ jol

JOLLER, -S n person who has a good time

JOLLEY, -S same as ▶ jolly

JOLLEYER

JOLLIED ▶ jolly

JOLLIER, -S n joker

JOLLIES ▶ jolly

JOLLIEST ▶ jolly

JOLLIFY vb be or cause to be jolly

JOLLILY ▶ jolly

JOLLING ▶ jol

JOLLITY n condition of being jolly

JOLLOP, -S n cream or unguent

JOLLS ▶ joll

JOLLY, JOLLIED, JOLLIES, JOLLIEST, -ING adj full of good humour ▷ adv extremely ▷ vb try to make or keep (someone) cheerful ▷ n festivity or celebration

JOLLYER, -S ▶ jol

JOLS ▶ jol

JOLT, -ED, -S n unpleasant surprise or shock ▷ vb surprise or shock

JOLTER -S

JOLTHEAD n fool

JOLTIER ▶ jolty

JOLTIEST ▶ jolty

JOLTILY ▶ jolty

JOLTING, -S n act of jolting

JOLTS ▶ jolt

JOLTY, JOLTIER, JOLTIEST ▶ jolty

JOMO, -S same as ▶ zo

JOMON, -S n particular era in Japanese history

JOMOS ▶ jomo

JONCANOE n Jamaican ceremony

JONES, -ED, -ES, -ING vb desire

JONG, -S n friend, often used in direct address

JONGLEUR n (in medieval France) an itinerant minstrel

JONGS ▶ jong

JONNOCK adj genuine ▷ adv honestly

JONQUIL, -S n fragrant narcissus

JONTY, JONTIES n petty officer

JOOK, -ED, -ING, -S vb poke or puncture (the skin) ▷ n jab or the resulting wound

JOOKERY n mischief

JOOKING ▶ jook

JOOKS ▶ jook

JOR, -S n movement in Indian music

JORAM, -S same as ▶ jorum

JORDAN, -S n chamber pot

JORDELOO same as ▶ gardyloo

JORS ▶ jor

JORUM, -S n large drinking bowl or vessel or its contents

JOSEPH, -S n woman's floor-length riding coat

JOSH, -ED, -ES vb tease ▷ n teasing or bantering joke

JOSHER -S

JOSHING, -S n act of joshing

JOSKIN, -S n bumpkin

JOSS, -ES n Chinese deity

JOSSER, -S n simpleton

JOSSES ▶ joss

JOSTLE, -D, -S, JOSTLING vb knock or push against ▷ n act of jostling

JOSTLER -S

JOT, -S, -TED vb write briefly ▷ n very small amount

JOTA, -S n Spanish dance

JOTS ▶ jot

JOTTED ▶ jot

JOTTER, -S n notebook

JOTTIER ▶ jotty

JOTTIEST ▶ jotty

JOTTING, -S ▶ jot

JOTTY, JOTTIER, JOTTIEST ▶ jot

JOTUN, -S n giant

JOTUNN, -S same as ▶ jotun

JOTUNS ▶ jotun

JOUAL, -S n nonstandard variety of Canadian French

JOUGS pl n iron ring for restraining an offender

JOUK, -ED, -ING, -S vb duck or dodge ▷ n sudden evasive movement

JOUKERY same as ▶ jookery

JOUKING ▶ jouk

JOUKS ▶ jouk

JOULE, -D, -S, JOULING n unit of work or energy ▷ vb knock

JOUNCE, -D, -S, JOUNCING vb shake or jolt or cause to shake or jolt ▷ n jolting movement

JOUNCIER ▶ jouncy

JOUNCING ▶ jounce

JOUNCY, JOUNCIER ▶ jounce

JOUR, -S n day

JOURNAL, -S n daily newspaper or magazine ▷ vb record in a journal

JOURNEY, -S n act of travelling from one place to another ▷ vb travel

JOURNO, -S n journalist

JOURS ▶ jour

JOUST, -ED, -S n combat between two knights ▷ vb fight on horseback using lances

JOUSTER -S

JOUSTING n act of jousting

JOUSTS ▶ joust

JOVIAL adj happy and cheerful

JOVIALLY

JOVIALTY

JOW, -ED, -ING, -S vb ring (a bell)

JOWAR, -S n variety of sorghum

JOWARI, -S same as ▶ jowar

JOWARS ▶ jowar

JOWED ▶ jow

JOWING ▶ jow

JOWL, -ING, -S n lower jaw ▷ vb knock

JOWLED

JOWLER, -S n dog with prominent jowls

JOWLIER ▶ jowly

JOWLIEST ▶ jowly

JOWLING ▶ jowl

JOWLS ▶ jowl

JOWLY, JOWLIER, JOWLIEST ▶ jowl

JOWS ▶ jow

JOY, -ED, -ING, -S n feeling of great delight or pleasure ▷ vb feel joy

JOYANCE, -S n joyous feeling or festivity

JOYED ▶ joy

JOYFUL adj feeling or bringing great joy

JOYFULLY

JOYING ▶ joy

JOYLESS adj feeling or bringing no joy

JOYOUS adj extremely happy and enthusiastic

JOYOUSLY

JOYPAD, -S n computer games console

JOYRIDE, -S, JOYRODE n drive in a car one has stolen ▷ vb take such a ride
JOYRIDER
JOYS ▸ joy
JOYSTICK n control device for an aircraft or computer
JUBA, -S n lively African-American dance
JUBATE adj possessing a mane
JUBBAH, -S n long loose outer garment with wide sleeves
JUBE, -S n part of a church or cathedral
JUBHAH, -S same as ▸ jubbah
JUBILANT adj feeling or expressing great joy
JUBILATE vb have or express great joy
JUBILE, -S same as ▸ jubilee
JUBILEE, -S n special anniversary, esp 25th or 50th
JUBILES ▸ jubile
JUCO, -S n junior college in America
JUD, -S n large block of coal
JUDAS, -ES n peephole
JUDDER, -ED, -S vb vibrate violently ▷ n violent vibration
JUDDERY adj shaky
JUDGE, -D, -S n public official ▷ vb act as a judge
JUDGER -S
JUDGING, -S n act of judging
JUDGMENT n opinion reached after careful thought
JUDICARE n (in Canada) state-paid legal services
JUDICIAL adj of or by a court or judge
JUDIES ▸ judy
JUDO, -S n type of sport
JUDOGI, -S n white two-piece cotton costume
JUDOIST, -S ▸ judo
JUDOKA, -S n competitor or expert in judo
JUDOS ▸ judo
JUDS ▸ jud
JUDY, JUDIES n woman
JUG, -GED, -GING, -GINGS, -S n container for liquids ▷ vb stew or boil (meat, esp hare) in an earthenware container
JUGA ▸ jugum
JUGAL, -S adj of or relating to the zygomatic bone ▷ n cheekbone
JUGATE adj having parts arranged in pairs
JUGFUL, -S, JUGSFUL same as ▸ jug
JUGGED ▸ jug
JUGGING ▸ jug
JUGGINGS ▸ jug

JUGGINS n silly person
JUGGLE, -D, -S, JUGGLING vb throw and catch (objects) to keep them in the air ▷ n act of juggling
JUGGLER, -S n person who juggles, esp a professional entertainer
JUGGLERY ▸ juggle
JUGGLES ▸ juggle
JUGGLING ▸ juggle
JUGHEAD, -S n clumsy person
JUGLET, -S n small jug
JUGS ▸ jug
JUGSFUL ▸ jugful
JUGULA ▸ jugulum
JUGULAR, -S n one of three large veins of the neck
JUGULATE vb check (a disease) by extreme measures or remedies
JUGULUM, JUGULA n lower throat
JUGUM, JUGA, -S n part of an insect's forewing
JUICE, -D, -S, JUICING n liquid part of vegetables, fruit, or meat ▷ vb extract juice from fruits and vegetables
JUICER, -S n kitchen appliance
JUICES ▸ juice
JUICIER ▸ juicy
JUICIEST ▸ juicy
JUICILY ▸ juicy
JUICING ▸ juice
JUICY, JUICIER, JUICIEST adj full of juice
JUJITSU, -S n Japanese martial art
JUJU, -S n W African magic charm or fetish
JUJUBE, -S n chewy sweet made of flavoured gelatine
JUJUISM, -S ▸ juju
JUJUIST, -S ▸ juju
JUJUS ▸ juju
JUJUTSU, -S same as ▸ jujitsu
JUKE, -D, -S, JUKING vb dance or play dance music
JUKEBOX n coin-operated music box
JUKED ▸ juke
JUKES ▸ juke
JUKING ▸ juke
JUKSKEI, -S n type of game
JUKU, -S n Japanese martial art
JULEP, -S n sweet alcoholic drink
JULIENNE adj (of vegetables or meat) cut into thin shreds ▷ n clear soup containing thinly shredded vegetables ▷ vb cut into thin pieces
JULIET, -S n code word for the letter J

JUMAR, -ED, -ING, -RED, -S n climbing tool ▷ vb climb (up a fixed rope) using jumars
JUMART, -S n mythical offspring of a bull and a mare
JUMBAL, -S same as ▸ jumble
JUMBIE, -S n Caribbean ghost
JUMBLE, -D, -S, JUMBLING n confused heap or state ▷ vb mix in a disordered way
JUMBLER -S
JUMBLIER ▸ jumbly
JUMBLING ▸ jumble
JUMBLY, JUMBLIER ▸ jumble
JUMBO, -S adj very large ▷ n large jet airliner
JUMBOISE same as ▸ jumboize
JUMBOIZE vb extend (a ship) by inserting a part between the bow and stern
JUMBOS ▸ jumbo
JUMBUCK, -S n sheep
JUMBY n Caribbean ghost
JUMELLE, -S n paired objects
JUMP, -ED, -S vb leap or spring into the air using the leg muscles ▷ n act of jumping
JUMPABLE
JUMPER, -S n sweater or pullover
JUMPIER ▸ jumpy
JUMPIEST ▸ jumpy
JUMPILY ▸ jumpy
JUMPING, -S ▸ jump
JUMPOFF, -S n round in a showjumping contest
JUMPROPE n rope held in the hands and jumped over
JUMPS ▸ jump
JUMPSHOT n type of shot in basketball in which a player jumps to reach the basket
JUMPSIES pl n game involving jumping over a straight rope
JUMPSUIT n one-piece garment of combined trousers and jacket or shirt
JUMPY, JUMPIER, JUMPIEST adj nervous
JUN variant of ▸ chon
JUNCATE, -S same as ▸ junket
JUNCO, -ES, -S n North American bunting
JUNCTION n place where routes, railway lines, or roads meet
JUNCTURE n point in time, esp a critical one
JUNCUS, -ES n type of rush
JUNGLE, -S n tropical forest of dense tangled vegetation
JUNGLED adj covered with jungle
JUNGLES ▸ jungle

JUNGLI, -S *n* uncultured person

JUNGLIER ▸ jungly

JUNGLIS ▸ jungli

JUNGLIST *n* jungle-music enthusiast

JUNGLY, JUNGLIER ▸ jungle

JUNIOR, -ED, -S *adj* of lower standing ▸ *n* junior person ▸ *vb* work as a junior

JUNIPER, -S *n* evergreen shrub with purple berries

JUNK, -ED, -ING, -S *n* discarded or useless objects ▸ *vb* discard as junk

JUNKANOO *n* Bahamian ceremony

JUNKED ▸ junk

JUNKER, -S *n* (formerly) young German nobleman

JUNKET, -ED, -S *n* excursion by public officials ▸ *vb* (of a public official, committee, etc) to go on a junket

JUNKETER

JUNKIE, -S *n* slang word for person addicted to something

JUNKIER ▸ junky

JUNKIES ▸ junkie

JUNKIEST ▸ junky

JUNKING ▸ junk

JUNKMAN, JUNKMEN *n* man who trades in discarded items

JUNKS ▸ junk

JUNKY, JUNKIER, JUNKIEST *adj* of low quality

JUNKYARD *n* place where junk is stored or collected for sale

JUNTA, -S *n* military officers holding power in a country

JUNTO, -S *same as* ▸ **junta**

JUPATI, -S *n* type of palm tree

JUPE, -S *n* sleeveless jacket

JUPON, -S *n* short sleeveless padded garment

JURA ▸ jus

JURAL *adj* of or relating to law or to the administration of justice

JURALLY

JURANT, -S *n* person taking oath

JURASSIC *adj* of the second period of the Mesozoic era

JURAT, -S *n* statement at the foot of an affidavit

JURATORY *adj* of, relating to, or expressed in an oath

JURATS ▸ jurat

JURE, -S *adv* by legal right ▸ *n* legal right

JUREL, -S *n* edible fish

JURES ▸ jure

JURIDIC *same as* > **juridical**

JURIED ▸ jury

JURIES ▸ jury

JURIST, -S *n* expert in law

JURISTIC *adj* of or relating to jurists

JURISTS ▸ jurist

JUROR, -S *n* member of a jury

JURY, JURIED, JURIES, -ING *n* group of people sworn to deliver a verdict in a court of law ▸ *adj* makeshift ▸ *vb* evaluate by jury

JURYLESS

JURYMAN, JURYMEN *n* member of a jury, esp a man

JURYMAST *n* replacement mast

JURYMEN ▸ juryman

JUS, JURA *n* right, power, or authority

JUSSIVE, -S *n* mood of verbs used for giving orders; imperative

JUST, -ED, -EST, -ING *adv* very recently ▸ *adj* fair or impartial in action or judgment ▸ *vb* joust

JUSTER -S

JUSTICE, -S *n* quality of being just

JUSTICER *n* magistrate

JUSTICES ▸ justice

JUSTIFY *vb* prove right or reasonable

JUSTING ▸ just

JUSTLE, -D, -S, JUSTLING *less common word for* ▸ **jostle**

JUSTLY ▸ just

JUSTNESS ▸ just

JUSTS *same as* ▸ **joust**

JUT, -S, -TED, -TING *vb* project or stick out ▸ *n* something that juts out

JUTE, -S *n* plant fibre, used for rope, canvas, etc

JUTELIKE

JUTS ▸ jut

JUTTED ▸ jut

JUTTIED ▸ jutty

JUTTIER ▸ jutty

JUTTIES ▸ jutty

JUTTIEST ▸ jutty

JUTTING ▸ jut

JUTTY, JUTTIED, JUTTIER, JUTTIES, JUTTIEST, -ING *vb* project beyond ▸ *adj* characterized by jutting

JUVE, -S *same as* ▸ **juvenile**

JUVENAL, -S *variant spelling* (*esp US*) *of* ▸ **juvenile**

JUVENILE *adj* young ▸ *n* young person or child

JUVES ▸ juve

JUVIE, -S *n* juvenile detention centre

JYMOLD *adj* having a hinge

JYNX, -ES *n* wryneck

This unusual word, another name for the bird known as a wryneck, is unique in combining J, Y and X without using any vowels.

J

Kk

Worth 5 points, **K** is a valuable tile to have in your rack. However, it's not the most useful tile for forming bonus words scoring that extra 50 points, so, as with the **J**, you will normally want to play it off fairly quickly. There are four two-letter words beginning with **K**: **ka, ki, ko** and **ky**. When it comes to three-letter words, remember **keg** (8 points), **ken** (7), **key** (10), **kex** (14), **kid** (8), **kin** (7), **kip** (9) and **kit** (7). Other three-letter words with **K** well worth remembering are **jak** (14) and **zek** (16).

KA, -ING, -S n (in ancient Egypt) type of spirit ▷ vb (in archaic usage) help
KAAL adj naked
KAAMA, -S n large African antelope with lyre-shaped horns
KAAS n Dutch cabinet or wardrobe
KAB, -S variant spelling of ► cab
KABAB, -BED, -S same as ► kebab
KABADDI, -S n type of game
KABAKA, -S n any of the former rulers of the Baganda people
KABALA, -S same as ► kabbalah
KABALISM
KABALIST
KABAR, -S archaic form of ► caber
KABAYA, -S n tunic
KABBALA, -S same as ► kabbalah
KABBALAH n ancient Jewish mystical tradition
KABBALAS ► kabbala
KABELE, -S same as ► kebele
KABELJOU n large fish that is an important food fish of South African waters
KABIKI, -S n fruit tree found in India
KABLOOEY interj expressing alarming or surprising abruptness
KABLOOIE same as ► kablooey
KABLOONA n (among Canadian Inuits) person who is not Inuit
KABOB, -BED, -S same as ► kebab

KABOCHA, -S n type of Japanese pumpkin
KABOODLE same as ► caboodle
KABOOM, -S n loud echoing explosive sound
KABS ► kab
KABUKI, -S n form of Japanese drama
KACCHA, -S n trousers worn traditionally by Sikhs
KACHA adj crude
KACHAHRI n Indian courthouse
KACHCHA same as ► kacha
KACHERI, -S same as ► kachahri
KACHINA, -S n type of supernatural being
KACHORI, -S n balls of fried dough with various fillings, eaten as a snack
KACK same as ► cack
KADAI, -S same as ► karahi
KADDISH n ancient Jewish liturgical prayer
KADE, -S same as ► ked
KADI, -S variant spelling of ► cadi
KAE, -D, -ING, -S n dialect word for jackdaw or jay ▷ vb (in archaic usage) help
KAF, -S n letter of the Hebrew alphabet
KAFFIR, -S n Southern African variety of sorghum
KAFFIYAH same as ► kaffiyeh
KAFFIYEH same as ► keffiyeh
KAFILA, -S n caravan
KAFIR, -S same as ► kaffir
KAFS ► kaf
KAFTAN, -S n long loose Eastern garment

KAFUFFLE n commotion or disorder
KAGO, -S n Japanese sedan chair
KAGOOL, -S variant spelling of ► cagoule
KAGOS ► kago
KAGOUL, -S variant spelling of ► cagoule
KAGOULE, -S same as ► kagoul
KAGOULS ► kagoul
KAGU, -S n crested nocturnal bird
KAHAL, -S n Jewish community
KAHAWAI, -S n food and game fish of New Zealand
KAHUNA, -S n Hawaiian priest, shaman, or expert
KAI, -S n food
KAIAK, -ED, -ING, -S same as ► kayak
KAID, -S n North African chieftain or leader
KAIE, -S archaic form of ► key
KAIF, -S same as ► kif
KAIK, -S same as ► kainga
KAIKA, -S same as ► kainga
KAIKAI, -S n food
KAIKAS ► kaika
KAIKS ► kaik
KAIL, -S same as ► kale
KAILYARD same as ► kaleyard
KAIM, -S same as ► kame
KAIMAKAM n Turkish governor
KAIMS ► kaim
KAIN, -S variant spelling of ► cain
KAING ► ka
KAINGA, -S n (in New Zealand) a Māori village or small settlement

KAINIT, -S same as ► **kainite**
KAINITE, -S n white mineral
KAINITS ► **kainit**
KAINS ► **kain**
KAIS ► **kai**
KAISER, -S n German or Austro-Hungarian emperor
KAISERIN n empress
KAISERS ► **kaiser**
KAIZEN, -S n type of philosophy
KAJAWAH, -S n type of seat or pannier used on a camel
KAJEPUT, -S n variety of Australian melaleuca
KAK, -S n South African slang word for faeces
KAKA, -S n parrot of New Zealand
KAKAPO, -S n nocturnal New Zealand parrot
KAKARIKI n green-feathered New Zealand parrot
KAKAS ► **kaka**
KAKEMONO n Japanese wall hanging
KAKI, -S n Asian persimmon tree
KAKIEMON n type of 17th century Japanese porcelain
KAKIS ► **kaki**
KAKIVAK, -S n fish spear used by Inuit people
KAKODYL, -S variant spelling of ► **cacodyl**
KAKS ► **kak**
KAKURO, -S n crossword-style puzzle with numbers
KALAM, -S n discussion and debate
KALAMATA n as in **kalamata olive** aubergine-coloured Greek olive
KALAMDAN n Persian box in which to keep pens
KALAMS ► **kalam**
KALE, -S n cabbage with crinkled leaves
KALENDAR variant form of ► **calendar**
KALENDS same as ► **calends**
KALES ► **kale**
KALEWIFE n Scots word for a female vegetable or cabbage seller
KALEYARD n vegetable garden
KALI, -S another name for ► **saltwort**
KALIAN, -S another name for ► **hookah**
KALIF, -S variant spelling of ► **caliph**
KALIFATE same as > **caliphate**

KALIFS ► **kalif**
KALIMBA, -S n musical instrument
KALINITE n alum
KALIPH, -S variant spelling of ► **caliph**
KALIS ► **kali**
KALIUM, -S n Latin for potassium
KALLIDIN n type of peptide
KALMIA, -S n evergreen ericaceous shrub
KALONG, -S n fruit bat
KALOOKI, -S n card game
KALOOKIE same as ► **kalooki**
KALOOKIS ► **kalooki**
KALOTYPE variant spelling of ► **calotype**
KALPA, -S n period in Hindu cosmology
KALPAC, -S same as ► **calpac**
KALPAK, -S variant spelling of ► **calpac**
KALPAS ► **kalpa**
KALPIS, -ES n Greek water jar
KALUKI, -S same as ► **kalooki**
KALUMPIT n type of Filipino fruit tree or its fruit
KALYPTRA n Greek veil
KAM Shakespearean word for ► **crooked**
KAMA, -S n large African antelope with lyre-shaped horns
KAMAAINA n Hawaiian local
KAMACITE n alloy of iron and nickel, occurring in meteorites
KAMAHI, -S n hardwood tree
KAMALA, -S n East Indian tree
KAMAS ► **kama**
KAME, -S n irregular mound of gravel, sand, etc
KAMEES, -ES same as ► **kameez**
KAMEEZ, -ES n long tunic
KAMELA, -S same as ► **kamala**
KAMERAD, -S interj shout of surrender ▷ vb surrender
KAMES ► **kame**
KAMI n divine being or spiritual force in Shinto
KAMICHI, -S n South American bird
KAMIK, -S n traditional Inuit boot
KAMIKAZE n Japanese pilot who performed a suicide mission ▷ adj undertaken in the knowledge that it will kill the person performing it
KAMIKS ► **kamik**
KAMILA, -S same as ► **kamala**

KAMIS, -ES same as ► **kameez**
KAMME same as ► **kam**
KAMOKAMO n kind of marrow found in New Zealand
KAMOTIK, -S n type of Inuit sled
KAMOTIQ, -S same as ► **kamotik**
KAMPONG, -S n (in Malaysia) village
KAMSEEN, -S same as ► **khamsin**
KAMSIN, -S same as ► **kamseen**
KANA, -S n Japanese syllabary
KANAE, -S n grey mullet
KANAKA, -S n Australian word for any native of the South Pacific
KANAS ► **kana**
KANBAN, -S n just-in-time manufacturing process
KANDY, KANDIES same as ► **candie**
KANE, -S n Hawaiian man or boy
KANEH, -S n 6-cubit Hebrew measure
KANES ► **kane**
KANG, -S n Chinese heatable platform
KANGA, -S n piece of gaily decorated thin cotton cloth
KANGAROO n Australian marsupial ▷ vb (of a car) move forward with sudden jerks
KANGAS ► **kanga**
KANGHA, -S n comb traditionally worn by Sikhs
KANGS ► **kang**
KANJI, -S n Japanese writing system
KANS, -ES n Indian wild sugar cane
KANT, -ED, -ING, -S archaic spelling of ► **cant**
KANTAR, -S n unit of weight
KANTED ► **kant**
KANTELA, -S same as ► **kantele**
KANTELE, -S n Finnish stringed instrument
KANTEN, -S same as ► **agar**
KANTHA, -S n Bengali embroidered quilt
KANTIKOY vb dance ceremonially
KANTING ► **kant**
KANTS ► **kant**
KANUKA, -S n New Zealand myrtaceous tree
KANZU, -S n long garment

K

KAOLIANG n any of various E Asian varieties of sorghum

KAOLIN, -S n fine white clay

KAOLINE, -S same as ► kaolin

KAOLINIC ► kaolin

KAOLINS ► kaolin

KAON, -S n type of meson
KAONIC

KAPA, -S n Hawaiian cloth made from beaten mulberry bark

KAPEYKA, KAPEEK n small currency unit of Belarus

KAPH, -S n 11th letter of the Hebrew alphabet

KAPOK, -S n fluffy fibre

KAPOW n sharp explosive sound

KAPPA, -S n tenth letter in the Greek alphabet

KAPU, -S n (in Hawaii) system of rules for daily life

KAPUKA, -S same as > **broadleaf**

KAPUS ► kapu

KAPUT adj ruined or broken

KAPUTT same as ► kaput

KARA, -S n steel bangle traditionally worn by Sikhs

KARAHI, -S n type of wok

KARAISM, -S n beliefs and doctrines of a Jewish sect

KARAIT, -S same as ► krait

KARAKA, -S n New Zealand tree

KARAKIA, -S n prayer

KARAKUL, -S n sheep of central Asia

KARAMU, -S n small New Zealand tree

KARANGA, -S n call or chant of welcome, sung by a female elder ▷ vb perform a karanga

KARAOKE, -S n form of entertainment

KARAS ► kara

KARAT, -S n measure of the proportion of gold in an alloy

KARATE, -S n Japanese system of unarmed combat

KARATEKA n competitor or expert in karate

KARATES ► karate

KARATS ► karat

KAREAREA n New Zealand falcon

KARENGO, -S n edible type of Pacific seaweed

KARITE, -S n shea tree

KARK, -ED, -ING, -S variant spelling of ► cark

KARMA, -S n person's actions affecting his or her fate in the next reincarnation
KARMIC

KARN, -S old word for ► cairn

KARO, -S n small New Zealand tree or shrub

KAROO, -S n high arid plateau

KARORO, -S n large seagull

KAROS ► karo

KAROSHI, -S n (in Japan) death caused by overwork

KAROSS, -ES n type of blanket

KARRI, -S n Australian eucalypt

KARROO, -S same as ► karoo

KARSEY, -S variant spelling of ► khazi

KARSIES ► karsy

KARST, -S n geological term
KARSTIC

KARSTIFY vb become karstic

KARSTS ► karst

KARSY, KARSIES variant spelling of ► khazi

KART, -S n light low-framed vehicle
KARTER -S

KARTING, -S ► kart

KARTS ► kart

KARYON, -S n nucleus of a cell

KARYOTIN less common word for > **chromatin**

KARZY, KARZIES variant spelling of ► khazi

KAS ► ka

KASBAH, -S n citadel of any of various North African cities

KASHA, -S n dish originating in Eastern Europe

KASHER, -ED, -S vb make fit for use

KASHMIR, -S variant spelling of ► cashmere

KASHRUS same as ► kashruth

KASHRUT, -S same as ► kashruth

KASHRUTH n condition of being fit for ritual use in general

KASHRUTS ► kashrut

KASME interj (in Indian English) I swear

KAT, -S same as ► khat

KATA, -S n form of exercise

KATAKANA n system of Japanese syllabic writing

KATAL, -S n SI unit of catalytic activity

KATANA, -S n Japanese samurai sword

KATAS ► kata

KATCHINA variant spelling of ► kachina

KATCINA, -S variant spelling of ► kachina

KATHAK, -S n form of dancing

KATHODAL ► kathode

KATHODE, -S variant spelling of ► cathode
KATHODIC

KATHUMP, -S n sound of a dull heavy blow

KATI, -S variant spelling of ► catty

KATION, -S variant spelling of ► cation

KATIPO, -S n small poisonous New Zealand spider

KATIS ► kati

KATORGA, -S n type of labour camp

KATS ► kat

KATSINA, -M, -S n (among the Hopi) doll representing spirit messengers

KATSURA, -S n Asian tree

KATTI, -S variant spelling of ► catty

KATYDID, -S n large green grasshopper of N America

KAUGH, -S same as ► kiaugh

KAUMATUA n senior member of a tribe

KAUPAPA, -S n strategy, policy, or cause

KAURI, -S n large NZ conifer

KAURIES ► kaury

KAURIS ► kauri

KAURU, -S n edible stem of the cabbage tree

KAURY, KAURIES variant spelling of ► kauri

KAVA, -S n Polynesian shrub

KAVAKAVA same as ► kava

KAVAL, -S n type of flute played in the Balkans

KAVAS, -S ► kava

KAVASS, -ES n armed Turkish constable

KAW, -ED, -ING, -S variant spelling of ► caw

KAWA, -S n protocol or etiquette

KAWAII, -S n (in Japan) quality of being lovable or cute

KAWAKAWA n aromatic shrub or small tree of New Zealand

KAWAS ► kawa

KAWAU, -S n New Zealand name for black shag

KAWED ► kaw

KAWING ► kaw

KAWS ► kaw

KAY, -S n name of the letter K

KAYAK, -ED, -S n Inuit canoe ▷ vb travel by kayak
KAYAKER -S

KAYAKING ► kayak

KAYAKS ► kayak

KAYLE n one of a set of ninepins

KAYLES pl n ninepins

KAYLIED adj intoxicated or drunk

KAYO, -ED, -ES, -S n another term for ▶ **knockout**

KAYOING -S

KAYS ▶ **kay**

KAZACHKI same as ▶ **kazachok**

KAZACHOC n Ukrainian folk dance

KAZACHOK n Russian folk dance

KAZATSKI same as ▶ **kazachok**

KAZATSKY same as ▶ **kazachok**

KAZATZKA same as ▶ **kazachok**

KAZI, -S variant spelling of ▶ **khazi**

KAZOO, -S n musical instrument

KBAR, -S n kilobar

KEA, -S n large brownish-green parrot of NZ

KEASAR, -S archaic variant of ▶ **kaiser**

KEAVIE, -S n archaic or dialect word for a type of crab

KEB, -BED, -BING, -S vb Scots word meaning miscarry or reject a lamb

KEBAB, -BED, -S n food grilled on a skewer ▷ vb skewer

KEBAR, -S n Scots word for beam or rafter

KEBBED ▶ keb

KEBBIE, -S n Scots word for shepherd's crook

KEBBING ▶ keb

KEBBOCK, -S n Scots word for a cheese

KEBBUCK, -S same as ▶ **kebbock**

KEBELE, -S n Ethiopian local council

KEBLAH, -S same as ▶ **kiblah**

KEBOB, -BED, -S same as ▶ **kebab**

KEBS ▶ keb

KECK, -ED, -ING vb retch or feel nausea

KECKLE, -D, -S Scots variant of ▶ **cackle**

KECKLING

KECKS, -ES pl n trousers

KECKSY, KECKSIES n dialect word meaning hollow plant stalk

KED, -S n as in **sheep ked** sheep tick

KEDDAH, -S same as ▶ **kheda**

KEDGE, -D, -S, KEDGING vb move (a ship) using cable attached to an anchor ▷ n light anchor used for kedging

KEDGER, -S n small anchor

KEDGEREE n dish of fish with rice and eggs

KEDGERS ▶ kedger

KEDGES ▶ kedge

KEDGIER ▶ kedgy

KEDGIEST ▶ kedgy

KEDGING ▶ kedge

KEDGY, KEDGIER, KEDGIEST adj dialect word for happy or lively

KEDS ▶ ked

KEECH, -ES n old word for lump of fat

KEEF, -S same as ▶ **kif**

KEEK, -ED, -ING, -S Scot word for ▶ **peep**

KEEKER -S

KEEL, -ED, -S n part of a ship ▷ vb mark with a stain

KEELAGE, -S n fee charged by certain ports

KEELBOAT n river boat with a shallow draught and a keel

KEELED ▶ keel

KEELER, -S n bargeman

KEELHALE same as ▶ **keelhaul**

KEELHAUL vb reprimand (someone) harshly

KEELIE, -S n kestrel

KEELING, -S ▶ keel

KEELLESS ▶ keel

KEELMAN, KEELMEN n bargeman

KEELS ▶ keel

KEELSON, -S n part of a ship

KEEMA, -S n (in Indian cookery) minced meat

KEEN, -ED, -EST, -S adj eager or enthusiastic ▷ vb wail over the dead ▷ n lament for the dead

KEENER -S

KEENING, -S ▶ keen

KEENLY ▶ keen

KEENNESS ▶ keen

KEENO, -S same as ▶ **keno**

KEENS ▶ keen

KEEP, -S, KEPT vb have or retain possession of ▷ n cost of food and everyday expenses

KEEPABLE

KEEPER, -S n person who looks after animals in a zoo

KEEPING, -S ▶ keep

KEEPNET, -S n cylindrical net used to keep fish alive

KEEPS ▶ keep

KEEPSAKE n gift treasured for the sake of the giver

KEEPSAKY

KEESHOND n breed of dog of the spitz type

KEESTER, -S same as ▶ **keister**

KEET, -S short for ▶ **parakeet**

KEEVE, -S n tub or vat

KEF, -S same as ▶ **kif**

KEFFEL, -S dialect word for ▶ **horse**

KEFFIYAH same as ▶ **kaffiyeh**

KEFFIYEH n cotton headdress worn by Arabs

KEFIR, -S n effervescent drink

KEFS ▶ kef

KEFTEDES n Greek dish of meatballs cooked with herbs and onions

KEFUFFLE same as > **kerfuffle**

KEG, -GED, -GING, -S n small metal beer barrel ▷ vb put in kegs

KEGELER, -S same as ▶ **kegler**

KEGGED ▶ keg

KEGGER, -S ▶ keg

KEGGING ▶ keg

KEGLER, -S n participant in a game of tenpin bowling

KEGLING, -S n bowling

KEGS ▶ keg

KEHUA, -S n ghost or spirit

KEIGHT ▶ ketch

KEIR, -S same as ▶ **kier**

KEIREN, -S n type of track cycling event

KEIRETSU n group of Japanese businesses

KEIRIN, -S n cycling race originating in Japan

KEIRS ▶ keir

KEISTER, -S n rump

KEITLOA, -S n type of rhinoceros

KEKENO, -S n New Zealand fur seal

KEKS same as ▶ **kecks**

KEKSYE, -S same as ▶ **kex**

KELEP, -S n large ant found in Central and South America

KELIM, -S same as ▶ **kilim**

KELL, -S dialect word for ▶ **hairnet**

KELLAUT, -S same as ▶ **khilat**

KELLIES ▶ kelly

KELLS ▶ kell

KELLY, KELLIES n part of a drill system

KELOID, -S n type of scar tissue

KELOIDAL

KELP, -ED, -ING, -S n large brown seaweed ▷ vb burn seaweed to make a type of ash

KELPER, -S n Falkland Islander

KELPFISH n type of fish that lives among kelp

KELPIE, -S n Australian sheepdog

KELPING ▸ kelp

KELPS ▸ kelp

KELPY same as ▸ **kelpie**

KELSON, -S same as ▸ **keelson**

KELT, -S n salmon that has recently spawned

KELTER, -S same as ▸ **kilter**

KELTIE variant spelling of ▸ **kelty**

KELTIES ▸ kelty

KELTS ▸ kelt

KELTY, KELTIES n old Scots word for a drink imposed on someone not thought to be drinking enough

KELVIN, -S n SI unit of temperature

KEMB, -ED, -ING, -S old word for ▸ **comb**

KEMBLA, -S n small change

KEMBO, -ED, -ING, -S same as ▸ **kimbo**

KEMBS ▸ kemb

KEMP, -ED, -S n coarse hair or strand of hair ▷ vb dialect word meaning to compete or try to come first

KEMPER -S

KEMPIER ▸ kempy

KEMPIEST ▸ kempy

KEMPING, -S ▸ kemp

KEMPLE, -S n variable Scottish measure for hay or straw

KEMPS ▸ kemp

KEMPT adj (of hair) tidy

KEMPY, KEMPIER, KEMPIEST ▸ **kemp**

KEN, -NED, -S vb know ▷ n range of knowledge or perception

KENAF, -S another name for ▸ **ambary**

KENCH, -ES n bin for salting and preserving fish

KENDO, -S n Japanese sport of fencing using wooden staves

KENDOIST n person who practises kendo

KENDOS ▸ kendo

KENNED ▸ ken

KENNEL, -ED, -S n hutlike shelter for a dog ▷ vb put or go into a kennel

KENNER, -S ▸ ken

KENNET, -S n old word for a small hunting dog

KENNETT, -S vb spoil or destroy ruthlessly

KENNING, -S ▸ ken

KENO, -S n game of chance similar to bingo

KENOSIS, KENOSES n Christ's renunciation of certain divine attributes

KENOTIC -S

KENOTRON n signal-amplifying device

KENS ▸ ken

KENSPECK adj Scots for easily seen or recognized

KENT, -ED, -ING, -S dialect word for ▸ **punt**

KENTE n brightly coloured handwoven cloth

KENTED ▸ kent

KENTES ▸ kente

KENTIA, -S n plant name

KENTING ▸ kent

KENTS ▸ kent

KEP, -PED, -PEN, -PING, -PIT, -S, KIPPEN vb catch

KEPHALIC variant spelling of ▸ **cephalic**

KEPHALIN same as ▸ **cephalin**

KEPHIR, -S same as ▸ **kefir**

KEPI, -S n French military cap with a flat top and a horizontal peak

KEPPED ▸ kep

KEPPEN ▸ kep

KEPPING ▸ kep

KEPPIT ▸ kep

KEPS ▸ kep

KEPT ▸ keep

KERAMIC rare variant of ▸ **ceramic**

KERAMICS rare variant of ▸ **ceramics**

KERATIN, -S n fibrous protein found in the hair and nails

KERATOID adj resembling horn

KERATOMA n horny growth on the skin

KERATOSE adj (esp of certain sponges) having a horny skeleton

KERB, -ED, -S n edging to a footpath ▷ vb provide with or enclose with a kerb

KERBAYA, -S n blouse worn by Malay women

KERBED ▸ kerb

KERBING, -S n material used for a kerb

KERBS ▸ kerb

KERBSIDE n edge of a pavement where it drops to the level of the road

KERCHIEF n piece of cloth worn over the head or round the neck

KERCHOO interj atishoo

KEREL, -S n chap or fellow

KERERU, -S n New Zealand pigeon

KERF, -ED, -ING, -S n cut made by a saw, an axe, etc ▷ vb cut

KERKY, KERKIER, KERKIEST adj stupid

KERMA, -S n quantity of radiation

KERMES, -ES n dried bodies of female scale insects

KERMESS same as ▸ **kermis**

KERMESSE same as ▸ **kermis**

KERMIS, -ES n (formerly) annual country festival or carnival

KERMODE, -S n type of black bear found in Canada

KERN, -S n projection of a printed character ▷ vb furnish (a typeface) with a kern

KERNE, -D, -S same as ▸ **kern**

KERNEL, -ED, -S n seed of a nut, cereal, or fruit stone ▷ vb form kernels

KERNELLY adj with or like kernels

KERNELS ▸ kernel

KERNES ▸ kerne

KERNING, -S n provision of kerns in printing

KERNISH adj resembling an armed foot soldier or peasant

KERNITE, -S n light soft colourless or white mineral

KERNS ▸ kern

KERO, -S short for ▸ **kerosene**

KEROGEN, -S n material that produces hydrocarbons when heated

KEROS ▸ kero

KEROSENE n liquid mixture distilled from petroleum and used as a fuel or solvent

KEROSINE same as ▸ **kerosene**

KERPLUNK vb land noisily

KERRIA, -S n type of shrub with yellow flowers

KERRY, KERRIES n breed of dairy cattle

KERSEY, -S n smooth woollen cloth

KERVE, -D, -S, KERVING dialect word for ▸ **carve**

KERYGMA, -S n Christian gospel

KESAR, -S old variant of ▸ **kaiser**

KESH n beard and uncut hair traditionally worn by Sikhs

KEST, -ING, -S old form of ▸ **cast**

KESTREL, -S n type of small falcon**

KESTS ► kest

KET, -S *n* dialect word for carrion

KETA, -S *n* type of salmon

KETAINE *adj* in poor taste

KETAMINE *n* drug used in medicine as an anaesthetic

KETAS ► keta

KETCH, KEIGHT, -ES, -ING *n* two-masted sailing vessel ▷ *vb* (in archaic usage) catch

KETCHUP, -S *n* thick cold sauce, usu made of tomatoes

KETCHUPY *adj* like ketchup

KETE, -S *n* basket woven from flax

KETENE, -S *n* colourless irritating toxic gas

KETES ► kete

KETMIA, -S *n as in* **bladder ketmia** plant with pale yellow flowers

KETO *adj as in* **keto form** form of tautomeric compounds

KETOL, -S *n* nitrogenous substance

KETONE, -S *n* type of organic solvent

KETONIC

KETOSE *n* any monosaccharide that contains a ketone group

KETOSIS, KETOSES *n* high concentration of ketone bodies in the blood

KETOTIC

KETOXIME *n* oxime formed by reaction between hydroxylamine and a ketone

KETS ► ket

KETTLE, -D, -S, KETTLING *n* container used for boiling water ▷ *vb* contain a public protest in an enclosed space

KETUBAH, -S, KETUBOT, KETUBOTH *n* Jewish marriage contract

KEVEL, -S *n* strong bitt or bollard for securing heavy hawsers

KEVIL, -S *old variant of* ► **kevel**

KEWL, -ER, -EST *nonstandard variant spelling of* ► **cool**

KEWPIE, -S *n* type of brightly coloured doll

KEX, -ES *n* any of several hollow-stemmed umbelliferous plants

This is another of the great high-scoring three-letter words that use X.

KEY, -ED *n* device for operating a lock by moving a bolt ▷ *adj* of great

importance ▷ *vb* enter (text) using a keyboard

KEYBOARD, -S *n* set of keys on a piano, computer, etc ▷ *vb* enter (text) using a keyboard

KEYBUGLE *n* bugle with keys

KEYCARD, -S *n* electronic card used as a key

KEYED ► key

KEYER, -S *n* device that keys signals or information into a device or computing system

KEYFRAME *n* image used to show the start and end of animation sequence

KEYHOLE, -S *n* opening for inserting a key into a lock

KEYING, -S ► key

KEYLESS ► key

KEYLINE, -S *n* outline image on artwork or plans to show where it is to be placed

KEYNOTE, -D, -S *adj* central or dominating ▷ *n* dominant idea of a speech etc ▷ *vb* deliver a keynote address to (a political convention, etc)

KEYNOTER *n* person delivering a keynote address

KEYNOTES ► keynote

KEYPAD, -S *n* small panel with a set of buttons

KEYPAL, -S *n* person one regularly exchanges emails with for fun

KEYPRESS *n* single depression of a keyboard key

KEYPUNCH *n* keyboard device to transfer data onto punched cards ▷ *vb* transfer (data) onto punched cards

KEYRING, -S *n* metal ring for keeping keys together

KEYS *interj* children's cry for truce

KEYSET, -S *n* set of computer keys used for a particular purpose

KEYSTER, -S *same as* ► **keister**

KEYSTONE *n* most important part of a process, organization, etc ▷ *vb* project or provide with a distorted image

KEYWAY, -S *n* engineering device

KEYWORD, -S *n* word or phrase used to find something on a computer

KGOTLA, -S *n* (in South African English) meeting place

KHADDAR, -S *n* cotton cloth

KHADI, -S *same as* ► **khaddar**

KHAF, -S *n* letter of the Hebrew alphabet

KHAKI, -S *adj* dull yellowish-brown ▷ *n* fabric of this colour used for military uniforms

KHALAT, -S *same as* ► **khilat**

KHALIF, -S *variant spelling of* ► **caliph**

KHALIFA, -S *same as* ► **caliph**

KHALIFAH *same as* ► **caliph**

KHALIFAS ► khalifa

KHALIFAT *same as* > **caliphate**

KHALIFS ► khalif

KHAMSEEN *same as* ► **khamsin**

KHAMSIN, -S *n* hot southerly wind

KHAN, -S *n* title of respect in Afghanistan and central Asia

KHANATE, -S *n* territory ruled by a khan

KHANDA, -S *n* double-edged sword

KHANGA, -S *same as* ► **kanga**

KHANJAR, -S *n* type of dagger

KHANS ► khan

KHANSAMA *same as* > **khansamah**

KHANUM, -S *feminine form of* ► **khan**

KHAPH, -S *n* letter of the Hebrew alphabet

KHARIF, -S *n* crop harvested at the beginning of winter

KHAT, -S *n* white-flowered evergreen shrub

KHAYA, -S *n* type of African tree

KHAYAL, -S *n* kind of Indian classical vocal music

KHAYAS ► khaya

KHAZEN, -IM, -S *same as* ► **chazan**

KHAZI, -S *n* lavatory

KHEDA, -S *n* enclosure used to capture wild elephants

KHEDAH, -S *same as* ► **kheda**

KHEDAS ► kheda

KHEDIVA, -S *n* khedive's wife

KHEDIVAL ► khedive

KHEDIVAS ► khediva

KHEDIVE, -S *n* viceroy of Egypt under Ottoman suzerainty

KHET, -S *n* Thai district

KHETH, -S *same as* ► **heth**

KHETS ► khet

KHI, -S *n* letter of the Greek alphabet

This is a letter of the Greek alphabet, also spelt **chi**. It is worth remembering as one of the higher-scoring

K

three-letter words starting with K.

KHILAFAT same as > caliphate

KHILAT, -S n (in the Middle East) gift given to someone as a mark of honour

KHILIM, -S same as ► kilim

KHIMAR, -S n type of headscarf worn by Muslim women

KHIRKAH, -S n dervish's woollen or cotton outer garment

KHIS ► khi

KHODJA, -S same as ► khoja

KHOJA, -S n teacher in a Muslim school

KHOR, -S n watercourse

KHOTBAH, -S same as ► khutbah

KHOTBEH, -S same as ► khutbah

KHOUM, -S n Mauritanian monetary unit

KHUD, -S n Indian ravine

KHURTA, -S same as ► kurta

KHUSKHUS n aromatic perennial Indian grass whose roots are woven into mats, fans, and baskets

KHUTBAH, -S n sermon in a Mosque, especially on a Friday

KI, -S n vital energy

KIAAT, -S n tropical African leguminous tree

KIACK, -S n N American fish of the herring family

KIANG, -S n variety of wild ass

KIAUGH, -S n (in Scots) anxiety

KIBBE, -S n Middle Eastern dish

KIBBEH, -S same as ► kibbe

KIBBES ► kibbe

KIBBI, -S same as ► kibbe

KIBBITZ same as ► kibitz

KIBBLE, -D, -S, KIBBLING n bucket used in wells or in mining for hoisting ▷ vb grind into small pieces

KIBBUTZ n communal farm or factory in Israel

KIBE, -S n chilblain

KIBEI, -S n someone of Japanese ancestry born in the US and educated in Japan

KIBES ► kibe

KIBITKA, -S n (in Russia) covered sledge or wagon

KIBITZ, -ED, -ES vb interfere or offer unwanted advice
KIBITZER

KIBLA, -S same as ► kiblah

KIBLAH, -S n direction of Mecca

KIBLAS ► kibla

KIBOSH, -ED, -ES vb put a stop to

KICK, -ED, -S vb drive, push, or strike with the foot ▷ n thrust or blow with the foot
KICKABLE

KICKBACK n money paid illegally for favours done ▷ vb have a strong reaction

KICKBALL n children's ball game or the large ball used in it

KICKBOX vb box with hands and feet

KICKDOWN n method of changing gear in a car with automatic transmission

KICKED ► kick

KICKER, -S n person or thing that kicks

KICKFLIP n type of skateboarding manoeuvre ▷ vb perform a kickflip in skateboarding

KICKIER ► kicky

KICKIEST ► kicky

KICKING, -S n act of kicking

KICKOFF, -S n kick that starts a game of football

KICKOUT, -S n (in basketball) instance of kicking the ball

KICKS ► kick

KICKSHAW n valueless trinket

KICKUP, -S n fuss

KICKY, KICKIER, KICKIEST adj excitingly unusual and different

KID, -DED, -S n child ▷ vb tease or deceive (someone) ▷ adj younger
KIDDER -S

KIDDIE same as ► kiddy

KIDDIED ► kiddy

KIDDIER, -S n old word for a market trader

KIDDIES ► kiddy

KIDDING, -S n act of kidding

KIDDISH ► kid

KIDDLE, -S n device for catching fish in a river or in the sea

KIDDO, -ES, -S n very informal term of address for a young person

KIDDUSH n (in Judaism) special blessing

KIDDY, KIDDIED, KIDDIES, -ING n affectionate word for a child ▷ vb tease or deceive

KIDEL, -S same as ► kiddle

KIDGE dialect word for ► lively

KIDGIE, -R, -ST adj dialect word for friendly and welcoming

KIDGLOVE adj overdelicate or overrefined

KIDLET, -S n humorous word for small child

KIDLIKE ► kid

KIDLING, -S n young kid

KIDLIT, -S n children's literature

KIDNAP, -ED, -S vb seize and hold (a person) to ransom
KIDNAPEE
KIDNAPER

KIDNEY, -S n either of the pair of organs that produce urine

KIDOLOGY n practice of bluffing or deception

KIDS ► kid

KIDSKIN, -S n soft smooth leather

KIDULT, -S n adult interested in entertainments intended for children ▷ adj aimed at or suitable for kidults, or both children and adults

KIDVID, -S n informal word for children's video or television

KIEF, -S same as ► kif

KIEKIE, -S n climbing bush plant of New Zealand

KIELBASA n Polish sausage

KIELBASI same as ► kielbasa

KIELBASY same as ► kielbasa

KIER, -S n vat in which cloth is bleached

KIERIE, -S n South African cudgel

KIERS ► kier

KIESTER, -S same as ► keister

KIEV, -S n type of chicken dish

KIEVE, -S same as ► keeve

KIEVS ► kiev

KIF, -S n marijuana

KIFF adj South African slang for excellent

KIFS ► kif

KIGHT, -S n archaic spelling of kite, the bird of prey

KIKOI, -S n piece of cotton cloth

KIKUMON, -S n emblem of the imperial family of Japan

KIKUYU, -S n type of grass

KILD old spelling of ► killed

KILERG, -S n 1000 ergs

KILEY, -S same as ► kylie

KILIM, -S n pileless woven rug

KILL, -ED, -S vb cause the death of ▷ n act of killing
KILLABLE

KILLADAR n fort commander or governor

KILLAS, -ES n Cornish clay slate

KILLCOW, -S n important person

KILLCROP n ever-hungry baby, thought to be a fairy changeling

KILLDEE, -S same as ► **killdeer**

KILLDEER n large brown-and-white North American plover with a noisy cry

KILLDEES ► **killdee**

KILLED ► **kill**

KILLER, -S n person or animal that kills, esp habitually

KILLICK, -S n small anchor, esp one made of a heavy stone

KILLIE, -S same as > **killifish**

KILLING, -S adj very tiring ▷ n sudden financial success

KILLJOY, -S n person who spoils others' pleasure

KILLOCK, -S same as ► **killick**

KILLOGIE n sheltered place in front of a kiln

KILLS ► **kill**

KILLUT, -S same as ► **khilat**

KILN, -ED, -ING, -S n type of oven ▷ vb fire or process in a kiln

KILO, -S n code word for the letter k

KILOBAR, -S n 1000 bars

KILOBASE n unit of measurement for DNA and RNA equal to 1000 base pairs

KILOBAUD n 1000 baud

KILOBIT, -S n 1024 bits

KILOBYTE n 1024 units of information

KILOGRAM n one thousand grams

KILOGRAY n 1000 gray

KILOMOLE n 1000 moles

KILOPOND n informal unit of gravitational force

KILORAD, -S n 1000 rads

KILOS ► **kilo**

KILOTON, -S n one thousand tons

KILOVOLT n one thousand volts

KILOWATT n one thousand watts

KILP, -S dialect form of ► **kelp**

KILT, -ED, -ING, -S n knee-length pleated tartan skirt-like garment ▷ vb put pleats in (cloth)

KILTED

KILTER, -S n working order or alignment

KILTIE, -S n someone wearing a kilt

KILTING, -S ► **kilt**

KILTLIKE ► **kilt**

KILTS ► **kilt**

KILTY same as ► **kiltie**

KIMBO, -ED, -ING, -S vb place akimbo

KIMCHEE, -S same as ► **kimchi**

KIMCHI, -S n Korean dish

KIMMER, -S same as ► **cummer**

KIMONO, -S n loose wide-sleeved Japanese robe

KIMONOED

KIN, -S n person's relatives collectively ▷ adj related by blood

KINA, -S n standard monetary unit of Papua New Guinea

KINAKINA same as ► **quinine**

KINARA, -S n African candle holder

KINAS ► **kina**

KINASE, -S n type of enzyme

KINCHIN, -S old slang word for ► **child**

KINCOB, -S n fine silk fabric

KIND, -ED, -EST, -ING, -S adj considerate, friendly, and helpful ▷ n class or group with common characteristics ▷ vb old word for beget or father

KINDA adv very informal shortening of kind of

KINDED ► **kind**

KINDER, -S adj more kind ▷ n kindergarten or nursery school

KINDEST ► **kind**

KINDIE same as ► **kindy**

KINDIES ► **kindy**

KINDING ► **kind**

KINDLE, -D, -S vb set (a fire) alight

KINDLER, -S

KINDLESS adj heartless

KINDLIER ► **kindly**

KINDLILY ► **kindly**

KINDLING n dry wood or straw for starting fires

KINDLY, KINDLIER adj having a warm-hearted nature ▷ adv in a considerate way

KINDNESS n quality of being kind

KINDRED, -S adj having similar qualities ▷ n blood relationship

KINDS ► **kind**

KINDY, KINDIES n kindergarten

KINE, -S pl n cows or cattle ▷ n Japanese pestle

KINEMA, -S same as ► **cinema**

KINES ► **kine**

KINESES ► **kinesis**

KINESIC adj of or relating to kinesics

KINESICS n study of the role of body movements in communication

KINESIS, KINESES n movement of an organism

KINETIC adj relating to or caused by motion

KINETICS n branch of mechanics concerned with the study of bodies in motion

KINETIN, -S n plant hormone

KINFOLK, -S another word for ► **kinsfolk**

KING, -ED, -ING, -S n male ruler of a monarchy ▷ vb make king

KINGBIRD n any of several large American flycatchers

KINGBOLT n pivot bolt that connects the body of a horse-drawn carriage to the front axle

KINGCUP, -S n yellow-flowered plant

KINGDOM, -S n state ruled by a king or queen

KINGED ► **king**

KINGFISH n food and game fish occurring in warm American Atlantic coastal waters

KINGHOOD ► **king**

KINGING ► **king**

KINGKLIP n edible eel-like marine fish of S Africa

KINGLE, -S n Scots word for a type of hard rock

KINGLESS ► **king**

KINGLET, -S n king of a small or insignificant territory

KINGLIER ► **kingly**

KINGLIKE ► **king**

KINGLING n minor king

KINGLY, KINGLIER adj appropriate to a king ▷ adv in a manner appropriate to a king

KINGPIN, -S n most important person in an organization

KINGPOST n vertical post connecting the apex of a triangular roof truss to the tie beam

KINGS ► **king**

KINGSHIP n position or authority of a king

KINGSIDE n side of the chessboard on which a particular king is at the start of a game

KINGWOOD n hard fine-grained violet-tinted wood of a Brazilian leguminous tree

KININ, -S n type of polypeptide

K

KINK, **-ED**, **-ING**, **-S** n twist or bend in rope, wire, hair, etc ▷ vb form or cause to form a kink

KINKAJOU n arboreal mammal of Central and South America

KINKED ► kink

KINKIER ► kinky

KINKIEST ► kinky

KINKILY ► kinky

KINKING ► kink

KINKLE, **-S** n little kink

KINKS ► kink

KINKY, **KINKIER**, **KINKIEST** adj tightly curled or looped

KINLESS adj without any relatives

KINO, **-S** same as ► keno

KINONE, **-S** n benzoquinone

KINOS ► kino

KINRED, **-S** old form of ► kindred

KINS ► kin

KINSFOLK pl n one's family or relatives

KINSHIP, **-S** n blood relationship

KINSMAN, **KINSMEN** n relative

KIORE, **-S** n small brown rat native to New Zealand

KIOSK, **-S** n small booth

KIP, **-PED**, **-PING**, **-S** vb sleep ▷ n sleep or slumber

KIPE, **-S** n dialect word for a basket for catching fish

KIPP, **-S** uncommon variant of ► kip

KIPPA, **-S** n skullcap worn by male Jews

KIPPAGE, **-S** n Scots word for a state of anger or excitement

KIPPAH, **-S** same as ► kippa

KIPPAS ► kippa

KIPPED ► kip

KIPPEN ► kep

KIPPER, **-S** n cleaned, salted, and smoked herring ▷ vb cure (a herring) by salting and smoking it

KIPPERED adj (of fish, esp herring) having been cleaned, salted, and smoked

KIPPERER ► kipper

KIPPERS ► kipper

KIPPING ► kip

KIPPS ► kipp

KIPS ► kip

KIPSKIN, **-S** same as ► kip

KIPUNJI, **-S** n Tanzanian species of monkey

KIR, **-S** n drink made from dry white wine and cassis

KIRANA, **-S** n small family-owned shop in India

KIRBEH, **-S** n leather bottle

KIRBY n as in kirby grip type of hairgrip

KIRIGAMI n art, originally Japanese, of folding and cutting paper into decorative shapes

KIRIMON, **-S** n Japanese imperial crest

KIRK, **-ED**, **-S** Scot word for ► church

KIRKING **-S**

KIRKMAN, **KIRKMEN** n member or strong upholder of the Kirk

KIRKS ► kirk

KIRKTON, **-S** n village or town with a parish church

KIRKWARD adv towards the church

KIRKYARD n churchyard

KIRMESS same as ► kermis

KIRN, **-ED**, **-ING**, **-S** dialect word for ► churn

KIRPAN, **-S** n short sword traditionally carried by Sikhs

KIRRI, **-S** n Hottentot stick

KIRS ► kir

KIRSCH, **-ES** n cherry brandy

KIRTAN, **-S** n devotional singing

KIRTLE, **-D**, **-S** n woman's skirt or dress ▷ vb dress with a kirtle

KIS ► ki

KISAN, **-S** n peasant or farmer

KISH, **-ES** n graphite formed on the surface of molten iron

KISHKA, **-S** same as ► kishke

KISHKE, **-S** n stuffed beef or fowl intestine, boiled and roasted

KISKADEE n large flycatcher of tropical America

KISMAT, **-S** same as ► kismet

KISMET, **-S** n fate or destiny

KISMETIC

KISS, **-ED**, **-ES**, **-ING** vb touch with the lips in affection or greeting ▷ n touch with the lips

KISSABLE

KISSABLY

KISSEL, **-S** n Russian dessert

KISSER, **-S** n mouth or face

KISSES ► kiss

KISSIER ► kissy

KISSIEST ► kissy

KISSING, **-S** ► kiss

KISSY, **KISSIER**, **KISSIEST** adj showing exaggerated affection

KIST, **-ED**, **-ING**, **-S** n large wooden chest ▷ vb place in a coffin

KISTFUL **-S**

KISTVAEN n stone tomb

KIT, **-S**, **-TED**, **-TING** n outfit or equipment for a specific purpose ▷ vb fit or provide

KITBAG, **-S** n bag for a soldier's or traveller's belongings

KITCHEN, **-S** n room used for cooking ▷ vb (in archaic usage) provide with food

KITE, **-D**, **-S** n light frame covered with a thin material ▷ vb soar and glide

KITELIKE

KITENGE, **-S** n thick cotton cloth

KITER, **-S** ► kite

KITES ► kite

KITH, **-S** n one's friends and acquaintances

KITHARA, **-S** variant of ► cithara

KITHE, **-D**, **-S**, **KITHING** same as ► kythe

KITHS ► kith

KITING, **-S** ► kite

KITLING, **-S** dialect word for ► kitten

KITS ► kit

KITSCH, **-ES** n art or literature with popular sentimental appeal ▷ n object or art that is tawdry, vulgarized, oversentimental or pretentious

KITSCHY

KITSET, **-S** n New Zealand word for furniture supplied in pieces

KITTED ► kit

KITTEL, **-S** n white garment worn for certain Jewish rituals or burial

KITTEN, **-ED**, **-S** n young cat ▷ vb (of cats) give birth

KITTENY

KITTIES ► kitty

KITTING ► kit

KITTLE, **-D**, **-R**, **-S**, **-ST**, **KITTLING** adj capricious and unpredictable ▷ vb be troublesome or puzzling to (someone)

KITTLIER ► kittly

KITTLING ► kittle

KITTLY, **KITTLIER** Scots word for ► ticklish

KITTUL, **-S** n type of palm from which jaggery sugar comes

KITTY, **KITTIES** n communal fund

KITUL, **-S** same as ► kittul

KIVA, **-S** n large room in a Pueblo Indian village

KIWI, -S n New Zealand flightless bird with a long beak and no tail

KLANG, -S n (in music) kind of tone

KLAP, -PED, -PING, -S vb slap or spank

KLATCH, -ES n gathering, especially over coffee

KLATSCH same as ▸ **klatch**

KLAVERN, -S n local Ku Klux Klan group

KLAVIER, -S same as ▸ **clavier**

KLAXON, -ED, -S n loud horn used on emergency vehicles ▷ vb hoot with a klaxon

KLEAGLE, -S n person with a particular rank in the Ku Klux Klan

KLEENEX n tradename for a kind of tissue

KLEFTIKO n type of Greek lamb dish

KLEPHT, -S n group of Greeks **KLEPHTIC**

KLEPTO, -S n compulsive thief

KLETT, -S n lightweight climbing boot

KLEZMER, -S n Jewish folk musician

KLICK, -S n kilometre

KLIEG, -S n as in **klieg light** intense carbon-arc light

KLIK, -S US military slang word for > **kilometre**

KLINKER, -S n type of brick used in paving

KLIPDAS n rock hyrax

KLISTER, -S n type of ski dressing for improving grip on snow

KLONDIKE same as ▸ **klondyke**

KLONDYKE n rich source of something ▷ vb transfer (bulk loads of fish) to factory ships at sea for processing

KLONG, -S n type of canal in Thailand

KLOOCH, -ES same as > **kloochman**

KLOOF, -S n mountain pass or gorge

KLOOTCH same as > **kloochman**

KLUDGE, -D, -S, KLUDGING n untidy solution ▷ vb cobble something together **KLUDGEY**

KLUDGIER ▸ **kludgy**

KLUDGING ▸ **kludge**

KLUDGY, KLUDGIER ▸ **kludge**

KLUGE, -D, -S, KLUGING same as ▸ **kludge**

KLUTZ, -ES n clumsy or stupid person **KLUTZY KLUTZIER**

KLYSTRON n electron tube for the amplification of microwaves

KNACK, -ING, -S n skilful way of doing something ▷ vb dialect word for crack or snap

KNACKED adj broken or worn out

KNACKER, -S n buyer of old horses for killing ▷ vb exhaust

KNACKERY n slaughterhouse for horses

KNACKIER ▸ **knacky**

KNACKING ▸ **knack**

KNACKISH adj old word meaning cunning or artful

KNACKS ▸ **knack**

KNACKY, KNACKIER adj old or dialect word for cunning or artful

KNAG, -S n knot in wood

KNAGGY, KNAGGIER adj knotty

KNAGS ▸ **knag**

KNAIDEL, -S same as ▸ **kneidel**

KNAP, -PED, -PING, -S n crest of a hill ▷ vb hit, hammer, or chip **KNAPPER -S**

KNAPPLE, -D, -S old word for ▸ **nibble**

KNAPS ▸ **knap**

KNAPSACK n soldier's or traveller's bag worn strapped on the back

KNAPWEED n plant with purplish thistle-like flowers

KNAR, -RING, -S old spelling of ▸ **gnar**

KNARL, -S old spelling of ▸ **gnarl**

KNARLIER ▸ **knarly**

KNARLS ▸ **knarl**

KNARLY, KNARLIER same as ▸ **gnarly**

KNARRED ▸ **knar**

KNARRIER ▸ **knarry**

KNARRING ▸ **knar**

KNARRY, KNARRIER ▸ **knar**

KNARS ▸ **knar**

KNAUR, -S variant form of ▸ **knur**

KNAVE, -S n jack at cards

KNAVERY n dishonest behaviour

KNAVES ▸ **knave**

KNAVISH ▸ **knave**

KNAWE, -S same as ▸ **knawel**

KNAWEL, -S n type of Old World plant

KNAWES ▸ **knawe**

KNEAD, -ED, -ING, -S vb work (dough) into a smooth mixture with the hands **KNEADER -S**

KNEE, -D, -ING, -S n joint between thigh and lower leg ▷ vb strike or push with the knee

KNEECAP, -S nontechnical name for ▸ **patella**

KNEED ▸ **knee**

KNEEHOLE n space for the knees, esp under a desk

KNEEING ▸ **knee**

KNEEJERK adj (of a reply or reaction) automatic and predictable

KNEEL, -ED, -ING, -S, KNELT vb fall or rest on one's knees ▷ n act or position of kneeling **KNEELER -S**

KNEEPAD, -S n protective covering for the knee

KNEEPAN, -S another word for ▸ **patella**

KNEEROOM n space to put one's knees

KNEES ▸ **knee**

KNEESIES n flirtatious touching of knees under table

KNEESOCK n type of sock that comes up to the knee

KNEIDEL, -S n (in Jewish cookery) small dumpling

KNELL, -ED, -ING, -S n sound of a bell, esp at a funeral or death ▷ vb ring a knell

KNELT ▸ **kneel**

KNESSET, -S n parliament or assembly

KNEVELL, -S vb old Scots word meaning beat

KNEW ▸ **know**

KNICKER n woman's or girl's undergarment

KNICKERS pl n woman's or girl's undergarment covering the lower trunk and having legs or legholes

KNICKS pl n knickers

KNIFE, -D, -S, KNIVES n sharp-edged blade with a handle ▷ vb cut or stab with a knife

KNIFEMAN, KNIFEMEN n man who is armed with a knife

KNIFER, -S ▸ **knife**

KNIFES ▸ **knife**

KNIFING, -S ▸ **knife**

KNIGHT, -ED, -S n man who has been given a knighthood ▷ vb award a knighthood to

KNIGHTLY adj of, resembling, or appropriate for a knight

KNIGHTS ▸ **knight**

K

K

KNISH, -ES *n* type of dish
KNIT, -S, -TED, -TING *vb* make (a garment) by interlocking a series of loops in wool or other yarn ▷ *n* fabric made by knitting
KNITBONE *n* comfrey
KNITCH, -ES *dialect word for* ▷ **bundle**
KNITS ▷ **knit**
KNITTED ▷ **knit**
KNITTER, -S ▷ **knit**
KNITTING ▷ **knit**
KNITTLE, -S *n* old word for string or cord
KNITWEAR *n* knitted clothes, such as sweaters
KNIVE, -D, KNIVING *rare variant of* ▷ **knife**
KNIVES ▷ **knife**
KNIVING ▷ **knive**
KNOB, -BED, -BING, -S *n* rounded projection, such as a switch on a radio ▷ *vb* supply with knobs
KNOBBER, -S *n* two-year-old male deer
KNOBBIER ▷ **knobby**
KNOBBING ▷ **knob**
KNOBBLE, -S *n* small knob ▷ *vb* dialect word meaning strike
KNOBBLED *same as* ▷ **knobbly**
KNOBBLES ▷ **knobble**
KNOBBLY *adj* covered with small bumps
KNOBBY, KNOBBIER ▷ **knob**
KNOBLIKE ▷ **knob**
KNOBS ▷ **knob**
KNOCK, -ED, -ING, -S *vb* give a blow or push to ▷ *n* blow or rap
KNOCKER, -S *n* metal fitting for knocking on a door
KNOCKING ▷ **knock**
KNOCKOFF *n* informal word for a cheap, often illegal, copy of something
KNOCKOUT *n* blow that renders an opponent unconscious ▷ *vb* render (someone) unconscious
KNOCKS ▷ **knock**
KNOLL, -ED, -ING, -S *n* small rounded hill ▷ *vb* (in archaic or dialect usage) knell
KNOLLER -S
KNOLLIER ▷ **knolly**
KNOLLING ▷ **knoll**
KNOLLS ▷ **knoll**
KNOLLY, KNOLLIER ▷ **knoll**
KNOP, -S *n* knob, esp an ornamental one
KNOPPED

KNOSP, -S *n* budlike architectural feature
KNOT, -S, -TED, -TING *n* type of fastening ▷ *vb* tie with or into a knot
KNOTHEAD *n* stupid person
KNOTHOLE *n* hole in a piece of wood where a knot has been
KNOTLESS ▷ **knot**
KNOTLIKE ▷ **knot**
KNOTS ▷ **knot**
KNOTTED ▷ **knot**
KNOTTER, -S ▷ **knot**
KNOTTIER ▷ **knotty**
KNOTTILY ▷ **knotty**
KNOTTING ▷ **knot**
KNOTTY, KNOTTIER *adj* full of knots
KNOTWEED *n* type of plant with small flowers and jointed stems
KNOTWORK *n* ornamentation consisting of a mass of intertwined and knotted cords
KNOUT, -ED, -ING, -S *n* stout whip ▷ *vb* whip
KNOW, KNEW, -S *vb* be or feel certain of the truth of (information etc)
KNOWABLE
KNOWE, -S *same as* ▷ **knoll**
KNOWER, -S ▷ **know**
KNOWES ▷ **knowe**
KNOWHOW, -S *n* ingenuity, knack, or skill
KNOWING, -S ▷ **know**
KNOWN, -S *n* fact or something that is known
KNOWS ▷ **know**
KNUB, -S *dialect word for* ▷ **knob**
KNUBBIER ▷ **knubby**
KNUBBLE, -D, -S *vb* dialect word for beat or pound using one's fists
KNUBBLY *adj* having small lumps or protuberances
KNUBBY, KNUBBIER *adj* knub
KNUBS ▷ **knub**
KNUCKLE, -D, -S *n* bone at the finger joint ▷ *vb* rub with the knuckles
KNUCKLER *n* type of pitch in baseball
KNUCKLES ▷ **knuckle**
KNUCKLY ▷ **knuckle**
KNUR, -S *n* knot or protuberance in a tree trunk or in wood
KNURL, -ED, -ING, -S *n* small ridge, often one of a series ▷ *vb* impress with a series of fine ridges or serrations
KNURLIER ▷ **knurly**
KNURLING ▷ **knurl**

KNURLS ▷ **knurl**
KNURLY, KNURLIER *rare word for* ▷ **gnarled**
KNURR, -S *same as* ▷ **knur**
KNURS ▷ **knur**
KNUT, -S *n* dandy
KO *n* (in New Zealand) traditional digging tool
KOA, -S *n* Hawaiian leguminous tree
KOALA, -S *n* tree-dwelling Australian marsupial with dense grey fur
KOAN, -S *n* (in Zen Buddhism) problem that admits no logical solution
KOAS ▷ **koa**
KOB, -S *n* any of several species of antelope
KOBAN, -S *n* old oval-shaped Japanese gold coin
KOBANG, -S *same as* ▷ **koban**
KOBANS ▷ **koban**
KOBO, -S *n* Nigerian monetary unit
KOBOLD, -S *n* mischievous household sprite
KOBOS ▷ **kobo**
KOBS ▷ **kob**
KOCHIA, -S *n* any of several plants whose foliage turns dark red
KOEKOEA, -S *n* long-tailed cuckoo of New Zealand
KOEL, -S *n* any of several parasitic cuckoos
KOFF, -S *n* Dutch masted merchant vessel
KOFTA, -S *n* Indian dish
KOFTGAR, -S *n* (in India) person skilled at inlaying steel with gold
KOFTGARI *n* ornamental Indian metalwork
KOFTGARS ▷ **koftgar**
KOFTWORK *same as* ▷ **koftgari**
KOGAL, -S *n* (in Japan) trendy teenage girl
KOHA, -S *n* gift or donation, esp of cash
KOHANIM ▷ **kohen**
KOHAS ▷ **koha**
KOHEKOHE *n* New Zealand tree with large glossy leaves and reddish wood
KOHEN, KOHANIM *n* member of the Jewish priestly caste
KOHL, -S *n* cosmetic powder
KOHLRABI *n* type of cabbage with an edible stem
KOHLS ▷ **kohl**
KOI, -S *n* any of various ornamental forms of the common carp**

KOINE, -S *n* common language among speakers of different languages

KOIS ► koi

KOJI, -S *n* Japanese steamed rice

KOKA, -S *n* former type of score in judo

KOKAKO, -S *n* type of crow

KOKAM, -S *same as* ► **kokum**

KOKANEE, -S *n* type of freshwater salmon

KOKAS ► koka

KOKER, -S *n* Guyanese sluice

KOKIRI, -S *n* type of rough-skinned New Zealand triggerfish

KOKOBEH *adj* (of certain fruit) having a rough skin

KOKOPU, -S *n* any of several small freshwater fish of New Zealand

KOKOWAI, -S *n* type of clay

KOKRA, -S *n* type of wood

KOKUM, -S *n* tropical tree

KOLA, -S *n as in* **kola nut** caffeine-containing seed used in medicine and soft drinks

KOLACKY *n* sweet bun with a fruit, jam, or nut filling

KOLAS ► kola

KOLBASI, -S *same as* ► **kolbassi**

KOLBASSA *same as* ► **kielbasa**

KOLBASSI *n* type of sausage

KOLHOZ, -ES *same as* ► **kolkhoz**

KOLHOZY ► kolhoz

KOLINSKI *same as* ► **kolinsky**

KOLINSKY *n* Asian mink

KOLKHOS, -Y *same as* ► **kolkhoz**

KOLKHOZ, -Y *n* (formerly) collective farm in the Soviet Union

KOLKOZ, -ES, -Y *same as* ► **kolkhoz**

KOLO, -S *n* Serbian folk dance

KOMATIK, -S *n* type of sledge

KOMBU, -S *n* dark brown seaweed

KOMISSAR *same as* > **commissar**

KOMITAJI *n* rebel or revolutionary

KOMONDOR *n* large powerful dog of an ancient Hungarian breed, originally used for sheep herding

KON, -D, -NING, -S *old word for* ► **know**

KONAKI, -S *same as* ► **koneke**

KONBU, -S *same as* ► **kombu**

KOND ► kon

KONDO, -S *n* (in Uganda) thief or armed robber

KONEKE, -S *n* type of farm vehicle

KONFYT, -S *n* South African fruit preserve

KONGONI *n* E African hartbeest

KONINI, -S *n* edible dark purple berry

KONK, -ED, -ING, -S *same as* ► **conk**

KONNING ► kon

KONS ► kon

KOODOO, -S *same as* ► **kudu**

KOOK, -ED, -ING, -S *n* eccentric person ▷ *vb* dialect word for vanish

KOOKIE *same as* ► **kooky**

KOOKIER ► kooky

KOOKIEST ► kooky

KOOKILY ► kooky

KOOKING ► kook

KOOKS ► kook

KOOKUM, -S *same as* ► **kokum**

KOOKY, KOOKIER, KOOKIEST *adj* crazy, eccentric, or foolish

KOOLAH, -S *old form of* ► **koala**

KOORI, -ES, -S *n* Australian Aborigine

KOP, -S *n* prominent isolated hill or mountain in southern Africa

KOPECK, -S *n* former Russian monetary unit

KOPEK, -S *same as* ► **kopeck**

KOPH, -S *n* 19th letter in the Hebrew alphabet

KOPIYKA, -S, KOPIYOK *n* monetary unit of Ukraine

KOPJE, -S *n* small hill

KOPPA, -S *n* consonantal letter in the Greek alphabet

KOPPIE, -S *same as* ► **kopje**

KOPS ► kop

KOR, -S *n* ancient Hebrew unit of capacity

KORA, -S *n* West African instrument

KORAI ► kore

KORARI, -S *n* native New Zealand flax plant

KORAS ► kora

KORAT, -S *n as in* **korat cat** rare blue-grey breed of cat

KORE, KORAI, -S *n* ancient Greek statue of a young woman wearing clothes

KORERO, -ED, -S *n* talk or discussion ▷ *vb* speak or converse

KORES ► kore

KORFBALL *n* game similar to basketball, in which each team consists of six men and six women

KORIMAKO *another name for* ► **bellbird**

KORKIR, -S *n* variety of lichen used in dyeing

KORMA, -S *n* type of mild Indian dish

KORO, -S *n* elderly Māori man

KOROMIKO *n* flowering New Zealand shrub

KORORA, -S *n* small New Zealand penguin

KOROS ► koro

KOROWAI, -S *n* decorative woven cloak worn by a Māori chief

KORS ► kor

KORU, -S *n* stylized curved pattern used esp in carving

KORUNA, KORUN, -S, KORUNY *n* standard monetary unit of the Czech Republic and Slovakia

KORUS ► koru

KOS, -ES *n* Indian unit of distance

KOSHER, -ED, -S *adj* conforming to Jewish religious law ▷ *n* kosher food ▷ *vb* prepare in accordance with Jewish dietary rules

KOSMOS, -ES *variant form of* ► **cosmos**

KOSS, -ES *same as* ► **kos**

KOTARE, -S *n* small greenish-blue kingfisher

KOTCH, -ED, -ES, -ING *vb* South African slang for vomit

KOTO, -S *n* Japanese stringed instrument

KOTOW, -ED, -ING, -S *same as* ► **kowtow**

KOTOWER -S

KOTTABOS *same as* ► **cottabus**

KOTUKU, -S *n* type of white heron

KOTWAL, -S *n* senior police officer or magistrate in an Indian town

KOULAN, -S *same as* ► **kulan**

KOUMIS, -ES *same as* ► **kumiss**

KOUMISS *same as* ► **kumiss**

KOUMYS, -ES *same as* ► **kumiss**

KOUMYSS *same as* ► **kumiss**

KOUPREY, -S *n* large wild SE Asian ox

KOURA, -S *n* New Zealand freshwater crayfish**

K

KOURBASH same as ► **kurbash**

KOUROS, KOUROI n ancient Greek statue of a young man

KOUSKOUS same as ► **couscous**

KOUSSO, -S n Abyssinian tree

KOW, -S old variant of ► **cow**

> This dialect variant of **cow** scores well for a three-letter word, and can be a good one to form when playing in more than one direction.

KOWHAI, -S n New Zealand tree

KOWS ► **kow**

KOWTOW, -ED, -S vb be servile (towards) ▷ n act of kowtowing

KOWTOWER

KRAAL, -ED, -ING, -S n S African village surrounded by a strong fence ▷ adj denoting or relating to the tribal aspects of the Black African way of life ▷ vb enclose (livestock) in a kraal

KRAB, -S same as ► **karabiner**

KRAFT, -S n strong wrapping paper

KRAI, -S n administrative division of Russia

KRAIT, -S n brightly coloured venomous snake of S and SE Asia

KRAKEN, -S n legendary sea monster

KRAMERIA another name for ► **rhatany**

KRANG, -S n dead whale from which the blubber has been removed

KRANS, -ES n sheer rock face

KRANTZ, -ES same as ► **krans**

KRANZ, -ES same as ► **krans**

KRATER, -S same as ► **crater**

KRAUT, -S n sauerkraut

KRAY, -S same as ► **krai**

KREASOTE same as ► **creosote**

KREATINE same as ► **creatine**

KREEP, -S n lunar substance

KREESE, -D, -S, KREESING same as ► **kris**

KREMLIN, -S n citadel of any Russian city

KRENG, -S same as ► **krang**

KREOSOTE same as ► **creosote**

KREPLACH pl n small filled dough casings usually served in soup

KREPLECH same as ► **kreplach**

KREUTZER n any of various former copper and silver coins of Germany or Austria

KREUZER, -S same as ► **kreutzer**

KREWE, -S n club taking part in New Orleans carnival parade

KRILL, -S n small shrimplike sea creature

KRIMMER, -S n tightly curled light grey fur

KRIS, -ED, -ES, -ING n type of Malayan and Indonesian knife ▷ vb stab or slash with a kris

KROMESKY n croquette consisting of a piece of bacon wrapped round minced meat or fish

KRONA, KRONOR, KRONUR n standard monetary unit of Sweden

KRONE, -N, -R n standard monetary unit of Norway and Denmark

KRONOR ► **krona**

KRONUR ► **krona**

KROON, -I, -S n standard monetary unit of Estonia

KRUBI, -S n aroid plant with an unpleasant smell

KRUBUT, -S same as ► **krubi**

KRULLER, -S variant spelling of ► **cruller**

KRUMHORN variant spelling of ► **crumhorn**

KRUMKAKE n Scandinavian biscuit

KRUMPER, -S ► **krumping**

KRUMPING n type of aggressive dance

KRUNK, -S n style of hip-hop music

KRUNKED same as ► **crunked**

KRUNKS ► **krunk**

KRYOLITE variant spelling of ► **cryolite**

KRYOLITH same as ► **cryolite**

KRYPSIS, KRYPSES n idea that Christ made secret use of his divine attributes

KRYPTON, -S n colourless gas

KRYTRON, -S n type of fast electronic gas-discharge switch

KSAR, -S old form of ► **tsar**

KUBASA, -S same as ► **kielbasa**

KUBIE, -S n Ukrainian roll filled with kielbasa

KUCCHA, -S same as ► **kaccha**

KUCHCHA same as ► **kacha**

KUCHEN, -S n breadlike cake

KUDLIK, -S n Inuit soapstone seal-oil lamp

KUDO variant of ► **kudos**

KUDOS, -ES n fame or credit

KUDU, -S n African antelope with spiral horns

KUDZU, -S n hairy leguminous climbing plant

KUE, -S n name of the letter Q

KUEH n (in Malaysia) any cake of Malay, Chinese, or Indian origin

KUES ► **kue**

KUFI, -S n cap for Muslim man

KUFIYAH, -S same as ► **keffiyeh**

KUGEL, -S n baked pudding in traditional Jewish cooking

KUIA, -S n Māori female elder or elderly woman

KUKRI, -S n heavy, curved knife used by Gurkhas

KUKU, -S n mussel

KULA, -S n ceremonial gift exchange among islanders in the W Pacific

KULAK, -I, -S n (formerly) property-owning Russian peasant

KULAN, -S n Asiatic wild ass

KULAS ► **kula**

KULBASA, -S same as ► **kielbasa**

KULFI, -S n Indian dessert

KULTUR, -S n German civilization

KUMARA, -S n tropical root vegetable with yellow flesh

KUMARI, -S n (in Indian English) maiden

KUMBALOI pl n worry beads

KUMERA, -S same as ► **kumara**

KUMIKUMI same as ► **kamokamo**

KUMIS, -ES same as ► **kumiss**

KUMISS, -ES n drink made from fermented mare's or other milk

KUMITE, -S n freestyle sparring or fighting

KUMKUM, -S n red pigment used by Hindu women to make a mark on the forehead

KUMMEL, -S n German liqueur

KUMQUAT, -S n citrus fruit resembling a tiny orange

KUMYS, -ES same as ► **kumiss**

KUNA, KUNE n standard monetary unit of Croatia

KUNEKUNE n feral pig

KUNJOOS adj (in Indian English) mean or stingy

KUNKAR, **-S** n type of limestone

KUNKUR, **-S** same as ► kunkar

KUNZITE, **-S** n variety of the mineral spodumene

KURBASH vb whip with a hide whip

KURGAN, **-S** n Russian burial mound

KURI, **-S** n mongrel dog

KURRE, **-S** old variant of ► cur

KURSAAL, **-S** n public room at a health resort

KURTA, **-S** n long loose garment

KURTOSIS, **KURTOSES** n measure of the concentration of a distribution around its mean

KURU, **-S** n degenerative disease of the nervous system

> This word for a kind of sickness found in New Guinea can give you something to play when you have two Us to dispose of.

KURUSH, **-ES** n small currency unit of Turkey

KURVEY, **-ED**, **-S** vb (in old South African English) transport goods by ox cart
KURVEYOR

KUSSO, **-S** variant spelling of ► kousso

KUTA, **-S** n (in Indian English) male dog

KUTCH, **-ES** same as ► catechu

KUTCHA adj makeshift or not solid

KUTCHES ► kutch

KUTI, **-S** n (in Indian English) female dog

KUTU, **-S** n body louse

KUVASZ, **-OK** n breed of dog from Hungary

KUZU, **-S** same as ► kudzu

> A Japanese climbing plant, this can be a great word for getting a high score out of a difficult rack.

KVAS, **-ES** same as ► kvass

KVASS, **-ES** n alcoholic drink

KVELL, **-ED**, **-ING**, **-S** vb US word meaning be happy

KVETCH, **-ED**, **-ES** vb complain or grumble
KVETCHER

KVETCHY adj tending to grumble or complain

KWACHA, **-S** n standard monetary unit of Zambia

KWAITO, **-S** n type of South African pop music

KWANZA, **-S** n standard monetary unit of Angola

KWELA, **-S** n type of pop music

KYACK, **-S** n type of pannier

KYAK, **-S** same as ► kayak

KYANG, **-S** same as ► kiang

KYANISE, **-D**, **-S** same as ► kyanize

KYANITE, **-S** n grey, green, or blue mineral
KYANITIC

KYANIZE, **-D**, **-S** vb treat (timber) with corrosive sublimate

KYAR, **-S** same as ► coir

KYAT, **-S** n standard monetary unit of Myanmar

KYBO, **-S** n temporary lavatory used when camping

KYBOSH, **-ED**, **-ES** same as ► kibosh

KYDST ► kythe

KYE, **-S** n Korean fundraising meeting

KYLE, **-S** n narrow strait or channel

KYLICES ► kylix

KYLIE, **-S** n type of boomerang

KYLIKES ► kylix

KYLIN, **-S** n (in Chinese art) mythical animal

KYLIX, **KYLICES**, **KYLIKES**, **-ES** n drinking vessel used in ancient Greece

KYLLOSIS, **KYLLOSES** n club foot

KYLOE, **-S** n breed of beef cattle

KYMOGRAM n image or other visual record created by a kymograph

KYND, **-ED**, **-ING**, **-S** old variant of ► kind

KYNDE, **-S** old variant of ► kind

KYNDED ► kynd

KYNDES ► kynde

KYNDING ► kynd

KYNDS ► kynd

KYNE pl n archaic word for cows

KYOGEN, **-S** n type of Japanese drama

KYPE, **-S** n hook on the lower jaw of a mature male salmon

KYPHOSIS, **KYPHOSES** n backward curvature of the thoracic spine
KYPHOTIC

KYRIE, **-S** n type of prayer

KYRIELLE n verse form of French origin characterized by repeated lines or words

KYRIES ► kyrie

KYTE, **-S** n belly

KYTHE, **KYDST**, **-D**, **-S**, **KYTHING** vb appear

KYU, **-S** n (in judo) one of the five student grades

> This means a novice grade in judo, and its unusual combination of letters makes it a useful word to remember when you have an unpromising set of letters on your rack.

K

LI

L can be a difficult letter to use well, especially when you need to play short words. Just three two-letter words begin with **L**: **la, li** and **lo**. Knowing this will save you valuable time in a game, especially when you are trying to fit words into a crowded board. There aren't very many three-letter words either, but don't forget common words like **lab** (5 points), **law** (6), **lay** (6), **low** (6) and **lye** (6). Try to remember the three-letter words that combine **L** with **X**: **lax, lex, lox** and **lux** (10 points each). These are particularly useful towards the end of a game if you have an **X** but little opportunity to play it. There is also the very useful **luz** for 12 points.

LA, -S n exclamation of surprise or emphasis ▷ n the sixth note of the musical scale

LAAGER, -ED, -S n (in Africa) a camp defended by a circular formation of wagons ▷ vb form (wagons) into a laager

LAARI, -S same as ► lari

LAB, -S n laboratory

LABARUM, LABARA, -S n standard carried in Christian processions

LABDA, -S same as ► lambda

LABDANUM n dark resinous juice obtained from various rockroses

LABDAS ► labda

LABEL, -ED, -ING, -LED, -S n piece of card fixed to an object ▷ vb give a label to

LABELER -S

LABELLA ► labellum

LABELLED ► label

LABELLER ► label

LABELLUM, LABELLA n lip-like part of certain plants

LABELS ► label

LABIA ► labium

LABIAL, -S adj of the lips ▷ n speech sound that involves the lips

LABIALLY

LABIATE, -S n plant with square stems, aromatic leaves, and a two-lipped flower ▷ adj of this family

LABIATED adj having a lip

LABIATES ► labiate

LABILE adj (of a compound) prone to chemical change

LABILITY

LABIS, -ES n cochlear

LABIUM, LABIA n lip or liplike structure

LABLAB, -S n twining leguminous plant

LABOR, -ING, -S same as ► labour

LABORED same as ► laboured

LABORER, -S same as ► labourer

LABORING ► labor

LABORISM same as ► labourism

LABORIST same as ► labourist

LABORITE n adherent of the Labour party

LABORS ► labor

LABOUR, -S n physical work or exertion ▷ vb work hard

LABOURED adj uttered or done with difficulty

LABOURER n person who labours, esp someone doing manual work for wages

LABOURS ► labour

LABRA ► labrum

LABRADOR n large retriever dog with a usu gold or black coat

LABRAL adj of or like a lip

LABRET, -S n piece of bone or shell

LABRID, -S same as ► labroid

LABROID, -S n type of fish ▷ adj of or relating to such fish

LABROSE adj thick-lipped

LABRUM, LABRA, -S n lip or liplike part

LABRUSCA n grape variety

LABRYS, -ES n type of axe

LABS ► lab

LABURNUM n ornamental tree with yellow hanging flowers

LAC, -S same as ► lakh

LACE, -D, -S n delicate fabric ▷ vb fasten with shoelaces, cords, etc

LACEBARK n small evergreen tree

LACED ► lace

LACELESS ► lace

LACELIKE ► lace

LACER, -S ► lace

LACERANT adj painfully distressing

LACERATE vb tear (flesh) ▷ adj having edges that are jagged or torn

LACERS ► lacer

LACERTID n type of lizard

LACES ► lace

LACET, -S n braidwork

LACEWING n any of various neuropterous insects

LACEWOOD n wood of sycamore tree

LACEWORK n work made from lace

LACEY same as ► lacy

LACHES, -ES n unreasonable delay in pursuing a legal remedy

LACIER ► lacy

LACIEST ► lacy

LACILY ► lacy

LACINESS ► lacy

LACING, -S ► lace

LACINIA, -E n narrow fringe on petal

LACK, -ED, -ING, -S n shortage of something needed ▷ vb need

LACKADAY another word for ► alas

LACKED ► **lack**

LACKER, **-ED**, **-S** variant spelling of ► **lacquer**

LACKEY, **-ED**, **-S** n servile follower ▷ vb act as a lackey (to)

LACKING ► **lack**

LACKLAND n fool

LACKS ► **lack**

LACMUS, **-ES** n old form of litmus

LACONIC adj using only a few words, terse

LACONISM n economy of expression

LACQUER, **-S** n hard varnish for wood or metal ▷ vb apply lacquer to

LACQUEY, **-S** same as ► **lackey**

LACRIMAL adj of tears or the glands which produce them ▷ n bone near tear gland

LACROSSE n sport in which teams catch and throw a ball using long sticks with a pouched net

LACRYMAL same as ► **lacrimal**

LACS ► **lac**

LACTAM, **-S** n any of a group of inner amides

LACTARY adj relating to milk

LACTASE, **-S** n any of a group of enzymes that hydrolyse lactose to glucose and galactose

LACTATE, **-D**, **-S** vb secrete milk ▷ n ester or salt of lactic acid

LACTEAL, **-S** adj of or like milk ▷ n any of the lymphatic vessels that convey chyle from the small intestine to the blood

LACTEAN another word for ► **lacteous**

LACTEOUS adj milky

LACTIC adj of or derived from milk

LACTIFIC adj yielding milk

LACTITOL n type of artificial sweetener

LACTONE, **-S** n any of a class of organic compounds **LACTONIC**

LACTOSE, **-S** n white crystalline sugar found in milk

LACUNA, **-E**, **-S** n gap or missing part, esp in a document or series **LACUNAL**

LACUNAR, **-S** n ceiling, soffit, or vault having coffers ▷ adj having a lacuna

LACUNARY ► **lacuna**

LACUNAS ► **lacuna**

LACUNATE ► **lacuna**

LACUNE, **-S** n hiatus

LACUNOSE ► **lacuna**

LACY, **LACIER**, **LACIEST** adj fine, like lace

LAD, **-S** n boy or young man

LADANUM, **-S** same as ► **labdanum**

LADDER, **-ED**, **-S** n frame of two poles connected by horizontal steps for climbing ▷ vb cause to have a line of undone stitches **LADDERY**

LADDIE, **-S** n familiar term for a male, esp a young man

LADDIER ► **laddy**

LADDIES ► **laddie**

LADDIEST ► **laddy**

LADDISH adj behaving in a macho or immature manner

LADDISM, **-S** n laddish attitudes and behaviour

LADDY, **LADDIER**, **LADDIEST** adj laddish

LADE, **-D**, **-S** vb put cargo on board ▷ n watercourse

LADEN, **-ED**, **-ING**, **-S** adj loaded ▷ vb load with cargo

LADER, **-S** ► **lade**

LADES ► **lade**

LADETTE, **-S** n young woman who behaves like a young man

LADHOOD, **-S** ► **lad**

LADIES n women's public toilet

LADIFY, **LADIFIED**, **LADIFIES** same as ► **ladyfy**

LADING, **-S** ► **lade**

LADINO, **-S** n Italian variety of white clover

LADLE, **-D**, **-S**, **LADLING** n long-handled spoon with a large bowl ▷ vb serve out **LADLEFUL**

LADLER, **-S** n person who serves with a ladle

LADLES ► **ladle**

LADLING ► **ladle**

LADRON, **-S** same as ► **ladrone**

LADRONE, **-S** n thief

LADRONS ► **ladron**

LADS ► **lad**

LADY n woman of good breeding or high rank ▷ adj female

LADYBIRD n small red beetle with black spots

LADYBUG, **-S** same as ► **ladybird**

LADYCOW, **-S** another word for ► **ladybird**

LADYFIED ► **ladyfy**

LADYFIES ► **ladyfy**

LADYFISH n type of game fish

LADYFLY another word for ► **ladybird**

LADYFY, **LADYFIED**, **LADYFIES** vb make a lady of (someone)

LADYHOOD ► **lady**

LADYISH ► **lady**

LADYISM, **-S** ► **lady**

LADYKIN, **-S** n endearing form of lady

LADYLIKE adj polite and dignified

LADYLOVE n beloved woman

LADYNESS n state of being a lady

LADYPALM n small palm, grown indoors

LADYSHIP n title of a peeress

LAER, **-ED**, **-ING**, **-S** another word for ► **laager**

LAESIE old form of ► **lazy**

LAETARE, **-S** n fourth Sunday of Lent

LAETRILE n drug used to treat cancer

LAEVO adj on the left

LAEVULIN n polysaccharide occurring in the tubers of certain helianthus plants

LAG, **-GED**, **-S** vb go too slowly, fall behind ▷ n delay between events

LAGAN, **-S** n goods or wreckage on the sea bed

LAGENA, **-S** n bottle with a narrow neck

LAGEND, **-S** same as ► **lagan**

LAGER, **-ED**, **-ING**, **-S** n light-bodied beer ▷ vb ferment into lager

LAGGARD, **-S** n person who lags behind ▷ adj sluggish, slow

LAGGED ► **lag**

LAGGEN, **-S** n spar of a barrel

LAGGER, **-S** n person who lags pipes

LAGGIN, **-S** same as ► **laggen**

LAGGING, **-S** ► **lag**

LAGGINS ► **laggin**

LAGNAPPE same as > **lagniappe**

LAGOON, **-S** n water cut off from the sea by reefs or sand bars **LAGOONAL**

LAGS ► **lag**

LAGUNA, **-S** n lagoon

LAGUNE, **-S** same as ► **lagoon**

LAH, **-S** n (in tonic sol-fa) sixth degree of any major scale

L

LAHAL, -S n game played by native peoples of the Pacific Northwest

LAHAR, -S n landslide of volcanic debris and water

LAHS ► lah

LAIC, -S adj laical ▷ n layman

LAICAL adj secular

LAICALLY ► laic

LAICH, -S n low-lying piece of land

LAICISE, -D, -S same as ► laicize

LAICISM, -S ► laic

LAICITY n state of being laical

LAICIZE, -D, -S vb remove ecclesiastical status from

LAICS ► laic

LAID, -ED, -ING, -S Scots form of ► load

LAIDLY, LAIDLIER adj very ugly

LAIDS ► laid

LAIGH, -ER, -EST, -S adj low-lying ▷ n area of low-lying ground

LAIK, -ED, -ING, -S vb play (a game, etc)

LAIKA, -S n type of small dog

LAIKED ► laik

LAIKER, -S ► laik

LAIKING ► laik

LAIKS ► laik

LAIN ► lie

LAIPSE, -D, -S, LAIPSING vb beat soundly

LAIR, -ED, -ING, -S n resting place of an animal ▷ vb retreat to or rest in a lair

LAIRAGE, -S n accommodation for farm animals

LAIRD, -S n Scottish landowner

LAIRDLY adj pertaining to laird(s)

LAIRDS ► laird

LAIRED ► lair

LAIRIER ► lairy

LAIRIEST ► lairy

LAIRING ► lair

LAIRISE, -D, -S same as ► lairize

LAIRIZE, -D, -S vb show off

LAIRS ► lair

LAIRY, LAIRIER, LAIRIEST adj gaudy or flashy

LAISSE, -S n type of rhyme scheme

LAITANCE n white film forming on drying concrete

LAITH Scots form of ► loath

LAITHLY same as ► laidly

LAITY, LAITIES n non-clergy

LAKE, -D, -S n expanse of water entirely surrounded

by land ▷ vb take time away from work

LAKEBED, -S n bed of lake

LAKED ► lake

LAKEFILL n area of land on a filled lake

LAKEHEAD n shore of a lake farthest from the outlet

LAKELAND n countryside with a lot of lakes

LAKELET, -S n small lake

LAKELIKE ► lake

LAKEPORT n port on lake

LAKER, -S n lake cargo vessel

LAKES ► lake

LAKESIDE n area at edge of lake

LAKEVIEW adj having a view of a lake

LAKEWARD same as > lakewards

LAKH, -S n (in India) 100 000, esp referring to this sum of rupees

LAKIER ► laky

LAKIEST ► laky

LAKIN, -S short form of ► ladykin

LAKING, -S ► lake

LAKINS ► lake

LAKISH adj similar to poetry of Lake poets

LAKSA, -S n (in Malaysia) Chinese dish of rice noodles in curry or hot soup

LAKY, LAKIER, LAKIEST adj of the reddish colour of the pigment lake

LALANG, -S n coarse weedy Malaysian grass

LALDIE, -S n great gusto

LALDY same as ► laldie

LALIQUE, -S n ornamental glass

LALL, -ED, -S vb make bad 'l' or 'r' sounds

LALLAN, -S n literary version of the English spoken in Lowland Scotland

LALLAND, -S same as ► lallan

LALLANS ► lallan

LALLED ► lall

LALLING, -S ► lall

LALLS ► lall

LALLYGAG vb loiter aimlessly

LAM, -MED, -S vb attack vigorously

LAMA, -S n Buddhist priest in Tibet or Mongolia

LAMANTIN another word for ► manatee

LAMAS ► lama

LAMASERY n monastery of lamas

LAMB, -ED, -S n young sheep ▷ vb give birth to a lamb or lambs

LAMBADA, -S n type of Brazilian dance

LAMBAST, -S vb beat or thrash

LAMBASTE same as ► lambast

LAMBASTS ► lambast

LAMBDA, -S n 11th letter of the Greek alphabet

LAMBDOID adj having the shape of the Greek letter lambda

LAMBED ► lamb

LAMBENCY ► lambent

LAMBENT adj (of a flame) flickering softly

LAMBER, -S n person that attends to lambing ewes

LAMBERT, -S n cgs unit of illumination, equal to 1 lumen per square centimetre

LAMBIE, -S same as ► lambkin

LAMBIER ► lamby

LAMBIES ► lambie

LAMBIEST ► lamby

LAMBING, -S n birth of lambs at the end of winter

LAMBKILL n N American dwarf shrub

LAMBKIN, -S n young lamb

LAMBLIKE ► lamb

LAMBLING n small lamb

LAMBOYS n skirt-like piece of armour made from metal strips

LAMBS ► lamb

LAMBSKIN n skin of a lamb, usually with the wool still on, used to make coats, slippers, etc

LAMBY, LAMBIER, LAMBIEST adj lamb-like

LAME, -R, -S, -ST, LAMING adj having an injured or disabled leg or foot ▷ vb make lame ▷ n fabric interwoven with gold or silver threads

LAMED, -S n 12th letter in the Hebrew alphabet

LAMEDH, -S same as ► lamed

LAMEDS ► lamed

LAMELLA, -E, -S n thin layer, plate, etc, like the calcified layers of which bone is formed

LAMELLAR

LAMELY ► lame

LAMENESS ► lame

LAMENT, -S vb feel or express sorrow (for) ▷ n passionate expression of grief

LAMENTED adj grieved for

LAMENTER ► lament
LAMENTS ► lament
LAMER ► lame
LAMES ► lame
LAMEST ► lame
LAMETER, -S *Scots form of* ► lamiger
LAMIA, -E, -S *n* female monster with a snake's body and a woman's head
LAMIGER, -S *n* disabled person
LAMINA, -E, -S *n* thin plate, esp of bone or mineral
LAMINAL, -S *n* consonant articulated with blade of tongue
LAMINAR ► lamina
LAMINARY ► lamina
LAMINAS ► lamina
LAMINATE *vb* make (a sheet of material) by sticking together thin sheets ▷ *n* laminated sheet ▷ *adj* composed of lamina
LAMING ► lame
LAMININ, -S *n* type of protein
LAMINOSE ► lamina
LAMINOUS ► lamina
LAMISH *adj* rather lame
LAMISTER *n* fugitive
LAMITER, -S *same as* ► lameter
LAMMED ► lam
LAMMER, -S *Scots word for* ► amber
LAMMIE *same as* ► lammy
LAMMIES ► lammy
LAMMIGER *same as* ► lamiger
LAMMING, -S ► lam
LAMMY, LAMMIES *n* thick woollen jumper
LAMP, -ED, -S *n* device which produces light from electricity, oil, or gas ▷ *vb* go quickly with long steps
LAMPAD, -S *n* candlestick
LAMPAS, -ES *n* swelling of the mucous membrane of the hard palate of horses
LAMPASSE *same as* ► lampas
LAMPED ► lamp
LAMPER, -S *n* lamprey
LAMPERN, -S *n* migratory European lamprey
LAMPERS ► lamper
LAMPHOLE *n* hole in ground for lowering lamp into sewer
LAMPING, -S ► lamp
LAMPION, -S *n* oil-burning lamp
LAMPLESS *adj* without a lamp
LAMPLIT *adj* lit by lamps

LAMPOON, -S *n* humorous satire ridiculing someone ▷ *vb* satirize or ridicule
LAMPPOST *n* post supporting a lamp in the street
LAMPREY, -S *n* eel-like fish with a round sucking mouth
LAMPS ► lamp
LAMPUKA, -S *same as* ► lampuki
LAMPUKI, -S *n* type of fish
LAMPYRID *n* firefly
LAMS ► lam
LAMSTER, -S *n* fugitive
LANA, -S *n* wood from genipap tree
LANAI, -S *Hawaiian word for* ► veranda
LANAS ► lana
LANATE *adj* having or consisting of a woolly covering of hairs
LANATED *same as* ► lanate
LANCE, -D, -S, LANCING *n* long spear used by a mounted soldier ▷ *vb* pierce (a boil or abscess) with a lancet
LANCEGAY *n* kind of ancient spear
LANCELET *n* type of marine invertebrate
LANCER *n* formerly, cavalry soldier armed with a lance
LANCERS *n* quadrille for eight or sixteen couples
LANCES ► lance
LANCET, -S *n* pointed two-edged surgical knife
LANCETED *adj* having one or more lancet arches or windows
LANCETS ► lancet
LANCH, -ED, -ES, -ING *obsolete form of* ► launch
LANCIERS *pl n* type of dance
LANCING ► lance
LAND *n* solid part of the earth's surface ▷ *vb* come or bring to earth after a flight, jump, or fall
LANDAU, -S *n* four-wheeled carriage with two folding hoods
LANDDROS *n* sheriff
LANDE, -S *n* type of moorland in SW France
LANDED *adj* possessing or consisting of lands
LANDER, -S *n* spacecraft which lands on a planet or other body
LANDES ► lande
LANDFALL *n* ship's first landing after a voyage

LANDFAST *adj* (of ice) attached to the shore
LANDFILL *n* disposing of rubbish by covering it with earth
LANDFORM *n* any natural feature of the earth's surface, such as valleys and mountains
LANDGRAB *n* sudden attempt to establish ownership of something
LANDING, -S *n* floor area at the top of a flight of stairs
LANDLADY *n* woman who owns and leases property
LANDLER, -S *n* Austrian country dance
LANDLESS ► land
LANDLINE *n* telecommunications cable laid over land
LANDLORD *n* person who rents out land, houses, etc
LANDMAN, LANDMEN *n* person who lives and works on land
LANDMARK *n* prominent object in or feature of a landscape
LANDMASS *n* large continuous area of land
LANDMEN ► landman
LANDMINE *n* type of bomb laid on or just under the surface of the ground ▷ *vb* lay (an area) with landmines
LANDRACE *n* white very long-bodied lop-eared breed of pork pig
LANDRAIL *n* type of bird
LANDS *pl n* holdings in land
LANDSIDE *n* part of an airport farthest from the aircraft
LANDSKIP *another word for* > landscape
LANDSLID > landslide
LANDSLIP *same as* > landslide
LANDSMAN, LANDSMEN *n* person who works or lives on land, as distinguished from a seaman
LANDWARD *same as* > landwards
LANDWASH *n* part of the shore between the high-water mark and the sea
LANDWIND *n* wind that comes from the land
LANE, -S *n* narrow road
LANELY *Scots form of* ► lonely
LANES ► lane
LANEWAY, -S *n* lane**

LANG, -EST *Scot word for* ► **long**

LANGAHA, -S *n* type of Madagascan snake

LANGAR, -S *n* dining hall in a gurdwara

LANGER *adj* comparative form of lang

LANGERED *adj* drunk

LANGEST ► **lang**

LANGLAUF *n* cross-country skiing

LANGLEY, -S *n* unit of solar radiation

LANGRAGE *n* shot consisting of scrap iron packed into a case, formerly used in naval warfare

LANGREL, -S *same as* ► **langrage**

LANGSHAN *n* breed of chicken

LANGSPEL *n* type of Scandinavian stringed instrument

LANGSPIL *n* type of Scandinavian stringed instrument

LANGSYNE *adv* long ago ► *n* times long past, esp those fondly remembered

LANGUAGE *n* system of sounds, symbols, etc for communicating thought ► *vb* express in language

LANGUE, -S *n* language considered as an abstract system

LANGUED *adj* having a tongue

LANGUES ► **langue**

LANGUET, -S *n* anything resembling a tongue

LANGUID *adj* lacking energy

LANGUISH *vb* suffer neglect or hardship

LANGUOR, -S *n* dreamy relaxation

LANGUR, -S *n* type of arboreal Old World monkey

LANIARD, -S *same as* ► **lanyard**

LANIARY *adj* adapted for tearing ► *n* tooth adapted for tearing

LANITAL, -S *n* fibre used in production of synthetic wool

LANK, -ED, -ER, -EST, -ING, -S *adj* straight and limp ► *vb* become lank

LANKIER ► **lanky**

LANKIEST ► **lanky**

LANKILY ► **lanky**

LANKING ► **lank**

LANKLY ► **lank**

LANKNESS ► **lank**

LANKS ► **lank**

LANKY, LANKIER, LANKIEST *adj* tall and thin

LANNER, -S *n* large falcon

LANNERET *n* male or tercel of the lanner falcon

LANNERS ► **lanner**

LANOLIN, -S *n* grease from sheep's wool used in ointments etc

LANOLINE *same as* ► **lanolin**

LANOLINS ► **lanolin**

LANOSE *same as* ► **lanate**

LANOSITY

LANT, -S *n* stale urine

LANTANA, -S *n* shrub with orange or yellow flowers

LANTERN, -S *n* light in a transparent protective case ► *vb* supply with a lantern

LANTHORN *archaic word for* ► **lantern**

LANTS ► **lant**

LANTSKIP *another word for* >**landscape**

LANUGO, -S *n* layer of fine hairs, esp the covering of the human fetus before birth

LANX *n* dish; plate

LANYARD, -S *n* neck cord to hold a knife or whistle

LAOGAI, -S *n* forced labour camp in China

LAP, -PED, -S *n* part between the waist and knees when sitting ► *vb* overtake so as to be one or more circuits ahead

LAPBOARD *n* flat board that can be used on the lap as a makeshift table or desk

LAPDOG, -S *n* small pet dog

LAPEL, -S *n* part of the front of a coat or jacket folded back towards the shoulders

LAPELED

LAPELLED

LAPFUL, -S *same as* ► **lap**

LAPHELD *adj* small enough to be used on one's lap

LAPIDARY *adj* of or relating to stones ► *n* person who cuts, polishes, sets, or deals in gemstones

LAPIDATE *vb* pelt with stones

LAPIDES ► **lapis**

LAPIDIFY *vb* change into stone

LAPIDIST *n* cutter and engraver of precious stones

LAPILLUS, LAPILLI *n* small piece of lava thrown from a volcano

LAPIN, -S *n* rabbit fur

LAPIS, LAPIDES, -ES *n as in* **lapis lazuli** brilliant blue mineral gemstone

LAPJE, -S *same as* ► **lappie**

LAPPED ► **lap**

LAPPEL, -S *same as* ► **lapel**

LAPPER, -ED, -S *n* one that laps ► *vb* curdle

LAPPET, -S *n* small hanging flap

LAPPETED

LAPPIE, -S *n* rag

LAPPING, -S ► **lap**

LAPS ► **lap**

LAPSABLE ► **lapse**

LAPSANG, -S *n* Chinese tea

LAPSE, -D, -S, LAPSING *n* temporary drop in a standard ► *vb* drop in standard

LAPSER -S

LAPSIBLE ► **lapse**

LAPSING ► **lapse**

LAPSTONE *n* device used by a cobbler on which leather is beaten

LAPSUS *n* lapse or error

LAPTOP, -S *adj* small enough to fit on a user's lap ► *n* small computer

LAPTRAY, -S *n* tray with a cushioned underside

LAPWING, -S *n* plover with a tuft of feathers on the head

LAPWORK, -S *n* work with lapping edges

LAR, -S *n* boy or young man

LARBOARD *n* port (side of a ship)

LARCENER ► **larceny**

LARCENY *n* theft

LARCH, -ES *n* deciduous coniferous tree

LARCHEN *adj* of larch

LARCHES ► **larch**

LARD, -ED, -ING, -S *n* soft white pig fat ► *vb* insert strips of bacon in before cooking

LARDER, -S *n* storeroom for food

LARDERER *n* person in charge of larder

LARDERS ► **larder**

LARDIER ► **lardy**

LARDIEST ► **lardy**

LARDING ► **lard**

LARDLIKE ► **lard**

LARDON, -S *n* strip or cube of fat or bacon used in larding meat

LARDOON, -S *same as* ► **lardon**

LARDS ► **lard**

LARDY, LARDIER, LARDIEST *adj* fat

LARE, -S *another word for* ► **lore**

LAREE, -S *n* Asian fish-hook

LARES ► **lare**

LARGANDO adv (music) growing slower and more marked

LARGE, -R, -S, -ST adj great in size, number ▷ n formerly, musical note

LARGELY adv principally

LARGEN, -ED, -S another word for ▸ enlarge

LARGER ▸ large

LARGES ▸ large

LARGESS same as ▸ largesse

LARGESSE n generous giving, esp of money

LARGEST ▸ large

LARGISH adj fairly large

LARGO, -S adv in a slow and dignified manner ▷ n performance piece in a slow manner

LARI, -S n monetary unit of Georgia

LARIAT, -ED, -S n lasso ▷ vb tether with lariat

LARIGAN, -S n type of tanned moccasin boot

LARINE adj of, relating to, or resembling a gull

LARIS ▸ lari

LARK, -ED, -ING, -S n small brown songbird ▷ vb frolic

LARKER -S

LARKIER ▸ larky

LARKIEST ▸ larky

LARKING ▸ lark

LARKISH ▸ lark

LARKS ▸ lark

LARKSOME adj mischievous

LARKSPUR n plant with spikes of blue, pink, or white flowers with spurs

LARKY, LARKIER, LARKIEST adj frolicsome

LARMIER, -S n pouch under lower eyelid of deer

LARN, -ED, -ING, -S, -T vb learn

LARNAX, LARNAKES n terracotta coffin

LARNED ▸ larn

LARNEY, LARNIER, LARNIEST adj (of clothes) smart

LARNING ▸ larn

LARNS ▸ larn

LARNT ▸ larn

LAROID adj relating to Larus genus of gull family

LARRIGAN n knee-high oiled leather moccasin boot worn by trappers, etc

LARRIKIN n mischievous or unruly person

LARRUP, -ED, -S vb beat or flog

LARRUPER

LARS ▸ lar

LARUM, -S archaic word for ▸ alarm

LARVA, -E, -S n immature insect

LARVAL

LARVATE adj masked; concealed

LARVATED same as ▸ larvate

LARYNGAL adj laryngeal ▷ n sound articulated in the larynx

LARYNX, LARYNGES, -ES n part of the throat containing the vocal cords

LAS ▸ la

LASAGNA, -S same as ▸ lasagne

LASAGNE, -S n sheet pasta

LASCAR, -S n East Indian seaman

LASE, -D, -S vb to be capable of acting as a laser

LASER, -ED, -ING, -S n device producing a very narrow intense beam of light ▷ vb use a laser on (something), esp as part of medical treatment

LASES ▸ lase

LASH, -ED, -ES, -ING n eyelash ▷ vb hit with a whip

LASHER -S

LASHINGS pl n great amount of

LASHINS variant of ▸ lashings

LASHKAR, -S n troop of Indian men with weapons

LASHLESS adj (of a whip) without a lash

LASING, -S ▸ lase

LASKET, -S n loop at the foot of a sail onto which an extra sail may be fastened

LASQUE, -S n flat-cut diamond

LASS, -ES n girl

LASSI, -S n cold drink made of yoghurt or buttermilk, flavoured with sugar, salt, or spice

LASSIE, -S n little lass

LASSIS ▸ lassi

LASSLORN adj abandoned by a young girl

LASSO, -ED, -ES, -S n rope with a noose ▷ vb catch with a lasso

LASSOCK, -S another word for ▸ lass

LASSOED ▸ lasso

LASSOER, -S ▸ lasso

LASSOES ▸ lasso

LASSOING n act of lassoing

LASSOS ▸ lasso

LASSU, -S n slow part of csárdás folk dance

LASSY n short for molasses

LAST, -ED, -S adv coming at the end or after all others ▷ adj only remaining ▷ n last person or thing ▷ vb continue

LASTAGE, -S n space for storing goods in ship

LASTBORN n last child to be born

LASTED ▸ last

LASTER, -S ▸ last

LASTING, -S adj remaining effective for a long time ▷ n strong durable fabric used for shoe uppers, etc

LASTLY adv at the end or at the last point

LASTS ▸ last

LAT, -I, -S n former coin of Latvia

LATAH, -S n psychological condition

LATAKIA, -S n Turkish tobacco

LATCH, -ED, -ES, -ING n fastening for a door with a bar and lever ▷ vb fasten with a latch

LATCHET, -S n shoe fastening

LATCHING ▸ latch

LATCHKEY n key for an outside door or gate, esp one that lifts a latch

LATE adj after the normal or expected time ▷ adv after the normal or expected time

LATED archaic word for ▸ belated

LATEEN, -S adj of a rig with a triangular sail bent to a yard hoisted to the head of a low mast

LATEENER n lateen-rigged ship

LATEENS ▸ lateen

LATELY adv in recent times

LATEN, -ED, -ING, -S vb become or cause to become late

LATENCE, -S ▸ latent

LATENCY, -S ▸ latent

LATENED ▸ laten

LATENESS ▸ late

LATENING ▸ laten

LATENS ▸ laten

LATENT, -S adj hidden and not yet developed ▷ n fingerprint that is not visible to the eye

LATENTLY

LATER adv afterwards

LATERAD adv towards the side

L

LATERAL, -S adj of or relating to the side or sides ▷ n lateral object, part, passage, or movement ▷ vb pass laterally

LATERISE same as ▶ **laterize**

LATERITE n any of a group of deposits consisting of residual insoluble ferric and aluminium oxides

LATERIZE vb develop into a laterite

LATEST, -S n the most recent news

LATEWAKE n vigil held over a dead body

LATEWOOD n wood formed later in tree's growing season

LATEX, -ES, LATICES n milky fluid found in some plants

LATH, -S n thin strip of wood ▷ vb attach laths to

LATHE, -D, -S n machine for turning wood or metal while it is being shaped ▷ vb shape, bore, or cut a screw thread in or on (a workpiece) on a lathe

LATHEE, -S same as ▶ **lathi**

LATHEN adj covered with laths

LATHER, -ED, -S n froth of soap and water ▷ vb make frothy
LATHERER
LATHERY

LATHES ▶ **lathe**

LATHI, -S n long heavy wooden stick used as a weapon in India

LATHIER ▶ **lathy**

LATHIEST ▶ **lathy**

LATHING, -S ▶ **lathe**

LATHIS ▶ **lathi**

LATHLIKE ▶ **lath**

LATHS ▶ **lath**

LATHWORK n work made of laths

LATHY, LATHIER, LATHIEST adj resembling a lath, esp in being tall and thin

LATHYRUS n genus of climbing plant

LATI ▶ **lat**

LATICES ▶ **latex**

LATIGO, -ES, -S n strap on horse's saddle

LATILLA, -S n stick making up part of ceiling

LATINA, -S n US female of Latin American origin

LATINISE same as ▶ **latinize**

LATINITY n facility in the use of Latin

LATINIZE vb translate into Latin

LATINO, -S n US male of Latin American origin

LATISH adv rather late ▷ adj rather late

LATITANT adj concealed

LATITAT, -S n writ presuming that person accused was hiding

LATITUDE n angular distance measured in degrees N or S of the equator

LATKE, -S n crispy Jewish pancake

LATOSOL, -S n type of deep, well-drained soil

LATRANT adj barking

LATRIA, -S n adoration that may be offered to God alone

LATRINE, -S n toilet in a barracks

LATRON, -S n bandit

LATS ▶ **lat**

LATTE, -S n coffee with hot milk

LATTEN, -S n metal or alloy, esp brass, made in thin sheets

LATTER, -S adj second of two ▷ n second of two people or things

LATTERLY adv recently

LATTERS ▶ **latter**

LATTES ▶ **latte**

LATTICE, -S n framework of intersecting strips of wood ▷ vb adorn with a lattice
LATTICED

LATTIN, -S n brass alloy beaten into a thin sheet

LATU, -S n type of edible Asian seaweed

LAUAN, -S n type of wood used in furniture-making

LAUCH, -ING, -S, LEUCH, LEUCHEN, LEUGH, LEUGHEN Scots form of ▶ **laugh**

LAUD, -ED, -ING vb praise or glorify ▷ n praise or glorification

LAUDABLE adj praiseworthy
LAUDABLY

LAUDANUM n opium-based sedative

LAUDATOR n one who praises highly

LAUDED ▶ **laud**

LAUDER, -S ▶ **laud**

LAUDING ▶ **laud**

LAUDS n traditional morning prayer of the Western Church

LAUF, -S n run in bobsleighing

LAUGH, -ED, -S vb make sounds with the voice expressing amusement ▷ n act of laughing
LAUGHER -S

LAUGHFUL ▶ **laugh**

LAUGHIER ▶ **laughy**

LAUGHING ▶ **laugh**

LAUGHS ▶ **laugh**

LAUGHTER n sound or action of laughing

LAUGHY, LAUGHIER adj laughing a lot

LAUNCE, -D, -S, LAUNCING old form of ▶ **lance**

LAUNCH, -ED, -ES vb put into the water for the first time ▷ n launching

LAUNCHER n device for launching projectiles

LAUNCHES ▶ **launch**

LAUNCING ▶ **launce**

LAUND, -S n open grassy space

LAUNDER, -S vb wash and iron ▷ n water trough

LAUNDRY n clothes for washing

LAUNDS ▶ **laund**

LAURA, -E, -S n group of monastic cells

LAUREATE adj crowned with laurel leaves as a sign of honour ▷ n person honoured with an award for art or science ▷ vb crown with laurel

LAUREL, -ED, -S n glossy-leaved shrub, bay tree ▷ vb crown with laurel

LAURIC adj as in **lauric acid** dodecanoic acid

LAURYL, -S n as in **lauryl alcohol** crystalline solid used to make detergents

LAUWINE, -S n avalanche

LAV, -S short for ▶ **lavatory**

LAVA, -S n molten rock thrown out by volcanoes

LAVABO, -ES, -S n ritual washing of priest's hands at Mass

LAVAFORM n in form of lava

LAVAGE, -S n washing out of a hollow organ

LAVALAVA n draped skirtlike garment worn by Polynesians

LAVALIER n decorative pendant worn on chain

LAVALIKE ▶ **lava**

LAVANDIN n hybrid of two varieties of the lavender plant

LAVAS ▶ **lava**

LAVASH, -ES n Armenian flat bread

LAVATERA n type of plant closely resembling the mallow

LAVATION n act or process of washing

LAVATORY n toilet

LAVE, -D, -S, LAVING archaic word for ► **wash**

LAVEER, -ED, -S vb (in sailing) tack

LAVEMENT n washing with injections of water

LAVENDER n shrub with fragrant flowers ▷ adj bluish-purple

LAVER, -S n priest's waterbasin for ritual ablutions

LAVEROCK Scot and northern English dialect word for ► **skylark**

LAVERS ► laver

LAVES ► lave

LAVING ► lave

LAVISH, -ED, -ES adj prolific ▷ vb give or spend generously

LAVISHER

LAVISHLY

LAVOLT, -ED, -S same as ► lavolta

LAVOLTA, -S n old Italian dance ▷ vb dance the lavolta

LAVOLTED ► lavolt

LAVOLTS ► lavolt

LAVRA, -S same as ► laura

LAVROCK, -S same as ► laverock

LAVS ► lav

LAVVY, LAVVIES n lavatory

LAW, -ED, -ER, -EST, -S n rule binding on a community ▷ vb prosecute ▷ adj (in archaic usage) low

LAWBOOK, -S n book on subject of law

LAWCOURT n court of law

LAWED ► law

LAWER ► law

LAWEST ► law

LAWFARE, -S n use of the law by a country against its enemies

LAWFUL adj allowed by law

LAWFULLY

LAWGIVER n giver of a code of laws

LAWIN, -S n bill or reckoning

LAWINE, -S n avalanche

LAWING, -S same as ► lawin

LAWINS ► lawin

LAWK interj used to show surprise

LAWKS same as ► lawk

LAWLAND, -S same as ► lowland

LAWLESS adj breaking the law

LAWLIKE ► law

LAWMAKER same as ► lawgiver

LAWMAN, LAWMEN n officer of the law

LAWN, -ING, -S n area of tended and mown grass ▷ vb create or make into a lawn

LAWNED adj having a lawn

LAWNIER ► lawny

LAWNIEST ► lawny

LAWNING ► lawn

LAWNS ► lawn

LAWNY, LAWNIER, LAWNIEST ► lawn

LAWS ► law

LAWSUIT, -S n court case

LAWYER, -ED, -S n professional legal expert ▷ vb act as lawyer

LAWYERLY

LAX, -ER, -ES, -EST adj not strict ▷ n laxative

LAXATION n act of making lax or the state of being lax

LAXATIVE adj (medicine) inducing the emptying of the bowels ▷ n medicine that induces the emptying of the bowels

LAXATOR, -S n muscle that loosens body part

LAXER ► lax

LAXES ► lax

LAXEST ► lax

LAXISM, -S ► laxist

LAXIST, -S n lenient or tolerant person

LAXITY, LAXITIES ► lax

LAXLY ► lax

LAXNESS ► lax

LAY, -S vb put in horizontal position

LAYABOUT n lazy person ▷ vb hit out with violent and repeated blows in all directions

LAYAWAY, -S n merchandise reserved for future delivery

LAYBACK, -S n technique for climbing cracks ▷ vb use layback technique

LAYDEEZ pl n jocular spelling of ladies

LAYER, -ED, -S n single thickness of some substance ▷ vb form a layer

LAYERAGE n covering stem or branch with soil to encourage new roots

LAYERED ► layer

LAYERING n act of arranging something in layers

LAYERS ► layer

LAYETTE, -S n clothes for a newborn baby

LAYIN, -S n basketball score

LAYING, -S ► lay

LAYINS ► layin

LAYLOCK, -S old form of ► lilac

LAYMAN, LAYMEN n person who is not a member of the clergy

LAYOFF, -S n act of suspending employees

LAYOUT, -S n arrangement, esp of printing matter

LAYOVER, -S n break in a journey

LAYS ► lay

LAYSHAFT n auxiliary shaft in a gearbox

LAYSTALL n place where waste is deposited

LAYTIME, -S n time allowed for loading cargo

LAYUP, -S n period of incapacity through illness

LAYWOMAN, LAYWOMEN n woman who is not a member of the clergy

LAZAR, -S archaic word for ► leper

LAZARET, -S same as > lazaretto

LAZARS ► lazar

LAZE, -D, -S, LAZING vb be idle or lazy ▷ n time spent lazing

LAZIED ► lazy

LAZIER ► lazy

LAZIES ► lazy

LAZIEST ► lazy

LAZILY ► lazy

LAZINESS ► lazy

LAZING ► laze

LAZO, -ED, -ES, -ING, -S another word for ► lasso

LAZULI, -S n lapis lazuli

LAZULITE n blue mineral

LAZURITE n rare blue mineral consisting of a sodium-calcium-aluminium silicate

LAZY, LAZIED, LAZIER, LAZIES, LAZIEST, -ING vb laze ▷ adj not inclined to work or exert oneself

LAZYISH

LAZZO, LAZZI n comic routine in the commedia dell'arte

LEA, -S n meadow

LEACH, -ED, -ES, -ING vb remove by passing a liquid through ▷ n act or process of leaching

LEACHATE n water that carries salts dissolved out of materials through which it has percolated

LEACHED ► leach

LEACHER, -S ► leach

LEACHES ► leach

LEACHIER ► leachy

LEACHING ► leach

LEACHY, LEACHIER adj porous

LEAD, -S, LED vb guide or conduct ▷ n first or most prominent place ▷ adj acting as a leader or lead

LEADABLE n able to be led

LEADED adj (of windows) made from many small panes of glass held together by lead strips

LEADEN, -ED, -S adj heavy or sluggish ▷ vb become or cause to become leaden

LEADENLY

LEADER, -S n person who leads

LEADIER ▶ leady

LEADIEST ▶ leady

LEADING, -S ▶ lead

LEADLESS adj without lead

LEADMAN, LEADMEN n man who leads

LEADOFF, -S n initial move

LEADS ▶ lead

LEADSMAN, LEADSMEN n sailor who takes soundings with a lead line

LEADWORK n maintenance work involving lead pipes, etc

LEADWORT n type of tropical or subtropical shrub with red, blue, or white flowers

LEADY, LEADIER, LEADIEST adj like lead

LEAF, -ED, -ING, -S, LEAVES n flat usu green blade attached to the stem of a plant ▷ vb turn (pages) cursorily

LEAFAGE, -S n leaves of plants

LEAFBUD, -S n bud producing leaves rather than flowers

LEAFED ▶ leaf

LEAFERY n foliage

LEAFIER ▶ leafy

LEAFIEST ▶ leafy

LEAFING ▶ leaf

LEAFLESS ▶ leaf

LEAFLET, -S n sheet of printed matter for distribution ▷ vb distribute leaflets (to)

LEAFLIKE ▶ leaf

LEAFMOLD n fungus on decayed leaves

LEAFROLL n viral disease of potatoes

LEAFS ▶ leaf

LEAFWORM n cotton plant pest

LEAFY, LEAFIER, LEAFIEST adj covered with leaves

LEAGUE, -D, -S, LEAGUING n association promoting the interests of its members

LEAGUER, -S vb harass; beset ▷ n encampment, esp of besiegers

LEAGUES ▶ league

LEAGUING ▶ league

LEAK, -ED, -ING, -S n hole or defect that allows the escape or entrance of liquid, gas, radiation, etc ▷ vb let liquid etc in or out

LEAKAGE, -S n act or instance of leaking

LEAKED ▶ leak

LEAKER, -S ▶ leak

LEAKIER ▶ leaky

LEAKIEST ▶ leaky

LEAKILY ▶ leaky

LEAKING ▶ leak

LEAKLESS ▶ leak

LEAKS ▶ leak

LEAKY, LEAKIER, LEAKIEST adj leaking

LEAL, -ER, -EST adj loyal

LEALLY

LEALTY LEALTIES

LEAM, -ED, -ING, -S vb shine

LEAN, -ED, -EST, -S, -T vb rest (against) ▷ adj thin but healthy-looking ▷ n lean part of meat

LEANER -S

LEANING, -S ▶ lean

LEANLY ▶ lean

LEANNESS ▶ lean

LEANS ▶ lean

LEANT ▶ lean

LEANY old form of ▶ lean

LEAP, -ED, -ING, -S, -T, LEPT vb make a sudden powerful jump ▷ n sudden powerful jump

LEAPER -S

LEAPFROG n game in which a player vaults over another bending down ▷ vb play leapfrog

LEAPING ▶ leap

LEAPROUS old form of ▶ leprous

LEAPS ▶ leap

LEAPT ▶ leap

LEAR, -ED, -ING, -S vb instruct

LEARE, -S same as ▶ lear

LEARED ▶ lear

LEARES ▶ leare

LEARIER ▶ leary

LEARIEST ▶ leary

LEARING ▶ lear

LEARN, -ED, -ING, -S, -T vb gain skill or knowledge by study, practice, or teaching

LEARNER, -S n someone who is learning something

LEARNING ▶ learn

LEARNS ▶ learn

LEARNT ▶ learn

LEARS ▶ lear

LEARY, LEARIER, LEARIEST same as ▶ leery

LEAS ▶ lea

LEASABLE ▶ lease

LEASE, -D, -S n contract by which land or property is rented for a stated time ▷ vb let or rent by lease

LEASER -S

LEASH, -ED, -ES, -ING n lead for a dog ▷ vb control by a leash

LEASING, -S ▶ lease

LEASOW, -ED, -S vb pasture

LEASOWE, -S same as ▶ leasow

LEASOWED ▶ leasow

LEASOWES ▶ leasowe

LEASOWS ▶ leasow

LEAST, -S n smallest amount ▷ adj smallest ▷ n smallest one ▷ adv in the smallest degree

LEASURE, -S old form of ▶ leisure

LEAT, -S n trench or ditch that conveys water to a mill wheel

LEATHER, -S n material made from treated animal skins ▷ adj of leather ▷ vb beat or thrash

LEATHERN adj made of or resembling leather

LEATHERS ▶ leather

LEATHERY adj like leather, tough

LEATS ▶ leat

LEAVE, LEAVING vb go away from ▷ n permission to be absent

LEAVED adj with leaves

LEAVEN, -ED, -S n substance that causes dough to rise ▷ vb raise with leaven

LEAVENER n person or thing that leavens

LEAVENS ▶ leaven

LEAVER, -S ▶ leave

LEAVES ▶ leaf

LEAVIER ▶ leavy

LEAVIEST ▶ leavy

LEAVING ▶ leave

LEAVINGS pl n something remaining, such as refuse

LEAVY, LEAVIER, LEAVIEST same as ▶ leafy

LEAZE, -S same as ▶ lease

LEBBEK, -S n type of timber tree

LEBEN, -S n semiliquid food made from curdled milk

LECANORA n type of lichen

LECCY, LECCIES n electricity

LECHAIM, -S interj drinking toast ▷ n drink for a toast

LECHAYIM same as ► **lechaim**

LECHWE, -S n African antelope

LECITHIN n yellow-brown compound found in plant and animal tissues

LECTERN, -S n reading desk

LECTIN, -S n type of protein

LECTION, -S n variant reading of a passage in a text

LECTOR, -S n university lecturer

LECTRESS n female reader

LECTURE, -D, -S n informative talk ▷ vb give a talk

LECTURER n person who lectures, esp in a university or college

LECTURES ► **lecture**

LECTURN, -S old form of ► **lectern**

LECYTHI ► **lecythus**

LECYTHIS n genus of very tall trees

LECYTHUS, LECYTHI n (in ancient Greece) a vase with a narrow neck

LED ► **lead**

LEDDEN, -S n language; speech

LEDE, -S n introductory part of a news story

LEDGE, -S n narrow shelf

LEDGED

LEDGER, -ED, -S n book of debit and credit accounts ▷ vb fish using a wire trace while the bait floats freely and the weight sinks

LEDGES ► **ledge**

LEDGY, LEDGIER, LEDGIEST ► **ledge**

LEDUM, -S n evergreen shrub

LEE, -D, -ING n sheltered side ▷ vb (Scots) lie

LEEAR, -S Scots form of ► **liar**

LEEBOARD n board lowered along the lee side of a vessel to reduce drift

LEECH, -ED, -ES, -ING n bloodsucking worm ▷ vb use leeches to suck the blood of

LEECHDOM n remedy

LEECHED ► **leech**

LEECHEE, -S same as ► **litchi**

LEECHES ► **leech**

LEECHING ► **leech**

LEED ► **lee**

LEEING ► **lee**

LEEK, -S n vegetable with a long bulb and thick stem

LEEP, -ED, -ING, -S vb boil; scald

LEER, -ED, -S vb look or grin at in a sneering manner ▷ n sneering look or grin

LEERIER ► **leery**

LEERIEST ► **leery**

LEERILY ► **leery**

LEERING, -S ► **leer**

LEERS ► **leer**

LEERY, LEERIER, LEERIEST adj suspicious or wary (of)

LEES pl n sediment of wine

LEESE, -S, LEESING old form of ► **loose**

LEET, -S n shortlist

LEETLE form of ► **little**

LEETS ► **leet**

LEEWARD n lee side ▷ adv towards this side ▷ adj towards where the wind blows

LEEWARDS adv towards the lee side

LEEWAY, -S n room for free movement within limits

LEEZE adj as in **leeze me** Scots for lief is me, an expression of affection

LEFT, -ER, -EST, -S adj on the opposite side from right ▷ n left side

LEFTE old past tense of ► **lift**

LEFTER ► **left**

LEFTEST ► **left**

LEFTIE same as ► **lefty**

LEFTIES ► **lefty**

LEFTISH ► **left**

LEFTISM, -S ► **leftist**

LEFTIST, -S adj of the political left ▷ n supporter of the political left

LEFTMOST ► **left**

LEFTOVER n unused portion of food or material ▷ adj left as an unused portion

LEFTS ► **left**

LEFTWARD same as > **leftwards**

LEFTWING adj of or relating to the leftist faction of a party, etc

LEFTY, LEFTIES n left-winger

LEG, -GED, -S n limb on which a person or animal walks, runs, or stands

LEGACY, LEGACIES n thing left in a will

LEGAL, -S adj established or permitted by law ▷ n legal expert

LEGALESE n conventional language in which legal documents are written

LEGALISE same as ► **legalize**

LEGALISM n strict adherence to the letter of the law

LEGALIST

LEGALITY n state or quality of being legal or lawful

LEGALIZE vb make legal

LEGALLY ► **legal**

LEGALS ► **legal**

LEGATARY n legatee

LEGATE, -D, -S, LEGATING n messenger or representative, esp from the Pope ▷ vb leave as legacy

LEGATEE, -S n recipient of a legacy

LEGATES ► **legate**

LEGATINE ► **legate**

LEGATING ► **legate**

LEGATION n diplomatic minister and his or her staff

LEGATO, -S adv smoothly ▷ n playing with no gaps between notes

LEGATOR, -S n person who gives a legacy or makes a bequest

LEGATOS ► **legato**

LEGEND, -S n traditional story

LEGENDRY

LEGER, -ING, -S variant of ► **ledger**

LEGERITY n agility

LEGERS ► **leger**

LEGES ► **lex**

LEGGE, -S vb lighten or lessen

LEGGED ► **leg**

LEGGER, -S n man who moves barge through tunnel using legs

LEGGES ► **legge**

LEGGIE, -S n leg spin bowler

LEGGIER ► **leggy**

LEGGIERO adj light; delicate

LEGGIES ► **leggie**

LEGGIEST ► **leggy**

LEGGIN, -S same as ► **legging**

LEGGING, -S n extra outer covering for the lower leg

LEGGINS ► **leggin**

LEGGISM, -S n blacklegging

LEGGO sentence substitute let go!

LEGGY, LEGGIER, LEGGIEST adj having long legs

LEGHOLD, -S n type of animal trap that clamps down on the animal's leg

LEGHORN, -S n Italian wheat straw woven into hats

LEGIBLE adj easily read

LEGIBLY

LEGION, -S n large military force ▷ adj very large or numerous

LEGIONED adj arranged in legions

LEGIONS ► **legion**

LEGIST, -S n legal mind

L

LEGIT, -S *n* legitimate drama ▷ *adj* legitimate

LEGITIM, -S *n* inheritance due to children from father

LEGITS ► legit

LEGLAN, -S *same as* ► leglin

LEGLEN, -S *same as* ► leglin

LEGLESS *adj* without legs

LEGLET, -S *n* leg jewellery

LEGLIKE ► leg

LEGLIN, -S *n* milk-pail

LEGMAN, LEGMEN *n* newsman who reports from the scene

LEGONG, -S *n* Indonesian dance

LEGROOM, -S *n* space to put one's legs

LEGS ► leg

LEGSIDE, -S *n* part of a cricket field to the left of a right-handed batsman as he faces the bowler

LEGUAAN, -S *n* S African lizard

LEGUAN, -S *same as* ► leguaan

LEGUME, -S *n* pod of a plant of the pea or bean family

LEGUMIN, -S *n* protein from leguminous plants

LEGWEAR, -S *n* clothing for legs

LEGWORK, -S *n* work that involves travelling on foot or as if on foot

LEHAIM, -S *same as* ► lechaim

LEHAYIM, -S *same as* ► lehaim

LEHR, -S *n* long tunnel-shaped oven used for annealing glass

LEHUA, -S *n* flower of Hawaii

LEI, -S *n* Hawaiian garland

LEIDGER, -S *same as* ► ledger

LEIGER, -S *same as* ► ledger

LEIPOA, -S *n* Australian bird

LEIR, -ED, -ING, -S *same as* ► lear

LEIS ► lei

LEISH, -ER, -EST *adj* agile

LEISLER, -S *n* small bat

LEISTER, -S *n* pronged fishing spear ▷ *vb* spear with a leister

LEISURE, -D, -S *n* time for relaxation or hobbies ▷ *vb* have leisure

LEK, -KED, -S, -U *n* bird display area ▷ *vb* gather at lek

LEKE old form of ► leak

LEKGOTLA *n* meeting place for village assemblies, court cases, and meetings of village leaders

LEKKED ► lek

LEKKER *adj* attractive or nice

LEKKING, -S ► lek

LEKS ► lek

LEKU ► lek

LEKVAR, -S *n* prune or apricot pie filling

LEKYTHOS, LEKYTHI, LEKYTHOI *n* Greek flask

LEKYTHUS *same as* ► lekythos

LEMAN, -S *n* beloved

LEME, -D, -S, LEMING *same as* ► leam

LEMEL, -S *n* metal filings

LEMES ► leme

LEMING ► leme

LEMMA, -S, -TA *n* word in its citation form

LEMME *vb* (short for) let me

LEMMING, -S *n* rodent of arctic regions

LEMNISCI > lemniscus

LEMON, -ED, -ING, -S *n* yellow oval fruit ▷ *adj* pale-yellow ▷ *vb* flavour with lemon

LEMONADE *n* lemon-flavoured soft drink, often fizzy

LEMONED ► lemon

LEMONIER ► lemony

LEMONING ► lemon

LEMONISH ► lemon

LEMONS ► lemon

LEMONY, LEMONIER *adj* like a lemon

LEMPIRA, -S *n* monetary unit of Honduras

LEMUR, -S *n* animal like a small monkey

LEMURES *pl n* spirits of the dead

LEMURIAN *same as* ► lemuroid

LEMURINE *same as* ► lemuroid

LEMUROID *adj* relating to the superfamily which includes the lemurs ▷ *n* animal that resembles or is closely related to a lemur

LEMURS ► lemur

LEND, -S, LENT *vb* give temporary use of

LENDABLE

LENDER -S

LENDING, -S ► lend

LENDS ► lend

LENES ► lenis

LENG, -ED, -ER, -EST, -ING, -S *vb* linger ▷ *adj* long

LENGTH, -S *n* extent or measurement from end to end

LENGTHEN *vb* make or become longer

LENGTHS ► length

LENGTHY *adj* very long

LENIENCE ► lenient

LENIENCY ► lenient

LENIENT, -S *adj* tolerant, not strict or severe ▷ *n* lenient person

LENIFY, LENIFIED, LENIFIES *vb* make lenient

LENIS, LENES *adj* pronounced with little muscular tension ▷ *n* consonant like this

LENITE, -D, -S, LENITING *vb* undergo lenition

LENITIES ► lenity

LENITING ► lenite

LENITION *n* weakening of consonant sound

LENITIVE *adj* soothing or alleviating of pain or distress ▷ *n* lenitive drug

LENITY, LENITIES *n* mercy or clemency

LENO, -S *n* weave in which the warp yarns are twisted in pairs between the weft

LENS, -ES *n* piece of glass or similar material with one or both sides curved

LENSE *same as* ► lens

LENSED *adj* incorporating a lens

LENSES ► lens

LENSING, -S *n* materials which colour and diffuse light

LENSLESS ► lens

LENSMAN, LENSMEN *n* camera operator

LENT ► lend

LENTANDO *adv* slowing down

LENTEN *adj* of or relating to Lent

LENTI ► lento

LENTIC *adj* of, relating to, or inhabiting still water

LENTICEL *n* any of numerous pores in the stem of a woody plant

LENTICLE *n* lens-shaped layer of mineral or rock embedded in a matrix of different constitution

LENTIGO *technical name for a* ► freckle

LENTIL, -S *n* edible seed

LENTISC, -S *same as* ► lentisk

LENTISK, -S *n* mastic tree

LENTO, LENTI, -S *adv* slowly ▷ *n* movement or passage performed slowly

LENTOID, -S *adj* lentiform ▷ *n* lentiform object

LENTOR, -S *n* lethargy

LENTOS ► lento

LENTOUS *adj* lethargic

LENVOY, -S *another word for* ► envoy

LEONE, -S *n* monetary unit of Sierra Leone

LEONINE *adj* like a lion

LEOPARD, -S *n* large spotted animal of the cat family

LEOTARD, -S *n* tight-fitting garment covering the upper body

LEP, -PED, -PING, -S *dialect word for* ► **leap**

LEPER, -S *n* person with leprosy

LEPID *adj* amusing

LEPIDOTE *adj* covered with scales, scaly leaves, or spots ▷ *n* lepidote person, creature, or thing

LEPORID, -S *adj* of the family of mammals including rabbits and hares ▷ *n* any animal belonging to this family

LEPORINE *adj* of, relating to, or resembling a hare

LEPPED ► **lep**

LEPPING ► **lep**

LEPRA, -S *n* leprosy

LEPROSE *adj* having or denoting a whitish scurfy surface

LEPROSY *n* disease attacking the nerves and skin

LEPROTIC *adj* relating to leprosy

LEPROUS *adj* having leprosy

LEPS ► **lep**

LEPT ► **leap**

LEPTA ► **lepton**

LEPTIN, -S *n* protein that regulates the amount of fat in the body

LEPTOME, -S *n* tissue of plant conducting food

LEPTON, LEPTA, -S *n* any of a group of elementary particles with weak interactions

LEPTONIC

LEQUEAR, -S *same as* ► **lacunar**

LERE, -D, -S, LERING *same as* ► **lear**

LERNAEAN *adj* relating to Lerna, the swamp in which dwelt the Hydra

LERP, -S *n* crystallized honeydew

LESBIAN, -S *n* homosexual woman ▷ *adj* of homosexual women

LESBIC *adj* relating to lesbians

LESION, -ED, -S *n* change in an organ of the body caused by injury ▷ *vb* cause lesions

LESS, -ES *n* smaller amount ▷ *adj* smaller in extent, degree, or duration ▷ *pron*

smaller part or quantity ▷ *adv* smaller extent or degree ▷ *prep* after deducting, minus

LESSEE, -S *n* person to whom a lease is granted

LESSEN, -ED, -S *vb* make or become smaller or not as much

LESSER *adj* not as great in quantity, size, or worth

LESSES ► **less**

LESSON, -ED, -S *n* class or single period of instruction in a subject ▷ *vb* censure or punish

LESSOR, -S *n* person who grants a lease of property

LEST, -ED, -ING, -S *conj* so as to prevent any possibility that ▷ *vb* listen

LESULA, -S *n* species of monkey inhabiting forests in DR Congo

LET, -S, -TED, LUITEN *n* act of letting property ▷ *vb* obstruct

LETCH, -ED, -ES, -ING *same as* ► **lech**

LETDOWN, -S *n* disappointment

LETHAL, -S *adj* deadly ▷ *n* weapon, etc capable of causing death

LETHALLY

LETHARGY *n* sluggishness or dullness

LETHE, -S *n* forgetfulness

LETHEAN

LETHEE, -S *n* life-blood

LETHES ► **lethe**

LETHIED *adj* forgetful

LETOUT, -S *n* circumstance that serves as an excuse not to do something

LETS ► **let**

LETTABLE ► **let**

LETTED ► **let**

LETTER *n* written message ▷ *vb* put letters on

LETTERED *adj* learned

LETTERER ► **letter**

LETTERN, -S *another word for* ► **lectern**

LETTERS *pl n* literary knowledge

LETTING, -S ► **let**

LETTRE, -S *n* letter

LETTUCE, -S *n* plant with large green leaves used in salads

LETUP, -S *n* lessening or abatement

LEU *n* monetary unit of Romania

LEUCEMIA *same as* ► **leukaemia**

LEUCEMIC *adj* of or like leucemia

LEUCH ► **lauch**

LEUCHEN ► **lauch**

LEUCIN, -S *same as* ► **leucine**

LEUCINE, -S *n* essential amino acid

LEUCINS ► **leucin**

LEUCITE, -S *n* grey or white mineral

LEUCITIC

LEUCO *n* as in **leuco base** colourless compound

LEUCOMA, -S *n* white opaque scar of the cornea

LEUCON, -S *n* type of sponge

LEUCOSES ► **leucosis**

LEUCOSIN *n* albumin in cereal grains

LEUCOSIS, LEUCOSES *same as* > **leukaemia**

LEUCOTIC *adj* of or relating to leucosis

LEUD, -ES, -S *Scots word for* ► **breadth**

LEUGH ► **lauch**

LEUGHEN ► **lauch**

LEUKEMIA *same as* > **leukaemia**

LEUKEMIC

LEUKOMA, -S *same as* ► **leucoma**

LEUKON, -S *n* white blood cell count

LEUKOSIS, LEUKOSES *n* abnormal growth of white blood cells

LEUKOTIC

LEV, -A, -S *n* monetary unit of Bulgaria

LEVANT, -ED, -S *n* leather made from the skins of goats, sheep, or seals ▷ *vb* bolt or abscond

LEVANTER *n* easterly wind in the W Mediterranean area, esp in the late summer

LEVANTS ► **levant**

LEVATOR, -S *n* muscle that raises a part of the body

LEVE, -S *adj* darling ▷ *adv* gladly

LEVEE, -D, -ING, -S *n* natural or artificial river embankment ▷ *vb* go to the reception of

LEVEL, -ED, -ING, -LED, -S *adj* horizontal ▷ *vb* make even or horizontal ▷ *n* horizontal line or surface

LEVELER, -S *same as* ► **leveller**

LEVELING ► **level**

LEVELLED ► **level**

LEVELLER *n* person or thing that levels

LEVELLY ► level

LEVELS ► level

LEVER, -ED, -ING, -S n handle used to operate machinery ▷ vb prise or move with a lever

LEVERAGE n action or power of a lever ▷ vb borrow capital required

LEVERED ► lever

LEVERET, -S n young hare

LEVERING ► lever

LEVERS ► lever

LEVES ► leve

LEVIABLE adj (of taxes, tariffs, etc) liable to be levied

LEVIED ► levy

LEVIER, -S ► levy

LEVIES ► levy

LEVIGATE vb grind into a fine powder or a smooth paste ▷ adj having a smooth polished surface

LEVIN, -S archaic word for > lightning

LEVIRATE n practice, required by Old Testament law, of marrying the widow of one's brother

LEVIS n jeans

LEVITATE vb rise or cause to rise into the air

LEVITE, -S n Christian clergyman

LEVITIC

LEVITY, LEVITIES n fickleness

LEVO adj anticlockwise

LEVODOPA n substance occurring naturally in the body and used to treat Parkinson's disease

LEVOGYRE n counterclockwise spiral

LEVS ► lev

LEVULIN, -S n substance obtained from certain bulbs

LEVULOSE n fructose

LEVY, LEVIED, LEVIES, -ING vb impose and collect (a tax) ▷ n imposition or collection of taxes

LEW adj tepid

LEWDSBY another word for ► lewdster

LEWDSTER n lewd person

LEWIS, -ES n lifting device for heavy stone or concrete blocks

LEWISIA, -S n type of herb

LEWISITE n colourless oily poisonous liquid

LEWISSON same as ► lewis

LEX, LEGES, -ES n system or body of laws

LEXEME, -S n minimal meaning ful unit of language

LEXEMIC

LEXES ► lex

LEXICA ► lexicon

LEXICAL adj relating to the vocabulary of a language

LEXICON, LEXICA, -S n dictionary

LEXIGRAM n figure or symbol that represents a word

LEXIS, -ES n totality of vocabulary in a language

LEY, -S n land under grass

LEYLANDI same as > leylandii

LEYS ► ley

LI n Chinese measurement of distance

LIABLE adj legally obliged or responsible

LIAISE, -D, -S, LIAISING vb establish and maintain communication

LIAISON, -S n communication and contact between groups

LIANA, -S n climbing plant

LIANE, -S same as ► liana

LIANG, -S n Chinese unit of weight

LIANOID ► liana

LIAR, -S n person who tells lies

LIARD, -S adj grey ▷ n former small coin

LIARS ► liar

LIART Scots form of ► liard

LIAS, -ES n lowest series of rocks of the Jurassic system

LIASSIC adj relating to the earliest epoch of the Jurassic period

LIATRIS n North American plant with white flowers

LIB, -BED, -BING, -S n informal word for liberation ▷ vb geld

LIBANT adj touching lightly

LIBATE, -D, -S, LIBATING vb offer as gift to the gods

LIBATION n drink poured as an offering to the gods

LIBATORY ► libate

LIBBARD, -S another word for ► leopard

LIBBED ► lib

LIBBER, -S n liberationist

LIBBING ► lib

LIBECCIO n strong westerly or southwesterly wind blowing onto the W coast of Corsica

LIBEL, -ED, -ING, -LED, -S n published statement falsely damaging a person's reputation ▷ vb falsely damage the reputation of

LIBELANT same as > libellant

LIBELED ► libel

LIBELEE, -S same as ► libellee

LIBELER, -S ► libel

LIBELING ► libel

LIBELIST ► libel

LIBELLED ► libel

LIBELLEE n person against whom a libel has been filed in an ecclesiastical court

LIBELLER ► libel

LIBELOUS ► libel

LIBELS ► libel

LIBER, -S, LIBRI n tome or book

LIBERAL, -S adj having social and political views that favour progress and reform ▷ n person with such views

LIBERATE vb set free

LIBERO, -S another name for ► sweeper

LIBERS ► liber

LIBERTY n freedom

LIBIDO, -S n psychic energy

LIBKEN, -S n lodging

LIBLAB, -S n 19th century British liberal

LIBRA, -E, -S n ancient Roman unit of weight

LIBRAIRE n bookseller

LIBRARY n room or building where books are kept

LIBRAS ► libra

LIBRATE, -D, -S vb oscillate or waver

LIBRETTO, LIBRETTI n words of an opera

LIBRI ► liber

LIBS ► lib

LICE ► louse

LICENCE, -D, -S n document giving official permission ▷ vb (in the US) give permission to

LICENCEE same as ► licensee

LICENCER ► licence

LICENCES ► licence

LICENSE, -D, -S vb grant or give a licence for

LICENSEE n holder of a licence

LICENSER ► license

LICENSES ► license

LICENSOR ► license

LICENTE adj permitted; allowed

LICH, -ES n dead body

LICHANOS n note played using forefinger

LICHEE, -S same as ► litchi

LICHEN, -S n small flowerless plant forming a crust on rocks, trees, etc ▷ vb cover with lichen

LICHENED

LICHENIN n complex polysaccharide occurring in certain species of moss

LICHENS ► lichen
LICHES ► lich
LICHGATE n roofed gate to a churchyard
LICHI, -S same as ► litchi
LICHT, -ED, -ER, -EST, -ING, -S Scot word for ► light
LICHTLY vb treat discourteously
LICHTS ► licht
LICHWAKE n night vigil over a dead body
LICHWAY, -S n path used to carry coffin into church
LICIT adj lawful, permitted
LICITLY
LICK, -ED, -S vb pass the tongue over ► n licking
LICKER -S
LICKING, -S n beating
LICKS ► lick
LICKSPIT n flattering or servile person
LICORICE same as > liquorice
LICTOR, -S n one of a group of ancient Roman officials
LID, -S n movable cover
LIDAR, -S n radar-type instrument
LIDDED ► lid
LIDDING, -S n lids
LIDGER, -S variant form of ► ledger
LIDLESS adj having no lid or top
LIDO, -S n open-air centre for swimming and water sports
LIDS ► lid
LIE, LAIN, -S vb make a false statement ► n falsehood
LIED, -ER n setting for solo voice and piano of a poem
LIEF, -ER, -EST, -S, LOOR adv gladly ► adj ready ► n beloved person
LIEFLY
LIEGE, -S adj bound to give or receive feudal service ► n lord
LIEGEDOM
LIEGEMAN, LIEGEMEN n (formerly) the subject of a sovereign or feudal lord
LIEGER, -S same as ► ledger
LIEGES ► liege
LIEN, -S n right to hold another's property until a debt is paid
LIENABLE adj that can be subject of a lien
LIENAL adj of or relating to the spleen
LIENEE, -S n person against whom a lien has been placed
LIENOR, -S n person who holds a lien

LIENS ► lien
LIENTERY n passage of undigested food in the faeces
LIER, -S n person who lies down
LIERNE, -S n short secondary rib that connects intersections of the primary ribs
LIERS ► lier
LIES ► lie
LIEU, -S n stead
LIEVE, -R, -S, -ST same as ► leve
LIFE, LIVES n state of living beings
LIFEBELT n ring filled with air, used to keep a person afloat when in danger of drowning
LIFEBOAT n boat used for rescuing people at sea
LIFEBUOY n any of various kinds of buoyant device for keeping people afloat
LIFECARE n care of person's health and welfare
LIFEFUL adj full of life
LIFEHACK n action that simplifies a task or reduces frustration in everyday life ► vb perform a lifehack
LIFEHOLD adj (of land) held while one is alive
LIFELESS adj dead
LIFELIKE adj closely resembling or representing life
LIFELINE n means of contact or support
LIFELONG adj lasting all of a person's life
LIFER, -S n prisoner sentenced to imprisonment for life
LIFES pl n as in **still lifes** paintings or drawings of inanimate objects
LIFESOME adj full of life
LIFESPAN n period of time during which a person or animal may be expected to live
LIFETIME n length of time a person is alive
LIFEWAY, -S n way of life
LIFEWORK n work to which a person has devoted their life
LIFT, -ED, -ING, -S vb move upwards in position, status, volume, etc ► n cage raised and lowered in a vertical shaft
LIFTABLE
LIFTBACK n hatchback
LIFTBOY, -S n person who operates a lift
LIFTED ► lift

LIFTER, -S ► lift
LIFTGATE n rear opening of hatchback
LIFTING ► lift
LIFTMAN, LIFTMEN same as ► liftboy
LIFTOFF, -S n moment a rocket leaves the ground ► vb (of a rocket) to leave its launch pad
LIFTS ► lift
LIFULL obsolete form of ► lifeful
LIG, -GED, -S n function with free entertainment and refreshments ► vb attend such a function
LIGAMENT n band of tissue joining bones
LIGAN, -S same as ► lagan
LIGAND, -S n atom, molecule, radical, or ion forming a complex with a central atom
LIGANS ► ligan
LIGASE, -S n any of a class of enzymes
LIGATE, -D, -S, LIGATING vb tie up or constrict (something) with a ligature
LIGATION
LIGATIVE
LIGATURE n link, bond, or tie ► vb bind with a ligature
LIGER, -S n hybrid offspring of a female tiger and a male lion
LIGGE, -S obsolete form of ► lie
LIGGED ► lig
LIGGER, -S ► lig
LIGGES ► ligge
LIGGING, -S ► lig
LIGHT, -ED, -EST, -ING, -S n electromagnetic radiation by which things are visible ► adj bright ► vb ignite ► adv with little luggage
LIGHTEN, -S vb make less dark
LIGHTER, -S n device for lighting cigarettes etc ► vb convey in a type of flat-bottomed barge
LIGHTEST ► light
LIGHTFUL adj full of light
LIGHTING ► light
LIGHTISH ► light
LIGHTLY adv in a light way ► vb belittle
LIGHTS ► light
LIGNAGE, -S another word for ► lineage
LIGNAN, -S n beneficial substance found in plants
LIGNE, -S n unit of measurement
LIGNEOUS adj of or like wood
LIGNES ► ligne

L

LIGNIFY vb become woody with the deposition of lignin in cell walls

LIGNIN, -S n complex polymer occurring in certain plant cell walls making the plant rigid

LIGNITE, -S n woody textured rock used as fuel
LIGNITIC

LIGNOSE, -S n explosive compound

LIGNUM, -S n wood

LIGROIN, -S n volatile fraction of petroleum

LIGROINE same as ► **ligroin**

LIGROINS ► **ligroin**

LIGS ► **lig**

LIGULA, -E, -S same as ► **ligule**
LIGULAR

LIGULATE adj having the shape of a strap

LIGULE, -S n membranous outgrowth between the leaf blade and sheath

LIGULOID ► **ligula**

LIGURE, -S n any of the 12 precious stones used in the breastplates of high priests

LIKABLE adj easy to like
LIKABLY

LIKE, -D, -S, -ST adj similar ▷ vb find enjoyable ▷ n favourable feeling, desire, or preference

LIKEABLE same as ► **likable**

LIKEABLY same as ► **likably**

LIKED ► **like**

LIKELY, LIKELIER adj tending or inclined ▷ adv probably

LIKEN, -ED, -ING, -S vb compare

LIKENESS n resemblance

LIKENING ► **liken**

LIKENS ► **liken**

LIKER, -S ► **like**

LIKES ► **like**

LIKEST ► **like**

LIKEWAKE same as ► **lykewake**

LIKEWALK same as ► **lykewake**

LIKEWISE adv similarly

LIKIN, -S n historically, Chinese tax

LIKING, -S n fondness

LIKINS ► **likin**

LIKUTA n coin in Zaïre

LILAC, -S n shrub with pale mauve flowers ▷ adj light-purple

LILIED adj decorated with lilies

LILIES ► **lily**

LILL, -ED, -ING, -S obsolete form of ► **loll**

LILLIPUT adj tiny ▷ n tiny person or being

LILLS ► **lill**

LILO, -S n inflatable mattress

LILT, -ED, -S n musical quality in speech ▷ vb speak with a lilt
LILTING

LILY, LILIES n plant which has large, often white, flowers

LILYLIKE adj resembling a lily

LIMA, -S n type of edible bean

LIMACEL, -S n small shell inside some kinds of slug

LIMACES ► **limax**

LIMACINE adj relating to slugs

LIMACON, -S n heart-shaped curve

LIMAIL, -S same as ► **lemel**

LIMAN, -S n lagoon

LIMAS ► **lima**

LIMATION n polishing

LIMAX, LIMACES n slug

LIMB, -ED, -ING, -S n arm, leg, or wing ▷ vb dismember

LIMBA, -S n type of African tree

LIMBATE adj having an edge or border of a different colour from the rest

LIMBEC, -S obsolete form of ► **alembic**

LIMBECK, -S obsolete form of ► **alembic**

LIMBECS ► **limbec**

LIMBED ► **limb**

LIMBER, -ED, -S vb loosen stiff muscles by exercising ▷ adj pliant or supple ▷ n part of a gun carriage
LIMBERER
LIMBERLY

LIMBI ► **limbus**

LIMBIC ► **limbus**

LIMBIER ► **limby**

LIMBIEST ► **limby**

LIMBING ► **limb**

LIMBLESS ► **limb**

LIMBMEAL adv piece by piece

LIMBO, -ED, -ES, -ING, -S n region between Heaven and Hell for the unbaptized ▷ vb perform a Caribbean dance that entails passing under a bar while leaning backwards

LIMBOUS adj with overlapping edges

LIMBS ► **limb**

LIMBUS, LIMBI, -ES n border

LIMBY, LIMBIER, LIMBIEST adj with long legs, stem, branches, etc

LIME, -D n calcium compound used as a fertilizer or in making cement ▷ vb spread a calcium compound upon

(land) ▷ adj having the flavour of lime fruit

LIMEADE, -S n drink made from sweetened lime juice and plain or carbonated water

LIMED ► **lime**

LIMEKILN n kiln in which calcium carbonate is burned to produce quicklime

LIMELESS ► **lime**

LIMELIT > **limelight**

LIMEN, -S, LIMINA another term for > **threshold**

LIMEPIT, -S n pit containing lime in which hides are placed to remove the hair

LIMERICK n humorous verse of five lines

LIMES, LIMITES n fortified boundary of the Roman Empire

LIMEWASH n mixture of lime and water used to whitewash walls, ceilings, etc

LIMEY, -S n British person ▷ adj British

LIMIER ► **limy**

LIMIEST ► **limy**

LIMINA ► **limen**

LIMINAL adj relating to the point beyond which a sensation becomes too faint to be experienced

LIMINESS ► **limy**

LIMING, -S ► **lime**

LIMIT, -ING, -S n ultimate extent, degree, or amount of something ▷ vb restrict or confine

LIMITARY adj of, involving, or serving as a limit

LIMITED, -S adj having a limit ▷ n limited train, bus, etc

LIMITER, -S n thing that limits something

LIMITES ► **limes**

LIMITING ► **limit**

LIMITS ► **limit**

LIMMA, -S n semitone

LIMMER, -S n scoundrel

LIMN, -ED, -ING, -S vb represent in drawing or painting

LIMNAEID n type of snail

LIMNED ► **limn**

LIMNER, -S ► **limn**

LIMNETIC adj of the open water of lakes down to the depth of light penetration

LIMNIC adj relating to lakes

LIMNING ► **limn**

LIMNS ► **limn**

LIMO, -S short for > **limousine**

LIMONENE n liquid optically active terpene with a lemon-like odour
LIMONITE n common brown, black, or yellow amorphous secondary mineral
LIMONIUM n sea plant with funnel-shaped flowers
LIMOS ▸ limo
LIMOSIS, LIMOSES n excessive hunger
LIMOUS adj muddy
LIMP, -ED, -EST, -S vb walk with an uneven step ▷ n limping walk ▷ adj without firmness or stiffness
LIMPA, -S n type of rye bread
LIMPED ▸ limp
LIMPER, -S ▸ limp
LIMPEST ▸ limp
LIMPET, -S n shellfish which sticks to rocks ▷ adj denoting weapons that are magnetically attached to their targets
LIMPID adj clear or transparent
LIMPIDLY
LIMPING, -S ▸ limp
LIMPKIN, -S n rail-like wading bird
LIMPLY ▸ limp
LIMPNESS ▸ limp
LIMPS ▸ limp
LIMPSEY same as ▸ limpsy
LIMPSY, LIMPSIER adj limp
LIMULI ▸ limulus
LIMULOID n type of crab
LIMULUS, LIMULI n horseshoe crab
LIMY, LIMIER, LIMIEST adj of, like, or smeared with birdlime
LIN, -NED, -NING, -S vb cease
LINABLE ▸ line
LINAC, -S n linear accelerator
LINAGE, -S n number of lines in written or printed matter
LINALOL, -S same as ▸ linalool
LINALOOL n optically active colourless fragrant liquid
LINCH, -ES n ledge
LINCHET, -S another word for ▸ linch
LINCHPIN n pin to hold a wheel on its axle
LINCTURE n medicine taken by licking
LINCTUS n cough medicine
LIND, -S variant of ▸ linden
LINDANE, -S n white poisonous crystalline powder
LINDEN, -S n large tree with heart-shaped leaves and fragrant yellowish flowers
LINDIED ▸ lindy

LINDIES ▸ lindy
LINDS ▸ lind
LINDWORM n wingless serpent-like dragon
LINDY, LINDIED, LINDIES, -ING n lively dance ▷ vb perform the lindy
LINE, -D, -S n long narrow mark ▷ vb mark with lines
LINEABLE
LINEAGE, -S n descent from an ancestor
LINEAL adj in direct line of descent
LINEALLY
LINEAR adj of or in lines
LINEARLY
LINEATE adj marked with lines
LINEATED same as ▸ lineate
LINEBRED adj having an ancestor that is common to sire and dam
LINECUT, -S n method of relief printing
LINED ▸ line
LINELESS ▸ line
LINELIKE ▸ line
LINEMAN, LINEMEN same as ▸ linesman
LINEMATE n ice hockey player on the same line as another
LINEMEN ▸ lineman
LINEN, -S n cloth or thread made from flax
LINENY
LINER, -S n large passenger ship
LINES ▸ line
LINESMAN, LINESMEN n (in some sports) an official who helps the referee or umpire
LINEUP, -S n row or arrangement of people or things
LINEY ▸ line
LING, -S n slender food fish
LINGA, -S same as ▸ lingam
LINGAM, -S n (in Sanskrit) masculine gender
LINGAS ▸ linga
LINGCOD, -S n type of food fish
LINGEL, -S n shoemaker's thread
LINGER, -ED, -S vb delay or prolong departure
LINGERER
LINGERIE n women's underwear or nightwear
LINGERS ▸ linger
LINGIER ▸ lingy
LINGIEST ▸ lingy
LINGLE, -S same as ▸ lingel
LINGO, -ES, -S n foreign or unfamiliar language or jargon

LINGOT, -S n ingot
LINGS ▸ ling
LINGSTER n person able to communicate with aliens
LINGUA, -E, -S n any tongue-like structure
LINGUAL, -S adj of the tongue ▷ n lingual consonant
LINGUAS ▸ lingua
LINGUICA n Portuguese sausage
LINGUINE n kind of pasta in the shape of thin flat strands
LINGUINI same as ▸ linguine
LINGUISA same as ▸ linguica
LINGUIST n person skilled in foreign languages
LINGULA, -E, -S n small tongue
LINGULAR
LINGY, LINGIER, LINGIEST adj heather-covered
LINHAY, -S n farm building with an open front
LINIER ▸ liny
LINIEST ▸ liny
LINIMENT n medicated liquid rubbed on the skin to relieve pain or stiffness
LININ, -S n network of viscous material in the nucleus of a cell
LINING, -S n layer of cloth attached to the inside of a garment etc
LININS ▸ linin
LINISH, -ED, -ES vb polish metal
LINISHER
LINK, -ED, -ING, -S n any of the rings forming a chain ▷ vb connect with or as if with links
LINKABLE
LINKAGE, -S n act of linking or the state of being linked
LINKBOY, -S n (formerly) a boy who carried a torch for pedestrians in dark streets
LINKED ▸ link
LINKER, -S n person or thing that links
LINKIER ▸ linky
LINKIEST ▸ linky
LINKING ▸ link
LINKMAN, LINKMEN same as ▸ linkboy
LINKROT, -S n state of having expired hyperlinks on a website
LINKS ▸ link
LINKSMAN, LINKSMEN same as ▸ linkboy
LINKSPAN n hinged bridge on a quay, used to move vehicles on or off a vessel

L

LINKSTER n interpreter

LINKUP, -S n establishing of a union between objects, groups, organizations, etc

LINKWORK n something made up of links

LINKY, LINKIER, LINKIEST adj (of countryside) consisting of links

LINN, -S n waterfall or a pool at the foot of it

LINNED ▸ lin

LINNET, -S n songbird of the finch family

LINNEY, -S same as ▸ linhay

LINNIES ▸ linny

LINNING ▸ lin

LINNS ▸ linn

LINNY, LINNIES same as ▸ linhay

LINO, -S same as ▸ linoleum

LINOCUT, -S n design cut in relief in lino mounted on a block of wood

LINOLEIC adj as in **linoleic acid** colourless oily essential fatty acid found in linseed

LINOLEUM n type of floor covering

LINOS ▸ lino

LINOTYPE n line of metal type produced by machine ▷ vb set as line of type

LINS ▸ lin

LINSANG, -S n any of several forest-dwelling viverrine mammals

LINSEED, -S n seed of the flax plant

LINSEY, -S n type of cloth

LINSTOCK n long staff holding a lighted match, formerly used to fire a cannon

LINT, -S n shreds of fibre, etc ▷ vb shed or remove lint

LINTED adj having lint

LINTEL, -S n horizontal beam at the top of a door or window

LINTELED adj (of a door or window) having a lintel

LINTELS ▸ lintel

LINTER, -S n machine for stripping the short fibres of ginned cotton seeds

LINTIE, -S Scot word for ▸ linnet

LINTIER ▸ linty

LINTIES ▸ lintie

LINTIEST ▸ linty

LINTING, -S n process of making lint

LINTLESS ▸ lint

LINTOL, -S same as ▸ lintel

LINTS ▸ lint

LINTSEED same as ▸ linseed

LINTY, LINTIER, LINTIEST ▸ lint

LINUM, -S n type of plant of temperate regions

LINURON, -S n type of herbicide

LINUX, -ES n nonproprietary computer operating system

LINY, LINIER, LINIEST ▸ line

LION, -S n large animal of the cat family

LIONCEL, -S n (in heraldry) small lion

LIONEL, -S same as ▸ lioncel

LIONESS n female lion

LIONET, -S n young lion

LIONFISH n any of various scorpion fishes of the Pacific

LIONHEAD n small breed of rabbit with long fur around the face

LIONISE, -D, -S same as ▸ lionize

LIONISER

LIONISM, -S n lion-like appearance of leprosy

LIONIZE, -D, -S vb treat as a celebrity

LIONIZER

LIONLIKE ▸ lion

LIONLY ▸ lion

LIONS ▸ lion

LIP, -PED, -S n either of the fleshy edges of the mouth ▷ vb touch with the lips

LIPA, -S n monetary unit of Croatia

LIPAEMIA n abnormally large amount of fat in the blood

LIPARITE n type of igneous rock

LIPAS ▸ lipa

LIPASE, -S n any of a group of enzymes that digest fat

LIPE, -S n lurching or jerking movement

LIPEMIA, -S same as ▸ lipaemia

LIPES ▸ lipe

LIPGLOSS n cosmetic for the lips to give a sheen

LIPID, -S n any of a group of organic compounds including fats, oils, waxes, and sterols

LIPIDE, -S same as ▸ lipid

LIPIDIC ▸ lipid

LIPIDS ▸ lipid

LIPIN, -S n family of nuclear proteins

LIPLESS ▸ lip

LIPLIKE ▸ lip

LIPLINER n cosmetic used to outline the lips

LIPO, -S n liposuction

LIPOCYTE n fat-storing cell

LIPOGRAM n piece of writing in which all words containing a particular letter have been omitted

LIPOIC adj as in **lipoic acid** sulphur-containing fatty acid

LIPOID, -S n fatlike substance, such as wax

LIPOIDAL

LIPOMA, -S, -TA n benign tumour composed of fatty tissue

LIPOS ▸ lipo

LIPOSOME n particle formed by lipids

LIPOSUCK vb subject to liposuction

LIPPED ▸ lip

LIPPEN, -ED, -S vb trust

LIPPER, -S Scots word for ▸ ripple

LIPPIE variant of ▸ lippy

LIPPIER ▸ lippy

LIPPIES ▸ lippy

LIPPIEST ▸ lippy

LIPPING, -S ▸ lip

LIPPY, LIPPIER, LIPPIES, LIPPIEST adj insolent or cheeky ▷ n lipstick

LIPREAD, -S vb follow what someone says by watching their lips

LIPS ▸ lip

LIPSALVE n substance used to prevent or relieve chapped lips

LIPSTICK n cosmetic in stick form, for colouring the lips ▷ vb put lipstick on

LIPURIA, -S n presence of fat in the urine

LIQUABLE adj that can be melted

LIQUATE, -D, -S vb separate one component of by heating until the more fusible part melts

LIQUEFY vb become liquid

LIQUESCE vb become liquid

LIQUEUR, -S n flavoured and sweetened alcoholic spirit ▷ vb flavour with liqueur

LIQUID, -S n substance in a physical state which can change shape but not size ▷ adj of or being a liquid

LIQUIDLY

LIQUIDUS n line on graph above which a substance is in liquid form

LIQUIDY adj having the nature of liquid

LIQUIFY same as ▸ liquefy

LIQUITAB n soluble plastic capsule containing liquid detergent or medicine

LIQUOR, -ED, -S *n* alcoholic drink ▷ *vb* steep in warm water to form wort in brewing

LIRA, -S, LIRE, LIRI, LIROT, LIROTH *n* monetary unit of Turkey, Malta, and formerly of Italy

LIRIOPE, -S *n* grasslike plant

LIRIPIPE *n* tip of a graduate's hood

LIRIPOOP *same as* ▸ **liripipe**

LIRK, -ED, -ING, -S *vb* wrinkle

LIROT ▸ **lira**

LIROTH ▸ **lira**

LIS, -SES *n* fleur-de-lis

LISENTE ▸ **sente**

LISK, -S *Yorkshire dialect for* ▸ **groin**

LISLE, -S *n* strong fine cotton thread or fabric

LISP, -ED, -S *n* speech defect in which s and z are pronounced th ▷ *vb* speak or utter with a lisp

LISPER -S

LISPING, -S ▸ **lisp**

LISPOUND *n* unit of weight

LISPS ▸ **lisp**

LISPUND, -S *same as* ▸ **lispound**

LISSES ▸ **lis**

LISSOM *adj* supple, agile

LISSOME *same as* ▸ **lissom**

LISSOMLY ▸ **lissom**

LIST, -ED, -ETH *n* item-by-item record of names or things, usu written one below another ▷ *vb* make a list of

LISTABLE

LISTBOX *n* small box on a computer screen, showing a list of options

LISTED ▸ **list**

LISTEE, -S *n* person on list

LISTEL, -S *another name for* ▸ **fillet**

LISTEN, -ED, -S *vb* concentrate on hearing something

LISTENER

LISTER, -S *n* plough with a double mouldboard to throw soil to sides of a central furrow

LISTERIA *n* type of rodlike Gram-positive bacterium

LISTERS ▸ **lister**

LISTETH ▸ **list**

LISTFUL *adj* paying attention

LISTING, -S *n* list or an entry in a list

LISTLESS *adj* lacking interest or energy

LISTS *pl n* field of combat in a tournament

LISTSERV *n* email service for those with similar interests

LIT, -S *n* archaic word for dye or colouring

LITAI ▸ **litas**

LITANY, LITANIES *n* prayer with responses from the congregation

LITAS, LITAI, LITU *n* monetary unit of Lithuania

LITCHI, -S *n* Chinese tree with round edible fruits

LITE, -D, -S, -ST, LITING *same as* ▸ **light**

LITENESS

LITER, -S *same as* ▸ **litre**

LITERACY *n* ability to read and write

LITERAL, -S *adj* according to the explicit meaning of a word or text ▷ *n* misspelling in a text

LITERARY *adj* of or knowledgeable about literature

LITERATE *adj* able to read and write ▷ *n* literate person

LITERATI, LITERATO *pl n* literary people

LITEROSE *adj* affectedly literary

LITERS ▸ **liter**

LITES ▸ **lite**

LITEST ▸ **lite**

LITH, -S *n* limb or joint

LITHARGE *n* lead monoxide

LITHATE, -S *n* salt of uric acid

LITHE, -D, -R, -S, -ST, LITHING *adj* flexible or supple, pliant ▷ *vb* listen

LITHELY

LITHEMIA *n* gout

LITHEMIC

LITHER ▸ **lithe**

LITHERLY *adj* crafty; cunning

LITHES ▸ **lithe**

LITHEST ▸ **lithe**

LITHIA, -S *n* lithium present in mineral waters as lithium salts

LITHIC *adj* of stone

LITHIFY *vb* turn into rock

LITHING ▸ **lithe**

LITHITE, -S *n* part of cell with sensory element

LITHIUM, -S *n* chemical element, the lightest known metal

LITHO, -ED, -ES, -ING, -S *n* lithography ▷ *vb* print using lithography

LITHOID *adj* resembling rock

LITHOING ▸ **litho**

LITHOPS *n* fleshy-leaved plant

LITHOS ▸ **litho**

LITHOSOL *n* type of azonal soil

LITHS ▸ **lith**

LITIGANT *n* person involved in a lawsuit ▷ *adj* engaged in litigation

LITIGATE *vb* bring or contest a law suit

LITING ▸ **lite**

LITMUS, -ES *n* soluble powder obtained from lichens

LITORAL *same as* ▸ **littoral**

LITOTES *n* ironical understatement used for effect

LITOTIC

LITRE, -S *n* unit of liquid measure

LITREAGE *n* volume in litres

LITRES ▸ **litre**

LITS ▸ **lit**

LITTEN *adj* lighted

LITTER, -ED, -S *n* untidy rubbish ▷ *vb* strew with litter

LITTERER *n* one who litters

LITTERS ▸ **litter**

LITTERY *adj* covered in litter

LITTLE, -R, -S, -ST *adj* small ▷ *adv* not a lot ▷ *n* small amount, extent, or duration

LITTLIE, -S *n* young child

LITTLIN, -S *same as* ▸ **littling**

LITTLING *n* child

LITTLINS ▸ **littlin**

LITTLISH *adj* rather small

LITTORAL *adj* of or by the seashore ▷ *n* coastal district

LITU ▸ **litas**

LITURGIC ▸ **liturgy**

LITURGY *n* prescribed form of public worship

LITUUS, -ES *n* curved trumpet

LIVABLE *adj* tolerable or pleasant to live (with)

LIVE, -D, -ST *vb* be alive ▷ *adj* living, alive ▷ *adv* in the form of a live performance

LIVEABLE *same as* ▸ **livable**

LIVEBLOG *vb* blog about (an event) as it happens

LIVED ▸ **live**

LIVEDO, -S *n* reddish discoloured patch on the skin

LIVELIER ▸ **lively**

LIVELILY ▸ **lively**

LIVELOD, -S *n* livelihood

LIVELONG *adj* long or seemingly long

LIVELOOD *n* livelihood

LIVELY, LIVELIER *adj* full of life or vigour

LIVEN, -ED, -ING, -S *vb* make or become lively

LIVENER -S

L

LIVENESS n state of being alive

LIVENING ► liven

LIVENS ► liven

LIVER, -S n person who lives in a specified way

LIVERED adj having liver

LIVERIED adj wearing livery

LIVERIES ► livery

LIVERING n process of liquid becoming lumpy

LIVERISH adj having a disorder of the liver

LIVERS ► liver

LIVERY, LIVERIES n distinctive dress ▷ adj of or resembling liver

LIVES ► life

LIVEST ► live

LIVETRAP n box constructed to trap an animal without injuring it

LIVEWARE n personnel working in a computer system

LIVEWELL n container of water on a fishing boat used to store live fish

LIVEYER, -S n (in Newfoundland) a full-time resident

LIVEYERE same as ► liveyer

LIVEYERS ► liveyer

LIVID, -ER, -EST adj angry or furious

LIVIDITY n state of being livid

LIVIDLY ► livid

LIVIER, -S same as ► liveyer

LIVING, -S adj possessing life, not dead or inanimate ▷ n condition of being alive

LIVINGLY

LIVOR, -S another word for ► lividity

LIVRE, -S n former French unit of money of account

LIVYER, -S same as ► liveyer

LIXIVIA ► lixivium

LIXIVIAL > lixiviate

LIXIVIUM, LIXIVIA n alkaline solution obtained by leaching wood ash with water

LIZARD, -S n four-footed reptile with a long body and tail

LIZZIE, -S n as in **tin lizzie** old or decrepit car

LLAMA, -S n woolly animal of the camel family

LLANERO, -S n native of llanos

LLANO, -S n extensive grassy treeless plain

LO interj look!

LOACH, -ES n carplike fish

LOAD n burden or weight ▷ vb put a load on or into

LOADABLE adj able to be loaded

LOADED adj containing a hidden trap

LOADEN, -ED, -S vb load

LOADER, -S n person who loads a gun or other firearm

LOADING, -S n load or burden

LOADS pl n lots or a lot

LOADSTAR same as ► lodestar

LOAF, -ED, -S, LOAVES n shaped mass of baked bread ▷ vb idle, loiter

LOAFER, -S n idler

LOAFING, -S ► loaf

LOAFS ► loaf

LOAM, -ED, -ING, -S n fertile soil ▷ vb cover, treat, or fill with loam

LOAMIER ► loamy

LOAMIEST ► loamy

LOAMING ► loam

LOAMLESS ► loam

LOAMS ► loam

LOAMY, LOAMIER, LOAMIEST ► loam

LOAN, -ED, -ING, -S n money lent at interest ▷ vb lend

LOANABLE

LOANBACK n facility by which an individual can borrow from his or her pension fund ▷ vb make use of this facility

LOANED ► loan

LOANEE, -S n sportsperson who is loaned out

LOANER, -S ► loan

LOANING, -S ► loan

LOANS ► loan

LOANWORD n word adopted from one language into another

LOAST ► lose

LOATH, -EST adj unwilling or reluctant (to)

LOATHE, -D, -S vb hate

LOATHER -S

LOATHEST ► loath

LOATHFUL adj causing loathing

LOATHING n strong disgust

LOATHLY adv with reluctance

LOATHY obsolete form of > loathsome

LOAVE, -D, LOAVING vb form a loaf

LOAVES ► loaf

LOAVING ► loave

LOB, -BED, -BING, -S n ball struck in a high arc ▷ vb strike in a high arc

LOBAR adj of or affecting a lobe

LOBATE adj with or like lobes

LOBATED same as ► lobate

LOBATELY ► lobate

LOBATION n division into lobes

LOBBED ► lob

LOBBER, -S n one who lobs

LOBBIED ► lobby

LOBBIES ► lobby

LOBBING ► lob

LOBBY, LOBBIED, LOBBIES, -ING n corridor into which rooms open ▷ vb try to influence (legislators) in the formulation of policy

LOBBYER -S

LOBBYGOW n errand boy

LOBBYING ► lobby

LOBBYISM ► lobbyist

LOBBYIST n person who lobbies on behalf of a particular interest

LOBE, -S n rounded projection

LOBED

LOBEFIN, -S n type of fish

LOBELESS adj having no lobes

LOBELET, -S n small lobe

LOBELIA, -S n garden plant

LOBELINE n crystalline alkaloid extracted from the seeds of the Indian tobacco plant

LOBES ► lobe

LOBI ► lobus

LOBING, -S n formation of lobes

LOBIPED adj with lobed toes

LOBLOLLY n southern US pine tree

LOBO, -S n timber wolf

LOBOLA, -S n (in African custom) price paid by a bridegroom's family to his bride's family

LOBOLO, -S same as ► lobola

LOBOS ► lobo

LOBOSE another word for ► lobate

LOBOTOMY n surgical incision into a lobe of the brain to treat certain disorders

LOBS ► lob

LOBSTER, -S n shellfish ▷ vb fish for lobsters

LOBSTICK n tree used as a landmark

LOBTAIL, -S vb (of a whale) hit a surface of water with the tail

LOBULAR ► lobule

LOBULATE ► lobule

LOBULE, -S n small lobe or a subdivision of a lobe

LOBULI ► lobulus

LOBULOSE ► lobule

LOBULUS, LOBULI n small lobe

LOBUS, LOBI n lobe
LOBWORM, -S same as ► **lugworm**
LOCA ► **locus**
LOCAL, -S adj of a particular place ▷ n person from a particular place
LOCALE, -S n scene of an event
LOCALISE same as ► **localize**
LOCALISM n pronunciation, phrase, etc, peculiar to a particular locality
LOCALIST
LOCALITE n resident of an area
LOCALITY n neighbourhood or area
LOCALIZE vb restrict to a particular area
LOCALLY adv within a particular area or place
LOCALS ► **local**
LOCATE, -D, -S, LOCATING vb discover the whereabouts of
LOCATER -S
LOCATION n site or position
LOCATIVE adj (of a word or phrase) indicating place or direction ▷ n locative case
LOCATOR, -S n part of index that shows where to find information
LOCAVORE n person who prefers locally produced food
LOCH, -S n lake
LOCHAN, -S n small inland loch
LOCHE, -S n freshwater fish of the cod family
LOCHS ► **loch**
LOCI ► **locus**
LOCIE, -S n type of logging engine
LOCK, -ED, -S n appliance for fastening a door, case, etc ▷ vb fasten or become fastened securely
LOCKABLE
LOCKAGE, -S n system of locks in a canal
LOCKAWAY n investment intended to be held for a relatively long time
LOCKBOX n system of collecting funds from companies by banks
LOCKDOWN n device used to secure equipment, etc
LOCKED ► **lock**
LOCKER, -S n small cupboard with a lock
LOCKET, -S n small hinged pendant for a portrait etc
LOCKFAST adj securely fastened with a lock

LOCKFUL, -S n sufficient to fill a canal lock
LOCKING, -S ► **lock**
LOCKJAW, -S n tetanus
LOCKLESS adj having no lock
LOCKMAN, LOCKMEN n lock-keeper
LOCKNUT, -S n nut screwed down on a primary nut to stop it from loosening
LOCKOUT, -S n closing of a workplace by an employer to force workers to accept terms
LOCKPICK another word for ► **picklock**
LOCKRAM, -S n type of linen cloth
LOCKS ► **lock**
LOCKSET, -S n hardware used to lock door
LOCKSMAN, LOCKSMEN same as ► **lockman**
LOCKSTEP n method of marching in step as closely as possible
LOCKUP, -S n prison
LOCO, -ED, -ES, -ING, -S n locomotive ▷ adj insane ▷ vb poison with locoweed
LOCOFOCO n match
LOCOING ► **loco**
LOCOISM, -S n disease of cattle, sheep, and horses caused by eating locoweed
LOCOMAN, LOCOMEN n railwayman
LOCOMOTE vb move from one place to another
LOCOS ► **loco**
LOCOWEED n any of several perennial leguminous plants
LOCULAR adj divided into compartments by septa
LOCULATE same as ► **locular**
LOCULE, -S n any of the chambers of an ovary or anther
LOCULED adj having locules
LOCULES ► **locule**
LOCULUS, LOCULI same as ► **locule**
LOCUM, -S n temporary stand-in for a doctor or clergyman
LOCUS, LOCA, LOCI n area or place where something happens
LOCUST, -ED, -S n destructive insect ▷ vb ravage, as locusts
LOCUSTA, -E n flower cluster unit in grasses
LOCUSTAL
LOCUSTED ► **locust**
LOCUSTS ► **locust**

LOCUTION n manner or style of speech
LOCUTORY adj room intended for conversation
LOD, -S n type of logarithm
LODE, -S n vein of ore
LODEN, -S n thick waterproof, woollen cloth
LODES ► **lode**
LODESMAN, LODESMEN n pilot
LODESTAR n star used in navigation or astronomy as a point of reference
LODGE, -D, -S n gatekeeper's house ▷ vb live in another's house at a fixed charge
LODGER, -S n tenant
LODGES ► **lodge**
LODGING n temporary residence
LODGINGS pl n rented room or rooms in which to live, esp in another person's house
LODGMENT n act of lodging or the state of being lodged
LODICULA n delicate scale in grass
LODICULE n minute scale at the base of the ovary in grass flowers
LODS ► **lod**
LOERIE, -S same as ► **lourie**
LOESS, -ES n fine-grained soil
LOESSAL
LOESSIAL
LOESSIC adj relating to or consisting of loess
LOFT, -ED, -ING, -S n space between the top storey and roof of a building ▷ vb strike, throw, or kick (a ball) high into the air
LOFTER, -S n type of golf club
LOFTIER ► **lofty**
LOFTIEST ► **lofty**
LOFTILY ► **lofty**
LOFTING ► **loft**
LOFTLESS ► **loft**
LOFTLIKE ► **loft**
LOFTS ► **loft**
LOFTSMAN, LOFTSMEN n person who reproduces in actual size a draughtsman's design for a ship or an aircraft
LOFTY, LOFTIER, LOFTIEST adj of great height
LOG, -GED, -S n portion of a felled tree stripped of branches ▷ vb saw logs from a tree
LOGAN, -S another name for ► **bogan**
LOGANIA, -S n type of Australian plant
LOGANS ► **logan**

L

LOGBOARD n board used for logging a ship's records

LOGBOOK, -S n book recording the details about a car or a ship's journeys

LOGE, -S n small enclosure or box in a theatre or opera house

LOGGAT, -S n small piece of wood

LOGGED ▸ log

LOGGER, -S n tractor or crane for handling logs

LOGGETS n old-fashioned game played with sticks

LOGGIA, -S, LOGGIE n covered gallery at the side of a building

LOGGIER ▸ loggy

LOGGIEST ▸ loggy

LOGGING, -S ▸ log

LOGGISH ▸ log

LOGGY, LOGGIER, LOGGIEST adj sluggish

LOGIA ▸ logion

LOGIC, -S n philosophy of reasoning

LOGICAL adj of logic

LOGICIST

LOGICIAN n person who specializes in or is skilled at logic

LOGICISE same as ▸ logicize

LOGICISM n philosophical theory that all of mathematics can be deduced from logic

LOGICIST

LOGICIZE vb present reasons for or against

LOGICS ▸ logic

LOGIE, -S n fire-place of a kiln

LOGIER ▸ logy

LOGIES ▸ logie

LOGIEST ▸ logy

LOGILY ▸ logy

LOGIN, -S n process by which a computer user logs on

LOGINESS ▸ logy

LOGINS ▸ login

LOGION, LOGIA, -S n saying of Christ regarded as authentic

LOGISTIC n uninterpreted calculus or system of symbolic logic ▷ adj (of a curve) having a particular form of equation

LOGJAM, -S n blockage of logs in a river ▷ vb cause a logjam

LOGJUICE n poor quality port wine

LOGLINE, -S n synopsis of screenplay

LOGLOG, -S n logarithm of a logarithm (in equations, etc)

LOGO same as ▸ logotype

LOGOED adj having a logo

LOGOFF, -S n process by which a computer user logs out

LOGOGRAM n single symbol representing an entire morpheme, word, or phrase

LOGOI ▸ logos

LOGOMACH n one who argues over words

LOGON, -S variant of ▸ login

LOGOS, LOGOI n reason expressed in words and things, argument, or justification

LOGOTYPE n piece of type with several uncombined characters cast on it

LOGOTYPY

LOGOUT, -S variant of ▸ logoff

LOGROLL, -S vb use logrolling in order to procure the passage of (legislation)

LOGS ▸ log

LOGWAY, -S another name for ▸ gangway

LOGWOOD, -S n tree of the Caribbean and Central America

LOGY, LOGIER, LOGIEST adj dull or listless

LOHAN, -S another word for ▸ arhat

LOIASIS, LOIASES n disease caused by a tropical eye worm

LOID, -ED, -ING, -S vb open (a lock) using a celluloid strip

LOIN n part of the body between the ribs and the hips

LOINS pl n hips and the inner surface of the legs

LOIPE, -N n cross-country skiing track

LOIR, -S n large dormouse

LOITER, -ED, -S vb stand or wait aimlessly or idly

LOITERER

LOKE, -S n track

LOKSHEN pl n noodles

LOLIGO, -S n type of squid

LOLIUM, -S n type of grass

LOLL, -ED, -ING, -S vb lounge lazily ▷ n act or instance of lolling

LOLLER -S

LOLLIES ▸ lolly

LOLLING ▸ loll

LOLLIPOP n boiled sweet on a small wooden stick

LOLLOP, -ED, -S vb move clumsily

LOLLOPY

LOLLS ▸ loll

LOLLY, LOLLIES n lollipop or ice lolly

LOLLYGAG same as ▸ lallygag

LOLLYPOP same as ▸ lollipop

LOLOG, -S same as ▸ loglog

LOLZ same as ▸ lulz

LOMA, -S, -TA n lobe

LOME, -S, LOMING vb cover with lome

LOMED

LOMEIN, -S n Chinese dish

LOMENT, -S n pod of certain leguminous plants

LOMENTA ▸ lomentum

LOMENTS ▸ loment

LOMENTUM, LOMENTA same as ▸ loment

LOMES ▸ lome

LOMING ▸ lome

LOMPISH another word for ▸ lumpish

LONE adj solitary

LONELIER ▸ lonely

LONELILY ▸ lonely

LONELY, LONELIER adj sad because alone

LONENESS ▸ lone

LONER, -S n solitary person

LONESOME adj lonely ▷ n own

LONG, -ED, -EST adj having length ▷ adv for a certain time ▷ vb have a strong desire (for)

LONGA, -S n long note

LONGAN, -S n sapindaceous tree of tropical and subtropical Asia

LONGAS ▸ longa

LONGBOAT n largest boat carried on a ship

LONGBOW, -S n large powerful bow

LONGCASE n as in **longcase clock** grandfather clock

LONGE, -ING, -S n rope used in training a horse ▷ vb train using a longe

LONGED ▸ long

LONGEING ▸ longe

LONGER, -S n line of barrels on a ship

LONGERON n main longitudinal structural member of an aircraft

LONGERS ▸ longer

LONGES ▸ longe

LONGEST ▸ long

LONGEVAL another word for > longaeval

LONGHAIR n cat with long hair

LONGHAND n ordinary writing, not shorthand or typing

LONGHEAD n person with long head**

LONGHORN n British breed of beef cattle with long curved horns

LONGIES n long johns

LONGING, -S n yearning ▷ adj having or showing desire

LONGISH adj rather long

LONGJUMP n jumping contest decided by length

LONGLEAF n North American pine tree

LONGLINE n (tennis) straight stroke played down court

LONGLIST n initial list from which a shortlist is selected ▷ vb include (eg a candidate) on a longlist

LONGLY ▶ long

LONGNECK n US, Canadian and Australian word for a 330-ml beer bottle with a long narrow neck

LONGNESS ▶ long

LONGS pl n full-length trousers

LONGSHIP n narrow open boat with oars and a square sail, used by the Vikings

LONGSOME adj slow; boring

LONGSPUR n any of various Arctic and North American buntings

LONGTIME adj of long standing

LONGUEUR n period of boredom or dullness

LONGWALL n long face in coal mine

LONGWAYS adv lengthways

LONGWISE same as ▶ longways

LONGWORM n as in **sea longworm** kind of marine worm

LONICERA n honeysuckle

LOO, -ED, -ING, -S n toilet ▷ vb Scots word meaning love

LOOBIER ▶ looby

LOOBIES ▶ looby

LOOBIEST ▶ looby

LOOBILY ▶ looby

LOOBY, LOOBIER, LOOBIES, LOOBIEST adj foolish ▷ n foolish or stupid person

LOOED ▶ loo

LOOEY, -S n lieutenant

LOOF, -S, LOOVES n part of ship's side

LOOFA, -S same as ▶ loofah

LOOFAH, -S n sponge made from the dried pod of a gourd

LOOFAS ▶ loofa

LOOFFUL, -S n handful

LOOFS ▶ loof

LOOIE, -S same as ▶ looey

LOOING ▶ loo

LOOK, -ED, -ING, -S vb direct the eyes or attention (towards) ▷ n instance of looking

LOOKDOWN n way paper appears when looked at under reflected light

LOOKED ▶ look

LOOKER, -S n person who looks

LOOKIE interj look (over here)

LOOKING ▶ look

LOOKISM, -S n discrimination because of appearance

LOOKIST -S

LOOKIT interj look at this

LOOKOUT, -S n act of watching for danger or for an opportunity ▷ vb be careful

LOOKOVER n inspection, esp a brief one

LOOKS ▶ look

LOOKSISM same as ▶ lookism

LOOKUP, -S n act of looking up information

LOOKY same as ▶ lookie

LOOM, -ED, -ING, -S n machine for weaving cloth ▷ vb appear dimly

LOON, -S n diving bird

LOONEY, -S same as ▶ loony

LOONIE n Canadian dollar coin

LOONIER ▶ loony

LOONIES ▶ loony

LOONIEST ▶ loony

LOONILY ▶ loony

LOONING, -S n cry of the loon

LOONS ▶ loon

LOONY, LOONIER, LOONIES, LOONIEST adj foolish or insane ▷ n foolish or insane person

LOOP, -ED, -S n round shape made by a curved line ▷ vb form with a loop

LOOPER, -S n person or thing that loops or makes loops

LOOPHOLE n means of evading a rule without breaking it ▷ vb provide with loopholes

LOOPIER ▶ loopy

LOOPIEST ▶ loopy

LOOPILY ▶ loopy

LOOPING, -S ▶ loop

LOOPS ▶ loop

LOOPY, LOOPIER, LOOPIEST adj slightly mad or crazy

LOOR ▶ lief

LOORD, -S obsolete word for ▶ lout

LOOS ▶ loo

LOOSE, -D, -R, -S, -ST adj not tight, fastened, fixed, or tense ▷ adv in a loose manner ▷ vb free

LOOSEBOX n enclosed stall with a door in which an animal can be kept

LOOSED ▶ loose

LOOSELY ▶ loose

LOOSEN, -ED, -S vb make loose

LOOSENER

LOOSER ▶ loose

LOOSES ▶ loose

LOOSEST ▶ loose

LOOSIE n informal word for loose forward

LOOSIES pl n cigarettes sold individually

LOOSING, -S n celebration of one's 21st birthday

LOOT, -ED, -S, LUTTEN vb pillage ▷ n goods stolen during pillaging

LOOTEN Scots past form of ▶ let

LOOTER, -S ▶ loot

LOOTING, -S ▶ loot

LOOTS ▶ loot

LOOVES ▶ loof

LOP, -PED, -S vb cut away ▷ n part(s) lopped off

LOPE, -D, -S, LOPING vb run with long easy strides ▷ n loping stride

LOPER -S

LOPGRASS n smooth-bladed grass

LOPING ▶ lope

LOPINGLY adv in a loping manner

LOPOLITH n saucer- or lens-shaped body of intrusive igneous rock

LOPPED ▶ lop

LOPPER, -ED, -S n tool for lopping ▷ vb curdle

LOPPET, -S n long-distance cross-country ski race

LOPPIER ▶ loppy

LOPPIES ▶ loppy

LOPPIEST ▶ loppy

LOPPING, -S ▶ lop

LOPPY, LOPPIER, LOPPIES, LOPPIEST adj floppy ▷ n ranch hand

LOPS ▶ lop

LOPSIDED adj greater in height, weight, or size on one side

LOPSTICK variant of ▶ lobstick

LOQUAT, -S n ornamental evergreen rosaceous tree

LOQUITUR n stage direction meaning he or she speaks

LOR interj exclamation of surprise or dismay

L

LORAL adj of part of side of bird's head

LORAN, -S n radio navigation system operating over long distances

LORATE adj like a strap

LORCHA, -S n junk-rigged vessel

LORD, -ED, -S n person with power over others ▷ vb act in a superior way

LORDING, -S n gentleman

LORDKIN, -S n little lord

LORDLESS ▶ lord

LORDLIER ▶ lordly

LORDLIKE ▶ lord

LORDLING n young lord

LORDLY, LORDLIER adj imperious, proud ▷ adv in the manner of a lord

LORDOMA, -S same as ▶ lordosis

LORDOSIS, LORDOSES n forward curvature of the lumbar spine

LORDOTIC

LORDS ▶ lord

LORDSHIP n position or authority of a lord

LORDY interj exclamation of surprise or dismay

LORE, -S n body of traditions

LOREAL adj concerning or relating to lore

LOREL, -S another word for ▶ losel

LORES ▶ lore

LORGNON, -S n monocle or pair of spectacles

LORIC, -S same as ▶ lorica

LORICA, -E, -S n hard outer covering of rotifers, ciliate protozoans, and similar organisms

LORICATE

LORICS ▶ loric

LORIES ▶ lory

LORIKEET n small brightly coloured Australian parrot

LORIMER, -S n (formerly) a person who made bits and spurs

LORINER, -S same as ▶ lorimer

LORING, -S n teaching

LORIOT, -S n golden oriole (bird)

LORIS, -ES n any of several prosimian primates

LORN adj forsaken or wretched

LORNNESS

LORRELL, -S obsolete word for ▶ losel

LORRY, LORRIES n large vehicle for transporting loads by road

LORY, LORIES n small parrot of Australia and Indonesia

LOS n approval

LOSABLE ▶ loose

LOSE, LOAST, -D, -S vb part with

LOSEL, -S n worthless person ▷ adj worthless

LOSEN same as ▶ lose

LOSER, -S n person or thing that loses

LOSES ▶ lose

LOSH interj lord

LOSING adj unprofitable; failing

LOSINGLY ▶ lose

LOSINGS pl n losses

LOSS, -ES n losing

LOSSIER ▶ lossy

LOSSIEST ▶ lossy

LOSSLESS ▶ loss

LOSSY, LOSSIER, LOSSIEST adj designed to have a high attenuation

LOST adj missing

LOSTNESS

LOT, -S, -TED, -TING pron great number ▷ n collection of people or things ▷ vb draw lots for

LOTA, -S n globular water container

LOTAH, -S same as ▶ lota

LOTAS ▶ lota

LOTE, -S another word for ▶ lotus

LOTH, -ER, -EST same as ▶ loath

LOTHARIO n rake, libertine, or seducer

LOTHER ▶ loth

LOTHEST ▶ loth

LOTHFULL obsolete form of ▶ loathful

LOTHNESS ▶ loth

LOTHSOME same as > loathsome

LOTI n monetary unit of Lesotho

LOTIC adj of communities living in rapidly flowing water

LOTION, -S n medical or cosmetic liquid for use on the skin

LOTO same as ▶ lotto

LOTOS, -ES same as ▶ lotus

LOTS ▶ lot

LOTSA determiner lots of

LOTTA n lot of

LOTTE, -S n type of fish

LOTTED ▶ lot

LOTTER, -S n someone who works an allotment

LOTTERY n method of raising money by selling tickets that win prizes by chance

LOTTES ▶ lotte

LOTTING ▶ lot

LOTTO, -S n game of chance

LOTUS, -ES n legendary plant whose fruit induces forgetfulness

LOU, -ED, -ING, -S Scot word for ▶ love

LOUCHE, -R, -ST adj shifty

LOUCHELY

LOUD, -ER, -EST adj noisy

LOUDEN, -ED, -S vb make louder

LOUDER ▶ loud

LOUDEST ▶ loud

LOUDISH adj fairly loud

LOUDLY, LOUDLIER ▶ loud

LOUDNESS ▶ loud

LOUED ▶ lou

LOUGH, -S n loch

LOUIE, -S same as ▶ looey

LOUING ▶ lou

LOUIS n former French gold coin

LOUMA, -S n market in developing countries

LOUN, -ED, -ING, -S same as ▶ lown

LOUND, -ED, -ING, -S same as ▶ loun

LOUNDER, -S vb beat severely

LOUNDING ▶ lound

LOUNDS ▶ lound

LOUNED ▶ loun

LOUNGE, -D, -S, LOUNGING n living room in a private house ▷ vb sit, lie, or stand in a relaxed manner

LOUNGER, -S n extending chair

LOUNGES ▶ lounge

LOUNGEY, LOUNGIER n suggestive of a lounge bar or easy-listening music

LOUNGING ▶ lounge

LOUNGY adj casual; relaxed

LOUNING ▶ loun

LOUNS ▶ loun

LOUP, -ED, -EN, -ING, -IT, -S Scot word for ▶ leap

LOUPE, -S n magnifying glass used by jewellers, horologists, etc

LOUPED ▶ loup

LOUPEN ▶ loup

LOUPES ▶ loupe

LOUPING ▶ loup

LOUPIT ▶ loup

LOUPS ▶ loup

LOUR, -ED, -S vb be overcast ▷ n menacing scowl

LOURE, -S n slow, former French dance

LOURED ► lour
LOURES ► loure
LOURIE, -S *n* type of African bird
LOURIER ► loury
LOURIES ► lourie
LOURIEST ► loury
LOURING, -S ► lour
LOURS ► lour
LOURY, LOURIER, LOURIEST *adj* sombre
LOUS ► lou
LOUSE, LICE, -D, -S *n* wingless parasitic insect ▷ *vb* ruin or spoil
LOUSER, -S *n* mean nasty person
LOUSES ► louse
LOUSIER ► lousy
LOUSIEST ► lousy
LOUSILY ► lousy
LOUSING, -S *n* act or instance of removing lice
LOUSY, LOUSIER, LOUSIEST *adj* mean or unpleasant
LOUT, -ED, -ING, -S *n* crude person ▷ *vb* bow or stoop
LOUTERY *n* crude or boorish behaviour
LOUTING ► lout
LOUTISH *adj* of a lout
LOUTS ► lout
LOUVAR, -S *n* large silvery whalelike scombroid fish
LOUVER, -S *same as* ► **louvre**
LOUVERED *same as* ► **louvred**
LOUVERS ► louver
LOUVRE, -S *n* one of a set of parallel slats slanted to admit air but not rain
LOUVRED *adj* having louvres
LOUVRES ► louvre
LOVABLE *adj* attracting or deserving affection
LOVABLY
LOVAGE, -S *n* European plant used for flavouring food
LOVAT, -S *n* yellowish-or bluish-green mixture in tweeds
LOVE, -D, -S *vb* have a great affection for ▷ *n* great affection
LOVEABLE *same as* ► **lovable**
LOVEABLY ► lovable
LOVEBIRD *n* small parrot
LOVEBITE *n* temporary red mark left on a person's skin by someone biting or sucking it
LOVEBUG, -S *n* small US flying insect
LOVED ► love
LOVEFEST *n* event when people talk about loving one another

LOVELESS *adj* without love
LOVELIER ► lovely
LOVELIES ► lovely
LOVELILY ► lovely
LOVELOCK *n* long lock of hair worn on the forehead
LOVELORN *adj* miserable because of unhappiness in love
LOVELY, LOVELIER, LOVELIES *adj* very attractive ▷ *n* attractive woman
LOVER, -S *n* person who loves something or someone
LOVERED *adj* having a lover
LOVERLY *adj* like a lover
LOVERS ► lover
LOVES ► love
LOVESEAT *n* armchair for two people
LOVESICK *adj* pining or languishing because of love
LOVESOME *adj* full of love
LOVEVINE *n* leafless parasitic vine
LOVEY, -S, LOVIER, LOVIEST *adj* loving; affectionate ▷ *n* affectionate person
LOVIE, -S *n* beloved person
LOVIER ► lovey
LOVIES ► lovie
LOVIEST ► lovey
LOVING, -S *adj* affectionate, tender ▷ *n* state of being in love
LOVINGLY
LOW, -ED, -EST, -S *adj* not high ▷ *adv* in a low position ▷ *n* low position ▷ *vb* moo
LOWAN, -S *n* type of Australian bird
LOWBALL, -S *vb* deliberately under-charge
LOWBORN *adj* of ignoble or common parentage
LOWBOY, -S *n* table fitted with drawers
LOWBRED *same as* ► **lowborn**
LOWBROW, -S *adj* with nonintellectual tastes and interests ▷ *n* person with nonintellectual tastes
LOWBUSH *n* type of blueberry bush
LOWDOWN, -S *n* inside info
LOWE, -S *variant of* ► **low**
LOWED ► low
LOWER, -ED, -S *adj* below one or more other things ▷ *vb* cause or allow to move down
LOWERIER ► lowery
LOWERING ► lower
LOWERS ► lower
LOWERY, LOWERIER *adj* sombre

LOWES ► lowe
LOWEST ► low
LOWING, -S ► low
LOWISH ► low
LOWLAND, -S *n* low-lying country ▷ *adj* of a lowland or lowlands
LOWLIER ► lowly
LOWLIEST ► lowly
LOWLIFE, -S, LOWLIVES *n* member or members of the underworld
LOWLIFER
LOWLIGHT *n* unenjoyable or unpleasant part of an event
LOWLILY ► lowly
LOWLIVES ► lowlife
LOWLY, LOWLIER, LOWLIEST *adj* modest, humble ▷ *adv* in a low or lowly manner
LOWN, -ED, -ING, -S *vb* calm
LOWND, -ED, -ING, -S *same as* ► **lown**
LOWNE, -S *same as* ► **loon**
LOWNED ► lown
LOWNES ► lowne
LOWNESS ► low
LOWNING ► lown
LOWNS ► lown
LOWP, -ED, -ING, -S *same as* ► **loup**
LOWPASS *adj* (of a filter) transmitting frequencies below a certain value
LOWPED ► lowp
LOWPING ► lowp
LOWPS ► lowp
LOWRIDER *n* car with body close to ground
LOWRIE *another name for* ► **lory**
LOWRY, LOWRIES *another name for* ► **lory**
LOWS ► low
LOWSE, -D, -R, -S, -ST, LOWSING *vb* release or loose ▷ *adj* loose
LOWSIT
LOWT, -ED, -ING, -S *same as* ► **lout**
LOWVELD, -S *n* low ground in S Africa
LOX, -ED, -ES, -ING *vb* load fuel tanks of spacecraft with liquid oxygen ▷ *n* kind of smoked salmon

A good word when you have an X to dispose of.

LOXYGEN, -S *n* liquid oxygen
LOY, -S *n* narrow spade with a single footrest
LOYAL, -ER, -EST, -LER *adj* faithful
LOYALISM ► loyalist

L

LOYALIST n patriotic supporter of the sovereign or government

LOYALLER ► loyal

LOYALLY ► loyal

LOYALTY n quality of being loyal

LOYS ► loy

LOZELL, -S n obsolete form of ► losel

LOZEN, -S n window pane

LOZENGE, -S n medicated tablet

LOZENGED adj decorated with lozenges

LOZENGES ► lozenge

LOZENGY adj divided by diagonal lines to form a lattice

LOZENS ► lozen

LUACH, LUCHOT, LUCHOTH n Jewish calendar

LUAU, -S n feast of Hawaiian food

LUBBARD, -S same as ► lubber

LUBBER, -S n big, awkward, or stupid person
LUBBERLY

LUBE, -D, -S, LUBING n lubricating oil ▷ vb lubricate with oil

LUBFISH n type of fish

LUBING ► lube

LUBRA, -S n Aboriginal woman

LUBRIC adj slippery

LUBRICAL same as ► lubric

LUCARNE, -S n type of dormer window

LUCE, -S another name for ► pike

LUCENCE, -S ► lucent

LUCENCY ► lucent

LUCENT adj brilliant
LUCENTLY

LUCERN, -S same as ► lucerne

LUCERNE, -S n alfalfa

LUCERNS ► lucern

LUCES ► luce

LUCHOT ► luach

LUCHOTH ► luach

LUCID, -ER, -EST adj clear
LUCIDITY
LUCIDLY

LUCIFER, -S n friction match

LUCIGEN, -S n type of lamp

LUCITE, -S n type of transparent acrylic-based plastic

LUCK, -ED, -ING, -S n fortune, good or bad ▷ vb have good fortune

LUCKEN adj shut

LUCKIE same as ► lucky

LUCKIER ► lucky

LUCKIES ► lucky

LUCKIEST ► lucky

LUCKILY ► lucky

LUCKING ► luck

LUCKLESS adj having bad luck

LUCKS ► luck

LUCKY, LUCKIER, LUCKIES, LUCKIEST adj having or bringing good luck ▷ n old woman

LUCRE, -S n money or wealth

LUCULENT adj easily understood

LUCUMA, -S n S American tree

LUCUMO, -S n Etruscan king

LUD, -S n lord ▷ interj exclamation of dismay or surprise

LUDERICK n Australian fish, usu black or dark brown in colour

LUDIC adj playful

LUDO, -S n game played with dice and counters on a board

LUDS ► lud

LUDSHIP, -S ► lud

LUES n any venereal disease

LUETIC adj

LUFF, -ED, -ING, -S vb sail (a ship) towards the wind ▷ n leading edge of a fore-and-aft sail

LUFFA, -S same as ► loofah

LUFFED ► luff

LUFFING ► luff

LUFFS ► luff

LUG, -GED, -GING, -S vb carry with great effort ▷ n projection serving as a handle

LUGE, -D, -S n racing toboggan ▷ vb ride on a luge

LUGEING -S

LUGER, -S n pistol

LUGES ► luge

LUGGABLE n unwieldy portable computer

LUGGAGE, -S n suitcases, bags, etc

LUGGED ► lug

LUGGER, -S n small working boat with an oblong sail

LUGGIE, -S n wooden bowl

LUGGING ► lug

LUGHOLE, -S informal word for ► ear

LUGING, -S ► luge

LUGS ► lug

LUGSAIL, -S n four-sided sail

LUGWORM, -S n large worm used as bait

LUIT Scots past form of ► let

LUITEN ► let

LUKE variant of ► lukewarm

LUKEWARM adj moderately warm, tepid

LULIBUB, -S obsolete form of ► lollipop

LULL, -ED, -ING, -S vb soothe (someone) by soft sounds or motions ▷ n brief time of quiet in a storm etc

LULLABY n quiet song ▷ vb quiet with a lullaby

LULLED ► lull

LULLER, -S ► lull

LULLING ► lull

LULLS ► lull

LULU, -S n person or thing deemed to be outstanding

LULZ pl n laughs at someone else's or one's own expense

LUM, -S n chimney

LUMA, -S n monetary unit of Armenia

LUMBAGO, -S n pain in the lower back

LUMBANG, -S n type of tree

LUMBAR, -S adj of the part of the body between the lowest ribs and the hipbones ▷ n old-fashioned kind of ship

LUMBER, -ED, -S n unwanted disused household articles ▷ vb burden with something unpleasant
LUMBERER

LUMBERLY adj heavy; clumsy

LUMBERS ► lumber

LUMBI ► lumbus

LUMBRICI > lumbricus

LUMBUS, LUMBI n part of the lower back and sides between the pelvis and the ribs

LUMEN, -S, LUMINA n derived SI unit of luminous flux
LUMENAL
LUMINAL

LUMINANT n something used to give light

LUMINARY n famous person ▷ adj of, involving, or characterized by light or enlightenment

LUMINE, -D, -S, LUMINING vb illuminate

LUMINISM n US artistic movement
LUMINIST

LUMINOUS adj reflecting or giving off light

LUMME interj exclamation of surprise or dismay

LUMMIER ► lummy

LUMMIEST ► lummy

LUMMOX, -ES n clumsy person

LUMMY, LUMMIER, LUMMIEST interj

LUMP, -ED, -ING, -S n shapeless mass ▷ vb consider as one group

LUMPEN, -S adj stupid or unthinking ▷ n member of underclass

LUMPENLY

LUMPER, -S n stevedore

LUMPFISH n North Atlantic scorpaenoid fish

LUMPIA, -S n type of Indonesian spring roll

LUMPIER ► lumpy

LUMPIEST ► lumpy

LUMPILY ► lumpy

LUMPING ► lump

LUMPISH adj stupid or clumsy

LUMPKIN, -S n lout

LUMPS ► lump

LUMPY, LUMPIER, LUMPIEST adj full of lumps

LUMS ► lum

LUN, -S n sheltered spot

LUNA, -S n large American moth

LUNACY, LUNACIES n foolishness

LUNANAUT same as > lunarnaut

LUNAR, -S adj relating to the moon ▷ n lunar distance

LUNARIAN n inhabitant of the moon

LUNARIES ► lunary

LUNARIST n one believing the moon influences weather

LUNARS ► lunar

LUNARY, LUNARIES n moonwort herb

LUNAS ► luna

LUNATE, -S adj shaped like a crescent ▷ n crescent-shaped bone forming part of the wrist

LUNATED variant of ► lunate

LUNATELY ► lunate

LUNATES ► lunate

LUNATIC, -S adj foolish ▷ n foolish person

LUNATION See ► month

LUNCH, -ED, -ES, -ING n meal at midday ▷ vb eat lunch

LUNCHBOX n container for carrying a packed lunch

LUNCHED ► lunch

LUNCHEON n formal lunch

LUNCHER, -S ► lunch

LUNCHES ► lunch

LUNCHING ► lunch

LUNE, -S same as ► lunette

LUNET, -S n small moon or satellite

LUNETTE, -S n anything that is shaped like a crescent

LUNG, -S n organ that allows an animal or bird to breathe air

LUNGAN, -S same as ► longan

LUNGE, -D, -ING, -S, LUNGING n sudden forward motion ▷ vb move with or make a lunge

LUNGEE, -S same as ► lungi

LUNGEING ► lunge

LUNGER, -S ► lunge

LUNGES ► lunge

LUNGFISH n freshwater bony fish with an air-breathing lung

LUNGFUL, -S ► lung

LUNGI, -S n cotton cloth worn as a loincloth, sash, or turban

LUNGIE, -S n guillemot

LUNGING ► lunge

LUNGIS ► lungi

LUNGLESS adj having no lungs

LUNGS ► lung

LUNGWORM n type of parasitic worm occurring in the lungs of mammals

LUNGWORT n plant with spotted leaves

LUNGYI, -S same as ► lungi

LUNIER ► luny

LUNIES ► luny

LUNIEST ► luny

LUNINESS ► luny

LUNK, -S n awkward person

LUNKER, -S n very large fish

LUNKHEAD n stupid person

LUNKS ► lunk

LUNS ► lun

LUNT, -ED, -ING, -S vb produce smoke

LUNULA, -E n white area at base of the fingernail

LUNULAR same as ► lunulate

LUNULATE adj having markings shaped like crescents

LUNULE, -S same as ► lunula

LUNY, LUNIER, LUNIES, LUNIEST same as ► loony

LUNYIE, -S same as ► lungie

LUPIN, -S n garden plant

LUPINE, -S adj like a wolf ▷ n lupin

LUPINS ► lupin

LUPOID adj suffering from lupus

LUPOUS adj relating to lupus

LUPPEN Scots past form of ► leap

LUPULIN, -S n resinous powder extracted from the female flowers of the hop plant

LUPULINE adj relating to lupulin

LUPULINS ► lupulin

LUPUS, -ES n ulcerous skin disease

LUR, -S n large bronze musical horn

LURCH, -ED, -ES vb tilt suddenly ▷ n lurching movement

LURCHER, -S n crossbred dog trained to hunt silently

LURCHES ► lurch

LURCHING ► lurch

LURDAN, -S n stupid or dull person ▷ adj dull or stupid

LURDANE, -S same as ► lurdan

LURDANS ► lurdan

LURDEN, -S same as ► lurdan

LURE, -D, -S, LURING vb tempt by promise of reward ▷ n person that lures

LURER -S

LUREX, -ES n thin glittery thread

LURGI, -S same as ► lurgy

LURGIES ► lurgy

LURGIS ► lurgi

LURGY, LURGIES n any undetermined illness

LURID, -ER, -EST adj sensational

LURIDLY

LURING, -S ► lure

LURINGLY ► lure

LURINGS ► luring

LURK, -ED, -S vb lie hidden

LURKER -S

LURKING, -S adj lingering

LURKS ► lurk

LURRY, LURRIES n confused jumble

LURS ► lur

LURVE, -S n love

LUSCIOUS adj extremely pleasurable to taste or smell

LUSER, -S n humorous term for computer user

LUSH, -ED, -ES, -EST, -ING adj growing thickly ▷ n alcoholic ▷ vb drink to excess

LUSHER, -S adj more lush ▷ n drunkard

LUSHES ► lush

LUSHEST ► lush

LUSHIER ► lushy

LUSHIES ► lushy

LUSHIEST ► lushy

LUSHING ► lush

LUSHLY ► lush

LUSHNESS ► lush

LUSHY, LUSHIER, LUSHIES, LUSHIEST adj slightly intoxicated ▷ n drunkard

LUSK, -ED, -ING, -S vb lounge around

LUSKISH adj lazy

LUSKS ▸ lusk

LUST, -ED, -ING, -S n strong desire ▷ vb have strong desire (for)

LUSTER, -ED, -S same as ▸ lustre

LUSTICK obsolete word for ▸ lusty

LUSTIER ▸ lusty

LUSTIEST ▸ lusty

LUSTILY ▸ lusty

LUSTING ▸ lust

LUSTIQUE obsolete word for ▸ lusty

LUSTLESS ▸ lust

LUSTRA ▸ lustrum

LUSTRAL adj of or relating to a ceremony of purification

LUSTRATE vb purify by means of religious rituals or ceremonies

LUSTRE, -D, -S n gloss, sheen ▷ vb make, be, or become lustrous

LUSTRINE same as ▸ lustring

LUSTRING n glossy silk cloth, formerly used for clothing, upholstery, etc

LUSTROUS ▸ lustre

LUSTRUM, LUSTRA, -S n period of five years

LUSTS ▸ lust

LUSTY, LUSTIER, LUSTIEST adj vigorous, healthy

LUSUS, -ES n freak, mutant

LUTANIST same as ▸ lutenist

LUTE, -D, -S n musical instrument r ▷ vb seal with cement and clay

LUTEA adj yellow

LUTEAL adj relating to the development of the corpus luteum

LUTECIUM same as ▸ lutetium

LUTED ▸ lute

LUTEFISK n Scandinavian fish dish

LUTEIN, -S n xanthophyll pigment

LUTENIST n person who plays the lute

LUTEOLIN n yellow crystalline compound found in many plants

LUTEOUS adj of a greenish-yellow colour

LUTER, -S n lute player

LUTES ▸ lute

LUTETIUM n silvery-white metallic element

LUTEUM adj yellow

LUTFISK, -S same as ▸ lutefisk

LUTHERN, -S another name for ▸ dormer

LUTHIER, -S n lute-maker

LUTING, -S n cement and clay

LUTIST, -S same as ▸ lutenist

LUTITE, -S another name for ▸ pelite

LUTTEN ▸ loot

LUTZ, -ES n skating jump

LUV, -S, -VED, -VING n love ▷ vb love

LUVVIE, -S n person who is involved in acting or the theatre

LUVVING ▸ luv

LUVVY same as ▸ luvvie

LUX, -ED, -ES, -ING n unit of illumination ▷ vb clean with a vacuum cleaner

> One of the key words using X.

LUXATE, -D, -S, LUXATING vb put (a shoulder, knee, etc) out of joint

LUXATION

LUXE, -R, -ST n as in **de luxe** luxuriousness ▷ adj luxury

LUXED ▸ lux

LUXER ▸ luxe

LUXES ▸ lux

LUXEST ▸ luxe

LUXING ▸ lux

LUXMETER n device for measuring light

LUXURIES ▸ luxury

LUXURIST n person who loves luxurious things

LUXURY, LUXURIES n enjoyment of rich, very comfortable living ▷ adj of or providing luxury

LUZ, -ZES n supposedly indestructible bone of the human body

> This very unusual word is very useful for playing the Z.

LUZERN, -S n alfalfa

LUZZES ▸ luz

LWEI, -S n Angolan monetary unit

LYAM, -S n leash

LYARD same as ▸ liard

LYART same as ▸ liard

LYASE, -S n any enzyme that catalyses the separation of two parts of a molecule

LYCAENID n type of butterfly

LYCEA ▸ lyceum

LYCEE, -S n secondary school

LYCEUM, LYCEA, -S n public building for concerts

LYCH, -ES same as ▸ lich

LYCHEE, -S same as ▸ litchi

LYCHES ▸ lych

LYCHGATE same as ▸ lichgate

LYCHNIS n plant with red, pink, or white flowers

LYCOPENE n red pigment

LYCOPOD, -S n type of moss

LYCOPSID n type of club moss

LYCRA, -S n type of elastic fabric used for tight-fitting garments

LYDDITE, -S n explosive consisting chiefly of fused picric acid

LYE, -S n caustic solution

LYFULL obsolete form of ▸ lifeful

LYING, -S ▸ lie

LYINGLY ▸ lie

LYINGS ▸ lying

LYKEWAKE n watch held over a dead person, often with festivities

LYKEWALK variant of ▸ lykewake

LYM, -S obsolete form of ▸ lyam

LYME, -S n as in **lyme grass** type of perennial dune grass

LYMITER, -S same as ▸ limiter

LYMPH n colourless bodily fluid

LYMPHAD, -S n ancient rowing boat

LYMPHOID adj of or resembling lymph, or relating to the lymphatic system

LYMPHOMA n any form of cancer of the lymph nodes

LYMPHOUS adj resembling lymph

LYMPHS ▸ lymph

LYMS ▸ lym

LYNAGE, -S obsolete form of ▸ lineage

LYNCEAN adj of a lynx

LYNCH, -ED, -ES vb put to death without a trial

LYNCHER -S

LYNCHET, -S n ridge formed by ploughing a hillside

LYNCHING ▸ lynch

LYNCHPIN same as ▸ linchpin

LYNE, -S n flax

LYNX, -ES n animal of the cat family

LYNXLIKE

LYOLYSIS, LYOLYSES n formation of an acid and a base from the interaction of a salt with a solvent

LYOPHIL same as > lyophilic

LYOPHILE same as > lyophilic

LYOPHOBE *same as*
> **lyophobic**
LYRA *n as in* **lyra viol** lutelike musical instrument
LYRATE *adj* shaped like a lyre
LYRATED *same as* ▶ **lyrate**
LYRATELY ▶ **lyrate**
LYRE, -S *n* ancient musical instrument
LYREBIRD *n* Australian bird, the male of which spreads its tail into the shape of a lyre
LYRES ▶ **lyre**
LYRIC, -S *adj* expressing emotion in songlike style ▷ *n* short poem in a songlike style
LYRICAL *same as* ▶ **lyric**
LYRICISE *same as* ▶ **lyricize**
LYRICISM *n* quality or style of lyric poetry
LYRICIST *n* person who writes the words of songs or musicals
LYRICIZE *vb* write lyrics

LYRICON, -S *n* wind synthesizer
LYRICS ▶ **lyric**
LYRIFORM *adj* lyre-shaped
LYRISM, -S *n* art or technique of playing the lyre
LYRIST, -S *same as* ▶ **lyricist**
LYSATE, -S *n* material formed by lysis
LYSE, -D, LYSING *vb* undergo lysis
LYSERGIC *adj as in* **lysergic acid** crystalline compound used in medical research
LYSES ▶ **lysis**
LYSIN, -S *n* antibodies that dissolute cells against which they are directed
LYSINE, -S *n* essential amino acid that occurs in proteins
LYSING ▶ **lyse**
LYSINS ▶ **lysin**
LYSIS, LYSES *n* destruction of cells by a lysin

LYSOGEN, -S *n* lysis-inducing agent
LYSOGENY
LYSOL, -S *n* antiseptic solution
LYSOSOME *n* any of numerous small particles that are present in the cytoplasm of most cells
LYSOZYME *n* enzyme occurring in tears, certain body tissues, and egg white
LYSSA, -S *less common word for* ▶ **rabies**
LYTE, -D, -S, LYTING *vb* dismount
LYTHE, -S *n* type of fish
LYTHRUM, -S *n* genus of plants including loosestrife
LYTIC *adj* relating to, causing, or resulting from lysis
LYTING ▶ **lyte**
LYTTA, -E, -S *n* mass of cartilage under the tongue in carnivores

L

Mm

M is a very useful letter when you need to form short words as it starts a two-letter word with every vowel, as well as with **Y** and with another **M**. Remembering this allows you to use **M** effectively when you're forming a word parallel to, and in contact with, a word that is already on the board. **M** also combines well with **X** and **Z**, so there is a lot of potential for high-scoring words. Keep **max**, **mix** and **mux** (12 points each) in mind, as well as **miz** and **moz** (14 each). It's also worth remembering the three-letter words ending in **W**: **maw**, **mew** and **mow** (8 points each). **Myc** is another useful word to remember when you are short of vowels.

MA, **-S** *n* mother
MAA, **-ED**, **-ING** *vb* (of goats) bleat
MAAR, **-E**, **-S** *n* coneless volcanic crater
MAAS, **-ES** *n* thick soured milk
MAATJES *n* pickled herring
MABE, **-S** *n* type of pearl
MABELA, **-S** *n* ground sorghum
MABES ► **mabe**
MAC, **-S** *n* macintosh
MACABER *same as* ► **macabre**
MACABRE *adj* strange and horrible, gruesome
MACACO, **-S** *n* type of lemur
MACADAM, **-S** *n* road surface
MACAHUBA *n* South American palm tree
MACALLUM *n* ice cream with raspberry sauce
MACAQUE, **-S** *n* monkey of Asia and Africa
MACARISE *vb* congratulate
MACARISM *n* blessing
MACARIZE *same as* ► **macarise**
MACARONI *n* pasta in short tube shapes
MACAROON *n* small biscuit or cake made with ground almonds
MACASSAR *n* oily preparation formerly put on the hair to make it smooth and shiny
MACAW, **-S** *n* large tropical American parrot
MACCABAW *same as* ► **maccaboy**
MACCABOY *n* dark rose-scented snuff

MACCHIA, **MACCHIE** *n* thicket in Italy
MACCOBOY *same as* ► **maccaboy**
MACE, **-D**, **-S**, **MACING** *n* club ▷ *vb* use a mace
MACER, **-S** *n* macebearer, esp (in Scotland) an official who acts as usher in a court of law
MACERAL, **-S** *n* any of the organic units that constitute coal
MACERATE *vb* soften by soaking
MACERS ► **macer**
MACES ► **mace**
MACH, **-S** *n* ratio of the speed of a body in a particular medium to the speed of sound in that medium
MACHACA, **-S** *n* Mexican dish of shredded dried beef
MACHAIR, **-S** *n* (in the western Highlands of Scotland) a strip of sandy, grassy land
MACHAN, **-S** *n* (in India) a raised platform used in tiger hunting
MACHE, **-S** *n* papier-mâché
MACHER, **-S** *n* important or influential person
MACHES ► **mache**
MACHETE, **-S** *n* broad heavy knife used for cutting or as a weapon
MACHI *n as in* **machi chips** in Indian English, fish and chips
MACHINE, **-D**, **-S** *n* apparatus designed to perform a task ▷ *vb* make or produce by machine

MACHISMO *n* exaggerated or strong masculinity
MACHO, **-S** *adj* strongly masculine ▷ *n* strong masculinity
MACHOISM
MACHREE, **-S** *n* Irish form of address meaning my dear
MACHS ► **mach**
MACHZOR, **-S** *n* Jewish prayer book
MACING ► **mace**
MACK, **-S** *same as* ► **mac**
MACKEREL *n* edible sea fish
MACKINAW *n* thick short double-breasted plaid coat
MACKLE, **-D**, **-S**, **MACKLING** *n* blurred impression ▷ *vb* mend hurriedly or in a makeshift way
MACKS ► **mack**
MACLE, **-S** *n* crystal consisting of two parts
MACLED
MACON, **-S** *n* wine from the Mâcon area
MACOYA, **-S** *n* South American tree
MACRAME, **-S** *n* ornamental work of knotted cord
MACRAMI, **-S** *same as* ► **macrame**
MACRO, **-S** *n* close-up lens
MACRON, **-S** *n* mark placed over a letter to represent a long vowel
MACROPOD *n* member of kangaroo family
MACROS ► **macro**
MACRURAL *adj* long-tailed
MACRURAN *n* type of decapod crustacean

MACS ▸ mac
MACULA, -E, -S n small spot like a freckle **MACULAR**
MACULATE vb spot, stain, or pollute ▷ adj spotted or polluted
MACULE, -S, MACULING same as ▸ **mackle** **MACULED**
MACULOSE adj having spots
MACUMBA, -S n religious cult in Brazil
MAD, -DED, -DEST, -DING, -S adj mentally deranged, insane ▷ vb make mad
MADAFU, -S n coconut milk
MADAM, -ED, -ING, -S, MESDAMES n polite term of address for a woman ▷ vb call someone madam
MADAME, -S n French title equivalent to Mrs
MADAMED ▸ madam
MADAMES ▸ madame
MADAMING ▸ madam
MADAMS ▸ madam
MADCAP, -S adj foolish or reckless ▷ n impulsive or reckless person
MADDED ▸ mad
MADDEN, -ED, -S vb infuriate or irritate
MADDER, -S n type of rose
MADDEST ▸ mad
MADDING ▸ mad
MADDISH ▸ mad
MADDOCK, -S same as ▸ **mattock**
MADE ▸ make
MADEFY, MADEFIED, MADEFIES vb make moist
MADEIRA, -S n kind of rich sponge cake
MADERISE vb become reddish
MADERIZE same as ▸ **maderise**
MADEUPPY adj artificial or contrived in an obvious way
MADGE, -S n type of hammer
MADHOUSE n place filled with uproar or confusion
MADID adj wet
MADISON, -S n type of cycle relay race
MADLING, -S n insane person
MADLY adv with great speed and energy
MADMAN, MADMEN n person who is insane
MADNESS n insanity
MADONNA, -S n picture or statue of the Virgin Mary
MADOQUA, -S n Ethiopian antelope

MADRAS, -ES n medium-hot curry
MADRASA, -S same as ▸ **madrasah**
MADRASAH n educational institution, particularly for Islamic religious instruction
MADRASAS ▸ madrasa
MADRASES ▸ madras
MADRASSA same as ▸ **madrasah**
MADRE, -S Spanish word for ▸ **mother**
MADRIGAL n 16th–17th-century part song for unaccompanied voices
MADRONA, -S n N American evergreen tree or shrub
MADRONE, -S same as ▸ **madrona**
MADRONO, -S same as ▸ **madrona**
MADS ▸ mad
MADTOM, -S n species of catfish
MADURO, -S adj (of cigars) dark and strong ▷ n cigar of this type
MADWOMAN, MADWOMEN n woman who is insane, esp one who behaves violently
MADWORT, -S n low-growing Eurasian plant with small blue flowers
MADZOON, -S same as ▸ **matzoon**
MAE, -S adj more
MAELID, -S n mythical spirit of apple tree
MAENAD, -ES, -S n female disciple of Dionysus **MAENADIC**
MAERL, -S n type of red coralline algae
MAES ▸ mae
MAESTOSO adv be performed majestically ▷ n piece or passage directed to be played in this way
MAESTRO, MAESTRI, -S n outstanding musician or conductor
MAFFIA, -S same as ▸ **mafia**
MAFFICK, -S vb celebrate extravagantly and publicly
MAFFLED adj baffled
MAFFLIN, -S n half-witted person
MAFFLING same as ▸ **mafflin**
MAFFLINS ▸ mafflin
MAFIA, -S n international secret organization founded in Sicily
MAFIC, -S n minerals present in igneous rock

MAFIOSO, MAFIOSI, -S n member of the Mafia
MAFTED adj suffering under oppressive heat
MAFTIR, -S n final section of the weekly Torah reading
MAG, -GED, -GING, -S vb talk ▷ n talk
MAGAININ n substance with antibacterial properties
MAGALOG, -S same as ▸ **magalogue**
MAGAZINE n periodical publication with articles by different writers
MAGE, -S archaic word for ▸ **magician**
MAGENTA, -S adj deep purplish-red ▷ n deep purplish red
MAGES ▸ mage
MAGESHIP ▸ mage
MAGG, -S same as ▸ **mag**
MAGGED ▸ mag
MAGGIE, -S n magpie
MAGGING ▸ mag
MAGGOT, -S n larva of an insect
MAGGOTY adj relating to, resembling, or ridden with maggots
MAGGS ▸ magg
MAGI ▸ magus
MAGIAN, -S ▸ magus
MAGIC, -KED, -S n supposed art of invoking supernatural powers to influence events ▷ vb transform or produce by or as if by magic ▷ adj of, using, or like magic **MAGICAL**
MAGICIAN n conjuror
MAGICKED ▸ magic
MAGICS ▸ magic
MAGILP, -S same as ▸ **megilp**
MAGISM, -S ▸ magus
MAGISTER n person entitled to teach in medieval university
MAGLEV, -S n type of high-speed train
MAGMA, -S, -TA n molten rock inside the earth's crust **MAGMATIC**
MAGNATE, -S n influential or wealthy person, esp in industry
MAGNES, -ES n magnetic iron ore
MAGNESIA n white tasteless substance used as an antacid and a laxative **MAGNESIC**
MAGNET, -S n piece of iron or steel capable of attracting

M

iron and pointing north when suspended

MAGNETAR *n* neutron star with intense magnetic field

MAGNETIC *adj* having the properties of a magnet

MAGNETO, -S *n* apparatus for ignition in an internal-combustion engine

MAGNETON *n* unit of magnetic moment

MAGNETOS ► magneto

MAGNETS ► magnet

MAGNIFIC *adj* magnificent, grandiose, or pompous

MAGNIFY *vb* increase in apparent size, as with a lens

MAGNOLIA *n* shrub or tree with showy white or pink flowers

MAGNON, -S *n* short for Cro-Magnon

MAGNOX, -ES *n* alloy used in fuel elements of some nuclear reactors

MAGNUM, -S *n* large wine bottle holding about 1.5 litres

MAGNUS *adj as in* **magnus hitch** knot similar to a clove hitch but having one more turn

MAGOT, -S *n* Chinese or Japanese figurine in a crouching position, usually grotesque

MAGPIE, -S *n* black-and-white bird

MAGS ► mag

MAGSMAN, MAGSMEN *n* raconteur

MAGUEY, -S *n* tropical American agave plant

MAGUS, MAGI *n* Zoroastrian priest of the ancient Medes and Persians

MAGYAR *adj* of or relating to a style of sleeve

MAHA *n as in* **maha yoga** form of yoga

MAHANT, -S *n* chief priest in a Hindu temple

MAHARAJA *same as* > **maharajah**

MAHARANI *n* wife of a maharaja

MAHATMA, -S *n* person revered for holiness and wisdom

MAHEWU, -S *n* (in South Africa) fermented liquid mealie-meal porridge

MAHIMAHI *n* Pacific fish

MAHJONG, -S *n* game of Chinese origin, using tiles

MAHJONGG *same as* ► **mahjong**

MAHJONGS ► mahjong

MAHMAL, -S *n* litter used in Muslim ceremony

MAHOE, -S *n* New Zealand tree

MAHOGANY *n* hard reddish-brown wood of several tropical trees ▷ *adj* reddish-brown

MAHONIA, -S *n* Asian and American evergreen shrub

MAHOUT, -S *n* (in India and the East Indies) elephant driver or keeper

MAHSEER, -S *n* large freshwater Indian fish

MAHSIR, -S *same as* ► **mahseer**

MAHUA, -S *n* Indian tree

MAHUANG, -S *n* herbal medicine from shrub

MAHUAS ► mahua

MAHWA, -S *same as* ► **mahua**

MAHZOR, -IM, -S *same as* > **machzor**

MAIASAUR *same as* > **maiasaura**

MAID, -ED, -ING, -S *n* female servant ▷ *vb* work as maid

MAIDAN, -S *n* (in Pakistan, India, etc) open area

MAIDED ► maid

MAIDEN, -S *n* young unmarried woman ▷ *adj* unmarried

MAIDENLY *adj* modest

MAIDENS ► maiden

MAIDHOOD ► maid

MAIDING ► maid

MAIDISH ► maid

MAIDISM, -S *n* pellagra

MAIDLESS ► maid

MAIDS ► maid

MAIEUTIC *adj* of or relating to the Socratic method of eliciting knowledge by a series of questions and answers

MAIGRE, -S *adj* not containing meat ▷ *n* species of fish

MAIHEM, -S *same as* ► **mayhem**

MAIK, -S *n* old halfpenny

MAIKO, -S *n* apprentice geisha

MAIKS ► maik

MAIL, -ED, -ING, -S *n* letters and packages transported and delivered by the post office ▷ *vb* send by mail

MAILABLE

MAILBAG, -S *n* large bag for transporting or delivering mail

MAILBOAT *n* boat that carries mail

MAILBOX *n* box into which letters and parcels are delivered

MAILCAR, -S *same as* > **mailcoach**

MAILE, -S *n* halfpenny

MAILED ► mail

MAILER, -S *n* person who addresses or mails letters, etc

MAILES ► maile

MAILGRAM *n* telegram

MAILING, -S ► mail

MAILL, -S *n* Scots word meaning rent

MAILLESS ► mail

MAILLOT, -S *n* tights worn for ballet, gymnastics, etc

MAILLS ► maill

MAILMAN, MAILMEN *n* postman

MAILROOM *n* room where mail to and from building is dealt with

MAILS ► mail

MAILSACK *same as* ► **mailbag**

MAILSHOT *n* posting of advertising material to many selected people at once

MAILVAN, -S *n* vehicle used to transport post

MAIM, -ED, -S *vb* cripple or mutilate ▷ *n* injury or defect

MAIMER -S

MAIMING, -S ► maim

MAIMS ► maim

MAIN, -ED, -ER, -EST, -ING, -S *adj* chief or principal ▷ *n* principal pipe or line carrying water, gas, or electricity ▷ *vb* lower sails

MAINBOOM *n* spar for mainsail

MAINDOOR *n* door from street into house

MAINED ► main

MAINER ► main

MAINEST ► main

MAINING ► main

MAINLAND *n* stretch of land which forms the main part of a country

MAINLINE *n* the trunk route between two points ▷ *adj* having an important position

MAINLY *adv* for the most part, chiefly

MAINMAST *n* chief mast of a ship

MAINOR, -S *n* act of doing something

MAINOUR, -S same as ▸ **mainor**

MAINS ▸ **main**

MAINSAIL n largest sail on a mainmast

MAINSTAY n chief support

MAINTAIN vb continue or keep in existence

MAINTOP, -S n top or platform at the head of the mainmast

MAINYARD n yard for a square mainsail

MAIOLICA same as ▸ **majolica**

MAIR, -S Scots form of ▸ **more**

MAIRE, -S n New Zealand tree

MAIREHAU n small aromatic shrub of New Zealand

MAIRES ▸ **maire**

MAIRS ▸ **mair**

MAISE, -S n measure of herring

MAIST, -S Scot word for ▸ **most**

MAISTER, -S Scots word for ▸ **master**

MAISTRY

MAISTS ▸ **maist**

MAIZE, -S n type of corn with spikes of yellow grains

MAJAGUA, -S same as ▸ **mahoe**

MAJESTIC adj beautiful, dignified, and impressive

MAJESTY n stateliness or grandeur

MAJLIS, -ES n (in Arab countries) an assembly

MAJOLICA n type of ornamented Italian pottery

MAJOR, -ED, -ING, -S adj greater in number, quality, or extent ▹ n middle-ranking army officer ▹ vb do one's principal study in (a particular subject)

MAJORAT, -S n estate, the right to which is that of the first born child of a family

MAJORED ▸ **major**

MAJORING ▸ **major**

MAJORITY n greater number

MAJORLY adv very

MAJORS ▸ **major**

MAK, -S Scot word for ▸ **make**

MAKABLE ▸ **make**

MAKAR, -S same as ▸ **maker**

MAKE, MADE, -S, MAKING vb create, construct, or establish ▹ n brand, type, or style

MAKEABLE

MAKEBATE n troublemaker

MAKEFAST n strong support to which a vessel is secured

MAKELESS ▸ **make**

MAKEOVER vb transfer the title of (property, etc) ▹ n alterations to improve me a person's appearance

MAKER, -S n person or company that makes something

MAKES ▸ **make**

MAKEUP, -S n cosmetics applied to the face

MAKHANI adj denoting an Indian dish made with butter or ghee

MAKI, -S n in Japanese cuisine, rice and other ingredients wrapped in a short seaweed roll

MAKIMONO n Japanese scroll

MAKING ▸ **make**

MAKINGS pl n potentials, qualities, or materials

MAKIS ▸ **maki**

MAKO, -S n powerful shark of the Atlantic and Pacific Oceans

MAKS ▸ **mak**

MAKUTA plural of ▸ **likuta**

MAKUTU, -ED, -S n Polynesian witchcraft ▹ vb cast a spell on

MAL, -S n illness

MALA, -S n string of beads or knots, used in praying and meditating

MALACCA, -S n stem of the rattan palm

MALACIA, -S n softening of an organ or tissue

MALADY, MALADIES n disease or illness

MALAISE, -S n something wrong which affects a section of society or area of activity

MALAM, -S same as ▸ **mallam**

MALAMUTE n Alaskan sled dog of the spitz type, having a dense usually greyish coat

MALANDER same as > **malanders**

MALANGA, -S same as ▸ **cocoyam**

MALAPERT adj saucy or impudent ▹ n saucy or impudent person

MALAPROP n word unintentionally confused with one of similar sound

MALAR, -S n cheekbone ▹ adj of or relating to the cheek or cheekbone

MALARIA, -S n infectious disease caused by mosquito bite

MALARIAL

MALARIAN

MALARKEY n nonsense or rubbish

MALARKY same as ▸ **malarkey**

MALAROMA n bad smell

MALARS ▸ **malar**

MALAS ▸ **mala**

MALATE, -S n any salt or ester of malic acid

MALAX, -ED, -ES, -ING vb soften

MALAXAGE

MALAXATE same as ▸ **malax**

MALAXED ▸ **malax**

MALAXES ▸ **malax**

MALAXING ▸ **malax**

MALE, -S adj of the sex which can fertilize reproductive cells ▹ n male person or animal

MALEATE, -S n any salt or ester of maleic acid

MALEDICT vb utter a curse against ▹ adj cursed or detestable

MALEFIC adj causing evil

MALEFICE n wicked deed

MALEIC adj as in **maleic acid** colourless soluble crystalline substance

MALEMIUT same as ▸ **malamute**

MALEMUTE same as ▸ **malamute**

MALENESS ▸ **male**

MALES ▸ **male**

MALFED adj having malfunctioned

MALGRADO prep in spite of

MALGRE, -D, -S, MALGRING same as ▸ **maugre**

MALI, -S n member of an Indian caste

MALIBU n as in **malibu board** lightweight surfboard

MALIC adj as in **malic acid** colourless crystalline compound occurring in apples

MALICE, -D, -S, MALICING n desire to cause harm to others ▹ vb wish harm to

MALICHO, -S n mischief

MALICING ▸ **malice**

MALIGN, -ED, -S vb slander or defame ▹ adj evil in influence or effect

MALIGNER

MALIGNLY

MALIHINI n (in Hawaii) a foreigner or stranger

M

MALIK, -S n person of authority in India

MALINE, -S n stiff net

MALINGER vb feign illness to avoid work

MALIS ▸ mali

MALISM, -S n belief that evil dominates world

MALISON, -S archaic or poetic word for ▸ **curse**

MALIST ▸ malism

MALKIN, -S archaic or dialect name for a ▸ **cat**

MALL, -ED, -S n street or shopping area closed to vehicles ▷ vb maul

MALLAM, -S n (in W Africa) expert in the Koran

MALLARD, -S n wild duck

MALLCORE n type of rock music combining heavy metal and hip-hop

MALLEATE vb hammer

MALLECHO same as ▸ **malicho**

MALLED, -S ▸ mall

MALLEE, -S n low-growing eucalypt in dry regions

MALLEI ▸ malleus

MALLEOLI > malleolus

MALLET, -S n (wooden) hammer

MALLEUS, MALLEI n small bone in the middle ear

MALLING, -S ▸ mall

MALLOW, -S n plant with pink or purple flowers

MALLS ▸ mall

MALM, -S n soft greyish limestone that crumbles easily

MALMAG, -S n Asian monkey

MALMIER ▸ malmy

MALMIEST ▸ malmy

MALMS ▸ malm

MALMSEY, -S n sweet Madeira wine

MALMY, MALMIER, MALMIEST adj looking like malm

MALODOR, -S same as ▸ **malodour**

MALODOUR n unpleasant smell

MALONATE n salt of malonic acid

MALONIC adj as in **malonic acid** colourless crystalline compound

MALOTI plural of ▸ **loti**

MALPOSED adj in abnormal position

MALS ▸ mal

MALSTICK same as > **maulstick**

MALT, -EDS, -S n grain, such as barley, dried in a kiln ▷ vb make into or make with malt

MALTASE, -S n enzyme that hydrolyses maltose to glucose

MALTED n malted milk drink

MALTEDS ▸ malt

MALTESE adj as in **maltese cross** cross-shaped part of a film projector

MALTHA, -S n any of various naturally occurring mixtures of hydrocarbons

MALTIER ▸ malty

MALTIEST ▸ malty

MALTING, -S n building in which malt is made or stored

MALTMAN, MALTMEN same as ▸ **maltster**

MALTOL, -S n food additive

MALTOSE, -S n sugar formed by the action of enzymes on starch

MALTREAT vb treat badly

MALTS ▸ malt

MALTSTER n person who makes or deals in malt

MALTWORM n heavy drinker

MALTY, MALTIER, MALTIEST adj of, like, or containing malt

MALUS, -ES n financial penalty incurred by an investor

MALVA, -S n mallow plant

MALVASIA n type of grape used to make malmsey

MALVESIE same as ▸ **malmsey**

MALWA, -S n Ugandan drink brewed from millet

MALWARE, -S n computer program designed to cause damage to a system

MALWAS ▸ malwa

MAM, -S same as ▸ **mother**

MAMA, -S n mother

MAMAGUY, -S vb deceive or tease ▷ n deception or flattery

MAMAKAU, -S same as ▸ **mamaku**

MAMAKO, -S same as ▸ **mamaku**

MAMAKU, -S n tall edible New Zealand tree fern

MAMALIGA same as ▸ **polenta**

MAMAS ▸ mama

MAMASAN, -S n (in Japan) woman in a position of authority

MAMATEEK n type of wigwam

MAMBA, -S n deadly S African snake

MAMBO, -ED, -ES, -ING, -S n Latin American dance resembling the rumba ▷ vb perform this dance

MAMEE, -S same as ▸ **mamey**

MAMELON, -S n small rounded hillock

MAMELUCO n Brazilian of mixed European and South American descent

MAMELUKE n member of a military class once ruling Egypt

MAMEY, -ES, -S n tropical tree

MAMIE, -S n tropical tree

MAMILLA, -E n nipple or teat

MAMILLAR adj of the breast

MAMLUK, -S same as ▸ **mameluke**

MAMMA, -E, -S n buxom and voluptuous woman

MAMMAL, -S n animal of the type that suckles its young

MAMMARY adj of the breasts or milk-producing glands ▷ n breast

MAMMAS ▸ mamma

MAMMATE adj having breasts

MAMMATUS, MAMMATI n breast-shaped cloud

MAMMEE, -S same as ▸ **mamey**

MAMMER, -ED, -S vb hesitate

MAMMET, -S same as ▸ **maumet**

MAMMETRY n worship of idols

MAMMETS ▸ mammet

MAMMEY, -S same as ▸ **mamey**

MAMMIE same as ▸ **mammy**

MAMMIES ▸ mammy

MAMMIFER same as ▸ **mammal**

MAMMILLA same as ▸ **mamilla**

MAMMITIS same as ▸ **mastitis**

MAMMOCK, -S n fragment ▷ vb tear or shred

MAMMON, -S n wealth regarded as a source of evil

MAMMOTH, -S n extinct elephant-like mammal ▷ adj colossal

MAMMY, MAMMIES same as ▸ **mother**

MAMPARA, -S n foolish person, idiot

MAMPOER, -S n home-distilled brandy

MAMS ▸ mam

MAMSELLE n mademoiselle

MAN, -D, -NED, -NING, -S, MEN n adult male ▷ vb supply with sufficient people for operation or defence

MANA, -S n authority, influence

MANACLE, -D, -S vb handcuff or fetter ▷ n metal ring or chain put round the wrists or ankles

MANAGE, -D, -S vb succeed in doing

MANAGER, -S n person in charge of a business, institution, actor, sports team, etc

MANAGES ▸ manage

MANAGING adj having administrative control or authority

MANAIA, -S n figure in Māori carving

MANAKIN, -S same as ▸ manikin

MANANA, -S n tomorrow ▷ adv tomorrow

MANAS ▸ mana

MANAT, -S n standard monetary unit of Azerbaijan

MANATEE, -S n large tropical plant-eating aquatic mammal

MANATI, -S same as ▸ manatee

MANATOID ▸ manatee

MANATS ▸ manat

MANATU, -S n large flowering deciduous New Zealand tree

MANAWA, -S in New Zealand, same as ▸ mangrove

MANBAG, -S n small handbag with a shoulder strap, carried by men

MANBAND, -S n boy band whose members have reached maturity

MANCALA, -S n African and Asian board game

MANCANDO adv musical direction meaning fading away

MANCHE, -S n long sleeve

MANCHET, -S n type of bread

MANCIPLE n steward who buys provisions, esp in a college, Inn of Court, or monastery

MANCUS, -ES n former English coin

MAND ▸ man

MANDALA, -S n circular design symbolizing the universe

MANDALIC

MANDAMUS n order of a superior court

MANDARIN n high-ranking government official

MANDATE, -D, -S n official or authoritative command ▷ vb give authority to

MANDATOR

MANDI, -S n (in India) a big market

MANDIBLE n lower jawbone or jawlike part

MANDIOC, -S same as ▸ manioc

MANDIOCA same as ▸ manioc

MANDIOCS ▸ mandioc

MANDIR, -S n Hindu or Jain temple

MANDIRA, -S same as ▸ mandir

MANDIRS ▸ mandir

MANDIS ▸ mandi

MANDOLA, -S n early type of mandolin

MANDOLIN n musical instrument with four pairs of strings

MANDOM, -S n mankind

MANDORA, -S n ancestor of mandolin

MANDORLA n area of light surrounding Christ in a painting

MANDRAKE n plant with a forked root

MANDREL, -S n shaft on which work is held in a lathe

MANDRIL, -S same as ▸ mandrel

MANDRILL n large blue-faced baboon

MANDRILS ▸ mandril

MANE n long hair on the neck of a horse, lion, etc

MANEB, -S n powdered fungicide

MANED ▸ mane

MANEGE, -D, -S, MANEGING n art of training horses and riders ▷ vb train horse

MANEH, -S same as ▸ mina

MANELESS ▸ mane

MANENT ▸ manet

MANES pl n spirits of the dead, often revered as minor deities

MANET, MANENT vb theatre direction, remain on stage

MANEUVER same as > manoeuvre

MANFUL adj determined and brave

MANFULLY

MANG, -ED, -ING, -S vb speak

MANGA, -S n type of Japanese comic book

MANGABEY n large African monkey

MANGABY same as ▸ mangabey

MANGAL, -S n Turkish brazier

MANGANIC adj of or containing manganese in the trivalent state

MANGANIN n copper-based alloy

MANGAS ▸ manga

MANGE, -S n skin disease of domestic animals

MANGEAO, -S n small New Zealand tree with glossy leaves

MANGED ▸ mang

MANGEL, -S n Eurasian variety of the beet plant

MANGER, -S n eating trough in a stable or barn

MANGES ▸ mange

MANGEY same as ▸ mangy

MANGIER ▸ mangy

MANGIEST ▸ mangy

MANGILY ▸ mangy

MANGING ▸ mang

MANGLE, -D, -S, MANGLING vb destroy by crushing and twisting ▷ n machine with rollers for squeezing water from washed clothes

MANGLER -S

MANGO, -ES, -S n tropical fruit with sweet juicy yellow flesh

MANGOLD, -S n type of root vegetable

MANGONEL n war engine for hurling stones

MANGOS ▸ mango

MANGROVE n tropical tree with exposed roots, which grows beside water

MANGS ▸ mang

MANGY, MANGIER, MANGIEST adj having mange

MANHOLE, -S n hole with a cover, through which a person can enter a drain or sewer

MANHOOD, -S n state or quality of being a man or being manly

MANHUNT, -S n organized search, usu by police, for a wanted man

MANI n place to pray

MANIA, -S n extreme enthusiasm

MANIAC, -S n mad person

MANIACAL adj affected with or characteristic of mania

MANIACS ▸ maniac

MANIAS ▸ mania

M

MANIC, -S adj extremely excited or energetic ▷ n person afflicted with mania

MANICURE n cosmetic care of the fingernails and hands ▷ vb care for (the fingernails and hands) in this way

MANIES ► many

MANIFEST adj easily noticed, obvious ▷ vb show plainly ▷ n list of cargo or passengers for customs

MANIFOLD adj numerous and varied ▷ n pipe with several outlets, esp in an internal-combustion engine ▷ vb duplicate (a page, book, etc)

MANIFORM adj like hand

MANIHOC, -S variation of ► manioc

MANIHOT, -S n tropical American plant

MANIKIN, -S n little man or dwarf

MANILA, -S n strong brown paper used for envelopes

MANILLA, -S n early currency in W Africa in the form of a small bracelet

MANILLE, -S n (in ombre and quadrille) the second best trump

MANIOC, -S same as ► cassava

MANIOCA, -S same as ► manioc

MANIOCS ► manioc

MANIPLE, -S n (in ancient Rome) a unit of 120 to 200 foot soldiers

MANIS, -ES n pangolin

MANITO, -S same as ► manitou

MANITOU, -S n Native American deified spirit or force

MANITU, -S same as ► manitou

MANJACK, -S n single individual

MANKIER ► manky

MANKIEST ► manky

MANKIND, -S n human beings collectively

MANKINI, -S n revealing man's swimming costume

MANKY, MANKIER, MANKIEST adj worthless, rotten, or in bad taste

MANLESS ► man

MANLIER ► manly

MANLIEST ► manly

MANLIKE adj resembling or befitting a man

MANLILY ► manly

MANLY, MANLIER, MANLIEST adj (possessing qualities) appropriate to a man

MANMADE adj made or produced by man

MANNA, -S n miraculous food which sustained the Israelites in the wilderness

MANNAN, -S n drug derived from mannose

MANNAS ► manna

MANNED ► man

MANNER n way a thing happens or is done

MANNERED adj affected

MANNERLY adj having good manners, polite ▷ adv with good manners

MANNERS pl n person's social conduct

MANNIKIN same as ► manikin

MANNING ► man

MANNISH adj like a man

MANNITE, -S same as ► mannitol

MANNITIC ► mannitol

MANNITOL n white crystalline water-soluble sweet-tasting substance

MANNOSE, -S n hexose sugar

MANO, -ES n stone for grinding grain

MANOAO, -S n New Zealand shrub

MANOES ► mano

MANOR, -S n large country house and its lands

MANORIAL

MANOS ► mano

MANPACK, -S n load carried by one person

MANPOWER n available number of workers

MANQUE, -S adj would-be ▷ n section on a roulette table

MANRED, -S n homage

MANRENT, -S same as ► manred

MANRIDER n train carrying miners in coal mine

MANROPE, -S n rope railing

MANS ► man

MANSARD, -S n type of sloping roof

MANSCAPE vb groom a man's bodily hair for aesthetics

MANSE, -S n house provided for a minister in some religious denominations

MANSHIFT n work done by one person in one shift

MANSION, -S n large house

MANSONRY n mansions collectively

MANSUETE adj gentle

MANSWORN adj perjured ▷ n someone who perjures

MANTA, -S n type of large ray with very wide winglike pectoral fins

MANTEAU, -S, -X n cloak or mantle

MANTEEL, -S n cloak

MANTEL, -S n structure round a fireplace ▷ vb construct a mantel

MANTELET n woman's short mantle, often lace-trimmed, worn in the mid-19th century

MANTELS ► mantel

MANTES ► mantis

MANTIC adj of or relating to divination and prophecy

MANTID, -S same as ► mantis

MANTIES ► manty

MANTILLA n (in Spain) a lace scarf covering a woman's head and shoulders

MANTIS, MANTES, -ES n carnivorous insect like a grasshopper

MANTISSA n part of a common logarithm consisting of the decimal point and the figures following it

MANTLE, -D, -S same as ► mantel

MANTLET, -S same as ► mantelet

MANTLING n drapery or scrollwork around a shield

MANTO, -ES, -S same as ► manteau

MANTRA, -S n any sacred word or syllable used as an object of concentration

MANTRAM, -S same as ► mantra

MANTRAP, -S n snare for catching people, esp trespassers

MANTRAS ► mantra

MANTRIC ► mantra

MANTUA, -S n loose gown of the 17th and 18th centuries

MANTY, MANTIES Scots variant of ► mantua

MANUAL, -S adj of or done with the hands ▷ n handbook

MANUALLY

MANUARY same as ► manual

MANUBRIA > manubrium

MANUCODE *n* bird of Paradise with blue-black plumage

MANUHIRI *n* visitor to a Māori marae

MANUKA, -S *n* New Zealand tree

MANUL, -S *n* Asian wildcat

MANUMEA, -S *n* pigeon of Samoa

MANUMIT, -S *vb* free from slavery

MANURE, -D, -S, MANURING *n* animal excrement used as a fertilizer ▷ *vb* fertilize (land) with this

MANURER -S

MANURIAL ▸ **manure**

MANURING ▸ **manure**

MANUS *n* wrist and hand

MANWARD *adv* towards humankind

MANWARDS *same as* ▸ **manward**

MANWISE *adv* in human way

MANY, MANIES *adj* numerous ▷ *n* large number

MANYATA, -S *same as* ▸ **manyatta**

MANYATTA *n* settlement of Masai people

MANYFOLD *adj* many in number

MANZELLO *n* instrument like saxophone

MAOMAO, -S *n* fish of New Zealand seas

MAORMOR, -S *same as* ▸ **mormaor**

MAP, -PED, -S *n* representation of the earth's surface or some part of it ▷ *vb* make a map of

MAPAU, -S *n* small New Zealand tree

MAPLE, -S *n* tree with broad leaves, a variety of which yields sugar

MAPLESS ▸ **map**

MAPLIKE ▸ **map**

MAPMAKER *n* person who draws maps

MAPPABLE ▸ **map**

MAPPED ▸ **map**

MAPPER, -S ▸ **map**

MAPPERY *n* making of maps

MAPPING, -S ▸ **map**

MAPPIST, -S ▸ **map**

MAPS ▸ **map**

MAPSTICK *same as* ▸ **mopstick**

MAPWISE *adv* like map

MAQUETTE *n* sculptor's small preliminary model or sketch

MAQUI *n* Chilean shrub

MAQUILA, -S *n* US-owned factory in Mexico

MAQUIS *n* French underground movement in World War II

MAR, -D, -RED, -RING, -S *vb* spoil or impair ▷ *n* disfiguring mark

MARA, -S *n* harelike S American rodent

MARABI, -S *n* kind of music popular in S African townships in the 1930s

MARABOU, -S *n* large black-and-white African stork

MARABOUT *n* Muslim holy man or hermit of North Africa

MARACA, -S *n* shaken percussion instrument

MARAE, -S *n* enclosed space in front of a Māori meeting house

MARAGING *adj as in* **maraging steel** strong low-carbon steel

MARAH, -S *n* bitterness

MARANTA, -S *n* tropical American plant

MARARI, -S *n* eel-like blennioid food fish

MARAS ▸ **mara**

MARASCA, -S *n* European cherry tree with red acid-tasting fruit

MARASMIC ▸ **marasmus**

MARASMUS *n* emaciation

MARATHON *n* long-distance race of 26 miles 385 yards (42.195 kilometres) ▷ *adj* of or relating to a race on foot of 26 miles 385 yards (42.195 kilometres)

MARAUD, -ED, -S *vb* wander or raid in search of plunder

MARAUDER

MARAVEDI *n* any of various Spanish coins of copper or gold

MARBLE, -D *n* kind of limestone with a mottled appearance ▷ *vb* mottle with variegated streaks in imitation of marble

MARBLER -S

MARBLES *n* game in which marble balls are rolled at one another

MARBLIER ▸ **marble**

MARBLING *n* mottled effect or pattern resembling marble

MARBLY ▸ **marble**

MARC, -S *n* remains of grapes or other fruit that have been pressed for wine-making

MARCATO, -S *adj* (of notes) heavily accented ▷ *adv* with each note heavily accented ▷ *n* heavily accented note

MARCEL, -S *n* hairstyle characterized by repeated regular waves ▷ *vb* make such waves in (the hair)

MARCELLA *n* type of fabric

MARCELS ▸ **marcel**

MARCH, -ED, -ES, -ING *vb* walk with a military step ▷ *n* action of marching

MARCHEN *n* German story

MARCHER, -S *n* person who marches

MARCHES ▸ **march**

MARCHESA *n* (in Italy) the wife or widow of a marchese

MARCHESE, MARCHESI *n* (in Italy) a nobleman ranking below a prince and above a count

MARCHING ▸ **march**

MARCHMAN, MARCHMEN *n* person living on border

MARCONI, -S *vb* communicate by wireless

MARCS ▸ **marc**

MARD ▸ **mar**

MARDY, MARDIED, MARDIER, MARDIES, MARDIEST, -ING *adj* (of a child) spoilt ▷ *vb* behave in mardy way

MARE, -S, MARIA *n* female horse or zebra

MAREMMA, -S, MAREMME *n* marshy unhealthy region near the shore, esp in Italy

MARENGO *adj* browned in oil and cooked with tomatoes, mushrooms, garlic, wine, etc

MARERO, -S *n* member of a C American organized criminal gang

MARES ▸ **mare**

MARG, -S *short for* ▸ **margarine**

MARGARIC *adj* of or resembling pearl

MARGARIN *n* ester of margaric acid

MARGATE, -S *n* greyish fish of W Atlantic

MARGAY, -S *n* feline mammal of Central and S America

MARGE, -S *n* margarine

MARGENT, -S *same as* ▸ **margin**

MARGES ▸ **marge**

MARGIN, -ED, -S *n* edge or border ▷ *vb* provide with a margin

M

MARGINAL adj insignificant, unimportant ▷ n marginal constituency

MARGINED ► margin

MARGINS ► margin

MARGOSA, -S n Indian tree

MARGRAVE n (formerly) a German nobleman ranking above a count

MARGS ► marg

MARIA ► mare

MARIACHI n small ensemble of street musicians in Mexico

MARID, -S n spirit in Muslim mythology

MARIES ► mary

MARIGOLD n plant with yellow or orange flowers

MARIGRAM n graphic record of the tide levels at a particular coastal station

MARIMBA, -S n Latin American percussion instrument

MARINA, -S n harbour for yachts and other pleasure boats

MARINADE n seasoned liquid in which fish or meat is soaked before cooking

MARINARA n Italian pasta sauce

MARINAS ► marina

MARINATE vb soak in marinade

MARINE, -S adj of the sea or shipping ▷ n (esp in Britain and the US) soldier trained for land and sea combat

MARINER, -S n sailor

MARINERA n folk dance of Peru

MARINERS ► mariner

MARINES ► marine

MARIPOSA n plant of southwestern US and Mexico

MARISH, -ES n marsh

MARITAGE n right of a lord to choose the spouses of his wards

MARITAL adj relating to marriage

MARITIME adj relating to shipping

MARJORAM n aromatic herb used for seasoning food and in salads

MARK, -S n line, dot, scar, etc visible on a surface ▷ vb make a mark on

MARKA, -S n unit of currency introduced as an interim currency in Bosnia-Herzegovina

MARKDOWN n price reduction ▷ vb reduce in price

MARKED adj noticeable **MARKEDLY**

MARKER, -S n object used to show the position of something

MARKET, -ED, -S n assembly or place for buying and selling ▷ vb offer or produce for sale **MARKETER**

MARKHOOR same as ► markhor

MARKHOR, -S n large wild Himalayan goat

MARKING, -S n arrangement of colours on an animal or plant

MARKKA, -A, -S n former standard monetary unit of Finland

MARKMAN, MARKMEN n person owning land

MARKS ► mark

MARKSMAN, MARKSMEN n person skilled at shooting

MARKUP, -S n percentage added to the cost of something to give the seller a profit

MARL, -ED, -S n soil formed of clay and lime, used as fertilizer ▷ vb fertilize (land) with marl

MARLE, -S same as ► marvel

MARLED ► marl

MARLES ► marle

MARLIER ► marly

MARLIEST ► marly

MARLIN, -S same as ► marline

MARLINE, -S n light rope, usually tarred, made of two strands laid left-handed

MARLING, -S same as ► marline

MARLINS ► marlin

MARLITE, -S n type of marl that contains clay and calcium carbonate **MARLITIC**

MARLS ► marl

MARLY, MARLIER, MARLIEST adj marl-like

MARM, -S same as ► madam

MARMEM n as in marmem alloy type of alloy

MARMITE, -S n large cooking pot

MARMOSE, -S n South American opossum

MARMOSET n small bushy-tailed monkey

MARMOT, -S n burrowing rodent

MARMS ► marm

MAROCAIN n fabric of ribbed crepe

MARON, -S n freshwater crustacean

MAROON, -ED, -S adj reddish-purple ▷ vb abandon ashore, esp on an island ▷ n exploding firework or flare used as a warning signal **MAROONER**

MAROQUIN n morocco leather

MAROR, -S n Jewish ceremonial dish of bitter herbs

MARPLOT, -S n person who spoils a plot

MARQUE, -S n brand of product, esp of a car

MARQUEE, -S n large tent used for a party or exhibition

MARQUES ► marque

MARQUESS n nobleman of the rank below a duke

MARQUIS n (in some European countries) nobleman of the rank above a count

MARQUISE same as ► marquee

MARRA, -S n (in N England) friend

MARRAM, -S n as in marram grass any of several grasses that grow on sandy shores

MARRANO, -S n Spanish or Portuguese Jew of the late Middle Ages who was converted to Christianity

MARRAS ► marra

MARRED ► mar

MARRELS same as ► merils

MARRER, -S ► mar

MARRI, -S n W Australian eucalyptus

MARRIAGE n state of being married

MARRIED ► marry

MARRIEDS pl n married people

MARRIER, -S ► marry

MARRIES ► marry

MARRING ► mar

MARRIS ► marri

MARRON, -S n large edible sweet chestnut

MARROW, -ED, -S n fatty substance inside bones ▷ vb be mate to **MARROWY**

MARRUM, -S same as ► marram

MARRY, MARRIED, MARRIES, -ING vb take as a

spouse ▷ *interj* exclamation of surprise or anger

MARS ▶ mar

MARSALA, -S *n* dark sweet dessert wine made in Sicily

MARSE, -S *same as* **▶ master**

MARSH, -ES *n* low-lying wet land

MARSHAL, -S *n* officer of the highest rank ▷ *vb* arrange in order

MARSHALL *n* shortened form of Marshall Plan

MARSHALS ▶ marshal

MARSHED *adj* having a marsh

MARSHES ▶ marsh

MARSHY, MARSHIER *adj* of, involving, or like a marsh

MARSPORT *n* spoilsport

MARSUPIA > marsupium

MART, -ED, -ING, -S *n* market ▷ *vb* sell or trade

MARTAGON *n* Eurasian lily plant cultivated for its mottled purplish-red flowers

MARTED ▶ mart

MARTEL, -S *n* hammer-shaped weapon ▷ *vb* use such a weapon

MARTELLO *n* small circular tower for coastal defence, formerly much used in Europe

MARTELS ▶ martel

MARTEN, -S *n* weasel-like animal

MARTEXT, -S *n* preacher who makes many mistakes

MARTIAL *adj* of war, warlike

MARTIALS *pl n as in* **court martials** military courts that try people subject to military law

MARTIAN, -S *n* inhabitant of Mars

MARTIN, -S *n* bird with a slightly forked tail

MARTINET *n* person who maintains strict discipline

MARTING ▶ mart

MARTINI, -S *n* cocktail of vermouth and gin

MARTINS ▶ martin

MARTLET, -S *n* footless bird often found in coats of arms

MARTS ▶ mart

MARTYR, -ED, -S *n* person who dies or suffers for his or her beliefs ▷ *vb* make a martyr of

MARTYRIA > martyrium

MARTYRLY ▶ martyr

MARTYRS ▶ martyr

MARTYRY *n* shrine or chapel erected in honour of a martyr

MARVEL, -ED, -S *vb* be filled with wonder ▷ *n* wonderful thing

MARVELER *n* (US) person who marvels

MARVELS ▶ marvel

MARVER, -ED, -S *vb* roll molten glass on slab

MARVY, MARVIER, MARVIEST *shortened form of* **> marvelous**

MARY, MARIES *n* woman

MARYBUD, -S *n* bud of marigold

MARYJANE *n* woman's shoe with strap over the top

MARZIPAN *n* paste of ground almonds, sugar, and egg whites ▷ *vb* cover with marzipan

MAS ▶ ma

MASA, -S *n* Mexican maize dough

MASALA, -S *n* mixture of spices ground into a paste ▷ *adj* spicy

MASAS ▶ masa

MASCARA, -S *n* cosmetic for darkening the eyelashes

MASCARON *n* in architecture, a face carved in stone or metal

MASCLE, -S *n* charge consisting of a lozenge with a lozenge-shaped hole in the middle

MASCLED

MASCON, -S *n* any of several lunar regions of high gravity

MASCOT, -S *n* person, animal, or thing supposed to bring good luck

MASCULY ▶ mascle

MASE, -D, -S, MASING *vb* function as maser

MASER, -S *n* device for amplifying microwaves

MASES ▶ mase

MASH, -ED, -ES *n* soft pulpy mass ▷ *vb* crush into a soft mass

MASHER -S

MASHGIAH *same as* **> mashgiach**

MASHIACH *n* messiah

MASHIE, -S *n* former golf club, used for approach shots

MASHIER ▶ mashy

MASHIES ▶ mashie

MASHIEST ▶ mashy

MASHING ▶ mash

MASHLAM, -S *same as* **▶ maslin**

MASHLIM, -S *same as* **▶ maslin**

MASHLIN, -S *same as* **▶ maslin**

MASHLOCH *same as* **▶ maslin**

MASHLUM, -S *same as* **▶ maslin**

MASHMAN, MASHMEN *n* brewery worker

MASHUA, -S *n* South American plant

MASHUP, -S *n* piece of music in which a producer or DJ blends together two or more tracks

MASHY, MASHIER, MASHIEST *adj* like mash

MASING ▶ mase

MASJID, -S *same as* **▶ mosque**

MASK, -S *n* covering for the face, as a disguise or protection ▷ *vb* cover with a mask

MASKABLE

MASKED *adj* disguised or covered by or as if by a mask

MASKEG, -S *n* North American bog

MASKER, -S *n* person who wears a mask or takes part in a masque

MASKING, -S *n* act or practice of masking

MASKLIKE ▶ mask

MASKS ▶ mask

MASLIN, -S *n* mixture of wheat, rye or other grain

MASON, -ED, -ING, -S *n* person who works with stone ▷ *vb* construct or strengthen with masonry

MASONIC *adj* of, characteristic of, or relating to Freemasons

MASONING ▶ mason

MASONITE *n* tradename for a kind of dark brown hardboard used for partitions, lining, etc

MASONRY *n* stonework

MASONS ▶ mason

MASOOLAH *n* Indian boat used in surf

MASQUE, -S *n* 16th–17th-century form of dramatic entertainment

MASQUER, -S *same as* **▶ masker**

MASQUES ▶ masque

MASS, -ING *n* coherent body of matter ▷ *adj* large-scale ▷ *vb* form into a mass

MASSA, -S *old fashioned variant of* **▶ master**

MASSACRE *n* indiscriminate killing of large numbers

of people ▷ *vb* kill in large numbers

MASSAGE, -D, -S *n* rubbing and kneading of parts of the body to reduce pain or stiffness ▷ *vb* give a massage to

MASSAGER

MASSAS ► **massa**

MASSCULT *n* culture of masses

MASSE *n* billiard stroke that makes the ball move in a curve around another ball

MASSED ► **mass**

MASSEDLY ► **mass**

MASSES *pl n* body of common people

MASSETER *n* muscle of the cheek used in moving the jaw, esp in chewing

MASSEUR, -S *n* person who gives massages

MASSEUSE *n* woman who gives massages, esp as a profession

MASSICOT *n* yellow earthy secondary mineral

MASSIER ► **massy**

MASSIEST ► **massy**

MASSIF, -S *n* connected group of mountains

MASSING ► **mass**

MASSIVE, -S *adj* large and heavy ▷ *n* group of friends or associates

MASSLESS ► **mass**

MASSOOLA *same as* ► **masoolah**

MASSTIGE *n* impression of exclusivity in mass-produced goods

MASSY, MASSIER, MASSIEST *literary word for* ► **massive**

MAST, -ED, -ING, -S *n* tall pole for supporting something, esp a ship's sails ▷ *vb* equip with a mast

MASTABA, -S *n* mud-brick superstructure above tombs in ancient Egypt

MASTABAH *same as* ► **mastaba**

MASTABAS ► **mastaba**

MASTED ► **mast**

MASTER, -ED, -S *n* person in control, such as an employer or an owner of slaves or animals ▷ *vb* acquire knowledge of or skill in

MASTERLY *adj* showing great skill

MASTERS ► **master**

MASTERY *n* expertise

MASTFUL ► **mast**

MASTHEAD *n* head of a mast ▷ *vb* send (a sailor) to the masthead as a punishment

MASTIC, -S *n* gum obtained from certain trees

MASTICH, -S *same as* ► **mastic**

MASTICHE *same as* ► **mastic**

MASTICHS ► **mastich**

MASTICOT *same as* ► **massicot**

MASTICS ► **mastic**

MASTIER ► **masty**

MASTIEST ► **masty**

MASTIFF, -S *n* large dog

MASTING ► **mast**

MASTITIC ► **mastitis**

MASTITIS *n* inflammation of a breast or udder

MASTIX, -ES *n* type of gum

MASTLESS ► **mast**

MASTLIKE ► **mast**

MASTODON *n* extinct elephant-like mammal

MASTOID, -S *n* projection of the bone behind the ear ▷ *adj* shaped like a nipple or breast

MASTS ► **mast**

MASTY, MASTIER, MASTIEST ► **mast**

MASU, -S *n* Japanese salmon

MASULA, -S *same as* ► **masoolah**

MASURIUM *n* silver-grey metallic element

MASUS ► **masu**

MAT, -S, -TED *n* piece of fabric used as a floor covering or to protect a surface ▷ *vb* tangle or become tangled into a dense mass ▷ *adj* having a dull, lustreless, or roughened surface

MATACHIN *n* dancer with sword

MATADOR, -S *n* man who kills the bull in bullfights

MATADORA *n* female matador

MATADORE *n* form of dominoes game

MATADORS ► **matador**

MATAI, -S *n* New Zealand tree, the wood of which is used for timber for building

MATAMATA (*in Malaysia*) *a former name for* ► **police**

MATATA, -S *same as* ► **fernbird**

MATATU, -S *n* type of shared taxi used in Kenya

MATCH, -ED, -ES *n* contest in a game or sport ▷ *vb* be exactly like, equal to, or in harmony with

MATCHBOX *n* small box for holding matches

MATCHED ► **match**

MATCHER, -S ► **match**

MATCHES ► **match**

MATCHET, -S *same as* ► **machete**

MATCHING ► **match**

MATCHUP, -S *n* sports match

MATE, -D, -S *n* friend ▷ *vb* pair (animals) or (of animals) be paired for reproduction

MATELESS

MATELOT, -S *n* sailor

MATELOTE *n* fish served with a sauce of wine, onions, seasonings, and fish stock

MATELOTS ► **matelot**

MATER, -S, MATRES *n* mother: often used facetiously

MATERIAL *n* substance of which a thing is made ▷ *adj* of matter or substance

MATERIEL *n* materials and equipment of an organization, esp a military force

MATERNAL *adj* of a mother

MATERS ► **mater**

MATES ► **mate**

MATESHIP *n* comradeship of friends, usually male, viewed as an institution

MATEY, -S, MATIER, MATIES, MATIEST *adj* friendly or intimate ▷ *n* friend or fellow: usually used in direct address

MATFELON *n* knapweed

MATGRASS *n* widespread European grass

MATH *same as* ► **maths**

MATHESIS, MATHESES *n* learning or wisdom

MATHS *n* science concerned with the study of numbers

MATICO, -S *n* Peruvian shrub

MATIER ► **matey**

MATIES ► **matey**

MATIEST ► **matey**

MATILDA, -S *n* bushman's swag

MATILY ► **matey**

MATIN *adj* of or relating to matins

MATINAL *same as* ► **matin**

MATINEE, -S *n* an afternoon performance in a theatre or cinema

MATINESS ► **maty**

MATING, -S ► **mate**

MATINS *pl n* early morning church service

MATIPO, -S *n* New Zealand shrub

MATJES *same as* ► **maatjes**

MATLESS ► mat
MATLO, -S same as ► matelot
MATLOW, -S same as ► matelot
MATOKE, -S n (in Uganda) the flesh of bananas, boiled and mashed as a food
MATOOKE, -S same as ► matoke
MATRASS n long-necked glass flask
MATRES ► mater
MATRIC, -S n matriculation
MATRICE same as ► matrix
MATRICES ► matrix
MATRICS ► matric
MATRIX, MATRICES, -ES n substance or situation in which something originates, takes form, or is enclosed
MATRON, -S n staid or dignified married woman
MATRONAL
MATRONLY adj (of a woman) middle-aged and plump
MATRONS ► matron
MATROSS n gunner's assistant
MATS ► mat
MATSAH, -S same as ► matzo
MATSURI, -S n Japanese religious ceremony
MATT, -S adj dull, not shiny ▷ n dull surface
MATTE, -S same as ► matt
MATTED ► mat
MATTEDLY ► mat
MATTER, -ED, -S n substance of which something is made ▷ vb be of importance
MATTERY adj discharging pus
MATTES ► matte
MATTIE, -S n young herring
MATTIFY vb make (the skin of the face) less oily or shiny using cosmetics
MATTIN same as ► matin
MATTING, -S ► mat
MATTINS same as ► matins
MATTOCK, -S n large pick with one of its blade ends flattened for loosening soil
MATTOID, -S n person displaying eccentric behaviour
MATTRASS same as ► matrass
MATTRESS n large stuffed flat case, often with springs, used on or as a bed
MATTS ► matt
MATURATE vb mature or bring to maturity

MATURE, -D, -S, -ST, MATURING adj fully developed or grown-up ▷ vb make or become mature
MATURELY
MATURER -S
MATURITY n state of being mature
MATUTINE same as > matutinal
MATWEED, -S n grass found on moors
MATY same as ► matey
MATZA, -S same as ► matzo
MATZAH, -S same as ► matzo
MATZAS ► matza
MATZO, -S, -T n large very thin biscuit of unleavened bread
MATZOH, -S, MATZOTH same as ► matzo
MATZOON, -S n fermented milk product similar to yogurt
MATZOS ► matzo
MATZOT ► matzo
MATZOTH ► matzoh
MAUBY, MAUBIES n Caribbean bittersweet drink
MAUD, -S n shawl or rug of grey wool plaid
MAUDLIN adj foolishly or tearfully sentimental
MAUDS ► maud
MAUGER same as ► maugre
MAUGRE, -D, -S, MAUGRING prep in spite of ▷ vb behave spitefully towards
MAUL, -ED, -S vb handle roughly ▷ n loose scrum
MAULER
MAULERS pl n hands
MAULGRE, -D, -S same as ► maugre
MAULING, -S n act of mauling
MAULS ► maul
MAULVI, -S n expert in Islamic law
MAUMET, -S n false god
MAUMETRY
MAUN dialect word for ► must
MAUND, -ED, -ING, -S n unit of weight used in Asia ▷ vb beg
MAUNDER, -S vb talk or act aimlessly or idly
MAUNDIES ► maundy
MAUNDING ► maund
MAUNDS ► maund
MAUNDY, MAUNDIES n ceremonial washing of the feet of poor people
MAUNGY, MAUNGIER adj (esp of a child) sulky, bad-tempered, or peevish

MAUNNA vb Scots term meaning must not
MAURI, -S n soul
MAUSIER ► mausy
MAUSIEST ► mausy
MAUSOLEA ► mausoleum
MAUSY, MAUSIER, MAUSIEST adj foggy; misty
MAUT, -S same as ► mahout
MAUTHER, -S n girl
MAUTS ► maut
MAUVAIS adj bad
MAUVAISE feminine form of ► mauvais
MAUVE, -R, -S, -ST adj pale purple ▷ n any of various pale purple colours
MAUVEIN, -S same as ► mauveine
MAUVEINE same as ► mauve
MAUVEINS ► mauvein
MAUVER ► mauve
MAUVES ► mauve
MAUVEST ► mauve
MAUVIN, -S same as ► mauveine
MAUVINE, -S same as ► mauveine
MAUVINS ► mauvin
MAUZY, MAUZIER, MAUZIEST adj foggy; misty
MAVEN, -S n expert or connoisseur
MAVERICK adj independent and unorthodox (person) ▷ n person of independent or unorthodox views ▷ vb take illegally
MAVIE, -S n type of thrush
MAVIN, -S same as ► maven
MAVIS, -ES n song thrush
MAW, -ED, -ING, -S n animal's mouth, throat, or stomach ▷ vb eat or bite
MAWBOUND adj (of cattle) constipated
MAWED ► maw
MAWGER adj (of persons or animals) thin or lean
MAWING ► maw
MAWK, -S n maggot
MAWKIER ► mawky
MAWKIEST ► mawky
MAWKISH adj foolishly sentimental
MAWKS ► mawk
MAWKY, MAWKIER, MAWKIEST ► mawk
MAWMET, -S same as ► maumet
MAWMETRY
MAWN, -S n measure of capacity
MAWPUS, -ES same as ► mopus**

M

M

MAWR, -S same as
► **mauther**
MAWS ► **maw**
MAWSEED, -S n poppy seed
MAWTHER, -S same as
► **mauther**
MAX, -ED, -ES, -ING vb reach
the full extent

Max is a short form of
maximum, and can also
be a verb giving **maxed,
maxes** and **maxing**.
Another of the key words
using X, and it can be
extended to **maxi**.

MAXI, -S adj (of a garment)
very long ▷ n type of large
racing yacht
MAXIBOAT n large racing
yacht
MAXICOAT n long coat
MAXILLA, -E, -S n upper
jawbone of a vertebrate
MAXILLAR
MAXIM, -S n general truth or
principle
MAXIMA ► **maximum**
MAXIMAL, -S adj maximum
▷ n maximum
MAXIMAND n something
that is to be maximized
MAXIMIN, -S n highest of a
set of minimum values
MAXIMISE same as
► **maximize**
MAXIMIST ► **maxim**
MAXIMITE n type of explosive
MAXIMIZE vb increase to a
maximum
MAXIMS ► **maxim**
MAXIMUM, MAXIMA, -S n
greatest possible (amount
or number) ▷ adj of, being,
or showing a maximum or
maximums
MAXIMUS n method rung on
twelve bells
MAXING ► **max**
MAXIS ► **maxi**
MAXIXE, -S n Brazilian dance
in duple time
MAXWELL, -S n cgs unit of
magnetic flux
**MAY, -ED, -ING, -S,
MIGHTEST, MIGHTST,
MOUGHT** vb used as
an auxiliary to express
possibility, permission,
opportunity, etc ▷ vb gather
may
MAYA, -S n illusion, esp the
material world of the senses
regarded as illusory
MAYAN
MAYAPPLE n American plant

MAYAS ► **maya**
MAYBE, -S adv perhaps,
possibly ▷ sentence substitute
possibly ▷ n possibility
MAYBIRD, -S n American
songbird
MAYBUSH n flowering shrub
MAYDAY, -S n international
radiotelephone distress
signal
MAYED ► **may**
MAYEST same as ► **mayst**
MAYFISH n type of
N American fish
MAYFLY, MAYFLIES n short-
lived aquatic insect
MAYHAP archaic word for
► **perhaps**
MAYHEM, -S n violent
destruction or confusion
MAYING, -S ► **may**
MAYO, -S n mayonnaise
MAYOR, -S n head of a
municipality
MAYORAL
MAYORESS n mayor's wife
MAYORS ► **mayor**
MAYOS ► **mayo**
MAYPOLE, -S n pole set up
for dancing round on the
first day of May to celebrate
spring
MAYPOP, -S n American wild
flower
MAYS ► **may**
MAYST singular form of the
present tense of ► **may**
MAYSTER, -S same as
► **master**
MAYVIN, -S same as
► **maven**
MAYWEED, -S n widespread
Eurasian weedy plant
MAZAEDIA > **mazaedium**
MAZARD, -S same as
► **mazer**
MAZARINE n blue colour
MAZE, -D, -S, MAZING n
complex network of paths
or lines
MAZEDLY adv in a bewildered
way
MAZEFUL ► **maze**
MAZELIKE ► **maze**
MAZELTOV interj
congratulations
MAZEMENT ► **maze**
MAZER, -S n large hardwood
drinking bowl
MAZES ► **maze**
MAZEY adj dizzy
MAZHBI, -S n low-caste Sikh
MAZIER ► **mazy**
MAZIEST ► **mazy**
MAZILY ► **mazy**
MAZINESS ► **mazy**

MAZING ► **maze**
MAZOURKA same as
► **mazurka**
MAZOUT, -S same as
► **mazut**
MAZUMA, -S n money
MAZURKA, -S n lively Polish
dance
MAZUT, -S n residue left after
distillation of petrol
MAZY, MAZIER, MAZIEST adj
of or like a maze
MAZZARD, -S same as
► **mazard**
MBAQANGA n style of Black
popular music of urban
South Africa
MBIRA, -S n African musical
instrument
ME, -S n (in tonic sol-fa) third
degree of any major scale
▷ pron refers to the speaker
or writer
MEACOCK, -S n timid person
MEAD, -S n alcoholic drink
made from honey
MEADOW, -S n piece of
grassland
MEADOWY
MEADS ► **mead**
MEAGER, -ER same as
► **meagre**
MEAGERLY ► **meagre**
MEAGRE, -R, -S, -ST adj
scanty or insufficient ▷ n
Mediterranean fish
MEAGRELY
MEAL, -ED, -ING, -S n
occasion when food is served
and eaten ▷ vb cover with
meal
MEALER, -S n person eating
but not lodging at boarding
house
MEALIE, -S n maize
MEALIER ► **mealy**
MEALIES ► **mealie**
MEALIEST ► **mealy**
MEALING ► **meal**
MEALLESS ► **meal**
MEALS ► **meal**
MEALTIME n time for meal
MEALWORM n larva of
various beetles which feeds
on meal, flour, and similar
stored foods
MEALY, MEALIER, MEALIEST
adj resembling meal
MEALYBUG n plant-eating
homopterous insect
MEAN, -EST, -S, -T vb intend
to convey or express ▷ adj
miserly, ungenerous, or petty
▷ n middle point between
two extremes

MEANDER, -S *vb* follow a winding course ▷ *n* winding course

MEANE, -D, -S *vb* moan

MEANER, -S ▶ **mean**

MEANES ▶ **meane**

MEANEST ▶ **mean**

MEANIE, -S *n* unkind or miserly person

MEANING, -S *n* what something means

MEANLY ▶ **mean**

MEANNESS ▶ **mean**

MEANS ▶ **mean**

MEANT ▶ **mean**

MEANTIME *n* intervening period ▷ *adv* meanwhile

MEANY *same as* ▶ **meanie**

MEARE, -S *same as* ▶ **mere**

MEARING *adj* forming boundary

MEASE, -D, -S, MEASING *vb* assuage

MEASLE, MEASLING *vb* infect with measles

MEASLED *adj* (of cattle, sheep, or pigs) infested with tapeworm larvae

MEASLES *n* infectious disease producing red spots

MEASLIER ▶ **measly**

MEASLING ▶ **measle**

MEASLY, MEASLIER *adj* meagre

MEASURE *n* size or quantity ▷ *vb* determine the size or quantity of

MEASURED *adj* slow and steady

MEASURER ▶ **measure**

MEASURES *pl n* rock strata that contain a particular type of deposit

MEAT, -S *n* animal flesh as food

MEATAL ▶ **meatus**

MEATAXE, -S *n* meat cleaver

MEATBALL *n* minced beef, shaped into a ball before cooking

MEATED *adj* fattened

MEATH, -S *same as* ▶ **mead**

MEATHE, -S *same as* ▶ **mead**

MEATHEAD *n* stupid person

MEATHES ▶ **meathe**

MEATHOOK *n* hook on which to hang meat

MEATHS ▶ **meath**

MEATIER ▶ **meaty**

MEATIEST ▶ **meaty**

MEATILY ▶ **meaty**

MEATLESS ▶ **meat**

MEATLOAF *n* chopped meat served in loaf-shaped mass

MEATMAN, MEATMEN *n* meat seller

MEATS ▶ **meat**

MEATUS, -ES *n* natural opening or channel

MEATY, MEATIER, MEATIEST *adj* (tasting) of or like meat

MEAWES *same as* ▶ **mews**

MEAZEL, -S *same as* ▶ **mesel**

MEBOS, -ES *n* South African dish of dried apricots

MECCA, -S *n* place that attracts many visitors

MECH, -S *n* mechanic

MECHANIC *n* person skilled in repairing or operating machinery

MECHITZA *n* screen in synagogue separating men and women

MECHOUI, -S *n* Canadian dish of meat roasted on a spit

MECHS ▶ **mech**

MECK, -S *same as* ▶ **maik**

MECONATE *n* salt of meconic acid

MECONIC *adj* derived from poppies

MECONIN, -S *n* substance found in opium

MECONIUM *n* dark green mucoid material that forms the first faeces of a newborn infant

MED, -S *n* doctor

MEDACCA, -S *n* Japanese freshwater fish

MEDAKA, -S *same as* ▶ **medacca**

MEDAL, -ED, -ING, -LED, -S *n* piece of metal with an inscription etc, given as a reward or memento ▷ *vb* honour with a medal

MEDALET, -S *n* small medal

MEDALING ▶ **medal**

MEDALIST *same as* > **medallist**

MEDALLED ▶ **medal**

MEDALLIC ▶ **medal**

MEDALS ▶ **medal**

MEDCINAL *same as* > **medicinal**

MEDDLE, -D, -S *vb* interfere annoyingly

MEDDLER -S

MEDDLING ▶ **meddle**

MEDEVAC, -S *n* evacuation of casualties ▷ *vb* transport (a wounded or sick person) to hospital

MEDFLY, MEDFLIES *n* Mediterranean fruit fly

MEDIA, -E, -S *n* medium of cultivation, conveyance, or expression

MEDIACY *n* quality or state of being mediate

MEDIAD *adj* situated near the median line or plane of an organism

MEDIAE ▶ **media**

MEDIAL, -S *adj* of or in the middle ▷ *n* speech sound between being fortis and lenis

MEDIALLY

MEDIAN, -S *n* middle (point or line) ▷ *adj* of, relating to, situated in, or directed towards the middle

MEDIANLY

MEDIANT, -S *n* third degree of a major or minor scale

MEDIAS ▶ **media**

MEDIATE, -D, -S *vb* intervene in a dispute to bring about agreement ▷ *adj* occurring as a result of or dependent upon mediation

MEDIATOR

MEDIC, -S *n* doctor or medical student

MEDICAID *n* US federal health insurance programme for persons on low income

MEDICAL, -S *adj* of the science of medicine ▷ *n* medical examination

MEDICANT *n* medicinal substance

MEDICARE *n* US federal health insurance programme for older people

MEDICATE *vb* treat with a medicinal substance

MEDICIDE *n* suicide assisted by doctor

MEDICINE *n* substance used to treat disease ▷ *vb* treat with medicine

MEDICK, -S *n* type of small leguminous plant with yellow or purple flowers

MEDICO, -S *n* doctor or medical student

MEDICS ▶ **medic**

MEDIEVAL *adj* of the Middle Ages ▷ *n* person living in medieval times

MEDIGAP, -S *n* private health insurance

MEDII ▶ **medius**

MEDINA, -S *n* ancient quarter of North African city

MEDIOCRE *adj* average in quality

MEDITATE *vb* reflect deeply, esp on spiritual matters

MEDIUM *adj* midway between extremes, average ▷ *n* middle state, degree, or condition

M

MEDIUMS pl n medium-dated gilt-edged securities

MEDIUS, MEDII, -ES n middle finger

MEDIVAC, -S variant spelling of ▶ medevac

MEDLAR, -S n apple-like fruit of a small tree

MEDLE, -D, -S, MEDLING same as ▶ meddle

MEDLEY, -S n miscellaneous mixture ▷ adj of, being, or relating to a mixture or variety

MEDLING ▶ medle

MEDRESA, -S same as ▶ madrasah

MEDRESE, -S same as ▶ madrasah

MEDS ▶ med

MEDULLA, -E, -S n marrow, pith, or inner tissue

MEDULLAR

MEDUSA, -E, -S n jellyfish

MEDUSAL

MEDUSAN -S

MEDUSOID same as ▶ medusa

MEE, -S n Malaysian noodle dish

MEED, -S n recompense

MEEK, -ER, -EST adj submissive or humble

MEEKEN, -ED, -S vb make meek

MEEKER ▶ meek

MEEKEST ▶ meek

MEEKLY ▶ meek

MEEKNESS ▶ meek

MEEMIE, -S n attack of hysteria

MEER, -ED, -ING, -S same as ▶ mere

MEERCAT, -S same as ▶ meerkat

MEERED ▶ meer

MEERING ▶ meer

MEERKAT, -S n S African mongoose

MEERS ▶ meer

MEES ▶ mee

MEET, -EST, -S vb come together (with) ▷ n meeting, esp a sports meeting ▷ adj fit or suitable

MEETER -S

MEETING, -S ▶ meet

MEETLY ▶ meet

MEETNESS n properness

MEETS ▶ meet

MEFF, -S dialect word for ▶ tramp

MEG, -S short for ▶ megabyte

MEGA adj extremely good, great, or successful

MEGABAR, -S n unit of million bars

MEGABIT, -S n one million bits

MEGABUCK n million dollars

MEGABYTE n 220 or 1 048 576 bytes

MEGACITY n city with over 10 million inhabitants

MEGADEAL n very good deal

MEGADOSE n very large dose, as of a medicine, vitamin, etc

MEGADYNE n unit of million dynes

MEGAFLOP n measure of a computer's processing speed

MEGAFOG, -S n amplified fog signal

MEGAHIT, -S n great success

MEGALITH n great stone, esp as part of a prehistoric monument

MEGALOPS n crab in larval stage

MEGAMALL n very large shopping mall

MEGAPLEX n large cinema complex

MEGAPOD, -S same as ▶ megapode

MEGAPODE n bird of Australia, New Guinea, and adjacent islands

MEGAPODS ▶ megapod

MEGARA ▶ megaron

MEGARAD, -S n unit of million rads

MEGARON, MEGARA, -S n tripartite rectangular room, found in Bronze Age Greece and Asia Minor

MEGASS, -ES another name for ▶ bagasse

MEGASSE same as ▶ megass

MEGASSES ▶ megass

MEGASTAR n very well-known personality in the entertainment business

MEGATON, -S n explosive power equal to that of one million tons of TNT

MEGAVOLT n one million volts

MEGAWATT n one million watts

MEGILLA, -S same as ▶ megillah

MEGILLAH n scroll of the Book of Esther, read on the festival of Purim

MEGILLAS ▶ megilla

MEGILP, -S n oil-painting medium of linseed oil mixed with mastic varnish or turpentine

MEGILPH, -S same as ▶ megilp

MEGILPS ▶ megilp

MEGOHM, -S n one million ohms

MEGRIM n caprice

MEGRIMS n fit of depression

MEGS ▶ meg

MEH interj expression of indifference or boredom

MEHNDI, -S n (esp in India) the practice of painting designs on the hands, feet, etc using henna

MEIKLE adj Scots word meaning large

MEIN, -ED, -ING, -S Scots word for ▶ moan

MEINEY, -S same as ▶ meiny

MEINIE same as ▶ meiny

MEINIES ▶ meiny

MEINING ▶ mein

MEINS ▶ mein

MEINT same as ▶ ming

MEINY, MEINIES n retinue or household

MEIOCYTE n cell that divides by meiosis to produce four haploid spores

MEIONITE n mineral containing silica

MEIOSIS, MEIOSES n type of cell division

MEIOTIC

MEISHI, -S n business card in Japan

MEISTER, -S n person who excels at a particular activity

MEITH, -S n landmark

MEJLIS, -ES same as ▶ majlis

MEKKA, -S same as ▶ mecca

MEL, -S n pure form of honey

MELA, -S n Asian cultural or religious fair or festival

MELAENA, -S n medical condition

MELAMED, MELAMDIM n Hebrew teacher

MELAMINE n colourless crystalline compound used in making synthetic resins

MELANGE, -S n mixture

MELANIAN n freshwater mollusc

MELANIC, -S adj relating to melanism or melanosis ▷ n darker form of creature

MELANIN, -S n dark pigment found in the hair, skin, and eyes

MELANISE same as ▶ melanize

MELANISM same as > melanosis

MELANIST

MELANITE n black variety of andradite garnet

MELANIZE vb turn into melanin

MELANO, -S n person with extremely dark skin

MELANOID adj resembling melanin ▷ n dark substance formed in skin

MELANOMA n tumour composed of dark-coloured cells, occurring in some skin cancers

MELANOS ▶ melano

MELANOUS adj having a dark complexion and black hair

MELAS ▶ mela

MELBA adj relating to a type of dessert sauce or toast

MELD, -ED, -ING, -S vb merge or blend ▷ n act of melding

MELDER -S

MELEE, -S n noisy confused fight or crowd

MELENA, -S n excrement stained by blood

MELIC, -S adj (of poetry, esp ancient Greek lyric poems) intended to be sung ▷ n type of grass

MELICK, -S n either of two pale green perennial grasses

MELICS ▶ melic

MELIK, -S same as ▶ malik

MELILITE n mineral containing calcium

MELILOT, -S n plant with small white or yellow fragrant flowers

MELINITE n high explosive made from picric acid

MELISMA n expressive vocal phrase or passage consisting of several notes sung to one syllable

MELITTIN n main toxic component in bee venom

MELL, -ED, -ING, -S vb mix

MELLAY, -S same as ▶ melee

MELLED ▶ mell

MELLIFIC adj forming or producing honey

MELLING ▶ mell

MELLITE, -S n soft yellow mineral

MELLITIC

MELLOW, -ED, -ER, -S adj soft, not harsh ▷ vb make or become mellow

MELLOWLY

MELLOWY same as ▶ mellow

MELLS ▶ mell

MELODEON n small accordion

MELODIA, -S same as ▶ melodica

MELODIC adj of melody

MELODICA n type of flute

MELODICS n study of melody

MELODIES ▶ melody

MELODION same as ▶ melodeon

MELODISE same as ▶ melodize

MELODIST n composer of melodies

MELODIZE vb provide with a melody

MELODY, MELODIES n series of musical notes which make a tune

MELOID, -S n type of long-legged beetle

MELON, -S n large round juicy fruit with a hard rind

MELONY adj like a melon

MELS ▶ mel

MELT, -ED, -S, MOLTEN vb (cause to) become liquid by heat ▷ n act or process of melting

MELTABLE

MELTAGE, -S n process or result of melting or the amount melted

MELTDOWN n (in a nuclear reactor) melting of the fuel rods, with the possible release of radiation

MELTED ▶ melt

MELTEMI, -S n northerly wind in the northeast Mediterranean

MELTER, -S ▶ melt

MELTIER ▶ melty

MELTIEST ▶ melty

MELTING, -S ▶ melt

MELTITH, -S n meal

MELTON, -S n heavy smooth woollen fabric with a short nap, used esp for overcoats

MELTS ▶ melt

MELTY, MELTIER, MELTIEST adj tending to melt

MEM, -S n 13th letter in the Hebrew alphabet, transliterated as m

MEMBER, -S n individual making up a body or society ▷ adj (of a country or group) belonging to an organization or alliance

MEMBERED adj having members

MEMBERS ▶ member

MEMBRAL adj of limbs

MEMBRANE n thin flexible tissue in a plant or animal body

MEME, -S n idea or element of social behaviour

MEMENTO, -S n thing serving to remind, souvenir

MEMES ▶ meme

MEMETIC adj of or relating to a meme

MEMETICS n study of genetic transmission of culture

MEMO, -S n memorandum

MEMOIR n biography or historical account based on personal knowledge

MEMOIRS pl n collection of reminiscences about a period or series of events

MEMORIAL n something serving to commemorate a person or thing ▷ adj serving as a memorial

MEMORIES ▶ memory

MEMORISE same as ▶ memorize

MEMORIZE vb commit to memory

MEMORY, MEMORIES n ability to remember

MEMOS ▶ memo

MEMS ▶ mem

MEMSAHIB n (formerly, in India) term of respect used for a European married woman

MEN ▶ man

MENACE, -D, -S, MENACING n threat ▷ vb threaten, endanger

MENACER -S

MENAD, -S same as ▶ maenad

MENAGE, -D, -S, MENAGING old form of ▶ manage

MENARCHE n first occurrence of menstruation

MENAZON, -S n type of insecticide

MEND, -ED, -S vb repair or patch ▷ n mended area

MENDABLE

MENDER -S

MENDIGO, -S n Spanish beggar or vagrant

MENDING, -S n something to be mended, esp clothes

MENDS ▶ mend

MENE, -D, -S, MENING Scots form of ▶ moan

MENEER, -S n S African title of address

MENES ▶ mene

MENFOLK pl n men collectively, esp the men of a particular family

MENFOLKS same as ▶ menfolk

MENG, -ED, -ING, -S vb mix

MENGE, -S same as ► **meng**
MENGED ► **meng**
MENGES ► **menge**
MENGING ► **meng**
MENGS ► **meng**
MENHADEN n marine N American fish, source of fishmeal, fertilizer, and oil
MENHIR, -S n single upright prehistoric stone
MENIAL, -S adj involving boring work of low status ▷ n person with a menial job
MENIALLY
MENILITE n liver opal
MENING ► **mene**
MENINX, MENINGES n one of three membranes that envelop the brain and spinal cord
MENISCAL ► **meniscus**
MENISCUS, MENISCI n curved surface of a liquid
MENO adv musical instruction indicating 'less'
MENOLOGY n ecclesiastical calendar of the months
MENOMINI same as > **menominee**
MENOPOME n American salamander
MENORAH, -S n seven-branched candelabrum used as an emblem of Judaism
MENSA, -S n faint constellation in the S hemisphere
MENSAE n star of the mensa constellation
MENSAL adj monthly
MENSAS ► **mensa**
MENSCH, -EN, -ES n decent person
MENSCHY adj decent
MENSE, -D, MENSING vb grace
MENSEFUL adj gracious
MENSES n menstruation
MENSH, -ED, -ES, -ING vb mention
MENSHEN n Chinese door god
MENSHES ► **mensh**
MENSHING ► **mensh**
MENSING ► **mense**
MENSTRUA > **menstruum**
MENSUAL same as ► **mensal**
MENSURAL adj of or involving measure
MENSWEAR n clothing for men
MENT same as ► **ming**
MENTA ► **mentum**
MENTAL adj of, in, or done by the mind
MENTALLY

MENTEE, -S n person trained by mentor
MENTHENE n liquid obtained from menthol
MENTHOL, -S n organic compound found in peppermint
MENTION, -S vb refer to briefly ▷ n brief reference
MENTO, -S n Jamaican song
MENTOR, -ED, -S n adviser or guide ▷ vb act as a mentor to (someone) ▷ vb act as mentor for
MENTOS ► **mento**
MENTUM, MENTA n chin
MENU, -S n list of dishes to be served, or from which to order
MENUDO, -S n Mexican soup
MENUS ► **menu**
MENYIE, -S same as ► **meinie**
MEOU, -ED, -ING, -S same as ► **meow**
MEOW, -ED, -ING, -S vb (of a cat) to make a characteristic crying sound ▷ interj imitation of this sound
MEPHITIC adj poisonous
MEPHITIS n foul-smelling discharge
MERANTI, -S n wood from any of several Malaysian trees
MERC, -ES, -S n mercenary
MERCADO, -S n market
MERCAPTO adj of a particular chemical group
MERCAT, -S Scots word for ► **market**
MERCER, -S n dealer in textile fabrics and fine cloth
MERCERY
MERCES ► **merc**
MERCH, -ES n merchandise
MERCHANT n person engaged in trade, wholesale trader ▷ adj of ships involved in commercial trade or their crews ▷ vb conduct trade in
MERCHES ► **merch**
MERCHET, -S n type of fine paid by feudal tenant to his lord
MERCHILD n mythical creature with upper body of child and lower body of fish
MERCIES ► **mercy**
MERCIFUL adj compassionate
MERCIFY vb show mercy to
MERCS ► **merc**
MERCURIC adj of or containing mercury in the divalent state

MERCURY n silvery liquid metal
MERCY, MERCIES n compassionate treatment
MERDE n French word for > **excrement**
MERE, -R, -S, -ST, MERING adj nothing more than ▷ n lake ▷ vb old form of survey
MERED adj forming a boundary
MEREL, -S same as ► **meril**
MERELL same as ► **meril**
MERELLS same as ► **merils**
MERELS ► **merel**
MERELY adv only
MERENGUE n type of lively dance music
MERER ► **mere**
MERES ► **mere**
MERESMAN, MERESMEN n man who decides on boundaries
MEREST ► **mere**
MERFOLK, -S n mermaids and mermen
MERGE, -D, -S vb combine or blend
MERGEE, -S n business taken over by merger
MERGENCE ► **merge**
MERGER, -S n combination of business firms into one
MERGES ► **merge**
MERGING, -S ► **merge**
MERGUEZ n heavily spiced N African sausage
MERI, -S n Māori war club
MERICARP n part of plant fruit
MERIDIAN n imaginary circle of the earth passing through both poles ▷ adj along or relating to a meridian
MERIL n counter used in merils
MERILS n old board game
MERIMAKE n merrymaking
MERING, -S ► **mere**
MERINGUE n baked mixture of egg whites and sugar
MERINO, -S n breed of sheep with fine soft wool
MERIS ► **meri**
MERISIS, MERISES n growth by division of cells
MERISM, -S n duplication of biological parts
MERISTEM n plant tissue responsible for growth
MERISTIC adj of or relating to the number of organs or parts in an animal or plant body**

MEUNIERE adj cooked in butter with lemon juice and parsley

MEUS ▸ meu

MEUSE, -D, -S, MEUSING n gap through which an animal passed ▷ vb go through this gap

MEVE, -D, -S, MEVING same as ▸ **move**

MEVROU, -S n S African title of address

MEW, -ED, -ING n cry of a cat ▷ vb utter this cry

MEWL, -ED, -ING, -S vb (esp of a baby) to cry weakly ▷ n weak or whimpering cry

MEWLER -S

MEWS, -ED, -ES, -ING same as ▸ **meuse**

MEYNT ▸ ming

MEZAIL, -S same as ▸ **mesail**

MEZCAL, -S variant spelling of ▸ **mescal**

MEZE, -S n type of hors d'oeuvre

MEZEREON same as ▸ **mezereum**

MEZEREUM n dried bark of certain shrubs, formerly used to treat arthritis

MEZES ▸ meze

MEZQUIT, -S same as ▸ **mesquite**

A **mezquit** is a kind of American tree, and makes a great bonus to play. Remember also that it takes an E to form the variant spelling **mezquite**.

MEZQUITE same as ▸ **mesquite**

MEZQUITS ▸ mezquit

MEZUZA, -S same as ▸ **mezuzah**

MEZUZAH, -S, MEZUZOT, MEZUZOTH n piece of parchment inscribed with biblical passages

MEZUZAS ▸ mezuza

MEZUZOT ▸ mezuzah

MEZUZOTH ▸ mezuzah

MEZZ same as > **mezzanine**

MEZZE, -S same as ▸ **meze**

MEZZO, -S adv moderately ▷ n singer with voice between soprano and contralto

MGANGA, -S n witch doctor

MHO, -S former name for ▸ **siemens**

MHORR, -S n African gazelle

MHOS ▸ mho

MI, -S n (in tonic sol-fa) the third degree of any major scale

MIAOU, -ED, -ING, -S same as ▸ **meow**

MIAOW, -ED, -ING, -S same as ▸ **meow**

MIASM, -S same as ▸ **miasma**

MIASMA, -S, -TA n unwholesome or foreboding atmosphere

MIASMAL

MIASMIC

MIASMOUS

MIASMS ▸ miasm

MIAUL, -ED, -ING, -S same as ▸ **meow**

MIB, -S n marble used in games

MIBUNA, -S n type of Japanese leafy vegetable

MIC, -S n microphone

MICA, -S n glasslike mineral used as an electrical insulator

MICATE, -D, -S, MICATING vb add mica to

MICAWBER n person who idles and trusts to fortune

MICE ▸ mouse

MICELL, -S same as ▸ **micelle**

MICELLA, -E, -S same as ▸ **micelle**

MICELLAR ▸ micelle

MICELLAS ▸ micella

MICELLE, -S n charged aggregate of molecules of colloidal size in a solution

MICELLS ▸ micell

MICH, -ED, -ES same as ▸ **mitch**

MICHAEL, -S n as in take the michael teasing

MICHE same as ▸ **mich**

MICHED ▸ mich

MICHER, -S ▸ mich

MICHES ▸ mich

MICHIGAN US name for > **newmarket**

MICHING, -S ▸ mich

MICHT, -S n Scots word for might

MICKERY n waterhole, esp in a dry riverbed

MICKEY, -ED, -S n young bull ▷ vb drug a person's drink

MICKIES ▸ micky

MICKLE, -R, -S, -ST adj large or abundant ▷ adv much ▷ n great amount

MICKY, MICKIES same as ▸ **mickey**

MICO, -S n marmoset

MICRA ▸ micron

MICRIFY vb make very small

MICRO, -S n small computer

MICROBAR n millionth of bar of pressure

MICROBE, -S n minute organism, esp one causing disease

MICROBIC

MICROBUS n small bus

MICROCAP adj (of investments) involving very small amounts of capital

MICROCAR n small car

MICRODOT n photographic copy of a document reduced to pinhead size

MICROHM, -S n millionth of ohm

MICROJET n light jet-propelled aircraft

MICROLUX n millionth of a lux

MICROMHO n millionth of mho

MICRON, MICRA, -S n unit of length equal to 10–6 metre

MICROS ▸ micro

MICRURGY n manipulation and examination of single cells under a microscope

MICS ▸ mic

MICTION, -S n urination

MID, -S adj intermediate, middle ▷ n middle ▷ prep amid

MIDAIR, -S n some point above ground level, in the air

MIDBAND adj using a range of frequencies between narrowband and broadband

MIDBRAIN n part of the brain that develops from the middle portion of the embryonic neural tube

MIDCAP adj (of investments) involving medium-sized amounts of capital

MIDCULT, -S n middlebrow culture

MIDDAY, -S n noon

MIDDEN, -S n rubbish heap

MIDDEST adj in middle

MIDDIE n glass or bottle containing 285ml of beer

MIDDIES ▸ middy

MIDDLE, -D, -S adj equidistant from two extremes ▷ n middle point or part ▷ vb place in the middle

MIDDLER, -S n pupil in middle years at school

MIDDLES ▸ middle

MIDDLING adj mediocre ▷ adv moderately

MIDDY, MIDDIES n middle-sized glass of beer

MIDFIELD n area between the two opposing defences

M

MIDGE, -S n small mosquito-like insect

MIDGET, -S n very small person or thing ▷ adj much smaller than normal

MIDGIE, -S n informal word for a small winged biting insect such as the midge or sandfly

MIDGIER ► midgy

MIDGIES ► midgie

MIDGIEST ► midgy

MIDGUT, -S n middle part of the digestive tract

MIDGY, MIDGIER, MIDGIEST ► midge

MIDI, -S adj (of a skirt, coat, etc) reaching to below the knee or midcalf ▷ n skirt, coat, etc reaching to below the knee or midcalf

MIDIRON, -S n golf club used for medium-length approach shots

MIDIS ► midi

MIDLAND, -S n middle part of a country

MIDLEG, -S n middle of leg

MIDLIFE, MIDLIVES n middle age

MIDLIFER n middle-aged person

MIDLINE, -S n line at middle of something

MIDLIST, -S n books in publisher's range that sell reasonably well

MIDLIVES ► midlife

MIDMONTH n middle of month

MIDMOST, -S adv in the middle or midst ▷ n the middle or midst

MIDNIGHT n twelve o'clock at night

MIDNOON, -S n noon

MIDPAY adj paying more than an unskilled job but less than a high-income one

MIDPOINT n point on a line equally distant from either end

MIDRANGE n part of loudspeaker

MIDRASH n homily on a Jewish scriptural passage

MIDRIB, -S n main vein of a leaf

MIDRIFF, -S n middle part of the body

MIDS ► mid

MIDSHIP adj in, of, or relating to the middle of a vessel ▷ n middle of a vessel

MIDSHIPS See > amidships

MIDSHORE adj between the inshore and the offshore

MIDSIZE adj medium-sized

MIDSIZED same as ► midsize

MIDSOLE, -S n layer between the inner and the outer sole of a shoe

MIDSPACE n area in middle of space

MIDST, -S See ► amid

MIDSTORY n level of forest trees between smallest and tallest

MIDSTS ► midst

MIDTERM, -S n middle of a term in a school, university, etc

MIDTOWN, -S n centre of a town

MIDWATCH n naval watch period beginning at midnight

MIDWATER n middle part of a body of water

MIDWAY, -S adv halfway ▷ adj in or at the middle of the distance ▷ n place in a fair, carnival, etc, where sideshows are located

MIDWEEK, -S n middle of the week

MIDWIFE, -D, -S, MIDWIVES n trained person who assists at childbirth ▷ vb act as midwife

MIDWIVE, -D vb act as midwife

MIDWIVES ► midwife

MIDYEAR, -S n middle of the year

MIELIE, -S same as ► mealie

MIEN, -S n person's bearing, demeanour, or appearance

MIEVE, -D, -S, MIEVING same as ► move

MIFF, -ED, -ING, -S vb take offence or offend ▷ n petulant mood

MIFFIER ► miffy

MIFFIEST ► miffy

MIFFILY ► miffy

MIFFING ► miff

MIFFS ► miff

MIFFY, MIFFIER, MIFFIEST adj easily upset

MIFTY same as ► miffy

MIG, -S n marble used in games

MIGAWD interj interjection used to express surprise

MIGG, -S same as ► mig

MIGGLE, -S n US word for playing marble

MIGGS ► migg

MIGHT, -S n physical strength

MIGHTEST ► may

MIGHTFUL same as ► mighty

MIGHTIER ► mighty

MIGHTILY adv great extent, amount, or degree

MIGHTS ► might

MIGHTST ► may

MIGHTY, MIGHTIER adj powerful ▷ adv very

MIGNON, -S adj small and pretty ▷ n tender boneless cut of meat

MIGNONNE

MIGRAINE n severe headache, often with nausea and visual disturbances

MIGRANT, -S n person or animal that moves from one place to another ▷ adj moving from one place to another

MIGRATE, -D, -S vb move from one place to settle in another

MIGRATOR

MIGS ► mig

MIHA, -S n young fern frond which has not yet opened

MIHI, -ED, -ING, -S n Māori ceremonial greeting ▷ vb greet

MIHRAB, -S n niche in a mosque showing the direction of Mecca

MIJNHEER same as ► mynheer

MIKADO, -S n Japanese emperor

MIKE, -D, -S, MIKING n microphone

MIKRON, MIKRA, -S same as ► micron

MIKVA, -S n place for ritual bathing by Orthodox Jews

MIKVAH, -S, MIKVOTH n pool used for ritual purification

MIKVAS ► mikva

MIKVEH, -S, MIKVOS, MIKVOT same as ► mikvah

MIKVOTH ► mikvah

MIL, -S n unit of length equal to one thousandth of an inch

MILADI, -S same as ► milady

MILADIES ► milady

MILADIS ► miladi

MILADY, MILADIES n (formerly) a continental title for an English gentlewoman

MILAGE, -S same as ► mileage

MILCH adj (of a cow) giving milk

MILCHIG same as ► milchik

MILCHIK adj containing or used in the preparation of milk products

MILD, -ED, -ER, -EST, -ING, -S *adj* not strongly flavoured ▷ *n* dark beer flavoured with fewer hops than bitter ▷ *vb* become gentle

MILDEN, -ED, -S *vb* make or become mild or milder

MILDER ▶ mild

MILDEST ▶ mild

MILDEW, -ED, -S *same as* ▶ mould **MILDEWY**

MILDING ▶ mild

MILDISH *adj* rather mild

MILDLY ▶ mild

MILDNESS ▶ mild

MILDS ▶ mild

MILE, -S *n* unit of length equal to 1760 yards or 1.609 kilometres

MILEAGE, -S *n* distance travelled in miles

MILEPOST *n* signpost that shows the distance in miles to or from a place

MILER, -S *n* athlete, horse, etc, that specializes in races of one mile

MILES ▶ mile

MILESIAN *adj* Irish

MILESIMO *n* Spanish word meaning thousandth

MILFOIL, -S *same as* ▶ yarrow

MILIA ▶ milium

MILIARIA *n* acute itching eruption of the skin, caused by blockage of the sweat glands

MILIARY *adj* resembling or relating to millet seeds

MILIEU, -S, -X *n* environment or surroundings

MILING, -S *n* activity of running one mile

MILITANT *adj* aggressive or vigorous in support of a cause ▷ *n* militant person

MILITAR *same as* ▶ military

MILITARY *adj* of or for soldiers, armies, or war ▷ *n* armed services

MILITATE *vb* have a strong influence or effect

MILITIA, -S *n* military force of trained citizens

MILIUM, MILIA *n* pimple

MILK, -ED, -ING, -S *n* white fluid produced by female mammals to feed their young ▷ *vb* draw milk from

MILKEN *adj* of or like milk

MILKER, -S *n* cow, goat, etc, that yields milk

MILKFISH *n* type of large silvery tropical food and game fish

MILKIER ▶ milky

MILKIEST ▶ milky

MILKILY ▶ milky

MILKING, -S ▶ milk

MILKLESS ▶ milk

MILKLIKE ▶ milk

MILKMAID *n* (esp in former times) woman who milks cows

MILKMAN, MILKMEN *n* man who delivers milk to people's houses

MILKO, -S *informal name for* ▶ milkman

MILKS ▶ milk

MILKSHED *n* area where milk is produced

MILKSOP, -S *n* feeble man

MILKWEED *n* monarch butterfly

MILKWOOD *n* tree producing latex

MILKWORT *n* plant with small flowers

MILKY, MILKIER, MILKIEST *adj* of or like milk

MILL, -S *n* factory ▷ *vb* grind, press, or process in or as if in a mill **MILLABLE**

MILLAGE, -S *adj* American tax rate calculated in thousandths per dollar

MILLCAKE *n* food for livestock

MILLDAM, -S *n* dam built to raise the water level to turn a millwheel

MILLE, -S *French word for* ▶ thousand

MILLED *adj* crushed or ground in a mill

MILLEPED *same as* > millepede

MILLER, -S *n* person who works in a mill

MILLES ▶ mille

MILLET, -S *n* type of cereal grass

MILLHAND *n* person who works in a mill

MILLIAMP *n* one thousandth of an ampere

MILLIARD *n* one thousand millions

MILLIARE *n* ancient Roman unit of distance

MILLIARY *adj* relating to or marking a distance equal to an ancient Roman mile of a thousand paces

MILLIBAR *n* unit of atmospheric pressure

MILLIE, -S *n* insulting name for a young working-class woman

MILLIEME *n* Tunisian monetary unit worth one thousandth of a dinar

MILLIER, -S *n* metric weight of million grams

MILLIES ▶ millie

MILLIGAL *n* unit of gravity

MILLILUX *n* thousandth of lux

MILLIME, -S *same as* ▶ millieme

MILLIMHO *n* thousandth of mho

MILLINE, -S *n* measurement of advertising space

MILLINER *n* maker or seller of women's hats

MILLINES ▶ milline

MILLING, -S *n* act or process of grinding, cutting, pressing, or crushing in a mill

MILLIOHM *n* thousandth of ohm

MILLION, -S *n* one thousand thousands

MILLIPED *same as* > millipede

MILLIREM *n* unit of radiation

MILLPOND *n* pool which provides water to turn a millwheel

MILLRACE *n* current of water that turns a millwheel

MILLRIND *n* iron support fitted across an upper millstone

MILLRUN, -S *same as* ▶ millrace

MILLS ▶ mill

MILLTAIL *n* channel carrying water away from mill

MILLWORK *n* work done in a mill

MILNEB, -S *n* type of pesticide

MILO, -S *n* variety of sorghum with heads of yellow or pinkish seeds

MILOR, -S *same as* ▶ milord

MILORD, -S *n* (formerly) a continental title used for an English gentleman

MILORS ▶ milor

MILOS ▶ milo

MILPA, -S *n* form of subsistence agriculture in Mexico

MILREIS *n* former monetary unit of Portugal and Brazil

MILS ▶ mil

MILSEY, -S *n* milk strainer

MILT, -ED, -ING, -S *n* reproductive fluid of male fish ▷ *vb* fertilize (the roe of a female fish) with milt

M

MILTER, -S n male fish that is mature and ready to breed

MILTIER ▶ milty

MILTIEST ▶ milty

MILTING ▶ milt

MILTONIA n tropical American orchid

MILTS ▶ milt

MILTY, MILTIER, MILTIEST adj full of milt

MILTZ, -ES same as ▶ milt

MILVINE adj of kites and related birds

MIM, -MER, -MEST adj prim, modest, or demure

MIMBAR, -S n pulpit in mosque

MIME, -D, -S, MIMING n acting without the use of words ▷ vb act in mime

MIMEO, -ED, -ING, -S vb mimeograph

MIMER, -S ▶ mime

MIMES ▶ mime

MIMESIS, MIMESES n imitative representation of nature or human behaviour

MIMESTER ▶ mime

MIMETIC adj imitating or representing something

MIMETITE n rare secondary mineral

MIMIC, -KED, -S vb imitate (a person or manner), esp for satirical effect ▷ n person or animal that is good at mimicking ▷ adj of, relating to, or using mimicry

MIMICAL

MIMICKER

MIMICRY n act or art of copying or imitating closely

MIMICS ▶ mimic

MIMING ▶ mime

MIMMER ▶ mim

MIMMEST ▶ mim

MIMMICK, -S same as ▶ minnick

MIMOSA, -E, -S n shrub with fluffy yellow flowers and sensitive leaves

MIMSEY same as ▶ mimsy

MIMSY, MIMSIER, MIMSIEST adj prim, underwhelming, and ineffectual

MIMULUS n plants cultivated for their yellow or red flowers

MINA, -E, -S n ancient unit of weight and money, used in Asia Minor

MINABLE ▶ mine

MINACITY > minacious

MINAE ▶ mina

MINAR, -S n tower

MINARET, -S n tall slender tower of a mosque

MINARS ▶ minar

MINAS ▶ mina

MINATORY adj threatening or menacing

MINBAR, -S same as ▶ mimbar

MINCE, -D, -S vb cut or grind into very small pieces ▷ n minced meat

MINCER, -S n machine for mincing meat

MINCES ▶ mince

MINCEUR adj (of food) low-fat

MINCIER ▶ mincy

MINCIEST ▶ mincy

MINCING adj affectedly elegant in manner

MINCY, MINCIER, MINCIEST adj excessively particular or fussy

MIND, -S n thinking faculties ▷ vb take offence at

MINDED adj having an inclination as specified

MINDEDLY adv in the manner of a person with the kind of mind specified

MINDER, -S n aide or bodyguard

MINDFUL adj heedful

MINDING, -S ▶ mind

MINDLESS adj stupid

MINDS ▶ mind

MINDSET, -S n ideas and attitudes with which a person approaches a situation

MINE, -D, -S pron belonging to me ▷ n deep hole for digging out coal, ores, etc ▷ vb dig for minerals

MINEABLE

MINEOLA, -S same as ▶ minneola

MINER, -S n person who works in a mine

MINERAL, -S n naturally occurring inorganic substance, such as metal ▷ adj of, containing, or like minerals

MINERS ▶ miner

MINES ▶ mine

MINETTE, -S n type of rock

MINEVER, -S same as ▶ miniver

MING, MEYNT, -ED, -S vb mix

MINGER, -S n insulting word for an unattractive person

MINGIER ▶ mingy

MINGIEST ▶ mingy

MINGILY adv in a miserly manner

MINGING adj unattractive or unpleasant

MINGLE, -D, -S, MINGLING vb mix or blend

MINGLER -S

MINGS ▶ ming

MINGY, MINGIER, MINGIEST adj miserly

MINI, -S same as ▶ minidress

MINIATE, -D, -S vb paint with minium

MINIBAR, -S n selection of drinks and confectionery provided in a hotel room

MINIBIKE n light motorcycle

MINIBUS n small bus

MINICAB, -S n ordinary car used as a taxi

MINICAM, -S n portable television camera

MINICAMP n period spent together in isolation by sports team

MINICAMS ▶ minicam

MINICAR, -S n small car

MINICOM, -S n device allowing typed telephone messages to be sent and received

MINIDISC n (esp formerly) small recordable compact disc

MINIDISH n small parabolic aerial for reception or transmission to a communications satellite

MINIDISK same as ▶ minidisc

MINIER ▶ miny

MINIEST ▶ miny

MINIFY, MINIFIED, MINIFIES vb minimize or lessen the size or importance of (something)

MINIGOLF n putting game played via various obstacles

MINIKIN, -S n small, dainty, or affected person or thing ▷ adj dainty, prim, or affected

MINILAB, -S n equipment for processing photographic film

MINIM, -S n note half the length of a semibreve ▷ adj very small

MINIMA ▶ minimum

MINIMAL, -S adj minimum ▷ n small surfboard

MINIMART n convenience store

MINIMAX n lowest of a set of maximum values ▷ vb make maximum as low as possible

MINIMENT same as ▶ muniment

MINIMILL n small mill

MINIMISE same as ▶ minimize

MINIMISM n desire to reduce to minimum
MINIMIST

MINIMIZE vb reduce to a minimum

MINIMOTO n reduced-size replica motorcycle used for racing

MINIMS ▶ minim

MINIMUM, MINIMA, -S n least possible (amount or number) ▷ adj of, being, or showing a minimum or minimums

MINIMUS adj youngest: used after the surname of a schoolboy with elder brothers at the same school

MINING, -S n act, process, or industry of extracting coal or ores from the earth

MINION, -S n servile assistant ▷ adj dainty, pretty, or elegant

MINIPARK n small park

MINIS ▶ mini

MINISH, -ED, -ES vb diminish

MINISKI, -S n short ski

MINISODE n episode of a television series shortened for broadcast on the internet

MINISTER n head of a government department ▷ vb attend to the needs of

MINISTRY n profession or duties of a clergyman

MINIUM, -S n bright red poisonous insoluble oxide of lead

MINIVAN, -S n small van, esp one with seats in the back for carrying passengers

MINIVER, -S n white fur, used in ceremonial costumes

MINIVET, -S n brightly coloured tropical Asian cuckoo shrike

MINK, -S n stoatlike animal

MINKE, -S n as in **minke whale** type of small whalebone whale or rorqual

MINKS ▶ mink

MINNEOLA n juicy citrus fruit that is a cross between a tangerine and a grapefruit

MINNICK, -S vb behave in fussy way

MINNIE, -S n mother

MINNOCK, -S same as **▶ minnick**

MINNOW, -S n small freshwater fish

MINNY same as **▶ minnie**

MINO, -S same as **▶ mynah**

MINOR, -ED, -ING, -S adj lesser ▷ n person regarded legally as a child ▷ vb take a minor

MINORCA, -S n breed of light domestic fowl

MINORED ▶ minor

MINORING ▶ minor

MINORITY n lesser number

MINORS ▶ minor

MINOS ▶ mino

MINOTAUR n as in **minotaur beetle** kind of dung-beetle

MINSHUKU n guesthouse in Japan

MINSTER, -S n cathedral or large church

MINSTREL n medieval singer or musician

MINT, -ED, -ING, -S n plant with aromatic leaves ▷ vb make (coins)

MINTAGE, -S n process of minting

MINTED ▶ mint

MINTER, -S ▶ mint

MINTIER ▶ minty

MINTIEST ▶ minty

MINTING ▶ mint

MINTS ▶ mint

MINTY, MINTIER, MINTIEST ▶ mint

MINUEND, -S n number from which another number is to be subtracted

MINUET, -ED, -S n stately dance ▷ vb dance the minuet

MINUS, -ES adj indicating subtraction ▷ n sign (-) denoting subtraction or a number less than zero ▷ prep reduced by the subtraction of

MINUTE, -D, -R, -ST, MINUTING n 60th part of an hour or degree ▷ vb record in the minutes ▷ adj very small

MINUTELY adv in great detail ▷ adj occurring every minute

MINUTER ▶ minute

MINUTES pl n official record of the proceedings of a meeting or conference

MINUTEST ▶ minute

MINUTIA singular noun of **▶ minutiae**

MINUTIAE pl n trifling or precise details
MINUTIAL

MINUTING ▶ minute

MINX, -ES n bold girl
MINXISH

MINY, MINIER, MINIEST adj of or like mines

MINYAN, -IM, -S n number of persons required by Jewish law to be present for a religious service

MIOCENE adj of, denoting, or formed in the fourth epoch of the Tertiary period

MIOMBO, -S n (in E Africa) a dry wooded area with sparse deciduous growth

MIOSIS, MIOSES, -ES n excessive contraction of the pupil of the eye
MIOTIC -S

MIPS n unit used to express the speed of a computer's central processing unit

MIQUELET n type of lock on old firearm

MIR, -I, -S n peasant commune in prerevolutionary Russia

MIRABLE adj wonderful

MIRACLE, -S n wonderful supernatural event

MIRADOR, -S n window, balcony, or turret

MIRAGE, -S n optical illusion, esp one caused by hot air

MIRBANE, -S n substance used in perfumes

MIRCHI Indian English word for **▶ hot**

MIRE, -D, -S, MIRING n swampy ground ▷ vb sink or be stuck in a mire

MIREPOIX n mixture of sautéed root vegetables

MIRES ▶ mire

MIREX, -ES n type of insecticide

MIRI ▶ mir

MIRID, -S n variety of leaf bug

MIRIER ▶ miry

MIRIEST ▶ miry

MIRIFIC adj achieving wonderful things

MIRIN, -S n Japanese rice wine

MIRINESS ▶ mire

MIRING ▶ mire

MIRINS ▶ mirin

MIRITI, -S n South American palm

MIRK, -ER, -EST, -S same as **▶ murk**

MIRKIER ▶ mirky

MIRKIEST ▶ mirky

MIRKILY ▶ mirk

MIRKS ▶ mirk

MIRKY, MIRKIER, MIRKIEST ▶ mirk

MIRLIER ▶ mirly

MIRLIEST ▶ mirly

MIRLITON another name (chiefly US) for **▶ chayote**

MIRLY, MIRLIER, MIRLIEST same as **▶ marly**

MIRO, -S n tall New Zealand tree

M

MIROMIRO n small New Zealand bird

MIROS ▸ miro

MIRROR, -ED, -S n coated glass surface for reflecting images ▷ vb reflect in or as if in a mirror

MIRS ▸ mir

MIRTH, -S n laughter, merriment, or gaiety

MIRTHFUL

MIRV, -ED, -ING, -S n missile that has several warheads, each one being directed to different enemy targets ▷ vb arm with mirvs

MIRY, MIRIER, MIRIEST ▸ mire

MIRZA, -S n title of respect placed before the surname of a distinguished man

MIS ▸ mi

MISACT, -ED, -S vb act wrongly

MISADAPT vb adapt badly

MISADD, -ED, -S vb add badly

MISAGENT n bad agent

MISAIM, -ED, -S vb aim badly

MISALIGN vb align badly

MISALLOT vb allot wrongly

MISALLY vb form unsuitable alliance

MISALTER vb alter wrongly

MISANDRY n hatred of men

MISAPPLY vb use something for a purpose for which it is not intended or is not suited

MISARRAY n disarray

MISASSAY vb assay wrongly

MISATE ▸ miseat

MISATONE vb atone wrongly

MISAVER, -S vb claim wrongly

MISAWARD vb award wrongly

MISBEGIN, MISBEGAN, MISBEGUN vb begin badly

MISBIAS vb prejudice wrongly

MISBILL, -S vb present inaccurate bill

MISBIND, -S, MISBOUND vb bind wrongly

MISBIRTH n abortion

MISBORN adj born prematurely

MISBOUND ▸ misbind

MISBRAND vb put misleading label on

MISBUILD, MISBUILT vb build badly

MISCALL, -S vb call by the wrong name

MISCARRY vb have a miscarriage

MISCAST, -S vb cast (a role or actor) inappropriately

MISCH adj as in **misch metal** alloy of cerium and other rare earth metals

MISCHIEF n annoying but not malicious behaviour

MISCHOSE ▸ mischoose

MISCIBLE adj able to be mixed

MISCITE, -D, -S vb cite wrongly

MISCLAIM vb claim wrongly

MISCLASS vb class badly

MISCODE, -D, -S vb code wrongly

MISCOIN, -S vb coin wrongly

MISCOLOR same as ▸ miscolour

MISCOOK, -S vb cook badly

MISCOPY vb copy badly

MISCOUNT vb count or calculate incorrectly ▷ n false count or calculation

MISCREED n false creed

MISCUE, -D, -S, MISCUING n faulty stroke in snooker, etc ▷ vb make a miscue

MISCUT, -S n cut wrongly

MISDATE, -D, -S vb date (a letter, event, etc) wrongly

MISDEAL, -S, -T vb deal out cards incorrectly ▷ n faulty deal

MISDEED, -S n wrongful act

MISDEEM, -S, MISDEMPT vb form bad opinion of

MISDIAL, -S vb dial telephone number incorrectly

MISDID ▸ misdo

MISDIET, -S n wrong diet ▷ vb diet or eat improperly

MISDIGHT adj done badly ▷ vb mismanage or treat badly

MISDO, MISDID, -ES, -ING vb do badly or wrongly

MISDOER -S

MISDONE adj done badly

MISDONNE same as ▸ misdone

MISDOUBT archaic word for ▸ doubt

MISDRAW, -N, -S, MISDREW vb draw poorly

MISDREAD n fear of approaching evil ▷ vb fear or dread

MISDREW ▸ misdraw

MISDRIVE, MISDROVE vb drive badly

MISE, -S n issue in the obsolete writ of right

MISEASE, -S n unease

MISEAT, MISATE, -EN, -S vb eat unhealthy food

MISEDIT, -S vb edit badly

MISENROL vb enrol wrongly

MISENTER vb enter wrongly

MISENTRY n wrong or mistaken entry

MISER, -S n person who hoards money and hates spending it

MISERE, -S n call in solo whist and other card games declaring a hand that will win no tricks

MISERERE n type of psalm

MISERES ▸ misere

MISERIES ▸ misery

MISERLY adj of or resembling a miser

MISERS ▸ miser

MISERY, MISERIES n great unhappiness

MISES ▸ mise

MISEVENT n mishap

MISFAITH n distrust

MISFALL, -S, MISFALNE, MISFELL vb happen as piece of bad luck

MISFARE, -D, -S vb get on badly

MISFEED, MISFED, -S vb feed wrongly

MISFEIGN vb feign with evil motive

MISFELL ▸ misfall

MISFIELD vb fail to field properly

MISFILE, -D, -S vb file (papers, records, etc) wrongly

MISFIRE, -D, -S vb (of a firearm or engine) fail to fire correctly ▷ n act or an instance of misfiring

MISFIT, -S n person not suited to his or her social environment ▷ vb fail to fit or be fitted

MISFOCUS n wrong or poor focus

MISFORM, -S vb form badly

MISFRAME vb frame wrongly

MISGAUGE vb gauge badly

MISGIVE, MISGAVE, -N, -S vb make or be apprehensive or suspicious

MISGO, -ES, -ING, -NE vb go wrong way

MISGRADE vb grade wrongly

MISGRAFF adj badly done

MISGRAFT vb graft wrongly

MISGROW, MISGREW, -N, -S vb grow in unsuitable way

MISGUESS vb guess wrongly

MISGUIDE vb guide or direct wrongly or badly

MISHAP, -S n minor accident ▷ vb happen as bad luck

MISHAPT same as ▸ misshapen

MISHEAR, -D, -S vb hear (what someone says) wrongly

MISHIT, -S n faulty shot, kick, or stroke ▷ vb hit or kick a ball with a faulty stroke

MISHMASH n confused collection or mixture

MISHMEE, -S n root of Asian plant

MISHMI, -S n evergreen perennial plant

MISHMOSH same as ▶ mishmash

MISHUGAS same as > meshugaas

MISINFER vb infer wrongly

MISINTER vb bury wrongly

MISJOIN, -S vb join badly

MISJUDGE vb judge wrongly or unfairly

MISKAL, -S n unit of weight in Iran

MISKEEP, -S, MISKEPT vb keep wrongly

MISKEN, -S, -T vb be unaware of

MISKEPT ▶ miskeep

MISKEY, -ED, -S vb key wrongly

MISKICK, -S vb fail to kick properly

MISKNOW, MISKNEW, -N, -S vb have wrong idea about

MISLABEL vb label badly

MISLABOR vb labour wrongly

MISLAY, MISLAID, MISLAIN, -S vb lose (something) temporarily

MISLAYER

MISLEAD, -S, MISLED vb give false or confusing information to

MISLEARN vb learn wrongly

MISLED ▶ mislead

MISLEEKE same as ▶ mislike

MISLETOE same as > mistletoe

MISLIE, -S, MISLYING vb lie wrongly

MISLIGHT, MISLIT vb use light to lead astray

MISLIKE, -D, -S vb dislike ▷ n dislike or aversion

MISLIKER

MISLIT ▶ mislight

MISLIVE, -D, -S vb live wickedly

MISLODGE vb lodge wrongly

MISLUCK, -S vb have bad luck

MISLYING ▶ mislie

MISMAKE, MISMADE, -S vb make badly

MISMARK, -S vb mark wrongly

MISMARRY vb make unsuitable marriage

MISMATCH vb form an unsuitable partner, opponent, or set ▷ n unsuitable match

MISMATE, -D, -S vb mate wrongly

MISMEET, -S, MISMET vb fail to meet

MISMETRE vb fail to follow the metre of a poem

MISMOVE, -D, -S vb move badly

MISNAME, -D, -S vb name badly

MISNOMER n incorrect or unsuitable name ▷ vb apply a misnomer to

MISO, -S n thick brown salty paste made from soya beans

MISOGAMY n hatred of marriage

MISOGYNY n hatred of women

MISOLOGY n hatred of reasoning or reasoned argument

MISORDER vb order badly

MISOS ▶ miso

MISPAGE, -D, -S vb page wrongly

MISPAINT vb paint badly or wrongly

MISPARSE vb parse wrongly

MISPART, -S vb part wrongly

MISPATCH vb patch wrongly

MISPEN, -S vb write wrongly

MISPLACE vb mislay

MISPLAN, -S vb plan badly or wrongly

MISPLANT vb plant badly or wrongly

MISPLAY, -S vb play badly or wrongly in games or sports ▷ n wrong or unskilful play

MISPLEAD, MISPLED vb plead incorrectly

MISPOINT vb punctuate badly

MISPOISE n lack of poise ▷ vb lack poise

MISPRICE vb give the wrong price to

MISPRINT n printing error ▷ vb print a letter incorrectly

MISPRISE same as ▶ misprize

MISPRIZE vb fail to appreciate the value of

MISPROUD adj undeservedly proud

MISQUOTE vb quote inaccurately

MISRAISE vb raise wrongly or excessively

MISRATE, -D, -S vb rate wrongly

MISREAD, -S vb misinterpret (a situation etc)

MISREFER vb refer wrongly

MISRELY vb rely wrongly

MISROUTE vb send wrong way

MISRULE, -D, -S vb govern inefficiently or unjustly ▷ n inefficient or unjust government

MISS, -ED, -ES vb fail to notice, hear, hit, reach, find, or catch ▷ n fact or instance of missing

MISSA, -E n Roman Catholic mass

MISSABLE ▶ miss

MISSAE ▶ missa

MISSAID ▶ missay

MISSAL, -S n book containing the prayers and rites of the Mass

MISSAW ▶ missee

MISSAY, MISSAID, -S vb say wrongly

MISSEAT, -S vb seat wrongly

MISSED ▶ miss

MISSEE, MISSAW, -N, -S vb see wrongly

MISSEEM, -S vb be unsuitable for

MISSEEN ▶ missee

MISSEES ▶ missee

MISSEL, -S adj as in **missel thrush** large European thrush

MISSELL, -S, MISSOLD vb sell (a product, esp a financial one) misleadingly

MISSELS ▶ missel

MISSEND, -S, MISSENT vb send wrongly

MISSENSE n type of genetic mutation ▷ vb give a wrong sense or meaning

MISSENT ▶ missend

MISSES ▶ miss

MISSET, -S vb set wrongly

MISSHAPE vb shape badly ▷ n something that is badly shaped

MISSHOD adj badly shod

MISSHOOD n state of being an unmarried woman

MISSIER ▶ missy

MISSIES ▶ missy

MISSIEST ▶ missy

MISSILE, -S n rocket with an exploding warhead

MISSILRY same as > missilery

MISSING adj lost or absent

MISSION, -S n specific task or duty ▷ vb direct a mission to or establish a mission in

MISSIS, -ES same as ▶ missus

MISSISH adj like a schoolgirl

MISSIVE, -S n letter ▷ adj sent or intended to be sent

MISSOLD ▶ missell

MISSORT, -S vb sort wrongly

MISSOUND vb sound wrongly

MISSOUT, -S n someone who has been overlooked

MISSPACE vb space out wrongly

MISSPEAK, MISSPOKE vb speak wrongly

MISSPELL, MISSPELT vb spell (a word) wrongly

MISSPEND, MISSPENT vb waste or spend unwisely

MISSPOKE ▶ misspeak

MISSTAMP vb stamp badly

MISSTART vb start wrongly

MISSTATE vb state incorrectly

MISSTEER vb steer badly

MISSTEP, -S n false step ▷ vb take a false step

MISSTOP, -S vb stop wrongly

MISSTYLE vb call by the wrong name

MISSUIT, -S vb be unsuitable for

MISSUS, -ES n one's wife or the wife of the person addressed or referred to

MISSY, MISSIER, MISSIES, MISSIEST n affectionate or disparaging form of address to a girl ▷ adj missish

MIST, -ED, -S n thin fog ▷ vb cover or be covered with mist

MISTAKE, -S n error or blunder ▷ vb misunderstand

MISTAKEN adj wrong in judgment or opinion

MISTAKER ▶ mistake

MISTAKES ▶ mistake

MISTAL, -S n cow shed

MISTBOW, -S same as ▶ fogbow

MISTEACH vb teach badly

MISTED ▶ mist

MISTELL, -S, MISTOLD vb tell wrongly

MISTEND, -S vb tend wrongly

MISTER, -ED, -S n informal form of address for a man ▷ vb call (someone) mister

MISTERM vb term badly

MISTERS ▶ mister

MISTERY same as ▶ mystery

MISTEUK Scots variant of ▶ mistook

MISTFUL ▶ mist

MISTHINK vb have poor opinion of

MISTHROW, MISTHREW vb fail to throw properly

MISTICO, -S n small Mediterranean sailing ship

MISTIER ▶ misty

MISTIEST ▶ misty

MISTILY ▶ misty

MISTIME, -D, -S vb do (something) at the wrong time

MISTING, -S n application of a fake suntan by spray

MISTITLE vb name badly

MISTLE, -D, -S, MISTLING same as ▶ mizzle

MISTOLD ▶ mistell

MISTOOK past tense of ▶ mistake

MISTOUCH vb fail to touch properly

MISTRACE vb trace wrongly

MISTRAIN vb train wrongly

MISTRAL, -S n strong dry northerly wind of S France

MISTREAT vb treat (a person or animal) badly

MISTRESS n woman in a position of authority, ownership, or control ▷ vb become a mistress

MISTRIAL n trial made void because of some error

MISTRUST vb have doubts or suspicions about ▷ n lack of trust

MISTRUTH n something untrue

MISTRYST vb fail to keep an appointment with

MISTS ▶ mist

MISTUNE, -D, -S vb fail to tune properly

MISTUTOR vb instruct badly

MISUNION n wrong or bad union

MISUSAGE ▶ misuse

MISUSE, -D, -S, MISUSING, MISUST n incorrect, improper, or careless use ▷ vb use wrongly

MISUSER, -S n abuse of some right, privilege, office, etc

MISUSES ▶ misuse

MISUSING ▶ misuse

MISUST ▶ misuse

MISVALUE vb value badly

MISWEEN, -S vb assess wrongly

MISWEND, -S, MISWENT vb become lost

MISWORD, -S vb word badly

MISWRITE, MISWRIT, MISWROTE vb write badly

MISYOKE, -D, -S vb join wrongly

MITCH, -ED, -ES, -ING vb play truant from school

MITE, -S n very small spider-like animal

MITER, -ED, -ING, -S same as ▶ mitre

MITERER -S

MITES ▶ mite

MITHER, -ED, -S vb fuss over or moan about something

MITICIDE n any drug or agent that destroys mites

MITIER ▶ mity

MITIEST ▶ mity

MITIGANT adj acting to mitigate ▷ n means of easing, lessening, or assuaging

MITIGATE vb make less severe

MITIS, -ES n malleable iron

MITOGEN, -S n any agent that induces mitosis

MITOSIS, MITOSES n type of cell division

MITOTIC

MITRAL adj of or like a mitre

MITRE, -D, -S, MITRING n bishop's pointed headdress ▷ vb join with a mitre joint

MITTS, -ENS, MITSVOTH same as ▶ mitzvah

MITT, -S same as ▶ mitten

MITTEN, -S n glove with one section for the thumb and one for the four fingers together

MITTENED adj wearing mittens

MITTENS ▶ mitten

MITTIMUS n warrant of commitment to prison

MITTS ▶ mitt

MITUMBA, -S n used clothes imported for sale in African countries

MITY, MITIER, MITIEST adj having mites

MITZVAH, -S, MITZVOTH n commandment or precept, esp one found in the Bible

MIURUS, -ES n type of rhythm in poetry

MIX, -ES, -T vb combine or blend into one mass ▷ n mixture

MIXABLE

MIXDOWN, -S n (in sound recording) the transfer of a multitrack master mix to two-track stereo tape

MIXED adj formed or blended together by mixing

MIXEDLY

MIXEN, -S n dunghill

M

MIXER, -S *n* kitchen appliance used for mixing foods

MIXES ► mix

MIXIBLE ► mix

MIXIER ► mixy

MIXIEST ► mixy

MIXING, -S *n* act of mixing

MIXOLOGY *n* art of mixing cocktails

MIXT ► mix

MIXTAPE, -S *n* compilation of songs from various sources

MIXTE *adj* of a type of bicycle frame

MIXTION, -S *n* amber-based mixture used in making gold leaf

MIXTURE, -S *n* something mixed

MIXUP, -S *n* something that is mixed up

MIXY, MIXIER, MIXIEST *adj* mixed

MIZ, -ZES *shortened form of* ► misery

> **Miz** is an informal short form of **misery**, very useful as a Z word. But you'll need a blank tile for the second Z if you want to form the plural **mizzes**.

MIZEN, -S *same as* ► **mizzen**

MIZMAZE, -S *n* maze

MIZUNA, -S *n* Japanese variety of lettuce

MIZZ *same as* ► **miz**

MIZZEN, -S *n* sail set on a mizzenmast ▷ *adj* of or relating to any kind of gear used with a mizzenmast

MIZZES ► miz

MIZZLE, -D, -S, MIZZLING *vb* decamp

MIZZLIER ► mizzly

MIZZLING ► mizzle

MIZZLY, MIZZLIER ► mizzle

MIZZY *adj as in* **mizzy maze** dialect expression meaning state of confusion

MM *interj* expression of enjoyment of taste or smell

MMM *interj* interjection expressing agreement or enjoyment

MNA, -S *same as* ► **mina**

MNEME, -S *n* ability to retain memory

MNEMIC

MNEMON, -S *n* unit of memory

MNEMONIC *adj* intended to help the memory ▷ *n* something, for instance a verse, intended to help the memory

MNEMONS ► mnemon

MO, -S *n* moment

MOA, -S *n* large extinct flightless New Zealand bird

MOAI *n* any of the gigantic carved stone figures found on Easter Island (Rapa Nui)

MOAN, -ED, -S *n* low cry of pain ▷ *vb* make or utter with a moan

MOANER -S

MOANFUL ► moan

MOANING, -S ► moan

MOANS ► moan

MOAS ► moa

MOAT, -ED, -ING, -S *n* deep wide ditch, esp around a castle ▷ *vb* surround with or as if with a moat

MOATLIKE

MOB, -BED, -S *n* disorderly crowd ▷ *vb* surround in a mob

MOBBER -S

MOBBIE *same as* ► **mobby**

MOBBIES ► mobby

MOBBING, -S ► mob

MOBBISH ► mob

MOBBISM, -S *n* behaviour as mob

MOBBLE, -D, -S, MOBBLING *same as* ► **moble**

MOBBY, MOBBIES *n* West Indian drink

MOBCAP, -S *n* woman's 18th-century cotton cap

MOBCAST, -S *vb* create and upload a podcast directly from a mobile phone

MOBE, -S *n* mobile phone

MOBEY, -S *same as* ► **moby**

MOBIE, -S *n* mobile phone

MOBILE, -S *adj* able to move ▷ *n* hanging structure designed to move in air currents

MOBILISE *same as* ► **mobilize**

MOBILITY *n* ability to move physically

MOBILIZE *vb* (of the armed services) prepare for active service

MOBISODE *n* episode of a TV show made for viewing on a mobile phone

MOBLE, -D, -S, MOBLING *vb* muffle

MOBLOG, -S *n* blog recorded in the form of mobile phone calls, text messages, and photographs

MOBOCRAT > mobocracy

MOBS ► mob

MOBSMAN, MOBSMEN *n* person in mob

MOBSTER, -S *n* member of a criminal organization

MOBY *n* mobile phone

MOC, -S *shortening of* ► **moccasin**

MOCASSIN *same as* ► **moccasin**

MOCCASIN *n* soft leather shoe

MOCCIES *pl n* informal Australian word for moccasins

MOCH, -ED, -ING, -S *n* spell of humid weather ▷ *vb* (of foods) become musty or spoiled

MOCHA, -S *n* kind of strong dark coffee

MOCHED ► moch

MOCHELL, -S *same as* ► **much**

MOCHI, -S *n* confection made with rice flour and sweetened bean paste

MOCHIE, -R, -ST *adj* damp or humid

MOCHILA, -S *n* South American shoulder bag

MOCHING ► moch

MOCHIS ► mochi

MOCHS ► moch

MOCHY *same as* ► **mochie**

MOCK, -ED, -S *vb* make fun of ▷ *adj* sham or imitation ▷ *n* act of mocking

MOCKABLE

MOCKADO *n* imitation velvet

MOCKAGE, -S *same as* ► **mockery**

MOCKED ► mock

MOCKER, -ED, -S *vb* dress up

MOCKERY *n* derision

MOCKING, -S ► mock

MOCKNEY *n* person who affects a cockney accent ▷ *adj* denoting an affected cockney accent or a person who has one

MOCKS ► mock

MOCKTAIL *n* cocktail without alcohol

MOCKUP, -S *n* working full-scale model of a machine, apparatus, etc, for testing, research, etc

MOCOCK, -S *n* Native American birchbark container

MOCS ► moc

MOCUCK, -S *same as* ► **mocock**

MOCUDDUM *same as* ► **muqaddam**

MOD, -DED, -S *n* member of a group of fashionable

M

young people, orig. in the 1960s ▷ *vb* modify (a piece of software or hardware)

MODAL, -S *adj* of or relating to mode or manner ▷ *n* modal word

MODALISM *n* type of Christian doctrine

MODALIST

MODALITY *n* condition of being modal

MODALLY ▶ modal

MODALS ▶ modal

MODDED ▶ mod

MODDER, -S *n* person who modifies a piece of hardware or software

MODDING, -S *n* practice of modifying a car to alter its appearance or performance

MODE, -S *n* method or manner

MODEL, -ED, -LED, -S *n* (miniature) representation ▷ *adj* excellent or perfect ▷ *vb* make a model of

MODELER -S

MODELING *same as* > **modelling**

MODELIST *same as* > **modellist**

MODELLED ▶ model

MODELLER ▶ model

MODELLO, MODELLI, -S *n* artist's preliminary sketch or model

MODELS ▶ model

MODEM, -ED, -ING, -S *n* device for connecting two computers by a telephone line ▷ *vb* send or receive by modem

MODENA, -S *n* popular variety of domestic fancy pigeon

MODER, -S *n* intermediate layer in humus

MODERATE *adj* not extreme ▷ *n* person of moderate views ▷ *vb* make or become less violent or extreme

MODERATO *adv* at a moderate speed ▷ *n* moderato piece

MODERN, -ER, -S *adj* of present or recent times ▷ *n* contemporary person

MODERNE, -S *n* style of architecture and design of the late 1920s and 1930s ▷ *adj* of or relating to this style of architecture and design

MODERNER ▶ modern

MODERNES ▶ moderne

MODERNLY ▶ modern

MODERNS ▶ modern

MODERS ▶ moder

MODES ▶ mode

MODEST, -ER *adj* not vain or boastful

MODESTLY

MODESTY *n* quality or condition of being modest

MODGE, -D, -S, MODGING *vb* do shoddily

MODI ▶ modus

MODICUM, MODICA, -S *n* small quantity

MODIFIED ▶ modify

MODIFIER *n* word that qualifies the sense of another

MODIFY, MODIFIED, MODIFIES *vb* change slightly

MODII ▶ modius

MODIOLAR ▶ modiolus

MODIOLUS, MODIOLI *n* central bony pillar of the cochlea

MODISH *adj* in fashion

MODISHLY

MODIST, -S *n* follower of fashion

MODISTE, -S *n* fashionable dressmaker or milliner

MODISTS ▶ modist

MODIUS, MODII *n* ancient Roman quantity measure

MODIWORT *Scots variant of* > **mouldwarp**

MODS ▶ mod

MODULAR, -S *adj* of, consisting of, or resembling a module or modulus ▷ *n* thing comprised of modules

MODULATE *vb* vary in tone

MODULE, -S *n* self-contained unit, section, or component with a specific function

MODULI ▶ modulus

MODULO *adv* with reference to modulus

MODULUS, MODULI *n* coefficient expressing a specified property

MODUS, MODI *n* way of doing something

MOE, -S *adv* more ▷ *n* wry face

MOELLON, -S *n* rubble

MOER, -ED, -ING, -S *n* in South Africa, slang word for the womb ▷ *vb* in South Africa, attack (someone or something) violently

MOES ▶ moe

MOFETTE, -S *n* opening in a region of nearly extinct volcanic activity, through which gases pass

MOFFETTE *same as* ▶ **mofette**

MOFUSSIL *n* provincial area in India

MOG, -GED, -GING, -S *vb* go away

MOGGAN, -S *n* stocking without foot

MOGGED ▶ mog

MOGGIE *same as* ▶ **moggy**

MOGGIES ▶ moggy

MOGGING ▶ mog

MOGGY, MOGGIES *n* cat

MOGHUL, -S *same as* ▶ **mogul**

MOGS ▶ mog

MOGUL, -S *n* important or powerful person

MOGULED *adj* having moguls

MOGULS ▶ mogul

MOHAIR, -S *n* fine hair of the Angora goat

MOHALIM *same as* ▶ **mohelim**

MOHAWK, -S *n* half turn from either edge of either skate to the corresponding edge of the other skate

MOHEL, -IM, -S *n* man qualified to conduct circumcisions

MOHICAN, -S *n* punk hairstyle

MOHO, -S *n* boundary between the earth's crust and mantle

MOHR, -S *same as* ▶ **mhorr**

MOHUA, -S *n* small New Zealand bird

MOHUR, -S *n* former Indian gold coin worth 15 rupees

MOI *pron* (used facetiously) me

MOIDER, -ED, -S *same as* ▶ **moither**

MOIDORE, -S *n* former Portuguese gold coin

MOIETY, MOIETIES *n* half

MOIL, -ED, -ING, -S *vb* moisten or soil or become moist, soiled, etc ▷ *n* toil

MOILE, -S *n* type of rice pudding made with almond milk

MOILED ▶ moil

MOILER, -S ▶ moil

MOILES ▶ moile

MOILING ▶ moil

MOILS ▶ moil

MOINEAU, -S *n* small fortification

Meaning a type of small fortification, this is another of those very useful 7-letter vowel dumps.

MOIRA, -I *n* fate

MOIRE, -S adj having a watered or wavelike pattern ▷ n any fabric that has such a pattern

MOISER, -S n informer

MOIST, -ED, -ER, -EST, -ING, -S adj slightly wet ▷ vb moisten

MOISTEN, -S vb make or become moist

MOISTER ► moist

MOISTEST ► moist

MOISTFUL adj full of moisture

MOISTIFY vb moisten

MOISTING ► moist

MOISTLY ► moist

MOISTS ► moist

MOISTURE n liquid diffused as vapour or condensed in drops

MOIT, -S same as ► mote

MOITHER, -S vb bother or bewilder

MOITS ► moit

MOJARRA, -S n tropical American sea fish

MOJITO, -S n rum-based cocktail

MOJO, -ES, -S n charm or magic spell

MOKADDAM same as ► muqaddam

MOKE, -S n donkey

MOKI, -S n edible sea fish of New Zealand

MOKIHI, -S n Māori raft

MOKIS ► moki

MOKO, -S n Māori tattoo or tattoo pattern

MOKOMOKO n type of skink found in New Zealand

MOKOPUNA n grandchild or young person

MOKORO, -S n (in Botswana) the traditional dugout canoe of the people of the Okavango Delta

MOKOS ► moko

MOKSHA, -S n freedom from the endless cycle of transmigration into a state of bliss

MOL, -S n the SI unit mole

MOLA, -S another name for ► sunfish

MOLAL adj of a solution containing one mole of solute per thousand grams of solvent

MOLALITY n measure of solvent concentration

MOLAR, -S n large back tooth used for grinding ▷ adj any of these teeth

MOLARITY n concentration

MOLARS ► molar

MOLAS ► mola

MOLASSE n sediment from the erosion of mountain ranges

MOLASSES n dark syrup, a by-product of sugar refining

MOLD, -ED, -S same as ► mould

MOLDABLE

MOLDER, -ED, -S same as ► moulder

MOLDIER ► moldy

MOLDIEST ► moldy

MOLDING, -S same as ► moulding

MOLDS ► mold

MOLDWARP same as > mouldwarp

MOLDY, MOLDIER, MOLDIEST same as ► mouldy

MOLE, -D, -S, MOLING n small dark raised spot on the skin ▷ vb as in **mole out** seek as if by burrowing

MOLECAST n molehill

MOLECULE n simplest freely existing chemical unit, composed of two or more atoms

MOLED ► mole

MOLEHILL n small mound of earth thrown up by a burrowing mole

MOLEHUNT n hunt for a mole

MOLES ► mole

MOLESKIN n dark grey dense velvety pelt of a mole, used as a fur

MOLEST, -ED, -S vb disturb or annoy

MOLESTER

MOLIES ► moly

MOLIMEN, -S n effort needed to perform bodily function

MOLINE, -S adj (of a cross) having arms of equal length, forked and curved back at the ends ▷ n moline cross

MOLINET, -S n stick for whipping chocolate

MOLING ► mole

MOLL, -S n gangster's female accomplice

MOLLA, -S same as ► mollah

MOLLAH, -S same as ► mullah

MOLLAS ► molla

MOLLIE same as ► molly

MOLLIES ► molly

MOLLIFY vb pacify or soothe

MOLLS ► moll

MOLLUSC, -S n soft-bodied, usu hard-shelled, animal

MOLLUSCA n molluscs collectively

MOLLUSCS ► mollusc

MOLLUSK, -S same as ► mollusc

MOLLY, MOLLIES n American freshwater fish

MOLOCH, -S n spiny Australian desert-living lizard

MOLOSSUS, MOLOSSI n division of metre in poetry

MOLS ► mol

MOLT, -ED, -ING, -S same as ► moult

MOLTEN ► melt

MOLTENLY ► melt

MOLTER, -S ► molt

MOLTING ► molt

MOLTO adv very

MOLTS ► molt

MOLY, MOLIES, -S n mythical magic herb

MOLYBDIC adj of or containing molybdenum in the trivalent or hexavalent state

MOLYS ► moly

MOM, -S same as ► mother

MOME, -S n fool

MOMENT, -S n short space of time

MOMENTA ► momentum

MOMENTLY same as ► moment

MOMENTO, -S same as ► memento

MOMENTS ► moment

MOMENTUM, MOMENTA n impetus to go forward, develop, or get stronger

MOMES ► mome

MOMI same as ► mom

MOMISM, -S n excessive domination of a child by his or her mother

MOMMA, -S same as ► mamma

MOMMET, -S same as ► mammet

MOMMY, MOMMIES same as ► mom

MOMOIR, -S n memoir written by a woman about motherhood

MOMS ► mom

MOMSERS ► momser

MOMUS, -ES n person who ridicules

MON, -S n dialect variant of ► man

MONA n W African guenon monkey

MONACHAL less common word for ► monastic

MONACID, -S same as ► monoacid

M

MONACT, -S adj (of sponge) with single-spiked structures in skeleton

MONAD, -S n any fundamental singular metaphysical entity

MONADAL

MONADES ► monas

MONADIC adj being or relating to a monad

MONADISM n doctrine that monads are the ultimate units of reality

MONADS ► monad

MONAL, -S n S Asian pheasant

MONAMINE n type of amine

MONANDRY n custom of having only one male partner over a period of time

MONARCH, -S n sovereign ruler of a state

MONARCHY n government by or a state ruled by a sovereign

MONARDA, -S n mintlike N American plant

MONAS, MONADES, -ES same as ► monad

MONASTIC adj of monks, nuns, or monasteries ▷ n person who is committed to this way of life, esp a monk

MONAUL, -S same as ► monal

MONAURAL adj relating to, having, or hearing with only one ear

MONAXIAL another word for ► uniaxial

MONAXON, -S n type of sponge

MONAZITE n yellow to reddish-brown mineral

MONDAIN, -S n man who moves in fashionable society ▷ adj characteristic of fashionable society

MONDAINE n woman who moves in fashionable society ▷ adj characteristic of fashionable society

MONDAINS ► mondain

MONDE, -S n French word meaning world or society

MONDIAL adj of or involving the whole world

MONDO, -S n Buddhist questioning technique

MONECIAN same as > **monecious**

MONELLIN n sweet protein

MONEME, -S less common word for ► **morpheme**

MONER, -A n hypothetical simple organism

MONERAN, -S n type of bacterium

MONERON same as ► **moner**

MONETARY adj of money or currency

MONETH, -S same as ► **month**

MONETISE same as ► **monetize**

MONETIZE vb establish as the legal tender of a country

MONEY, -MEN, -S, MONIES n medium of exchange, coins or banknotes

MONEYBAG n bag for money

MONEYBOX n box for keeping money in

MONEYED adj rich

MONEYER, -S n person who coins money

MONEYMAN n person supplying money

MONEYMEN ► money

MONEYS ► money

MONGCORN same as ► **maslin**

MONGEESE ► mongoose

MONGER, -ED, -S n trader or dealer ▷ vb deal in

MONGERY

MONGO, -S same as ► **mungo**

MONGOE, -S same as ► **mongo**

MONGOOSE, MONGEESE n stoatlike mammal of Asia and Africa that kills snakes

MONGOS ► mongo

MONGREL, -S n animal, esp a dog, of mixed breed ▷ adj of mixed breed or origin

MONGST short for ► **amongst**

MONIAL, -S n mullion

MONIC adj denoting a type of polynomial

MONICKER same as ► **moniker**

MONIE Scots word for ► **many**

MONIED same as ► **moneyed**

MONIES ► money

MONIKER, -S n person's name or nickname

MONILIA, -E, -S n type of fungus

MONILIAL adj denoting a thrush infection caused by a fungus

MONILIAS ► monilia

MONIMENT same as ► **monument**

MONISH, -ED, -ES same as ► **admonish**

MONISM, -S n doctrine that reality consists of only one basic substance or element

MONIST -S

MONISTIC

MONITION n warning or caution

MONITIVE adj reproving

MONITOR, -S n person or device that checks, controls, warns, or keeps a record of something ▷ vb watch and check on

MONITORY adj acting as or giving a warning ▷ n letter containing a monition

MONK, -S n member of an all-male religious community

MONKEY, -ED, -S n long-tailed primate ▷ vb meddle or fool

MONKFISH n type of fish

MONKHOOD n condition of being a monk

MONKISH adj of, relating to, or resembling a monk or monks

MONKS ► monk

MONO, -S n monophonic sound

MONOACID adj base which is capable of reacting with only one molecule of a monobasic acid

MONOAO, -S n New Zealand plant with rigid leaves

MONOBLOC adj made from a single piece of something

MONOBROW n appearance of a single eyebrow as a result of the eyebrows joining above a person's nose

MONOCARP n plant that is monocarpic

MONOCLE, -S n eyeglass for one eye only

MONOCLED

MONOCOT, -S n type of flowering plant with a single embryonic seed leaf

MONOCRAT ► monocracy

MONOCROP vb plant the same crop in a field every year

MONOCYTE n large phagocytic leucocyte with a spherical nucleus and clear cytoplasm

MONODIC ► monody

MONODIES ► monody

MONODIST ► monody

MONODONT adj (of certain animals, esp the male narwhal) having a single tooth throughout life

MONODY, MONODIES n (in Greek tragedy) an ode sung by a single actor

MONOECY same as > **monoecism**

MONOFIL, -S n synthetic thread or yarn composed of a single strand rather than twisted fibres

MONOFUEL n single type of fuel

MONOGAMY n custom of being married to one person at a time

MONOGENY n the hypothetical descent of all organisms from a single cell or organism

MONOGERM adj containing single seed

MONOGLOT n person speaking only one language

MONOGONY n asexual reproduction

MONOGRAM n design of combined letters, esp a person's initials ▷ vb decorate (clothing, stationery, etc) with a monogram

MONOGYNY n custom of having only one female partner over a period of time

MONOHULL n sailing vessel with a single hull

MONOKINE n type of protein

MONOKINI n bottom half of a bikini

MONOLINE adj as in **monoline insurer** insurer who pays the principal and interest on a bond in the event of a default

MONOLITH n large upright block of stone

MONOLOG, -S same as > **monologue**

MONOLOGY > **monologue**

MONOMARK n series of letters or figures to identify goods, personal articles, etc

MONOMER, -S n compound whose molecules can join together to form a polymer

MONOMIAL n expression consisting of a single term, such as 5ax ▷ adj consisting of a single algebraic term

MONOMODE adj denoting a type of optical fibre

MONONYM, -S n person who is famous enough to be known only by one name

MONOPOD, -S same as ▶ **monopode**

MONOPODE n member of a legendary one-legged race of Africa

MONOPODS ▶ monopod

MONOPODY n single-foot measure in poetry

MONOPOLE n magnetic pole considered in isolation

MONOPOLY n exclusive possession of or right to do something

MONORAIL n single-rail railway

MONOS ▶ mono

MONOSEMY n fact of having only a single meaning

MONOSES ▶ monosis

MONOSIES ▶ monosy

MONOSIS, MONOSES n abnormal separation

MONOSKI, -S n wide ski on which the skier stands with both feet ▷ vb ski on a monoski

MONOSOME n unpaired chromosome, esp an X-chromosome in an otherwise diploid cell

MONOSOMY n condition with a missing pair of chromosomes

MONOSY, MONOSIES same as ▶ **monosis**

MONOTASK vb perform only one task at a time

MONOTINT n black-and-white photograph or transparency

MONOTONE n unvaried pitch in speech or sound ▷ adj unvarying ▷ vb speak in monotone

MONOTONY n wearisome routine, dullness

MONOTYPE n single print made from a metal or glass plate on which a picture has been painted

MONOXIDE n oxide that contains one oxygen atom per molecule

MONS ▶ mon

MONSIEUR n French title of address equivalent to sir or Mr

MONSOON, -S n seasonal wind of SE Asia

MONSTER, -S n imaginary, usu frightening, beast ▷ adj huge ▷ vb criticize (a person or group) severely

MONSTERA n type of tropical climbing plant

MONSTERS ▶ monster

MONTAGE, -D, -S n (making of) a picture composed from pieces of others ▷ vb make as a montage

MONTAN adj as in **montan wax** hard wax obtained from lignite and peat

MONTANE, -S n area of mountain dominated by vegetation ▷ adj of or inhabiting mountainous regions

MONTANT, -S n vertical part in woodwork

MONTANTO n rising blow

MONTANTS ▶ montant

MONTARIA n Brazilian canoe

MONTE, -S n gambling card game of Spanish origin

MONTEITH n large ornamental bowl

MONTEM, -S n former money-raising practice at Eton school

MONTERO, -S n round cap with a flap at the back worn by hunters

MONTES ▶ monte

MONTH, -S n one of the twelve divisions of the calendar year

MONTHLY adj happening or payable once a month ▷ adv once a month ▷ n monthly magazine

MONTHS ▶ month

MONTICLE same as > **monticule**

MONTIES ▶ monty

MONTRE, -S n pipes of organ

MONTURE, -S n mount or frame

MONTY, MONTIES n complete form of something

MONUMENT n something, esp a building or statue, that commemorates something

MONURON, -S n type of weedkiller

MONY Scot word for ▶ **many**

MOO, -ED, -ING, -S n long deep cry of a cow ▷ vb make this noise ▷ interj instance or imitation of this sound

MOOCH, -ED, -ES, -ING vb loiter about aimlessly

MOOCHER -S

MOOD, -S n temporary (gloomy) state of mind

MOODIED ▶ moody

MOODIER ▶ moody

MOODIES ▶ moody

MOODIEST ▶ moody

MOODILY ▶ moody

MOODS ▶ mood

MOODY, MOODIED, MOODIER, MOODIES,

M

MOODIEST, -ING adj sullen or gloomy ▷ vb flatter

MOOED ► moo

MOOI adj pleasing or nice

MOOING ► moo

MOOK, -S n person regarded with contempt, esp a stupid person

MOOKTAR, -S same as ► mukhtar

MOOL, -ED, -ING, -S same as ► mould

MOOLA, -S same as ► moolah

MOOLAH, -S slang word for ► money

MOOLAS ► moola

MOOLED ► mool

MOOLEY, -S same as ► mooly

MOOLI, -S n type of large white radish

MOOLIES ► mooly

MOOLING ► mool

MOOLIS ► mooli

MOOLOO, -S n person from the Waikato

MOOLS ► mool

MOOLVI, -S same as ► moolvie

MOOLVIE, -S n (esp in India) Muslim learned man

MOOLVIS ► moolvi

MOOLY, MOOLIES same as ► muley

MOON, -ING, -S n natural satellite of the earth ▷ vb be idle in a listless or dreamy way

MOONBEAM n ray of moonlight

MOONBOW, -S n rainbow made by moonlight

MOONCAKE n type of round Chinese cake

MOONCALF n person who idles time away

MOONDOG, -S n bright spot in the sky caused by moonlight

MOONDUST n dust on surface of moon

MOONED adj decorated with a moon

MOONER, -S ► moon

MOONEYE, -S n N American large-eyed freshwater fish

MOONFACE n big round face ▷ vb have a moon face

MOONFISH n type of tropical fish

MOONG n as in moong bean kind of bean

MOONGATE n circular gateway in a wall

MOONIER ► moony

MOONIES ► moony

MOONIEST ► moony

MOONILY ► moony

MOONING ► moon

MOONISH ► moon

MOONLESS ► moon

MOONLET, -S n small moon

MOONLIKE ► moon

MOONLIT adj illuminated by the moon

MOONPORT n place from which flights leave for moon

MOONRISE n moment when the moon appears above the horizon

MOONROCK n rock from moon

MOONROOF same as ► sunroof

MOONS ► moon

MOONSAIL n small sail high on a mast

MOONSEED n type of climbing plant with red or black fruits

MOONSET, -S n moment when the moon disappears below the horizon

MOONSHEE same as ► munshi

MOONSHIP n lunar module

MOONSHOT n launching of a spacecraft to the moon

MOONWALK n instance of walking on the moon

MOONWARD adj towards moon

MOONWORT n type of fern with crescent-shaped leaflets

MOONY, MOONIER, MOONIES, MOONIEST adj dreamy or listless ▷ n crazy or foolish person

MOOP, -ED, -ING, -S same as ► moup

MOOR, -ED, -S n tract of open uncultivated ground covered with grass and heather ▷ vb secure (a ship) with ropes etc

MOORAGE, -S n place for mooring a vessel

MOORBURN n practice of burning off old growth on a heather moor

MOORCOCK n male of the red grouse

MOORED ► moor

MOORFOWL n red grouse

MOORHEN, -S n small black water bird

MOORIER ► moory

MOORIEST ► moory

MOORILL, -S n disease of cattle on moors

MOORING n place for mooring a ship

MOORINGS pl n ropes and anchors used in mooring a vessel

MOORISH adj of or relating to the Moor people of North Africa

MOORLAND n area of moor

MOORLOG, -S n rotted wood below the surface of a moor

MOORMAN, MOORMEN n person living on a moor

MOORS ► moor

MOORVA, -S same as ► murva

MOORWORT n low-growing pink-flowered shrub that grows in peaty bogs

MOORY, MOORIER, MOORIEST ► moor

MOOS ► moo

MOOSE n large N American deer

MOOT, -ED, -EST, -S adj debatable ▷ vb bring up for discussion ▷ n (in Anglo-Saxon England) a local administrative assembly

MOOTABLE

MOOTER -S

MOOTING, -S ► moot

MOOTMAN, MOOTMEN n person taking part in a moot

MOOTNESS ► moot

MOOTS ► moot

MOOVE, -D, -S, MOOVING same as ► move

MOP, -PED, -PING, -S n long stick with twists of cotton or a sponge on the end, used for cleaning ▷ vb clean or soak up with or as if with a mop

MOPANE, -S same as ► mopani

MOPANI, -S n S African tree that is highly resistant to drought

MOPBOARD n wooden border fixed round the base of an interior wall

MOPE, -S, MOPING, MOPISHLY vb be gloomy and apathetic ▷ n gloomy person

MOPED, -S n light motorized cycle

MOPEHAWK same as ► mopoke

MOPER, -S ► mope

MOPERIES ► mopery

MOPERS ► moper

MOPERY, MOPERIES n gloominess

MOPES ► mope

MOPEY same as ► mopy

MOPHEAD, -S n person with shaggy hair

MOPIER ► mopy
MOPIEST ► mopy
MOPILY ► mopy
MOPINESS ► mopy
MOPING ► mope
MOPINGLY ► mope
MOPISH ► mope
MOPISHLY ► mope
MOPOKE, -S n species of owl
MOPPED ► mop
MOPPER, -S ► mop
MOPPET, -S same as
  ► poppet
MOPPIER ► moppy
MOPPIEST ► moppy
MOPPING ► mop
MOPPY, MOPPIER,
  MOPPIEST adj (of hair) thick,
  dishevelled
MOPS ► mop
MOPSIES ► mopsy
MOPSTICK n mop handle
MOPSY, MOPSIES n untidy or
  dowdy person
MOPUS, -ES n person who
  mopes
MOPY, MOPIER, MOPIEST
  ► mope
MOQUETTE n thick velvety
  fabric used for carpets and
  upholstery
MOR, -S n layer of acidic
  humus formed in cool moist
  areas
MORA, -E, -S n quantity of a
  short syllable in verse
MORAINAL ► moraine
MORAINE, -S n accumulated
  mass of debris deposited by
  a glacier
MORAINIC
MORAL, -S adj concerned
  with right and wrong
  conduct ▷ n lesson to be
  obtained from a story or
  event ▷ vb moralize
MORALE, -S n degree of
  confidence or hope of a
  person or group
MORALISE same as
  ► moralize
MORALISM n habit or
  practice of moralizing
MORALIST n person with
  a strong sense of right and
  wrong
MORALITY n good moral
  conduct
MORALIZE vb make moral
  pronouncements
MORALL, -ED, -S same as
  ► mural
MORALLER ► moral
MORALLS ► morall
MORALLY ► moral
MORALS ► moral

MORAS ► mora
MORASS, -ES n marsh
  MORASSY
MORAT, -S n drink containing
  mulberry juice
MORATORY > moratoria
MORATS ► morat
MORAY, -S n large voracious
  eel
MORBID, -ER adj unduly
  interested in death or
  unpleasant events
  MORBIDLY
MORBIFIC adj causing
  disease
MORBILLI same as
  ► measles
MORBUS, -ES n disease
MORCEAU, -X n fragment
  or morsel
MORCHA, -S n (in India)
  hostile demonstration
MORDANCY ► mordant
MORDANT, -S adj sarcastic
  or scathing ▷ n substance
  used to fix dyes ▷ vb treat
  (a fabric, yarn, etc) with a
  mordant
MORDENT, -S n melodic
  ornament in music
MORE adj greater in amount
  or degree ▷ adv greater
  extent ▷ pron greater
  or additional amount or
  number
MOREEN, -S n heavy, usually
  watered, fabric of wool or
  wool and cotton
MOREISH adj (of food)
  causing a desire for more
MOREL, -S n edible
  mushroom with a pitted cap
MORELLE, -S n nightshade
MORELLO, -S n variety of
  small very dark sour cherry
MORELS ► morel
MORENDO, -S adv (in music)
  dying away ▷ n gentle
  decrescendo at the end of a
  musical strain
MORENESS ► more
MOREOVER adv in addition
  to what has already been said
MOREPORK same as
  ► mopoke
MORES pl n customs and
  conventions embodying
  the fundamental values of a
  community
MORESQUE adj (esp of
  decoration and architecture)
  of Moorish style ▷ n Moorish
  design or decoration
MORGAN, -S n American
  breed of small compact
  saddle horse

MORGAY, -S n small dogfish
MORGEN, -S n South African
  unit of area
MORGUE, -S same as
  ► mortuary
MORIA, -S n folly
MORIBUND adj without force
  or vitality
MORICHE, -S same as
  ► miriti
MORION, -S n 16th-century
  helmet with a brim and wide
  comb
MORISCO, -S n morris dance
MORISH same as ► moreish
MORKIN, -S n animal dying in
  accident
MORLING, -S n sheep killed
  by disease
MORMAOR, -S n former high-
  ranking Scottish nobleman
MORN, -S n morning
MORNAY, -S adj served with a
  cheese sauce
MORNE, -D, -S same as
  ► mourn
MORNING, -S n part of the
  day before noon
MORNS ► morn
MOROCCO, -S n goatskin
  leather
MORON, -S n insulting term
  for a foolish or stupid person
  MORONIC
  MORONISM
  MORONITY
MOROSE, -R, -ST adj sullen
  or moody
  MOROSELY
  MOROSITY
MORPH, -ED, -S n
  phonological representation
  of a morpheme ▷ vb
  undergo or cause to undergo
  morphing
MORPHEAN adj of or relating
  to Morpheus, the god of
  sleep and dreams
MORPHED ► morph
MORPHEME n speech
  element that cannot be
  subdivided
MORPHEW, -S n blemish
  on skin
MORPHIA, -S same as
  ► morphine
MORPHIC adj as in morphic
  resonance idea that an
  event can lead to similar
  events in the future through
  a telepathic effect
MORPHIN, -S variant form of
  ► morphine
MORPHINE n drug extracted
  from opium, used as an
  anaesthetic and sedative

M

MORPHING n one image changing to another by small gradual steps using computer animation

MORPHINS ► morphin

MORPHO, -S n type of butterfly

MORPHS ► morph

MORRA, -S same as ► **mora**

MORRELL, -S n tall SW Australian eucalyptus with pointed buds

MORRHUA, -S n cod

MORRICE, -S same as ► **morris**

MORRION, -S same as ► **morion**

MORRIS, -ED, -ES vb perform morris dance

MORRO, -S n rounded hill or promontory

MORROW, -S n next day

MORS ► mor

MORSAL, -S same as ► **morsel**

MORSE n clasp or fastening on a cope

MORSEL, -ED, -S n small piece, esp of food ▷ vb divide into morsels

MORSES ► morse

MORSURE, -S n bite

MORT, -S n call blown on a hunting horn to signify the death of the animal hunted

MORTAL, -S adj subject to death ▷ n human being

MORTALLY

MORTAR, -ED, -S n small cannon with a short range ▷ vb fire on with mortars

MORTARY adj of or like mortar

MORTBELL n bell rung for funeral

MORTGAGE n conditional pledging of property as security for the repayment of a loan ▷ vb pledge (property) as security thus ▷ adj of or relating to a mortgage

MORTICE, -D, -S same as ► **mortise**

MORTICER

MORTIFIC adj causing death

MORTIFY vb humiliate

MORTISE, -D, -S n slot cut into a piece of wood, stone, etc ▷ vb cut a slot in (a piece of wood, stone, etc)

MORTISER

MORTLING n dead body

MORTMAIN n status of lands held inalienably by a church

MORTS ► mort

MORTSAFE n cage placed over a grave to deter body snatchers

MORTUARY n building where corpses are kept before burial or cremation ▷ adj of or relating to death or burial

MORULA, -E, -S n solid ball of cells resulting from the splitting of a fertilized ovum

MORULAR

MORWONG, -S n food fish of Australasian coastal waters

MORYAH interj exclamation of annoyance, disbelief, etc

MOS ► mo

MOSAIC, -S n design or decoration using small pieces of coloured stone or glass

MOSASAUR n type of extinct Cretaceous giant marine lizard, typically with paddle-like limbs

MOSCATO, -S n type of sweet dessert wine

MOSCHATE n odour like musk

MOSE, -D, -S, MOSING vb have glanders

MOSELLE, -S n German white wine from the Moselle valley

MOSES ► mose

MOSEY, -ED, -ING, -S vb walk in a leisurely manner

MOSH, -ED, -ES n dance performed to loud rock music ▷ vb dance in this manner

MOSHAV, -IM n cooperative settlement in Israel

MOSHED ► mosh

MOSHER, -S ► mosh

MOSHES ► mosh

MOSHING, -S ► mosh

MOSING ► mose

MOSK, -S same as ► **mosque**

MOSLINGS n shavings from animal skin being prepared

MOSQUE, -S n Muslim temple

MOSQUITO n blood-sucking flying insect

MOSS, -ED, -ES, -ING n small flowerless plant growing in masses on moist surfaces ▷ vb gather moss

MOSSBACK n old turtle, shellfish, etc, that has a growth of algae on its back

MOSSED ► moss

MOSSER, -S ► moss

MOSSES ► moss

MOSSIE, -S n common sparrow

MOSSIER ► mossy

MOSSIES ► mossie

MOSSIEST ► mossy

MOSSING ► moss

MOSSLAND n land covered in peat

MOSSLIKE ► moss

MOSSO adv to be performed with rapidity

MOSSY, MOSSIER, MOSSIEST ► moss

MOST, -S n greatest number or degree ▷ adj greatest in number or degree ▷ adv in the greatest degree

MOSTE ► mote

MOSTEST, -S ► most

MOSTLY adv for the most part, generally

MOSTS ► most

MOSTWHAT adv mostly

MOT, -S n girl or young woman, esp one's girlfriend

MOTE, -D, -S n tiny speck ▷ vb may or might

MOTED adj containing motes

MOTEL, -S n roadside hotel for motorists

MOTELIER n person running motel

MOTELS ► motel

MOTEN ► mote

MOTES ► mote

MOTET, -S n short sacred choral song

MOTETT, -S same as ► **motet**

MOTEY, -S, MOTIER, MOTIEST adj containing motes ▷ n pigment made from earth

MOTH, -S n nocturnal insect like a butterfly

MOTHBALL n small ball of camphor or naphthalene used to repel moths from stored clothes ▷ vb store (something operational) for future use

MOTHED adj damaged by moths

MOTHER, -ED, -S n female parent ▷ adj native or inborn ▷ vb look after as a mother

MOTHERLY adj of or resembling a mother, esp in warmth, or protectiveness

MOTHERS ► mother

MOTHERY ► mother

MOTHIER ► mothy

MOTHIEST ► mothy

MOTHLIKE ► moth

MOTHS ► moth

MOTHY, MOTHIER, MOTHIEST adj ragged

MOTIER ► motey

MOTIEST ► motey

MOTIF, -S n (recurring) theme or design

MOTIFIC adj causing motion

MOTIFS ► motif

MOTILE, -S adj capable of independent movement ▷ n person whose mental imagery strongly reflects movement
MOTILITY
MOTION, -ED, -S n process, action, or way of moving ▷ vb direct (someone) by gesture
MOTIONAL
MOTIONER
MOTIVATE vb give incentive to
MOTIVE, -D, -S, MOTIVING n reason for a course of action ▷ adj causing motion ▷ vb motivate
MOTIVIC adj of musical motif
MOTIVING ▶ motive
MOTIVITY n power of moving or of initiating motion
MOTLEY, -ER, -S, MOTLIER, MOTLIEST adj miscellaneous ▷ n costume of a jester
MOTMOT, -S n tropical American bird with a long tail and blue and brownish-green plumage
MOTOR, -ED, -ING, -S n engine, esp of a vehicle ▷ vb travel by car ▷ adj of or relating to cars and other vehicles powered by engines
MOTORAIL n transport of cars by train
MOTORBUS n bus driven by an internal-combustion engine
MOTORCAR n self-propelled electric railway car
MOTORDOM n world of motor cars
MOTORED ▶ motor
MOTORIAL ▶ motor
MOTORIC ▶ motor
MOTORING ▶ motor
MOTORISE same as ▶ motorize
MOTORIST n driver of a car
MOTORIUM n area of nervous system involved in movement
MOTORIZE vb equip with a motor
MOTORMAN, MOTORMEN n driver of an electric train
MOTORS ▶ motor
MOTORWAY n main road for fast-moving traffic
MOTORY ▶ motor
MOTS ▶ mot
MOTSER, -S n large sum of money, esp a gambling win
MOTT, -S n clump of trees

MOTTE, -S n mound on which a castle was built
MOTTIER ▶ motty
MOTTIES ▶ motty
MOTTIEST ▶ motty
MOTTLE, -D, -S, MOTTLING vb colour with streaks or blotches of different shades ▷ n mottled appearance, as of the surface of marble
MOTTLER, -S n paintbrush for mottled effects
MOTTLES ▶ mottle
MOTTLING ▶ mottle
MOTTO, -ES, -S n saying expressing an ideal or rule of conduct
MOTTOED adj having motto
MOTTOES ▶ motto
MOTTOS ▶ motto
MOTTS ▶ mott
MOTTY, MOTTIER, MOTTIES, MOTTIEST n target at which coins are aimed in pitch-and-toss ▷ adj containing motes
MOTUCA, -S n Brazilian fly
MOTZA, -S same as ▶ motser
MOU, -S Scots word for ▶ mouth
MOUCH, -ED, -ES, -ING same as ▶ mooch
MOUCHARD n police informer
MOUCHED ▶ mouch
MOUCHER, -S ▶ mouch
MOUCHES ▶ mouch
MOUCHING ▶ mouch
MOUCHOIR n handkerchief
MOUE, -S n disdainful or pouting look
MOUFFLON same as ▶ mouflon
MOUFLON, -S n wild mountain sheep of Corsica and Sardinia
MOUGHT ▶ may
MOUILLE adj palatalized, as in the sounds represented by Spanish ll or ñ
MOUJIK, -S same as ▶ muzhik
MOULAGE, -S n mould making
MOULD, -ED, -S n hollow container in which metal etc is cast ▷ vb shape
MOULDER, -S vb decay into dust ▷ n person who moulds or makes moulds
MOULDIER ▶ mouldy
MOULDING n moulded ornamental edging
MOULDS ▶ mould
MOULDY, MOULDIER adj stale or musty
MOULIN, -S n vertical shaft in a glacier

MOULINET n device for bending crossbow
MOULINS ▶ moulin
MOULS Scots word for ▶ mould
MOULT, -ED, -ING, -S vb shed feathers, hair, or skin to make way for new growth ▷ n process of moulting
MOULTEN adj having moulted
MOULTER, -S ▶ moult
MOULTING ▶ moult
MOULTS ▶ moult
MOUND, -ED, -ING, -S n heap, esp of earth or stones ▷ vb gather into a mound
MOUNSEER same as ▶ monsieur
MOUNT, -S vb climb or ascend ▷ n backing or support on which something is fixed
MOUNTAIN n hill of great size ▷ adj of, found on, or for use on a mountain or mountains
MOUNTANT n adhesive for mounting pictures
MOUNTED adj riding horses
MOUNTER, -S ▶ mount
MOUNTING same as ▶ mount
MOUNTS ▶ mount
MOUP, -ED, -ING, -S n nibble
MOURN, -ED, -S vb feel or express sorrow for (a dead person or lost thing)
MOURNER, -S n person attending a funeral
MOURNFUL adj sad or dismal
MOURNING n grieving ▷ adj of or relating to mourning
MOURNS ▶ mourn
MOUS ▶ mou
MOUSAKA, -S same as ▶ moussaka
MOUSE, MICE, -D, -S n small long-tailed rodent ▷ vb stalk and catch mice
MOUSEKIN n little mouse
MOUSEMAT n piece of material on which a computer mouse is moved
MOUSEPAD n pad for computer mouse
MOUSER, -S n cat used to catch mice
MOUSERY n place infested with mice
MOUSES ▶ mouse
MOUSEY same as ▶ mousy
MOUSIE, -S n little mouse
MOUSIER ▶ mousy
MOUSIES ▶ mousie
MOUSIEST ▶ mousy
MOUSILY ▶ mousy
MOUSING, -S n device for closing off a hook

M

M

MOUSLE, -D, -S, MOUSLING vb handle roughly

MOUSME, -S n Japanese girl

MOUSMEE, -S same as ► mousme

MOUSMES ► mousme

MOUSSAKA n dish made with meat, aubergines, and tomatoes, topped with cheese sauce

MOUSSE, -D, -S, MOUSSING n dish of flavoured cream whipped and set ▷ vb apply mousse to

MOUSSEUX n type of sparkling wine

MOUSSING ► mousse

MOUST, -ED, -ING, -S same as ► must

MOUSY, MOUSIER, MOUSIEST adj like a mouse, esp in hair colour

MOUTAN, -S n variety of peony

MOUTER, -ED, -S same as ► multure

MOUTERER

MOUTH, -ED, -ING, -S n opening in the head for eating and issuing sounds ▷ vb form (words) with the lips without speaking

MOUTHER -S

MOUTHFUL n amount of food or drink put into the mouth at any one time when eating or drinking

MOUTHIER ► mouthy

MOUTHILY ► mouthy

MOUTHING ► mouth

MOUTHS ► mouth

MOUTHY, MOUTHIER adj bombastic

MOUTON, -S n sheepskin processed to resemble the fur of another animal

MOVABLE, -S adj able to be moved or rearranged ▷ n movable article, esp a piece of furniture

MOVABLY

MOVANT, -S n person who applies to a court of law

MOVE, -D, -S vb change in place or position ▷ n moving

MOVEABLE same as ► movable

MOVEABLY

MOVED ► move

MOVELESS adj immobile

MOVEMENT n action or process of moving

MOVER, -S n person or animal that moves in a particular way

MOVES ► move

MOVIE, -S n cinema film

MOVIEDOM n world of cinema

MOVIEOKE n entertainment in which people act out scenes from movies

MOVIEOLA same as ► moviola

MOVIES ► movie

MOVING adj arousing or touching the emotions

MOVINGLY

MOVIOLA, -S n viewing machine used in cutting and editing film

MOW, -ED, -N, -S vb cut (grass or crops) ▷ n part of a barn where hay, straw, etc, is stored

MOWA, -S same as ► mahua

MOWBURN, -S vb heat up in mow

MOWBURNT adj (of hay, straw, etc) damaged by overheating in a mow

MOWDIE, -S Scot words for ► mole

MOWED ► mow

MOWER, -S ► mow

MOWING, -S ► mow

MOWN ► mow

MOWRA, -S same as ► mahua

MOWS ► mow

MOXA, -S n downy material obtained from various plants

MOXIE, -S n courage, nerve, or vigour

MOY, -S n coin

MOYA, -S n mud emitted from a volcano

MOYITY, MOYITIES same as ► moiety

MOYL, -S same as ► moyle

MOYLE, -D, -S, MOYLING vb toil

MOYLS ► moyl

MOYS ► moy

MOZ, -ES n hex

This unusual word, Australian slang for bad luck, is another of the very useful short words that use the Z, and it can be extended to **moze** or **mozo**.

MOZE, -D, MOZING vb give nap to

MOZES ► moz

MOZETTA, -S, MOZETTE same as ► mozzetta

MOZING ► moze

MOZO, -S n porter in southwest USA

MOZZ, -ES same as ► moz

MOZZETTA, MOZZETTE n short hooded cape worn by the pope, cardinals, etc

MOZZIE, -S same as ► mossie

MOZZLE, -D, -S, MOZZLING n luck ▷ vb hamper or impede (someone)

MPRET, -S n former Albanian ruler

MRIDANG, -S n drum used in Indian music

MRIDANGA same as ► mridang

MRIDANGS ► mridang

MU, -S n 12th letter in the Greek alphabet

MUCATE, -S n salt of mucic acid

MUCH, -ES adj large amount or degree of ▷ n large amount or degree ▷ adv great degree

MUCHACHA n (in Spain etc) young woman or female servant

MUCHACHO n young man

MUCHEL, -S same as ► much

MUCHELL, -S same as ► much

MUCHELS ► muchel

MUCHES ► much

MUCHLY ► much

MUCHNESS n magnitude

MUCHO adv Spanish for very

MUCIC adj as in mucic acid colourless crystalline solid carboxylic acid

MUCID adj mouldy, musty, or slimy

MUCIDITY

MUCIGEN, -S n substance present in mucous cells that is converted into mucin

MUCILAGE n gum or glue

MUCIN, -S n any of a group of nitrogenous mucoproteins occurring in saliva, skin, tendon, etc

MUCINOID adj of or like mucin

MUCINOUS ► mucin

MUCINS ► mucin

MUCK, -ED, -ING, -S n dirt, filth

MUCKER, -ED, -S n person who shifts broken rock or waste ▷ vb hoard

MUCKHEAP n dunghill

MUCKIER ► mucky

MUCKIEST ► mucky

MUCKILY ► mucky

MUCKING ► muck

MUCKLE, -S same as ► mickle

MUCKLUCK same as ► mukluk

MUCKRAKE n agricultural rake for spreading manure ▷ vb seek out and expose scandal, esp concerning public figures

MUCKS ► muck

MUCKWORM n any larva or worm that lives in mud

MUCKY, MUCKIER, MUCKIEST adj dirty or muddy

MUCLUC, -S same as ▶ mukluk

MUCOID, -S adj of the nature of or resembling mucin ▷ n substance like mucin

MUCOIDAL same as ▶ mucoid

MUCOIDS ▶ mucoid

MUCOR, -S n type of fungus

MUCOSA, -E, -S n mucus-secreting membrane that lines body cavities

MUCOSAL

MUCOSE same as ▶ mucous

MUCOSITY ▶ mucous

MUCOUS adj of, resembling, or secreting mucus

MUCRO, -NES, -S n short pointed projection from certain parts or organs

MUCULENT adj like mucus

MUCUS, -ES n slimy secretion of the mucous membranes

MUD, -DED, -DING, -S n wet soft earth ▷ vb cover in mud

MUDBANK, -S n sloping area of mud beside a body of water

MUDBATH, -S n medicinal bath in heated mud

MUDBUG, -S n crayfish

MUDCAP, -S vb use explosive charge in blasting

MUDCAT, -S n any of several large North American catfish

MUDDED ▶ mud

MUDDER, -S n horse that runs well in mud

MUDDIED ▶ muddy

MUDDIER ▶ muddy

MUDDIES ▶ muddy

MUDDIEST ▶ muddy

MUDDILY ▶ muddy

MUDDING ▶ mud

MUDDLE, -D, -S vb confuse ▷ n state of confusion

MUDDLER, -S n person who muddles or muddles through

MUDDLES ▶ muddle

MUDDLIER ▶ muddly

MUDDLING ▶ muddle

MUDDLY, MUDDLIER ▶ muddle

MUDDY, MUDDIED, MUDDIER, MUDDIES, MUDDIEST, -ING adj covered or filled with mud ▷ vb make muddy

MUDEJAR n Spanish Moor ▷ adj of or relating to a style of architecture

MUDEYE, -S n larva of the dragonfly

MUDFISH n fish that lives at the muddy bottoms of rivers, lakes, etc

MUDFLAP, -S n flap above wheel to deflect mud

MUDFLAT, -S n tract of low muddy land

MUDFLOW, -S n flow of soil mixed with water down a steep unstable slope

MUDGE, -D, -S, MUDGING vb speak vaguely

MUDGER -S

MUDGUARD n cover over a wheel to prevent mud or water being thrown up by it

MUDHEN, -S n water bird living in muddy place

MUDHOLE, -S n hole with mud at bottom

MUDHOOK, -S n anchor

MUDIR, -S n local governor

MUDIRIA, -S n province of mudir

MUDIRIEH same as ▶ mudiria

MUDIRS ▶ mudir

MUDLARK, -S n street urchin ▷ vb play in mud

MUDPACK, -S n cosmetic paste applied to the face

MUDPIE, -S n small mass of mud moulded into a pie shape

MUDPUPPY n type of salamander

MUDRA, -S n hand movement in Hindu religious dancing

MUDROCK, -S n type of sedimentary rock

MUDROOM, -S n room where muddy shoes may be left

MUDS ▶ mud

MUDSCOW, -S n boat for travelling over mudflats

MUDSILL, -S n support for building at or below ground

MUDSLIDE n landslide of mud

MUDSLING, MUDSLUNG vb make accusations against a rival candidate

MUDSTONE n dark grey clay rock similar to shale but with the lamination less well developed

MUDWORT, -S n plant growing in mud

MUEDDIN, -S same as ▶ muezzin

MUENSTER n whitish-yellow semihard whole milk cheese, often flavoured with caraway or aniseed

MUESLI, -S n mixture of grain, nuts, and dried fruit

MUEZZIN, -S n official who summons Muslims to prayer

MUFF, -ED, -ING, -S n tube-shaped covering to keep the hands warm ▷ vb bungle (an action)

MUFFIN, -S n light round flat yeast cake

MUFFING ▶ muff

MUFFINS ▶ muffin

MUFFISH ▶ muff

MUFFLE, -D, -S, MUFFLING vb wrap up for warmth or to deaden sound ▷ n something that muffles

MUFFLER, -S n scarf

MUFFLES ▶ muffle

MUFFLING ▶ muffle

MUFFS ▶ muff

MUFLON, -S same as ▶ moufflon

MUFTI, -S n civilian clothes worn by a person who usually wears a uniform

MUG, -GED, -S n large drinking cup ▷ vb attack in order to rob

MUGFUL, -S same as ▶ mug

MUGG, -S same as ▶ mug

MUGGA, -S n Australian eucalyptus tree

MUGGAR, -S same as ▶ mugger

MUGGAS ▶ mugga

MUGGED ▶ mug

MUGGEE, -S n mugged person

MUGGER, -S n person who commits robbery with violence

MUGGIER ▶ muggy

MUGGIEST ▶ muggy

MUGGILY ▶ muggy

MUGGING, -S ▶ mug

MUGGINS n stupid or gullible person

MUGGISH same as ▶ muggy

MUGGLE, -S n person who does not possess supernatural powers

MUGGS ▶ mugg

MUGGUR, -S same as ▶ mugger

MUGGY, MUGGIER, MUGGIEST adj (of weather) damp and stifling

MUGHAL, -S same as ▶ mogul

MUGS ▶ mug

MUGSHOT, -S n police photograph of person's face

MUGWORT, -S n N temperate herbaceous plant with aromatic leaves

MUGWUMP, -S n neutral or independent person

MUHLY, MUHLIES n American grass

MUID, -S *n* former French measure of capacity

MUIL, -S *same as* ► **mule**

MUIR, -S *same as* ► **moor**

MUIRBURN *same as* ► **moorburn**

MUIRS ► **muir**

MUIST, -ED, -ING, -S *same as* ► **must**

MUJIK, -S *same as* ► **muzhik**

MUKHTAR, -S *n* lawyer in India

MUKLUK, -S *n* soft boot, usually of sealskin

MUKTUK, -S *n* thin outer skin of the beluga, used as food

MULATTO *adj* of a light brown colour

MULBERRY *n* tree whose leaves are used to feed silkworms ▷ *adj* dark purple

MULCH, -ED, -ES, -ING *n* mixture of wet straw, leaves, etc ▷ *vb* cover (land) with mulch

MULCT, -ED, -ING, -S *vb* cheat or defraud ▷ *n* fine or penalty

MULE, -D, MULING *n* offspring of a horse and a donkey ▷ *vb* strike coin with different die on each side

MULES, -ED, -ES, -ING *vb* surgically remove folds of skin from a sheep

MULETA, -S *n* small cape attached to a stick used by a matador

MULETEER *n* mule driver

MULEY, -S *adj* (of cattle) having no horns ▷ *n* any hornless cow

MULGA, -S *n* Australian acacia shrub growing in desert regions

MULIE, -S *n* type of N American deer

MULING ► **mule**

MULISH *adj* obstinate
MULISHLY

MULL, -ED, -ING, -S *vb* think (over) or ponder ▷ *n* promontory or headland

MULLA, -S *same as* ► **mullah**

MULLAH, -S *n* Muslim scholar, teacher, or religious leader

MULLAHED *same as* ► **mullered**

MULLAHS ► **mullah**

MULLARKY *same as* ► **malarkey**

MULLAS ► **mulla**

MULLED ► **mull**

MULLEIN, -S *n* type of European plant

MULLEN, -S *same as* ► **mullein**

MULLER, -S *n* flat heavy implement used to grind material ▷ *vb* beat up or defeat thoroughly

MULLERED *adj* drunk

MULLERS ► **muller**

MULLET, -S *n* edible sea fish

MULLEY, -S *same as* ► **muley**

MULLIGAN *n* stew made from odds and ends of food

MULLING ► **mull**

MULLION, -S *n* vertical dividing bar in a window ▷ *vb* furnish with mullions

MULLITE, -S *n* colourless mineral

MULLOCK, -S *n* waste material from a mine

MULLOCKY

MULLOWAY *n* large Australian sea fish, valued for sport and food

MULLS ► **mull**

MULMUL, -S *n* muslin

MULMULL, -S *same as* ► **mulmul**

MULMULS ► **mulmul**

MULSE, -S *n* drink containing honey

MULSH, -ED, -ES, -ING *same as* ► **mulch**

MULTEITY *n* manifoldness

MULTIAGE *adj* involving different age groups

MULTICAR *adj* involving several cars

MULTIDAY *adj* involving more than one day

MULTIFID *adj* having or divided into many lobes or similar segments

MULTIFIL *n* fibre made up of many filaments

MULTIGYM *n* exercise apparatus incorporating a variety of weights, used for toning the muscles

MULTIJET *adj* involving more than one jet

MULTIPED *adj* having many feet ▷ *n* insect or animal having many feet

MULTIPLE *adj* having many parts ▷ *n* quantity which contains another an exact number of times

MULTIPLY *vb* increase in number or degree

MULTITON *adj* weighing several tons

MULTIUSE *adj* suitable for more than one use

MULTIWAY *adj* having several paths or routes

MULTUM, -S *n* substance used in brewing

MULTURE, -D, -S *n* fee formerly paid to a miller for grinding grain ▷ *vb* take multure

MULTURER

MUM, -MED, -S *n* mother ▷ *vb* act in a mummer's play

MUMBLE, -D, -S *vb* speak indistinctly, mutter ▷ *n* indistinct utterance

MUMBLER -S

MUMBLIER ► **mumbly**

MUMBLING ► **mumble**

MUMBLY, MUMBLIER ► **mumble**

MUMM, -S *same as* ► **mum**

MUMMED ► **mum**

MUMMER, -ED, -S *n* actor in a traditional English folk play ▷ *vb* perform as a mummer

MUMMERY *n* performance by mummers

MUMMIA, -S *n* mummified flesh used as medicine

MUMMIED ► **mummy**

MUMMIES ► **mummy**

MUMMIFY *vb* preserve a body as a mummy

MUMMING, -S ► **mum**

MUMMOCK, -S *same as* ► **mammock**

MUMMS ► **mumm**

MUMMY, MUMMIED, MUMMIES, -ING *n* body embalmed and wrapped for burial in ancient Egypt ▷ *vb* mummify

MUMP, -ED, -ING *vb* be silent

MUMPER -S

MUMPISH ► **mumps**

MUMPS *n* infectious disease with swelling in the glands of the neck

MUMS ► **mum**

MUMSY, MUMSIER, MUMSIEST *adj* (of a woman) wearing clothes that are old-fashioned and unflattering ▷ *n* mother

MUMU, -S *n* oven in Papua New Guinea

MUN, -S *same as* ► **maun**

MUNCH, -ED, -ES, -ING *vb* chew noisily and steadily

MUNCHER -S

MUNCHIE *n* small amount of food eaten between meals

MUNCHIER ► **munchy**

MUNCHIES *pl n* craving for food

MUNCHING ► **munch**

MUNCHKIN *n* undersized person or a child, esp an appealing one

MUNCHY, MUNCHIER *adj* suitable for snacking

MUNDANE, -R adj everyday

MUNDIC, -S n iron pyrites

MUNDIFY vb cleanse

MUNDUNGO n tripe in Spain

MUNG, -ED, -ING, -S vb process (computer data)

MUNGA, -S n army canteen

MUNGCORN n maslin

MUNGE, -S vb modify a password into an unguessable state

MUNGED ► mung

MUNGES ► munge

MUNGING ► mung

MUNGO, -ES, -S n cheap felted fabric made from waste wool

MUNGOOSE same as ► mongoose

MUNGOS ► mungo

MUNGS ► mung

MUNI, -S n municipal radio broadcast

MUNIFY, MUNIFIED, MUNIFIES vb fortify

MUNIMENT n means of defence

MUNIS ► muni

MUNITE, -D, -S, MUNITING vb strengthen

MUNITION vb supply with munitions

MUNNION, -S archaic word for ► mullion

MUNS ► mun

MUNSHI, -S n secretary in India

MUNSTER, -S variant of ► muenster

MUNTED adj destroyed or ruined

MUNTER n insulting word for an unattractive person

MUNTIN, -S n supporting or strengthening bar

MUNTINED adj having a muntin

MUNTING, -S same as ► muntin

MUNTINS ► muntin

MUNTJAC, -S n small Asian deer

MUNTJAK, -S same as ► muntjac

MUNTRIE, -S n Australian shrub with green-red edible berries

MUON, -S n elementary particle with a mass 207 times that of an electron

MUONIC

MUONIUM, -S n form of hydrogen

MUONS ► muon

MUPPET, -S n stupid person

MUQADDAM n person of authority in India

MURA, -S n group of people living together in Japanese countryside

MURAENA, -S n moray eel

MURAENID n eel of moray family

MURAGE, -S n tax levied for the construction or maintenance of town walls

MURAL, -S n painting on a wall ▷ adj of or relating to a wall

MURALED same as ► muralled

MURALIST ► mural

MURALLED adj decorated with mural

MURALS ► mural

MURAS ► mura

MURDABAD interj down with

MURDER, -ED, -S n unlawful intentional killing of a human being ▷ vb kill in this way

MURDEREE n murder victim

MURDERER ► murder

MURDERS ► murder

MURE, -D, -S, MURING archaic or literary word for ► immure

MUREIN, -S n polymer found in cells

MURENA, -S same as ► muraena

MURES ► mure

MUREX, -ES, MURICES n marine gastropod formerly used as a source of purple dye

MURGEON, -S vb grimace at

MURIATE, -S obsolete name for a ► chloride

MURIATED

MURIATIC adj as in **muriatic acid** former name for a strong acid used in many industrial processes

MURICATE adj having a surface roughened by numerous short points

MURICES ► murex

MURID, -S n animal of mouse family

MURIFORM adj like mouse

MURINE, -S n animal belonging to the family that includes rats and mice

MURING ► mure

MURK, -ED, -ER, -EST, -ING, -S n thick darkness ▷ adj dark or gloomy ▷ vb murder (a person)

MURKIER ► murky

MURKIEST ► murky

MURKILY ► murky

MURKING ► murk

MURKISH ► murk

MURKLY ► murk

MURKS ► murk

MURKSOME ► murk

MURKY, MURKIER, MURKIEST adj dark or gloomy

MURL, -ED, -ING, -S vb crumble

MURLAIN, -S n type of basket

MURLAN, -S same as ► murlain

MURLED ► murl

MURLIER ► murly

MURLIEST ► murly

MURLIN, -S same as ► murlain

MURLING ► murl

MURLINS ► murlin

MURLS ► murl

MURLY, MURLIER, MURLIEST ► murl

MURMUR, -ED, -S vb speak or say in a quiet indistinct way ▷ n continuous low indistinct sound

MURMURER

MURPHY, MURPHIES dialect or informal word for ► potato

MURR, -S n former name for a cold

MURRA, -S same as ► murrhine

MURRAGH, -S n type of large caddis fly

MURRAIN, -S n cattle plague

MURRAM, -S n type of gravel

MURRAS ► murra

MURRAY, -S n large Australian freshwater fish

MURRE, -S n type of guillemot

MURREE, -S n native Australian

MURRELET n type of small diving bird related to the auks

MURREN, -S same as ► murrain

MURRES ► murre

MURREY, -S adj mulberry colour

MURRHA, -S same as ► murra

MURRHINE adj of or relating to an unknown substance used in ancient Rome to make vases, cups, etc ▷ n substance so used

MURRI, -S same as ► murree

MURRIES ► murry

MURRIN, -S same as ► murrain

MURRINE, -S same as ► murrhine

MURRINS ► murrin

MURRION, -S same as ► murrain

MURRIS ► murri

MURRS ► murr

M

MURRY, MURRIES same as
▶ moray

MURTHER, -S same as
▶ murder

MURTI, -S n image of a deity, which itself is considered divine

MURVA, -S n type of hemp

MUS ▶ mu

MUSANG, -S n catlike animal of Malaysia

MUSAR, -S n rabbinic literature concerned with ethics

MUSCA, -E n small constellation in the S hemisphere

MUSCADEL same as
▶ muscatel

MUSCADET n white grape, used for making wine

MUSCADIN n Parisian dandy

MUSCAE ▶ musca

MUSCAT, -S same as
▶ muscatel

MUSCATEL n rich sweet wine made from muscat grapes

MUSCATS ▶ muscat

MUSCID, -S n type of fly

MUSCLE, -D, -S, MUSCLING n tissue in the body which produces movement ▷ vb force one's way (in)

MUSCLEY adj of a muscular build

MUSCLIER ▶ muscly

MUSCLING ▶ muscle

MUSCLY, MUSCLIER same as
▶ muscley

MUSCOID, -S adj moss-like ▷ n moss-like plant

MUSCONE, -S same as
▶ muskone

MUSCOSE adj like moss

MUSCOVY adj as in **muscovy duck** a kind of duck

MUSCULAR adj with well-developed muscles

MUSE, -D, -S vb ponder quietly ▷ n state of abstraction
MUSEFUL
MUSER, -S

MUSET, -S same as ▶ musit

MUSETTE, -S n type of bagpipe formerly popular in France

MUSEUM, -S n building where objects are exhibited and preserved

MUSH, -D, -ES n soft pulpy mass ▷ interj order to dogs in a sled team to start up or go faster ▷ vb travel by or drive a dogsled

MUSHA interj Irish exclamation of surprise

MUSHED ▶ mush

MUSHER, -S ▶ mush

MUSHES ▶ mush

MUSHIER ▶ mushy

MUSHIEST ▶ mushy

MUSHILY ▶ mushy

MUSHING, -S n act of mushing

MUSHRAT same as ▶ muskrat

MUSHRATS same as
▶ mushrat

MUSHROOM n edible fungus with a stem and cap ▷ vb grow rapidly

MUSHY, MUSHIER, MUSHIEST adj soft and pulpy

MUSIC, -KED, -S n art form using a melodious and harmonious combination of notes ▷ vb play music

MUSICAL, -S adj of or like music ▷ n play or film with songs and dancing

MUSICALE n party or social evening with a musical programme

MUSICALS ▶ musical

MUSICIAN n person who plays or composes music, esp as a profession

MUSICK, -S same as ▶ music

MUSICKED ▶ music

MUSICKER ▶ music

MUSICKS ▶ musick

MUSICS ▶ music

MUSIMON, -S same as
▶ moufflon

MUSING, -S ▶ muse

MUSINGLY ▶ muse

MUSINGS ▶ musing

MUSIT, -S n gap in fence

MUSIVE adj mosaic

MUSJID, -S same as ▶ masjid

MUSK, -ED, -ING, -S n scent obtained from a gland of the musk deer or produced synthetically ▷ vb perfume with musk

MUSKEG, -S n area of undrained boggy land

MUSKET, -S n long-barrelled gun

MUSKETRY n (use of) muskets

MUSKETS ▶ musket

MUSKIE, -S n large North American freshwater game fish

MUSKIER ▶ musky

MUSKIES ▶ muskie

MUSKIEST ▶ musky

MUSKILY ▶ musky

MUSKING ▶ musk

MUSKIT, -S same as
▶ mesquite

MUSKLE, -S same as
▶ mussel

MUSKONE, -S n substance in musk

MUSKOX, -EN n large Canadian mammal

MUSKRAT, -S n N American beaver-like rodent

MUSKROOT same as
> moschatel

MUSKS ▶ musk

MUSKY, MUSKIER, MUSKIEST adj smelling of musk

MUSLIN, -S n fine cotton fabric

MUSLINED adj wearing muslin

MUSLINET n coarse muslin

MUSLINS ▶ muslin

MUSMON, -S same as
▶ musimon

MUSO, -S n musician who is concerned with technique rather than content or expression

MUSPIKE, -S n Canadian freshwater fish

MUSQUASH same as
▶ muskrat

MUSROL, -S n part of bridle

MUSS, -ED, -ES, -ING vb make untidy ▷ n state of disorder

MUSSE same as ▶ muss

MUSSED ▶ muss

MUSSEL, -S n edible shellfish with a dark hinged shell

MUSSES ▶ muss

MUSSIER ▶ mussy

MUSSIEST ▶ mussy

MUSSILY ▶ mussy

MUSSING ▶ muss

MUSSY, MUSSIER, MUSSIEST adj untidy or disordered

MUST, -ED, -ING, -S vb used as an auxiliary to express obligation, certainty, or resolution ▷ n essential or necessary thing

MUSTACHE same as
> moustache

MUSTANG, -S n wild horse of SW USA

MUSTARD, -S n paste made from the powdered seeds of a plant ▷ adj brownish-yellow
MUSTARDY

MUSTED ▶ must

MUSTELID n member of weasel family

MUSTER, -ED, -S vb summon up ▷ n assembly of military personnel
MUSTERER

MUSTH, -S n state of frenzied excitement in the males of certain large mammals

MUSTIER ▶ musty

MUSTIEST ▶ musty

MUSTILY ▸ musty

MUSTING ▸ must

MUSTS ▸ must

MUSTY, MUSTIER, MUSTIEST adj smelling mouldy and stale

MUT, -S another word for ▸ **em**

MUTABLE adj liable to change **MUTABLY**

MUTAGEN, -S n any substance that can induce genetic mutation

MUTANDUM, MUTANDA n something to be changed

MUTANT, -S n mutated animal, plant, etc ▸ adj of or resulting from mutation

MUTASE, -S n type of enzyme

MUTATE, -D, -S, MUTATING vb (cause to) undergo mutation

MUTATION same as ▸ **mutant**

MUTATIVE ▸ mutate

MUTATOR, -S n something that causes a mutation

MUTATORY adj subject to change

MUTCH, -ED, -ES, -ING n close-fitting linen cap ▸ vb cadge

MUTCHKIN n Scottish unit of liquid measure equal to slightly less than one pint

MUTE, -R, -S, -ST, MUTING adj silent ▸ n person who is unable to speak ▸ vb reduce the volume or soften the tone of a musical instrument

MUTED adj (of sound or colour) softened

MUTEDLY

MUTELY ▸ mute

MUTENESS ▸ mute

MUTER ▸ mute

MUTES ▸ mute

MUTEST ▸ mute

MUTI, -S n medicine, esp herbal medicine

MUTICATE same as ▸ **muticous**

MUTICOUS adj lacking an awn, spine, or point

MUTILATE vb deprive of a limb or other part

MUTINE, -D, -S, MUTINING vb mutiny

MUTINEER n person who mutinies

MUTINES ▸ mutine

MUTING ▸ mute

MUTINIED ▸ mutiny

MUTINIES ▸ mutiny

MUTINING ▸ mutine

MUTINOUS adj openly rebellious

MUTINY, MUTINIED, MUTINIES n rebellion against authority, esp by soldiers or sailors ▸ vb commit mutiny

MUTIS ▸ muti

MUTISM, -S n state of being mute

MUTON, -S n part of gene

MUTS ▸ mut

MUTT, -S n mongrel dog

MUTTER, -ED, -S vb utter or speak indistinctly ▸ n muttered sound or grumble

MUTTERER

MUTTON, -S n flesh of sheep, used as food

MUTTONY

MUTTS ▸ mutt

MUTUAL, -S adj felt or expressed by each of two people about the other ▸ n mutual company

MUTUALLY

MUTUCA, -S same as ▸ **motuca**

MUTUEL, -S n system of betting

MUTULAR ▸ mutule

MUTULE, -S n flat block in a Doric cornice

MUTUUM, -S n contract for loan of goods

MUUMUU, -S n loose brightly-coloured dress worn by women in Hawaii

MUX, -ED, -ES, -ING vb spoil

This word meaning to spoil or botch is very useful not only because it contains an X, but because its verb forms can enable you to clear your rack of unpromising letters.

MUZAK, -S n piped background music

MUZAKY adj having a bland sound

MUZHIK, -S n Russian peasant, esp under the tsars

MUZJIK, -S same as ▸ **muzhik**

Meaning a Russian peasant, this is a wonderful high-scoring word, combining Z, J and K, and if you can play the plural using all of your tiles, you'll gain a bonus of 50 points.

MUZZ, -ED, -ES, -ING vb make (something) muzzy

MUZZIER ▸ muzzy

MUZZIEST ▸ muzzy

MUZZILY ▸ muzzy

MUZZING ▸ muzz

MUZZLE, -D, -S, MUZZLING n animal's mouth and nose ▸ vb prevent from being heard or noticed

MUZZLER -S

MUZZY, MUZZIER, MUZZIEST adj confused or muddled

MVULE, -S n tropical African tree

MWAH interj representation of the sound of a kiss

MWALIMU, -S n teacher

MY adj belonging to me ▸ interj exclamation of surprise or awe

MYAL ▸ myalism

MYALGIA, -S n pain in a muscle or a group of muscles

MYALGIC

MYALISM, -S n kind of witchcraft

MYALIST -S

MYALL, -S n Australian acacia with hard scented wood

MYASIS, MYASES same as ▸ **myiasis**

MYC, -S n oncogene that aids the growth of tumorous cells

MYCELE, -S n microscopic spike-like structure in mucus

MYCELIA ▸ mycelium

MYCELIAL ▸ mycelium

MYCELIAN ▸ mycelium

MYCELIUM, MYCELIA n mass forming the body of a fungus

MYCELLA, -S n blue-veined Danish cream cheese

MYCELOID ▸ mycelium

MYCETES ▸ myc

MYCETOMA n chronic fungal infection

MYCOLOGY n study of fungi

MYCOSIS, MYCOSES n any infection or disease caused by fungus

MYCOTIC

MYCS ▸ myc

MYELIN, -S n white tissue forming an insulating sheath around certain nerve fibres

MYELINE, -S same as ▸ **myelin**

MYELINIC ▸ myelin

MYELINS ▸ myelin

MYELITIS, MYELITES n inflammation of the spinal cord or of the bone marrow

MYELOID adj of or relating to the spinal cord or the bone marrow

MYELOMA, -S n tumour of the bone marrow

MYELON, -S n spinal cord

M

MYGALE, -S *n* large American spider

MYIASIS, MYIASES *n* infestation of the body by the larvae of flies

MYLAR, -S *n* tradename for a kind of strong polyester film

MYLODON, -S *n* prehistoric giant sloth

MYLODONT *same as* ▸ **mylodon**

MYLONITE *n* fine-grained metamorphic rock

MYNA, -S *same as* ▸ **mynah**

MYNAH, -S *n* tropical Asian starling which can mimic human speech

MYNAS ▸ **myna**

MYNHEER, -S *n* Dutch title of address

MYOBLAST *n* cell from which muscle develops

MYOGEN, -S *n* albumin found in muscle

MYOGENIC *adj* originating in or forming muscle tissue

MYOGENS ▸ **myogen**

MYOGRAM, -S *n* tracings of muscular contractions

MYOGRAPH *n* instrument for recording tracings of muscular contractions

MYOID, -S *adj* like muscle ▸ *n* section of a retinal cone or rod which is sensitive to changes in light intensity

MYOLOGIC ▸ **myology**

MYOLOGY *n* study of the structure and diseases of muscles

MYOMA, -S, -TA *n* benign tumour composed of muscle tissue

MYOMANCY *n* divination through observing mice

MYOMAS ▸ **myoma**

MYOMATA ▸ **myoma**

MYOMERE, -S *n* part of a vertebrate embryo

MYOPATHY *n* any disease affecting muscles or muscle tissue

MYOPE, -S *n* any person afflicted with myopia

MYOPHILY *n* pollination of plants by flies

MYOPIA, -S *n* short-sightedness

MYOPIC, -S *n* shortsighted person

MYOPIES ▸ **myopy**

MYOPS, -ES *same as* ▸ **myope**

MYOPY, MYOPIES *same as* ▸ **myopia**

MYOSCOPE *n* electrical instrument for stimulating muscles

MYOSES ▸ **myosis**

MYOSIN, -S *n* protein found in muscle

MYOSIS, MYOSES, -ES *same as* ▸ **miosis**

MYOSITIS *n* inflammation of muscle

MYOSOTE, -S *same as* ▸ **myosotis**

MYOSOTIS *n* type of hairy-leaved flowering plant, such as the forget-me-not

MYOTIC, -S ▸ **miosis**

MYOTOME, -S *n* any segment of embryonic mesoderm that develops into skeletal muscle

MYOTONIA *n* lack of muscle tone, frequently including muscle spasm or rigidity

MYOTONIC

MYOTUBE, -S *n* cylindrical cell in muscle

MYRBANE, -S *same as* ▸ **mirbane**

MYRIAD, -S *adj* innumerable ▸ *n* large indefinite number

MYRIADTH

MYRIAPOD *n* type of invertebrate with a long segmented body and many legs, such as a centipede

MYRICA, -S *n* dried root bark of the wax myrtle

MYRINGA, -S *n* eardrum

MYRIOPOD *same as* ▸ **myriapod**

MYRISTIC *adj* of nutmeg plant family

MYRMIDON *n* follower or henchman

MYRRH, -S *n* aromatic gum used in perfume, incense, and medicine

MYRRHIC

MYRRHINE ▸ **murra**

MYRRHOL, -S *n* oil of myrrh

MYRRHS ▸ **myrrh**

MYRRHY *adj* of or like myrrh

MYRTLE, -S *n* flowering evergreen shrub

MYSELF *pron* reflexive form of I or me

MYSID, -S *n* small shrimplike crustacean

MYSOST, -S *n* Norwegian cheese

MYSPACE, -D, -S *vb* search for (someone) on the MySpace website

MYSTAGOG *n* person instructing others in religious mysteries

MYSTERY *n* strange or inexplicable thing

MYSTIC, -S *n* person who seeks spiritual knowledge ▸ *adj* mystical

MYSTICAL *adj* having a spiritual or religious significance beyond human understanding

MYSTICLY ▸ **mystic**

MYSTICS ▸ **mystic**

MYSTIFY *vb* bewilder or puzzle

MYSTIQUE *n* aura of mystery or power

MYTH, -S *n* tale with supernatural characters

MYTHI ▸ **mythus**

MYTHIC *same as* ▸ **mythical**

MYTHICAL *adj* of or relating to myth

MYTHIER ▸ **mythy**

MYTHIEST ▸ **mythy**

MYTHISE, -D, -S *same as* ▸ **mythize**

MYTHISM, -S *same as* > **mythicism**

MYTHIST -S

MYTHIZE, -D, -S *same as* > **mythicize**

MYTHOS, MYTHOI *n* beliefs of a specific group or society

MYTHS ▸ **myth**

MYTHUS, MYTHI *same as* ▸ **mythos**

MYTHY, MYTHIER, MYTHIEST *adj* of or like myth

MYTILOID *adj* like mussel

MYXAMEBA *same as* > **myxamoeba**

MYXEDEMA *same as* > **myxoedema**

MYXO, -S *n* viral disease of rabbits

MYXOCYTE *n* cell in mucous tissue

MYXOID *adj* containing mucus

MYXOMA, -S, -TA *n* tumour composed of mucous connective tissue

MYXOS ▸ **myxo**

MZEE, -S *n* old person ▸ *adj* advanced in years

MZUNGU, -S *n* (in E Africa) White person

Nn

Along with **R** and **T**, **N** is one of the most common consonants in Scrabble. As you'll often have it on your rack, it's well worth learning what **N** can do in different situations. **N** is useful when you need short words, as it begins two-letter words with every vowel except **I**, and with **Y** as well. There are plenty of three-letter words starting with **N**, but there aren't many high-scoring ones apart from **nix** and **nox** for 10 points each, **nym** for 8 points and **nek** for 7 points. Remember words like **nab** (5 points), **nag** (4), **nap** (5), **nav** (6), **nay** (6), **new** (6), **nib** (5), **nob** (5), **nod** (4), **now** (6) and **nug** (4).

NA *same as* ► **nae**
NAAM, -S *same as* ► **nam**
NAAN, -S *n* slightly leavened flat Indian bread
NAARTJE, -S *same as* ► **naartjie**
NAARTJIE *n* tangerine
NAB, -BED, -BING, -S *vb* arrest (someone)
NABBER, -S *n* thief
NABBING ► **nab**
NABE, -S *n* Japanese hotpot
NABIS *n* Parisian art movement
NABK, -S *n* edible berry
NABLA, -S *another name for* ► **del**
NABOB, -S *n* rich, powerful, or important man
NABOBERY
NABOBESS
NABOBISH
NABOBISM
NABS ► **nab**
NACARAT, -S *n* red-orange colour
NACELLE, -S *n* streamlined enclosure on an aircraft
NACH *n* Indian dance
NACHAS *n* pleasure
NACHE, -S *n* rump
NACHO, -S *n* snack of a piece of tortilla with a topping
NACKET, -S *n* light lunch, snack
NACRE, -S *n* mother of pearl
NACRED
NACREOUS
NACRITE, -S *n* mineral
NACROUS ► **nacre**
NADA, -S *n* nothing

NADIR, -S *n* point in the sky opposite the zenith
NADIRAL
NAE, -S *Scot word for* ► **no**
NAEBODY *Scots variant of* ► **nobody**
NAES ► **nae**
NAETHING *Scots variant of* ► **nothing**
NAEVE, -S *n* birthmark
NAEVI ► **naevus**
NAEVOID ► **naevus**
NAEVUS, NAEVI *n* birthmark or mole
NAFF, -ED, -ER, -EST, -ING, -S *adj* lacking quality or taste ▷ *vb* go away
NAFFLY
NAFFNESS
NAG, -GED, -GING, -S *vb* scold or find fault constantly ▷ *n* person who nags
NAGA, -S *n* cobra
NAGANA, -S *n* disease of all domesticated animals of central and southern Africa
NAGAPIE, -S *n* bushbaby
NAGARI, -S *n* scripts for writing several languages of India
NAGAS ► **naga**
NAGGED ► **nag**
NAGGER, -S ► **nag**
NAGGIER ► **naggy**
NAGGIEST ► **naggy**
NAGGING, -S ► **nag**
NAGGY, NAGGIER, NAGGIEST ► **nag**
NAGMAAL, -S *n* Communion
NAGOR, -S *another name for* ► **reedbuck**
NAGS ► **nag**

NAGWARE, -S *n* software that is initially free and then requires payment
NAH *same as* ► **no**
NAHAL, -S *n* agricultural settlement run by an Israeli military youth organization
NAIAD, -ES, -S *n* nymph living in a lake or river
NAIANT *adj* swimming
NAIF, -ER, -EST, -S *less common word for* ► **naive**
NAIFLY
NAIFNESS
NAIK, -S *n* chief
NAIL, -ED, -S *n* pointed piece of metal used to join two objects together ▷ *vb* attach (something) with nails
NAILER -S
NAILERY *n* nail factory
NAILFILE *n* small metal file used to shape and smooth the nails
NAILFOLD *n* skin at base of fingernail
NAILHEAD *n* decorative device, as on tooled leather, resembling the round head of a nail
NAILING, -S ► **nail**
NAILLESS ► **nail**
NAILS ► **nail**
NAILSET, -S *n* punch for driving down the head of a nail
NAIN *adj* own
NAINSELL *n* own self
NAINSOOK *n* light soft plain-weave cotton fabric, used esp for babies' wear

NAIRA, -S n standard monetary unit of Nigeria, divided into 100 kobo

NAIRU, -S n Non-Accelerating Inflation Rate of Unemployment

NAISSANT adj (of a beast) having only the forepart shown above a horizontal division of a shield

NAIVE, -R, -S, -ST adj innocent and gullible ▷ n person who is naive, esp in artistic style

NAIVELY

NAIVETE, -S variant of ▸ naivety

NAIVETY n state or quality of being naive

NAIVIST ▸ naive

NAKED, -ER, -EST adj without clothes

NAKEDLY

NAKER, -S n small kettledrum used in medieval music

NAKFA, -S n standard currency unit of Eritrea

NALA, -S n ravine

NALED, -S n type of insecticide

NALLA, -S n ravine

NALLAH, -S same as ▸ nalla

NALLAS ▸ nalla

NALOXONE n substance that counteracts opiates

NAM, -S n distraint

NAMABLE ▸ name

NAMASKAR n salutation used in India

NAMASTE, -S n Indian greeting

NAME, -D, -S n word by which a person or thing is known ▷ vb give a name to

NAMEABLE

NAMELESS adj without a name

NAMELY adv that is to say

NAMER, -S ▸ name

NAMES ▸ name

NAMESAKE n person with the same name as another

NAMETAG, -S n identification badge

NAMETAPE n narrow cloth tape bearing the owner's name and attached to an article

NAMING, -S ▸ name

NAMMA adj as in **namma hole** Australian word for a natural well in rock

NAMS ▸ nam

NAMU, -S n black New Zealand sandfly

NAN, -S n grandmother

NANA, -S same as ▸ nan

NANDIN, -S same as ▸ nandina

NANDINA, -S n type of shrub

NANDINE, -S n African palm civet

NANDINS ▸ nandin

NANDOO, -S same as ▸ nandu

NANDU, -S n type of ostrich

NANE Scot word for ▸ none

NANG adj excellent; cool

NANISM, -S n dwarfism

NANITE, -S n microscopically small machine or robot

NANKEEN, -S n hard-wearing buff-coloured cotton fabric

NANKIN, -S same as ▸ nankeen

NANNA, -S same as ▸ nan

NANNIE same as ▸ nanny

NANNY, NANNIED, NANNIES n woman whose job is looking after young children ▷ vb be too protective towards

NANNYGAI n edible sea fish of Australia which is red in colour and has large prominent eyes

NANNYING n act of nannying

NANNYISH ▸ nanny

NANO, -S n science concerned with materials on a molecular scale

NANOBE, -S n microbe that is smaller than the smallest known bacterium

NANOBEE, -S n artificial nanoparticle

NANOBES ▸ nanobe

NANOBOT, -S n microscopically small robot

NANODOT, -S n microscopic cluster of atoms used to store data in a computer chip

NANOGRAM n unit of measurement

NANOOK, -S n polar bear

NANOPORE n microscopically small pore in an electrically insulating membrane

NANOS ▸ nano

NANOTECH n technology of very small objects

NANOTUBE n cylindrical molecule of carbon

NANOWATT n unit of measurement

NANOWIRE n microscopically thin wire

NANS ▸ nan

NANUA, -S same as ▸ moki

NAOS, NAOI, -ES n ancient classical temple

NAP, -PED, -PING, -S n short sleep ▷ vb have a short sleep

NAPA, -S n type of leather

NAPALM, -ED, -S n highly inflammable jellied petrol, used in bombs ▷ vb attack (people or places) with napalm

NAPAS ▸ napa

NAPE, -D, -S, NAPING n back of the neck ▷ vb attack with napalm

NAPERY, NAPERIES n household linen, esp table linen

NAPES ▸ nape

NAPHTHA, -S n liquid mixture used as a solvent and in petrol

NAPHTHOL n white crystalline solid used in dyes

NAPHTHYL n type of monovalent radical

NAPHTOL, -S same as ▸ naphthol

NAPIFORM adj shaped like a turnip

NAPING ▸ nape

NAPKIN, -S same as ▸ nappy

NAPLESS adj threadbare

NAPOLEON n former French gold coin worth 20 francs

NAPOO, -ED, -ING, -S vb military slang meaning kill

NAPPA, -S n soft leather

NAPPE, -S n mass of rock that has been thrust from its original position by earth movements

NAPPED ▸ nap

NAPPER, -S n person or thing that raises the nap on cloth

NAPPES ▸ nappe

NAPPIE same as ▸ nappy

NAPPIER ▸ nappy

NAPPIES ▸ nappy

NAPPIEST ▸ nappy

NAPPING ▸ nap

NAPPY, NAPPIER, NAPPIES, NAPPIEST n piece of absorbent material fastened round a baby's lower torso ▷ adj having a nap

NAPRON, -S same as ▸ apron

NAPROXEN n pain-killing drug

NAPS ▸ nap

NARAS, -ES same as ▸ narras

NARCEEN, -S same as ▸ narceine

NARCEIN, -S same as ▸ narceine

NARCEINE n narcotic alkaloid that occurs in opium

NARCEINS ▸ narcein

NARCISM, -S n exceptional admiration for oneself

NARCISSI ▶ **narcissus**

NARCIST, -S n narcissist

NARCOMA, -S n coma caused by intake of narcotic drugs

NARCOSE same as ▶ **narcosis**

NARCOSIS, NARCOSES n effect of a narcotic

NARCOTIC adj of a drug which produces numbness and drowsiness ▷ n such a drug

NARD, -ED, -ING, -S n any of several plants with aromatic roots ▷ vb anoint with nard oil

NARDINE

NARDOO, -S n cloverlike fern which grows in swampy areas

NARDS ▶ **nard**

NARES, NARIS pl n nostrils

NARGHILE another name for ▶ **hookah**

NARGHILY same as ▶ **narghile**

NARGILE, -S same as ▶ **narghile**

NARGILEH same as ▶ **narghile**

NARGILES ▶ **nargile**

NARGILY same as ▶ **narghile**

NARIAL adj of or relating to the nares

NARICORN n bird's nostril

NARINE same as ▶ **narial**

NARIS ▶ **nares**

NARK, -ED, -ING, -S vb annoy ▷ n informer or spy

NARKIER ▶ **narky**

NARKIEST ▶ **narky**

NARKING ▶ **nark**

NARKS ▶ **nark**

NARKY, NARKIER, NARKIEST adj irritable or complaining

NARQUOIS adj malicious

NARRAS, -ES n type of shrub

NARRATE, -D, -S vb tell (a story)

NARRATER same as ▶ **narrator**

NARRATES ▶ **narrate**

NARRATOR n person who tells a story or gives an account of something

NARRE adj nearer

NARROW, -ED, -ER adj small in breadth in comparison to length ▷ vb make or become narrow

NARROWLY

NARROWS pl n narrow part of a strait, river, or current

NARTHEX n portico at the west end of a basilica or church

NARTJIE, -S same as ▶ **naartjie**

> This word for a small sweet orange is one to look out for when you have the J with the good letters of 'retain'. And it has alternative spellings **naartje** and **naartjie**.

NARWAL, -S same as ▶ **narwhal**

NARWHAL, -S n arctic whale with a long spiral tusk

NARWHALE same as ▶ **narwhal**

NARWHALS ▶ **narwhal**

NARY adv not

NAS vb has not

NASAL, -S adj of the nose ▷ n nasal speech sound, such as English m, n, or ng

NASALISE same as ▶ **nasalize**

NASALISM n nasal pronunciation

NASALITY ▶ **nasal**

NASALIZE vb pronounce nasally

NASALLY ▶ **nasal**

NASALS ▶ **nasal**

NASARD, -S n organ stop

NASCENCE ▶ **nascent**

NASCENCY ▶ **nascent**

NASCENT adj starting to grow or develop

NASHGAB, -S n chatter

NASHI, -S n fruit of the Japanese pear

NASIAL ▶ **nasion**

NASION, -S n craniometric point where the top of the nose meets the ridge of the forehead

NASSELLA n as in **nassella tussock** type of tussock grass

NASTALIK n type of script

NASTIC adj (of movement of plants) independent of the direction of the external stimulus

NASTIER ▶ **nasty**

NASTIES ▶ **nasty**

NASTIEST ▶ **nasty**

NASTILY ▶ **nasty**

NASTY, NASTIER, NASTIES, NASTIEST adj unpleasant ▷ n something unpleasant

NASUTE, -S n type of termite

NAT, -S n supporter of nationalism

NATAL adj of or relating to birth

NATALITY n birth rate in a given place

NATANT adj (of aquatic plants) floating on the water

NATANTLY adv in a floating manner

NATATION n swimming

NATATORY adj of or relating to swimming

NATCH, -ES sentence substitute naturally ▷ n notch

NATES, NATIS pl n buttocks

NATHEMO same as > **nathemore**

NATHLESS same as > **natheless**

NATIFORM adj resembling buttocks

NATION, -S n people of one or more cultures or races organized as a single state

NATIONAL adj of or serving a nation as a whole ▷ n citizen of a nation

NATIONS ▶ **nation**

NATIS ▶ **nates**

NATIVE, -S adj relating to a place where a person was born ▷ n person born in a place

NATIVELY

NATIVISM n policy of favouring the natives of a country over the immigrants

NATIVIST

NATIVITY n birth or origin

NATRIUM, -S obsolete name for ▶ **sodium**

NATRON, -S n whitish or yellow mineral

NATS ▶ **nat**

NATTER, -ED, -S vb talk idly or chatter ▷ n long idle chat

NATTERER

NATTERY adj irritable

NATTIER ▶ **natty**

NATTIEST ▶ **natty**

NATTILY ▶ **natty**

NATTY, NATTIER, NATTIEST adj smart and spruce

NATURA, -E n nature

NATURAL, -S adj normal or to be expected ▷ n person with an inborn talent or skill

NATURE, -S n whole system of the physical world not controlled by human beings

NATURED adj having a certain disposition

NATURES ▶ **nature**

NATURING adj creative

NATURISM n nudism

NATURIST

N

NAUCH, -ES same as
► **nautch**
NAUGHT, -S n nothing ▷ adv
not at all
NAUGHTY adj disobedient or
mischievous
NAUMACHY same as
> **naumachia**
NAUNT, -S n aunt
NAUPLIAL adj of or like a
nauplius, the larval form of
certain crustaceans
NAUPLIUS, NAUPLII n larva
of many crustaceans
NAUSEA, -S n feeling of being
about to vomit
NAUSEANT n substance
inducing nausea
NAUSEAS ► **nausea**
NAUSEATE vb make
(someone) feel sick
NAUSEOUS adj as if about
to vomit
NAUTCH, -ES n intricate
traditional Indian dance
NAUTIC same as ► **nautical**
NAUTICAL adj of the sea or
ships
NAUTICS n science of
navigation
NAUTILUS, NAUTILI n
shellfish with many tentacles
NAV, -S n (short for)
navigation
NAVAID, -S n navigational aid
NAVAL adj of or relating to a
navy or ships
NAVALISM n domination of
naval interests
NAVALLY ► **naval**
NAVAR, -S n system of air
navigation
NAVARCH, -S n admiral
NAVARCHY n navarch's term
of office
NAVARHO, -S n aircraft
navigation system
NAVARIN, -S n stew of
mutton or lamb with root
vegetables
NAVARS ► **navar**
NAVE, -S n long central part
of a church
NAVEL, -S n hollow in the
middle of the abdomen
NAVES ► **nave**
NAVETTE, -S n gem cut
NAVEW, -S another name for
► **turnip**
NAVICERT n certificate
specifying the contents of a
neutral ship's cargo
NAVICULA n incense holder
NAVIES ► **navy**

NAVIGATE vb direct or plot
the path or position of a ship,
aircraft, or car
NAVS ► **nav**
**NAVVY, NAVVIED, NAVVIES,
-ING** n labourer employed on
a road or a building site ▷ vb
work as a navvy
NAVY, NAVIES n warships
with their crews and
organization ▷ adj navy-blue
NAW same as ► **no**
NAWAB, -S n (formerly) a
Muslim ruler or landowner
in India
NAY, -S interj no ▷ n person
who votes against a motion
▷ adv used for emphasis
▷ sentence substitute no
NAYSAY, NAYSAID, -S vb
say no
NAYSAYER
NAYTHLES same as
> **natheless**
NAYWARD n towards denial
NAYWARDS same as
► **nayward**
NAYWORD, -S n proverb
NAZE, -S n flat marshy
headland
NAZI, -S n person who
thinks or acts in a brutal or
dictatorial way
NAZIFY, NAZIFIED, NAZIFIES
vb make nazi in character
NAZIR, -S n Muslim official
NAZIS ► **nazi**
NE conj nor
NEAFE, -S same as ► **nieve**
NEAFFE, -S same as ► **nieve**
NEAL, -ED, -ING, -S same as
► **anneal**
NEANIC adj of or relating to
the early stages in a life cycle
NEAP, -ED, -ING, -S adj of,
relating to, or constituting a
neap tide ▷ vb be grounded
by a neap tide
NEAR, -ED, -ER, -EST, -ING, -S
adj indicating a place or time
not far away ▷ vb draw close
(to) ▷ prep at or to a place or
time not far away from ▷ adv
at or to a place or time not far
away ▷ n left side of a horse
or vehicle
NEARBY adj not far away
▷ adv close at hand
NEARED ► **near**
NEARER ► **near**
NEAREST ► **near**
NEARING ► **near**
NEARISH adj quite near
NEARLY, NEARLIER adv
almost
NEARNESS ► **near**

NEARS ► **near**
NEARSIDE n side of a vehicle
that is nearer the kerb
NEAT, -ER, -EST, -S adj tidy
and clean ▷ n domestic
bovine animal
NEATEN, -ED, -S vb make neat
NEATER ► **neat**
NEATEST ► **neat**
NEATH short for ► **beneath**
NEATHERD n cowherd
NEATLY ► **neat**
NEATNESS ► **neat**
NEATNIK, -S n very neat and
tidy person
NEATS ► **neat**
NEB, -BED, -BING, -S n beak
of a bird or the nose of an
animal ▷ vb look around
nosily
NEBBICH, -S same as
► **nebbish**
NEBBING ► **neb**
NEBBISH n timid man
NEBBISHE same as
► **nebbish**
NEBBISHY adj timid
NEBBUK, -S n type of shrub
NEBECK, -S same as
► **nebbuk**
NEBEK, -S same as ► **nebbuk**
NEBEL, -S n Hebrew musical
instrument
NEBISH, -ES same as
► **nebbish**
NEBRIS, -ES n fawn-skin
NEBS ► **neb**
NEBULA, -E, -S n hazy cloud of
particles and gases
NEBULAR
NEBULE, -S n cloud
NEBULISE same as
► **nebulize**
NEBULIUM n element
NEBULIZE vb turn (a liquid)
into a fine spray
NEBULOSE same as
► **nebulous**
NEBULOUS adj vague and
unclear
NEBULY adj wavy
NECK, -ED, -S n part of the
body joining the head to
the shoulders ▷ vb kiss and
cuddle
NECKATEE n piece of
ornamental cloth worn
around the neck
NECKBAND n band around
the neck of a garment
NECKBEEF n cheap cattle
flesh
NECKED ► **neck**
NECKER, -S ► **neck**
NECKGEAR n any neck
covering

NECKING, -S n activity of kissing and embracing passionately

NECKLACE n decorative piece of jewellery worn around the neck

NECKLESS ▸ neck

NECKLET, -S n ornament worn round the neck

NECKLIKE ▸ neck

NECKLINE n shape or position of the upper edge of a dress or top

NECKS ▸ neck

NECKSHOT n shot in the neck of an animal

NECKTIE, -S same as ▸ tie

NECKWEAR n articles of clothing, such as ties, scarves, etc, worn about the neck

NECKWEED n type of plant

NECROPSY n postmortem examination ▷ vb carry out a necropsy

NECROSE, -D, -S vb cause or undergo necrosis

NECROSIS n death of cells in the body
NECROTIC

NECTAR, -S n sweet liquid collected from flowers by bees

NECTARED adj filled with nectar

NECTARS ▸ nectar

NECTARY n structure secreting nectar in a plant

NED, -S n derogatory name for an adolescent hooligan

NEDDIER ▸ neddy

NEDDIES ▸ neddy

NEDDIEST ▸ neddy

NEDDISH ▸ ned

NEDDY, NEDDIER, NEDDIES, NEDDIEST n donkey ▷ adj of or relating to neds

NEDETTE, -S n derogatory name for a female adolescent hooligan

NEDS ▸ ned

NEE prep indicating the maiden name of a married woman ▷ adj indicating the maiden name of a married woman

NEED, -ED, -ING vb require or be in want of ▷ n condition of lacking something
NEEDER -S

NEEDFIRE n beacon

NEEDFUL adj necessary or required

NEEDFULS n must-haves

NEEDIER ▸ needy

NEEDIEST ▸ needy

NEEDILY ▸ needy

NEEDING ▸ need

NEEDLE, -D, -S, NEEDLING n thin pointed piece of metal with an eye through which thread is passed for sewing ▷ vb goad or provoke

NEEDLER, -S n needle maker

NEEDLES ▸ needle

NEEDLESS adj unnecessary

NEEDLIER ▸ needly

NEEDLING ▸ needle

NEEDLY, NEEDLIER adj like or full of needles

NEEDMENT n a necessity

NEEDS adv necessarily ▷ pl n what is required

NEEDY, NEEDIER, NEEDIEST adj poor, in need of financial support

NEELD, -S same as ▸ needle

NEELE, -S same as ▸ needle

NEEM, -S n type of large Indian tree

NEEMB, -S same as ▸ neem

NEEMS ▸ neem

NEEP, -S dialect name for ▸ turnip

NEESE, -D, -S, NEESING same as ▸ neeze

NEEZE, -D, -S, NEEZING vb sneeze

NEF, -S n church nave

NEFAST adj wicked

NEFS ▸ nef

NEG, -S n photographic negative

NEGATE, -D, -S, NEGATING vb invalidate
NEGATER -S

NEGATION n opposite or absence of something

NEGATIVE adj expressing a denial or refusal ▷ n negative word or statement

NEGATON, -S same as ▸ negatron

NEGATOR, -S ▸ negate

NEGATORY adj relating to the act of negation

NEGATRON obsolete word for ▸ electron

NEGLECT, -S vb take no care of ▷ n neglecting or being neglected

NEGLIGE, -S variant of ▸ negligee

NEGLIGEE n woman's lightweight usu lace-trimmed dressing gown

NEGLIGES ▸ neglige

NEGRONI, -S n type of cocktail

NEGS ▸ neg

NEGUS, -ES n hot drink of port and lemon juice

NEIF, -S same as ▸ nieve

NEIGH, -ED, -S n loud high-pitched sound made by a horse ▷ vb make this sound

NEIGHBOR same as > neighbour

NEIGHED ▸ neigh

NEIGHING n act of neighing

NEIGHS ▸ neigh

NEINEI, -S n type of plant

NEIST Scots variant of ▸ next

NEITHER pron not one nor the other ▷ adj not one nor the other (of two)

NEIVE, -S same as ▸ nieve

NEK, -S n mountain pass

NEKTON, -S n free-swimming animals in the middle depths of a sea or lake
NEKTONIC

NELIES same as ▸ nelis

NELIS n type of pear

NELLIE, -S n type of albatross

NELLY n as in not on your nelly not under any circumstances

NELSON, -S n type of wrestling hold

NELUMBO, -S n type of aquatic plant

NEMA, -S n filament

NEMATIC, -S n substance having a mesomorphic state

NEMATODE n slender cylindrical unsegmented worm
NEMATOID

NEMESES ▸ nemesis

NEMESIA, -S n type of southern African plant

NEMESIS, NEMESES n retribution or vengeance

NEMN, -ED, -ING, -S vb name

NEMORAL adj of a wood

NEMOROUS adj woody

NEMPT adj named

NENE, -S n rare black-and-grey short-winged Hawaiian goose

NENNIGAI same as ▸ nannygai

NENUPHAR n type of water lily

NEOBLAST n worm cell

NEOCON, -S n supporter of conservative politics

NEOGENE adj of, denoting, or formed during the Miocene and Pliocene epochs

NEOLITH, -S n Neolithic stone implement

NEOLOGIC > neologism

NEOLOGY same as > neologism

NEOMORPH n genetic component

N

NEOMYCIN n type of antibiotic obtained from a bacterium

NEON, -S n element used in illuminated signs and lights ▷ adj of or illuminated by neon

NEONATAL adj relating to the first few weeks of a baby's life

NEONATE, -S n newborn child

NEONED adj lit with neon

NEONS ► neon

NEOPAGAN n advocate of the revival of paganism

NEOPHILE n person who welcomes new things

NEOPHOBE > neophobia

NEOPHYTE n beginner or novice

NEOPLASM n any abnormal new growth of tissue

NEOPRENE n synthetic rubber used in waterproof products

NEOSOUL, -S n soul music combined with other genres

NEOTENIC ► neoteny

NEOTENY n persistence of larval or fetal features in the adult form of an animal

NEOTERIC adj belonging to a new fashion or trend ▷ n new writer or philosopher

NEOTOXIN n harmful agent

NEOTYPE, -S n specimen selected to replace a type specimen that has been lost or destroyed

NEP, -S n catmint

NEPENTHE n drug that ancient writers referred to as a means of forgetting grief or trouble

NEPER, -S n unit expressing the ratio of two quantities

NEPETA, -S same as ► catmint

NEPHEW, -S n son of one's sister or brother

NEPHRIC adj renal

NEPHRISM n chronic kidney disease

NEPHRITE n tough fibrous amphibole mineral

NEPHROID adj kidney-shaped

NEPHRON, -S n urine-secreting tubule in the kidney

NEPIONIC adj of or relating to the juvenile period in the life cycle of an organism

NEPIT, -S n unit of information equal to 1.44 bits

NEPOTIC ► nepotism

NEPOTISM n favouritism in business shown to relatives and friends

NEPOTIST

NEPS ► nep

NERAL, -S n isomer of citral

NERD, -S n boring person obsessed with a particular subject

NERDIC, -S same as > geekspeak

NERDIER ► nerdy

NERDIEST ► nerdy

NERDISH ► nerd

NERDS ► nerd

NERDY, NERDIER, NERDIEST adj clumsy, socially inept

NEREID, -ES, -S n sea nymph in Greek mythology

NEREIS n type of marine worm

NERINE, -S n type of S African plant related to the amaryllis

NERITE, -S n type of sea snail

NERITIC adj of or formed in shallow seas near a coastline

NERK, -S n fool

NERKA, -S n type of salmon

NERKS ► nerk

NEROL, -S n scented liquid

NEROLI, -S n brown oil used in perfumery

NEROLS ► nerol

NERTS interj nuts

NERTZ same as ► nerts

NERVAL ► nerve

NERVATE adj (of leaves) with veins

NERVE, -D, -S n bundle of fibres that conducts impulses between the brain and body ▷ vb give courage to oneself

NERVELET n small nerve

NERVER, -S n someone or something which nerves

NERVES ► nerve

NERVIER ► nervy

NERVIEST ► nervy

NERVILY ► nervy

NERVINE, -S adj having a soothing effect upon the nerves ▷ n nervine drug or agent

NERVING, -S ► nerve

NERVOUS adj apprehensive or worried

NERVULAR adj relating to a nervule

NERVULE, -S n small vein

NERVURE, -S n stiff rod in an insect's wing

NERVY, NERVIER, NERVIEST adj excitable or nervous

NESCIENT > nescience

NESH, -ER, -EST adj sensitive to the cold

NESHNESS

NESS, -ES n headland, cape

NEST, -ED n place or structure in which birds or certain animals lay eggs or give birth to young ▷ vb make or inhabit a nest

NESTABLE

NESTER -S

NESTFUL, -S n the contents of a nest

NESTING, -S ► nest

NESTLE, -D, -S vb snuggle

NESTLER -S

NESTLIKE ► nest

NESTLING n bird too young to leave the nest

NESTMATE n bird that shares a nest with another bird

NESTOR, -S n wise old man

NESTS ► nest

NET, -S, -TED n fabric of meshes of string, thread, or wire with many openings ▷ vb catch (a fish or animal) in a net ▷ adj left after all deductions

NETBALL, -S n team game in which a ball has to be thrown through a high net

NETBOOK, -S n type of small laptop computer

NETE, -S n lyre string

NETFUL, -S n the contents of a net

NETHEAD, -S n expert on the internet

NETHER adj lower

NETIZEN, -S n person who regularly uses the internet

NETLESS adj without a net

NETLIKE adj resembling a net

NETOP, -S n friend

NETROOT, -S n activist who promotes a cause via the internet

NETS ► net

NETSPEAK n jargon, abbreviations, and emoticons typically used by frequent internet users

NETSUKE, -S n (in Japan) a carved ornamental toggle

NETSURF, -S vb browse the internet for information

NETT, -S same as ► net

NETTABLE adj that can be netted

NETTED ► net

NETTER, -S n person that makes nets

NETTIE n enthusiastic user of the internet

NETTIER ► netty

NETTIES ► **netty**

NETTIEST ► **netty**

NETTING, -S ► **net**

NETTLE, -D, -S, NETTLING *n* plant with stinging hairs on the leaves ▷ *vb* bother or irritate

NETTLER, -S *n* one that nettles

NETTLES ► **nettle**

NETTLIER ► **nettly**

NETTLING ► **nettle**

NETTLY, NETTLIER *adj* like a nettle

NETTS ► **nett**

NETTY, NETTIER, NETTIES, NETTIEST *n* lavatory ▷ *adj* resembling a net

NETWORK, -S *n* system of intersecting lines, roads, etc ▷ *vb* broadcast (a programme) over a network

NEUK, -S *Scot word for* ► **nook**

NEUM, -S *same as* ► **neume**

NEUMATIC *adj* relating to a neume

NEUME, -S *n* notational symbol

NEUMIC

NEUMS ► **neum**

NEURAL *adj* of a nerve or the nervous system

NEURALLY

NEURAXON *n* biological cell component

NEURINE, -S *n* poisonous alkaloid

NEURISM, -S *n* nerve force

NEURITE, -S *n* biological cell component

NEURITIC ► **neuritis**

NEURITIS *n* inflammation of a nerve or nerves

NEUROID, -S *adj* nervelike ▷ *n* either of the halves of a neural arch

NEUROMA, -S *n* any tumour composed of nerve tissue

NEURON, -S *same as* ► **neurone**

NEURONAL ► **neurone**

NEURONE, -S *n* cell specialized to conduct nerve impulses

NEURONIC

NEURONS ► **neuron**

NEUROPIL *n* dense network of neurons and glia in the central nervous system

NEUROSAL *adj* relating to neurosis

NEUROSIS, NEUROSES *n* mental disorder producing hysteria, anxiety, depression, or obsessive behaviour

NEUROTIC *adj* emotionally unstable ▷ *n* neurotic person

NEURULA, -S *n* stage of embryonic development

NEURULAE

NEURULAR

NEUSTIC ► **neuston**

NEUSTON, -S *n* organisms that float on the surface of open water

NEUTER, -ED, -S *adj* belonging to a particular class of grammatical inflections in some languages ▷ *vb* castrate (an animal) ▷ *n* neuter gender

NEUTRAL, -S *adj* taking neither side in a war or dispute ▷ *n* neutral person or nation

NEUTRINO *n* elementary particle with no mass or electrical charge

NEUTRON, -S *n* electrically neutral elementary particle

NEVE, -S *n* mass of porous ice, formed from snow

NEVEL, -LED, -S *vb* beat with the fists

NEVER *adv* at no time ▷ *sentence substitute* at no time ▷ *interj* surely not!

NEVES ► **neve**

NEVI ► **nevus**

NEVOID ► **naevus**

NEVUS, NEVI *same as* ► **naevus**

NEW, -ED, -ER, -EST, -ING *adj* not existing before ▷ *adv* recently ▷ *vb* make new

NEWB, -S *n* newbie

NEWBIE, -S *n* person new to a job, club, etc

NEWBORN, -S *adj* recently or just born ▷ *n* newborn baby

NEWBS ► **newb**

NEWCOME *adj* recently arrived

NEWCOMER *n* recent arrival or participant

NEWED ► **new**

NEWEL, -S *n* post at the top or bottom of a flight of stairs

NEWELL, -S *n* new thing

NEWELLED ► **newel**

NEWELLS ► **newell**

NEWELS ► **newel**

NEWER ► **new**

NEWEST ► **new**

NEWFOUND *adj* newly or recently discovered

NEWIE, -S *n* fresh idea or thing

NEWING ► **new**

NEWISH *adj* fairly new

NEWISHLY

NEWLY *adv* recently

NEWLYWED *n* recently married person

NEWMOWN *adj* freshly cut

NEWNESS ► **new**

NEWS, -ED, -ES, -ING *n* important or interesting new happenings ▷ *vb* report

NEWSBEAT *n* particular area of news reporting

NEWSBOY, -S *n* boy who sells or delivers newspapers

NEWSCAST *n* radio or television broadcast of the news

NEWSCLIP *n* brief extract from news broadcast

NEWSDESK *n* news gathering and reporting department

NEWSED ► **news**

NEWSES ► **news**

NEWSFEED *n* service that provides news articles for distribution

NEWSGIRL *n* female newsreader or reporter

NEWSHAWK *n* newspaper reporter

NEWSIE *same as* ► **newsy**

NEWSIER ► **newsy**

NEWSIES ► **newsy**

NEWSIEST ► **newsy**

NEWSING ► **news**

NEWSLESS ► **news**

NEWSMAN, NEWSMEN *n* male newsreader or reporter

NEWSPEAK *n* deliberately ambiguous and misleading language of politicians and officials

NEWSREEL *n* short film giving news

NEWSROOM *n* room where news is received and prepared for publication or broadcasting

NEWSWIRE *n* electronic means of delivering up-to-the-minute news

NEWSY, NEWSIER, NEWSIES, NEWSIEST *adj* full of news ▷ *n* newsagent

NEWT, -S *n* small amphibious creature

NEWTON, -S *n* unit of force

NEWTS ► **newt**

NEWWAVER *n* member of new wave

NEXT, -S *adv* immediately following ▷ *n* next person or thing

NEXTDOOR *adj* in or at the adjacent house or building

NEXTLY ► **next**

NEXTNESS ► **next**

NEXTS ► **next**

N

NEXUS, -ES n connection or link

NGAI n clan or tribe

NGAIO, -S n small New Zealand tree

NGANA, -S same as ► **nagana**

NGARARA, -S n lizard found in New Zealand

NGATI, -S n (occurring as part of the tribe name) a tribe or clan

NGOMA, -S n type of drum

NGULTRUM n standard monetary unit of Bhutan, divided into 100 chetrum

NGWEE, -S n Zambian monetary unit

NHANDU, -S n type of spider

NIACIN, -S n vitamin of the B complex

NIAGARA, -S n deluge or outpouring

NIB, -BED, -BING, -S n writing point of a pen ▷ vb provide with a nib

NIBBLE, -D, -S, NIBBLING vb take little bites (of) ▷ n little bite

NIBBLER, -S n person, animal, or thing that nibbles

NIBBLES ► nibble

NIBBLIES ► nibbly

NIBBLING ► nibble

NIBBLY, NIBBLIES n small item of food

NIBLET, -S n very small piece of food

NIBLICK, -S n former golf club giving a great deal of lift

NIBLIKE ► nib

NIBS ► nib

NICAD, -S n rechargeable dry-cell battery

NICE, -R, -ST adj pleasant
NICEISH
NICELY
NICENESS

NICETY, NICETIES n subtle point

NICHE, -D, -S, NICHING n hollow area in a wall ▷ adj of or aimed at a specialist group or market ▷ vb place (a statue) in a niche

NICHER, -ED, -S vb snigger

NICHES ► niche

NICHING ► niche

NICHROME n (tradename) alloy of nickel and chrome

NICHT, -S Scot word for ► **night**

NICISH ► nice

NICK, -ED, -ING, -S vb make a small cut in ▷ n small cut

NICKAR, -S n hard seed

NICKED ► nick

NICKEL, -ED, -S n silvery-white metal often used in alloys ▷ vb plate with nickel

NICKELIC adj of or containing metallic nickel

NICKELS ► nickel

NICKER, -ED, -S n pound sterling ▷ vb (of a horse) to neigh softly

NICKING ► nick

NICKLE, -D, -S, NICKLING same as ► **nickel**

NICKNACK n cheap ornament or trinket

NICKNAME n familiar name given to a person or place ▷ vb call by a nickname

NICKS ► nick

NICKUM, -S n mischievous person

NICOISE adj prepared with tomatoes, black olives, garlic and anchovies

NICOL, -S n device for producing plane-polarized light

NICOTIAN n tobacco user

NICOTIN same as ► **nicotine**

NICOTINE n poisonous substance found in tobacco

NICOTINS same as ► **nicotin**

NICTATE, -D, -S same as ► **nictitate**

NID, -S same as ► **nide**

NIDAL ► nidus

NIDATE, -D, -S, NIDATING vb undergo nidation

NIDATION n implantation

NIDDICK, -S n nape of the neck

NIDE, -D, -S vb nest

NIDERING same as ► **niddering**

NIDES ► nide

NIDGET, -ED, -S n type of hoe ▷ vb assist a woman in labour

NIDI ► nidus

NIDIFY, NIDIFIED, NIDIFIES vb (of a bird) to make or build a nest

NIDING, -S n coward

NIDOR, -S n cooking smell
NIDOROUS

NIDS ► nid

NIDUS, NIDI, -ES n nest in which insects or spiders deposit their eggs

NIE, -D, -S archaic spelling of ► **nigh**

NIECE, -S n daughter of one's sister or brother

NIED ► nie

NIEF, -S same as ► **nieve**

NIELLI ► niello

NIELLIST ► niello

NIELLO, NIELLI, -ED, -S n black compound of sulphur and silver, lead, or copper ▷ vb decorate or treat with niello

NIENTE adv softly fading away

NIES ► nie

NIEVE, -S n closed hand

NIEVEFUL n closed handful

NIEVES ► nieve

NIFE, -S n earth's core

NIFF, -ED, -ING, -S n stink ▷ vb stink

NIFFER, -ED, -S vb barter

NIFFIER ► niffy

NIFFIEST ► niffy

NIFFING ► niff

NIFFNAFF vb trifle

NIFFS ► niff

NIFFY, NIFFIER, NIFFIEST ► **niff**

NIFTIER ► nifty

NIFTIES ► nifty

NIFTIEST ► nifty

NIFTILY ► nifty

NIFTY, NIFTIER, NIFTIES, NIFTIEST adj neat or smart ▷ n nifty thing

NIGELLA, -S n type of Mediterranean plant

NIGGARD, -S n stingy person ▷ adj miserly ▷ vb act in a niggardly way

NIGGLE, -D, -S vb worry slightly ▷ n small worry or doubt

NIGGLER -S

NIGGLIER ► niggly

NIGGLING adj petty ▷ n act or instance of niggling

NIGGLY, NIGGLIER ► niggle

NIGH, -ED, -ER, -EST, -ING, -S prep near ▷ adv nearly ▷ adj near ▷ vb approach
NIGHLY
NIGHNESS

NIGHT n time of darkness between sunset and sunrise ▷ adj of, occurring, or working at night

NIGHTCAP n drink taken just before bedtime

NIGHTED adj darkened

NIGHTIE, -S n nightgown

NIGHTJAR n nocturnal bird with a harsh cry

NIGHTLY adv (happening) each night ▷ adj happening each night

NIGHTS adv at night or on most nights

NIGHTY same as ► **nightie**

NIGIRI, -S n small oval block of cold rice, wasabi and fish

NIGRIFY vb blacken

NIGROSIN same as
> nigrosine
NIHIL, -S n nil
NIHILISM n rejection of all
established authority and
institutions
NIHILIST
NIHILITY n state or condition
of being nothing
NIHILS ► nihil
NIHONGA, -S n Japanese form
of painting
NIKAB, -S same as ► niqab
NIKAH, -S n Islamic marriage
contract
NIKAU, -S n palm tree native
to New Zealand
NIL, -S n nothing, zero
NILGAI, -S n large Indian
antelope
NILGAU, -S same as
► nilghau
NILGHAI, -S same as ► nilgai
NILGHAU, -S same as
► nilgai
NILL, -ED, -ING, -S vb be
unwilling
NILS ► nil
NIM, -MED, -MING, -S n game
involving removing one
or more small items from
several rows or piles ▷ vb
steal
NIMB, -S n halo
NIMBED
NIMBI ► nimbus
NIMBLE, -R, -ST adj agile and
quick
NIMBLY
NIMBS ► nimb
NIMBUS, NIMBI, -ES n dark
grey rain cloud
NIMBUSED
NIMBYISM n practice of
objecting to something that
will affect one or take place in
one's locality
NIMIETY rare word for
► excess
NIMIOUS
NIMMED ► nim
NIMMER, -S ► nim
NIMMING ► nim
NIMONIC adj as in **nimonic
alloy** type of nickel-based
alloy
NIMPS adj easy
NIMROD, -S n hunter
NIMS ► nim
NINCOM, -S same as
> nicompoop
NINCUM, -S same as
> nicompoop
NINE, -S n one more than
eight

NINEBARK n North American
shrub
NINEFOLD adj having nine
times as many or as much
▷ adv by nine times as much
or as many
NINEPIN n skittle used in
ninepins
NINEPINS n game of skittles
NINER, -S n (US) student in
the ninth grade
NINES ► nine
NINETEEN n ten and nine
NINETY, NINETIES n ten
times nine ▷ determiner
amounting to ninety
NINJA, -S n person skilled in
ninjutsu
NINJITSU same as ► ninjutsu
NINJUTSU n Japanese martial
art
NINNY, NINNIES n stupid
person
NINNYISH
NINON, -S n fine strong silky
fabric
NINTH, -S n (of) number nine
in a series ▷ adj coming after
the eighth ▷ adv after the
eighth
NINTHLY same as ► ninth
NINTHS ► ninth
NIOBATE, -S n type of salt
crystal
NIOBIC adj of or containing
niobium in the pentavalent
state
NIOBITE, -S another name for
> columbite
NIOBIUM, -S n white metallic
element
NIOBOUS adj of or containing
niobium in the trivalent state
NIP, -PED, -PING, -S vb hurry
▷ n pinch or light bite
NIPA, -S n palm tree of S and
SE Asia
NIPPED ► nip
NIPPER, -ED n small child
▷ vb secure with rope
NIPPERS pl n instrument
or tool for pinching or
squeezing
NIPPIER ► nippy
NIPPIEST ► nippy
NIPPILY ► nippy
NIPPING ► nip
NIPPLE, -D, -S, NIPPLING n
projection in the centre of
a breast ▷ vb provide with
a nipple
NIPPY, NIPPIER, NIPPIEST adj
frosty or chilly
NIPS ► nip
NIPTER, -S n type of religious
ceremony

NIQAAB, -S n veil worn by
some Muslim women
NIQAB, -S n type of veil worn
by some Muslim women

> One of those invaluable
> words allowing you to play
> the Q without a U. It can
> also be spelt **nikab**.

NIRAMIAI n sumo wrestling
procedure
NIRL, -ED, -ING, -IT, -S vb
shrivel
NIRLIE variant of ► nirly
NIRLIER ► nirly
NIRLIEST ► nirly
NIRLING ► nirl
NIRLIT ► nirl
NIRLS ► nirl
NIRLY, NIRLIER, NIRLIEST adj
shrivelled
NIRVANA, -S n absolute
spiritual enlightenment
and bliss
NIRVANIC
NIS n friendly goblin
NISBERRY same as
> naseberry
NISEI, -S n native-born citizen
of the US or Canada whose
parents were Japanese
NISGUL, -S n smallest and
weakest bird in a brood of
chickens
NISH, -ES n nothing
NISI adj (of a court order)
coming into effect on a
specified date
NISSE, -S same as ► nis
NISUS n impulse towards or
striving after a goal
NIT, -S n egg or larva of a louse
NITE, -S variant of ► night
NITER, -S same as ► nitre
NITERIE, -S n nightclub
NITERS ► niter
NITERY ► niter
NITES ► nite
NITHER, -ED, -S vb shiver
NITHING, -S n coward
NITID adj bright
NITINOL, -S n metal alloy
NITON, -S less common name
for ► radon
NITPICK, -S vb criticize
unnecessarily
NITPICKY
NITRATE, -D, -S n compound
of nitric acid, used as a
fertilizer ▷ vb treat with
nitric acid or a nitrate
NITRATOR
NITRE, -S n potassium nitrate
NITREOUS adj as in **nitreous
silica** another name for
quartz glass

N

NITRES ▶ nitre
NITRIC adj of or containing nitrogen
NITRID, -S same as ▶ nitride
NITRIDE, -D, -S n compound of nitrogen ▷ vb make into a nitride
NITRIDS ▶ nitrid
NITRIFY vb treat or cause to react with nitrogen
NITRIL, -S same as ▶ nitrile
NITRILE, -S n any one of a particular class of organic compounds
NITRILS ▶ nitril
NITRITE, -S n salt or ester of nitrous acid
NITRO, -S n nitroglycerine
NITROGEN n colourless odourless gas that forms four fifths of the air
NITROLIC adj pertaining to a group of acids
NITROS ▶ nitro
NITROSO adj of a particular monovalent group
NITROSYL another word for ▶ nitroso
NITROUS adj derived from or containing nitrogen in a low valency state
NITROX, -ES n mixture of nitrogen and oxygen used in diving
NITROXYL n type of chemical
NITRY adj nitrous
NITRYL, -S n chemical compound
NITS ▶ nit
NITTY, NITTIER, NITTIEST adj infested with nits
NITWIT, -S n stupid person
NIVAL adj of or growing in or under snow
NIVATION n weathering of rock around a patch of snow by alternate freezing and thawing
NIVEOUS adj resembling snow, esp in colour
NIX, -ED, -ES, -ING sentence substitute be careful! watch out! ▷ n rejection or refusal ▷ vb veto, deny, reject, or forbid (plans, suggestions, etc)

> This is a handy little word, combining X with two of the most common tiles in the game.

NIXE n water sprite
NIXED ▶ nix
NIXER, -S n spare-time job
NIXES ▶ nix

NIXIE, -S n female water sprite, usually unfriendly to humans
NIXING ▶ nix
NIXY same as ▶ nixie
NIZAM, -S n (formerly) a Turkish regular soldier
NIZAMATE n territory of the nizam
NIZAMS ▶ nizam
NKOSI, -S n term of address to a superior
NO, -ES, -S interj expresses denial, disagreement, or refusal ▷ adj not any, not a ▷ adv not at all ▷ n answer or vote of 'no'
NOAH, -S n shark
NOB, -S n person of wealth or social distinction
NOBBIER ▶ nobby
NOBBIEST ▶ nobby
NOBBILY ▶ nob
NOBBLE, -D, -S, NOBBLING vb attract the attention of
NOBBLER -S
NOBBUT adv nothing but
NOBBY, NOBBIER, NOBBIEST ▶ nob
NOBELIUM n artificially-produced radioactive element
NOBILITY n quality of being noble
NOBLE, -R, -S, -ST adj showing or having high moral qualities ▷ n member of the nobility
NOBLEMAN, NOBLEMEN n person of noble rank
NOBLER ▶ noble
NOBLES ▶ noble
NOBLESSE n noble birth or condition
NOBLEST ▶ noble
NOBLY ▶ noble
NOBODY, NOBODIES pron no person ▷ n person of no importance
NOBS ▶ nob
NOCAKE, -S n Indian meal made from dried corn
NOCEBO, -S n harmless substance that causes harmful effects in patients who expect it to be harmful
NOCENT, -S n guilty person
NOCENTLY
NOCHEL, -S same as ▶ notchel
NOCHELED same as > notcheled
NOCHELS ▶ nochel
NOCK, -ED, -ING, -S n notch on an arrow or a bow for the

bowstring ▷ vb fit (an arrow) on a bowstring
NOCKET, -S same as ▶ nacket
NOCKING ▶ nock
NOCKS ▶ nock
NOCTILIO n type of bat
NOCTUA, -S n type of moth
NOCTUARY n nightly journal
NOCTUAS ▶ noctua
NOCTUID, -S n type of nocturnal moth ▷ adj of or relating to this type of moth
NOCTULE, -S n any of several large Old World insectivorous bats
NOCTUOID adj of or like a noctuid ▷ n member of the family of moths Noctuidae
NOCTURIA n excessive urination during the night
NOCTURN, -S n any of the main sections of the office of matins
NOCTURNE n short dreamy piece of music
NOCTURNS ▶ nocturn
NOCUOUS adj harmful
NOD, -DED, -S vb lower and raise (one's head) briefly in agreement or greeting ▷ n act of nodding
NODAL adj of or like a node
NODALISE same as ▶ nodalize
NODALITY ▶ nodal
NODALIZE vb make something nodal
NODALLY ▶ nodal
NODATED adj knotted
NODATION n knottiness
NODDED ▶ nod
NODDER, -S ▶ nod
NODDIER ▶ noddy
NODDIES ▶ noddy
NODDIEST ▶ noddy
NODDING, -S ▶ nod
NODDLE, -D, -S, NODDLING n head ▷ vb nod (the head), as through drowsiness
NODDY, NODDIER, NODDIES, NODDIEST n tropical tern with a dark plumage ▷ adj very easy to use or understand
NODE, -S n point on a plant stem from which leaves grow
NODI ▶ nodus
NODICAL adj of or relating to the nodes of a celestial body
NODOSE adj having nodes or knotlike swellings
NODOSITY
NODOUS same as ▶ nodose
NODS ▶ nod
NODULAR ▶ nodule

NODULE, -S n small knot or lump
NODULED
NODULOSE
NODULOUS
NODUS, NODI n problematic idea, situation, etc
NOEL, -S n Christmas
NOES ▶ no
NOESIS, NOESES, -ES n exercise of reason
NOETIC adj of or relating to the mind
NOG, -S same as ▶ nogging
NOGAKU n Japanese style of drama
NOGG, -S same as ▶ nog
NOGGED adj built with timber and brick
NOGGIN, -S n head
NOGGING, -S n short horizontal timber member
NOGGINS ▶ noggin
NOGGS ▶ nogg
NOGS ▶ nog
NOH n stylized classic drama of Japan
NOHOW adv under any conditions
NOHOWISH
NOIL, -S n short or knotted fibres that are separated from the long fibres by combing
NOILIER ▶ noily
NOILIES ▶ noily
NOILIEST ▶ noily
NOILS ▶ noil
NOILY, NOILIER, NOILIES, NOILIEST n dry white vermouth drink from France ▷ adj resembling a noil
NOINT, -ED, -ING, -S vb anoint
NOINTER, -S n mischievous child
NOINTING ▶ noint
NOINTS ▶ noint
NOIR, -S adj (of a film) showing characteristics of a film noir, in plot or style ▷ n film noir
NOIRISH
NOISE, -D, -S, NOISING n sound, usu a loud or disturbing one ▷ vb spread (news or gossip)
NOISEFUL
NOISENIK n rock musician who performs loud harsh music
NOISES ▶ noise
NOISETTE n hazelnut chocolate ▷ adj flavoured or made with hazelnuts
NOISIER ▶ noisy

NOISIEST ▶ noisy
NOISILY ▶ noisy
NOISING ▶ noise
NOISOME adj (of smells) offensive
NOISY, NOISIER, NOISIEST adj making a lot of noise
NOLE, -S same as ▶ noll
NOLITION n unwillingness
NOLL, -S n head
NOLO, -S as in **nolo contendere** plea indicating that the defendant does not wish to contest the case
NOM, -S n name
NOMA, -S n gangrenous inflammation of the mouth
NOMAD, -S n member of a tribe with no fixed dwelling place
NOMADE, -S same as ▶ nomad
NOMADIC adj relating to or characteristic of nomads
NOMADIES ▶ nomady
NOMADISE same as ▶ nomadize
NOMADISM ▶ nomad
NOMADIZE vb live as nomads
NOMADS ▶ nomad
NOMADY, NOMADIES n practice of living like nomads
NOMARCH, -S n head of an ancient Egyptian nome
NOMARCHY n any of the provinces of modern Greece
NOMAS ▶ noma
NOMBLES variant spelling of ▶ numbles
NOMBRIL, -S n point on a shield
NOME, -S n any of the former provinces of modern Greece
NOMEN, -S, NOMINA n ancient Roman's second name
NOMES ▶ nome
NOMIC adj normal or habitual
NOMINA ▶ nomen
NOMINAL, -S adj in name only ▷ n nominal element
NOMINATE vb suggest as a candidate ▷ adj having a particular name
NOMINEE, -S n candidate
NOMISM, -S n adherence to laws as a primary exercise of religion
NOMISTIC
NOMOGENY n law of life originating as a natural process
NOMOGRAM n arrangement of two linear or logarithmic scales
NOMOI ▶ nomos

NOMOLOGY n science of law and law-making
NOMOS, NOMOI n convention
NOMS ▶ nom
NON adv not
NONA n sleeping sickness
NONACID, -S adj not acid ▷ n nonacid substance
NONACTOR n person who is not an actor
NONADULT n person who is not an adult
NONAGE, -D, -S n state of being under full legal age
NONAGON, -S n geometric figure with nine sides
NONANE, -S n type of chemical compound
NONANOIC adj as in **nonanoic acid** colourless oily fatty acid with a rancid odour
NONARIES ▶ nonary
NONART, -S n something that does not constitute art
NONARY, NONARIES n set or group of nine
NONAS same as ▶ nones
NONBANK, -S n business or institution that is not a bank but provides similar services
NONBASIC adj not basic
NONBEING n philosophical problem relating to the question of existence
NONBLACK n person who is not Black
NONBODY n nonphysical nature of a person
NONBOOK, -S n book with little substance
NONBRAND adj not produced by a well-known company
NONCASH adj other than cash
NONCE, -S n present time or occasion
NONCLASS n lack of class
NONCLING adj not liable to stick
NONCOLA, -S n soft drink other than cola
NONCOLOR same as > noncolour
NONCOM, -S n person not involved in combat
NONCORE adj not central or essential
NONCOUNT adj not capable of being counted
NONCRIME n incident that is not a crime
NONDAIRY adj not containing dairy products**

N

NONDANCE n series of movements that do not constitute a dance

NONDRIP adj (of paint) specially formulated to minimize dripping during application

NONDRUG adj not involving the use of drugs

NONE pron not any

NONEGO, -S n everything that is outside one's conscious self

NONELECT n person not chosen

NONELITE adj not elite

NONEMPTY adj mathematical term

NONENTRY n failure to enter

NONEQUAL adj not equal ▷ n person who is not the equal of another person

NONES n (in the Roman calendar) the ninth day before the ides of each month

NONESUCH n matchless person or thing

NONET, -S n piece of music composed for a group of nine instruments

NONETTE, -S same as ▶ nonet

NONETTO, NONETTI, -S same as ▶ nonet

NONEVENT n disappointing or insignificant occurrence

NONFACT, -S n event or thing not provable

NONFAN, -S n person who is not a fan

NONFARM adj not connected with a farm

NONFAT adj fat free

NONFATAL adj not resulting in or capable of causing death

NONFATTY adj not fatty

NONFINAL adj not final

NONFLUID adj not fluid ▷ n something that is not a fluid

NONFOCAL adj not focal

NONFOOD, -S n item that is not food ▷ adj relating to items other than food

NONFUEL, -S adj not relating to fuel ▷ n energy not used for generating heat, power, or electricity

NONG, -S n stupid or incompetent person

NONGAME adj not pursued for competitive sport purposes

NONGAY, -S n person who is not gay

NONGLARE adj not causing glare ▷ n any of various nonglare materials

NONGREEN adj not green

NONGS ▶ nong

NONGUEST n person who is not a guest

NONGUILT n state of being innocent

NONHARDY adj fragile

NONHEME adj of dietary iron, obtained from vegetable foods

NONHERO n person who is not a hero

NONHOME adj not of the home

NONHUMAN n something not human

NONI, -S n tree of SE Asia and the Pacific islands

NONIDEAL adj not ideal

NONIMAGE n person who is not a celebrity

NONINERT adj not inert

NONIONIC adj not ionic

NONIRON adj not requiring ironing

NONIS ▶ noni

NONISSUE n matter of little importance

NONJUROR n person who refuses to take an oath, as of allegiance

NONJURY n trial without a jury

NONLABOR same as > nonlabour

NONLEAFY adj not leafy

NONLEGAL adj not legal

NONLEVEL adj not level

NONLIFE, NONLIVES n matter which is not living

NONLOCAL adj not of, affecting, or confined to a limited area or part ▷ n person who is not local to an area

NONLOYAL adj not loyal

NONLYRIC adj without lyrics

NONMAJOR n student who is not majoring in a specified subject

NONMAN, NONMEN n being that is not a man

NONMEAT, -S n substance that does not contain meat ▷ adj not containing meat

NONMEN ▶ nonman

NONMETAL n chemical element that forms acidic oxides and is a poor conductor of heat and electricity

NONMETRO adj not metropolitan

NONMODAL adj not modal

NONMONEY adj not involving money

NONMORAL adj not involving morality

NONMUSIC n (unpleasant) noise

NONNASAL adj not nasal

NONNAVAL adj not belonging to the navy

NONNEWS adj not concerned with news

NONNIES ▶ nonny

NONNOBLE adj not noble

NONNOVEL n literary work that is not a novel

NONNY, NONNIES n meaningless word

NONOBESE adj not obese

NONOHMIC adj not having electrical resistance

NONOILY adj not oily

NONORAL adj not oral

NONOWNER n person who is not an owner

NONPAGAN n person who is not a pagan

NONPAID adj without payment

NONPAPAL adj not of the pope

NONPAR adj nonparticipating

NONPARTY adj not connected with a political party

NONPAST, -S n grammatical term

NONPEAK, -S n period of low demand

NONPLAY, -S n social behaviour that is not classed as play

NONPLUS vb put at a loss ▷ n state of utter perplexity prohibiting action or speech

NONPOINT adj without a specific site

NONPOLAR adj not polar

NONPOOR, -S adj not poor ▷ n person who is not poor

NONPRINT adj published in a format other than print on paper

NONPROS vb enter a judgment of non prosequitur

NONQUOTA adj not included in a quota

NONRATED adj not rated

NONRIGID adj not rigid

NONRIVAL n person or thing not competing for success

NONROYAL adj not royal ▷ n person who is not a member of a royal family

NONRUN adj (of tights) not laddering

NONRURAL adj not rural

NONSELF n foreign molecule in the body

NONSENSE n something that has or makes no sense ▷ interj exclamation of disagreement

NONSKED, -S n non-scheduled aeroplane

NONSKID adj designed to reduce skidding

NONSKIER n person who does not ski

NONSLIP adj designed to prevent slipping

NONSOLAR adj not related to the sun

NONSOLID n substance that is not a solid

NONSTICK adj coated with a substance that food will not stick to when cooked

NONSTOP, -S adv without a stop ▷ adj without a stop ▷ n nonstop flight

NONSTORY n story of little substance or importance

NONSTYLE n style that cannot be identified

NONSUCH same as ▶ nonesuch

NONSUGAR n substance that is not a sugar

NONSUIT, -S n order of a judge dismissing a suit ▷ vb order the dismissal of the suit of (a person)

NONTAX, -ES n tax that has little real effect

NONTIDAL adj not having a tide

NONTITLE adj without title

NONTONAL adj not written in a key

NONTONIC adj not tonic

NONTOXIC adj not poisonous

NONTRUMP adj not of the trump suit

NONTRUTH same as ▶ untruth

NONUNION adj (of a company) not employing trade union members ▷ n failure of broken bones or bone fragments to heal

NONUPLE, -S adj ninefold ▷ n ninefold number

NONUPLET n child born in a multiple birth of nine siblings

NONURBAN adj rural

NONUSE, -S n failure to use

NONUSER -S

NONUSING ▶ nonuse

NONVALID adj not valid

NONVIRAL adj not caused by a virus

NONVITAL adj not vital

NONVOCAL n music track without singing

NONVOTER n person who does not vote

NONWAGE adj not part of wages

NONWAR, -S n state of nonviolence

NONWHITE n person who is not White

NONWOODY adj not woody

NONWOOL adj not wool

NONWORD, -S n series of letters not recognised as a word

NONWORK, -S adj not involving work ▷ n part of life which does not involve work

NONWOVEN n material made by a method other than weaving

NONYL, -S n type of chemical

NONZERO adj not equal to zero

NOO n type of Japanese musical drama

NOOB, -S same as ▶ newbie

NOODGE, -D, -S, NOODGING vb annoy persistently

NOODLE, -D, -S n ribbon-like strip of pasta ▷ vb improvise aimlessly on a musical instrument

NOODLING n aimless musical improvisation

NOOGIE, -S n act of inflicting pain by rubbing head hard

NOOIT interj South African exclamation of surprise

NOOK, -S n corner or recess

NOOKIER ▶ nooky

NOOKIEST ▶ nooky

NOOKLIKE ▶ nook

NOOKS ▶ nook

NOOKY, NOOKIER, NOOKIEST adj resembling a nook

NOOLOGY n study of intuition

NOOMETRY n mind measurement

NOON, -ED, -S n twelve o'clock midday ▷ vb take a rest at noon

NOONDAY, -S adj happening at noon ▷ n middle of the day

NOONED ▶ noon

NOONER, -S n event taking place in the middle of the day

NOONING, -S n midday break for rest or food

NOONS ▶ noon

NOONTIDE same as ▶ noontime

NOONTIME n middle of the day

NOOP, -S n point of the elbow

NOOSE, -D, -S, NOOSING n loop in the end of a rope, tied with a slipknot ▷ vb catch in a noose

NOOSER, -S n person who uses a noose

NOOSES ▶ noose

NOOSING ▶ noose

NOPAL, -ES, -S n type of cactus

NOPALITO n small cactus

NOPALS ▶ nopal

NOPE interj no

NOPLACE same as ▶ nowhere

NOR prep and not

NORDIC adj of competitions in cross-country racing and ski-jumping

NORI, -S n edible seaweed

NORIA, -S n water wheel with buckets attached to its rim

NORIMON, -S n Japanese passenger vehicle

NORIS ▶ nori

NORITE, -S n variety of gabbro

NORITIC

NORLAND, -S n north part of a country on the earth

NORM, -S n standard that is regarded as normal

NORMA, -S n norm or standard

NORMAL, -S adj usual, regular, or typical ▷ n usual or regular state, degree or form

NORMALCY

NORMALLY adv as a rule

NORMALS ▶ normal

NORMAN, -S n post used for winding on a ship

NORMANDE n type of cattle

NORMANS ▶ norman

NORMAS ▶ norma

NORMED n mathematical term

NORMLESS adj without a norm

NORMS ▶ norm

NORSEL, -S vb fit with short lines for fastening hooks

NORTENA, -S same as ▶ norteno

NORTENO, -S n type of Mexican music

NORTH, -ED, -S n direction towards the North Pole, opposite south ▷ adj in

N

the north ▷ *adv* in, to, or towards the north ▷ *vb* move north

NORTHER, **-S** *n* wind or storm from the north ▷ *vb* move north

NORTHERN *adj* situated in or towards the north ▷ *n* person from the north

NORTHERS ▸ **norther**

NORTHING *n* movement or distance covered in a northerly direction

NORTHS ▸ **north**

NORWARD *same as* > **northward**

NORWARDS *same as* ▸ **norward**

NOS ▸ **no**

NOSE, **-D**, **-S** *n* organ of smell, used also in breathing ▷ *vb* move forward slowly and carefully

NOSEAN, **-S** *n* type of mineral

NOSEBAG, **-S** *n* bag containing feed fastened round a horse's head

NOSEBAND *n* part of a horse's bridle that goes around the nose

NOSED ▸ **nose**

NOSEDIVE, **NOSEDOVE** *vb* (of an aircraft) plunge suddenly with the nose pointing downwards

NOSEGAY, **-S** *n* small bunch of flowers

NOSELESS ▸ **nose**

NOSELIKE ▸ **nose**

NOSELITE *same as* ▸ **nosean**

NOSER, **-S** *n* strong headwind

NOSES ▸ **nose**

NOSEY, **-S** *adj* prying or inquisitive ▷ *n* nosey person

NOSH, **-ED**, **-ES**, **-ING** *n* food ▷ *vb* eat

NOSHER **-S**

NOSHERIE *same as* ▸ **noshery**

NOSHERS ▸ **nosher**

NOSHERY *n* restaurant or other place where food is served

NOSHES ▸ **nosh**

NOSHING ▸ **nosh**

NOSIER ▸ **nosy**

NOSIES ▸ **nosy**

NOSIEST ▸ **nosy**

NOSILY ▸ **nosy**

NOSINESS ▸ **nosy**

NOSING, **-S** *n* edge of a step or stair tread

NOSODE, **-S** *n* homeopathic remedy

NOSOLOGY *n* branch of medicine concerned with the classification of diseases

NOSTOC, **-S** *n* type of bacterium occurring in moist places

NOSTOS, **NOSTOI** *n* story of a return home

NOSTRIL, **-S** *n* one of the two openings at the end of the nose

NOSTRO *adj as in* **nostro account** bank account conducted by a British bank with a foreign bank

NOSTRUM, **-S** *n* quack medicine

NOSY, **NOSIER**, **NOSIES**, **NOSIEST** *adj* prying or inquisitive ▷ *n* inquisitive person

NOT *adv* expressing negation, refusal, or denial

NOTA ▸ **notum**

NOTABLE, **-S** *adj* worthy of being noted, remarkable ▷ *n* person of distinction

NOTABLY *adv* particularly or especially

NOTAEUM, **-S** *n* back of a bird's body

NOTAIRE, **-S** *n* (in France) notary

NOTAL ▸ **notum**

NOTANDUM, **NOTANDA** *n* notable fact

NOTARIAL ▸ **notary**

NOTARIES ▸ **notary**

NOTARISE *same as* ▸ **notarize**

NOTARIZE *vb* attest to or authenticate (a document, contract, etc), as a notary

NOTARY, **NOTARIES** *n* person authorized to witness legal documents

NOTATE, **-D**, **-S**, **NOTATING** *vb* write (esp music) in notation

NOTATION *n* representation of numbers or quantities in a system by a series of symbols

NOTATOR, **-S** *n* person who notates

NOTCH, **-ED**, **-ES**, **-ING** *n* V-shaped cut ▷ *vb* make a notch in

NOTCHEL, **-S** *vb* refuse to pay another person's debts

NOTCHER, **-S** *n* person who cuts notches

NOTCHES ▸ **notch**

NOTCHIER ▸ **notchy**

NOTCHING ▸ **notch**

NOTCHY, **NOTCHIER** *adj* (of a motor vehicle gear mechanism) requiring careful gear-changing

NOTE, **-S**, **NOTING** *n* short letter ▷ *vb* notice, pay attention to

NOTEBOOK *n* book for writing in

NOTECARD *n* greetings card with space to write note

NOTECASE *same as* ▸ **wallet**

NOTED *adj* well-known

NOTEDLY

NOTELESS ▸ **note**

NOTELET, **-S** *n* small folded card with a design on the front

NOTEPAD, **-S** *n* number of sheets of paper fastened together

NOTER, **-S** *n* person who takes notes

NOTES ▸ **note**

NOTHER *same as* ▸ **other**

NOTHING, **-S** *pron* not anything ▷ *adv* not at all ▷ *n* person or thing of no importance

NOTICE, **-D**, **-S**, **NOTICING** *n* observation or attention ▷ *vb* observe, become aware of

NOTICER, **-S** *n* person who takes notice

NOTICES ▸ **notice**

NOTICING ▸ **notice**

NOTIFIED ▸ **notify**

NOTIFIER ▸ **notify**

NOTIFY, **NOTIFIED**, **NOTIFIES** *vb* inform

NOTING ▸ **note**

NOTION, **-S** *n* idea or opinion

NOTIONAL *adj* speculative, imaginary, or unreal

NOTIONS ▸ **notion**

NOTITIA, **-E**, **-S** *n* register or list, esp of ecclesiastical districts

NOTORNIS *n* rare flightless rail of New Zealand

NOTOUR *adj* notorious

NOTT *same as* ▸ **not**

NOTTURNO, **NOTTURNI** *n* piece of music

NOTUM, **NOTA** *n* cuticular plate on an insect

NOUGAT, **-S** *n* chewy sweet containing nuts and fruit

NOUGHT, **-S** *n* figure o

NOUL, **-S** *same as* ▸ **noll**

NOULD *vb* would not

NOULDE *same as* ▸ **nould**

NOULE, **-S** *same as* ▸ **noll**

NOULS ▸ **noul**

NOUMENA ▸ **noumenon**

NOUMENAL ▸ **noumenon**

NOUMENON, NOUMENA n thing as it is in itself

NOUN, -S n word that refers to a person, place, or thing

NOUNAL

NOUNALLY

NOUNIER ▸ nouny

NOUNIEST ▸ nouny

NOUNLESS ▸ noun

NOUNS ▸ noun

NOUNY, NOUNIER, NOUNIEST adj nounlike

NOUP, -S n steep headland

NOURICE, -S n nurse

NOURISH vb feed

NOURSLE, -D, -S vb nurse

NOUS, -ES n common sense

NOUSELL, -S vb foster

NOUSES ▸ nous

NOUSLE, -D, -S, NOUSLING vb nuzzle

NOUT same as ▸ **nought**

NOUVEAU adj having recently become the thing specified

NOUVEAUX same as ▸ **nouveau**

NOUVELLE n long short story

NOVA, -E, -S n type of star

NOVALIA n newly reclaimed land

NOVALIKE adj resembling a nova

NOVAS ▸ nova

NOVATE, -S, NOVATING vb substitute one thing in place of another

NOVATED adj as in **novated lease** Australian system of employer-aided car purchase

NOVATES ▸ novate

NOVATING ▸ novate

NOVATION n substitution of a new obligation for an old one by mutual agreement

NOVEL, -S n long fictitious story in book form ▷ adj fresh, new, or original

NOVELDOM n realm of fiction

NOVELESE n style of writing characteristic of poor novels

NOVELISE same as ▸ **novelize**

NOVELISH adj resembling a novel

NOVELISM n innovation

NOVELIST n writer of novels

NOVELIZE vb convert (a true story, film, etc) into a novel

NOVELLA, -E, -S, NOVELLE n short novel

NOVELLY ▸ novel

NOVELS ▸ novel

NOVELTY n newness

NOVEMBER n code word for the letter N

NOVENA, -E, -S n set of prayers or services on nine consecutive days

NOVENARY n set of nine

NOVENAS ▸ novena

NOVERCAL adj stepmotherly

NOVERINT n writ

NOVICE, -S n beginner

NOVITY, NOVITIES n novelty

NOVUM, -S n game played with dice

NOW, -S adv at or for the present time

NOWADAYS adv in these times

NOWAY adv in no manner

NOWAYS same as ▸ **noway**

NOWCAST, -S n report on current weather conditions

NOWED adj knotted

NOWHENCE adv from no place

NOWHERE, -S adv not anywhere ▷ n nonexistent or insignificant place

NOWISE another word for ▸ **noway**

NOWL, -S n crown of the head

NOWN same as ▸ **own**

NOWNESS

NOWS ▸ now

NOWT, -S n nothing

NOWTIER ▸ nowty

NOWTIEST ▸ nowty

NOWTS ▸ nowt

NOWTY, NOWTIER, NOWTIEST adj bad-tempered

NOWY adj having a small projection at the centre (of a cross)

NOX, -ES n nitrogen oxide

> Meaning nitrogen oxide, this is another of those very useful short words containing X.

NOXAL adj relating to damage done by something belonging to another

NOXES ▸ nox

NOXIOUS adj poisonous or harmful

NOY, -ED, -ING, -S vb harass

NOYADE, -S n execution by drowning

NOYANCE, -S n nuisance

NOYAU, -S, -X n brandy-based liqueur

NOYED ▸ noy

NOYES, -ES archaic form of ▸ **noise**

NOYING ▸ noy

NOYOUS ▸ noy

NOYS ▸ noy

NOYSOME ▸ noy

NOZZER, -S n new recruit (in the Navy)

NOZZLE, -S n projecting spout through which fluid is discharged

NTH adj of an unspecified number

> A good word to remember for awkward situations on the board, as it's one of very few three-letter words that doesn't contain a vowel.

NU, -S n 13th letter in the Greek alphabet

NUANCE, -D, -S, NUANCING n subtle difference in colour, meaning, or tone ▷ vb give subtle differences to

NUB, -S n point or gist (of a story etc) ▷ vb hang from the gallows

NUBBED ▸ nub

NUBBIER ▸ nubby

NUBBIEST ▸ nubby

NUBBIN, -S n something small or undeveloped, esp a fruit or ear of corn

NUBBING, -S n act of hanging (a criminal)

NUBBINS ▸ nubbin

NUBBLE, -D, -S, NUBBLING n small lump ▷ vb dialect word for beat or pound using one's fists

NUBBLIER ▸ nubbly

NUBBLING ▸ nubble

NUBBLY, NUBBLIER ▸ **nubble**

NUBBY, NUBBIER, NUBBIEST adj having small lumps or protuberances

NUBECULA n small irregular galaxy near the S celestial pole

NUBIA, -S n fleecy scarf for the head, worn by women

NUBIFORM adj cloudlike

NUBILE adj (of a girl or woman) mature enough for marriage

NUBILITY

NUBILOSE same as ▸ **nubilous**

NUBILOUS adj cloudy

NUBS ▸ nub

NUBUCK, -S n type of leather with a velvety finish

NUCELLAR ▸ nucellus

NUCELLUS, NUCELLI n central part of a plant ovule containing the embryo sac

NUCHA, -E n back or nape of the neck

NUCHAL, -S n scale on a reptile's neck

N

NUCLEAL ▶ nucleus

NUCLEAR adj of nuclear weapons or energy

NUCLEASE n any of a group of enzymes that hydrolyse nucleic acids to simple nucleotides

NUCLEATE adj having a nucleus ▷ vb form a nucleus

NUCLEI ▶ nucleus

NUCLEIC adj as in **nucleic acid** type of complex compound that is a vital constituent of living cells

NUCLEIDE same as ▶ **nuclide**

NUCLEIN, -S n protein that occurs in the nuclei of living cells

NUCLEOID n component of a bacterium

NUCLEOLE variant of > nucleolus

NUCLEOLI > nucleolus

NUCLEON, -S n proton or neutron

NUCLEUS, NUCLEI n centre, esp of an atom or cell

NUCLIDE, -S n species of atom characterized by its atomic number and its mass number

NUCLIDIC

NUCULE, -S n small seed

NUDATION n act of removing a covering

NUDDY, NUDDIES n as in **in the nuddy** in the nude

NUDE, -R, -S, -ST adj naked ▷ n naked figure in painting, sculpture, or photography

NUDELY

NUDENESS

NUDGE, -D, -S, NUDGING vb push gently, esp with the elbow ▷ n gentle push or touch

NUDGER -S

NUDICAUL adj (of plants) having stems without leaves

NUDISM, -S n practice of not wearing clothes

NUDIST, -S

NUDITY, NUDITIES n state or fact of being nude

NUDNICK, -S same as ▶ **nudnik**

NUDNIK, -S n boring person

NUDZH, -ED, -ES, -ING same as ▶ **nudge**

NUFF, -S slang form of ▶ **enough**

NUFFIN, -S slang form of ▶ **nothing**

NUFFS ▶ nuff

NUG, -S n lump of wood sawn from a log

NUGAE n jests

NUGATORY adj of little value

NUGGAR, -S n sailing boat used to carry cargo on the Nile

NUGGET, -ED, -S n small lump of gold in its natural state ▷ vb polish footwear

NUGGETY adj of or resembling a nugget

NUGS ▶ nug

NUISANCE n something or someone that causes annoyance or bother

NUKE, -D, -S, NUKING vb attack with nuclear weapons ▷ n nuclear weapon

NULL, -S adj without legal force ▷ vb make negative

NULLA, -S same as ▶ **nullah**

NULLAH, -S n stream or drain

NULLAS ▶ nulla

NULLED ▶ null

NULLIFY vb make ineffective

NULLING, -S n knurling

NULLITY n state of being null

NULLNESS ▶ null

NULLS ▶ null

NUMB, -ED, -EST, -ING, -S adj without feeling, as through cold, shock, or fear ▷ vb make numb

NUMBAT, -S n small Australian marsupial

NUMBED ▶ numb

NUMBER, -ED, -S n sum or quantity ▷ vb count

NUMBERER n person who numbers

NUMBERS ▶ number

NUMBEST ▶ numb

NUMBFISH n any of several electric ray fish

NUMBHEAD n insulting word for a stupid person

NUMBING ▶ numb

NUMBLES n animal organs, cooked for food

NUMBLY ▶ numb

NUMBNESS ▶ numb

NUMBNUT n insulting word for a stupid person

NUMBNUTS n insulting word for a stupid person

NUMBS ▶ numb

NUMCHUCK same as ▶ **nunchaku**

NUMDAH, -S n coarse felt made esp in India

NUMEN n deity or spirit presiding over a thing or place

NUMERACY n ability to use numbers, esp in arithmetical operations

NUMERAL, -S n word or symbol used to express a sum or quantity ▷ adj of, consisting of, or denoting a number

NUMERARY adj of or relating to numbers

NUMERATE adj able to do basic arithmetic ▷ vb read (a numerical expression)

NUMERIC, -S n number or numeral

NUMEROUS adj existing or happening in large numbers

NUMINA plural of ▶ **numen**

NUMINOUS adj arousing religious or spiritual emotions ▷ n something that arouses religious or spiritual emotions

NUMMARY adj of or relating to coins

NUMMIER ▶ nummy

NUMMIEST ▶ nummy

NUMMULAR adj shaped like a coin

NUMMY, NUMMIER, NUMMIEST adj delicious

NUMNAH, -S same as ▶ **numdah**

NUMPKIN, -S n stupid person

NUMPTY, NUMPTIES n stupid person

NUMSKULL same as > **numbskull**

NUN, -S n female member of a religious order

NUNATAK, -S n isolated mountain peak projecting through glacial ice

NUNCHAKU n rice flail used as a weapon

NUNCHEON n light snack

NUNCHUK, -S n type of weapon used in martial arts

NUNCIO, -S n pope's ambassador

NUNCLE, -S archaic or dialect word for ▶ **uncle**

NUNDINAL ▶ nundine

NUNDINE, -S n market day

NUNHOOD, -S n condition, practice, or character of a nun

NUNLIKE ▶ nun

NUNNERY n convent

NUNNISH ▶ nun

NUNNY n as in **nunny bag** small sealskin haversack used in Canada

NUNS ▶ nun

NUNSHIP, -S ▶ nun

NUPTIAL adj relating to marriage

NUPTIALS pl n wedding

NUR, -S n wooden ball

NURAGHE, NURAGHI *n* Sardinian round tower
NURAGHIC
NURD, -S *same as* ▶ **nerd**
NURDIER ▶ **nurdy**
NURDIEST ▶ **nurdy**
NURDISH ▶ **nerd**
NURDLE, -D, -S, NURDLING *vb* score runs in cricket by soft deflections
NURDS ▶ **nurd**
NURDY, NURDIER, NURDIEST ▶ **nurd**
NURHAG, -S *n* Sardinian round tower
NURL, -ED, -ING, -S *variant of* ▶ **knurl**
NURR, -S *n* wooden ball
NURS ▶ **nur**
NURSE, -D, -S *n* person employed to look after sick people ▷ *vb* look after (a sick person)
NURSER, -S *n* person who treats something carefully
NURSERY *n* room where children sleep or play
NURSES ▶ **nurse**
NURSING, -S *n* practice or profession of caring for the sick and injured
NURSLE, -D, -S *vb* nuzzle
NURSLING *n* child or young animal that is being suckled, nursed, or fostered
NURTURAL ▶ **nurture**
NURTURE, -D, -S *n* act or process of promoting development ▷ *vb* promote or encourage development
NURTURER
NUS ▶ **nu**
NUT, -S, -TED *n* fruit consisting of a hard shell and a kernel ▷ *vb* gather nuts
NUTANT *adj* having the apex hanging down
NUTARIAN *n* person whose diet is based around nuts
NUTATE, -D, -S, NUTATING *vb* nod
NUTATION *n* periodic variation in the precession of the earth's axis
NUTBAR, -S *n* bar made from chopped nuts
NUTBROWN *adj* of a brownish colour, esp a reddish-brown

NUTCASE, -S *n* slang word for a foolish or crazy person
NUTGALL, -S *n* nut-shaped gall caused by gall wasps on the oak and other trees
NUTGRASS *n* type of plant
NUTHATCH *n* small songbird
NUTHIN *n* nothing
NUTJOB, -S *n* slang word for a foolish or crazy person
NUTLET, -S *n* portion of a fruit that fragments when mature
NUTLIKE ▶ **nut**
NUTLOAF *n* savoury loaf made from nuts
NUTMEAL, -S *n* type of grain
NUTMEAT, -S *n* kernel of a nut
NUTMEG, -S *n* spice made from the seed of a tropical tree ▷ *vb* kick or hit the ball between the legs of (an opposing player)
NUTMEGGY *adj* of or similar to nutmeg
NUTMEGS ▶ **nutmeg**
NUTPICK, -S *n* tool used to dig the meat from nuts
NUTRIA, -S *n* fur of the coypu
NUTRIENT *n* substance that provides nourishment ▷ *adj* providing nourishment
NUTS ▶ **nut**
NUTSEDGE *same as* ▶ **nutgrass**
NUTSHELL *n* shell around the kernel of a nut
NUTSIER ▶ **nutsy**
NUTSIEST ▶ **nutsy**
NUTSO, -S *n* slang word for a foolish or crazy person
NUTSY, NUTSIEST *adj* slang word for foolish or crazy
NUTTED ▶ **nut**
NUTTER, -S *n* slang word for a foolish or crazy person
NUTTERY *n* place where nut trees grow
NUTTIER ▶ **nutty**
NUTTIEST ▶ **nutty**
NUTTILY ▶ **nutty**
NUTTING, -S *n* act of gathering nuts
NUTTY, NUTTIER, NUTTIEST *adj* containing or resembling nuts
NUTWOOD, -S *n* any of various nut-bearing trees, such as walnut

NUZZER, -S *n* present given to a superior in India
NUZZLE, -D, -S, NUZZLING *vb* push or rub gently with the nose or snout
NUZZLER, -S *n* person or thing that nuzzles
NUZZLES ▶ **nuzzle**
NUZZLING ▶ **nuzzle**
NY, -S *same as* ▶ **nigh**
NYAFF, -ED, -ING, -S *n* small or contemptible person ▷ *vb* yelp like a small dog
NYAH *interj* interjection used to express contempt
NYALA, -S *n* spiral-horned southern African antelope
NYANZA, -S *n* (in E Africa) a lake
NYAS, -ES *n* young hawk
NYBBLE, -S *n* small byte
NYE, -D, -S, NYING *n* flock of pheasants ▷ *vb* near
NYLGHAI, -S *same as* ▶ **nilgai**
NYLGHAU, -S *same as* ▶ **nilgai**
NYLON *n* synthetic material used for clothing etc
NYLONED *adj* wearing nylons
NYLONS *pl n* stockings made of nylon
NYM *adj as in* **nym war** dispute about publishing material online under a pseudonym
NYMPH, -ED, -ING, -S *n* mythical spirit of nature, represented as a beautiful young woman ▷ *vb* fish with a particular type of fly on the hook
NYMPHA, -E *n* either one of the labia minora
NYMPHAEA *n* water lily
NYMPHAL ▶ **nymph**
NYMPHEAN ▶ **nymph**
NYMPHED ▶ **nymph**
NYMPHIC ▶ **nymph**
NYMPHING ▶ **nymph**
NYMPHISH ▶ **nymph**
NYMPHLY ▶ **nymph**
NYMPHS ▶ **nymph**
NYS ▶ **ny**
NYSSA, -S *n* type of tree
NYSTATIN *n* type of antibiotic obtained from a bacterium

N

Oo

With eight **O**s in the bag, you're likely to have at least one on your rack during a game. There are plenty of good two-letter words starting with **O**. It's worth knowing that **O** will form a two-letter word in front of every other vowel except **A**, as well as in front of **Y**. **O** also combines well with **X**, with **ox** (9 points) as the obvious starting point, and several words that refer to **oxygen** (17), including **oxo** (10) and **oxy** (13). Don't forget the short everyday words that begin with **O**. While **on** and **or** (2 each) won't earn you many points, they can be very helpful when you are trying to score in more than one direction at a time. **Of** and **oh** (5 each) can also prove very useful.

OAF, -S, OAVES *n* stupid or clumsy person

OAFISH

OAFISHLY

OAK, -S *n* deciduous forest tree

OAKED *adj* relating to wine that is stored for a time in oak barrels prior to bottling

OAKEN *adj* made of the wood of the oak

OAKER, -S *same as* ▶ **ochre**

OAKIER ▶ **oaky**

OAKIES ▶ **oaky**

OAKIEST ▶ **oaky**

OAKINESS *n* quality of being oaky

OAKLEAF *n* the leaf of the oak

OAKLIKE ▶ **oak**

OAKLING, -S *n* young oak

OAKMOSS *n* type of lichen

OAKS ▶ **oak**

OAKUM, -S *n* fibre obtained by unravelling old rope

OAKWOOD, -S *n* the wood of the oak

OAKY, OAKIER, OAKIES, OAKIEST *adj* hard like the wood of an oak ▷ *n* ice cream

OANSHAGH *n* foolish girl or woman

OAR, -ING, -S *n* pole with a broad blade, used for rowing a boat ▷ *vb* propel with oars

OARAGE, -S *n* use or number of oars

OARED *adj* equipped with oars

OARFISH *n* very long ribbonfish with long slender ventral fins

OARIER ▶ **oary**

OARIEST ▶ **oary**

OARING ▶ **oar**

OARLESS ▶ **oar**

OARLIKE ▶ **oar**

OARLOCK, -S *n* swivelling device that holds an oar in place

OARS ▶ **oar**

OARSMAN, OARSMEN *n* person who rows

OARWEED, -S *n* type of brown seaweed

OARY, OARIER, OARIEST *adj* of or like an oar

OASIS, OASES *n* fertile area in a desert

OAST, -S *n* oven for drying hops

OAT, -S *n* hard cereal grown as food

OATCAKE, -S *n* thin flat biscuit of oatmeal

OATEN *adj* made of oats or oat straw

OATER, -S *n* film about the American Wild West

OATH, -S *n* solemn promise, esp to be truthful in court

OATHABLE *adj* able to take an oath

OATHS ▶ **oath**

OATIER ▶ **oaty**

OATIEST ▶ **oaty**

OATLIKE ▶ **oat**

OATMEAL, -S *n* coarse flour made from oats ▷ *adj* pale brownish-cream

OATS ▶ **oat**

OATY, OATIER, OATIEST *adj* of, like, or containing oats

OAVES ▶ **oaf**

OB, -S *n* expression of opposition

OBA, -S *n* (in W Africa) a Yoruba chief or ruler

OBANG, -S *n* former Japanese coin

OBAS ▶ **oba**

OBCONIC *adj* shaped like a cone and attached at the pointed end

OBDURACY ▶ **obdurate**

OBDURATE *adj* hardhearted or stubborn ▷ *vb* make obdurate

OBDURE, -D, -S, OBDURING *vb* make obdurate

OBE, -S *n* ancient Laconian village

OBEAH, -ED, -ING, -S *vb* cast spell on

OBEAHISM

OBECHE, -S *n* African tree

OBEDIENT *adj* obeying or willing to obey

OBEISANT > **obeisance**

OBEISM, -S *n* belief in obeah

OBELI ▶ **obelus**

OBELIA, -S *n* type of jellyfish

OBELION *n* area of skull

OBELISE, -D, -S *same as* ▶ **obelize**

OBELISK, -S *n* stone column tapering to a pyramid at the top

OBELISM, -S *n* practice of marking passages in text

OBELIZE, -D, -S *vb* mark (a word or passage) with an obelus

OBELUS, OBELI *n* mark used to indicate spurious words or passages

OBENTO, -S n Japanese lunch box

OBES ▶ obe

OBESE, -R, -ST adj very fat
OBESELY
OBESITY

OBESOGEN n agent causing obesity

OBEY, -ED, -ING, -S vb carry out instructions or orders
OBEYABLE
OBEYER -S

OBI, -ED, -ING, -S n broad sash tied in a large flat bow at the back ▷ vb bewitch

OBIA, -S same as ▶ obeah

OBIED ▶ obi

OBIING ▶ obi

OBIISM, -S ▶ obi

OBIIT vb died

OBIS ▶ obi

OBIT, -S n memorial service

OBITAL adj of obits

OBITER adv by the way

OBITS ▶ obit

OBITUAL adj of obits

OBITUARY n announcement of someone's death, esp in a newspaper

OBJECT, -ED, -S n physical thing ▷ vb express disapproval
OBJECTOR

OBJET, -S n object

OBJURE, -D, -S, OBJURING vb put on oath

OBLAST, -I, -S n administrative division of the constituent republics of Russia

OBLATE, -S adj (of a sphere) flattened at the poles ▷ n person dedicated to a monastic or religious life
OBLATELY

OBLATION n religious offering
OBLATORY

OBLIGANT n person promising to pay a sum

OBLIGATE vb compel, constrain, or oblige morally or legally ▷ adj compelled, bound, or restricted

OBLIGATO, OBLIGATI same as > obbligato

OBLIGE, -D, -S vb compel (someone) morally or by law

OBLIGEE, -S n person in whose favour an obligation, contract, or bond is created

OBLIGER, -S ▶ oblige

OBLIGES ▶ oblige

OBLIGING adj ready to help other people

OBLIGOR, -S n person who binds himself by contract

OBLIQUE, -D, -R, -S adj slanting ▷ n symbol (/) ▷ vb take or have an oblique direction

OBLIQUID adj oblique

OBLIVION n state of being forgotten

OBLONG, -S adj having two long sides, two short sides, and four right angles ▷ n oblong figure
OBLONGLY

OBLOQUY n verbal abuse

OBO, -S n ship carrying oil and ore

OBOE, -S n double-reeded woodwind instrument
OBOIST -S

OBOL, -S same as ▶ obolus

OBOLARY adj very poor

OBOLE, -S n former weight unit in pharmacy

OBOLI ▶ obolus

OBOLS ▶ obol

OBOLUS, OBOLI n Greek unit of weight

OBOS ▶ obo

OBOVATE adj shaped like the longitudinal section of an egg

OBOVOID adj (of a fruit) egg-shaped with the narrower end at the base

OBS ▶ ob

OBSCENE, -R adj indecent

OBSCURE, -D, -R, -S adj not well known ▷ vb make (something) obscure

OBSEQUIE same as ▶ obsequy

OBSEQUY singular of > obsequies

OBSERVE, -D, -S vb see or notice

OBSERVER n person who observes, esp one who watches someone or something carefully

OBSERVES ▶ observe

OBSESS, -ED, -ES vb preoccupy (someone) compulsively
OBSESSOR

OBSIDIAN n dark glassy volcanic rock

OBSIGN, -ED, -S vb confirm

OBSOLETE adj no longer in use ▷ vb make obsolete

OBSTACLE n something that makes progress difficult

OBSTRUCT vb block with an obstacle

OBTAIN, -ED, -S vb acquire intentionally
OBTAINER

OBTECT adj (of a pupa) encased in a hardened secretion

OBTECTED same as ▶ obtect

OBTEMPER vb comply (with)

OBTEND, -ED, -S vb put forward

OBTEST, -ED, -S vb beg (someone) earnestly

OBTRUDE, -D, -S vb push oneself or one's ideas on others
OBTRUDER

OBTUND, -ED, -S vb deaden or dull

OBTURATE vb stop up (an opening, esp the breech of a gun)

OBTUSE, -R, -ST adj not sharp or pointed
OBTUSELY
OBTUSITY

OBVERSE, -S n opposite way of looking at an idea ▷ adj facing or turned towards the observer

OBVERT, -ED, -S vb deduce the obverse of (a proposition)

OBVIATE ▶ obviate

OBVIATE, -D, -S vb make unnecessary
OBVIATOR

OBVIOUS adj easy to see or understand, evident

OBVOLUTE adj (of leaves or petals in the bud) folded so that the margins overlap each other

OBVS adv obviously

OCA, -S n any of various South American herbaceous plants

OCARINA, -S n small oval wind instrument

OCAS ▶ oca

OCCAM, -S n computer programming language

OCCAMIES ▶ occamy

OCCAMS ▶ occam

OCCAMY, OCCAMIES n type of alloy

OCCASION n time at which a particular thing happens ▷ vb cause

OCCIDENT literary or formal word for ▶ west

OCCIES ▶ occy

OCCIPUT, OCCIPITA, -S n back of the head

OCCLUDE, -D, -S vb obstruct
OCCLUDER

OCCLUSAL > occlusion

OCCLUSOR n muscle for closing opening

OCCULT, -ED, -S adj relating to the supernatural ▷ vb

(of a celestial body) to hide (another celestial body) from view

OCCULTER n something that obscures

OCCULTLY ► occult

OCCULTS ► occult

OCCUPANT n person occupying a specified place

OCCUPATE same as ► occupy

OCCUPIED ► occupy

OCCUPIER n person who lives in a particular house, whether as owner or tenant

OCCUPY, OCCUPIED, OCCUPIES vb live or work in (a building)

OCCUR, -RED, -S vb happen

OCCY, OCCIES n as in **all over the occy** dialect expression meaning in every direction

OCEAN, -S n vast area of sea between continents

OCEANAUT n undersea explorer

OCEANIC adj of or relating to the ocean

OCEANID, -S n ocean nymph in Greek mythology

OCEANS ► ocean

OCELLAR ► ocellus

OCELLATE ► ocellus

OCELLUS, OCELLI n simple eye of insects and some other invertebrates

OCELOID adj of or like an ocelot

OCELOT, -S n American wild cat with a spotted coat

OCH interj expression of surprise, annoyance, or disagreement

OCHE, -S n (in darts) mark behind which a player must stand

OCHER, -ED, -ING, -S same as ► ochre

OCHERISH adj (US) resembling ochre

OCHEROID adj (US) of or like ochre

OCHEROUS ► ocher

OCHERS ► ocher

OCHERY ► ocher

OCHES ► oche

OCHIDORE n type of crab

OCHONE interj expression of sorrow or regret

OCHRE, -D, -S, OCHRING n brownish-yellow earth ▷ adj moderate yellow-orange to orange ▷ vb colour with ochre

OCHREA, -E, -S n cup-shaped structure that sheathes the stems of certain plants

OCHREATE same as ► ocreate

OCHRED ► ochre

OCHREOUS ► ochre

OCHRES ► ochre

OCHREY ► ochre

OCHRING ► ochre

OCHROID ► ochre

OCHROUS ► ochre

OCHRY ► ochre

OCICAT, -S n breed of cat with a spotted coat

OCKER, -S n uncultivated or boorish Australian

OCKERISM n Australian boorishness

OCKERS ► ocker

OCKODOLS pl n one's feet when wearing boots

OCOTILLO n cactus-like tree

OCREA, -E, -S same as ► ochrea

OCREATE adj possessing an ocrea

OCTA, -S same as ► okta

OCTAD, -S n group or series of eight

OCTADIC

OCTAGON, -S n geometric figure with eight sides

OCTAL, -S n number system with a base 8

OCTAN, -S n illness that occurs weekly

OCTANE, -S n hydrocarbon found in petrol

OCTANGLE same as ► octagon

OCTANOL, -S n alcohol containing eight carbon atoms

OCTANS ► octan

OCTANT, -S n any of the eight parts into which the three planes containing the Cartesian coordinate axes divide space

OCTANTAL

OCTAPLA, -S n book with eight texts

OCTAPODY n line of verse with eight metrical feet

OCTARCHY n government by eight rulers

OCTAS ► octa

OCTAVAL ► octave

OCTAVE, -S n (interval between the first and) eighth note of a scale ▷ adj consisting of eight parts

OCTAVO, -S n book size in which the sheets are folded into eight leaves

OCTET, -S n group of eight performers

OCTETT, -S same as ► octet

OCTETTE, -S same as ► octet

OCTETTS ► octett

OCTOFID adj divided into eight

OCTONARY adj relating to or based on the number eight ▷ n stanza of eight lines

OCTOPI ► octopus

OCTOPOD, -S n type of mollusc ▷ adj of these molluscs

OCTOPOID adj of or like an octopus

OCTOPUS, OCTOPI n sea creature with a soft body and eight tentacles

OCTOPUSH n hockey-like game played underwater

OCTROI, -S n duty on various goods brought into certain European towns

OCTUOR, -S n octet

OCTUPLE, -D, -S n quantity or number eight times as great as another ▷ adj eight times as much or as many ▷ vb multiply by eight

OCTUPLET n one of eight offspring from one birth

OCTUPLEX n something made up of eight parts

OCTUPLY adv by eight times

OCTYL, -S n group of atoms

OCULAR, -S adj relating to the eyes or sight ▷ n lens in an optical instrument

OCULARLY

OCULATE adj possessing eyes

OCULATED same as ► oculate

OCULI ► oculus

OCULIST, -S n ophthalmologist

OCULUS, OCULI n round window

OD, -S n hypothetical force

ODA, -S n room or chamber

ODAH, -S same as ► oda

ODAL, -S same as ► udal

ODALLER -S

ODAS ► oda

ODD, -ER, -EST adj unusual

ODDBALL, -S n eccentric person ▷ adj strange or peculiar

ODDER ► odd

ODDEST ► odd

ODDISH ► odd

ODDITY, ODDITIES n odd person or thing

ODDLY ► odd

ODDMENT, -S n odd piece or thing

ODDNESS ▸ odd

ODDS pl n probability of something happening

ODDSMAN, ODDSMEN n umpire

ODE, -S n lyric poem, usu addressed to a particular subject

ODEA ▸ odeum

ODEON, -S same as ▸ **odeum**

ODES ▸ ode

ODEUM, ODEA, -S n ancient building for musical performances

ODIC ▸ od

ODIOUS adj offensive
ODIOUSLY

ODISM, -S ▸ od

ODIST, -S ▸ od

ODIUM, -S n widespread dislike

ODOGRAPH same as ▸ **odometer**

ODOMETER n device that records the number of miles that a bicycle or motor vehicle has travelled
ODOMETRY

ODONATA pl n insects of an order that includes dragonflies

ODONATE, -S n dragonfly or related insect

ODONTIC adj of teeth

ODONTIST n dentist

ODONTOID adj toothlike ▷ n bone in the spine

ODONTOMA n tumour near teeth

ODOR, -S same as ▸ **odour**

ODORANT, -S n something with a strong smell

ODORATE adj having a strong smell

ODORED same as ▸ **odoured**

ODORFUL same as ▸ **odourful**

ODORISE, -D, -S same as ▸ **odorize**

ODORISER same as ▸ **odorizer**

ODORISES ▸ odorise

ODORIZE, -D, -S vb give an odour to

ODORIZER n something that odorizes

ODORIZES ▸ odorize

ODORLESS ▸ odor

ODOROUS adj having or emitting a characteristic smell

ODORS ▸ odor

ODOUR, -S n particular smell

ODOURED adj having an odour

ODOURFUL adj full of odour

ODOURS ▸ odour

ODS ▸ od

ODSO n cry of surprise

ODYL, -S same as ▸ **od**

ODYLE, -S same as ▸ **od**

ODYLISM, -S ▸ odyl

ODYLS ▸ odyl

ODYSSEAN adj of or like an odyssey

ODYSSEY, -S n long eventful journey

ODZOOKS interj cry of surprise

OE, -S n grandchild

OECIST, -S n colony founder

OECOLOGY less common spelling of ▸ **ecology**

OEDEMA, -S, -TA n abnormal swelling

OEDIPAL adj relating to a complex whereby a male child wants to replace his father

OEDIPEAN same as ▸ **oedipal**

OEILLADE n suggestive glance

OENOLOGY n study of wine

OENOMEL, -S n drink made of wine and honey

OENOPHIL same as > **oenophile**

OERLIKON n type of cannon

OERSTED, -S n cgs unit of magnetic field strength

OES ▸ oe

OESTRAL ▸ oestrus

OESTRIN, -S obsolete term for > **oestrogen**

OESTRIOL n weak oestrogenic hormone secreted by the mammalian ovary

OESTRONE n weak oestrogenic hormone secreted by the mammalian ovary

OESTROUS ▸ oestrus

OESTRUAL adj relating to oestrus

OESTRUM, -S same as ▸ **oestrus**

OESTRUS n regularly occurring period of fertility in female mammals

OEUVRE, -S n work of art, literature, music, etc

OF prep belonging to

OFF, -ED, -S prep away from ▷ adv away ▷ adj not operating ▷ n side of the field to which the batsman's feet point ▷ vb take off

OFFA prep off

OFFAL, -S n edible organs of an animal, such as liver or kidneys

OFFBEAT, -S adj unusual or eccentric ▷ n any of the normally unaccented beats in a bar

OFFCAST, -S n cast-off

OFFCUT, -S n piece remaining after the required parts have been cut out

OFFED ▸ off

OFFENCE, -S n (cause of) hurt feelings or annoyance

OFFEND, -ED, -S vb hurt the feelings of, insult
OFFENDER

OFFENSE, -S same as ▸ **offence**

OFFER, -ED, -S vb present (something) for acceptance or rejection ▷ n something offered

OFFEREE, -S n person to whom an offer is made

OFFERER, -S ▸ offer

OFFERING n thing offered

OFFEROR, -S ▸ offer

OFFERS ▸ offer

OFFHAND adj casual, curt ▷ adv without preparation

OFFICE, -S n room or building where people work at desks

OFFICER, -S n person in authority in the armed services ▷ vb furnish with officers

OFFICES ▸ office

OFFICIAL adj of a position of authority ▷ n person who holds a position of authority

OFFIE, -S n off-licence

OFFING, -S n area of the sea visible from the shore

OFFISH adj aloof or distant in manner
OFFISHLY

OFFKEY adj out of tune

OFFLINE adj disconnected from a computer or the internet

OFFLOAD, -S vb pass responsibility to someone else

OFFPEAK adj relating to times outside periods of intensive use

OFFPRINT n separate reprint of an article that originally appeared in a larger publication ▷ vb reprint (an article taken from a larger publication) separately

OFFPUT, -S n act of putting off

O

OFFRAMP, -S n road allowing traffic to leave a motorway

OFFS ▶ off

OFFSCUM, -S n scum

OFFSET, -S vb cancel out ▷ n printing method

OFFSHOOT n something developed from something else

OFFSHORE adv away from or at some distance from the shore ▷ adj sited or conducted at sea ▷ n company operating abroad where the tax system is more advantageous than at home ▷ vb transfer (work) to another country where wages are lower

OFFSIDE, -S adv (positioned) illegally ahead of the ball ▷ n side of a vehicle nearest the centre of the road

OFFSIDER n partner or assistant

OFFSIDES ▶ offside

OFFSTAGE adv out of the view of the audience ▷ n something that happens offstage

OFFTAKE, -S n act of taking off

OFFTRACK adj not at a racetrack

OFFY same as ▶ offie

OFLAG, -S n prisoner-of-war camp for officers in World War II

OFT, -ER, -EST adv often

OFTEN, -ER, -EST adv frequently, much of the time

OFTER ▶ oft

OFTEST ▶ oft

OFTTIMES same as ▶ often

OGAM, -S same as ▶ ogham **OGAMIC**

OGDOAD, -S n group of eight

OGEE, -S n moulding having a cross section in the form of a letter S

OGEED adj (of an arch or moulding) having an ogee

OGEES ▶ ogee

OGGIN, -S n sea

OGHAM, -S n ancient writing system used by the Celts **OGHAMIC** **OGHAMIST**

OGIVAL ▶ ogive

OGIVE, -S n diagonal rib or groin of a Gothic vault

OGLE, -D, -S vb stare or gape at ▷ n flirtatious look **OGLER -S**

OGLING, -S ▶ ogle

OGMIC ▶ ogam

OGRE, -S n giant that eats human flesh

OGREISH

OGREISM -S

OGRESS, -ES ▶ ogre

OGRISH ▶ ogre

OGRISHLY ▶ ogre

OGRISM, -S ▶ ogre

OH, -ED, -ING, -S interj exclamation of surprise, pain, etc ▷ vb say oh

OHIA, -S n Hawaiian plant

OHING ▶ oh

OHM, -S n unit of electrical resistance

OHMAGE, -S n electrical resistance in ohms

OHMIC adj of or relating to a circuit element

OHMMETER n instrument for measuring electrical resistance

OHMS ▶ ohm

OHO n exclamation expressing surprise, exultation, or derision

OHONE same as ▶ ochone

OHS ▶ oh

OI, -S interj shout to attract attention ▷ n grey-faced petrel

OIDIA ▶ oidium

OIDIOID ▶ oidium

OIDIUM, OIDIA n type of fungal spore

OIK, -S n insulting word for person regarded as inferior because ignorant or lower-class

OIKIST, -S same as ▶ oecist

OIKS ▶ oik

OIL, -ED, -ING, -S n viscous liquid, insoluble in water and usu flammable ▷ vb lubricate (a machine) with oil

OILBIRD, -S n type of nocturnal gregarious cave-dwelling bird

OILCAMP, -S n camp for oilworkers

OILCAN, -S n container with a long nozzle for applying oil to machinery

OILCLOTH n waterproof material

OILCUP, -S n cup-shaped oil reservoir in a machine providing continuous lubrication for a bearing

OILED ▶ oil

OILER, -S n person, device, etc, that lubricates or supplies oil

OILERIES ▶ oilery

OILERS ▶ oiler

OILERY, OILERIES n oil business

OILFIELD n area containing oil reserves

OILFIRED adj using oil as fuel

OILGAS, -ES n gaseous mixture of hydrocarbons used as a fuel

OILHOLE, -S n hole for oil

OILIER ▶ oily

OILIEST ▶ oily

OILILY ▶ oily

OILINESS ▶ oily

OILING ▶ oil

OILLET, -S same as ▶ eyelet

OILMAN, OILMEN n person who owns or operates oil wells

OILNUT, -S n nut from which oil is extracted

OILPAN, -S n sump

OILPAPER n oiled paper

OILPROOF adj resistant to oil

OILS ▶ oil

OILSEED, -S n seed from which oil is extracted

OILSKIN, -S n (garment made from) waterproof material

OILSTONE n stone with a fine grain lubricated with oil and used for sharpening cutting tools

OILTIGHT adj not allowing oil through

OILWAY, -S n channel for oil

OILY, OILIER, OILIEST adj soaked or covered with oil

OINK, -ED, -ING, -S n grunt of a pig or an imitation of this ▷ interj imitation or representation of the grunt of a pig ▷ vb make noise of pig

OINOLOGY same as ▶ oenology

OINOMEL, -S same as ▶ oenomel

OINT, -ED, -ING, -S vb anoint

OINTMENT n greasy substance used for healing skin or as a cosmetic

OINTS ▶ oint

OIS ▶ oi

OITICICA n South American tree

OJIME, -S n Japanese bead used to secure cords

OKA, -S n unit of weight used in Turkey

OKAPI, -S n African animal related to the giraffe but with a shorter neck

OKAS ▶ oka

OKAY, -ED, -ING, -S adj satisfactory ▷ vb approve or endorse ▷ n approval or agreement ▷ *interj* expression of approval

OKE, -S *same as* ▶ **oka**

OKEH, -S *variant of* ▶ **okay**

OKES ▶ **oke**

OKEYDOKE *variant of* ▶ **okay**

OKIMONO, -S *n* Japanese ornamental item

OKRA, -S *n* tropical plant with edible green pods

OKTA, -S *n* unit used in meteorology to measure cloud cover

OLD, -EST, -S *adj* having lived or existed for a long time ▷ *n* earlier or past time

OLDE *adj* old-world or quaint, used facetiously

OLDEN, -ED, -ING, -S *adj* old ▷ *vb* grow old

OLDER *adj* having lived or existed longer

OLDEST ▶ **old**

OLDIE, -S *n* old but popular song or film

OLDISH ▶ **old**

OLDNESS ▶ **old**

OLDS ▶ **old**

OLDSQUAW *n* type of long-tailed sea duck

OLDSTER, -S *n* older person

OLDSTYLE *n* printing type style

OLDWIFE, OLDWIVES *n* any of various fishes, esp the menhaden or the alewife

OLDY *same as* ▶ **oldie**

OLE, -S *interj* exclamation of approval or encouragement customary at bullfights ▷ *n* cry of olé

OLEA ▶ **oleum**

OLEANDER *n* Mediterranean flowering evergreen shrub

OLEARIA, -S *n* daisy bush

OLEASTER *n* type of shrub with silver-white twigs and yellow flowers

OLEATE, -S *n* any salt or ester of oleic acid

OLEFIANT *adj* forming oil

OLEFIN, -S *same as* ▶ **olefine**

OLEFINE *n* another name for ▶ **alkene**

OLEFINIC

OLEFINS ▶ **olefin**

OLEIC *adj as in* **oleic acid** colourless oily liquid used in making soap

OLEIN, -S *another name for* ▶ **triolein**

OLEINE, -S *same as* ▶ **olein**

OLEINS ▶ **olein**

OLENT *adj* having smell

OLEO, -S *n as in* **oleo oil** oil extracted from beef fat

OLES ▶ **ole**

OLESTRA, -S *n* trademark term for an artificial fat

OLEUM, OLEA, -S *n* type of sulphuric acid

OLFACT, -ED, -S *vb* smell something

OLIBANUM *n* frankincense

OLICOOK, -S *n* doughnut

OLID *adj* foul-smelling

OLIGARCH *n* member of an oligarchy

OLIGEMIA *same as* ▷ **oligaemia**

OLIGEMIC ▷ **oligaemia**

OLIGIST, -S *n* type of iron ore

OLIGOMER *n* compound of relatively low molecular weight containing up to five monomer units

OLIGURIA *n* excretion of an abnormally small volume of urine

OLIGURIC *adj* relating to oliguria

OLINGO, -S *n* South American mammal

OLIO, -S *n* dish of many different ingredients

OLIPHANT *archaic variant of* ▶ **elephant**

OLITORY *n* kitchen garden

OLIVARY *adj* shaped like an olive

OLIVE, -S *n* small green or black fruit used as food or pressed for its oil ▷ *adj* greyish-green

OLIVER, -S *n as in* **Bath oliver** type of unsweetened biscuit

OLIVES ▶ **olive**

OLIVET, -S *n* button shaped like olive

OLIVINE, -S *n* olive-green mineral of the olivine group

OLIVINIC *adj* containing olivine

OLLA, -S *n* cooking pot

OLLAMH, -S *n* old Irish term for a wise man

OLLAS ▶ **olla**

OLLAV, -S *same as* ▶ **ollamh**

OLLER, -S *n* waste ground

OLLIE, -D, -ING, -S *n* type of skateboarding jump ▷ *vb* perform an ollie

OLM, -S *n* pale blind eel-like salamander

OLOGIES ▶ **ology**

OLOGIST, -S *n* scientist

OLOGOAN, -S *vb* complain loudly without reason

OLOGY, OLOGIES *n* science or other branch of knowledge

OLOROSO, -S *n* golden-coloured sweet sherry

OLPE, OLPAE, -S *n* ancient Greek jug

OLYCOOK, -S *same as* ▶ **olykoek**

OLYKOEK, -S *n* American type of doughnut

OLYMPIAD *n* staging of the modern Olympic Games

OLYMPICS *pl n* modern revival of the ancient Greek games, featuring sporting contests

OM, -S *n* sacred syllable in Hinduism

OMA, -S *n* grandmother

OMADHAUN *n* foolish man or boy

OMAS ▶ **oma**

OMASA ▶ **omasum**

OMASAL ▶ **omasum**

OMASUM, OMASA *n* compartment in the stomach of a ruminant animal

OMBER, -S *same as* ▶ **ombre**

OMBRE, -S *n* 18th-century card game

OMBRELLA *old form of* ▶ **umbrella**

OMBRES ▶ **ombre**

OMBU, -S *n* South American tree

OMEGA, -S *n* last letter in the Greek alphabet

OMELET, -S *same as* ▶ **omelette**

OMELETTE *n* dish of eggs beaten and fried

OMEN, -ED, -ING, -S *n* happening or object thought to foretell success or misfortune ▷ *vb* portend

OMENTA ▶ **omentum**

OMENTAL ▶ **omentum**

OMENTUM, OMENTA, -S *n* double fold of the peritoneum

OMER, -S *n* ancient Hebrew unit of dry measure

OMERTA, -S *n* conspiracy of silence

OMICRON, -S *n* 15th letter in the Greek alphabet

OMIKRON, -S *same as* ▶ **omicron**

OMINOUS *adj* worrying, seeming to foretell misfortune

OMISSION *n* something that has been left out or passed over

OMISSIVE

OMIT, -S, -TED, -TING *vb* leave out

OMITTER -S

O

OMLAH, -S n staff team in India

OMMATEUM, OMMATEA n insect eye

OMNEITY n state of being all

OMNIANA n miscellaneous collection

OMNIARCH n ruler of everything

OMNIBUS n several books or TV or radio programmes made into one ▷ adj consisting of or dealing with several different things at once

OMNIETY same as ▸ omneity

OMNIFIC adj creating all things

OMNIFIED ▸ omnify

OMNIFIES ▸ omnify

OMNIFORM adj of all forms

OMNIFY, OMNIFIED, OMNIFIES vb make something universal

OMNIMODE adj of all functions

OMNIUM, -S n total value

OMNIVORA n group of omnivorous mammals

OMNIVORE n omnivorous animal

OMNIVORY n state of being omnivorous

OMOHYOID n muscle in shoulder

OMOPHAGY same as ▸ omophagia

OMOPLATE n shoulder blade

OMOV, -S n voting system in which each voter has one vote to cast

OMPHALI ▸ omphalos

OMPHALIC ▸ omphalos

OMPHALOS, OMPHALI, OMPHALOI n (in the ancient world) a sacred conical object, esp a stone

OMRAH, -S n Muslim noble

OMS ▸ om

ON, -NED, -NING, -S prep indicating position above, attachment, closeness, etc ▷ adv in operation ▷ adj operating ▷ n side of the field on which the batsman stands ▷ vb go on

ONAGER, -S, ONAGRI n wild ass of Persia

ONBEAT, -S n first and third beats in a bar of four-four time

ONBOARD adj on a ship or other craft

ONCE, -S adv on one occasion ▷ n one occasion

ONCER, -S n (formerly) a one-pound note

ONCES ▸ once

ONCET dialect form of ▸ once

ONCIDIUM n American orchid

ONCOGEN, -S n substance causing tumours to form

ONCOGENE n gene that can cause cancer when abnormally activated

ONCOGENS ▸ oncogen

ONCOLOGY n branch of medicine concerned with the study, classification, and treatment of tumours

ONCOME, -S n act of coming on

ONCOMICE ▸ oncomouse

ONCOMING adj approaching from the front ▷ n approach or onset

ONCOST, -S same as ▸ overheads

ONCOTOMY n surgical cutting of a tumour

ONCUS same as ▸ onkus

ONDATRA, -S same as ▸ musquash

ONDINE, -S same as ▸ undine

ONDING, -S Scots word for ▸ onset

ONDOGRAM n record made by ondograph

ONE, -S adj single, lone ▷ n number or figure 1 ▷ pron any person

ONEFOLD adj simple

ONEIRIC adj of or relating to dreams

ONELY same as ▸ only

ONENESS n unity

ONER, -S n single continuous action

ONERIER ▸ onery

ONERIEST ▸ onery

ONEROUS adj (of a task) difficult to carry out

ONERS ▸ oner

ONERY, ONERIER, ONERIEST same as ▸ ornery

ONES ▸ one

ONESELF pron reflexive form of one

ONESIE, -S n one-piece garment combining a top with trousers

ONETIME adj at some time in the past

ONEYER, -S old form of ▸ one

ONEYRE, -S same as ▸ oneyer

ONFALL, -S n attack or onset

ONFLOW, -S n flowing on

ONGAONGA n New Zealand nettle with a severe or fatal sting

ONGOING adj in progress, continuing

ONGOINGS pl n things that are happening

ONIE variant spelling of ▸ ony

ONION, -ED, -ING, -S n strongly flavoured edible bulb ▷ vb add onion to

ONIONIER ▸ oniony

ONIONING ▸ onion

ONIONS ▸ onion

ONIONY, ONIONIER ▸ onion

ONIRIC same as ▸ oneiric

ONISCOID adj of or like woodlice

ONIUM, -S n as in **onium compound** type of chemical salt

ONKUS adj bad

ONLAY, -S n artificial veneer for a tooth

ONLIEST same as ▸ only

ONLINE adj connected to a computer or the internet

ONLINER, -S n person who uses the internet regularly

ONLOAD, -ED, -S vb load files on to a computer

ONLOOKER n person who watches without taking part

ONLY adj alone of its kind ▷ adv exclusively

ONNED ▸ on

ONNING ▸ on

ONO, -S n Hawaiian fish

ONOMAST, -S n person who studies proper names

ONOS ▸ ono

ONRUSH, -ES n forceful forward rush or flow

ONS ▸ on

ONSCREEN adj appearing on screen

ONSET, -S n beginning

ONSETTER n attacker

ONSHORE adv towards the land

ONSIDE, -S adv (of a player in various sports) in a legal position ▷ adj taking one's part or side ▷ n part of cricket field where a batsman stands

ONST same as ▸ once

ONSTAGE adj visible by audience

ONSTEAD, -S Scots word for ▸ farmstead

ONSTREAM adj in operation

ONTIC adj having real existence

ONTO prep a position on

ONTOGENY n entire sequence of events involved in the development of an individual organism

ONTOLOGY n branch of philosophy concerned with existence

ONUS, -ES n responsibility or burden

ONWARD same as ► onwards

ONWARDLY

ONWARDS adv at or towards a point or position ahead

ONY Scots word for ► any

ONYCHA, -S n part of mollusc

ONYCHIA, -S n inflammation of the nails or claws of animals

ONYCHITE n type of stone

ONYCHIUM n part of insect foot

ONYMOUS adj (of a book) bearing its author's name

ONYX, -ES n type of quartz with coloured layers

OO, -S Scots word for ► wool

OOBIT, -S n hairy caterpillar

OOCYST, -S n type of zygote

OOCYTE, -S n immature female germ cell that gives rise to an ovum

OODLES pl n great quantities

OODLINS same as ► oodles

OOF, -S n money

OOFIER ► oofy

OOFIEST ► oofy

OOFS ► oof

OOFTISH n money

OOFY, OOFIER, OOFIEST ► oof

OOGAMETE n female gamete

OOGAMIES ► oogamy

OOGAMOUS ► oogamy

OOGAMY, OOGAMIES n type of reproduction

OOGENY, OOGENIES same as > oogenesis

OOGONIA ► oogonium

OOGONIAL ► oogonium

OOGONIUM, OOGONIA n immature female germ cell forming oocytes by repeated divisions

OOH, -ED, -S interj exclamation of surprise, pleasure, pain, etc ▷ vb say ooh

OOHING, -S n act of exclaiming 'ooh'

OOHS ► ooh

OOIDAL adj shaped like egg

OOLACHAN same as ► eulachon

OOLAKAN, -S same as ► eulachon

OOLICHAN n north Pacific candlefish

OOLITE, -S n limestone made up of tiny grains of calcium carbonate

OOLITH, -S n tiny spherical grain of sedimentary rock

OOLITIC ► oolite

OOLOGIC ► oology

OOLOGIES ► oology

OOLOGIST ► oology

OOLOGY, OOLOGIES n study of birds' eggs

OOLONG, -S n kind of dark tea

OOM, -S n title of respect used to refer to an elderly man

OOMIAC, -S same as ► umiak

OOMIACK, -S same as ► umiak

OOMIACS ► oomiac

OOMIAK, -S same as ► umiak

OOMPAH, -ED, -S n representation of the sound made by a deep brass instrument ▷ vb make the noise of a brass instrument

OOMPH, -S n enthusiasm, vigour, or energy

OOMS ► oom

OOMYCETE n organism formerly classified as fungi

OON, -S Scots word for ► oven

OONT, -S n camel

OOP, -ED, -ING vb Scots word meaning to bind

OOPHORON n ovary

OOPHYTE, -S n gametophyte in mosses, liverworts, and ferns

OOPHYTIC

OOPING ► oop

OOPS interj exclamation of surprise or apology

OOR Scots form of ► our

OORALI, -S n member of Indian people

OORIAL, -S n Himalayan sheep

OORIE, -R, -ST adj Scots word meaning shabby

This Scots word is one of the classic 5-letter vowel dumps. It has almost equally useful variants **ourie** and **owrie**.

OOS ► oo

OOSE, -S n dust

OOSIER ► oosy

OOSIEST ► oosy

OOSPERM, -S n fertilized ovum

OOSPHERE n large female gamete produced in the oogonia of algae and fungi

OOSPORE, -S n thick-walled spore developed from a fertilized oosphere

OOSPORIC

OOSY, OOSIER, OOSIEST ► oose

OOT, -S Scots word for ► out

OOTHECA, -E n capsule containing eggs

OOTHECAL

OOTID, -S n immature female gamete that develops into an ovum

OOTS ► oot

OOZE, -D, -S, OOZING vb flow slowly ▷ n sluggish flow

OOZIER ► oozy

OOZIEST ► oozy

OOZILY ► oozy

OOZINESS ► oozy

OOZING ► ooze

OOZY, OOZIER, OOZIEST adj moist or dripping

OP, -S n operation

OPA, -S n grandfather

OPACIFY vb become or make opaque

OPACITY n state or quality of being opaque

OPACOUS same as ► opaque

OPAH, -S n large soft-finned deep-sea fish

OPAL, -S n iridescent precious stone

OPALED adj made like opal

OPALESCE vb exhibit a milky iridescence

OPALINE, -S adj opalescent ▷ n opaque or semiopaque whitish glass

OPALISED same as ► opalized

OPALIZED adj made into opal

OPALS ► opal

OPAQUE, -D, -R, -S, -ST, OPAQUING adj not able to be seen through, not transparent ▷ n opaque pigment used to block out particular areas on a negative ▷ vb make opaque

OPAQUELY

OPAS ► opa

OPCODE, -S n computer code containing operating instructions

OPE, -D, -S, OPING archaic or poetic word for ► open

OPEN, -ED, -EST, -S adj not closed ▷ vb (cause to) become open ▷ n competition which all may enter

OPENABLE

O

OPENCAST n as in **opencast mining** mining by excavating from the surface

OPENED ▶ open

OPENER, -S n tool for opening cans and bottles

OPENEST ▶ open

OPENING, -S n beginning ▷ adj first

OPENLY ▶ open

OPENNESS ▶ open

OPENS ▶ open

OPENSIDE n in rugby, flanker who plays on the open side of the scrum

OPENWORK n ornamental work, as of metal or embroidery, having a pattern of openings or holes

OPEPE, -S n African tree

OPERA, -S n drama in which the text is sung to an orchestral accompaniment

OPERABLE adj capable of being treated by a surgical operation

OPERABLY

OPERAND, -S n quantity, variable, or function upon which an operation is performed

OPERANT, -S adj producing effects ▷ n person or thing that operates

OPERAS ▶ opera

OPERATE, -D, -S vb (cause to) work

OPERATIC adj of or relating to opera

OPERATOR n person who operates a machine or instrument

OPERCELE same as ▶ opercule

OPERCULA > operculum

OPERCULE n gill cover

OPERETTA n light-hearted comic opera

OPERON, -S n group of adjacent genes in bacteria

OPEROSE adj laborious

OPES ▶ ope

OPHIDIAN n reptile of the suborder which comprises the snakes

OPHITE, -S n any of several greenish mottled rocks

OPHITIC adj having small elongated feldspar crystals enclosed

OPHIURA n sea creature like a starfish

OPHIURAN same as ▶ ophiura

OPHIURAS ▶ ophiura

OPHIURID same as ▶ ophiura

OPIATE, -D, -S, OPIATING n narcotic drug containing opium ▷ adj containing or consisting of opium ▷ vb treat with an opiate

OPIFICER n craftsman

OPINABLE adj thinkable

OPINE, -D, -S, OPINING vb express an opinion

OPING ▶ ope

OPINICUS n mythical monster

OPINING ▶ opine

OPINION, -S n personal belief or judgment

OPIOID, -S n substance that resembles morphine

OPIUM, -S n addictive narcotic drug made from poppy seeds

OPIUMISM n addiction to opium

OPIUMS ▶ opium

OPOPANAX n medical resin from plant

OPORICE, -S n former medicine made from fruit

OPOSSUM, -S n small marsupial of America or Australasia

OPPIDAN, -S adj of a town ▷ n person living in a town

OPPILANT ▶ oppilate

OPPILATE vb block (the pores, bowels, etc)

OPPO, -S n counterpart in another organization

OPPONENS n muscle of the thumb

OPPONENT n person one is working against in a contest, battle, or argument ▷ adj opposite, as in position

OPPOS ▶ oppo

OPPOSE, -D, -S vb work against

OPPOSER -S

OPPOSING ▶ oppose

OPPOSITE adj situated on the other side ▷ n person or thing that is opposite ▷ prep facing ▷ adv on the other side

OPPRESS vb control by cruelty or force

OPPUGN, -ED, -S vb call into question

OPPUGNER

OPS ▶ op

OPSIMATH n person who learns late in life

OPSIN, -S n type of protein

OPSONIC ▶ opsonin

OPSONIFY same as ▶ opsonize

OPSONIN, -S n constituent of blood serum

OPSONISE same as ▶ opsonize

OPSONIUM n relish eaten with bread

OPSONIZE vb subject (bacteria) to the action of opsonins

OPT, -ED, -ING, -S vb show a preference, choose

OPTANT, -S n person who opts

OPTATIVE adj indicating or expressing choice, preference, or wish ▷ n optative mood

OPTED ▶ opt

OPTER, -S ▶ opt

OPTIC adj relating to the eyes or sight

OPTICAL adj of or involving light or optics

OPTICIAN n person qualified to prescribe glasses

OPTICIST n optics expert

OPTICS n science of sight and light

OPTIMA ▶ optimum

OPTIMAL adj best or most favourable

OPTIMATE n Roman aristocrat

OPTIME, -S n mathematics student at Cambridge University

OPTIMISE same as ▶ optimize

OPTIMISM n tendency to take the most hopeful view

OPTIMIST

OPTIMIZE vb make the most of

OPTIMUM, OPTIMA, -S n best possible conditions ▷ adj most favourable

OPTING ▶ opt

OPTION, -ED, -S n choice ▷ vb obtain an option on

OPTIONAL adj possible but not compulsory ▷ n optional thing

OPTIONED ▶ option

OPTIONEE n holder of a financial option

OPTIONS ▶ option

OPTOLOGY n science of sight

OPTRONIC adj relating to optronics

OPTS ▶ opt

OPULENCE ▶ opulent

OPULENCY ▶ opulent

OPULENT adj having or indicating wealth

OPULUS, -ES n flowering shrub

OPUNTIA, -S n type of cactus

OPUS, -ES n artistic creation, esp a musical work

OPUSCLE, -S same as ▸ opuscule

OPUSCULA ▸ opusculum

OPUSCULE n small or insignificant artistic work

OPUSES ▸ opus

OQUASSA, -S n American trout

OR, -S prep before ▷ adj of the metal gold ▷ n gold

ORA ▸ os

ORACH same as ▸ orache

ORACHE, -S n type of plant

ORACIES ▸ oracy

ORACLE, -D, -S, ORACLING n shrine of an ancient god ▷ vb utter as an oracle

ORACULAR adj of or like an oracle

ORACY, ORACIES n capacity to use speech

ORAD adv towards the mouth

ORAGIOUS adj stormy

ORAL, -S adj spoken ▷ n spoken examination

ORALISM, -S n oral method of communicating with deaf people

ORALIST -S

ORALITY n state of being oral

ORALLY ▸ oral

ORALS ▸ oral

ORANG, -S n orangutan

ORANGE, -R, -S, -ST n reddish-yellow citrus fruit ▷ adj reddish-yellow

ORANGERY n greenhouse for growing orange trees

ORANGES ▸ orange

ORANGEST ▸ orange

ORANGEY ▸ orange

ORANGIER ▸ orangy

ORANGISH ▸ orange

ORANGS ▸ orang

ORANGY, ORANGIER ▸ orange

ORANT, -S n artistic representation of worshipper

ORARIA ▸ orarium

ORARIAN, -S n person who lives on the coast

ORARION, -S n garment worn by Greek clergyman

ORARIUM, ORARIA, -S n handkerchief

ORATE, -D, -S, ORATING vb make or give an oration

ORATION, -S n formal speech

ORATOR, -S n skilful public speaker

ORATORIO n musical composition for choir and orchestra

ORATORS ▸ orator

ORATORY n art of making speeches

ORATRESS n female orator

ORATRIX n female orator

ORATURE, -S n oral forms of literature

ORB, -ED, -ING, -S n ceremonial decorated sphere ▷ vb make or become circular or spherical

ORBIER ▸ orby

ORBIEST ▸ orby

ORBING ▸ orb

ORBIT, -ED, -ING, -S n curved path ▷ vb move in an orbit around

ORBITA, -S same as ▸ orbit

ORBITAL, -S adj of or denoting an orbit ▷ n region surrounding an atomic nucleus

ORBITAS ▸ orbita

ORBITED ▸ orbit

ORBITER, -S n spacecraft or satellite designed to orbit a planet without landing on it

ORBITIES ▸ orbity

ORBITING ▸ orbit

ORBITS ▸ orbit

ORBITY, ORBITIES n bereavement

ORBLESS ▸ orb

ORBS ▸ orb

ORBY, ORBIER, ORBIEST adj orb-shaped

ORC, -S n any of various whales, such as the killer and grampus

ORCA, -S n killer whale

ORCEIN, -S n brown crystalline material

ORCHARD, -S n area where fruit trees are grown

ORCHAT, -S same as ▸ orchard

ORCHEL, -S same as ▸ orchil

ORCHELLA same as ▸ orchil

ORCHELS ▸ orchel

ORCHESIS, ORCHESES n art of dance

ORCHID, -S n plant with flowers that have unusual lip-shaped petals

ORCHIL, -S n any of various lichens

ORCHILLA same as ▸ orchil

ORCHILS ▸ orchil

ORCHIS, -ES n type of orchid

ORCHITIC ▸ orchitis

ORCHITIS n inflammation of one or both testicles

ORCIN, -S same as ▸ orcinol

ORCINE, -S same as ▸ orcinol

ORCINOL, -S n colourless crystalline water-soluble solid

ORCINS ▸ orcin

ORCS ▸ orc

ORD, -S n pointed weapon

ORDAIN, -ED, -S vb make (someone) a member of the clergy

ORDAINER

ORDALIAN adj of an ordeal

ORDALIUM same as ▸ ordeal

ORDEAL, -S n painful or difficult experience

ORDER, -ED, -ING, -S n instruction to be carried out ▷ vb give an instruction to

ORDERER -S

ORDERLY adj well-organized ▷ n hospital attendant ▷ adv according to custom or rule

ORDERS ▸ order

ORDINAL, -S adj denoting a certain position in a sequence of numbers ▷ n book containing the forms of services for the ordination of ministers

ORDINAND n candidate for ordination

ORDINANT n person who ordains

ORDINAR, -S Scots word for ▸ ordinary

ORDINARY adj usual or normal

ORDINATE n vertical coordinate of a point in a two-dimensional system of coordinates ▷ vb ordain

ORDINEE, -S n person being ordained

ORDINES ▸ ordo

ORDNANCE n weapons and military supplies

ORDO, ORDINES, -S n religious order

ORDS ▸ ord

ORDURE, -S n excrement

ORDUROUS

ORE, -S n (rock containing) a mineral which yields metal

OREAD, -ES, -S n mountain nymph

OREBODY n mass of ore in a mine

ORECTIC adj of or relating to the desires

ORECTIVE ▸ orexis

OREGANO, -S n sweet-smelling herb used in cooking

OREIDE, -S same as ▸ oroide

OREODONT n extinct prehistoric mammal

O

OREOLOGY same as ► orology

ORES ► ore

OREWEED, -S n seaweed

OREXIN, -S n hormone that promotes wakefulness and stimulates the appetite

OREXIS, -ES n appetite

ORF, -S n infectious disease of sheep

ORFE, -S n small slender European fish

ORFRAY, -S same as ► orphrey

ORFS ► orf

ORG, -S n organization

ORGAN, -S n part of an animal or plant that has a particular function

ORGANA ► organon

ORGANDIE n fine cotton fabric

ORGANDY same as ► organdie

ORGANIC, -S adj of or produced from animals or plants ▷ n substance that is derived from animal or vegetable matter

ORGANISE same as ► organize

ORGANISM n any living animal or plant

ORGANIST n organ player

ORGANITY same as ► organism

ORGANIZE vb make arrangements for

ORGANON, ORGANA, -S n system of logical or scientific rules

ORGANS ► organ

ORGANUM, -S same as ► organon

ORGANZA, -S n thin stiff fabric of silk, cotton, or synthetic fibre

ORGEAT, -S n drink made with orange flower water

ORGIA, -S same as ► orgy

ORGIAC ► orgy

ORGIAS ► orgia

ORGIAST, -S n person who indulges immoderately in an activity

ORGIC ► orgy

ORGIES ► orgy

ORGONE, -S n substance claimed to be needed for mental health

ORGS ► org

ORGUE, -S n number of stakes lashed together

ORGULOUS adj proud

ORGY, ORGIES n act of immoderate indulgence

ORIBATID n type of mite

ORIBI, -S n small African antelope

ORICHALC n type of alloy

ORIEL, -S n type of bay window

ORIELLED adj having an oriel

ORIELS ► oriel

ORIENCY n state of being iridescent

ORIENT, -ED, -S vb position (oneself) according to one's surroundings ▷ n eastern sky or the dawn ▷ adj eastern

ORIENTAL adj eastern ▷ n native of the orient

ORIENTED ► orient

ORIENTER ► orient

ORIENTS ► orient

ORIFEX, -ES same as ► orifice

ORIFICE, -S n opening or hole

ORIGAMI, -S n Japanese decorative art of paper folding

ORIGAN, -S another name for ► marjoram

ORIGANE, -S same as ► origan

ORIGANS ► origan

ORIGANUM n type of aromatic plant

ORIGIN, -S n point from which something develops

ORIGINAL adj first or earliest ▷ n first version, from which others are copied

ORIGINS ► origin

ORIHOU, -S n small New Zealand tree

ORILLION n part of bastion

ORINASAL adj pronounced with simultaneous oral and nasal articulation ▷ n orinasal speech sound

ORIOLE, -S n tropical or American songbird

ORISHA, -S n any of the minor gods or spirits of traditional Yoruba religion

ORISON, -S another word for ► prayer

ORIXA, -S same as ► orisha

ORLE, -S n border around a shield

ORLEANS n type of fabric

ORLES ► orle

ORLISTAT n drug used for slimming

ORLON, -S n crease-resistant acrylic fibre or fabric

ORLOP, -S n (in a vessel with four or more decks) the lowest deck

ORMER, -S n edible marine mollusc

ORMOLU, -S n gold-coloured alloy used for decoration

ORNAMENT n decorative object ▷ vb decorate

ORNATE, -R, -ST adj highly decorated, elaborate

ORNATELY

ORNERY, ORNERIER adj stubborn or vile-tempered

ORNIS, -ES less common word for ► avifauna

ORNITHES n birds in Greek myth

ORNITHIC adj of or relating to birds or a bird fauna

OROGEN, -S n part of earth subject to orogeny

OROGENIC ► orogeny

OROGENS ► orogen

OROGENY n formation of mountain ranges

OROIDE, -S n alloy containing copper, tin, and other metals

OROLOGY same as > orography

OROMETER n aneroid barometer with an altitude scale

ORONASAL adj of or relating to the mouth and nose

OROPESA, -S n float used in minesweeping

OROTUND adj (of the voice) resonant and booming

ORPHAN, -ED, -S n child whose parents are dead ▷ vb deprive of parents

ORPHIC adj mystical or occult

ORPHICAL same as ► orphic

ORPHISM, -S n style of abstract art

ORPHREY, -S n richly embroidered band or border

ORPIMENT n yellow mineral

ORPIN, -S same as ► orpine

ORPINE, -S n type of plant

ORPINS ► orpin

ORRA adj odd or unmatched

ORRAMAN, ORRAMEN n man who does odd jobs

ORRERY, ORRERIES n mechanical model of the solar system

ORRICE, -S same as ► orris

ORRIS, -ES n kind of iris

ORS ► or

ORSEILLE same as ► orchil

ORSELLIC

ORT n fragment

ORTHIAN adj having high pitch

ORTHICON n type of television camera tube

ORTHO, -S n type of photographic plate
ORTHODOX adj conforming to established views
ORTHOEPY n study of correct or standard pronunciation
ORTHOPOD n surgeon
ORTHOS ▸ ortho
ORTHOSIS, ORTHOSES n artificial or mechanical aid to support a weak part of the body
ORTHOTIC > orthotics
ORTHROS n canonical hour in the Greek Church
ORTOLAN, -S n small European songbird eaten as a delicacy
ORTS pl n scraps or leavings
ORVAL, -S n plant of sage family
ORYX, -ES n large African antelope
ORZO, -S n pasta in small grain shapes
OS, ORA, -AR, -SA n mouth or mouthlike part or opening
OSCAR, -S n cash
OSCHEAL adj of the scrotum
OSCINE, -S n songbird ▷ adj of songbirds
OSCININE
OSCITANT > oscitancy
OSCITATE vb yawn
OSCULA ▸ osculum
OSCULANT adj possessing some of the characteristics of two different taxonomic groups
OSCULAR adj of or relating to an osculum
OSCULATE vb kiss
OSCULE, -S n small mouth or opening
OSCULUM, OSCULA n mouthlike aperture
OSE, -S same as ▸ esker
OSETRA, -S n type of caviar
OSHAC n plant smelling of ammonia
OSIER, -S n willow tree
OSIERED adj covered with osiers
OSIERIES ▸ osiery
OSIERS ▸ osier
OSIERY, OSIERIES n work done with osiers
OSMATE, -S n salt of osmic acid
OSMATIC adj relying on sense of smell
OSMIATE, -S same as ▸ osmate
OSMIC adj of or containing osmium in a high valence state

OSMICS n science of smell
OSMIOUS same as ▸ osmous
OSMIUM, -S n heaviest known metallic element
OSMOL, -S same as ▸ osmole
OSMOLAL ▸ osmole
OSMOLAR adj containing one osmole per litre
OSMOLE, -S n unit of osmotic pressure
OSMOLS ▸ osmol
OSMOSE, -D, -S, OSMOSING vb undergo or cause to undergo osmosis
OSMOSIS n movement of a liquid through a membrane
OSMOTIC
OSMOUS adj of or containing osmium in a low valence state
OSMUND, -S same as ▸ osmunda
OSMUNDA, -S n type of fern
OSMUNDS ▸ osmund
OSNABURG n coarse plain-woven cotton used for sacks, furnishings, etc
OSPREY, -S n large fish-eating bird of prey
OSSA ▸ os
OSSARIUM same as ▸ ossuary
OSSATURE n skeleton
OSSEIN, -S n protein that forms the organic matrix of bone
OSSELET, -S n growth on knee of horse
OSSEOUS adj consisting of or like bone
OSSETER, -S n sturgeon
OSSETRA, -S same as ▸ osetra
OSSIA, -S n alternate version or passage ▷ conj or
OSSICLE, -S n small bone, esp one of those in the middle ear
OSSIFIC adj making something turn to bone
OSSIFIED adj converted into bone
OSSIFIER ▸ ossify
OSSIFY, OSSIFIES vb (cause to) become bone, harden
OSSOBUCO n Italian dish of veal shank and vegetables stewed in wine
OSSUARY n any container for the burial of human bones, such as an urn or vault
OSTEAL adj of or relating to bone or to the skeleton
OSTEITIC ▸ osteitis
OSTEITIS n inflammation of a bone

OSTENT, -ED, -S n appearance ▷ vb display boastfully
OSTEOGEN n material from which bone forms
OSTEOID, -S adj of or resembling bone ▷ n bony deposit
OSTEOMA, -S n tumour composed of bone or bonelike tissue
OSTEOSIS, OSTEOSES n forming of bony tissue
OSTIA ▸ ostium
OSTIAL ▸ ostium
OSTIARY another word for ▸ porter
OSTIATE adj having ostium
OSTINATO, OSTINATI n persistently repeated phrase or rhythm
OSTIOLAR ▸ ostiole
OSTIOLE, -S n pore in the reproductive bodies of certain algae and fungi
OSTIUM, OSTIA n pore in sponges through which water enters the body
OSTLER, -S n stableman at an inn
OSTMARK, -S n currency of the former East Germany
OSTOMATE n person with an ostomy
OSTOMY, OSTOMIES n surgically made opening
OSTOSIS, OSTOSES n formation of bone
OSTRACA ▸ ostracon
OSTRACOD n type of minute crustacean
OSTRACON, OSTRACA n (in ancient Greece) a potsherd used for ostracizing
OSTRAKON, OSTRAKA same as ▸ ostracon
OSTREGER n keeper of hawks
OSTRICH n large African bird that runs fast but cannot fly
OTAKU, -S n Japanese computer geek
OTALGIA, -S technical name for ▸ earache
OTALGIC
OTALGY, OTALGIES same as ▸ otalgia
OTARID adj of or like an otary, an eared seal
OTARIES ▸ otary
OTARINE ▸ otary

O

This means like an otary or eared seal, and is perhaps the most commonly played of all 7-letter bonus words, so well worth learning for that extra 50 points it can give you.

OTARY, OTARIES n seal with ears

OTHER, -S adj remaining in a group of which one or some have been specified ▷ n other person or thing

OTIC adj of or relating to the ear

OTIOSE adj not useful
OTIOSELY
OTIOSITY

OTITIC ▸ otitis

OTITIS, OTITIDES, -ES n inflammation of the ear

OTOCYST, -S n embryonic structure in vertebrates that develops into the inner ear

OTOLITH, -S n granule of calcium carbonate in the inner ear of vertebrates

OTOLOGIC adj relating to otology

OTOLOGY n branch of medicine concerned with the ear

OTOSCOPE another name for > auriscope

OTOSCOPY n examination of ear using otoscope

OTOTOXIC adj toxic to the ear

OTTAR, -S variant of ▸ attar

OTTAVA, -S n interval of an octave

OTTAVINO n piccolo

OTTER, -ED, -ING, -S n small brown freshwater mammal that eats fish ▷ vb fish using an otter board

OTTO, -S another name for ▸ attar

OTTOMAN, -S n storage chest with a padded lid for use as a seat

OTTOS ▸ otto

OU, -ENS, -S interj expressing concession ▷ n man, bloke, or chap

OUABAIN, -S n poisonous white crystalline glycoside

OUAKARI, -S n South American monkey

OUBAAS, -ES n man in authority

OUBIT, -S n hairy caterpillar

OUCH, -ED, -ES, -ING interj exclamation of sudden pain ▷ n brooch or clasp set with gems ▷ vb say ouch

OUCHT, -S Scots word for ▸ anything

OUD, -S n Arabic stringed musical instrument

OUENS ▸ ou

OUGHLY, OUGHLIED, OUGHLIES variant of ▸ ugly

OUGHT, -ED, -ING, -S vb have an obligation ▷ n zero

OUGIYA, -S n monetary unit of Mauretania

OUGLIE, -D, -S variant of ▸ ugly

OUGUIYA, -S n standard monetary unit of Mauritania

OUIJA, -S n tradename for a board through which spirits supposedly answer questions

OUISTITI n marmoset

OUK, -S Scots word for ▸ week

OULACHON same as ▸ eulachon

OULAKAN, -S same as ▸ eulachon

OULD, -ER, -EST Scots or Irish form of ▸ old

OULK, -S Scots form of ▸ week

OULONG, -S same as ▸ oolong

OUMA, -S n grandmother, often as a title with a surname

OUNCE, -S n unit of weight equal to one sixteenth of a pound

OUNDY, OUNDIER, OUNDIEST adj wavy

OUP, -ED, -ING, -S same as ▸ oop

OUPA, -S n grandfather, often as a title with a surname

OUPED ▸ oup

OUPH, -S same as ▸ oaf

OUPHE, -S same as ▸ oaf

OUPHS ▸ ouph

OUPING ▸ oup

OUPS ▸ oup

OUR adj belonging to us ▷ determiner of, belonging to, or associated in some way with us

OURALI, -S n plant from which curare comes

OURANG, -S same as ▸ orang

OURARI, -S same as ▸ ourali

OUREBI, -S same as ▸ oribi

OURIE, -R, -ST same as ▸ oorie

OURN dialect form of ▸ our

OUROLOGY same as ▸ urology

OURS pron thing(s) belonging to us

OURSELF pron formal word for myself used by monarchs

OUS ▸ ou

OUSEL, -S same as ▸ ouzel

OUST, -ED, -ING, -S vb force (someone) out, expel

OUSTER, -S n act of forcing someone out of a position

OUSTING ▸ oust

OUSTITI, -S n device for opening locked door

OUSTS ▸ oust

OUT, -ED, -S adj denoting movement or distance away from ▷ vb put or throw out

OUTA prep informal contraction of out of

OUTACT, -ED, -S vb surpass in acting

OUTADD, -ED, -S vb beat or surpass at adding

OUTAGE, -S n period of power failure

OUTARGUE vb defeat in argument

OUTASITE adj amazing, excellent

OUTASK, -ED, -S vb declare wedding banns

OUTATE ▸ outeat

OUTBACK, -S n remote bush country of Australia

OUTBAKE, -D, -S vb bake more or better than

OUTBAR, -S vb keep out

OUTBARK, -S vb bark more or louder than

OUTBARS ▸ outbar

OUTBAWL, -S vb bawl more or louder than

OUTBEAM, -S vb beam more or brighter than

OUTBEG, -S vb beg more or better than

OUTBID, -S vb offer a higher price than

OUTBITCH vb bitch more or better than

OUTBLAZE vb blaze more or hotter than

OUTBLEAT vb bleat more or louder than

OUTBLESS vb bless more than

OUTBLOOM vb bloom more or better than

OUTBLUFF vb surpass in bluffing

OUTBLUSH vb blush more than

OUTBOARD adj (of a boat's engine) portable, with its own propeller ▷ adv away from the centre line of a vessel or aircraft ▷ n outboard motor

OUTBOAST vb surpass in boasting

OUTBOUND adj going out

OUTBOX, -ED, -ES vb surpass in boxing

OUTBRAG, -S vb brag more or better than

OUTBRAVE vb surpass in bravery

OUTBRAWL vb defeat in a brawl

OUTBREAK, OUTBROKE n sudden occurrence (of something unpleasant) ▷ vb break out

OUTBREED, OUTBRED vb produce offspring outside a particular family or tribe

OUTBRIBE vb bribe more than

OUTBROKE ▸ outbreak

OUTBUILD, OUTBUILT vb exceed in building

OUTBULGE vb bulge outwards

OUTBULK, -S vb exceed in bulk

OUTBULLY vb exceed in bullying

OUTBURN, -S, -T vb burn longer or brighter than

OUTBURST n sudden expression of emotion ▷ vb burst out

OUTBUY, -S vb buy more than

OUTBY adv outside

OUTBYE same as ▸ outby

OUTCALL, -S n visit to customer's home by professional ▷ vb bid higher than another player in a card game

OUTCAPER vb exceed in capering

OUTCAST, -S n person rejected by a particular group ▷ adj rejected, abandoned, or discarded

OUTCASTE n person who has been expelled from a caste ▷ vb cause (someone) to lose his or her caste

OUTCASTS ▸ outcast

OUTCATCH vb catch more than

OUTCAVIL vb exceed in cavilling

OUTCHARM vb exceed in charming

OUTCHEAT vb exceed in cheating

OUTCHIDE, OUTCHID vb exceed in chiding

OUTCITY n anywhere outside a city's confines

OUTCLASS vb surpass in quality

OUTCLIMB, OUTCLOMB vb exceed in climbing

OUTCOACH vb exceed in coaching

OUTCOME, -S n result

OUTCOOK, -S vb cook more or better than

OUTCOUNT vb exceed in counting

OUTCRAWL vb crawl further or faster than

OUTCRIED ▸ outcry

OUTCRIES ▸ outcry

OUTCROP, -S n part of a rock formation that sticks out of the earth ▷ vb (of rock strata) to protrude through the surface of the earth

OUTCROSS vb breed (animals or plants of the same breed but different strains) ▷ n animal or plant produced as a result of outcrossing

OUTCROW, -S vb exceed in crowing

OUTCROWD vb have more crowd than

OUTCROWS ▸ outcrow

OUTCRY, OUTCRIED, OUTCRIES n vehement or widespread protest ▷ vb cry louder or make more noise than (someone or something)

OUTCURSE vb exceed in cursing

OUTCURVE n baseball thrown to curve away from batter

OUTDANCE vb surpass in dancing

OUTDARE, -D, -S vb be more brave than

OUTDATE, -S vb make or become old-fashioned or obsolete

OUTDATED adj old-fashioned

OUTDATES ▸ outdate

OUTDO, OUTDID, -ES, -ING, -NE vb surpass in performance

OUTDODGE vb surpass in dodging

OUTDOER, -S ▸ outdo

OUTDOES ▸ outdo

OUTDOING ▸ outdo

OUTDONE ▸ outdo

OUTDOOR adj taking place in the open air

OUTDOORS adv in(to) the open air ▷ n open air

OUTDRAG, -S vb beat in drag race

OUTDRANK ▸ outdrink

OUTDRAW, -N, -S, OUTDREW vb draw (a gun) faster than

OUTDREAM vb exceed in dreaming

OUTDRESS vb dress better than

OUTDREW ▸ outdraw

OUTDRINK, OUTDRANK, OUTDRUNK vb drink more alcohol than

OUTDRIVE, OUTDROVE vb exceed in driving

OUTDROP, -S same as ▸ outcrop

OUTDROVE ▸ outdrive

OUTDRUNK ▸ outdrink

OUTDUEL, -S vb defeat in duel

OUTDURE, -D, -S vb last longer than

OUTDWELL, OUTDWELT vb live outside something

OUTEARN, -S vb earn more than

OUTEAT, OUTATE, -EN, -S vb eat more than

OUTECHO vb echo more than

OUTED ▸ out

OUTEDGE, -S n furthest limit

OUTER, -S adj on the outside ▷ n white outermost ring on a target

OUTFABLE vb exceed in creating fables

OUTFACE, -D, -S vb subdue or disconcert by staring

OUTFALL, -S n mouth of a river or drain

OUTFAST, -S vb fast longer than

OUTFAWN, -S vb exceed in fawning

OUTFEAST vb exceed in feasting

OUTFEEL, -S, OUTFELT vb exceed in feeling

OUTFENCE vb surpass at fencing

OUTFIELD n area far from the pitch

OUTFIGHT vb surpass in fighting

OUTFIND, -S, OUTFOUND vb exceed in finding

OUTFIRE, -D, -S vb exceed in firing

OUTFISH vb catch more fish than

OUTFIT, -S n matching set of clothes ▷ vb furnish or be furnished with an outfit

OUTFLANK vb get round the side of (an enemy army)

OUTFLASH vb be flashier than

OUTFLEW ▸ outfly

OUTFLIES ▸ outfly

OUTFLING, OUTFLUNG n cutting remark ▷ vb whip out

OUTFLOAT vb surpass at floating

OUTFLOW, -S n anything that flows out, such as liquid or money ▷ vb flow faster than

OUTFLOWN ► outfly
OUTFLOWS ► outflow
OUTFLUNG ► outfling
OUTFLUSH n burst of light
OUTFLY, OUTFLEW, OUTFLIES, OUTFLOWN vb fly better or faster than
OUTFOOL, -S vb be more foolish than
OUTFOOT, -S vb (of a boat) to go faster than (another boat)
OUTFOUND ► outfind
OUTFOX, -ED, -ES vb defeat or foil by being more cunning
OUTFROWN vb dominate by frowning more than
OUTGAIN, -S vb gain more than
OUTGAS, -ES vb undergo the removal of adsorbed or absorbed gas from solids
OUTGATE, -S n way out
OUTGAVE ► outgive
OUTGAZE, -D, -S vb gaze beyond
OUTGIVE, OUTGAVE, -N, -S vb exceed in giving
OUTGLARE vb exceed in glaring
OUTGLEAM vb gleam more than
OUTGLOW, -S vb glow more than
OUTGNAW, -N, -S vb exceed in gnawing
OUTGO, -ES, -NE, OUTWENT vb exceed or outstrip ▷ n cost
OUTGOER -S
OUTGOING adj leaving ▷ n act of going out
OUTGONE ► outgo
OUTGREW ► outgrow
OUTGRIN, -S vb exceed in grinning
OUTGROSS vb earn more than
OUTGROUP n group of people outside one's own group of people
OUTGROW, OUTGREW, -N, -S vb become too large or too old for
OUTGUARD n guard furthest away from main party
OUTGUESS vb surpass in guessing
OUTGUIDE n folder in filing system ▷ vb beat or surpass at guiding
OUTGUN, -S vb surpass in fire power
OUTGUSH vb gush out
OUTHAUL, -S n line or cable for tightening the foot of a sail

OUTHEAR, -D, -S vb exceed in hearing
OUTHER same as ► other
OUTHIRE, -D, -S vb hire out
OUTHIT, -S vb hit something further than (someone else)
OUTHOMER vb score more home runs than
OUTHOUSE n building near a main building
OUTHOWL, -S vb exceed in howling
OUTHUMOR same as > outhumour
OUTHUNT, -S vb exceed in hunting
OUTHYRE, -D, -S same as ► outhire
OUTING, -S n leisure trip
OUTJEST, -S vb exceed in jesting
OUTJET, -S n projecting part
OUTJINX vb exceed in jinxing

If someone else plays **jinx**, you can outjinx them by adding O, U and T! And if you can form the whole word using all of your letters, you'll get a 50-point bonus.

OUTJUMP, -S vb jump higher or farther than
OUTJUT, -S vb jut out ▷ n projecting part
OUTKEEP, -S, OUTKEPT vb beat or surpass at keeping
OUTKICK, -S vb exceed in kicking
OUTKILL, -S vb exceed in killing
OUTKISS vb exceed in kissing
OUTLAID ► outlay
OUTLAIN ► outlay
OUTLAND, -S adj outlying or distant ▷ n outlying areas of a country or region
OUTLASH n sudden attack ▷ vb shed tears
OUTLAST, -S vb last longer than
OUTLAUGH vb laugh longer or louder than
OUTLAW, -ED, -S n criminal deprived of legal protection, bandit ▷ vb make illegal
OUTLAWRY n act of outlawing or the state of being outlawed
OUTLAWS ► outlaw
OUTLAY, OUTLAID, OUTLAIN, -S n expenditure ▷ vb spend (money)
OUTLEAD, OUTLED vb be better leader than
OUTLEAP, -S, -T vb leap higher or farther than

OUTLEARN vb exceed in learning
OUTLED ► outlead
OUTLER, -S n farm animal kept out of doors
OUTLET, -S n means of expressing emotion
OUTLIE, -D, -S vb lie outside a particular place
OUTLIER, -S n outcrop of rocks that is entirely surrounded by older rocks
OUTLIES ► outlie
OUTLINE, -D, -S n short general explanation ▷ vb summarize
OUTLINER
OUTLIVE, -D, -S vb live longer than
OUTLIVER
OUTLOOK, -S n attitude ▷ vb look out
OUTLOVE, -D, -S vb exceed in loving
OUTLYING adj distant from the main area
OUTMAN, -S vb surpass in manpower
OUTMARCH vb exceed in marching
OUTMATCH vb surpass or outdo (someone)
OUTMODE, -S vb make unfashionable
OUTMODED adj no longer fashionable or accepted
OUTMODES ► outmode
OUTMOST another word for > outermost
OUTMOVE, -D, -S vb move faster or better than
OUTNAME, -D, -S vb be more notorious than
OUTNESS n state or quality of being external
OUTNIGHT vb refer to night more often than
OUTPACE, -D, -S vb go faster than (someone)
OUTPAINT vb exceed in painting
OUTPART, -S n remote region
OUTPASS vb exceed in passing
OUTPEEP, -S vb peep out
OUTPEER, -S vb surpass
OUTPITCH vb exceed in pitching
OUTPITY vb exceed in pitying
OUTPLACE vb find job for ex-employee
OUTPLAN, -S vb exceed in planning
OUTPLAY, -S vb perform better than one's opponent

OUTPLOD, -S vb exceed in plodding

OUTPLOT, -S vb exceed in plotting

OUTPOINT vb score more points than

OUTPOLL, -S vb win more votes than

OUTPORT, -S n isolated fishing village, esp in Newfoundland

OUTPOST, -S n outlying settlement

OUTPOUR, -S n act of flowing or pouring out ▷ vb pour or cause to pour out freely or rapidly

OUTPOWER vb have more power than

OUTPRAY, -S vb exceed in praying

OUTPREEN vb exceed in preening

OUTPRESS vb exceed in pressing

OUTPRICE vb sell at better price than

OUTPRIZE vb prize more highly than

OUTPSYCH vb defeat by psychological means

OUTPULL, -S vb exceed in pulling

OUTPUNCH vb punch better than

OUTPUPIL n student sent to a different school to the one he or she would normally attend

OUTPUSH vb exceed in pushing

OUTPUT, -S n amount produced ▷ vb produce (data) at the end of a process

OUTQUOTE vb exceed in quoting

OUTRACE, -D, -S vb surpass in racing

OUTRAGE, -D, -S n great moral indignation ▷ vb offend morally

OUTRAISE vb raise more money than

OUTRAN ▸ outrun

OUTRANCE n furthest extreme

OUTRANG ▸ outring

OUTRANGE vb have a greater range than

OUTRANK, -S vb be of higher rank than (someone)

OUTRATE, -D, -S vb offer better rate than

OUTRAVE, -D, -S vb outdo in raving

OUTRE adj shockingly eccentric

OUTREACH vb surpass in reach ▷ n act or process of reaching out

OUTREAD, -S vb outdo in reading

OUTRED, -S vb be redder than

OUTREIGN vb reign for longer than

OUTREMER n land overseas

OUTRIDE, -S, OUTRODE vb outdo by riding faster, farther, or better than ▷ n extra unstressed syllable within a metrical foot

OUTRIDER n motorcyclist acting as an escort

OUTRIDES ▸ outride

OUTRIG, -S vb supply with outfit

OUTRIGHT adv absolute(ly) ▷ adj complete

OUTRIGS ▸ outrig

OUTRING, OUTRANG, -S, OUTRUNG vb exceed in ringing

OUTRIVAL vb surpass

OUTRO, -S n instrumental passage that concludes a piece of music

OUTROAR, -S vb roar louder than

OUTROCK, -S vb outdo in rocking

OUTRODE ▸ outride

OUTROLL, -S vb exceed in rolling

OUTROOP, -S n auction

OUTROOT, -S vb root out

OUTROPE, -S same as ▸ outroop

OUTROPER

OUTROS ▸ outro

OUTROW, -ED, -S vb outdo in rowing

OUTRUN, OUTRAN, -S vb run faster than

OUTRUNG ▸ outring

OUTRUNS ▸ outrun

OUTRUSH n flowing or rushing out ▷ vb rush out

OUTS ▸ out

OUTSAID ▸ outsay

OUTSAIL, -S vb sail better than

OUTSANG ▸ outsing

OUTSAT ▸ outsit

OUTSAVOR same as ▸ outsavour

OUTSAW ▸ outsee

OUTSAY, OUTSAID, -S vb say something out loud

OUTSCOLD vb outdo in scolding

OUTSCOOP vb outdo in achieving scoops

OUTSCORE vb score more than

OUTSCORN vb defy with scorn

OUTSEE, OUTSAW, -N, -S vb exceed in seeing

OUTSELL, -S, OUTSOLD vb be sold in greater quantities than

OUTSERT, -S another word for ▸ wraparound

OUTSERVE vb serve better at tennis than

OUTSET, -S n beginning

OUTSHAME vb greatly shame

OUTSHINE, OUTSHONE vb surpass (someone) in excellence

OUTSHOOT vb surpass or excel in shooting ▷ n thing that projects or shoots out

OUTSHOT, -S n projecting part

OUTSHOUT vb shout louder than

OUTSIDE, -S adv indicating movement to or position on the exterior ▷ adj unlikely ▷ n external area or surface

OUTSIDER n person outside a specific group

OUTSIDES ▸ outside

OUTSIGHT n power of seeing

OUTSIN, -S vb sin more than

OUTSING, OUTSANG, -S, OUTSUNG vb sing better or louder than

OUTSINS ▸ outsin

OUTSIT, OUTSAT, -S vb sit longer than

OUTSIZE, -S adj larger than normal ▷ n outsize garment

OUTSIZED same as ▸ outsize

OUTSIZES ▸ outsize

OUTSKATE vb skate better than

OUTSKIRT singular of ▸ outskirts

OUTSLEEP, OUTSLEPT vb sleep longer than

OUTSLICK vb outsmart

OUTSMART vb outwit

OUTSMELL, OUTSMELT vb surpass in smelling

OUTSMILE vb outdo in smiling

OUTSMOKE vb smoke more than

OUTSNORE vb outdo in snoring

OUTSOAR, -S vb fly higher than

OUTSOLD ▸ outsell

OUTSOLE, -S n outermost sole of a shoe

OUTSPAN, -S vb relax

O

OUTSPEAK, OUTSPOKE *vb* speak better or louder than

OUTSPEED, OUTSPED *vb* go faster than

OUTSPELL, OUTSPELT *vb* exceed at spelling

OUTSPEND, OUTSPENT *vb* spend more than

OUTSPOKE ► outspeak

OUTSPORT *vb* sport in excess of

OUTSTAND, OUTSTOOD *vb* be outstanding or excel

OUTSTARE *vb* stare longer than

OUTSTART *vb* jump out ▷ *n* outset

OUTSTATE *vb* surpass in stating

OUTSTAY, -S *vb* overstay

OUTSTEER *vb* steer better than

OUTSTEP, -S *vb* step farther than

OUTSTOOD ► outstand

OUTSTRIP *vb* surpass

OUTSTUDY *vb* outdo in studying

OUTSTUNT *vb* outdo in performing stunts

OUTSULK, -S *vb* outdo in sulking

OUTSUM, -S *vb* add up to more than

OUTSUNG ► outsing

OUTSWAM ► outswim

OUTSWEAR, OUTSWARE, OUTSWORE, OUTSWORN *vb* swear more than

OUTSWEEP *n* outward movement of arms in swimming breaststroke

OUTSWELL *vb* exceed in swelling

OUTSWEPT *adj* curving outwards

OUTSWIM, OUTSWAM, -S, OUTSWUM *vb* outdo in swimming

OUTSWING *n* (in cricket) movement of a ball from leg to off through the air

OUTSWORE ► outswear

OUTSWORN ► outswear

OUTSWUM ► outswim

OUTSWUNG *adj* made to curve outwards

OUTTA *prep* informal contraction of out of

OUTTAKE, -N, -S, OUTTOOK *n* unreleased take from a recording session, film, or TV programme ▷ *vb* take out

OUTTALK, -S *vb* talk more, longer, or louder than (someone)

OUTTASK, -S *vb* assign task to staff outside organization

OUTTELL, -S, OUTTOLD *vb* make known

OUTTHANK *vb* outdo in thanking

OUTTHINK *vb* outdo in thinking

OUTTHREW ► outthrow

OUTTHROB *vb* outdo in throbbing

OUTTHROW, OUTTHREW *vb* throw better than

OUTTOLD ► outtell

OUTTOOK ► outtake

OUTTOP, -S *vb* rise higher than

OUTTOWER *vb* tower over

OUTTRADE *vb* surpass in trading

OUTTRICK *vb* outdo in trickery

OUTTROT, -S *vb* exceed at trotting

OUTTRUMP *vb* count for more than

OUTTURN, -S *same as* ► output

OUTVALUE *vb* surpass in value

OUTVAUNT *vb* outdo in boasting

OUTVENOM *vb* surpass in venomousness

OUTVIE, -D, -S, OUTVYING *vb* outdo in competition

OUTVOICE *vb* surpass in noise

OUTVOTE, -D, -S *vb* defeat by getting more votes than **OUTVOTER**

OUTVYING ► outvie

OUTWAIT, -S *vb* wait longer than

OUTWALK, -S *vb* walk farther or longer than

OUTWAR, -S *vb* surpass or exceed in warfare

OUTWARD *same as* ► outwards

OUTWARDS *adv* towards the outside

OUTWARS ► outwar

OUTWASH *n* gravel carried and deposited by water from melting glaciers

OUTWASTE *vb* outdo in wasting

OUTWATCH *vb* surpass in watching

OUTWEAR, -S, OUTWORE *vb* use up or destroy by wearing

OUTWEARY *vb* exhaust

OUTWEED, -S *vb* root out

OUTWEEP, -S, OUTWEPT *vb* outdo in weeping

OUTWEIGH *vb* be more important, significant, or influential than

OUTWELL, -S *vb* pour out

OUTWENT ► outgo

OUTWEPT ► outweep

OUTWHIRL *vb* surpass at whirling

OUTWICK, -S *vb* move one curling stone by striking with another

OUTWILE, -D, -S *vb* surpass in cunning

OUTWILL, -S *vb* demonstrate stronger will than

OUTWIN, -S, OUTWON *vb* get out of

OUTWIND, -S, OUTWOUND *vb* unwind

OUTWING, -S *vb* surpass in flying

OUTWINS ► outwin

OUTWISH *vb* surpass in wishing

OUTWIT, -S *vb* get the better of (someone) by cunning

OUTWITH *prep* outside

OUTWITS ► outwit

OUTWON ► outwin

OUTWORE ► outwear

OUTWORK, -S *n* defences which lie outside main defensive works ▷ *vb* work better, harder, etc, than

OUTWORN *adj* no longer in use

OUTWORTH *vb* be more valuable than

OUTWOUND ► outwind

OUTWREST *vb* extort

OUTWRITE, OUTWRIT, OUTWROTE *vb* outdo in writing

OUTYELL, -S *vb* outdo in yelling

OUTYELP, -S *vb* outdo in yelping

OUTYIELD *vb* yield more than

OUVERT *adj* open

OUVERTE *feminine form of* ► ouvert

OUVRAGE, -S *n* work

OUVRIER, -S *n* worker

OUVRIERE *feminine form of* ► ouvrier

OUVRIERS ► ouvrier

OUZEL, -S *n* type of bird

OUZO, -S *n* strong aniseed-flavoured spirit from Greece

OVA ► ovum

OVAL, -S *adj* egg-shaped ▷ *n* anything that is oval in shape **OVALITY**

OVALLY

OVALNESS

OVARIAL ► ovary

OVARIAN ► ovary

OVARIES ► ovary

OVARIOLE n tube in insect ovary

OVARIOUS adj of eggs

OVARITIS n inflammation of an ovary

OVARY, OVARIES n female egg-producing organ

OVATE, -D, -S, OVATING adj shaped like an egg ▷ vb give ovation

OVATELY

OVATION, -S n enthusiastic round of applause

OVATOR, -S ► ovate

OVEL, -S n mourner, esp during the first seven days after a death

OVEN, -ED, -ING, -S n heated compartment or container for cooking ▷ vb cook in an oven

OVENABLE adj (of food) suitable for cooking in an oven

OVENBIRD n type of small brownish South American bird

OVENED ► oven

OVENING ► oven

OVENLIKE ► oven

OVENS ► oven

OVENWARE n heat-resistant dishes in which food can be both cooked and served

OVENWOOD n pieces of wood for burning in an oven

OVER, -ED, -ING, -S adv indicating position on the top of, amount greater than, etc ▷ adj finished ▷ n (in cricket) series of six balls bowled from one end ▷ vb jump over

OVERABLE adj too able

OVERACT, -S vb act in an exaggerated way

OVERAGE, -S adj beyond a specified age ▷ n amount beyond given limit

OVERAGED adj very old

OVERAGES ► overage

OVERALL, -S adv in total ▷ n coat-shaped protective garment ▷ adj from one end to the other

OVERAPT adj tending excessively

OVERARCH vb form an arch over

OVERARM, -S adv with the arm above the shoulder ▷ adj bowled, thrown, or performed with the arm raised above the shoulder ▷ vb throw (a ball) overarm

OVERATE ► overeat

OVERAWE, -D, -S vb affect (someone) with an overpowering sense of awe

OVERBAKE vb bake too long

OVERBANK n sediment deposited on the flood plain of a river

OVERBEAR, OVERBORE, OVERBORN vb dominate or overcome

OVERBEAT vb beat too much

OVERBED adj fitting over bed

OVERBET, -S vb bet too much

OVERBID, -S vb bid for more tricks than one can expect to win ▷ n bid higher than someone else's bid

OVERBIG adj too big

OVERBILL vb charge too much money

OVERBITE n extension of the upper front teeth over the lower front teeth when the mouth is closed

OVERBLOW, OVERBLEW vb blow into (a wind instrument) with greater force than normal

OVERBOIL vb boil too much

OVERBOLD adj too bold

OVERBOOK vb accept too many bookings

OVERBOOT n protective boot worn over an ordinary boot or shoe

OVERBORE ► overbear

OVERBORN ► overborn

OVERBRED adj produced by too selective breeding

OVERBRIM vb overflow

OVERBROW vb hang over

OVERBULK vb loom large over

OVERBURN vb (formerly) copy information onto CD

OVERBUSY adj too busy ▷ vb make too busy

OVERBUY, -S vb buy too much or too many

OVERBY adv Scots expression meaning over the road or across the way

OVERCALL n bid higher than the preceding one ▷ vb bid higher than (an opponent)

OVERCAME ► overcome

OVERCAST adj (of the sky) covered by clouds ▷ vb make or become overclouded or gloomy ▷ n covering, as of clouds or mist

OVERCLAD adj wearing too many clothes

OVERCLOY vb weary with excess

OVERCLUB vb (in golf) use a club which causes the shot to go too far

OVERCOAT n heavy coat

OVERCOLD adj too cold

OVERCOME, OVERCAME vb gain control over after an effort

OVERCOOK vb spoil food by cooking it for too long

OVERCOOL vb cool too much

OVERCOY adj too modest

OVERCRAM vb fill too full

OVERCRAW ► overcrow

OVERCROP vb exhaust (land) by excessive cultivation

OVERCROW vb crow over

OVERCURE vb take curing process too far

OVERCUT, -S vb cut too much

OVERDARE vb dare too much

OVERDEAR adj too dear

OVERDECK n upper deck

OVERDO, OVERDID, -ES, -NE vb do to excess

OVERDOER

OVERDOG, -S n person or side in an advantageous position

OVERDONE ► overdo

OVERDOSE n excessive dose of a drug ▷ vb take an overdose

OVERDRAW, OVERDREW vb withdraw more money than is in (one's bank account)

OVERDRY vb dry too much

OVERDUB, -S vb add (new sounds) to an audio recording so that the old and the new sounds can be heard ▷ n sound or series of sounds added by this method

OVERDUE adj still due after the time allowed

OVERDUST vb dust too much

OVERDYE, -D, -S vb dye (a fabric, yarn, etc) excessively

OVERDYER

OVEREASY adj too easy

OVEREAT, OVERATE, -S vb eat more than is necessary or healthy

OVERED ► over

OVEREDIT vb edit too much

OVEREGG, -S vb exaggerate absurdly

OVEREYE, -D, -S vb survey

OVERFALL, OVERFELL n turbulent stretch of water caused by marine currents over an underwater ridge ▷ vb fall over

OVERFAR adv too far

OVERFAST adj too fast

OVERFAT adj too fat

O

OVERFEAR vb fear too much
OVERFEED, OVERFED vb give (a person, plant, or animal) more food than is necessary or healthy
OVERFELL ▸ overfall
OVERFILL vb put more into (something) than there is room for
OVERFINE adj too fine
OVERFISH vb fish too much
OVERFIT adj too fit
OVERFLEW ▸ overfly
OVERFLOW vb flow over ▹ n something that overflows
OVERFLY, OVERFLEW vb fly over (a territory) or past (a point)
OVERFOLD n fold in which one or both limbs have been inclined more than 90°
OVERFOND adj excessively keen (on)
OVERFOUL adj too foul
OVERFREE adj too forward
OVERFULL adj excessively full
OVERFUND vb supply with too much money
OVERGALL vb make sore all over
OVERGANG vb dominate
OVERGAVE ▸ overgive
OVERGEAR vb cause (a company) to have too high a proportion of loan stock
OVERGET, -S, OVERGOT vb overtake
OVERGILD, OVERGILT vb gild too much
OVERGIRD, OVERGIRT vb gird too tightly
OVERGIVE, OVERGAVE vb give up
OVERGLAD adj too glad
OVERGO, -ES, -NE, OVERWENT vb go beyond
OVERGOAD vb goad too much
OVERGOES ▸ overgo
OVERGONE ▸ overgo
OVERGOT ▸ overget
OVERGROW, OVERGREW vb grow over or across (an area, path, lawn, etc)
OVERHAIR n outer coat of animal
OVERHALE same as
> **overhaile**
OVERHAND adj thrown or performed with the hand raised above the shoulder ▹ adv with the hand above the shoulder ▹ vb sew with the thread passing over two edges in one direction

OVERHANG, OVERHUNG vb project overhanging something ▹ n overhanging part
OVERHARD adj too hard
OVERHATE vb hate too much
OVERHAUL vb examine and repair ▹ n examination and repair
OVERHEAD adj above one's head ▹ adv over or above head height ▹ n stroke in racket games played from above head height
OVERHEAP vb supply too much
OVERHEAR vb hear (a speaker or remark) unintentionally
OVERHEAT vb make or become excessively hot ▹ n condition of being overheated
OVERHELD ▸ overhold
OVERHENT vb overtake
OVERHIGH adj too high
OVERHIT, -S vb hit too strongly
OVERHOLD, OVERHELD vb value too highly
OVERHOLY adj too holy
OVERHOPE vb hope too much
OVERHOT adj too hot
OVERHUNG ▸ overhang
OVERHUNT vb hunt too much
OVERHYPE vb hype too much
OVERIDLE adj too idle
OVERING ▸ over
OVERJOY, -S vb give great delight to
OVERJUMP vb jump too far
OVERJUST adj too just
OVERKEEN adj too keen
OVERKEEP, OVERKEPT vb keep too long
OVERKEST same as
> **overcast**
OVERKILL n treatment that is greater than required
OVERKIND adj too kind
OVERKING n supreme king
OVERKNEE adj reaching to above knee
OVERLADE vb overburden
OVERLAID ▸ overlay
OVERLAIN ▸ overlie
OVERLAND adv by land ▹ vb drive (cattle or sheep) overland
OVERLAP, -S vb share part of the same space or period of time (as) ▹ n area overlapping
OVERLARD vb cover with lard
OVERLATE adj too late

OVERLAX adj too lax
OVERLAY, OVERLAID, -S vb cover with a thin layer ▹ n something that is laid over something else
OVERLEAF adv on the back of the current page
OVERLEAP vb leap too far
OVERLEND, OVERLENT vb lend too much
OVERLET, -S vb let to too many
OVERLEWD adj too lewd
OVERLIE, OVERLAIN, -S vb lie on or cover (something or someone)
OVERLIER
OVERLIT > overlight
OVERLIVE vb live too much
OVERLOAD vb put too large a load on or in ▹ n excessive load
OVERLOCK vb sew fabric with interlocking stitch
OVERLONG adj too or excessively long
OVERLOOK vb fail to notice ▹ n high place affording a view
OVERLORD n supreme lord or master
OVERLOUD adj too loud
OVERLOVE vb love too much
OVERLUSH adj too lush
OVERLY adv excessively
OVERMAN, -S, OVERMEN vb provide with too many staff ▹ n man who oversees others
OVERMANY adj too many ▹ n excess of people
OVERMAST vb provide mast that is too big
OVERMEEK adj too meek
OVERMELT vb melt too much
OVERMEN ▸ overman
OVERMILD adj too mild
OVERMILK vb milk too much
OVERMINE vb mine too much
OVERMIX vb mix too much
OVERMUCH adj too much ▹ n excessive amount
OVERNAME vb repeat (someone's) name
OVERNEAR adj too near
OVERNEAT adj too neat
OVERNET, -S vb cover with net
OVERNEW adj too new
OVERNICE adj too fastidious, precise, etc
OVERPACK vb pack too much
OVERPAGE same as
▸ **overleaf**
OVERPAID ▸ overpay

O

OVERPART vb give an actor too difficult a role

OVERPASS, OVERPAST vb pass over, through, or across

OVERPAY, OVERPAID, -S vb pay (someone) at too high a rate

OVERPEER vb look down over

OVERPERT adj too insolent

OVERPLAN vb plan excessively

OVERPLAY same as ▸ **overact**

OVERPLOT vb plot onto existing graph or map

OVERPLUS n surplus or excess quantity

OVERPLY vb ply too much

OVERPOST vb hurry over

OVERPUMP vb pump too much

OVERRACK vb strain too much

OVERRAKE vb rake over

OVERRAN ▸ **overrun**

OVERRANK adj too rank ▸ vb assign an unnecessarily high rank to

OVERRASH adj too rash

OVERRATE vb have too high an opinion of

OVERREAD vb read over

OVERRED, -S vb paint over in red

OVERREN, -S same as ▸ **overrun**

OVERRICH adj (of food) excessively flavoursome or fatty

OVERRIDE, OVERRODE vb overrule ▸ n device or system that can override an automatic control

OVERRIFE adj too rife

OVERRIPE adj (of a fruit or vegetable) so ripe that it has started to decay

OVERRODE ▸ **override**

OVERRUDE adj very rude

OVERRUFF vb defeat trump card by playing higher trump

OVERRULE vb reverse the decision of (a person with less power)

OVERRUN, OVERRAN, -S vb conquer rapidly ▸ n act or an instance of overrunning

OVERS ▸ **over**

OVERSAD adj too sad

OVERSAIL vb project beyond

OVERSALE n selling of more than is available

OVERSALT vb put too much salt in

OVERSAVE vb put too much money in savings

OVERSAW ▸ **oversee**

OVERSEA same as ▸ **overseas**

OVERSEAS adj to, of, or from a distant country ▸ adv across the sea ▸ n foreign country or foreign countries collectively

OVERSEE, OVERSAW, -N, -S vb watch over from a position of authority

OVERSEED vb plant too much seed in

OVERSEEN ▸ **oversee**

OVERSEER n person who oversees others, esp workmen

OVERSEES ▸ **oversee**

OVERSELL, OVERSOLD vb exaggerate the merits or abilities of

OVERSET, -S vb disturb or upset

OVERSEW, -N, -S vb sew (two edges) with stitches that pass over them both

OVERSHOE n protective shoe worn over an ordinary shoe

OVERSHOT adj (of a water wheel) driven by a flow of water that passes over the wheel ▸ n type of fishing rod

OVERSICK adj too sick

OVERSIDE adv over the side (of a ship) ▸ n top side

OVERSIZE adj larger than the usual size ▸ n size larger than the usual or proper size

OVERSKIP vb skip over

OVERSLIP vb slip past

OVERSLOW adj too slow

OVERSMAN, OVERSMEN n overseer

OVERSOAK vb soak too much

OVERSOFT adj too soft

OVERSOLD ▸ **oversell**

OVERSOON adv too soon

OVERSOUL n universal divine essence

OVERSOW, -N, -S vb sow again after first sowing

OVERSPIN n forward spinning motion

OVERSTAY vb stay beyond the limit or duration of

OVERSTEP vb go beyond (a certain limit)

OVERSTIR vb stir too much

OVERSUDS vb produce too much lather

OVERSUP, -S vb sup too much

OVERSURE adj too sure

OVERSWAM ▸ **overswim**

OVERSWAY vb overrule

OVERSWIM, OVERSWAM, OVERSWUM vb swim across

OVERT adj open, not hidden

OVERTAKE, OVERTOOK vb move past (a vehicle or person) travelling in the same direction

OVERTALK vb talk over

OVERTAME adj too tame

OVERTART adj too bitter

OVERTASK vb impose too heavy a task upon

OVERTAX vb put too great a strain on

OVERTEEM vb be too full of something

OVERTHIN adj too thin

OVERTIME adv in addition to one's normal working hours ▸ n work at a regular job done in addition to regular working hours ▸ vb exceed the required time for (a photographic exposure)

OVERTIP, -S vb give too much money as a tip

OVERTIRE vb make too tired

OVERTLY ▸ **overt**

OVERTOIL vb work too hard

OVERTONE n additional meaning

OVERTOOK ▸ **overtake**

OVERTOP, -S vb exceed in height

OVERTRIM vb trim too much

OVERTRIP vb tread lightly over

OVERTURE n orchestral introduction ▸ vb make or present an overture to

OVERTURN vb turn upside down ▸ n act of overturning or the state of being overturned

OVERTYPE vb type over existing text

OVERURGE vb urge too strongly

OVERUSE, -D, -S vb use excessively ▸ n excessive use

OVERVEIL vb cover over

OVERVIEW n general survey

OVERVOTE vb vote more times than is allowed

OVERWARM vb make too warm

OVERWARY adj excessively wary

OVERWASH n act of washing over something

OVERWEAK adj too weak

OVERWEAR, OVERWORE, OVERWORN vb wear out

OVERWEEN vb think too highly of

O

OVERWENT ▶ overgo

OVERWET, -S vb make too wet

OVERWIDE adj too wide

OVERWILY adj too crafty

OVERWIND vb wind (a watch) beyond the proper limit

OVERWING vb fly above

OVERWISE adj too wise

OVERWORD n repeated word or phrase

OVERWORE ▶ overwear

OVERWORK vb work too much ▷ n excessive work

OVERWORN ▶ overwear

OVERWRAP vb cover with a wrapping

OVERYEAR vb keep for later year

OVERZEAL n excess of zeal

OVIBOS, -ES n type of ox

OVICIDAL ▶ ovicide

OVICIDE, -S n killing of sheep

OVIDUCAL ▶ oviduct

OVIDUCT, -S n tube through which eggs are conveyed

OVIFORM adj shaped like an egg

OVINE, -S adj of or like a sheep ▷ n member of sheep family

OVIPARA n all oviparous animals

OVIPOSIT vb (of insects and fishes) to deposit eggs through an ovipositor

OVISAC, -S n capsule or sac in which egg cells are produced

OVIST, -S n person believing ovum contains all subsequent generations

OVOID, -S adj egg-shaped ▷ n something that is ovoid

OVOIDAL, -S adj ovoid ▷ n something that is ovoid

OVOIDS ▶ ovoid

OVOLO, OVOLI, -S n type of convex moulding

> Two Os on your rack can normally be dealt with; three is a bit much, but this word for a moulding can handle them. Note that the plural can be **ovolos** or **ovoli**.

OVONIC adj using particular electronic storage batteries

OVONICS n science of ovonic equipment

OVULAR ▶ ovule

OVULARY ▶ ovule

OVULATE, -D, -S vb produce or release an egg cell from an ovary

OVULE, -S n plant part that contains the egg cell

OVUM, OVA n unfertilized egg cell

OW interj exclamation of pain

OWCHE, -S same as ▶ ouch

OWE, -D, -S, OWING vb be obliged to pay (a sum of money) to (a person)

OWELTY, OWELTIES n equality, esp in financial transactions

OWER Scots word for ▶ over

OWERBY adv over there

OWERLOUP n Scots word meaning encroachment

OWES ▶ owe

OWING ▶ owe

OWL, -ED, -ING, -S n night bird of prey ▷ vb act like an owl

OWLER, -S n smuggler

OWLERIES ▶ owlery

OWLERS ▶ owler

OWLERY, OWLERIES n place where owls live

OWLET, -S n young or nestling owl

OWLIER ▶ owly

OWLIEST ▶ owly

OWLING ▶ owl

OWLISH adj like an owl **OWLISHLY**

OWLLIKE ▶ owl

OWLS ▶ owl

OWLY, OWLIER, OWLIEST same as ▶ owlish

OWN, -ED, -ING, -S adj used to emphasize possession ▷ pron thing(s) belonging to a particular person ▷ vb possess

OWNABLE adj able to be owned

OWNED ▶ own

OWNER, -S n person who owns

OWNING ▶ own

OWNS ▶ own

OWNSOME, -S n solitary state

OWRE, -S same as ▶ ower

OWRECOME, OWRECAME n chorus of song ▷ vb overcome

OWRELAY, -S Scots form of ▶ overlay

OWRES ▶ owre

OWREWORD variant of ▶ overword

OWRIE, -R, -ST same as ▶ oorie

OWSE Scots form of ▶ ox

OWSEN Scots word for ▶ oxen

OWT, -S dialect word for ▶ anything

OX, -EN, -ES n castrated bull

OXALATE, -D, -S n salt or ester of oxalic acid ▷ vb treat with oxalate

OXALIC adj as in **oxalic acid** poisonous acid found in many plants

OXALIS, -ES n type of plant

OXAZEPAM n drug used to relieve anxiety

OXAZINE, -S n type of chemical compound

OXAZOLE, -S n type of liquid chemical compound

OXBLOOD, -S n dark reddish-brown colour ▷ adj of this colour

OXBOW, -S n piece of wood fitted around the neck of a harnessed ox

OXCART, -S n cart pulled by ox

OXEN ▶ ox

OXER, -S n high fence

OXES ▶ ox

OXEYE, -S n daisy-like flower

OXFORD, -S n type of stout laced shoe with a low heel

OXGANG, -S n old measure of farmland

OXGATE, -S same as ▶ oxgang

OXHEAD, -S n head of an ox

OXHEART, -S n heart-shaped cherry

OXHERD, -S n person who tends oxen

OXHIDE, -S n leather made from the hide of an ox

OXIC adj involving oxygen

OXID, -S same as ▶ oxide

OXIDABLE adj able to undergo oxidation

OXIDANT, -S n substance that acts or is used as an oxidizing agent

OXIDASE, -S n enzyme that brings about oxidation

OXIDASIC

OXIDATE, -D, -S another word for ▶ oxidize

OXIDE, -S n compound of oxygen and one other element

OXIDIC

OXIDISE, -D, -S same as ▶ oxidize

OXIDISER same as ▶ oxidizer

OXIDISES ▶ oxidise

OXIDIZE, -D, -S vb combine chemically with oxygen

OXIDIZER same as ▶ oxidant

OXIDIZES ▶ oxidize

OXIDS ▶ oxid

OXIES ► oxy

OXIM, -S *same as* **►** oxime

OXIME, -S *n* type of chemical compound

OXIMETER *n* instrument for measuring oxygen in blood
OXIMETRY

OXIMS ► oxim

OXLAND, -S *same as*
► oxgang

OXLIKE ► ox

OXLIP, -S *n* type of woodland plant

OXO *n as in* **oxo acid** acid that contains oxygen

OXONIUM, -S *n as in*
oxonium compound
type of salt derived from an organic ether

OXPECKER *n* type of African starling

OXSLIP, -S *same as* **►** oxlip

OXTAIL, -S *n* tail of an ox, used in soups and stews

OXTER, -ED, -ING, -S *n* armpit
▷ *vb* grip under arm

OXTONGUE *n* type of plant

OXY, OXIES ► ox

OXYACID, -S *n* any acid that contains oxygen

OXYGEN, -S *n* gaseous element essential to life and combustion
OXYGENIC

OXYMEL, -S *n* mixture of vinegar and honey

OXYMORON, OXYMORA
n figure of speech that combines two apparently contradictory ideas

OXYNTIC *adj* of or denoting stomach cells that secrete acid

OXYPHIL, -S *n* type of cell found in glands

OXYPHILE *same as* **►** oxyphil

OXYPHILS ► oxyphil

OXYSALT, -S *n* any salt of an oxyacid

OXYSOME, -S *n* group of molecules

OXYTOCIC *adj* accelerating childbirth by stimulating uterine contractions ▷ *n* oxytocic drug or agent

OXYTOCIN *n* hormone that stimulates the ejection of milk in mammals

OXYTONE, -S *adj* having an accent on the final syllable
▷ *n* oxytone word

OXYTONIC *adj* (of a word) having the stress or acute accent on the last syllable

OXYTROPE *n* type of flowering plant

OY, -S *n* grandchild

OYE *same as* **►** oy

OYER, -S *n* (in the 13th century) an assize

OYES, -ES, -SES *same as*
► oyez

OYEZ, -ES *interj* shouted three times by a public crier calling for attention ▷ *n* such a cry

OYS ► oy

OYSTER, -ED, -S *n* edible shellfish ▷ *vb* dredge for, gather, or raise oysters

OYSTERER *n* person fishing for oysters

OYSTERS ► oyster

OYSTRIGE *archaic variant of*
► ostrich

OZAENA, -S *n* inflammation of nasal mucous membrane

OZALID, -S *n* method of duplicating writing or illustrations

OZEKI, -S *n* sumo wrestling champion

OZONATE, -D, -S *vb* add ozone to

OZONE, -S *n* strong-smelling form of oxygen
OZONIC

OZONIDE, -S *n* type of unstable explosive compound

OZONISE, -D, -S *same as*
► ozonize
OZONISER

OZONIZE, -D, -S *vb* convert (oxygen) into ozone
OZONIZER

OZONOUS ► ozone

OZZIE, -S *n* hospital

O

Pp

P forms a two-letter word in front of every vowel except **U**, which makes it very useful for joining a new word to one already on the board. It also forms several three-letter words with **X**: **pax, pix, pox** (12 points each) and **pyx** (15). Other three-letter words with **P** well worth remembering are **zap, zep** and **zip** for 14 points each and **jap** for 12 points.

PA *n* (formerly) fortified Māori settlement

PAAL, -S *n* stake driven into the ground

PAAN, -S *n* leaf of the betel tree

PABLUM, -S *same as* ▷ **pabulum**

PABOUCHE *n* soft shoe

PABULAR ▷ **pabulum**

PABULOUS ▷ **pabulum**

PABULUM, -S *n* food

PAC, -S *n* soft shoe

PACA, -S *n* large burrowing rodent

PACABLE *adj* easily appeased

PACAS ▷ **paca**

PACATION *n* act of making peace

PACE, -D, -S *n* single step in walking ▷ *vb* walk up and down, esp in anxiety ▷ *prep* with due respect to: used to express polite disagreement

PACEMAN, PACEMEN *n* (in cricket) fast bowler

PACER, -S *n* horse trained to move at a special gait, esp for racing

PACES ▷ **pace**

PACEWAY, -S *n* racecourse for trotting and pacing

PACEY *adj* fast-moving, quick, lively

PACHA, -S *same as* ▷ **pasha**

PACHADOM *n* rank of pacha

PACHAK, -S *n* fragrant roots of Asian plant

PACHALIC *n* jurisdiction of pasha

PACHAS ▷ **pacha**

PACHINKO *n* Japanese game similar to pinball

PACHISI, -S *n* Indian game resembling backgammon

PACHOULI *same as* ▷ **patchouli**

PACHUCO, -S *n* young Mexican living in the US

PACIER ▷ **pacy**

PACIEST ▷ **pacy**

PACIFIC *adj* tending to bring peace

PACIFIED ▷ **pacify**

PACIFIER *n* baby's dummy

PACIFIES ▷ **pacify**

PACIFISM *n* belief that violence is unjustifiable

PACIFIST *n* person who refuses on principle to take part in war ▷ *adj* advocating, relating to, or characterized by pacifism

PACIFY, PACIFIED, PACIFIES *vb* soothe, calm

PACING, -S *n* act of pacing

PACK, -S *vb* put (clothes etc) together in a suitcase or bag ▷ *n* bag carried on a person's or animal's back

PACKABLE

PACKAGE, -D, -S *same as* ▷ **packet**

PACKAGER *n* independent firm specializing in design and production

PACKAGES ▷ **package**

PACKED *adj* completely filled

PACKER, -S *n* person or company who packs goods

PACKET, -ED, -S *n* small container (and contents) ▷ *vb* wrap up in a packet or as a packet

PACKFONG *n* Chinese alloy

PACKING, -S *n* material, such as paper or plastic, used to protect packed goods

PACKMAN, PACKMEN *n* man carrying a pack

PACKMULE *n* mule used to carry burdens

PACKNESS ▷ **pack**

PACKS ▷ **pack**

PACKSACK *n* bag carried strapped on the back or shoulder

PACKWAX *n* neck ligament

PACKWAY, -S *n* path for pack animals

PACO, -S *n* S American mammal

PACS ▷ **pac**

PACT, -S *n* formal agreement

PACTA ▷ **pactum**

PACTION, -S *vb* concur with

PACTS ▷ **pact**

PACTUM, PACTA *n* pact

PACY, PACIER, PACIEST *same as* ▷ **pacey**

PACZKI, -S *n* round filled doughnut

PAD, -DED, -S *n* piece of soft material used for protection, support, absorption of liquid, etc ▷ *vb* protect or fill with soft material

PADANG, -S *n* (in Malaysia) playing field

PADAUK, -S *n* tropical African or Asian tree

PADDED ▷ **pad**

PADDER, -S *n* highwayman who robs on foot

PADDIES ▷ **paddy**

PADDING, -S ▷ **pad**

PADDLE, -D, -S, PADDLING *n* short oar with a broad blade at one or each end ▷ *vb* move (a canoe etc) with a paddle

PADDLER -S

PADDOCK, -S *n* small field or enclosure for horses ▷ *vb* place (a horse) in a paddock

PADDY, PADDIES *n* fit of temper

PADELLA, -S *n* type of candle

PADERERO *same as* ▷ **paterero**

PADI, -S *same as* ▷ **paddy**

PADISHAH n Iranian ruler

PADKOS n snacks and provisions for a journey

PADLE, -S another name for ▸ **lumpfish**

PADLOCK, -S n detachable lock with a hinged hoop ▹ vb fasten (something) with a padlock

PADMA, -S n type of lotus

PADNAG, -S n ambling horse

PADOUK, -S same as ▸ **padauk**

PADRE, -S, PADRI n chaplain to the armed forces

PADRONA, -S n female boss or employer

PADRONE, -S, PADRONI n owner or proprietor of an inn, esp in Italy

PADS ▸ **pad**

PADSAW, -S n small narrow saw used for cutting curves

PADSHAH, -S same as ▸ **padishah**

PADUASOY n rich strong silk fabric used for hangings, vestments, etc

PAEAN, -S n song of triumph or thanksgiving

PAEANISM

PAELLA, -S n Spanish dish of rice, chicken, shellfish, and vegetables

PAENULA, -E, -S n ancient Roman cloak

PAEON, -S n metrical foot of four syllables

PAEONIC -S

PAEONIES ▸ **paeony**

PAEONS ▸ **paeon**

PAEONY, PAEONIES same as ▸ **peony**

PAESAN, -S n fellow countryman

PAESANO, PAESANI, -S n Italian-American man

PAESANS ▸ **paesan**

PAGAN, -S adj not belonging to one of the world's main religions ▹ n pagan person

PAGANDOM

PAGANISE same as ▸ **paganize**

PAGANISH ▸ **pagan**

PAGANISM ▸ **pagan**

PAGANIST ▸ **pagan**

PAGANIZE vb become pagan, render pagan, or convert to paganism

PAGANS ▸ **pagan**

PAGE, -D, -S n (one side of) sheet of paper forming a book etc ▹ vb summon (someone) by bleeper or loudspeaker

PAGEANT, -S n parade or display of people in costume

PAGEBOY, -S n type of hairstyle

PAGED ▸ **page**

PAGEFUL, -S n amount (of text, etc) that a page will hold

PAGEHOOD n state of being a page

PAGER, -S n small electronic device, capable of receiving short messages

PAGES ▸ **page**

PAGEVIEW n electronic page of information displayed at the request of a user

PAGINAL adj page-for-page

PAGINATE vb number the pages of (a book, manuscript, etc) in sequence

PAGING, -S ▸ **page**

PAGLE, -S same as ▸ **paigle**

PAGOD, -S n oriental idol

PAGODA, -S n pyramid-shaped Asian temple or tower

PAGODITE n type of soft mineral used for carving

PAGODS ▸ **pagod**

PAGRI, -S n type of turban

PAGURIAN n type of decapod crustacean of the family which includes the hermit crabs

PAGURID, -S same as ▸ **pagurian**

PAH, -S same as ▸ **pa**

PAHAUTEA same as > **kaikawaka**

PAHLAVI, -S n Iranian coin

PAHOEHOE n hardened lava

PAHS ▸ **pah**

PAID ▸ **pay**

PAIDLE, -S Scots variant of ▸ **paddle**

PAIGLE, -S n cowslip

PAIK, -ED, -ING, -S vb thump or whack

PAIL, -S n bucket

PAILFUL, -S, PAILSFUL same as ▸ **pail**

PAILLARD n thin slice of meat

PAILLON, -S n thin leaf of metal

PAILS ▸ **pail**

PAILSFUL ▸ **pailful**

PAIN, -ING n physical or mental suffering ▹ vb cause (someone) mental or physical suffering

PAINCH, -ES Scots variant of ▸ **paunch**

PAINED adj having or suggesting pain or distress

PAINFUL adj causing pain or distress

PAINIM, -S n heathen or pagan

PAINING ▸ **pain**

PAINLESS adj not causing pain or distress

PAINS pl n care or trouble

PAINT, -ED, -S n coloured substance, spread on a surface with a brush or roller ▹ vb colour or coat with paint

PAINTBOX n box containing a tray of dry watercolour paints

PAINTED ▸ **paint**

PAINTER, -S n rope at the front of a boat, for tying it up

PAINTIER ▸ **painty**

PAINTING n picture produced by using paint

PAINTPOT n pot for holding paint

PAINTS ▸ **paint**

PAINTURE n art of painting

PAINTY, PAINTIER ▸ **paint**

PAIOCK, -S obsolete word for ▸ **peacock**

PAIOCKE, -S obsolete word for ▸ **peacock**

PAIOCKS ▸ **paiock**

PAIR, -ED, -ER, -EST, -S n set of two things matched for use together ▹ vb group or be grouped in twos

PAIRE, -S obsolete spelling of ▸ **pair**

PAIRED ▸ **pair**

PAIRER ▸ **pair**

PAIRES ▸ **paire**

PAIREST ▸ **pair**

PAIRIAL, -S variant of ▸ **prial**

PAIRING, -S ▸ **pair**

PAIRS ▸ **pair**

PAIRWISE adv in pairs

PAIS n country

PAISA, -S, PAISE n monetary unit of Bangladesh, Bhutan, India, Nepal, and Pakistan

PAISAN, -S n fellow countryman

PAISANA, -S n female peasant

PAISANO, -S n friend

PAISANS ▸ **paisan**

PAISAS ▸ **paisa**

PAISE ▸ **paisa**

PAISLEY, -S n pattern of small curving shapes with intricate detailing

PAITRICK Scots word for > **partridge**

PAJAMA, -S same as ▸ **pyjama**

PAJAMAED adj wearing pajamas

PAJAMAS ▸ **pajama**

PAJOCK, -S obsolete word for ▸ **peacock**

P

PAJOCKE, -S obsolete word for ▸ peacock

PAJOCKS ▸ pajock

PAK, -S n pack

PAKAHI, -S n acid land that is unsuitable for cultivation

PAKAPOO, -S n Chinese lottery

PAKEHA, -S n person of European descent, as distinct from a Māori

PAKFONG, -S same as ▸ packfong

PAKIHI, -S n area of swampy infertile land

PAKKA variant of ▸ pukka

PAKOKO, -S n small freshwater fish

PAKORA, -S n fried battered pieces of vegetable, chicken, etc

PAKS ▸ pak

PAKTHONG n white alloy containing copper, zinc, and nickel

PAKTONG, -S same as ▸ pakthong

PAL, -S n friend ▹ vb associate as friends

PALABRA, -S n word

PALACE, -S n residence of a king, bishop, etc

PALACED adj having palaces

PALACES ▸ palace

PALADIN, -S n knight who did battle for a monarch

PALAGI, -S n (in Samoa) European

PALAIS n dance hall

PALAMA, -E n webbing on bird's feet

PALAMATE

PALAMINO same as ▸ palomino

PALAPA, -S n open-sided tropical building

PALAS, -ES n East Indian tree

PALATAL, -S adj of or relating to the palate ▹ n bony plate that forms the palate

PALATE, -D, -S, PALATING n roof of the mouth ▹ vb perceive by taste

PALATIAL adj like a palace, magnificent

PALATINE same as ▸ palatal

PALATING ▸ palate

PALAVER, -S n time-wasting fuss ▹ vb (often used humorously) have a conference

PALAY, -S n type of rubber

PALAZZO, PALAZZI, -S n Italian palace

PALE, -D, -R, -S, -ST adj light, whitish ▹ vb become pale

▹ n wooden or metal post used in fences

PALEA, -E n bract in a grass spikelet

PALEAL

PALEATE adj having scales

PALEBUCK n small African antelope

PALED ▸ pale

PALELY ▸ pale

PALENESS ▸ pale

PALEOCON n extremely right-wing conservative

PALEOSOL n ancient soil horizon

PALER ▸ pale

PALES ▸ pale

PALEST ▸ pale

PALESTRA same as > palaestra

PALET, -S n perpendicular band on escutcheon

PALETOT, -S n loose outer garment

PALETS ▸ palet

PALETTE, -S n artist's flat board for mixing colours on

PALEWAYS same as ▸ palewise

PALEWISE adv by perpendicular lines

PALFREY, -S n light saddle horse, esp ridden by women

PALI, -S n cliff in Hawaii

PALIER ▸ paly

PALIEST ▸ paly

PALIFORM adj resembling coral

PALIKAR, -S n Greek soldier

PALIMONY n alimony awarded to a nonmarried partner after the break-up of a long-term relationship

PALING, -S n wooden or metal post used in fences

PALINKA n type of apricot brandy

PALINODE n poem in which the poet recants something he or she has said in a former poem

PALINODY

PALIS ▸ pali

PALISADE n fence made of wooden posts driven into the ground ▹ vb enclose with a palisade

PALISADO same as ▸ palisade

PALISH adj rather pale

PALKEE, -S n covered Oriental litter

PALKI, -S same as ▸ palkee

PALL, -ED, -ING, -S n cloth spread over a coffin ▹ vb become boring

PALLA, -E n ancient Roman cloak

PALLADIA > palladium

PALLADIC adj of or containing palladium in the trivalent or tetravalent state

PALLAE ▸ palla

PALLAH, -S n S African antelope

PALLED ▸ pall

PALLET, -ED, -S same as ▸ palette

PALLETTE n armpit plate of a suit of armour

PALLIA ▸ pallium

PALLIAL adj relating to cerebral cortex

PALLIARD n person who begs

PALLIATE vb lessen the severity of (something) without curing it

PALLID, -ER adj pale, esp because ill or weak

PALLIDLY

PALLIED ▸ pally

PALLIER ▸ pally

PALLIES ▸ pally

PALLIEST ▸ pally

PALLING ▸ pall

PALLIUM, PALLIA, -S n garment worn by men in ancient Greece or Rome

PALLONE, -S n Italian ball game

PALLOR, -S n paleness of complexion

PALLS ▸ pall

PALLY, PALLIED, PALLIER, PALLIES, PALLIEST, -ING adj on friendly terms ▹ vb as in **pally up** become friends with

PALM, -ED, -ING, -S n inner surface of the hand ▹ vb conceal in or about the hand, as in sleight-of-hand tricks

PALMAR adj of or relating to the palm of the hand

PALMARY adj worthy of praise

PALMATE adj shaped like an open hand

PALMATED same as ▸ palmate

PALMBALL n baseball pitched from the palm and thumb

PALMED ▸ palm

PALMER, -S n medieval pilgrim

PALMETTE n ornament or design resembling the palm leaf

PALMETTO n small palm tree with fan-shaped leaves

PALMFUL, -S n amount that can be held in the palm of a hand

PALMIE, -S n palmtop computer

PALMIER, -S n type of French pastry

PALMIES ▶ palmie

PALMIEST ▶ palmy

PALMIET, -S n South African rush

PALMING ▶ palm

PALMIPED n web-footed bird

PALMIST > palmistry

PALMISTS > palmistry

PALMITIC adj as in **palmitic acid** white crystalline solid that is a saturated fatty acid

PALMITIN n colourless glyceride of palmitic acid

PALMLIKE ▶ palm

PALMS ▶ palm

PALMTOP, -S adj small enough to be held in the hand ▷ n computer small enough to be held in the hand

PALMY, PALMIEST adj successful, prosperous and happy

PALMYRA, -S n tall tropical Asian palm

PALOLO, -S n polychaete worm of the S Pacific Ocean

PALOMINO, -S n gold-coloured horse with a white mane and tail

PALOOKA, -S n stupid or clumsy boxer or other person

PALP, -ED, -ING, -S n sensory appendage in crustaceans and insects ▷ vb feel

PALPABLE adj obvious **PALPABLY**

PALPAL ▶ palp

PALPATE, -D, -S vb examine (an area of the body) by touching ▷ adj of, relating to, or possessing a palp or palps

PALPATOR n type of beetle

PALPEBRA n eyelid

PALPED ▶ palp

PALPI ▶ palpus

PALPING ▶ palp

PALPS ▶ palp

PALPUS, PALPI, -ES same as ▶ palp

PALS ▶ pal

PALSA, -S n landform of subarctic regions

PALSHIP, -S n state of being pals

PALSIED ▶ palsy

PALSIER ▶ palsy

PALSIES ▶ palsy

PALSIEST ▶ palsy

PALSTAFF variant of ▶ palstave

PALSTAVE n chisel made to fit into a split wooden handle

PALSY, PALSIER, PALSIES, PALSIEST, -ING n paralysis ▷ vb paralyse ▷ adj friendly

PALTER, -ED, -S vb act or talk insincerely **PALTERER**

PALTRIER ▶ paltry

PALTRILY ▶ paltry

PALTRY, PALTRIER adj insignificant

PALUDAL adj of, relating to, or produced by marshes

PALUDIC adj of malaria

PALUDINE adj relating to marsh

PALUDISM rare word for ▶ malaria

PALUDOSE adj growing or living in marshes

PALUDOUS adj marshy

PALY, PALIER, PALIEST adj vertically striped

PAM, -S n knave of clubs

PAMPA n grassland area

PAMPAS, -ES pl n vast grassy plains in S America **PAMPEAN -S**

PAMPER, -ED, -S vb treat (someone) with great indulgence, spoil **PAMPERER**

PAMPERO, -S n dry cold wind in South America

PAMPERS ▶ pamper

PAMPHLET n thin paper-covered booklet ▷ vb produce pamphlets

PAMPHREY n cabbage

PAMPOEN, -S n pumpkin

PAMS ▶ pam

PAN, -NED, -S n wide long-handled metal container used in cooking ▷ vb sift gravel from (a river) in a pan to search for gold

PANACEA, -S n remedy for all diseases or problems **PANACEAN**

PANACHE, -S n confident elegant style

PANADA, -S n mixture used as a thickening in cookery

PANAMA, -S n hat made of plaited leaves

PANARY, PANARIES n storehouse for bread

PANATELA same as > panatella

PANAX, -ES n genus of perennial herbs

PANBROIL vb broil in a pan

PANCAKE, -D, -S n thin flat circle of fried batter ▷ vb cause (an aircraft) to make a pancake landing

PANCE, -S n pansy

PANCETTA n lightly spiced cured bacon from Italy

PANCHAX n brightly coloured tropical Asian cyprinodont fish

PANCHEON n shallow bowl

PANCHION same as ▶ pancheon

PANCREAS n large gland behind the stomach that produces insulin and helps digestion

PAND, -S n valance

PANDA, -S n large black-and-white bearlike mammal from China

PANDAN, -S n type of palm of S E Asia

PANDANI, -S n tropical tree

PANDANS ▶ pandan

PANDANUS n Old World tropical palmlike plant

PANDAR, -ED, -S rare variant of ▶ pander

PANDAS ▶ panda

PANDECT, -S n treatise covering all aspects of a particular subject

PANDEMIA n epidemic affecting everyone

PANDEMIC adj (of a disease) occurring over a wide area ▷ n pandemic disease

PANDER, -ED, -S vb indulge (a person his or her desires) ▷ n someone who indulges a person in his or her desires

PANDERER n someone who indulges a person in his or her desires

PANDERLY ▶ pander

PANDERS ▶ pander

PANDIED ▶ pandy

PANDIES ▶ pandy

PANDIT, -S same as ▶ pundit

PANDOOR, -S same as ▶ pandour

PANDORA, -S n handsome red sea bream

PANDORE, -S another word for ▶ bandore

PANDOUR, -S n one of an 18th-century force of Croatian soldiers

PANDOWDY n deep-dish pie made from fruit, esp apples, with a cake topping

PANDROP, -S n hard mint-flavoured sweet

PANDS ▶ pand

P

PANDURA, -S *n* ancient stringed instrument

PANDY, PANDIED, PANDIES, -ING *n* (in schools) stroke on the hand with a strap as a punishment ▷ *vb* punish with such strokes

PANE, -D, -S, PANING *n* sheet of glass in a window or door ▷ *adj* (of fish, meat, etc) dipped in or rolled in breadcrumbs before cooking

PANEER, -S *n* soft white cheese, used in Indian cookery

PANEGYRY *n* formal public commendation; panegyric

PANEITY *n* state of being bread

PANEL, -ED, -LED, -S *n* flat distinct section of a larger surface, for example in a door ▷ *vb* cover or decorate with panels ▷ *adj* of a group acting as a panel

PANELESS ▶ **pane**

PANELING *same as* > **panelling**

PANELIST *same as* > **panellist**

PANELLED ▶ **panel**

PANELS ▶ **panel**

PANES ▶ **pane**

PANETELA *same as* ▶ **panatela**

PANFISH *n* small food fish ▷ *vb* fish for panfish

PANFORTE *n* hard spicy cake

PANFRY, PANFRIED, PANFRIES *vb* fry in a pan

PANFUL, -S *n* the contents of a pan

PANG, -ED, -ING, -S *n* sudden sharp feeling of pain or sadness ▷ *vb* cause pain

PANGA, -S *n* broad heavy knife of E Africa, used as a tool or weapon

PANGAMIC *adj* relating to pangamy

PANGAMY *n* unrestricted mating

PANGAS ▶ **panga**

PANGED ▶ **pang**

PANGEN, -S *same as* ▶ **pangene**

PANGENE, -S *n* hypothetical particle of protoplasm

PANGENS ▶ **pangene**

PANGING ▶ **pang**

PANGLESS *adj* without pangs

PANGOLIN *n* mammal with very long snout

PANGRAM, -S *n* sentence incorporating all the letters of the alphabet

PANGS ▶ **pang**

PANHUMAN *adj* relating to all humanity

PANIC, -KED, -S *n* sudden overwhelming fear ▷ *vb* feel or cause to feel panic ▷ *adj* of or resulting from such terror

PANICK, -S *old word for* ▶ **panic**

PANICKED ▶ **panic**

PANICKS ▶ **panick**

PANICKY ▶ **panic**

PANICLE, -S *n* loose, irregularly branched cluster of flowers

PANICLED

PANICS ▶ **panic**

PANICUM, -S *n* type of grass

PANIER, -S *same as* ▶ **pannier**

PANIM, -S *n* heathen or pagan

PANING ▶ **pane**

PANINO, PANINI *n* Italian sandwich

PANISC, -S *n* faun; attendant of Pan

PANISK, -S *same as* ▶ **panisc**

PANISLAM *n* all of Islam or the Muslim world

PANKO, -S *n* flaky breadcrumbs used in Japanese cookery

PANLIKE *adj* resembling a pan

PANMIXES ▶ **panmixis**

PANMIXIA *n* (in population genetics) random mating within an interbreeding population

PANMIXIS, PANMIXES *same as* ▶ **panmixia**

PANNAGE, -S *n* pasturage for pigs, esp in a forest

PANNE, -S *n* lightweight velvet fabric

PANNED ▶ **pan**

PANNER, -S ▶ **pan**

PANNES ▶ **panne**

PANNICK, -S *old spelling of the noun* ▶ **panic**

PANNICLE *n* thin layer of body tissue

PANNIER, -S *n* bag fixed on the back of a cycle

PANNIKEL *n* skull

PANNIKIN *n* small metal cup or pan

PANNING, -S ▶ **pan**

PANNIST, -S *n* person who plays a steel drum

PANNOSE *adj* like felt

PANNUS, -ES *n* inflammatory fleshy lesion on the surface of the eye

PANOCHA, -S *n* coarse grade of sugar made in Mexico

PANOCHE, -S *n* type of dark sugar

PANOPLY *n* magnificent array

PANOPTIC *adj* taking in all parts, aspects, etc, in a single view

PANORAMA *n* wide unbroken view of a scene

PANPIPE, -S *n* wind instrument

PANS ▶ **pan**

PANSIED *adj* covered with pansies

PANSIES ▶ **pansy**

PANSOPHY *n* universal knowledge

PANSTICK *n* type of cosmetic in stick form

PANSY, PANSIES *n* small garden flower

PANT, -ED *vb* breathe quickly and noisily during or after exertion ▷ *n* act of panting

PANTABLE *n* soft shoe

PANTALET *same as* > **pantalets**

PANTALON *n* keyboard instrument

PANTED ▶ **pant**

PANTER, -S *n* person who pants

PANTHEON *n* (in ancient Greece and Rome) temple built to honour all the gods

PANTHER, -S *n* leopard, esp a black one

PANTIE *same as* ▶ **panty**

PANTIES *pl n* women's underpants

PANTILE, -D, -S *n* roofing tile with an S-shaped cross section ▷ *vb* tile roof with pantiles

PANTINE, -S *n* pasteboard puppet

PANTING, -S ▶ **pant**

PANTLEG, -S *n* leg part of a pair of trousers

PANTLER, -S *n* pantry servant

PANTO, -S *same as* > **pantomime**

PANTOFLE *n* kind of slipper

PANTON, -S *n* type of horseshoe

PANTOS ▶ **panto**

PANTOUM, -S *n* verse form

PANTRY, PANTRIES *n* small room or cupboard for storing food

PANTS *pl n* undergarment for the lower part of the body

PANTSUIT *n* woman's suit of a jacket or top and trousers

PANTUN, -S *n* Malayan poetry

PANTY *n* woman's undergarment

P

PANZER, -S n German tank

PAOLO, PAOLI n Italian silver coin

PAP, -PED, -PING, -S n soft food for babies or invalids ▷ vb (of the paparazzi) to follow and photograph (a famous person) ▷ vb feed with pap

PAPA, -S n father

PAPABLE adj suitable for papacy

PAPACY, PAPACIES n position or term of office of a pope

PAPADAM, -S variant of ▶ poppadom

PAPADOM, -S variant of ▶ poppadom

PAPADUM, -S variant of ▶ poppadom

PAPAIN, -S n enzyme in the unripe fruit of the papaya

PAPAL adj of the pope

PAPALISE same as ▶ papalize

PAPALISM n papal system

PAPALIST n supporter of a pope

PAPALIZE vb make papal

PAPALLY ▶ papal

PAPAS ▶ papa

PAPAUMA, -S n New Zealand word for broadleaf

PAPAVER, -S n genus of poppies

PAPAW, -S same as ▶ papaya

PAPAYA, -S n large sweet West Indian fruit

PAPAYAN

PAPE, -S n spiritual father

PAPER, -ED, -ING, -S n material made in sheets from wood pulp or other fibres ▷ vb cover (walls) with wallpaper

PAPERBOY n boy employed to deliver newspapers to people's homes

PAPERED ▶ paper

PAPERER, -S ▶ paper

PAPERIER ▶ papery

PAPERING ▶ paper

PAPERS ▶ paper

PAPERY, PAPERIER adj like paper, esp in thinness, flimsiness, or dryness

PAPES ▶ pape

PAPILIO, -S n butterfly

PAPILLA, -E n small projection of tissue

PAPILLAR

PAPILLON n breed of toy spaniel with large ears

PAPOOSE, -S n Native American child

PAPPADAM same as ▶ poppadom

PAPPADOM same as ▶ poppadom

PAPPADUM n thin circle of dough fried in oil until crisp

PAPPED ▶ pap

PAPPI ▶ pappus

PAPPIER ▶ pappy

PAPPIES ▶ pappy

PAPPIEST ▶ pappy

PAPPING ▶ pap

PAPPOOSE same as ▶ papoose

PAPPOSE ▶ pappus

PAPPOUS ▶ pappus

PAPPUS, PAPPI, -ES n ring of hairs surrounding the fruit in composite plants

PAPPY, PAPPIER, PAPPIES, PAPPIEST adj resembling pap

PAPRICA, -S same as ▶ paprika

PAPRIKA, -S n mild powdered seasoning

PAPS ▶ pap

PAPULA, -E, -S same as ▶ papule

PAPULAR ▶ papule

PAPULAS ▶ papula

PAPULE, -S n small solid usually round elevation of the skin

PAPULOSE

PAPULOUS

PAPYRAL ▶ papyrus

PAPYRI ▶ papyrus

PAPYRIAN ▶ papyrus

PAPYRINE ▶ papyrus

PAPYRUS, PAPYRI n tall water plant

PAR, -RED, -RING, -S n usual or average condition ▷ vb play (a golf hole) in par

PARA, -S n paratrooper

PARABEMA n architectural feature

PARABEN, -S n carcinogenic ester

PARABLE, -D, -S n story that illustrates a religious teaching ▷ vb write a parable

PARABOLA n regular curve resembling the course of an object thrown forward and up

PARABOLE n similitude

PARACHOR n quantity constant over range of temperatures

PARACME, -S n phase where fever lessens

PARADE, -D, -S, PARADING n procession or march

▷ vb display or flaunt

PARADER -S

PARADING ▶ parade

PARADISE n heaven

PARADOR, -S n state-run hotel in Spain

PARADOS n bank behind a trench or other fortification

PARADOX n person or thing made up of contradictory elements

PARADOXY n state of being paradoxical

PARADROP n delivery of personnel or equipment from an aircraft by parachute

PARAE n type of fish

PARAFFIN n liquid mixture distilled from petroleum and used as a fuel or solvent ▷ vb treat with paraffin or paraffin wax

PARAFFLE n extravagant display

PARAFLE, -S same as ▶ paraffle

PARAFOIL n airfoil used on a paraglider

PARAFORM n paraformaldehyde

PARAGE, -S n type of feudal land tenure

PARAGOGE n addition of a sound or a syllable to the end of a word

PARAGON, -S n model of perfection ▷ vb equal or surpass

PARAGRAM n pun

PARAKEET n small long-tailed parrot

PARAKITE n series of linked kites

PARALLAX n apparent change in an object's position due to a change in the observer's position

PARALLEL adj separated by an equal distance at every point ▷ n line separated from another by an equal distance at every point ▷ vb correspond to

PARALOGY n anatomical similarity

PARALYSE vb affect with paralysis

PARALYZE same as ▶ paralyse

PARAMENT n ecclesiastical vestment or decorative hanging

PARAMESE n note in ancient Greek music

P

PARAMO, -S n high plateau in the Andes

PARAMOUR n lover

PARANETE n note in ancient Greek music

PARANG, -S n knife used by the Dyaks of Borneo

PARANOEA same as ▸ **paranoia**

PARANOIA n mental illness causing delusions of grandeur or persecution **PARANOIC**

PARANOID adj of, characterized by, or resembling paranoia ▸ n person who shows the behaviour patterns associated with paranoia

PARANYM, -S n euphemism

PARAPARA n small carnivorous New Zealand tree

PARAPET, -S n low wall or railing along the edge of a balcony or roof ▸ vb provide with a parapet

PARAPH, -ED, -S n flourish after a signature ▸ vb embellish signature

PARAQUAT n yellow extremely poisonous soluble solid used in solution as a weedkiller

PARAQUET n long-tailed parrot

PARAS ▸ **para**

PARASAIL vb glide through air on parachute towed by boat

PARASANG n Persian unit of distance equal to about 5.5 km or 3.4 miles

PARASHAH, PARASHOT n section of the Torah read in the synagogue

PARASITE n animal or plant living in or on another

PARASOL, -S n umbrella-like sunshade

PARATHA, -S n (in Indian cookery) flat unleavened bread

PARAVAIL adj lowest

PARAVANE n device that cuts the anchors of moored mines

PARAVANT adv pre-eminently ▸ n pre-eminent person or thing

PARAWING n paraglider

PARAXIAL adj (of a light ray) parallel to the axis of an optical system

PARAZOAN, PARAZOA n sea sponge

PARAZOON n parasitic animal

PARBAKE, -D, -S vb partially bake

PARBOIL, -S vb boil until partly cooked

PARBREAK vb vomit

PARCEL, -ED, -S n something wrapped up, package ▸ vb wrap up

PARCENER n person who takes an equal share with another or others

PARCH, -ED, -ES, -ING vb make very hot and dry

PARCHESI same as ▹ **parcheesi**

PARCHING ▸ **parch**

PARCHISI same as ▹ **parcheesi**

PARCLOSE n screen or railing in a church separating off an altar, chapel, etc

PARD, -S n leopard or panther

PARDAH, -S same as ▸ **purdah**

PARDAL, -S variant spelling of ▸ **pardale**

PARDALE, -S n leopard

PARDALIS n leopard

PARDALS ▸ **pardal**

PARDED adj having spots

PARDEE adv certainly

PARDI same as ▸ **pardee**

PARDIE same as ▸ **pardee**

PARDINE adj spotted

PARDNER, -S n friend or partner: used as a term of address

PARDON, -ED, -S vb forgive, excuse ▸ n forgiveness ▸ interj sorry ▸ sentence substitute sorry

PARDONER n (before the Reformation) person licensed to sell ecclesiastical indulgences

PARDONS ▸ **pardon**

PARDS ▸ **pard**

PARDY same as ▸ **pardee**

PARE, -D, -S vb cut off the skin or top layer of

PARECISM n state of having male and female organs close together

PARED ▸ **pare**

PAREIRA, -S n root of a South American climbing plant

PARELLA, -S n type of lichen

PARELLE, -S same as ▸ **parella**

PAREN, -S n parenthesis

PARENT, -ED, -S n father or mother ▸ vb raise offspring

PARENTAL adj of or relating to a parent or parenthood

PARENTED ▸ **parent**

PARENTS ▸ **parent**

PAREO, -S same as ▸ **pareu**

PARER, -S ▸ **pare**

PARERA, -S n New Zealand duck

PARERGON, PARERGA n work that is not one's main employment

PARERS ▸ **parer**

PARES ▸ **pare**

PARESIS, PARESES n incomplete or slight paralysis of motor functions **PARETIC -S**

PAREU, -S n Polynesian skirt or loincloth

PAREV adj containing neither meat nor milk products

PAREVE same as ▸ **parev**

PARFAIT, -S n dessert consisting of layers of ice cream, fruit, and sauce

PARFLESH same as ▹ **parfleche**

PARFOCAL adj with focal points in the same plane

PARGANA, -S n Indian sub-district

PARGE, -D, -S vb coat with plaster

PARGET, -ED, -S n plaster, mortar, etc, used to line chimney flues or cover walls ▸ vb cover or decorate with parget

PARGETER n one who pargets

PARGETS ▸ **parget**

PARGING, -S ▸ **parge**

PARGO, -ES, -S n sea bream

PARHELIA ▸ **parhelion**

PARHELIC ▹ **parhelion**

PARIAH, -S n social outcast

PARIAL, -S n pair royal of playing cards

PARIAN, -S n type of marble or porcelain

PARIES, PARIETES n wall of an organ or bodily cavity

PARIETAL adj of the walls of a body cavity such as the skull ▸ n parietal bone

PARIETES ▸ **paries**

PARING, -S n piece pared off

PARIS, -ES n type of herb

PARISH, -ES n area that has its own church and a priest or pastor

PARISHAD n Indian assembly

PARISHEN n member of parish

PARISHES ▸ **parish**

PARISON, -S n unshaped mass of glass

PARITIES ▸ **parity**

PARITOR, -S n official who summons witnesses

PARITY, PARITIES n equality or equivalence

PARK, -ED, -S n area of open land for recreational use by the public ▷ vb stop and leave (a vehicle) temporarily

PARKA, -S n large waterproof jacket with a hood

PARKADE, -S n building used as a car park

PARKAS ▶ parka

PARKED ▶ park

PARKEE, -S n Inuit outer garment

PARKER, -S ▶ park

PARKETTE n small public car park

PARKI, -S variant of ▶ parka

PARKIE, -S n park keeper

PARKIER ▶ parky

PARKIES ▶ parkie

PARKIEST ▶ parky

PARKIN, -S n moist spicy ginger cake

PARKING, -S ▶ park

PARKINS ▶ parkin

PARKIS ▶ parki

PARKISH adj like a park

PARKLAND n grassland with scattered trees

PARKLIKE ▶ park

PARKLY adj having many parks or resembling a park

PARKOUR, -S n sport of running in urban areas over obstacles

PARKS ▶ park

PARKWARD adv towards a park

PARKWAY, -S n wide road planted with trees, turf, etc

PARKY, PARKIER, PARKIEST adj (of the weather) chilly

PARLANCE n particular way of speaking, idiom

PARLANDO adv to be performed as though speaking

PARLANTE same as ▶ parlando

PARLAY, -ED, -S vb stake (winnings from one bet) on a subsequent wager ▷ n bet in which winnings are parlayed

PARLE, -D, -S, PARLING vb speak

PARLEY, -ED, -S n meeting between opponents to discuss terms ▷ vb have a parley

PARLEYER

PARLIES pl n small Scottish biscuits

PARLING ▶ parle

PARLOR, -S same as ▶ parlour

PARLOUR, -S n living room for receiving visitors

PARLOUS adj dire ▷ adv extremely

PARLY n short form of parliament

PARMESAN n Italian hard cheese

PAROCHIN n old Scottish parish

PARODIC ▶ parody

PARODIED ▶ parody

PARODIES ▶ parody

PARODIST ▶ parody

PARODOI n path leading to Greek theatre

PARODOS n ode sung by Greek chorus

PARODY, PARODIED, PARODIES n exaggerated and amusing imitation of someone else's style ▷ vb make a parody of

PAROEMIA n proverb

PAROL, -S n (formerly) pleadings in an action when presented by word of mouth ▷ adj (of a contract, lease, etc) not made under seal

PAROLE, -D, -S, PAROLING n early freeing of a prisoner on condition that he or she behaves well ▷ vb put on parole

PAROLEE -S

PAROLS ▶ parol

PARONYM, -S n cognate word

PARONYMY

PAROQUET n small long-tailed parrot

PARORE, -S n type of fish found around Australia and New Zealand

PAROSMIA n any disorder of the sense of smell

PAROTIC adj situated near the ear

PAROTID, -S adj relating to or situated near the parotid gland ▷ n parotid gland

PAROTIS n parotid gland

PAROTOID n poison gland on certain toads and salamanders ▷ adj resembling a parotoid gland

PAROUS adj having given birth

PAROUSIA n Second Coming

PAROXYSM n uncontrollable outburst of rage, delight, etc

PARP, -ED, -ING, -S vb make a honking sound

PARPANE, -S n parapet on bridge

PARPED ▶ parp

PARPEN, -S same as ▶ parpend

PARPEND, -S same as ▶ perpend

PARPENS ▶ parpen

PARPENT, -S n parapet on bridge

PARPING ▶ parp

PARPOINT n parapet on bridge

PARPS ▶ parp

PARQUET, -S n floor covering made of wooden blocks ▷ vb cover with parquet

PARR, -S n salmon up to two years of age

PARRA, -S n tourist or non-resident on a beach

PARRAL, -S same as ▶ parrel

PARRAS ▶ parra

PARRED ▶ par

PARREL, -S n ring that holds the jaws of a boom to the mast

PARRIDGE Scottish variant of ▶ porridge

PARRIED ▶ parry

PARRIER, -S ▶ parry

PARRIES ▶ parry

PARRING ▶ par

PARRITCH Scottish variant of ▶ porridge

PARROCK, -S vb put (an animal) in a small field

PARROKET n small long-tailed parrot

PARROT, -ED, -S n tropical bird with a short hooked beak ▷ vb repeat (someone else's words) without thinking

PARROTER n person who repeats what is said

PARROTRY ▶ parrot

PARROTS ▶ parrot

PARROTY adj like a parrot; chattering

PARRS ▶ parr

PARRY, PARRIED, PARRIES, -ING vb ward off (an attack) ▷ n parrying

PARS ▶ par

PARSABLE ▶ parse

PARSE, -D, -S vb analyse (a sentence) in terms of grammar

PARSEC, -S n unit of astronomical distance

PARSED ▶ parse

PARSER, -S n program that interprets input to a computer

PARSES ▶ parse

PARSING, -S ▶ parse

PARSLEY, -S, PARSLIED n herb used for seasoning and

P

decorating food ▷ *vb* garnish with parsley

PARSNEP, -S same as ► **parsnip**

PARSNIP, -S *n* long tapering cream-coloured root vegetable

PARSON, -S *n* Anglican parish priest

PARSONIC

PART *n* one of the pieces that make up a whole ▷ *vb* divide or separate

PARTAKE, -N, -S, PARTOOK *vb* take (food or drink)

PARTAKER

PARTAN, -S *Scottish word for* ► **crab**

PARTED *adj* divided almost to the base

PARTER, -S *n* thing that parts

PARTERRE *n* formally patterned flower garden

PARTERS ► **parter**

PARTI, -S *n* concept of architectural design

PARTIAL, -S *adj* not complete ▷ *n* any of the component tones of a single musical sound ▷ *vb* remove (a factor) from a set of statistics

PARTIBLE *adj* (esp of property or an inheritance) divisible

PARTICLE *n* extremely small piece or amount

PARTIED ► **party**

PARTIER, -S *n* person who parties

PARTIES ► **party**

PARTIM *adv* in part

PARTIS ► **parti**

PARTISAN *n* strong supporter of a party or group ▷ *adj* prejudiced or one-sided

PARTITA, -S *n* type of suite

PARTITE *adj* composed of or divided into a specified number of parts

PARTIZAN same as ► **partisan**

PARTLET, -S *n* woman's garment

PARTLY *adv* not completely

PARTNER, -S *n* either member of a couple in a relationship or activity ▷ *vb* be the partner of

PARTON, -S *n* hypothetical elementary particle

PARTOOK ► **partake**

PARTS *pl n* abilities or talents

PARTURE, -S *n* departure

PARTWAY *adv* some of the way

PARTWORK *n* series of magazines issued at regular intervals

PARTY, PARTIED, PARTIES *n* social gathering for pleasure ▷ *vb* celebrate, have fun ▷ *adj* (of a shield) divided vertically into two

PARTYER, -S *n* person who parties

PARTYING *n* act of partying

PARTYISM *n* devotion to political party

PARULIS another name for ► **gumboil**

PARURA, -S same as ► **parure**

PARURE, -S *n* set of jewels or other ornaments

PARVE same as ► **parev**

PARVENU, -S *n* person newly risen to a position of power or wealth ▷ *adj* of or characteristic of a parvenu

PARVENUE *n* woman newly risen to a position of power or wealth ▷ *adj* of a parvenue

PARVENUS ► **parvenu**

PARVIS *n* court or portico in front of a building, esp a church

PARVISE, -S same as ► **parvis**

PARVO, -S *n* disease of cattle and dogs

PARVOLIN *n* substance resulting from the putrefaction of flesh

PARVOS ► **parvo**

PAS *n* dance step or movement, esp in ballet

PASCAL, -S *n* unit of pressure

PASCHAL, -S *adj* of the Passover or Easter ▷ *n* Passover or Easter

PASCUAL, -S *adj* relating to pasture ▷ *n* plant that grows in pasture

PASE, -S *n* movement of the cape or muleta by a matador

PASEAR, -ED, -S *vb* go for a rambling walk

PASELA, -S same as ► **bonsela**

PASEO, -S *n* bullfighters' procession

PASES ► **pase**

PASH, -ED, -ES, -ING *n* infatuation ▷ *vb* throw or be thrown and break or be broken to bits

PASHA, -S *n* high official of the Ottoman Empire

PASHADOM *n* territory of a pasha

PASHALIC same as ► **pashalik**

PASHALIK *n* province or jurisdiction of a pasha

PASHAS ► **pasha**

PASHED ► **pash**

PASHES ► **pash**

PASHIM, -S same as ► **pashm**

PASHING ► **pash**

PASHKA, -S *n* rich Russian dessert

PASHM, -S *n* underfur of various Tibetan animals, esp goats, used for cashmere shawls

PASHMINA *n* type of cashmere scarf or shawl made from the underfur of Tibetan goats

PASHMS ► **pashm**

PASKA, -S same as ► **paskha**

PASKHA, -S *n* Russian dessert eaten at Easter

PASPALUM *n* type of grass with wide leaves

PASPY, PASPIES *n* piece of music in triple time

PASQUIL, -S *n* abusive lampoon or satire ▷ *vb* ridicule with pasquil

PASS, -ED, -ES *vb* go by, past, or through ▷ *n* successful result in a test or examination

PASSABLE *adj* (just) acceptable

PASSABLY *adv* fairly

PASSADE, -S *n* act of moving back and forth in the same place

PASSADO, -S *n* forward thrust with sword

PASSAGE, -D, -S *n* channel or opening providing a way through ▷ *vb* move or cause to move at a passage

PASSAGER *n as in* **passager hawk** young hawk or falcon caught while on migration

PASSAGES ► **passage**

PASSANT *adj* (of a heraldic beast) walking

PASSATA, -S *n* sauce made from sieved tomatoes

PASSBAND *n* frequency band within which signals are transmitted by a filter

PASSBOOK *n* record of a person's bank transactions

PASSE *adj* out-of-date

PASSED ► **pass**

PASSEE *adj* out-of-date

PASSEL, -S *n* group or quantity of no fixed number

PASSER, -S *n* person or thing that passes

PASSERBY n person that is passing or going by, esp on foot

PASSERS ▶ passer

PASSES ▶ pass

PASSIBLE adj susceptible to emotion or suffering

PASSIBLY

PASSIM adv everywhere, throughout

PASSING, -S adj brief or transitory ▷ n death

PASSION, -S n intense love ▷ vb give passionate character to

PASSIVE, -S adj not playing an active part ▷ n passive form of a verb

PASSKEY, -S n private key

PASSLESS adj having no pass

PASSMAN, PASSMEN n student who passes without honours

PASSMENT same as
> **passement**

PASSOUT, -S n (in ice hockey) pass by an attacking player from behind the opposition goal line

PASSOVER n lamb eaten during Passover

PASSPORT n official document of nationality granting permission to travel abroad

PASSUS, -ES n division or section of a poem, story, etc

PASSWORD n secret word or phrase that ensures admission

PAST, -S adj of the time before the present ▷ n period of time before the present ▷ adv ago ▷ prep beyond

PASTA, -S n type of food that is made from flour and water

PASTANCE n activity that passes time

PASTAS ▶ pasta

PASTE, -D, -S n moist soft mixture, such as toothpaste ▷ vb fasten with paste

PASTEL, -S n coloured chalk crayon for drawing ▷ adj pale and delicate in colour

PASTER, -S n person or thing that pastes

PASTERN, -S n part of a horse's foot

PASTERS ▶ paster

PASTES ▶ paste

PASTEUP, -S n material pasted on a sheet of paper or board

PASTICCI > pasticcio

PASTICHE n work of art that mixes styles or copies the style of another artist

PASTIER ▶ pasty

PASTIES ▶ pasty

PASTIEST ▶ pasty

PASTIL, -S same as ▶ **pastille**

PASTILLE n small fruit-flavoured and sometimes medicated sweet

PASTILS ▶ pastil

PASTILY ▶ pasty

PASTIME, -S n activity that makes time pass pleasantly

PASTINA, -S n small pieces of pasta

PASTING, -S n heavy defeat

PASTIS, -ES n anise-flavoured alcoholic drink

PASTITSO n Greek dish of baked pasta

PASTLESS adj having no past

PASTNESS n quality of being past

PASTOR, -ED, -S n member of the clergy in charge of a congregation ▷ vb act as a pastor

PASTORAL adj of or depicting country life ▷ n poem or picture portraying country life

PASTORED ▶ pastor

PASTORLY ▶ pastor

PASTORS ▶ pastor

PASTRAMI n highly seasoned smoked beef

PASTRIES ▶ pastry

PASTROMI same as
▶ **pastrami**

PASTRY, PASTRIES n baking dough made of flour, fat, and water

PASTS ▶ past

PASTURAL adj of pasture

PASTURE, -D, -S n grassy land for farm animals to graze on ▷ vb cause (livestock) to graze

PASTURER n person who tends cattle

PASTURES ▶ pasture

PASTY, PASTIER, PASTIES, PASTIEST adj (of a complexion) pale and unhealthy ▷ n round of pastry folded over a savoury filling

PAT, -S, -TED, -TEST, -TING vb tap lightly ▷ n gentle tap or stroke ▷ adj quick, ready, or glib

PATACA, -S n monetary unit of Macao

PATAGIA ▶ patagium

PATAGIAL ▶ patagium

PATAGIUM, PATAGIA n web of skin acting as wings in bats

PATAKA, -S n building on stilts, used for storing provisions

PATAMAR, -S n type of boat

PATBALL, -S n game like squash but using hands

PATCH, -ED, -ES, -ING n piece of material sewn on a garment ▷ vb mend with a patch

PATCHER -S

PATCHERY n bungling work

PATCHES ▶ patch

PATCHIER ▶ patchy

PATCHILY ▶ patchy

PATCHING ▶ patch

PATCHY, PATCHIER adj of uneven quality or intensity

PATE, -S n head

PATED

PATELLA, -E, -S n kneecap

PATELLAR

PATEN, -S n plate used for the bread at Communion

PATENCY n condition of being obvious

PATENS ▶ paten

PATENT, -ED, -S n document giving the exclusive right to make or sell an invention ▷ adj open to public inspection ▷ vb obtain a patent for

PATENTEE n person, group, company, etc, that has been granted a patent

PATENTLY adv obviously

PATENTOR n person who or official body that grants a patent or patents

PATENTS ▶ patent

PATER, -S n father

PATERA, -E n shallow ancient Roman bowl

PATERERO n type of cannon

PATERNAL adj fatherly

PATERS ▶ pater

PATES ▶ pate

PATH, -ED, -ING, -S n surfaced walk or track ▷ vb make a path

PATHETIC adj causing feelings of pity or sadness ▷ pl n pathetic sentiments ▷ n pathetic person

PATHIC, -S n person who suffers ▷ adj of or relating to suffering

PATHING ▶ path

PATHLESS ▶ path

PATHNAME n description of where a file is found in a hierarchy of directories

P

PATHOGEN n thing that causes disease

PATHOS, -ES n power of arousing pity or sadness

PATHS ▸ path

PATHWAY, -S n path

PATIBLE adj endurable

PATIENCE n quality of being patient

PATIENT, -S adj enduring difficulties or delays calmly ▷ n person receiving medical treatment ▷ vb make calm

PATIKI, -S n New Zealand sand flounder or dab

PATIN, -S same as ▸ paten

PATINA, -E, -S n fine layer on a surface

PATINAED adj having a patina

PATINAS ▸ patina

PATINATE vb coat with patina

PATINE, -D, -S, PATINING vb cover with patina

PATINISE same as ▸ patinize

PATINIZE vb coat with patina

PATINS ▸ patin

PATIO, -S n paved area adjoining a house

PATKA, -S n head covering worn by Sikh men

PATLY adv fitly

PATNESS n appropriateness

PATOIS n regional dialect, esp of French

PATONCE adj (of cross) with limbs which broaden from centre

PATOOT, -S same as ▸ patootie

PATOOTIE n person's bottom

PATOOTS ▸ patoot

PATRIAL, -S n (in Britain, formerly) person with a right to live in the United Kingdom

PATRIATE vb bring under the authority of an autonomous country

PATRICK, -S n former Irish coin

PATRICO, -S n fraudulent priest

PATRIOT, -S n person who loves his or her country

PATROL, -S n regular circuit by a guard ▷ vb go round on guard, or reconnoitring

PATRON, -S n person who gives financial support

PATRONAL > patroness

PATRONLY > patroness

PATRONNE n woman who owns or manages a hotel, restaurant, or bar

PATRONS ▸ patron

PATROON, -S n Dutch land-holder in New Netherland and New York

PATS ▸ pat

PATSY, PATSIES n person who is easily cheated, victimized, etc

PATTAMAR n Indian courier

PATTE, -S n band keeping belt in place

PATTED ▸ pat

PATTEE adj (of a cross) having triangular arms widening outwards

PATTEN, -ED, -S n wooden clog or sandal ▷ vb wear pattens

PATTER, -ED, -S vb make repeated soft tapping sounds ▷ n quick succession of taps

PATTERER

PATTERN, -S n arrangement of repeated parts or decorative designs ▷ vb model

PATTERS ▸ patter

PATTES ▸ patte

PATTEST ▸ pat

PATTIE same as ▸ patty

PATTIES ▸ patty

PATTING ▸ pat

PATTLE, -S dialect for ▸ paddle

PATTRESS n box for the space behind electrical sockets and switches

PATTY, PATTIES n small flattened cake of minced food

PATTYPAN n small round flattish squash

PATU, -S n short Māori club, now used ceremonially

PATULENT adj spreading widely

PATULIN, -S n toxic antibiotic

PATULOUS adj spreading widely or expanded

PATUS ▸ patu

PATUTUKI n blue cod

PATY adj (of cross) having arms of equal length

PATZER, -S n novice chess player

PAUA, -S n edible shellfish of New Zealand

PAUCAL, -S n grammatical number for words in contexts where a few of their referents are described ▷ adj relating to or inflected for this number

PAUCITY n scarcity

PAUGHTY Scots word for ▸ haughty

PAUL, -S same as ▸ pawl

PAULDRON n either of two metal plates worn with armour to protect the shoulders

PAULIN, -S n tarpaulin

PAULS ▸ paul

PAUNCE, -S n pansy

PAUNCH, -ED, -ES n protruding belly ▷ vb stab in the stomach

PAUNCHY adj having a protruding belly or abdomen

PAUPER, -ED, -S n very poor person ▷ vb reduce to beggary

PAURAQUE n type of long-tailed nocturnal bird

PAUROPOD n minute myriapod

PAUSAL ▸ pause

PAUSE, -D, -S vb stop for a time ▷ n stop or rest in speech or action

PAUSEFUL adj taking pauses

PAUSER, -S ▸ pause

PAUSES ▸ pause

PAUSING, -S ▸ pause

PAV, -S short for ▸ pavlova

PAVAGE, -S n tax towards paving streets

PAVAN, -S same as ▸ pavane

PAVANE, -S n slow and stately dance

PAVANS ▸ pavan

PAVE, -D, -S vb form (a surface) with stone or brick ▷ n paved surface, esp an uneven one

PAVEED adj (of jewels) set close together

PAVEMENT n paved path for pedestrians ▷ vb provide with pavement

PAVEN, -S same as ▸ pavane

PAVER, -S ▸ pave

PAVES ▸ pave

PAVID adj fearful

PAVILION n building on a playing field etc ▷ vb place or set in or as if in a pavilion

PAVILLON n bell of wind instrument

PAVIN, -S same as ▸ pavane

PAVING, -S n paved surface ▷ adj of or for a paved surface or pavement

PAVINS ▸ pavin

PAVIOR, -S same as ▸ paviour

PAVIOUR, -S n person who lays paving

PAVIS n large square shield

PAVISE, -S same as ▸ pavis

PAVISER, -S n soldier holding a pavis

PAVISES ▸ pavise

PAVISSE, -S same as ► pavis

PAVLOVA, -S n meringue cake topped with whipped cream and fruit

PAVONE, -S n peacock

PAVONIAN same as ► pavonine

PAVONINE adj of or resembling a peacock or the colours, design, or iridescence of a peacock's tail

PAVS ► pav

PAW, -ED, -ING, -S n animal's foot with claws and pads ▷ vb scrape with the paw or hoof

PAWA, -S old word for ► peacock

PAWAW, -ED, -ING, -S vb recite N American incantation

PAWED ► paw

PAWER, -S n person or animal that paws

PAWING ► paw

PAWK, -S Scots word for ► trick

PAWKIER ► pawky

PAWKIEST ► pawky

PAWKILY ► pawky

PAWKS ► pawk

PAWKY, PAWKIER, PAWKIEST adj having or characterized by a dry wit

PAWL, -S n pivoted lever shaped to engage with a ratchet

PAWN, -ED, -ING, -S vb deposit (an article) as security for money borrowed ▷ n chessman of the lowest value

PAWNABLE

PAWNAGE -S

PAWNCE, -S old word for ► pansy

PAWNED ► pawn

PAWNEE, -S n one who accepts goods in pawn

PAWNER, -S n one who pawns his or her possessions

PAWNING ► pawn

PAWNOR, -S same as ► pawner

PAWNS ► pawn

PAWNSHOP n premises of a pawnbroker

PAWPAW, -S same as ► papaw

PAWS ► paw

PAX, -ES n peace ▷ interj call signalling a desire to end hostilities

Latin for peace, this is yet another of those very useful short words containing X.

PAXIUBA, -S n tropical tree

PAXWAX, -ES n strong ligament in the neck of many mammals

PAY, PAID, -ED, -S vb give money etc in return for goods or services ▷ n wages or salary

PAYABLE, -S adj due to be paid ▷ n debt to be paid

PAYABLY

PAYBACK, -S n return on an investment

PAYCHECK n payment for work done

PAYDAY, -S n day on which wages or salaries are paid

PAYDOWN, -S n reduction of debt through repayment

PAYED ► pay

PAYEE, -S n person to whom money is paid or due

PAYER, -S n person who pays

PAYESS pl n uncut sideburns worn by some Jewish men

PAYFONE, -S US spelling of ► payphone

PAYGRADE n military rank

PAYING, -S ► pay

PAYLIST, -S n list of people to be paid

PAYLOAD, -S n passengers or cargo of an aircraft

PAYMENT, -S n act of paying

PAYNIM, -S n heathen or pagan

PAYNIMRY n state of being heathen

PAYNIMS ► paynim

PAYOFF, -S n final settlement, esp in retribution

PAYOLA, -S n bribe to promote a commercial product

PAYOR, -S same as ► payer

PAYOUT, -S n sum of money paid out

PAYPHONE n coin-operated telephone

PAYROLL, -S n list of employees who receive regular pay

PAYS ► pay

PAYSAGE, -S n landscape

PAYSD Spenserian form of ► poised

PAYSLIP, -S n note of payment given to employee

PAYWALL, -S n system that denies access to a website unless a payment is made

PAZAZZ, -ES same as ► pizzazz

PAZZAZZ same as ► pizzazz

PE n 17th letter of the Hebrew alphabet, transliterated as p

PEA, -S n climbing plant with seeds growing in pods

PEABERRY n coffee berry containing one seed

PEABRAIN n stupid person

PEACE, -D, -S, PEACING n calm, quietness

PEACEFUL adj not in a state of war or disagreement

PEACENIK n activist who opposes war

PEACES ► peace

PEACH, -ED, -ES, -ING n soft juicy fruit ▷ adj pinkish-orange ▷ vb inform against an accomplice

PEACHER -S

PEACHICK n young peafowl

PEACHIER ► peachy

PEACHILY ► peachy

PEACHING ► peach

PEACHY, PEACHIER adj of or like a peach, esp in colour or texture

PEACING ► peace

PEACOAT, -S n woollen jacket

PEACOCK, -S n large male bird with a brilliantly coloured fanlike tail ▷ vb display (oneself) proudly

PEACOCKY

PEACOD, -S same as ► peacod

PEAFOWL, -S n peacock or peahen

PEAG, -S n (formerly) money used by Native Americans

PEAGE, -S same as ► peag

PEAGS ► peag

PEAHEN, -S ► peacock

PEAK, -S n pointed top, esp of a mountain ▷ vb form or reach a peak ▷ adj of or at the point of greatest demand

PEAKED adj having a peak

PEAKIER ► peaky

PEAKIEST ► peaky

PEAKING, -S n act of peaking

PEAKISH adj sickly

PEAKLESS adj without a peak

PEAKLIKE ► peak

PEAKS ► peak

PEAKY, PEAKIER, PEAKIEST ► peak

PEAL, -ED, -ING, -S n long loud echoing sound, esp of bells or thunder ▷ vb sound with a peal or peals

PEALIKE ► pea

PEALING ► peal

PEALS ► peal

PEAN, -ED, -ING, -S same as ► peen

PEANUT, -S n pea-shaped nut that ripens underground

PEANUTTY adj having the taste of peanuts

PEAPOD, -S n pod of the pea plant

PEAR, -S n sweet juicy fruit with a narrow top and rounded base

PEARCE, -D, -S, PEARCING old spelling of ▸ **pierce**

PEARE, -S obsolete spelling of ▸ **pear**

PEARL, -ED, -ING, -S same as ▸ **purl**

PEARLASH n granular crystalline form of potassium carbonate

PEARLED ▸ **pearl**

PEARLER, -S n person who dives for or trades in pearls ▷ adj excellent

PEARLIER ▸ **pearly**

PEARLIES ▸ **pearly**

PEARLIN n type of lace used to trim clothes

PEARLING ▸ **pearl**

PEARLINS n type of lace

PEARLITE same as ▸ **perlite**

PEARLS ▸ **pearl**

PEARLY, PEARLIER, PEARLIES adj resembling a pearl, esp in lustre ▷ n London costermonger who wears pearl buttons

PEARMAIN n any of several varieties of apple having a red skin

PEARS ▸ **pear**

PEARST archaic variant of ▸ **pierced**

PEART, -ER, -EST adj lively **PEARTLY**

PEARWOOD n wood from pear tree

PEAS ▸ **pea**

PEASANT, -S n person working on the land

PEASANTY adj having qualities ascribed to traditional country life or people

PEASCOD, -S same as ▸ **cod**

PEASE, -D, -S, PEASING n archaic or dialect word for pea ▷ vb appease

PEASECOD n pod of a pea plant

PEASED ▸ **pease**

PEASEN obsolete plural of ▸ **pease**

PEASES ▸ **pease**

PEASING ▸ **pease**

PEASON obsolete plural of ▸ **pease**

PEAT, -S n decayed vegetable material found in bogs

PEATARY n area covered with peat

PEATERY same as ▸ **peatary**

PEATIER ▸ **peaty**

PEATIEST ▸ **peaty**

PEATLAND n area of land consisting of peat bogs

PEATMAN, PEATMEN n person who collects peat

PEATS ▸ **peat**

PEATSHIP n ship carrying peat

PEATY, PEATIER, PEATIEST ▸ **peat**

PEAVEY, -S n wooden lever used for handling logs

PEAVY, PEAVIES same as ▸ **peavey**

PEAZE, -D, -S, PEAZING same as ▸ **pease**

PEBA, -S n type of armadillo

PEBBLE, -D, -S n small roundish stone ▷ vb cover with pebbles

PEBBLIER ▸ **pebbly**

PEBBLING n (in curling) act of spraying the rink with drops of hot water to slow down the stone

PEBBLY, PEBBLIER ▸ **pebble**

PEBRINE, -S n disease of silkworms

PEC n pectoral muscle

PECAN, -S n edible nut of a N American tree

PECCABLE adj liable to sin

PECCANCY ▸ **peccant**

PECCANT adj guilty of an offence

PECCARY n piglike animal of American forests

PECCAVI, -S n confession of guilt

PECH, -ED, -ING, -S Scottish word for ▸ **pant**

PECHAN, -S Scots word for ▸ **stomach**

PECHED ▸ **pech**

PECHING ▸ **pech**

PECHS ▸ **pech**

PECK, -ED, -S vb strike or pick up with the beak ▷ n pecking movement

PECKE, -S n quarter of bushel

PECKED ▸ **peck**

PECKER, -S n short for woodpecker

PECKES ▸ **pecke**

PECKIER ▸ **pecky**

PECKIEST ▸ **pecky**

PECKING, -S ▸ **peck**

PECKISH adj slightly hungry

PECKS ▸ **peck**

PECKY, PECKIER, PECKIEST adj discoloured

PECORINO, PECORINI n Italian cheese made from ewes' milk

PECS pl n pectoral muscles

PECTASE, -S n enzyme occurring in certain ripening fruits

PECTATE, -S n salt or ester of pectic acid

PECTEN, -S, PECTINES n comblike structure in the eye of birds and reptiles

PECTIC ▸ **pectin**

PECTIN, -S n substance in fruit that makes jam set

PECTINAL adj resembling a comb ▷ n fish with bones or a spine resembling a comb

PECTINES ▸ **pecten**

PECTINS ▸ **pectin**

PECTISE, -D, -S same as ▸ **pectize**

PECTIZE, -D, -S vb change into a jelly

PECTORAL adj of the chest or thorax ▷ n pectoral muscle or fin

PECTOSE, -S n insoluble carbohydrate found in unripe fruit

PECULATE vb embezzle (public money)

PECULIA ▸ **peculium**

PECULIAR adj strange ▷ n special sort, esp an accented letter

PECULIUM, PECULIA n property that a father or master allowed his child or slave to hold as his own

PED, -S n pannier

PEDAGOG, -S same as ▸ **pedagogue**

PEDAGOGY n principles, practice, or profession of teaching

PEDAL, -ED, -ING, -LED, -S n foot-operated lever ▷ vb propel (a bicycle) by using its pedals ▷ adj of or relating to the foot or the feet

PEDALCAR n child's vehicle that is operated by pedals

PEDALED ▸ **pedal**

PEDALER, -S ▸ **pedal**

PEDALFER n type of zonal soil deficient in lime but containing deposits of aluminium and iron

PEDALIER n pedal piano

PEDALING ▸ **pedal**

PEDALLED ▸ **pedal**

PEDALLER n person who pedals

PEDALO, -ES, -S n pedal-operated pleasure craft

PEDALS ▶ pedal

PEDANT, -S n person who is excessively concerned with details and rules

PEDANTIC adj of, relating to, or characterized by pedantry

PEDANTRY n practice of being a pedant, esp in the minute observance of petty rules or details

PEDANTS ▶ pedant

PEDATE adj (of a plant leaf) divided into several lobes arising at a common point **PEDATELY**

PEDDER, -S old form of ▶ pedlar

PEDDLE, -D, -S, PEDDLING vb sell (goods) from door to door

PEDDLER, -S same as ▶ pedlar

PEDDLERY n business of peddler

PEDDLES ▶ peddle

PEDDLING ▶ peddle

PEDERERO n type of cannon

PEDES ▶ pes

PEDESIS, PEDESES n random motion of small particles

PEDESTAL n base supporting a column, statue, etc

PEDETIC adj of feet

PEDICAB, -S n pedal-operated tricycle, available for hire

PEDICEL, -S n stalk bearing a single flower of an inflorescence

PEDICLE, -S n any small stalk **PEDICLED**

PEDICULI > pediculus

PEDICURE n medical or cosmetic treatment of the feet ▷ vb give a pedicure

PEDIFORM adj shaped like a foot

PEDIGREE n register of ancestors, esp of a purebred animal

PEDIMENT n triangular part over a door etc

PEDIPALP n either member of the second pair of head appendages of arachnids

PEDLAR, -S n person who sells goods from door to door

PEDLARY same as ▶ pedlery

PEDLER, -S same as ▶ pedlar

PEDLERY n business of pedler

PEDOCAL, -S n type of soil that is rich in lime

PEDOLOGY same as > paedology

PEDRAIL, -S n device replacing wheel on rough surfaces

PEDRERO, -S n type of cannon

PEDRO, -S n card game

PEDS ▶ ped

PEDUNCLE same as ▶ pedicel

PEDWAY, -S n walkway for pedestrians only

PEE, -D, -ING, -S vb urinate ▷ n urine

PEEBEEN, -S n type of large evergreen

PEECE, -S obsolete variant of ▶ piece

PEED ▶ pee

PEEING ▶ pee

PEEK, -ED, -ING, -S n peep or glance ▷ vb glance quickly or secretly

PEEKABO, -S same as ▶ peekaboo

PEEKABOO n game in which one person hides his or her face and suddenly reveals it ▷ adj made of fabric that is almost transparent

PEEKABOS ▶ peekabo

PEEKAPOO n dog which is cross between Pekingese and poodle

PEEKED ▶ peek

PEEKING ▶ peek

PEEKS ▶ peek

PEEL, -ED, -S vb remove the skin or rind of (a vegetable or fruit) ▷ n rind or skin **PEELABLE**

PEELER, -S n device for peeling vegetables, fruit, etc

PEELING, -S n strip that has been peeled off

PEELS ▶ peel

PEEN, -ED, -S n end of a hammer head opposite the striking face ▷ vb strike with the peen of a hammer

PEENGE, -D, -S, PEENGING vb complain

PEENING, -S n act of peening

PEENS ▶ peen

PEEOY, -S n homemade firework

PEEP, -ED, -ING, -S vb look slyly or quickly ▷ n peeping look

PEEPBO, -S n game of peekaboo

PEEPE old spelling of ▶ pip

PEEPED ▶ peep

PEEPER, -S n person who peeps

PEEPES archaic spelling of ▶ peeps

PEEPHOLE n small aperture for observation

PEEPING ▶ peep

PEEPS ▶ peep

PEEPSHOW n box containing a series of pictures that can be seen through a small hole

PEEPTOE adj of a shoe in which the toe is not covered

PEEPUL, -S n Indian moraceous tree

PEER, -ED, -ING, -S n (in Britain) member of the nobility ▷ vb look closely and intently

PEERAGE, -S n whole body of peers

PEERED ▶ peer

PEERESS n (in Britain) woman holding the rank of a peer

PEERIE, -R, -S, -ST n spinning top ▷ adj small

PEERING ▶ peer

PEERLESS adj unequalled, unsurpassed

PEERS ▶ peer

PEERY n child's spinning top

PEES ▶ pee

PEESWEEP n early spring storm

PEETWEET n spotted sandpiper

PEEVE, -S, PEEVING vb irritate or annoy ▷ n something that irritates **PEEVED**

PEEVER, -S n hopscotch

PEEVES ▶ peeve

PEEVING ▶ peeve

PEEVISH adj fretful or irritable

PEEWEE, -S same as ▶ pewee

PEEWIT, -S same as ▶ lapwing

PEG, -GED, -S n pin or clip for joining, fastening, marking, etc ▷ vb fasten with pegs

PEGASUS n winged horse

PEGBOARD n board with holes into which pegs can be fitted

PEGBOX, -ES n part of stringed instrument that holds tuning pegs

PEGGED ▶ peg

PEGGIER ▶ peggy

PEGGIES ▶ peggy

PEGGIEST ▶ peggy

PEGGING, -S ▶ peg

PEGGY, PEGGIER, PEGGIES, PEGGIEST n type of small warbler ▷ adj resembling a peg

PEGH, -ED, -ING, -S variant of ▶ pech

PEGLESS ▶ peg

PEGLIKE ▶ peg

PEGS ▶ peg

PEGTOP, -S n type of spinning top

P

PEH, -S *same as* ▶ **pe**

PEIGNOIR *n* woman's light dressing gown

PEIN, -ED, -ING, -S *same as* ▶ **peen**

PEINCT, -ED, -S *vb* paint

PEINED ▶ **pein**

PEINING ▶ **pein**

PEINS ▶ **pein**

PEISE, -D, -S, PEISING *same as* ▶ **peize**

PEISHWA, -S *n* Indian leader

PEISHWAH *same as* ▶ **peishwa**

PEISHWAS ▶ **peishwa**

PEISING ▶ **peise**

PEIZE, -D, -S, PEIZING *vb* weight or poise

PEJORATE *vb* change for the worse

PEKAN, -S *n* large North American marten

PEKE, -S *n* Pekingese dog

PEKEPOO, -S *same as* ▶ **peekapoo**

PEKES ▶ **peke**

PEKIN, -S *n* silk fabric

PEKOE, -S *n* high-quality tea

PEL, -S *n* pixel

PELA, -S *n* insect living on wax

PELAGE, -S *n* coat of a mammal, consisting of hair, wool, fur, etc

PELAGIAL *adj* of the open sea ▷ *n* open body of water such as a lake or the sea

PELAGIAN *adj* of or inhabiting the open sea ▷ *n* pelagic creature

PELAGIC, -S *adj* of or relating to the open sea ▷ *n* any pelagic creature

PELAS ▶ **pela**

PELAU, -S *n* dish made with meat, rice, and pigeon peas

PELE, -S *Spenserian variant of* ▶ **peal**

PELERINE *n* woman's narrow cape with long pointed ends in front

PELES ▶ **pele**

PELF, -S *n* money or wealth

PELHAM, -S *n* horse's bit for a double bridle

PELICAN, -S *n* large water bird with a pouch beneath its bill

PELISSE, -S *n* cloak or loose coat which is usually fur-trimmed

PELITE, -S *n* any argillaceous rock such as shale

PELITIC

PELL, -ED, -ING, -S *n* hide of an animal ▷ *vb* hit violently

PELLACH, -S *same as* ▶ **pellack**

PELLACK, -S *n* porpoise

PELLAGRA *n* disease caused by lack of vitamin B

PELLED ▶ **pell**

PELLET, -ED, -S *n* small ball of something ▷ *vb* strike with pellets

PELLETAL

PELLICLE *n* thin skin or film

PELLING ▶ **pell**

PELLMELL *n* disorder

PELLOCK, -S *n* porpoise

PELLS ▶ **pell**

PELLUCID *adj* very clear

PELLUM, -S *n* dust

PELMA, -S *n* sole of the foot

PELMATIC

PELMET, -S *n* ornamental drapery or board, concealing a curtain rail

PELOID, -S *n* mud used therapeutically

PELOLOGY *n* study of therapeutic uses of mud

PELON, -S *adj* hairless ▷ *n* hairless person or animal

PELORIA, -S *n* abnormal production of flowers in a plant

PELORIAN

PELORIC

PELORIES ▶ **pelory**

PELORISM *n* floral mutation

PELORUS *n* sighting device

PELORY, PELORIES *n* floral mutation

PELOTA, -S *n* game where players propel a ball against a wall

PELOTON, -S *n* main field of riders in a bicycle road race

PELS ▶ **pel**

PELT, -ED, -S *vb* throw missiles at ▷ *n* skin of a fur-bearing animal

PELTA, -E, -S *n* small ancient shield

PELTAST, -S *n* (in ancient Greece) lightly armed foot soldier

PELTATE *adj* (of leaves) having the stalk attached to the centre of the lower surface

PELTED ▶ **pelt**

PELTER, -ED, -S *vb* rain heavily

PELTING, -S ▶ **pelt**

PELTLESS ▶ **pelt**

PELTRY, PELTRIES *n* pelts of animals collectively

PELTS ▶ **pelt**

PELVES ▶ **pelvis**

PELVIC, -S *adj* of, near, or relating to the pelvis ▷ *n* pelvic bone

PELVIS, PELVES, -ES *n* framework of bones at the base of the spine

PEMBINA, -S *n* type of cranberry

PEMBROKE *n* small table

PEMICAN, -S *same as* ▶ **pemmican**

PEMMICAN *n* pressed cake of meat with fat and berries or dried fruits

PEMOLINE *n* mild stimulant

PEMPHIGI ▶ **pemphigus**

PEMPHIX *n* type of crustacean

PEN, -NED, -NING, -S *n* instrument for writing in ink ▷ *vb* write or compose

PENAL *adj* of or used in punishment

PENALISE *same as* ▶ **penalize**

PENALITY ▶ **penal**

PENALIZE *vb* impose a penalty on

PENALLY ▶ **penal**

PENALTY *n* punishment for a crime or offence

PENANCE, -D, -S *n* voluntary self-punishment ▷ *vb* impose a penance upon (a sinner)

PENANG, -S *variant of* ▶ **pinang**

PENATES *pl n* household gods

PENCE ▶ **penny**

PENCEL, -S *n* small pennon

PENCHANT *n* inclination or liking

PENCIL, -ED, -S *n* thin cylindrical instrument for writing or drawing ▷ *vb* draw, write, or mark with a pencil

PENCILER

PENCRAFT *n* skill in writing

PEND, -ED, -S *vb* await judgment or settlement ▷ *n* archway or vaulted passage

PENDANT, -S *n* ornament worn on a chain round the neck

PENDED ▶ **pend**

PENDENCY ▶ **pendent**

PENDENT, -S *adj* hanging ▷ *n* pendant

PENDICLE *n* something dependent on another

PENDING *prep* while waiting for ▷ *adj* not yet decided or settled

PENDS ▶ **pend**

PENDU *adj* in informal Indian English, culturally backward

PENDULAR *adj* pendulous

PENDULE, -S n type of climbing manoeuvre
PENDULUM same as ▸ pendule
PENE, -D, PENING variant of ▸ peen
PENES ▸ penis
PENFOLD, -S same as ▸ pinfold
PENFUL, -S n contents of pen
PENGO, -S n former monetary unit of Hungary
PENGUIN, -S n flightless black-and-white sea bird
PENI old spelling of ▸ penny
PENIAL ▸ penis
PENICIL, -S n small pad for wounds
PENIE, -S old spelling of ▸ penny
PENILE adj of or relating to the penis
PENILL > penillion
PENING ▸ pene
PENIS, PENES, -ES n organ of copulation and urination in male mammals
PENITENT adj feeling sorry for having done wrong ▷ n someone who is penitent
PENK, -S n small fish
PENKNIFE n small knife with blade(s) that fold into the handle
PENKS ▸ penk
PENLIGHT n small thin flashlight
PENLITE, -S same as ▸ penlight
PENMAN, PENMEN n person skilled in handwriting
PENNA, -E n large feather
PENNAL, -S n first-year student of Protestant university
PENNAME, -S n author's pseudonym
PENNANT, -S same as ▸ pendant
PENNATE adj having feathers, wings, or winglike structures
PENNATED same as ▸ pennate
PENNE, -S n pasta in the form of short tubes
PENNED ▸ pen
PENNEECH n card game
PENNEECK same as ▸ penneech
PENNER, -S n person who writes
PENNES ▸ penne
PENNI, -A, -S n former Finnish monetary unit
PENNIED adj having money
PENNIES ▸ penny

PENNILL n stanza in a Welsh poem
PENNINE, -S n mineral found in the Pennine Alps
PENNING ▸ pen
PENNIS ▸ penni
PENNON, -S n triangular or tapering flag
PENNONED n equipped with a pennon
PENNONS ▸ pennon
PENNY, PENCE, PENNIES n coin worth one hundredth of a pound
PENNYBOY n employee whose duties include menial tasks, such as running errands
PENNYFEE n small payment
PENOCHE, -S n type of fudge
PENOLOGY n study of punishment and prison management
PENONCEL n small narrow flag
PENPOINT n tip of pen
PENS ▸ pen
PENSEE, -S n thought put down on paper
PENSEL, -S same as ▸ pencel
PENSIL, -S same as ▸ pencel
PENSILE adj designating or building a hanging nest
PENSILS ▸ pensil
PENSION, -S n regular payment to people above a certain age, etc ▷ vb grant a pension to
PENSIONE, PENSIONI n Italian boarding house
PENSIONS ▸ pension
PENSIVE adj deeply thoughtful, often with a tinge of sadness
PENSTER, -S n writer
PENSTOCK n conduit that supplies water to a hydroelectric power plant
PENSUM, -S n school exercise
PENT, -S n penthouse
PENTACLE same as > pentagram
PENTACT, -S n sponge spicule with five rays
PENTAD, -S n group or series of five
PENTADIC
PENTAGON n geometric figure with five sides
PENTANE, -S n alkane hydrocarbon with three isomers
PENTANOL n colourless oily liquid
PENTARCH n member of pentarchy

PENTENE, -S n colourless flammable liquid alkene
PENTHIA, -S n child born fifth
PENTICE, -D, -S vb accommodate in a penthouse
PENTISE, -D, -S same as ▸ pentice
PENTITO, PENTITI n criminal who offers information to the police
PENTODE, -S n electronic valve having five electrodes
PENTOMIC adj denoting the subdivision of an army division into five battle groups
PENTOSAN n polysaccharide occurring in plants, humus, etc
PENTOSE, -S n monosaccharide containing five atoms of carbon per molecule
PENTROOF n lean-to
PENTS ▸ pent
PENTYL, -S n one of a particular chemical group
PENUCHE, -S same as ▸ panocha
PENUCHI, -S same as ▸ panocha
PENUCHLE same as ▸ pinochle
PENUCKLE same as ▸ penuchle
PENULT, -S n last syllable but one in a word
PENUMBRA n (in an eclipse) partially shadowed region which surrounds the full shadow
PENURY, PENURIES n extreme poverty
PENWIPER n something for cleaning the ink from a pen
PENWOMAN, PENWOMEN n female writer
PEON, -ES, -S n Spanish-American farm labourer or unskilled worker
PEONAGE, -S n state of being a peon
PEONES ▸ peon
PEONIES ▸ peony
PEONISM, -S same as ▸ peonage
PEONS ▸ peon
PEONY, PEONIES n garden plant
PEOPLE, -D, -S, PEOPLING pl n persons generally ▷ vb provide with inhabitants
PEOPLER, -S n settler
PEOPLES ▸ people
PEOPLING ▸ people

P

PEP, -PED, -PING, -S *n* high spirits, energy, or enthusiasm ▷ *vb* liven by imbuing with new vigour

PEPERINO *n* type of volcanic rock

PEPERONI *same as* > **pepperoni**

PEPFUL *adj* full of vitality

PEPINO, -S *n* purple-striped yellow fruit

PEPITA, -S *n* edible dried seed of a squash

PEPLA ▸ **peplum**

PEPLOS, -ES *n* part of a woman's attire in ancient Greece

PEPLUM, PEPLA, -S *same as* ▸ **peplos**

PEPLUMED

PEPLUS, -ES *same as* ▸ **peplos**

PEPO, -S *n* fruit such as the melon, squash, cucumber, or pumpkin

PEPONIDA *variant of* ▸ **pepo**

PEPONIUM *variant of* ▸ **pepo**

PEPOS ▸ **pepo**

PEPPED ▸ **pep**

PEPPER, -ED, -S *n* sharp hot condiment ▷ *vb* season with pepper

PEPPERER

PEPPERY *adj* tasting of pepper

PEPPIER ▸ **peppy**

PEPPIEST ▸ **peppy**

PEPPILY ▸ **peppy**

PEPPING ▸ **pep**

PEPPY, PEPPIER, PEPPIEST *adj* full of vitality

PEPS ▸ **pep**

PEPSI, -S *n* (tradename) brand of soft drink

PEPSIN, -S *n* enzyme produced in the stomach

PEPSINE, -S *same as* ▸ **pepsin**

PEPSINS ▸ **pepsin**

PEPSIS ▸ **pepsi**

PEPTALK, -S *n* talk meant to inspire ▷ *vb* give a peptalk to

PEPTIC, -S *adj* relating to digestion or the digestive juices ▷ *n* substance that aids digestion

PEPTID, -S *variant of* ▸ **peptide**

PEPTIDE, -S *n* organic chemical compound

PEPTIDIC *adj* of peptides

PEPTIDS ▸ **peptid**

PEPTISE, -D, -S *same as* ▸ **peptize**

PEPTISER

PEPTIZE, -D, -S *vb* disperse into a colloidal state

PEPTIZER

PEPTONE, -S *n* any of a group of organic compounds

PEPTONIC

PEQUISTE *n* in Canada, member or supporter of the Parti Québécois

PER *prep* for each

PERACID, -S *n* acid in which the element forming the acid radical exhibits its highest valency

PERACUTE *adj* very acute

PERAEON, PERAEA, -S *same as* ▸ **pereion**

PERAI, -S *another name for* ▸ **piranha**

PERC, -S *n* perchloride

PERCALE, -S *n* close-textured woven cotton fabric

PERCASE *adv* perchance

PERCE, -D, -N, -S, PERCING *obsolete word for* ▸ **pierce**

PERCEANT *adj* piercing

PERCED ▸ **perce**

PERCEIVE *vb* become aware of (something) through the senses

PERCEN ▸ **perce**

PERCENT, -S *n* percentage or proportion

PERCEPT, -S *n* concept that depends on recognition of some external object or phenomenon

PERCES ▸ **perce**

PERCH, -ED, -ES, -ING *n* resting place for a bird ▷ *vb* alight, rest, or place on or as if on a perch

PERCHER -S

PERCHERY *n* barn in which hens are allowed to move without restriction

PERCHES ▸ **perch**

PERCHING ▸ **perch**

PERCID, -S *n* type of freshwater fish

PERCINE, -S *adj* of perches ▷ *n* type of perch-like fish

PERCING ▸ **perce**

PERCOCT, -S *adj* well-cooked ▷ *vb* cook thoroughly

PERCOID, -S *n* type of spiny-finned teleost fish

PERCOLIN *n* pain-relieving drug

PERCS ▸ **perc**

PERCUSS *vb* strike sharply, rapidly, or suddenly

PERDENDO *adj* (of music) getting gradually quieter and slower

PERDIE *adv* certainly

PERDU, -S *adj* (of a soldier) placed on hazardous sentry duty ▷ *n* soldier placed on hazardous sentry duty

PERDUE, -S *same as* ▸ **perdu**

PERDURE, -D, -S *vb* last for long time

PERDUS ▸ **perdu**

PERDY *adv* certainly

PERE, -S *n* addition to a French surname to specify the father

PEREA ▸ **pereon**

PEREGAL, -S *adj* equal ▷ *n* equal

PEREGRIN *variant spelling of* > **peregrine**

PEREION, PEREIA, -S *n* thorax of some crustaceans

PEREIRA, -S *n* bark of a South American apocynaceous tree

PERENTIE *n* large dark-coloured Australian monitor lizard

PERENTY *same as* ▸ **perentie**

PEREON, PEREA, -S *same as* ▸ **pereion**

PEREOPOD *same as* > **pereiopod**

PERES ▸ **pere**

PERFAY *interj* by my faith

PERFECT, -S *adj* having all the essential elements ▷ *n* perfect tense ▷ *vb* improve

PERFECTA *n* bet on the order of the first and second in a race

PERFECTI *n* ascetic group of elite Cathars

PERFECTO *n* large cigar that is tapered from both ends

PERFECTS ▸ **perfect**

PERFET *obsolete variant of* ▸ **perfect**

PERFIDY *n* perfidious act

PERFIN, -S *former name for* ▸ **spif**

PERFING, -S *n* practice of taking early retirement from the police force

PERFINS ▸ **perfin**

PERFORCE *adv* of necessity

PERFORM, -S *vb* carry out (an action)

PERFUME, -D, -S *n* liquid cosmetic worn for its pleasant smell ▷ *vb* give a pleasant smell to

PERFUMER *n* person who makes or sells perfume

PERFUMES ▸ **perfume**

PERFUMY *adj* like perfume

PERFUSE, -D, -S *vb* permeate through or over

PERGOLA, -S n framework of trellis supporting climbing plants

PERHAPS adv possibly, maybe ▷ sentence substitute it may happen, be so, etc ▷ n something that might have happened

PERI, -S n (in Persian folklore) one of a race of beautiful supernatural beings

PERIAGUA n dugout canoe

PERIANTH n outer part of a flower

PERIAPT, -S n charm or amulet

PERIBLEM n layer of meristematic tissue in stems and roots that gives rise to the cortex

PERIBOLI > peribolos

PERICARP n part of a fruit enclosing the seed that develops from the wall of the ovary

PERICON n Argentinian dance

PERICOPE n selection from a book, esp a passage from the Bible read at religious services

PERIDERM n outer corky protective layer of woody stems and roots

PERIDIA ▶ peridium

PERIDIAL ▶ peridium

PERIDIUM, PERIDIA n distinct outer layer of the spore-bearing organ in many fungi

PERIDOT, -S n pale green transparent gemstone

PERIDOTE same as ▶ peridot

PERIDOTS ▶ peridot

PERIGEAL ▶ perigee

PERIGEAN ▶ perigee

PERIGEE, -S n point in the orbit of the moon or a satellite that is nearest the earth

PERIGON, -S n angle of 360°

PERIGONE n part enclosing the essential organs of a flower

PERIGONS ▶ perigon

PERIGYNY n condition of having the stamens and other floral parts at the same level as the carpels

PERIL, -ED, -ING, -LED, -S n great danger ▷ vb expose to danger

PERILLA, -S n type of mint

PERILLED ▶ peril

PERILOUS adj very hazardous or dangerous

PERILS ▶ peril

PERILUNE n point in a lunar orbit when a spacecraft launched from the moon is nearest the moon

PERINEA ▶ perineum

PERINEAL ▶ perineum

PERINEUM, PERINEA n region of the body between the anus and the genitals

PERIOD, -ED, -S n particular portion of time ▷ adj (of furniture, dress, a play, etc) dating from or in the style of an earlier time ▷ vb divide into periods

PERIODIC adj recurring at intervals

PERIODID n kind of iodide

PERIODS ▶ period

PERIOST, -S n thick fibrous two-layered membrane covering the surface of bones

PERIOTIC adj of or relating to the structures situated around the internal ear ▷ n periotic bone

PERIPETY n abrupt turn of events or reversal of circumstances

PERIPLUS n circumnavigation

PERIPTER n type of ancient temple

PERIQUE, -S n strong highly-flavoured tobacco

PERIS ▶ peri

PERISARC n outer chitinous layer secreted by colonial hydrozoan coelenterates

PERISH, -ES vb be destroyed or die

PERISHED adj (of a person, part of the body, etc) extremely cold

PERISHER n mischievous person

PERISHES ▶ perish

PERITUS, PERITI n Catholic theology consultant

PERIWIG, -S same as ▶ peruke

PERJINK adj prim or finicky

PERJURE, -S vb render (oneself) guilty of perjury

PERJURED adj having sworn falsely

PERJURER ▶ perjure

PERJURES ▶ perjure

PERJURY n act or crime of lying while under oath in a court

PERK, -ED, -ING, -S n incidental benefit gained from a job, such as a company car ▷ adj pert ▷ vb (of coffee) percolate

PERKIER ▶ perky

PERKIEST ▶ perky

PERKILY ▶ perky

PERKIN, -S same as ▶ parkin

PERKING ▶ perk

PERKINS ▶ perkin

PERKISH adj perky

PERKS ▶ perk

PERKY, PERKIER, PERKIEST adj lively or cheerful

PERLITE, -S n variety of obsidian

PERLITIC

PERLOUS same as ▶ perilous

PERM, -ED, -ING, -S n long-lasting curly hairstyle ▷ vb give (hair) a perm

PERMATAN n permanent tan, esp artificial

PERMEANT > permeance

PERMEASE n carrier protein

PERMEATE vb pervade or pass through the whole of (something)

PERMED ▶ perm

PERMIAN adj of, denoting, or formed in the last period of the Palaeozoic era

PERMIE, -S n person, esp an office worker, employed by a firm on a permanent basis

PERMING ▶ perm

PERMIT, -S vb give permission, allow ▷ n document giving permission to do something

PERMS ▶ perm

PERMUTE, -D, -S vb change the sequence of

PERN, -ED, -ING, -S n type of buzzard ▷ vb spin

PERNANCY n receiving of rents

PERNED ▶ pern

PERNING ▶ pern

PERNIO n chilblain

PERNOD, -S n aniseed-flavoured aperitif from France

PERNS ▶ pern

PEROG, -S same as ▶ pirog

PEROGI, -ES, -S n type of Polish dumpling

PEROGIE same as ▶ perogi

PEROGIES ▶ perogi

PEROGIS ▶ perogi

PEROGS ▶ perog

PEROGY same as ▶ perogi

PERONE, -S n fibula

PERONEAL adj of or relating to the fibula or the outer side of the leg

PERONES ▶ perone

PERONEUS n lateral muscle of the leg

PERORAL adj administered through mouth

P

PERORATE vb speak at length, esp in a formal manner

PEROXID, -S variant of ► **peroxide**

PEROXIDE n hydrogen peroxide used as a hair bleach ▷ adj bleached with or resembling peroxide ▷ vb bleach (the hair) with peroxide

PEROXIDS ► **peroxid**

PEROXO n type of acid

PEROXY adj containing the peroxide group

PERP, -S n someone who has committed a crime

PERPEND, -S n large stone that passes through a wall from one side to the other ▷ vb ponder

PERPENT, -S same as ► **perpend**

PERPLEX vb puzzle, bewilder

PERPS ► **perp**

PERRADII ► **perradius**

PERRIER, -S n short mortar

PERRIES ► **perry**

PERRON, -S n external flight of steps

PERRUQUE old spelling of ► **peruke**

PERRY, PERRIES n alcoholic drink made from fermented pears

PERSALT, -S n any salt of a peracid

PERSANT adj piercing

PERSAUNT adj piercing

PERSE, -D, -S, PERSING old variant of ► **pierce**

PERSEITY n quality of having substance independently of real objects

PERSES ► **perse**

PERSICO, -S same as ► **persicot**

PERSICOT n cordial made from apricots

PERSING ► **perse**

PERSIST, -S vb continue to be or happen, last

PERSON, -S n human being

PERSONA, -E, -S n someone's personality as presented to others

PERSONAL adj individual or private ▷ n item of movable property

PERSONAS ► **persona**

PERSONS ► **person**

PERSPEX n any of various clear acrylic resins

PERSPIRE vb sweat

PERSPIRY adj perspiring

PERST adj perished

PERSUADE vb make (someone) do something by argument, charm, etc

PERSUE, -D, -S, PERSUING obsolete form of ► **pursue**

PERSWADE obsolete form of ► **persuade**

PERT, -ER, -EST, -S adj saucy and cheeky ▷ n pert person

PERTAIN, -S vb belong or be relevant (to)

PERTAKE, -N, -S, PERTOOK obsolete form of ► **partake**

PERTER ► **pert**

PERTEST ► **pert**

PERTHITE n type of feldspar

PERTLY ► **pert**

PERTNESS ► **pert**

PERTOOK ► **pertake**

PERTS ► **pert**

PERTURB, -S vb disturb greatly

PERTUSE adj having holes

PERTUSED adj having holes

PERUKE, -S n wig for men worn in the 17th and 18th centuries

PERUKED adj wearing wig

PERUKES ► **peruke**

PERUSAL, -S ► **peruse**

PERUSE, -D, -S, PERUSING vb read in a careful or leisurely manner

PERUSER -S

PERVADE, -D, -S vb spread right through (something)

PERVADER

PERVERSE adj deliberately doing something different from what is thought normal or proper

PERVERT, -S vb use or alter for a wrong purpose

PERVIATE vb perforate or burrow

PERVIOUS adj able to be penetrated, permeable

PES, PEDES n animal part corresponding to the foot

PESADE, -S n position in which the horse stands on the hind legs with the forelegs in the air

PESANT, -S obsolete spelling of ► **peasant**

PESANTE adv to be performed clumsily

PESANTS ► **pesant**

PESAUNT, -S obsolete spelling of ► **peasant**

PESETA, -S n former monetary unit of Spain

PESEWA, -S n Ghanaian monetary unit

PESHWA, -S same as ► **peishwa**

PESKIER ► **pesky**

PESKIEST ► **pesky**

PESKILY ► **pesky**

PESKY, PESKIER, PESKIEST adj troublesome

PESO, -S n monetary unit of Argentina, Mexico, etc

PESSIMA n lowest point

PESSIMAL adj (of animal's environment) least favourable for survival

PESSIMUM same as ► **pessimal**

PEST, -S n annoying person

PESTER, -ED, -S vb annoy or nag continually

PESTERER

PESTFUL adj causing annoyance

PESTHOLE n breeding ground for disease

PESTIER ► **pesty**

PESTIEST ► **pesty**

PESTLE, -D, -S, PESTLING n club-shaped implement for grinding ▷ vb pound with or as if with a pestle

PESTO, -S n sauce for pasta

PESTS ► **pest**

PESTY, PESTIER, PESTIEST adj persistently annoying

PET, -S, -TED n animal kept for pleasure and companionship ▷ adj kept as a pet ▷ vb treat as a pet

PETABYTE n in computing, 1015 or 250 bytes

PETAFLOP n (in computing) unit of processing speed

PETAL, -S n one of the brightly coloured outer parts of a flower

PETALED

PETALINE

PETALISM n ostracism in ancient Syracuse

PETALLED ► **petal**

PETALODY n condition in which stamens or other flower parts assume the form and function of petals

PETALOID adj resembling a petal, esp in shape

PETALOUS adj bearing or having petals

PETALS ► **petal**

PETANQUE n French game similar to bowls

PETAR, -S obsolete variant of ► **petard**

PETARA, -S n clothes basket

PETARD, -S n device containing explosives

PETARIES ► **petary**

PETARS ► **petar**

PETARY, PETARIES n weapon for hurling stones

PETASOS same as ▸ **petasus**

PETASUS n broad-brimmed hat worn by the ancient Greeks

PETCHARY n type of kingbird

PETCOCK, -S n small valve

PETECHIA n small discoloured spot on the skin

PETER, -ED, -ING, -S vb fall (off) in volume, intensity, etc, and finally cease ▷ n act of petering

PETERMAN, PETERMEN n burglar skilled in safe-breaking

PETERS ▸ **peter**

PETHER, -S old variant of ▸ **pedlar**

PETIOLAR ▸ **petiole**

PETIOLE, -S n stalk which attaches a leaf to a plant **PETIOLED**

PETIT adj of little or lesser importance

PETITE, -S adj (of a woman) small and dainty ▷ n clothing size for small women

PETITION n formal request, esp one signed by many people and presented to parliament ▷ vb present a petition to

PETITORY adj soliciting

PETNAP, -S vb steal pet **PETNAPER**

PETRALE, -S n type of sole

PETRARY n weapon for hurling stones

PETRE, -S same as > **saltpetre**

PETREL, -S n sea bird with a hooked bill and tubular nostrils

PETRES ▸ **petre**

PETRI n as in **petri dish** shallow glass dish used for cultures of bacteria

PETRIFIC adj petrifying

PETRIFY vb frighten severely

PETROL, -S n flammable liquid obtained from petroleum ▷ vb supply with petrol

PETROLIC adj of, relating to, containing, or obtained from petroleum

PETROLS ▸ **petrol**

PETRONEL n obsolete cavalry firearm

PETROSAL adj of the dense part of the temporal bone that surrounds the inner ear ▷ n petrosal bone

PETROUS adj denoting the dense part of the temporal bone around the inner ear

PETS ▸ **pet**

PETSAI, -S n Chinese cabbage

PETTABLE ▸ **pet**

PETTED ▸ **pet**

PETTEDLY ▸ **pet**

PETTER, -S ▸ **pet**

PETTI, -ES ▸ **petto**

PETTIER ▸ **petty**

PETTIES ▸ **petti**

PETTIEST ▸ **petty**

PETTIFOG vb quibble or fuss over details

PETTILY ▸ **petty**

PETTING, -S ▸ **pet**

PETTISH adj peevish or fretful

PETTLE, -D, -S, PETTLING vb pat animal

PETTO, PETTI n breast of an animal

PETTY, PETTIER, PETTIEST adj unimportant, trivial

PETULANT adj childishly irritable or peevish

PETUNIA, -S n garden plant with funnel-shaped flowers

PETUNTSE n fusible feldspathic mineral used in hard-paste porcelain

PETUNTZE same as ▸ **petuntse**

PEW, -S n fixed benchlike seat in a church

PEWEE, -S n small N American flycatcher

PEWIT, -S another name for ▸ **lapwing**

PEWS ▸ **pew**

PEWTER, -S n greyish metal made of tin and lead **PEWTERER**

PEWTERY adj of or like pewter

PEYOTE, -S another name for ▸ **mescal**

PEYOTISM n ritual use of peyote

PEYOTIST n person who uses peyote

PEYOTL, -S same as ▸ **peyote**

PEYSE, -D, -S, PEYSING vb weight or poise

PEYTRAL, -S same as ▸ **peytrel**

PEYTREL, -S n breastplate of horse's armour

PEZANT, -S obsolete spelling of ▸ **peasant**

PEZIZOID adj having cup-like form

PFENNIG, -E, -S n former German monetary unit

PFENNING old variant of ▸ **pfennig**

PFFT interj sound indicating sudden disappearance of something

PFUI interj phooey

PHABLET, -S n type of handheld personal computer

PHACELIA n plant grown for its large, deep blue bell flowers

PHACOID adj lentil- or lens-shaped

PHAEIC adj (of animals) having dusky coloration

PHAEISM -S

PHAETON, -S n light four-wheeled horse-drawn carriage

PHAGE, -S n parasitic virus that destroys its host

PHALANGE another name for ▸ **phalanx**

PHALANX n closely grouped mass of people

PHALLI ▸ **phallus**

PHALLIC adj of or resembling a penis

PHALLIN, -S n poisonous substance from mushroom

PHALLOID adj resembling a penis

PHALLUS, PHALLI n penis

PHANG, -ED, -ING, -S old variant spelling of ▸ **fang**

PHANTASM n unreal vision, illusion

PHANTAST same as ▸ **fantast**

PHANTASY same as ▸ **fantasy**

PHANTOM, -S n ghost ▷ adj deceptive or unreal

PHANTOMY adj of phantoms

PHARAOH, -S n ancient Egyptian king

PHARE, -S n beacon tower

PHARISEE n self-righteous or hypocritical person

PHARM, -ED, -S vb redirect (a website user) to another, bogus website

PHARMA, -S n pharmaceutical companies considered together as an industry

PHARMACY n preparation and dispensing of drugs and medicines

PHARMAS ▸ **pharma**

PHARMED ▸ **pharm**

PHARMER, -S n person who pharms

PHARMING n rearing or growing genetically-modified animals or plants in order to develop pharmaceuticals

P

PHARMS ▸ pharm

PHAROS, -ES n lighthouse

PHARYNX n cavity forming the back part of the mouth

PHASE, -D, -S n distinct or characteristic stage in a development or chain of events ▷ vb arrange or carry out in stages

PHASEAL

PHASEOUT n gradual reduction

PHASER, -S n type of science-fiction weapon

PHASES ▸ phase

PHASIC ▸ phase

PHASING, -S n effect achieved by varying the phase relationship of two similar audio signals

PHASIS another word for ▸ **phase**

PHASMID, -S n stick insect or leaf insect

PHASOR, -S n rotating vector representing a quantity that varies sinusoidally

PHAT, -TER, -TEST adj terrific

PHATIC adj (of speech) used to express sociability rather than specific meaning

PHATTER ▸ phat

PHATTEST ▸ phat

PHEASANT n game bird with bright plumage

PHEAZAR, -S old variant of ▸ **vizier**

PHEER, -S same as ▸ **fere**

PHEERE, -S same as ▸ **fere**

PHEERS ▸ pheer

PHEESE, -D, -S, PHEESING vb worry

PHEEZE, -D, -S, PHEEZING same as ▸ **pheese**

PHELLEM, -S n technical name for ▸ **cork**

PHELLOID adj like cork

PHELONIA > phelonion

PHENATE, -S n ester or salt of phenol

PHENAZIN same as > **phenazine**

PHENE, -S n genetically determined characteristic of organism

PHENETIC > phenetics

PHENETOL same as > **phenetole**

PHENGITE n type of alabaster

PHENIC adj of phenol

PHENIX, -ES same as ▸ **phoenix**

PHENOGAM same as > **phaenogam**

PHENOL, -S n chemical used in disinfectants and antiseptics

PHENOLIC adj of, containing, or derived from phenol ▷ n derivative of phenol

PHENOLS ▸ phenol

PHENOM, -S n person or thing of outstanding abilities

PHENOME, -S n full complement of phenotypical traits of an organism, species, etc

PHENOMS ▸ phenom

PHENOXY modifier as in **phenoxy resin** any of a class of resins derived from polyhydroxy ethers

PHENYL, -S n chemical substance

PHENYLIC

PHEON, -S n barbed iron head of dart

PHERESIS, PHERESES n specialized form of blood donation

PHESE, -D, -S, PHESING same as ▸ **pheese**

PHEW interj exclamation of relief, surprise, etc

PHI, -S n 21st letter in the Greek alphabet

PHIAL, -LED, -S n small bottle for medicine etc ▷ vb put in phial

PHILABEG same as ▸ **filibeg**

PHILAMOT variant of ▸ **filemot**

PHILIBEG variant spelling of ▸ **filibeg**

PHILOMEL n nightingale

PHILOMOT n colour of dead leaf

PHILTER, -S same as ▸ **philtre**

PHILTRA ▸ philtrum

PHILTRE, -D, -S n magic drink supposed to arouse love in the person who drinks it ▷ vb mix with love potion

PHILTRUM, PHILTRA n indentation above the upper lip

PHINNOCK variant spelling of ▸ **finnock**

PHIS ▸ phi

PHISH, -ED, -ES vb engage in phishing

PHISHER, -S n person who phishes

PHISHES ▸ phish

PHISHING n internet fraud to extract personal and financial details

PHISNOMY n physiognomy

PHIZ, -ES, -ZES n face or a facial expression

PHIZOG, -S same as ▸ **phiz**

PHIZZ n face

PHIZZES ▸ phiz

PHLEGM, -S n thick yellowish substance formed in the nose and throat during a cold

PHLEGMON n inflammatory mass that may progress to abscess

PHLEGMS ▸ phlegm

PHLEGMY ▸ phlegm

PHLOEM, -S n plant tissue that acts as a path for the distribution of food

PHLOMIS n plant of Phlomis genus

PHLOX, -ES n flowering garden plant

PHO, -S n Vietnamese noodle soup

PHOBIA, -S n intense and unreasoning fear or dislike

PHOBIC, -S adj of, relating to, or arising from a phobia ▷ n person suffering from a phobia

PHOBISM, -S n phobia

PHOBIST -S

PHOCA, -E, -S n genus of seals

PHOCINE adj of, relating to, or resembling a seal

PHOEBE, -S n greyish-brown North American flycatcher

PHOEBUS n sun

PHOENIX n legendary bird said to set fire to itself and rise anew from its ashes

PHOH variant of ▸ **foh**

PHOLAS, PHOLADES n type of bivalve mollusc

PHON, -S n unit of loudness

PHONAL adj relating to voice

PHONATE, -D, -S vb articulate speech sounds

PHONE, -D, -S, PHONING vb telephone ▷ n single uncomplicated speech sound

PHONECAM n digital camera incorporated in a mobile phone

PHONED ▸ phone

PHONEME, -S n one of the set of speech sounds in a language

PHONEMIC adj of or relating to the phoneme

PHONER, -S n person making a telephone call

PHONES ▸ phone

PHONETIC adj of speech sounds

PHONEY, -ED, -S adj not genuine ▷ n phoney person or thing ▷ vb fake

PHONIC ▸ phonics

PHONICS n method of teaching people to read
PHONIED ► phony
PHONIER ► phony
PHONIES ► phony
PHONIEST ► phony
PHONILY ► phony
PHONING ► phone
PHONO, -S n phonograph
PHONON, -S n quantum of vibrational energy
PHONOS ► phono
PHONS ► phon
PHONY, PHONIED, PHONIER, PHONIES, PHONIEST, -ING vb fake
PHOOEY interj exclamation of scorn or contempt
PHORATE, -S n type of insecticide
PHORESY n association in which one animal clings to another to ensure movement from place to place
PHORETIC adj relating to phoresy
PHORMINX n ancient Greek stringed instrument
PHORMIUM n New Zealand plant
PHORONID n small wormlike marine animal
PHOS ► pho
PHOSGENE n poisonous gas used in warfare
PHOSPHID same as ► phosphide
PHOSPHIN same as ► phosphine
PHOSPHOR n synthetic fluorescent or phosphorescent substance
PHOSSY adj as in phossy jaw gangrenous condition of the lower jawbone
PHOT, -S n unit of illumination
PHOTIC adj of or concerned with light
PHOTICS n science of light
PHOTINIA n genus of garden plants
PHOTINO, -S n hypothetical elementary particle
PHOTISM, -S n sensation of light or colour caused by stimulus of another sense
PHOTO, -ED, -ING, -S n photograph ▷ vb take a photograph of
PHOTOFIT n combining of photographs of facial features into a composite picture of a face
PHOTOG, -S n photograph
PHOTOGEN same as > photogene

PHOTOGS ► photog
PHOTOING ► photo
PHOTOMAP n map constructed by adding grid lines, place names, etc, to aerial photographs ▷ vb map (an area) using aerial photography
PHOTON, -S n quantum of electromagnetic radiation energy
PHOTONIC
PHOTOPIA n normal adaptation of the eye to light
PHOTOPIC
PHOTOPSY same as > photopsia
PHOTOS ► photo
PHOTOSET vb set (type matter) by photosetting
PHOTS ► phot
PHPHT interj expressing irritation or reluctance
PHRASAL adj of, relating to, or composed of phrases
PHRASE, -D, -S n group of words forming a unit of meaning, esp within a sentence ▷ vb express in words
PHRASER -S
PHRASIER ► phrasy
PHRASING n exact words used to say or write something
PHRASY, PHRASIER adj containing phrases
PHRATRAL ► phratry
PHRATRIC ► phratry
PHRATRY n group of people within a tribe who have a common ancestor
PHREAK, -ED, -S vb hack into a telecommunications system
PHREAKER
PHREATIC adj of or relating to ground water occurring below the water table
PHRENIC, -S adj of or relating to the diaphragm ▷ n (a nerve, blood vessel, etc) located in the diaphragm
PHRENISM, -S n belief in non-physical life force
PHRENSY obsolete spelling of ► frenzy
PHRYGANA another name for ► garigue
PHT same as ► phpht

> It is easy to overlook this little word, that may offer a way out when your rack seems hopelessly clogged with consonants.

PHTHALIC adj as in phthalic anhydride white crystalline substance used mainly in producing dyestuffs
PHTHALIN n colourless compound formed by reduction of phthalein
PHTHISES ► phthisis
PHTHISIC adj relating to or affected with phthisis ▷ n person suffering from phthisis
PHTHISIS, PHTHISES n any disease that causes wasting of the body, esp pulmonary tuberculosis
PHUT, -S, -TED, -TING vb make muffled explosive sound
PHWOAH same as ► phwoar
PHWOAR interj expression of attraction
PHYLA ► phylum
PHYLAE ► phyle
PHYLAR ► phylum
PHYLARCH n chief of tribe
PHYLAXIS n protection against infection
PHYLE, PHYLAE n tribe or clan of an ancient Greek people
PHYLESIS, PHYLESES n evolutionary events that modify taxon without causing speciation
PHYLETIC adj of or relating to the evolution of a species or group of organisms
PHYLIC ► phyle
PHYLLARY n bract subtending flower head of composite plant
PHYLLID, -S n leaf of a liverwort or moss
PHYLLITE n compact lustrous metamorphic rock
PHYLLO, -S variant of ► filo
PHYLLODE n flattened leafstalk that resembles and functions as a leaf
PHYLLODY n abnormal development of leaves from parts of flower
PHYLLOID adj resembling a leaf ▷ n leaf-like organ
PHYLLOME n leaf or a leaflike organ
PHYLLOS ► phyllo
PHYLON n tribe
PHYLUM, PHYLA n major taxonomic division of animals and plants
PHYSALIA n Portuguese man-of-war
PHYSALIS n strawberry tomato

P

PHYSED, -S n physical education

PHYSES ▸ physis

PHYSETER n machine for filtering

PHYSIC n medicine or drug, esp a cathartic or purge ▷ vb treat (a patient) with medicine

PHYSICAL adj of the body, as contrasted with the mind or spirit

PHYSICKY ▸ physic

PHYSICS n science of the properties of matter and energy

PHYSIO, -S n physiotherapist

PHYSIQUE n person's bodily build and muscular development

PHYSIS, PHYSES n part of bone responsible for lengthening

PHYTANE, -S n hydrocarbon found in fossilised plant remains

PHYTIN, -S n substance from plants used as an energy supplement

PHYTOID adj resembling plant

PHYTOL, -S n alcohol used to synthesize some vitamins

PHYTON, -S n unit of plant structure

PHYTONIC

PHYTOSIS, PHYTOSES n disease caused by vegetable parasite

PI, -ED, -ING, -S n sixteenth letter in the Greek alphabet ▷ vb spill and mix (set type) indiscriminately

PIA, -S n innermost of the three membranes that cover the brain and the spinal cord

PIACULAR adj making expiation for a sacrilege

PIAFFE, -D, -S, PIAFFING n passage done on the spot ▷ vb strut on the spot

PIAFFER -S

PIAL adj relating to pia mater

PIAN, -S n contagious tropical skin disease

PIANETTE n small piano

PIANI ▸ piano

PIANIC adj of piano

PIANINO, -S n small upright piano

PIANISM, -S n technique, skill, or artistry in playing the piano

PIANIST, -S n person who plays the piano

PIANISTE variant of ▸ pianist

PIANISTS ▸ pianist

PIANO, PIANI, -S n musical instrument with strings which are struck by hammers worked by a keyboard ▷ adv quietly

PIANOLA, -S n type of player piano

PIANOS ▸ piano

PIANS ▸ pian

PIARIST, -S n member of a Roman religious order

PIAS ▸ pia

PIASABA, -S same as ▸ piassava

PIASAVA, -S same as ▸ piassava

PIASSABA same as ▸ piassava

PIASSAVA n South American palm tree

PIASTER, -S same as ▸ piastre

PIASTRE, -S n fractional monetary unit of Egypt, Lebanon, Sudan, South Sudan, and Syria

PIAZZA, -S, PIAZZE n square or marketplace, esp in Italy

PIAZZIAN

PIBAL, -S n method of measuring wind

PIBROCH, -S n form of bagpipe music

PIC, -S n photograph or illustration

PICA, -S n abnormal craving to ingest substances

PICACHO, -S n pointed solitary mountain

PICADOR, -S n mounted bullfighter with a lance

PICAL adj relating to pica

PICAMAR, -S n hydrocarbon extract of beechwood tar

PICANTE adj spicy

PICARA, -S n female adventurer

PICARIAN n tree-haunting bird

PICARO, -S n roguish adventurer

PICAROON n adventurer or rogue

PICAROS ▸ picaro

PICAS ▸ pica

PICAYUNE adj of small value or importance ▷ n any coin of little value, such as a five-cent piece

PICCATA, -S adj sautéed and served in a lemon sauce ▷ n dish of food sautéed and served in a lemon sauce

PICCIES ▸ piccy

PICCOLO, -S n small flute

PICCY, PICCIES n picture or photograph

PICE n former Indian coin worth one sixty-fourth of a rupee

PICENE, -S n type of hydrocarbon

PICEOUS adj of, relating to, or resembling pitch

PICHURIM n S American laurel tree

PICIFORM adj relating to certain tree-haunting birds

PICINE adj relating to woodpeckers

PICK, -ED, -ING, -S vb choose ▷ n choice

PICKABLE

PICKADIL same as ▸ piccadill

PICKAX same as ▸ pickaxe

PICKAXE, -D, -S n large pick ▷ vb use a pickaxe on (earth, rocks, etc)

PICKBACK vb carry by piggyback

PICKED ▸ pick

PICKEER, -S vb make raid for booty

PICKER, -S n person or thing that picks

PICKEREL n North American freshwater game fish

PICKERS ▸ picker

PICKERY n petty theft

PICKET, -ED, -S n person or group standing outside a workplace during a strike ▷ vb form a picket outside (a workplace)

PICKETER

PICKIER ▸ picky

PICKIEST ▸ picky

PICKILY ▸ picky

PICKIN, -S n small child

PICKING ▸ pick

PICKINGS pl n money easily acquired

PICKINS ▸ pickin

PICKLE, -S, PICKLING n food preserved in vinegar or salt water ▷ vb preserve in vinegar or salt water

PICKLED adj (of food) preserved

PICKLER, -S ▸ pickle

PICKLES ▸ pickle

PICKLING ▸ pickle

PICKLOCK n person who picks locks, esp one who gains unlawful access to premises by this means

PICKMAW, -S n type of gull

PICKNEY, -S n (in Jamaica) child

PICKOFF, -S n baseball play

PICKS ▸ pick

PICKUP, -S n small truck with an open body and low sides

PICKWICK n tool for raising the short wick of an oil lamp

PICKY, PICKIER, PICKIEST adj fussy

PICLORAM n type of herbicide

PICNIC, -S n informal meal out of doors ▷ vb have a picnic
PICNICKY

PICOGRAM n trillionth of gram

PICOLIN, -S variant of ▸ picoline

PICOLINE n liquid derivative of pyridine found in bone oil and coal tar

PICOLINS ▸ picolin

PICOMOLE n trillionth of a mole

PICONG, -S n any teasing or satirical banter

PICOT, -ED, -ING, -S n any of pattern of small loops, as on lace ▷ vb decorate material with small loops

PICOTE adj (of material) picoted

PICOTED ▸ picot

PICOTEE, -S n type of carnation

PICOTING ▸ picot

PICOTITE n dark-brown mineral

PICOTS ▸ picot

PICOWAVE vb treat food with gamma waves

PICQUET, -S vb provide early warning of attack

PICRA, -S n powder of aloes and canella

PICRATE, -S n any salt or ester of picric acid

PICRATED adj containing picrate

PICRATES ▸ picrate

PICRIC adj as in picric acid toxic sparingly soluble crystalline yellow acid

PICRITE, -S n coarse-grained ultrabasic igneous rock
PICRITIC

PICS ▸ pic

PICTURAL n picture

PICTURE, -D, -S n drawing or painting ▷ vb visualize, imagine

PICUL, -S n unit of weight, used in China, Japan, and SE Asia

PICULET, -S n small tropical woodpecker with a short tail

PICULS ▸ picul

PIDDLE, -D, -S vb urinate
PIDDLER -S

PIDDLIER ▸ piddly

PIDDLING adj small or unimportant

PIDDLY, PIDDLIER adj trivial

PIDDOCK, -S n marine bivalve that bores into rock, clay, or wood

PIDGEON, -S variant of ▸ pidgin

PIDGIN, -S n language made up of elements of other languages

PIE, -S n dish of meat, fruit, etc baked in pastry

PIEBALD, -S adj (horse) with irregular black-and-white markings ▷ n black-and-white horse

PIECE, -D, -S n separate bit or part

PIECEN, -ED, -S vb join broken threads
PIECENER

PIECER, -S n person who mends, repairs, or joins something

PIECES ▸ piece

PIECING, -S ▸ piece

PIECRUST n pastry used for making pies

PIED ▸ pi

PIEDFORT n coin thicker than normal

PIEDISH n container for baking pies

PIEDMONT adj (of glaciers, plains, etc) formed or situated at the foot of a mountain or mountain range ▷ n gentle slope leading from mountains to flat land

PIEDNESS n state of being pied

PIEFORT, -S same as ▸ piedfort

PIEHOLE, -S n person's mouth

PIEING, -S n act of pushing a pie into a person's face

PIEMAN, PIEMEN n seller of pies

PIEND, -S n salient angle

PIEPLANT n rhubarb

PIER, -S n platform on stilts sticking out into the sea

PIERAGE, -S n accommodation for ships at piers

PIERCE, -D, -S vb make a hole in or through with a sharp instrument
PIERCER -S

PIERCING adj (of a sound) shrill and high-pitched ▷ n art or practice of piercing body parts for the insertion of jewellery

PIERHEAD n end of a pier farthest from the shore

PIERID, -S n type of butterfly

PIERIS, -ES n American or Asiatic shrub

PIEROG, -S same as ▸ pirog

PIEROGI n Polish dumpling

PIEROGS ▸ pierog

PIERROT, -S n clown or masquerader with a whitened face

PIERS ▸ pier

PIERST archaic spelling of ▸ pierced

PIERT, -S n small plant with small greenish flowers

PIES ▸ pie

PIET, -S n magpie

PIETA, -S n sculpture, painting, or drawing of the dead Christ, supported by the Virgin Mary

PIETIES ▸ piety

PIETISM, -S n exaggerated piety

PIETIST -S

PIETS ▸ piet

PIETY, PIETIES n deep devotion to God and religion

PIEZO adj piezoelectric

PIFFERO, -S n small rustic flute

PIFFLE, -D, -S n nonsense ▷ vb talk or behave feebly

PIFFLER, -S n talker of nonsense

PIFFLES ▸ piffle

PIFFLING adj worthless

PIG, -GED, -S n animal kept and killed for pork, ham, and bacon ▷ vb eat greedily

PIGBOAT, -S n submarine

PIGEON, -ED, -S n bird with a heavy body and short legs ▷ vb pigeonhole

PIGEONRY n loft for keeping pigeons

PIGEONS ▸ pigeon

PIGFACE, -S n creeping succulent plant

PIGFEED, -S n food for pigs

PIGFISH n grunting fish of the North American Atlantic coast

PIGGED ▸ pig

PIGGERY n place for keeping and breeding pigs

PIGGIE same as ▸ piggy

PIGGIER ▸ piggy

PIGGIES ▸ piggy

PIGGIEST ▸ piggy

PIGGIN, -S n small wooden bucket or tub

PIGGING, -S ▸ pig

PIGGINS ▸ piggin

P

PIGGISH adj like a pig, esp in appetite or manners

PIGGY, PIGGIER, PIGGIES, PIGGIEST n child's word for a pig ▷ adj like a pig

PIGHT, -ED, -ING, -S vb pierce

PIGHTLE, -S n small enclosure

PIGHTS ▶ pight

PIGLET, -S n young pig

PIGLIKE ▶ pig

PIGLING, -S n young pig

PIGMAEAN same as ▶ pygmaean

PIGMAN, PIGMEN n male pig farmer

PIGMEAN same as ▶ pygmaean

PIGMEAT, -S less common name for ▶ pork

PIGMEN ▶ pigman

PIGMENT, -S n colouring matter, paint or dye ▷ vb colour with pigment

PIGMIES ▶ pigmy

PIGMOID, -S adj of pygmies ▷ n pygmy

PIGMY, PIGMIES same as ▶ pygmy

PIGNOLI, -S same as ▶ pignolia

PIGNOLIA n edible seed of nut pine

PIGNOLIS ▶ pignoli

PIGNUS, PIGNORA n pawn or pledge

PIGNUT, -S n bitter nut of hickory trees

PIGOUT, -S n binge

PIGPEN, -S same as ▶ pigsty

PIGS ▶ pig

PIGSKIN, -S n skin of the domestic pig ▷ adj made of pigskin

PIGSNEY, -S same as ▶ pigsny

PIGSNIE, -S same as ▶ pigsny

PIGSNY n former pet name for girl

PIGSTICK, PIGSTUCK vb (esp in India) hunt and spear wild boar, esp from horseback

PIGSTIES ▶ pigsty

PIGSTUCK ▶ pigstick

PIGSTY, PIGSTIES same as ▶ pigpen

PIGSWILL n waste food or other edible matter fed to pigs

PIGTAIL, -S n plait of hair hanging from the back or either side of the head

PIGWASH n wet feed for pigs

PIGWEED, -S n coarse North American weed

PIHOIHOI n variety of New Zealand pipit

PIING ▶ pi

PIKA, -S n burrowing mammal

PIKAKE, -S n type of Asian vine

PIKAS ▶ pika

PIKAU, -S n pack, knapsack, or rucksack

PIKE, -D, -S n large predatory freshwater fish ▷ vb stab or pierce using a pike ▷ adj (of the body position of a diver) bent at the hips but with the legs straight

PIKELET, -S n small thick pancake

PIKEMAN, PIKEMEN n (formerly) soldier armed with a pike

PIKER, -S n shirker

PIKES ▶ pike

PIKI, -S n bread made from blue cornmeal

PIKING, -S ▶ pike

PIKIS ▶ piki

PIKUL, -S same as ▶ picul

PILA, -E n pillar-like anatomical structure

PILAF, -S same as ▶ pilau

PILAFF, -S same as ▶ pilau

PILAFS ▶ pilaf

PILAO, -S same as ▶ pilau

PILAR adj relating to hair

PILASTER, -S n square column, usu set in a wall

PILAU, -S n Middle Eastern dish

PILAW, -S same as ▶ pilau

PILCH, -ES n outer garment, originally one made of skin

PILCHARD n small edible sea fish of the herring family

PILCHER, -S n scabbard for sword

PILCHES ▶ pilch

PILCORN, -S n type of oat

PILCROW, -S n paragraph mark

PILE, -D n number of things lying on top of each other ▷ vb collect into a pile

PILEA, -S n plant which releases a cloud of pollen when shaken

PILEATE adj (of birds) having a crest

PILEATED same as ▶ pileate

PILED ▶ pile

PILEI ▶ pileus

PILELESS ▶ pile

PILEOUS adj hairy

PILER, -S n placer of things on pile

PILES pl n swollen veins in the rectum, haemorrhoids

PILEUM n top of a bird's head

PILEUP, -S n multiple collision of vehicles

PILEUS, PILEI n upper cap-shaped part of a mushroom

PILEWORK n construction built from heavy stakes or cylinders

PILEWORT n plant used to treat piles

PILFER, -ED, -S vb steal in small quantities

PILFERER

PILFERY n theft

PILGRIM, -S n person who journeys to a holy place ▷ vb travel as a pilgrim

PILI, -S, PILUS n Philippine tree with edible seeds resembling almonds

PILIFORM adj resembling a long hair

PILING, -S n act of driving piles

PILINUT, -S n type of nut found in the Philippines

PILIS ▶ pili

PILL, -ED, -S n small ball of medicine swallowed whole ▷ vb peel or skin (something)

PILLAGE, -D, -S vb steal property by violence in war ▷ n violent seizure of goods, esp in war

PILLAGER

PILLAR, -ED, -S n upright post, usu supporting a roof ▷ vb provide or support with pillars

PILLAU, -S same as ▶ pilau

PILLBOX n small box for pills

PILLBUG, -S n type of woodlouse

PILLED ▶ pill

PILLIE, -S n pilchard

PILLING, -S ▶ pill

PILLION, -S n seat for a passenger behind the rider of a motorcycle ▷ adv on a pillion ▷ vb ride pillion

PILLOCK, -S n stupid or annoying person

PILLORY n frame in which an offender was locked and exposed to public abuse ▷ vb ridicule publicly

PILLOW, -ED, -S n stuffed cloth bag for supporting the head in bed ▷ vb rest as if on a pillow

PILLOWY

PILLS ▶ pill

PILLWORM n worm that rolls up spirally

PILLWORT n small Eurasian water fern

PILOSE *adj* covered with fine soft hairs
PILOSITY
PILOT, -ED, -S *n* person qualified to fly an aircraft or spacecraft ▷ *adj* experimental and preliminary ▷ *vb* act as the pilot of
PILOTAGE *n* act of piloting an aircraft or ship
PILOTED ▸ pilot
PILOTING *n* navigational handling of a ship near land
PILOTIS *pl n* posts raising a building up from the ground
PILOTMAN, PILOTMEN *n* railway worker who directs trains through hazardous stretches of track
PILOTS ▸ pilot
PILOUS *same as* ▸ **pilose**
PILOW, -S *same as* ▸ **pilau**
PILSENER *same as* ▸ **pilsner**
PILSNER, -S *n* type of pale beer with a strong flavour of hops
PILULA, -E, -S *n* pill
PILULAR ▸ pilule
PILULAS ▸ pilula
PILULE, -S *n* small pill
PILUM *n* ancient Roman javelin
PILUS ▸ pili
PILY *adj* like wool or pile
PIMA, -S *n* type of cotton
PIMENT, -S *n* wine flavoured with spices
PIMENTO, -S *same as* ▸ **pimiento**
PIMENTON *n* smoked chilli powder
PIMENTOS ▸ pimento
PIMENTS ▸ piment
PIMIENTO *n* Spanish pepper with a red fruit used as a vegetable
PIMP, -ED, -S *vb* embellish
PIMPING, -S
PIMPLE, -S *n* small pus-filled spot on the skin
PIMPLED
PIMPLY PIMPLIER
PIMPS ▸ pimp
PIN, -NED, -S *n* short thin piece of stiff wire with a point and head, for fastening things ▷ *vb* fasten with a pin
PINA, -S *n* cone of silver amalgam
PINACOID *n* pair of opposite parallel faces of crystal
PINAFORE *n* apron
PINAKOID *same as* ▸ **pinacoid**
PINANG, -S *n* areca tree

PINAS ▸ pina
PINASTER *n* Mediterranean pine tree
PINATA, -S *n* papier-mâché party decoration filled with sweets
PINBALL, -S *vb* ricochet
PINBOARD *n* cork board for pinning notices, messages etc on
PINBONE, -S *n* part of sirloin
PINCASE, -S *n* case for holding pins
PINCER, -ED *vb* grip with pincers
PINCERS *pl n* tool consisting of two hinged arms, for gripping
PINCH, -ED, -ES, -ING *vb* squeeze between finger and thumb ▷ *n* act of pinching
PINCHBUG *n* type of crab
PINCHECK *n* small check woven into fabric
PINCHED ▸ pinch
PINCHER, -S ▸ pinch
PINCHES ▸ pinch
PINCHGUT *n* miserly person
PINCHING ▸ pinch
PINCURL, -S *n* curl secured by a hairpin
PINDAN, -S *n* desert region of Western Australia
PINDAREE *same as* ▸ **pindari**
PINDARI, -S *n* former irregular Indian horseman
PINDER, -S *n* person who impounds
PINDLING *adj* peevish or fractious
PINDOWN, -S *n* wrestling manoeuvre
PINE, -D, -S, PINING *n* evergreen coniferous tree ▷ *vb* feel great longing (for)
PINEAL, -S *adj* resembling a pine cone ▷ *n* pineal gland
PINECONE *n* seed-producing structure of a pine tree
PINED ▸ pine
PINELAND *n* area covered with pine forest
PINELIKE ▸ pine
PINENE, -S *n* isomeric terpene found in many essential oils
PINERY, PINERIES *n* place, esp a hothouse, where pineapples are grown
PINES ▸ pine
PINESAP, -S *n* red herb of N America
PINETUM, PINETA *n* area of land where pine trees are grown
PINEWOOD *n* wood of pine trees

PINEY ▸ pine
PINFALL, -S *another name for* ▸ **fall**
PINFISH *n* small porgy of the Atlantic
PINFOLD, -S *n* pound for stray cattle ▷ *vb* gather or confine in or as if in a pinfold
PING, -ED, -S *n* short high-pitched sound ▷ *vb* make such a noise
PINGER, -S *n* device, esp a timer, that makes a pinging sound
PINGING ▸ ping
PINGLE, -D, -S, PINGLING *vb* enclose small area of ground
PINGLER, -S
PINGO, -ES, -S *n* mound of earth or gravel formed in Arctic regions
PINGPONG *n* Australian football
PINGRASS *n* weed with fernlike leaves
PINGS ▸ ping
PINGUEFY *vb* become greasy or fat
PINGUID *adj* fatty, oily, or greasy
PINGUIN, -S *same as* ▸ **penguin**
PINHEAD, -S *n* head of a pin
PINHOLE, -S *n* small hole made with or as if with a pin
PINIER ▸ piny
PINIES ▸ piny
PINIEST ▸ piny
PINING ▸ pine
PINION, -ED, -S *n* bird's wing ▷ *vb* immobilize (someone) by tying or holding his or her arms
PINITE, -S *n* greyish-green or brown mineral
PINITOL *n* compound found in pinewood
PINK, -ED, -EST, -S *n* pale reddish colour ▷ *adj* of the colour pink ▷ *vb* (of an engine) make a metallic noise because not working properly
PINKEN, -ED, -S *vb* turn pink
PINKER, -S *n* something that pinks
PINKEST ▸ pink
PINKEY, -S *n* type of ship
PINKEYE, -S *n* acute inflammation of the conjunctiva of the eye
PINKEYS ▸ pinkey
PINKIE, -S *n* little finger
PINKIER ▸ pinky
PINKIES ▸ pinkie
PINKIEST ▸ pinky

P

PINKING, -S ▸ pink
PINKISH ▸ pink
PINKLY ▸ pink
PINKNESS ▸ pink
PINKO, -ES, -S n person regarded as mildly left-wing
PINKROOT n plant with red-and-yellow flowers and pink roots
PINKS ▸ pink
PINKY, PINKIER, PINKIEST adj of a pink colour
PINLESS adj without a pin
PINNA, -E, -S n external part of the ear
PINNACE, -S n ship's boat
PINNACLE n highest point of fame or success ▷ vb set on or as if on a pinnacle
PINNAE ▸ pinna
PINNAL ▸ pinna
PINNAS ▸ pinna
PINNATE adj (of compound leaves) having leaflets growing opposite each other in pairs
PINNATED same as ▸ pinnate
PINNED ▸ pin
PINNER, -S n person or thing that pins
PINNET, -S n pinnacle
PINNIE, -S same as ▸ pinny
PINNING, -S ▸ pin
PINNIPED n aquatic placental mammal such as the seal, sea lion, walrus, etc
PINNOCK, -S n small bird
PINNOED adj held or bound by the arms
PINNULA, -E, -S same as ▸ pinnule
PINNULAR ▸ pinnule
PINNULAS ▸ pinnula
PINNULE, -S n lobe of a leaflet of a pinnate compound leaf
PINNY informal or child's name for ▸ pinafore
PINOCHLE n card game for two to four players similar to bezique
PINOCLE, -S same as ▸ pinochle
PINOLE, -S n flour made in the southwestern United States
PINON, -ES, -S n low-growing pine
PINOT, -S n any of several grape varieties
PINOTAGE n variety of red grape
PINOTS ▸ pinot
PINPOINT vb locate or identify exactly ▷ adj exact ▷ n insignificant or trifling thing

PINPRICK n small irritation or annoyance ▷ vb puncture with or as if with a pin
PINS ▸ pin
PINSCHER n breed of dog
PINSPOT, -S vb illuminate with a small spotlight
PINSWELL n small boil
PINT, -S n liquid measure, 1/8 gallon (.568 litre)
PINTA, -S n pint of milk
PINTABLE n pinball machine
PINTADA, -S same as ▸ pintado
PINTADO, -S n species of seagoing petrel
PINTAIL, -S n greyish-brown duck with a pointed tail
PINTANO, -S n tropical reef fish
PINTAS ▸ pinta
PINTLE, -S n pin or bolt forming the pivot of a hinge
PINTO, -ES, -S adj marked with patches of white ▷ n pinto horse
PINTS ▸ pint
PINTSIZE same as > pintsized
PINTUCK, -S vb tuck with a narrow fold of fabric
PINUP, -S n picture of a physically attractive person
PINWALE, -S n fabric with narrow ridges
PINWEED, -S n herb with tiny flowers
PINWHEEL n cogwheel whose teeth are formed by small pins
PINWORK, -S n (in needlepoint lace) fine raised stitches
PINWORM, -S n parasitic nematode worm
PINXIT vb (he or she) painted (it)
PINY, PINIER, PINIES, PINIEST variant of ▸ peony
PINYIN, -S n system of romanized spelling for the Chinese language
PINYON, -S n low-growing pine
PIOLET, -S n type of ice axe
PION, -S n type of subatomic particle
PIONED adj abounding in marsh marigolds
PIONEER, -S n explorer or early settler of a new country ▷ vb be the pioneer or leader of
PIONER, -S obsolete spelling of ▸ pioneer
PIONEY, -S same as ▸ peony

PIONIC ▸ pion
PIONIES ▸ piony
PIONING, -S n work of pioneers
PIONS ▸ pion
PIONY, PIONIES same as ▸ peony
PIOPIO, -S n New Zealand thrush, thought to be extinct
PIOSITY n grandiose display of piety
PIOTED adj pied
PIOUS adj deeply religious, devout
PIOUSLY
PIOY, -S variant of ▸ peeoy
PIOYE, -S variant of ▸ peeoy
PIOYS ▸ pioy
PIP, -PED, -PING, -S n small seed in a fruit ▷ vb chirp
PIPA, -S n tongueless S American toad
PIPAGE, -S n pipes collectively
PIPAL, -S same as ▸ peepul
PIPAS ▸ pipa
PIPE, -D, -S n tube for conveying liquid or gas ▷ vb play on a pipe
PIPEAGE, -S same as ▸ pipage
PIPECLAY n fine white clay used in tobacco pipes ▷ vb whiten with pipeclay
PIPED ▸ pipe
PIPEFISH n fish with a long tubelike snout and an elongated body
PIPEFUL, -S n as much tobacco, etc as will fill a pipe
PIPELESS ▸ pipe
PIPELIKE ▸ pipe
PIPELINE n long pipe for transporting oil, water, etc
PIPER, -S n player on a pipe or bagpipes
PIPERIC ▸ piperine
PIPERINE n crystalline insoluble alkaloid that is the active ingredient of pepper
PIPERS ▸ piper
PIPES ▸ pipe
PIPESTEM n hollow stem of pipe
PIPET, -S same as ▸ pipette
PIPETTE, -D, -S n slender glass tube used to transfer or measure fluids ▷ vb transfer or measure out (a liquid) using a pipette
PIPEWORK n stops and flues on pipe organ
PIPEWORT n perennial plant with a twisted flower stalk and a greenish-grey scaly flower head

PIPI, -S n edible mollusc often used as bait
PIPIER ▸ pipy
PIPIEST ▸ pipy
PIPINESS n material's suitability for use as pipe
PIPING, -S n system of pipes
PIPINGLY
PIPIS ▸ pipi
PIPIT, -S n small brownish songbird
PIPKIN, -S same as ▸ **piggin**
PIPLESS ▸ pip
PIPPED ▸ pip
PIPPIER ▸ pippy
PIPPIEST ▸ pippy
PIPPIN, -S n type of eating apple
PIPPING ▸ pip
PIPPINS ▸ pippin
PIPPY, PIPPIER, PIPPIEST adj containing many pips
PIPS ▸ pip
PIPUL, -S n Indian fig tree
PIPY, PIPIER, PIPIEST ▸ pipe
PIQUANCE same as ▸ **piquant**
PIQUANCY ▸ piquant
PIQUANT adj having a pleasant spicy taste
PIQUE, -D, -S, PIQUING n feeling of hurt pride, baffled curiosity, or resentment ▷ vb hurt the pride of
PIQUET, -ED, -S n card game for two ▷ vb play game of piquet
PIQUILLO n variety of sweet red pepper
PIQUING ▸ pique
PIR, -S n Sufi master
PIRACY, PIRACIES n robbery on the seas
PIRAGUA, -S same as ▸ **pirogue**
PIRAI, -S n large S American fish
PIRANA, -S same as ▸ **piranha**
PIRANHA, -S n fierce fish of tropical America
PIRARUCU n large S American food fish
PIRATE, -D, -S n sea robber ▷ vb sell or reproduce (artistic work etc) illegally
PIRATIC
PIRATING n act of pirating
PIRAYA, -S same as ▸ **pirai**
PIRIFORM adj shaped like pear
PIRL, -S n ripple in water
PIRLICUE same as ▸ **purlicue**
PIRLS ▸ pirl
PIRN, -S n reel or bobbin
PIRNIE, -S n stripy nightcap

PIRNIT adj striped
PIRNS ▸ pirn
PIROG, -HI, -I, -IES n type of large Russian pie
PIROGEN n turnovers made from kneaded dough
PIROGHI ▸ pirog
PIROGI ▸ pirog
PIROGIES ▸ pirog
PIROGUE, -S n any of various kinds of dugout canoes
PIROJKI same as ▸ **piroshki**
PIROQUE, -S same as ▸ **pirogue**
PIROSHKI same as ▸ **pirozhki**
PIROZHOK, PIROZHKI n small triangular pastry filled with meat, vegetables, etc
PIRS ▸ pir
PIS ▸ pi
PISCARY n place where fishing takes place
PISCATOR n fisherman
PISCINA, -E, -S n stone basin where water used at Mass is poured away
PISCINAL
PISCINE, -S n pond or pool
PISCO, -S n S American brandy
PISE, -S n rammed earth or clay used to make floors or walls
PISH, -ED, -ES, -ING interj exclamation of impatience or contempt ▷ vb make this exclamation at (someone or something)
PISHEOG, -S same as ▸ **pishogue**
PISHER, -S n Yiddish term for small boy
PISHES ▸ pish
PISHING ▸ pish
PISHOGE, -S same as ▸ **pishogue**
PISHOGUE n sorcery
PISIFORM adj resembling a pea ▷ n small pealike bone on the ulnar side of the carpus
PISKY, PISKIES n Cornish fairy
PISMIRE, -S archaic or dialect word for ▸ **ant**
PISO, -S n peso of the Philippines
PISOLITE n sedimentary rock
PISOLITH same as ▸ **pisolite**
PISOS ▸ piso
PISTACHE n tree yielding pistachio nut
PISTE, -S n ski slope
PISTED adj marked off into pistes
PISTES ▸ piste

PISTIL, -S n seed-bearing part of a flower
PISTOL, -ED, -S n short-barrelled handgun ▷ vb shoot with a pistol
PISTOLE, -S n gold coin formerly used in Europe
PISTOLED ▸ pistol
PISTOLES ▸ pistole
PISTOLET n small pistol
PISTOLS ▸ pistol
PISTON, -S n cylindrical part in an engine that slides to and fro in a cylinder
PISTOU, -S n French sauce
PIT, -S, -TED n deep hole in the ground ▷ vb mark with small dents or scars
PITA, -S n any of several agave plants yielding a strong fibre
PITAHAYA n any giant cactus of Central America and the SW United States
PITAPAT, -S adv with quick light taps ▷ n such taps ▷ vb make quick light taps or beats
PITARA, -S variant of ▸ **petara**
PITARAH, -S variant of ▸ **petara**
PITARAS ▸ pitara
PITAS ▸ pita
PITAYA, -S same as ▸ **pitahaya**
PITCH, -ED, -ES, -ING vb throw, hurl ▷ n area marked out for playing sport
PITCHER, -S n large jug with a narrow neck
PITCHES ▸ pitch
PITCHIER ▸ pitchy
PITCHILY ▸ pitchy
PITCHING ▸ pitch
PITCHMAN, PITCHMEN n itinerant pedlar of small merchandise who operates from a stand at a fair, etc
PITCHOUT n type of baseball pitch
PITCHY, PITCHIER adj full of or covered with pitch
PITEOUS adj arousing pity
PITFALL, -S n hidden difficulty or danger
PITH, -ED, -ING, -S n soft white lining of the rind of oranges etc ▷ vb destroy the brain and spinal cord of a laboratory animal
PITHBALL n type of conductor
PITHEAD, -S n top of a mine shaft and the buildings and hoisting gear around it
PITHED ▸ pith
PITHFUL ▸ pith

P

PITHIER ► pithy
PITHIEST ► pithy
PITHILY ► pithy
PITHING ► pith
PITHLESS ► pith
PITHLIKE ► pith
PITHOS, PITHOI *n* large ceramic container for oil or grain
PITHS ► pith
PITHY, PITHIER, PITHIEST *adj* short and full of meaning
PITIABLE *adj* arousing or deserving pity or contempt
PITIABLY
PITIED ► pity
PITIER, -S ► pity
PITIES ► pity
PITIETH *vb as in* **it pitieth me** archaic inflection of 'pity'
PITIFUL *adj* arousing pity
PITIKINS *n as in* **ods pitikins** mild oath
PITILESS *adj* feeling no pity or mercy
PITMAN, -S, PITMEN *n* coal miner ▷ *n* connecting rod (in a machine)
PITON, -S *n* metal spike used in climbing to secure a rope
PITOT, -S *n* tube used to measure the pressure of a liquid stream
PITPROP, -S *n* support beam in mine shaft
PITS ► pit
PITSAW, -S *n* large saw formerly used for cutting logs into planks
PITTA, -S *n* small brightly coloured ground-dwelling tropical bird
PITTANCE *n* very small amount of money
PITTAS ► pitta
PITTED ► pit
PITTEN *adj* having been put
PITTER, -ED, -S *vb* make pattering sound
PITTING, -S ► pit
PITTITE, -S *n* occupant of a theatre pit
PITUITA, -S *n* thick nasal secretion
PITUITE, -S *n* mucus
PITURI, -S *n* Australian solanaceous shrub
PITY, PITIED, PITIES *n* sympathy or sorrow for others' suffering ▷ *vb* feel pity for
PITYING
PITYROID *adj* resembling bran
PIU *adv* more (quickly, softly, etc)

PIUM, -S *n* stinging insect
PIUPIU, -S *n* skirt worn by Māoris on ceremonial occasions
PIVOT, -ED, -ING, -S *n* central shaft on which something turns ▷ *vb* provide with or turn on a pivot
PIVOTAL *adj* of crucial importance
PIVOTED ► pivot
PIVOTER, -S ► pivot
PIVOTING ► pivot
PIVOTMAN, PIVOTMEN *n* person in rank around whom others wheel
PIVOTS ► pivot
PIX, -ES *less common spelling of* ► **pyx**
PIXEL, -S *n* any of a number of very small picture elements
PIXELATE *vb* divide an image into pixels
PIXELS ► pixel
PIXES ► pix
PIXIE *n* (in folklore) fairy
PIXIEISH
PIXIES ► pixy
PIXILATE *same as* ► **pixelate**
PIXINESS ► pixie
PIXY, PIXIES *same as* ► **pixie**
PIXYISH
PIZAZZ, -ES *same as* ► **pizzazz**
PIZAZZY
PIZE, -D, -S, PIZING *vb* strike (someone a blow)
PIZZA, -S *n* flat disc of dough covered with a wide variety of savoury toppings and baked
PIZZAZ, -ES *same as* ► **pzazz**
PIZZAZZ *n* attractive combination of energy and style
PIZZAZZY
PIZZELLE *n* Italian sweet wafer
PIZZERIA *n* place where pizzas are made, sold, or eaten
PIZZLE, -S *n* penis of an animal, esp a bull
PLAAS, -ES *n* farm
PLACABLE *adj* easily placated or appeased
PLACABLY
PLACARD, -S *n* notice that is carried or displayed in public ▷ *vb* attach placards to
PLACATE, -D, -S *vb* make (someone) stop feeling angry or upset
PLACATER
PLACCAT, -S *variant of* ► **placket**

PLACCATE *variant of* ► **placket**
PLACCATS ► placcat
PLACE, -D, -S *n* particular part of an area or space ▷ *vb* put in a particular place
PLACEBO, -S *n* pill given to a patient instead of an active drug
PLACED ► place
PLACEMAN, PLACEMEN *n* person who holds a public office as a reward for political support
PLACEMAT *n* table mat for a person to put their plate on
PLACEMEN ► placeman
PLACENTA *n* organ formed in the womb during pregnancy, providing nutrients for the fetus
PLACER, -S *n* surface sediment containing particles of gold or some other valuable mineral
PLACES ► place
PLACET, -S *n* vote or expression of assent
PLACID, -ER *adj* not easily excited or upset, calm
PLACIDLY
PLACING, -S *n* method of issuing securities to the public using an intermediary
PLACIT, -S *n* decree or dictum
PLACITA ► placitum
PLACITS ► placit
PLACITUM, PLACITA *n* court or assembly in Middle Ages
PLACK, -S *n* small former Scottish coin
PLACKET, -S *n* opening at the waist of a dress or skirt
PLACKS ► plack
PLACOID, -S *adj* platelike or flattened ▷ *n* fish with placoid scales
PLAFOND, -S *n* ceiling, esp one having ornamentation
PLAGAL *adj* (of a cadence) progressing from the subdominant to the tonic chord
PLAGE, -S *n* bright patch in the sun's chromosphere
PLAGIARY *n* person who plagiarizes or a piece of plagiarism
PLAGIUM, -S *n* crime of kidnapping
PLAGUE, -D, -S, PLAGUING *n* fast-spreading fatal disease ▷ *vb* trouble or annoy continually
PLAGUER -S

P

PLAGUEY, PLAGUIER same as ▸ **plaguy**

PLAGUILY ▸ **plaguy**

PLAGUING ▸ **plague**

PLAGUY adj disagreeable or vexing ▹ adv disagreeably or annoyingly

PLAICE, -S n edible European flatfish

PLAID, -ED, -ING, -S n long piece of tartan cloth worn as part of Highland dress ▹ vb weave cloth into plaid

PLAIDMAN, PLAIDMEN n wearer of plaid

PLAIDS ▸ **plaid**

PLAIN, -ED, -ER, -EST, -ING adj easy to see or understand ▹ n large stretch of level country ▹ adv clearly or simply ▹ vb complain

PLAINANT n plaintiff

PLAINED ▸ **plain**

PLAINER ▸ **plain**

PLAINEST ▸ **plain**

PLAINFUL adj apt to complain

PLAINING ▸ **plain**

PLAINISH ▸ **plain**

PLAINLY ▸ **plain**

PLAINS pl n extensive tracts of flat treeless countryside

PLAINT, -S n complaint or lamentation

PLAISTER n plaster

PLAIT, -ED, -ING, -S n intertwined length of hair ▹ vb intertwine separate strands in a pattern

PLAITER -S

PLAN, -NED, -NING, -S n way thought out to do or achieve something ▹ vb arrange beforehand

PLANAR adj of or relating to a plane

PLANARIA n type of flatworm

PLANATE adj having been flattened

PLANCH, -ED, -ES vb cover with planks

PLANCHE same as ▸ **planch**

PLANCHED ▸ **planch**

PLANCHES ▸ **planch**

PLANCHET n piece of metal ready to be stamped as a coin, medal, etc

PLANE, -D, -S, PLANING n aeroplane ▹ adj perfectly flat or level ▹ vb glide or skim

PLANER, -S n machine with a cutting tool that makes repeated horizontal strokes

PLANES ▸ **plane**

PLANET, -S n large body in space that revolves round the sun or another star

PLANFORM n outline or silhouette of an object, esp an aircraft, as seen from above

PLANGENT adj (of sounds) mournful and resounding

PLANING ▸ **plane**

PLANISH vb give a smooth surface to (a metal)

PLANK, -ED, -S n long flat piece of sawn timber ▹ vb cover or provide (an area) with planks

PLANKING n number of planks

PLANKS ▸ **plank**

PLANKTER n organism in plankton

PLANKTIC adj relating to plankton

PLANKTON n minute animals and plants floating in the surface water of a sea or lake

PLANLESS adj having no plan

PLANNED ▸ **plan**

PLANNER, -S n person who makes plans

PLANNING ▸ **plan**

PLANOSOL n soil of humid or subhumid uplands

PLANS ▸ **plan**

PLANT, -ED, -ING, -S n living organism that grows in the ground and has no power to move ▹ vb put in the ground to grow

PLANTA, -E, -S n sole of foot

PLANTAGE n plants

PLANTAIN n low-growing wild plant with broad leaves

PLANTAR adj of, relating to, or occurring on the sole of the foot

PLANTAS ▸ **planta**

PLANTED ▸ **plant**

PLANTER, -S n owner of a plantation

PLANTING ▸ **plant**

PLANTLET n small plant

PLANTS ▸ **plant**

PLANTULE n embryo in act of germination

PLANULA, -E n free-swimming larva of hydrozoan coelenterates

PLANULAR

PLANURIA n expulsion of urine from abnormal opening

PLANURY another name for ▸ **planuria**

PLANXTY n Celtic melody for harp

PLAP, -PED, -PING, -S same as ▸ **plop**

PLAQUE, -S n inscribed commemorative stone or metal plate

PLASH, -ED, -ES, -ING same as ▸ **pleach**

PLASHER, -S n type of farm tool

PLASHES ▸ **plash**

PLASHET, -S n small pond

PLASHIER ▸ **plashy**

PLASHING ▸ **plash**

PLASHY, PLASHIER adj wet or marshy

PLASM, -S same as ▸ **plasma**

PLASMA, -S n clear liquid part of blood

PLASMIC

PLASMID, -S n small circle of bacterial DNA

PLASMIN, -S n proteolytic enzyme that causes fibrinolysis in blood clots

PLASMOID n section of a plasma having a characteristic shape

PLASMON, -S n sum total of plasmagenes in a cell

PLASMS ▸ **plasm**

PLAST archaic past participle of ▸ **place**

PLASTE archaic past participle of ▸ **place**

PLASTER, -S n mixture of lime, sand, etc for coating walls ▹ vb cover with plaster

PLASTERY

PLASTIC, -S n synthetic material that can be moulded when soft but sets in a hard long-lasting shape ▹ adj made of plastic

PLASTID, -S n small particle in the cells of plants and some animals

PLASTRAL ▸ **plastron**

PLASTRON, PLASTRUM n bony plate forming the ventral part of the shell of a tortoise or turtle

PLAT, -S, -TED, -TING n small area of ground

PLATAN, -S n plane tree

PLATANE, -S same as ▸ **platan**

PLATANNA n S African frog

PLATANS ▸ **platan**

PLATBAND n border of flowers in garden

PLATE, -S n shallow dish for holding food ▹ vb cover with a thin coating of gold, silver, or other metal

PLATEASM n talking with mouth open too wide

P

PLATEAU, -S, -X *n* area of level high land ▷ *vb* remain stable for a long period

PLATED *adj* coated with a layer of metal

PLATEFUL *same as* ▶ **plate**

PLATELET *n* minute particle occurring in blood of vertebrates and involved in clotting of blood

PLATEMAN, PLATEMEN *n* one of crew of steam train

PLATEN, -S *n* roller of a typewriter, against which the paper is held

PLATER, -S *n* person or thing that plates

PLATES ▶ **plate**

PLATFORM *n* raised floor

PLATIER ▶ **platy**

PLATIES ▶ **platy**

PLATIEST ▶ **platy**

PLATINA, -S *n* alloy of platinum and several other metals

PLATING, -S *n* coating of metal

PLATINIC *adj* of or containing platinum, esp in the tetravalent state

PLATINUM *n* valuable silvery-white metal

PLATONIC *adj* (of a relationship) friendly or affectionate but not romantic ▷ *n* platonic friend

PLATOON, -S *n* smaller unit within a company of soldiers ▷ *vb* organise into platoons

PLATS ▶ **plat**

PLATT *adj as in* **scale and platt** denoting a modern straight staircase with landings as opposed to a spiral staircase

PLATTED ▶ **plat**

PLATTER, -S *n* large dish

PLATTING ▶ **plat**

PLATY, PLATIER, PLATIES, PLATIEST, -S *adj* of, relating to, or designating rocks the constituents of which occur in flaky layers ▷ *n* brightly coloured freshwater fish

PLATYPUS, PLATYPI *n* Australian egg-laying amphibious mammal

PLATYS ▶ **platy**

PLATYSMA *n* muscle located on side of neck

PLAUDIT, -S *n* expression of enthusiastic approval

PLAUDITE *interj* give a round of applause!

PLAUDITS ▶ **plaudit**

PLAUSIVE *adj* expressing praise or approval

PLAY, -ED, -S *vb* occupy oneself in (a game or recreation) ▷ *n* story performed on stage or broadcast

PLAYA, -S *n* (in the US) temporary lake in a desert basin

PLAYABLE ▶ **play**

PLAYACT, -S *vb* pretend or make believe

PLAYAS ▶ **playa**

PLAYBACK *n* reproducing of a recording, esp formerly on magnetic tape ▷ *vb* listen to or watch (something recorded)

PLAYBILL *n* poster or bill advertising a play

PLAYBOOK *n* book containing a range of possible set plays

PLAYBOY, -S *n* rich man who lives only for pleasure

PLAYBUS *n* mobile playground in a bus

PLAYDATE *n* gathering of children at house for play

PLAYDAY, -S *n* day given to play

PLAYDOWN *same as* ▶ **playoff**

PLAYED ▶ **play**

PLAYER, -S *n* person who plays a game or sport

PLAYFUL *adj* lively

PLAYGIRL *n* rich woman devoted to pleasure

PLAYGOER *n* person who goes often to the theatre

PLAYING, -S *n* act of playing

PLAYLAND *n* playground

PLAYLESS ▶ **play**

PLAYLET, -S *n* short play

PLAYLIKE ▶ **play**

PLAYLIST *n* list of songs chosen for playing, such as on a radio station ▷ *vb* put (a song) on a playlist

PLAYMATE *n* companion in play

PLAYOFF, -S *n* extra contest to decide the winner when two or more competitors are tied

PLAYPEN, -S *n* small portable enclosure in which a young child can safely be left to play

PLAYROOM *n* recreation room, esp for children

PLAYS ▶ **play**

PLAYSET, -S *n* outdoor equipment for children to play on

PLAYSLIP *n* form used to select numbers in a lottery draw

PLAYSOME *adj* playful

PLAYSUIT *n* woman's or child's outfit, usually comprising shorts and a top

PLAYTIME *n* time for play or recreation, such as a school break

PLAYWEAR *n* clothes suitable for playing in

PLAZA, -S *n* open space or square

PLEA, -ED, -ING, -S *n* serious or urgent request, entreaty ▷ *vb* entreat

PLEACH, -ED, -ES *vb* interlace the stems or boughs of (a tree or hedge)

PLEAD, -ED, -ING, -S, PLED *vb* ask urgently or with deep feeling

PLEADER -S

PLEAED ▶ **plea**

PLEAING ▶ **plea**

PLEAS ▶ **plea**

PLEASANT *adj* pleasing, enjoyable

PLEASE, -S *vb* give pleasure or satisfaction to ▷ *adv* polite word of request

PLEASED

PLEASER -S

PLEASETH *obsolete inflection of* ▶ **please**

PLEASING *adj* giving pleasure or satisfaction ▷ *n* act of giving pleasure

PLEASURE *n* feeling of happiness and satisfaction ▷ *vb* give pleasure to or take pleasure (in)

PLEAT, -ED, -S *n* fold made by doubling material back on itself ▷ *vb* arrange (material) in pleats

PLEATER, -S *n* attachment on a sewing machine that makes pleats

PLEATHER *n* synthetic leather

PLEATING *n* act of pleating

PLEATS ▶ **pleat**

PLEB *n* common vulgar person

PLEBBY, PLEBBIER *adj* common or vulgar

PLEBE, -S *n* member of the lowest class at the US Naval Academy or Military Academy

PLEBEAN *old variant of* ▶ **plebeian**

PLEBEIAN *adj* of the lower social classes ▷ *n* member of the lower social classes

PLEBES ▸ plebe

PLEBIFY vb make plebeian

PLEBS n common people

PLECTRA ▸ plectrum

PLECTRE, -S variant of ▸ **plectrum**

PLECTRON same as ▸ **plectrum**

PLECTRUM, PLECTRA n small implement for plucking the strings of a guitar etc

PLED ▸ plead

PLEDGE, -D, -S, PLEDGING n solemn promise ▷ vb promise solemnly

PLEDGEE, -S n person to whom a pledge is given

PLEDGEOR same as ▸ **pledgor**

PLEDGER, -S same as ▸ **pledgor**

PLEDGES ▸ pledge

PLEDGET, -S n small flattened pad of wool, cotton, etc

PLEDGING ▸ pledge

PLEDGOR, -S n person who gives or makes a pledge

PLEIAD, -ES, -S n brilliant or talented group, esp one with seven members

PLENA ▸ plenum

PLENARTY n state of endowed church office when occupied

PLENARY adj (of a meeting) attended by all members ▷ n book read at the Eucharist

PLENCH, -ES n tool combining wrench and pliers

PLENIPO, -S n plenipotentiary diplomat

PLENISH vb fill, stock, or resupply

PLENISM, -S n philosophical theory

PLENIST -S

PLENTY, PLENTIES n large amount or number ▷ adj very many ▷ adv more than adequately

PLENUM, PLENA, -S n enclosure containing gas at a high pressure

PLEON, -S n abdomen of crustacean

PLEONAL adj of the abdomen of a crustacean

PLEONASM n use of more words than necessary

PLEONAST n person using more words than necessary

PLEONIC ▸ pleon

PLEONS ▸ pleon

PLEOPOD, -S another name for ▸ **swimmeret**

PLERION, -S n filled-centre supernova remnant

PLEROMA, -S n abundance

PLEROME, -S n central column in growing stem or root

PLESH, -ES n small pool

PLESSOR, -S same as ▸ **plexor**

PLETHORA n excess

PLEUCH, -ED, -S same as ▸ **pleugh**

PLEUGH, -ED, -S Scottish word for ▸ **plough**

PLEURA, -E, -S n membrane covering the lungs

PLEURAL

PLEURISY n inflammation of the membrane covering the lungs

PLEURON n part of the cuticle of arthropods

PLEUSTON n mass of small organisms, esp algae, floating at the surface of shallow pools

PLEW, -S n (formerly in Canada) beaver skin used as a standard unit of value in the fur trade

PLEX, -ED, -ES, -ING n shortening of multiplex ▷ vb make a plexus

PLEXAL ▸ plexus

PLEXED ▸ plex

PLEXES ▸ plex

PLEXING ▸ plex

PLEXOR, -S n small hammer with a rubber head

PLEXURE, -S n act of weaving together

PLEXUS, -ES n complex network of nerves or blood vessels

PLIABLE adj easily bent

PLIABLY

PLIANCY ▸ pliant

PLIANT adj pliable

PLIANTLY

PLICA, -E, -S n folding over of parts, such as a fold of skin, muscle, peritoneum, etc

PLICAL

PLICATE, -D, -S adj having or arranged in parallel folds or ridges ▷ vb arrange into parallel folds

PLIE n classic ballet practice posture with back erect and knees bent

PLIED ▸ ply

PLIER n person who plies a trade

PLIERS pl n tool with hinged arms and jaws for gripping

PLIES ▸ ply

PLIGHT, -ED, -S n difficult or dangerous situation

PLIGHTER

PLIM, -MED, -MING, -S vb swell with water

PLIMSOL, -S same as ▸ **plimsole**

PLIMSOLE same as ▸ **plimsoll**

PLIMSOLL n light rubber-soled canvas shoe worn for various sports

PLIMSOLS ▸ plimsol

PLING, -ED, -ING, -S n (in computer jargon) an exclamation mark ▷ vb beg from

PLINK, -ED, -S n short sharp often metallic sound ▷ vb make such a noise

PLINKER -S

PLINKIER ▸ plinky

PLINKING ▸ plink

PLINKS ▸ plink

PLINKY, PLINKIER adj (of a sound) short, sharp, and often metallic

PLINTH, -S n slab forming the base of a statue, column, etc

PLIOCENE adj of the Pliocene geological time period

PLIOFILM n transparent plastic material

PLIOSAUR n type of dinosaur

PLIOTRON n type of vacuum tube

PLISKIE, -R, -S n practical joke ▷ adj tricky or mischievous

PLISKY same as ▸ **pliskie**

PLISSE, -S n fabric with a wrinkled finish, achieved by treatment involving caustic soda

PLOAT, -ED, -ING, -S vb thrash

PLOD, -DED, -S vb walk with slow heavy steps ▷ n act of plodding

PLODDER, -S n person who plods

PLODDING ▸ plod

PLODGE, -D, -S, PLODGING vb wade in water, esp the sea ▷ n act of wading

PLODS ▸ plod

PLOIDY, PLOIDIES n number of copies of set of chromosomes in cell

PLONG, -D, -S obsolete variant of ▸ **plunge**

PLONGE, -D, -S, PLONGING same as ▸ **plunge**

PLONGS ▸ plong

PLONK, -ED, -ING, -S vb put (something) down heavily and carelessly ▷ n act of plonking ▷ interj

exclamation imitative of this sound
PLONKER, -S n stupid person
PLONKIER ▸ plonky
PLONKING ▸ plonk
PLONKO, -S n alcoholic, esp one who drinks wine
PLONKS ▸ plonk
PLONKY, PLONKIER ▸ plonk
PLOOK, -S same as ▸ **plouk**
PLOOKIE same as ▸ **plouky**
PLOOKIER ▸ plooky
PLOOKS ▸ plook
PLOOKY, PLOOKIER ▸ plook
PLOP, -PED, -PING, -S n sound of an object falling into water without a splash ▷ vb make this sound ▷ interj exclamation imitative of this sound
PLOSION, -S n sound of an abrupt break or closure, esp the audible release of a stop
PLOSIVE, -S adj pronounced with a sudden release of breath ▷ n plosive consonant
PLOT, -S, -TED, -TING n secret plan to do something illegal or wrong ▷ vb plan secretly, conspire
PLOTFUL
PLOTLESS
PLOTLINE n literary or dramatic plot
PLOTS ▸ plot
PLOTTAGE n land that makes up plot
PLOTTED ▸ plot
PLOTTER, -S same as ▸ **plouter**
PLOTTIE, -S n hot spiced drink
PLOTTIER ▸ plotty
PLOTTIES ▸ plottie
PLOTTING ▸ plot
PLOTTY, PLOTTIER adj intricately plotted
PLOTZ, -ED, -ES, -ING vb faint or collapse
PLOUGH, -ED, -S n agricultural tool for turning over soil ▷ vb turn over (earth) with a plough
PLOUGHER
PLOUK, -S n pimple
PLOUKIE
PLOUKIER ▸ plouky
PLOUKS ▸ plouk
PLOUKY, PLOUKIER ▸ plouk
PLOUTER, -S same as ▸ **plowter**
PLOVER, -S n shore bird with a straight bill and long pointed wings
PLOVERY

PLOW, -ED, -S same as ▸ **plough**
PLOWABLE
PLOWBACK n reinvestment of profits
PLOWBOY, -S same as > **ploughboy**
PLOWED ▸ plow
PLOWER, -S ▸ plow
PLOWHEAD n draught iron of plow
PLOWING, -S > ploughing
PLOWLAND n land plowed
PLOWMAN, PLOWMEN same as > **ploughman**
PLOWS ▸ plow
PLOWTAIL n the end of a plough where the handles are
PLOWTER, -S vb work or play in water or mud ▷ n act of plowtering
PLOWWISE adv as in ploughing
PLOY, -ED, -ING, -S n manoeuvre designed to gain an advantage ▷ vb form a column from a line of troops
PLOYE, -S n buckwheat pancake
PLOYED ▸ ploy
PLOYES ▸ ploye
PLOYING ▸ ploy
PLOYS ▸ ploy
PLU same as ▸ **plew**
PLUCK, -ED, -ING, -S vb pull or pick off ▷ n courage
PLUCKER -S
PLUCKIER ▸ plucky
PLUCKILY ▸ plucky
PLUCKING ▸ pluck
PLUCKS ▸ pluck
PLUCKY, PLUCKIER adj brave
PLUE, -S same as ▸ **plew**
PLUFF, -ED, -ING, -S vb expel in puffs
PLUFFIER ▸ pluffy
PLUFFING ▸ pluff
PLUFFS ▸ pluff
PLUFFY, PLUFFIER ▸ pluff
PLUG, -GED, -GING, -S n thing fitting into and filling a hole ▷ vb block or seal (a hole or gap) with a plug
PLUGGER -S
PLUGHOLE n hole at the bottom of a bath or sink which can be closed with a plug
PLUGLESS ▸ plug
PLUGOLA, -S n plugging of products on television
PLUGS ▸ plug
PLUGUGLY n city tough; ruffian

PLUM, -MER, -MEST, -S n oval usu dark red fruit with a stone in the middle ▷ adj dark purplish-red
PLUMAGE, -S n bird's feathers
PLUMAGED
PLUMATE adj of, relating to, or possessing one or more feathers or plumes
PLUMB, -ED, -S vb understand (something obscure) ▷ adv exactly ▷ n weight suspended at the end of a line
PLUMBAGO n plant of warm regions with clusters of blue, white, or red flowers
PLUMBATE n compound formed from lead oxide
PLUMBED ▸ plumb
PLUMBER, -S n person who fits and repairs pipes and fixtures for water and drainage systems
PLUMBERY same as ▸ **plumbing**
PLUMBIC adj of or containing lead in the tetravalent state
PLUMBING n pipes and fixtures used in water and drainage systems
PLUMBISM n chronic lead poisoning
PLUMBITE n substance containing lead oxide
PLUMBOUS adj of or containing lead in the divalent state
PLUMBS ▸ plumb
PLUMBUM, -S n obsolete name for lead (the metal)
PLUMCAKE n cake with raisins in it
PLUMCOT, -S n hybrid of apricot and plum
PLUME, -D, -S, PLUMING n feather, esp one worn as an ornament ▷ vb adorn or decorate with feathers or plumes
PLUMELET n small plume
PLUMERIA n tropical tree with candelabra-like branches
PLUMERY n plumes collectively
PLUMES ▸ plume
PLUMIER ▸ plumy
PLUMIEST ▸ plumy
PLUMING ▸ plume
PLUMIPED n bird with feathered feet
PLUMIST, -S n person who makes plumes
PLUMLIKE ▸ plum
PLUMMER ▸ plum

PLUMMEST ▶ plum
PLUMMET, -S vb plunge downward ▷ n weight on a plumb line or fishing line
PLUMMY, PLUMMIER adj of, full of, or like plums
PLUMOSE same as ▶ plumate
PLUMOUS adj having plumes or feathers
PLUMP, -ED, -EST, -ING, -S adj moderately or attractively fat ▷ vb sit or fall heavily and suddenly ▷ n heavy abrupt fall or the sound of this ▷ adv suddenly or heavily
PLUMPEN, -S vb make or become plump
PLUMPER, -S n pad carried in the mouth by actors to round out the cheeks
PLUMPEST ▶ plump
PLUMPIE same as ▶ plumpy
PLUMPIER ▶ plumpy
PLUMPING ▶ plump
PLUMPISH adj on the plump side
PLUMPLY ▶ plump
PLUMPS ▶ plump
PLUMPY, PLUMPIER adj plump
PLUMS ▶ plum
PLUMULA, -E n down feather
PLUMULAR ▶ plumule
PLUMULE, -S n embryonic shoot of seed-bearing plants
PLUMY, PLUMIER, PLUMIEST adj like a feather
PLUNDER, -S vb take by force, esp in time of war ▷ n things plundered, spoils
PLUNGE, -D, -S, PLUNGING vb put or throw forcibly or suddenly (into) ▷ n plunging dive
PLUNGER, -S n rubber suction cup used to clear blocked pipes
PLUNGES ▶ plunge
PLUNGING ▶ plunge
PLUNK, -ED, -ING, -S vb pluck the strings of (a banjo etc) to produce a twanging sound ▷ n act or sound of plunking ▷ interj exclamation imitative of the sound of something plunking ▷ adv exactly
PLUNKER -S
PLUNKIER ▶ plunky
PLUNKING ▶ plunk
PLUNKS ▶ plunk
PLUNKY, PLUNKIER adj sounding like plucked banjo string

PLUOT, -S n hybrid fruit of the plum and apricot
PLURAL, -S adj of or consisting of more than one ▷ n word indicating more than one
PLURALLY
PLURISIE same as ▶ pleurisy
PLURRY euphemism for ▶ bloody
PLUS, -ED, -ES, -ING, -SED, -SES, -SING vb make or become greater in value
PLUSAGE, -S same as ▶ plussage
PLUSED ▶ plus
PLUSES ▶ plus
PLUSH, -ER, -ES, -EST n fabric with long velvety pile ▷ adj luxurious
PLUSHED adj showily luxurious
PLUSHER ▶ plush
PLUSHES ▶ plush
PLUSHEST ▶ plush
PLUSHIER ▶ plushy
PLUSHILY ▶ plushy
PLUSHLY ▶ plush
PLUSHY, PLUSHIER same as ▶ plush
PLUSING ▶ plus
PLUSSAGE n amount over and above another amount
PLUSSED ▶ plus
PLUSSES ▶ plus
PLUSSING ▶ plus
PLUTEAL ▶ pluteus
PLUTEUS, PLUTEI n larva of sea urchin
PLUTOID, -S n dwarf planet whose orbit is beyond Neptune's
PLUTON, -S n any mass of igneous rock that has solidified below the surface of the earth
PLUTONIC adj formed from molten rock below the earth's surface
PLUTONS ▶ pluton
PLUVIAL, -S n period of high rainfall
PLUVIAN, -S n crocodile bird
PLUVIOSE same as ▶ pluvious
PLUVIOUS adj of or relating to rain
PLUVIUS adj as in **pluvius insurance** insurance against rain
PLY, PLIED, PLIES, -ING vb work at (a job or trade) ▷ n thickness of wool, fabric, etc
PLYER, -S n person who plies trade

PLYING ▶ ply
PLYINGLY ▶ ply
PLYWOOD, -S n board made of thin layers of wood glued together
PNEUMA, -S n person's vital spirit, soul, or creative energy
PO, -S n chamber pot
POA, -S n type of grass
POACEOUS adj relating to the plant family which comprises grasses
POACH, -ED, -ES, -ING vb catch (animals) illegally on someone else's land
POACHER, -S n person who catches animals illegally on someone else's land
POACHES ▶ poach
POACHIER ▶ poachy
POACHING ▶ poach
POACHY, POACHIER adj (of land) wet and soft
POAKA, -S n type of stilt (bird) native to New Zealand
POAKE, -S n waste matter from tanning of hides
POAS ▶ poa
POBLANO, -S n variety of chilli pepper
POBOY, -S n New Orleans sandwich
POCHARD, -S n European diving duck
POCHAY, -ED, -S n closed horse-drawn four-wheeled coach ▷ vb transport by pochay
POCHETTE n envelope-shaped handbag used by women and men
POCHOIR, -S n print made from stencils
POCK, -ED, -ING, -S n pus-filled blister resulting from smallpox ▷ vb mark with scars
POCKARD, -S variant of ▶ pochard
POCKED ▶ pock
POCKET, -ED, -S n small bag sewn into clothing for carrying things ▷ vb put into one's pocket ▷ adj small
POCKETER
POCKIER ▶ pocky
POCKIES pl n woollen mittens
POCKIEST ▶ pocky
POCKILY ▶ pock
POCKING ▶ pock
POCKMARK n pitted scar left on the skin after the healing of a smallpox or similar pustule ▷ vb scar or pit (a surface) with pockmarks

P

POCKPIT, -S n mark left on skin after a pock has gone

POCKS ▸ pock

POCKY, POCKIER, POCKIEST ▸ pock

POCO adv little

POCOSEN, -S same as ▸ pocosin

POCOSIN, -S n swamp in US upland coastal region

POCOSON, -S same as ▸ pocosin

POD, -DED, -DING, -S n long narrow seed case of peas, beans, etc ▷ vb remove the pod from

PODAGRA, -S n gout of the foot or big toe

PODAGRAL

PODAGRIC

PODAL adj relating to feet

PODALIC adj relating to feet

PODARGUS n bird of SE Asia and Australia

PODCAST, -S n audio file able to be downloaded and listened to on a computer or MP3 player ▷ vb make available in this format

PODDED ▸ pod

PODDIE n user of or enthusiast for the iPod, a portable digital music player

PODDIER ▸ poddy

PODDIES ▸ poddy

PODDIEST ▸ poddy

PODDING ▸ pod

PODDLE, -D, -S, PODDLING vb move or travel in a leisurely manner

PODDY, PODDIER, PODDIES, PODDIEST n handfed calf or lamb ▷ adj fat

PODESTA, -S n (in modern Italy) subordinate magistrate in some towns

PODEX, -ES n posterior

PODGE, -S n short chubby person

PODGIER ▸ podgy

PODGIEST ▸ podgy

PODGILY ▸ podgy

PODGY, PODGIER, PODGIEST adj short and fat

PODIA ▸ podium

PODIAL ▸ podium

PODIATRY another word for > chiropody

PODITE, -S n crustacean leg

PODITIC adj similar to the limb segment of an arthropod

PODIUM, PODIA, -ED, -S n small raised platform for a conductor or speaker ▷ vb

finish in the top three places in a sporting competition

PODLEY, -S n young coalfish

PODLIKE ▸ pod

PODOCARP n stem supporting fruit

PODOLOGY n study of feet

PODOMERE n segment of limb of arthropod

PODS ▸ pod

PODSOL, -S same as ▸ podzol

PODSOLIC ▸ podzol

PODSOLS ▸ podsol

PODUNK, -S adj small or unimportant ▷ n small or unimportant thing

PODZOL, -S n type of soil characteristic of coniferous forest regions

PODZOLIC

POECHORE n dry region

POEM, -S n imaginative piece of writing in rhythmic lines

POEMATIC adj of poetry

POEMS ▸ poem

POEP, -ED, -ING, -S n emission of gas from the anus ▷ vb break wind

POEPS ▸ poep

POESY, POESIED, POESIES, -ING n poetry ▷ vb write poems

POET, -S n writer of poems

POETESS n female poet

POETIC adj of or like poetry

POETICAL n poet

POETICS n principles and forms of poetry or the study of these

POETISE, -D, -S same as > poeticize

POETISER

POETIZE, -D, -S same as > poeticize

POETIZER

POETLESS ▸ poet

POETLIKE ▸ poet

POETRY, POETRIES n poems

POETS ▸ poet

POETSHIP n state of being poet

POFFLE, -S n small piece of land

POGEY, -S n financial or other relief given to the unemployed by the government

POGGE, -S n European marine scorpaenoid fish

POGIES ▸ pogy

POGO, -ED, -ES, -ING, -S vb jump up and down on one spot

POGOER -S

POGONIA, -S n orchid with pink or white fragrant flowers

POGONIP, -S n icy winter fog

POGOS ▸ pogo

POGROM, -ED, -S n organized persecution and massacre ▷ vb carry out a pogrom

POGY, POGIES same as ▸ pogey

POH, -ED, -ING, -S interj exclamation expressing contempt or disgust ▷ vb reject contemptuously

POHIRI, -S variant spelling of ▸ powhiri

POHS ▸ poh

POI, -S n ball of woven flax swung rhythmically by Māori women during poi dances

POIGNADO old variant of ▸ poniard

POIGNANT adj sharply painful to the feelings

POILU, -S n infantryman in the French Army

POINADO old variant of ▸ poniard

POIND, -ED, -ING, -S vb take (property of a debtor) in execution or by way of distress

POINDER -S

POINT, -S n main idea in a discussion ▷ vb show the position of something by extending a finger towards it

POINTE, -S n tip of the toe

POINTED adj having a sharp end

POINTEL, -S n engraver's tool

POINTER, -S n helpful hint

POINTES ▸ pointe

POINTIER ▸ pointy

POINTING n insertion of mortar between the joints in brickwork

POINTMAN, POINTMEN n soldier who walks at the front of an infantry patrol in combat

POINTS ▸ point

POINTY, POINTIER adj having a sharp point or points

POIS ▸ poi

POISE, -S, POISING n calm dignified manner ▷ vb be balanced or suspended

POISED adj absolutely ready

POISER, -S n balancing organ of some insects

POISES ▸ poise

POISHA, -S n monetary unit of Bangladesh

POISING ▸ poise

POISON, -ED, -S *n* substance that kills or injures when swallowed or absorbed ▷ *vb* give poison to
POISONER

POISSON, -S *n* fish

POITIN, -S *variant spelling of* ▷ **poteen**

POITREL, -S *n* breastplate of horse's armour

POITRINE *n* woman's bosom

POKABLE ▷ **poke**

POKAL, -S *n* tall drinking cup

POKE, -D, -S, POKING *vb* jab or prod with one's finger, a stick, etc ▷ *n* poking

POKEFUL, -S *n* contents of small bag

POKER, -S *n* metal rod for stirring a fire

POKERISH *adj* stiff like poker

POKEROOT *same as* ▷ **pokeweed**

POKERS ▷ **poker**

POKES ▷ **poke**

POKEWEED *n* plant with a poisonous root used medicinally

POKEY, -S *same as* ▷ **pokie**

POKIE *n* poker machine

POKIER ▷ **poky**

POKIES ▷ **poky**

POKIEST ▷ **poky**

POKILY ▷ **poky**

POKINESS ▷ **poky**

POKING ▷ **poke**

POKY, POKIER, POKIES, POKIEST *adj* small and cramped

POL, -S *n* political campaigner

POLACCA, -S *same as* ▷ **polacre**

POLACRE, -S *n* three-masted sailing vessel

POLAR, -S *adj* of or near either of the earth's poles ▷ *n* type of line in geometry

POLARISE *same as* ▷ **polarize**

POLARITY *n* state of having two directly opposite tendencies or opinions

POLARIZE *vb* form or cause to form into groups with directly opposite views

POLARON, -S *n* kind of electron

POLARS ▷ **polar**

POLDER, -ED, -S *n* land reclaimed from the sea, esp in the Netherlands ▷ *vb* reclaim land from the sea

POLE, -D, -S *n* long rounded piece of wood etc ▷ *vb* strike or push with a pole

POLEAX *same as* ▷ **poleaxe**

POLEAXE, -D, -S *vb* hit or stun with a heavy blow ▷ *n* axe formerly used in battle or used by a butcher

POLECAT, -S *n* small animal of the weasel family

POLED ▷ **pole**

POLEIS ▷ **polis**

POLELESS ▷ **pole**

POLEMIC *n* fierce attack on or defence of a particular opinion, belief, etc ▷ *adj* of or involving dispute or controversy

POLEMICS *n* art of dispute

POLEMISE *same as* ▷ **polemize**

POLEMIST ▷ **polemic**

POLEMIZE *vb* engage in controversy

POLENTA, -S *n* thick porridge made in Italy, usually from maize

POLER, -S *n* person or thing that poles, esp a punter

POLES ▷ **pole**

POLESTAR *n* guiding principle, rule, standard, etc

POLEWARD *adv* towards a pole

POLEY, -S *adj* (of cattle) hornless or polled ▷ *n* animal with horns removed

POLEYN, -S *n* piece of armour for protecting the knee

POLEYS ▷ **poley**

POLICE, -D, -S, POLICING *n* organized force in a state which keeps law and order ▷ *vb* control or watch over with police or a similar body

POLICER, -S *n* computer device controlling use

POLICES ▷ **police**

POLICIER *n* film featuring police investigating crimes

POLICIES ▷ **policy**

POLICING ▷ **police**

POLICY, POLICIES *n* plan of action adopted by a person, group, or state

POLIES ▷ **poly**

POLING, -S ▷ **pole**

POLIO, -S *n* acute viral disease

POLIS, POLEIS, -ES *n* ancient Greek city-state

POLISH, -ES *vb* make smooth and shiny by rubbing ▷ *n* substance used for polishing

POLISHED *adj* accomplished

POLISHER ▷ **polish**

POLISHES ▷ **polish**

POLITE, -R, -ST *adj* showing consideration for others in one's manners, speech, etc

POLITELY

POLITIC *adj* wise and likely to prove advantageous

POLITICK *vb* engage in politics

POLITICO *n* politician

POLITICS *n* winning and using of power to govern society

POLITY, POLITIES *n* politically organized state, church, or society

POLJE, -S *n* large elliptical depression in karst regions

POLK, -ED, -ING, -S *vb* dance a polka

POLKA, -ED, -ING, -S *n* lively 19th-century dance ▷ *vb* dance a polka

POLKED ▷ **polk**

POLKING ▷ **polk**

POLKS ▷ **polk**

POLL, -S *n* questioning of a random sample of people to find out general opinion ▷ *vb* receive (votes)

POLLACK, -S *n* food fish related to the cod, found in northern seas

POLLAN, -S *n* whitefish that occurs in lakes in Northern Ireland

POLLARD, -S *n* animal that has shed its horns or has had them removed ▷ *vb* cut off the top of (a tree) to make it grow bushy

POLLAXE, -D, -S *same as* ▷ **poleaxe**

POLLED *adj* (of animals, esp cattle) having the horns cut off or being naturally hornless

POLLEE, -S ▷ **poll**

POLLEN, -ED, -S *n* fine dust produced by flowers to fertilize other flowers ▷ *vb* collect pollen

POLLENT *adj* strong

POLLER, -S ▷ **poll**

POLLEX, POLLICES *n* first digit of the forelimb of amphibians, reptiles, birds, and mammals

POLLICAL

POLLICIE *obsolete spelling of* ▷ **policy**

POLLICY *obsolete spelling of* ▷ **policy**

POLLIES ▷ **polly**

POLLING, -S *n* casting or registering of votes at an election

POLLINIA > **pollinium**

POLLINIC ▷ **pollen**

POLLIST, -S *n* one advocating the use of polls**

POLLIWIG same as ▸ **polliwog**

POLLIWOG n sailor who has not crossed the equator

POLLMAN, POLLMEN n one passing a degree without honours

POLLOCK, -S same as ▸ **pollack**

POLLS ▸ **poll**

POLLSTER n person who conducts opinion polls

POLLUTE, -S vb contaminate with something poisonous or harmful

POLLUTED adj made unclean or impure

POLLUTER ▸ **pollute**

POLLUTES ▸ **pollute**

POLLY, POLLIES n politician

POLLYWIG same as ▸ **polliwog**

POLLYWOG same as ▸ **polliwog**

POLO, -S n game like hockey played by teams of players on horseback

POLOIDAL adj relating to a type of magnetic field

POLOIST, -S n devotee of polo

POLONIE same as ▸ **polony**

POLONIES ▸ **polony**

POLONISE same as ▸ **polonize**

POLONISM

POLONIUM n radioactive element that occurs in trace amounts in uranium ores

POLONIZE vb make Polish

POLONY, POLONIES n bologna sausage

POLOS ▸ **polo**

POLS ▸ **pol**

POLT, -ED, -ING, -S n thump or blow ▷ vb strike

POLTFOOT, POLTFEET adj having a club foot ▷ n club foot

POLTING ▸ **polt**

POLTROON n utter coward

POLTS ▸ **polt**

POLY, POLIES, -S n polytechnic

POLYACID adj having two or more hydroxyl groups ▷ n compound made up of two or more hydroxyl groups

POLYACT adj (of a sea creature) having many tentacles or limb-like protrusions

POLYADIC adj (of a relation, operation, etc) having several argument places

POLYARCH n member of polyarchy

POLYAXON n nerve cell with multiple branches

POLYBAG, -S vb put into a polythene bag

POLYBRID n hybrid plant with more than two parental groups

POLYCOT, -S n plant that has or appears to have more than two cotyledons

POLYDRUG adj relating to using several drugs together

POLYENE, -S n organic chemical compound

POLYENIC

POLYGALA n herbaceous plant or small shrub

POLYGAM, -S n plant of the Polygamia class

POLYGAMY n practice of having more than one husband or wife at the same time

POLYGENE n any of a group of genes that each produce a small effect on a particular characteristic of the phenotype

POLYGENY > polygenic

POLYGLOT adj (person) able to speak or write several languages ▷ n person who can speak many languages

POLYGON, -S n geometrical figure with three or more angles and sides

POLYGONY

POLYGYNE adj (of a colony of insects) having more than one egg-laying queen

POLYGYNY n practice of having more than one female partner at the same time

POLYMATH n person of great and varied learning

POLYMER, -S n chemical compound with large molecules made of simple molecules of the same kind

POLYMERY

POLYNIA, -S same as ▸ **polynya**

POLYNYA, -S, POLYNYI n stretch of open water surrounded by ice

POLYOL, -S n type of alcohol

POLYOMA, -S n type of tumour caused by virus

POLYONYM n object with many names

POLYP, -S n small simple sea creature with a hollow cylindrical body

POLYPARY n common base and connecting tissue of

a colony of coelenterate polyps, esp coral

POLYPE, -S variant of ▸ **polyp**

POLYPED, -S same as ▸ **polypod**

POLYPES ▸ **polype**

POLYPHON n musical instrument resembling a lute

POLYPI ▸ **polypus**

POLYPIDE n polyp forming part of a colonial animal

POLYPILL n pill containing a number of medicines that all treat the same condition

POLYPINE adj of or relating to polyps

POLYPITE same as ▸ **polypide**

POLYPNEA n rapid breathing

POLYPOD, -S adj (esp of insect larvae) having many legs or similar appendages ▷ n animal of this type

POLYPODY n fern with deeply divided leaves and round naked sori

POLYPOID ▸ **polyp**

POLYPORE n type of fungi

POLYPOUS ▸ **polyp**

POLYPS ▸ **polyp**

POLYPUS, POLYPI same as ▸ **polyp**

POLYS ▸ **poly**

POLYSEME n word with many meanings

POLYSEMY n existence of several meanings in a single word

POLYSOME n assemblage of ribosomes associated with a messenger RNA molecule

POLYSOMY

POLYTENE adj denoting a type of giant-size chromosome

POLYTENY

POLYTYPE n crystal occurring in more than one form ▷ vb produce by use of a polytype

POLYURIA n state of discharging abnormally large quantities of urine

POLYURIC

POLYZOA n small mosslike aquatic creatures

POLYZOAN another word for ▸ **bryozoan**

POLYZOIC adj (of certain colonial animals) having many zooids or similar polyps

POLYZOON n individual zooid within polyzoan

POM, -S same as ▸ **pommy**

POMACE, -S n apple pulp left after pressing for juice

POMADE, -D, -S, POMADING n perfumed oil put on the hair to make it smooth and shiny ▷ vb put pomade on

POMANDER n mixture of sweet-smelling petals, herbs, etc

POMATO, -ES n hybrid of tomato and potato

POMATUM, -S same as ▸ pomade

POMBE, -S n any alcoholic drink

POME, -S n fleshy fruit of the apple and related plants

POMELO, -S n edible yellow fruit, like a grapefruit

POMEROY, -S n bullet used to down airships

POMES ▸ pome

POMFRET, -S n small black rounded liquorice sweet

POMMEE adj (of cross) having end of each arm ending in disk

POMMEL, -ED, -S same as ▸ pummel

POMMELE adj having a pommel

POMMELED ▸ pommel

POMMELS ▸ pommel

POMMETTY adj having a pommel

POMMIE same as ▸ pommy

POMMY, POMMIES n word used by Australians and New Zealanders for a British person

POMO, -S n postmodernist

POMOLOGY n branch of horticulture that is concerned with the study and cultivation of fruit

POMOS ▸ pomo

POMP, -S n stately display or ceremony

POMPANO, -S n deep-bodied carangid food fish

POMPELO, -S n large Asian citrus fruit

POMPEY, -ED, -S vb mollycoddle

POMPIER, -S adj slavishly conventional ▷ n conventional or imitative artist

POMPILID n spider-hunting wasp

POMPION, -S n pumpkin

POMPOM, -S n decorative ball of tufted wool, silk, etc

POMPON, -S same as ▸ pompom

POMPOON, -S variant of ▸ pompom

POMPOSO adj (of music) to be played in a ceremonial manner

POMPOUS adj foolishly serious and grand, self-important

POMPS ▸ pomp

POMROY, -S variant of ▸ pomeroy

POMS ▸ pom

POMWATER n kind of apple

PONCE, -D, -S, PONCING vb act stupidly or waste time

PONCEAU, -S, -X n scarlet red

PONCED ▸ ponce

PONCES ▸ ponce

PONCEY, PONCIER, PONCIEST adj ostentatious or pretentious

PONCHO, -S n loose circular cloak with a hole for the head

PONCHOED adj wearing poncho

PONCHOS ▸ poncho

PONCIER ▸ poncey

PONCIEST ▸ poncey

PONCING ▸ ponce

PONCY same as ▸ poncey

POND, -ED, -S n small area of still water ▷ vb hold back (flowing water)

PONDAGE, -S n water held in reservoir

PONDED ▸ pond

PONDER, -ED, -S vb think thoroughly or deeply (about)

PONDERAL adj relating to weight

PONDERED ▸ ponder

PONDERER ▸ ponder

PONDERS ▸ ponder

PONDING ▸ pond

PONDOK, -S n (in southern Africa) crudely made house or shack

PONDS ▸ pond

PONDWEED n plant that grows in ponds

PONE, -S n bread made of maize

PONENT, -S adj westerly ▷ n the west

PONES ▸ pone

PONEY, -S same as ▸ pony

PONG, -ED, -ING, -S n strong unpleasant smell ▷ vb give off a strong unpleasant smell

PONGA, -S n tall New Zealand tree fern

PONGAL, -S n Indian dish of cooked rice

PONGAS ▸ ponga

PONGED ▸ pong

PONGEE, -S n thin plain-weave silk fabric

PONGID, -S n primate of the family which includes the gibbons and the great apes

PONGIER ▸ pongy

PONGIEST ▸ pongy

PONGING ▸ pong

PONGO, -ES, -S n anthropoid ape, esp an orang-utan or (formerly) a gorilla

PONGS ▸ pong

PONGY, PONGIER, PONGIEST ▸ pong

PONIARD, -S n small slender dagger ▷ vb stab with a poniard

PONIED ▸ pony

PONIES ▸ pony

PONK, -ED, -ING, -S n evil spirit ▷ vb stink

PONS, PONTES n bridge of connecting tissue

PONT, -S n (in South Africa) river ferry

PONTAGE, -S n tax paid for repairing bridge

PONTAL adj of or relating to the pons

PONTES ▸ pons

PONTIC adj of or relating to the pons

PONTIE same as ▸ ponty

PONTIES ▸ ponty

PONTIFEX n (in ancient Rome) any of the senior members of the Pontifical College

PONTIFF, -S n Pope

PONTIFIC ▸ pontify

PONTIFY vb speak or behave in a pompous or dogmatic manner

PONTIL, -S same as ▸ punty

PONTILE, -S adj relating to pons ▷ n metal bar used in glass-making

PONTILS ▸ pontil

PONTINE adj of or relating to bridges

PONTON, -S variant of ▸ pontoon

PONTOON, -S n floating platform supporting a temporary bridge ▷ vb cross a river using pontoons

PONTS ▸ pont

PONTY, PONTIES n rod used for shaping molten glass

PONY, PONIED, PONIES, -ING n small horse ▷ vb settle bill or debt

PONYSKIN n leather from pony hide

PONYTAIL n long hair tied in one bunch at the back of the head

PONZU, -S *n* type of Japanese dipping sauce

POO, -ED, -ING, -S *vb* defecate

POOBAH, -S *n* influential person

POOCH, -ED, -ES, -ING *n* slang word for dog ▷ *vb* bulge or protrude

POOD, -S *n* unit of weight, used in Russia

POODLE, -S *n* dog with curly hair often clipped fancifully

POODS ► pood

POOED ► poo

POOGYE, -S *n* Hindu nose-flute

POOH, -ED, -ING, -S *interj* exclamation of disdain, contempt, or disgust ▷ *vb* make such an exclamation

POOING ► poo

POOJA, -S *variant of* ► puja

POOJAH, -S *variant of* ► puja

POOJAS ► pooja

POOK, -ING, -IT, -S *vb* pluck

POOKA, -S *n* malevolent Irish spirit

POOKING ► pook

POOKIT ► pook

POOKS ► pook

POOL, -ED, -ING *n* small body of still water ▷ *vb* put in a common fund

POOLER, -S *n* person taking part in pool

POOLHALL *n* room containing pool tables

POOLING ► pool

POOLROOM *n* hall or establishment where pool, billiards, etc, are played

POOLS *pl n* organized nationwide gambling pool

POOLSIDE *n* area surrounding swimming pool

POON, -S *n* SE Asian tree

POONAC, -S *n* coconut residue

POONS ► poon

POOP, -ED, -ING, -S *n* raised part at the back of a sailing ship ▷ *vb* (of a wave or sea) break over the stern of (a vessel)

POOPER, -S *n as in* **party pooper** person who spoils other people's enjoyment

POOPIER ► poopy

POOPIEST ► poopy

POOPING ► poop

POOPS ► poop

POOPY, POOPIER, POOPIEST *adj* stupid or ineffectual

POOR, -ER, -EST *adj* having little money and few possessions

POORBOX *n* box used for the collection of money for the poor

POORER ► poor

POOREST ► poor

POORI, -S *n* unleavened Indian bread

POORISH ► poor

POORLY, POORLIER *adv* in a poor manner ▷ *adj* not in good health

POORNESS ► poor

POORT, -S *n* (in South Africa) steep narrow mountain pass

POORTITH *same as* ► puirtith

POORTS ► poort

POORWILL *n* bird of N America

POOS ► poo

POOT, -ED, -ING, -S *vb* break wind

POOTER -S

POOTLE, -D, -S, POOTLING *vb* travel or go in a relaxed or leisurely manner

POOTS ► poot

POP, -PED, -PING, -S *vb* make or cause to make a small explosive sound ▷ *n* small explosive sound ▷ *adj* popular

POPADUM, -S *same as* ► poppadom

POPCORN, -S *n* grains of maize heated until they puff up and burst

POPE, -S *n* bishop of Rome as head of the Roman Catholic Church

POPEDOM, -S *n* office or dignity of a pope

POPEHOOD ► pope

POPELESS ► pope

POPELIKE ► pope

POPERA, -S *n* music drawing on opera or classical music and aiming for popular appeal

POPERIN, -S *n* kind of pear

POPES ► pope

POPESEYE *adj* denoting a cut of steak

POPESHIP ► pope

POPETTE, -S *n* young female fan or performer of pop music

POPEYED *adj* staring in astonishment

POPGUN, -S *n* toy gun that fires a pellet or cork by means of compressed air

POPINAC, -S *n* type of thorny shrub

POPINACK *same as* ► popinac

POPINACS ► popinac

POPINJAY *n* conceited, foppish, or overly talkative person

POPJOY, -ED, -S *vb* amuse oneself

POPLAR, -S *n* tall slender tree

POPLIN, -S *n* ribbed cotton material

POPLITEI > popliteus

POPLITIC *same as* > popliteal

POPOUT, -S *n* type of out in baseball

POPOVER, -S *n* individual Yorkshire pudding, often served with roast beef

POPPA, -S *same as* ► papa

POPPADOM *n* thin round crisp Indian bread

POPPADUM *same as* ► poppadom

POPPAS ► poppa

POPPED ► pop

POPPER, -S *n* press stud

POPPET, -S *n* term of affection for a small child or sweetheart

POPPIED *adj* covered with poppies

POPPIER ► poppy

POPPIES ► poppy

POPPIEST ► poppy

POPPING ► pop

POPPISH *adj* like pop music

POPPIT, -S *n* bead used to form necklace

POPPLE, -D, -S, POPPLING *vb* (of boiling water or a choppy sea) to heave or toss

POPPLIER ► popply

POPPLING ► popple

POPPLY, POPPLIER *adj* covered in small bumps

POPPY, POPPIER, POPPIES, POPPIEST *n* plant with a large red flower ▷ *adj* reddish-orange

POPRIN *same as* ► poperin

POPS ► pop

POPSICLE *n* tradename for a kind of ice lolly

POPSIE *same as* ► popsy

POPSIES ► popsy

POPSOCK, -S *n* women's knee-length nylon stocking

POPSTER, -S *n* pop star

POPSTREL *n* young, attractive female pop star

POPSY, POPSIES *n* attractive young woman

POPULACE *n* ordinary people

POPULAR, -S *adj* widely liked and admired ▷ *n* cheap newspapers with mass circulation

POPULATE *vb* live in, inhabit

POPULISM n political strategy based on an appeal to the prejudices of ordinary people

POPULIST adj appealing to the interests or prejudices of ordinary people ⊳ n person who appeals to the interests or prejudices of ordinary people

POPULOUS adj densely populated

PORAE, -S n large edible sea fish of New Zealand waters

PORAL adj relating to pores

PORANGI adj crazy

PORCH, -ES n covered approach to the entrance of a building

PORCHED adj having a porch

PORCHES ► porch

PORCINE adj of or like a pig

PORCINO, PORCINI n edible woodland fungus

PORE, -D, -S, PORING n tiny opening in the skin or in the surface of a plant ⊳ vb make a close intent examination or study

PORER, -S n person who pores

PORES ► pore

PORGE, -D, -S, PORGING vb cleanse (slaughtered animal) ceremonially

PORGIE same as ► porgy

PORGIES ► porgy

PORGING ► porge

PORGY, PORGIES n any of various sparid fishes

PORIER ► pory

PORIEST ► pory

PORIFER, -S n type of invertebrate

PORIN, -S n protein through which molecules can pass

PORINA, -S n moth the larva of which causes damage to grassland

PORINESS ► pory

PORING ► pore

PORINS ► porin

PORISM, -S n type of mathematical proposition **PORISTIC**

PORK, -ED, -ING, -S vb eat ravenously ⊳ n the flesh of pigs used as food

PORKER, -S n pig raised for food

PORKIER ► porky

PORKIES ► porky

PORKIEST ► porky

PORKING ► pork

PORKLING n pig

PORKPIE, -S n hat with a round flat crown and a brim that can be turned up or down

PORKS ► pork

PORKWOOD n wood of small American tree

PORKY, PORKIER, PORKIES, PORKIEST adj of or like pork ⊳ n lie

PORLOCK, -S vb interrupt or intrude at an awkward moment

POROGAMY n fertilization of seed plants

POROSE adj pierced with small pores

POROSIS, POROSES n porous condition of bones

POROSITY n state or condition of being porous

POROUS adj allowing liquid to pass through gradually **POROUSLY**

PORPESS n type of fish

PORPESSE same as ► porpoise

PORPHYRY n reddish rock with large crystals in it

PORPOISE n fishlike sea mammal ⊳ vb (of an aeroplane) nose-dive during landing

PORRECT, -S adj extended forwards ⊳ vb stretch forward

PORRIDGE n breakfast food made of oatmeal cooked in water or milk **PORRIDGY**

PORRIGO, -S n disease of the scalp

PORT, -ED, -IER, -ING, -S same as ► porthole

PORTA, -S n aperture in an organ

PORTABLE adj easily carried ⊳ n article designed to be easily carried, such as a television or typewriter **PORTABLY**

PORTAGE, -D, -S n (route for) transporting boats overland ⊳ vb transport (boats) in this way

PORTAGUE n former Portuguese gold coin

PORTAL, -S n large imposing doorway or gate **PORTALED**

PORTANCE n person's bearing

PORTAPAK same as > portapack

PORTAS ► porta

PORTASES variant of ► portesse

PORTATE adj diagonally athwart escutcheon

PORTED ► port

PORTEND, -S vb be a sign of

PORTENT, -S n sign of a future event

PORTEOUS variant of ► portesse

PORTER, -ED, -S n man who carries luggage ⊳ vb carry luggage

PORTERLY adj like a porter

PORTERS ► porter

PORTESS variant of ► portesse

PORTESSE n prayer book

PORTFIRE n slow-burning fuse formerly used in fireworks

PORTHOLE n small round window in a ship or aircraft

PORTHORS same as ► portesse

PORTHOS same as ► portesse

PORTICO, -S n porch or covered walkway with columns supporting the roof

PORTIER ► port

PORTIERE n curtain hung in a doorway

PORTIEST ► porty

PORTIGUE same as ► portague

PORTING ► port

PORTION, -S n part or share ⊳ vb divide (something) into shares

PORTLAND n type of rose

PORTLAST n gunwale of ship

PORTLESS ► port

PORTLY, PORTLIER adj rather fat

PORTMAN, PORTMEN n inhabitant of port

PORTOISE same as ► portlast

PORTOLAN n book of sailing charts

PORTOUS variant of ► portesse

PORTRAIT n picture of a person ⊳ adj (of a publication or an illustration in a publication) of greater height than width

PORTRAY, -S vb describe or represent by artistic means, as in writing or film

PORTRESS n female porter, esp a doorkeeper

PORTS ► port

PORTSIDE adj beside port

PORTULAN same as ► portolan

P

PORTY, **PORTIEST** adj like port

PORY, **PORIER**, **PORIEST** adj containing pores

POS ► **po**

POSABLE ► **pose**

POSADA, **-S** n inn in a Spanish-speaking country

POSAUNE, **-S** n organ chorus reed

POSE, **-D**, **-S** vb place in or take up a particular position to be photographed or drawn ▷ n position while posing

POSEABLE adj able to be manipulated into poses

POSED ► **pose**

POSER, **-S** n puzzling question

POSERISH same as ► **posey**

POSERS ► **poser**

POSES ► **pose**

POSEUR, **-S** n person who behaves in an affected way to impress others

POSEUSE, **-S** n female poseur

POSEY adj (of a place) for, characteristic of, or full of posers

POSH, **-ED**, **-ER**, **-ES**, **-EST**, **-ING** adj smart, luxurious ▷ adv in a manner associated with the upper class ▷ vb make posh

POSHLY

POSHNESS

POSHO, **-S** n corn meal

POSHTEEN same as ► **posteen**

POSIER ► **posy**

POSIES ► **posy**

POSIEST ► **posy**

POSING, **-S** ► **pose**

POSINGLY ► **pose**

POSINGS ► **posing**

POSIT, **-ED**, **-ING**, **-S** vb lay down as a basis for argument ▷ n fact, idea, etc, that is posited

POSITIF, **-S** n (on older organs) manual controlling soft stops

POSITING ► **posit**

POSITION n place ▷ vb place

POSITIVE same as ► **plus**

POSITON, **-S** n part of chromosome

POSITRON n particle with same mass as electron but positive charge

POSITS ► **posit**

POSNET, **-S** n small basin or dish

POSOLE, **-S** n Central American stew

POSOLOGY n branch of medicine concerned with appropriate doses of drugs

POSS, **-ED**, **-ING** vb wash (clothes) by agitating them with a long rod, pole, etc

POSSE, **-S** n group of men organized to maintain law and order

POSSED ► **poss**

POSSER, **-S** n short stick used for stirring clothes in a washtub

POSSES ► **posse**

POSSESS vb have as one's property

POSSET, **-ED**, **-S** n drink of hot milk curdled with ale, beer, etc, flavoured with spices ▷ vb treat with a posset

POSSIBLE adj able to exist, happen, or be done ▷ n person or thing that might be suitable or chosen

POSSIBLY adv perhaps, not necessarily

POSSIE, **-S** n place

POSSING ► **poss**

POSSUM, **-ED**, **-S** vb pretend to be dead, asleep, ignorant, etc

POST, **-ED**, **-S** n official system of delivering letters and parcels ▷ vb send by post

POSTAGE, **-S** n charge for sending a letter or parcel by post

POSTAL, **-S** adj of a Post Office or the mail-delivery service ▷ n postcard

POSTALLY

POSTANAL adj behind the anus

POSTBAG, **-S** n postman's bag

POSTBASE n morpheme used as a suffix on a root word

POSTBOX n box into which mail is put for collection by the postal service

POSTBOY, **-S** n man or boy who brings the post round to offices

POSTBURN adj after injury from burns

POSTBUS n vehicle carrying the mail that also carries passengers

POSTCARD n card for sending a message by post without an envelope

POSTCAVA n inferior vena cava

POSTCODE n system of letters and numbers used to aid the sorting of mail ▷ vb put a postcode on a letter

POSTCOUP adj after a coup

POSTDATE vb write a date on (a cheque) that is later than the actual date

POSTDIVE adj following a dive

POSTDOC, **-S** n postdoctoral degree

POSTDRUG adj of time after drug has been taken

POSTED ► **post**

POSTEEN, **-S** n Afghan leather jacket

POSTER, **-ED**, **-S** n large picture or notice stuck on a wall ▷ vb cover with posters

POSTERN, **-S** n small back door or gate ▷ adj situated at the rear or on the side

POSTERS ► **poster**

POSTFACE n note added to the end of a text

POSTFIRE adj of the period after a fire

POSTFIX vb add or append at the end of something

POSTFORM vb mould or shape (plastic) while it hot from reheating

POSTGAME adj of period after sports match

POSTGRAD n graduate taking further degree

POSTHEAT n industrial heating process ▷ vb heat a material after welding to relieve stresses

POSTHOLE n hole dug in ground to hold fence post

POSTICAL adj (of the position of plant parts) behind another part

POSTICHE adj (of architectural ornament) inappropriately applied ▷ n imitation, counterfeit, or substitute

POSTIE, **-S** n postman

POSTIL, **-ED**, **-S** n commentary or marginal note, as in a Bible ▷ vb annotate (a biblical passage)

POSTIN, **-S** variant of ► **posteen**

POSTING, **-S** n job to which someone is assigned

POSTINS ► **postin**

POSTIQUE variant of ► **postiche**

POSTLUDE n final or concluding piece or movement

POSTMAN, **POSTMEN** n person who collects and delivers post

POSTMARK n official mark stamped on letters showing

place and date of posting ▷ vb put such a mark on (mail)

POSTMEN ▸ postman

POSTNATI pl n those born in Scotland after its union with England

POSTOP, -S n person recovering from surgery

POSTORAL adj situated at the back of the mouth

POSTPAID adj with the postage prepaid

POSTPONE vb put off to a later time

POSTPOSE vb place (word or phrase) after other constituents in sentence

POSTPUNK adj (of pop music) belonging to a style that followed punk rock ▷ n musician of the musical trend after punk

POSTRACE adj of the period after a race

POSTRIOT adj of the period after a riot

POSTS ▸ post

POSTSHOW adj of the period after a show

POSTSYNC vb add a sound recording to (and synchronize with) an existing video or film recording

POSTTAX adj of the period after tax is paid

POSTTEEN n young adult

POSTTEST n test taken after a lesson

POSTURAL ▸ posture

POSTURE, -D, -S n position or way in which someone stands, walks, etc ▷ vb behave in an exaggerated way to get attention

POSTURER

POSTWAR adj occurring or existing after a war

POSY, POSIER, POSIES, POSIEST n small bunch of flowers

POT, -S, -TED, -TING n round deep container ▷ vb plant in a pot

POTABLE, -S adj drinkable ▷ n something fit to drink

POTAE, -S n hat

POTAGE, -S n thick soup

POTAGER, -S n small kitchen garden

POTAGES ▸ potage

POTALE, -S n residue from a grain distillery, used as animal feed

POTAMIC adj of or relating to rivers

POTASH, -ED, -ES n white powdery substance obtained from ashes and used as fertilizer ▷ vb treat with potash

POTASS, -ES abbreviated form of > **potassium**

POTASSA, -S n potassium oxide

POTASSES ▸ potass

POTASSIC > potassium

POTATION n act of drinking

POTATO, -ES n roundish starchy vegetable that grows underground

POTATORY adj of, relating to, or given to drinking

POTBELLY n bulging belly

POTBOIL, -S vb boil in a pot

POTBOUND adj (of plant) unable to grow because pot is too small

POTBOY, -S n (esp formerly) youth or man employed at a public house to serve beer, etc

POTCH, -ES n inferior quality opal used in jewellery for mounting precious opals

POTCHE, -D, POTCHING vb stab

POTCHER -S

POTCHES ▸ potch

POTCHING ▸ potche

POTE, -D, -S, POTING vb push

POTEEN, -S n (in Ireland) illegally made alcoholic drink

POTENCE, -S same as ▸ **potency**

POTENCY n state or quality of being potent

POTENT, -S adj having great power or influence ▷ n potentate or ruler

POTENTLY

POTES ▸ pote

POTFUL, -S n amount held by a pot

POTGUN, -S n pot-shaped mortar

POTHEEN, -S rare variant of ▸ **poteen**

POTHER, -ED, -S n fuss or commotion ▷ vb make or be troubled or upset

POTHERB, -S n plant whose leaves, flowers, or stems are used in cooking

POTHERED ▸ pother

POTHERS ▸ pother

POTHERY adj stuffy

POTHOLE, -D, -S n hole in the surface of a road

POTHOLER > potholing

POTHOLES ▸ pothole

POTHOOK, -S n S-shaped hook for suspending a pot over a fire

POTHOS n climbing plant

POTHOUSE n (formerly) small tavern or pub

POTICARY obsolete spelling of > **pothecary**

POTICHE, -S n tall vase or jar that narrows towards the neck

POTIN, -S n bronze alloy with high tin content

POTING ▸ pote

POTINS ▸ potin

POTION, -S n dose of medicine or poison

POTJIE, -S n three-legged iron pot used for cooking

POTLACH same as ▸ **potlatch**

POTLACHE same as ▸ **potlatch**

POTLATCH n competitive ceremonial activity among certain Native American tribes

POTLIKE ▸ pot

POTLINE, -S n row of electrolytic cells for reducing metals

POTLUCK, -S n whatever food happens to be available without special preparation

POTMAN, POTMEN same as ▸ **potboy**

POTOO, -S n nocturnal tropical bird

POTOROO, -S n Australian leaping rodent

POTPIE, -S n meat and vegetable stew with a pie crust on top

POTS ▸ pot

POTSHARD same as ▸ **potsherd**

POTSHARE same as ▸ **potsherd**

POTSHERD n broken fragment of pottery

POTSHOP, -S n public house

POTSHOT, -S n shot taken without careful aim

POTSIE same as ▸ **potsy**

POTSIES ▸ potsy

POTSTONE n impure massive variety of soapstone, formerly used for making cooking vessels

POTSY, POTSIES n hopscotch

POTT, -S old variant of ▸ **pot**

POTTABLE adj (esp of a snooker ball) easily potted

POTTAGE, -S n thick soup or stew

POTTED ▸ pot

P

POTTEEN, -S same as ► poteen

POTTER, -ED, -S same as ► putter

POTTERER

POTTERY n articles made from baked clay

POTTIER ► potty

POTTIES ► potty

POTTIEST ► potty

POTTING ► pot

POTTLE, -S n liquid measure equal to half a gallon

POTTO, -S n short-tailed prosimian primate

POTTS ► pott

POTTY, POTTIER, POTTIES, POTTIEST adj silly or eccentric ▷ n bowl used by a small child as a toilet

POTZER, -S same as ► patzer

POUCH, -ED, -ES, -ING n small bag ▷ vb place in or as if in a pouch

POUCHFUL n amount a pouch will hold

POUCHIER ► pouchy

POUCHING ► pouch

POUCHY, POUCHIER ► pouch

POUDER, -S obsolete spelling of ► powder

POUDRE, -S old spelling of ► powder

POUF, -ED, -ING, -S n large solid cushion used as a seat ▷ vb pile up hair into rolled puffs

POUFF, -S same as ► pouf

POUFFE, -D, -S, POUFFING same as ► pouf

POUFFS ► pouff

POUFING ► pouf

POUFS ► pouf

POUK, -ING, -S Scots variant of ► poke

POUKE, -S n mischievous spirit

POUKING ► pouk

POUKIT ► pouk

POUKS ► pouk

POULAINE n tapering toe of shoe

POULARD, -S n hen that has been spayed for fattening

POULARDE same as ► poulard

POULARDS ► poulard

POULDER, -S obsolete spelling of ► powder

POULDRE, -S archaic spelling of ► powder

POULDRON same as ► pauldron

POULE, -S n fowl suitable for slow stewing

POULP, -S n octopus

POULPE, -S variant of ► poulp

POULPS ► poulp

POULT, -S n young of a gallinaceous bird

POULTER, -S n poultry dealer

POULTICE n moist dressing, often heated, applied to inflamed skin ▷ vb apply poultice to

POULTRY n domestic fowls

POULTS ► poult

POUNCE, -D, -S, POUNCING vb spring upon suddenly to attack or capture ▷ n pouncing

POUNCER -S

POUNCET, -S n box with a perforated top used for perfume

POUNCING ► pounce

POUND, -ED, -ING, -S n monetary unit of Britain and some other countries ▷ vb hit heavily and repeatedly

POUNDAGE n charge of so much per pound of weight or sterling

POUNDAL, -S n fps unit of force

POUNDED ► pound

POUNDER, -S ► pound

POUNDING ► pound

POUNDS ► pound

POUPE, -D, -S, POUPING, POUPT vb make sudden blowing sound

POUR, -ED, -S vb flow or cause to flow out in a stream

POURABLE

POURER -S

POURIE, -S n jug

POURING, -S ► pour

POURS ► pour

POURSEW, -S obsolete spelling of ► pursue

POURSUE, -D, -S obsolete spelling of ► pursue

POURSUIT same as ► pursuit

POURTRAY obsolete spelling of ► portray

POUSADA, -S n traditional Portuguese hotel

POUSSE, -S same as ► pease

POUSSIE, -S old variant of ► pussy

POUSSIN, -S n young chicken reared for eating

POUT, -ED, -S vb thrust out one's lips, look sulky ▷ n pouting look

POUTER, -S n pigeon that can puff out its crop

POUTFUL adj tending to pout

POUTHER, -S Scots variant of ► powder

POUTIER ► pouty

POUTIEST ► pouty

POUTINE, -S n dish of chipped potatoes topped with cheese and sauce

POUTING, -S ► pout

POUTS ► pout

POUTY, POUTIER, POUTIEST ► pout

POVERTY n state of being without enough food or money

POW, -S interj exclamation to indicate that a collision or explosion has taken place ▷ n head or a head of hair

POWAN, -S n type of freshwater whitefish occurring in some Scottish lakes

POWDER, -ED, -S n substance in the form of tiny loose particles ▷ vb apply powder to

POWDERER

POWDERY

POWER, -ED, -ING, -S n ability to do or act ▷ vb give or provide power to

POWERFUL adj having great power or influence ▷ adv extremely

POWERING ► power

POWERS ► power

POWHIRI, -S n Māori ceremony of welcome, esp to a marae

POWIN, -S n peacock

POWN, -S variant of ► powin

POWND, -ED, -ING, -S obsolete spelling of ► pound

POWNEY, -S old Scots spelling of ► pony

POWNIE, -S old Scots spelling of ► pony

POWNS ► pown

POWNY old Scots spelling of ► pony

POWRE, -D, -S, POWRING obsolete spelling of ► power

POWS ► pow

POWSOWDY same as > pousowdie

POWTER, -ED, -S vb scrabble about

POWWAW interj expression of disbelief or contempt

POWWOW, -ED, -S n talk or conference ▷ vb hold a powwow

POX, -ED, -ES, -ING n disease in which skin pustules form ▷ vb infect with pox

POXIER ► poxy

POXIEST ▶ poxy

POXING ▶ pox

POXVIRUS n virus such as smallpox

POXY, POXIER, POXIEST adj of poor quality; rotten

POYNANT old variant of ▶ poignant

POYNT, -ED, -ING, -S obsolete spelling of ▶ point

POYOU, -S n type of armadillo

POYSE, -D, -S, POYSING obsolete variant of ▶ poise

POYSON, -ED, -S obsolete spelling of ▶ poison

POZ adj positive

> **Poz** is an old-fashioned short form of **positive**, and one of the most frequently played short Z words.

POZOLE, -S same as ▶ posole

POZZ adj positive

POZZIES ▶ pozzy

POZZOLAN same as > pozzolana

POZZY, POZZIES same as ▶ possie

PRAAM, -S same as ▶ pram

PRABBLE, -S variant of ▶ brabble

PRACTIC, -S adj practical ▷ n practice ▷ vb put (a theory) into practice

PRACTICE same as ▶ practise

PRACTICK obsolete word for ▶ practice

PRACTICS ▶ practic

PRACTISE vb do repeatedly so as to gain skill

PRACTIVE obsolete word for ▶ active

PRAD, -S n horse

PRAECIPE n written request addressed to court

PRAEDIAL adj of or relating to land, farming, etc ▷ n slave attached to a farm

PRAEFECT same as ▶ prefect

PRAELECT same as ▶ prelect

PRAESES n Roman governor

PRAETOR, -S n (in ancient Rome) senior magistrate ranking just below the consuls

PRAHU, -S same as ▶ proa

PRAIRIE, -S n large treeless area of grassland

PRAIRIED

PRAISE, -D, -S, PRAISING vb express approval of (someone or something) ▷ n something said or written to show approval

PRAISER -S

PRAJNA, -S n wisdom or understanding

PRALINE, -S n sweet made of nuts and caramelized sugar

PRAM, -S n four-wheeled carriage for a baby, pushed by hand

PRANA, -S n cosmic energy believed to come from the sun

PRANCE, -D, -S, PRANCING vb walk with exaggerated bouncing steps ▷ n act of prancing

PRANCER -S

PRANCK, -S obsolete variant of ▶ prank

PRANCKE, -S obsolete variant of ▶ prank

PRANCKED ▶ pranck

PRANCKES ▶ prancke

PRANCKS ▶ pranck

PRANDIAL adj of or relating to a meal

PRANG, -ED, -ING, -S n crash in a car or aircraft ▷ vb crash or damage (an aircraft or car)

PRANK, -ED, -ING, -S n mischievous trick ▷ vb dress or decorate showily or gaudily

PRANKFUL

PRANKIER ▶ pranky

PRANKING ▶ prank

PRANKISH ▶ prank

PRANKLE, -D, -S obsolete variant of ▶ prance

PRANKS ▶ prank

PRANKY, PRANKIER ▶ prank

PRAO, -S same as ▶ proa

PRASE, -S n light green translucent variety of chalcedony

PRAT, -S n stupid person

PRATE, -D, -S vb talk idly and at length ▷ n chatter

PRATER -S

PRATIE, -S n potato

PRATING, -S ▶ prate

PRATIQUE n formal permission given to a vessel to use a foreign port

PRATS ▶ prat

PRATT, -ED, -ING, -S n buttocks ▷ vb hit on the buttocks

PRATTLE, -D, -S vb chatter in a childish or foolish way ▷ n childish or foolish talk

PRATTLER

PRATTS ▶ pratt

PRATY obsolete variant of ▶ pretty

PRAU, -S same as ▶ proa

PRAUNCE, -D, -S obsolete variant of ▶ prance

PRAUS ▶ prau

PRAVITY n moral degeneracy

PRAWLE, -S n Shakespearian spelling of "brawl"

PRAWLIN, -S variant of ▶ praline

PRAWN, -ED, -ING, -S n edible shellfish like a large shrimp ▷ vb catch prawns

PRAWNER -S

PRAXIS, PRAXES, -ES n practice as opposed to theory

PRAY, -ED, -S vb say prayers ▷ adv I beg you ▷ interj I beg you

PRAYER, -S n thanks or appeal addressed to one's God

PRAYING, -S ▶ pray

PRAYS ▶ pray

PRE prep before

PREACE, -D, -S, PREACING obsolete variant of ▶ press

PREACH, -ED, -ES vb give a talk on a religious theme as part of a church service

PREACHER n person who preaches, esp in church

PREACHES ▶ preach

PREACHY adj inclined to or marked by preaching

PREACING ▶ preace

PREACT, -ED, -S vb act beforehand

PREADAPT vb adapt beforehand

PREADMIT vb prepare patient prior to treatment

PREADOPT vb adopt in advance

PREADULT n animal or person who has not reached adulthood

PREAGED adj treated to appear older

PREALLOT vb allot beforehand

PREALTER vb alter beforehand

PREAMBLE n introductory part to something said or written ▷ vb write a preamble

PREAMP, -S n electronic amplifier

PREANAL adj situated in front of anus

PREAPPLY vb apply beforehand

PREARM, -ED, -S vb arm beforehand

PREASE, -D, -S, PREASING vb crowd or press

P

PREASSE, -D, -S obsolete spelling of ▶ **press**

PREAUDIT n examination of contracts before a transaction

PREAVER, -S vb aver in advance

PREAXIAL adj situated or occurring in front of the axis of the body

PREBADE ▶ **prebid**

PREBAKE, -D, -S vb bake before further cooking

PREBASAL adj in front of a base

PREBEND, -S n allowance paid to a canon or member of the cathedral chapter

PREBID, PREBADE, -S vb bid beforehand

PREBILL, -S vb issue an invoice before the service has been provided

PREBIND, -S, PREBOUND vb bind a book in a hard-wearing binding

PREBIRTH n period of life before birth

PREBLESS vb bless a couple before they marry

PREBOARD vb board an aircraft before other passengers

PREBOIL, -S vb boil beforehand

PREBOOK, -S vb book well in advance

PREBOOM adj of the period before an economic boom

PREBORN adj unborn

PREBOUND ▶ **prebind**

PREBUILD, PREBUILT vb build beforehand

PREBUY, -S vb buy in advance

PRECAST, -S adj cast in a particular form before being used ▷ vb cast (concrete) in a particular form before use

PRECAVA, -E n superior vena cava

PRECAVAL

PRECEDE, -D, -S vb go or be before

PRECEESE Scots variant of ▶ **precise**

PRECENT, -S vb issue a command or law

PRECEPIT old word for > **precipice**

PRECEPT, -S n rule of behaviour

PRECES pl n prayers

PRECESS vb undergo or cause to undergo precession

PRECHECK vb check beforehand

PRECHILL vb chill beforehand

PRECHOSE > **prechoose**

PRECIEUX n pretentious male

PRECINCT n area in a town closed to traffic

PRECIOUS adj of great value and importance ▷ adv very

PRECIP, -S n precipitation

PRECIPE, -S n type of legal document

PRECIPS ▶ **precip**

PRECIS, -ED, -ES n short written summary of a longer piece ▷ vb make a precis of

PRECISE, -R adj exact, accurate in every detail

PRECISED ▶ **precis**

PRECISER ▶ **precise**

PRECISES ▶ **precis**

PRECITED adj cited previously

PRECLEAN vb clean beforehand

PRECLEAR vb approve in advance

PRECLUDE vb make impossible to happen

PRECODE, -D, -S vb code beforehand

PRECOOK, -S vb cook (food) beforehand

PRECOOL, -S vb cool in advance

PRECOUP adj of the period before a coup

PRECRASH adj of the period before a crash

PRECURE, -D, -S vb cure in advance

PRECURSE n forerunning ▷ vb be a precursor of

PRECUT, -S vb cut in advance

PRECYCLE vb preemptive approach to waste reduction involving minimal use of packaging

PREDATE, -D, -S vb occur at an earlier date than

PREDATOR n predatory animal

PREDAWN, -S n period before dawn

PREDEATH n period immediately before death

PREDELLA, PREDELLE n series of small paintings or sculptures in a long narrow strip on an altarpiece

PREDIAL, -S same as ▶ **praedial**

PREDICT, -S vb tell about in advance, prophesy

PREDIED ▶ **predy**

PREDIES ▶ **predy**

PREDIVE adj happening before a dive

PREDOOM, -S vb pronounce (someone or something's) doom beforehand

PREDRAFT adj before a draft ▷ n preliminary draft prior to an official draft

PREDRIED ▶ **predry**

PREDRIES ▶ **predry**

PREDRILL vb drill in advance

PREDRY, PREDRIED, PREDRIES vb dry beforehand

PREDUSK, -S n period before dusk

PREDY, PREDIED, PREDIES, -ING vb prepare for action

PREE, -D, -ING, -S vb try or taste

PREEDIT, -S vb edit beforehand

PREEING ▶ **pree**

PREELECT vb elect beforehand

PREEMIE, -S n premature infant

PREEMPT, -S vb acquire in advance of or to the exclusion of others

PREEN, -ED, -ING, -S vb (of a bird) clean or trim (feathers) with the beak ▷ n pin, esp a decorative one

PREENACT vb enact beforehand

PREENED ▶ **preen**

PREENER, -S ▶ **preen**

PREENING ▶ **preen**

PREENS ▶ **preen**

PREERECT vb erect beforehand

PREES ▶ **pree**

PREEVE, -D, -S, PREEVING old form of ▶ **prove**

PREEXIST vb exist beforehand

PREFAB, -S n prefabricated house ▷ vb manufacture sections of (building) in factory

PREFACE, -D, -S n introduction to a book ▷ vb serve as an introduction to (a book, speech, etc)

PREFACER

PREFADE, -D, -S vb fade beforehand

PREFARD vb old form of preferred

PREFECT, -S n senior pupil in a school, with limited power over others

PREFER, -S vb like better

PREFIGHT adj of the period before a boxing match

PREFILE, -D, -S vb file beforehand

PREFIRE, -D, -S vb fire beforehand

PREFIX, -ED, -ES n letters put at the beginning of a word to make a new word ▷ vb put as an introduction or prefix (to)

PREFIXAL

PREFLAME adj of the period before combustion

PREFOCUS vb focus in advance

PREFORM, -S vb form beforehand

PREFRANK vb frank in advance

PREFROZE > prefreeze

PREFUND, -S vb pay for in advance

PREGAME, -S adj of the period before a sports match ▷ n such a period

PREGGERS informal word for ▶ pregnant

PREGGY, PREGGIER informal word for ▶ pregnant

PREGNANT adj carrying a fetus in the womb

PREGUIDE vb give guidance in advance

PREHAB, -S n any programme of training designed to prevent sports injury

PREHEAT, -S vb heat (an oven, grill, pan, etc) beforehand

PREHEND, -S vb take hold of

PREHNITE n green mineral

PREHUMAN n hominid that predates man

PREIF, -S old form of ▶ proof

PREIFE, -S old form of ▶ proof

PREIFS ▶ preif

PREJINK variant of ▶ perjink

PREJUDGE vb judge beforehand without sufficient evidence

PRELACY n office or status of a prelate

PRELATE, -S n bishop or other churchman of high rank

PRELATIC

PRELATY n prelacy

PRELAW adj before taking up study of law

PRELECT, -S vb lecture or discourse in public

PRELEGAL adj of the period before the start of a law course

PRELIFE, PRELIVES n life lived before one's life on earth

PRELIM n event which precedes another

PRELIMIT vb limit beforehand

PRELIMS pl n pages of a book which come before the main text

PRELIVES ▶ prelife

PRELOAD, -S vb load beforehand

PRELOVED adj previously owned or used

PRELUDE, -D, -S n introductory movement in music ▷ vb act as a prelude to (something)

PRELUDER

PRELUDIO, PRELUDI n musical prelude

PRELUNCH adj of the period before lunch

PREM, -S n informal word for a premature infant

PREMADE adj made in advance

PREMAN, PREMEN n hominid

PREMEAL adj of the period before a meal

PREMED, -S n premedical student

PREMEDIC same as ▶ premed

PREMEDS ▶ premed

PREMEET adj happening before a meet

PREMEN ▶ preman

PREMIA ▶ premium

PREMIE, -S same as ▶ preemie

PREMIER, -S n prime minister ▷ adj chief, leading

PREMIERE n first performance of a play, film, etc ▷ vb give, or (of a film, play, or opera) be, a premiere

PREMIERS ▶ premier

PREMIES ▶ premie

PREMISE, -D, -S n statement used as the basis of reasoning ▷ vb state or assume (a proposition) as a premise

PREMISS same as ▶ premise

PREMIUM, PREMIA, -S n additional sum of money, as on a wage or charge

PREMIX, -ED, -ES, -T vb mix beforehand

PREMOLAR n tooth between the canine and first molar in adult humans ▷ adj situated before a molar tooth

PREMOLD, -S same as ▶ premould

PREMOLT same as ▶ premoult

PREMORAL adj not governed by sense of right and wrong

PREMORSE adj appearing as though the end had been bitten off

PREMOTOR adj relating to a part of the frontal lobe of the brain

PREMOULD vb mould in advance

PREMOULT adj happening in the period before an animal moults

PREMOVE, -D, -S vb prompt to action

PREMS ▶ prem

PREMUNE adj having immunity to a disease as a result of latent infection

PREMY variant of ▶ preemie

PRENAME, -S n forename

PRENASAL n bone in the front of the nose

PRENATAL adj before birth, during pregnancy ▷ n prenatal examination

PRENEED adj arranged in advance of eventual requirements

PRENOMEN less common spelling of > praenomen

PRENOON adj of the period before noon

PRENT, -ED, -ING, -S Scots variant of ▶ print

PRENTICE vb bind as an apprentice

PRENTING ▶ prent

PRENTS ▶ prent

PRENUP, -S n prenuptial agreement

PRENZIE adj Shakespearian word supposed by some to mean "princely"

PREON, -S n (in particle physics) hypothetical subcomponent of a quark

PREOP, -S n patient being prepared for surgery

PREORAL adj situated in front of mouth

PREORDER vb order in advance

PREOWNED adj second-hand

PREP, -PED, -PING, -S vb prepare

PREPACK, -S vb pack in advance of sale

PREPAID ▶ prepay

PREPARE, -D, -S vb make or get ready

PREPARER

PREPASTE vb paste in advance

PREPAVE, -D, -S vb pave beforehand

PREPAY, PREPAID, -S vb pay for in advance

P

PREPENSE adj (usually in legal contexts) arranged in advance ▷ vb consider beforehand

PREPLACE vb place in advance

PREPLAN, -S vb plan beforehand

PREPLANT adj planted in advance

PREPONE, -D, -S vb bring forward to an earlier time

PREPOSE, -D, -S vb place before

PREPPED ▸ prep

PREPPIE same as ▸ **preppy**

PREPPIER ▸ preppy

PREPPIES ▸ preppy

PREPPILY ▸ preppy

PREPPING ▸ prep

PREPPY, PREPPIER, PREPPIES adj denoting a fashion style of neat, understated clothes ▷ n person exhibiting such style

PREPREG, -S n material already impregnated with synthetic resin

PREPRESS adj before printing

PREPRICE vb price in advance

PREPRINT vb print in advance

PREPS ▸ prep

PREPUBIS, PREPUBES n animal hip bone

PREPUCE, -S n foreskin

PREPUNCH vb pierce with holes in advance

PREPUPA, -E, -S n insect in stage of life before pupa

PREPUPAL adj of the period between the larval and pupal stages

PREPUPAS ▸ prepupa

PREQUEL, -S n film or book about an earlier stage of a story

PRERACE adj of the period before a race

PRERADIO adj before the invention of radio

PRERENAL adj anterior to kidney

PRERINSE vb treat before rinsing

PRERIOT adj of the period before a riot

PREROCK adj of the era before rock music

PRERUPT adj abrupt

PRESA, PRESE n musical sign or symbol to indicate the entry of a part

PRESAGE, -D, -S vb be a sign or warning of ▷ n omen

PRESAGER

PRESALE, -S n practice of arranging the sale of a product before it is available

PRESBYTE n person with presbyopy

PRESCIND vb withdraw attention (from something)

PRESCORE vb record (the score of a film) before shooting

PRESCUTA > prescutum

PRESE ▸ presa

PRESELL, -S, PRESOLD vb promote in advance of appearance

PRESENCE n fact of being in a specified place

PRESENT adj being in a specified place ▷ n present time or tense ▷ vb introduce formally or publicly

PRESENTS pl n used in a deed or document to refer to itself

PRESERVE vb keep from being damaged, changed, or ended ▷ n area of interest restricted to a particular person or group

PRESES variant of ▸ **praeses**

PRESET, -S vb set a timer so that equipment starts to work at a specific time ▷ adj (of equipment) with the controls set in advance ▷ n control that is used to set initial conditions

PRESHAPE vb shape beforehand

PRESHIP, -S vb ship in advance

PRESHOW, -N, -S vb show in advance

PRESIDE, -D, -S vb be in charge, esp of a meeting

PRESIDER

PRESIDIA > presidium

PRESIDIO n military post or establishment, esp in countries formerly under Spanish control

PRESIFT, -S vb sift beforehand

PRESLEEP adj of the period before sleep

PRESLICE vb slice in advance

PRESOAK, -S vb soak beforehand

PRESOLD ▸ presell

PRESOLVE vb solve beforehand

PRESONG adj of the period before a song is sung

PRESORT, -S vb sort in advance

PRESPLIT adj of the period prior to a split

PRESS, -ED, -ES vb apply force or weight to ▷ n printing machine

PRESSER -S

PRESSFAT n wine vat

PRESSFUL ▸ press

PRESSIE, -S informal word for ▸ **present**

PRESSING adj urgent ▷ n large number of gramophone records produced at one time

PRESSION n act of pressing

PRESSMAN, PRESSMEN n person who works for the press

PRESSOR, -S n something that produces an increase in blood pressure

PRESSRUN n number of books printed at one time

PRESSURE n force produced by pressing ▷ vb persuade forcefully

PRESSY same as ▸ **pressie**

PREST, -ED, -ING, -S adj prepared for action or use ▷ n loan of money ▷ vb give as a loan

PRESTAMP vb stamp in advance

PRESTED ▸ prest

PRESTER, -S ▸ prest

PRESTIGE n high status or respect resulting from success or achievements

PRESTING ▸ prest

PRESTO, -S adv very quickly ▷ n passage to be played very quickly

PRESTORE vb store in advance

PRESTOS ▸ presto

PRESTS ▸ prest

PRESUME, -D, -S vb suppose to be the case

PRESUMER

PRETAPE, -D, -S vb (formerly) tape in advance

PRETASTE vb taste in advance

PRETAX adj before tax

PRETEEN, -S n boy or girl approaching his or her teens

PRETELL, -S, PRETOLD vb predict

PRETENCE n behaviour intended to deceive, pretending

PRETEND, -S vb claim (something untrue) ▷ adj fanciful

PRETENSE same as ▸ **pretence**

PRETERIT same as > **preterite**

PRETERM, -S n premature baby

PRETEST, -S *vb* test (something) before presenting it to its intended public or client ▷ *n* act or instance of pretesting

PRETEXT, -S *n* false reason given to hide the real one ▷ *vb* get personal information under false pretences

PRETOLD ▶ pretell

PRETONIC *adj* relating to the syllable before the one bearing the primary stress in a word

PRETOR, -S *same as* ▶ **praetor**

PRETRAIN *vb* train in advance

PRETREAT *vb* treat in advance

PRETRIAL *n* hearing prior to a trial

PRETRIM, -S *vb* trim in advance

PRETTIED ▶ pretty

PRETTIER ▶ pretty

PRETTIES ▶ pretty

PRETTIFY *vb* make pretty

PRETTILY ▶ pretty

PRETTY, PRETTIED, PRETTIER, PRETTIES *adj* pleasing to look at ▷ *adv* fairly, moderately ▷ *vb* pretty

PRETYPE, -D, -S *vb* type in advance

PRETZEL, -S *n* brittle salted biscuit ▷ *vb* bend or twist

PREUNION *n* early form of trade union

PREUNITE *vb* unite in advance

PREVAIL, -S *vb* gain mastery

PREVALUE *vb* value beforehand

PREVE, -D, -S, PREVING *vb* prove

PREVENE, -D, -S *vb* come before

PREVENT, -S *vb* keep from happening or doing

PREVERB, -S *n* particle preceding root of verb

PREVES ▶ preve

PREVIEW, -S *n* advance showing of a film or exhibition before it is shown to the public ▷ *vb* view in advance

PREVING ▶ preve

PREVIOUS *adj* coming or happening before

PREVISE, -D, -S *vb* predict or foresee

PREVISIT *vb* visit beforehand

PREVISOR ▶ previse

PREVUE, -D, -S, PREVUING *same as* ▶ **preview**

PREWAR *adj* relating to the period before a war, esp before World War I or II

PREWARM, -S *vb* warm beforehand

PREWARN, -S *vb* warn in advance

PREWASH *vb* give a preliminary wash to (clothes) ▷ *n* preliminary wash

PREWEIGH *vb* weigh beforehand

PREWIRE, -D, -S *vb* wire beforehand

PREWORK, -S *vb* work in advance

PREWORN *adj* (of clothes) second-hand

PREWRAP, -S *vb* wrap in advance

PREWYN, -S *obsolete spelling of* ▶ **prune**

PREX, -ES *same as* ▶ **prexy**

PREXIE *same as* ▶ **prexy**

PREXY, PREXIES *n* US college president

PREY, -ED, -ING, -S *n* animal hunted and killed for food by another animal ▷ *vb* hunt or seize food by killing other animals

PREYER -S

PREYFUL *adj* rich in prey

PREYING ▶ prey

PREYS ▶ prey

PREZ, -ES *n* president

PREZZIE, -S *same as* ▶ **pressie**

PRIAL, -S *n* pair royal of cards

PRIAPEAN *same as* ▶ **priapic**

PRIAPI ▶ priapus

PRIAPIC *adj* phallic

PRIAPUS, PRIAPI *n* representation of the penis

PRIBBLE, -S *variant of* ▶ **prabble**

PRICE, -D, -S *n* amount of money for which a thing is bought or sold ▷ *vb* fix or ask the price of

PRICER -S

PRICEY *adj* expensive

PRICIER ▶ pricy

PRICIEST ▶ pricy

PRICILY ▶ pricey

PRICING, -S ▶ price

PRICK, -ED, -ING, -S *vb* pierce lightly with a sharp point ▷ *n* sudden sharp pain caused by pricking

PRICKER, -S *n* person or thing that pricks

PRICKET, -S *n* male deer in the second year of life

PRICKIER ▶ pricky

PRICKING ▶ prick

PRICKLE, -D, -S *n* thorn or spike on a plant ▷ *vb* have a tingling or pricking sensation

PRICKLY *adj* having prickles

PRICKS ▶ prick

PRICKY, PRICKIER *adj* covered with pricks

PRICY, PRICIER, PRICIEST *same as* ▶ **pricey**

PRIDE, -D, -S, PRIDING *n* feeling of pleasure and satisfaction when one has done well

PRIDEFUL

PRIDIAN *adj* relating to yesterday

PRIDING ▶ pride

PRIED ▶ pry

PRIEDIEU *n* piece of furniture for use when kneeling to pray

PRIEF, -S *obsolete variant of* ▶ **proof**

PRIEFE, -S *obsolete variant of* ▶ **proof**

PRIEFS ▶ prief

PRIER, -S *n* person who pries

PRIES ▶ pry

PRIEST, -ED, -S *n* (in the Christian church) person who can administer the sacraments and preach ▷ *vb* make a priest

PRIESTLY *adj* of, relating to, characteristic of, or befitting a priest

PRIESTS ▶ priest

PRIEVE, -D, -S, PRIEVING *obsolete variant of* ▶ **proof**

PRIG, -GED, -GING, -S *n* self-righteous person who acts as if superior to others

PRIGGER, -S *n* thief

PRIGGERY ▶ prig

PRIGGING ▶ prig

PRIGGISH ▶ prig

PRIGGISM ▶ prig

PRIGS ▶ prig

PRILL, -ED, -ING, -S *vb* convert (a material) into a granular free-flowing form ▷ *n* prilled material

PRIM, -MED, -MEST, -MING, -S *adj* formal, proper, and rather prudish ▷ *vb* make prim

PRIMA, -S *same as* ▶ **primo**

PRIMACY *n* state of being first in rank, grade, etc

PRIMAGE, -S *n* tax added to customs duty

PRIMAL *adj* of basic causes or origins

PRIMALLY

PRIMARY *adj* chief, most important ▷ *n* person or

thing that is first in position, time, or importance

PRIMAS ▸ prima

PRIMATAL n primate

PRIMATE, -S n member of an order of mammals including monkeys and humans

PRIMATIC

PRIME, -D, -S adj main, most important ▷ n time when someone is most vigorous ▷ vb give (someone) information in advance

PRIMELY

PRIMER, -S n special paint applied to bare wood etc before the main paint

PRIMERO, -S n 16th- and 17th-century card game

PRIMERS ▸ primer

PRIMES ▸ prime

PRIMEUR, -S n anything (esp fruit) produced early

PRIMEVAL adj of the earliest age of the world

PRIMI ▸ primo

PRIMINE, -S n integument surrounding an ovule or the outer of two such integuments

PRIMING, -S same as ▸ primer

PRIMLY ▸ prim

PRIMMED ▸ prim

PRIMMER, -S n elementary textbook

PRIMMEST ▸ prim

PRIMMING ▸ prim

PRIMNESS ▸ prim

PRIMO, PRIMI, -S n upper or right-hand part in a piano duet

PRIMP, -ED, -ING, -S vb tidy (one's hair or clothes) fussily

PRIMROSE n pale yellow spring flower ▷ adj pale yellow

PRIMROSY

PRIMS ▸ prim

PRIMSIE, -R Scots variant of ▸ prim

PRIMULA, -S n type of primrose with brightly coloured flowers

PRIMUS, -ES n presiding bishop in the Synod

PRIMY adj prime

PRINCE, -D, -S, PRINCING n son of a king or queen ▷ vb act like a prince

PRINCELY adj of or like a prince ▷ adv in a princely manner

PRINCES ▸ prince

PRINCESS n female member of a royal family, esp the daughter of the king or queen

PRINCING ▸ prince

PRINCIPE, PRINCIPI n prince

PRINCOCK same as ▸ princox

PRINCOX n pert youth

PRINK, -ED, -ING, -S vb dress (oneself) finely

PRINKER -S

PRINT, -ED, -S vb reproduce (a newspaper, book, etc) in large quantities by mechanical or electronic means ▷ n printed words etc

PRINTER, -S n person or company engaged in printing

PRINTERY n establishment in which printing is carried out

PRINTING n process of producing printed matter

PRINTOUT n printed information produced by a computer output device

PRINTS ▸ print

PRION, -S n dovelike petrel with a serrated bill

PRIOR, -S adj earlier ▷ n head monk in a priory

PRIORATE n office, status, or term of office of a prior

PRIORESS n deputy head nun in a convent

PRIORIES ▸ priory

PRIORITY n most important thing that must be dealt with first

PRIORLY ▸ prior

PRIORS ▸ prior

PRIORY, PRIORIES n place where certain orders of monks or nuns live

PRISAGE, -S n customs duty levied until 1809 upon wine imported into England

PRISE, -D, -S, PRISING same as ▸ pry

PRISER -S

PRISERE, -S n primary sere or succession from bare ground to the community climax

PRISERS ▸ priser

PRISES ▸ prise

PRISING ▸ prise

PRISM, -S n transparent block used to disperse light into a spectrum

PRISMOID n prism-like geometrical shape

PRISMS ▸ prism

PRISMY ▸ prism

PRISON, -ED, -S n building where criminals and accused people are held ▷ vb imprison

PRISONER n person held captive

PRISONS ▸ prison

PRISS, -ED, -ES, -ING n prissy person ▷ vb act prissily

PRISSIER ▸ prissy

PRISSIES ▸ prissy

PRISSILY ▸ prissy

PRISSING ▸ priss

PRISSY, PRISSIER, PRISSIES adj prim, correct, and easily shocked ▷ n prissy person

PRISTANE n colourless combustible liquid

PRISTINE adj clean, new, and unused

PRITHEE interj pray thee

PRIVACY n condition of being private

PRIVADO, -S n close friend

PRIVATE, -R, -S adj for the use of one person or group only ▷ n soldier of the lowest rank

PRIVET, -S n bushy evergreen shrub used for hedges

PRIVIER ▸ privy

PRIVIES ▸ privy

PRIVIEST ▸ privy

PRIVILY adv in a secret way

PRIVITY n legally recognized relationship between two parties

PRIVY, PRIVIER, PRIVIES, PRIVIEST adj sharing knowledge of something secret ▷ n toilet, esp an outside one

PRIZABLE adj of worth

PRIZE, -D, -S, PRIZING n reward given for success in a competition etc ▷ adj winning or likely to win a prize ▷ vb value highly

PRIZEMAN, PRIZEMEN n winner of prize

PRIZER, -S n contender for prize

PRIZES ▸ prize

PRIZING ▸ prize

PRO, -S prep in favour of ▷ n professional ▷ adv in favour of a motion etc

PROA, -S n canoe-like boat used in the South Pacific

PROB, -S n problem

PROBABLE adj likely to happen or be true ▷ n person who is likely to be chosen for a team, event, etc

PROBABLY adv in all likelihood ▷ sentence substitute I believe such a thing or situation may be the case

PROBALL adj believable

PROBAND, -S n first patient to be investigated in a family study

PROBANG, -S n long flexible rod used to apply medication

PROBATE, -D, -S n process of proving the validity of a will ▷ vb establish officially the authenticity and validity of (a will)

PROBE, -D, -S vb search into or examine closely ▷ n surgical instrument used to examine a wound, cavity, etc

PROBER -S

PROBING, -S n act of making a thorough enquiry

PROBIT, -S n statistical measurement

PROBITY n honesty, integrity

PROBLEM, -S n something difficult to deal with or solve ▷ adj of a literary work that deals with difficult moral questions

PROBS ▸ prob

PROCAINE n colourless or white crystalline water-soluble substance

PROCARP, -S n female reproductive organ in red algae

PROCEED vb start or continue doing

PROCEEDS pl n money obtained from an event or activity

PROCESS n series of actions or changes ▷ vb handle or prepare by a special method of manufacture

PROCHAIN variant of ▸ prochein

PROCHEIN adj next or nearest

PROCINCT n state of preparedness

PROCLAIM vb declare publicly

PROCLIVE adj prone

PROCTAL adj relating to the rectum

PROCTOR, -S n university worker who enforces discipline ▷ vb invigilate (an examination)

PROCURAL ▸ procure

PROCURE, -D, -S vb get, provide

PROCURER n person who provides something

PROCURES ▸ procure

PROD, -DED, -S vb poke with something pointed ▷ n prodding

PRODDER -S

PRODDING n act of prodding

PRODIGAL adj recklessly extravagant, wasteful ▷ n person who spends lavishly or squanders money

PRODIGY n person with some marvellous talent

PRODITOR n traitor

PRODNOSE vb make uninvited inquiries (about someone else's business, for example)

PRODROMA n symptom that signals the onset of a disease

PRODROME, PRODROMI n any symptom that signals the impending onset of a disease

PRODRUG, -S n compound that is metabolized in the body to produce an active drug

PRODS ▸ prod

PRODUCE, -D, -S vb bring into existence ▷ n food grown for sale

PRODUCER n person with control over the making of a film, record, etc

PRODUCES ▸ produce

PRODUCT, -S n something produced

PROEM, -S n introduction or preface

PROEMIAL

PROETTE, -S n female golfing professional

PROF, -S short for ▸ professor

PROFACE interj much good may it do you

PROFANE, -D, -S adj showing disrespect for religion or holy things ▷ vb treat (something sacred) irreverently, desecrate

PROFANER

PROFESS vb state or claim (something as true), sometimes falsely

PROFFER, -S vb offer ▷ n act of proffering

PROFILE, -D, -S n outline, esp of the face, as seen from the side ▷ vb draw, write, or make a profile of

PROFILER n device that creates a profile

PROFILES ▸ profile

PROFIT, -ED, -S n money gained ▷ vb gain or benefit

PROFITER

PROFORMA n invoice issued before an order is placed

PROFOUND adj showing or needing great knowledge ▷ n great depth

PROFS ▸ prof

PROFUSE adj plentiful

PROFUSER

PROG, -GED, -GING, -S vb prowl about for or as if for food or plunder ▷ n food obtained by begging

PROGENY n children

PROGERIA n premature old age in children

PROGGED ▸ prog

PROGGER, -S n fan of progressive rock

PROGGING ▸ prog

PROGGINS n proctor

PROGNOSE vb predict course of disease

PROGRADE vb (of beach) advance towards sea

PROGRAM, -S same as ▸ programme

PROGRESS n improvement, development ▷ vb become more advanced or skilful

PROGS ▸ prog

PROGUN adj in favour of public owning firearms

PROHIBIT vb forbid or prevent from happening

PROIGN, -ED, -S same as ▸ proin

PROIN, -ED, -ING, -S vb trim or prune

PROINE, -S same as ▸ proin

PROINED ▸ proin

PROINES ▸ proine

PROINING ▸ proin

PROINS ▸ proin

PROJECT, -S n planned scheme to do or examine something over a period ▷ vb make a forecast based on known data

PROJET, -S n draft of a proposed treaty

PROKE, -D, -S, PROKING vb thrust or poke

PROKER -S

PROLABOR adj favouring the Labor party

PROLAMIN same as ▸ prolamine

PROLAN, -S n constituent of human pregnancy urine

PROLAPSE n slipping down of an internal organ of the body from its normal position ▷ vb (of an internal organ) slip from its normal position

PROLATE, -D, -S adj having a polar diameter which is longer than the equatorial diameter ▷ vb pronounce or utter

PROLE, -D, -S, PROLING old form of ▸ prowl

P

PROLEG, -S n appendage on abdominal segment of a caterpillar

PROLER, -S n prowler

PROLES ► **prole**

PROLIFIC adj very productive

PROLINE, -S n nonessential amino acid that occurs in protein

PROLING ► **prole**

PROLIX adj (of speech or a piece of writing) overlong and boring

PROLIXLY

PROLL, -ED, -ING, -S vb prowl or search

PROLLER -S

PROLLY adv probably

PROLOG, -ED, -S same as ► **prologue**

PROLOGUE n introduction to a play or book ▷ vb introduce or preface with or as if with a prologue

PROLONG, -S vb make (something) last longer

PROLONGE n (formerly) rope used as part of the towing equipment of a gun carriage

PROLONGS ► **prolong**

PROM, -S n formal dance held at a high school or college

PROMETAL n type of cast iron

PROMINE, -S n substance promoting cell growth

PROMISE, -D, -S vb say that one will definitely do or not do something ▷ n undertaking to do or not to do something

PROMISEE n person to whom a promise is made

PROMISER ► **promise**

PROMISES ► **promise**

PROMISOR n person who makes a promise

PROMMER, -S n spectator at promenade concert

PROMO, -ED, -ING, -S vb promote (something)

PROMOTE, -D, -S vb help to make (something) happen or increase

PROMOTER n person who organizes or finances an event etc

PROMOTES ► **promote**

PROMOTOR variant of ► **promoter**

PROMPT, -ED, -S vb cause (an action) ▷ adj done without delay ▷ adv exactly ▷ n anything that serves to remind

PROMPTER n person offstage who prompts actors

PROMPTLY ► **prompt**

PROMPTS ► **prompt**

PROMS ► **prom**

PROMULGE vb bring to public knowledge

PRONAOS, PRONAOI n inner area of the portico of a classical temple

PRONATE, -D, -S vb turn (a limb, hand, or foot) so that the palm or sole is directed downwards

PRONATOR n any muscle whose contractions produce or affect pronation

PRONE, -R, -S, -ST n sermon

PRONELY

PRONEUR, -S n flatterer

PRONG, -ED, -ING, -S n one spike of a fork or similar instrument ▷ vb prick or spear with or as if with a prong

PRONOTA ► **pronotum**

PRONOTAL ► **pronotum**

PRONOTUM, PRONOTA n notum of the prothorax of an insect

PRONOUN, -S n word, such as she or it, used to replace a noun

PRONTO adv at once

PROO interj (to a horse) stop!

PROOF, -ED, -ING, -S n evidence that shows that something is true or has happened ▷ adj able to withstand ▷ vb take a proof from (type matter)

PROOFER, -S n reader of proofs

PROOFING ► **proof**

PROOFS ► **proof**

PROOTIC, -S n bone in front of ear

PROP, -PED, -PING, -S vb support (something) so that it stays upright or in place ▷ n pole, beam, etc used as a support

PROPAGE, -D, -S vb propagate

PROPALE, -D, -S vb publish (something)

PROPANE, -S n flammable gas found in petroleum and used as a fuel

PROPANOL n colourless alcohol

PROPEL, -S vb cause to move forward

PROPENAL n type of aldehyde used as a herbicide and tear gas

PROPEND, -S vb be inclined or disposed

PROPENE, -S n colourless gaseous alkene obtained by cracking petroleum

PROPENOL n liquid used to make allylic alcohol

PROPENSE adj inclining forward

PROPENYL n three-carbon radical

PROPER, -ER, -S adj real or genuine ▷ n service or psalm regarded as appropriate to a specific day, season, etc

PROPERLY

PROPERTY same as ► **proprium**

PROPHAGE n type of virus in a bacterial cell

PROPHASE n first stage of mitosis

PROPHECY n prediction

PROPHESY vb foretell

PROPHET, -S n person chosen by God to spread His word

PROPHYLL n leaf-shaped plant structure

PROPINE, -D, -S vb drink a toast to

PROPJET, -S another name for > **turboprop**

PROPMAN, PROPMEN n member of the stage crew in charge of the stage props

PROPOLIS n resinous aromatic substance collected by bees from trees

PROPONE, -D, -S vb propose or put forward, esp before a court

PROPOSAL n act of proposing

PROPOSE, -D, -S vb put forward for consideration

PROPOSER

PROPOUND vb put forward for consideration

PROPPANT n material used in the oil extraction process

PROPPED ► **prop**

PROPPING ► **prop**

PROPRIUM, PROPRIA n attribute that is not essential to a species but is common and peculiar to it

PROPS ► **prop**

PROPYL, -S n the monovalent group of atoms C_3H_7-

PROPYLA ► **propylon**

PROPYLIC ► **propyl**

PROPYLON, PROPYLA n portico, esp one that forms the entrance to a temple

PROPYLS ► **propyl**

PROPYNE, -S n type of gaseous methyl acetylene

PRORATE, -D, -S vb divide, assess, or distribute (something) proportionately

PRORE, -S n forward part of ship

PROROGUE vb suspend (parliament) without dissolving it

PROS ▸ pro

PROSAIC adj lacking imagination, dull

PROSAISM n prosaic quality or style

PROSAIST

PROSE, -D, -S n ordinary speech or writing in contrast to poetry ▸ vb speak or write in a tedious style

PROSECCO n Italian sparkling white wine

PROSECT, -S vb dissect a cadaver for a public demonstration

PROSED ▸ prose

PROSEMAN, PROSEMEN n writer of prose

PROSER, -S n writer of prose

PROSES ▸ prose

PROSIER ▸ prosy

PROSIEST ▸ prosy

PROSIFY vb write prose

PROSILY ▸ prosy

PROSING, -S ▸ prose

PROSIT interj good health! cheers!

PROSO, -S n millet

PROSODIC ▸ prosody

PROSODY n study of poetic metre and techniques

PROSOMA, -S n head and thorax of an arachnid

PROSOMAL

PROSOPON n (in Christianity) manifestation of any of the persons of the Trinity

PROSOS ▸ proso

PROSPECT n something anticipated ▸ vb explore, esp for gold

PROSPER, -S vb be successful

PROST same as ▸ prosit

PROSTATE n gland in male mammals that surrounds the neck of the bladder ▸ adj of or relating to the prostate gland

PROSTYLE adj (of a building) having a row of columns in front ▸ n prostyle building, portico, etc

PROSUMER n amateur user of electronic equipment suitable for professionals

PROSY, PROSIER, PROSIEST adj dull and long-winded

PROTAMIN same as ▸ protamine

PROTASIS, PROTASES n antecedent of a conditional statement

PROTATIC

PROTEA, -S n African shrub with showy flowers

PROTEAN, -S adj constantly changing ▸ n creature that can change shape

PROTEAS ▸ protea

PROTEASE n any enzyme involved in proteolysis

PROTECT, -S vb defend from trouble, harm, or loss

PROTEGE, -S n person who is protected and helped by another

PROTEGEE n woman or girl who is protected and helped by another

PROTEGES ▸ protege

PROTEI ▸ proteus

PROTEID, -S n protein

PROTEIDE variant of ▸ proteid

PROTEIDS ▸ proteid

PROTEIN, -S n any of a group of complex organic compounds that are essential for life

PROTEND, -S vb hold out or stretch

PROTENSE n extension

PROTEOME n full complement of proteins that occur within a cell, tissue, or organism

PROTEOSE n compound formed during proteolysis

PROTEST, -S n declaration or demonstration of objection ▸ vb object, disagree

PROTEUS, PROTEI n aerobic bacterium

PROTHYL, -S variant of ▸ protyle

PROTIST, -S n organism belonging to the protozoans, unicellular algae, and simple fungi

PROTIUM, -S n most common isotope of hydrogen

PROTO adj as in **proto team** team of people trained to deal with underground rescues, etc

PROTOCOL, -S n rules of behaviour for formal occasions

PROTON, -S n positively charged particle in the nucleus of an atom

PROTONIC adj (of a solvent, such as water) able to donate hydrogen ions to solute molecules

PROTONS ▸ proton

PROTOPOD n part of crustacean's leg

PROTORE, -S n primary mineral deposit

PROTOXID variant of ▸ protoxide

PROTOZOA ▸ protozoan

PROTRACT vb lengthen or extend (a situation etc)

PROTRADE adj in favour of trade

PROTRUDE vb stick out, project

PROTURAN n any of an order of white wingless insects

PROTYL, -S same as ▸ protyle

PROTYLE, -S n hypothetical primitive substance

PROTYLS ▸ protyl

PROUD, -ER, -EST adj feeling pleasure and satisfaction

PROUDFUL adj full of pride

PROUDISH adj rather proud

PROUDLY ▸ proud

PROUL, -ED, -ING, -S variant of ▸ prowl

PROULER, -S Scots variant of ▸ prowler

PROULING ▸ proul

PROULS ▸ proul

PROUNION adj in favour of or supporting the constitutional union between two or more countries

PROVABLE ▸ prove

PROVABLY ▸ prove

PROVAND, -S n food

PROVANT, -S adj supplied with provisions ▸ vb supply with provisions

PROVE, -D, -N, -S vb establish the validity of

PROVEDOR variant of ▸ provedore

PROVEN ▸ prove

PROVEND, -S same as ▸ provand

PROVENLY ▸ prove

PROVER, -S ▸ prove

PROVERB, -S n short saying that expresses a truth or gives a warning ▸ vb utter or describe (something) in the form of a proverb

PROVERS ▸ prover

PROVES ▸ prove

PROVIANT variant of ▸ provand

PROVIDE, -D, -S vb make available

PROVIDER

P

P

PROVIDOR variant of
> **provedore**

PROVINCE n area governed as
a unit of a country or empire

PROVINE, -D, -S vb plant
branch of vine in ground for
propagation

PROVING, -S ► **prove**

PROVIRAL ► **provirus**

PROVIRUS n inactive form of
a virus in a host cell

PROVISO, -S n condition,
stipulation

PROVISOR n person who
receives provision

PROVISOS ► **proviso**

PROVOKE, -D, -S vb
deliberately anger
PROVOKER

PROVOST, -S n head of
certain university colleges
in Britain

PROW, -ER, -EST, -S n bow of
a vessel ▷ adj gallant

PROWAR adj in favour of or
supporting war

PROWER ► **prow**

PROWESS n superior skill or
ability

PROWEST ► **prow**

PROWL, -ED, -ING, -S vb
move stealthily around a
place as if in search of prey or
plunder ▷ n prowling
PROWLER -S

PROWS ► **prow**

PROXEMIC > **proxemics**

PROXIES ► **proxy**

PROXIMAL same as
> **proximate**

PROXIMO adv in or during the
next or coming month

PROXY, PROXIES n person
authorized to act on behalf of
someone else

PROYN, -ED, -ING, -S obsolete
spelling of ► **prune**

PROYNE, -S obsolete spelling
of ► **prune**

PROYNED ► **proyn**

PROYNES ► **proyne**

PROYNING ► **proyn**

PROYNS ► **proyn**

PRUDE, -S n person who is
excessively modest, prim,
or proper

PRUDENCE n caution in
practical affairs

PRUDENT adj cautious,
discreet, and sensible

PRUDERY ► **prude**

PRUDES ► **prude**

PRUDISH ► **prude**

PRUH variant of ► **proo**

PRUINA, -S n woolly white
covering on some lichens

PRUINE, -S obsolete spelling
of ► **prune**

PRUINOSE adj coated with a
powdery or waxy bloom

PRUNABLE ► **prune**

PRUNE, -D, -S n dried plum
▷ vb cut off dead parts or
excessive branches from (a
tree or plant)

PRUNELLA n strong fabric,
esp a twill-weave worsted,
used for gowns and the
uppers of some shoes

PRUNELLE same as
► **prunella**

PRUNELLO same as
► **prunella**

PRUNER, -S ► **prune**

PRUNES ► **prune**

**PRUNEY, PRUNIER,
PRUNIEST** adj resembling
a prune

PRUNING, -S ► **prune**

PRUNT, -S n glass
ornamentation
PRUNTED

PRUNUS, -ES n type of
ornamental tree or shrub

PRURIGO, -S n chronic
inflammatory disease of
the skin

PRURITIC ► **pruritus**

PRURITUS n any intense
sensation of itching

PRUSIK, -ED, -S n sliding knot
used in climbing ▷ vb climb
(up a rope) using prusiks

PRUSSIAN adj as in **prussian
blue** colour pigment,
discovered in Berlin

PRUSSIC adj as in **prussic
acid** weakly acidic extremely
poisonous aqueous solution
of hydrogen cyanide

PRUTA same as ► **prutah**

PRUTAH, PRUTOT, PRUTOTH
n former Israeli coin

PRY, PRIED, PRIES vb make
an impertinent or uninvited
inquiry into a private matter
▷ n act of prying

PRYER, -S same as ► **prier**

PRYING, -S ► **pry**

PRYINGLY ► **pry**

PRYINGS ► **prying**

PRYS old variant of ► **price**

PRYSE, -D, -S, PRYSING old
variant of ► **price**

PRYTANEA ► **prytaneum**

PRYTHEE same as ► **prithee**

PSALM, -ED, -ING, -S n sacred
song ▷ vb sing a psalm
PSALMIC

PSALMIST n writer of psalms

PSALMODY n singing of
sacred music

PSALMS ► **psalm**

PSALTER, -S n book
containing a version of
Psalms

PSALTERY n ancient
instrument played by
plucking strings

PSALTRY same as ► **psaltery**

PSAMMITE rare name for
> **sandstone**

PSAMMON, -S n microscopic
life forms living between
grains of sand

PSCHENT, -S n ancient
Egyptian crown

PSELLISM n stammering

PSEPHISM n proposition
adopted by a majority vote

PSEPHITE n any rock that
consists of large fragments
embedded in a finer matrix

PSEUD, -S n pretentious
person

PSEUDERY n pretentious talk

PSEUDISH ► **pseud**

PSEUDO, -S n pretentious
person

PSEUDS ► **pseud**

PSHAW, -ED, -ING, -S n
exclamation of disgust,
impatience, disbelief, etc
▷ vb make this exclamation

PSI, -S n 23rd letter of the
Greek alphabet

PSILOCIN n hallucinogenic
substance

PSILOSIS, PSILOSES n disease
of the small intestine

PSILOTIC

PSION, -S n type of
elementary particle

PSIONIC ► **psionics**

PSIONICS n study of the
practical use of psychic
powers

PSIONS ► **psion**

PSIS ► **psi**

PSOAS, PSOAE, PSOAI, -ES n
either of two muscles of the
loins that aid in flexing and
rotating the thigh
PSOATIC

PSOCID, -S n tiny wingless
insect

PSORA, -S n itching skin
complaint

PSORALEA n type of tropical
and subtropical plant with
curly leaves and white or
purple flowers

PSORALEN n treatment for
some skin diseases

PSORAS ► **psora**

PSORIC ► **psora**

PSST interj sound made to
attract someone's attention

PST *interj* sound made to attract someone's attention

You would need to be fairly desperate to use good letters to play this exclamation, but sometimes with no vowels on your rack things can be that desperate.

PSYCH, -ED, -ES, -ING, -S *vb* psychoanalyse

PSYCHE *same as* ► **psych**

PSYCHED ► **psych**

PSYCHES ► **psych**

PSYCHIC, -S *adj* having mental powers which cannot be explained by natural laws ▷ *n* person with psychic powers

PSYCHING ► **psych**

PSYCHISM *n* belief in a universal soul

PSYCHIST

PSYCHOID *n* name for an animal's innate impetus to perform actions

PSYCHS ► **psych**

PSYLLA, -S *same as* ► **psyllid**

PSYLLID, -S *n* type of insect of the family which comprises the jumping plant lice

PSYLLIUM *n* grain, the husks of which are used as a laxative

PSYOP, -S *n* psychological operation

PSYWAR, -S *n* psychological warfare

PTARMIC, -S *n* material that causes sneezing

PTERIA ► **pterion**

PTERIN, -S *n* compound such as folic acid

PTERION, PTERIA *n* point on the side of the skull where a number of bones meet

PTEROIC *adj as in* **pteroic acid** a kind of acid found in spinach

PTEROPOD *n* small marine gastropod mollusc

PTERYGIA > **pterygium**

PTERYLA, -E *n* any of the tracts of skin that bear contour feathers

PTILOSIS, PTILOSES *n* falling out of eye lashes

PTISAN, -S *n* grape juice drained off without pressure

PTOMAIN, -S *same as* ► **ptomaine**

PTOMAINE *n* any of a group of poisonous alkaloids found in decaying matter

PTOMAINS ► **ptomain**

PTOOEY *interj* imitation of the sound of spitting

PTOSIS, PTOSES *n* prolapse or drooping of a part, esp the eyelid

PTOTIC

PTUI *same as* ► **ptooey**

PTYALIN, -S *n* amylase secreted in the saliva of man and other animals

PTYALISE *same as* ► **ptyalize**

PTYALISM *n* excessive secretion of saliva

PTYALIZE *vb* expel saliva from the mouth

PTYXIS, PTYXES, -ES *n* folding of a leaf in a bud

PUB, -BED, -BING, -S *n* building with a bar licensed to sell alcoholic drinks ▷ *vb* visit a pub or pubs

PUBBINGS ► **pubbing**

PUBCO, -S *n* company operating a chain of pubs

PUBERAL *adj* relating to puberty

PUBERTAL ► **puberty**

PUBERTY *n* period at the beginning of adolescence

PUBIC *adj* of the lower abdomen

PUBIS, -ES *n* one of the three sections of the hipbone that forms part of the pelvis

PUBLIC, -S *adj* of or concerning the people as a whole ▷ *n* community, people in general

PUBLICAN *n* person who owns or runs a pub

PUBLICLY *adv* in a public manner

PUBLICS ► **public**

PUBLISH *vb* produce and issue (printed matter) for sale

PUBS ► **pub**

PUCAN, -S *n* traditional Connemara open sailing boat

PUCCOON, -S *n* N American plant that yields a red dye

PUCE, -R, -S, -ST *adj* purplish-brown ▷ *n* colour varying from deep red to dark purplish-brown

PUCELAGE *n* state of being a maid or girl

PUCELLE, -S *n* maid or girl

PUCER ► **puce**

PUCES ► **puce**

PUCEST ► **puce**

PUCK, -ED, -ING, -S *n* mischievous or evil spirit ▷ *vb* strike (the ball) in hurling

PUCKA *same as* ► **pukka**

PUCKED ► **puck**

PUCKER, -ED, -S *vb* gather into wrinkles ▷ *n* wrinkle or crease

PUCKERER

PUCKERY *adj* tending to pucker ▷ *n* puckishness

PUCKFIST *n* puffball

PUCKING ► **puck**

PUCKISH ► **puck**

PUCKLE, -S *n* early type of machine gun

PUCKOUT, -S *n* (in hurling) free hit made by the goalkeeper

PUCKS ► **puck**

PUCKSTER *n* hockey player

PUD, -S *short for* ► **pudding**

PUDDEN, -S *dialect spelling of* ► **pudding**

PUDDER, -ED, -S *vb* make bother or fuss

PUDDIER ► **puddy**

PUDDIES ► **puddy**

PUDDIEST ► **puddy**

PUDDING, -S *n* dessert, esp a cooked one served hot

PUDDINGY

PUDDLE, -D, -S *n* small pool of water, esp of rain ▷ *vb* make (clay etc) into puddle

PUDDLER -S

PUDDLIER ► **puddly**

PUDDLING *n* process for converting pig iron into wrought iron

PUDDLY, PUDDLIER ► **puddle**

PUDDOCK, -S *same as* ► **paddock**

PUDDY, PUDDIER, PUDDIES, PUDDIEST *n* paw ▷ *adj* short and podgy

PUDENCY *n* modesty, shame, or prudishness

PUDENDA ► **pudendum**

PUDENDAL ► **pudendum**

PUDENDUM, PUDENDA *n* human external genital organs collectively, esp of a female

PUDENT *adj* lacking in ostentation; humble

PUDEUR, -S *n* sense of shame or embarrassment

PUDGE, -S *same as* ► **podge**

PUDGIER ► **pudgy**

PUDGIEST ► **pudgy**

PUDGILY ► **pudgy**

PUDGY, PUDGIER, PUDGIEST *adj* podgy

PUDIBUND *adj* prudish

PUDIC ► **pudendum**

PUDICITY *n* modesty

PUDOR, -S *n* sense of shame

PUDS ► **pud**

PUDSEY *variant of* ► **pudsy**

PUDSY, PUDSIER, PUDSIES, PUDSIEST adj plump ▷ n plump person

PUDU, -S n diminutive Andean antelope

PUEBLO, -S n communal village of flat-roofed houses

PUER, -ED, -ING, -S vb steep hides in an alkaline substance from the dung of dogs

PUERILE adj silly and childish

PUERING ▸ puer

PUERPERA n woman who has recently given birth

PUERS ▸ puer

PUFF, -ED, -S n (sound of) short blast of breath, wind, etc ▷ vb blow or breathe in short quick draughts

PUFFA adj type of quilted and padded jacket

PUFFBACK n type of small African bird

PUFFBALL n ball-shaped fungus

PUFFBIRD n brownish tropical American bird with a large head

PUFFED ▸ puff

PUFFER, -S n person or thing that puffs

PUFFERY n exaggerated praise, esp in publicity or advertising

PUFFIER ▸ puffy

PUFFIEST ▸ puffy

PUFFILY ▸ puffy

PUFFIN, -S n sea bird with a brightly-coloured beak

PUFFING, -S ▸ puff

PUFFINS ▸ puffin

PUFFS ▸ puff

PUFFY, PUFFIER, PUFFIEST adj short of breath

PUG, -GED, -S n small snub-nosed dog ▷ vb mix or knead (clay) with water to form a malleable mass or paste

PUGAREE, -S same as ▸ puggree

PUGGAREE same as ▸ puggree

PUGGED ▸ pug

PUGGERY same as ▸ puggree

PUGGIE, -S n Scottish word for fruit machine

PUGGIER ▸ puggy

PUGGIES ▸ puggie

PUGGIEST ▸ puggy

PUGGING, -S ▸ pug

PUGGISH ▸ pug

PUGGLE, -D, -S, PUGGLING vb stir up by poking

PUGGREE, -S n scarf, usually pleated, around the crown of some hats, esp sun helmets

PUGGRY, PUGGRIES same as ▸ puggree

PUGGY, PUGGIER, PUGGIEST adj sticky, claylike ▷ n term of endearment

PUGH interj exclamation of disgust

PUGIL, -S n pinch or small handful

PUGILISM n art, practice, or profession of fighting with the fists

PUGILIST

PUGILS ▸ pugil

PUGMARK, -S n trail of an animal

PUGREE, -S same as ▸ puggree

PUGS ▸ pug

PUH interj exclamation expressing contempt or disgust

PUHA, -S n sow thistle

PUIR, -ER, -EST Scottish word for ▸ poor

PUIRTITH n poverty

PUISNE, -S adj (esp of a subordinate judge) of lower rank ▷ n judge of lower rank

PUISNY adj younger or inferior

PUISSANT adj powerful

PUJA, -S n ritual in honour of the gods, performed either at home or in the mandir (temple)

PUJAH, -S same as ▸ puja

PUJARI, -S n Hindu priest

PUJAS ▸ puja

PUKA, -S in New Zealand English, same as > broadleaf

PUKATEA, -S n aromatic New Zealand tree

PUKE, -D, -S, PUKING vb vomit ▷ n act of vomiting

PUKEKO, -S n brightly coloured New Zealand wading bird

PUKER, -S n person who vomits

PUKES ▸ puke

PUKEY, PUKIER, PUKIEST adj of or like vomit

PUKING ▸ puke

PUKKA adj properly done, constructed, etc

PUKKAH adj genuine

PUKU, -S n belly or stomach

PUKY same as ▸ pukey

PUL, -IK, -S n Afghan monetary unit

PULA, -S n standard monetary unit of Botswana

PULAO, -S same as ▸ pilau

PULAS ▸ pula

PULDRON, -S same as ▸ pauldron

PULE, -D, -S vb whine or whimper

PULER -S

PULI, -S n Hungarian sheepdog

PULICENE adj flea-ridden

PULICIDE n flea-killing substance

PULIER ▸ puly

PULIEST ▸ puly

PULIK ▸ pul

PULING, -S ▸ pule

PULINGLY ▸ pule

PULINGS ▸ puling

PULIS ▸ puli

PULK, -S same as ▸ pulka

PULKA, -S n reindeer-drawn sleigh

PULKHA, -S same as ▸ pulka

PULKS ▸ pulk

PULL, -ED, -ING, -S vb exert force on (an object) to move it towards the source of the force ▷ n act of pulling

PULLBACK n act of pulling back

PULLED ▸ pull

PULLER, -S ▸ pull

PULLET, -S n young hen

PULLEY, -ED, -S n device for lifting weights by a downward pull ▷ vb lift with a pulley

PULLI ▸ pullus

PULLIES ▸ pully

PULLING ▸ pull

PULLMAN, -S n luxurious railway coach, esp a sleeping car

PULLORUM n as in **pullorum disease** acute serious bacterial disease of very young birds

PULLOUT, -S n removable section of a magazine, etc

PULLOVER n sweater that is pulled on over the head

PULLS ▸ pull

PULLUP, -S n exercise in which the body is raised by the arms pulling on a horizontal bar

PULLUS, PULLI n technical term for a chick or young bird

PULLY, PULLIES n pullover

PULMO, -NES n lung

PULMONIC adj of or relating to the lungs ▷ n person with lung disease

PULMOTOR n apparatus for pumping oxygen into the lungs during artificial respiration

PULP, -ED, -S n soft wet substance made from crushed or beaten matter ▷ vb reduce to pulp
PULPAL
PULPALLY
PULPER -S

PULPIER ▶ pulpy

PULPIEST ▶ pulpy

PULPIFY vb reduce to pulp

PULPILY ▶ pulpy

PULPING, -S n act of pulping

PULPIT, -S n raised platform for a preacher
PULPITAL
PULPITED

PULPITER n preacher

PULPITRY n art of delivering sermons

PULPITS ▶ pulpit

PULPITUM n stone screen dividing nave and choir

PULPLESS ▶ pulp

PULPMILL n mill making raw material for paper

PULPOUS n soft and yielding

PULPS ▶ pulp

PULPWOOD n pine, spruce, or any other soft wood used to make paper

PULPY, PULPIER, PULPIEST adj having a soft or soggy consistency

PULQUE, -S n light alcoholic drink from Mexico

PULS ▶ pul

PULSANT adj vibrant

PULSAR, -S n small dense star which emits regular bursts of radio waves

PULSATE, -D, -S vb throb, quiver

PULSATOR n device that stimulates rhythmic motion of a body

PULSE, -D, -S, PULSING n regular beating of blood through the arteries at each heartbeat ▷ vb beat, throb, or vibrate

PULSEJET n type of ramjet engine

PULSER, -S n thing that pulses

PULSES ▶ pulse

PULSIDGE archaic word for ▶ pulse

PULSIFIC adj causing the pulse to increase

PULSING ▶ pulse

PULSION, -S n act of driving forward

PULSOJET same as ▶ pulsejet

PULTAN, -S n native Indian regiment

PULTON, -S same as ▶ pultan

PULTOON, -S same as ▶ pultan

PULTRUDE vb produce reinforced plastic process by pultrusion

PULTUN, -S same as ▶ pultan

PULTURE, -S n food and drink claimed by foresters

PULU, -S n substance used for stuffing cushions

PULVER, -ED, -S vb make into powder

PULVIL, -S vb apply perfumed powder

PULVILIO n perfumed powder

PULVILLE same as ▶ pulvil

PULVILLI > pulvillus

PULVILS ▶ pulvil

PULVINAR n part of the thalamus

PULVINUS, PULVINI n swelling at the base of a leafstalk

PULWAR, -S n light Indian river boat

PULY, PULIER, PULIEST adj whiny

PUMA, -S n large American wild cat with a greyish-brown coat

PUMELO, -S same as ▶ pomelo

PUMICATE vb pound fruit with pumice to make juice

PUMICE, -D, -S, PUMICING n light porous stone used for scouring ▷ vb rub or polish with pumice
PUMICER -S

PUMICITE n fine-grained variety of pumice

PUMIE, -S n small stone

PUMMEL, -ED, -S vb strike repeatedly with or as if with the fists

PUMMELO, -S same as ▶ pomelo

PUMMELS ▶ pummel

PUMP, -ED, -ING, -S n machine used to force a liquid or gas to move in a particular direction ▷ vb raise or drive with a pump

PUMPABLE adj capable of being pumped

PUMPED ▶ pump

PUMPER, -S ▶ pump

PUMPHOOD n cover for the upper wheel of a chain pump

PUMPING, -S ▶ pump

PUMPION, -S archaic word for ▶ pumpkin

PUMPJACK n pumping apparatus at an oil well

PUMPKIN, -S n large round fruit with an orange rind

PUMPKING n programmer with authority to change the master source code

PUMPKINS ▶ pumpkin

PUMPLESS ▶ pump

PUMPLIKE ▶ pump

PUMPS ▶ pump

PUMY adj large and round

PUN, -NED, -S n use of words to exploit double meanings for humorous effect ▷ vb make puns

PUNA, -S n high cold dry plateau, esp in the Andes

PUNALUA, -S n marriage between the sisters of one family to the brothers of another
PUNALUAN

PUNAS ▶ puna

PUNCE, -D, -S, PUNCING n kick ▷ vb kick

PUNCH, -ED, -ES, -ING vb strike at with a clenched fist ▷ n blow with a clenched fist

PUNCHBAG n stuffed bag punched for boxing training

PUNCHED ▶ punch

PUNCHEON n large cask of variable capacity, usually between 70 and 120 gallons

PUNCHER, -S ▶ punch

PUNCHES ▶ punch

PUNCHIER ▶ punchy

PUNCHILY ▶ punchy

PUNCHING ▶ punch

PUNCHOUT n fist fight

PUNCHY, PUNCHIER adj forceful

PUNCING ▶ punce

PUNCTA ▶ punctum

PUNCTATE adj having or marked with minute spots, holes, or depressions

PUNCTO, -S n tip of a fencing sword

PUNCTUAL adj arriving or taking place at the correct time

PUNCTULE n very small opening

PUNCTUM, PUNCTA n tip or small point

PUNCTURE n small hole made by a sharp object, esp in a tyre ▷ vb pierce a hole in

PUNDIT, -S n expert who speaks publicly on a subject

PUNDITIC adj of or relating to pundits

PUNDITRY n expressing of expert opinions

PUNDITS ► pundit

PUNDONOR n point of honour

PUNG, -S n horse-drawn sleigh with a boxlike body on runners

PUNGA, -S variant spelling of ► ponga

PUNGENCE n pungency

PUNGENCY ► pungent

PUNGENT adj having a strong sharp bitter flavour

PUNGLE, -D, -S, PUNGLING vb make payment

PUNGS ► pung

PUNIER ► puny

PUNIEST ► puny

PUNILY ► puny

PUNINESS ► puny

PUNISH, -ED, -ES vb cause (someone) to suffer or undergo a penalty for some wrongdoing

PUNISHER

PUNITION n punishment

PUNITIVE adj relating to punishment

PUNITORY same as ► punitive

PUNJI, -ED, -ES, -ING, -S n sharpened bamboo stick ► vb fortify with punjis

PUNK, -ER, -ERS, -EST, -S n style of rock music of the late 1970s ► adj relating to the punk movement

PUNKA, -S n fan made of a palm leaf or leaves

PUNKAH, -S same as ► punka

PUNKAS ► punka

PUNKER ► punk

PUNKERS ► punk

PUNKEST ► punk

PUNKETTE n female follower of punk music

PUNKEY, -S n small winged insect

PUNKIE, -S same as ► punkey

PUNKIER ► punky

PUNKIES ► punkie

PUNKIEST ► punky

PUNKIN, -S same as ► pumpkin

PUNKISH ► punk

PUNKS ► punk

PUNKY, PUNKIER, PUNKIEST adj of punk music

PUNNED ► pun

PUNNER, -S ► pun

PUNNET, -S n small basket for fruit

PUNNIER ► punny

PUNNIEST ► punny

PUNNING, -S ► pun

PUNNY, PUNNIER, PUNNIEST adj of puns

PUNS ► pun

PUNSTER, -S n person who is fond of making puns

PUNT, -ED, -ING, -S n open flat-bottomed boat propelled by a pole ► vb travel in a punt

PUNTEE, -S same as ► punty

PUNTER, -S n informal word for a member of the public

PUNTIES ► punty

PUNTING ► punt

PUNTO, -S n hit in fencing

PUNTS ► punt

PUNTSMAN, PUNTSMEN n man in charge of a river punt

PUNTY, PUNTIES n long iron rod used in the finishing process of glass-blowing

PUNY, PUNIER, PUNIEST adj small and feeble

PUP, -PED, -PING, -S n young of certain animals, such as dogs and seals ► vb (of dogs, seals, etc) to give birth to pups

PUPA, -E, -S n insect at the stage of development between a larva and an adult

PUPAL

PUPARIA ► puparium

PUPARIAL ► puparium

PUPARIUM, PUPARIA n case enclosing the pupae of certain insects

PUPAS ► pupa

PUPATE, -D, -S, PUPATING vb (of an insect larva) to develop into a pupa

PUPATION

PUPFISH n type of small fish

PUPIL, -S n person who is taught by a teacher

PUPILAGE same as > pupillage

PUPILAR ► pupil

PUPILARY same as > pupillary

PUPILLAR ► pupil

PUPILS ► pupil

PUPPED ► pup

PUPPET, -S n small doll or figure moved by strings or by the operator's hand

PUPPETRY n art of making and manipulating puppets and presenting puppet shows

PUPPETS ► puppet

PUPPIED ► puppy

PUPPIES ► puppy

PUPPING ► pup

PUPPODUM same as ► poppadom

PUPPY, PUPPIED, PUPPIES, -ING n young dog ► vb have puppies

PUPPYDOM n state of being a puppy

PUPPYING ► puppy

PUPPYISH ► puppy

PUPPYISM n impudence

PUPS ► pup

PUPU, -S n Hawaiian dish

PUPUNHA, -S n fruit of a type of palm tree

PUPUS ► pupu

PUR, -S same as ► purr

PURANA, -S n type of Sanskrit sacred writing

PURANIC

PURBLIND adj partly or nearly blind

PURCHASE vb obtain by payment ► n thing that is bought

PURDA, -S same as ► purdah

PURDAH, -S n Muslim and Hindu custom of keeping women in seclusion

PURDAHED

PURDAS ► purda

PURE, -D, -R, -S, -ST, PURING adj unmixed, untainted ► vb make pure

PUREBRED adj denoting a pure strain obtained through many generations of controlled breeding ► n purebred animal

PURED ► pure

PUREE, -D, -ING, -S n smooth thick pulp of cooked and sieved fruit, vegetables, meat, or fish ► vb make (cooked foods) into a puree

PURELY adv in a pure manner

PURENESS ► pure

PURER ► pure

PURES ► pure

PUREST ► pure

PURFLE, -D, -S n ruffled or curved ornamental band ► vb decorate with such a band or bands

PURFLER -S

PURFLING same as ► purfle

PURFLY ► purfle

PURGE, -D, -S vb rid (a thing or place) of (unwanted things or people) ► n purging

PURGER -S

PURGING, -S ► purge

PURI, -S n unleavened flaky Indian bread, that is deep-fried in ghee and served hot

PURIFIED ► purify

PURIFIER n device or substance that frees something of extraneous, contaminating, or debasing matter

PURIFY, PURIFIED, PURIFIES vb make or become pure

PURIN, -S same as ▸ **purine**

PURINE n colourless crystalline solid that can be prepared from uric acid

PURING ▸ **pure**

PURINS ▸ **purin**

PURIRI, -S n forest tree of New Zealand

PURIS ▸ **puri**

PURISM, -S n strict insistence on the correct usage or style
PURIST -S
PURISTIC

PURITAN, -S n person who follows strict moral or religious principles ▷ adj of or like a puritan

PURITY, PURITIES n state or quality of being pure

PURL, -ED, -S n stitch made by knitting a plain stitch backwards ▷ vb knit in purl

PURLER, -S n headlong or spectacular fall

PURLICUE vb finish a pen stroke with a flourish

PURLIEU, -S, -X n land on the edge of a royal forest

PURLIN, -S n horizontal beam that supports the rafters of a roof

PURLINE, -S same as ▸ **purlin**

PURLING, -S ▸ **purl**

PURLINS ▸ **purlin**

PURLOIN, -S vb steal

PURLS ▸ **purl**

PURPIE, -S old Scots word for ▸ **purslane**

PURPLE, -D, -R, -S, -ST, PURPLING n colour between red and blue ▷ adj of a colour between red and blue ▷ vb make purple

PURPLY ▸ **purple**

PURPLING ▸ **purple**

PURPLISH ▸ **purple**

PURPLY, PURPLIER ▸ **purple**

PURPORT, -S vb claim (to be or do something) ▷ n apparent meaning, significance

PURPOSE, -D, -S n reason for which something is done or exists

PURPURA, -S n blood disease causing purplish spots

PURPURE, -S n purple

PURPURIC ▸ **purpura**

PURPURIN n red crystalline compound used as a stain for biological specimens

PURPY variant of ▸ **purpie**

PURR, -ED, -S vb (of cats) make low vibrant sound, usu when pleased ▷ n this sound

PURRING -S

PURS ▸ **pur**

PURSE, -D, -S, PURSING n small bag for money ▷ vb draw (one's lips) together into a small round shape

PURSEFUL n that which can be contained in purse

PURSER, -S n ship's officer who keeps the accounts

PURSES ▸ **purse**

PURSEW, -ED, -S archaic spelling of ▸ **pursue**

PURSIER ▸ **pursy**

PURSIEST ▸ **pursy**

PURSILY ▸ **pursy**

PURSING ▸ **purse**

PURSLAIN same as ▸ **purslane**

PURSLANE n weedy plant used in salads

PURSUAL, -S n act of pursuit

PURSUANT adj in agreement or conformity

PURSUE, -D, -S, PURSUING vb chase

PURSUER -S

PURSUIT, -S n pursuing

PURSY, PURSIER, PURSIEST adj short-winded

PURTIER ▸ **purty**

PURTIEST ▸ **purty**

PURTRAID variant of ▸ **purtrayd**

PURTRAYD adj archaic spelling of portrayed

PURTY, PURTIER, PURTIEST adj pretty

PURULENT adj of or containing pus

PURVEY, -ED, -S vb supply (provisions) ▷ n food and drink laid on at a wedding reception, etc

PURVEYOR n person, organization, etc, that supplies food and provisions

PURVEYS ▸ **purvey**

PURVIEW, -S n scope or range of activity or outlook

PUS, -ES n yellowish matter produced by infected tissue

PUSH, -ES vb move or try to move by steady force ▷ n act of pushing

PUSHBACK n negative or unfavourable response

PUSHBALL n game in which two teams try to push a

heavy ball towards opposite goals

PUSHBIKE n pedal-driven bicycle

PUSHCART n handcart, typically having two wheels and a canvas roof, used esp by street vendors

PUSHDOWN n list in which the last item added is at the top

PUSHED adj short of

PUSHER, -S n person who or thing that pushes

PUSHES ▸ **push**

PUSHFUL ▸ **push**

PUSHIER ▸ **pushy**

PUSHIEST ▸ **pushy**

PUSHILY ▸ **pushy**

PUSHING prep almost or nearly (a certain age, speed, etc) ▷ adj aggressively ambitious ▷ adv almost or nearly (a certain age, speed, etc)

PUSHOVER n something easily achieved

PUSHPIN, -S n pin with a small ball-shaped head

PUSHPIT, -S n safety rail at the stern of a boat

PUSHROD, -S n metal rod transmitting motion in an engine

PUSHUP, -S n exercise in which the body is raised and lowered to the floor by the arms

PUSHY, PUSHIER, PUSHIEST adj too assertive or ambitious

PUSLE, -D, -S, PUSLING old spelling of ▸ **puzzle**

PUSLEY, -S same as ▸ **purslane**

PUSLIKE ▸ **pus**

PUSLING ▸ **pusle**

PUSS, -ES same as ▸ **pussy**

PUSSEL, -S n girl

PUSSER, -S n naval purser

PUSSES ▸ **puss**

PUSSIER ▸ **pussy**

PUSSIES ▸ **pussy**

PUSSIEST ▸ **pussy**

PUSSLEY, -S n weedy trailing herb

PUSSLIES ▸ **pussly**

PUSSLIKE ▸ **puss**

PUSSLY, PUSSLIES variant of ▸ **pussley**

PUSSY, PUSSIER, PUSSIES, PUSSIEST n cat ▷ adj containing or full of pus

PUSSYCAT same as ▸ **pussy**

PUSTULAR ▸ **pustule**

P

PUSTULE, -S n pimple containing pus
PUSTULED
PUT, -S vb cause to be (in a position, state, or place) ▷ n throw in putting the shot
PUTAMEN, -S, PUTAMINA n hard endocarp or stone of fruit
PUTATIVE adj reputed, supposed
PUTCHEON n trap for catching salmon
PUTCHER, -S n trap for catching salmon
PUTCHOCK same as ▸ **pachak**
PUTCHUK, -S same as ▸ **pachak**
PUTDOWN, -S n snub or insult
PUTEAL, -S n enclosure around a well
PUTELI, -S n (in India) type of boat
PUTID adj having an unpleasant odour
PUTLOCK, -S same as ▸ **putlog**
PUTLOG, -S n short horizontal beam that with others supports the floor planks of a scaffold
PUTOFF, -S n pretext or delay
PUTOIS n brush to paint pottery
PUTON, -S n hoax or piece of mockery
PUTOUT, -S n baseball play in which the batter or runner is put out
PUTREFY vb rot and produce an offensive smell
PUTRID, -ER adj rotten and foul-smelling
PUTRIDLY
PUTS ▸ put
PUTSCH, -ES n sudden violent attempt to remove a government from power
PUTT, -ED, -S n stroke on the putting green to roll the ball into or near the hole ▷ vb strike (the ball) in this way
PUTTEE, -S n strip of cloth worn wound around the leg
PUTTEN old Scots past participle of ▸ **put**
PUTTER, -ED, -S n golf club for putting ▷ vb busy oneself in a desultory though agreeable manner
PUTTERER
PUTTI ▸ putto
PUTTIE same as ▸ **puttee**
PUTTIED ▸ putty

PUTTIER, -S n glazier
PUTTIES ▸ putty
PUTTING, -S ▸ put
PUTTO, PUTTI n representation of a small boy
PUTTOCK, -S n type of bird of prey
PUTTS ▸ putt
PUTTY, PUTTIED, PUTTIES, -ING n stiff paste of whiting and linseed oil ▷ vb fill, fix, or coat with putty
PUTURE, -S n claim of foresters for food
PUTZ, -ED, -ES, -ING n despicable or stupid person ▷ vb waste time
PUY, -S n small volcanic cone
PUZEL, -S same as ▸ **pucelle**
PUZZEL, -S same as ▸ **pucelle**
PUZZLE, -D, -S vb perplex and confuse or be perplexed or confused ▷ n problem that cannot be easily solved
PUZZLER, -S n person or thing that puzzles
PUZZLES ▸ puzzle
PUZZLING ▸ puzzle
PWN, -ED, -ING, -S vb defeat (an opponent) in conclusive and humiliating fashion
PYA, -S n monetary unit of Myanmar worth one hundredth of a kyat
PYAEMIA, -S n blood poisoning with pus-forming microorganisms in the blood
PYAEMIC
PYAS ▸ pya
PYAT, -S n magpie ▷ adj pied
PYCNIC same as ▸ **pyknic**
PYCNIDIA ▸ pycnidium
PYCNITE, -S n variety of topaz
PYCNON, -S old word for ▸ **semitone**
PYCNOSIS, PYCNOSES n process of shrinking in a cell nucleus
PYCNOTIC
PYE, -ING, -S same as ▸ **pie**
PYEBALD, -S same as ▸ **piebald**
PYEING ▸ pye
PYELITIC ▸ pyelitis
PYELITIS n inflammation of the pelvis of the kidney
PYEMIA, -S same as ▸ **pyaemia**
PYEMIC ▸ pyaemia
PYENGADU variant of ▸ **pyinkado**
PYES ▸ pye
PYET, -S same as ▸ **pyat**
PYGAL, -S n rear part
PYGARG, -S n type of horned mammal

PYGARGUS n white-tailed bird of prey
PYGIDIA ▸ pygidium
PYGIDIAL ▸ pygidium
PYGIDIUM, PYGIDIA n terminal division in certain invertebrates
PYGMAEAN ▸ pygmy
PYGMEAN ▸ pygmy
PYGMIES ▸ pygmy
PYGMOID, -S adj of or like pygmies ▷ n pygmy
PYGMY, PYGMIES n something that is a very small example of its type ▷ adj very small
PYGMYISH
PYGMYISM
PYIC adj relating to pus
PYIN, -S n constituent of pus
PYINKADO n leguminous tree native to India and Myanmar
PYINS ▸ pyin
PYJAMA same as ▸ **pyjamas**
PYJAMAED ▸ pyjamas
PYJAMAS pl n loose-fitting trousers and top worn in bed
PYKNIC, -S adj characterized by a broad squat fleshy physique ▷ n person with this physical type
PYKNOSIS, PYKNOSES n thickening of a cell
PYKNOTIC
PYLON, -S n steel tower-like structure supporting electrical cables
PYLORI ▸ pylorus
PYLORIC ▸ pylorus
PYLORUS, PYLORI n small circular opening at the base of the stomach
PYNE, -D, -S, PYNING archaic variant of ▸ **pine**
PYODERMA n any skin eruption characterized by pustules or the formation of pus
PYOGENIC adj of or relating to the formation of pus
PYOID adj resembling pus
PYONER, -S old variant of ▸ **pioneer**
PYONINGS n old term for the work of pioneers
PYORRHEA same as ▸ **pyorrhoea**
PYOSIS, PYOSES n formation of pus
PYOT, -S same as ▸ **pyat**
PYRAL ▸ pyre
PYRALID, -S n tropical moth
PYRALIS same as ▸ **pyralid**
PYRAMID, -S n solid figure with a flat base and

triangular sides sloping upwards to a point ▷ vb build up or be arranged in the form of a pyramid
PYRAMIS n pyramid-shaped structure
PYRAN, -S n unsaturated heterocyclic organic compound
PYRANOID
PYRANOSE n structure in many sugars
PYRANS ► **pyran**
PYRAZOLE n crystalline soluble basic heterocyclic compound
PYRE, -S n pile of wood for burning a corpse on
PYRENE, -S n solid polynuclear aromatic hydrocarbon extracted from coal tar
PYRENOID n any of various small protein granules that occur in certain algae
PYRES ► **pyre**
PYRETIC adj of, relating to, or characterized by fever
PYREX, -ES n tradename for glass used in cookery and chemical apparatus
PYREXIA, -S technical name for ► **fever**
PYREXIAL
PYREXIC
PYRIC adj of or relating to burning
PYRIDIC ► **pyridine**
PYRIDINE n colourless hygroscopic liquid with a characteristic odour
PYRIFORM adj (esp of organs of the body) pear-shaped
PYRITE n yellow mineral consisting of iron sulphide in cubic crystalline form
PYRITES same as ► **pyrite**
PYRITIC ► **pyrite**

PYRITISE same as ► **pyritize**
PYRITIZE vb convert into pyrites
PYRITOUS ► **pyrite**
PYRO, -S n pyromaniac
PYROGEN, -S n any of a group of substances that cause a rise in temperature in an animal body
PYROGY, PYROGIES same as ► **pierogi**
PYROHY, PYROHIES same as ► **perogi**
PYROLA, -S n evergreen perennial
PYROLISE same as ► **pyrolize**
PYROLIZE vb subject to pyrolysis
PYROLOGY n study of heat
PYROLYSE vb subject to pyrolysis
PYROLYZE same as ► **pyrolyse**
PYRONE, -S n type of heterocyclic compound
PYRONIN, -S n red dye used as a biological stain
PYRONINE same as ► **pyronin**
PYRONINS ► **pyronin**
PYROPE, -S n deep yellowish-red garnet used as a gemstone
PYROPUS variant of ► **pyrope**
PYROS ► **pyro**
PYROSIS, PYROSES technical name for > **heartburn**
PYROSOME n tube-shaped glowing marine creature
PYROSTAT n device that activates an alarm or extinguisher in the event of a fire
PYROXENE n silicate mineral
PYROXYLE same as > **pyroxylin**

PYRRHIC, -S n metrical foot of two short or unstressed syllables ▷ adj of or relating to such a metrical foot
PYRRHOUS adj ruddy or reddish
PYRROL, -S same as ► **pyrrole**
PYRROLE, -S n colourless insoluble toxic liquid
PYRROLIC
PYRROLS ► **pyrrol**
PYRUVATE n ester or salt of pyruvic acid
PYRUVIC adj as in **pyruvic acid** colourless pleasant-smelling liquid
PYSANKA, PYSANKY n hand-painted Ukrainian Easter egg
PYTHIUM, -S n type of fungi
PYTHON, -S n large nonpoisonous snake that crushes its prey
PYTHONIC
PYURIA, -S n any condition characterized by the presence of pus in the urine
PYX, -ED, -ES, -ING n any receptacle for the Eucharistic Host ▷ vb put (something) in a pyx

This word can also be spelt **pix**. It's a great word to know as it can earn a good score from a rack that is short of vowels.

PYXIDES ► **pyxis**
PYXIDIUM, PYXIDIA n dry fruit of such plants as the plantain
PYXIE, -S n creeping evergreen shrub of the eastern US
PYXING ► **pyx**
PYXIS, PYXIDES same as ► **pyxidium**
PZAZZ, -ES same as ► **pizzazz**

P

Qq

With a value of 10 points, **Q** can help you to achieve some good scores, but it can also be a very awkward tile, making it difficult to get bonus words scoring that extra 50 points, and you will normally want to play it off quickly. Often you will not have a **U** to go with it, so it's a good idea to remember the short words beginning with **Q** that don't need a **U**. This is easy, as there's only one two-letter word starting with **Q**: **qi** (11 points). There are four three-letter words, only one of which needs a **U**: **qua** (12). The other three are **qat, qin** and **qis** (12 each). If you do have a **U**, remember **quiz** (22), which is a very useful word, and can take an **S** at the front to make **squiz**. Don't forget **quartz** (24) either, or the useful **suq** (12 points) that is easily overlooked.

QABALA, -S *same as*
► **kabbalah**
QABALAH, -S *same as*
► **kabbalah**
QABALAS ► **qabala**
QABALISM ► **qabalah**
QABALIST ► **qabalah**
QADI, -S *variant spelling of*
► **cadi**
QAID, -S *n* chief

> An Arabic word, this and its variant **qadi** are two of the most frequently played words in Scrabble. There are also alternative spellings **cadi, caid, kadi** and **kaid**.

QAIMAQAM *n* Turkish officer or official
QAJAQ, -S *n* kayak
QALAMDAN *n* writing case
QAMUTIK, -S *n* sled with wooden runners
QANAT, -S *n* underground irrigation channel

> This word comes up many times as one of the words allowing you to play the Q without a U.

QASIDA, -S *n* Arabic verse form
QAT, -S *variant spelling of*
► **khat**

> The leaves of this shrub are chewed as a stimulant, and it's certainly been a stimulus for Scrabble, being one of the three three-letter words that can be played without a U: the others are **qin** and **qis**.

QAWWAL, -S *n* qawwali singer
QAWWALI, -S *n* Islamic religious song, esp in Asia
QAWWALS ► **qawwal**
QI, -S *n* vital energy
QIBLA, -S *variant of*
► **kiblah**

> The direction in which Muslims turn to pray, a useful word allowing the Q to be played without the U. It can also be spelt **keblah, kibla** and **kiblah**.

QIGONG, -S *n* system of breathing and exercise
QIN, -S *n* Chinese stringed instrument related to the zither

> This Chinese musical instrument is another indispensable word as, like **qat**, it combines Q with two of the most common letters in the game.

QINDAR, -KA, -S *n* Albanian monetary unit
QINS ► **qin**
QINTAR, -KA, -S *same as*
► **qindar**
QIS ► **qi**
QIVIUT, -S *n* soft muskox wool
QOPH, -S *variant of* ► **koph**

> A letter of the Hebrew alphabet, also spelt **koph**. The Hebrew alphabet, like the Greek alphabet, is well worth studying from the Scrabble point of view, as it gives us many other useful short words like **ayin, beth, heth, kaph** and **lamedh**.

QORMA, -S *variant spelling of*
► **korma**
QUA *prep* in the capacity of

> This is the only three-letter word beginning with Q that needs a U. It is played so often that it is well worth mastering all the hooks to this: it takes A at the front to make **aqua** and D, G, I, T and Y at the back to make **quad, quag, quai, quat** and **quay**.

QUAALUDE *n* methaqualone
QUACK, -ED, -ING, -S *vb* (of a duck) utter a harsh guttural sound ▷ *n* unqualified person who claims medical knowledge
QUACKER -S
QUACKERY *n* activities or methods of a quack
QUACKIER ► **quacky**
QUACKING ► **quack**
QUACKISH ► **quack**
QUACKISM *same as*
► **quackery**
QUACKLE, -D, -S *same as*
► **quack**
QUACKS ► **quack**
QUACKY, QUACKIER
► **quack**
QUAD, -S *n* quadrangle
QUADDED *adj* formed of multiple quads

QUADDING n birdwatching in a specified area

QUADPLAY same as ► **fourplay**

QUADPLEX n apartment on four floors

QUADRANS n Roman coin

QUADRANT n quarter of a circle

QUADRAT, -S n area marked out for study of the plants in the surrounding area

QUADRATE n cube or square, or a square or cubelike object ▷ vb make square or rectangular ▷ adj of or relating to this bone

QUADRATI > **quadratus**

QUADRATS ► **quadrat**

QUADRIC, -S adj having or characterized by an equation of the second degree ▷ n quadric curve, surface, or function

QUADRIGA n (in the classical world) a two-wheeled chariot drawn by four horses abreast

QUADS ► **quad**

QUAERE, -D, -S n query or question ▷ interj ask or inquire ▷ vb ask

QUAESTOR n any of several magistrates of ancient Rome, usually a financial administrator

QUAFF, -ED, -ING, -S vb drink heartily or in one draught **QUAFFER -S**

QUAG, -S another word for ► **quagmire**

QUAGGA, -S n recently extinct zebra

QUAGGY, QUAGGIER adj resembling a marsh or quagmire

QUAGMIRE n soft wet area of land ▷ vb bog down **QUAGMIRY**

QUAGS ► **quag**

QUAHAUG, -S same as ► **quahog**

QUAHOG, -S n edible clam

QUAI, -S same as ► **quay**

QUAICH, -ES, -S n small shallow drinking cup

QUAIGH, -S same as ► **quaich**

QUAIL, -ED, -ING, -S n small game bird of the partridge family ▷ vb shrink back with fear

QUAINT, -ER adj attractively unusual, esp in an old-fashioned style **QUAINTLY**

QUAIR, -S n book

QUAIS ► **quai**

QUAKE, -D, -S, QUAKING, QUAKINGS vb shake or tremble with or as if with fear ▷ n earthquake

QUAKER -S

QUAKIER ► **quaky**

QUAKIEST ► **quaky**

QUAKILY ► **quaky**

QUAKING ► **quake**

QUAKINGS ► **quake**

QUAKY, QUAKIER, QUAKIEST adj inclined to quake

QUALE, QUALIA n essential property or quality

QUALIFY vb provide or be provided with the abilities necessary

QUALITY n degree or standard of excellence ▷ adj excellent or superior

QUALM, -S n pang of conscience

QUALMIER ► **qualmy**

QUALMING adj having a qualm ▷ n state of having a qualm

QUALMISH ► **qualm**

QUALMS ► **qualm**

QUALMY, QUALMIER ► **qualm**

QUAMASH another name for ► **camass**

QUANDANG same as ► **quandong**

QUANDARY n difficult situation or dilemma

QUANDONG n small Australian tree with edible fruit and nuts used in preserves

QUANGO, -S n partly independent official body set up by a government

QUANNET, -S n flat file with handle at one end

QUANT, -ED, -ING, -S n long pole for propelling a boat ▷ vb propel (a boat) with a quant

QUANTA ► **quantum**

QUANTAL adj of or relating to a quantum or an entity that is quantized

QUANTED ► **quant**

QUANTIC, -S n mathematical function

QUANTIFY vb discover or express the quantity of

QUANTILE n element of a division

QUANTING ► **quant**

QUANTISE same as ► **quantize**

QUANTITY n specified or definite amount or number

QUANTIZE vb restrict (a physical quantity) to one of a set of values characterized by quantum numbers

QUANTONG same as ► **quandong**

QUANTS ► **quant**

QUANTUM, QUANTA, -S n desired or required amount ▷ adj of or designating a major breakthrough

QUARE, -R, -ST adj remarkable or strange

QUARK, -S n subatomic particle thought to be the fundamental unit of matter

This subatomic particle appears in the Scrabble cloud-chamber fairly often, and when it does, remember that you can put an S on the front of it to make **squark**.

QUARREL, -S n angry disagreement ▷ vb have a disagreement or dispute

QUARRIAN n cockatiel of scrub and woodland regions of inland Australia

QUARRIED ► **quarry**

QUARRIER another word for > **quarryman**

QUARRIES ► **quarry**

QUARRION same as ► **quarrian**

QUARRY, QUARRIED, QUARRIES n place where stone is dug from the surface of the earth ▷ vb extract (stone) from a quarry

QUART, -S n unit of liquid measure equal to two pints (1.136 litres)

QUARTAN, -S adj (esp of a malarial fever) occurring every third day ▷ n quartan malaria

QUARTE, -S n fourth of eight basic positions from which a parry or attack can be made in fencing

QUARTER n one of four equal parts of something ▷ vb divide into four equal parts ▷ adj being or consisting of one of four equal parts

QUARTERN n fourth part of certain weights or measures, such as a peck or a pound

QUARTERS pl n accommodation, esp as provided for military personnel

Q

QUARTES ▸ quarte
QUARTET, -S n group of four performers
QUARTETT same as ▸ **quartet**
QUARTIC, -S n biquadratic equation
QUARTIER n city district
QUARTILE n one of three values of a variable dividing its distribution into four groups with equal frequencies ▷ adj of a quartile
QUARTO, -S n book size in which the sheets are folded into four leaves
QUARTS ▸ quart
QUARTZ, -ES n hard glossy mineral
QUARTZY
QUASAR, -S n extremely distant starlike object that emits powerful radio waves
QUASH, -ED, -ES, -ING vb annul or make void
QUASHER -S
QUASI adv as if
QUASS, -ES variant of ▸ **kvass**
QUASSIA, -S n tropical American tree
QUASSIN, -S n bitter crystalline substance
QUAT, -S, -TED, -TING n spot ▷ vb beat down or squash
QUATCH, -ED, -ES vb move
QUATE, -S n fortune
QUATORZE n cards worth 14 points in piquet
QUATRAIN n stanza or poem of four lines
QUATRE, -S n playing card with four pips
QUATS ▸ quat
QUATTED ▸ quat
QUATTING ▸ quat
QUAVER, -ED, -S vb (of a voice) quiver or tremble ▷ n note half the length of a crotchet
QUAVERER
QUAVERY
QUAY, -S n wharf built parallel to the shore
QUAYAGE, -S n system of quays
QUAYD archaic past participle of ▸ **quail**
Meaning daunted, this Spenserian word makes a surprising hook for **quay**.

QUAYLIKE ▸ quay
QUAYS ▸ quay
QUAYSIDE n edge of a quay along the water

QUAZZY, QUAZZIER adj unwell
QUBIT, -S n quantum bit
QUBYTE, -S n unit of eight qubits
QUEACH, -ES n thicket
QUEACHY adj unwell
QUEAN, -S n Scots word for a young unmarried woman
QUEASIER ▸ queasy
QUEASILY ▸ queasy
QUEASY, QUEASIER adj having the feeling that one is about to vomit
QUEAZY, QUEAZIER same as ▸ **queasy**
QUEBEC, -S n code word for the letter Q
QUEECHY same as ▸ **queachy**
QUEEN, -ED, -ING, -S n female sovereign who is the official ruler or head of state ▷ vb crown as queen
QUEENCUP n type of flowering plant
QUEENDOM n territory, state, people, or community ruled over by a queen
QUEENED ▸ queen
QUEENIE, -S n scallop
QUEENIER ▸ queeny
QUEENIES ▸ queenie
QUEENING ▸ queen
QUEENITE n supporter of a queen
QUEENLET n queen of a small realm
QUEENLY adj resembling or appropriate to a queen ▷ adv in a manner appropriate to a queen
QUEENS ▸ queen
QUEENY, QUEENIER adj resembling a queen
QUEER, -ED, -ER, -EST, -ING, -S adj not normal or usual ▷ vb spoil or thwart
QUEERISH
QUEERITY
QUEERLY
QUEEST, -S n wood pigeon
QUEINT same as ▸ **quaint**
QUELCH, -ED, -ES same as ▸ **squelch**
QUELEA, -S n East African weaver bird
QUELL, -ED, -ING, -S vb suppress
QUELLER -S
QUEME, -D, -S, QUEMING vb please
QUENA, -S n Andean flute
QUENCH, -ED, -ES vb satisfy (one's thirst)
QUENCHER

QUENELLE n finely sieved mixture of cooked meat or fish shaped into various forms
QUEP interj expression of derision
QUERCINE adj of or relating to oak trees
QUERIDA, -S n sweetheart
QUERIED ▸ query
QUERIER, -S ▸ query
QUERIES ▸ query
QUERIST, -S n person who makes inquiries or queries
QUERN, -S n stone hand mill for grinding corn
QUERY, QUERIED, QUERIES, -ING n question, esp one raising doubt ▷ vb express uncertainty, doubt, or an objection
QUEST, -ED, -S n long and difficult search ▷ vb go in search of
QUESTANT n one who quests
QUESTED ▸ quest
QUESTER, -S ▸ quest
QUESTING ▸ quest
QUESTION n form of words addressed to a person in order to obtain an answer ▷ vb put a question or questions to (a person)
QUESTOR, -S same as ▸ **quaestor**
QUESTS ▸ quest
QUETCH, -ED, -ES vb move
QUETHE, -S, QUETHING vb say
QUETSCH n plum brandy
QUETZAL, -S n crested bird of Central and N South America

This is a great word if you can get the tiles for it, so it's well worth remembering both spellings – it can also be **quezal** – and the four plural forms, which are **quetzals** or **quetzales** and **quezals** or **quezales**.

QUEUE, -D, -ING, -S, QUEUING, QUEUINGS n line of people or vehicles waiting for something ▷ vb form or remain in a line while waiting
QUEUER -S
QUEY, -S n young cow
QUEYN, -S n girl
QUEYNIE, -S same as ▸ **queyn**
QUEYNS ▸ queyn
QUEYS ▸ quey
QUEZAL, -ES, -S same as ▸ **quetzal**

QUIBBLE, -D, -S vb make trivial objections ▷ n trivial objection
QUIBBLER
QUIBLIN, -S same as ▸ quibble
QUICH, -ED, -ING vb move
QUICHE, -S n savoury flan with an egg custard filling
QUICHED ▸ quich
QUICHES ▸ quiche
QUICHING ▸ quich
QUICK, -ER, -EST, -S adj speedy, fast ▷ n area of sensitive flesh under a nail ▷ adv in a rapid manner
QUICKEN, -S vb make or become faster ▷ n rowan tree
QUICKER ▸ quick
QUICKEST ▸ quick
QUICKIE, -S n anything done or made hurriedly ▷ adj made or done rapidly
QUICKLY ▸ quick
QUICKS ▸ quick
QUICKSET adj (of plants or cuttings) planted so as to form a hedge ▷ n hedge composed of such plants
QUICKY same as ▸ quickie
QUID, -S n pound (sterling)
QUIDAM, -S n specified person
QUIDDANY n quince jelly ▷ vb make into quince jelly
QUIDDIT, -S same as ▸ quiddity
QUIDDITY n essential nature of something
QUIDDLE, -D, -S vb waste time
QUIDDLER
QUIDNUNC n person eager to learn news and scandal
QUIDS ▸ quid
QUIESCE, -D, -S vb quieten
QUIET, -ED, -ER, -ERS, -EST, -ING, -S adj with little noise ▷ n quietness ▷ vb make or become quiet
QUIETEN, -S vb make or become quiet
QUIETER ▸ quiet
QUIETERS ▸ quiet
QUIETEST ▸ quiet
QUIETING ▸ quiet
QUIETISM n passivity and calmness of mind towards external events
QUIETIST
QUIETIVE n sedative drug
QUIETLY ▸ quiet
QUIETS ▸ quiet
QUIETUDE n quietness, peace, or tranquillity

QUIETUS n release from life
QUIFF, -S n tuft of hair brushed up above the forehead
QUIFFED adj having a quiff
QUIFFS ▸ quiff
QUIGHT, -ED, -S vb quit
QUILL, -ED, -S n pen made from the feather of a bird's wing or tail ▷ vb wind (thread, yarn, etc) onto a spool or bobbin
QUILLAI, -S another name for ▸ soapbark
QUILLAIA same as ▸ quillai
QUILLAIS ▸ quillai
QUILLAJA same as ▸ quillai
QUILLED ▸ quill
QUILLET, -S n quibble or subtlety
QUILLING n craftwork in which material is formed into small bands that form the basis of a design
QUILLMAN, QUILLMEN n clerk
QUILLON, -S n either half of the extended crosspiece of a sword or dagger
QUILLOW, -S n quilt folded to make a pillow
QUILLS ▸ quill
QUILT, -ED, -S n padded covering for a bed ▷ vb stitch together two layers of (fabric) with padding between them
QUILTER, -S
QUILTING n material used for making a quilt
QUILTS ▸ quilt
QUIN, -S n short for quintuplet
QUINA, -S n quinine
QUINARY adj consisting of fives or by fives ▷ n set of five
QUINAS ▸ quina
QUINATE adj arranged in or composed of five parts
QUINCE, -S n acid-tasting pear-shaped fruit
QUINCHE, -D, -S vb move
QUINCUNX n five objects arranged in the shape of a rectangle with the fifth in the centre
QUINE, -S variant of ▸ quean
QUINELA, -S same as ▸ quinella
QUINELLA n form of betting in which the punter bets on selecting the first and second place-winners in any order
QUINES ▸ quine
QUINIC adj as in quinic acid white crystalline soluble

optically active carboxylic acid
QUINIE, -S n girl
QUINIELA same as ▸ quinella
QUINIES ▸ quinie
QUININ, -S same as ▸ quinine
QUININA, -S same as ▸ quinine
QUININE, -S n bitter drug used as a tonic and formerly to treat malaria
QUININS ▸ quinin
QUINNAT, -S n Pacific salmon
QUINO, -S same as ▸ keno
QUINOA, -S n type of grain high in nutrients
QUINOID, -S same as > quinonoid
QUINOL, -S n white crystalline soluble phenol used as a photographic developer
QUINOLIN same as > quinoline
QUINOLS ▸ quinol
QUINONE, -S n yellow crystalline water-soluble unsaturated ketone
QUINOS ▸ quino
QUINS ▸ quin
QUINSIED ▸ quinsy
QUINSY, QUINSIES n inflammation of the throat or tonsils
QUINT, -S same as ▸ quin
QUINTA, -S n Portuguese vineyard where grapes for wine or port are grown
QUINTAIN n post or target set up for tilting exercises for mounted knights or foot soldiers
QUINTAL, -S n unit of weight
QUINTAN, -S adj (of a fever) occurring every fourth day ▷ n quintan fever
QUINTAR, -S n Albanian unit of currency
QUINTAS ▸ quinta
QUINTE, -S n fifth of eight basic positions from which a parry or attack can be made in fencing
QUINTET, -S n group of five performers
QUINTETT same as ▸ quintet
QUINTIC, -S adj of or relating to the fifth degree ▷ n mathematical function
QUINTILE n aspect of 72° between two heavenly bodies

Q

QUINTIN, -S *same as*
▸ **quintain**

QUINTS ▸ **quint**

QUINZE, -S *n* card game
where players aim to score 15

> Deriving from the French
> word for fifteen, this makes
> a high-scoring word that
> you may well get to play,
> and if you can use all your
> tiles to form the plural, you'll
> get a 50-point bonus.

QUINZHEE *n* shelter made
from hollowed-out snow

QUINZIE, -S *same as*
▸ **quinzhee**

QUIP, -PED, -PING, -S *n* witty
saying ▷ *vb* make a quip

QUIPO, -S *same as* ▸ **quipu**

QUIPPED ▸ **quip**

QUIPPER, -S ▸ **quip**

QUIPPIER ▸ **quippy**

QUIPPING ▸ **quip**

QUIPPISH ▸ **quip**

QUIPPU, -S *same as* ▸ **quipu**

QUIPPY, QUIPPIER ▸ **quip**

QUIPS ▸ **quip**

QUIPSTER *n* person inclined
to make sarcastic or witty
remarks

QUIPU, -S *n* device of
the Incas used to record
information using knotted
cords

QUIRE, -D, -S, QUIRING *n* set
of 24 or 25 sheets of paper
▷ *vb* arrange in quires

QUIRK, -ED, -ING, -S *n*
peculiarity of character ▷ *vb*
quip

QUIRKIER ▸ **quirky**

QUIRKILY ▸ **quirk**

QUIRKING ▸ **quirk**

QUIRKISH ▸ **quirk**

QUIRKS ▸ **quirk**

QUIRKY, QUIRKIER
▸ **quirk**

QUIRT, -ED, -ING, -S *n* whip
with a leather thong at one
end ▷ *vb* strike with a quirt

QUISLING *n* traitor who aids
an occupying enemy force

QUIST, -S *n* wood pigeon

QUIT, -S, -TED, -TING *vb* stop
(doing something) ▷ *adj* free
(from)

QUITCH, -ED, -ES *vb* move

QUITE, -D, -S, QUITING
archaic form of ▸ **quit**

QUITRENT *n* former rent
payable by a freeholder to his
lord that released him from
performing services

QUITS ▸ **quit**

QUITTAL, -S *n* repayment
of an action with a similar
action

QUITTED ▸ **quit**

QUITTER, -S *n* person who
lacks perseverance

QUITTING ▸ **quit**

QUITTOR, -S *n* infection of
the cartilages on the side of a
horse's foot

QUIVER, -ED, -S *vb* shake
with a tremulous movement
▷ *n* shaking or trembling

QUIVERER

QUIVERY

QUIXOTE, -S *n* impractical
idealist

> Using the Q and X, this word
> for an impractical dreamer
> has a reasonable chance of
> coming up, so keeping an
> eye open for it is not that
> quixotic!

QUIXOTIC *adj* romantic and
unrealistic

QUIXOTRY ▸ **quixote**

QUIZ, -ZED, -ZES, -ZING *n*
entertainment in which the
knowledge of the players
is tested by a series of
questions ▷ *vb* investigate
by close questioning

QUIZZER -S

QUIZZERY ▸ **quiz**

QUIZZES ▸ **quiz**

QUIZZIFY ▸ **quiz**

QUIZZING ▸ **quiz**

QULLIQ, -S *n* type of oil lamp
used by Inuit people

QUOAD *adv* as far as

QUOD, -DED, -DING, -S *n* jail
▷ *vb* say

QUODLIN, -S *n* cooking apple

QUODS ▸ **quod**

QUOHOG, -S *n* edible clam

QUOIF, -ED, -ING, -S *vb*
arrange (the hair)

QUOIN, -ED, -ING, -S *n*
external corner of a building
▷ *vb* wedge

QUOIST, -S *n* wood pigeon

QUOIT, -ED, -ING *n* large ring
used in the game of quoits
▷ *vb* throw as a quoit

QUOITER -S

QUOITS *n* game in which
quoits are tossed at a stake in
the ground

QUOKKA, -S *n*
small Australian wallaby

QUOLL, -S *n* Australian
catlike carnivorous
marsupial

QUOMODO, -S *n* manner

QUONDAM *adj* of an earlier
time

QUONK, -ED, -ING, -S *vb*
make an accidental noise
while broadcasting

QUOOKE *archaic past
participle of* ▸ **quake**

QUOP, -PED, -PING, -S *vb*
pulsate or throb

QUORATE *adj* having or being
a quorum

QUORUM, -S *n* minimum
number of people required to
be present at a meeting

QUOTA, -S *n* share that is due
from, due to, or allocated to a
group or person

QUOTABLE *adj* apt or suitable
for quotation

QUOTABLY

QUOTAS ▸ **quota**

QUOTE, -D, -S, QUOTING
vb repeat (words) exactly
▷ *n* quotation ▷ *interj*
expression used to indicate
that the words that follow
form a quotation

QUOTER -S

QUOTH *vb* said

QUOTHA *interj* expression of
mild sarcasm, used in picking
up a word or phrase used by
someone else

QUOTIENT *n* result of the
division of one number or
quantity by another

QUOTING ▸ **quote**

QUOTUM, -S *same as*
▸ **quota**

QURSH, -ES *same as*
▸ **qurush**

QURUSH, -ES *n* former
Saudi Arabian currency
unit

QUYTE, -D, -S, QUYTING
same as ▸ **quit**

QWERTY, QWERTIES, -S *n*
standard English-language
typewriter or computer
keyboard

Q

Rr

R is one of the most common consonants in Scrabble, along with **N** and **T**. Despite this, however, there is only one two-letter word beginning with **R**: **re** (2 points). This is worth remembering, as you won't need to waste time trying to think of others. There are some good three-letter words with **R**, however, some of which are quite unusual: **raj, rax** and **rex** (10 each), and **rez** and **riz** (12 each). Also, don't forget common words like **raw, ray** and **row** (6 each).

RABANNA, -S n Madagascan woven raffia
RABASKA, -S n large canoe
RABAT, -S, -TED vb rotate so that the plane rotated coincides with another
RABATINE n type of collar
RABATO, -ES, -S n wired or starched collar
RABATS ▸ rabat
RABATTE, -S same as ▸ rabat
RABATTED ▸ rabat
RABATTES ▸ rabatte
RABBET, -ED, -S n recess cut into a surface ▷ vb cut or form a rabbet in (timber)
RABBI, -ES, -S n Jewish spiritual leader
RABBIN, -S same as ▸ rabbi
RABBINIC adj of or relating to the rabbis, their teachings, writings, views, language, etc
RABBINS ▸ rabbin
RABBIS ▸ rabbi
RABBIT, -ED, -S n small burrowing mammal with long ears ▷ vb talk too much
RABBITER n person who traps and sells rabbits
RABBITO, -S same as ▸ rabbitoh
RABBITOH n (formerly) an itinerant seller of rabbits for eating
RABBITOS ▸ rabbito
RABBITRY n place where tame rabbits are kept and bred
RABBITS ▸ rabbit
RABBITY adj rabbitlike
RABBLE, -D, -S, RABBLING n disorderly crowd of noisy people ▷ vb stir, mix, or skim

(the molten charge) in a roasting furnace
RABBLER, -S n device for stirring, mixing, or skimming a molten charge in a furnace
RABBLES ▸ rabble
RABBLING ▸ rabble
RABBONI, -S n very respectful Jewish title or form of address
RABI, -S n (in Pakistan, India, etc) a crop that is harvested at the end of winter
RABIC ▸ rabies
RABID, -ER, -EST adj fanatical
RABIDITY
RABIDLY
RABIES n usu fatal viral disease transmitted by dogs and certain other animals
RABIETIC
RABIS ▸ rabi
RACA adj biblical word meaning worthless or empty-headed
RACAHOUT n acorn flour or drink made from it
RACCOON, -S n small N American mammal with a long striped tail
RACE, -D, -S n contest of speed ▷ vb compete with in a race
RACEABLE adj fit for racing
RACECARD n card providing information about a race meeting
RACED ▸ race
RACEGOER n one who attends a race meeting, esp a habitual frequenter of race meetings
RACEMATE n racemic compound

RACEME, -S n cluster of flowers along a central stem, as in the foxglove
RACEMED adj with or in racemes
RACEMES ▸ raceme
RACEMIC adj being a mixture of equal amounts of enantiomers
RACEMISE same as ▸ racemize
RACEMISM ▸ racemic
RACEMIZE vb change or cause to change into a racemic mixture
RACEMOID adj resembling a raceme
RACEMOSE adj being or resembling a raceme
RACEMOUS same as ▸ racemose
RACEPATH same as > racetrack
RACER, -S n person, animal, or machine that races
RACES ▸ race
RACEWALK vb race by walking fast rather than running
RACEWAY, -S n racetrack, esp one for banger racing
RACH, -ES n scent hound
RACHE same as ▸ rach
RACHES ▸ rach
RACHET, -ED, -S same as ▸ ratchet
RACHIAL ▸ rachis
RACHIDES ▸ rachis
RACHILLA n (in grasses) the short stem of a spikelet that bears the florets
RACHIS, RACHIDES, -ES n main axis or stem of an inflorescence or compound leaf

RACHITIC ▸ rachitis

RACHITIS *another name for* ▸ **rickets**

RACIAL *adj* relating to the division of the human species into races

RACIALLY

RACIER ▸ racy

RACIEST ▸ racy

RACILY ▸ racy

RACINESS ▸ racy

RACING, -S *adj* denoting or associated with horse races ▷ *n* practice of engaging in contests of speed

RACINO, -S *n* combined racetrack and casino

RACISM, -S *n* hostile attitude or behaviour to members of other races

RACIST -S

RACK, -ED, -ING, -INGS, -S *n* framework for holding particular articles, such as coats or luggage ▷ *vb* cause great suffering to

RACKER -S

RACKET, -ED *n* bat with strings stretched in an oval frame, used in tennis etc ▷ *vb* strike with a racket

RACKETEER *n* someone making a racket

RACKETRY *n* noise and commotion

RACKETS *n* ball game played in a paved walled court

RACKETT, -S *n* early double-reeded wind instrument

RACKETY *adj* involving noise, commotion and excitement

RACKFUL, -S ▸ rack

RACKING ▸ rack

RACKINGS ▸ rack

RACKLE, -S *n* (Scot) chain

RACKS ▸ rack

RACKWORK *n* mechanism with a rack and pinion

RACLETTE *n* Swiss dish of melted cheese served on boiled potatoes

RACLOIR, -S *n* scraper

RACON, -S *n* radar beacon

RACOON, -S *same as* ▸ **raccoon**

RACQUET, -S *same as* ▸ **racket**

RACY, RACIER, RACIEST *adj* slightly shocking

RAD, -DED, -DER, -DEST, -DING, -S *n* former unit of absorbed ionizing radiation dose ▷ *vb* fear ▷ *adj* slang term for great

RADAR, -S *n* device for tracking distant objects

RADDED ▸ rad

RADDER ▸ rad

RADDEST ▸ rad

RADDING ▸ rad

RADDLE, -S, RADDLING *same as* ▸ **ruddle**

RADDLED *adj* (of a person) unkempt or run-down in appearance

RADDLES ▸ raddle

RADDLING ▸ raddle

RADDOCKE *same as* ▸ **ruddock**

RADE (*in Scots dialect*) *past tense of* ▸ **ride**

RADGE, -R, -S, -ST *adj* angry or uncontrollable ▷ *n* person acting in such a way

RADIABLE *adj* able to be x-rayed

RADIAL, -S *adj* spreading out from a common central point ▷ *n* radial-ply tyre

RADIALE, RADIALIA *n* bone in the wrist

RADIALLY ▸ radial

RADIALS ▸ radial

RADIAN, -S *n* unit for measuring angles, equal to 57.296°

RADIANCE *n* quality or state of being radiant

RADIANCY *same as* ▸ **radiance**

RADIANS ▸ radian

RADIANT, -S *adj* looking happy ▷ *n* point or object that emits radiation

RADIATA, -S *adj as in* **radiata pine** type of pine tree

RADIATE, -D, -S *vb* spread out from a centre ▷ *adj* having rays or a radial structure

RADIATOR *n* arrangement of pipes containing hot water or steam to heat a room

RADICAL, -S *adj* fundamental ▷ *n* person advocating fundamental (political) change

RADICAND *n* number from which a root is to be extracted

RADICANT *adj* forming roots from the stem

RADICATE *vb* root or cause to take root

RADICEL, -S *n* very small root

RADICES ▸ radix

RADICLE, -S *n* small or developing root

RADICULE *same as* ▸ **radicle**

RADII ▸ radius

RADIO, -ED, -ING, -S *n* use of electromagnetic waves for broadcasting, communication, etc ▷ *vb* transmit (a message) by radio ▷ *adj* of, relating to, or using radio

RADIOES *less common spelling of* ▸ **radios**

RADIOING ▸ radio

RADIOMAN, RADIOMEN *n* radio operator

RADIOS ▸ radio

RADISH, -ES *n* small hot-flavoured root vegetable eaten raw in salads

RADIUM, -S *n* radioactive metallic element

RADIUS, RADII, -ED, -ES *n* (length of) a straight line from the centre to the circumference of a circle ▷ *vb* give a round shape

RADIX, RADICES, -ES *n* any number that is the base of a number system or of a system of logarithms

RADOME, -S *n* protective housing for a radar antenna

RADON, -S *n* radioactive gaseous element

RADS ▸ rad

RADULA, -E, -S *n* horny tooth-bearing strip on the tongue of molluscs

RADULAR

RADULATE

RADWASTE *n* radioactive wast

RAFALE, -S *n* burst of artillery fire

RAFF, -S *n* rubbish

RAFFIA, -S *n* prepared palm fibre for weaving mats etc

RAFFISH *adj* slightly disreputable

RAFFLE, -D, -S, RAFFLING *n* lottery with goods as prizes ▷ *vb* offer as a prize in a raffle

RAFFLER -S

RAFFS ▸ raff

RAFT, -ED, -S *n* floating platform of logs, planks, etc ▷ *vb* convey on or travel by raft, or make a raft from

RAFTER, -ED, -S *n* one of the main beams of a roof ▷ *vb* fit with rafters

RAFTING, -S ▸ raft

RAFTMAN, RAFTMEN *same as* ▸ **raftsman**

RAFTS ▸ raft

RAFTSMAN, RAFTSMEN *n* someone who does rafting

RAG, -GEDER, -S *n* fragment of cloth ▷ *vb* tease ▷ *adj* of various charitable events at a British university

R

RAGA, -S n pattern of melody and rhythm in Indian music

RAGBAG, -S n confused assortment, jumble

RAGBOLT, -S n bolt that has angled projections on it

RAGDE archaic past form of ▸ **rage**

RAGE, -D, -S n violent anger or passion ▷ vb speak or act with fury

RAGEE, -S same as ▸ **ragi**

RAGEFUL ▸ **rage**

RAGER, -S ▸ **rage**

RAGES ▸ **rage**

RAGG, -S same as ▸ **ragstone**

RAGGA, -S n dance-oriented style of reggae

RAGGED ▸ **rag**

RAGGEDER ▸ **rag**

RAGGEDLY ▸ **rag**

RAGGED adj somewhat ragged

RAGGEE, -S same as ▸ **ragi**

RAGGERY n rags

RAGGIER ▸ **raggy**

RAGGIES ▸ **raggy**

RAGGIEST ▸ **raggy**

RAGGING, -S ▸ **rag**

RAGGLE, -D, -S, RAGGLING n thin groove cut in stone or brickwork ▷ vb cut a raggle in

RAGGS ▸ **ragg**

RAGGY, RAGGIER, RAGGIES, RAGGIEST adj raglike ▷ n cereal grass cultivated in Africa and Asia for its edible grain

RAGI, -S n cereal grass cultivated in Africa and Asia for its edible grain

RAGING, -S ▸ **rage**

RAGINGLY ▸ **rage**

RAGINGS ▸ **raging**

RAGINI n Indian musical form related to a raga

RAGIS ▸ **ragi**

RAGLAN, -S adj (of a sleeve) joined to a garment from the neck to the underarm ▷ n coat with sleeves that continue to the collar

RAGMAN, -S, RAGMEN n rag-and-bone man

RAGMENT, -S n statute, roll, or list

RAGOUT, -ED, -S n richly seasoned stew of meat and vegetables ▷ vb make into a ragout

RAGS ▸ **rag**

RAGSTONE n hard sandstone or limestone, esp when used for building

RAGTAG, -S n disparaging term for common people

RAGTAIL adj ragged; shabby

RAGTIME, -S n style of jazz piano music

RAGTIMER

RAGTOP, -S n informal word for a car with a folding or removable roof

RAGU, -S n Italian meat and tomato sauce

RAGULED same as ▸ **raguly**

RAGULY adj (in heraldry) having toothlike or stublike projections

RAGUS ▸ **ragu**

RAGWEED, -S n any of several plants

RAGWHEEL n toothed wheel

RAGWORK, -S n weaving or needlework using rags

RAGWORM, -S n type of worm that lives chiefly in burrows in sand or mud

RAGWORT, -S n plant with ragged leaves and yellow flowers

RAH, -ED, -ING, -S informal US word for ▸ **cheer**

RAHUI, -S n Māori prohibition

RAI, -S n type of Algerian popular music

RAIA, -S same as ▸ **rayah**

RAID, -ED, -S n sudden surprise attack or search ▷ vb make a raid on

RAIDER, -S

RAIDING, -S ▸ **raid**

RAIDS ▸ **raid**

RAIK, -ED, -ING, -S n wander ▷ vb wander

RAIL, -ED, -S n horizontal bar, esp as part of a fence or track ▷ vb complain bitterly or loudly

RAILAGE, -S n cost of transporting goods by rail

RAILBED, -S n ballast layer supporting the sleepers of a railway track

RAILBIRD n racing aficionado

RAILBUS n buslike vehicle for use on railway lines

RAILCAR, -S n passenger-carrying railway vehicle consisting of a single coach

RAILCARD n card entitling the holder to cheaper rail travel

RAILCARS ▸ **railcar**

RAILE, -S archaic spelling of ▸ **rail**

RAILED ▸ **rail**

RAILER, -S ▸ **rail**

RAILES ▸ **raile**

RAILHEAD n terminal of a railway

RAILING, -S n fence made of rails supported by posts

RAILLERY n teasing or joking

RAILLESS ▸ **rail**

RAILLY, RAILLIES old word for ▸ **mock**

RAILMAN, RAILMEN n railway employee

RAILROAD same as ▸ **railway**

RAILS ▸ **rail**

RAILWAY, -S n track of iron rails on which trains run

RAIMENT, -S n clothing

RAIN, -ED, -ING, -S n water falling in drops from the clouds ▷ vb fall or pour down as rain

RAINBAND n dark band in the solar spectrum caused by water in the atmosphere

RAINBIRD n bird whose call is believed to be a sign of impending rain

RAINBOW, -S n arch of colours in the sky

RAINBOWY

RAINCOAT n water-resistant overcoat

RAINDATE n US term for an alternative date in case of rain

RAINDROP n water droplet that falls from the sky when it is raining

RAINE, -S archaic spelling of ▸ **reign**

RAINED ▸ **rain**

RAINES ▸ **raine**

RAINFALL n amount of rain

RAINIER ▸ **rainy**

RAINIEST ▸ **rainy**

RAINILY ▸ **rainy**

RAINING ▸ **rain**

RAINLESS ▸ **rain**

RAINOUT, -S n radioactive fallout or atmospheric pollution carried to the earth by rain

RAINS ▸ **rain**

RAINSUIT n waterproof jacket and trousers

RAINWASH n action of rain ▷ vb erode or wet as a result of rain

RAINWEAR n protective garments intended for use in wet weather

RAINY, RAINIER, RAINIEST adj characterized by a large rainfall

RAIRD, -S same as ▸ **reird**

RAIS ▸ **rai**

RAISABLE ▸ **raise**

RAISE, -D, -S vb lift up ▷ n increase in pay
RAISER -S
RAISIN, -S n dried grape
RAISING, -S n rule that moves a constituent from an embedded clause into the main clause
RAISINS ▶ raisin
RAISINY ▶ raisin
RAISONNE adj carefully thought out
RAIT, -ED, -ING, -S same as ▶ ret
RAITA, -S n Indian dish of chopped cucumber, mint, etc, in yogurt
RAITED ▶ rait
RAITING ▶ rait
RAITS ▶ rait
RAIYAT, -S same as ▶ ryot
RAJ, -ES n (in India) government

This Indian word for rule or empire is one of the essential short words that use a J. Remember that it can be extended to **raja**.

RAJA, -S same as ▶ rajah
RAJAH, -S n Indian ruler
RAJAS ▶ raja
RAJASHIP ▶ raja
RAJES ▶ raj
RAKE, -D, -S n tool used for smoothing earth or gathering leaves, hay, etc ▷ vb gather or smooth with a rake
RAKEE, -S same as ▶ raki
RAKEOFF, -S n share of profits, esp one that is illegal or given as a bribe
RAKER, -S n person who rakes
RAKERIES ▶ rakery
RAKERS ▶ raker
RAKERY, RAKERIES n rakish behaviour
RAKES ▶ rake
RAKI, -S n strong spirit distilled from grain
RAKIA, -S n strong fruit-based alcoholic drink popular in the Balkans
RAKIJA, -S same as ▶ rakia
RAKING, -S n (in rugby) offence of scraping an opponent with the studs
RAKIS ▶ raki
RAKISH adj dashing or jaunty
RAKISHLY
RAKSHAS same as ▶ rakshasa
RAKSHASA n Hindu demon

RAKU, -S n type of Japanese pottery
RALE, -S n abnormal coarse crackling sound heard on auscultation of the chest
RALLIED ▶ rally
RALLIER, -S ▶ rally
RALLIES ▶ rally
RALLINE adj relating to a family of birds that includes the rails, crakes, and coots
RALLY, RALLIED, RALLIES, -ING n large gathering of people for a meeting ▷ vb bring or come together after dispersal or for a common cause
RALLYE, -S US variant of ▶ rally
RALLYING ▶ rally
RALLYIST ▶ rally
RALPH, -ED, -ING, -S vb slang word meaning vomit
RAM, -MED, -MING, -S n male sheep ▷ vb strike against with force
RAMADA, -S n outdoor eating area with roof but open sides
RAMAKIN, -S same as ▶ ramekin
RAMAL adj relating to a branch or branches
RAMATE adj with branches
RAMBLA, -S n dried-up riverbed
RAMBLE, -D, -S vb walk without a definite route ▷ n walk, esp in the country
RAMBLER, -S n person who rambles
RAMBLES ▶ ramble
RAMBLING adj large and irregularly shaped ▷ n activity of going for long walks in the country
RAMBUTAN n SE Asian tree that has bright red edible fruit
RAMCAT, -S n dialect word for a male cat
RAMEAL same as ▶ ramal
RAMEE, -S same as ▶ ramie
RAMEKIN, -S n small ovenproof dish for a single serving of food
RAMEN, -S n Japanese dish consisting of a clear broth containing thin white noodles
RAMENTUM, RAMENTA n any of the thin brown scales that cover the stems and leaves of young ferns
RAMEOUS same as ▶ ramal
RAMEQUIN same as ▶ ramekin

RAMET, -S n any of the individuals in a group of clones
RAMI, -S same as ▶ ramie
RAMIE, -S n woody Asian shrub with broad leaves
RAMIFIED ▶ ramify
RAMIFIES ▶ ramify
RAMIFORM adj having a branchlike shape
RAMIFY, RAMIFIED, RAMIFIES vb become complex
RAMILIE, -S same as ▶ ramillie
RAMILLIE n wig with a plait at the back fashionable in the 18th century
RAMIN, -S n swamp-growing tree found in Malaysia and Indonesia
RAMIS ▶ rami
RAMJET, -S n type of jet engine
RAMMED ▶ ram
RAMMEL, -S n discarded or waste matter
RAMMER, -S ▶ ram
RAMMIER ▶ rammy
RAMMIES ▶ rammy
RAMMIEST ▶ rammy
RAMMING ▶ ram
RAMMISH adj like a ram, esp in being foul-smelling
RAMMLE, -S n collection of items saved in case they become useful
RAMMY, RAMMIER, RAMMIES, RAMMIEST n noisy disturbance or free-for-all ▷ vb make a rammy ▷ adj like a ram
RAMONA, -S same as > sagebrush
RAMOSE adj having branches
RAMOSELY
RAMOSITY
RAMOUS same as ▶ ramose
RAMOUSLY ▶ ramose
RAMP, -ED, -S n slope joining two level surfaces ▷ vb (esp of animals) to rush around in a wild excited manner
RAMPAGE, -D, -S vb dash about violently
RAMPAGER
RAMPANCY ▶ rampant
RAMPANT adj growing or spreading uncontrollably
RAMPART, -S n mound or wall for defence ▷ vb provide with a rampart
RAMPAUGE Scots variant of ▶ rampage
RAMPED ▶ ramp
RAMPER, -S ▶ ramp

R

RAMPICK, -S same as
▶ rampike

RAMPIKE, -S n US or dialect
word for a dead tree

RAMPING, -S ▶ ramp

RAMPION, -S n European
and Asian plant

RAMPIRE n archaic variant
of ▶ rampart
RAMPIRED

RAMPOLE, -S same as
▶ rampike

RAMPS ▶ ramp

RAMPSMAN, RAMPSMEN n
mugger

RAMROD, -S n long thin rod
used for cleaning the barrel
of a gun ▷ adj (of someone's
posture) very straight and
upright ▷ vb drive

RAMS ▶ ram

RAMSHORN n as in
ramshorn snail any of
various freshwater snails

RAMSON, -S n type of garlic

RAMSTAM adv headlong
▷ adj headlong

RAMTIL, -S n African plant
grown in India esp for its oil

RAMTILLA same as ▶ ramtil

RAMTILS ▶ ramtil

RAMULAR adj relating to a
branch or branches

RAMULI ▶ ramulus

RAMULOSE adj (of the parts
or organs of animals and
plants) having many small
branches

RAMULOUS same as
▶ ramulose

RAMULUS, RAMULI n small
branch

RAMUS n barb of a bird's
feather

RAN ▶ run

RANA, -S n genus of frogs

RANARIAN adj of or relating
to frogs

RANARIUM n place for
keeping frogs

RANAS ▶ rana

RANCE, -D, -S, RANCING
Scots word for ▶ prop

RANCEL, -S vb (in Shetland
and Orkney) carry out a
search

RANCES ▶ rance

RANCH, -ED, -ES, -ING n large
cattle farm in the American
West ▷ vb run a ranch

RANCHER, -S n person who
owns, manages, or works on
a ranch

RANCHERA n type of Mexican
country music

RANCHERO another word for
▶ rancher

RANCHERS ▶ rancher

RANCHES ▶ ranch

RANCHING ▶ ranch

RANCHMAN, RANCHMEN n
man who owns, manages, or
works on a ranch

RANCHO, -S n hut or group
of huts for housing ranch
workers

RANCID, -ER adj (of butter,
bacon, etc) stale and having
an offensive smell
RANCIDLY

RANCING ▶ rance

RANCOR, -S same as
▶ rancour
RANCORED

RANCOUR, -S n deep bitter
hate

RAND, -ED, -ING, -S n leather
strip on the heel of a shoe
▷ vb cut into rands

RANDAN, -S n boat rowed by
three people

RANDED ▶ rand

RANDEM, -S adv with three
horses harnessed together as
a team ▷ n carriage or team
of horses so driven

RANDIE same as ▶ randy

RANDIER ▶ randy

RANDIES ▶ randy

RANDIEST ▶ randy

RANDILY ▶ randy

RANDING ▶ rand

RANDLORD n mining
magnate during the
19th-century gold boom in
Johannesburg

RANDOM, -S adj made or
done by chance or without
plan ▷ n (in mining) the
course of a vein of ore
RANDOMLY

RANDON, -S old variant of
▶ random

RANDS ▶ rand

**RANDY, RANDIER, RANDIES,
RANDIEST** adj rude or
reckless ▷ n rude or reckless
person

RANEE, -S same as ▶ rani

RANG, -S n (Scot) rank

RANGE, -D, -S n limits of
effectiveness or variation
▷ vb vary between one point
and another

RANGER, -S n official in
charge of a nature reserve etc

RANGES ▶ range

RANGI, -S n sky

RANGIER ▶ rangy

RANGIEST ▶ rangy

RANGILY ▶ rangy

RANGING, -S ▶ range

RANGIORA n evergreen New
Zealand shrub or small tree

RANGIS ▶ rangi

RANGOLI, -S n traditional
Indian ground decoration

RANGS ▶ rang

**RANGY, RANGIER,
RANGIEST** adj having long
slender limbs

RANI, -S n wife or widow of
a rajah

RANID, -S n frog

RANIFORM adj froglike

RANINE adj relating to frogs

RANIS ▶ rani

RANK, -ED, -EST, -S n relative
place or position ▷ vb have a
specific rank or position ▷ adj
complete or absolute

RANKE, -S archaic variant of
▶ rank

RANKED ▶ rank

RANKER, -S n soldier in the
ranks

RANKES ▶ ranke

RANKEST ▶ rank

RANKING, -S adj prominent
▷ n position on a scale

RANKISH adj old word
meaning rather rank

RANKISM, -S n discrimination
against people on the
grounds of rank

RANKIST, -S n person who
discriminates on the grounds
of rank

RANKLE, -D, -S, RANKLING
vb continue to cause
resentment or bitterness

RANKLESS ▶ rank

RANKLING ▶ rankle

RANKLY ▶ rank

RANKNESS ▶ rank

RANKS ▶ rank

RANPIKE, -S same as
▶ rampike

RANSACK, -S vb search
thoroughly

RANSEL, -S same as ▶ rancel

RANSOM, -ED, -S n money
demanded for the release of
a kidnapped person ▷ vb pay
money to obtain the release
of a captive
RANSOMER

RANT, -ED, -S vb talk in a loud
and excited way ▷ n loud
excited speech
RANTER -S

RANTING, -S ▶ rant

RANTS ▶ rant

RANULA, -S n saliva-filled
cyst that develops under the
tongue

R

RANULAR adj of a cyst under the tongue

RANULAS ▸ ranula

RANZEL, -S same as ▸ **rancel**

RAOULIA, -S n flowering plant of New Zealand

RAP, -PED, -S vb hit with a sharp quick blow ▷ n quick sharp blow

RAPACITY > rapacious

RAPE, -D, -S, RAPING n violent sexual crime ▷ vb commit rape

RAPER -S

RAPESEED n seed of the oilseed rape plant

RAPHAE ▸ raphe

RAPHANIA n type of ergotism possibly resulting from consumption of radish seeds

RAPHE, RAPHAE, -S n elongated ridge of conducting tissue along the side of certain seeds

RAPHIA, -S same as ▸ **raffia**

RAPHIDE, -S n needle-shaped crystal that occurs in many plant cells

RAPHIS same as ▸ **raphide**

RAPID, -ER, -EST adj quick, swift

RAPIDITY

RAPIDLY

RAPIDS pl n part of a river with a fast turbulent current

RAPIER, -S n fine-bladed sword

RAPIERED adj carrying a rapier

RAPIERS ▸ rapier

RAPINE, -S n pillage or plundering

RAPING ▸ rape

RAPINI, -S n type of leafy vegetable

RAPIST, -S n person who commits rape

RAPLOCH, -S n Scots word for homespun woollen material ▷ adj Scots word meaning coarse or homemade

RAPPAREE n Irish irregular soldier of the late 17th century

RAPPE, -S n Arcadian dish of grated potatoes and pork or chicken

RAPPED ▸ rap

RAPPEE, -S n moist English snuff of the 18th and 19th centuries

RAPPEL, -ED, -S n (formerly) a drumbeat to call soldiers to arms ▷ vb abseil

RAPPEN n Swiss coin equal to one hundredth of a franc

RAPPER, -S n something used for rapping, such as a knocker on a door

RAPPES ▸ rappe

RAPPING, -S ▸ rap

RAPPINI same as ▸ **rapini**

RAPPORT, -S n harmony or agreement

RAPS ▸ rap

RAPT adj engrossed or spellbound

RAPTLY

RAPTNESS

RAPTOR, -S n any bird of prey

RAPTURE, -D, -S n ecstasy ▷ vb entrance

RARE, -D, -R, -S, -ST adj uncommon ▷ vb rear

RAREBIT, -S n as in **Welsh rarebit** dish made from melted cheese served on toast

RARED ▸ rare

RAREE n as in **raree show** street show or carnival

RAREFIED adj highly specialized, exalted

RAREFIER ▸ rarefy

RAREFY, RAREFIES vb make or become rarer or less dense

RARELY adv seldom

RARENESS ▸ rare

RARER ▸ rare

RARERIPE adj ripening early ▷ n fruit or vegetable that ripens early

RARES ▸ rare

RAREST ▸ rare

RARIFIED same as ▸ **rarefied**

RARIFY, RARIFIES same as ▸ **rarefy**

RARING adj ready

RARITY, RARITIES n something that is valuable because it is unusual

RARK, -ED, -ING, -S vb as in **rark up** informal New Zealand expression meaning reprimand severely

RAS n headland

RASBORA, -S n often brightly coloured tropical fish

RASCAL, -S n rogue ▷ adj belonging to the mob or rabble

RASCALLY adj dishonest or mean ▷ adv in a dishonest or mean fashion

RASCALS ▸ rascal

RASCASSE n any of various fishes with venomous spines on the fins

RASCHEL, -S n type of loosely knitted fabric

RASE, -D, -S, RASING same as ▸ **raze**

RASER -S

RASH, -ED, -ES, -EST, -ING adj hasty, reckless, or incautious ▷ n eruption of spots or patches on the skin ▷ vb (in old usage) cut

RASHER, -S n thin slice of bacon

RASHES ▸ rash

RASHEST ▸ rash

RASHIE, -S n protective shirt worn by surfers

RASHING ▸ rash

RASHLIKE ▸ rash

RASHLY ▸ rash

RASHNESS ▸ rash

RASING ▸ rase

RASMALAI n Indian dessert made from cheese, milk, and almonds

RASORIAL adj (of birds such as domestic poultry) adapted for scratching the ground for food

RASP, -ED, -S n harsh grating noise ▷ vb speak in a grating voice

RASPER -S

RASPIER ▸ raspy

RASPIEST ▸ raspy

RASPING adj (esp of a noise) harsh or grating

RASPINGS pl n browned breadcrumbs for coating fish and other foods before frying, baking, etc

RASPISH ▸ rasp

RASPS ▸ rasp

RASPY, RASPIER, RASPIEST same as ▸ **rasping**

RASSE, -S n small S Asian civet

RASSLE, -D, -S, RASSLING dialect variant of ▸ **wrestle**

RASSLER, -S n wrestler

RASSLES ▸ rassle

RASSLING ▸ rassle

RAST archaic past form of ▸ **race**

RASTA adj of a member of a particular Black religious movement

RASTER, -ED, -S n image consisting of rows of pixel information ▷ vb turn a digital image into a large picture

RASTRUM, -S n pen for drawing the five lines of a musical stave simultaneously

RASURE, -S n scraping

RAT, -S, -TED n small rodent ▷ vb inform (on)

RATA, -S n New Zealand hardwood forest tree

R

RATABLE adj able to be rated or evaluated ▷ n something that can be rated or evaluated

RATABLES pl n property that is liable to rates

RATABLY ▶ ratable

RATAFEE, -S same as ▶ ratafia

RATAFIA, -S n liqueur made from fruit

RATAL, -S n amount on which rates are assessed ▷ adj of or relating to rates (local taxation)

RATAN, -S same as ▶ rattan

RATANIES ▶ ratany

RATANS ▶ ratan

RATANY, RATANIES n flowering desert shrub

RATAPLAN n drumming sound ▷ vb drum

RATAS ▶ rata

RATATAT, -S n sound of knocking on a door

RATBAG, -S n insulting term for an eccentric or unreliable person

RATBITE n as in **ratbite fever** acute infectious disease that can be caught from rats

RATCH, -ED, -ES, -ING same as ▶ ratchet

RATCHET, -S n set of teeth on a bar or wheel allowing motion in one direction only ▷ vb move using or as if using a ratchet system

RATCHING ▶ ratch

RATE, -D n degree of speed or progress ▷ vb consider or value

RATEABLE same as ▶ ratable

RATEABLY

RATED ▶ rate

RATEEN, -S same as ▶ ratine

RATEL, -S n large African and S Asian musteline mammal

RATER, -S ▶ rate

RATES pl n (in some countries) a tax on property levied by a local authority

RATFINK, -S n contemptible or undesirable person

RATFISH n deep-sea fish with a whiplike tail

RATH, -S same as ▶ rathe

RATHA, -S n (in India) a four-wheeled carriage drawn by horses or bullocks

RATHE adj blossoming or ripening early in the season

RATHER adv some extent ▷ interj expression of strong affirmation ▷ sentence substitute expression of

strong affirmation, often in answer to a question

RATHEST adv dialect or archaic word meaning soonest

RATHOLE, -S n rat's hiding place or burrow

RATHRIPE adj dialect word meaning mature or ripe ahead of time ▷ n variety of apple or other fruit that is quick to ripen

RATHS ▶ rath

RATICIDE n rat poison

RATIFIED ▶ ratify

RATIFIER ▶ ratify

RATIFY, RATIFIED, RATIFIES vb give formal approval to

RATINE, -S n coarse loosely woven cloth

RATING, -S n valuation or assessment

RATIO, -S n relationship between two numbers or amounts expressed as a proportion

RATION, -ED n fixed allowance of food etc ▷ vb limit to a certain amount per person

RATIONAL adj reasonable, sensible ▷ n rational number

RATIONED ▶ ration

RATIONS pl n fixed daily allowance of food

RATIOS ▶ ratio

RATITE, -S n (of flightless birds) having a breastbone that lacks a keel ▷ n bird that belongs to this group

RATLIKE ▶ rat

RATLIN, -S same as ▶ ratline

RATLINE, -S n light line tied across the shrouds of a sailing vessel

RATLING, -S n young rat

RATLINS ▶ ratlin

RATO, -S n rocket-assisted take-off

RATOO, -S same as ▶ ratu

RATOON, -ED, -S n new shoot that grows from near the root or crown of crop plants ▷ vb propagate by such a growth

RATOONER n plant that spreads by ratooning

RATOONS ▶ ratoon

RATOOS ▶ ratoo

RATOS ▶ rato

RATPACK, -S n members of the press who pursue celebrities

RATPROOF adj impenetrable by rats

RATS ▶ rat

RATSBANE n rat poison, esp arsenic oxide

RATTAIL, -S n type of fish

RATTAN, -S n climbing palm with jointed stems used for canes

RATTED ▶ rat

RATTEEN, -S same as ▶ ratine

RATTEN, -ED, -S vb sabotage or steal tools in order to disrupt the work of **RATTENER**

RATTER, -S n dog or cat that catches and kills rats

RATTERY n rats' dwelling area

RATTIER ▶ ratty

RATTIEST ▶ ratty

RATTILY ▶ ratty

RATTING, -S ▶ rat

RATTISH adj of, resembling, or infested with rats

RATTLE, -D, -S vb give out a succession of short sharp sounds ▷ n short sharp sound

RATTLER, -S n something that rattles

RATTLES ▶ rattle

RATTLIER ▶ rattly

RATTLIN, -S same as ▶ ratline

RATTLINE same as ▶ ratline

RATTLING adv exceptionally, very ▷ n succession of short sharp sounds

RATTLINS ▶ rattlin

RATTLY, RATTLIER adj having a rattle

RATTON, -S n dialect word for a little rat

RATTOON, -S same as ▶ ratoon

RATTRAP, -S n device for catching rats

RATTY, RATTIER, RATTIEST adj bad-tempered, irritable

RATU, -S n title used by Fijian chiefs or nobles

RAUCID adj raucous

RAUCITY ▶ raucous

RAUCLE, -R, -ST adj Scots word for rough or tough

RAUCOUS adj hoarse or harsh

RAUGHT archaic past form of ▶ reach

RAUN, -S n fish roe or spawn

RAUNCH, -ED, -ES n lack of polish or refinement ▷ vb behave in a raunchy manner

RAUNCHY adj earthy, sexy

RAUNGE, -D, -S, RAUNGING archaic word for ▶ range

RAUNS ▶ raun

RAUPATU, -S n confiscation or seizure of land

R

RAUPO, -S n New Zealand bulrush

RAURIKI, -S n any of various plants with prickly leaves

RAV, -S n Hebrew word for rabbi

RAVAGE, -D, -S, RAVAGING vb cause extensive damage to ▷ n destructive action

RAVAGER -S

RAVE, -D, -S vb talk wildly or with enthusiasm ▷ n enthusiastically good review

RAVEL, -ED, -ING, -LED, -S vb tangle or become entangled ▷ n tangle or complication

RAVELER -S

RAVELIN, -S n outwork having two embankments at a salient angle

RAVELING ▸ ravel

RAVELINS ▸ ravelin

RAVELLED ▸ ravel

RAVELLER ▸ ravel

RAVELLY ▸ ravel

RAVELS ▸ ravel

RAVEN, -ED, -S n black bird like a large crow ▷ adj (of hair) shiny black ▷ vb seize or seek (plunder, prey, etc)

RAVENER -S

RAVENING adj (of animals) hungrily searching for prey

RAVENOUS adj very hungry

RAVENS ▸ raven

RAVER, -S n person who leads a wild or uninhibited social life

RAVES ▸ rave

RAVEY, RAVIER, RAVIEST adj characteristic of a rave

RAVIGOTE n rich white sauce with herbs and shallots

RAVIN, -ED, -ING, -S archaic spelling of ▸ raven

RAVINE, -S n narrow steep-sided valley worn by a stream

RAVINED ▸ ravin

RAVINES ▸ ravine

RAVING, -S adj delirious ▷ n frenzied, irrational, or wildly extravagant talk or utterances

RAVINGLY

RAVINING ▸ ravin

RAVINS ▸ ravin

RAVIOLI, -S n small squares of pasta with a savoury filling

RAVISH, -ED, -ES vb enrapture

RAVISHER

RAVS ▸ rav

RAW, -ER, -EST, -S n as in **in the raw** without clothes ▷ adj uncooked

RAWARU, -S n New Zealand name for blue cod

RAWBONE archaic variant of ▸ rawboned

RAWBONED adj having a lean bony physique

RAWER ▸ raw

RAWEST ▸ raw

RAWHEAD, -S n bogeyman

RAWHIDE, -D, -S n untanned hide ▷ vb whip

RAWIN, -S n monitoring of winds in the upper atmosphere using radar and a balloon

RAWING, -S (in dialect) same as ▸ rowen

RAWINS ▸ rawin

RAWISH ▸ raw

RAWLY ▸ raw

RAWMAISH n Irish word for foolish or exaggerated talk

RAWN, -S (in dialect) same as ▸ rowen

RAWNESS ▸ raw

RAWNS ▸ rawn

RAWS ▸ raw

RAX, -ED, -ES, -ING vb stretch or extend ▷ n act of stretching or straining

A dialect word meaning to stretch or strain, and one of the essential short words to know for using the X.

RAY, -ED, -ING, -S n single line or narrow beam of light ▷ vb (of an object) to emit (light) in rays or (of light) to issue in the form of rays

RAYA, -S same as ▸ rayah

RAYAH, -S n (formerly) a non-Muslim subject of the Ottoman Empire

RAYAS ▸ raya

RAYED ▸ ray

RAYGRASS same as ▸ ryegrass

RAYING ▸ ray

RAYLE, -D, -S, RAYLING archaic spelling of ▸ rail

RAYLESS adj dark

RAYLET, -S n small ray

RAYLIKE adj resembling a ray

RAYLING ▸ rayle

RAYNE, -S archaic spelling of ▸ reign

RAYON, -S n (fabric made of) a synthetic fibre

RAYS ▸ ray

RAZE, -D, -S, RAZING vb destroy (buildings or a town) completely

RAZEE, -D, -ING, -S n sailing ship that has had its upper deck or decks removed ▷ vb remove the upper deck or decks of (a sailing ship)

RAZER, -S ▸ raze

RAZES ▸ raze

RAZING ▸ raze

RAZMATAZ n noisy or showy fuss or activity

RAZOO, -S n imaginary coin

RAZOR, -ED, -ING, -S n sharp instrument for shaving ▷ vb cut or shave with a razor

RAZURE, -S same as ▸ rasure

RAZZ, -ED, -ES vb make fun of

RAZZIA, -S n raid for plunder or slaves

RAZZING, -S n act of making fun of someone

RAZZLE, -S n as in **on the razzle** out enjoying oneself or celebrating

RE prep concerning ▷ n the second note of the musical scale

REABSORB vb absorb again

REACCEDE vb accede again

REACCENT vb accent again

REACCEPT vb accept again

REACCUSE vb accuse again

REACH, -ED, -ES, -ING vb arrive at ▷ n distance that one can reach

REACHER -S

REACT, -ED, -ING, -S vb act in response (to)

REACTANT n substance that participates in a chemical reaction

REACTED ▸ react

REACTING ▸ react

REACTION n physical or emotional response to a stimulus

REACTIVE adj chemically active

REACTOR, -S n apparatus in which a nuclear reaction is controlled to produce energy

REACTS ▸ react

READ, -S vb look at and understand or take in (written or printed matter) ▷ n matter suitable for reading

READABLE adj enjoyable to read

READABLY

READAPT, -S vb adapt again

READD, -ED, -ING, -S vb add again

READDICT vb cause to become addicted again

READDING ▸ readd

READDS ▸ readd

READER, -S n person who reads

READERLY adj pertaining to or suitable for a reader

READERS ▸ reader

READIED ▸ ready

READIER ▸ ready

READIES pl n ready money
READIEST ▶ ready
READILY adv promptly
READING, -S ▶ read
READJUST vb adapt to a new situation
README n document which accompanies computer files or software
READMIT, -S vb let (a person, country, etc) back in to a place or organization
READOPT, -S vb adopt again
READORN, -S vb adorn again
READOUT, -S n act of retrieving information from a computer memory or storage device
READS ▶ read
READVISE vb advise again
READY, READIED, READIER, READIEST, -ING adj prepared for use or action ▷ vb prepare
REAEDIFY vb rebuild
REAFFIRM vb state again, confirm
REAFFIX vb affix again
REAGENCY ▶ reagent
REAGENT, -S n chemical substance that reacts with another
REAGIN, -S n type of antibody that is formed against an allergen
REAGINIC
REAK, -ED, -ING, -S same as ▶ reck
REAL, -ER, -ES, -EST, -S adj existing in fact ▷ n standard monetary unit of Brazil
REALGAR, -S n rare orange-red soft mineral
REALIA pl n real-life facts and material used in teaching
REALIGN, -S vb change or put back to a new or former place or position
REALISE, -D, -S same as ▶ realize
REALISER
REALISM, -S n awareness or acceptance of things as they are
REALIST, -S n person who accepts events, etc, as they are
REALITY n state of things as they are
REALIZE, -D, -S vb become aware or grasp the significance of
REALIZER
REALLIE old or dialect variant of ▶ really
REALLIED ▶ really

REALLIES ▶ really
REALLOT, -S vb allot again
REALLY, REALLIED, REALLIES adv very ▷ interj exclamation of dismay, doubt, or surprise ▷ vb (in archaic usage) rally
REALM, -S n kingdom
REALNESS ▶ real
REALO, -S n member of the German Green party with moderate views

A **realo** is a member of the less radical section of the German Green party. It is important to know not because it scores well, but because it provides an easily overlooked hook by allowing you to add O to **real**.

REALS ▶ real
REALTER, -S vb alter again
REALTIE n archaic word meaning sincerity
REALTIES ▶ realty
REALTIME adj (of a data-processing system) constantly updating to reflect the latest changes in data
REALTONE n audio clip of an original recording, used as a mobile phone ringtone
REALTOR, -S n estate agent
REALTY, REALTIES n immovable property
REAM, -ED, -ING, -S n twenty quires of paper, generally 500 sheets ▷ vb enlarge (a hole) by use of a reamer
REAME, -S archaic variant of ▶ realm
REAMED ▶ ream
REAMEND, -S vb amend again
REAMER, -S n tool used for smoothing the bores of holes accurately to size
REAMES ▶ reame
REAMIER ▶ reamy
REAMIEST ▶ reamy
REAMING ▶ ream
REAMS ▶ ream
REAMY, REAMIER, REAMIEST Scots for ▶ creamy
REAN, -S same as ▶ reen
REANNEX vb annex again
REANOINT vb anoint again
REANS ▶ rean
REANSWER vb answer again
REAP, -ED, -S vb cut and gather (a harvest)
REAPABLE

REAPER, -S n person who reaps or machine for reaping
REAPHOOK n sickle
REAPING, -S n act of reaping
REAPPEAR vb appear again
REAPPLY vb put or spread (something) on again
REAPS ▶ reap
REAR, -ED, -S n back part ▷ vb care for and educate (children)
REARER, -S
REARGUE, -D, -S vb argue again
REARING, -S n act of rearing
REARISE, -N, -S, REAROSE vb arise again
REARLY old word for ▶ early
REARM, -ED, -ING, -S vb arm again
REARMICE > rearmouse
REARMING ▶ rearm
REARMOST adj nearest the back
REARMS ▶ rearm
REAROSE ▶ rearise
REAROUSE vb arouse again
REARREST vb arrest again
REARS ▶ rear
REARWARD adj in the rear ▷ adv towards the rear ▷ n position in the rear, esp the rear division of a military formation
REASCEND vb ascend again
REASCENT n new ascent
REASON, -S n cause or motive ▷ vb think logically in forming conclusions
REASONED adj well thought out or well presented
REASONER ▶ reason
REASONS ▶ reason
REASSAIL vb assail again
REASSERT vb assert (rights, claims, etc) again
REASSESS vb reconsider the value or importance of
REASSIGN vb move (personnel, resources, etc) to a new post, department, location, etc
REASSORT vb assort again
REASSUME vb assume again
REASSURE vb restore confidence to
REAST, -ED, -ING, -S same as ▶ reest
REASTIER ▶ reasty
REASTING ▶ reast
REASTS ▶ reast
REASTY, REASTIER adj (in dialect) rancid
REATA, -S n lasso
REATE, -S n type of crowfoot
REATTACH vb attach again

R

REATTACK vb attack again

REATTAIN vb attain again

REAVAIL, -S vb avail again

REAVE, -D, -S, REAVING, REFT vb carry off (property, prisoners, etc) by force

REAVER -S

REAVOW, -ED, -S vb avow again

REAWAKE, -D, -S, REAWOKE, REAWOKEN vb awake again

REAWAKEN vb emerge or rouse from sleep

REAWAKES ▸ reawake

REAWOKE ▸ reawake

REAWOKEN ▸ reawake

REB, -S n Confederate soldier in the American Civil War

REBACK, -ED, -S vb provide with a new back, backing, or lining

REBADGE, -D, -S vb relaunch (a product) under a new name, brand, or logo

REBAIT, -ED, -S vb bait again

REBAR, -S n rod providing reinforcement in concrete structures

REBASE, -D, -S, REBASING vb set on a new foundation

REBATE, -D, -S, REBATING n discount or refund ▷ vb cut a rabbet in

REBATER -S

REBATO, -ES, -S same as ▸ rabato

REBBE, -S n individual's chosen spiritual mentor

REBEC, -S n medieval stringed instrument resembling the violin

REBECK, -S same as ▸ rebec

REBECS ▸ rebec

REBEGIN, REBEGAN, -S, REBEGUN vb begin again

REBEL, -LED, -S vb revolt against the ruling power ▷ n person who rebels ▷ adj rebelling

REBELDOM

REBELLER

REBELLOW vb re-echo loudly

REBELS ▸ rebel

REBID, -DEN, -S vb bid again

REBILL, -ED, -S vb bill again

REBIND, -S vb bind again

REBIRTH, -S n revival or renaissance

REBITE, REBIT, -S, REBITING, REBITTEN vb (in printing) to give another application of acid

REBLEND, -S vb blend again

REBLENT same as ▸ reblend

REBLOOM, -S vb bloom again

REBOANT adj resounding or reverberating

REBOARD, -S vb board again

REBODY, REBODIED, REBODIES vb give a new body to

REBOIL, -ED, -S vb boil again

REBOOK, -ED, -S vb book again

REBOOT, -ED, -S vb shut down and then restart (a computer system)

REBOP, -S same as ▸ bebop

REBORE, -D, -S, REBORING n boring of a cylinder to restore its true shape ▷ vb carry out this process

REBORN adj active again after a period of inactivity

REBORROW vb borrow again

REBOTTLE vb bottle again

REBOUGHT ▸ rebuy

REBOUND, -S vb spring back ▷ n act of rebounding

REBOZO, -S n long scarf covering the shoulders and head

REBRACE, -D, -S vb brace again

REBRANCH vb branch again

REBRAND, -S vb change or update the image of (an organization or product)

REBREED, REBRED, -S vb breed again

REBS ▸ reb

REBUFF, -ED, -S vb reject or snub ▷ n blunt refusal, snub

REBUILD, -S, REBUILT vb build (a building or town) again, after severe damage

REBUKE, -D, -S, REBUKING vb scold sternly ▷ n stern scolding

REBUKER -S

REBURIAL ▸ rebury

REBURY, REBURIED, REBURIES vb bury again

REBUS, -ES n puzzle consisting of pictures and symbols representing words or syllables

REBUT, -S, -TED vb prove that (a claim) is untrue

REBUTTAL

REBUTTER n defendant's pleading in reply to a claimant's surrejoinder

REBUTTON vb button again

REBUY, REBOUGHT, -ING, -S vb buy again

REC, -S n short for recreation

RECAL, -S same as ▸ recall

RECALL, -ED, -S vb recollect or remember ▷ n ability to remember

RECALLER

RECALS ▸ recal

RECAMIER n shade of pink

RECANE, -D, -S, RECANING vb cane again

RECANT, -ED, -S vb withdraw (a statement or belief) publicly

RECANTER

RECAP, -PED, -S vb recapitulate ▷ n recapitulation

RECAPTOR > recapture

RECARPET vb replace one carpet with another

RECARRY vb carry again

RECAST, -S vb organize or set out in a different way

RECATCH, RECAUGHT vb catch again

RECCE, -D, -ED, -ING, -S vb reconnoitre ▷ n reconnaissance

RECCIED ▸ reccy

RECCIES ▸ reccy

RECCO, -S same as ▸ recce

RECCY, RECCIED, RECCIES, -ING same as ▸ recce

RECEDE, -D, -S, RECEDING vb move to a more distant place

RECEIPT, -S n written acknowledgment of money or goods received ▷ vb acknowledge payment of (a bill), as by marking it

RECEIVAL n act of receiving or state of being received

RECEIVE, -S vb take, accept, or get

RECEIVED adj generally accepted

RECEIVER n part of telephone that is held to the ear

RECEIVES ▸ receive

RECEMENT vb cement again

RECENCY ▸ recent

RECENSE, -D, -S vb revise

RECENSOR vb censor again

RECENT, -ER adj having happened lately

RECENTLY

RECENTRE vb centre again

RECEPT, -S n idea or image formed in the mind by repeated experience

RECEPTOR n sensory nerve ending that changes specific stimuli into nerve impulses

RECEPTS ▸ recept

RECESS, -ED, -ES n niche or alcove ▷ vb place or set (something) in a recess

RECHANGE vb change again

RECHARGE vb cause (a battery etc) to take in and store electricity again

RECHART, -S vb chart again

RECHATE, -S same as ▸ recheat

RECHEAT, -S n (in a hunt) sounding of the horn to call back the hounds ▷ vb sound the horn to call back the hounds

RECHECK, -S vb check again

RECHEW, -ED, -S vb chew again

RECHIE adj smoky

RECHIP, -S vb put a new chip into (a stolen mobile phone) so it can be reused

RECHOOSE, RECHOSE, RECHOSEN vb choose again

RECIPE, -S n directions for cooking a dish

RECIRCLE vb circle again

RECISION n act of cancelling or rescinding

RECIT, -S n narrative

RECITAL, -S n musical performance by a soloist or soloists

RECITE, -D, -S, RECITING vb repeat (a poem, story, etc) aloud to an audience

RECITER -S

RECITS ▶ recit

RECK, -ED, -ING, -S vb mind or care about (something)

RECKAN, -S adj strained, tormented, or twisted ▷ n chain or hook for hanging a pot over a fire

RECKED ▶ reck

RECKING ▶ reck

RECKLESS adj heedless of danger

RECKLING dialect word for ▶ runt

RECKON, -ED, -S vb consider or think

RECKONER n any of various devices or tables used to facilitate reckoning, esp a ready reckoner

RECKONS ▶ reckon

RECKS ▶ reck

RECLAD, -S vb cover in a different substance

RECLAIM, -S vb regain possession of ▷ n act of reclaiming or state of being reclaimed

RECLAME, -S n public acclaim or attention

RECLASP, -S vb clasp again

RECLEAN, -S vb clean again

RECLIMB, -S vb climb again

RECLINE, -D, -S vb rest in a leaning position

RECLINER n armchair with adjustable back

RECLINES ▶ recline

RECLOSE, -D, -S vb close again

RECLOTHE vb clothe again

RECLUSE, -S n person who avoids other people ▷ adj solitary

RECOAL, -S vb supply or be supplied with fresh coal

RECOAT, -ED, -S vb coat again

RECOCK, -ED, -S vb cock again

RECODE, -D, -S, RECODING vb put into a new code

RECODIFY vb codify again

RECODING ▶ recode

RECOIL, -ED, -S vb jerk or spring back ▷ n backward jerk

RECOILER

RECOIN, -ED, -S vb coin again

RECOLLET n member of a particular Franciscan order

RECOLOR, -S same as ▶ recolour

RECOLOUR vb give a new colour to

RECOMB, -ED, -S vb comb again

RECOMMIT vb send (a bill) back to a committee for further consideration

RECON, -NED, -S vb make a preliminary survey

RECONFER vb confer again

RECONNED ▶ recon

RECONS ▶ recon

RECONVEY vb convey again

RECOOK, -ED, -S vb cook again

RECOPY, RECOPIED, RECOPIES vb copy again

RECORD, -ED, -S n document or other thing that preserves information ▷ vb put in writing

RECORDER n person or machine that records, esp audio or video material

RECORDS ▶ record

RECORK, -ED, -S vb cork again

RECOUNT, -S vb tell in detail

RECOUP, -ED, -S vb regain or make good (a loss)

RECOUPE, -S vb (in law) keep back or withhold

RECOUPED ▶ recoup

RECOUPES ▶ recoupe

RECOUPLE vb couple again

RECOUPS ▶ recoup

RECOURE, -D, -S archaic variant of ▶ recover

RECOURSE archaic word for ▶ return

RECOVER, -S vb become healthy again

RECOVERY n act of recovering from sickness, a shock, or a setback

RECOWER, -S archaic variant of ▶ recover

RECOYLE, -D, -S archaic spelling of ▶ recoil

RECRATE, -D, -S vb crate again

RECREANT n disloyal or cowardly person ▷ adj cowardly

RECREATE vb amuse (oneself or someone else)

RECROSS vb move or go across (something) again

RECROWN, -S vb crown again

RECRUIT, -S vb enlist (new soldiers, members, etc) ▷ n newly enlisted soldier

RECS ▶ rec

RECTA ▶ rectum

RECTAL adj of the rectum **RECTALLY**

RECTI ▶ rectus

RECTIFY vb put right, correct

RECTION, -S n (in grammar) the determination of the form of one word by another word

RECTITIC ▶ rectitis

RECTITIS n inflammation of the rectum

RECTO, -S n right-hand page of a book

RECTOR, -S n clergyman in charge of a parish

RECTORAL adj of or relating to God's rule or to a rector

RECTORS ▶ rector

RECTORY n rector's house

RECTOS ▶ recto

RECTRESS same as > rectoress

RECTRIX n any of the large stiff feathers of a bird's tail

RECTUM, RECTA, -S n final section of the large intestine

RECTUS, RECTI n straight muscle

RECUILE, -D, -S archaic variant of ▶ recoil

RECULE, -D, -S, RECULING archaic variant of ▶ recoil

RECUR, -RED, -S vb happen again

RECURE, -D, -S, RECURING vb archaic word for cure or recover

RECURRED ▶ recur

RECURS ▶ recur

RECURVE, -D, -S vb curve or bend (something) back or down

RECUSAL, -S n withdrawal of a judge from a case

R

RECUSANT n Roman Catholic who did not attend the services of the Church of England ▷ adj (formerly, of Catholics) refusing to attend services of the Church of England

RECUSE, -D, -S, RECUSING vb (in law) object to or withdraw (a judge)

RECUT, -S vb cut again

RECYCLE, -D, -S vb reprocess (used materials) for further use ▷ n repetition of a fixed sequence of events
RECYCLER

RED, -DEST, -S adj of a colour varying from crimson to orange and seen in blood, fire, etc ▷ n red colour

REDACT, -ED, -S vb compose or draft (an edict, proclamation, etc)
REDACTOR

REDAMAGE vb damage again

REDAN, -S n fortification of two parapets at a salient angle

REDARGUE vb archaic word for disprove or refute

REDATE, -D, -S, REDATING vb change date of

REDBACK, -S n small venomous Australian spider

REDBAIT, -S vb harass those with leftwing leanings

REDBAY, -S n type of tree

REDBELLY n any of various animals having red underparts

REDBIRD, -S n type of bird, the male of which has bright red plumage

REDBONE, -S n type of American dog

REDBRICK adj founded in the late 19th or early 20th century ▷ n denoting a provincial British university of relatively recent foundation

REDBUD, -S n American tree with heart-shaped leaves

REDBUG, -S another name for ► chigger

REDCAP, -S n military policeman

REDCOAT, -S n British soldier

REDD, -ED, -S vb bring order to ▷ n act or an instance of redding

REDDEN, -ED, -S vb make or become red

REDDENDA > reddendum

REDDENDO n Scottish legal clause specifying what duties are required in exchange for something

REDDENED ► redden

REDDENS ► redden

REDDER, -S ► redd

REDDEST ► red

REDDIER ► reddy

REDDIEST ► reddy

REDDING, -S ► redd

REDDISH adj somewhat red

REDDLE, -D, -S, REDDLING same as ► ruddle

REDDS ► redd

REDDY, REDDIER, REDDIEST adj reddish

REDE, -D, -S, REDING n advice or counsel ▷ vb advise

REDEAL, -S, -T vb deal again

REDEAR, -S n variety of sunfish with a red flash above the gills

REDECIDE vb decide again

REDED ► rede

REDEEM, -ED, -S vb make up for
REDEEMER

REDEFEAT vb defeat again

REDEFECT vb defect back or again

REDEFIED ► redefy

REDEFIES ► redefy

REDEFINE vb define (something) again or differently

REDEFY, REDEFIED, REDEFIES vb defy again

REDELESS ► rede

REDEMAND vb demand again

REDENY, REDENIED, REDENIES vb deny again

REDEPLOY vb assign to a new position or task

REDES ► rede

REDESIGN vb change the design of (something) ▷ n something that has been redesigned

REDEYE, -S n inferior whiskey

REDFIN, -S n any of various small fishes with reddish fins that are popular aquarium fishes

REDFISH n male salmon that has recently spawned

REDFOOT, -S n fatal disease of newborn lambs

REDHEAD, -S n person with reddish hair

REDHORSE n type of fish

REDIA, -E, -S n parasitic larva of flukes

REDIAL, -ED, -S vb dial (a telephone number) again

REDIAS ► redia

REDID ► redo

REDIGEST vb digest again

REDING ► rede

REDIP, -PED, -S vb dip again

REDIPT archaic past form of ► redip

REDIRECT vb send in a new direction or course

REDISTIL vb distil again

REDIVIDE vb divide again

REDLINE, -D, -S vb refuse a loan to (a person or country) because of the presumed risks involved

REDLINER

REDLY ► red

REDNESS ► red

REDO, REDID, -ES, -ING, -NE, -S vb do over again in order to improve ▷ n instance of redoing something

REDOCK, -ED, -S vb dock again

REDOES ► redo

REDOING ► redo

REDOLENT adj reminiscent (of)

REDON, -NED, -S vb don again

REDONE ► redo

REDONNED ► redon

REDONS ► redon

REDOS ► redo

REDOUBLE vb increase, multiply, or intensify ▷ n act of redoubling

REDOUBT, -S n small fort defending a hilltop or pass ▷ vb fear

REDOUND, -S vb cause advantage or disadvantage (to)

REDOUT, -S n reddened vision caused by a rush of blood to the head

REDOWA, -S n Bohemian folk dance similar to the waltz

REDOX, -ES n chemical reaction in which one substance is reduced and the other is oxidized

REDPOLL, -S n mostly grey-brown finch with a red crown and pink breast

REDRAFT, -S vb write a second copy of (a letter, proposal, essay, etc) ▷ n second draft

REDRAW, -N, -S, REDREW vb draw up (something) again or differently
REDRAWER

REDREAM, -S, -T vb dream again

REDRESS vb make amends for ▷ n compensation or amends

REDREW ► redraw
REDRIED ► redry
REDRIES ► redry
REDRILL, -S vb drill again
REDRIVE, -N, -S, REDROVE vb drive again
REDROOT, -S n yellow-flowered bog plant whose roots yield a red dye
REDROVE ► redrive
REDRY, REDRIED, REDRIES, -ING vb dry again
REDS ► red
REDSEAR same as ► redshort
REDSHANK n large Eurasian sandpiper with red legs
REDSHARE n red algae
REDSHIFT n shift in the lines of the spectrum of an astronomical object
REDSHIRE same as ► redshare
REDSHIRT vb take a year out of a sports team
REDSHORT vb become brittle at red-hot temperatures
REDSTART n European bird of the thrush family
REDTAIL, -S n variety of bird with red colouring on its tail
REDTOP, -S n sensationalist tabloid newspaper
REDUB, -BED, -S vb fix or repair
REDUCE, -D, -S, REDUCING vb bring down, lower
REDUCER, -S n chemical solution used to lessen the density of a negative or print
REDUCES ► reduce
REDUCING ► reduce
REDUCTOR n apparatus in which substances can be reduced
REDUIT, -S n fortified part from which a garrison may fight on once an enemy has taken outworks
REDUVIID n type of insect
REDUX adj brought back or returned
REDWARE, -S another name for ► kelp
REDWATER n tick-borne disease of cattle
REDWING, -S n small European thrush
REDWOOD, -S n giant Californian conifer with reddish bark
REDYE, -D, -ING, -S vb dye again
REE, -S n Scots word for walled enclosure

REEARN, -ED, -S vb earn again
REEBOK, -S same as ► rhebok
REECH, -ED, -ES, -ING vb (in dialect) smoke
REECHIE same as ► reechy
REECHIER ► reechy
REECHING ► reech
REECHO, -ED, -ES vb echo again
REECHY, REECHIER adj (in dialect) smoky
REED, -ED, -S n tall grass that grows in swamps and shallow water
REEDBED, -S n area of wetland with reeds growing in it
REEDBIRD n any of several birds that frequent reed beds, esp (in the US and Canada) the bobolink
REEDBUCK n buff-coloured African antelope with inward-curving horns
REEDE, -S obsolete variant of ► red
REEDED ► reed
REEDEN adj of or consisting of reeds
REEDER, -S n thatcher
REEDES ► reede
REEDIER ► reedy
REEDIEST ► reedy
REEDIFY vb edify again or rebuild
REEDILY ► reedy
REEDING, -S n set of small semicircular architectural mouldings
REEDIT, -ED, -S vb edit again
REEDLIKE adj resembling a reed
REEDLING n tawny titlike Eurasian songbird common in reed beds
REEDMAN, REEDMEN n musician who plays a wind instrument that has a reed
REEDS ► reed
REEDSTOP n organ stop that controls a rank of reed pipes
REEDY, REEDIER, REEDIEST adj harsh and thin in tone
REEF, -ED, -S n ridge of rock or coral near the surface of the sea ▷ vb roll up part of a sail
REEFABLE
REEFER, -S n short thick jacket worn esp by sailors
REEFIER ► reefy
REEFIEST ► reefy
REEFING, -S ► reef
REEFS ► reef

REEFY, REEFIER, REEFIEST adj with reefs
REEJECT, -S vb eject again
REEK, -ED, -S vb smell strongly ▷ n strong unpleasant smell
REEKER -S
REEKIE same as ► reeky
REEKIER ► reeky
REEKIEST ► reeky
REEKING ► reek
REEKS ► reek
REEKY, REEKIER, REEKIEST adj steamy or smoky
REEL, -ED, -S n (formerly) cylindrical object on which film, tape, thread, or wire is wound ▷ vb stagger, sway, or whirl
REELABLE
REELECT, -S vb elect again
REELED ► reel
REELER, -S ► reel
REELING, -S ► reel
REELMAN, REELMEN n (formerly) member of a beach life-saving team operating a winch
REELS ► reel
REEMBARK vb embark again
REEMBODY vb embody again
REEMERGE vb emerge again
REEMIT, -S vb emit again
REEMPLOY vb employ again
REEN, -S n ditch, esp a drainage channel
REENACT, -S vb enact again
REENDOW, -S vb endow again
REENGAGE vb engage again
REENJOY, -S vb enjoy again
REENLIST vb enlist again
REENROLL vb enrol again
REENS ► reen
REENTER, -S vb enter again
REENTRY n return of a spacecraft into the earth's atmosphere
REEQUIP, -S vb equip again
REERECT, -S vb erect again
REES ► ree
REEST, -ED, -ING, -S vb (esp of horses) to be noisily uncooperative
REESTIER ► reesty
REESTING ► reest
REESTS ► reest
REESTY, REESTIER same as ► reasty
REEVE, -D, -S, REEVING n local representative of the king in a shire until the early 11th century ▷ vb pass (a rope or cable) through an eye or other narrow opening

REEVOKE, -D, -S vb evoke again

REEXPEL, -S vb expel again

REEXPORT vb export again

REEXPOSE vb expose again

REF, -FED, -S n referee in sport ▷ vb referee

REFACE, -D, -S, REFACING vb repair or renew the facing of (a wall)

REFALL, -EN, -S, REFELL vb fall again

REFASTEN vb fasten again

REFECT, -ED, -S vb archaic word for restore or refresh with food and drink

REFEED, REFED, -S vb feed again

REFEEL, -S, REFELT vb feel again

REFEL, -LED, -S vb refute

REFELL ▶ refall

REFELLED ▶ refel

REFELS ▶ refel

REFELT ▶ refeel

REFENCE, -D, -S vb fence again

REFER, -RED, -S vb allude (to)

REFEREE, -D, -S n umpire in sports, esp soccer or boxing ▷ vb act as referee of

REFERENT n object or idea to which a word or phrase refers

REFERRAL ▶ refer

REFERRED ▶ refer

REFERRER ▶ refer

REFERS ▶ refer

REFFED ▶ ref

REFFING, -S n act or instance of refereeing a sports match

REFI, -S n refinancing of a debt

REFIGHT, -S, REFOUGHT vb fight again ▷ n second or new fight

REFIGURE vb figure again

REFILE, -D, -S, REFILING vb file again

REFILL, -ED, -S vb fill again ▷ n second or subsequent filling

REFILM, -ED, -S vb film again

REFILTER vb filter again

REFIND, -S vb find again

REFINE, -S, REFINING vb purify

REFINED adj cultured or polite

REFINER, -S n person, device, or substance that removes impurities, etc

REFINERY n place where sugar, oil, etc is refined

REFINES ▶ refine

REFINING ▶ refine

REFINISH vb finish again

REFIRE, -D, -S, REFIRING vb fire again

REFIS ▶ refi

REFIT, -S, -TED vb make ready for use again by repairing or re-equipping ▷ n repair or re-equipping for further use

REFIX, -ED, -ES, -ING vb fix again

REFLAG, -S vb flag again

REFLATE, -D, -S vb inflate or be inflated again

REFLECT, -S vb throw back, esp rays of light, heat, etc

REFLET, -S n iridescent glow or lustre, as on ceramic ware

REFLEW ▶ refly

REFLEX, -ED, -ES n involuntary response to a stimulus or situation ▷ adj (of a muscular action) involuntary ▷ vb bend, turn, or reflect backwards

REFLEXLY

REFLIES ▶ refly

REFLOAT, -S vb float again

REFLOOD, -S vb flood again

REFLOW, -ED, -S vb flow again

REFLOWER vb flower again

REFLOWN ▶ refly

REFLOWS ▶ reflow

REFLUENT adj flowing back

REFLUX, -ED, -ES vb boil in a vessel attached to a condenser, so that the vapour condenses and flows back in ▷ n act of refluxing

REFLY, REFLEW, REFLIES, REFLOWN, -ING vb fly again

REFOCUS vb focus again or anew

REFOLD, -ED, -S vb fold again

REFOOT, -ED, -S vb foot again

REFOREST vb replant (an area that was formerly forested) with trees

REFORGE, -D, -S vb forge again

REFORM, -ED, -S n improvement ▷ vb improve

REFORMAT vb format again

REFORMED ▶ reform

REFORMER ▶ reform

REFORMS ▶ reform

REFOUGHT ▶ refight

REFOUND, -S vb found again

REFRACT, -S vb change the course of (light etc) passing from one medium to another

REFRAIN, -S n frequently repeated part of a song ▷ vb abstain (from action)

REFRAME, -D, -S vb support or enclose (a picture, photograph, etc) in a new or different frame

REFREEZE, REFROZE, REFROZEN vb freeze or be frozen again after having defrosted

REFRESH vb revive or reinvigorate, as through food, drink, or rest

REFRIED ▶ refry

REFRIES ▶ refry

REFRINGE formerly used to mean ▶ refract

REFRONT, -S vb put a new front on

REFROZE ▶ refreeze

REFROZEN ▶ refreeze

REFRY, REFRIED, REFRIES, -ING vb fry again

REFS ▶ ref

REFT ▶ reave

REFUEL, -ED, -S vb supply or be supplied with fresh fuel

REFUGE, -D, -S, REFUGING n (source of) shelter or protection ▷ vb take refuge or give refuge to

REFUGEE, -S n person who seeks refuge, esp in a foreign country

REFUGES ▶ refuge

REFUGIA ▶ refugium

REFUGING ▶ refuge

REFUGIUM, REFUGIA n region that has remained unaltered by a climatic change affecting surrounding regions

REFUND, -ED, -S vb pay back ▷ n return of money

REFUNDER

REFURB, -ED, -S vb refurbish ▷ n (act or instance of) refurbishment

REFUSAL, -S n denial of anything demanded or offered

REFUSE, -D, -S, REFUSING vb decline, deny, or reject ▷ n rubbish or useless matter

REFUSER -S

REFUSION n new or further fusion

REFUSNIK same as ▷ **refusenik**

REFUTAL, -S n act or process of refuting

REFUTE, -D, -S, REFUTING vb disprove

REFUTER -S

REG, -S n large expanse of stony desert terrain

REGAIN, -ED, -S vb get back or recover ▷ n process of getting something back, esp lost weight

REGAINER

REGAL, -S adj of or like a king or queen ▷ n portable organ equipped only with small reed pipes

REGALE, -D, -S, REGALING vb entertain (someone) with stories etc ▷ n feast
REGALER -S
REGALIA, -S pl n ceremonial emblems of royalty or high office
REGALIAN adj royal
REGALIAS ▶ regalia
REGALING ▶ regale
REGALISM n principle that the sovereign has supremacy in church affairs
REGALIST
REGALITY n state or condition of being royal
REGALLY ▶ regal
REGALS ▶ regal
REGAR, -S same as ▶ regur
REGARD, -ED, -S vb consider ▷ n respect or esteem
REGARDER
REGARS ▶ regar
REGATHER vb gather again
REGATTA, -S n meeting for yacht or boat races
REGAUGE, -D, -S vb gauge again
REGAVE ▶ regive
REGEAR, -ED, -S vb readjust
REGELATE vb undergo or cause to undergo regelation
REGENCE, -S old variant of ▶ regency
REGENCY n status or period of office of a regent
REGENT, -S n ruler of a kingdom during the absence, childhood, or illness of its monarch ▷ adj ruling as a regent
REGENTAL
REGES ▶ rex
REGEST, -ED, -S n archaic word for register ▷ vb register
REGGAE, -S n style of Jamaican popular music with a strong beat
REGGO, -S same as ▶ rego
REGICIDE n killing of a king
REGIE, -S n government-directed management or government monopoly
REGIFT, -ED, -S vb give (a previously received gift) to someone else
REGIFTER n person who regifts something
REGIFTS ▶ regift
REGILD, -ED, -S vb gild again
REGILT archaic past form of ▶ regild
REGIME, -S n system of government

REGIMEN, -S n prescribed system of diet etc
REGIMENT n organized body of troops as a unit of the army ▷ vb force discipline or order on, esp in a domineering manner
REGIMES ▶ regime
REGINA, -E, -S n queen
REGINAL adj queenly
REGINAS ▶ regina
REGION, -S n administrative division of a country
REGIONAL adj of, characteristic of, or limited to a region ▷ n regional heat of a competition
REGIONS ▶ region
REGISTER n (book containing) an official list or record of things ▷ vb enter in a register or set down in writing
REGISTRY n place where official records are kept
REGIUS adj as in **regius professor** Crown-appointed holder of a university chair
REGIVE, REGAVE, -N, -S, REGIVING vb give again or back
REGLAZE, -D, -S vb glaze again
REGLET, -S n flat narrow architectural moulding
REGLOSS vb gloss again or give a new gloss to
REGLOW, -ED, -S vb glow again
REGLUE, -D, -S, REGLUING vb glue again
REGMA, -TA n type of fruit with cells that break open and break away when ripe
REGMAKER n drink taken to relieve the symptoms of a hangover
REGMATA ▶ regma
REGNA ▶ regnum
REGNAL adj of a sovereign, reign, or kingdom
REGNANCY ▶ regnant
REGNANT adj reigning
REGNUM, REGNA n reign or rule
REGO, -S n registration of a motor vehicle
REGOLITH n layer of loose material covering the bedrock of the earth and moon
REGORGE, -D, -S vb vomit up
REGOS ▶ rego
REGOSOL, -S n type of azonal soil

REGRADE, -D, -S vb grade again
REGRAFT, -S vb graft again
REGRANT, -S vb grant again
REGRATE, -D, -S vb buy up (commodities) in advance so as to raise their price for resale
REGRATER
REGRATOR
REGREDE, -D, -S vb go back
REGREEN, -S vb green again
REGREET, -S vb greet again or return greetings of
REGRESS vb revert to a former worse condition ▷ n return to a former and worse condition
REGRET, -S vb feel sorry about ▷ n feeling of repentance, guilt, or sorrow
REGREW ▶ regrow
REGRIND, -S, REGROUND vb grind again
REGROOM, -S vb groom again
REGROOVE vb groove again
REGROUND ▶ regrind
REGROUP, -S vb reorganize (military forces) after an attack or defeat
REGROW, REGREW, -N, -S vb grow or be grown again after having been cut or having died or withered
REGROWTH n growing back of hair, plants, etc
REGS ▶ reg
REGULA, -E n rule
REGULAR, -S adj normal, customary, or usual ▷ n regular soldier
REGULATE vb control, esp by rules
REGULI ▶ regulus
REGULINE ▶ regulus
REGULISE variant spelling of ▶ regulize
REGULIZE vb turn into regulus
REGULO, -S n any of a number of temperatures to which a gas oven may be set
REGULUS, REGULI n impure metal forming beneath the slag during the smelting of ores
REGUR, -S n black loamy Indian soil
REH, -S n (in India) salty surface crust on the soil
REHAB, -BED, -S vb help (a person) to readapt to society or a new job ▷ n treatment or help given to an addict, etc
REHABBER

R

REHAMMER vb hammer again

REHANDLE vb handle again

REHANG, -ED, -S, REHUNG vb hang again

REHARDEN vb harden again

REHASH, -ED, -ES vb rework or reuse ▷ n old ideas presented in a new form

REHEAR, -D, -S vb hear again

REHEARSE vb practise (a play, concert, etc)

REHEAT, -ED, -S vb heat or be heated again
REHEATER

REHEEL, -ED, -S vb put a new heel or new heels on

REHEM, -MED, -S vb hem again

REHINGE, -D, -S vb put a new hinge or new hinges on

REHIRE, -D, -S, REHIRING vb hire again

REHOBOAM n wine bottle holding the equivalent of six normal bottles (approximately 156 ounces)

REHOME, -D, -S vb find a new home for (esp a pet)

REHOMING n act of rehoming

REHOUSE, -D, -S vb provide with a new (and better) home

REHS ▶ reh

REHUNG ▶ rehang

REI n name for a former Portuguese coin

REIF, -S n Scots word meaning robbery or plunder

REIFIED ▶ reify

REIFIER, -S ▶ reify

REIFIES ▶ reify

REIFS ▶ reif

REIFY, REIFIED, REIFIES, -ING vb consider or make (an abstract idea or concept) real or concrete

REIGN, -ED, -ING, -S n period of a sovereign's rule ▷ vb rule (a country)

REIGNITE vb catch fire or cause to catch fire again

REIGNS ▶ reign

REIK, -S Scots word for ▶ smoke

REIKI, -S n form of therapy to encourage healing or restore wellbeing

REIKS ▶ reik

REILLUME vb relight

REIMAGE, -D, -S vb image again

REIMPORT vb import (goods manufactured from exported raw materials) ▷ n act of reimporting

REIMPOSE vb establish previously imposed laws, controls, etc, again

REIN, -ED, -ING vb check or manage with reins

REINCITE vb incite again

REINCUR, -S vb incur again

REINDEER n deer of arctic regions with large branched antlers

REINDEX vb index again

REINDICT vb indict again

REINDUCE vb induce again

REINDUCT vb induct again

REINED ▶ rein

REINETTE n variety of apple

REINFECT vb infect or contaminate again

REINFORM vb inform again

REINFUND vb archaic word for pour in again

REINFUSE vb infuse again

REINING ▶ rein

REINJECT vb inject again

REINJURE vb injure again

REINJURY n further injury

REINK, -ED, -ING, -S vb ink again

REINLESS ▶ rein

REINS pl n narrow straps attached to a bit to guide a horse

REINSERT vb insert again

REINSMAN, REINSMEN n driver in a trotting race

REINSTAL same as > reinstall

REINSURE vb insure again

REINTER, -S vb inter again

REINVADE vb invade again

REINVENT vb replace (a product, etc) with an entirely new version

REINVEST vb put back profits from a previous investment into the same enterprise

REINVITE vb invite again

REINVOKE vb invoke again

REIRD, -S Scots word for ▶ din

REIS, -ES n small branch

REISHI, -S n type of mushroom with a shiny cap

REISSUE, -D, -S n book, record, etc, that is released again after being unavailable ▷ vb release (a book, record, etc) again after a period of unavailability
REISSUER

REIST, -ED, -ING, -S same as ▶ reest

REITBOK, -S same as ▶ reedbuck

REITER, -ED, -S n soldier in the German cavalry ▷ vb repeat something

REIVE, -D, -S vb go on a plundering raid
REIVER -S

REIVING, -S n act of going on a plundering raid

REJACKET n put a new jacket on

REJECT, -ED, -S vb refuse to accept or believe ▷ n person or thing rejected as not up to standard

REJECTEE n someone who has been rejected

REJECTER ▶ reject

REJECTOR ▶ reject

REJECTS ▶ reject

REJIG, -GED, -S vb re-equip (a factory or plant) ▷ n act or process of rejigging
REJIGGER

REJOICE, -D, -S vb feel or express great happiness
REJOICER

REJOIN, -ED, -S vb join again

REJON, -ES n bullfighting lance

REJONEO, -S n bullfighting activity in which a mounted bullfighter spears the bull with lances

REJONES ▶ rejon

REJOURN, -S vb archaic word meaning postpone or adjourn

REJUDGE, -D, -S vb judge again

REJUGGLE vb juggle again

REKE, -D, -S, REKING same as ▶ reck

REKEY, -ED, -ING, -S vb key again

REKINDLE vb arouse former emotions or interests

REKING ▶ reke

REKNIT, -S vb knit again

REKNOT, -S vb knot again

RELABEL, -S vb label again

RELACE, -D, -S, RELACING vb lace again

RELACHE, -S n break

RELACING ▶ relace

RELAID ▶ relay

RELAND, -ED, -S vb land again

RELAPSE, -D, -S vb fall back into bad habits, illness, etc ▷ n return of bad habits, illness, etc
RELAPSER

RELATA ▶ relatum

RELATE, -S, RELATING vb establish a relation between

RELATED adj linked by kinship or marriage

RELATER, -S ▶ relate

RELATES ▶ relate

RELATING ► relate

RELATION n connection between things

RELATIVE adj true to a certain degree or extent ▷ n person connected by blood or marriage

RELATOR, -S n person who relates a story

RELATUM, RELATA n one of the objects between which a relation is said to hold

RELAUNCH vb launch again ▷ n another launching, or something that is relaunched

RELAX, -ES, -ING vb make or become looser, less tense, or less rigid

RELAXANT n drug or agent that relaxes, esp one that relaxes tense muscles ▷ adj of, relating to, or tending to produce relaxation

RELAXED ► relax

RELAXER, -S n person or thing that relaxes

RELAXES ► relax

RELAXIN, -S n hormone secreted during pregnancy

RELAXING ► relax

RELAXINS ► relaxin

RELAY, RELAID, -ED, -ING, -S n fresh set of people or animals relieving others ▷ vb pass on (a message)

RELEARN, -S, -T vb learn (something previously known) again

RELEASE, -D, -S vb set free ▷ n setting free

RELEASEE n someone to whom an estate is released or someone released from captivity

RELEASER ► release

RELEASES ► release

RELEASOR n someone releasing an estate to someone else

RELEGATE vb put in a less important position

RELEND, -S vb lend again

RELENT, -ED, -S vb give up a harsh intention, become less severe

RELET, -S vb let again

RELETTER vb redo lettering of

RELEVANT adj do with the matter in hand

RELEVE, -S n dance move in which heels are off the ground

RELIABLE adj able to be trusted, dependable ▷ n something or someone

believed to be reliable

RELIABLY

RELIANCE n dependence, confidence, or trust

RELIANT

RELIC, -S n something that has survived from the past

RELICT, -S n relic

RELIDE archaic past form of ► rely

RELIE archaic spelling of ► rely

RELIED ► rely

RELIEF, -S n gladness at the end or removal of pain, distress, etc

RELIER, -S n ► rely

RELIES ► rely

RELIEVE, -S vb bring relief to

RELIEVED adj experiencing relief, esp from worry or anxiety

RELIEVER n person or thing that relieves

RELIEVES ► relieve

RELIEVO, -S same as ► relief

RELIGHT, -S, RELIT vb ignite or cause to ignite again

RELIGION n system of belief in and worship of a supernatural power or god

RELINE, -D, -S, RELINING vb line again or anew

RELINK, -ED, -S vb link again

RELIQUE, -S archaic spelling of ► relic

RELISH, -ED, -ES vb enjoy, like very much ▷ n liking or enjoyment

RELIST, -ED, -S vb list again

RELIT ► relight

RELIVE, -D, -S, RELIVING vb experience (a sensation etc) again, esp in the imagination

RELIVER, -S vb deliver up again

RELIVES ► relive

RELIVING ► relive

RELLENO, -S n Mexican dish of stuffed vegetable

RELLIE n relative

RELLIES pl n relatives or relations

RELLISH (in music) variant of ► relish

RELOAD, -ED, -S vb put fresh ammunition into (a firearm)

RELOADER

RELOAN, -ED, -S vb loan again

RELOCATE vb move to a new place to live or work

RELOCK, -ED, -S vb lock again

RELOOK, -ED, -S vb look again

RELUCENT adj bright

RELUCT, -ED, -S vb struggle or rebel

RELUME, -D, -S, RELUMING vb light or brighten again

RELUMINE same as ► relume

RELUMING ► relume

RELY, RELIED, RELIES, -ING vb depend (on)

REM, -S n dose of ionizing radiation

REMADE, -S n object that has been reconstructed from original materials

REMAIL, -ED, -S vb mail again

REMAILER n internet service that forwards emails anonymously

REMAILS ► remail

REMAIN, -ED vb continue

REMAINS pl n relics, esp of ancient buildings

REMAKE, -S, REMAKING vb make again in a different way ▷ n new version of an old film

REMAKER -S

REMAN, -NED, -S vb man again or afresh

REMAND, -ED, -S vb send back into custody or put on bail before trial

REMANENT adj remaining or left over ▷ n archaic word meaning remainder

REMANET, -S n something left over

REMANIE, -S n fragments and fossils of older origin found in a more recent deposit

REMANNED ► reman

REMANS ► reman

REMAP, -PED, -S vb map again

REMARK, -ED, -S vb make a casual comment (on) ▷ n observation or comment

REMARKER

REMARKET vb market again

REMARKS ► remark

REMARQUE n printing mark in the margin of a plate

REMARRY vb marry again

REMASTER vb make a new master audio recording from an earlier recording

REMATCH n second or return game or contest between two players ▷ vb match (two contestants) again

REMATE, -D, -S, REMATING vb mate (animals) again ▷ n finishing pass in bullfighting

REMBLAI, -S n earth used for an embankment or rampart

REMBLE, -D, -S, REMBLING dialect word for ► remove

R

REMEAD, -ED, -S archaic or dialect word for ► **remedy**

REMEDE, -D, -S, REMEDING archaic or dialect word for ► **remede**

REMEDIAL adj intended to correct a specific disability, etc

REMEDIAT archaic word for ► **remedial**

REMEDIED ► **remedy**

REMEDIES ► **remedy**

REMEDING ► **remede**

REMEDY, REMEDIED, REMEDIES n means of curing pain or disease ▷ vb put right

REMEET, -S, REMET vb meet again

REMEID, -ED, -S archaic or dialect word for ► **remedy**

REMELT, -ED, -S vb melt again

REMEMBER vb retain in or recall to one's memory

REMEN, -S n ancient Egyptian measurement unit

REMEND, -ED, -S vb mend again

REMENS ► **remen**

REMERCY vb archaic word for thank

REMERGE, -D, -S vb merge again

REMET ► **remeet**

REMEX, REMIGES n any of the large flight feathers of a bird's wing

REMIGATE vb row

REMIGES ► **remex**

REMIGIAL ► **remex**

REMIND, -ED, -S vb cause to remember

REMINDER n something that recalls the past

REMINDS ► **remind**

REMINT, -ED, -S vb mint again

REMISE, -D, -S, REMISING vb give up or relinquish (a right, claim, etc) ▷ n second thrust made on the same lunge after the first has missed

REMISS adj negligent or careless

REMISSLY

REMIT, -S, -TED vb send (money) for goods, services, etc, esp by post ▷ n area of competence or authority

REMITTAL

REMITTEE n recipient of a remittance

REMITTER n person who remits

REMITTOR same as ► **remitter**

REMIX, -ED, -ES, -ING vb change the relative prominence of each performer's part of (a recording) ▷ n remixed version of a recording

REMIXER, -S n person who remixes a recording

REMIXES ► **remix**

REMIXING ► **remix**

REMIXT informal past form of ► **remix**

REMNANT, -S n small piece, esp of fabric, left over ▷ adj remaining

REMODEL, -S vb give a different shape or form to ▷ n something that has been remodelled

REMODIFY vb modify again

REMOLADE same as > **remoulade**

REMOLD, -ED, -S US spelling of ► **remould**

REMORA, -S n spiny-finned fish

REMORID

REMORSE, -S n feeling of sorrow and regret for something one did

REMOTE, -R, -S, -ST adj far away, distant ▷ n (in informal usage) remote control

REMOTELY

REMOTION n removal

REMOUD Spenserian variant of ► **removed**

REMOULD, -S vb change completely ▷ n renovated tyre

REMOUNT, -S vb get on (a horse, bicycle, etc) again ▷ n fresh horse

REMOVAL, -S n removing, esp changing residence

REMOVE, -S, REMOVING vb take away or off ▷ n degree of difference

REMOVED adj very different or distant

REMOVER, -S ► **remove**

REMOVES ► **remove**

REMOVING ► **remove**

REMS ► **rem**

REMUAGE, -S n process of turning wine bottles to let the sediment out

REMUDA, -S n stock of horses enabling riders to change mounts

REMUEUR, -S n person carrying out remuage

REMURMUR vb murmur again or murmur in reply

REN, -NED, -S archaic variant of ► **run**

RENAGUE, -D, -S same as ► **renege**

RENAIL, -ED, -S vb nail again

RENAL adj of the kidneys

RENAME, -D, -S, RENAMING vb change the name of (someone or something)

RENATURE vb return to natural state

RENAY, -ED, -ING, -S vb archaic word meaning renounce

REND, -ED, -ING, -S vb tear or wrench apart

RENDER, -ED, -S vb cause to become ▷ n first thin coat of plaster applied to a surface

RENDERER

RENDIBLE ► **rend**

RENDING ► **rend**

RENDS ► **rend**

RENDZINA n dark soil found in grassy or formerly grassy areas of moderate rainfall

RENEAGUE same as ► **renege**

RENEGADE n person who deserts a cause ▷ vb become a renegade

RENEGADO archaic word for ► **renegade**

RENEGATE old variant of ► **renegade**

RENEGE, -D, -S, RENEGING vb go back (on a promise etc)

RENEGER -S

RENEGUE, -D, -S same as ► **renege**

RENEGUER ► **renegue**

RENEGUES ► **renegue**

RENEST, -ED, -S vb nest again or form a new nest

RENEW, -ED, -ING, -S vb begin again

RENEWAL, -S n act of renewing or state of being renewed

RENEWED ► **renew**

RENEWER, -S ► **renew**

RENEWING ► **renew**

RENEWS ► **renew**

RENEY, -ED, -ING, -S same as ► **renay**

RENFORCE, RENFORST vb archaic word for reinforce

RENGA, -S n type of collaborative poetry found in Japan

RENIED ► **reny**

RENIES ► **reny**

RENIFORM adj having the shape or profile of a kidney

RENIG, -GED, -S same as ► **renege**

RENIN, -S n enzyme secreted by the kidneys
RENITENT adj reluctant
RENK, -ER, -EST adj unpleasant
RENMINBI same as ▸ **yuan**
RENNASE, -S same as ▸ **rennin**
RENNE, -S archaic variant of ▸ **run**
RENNED ▸ **ren**
RENNES ▸ **renne**
RENNET, -S n substance for curdling milk to make cheese
RENNIN, -S n enzyme that occurs in gastric juice
RENNING, -S ▸ **ren**
RENNINS ▸ **rennin**
RENO, -S n renovated house
RENOGRAM n X-ray kidney image
RENOS ▸ **reno**
RENOTIFY vb notify again
RENOUNCE vb give up (a belief, habit, etc) voluntarily ▷ n failure to follow suit in a card game
RENOVATE vb restore to good condition
RENOWN, -S n widespread good reputation ▷ vb make famous
RENOWNED adj famous
RENOWNER n renown giver
RENOWNS ▸ **renown**
RENS ▸ **ren**
RENT, -ED, -S n payment made by a tenant to a landlord or owner of a property ▷ vb grant the right to use one's property for payment
RENTABLE ▸ **rend**
RENTAL, -S n sum payable as rent ▷ adj of or relating to rent
RENTE, -S n annual income from capital investment
RENTED ▸ **rent**
RENTER, -S n person who lets his or her property in return for rent
RENTES ▸ **rente**
RENTIER, -S n person who lives off unearned income such as rents or interest
RENTING, -S ▸ **rent**
RENTS ▸ **rent**
RENUMBER vb number again or afresh
RENVERSE, RENVERST vb archaic word meaning overturn
RENVOI, -S n referring of a dispute to a jurisdiction other than that in which it arose

RENVOY, -S old variant of ▸ **renvoi**
RENY, RENIED, RENIES, -ING same as ▸ **renay**
REO, -S n New Zealand language
REOBJECT vb object again
REOBTAIN vb obtain again
REOCCUPY vb occupy (a building, area, etc) again
REOCCUR, -S vb happen, take place, or come about again
REOFFEND vb commit another offence
REOFFER, -S vb offer again
REOIL, -ED, -ING, -S vb oil again
REOPEN, -ED, -S vb open again after a period of being closed or suspended
REOPENER n clause in a legal document allowing for an issue to be revisited at a subsequent date
REOPENS ▸ **reopen**
REOPPOSE vb oppose again
REORDAIN vb ordain again
REORDER, -S vb change the order of
REORG, -ED, -ING, -S vb reorganize
REORIENT vb adjust or align (something) in a new or different way
REOS ▸ **reo**
REOUTFIT vb outfit again
REOVIRUS n type of virus
REP, -PED, -S n sales representative ▷ vb work as a representative
REPACIFY vb pacify again
REPACK, -ED, -S vb place or arrange (articles) in (a container) again or in a different way
REPAID ▸ **repay**
REPAINT, -S vb apply a new or fresh coat of paint
REPAIR, -ED, -S vb restore to good condition, mend ▷ n act of repairing
REPAIRER
REPAND adj having a wavy margin
REPANDLY
REPANEL, -S vb panel again or anew
REPAPER, -S vb paper again or afresh
REPARK, -ED, -S vb park again
REPARTEE n interchange of witty retorts ▷ vb retort
REPASS, -ED, -ES vb pass again
REPAST, -ED, -S n meal ▷ vb feed (on)

REPATCH vb patch again
REPAVE, -D, -S, REPAVING vb pave again
REPAY, REPAID, -ING, -S vb pay back, refund
REPEAL, -ED, -S vb cancel (a law) officially ▷ n act of repealing
REPEALER
REPEAT, -S vb say or do again ▷ n act or instance of repeating
REPEATED adj done, made, or said again and again
REPEATER n firearm that may be discharged many times without reloading
REPEATS ▸ **repeat**
REPEG, -GED, -S vb peg again
REPEL, -LED, -S vb be disgusting to
REPELLER
REPENT, -ED, -S vb feel regret for (a deed or omission) ▷ adj lying or creeping along the ground
REPENTER
REPEOPLE vb people again
REPEREPE n New Zealand word for the elephant fish
REPERK, -ED, -S vb perk again
REPERUSE vb peruse again
REPETEND n digit or series of digits in a recurring decimal that repeats itself
REPHRASE vb express in different words
REPIN, -NED, -S vb pin again
REPINE, -D, -S, REPINING vb fret or complain
REPINER -S
REPINNED ▸ **repin**
REPINS ▸ **repin**
REPIQUE, -D, -S n score of 30 in the card-game piquet ▷ vb score a repique against (someone)
REPLA ▸ **replum**
REPLACE, -D, -S vb substitute for
REPLACER
REPLAN, -S vb plan again
REPLANT, -S vb plant again
REPLATE, -D, -S vb plate again
REPLAY, -ED, -S n immediate reshowing on TV of an incident in sport ▷ vb play (a match, recording, etc) again
REPLEAD, -S, REPLED vb plead again
REPLEDGE vb pledge again
REPLETE, -D, -S adj filled or gorged ▷ vb fill again
REPLEVIN n recovery of goods unlawfully taken

REPLEVY vb recover possession of (goods) by replevin

REPLICA, -S n exact copy

REPLICON n region of a DNA molecule that is replicated from a single origin

REPLIED ▶ reply

REPLIER, -S ▶ reply

REPLIES ▶ reply

REPLOT, -S vb plot again

REPLOUGH vb plough again

REPLOW, -ED, -S vb plow again

REPLUM, REPLA n internal separating wall in some fruits

REPLUMB, -S vb plumb again

REPLUNGE vb plunge again

REPLY, REPLIED, REPLIES, -ING vb answer or respond ▷ n answer or response

REPO, -S n act of repossessing

REPOINT, -S vb repair the joints of (brickwork, masonry, etc) with mortar or cement

REPOLISH vb polish again

REPOLL, -ED, -S vb poll again

REPOMAN, REPOMEN n man employed to repossess goods in cases of non-payment

REPONE, -D, -S, REPONING vb restore (someone) to his or her former status, office, etc

REPORT, -ED, -S vb give an account of ▷ n account or statement

REPORTER n person who gathers news for a newspaper, TV, etc

REPORTS ▶ report

REPOS ▶ repo

REPOSAL, -S n repose

REPOSALL archaic spelling of ▶ reposal

REPOSALS ▶ reposal

REPOSE, -D, -S, REPOSING n peace ▷ vb lie or lay at rest

REPOSER -S

REPOSIT, -S vb put away, deposit, or store up

REPOST, -ED, -S vb post again

REPOSURE old word for ▶ repose

REPOT, -S, -TED vb put (a house plant) into a new usually larger pot

REPOUR, -ED, -S vb pour back or again

REPOUSSE adj raised in relief ▷ n design or surface made in this way

REPOWER, -S vb put new engine in

REPP, -S same as ▶ rep

REPPED ▶ rep

REPPING, -S ▶ rep

REPPS ▶ repp

REPREEVE archaic spelling of ▶ reprieve

REPRESS vb keep (feelings) in check

REPRICE, -D, -S vb price again

REPRIEFE n (in archaic usage) reproof

REPRIEVE vb postpone the execution of (a condemned person) ▷ n (document granting) postponement or cancellation of a punishment

REPRIME, -D, -S vb prime again

REPRINT, -S vb print further copies of (a book) ▷ n reprinted copy

REPRISAL n retaliation

REPRISE, -D, -S n repeating of an earlier theme ▷ vb repeat an earlier theme

REPRIVE, -D, -S archaic spelling of ▶ reprieve

REPRIZE, -D, -S archaic spelling of ▶ reprise

REPRO, -S n imitation or facsimile of a work of art; reproduction

REPROACH vb blame, rebuke

REPROBE, -D, -S vb probe again

REPROOF, -S n severe blaming of someone for a fault ▷ vb treat (a coat, jacket, etc) so as to renew its texture, etc

REPROS ▶ repro

REPROVAL same as ▶ reproof

REPROVE, -D, -S vb speak severely to (someone) about a fault

REPROVER

REPRYVE, -D, -S archaic spelling of ▶ reprieve

REPS ▶ rep

REPTANT adj creeping, crawling, or lying along the ground

REPTILE, -S n cold-blooded egg-laying vertebrate with horny scales or plates ▷ adj creeping, crawling, or squirming

REPTILIA > reptilium

REPUBLIC n government in which the people possess the supreme power

REPUGN, -ED, -S vb oppose or conflict (with)

REPULP, -ED, -S vb pulp again

REPULSE, -D, -S vb be disgusting to ▷ n driving back

REPULSER

REPUMP, -ED, -S vb pump again

REPUNIT, -S n any number that consists entirely of the same repeated digits

REPURE, -D, -S, REPURING archaic word meaning make pure again

REPURIFY vb purify again

REPURING ▶ repure

REPURSUE vb pursue again

REPUTE, -S, REPUTING n reputation ▷ vb consider (a person or thing) to be as specified

REPUTED adj supposed

REPUTES ▶ repute

REPUTING ▶ repute

REQUERE, -D, -S archaic variant of ▶ require

REQUEST, -S vb ask ▷ n asking

REQUIEM, -S n Mass celebrated for the dead

REQUIGHT archaic spelling of ▶ requite

REQUIN, -S vb type of shark

REQUINTO n type of small guitar

REQUIRE, -D, -S vb want or need

REQUIRER

REQUIT, -S vb quit again

REQUITAL n act or an instance of requiting

REQUITE, -D, -S vb return to someone (the same treatment or feeling as received)

REQUITER

REQUITS ▶ requit

REQUOTE, -D, -S vb quote again

REQUOYLE archaic spelling of ▶ recoil

RERACK, -ED, -S vb rack again

RERAIL, -ED, -S vb put back on a railway line

RERAISE, -D, -S vb raise again

RERAN ▶ rerun

REREAD, -S vb read (something) again

RERECORD vb record again

REREDOS n ornamental screen behind an altar

REREMAI, -S n New Zealand word for the basking shark

REREMICE > reremouse

REREMIND vb remind again

RERENT, -ED, -S vb rent again

REREPEAT vb repeat again

REREVIEW vb review again

REREVISE vb revise again

REREWARD archaic spelling of ▶ rearward

RERIG, -GED, -S vb rig again

R

RERISE, -N, -S, RERISING, REROSE *vb* rise again

REROLL, -ED, -S *vb* roll again **REROLLER**

REROOF, -ED, -S *vb* put a new roof or roofs on

REROSE ▸ rerise

REROUTE, -D, -S *vb* send or direct by a different route

RERUN, RERAN, -S *n* film or programme that is broadcast again, repeat ▷ *vb* put on (a film or programme) again

RES, -ES *informal word for* > residence

RESADDLE *vb* saddle again

RESAID ▸ resay

RESAIL, -ED, -S *vb* sail again

RESALE, -S *n* selling of something purchased earlier

RESALGAR *archaic variant of* ▸ realgar

RESALUTE *vb* salute back or again

RESAMPLE *vb* (in graphics or digital photography) change the size or resolution of

RESAT ▸ resit

RESAW, -ED, -ING, -N, -S *vb* saw again

RESAY, RESAID, -ING, -S *vb* say again or in response

RESCALE, -D, -S *vb* resize

RESCHOOL *vb* retrain

RESCIND, -S *vb* annul or repeal

RESCORE, -D, -S *vb* score afresh

RESCREEN *vb* screen again

RESCRIPT *n* ordinance taking the form of a reply by the Roman emperor to a point of law

RESCUE, -D, -S, RESCUING *vb* deliver from danger or trouble, save ▷ *n* rescuing

RESCUEE, -S *n* person who is rescued

RESCUER, -S ▸ rescue

RESCUES ▸ rescue

RESCUING ▸ rescue

RESCULPT *vb* sculpt again

RESEAL, -ED, -S *vb* close or secure tightly again

RESEARCH *n* systematic investigation to discover facts or collect information ▷ *vb* carry out investigations

RESEASON *vb* season again

RESEAT, -ED, -S *vb* show (a person) to a new seat

RESEAU, -S, -X *n* mesh background to a lace or other pattern

RESECT, -ED, -S *vb* cut out part of (a bone, an organ, or other structure or part)

RESECURE *vb* secure again

RESEDA, -S *n* plant that has small spikes of grey-green flowers ▷ *adj* of a greyish-green colour

RESEE, -ING, -N, -S *vb* see again

RESEED, -ED, -S *vb* form seed and reproduce naturally, forming a constant plant population

RESEEING ▸ resee

RESEEK, -S, RESOUGHT *vb* seek again

RESEEN ▸ resee

RESEES ▸ resee

RESEIZE, -D, -S *vb* seize again

RESELECT *vb* choose (someone or something) again

RESELL, -S, RESOLD *vb* sell (something) one has previously bought **RESELLER**

RESEMBLE *vb* be or look like

RESEND, -S *vb* send again

RESENT, -ED, -S *vb* feel bitter about **RESENTER**

RESERVE, -S *vb* set aside, keep for future use ▷ *n* something, esp money or troops, kept for emergencies

RESERVED *adj* not showing one's feelings, lacking friendliness

RESERVER ▸ reserve

RESERVES ▸ reserve

RESES ▸ res

RESET, -S *vb* set again (a broken bone, matter in type, a gemstone, etc) ▷ *n* act or an instance of setting again

RESETTED *same as* ▸ **reset**

RESETTER ▸ reset

RESETTLE *vb* settle to live in a different place

RESEW, -ED, -ING, -N, -S *vb* sew again

RESH, -ES *n* 20th letter of the Hebrew alphabet

RESHAPE, -D, -S *vb* shape (something) again or differently **RESHAPER**

RESHAVE, -D, -N, -S *vb* shave again

RESHES ▸ resh

RESHINE, -D, -S, RESHONE *vb* shine again

RESHIP, -S *vb* ship again

RESHOE, RESHOD, -D, -S *vb* put a new shoe or shoes on

RESHONE ▸ reshine

RESHOOT, -S, RESHOT *vb* shoot again

RESHOW, -ED, -N, -S *vb* show again

RESHOWER *vb* have another shower

RESHOWN ▸ reshow

RESHOWS ▸ reshow

RESIANCE *archaic word for* > residence

RESIANT, -S *archaic word for* ▸ resident

RESID, -S *n* residual oil left over from the petroleum distillation process

RESIDE, -D, -S, RESIDING *vb* dwell permanently

RESIDENT *n* person who lives in a place ▷ *adj* living in a place

RESIDER, -S ▸ reside

RESIDES ▸ reside

RESIDING ▸ reside

RESIDS ▸ resid

RESIDUA ▸ residuum

RESIDUAL *adj* of or being a remainder ▷ *n* something left over as a residue

RESIDUE, -S *n* what is left, remainder

RESIDUUM, RESIDUA *n* residue

RESIFT, -ED, -S *vb* sift again

RESIGHT, -S *vb* sight again

RESIGN, -S *vb* give up office, a job, etc

RESIGNED *adj* content to endure

RESIGNER ▸ resign

RESIGNS ▸ resign

RESILE, -D, -S, RESILING *vb* spring or shrink back

RESILIN, -S *n* substance found in insect bodies

RESILING ▸ resile

RESILINS ▸ resilin

RESILVER *vb* silver again

RESIN, -ED, -ING, -S *n* sticky substance from plants, esp pines ▷ *vb* treat or coat with resin

RESINATA *n* type of wine

RESINATE *vb* impregnate with resin

RESINED ▸ resin

RESINER, -S *n* applier or collector of resin

RESINIFY *vb* become or cause to be resinous

RESINING ▸ resin

RESINISE *variant spelling of* ▸ resinize

RESINIZE *vb* apply resin to

RESINOID *adj* resembling, characteristic of, or

R

containing resin ▷ *n* any resinoid substance, esp a synthetic compound

RESINOUS ► resin

RESINS ► resin

RESINY *adj* resembling, containing or covered with resin

RESIST, -ED, -S *vb* withstand or oppose ▷ *n* substance used to protect something **RESISTER**

RESISTOR *n* component of an electrical circuit producing resistance

RESISTS ► resist

RESIT, RESAT, -S *vb* take (an exam) again ▷ *n* exam that has to be taken again

RESITE, -D, -S, RESITING *vb* move to a different site

RESITS ► resit

RESIZE, -D, -S, RESIZING *vb* change size of

RESKETCH *vb* sketch again

RESKEW, -ED, -S *archaic spelling of* ► rescue

RESKILL, -S *vb* train (workers) to acquire new skills

RESKIN, -S *vb* replace the outermost layer of an aircraft

RESKUE, -D, -S, RESKUING *archaic spelling of* ► rescue

RESLATE, -D, -S *vb* slate again

RESMELT, -S *vb* smelt again

RESMOOTH *vb* smooth again

RESOAK, -ED, -S *vb* soak again

RESOD, -DED, -S *vb* returf

RESOFTEN *vb* soften again

RESOJET, -S *n* type of jet engine

RESOLD ► resell

RESOLDER *vb* solder again

RESOLE, -D, -S, RESOLING *vb* put a new sole or new soles on

RESOLUTE *adj* firm in purpose ▷ *n* someone resolute

RESOLVE, -S *vb* decide with an effort of will ▷ *n* absolute determination

RESOLVED *adj* determined

RESOLVER ► resolve

RESOLVES ► resolve

RESONANT *adj* resounding or re-echoing ▷ *n* type of unobstructed speech sound

RESONATE *vb* resound or cause to resound

RESORB, -ED, -S *vb* absorb again

RESORCIN *n* substance used principally in dyeing

RESORT, -ED, -S *vb* have recourse (to) for help etc

▷ *n* place for holidays

RESORTER

RESOUGHT ► reseek

RESOUND, -S *vb* echo or ring with sound

RESOURCE *n* thing resorted to for support ▷ *vb* provide funding or other resources for

RESOW, -ED, -ING, -N, -S *vb* sow again

RESPACE, -D, -S *vb* change the spacing of

RESPADE, -D, -S *vb* dig over

RESPEAK, -S, RESPOKE, RESPOKEN *vb* speak further

RESPECT, -S *n* consideration ▷ *vb* treat with esteem

RESPELL, -S, RESPELT *vb* spell again

RESPIRE, -D, -S *vb* breathe

RESPITE, -D, -S *n* pause, interval of rest ▷ *vb* grant a respite to

RESPLEND *vb* be resplendent

RESPLICE *vb* splice again

RESPLIT, -S *vb* split again

RESPOKE ► respeak

RESPOKEN ► respeak

RESPOND, -S *vb* answer ▷ *n* pilaster or an engaged column that supports an arch or a lintel

RESPONSA *n* that part of rabbinic literature concerned with written rulings in answer to questions

RESPONSE *n* answer

RESPOOL, -S *vb* rewind onto spool

RESPOT, -S *vb* (in billiards) replace on one of the spots

RESPRANG ► respring

RESPRAY, -S *n* new coat of paint applied to a car, van, etc ▷ *vb* spray (a car, wheels, etc) with a new coat of paint

RESPREAD *vb* spread again

RESPRING, RESPRANG, RESPRUNG *vb* put new springs in

RESPROUT *vb* sprout again

RESPRUNG ► respring

REST, -ED, -S *n* freedom from exertion etc ▷ *vb* take a rest

RESTABLE *vb* put in stable again or elsewhere

RESTACK, -S *vb* stack again

RESTAFF, -S *vb* staff again

RESTAGE, -D, -S *vb* produce or perform a new production of (a play)

RESTAMP, -S *vb* stamp again

RESTART, -S *vb* commence (something) or set (something) in motion again

▷ *n* act or an instance of starting again

RESTATE, -D, -S *vb* state or affirm (something) again or in a different way

RESTED ► rest

RESTEM, -S *vb* stem again

RESTER, -S ► rest

RESTFUL *adj* relaxing or soothing

RESTIER ► resty

RESTIEST ► resty

RESTIFF *same as* ► restive

RESTING, -S ► rest

RESTITCH *vb* stitch again

RESTIVE *adj* restless or impatient

RESTLESS *adj* bored or dissatisfied

RESTO, -S *n* restored antique, vintage car, etc

RESTOCK, -S *vb* replenish stores or supplies

RESTOKE, -D, -S *vb* stoke again

RESTORAL *n* restoration

RESTORE, -D, -S *vb* return (a building, painting, etc) to its original condition

RESTORER

RESTOS ► resto

RESTRAIN *vb* hold (someone) back from action

RESTRESS *vb* stress again or differently

RESTRICT *vb* confine to certain limits

RESTRIKE, RESTRUCK *vb* strike again

RESTRING, RESTRUNG *vb* string again or anew

RESTRIVE, RESTROVE *vb* strive again

RESTROOM *n* room in a public building having lavatories and washing facilities

RESTROVE ► restrive

RESTRUCK ► restrike

RESTRUNG ► restring

RESTS ► rest

RESTUDY *vb* study again

RESTUFF, -S *vb* put new stuffing in

RESTUMP, -S *vb* provide with new stumps

RESTY, RESTIER, RESTIEST *adj* restive

RESTYLE, -D, -S *vb* style again

RESUBMIT *vb* submit again

RESULT, -ED, -S *n* outcome or consequence ▷ *vb* be the outcome or consequence (of)

RESUME, -D, -S, RESUMING *vb* begin again ▷ *n* summary

RESUMER, -S

RESUMMON vb summon again

RESUPINE adj lying on the back

RESUPPLY vb provide (with something) again

RESURGE, -D, -S vb rise again from or as if from the dead

RESURVEY vb survey again

RESUS, -ES, -SES n (short for) resuscitation room

RET, -S, -TED, -TING vb moisten or soak (flax, hemp, jute, etc) to facilitate separation of fibres

RETABLE, -S n ornamental screenlike structure above and behind an altar

RETABLO, -S n shelf for panels behind an altar

RETACK, -ED, -S vb tack again

RETACKLE vb tackle again

RETACKS ▸ retack

RETAG, -GED, -S vb tag again

RETAIL, -ED, -S n selling of goods individually or in small amounts to the public ▷ adj of or engaged in such selling ▷ adv by retail ▷ vb sell or be sold retail

RETAILER

RETAILOR vb tailor afresh

RETAILS ▸ retail

RETAIN, -ED, -S vb keep in one's possession

Perhaps the most important word in Scrabble, because its letters combine with every other letter apart from A, Q, V, X, Y and Z to form a 7-letter bonus word that will score you an extra 50 points, so if you have these six letters on your rack you know that a bonus is either available or close. And if you have an S as well, so much the better, because not only does this rack offer you 11 different words to choose from, but if none of those can be fitted in then **retains** combines with every other letter except for Q, V, X, Y and Z to form at least one 8-letter word.

RETAINER n fee to retain someone's services

RETAINS ▸ retain

RETAKE, -N, -S, RETAKING, RETOOK vb recapture ▷ n act of rephotographing a scene

RETAKER -S

RETALLY vb count up again

RETAMA, -S n type of shrub

RETAPE, -D, -S, RETAPING vb tape again

RETARD, -ED, -S vb delay or slow (progress or development)

RETARDER n substance that slows down chemical change

RETARDS ▸ retard

RETARGET vb target afresh or differently

RETASTE, -D, -S vb taste again

RETAUGHT ▸ reteach

RETAX, -ED, -ES, -ING vb tax again

RETCH, -ED, -ES vb try to vomit ▷ n involuntary spasm of the stomach

RETCHING n act of retching

RETE, RETIA n any network of nerves or blood vessels

RETEACH, RETAUGHT vb teach again

RETEAM, -ED, -S vb team up again

RETEAR, -S, RETORE, RETORN vb tear again

RETELL, -S, RETOLD vb relate (a story, etc) again or differently

RETELLER

RETEM, -S n type of shrub

RETEMPER vb temper again

RETEMS ▸ retem

RETENE, -S n yellow crystalline hydrocarbon found in tar oils

RETEST, -ED, -S vb test (something) again or differently

RETHINK, -S vb consider again, esp with a view to changing one's tactics ▷ n act or an instance of thinking again

RETHREAD vb thread again

RETIA ▸ rete

RETIAL ▸ rete

RETIARII > retiarius

RETIARY adj of, relating to, or resembling a net or web

RETICENT adj uncommunicative, reserved

RETICLE, -S n network of fine lines, wires, etc, used in optical instruments

RETICULA > reticulum

RETICULE same as ▸ **reticle**

RETIE, -D, -ING, -S, RETYING vb tie again

RETIFORM adj netlike

RETILE, -D, -S, RETILING vb put new tiles in or on

RETALLY vb count up again

RETIME, -D, -S, RETIMING vb time again or alter time of

RETINA, -E, -S n light-sensitive membrane at the back of the eye

RETINAL, -S adj of or relating to the retina ▷ n aldehyde form of the polyene retinol

RETINAS ▸ retina

RETINE, -S n chemical found in body cells that slows cell growth and division

RETINENE n aldehyde form of the polyene retinol

RETINES ▸ retine

RETINITE n any of various resins of fossil origin, esp one derived from lignite

RETINOIC adj containing or derived from retinoid

RETINOID adj resinlike ▷ n derivative of vitamin A

RETINOL, -S n another name for vitamin A and rosin oil

RETINT, -ED, -S vb tint again or change tint of

RETINUE, -S n band of attendants

RETINUED

RETINULA n part of the compound eye in certain arthropods

RETIRACY n (in US English) retirement

RETIRAL, -S n act of retiring from office, one's work, etc

RETIRANT n (in US English) retired person

RETIRE, -S vb (cause to) give up office or work, esp through age

RETIRED adj having retired from work etc

RETIREE, -S n person who has retired from work

RETIRER, -S ▸ retire

RETIRES ▸ retire

RETIRING adj shy

RETITLE, -D, -S vb give a new title to

RETOLD ▸ retell

RETOOK ▸ retake

RETOOL, -ED, -S vb replace, re-equip, or rearrange the tools in (a factory, etc)

RETORE ▸ retear

RETORN ▸ retear

RETORT, -ED, -S vb reply quickly, wittily, or angrily ▷ n quick, witty, or angry reply

RETORTER

RETOTAL, -S vb add up again

RETOUCH vb restore or improve by new touches, esp of paint ▷ n art or practice of retouching

R

RETOUR, **-ED**, **-S** *vb* (in Scottish law) to return as heir

RETOX, **-ED**, **-ES**, **-ING** *vb* embark on a binge of something unhealthy after a period of abstinence

RETRACE, **-D**, **-S** *vb* go back over (a route etc) again

RETRACER

RETRACK, **-S** *vb* track again

RETRACT, **-S** *vb* withdraw (a statement etc)

RETRAICT *archaic form of* ▸ **retreat**

RETRAIN, **-S** *vb* train to do a new or different job

RETRAIT, **-S** *archaic form of* ▸ **retreat**

RETRAITE *archaic form of* ▸ **retreat**

RETRAITS ▸ **retrait**

RETRAITT *n* archaic word meaning portrait

RETRAL *adj* at, near, or towards the back

RETRALLY

RETRATE, **-D**, **-S** *archaic form of* ▸ **retreat**

RETREAD, **-S**, **RETROD** *n* remould ▸ *vb* remould

RETREAT, **-S** *vb* move back from a position, withdraw ▸ *n* act of or military signal for retiring or withdrawal

RETREE, **-S** *n* imperfectly made paper

RETRENCH *vb* reduce expenditure, cut back

RETRIAL, **-S** *n* second trial of a case or defendant in a court of law

RETRIED ▸ **retry**

RETRIES ▸ **retry**

RETRIEVE *vb* fetch back again ▸ *n* chance of being retrieved

RETRIM, **-S** *vb* trim again

RETRO, **-S** *adj* associated with or revived from the past ▸ *n* a retro style of art

RETROACT *vb* act in opposition

RETROD ▸ **retread**

RETROFIT *vb* equip (a piece of equipment) with new parts after manufacture

RETRONYM *n* word coined for existing thing to distinguish it from new thing

RETRORSE *adj* (esp of plant parts) pointing backwards or in a direction opposite to normal

RETROS ▸ **retro**

RETRY, **RETRIED**, **RETRIES**, **-ING** *vb* try again (a case already determined)

RETS ▸ **ret**

RETSINA, **-S** *n* Greek wine flavoured with resin

RETTED ▸ **ret**

RETTERY *n* flax-retting place

RETTING ▸ **ret**

RETUND, **-ED**, **-S** *vb* weaken or blunt

RETUNE, **-D**, **-S**, **RETUNING** *vb* tune (a musical instrument) differently or again

RETURF, **-ED**, **-S** *vb* turf again

RETURN, **-ED**, **-S** *vb* go or come back ▸ *n* returning ▸ *adj* of or being a return

RETURNEE *n* person who returns to his or her native country, esp after war service

RETURNER *n* person or thing that returns

RETURNIK *n* someone returning to the former Soviet Union

RETURNS ▸ **return**

RETUSE *adj* having a rounded apex and a central depression

RETWEET, **-S** *vb* post (another user's post) on the Twitter website for one's own followers

RETWIST, **-S** *vb* twist again

RETYING ▸ **retie**

RETYPE, **-D**, **-S**, **RETYPING** *vb* type again

REUNIFY *vb* bring together again something previously divided

REUNION, **-S** *n* meeting of people who have been apart

REUNITE, **-D**, **-S** *vb* bring or come together again after a separation

REUNITER

REUPTAKE, **REUPTOOK** *vb* absorb again ▸ *n* act of reabsorbing

REURGE, **-D**, **-S**, **REURGING** *vb* urge again

REUSABLE *adj* able to be used more than once

REUSE, **-D**, **-S**, **REUSING** *vb* use again ▸ *n* act of using something again

REUTTER, **-S** *vb* utter again

REV, **-S**, **-VED**, **-VING** *n* revolution (of an engine) ▸ *vb* increase the speed of revolution of (an engine)

REVALUE, **-D**, **-S** *vb* adjust the exchange value of (a currency) upwards

REVAMP, **-ED**, **-S** *vb* renovate or restore ▸ *n* something that has been renovated or revamped

REVAMPER

REVANCHE *n* revenge

REVEAL, **-ED**, **-S** *vb* make known ▸ *n* vertical side of an opening in a wall

REVEALER

REVEHENT *adj* (in anatomy) carrying back

REVEILLE *n* morning bugle call to waken soldiers

REVEL, **-ED**, **-ING**, **-LED**, **-S** *vb* take pleasure (in) ▸ *n* occasion of noisy merrymaking

REVELER **-S**

REVELLER ▸ **revel**

REVELRY *n* festivity

REVELS ▸ **revel**

REVENANT *n* something, esp a ghost, that returns

REVENGE, **-D**, **-S** *n* retaliation for wrong done ▸ *vb* make retaliation for

REVENGER

REVENUAL ▸ **revenue**

REVENUE, **-S** *n* income, esp of a state

REVENUED

REVENUER *n* revenue officer or cutter

REVENUES ▸ **revenue**

REVERB, **-ED**, **-S** *n* electronic device that creates artificial acoustics ▸ *vb* reverberate

REVERE, **-D**, **-S**, **REVERING** *vb* be in awe of and respect greatly

REVEREND *adj* worthy of reverence ▸ *n* clergyman

REVERENT *adj* showing reverence

REVERER, **-S** ▸ **revere**

REVERES ▸ **revere**

REVERIE, **-S** *n* absent-minded daydream

REVERIFY *vb* verify again

REVERING ▸ **revere**

REVERIST *n* someone given to reveries

REVERS *n* turned back part of a garment, such as the lapel

REVERSAL *n* act or an instance of reversing

REVERSE, **-D**, **-S** *vb* turn upside down or the other way round ▸ *n* opposite ▸ *adj* opposite or contrary

REVERSER

REVERSI *n* game played on a draughtboard

REVERSIS *n* type of card game

REVERSO, **-S** *another name for* ▸ **verso**

REVERT, **-ED**, **-S** *vb* return to a former state

REVERTER

REVERY *same as* ▸ **reverie**

REVEST, -ED, -S vb restore (former power, authority, status, etc, to a person)

REVESTRY same as ▸ **vestry**

REVESTS ▸ **revest**

REVET, -S, -TED vb face (a wall or embankment) with stones

REVEUR, -S n daydreamer

REVEUSE, -S n female daydreamer

REVIE, -D, -S, REVYING vb archaic cards term meaning challenge by placing a larger stake

REVIEW, -ED, -S n critical assessment of a book, concert, etc ▷ vb hold or write a review of

REVIEWAL same as ▸ **review**

REVIEWED ▸ **review**

REVIEWER ▸ **review**

REVIEWS ▸ **review**

REVILE, -D, -S, REVILING vb be abusively scornful of

REVILER -S

REVISAL, -S ▸ **revise**

REVISE, -D, -S, REVISING vb change or alter ▷ n act, process, or result of revising

REVISER -S

REVISION n act of revising

REVISIT, -S vb visit again

REVISOR, -S ▸ **revise**

REVISORY adj of or having the power of revision

REVIVAL, -S n reviving or renewal

REVIVE, -D, -S vb bring or come back to life, vigour, use, etc

REVIVER -S

REVIVIFY vb give new life to

REVIVING ▸ **revive**

REVIVOR, -S n means of reviving a lawsuit that has been suspended

REVOICE, -D, -S vb utter again

REVOKE, -D, -S, REVOKING vb cancel (a will, agreement, etc) ▷ n act of revoking

REVOKER -S

REVOLT, -S n uprising against authority ▷ vb rise in rebellion

REVOLTER

REVOLUTE adj (esp of the margins of a leaf) rolled backwards and downwards

REVOLVE, -D, -S vb turn round, rotate ▷ n circular section of a stage that can be rotated

REVOLVER n repeating pistol

REVOLVES ▸ **revolve**

REVOTE, -D, -S, REVOTING vb decide or grant again by a new vote

REVS ▸ **rev**

REVUE, -S n theatrical entertainment with topical sketches and songs

REVUIST -S

REVULSED adj filled with disgust

REVVED ▸ **rev**

REVVING ▸ **rev**

REVYING ▸ **revie**

REW, -S archaic spelling of ▸ **rue**

REWAKE, -D, -S, REWAKING, REWOKE, REWOKEN vb awaken again

REWAKEN, -S vb awaken again

REWAKES ▸ **rewake**

REWAKING ▸ **rewake**

REWAN archaic past form of ▸ **rewin**

REWARD, -ED, -S n something given in return for a service ▷ vb pay or give something to (someone) for a service, information, etc

REWARDER

REWAREWA n New Zealand tree

REWARM, -ED, -S vb warm again

REWASH, -ED, -ES vb wash again

REWATER, -S vb water again

REWAX, -ED, -ES, -ING vb wax again

REWEAR, -S, REWORE, REWORN vb wear again

REWEAVE, -D, -S, REWOVE, REWOVEN vb weave again

REWED, -DED, -S vb wed again

REWEIGH, -S vb weigh again

REWELD, -ED, -S vb weld again

REWET, -S, -TED vb wet again

REWIDEN, -S vb widen again

REWILD, -ED, -S vb return areas of land to a wild state

REWIN, -S, REWON vb win again

REWIND, -ED, -S, REWOUND vb wind again

REWINDER

REWINS ▸ **rewin**

REWIRE, -D, -S vb provide (a house, engine, etc) with new wiring

REWIRING n act of rewiring

REWOKE ▸ **rewake**

REWOKEN ▸ **rewake**

REWON ▸ **rewin**

REWORD, -ED, -S vb alter the wording of

REWORE ▸ **rewear**

REWORK, -ED, -S vb improve or bring up to date

REWORN ▸ **rewear**

REWOUND ▸ **rewind**

REWOVE ▸ **reweave**

REWOVEN ▸ **reweave**

REWRAP, -S, -T vb wrap again

REWRITE, -S, REWROTE vb write again in a different way ▷ n something rewritten

REWRITER

REWS ▸ **rew**

REWTH, -S archaic variant of ▸ **ruth**

REX, REGES, -ES n king

> **Rex** is a Latin word for **king**, a very commonly played X word.

REXINE, -S n tradename for a form of artificial leather

REYNARD, -S n fox

REZ, -ES, -ZES n informal word for an instance of reserving; reservation

> **Rez** is a short informal word for **reservation**, and is one of the most commonly played Z words.

REZERO, -ED, -ES, -S vb reset to zero

REZES ▸ **rez**

REZONE, -D, -S, REZONING vb zone again

REZZES ▸ **rez**

RHABDOID adj rod-shaped ▷ n rod-shaped structure found in cells of some plants and animals

RHABDOM, -S n rodlike structures found in the eye of insects

RHABDOME same as ▸ **rhabdom**

RHABDOMS ▸ **rhabdom**

RHABDUS n sponge spicule

RHACHIAL ▸ **rachis**

RHACHIS same as ▸ **rachis**

RHAGADES pl n cracks found in the skin

RHAMNOSE n type of plant sugar

RHAMNUS n buckthorn

RHAPHE, RHAPHAE, -S same as ▸ **raphe**

RHAPHIDE same as ▸ **raphide**

RHAPHIS same as ▸ **raphide**

RHAPSODE n (in ancient Greece) professional reciter of poetry

R

RHAPSODY n freely structured emotional piece of music

RHATANY n South American leguminous shrub

RHEA, -S n S American three-toed ostrich

RHEBOK, -S n woolly brownish-grey southern African antelope

RHEMATIC adj of or relating to word formation

RHEME, -S n constituent of a sentence that adds most new information

RHENIUM, -S n silvery-white metallic element with a high melting point

RHEOBASE n minimum nerve impulse required to elicit a response from a tissue

RHEOCORD same as > rheochord

RHEOLOGY n branch of physics concerned with the flow and change of shape of matter

RHEOPHIL adj liking flowing water

RHEOSTAT n instrument for varying the resistance of an electrical circuit

RHEOTOME n interrupter

RHESUS, -ES n macaque monkey

RHETOR, -S n teacher of rhetoric

RHETORIC n art of effective speaking or writing

RHETORS ▸ rhetor

RHEUM, -S n watery discharge from the eyes or nose

RHEUMED adj rheumy

RHEUMIC adj of or relating to rheum

RHEUMIER ▸ rheumy

RHEUMS ▸ rheum

RHEUMY, RHEUMIER adj of the nature of rheum

RHEXIS, RHEXES, -ES n rupture

RHIES ▸ rhy

RHIME, -S old spelling of ▸ rhyme

RHINAL adj of or relating to the nose

RHINE, -S n dialect word for a ditch

RHINITIC ▸ rhinitis

RHINITIS n inflammation of the mucous membrane that lines the nose

RHINO, -S n rhinoceros

RHIZIC adj of or relating to the root of an equation

RHIZINE, -S same as ▸ rhizoid

RHIZOBIA > rhizobium

RHIZOID, -S n hairlike structure in mosses, ferns, and related plants

RHIZOMA same as ▸ rhizome

RHIZOME, -S n thick underground stem producing new plants

RHIZOMIC

RHIZOPI ▸ rhizopus

RHIZOPOD n type of protozoan of the phylum which includes the amoebas

RHIZOPUS, RHIZOPI n type of fungus

RHO, -S n 17th letter in the Greek alphabet

It's useful to remember words that start with RH, as they can come in useful. If you or someone else plays **rho**, which is a Greek letter, remember that it can be expanded to, for example, **rhody, rhomb, rhodium, rhombus** or **rhomboid**.

RHODAMIN same as > rhodamine

RHODANIC adj of or relating to sulphocyanic acid

RHODIC adj of or containing rhodium, esp in the tetravalent state

RHODIE same as ▸ rhody

RHODIES ▸ rhody

RHODINAL n substance with a lemon-like smell found esp in citronella and certain eucalyptus oils

RHODIUM, -S n hard metallic element

RHODORA, -S n type of shrub

RHODOUS adj of or containing rhodium (but proportionally more than a rhodic compound)

RHODY, RHODIES n rhododendron

RHOMB, -S same as ▸ rhombus

RHOMBI ▸ rhombus

RHOMBIC adj relating to or having the shape of a rhombus

RHOMBOI ▸ rhombos

RHOMBOID n parallelogram with adjacent sides of unequal length ▷ adj having such a shape

RHOMBOS, RHOMBOI n wooden slat attached to a thong that makes a roaring sound when the thong is whirled

RHOMBS ▸ rhomb

RHOMBUS, RHOMBI n diamond-shaped figure

RHONCHAL ▸ rhonchus

RHONCHUS, RHONCHI n respiratory sound resembling snoring

RHONCUS n rattling or whistling respiratory sound resembling snoring

RHONE, -S same as ▸ rone

RHOPALIC adj (of verse) with each word having one more syllable than the word before

RHOS ▸ rho

RHOTIC adj denoting or speaking a dialect of English in which postvocalic r s are pronounced

RHUBARB, -S n garden plant with fleshy stalks ▷ interj noise made by actors to simulate conversation ▷ vb simulate conversation in this way

RHUBARBY

RHUMB, -S n as in rhumb line imaginary line on the surface of a sphere that intersects all meridians at the same angle

RHUMBA, -ED, -S same as ▸ rumba

RHUMBS ▸ rhumb

RHUS, -ES n genus of shrubs and small trees

RHY, RHIES archaic spelling of ▸ rye

This alternative spelling of **rye** can come in useful when you are short of vowels.

RHYME, -D, -S, RHYMING n sameness of the final sounds at the ends of lines of verse, or in words ▷ vb make a rhyme

RHYMER, -S same as > rhymester

RHYMES ▸ rhyme

RHYMING ▸ rhyme

RHYMIST, -S ▸ rhyme

RHYNE, -S same as ▸ rhine

RHYOLITE n fine-grained igneous rock

RHYTA ▸ rhyton

RHYTHM, -S n any regular movement or beat

RHYTHMAL adj rhythmic

RHYTHMED ▸ rhythm

RHYTHMI ▸ rhythmus

RHYTHMIC adj of, relating to, or characterized by rhythm, as in movement or sound

RHYTHMS ▸ rhythm

R

RHYTHMUS, RHYTHMI n rhythm

RHYTINA, -S n type of sea cow

RHYTON, RHYTA, -S n (in ancient Greece) horn-shaped drinking vessel

RIA, -S n long narrow inlet of the seacoast

RIAD, -S n traditional Moroccan house with an interior garden

RIAL, -S n standard monetary unit of Iran

RIALTO, -S n market or exchange

RIANCY, RIANCIES ▶ riant

RIANT adj laughing **RIANTLY**

RIAS ▶ ria

RIATA, -S same as ▶ **reata**

RIB, -BED, -S n one of the curved bones forming the framework of the upper part of the body ▷ vb provide or mark with ribs

RIBA, -S n (in Islam) interest or usury

RIBALD, -ER, -S adj humorously or mockingly rude ▷ n ribald person **RIBALDLY**

RIBALDRY n ribald language or behaviour

RIBALDS ▶ ribald

RIBAND, -S n ribbon awarded for some achievement

RIBAS ▶ riba

RIBAUD, -S archaic variant of ▶ **ribald**

RIBAUDRY archaic variant of ▶ **ribaldry**

RIBAUDS ▶ ribaud

RIBBAND, -S same as ▶ **riband**

RIBBED ▶ rib

RIBBER, -S n someone who ribs

RIBBIE, -S n baseball run batted in

RIBBIER ▶ ribby

RIBBIES ▶ ribbie

RIBBIEST ▶ ribby

RIBBING, -S ▶ rib

RIBBIT, -S n sound a frog makes

RIBBON, -ED, -S n narrow band of fabric used for trimming, tying, etc ▷ vb adorn with a ribbon or ribbons

RIBBONRY n ribbons or ribbon work

RIBBONS ▶ ribbon

RIBBONY ▶ ribbon

RIBBY, RIBBIER, RIBBIEST adj with noticeable ribs

RIBCAGE, -S n bony structure of ribs enclosing the lungs

RIBES n genus of shrubs that includes currants

RIBEYE, -S n beefsteak cut from the outer side of the rib section

RIBGRASS same as ▶ **ribwort**

RIBIBE, -S n rebeck

RIBIBLE, -S same as ▶ **ribibe**

RIBIER, -S n variety of grape

RIBLESS ▶ rib

RIBLET, -S n small rib

RIBLIKE ▶ rib

RIBOSE, -S n pentose sugar that occurs in RNA and riboflavin

RIBOSOME n any of numerous minute particles in the cytoplasm of cells

RIBOZYME n RNA molecule capable of catalysing a chemical reaction

RIBS ▶ rib

RIBSTON, -S n variety of apple

RIBSTONE same as ▶ **ribston**

RIBSTONS ▶ ribston

RIBULOSE n type of sugar

RIBWORK, -S n work or structure involving ribs

RIBWORT, -S n Eurasian plant with lancelike ribbed leaves

RICE, -D, -S, RICING n cereal plant grown on wet ground in warm countries ▷ vb sieve (vegetables) to a coarse mashed consistency

RICEBIRD, -S n any of various birds frequenting rice fields, esp the Java sparrow

RICED ▶ rice

RICER, -S n kitchen utensil through which soft foods are pressed to form a coarse mash

RICERCAR same as > **ricercare**

RICERS ▶ ricer

RICES ▶ rice

RICEY adj resembling or containing rice

RICH, -ED, -ER, -EST, -ING adj owning a lot of money or property, wealthy ▷ vb (in archaic usage) enrich

RICHEN, -ED, -S vb enrich

RICHER ▶ rich

RICHES pl n wealth

RICHESSE n wealth or richness

RICHEST ▶ rich

RICHING ▶ rich

RICHLY adv elaborately

RICHNESS n state or quality of being rich

RICHT, -ED, -ER, -EST, -ING, -S adj right ▷ adv right ▷ n right ▷ vb right

RICHWEED n type of plant

RICIER ▶ ricy

RICIEST ▶ ricy

RICIN, -S n highly toxic protein, a lectin, derived from castor-oil seeds

RICING ▶ rice

RICINS ▶ ricin

RICINUS n genus of plants

RICK, -ED, -ING, -S n stack of hay etc ▷ vb wrench or sprain (a joint)

RICKER, -S n young kauri tree of New Zealand

RICKET n mistake

RICKETS n disease of children marked by softening of the bones, bow legs, etc

RICKETTY same as ▶ **rickety**

RICKETY adj shaky or unstable

RICKEY, -S n cocktail consisting of gin or vodka, lime juice, and soda water, served iced

RICKING ▶ rick

RICKLE, -S n unsteady or shaky structure

RICKLY, RICKLIER adj archaic word for run-down or rickety

RICKRACK n zigzag braid used for trimming

RICKS ▶ rick

RICKSHA, -S same as ▶ **rickshaw**

RICKSHAW n light two-wheeled man-drawn Asian vehicle

RICKYARD n place where hayricks are put

RICOCHET vb (of a bullet) rebound from a solid surface ▷ n such a rebound

RICOTTA, -S n soft white unsalted Italian cheese made from sheep's milk

RICRAC, -S same as ▶ **rickrack**

RICTAL ▶ rictus

RICTUS, -ES n gape or cleft of an open mouth or beak

RICY, RICIER, RICIEST same as ▶ **ricey**

RID, -DED, -S vb clear or relieve (of)

RIDABLE ▶ ride

RIDDANCE n act of getting rid of something undesirable or unpleasant

RIDDED ▶ rid

RIDDEN ▶ ride

R

RIDDER, -S ► rid
RIDDING ► rid
RIDDLE, -D, -S, RIDDLING
n question made puzzling
to test one's ingenuity ▷ *vb*
speak in riddles
RIDDLER -S
RIDE, RIDDEN, -S *vb* sit
on and control or propel
(a horse, bicycle, etc) ▷ *n*
journey on a horse etc
RIDEABLE
RIDENT *adj* laughing, smiling,
or happy
RIDER, -S *n* person who rides
RIDERED
RIDES ► ride
RIDGE, -D, -S *n* long narrow
hill ▷ *vb* form into a ridge
or ridges
RIDGEL, -S *same as*
> ridgeling
RIDGER, -S *n* plough used to
form furrows and ridges
RIDGES ► ridge
RIDGETOP *n* summit of ridge
RIDGEWAY *n* road or track
along a ridge, esp one of
great antiquity
RIDGIER ► ridgy
RIDGIEST ► ridgy
RIDGIL, -S *same as*
> ridgeling
RIDGING, -S ► ridge
RIDGLING *same as*
> ridgeling
RIDGY, RIDGIER, RIDGIEST
► ridge
RIDIC *adj* ridiculous
RIDICULE *n* treatment of a
person or thing as ridiculous
▷ *vb* laugh at, make fun of
RIDING, -S ► ride
RIDLEY, -S *n* marine turtle
RIDOTTO, -S *n* entertainment
with music and dancing,
often in masquerade
RIDS ► rid
RIEL, -S *n* standard monetary
unit of Cambodia
RIEM, -S *n* strip of hide
RIEMPIE, -S *n* leather thong
or lace used mainly to make
chair seats
RIEMS ► riem
RIESLING *n* type of white
wine
RIEVE, -S, RIEVING *n* archaic
word for rob or plunder
RIEVER, -S *n* archaic word for
robber or plunderer
RIEVES ► rieve
RIEVING ► rieve
RIF, -S *vb* lay off
RIFAMPIN *n* drug used in the
treatment of tuberculosis,
meningitis, and leprosy

RIFE, -R, -ST *adj* widespread
or common
RIFELY
RIFENESS
RIFF, -ED, -ING, -S *n* short
repeated melodic figure ▷ *vb*
play or perform riffs in jazz or
rock music
RIFFAGE, -S *n* (in jazz or rock
music) act or an instance
of playing a short series of
chords
RIFFED ► riff
RIFFING ► riff
RIFFLE, -D, -S, RIFFLING *vb*
flick through (pages etc)
quickly ▷ *n* rapid in a stream
RIFFLER, -S *n* file with a
curved face for filing concave
surfaces
RIFFLES ► riffle
RIFFLING ► riffle
RIFFOLA, -S *n* use of an
abundance of dominant riffs
RIFFRAFF *n* rabble,
disreputable people
RIFFS ► riff
RIFLE, -D, -S *n* firearm with
a long barrel ▷ *vb* cut spiral
grooves inside the barrel
of a gun
RIFLEMAN, RIFLEMEN *n*
person skilled in the use of a
rifle, esp a soldier
RIFLER, -S ► rifle
RIFLERY *n* rifle shots
RIFLES ► rifle
RIFLING, -S *n* cutting of spiral
grooves on the inside of a
firearm's barrel
RIFLIP, -S *n* genetic difference
between two individuals
RIFS ► rif
RIFT, -ED, -ING, -S *n* break in
friendly relations ▷ *vb* burst
or cause to burst open
RIFTE *archaic word for* ► rift
RIFTED ► rift
RIFTIER ► rifty
RIFTIEST ► rifty
RIFTING ► rift
RIFTLESS ► rift
RIFTS ► rift
RIFTY, RIFTIER, RIFTIEST
► rift
RIG, -GED, -S *vb* arrange
in a dishonest way ▷ *n*
apparatus for drilling for oil
and gas
RIGADOON *n* old Provençal
couple dance, light and
graceful, in lively duple time
RIGATONI *n* macaroni in the
form of short ridged often
slightly curved pieces
RIGAUDON *same as*
► rigadoon

RIGG, -S *n* type of fish
RIGGALD, -S *same as*
> ridgeling
RIGGED ► rig
RIGGER, -S *n* workman who
rigs vessels, etc
RIGGING, -S ► rig
RIGGS ► rigg
RIGHT, -ED, -EST, -ING, -S
adj just ▷ *adv* correctly ▷ *n*
claim, title, etc allowed or
due ▷ *vb* bring or come back
to a normal or correct state
RIGHTEN, -S *vb* set right
RIGHTER, -S ► right
RIGHTEST ► right
RIGHTFUL *adj* in accordance
with what is right
RIGHTIER ► righty
RIGHTIES ► righty
RIGHTING ► right
RIGHTISH *adj* somewhat
right, esp politically
RIGHTISM ► rightist
RIGHTIST *adj* on the political
right ▷ *n* supporter of the
political right
RIGHTLY *adv* in accordance
with the true facts or justice
RIGHTO *interj* expression of
agreement or compliance
RIGHTS ► right
**RIGHTY, RIGHTIER,
RIGHTIES** *n* right-handed
person ▷ *adj* right-handed
RIGID, -ER, -EST, -S *adj*
inflexible or strict ▷ *adv*
completely or excessively ▷ *n*
strict and unbending person
RIGIDIFY *vb* make or become
rigid
RIGIDISE *same as* ► rigidize
RIGIDITY ► rigid
RIGIDIZE *vb* make or become
rigid
RIGIDLY ► rigid
RIGIDS ► rigid
RIGLIN, -S *same as*
> ridgeling
RIGLING, -S *same as*
> ridgeling
RIGLINS ► riglin
RIGOL, -S *n* (in dialect) ditch
or gutter
RIGOLL, -S *same as* ► rigol
RIGOLS ► rigol
RIGOR, -S *same as* ► rigour
RIGORISM *n* strictness in
judgment or conduct
RIGORIST
RIGOROUS *adj* harsh, severe,
or stern
RIGORS ► rigor
RIGOUR, -S *n* harshness,
severity, or strictness
RIGOUT, -S *n* person's
clothing

RIGS ▸ rig

RIKISHA, -S *same as* ▸ **rickshaw**

RIKISHI *n* sumo wrestler

RIKSHAW, -S *same as* ▸ **rickshaw**

RILE, -D, -S, RILING *vb* anger or annoy

RILEY, RILIER, RILIEST *adj* cross or irritable

RILIEVO, RILIEVI *same as* ▸ **relief**

RILING ▸ rile

RILL, -ED, -ING, -S *n* small stream ▷ *vb* trickle

RILLE, -S *same as* ▸ **rill**

RILLED ▸ rill

RILLES ▸ rille

RILLET *n* little rill

RILLING ▸ rill

RILLMARK *n* mark left by the trickle of a rill

RILLS ▸ rill

RIM, -MED, -S *n* edge or border ▷ *vb* put a rim on (a pot, cup, wheel, etc)

RIMA, -E *n* long narrow opening

RIMAYE, -S *n* crevasse at the head of a glacier

RIME, -D, -S, RIMING *same as* ▸ **rhyme**

RIMELESS ▸ rhyme

RIMER, -S *same as* > **rhymester**

RIMES ▸ rime

RIMESTER *same as* > **rhymester**

RIMFIRE, -S *adj* (of a cartridge) having the primer in the rim of the base ▷ *n* cartridge of this type

RIMIER ▸ rimy

RIMIEST ▸ rimy

RIMINESS ▸ rimy

RIMING ▸ rime

RIMLAND, -S *n* area situated on the outer edges of a region

RIMLESS ▸ rim

RIMMED ▸ rim

RIMMER, -S *n* tool for shaping the edge of something

RIMMING, -S ▸ rim

RIMOSE *adj* (esp of plant parts) having the surface marked by a network of intersecting cracks

RIMOSELY

RIMOSITY

RIMOUS *same as* ▸ **rimose**

RIMPLE, -D, -S, RIMPLING *vb* crease or wrinkle

RIMROCK, -S *n* rock forming the boundaries of a sandy or gravelly alluvial deposit

RIMS ▸ rim

RIMSHOT, -S *n* deliberate simultaneous striking of skin and rim of drum

RIMU, -S *n* New Zealand tree

RIMY, RIMIER, RIMIEST *adj* coated with rime

RIN, -NING, -S *Scots variant of* ▸ **run**

RIND, -ED, -ING, -S *n* tough outer coating of fruits, cheese, or bacon ▷ *vb* take the bark off

RINDIER ▸ rindy

RINDIEST ▸ rindy

RINDING ▸ rind

RINDLESS ▸ rind

RINDS ▸ rind

RINDY, RINDIER, RINDIEST *adj* with a rind or rindlike skin

RINE, -S *archaic variant of* ▸ **rind**

RING, -ED, -S *vb* give out a clear resonant sound, as a bell ▷ *n* ringing

RINGBARK *same as* ▸ **ring**

RINGBIT, -S *n* type of bit worn by a horse

RINGBOLT *n* bolt with a ring fitted through an eye attached to the bolt head

RINGBONE *n* abnormal bony growth affecting the pastern of a horse, often causing lameness

RINGDOVE *n* large Eurasian pigeon with white patches on the wings and neck

RINGED ▸ ring

RINGENT *adj* (of the corolla of plants) consisting of two gaping lips

RINGER, -S *n* person or thing apparently identical to another

RINGETTE *n* team sport played on ice, using straight sticks to control a rubber ring

RINGGIT, -S *n* standard monetary unit of Malaysia

RINGHALS *n* variety of cobra

RINGING, -S ▸ ring

RINGLESS ▸ ring

RINGLET, -S *n* curly lock of hair

RINGLETY *adj* resembling a ringlet

RINGLIKE ▸ ring

RINGMAN, RINGMEN *n* (in dialect) ring finger

RINGNECK *n* any bird that has ringlike markings round its neck

RINGS ▸ ring

RINGSIDE *n* row of seats nearest a boxing or circus ring ▷ *adj* providing a close uninterrupted view

RINGSTER *n* member of a ring controlling a market in antiques, art treasures, etc

RINGTAIL *n* possum with a curling tail used to grip branches while climbing

RINGTAW, -S *n* game in which the aim is to knock marbles out of a ring

RINGTONE *n* musical tune played by a mobile phone when a call is received

RINGTOSS *n* game in which participants try to throw hoops onto an upright stick

RINGWAY, -S *n* bypass

RINGWISE *adj* used to being in the ring and able to respond appropriately

RINGWOMB *n* complication at lambing resulting from failure of the cervix to open

RINGWORK *n* circular earthwork

RINGWORM *n* fungal skin disease in circular patches

RINK, -ED, -ING, -S *n* sheet of ice for skating or curling ▷ *vb* skate on a rink

RINKHALS *n* S African cobra that can spit venom

RINKING ▸ rink

RINKS ▸ rink

RINKSIDE *n* area at the side of a rink

RINNING ▸ rin

RINS ▸ rin

RINSABLE ▸ rinse

RINSE, -D, -S *vb* remove soap from (washed clothes, hair, etc) by applying clean water ▷ *n* rinsing

RINSER -S

RINSIBLE ▸ rinse

RINSING, -S ▸ rinse

RIOJA, -S *n* red or white Spanish wine with a vanilla bouquet and flavour

RIOT, -ED, -S *n* disorderly unruly disturbance ▷ *vb* take part in a riot

RIOTER -S

RIOTING, -S ▸ riot

RIOTISE, -S *n* archaic word for riotous behaviour and excess

RIOTIZE, -S *same as* ▸ **riotise**

RIOTOUS *adj* unrestrained

RIOTRY, RIOTRIES *n* riotous behaviour

RIOTS ▸ riot

RIP, -PED, -PING, -S *vb* tear violently ▷ *n* split or tear

RIPARIAL *adj* riparian

RIPARIAN *adj* of or on the banks of a river ▷ *n* person who owns land on a river bank

R

RIPCORD, -S n cord pulled to open a parachute

RIPE, -D, -S, -ST, RIPING adj ready to be reaped, eaten, etc ▷ vb ripen

RIPECK, -S same as ▸ ryepeck

RIPED ▸ ripe

RIPELY ▸ ripe

RIPEN, -ED, -ING, -S vb grow ripe

RIPENER -S

RIPENESS ▸ ripe

RIPENING ▸ ripen

RIPENS ▸ ripen

RIPER, -S adj more ripe ▷ n old Scots word meaning plunderer

RIPES ▸ ripe

RIPEST ▸ ripe

RIPIENO, RIPIENI, -S n (in baroque concertos and concerti grossi) the full orchestra

RIPING ▸ ripe

RIPOFF, -S n grossly overpriced article

RIPOST, -S same as ▸ riposte

RIPOSTE, -D, -S n verbal retort ▷ vb make a riposte

RIPOSTS ▸ ripost

RIPP, -S n old Scots word for a handful of grain

RIPPABLE ▸ rip

RIPPED ▸ rip

RIPPER, -S n person who rips

RIPPIER, -S n archaic word for fish seller

RIPPING, -S ▸ rip

RIPPLE, -D, -S n slight wave or ruffling of a surface ▷ vb flow or form into little waves (on)

RIPPLER -S

RIPPLET, -S n tiny ripple

RIPPLIER ▸ ripply

RIPPLING ▸ ripple

RIPPLY, RIPPLIER ▸ ripple

RIPPS ▸ ripp

RIPRAP, -S vb deposit broken stones in or on

RIPS ▸ rip

RIPSAW, -ED, -N, -S n handsaw for cutting along the grain of timber ▷ vb saw with a ripsaw

RIPSTOP, -S n tear-resistant cloth

RIPT archaic past form of ▸ rip

RIPTIDE, -S n stretch of turbulent water in the sea

RIRORIRO n small NZ bush bird that hatches the eggs of the shining cuckoo

RISALDAR n Indian cavalry officer

RISE, -N, -S vb get up from a lying, sitting, or kneeling position ▷ n rising

RISER, -S n person who rises, esp from bed

RISES ▸ rise

RISHI, -S n Indian seer or sage

RISIBLE adj causing laughter, ridiculous

RISIBLES pl n sense of humour

RISIBLY ▸ risible

RISING, -S ▸ rise

RISK, -ED, -ING, -S n chance of disaster or loss ▷ vb act in spite of the possibility of (injury or loss)

RISKER -S

RISKFUL ▸ risk

RISKIER ▸ risky

RISKIEST ▸ risky

RISKILY ▸ risky

RISKING ▸ risk

RISKLESS ▸ risk

RISKS ▸ risk

RISKY, RISKIER, RISKIEST adj full of risk, dangerous

RISOLUTO adj musical term meaning firm and decisive ▷ adv firmly and decisively

RISORIUS, RISORII n facial muscle responsible for smiling

RISOTTO, -S n dish of rice cooked in stock with vegetables, meat, etc

RISP, -ED, -S vb Scots word meaning rasp

RISPETTO, RISPETTI n kind of folk song

RISPING, -S ▸ risp

RISPS ▸ risp

RISQUE, -S same as ▸ risk

RISSOLE, -S n cake of minced meat, coated with breadcrumbs and fried

RISTRA, -S n string of dried chilli peppers

RISUS, -ES n involuntary grinning expression

RIT, -S, -TED, -TING vb Scots word for cut or slit

RITARD, -S n (in music) a slowing down

RITE, -S n formal practice or custom, esp religious

RITELESS

RITENUTO adv held back momentarily ▷ n (in music) a slowing down

RITES ▸ rite

RITORNEL n (in music) orchestral passage

RITS ▸ rit

RITT, -S same as ▸ rit

RITTED ▸ rit

RITTER, -S n knight or horseman

RITTING ▸ rit

RITTS ▸ ritt

RITUAL, -S n prescribed order of rites ▷ adj concerning rites

RITUALLY

RITZ, -ES modifier as in **put on the ritz** assume a superior air or make an ostentatious display

RITZIER ▸ ritzy

RITZIEST ▸ ritzy

RITZILY ▸ ritzy

RITZY, RITZIER, RITZIEST adj luxurious or elegant

RIVA, -S n rock cleft

RIVAGE, -S n bank, shore, or coast

RIVAL, -ED, -ING, -LED, -S n person or thing that competes with another ▷ adj in the position of a rival ▷ vb (try to) equal

RIVALESS n female rival

RIVALING ▸ rival

RIVALISE same as ▸ rivalize

RIVALITY ▸ rival

RIVALIZE vb become a rival

RIVALLED ▸ rival

RIVALRY n keen competition

RIVALS ▸ rival

RIVAS ▸ riva

RIVE, -D, -N, -S, RIVING vb split asunder

RIVEL, -LED, -S vb archaic word meaning wrinkle

RIVEN ▸ rive

RIVER, -S n large natural stream of water

RIVERAIN same as ▸ riparian

RIVERBED n bed of a river

RIVERED adj with a river or rivers

RIVERET, -S n archaic word for rivulet or stream

RIVERINE same as ▸ riparian

RIVERMAN, RIVERMEN n boatman or man earning his living working on a river

RIVERS ▸ river

RIVERWAY n river serving as a waterway

RIVERY adj riverlike

RIVES ▸ rive

RIVET, -ED, -ING, -S, -TED n bolt for fastening metal plates ▷ vb fasten with rivets

RIVETER -S

RIVIERA, -S n coastline resembling the Mediterranean Riviera

RIVIERE, -S n necklace of diamonds which gradually increase in size

RIVING ▸ rive

RIVLIN, -S n Scots word for rawhide shoe

RIVO interj (in the past) an informal toast

RIVULET, -S n small stream

RIVULOSE adj having meandering lines

RIVULUS n type of small tropical American fish

RIYAL, -S n standard monetary unit of Qatar, divided into 100 dirhams

RIZ (in some dialects) past form of ► **rise**

This unusual past tense of **rise** is one of the essential Z words.

RIZA, -S n partial icon cover made from precious metal

RIZARD, -S n redcurrant

RIZAS ► **riza**

RIZZAR, -ED, -S Scots word for redcurrant ▷ vb Scots word for sun-dry

RIZZART, -S n Scots word for redcurrant

RIZZER, -ED, -S same as ► **rizzar**

RIZZOR, -ED, -S vb dry

ROACH, -ES, -ING n Eurasian freshwater fish ▷ vb clip (mane) short so that it stands upright

ROACHED adj arched convexly, as the back of certain breeds of dog, such as the whippet

ROACHES ► **roach**

ROACHING ► **roach**

ROAD, -S n way prepared for passengers, vehicles, etc

ROADBED, -S n material used to make a road

ROADEO, -S n competition testing driving skills

ROADHOG, -S n selfish or aggressive driver

ROADIE, -S n person who transports and sets up equipment for a band

ROADING, -S n road building

ROADKILL n remains of an animal or animals killed on the road by motor vehicles

ROADLESS ► **road**

ROADMAN, ROADMEN n someone involved in road repair or construction

ROADS ► **road**

ROADSHOW n radio show broadcast live from a place being visited by a touring disc jockey

ROADSIDE n side of a road ▷ adj situated beside a road

ROADSMAN, ROADSMEN same as ► **roadman**

ROADSTER n open car with only two seats

ROADWAY, -S n part of a road used by vehicles

ROADWORK n sports training by running along roads

ROAM, -ED, -S vb wander about ▷ n act of roaming

ROAMER -S

ROAMING, -S ► **roam**

ROAMS ► **roam**

ROAN, -S adj (of a horse) having a brown or black coat sprinkled with white hairs ▷ n roan horse

ROANPIPE n drainpipe leading down from a gutter

ROANS ► **roan**

ROAR, -ED, -S vb make or utter a loud deep hoarse sound like that of a lion ▷ n such a sound

ROARER -S

ROARIE Scots word for ► **noisy**

ROARIER ► **roary**

ROARIEST ► **roary**

ROARING, -S ► **roar**

ROARMING adj severe

ROARS ► **roar**

ROARY, ROARIER, ROARIEST adj roarlike or tending to roar

ROAST, -ED, -S vb cook by dry heat, as in an oven ▷ n roasted joint of meat ▷ adj roasted

ROASTER, -S n person or thing that roasts

ROASTIE, -S n roast potato

ROASTING adj extremely hot ▷ n severe criticism or scolding

ROASTS ► **roast**

ROATE, -D, -S, ROATING archaic form of ► **rote**

ROB, -BED, -BING, -S vb steal from

ROBALO, -S n tropical fish

ROBAND, -S n piece of marline used for fastening a sail to a spar

ROBATA, -S n grill used for Japanese cooking

ROBBED ► **rob**

ROBBER, -S ► **rob**

ROBBERY n stealing of property from a person by using or threatening to use force

ROBBIN, -S same as ► **roband**

ROBBING ► **rob**

ROBBINS ► **robbin**

ROBE, -D, -S n long loose outer garment ▷ vb put a robe on

ROBIN, -S n small brown bird with a red breast

ROBING, -S ► **robe**

ROBINIA, -S n type of leguminous tree

ROBINS ► **robin**

ROBLE, -S n oak tree

ROBOCALL n automated telephone call that delivers a message to a large number of people

ROBORANT adj tending to fortify or increase strength ▷ n drug or agent that increases strength

ROBOT, -S n automated machine, esp one performing functions in a human manner

ROBOTIC

ROBOTICS n science of designing and using robots

ROBOTISE same as ► **robotize**

ROBOTISM ► **robot**

ROBOTIZE vb automate

ROBOTRY ► **robot**

ROBOTS ► **robot**

ROBS ► **rob**

ROBURITE n flameless explosive

ROBUST, -ER adj very strong and healthy

ROBUSTA, -S n species of coffee tree

ROBUSTER ► **robust**

ROBUSTLY ► **robust**

ROC, -S n monstrous bird of Arabian mythology

ROCAILLE n decorative rock or shell work

ROCH, -ES same as ► **rotch**

ROCHET, -S n white surplice with tight sleeves, worn by Church dignitaries

ROCK, -ED, -S n hard mineral substance that makes up part of the earth's crust, stone ▷ vb (cause to) sway to and fro ▷ adj of or relating to rock music

ROCKABLE

ROCKABY same as ► **rockabye**

ROCKABYE n lullaby or rocking motion used with a baby during lullabies

ROCKAWAY n four-wheeled horse-drawn carriage, usually with two seats and a hard top

ROCKED ► **rock**

ROCKER, -S n rocking chair

ROCKERY n mound of stones in a garden for rock plants

R

ROCKET, -ED, -S n self-propelling device powered by the burning of explosive contents ▷ vb move fast, esp upwards

ROCKETER n bird that launches itself into the air like a rocket when flushed

ROCKETRY n science and technology of the design and operation of rockets

ROCKETS ▶ rocket

ROCKFALL n instance of rocks breaking away and falling from an outcrop

ROCKFISH n any of various fishes that live among rocks

ROCKIER, -S n archaic or dialect word for rock pigeon

ROCKIEST ▶ rocky

ROCKILY ▶ rocky

ROCKING, -S ▶ rock

ROCKLAY, -S same as ▶ rokelay

ROCKLESS ▶ rock

ROCKLIKE ▶ rock

ROCKLING n any of various small sea fishes having an elongated body and barbels around the mouth

ROCKOON, -S n rocket fired from a balloon at high altitude

ROCKROSE n any of various shrubs or herbaceous plants cultivated for their roselike flowers

ROCKS ▶ rock

ROCKWEED n any of various seaweeds that grow on rocks exposed at low tide

ROCKWOOL n mineral wool used for insulation

ROCKWORK n structure made of rock

ROCKY, ROCKIEST adj having many rocks

ROCOCO, -S adj (of furniture, architecture, etc) having much elaborate decoration ▷ n style of architecture and decoration characterized by elaborate ornamentation

ROCQUET, -S n another name for the salad plant rocket

ROCS ▶ roc

ROD, -DED, -S n slender straight bar, stick ▷ vb clear with a rod

RODDING -S

RODE, -D, -S vb (of the male woodcock) to perform a display flight

RODENT, -S n animal with teeth specialized for gnawing

RODEO, -ED, -ING, -S n display of skill by cowboys,

such as bareback riding ▷ vb take part in a rodeo

RODES ▶ rode

RODEWAY, -S archaic spelling of ▶ roadway

RODING, -S ▶ rode

RODLESS ▶ rod

RODLIKE ▶ rod

RODMAN, RODMEN n someone who uses or fishes with a rod

RODNEY, -S n type of small fishing boat used in Canada

RODS ▶ rod

RODSMAN, RODSMEN same as ▶ rodman

RODSTER, -S n angler

ROE, -S n mass of eggs in a fish, sometimes eaten as food

ROEBUCK, -S n male of the roe deer

ROED adj with roe inside

ROEMER, -S n drinking glass, typically having an ovoid bowl on a short stem

ROENTGEN n unit measuring a radiation dose

ROES ▶ roe

ROESTI, -S same as ▶ rosti

ROESTONE same as ▶ oolite

ROGALLO, -S n flexible fabric delta wing

ROGATION n solemn supplication, esp in a form of ceremony prescribed by the Church

ROGATORY adj (esp in legal contexts) seeking or authorized to seek information

ROGER, -ED, -ING, -S interj (used in signalling) message received ▷ vb acknowledge a received message

ROGNON, -S n isolated rock outcrop on a glacier

ROGUE, -D, -ING, -S, ROGUING n dishonest or unprincipled person ▷ adj (of a wild beast) living apart from the herd ▷ vb rid (a field or crop) of inferior or unwanted plants

ROGUER, -S n rogue

ROGUERY n dishonest or immoral behaviour

ROGUES ▶ rogue

ROGUING ▶ rogue

ROGUISH adj dishonest or unprincipled

ROGUY same as ▶ roguish

ROID adj as in **roid rage** angry and aggressive behaviour caused by the use of anabolic steroids

ROIL, -ED, -ING, -S vb make (a liquid) cloudy or turbid by stirring up dregs or sediment

ROILIER ▶ roily

ROILIEST ▶ roily

ROILING ▶ roil

ROILS ▶ roil

ROILY, ROILIER, ROILIEST adj cloudy or muddy

ROIN, -ED, -ING, -S same as ▶ royne

ROINISH same as ▶ roynish

ROINS ▶ roin

ROIST, -ED, -ING, -S archaic variant of ▶ roister

ROISTER, -S vb make merry noisily or boisterously

ROISTING ▶ roist

ROISTS ▶ roist

ROJAK, -S n (in Malaysia) a salad dish served in chilli sauce

ROJI, -S n Japanese tea garden or its path of stones

ROK, -S same as ▶ roc

> **Rok** is an alternative spelling of **roc**, the mythical bird. Other spellings are **ruc** and **rukh**.

ROKE, -D, -S, ROKING vb (in dialect) steam or smoke

ROKELAY, -S n type of cloak

ROKER, -S n variety of ray

ROKES ▶ roke

ROKIER ▶ roky

ROKIEST ▶ roky

ROKING ▶ roke

ROKKAKU n hexagonal Japanese kite

ROKS ▶ rok

ROKY, ROKIER, ROKIEST adj (in dialect) steamy or smoky

ROLAG, -S n roll of carded wool ready for spinning

ROLAMITE n type of bearing using two rollers and a moving flexible band

ROLE, -S n task or function

ROLF, -ED, -ING, -INGS, -S vb massage following a particular technique

ROLFER -S

ROLL, -ED, -S vb move by turning over and over ▷ n act of rolling over or from side to side

ROLLABLE

ROLLAWAY n mounted on rollers so as to be easily moved, esp to be stored away after use

ROLLBACK n reduction to a previous price

ROLLBAR, -S n bar that reinforces the frame of a car

ROLLED ▶ roll

ROLLER, **-S** n rotating cylinder

ROLLICK, **-S** vb behave in a boisterous manner ▷ n boisterous or carefree escapade

ROLLICKY adj rollicking

ROLLIE, **-S** n hand-rolled cigarette

ROLLING, **-S** ▶ **roll**

ROLLMOP, **-S** n herring fillet rolled round onion slices and pickled

ROLLNECK adj (of a garment) having a high neck that is worn rolled over ▷ n rollneck sweater or other garment

ROLLOCK, **-S** same as ▶ **rowlock**

ROLLOUT, **-S** n presentation to the public of a new aircraft, product, etc; launch

ROLLOVER n instance of a prize continuing in force for an additional period

ROLLS ▶ **roll**

ROLLTOP n as in **rolltop desk** desk having a slatted wooden panel that can be pulled down over the writing surface

ROLLUP, **-S** n something rolled into a tube shape

ROLLWAY n incline down which logs are rolled

ROM, **-S** n male gypsy

ROMA n gypsy

ROMAGE, **-S** archaic variant of ▶ **rummage**

ROMAIKA, **-S** n Greek dance

ROMAINE, **-S** n usual US and Canadian name for 'cos' (lettuce)

ROMAJI, **-S** n Roman alphabet as used to write Japanese

ROMAL, **-S** same as ▶ **rumal**

ROMAN, **-S** adj in or relating to the vertical style of printing type used for most printed matter ▷ n roman type

ROMANCE, **-D**, **-S** n love affair ▷ vb exaggerate or fantasize

ROMANCER

ROMANISE same as ▶ **romanize**

ROMANIZE vb impart a Roman Catholic character to (a ceremony, practice, etc)

ROMANO, **-S** n hard light-coloured sharp-tasting cheese

ROMANS ▶ **roman**

ROMANTIC adj of or dealing with love ▷ n romantic person or artist

ROMANZA, **-S** n short instrumental piece of song-like character

ROMAUNT, **-S** n verse romance

ROMCOM, **-S** n comedy based around the romantic relationships of the characters

ROMEO, **-S** n male sweetheart

ROMNEYA, **-S** n bushy type of poppy

ROMP, **-ED**, **-ING**, **-S** vb play wildly and joyfully ▷ n boisterous activity

ROMPER n playful or boisterous child

ROMPERS pl n child's overalls

ROMPING ▶ **romp**

ROMPISH adj inclined to romp

ROMPS ▶ **romp**

ROMS ▶ **rom**

RONCADOR n any of several types of fish

RONDACHE n round shield

RONDAVEL n circular building, often thatched

RONDE, **-S** n round dance

RONDEAU, **-X** n poem with the opening words of the first line used as a refrain

RONDEL, **-S** n rondeau with a two-line refrain appearing twice or three times

RONDELET n brief rondeau, having five or seven lines and a refrain taken from the first line

RONDELLE n type of bead

RONDELS ▶ **rondel**

RONDES ▶ **ronde**

RONDINO, **-S** n short rondo

RONDO, **-S** n piece of music with a leading theme continually returned to

RONDURE, **-S** n circle or curve

RONE, **-S** n drainpipe or gutter for carrying rainwater from a roof

RONEO, **-ED**, **-ING**, **-S** vb duplicate (a document) from a stencil ▷ n document reproduced by this process

RONEPIPE same as ▶ **rone**

RONES ▶ **rone**

RONG archaic past participle of ▶ **ring**

RONGGENG n Malay traditional dance

RONIN, **-S** n lordless samurai, esp one whose feudal lord had been deprived of his territory

RONNE, **RONNING** archaic form of ▶ **run**

RONNEL, **-S** n type of pesticide

RONNIE, **-S** n Dublin slang word for moustache

RONNING ▶ **ronne**

RONT, **-S** archaic variant of ▶ **runt**

RONTE, **-S** archaic variant of ▶ **runt**

RONTGEN, **-S** variant spelling of ▶ **roentgen**

RONTS ▶ **ront**

RONZ n rest of New Zealand

RONZER, **-S** n New Zealand word for a New Zealander not from Auckland

ROO, **-S** n kangaroo

ROOD, **-S** n Cross

ROOF, **-ED**, **-S** n outside upper covering of a building, car, etc ▷ vb put a roof on

ROOFER **-S**

ROOFIE, **-S** n tablet of sedative drug

ROOFIER ▶ **roofy**

ROOFIES ▶ **roofie**

ROOFIEST ▶ **roofy**

ROOFING, **-S** n material used to build a roof

ROOFLESS ▶ **roof**

ROOFLIKE ▶ **roof**

ROOFLINE n uppermost edge of a roof

ROOFS ▶ **roof**

ROOFTOP, **-S** n outside part of the roof of a building

ROOFTREE same as > **ridgepole**

ROOFY, **ROOFIER**, **ROOFIEST** adj with roofs

ROOIBOS, **-ES** n tea prepared from the dried leaves of an African plant

ROOIKAT, **-S** n South African lynx

ROOK, **-ED**, **-ING**, **-S** n Eurasian bird of the crow family ▷ vb swindle

ROOKERY n colony of rooks, penguins, or seals

ROOKIE, **-S** n new recruit

ROOKIER ▶ **rooky**

ROOKIES ▶ **rookie**

ROOKIEST ▶ **rooky**

ROOKING ▶ **rook**

ROOKISH ▶ **rook**

ROOKS ▶ **rook**

ROOKY, **ROOKIER**, **ROOKIEST** adj abounding in rooks

ROOM, **-ED**, **-ING**, **-S** n enclosed area in a building ▷ vb occupy or share a room

ROOMER **-S**

ROOMETTE n self-contained compartment in a railway sleeping car

R

ROOMFUL, -S, ROOMSFUL *n* number or quantity sufficient to fill a room

ROOMIE, -S *n* roommate

ROOMIER ► roomy

ROOMIES ► roomie

ROOMIEST ► roomy

ROOMILY ► roomy

ROOMING ► room

ROOMMATE *n* person with whom one shares a room or apartment

ROOMS ► room

ROOMSFUL ► roomful

ROOMSOME *adj* archaic word meaning roomy

ROOMY, ROOMIER, ROOMIEST *adj* spacious

ROON, -S *n* Scots word for shred or strip

ROOP, -ED, -ING, -S *same as* ► **roup**

ROOPIER ► roopy

ROOPIEST ► roopy

ROOPING ► roop

ROOPIT *same as* ► **roopy**

ROOPS ► roop

ROOPY, ROOPIER, ROOPIEST *adj* (in dialect) hoarse

ROORBACH *same as* ► **roorback**

ROORBACK *n* false or distorted report or account, used to obtain political advantage

ROOS ► roo

ROOSA, -S *n* type of grass

ROOSE, -D, -S, ROOSING *vb* flatter

ROOSER -S

ROOST, -ED, -ING, -S *n* perch for fowls ▷ *vb* perch

ROOSTER, -S *n* domestic cock

ROOSTING ► roost

ROOSTS ► roost

ROOT, -ED *n* part of a plant that grows down into the earth obtaining nourishment ▷ *vb* establish a root and start to grow

ROOTAGE, -S *n* root system

ROOTBALL *n* mass of the roots of a plant

ROOTCAP, -S *n* layer of cells at root tip

ROOTED ► root

ROOTEDLY ► root

ROOTER, -S ► root

ROOTHOLD ► root

ROOTIER ► rooty

ROOTIES ► rooty

ROOTIEST ► rooty

ROOTING, -S ► root

ROOTKIT, -S *n* set of programs used to gain unauthorized access to a computer system

ROOTLE, -D, -S, ROOTLING *same as* ► **root**

ROOTLESS *adj* having no sense of belonging

ROOTLET, -S *n* small root or branch of a root

ROOTLIKE ► root

ROOTLING ► rootle

ROOTS *adj* (of popular music) going back to the origins of a style

ROOTSY ROOTSIER

ROOTWORM *n* beetle larva feeding on roots

ROOTY, ROOTIER, ROOTIES, ROOTIEST *adj* rootlike ▷ *n* (in military slang) bread

ROPABLE *adj* capable of being roped

ROPE, -D, -S *n* thick cord ▷ *n* bind or fasten with rope

ROPEABLE *same as* ► **ropable**

ROPED ► rope

ROPELIKE ► rope

ROPER, -S *n* someone who makes ropes

ROPERIES ► ropery

ROPERS ► roper

ROPERY, ROPERIES *n* place where ropes are made

ROPES ► rope

ROPEWALK *n* long narrow usually covered path or shed where ropes are made

ROPEWAY, -S *n* type of aerial lift

ROPEWORK *n* making, mending, or tying ropes

ROPEY *adj* inferior or inadequate

ROPIER ► ropy

ROPIEST ► ropy

ROPILY ► ropey

ROPINESS ► ropey

ROPING, -S ► rope

ROPY, ROPIER, ROPIEST *same as* ► **ropey**

ROQUE, -S *n* game developed from croquet

ROQUET, -ED, -S *vb* drive one's ball against (another person's ball) in croquet ▷ *n* act of roqueting

ROQUETTE *n* another name for the salad plant rocket

RORAL *archaic word for* ► **dewy**

RORE, -S *archaic spelling of* ► **roar**

RORIC *same as* ► **roral**

RORID *same as* ► **roral**

RORIE *same as* ► **roary**

RORIER ► rory

RORIEST ► rory

RORQUAL, -S *n* toothless whale with a dorsal fin

RORT, -ED, -ING, -S *n* dishonest scheme ▷ *vb* take unfair advantage of something

RORTER, -S *n* small-scale confidence trickster

RORTIER ► rorty

RORTIEST ► rorty

RORTING, -S ► rort

RORTS ► rort

RORTY, RORTIER, RORTIEST ► **rort**

RORY, RORIER, RORIEST *adj* dewy

ROSACE, -S *another name for* ► **rosette**

ROSACEA, -S *n* chronic inflammatory disease affecting the skin of the face

ROSACES ► rosace

ROSAKER, -S *archaic word for* ► **realgar**

ROSALIA, -S *n* melody which is repeated but at a higher pitch each time

ROSARIA ► rosarium

ROSARIAN *n* person who cultivates roses, esp professionally

ROSARIES ► rosary

ROSARIUM, ROSARIA *n* rose garden

ROSARY, ROSARIES *n* series of prayers

ROSBIF, -S *n* term used in France for an English person

ROSCID *adj* dewy

ROSCOE, -S *slang word for* ► **gun**

ROSE, -D, -S, ROSING *n* flowering plant ▷ *vb* cause to redden

ROSEAL *adj* rosy or roselike

ROSEATE *adj* rose-coloured

ROSEBAY, -S *n as in* **rosebay willowherb** perennial plant with spikes of deep pink flowers

ROSEBED, -S *n* part of a garden where roses grow

ROSEBOWL *n* bowl for displaying roses or other flowers

ROSEBUD, -S *n* rose which has not yet fully opened

ROSEBUSH *n* flowering shrub

ROSED ► rose

ROSEFISH *n* red food fish of North Atlantic coastal waters

ROSEHIP, -S *n* berry-like fruit of a rose plant

ROSELESS ► rise

ROSELIKE ► rise

ROSELLA, -S *n* type of Australian parrot

ROSELLE, -S *n* Indian flowering plant

ROSEMARY *n* fragrant flowering shrub

ROSEOLA, -S *n* feverish condition of young children caused by a virus

ROSEOLAR

ROSERIES ▶ rosery

ROSEROOT *n* Eurasian mountain plant

ROSERY, ROSERIES *n* bed or garden of roses

ROSES ▶ rose

ROSESLUG *n* one of various types of pest that feed on roses

ROSET, -ED, -ING, -S, -TED *n* Scots word meaning rosin ▷ *vb* rub rosin on

ROSETTE, -S *n* rose-shaped ornament

ROSETTED ▶ roset

ROSETTES ▶ rosette

ROSETTY ▶ roset

ROSETY ▶ roset

ROSEWOOD *n* fragrant wood used to make furniture

ROSHAMBO *n* the game of rock-paper-scissors

ROSHI, -S *n* teacher of Zen Buddhism

ROSIED ▶ rosy

ROSIER, -S *archaic word for* ▶ **rosebush**

ROSIERE, -S *archaic word for* ▶ **rosebush**

ROSIERS ▶ rosier

ROSIES ▶ rosy

ROSIEST ▶ rosy

ROSILY ▶ rosy

ROSIN, -ED, -ING, -S *n* resin used for treating the bows of violins etc ▷ *vb* apply rosin to

ROSINATE *n* chemical compound

ROSINED ▶ rosin

ROSINER, -S *n* strong alcoholic drink

ROSINESS ▶ rosy

ROSING ▶ rose

ROSINING ▶ rosin

ROSINOL, -S *n* yellowish fluorescent oily liquid obtained from certain resins

ROSINOUS *adj* rosiny

ROSINS ▶ rosin

ROSINY ▶ rosin

ROSIT, -ED, -ING, -S *same as* ▶ **roset**

ROSOGLIO *same as* ▶ **rosolio**

ROSOLIO, -S *n* type of cordial

ROSSER, -S *n* bark-removing machine

ROST, -ED, -ING, -S *archaic spelling of* ▶ **roast**

ROSTELLA ▶ rostellum

ROSTER, -ED, -S *n* list of people and their turns of duty ▷ *vb* place on a roster

ROSTI, -S *n* cheese-topped fried Swiss dish of grated potato

ROSTING ▶ rost

ROSTIS ▶ rosti

ROSTRA ▶ rostrum

ROSTRAL *adj* of or like a beak or snout

ROSTRATE *adj* having a beak or beaklike process

ROSTRUM, ROSTRA, -S *n* platform or stage

ROSTS ▶ rost

ROSULA, -S *n* rosette

ROSULATE *adj* in the form of a rose

ROSY, ROSIED, ROSIES, ROSIEST, -ING *adj* pink-coloured ▷ *vb* redden or make pink

ROT, -S, -TED, -TING *vb* decompose or decay ▷ *n* decay

ROTA, -S *n* list of people who take it in turn to do a particular task

ROTAL *adj* of or relating to wheels or rotation

ROTAN, -S *another name for* ▶ **rattan**

ROTARY, ROTARIES *adj* revolving ▷ *n* traffic roundabout

ROTAS ▶ rota

ROTATE, -D, -S *vb* (cause to) move around a centre or on a pivot ▷ *adj* designating a corolla the united petals of which radiate from a central point

ROTATING *adj* revolving around a central axis, line, or point

ROTATION *n* act of rotating

ROTATIVE *same as* ▶ **rotatory**

ROTATOR, -S *n* person, device, or part that rotates or causes rotation

ROTATORY *adj* of, relating to, possessing, or causing rotation

ROTAVATE *same as* ▶ **rotovate**

ROTCH, -ES *n* little auk

ROTCHE *same as* ▶ **rotch**

ROTCHES ▶ rotch

ROTCHIE, -S *same as* ▶ **rotch**

ROTE, -D, -S, ROTING *n* mechanical repetition ▷ *vb* learn by rote

ROTENONE *n* white odourless crystalline substance

ROTES ▶ rote

ROTGRASS *n* type of grass blamed for sheeprot

ROTGUT, -S *n* alcoholic drink of inferior quality

ROTHER, -S *dialect word for* ▶ **ox**

ROTI, -S *n* (in India and the Caribbean) a type of unleavened bread

ROTIFER, -S *n* minute aquatic multicellular invertebrate

ROTIFORM *adj* in the shape of a wheel

ROTING ▶ rote

ROTINI, -S *n* type of small spiral-shaped pasta

ROTIS ▶ roti

ROTL, -S *n* unit of weight used in Muslim countries

ROTO, -S *n* printing process using a cylinder etched with many small recesses in a rotary press

ROTOLO, -S *n* (in Italian cuisine) a roll

ROTON, -S *n* quantum of vortex motion

ROTOR, -S *n* revolving portion of a dynamo, motor, or turbine

ROTOS ▶ roto

ROTOTILL *vb* break up the soil using a rototiller

ROTOVATE *vb* break up (the surface of the earth, or an area of ground) using a rotavator

ROTPROOF *adj* proof against rot

ROTS ▶ rot

ROTTAN, -S *n* (in dialect) a rat

ROTTE, -S *n* ancient stringed instrument

ROTTED ▶ rot

ROTTEN, -ER, -S *adj* decaying ▷ *adv* extremely ▷ *n* (in dialect) a rat

ROTTENLY

ROTTER, -S *n* despicable person

ROTTES ▶ rotte

ROTTING ▶ rot

ROTULA, -E, -S *n* kneecap

ROTUND, -ED, -ER, -S *adj* round and plump ▷ *vb* make round

ROTUNDA, -S *n* circular building or room, esp with a dome

ROTUNDED ▶ rotund

ROTUNDER ▶ rotund

ROTUNDLY ▶ rotund

ROTUNDS ▶ rotund

R

ROTURIER n freeholder or ordinary person

ROUBLE, -S n monetary unit of Russia, Belarus, and Tajikistan

ROUCHE, -S same as ▶ **ruche**

ROUCHED adj trimmed with a rouche

ROUCHES ▶ **rouche**

ROUCHING n lace trimming

ROUCOU, -S another name for ▶ **annatto**

ROUE, -S n man given to immoral living

ROUEN, -S n breed of duck

ROUES ▶ **roue**

ROUGE, -D, -S, ROUGING n red cosmetic used to colour the cheeks ▷ vb apply rouge to

ROUGH, -ED, -EST, -S adj uneven or irregular ▷ vb make rough ▷ n rough state or area

ROUGHAGE n indigestible constituents of food which aid digestion

ROUGHDRY vb dry (clothes or linen) without smoothing

ROUGHED ▶ **rough**

ROUGHEN, -S vb make or become rough

ROUGHER, -S n person that does the rough preparatory work on something ▷ adj more rough

ROUGHEST ▶ **rough**

ROUGHHEW vb cut or hew (timber, stone, etc) roughly without finishing the surface

ROUGHIE, -S n small food fish found in Australian waters

ROUGHING n (in ice hockey) excessive use of force

ROUGHISH adj somewhat rough

ROUGHLEG n any of several kinds of large hawk with feathered legs

ROUGHLY adv without being exact or fully authenticated

ROUGHOUT n unfinished roughly-shaped artifact

ROUGHS ▶ **rough**

ROUGHT archaic past form of ▶ **reach**

ROUGHY spelling variant of ▶ **roughie**

ROUGING ▶ **rouge**

ROUILLE, -S n kind of sauce

ROUL, -S archaic form of ▶ **roll**

ROULADE, -S n slice of meat rolled and cooked

ROULE, -S archaic form of ▶ **roll**

ROULEAU, -S, -X n roll of paper containing coins

ROULES ▶ **roule**

ROULETTE n gambling game played with a revolving wheel and a ball ▷ vb use a toothed wheel on (something), as in engraving, making stationery, etc

ROULS ▶ **roul**

ROUM, -S archaic spelling of ▶ **room**

ROUMING, -S n pasture given for an animal

ROUMS ▶ **roum**

ROUNCE, -S n handle that is turned to move paper and plates on a printing press

ROUNCY, ROUNCIES archaic word for ▶ **horse**

ROUND, -EST, -S adj spherical, cylindrical, circular, or curved ▷ prep indicating an encircling movement, presence on all sides, etc ▷ vb move round ▷ n round shape

ROUNDED adj round or curved

ROUNDEL, -S same as ▷ **roundelay**

ROUNDER n run round all four bases after one hit in rounders

ROUNDERS n bat-and-ball team game

ROUNDEST ▶ **round**

ROUNDING n process in which a number with a fraction is approximated as the closest number up or down

ROUNDISH adj somewhat round

ROUNDLE, -S same as ▶ **roundel**

ROUNDLET n small circle

ROUNDLY adv thoroughly

ROUNDS ▶ **round**

ROUNDUP, -S n act of gathering together

ROUNDURE n archaic word meaning roundness

ROUP, -ED, -ING, -S n any of various chronic respiratory diseases of birds, esp poultry ▷ vb sell by auction

ROUPET adj Scots word meaning hoarse or croaky

ROUPIER ▶ **roupy**

ROUPIEST ▶ **roupy**

ROUPILY ▶ **roup**

ROUPING ▶ **roup**

ROUPIT same as ▶ **roupet**

ROUPS ▶ **roup**

ROUPY, ROUPIER, ROUPIEST ▶ **roup**

ROUSABLE adj capable of being roused

ROUSANT adj (in heraldry) rising

ROUSE, -D, -S same as ▶ **reveille**

ROUSER, -S n person or thing that rouses people

ROUSES ▶ **rouse**

ROUSING adj lively, vigorous

ROUSSEAU n pemmican fried in its own fat

ROUST, -ED, -ING, -S vb rout or stir, as out of bed

ROUSTER, -S n unskilled labourer on an oil rig

ROUSTING ▶ **roust**

ROUSTS ▶ **roust**

ROUT, -S n overwhelming defeat ▷ vb defeat and put to flight

ROUTE, -D, -ING, -S n roads taken to reach a destination ▷ vb send by a particular route

ROUTEMAN, ROUTEMEN n (in US English) delivery man or salesman doing a particular round

ROUTER, -S n device that allows data to be moved between points on a network

ROUTES ▶ **route**

ROUTEWAY n track, road, or waterway, etc, used as a route to somewhere

ROUTH, -S n abundance ▷ adj abundant

ROUTHIE, -R adj abundant, plentiful, or well filled

ROUTHS ▶ **routh**

ROUTINE, -S n usual or regular method of procedure ▷ adj ordinary or regular

ROUTING, -S ▶ **rout**

ROUTOUS ▶ **rout**

ROUTS ▶ **rout**

ROUX n fat and flour cooked together as a basis for sauces

ROVE, -D, -N, -S, ROVING, ROVINGS vb wander about

ROVER, -S n wanderer, traveller

ROVES ▶ **rove**

ROVING ▶ **rove**

ROVINGLY ▶ **rove**

ROVINGS ▶ **rove**

ROW, -ED, -S n straight line of people or things ▷ vb propel (a boat) by oars

ROWABLE

ROWAN, -S n tree producing bright red berries, mountain ash

ROWBOAT, -S n small boat propelled by one or more pairs of oars

ROWDEDOW *same as* ► **rowdydow**
ROWDIER ► **rowdy**
ROWDIES ► **rowdy**
ROWDIEST ► **rowdy**
ROWDILY ► **rowdy**
ROWDY, ROWDIER, ROWDIES, ROWDIEST *adj* disorderly, noisy, and rough ▷ *n* person like this
ROWDYDOW *n* hullabaloo ▷ *vb* make noise
ROWDYISH ► **rowdy**
ROWDYISM *n* rowdy behaviour or tendencies or a habitual pattern of rowdy behaviour
ROWED ► **row**
ROWEL, -ED, -ING, -LED, -S *n* small spiked wheel on a spur ▷ *vb* goad (a horse) using a rowel
ROWEN, -S *another word for* > **aftermath**
ROWER, -S ► **row**
ROWIE, -S *n* Scottish bread roll made with butter and fat
ROWING, -S ► **row**
ROWLOCK, -S *n* device on a boat that holds an oar in place
ROWME, -S *archaic variant of* ► **room**
ROWND, -ED, -ING, -S *archaic variant of* ► **round**
ROWNDELL *archaic variant of* ► **roundel**
ROWNDING ► **rownd**
ROWNDS ► **rownd**
ROWOVER, -S *n* act of winning a rowing race unopposed
ROWS ► **row**
ROWT, -ED, -ING, -S *archaic variant of* ► **rout**
ROWTH, -S *same as* ► **routh**
ROWTING ► **rowt**
ROWTS ► **rowt**
ROYAL, -LER, -S *adj* of, befitting, or supported by a king or queen ▷ *n* member of a royal family
ROYALET, -S *n* minor king
ROYALISE *same as* ► **royalize**
ROYALISM ► **royalist**
ROYALIST *n* supporter of monarchy ▷ *adj* of or relating to royalists
ROYALIZE *vb* make royal
ROYALLER ► **royal**
ROYALLY ► **royal**
ROYALS ► **royal**
ROYALTY *n* royal people
ROYNE, -D, -S, ROYNING *archaic word for* ► **gnaw**

ROYNISH *archaic word for* ► **mangy**
ROYST, -ED, -ING, -S *same as* ► **roist**
ROYSTER, -S *same as* ► **roister**
ROYSTING ► **royst**
ROYSTS ► **royst**
ROZELLE, -S *same as* ► **roselle**
ROZET, -ED, -ING, -S *same as* ► **roset**
ROZIT, -ED, -ING, -S *same as* ► **roset**
ROZZER, -S *n* policeman
RUANA, -S *n* woollen wrap resembling a poncho
RUB, -BED, -S *vb* apply pressure with a circular or backwards-and-forwards movement ▷ *n* act of rubbing
RUBABOO, -S *n* soup or stew made by boiling pemmican with, if available, flour and vegetables
RUBACE, -S *same as* ► **rubasse**
RUBAI, -S *n* verse form of Persian origin consisting of four-line stanzas
RUBAIYAT *n* (in Persian poetry) a verse form consisting of four-line stanzas
RUBASSE, -S *n* type of quartz containing red haematite
RUBATO, RUBATI, -S *n* (with) expressive flexibility of tempo ▷ *adv* be played with a flexible tempo
RUBBABOO *same as* ► **rubaboo**
RUBBED ► **rub**
RUBBER, -ED, -S *n* strong waterproof elastic material ▷ *adj* made of or producing rubber ▷ *vb* provide with rubber coating
RUBBERY *adj* having the texture of or resembling rubber, esp in flexibility or toughness
RUBBET *old Scots past form of* ► **rob**
RUBBIDY *same as* ► **rubbity**
RUBBIES ► **rubby**
RUBBING, -S ► **rub**
RUBBISH *n* waste matter ▷ *vb* criticize
RUBBISHY *adj* worthless, of poor quality, or useless
RUBBIT *old Scots past form of* ► **rob**
RUBBITY *n* pub
RUBBLE, -D, -S, RUBBLING *n* fragments of broken stone,

brick, etc ▷ *vb* turn into rubble
RUBBLIER ► **rubbly**
RUBBLING ► **rubble**
RUBBLY, RUBBLIER ► **rubble**
RUBBOARD *n* board for scrubbing clothes on
RUBBY, RUBBIES *n* slang word for rubbing alcohol
RUBBYDUB *n* person who drinks cheap alcohol mixtures
RUBDOWN, -S *n* act of drying or cleaning vigorously
RUBE, -S *n* unsophisticated countryman
RUBEFY, RUBEFIED, RUBEFIES *vb* make red
RUBEL, -S *n* currency unit of Belarus
RUBELLA, -S *n* mild contagious viral disease
RUBELLAN *n* red-coloured mineral
RUBELLAS ► **rubella**
RUBELS ► **rubel**
RUBEOLA, -S *technical name for* ► **measles**
RUBEOLAR
RUBES ► **rube**
RUBICON, -S *n* point of no return ▷ *vb* (in bezique) to beat before the loser has managed to gain as many as 1000 points
RUBICUND *adj* ruddy
RUBIDIC ► **rubidium**
RUBIDIUM *n* soft highly reactive radioactive element
RUBIED ► **ruby**
RUBIER ► **ruby**
RUBIES ► **ruby**
RUBIEST ► **ruby**
RUBIFY, RUBIFIED, RUBIFIES *same as* ► **rubefy**
RUBIN, -S *archaic word for* ► **ruby**
RUBINE, -S *archaic word for* ► **ruby**
RUBINS ► **rubin**
RUBIOUS *adj* of the colour ruby
RUBLE, -S, RUBLI *same as* ► **rouble**
RUBOFF, -S *n* resulting effect on something else; consequences
RUBRIC, -S *n* set of rules for behaviour ▷ *adj* written, printed, or marked in red
RUBRICAL
RUBS ► **rub**
RUBSTONE *n* stone used for sharpening or smoothing, esp a whetstone
RUBUS, -ES *n* fruit-bearing genus of shrubs

R

RUBY, RUBIED, RUBIER, RUBIES, RUBIEST, -ING n red precious gemstone ▷ adj deep red ▷ vb redden

RUBYLIKE

RUC, -S same as ▸ roc

RUCHE, -D, -S n pleat or frill of lace etc as a decoration ▷ vb put a ruche on

RUCHING, -S n material used for a ruche

RUCK, -ED, -ING, -S n rough crowd of common people ▷ vb wrinkle or crease

RUCKLE, -D, -S, RUCKLING another word for ▸ ruck

RUCKMAN, RUCKMEN n person who plays in the ruck

RUCKS ▸ ruck

RUCKSACK n large pack carried on the back

RUCKSEAT n seat fixed to or forming part of a rucksack

RUCKUS, -ES n uproar

RUCOLA, -S n another name for the salad plant rocket

RUCS ▸ ruc

RUCTION, -S n uproar

RUCTIOUS adj tending or likely to cause ructions

RUD, -DED, -DING, -S n red or redness ▷ vb redden

RUDAS, -ES n Scots word for a coarse, rude old woman

RUDD, -S n European freshwater fish

RUDDED ▸ rud

RUDDER, -S n device for steering a boat or aircraft

RUDDIED ▸ ruddy

RUDDIER ▸ ruddy

RUDDIES ▸ ruddy

RUDDIEST ▸ ruddy

RUDDILY ▸ ruddy

RUDDING ▸ rud

RUDDLE, -D, -S, RUDDLING n red ochre, used esp to mark sheep ▷ vb mark (sheep) with ruddle

RUDDOCK, -S dialect name for the ▸ robin

RUDDS ▸ rudd

RUDDY, RUDDIED, RUDDIER, RUDDIES, RUDDIEST, -ING adj of a fresh healthy red colour ▷ adv bloody ▷ vb redden

RUDE, -R, -S, -ST archaic spelling of ▸ rood

RUDELY

RUDENESS

RUDERAL, -S n plant that grows on waste ground ▷ adj growing in waste places

RUDERY, RUDERIES ▸ rude

RUDES ▸ rude

RUDESBY n archaic word for rude person

RUDEST ▸ rude

RUDI, -S same as ▸ rudie

RUDIE, -S n member of a youth movement originating in the 1960s

RUDIMENT n first principles or elementary stages of a subject

RUDIS ▸ rudi

RUDISH adj somewhat rude

RUDIST, -S n cone-shaped extinct mollusc

RUDISTID same as ▸ rudist

RUDISTS ▸ rudist

RUDS ▸ rud

RUDY same as ▸ rudie

RUE, -D, -S vb feel regret for ▷ n plant with evergreen bitter leaves

RUEDA, -S n type of Cuban round dance

RUEFUL adj regretful or sorry

RUEFULLY

RUEING, -S ▸ rue

RUELLE, -S n area between bed and wall

RUELLIA, -S n genus of plants

RUER, -S ▸ rue

RUES ▸ rue

RUFF, -ED, -ING, -S n circular pleated, gathered, or fluted collar ▷ vb trump

RUFFE, -S n European freshwater fish

RUFFED ▸ ruff

RUFFES ▸ ruffe

RUFFIAN, -S n violent lawless person ▷ vb act like a ruffian

RUFFIN, -S archaic name for ▸ ruffe

RUFFING ▸ ruff

RUFFINS ▸ ruffin

RUFFLE, -D, -S, RUFFLING vb disturb the calm of ▷ n frill or pleat

RUFFLER, -S n person or thing that ruffles

RUFFLES ▸ ruffle

RUFFLIER ▸ ruffly

RUFFLIKE ▸ ruff

RUFFLING ▸ ruffle

RUFFLY, RUFFLIER adj ruffled

RUFFS ▸ ruff

RUFIYAA, -S n standard monetary unit of the Maldives

RUFOUS, -ES n reddish-brown colour

RUG, -S n small carpet ▷ vb (in dialect) tug

RUGA, -E n fold, wrinkle, or crease

RUGAL adj (in anatomy) with ridges or folds

RUGALACH same as ▸ rugelach

RUGATE same as ▸ rugose

RUGBY, RUGBIES n form of football played with an oval ball which may be handled by the players

RUGELACH n fruit and nut pastry shaped like a croissant

RUGGED, -ER adj rocky or steep

RUGGEDLY

RUGGER, -S same as ▸ rugby

RUGGIER ▸ ruggy

RUGGIEST ▸ ruggy

RUGGING, -S ▸ rug

RUGGY, RUGGIER, RUGGIEST adj (in dialect) rough or rugged

RUGLIKE ▸ rug

RUGOLA, -S n another name for the salad plant rocket

RUGOSA, -S n any of various shrubs descended from a particular type of wild rose

RUGOSE adj wrinkled

RUGOSELY

RUGOSITY

RUGOUS same as ▸ rugose

RUGRAT, -S n young child

RUGS ▸ rug

RUGULOSE adj with little wrinkles

RUIN, -ED, -S vb destroy or spoil completely ▷ n destruction or decay

RUINABLE

RUINATE, -D, -S vb archaic word for bring or come to ruin

RUINED ▸ ruin

RUINER, -S ▸ ruin

RUING, -S ▸ rue

RUINING, -S ▸ ruin

RUINOUS adj causing ruin

RUINS ▸ ruin

RUKH, -S same as ▸ roc

RULABLE ▸ rule

RULE, -D, -S n statement of what is allowed, for example in a game or procedure ▷ vb govern

RULELESS

RULER, -ED, -ING, -S n person who governs ▷ vb punish by hitting with a ruler

RULES ▸ rule

RULESSE adj archaic word meaning ruleless or without rules

RULIER ▸ ruly

RULIEST ▸ ruly

RULING, -S n formal decision ▷ adj controlling or exercising authority

RULLION, -S n Scots word for rawhide shoe

RULLOCK, -S same as ▶ **rowlock**

RULY, RULIER, RULIEST adj orderly

RUM, -MEST, -S n alcoholic drink distilled from sugar cane ▷ adj odd, strange

RUMAKI, -S n savoury of chicken liver and sliced water chestnut wrapped in bacon

RUMAL, -S n handkerchief or type of cloth

RUMBA, -ED, -ING, -S n lively ballroom dance of Cuban origin ▷ vb dance the rumba

RUMBELOW n nonsense word used in the refrain of certain sea shanties

RUMBLE, -D, -S vb make a low continuous noise ▷ n deep resonant sound

RUMBLER -S

RUMBLIER ▶ **rumbly**

RUMBLING ▶ **rumble**

RUMBLY, RUMBLIER adj rumbling or liable to rumble

RUMBO, -S n rum-based cocktail

RUMDUM, -S n alcoholic

RUME, -S archaic form of ▶ **rheum**

RUMEN, -S, RUMINA n first compartment of the stomach of ruminants

RUMES ▶ **rume**

RUMINA ▶ **rumen**

RUMINAL ▶ **rumen**

RUMINANT n cud-chewing (animal, such as a cow, sheep, or deer) ▷ adj of ruminants

RUMINATE vb chew the cud

RUMKIN, -S n archaic term for a drinking vessel

RUMLY ▶ **rum**

RUMMAGE, -D, -S vb search untidily and at length ▷ n untidy search through a collection of things

RUMMAGER

RUMMER, -S n drinking glass

RUMMEST ▶ **rum**

RUMMIER ▶ **rummy**

RUMMIES ▶ **rummy**

RUMMIEST ▶ **rummy**

RUMMILY ▶ **rummy**

RUMMISH adj rather strange, peculiar, or odd ▷ vb roar or protest

RUMMY, RUMMIER, RUMMIES, RUMMIEST n card game in which players try to collect sets or sequences ▷ adj of or like rum in taste or smell

RUMNESS ▶ **rum**

RUMOR, -ED, -ING, -S same as ▶ **rumour**

RUMORER, -S n person given to spreading rumours

RUMORING ▶ **rumor**

RUMOROUS adj involving or containing rumours

RUMORS ▶ **rumor**

RUMOUR, -ED, -S n unproved statement ▷ vb pass around or circulate in the form of a rumour

RUMOURER n someone given to spreading rumours

RUMOURS ▶ **rumour**

RUMP, -ED, -ING, -S n buttocks ▷ vb turn back on

RUMPIES ▶ **rumpy**

RUMPING ▶ **rump**

RUMPLE, -D, -S, RUMPLING vb make untidy, crumpled, or dishevelled ▷ n wrinkle, fold, or crease

RUMPLESS ▶ **rump**

RUMPLIER ▶ **rumply**

RUMPLING ▶ **rumple**

RUMPLY, RUMPLIER ▶ **rumple**

RUMPOT, -S n alcoholic

RUMPS ▶ **rump**

RUMPUS, -ES n noisy commotion

RUMPY, RUMPIES n tailless Manx cat ▷ adj with a large or noticeable rump

RUMS ▶ **rum**

RUN, RAN, -S vb move with a more rapid gait than walking ▷ n act or spell of running

RUNABOUT n small car used for short journeys ▷ vb move busily from place to place

RUNAGATE n vagabond, fugitive, or renegade

RUNANGA, -S n Māori assembly or council

RUNAWAY, -S n person or animal that runs away

RUNBACK, -S n (in tennis) the areas behind the baselines of the court

RUNCH, -ES n another name for white charlock

RUNCIBLE adj as in **runcible spoon** forklike utensil with two prongs and one sharp curved prong

RUND, -S same as ▶ **roon**

RUNDALE, -S n system of land tenure in Ireland

RUNDLE, -S n rung of a ladder

RUNDLED adj rounded

RUNDLES ▶ **rundle**

RUNDLET, -S n liquid measure, generally about 15 gallons

RUNDOWN, -S adj tired; exhausted ▷ n brief review, résumé, or summary

RUNDS ▶ **rund**

RUNE, -S n any character of the earliest Germanic alphabet

RUNED n with runes on

RUNELIKE adj resembling a rune or runes

RUNES ▶ **rune**

RUNFLAT, -S adj having a safety feature that prevents tyres becoming dangerous when flat

RUNG, -S n crosspiece on ladder

RUNGED adj having rungs

RUNGLESS ▶ **rung**

RUNGS ▶ **rung**

RUNIC ▶ **rune**

RUNKLE, -D, -S, RUNKLING vb (in dialect) crease or wrinkle

RUNLESS ▶ **run**

RUNLET, -S n cask for wine, beer, etc

RUNNABLE ▶ **run**

RUNNEL, -S n small brook

RUNNER, -S n competitor in a race

RUNNET, -S dialect word for ▶ **rennet**

RUNNIER ▶ **runny**

RUNNIEST ▶ **runny**

RUNNING, -S ▶ **run**

RUNNY, RUNNIER, RUNNIEST adj tending to flow

RUNOFF, -S n extra race to decide the winner after a tie

RUNOUT, -S n dismissal of a batsman by running him out

RUNOVER, -S n incident in which someone is run over by a vehicle

RUNPROOF adj (of stockings or tights) designed to be especially resistant to being ripped

RUNRIG, -S same as ▶ **rundale**

RUNROUND same as > **runaround**

RUNS ▶ **run**

RUNT, -S n smallest animal in a litter

RUNTED adj stunted

RUNTIER ▶ **runty**

RUNTIEST ▶ **runty**

RUNTISH ▶ **runt**

RUNTS ▶ **runt**

RUNTY, RUNTIER, RUNTIEST ▶ **runt**

RUNWAY, -S n hard level roadway where aircraft take off and land

R

RUPEE, -S n monetary unit of India and Pakistan

RUPIA, -S n type of skin eruption

RUPIAH, -S n standard monetary unit of Indonesia

RUPIAS ▶ rupia

RUPTURE, -D, -S n breaking, breach ▷ vb break, burst, or sever

RURAL, -S adj in or of the countryside ▷ n country dweller

RURALISE same as **▶ ruralize**

RURALISM ▶ rural

RURALIST ▶ rural

RURALITE ▶ rural

RURALITY ▶ rural

RURALIZE vb make rural in character, appearance, etc

RURALLY ▶ rural

RURALS ▶ rural

RURBAN adj part country, part urban

RURP, -S n very small piton

RURU, -S another name for **▶ mopoke**

RUSA, -S n type of deer with a mane

RUSALKA, -S n water nymph or spirit

RUSAS ▶ rusa

RUSCUS, -ES n type of shrub

RUSE, -S n stratagem or trick

RUSH, -ED vb move or do very quickly ▷ n sudden quick or violent movement ▷ adj done with speed, hasty

RUSHEE, -S n someone interested in gaining fraternity or sorority membership

RUSHEN adj made of rushes

RUSHER, -S ▶ rush

RUSHES pl n (in film-making) the initial prints of a scene or scenes before editing

RUSHIER ▶ rushy

RUSHIEST ▶ rushy

RUSHING, -S ▶ rush

RUSHLIKE ▶ rush

RUSHY, RUSHIER, RUSHIEST adj full of rushes

RUSINE adj of or relating to rusa deer

RUSK, -S n hard brown crisp biscuit, used esp for feeding babies

RUSMA, -S n Turkish depilatory

RUSSE adj as in **charlotte russe** cold dessert made from cream, etc, surrounded by sponge fingers

RUSSEL, -S n type of woollen fabric

RUSSET, -ED, -S adj reddish-brown ▷ n apple with rough reddish-brown skin ▷ vb become russet-coloured

RUSSETY

RUSSIA, -S n Russia leather

RUSSIFY vb cause to become Russian in character

RUSSULA, -E, -S n type of fungus, typically of toadstool shape

RUST, -ED, -S n reddish-brown coating formed on iron etc that has been exposed to moisture ▷ adj reddish-brown ▷ vb become coated with rust

RUSTABLE adj liable to rust

RUSTED ▶ rust

RUSTIC, -S adj of or resembling country people ▷ n person from the country

RUSTICAL n rustic

RUSTICLY ▶ rustic

RUSTICS ▶ rustic

RUSTIER ▶ rusty

RUSTIEST ▶ rusty

RUSTILY ▶ rusty

RUSTING, -S ▶ rust

RUSTLE, -D, -S n (make) a low whispering sound ▷ vb steal (cattle)

RUSTLER, -S n cattle thief

RUSTLES ▶ rustle

RUSTLESS ▶ rustle

RUSTLING ▶ rustle

RUSTRE, -S n (in heraldry) lozenge with a round hole in the middle showing the background colour

RUSTRED

RUSTS ▶ rust

RUSTY, RUSTIER, RUSTIEST adj coated with rust

RUT, -S, -TED n furrow made by wheels ▷ vb make ruts in

RUTABAGA n plant with a bulbous edible root

RUTH, -S n pity

RUTHENIC adj of or containing ruthenium, esp in a high valency state

RUTHER adv rather

RUTHFUL adj full of or causing sorrow or pity

RUTHLESS adj pitiless, merciless

RUTHS ▶ ruth

RUTILANT adj of a reddish colour or glow

RUTILE, -S n black, yellowish, or reddish-brown mineral

RUTIN, -S n bioflavonoid found in various plants including rue

RUTS ▶ rut

RUTTED ▶ rut

RUTTER, -S n (in history) type of cavalry soldier

RUTTIER ▶ rutty

RUTTIEST ▶ rutty

RUTTILY ▶ rutty

RUTTING, -S ▶ rut

RUTTISH adj (of an animal) in a condition of rut

RUTTY, RUTTIER, RUTTIEST adj full of ruts or holes

RYA, -S n type of rug originating in Scandinavia

RYAL, -S n one of several old coins

RYAS ▶ rya

RYBAT, -S n polished stone piece forming the side of a window or door

RYE, -S n kind of grain used for fodder and bread

RYEBREAD n bread made from rye flour

RYEFLOUR n flour made from rye

RYEGRASS n type of grass, widely cultivated as a forage crop

RYEPECK, -S n punt-mooring pole

RYES ▶ rye

RYFE archaic variant of **▶ rife**

RYKE, -D, -S, RYKING Scots variant of **▶ reach**

RYMME, -D, -S, RYMMING same as **▶ rim**

RYND, -S n (in milling) crossbar piece forming part of the support structure of the upper millstone

RYOKAN, -S n traditional Japanese inn

RYOT, -S n (in India) a peasant or tenant farmer

RYOTWARI n (in India) system of land tenure in which land taxes are paid to the state

RYPE, -R n ptarmigan

RYPECK, -S same as **▶ ryepeck**

RYPER ▶ rype

RYU, -S n school of Japanese martial arts

R

Ss

S begins only four two-letter words, **sh** (5 points), **si, so** and **st** (2 each). These are easy to remember, and it's worth noting that two of them, **sh** and **st**, don't use any vowels. Interestingly, there are quite a few three-letter words beginning with **S** that don't contain vowels, some of which give good scores. These are **shh** (9), **shy** (9), **sky** (10), **sly** (6), **sny** (6), **spy** (8), **sty** (6), **swy** (9) and **syn** (6). **S** also forms a number of three-letter words with **X**. These are easy to remember as they use every vowel except **U**: **sax, sex, six** and **sox** (10 each). When it comes to **Z**, you will find **saz, sez** and **soz** (12 each) very useful, and the same applies to **suq** (12 points).

SAAG, -S *n* (in Indian cookery) spinach

SAB, -BED, -BING, -S *n* person engaged in direct action to prevent a targeted activity taking place ▷ *vb* take part in such action

SABAL, -S *n* variety of palm tree

SABATON, -S *n* foot covering in suit of armour

SABAYON, -S *n* dessert or sweet sauce made with egg yolks, sugar, and wine

SABBAT, -S *n* midnight meeting of witches

SABBATH, -S *n* period of rest

SABBATIC *n* period of leave granted to university staff

SABBATS ▶ **sabbat**

SABBED ▶ **sab**

SABBING, -S ▶ **sab**

SABE, -D, -ING, -S *n* very informal word meaning sense or savvy ▷ *vb* very informal word meaning know or savvy

SABELLA, -S *n* marine worm

SABER, -ED, -ING, -S *same as* ▶ **sabre**

SABES ▶ **sabe**

SABHA, -S *n* set of Muslim prayer beads

SABICU, -S *n* type of Caribbean tree

SABIN, -S *n* unit of acoustic absorption

SABINE, -S *variant of* ▶ **savin**

SABINS ▶ **sabin**

SABIR, -S *n* member of ancient Turkic people

SABKHA, -S *n* flat coastal plain with a salt crust, common in Arabia

SABKHAH, -S *n* sabkha

SABKHAS ▶ **sabkha**

SABKHAT, -S *n* sabkha

SABLE, -D, -S, SABLING *n* dark fur from a small weasel-like Arctic animal ▷ *adj* black

SABOT, -S *n* wooden shoe traditionally worn by peasants in France

SABOTAGE *n* intentional damage done to machinery, systems, etc ▷ *vb* damage intentionally

SABOTED *adj* wearing sabots

SABOTEUR *n* person who commits sabotage

SABOTIER *n* wearer of wooden clogs

SABOTS ▶ **sabot**

SABRA, -S *n* native-born Israeli Jew

SABRE, -D, -S, SABRING *n* curved cavalry sword ▷ *vb* injure or kill with a sabre

SABREUR, -S *n* person wielding sabre

SABRING ▶ **sabre**

SABS ▶ **sab**

SABULINE *same as* ▶ **sabulous**

SABULOSE *same as* ▶ **sabulous**

SABULOUS *adj* like sand in texture

SABURRA, -S *n* granular deposit

SABURRAL

SAC, -S *n* pouchlike structure in an animal or plant

SACATON, -S *n* coarse grass of the southwestern US and Mexico

SACBUT, -S *n* medieval trombone

SACCADE, -S *n* movement of the eye when it makes a sudden change of fixation, as in reading

SACCADIC

SACCATE *adj* in the form of a sac

SACCOS, SACCOI, -ES *n* bishop's garment in the Orthodox Church

SACCULAR *adj* of or resembling a sac

SACCULE, -S *n* small sac

SACCULUS, SACCULI *same as* ▶ **saccule**

SACELLUM, SACELLA *n* tomb within a church

SACHEM, -S *same as* ▶ **sagamore**

SACHEMIC

SACHET, -S *n* small envelope or bag containing a single portion

SACHETED *adj* contained in a sachet

SACHETS ▶ **sachet**

SACK, -ED, -S *n* large bag made of coarse material ▷ *vb* dismiss

SACKABLE *adj* of an offence that is sufficiently serious to warrant dismissal from a job

SACKAGE, -D, -S *n* act of sacking a place ▷ *vb* sack or plunder

SACKBUT, -S *n* medieval form of trombone

SACKED ▶ **sack**

SACKER, -S ► sack
SACKFUL, -S, SACKSFUL ► sack
SACKING, -S n rough woven material used for sacks
SACKLESS adj old word meaning innocent
SACKLIKE ► sack
SACKLOAD n amount of something that a sack contains
SACKS ► sack
SACKSFUL ► sackful
SACLESS adj old word meaning unchallengeable
SACLIKE ► sac
SACQUE, -S same as ► sack
SACRA ► sacrum
SACRAL, -S adj of or associated with sacred rites ▷ n sacral vertebra
SACRARIA > sacrarium
SACRED, -ER adj holy
SACREDLY
SACRIFY vb old form of sacrifice
SACRING, -S n act or ritual of consecration
SACRIST, -S same as > sacristan
SACRISTY n room in a church where sacred objects are kept
SACRUM, SACRA, -S n wedge-shaped bone at the base of the spine
SACS ► sac
SAD, -DED, -DER, -DEST, -DING, -S adj sorrowful, unhappy ▷ vb New Zealand word meaning express sadness or displeasure strongly
SADDEN, -ED, -S vb make (someone) sad
SADDER ► sad
SADDEST ► sad
SADDHU, -S same as ► sadhu
SADDIE, -S same as ► saddo
SADDING ► sad
SADDISH ► sad
SADDLE, -D, -S, SADDLING n rider's seat on a horse or bicycle ▷ vb put a saddle on (a horse)
SADDLER, -S n maker or seller of saddles
SADDLERY n saddles and harness for horses collectively
SADDLES ► saddle
SADDLING ► saddle
SADDO, -ES, -S vb make sad ▷ n socially inadequate or pathetic person
SADE, -S same as ► sadhe

SADHANA, -S n one of a number of spiritual practices which lead to perfection
SADHE, -S n 18th letter in the Hebrew alphabet
SADHU, -S n Hindu wandering holy man
SADI, -S variant of ► sadhe
SADIRON, -S n heavy iron pointed at both ends, for pressing clothes
SADIS ► sadi
SADISM, -S n gaining of pleasure from inflicting suffering
SADIST -S
SADISTIC
SADLY ► sad
SADNESS ► sad
SADO, -S variant of ► chado
SADS ► sad
SADZA, -S n southern African porridge
SAE Scot word for ► so
SAECULUM, SAECULA n age in astronomy
SAETER, -S n upland pasture in Norway
SAFARI, -ED, -S n expedition to hunt or observe wild animals, esp in Africa ▷ vb go on safari
SAFARIST n person on safari
SAFE, -D, -R, -S, -ST, SAFING adj secure, protected ▷ n strong lockable container ▷ vb make safe
SAFELY
SAFENESS
SAFETY, SAFETIED, SAFETIES n state of being safe ▷ vb make safe
SAFFIAN, -S n leather tanned with sumach and usually dyed a bright colour
SAFFRON, -S n orange-coloured flavouring obtained from a crocus ▷ adj orange
SAFFRONY adj like saffron
SAFING ► safe
SAFRANIN same as > safranine
SAFROL, -S n oily liquid obtained from sassafras
SAFROLE, -S n colourless or yellowish oily water-insoluble liquid
SAFROLS ► safrol
SAFRONAL n oily liquid derived from saffron
SAFT, -ER, -EST Scot word for ► soft
SAG, -GED, -S vb sink in the middle ▷ n droop
SAGA, -S n legend of Norse heroes

SAGACITY n foresight, discernment, or keen perception
SAGAMAN, SAGAMEN n person reciting Norse sagas
SAGAMORE n (among some Native Americans) a chief or eminent man
SAGANASH n Algonquian term for an Englishman
SAGAS ► saga
SAGATHY n type of light fabric
SAGBUT, -S n medieval trombone
SAGE, -R, -S, -ST n very wise man ▷ adj wise
SAGEHOOD n state of being wise
SAGELY ► sage
SAGENE, -S n fishing net
SAGENESS ► sage
SAGENITE n mineral found in crystal form
SAGER ► sage
SAGES ► sage
SAGEST ► sage
SAGGAR, -ED, -S n box in which fragile ceramic wares are placed for protection ▷ vb put in a saggar
SAGGARD, -S n saggar
SAGGARED ► saggar
SAGGARS ► saggar
SAGGED ► sag
SAGGER, -ED, -S same as ► saggar
SAGGIER ► saggy
SAGGIEST ► saggy
SAGGING, -S ► sag
SAGGY, SAGGIER, SAGGIEST adj tending to sag
SAGIER ► sagy
SAGIEST ► sagy
SAGINATE vb fatten livestock
SAGITTA, -S n sine of an arc
SAGITTAL adj resembling an arrow
SAGITTAS ► sagitta
SAGO, -S n starchy cereal from the powdered pith of the sago palm tree
SAGOIN, -S n South American monkey
SAGOS ► sago
SAGOUIN, -S n South American monkey
SAGRADA adj as in cascara sagrada dried bark of the cascara buckthorn
SAGS ► sag
SAGUARO, -S n giant cactus of desert regions
SAGUIN, -S n South American monkey
SAGUM n Roman soldier's cloak

S

SAGY, SAGIER, SAGIEST *adj* like or containing sage

SAHEB, -S *same as* ▶ **sahib**

SAHIB, -S *n* Indian term of address placed after a man's name as a mark of respect

SAHIBA, -S *n* respectful Indian term of address for woman

SAHIBAH, -S *n* sahiba

SAHIBAS ▶ **sahiba**

SAHIBS ▶ **sahib**

SAHIWAL, -S *n* breed of cattle in India

SAHUARO, -S *same as* ▶ **saguaro**

SAI, -S *n* South American monkey

SAIBLING *n* freshwater fish

SAIC, -S *n* boat of eastern Mediterranean

SAICE, -S *same as* ▶ **syce**

SAICK, -S *n* boat of eastern Mediterranean

SAICS ▶ **saic**

SAID, -S *same as* ▶ **sayyid**

SAIDEST ▶ **say**

SAIDS ▶ **said**

SAIDST ▶ **say**

SAIGA, -S *n* either of two antelopes of the plains of central Asia

SAIKEI, -S *n* Japanese ornamental miniature landscape

SAIKLESS *old Scots word for* ▶ **innocent**

SAIL, -ED, -S *n* sheet of fabric stretched to catch the wind for propelling a sailing boat ▷ *vb* travel by water

SAILABLE

SAILBOAT *n* boat propelled chiefly by sail

SAILED ▶ **sail**

SAILER, -S *n* vessel, esp one equipped with sails, with specified sailing characteristics

SAILFISH *n* large tropical game fish, with a long sail-like fin on its back

SAILING, -S *n* practice, art, or technique of sailing a vessel

SAILLESS ▶ **sail**

SAILOR, -S *n* member of a ship's crew

SAILORLY

SAILPAST *n* sailing of ships past a particular place

SAILROOM *n* space on ship for storing sails

SAILS ▶ **sail**

SAIM, -S *Scots word for* ▶ **lard**

SAIMIN, -S *n* Hawaiian dish of noodles

SAIMIRI, -S *n* South American monkey

SAIMS ▶ **saim**

SAIN, -ED, -ING, -S *vb* make the sign of the cross over so as to bless or protect from evil or sin

SAINE *vb* old form of say

SAINED ▶ **sain**

SAINFOIN *n* Eurasian plant with pink flowers, widely grown as feed for grazing farm animals

SAINING ▶ **sain**

SAINS ▶ **sain**

SAINT, -ING, -S *n* person venerated after death as specially holy ▷ *vb* canonize

SAINTDOM

SAINTED *adj* formally recognized by a Christian Church as a saint

SAINTESS *n* female saint

SAINTING ▶ **saint**

SAINTISH ▶ **saint**

SAINTISM *n* quality of being saint

SAINTLY *adj* behaving in a very good, patient, or holy way

SAINTS ▶ **saint**

SAIQUE, -S *n* boat in eastern Mediterranean

SAIR, -ED, -ER, -EST, -ING, -S *Scot word for* ▶ **sore**

SAIS ▶ **sai**

SAIST ▶ **say**

SAITH, -S *form of the present tense (indicative mood) of* ▶ **say**

SAITHE, -S *n* dark-coloured food fish found in northern seas

SAITHS ▶ **saith**

SAIYID, -S *n* Muslim descended from Mohammed's grandson

SAJOU, -S *n* South American monkey

SAKAI, -S *n* Malaysian aborigine

SAKE, -S *n* benefit

SAKER, -S *n* large falcon of E Europe and central Asia

SAKERET, -S *n* male saker

SAKERS ▶ **saker**

SAKES ▶ **sake**

SAKI, -S *n* small arboreal monkey

SAKIA, -S *n* water wheel in Middle East

SAKIEH, -S *n* water wheel in Middle East

SAKIS ▶ **saki**

SAKIYEH, -S *n* water wheel in Middle East

SAKKOS, SAKKOI, -ES *n* bishop's garment in Orthodox Church

SAKSAUL, -S *n* Asian tree

SAKTI, -S *n* wife of a Hindu god

SAL, -S *pharmacological term for* ▶ **salt**

SALAAM, -ED, -S *n* low bow of greeting among Muslims ▷ *vb* make a salaam

SALABLE *same as* ▶ **saleable**

SALABLY ▶ **saleably**

SALAD, -S *n* dish of raw vegetables, eaten as a meal or part of a meal

SALADANG *n* variety of ox

SALADE, -S *same as* ▶ **sallet**

SALADING *n* ingredients for salad

SALADS ▶ **salad**

SALAL, -S *n* North American shrub

SALAMI, -S *n* highly spiced sausage

SALAMON, -S *n* word used in old oaths

SALARIAT *n* salary-earning class

SALARIED *adj* earning or providing a salary

SALARY, SALARIES *n* fixed regular payment, usu monthly, to an employee ▷ *vb* pay a salary to

SALAT, -S *n* obligatory series of Islamic prayers facing towards Mecca

SALBAND, -S *n* coating of mineral

SALCHOW, -S *n* type of figure-skating jump

SALE, -S *n* exchange of goods for money

SALEABLE *adj* fit or likely to be sold

SALEABLY

SALEP, -S *n* dried ground starchy tubers of various orchids

SALERING *n* enclosed area for livestock at market

SALEROOM *n* place where goods are sold by auction

SALES ▶ **sale**

SALESMAN, SALESMEN *n* person who sells goods

SALET, -S *same as* ▶ **sallet**

SALEWD ▶ **salue**

SALEYARD *n* area with pens for holding animals before auction

SALFERN, -S *n* plant of borage family

S

SALIC adj (of rocks and minerals) having a high content of silica and alumina

SALICES ► salix

SALICET, -S n soft-toned organ stop

SALICETA > salicetum

SALICETS ► salicet

SALICIN, -S n colourless or white crystalline water-soluble glucoside

SALICINE same as ► salicin

SALICINS ► salicin

SALIENCE ► salient

SALIENCY n quality of being prominent

SALIENT, -S adj prominent, noticeable ▷ n projecting part of a front line

SALIFY, SALIFIED, SALIFIES vb treat, mix with, or cause to combine with a salt

SALIGOT, -S n water chestnut

SALINA, -S n salt marsh, lake, or spring

SALINE, -S adj containing salt ▷ n solution of sodium chloride and water

SALINISE same as ► salinize

SALINITY ► saline

SALINIZE vb treat with salt

SALIVA, -S n liquid that forms in the mouth, spittle

SALIVAL

SALIVARY

SALIVATE vb produce saliva

SALIX, SALICES n plant or tree of willow family

SALL archaic form of ► shall

SALLAD, -S old spelling of ► salad

SALLAL, -S n North American shrub

SALLE, -S n hall

SALLEE, -S n SE Australian eucalyptus

SALLES ► salle

SALLET, -S n light round helmet

SALLIED ► sally

SALLIER, -S ► sally

SALLIES ► sally

SALLOW, -ED, -ER, -S adj of an unhealthy pale or yellowish colour ▷ vb make sallow ▷ n any of several small willow trees

SALLOWLY

SALLOWY

SALLY, SALLIED, SALLIES, -ING n violent excursion ▷ vb set or rush out

SALMI n ragout of game stewed in a rich brown sauce

SALMIS same as ► salmi

SALMON, -S n large fish with orange-pink flesh valued as food ▷ adj orange-pink

SALMONET n young salmon

SALMONID n type of soft-finned fish of the family which includes the salmon

SALMONS ► salmon

SALMONY adj of or like a salmon

SALOL, -S n white sparingly soluble compound

SALON, -S n commercial premises of a hairdresser, beautician, etc

SALOON, -S n closed car with four or more seats

SALOOP, -S n infusion of aromatic herbs or other plant parts formerly used as a tonic or cure

SALOP, -S variant of ► saloop

SALOPIAN ► saloop

SALOPS ► salop

SALP, -S n minute animal floating in sea

SALPA, -E, -S n any of various minute floating animals of warm oceans

SALPIAN, -S n minute animal floating in sea

SALPICON n mixture of chopped fish, meat, or vegetables in a sauce

SALPID, -S n minute animal floating in sea

SALPINX n Fallopian tube or Eustachian tube

SALPS ► salp

SALS ► sal

SALSA, -ED, -ING, -S n lively Puerto Rican dance ▷ vb dance the salsa

SALSE, -S n volcano expelling mud

SALSIFY n Mediterranean plant with a long white edible root

SALSILLA n tropical American vine

SALT, -EST, -S n white crystalline substance used to season food ▷ vb season or preserve with salt

SALTANDO n staccato piece of violin playing

SALTANT, -S adj (of an organism) differing from others of its species because of a saltation ▷ n saltant organism

SALTATE, -D, -S vb go through saltation

SALTATO, -S n saltando

SALTBOX n box for salt with a sloping lid

SALTBUSH n shrub that grows in alkaline desert regions

SALTCAT, -S n salty medicine for pigeons

SALTED adj seasoned, preserved, or treated with salt

SALTER, -S n person who deals in or manufactures salt

SALTERN, -S n place where salt is obtained from pools of evaporated sea water

SALTERS ► salter

SALTERY n factory where fish is salted for storage

SALTEST ► salt

SALTFISH n salted cod

SALTIE, -S n saltwater crocodile

SALTIER, -S same as ► saltire

SALTIES ► saltie

SALTIEST ► salty

SALTILY ► salty

SALTINE, -S n salty biscuit

SALTING, -S n area of low ground regularly inundated with salt water

SALTIRE, -S n diagonal cross on a shield

SALTISH ► salt

SALTLESS ► salt

SALTLIKE ► salt

SALTLY ► salt

SALTNESS ► salt

SALTO, -ED, -ING, -S n daring jump ▷ vb perform a daring jump

SALTPAN, -S n shallow basin containing salt from an evaporated salt lake

SALTS ► salt

SALTUS, -ES n break in the continuity of a sequence

SALTWORK n place where salt is refined

SALTWORT n any of several chenopodiaceous plants

SALTY, SALTIEST adj of, tasting of, or containing salt

SALUE, SALEWD, -D, -S, SALUING vb old word meaning salute

SALUKI, -S n type of tall hound with a smooth coat

SALUT interj cheers!

SALUTARY adj producing a beneficial result

SALUTE, -D, -S, SALUTING n motion of the arm as a formal military sign of respect ▷ vb greet with a salute

SALUTER -S

SALVABLE adj capable of or suitable for being saved or salvaged

SALVABLY

SALVAGE, -D, -S *n* saving of a ship or other property from destruction ▷ *vb* save from destruction or waste

SALVAGEE *n* rope on sailing ship

SALVAGER ▶ salvage

SALVAGES ▶ salvage

SALVE, -D, -S *n* healing or soothing ointment ▷ *vb* soothe or appease

SALVER, -S *same as* ▶ **salvor**

SALVES ▶ salve

SALVETE, -S *n* Latin greeting

SALVIA, -S *n* plant with blue or red flowers

SALVIFIC *adj* acting to salve

SALVING, -S ▶ salve

SALVO, -ED, -ES, -ING, -S *n* simultaneous discharge of guns etc ▷ *vb* attack with a salvo

SALVOR, -S *n* person instrumental in salvaging a vessel or its cargo

SALVOS ▶ salvo

SALWAR, -S *n as in* **salwar kameez** long tunic worn over a pair of baggy trousers

SAM, -MED, -MING, -S *vb* collect

SAMA, -S *n* Japanese title of respect

SAMAAN, -S *n* South American tree

SAMADHI, -S *n* state of deep meditative contemplation

SAMAN, -S *n* South American tree

SAMARA, -S *n* dry indehiscent one-seeded fruit

SAMARIUM *n* silvery metallic element

SAMAS ▶ sama

SAMBA, -ED, -ING, -S *n* lively Brazilian dance ▷ *vb* perform such a dance

SAMBAL, -S *n* Malaysian dish

SAMBAR, -S *n* S Asian deer with three-tined antlers

SAMBAS ▶ samba

SAMBHAR, -S *n* Indian dish

SAMBHUR, -S *n* Asian deer

SAMBUCA, -S *n* Italian liqueur

SAMBUKE, -S *n* ancient Greek stringed instrument

SAMBUR, -S *same as* ▶ **sambar**

SAME, -S *adj* identical, not different, unchanged ▷ *n* something identical

SAMECH, -S *n* letter in Hebrew alphabet

SAMEK, -S *variant of* ▶ **samekh**

SAMEKH, -S *n* 15th letter in the Hebrew alphabet

SAMEKS ▶ samek

SAMEL *adj* of brick, not sufficiently fired

SAMELY *adj* the same

SAMEN *old Scots form of* ▶ **same**

SAMENESS *n* state or quality of being the same

SAMES ▶ same

SAMEY, SAMIER, SAMIEST *adj* monotonous

SAMFOO, -S *n* style of casual dress worn by Chinese women

SAMFU, -S *n* Chinese female outfit

SAMIEL, -S *same as* ▶ **simoom**

SAMIER ▶ samey

SAMIEST ▶ samey

SAMISEN, -S *n* Japanese plucked stringed instrument with a long neck

SAMITE, -S *n* heavy fabric of silk used in the Middle Ages

SAMITHI, -S *same as* ▶ **samiti**

SAMITI, -S *n* (in India) an association, esp one formed to organize political activity

SAMIZDAT *n* system of secret printing and distribution of banned literature in the former USSR

SAMLET, -S *n* young salmon

SAMLOR, -S *n* motor vehicle in Thailand

SAMMED ▶ sam

SAMMIES ▶ sammy

SAMMING ▶ sam

SAMMY, SAMMIES *n* (in South Africa) an Indian fruit and vegetable vendor

SAMNITIS *n* poisonous plant mentioned by Spenser

SAMOSA, -S *n* (in Indian cookery) a small fried triangular spiced meat or vegetable pasty

SAMOVAR, -S *n* Russian tea urn

SAMOYED, -S *n* Siberian breed of dog with a tightly curled tail

SAMP, -S *n* crushed maize used for porridge

SAMPAN, -S *n* small boat with oars used in China

SAMPHIRE *n* plant found on rocks by the seashore

SAMPI, -S *n* old Greek number character

SAMPIRE, -S *n* samphire

SAMPIS ▶ sampi

SAMPLE, -D, -S *n* part taken as representative of a whole ▷ *vb* take and test a sample of

SAMPLER, -S *n* piece of embroidery showing the embroiderer's skill

SAMPLERY *n* making of samplers

SAMPLES ▶ sample

SAMPLING *n* process of selecting a random sample

SAMPS ▶ samp

SAMS ▶ sam

SAMSARA, -S *n* endless cycle of birth, death, and rebirth

SAMSARIC *adj* relating to the eternal cycle of birth, suffering, death and rebirth in Indian religions

SAMSHOO, -S *n* Chinese alcoholic drink

SAMSHU, -S *n* alcoholic drink made from fermented rice

SAMSKARA *n* Hindu purification ceremony

SAMURAI, -S *n* member of an ancient Japanese warrior caste

SAN *n* sanatorium

SANATIVE *less common word for* ▶ **curative**

SANATORY *adj* healing

SANCAI, -S *n* glaze in Chinese pottery

SANCHO, -S *n* African stringed instrument

SANCTA ▶ sanctum

SANCTIFY *vb* make holy

SANCTION *n* permission, authorization ▷ *vb* allow, authorize

SANCTITY *n* sacredness, inviolability

SANCTUM, SANCTA, -S *n* sacred place

SAND, -ED, -S *n* substance consisting of small grains of rock, esp on a beach or in a desert ▷ *vb* smooth with sandpaper

SANDABLE

SANDAL, -S *n* light shoe consisting of a sole attached by straps ▷ *vb* put sandals on

SANDALED

SANDARAC *n* either of two coniferous trees having hard fragrant dark wood

SANDBAG, -S *n* bag filled with sand, used as protection against flood water ▷ *vb* protect with sandbags

SANDBANK *n* bank of sand below the surface of a river or sea

S

SANDBAR, -S n ridge of sand in a river or sea, often exposed at low tide

SANDBOX n container on a locomotive from which sand is released onto the rails

SANDBOY, -S n as in **happy as a sandboy** very happy or high-spirited

SANDBUR, -S n variety of wild grass

SANDBURR n variety of wild grass

SANDBURS ▶ sandbur

SANDDAB, -S n type of small Pacific flatfish

SANDED ▶ sand

SANDEK, -S n man who holds a baby being circumcised

SANDER, -S n power tool for smoothing surfaces

SANDFISH n burrowing Pacific fish

SANDFLY n any of various small mothlike flies

SANDHEAP n heap of sand

SANDHI, -S n modification of a word under the influence of an adjacent word

SANDHILL n hill of sand

SANDHIS ▶ sandhi

SANDHOG, -S n person who works in underground or underwater construction projects

SANDIER ▶ sandy

SANDIEST ▶ sandy

SANDING, -S ▶ sand

SANDIVER n scum forming on molten glass

SANDLESS ▶ sand

SANDLIKE ▶ sand

SANDLING n sand eel

SANDLOT, -S n area of vacant ground used for children's games

SANDMAN, SANDMEN n (in folklore) a magical person supposed to put children to sleep

SANDPEEP n small sandpiper

SANDPILE n pile of sand

SANDPIT, -S n shallow pit or container holding sand for children to play in

SANDPUMP n pump for wet sand

SANDS ▶ sand

SANDSHOE n light canvas shoe with a rubber sole

SANDSOAP n gritty general-purpose soap

SANDSPIT n small point of land created by sand dunes

SANDSPUR n American wild grass

SANDWICH n two slices of bread with a layer of food between ▷ vb insert between two other things

SANDWORM n any of various polychaete worms that live in burrows on sandy shores, esp the lugworm

SANDWORT n any of numerous caryophyllaceous plants

SANDY, SANDIER, SANDIEST adj covered with sand

SANDYISH adj somewhat sandy or covered with sand

SANE, -D, -R, -S, -ST, SANING adj of sound mind ▷ vb heal

SANELY

SANENESS

SANG, -S Scots word for ▶ song

SANGA, -S n Ethiopian ox

SANGAR, -S n breastwork of stone or sods

SANGAREE n spiced drink similar to sangria

SANGARS ▶ sangar

SANGAS ▶ sanga

SANGEET, -S n Indian pre-wedding celebration

SANGER, -S n sandwich

SANGH, -S n Indian union or association

SANGHA, -S n Buddhist monastic order or community

SANGHAT, -S n local Sikh community or congregation

SANGHS ▶ sangh

SANGLIER n wild boar

SANGO, -S same as ▶ sanger

SANGOMA, -S n witch doctor or herbalist

SANGOS ▶ sango

SANGRAIL n legendary cup used by Christ at the Last Supper

SANGREAL same as ▶ sangrail

SANGRIA, -S n Spanish drink of red wine and fruit

SANGS ▶ sang

SANGUIFY vb turn into blood

SANGUINE adj cheerful, optimistic ▷ n red pencil containing ferric oxide, used in drawing

SANICLE, -S n type of plant with clusters of small white flowers

SANIDINE n alkali feldspar that is found in lavas

SANIES n thin greenish foul-smelling discharge from a wound, etc

SANIFY, SANIFIED, SANIFIES vb make healthy

SANING ▶ sane

SANIOUS ▶ sanies

SANITARY adj promoting health by getting rid of dirt and germs

SANITATE vb make sanitary

SANITIES ▶ sanity

SANITISE same as ▶ sanitize

SANITIZE vb omit unpleasant details to make (news) more acceptable

SANITY, SANITIES n state of having a normal healthy mind

SANJAK, -S n (in the Turkish Empire) a subdivision of a vilayet

SANK ▶ sink

SANKO, -S n African stringed instrument

SANNIE, -S Scots word for ▶ sandshoe

SANNOP, -S n Native American married man

SANNUP, -S n Native American married man

SANNYASI n Brahman who having attained the last stage of life as a beggar will not be reborn

SANPAN, -S n sampan

SANPRO, -S n sanitary-protection products, collectively

SANS archaic word for ▶ without

SANSA, -S n African musical instrument

SANSAR, -S n name of a wind that blows in Iran

SANSAS ▶ sansa

SANSEI, -S n American whose parents were Japanese immigrants

SANSERIF n style of printer's typeface

SANT, -S n devout person in India

SANTAL, -S n sandalwood

SANTALIC adj of sandalwood

SANTALIN n substance giving sandalwood its colour

SANTALOL n liquid from sandalwood used in perfume

SANTALS ▶ santal

SANTERA, -S n priestess of santeria

SANTERIA n Caribbean religious cult

SANTERO, -S n priest of santeria

SANTIM n coin formerly used in Latvia

SANTIMS, SANTIMI n former money unit in Latvia

SANTIMU same as ▸ **santims**

SANTIR, -S n Middle Eastern stringed instrument

SANTO, -S n saint or representation of one

SANTOL, -S n fruit from Southeast Asia

SANTON, -S n French figurine

SANTONIN n soluble substance extracted from santonica

SANTONS ▸ **santon**

SANTOOR, -S same as ▸ **santir**

SANTOS ▸ **santo**

SANTOUR, -S n Middle Eastern stringed instrument

SANTS ▸ **sant**

SANTUR, -S n Middle Eastern stringed instrument

SANYASI same as ▸ **sannyasi**

SAOLA, -S n small, very rare bovine mammal of Vietnam and Laos

SAOUARI, -S n tropical American tree

SAP, -PED, -S n moisture that circulates in plants ▷ vb undermine

SAPAJOU, -S n capuchin monkey

SAPAN, -S n tropical tree

SAPEGO, -ES n skin disease

SAPELE, -S n type of W African tree

SAPFUL adj full of sap

SAPHEAD, -S n simpleton, idiot, or fool

SAPHENA, -E, -S n either of two large superficial veins of the legs

SAPID adj having a pleasant taste

SAPIDITY

SAPIENCE ▸ **sapient**

SAPIENCY ▸ **sapient**

SAPIENS adj relating to or like modern human beings

SAPIENT, -S adj wise, shrewd ▷ n wise person

SAPLESS ▸ **sap**

SAPLING, -S n young tree

SAPONIFY vb convert (a fat) into a soap by treatment with alkali

SAPONIN, -S n any of a group of plant glycosides

SAPONINE n saponin

SAPONINS ▸ **saponin**

SAPONITE n type of clay mineral

SAPOR, -S n quality in a substance that is perceived by the sense of taste

SAPOROUS

SAPOTA, -S same as ▸ **sapodilla**

SAPOTE, -S n Central American tree

SAPOUR, -S variant of ▸ **sapor**

SAPPAN, -S n tropical tree

SAPPED ▸ **sap**

SAPPER, -S n soldier in an engineering unit

SAPPHIC, -S adj lesbian ▷ n verse written in a particular form

SAPPHIRE n blue precious stone ▷ adj deep blue

SAPPHISM n lesbianism

SAPPHIST n lesbian

SAPPIER ▸ **sappy**

SAPPIEST ▸ **sappy**

SAPPILY ▸ **sappy**

SAPPING, -S n act of sapping

SAPPLE, -D, -S, SAPPLING vb Scots word meaning wash in water

SAPPY, SAPPIER, SAPPIEST adj (of plants) full of sap

SAPREMIA American spelling of ▸ **sapraemia**

SAPREMIC

SAPROBE, -S n organism that lives on decaying organisms

SAPROBIC

SAPROPEL n decomposed remains of aquatic organisms at the bottoms of lakes and oceans

SAPS ▸ **sap**

SAPSAGO, -S n hard greenish Swiss cheese

SAPUCAIA n Brazilian tree

SAPWOOD, -S n soft wood, just beneath the bark in tree trunks, that consists of living tissue

SAR, -ED, -ING, -S n marine fish ▷ vb Scots word meaning savour

SARABAND same as ▸ **sarabande**

SARAFAN, -S n Russian woman's cloak

SARAN, -S n any one of a class of thermoplastic resins

SARANGI, -S n stringed instrument of India played with a bow

SARANS ▸ **saran**

SARAPE, -S n serape

SARCASM, -S n (use of) bitter or wounding ironic language

SARCENET n fine soft silk fabric formerly from Italy and used for clothing, ribbons, etc

SARCINA, -E, -S n type of bacterium

SARCODE, -S n material making up living cell

SARCODIC

SARCOID, -S adj of, relating to, or resembling flesh ▷ n tumour resembling a sarcoma

SARCOMA, -S n malignant tumour beginning in connective tissue

SARCONET n type of silk

SARCOUS adj (of tissue) muscular or fleshy

SARD, -S n orange, red, or brown variety of chalcedony

SARDANA, -S n Catalan dance

SARDAR, -S n title used before the name of Sikh men

SARDEL, -S n small fish

SARDELLE n small fish

SARDELS ▸ **sardel**

SARDINE, -D, -S n small fish of the herring family ▷ vb cram together

SARDIUS same as ▸ **sard**

SARDONIC adj mocking or scornful

SARDONYX n brown-and-white gemstone

SARDS ▸ **sard**

SARED ▸ **sar**

SAREE, -S same as ▸ **sari**

SARGASSA ▸ **sargassum**

SARGASSO same as ▸ **sargassum**

SARGE, -S n sergeant

SARGO same as ▸ **sargus**

SARGOS, -ES variant of ▸ **sargus**

SARGUS, -ES n species of sea fish

SARI, -S n long piece of cloth draped around the body and over one shoulder

SARIN, -S n chemical used in warfare as a lethal nerve gas producing asphyxia

SARING ▸ **sar**

SARINS ▸ **sarin**

SARIS ▸ **sari**

SARK, -S n shirt or (formerly) chemise

SARKIER ▸ **sarky**

SARKIEST ▸ **sarky**

SARKILY ▸ **sarky**

SARKING, -S n flat planking supporting the roof cladding of a building

SARKS ▸ **sark**

SARKY, SARKIER, SARKIEST adj sarcastic

S

SARMENT, -S n thin twig
SARMENTA ▷ sarmentum
SARMENTS ▷ sarment
SARMIE, -S n sandwich
SARNEY, -S n sandwich
SARNIE, -S n sandwich
SAROD, -S n Indian stringed musical instrument
SARODE, -S n Indian stringed instrument
SARODIST n sarod player
SARODS ▷ sarod
SARONG, -S n long piece of cloth tucked around the waist or under the armpits
SARONIC ▷ saros
SAROS, -ES n cycle in which eclipses of the sun and moon occur in the same sequence
SARPANCH n head of a panchayat
SARRASIN n buckwheat
SARRAZIN same as ▷ sarrasin
SARS ▷ sar
SARSAR, -S same as ▷ sansar
SARSDEN, -S n sarsen
SARSEN, -S n boulder of silicified sandstone
SARSENET same as ▷ sarcenet
SARSENS ▷ sarsen
SARSNET, -S n type of silk
SARTOR, -S humorous or literary word for ▷ tailor
SARTORII ▷ sartorius
SARTORS ▷ sartor
SARUS, -ES n Indian bird of crane family
SASANQUA n type of camellia
SASARARA n scolding
SASER, -S n device for amplifying ultrasound
SASH, -ED, -ES, -ING n decorative strip of cloth worn round the waist or over one shoulder ▷ vb furnish with a sash, sashes, or sash windows
SASHAY, -ED, -S vb move or walk in a casual or a showy manner
SASHED ▷ sash
SASHES ▷ sash
SASHIMI, -S n Japanese dish of thin fillets of raw fish
SASHING ▷ sash
SASHLESS ▷ sash
SASIN, -S another name for ▷ blackbuck
SASINE, -S n granting of legal possession of feudal property
SASINS ▷ sasin
SASS, -ED, -ES, -ING n insolent or impudent talk

or behaviour ▷ vb talk or answer back in such a way
SASSABY n African antelope of grasslands and semideserts
SASSE n old word meaning canal lock
SASSED ▷ sass
SASSES ▷ sass
SASSIER ▷ sassy
SASSIES ▷ sassy
SASSIEST ▷ sassy
SASSILY ▷ sassy
SASSING ▷ sass
SASSOLIN n boric acid
SASSWOOD same as ▷ sassy
SASSY, SASSIER, SASSIES, SASSIEST adj insolent, impertinent ▷ n W African leguminous tree with poisonous bark
SASTRA, -S same as ▷ shastra
SASTRUGA, SASTRUGI n ridge on a snow-covered plain
SAT ▷ sit
SATAI, -S same as ▷ satay
SATANG, -S n monetary unit of Thailand worth one hundredth of a baht
SATANIC adj of Satan
SATANISM n worship of the devil
SATANIST
SATANITY n quality of being satanic
SATARA, -S n type of cloth
SATAY, -S n Indonesian and Malaysian dish
SATCHEL, -S n bag, usu with a shoulder strap, for carrying books
SATCOM, -S n satellite communications
SATE, -D, -S, SATING vb satisfy (a desire or appetite) fully
SATEEN, -S n glossy linen or cotton fabric, woven in such a way that it resembles satin
SATELESS adj old word meaning insatiable
SATELLES n species of bacteria
SATEM adj denoting or belonging to a particular group of Indo-European languages
SATES ▷ sate
SATI, -S n Indian widow suicide
SATIABLE adj capable of being satiated
SATIABLY

SATIATE, -D, -S vb provide with more than enough, so as to disgust
SATIETY n feeling of having had too much
SATIN, -ED, -ING, -S n silky fabric with a glossy surface on one side ▷ adj like satin in texture ▷ vb cover with satin
SATINET, -S n thin or imitation satin
SATING ▷ sate
SATINING ▷ satin
SATINPOD n honesty (the plant)
SATINS ▷ satin
SATINY ▷ satin
SATIRE, -S n use of ridicule to expose vice or folly
SATIRIC same as ▷ satirical
SATIRISE same as ▷ satirize
SATIRIST n writer of satire
SATIRIZE vb ridicule by means of satire
SATIS ▷ sati
SATISFY vb please, content
SATIVE adj old word meaning cultivated
SATNAV, -S n satellite navigation system
SATORI, -S n state of sudden indescribable intuitive enlightenment
SATRAP, -S n (in ancient Persia) a provincial governor or subordinate ruler
SATRAPAL
SATRAPY n province, office, or period of rule of a satrap
SATSANG, -S n sacred gathering in Hinduism
SATSUMA, -S n kind of small orange
SATURANT n substance that causes a solution, etc, to be saturated ▷ adj (of a substance) causing saturation
SATURATE vb soak thoroughly
SATURNIC adj poisoned by lead
SATYR, -S n woodland god, part man, part goat
SATYRA, -S n female satyr
SATYRAL, -S n mythical beast in heraldry
SATYRAS ▷ satyra
SATYRE, -S n as in **sea satyre** sea creature mentioned in Spenser's poetry
SATYRESS n female satyr
SATYRIC ▷ satyr
SATYRID, -S n butterfly with typically brown or dark wings with paler markings

SATYRISK n small satyr
SATYRS ▸ satyr
SAU archaic past tense of
▸ **see**
SAUBA, -S n South American ant
SAUCE, -D, -S, SAUCING n liquid added to food to enhance flavour ▷ vb prepare (food) with sauce
SAUCEBOX n saucy person
SAUCED ▸ sauce
SAUCEPAN n cooking pot with a long handle
SAUCEPOT n cooking pot with lid
SAUCER, -S n small round dish put under a cup
SAUCES ▸ sauce
SAUCH, -S n sallow or willow
SAUCIER, -S n chef who makes sauces
SAUCIEST ▸ saucy
SAUCILY ▸ saucy
SAUCING ▸ sauce
SAUCISSE n type of explosive fuse
SAUCY, SAUCIEST adj impudent
SAUFGARD old form of
> **safeguard**
SAUGER, -S n small North American pikeperch
SAUGH, -S same as ▸ **sauch**
SAUGHY adj Scots word meaning made of willow
SAUL, -S Scots word for
▸ **soul**
SAULGE, -S n old word for sage plant
SAULIE, -S n Scots word meaning professional mourner
SAULS ▸ saul
SAULT, -S n waterfall in Canada
SAUNA, -ED, -ING, -S n Finnish-style steam bath ▷ vb have a sauna
SAUNT, -ED, -ING, -S Scots form of ▸ **saint**
SAUNTER, -S vb walk in a leisurely manner, stroll ▷ n leisurely walk
SAUNTING ▸ saunt
SAUNTS ▸ saunt
SAUREL, -S n type of mackerel
SAURIAN, -S n lizard
SAURIES ▸ saury
SAUROID, -S adj like a lizard ▷ n type of fish
SAUROPOD n type of herbivorous dinosaur including the brontosaurus and the diplodocus

SAURY, SAURIES n type of fish of tropical and temperate seas
SAUSAGE, -S n minced meat in an edible tube-shaped skin
SAUT, -ED, -ING, -S Scot word for ▸ **salt**
SAUTE, -ED, -ING, -S vb fry quickly in a little fat ▷ n dish of sautéed food ▷ adj sautéed until lightly brown
SAUTED ▸ saut
SAUTEED ▸ saute
SAUTEING ▸ saute
SAUTERNE n sauternes
SAUTES ▸ saute
SAUTING ▸ saut
SAUTOIR, -S n long necklace or pendant
SAUTOIRE variant of
▸ **sautoir**
SAUTOIRS ▸ sautoir
SAUTS ▸ saut
SAV, -S short for ▸ **saveloy**
SAVABLE ▸ save
SAVAGE, -D, -R, -S, -ST, SAVAGING adj wild, untamed ▷ n uncivilized person ▷ vb attack ferociously
SAVAGELY
SAVAGERY n viciousness and cruelty
SAVAGES ▸ savage
SAVAGEST ▸ savage
SAVAGING ▸ savage
SAVAGISM ▸ savage
SAVANNA, -S n open grasslands of tropical Africa
SAVANNAH same as
▸ **savanna**
SAVANNAS ▸ savanna
SAVANT, -S n learned person
SAVANTE -S
SAVARIN, -S n type of cake
SAVATE, -S n form of boxing in which blows may be delivered with the feet
SAVE, -D, -S vb rescue or preserve from harm, protect ▷ n act of preventing a goal ▷ prep except
SAVEABLE
SAVEGARD vb old word meaning protect
SAVELOY, -S n spicy smoked sausage
SAVER, -S ▸ save
SAVES ▸ save
SAVEY, -ED, -ING, -S vb understand
SAVIN, -S n small spreading juniper bush of Europe, N Asia, and North America
SAVINE, -S same as ▸ **savin**

SAVING, -S n economy ▷ prep except ▷ adj tending to save or preserve
SAVINGLY
SAVINS ▸ savin
SAVIOR, -S same as
▸ **saviour**
SAVIOUR, -S n person who rescues another
SAVOR, -ED, -ING, -S same as
▸ **savour**
SAVORER -S
SAVORIER ▸ savory
SAVORIES ▸ savory
SAVORILY ▸ savour
SAVORING ▸ savor
SAVOROUS ▸ savour
SAVORS ▸ savor
SAVORY, SAVORIER, SAVORIES same as
▸ **savoury**
SAVOUR, -ED, -S vb enjoy, relish ▷ n characteristic taste or odour
SAVOURER
SAVOURLY adv old word meaning refreshingly
SAVOURS ▸ savour
SAVOURY adj salty or spicy ▷ n savoury dish served before or after a meal
SAVOY, -S n variety of cabbage
SAVOYARD n person keenly interested in the operettas of Gilbert and Sullivan
SAVOYS ▸ savoy
SAVS ▸ sav
SAVVEY, -ED, -S vb understand
SAVVIED ▸ savvy
SAVVIER ▸ savvy
SAVVIES ▸ savvy
SAVVIEST ▸ savvy
SAVVILY ▸ savvy
SAVVY, SAVVIED, SAVVIER, SAVVIES, SAVVIEST, -ING vb understand ▷ n understanding, intelligence ▷ adj shrewd
SAW, -ED, -S n hand tool for cutting wood and metal ▷ vb cut with a saw
SAWAH, -S n paddyfield
SAWBILL, -S n type of hummingbird
SAWBLADE n blade of a saw
SAWBONES n surgeon or doctor
SAWBUCK, -S n sawhorse, esp one having an X-shaped supporting structure
SAWDER, -ED, -S n flattery ▷ vb flatter
SAWDUST, -S n fine wood fragments made in sawing

S

▷ *vb* cover with sawdust
SAWDUSTY
SAWED, -S ▸ saw
SAWER, -S ▸ saw
SAWFISH *n* fish with a long toothed snout
SAWFLY, SAWFLIES *n* any of various hymenopterous insects
SAWGRASS *n* type of sedge with serrated leaves
SAWHORSE *n* structure for supporting wood that is being sawn
SAWING, -S ▸ saw
SAWLIKE ▸ saw
SAWLOG, -S *n* log suitable for sawing
SAWMILL, -S *n* mill where timber is sawn into planks
SAWN *past participle of* ▸ saw
SAWNEY, -S *n* derogatory word for a fool
SAWPIT, -S *n* pit above which a log is sawn into planks
SAWS ▸ saw
SAWSHARK *n* shark with long sawlike snout
SAWTOOTH, SAWTEETH *adj* (of a waveform) having an amplitude that varies linearly with time between two values
SAWYER, -S *n* person who saws timber for a living
SAX, -ES *same as* > saxophone
SAXATILE *adj* living among rocks
SAXAUL, -S *n* Asian tree
SAXE *adj as in* **saxe blue** light greyish-blue colour
SAXES ▸ sax
SAXHORN, -S *n* valved brass instrument used chiefly in brass and military bands
SAXICOLE *variant of* ▸ saxatile
SAXIST, -S *n* saxophone player
SAXMAN, SAXMEN *n* saxophone player
SAXONIES ▸ saxony
SAXONITE *n* igneous rock
SAXONY, SAXONIES *n* fine 3-ply yarn used for knitting and weaving
SAXTUBA, -S *n* bass saxhorn
SAY, SAIDEST, SAIDST, SAIST, -EST, -NE, -S, -ST *vb* speak or utter ▷ *n* right or chance to speak
SAYABLE
SAYED, -S *same as* ▸ sayyid
SAYER, -S ▸ say
SAYEST ▸ say

SAYID, -S *same as* ▸ sayyid
SAYING, -S ▸ say
SAYNE ▸ say
SAYON, -S *n* type of tunic
SAYONARA *n* Japanese farewell
SAYONS ▸ sayon
SAYS ▸ say
SAYST ▸ say
SAYYID, -S *n* Muslim claiming descent from Mohammed's grandson Husain
SAZ, -ES, -ZES *n* Middle Eastern stringed instrument

This musical instrument is one of the most frequently played Z words.

SAZERAC, -S *n* mixed drink of whisky, Pernod, syrup, bitters, and lemon
SAZES ▸ saz
SAZHEN, -S *n* Russian measure of length
SAZZES ▸ saz
SBIRRO, SBIRRI *n* Italian police officer
SCAB, -BED, -BING, -S *n* crust formed over a wound ▷ *vb* become covered with a scab
SCABBARD *n* sheath for a sword or dagger
SCABBED ▸ scab
SCABBIER ▸ scabby
SCABBILY ▸ scabby
SCABBING ▸ scab
SCABBLE, -D, -S *vb* shape (stone) roughly
SCABBY, SCABBIER *adj* covered with scabs
SCABIES *n* itchy skin disease
SCABIOSA *n* flowering plant
SCABIOUS *n* plant with showy blue, red, or whitish dome-shaped flower heads ▷ *adj* having or covered with scabs
SCABLAND *n* barren rocky land
SCABLIKE ▸ scab
SCABRID *adj* having a rough or scaly surface
SCABROUS *adj* rough and scaly
SCABS ▸ scab
SCAD *n* any of various carangid fishes
SCADS *pl n* large amount or number
SCAFF, -ED, -ING, -S *n* Scots word meaning food ▷ *vb* ask for (food) in a mean or rude manner
SCAFFIE, -S *n* Scots word meaning street cleaner
SCAFFIER ▸ scaffy

SCAFFIES ▸ scaffie
SCAFFING ▸ scaff
SCAFFOLD *n* temporary platform for workmen ▷ *vb* provide with a scaffold
SCAFFS ▸ scaff
SCAFFY, SCAFFIER *adj* having little value, cheap
SCAG, -GED, -GING, -S *n* tear in a garment or piece of cloth ▷ *vb* make a tear in (cloth)
SCAGLIA, -S *n* type of limestone
SCAGS ▸ scag
SCAIL, -ED, -ING, -S *vb* Scots word meaning disperse
SCAITH, -ED, -S *vb* old word meaning injure
SCALA, -E *n* passage inside the cochlea
SCALABLE *adj* capable of being scaled or climbed
SCALABLY
SCALADE, -S *short for* ▸ escalade
SCALADO, -S *same as* ▸ scalade
SCALAE ▸ scala
SCALAGE, -S *n* percentage deducted from the price of goods liable to shrink or leak
SCALAR, -S *adj* having magnitude but no direction ▷ *n* quantity that has magnitude but not direction
SCALARE, -S *another name for* > angelfish
SCALARS ▸ scalar
SCALAWAG *same as* > scallywag
SCALD, -ED, -ING, -S *same as* ▸ skald
SCALDER -S
SCALDIC ▸ skald
SCALDING ▸ scald
SCALDINO, SCALDINI *n* Italian brazier
SCALDS ▸ scald
SCALE, -D, -S *n* one of the thin overlapping plates covering fishes and reptiles ▷ *vb* remove scales from
SCALENE, -S *n* triangle with three unequal sides
SCALENUS, SCALENI *n* any one of the three muscles situated on each side of the neck
SCALEPAN *n* part of scales holding weighed object
SCALER, -S *n* person or thing that scales
SCALES ▸ scale
SCALEUP, -S *n* increase
SCALIER ▸ scaly
SCALIEST ▸ scaly

SCALING, -S ▸ scale

SCALL, -S *n* disease of the scalp characterized by itching and scab formation **SCALLED**

SCALLIES ▸ scally

SCALLION *same as* ▸ shallot

SCALLOP, -S *n* edible shellfish with two fan-shaped shells ▷ *vb* decorate (an edge) with scallops

SCALLS ▸ scall

SCALLY, SCALLIES *n* rascal

SCALP, -ED, -S *n* skin and hair on top of the head ▷ *vb* cut off the scalp of

SCALPEL, -S *n* small surgical knife

SCALPER, -S ▸ scalp

SCALPING *n* process in which the top portion of a metal ingot is machined away before use

SCALPINS *n* small stones

SCALPRUM *n* large scalpel

SCALPS ▸ scalp

SCALY, SCALIER, SCALIEST *adj* resembling or covered in scales

SCAM, -MED, -MING, -S *n* dishonest scheme ▷ *vb* swindle (someone) by means of a trick

SCAMBLE, -D, -S *vb* scramble **SCAMBLER**

SCAMEL, -S *n* Shakespearian word of uncertain meaning

SCAMMED ▸ scam

SCAMMER, -S *n* person who perpetrates a scam

SCAMMING ▸ scam

SCAMMONY *n* twining Asian convolvulus plant

SCAMP, -ED, -ING, -S *n* mischievous child ▷ *vb* perform without care

SCAMPER, -S *vb* run about hurriedly or in play ▷ *n* scampering

SCAMPI, -ES, -S *pl n* large prawns

SCAMPING ▸ scamp

SCAMPIS ▸ scampi

SCAMPISH ▸ scamp

SCAMPS ▸ scamp

SCAMS ▸ scam

SCAMSTER *same as* ▸ scammer

SCAMTO, -S *n* argot of urban Black people in South Africa

SCAN, -D, -NED, -NING, -S *vb* scrutinize carefully ▷ *n* scanning

SCANDAL, -S *n* disgraceful action or event ▷ *vb* disgrace

SCANDENT *adj* (of plants) having a climbing habit

SCANDIA, -S *n* scandium oxide

SCANDIC *adj* of or containing scandium

SCANDIUM *n* rare silvery-white metallic element

SCANNED ▸ scan

SCANNER, -S *n* electronic device used for scanning

SCANNING ▸ scan

SCANS ▸ scan

SCANSION *n* metrical scanning of verse

SCANT, -ED, -ER, -EST, -ING, -S *adj* barely sufficient, meagre ▷ *vb* limit in size or quantity ▷ *adv* scarcely

SCANTIER ▸ scanty

SCANTIES *n* women's underwear

SCANTILY ▸ scanty

SCANTING ▸ scant

SCANTITY *n* quality of being scant

SCANTLE, -D, -S *vb* stint

SCANTLY ▸ scant

SCANTS ▸ scant

SCANTY, SCANTIER *adj* barely sufficient or not sufficient

SCAPA, -ED, -ING, -S *variant of* ▸ scarper

SCAPE, -D, -S, SCAPING *n* leafless stalk in plants ▷ *vb* archaic word for escape

SCAPHOID *obsolete word for* > navicular

SCAPI ▸ scapus

SCAPING ▸ scape

SCAPOSE ▸ scape

SCAPPLE, -D, -S *vb* shape roughly

SCAPULA, -E, -S *n* shoulder blade

SCAPULAR *adj* of the scapula ▷ *n* loose sleeveless garment worn by monks over their habits

SCAPULAS ▸ scapula

SCAPUS, SCAPI *n* flower stalk

SCAR, -RED, -RING, -S *n* mark left by a healed wound ▷ *vb* mark or become marked with a scar

SCARAB, -S *n* sacred beetle of ancient Egypt

SCARABEE *n* old word for scarab beetle

SCARABS ▸ scarab

SCARCE, -R, -ST *adj* insufficient to meet demand

SCARCELY *adv* hardly at all

SCARCER ▸ scarce

SCARCEST ▸ scarce

SCARCITY *n* inadequate supply

SCARE, -DER, -S, SCARING *vb* frighten or be frightened ▷ *n* fright, sudden panic ▷ *adj* causing (needless) fear or alarm

SCARED

SCAREDY *n* someone who is easily frightened

SCARER, -S ▸ scare

SCARES ▸ scare

SCAREY *adj* frightening

SCARF, -ED, -ING, -S, SCARVES *n* piece of material worn round the neck, head, or shoulders ▷ *vb* join in this way

SCARFER -S

SCARFISH *n* type of fish

SCARFPIN *n* decorative pin securing scarf

SCARFS ▸ scarf

SCARIER ▸ scary

SCARIEST ▸ scary

SCARIFY *vb* scratch or cut slightly all over

SCARILY ▸ scary

SCARING ▸ scare

SCARIOSE *same as* ▸ scarious

SCARIOUS *adj* (of plant parts) membranous, dry, and brownish in colour

SCARLESS ▸ scar

SCARLET, -S *n* brilliant red ▷ *adj* bright red ▷ *vb* make scarlet

SCARMOGE *n* old form of skirmish

SCARP, -ED, -ING, -S *n* steep slope ▷ *vb* wear or cut so as to form a steep slope

SCARPA, -ED, -S *vb* run away

SCARPED ▸ scarp

SCARPER, -S *vb* run away ▷ *n* hasty departure

SCARPH, -ED, -S *vb* join with scarf joint

SCARPING ▸ scarp

SCARPS ▸ scarp

SCARRE, -S *n* Shakespearian word of unknown meaning

SCARRED ▸ scar

SCARRES ▸ scarre

SCARRIER ▸ scarry

SCARRING ▸ scar

SCARRY, SCARRIER ▸ scar

SCARS ▸ scar

SCART, -ED, -ING, -S *vb* scratch or scrape ▷ *n* scratch or scrape

SCARTH, -S *Scots word for* > cormorant

SCARTING ▸ scart

SCARTS ▸ scart

S

SCARVED adj wearing a scarf
SCARVES ► scarf
SCARY, SCARIER, SCARIEST adj frightening
SCAT, -S, -TED, -TING vb go away ▷ n jazz singing using improvised vocal sounds instead of words
SCATBACK n American football player
SCATCH, -ES same as ► stilt
SCATH, -S vb old word meaning injure
SCATHE, -D, -S vb attack with severe criticism ▷ n harm
SCATHING adj harshly critical
SCATHS ► scath
SCATOLE, -S n substance found in coal
SCATS ► scat
SCATT, -S n old word meaning tax ▷ vb tax
SCATTED ► scat
SCATTER, -S vb throw about in various directions ▷ n scattering
SCATTERY adj dispersed
SCATTIER ► scatty
SCATTILY ► scatty
SCATTING ► scat
SCATTS ► scatt
SCATTY, SCATTIER adj empty-headed
SCAUD, -ED, -ING, -S Scot word for ► scald
SCAUP, -ED, -ING, -S variant of ► scalp
SCAUPER, -S same as ► scorper
SCAUPING ► scaup
SCAUPS ► scaup
SCAUR, -ED, -ING, -S same as ► scar
SCAURIES ► scaury
SCAURING ► scaur
SCAURS ► scaur
SCAURY, SCAURIES n young seagull
SCAVAGE, -D, -S n old word meaning toll ▷ vb scavenge
SCAVAGER
SCAVENGE vb search for (anything usable) among discarded material
SCAW, -S n headland
SCAWTITE n mineral containing calcium
SCAZON, -S n metre in poetry
SCEAT, -TAS n Anglo-Saxon coin
SCEATT same as ► sceat
SCEATTAS ► sceat
SCEDULE, -D, -S old spelling of ► schedule
SCELERAT n villain

SCENA, -S n scene in an opera, usually longer than a single aria
SCENARIO n summary of the plot of a play or film
SCENARY n scenery
SCENAS ► scena
SCEND, -ED, -ING, -S vb (of a vessel) to surge upwards in a heavy sea ▷ n upward heaving of a vessel pitching
SCENE, -D, -S, SCENING n place of action of a real or imaginary event ▷ vb set in a scene
SCENEMAN, SCENEMEN n person shifting stage scenery
SCENERY n natural features of a landscape
SCENES ► scene
SCENIC, -S adj picturesque ▷ n something scenic
SCENICAL ► scene
SCENICS ► scenic
SCENING ► scene
SCENT, -ING, -S n pleasant smell ▷ vb detect by smell
SCENTED
SCENTFUL adj old word meaning having scent
SCENTING ► scent
SCENTS ► scent
SCEPSIS n doubt
SCEPTER, -S same as ► sceptre
SCEPTIC, -S n person who habitually doubts generally accepted beliefs ▷ adj of or relating to sceptics
SCEPTRAL adj royal
SCEPTRE, -S n ornamental rod symbolizing royal power ▷ vb invest with authority
SCEPTRED
SCEPTRY adj having sceptre
SCERNE, -D, -S, SCERNING vb old word meaning discern
SCHANSE, -S ► schantze
SCHANTZE n stones heaped to shelter soldier in battle
SCHANZE, -S same as ► schantze
SCHAPPE, -D, -S n yarn or fabric made from waste silk
SCHAPSKA n cap worn by lancer
SCHAV, -S n Polish soup
SCHEDULE n plan of procedure for a project ▷ vb plan to occur at a certain time
SCHELLUM n Scots word meaning rascal
SCHELLY n freshwater whitefish of the English Lake District

SCHELM, -S n South African word meaning rascal
SCHEMA, -S, -TA n overall plan or diagram
SCHEME, -D, -S n systematic plan ▷ vb plan in an underhand manner
SCHEMER -S
SCHEMIE, -S n insulting Scots word for a resident of a housing scheme
SCHEMING adj given to making plots ▷ n intrigues
SCHERZO, SCHERZI, -S n brisk lively piece of music
SCHIEDAM n type of gin produced in the Netherlands
SCHILLER n unusual iridescent or metallic lustre in some minerals
SCHIMMEL n roan horse
SCHISM, -S n (group resulting from) division in an organization
SCHISMA, -S n musical term
SCHISMS ► schism
SCHIST, -S n crystalline rock which splits into layers
SCHIZOID adj abnormally introverted ▷ n schizoid person
SCHIZONT n cell formed from a trophozoite during the asexual stage of the life cycle of sporozoan protozoans
SCHLAGER n German duelling sword
SCHLEP, -S vb drag or lug (oneself or an object) with difficulty ▷ n arduous journey or procedure
SCHLEPP, -S vb schlep
SCHLEPPY same as ► shleppy
SCHLEPS ► schlep
SCHLICH, -S n finely crushed ore
SCHLIERE n (in physics or geology) streak of different density or composition from surroundings
SCHLOCK, -S n goods or produce of cheap or inferior quality ▷ adj cheap, inferior, or trashy
SCHLOCKY adj of poor quality
SCHLOSS n German castle
SCHLUB, -S n coarse or contemptible person
SCHLUMP, -S vb move in lazy way
SCHLUMPY
SCHMALTZ n excessive sentimentality
SCHMALZ same as ► schmaltz

SCHMALZY adj schmaltzy

SCHMATTE same as > schmutter

SCHMEAR, -S n situation, matter, or affair ▷ vb spread or smear

SCHMECK, -S n taste ▷ vb taste good

SCHMEER, -S same as ► schmear

SCHMELZ n ornamental glass

SCHMELZE variant of ► schmelz

SCHMICK adj (in Australia) excellent, elegant, or stylish

SCHMO, -ES, -S n dull, stupid, or boring person

SCHMOCK, -S n stupid person

SCHMOE n stupid person

SCHMOES ► schmo

SCHMOOS variant of ► schmoose

SCHMOOSE vb chat

SCHMOOZ n chat

SCHMOOZE vb chat or gossip ▷ n trivial conversation **SCHMOOZY**

SCHMOS ► schmo

SCHMUCK, -S n stupid or contemptible person ▷ vb act as a schmuck

SCHMUCKY adj foolish

SCHMUTZ n dirt; grime

SCHNAPPS n strong alcoholic spirit

SCHNAPS same as ► schnapps

SCHNECKE > schnecken

SCHNELL adj German word meaning quick

SCHNOOK, -S n stupid or gullible person

SCHNORR, -S vb beg

SCHNOZ, -ES n nose

SCHNOZZ n nose

SCHOLAR, -S n learned person

SCHOLIA ► scholium

SCHOLION n scholarly annotation

SCHOLIUM, SCHOLIA n commentary or annotation, esp on a classical text

SCHOOL, -ED, -S n place where children are taught or instruction is given in a subject ▷ vb educate or train

SCHOOLE, -S n old form of shoal

SCHOOLED ► school

SCHOOLER n pupil at a school of a specified kind

SCHOOLES ► schoole

SCHOOLIE n schoolteacher or a high-school student

SCHOOLS ► school

SCHOONER n sailing ship rigged fore-and-aft

SCHORL, -S n type of black tourmaline

SCHOUT, -S n council officer in Netherlands

SCHRIK, -S variant of ► skrik

SCHROD, -S n young cod

SCHTICK, -S same as ► shtick

SCHTIK, -S n schtick

SCHTOOK, -S n trouble

SCHTOOM adj silent

SCHTUCK, -S n trouble

SCHTUM adj silent or dumb

SCHUIT, -S n Dutch boat with flat bottom

SCHUL, -N, -S same as ► shul

SCHUSS, -ED, -ES n straight high-speed downhill run ▷ vb perform a schuss **SCHUSSER**

SCHUYT, -S n Dutch boat with flat bottom

SCHVITZ same as ► shvitz

SCHWA, -S n vowel representing the sound in unstressed syllables

SCHWAG, -S n promotional material given away for free

SCHWAS ► schwa

SCIAENID adj of or relating to a family of mainly tropical and subtropical marine percoid fishes ▷ n any of these fish

SCIARID, -S n small fly

SCIATIC, -S adj of the hip ▷ n sciatic part of the body

SCIATICA n severe pain in the large nerve in the back of the leg

SCIATICS ► sciatic

SCIENCE, -S n systematic study and knowledge of natural or physical phenomena

SCIENCED adj old word meaning learned

SCIENCES ► science

SCIENT adj old word meaning scientific

SCIENTER adv knowingly

SCILICET adv namely

SCILLA, -S n plant with small bell-shaped flowers

SCIMETAR n scimitar

SCIMITAR n curved oriental sword

SCIMITER n scimitar

SCINCOID adj of, relating to, or resembling a skink ▷ n any animal, esp a lizard, resembling a skink

SCIOLISM n practice of opinionating on subjects of which one has only

superficial knowledge

SCIOLIST

SCIOLOUS

SCIOLTO adv musical direction meaning freely

SCION, -S n descendant or heir

SCIROC, -S ► scirocco

SCIROCCO n hot Mediterranean wind

SCIROCS ► sciroc

SCIRRHUS, SCIRRHI n hard cancerous growth composed of fibrous tissues

SCISSEL, -S n waste metal left over from sheet metal after discs have been punched out of it

SCISSIL, -S n scissel

SCISSILE adj capable of being cut or divided

SCISSILS ► scissil

SCISSION n act or an instance of cutting, splitting, or dividing

SCISSOR vb cut (an object) with scissors

SCISSORS pl n cutting instrument with two crossed pivoted blades

SCISSURE n longitudinal cleft

SCIURID, -S n squirrel or related rodent

SCIURINE adj relating to a family of rodents that includes squirrels, marmots, and chipmunks ▷ n any sciurine animal

SCIUROID adj (of an animal) resembling a squirrel

SCLAFF, -ED, -S vb cause (the club) to hit (the ground behind the ball) when making a stroke ▷ n sclaffing stroke or shot **SCLAFFER**

SCLATE, -D, -S, SCLATING vb (Scots) slate ▷ n (Scots) slate

SCLAVE, -S n old form of slave

SCLERA, -E, -S n tough white substance that forms the outer covering of the eyeball **SCLERAL**

SCLERE, -S n supporting anatomical structure

SCLEREID n type of biological cell

SCLEREMA n condition in which body tissues harden

SCLERES ► sclere

SCLERITE n any of the hard chitinous plates that make up the exoskeleton of an arthropod

S

SCLEROID adj (of organisms and their parts) hard or hardened

SCLEROMA n any small area of abnormally hard tissue, esp in a mucous membrane

SCLEROSE vb affect with sclerosis

SCLEROUS adj hard

SCLIFF, -S n Scots word for small piece

SCLIM, -MED, -S vb Scots word meaning climb

SCODY, SCODIER, SCODIEST adj unkempt

SCOFF, -ED, -S vb express derision ▷ n mocking expression

SCOFFER -S

SCOFFING ▶ **scoff**

SCOFFLAW n person who habitually flouts or violates the law

SCOFFS ▶ **scoff**

SCOG, -GED, -GING, -S vb shelter

SCOINSON n part of door or window frame

SCOLD, -ED, -S vb find fault with, reprimand ▷ n person who scolds

SCOLDER -S

SCOLDING ▶ **scold**

SCOLDS ▶ **scold**

SCOLECES ▶ **scolex**

SCOLECID n variety of worm

SCOLEX, SCOLECES, SCOLICES n headlike part of a tapeworm

SCOLIA ▶ **scolion**

SCOLICES ▶ **scolex**

SCOLIOMA n condition with abnormal curvature of spine

SCOLION, SCOLIA n ancient Greek drinking song

SCOLLOP, -S variant of ▶ **scallop**

SCOLYTID n type of beetle

SCOMBRID n fish of mackerel family

SCOMFISH vb Scots word meaning stifle

SCONCE, -D, -S, SCONCING n bracket on a wall for holding candles or lights ▷ vb challenge (a fellow student) to drink a large quantity of beer

SCONE, -S n small plain cake baked in an oven or on a griddle

SCONTION n part of door or window frame

SCOOBY, SCOOBIES n clue; notion

SCOOCH, -ED, -ES vb compress one's body into smaller space

SCOOG, -ED, -ING, -S vb shelter

SCOOP, -ED, -ING, -S n shovel-like tool for ladling or hollowing out ▷ vb take up or hollow out with or as if with a scoop

SCOOPER -S

SCOOPFUL ▶ **scoop**

SCOOPING ▶ **scoop**

SCOOPS ▶ **scoop**

SCOOSH, -ED, -ES vb squirt ▷ n squirt or rush of liquid

SCOOT, -ED, -ING, -S vb leave or move quickly ▷ n act of scooting

SCOOTCH same as ▶ **scooch**

SCOOTED ▶ **scoot**

SCOOTER, -S n child's vehicle propelled by pushing on the ground with one foot ▷ vb go on a scooter

SCOOTING ▶ **scoot**

SCOOTS ▶ **scoot**

SCOP, -S n (in Anglo-Saxon England) a bard or minstrel

SCOPA, -E, -S n tuft of hairs on the abdomen or hind legs of bees

SCOPATE adj having tuft

SCOPE, -D, -S, SCOPING n opportunity for using abilities ▷ vb look at or examine carefully

SCOPELID n deep-sea fish

SCOPES ▶ **scope**

SCOPING ▶ **scope**

SCOPS ▶ **scop**

SCOPULA, -E, -S n small tuft of dense hairs on the legs and chelicerae of some spiders

SCORCH, -ED, -ES vb burn on the surface ▷ n slight burn

SCORCHER n very hot day

SCORCHES ▶ **scorch**

SCORDATO adj musical term meaning out of tune

SCORE, -D, -S n points gained in a game or competition ▷ vb gain (points) in a game

SCOREPAD n pad for recording score in game

SCORER, -S ▶ **score**

SCORES ▶ **score**

SCORIA, -E n mass of solidified lava containing many cavities

SCORIAC

SCORIFY vb remove (impurities) from metals by forming scoria

SCORING, -S n act or practice of scoring

SCORIOUS ▶ **scoria**

SCORN, -ED, -ING, -S n open contempt ▷ vb despise

SCORNER -S

SCORNFUL ▶ **scorn**

SCORNING ▶ **scorn**

SCORNS ▶ **scorn**

SCORPER, -S n kind of fine chisel with a square or curved tip

SCORPION n small lobster-shaped animal with a sting at the end of a jointed tail

SCORSE, -D, -S, SCORSING vb exchange

SCORSER -S

SCOT, -S n payment or tax

SCOTCH, -ED, -ES vb put an end to ▷ n gash

SCOTER, -S n type of sea duck

SCOTIA, -S n deep concave moulding

SCOTOMA, -S n blind spot

SCOTOMIA n dizziness

SCOTOMY n dizziness

SCOTOPIA n ability of the eye to adjust for night vision

SCOTOPIC

SCOTS ▶ **scot**

SCOTTIE, -S n type of small sturdy terrier

SCOUG, -ED, -ING, -S vb shelter

SCOUP, -ED, -ING, -S vb Scots word meaning jump

SCOUR, -ED, -ING, -S vb clean or polish by rubbing with something rough ▷ n scouring

SCOURER -S

SCOURGE, -D, -S n person or thing causing severe suffering ▷ vb cause severe suffering to

SCOURGER -S

SCOURIE, -S n young seagull

SCOURING ▶ **scour**

SCOURS ▶ **scour**

SCOURSE, -D, -S vb exchange

SCOUSE, -S n stew made from left-over meat

SCOUSER, -S n inhabitant of Liverpool

SCOUSES ▶ **scouse**

SCOUT, -ED, -ING, -S n person sent out to reconnoitre ▷ vb act as a scout

SCOUTER -S

SCOUTH, -S n Scots word meaning plenty of scope

SCOUTHER vb Scots word meaning scorch

SCOUTHS ▶ **scouth**

SCOUTING ▶ **scout**

SCOUTS ▶ **scout**

S

SCOW, -ED, -ING, -S *n* unpowered barge used for carrying freight ▷ *vb* transport by scow

SCOWDER, -S *vb* Scots word meaning scorch

SCOWED ▸ scow

SCOWING ▸ scow

SCOWL, -ED, -ING, -S *n, vb* (have an) angry or sullen expression

SCOWLER, -S *n* person who scowls

SCOWLING ▸ scowl

SCOWLS ▸ scowl

SCOWP, -ED, -ING, -S *vb* Scots word meaning jump

SCOWRER, -S *n* old word meaning hooligan

SCOWRIE, -S *n* young seagull

SCOWS ▸ scow

SCOWTH, -S *n* Scots word meaning plenty of scope

SCOWTHER *vb* Scots word meaning scorch

SCOWTHS ▸ scowth

SCOZZA, -S *n* rowdy person, esp one who drinks a lot of alcohol

SCRAB, -BED, -S *vb* scratch

SCRABBLE *vb* scrape at with the hands, feet, or claws ▷ *n* board game in which words are formed by letter tiles

SCRABBLY *adj* covered with stunted trees

SCRABS ▸ scrab

SCRAE, -S *Scots word for* ▸ **scree**

SCRAG, -GED, -S *n* thin end of a neck of mutton ▷ *vb* wring the neck of

SCRAGGLY *adj* untidy or irregular

SCRAGGY *adj* thin, bony

SCRAGS ▸ scrag

SCRAICH, -S *vb* Scots word meaning scream

SCRAIGH, -S *vb* Scots word meaning scream

SCRAM, -MED, -S *vb* go away quickly ▷ *n* emergency shutdown of a nuclear reactor

SCRAMB, -ED, -S *vb* scratch with nails or claws

SCRAMBLE *vb* climb or crawl hastily or awkwardly ▷ *n* scrambling

SCRAMBS ▸ scramb

SCRAMJET *n* type of jet engine

SCRAMMED ▸ scram

SCRAMS ▸ scram

SCRAN, -S *n* food

SCRANCH *vb* crunch

SCRANNEL *adj* thin ▷ *n* thin person or thing

SCRANNY *adj* scrawny

SCRANS ▸ scran

SCRAP, -PED, -S *n* small piece ▷ *vb* discard as useless

SCRAPE, -D, -S *vb* rub with something rough or sharp ▷ *n* act or sound of scraping

SCRAPER -S

SCRAPIE, -S *n* disease of sheep and goats

SCRAPING *n* act of scraping

SCRAPPED ▸ scrap

SCRAPPER *n* person who scraps

SCRAPPLE *n* scraps of pork cooked with cornmeal and formed into a loaf

SCRAPPY *adj* fragmentary, disjointed

SCRAPS ▸ scrap

SCRAT, -S, -TED *vb* scratch

SCRATCH *vb* mark or cut with anything rough or sharp ▷ *n* wound, mark, or sound made by scratching ▷ *adj* put together at short notice

SCRATCHY

SCRATS ▸ scrat

SCRATTED ▸ scrat

SCRATTLE *vb* dialect word meaning scratch

SCRAUCH, -S *vb* squawk

SCRAUGH, -S *vb* squawk

SCRAVEL, -S *vb* move quickly

SCRAW, -S *n* sod from the surface of a peat bog or from a field

SCRAWB, -ED, -S *same as* ▸ **scrob**

SCRAWL, -ED, -S *vb* write carelessly or hastily ▷ *n* scribbled writing

SCRAWLER

SCRAWLY

SCRAWM, -ED, -S *vb* dialect word meaning scratch

SCRAWNY *adj* thin and bony

SCRAWP, -ED, -S *vb* scratch (the skin) to relieve itching

SCRAWS ▸ scraw

SCRAY, -S *n* tern

SCRAYE, -S *n* tern

SCRAYS ▸ scray

SCREAK, -ED, -S *vb* screech or creak ▷ *n* screech or creak

SCREAKY

SCREAM, -ED, -S *vb* utter a piercing cry, esp of fear or pain ▷ *n* shrill piercing cry

SCREAMER *n* person or thing that screams

SCREAMO, -S *n* type of emo music featuring screaming vocals

SCREAMS ▸ scream

SCREE, -S *n* slope of loose shifting stones

SCREECH *n* (utter) a shrill cry ▷ *vb* utter a shrill cry

SCREECHY *adj* loud and shrill

SCREED, -ED, -S *n* long tedious piece of writing ▷ *vb* rip

SCREEDER

SCREEN, -ED, -S *n* surface of a television set, VDU, etc ▷ *vb* shelter or conceal with or as if with a screen

SCREENER

SCREENIE *n* informal Australian word for screensaver

SCREENS ▸ screen

SCREES ▸ scree

SCREET, -ED, -S *vb* shed tears ▷ *n* act or sound of crying

SCREEVE, -D, -S *vb* write

SCREEVER

SCREICH, -S *same as* ▸ **screigh**

SCREIGH, -S *Scot word for* ▸ **screech**

SCREW, -ING, -S *n* metal pin with a spiral ridge along its length ▷ *vb* turn (a screw)

SCREWED *adj* fastened by a screw or screws

SCREWER, -S ▸ screw

SCREWIER ▸ screwy

SCREWING ▸ screw

SCREWS ▸ screw

SCREWTOP *n* lid with a threaded rim that is turned to close it securely

SCREWUP, -S *n* something done badly

SCREWY, SCREWIER *adj* crazy or eccentric

SCRIBAL ▸ scribe

SCRIBBLE *vb* write hastily or illegibly ▷ *n* something scribbled

SCRIBBLY

SCRIBE, -D, -S, SCRIBING *n* person who copies documents ▷ *vb* score a line with a pointed instrument

SCRIBER, -S *n* pointed steel tool used to score materials as a guide to cutting, etc

SCRIBES ▸ scribe

SCRIBING ▸ scribe

SCRIBISM ▸ scribe

SCRIECH, -S *vb* Scots word meaning screech

SCRIED ▸ scry

SCRIENE, -S *n* old form of screen

SCRIES ▸ scry

S

SCRIEVE, -D, -S vb Scots word meaning write

SCRIGGLE vb wriggle **SCRIGGLY**

SCRIKE, -D, -S, SCRIKING vb old word meaning shriek

SCRIM, -S n open-weave muslin or hessian fabric

SCRIMP, -ED, -S vb be very economical **SCRIMPER**

SCRIMPIT adj Scots word meaning ungenerous

SCRIMPLY adv sparingly

SCRIMPS ► scrimp

SCRIMPY ► scrimp

SCRIMS ► scrim

SCRIMURE old word for **► fencer**

SCRINE, -S n old form of shrine

SCRIP, -S n certificate representing a claim to stocks or shares

SCRIPT, -ED, -S n text of a film, play, or TV programme ▷ vb write a script for

SCRIPTER n person who writes scripts for films, play, or television dramas

SCRIPTS ► script

SCRITCH vb screech

SCRIVE, -D, -S, SCRIVING Scots word for **► write**

SCROB, -BED, -S vb scrape with claws

SCROBBLE vb record a person's music preferences in order to recommend similar music

SCROBE, -S n groove

SCROBS ► scrob

SCROD, -S n young cod or haddock

SCROFULA n tuberculosis of the lymphatic glands

SCROG, -S n Scots word meaning small tree

SCROGGIE adj having scrogs upon it

SCROGGIN n mixture of nuts and dried fruits

SCROGGY variant of **► scroggie**

SCROGS ► scrog

SCROLL, -ED, -S n roll of parchment or paper ▷ vb move (text) up or down on a VDU screen

SCROLLER n person or thing that scrolls

SCROLLS ► scroll

SCROME, -D, -S, SCROMING vb crawl or climb

SCROOCH vb scratch (the skin) to relieve itching

SCROOGE, -D, -S variant of **► scrouge**

SCROOP, -ED, -S vb emit a grating or creaking sound ▷ n such a sound

SCROOTCH vb hunch up

SCRORP, -S n deep scratch or weal

SCROTA ► scrotum

SCROTAL ► scrotum

SCROTUM, SCROTA, -S n pouch of skin containing the testicles

SCROUGE, -D, -S vb crowd or press

SCROUGER n American word meaning whopper

SCROUGES ► scrouge

SCROUNGE vb get by cadging or begging

SCROUNGY adj shabby

SCROW, -S n scroll

SCROWDGE vb squeeze

SCROWL, -ED, -S vb old form of scroll

SCROWLE, -S vb old form of scroll

SCROWLED ► scrowl

SCROWLES ► scrowle

SCROWLS ► scrowl

SCROWS ► scrow

SCROYLE, -S n old word meaning wretch

SCRUB, -BED, -S vb clean by rubbing, often with a hard brush and water ▷ n scrubbing ▷ adj stunted or inferior

SCRUBBER n person or thing that scrubs

SCRUBBY adj covered with scrub

SCRUBS ► scrub

SCRUFF, -ED, -S same as **► scum**

SCRUFFY adj unkempt or shabby

SCRUM, -MED, -S n restarting of play in rugby ▷ vb form a scrum

SCRUMMIE n informal word for scrum half

SCRUMMY adj delicious

SCRUMP, -ED, -S vb steal (apples) from an orchard or garden

SCRUMPLE vb crumple or crush

SCRUMPOX n skin infection spread among players in scrum

SCRUMPS ► scrump

SCRUMPY n rough dry cider

SCRUMS ► scrum

SCRUNCH vb crumple or crunch or be crumpled or

crunched ▷ n act or sound of scrunching

SCRUNCHY adj crunchy

SCRUNT, -S n Scots word meaning stunted thing **SCRUNTY**

SCRUPLE, -D, -S n doubt produced by one's conscience or morals ▷ vb have doubts on moral grounds **SCRUPLER**

SCRUTINY n close examination

SCRUTO, -S n trapdoor on stage

SCRUZE, -D, -S, SCRUZING vb old word meaning squeeze

SCRY, SCRIED, SCRIES, -DE vb divine, esp by crystal gazing

SCRYER -S

SCRYING, -S ► scry

SCRYNE, -S n old form of shrine

SCUBA, -ED, -ING, -S n apparatus used in diving ▷ vb dive using scuba equipment

SCUCHIN, -S n old form of scutcheon

SCUD, -DED, -DING, -S vb move along swiftly ▷ n act of scudding

SCUDDER -S

SCUDDLE, -D, -S vb scuttle

SCUDI ► scudo

SCUDLER, -S n Scots word meaning leader of festivities

SCUDO, SCUDI n any of several former Italian coins

SCUDS ► scud

SCUFF, -ED, -ING, -S vb drag (the feet) while walking ▷ n mark caused by scuffing

SCUFFER, -S n type of sandal

SCUFFING ► scuff

SCUFFLE, -D, -S vb fight in a disorderly manner ▷ n disorderly struggle **SCUFFLER**

SCUFFS ► scuff

SCUFT, -S n dialect word meaning nape of neck

SCUG, -GED, -GING, -S vb shelter

SCUL, -S n old form of school

SCULCH, -ES n rubbish

SCULK, -ED, -ING, -S vb old form of skulk

SCULKER -S

SCULL, -ED, -ING, -S n small oar ▷ vb row (a boat) using sculls

SCULLE, -S n old form of school

SCULLED ► scull

SCULLER, -S ► scull

SCULLERY n small room where washing-up and other kitchen work is done

SCULLES ► sculle

SCULLING ► scull

SCULLION n servant employed to do the hard work in a kitchen

SCULLS ► scull

SCULP, -ED, -ING, -S variant of > sculpture

SCULPIN, -S n type of fish of the family which includes bullheads and sea scorpions

SCULPING ► sculp

SCULPINS ► sculpin

SCULPS ► sculp

SCULPSIT vb (he or she) sculptured it: used formerly on sculptures next to a sculptor's name

SCULPT, -ED, -S same as > sculpture

SCULPTOR n person who makes sculptures

SCULPTS ► sculpt

SCULS ► scul

SCULTCH same as ► sculch

SCUM, -MED, -MING, -S n impure or waste matter on the surface of a liquid ▷ vb remove scum from

SCUMBER, -S vb old word meaning defecate

SCUMBLE, -D, -S vb soften or blend (an outline or colour) with a thin upper coat of opaque colour ▷ n upper layer of colour applied in this way

SCUMFISH vb Scots word meaning disgust

SCUMLESS ► scum

SCUMLIKE ► scum

SCUMMED ► scum

SCUMMER, -S ► scum

SCUMMIER ► scummy

SCUMMILY ► scummy

SCUMMING ► scum

SCUMMY, SCUMMIER adj of, resembling, consisting of, or covered with scum

SCUMS ► scum

SCUNGE, -D, -S, SCUNGING vb borrow ▷ n dirty or worthless person

SCUNGIER ► scungy

SCUNGILE same as > scungille

SCUNGILI same as > scungilli

SCUNGING ► scunge

SCUNGY, SCUNGIER adj sordid or dirty

SCUNNER, -S vb feel aversion ▷ n strong aversion

SCUP, -S n common sparid fish of American coastal regions of the Atlantic

SCUPPAUG n sea fish

SCUPPER, -S vb defeat or ruin ▷ n drain in the side of a ship

SCUPS ► scup

SCUR, -RED, -RING, -S n small unattached growth of horn at the site of a normal horn in cattle

SCURF, -S n flaky skin on the scalp

SCURFIER ► scurfy

SCURFS ► scurf

SCURFY, SCURFIER ► scurf

SCURRED ► scur

SCURRIED ► scurry

SCURRIER n old word meaning scout

SCURRIES ► scurry

SCURRIL adj old word meaning vulgar

SCURRILE adj old word meaning vulgar

SCURRING ► scur

SCURRY, SCURRIED, SCURRIES vb move hastily ▷ n act or sound of scurrying

SCURS ► scur

SCURVIER ► scurvy

SCURVIES ► scurvy

SCURVILY ► scurvy

SCURVY, SCURVIER, SCURVIES n disease caused by lack of vitamin C ▷ adj mean and despicable

SCUSE, -D, -S, SCUSING shortened form of ► excuse

SCUT, -S n short tail of the hare, rabbit, or deer

SCUTA ► scutum

SCUTAGE, -S n payment to a lord from his vassal in lieu of military service

SCUTAL ► scute

SCUTATE adj (of animals) having or covered with large bony or horny plates

SCUTCH, -ED, -ES vb separate the fibres from the woody part of (flax) by pounding ▷ n tool used for this

SCUTCHER same as ► scutch

SCUTCHES ► scutch

SCUTE, -S n horny or chitinous plate that makes up part of the exoskeleton in armadillos, etc

SCUTELLA > scutellum

SCUTES ► scute

SCUTIGER n species of centipede

SCUTS ► scut

SCUTTER, -S informal word for ► scurry

SCUTTLE, -D, -S n fireside container for coal ▷ vb run with short quick steps

SCUTTLER

SCUTUM, SCUTA n middle of three plates into which the notum of an insect's thorax is divided

SCUTWORK n menial or dull work

SCUZZ, -ES n dirt

SCUZZY, SCUZZIER adj unkempt, dirty, or squalid

SCYBALUM, SCYBALA n hard faeces in stomach

SCYE, -S n Scots word meaning sleeve-hole

SCYPHATE adj shaped like cup

SCYPHUS, SCYPHI n ancient Greek two-handled drinking cup

SCYTALE, -S n coded message in ancient Sparta

SCYTHE, -D, -S, SCYTHING n long-handled tool with a curved blade for cutting grass ▷ vb cut with a scythe

SCYTHER ► scythe

SDAINE, -D, -S, SDAINING vb old form of disdain

SDAYN, -ED, -ING, -S vb old form of disdain

SDEIGN, -ED, -S vb old form of disdain

SDEIGNE, -S vb old form of disdain

SDEIGNED ► sdeign

SDEIGNES ► sdeigne

SDEIGNS ► sdeign

SDEIN, -ED, -ING, -S vb old form of disdain

SEA, -S n mass of salt water covering three quarters of the earth's surface

SEABAG, -S n canvas bag for holding a sailor's belongings

SEABANK, -S n sea shore

SEABEACH n beach at seaside

SEABED, -S n bottom of sea

SEABIRD, -S n bird that lives on the sea

SEABLITE n prostrate annual plant of the goosefoot family

SEABOARD n coast

SEABOOT, -S n sailor's waterproof boot

SEABORNE adj carried on or by the sea

SEACOAST n land bordering on the sea

SEACOCK, -S n valve in the hull of a vessel below the water line

SEACRAFT n skill as sailor

SEACUNNY n quartermaster on Indian ship

SEADOG, -S another word for
▶ **fogbow**
SEADROME n aerodrome
floating on sea
SEAFARER n traveller who
goes by sea
SEAFLOOR n bottom of
the sea
SEAFOAM, -S n foam formed
on the sea
SEAFOLK, -S n people who
sail sea
SEAFOOD, -S n edible
saltwater fish or shellfish
SEAFOWL, -S n seabird
SEAFRONT n built-up area
facing the sea
SEAGIRT adj surrounded by
the sea
SEAGOING adj built for
travelling on the sea
SEAGRASS n grass which
grows by or in the sea
SEAGULL, -S n gull
SEAHAWK, -S n skua
SEAHOG, -S n porpoise
SEAHORSE n marine fish with
a horselike head that swims
upright
SEAHOUND n dogfish
SEAKALE, -S n European
coastal plant
SEAL, -S n piece of wax, etc
attached to a document as a
mark of authentication ▷ vb
close with or as if with a seal
SEALABLE
SEALANT, -S n any substance
used for sealing
SEALCH, -S Scots word for
▶ **seal**
SEALED adj (of a road) having
a hard surface
SEALER, -S n person or thing
that seals
SEALERY n occupation of
hunting seals
SEALGH, -S Scots word for
▶ **seal**
SEALIFT, -S vb transport
by ship
SEALINE, -S n company
running regular sailings
SEALING, -S ▶ **seal**
SEALLIKE adj resembling
a seal
SEALS ▶ **seal**
SEALSKIN n skin or prepared
fur of a seal, used to make
coats
SEALWAX n sealing wax
SEALYHAM n type of short-
legged terrier
SEAM, -ED, -ING, -S n line
where two edges are joined,

as by stitching ▷ vb mark
with furrows or wrinkles
SEAMAID, -S n mermaid
SEAMAN, SEAMEN n sailor
SEAMANLY
SEAMARK, -S n conspicuous
object on a shore used as
a guide
SEAME, -S n old word
meaning grease
SEAMED ▶ **seam**
SEAMEN ▶ **seaman**
SEAMER, -S n bowler who
makes the ball bounce on
its seam
SEAMES ▶ **seame**
SEAMFREE adj having no
seam
SEAMIER ▶ **seamy**
SEAMIEST ▶ **seamy**
SEAMING, -S ▶ **seam**
SEAMLESS adj (of a garment)
without seams
SEAMLIKE ▶ **seam**
SEAMOUNT n submarine
mountain rising more than
1000 metres above the
surrounding ocean floor
SEAMS ▶ **seam**
SEAMSET, -S n tool for
flattening seams in metal
SEAMSTER n person who
sews
SEAMY, SEAMIER, SEAMIEST
adj sordid
SEAN, -ED, -ING, -S vb fish
with seine net
SEANCE, -S n meeting at
which spiritualists attempt
to communicate with the
dead
SEANED ▶ **sean**
SEANING ▶ **sean**
SEANS ▶ **sean**
SEAPIECE n artwork
depicting sea
SEAPLANE n aircraft designed
to take off from and land on
water
SEAPORT, -S n town or city
with a harbour for boats
and ships
SEAQUAKE n agitation and
disturbance of the sea caused
by an earthquake at the
sea bed
SEAR, -ED, -ER, -EST, -S vb
scorch, burn the surface of
▷ n mark caused by searing
▷ adj dried up
SEARAT, -S n pirate
SEARCE, -D, -S, SEARCING
vb sift
SEARCH, -ED, -ES vb examine
closely in order to find

something ▷ n searching
SEARCHER
SEARCING ▶ **searce**
SEARE adj old word meaning
dry and withered
SEARED ▶ **sear**
SEARER ▶ **sear**
SEAREST ▶ **sear**
SEARING, -S ▶ **sear**
SEARNESS ▶ **sear**
SEAROBIN n type
of American gurnard
SEARS ▶ **sear**
SEAS ▶ **sea**
SEASCAPE n picture of a
scene at sea
SEASCOUT n member of
seagoing scouts
SEASE, -D, -S, SEASING vb old
form of seize
SEASHELL n empty shell of a
mollusc
SEASHORE n land bordering
on the sea
SEASICK adj suffering from
nausea caused by the motion
of a ship
SEASIDE, -S n area, esp a
holiday resort, on the coast
SEASING ▶ **sease**
SEASON, -S n one of four
divisions of the year ▷ vb
flavour with salt, herbs, etc
SEASONAL adj depending on
or varying with the seasons
▷ n seasonal thing
SEASONED ▶ **season**
SEASONER ▶ **season**
SEASONS ▶ **season**
SEASPEAK n language used
by sailors
SEASURE, -S n old form of
seizure
SEAT, -ED, -S n thing designed
or used for sitting on ▷ vb
cause to sit
SEATBACK n back of seat
SEATBELT n safety belt in
vehicle
SEATED ▶ **seat**
SEATER, -S n person or thing
that seats
SEATING, -S n supply or
arrangement of seats ▷ adj
of or relating to the provision
of places to sit
SEATLESS ▶ **seat**
SEATMATE n person sitting in
next seat
SEATRAIN n ship that can
carry a train
SEATROUT n trout living in
the sea
SEATS ▶ **seat**
SEATWORK n school work
done at pupils' desks

SEAWALL, -S *n* wall built to prevent encroachment or erosion by the sea

SEAWAN, -S *n* shell beads used by certain Native Americans as money

SEAWANT, -S *n* Native American name for silver coins

SEAWARD *same as* ► **seawards**

SEAWARDS *adv* towards the sea

SEAWARE, -S *n* any of numerous large coarse seaweeds

SEAWATER *n* water from sea

SEAWAY, -S *n* waterway giving access to an inland port

SEAWEED, -S *n* plant growing in the sea

SEAWEEDY *adj* full of seaweed

SEAWIFE, SEAWIVES *n* variety of sea fish

SEAWOMAN, SEAWOMEN *n* mermaid

SEAWORM, -S *n* marine worm

SEAZE, -D, -S, SEAZING *vb* old form of seize

SEBACIC *adj* derived from sebacic acid, a white crystalline acid

SEBASIC *same as* ► **sebacic**

SEBATE, -S *n* salt of sebacic acid

SEBESTEN *n* Asian tree

SEBIFIC *adj* producing fat

SEBUM, -S *n* oily substance secreted by the sebaceous glands

SEBUNDY *n* irregular soldier in India

SEC, -S *same as* ► **secant**

SECALOSE *n* type of sugar

SECANT, -S *n* the ratio of the length of the hypotenuse to the length of the adjacent side

SECANTLY

SECATEUR *n* secateurs

SECCO, -S *n* wall painting done on dried plaster with tempera

SECEDE, -D, -S, SECEDING *vb* withdraw formally from a political alliance or federation

SECEDER -S

SECERN, -ED, -S *vb* (of a gland or follicle) to secrete

SECESH, -ES *n* secessionist in US Civil War

SECESHER *n* secessionist in US Civil War

SECESHES ► **secesh**

SECH, -S *n* hyperbolic secant

SECKEL, -S *variant of* ► **seckle**

SECKLE, -S *n* type of pear

SECLUDE, -S *vb* keep (a person) from contact with others

SECLUDED *adj* private, sheltered

SECLUDES ► **seclude**

SECO *adj* (of wine) dry

SECODONT *n* animal with cutting back teeth

SECONAL, -S *n* tradename for secobarbital

SECOND, -ED, -S *adj* coming directly after the first ▷ *n* person or thing coming second ▷ *vb* express formal support for (a motion proposed in a meeting)

SECONDE, -S *n* second of eight positions from which a parry or attack can be made in fencing

SECONDED ► **second**

SECONDEE *n* person who is seconded

SECONDER ► **second**

SECONDES ► **seconde**

SECONDI ► **secondo**

SECONDLY *same as* ► **second**

SECONDO, SECONDI *n* left-hand part in a piano duet

SECONDS ► **second**

SECPAR, -S *n* distance unit in astronomy

SECRECY *n* state of being secret

SECRET, -ER, -S *adj* kept from the knowledge of others ▷ *n* something kept secret

SECRETA *n* secretions

SECRETE, -D, -S *vb* (of an organ, gland, etc) produce and release (a substance)

SECRETER ► **secret**

SECRETES ► **secrete**

SECRETIN *n* peptic hormone secreted by the mucosae of the duodenum and jejunum

SECRETLY ► **secret**

SECRETOR ► **secrete**

SECRETS ► **secret**

SECS ► **sec**

SECT, -S *n* subdivision of a religious or political group

SECTARY *n* member of a sect

SECTATOR *n* member of sect

SECTILE *adj* able to be cut smoothly

SECTION, -S *n* part cut off ▷ *vb* cut or divide into sections

SECTOR, -ED, -S *n* part or subdivision of a sector ▷ *vb* divide into sectors

SECTORAL

SECTS ► **sect**

SECULA ► **seculum**

SECULAR, -S *adj* worldly, as opposed to sacred ▷ *n* member of the secular clergy

SECULUM, SECULA, -S *n* age in astronomy

SECUND *adj* having or designating parts arranged on or turned to one side of the axis

SECUNDLY

SECUNDUM *adj* according to

SECURE, -D, -S, -ST, SECURING *adj* free from danger ▷ *vb* obtain

SECURELY

SECURER -S

SECURITY *n* precautions against theft, espionage, or other danger

SED *old spelling of* ► **said**

SEDAN, -S *same as* ► **saloon**

SEDARIM ► **seder**

SEDATE, -D, -R, -S, -ST, SEDATING *adj* calm and dignified ▷ *vb* give a sedative drug to

SEDATELY

SEDATION *n* state of calm, esp when brought about by sedatives

SEDATIVE *adj* having a soothing or calming effect ▷ *n* sedative drug

SEDENT *adj* seated

SEDER, SEDARIM, -S *n* Jewish ceremonial meal held on the first night or first two nights of Passover

SEDERUNT *n* sitting of an ecclesiastical assembly, court, etc

SEDES *Latin word for* ► **seat**

SEDGE, -S *n* coarse grasslike plant growing on wet ground

SEDGED *adj* having sedge

SEDGES ► **sedge**

SEDGY, SEDGIER, SEDGIEST ► **sedge**

SEDILE *n* seat for clergy in church

SEDILIA *n* group of three seats where the celebrant and ministers sit during High Mass

SEDILIUM *n* seat for clergy in church

S

SEDIMENT n matter which settles to the bottom of a liquid

SEDITION n speech or action encouraging rebellion against the government

SEDUCE, -D, -S, SEDUCING vb win over or attract

SEDUCER, -S n person who entices, allures, or seduces

SEDUCES ▶ seduce

SEDUCING ▶ seduce

SEDUCIVE adj seductive

SEDUCTOR n person who seduces

SEDULITY ▶ sedulous

SEDULOUS adj diligent or persevering

SEDUM, -S n rock plant

SEE, -N, -S vb perceive with the eyes or mind ▷ n diocese of a bishop

SEEABLE

SEECATCH n male seal in Aleutians

SEED, -ED, -S n mature fertilized grain of a plant ▷ vb sow with seed

SEEDBED, -S n area of soil prepared for the growing of seedlings before they are transplanted

SEEDBOX n part of plant that contains seeds

SEEDCAKE n sweet cake flavoured with caraway seeds and lemon rind or essence

SEEDCASE n part of a fruit enclosing the seeds

SEEDED ▶ seed

SEEDER, -S n person or thing that seeds

SEEDHEAD n flowerhead in a seed

SEEDIER ▶ seedy

SEEDIEST ▶ seedy

SEEDILY ▶ seedy

SEEDING, -S ▶ seed

SEEDLESS ▶ seed

SEEDLIKE ▶ seed

SEEDLING n young plant raised from a seed

SEEDLIP, -S n basket holding seeds to be sown

SEEDMAN, SEEDMEN n seller of seeds

SEEDNESS n old word meaning sowing of seeds

SEEDPOD, -S n carpel enclosing the seeds of a flowering plant

SEEDS ▶ seed

SEEDSMAN, SEEDSMEN n seller of seeds

SEEDTIME n season when seeds are sown

SEEDY, SEEDIER, SEEDIEST adj shabby

SEEING, -S ▶ see

SEEK, -ING, -S, SOUGHT vb try to find or obtain

SEEKER -S

SEEL, -ED, -S vb sew up the eyelids of (a hawk or falcon) so as to render it quiet and tame

SEELD adj old word meaning rare

SEELED ▶ seel

SEELIE pl n good benevolent fairies

SEELIER ▶ seely

SEELIEST ▶ seely

SEELING, -S ▶ seel

SEELS ▶ seel

SEELY, SEELIER, SEELIEST adj old word meaning happy

SEEM, -ED, -S vb appear to be

SEEMER -S

SEEMING, -S adj apparent but not real ▷ n outward or false appearance

SEEMLESS adj old word meaning unseemly

SEEMLY, SEEMLIER adj proper or fitting ▷ adv properly or decorously

SEEMS ▶ seem

SEEN ▶ see

SEEP, -ED, -ING, -S vb trickle through slowly, ooze ▷ n small spring or place where water, oil, etc, has oozed through the ground

SEEPAGE, -S n act or process of seeping

SEEPED ▶ seep

SEEPIER ▶ seepy

SEEPIEST ▶ seepy

SEEPING ▶ seep

SEEPS ▶ seep

SEEPY, SEEPIER, SEEPIEST adj tending to seep

SEER, -S n person who sees

SEERESS

SEES ▶ see

SEESAW, -ED, -S n plank balanced in the middle so that two people seated on either end ride up and down alternately ▷ vb move up and down

SEETHE, -D, -S vb be very agitated ▷ n act or state of seething

SEETHER -S

SEETHING adj boiling or foaming as if boiling

SEEWING, -S n suing

SEFER, SIFREI n scrolls of the Law

SEG, -S n metal stud on shoe sole

SEGAR, -S n cigar

SEGETAL adj (of weeds) growing amongst crops

SEGGAR, -S n box in which pottery is baked

SEGHOL, -S n pronunciation mark in Hebrew

SEGMENT, -S n one of several sections into which something may be divided ▷ vb divide into segments

SEGNO, SEGNI, -S n sign at the beginning or end of a section directed to be repeated

SEGO, -S n American variety of lily

SEGOL, -S variant of ▶ seghol

SEGOLATE variant of > segholate

SEGOLS ▶ segol

SEGOS ▶ sego

SEGREANT adj having raised wings in heraldry

SEGS ▶ seg

SEGUE, -D, -ING, -S vb proceed from one section or piece of music to another without a break ▷ n practice or an instance of playing music in this way

SEGUGIO, -S n Italian breed of dog

SEHRI, -S n meal eaten before sunrise by Muslims fasting during Ramadan

SEI, -S n type of rorqual

SEICENTO n 17th century with reference to Italian art and literature

SEICHE, -S n periodic oscillation of the surface of an enclosed or semienclosed body of water

SEIDEL, -S n vessel for drinking beer

SEIF, -S n long ridge of blown sand in a desert

SEIGNEUR n feudal lord

SEIGNIOR n (in England) the lord of a seigniory

SEIGNORY n lordship

SEIK, -ER, -EST Scot word for ▶ sick

SEIL, -ED, -ING, -S vb dialect word meaning strain

SEINE, -D, -S n large fishing net that hangs vertically from floats ▷ vb catch (fish) using this net

SEINER -S

SEINING, -S ▶ seine

SEIR, -S n fish of Indian seas

SEIS ▶ sei

SEISABLE ► seise
SEISE, -D, -S vb put into legal possession of (property, etc)
SEISER -S
SEISIN, -S n feudal possession of an estate in land
SEISING, -S ► seise
SEISINS ► seisin
SEISM, -S n earthquake
SEISMAL adj of earthquakes
SEISMIC adj relating to earthquakes
SEISMISM n occurrence of earthquakes
SEISMS ► seism
SEISOR, -S n person who takes seisin
SEISURE, -S n act of seisin
SEITAN, -S same as ► seiten
SEITEN, -S n gluten from wheat
SEITY, SEITIES n selfhood
SEIZA, -S n traditional Japanese kneeling position
SEIZABLE ► seize
SEIZAS ► seiza
SEIZE, -D, -S vb take hold of forcibly or quickly
SEIZER -S
SEIZIN, -S same as ► seisin
SEIZING, -S n binding used for holding together two ropes, two spars, etc
SEIZINS ► seizin
SEIZOR, -S n person who takes seisin
SEIZURE, -S n sudden violent attack of an illness
SEJANT adj (of a beast) shown seated
SEJEANT same as ► sejant
SEKOS, -ES n holy place
SEKT, -S n German sparkling wine
SEL, -S Scot word for ► self
SELADANG n Malaysian tapir
SELAH, -S n Hebrew word of unknown meaning occurring in the Old Testament psalms
SELAMLIK n men's quarters in Turkish house
SELCOUTH adj old word meaning strange
SELD adj old word meaning rare
SELDOM adv not often, rarely
SELDOMLY
SELDSEEN adj old word meaning seldom seen
SELE, -S n old word meaning happiness
SELECT, -ED, -S vb pick out or choose ▷ adj chosen in preference to others
SELECTA, -S n disc jockey
SELECTED ► select

SELECTEE n person who is selected, esp for military service
SELECTLY ► select
SELECTOR n person or thing that selects
SELECTS ► select
SELENATE n any salt or ester formed by replacing one or both of the hydrogens of selenic acid with metal ions or organic groups
SELENIAN adj of the moon
SELENIC adj of or containing selenium, esp in the hexavalent state
SELENIDE n compound containing selenium
SELENITE n colourless glassy variety of gypsum
SELENIUM n nonmetallic element with photoelectric properties
SELENOUS same as > selenious
SELES ► sele
SELF, -ED, -S, SELVES n distinct individuality or identity of a person or thing ▷ pron myself, yourself, himself, or herself ▷ vb reproduce by oneself
SELFDOM, -S n selfhood
SELFED ► self
SELFHEAL n low-growing European herbaceous plant
SELFHOOD n state of having a distinct identity
SELFIE, -S n photograph taken by pointing a camera at oneself
SELFING, -S ► self
SELFISH adj caring too much about oneself and not enough about others
SELFISM, -S n emphasis on self
SELFIST -S
SELFLESS adj unselfish
SELFNESS n egotism
SELFS ► self
SELFSAME adj very same
SELFWARD adj toward self
SELICTAR n Turkish sword-bearer
SELKIE, -S same as ► silkie
SELL, -S vb exchange (something) for money ▷ n manner of selling
SELLA, -E, -S n area of bone in body
SELLABLE ► sell
SELLAE ► sella
SELLAS ► sella
SELLE, -S n old word meaning seat

SELLER, -S n person who sells
SELLES ► selle
SELLING, -S n providing goods or services to customers in exchange for money
SELLOFF, -S n act of selling cheaply
SELLOUT, -S n performance of a show etc for which all the tickets are sold
SELLS ► sell
SELS ► sel
SELSYN, -S same as ► synchro
SELTZER, -S n natural effervescent water containing minerals
SELVA, -S n dense equatorial forest
SELVAGE, -D, -S n edge of cloth, woven so as to prevent unravelling ▷ vb edge or border
SELVAGEE n rope used as strap
SELVAGES ► selvage
SELVAS ► selva
SELVEDGE same as ► selvage
SELVES ► self
SEMANTIC adj relating to the meaning of words
SEMANTRA > semantron
SEMATIC adj acting as a warning, esp to potential predators
SEMBLANT n semblance
SEMBLE, -D, -S, SEMBLING vb seem
SEME, -S adj dotted (with)
SEMEE variant of ► seme
SEMEED adj seme
SEMEION, SEMEIA n unit of metre in ancient poetry
SEMEME, -S n meaning of a morpheme
SEMEMIC
SEMEN, -S, SEMINA n sperm-carrying fluid produced by male animals
SEMES ► seme
SEMESTER n either of two divisions of the academic year
SEMI n semidetached house
SEMIARID adj denoting land that lies on the edges of a desert but has a slightly higher rainfall
SEMIBALD adj partly bald
SEMIBOLD adj denoting a weight of typeface between medium and bold face ▷ n semibold type
SEMIBULL n papal bull issued before coronation

S

SEMICOMA n condition similar to a coma

SEMIDEAF adj partly deaf

SEMIDOME n half-dome, esp one used to cover a semicircular apse

SEMIDRY adj partly dry

SEMIE, **-S** n historical name for a student in second year at a Scottish university

SEMIFIT adj not fully fit

SEMIGALA adj characterized by quite a lot of celebration and fun ▷ n occasion that is festive but not to the degree of a gala

SEMIHARD adj partly hard

SEMIHIGH adj moderately high

SEMIHOBO n person looking almost like hobo

SEMILLON n grape used to make wine

SEMILOG adj semilogarithmic

SEMILUNE n half-moon shape

SEMIMAT adj semimatt

SEMIMATT adj with surface midway between matt and gloss

SEMIMILD adj somewhat mild

SEMIMUTE adj having speech impairment through hearing loss ▷ n person who is semimute

SEMINA ▶ **semen**

SEMINAL adj original and influential

SEMINAR, **-S** n meeting of a group of students for discussion

SEMINARY n college for priests

SEMINATE vb sow

SEMINUDE adj partly nude

SEMIOPEN adj half-open

SEMIOSIS, **SEMIOSES** n action involving establishing relationship between signs

SEMIOTIC adj relating to signs and symbols, esp spoken or written signs

SEMIOVAL adj shaped like half of oval

SEMIPED, **-S** n measure in poetic metre

SEMIPRO, **-S** n semiprofessional

SEMIRAW adj not fully cooked or processed

SEMIS, **-ES** n ancient Roman coin

SEMISOFT adj partly soft

SEMITAR, **-S** old spelling of ▶ scimitar

SEMITAUR old spelling of ▶ scimitar

SEMITIST n student of Semitic languages and culture

SEMITONE n smallest interval between two notes in Western music

SEMIWILD adj not fully domesticated

SEMMIT, **-S** n vest

SEMOLINA n hard grains of wheat left after the milling of flour, used to make puddings and pasta

SEMPER adv Latin word meaning always

SEMPLE, **-R**, **-ST** adj Scots word meaning simple

SEMPLICE adv be performed in a simple manner

SEMPRE adv (preceding a tempo or dynamic marking) always

SEMPSTER n person who sews

SEMSEM, **-S** n sesame

SEMUNCIA n ancient Roman coin

SEN, **-S** n monetary unit of Brunei, Cambodia, Indonesia, Malaysia, and formerly of Japan

SENA, **-S** n (in India) the army

SENARIES ▶ **senary**

SENARIUS, **SENARII** n type of poem

SENARY, **SENARIES** adj of or relating to the number six

SENAS ▶ **sena**

SENATE, **-S** n main governing body at some universities

SENATOR, **-S** n member of a senate

SEND, **-S** vb cause (a person or thing) to go to or be taken or transmitted to a place

SENDABLE

SENDAL, **-S** n fine silk fabric used for ceremonial clothing, etc

SENDED vb old word meaning sent

SENDER, **-S** ▶ **send**

SENDING, **-S** ▶ **send**

SENDOFF, **-S** n demonstration of good wishes at a person's departure ▷ vb dispatch (something, such as a letter)

SENDS ▶ **send**

SENDUP, **-S** n parody or imitation

SENE, **-S** n money unit in Samoa

SENECA, **-S** variant of ▶ senega

SENECIO, **-S** n type of plant of the genus which includes groundsels and ragworts

SENEGA, **-S** n milkwort plant of the eastern US

SENES ▶ **sene**

SENESCE, **-D**, **-S** vb grow old

SENGI, **-S** n African shrew

SENGREEN n house leek

SENHOR, **-ES**, **-S** n Portuguese term of address for man

SENHORA, **-S** n Portuguese term of address for woman

SENHORES ▶ **senhor**

SENHORS ▶ **senhor**

SENILE, **-S** adj mentally or physically weak because of old age ▷ n senile person

SENILELY

SENILITY

SENIOR, **-S** adj superior in rank or standing ▷ n senior person

SENITI, **-S** n money unit in Tonga

SENNA, **-S** n tropical plant

SENNET, **-S** n fanfare: used as a stage direction in Elizabethan drama

SENNIGHT archaic word for ▶ week

SENNIT, **-S** n flat braided cordage used on ships

SENOPIA, **-S** n short-sightedness in old age

SENOR, **-ES**, **-S** n Spanish term of address equivalent to sir or Mr

SENORA, **-S** n Spanish term of address equivalent to madam or Mrs

SENORES ▶ **senor**

SENORITA n Spanish term of address equivalent to madam or Miss

SENORS ▶ **senor**

SENRYU n Japanese short poem

SENS ▶ **sen**

SENSA ▶ **sensum**

SENSATE, **-D**, **-S** adj perceived by the senses ▷ vb make sensate

SENSE, **-D**, **-S** n any of the faculties of perception or feeling ▷ vb perceive

SENSEFUL adj full of sense

SENSEI, **-S** n martial arts teacher

SENSES ▶ **sense**

SENSI, **-S** same as ▶ **sensei**

SENSIBLE adj having or showing good sense ▷ n sensible thing or person

SENSIBLY

SENSILE adj capable of feeling

SENSILLA > sensillum

SENSING, -S > sense

SENSIS > sensi

SENSISM, -S n theory that ideas spring from senses

SENSIST -S

SENSOR, -S n device that detects or measures the presence of something, such as radiation

SENSORIA > sensorium

SENSORS > sensor

SENSORY adj of the senses or sensation

SENSUAL adj giving pleasure to the body and senses rather than the mind

SENSUM, SENSA n sensation detached from the information it conveys

SENSUOUS adj pleasing to the senses

SENT, -ED, -I, -ING, -S n former monetary unit of Estonia ▷ vb old spelling of scent

SENTE, LISENTE n money unit in Lesotho

SENTED > sent

SENTENCE n sequence of words capable of standing alone as a statement, question, or command ▷ vb pass sentence on (a convicted person)

SENTI > sent

SENTIENT adj capable of feeling ▷ n sentient person or thing

SENTIMO, -S n money unit in Philippines

SENTINEL n sentry ▷ vb guard as a sentinel

SENTING > sent

SENTRY, SENTRIES n soldier on watch

SENTS > sent

SENVY, SENVIES n mustard

SENZA prep without

SEPAD, -DED, -S vb suppose

SEPAL, -S n leaflike division of the calyx of a flower

SEPALED

SEPALINE same as ▸ sepaloid

SEPALLED > sepal

SEPALODY n changing of flower part into sepal

SEPALOID adj (esp of petals) resembling a sepal in structure and function

SEPALOUS adj with sepals

SEPALS > sepal

SEPARATA > separatum

SEPARATE vb act as a barrier between ▷ adj not the same, different ▷ n item of clothing that only covers half the body

SEPHEN, -S n stingray

SEPIA, -S n reddish-brown pigment ▷ adj dark reddish-brown

SEPIC adj of sepia

SEPIMENT n hedge

SEPIOST, -S n cuttlefish bone

SEPIUM, -S n cuttlefish bone

SEPMAG adj designating a film, etc for which the sound is recorded on separate magnetic material

SEPOY, -S n (formerly) Indian soldier in the service of the British

SEPPUKU, -S n Japanese ritual suicide

SEPS n species of lizard

SEPSIS, SEPSES n poisoning caused by pus-forming bacteria

SEPT, -S n clan, esp in Ireland or Scotland

SEPTA > septum

SEPTAGE, -S n waste removed from septic tank

SEPTAL adj of or relating to a septum

SEPTARIA > septarium

SEPTATE adj divided by septa

SEPTET, -S n group of seven performers

SEPTETTE same as ▸ septet

SEPTIC, -S adj (of a wound) infected ▷ n infected wound

SEPTICAL

SEPTIMAL adj of number seven

SEPTIME, -S n seventh of eight basic positions from which a parry can be made in fencing

SEPTLEVA n gambling term from old card game

SEPTORIA n any of various parasitic fungi

SEPTS > sept

SEPTUM, SEPTA, -S n dividing partition between two cavities in the body

SEPTUOR, -S n group of seven musicians

SEPTUPLE vb multiply by seven ▷ adj seven times as much or as many ▷ n quantity or number seven times as great as another

SEQUEL, -S n novel, play, or film that continues the story of an earlier one

SEQUELA, -E n disease related to or arising from a pre-existing disease

SEQUELS > sequel

SEQUENCE n arrangement of two or more things in successive order ▷ vb arrange in a sequence

SEQUENCY n number of changes in mathematical list

SEQUENT, -S adj following in order or succession ▷ n something that follows

SEQUIN, -ED, -S n small ornamental metal disc on a garment ▷ vb apply sequins

SEQUITUR n conclusion that follows from the premises

SEQUOIA, -S n giant Californian coniferous tree

> This word for a redwood tree is one of the most frequently played bonuses using the Q, a great one to remember as it also clears out a surplus of vowels.

SER, -S n unit of weight used in India

SERA > serum

SERAC, -S n pinnacle of ice among crevasses on a glacier, usually on a steep slope

SERAFILE n line of soldiers

SERAFIN, -S n old silver coin of Goa

SERAGLIO n sultan's palace

SERAI, -S n caravanserai or inn

SERAIL, -S same as ▸ seraglio

SERAIS > serai

SERAL > sere

SERANG, -S n native captain of a crew of sailors in the East Indies

SERAPE, -S n blanket-like shawl often of brightly-coloured wool

SERAPH, -IM, -S n member of the highest order of angels

SERAPHIC adj of or resembling a seraph

SERAPHIM > seraph

SERAPHIN n angel

SERAPHS > seraph

SERDAB, -S n secret chamber in an ancient Egyptian tomb

SERE, -D, -R, -S, -ST, SERING adj dried up or withered ▷ n series of changes occurring in the ecological succession of a particular community ▷ vb sear

SEREIN, -S n fine rain falling from a clear sky after sunset

S

SERENADE n music played or sung to a woman by an admirer ▷ vb sing or play a serenade to (someone)

SERENATA n 18th-century cantata, often dramatic in form

SERENATE n old form of serenade ▷ vb make serene

SERENE, -D, -R, -S, -ST, SERENING adj calm, peaceful ▷ vb make serene

SERENELY

SERENITY n state or quality of being serene

SERER ► sere

SERES ► sere

SEREST ► sere

SERF, -S n medieval farm labourer who could not leave the land he worked on

SERFAGE -S

SERFDOM, -S ► serf

SERFHOOD ► serf

SERFISH ► serf

SERFLIKE ► serf

SERFS ► serf

SERFSHIP ► serf

SERGE, -S n strong woollen fabric

SERGEANT n noncommissioned officer in the army

SERGED adj with sewn seam

SERGER, -S n sewing machine attachment for finishing seams

SERGES ► serge

SERGING, -S n type of sewing

SERIAL, -S n story or play produced in successive instalments ▷ adj of or forming a series

SERIALLY

SERIATE, -D, -S adj forming a series ▷ vb form into a series

SERIATIM adv in a series

SERIC adj of silk

SERICIN, -S n gelatinous protein found on the fibres of raw silk

SERICITE n type of mica

SERICON, -S n solution used in alchemy

SERIEMA, -S n either of two cranelike South American birds

SERIES n group or succession of related things, usu arranged in order

SERIF, -S n small line at the extremities of a main stroke in a type character

SERIFED adj having serifs

SERIFFED adj having serifs

SERIFS ► serif

SERIN, -S n any of various small yellow-and-brown finches

SERINE, -S n sweet-tasting amino acid

SERING ► sere

SERINGA, -S n any of several trees that yield rubber

SERINS ► serin

SERIOUS adj giving cause for concern

SERIPH, -S same as ► serif

SERJEANT same as ► sergeant

SERK, -S Scots word for ► shirt

SERKALI, -S n government in Africa

SERKS ► serk

SERMON, -ED, -S n speech on a religious or moral subject ▷ vb deliver a sermon

SERMONER variant of > sermoneer

SERMONET n short sermon

SERMONIC ► sermon

SERMONS ► sermon

SEROLOGY n science concerned with serums

SERON, -S n crate

SEROON, -S n crate

SEROPUS n liquid consisting of serum and pus

SEROSA, -E, -S n one of the thin membranes surrounding the embryo in an insect's egg

SEROSAL

SEROSITY ► serous

SEROTINE adj produced, flowering, or developing late in the season ▷ n either of two insectivorous bats

SEROTINY n state of being serotinous

SEROTYPE n category into which material is placed based on its serological activity ▷ vb class according to serotype

SEROUS adj of, containing, or like serum

SEROVAR, -S n subdivision of species

SEROW, -S n either of two antelopes of mountainous regions of S and SE Asia

SERPENT, -S n snake

SERPIGO, -S n any progressive skin eruption

SERPULA, -E, -S n type of marine mollusc

SERPULID n marine polychaete worm

SERR, -S vb press close together

SERRA, -E, -S n sawlike part or organ

SERRAN, -S n species of fish

SERRANID n type of marine fish of the family which includes the sea bass and sea perch

SERRANO, -S n type of Spanish ham

SERRANS ► serran

SERRAS ► serra

SERRATE, -S adj (of leaves) having a margin of forward pointing teeth ▷ vb make serrate

SERRATED adj having a notched or sawlike edge

SERRATES ► serrate

SERRATUS, SERRATI n muscle in thorax

SERRE, -D, -S, SERRING vb press close together

SERRIED adj in close formation

SERRIES ► serry

SERRING ► serre

SERRS ► serr

SERRY, SERRIES, -ING vb close together

SERS ► ser

SERUEWE, -D, -S vb old word meaning survey

SERUM, SERA, -S n watery fluid left after blood has clotted

SERUMAL

SERVABLE ► serve

SERVAL, -S n feline African mammal

SERVANT, -S n person employed to do household work for another ▷ vb work as a servant

SERVE, -D, -S vb work for (a person, community, or cause) ▷ n act of serving the ball

SERVER, -S n player who serves in racket games

SERVERY n room from which food is served

SERVES ► serve

SERVEWE, -D, -S vb old word meaning survey

SERVICE, -D, -S n serving ▷ adj serving the public rather than producing goods ▷ vb provide a service or services to

SERVICER

SERVIENT adj subordinate

SERVILE, -S adj too eager to obey people, fawning ▷ n servile person

SERVING, -S n portion of food

SERVITOR *n* servant or attendant

SERVLET, -S *n* small program that runs on a web server

SERVO, -S *n* servomechanism ▷ *adj* of a servomechanism

SERVQUAL *n* provision of high-quality products backed by a high level of customer service

SESAME, -S *n* plant cultivated for its seeds and oil

SESAMOID *adj* of or relating to various small bones formed in tendons ▷ *n* sesamoid bone

SESE *interj* exclamation found in Shakespeare

SESELI, -S *n* garden plant

SESEY *interj* exclamation found in Shakespeare

SESH, -ES *short for* ▸ **session**

SESS, -ED, -ES, -ING *n* old word meaning tax ▷ *vb* assess or impose (a tax)

SESSA *interj* exclamation found in Shakespeare

SESSED ▸ **sess**

SESSES ▸ **sess**

SESSILE *adj* (of flowers or leaves) having no stalk

SESSING ▸ **sess**

SESSION, -S *n* period spent in an activity

SESSPOOL *n* cesspool

SESTERCE *n* silver or, later, bronze coin of ancient Rome worth a quarter of a denarius

SESTET, -S *n* last six lines of a sonnet

SESTETT, -S *n* group of six

SESTETTE *n* group of six

SESTETTO *n* composition for six musicians

SESTETTS ▸ **sestett**

SESTINA, -S *n* elaborate verse form of Italian origin

SESTINE, -S *n* poem of six lines

SESTON, -S *n* type of plankton

SET, -S *vb* put in a specified position or state ▷ *n* setting or being set ▷ *adj* fixed or established beforehand

SETA, -E *n* bristle or bristle-like appendage

SETAL

SETBACK, -S *n* anything that delays progress

SETENANT *n* pair of postage stamps of different values joined together

SETIFORM *adj* shaped like a seta

SETLINE, -S *n* any of various types of fishing line

SETNESS ▸ **set**

SETOFF, -S *n* counterbalance

SETON, -S *n* surgical thread inserted below the skin

SETOSE *adj* covered with setae

SETOUS ▸ **seta**

SETOUT, -S *n* beginning or outset

SETS ▸ **set**

SETSCREW *n* screw that fits into the boss or hub of a wheel

SETT, -S *n* badger's burrow

SETTEE, -S *n* couch

SETTER, -ED, -S *n* long-haired gun dog ▷ *vb* treat with a piece of setterwort

SETTING, -S ▸ **set**

SETTLE, -D, -S, SETTLING *vb* arrange or put in order ▷ *n* long wooden bench with high back and arms

SETTLER, -S *n* colonist

SETTLES ▸ **settle**

SETTLING ▸ **settle**

SETTLOR, -S *n* person who settles property on someone

SETTS ▸ **sett**

SETUALE, -S *n* valerian

SETULE, -S *n* small bristle

SETULOSE

SETULOUS

SETUP, -S *n* way in which anything is organized or arranged

SETWALL, -S *n* valerian

SEV, -S *n* Indian snack of deep-fried noodles

SEVEN *n* one more than six ▷ *adj* amounting to seven ▷ *determiner* amounting to seven

SEVENS *n* Rugby Union match or series of matches played with seven players on each side

SEVENTH, -S *n* number seven in a series ▷ *adj* coming after the sixth and before the eighth ▷ *adv* after the sixth person, position, event, etc

SEVENTY *n* ten times seven ▷ *adj* amounting to seventy ▷ *determiner* amounting to seventy

SEVER, -ED, -ING, -S *vb* cut through or off

SEVERAL, -S *adj* some, a few ▷ *n* individual person

SEVERE, -R, -ST *adj* strict or harsh

SEVERED ▸ **sever**

SEVERELY ▸ **severe**

SEVERER ▸ **severe**

SEVEREST ▸ **severe**

SEVERIES ▸ **severy**

SEVERING ▸ **sever**

SEVERITY ▸ **severe**

SEVERS ▸ **sever**

SEVERY, SEVERIES *n* part of vaulted ceiling

SEVICHE, -S *n* Mexican fish dish

SEVRUGA, -S *n* species of sturgeon

SEVS ▸ **sev**

SEW, -ED, -N, -S *vb* join with thread repeatedly passed through with a needle

SEWABLE

SEWAGE, -S *n* waste matter carried away in sewers

SEWAN, -S *same as* ▸ **seawan**

SEWAR, -S *n* Asian dagger

SEWED ▸ **sew**

SEWEL, -S *n* scarecrow

SEWELLEL *n* mountain beaver

SEWELS ▸ **sewel**

SEWEN, -S *same as* ▸ **sewin**

SEWER, -ED, -ING, -S *n* drain to remove waste water and sewage ▷ *vb* provide with sewers

SEWERAGE *n* system of sewers

SEWERED ▸ **sewer**

SEWERING ▸ **sewer**

SEWERS ▸ **sewer**

SEWIN, -S *n* sea trout

SEWING, -S ▸ **sew**

SEWINS ▸ **sewin**

SEWN ▸ **sew**

SEWS ▸ **sew**

SEX, -ED, -ES, -ING *n* state of being male or female ▷ *vb* find out the sex of

SEXER, -S *n* person checking the gender of chickens

SEXES ▸ **sex**

SEXFID *adj* split into six

SEXFOIL, -S *n* flower with six petals or leaves

SEXIER ▸ **sexy**

SEXIEST ▸ **sexy**

SEXILY ▸ **sexy**

SEXINESS ▸ **sexy**

SEXING, -S ▸ **sex**

SEXISM, -S *n* discrimination on the basis of a person's gender

SEXIST -S

SEXLESS *adj* neither male nor female

SEXTAIN, -S *same as* ▸ **sestina**

SEXTAN *adj* (of a fever) marked by paroxysms that recur after an interval of five days

SEXTANS *n* ancient Roman coin

S

SEXTANT, -S n navigator's instrument for measuring angles

SEXTARII ▶ sextarius

SEXTET, -S n group of six performers

SEXTETT, -S n sextet

SEXTETTE same as ▶ **sextet**

SEXTETTS ▶ sextett

SEXTILE, -S n value of a variable dividing its distribution into six groups with equal frequencies

SEXTO, -S same as ▶ **sixmo**

SEXTOLET n group of six musical notes

SEXTON, -S n official in charge of a church and churchyard

SEXTOS ▶ sexto

SEXTUOR, -S n sextet

SEXTUPLE vb multiply by six ▷ adj six times as much or as many ▷ n quantity or number six times as great as another

SEXTUPLY

SEXUAL adj of or characterized by sex

SEXUALLY

SEXY, SEXIER, SEXIEST adj exciting or attractive

SEY, -S n Scots word meaning part of cow carcase

SEYEN, -S n old form of scion

SEYS ▶ sey

SEYSURE, -S n old form of seizure

SEZ vb informal spelling of 'says'

> **Sez** is a short informal form of **says**, very useful for disposing of the Z.

SFERICS same as ▶ **spherics**

SFORZATO, SFORZATI same as > **sforzando**

SFUMATO, -S n gradual transition between areas of different colour in painting

SH interj hush

SHA interj be quiet

SHABASH interj (in Indian English) bravo or well done

SHABBIER ▶ shabby

SHABBILY ▶ shabby

SHABBLE, -S n Scots word meaning old sword

SHABBY, SHABBIER adj worn or dilapidated in appearance

SHABRACK n cavalryman's saddle cloth

SHACK, -ED, -ING, -S n rough hut ▷ vb evade (work or responsibility)

SHACKIER ▶ shacky

SHACKING ▶ shack

SHACKLE, -D, -S n metal ring for securing a person's wrists or ankles ▷ vb fasten with shackles

SHACKLER

SHACKO, -ES, -S same as ▶ **shako**

SHACKS ▶ shack

SHACKY, SHACKIER adj resembling a shack; dilapidated

SHAD, -S n herring-like fish

SHADBLOW n type of shrub

SHADBUSH n type of N American tree or shrub

SHADCHAN n Jewish marriage broker

SHADDOCK another name for ▶ **pomelo**

SHADDUP interj shut up

SHADE, -D n relative darkness ▷ vb screen from light

SHADER -S

SHADES pl n gathering darkness at nightfall

SHADFLY American name for ▶ **mayfly**

SHADIER ▶ shady

SHADIEST ▶ shady

SHADILY ▶ shady

SHADING, -S n graded areas of tone indicating tone and dark in a painting or drawing

SHADKHAN same as ▶ **shadchan**

SHADOOF, -S n mechanism for raising water

SHADOW, -ED, -S n dark shape cast on a surface when something stands between a light and the surface ▷ vb cast a shadow over

SHADOWER

SHADOWY adj (of a place) full of shadows

SHADRACH n lump of iron that has not been melted in the furnace

SHADS ▶ shad

SHADUF, -S same as ▶ **shadoof**

SHADY, SHADIER, SHADIEST adj situated in or giving shade

SHAFT, -ED, -S n long narrow straight handle of a tool or weapon ▷ vb treat badly

SHAFTER -S

SHAFTING n assembly of rotating shafts for transmitting power

SHAFTS ▶ shaft

SHAG, -GING, -S n cormorant ▷ adj (of a carpet) having a long pile ▷ vb make shaggy

SHAGBARK n North American hickory tree

SHAGGED ▶ shagged

SHAGGIER ▶ shaggy

SHAGGILY ▶ shaggy

SHAGGING ▶ shag

SHAGGY, SHAGGIER adj covered with rough hair or wool

SHAGPILE adj (of carpet) having long fibres

SHAGREEN n sharkskin

SHAGROON n nineteenth-century Australian settler in Canterbury

SHAGS ▶ shagnoun

SHAH, -S n formerly, ruler of Iran

SHAHADA, -S n Islamic declaration of faith

SHAHADAH same as ▶ **shahada**

SHAHADAS ▶ shahada

SHAHDOM, -S ▶ shah

SHAHEED, -S same as ▶ **shahid**

SHAHID, -S n Muslim martyr

SHAHS ▶ shah

SHAIKH, -S n sheikh

SHAIRD, -S n Scots word meaning shred

SHAIRN, -S Scots word for ▶ **dung**

SHAITAN, -S n (in Muslim countries) an evil spirit

SHAKABLE ▶ shake

SHAKE, -N, -S vb move quickly up and down or back and forth ▷ n shaking

SHAKED vb old form of shook

SHAKEN ▶ shake

SHAKEOUT n process of reducing the number of people in a workforce

SHAKER, -S n container in which drinks are mixed or from which powder is shaken

SHAKES ▶ shake

SHAKEUP, -S n radical reorganization

SHAKIER ▶ shaky

SHAKIEST ▶ shaky

SHAKILY ▶ shaky

SHAKING, -S ▶ shake

SHAKO, -ES, -S n tall cylindrical peaked military hat with a plume

SHAKT vb old form of shook

SHAKUDO, -S n Japanese alloy of copper and gold

SHAKY, SHAKIER, SHAKIEST adj unsteady

SHALE, -D, -S, SHALING n flaky sedimentary rock

SHALEY

SHALIER ▶ shaly

SHALIEST ▸ shaly

SHALING ▸ shale

SHALL, SHOULD *vb* used as an auxiliary to make the future tense

SHALLI, -S *n* type of fabric

SHALLON, -S *n* American shrub

SHALLOON *n* light twill-weave woollen fabric used chiefly for coat linings, etc

SHALLOP, -S *n* light boat used for rowing in shallow water

SHALLOT, -S *n* kind of small onion

SHALLOW, -S *adj* not deep ▷ *n* shallow place in a body of water ▷ *vb* make or become shallow

SHALM, -S *n* old woodwind instrument

SHALOM, -S *n* Jewish greeting meaning 'peace be with you'

SHALOT, -S *n* shallot

SHALT singular form of the present tense (indicative mood) of ▸ **shall**

SHALWAR, -S *n* pair of loose-fitting trousers tapering to a narrow fit around the ankles

SHALY, SHALIER, SHALIEST ▸ shale

SHAM, -MED, -MING, -S *n* thing or person that is not genuine ▷ *adj* not genuine ▷ *vb* fake, feign

SHAMA, -S *n* Indian songbird

SHAMABLE ▸ shame

SHAMABLY ▸ shame

SHAMAL, -S *n* hot northwesterly wind

SHAMAN, -S *n* priest of shamanism

SHAMANIC

SHAMAS ▸ shama

SHAMBA, -S *n* (in E Africa) any field used for growing crops

SHAMBLE, -D *vb* walk in a shuffling awkward way ▷ *n* awkward or shuffling walk

SHAMBLES *n* disorderly event or place

SHAMBLY ▸ shamble

SHAME, -D, -S, SHAMING *n* painful emotion caused by awareness of having done something foolish ▷ *vb* cause to feel shame

SHAMEFUL *adj* causing or deserving shame

SHAMER, -S *n* cause of shame

SHAMES ▸ shame

SHAMIANA *n* tent in India

SHAMINA, -S *n* wool blend of pashm and shahtoosh

SHAMING ▸ shame

SHAMISEN *n* Japanese stringed instrument

SHAMMAS same as ▸ **shammes**

SHAMMASH same as ▸ **shammes**

SHAMMED ▸ sham

SHAMMER, -S ▸ sham

SHAMMES *n* official acting as the beadle, sexton, and caretaker of a synagogue

SHAMMIED ▸ shammy

SHAMMIES ▸ shammy

SHAMMING ▸ sham

SHAMMOS same as ▸ **shammes**

SHAMMY, SHAMMIED, SHAMMIES *n* piece of chamois leather ▷ *vb* rub with a shammy

SHAMOIS *n* chamois ▷ *vb* clean with shamois

SHAMOS same as ▸ **shammes**

SHAMOY, -ED, -S *n* chamois ▷ *vb* rub with a shamoy

SHAMPOO, -S *n* liquid soap for washing hair, carpets, or upholstery ▷ *vb* wash with shampoo

SHAMROCK *n* clover leaf, esp as the Irish emblem

SHAMS ▸ sham

SHAMUS, -ES *n* police or private detective

SHAN, -S variant of ▸ **shand**

SHAND, -S *n* old word meaning fake coin

SHANDIES ▸ shandy

SHANDRY *n* light horse-drawn cart

SHANDS ▸ shand

SHANDY, SHANDIES *n* drink made of beer and lemonade

SHANGHAI *vb* force or trick (someone) into doing something ▷ *n* catapult

SHANK, -ED, -ING, -S *n* lower leg ▷ *vb* (of fruits, roots, etc) to show disease symptoms

SHANNY, SHANNIES *n* European blenny of rocky coastal waters

SHANS ▸ shan

SHANTEY, -S same as ▸ **shanty**

SHANTI, -S *n* peace

SHANTIES ▸ shanty

SHANTIH, -S same as ▸ **shanti**

SHANTIS ▸ shanti

SHANTUNG *n* soft Chinese silk with a knobbly surface

SHANTY, SHANTIES *n* shack or crude dwelling

SHAPABLE ▸ shape

SHAPE, -D, -S *n* outward form of an object ▷ *vb* form or mould

SHAPELY *adj* having an attractive shape

SHAPEN, -ED, -S *vb* shape

SHAPER, -S ▸ shape

SHAPES ▸ shape

SHAPEUP, -S *n* system of hiring dockers for a day's work

SHAPING, -S ▸ shape

SHAPS *n* leather over-trousers worn by cowboys

SHARABLE ▸ share

SHARD, -S *n* broken piece of pottery or glass

SHARDED *adj* old word meaning hidden under dung

SHARDS ▸ shard

SHARE, -D, -S *n* part of something that belongs to or is contributed by a person ▷ *vb* give or take a share of (something)

SHAREMAN, SHAREMEN *n* member of fishing-boat crew who shares profits

SHARER, -S ▸ share

SHARES ▸ share

SHARIA, -S *n* body of doctrines that regulate the lives of Muslims

SHARIAH, -S same as ▸ **sharia**

SHARIAS ▸ sharia

SHARIAT, -S *n* Islamic religious law

SHARIF, -S same as ▸ **sherif**

SHARING, -S ▸ share

SHARK, -ED, -ING, -S *n* large usu predatory sea fish ▷ *vb* obtain (something) by cheating or deception

SHARKER, -S *n* shark hunter

SHARKING ▸ shark

SHARKISH *adj* resembling or behaving like a shark

SHARKS ▸ shark

SHARN, -S Scots word for ▸ **dung**

SHARNIER ▸ sharny

SHARNIES ▸ sharny

SHARNS ▸ sharn

SHARNY, SHARNIER, SHARNIES *n* (Scot) person who cleans a cow-house ▷ *adj* (Scot) covered in dung

SHARON *n* as in **sharon fruit** persimmon

SHARP, -ED, -EST, -ING, -S *adj* having a keen cutting edge or fine point ▷ *adv* promptly ▷ *n* symbol raising a note one semitone above natural pitch ▷ *vb* make sharp

S

SHARPEN, -S vb make or become sharp or sharper

SHARPER, -S n person who cheats

SHARPEST ▶ sharp

SHARPIE, -S n member of a teenage group having short hair and distinctive clothes

SHARPING ▶ sharp

SHARPISH adj fairly sharp ▷ adv promptly

SHARPLY ▶ sharp

SHARPS ▶ sharp

SHARPY n swindler

SHASH, -ED, -ES, -ING vb old form of sash

SHASHLIK n type of kebab

SHASLIK, -S n type of kebab

SHASTA, -S n plant of the daisy family

SHASTER, -S same as ▶ shastra

SHASTRA, -S n any of the sacred writings of Hinduism

SHATOOSH same as > shahtoosh

SHATTER, -S vb break into pieces ▷ n fragment

SHATTERY adj liable to shatter

SHAUCHLE vb Scots word meaning shuffle

SHAUCHLY

SHAUGH, -S n old word meaning small wood

SHAUL, -ED, -ING, -S vb old form of shawl

SHAVABLE ▶ shave

SHAVE, -D, -S vb remove (hair) from (the face, head, or body) with a razor or shaver ▷ n shaving

SHAVEN adj closely shaved or tonsured

SHAVER, -S n electric razor

SHAVES ▶ shave

SHAVIE, -S n Scots word meaning trick

SHAVING, -S ▶ shave

SHAW, -ED, -ING, -S n small wood ▷ vb show

SHAWARMA n strips of lamb, usu served in a pitta

SHAWED ▶ shaw

SHAWING ▶ shaw

SHAWL, -ED, -ING, -S n piece of cloth worn over a woman's shoulders or wrapped around a baby ▷ vb cover with a shawl

SHAWLEY, -S same as ▶ shawlie

SHAWLIE, -S n insulting term for a working-class woman who wears a shawl

SHAWLING ▶ shawl

SHAWLS ▶ shawl

SHAWM, -S n medieval form of the oboe with a conical bore and flaring bell

SHAWN variant of ▶ shawm

SHAWS ▶ shaw

SHAY, -S dialect word for ▶ chaise

SHAYA, -S n Indian plant

SHAYKH, -S same as ▶ sheikh

SHAYS ▶ shay

SHAZAM interj magic slogan

SHCHI, -S n Russian cabbage soup

SHE, -S pron female person or animal previously mentioned ▷ n female person or animal

SHEA, -S n tropical African tree

SHEADING n any of the six subdivisions of the Isle of Man

SHEAF, -ED, -ING, -S, SHEAVES n bundle of papers ▷ vb tie into a sheaf

SHEAFIER ▶ sheafy

SHEAFING ▶ sheaf

SHEAFS ▶ sheaf

SHEAFY, SHEAFIER ▶ sheaf

SHEAL, -ED, -ING, -S vb old word meaning shell

SHEAR, -ED, -ING, -S vb clip hair or wool from ▷ n breakage caused through strain or twisting

SHEARER -S

SHEARLEG n one spar of shearlegs

SHEARMAN, SHEARMEN n person who trims cloth

SHEARS ▶ shear

SHEAS ▶ shea

SHEATH, -S n close-fitting cover, esp for a knife or sword

SHEATHE, -D, -S vb put into a sheath

SHEATHER

SHEATHS ▶ sheath

SHEATHY ▶ sheathe

SHEAVE, -D, SHEAVING vb gather or bind into sheaves ▷ n wheel with a grooved rim

SHEAVES ▶ sheaf

SHEAVING ▶ sheave

SHEBANG, -S n situation, matter, or affair

SHEBEAN, -S same as ▶ shebeen

SHEBEEN, -S n place where alcohol is sold illegally ▷ vb run a shebeen

SHECHITA n Jewish method of killing animals for food

SHED, -DED, -S n building used for storage or shelter or as a workshop ▷ vb get rid of

SHEDABLE

SHEDDER, -S n person or thing that sheds

SHEDDING ▶ shed

SHEDFUL, -S n quantity or amount contained in a shed

SHEDHAND n labourer working in a shearing shed

SHEDLIKE ▶ shed

SHEDLOAD n very large amount or number

SHEDS ▶ shed

SHEEL, -ED, -ING, -S vb old word meaning shell

SHEEN, -ED, -ING, -S n glistening brightness on the surface of something ▷ adj shining and beautiful ▷ vb give a sheen to

SHEENFUL

SHEENIER ▶ sheeny

SHEENING ▶ sheen

SHEENS ▶ sheen

SHEENY, SHEENIER ▶ sheen

SHEEP n ruminant animal bred for wool and meat

SHEEPCOT n sheepcote

SHEEPDOG n dog used for herding sheep

SHEEPIER ▶ sheepy

SHEEPISH adj embarrassed because of feeling foolish

SHEEPLE pl n people who follow the majority in matters of opinion, taste, etc

SHEEPMAN, SHEEPMEN n person who keeps sheep

SHEEPO, -S n person employed to bring sheep to the catching pen in a shearing shed

SHEEPY, SHEEPIER ▶ sheep

SHEER, -ED, -ER, -EST, -ING, -S adj absolute, complete ▷ adv steeply ▷ vb change course suddenly ▷ n any transparent fabric used for making garments

SHEERLEG n one spar of sheerlegs

SHEERLY ▶ sheer

SHEERS ▶ sheer

SHEESH interj exclamation of surprise or annoyance

SHEESHA, -S n Oriental water-pipe for smoking tobacco

SHEET, -ED, -S n large piece of cloth used as an inner bed cover ▷ vb provide with, cover, or wrap in a sheet

SHEETER -S

SHEETFED adj printing on separate sheets of paper

SHEETIER ▶ sheety

SHEETING n material from which sheets are made

SHEETS ▶ sheet

SHEETY, SHEETIER ▸ sheet
SHEEVE, -S n part of mine winding gear
SHEHITA, -S n slaughter of animal according to Jewish religious law
SHEHITAH n slaughter of animal according to Jewish religious law
SHEHITAS ▸ shehita
SHEHNAI, -S n Indian wind instrument
SHEIK, -S same as ▸ **sheikh**
SHEIKDOM same as > **sheikhdom**
SHEIKH, -S n Arab chief
SHEIKHA, -S n chief wife of sheikh
SHEIKHS ▸ sheikh
SHEIKS ▸ sheik
SHEILA, -S n girl or woman
SHEILING n hut used by shepherds
SHEITAN, -S n Muslim demon
SHEITEL, -S n traditional wig worn by Orthodox Jewish women
SHEKEL, SHEKALIM, -IM, -S n monetary unit of Israel
SHELDUCK n large brightly coloured wild duck of Europe and Asia
SHELF, -ED, -ING, -S, SHELVES n board fixed horizontally for holding things ▷ vb put on a shelf
SHELFFUL
SHELFIER ▸ shelfy
SHELFING ▸ shelf
SHELFS ▸ shelf
SHELFY, SHELFIER ▸ shelf
SHELL, -ED, -ING, -S n hard outer covering of an egg, nut, or certain animals ▷ vb take the shell from
SHELLAC, -S n resin used in varnishes ▷ vb coat with shellac
SHELLACK vb shellac
SHELLACS ▸ shellac
SHELLED ▸ shell
SHELLER, -S ▸ shell
SHELLFUL ▸ shell
SHELLIER ▸ shelly
SHELLING ▸ shell
SHELLS ▸ shell
SHELLY, SHELLIER ▸ shell
SHELTA, -S n secret language used by some travelling people in Britain and Ireland
SHELTER, -S n structure providing protection from danger or the weather ▷ vb give shelter to
SHELTERY

SHELTIE n small dog similar to a collie
SHELTY, SHELTIES same as ▸ **sheltie**
SHELVE, -D vb put aside or postpone
SHELVER -S
SHELVES ▸ shelf
SHELVIER ▸ shelvy
SHELVING n (material for) shelves
SHELVY, SHELVIER adj having shelves
SHEN n (in Chinese thought) spiritual element of the psyche
SHENAI, -S same as ▸ **shehnai**
SHEND, -ING, -S, SHENT vb put to shame
SHEOL, -S n hell
SHEPHERD n person who tends sheep ▷ vb guide or watch over (people)
SHEQALIM n plural of sheqel
SHEQEL, -S same as ▸ **shekel**
SHERANG, -S n person in charge
SHERBERT same as ▸ **sherbet**
SHERBET, -S n fruit-flavoured fizzy powder
SHERD, -S same as ▸ **shard**
SHERE old spelling of ▸ **sheer**
SHEREEF, -S same as ▸ **sherif**
SHERIA, -S same as ▸ **sharia**
SHERIAT, -S n Muslim religious law
SHERIF, ASHRAF, -S n descendant of Mohammed through his daughter Fatima
SHERIFF, -S n (in the US) chief law enforcement officer of a county
SHERIFS ▸ sherif
SHERLOCK n detective ▷ vb investigate (something)
SHERO, -ES n woman considered a hero
SHEROOT, -S n cheroot
SHERPA, -S n official who assists at a summit meeting
SHERRIED adj flavoured with sherry
SHERRIES ▸ sherry
SHERRIS n old form of sherry
SHERRY, SHERRIES n pale or dark brown fortified wine
SHERWANI n long coat closed up to the neck, worn by men in India
SHES ▸ she
SHET, -S, -TING vb old form of shut
SHETLAND n type of wool spun in the Shetland islands

SHETS ▸ shet
SHETTING ▸ shet
SHEUCH, -ED, -S n ditch or trough ▷ vb dig
SHEUGH, -ED, -S same as ▸ **sheuch**
SHEVA, -S n mark in Hebrew writing
SHEW, -ED, -ING, -N, -S archaic spelling of ▸ **show**
SHEWEL, -S n old word meaning scarecrow
SHEWER, -S ▸ shew
SHEWING ▸ shew
SHEWN ▸ shew
SHEWS ▸ shew
SHH interj sound made to ask for silence
SHHH interj interjection requesting quietness
SHIAI, -S n judo contest
SHIATSU, -S n type of massage
SHIATZU, -S n shiatsu
SHIBAH, -S n Jewish period of mourning
SHICKER, -S n alcoholic drink
SHIDDER, -S n old word meaning female animal
SHIDDUCH n arranged marriage
SHIED ▸ shy
SHIEL, -ED, -S vb sheal
SHIELD, -ED, -S n piece of armour carried on the arm to protect the body from blows or missiles ▷ vb protect
SHIELDER
SHIELED ▸ shiel
SHIELING n rough hut or shelter used by people tending cattle on high or remote ground
SHIELS ▸ shiel
SHIER, -S n horse that shies habitually
SHIES ▸ shy
SHIEST ▸ shy
SHIFT, -ED, -ING, -S vb move ▷ n shifting
SHIFTER -S
SHIFTIER ▸ shifty
SHIFTILY ▸ shifty
SHIFTING ▸ shift
SHIFTS ▸ shift
SHIFTY, SHIFTIER adj evasive or untrustworthy
SHIGELLA n type of rod-shaped Gram-negative bacterium
SHIITAKE n kind of mushroom widely used in Oriental cookery
SHIKAR, -S n hunting, esp big-game hunting ▷ vb hunt (game, esp big game)

S

SHIKARA, -S n (in Kashmir) light, flat-bottomed boat

SHIKAREE same as ▸ shikari

SHIKARI, -S n (in India) a hunter

SHIKARS ▸ shikar

SHIKKER, -S n Yiddish term for drunk person

SHIKRA, -S n small Asian sparrowhawk

SHILINGI n money unit in Tanzania

SHILL, -ED, -S n confidence trickster's assistant ▷ vb act as a shill

SHILLALA n short Irish club or cudgel

SHILLED ▸ shill

SHILLING n former British coin

SHILLS ▸ shill

SHILPIT adj puny

SHILY ▸ shy

SHIM, -MED, -MING, -S n thin strip of material placed between two close surfaces to fill a gap ▷ vb fit or fill up with a shim

SHIMAAL, -S n hot Middle Eastern wind

SHIMMED ▸ shim

SHIMMER, -S n (shine with) a faint unsteady light ▷ vb shine with a faint unsteady light

SHIMMERY adj shining with a glistening or tremulous light

SHIMMEY, -S n chemise

SHIMMIED ▸ shimmy

SHIMMIES ▸ shimmy

SHIMMING ▸ shim

SHIMMY, SHIMMIED, SHIMMIES n American ragtime dance ▷ vb dance the shimmy

SHIMS ▸ shim

SHIN, -NED, -NING, -S n front of the lower leg ▷ vb climb by using the hands or arms and legs

SHINBONE n tibia

SHINDIES ▸ shindy

SHINDIG, -S n noisy party

SHINDY, SHINDIES, -S n quarrel or commotion

SHINE, -D, -S, SHINING, SHONE vb give out or reflect light; cause to gleam ▷ n brightness or lustre

SHINER, -S n black eye

SHINES ▸ shine

SHINESS ▸ shy

SHINGLE, -D n wooden roof tile ▷ vb cover (a roof) with shingles

SHINGLER

SHINGLES n disease causing a rash of small blisters along a nerve

SHINGLY ▸ shingle

SHINIER ▸ shiny

SHINIES ▸ shiny

SHINIEST ▸ shiny

SHINILY ▸ shiny

SHINING ▸ shine

SHINKIN, -S n worthless person

SHINLEAF n wintergreen

SHINNE, -S n old form of chin

SHINNED ▸ shin

SHINNERY n American oak tree

SHINNES ▸ shinne

SHINNEY, -S vb climb with hands and legs

SHINNIED ▸ shinny

SHINNIES ▸ shinny

SHINNING ▸ shin

SHINNY, SHINNIED, SHINNIES same as ▸ shinty

SHINOLA, -S n tradename of a kind of boot polish

SHINS ▸ shin

SHINTY, SHINTIED, SHINTIES n game like hockey ▷ vb play shinty

SHINY, SHINIER, SHINIES, SHINIEST adj bright and polished

SHIP, -PED, -PING, -S n large seagoing vessel ▷ vb send or transport by carrier, esp a ship

SHIPFUL, -S n amount carried by ship

SHIPLAP, -S n method of constructing ship hull

SHIPLESS ▸ ship

SHIPLOAD n quantity carried by a ship

SHIPMAN, SHIPMEN n master or captain of a ship

SHIPMATE n sailor serving on the same ship as another

SHIPMEN ▸ shipman

SHIPMENT n act of shipping cargo

SHIPPED ▸ ship

SHIPPEN, -S n dialect word for cattle shed

SHIPPER, -S n person or company that ships

SHIPPING ▸ ship

SHIPPO, -S n Japanese enamel work

SHIPPON, -S n dialect word for cattle shed

SHIPPOS ▸ shippo

SHIPS ▸ ship

SHIPSIDE n part of wharf next to ship

SHIPTIME n arrival time of a supply ship

SHIPWAY, -S n structure on which a vessel is built, then launched

SHIPWORM n type of wormlike marine bivalve mollusc

SHIPYARD n place where ships are built

SHIR, -S n gathering in material

SHIRALEE n swag

SHIRAZ, -ES n variety of black grape used for wine

SHIRE, -D, -S, SHIRING n county ▷ vb refresh or rest

SHIREMAN, SHIREMEN n sheriff

SHIRES ▸ shire

SHIRING ▸ shire

SHIRK, -ED, -ING, -S vb avoid (duty or work) ▷ n person who shirks

SHIRKER -S

SHIRR, -ED, -ING, -S vb gather (fabric) into parallel rows to decorate a dress, etc ▷ n series of gathered rows decorating a dress, etc

SHIRRA, -S old Scots word for ▸ sheriff

SHIRRED ▸ shirr

SHIRRING ▸ shirr

SHIRRS ▸ shirr

SHIRS ▸ shir

SHIRT, -ED, -S n garment for the upper part of the body ▷ vb put a shirt on

SHIRTIER ▸ shirty

SHIRTILY ▸ shirty

SHIRTING n fabric used in making men's shirts

SHIRTS ▸ shirt

SHIRTY, SHIRTIER adj bad-tempered or annoyed

SHISH adj as in shish kebab dish of meat and vegetables grilled on skewers

SHISHA, -S same as ▸ hookah

SHISO, -S n Asian plant with aromatic leaves

SHIST, -S n schist

SHITAKE, -S same as ▸ shiitake

SHITTAH, -S, SHITTIM n tree mentioned in the Old Testament

SHITWORK n work considered to be menial or routine

SHITZU, -S n breed of small dog with long, silky fur

SHIUR, -IM n lesson in which a passage of the Talmud is studied

SHIV, -S, -VED, -VING variant spelling of ► chiv

SHIVA, -S variant of ► shivah

SHIVAH, -S n Jewish period of formal mourning

SHIVAREE n discordant mock serenade to newlyweds, made with pans, kettles, etc

SHIVAS ► shiva

SHIVE, -S n flat cork or bung for wide-mouthed bottles

SHIVER, -ED n vb tremble, as from cold or fear ▷ n shivering
SHIVERER

SHIVERY adj inclined to shiver or tremble

SHIVES ► shive

SHIVITI, -S n Jewish decorative plaque with religious message

SHIVOO, -S n Australian word meaning rowdy party

SHIVS ► shiv

SHIVVED ► shiv

SHIVVING ► shiv

SHIZZLE, -S n form of US rap slang

SHLEMIEL same as ► schlemiel

SHLEP, -PED, -S vb schlep

SHLEPP, -S vb schlep

SHLEPPED ► shlep

SHLEPPER ► shlep

SHLEPPS ► shlepp

SHLEPPY adj dingy, shabby, or rundown

SHLEPS ► shlep

SHLOCK, -S n something of poor quality
SHLOCKY

SHLOSHIM n period of thirty days' deep mourning following a death

SHLUB, -S same as ► schlub

SHLUMP, -ED, -S vb move in lazy way
SHLUMPY

SHMALTZ n schmaltz
SHMALTZY

SHMATTE, -S n rag

SHMEAR, -ED, -S same as ► schmear

SHMEER, -ED, -S same as ► schmear

SHMEK, -S n smell

SHMO, -ES same as ► schmo

SHMOCK, -S n despicable person

SHMOE same as ► schmoe

SHMOES ► shmo

SHMOOSE, -D, -S variant of ► schmooze

SHMOOZE, -D, -S variant of ► schmooze

SHMOOZER same as > schmoozer

SHMOOZES ► shmooze

SHMOOZY adj talking casually, gossipy

SHMUCK, -S n despicable person

SHMUCKY same as ► schmucky

SHNAPPS same as ► schnapps

SHNAPS n schnapps

SHNOOK, -S n stupid person

SHNORRER same as > schnorrer

SHO adj sure, as pronounced in southern US

SHOAL, -ED, -ER, -EST, -ING, -S n large number of fish swimming together ▷ vb make or become shallow ▷ adj (of the draught of a vessel) drawing little water

SHOALIER ► shoaly

SHOALING ► shoal

SHOALS ► shoal

SHOALY, SHOALIER adj shallow

SHOAT, -S n piglet that has recently been weaned

SHOCHET, -S n (in Judaism) a person licensed to slaughter animals and birds

SHOCHU, -S n type of Japanese alcoholic spirit

SHOCK, -ED, -S vb horrify, disgust, or astonish ▷ n sudden violent emotional disturbance ▷ adj bushy

SHOCKER, -S n person or thing that shocks or horrifies

SHOCKING adj causing horror, disgust, or astonishment

SHOCKS ► shock

SHOD ► shoe

SHODDEN vb old form of shod

SHODDIER ► shoddy

SHODDIES ► shoddy

SHODDILY ► shoddy

SHODDY, SHODDIER, SHODDIES adj made or done badly ▷ n yarn or fabric made from wool waste or clippings

SHODER, -S n skins used in making gold leaf

SHOE, SHOD, -D, -S n outer covering for the foot, ending below the ankle ▷ vb fit with a shoe or shoes

SHOEBILL n large wading bird of tropical E African swamps

SHOEBOX n cardboard box for shoes

SHOED ► shoe

SHOEHORN n smooth curved implement inserted at the heel of a shoe to ease the foot into it ▷ vb cram (people or things) into a very small space

SHOEING, -S ► shoe

SHOELACE n cord for fastening shoes

SHOELESS ► shoe

SHOEPAC, -S n waterproof boot

SHOEPACK n waterproof boot

SHOEPACS ► shoepac

SHOER, -S n person who shoes horses

SHOES ► shoe

SHOETREE n piece of metal, wood, or plastic inserted in a shoe to keep its shape

SHOFAR, -S, SHOFROTH n ram's horn sounded in Jewish synagogue

SHOG, -GED, -GING, -S vb shake

SHOGGLE, -D, -S vb shake
SHOGGLY

SHOGI, -S n Japanese chess

SHOGS ► shog

SHOGUN, -S n Japanese chief military commander
SHOGUNAL

SHOJI, -S n Japanese rice-paper screen in a sliding wooden frame

SHOJO n genre of Japanese comics intended for girls

SHOLA, -S n Indian plant

SHOLOM, -S n Hebrew greeting

SHONE ► shine

SHONEEN, -S n Irishman who imitates English ways

SHONKY, SHONKIER adj unreliable or unsound

SHOO, -ED, -ING, -S interj go away! ▷ vb drive away as by saying 'shoo'

SHOOFLY n as in shoofly pie US dessert similar to treacle tart

SHOOGIE, -D, -S vb Scots word meaning swing

SHOOGLE, -D, -S vb shake, sway, or rock back and forth ▷ n rocking motion
SHOOGLY

SHOOING ► shoo

SHOOK, -S n set of parts ready for assembly

SHOOL, -ED, -ING, -S dialect word for ► shovel

SHOOLE, -S *dialect word for*
► **shovel**
SHOOLED ► **shool**
SHOOLES ► **shoole**
SHOOLING ► **shool**
SHOOLS ► **shool**
SHOON *plural of* ► **shoe**
SHOORA, -S *same as* ► **shura**
SHOOS ► **shoo**
SHOOSH, -ED, -ES *vb* make a
rushing sound when moving
SHOOT, -ING, -S *vb* hit,
wound, or kill with a missile
fired from a weapon ▷ *n* new
branch or sprout of a plant
SHOOTER, -S *n* person or
thing that shoots
SHOOTIE, -S *n* type of shoe
that covers the ankle
SHOOTING ► **shoot**
SHOOTIST *n* person who
shoots
SHOOTOUT *n* conclusive
gunfight
SHOOTS ► **shoot**
SHOP, -PED, -PING, -S *n* place
for sale of goods and services
▷ *vb* visit a shop or shops to
buy goods
SHOPBOT, -S *n* price-
comparison website
SHOPBOY, -S *n* boy working
in shop
SHOPE *n* old form of shape
SHOPFUL, -S *n* amount
stored in shop
SHOPGIRL *n* girl working
in shop
SHOPHAR, -S *same as*
► **shofar**
SHOPLESS *adj* (of an area)
having no shops
SHOPLIFT *vb* steal from shop
SHOPMAN, SHOPMEN *n*
man working in shop
SHOPPE, -S *old-fashioned
spelling of* ► **shop**
SHOPPED ► **shop**
SHOPPER, -S *n* person who
buys goods in a shop
SHOPPES ► **shoppe**
SHOPPIER ► **shoppy**
SHOPPIES ► **shoppy**
SHOPPING ► **shop**
**SHOPPY, SHOPPIER,
SHOPPIES** *adj* of a shop ▷ *n*
shop assistant
SHOPS ► **shop**
SHOPTALK *n* conversation
about one's work, carried on
outside working hours
SHOPWORN *adj* worn or
faded from being displayed
in a shop
SHORAN, -S *n* short-range
radar system

SHORE, -D, -S *n* edge of a sea
or lake ▷ *vb* prop or support
SHOREMAN, SHOREMEN *n*
person who lives on shore
SHORER, -S ► **shore**
SHORES ► **shore**
SHORING, -S ► **shore**
SHORL, -S *n* black mineral
SHORN *past participle of*
► **shear**
SHORT, -ED, -ER, -EST, -ING
adj not long ▷ *adv* abruptly
▷ *n* drink of spirits ▷ *vb*
short-circuit
SHORTAGE *n* deficiency
SHORTARM *adj* (of a punch)
with the arm bent
SHORTCUT *n* route that is
shorter than the usual one
SHORTED ► **short**
SHORTEN, -S *vb* make or
become shorter
SHORTER ► **short**
SHORTEST ► **short**
SHORTIA, -S *n* American
flowering plant
SHORTIE, -S *n* person or thing
that is extremely short
SHORTING ► **short**
SHORTISH ► **short**
SHORTLY *adv* soon
SHORTS *pl n* trousers
reaching the top of the thigh
or partway to the knee
SHORTY *same as* ► **shortie**
SHOT, -S, -TED, -TING *vb* load
with shot
SHOTE, -S *same as* ► **shoat**
SHOTGUN, -S *n* gun for
firing a charge of shot at
short range ▷ *adj* involving
coercion or duress ▷ *vb*
shoot or threaten with or as if
with a shotgun
SHOTHOLE *n* drilled hole in
to which explosive is put for
blasting
SHOTS ► **shot**
SHOTT, -S *n* shallow
temporary salt lake or marsh
in the North African desert
SHOTTE, -S *n* old form of
shoat
SHOTTED ► **shot**
SHOTTEN *adj* (of fish, esp
herring) having recently
spawned
SHOTTES ► **shotte**
SHOTTING ► **shot**
SHOTTLE, -S *n* small drawer
SHOTTS ► **shott**
SHOUGH, -S *n* old word
meaning lapdog
SHOULD ► **shall**
SHOULDER *n* part of the body
to which an arm, foreleg, or

wing is attached ▷ *vb* bear (a
burden or responsibility)
SHOULDST *form of the past
tense of* ► **shall**
SHOUSE, -S *n* toilet ▷ *adj*
unwell or in poor spirits
SHOUT, -ED, -ING, -S *n* loud
cry ▷ *vb* cry out loudly
SHOUTER -S
SHOUTHER *Scots form of*
► **shoulder**
SHOUTIER ► **shouty**
SHOUTING ► **shout**
SHOUTOUT *n* public greeting,
esp one broadcast via
television or radio
SHOUTS ► **shout**
SHOUTY, SHOUTIER *adj*
characterized by or involving
shouting
SHOVE, -D, -S *vb* push roughly
▷ *n* rough push
SHOVEL, -ED, -S *n* tool for
lifting or moving loose
material ▷ *vb* lift or move as
with a shovel
SHOVELER *n* type of duck
SHOVELS ► **shovel**
SHOVER, -S ► **shove**
SHOVES ► **shove**
SHOVING, -S *n* act of pushing
hard
SHOW, -ED, -N, -S *vb* make,
be, or become noticeable or
visible ▷ *n* public exhibition
SHOWABLE
SHOWBIZ *n* entertainment
industry including theatre,
films, and TV
SHOWBOAT *n* paddle-wheel
river steamer with a theatre
and a repertory company
▷ *vb* perform or behave in a
showy and flamboyant way
SHOWBOX *n* box containing
showman's material
SHOWCASE *n* situation in
which something is displayed
to best advantage ▷ *vb*
exhibit or display ▷ *adj*
displayed or meriting display
as in a showcase
SHOWD, -ED, -ING, -S *vb*
rock or sway to and fro ▷ *n*
rocking motion
SHOWDOWN *n*
confrontation that settles a
dispute
SHOWDS ► **showd**
SHOWED ► **show**
SHOWER, -ED, -S *n* kind
of bath in which a person
stands while being sprayed
with water ▷ *vb* wash in a
shower
SHOWERER
SHOWERY

SHOWGHE, -S *n* old word meaning lapdog

SHOWGIRL *n* girl who appears in shows, etc, esp as a singer or dancer

SHOWGOER *n* member of the audience of a play, film, or show

SHOWIER ▸ showy

SHOWIEST ▸ showy

SHOWILY ▸ showy

SHOWING, -S ▸ show

SHOWJUMP *vb* take part in a showjumping competition

SHOWMAN, SHOWMEN *n* man skilled at presenting anything spectacularly

SHOWN ▸ show

SHOWOFF, -S *n* person who makes a vain display of himself or herself

SHOWRING *n* area where animals are displayed for sale or competition

SHOWROOM *n* room in which goods for sale are on display

SHOWS ▸ show

SHOWTIME *n* time when show begins

SHOWY, SHOWIER, SHOWIEST *adj* gaudy

SHOWYARD *n* yard where cattle are displayed

SHOYU, -S *n* Japanese variety of soy sauce

SHRADDHA *n* Hindu offering to an ancestor

SHRANK ▸ shrink

SHRAPNEL *n* artillery shell filled with pellets which scatter on explosion

SHRED, -DED, -S *n* long narrow strip torn from something ▷ *vb* tear to shreds

SHREDDER

SHREDDY

SHREEK, -ED, -S old spelling of ▸ shriek

SHREIK, -ED, -S old spelling of ▸ shriek

SHREW, -ED, -ING, -S *n* small mouselike animal ▷ *vb* curse or damn

SHREWD, -ER *adj* clever and perceptive

SHREWDIE *n* shrewd person

SHREWDLY ▸ shrewd

SHREWED ▸ shrew

SHREWING ▸ shrew

SHREWISH *adj* bad-tempered and nagging

SHREWS ▸ shrew

SHRI, -S *n* Indian title of respect

SHRIECH old spelling of ▸ shriek

SHRIEK, -ED, -S *n* shrill cry ▷ *vb* utter (with) a shriek

SHRIEKER

SHRIEKY

SHRIEVAL *adj* of or relating to a sheriff

SHRIEVE, -D, -S archaic word for ▸ sheriff

SHRIFT, -S *n* act or an instance of shriving or being shriven

SHRIGHT, -S *n* old word meaning shriek

SHRIKE, -D, -S, SHRIKING *n* songbird with a heavy hooked bill ▷ *vb* archaic word for shriek

SHRILL, -ED, -ER, -S *adj* (of a sound) sharp and high-pitched ▷ *vb* utter shrilly

SHRILLY

SHRIMP, -ED, -S *n* small edible shellfish ▷ *vb* fish for shrimps

SHRIMPER

SHRIMPY

SHRINAL ▸ shrine

SHRINE, -D, -S, SHRINING *n* place of worship associated with a sacred person or object ▷ *vb* enshrine

SHRINK, SHRANK, -S, SHRUNK *vb* become or make smaller ▷ *n* psychiatrist

SHRINKER

SHRIS ▸ shri

SHRITCH *vb* old word meaning shriek

SHRIVE, -D, -N, -S, SHRIVING *vb* hear the confession of (a penitent)

SHRIVEL, -S *vb* shrink and wither

SHRIVEN ▸ shrive

SHRIVER, -S ▸ shrive

SHRIVES ▸ shrive

SHRIVING ▸ shrive

SHROFF, -ED, -S *n* (in China and Japan) expert employed to identify counterfeit money ▷ *vb* test (money) and separate out the counterfeit and base

SHROUD, -ED, -S *n* piece of cloth used to wrap a dead body ▷ *vb* conceal

SHROUDY

SHROVE, -D, -S, SHROVING *vb* dialect word meaning to observe Shrove-tide

SHROW, -ED, -ING, -S *vb* old form of shrew

SHROWD *adj* old form of shrewd

SHROWED ▸ shrow

SHROWING ▸ shrow

SHROWS ▸ shrow

SHRUB, -BED, -S *n* woody plant smaller than a tree ▷ *vb* plant shrubs

SHRUBBY *adj* consisting of, planted with, or abounding in shrubs

SHRUBS ▸ shrub

SHRUG, -GED, -S *vb* raise and then drop (the shoulders) as a sign of indifference or doubt ▷ *n* shrugging

SHRUNK ▸ shrink

SHRUNKEN *adj* reduced in size

SHTCHI, -S *n* Russian cabbage soup

SHTETEL, -S same as ▸ shtetl

SHTETL, -S *n* Jewish community in Eastern Europe

SHTICK, -S *n* comedian's routine

SHTICKY

SHTIK, -S *n* shtick

SHTOOK, -S ▸ took

SHTOOM *adj* silent

SHTUCK, -S *n* trouble

SHTUM *adj* silent

SHTUMM *adj* silent

SHUCK, -ED, -ING *n* outer covering of something ▷ *vb* remove the shucks from

SHUCKER -S

SHUCKS *pl n* something of little value ▷ *interj* exclamation of disappointment, annoyance, etc

SHUDDER, -S *vb* shake or tremble violently, esp with horror ▷ *n* shaking or trembling

SHUDDERY

SHUFFLE, -D, -S *vb* walk without lifting the feet ▷ *n* shuffling

SHUFFLER

SHUFTI, -S same as ▸ shufty

SHUFTIES ▸ shufty

SHUFTIS ▸ shufti

SHUFTY, SHUFTIES *n* look

SHUGGY, SHUGGIES *n* swing, as at a fairground

SHUL, -N, -S *n* Yiddish word for > synagogue

SHULE, -D, -S, SHULING *vb* saunter

SHULN ▸ shul

SHULS ▸ shul

SHUMAI *pl n* (in Japan) small stuffed dumplings

SHUN, -NED, -NING, -S *vb* avoid

SHUNLESS adj old word meaning not to be shunned
SHUNNED ► shun
SHUNNER, -S ► shun
SHUNNING ► shun
SHUNPIKE vb take side road to avoid toll at turnpike
SHUNS ► shun
SHUNT, -ED, -ING, -S vb move (objects or people) to a different position ▷ n shunting
SHUNTER, -S n small railway locomotive used for manoeuvring coaches
SHUNTING ► shunt
SHUNTS ► shunt
SHURA, -S n consultative council or assembly
SHURIKEN n Japanese weapon with blades or points, thrown by hand
SHUSH, -ED, -ES, -ING interj be quiet! ▷ vb quiet by saying 'shush'
SHUSHER -S
SHUT, -S, -TING vb bring together or fold, close
SHUTDOWN n closing of a factory, shop, or other business ▷ vb discontinue operations permanently
SHUTE, -D, -S, SHUTING variant of ► chute
SHUTEYE, -S n sleep
SHUTING ► shute
SHUTOFF, -S n device that shuts something off
SHUTOUT, -S n game in which the opposing team does not score
SHUTS ► shut
SHUTTER, -S n hinged doorlike cover for closing off a window ▷ vb close or equip with a shutter
SHUTTING ► shut
SHUTTLE, -D, -S n bobbin-like device used in weaving ▷ vb move by or as if by a shuttle
SHUTTLER
SHVITZ, -ED, -ES vb sweat
SHWA, -S same as ► schwa
SHWANPAN same as ► swanpan
SHWAS ► shwa
SHWESHWE n African cotton print fabric
SHY, SHIED, SHIES, SHIEST, -EST, -ING adj not at ease in company ▷ vb start back in fear ▷ n throw
SHYER -S
SHYISH ► shy

SHYLOCK, -S vb lend money at an exorbitant rate of interest
SHYLY ► shy
SHYNESS ► shy
SHYPOO, -S n liquor of poor quality
SHYSTER, -S n person who uses discreditable or unethical methods
SI same as ► te
SIAL, -S n silicon-rich and aluminium-rich rocks of the earth's continental upper crust
SIALIC
SIALID, -S n species of fly
SIALIDAN
SIALOID adj resembling saliva
SIALON, -S n type of ceramic
SIALS ► sial
SIAMANG, -S n large black gibbon
SIAMESE, -D, -S variant of ► siameze
SIAMEZE, -D, -S vb join together
SIB, -S n blood relative
SIBB, -S n sib
SIBILANT adj hissing ▷ n consonant pronounced with a hissing sound
SIBILATE vb pronounce or utter (words or speech) with a hissing sound
SIBILOUS ► sibilant
SIBLING, -S n brother or sister
SIBS ► sib
SIBSHIP, -S n group of children of the same parents
SIBYL, -S n (in ancient Greece and Rome) prophetess
SIBYLIC
SIBYLLIC
SIC, -CED, -CING, -S adv thus ▷ vb attack
SICARIO, -S n hired gunman, esp in Latin America
SICCAN adj Scots word meaning such
SICCAR adj sure
SICCED ► sic
SICCING ► sic
SICCITY n dryness
SICE, -S same as ► syce
SICH adj old form of such
SICHT, -ED, -ING, -S Scot word for ► sight
SICK, -ED, -ER, -EST, -ING, -S adj vomiting or likely to vomit ▷ n vomit ▷ vb vomit
SICKBAY, -S n room for the treatment of sick people
SICKBED, -S n bed where sick person lies
SICKED ► sick

SICKEE, -S n person off work through illness
SICKEN, -ED, -S vb make nauseated or disgusted
SICKENER n something that induces sickness or nausea
SICKENS ► sicken
SICKER ► sick
SICKERLY adv Scots word meaning surely
SICKEST ► sick
SICKIE, -S n day of sick leave from work
SICKING ► sick
SICKISH ► sick
SICKLE, -D, -S, SICKLING n tool with a curved blade for cutting grass or grain ▷ vb cut with a sickle
SICKLIED ► sickly
SICKLIER ► sickly
SICKLIES ► sickly
SICKLILY ► sickly
SICKLING ► sickle
SICKLY, SICKLIED, SICKLIER, SICKLIES adj unhealthy, weak ▷ adv suggesting sickness ▷ vb make sickly
SICKNESS n particular illness or disease
SICKOUT, -S n industrial action in which all workers report sick simultaneously
SICKROOM n room to which a person who is ill is confined
SICKS ► sick
SICKY n day off work due to illness
SICLIKE adj Scots word meaning suchlike
SICS ► sic
SIDA, -S n Australian hemp plant
SIDALCEA n type of perennial N American plant
SIDAS ► sida
SIDDHA, -S n (in Hinduism) person who has achieved perfection
SIDDHI, -S n (in Hinduism) power attained with perfection
SIDDUR, -IM, -S n Jewish prayer book
SIDE, -D, -S n line or surface that borders anything ▷ adj at or on the side
SIDEARM, -S n weapon worn on belt ▷ vb provide with a sidearm
SIDEBAND n frequency band either above or below the carrier frequency

SIDEBAR, **-S** n small newspaper article beside larger one

SIDEBONE n damage to the cartilage in a horse's hoof

SIDEBURN n strip of whiskers down one side of a man's face

SIDECAR, **-S** n small passenger car on the side of a motorcycle

SIDED ▷ side

SIDEDLY adv pertaining to given number of sides

SIDEHILL n side of hill

SIDEKICK n close friend or associate

SIDELESS adj without sides

SIDELINE n subsidiary interest or source of income ▷ vb prevent (a player) from taking part in a game

SIDELING adj to one side ▷ adv sideways ▷ n slope, esp on the side of a road

SIDELOCK n long lock of hair on side of head

SIDELONG adj sideways ▷ adv obliquely

SIDEMAN, **SIDEMEN** n member of a dance band or a jazz group other than the leader

SIDEMEAT n meat from the side of a pig

SIDEMEN ▷ sideman

SIDENOTE n note written in margin

SIDEPATH n minor path

SIDER, **-S** n one who sides with another

SIDERAL adj from the stars

SIDERATE vb strike violently

SIDEREAL adj of or determined with reference to the stars

SIDERITE n pale yellow to brownish-black mineral

SIDEROAD n (esp in Ontario) a road going at right angles to concession roads

SIDERS ▷ sider

SIDES ▷ side

SIDESHOW n entertainment offered along with the main show

SIDESLIP same as ▷ slip

SIDESMAN, **SIDESMEN** n man elected to help the parish church warden

SIDESPIN n horizontal spin put on ball

SIDESTEP vb dodge (an issue) ▷ n movement to one side, such as in dancing or boxing

SIDEWALK n paved path for pedestrians, at the side of a road

SIDEWALL n either of the sides of a pneumatic tyre between the tread and the rim

SIDEWARD adj directed or moving towards one side ▷ adv towards one side

SIDEWAY variant of ▷ sideways

SIDEWAYS adv or from the side ▷ adj moving or directed to or from one side

SIDEWISE adv sideways

SIDH pl n fairy people

SIDHA, **-S** n (in Hinduism) person who has achieved perfection

SIDHE pl n inhabitants of fairyland

SIDING, **-S** n short stretch of railway track on which trains are shunted from the main line

SIDLE, **-D**, **-S**, **SIDLING** vb walk in a furtive manner ▷ n sideways movement

SIDLER **-S**

SIECLE, **-S** n century, period, or era

SIEGE, **-D**, **-S**, **SIEGING** n surrounding and blockading of a place ▷ vb lay siege to

SIEGER, **-S** n person who besieges

SIEGES ▷ siege

SIEGING ▷ siege

SIELD adj (archaic) provided with a ceiling

SIEMENS n SI unit of electrical conductance

SIEN, **-S** n old word meaning scion

SIENITE, **-S** n type of igneous rock

SIENNA, **-S** n reddish- or yellowish-brown pigment made from natural earth

SIENS ▷ sien

SIENT, **-S** n old word meaning scion

SIEROZEM n type of soil

SIERRA, **-S** n range of mountains in Spain or America with jagged peaks

SIERRAN

SIES interj in South Africa, an exclamation of disgust

SIESTA, **-S** n afternoon nap, taken in hot countries

SIETH, **-S** n old form of scythe

SIEUR, **-S** n French word meaning lord

SIEVE, **-D**, **-S**, **SIEVING** n utensil with mesh through which a substance is sifted or strained ▷ vb sift or strain through a sieve

SIEVERT, **-S** n derived SI unit of dose equivalent, equal to 1 joule per kilogram

SIEVES ▷ sieve

SIEVING ▷ sieve

SIF adj South African slang for disgusting

SIFAKA, **-S** n either of two large rare arboreal lemuroid primates

SIFFLE, **-D**, **-S**, **SIFFLING** vb whistle

SIFFLEUR n male professional whistler

SIFFLING ▷ siffle

SIFREI ▷ sefer

SIFT, **-ED**, **-ING**, **-S** vb remove the coarser particles from a substance with a sieve

SIFTER **-S**

SIFTINGS pl n material or particles separated out by or as if by a sieve

SIFTS ▷ sift

SIG, **-S** n short for signature

SIGANID, **-S** n tropical fish

SIGH, **-ED**, **-S** n long audible breath expressing sadness, tiredness, relief, or longing ▷ vb utter a sigh

SIGHER **-S**

SIGHFUL ▷ sigh

SIGHING, **-S** n act of sighing

SIGHLESS ▷ sigh

SIGHLIKE ▷ sigh

SIGHS ▷ sigh

SIGHT, **-ING**, **-S** n ability to see ▷ vb catch sight of

SIGHTED adj not blind

SIGHTER, **-S** n any of six practice shots allowed to each competitor in a tournament

SIGHTING ▷ sight

SIGHTLY adj pleasing or attractive to see

SIGHTS ▷ sight

SIGHTSEE, **SIGHTSAW** vb visit the famous or interesting sights of (a place)

SIGIL, **-S** n seal or signet

SIGISBEO, **SIGISBEI** n male escort for a married woman

SIGLA, **-S** n list of symbols used in a book

SIGLOS, **SIGLOI** n silver coin of ancient Persia

SIGLUM n symbol used in book

SIGMA, **-S** n 18th letter in the Greek alphabet

S

SIGMATE, -D, -S adj shaped like the Greek letter sigma or the Roman S ⊳ n sigmate thing ⊳ vb add a sigma
SIGMATIC
SIGMOID, -S adj shaped like the letter S ⊳ n S-shaped bend in the final portion of the large intestine
SIGN, -ED, -S n indication of something not immediately or outwardly observable ⊳ vb write (one's name) on (a document or letter) to show its authenticity
SIGNA pl n symbols
SIGNABLE ▶ sign
SIGNAGE, -S n signs collectively
SIGNAL, -ED, -S n sign or gesture to convey information ⊳ adj very important ⊳ vb convey (information) by signal
SIGNALER
SIGNALLY adv conspicuously or especially
SIGNALS ▶ signal
SIGNARY n set of symbols
SIGNED ▶ sign
SIGNEE, -S n person signing document
SIGNER, -S n person who signs something
SIGNET, -ED, -S n small seal used to authenticate documents ⊳ vb stamp or authenticate with a signet
SIGNEUR old spelling of **▶ senior**
SIGNIEUR n old word meaning lord
SIGNIFY vb indicate or suggest
SIGNING, -S n system of communication using hand and arm movements
SIGNIOR, -I, -S same as **▶ signor**
SIGNIORY n old word meaning lordship
SIGNLESS ▶ sign
SIGNOR, -S n Italian term of address equivalent to sir or Mr
SIGNORA, -S n Italian term of address equivalent to madam or Mrs
SIGNORE, -S, SIGNORI n Italian man: a title of respect equivalent to sir
SIGNORIA n government of Italian city
SIGNORS ▶ signor
SIGNORY same as **> seigniory**

SIGNPOST n post bearing a sign that shows the way ⊳ vb mark with signposts
SIGNS ▶ sign
SIGS ▶ sig
SIJO, -S n Korean poem
SIK adj excellent
SIKA, -S n Japanese forest-dwelling deer
SIKE, -S n small stream
SIKER adj old spelling of sicker
SIKES ▶ sike
SIKORSKY n type of helicopter
SIKSIK, -S n Arctic ground squirrel
SILAGE, -D, -S, SILAGING n fodder crop harvested while green and partially fermented in a silo ⊳ vb make silage
SILANE, -S n gas containing silicon
SILASTIC n tradename for a type of flexible silicone rubber
SILD, -S n any of various small young herrings
SILE, -D, -S, SILING vb pour with rain
SILEN, -S n god of woodland
SILENCE, -S n absence of noise or speech ⊳ vb make silent
SILENCED adj (of a member of the clergy) forbidden to preach or perform clerical functions
SILENCER n device to reduce the noise of an engine exhaust or gun
SILENCES ▶ silence
SILENE, -S n type of plant with mostly red or pink flowers, often grown as a garden plant
SILENI ▶ silenus
SILENS ▶ silen
SILENT, -ER, -S adj tending to speak very little ⊳ n silent film
SILENTLY
SILENUS, SILENI n woodland deity
SILER, -S n strainer
SILES ▶ sile
SILESIA, -S n twill-weave fabric of cotton or other fibre
SILEX, -ES n type of heat-resistant glass made from fused quartz
SILICA, -S n hard glossy mineral found as quartz and in sandstone
SILICATE n compound of silicon, oxygen, and a metal

SILICIC adj of, concerned with, or containing silicon or an acid obtained from silicon
SILICIDE n any one of a class of binary compounds formed between silicon and certain metals
SILICIFY vb convert or be converted into silica
SILICIUM rare name for **▶ silicon**
SILICLE, -S same as **▶ silicula**
SILICON, -S n brittle nonmetallic element ⊳ adj denoting an area that contains much high-technology industry
SILICONE n tough synthetic substance made from silicon and used in lubricants
SILICONS ▶ silicon
SILICULA n short broad siliqua occurring in cruciferous plants
SILICULE same as **▶ silicula**
SILING ▶ sile
SILIQUA, -E, -S n long dry dehiscent fruit of cruciferous plants such as the wallflower
SILIQUE, -S same as **▶ siliqua**
SILK, -ED, -ING, -S n fibre made by the larva of a certain moth ⊳ vb (of maize) develop long hairlike styles
SILKEN, -ED, -S adj made of silk ⊳ vb make like silk
SILKIE, -S n Scots word for a seal
SILKIER ▶ silky
SILKIES ▶ silkie
SILKIEST ▶ silky
SILKILY ▶ silky
SILKING ▶ silk
SILKLIKE ▶ silk
SILKS ▶ silk
SILKTAIL n waxwing
SILKWEED another name for **▶ milkweed**
SILKWORM n caterpillar that spins a cocoon of silk
SILKY, SILKIER, SILKIEST adj of or like silk
SILL, -S n ledge at the bottom of a window or door
SILLABUB same as **▶ syllabub**
SILLADAR n Indian irregular cavalryman
SILLER, -S n silver ⊳ adj silver
SILLIBUB n syllabub
SILLIER ▶ silly
SILLIES ▶ silly
SILLIEST ▶ silly
SILLILY ▶ silly
SILLOCK, -S n young coalfish
SILLS ▶ sill

SILLY, SILLIER, SILLIES, SILLIEST *adj* foolish ▷ *n* foolish person

SILO, -ED, -ING, -S *n* pit or airtight tower for storing silage or grains ▷ *vb* put in a silo

SILOXANE *n* any of a class of compounds containing alternate silicon and oxygen atoms

SILPHIUM, SILPHIA *n* American flowering wild plant

SILT, -ED, -ING, -S *n* mud deposited by moving water ▷ *vb* fill or be choked with silt

SILTIER ► silty

SILTIEST ► silty

SILTING ► silt

SILTS ► silt

SILTY, SILTIER, SILTIEST ► silt

SILURIAN *adj* formed in the third period of the Palaeozoic

SILURID, -S *n* type of freshwater fish of the family which includes catfish

SILURIST *n* member of ancient Silurian tribe

SILUROID *n* freshwater fish

SILVA, -E, -S *same as* ► **sylva**

SILVAN, -S *same as* ► **sylvan**

SILVAS ► silva

SILVATIC *adj* wild, not domestic

SILVER, -ED, -S *n* white precious metal ▷ *adj* made of or of the colour of silver ▷ *vb* coat with silver

SILVERER

SILVERLY *adv* like silver

SILVERN *adj* silver

SILVERS ► silver

SILVERY *adj* like silver

SILVEX, -ES *n* type of weedkiller

SILVICAL *adj* of trees

SILVICS *n* study of trees

SIM, -S *n* computer game that simulates an activity

SIMA, -S *n* silicon-rich and magnesium-rich rocks of the earth's oceanic crust

SIMAR, -S *variant spelling of* ► **cymar**

SIMARRE, -S *n* woman's loose gown

SIMARS ► simar

SIMARUBA *same as* > **simarouba**

SIMAS ► sima

SIMATIC ► sima

SIMAZINE *n* organic weedkiller

SIMBA, -S *E African word for* ► **lion**

SIMCHA, -S *n* Jewish celebration or festival

SIMI, -S *n* East African sword

SIMIAL *adj* of apes

SIMIAN, -S *n* monkey or ape ▷ *adj* of or resembling a monkey or ape

SIMILAR *adj* alike but not identical

SIMILE, -S *n* figure of speech comparing one thing to another, using 'as' or 'like'

SIMILISE *same as* ► **similize**

SIMILIZE *vb* use similes

SIMILOR, -S *n* alloy used in cheap jewellery

SIMIOID *adj* of apes

SIMIOUS *adj* of apes

SIMIS ► simi

SIMITAR, -S *same as* ► **scimitar**

SIMKIN, -S *word used in India for* ► **champagne**

SIMLIN, -S *n* American variety of squash plant

SIMMER, -ED, -S *vb* cook gently at just below boiling point ▷ *n* state of simmering

SIMNEL, -S *n as in* **simnel cake** fruit cake with marzipan eaten at Easter

SIMOLEON *n* American slang for dollar

SIMONIAC *n* person who is guilty of practising simony

SIMONIES ► simony

SIMONISE *same as* ► **simonize**

SIMONIST ► simony

SIMONIZE *vb* polish with wax

SIMONY, SIMONIES *n* practice of buying or selling Church benefits

SIMOOM, -S *n* hot suffocating sand-laden desert wind

SIMOON, -S *same as* ► **simoom**

SIMORG, -S *n* bird in Persian myth

SIMP, -S *short for* > **simpleton**

SIMPAI, -S *n* Indonesian monkey

SIMPER, -ED, -S *vb* smile in a silly or affected way ▷ *n* simpering smile

SIMPERER

SIMPKIN, -S *word used in India for* > **champagne**

SIMPLE, -D, -S, -ST, SIMPLING *adj* easy to understand or do ▷ *n* simpleton ▷ *vb* archaic word meaning to look for medicinal herbs

SIMPLER -S

SIMPLEX *adj* permitting the transmission of signals in only one direction in a radio circuit ▷ *n* simple not a compound word

SIMPLIFY *vb* make less complicated

SIMPLING ► simple

SIMPLISM *n* quality of being extremely naive

SIMPLIST *n* old word meaning expert in herbal medicine

SIMPLY *adv* in a simple manner

SIMPS ► simp

SIMS ► sim

SIMUL, -S *adj* simultaneous ▷ *n* simultaneous broadcast

SIMULANT *adj* simulating ▷ *n* simulant thing

SIMULAR, -S *n* person or thing that simulates or imitates ▷ *adj* fake

SIMULATE *vb* make a pretence of ▷ *adj* assumed or simulated

SIMULIUM *n* tropical fly

SIMULS ► simul

SIMURG, -S *same as* ► **simurgh**

SIMURGH, -S *n* bird in Persian myth

SIMURGS ► simurg

SIN, -NED, -NING, -S *n* offence or transgression ▷ *vb* commit a sin

SINAPISM *n* mixture of black mustard seeds and an adhesive, applied to the skin

SINCE *prep* during the period of time after ▷ *adv* from that time

SINCERE, -R *adj* without pretence or deceit

SINCIPUT *n* forward upper part of the skull

SIND, -ED, -S *variant of* ► **syne**

SINDING -S

SINDON, -S *n* type of cloth

SINDS ► sind

SINE, -D, -S, SINING *same as* ► **syne**

SINECURE *n* paid job with minimal duties

SINED ► sine

SINES ► sine

SINEW, -ING, -S *n* tough fibrous tissue joining muscle to bone ▷ *vb* make strong

SINEWED *adj* having sinews

SINEWIER ► sinewy

SINEWING ► sinew

SINEWS ► sinew

SINEWY, SINEWIER *adj* lean and muscular**

S

SINFONIA, SINFONIE n symphony orchestra

SINFUL adj guilty of sin

SINFULLY

SING, -S, SUNG vb make musical sounds with the voice ▷ n act or performance of singing

SINGABLE

SINGE, -D, -ING, -S vb burn the surface of ▷ n superficial burn

SINGER, -S n person who sings, esp professionally

SINGES ► singe

SINGING, -S ► sing

SINGLE, -D, SINGLING adj one only ▷ n single thing ▷ vb pick out from others

SINGLES pl n match played with one person on each side

SINGLET, -S n sleeveless vest

SINGLING ► single

SINGLY adv one at a time

SINGS ► sing

SINGSONG n informal singing session ▷ adj (of the voice) repeatedly rising and falling in pitch

SINGULAR adj (of a word or form) denoting one person or thing ▷ n singular form of a word

SINGULT, -S n old word meaning sob

SINH, -S n hyperbolic sine

SINICAL ► sine

SINICISE same as ► sinicize

SINICIZE vb make Chinese

SINING ► sine

SINISTER adj threatening or suggesting evil or harm

SINK, SANK, -S vb submerge (in liquid) ▷ n fixed basin with a water supply and drainage pipe

SINKABLE

SINKAGE, -S n act of sinking or degree to which something sinks or has sunk

SINKER, -S n weight for a fishing line

SINKFUL, -S n amount that can be held in a sink

SINKHOLE n depression in the ground surface where a stream disappears underground

SINKIER ► sinky

SINKIEST ► sinky

SINKING, -S ► sink

SINKS ► sink

SINKY, SINKIER, SINKIEST adj giving underfoot

SINLESS adj free from sin or guilt

SINNED ► sin

SINNER, -ED, -S n person that sins ▷ vb behave like a sinner

SINNET, -S n braided rope

SINNING ► sin

SINOLOGY n study of Chinese culture, etc

SINOPIA, -S, SINOPIE n pigment made from iron ore

SINOPIS n pigment made from iron ore

SINOPITE n iron ore

SINS ► sin

SINSYNE adv Scots word meaning since

SINTER, -ED, -S n whitish porous incrustation deposited from hot springs ▷ vb form large particles from (powders) by heating or pressure

SINTERY

SINUATE, -S vb wind

SINUATED same as ► sinuate

SINUATES ► sinuate

SINUITIS variant of > sinusitis

SINUOSE adj sinuous

SINUOUS adj full of turns or curves

SINUS, -ES n hollow space in a bone, esp an air passage opening into the nose

SINUSOID n blood vessel in certain organs ▷ adj resembling a sinus

SIP, -PED, -PING, -S vb drink in small mouthfuls ▷ n amount sipped

SIPE, -D, -S, SIPING vb soak

SIPHON, -ED, -S n bent tube which uses air pressure to draw liquid from a container ▷ vb draw off thus

SIPHONAL adj like a siphon

SIPHONED ► siphon

SIPHONET n sucking tube on an aphid

SIPHONIC same as ► siphonal

SIPHONS ► siphon

SIPING ► sipe

SIPPABLE adj able to be sipped

SIPPED ► sip

SIPPER, -S ► sip

SIPPET, -S n small piece of toast eaten with soup or gravy

SIPPING ► sip

SIPPLE, -D, -S, SIPPLING vb sip

SIPPY adj as in **sippy cup** infant's drinking cup with a tight-fitting lid and perforated spout

SIPS ► sip

SIR, -RED, -RING, -S n polite term of address for a man ▷ vb call someone 'sir'

SIRCAR, -S n government in India

SIRDAR, -S same as ► sardar

SIRE, -D, -S, SIRING n male parent of a horse or other domestic animal ▷ vb father

SIREE, -S emphasized form of ► sir

SIREN, -S n device making a loud wailing noise as a warning

SIRENIAN n animal such as the dugong and manatee

SIRENIC ► siren

SIRENISE variant of ► sirenize

SIRENIZE vb bewitch

SIRENS ► siren

SIRES ► sire

SIRGANG, -S n Asian bird

SIRI, -S ► betel

SIRIASIS, SIRIASES n sunstroke

SIRIH, -S n betel

SIRING, -S ► sire

SIRIS ► siri

SIRKAR, -S n government in India

SIRLOIN, -S n prime cut of loin of beef

SIRNAME, -D, -S vb old form of surname

SIROC, -S n sirocco

SIROCCO, -S n hot wind blowing from N Africa into S Europe

SIROCS ► siroc

SIRONISE same as ► sironize

SIRONIZE vb treat (a woollen fabric) chemically to prevent it wrinkling after being washed

SIROSET adj of the chemical treatment of woollen fabrics to give a permanent-press effect

SIRRA, -S disrespectful form of ► sir

SIRRAH, -S n contemptuous term used in addressing a man or boy

SIRRAS ► sirra

SIRRED ► sir

SIRREE, -S n form of 'sir' used for emphasis

SIRRING ► sir

SIRS ► sir

SIRTUIN, -S n protein that regulates cell metabolism and ageing

SIRUP, -ED, -ING, -S same as ► syrup

SIRUPIER ► sirupy
SIRUPING ► sirup
SIRUPS ► sirup
SIRUPY, SIRUPIER ► sirup
SIRVENTE n verse form employed by the troubadours of Provence to satirize political themes
SIS, -ES n sister
SISAL, -S n (fibre of) plant used in making ropes
SISERARY n scolding
SISES ► sis
SISKIN, -S n yellow-and-black finch
SISS, -ES shortening of ► sister
SISSIER ► sissy
SISSIES ► sissy
SISSIEST ► sissy
SISSOO, -S n Indian tree
SISSY, SISSIER, SISSIES, SISSIEST n weak or cowardly (person) ▷ adj weak or cowardly
SISSYISH
SIST, -ED, -ING, -S vb Scottish law term meaning stop
SISTER, -ED, -S n girl or woman with the same parents as another person ▷ adj closely related, similar ▷ vb be or be like a sister
SISTERLY adj of or like a sister
SISTERS ► sister
SISTING ► sist
SISTRA ► sistrum
SISTROID adj contained between the convex sides of two intersecting curves
SISTRUM, SISTRA, -S n musical instrument of ancient Egypt consisting of a metal rattle
SISTS ► sist
SIT, SAT, -S vb rest one's body upright on the buttocks
SITAR, -S n Indian stringed musical instrument
SITARIST
SITCOM, -S n situation comedy
SITE, -D, -S n place where something is, was, or is intended to be located ▷ vb provide with a site
SITELLA, -S n type of small generally black-and-white bird
SITES ► site
SITFAST, -S n sore on a horse's back caused by rubbing of the saddle
SITH archaic word for ► since
SITHE, -D, -S, SITHING vb old form of scythe

SITHEE interj look here! listen!
SITHEN adv old word meaning since
SITHENCE adv old word meaning since
SITHENS adv old word meaning since
SITHES ► sithe
SITHING ► sithe
SITING, -S n act of siting
SITKA modifier as in sitka spruce tall North American spruce tree
SITKAMER n sitting room
SITOLOGY n scientific study of food, diet, and nutrition
SITREP, -S n military situation report
SITS ► sit
SITTAR, -S n sitar
SITTELLA variant spelling of ► sitella
SITTEN adj dialect word for in the saddle
SITTER, -S n baby-sitter
SITTINE, -S adj of nuthatch bird family ▷ n type of nuthatch
SITTING, -S ► sit
SITUATE, -D, -S vb place ▷ adj (now used esp in legal contexts) situated
SITULA, -E n bucket-shaped container
SITUP, -S n exercise in which the body is brought into a sitting position
SITUS, -ES n position or location
SITZ n as in sitz bath bath in which the buttocks and hips are immersed in hot water
SITZMARK n depression in the snow where a skier has fallen
SIVER, -S same as ► syver
SIWASH, -ED, -ES vb (in the Pacific Northwest) to camp out with only natural shelter
SIX, -ES n one more than five
SIXAIN, -S n stanza or poem of six lines
SIXAINE, -S n six-line stanza of poetry
SIXAINS ► sixain
SIXER, -S same as ► six
SIXES ► six
SIXFOLD adj having six times as many or as much ▷ adv by six times as many or as much
SIXISH adj around six years of age
SIXMO, -S n book size resulting from folding a sheet of paper into six leaves

SIXPENCE n former British and Australian coin worth six pennies
SIXPENNY adj (of a nail) two inches in length
SIXSCORE n hundred and twenty
SIXTE, -S n sixth of eight basic positions from which a parry or attack can be made in fencing
SIXTEEN, -S n six and ten ▷ adj amounting to sixteen ▷ determiner amounting to sixteen
SIXTES ► sixte
SIXTH, -S n (of) number six in a series ▷ adj coming after the fifth and before the seventh in numbering order ▷ adv after the fifth person, position, etc
SIXTHLY same as ► sixth
SIXTHS ► sixth
SIXTIES ► sixty
SIXTIETH adj being the ordinal number of sixty in numbering order ▷ n one of 60 approximately equal parts of something
SIXTY, SIXTIES n six times ten ▷ adj amounting to sixty
SIXTYISH
SIZABLE adj quite large
SIZABLY ► sizable
SIZAR, -S n undergraduate receiving a maintenance grant from the college
SIZE, -S n dimensions, bigness ▷ vb arrange according to size
SIZEABLE same as ► sizable
SIZEABLY ► sizable
SIZED adj of a specified size
SIZEISM, -S n discrimination on the basis of a person's size
SIZEIST, -S
SIZEL, -S n scrap metal clippings
SIZER, -S ► size
SIZES ► size
SIZIER ► sizy
SIZIEST ► sizy
SIZINESS ► size
SIZING, -S ► size
SIZISM, -S n discrimination against people because of weight
SIZIST, -S
SIZY, SIZIER, SIZIEST ► size
SIZZLE, -D, -S vb make a hissing sound like frying fat ▷ n hissing sound
SIZZLER, -S n something that sizzles
SIZZLES ► sizzle

S

SIZZLING adj extremely hot

SJAMBOK, -S n whip or riding crop made of hide ▷ vb beat with a sjambok

SJOE interj South African exclamation of surprise, admiration, exhaustion, etc

SKA, -S n type of West Indian pop music of the 1960s

SKAG, -S same as ▶ scag

SKAIL, -ED, -ING, -S vb Scots word meaning disperse

SKAITH, -ED, -S vb Scots word meaning injure

SKALD, -S n (in ancient Scandinavia) a bard or minstrel

SKALDIC

SKANGER n insulting Irish word for a young working-class person who wears casual sports clothes

SKANK, -ED, -ING, -S n fast dance to reggae music ▷ vb perform this dance

SKANKER -S

SKANKIER ▶ skanky

SKANKING ▶ skank

SKANKS ▶ skank

SKANKY, SKANKIER adj dirty or unattractive

SKART, -S Scots word for > cormorant

SKARTH, -S Scots word for > cormorant

SKARTS ▶ skart

SKAS ▶ ska

SKAT, -S n three-handed card game using 32 cards

SKATE, -D, -S n boot with a steel blade or sets of wheels attached to the sole ▷ vb glide on or as if on skates

SKATER, -S n person who skates

SKATES ▶ skate

SKATING, -S ▶ skate

SKATOL, -S n skatole

SKATOLE, -S n white or brownish crystalline solid

SKATOLS ▶ skatol

SKATS ▶ skat

SKATT, -S n dialect word meaning throw

SKAW, -S variant of ▶ scaw

SKEAN, -S n kind of double-edged dagger

SKEANE, -S same as ▶ skein

SKEANS ▶ skean

SKEAR, -ED, -ING, -S dialect form of ▶ scare

SKEARIER ▶ skeary

SKEARING ▶ skear

SKEARS ▶ skear

SKEARY, SKEARIER dialect form of ▶ scary

SKED, -DED, -DING, -S vb short for schedule

SKEE, -D, -ING, -S variant spelling of ▶ ski

SKEECHAN n old Scots type of beer

SKEED ▶ skee

SKEEF adj, adv South African slang for at an oblique angle

SKEEING ▶ skee

SKEELY, SKEELIER adj Scots word meaning skilful

SKEEN, -S n type of ibex

SKEER, -ED, -ING, -S dialect form of ▶ scare

SKEERIER ▶ skeery

SKEERING ▶ skeer

SKEERS ▶ skeer

SKEERY, SKEERIER dialect form of ▶ scary

SKEES ▶ skee

SKEET, -S n form of clay-pigeon shooting

SKEETER, -S informal word for ▶ mosquito

SKEETS ▶ skeet

SKEEVY, SKEEVIER adj repulsive

SKEG, -S n reinforcing brace between the after end of a keel and the rudderpost

SKEGG, -S n skeg

SKEGGER, -S n young salmon

SKEGGS ▶ skegg

SKEGS ▶ skeg

SKEIGH, -ER adj Scots word meaning shy

SKEIN, -ED, -ING, -S n yarn wound in a loose coil ▷ vb wind into a skein

SKELDER, -S vb beg

SKELETAL ▶ skeleton

SKELETON n framework of bones inside a person's or animal's body ▷ adj reduced to a minimum

SKELF, -S n splinter of wood, esp when embedded accidentally in the skin

SKELL, -S n homeless person

SKELLIE adj skelly

SKELLIED ▶ skelly

SKELLIER ▶ skelly

SKELLIES ▶ skelly

SKELLOCH n Scots word meaning scream

SKELLS ▶ skell

SKELLUM, -S n rogue

SKELLY, SKELLIED, SKELLIER, SKELLIES n whitefish of certain lakes in the Lake District ▷ vb look sideways or squint ▷ adj cross-eyed

SKELM, -S n villain or crook

SKELP, -ED, -ING, -S vb slap ▷ n slap

SKELPIT vb Scots word meaning skelped

SKELPS ▶ skelp

SKELTER, -S vb scurry

SKELUM, -S n Scots word meaning rascal

SKEN, -NED, -NING, -S vb squint or stare

SKENE, -S n Scots word meaning dagger

SKENNED ▶ sken

SKENNING ▶ sken

SKENS ▶ sken

SKEO, -ES, -S n Scots dialect word meaning hut

SKEP, -PED, -PING, -S n beehive, esp one constructed of straw ▷ vb gather into a hive

SKEPFUL, -S n amount skep will hold

SKEPPED ▶ skep

SKEPPING ▶ skep

SKEPS ▶ skep

SKEPSIS n doubt

SKEPTIC, -S same as ▶ sceptic

SKER, -RED, -RING, -S vb scour

SKERRICK n small fragment or amount

SKERRIES ▶ skerry

SKERRING ▶ sker

SKERRY, SKERRIES n rocky island or reef

SKERS ▶ sker

SKET, -S, -TED, -TING vb splash (water)

SKETCH, -ED, -ES n rough drawing ▷ vb make a sketch (of)

SKETCHER

SKETCHY adj incomplete or inadequate

SKETS ▶ sket

SKETTED ▶ sket

SKETTING ▶ sket

SKEW, -ED, -EST, -ING, -S vb make slanting or crooked ▷ adj slanting or crooked ▷ n slanting position

SKEWBACK n sloping surface on both sides of a segmental arch that takes the thrust

SKEWBALD adj (horse) marked with patches of white and another colour ▷ n horse with this marking

SKEWED ▶ skew

SKEWER, -ED, -S n pin to hold meat together during cooking ▷ vb fasten with a skewer

SKEWEST ▶ skew

SKEWING ▶ skew

SKEWNESS n quality or condition of being skew

SKEWS ▶ skew

SKI, -S n one of a pair of long runners fastened to boots for gliding over snow or water ▷ vb travel on skis
SKIABLE

SKIAGRAM n picture made from shadows

SKIATRON n type of cathode ray tube

SKIBOB, -S n vehicle made of two short skis for gliding down snow slopes

SKID, -DED, -S vb (of a moving vehicle) slide sideways uncontrollably ▷ n skidding
SKIDDER -S

SKIDDIER ▶ skiddy

SKIDDING n act of skidding

SKIDDOO, -S vb go away quickly

SKIDDY, SKIDDIER ▶ skid

SKIDLID, -S n crash helmet

SKIDMARK n mark left by a skid

SKIDOO, -ED, -S n snowmobile ▷ vb travel on a skidoo

SKIDOOER n person who rides a skidoo

SKIDOOS ▶ skidoo

SKIDPAD, -S n area of road used to test skidding

SKIDPAN, -S n area made slippery so that vehicle drivers can practise controlling skids

SKIDS ▶ skid

SKIDWAY, -S n platform on which logs ready for sawing are piled

SKIED ▶ sky

SKIER, -S ▶ ski

SKIES ▶ sky

SKIEY, -ER, -EST adj of the sky

SKIFF, -ED, -ING, -S n small boat ▷ vb travel in a skiff

SKIFFLE, -D, -S n style of popular music of the 1950s ▷ vb play this style of music

SKIFFS ▶ skiff

SKIING, -S ▶ ski

SKIJORER > skijoring

SKILFUL adj having or showing skill

SKILFULL less common spelling of ▶ skilful

SKILL, -S n special ability or expertise

SKILLED adj possessing or demonstrating skill, or special training

SKILLESS ▶ skill

SKILLET, -S n small frying pan or shallow cooking pot

SKILLFUL same as ▶ skilful

SKILLIER ▶ skilly

SKILLIES ▶ skilly

SKILLING n former Scandinavian coin of low denomination

SKILLION n part of a building having a lower, esp sloping, roof

SKILLS ▶ skill

SKILLY, SKILLIER, SKILLIES n thin soup or gruel ▷ adj skilled

SKIM, -MED, -MING, -S vb remove floating matter from the surface of (a liquid) ▷ n act or process of skimming

SKIMMER, -S n person or thing that skims

SKIMMIA, -S n shrub of S and SE Asia

SKIMMING ▶ skim

SKIMP, -ED, -ING, -S vb not invest enough time, money, material, etc

SKIMPIER ▶ skimpy

SKIMPILY ▶ skimpy

SKIMPING ▶ skimp

SKIMPS ▶ skimp

SKIMPY, SKIMPIER adj scanty or insufficient

SKIMS ▶ skim

SKIN, -NED, -NING, -S n outer covering of the body ▷ vb remove the skin of

SKINCARE n use of cosmetics in taking care of skin

SKINFOOD n cosmetic cream for the skin

SKINFUL, -S n sufficient alcoholic drink to make one drunk

SKINHEAD n youth with very short hair

SKINK, -ED, -ING, -S n type of lizard with reduced limbs and smooth scales ▷ vb serve a drink
SKINKER -S

SKINLESS ▶ skin

SKINLIKE ▶ skin

SKINNED ▶ skin

SKINNER, -S n person who prepares or deals in animal skins

SKINNIER ▶ skinny

SKINNIES ▶ skinny

SKINNING ▶ skinny

SKINNY, SKINNIER, SKINNIES adj thin ▷ n information

SKINS ▶ skin

SKINSUIT n skintight one-piece garment worn by cyclists to reduce friction

SKINT, -ER, -EST adj having no money

SKIO, -ES, -S n Scots dialect word meaning hut

SKIORER, -S n one who engages in the sport of skioring

SKIORING n sport of being towed on skis by horse

SKIOS ▶ skio

SKIP, -PED, -PING, -S vb leap lightly from one foot to the other ▷ n skipping

SKIPJACK n important food fish of tropical seas

SKIPLANE n aircraft fitted with skis to enable it to land on and take off from snow

SKIPPED ▶ skip

SKIPPER, -S vb captain ▷ n captain of a ship or aircraft

SKIPPET, -S n small round box for preserving a document or seal

SKIPPIER ▶ skippy

SKIPPING ▶ skip

SKIPPY, SKIPPIER adj in high spirits

SKIPS ▶ skip

SKIRL, -ED, -ING, -S n sound of bagpipes ▷ vb (of bagpipes) to give out a shrill sound

SKIRMISH n brief or minor fight or argument ▷ vb take part in a skirmish

SKIRR, -ED, -ING, -S vb move, run, or fly rapidly ▷ n whirring or grating sound, as of the wings of birds in flight

SKIRRET, -S n umbelliferous Old World plant

SKIRRING ▶ skirr

SKIRRS ▶ skirr

SKIRT, -ED, -S n woman's garment hanging from the waist ▷ vb border

SKIRTER, -S n man who skirts fleeces

SKIRTING n border fixed round the base of an interior wall to protect it from kicks, dirt, etc

SKIRTS ▶ skirt

SKIS ▶ ski

SKIT, -S n brief satirical sketch

SKITCH, -ED, -ES vb (of a dog) to attack

SKITE, -D, -S, SKITING n boast ▷ vb boast

SKITS ▶ skit

SKITTER, -S vb move or run rapidly or lightly

S

SKITTERY adj moving lightly and rapidly

SKITTISH adj playful or lively

SKITTLE, -D, -S n bottle-shaped object used as a target in some games ▷ vb play skittles

SKIVE, -D, -S vb evade work or responsibility

SKIVER, -ED, -S n tanned outer layer split from a skin ▷ vb cut leather

SKIVES ► skive

SKIVIE, -R, -ST adj old Scots word meaning disarranged

SKIVING, -S ► skive

SKIVVY, SKIVVIED, SKIVVIES n female servant who does menial work ▷ vb work as a skivvy

SKIVY ► skive

SKIWEAR n clothes for skiing in

SKLATE, -D, -S, SKLATING Scots word for ► slate

SKLENT, -ED, -S Scots word for ► slant

SKLIFF, -ED, -S n Scots word meaning little piece ▷ vb shuffle (the feet)

SKLIM, -MED, -S vb Scots word meaning climb

SKOAL, -ED, -ING, -S same as ► skol

SKOFF, -ED, -ING, -S vb eat greedily

SKOG, -GED, -GING, -S same as ► scog

SKOKIAAN n (in South Africa) a potent alcoholic beverage

SKOL, -ED, -ING, -LED, -LING, -S sentence substitute good health! (a drinking toast) ▷ vb down (an alcoholic drink) in one go

SKOLIA ► skolion

SKOLING ► skol

SKOLION, SKOLIA n ancient Greek drinking song

SKOLLED ► skol

SKOLLIE same as ► skolly

SKOLLIES ► skolly

SKOLLING ► skol

SKOLLY, SKOLLIES n hooligan, usually one of a gang

SKOLS ► skol

SKOOKUM, -S adj strong or brave ▷ n strong or brave person

SKOOL, -S ironically illiterate or childish spelling of ► school

SKOOSH, -ED, -ES vb Scots word meaning squirt

SKORT, -S n pair of shorts with a front panel which gives the appearance of a skirt

SKOSH, -ES n little bit

SKRAN, -S n food

SKREEGH, -S vb Scots word meaning screech

SKREEN, -S n screen

SKREIGH, -S vb Scots word meaning screech

SKRIECH, -S vb Scots word meaning screech

SKRIED ► skry

SKRIEGH, -S vb Scots word meaning screech

SKRIES ► skry

SKRIK, -S n South African word meaning fright

SKRIKE, -D, -S, SKRIKING vb cry

SKRIKS ► skrik

SKRIMP, -ED, -S vb steal apples

SKRONK, -S n type of dissonant, grating popular music

SKRUMP, -ED, -S vb steal apples

SKRY, SKRIED, SKRIES, -ING vb try to tell future

SKRYER -S

SKUA, -S n large predatory gull

SKUDLER, -S n Scots word meaning leader of festivities

SKUG, -GED, -GING, -S vb shelter

SKULK, -ED, -ING, -S vb move stealthily ▷ n person who skulks

SKULKER -S

SKULL, -ED, -ING, -S n bony framework of the head ▷ vb strike on the head

SKULLCAP n close-fitting brimless cap

SKULLED ► skull

SKULLING ► skull

SKULLS ► skull

SKULPIN, -S n North American fish

SKUMMER, -S same as ► scumber

SKUNK, -ED, -ING, -S n small mammal which emits a foul-smelling fluid when attacked ▷ vb defeat overwhelmingly in a game

SKUNKIER ► skunky

SKUNKING ► skunk

SKUNKS ► skunk

SKUNKY, SKUNKIER ► skunk

SKURRY, SKURRIED, SKURRIES vb scurry

SKUTTLE, -D, -S vb scuttle

SKY, SKIED, SKIES, -ED, -ING n upper atmosphere as seen from the earth ▷ vb hit high in the air

SKYBOARD n small board used for skysurfing

SKYBORN adj born in heaven

SKYBORNE adj flying through sky

SKYBOX, -ES n luxurious suite high up in the stand of a sports stadium

SKYCAP, -S n luggage porter at American airport

SKYCLAD adj naked

SKYDIVE, -D, -S, SKYDOVE vb take part in skydiving

SKYDIVER

SKYED ► sky

SKYER, -S n cricket ball hit up into air

SKYEY, SKYIER, SKYIEST adj of the sky

SKYF, -ED, -ING, -S n South African slang for a cigarette or substance for smoking ▷ vb smoke a cigarette

SKYGLOW, -S n glow in the night sky caused by urban lights

SKYHOME, -S n Australian slang for a sub-penthouse flat in a tall building

SKYHOOK, -S n hook hung from helicopter

SKYIER ► skyey

SKYIEST ► skyey

SKYING ► sky

SKYISH ► sky

SKYJACK, -S vb hijack (an aircraft)

SKYLAB, -S n orbiting space station

SKYLARK, -S n lark that sings while soaring at a great height ▷ vb play or frolic

SKYLESS adj having no sky

SKYLIGHT n window in a roof or ceiling

SKYLIKE ► sky

SKYLINE, -S n outline of buildings, trees, etc against the sky

SKYLIT adj having skylight

SKYMAN, SKYMEN n paratrooper

SKYPHOS, SKYPHOI n ancient Greek drinking cup

SKYR, -S n Scandinavian cheese

SKYRE, -D, -S, SKYRING vb Scots word meaning shine

SKYRMION n (in theoretical physics) mathematical model used to model baryons

SKYRS ► **skyr**

SKYSAIL, -S n square sail set above the royal on a square-rigger

SKYSCAPE n painting, drawing, photograph, etc, representing or depicting the sky

SKYSURF, -S vb perform freefall aerobatics

SKYTE, -D, -S, SKYTING vb Scots word meaning slide

SKYWALK, -S n tightrope walk at great height

SKYWARD adj towards the sky ▷ adv towards the sky

SKYWARDS same as ► **skyward**

SKYWATCH vb watch the sky in search of celestial bodies or aircraft

SKYWAY, -S n air route

SKYWRITE, SKYWROTE vb write message in sky with smoke from aircraft

SLAB, -BED, -S n broad flat piece ▷ vb cut or make into a slab or slabs

SLABBER, -S vb dribble from the mouth

SLABBERY

SLABBIER ► **slabby**

SLABBING n act of slabbing

SLABBY, SLABBIER ► **slab**

SLABLIKE ► **slab**

SLABS ► **slab**

SLACK, -ED, -EST, -ING same as ► **slake**

SLACKEN, -S vb make or become slack

SLACKER, -S n person who evades work or duty

SLACKEST ► **slack**

SLACKING ► **slack**

SLACKLY ► **slack**

SLACKS pl n casual trousers

SLADANG, -S n Malayan tapir

SLADE, -S n little valley

SLAE, -S Scots word for ► **sloe**

SLAG, -GED, -S n waste left after metal is smelted ▷ vb criticize

SLAGGIER ► **slaggy**

SLAGGING ► **slag**

SLAGGY, SLAGGIER ► **slag**

SLAGS ► **slag**

SLAHAL, -S same as ► **lahal**

SLAID, -S vb (Scot) sledge

SLAIN ► **slay**

SLAINTE interj cheers!

SLAIRG, -ED, -S Scots word for ► **spread**

SLAISTER vb cover with a sloppy mess ▷ n sloppy mess

SLAKABLE ► **slake**

SLAKE, -D, -S, SLAKING vb satisfy (thirst or desire)

SLAKER -S

SLALOM, -ED, -S n skiing or canoeing race over a winding course ▷ vb take part in a slalom

SLALOMER

SLAM, -MED, -MING, -S vb shut, put down, or hit violently and noisily ▷ n act or sound of slamming

SLAMMER, -S n prison

SLAMMING ► **slam**

SLAMS ► **slam**

SLANDER, -S n false and malicious statement about a person ▷ vb utter slander about

SLANE, -S n spade for cutting turf

SLANG, -ED, -ING, -S n very informal language ▷ vb use insulting language to (someone)

SLANGER, -S n street vendor

SLANGIER ► **slangy**

SLANGILY ► **slang**

SLANGING ► **slang**

SLANGISH ► **slang**

SLANGS ► **slang**

SLANGY, SLANGIER ► **slang**

SLANK dialect word for ► **lank**

SLANT, -ED, -S vb lean at an angle, slope ▷ n slope

SLANTER, -S same as ► **slinter**

SLANTIER ► **slanty**

SLANTING ► **slant**

SLANTLY ► **slant**

SLANTS ► **slant**

SLANTY, SLANTIER adj slanting

SLAP, -PED, -S n blow with the open hand or a flat object ▷ vb strike with the open hand or a flat object

SLAPDASH adj careless and hasty ▷ adv carelessly or hastily ▷ n slapdash activity or work ▷ vb do in a hurried and careless manner

SLAPHEAD n derogatory term for a bald person

SLAPJACK n simple card game

SLAPPED ► **slap**

SLAPPER, -S ► **slap**

SLAPPING ► **slap**

SLAPS ► **slap**

SLAPSHOT n hard, fast, often wild, shot executed with a powerful downward swing

SLART, -ED, -ING, -S vb spill (something)

SLASH, -ED, -ES vb cut with a sweeping stroke ▷ n sweeping stroke

SLASHER, -S n machine used for cutting scrub or undergrowth in the bush

SLASHES ► **slash**

SLASHING adj aggressively critical ▷ n act of slashing

SLAT, -S, -TED, -TING n narrow strip of wood or metal ▷ vb provide with slats

SLATCH, -ES n slack part of rope

SLATE, -D, -S n rock which splits easily into thin layers ▷ vb cover with slates ▷ adj dark grey

SLATER, -S n person trained in laying roof slates

SLATES ► **slate**

SLATEY adj slightly mad

SLATHER, -S vb spread quickly or lavishly

SLATIER ► **slaty**

SLATIEST ► **slaty**

SLATING, -S n act or process of laying slates

SLATS ► **slat**

SLATTED ► **slat**

SLATTER, -S vb be slovenly

SLATTERY adj slovenly

SLATTING ► **slat**

SLATY, SLATIER, SLATIEST adj consisting of or resembling slate

SLAVE, -D, -S, SLAVING n person owned by another for whom he or she has to work ▷ vb work like a slave

SLAVER, -ED, -S n person or ship engaged in the slave trade ▷ vb dribble saliva from the mouth

SLAVERER

SLAVERY n state or condition of being a slave

SLAVES ► **slave**

SLAVEY, -S n female general servant

SLAVING ► **slave**

SLAVISH adj of or like a slave

SLAW, -S short for ► **coleslaw**

SLAY, SLAIN, -ED, -S vb kill

SLAYABLE

SLAYER -S

SLAYING, -S n act of slaying

SLAYS ► **slay**

SLEAVE, -D, -S, SLEAVING n tangled thread ▷ vb disentangle (twisted thread, etc)

S

SLEAZE, -D, -S, SLEAZING
n behaviour considered
dishonest or disreputable
▷ vb behave in a sleazy
manner
SLEAZIER ▸ sleazy
SLEAZILY ▸ sleazy
SLEAZING ▸ sleaze
SLEAZY, SLEAZIER adj run-
down or sordid
SLEB, -S n celebrity
SLED, -DED, -DING, -ED, -S
same as ▸ sledge
SLEDDER -S
SLEDGE, -D, -S, SLEDGING
n carriage on runners for
sliding on snow ▷ vb travel
by sledge
SLEDGER -S
SLEDS ▸ sled
SLEE, -R, -ST Scots word for
▸ sly
SLEECH, -ES n slippery mud
SLEECHY
SLEEK, -ED, -EST, -ING, -S adj
glossy, smooth, and shiny
▷ vb make smooth and
glossy, as by grooming, etc
SLEEKEN, -S vb make sleek
SLEEKER, -S ▸ sleek
SLEEKEST ▸ sleek
SLEEKIER ▸ sleeky
SLEEKING ▸ sleek
SLEEKIT adj smooth
SLEEKLY ▸ sleek
SLEEKS ▸ sleek
SLEEKY, SLEEKIER ▸ sleek
SLEEP, -ING, -S, SLEPT n
state of rest characterized by
unconsciousness ▷ vb be in
or as if in a state of sleep
SLEEPER, -S n railway car
fitted for sleeping in
SLEEPERY Scots word for
▸ sleepy
SLEEPIER ▸ sleepy
SLEEPILY ▸ sleepy
SLEEPING ▸ sleep
SLEEPOUT n small building
for sleeping in
SLEEPRY Scots word for
▸ sleepy
SLEEPS ▸ sleep
SLEEPY, SLEEPIER adj
needing sleep
SLEER ▸ slee
SLEEST ▸ slee
SLEET, -ED, -ING, -S n rain and
snow or hail falling together
▷ vb fall as sleet
SLEETIER ▸ sleety
SLEETING ▸ sleet
SLEETS ▸ sleet
SLEETY, SLEETIER ▸ sleet

SLEEVE, -D, -S n part of a
garment which covers the
arm
SLEEVEEN n sly obsequious
smooth-tongued person
SLEEVER, -S n old beer
measure
SLEEVES ▸ sleeve
SLEEVING n tubular flexible
insulation into which bare
wire can be inserted
SLEEZY, SLEEZIER adj sleazy
SLEIDED adj old word
meaning separated
SLEIGH, -ED, -S same as
▸ sledge
SLEIGHER
SLEIGHT, -S n skill or cunning
SLENDER adj slim
SLENTER, -S same as
▸ slinter
SLEPT ▸ sleep
SLEUTH, -ED, -S n detective
▷ vb track or follow
SLEW, -ED, -ING, -S vb twist
sideways, esp awkwardly
SLEY, -S n weaver's tool for
separating threads
SLICE, -D, -S n thin flat piece
cut from something ▷ vb cut
into slices
SLICER -S
SLICING, -S ▸ slice
SLICK, -ED, -EST, -ING, -S
adj persuasive and glib ▷ n
patch of oil on water ▷ vb
make smooth or sleek
SLICKEN, -S vb make smooth
SLICKER, -S n sly or
untrustworthy person
SLICKEST ▸ slick
SLICKING ▸ slick
SLICKLY ▸ slick
SLICKS ▸ slick
SLID ▸ slide
SLIDABLE ▸ slide
SLIDDEN ▸ slide
SLIDDER, -S vb slip
SLIDDERY adj slippery
**SLIDE, SLID, SLIDDEN, -D,
-S** vb slip smoothly along (a
surface) ▷ n sliding
SLIDER -S
SLIDEWAY n sloping channel
down which things are slid
SLIDING, -S ▸ slide
SLIER ▸ sly
SLIEST ▸ sly
SLIEVE, -S n Irish mountain
SLIGHT, -ED, -ER, -S adj small
in quantity or extent ▷ n
snub ▷ vb insult (someone)
by behaving rudely
SLIGHTLY adv in small
measure or degree
SLIGHTS ▸ slight

SLILY ▸ sly
SLIM, -MED, -MEST, -MING, -S
adj not heavy or stout, thin
▷ vb make or become slim by
diet and exercise
SLIMDOWN n instance of an
organization cutting staff
SLIME, -D, -S, SLIMING n
unpleasant thick slippery
substance ▷ vb cover with
slime
SLIMIER ▸ slimy
SLIMIEST ▸ slimy
SLIMILY ▸ slimy
SLIMING ▸ slime
SLIMLINE adj slim
SLIMLY ▸ slim
SLIMMED ▸ slim
SLIMMER, -S ▸ slim
SLIMMEST ▸ slim
SLIMMING ▸ slim
SLIMMISH ▸ slim
SLIMNESS ▸ slim
SLIMPSY adj thin and flimsy
SLIMS ▸ slim
SLIMSY, SLIMSIER adj frail
SLIMY, SLIMIER, SLIMIEST
adj of, like, or covered with
slime
SLING, -ING, -S, SLUNG n
bandage hung from the neck
to support an injured hand or
arm ▷ vb throw
SLINGER -S
SLINK, -ED, -ING, -S, SLUNK
vb move furtively or guiltily
▷ n animal, esp a calf, born
prematurely
SLINKER -S
SLINKIER ▸ slinky
SLINKILY ▸ slinky
SLINKING ▸ slink
SLINKS ▸ slink
SLINKY, SLINKIER adj (of
clothes) figure-hugging
SLINTER, -S n dodge, trick, or
stratagem
SLIOTAR, -S n ball used in
hurling
SLIP, -PED, -PING, -S vb
lose balance by sliding ▷ n
slipping
SLIPCASE n protective case
for a book
SLIPE, -D, -S, SLIPING n wool
removed from the pelt of
a slaughtered sheep ▷ vb
remove skin
SLIPFORM n mould used in
building
SLIPING ▸ slipe
SLIPKNOT n knot tied so that
it will slip along the rope
round which it is made
SLIPLESS ▸ slip

SLIPOUT, -S n instance of slipping out

SLIPOVER adj of or denoting a garment that can be put on easily over the head ▷ n such a garment, esp a sleeveless pullover

SLIPPAGE n act or an instance of slipping

SLIPPED ► slip

SLIPPER, -S n light shoe for indoor wear ▷ vb hit or beat with a slipper

SLIPPERY adj so smooth or wet as to cause slipping or be difficult to hold

SLIPPIER ► slippy

SLIPPILY ► slippy

SLIPPING ► slip

SLIPPY, SLIPPIER adj slippery

SLIPRAIL n rail in a fence that can be slipped out of place to make an opening

SLIPS ► slip

SLIPSHOD adj (of an action) careless

SLIPSLOP n weak or unappetizing food or drink

SLIPSOLE n separate sole on shoe

SLIPT vb old form of slipped

SLIPUP, -S n mistake or mishap

SLIPWARE n pottery that has been decorated with slip

SLIPWAY, -S n launching slope on which ships are built or repaired

SLISH, -ES n old word meaning cut

SLIT, -S, -TED, -TING n long narrow cut or opening ▷ vb make a long straight cut in

SLITHER, -S vb slide unsteadily ▷ n slithering movement

SLITHERY adj moving with a slithering motion

SLITLESS ► slit

SLITLIKE ► slit

SLITS ► slit

SLITTED ► slit

SLITTER, -S ► slit

SLITTIER ► slitty

SLITTING ► slit

SLITTY, SLITTIER ► slit

SLIVE, -D, -N, -S, SLIVING, SLOVE vb slip

SLIVER, -ED, -S n small thin piece ▷ vb cut into slivers

SLIVERER

SLIVES ► slive

SLIVING ► slive

SLIVOVIC n plum brandy

SLOAN, -S n severe telling-off

SLOB, -BED, -BING, -S n lazy and untidy person ▷ vb behave like a slob

SLOBBER, -S vb dribble or drool ▷ n liquid or saliva spilt from the mouth

SLOBBERY

SLOBBIER ► slobby

SLOBBING ► slob

SLOBBISH ► slob

SLOBBY, SLOBBIER ► slob

SLOBLAND n muddy ground

SLOBS ► slob

SLOCKEN, -S vb Scots word meaning slake

SLOE, -S n sour blue-black fruit

SLOEBUSH n bush on which sloes grow

SLOES ► sloe

SLOETREE n sloe plant

SLOG, -GED, -GING, -S vb work hard and steadily ▷ n long and exhausting work or walk

SLOGAN, -S n catchword or phrase used in politics or advertising

SLOGANED adj having a slogan

SLOGANS ► slogan

SLOGGED ► slog

SLOGGER, -S ► slog

SLOGGING ► slog

SLOGS ► slog

SLOID, -S n Swedish woodwork

SLOJD, -S same as ► **sloid**

SLOKEN, -ED, -S vb Scots word meaning slake

SLOMMOCK vb walk assertively with a hip-rolling gait

SLOMO, -S n slow-motion sequence in a film

SLOOM, -ED, -ING, -S vb slumber

SLOOMIER ► sloomy

SLOOMING ► sloom

SLOOMS ► sloom

SLOOMY, SLOOMIER ► sloom

SLOOP, -S n small single-masted ship

SLOOSH, -ED, -ES vb wash with water

SLOOT, -S n ditch for irrigation or drainage

SLOP, -PED, -PING, -S vb splash or spill ▷ n spilt liquid

SLOPE, -D, -S vb slant ▷ n sloping surface

SLOPER -S

SLOPIER ► slopy

SLOPIEST ► slopy

SLOPING ► slope

SLOPPED ► slop

SLOPPIER ► sloppy

SLOPPILY ► sloppy

SLOPPING ► slop

SLOPPY, SLOPPIER adj careless or untidy

SLOPS ► slop

SLOPWORK n manufacture of cheap shoddy clothing or the clothes so produced

SLOPY, SLOPIER, SLOPIEST ► slope

SLORM, -ED, -ING, -S vb wipe carelessly

SLOSH, -ED, -ES, -ING vb pour carelessly ▷ n splashing sound

SLOSHIER ► sloshy

SLOSHING ► slosh

SLOSHY, SLOSHIER ► slosh

SLOT, -S, -TED, -TING n narrow opening for inserting something ▷ vb make a slot or slots in

SLOTBACK n American football player

SLOTH, -ED, -ING, -S n slow-moving animal of tropical America ▷ vb be lazy

SLOTHFUL adj lazy or idle

SLOTHING ► sloth

SLOTHS ► sloth

SLOTS ► slot

SLOTTED ► slot

SLOTTER, -S ► slot

SLOTTING ► slot

SLOUCH, -ED, -ES vb sit, stand, or move with a drooping posture ▷ n drooping posture

SLOUCHER

SLOUCHY adj slouching

SLOUGH, -ED, -S n bog ▷ vb (of a snake) shed (its skin)

SLOUGHI, -S n N African breed of dog resembling a greyhound

SLOUGHS ► slough

SLOUGHY ► slough

SLOVE ► slive

SLOVEN, -S n habitually dirty or untidy person

SLOVENLY adj dirty or untidy ▷ adv in a slovenly manner

SLOVENRY n quality of being slovenly

SLOVENS ► sloven

SLOW, -ED, -ER, -EST, -S adj taking a longer time than is usual or expected ▷ adv slowly ▷ vb reduce the speed (of)

SLOWBACK n lazy person

SLOWDOWN n any slackening of pace

SLOWED ► slow

S

SLOWER ► slow

SLOWEST ► slow

SLOWING, -S ► slow

SLOWISH ► slow

SLOWLY ► slow

SLOWNESS ► slow

SLOWPOKE same as
> slowcoach

SLOWS ► slow

SLOWWORM n small legless
lizard

SLOYD, -S n Swedish
woodwork

SLUB, -BED, -BING, -S n lump
in yarn or fabric ▷ vb draw
out and twist (a sliver of fibre)
before spinning ▷ adj (of
material) having an irregular
appearance

SLUBB, -S same as ► slub

SLUBBED ► slub

SLUBBER, -S vb smear

SLUBBIER ► slubby

SLUBBING ► slub

SLUBBS ► slubb

SLUBBY, SLUBBIER ► slub

SLUBS ► slub

SLUDGE, -D, -S, SLUDGING n
thick mud ▷ vb convert into
sludge

SLUDGIER ► sludgy

SLUDGING ► sludge

SLUDGY, SLUDGIER adj
consisting of, containing, or
like sludge

SLUE, -D, -ING, -S, SLUING
same as ► slew

SLUFF, -ED, -ING, -S same as
► slough

SLUG, -GED, -GING, -S n land
snail with no shell ▷ vb hit
hard

SLUGABED n person who
remains in bed through
laziness

SLUGFEST n fist fight

SLUGGARD n lazy person
▷ adj lazy

SLUGGED ► slug

SLUGGER, -S n (esp in boxing,
baseball, etc) a person who
strikes hard

SLUGGING ► slug

SLUGGISH adj slow-moving,
lacking energy

SLUGHORN same as
► slogan

SLUGS ► slug

SLUICE, -D, -S, SLUICING n
channel that carries a rapid
current of water ▷ vb drain
water by means of a sluice

SLUICIER ► sluicy

SLUICING ► sluice

SLUICY, SLUICIER ► sluice

SLUING ► slue

SLUIT, -S n water channel in
South Africa

SLUM, -MED, -MING, -S n
squalid overcrowded house
or area ▷ vb experience
poorer places or conditions
than usual

SLUMBER, -S n sleep ▷ vb
sleep

SLUMBERY adj sleepy

SLUMBRY same as
► slumbery

SLUMGUM, -S n material left
after wax is extracted from
honeycomb

SLUMISM, -S n existence of
slums

SLUMLORD n absentee
landlord of slum property,
esp one who profiteers

SLUMMED ► slum

SLUMMER, -S ► slum

SLUMMIER ► slummy

SLUMMING ► slum

SLUMMOCK vb move slowly
and heavily

SLUMMY, SLUMMIER
► slum

SLUMP, -ED, -ING, -S vb (of
prices or demand) decline
suddenly ▷ n sudden decline
in prices or demand

SLUMPIER ► slumpy

SLUMPING ► slump

SLUMPS ► slump

SLUMPY, SLUMPIER adj
boggy

SLUMS ► slum

SLUNG ► sling

SLUNK ► slink

SLUR, -RED, -RING, -S vb
pronounce or utter (words)
indistinctly ▷ n slurring of
words

SLURB, -S n suburban slum

SLURBAN

SLURP, -ED, -ING, -S vb eat
or drink noisily ▷ n slurping
sound

SLURPER -S

SLURPIER ► slurpy

SLURPING ► slurp

SLURPS ► slurp

SLURPY, SLURPIER adj
making a slurping noise

SLURRED ► slur

SLURRIED ► slurry

SLURRIES ► slurry

SLURRING ► slur

**SLURRY, SLURRIED,
SLURRIES** n muddy liquid
mixture ▷ vb spread slurry

SLURS ► slur

SLURVE, -S n pitch in baseball
combining elements of the
slider and the curveball

SLUSE, -S same as ► sluice

SLUSH, -ED, -ES, -ING n
watery muddy substance
▷ vb make one's way through
or as if through slush

SLUSHIER ► slushy

SLUSHIES ► slushy

SLUSHILY ► slushy

SLUSHING ► slush

**SLUSHY, SLUSHIER,
SLUSHIES** adj of,
resembling, or consisting of
slush ▷ n unskilled kitchen
assistant

SLUTCH, -ES n mud

SLUTCHY

SLY, SLIER, SLIEST, -ER, -EST
adj crafty

SLYBOOTS pl n person who
is sly

SLYER ► sly

SLYEST ► sly

SLYISH ► sly

SLYLY ► sly

SLYNESS ► sly

SLYPE, -S n covered
passageway in a church

SMA Scots word for ► small

SMAAK, -ED, -ING, -S vb
South African slang for like
or love

SMACK, -ED, -S vb slap
sharply ▷ n sharp slap ▷ adv
squarely or directly

SMACKER, -S n loud kiss

SMACKING adj brisk

SMACKS ► smack

SMAIK, -S n Scots word
meaning rascal

**SMALL, -ED, -ER, -EST, -ING,
-S** adj not large in size,
number, or amount ▷ n
narrow part of the lower
back ▷ adv into small pieces
▷ vb make small

SMALLAGE n wild celery

SMALLBOY n steward's
assistant or deputy steward
in European households in
W Africa

SMALLED ► small

SMALLER ► small

SMALLEST ► small

SMALLING ► small

SMALLISH ► small

SMALLPOX n contagious
disease with blisters that
leave scars

SMALLS ► small

SMALLSAT n small
communications satellite

SMALM, -ED, -ING, -S same as
► smarm

SMALMIER ► smalmy

SMALMILY ► smalmy

SMALMING ► smalm

SMALMS ► smalm

SMALMY, SMALMIER *same as* ► **smarmy**

SMALT, -S *n* type of silica glass coloured deep blue with cobalt oxide

SMALTI ► smalto

SMALTINE *n* mineral containing cobalt

SMALTITE *n* silver-white to greyish mineral

SMALTO, SMALTI, -S *n* coloured glass, etc, used in mosaics

SMALTS ► smalt

SMARAGD, -S *n* any green gemstone, such as the emerald

SMARAGDE *same as* ► **smaragd**

SMARAGDS ► smaragd

SMARM, -ED, -ING, -S *vb* bring (oneself) into favour (with) ▷ *n* obsequious flattery

SMARMIER ► smarmy

SMARMILY ► smarmy

SMARMING ► smarm

SMARMS ► smarm

SMARMY, SMARMIER *adj* unpleasantly suave or flattering

SMART, -ED, -ER, -EST, -ING *adj* well-kept and neat ▷ *vb* feel or cause stinging pain ▷ *n* stinging pain ▷ *adv* in a smart manner

SMARTEN, -S *vb* make or become smart

SMARTER ► smart

SMARTEST ► smart

SMARTIE *same as* ► **smarty**

SMARTIES ► smarty

SMARTING ► smart

SMARTISH ► smart

SMARTLY ► smart

SMARTS *pl n* know-how, intelligence, or wits

SMARTY, SMARTIES *n* would-be clever person

SMASH, -ED, -ES *vb* break violently and noisily ▷ *n* act or sound of smashing ▷ *adv* with a smash

SMASHER, -S *n* attractive person or thing

SMASHES ► smash

SMASHING *adj* excellent

SMASHUP, -S *n* bad collision of cars

SMATCH, -ED, -ES *less common word for* ► **smack**

SMATTER, -S *n* smattering ▷ *vb* prattle

SMAZE, -S *n* smoky haze, less damp than fog

SMEAR, -ED, -ING, -S *vb* spread with a greasy or sticky substance ▷ *n* dirty mark or smudge

SMEARER -S

SMEARIER ► smeary

SMEARILY ► smeary

SMEARING ► smear

SMEARS ► smear

SMEARY, SMEARIER *adj* smeared, dirty

SMEATH, -S *n* duck

SMECTIC *adj* (of a substance) existing in state in which the molecules are oriented in layers

SMECTITE *n* type of clay mineral

SMEDDUM, -S *n* any fine powder

SMEE, -S *n* duck

SMEECH, -ED, -ES *Southwest English dialect form of* ► **smoke**

SMEEK, -ED, -ING, -S *vb* smoke

SMEES ► smee

SMEETH, -ED, -S *n* duck ▷ *vb* make smooth

SMEGMA, -S *n* whitish sebaceous secretion that accumulates beneath the prepuce

SMEIK, -ED, -S *same as* ► **smeke**

SMEIKING *same as* ► **smeking**

SMEIKS ► smeik

SMEKE, -D, -S, SMEKING *n* smoke ▷ *vb* smoke

SMELL, -ED, -ING, -S *vb* perceive (a scent or odour) by means of the nose ▷ *n* ability to perceive odours by the nose

SMELLER -S

SMELLIER ► smelly

SMELLIES *pl n* pleasant-smelling products such as perfumes, body lotions, bath salts, etc

SMELLING ► smell

SMELLS ► smell

SMELLY, SMELLIER *adj* having a nasty smell

SMELT, -ED, -ING, -S *vb* extract metal from an ore

SMELTER, -S *n* industrial plant where smelting is carried out

SMELTERY *variant of* ► **smelter**

SMELTING ► smelt

SMELTS ► smelt

SMERK, -ED, -ING, -S *same as* ► **smirk**

SMEUSE, -S *n* way through hedge

SMEW, -S *n* duck of N Europe and Asia

SMICKER, -S *vb* smirk

SMICKET, -S *n* smock

SMIDDY, SMIDDIED, SMIDDIES *Scots word for* ► **smithy**

SMIDGE, -S *n* very small amount or part

SMIDGEN, -S *n* very small amount or part

SMIDGEON *same as* ► **smidgen**

SMIDGES ► smidge

SMIDGIN, -S *same as* ► **smidgen**

SMIGHT, -S *same as* ► **smite**

SMILAX, -ES *n* type of climbing shrub

SMILE, -D, -S *n* turning up of the corners of the mouth to show pleasure or friendliness ▷ *vb* give a smile

SMILEFUL *adj* full of smiles

SMILER, -S ► smile

SMILES ► smile

SMILET, -S *n* little smile

SMILEY, -S, SMILIER, SMILIES, SMILIEST *n* symbol depicting a smile or other facial expression, used in e-mail ▷ *adj* cheerful

SMILING, -S ► smile

SMILODON *n* extinct sabre-toothed tiger

SMIR, -S *n* drizzly rain ▷ *vb* drizzle lightly

SMIRCH, -ED, -ES *n* stain ▷ *vb* disgrace

SMIRCHER

SMIRK, -ED, -S *n* smug smile ▷ *vb* give a smirk

SMIRKER -S

SMIRKIER ► smirky

SMIRKILY ► smirk

SMIRKING ► smirk

SMIRKS ► smirk

SMIRKY, SMIRKIER ► smirk

SMIRR, -ED, -ING, -S *same as* ► **smir**

SMIRRIER ► smirry

SMIRRING ► smirr

SMIRRS ► smirr

SMIRRY, SMIRRIER ► smirry

SMIRS ► smir

SMIRTING *n* flirting amongst those smoking outside a non-smoking office, pub, etc

SMITE, SMIT, -S, SMITING, SMITTEN, SMOTE *vb* strike hard

SMITER -S

SMITH, -ED, -S *n* worker in metal ▷ *vb* work in metal

SMITHERS pl n little shattered pieces

SMITHERY n trade or craft of a blacksmith

SMITHIED ► smithy

SMITHIES ► smithy

SMITHING n act of working as a smith

SMITHS ► smith

SMITHY, SMITHIED, SMITHIES n blacksmith's workshop ▷ vb work as a smith

SMITING ► smite

SMITS ► smit

SMITTED ► smit

SMITTEN ► smite

SMITTING ► smit

SMITTLE adj infectious

SMOCK, -ED, -S n loose overall ▷ vb gather (material) by sewing in a honeycomb pattern

SMOCKING n ornamental needlework used to gather material

SMOCKS ► smock

SMOG, -S n mixture of smoke and fog

SMOGGY SMOGGIER SMOGLESS

SMOILE, -D, -S, SMOILING same as ► smile

SMOKABLE ► smoke

SMOKE, -D, -S, SMOKING n cloudy mass that rises from something burning ▷ vb give off smoke or treat with smoke

SMOKEBOX n part of a steam engine or boiler

SMOKED ► smoke

SMOKEHO, -S same as ► smoko

SMOKEPOT n device for producing smoke

SMOKER, -S n person who habitually smokes tobacco

SMOKES ► smoke

SMOKEY, -S ► smoky

SMOKIE n smoked haddock

SMOKIER ► smoky

SMOKIES ► smoky

SMOKIEST ► smoky

SMOKILY ► smoky

SMOKING, -S ► smoke

SMOKO, -S n short break from work for tea or a cigarette

SMOKY, SMOKIER, SMOKIES, SMOKIEST adj filled with or giving off smoke, sometimes excessively ▷ n haddock that has been smoked

SMOLDER, -S same as ► smoulder

SMOLT, -S n young salmon at the stage when it migrates to the sea

SMOOCH, -ED, -ES vb kiss and cuddle ▷ n smooching

SMOOCHER

SMOOCHY adj romantic

SMOODGE, -D, -S same as ► smooch

SMOOGE, -D, -S, SMOOGING same as ► smooch

SMOOR, -ED, -ING, -S vb Scots word meaning put out fire

SMOOSH, -ED, -ES vb paint to give softened look

SMOOT, -ED, -ING, -S vb work as printer

SMOOTH, -ED, -ES, -S adj even in surface, texture, or consistency ▷ vb make smooth ▷ adv in a smooth manner ▷ n smooth part of something

SMOOTHE same as ► smooth

SMOOTHED ► smooth

SMOOTHEN vb make or become smooth

SMOOTHER ► smooth

SMOOTHES ► smooth

SMOOTHIE n smooth thick drink made with fruit and milk and sometimes ice cream

SMOOTHLY ► smooth

SMOOTHS ► smooth

SMOOTHY same as ► smoothie

SMOOTING ► smoot

SMOOTS ► smoot

SMORBROD n Danish hors d'oeuvre

SMORE, -D, -S, SMORING same as ► smoor

SMORG, -S n short for smorgasbord

SMORING ► smore

SMORZATO same as > smorzando

SMOTE ► smite

SMOTHER, -S vb suffocate or stifle ▷ n anything, such as a cloud of smoke, that stifles

SMOTHERY

SMOUCH, -ED, -ES vb kiss

SMOULDER vb burn slowly with smoke but no flame ▷ n dense smoke, as from a smouldering fire

SMOULDRY adj smouldering

SMOUSE, -D, -S, SMOUSING vb South African word meaning peddle

SMOUSER -S

SMOUT, -ED, -ING, -S n child or undersized person ▷ vb creep or sneak

SMOWT, -S same as ► smout

SMOYLE, -D, -S, SMOYLING same as ► smile

SMRITI, -S n class of Hindu sacred literature

SMUDGE, -D, -S, SMUDGING vb make or become smeared or soiled ▷ n dirty mark

SMUDGER -S

SMUDGIER ► smudgy

SMUDGILY ► smudge

SMUDGING ► smudge

SMUDGY, SMUDGIER adj smeared, blurred, or soiled, or likely to become so

SMUG, -GED, -GER, -GEST, -GING, -S adj self-satisfied ▷ vb make neat

SMUGGERY n condition or an instance of being smug

SMUGGEST ► smug

SMUGGING ► smug

SMUGGLE, -D, -S vb import or export (goods) secretly and illegally

SMUGGLER

SMUGLY ► smug

SMUGNESS ► smug

SMUGS ► smug

SMUR, -RED, -RING, -S same as ► smir

SMURFING n intentionally overwhelming a computer network with messages

SMURRED ► smur

SMURRIER ► smurry

SMURRING ► smur

SMURRY, SMURRIER ► smur

SMURS ► smur

SMUSH, -ED, -ES, -ING vb crush

SMUT, -S, -TED, -TING n small dark smudge or stain ▷ vb mark or become marked or smudged

SMUTCH, -ED, -ES vb smudge ▷ n mark

SMUTCHY

SMUTS ► smut

SMUTTED ► smut

SMUTTIER ► smutty

SMUTTILY ► smut

SMUTTING ► smut

SMUTTY, SMUTTIER ► smut

SMYTRIE, -S n Scots word meaning collection

SNAB, -S same as ► snob

SNABBLE, -D, -S same as ► snaffle

SNABS ► snab

SNACK, -ED, -ING, -S *n* light quick meal ▷ *vb* eat a snack
SNACKER -S
SNACKIER ▶ snacky
SNACKING ▶ snack
SNACKS ▶ snack
SNACKY, SNACKIER *adj* of the nature of a snack
SNAFFLE, -D, -S *n* jointed bit for a horse ▷ *vb* steal
SNAFU, -ED, -ING, -S *n* confusion or chaos regarded as the normal state ▷ *adj* confused or muddled up, as usual ▷ *vb* throw into chaos
SNAG, -GED, -GING, -S *n* difficulty or disadvantage ▷ *vb* catch or tear on a point
SNAGGER, -S *n* type of fishing hook
SNAGGIER ▶ snaggy
SNAGGING ▶ snag
SNAGGLE, -S *n* tangled mass
SNAGGY, SNAGGIER *adj* having sharp protuberances
SNAGLIKE ▶ snag
SNAGS ▶ snag
SNAIL, -ED, -ING, -S *n* slow-moving mollusc with a spiral shell ▷ *vb* move slowly
SNAILERY *n* place where snails are bred
SNAILIER ▶ snaily
SNAILING ▶ snail
SNAILS ▶ snail
SNAILY, SNAILIER ▶ snail
SNAKE, -D, -S, SNAKING *n* long thin scaly limbless reptile ▷ *vb* move in a winding course like a snake
SNAKEBIT *adj* bitten by snake
SNAKED ▶ snake
SNAKEPIT *n* pit filled with snakes
SNAKES ▶ snake
SNAKEY *same as* ▶ **snaky**
SNAKIER ▶ snaky
SNAKIEST ▶ snaky
SNAKILY ▶ snaky
SNAKING ▶ snake
SNAKISH ▶ snake
SNAKY, SNAKIER, SNAKIEST *adj* twisted or winding
SNAP, -PED, -PING, -S *vb* break suddenly ▷ *n* act or sound of snapping ▷ *adj* made on the spur of the moment ▷ *adv* with a snap
SNAPBACK *n* sudden rebound or change in direction
SNAPLESS ▶ snap
SNAPLINK *n* metal link used in mountaineering
SNAPPED ▶ snap

SNAPPER, -S *n* food fish of Australia and New Zealand ▷ *vb* stumble
SNAPPIER ▶ snappy
SNAPPILY ▶ snappy
SNAPPING ▶ snap
SNAPPISH *same as* ▶ **snappy**
SNAPPY, SNAPPIER *adj* irritable
SNAPS ▶ snap
SNAPSHOT *n* informal photograph
SNAPTIN, -S *n* container for food
SNAPWEED *n* impatiens
SNAR, -RED, -RING, -S *same as* ▶ **snarl**
SNARE, -D, -S *n* trap with a noose ▷ *vb* catch in or as if in a snare
SNARER -S
SNARF, -ED, -ING, -S *vb* eat or drink greedily
SNARFLE, -D, -S *vb* (of an animal) grunt and snort while rooting for food
SNARFS ▶ snarf
SNARIER ▶ snary
SNARIEST ▶ snary
SNARING, -S ▶ snare
SNARK, -S *n* imaginary creature in Lewis Carroll's poetry
SNARKIER ▶ snarky
SNARKILY ▶ snarky
SNARKS ▶ snark
SNARKY, SNARKIER *adj* unpleasant and scornful
SNARL, -ED, -S *vb* (of an animal) growl with bared teeth ▷ *n* act or sound of snarling
SNARLER -S
SNARLIER ▶ snarly
SNARLING ▶ snarl
SNARLS ▶ snarl
SNARLY, SNARLIER ▶ snarl
SNARRED ▶ snar
SNARRING ▶ snar
SNARS ▶ snar
SNARY, SNARIER, SNARIEST ▶ snare
SNASH, -ED, -ES, -ING *vb* Scots word meaning speak cheekily
SNASTE, -S *n* candle wick
SNATCH, -ED, -ES *vb* seize or try to seize suddenly ▷ *n* snatching
SNATCHER
SNATCHY *adj* disconnected or spasmodic
SNATH, -S *n* handle of a scythe
SNATHE, -S *same as* ▶ **snath**
SNATHS ▶ snath

SNAW, -ED, -ING, -S *Scots variant of* ▶ **snow**
SNAZZIER ▶ snazzy
SNAZZILY ▶ snazzy
SNAZZY, SNAZZIER *adj* stylish and flashy
SNEAD, -S *n* scythe handle
SNEAK, -ED, -S *vb* move furtively ▷ *n* cowardly or underhand person ▷ *adj* without warning
SNEAKBOX *n* small camouflaged boat, used for wildfowl hunting
SNEAKED ▶ sneak
SNEAKER *n* canvas shoe with rubber sole
SNEAKERS ▶ sneaker
SNEAKEUP *n* sneaky person
SNEAKIER ▶ sneaky
SNEAKILY ▶ sneak
SNEAKING *adj* slight but persistent
SNEAKISH *adj* typical of a sneak
SNEAKS ▶ sneak
SNEAKSBY *n* sneak
SNEAKY, SNEAKIER ▶ sneak
SNEAP, -ED, -ING, -S *vb* nip
SNEATH, -S *same as* ▶ **snath**
SNEB, -BED, -BING, -S *same as* ▶ **snib**
SNEBBE, -S *same as* ▶ **snub**
SNEBBED ▶ sneb
SNEBBES ▶ snebbe
SNEBBING ▶ sneb
SNEBS ▶ sneb
SNECK, -ED, -ING, -S *n* small squared stone used in a rubble wall to fill spaces between stones ▷ *vb* fasten (a latch)
SNED, -DED, -DING, -S *vb* prune or trim
SNEE, -D, -ING, -S *vb* cut
SNEER, -ED, -S *n* contemptuous expression or remark ▷ *vb* show contempt by a sneer
SNEERER -S
SNEERFUL ▶ sneer
SNEERIER ▶ sneery
SNEERING ▶ sneer
SNEERS ▶ sneer
SNEERY, SNEERIER *adj* contemptuous or scornful
SNEES ▶ snee
SNEESH, -ED, -ES *n* Scots word meaning pinch of snuff ▷ *vb* take snuff
SNEESHAN *n* Scots word meaning pinch of snuff
SNEESHED ▶ sneesh
SNEESHES ▶ sneesh
SNEESHIN *same as* ▶ **sneeshan**

S

SNEEZE, -D, -S, SNEEZING
vb expel air from the nose
suddenly, involuntarily, and
noisily ▷ *n* act or sound of
sneezing

SNEEZER -S

SNEEZIER ► sneezy

SNEEZING ► sneeze

SNEEZY, SNEEZIER ► sneeze

SNELL, -ED, -ER, -EST, -ING, -S
adj biting ▷ *vb* attach hook
to fishing line

SNELLY

SNIB, -BED, -BING, -S *n* catch
of a door or window ▷ *vb*
bolt or fasten (a door)

SNICK, -ED, -ING, -S *n* (make)
a small cut or notch ▷ *vb*
make a small cut or notch in
(something)

SNICKER, -S *same as*
► **snigger**

SNICKERY

SNICKET, -S *n* passageway
between walls or fences

SNICKING ► snick

SNICKS ► snick

**SNIDE, -D, -R, -S, -ST,
SNIDING** *adj* critical in an
unfair and nasty way ▷ *n*
sham jewellery ▷ *vb* fill or
load

SNIDELY

SNIDEY, SNIDIER, SNIDIEST
same as ► **snide**

SNIDING ► snide

SNIES ► sny

SNIFF, -ED, -S *vb* inhale
through the nose in short
audible breaths ▷ *n* act or
sound of sniffing

SNIFFER, -S *n* device for
detecting hidden substances
such as drugs

SNIFFIER ► sniffy

SNIFFILY ► sniffy

SNIFFING ► sniff

SNIFFISH *adj* disdainful

SNIFFLE, -D, -S *vb* sniff
repeatedly, as when suffering
from a cold ▷ *n* slight cold

SNIFFLER

SNIFFLY

SNIFFS ► sniff

SNIFFY, SNIFFIER *adj*
contemptuous or scornful

SNIFT, -ED, -ING, -S *same as*
► **sniff**

SNIFTER, -S *n* small quantity
of alcoholic drink ▷ *vb* sniff

SNIFTIER ► snifty

SNIFTING ► snift

SNIFTS ► snift

SNIFTY, SNIFTIER *adj* slang
word meaning excellent

SNIG, -GED, -GING, -S *vb*
drag (a felled log) by a chain
or cable

SNIGGER, -S *n* sly laugh ▷ *vb*
laugh slyly

SNIGGING ► snig

SNIGGLE, -D, -S *vb* fish for
eels by dangling or thrusting
a baited hook into cavities
▷ *n* baited hook used for
sniggling eels

SNIGGLER

SNIGLET, -S *n* invented word

SNIGS ► snig

SNIP, -PED, -PING, -S *vb*
cut in small quick strokes
with scissors or shears
▷ *n* bargain ▷ *interj*
representation of the sound
of scissors or shears closing

SNIPE, -D, -S *n* wading bird
with a long straight bill ▷ *vb*
shoot at (a person) from
cover

SNIPER, -S *n* person who
shoots at someone from
cover

SNIPES ► snipe

SNIPIER ► snipy

SNIPIEST ► snipy

SNIPING, -S ► snipe

SNIPPED ► snip

SNIPPER, -S ► snip

SNIPPET, -S *n* small piece

SNIPPETY

SNIPPIER ► snippy

SNIPPILY ► snippy

SNIPPING ► snip

SNIPPY, SNIPPIER *adj*
scrappy

SNIPS ► snip

SNIPY, SNIPIER, SNIPIEST *adj*
like a snipe

SNIRT, -ED, -ING, -S *n* Scots
word meaning suppressed
laugh ▷ *vb* to snigger

SNIRTLE, -D, -S *vb* Scots word
meaning snicker

SNIRTS ► snirt

SNIT, -S *n* fit of temper

SNITCH, -ED, -ES *vb* act as an
informer ▷ *n* informer

SNITCHER

SNITCHY *adj* bad-tempered
or irritable

SNITS ► snit

SNITTY, SNITTIER *adj* cross
or irritable

SNIVEL, -ED, -S *vb* cry in a
whining way ▷ *n* act of
snivelling

SNIVELER

SNIVELLY

SNIVELY *same as* ► **snivelly**

SNOB, -S *n* person who judges
others by social rank

SNOBBERY

SNOBBIER ► snobby

SNOBBILY ► snob

SNOBBISH ► snob

SNOBBISM ► snob

SNOBBY, SNOBBIER ► snob

SNOBLING *n* little snob

SNOBS ► snob

SNOCOACH *n* bus-like vehicle
for travelling on snow

**SNOD, -DED, -DER, -DEST,
-DING, -DIT, -S** *adj* Scots
word meaning tidy ▷ *vb*
make tidy

SNOEK, -S *n* edible marine fish

SNOEP *adj* mean or tightfisted

SNOG, -GED, -GING, -S *vb* kiss
and cuddle ▷ *n* act of kissing
and cuddling

SNOGGER, -S *n* person who
snogs

SNOGGING ► snog

SNOGS ► snog

SNOKE, -D, -S, SNOKING
same as ► **snook**

SNOOD, -ED, -ING, -S *n* pouch
loosely holding a woman's
hair at the back ▷ *vb* hold
(the hair) in a snood

SNOOK, -ED, -ING, -S *n* any
of several large game fishes
▷ *vb* lurk

SNOOKER, -S *n* game played
on a billiard table ▷ *vb* leave
(a snooker opponent) unable
to hit the target ball

SNOOKING ► snook

SNOOKS ► snook

SNOOL, -ED, -ING, -S *vb* Scots
word meaning dominate

SNOOP, -ED, -ING, -S *vb* pry
▷ *n* snooping

SNOOPER, -S *n* person who
snoops

SNOOPIER ► snoopy

SNOOPILY ► snoop

SNOOPING ► snoop

SNOOPS ► snoop

SNOOPY, SNOOPIER
► **snoop**

SNOOSE, -S *n* snuff

SNOOT, -ED, -ING, -S *n* nose
▷ *vb* look contemptuously at

SNOOTFUL *n* enough alcohol
to make someone drunk

SNOOTIER ► snooty

SNOOTILY ► snooty

SNOOTING ► snoot

SNOOTS ► snoot

SNOOTY, SNOOTIER *adj*
haughty

SNOOZE, -D, -S, SNOOZING
vb take a brief light sleep

▷ *n* brief light sleep

SNOOZER -S

SNOOZIER ▸ snoozy

SNOOZING ▸ snooze

SNOOZLE, -D, -S *vb* cuddle and sleep

SNOOZY, SNOOZIER ▸ **snooze**

SNORE, -D, -S *vb* make snorting sounds while sleeping ▷ *n* sound of snoring

SNORER -S

SNORING, -S ▸ snore

SNORKEL, -S *n* tube allowing a swimmer to breathe ▷ *vb* swim using a snorkel

SNORT, -ED, -S *vb* exhale noisily through the nostrils ▷ *n* act or sound of snorting

SNORTER, -S *n* person or animal that snorts

SNORTIER ▸ snorty

SNORTING ▸ snort

SNORTS ▸ snort

SNORTY, SNORTIER ▸ snort

SNOT, -S, -TED, -TING *n* mucus from the nose ▷ *vb* blow one's nose

SNOTRAG, -S *n* handkerchief

SNOTS ▸ snot

SNOTTED ▸ snot

SNOTTER, -S *vb* breathe through obstructed nostrils

SNOTTERY *n* snot

SNOTTIE *n* midshipman

SNOTTIER ▸ snotty

SNOTTIES ▸ snotty

SNOTTILY ▸ snotty

SNOTTING ▸ snot

SNOTTY, SNOTTIER, SNOTTIES *adj* covered with mucus from the nose

SNOUT, -ING, -S *n* animal's projecting nose and jaws ▷ *vb* have or give a snout

SNOUTED

SNOUTIER ▸ snouty

SNOUTING ▸ snout

SNOUTISH ▸ snout

SNOUTS ▸ snout

SNOUTY, SNOUTIER ▸ **snout**

SNOW, -ED, -ING, -S *n* frozen vapour falling from the sky in flakes ▷ *vb* fall as or like snow

SNOWBALL *n* snow pressed into a ball for throwing ▷ *vb* increase rapidly

SNOWBANK *n* bank of snow

SNOWBELL *n* Asian shrub

SNOWBELT *n* northern states of USA

SNOWBIRD *n* bird of arctic regions

SNOWBOOT *n* boot for walking in snow

SNOWBUSH *n* North American plant

SNOWCAP, -S *n* cap of snow on top of a mountain

SNOWCAT, -S *n* tracked vehicle for travelling over snow

SNOWDOME *n* leisure centre with facilities for skiing, skating, etc

SNOWDROP *n* small white bell-shaped spring flower

SNOWED ▸ snow

SNOWFALL *n* fall of snow

SNOWFLEA *n* wingless insect that lives on or in snow

SNOWIER ▸ snowy

SNOWIEST ▸ snowy

SNOWILY ▸ snowy

SNOWING ▸ snow

SNOWISH *adj* like snow

SNOWK, -ED, -ING, -S *same as* ▸ **snook**

SNOWLAND *n* area where snow lies

SNOWLESS ▸ snow

SNOWLIKE ▸ snow

SNOWLINE *n* limit of permanent snow

SNOWMAN, SNOWMEN *n* figure shaped out of snow

SNOWMELT *n* melting of snow in spring

SNOWMEN ▸ snowman

SNOWMOLD *same as* > **snowmould**

SNOWPACK *n* body of hard-packed snow

SNOWPLOW *n* implement or vehicle for clearing snow away

SNOWS ▸ snow

SNOWSHED *n* shelter built over an exposed section of railway track

SNOWSHOE *n* racket-shaped frame with a network of thongs stretched across it for walking on snow ▷ *vb* walk using snowshoes

SNOWSLIP *n* small snow avalanche

SNOWSUIT *n* one-piece winter outer garment for child

SNOWY, SNOWIER, SNOWIEST *adj* covered with or abounding in snow

SNUB, -BED, -BING, -S *vb* insult deliberately ▷ *n* deliberate insult ▷ *adj* (of a nose) short and blunt

SNUBBE, -S *n* stub

SNUBBED ▸ snub

SNUBBER, -S ▸ snub

SNUBBES ▸ snubbe

SNUBBIER ▸ snubby

SNUBBING ▸ snub

SNUBBISH ▸ snub

SNUBBY, SNUBBIER ▸ snub

SNUBFIN *adj as in* **snubfin dolphin** Australian dolphin with a small dorsal fin

SNUBNESS ▸ snub

SNUBS ▸ snub

SNUCK *past tense and past participle of* ▸ **sneak**

SNUDGE, -D, -S, SNUDGING *vb* be miserly

SNUFF, -ED, -ING, -S *n* powdered tobacco for sniffing up the nostrils ▷ *vb* extinguish (a candle)

SNUFFBOX *n* small container for holding snuff

SNUFFED ▸ snuff

SNUFFER, -S ▸ snuff

SNUFFIER ▸ snuffy

SNUFFILY ▸ snuffy

SNUFFING ▸ snuff

SNUFFLE, -D *vb* breathe noisily or with difficulty ▷ *n* act or the sound of snuffling

SNUFFLER

SNUFFLES *same as* ▸ **sniffles**

SNUFFLY ▸ snuffle

SNUFFS ▸ snuff

SNUFFY, SNUFFIER *adj* of, relating to, or resembling snuff

SNUG, -GED, -GER, -GEST, -GING, -S *adj* warm and comfortable ▷ *n* small peg that stops a bolt from turning ▷ *vb* make or become comfortable and warm

SNUGGERY *n* cosy and comfortable place or room

SNUGGEST ▸ snug

SNUGGIES *pl n* specially warm underwear

SNUGGING ▸ snug

SNUGGLE, -D, -S *vb* nestle into a person or thing for warmth or from affection ▷ *n* act of snuggling

SNUGGLY *adj* comfortably warm and suitable for snuggling

SNUGLY ▸ snug

SNUGNESS ▸ snug

SNUGS ▸ snug

SNUSH, -ED, -ES, -ING *vb* take snuff

SNUZZLE, -D, -S *vb* root in ground

SNY, SNIES *same as* ▸ **snye**

A side channel of a river, that can be useful when you are short of vowels. And note that it can be extended to form **snye**.

SNYE, -S *n* side channel of a river

SO, -S *adv* such an extent ▷ *interj* exclamation of surprise, triumph, or realization ▷ *n* the fifth note of the musical scale

SOAK, -ED, -EN, -S *vb* make wet ▷ *n* soaking

SOAKAGE, -S *n* process or a period in which a permeable substance is soaked in a liquid

SOAKAWAY *n* pit filled with rubble, etc, into which rain or waste water drains

SOAKED ▸ soak

SOAKEN ▸ soak

SOAKER, -S ▸ soak

SOAKING, -S ▸ soak

SOAKS ▸ soak

SOAP, -ED, -ING, -S *n* compound of alkali and fat, used with water as a cleaning agent ▷ *vb* apply soap to

SOAPBARK *n* W South American rosaceous tree

SOAPBOX *n* crate used as a platform for speech-making ▷ *vb* deliver a speech from a soapbox

SOAPDISH *n* dish for holding soap

SOAPED ▸ soap

SOAPER, -S *n* soap opera

SOAPFISH *n* tropical fish with toxic mucus

SOAPIE, -S *n* soap opera

SOAPIER ▸ soapie

SOAPIES ▸ soapie

SOAPIEST ▸ soapy

SOAPILY ▸ soapy

SOAPING ▸ soap

SOAPLESS ▸ soap

SOAPLIKE ▸ soap

SOAPROOT *n* plant with roots used as soap substitute

SOAPS ▸ soap

SOAPSUDS *pl n* foam or lather produced when soap is mixed with water

SOAPWORT *n* Eurasian plant with clusters of fragrant pink or white flowers

SOAPY, SOAPIER, SOAPIEST *adj* covered with soap

SOAR, -ED, -S *vb* rise or fly upwards ▷ *n* act of soaring

SOARAWAY *adj* exceedingly successful

SOARE, -S *n* young hawk

SOARED ▸ soar

SOARER, -S ▸ soar

SOARES ▸ soare

SOARING, -S ▸ soar

SOARS ▸ soar

SOAVE, -S *n* dry white Italian wine

SOB, -BED, -S *vb* weep with convulsive gasps ▷ *n* act or sound of sobbing

SOBA, -S *n* (in Japanese cookery) noodles made from buckwheat flour

SOBBED ▸ sob

SOBBER, -S ▸ sob

SOBBING, -S ▸ sob

SOBEIT *conj* provided that

SOBER, -ED, -ER, -EST, -S *adj* not drunk ▷ *vb* make or become sober

SOBERING

SOBERISE *same as* ▸ soberize

SOBERIZE *vb* make sober

SOBERLY ▸ sober

SOBERS ▸ sober

SOBFUL *adj* tearful

SOBOLE, -S *n* creeping underground stem that produces roots and buds

SOBRIETY *n* state of being sober

SOBS ▸ sob

SOC, -ES, -S *n* feudal right to hold court

SOCA, -S *n* mixture of soul and calypso music

SOCAGE, -S *n* tenure of land by certain services

SOCAGER -S

SOCAS ▸ soca

SOCCAGE, -S *same as* ▸ socage

SOCCER, -S *n* football played by two teams of eleven kicking a spherical ball

SOCES ▸ soc

SOCIABLE *adj* friendly or companionable ▷ *n* type of open carriage with two seats facing each other

SOCIABLY

SOCIAL, -S *adj* living in a community ▷ *n* informal gathering

SOCIALLY

SOCIATE, -S *n* associate

SOCIETAL *adj* of or relating to society, esp human society or social relations

SOCIETY *n* human beings considered as a group

SOCK, -ED, -ING, -S *n* knitted covering for the foot ▷ *vb* hit hard

SOCKET, -ED, -S *n* hole or recess into which something

fits ▷ *vb* furnish with or place into a socket

SOCKETTE *n* sock not covering ankle

SOCKEYE, -S *n* Pacific salmon with red flesh

SOCKING ▸ sock

SOCKLESS ▸ sock

SOCKMAN, SOCKMEN *same as* ▸ socman

SOCKO *adj* excellent

SOCKS ▸ sock

SOCLE, -S *another name for* ▸ plinth

SOCMAN, SOCMEN *n* tenant holding land by socage

SOCS ▸ soc

SOD, -DED, -S *n* (piece of) turf ▷ *vb* cover with sods

SODA, -S *n* compound of sodium

SODAIC *adj* containing soda

SODAIN *same as* ▸ sudden

SODAINE *same as* ▸ sudden

SODALESS ▸ soda

SODALIST *n* member of sodality

SODALITE *n* blue, grey, yellow, or colourless mineral

SODALITY *n* religious or charitable society

SODAMIDE *n* white crystalline compound used as a dehydrating agent

SODAS ▸ soda

SODDED ▸ sod

SODDEN, -ED, -S *adj* soaked ▷ *vb* make or become sodden

SODDENLY

SODDIE, -S *n* house made of sod

SODDIER ▸ soddy

SODDIES ▸ soddie

SODDIEST ▸ soddy

SODDING ▸ sod

SODDY, SODDIER, SODDIEST *adj* covered with turf

SODGER, -ED, -S *dialect variant of* ▸ soldier

SODIC *adj* containing sodium

SODICITY

SODIUM, -S *n* silvery-white metallic element

SODS ▸ sod

SOEVER *adv* in any way at all

SOFA, -S *n* couch

SOFABED, -S *n* sofa that converts into a bed

SOFAR, -S *n* system for determining a position at sea

SOFAS ▸ sofa

SOFFIONI *n* holes in volcano that emit steam

SOFFIT, -S *n* underside of a part of a building or a structural component

SOFT, -ED, -ER, -EST, -ING, -S adj easy to shape or cut ▷ adv softly ▷ vb soften
SOFTA, -S n Muslim student of divinity and jurisprudence
SOFTBACK n paperback
SOFTBALL n game similar to baseball, played using a larger softer ball
SOFTED ▸ soft
SOFTEN, -ED, -S vb make or become soft or softer
SOFTENER n substance added to another substance to increase its softness
SOFTENS ▸ soften
SOFTER ▸ soft
SOFTEST ▸ soft
SOFTHEAD n insulting word for a stupid person
SOFTIE n person who is easily upset
SOFTIES ▸ softy
SOFTING ▸ soft
SOFTISH ▸ soft
SOFTLING n weakling
SOFTLY ▸ soft
SOFTNESS n quality or an instance of being soft
SOFTS ▸ soft
SOFTWARE n computer programs
SOFTWOOD n wood of a coniferous tree
SOFTY, SOFTIES same as ▸ softie
SOG, -GED, -S vb soak
SOGER, -S same as ▸ sodger
SOGGED ▸ sog
SOGGIER ▸ soggy
SOGGIEST ▸ soggy
SOGGILY ▸ soggy
SOGGING, -S ▸ sog
SOGGY, SOGGIER, SOGGIEST adj soaked
SOGS ▸ sog
SOH, -S n (in tonic sol-fa) fifth degree of any major scale
SOHO interj exclamation announcing the sighting of a hare
SOHS ▸ soh
SOHUR, -S same as ▸ suhur
SOIGNE adj well-groomed, elegant
SOIGNEE variant of ▸ soigne
SOIL, -ED, -S n top layer of earth ▷ vb make or become dirty
SOILAGE, -S n green fodder
SOILED ▸ soil
SOILIER ▸ soily
SOILIEST ▸ soily
SOILING, -S ▸ soil
SOILLESS ▸ soil
SOILS ▸ soil

SOILURE, -S n act of soiling or the state of being soiled
SOILY, SOILIER, SOILIEST ▸ soil
SOIREE, -S n evening party or gathering
SOJA, -S same as ▸ soya
SOJOURN, -S n temporary stay ▷ vb stay temporarily
SOJU, -S n type of Korean vodka
SOKAH, -S same as ▸ soca
SOKAIYA n Japanese extortionist
SOKE, -S n right to hold a local court
SOKEMAN, SOKEMEN same as ▸ socman
SOKEN, -S n feudal district
SOKES ▸ soke
SOKOL, -S n Czech gymnastic association
SOL, -S n liquid colloidal solution
SOLA, -S n Indian plant
SOLACE, -D, -S, SOLACING vb comfort in distress ▷ n comfort in misery or disappointment
SOLACER -S
SOLAH, -S n Indian plant
SOLAN, -S archaic name for ▸ gannet
SOLAND, -S n solan goose
SOLANDER n box for specimens, maps, etc, in the form of a book with a lid
SOLANDS ▸ soland
SOLANIN, -S same as ▸ solanine
SOLANINE n poisonous alkaloid found in various solanaceous plants
SOLANINS ▸ solanin
SOLANO, -S n hot wind in Spain
SOLANS ▸ solan
SOLANUM, -S n any plant of the genus that includes the potato
SOLAR, -S adj of the sun ▷ n upper room
SOLARIA ▸ solarium
SOLARISE same as ▸ solarize
SOLARISM n explanation of myths in terms of the movements and influence of the sun
SOLARIST
SOLARIUM, SOLARIA n place with beds and ultraviolet lights used for acquiring an artificial suntan
SOLARIZE vb treat by exposure to the sun's rays
SOLARS ▸ solar

SOLAS ▸ sola
SOLATE, -D, -S, SOLATING vb change from gel to liquid
SOLATIA ▸ solatium
SOLATING ▸ solate
SOLATION n liquefaction of a gel
SOLATIUM, SOLATIA n compensation awarded for injury to the feelings
SOLD, -S n obsolete word for salary
SOLDADO, -S n soldier
SOLDAN, -S archaic word for ▸ sultan
SOLDE, -S n wages
SOLDER, -ED, -S n soft alloy used to join two metal surfaces ▷ vb join with solder
SOLDERER
SOLDES ▸ solde
SOLDI ▸ soldo
SOLDIER, -S n member of an army ▷ vb serve in an army
SOLDIERY n soldiers collectively
SOLDO, SOLDI n former Italian copper coin
SOLDS ▸ sold
SOLE, -D, -S, SOLING adj one and only ▷ n underside of the foot ▷ vb provide (a shoe) with a sole
SOLECISE variant of ▸ solecize
SOLECISM n minor grammatical mistake
SOLECIST
SOLECIZE vb commit a solecism
SOLED ▸ sole
SOLEI ▸ soleus
SOLEIN same as ▸ sullen
SOLELESS ▸ sole
SOLELY adv only, completely
SOLEMN, -ER adj serious, deeply sincere
SOLEMNLY
SOLENESS ▸ sole
SOLENOID n coil of wire magnetized by passing a current through it
SOLER, -S same as ▸ sole
SOLERA, -S n system for aging sherry and other fortified wines
SOLERET, -S n armour for foot
SOLERS ▸ soler
SOLES ▸ sole
SOLEUS, SOLEI, -ES n muscle in calf of leg
SOLFEGE, -S variant of >solfeggio
SOLFEGGI >solfeggio

S

SOLGEL adj changing between sol and gel

SOLI adv to be performed by or with soloists

SOLICIT, -S vb request

SOLICITY n act of making a request

SOLID, -ER, -EST, -S adj (of a substance) keeping its shape ▷ n three-dimensional shape

SOLIDAGO n chiefly American plant of the genus which includes the goldenrods

SOLIDARE n old coin

SOLIDARY adj marked by unity of interests, responsibilities, etc

SOLIDATE vb consolidate

SOLIDER ► solid

SOLIDEST ► solid

SOLIDI ► solidus

SOLIDIFY vb make or become solid or firm

SOLIDISH ► solid

SOLIDISM n belief that diseases spring from damage to solid parts of body

SOLIDIST

SOLIDITY ► solid

SOLIDLY ► solid

SOLIDS ► solid

SOLIDUM, -S n part of pedestal

SOLIDUS, SOLIDI same as ► slash

SOLING ► sole

SOLION, -S n amplifier used in chemistry

SOLIPED, -S n animal whose hooves are not cloven

SOLIQUID n semi-solid, semi-liquid solution

SOLITARY adj alone, single ▷ n hermit

SOLITO adv musical instruction meaning play in usual manner

SOLITON, -S n type of isolated particle-like wave

SOLITUDE n state of being alone

SOLIVE, -S n type of joist

SOLLAR, -ED, -S n archaic word meaning attic ▷ vb put in a sollar

SOLLER, -S same as ► sollar

SOLLERET n protective covering for the foot consisting of riveted plates of armour

SOLLERS ► soller

SOLO, -ED, -ES, -ING, -S n music for one performer ▷ adj done alone ▷ adv by oneself, alone ▷ vb undertake a venture alone

SOLOIST, -S n person who performs a solo

SOLON, -S n US congressman

SOLONETS same as ► solonetz

SOLONETZ n type of intrazonal soil with a high saline content characterized by leaching

SOLONS ► solon

SOLOS ► solo

SOLPUGID n venomous arachnid

SOLS ► sol

SOLSTICE n either the shortest (in winter) or longest (in summer) day of the year

SOLUBLE, -S adj able to be dissolved ▷ n soluble substance

SOLUBLY

SOLUM, -S n upper layers of the soil profile

SOLUNAR adj relating to sun and moon

SOLUS, -ES n advert printed or published separately from others

SOLUTAL adj relating to a solute

SOLUTE, -S n substance in a solution that is dissolved ▷ adj loose or unattached

SOLUTION n answer to a problem

SOLUTIVE adj dissolving ▷ n solvent or laxative

SOLVABLE adj capable of being solved

SOLVATE, -D, -S vb undergo, cause to undergo, or partake in solvation

SOLVE, -D, -S, SOLVING vb find the answer to (a problem)

SOLVENCY n ability to pay all debts

SOLVENT, -S adj having enough money to pay one's debts ▷ n liquid capable of dissolving other substances

SOLVER, -S ► solve

SOLVES ► solve

SOLVING ► solve

SOM, -S, -Y n currency of Kyrgyzstan and Uzbekistan

SOMA, -S, -TA n body of an organism as distinct from the germ cells

SOMAN, -S n compound developed as a nerve gas

SOMAS ► soma

SOMATA ► soma

SOMATIC adj of the body, as distinct from the mind

SOMATISM n materialism

SOMATIST

SOMBER, -ED, -ER, -S adj (in the US) sombre ▷ vb (in the US) make sombre

SOMBERLY

SOMBRE, -D, -R, -S, -ST, SOMBRING adj dark, gloomy ▷ vb make sombre

SOMBRELY

SOMBRERO n wide-brimmed Mexican hat

SOMBRES ► sombre

SOMBREST ► sombre

SOMBRING ► sombre

SOMBROUS ► sombre

SOME adj unknown or unspecified ▷ pron certain unknown or unspecified people or things ▷ adv approximately ▷ determiner (a) certain unknown or unspecified

SOMEBODY pron some person ▷ n important person

SOMEDAY adv at some unspecified time in the future

SOMEDEAL adv to some extent ▷ n some part of something

SOMEDELE same as ► somedeal

SOMEGATE adv Scots word meaning somehow

SOMEHOW adv in some unspecified way

SOMEONE, -S pron somebody ▷ n significant or important person

SOMERSET n somersault

SOMETIME adv at some unspecified time ▷ adj former

SOMEWAY adv in some unspecified manner

SOMEWAYS same as ► someway

SOMEWHAT adv some extent, rather ▷ n vague amount

SOMEWHEN adv at some time

SOMEWHY adv for some reason

SOMEWISE adv in some way or to some degree

SOMITAL ► somite

SOMITE, -S n segment of mesoderm in vertebrate embryos

SOMITIC

SOMNIAL adj of dreams

SOMNIATE vb dream

SOMNIFIC adj inducing sleep

SOMONI, -S n monetary unit of Tajikistan

SOMS ► som

SOMY ► som

SON, -S n male offspring

SONANCE, -S same as ► sonant

SONANCY ► sonant

SONANT, -S n voiced sound able to form a syllable or syllable nucleus ▷ adj denoting a voiced sound like this

SONANTAL

SONANTIC

SONAR, -S n device for detecting underwater objects by the reflection of sound waves

SONARMAN, SONARMEN n sonar operator

SONARS ► sonar

SONATA, -S n piece of music in several movements for one instrument

SONATINA n short sonata

SONATINE same as ► sonatina

SONCE, -S n Scots word meaning good luck

SONDAGE, -S n deep trial trench for inspecting stratigraphy

SONDE, -S n rocket, balloon, or probe used for observing in the upper atmosphere

SONDELI, -S n Indian shrew

SONDER, -S n yacht category

SONDES ► sonde

SONE, -S n subjective unit of loudness

SONERI, -S n Indian cloth of gold

SONES ► sone

SONG, -S n music for the voice

SONGBIRD n any bird with a musical call

SONGBOOK n book of songs

SONGFEST n event with many songs

SONGFUL adj tuneful

SONGKOK, -S n (in Malaysia and Indonesia) a kind of oval brimless hat, resembling a skull

SONGLESS ► song

SONGLIKE ► song

SONGMAN, SONGMEN n singer

SONGS ► song

SONGSTER n singer

SONHOOD, -S ► son

SONIC adj of or producing sound

SONICATE vb subject to sound waves

SONICS n study of mechanical vibrations in matter

SONLESS ► son

SONLIKE ► son

SONLY adj like a son

SONNE, -S same as ► son

SONNET, -ED, -S n fourteen-line poem ▷ vb compose sonnets

SONNY, SONNIES n term of address to a boy

SONOBUOY n buoy equipped to detect underwater noises and transmit them by radio

SONOGRAM n three-dimensional representation of a sound signal

SONORANT n type of frictionless continuant or nasal

SONORITY ► sonorous

SONOROUS adj (of sound) deep or resonant

SONOVOX n device used to alter sound of human voice in music recordings

SONS ► son

SONSE, -S same as ► sonce

SONSHIP, -S ► son

SONSIE same as ► sonsy

SONSY, SONSIER, SONSIEST adj plump

SONTAG, -S n type of knitted women's cape

SONTIES n Shakespearian oath

SOOCHONG same as ► souchong

SOOEY interj call used to summon pigs

SOOGEE, -D, -S vb clean ship using a special solution

SOOGIE, -D, -S same as ► soogee

SOOJEY, -S same as ► soogee

SOOK, -ED, -ING, -S n baby ▷ vb suck

SOOL, -ED, -ING, -S vb incite (a dog) to attack

SOOLE, -S same as ► sool

SOOLED ► sool

SOOLER, -S n person who incites a dog to attack

SOOLES ► soole

SOOLING ► sool

SOOLS ► sool

SOOM, -ED, -ING, -S Scots word for ► swim

SOON adv in a short time

SOONER, -S adv rather ▷ n idler or shirker

SOONEST adv as soon as possible

SOONISH adj somewhat soon

SOOP, -ED, -S Scots word for ► sweep

SOOPING -S

SOOT, -ED, -ES, -S n black powder formed by the incomplete burning of an organic substance ▷ vb cover with soot

SOOTE n sweet

SOOTED ► soot

SOOTES ► soot

SOOTH, -EST, -S n truth or reality ▷ adj true or real

SOOTHE, -D, -S vb make calm

SOOTHER, -S vb flatter

SOOTHES ► soothe

SOOTHEST ► sooth

SOOTHFUL adj truthful

SOOTHING adj having a calming, assuaging, or relieving effect

SOOTHLY ► sooth

SOOTHS ► sooth

SOOTHSAY vb predict the future

SOOTIER ► sooty

SOOTIEST ► sooty

SOOTILY ► sooty

SOOTING, -S n state of becoming covered with soot

SOOTLESS ► soot

SOOTS ► soot

SOOTY, SOOTIER, SOOTIEST adj covered with soot

SOP, -PED, -S n concession to pacify someone ▷ vb mop up or absorb (liquid)

SOPH, -S shortened form of > sophomore

SOPHERIC ► sopherim

SOPHERIM n Jewish scribes

SOPHIES ► sophy

SOPHISM, -S n argument that seems reasonable but is actually false and misleading

SOPHIST, -S n person who uses clever but invalid arguments

SOPHS ► soph

SOPHY, SOPHIES n title of the Persian monarchs

SOPITE, -D, -S, SOPITING vb lull to sleep

SOPOR, -S n abnormally deep sleep

SOPOROSE adj sleepy

SOPOROUS same as ► soporose

SOPORS ► sopor

SOPPED ► sop

SOPPIER ► soppy

SOPPIEST ► soppy

SOPPILY ► soppy

SOPPING, -S ► sop

SOPPY, SOPPIER, SOPPIEST adj over-sentimental

S

SOPRA *adv* musical instruction meaning above

SOPRANO, SOPRANI, -S *n* singer with the highest female or boy's voice ▷ *adj* of a musical instrument that is the highest or second highest pitched in its family

SOPS ▷ sop

SORA, -S *n* North American rail with a yellow bill

SORAGE, -S *n* first year in hawk's life

SORAL ▷ sorus

SORAS ▷ sora

SORB, -ED, -ING, -S *n* any of various related trees, esp the mountain ash ▷ *vb* absorb or adsorb

SORBABLE

SORBARIA *n* Asian shrub

SORBATE, -S *n* salt of sorbic acid

SORBED ▷ sorb

SORBENT, -S ▷ sorb

SORBET, -S *same as* ▷ **sherbet**

SORBIC ▷ sorb

SORBING ▷ sorb

SORBITAN *n* any of a group of compounds derived from sorbitol

SORBITE, -S *n* mineral found in steel

SORBITIC

SORBITOL *n* white water-soluble crystalline alcohol with a sweet taste

SORBO *n as in* **sorbo rubber** spongy form of rubber

SORBOSE, -S *n* sugar derived from the berries of the mountain ash

SORBS ▷ sorb

SORBUS, -ES *n* rowan or related tree

SORCERER *n* magician

SORCERY *n* witchcraft or magic

SORD, -ED, -ING, -S *n* flock of mallard ducks ▷ *vb* ascend in flight

SORDA *n* deaf woman

SORDED ▷ sord

SORDES *pl n* dark incrustations on the lips and teeth of patients with prolonged fever

SORDID, -ER *adj* dirty, squalid

SORDIDLY

SORDINE, -S *same as* ▷ **sordino**

SORDING ▷ sord

SORDINO, SORDINI *n* mute for a stringed or brass musical instrument

SORDO *n* deaf man

SORDOR, -S *n* sordidness

SORDS ▷ sord

SORE, -D, -R, -S, -ST *adj* painful ▷ *n* painful area on the body ▷ *adv* greatly ▷ *vb* make sore

SOREDIA ▷ soredium

> This is the plural of **soredium**, a reproductive body in lichens. It is a very frequently played bonus, and it has a 'twin': **roadies**. It is a good idea to become familiar with at least the higher probability twin sevens and eights, since the thought of one will often prompt the other, and it may well be that one twin will fit on the board where the other would not.

SOREDIAL ▷ soredium

SOREDIUM, SOREDIA *n* organ of vegetative reproduction in lichens

SOREE, -S *same as* ▷ **sora**

SOREHEAD *n* peevish or disgruntled person

SOREHON, -S *n* old Irish feudal right

SOREL, -S *variant of* ▷ **sorrel**

SORELL, -S *same as* ▷ **sorrel**

SORELS ▷ sorel

SORELY *adv* greatly

SORENESS ▷ sore

SORER ▷ sore

SORES ▷ sore

SOREST ▷ sore

SOREX, -ES *n* shrew or related animal

SORGHO, -S *same as* ▷ **sorgo**

SORGHUM, -S *n* kind of grass cultivated for grain

SORGO, -S *n* any of several varieties of sorghum that have watery sweet juice

SORI ▷ sorus

SORICINE *adj* of or resembling a shrew

SORICOID *same as* ▷ **soricine**

SORING, -S ▷ sore

SORITES *n* type of syllogism in which only the final conclusion is stated

SORITIC

SORN, -ED, -S *vb* obtain food, etc, from another person by presuming on his or her generosity

SORNER -S

SORNING, -S ▷ sorn

SORNS ▷ sorn

SOROBAN, -S *n* Japanese abacus

SOROCHE, -S *n* altitude sickness

SORORAL *adj* of sister

SORORATE *n* custom in some societies of a widower marrying his deceased wife's younger sister

SORORIAL *same as* ▷ **sororal**

SORORISE *same as* ▷ **sororize**

SORORITY *n* society for female students

SORORIZE *vb* socialize in sisterly way

SOROSIS, SOROSES *n* fleshy multiple fruit

SORPTION *n* process in which one substance takes up or holds another

SORPTIVE

SORRA, -S *Irish word for* ▷ **sorrow**

SORREL, -S *n* bitter-tasting plant

SORRIER ▷ sorry

SORRIEST ▷ sorry

SORRILY ▷ sorry

SORROW, -ED, -S *n* grief or sadness ▷ *vb* grieve

SORROWER

SORRY, SORRIER, SORRIEST *adj* feeling pity or regret ▷ *interj* exclamation expressing apology or asking someone to repeat what he or she has said

SORRYISH

SORT, -S *n* group all sharing certain qualities or characteristics ▷ *vb* arrange according to kind

SORTA *adv* phonetic representation of 'sort of'

SORTABLE ▷ sort

SORTABLY ▷ sort

SORTAL, -S *n* type of logical or linguistic concept

SORTANCE *n* suitableness

SORTED *interj* exclamation of satisfaction, approval, etc ▷ *adj* having been corrected or made ready

SORTER, -S ▷ sort

SORTES *n* divination by opening book at random

SORTIE, -D, -S *n* relatively short return trip ▷ *vb* make a sortie

SORTING, -S ▷ sort

SORTMENT *n* assortment

SORTS ▷ sort

SORUS, SORI *n* cluster of sporangia on the

undersurface of certain fern leaves

SOS, **-es** ► so

SOSATIE, **-S** n skewer of curried meat pieces

SOSS, **-ED**, **-ES** vb make dirty or muddy

SOSSING -S

SOT, **-S**, **-TED** n habitual drunkard ▷ adv indeed: used to contradict a negative statement ▷ vb be a drunkard

SOTERIAL adj of salvation

This means pertaining to salvation, and is one of the most important 8-letter words to know because the chance to play it as a bonus comes up so often.

SOTH, **-S** archaic variant of ► sooth

SOTOL, **-S** n American plant related to agave

SOTS ► sot

SOTTED ► sot

SOTTEDLY ► sot

SOTTING, **-S** ► sot

SOTTISH ► sot

SOU, **-S** n former French coin

SOUARI, **-S** n tree of tropical America

SOUBISE, **-S** n purée of onions mixed into a thick white sauce and served over eggs, fish, etc

SOUCAR, **-S** n Indian banker

SOUCE, **-D**, **-S**, **SOUCING**, **SOUCT** same as ► souse

SOUCHONG n black tea with large leaves

SOUCING ► souce

SOUCT ► souce

SOUDAN, **-S** obsolete variant of ► sultan

SOUFFLE, **-S** n light fluffy dish made with beaten egg whites ▷ adj made light and fluffy

SOUFFLED

SOUGH, **-ED**, **-ING**, **-S** vb (of the wind) make a sighing sound ▷ n soft continuous murmuring sound

SOUGHT ► seek

SOUK, **-ED**, **-ING**, **-S** same as ► sook

SOUKOUS n style of African popular music

SOUKS ► souk

SOUL, **-S** n spiritual and immortal part of a human being

SOULDAN, **-S** same as ► soldan

SOULDIER same as ► soldier

SOULED adj having soul

SOULFUL adj full of emotion

SOULLESS adj lacking human qualities, mechanical

SOULLIKE adj resembling a soul

SOULMATE n person with whom one has most affinity

SOULS ► soul

SOULSTER n soul music singer

SOUM, **-ED**, **-S** vb decide how many animals can graze particular pasture

SOUMING -S

SOUND, **-ED**, **-EST**, **-S** n something heard, noise ▷ vb make or cause to make a sound ▷ adj in good condition ▷ adv soundly

SOUNDBOX n resonating chamber of the hollow body of a violin, guitar, etc

SOUNDED ► sound

SOUNDER, **-S** n device formerly used to convert electric signals into sounds

SOUNDEST ► sound

SOUNDING adj resounding

SOUNDLY ► sound

SOUNDMAN, **SOUNDMEN** n sound recorder in television crew

SOUNDS ► sound

SOUP, **-ED**, **-ING**, **-S** n liquid food made from meat, vegetables, etc ▷ vb give soup to

SOUPCON, **-S** n small amount

SOUPED ► soup

SOUPER, **-S** n person dispensing soup

SOUPFIN, **-S** n Pacific requiem shark valued for its fins

SOUPIER ► soupy

SOUPIEST ► soupy

SOUPILY adv in a soupy manner

SOUPING ► soup

SOUPLE, **-D**, **-S**, **SOUPLING** same as ► supple

SOUPLESS ► soup

SOUPLIKE ► soup

SOUPLING ► souple

SOUPS ► soup

SOUPY, **SOUPIER**, **SOUPIEST** adj having the appearance or consistency of soup

SOUR, **-ED**, **-ER**, **-EST**, **-S** adj sharp-tasting ▷ vb make or become sour

SOURBALL n tart-flavoured boiled sweet

SOURCE, **-D**, **-S**, **SOURCING** n origin or starting point

▷ vb establish a supplier of (a product, etc)

SOURDINE n soft stop on an organ or harmonium

SOURED ► sour

SOURER ► sour

SOUREST ► sour

SOURGUM, **-S** n tree of eastern N America

SOURING, **-S** ► sour

SOURISH ► sour

SOURLY ► sour

SOURNESS ► sour

SOUROCK, **-S** n Scots word for sorrel plant

SOURPUSS n person who is always gloomy, pessimistic, or bitter

SOURS ► sour

SOURSE, **-S** same as ► source

SOURSOP, **-S** n small West Indian tree

SOURVELD n grazing field with long coarse grass

SOURWOOD n sorrel tree

SOUS ► sou

SOUSE, **-D**, **-S** vb plunge (something) into liquid ▷ n liquid used in pickling

SOUSER, **-S** n person who frequently gets drunk

SOUSES ► souse

SOUSING, **-S** ► souse

SOUSLIK, **-S** same as ► suslik

SOUT, **-S** same as ► soot

SOUTACHE n narrow braid used as a decorative trimming

SOUTANE, **-S** n Roman Catholic priest's cassock

SOUTAR, **-S** same as ► souter

SOUTER, **-S** n shoemaker or cobbler

SOUTERLY

SOUTH, **-ED**, **-S** n direction towards the South Pole, opposite north ▷ adj in the south ▷ adv in, to, or towards the south ▷ vb turn south

SOUTHER, **-S** n strong wind or storm from the south ▷ vb turn south

SOUTHERN adj situated in or towards the south ▷ n southerner

SOUTHERS ► souther

SOUTHING n movement, deviation, or distance covered in a southerly direction

SOUTHPAW n left-handed person, esp a boxer ▷ adj left-handed

S

SOUTHRON n southerner
SOUTHS ► south
SOUTHSAY same as
► soothsay
SOUTS ► sout
SOUVENIR n keepsake,
memento ▷ vb steal or keep
(something, esp a small
article) for one's own use
SOUVLAKI same as
> souvlakia
SOV, -S shortening of
> sovereign
SOVIET, -S n formerly, elected
council in the USSR ▷ adj of
the former USSR
SOVIETIC
SOVKHOZ, -Y n large
mechanized farm in former
USSR
SOVRAN, -S literary word for
> sovereign
SOVRANLY
SOVRANTY
SOVS ► sov
SOW, -ED, -N, -S vb scatter
or plant (seed) in or on (the
ground) ▷ n female adult pig
SOWABLE
SOWANS same as ► sowens
SOWAR, -S n Indian
cavalryman
SOWARREE n Indian
mounted escort
SOWARRY same as
► sowarree
SOWARS ► sowar
SOWBACK, -S another name
for ► hogback
SOWBELLY n salt pork from
pig's belly
SOWBREAD n S European
primulaceous plant
SOWBUG, -S n (in N America)
woodlouse
SOWCAR, -S same as
► soucar
SOWCE, -D, -S, SOWCING
same as ► souse
SOWDER, -S same as
► sawder
SOWED ► sow
SOWENS n pudding made
from oatmeal husks steeped
and boiled
SOWER, -S ► sow
SOWF, -ED, -ING, -S same as
► sowth
SOWFF, -ED, -ING, -S same as
► sowth
SOWFING ► sowf
SOWFS ► sowf
SOWING ► sow
SOWL, -ED, -ING, -S same as
► sole
SOWLE, -S same as ► sole

SOWLED ► sowl
SOWLES ► sowle
SOWLING ► sowl
SOWLS ► sowl
SOWM, -ED, -ING; -S same as
► soum
SOWN ► sow
SOWND, -ED, -ING, -S vb
wield
SOWNE, -S same as ► sound
SOWP, -ED, -ING, -S n
spoonful ▷ vb soak
SOWS ► sow
SOWSE, -D, -S, SOWSING
same as ► souse
SOWSSE, -D, -S, SOWSSING
same as ► souse
SOWTER, -S same as
► souter
SOWTH, -ED, -ING, -S vb
Scots word meaning whistle
SOX pl n informal spelling of
'socks'

> This informal word for
> **socks** is one of the key short
> words to remember for
> using the X.

SOY, -S n as in **soy sauce** salty
dark brown sauce made from
soya beans
SOYA, -S n plant whose edible
bean is used for food and as a
source of oil
SOYBEAN, -S n soya bean
SOYLE, -D, -S, SOYLING n
body ▷ vb elucidate
SOYMEAL, -S n foodstuff
made from soybeans
SOYMILK, -S n milk substitute
made from soya
SOYS ► soy
SOYUZ, -ES n Russian
spacecraft
SOZ interj (slang) sorry
SOZIN, -S n form of protein
SOZINE, -S same as ► sozin
SOZINS ► sozin
SOZZLE, -S, SOZZLING vb
make wet
SOZZLED adj drunk
SOZZLES ► sozzle
SOZZLIER ► sozzly
SOZZLING ► sozzle
SOZZLY, SOZZLIER adj wet
SPA, -S n resort with a
mineral-water spring ▷ vb
visit a spa
SPACE, -D, -S n unlimited
expanse in which all objects
exist and move ▷ vb place at
intervals
SPACELAB n laboratory
in space where scientific
experiments are performed

SPACEMAN, SPACEMEN n
person who travels in space
SPACER, -S n piece of material
used to create or maintain a
space between two things
SPACES ► space
SPACEY, SPACIER, SPACIEST
adj vague and dreamy
SPACIAL same as ► spatial
SPACIER ► spacey
SPACIEST ► spacey
SPACING, -S n arrangement of
letters, words, etc, on a page
in order to achieve legibility
SPACIOUS adj having a large
capacity or area
SPACKLE, -D, -S vb fill holes
in plaster
SPACY same as ► spacey
SPADE, -D, -S, SPADING n
tool for digging
SPADEFUL n amount spade
will hold
SPADEMAN, SPADEMEN n
man who works with spade
SPADER, -S ► spade
SPADES ► spade
SPADGER, -S n sparrow
SPADICES ► spadix
SPADILLE n (in ombre and
quadrille) the ace of spades
SPADILLO same as ► spadille
SPADING ► spade
SPADIX, SPADICES, -ES n
spike of small flowers on a
fleshy stem
SPADO, -ES, -NES, -S n
neutered animal
SPADROON n type of sword
SPAE, -D, -S vb foretell (the
future)
SPAEING, -S
SPAEMAN, SPAEMEN n man
who can supposedly foretell
the future
SPAER, -S ► spae
SPAES ► spae
SPAETZLE n German noodle
dish
SPAEWIFE n woman who can
supposedly foretell the future
SPAG, -GED, -GING, -S vb (of
a cat) to scratch (a person)
with the claws
SPAGERIC same as
► spagyric
SPAGGED ► spag
SPAGGING ► spag
SPAGIRIC same as
► spagyric
SPAGS ► spag
SPAGYRIC adj of or relating to
alchemy ▷ n alchemist
SPAHEE, -S same as ► spahi

SPAHI, -S *n* (formerly) an irregular cavalryman in the Turkish armed forces

SPAIL, -S *Scots word for* ► **spall**

SPAIN, -ED, -ING, -S *variant of* ► **spane**

SPAING, -S ► **spa**

SPAINING ► **spain**

SPAINS ► **spain**

SPAIRGE, -D, -S *Scots word for* ► **sparge**

SPAIT, -S *same as* ► **spate**

SPAKE *past tense of* ► **speak**

SPALD, -S *same as* ► **spauld**

SPALDEEN *n* ball used in street game

SPALDS ► **spald**

SPALE, -S *Scots word for* ► **spall**

SPALL, -ED, -ING, -S *n* splinter or chip of ore, rock, or stone ▷ *vb* split or cause to split into such fragments

SPALLE, -S *same as* ► **spauld**

SPALLED ► **spall**

SPALLER, -S ► **spall**

SPALLES ► **spalle**

SPALLING ► **spall**

SPALLS ► **spall**

SPALPEEN *n* itinerant seasonal labourer

SPALT, -ED, -ING, -S *vb* split

SPAM, -MED, -MING, -S *vb* send unsolicited e-mail simultaneously to a number of newsgroups on the internet ▷ *n* unsolicited electronic mail or text messages sent in this way

SPAMBOT, -S *n* computer program that sends spam

SPAMMED ► **spam**

SPAMMER, -S ► **spam**

SPAMMIE, -S *n* love bite

SPAMMIER ► **spammy**

SPAMMIES ► **spammie**

SPAMMING ► **spam**

SPAMMY, SPAMMIER *adj* bland

SPAMS ► **spam**

SPAN, -NED, -NING, -S *n* space between two points ▷ *vb* stretch or extend across

SPANCEL, -S *n* length of rope for hobbling an animal ▷ *vb* hobble (an animal) with a loose span

SPANDEX *n* type of synthetic stretch fabric made from polyurethane fibre

SPANDREL *n* triangular surface bounded by the outer curve of an arch and the adjacent wall

SPANDRIL *same as* ► **spandrel**

SPANE, -D, -S, SPANING *vb* Scots word meaning wean

SPANG, -ED, -ING, -S *adv* exactly, firmly, or straight ▷ *vb* dash

SPANGHEW *vb* throw in air

SPANGING ► **spang**

SPANGLE, -D, -S *n* small shiny metallic ornament ▷ *vb* decorate with spangles

SPANGLER

SPANGLET *n* little spangle

SPANGLY ► **spangle**

SPANGS ► **spang**

SPANIEL, -S *n* dog with long ears and silky hair

SPANING ► **spane**

SPANK, -ED, -S *vb* slap with the open hand, on the buttocks or legs ▷ *n* such a slap

SPANKER, -S *n* fore-and-aft sail or a mast that is aftermost in a sailing vessel

SPANKING *adj* outstandingly fine or smart ▷ *n* series of spanks, usually as a punishment for children

SPANKS ► **spank**

SPANLESS *adj* impossible to span

SPANNED ► **span**

SPANNER, -S *n* tool for gripping and turning a nut or bolt

SPANNING ► **span**

SPANS ► **span**

SPANSPEK *n* cantaloupe melon

SPANSULE *n* modified-release capsule of a drug

SPANWORM *n* larva of a type of moth

SPAR, -RED, -RING, -S *n* pole used as a ship's mast, boom, or yard ▷ *vb* box or fight using light blows for practice

SPARABLE *n* small nail with no head, used for fixing the soles and heels of shoes

SPARAXIS *n* type of plant with dainty spikes of star-shaped purple, red, or orange flowers

SPARE, SPARD, -D, -S, -ST *adj* extra ▷ *n* duplicate kept in case of damage or loss ▷ *vb* refrain from punishing or harming

SPARELY

SPARER -S

SPARERIB *n* cut of pork ribs with most of the meat trimmed off

SPARERS ► **sparer**

SPARES ► **spare**

SPAREST ► **spare**

SPARGE, -D, -S, SPARGING *vb* sprinkle or scatter (something)

SPARGER -S

SPARID, -S *n* type of marine percoid fish ▷ *adj* of or belonging to this family of fish

SPARING *adj* economical

SPARK, -ED, -ING *n* fiery particle thrown out from a fire or caused by friction ▷ *vb* give off sparks

SPARKE, -S *n* weapon

SPARKED ► **spark**

SPARKER, -S ► **spark**

SPARKES ► **sparke**

SPARKIE, -S *n* electrician

SPARKIER ► **sparky**

SPARKIES ► **sparkie**

SPARKILY ► **sparky**

SPARKING ► **spark**

SPARKISH ► **spark**

SPARKLE, -D, -S *vb* glitter with many points of light ▷ *n* sparkling points of light

SPARKLER *n* hand-held firework that emits sparks

SPARKLES ► **sparkle**

SPARKLET *n* little spark

SPARKLY *adj* sparkling ▷ *n* sparkling thing

SPARKS *n* electrician

SPARKY, SPARKIER *adj* lively

SPARLIKE ► **spar**

SPARLING *n* European smelt

SPAROID, -S *same as* ► **sparid**

SPARRE, -S *same as* ► **spar**

SPARRED ► **spar**

SPARRER, -S ► **spar**

SPARRES ► **sparre**

SPARRIER ► **sparry**

SPARRING ► **spar**

SPARROW, -S *n* small brownish bird

SPARRY, SPARRIER *adj* (of minerals) containing, relating to, or resembling spar

SPARS ► **spar**

SPARSE, -R, -ST *adj* thinly scattered

SPARSELY

SPARSITY

SPART, -S *n* esparto

SPARTAN, -S *adj* strict and austere ▷ *n* disciplined or brave person

SPARTH, -S *n* type of battle-axe

SPARTHE, -S *same as* ► **sparth**

SPARTHS ► **sparth**

S

SPARTINA n grass growing in salt marshes

SPARTS ▶ spart

SPAS ▶ spa

SPASM, -ED, -ING, -S n involuntary muscular contraction ▷ vb go into spasm

SPASMIC

SPASTIC adj affected by spasms

SPAT, -S, -TED, -TING vb have a quarrel

SPATE, -S n large number of things happening within a period of time

SPATFALL n mass of larvae on sea bed

SPATHAL ▶ spathe

SPATHE, -S n large sheathlike leaf enclosing a flower cluster

SPATHED

SPATHIC adj (of minerals) resembling spar

SPATHOSE same as ▶ spathic

SPATIAL adj of or in space

SPATLESE n type of German wine, usu white

SPATS ▶ spat

SPATTED ▶ spat

SPATTEE, -S n type of gaiter

SPATTER, -S vb scatter or be scattered in drops over (something) ▷ n spattering sound

SPATTING ▶ spat

SPATULA, -S n utensil with a broad flat blade for spreading or stirring

SPATULAR

SPATULE, -S n spatula

SPATZLE, -S same as ▶ spaetzle

SPAUL, -S same as ▶ spauld

SPAULD, -S n shoulder

SPAULS ▶ spaul

SPAVIE, -S Scots variant of ▶ spavin

SPAVIET adj Scots word meaning spavined

SPAVIN, -S n enlargement of the hock of a horse by a bony growth

SPAVINED adj affected with spavin

SPAVINS ▶ spavin

SPAW, -S same as ▶ spa

SPAWL, -ED, -ING, -S vb spit

SPAWN, -ED, -ING, -S n jelly-like mass of eggs of fish, frogs, or molluscs ▷ vb (of fish, frogs, or molluscs) lay eggs

SPAWNER -S

SPAWNIER ▶ spawny

SPAWNING ▶ spawn

SPAWNS ▶ spawn

SPAWNY, SPAWNIER adj like spawn

SPAWS ▶ spaw

SPAY, -ED, -ING, -S vb remove the ovaries from (a female animal)

SPAYAD, -S n male deer

SPAYD, -S same as ▶ spayad

SPAYED ▶ spay

SPAYING ▶ spay

SPAYS ▶ spay

SPAZA adj as in spaza shop South African slang for a small shop in a township

SPEAK, -ING, -S, SPOKEN vb say words, talk

SPEAKER, -S n person who speaks, esp at a formal occasion

SPEAKING ▶ speak

SPEAKOUT n firm or brave statement of one's beliefs

SPEAKS ▶ speak

SPEAL, -S same as ▶ spule

SPEAN, -ED, -ING, -S same as ▶ spane

SPEAR, -ED, -S n weapon consisting of a long shaft with a sharp point ▷ vb pierce with or as if with a spear

SPEARER -S

SPEARGUN n device for shooting spears underwater

SPEARIER ▶ speary

SPEARING n act of spearing

SPEARMAN, SPEARMEN n soldier armed with a spear

SPEARS ▶ spear

SPEARY, SPEARIER ▶ spear

SPEAT, -S same as ▶ spate

SPEC, -CED, -CING vb set specifications

SPECCIER ▶ speccy

SPECCIES ▶ speccy

SPECCING ▶ spec

SPECCY, SPECCIER, SPECCIES n person wearing spectacles ▷ adj wearing spectacles

SPECIAL, -S adj distinguished from others of its kind ▷ n product, programme, etc which is only available at a certain time ▷ vb advertise and sell (an item) at a reduced price

SPECIATE vb form or develop into a new biological species

SPECIE n coins as distinct from paper money

SPECIES n group of plants or animals that are related

closely enough to interbreed naturally

SPECIFIC adj particular, definite ▷ n drug used to treat a particular disease

SPECIFY vb refer to or state specifically

SPECIMEN n individual or part typifying a whole

SPECIOUS adj apparently true, but actually false

SPECK, -ED, -ING, -S n small spot or particle ▷ vb mark with specks or spots

SPECKIER ▶ specky

SPECKIES ▶ specky

SPECKING ▶ speck

SPECKLE, -S n small spot ▷ vb mark with speckles

SPECKLED

SPECKS ▶ speck

SPECKY, SPECKIER, SPECKIES same as ▶ speccy

SPECS pl n spectacles

SPECT, -ED, -ING, -S vb expect

SPECTATE vb watch

SPECTED ▶ spect

SPECTER, -S same as ▶ spectre

SPECTING ▶ spect

SPECTRA ▶ spectrum

SPECTRAL adj of or like a spectre

SPECTRE, -S n ghost

SPECTRIN n any one of a class of fibrous proteins found in the membranes of red blood cells

SPECTRUM, SPECTRA n range of different colours, radio waves, etc in order of their wavelengths

SPECTS ▶ spect

SPECULA ▶ speculum

SPECULAR adj of, relating to, or having the properties of a mirror

SPECULUM, SPECULA n medical instrument for examining body cavities

SPED ▶ speed

SPEECH, -ED, -ES n act, power, or manner of speaking ▷ vb make a speech

SPEED, SPED, -ED, -ING, -S n swiftness ▷ vb go quickly

SPEEDER -S

SPEEDFUL ▶ speed

SPEEDIER ▶ speedy

SPEEDILY ▶ speedy

SPEEDING ▶ speed

SPEEDO, -S n speedometer

SPEEDS ▶ speed

SPEEDUP, -S n acceleration

SPEEDWAY n track for motorcycle racing

SPEEDY, SPEEDIER adj prompt

SPEEL, -ED, -ING, -S n splinter of wood ▷ vb Scots meaning climb

SPEELER -S

SPEER, -ED, -ING, -S same as ▶ speir

SPEIL, -ED, -ING, -S dialect word for ▶ climb

SPEIR, -ED, -ING, -S vb ask

SPEISE, -S same as ▶ speiss

SPEISS, -ES n compounds formed when ores containing arsenic or antimony are smelted

SPEK, -S n bacon, fat, or fatty pork used for larding venison or other game

SPEKBOOM n South African shrub

SPEKS ▶ spek

SPELAEAN adj of, found in, or inhabiting caves

SPELD, -ED, -ING, -S vb Scots word meaning spread

SPELDER, -S same as ▶ speld

SPELDIN, -S n fish split and dried

SPELDING same as ▶ speldin

SPELDINS ▶ speldin

SPELDRIN same as ▶ speldin

SPELDS ▶ speld

SPELEAN same as ▶ spelaean

SPELK, -S n splinter of wood

SPELL, -ED, -ING, -S vb give in correct order the letters that form (a word) ▷ n formula of words supposed to have magic power

SPELLER, -S n person who spells words in the manner specified

SPELLFUL adj magical

SPELLING ▶ spell

SPELLS ▶ spell

SPELT, -S n wheat variety

SPELTER, -S n impure zinc, usually containing about 3 per cent of lead and other impurities

SPELTS ▶ spelt

SPELTZ, -ES n wheat variety

SPELUNK, -S vb explore caves

SPENCE, -S n larder or pantry

SPENCER, -S n short fitted coat or jacket

SPENCES ▶ spence

SPEND, -ING, -S, SPENT vb pay out (money)

SPENDALL n spendthrift

SPENDER, -S n person who spends money in a manner specified

SPENDIER ▶ spendy

SPENDING ▶ spend

SPENDS ▶ spend

SPENDY, SPENDIER adj expensive

SPENSE, -S same as ▶ spence

SPENT ▶ spend

SPEOS, -ES n (esp in ancient Egypt) a temple or tomb cut into a rock face

SPERLING same as ▶ sparling

SPERM, -S n male reproductive cell

SPERMARY n any organ in which sperm are produced

SPERMIC same as > spermatic

SPERMINE n colourless basic water-soluble amine

SPERMOUS same as > spermatic

SPERMS ▶ sperm

SPERRE, -D, -S, SPERRING vb bolt

SPERSE, -D, -S, SPERSING, SPERST vb disperse

SPERTHE, -S same as ▶ sparth

SPET, -S, -TING same as ▶ spit

SPETCH, -ED, -ES n piece of animal skin

SPETS ▶ spet

SPETSNAZ n Soviet intelligence force

SPETTING ▶ spet

SPETZNAZ same as ▶ spetsnaz

SPEUG, -S n sparrow

SPEW, -ED, -ING, -S vb vomit ▷ n something ejected from the mouth

SPEWER -S

SPEWIER ▶ spewy

SPEWIEST ▶ spewy

SPEWING ▶ spew

SPEWS ▶ spew

SPEWY, SPEWIER, SPEWIEST adj marshy

SPHAER, -S same as ▶ sphere

SPHAERE, -S same as ▶ sphere

SPHAERS ▶ sphaer

SPHAGNUM n moss found in bogs

SPHAIREE n game resembling tennis played with wooden bats and a perforated plastic ball

SPHEAR, -S same as ▶ sphere

SPHEARE, -S same as ▶ sphere

SPHEARS ▶ sphear

SPHENE, -S n brown, yellow, green, or grey lustrous mineral

SPHENIC adj having the shape of a wedge

SPHENOID adj wedge-shaped ▷ n wedge-shaped thing

SPHERAL adj of or shaped like a sphere

SPHERE, -D, -S, SPHERING n perfectly round solid object ▷ vb surround or encircle

SPHERIC same as > spherical

SPHERICS n geometry and trigonometry of figures on the surface of a sphere

SPHERIER ▶ sphery

SPHERING ▶ sphere

SPHEROID n solid figure that is almost but not exactly a sphere

SPHERULE n very small sphere or globule

SPHERY, SPHERIER adj resembling a sphere

SPHINGES ▶ sphinx

SPHINGID n hawk moth

SPHINX, SPHINGES, -ES n huge statue built by the ancient Egyptians

SPHYGMIC adj of or relating to the pulse

SPHYGMUS n person's pulse

SPHYNX, -ES n breed of cat

SPIAL, -S n observation

SPICA, -E, -S n spiral bandage formed by a series of overlapping figure-of-eight turns

SPICATE adj having, arranged in, or relating to spikes

SPICATED same as ▶ spicate

SPICCATO n style of playing a stringed instrument in which the bow bounces lightly off the strings ▷ adv be played in this manner

SPICE, -D, -S, SPICING n aromatic substance used as flavouring ▷ vb flavour with spices

SPICER -S

SPICERY n spices collectively

SPICES ▶ spice

SPICEY same as ▶ spicy

SPICIER ▶ spicy

SPICIEST ▶ spicy

SPICILY ▶ spicy

SPICING ▶ spice

SPICK, -ER, -EST adj neat and clean

SPICKNEL same as ▶ spignel

S

SPICULA, -E same as
► **spiculum**

SPICULAR ► spiculum

SPICULE, -S n small slender
pointed structure or crystal

SPICULUM, -S same as ► spicule

SPICY, SPICIER, SPICIEST adj
flavoured with spices

SPIDE, -S n insulting Irish
word for a young working-
class man who dresses in
casual sports clothes

SPIDER, -ED, -S n small eight-
legged creature which spins a
web to catch insects for food
▷ vb follow internet links to
gather information

SPIDERY adj thin and angular
like a spider's legs

SPIDES ► spide

SPIE same as ► spy

SPIED ► spy

SPIEGEL, -S n manganese-
rich pig iron

SPIEL, -ED, -ING, -S n speech
made to persuade someone
to do something ▷ vb deliver
a prepared spiel

SPIELER -S

SPIER, -ED, -ING, -S variant
of ► speir

SPIES ► spy

SPIF, -S n postage stamp
perforated with the initials
of a firm to avoid theft by
employees

SPIFF, -ED, -S vb make smart

SPIFFIED ► spiffy

SPIFFIER ► spiffy

SPIFFIES ► spiffy

SPIFFILY ► spiffy

SPIFFING adj excellent

SPIFFS ► spiff

**SPIFFY, SPIFFIED, SPIFFIER,
SPIFFIES** adj smart ▷ n
smart thing or person ▷ vb
smarten

SPIFS ► spif

SPIGHT, -ED, -S same as
► spite

SPIGNEL, -S n European
umbelliferous plant

SPIGOT, -S n stopper for, or
tap fitted to, a cask

SPIKE, -D, -S, SPIKING n sharp
point ▷ vb put spikes on

SPIKELET n unit of a grass
inflorescence

SPIKER, -S ► spike

SPIKERY n High-
Church Anglicanism

SPIKES ► spike

SPIKEY same as ► spiky

SPIKIER ► spiky

SPIKIEST ► spiky

SPIKILY ► spiky

SPIKING ► spike

SPIKY, SPIKIER, SPIKIEST adj
resembling a spike

SPILE, -D, -S n heavy timber
stake or pile ▷ vb provide or
support with a spile

SPILIKIN same as > **spillikin**

SPILING, -S ► spile

SPILITE, -S n type of igneous
rock

SPILITIC

SPILL, -ED, -ING, -S, SPILT
vb pour from or as if from a
container ▷ n fall

SPILLAGE n instance or the
process of spilling

SPILLED ► spill

SPILLER, -S ► spill

SPILLING ► spill

SPILLS ► spill

SPILLWAY n channel that
carries away surplus water,
as from a dam

SPILT ► spill

SPILTH, -S n something spilled

SPIM, -S n spam sent and
received via an instant-
messaging system

SPIMMER, -S n person who
sends spam via an instant-
messaging system

SPIMMING n the sending
of spam via an instant-
messaging system

SPIMS ► spim

SPIN, -NING, -S, SPUN vb
revolve or cause to revolve
rapidly ▷ n revolving motion

SPINA, -E, -S n spine

SPINACH n dark green leafy
vegetable

SPINACHY

SPINAE ► spina

SPINAGE, -S same as
► spinach

SPINAL, -S adj of the spine ▷ n
anaesthetic administered in
the spine

SPINALLY

SPINAR, -S n fast-spinning
star

SPINAS ► spina

SPINATE adj having a spine

SPINDLE, -D, -S n rotating
rod that acts as an axle ▷ vb
form into a spindle or equip
with spindles

SPINDLER

SPINDLY adj long, slender,
and frail

SPINE, -S n backbone

SPINED

SPINEL, -S n any of a group
of hard glassy minerals of
variable colour

SPINELLE same as ► spinel

SPINELS ► spinel

SPINES ► spine

SPINET, -S n small
harpsichord

SPINETTE same as ► spinet

SPINIER ► spiny

SPINIEST ► spiny

SPINIFEX n coarse
spiny Australian grass

SPINK, -ED, -ING, -S n finch
▷ vb (of a finch) chirp

SPINLESS ► spin

SPINNER, -S n bowler who
makes the ball change
direction when it bounces

SPINNERY n spinning mill

SPINNET, -S same as ► spinet

SPINNEY, -S n small wood

SPINNIER ► spinny

SPINNIES ► spinny

SPINNING ► spin

SPINNY, SPINNIER, SPINNIES
adj crazy

SPINODE, -S another name
for ► cusp

SPINOFF, -S n development
derived incidentally from an
existing enterprise

SPINONE, SPINONI n as in
Italian spinone wiry-coated
gun dog

SPINOR, -S n type of
mathematical object

SPINOSE adj (esp of plants)
bearing many spines

SPINOUS adj resembling a
spine or thorn

SPINOUT, -S n spinning skid
that causes a car to run off
the road

SPINS ► spin

SPINSTER n unmarried
woman

SPINTEXT n preacher

SPINTO, -S n lyrical singing
voice

SPINULA, -E n small spine

SPINULE, -S n very small
spine, thorn, or prickle

SPINY, SPINIER, SPINIEST adj
covered with spines

SPIRACLE n small blowhole
for breathing through, such
as that of a whale

SPIRAEA, -S n plant with
small white or pink flowers

SPIRAL, -ED, -S n continuous
curve formed by a point
winding about a central axis
▷ vb move in a spiral ▷ adj
having the form of a spiral

SPIRALLY

SPIRANT, -S n fricative
consonant

SPIRATED adj twisted in spiral

SPIRE, -D, -S, SPIRING *n* pointed part of a steeple ▷ *vb* assume the shape of a spire

SPIREA, -S *same as* ▸ **spiraea**

SPIRED ▸ **spire**

SPIRELET *another name for* ▸ **fleche**

SPIREM, -S *same as* ▸ **spireme**

SPIREME, -S *n* tangled mass of chromatin threads

SPIREMS ▸ **spirem**

SPIRES ▸ **spire**

SPIRIC, -S *n* type of curve

SPIRIER ▸ **spiry**

SPIRIEST ▸ **spiry**

SPIRILLA > **spirillum**

SPIRING ▸ **spire**

SPIRIT, -S *n* nonphysical aspect of a person concerned with profound thoughts ▷ *vb* carry away mysteriously

SPIRITED *adj* lively

SPIRITS ▸ **spirit**

SPIRITUS *n* spirit

SPIRITY *adj* spirited

SPIRLING *same as* ▸ **sparling**

SPIROID *adj* resembling a spiral or displaying a spiral form

SPIRT, -ED, -ING, -S *same as* ▸ **spurt**

SPIRTLE, -S *same as* ▸ **spurtle**

SPIRTS ▸ **spirt**

SPIRULA, -E, -S *n* tropical cephalopod mollusc

SPIRY, SPIRIER, SPIRIEST ▸ **spire**

SPIT, -S, -TED, -TEN, -TING *vb* eject (saliva or food) from the mouth ▷ *n* saliva

SPITAL, -S *n* obsolete word for hospital

SPITBALL *n* small missile made from chewed paper ▷ *vb* make suggestions

SPITCHER *adj* doomed ▷ *vb* be doomed

SPITE, -D, -S, SPITING *n* deliberate nastiness ▷ *vb* annoy or hurt from spite

SPITEFUL *adj* full of or motivated by spite

SPITES ▸ **spite**

SPITFIRE *n* person with a fiery temper

SPITING ▸ **spite**

SPITS ▸ **spit**

SPITTED ▸ **spit**

SPITTEN ▸ **spit**

SPITTER, -S ▸ **spit**

SPITTIER ▸ **spitty**

SPITTING ▸ **spit**

SPITTLE, -S *n* fluid produced in the mouth, saliva

SPITTLY *adj* covered with spittle

SPITTOON *n* bowl to spit into

SPITTY, SPITTIER *adj* covered with saliva

SPITZ, -ES *n* stockily built dog with a tightly curled tail

SPIV, -S *n* smartly dressed man who makes a living by shady dealings

SPIVVERY *n* behaviour of spivs

SPIVVIER ▸ **spivvy**

SPIVVISH *adj* characteristic of a spiv

SPIVVY, SPIVVIER ▸ **spiv**

SPLAKE, -S *n* type of hybrid trout bred by Canadian zoologists

SPLASH, -ED, -ES *vb* scatter liquid on (something) ▷ *n* splashing sound

SPLASHER *n* anything used for protection against splashes

SPLASHES ▸ **splash**

SPLASHY *adj* having irregular marks

SPLAT, -S, -TED *n* wet slapping sound ▷ *vb* make wet slapping sound

SPLATCH *vb* splash

SPLATS ▸ **splat**

SPLATTED ▸ **splat**

SPLATTER *n* splash ▷ *vb* splash (something or someone) with small blobs

SPLAY, -ED, -ING, -S *vb* spread out, with ends spreading in different directions ▷ *adj* spread out ▷ *n* surface of a wall that forms an oblique angle to the main flat surfaces

SPLEEN, -S *n* abdominal organ which filters bacteria from the blood

SPLEENY

SPLENDID *adj* excellent

SPLENDOR *same as* > **splendour**

SPLENIA ▸ **splenium**

SPLENIAL ▸ **splenius**

SPLENIC *adj* of, relating to, or in the spleen

SPLENII ▸ **splenius**

SPLENIUM, SPLENIA *n* structure in brain

SPLENIUS, SPLENII *n* either of two flat muscles situated at the back of the neck

SPLENT, -S *same as* ▸ **splint**

SPLICE, -D, -S, SPLICING *vb* join by interweaving or overlapping ends

SPLICER -S

SPLINE, -D, -S, SPLINING *n* type of narrow key around a shaft that fits into a corresponding groove ▷ *vb* provide (a shaft, part, etc) with splines

SPLINT, -ED, -S *n* rigid support for a broken bone ▷ *vb* apply a splint to (a broken arm, etc)

SPLINTER *n* thin sharp piece broken off, esp from wood ▷ *vb* break into fragments

SPLINTS ▸ **splint**

SPLISH, -ED, -ES *vb* splash

SPLIT, -S, -TED *vb* break into separate pieces ▷ *n* splitting

SPLITTER

SPLODGE, -D, -S *n* large uneven spot or stain ▷ *vb* mark (something) with a splodge or splodges

SPLODGY

SPLOG, -S *n* spam blog

SPLOOSH *vb* splash or cause to splash about uncontrollably ▷ *n* instance or sound of splooshing

SPLORE, -S *n* revel

SPLOSH, -ED, -ES *vb* scatter (liquid) vigorously about in blobs ▷ *n* instance or sound of sploshing

SPLOTCH *vb* splash, daub

SPLOTCHY

SPLURGE, -D, -S *vb* spend money extravagantly ▷ *n* bout of extravagance

SPLURGER

SPLURGY

SPLURT, -ED, -S *vb* gush out

SPLUTTER *vb* utter with spitting or choking sounds ▷ *n* spluttering

SPOD, -S *adj* boring, unattractive, or overly studious

SPODDY SPODDIER

SPODE, -S *n* type of English china or porcelain

SPODIUM, -S *n* black powder

SPODOSOL *n* ashy soil

SPODS ▸ **spod**

SPOFFISH *adj* officious

SPOFFY *same as* ▸ **spoffish**

SPOIL, -ED, -ING, -S, -T *vb* damage

SPOILAGE *n* amount of material that has been spoilt

SPOILED ▸ **spoil**

SPOILER, -S *n* device on an aircraft or car to increase drag

SPOILFUL *adj* taking spoils

SPOILING ▸ **spoil**

SPOILS ▸ **spoil**

S

S

SPOILT ▸ spoil
SPOKE, -D, -S, SPOKING *n* radial member of a wheel ▷ *vb* equip with spokes
SPOKEN ▸ speak
SPOKES ▸ spoke
SPOKING ▸ spoke
SPOLIATE *less common word for* ▸ **despoil**
SPONDAIC *adj* of, relating to, or consisting of spondees ▷ *n* spondaic line
SPONDEE, -S *n* metrical foot of two long syllables
SPONDYL, -S *n* vertebra
SPONGE, -D, -S, SPONGING *n* sea animal with a porous absorbent skeleton ▷ *vb* wipe with a sponge
SPONGER, -S *n* person who sponges on others
SPONGES ▸ sponge
SPONGIER ▸ spongy
SPONGILY ▸ spongy
SPONGIN, -S *n* fibrous horny protein in sponges
SPONGING ▸ sponge
SPONGINS ▸ spongin
SPONGOID ▸ sponge
SPONGY, SPONGIER *adj* of or resembling a sponge
SPONSAL *n* marriage
SPONSING *same as* ▸ **sponson**
SPONSION *n* act or process of becoming surety
SPONSON, -S *n* outboard support for a gun enabling it to fire fore and aft
SPONSOR, -S *n* person who promotes something ▷ *vb* act as a sponsor for
SPONTOON *n* infantry weapon used in the 18th and 19th centuries
SPOOF, -ED, -ING, -S *n* mildly satirical parody ▷ *vb* fool (a person) with a trick or deception
SPOOFER -S
SPOOFERY ▸ spoof
SPOOFIER ▸ spoofy
SPOOFING ▸ spoof
SPOOFS ▸ spoof
SPOOFY, SPOOFIER ▸ spoof
SPOOK, -ED, -ING, -S *n* ghost ▷ *vb* frighten
SPOOKERY *n* spooky events
SPOOKIER ▸ spooky
SPOOKILY ▸ spooky
SPOOKING ▸ spook
SPOOKISH ▸ spook
SPOOKS ▸ spook
SPOOKY, SPOOKIER *adj* ghostly or eerie

SPOOL, -ED, -ING, -S *n* cylinder round which something can be wound ▷ *vb* wind or be wound onto a spool or reel
SPOOLER -S
SPOOM, -ED, -ING, -S *vb* sail fast before wind
SPOON, -ED, -ING, -S *n* shallow bowl attached to a handle for eating, stirring, or serving food ▷ *vb* lift with a spoon
SPOONER, -S *n* person who engages in spooning
SPOONEY, -S *same as* ▸ **spoony**
SPOONFED *adj* having been given someone else's opinions
SPOONFUL *n* amount that a spoon is able to hold
SPOONIER ▸ spoony
SPOONIES ▸ spoony
SPOONILY ▸ spoony
SPOONING ▸ spoon
SPOONS ▸ spoon
SPOONY, SPOONIER, SPOONIES *adj* foolishly or stupidly in love ▷ *n* fool or silly person, esp one in love
SPOOR, -ED, -ING, -S *n* trail of an animal ▷ *vb* track (an animal) by following its trail
SPOORER -S
SPOOT, -S *n* razor shell
SPORADIC *adj* intermittent, scattered
SPORAL ▸ spore
SPORE, -D, -S, SPORING *n* minute reproductive body of some plants ▷ *vb* produce, carry, or release spores
SPORIDIA > sporidium
SPORING ▸ spore
SPORK, -S *n* spoon-shaped piece of cutlery with tines like a fork
SPOROID *adj* of or like a spore
SPOROZOA *n* class of microscopic creature
SPORRAN, -S *n* pouch worn in front of a kilt
SPORT, -ED *n* activity for pleasure, competition, or exercise ▷ *vb* wear proudly
SPORTER -S
SPORTFUL ▸ sport
SPORTIER ▸ sporty
SPORTIES ▸ sporty
SPORTIF, -S *adj* sporty ▷ *n* sporty person
SPORTILY ▸ sporty
SPORTING *adj* of sport
SPORTIVE *adj* playful

SPORTS *adj* of or used in sports ▷ *n* meeting held at a school or college for competitions in athletic events
SPORTY, SPORTIER, SPORTIES *adj* (of a person) interested in sport ▷ *n* young person who takes an interest in sport and fitness
SPORULAR ▸ sporule
SPORULE, -S *n* spore, esp a very small spore
SPOSH, -ES *n* slush
SPOSHY SPOSHIER
SPOT, -S, -TED, -TING *n* small mark on a surface ▷ *vb* notice
SPOTLESS *adj* absolutely clean
SPOTLIT > spotlight
SPOTS ▸ spot
SPOTTED ▸ spot
SPOTTER, -S *n* person who notes numbers or types of trains or planes
SPOTTIE, -S *n* young deer of up to three months of age
SPOTTIER ▸ spotty
SPOTTIES ▸ spottie
SPOTTILY ▸ spotty
SPOTTING ▸ spot
SPOTTY, SPOTTIER *adj* with spots
SPOUSAGE *n* marriage
SPOUSAL, -S *n* marriage ceremony ▷ *adj* of or relating to marriage
SPOUSE, -D, -S, SPOUSING *n* person to whom one is married ▷ *vb* marry
SPOUT, -ED, -S *vb* pour out in a stream or jet ▷ *n* projecting tube or lip for pouring liquids
SPOUTER -S
SPOUTIER ▸ spouty
SPOUTING *n* rainwater downpipe on the outside of a building
SPOUTS ▸ spout
SPOUTY, SPOUTIER ▸ spout
SPRACK *adj* vigorous
SPRACKLE *vb* clamber
SPRAD ▸ spread
SPRADDLE *n* disease of fowl preventing them from standing
SPRAG, -GED, -S *n* device used to prevent a vehicle from running backwards on an incline ▷ *vb* use sprag to prevent vehicle from moving
SPRAID *vb* chapped
SPRAIN, -ED, -S *vb* injure (a joint) by a sudden twist ▷ *n* such an injury**

SPRAINT, -S n piece of otter's dung

SPRANG, -S n branch

SPRANGLE vb sprawl

SPRANGS ► sprang

SPRAT, -S n small sea fish

SPRATTLE vb scramble

SPRAUNCY adj smart

SPRAWL, -ED, -S vb lie or sit with the limbs spread out ▷ n part of a city that has spread untidily over a large area
SPRAWLER
SPRAWLY

SPRAY, -ED, -IER, -ING, -S n (device for producing) fine drops of liquid ▷ vb scatter in fine drops
SPRAYER -S

SPRAYEY ► spray

SPRAYIER ► spray

SPRAYING ► spray

SPRAYS ► spray

SPREAD, SPRAD, -S vb open out or be displayed to the fullest extent ▷ n spreading ▷ adj extended or stretched out, esp to the fullest extent
SPREADER n machine or device used for scattering bulk materials over a relatively wide area

SPREADS ► spread

SPREAGH, -S n cattle raid

SPREATHE vb chap

SPREAZE, -S same as ► spreathe

SPREAZED same as > spreathed

SPREAZES ► spreaze

SPRED, -S same as ► spread

SPREDD, -S same as ► spread

SPREDDE, -N, -S same as ► spread

SPREDDS ► spredd

SPREDS ► spred

SPREE, -D, -ING, -S n session of overindulging, usu in drinking or spending money ▷ vb go on a spree

SPREETHE same as ► spreathe

SPREEZE, -D, -S same as ► spreathe

SPRENT, -ED, -S adj sprinkled ▷ vb leap forward in an agile manner

SPREW, -S same as ► sprue

SPRIER ► spry

SPRIEST ► spry

SPRIG, -GED, -S n twig or shoot ▷ vb fasten or secure with sprigs
SPRIGGER
SPRIGGY

SPRIGHT, -S same as ► sprite

SPRIGS ► sprig

SPRING, -S, SPRONG, SPRUNG vb move suddenly upwards or forwards in a single motion, jump ▷ n season between winter and summer

SPRINGAL n young man

SPRINGE, -D, -S n type of snare for catching small wild animals or birds ▷ vb set such a snare

SPRINGER n small spaniel

SPRINGES ► springe

SPRINGLE same as ► springe

SPRINGS ► spring

SPRINGY adj elastic

SPRINKLE vb scatter (liquid or powder) in tiny drops or particles over (something) ▷ n act or an instance of sprinkling or a quantity that is sprinkled

SPRINT, -ED, -S n short race run at top speed ▷ vb run a short distance at top speed
SPRINTER

SPRIT, -S n small spar set diagonally across a sail to extend it

SPRITE, -S n elf

SPRITELY same as > sprightly

SPRITES ► sprite

SPRITS ► sprit

SPRITZ, -ED, -ES vb spray liquid

SPRITZER n tall drink of wine and soda water

SPRITZES ► spritz

SPRITZIG adj (of wine) sparkling ▷ n sparkling wine

SPRITZY adj fizzy

SPROCKET n wheel with teeth on the rim, that drives or is driven by a chain

SPROD, -S n young salmon

SPROG, -S n child

SPROGLET n small child

SPROGS ► sprog

SPRONG ► spring

SPROUT, -ED, -S vb put forth shoots ▷ n shoot

SPRUCE, -D, -R, -S, -ST, SPRUCING n kind of fir ▷ adj neat and smart
SPRUCELY

SPRUCIER ► sprucy

SPRUCING ► spruce

SPRUCY, SPRUCIER ► spruce

SPRUE, -S n vertical channel in a mould

SPRUG, -S n sparrow

SPRUIK, -ED, -S vb speak in public (used esp of a showman or salesman)
SPRUIKER

SPRUIT, -S n small tributary stream or watercourse

SPRUNG ► spring

SPRUSH, -ED, -ES Scots form of ► spruce

SPRY, SPRIER, SPRIEST, -ER, -EST adj active or nimble
SPRYLY
SPRYNESS

SPUD, -DED, -DING, -S n potato ▷ vb remove (bark) or eradicate (weeds) with a spud

SPUDDER, -S same as ► spud

SPUDDIER ► spuddy

SPUDDING ► spud

SPUDDLE, -S n feeble movement

SPUDDY, SPUDDIER adj short and fat

SPUDGEL, -S n bucket on a long handle

SPUDS ► spud

SPUE, -D, -ING, -S, SPUING same as ► spew
SPUER -S

SPUG, -S same as ► spuggy

SPUGGY, SPUGGIES n house sparrow

SPUGS ► spug

SPUILZIE vb plunder

SPUING ► spue

SPULE, -S Scots word for ► shoulder

SPULYE, -D, -S same as ► spuilzie

SPULYIE, -D, -S same as ► spuilzie

SPULZIE, -D, -S same as ► spuilzie

SPUMANTE n Italian sparkling wine

SPUME, -D, -S, SPUMING vb froth ▷ n foam or froth on the sea

SPUMIER ► spumy

SPUMIEST ► spumy

SPUMING ► spume

SPUMONE, -S n creamy Italian ice cream

SPUMONI, -S same as ► spumone

SPUMOUS ► spume

SPUMY, SPUMIER, SPUMIEST ► spume

SPUN ► spin

SPUNGE, -S same as ► sponge

SPUNK, -ED, -ING, -S n courage, spirit ▷ vb catch fire

SPUNKIE, -S n will-o'-the-wisp

SPUNKIER ► spunky
SPUNKIES ► spunkie
SPUNKILY ► spunk
SPUNKING ► spunk
SPUNKS ► spunk
SPUNKY, SPUNKIER ► spunk
SPUNYARN n small stuff made from rope yarns twisted together
SPUR, -RED, -RING, -S n stimulus or incentive ▷ vb urge on, incite (someone)
SPURDOG, -S n the dogfish
SPURGALL vb prod with spur
SPURGE, -S n plant with milky sap
SPURIAE n type of bird feathers
SPURIOUS adj not genuine
SPURLESS ► spur
SPURLING same as ► sparling
SPURN, -ED, -ING, -S vb reject with scorn ▷ n instance of spurning
SPURNE, -S vb spur
SPURNED ► spurn
SPURNER, -S ► spurn
SPURNES ► spurne
SPURNING ► spurn
SPURNS ► spurn
SPURRED ► spur
SPURRER, -S ► spur
SPURREY, -S n any of several low-growing European plants
SPURRIER n maker of spurs
SPURRIES ► spurry
SPURRING ► spur
SPURRY, SPURRIES n spurrey ▷ adj resembling a spur
SPURS ► spur
SPURT, -ED, -ING, -S vb gush or cause to gush out in a jet ▷ n short sudden burst of activity or speed
SPURTER -S
SPURTLE, -S n wooden spoon for stirring porridge
SPURTS ► spurt
SPURWAY, -S n path used by riders
SPUTA ► sputum
SPUTNIK, -S n early Soviet artificial satellite
SPUTTER, -S n splutter ▷ vb splutter
SPUTTERY
SPUTUM, SPUTA n spittle, usu mixed with mucus
SPY, SPIED, SPIES n person employed to obtain secret information ▷ vb act as a spy
SPYAL, -S n spy
SPYCAM, -S n camera used for covert surveillance
SPYGLASS n small telescope

SPYHOLE, -S n small hole in a door, etc through which one may watch secretly
SPYING, -S ► spy
SPYPLANE n military aeroplane used to spy on enemy
SPYRE, -S same as ► spire
SPYWARE, -S n software used to gain information about a computer user
SQUAB, -BED, -BER, -S n young bird yet to leave the nest ▷ adj (of birds) recently hatched and still unfledged ▷ vb fall
SQUABASH vb crush
SQUABBED ► squab
SQUABBER ► squab
SQUABBLE n (engage in) a petty or noisy quarrel ▷ vb quarrel over a small matter
SQUABBY ► squab
SQUABS ► squab
SQUACCO, -S n S European heron
SQUAD, -DED, -S n small group of people working or training together ▷ vb set up squads
SQUADDIE n private soldier
SQUADDY same as ► squaddie
SQUADRON n division of an air force, fleet, or cavalry regiment ▷ vb assign to squadrons
SQUADS ► squad
SQUAIL, -ED, -S vb throw sticks at
SQUAILER
SQUALENE n terpene first found in the liver of sharks
SQUALID adj dirty and unpleasant
SQUALL, -ED, -S n sudden strong wind ▷ vb cry noisily, yell
SQUALLER
SQUALLY
SQUALOID adj of or like a shark
SQUALOR, -S n disgusting dirt and filth
SQUAMA, -E n scale or scalelike structure
SQUAMATE
SQUAME, -S same as ► squama
SQUAMOSE same as ► squamous
SQUAMOUS adj (of epithelium) consisting of one or more layers of flat platelike cells
SQUAMULA same as > squamella

SQUAMULE same as > squamella
SQUANDER vb waste (money or resources) ▷ n extravagance or dissipation
SQUARE, -D, -S, -ST, SQUARING n geometric figure with four equal sides and four right angles ▷ adj square in shape ▷ vb multiply (a number) by itself ▷ adv squarely, directly
SQUARELY adv in a direct way
SQUARER, -S ► square
SQUARES ► square
SQUAREST ► square
SQUARIAL n type of square dish for receiving satellite television
SQUARING ► square
SQUARISH ► square
SQUARK, -S n hypothetical boson partner of a quark
SQUARSON n clergyman who is also landowner
SQUASH, -ED, -ES vb crush flat ▷ n sweet fruit drink diluted with water
SQUASHER
SQUASHY adj soft and easily squashed
SQUAT, -S, -TED vb crouch with the knees bent and the weight on the feet ▷ n place where squatters live ▷ adj short and broad
SQUATLY
SQUATTER n illegal occupier of unused premises ▷ vb splash along
SQUATTLE vb squat
SQUATTY adj short and broad
SQUAWK, -ED, -S n loud harsh cry ▷ vb utter a squawk
SQUAWKER
SQUAWKY
SQUEAK, -ED, -S n short shrill cry or sound ▷ vb make or utter a squeak
SQUEAKER
SQUEAKY
SQUEAL, -ED, -S n long shrill cry or sound ▷ vb make or utter a squeal
SQUEALER
SQUEEGEE n tool with a rubber blade for clearing water from a surface ▷ vb remove (water or other liquid) from (something) by use of a squeegee
SQUEEZE, -D, -S vb grip or press firmly ▷ n squeezing
SQUEEZER
SQUEEZY

SQUEG, -GED, -S vb oscillate
SQUEGGER

SQUELCH vb make a wet sucking sound, as by walking through mud ▷ n squelching sound
SQUELCHY

SQUIB, -BED, -S n small firework that hisses before exploding

SQUIBBER n (in baseball) ground ball that becomes a base hit

SQUIBS ▶ squib

SQUID, -DED, -S n sea creature with tentacles ▷ vb (of a parachute) to assume an elongated shape

SQUIDGE, -D, -S vb squash

SQUIDGY adj soft, moist, and squashy

SQUIDS ▶ squid

SQUIER, -S same as ▶ **squire**

SQUIFF same as ▶ **squiffy**

SQUIFFED same as ▶ **squiffy**

SQUIFFER n concertina

SQUIFFY adj slightly drunk

SQUIGGLE n wavy line ▷ vb wriggle
SQUIGGLY

SQUILGEE same as ▶ **squeegee**

SQUILL, -S n Mediterranean plant of the lily family

SQUILLA, -E, -S n type of mantis shrimp

SQUILLS ▶ squill

SQUINCH n small arch across an interior corner of a tower ▷ vb squeeze

SQUINIED ▶ squiny

SQUINIES ▶ squiny

SQUINNY vb squint ▷ adj squint

SQUINT, -ED, -S vb have eyes which face in different directions ▷ n squinting condition of the eye ▷ adj crooked
SQUINTER
SQUINTY

SQUINY, SQUINIED, SQUINIES same as ▶ **squinny**

SQUIRAGE n body of squires

SQUIRE, -D, -S, SQUIRING n country gentleman, usu the main landowner in a community ▷ vb (of a man) escort (a woman)

SQUIREEN n petty squire

SQUIRELY ▶ squire

SQUIRES ▶ squire

SQUIRESS n wife of squire

SQUIRING ▶ squire

SQUIRISH ▶ squire

SQUIRL, -S n decorative flourish in handwriting

SQUIRM, -ED, -S vb wriggle, writhe ▷ n wriggling movement
SQUIRMER

SQUIRMY adj moving with a wriggling motion

SQUIRR, -ED, -S same as ▶ **skirr**

SQUIRREL n small bushy-tailed tree-living animal ▷ vb store for future use

SQUIRRS ▶ squirr

SQUIRT, -ED, -S vb force (a liquid) or (of a liquid) be forced out of a narrow opening ▷ n jet of liquid
SQUIRTER

SQUISH, -ED, -ES n soft squelching sound ▷ vb crush (something) with a soft squelching sound

SQUISHY adj soft and yielding to the touch

SQUIT, -S n insignificant person

SQUITCH n couch grass

SQUITS ▶ squit

SQUIZ, -ZES n look or glance, esp an inquisitive one

The word **quiz** comes up surprisingly often, so it is useful to remember that you can put an S on the front of it to form this Australian slang word for a quick look.

SQUOOSH vb squash
SQUOOSHY

SQUOOSH, -ED, -ES same as ▶ **squoosh**

SRADDHA, -S n Hindu offering to ancestor

SRADHA, -S same as ▶ **sraddha**

SRI, -S n title of respect used when addressing a Hindu

ST interj exclamation to attract attention

STAB, -BED, -BING, -S vb pierce with something pointed ▷ n stabbing
STABBER -S

STABILE, -S n stationary abstract construction, usually of wire, metal, wood, etc ▷ adj fixed

STABLE, -D, -S, -ST n building in which horses are kept ▷ vb put or keep (a horse) in a stable ▷ adj firmly fixed or established

STABLER, -S n stable owner

STABLES ▶ stable

STABLEST ▶ stable

STABLING n stable buildings or accommodation

STABLISH archaic variant of ▷ **establish**

STABLY ▶ stable

STABS ▶ stab

STACCATO, STACCATI adv with the notes sharply separated ▷ adj consisting of short abrupt sounds ▷ n staccato note

STACHYS n type of plant of the genus which includes lamb's ears and betony

STACK, -ED, -S n ordered pile ▷ vb pile in a stack
STACKER -S

STACKET, -S n fence of wooden posts

STACKING n arrangement of aircraft traffic in busy flight lanes

STACKS ▶ stack

STACKUP, -S n number of aircraft waiting to land

STACTE, -S n one of several sweet-smelling spices used in incense

STADDA, -S n type of saw

STADDLE, -S n type of support or prop

STADE, -S same as ▶ **stadium**

STADIA, -S n instrument used in surveying

STADIAL, -S n stage in development of glacier

STADIAS ▶ stadia

STADIUM, -S n sports arena with tiered seats for spectators

STAFF, -ED, -S n people employed in an organization ▷ vb supply with personnel

STAFFAGE n ornamentation in work of art

STAFFED ▶ staff

STAFFER, -S n member of staff, esp, in journalism, of editorial staff

STAFFING n act of hiring employees

STAFFMAN, STAFFMEN n person who holds the levelling staff when a survey is being made

STAFFS ▶ staff

STAG, -GED, -GING, -S n adult male deer ▷ adv without a female escort ▷ vb apply for (shares) with the intention of selling them for quick profit

STAGE, -D, -S n step or period of development ▷ vb put (a play) on stage

S

STAGEFUL n amount that can appear on stage

STAGER, -S n person of experience

STAGERY n theatrical effects or techniques

STAGES ► stage

STAGETTE n young unmarried professional woman

STAGEY same as ► stagy

STAGGARD n male red deer in the fourth year of life

STAGGART same as ► staggard

STAGGED ► stag

STAGGER vb walk unsteadily ▷ n staggering

STAGGERS n disease of horses and other domestic animals that causes staggering

STAGGERY ► stagger

STAGGIE, -S n little stag

STAGGIER ► staggy

STAGGIES ► staggie

STAGGING ► stag

STAGGY, STAGGIER ► stag

STAGHORN n as in **staghorn fern** type of fern with fronds that resemble antlers

STAGIER ► stagy

STAGIEST ► stagy

STAGILY ► stagy

STAGING, -S n temporary support used in building

STAGNANT adj (of water or air) stale from not moving

STAGNATE vb be stagnant

STAGS ► stag

STAGY, STAGIER, STAGIEST adj too theatrical or dramatic

STAID, -ER, -EST adj sedate, serious, and rather dull

STAIDLY

STAIG, -S Scots variant of ► stag

STAIN, -ED, -ING, -S vb discolour, mark ▷ n discoloration or mark

STAINER -S

STAIR n one step in a flight of stairs

STAIRED adj having stairs

STAIRS pl n flight of steps between floors, usu indoors

STAIRWAY n staircase

STAITH, -S same as ► staithe

STAITHE, -S n wharf

STAITHS ► staith

STAKE, -D, -S, STAKING n pointed stick or post driven into the ground as a support or marker ▷ vb support or mark out with stakes

STAKEOUT n police surveillance of an area or house ▷ vb keep an area or house under surveillance

STAKER, -S n person who marks off an area with stakes

STAKES ► stake

STAKING ► stake

STALAG, -S n German prisoner-of-war camp

STALAGMA ► stalagmite

STALAGS ► stalag

STALE, -D, -R, -S, -ST, STALING adj not fresh ▷ vb make or become stale ▷ n urine of horses or cattle

STALELY

STALK, -ED, -ING, -S n plant's stem ▷ vb follow or approach stealthily

STALKER -S

STALKIER ► stalky

STALKILY ► stalky

STALKING ► stalk

STALKO, -ES, -S n idle gentleman

STALKS ► stalk

STALKY, STALKIER adj like a stalk

STALL, -ED, -ING, -S n small stand for the display and sale of goods ▷ vb (of a motor vehicle or engine) stop accidentally

STALLAGE n rent paid for market stall

STALLED ► stall

STALLING ► stall

STALLION n uncastrated male horse

STALLMAN, STALLMEN n keeper of a stall

STALLS ► stall

STALWART adj strong and sturdy ▷ n stalwart person

STAMEN, -S n pollen-producing part of a flower

STAMENED adj having stamen

STAMENS ► stamen

STAMINA, -S n enduring energy and strength

STAMINAL

STAMMEL, -S n coarse woollen cloth in former use for undergarments

STAMMER, -S vb speak or say with involuntary pauses or repetition of syllables ▷ n tendency to stammer

STAMNOS, STAMNOI n ancient Greek jar

STAMP, -ED, -ING, -S n piece of gummed paper stuck to an envelope or parcel ▷ vb bring (one's foot) down forcefully

STAMPEDE n sudden rush of frightened animals or of a crowd ▷ vb (cause to) take part in a stampede

STAMPEDO same as ► stampede

STAMPER, -S ► stamp

STAMPING ► stamp

STAMPS ► stamp

STANCE, -S n attitude

STANCH, -ED, -ES vb stem the flow of (a liquid, esp blood) ▷ adj loyal and dependable

STANCHEL same as > stanchion

STANCHER ► stanch

STANCHES ► stanch

STANCHLY ► stanch

STANCK adj faint

STAND, -EN, -ING, -S, STOOD, STOODEN, STUDDEN vb be in, rise to, or place in an upright position ▷ n stall for the sale of goods

STANDARD n level of quality ▷ adj usual, regular, or average

STANDBY, -S n person or thing that is ready for use

STANDEE, -S n person who stands

STANDEN ► stand

STANDER, -S ► stand

STANDING ► stand

STANDISH n stand, usually of metal, for pens, ink bottles, etc

STANDOFF n act or an instance of standing off or apart ▷ vb stay at a distance

STANDOUT n distinctive or outstanding person or thing

STANDPAT n (in poker) refusal to change one's card

STANDS ► stand

STANDUP, -S n comedian who performs solo

STANE, -D, -S, STANING Scot word for ► stone

STANG, -ED, -ING, -S vb sting

STANHOPE n light one-seater carriage with two or four wheels

STANIEL, -S n kestrel

STANINE, -S n scale of nine levels

STANING ► stane

STANK, -ED, -ING, -S vb dam

STANNARY n place or region where tin is mined or worked

STANNATE n salt of stannic acid

STANNEL, -S same as ► staniel

STANNIC adj of or containing tin, esp in the tetravalent state

STANNITE n grey metallic mineral

STANNOUS adj of or containing tin, esp in the divalent state

STANNUM, -S n tin (the metal)

STANOL, -S n drug taken to prevent heart disease

STANYEL, -S same as
▶ **staniel**

STANZA, -S n verse of a poem
STANZAED
STANZAIC

STANZE, -S same as ▶ **stanza**

STANZO, -ES, -S same as
▶ **stanza**

STAP, -PED, -PING, -S same as ▶ **stop**

STAPEDES ▶ **stapes**

STAPEDII > **stapedius**

STAPELIA n fleshy cactus-like leafless African plant

STAPES, STAPEDES n stirrup-shaped bone in the middle ear of mammals

STAPH, -S n staphylococcus

STAPLE, -D, -S n U-shaped piece of metal used to fasten papers ▷ vb fasten with staples ▷ adj of prime importance

STAPLER, -S n small device for fastening papers together

STAPLES ▶ **staple**

STAPLING n as in **stomach stapling** surgical treatment for obesity

STAPPED ▶ **stap**

STAPPING ▶ **stap**

STAPPLE, -S same as
▶ **stopple**

STAPS ▶ **stap**

STAR, -RED, -RING, -S n hot gaseous mass in space, visible in the night sky as a point of light ▷ vb feature or be featured as a star ▷ adj leading, famous

STARAGEN n tarragon

STARCH, -ED, -ES n carbohydrate forming the main food element in bread, potatoes, etc ▷ vb stiffen (fabric) with starch ▷ adj (of a person) formal
STARCHER

STARCHY adj containing starch

STARDOM, -S n status of a star in the entertainment or sports world

STARDUST n dusty material found between the stars

STARE, -D, -S vb look or gaze fixedly (at) ▷ n fixed gaze
STARER -S

STARETS, STARTSY n Russian holy man

STARETZ same as ▶ **starets**

STARFISH n star-shaped sea creature

STARGAZE vb observe the stars

STARING, -S ▶ **stare**

STARK, -ED, -ER, -EST, -ING, -S adj harsh, unpleasant, and plain ▷ adv completely ▷ vb stiffen

STARKEN, -S vb become or make stark

STARKER ▶ **stark**

STARKERS adj completely naked

STARKEST ▶ **stark**

STARKING ▶ **stark**

STARKLY ▶ **stark**

STARKS ▶ **stark**

STARLESS ▶ **star**

STARLET, -S n young actress presented as a future star

STARLIKE ▶ **star**

STARLING n songbird with glossy black speckled feathers

STARLIT same as > **starlight**

STARN, -ED, -ING, -S same as
▶ **stern**

STARNIE, -S n Scots word for little star

STARNING ▶ **starn**

STARNOSE n American mole with starlike nose

STARNS ▶ **starn**

STAROSTA n headman of Russian village

STAROSTY n estate of Polish nobleman

STARR, -S n (in Judaism) release from a debt

STARRED ▶ **star**

STARRIER ▶ **starry**

STARRILY ▶ **starry**

STARRING ▶ **star**

STARRS ▶ **starr**

STARRY, STARRIER adj full of or like stars

STARS ▶ **star**

STARSHIP n spacecraft in science fiction

STARSPOT n dark patch on surface of star

START, -ED, -ING, -S vb take the first step, begin ▷ n first part of something

STARTER, -S n first course of a meal

STARTFUL adj tending to start

STARTING ▶ **start**

STARTISH same as ▶ **startful**

STARTLE, -D, -S vb slightly surprise or frighten
STARTLER

STARTLY same as > **startlish**

STARTS ▶ **start**

STARTSY ▶ **starets**

STARTUP, -S n business enterprise that has been launched recently

STARVE, -D, -S, STARVING vb die or suffer or cause to die or suffer from hunger

STARVER -S

STARWORT n plant with star-shaped flowers

STASES ▶ **stasis**

STASH, -ED, -ES, -ING vb store in a secret place ▷ n secret store

STASHIE, -S same as
▶ **stushie**

STASHING ▶ **stash**

STASIMON, STASIMA n ode sung in Greek tragedy

STASIS, STASES n stagnation in the normal flow of bodily fluids

STAT, -S n statistic

STATABLE ▶ **state**

STATAL adj of a federal state

STATANT adj (of an animal) in profile with all four feet on the ground

STATE, -S, STATING n condition of a person or thing ▷ adj of or concerning the State ▷ vb express in words

STATED adj (esp of a sum) determined by agreement
STATEDLY

STATELET n small state

STATELY adj dignified or grand ▷ adv in a stately manner

STATER, -S n any of various usually silver coins of ancient Greece

STATES ▶ **state**

STATIC adj stationary or inactive ▷ n crackling sound or speckled picture caused by interference in radio or TV reception
STATICAL

STATICE, -S n plant name formerly used for both thrift and sea lavender

STATICKY ▶ **static**

STATICS n study of the forces producing a state of equilibrium

STATIM adv right away

STATIN, -S n type of drug that lowers the levels of

S

low-density lipoproteins in the blood

STATING ► state

STATINS ► statin

STATION, -S n place where trains stop for passengers ▷ vb assign (someone) to a particular place

STATISM, -S n theory or practice of concentrating economic and political power in the state

STATIST, -S n advocate of statism ▷ adj of, characteristic of, advocating, or relating to statism

STATIVE, -S adj denoting a verb describing a state rather than an activity, act, or event ▷ n stative verb

STATOR, -S n stationary part of a rotary machine or device

STATS ► stat

STATTO, -S n person preoccupied with the facts and figures of a subject

STATUA, -S same as ► statue

STATUARY n statues collectively ▷ adj of, relating to, or suitable for statues

STATUAS ► statua

STATUE, -S n large sculpture of a human or animal figure

STATUED adj decorated with or portrayed in a statue or statues

STATUES ► statue

STATURE, -S n person's height

STATURED adj having stature

STATURES ► stature

STATUS, -ES n social position

STATUSY adj conferring or having status

STATUTE, -S n written law

STAUMREL n stupid person

STAUN, -ING, -S Scot word for ► stand

STAUNCH same as ► stanch

STAUNING ► staun

STAUNS ► staun

STAVE, -D, -S, STAVING same as ► staff

STAW, -ED, -ING, -S Scots form of ► stall

STAY, -ED, -ING vb remain in a place or condition ▷ n period of staying in a place

STAYAWAY n strike in South Africa

STAYED ► stay

STAYER, -S n person or thing that stays

STAYING ► stay

STAYLESS adj with no stays or support

STAYNE, -D, -S, STAYNING same as ► stain

STAYRE, -S same as ► stair

STAYS pl n old-fashioned corsets with bones in them

STAYSAIL n sail fastened on a stay

STEAD, -ED, -S n place or function that should be taken by another ▷ vb help or benefit

STEADIED ► steady

STEADIER ► steady

STEADIES ► steady

STEADILY ► steady

STEADING n farmstead

STEADS ► stead

STEADY, STEADIED, STEADIES adj not shaky or wavering ▷ vb make steady ▷ adv in a steady manner

STEAK, -S n thick slice of meat, esp beef

STEAL, -ED, -ING, -S, -T, STOLEN, STOLN, STOWN vb take unlawfully or without permission

STEALAGE n theft

STEALE, -S n handle

STEALED ► steal

STEALER, -S n person who steals something

STEALES ► steale

STEALING ► steal

STEALS ► steal

STEALT ► steal

STEALTH, -S n moving carefully and quietly ▷ adj (of technology) able to render an aircraft almost invisible to radar ▷ vb approach undetected

STEALTHY adj characterized by great caution, secrecy, etc

STEAM, -ED, -S n vapour into which water changes when boiled ▷ vb give off steam

STEAMER, -S n steam-propelled ship ▷ vb travel by steamer

STEAMIE, -S n public wash house

STEAMIER ► steamy

STEAMIES ► steamie

STEAMILY ► steamy

STEAMING adj very hot ▷ n robbery by a large gang of youths

STEAMS ► steam

STEAMY, STEAMIER adj full of steam

STEAN, -S n earthenware vessel

STEANE, -D, -S, STEANING same as ► steen

STEANS ► stean

STEAPSIN n pancreatic lipase

STEAR, -D, -ING, -S same as ► steer

STEARAGE same as ► steerage

STEARATE n any salt or ester of stearic acid

STEARD ► stear

STEARE, -D, -S same as ► steer

STEARIC adj of or relating to suet or fat

STEARIN, -S n colourless crystalline ester of glycerol and stearic acid

STEARINE same as ► stearin

STEARING ► stear

STEARINS ► stearin

STEARS ► stear

STEATITE same as > soapstone

STEATOMA n tumour of sebaceous gland

STED, -DED, -DING, -S same as ► stead

STEDD, -S same as ► stead

STEDDE, -S same as ► stead

STEDDED ► sted

STEDDES ► stedde

STEDDIED ► steddy

STEDDIES ► steddy

STEDDING ► sted

STEDDS ► stedd

STEDDY, STEDDIED, STEDDIES same as ► steady

STEDE, -D, -S, STEDING same as ► stead

STEDFAST same as > steadfast

STEDING ► stede

STEDS ► sted

STEED, -ED, -ING, -S same as ► stead

STEEDIED ► steedy

STEEDIES ► steedy

STEEDING ► steed

STEEDS ► steed

STEEDY, STEEDIED, STEEDIES same as ► steady

STEEK, -ED, -ING, -IT, -S vb Scots word meaning shut

STEEL, -D, -ED, -ING n hard malleable alloy of iron and carbon ▷ vb prepare (oneself) for something unpleasant

STEELBOW n material lent to tenant by landlord

STEELD ► steel

STEELED ► steel

STEELIE, -S n steel ball bearing used as marble

STEELIER ► steely

STEELIES ► steelie

STEELING ► steel

STEELMAN, STEELMEN *n* person working in steel industry

STEELS *pl n* shares and bonds of steel companies

STEELY, STEELIER ► **steel**

STEEM, -ED, -ING, -S variant of ► **esteem**

STEEN, -ED, -ING, -S *vb* line with stone

STEENBOK *n* small antelope of central and southern Africa

STEENED ► **steen**

STEENING ► **steen**

STEENS ► **steen**

STEEP, -ED, -EST, -ING, -S *adj* sloping sharply ▷ *vb* soak or be soaked in liquid ▷ *n* instance or the process of steeping

STEEPEN, -S *vb* become steep or steeper

STEEPER, -S ► **steep**

STEEPEST ► **steep**

STEEPUP *adj* very steep

STEEPIER ► **steepy**

STEEPING ► **steep**

STEEPISH ► **steep**

STEEPLE, -S same as ► **spire**
STEEPLED

STEEPLY ► **steep**

STEEPS ► **steep**

STEEPUP *adj* very steep

STEEPY, STEEPIER same as ► **steep**

STEER, -ED, -ING, -S *vb* direct the course of (a vehicle or ship) ▷ *n* castrated male ox

STEERAGE *n* cheapest accommodation on a passenger ship

STEERED ► **steer**

STEERER, -S ► **steer**

STEERIER ► **steery**

STEERIES ► **steery**

STEERING ► **steer**

STEERS ► **steer**

STEERY, STEERIER, STEERIES *n* commotion ▷ *adj* busy or bustling

STEEVE, -D, -R, -S, -ST, STEEVING *n* spar having a pulley block at one end ▷ *vb* stow (cargo) securely in the hold of a ship
STEEVELY

STEGODON *n* mammal of Pliocene to Pleistocene times, similar to the mastodon

STEIL, -S same as ► **steal**

STEIN, -ED, -ING, -S same as ► **steen**

STEINBOK same as ► **steenbok**

STEINED ► **stein**

STEINING ► **stein**

STEINS ► **stein**

STELA, -E, -I same as ► **stele**

STELAR ► **stele**

STELE, -S *n* upright stone slab or column decorated with figures or inscriptions
STELENE
STELIC

STELL, -ED, -ING, -S *n* shelter for cattle or sheep built on moorland or hillsides ▷ *vb* position or place

STELLA, -S *n* star or something star-shaped

STELLAR *adj* of stars

STELLAS ► **stella**

STELLATE *adj* resembling a star in shape

STELLED ► **stell**

STELLIFY *vb* change or be changed into a star

STELLING ► **stell**

STELLIO *n* as in **stellio lizard** denoting type of lizard

STELLION *n* Mediterranean lizard

STELLITE *n* alloy containing cobalt, chromium, carbon, tungsten, and molybdenum

STELLS ► **stell**

STEM, -MED, -MING, -S *vb* stop (the flow of something) ▷ *n* main axis of a plant, which bears the leaves, axillary buds, and flowers

STEMBOK, -S same as ► **steenbok**

STEMBUCK same as ► **steenbok**

STEME, -D, -S, STEMING same as ► **steam**

STEMHEAD *n* head of the stem of a vessel

STEMING ► **steme**

STEMLESS ► **stem**

STEMLET, -S *n* little stem

STEMLIKE ► **stem**

STEMMA, -S, -TA *n* family tree

STEMME, -S archaic variant of ► **stem**

STEMMED ► **stem**

STEMMER, -S ► **stem**

STEMMERY *n* tobacco factory

STEMMES ► **stemme**

STEMMIER ► **stemmy**

STEMMING ► **stem**

STEMMY, STEMMIER *adj* (of wine) young and raw

STEMPEL, -S *n* timber support

STEMPLE, -S same as ► **stempel**

STEMS ► **stem**

STEMSON, -S *n* curved timber at the bow of a wooden vessel

STEMWARE *n* collective term for glasses, goblets, etc, with stems

STEN, -NED, -NING, -S *vb* stride

STENCH, -ED, -ES *n* foul smell ▷ *vb* cause to smell
STENCHY

STENCIL, -S *n* thin sheet through which ink passes to form a pattern on the surface below ▷ *vb* make (a pattern) with a stencil

STEND, -ED, -ING, -S *vb* Scots word meaning bound

STENGAH, -S same as ► **stinger**

STENLOCK *n* fish of northern seas

STENNED ► **sten**

STENNING ► **sten**

STENO, -S *n* stenographer

STENOKY *n* survival dependent on conditions remaining within a narrow range of variables

STENOS ► **steno**

STENOSED *adj* abnormally contracted

STENOSIS, STENOSES *n* abnormal narrowing of a bodily canal or passage
STENOTIC

STENS ► **sten**

STENT, -ED, -ING, -S *n* surgical implant used to keep an artery open ▷ *vb* assess

STENTOR, -S *n* person with an unusually loud voice

STENTOUR *n* tax assessor

STENTS ► **stent**

STEP, -PED, -PING, -S, -T *vb* move and set down the foot, as when walking ▷ *n* stepping

STEPDAD, -S *n* stepfather

STEPDAME *n* woman married to one's father

STEPHANE *n* ancient Greek headdress

STEPLESS *adj* without steps

STEPLIKE ► **step**

STEPMOM, -S *n* stepmother

STEPNEY, -S *n* spare wheel

STEPOVER *n* (in football) instance of raising the foot over the ball as a feint

STEPPE, -S *n* extensive grassy plain usually without trees

STEPPED ► **step**

STEPPER, -S *n* person who or animal that steps, esp a horse or a dancer

S

STEPPES ► steppe

STEPPING ► step

STEPS ► step

STEPSON, -S *n* son of one's spouse by an earlier relationship

STEPT ► step

STEPWISE *adj* arranged in the manner of or resembling steps ▷ *adv* with the form or appearance of steps

STERANE, -S *n* any of a class of hydrocarbons found in crude oils

STERE, -S *n* unit used to measure volumes of stacked timber

STEREO, -ED, -S *n* stereophonic record player ▷ *adj* feeding two loudspeakers through separate channels ▷ *vb* make stereophonic

STEREOME *n* tissue of a plant that provides mechanical support

STEREOS ► stereo

STERES ► stere

STERIC *adj* of or caused by the spatial arrangement of atoms in a molecule

STERICAL *same as* ► **steric**

STERIGMA *n* minute stalk bearing a spore or chain of spores in certain fungi

STERILE *adj* free from germs

STERLET, -S *n* small sturgeon of N Asia and E Europe

STERLING *n* British money system ▷ *adj* genuine and reliable

STERN, -ED, -ER, -EST, -ING, -S *adj* severe, strict ▷ *n* rear part of a ship ▷ *vb* row boat backward

STERNA ► sternum

STERNAGE *n* sterns

STERNAL ► sternum

STERNED ► stern

STERNER ► stern

STERNEST ► stern

STERNING ► stern

STERNITE *n* part of an arthropod

STERNLY ► stern

STERNS ► stern

STERNSON *n* timber bolted to the sternpost and keelson at the stern of a wooden vessel

STERNUM, STERNA, -S *n* long flat bone to which most of the ribs are attached

STERNWAY *n* movement of a vessel sternforemost

STEROID, -S *n* organic compound containing a carbon ring system

STEROL, -S *n* natural insoluble alcohol such as cholesterol and ergosterol

STERTOR, -S *n* laborious or noisy breathing

STERVE, -D, -S, STERVING *same as* ► **starve**

STET, -S, -TED, -TING *interj* instruction to ignore an alteration previously made ▷ *vb* indicate to a printer that deleted matter is to be kept ▷ *n* mark indicating that deleted matter is to be kept

STETSON, -S *n* cowboy hat

STETTED ► stet

STETTING ► stet

STEVEN, -S *n* voice

STEVIA, -S *n* any of a genus of plant with sweet leaves

STEW, -S *n* food cooked slowly in a closed pot ▷ *vb* cook slowly in a closed pot

STEWABLE

STEWARD, -S *n* person who looks after passengers on a ship or aircraft ▷ *vb* act as a steward (of)

STEWED *adj* (of food) cooked by stewing

STEWER, -S ► stew

STEWIER ► stewy

STEWIEST ► stewy

STEWING, -S ► stew

STEWPAN, -S *n* pan used for making stew

STEWPOND *n* fishpond

STEWPOT, -S *n* pot used for making stew

STEWS ► stew

STEWY, STEWIER, STEWIEST ► stew

STEY, -ER, -EST, -S *adj* (Scots) steep ▷ *n* ladder

STHENIA, -S *n* abnormal strength

STHENIC *adj* abounding in energy or bodily strength

STIBBLE, -S *Scots form of* ► **stubble**

STIBBLER *n* horse allowed to eat stubble

STIBBLES ► stibble

STIBIAL ► stibium

STIBINE, -S *n* colourless slightly soluble poisonous gas

STIBIUM, -S *obsolete name for* ► **antimony**

STIBNITE *n* soft greyish mineral

STICCADO *n* type of xylophone

STICCATO *same as* ► **sticcado**

STICH, -S *n* line of poetry

STICHERA > sticheron

STICHIC ► stich

STICHOS, STICHOI *n* line of poem

STICHS ► stich

STICK, -ED, -ING, -S *n* long thin piece of wood ▷ *vb* push (a pointed object) into (something)

STICKER, -S *n* adhesive label or sign ▷ *vb* put stickers on

STICKFUL ► stick

STICKIE, -S *n* notepaper with an adhesive strip

STICKIED ► sticky

STICKIER ► sticky

STICKIES ► stickie

STICKILY ► sticky

STICKING ► stick

STICKIT *Scots form of* ► **stuck**

STICKJAW *n* stodgy food

STICKLE, -D, -S *vb* dispute stubbornly, esp about minor points

STICKLER *n* person who insists on something

STICKLES ► stickle

STICKMAN, STICKMEN *n* human figure drawn in thin strokes

STICKOUT *n* conspicuous person or thing

STICKPIN *n* tiepin

STICKS ► stick

STICKUM, -S *n* adhesive

STICKUP, -S *n* robbery at gun-point

STICKY, STICKIED, STICKIER *adj* covered with an adhesive substance ▷ *vb* make sticky ▷ *n* inquisitive look or stare

STICTION *n* frictional force to be overcome to set one object in motion when it is in contact with another

STIDDIE, -D, -S *same as* ► **stithy**

STIE *same as* ► **sty**

STIED ► sty

STIES ► sty

STIEVE, -R, -ST *same as* ► **steeve**

STIEVELY

STIFF, -ED, -ER, -EST, -ING, -S *adj* not easily bent or moved ▷ *n* loser or failure ▷ *adv* completely or utterly ▷ *vb* fail completely

STIFFEN, -S *vb* make or become stiff

STIFFER ► stiff

STIFFEST ► stiff

STIFFING ► stiff

STIFFISH ► stiff
STIFFLY ► stiffy
STIFFS ► stiff
STIFLE, -D, -S *vb* suppress ▷ *n* joint in the hind leg of a horse, dog, etc
STIFLER -S
STIFLING *adj* uncomfortably hot and stuffy
STIGMA, -S, -TA *n* mark of social disgrace
STIGMAL *adj* of part of insect wing
STIGMAS ► stigma
STIGMATA ► stigma
STIGME, -S *n* dot in Greek punctuation
STILB, -S *n* unit of luminance
STILBENE *n* colourless or slightly yellow crystalline hydrocarbon used in the manufacture of dyes
STILBITE *n* white or yellow zeolite mineral
STILBS ► stilb
STILE, -D, -S, STILING *same as* ► **style**
STILET, -S *same as* ► **stylet**
STILETTO *n* small narrow dagger ▷ *vb* stab with a stiletto
STILING ► stile
STILL, -ED, -EST, -ING, -S *adv* now or in the future as before ▷ *adj* motionless ▷ *n* calmness; apparatus for distillation ▷ *vb* make still
STILLAGE *n* frame or stand for keeping things off the ground, such as casks in a brewery
STILLED ► still
STILLER, -S ► still
STILLEST ► still
STILLIER ► stilly
STILLING ► still
STILLION *n* stand for cask
STILLMAN, STILLMEN *n* someone involved in the operation of a still
STILLS ► still
STILLSON *n* type of wrench
STILLY, STILLIER *adv* quietly or calmly ▷ *adj* still, quiet, or calm
STILT, -ING, -S *n* either of a pair of long poles with footrests for walking raised from the ground ▷ *vb* raise or place on or as if on stilts
STILTED *adj* stiff and formal in manner
STILTER, -S ► stilt
STILTIER ► stilty
STILTING ► stilt
STILTISH ► stilt

STILTS ► stilt
STILTY, STILTIER ► stilt
STIM, -S *n* very small amount
STIME, -D, -S, STIMING *same as* ► **styme**
STIMIE, -D, -S *same as* ► **stymie**
STIMING ► stime
STIMS ► stim
STIMULUS, STIMULI *n* something that rouses a person or thing to activity
STIMY, -ING *same as* ► **stymie**
STING, -ED, -S, STONG, STUNG *vb* (of certain animals or plants) wound by injecting with poison ▷ *n* wound or pain caused by or as if by stinging
STINGE, -S *n* stingy or miserly person
STINGED ► sting
STINGER, -S *n* person, plant, animal, etc, that stings or hurts
STINGES ► stinge
STINGIER ► stingy
STINGIES ► stingy
STINGILY ► stingy
STINGING ► sting
STINGO, -S *n* strong alcohol
STINGRAY *n* flatfish capable of inflicting painful wounds
STINGS ► sting
STINGY, STINGIER, STINGIES *adj* mean or miserly ▷ *n* stinging nettle
STINK, -ING, -S, STUNK *n* strong unpleasant smell ▷ *vb* give off a strong unpleasant smell
STINKARD *n* smelly person
STINKBUG *n* type of insect that releases an unpleasant odour
STINKER, -S *n* difficult or unpleasant person or thing
STINKIER ► stinky
STINKING ► stink
STINKO *adj* drunk
STINKPOT *n* thing that stinks
STINKS ► stink
STINKY, STINKIER *adj* having a foul smell
STINT, -ED, -ING, -S *vb* be miserly with (something) ▷ *n* allotted amount of work
STINTER -S
STINTIER ► stinty
STINTING ► stint
STINTS ► stint
STINTY, STINTIER ► stint
STIPA, -S *n* variety of grass
STIPE *n* stalk in plants that bears reproductive structures

STIPED *same as* ► **stipitate**
STIPEL, -S *n* small paired leaflike structure at the base of certain leaflets
STIPEND, -S *n* regular allowance or salary
STIPES, STIPITES *n* second maxillary segment in insects and crustaceans
STIPPLE, -D, -S *vb* paint, draw, or engrave using dots ▷ *n* technique of stippling
STIPPLER
STIPULAR ► stipule
STIPULE, -S *n* small paired usually leaflike outgrowth occurring at the base of a leaf or its stalk
STIPULED
STIR, -RED, -RING, -S *vb* mix up (a liquid) by moving a spoon etc around in it ▷ *n* stirring
STIRE, -D, -S, STIRING *same as* ► **steer**
STIRK, -S *n* heifer of 6 to 12 months old
STIRLESS ► stir
STIRP *same as* ► **stirps**
STIRPS, STIRPES *n* line of descendants from an ancestor
STIRRA, -S *same as* ► **sirra**
STIRRAH, -S *same as* ► **sirrah**
STIRRAS ► stirra
STIRRE, -S *same as* ► **steer**
STIRRED ► stir
STIRRER, -S *n* person who deliberately causes trouble
STIRRES ► stirre
STIRRING ► stir
STIRRUP, -S *n* metal loop attached to a saddle for supporting a rider's foot
STIRS ► stir
STISHIE, -S *same as* ► **stushie**
STITCH, -ED, -ES *n* link made by drawing thread through material with a needle ▷ *vb* sew
STITCHER
STITHY, STITHIED, STITHIES *n* forge or anvil ▷ *vb* forge on an anvil
STIVE, -D, -S, STIVING *vb* stifle
STIVER, -S *n* former Dutch coin
STIVES ► stive
STIVIER ► stivy
STIVIEST ► stivy
STIVING ► stive
STIVY, STIVIER, STIVIEST *adj* stuffy

S

STOA, -E, -I, -S *n* covered walk that has a colonnade on one or both sides

STOAT, -S *n* small mammal of the weasel family

STOB, -BED, -BING, -S same as ▶ **stab**

STOBIE *adj* as in **stobie pole** steel and concrete pole for supporting electricity wires

STOBS ▶ **stob**

STOCCADO *n* fencing thrust

STOCCATA same as ▶ **stoccado**

STOCIOUS same as ▶ **stotious**

STOCK, -ED *n* total amount of goods available for sale in a shop ▷ *adj* kept in stock, standard ▷ *vb* keep for sale or future use

STOCKADE *n* enclosure or barrier made of stakes ▷ *vb* surround with a stockade

STOCKAGE *n* livestock put to graze on crops

STOCKCAR *n* car that has been strengthened for a form of racing in which the cars often collide

STOCKED ▶ **stock**

STOCKER, -S ▶ **stock**

STOCKIER ▶ **stocky**

STOCKILY ▶ **stocky**

STOCKING *n* close-fitting covering for the foot and leg

STOCKISH *adj* stupid or dull

STOCKIST *n* dealer who stocks a particular product

STOCKMAN, STOCKMEN *n* man engaged in the rearing or care of farm livestock, esp cattle

STOCKPOT *n* pot in which stock for soup is made

STOCKS *pl n* instrument of punishment in which an offender was locked

STOCKY, STOCKIER *adj* (of a person) broad and sturdy

STODGE, -D, -S, STODGING *n* heavy starchy food ▷ *vb* stuff (oneself or another) with food

STODGER, -S *n* dull person

STODGES ▶ **stodge**

STODGIER ▶ **stodgy**

STODGILY ▶ **stodgy**

STODGING ▶ **stodge**

STODGY, STODGIER *adj* (of food) heavy and starchy

STOEP, -S *n* verandah

STOGEY, -S same as ▶ **stogy**

STOGIE same as ▶ **stogy**

STOGY, STOGIES *n* any long cylindrical inexpensive cigar

STOIC, -S *n* person who suffers hardship without showing his or her feelings ▷ *adj* suffering hardship without showing one's feelings

STOICAL *adj* suffering great difficulties without showing one's feelings

STOICISM *n* indifference to pleasure and pain

STOICS ▶ **stoic**

STOIT, -ED, -ING, -S *vb* bounce

STOITER, -S *vb* stagger

STOITING ▶ **stoit**

STOITS ▶ **stoit**

STOKE, STOKING *vb* feed and tend (a fire or furnace)

STOKED *adj* very pleased

STOKER, -S *n* person employed to tend a furnace on a ship or train powered by steam

STOKES *n* cgs unit of kinematic viscosity

STOKESIA *n* American flowering plant

STOKING ▶ **stoke**

STOKVEL, -S *n* (in S Africa) informal savings pool or syndicate

STOLE, -S *n* long scarf or shawl

STOLED *adj* wearing a stole

STOLEN ▶ **steal**

STOLES ▶ **stole**

STOLID, -ER *adj* showing little emotion or interest

STOLIDLY

STOLLEN, -S *n* rich sweet bread containing nuts, raisins, etc

STOLN ▶ **steal**

STOLON, -S *n* long horizontal stem that grows along the surface of the soil

STOLONIC

STOLPORT *n* airport for short take-off aircraft

STOMA, -S, -TA *n* pore in a plant leaf that controls the passage of gases

STOMACH, -S *n* organ in the body which digests food ▷ *vb* put up with

STOMACHY *adj* having a large belly

STOMACK, -S *n* as in **have a stomack** (in E Africa) be pregnant

STOMAL ▶ **stoma**

STOMAS ▶ **stoma**

STOMATA ▶ **stoma**

STOMATAL *adj* of, relating to, or possessing stomata or a stoma

STOMATE, -S *n* opening on leaf through which water evaporates

STOMATIC *adj* of or relating to a mouth or mouthlike part

STOMIUM, STOMIA, -S *n* part of the sporangium of ferns that ruptures to release the spores

STOMODEA > **stomodeum**

STOMP, -ED, -ING, -S *vb* tread heavily ▷ *n* rhythmic stamping jazz dance

STOMPER, -S *n* song with a strong beat

STOMPIE, -S *n* cigarette butt

STOMPIER ▶ **stompy**

STOMPIES ▶ **stompie**

STOMPING ▶ **stomp**

STOMPS ▶ **stomp**

STOMPY, STOMPIER *adj* (of music) encouraging stomping of the feet

STONABLE ▶ **stone**

STOND, -S same as ▶ **stand**

STONE, -D, -S *n* material of which rocks are made ▷ *vb* throw stones at

STONECUT *n* (print made from) a carved block of stone

STONED ▶ **stone**

STONEFLY *n* type of insect whose larvae are aquatic

STONEN *adj* of stone

STONER, -S *n* device for removing stones from fruit

STONERAG *n* type of lichen

STONERAW same as ▶ **stonerag**

STONERN same as ▶ **stonen**

STONERS ▶ **stoner**

STONES ▶ **stone**

STONEY same as ▶ **stony**

STONG ▶ **sting**

STONIED ▶ **stony**

STONIER ▶ **stony**

STONIES ▶ **stony**

STONIEST ▶ **stony**

STONILY ▶ **stony**

STONING, -S ▶ **stone**

STONISH same as ▶ **astonish**

STONK, -ED, -ING, -S *vb* bombard (soldiers, buildings, etc) with artillery ▷ *n* concentrated bombardment

STONKER, -S *vb* destroy

STONKING ▶ **stonk**

STONKS ▶ **stonk**

STONN, -ING, -S same as ▶ **stun**

STONNE, -D, -S same as ▶ **stun**

STONNING ▶ **stonn**

STONNS ▸ stonn

STONY, STONIED, STONIER, STONIES, STONIEST, -ING *adj* of or like stone ▹ *vb* astonish

STOOD ▸ stand

STOODEN ▸ stand

STOOGE, -D, -S, STOOGING *n* actor who feeds lines to a comedian ▹ *vb* act as a stooge

STOOK, -ED, -S *n* number of sheaves set upright in a field to dry ▹ *vb* set up (sheaves) in stooks

STOOKER -S

STOOKIE, -S *n* stucco

STOOKING *n* act of stooking

STOOKS ▸ stook

STOOL, -ED, -ING, -S *n* chair without arms or back ▹ *vb* (of a plant) send up shoots from the base of the stem

STOOLIE, -S *n* police informer

STOOLING ▸ stool

STOOLS ▸ stool

STOOLY *n* (US) informant for the police

STOOP, -ED, -S *vb* bend forward and downward

STOOPE, -S *same as* ▸ stoup

STOOPED ▸ stoop

STOOPER, -S ▸ stoop

STOOPES ▸ stoope

STOOPING ▸ stoop

STOOPS ▸ stoop

STOOR, -S *same as* ▸ stour

STOOSHIE *same as* ▸ stushie

STOOZE, -D, -S, STOOZING *vb* borrow money cheaply and invest it to make a profit

STOOZER, -S *n* person who stoozes

STOOZES ▸ stooze

STOOZING ▸ stooze

STOP, -PED, -PING, -S, -T *vb* cease or cause to cease from doing (something) ▹ *n* stopping or being stopped

STOPBAND *n* band of frequencies stopped by a filter

STOPBANK *n* embankment to prevent flooding

STOPCOCK *n* valve to control or stop the flow of fluid in a pipe

STOPE, -D, -S *n* steplike excavation made in a mine to extract ore ▹ *vb* mine (ore, etc) by cutting stopes

STOPER, -S *n* drill used in mining

STOPES ▸ stope

STOPGAP, -S *n* temporary substitute

STOPING, -S *n* process by which country rock is broken up and engulfed by magma

STOPLESS ▸ stop

STOPOFF, -S *n* break in a journey

STOPOVER *n* short break in a journey ▹ *vb* make a stopover

STOPPAGE *n* act of stopping something or the state of being stopped

STOPPED ▸ stop

STOPPER, -S *n* plug for closing a bottle etc ▹ *vb* close or fit with a stopper

STOPPING ▸ stop

STOPPLE, -D, -S *same as* ▸ stopper

STOPS ▸ stop

STOPT ▸ stop

STOPWORD *n* common word not used in computer search engines

STORABLE ▸ store

STORAGE, -S *n* storing

STORAX, -ES *n* type of tree or shrub with white flowers

STORE, -D, STORING *vb* collect and keep (things) for future use ▹ *n* shop

STOREMAN, STOREMEN *n* man looking after storeroom

STORER, -S ▸ store

STORES *pl n* supply of food and essentials for a journey

STOREY, -S *n* floor or level of a building

STOREYED *adj* having a storey or storeys

STOREYS ▸ storey

STORGE, -S *n* affection

STORIED ▸ story

STORIES ▸ story

STORING ▸ store

STORK, -S *n* large wading bird

STORM, -ED, -S *n* violent weather with wind, rain, or snow ▹ *vb* attack or capture (a place) suddenly

STORMER, -S *n* outstanding example of its kind

STORMFUL ▸ storm

STORMIER ▸ stormy

STORMILY ▸ stormy

STORMING *adj* characterized by or displaying dynamism, speed, and energy

STORMS ▸ storm

STORMY, STORMIER *adj* characterized by storms

STORY, STORIED, STORIES, -ING *n* narration of a chain of events ▹ *vb* decorate with scenes from history

STOSS, -ES *adj* (of the side of a hill) facing the onward flow of a glacier ▹ *n* hillside facing glacier flow

STOT, -S, -TED, -TING *n* bullock ▹ *vb* bounce or cause to bounce

STOTIN, -OV, -S *n* former monetary unit of Slovenia

STOTINKA, STOTINKI *n* monetary unit of Bulgaria, worth one hundredth of a lev

STOTINOV ▸ stotin

STOTINS ▸ stotin

STOTIOUS *adj* drunk

STOTS ▸ stot

STOTT, -S *same as* ▸ stot

STOTTED ▸ stot

STOTTER, -S *same as* ▸ stot

STOTTIE, -S *n* wedge of bread cut from a flat round loaf

STOTTING ▸ stot

STOTTS ▸ stot

STOTTY *same as* ▸ stottie

STOUN, -ING, -S *same as* ▸ stun

STOUND, -ED, -S *n* short while ▹ *vb* ache

STOUNING ▸ stoun

STOUNS ▸ stoun

STOUP, -S *n* small basin for holy water

STOUR, -S *n* turmoil or conflict

STOURE, -S *same as* ▸ stour

STOURIE *same as* ▸ stoury

STOURIER ▸ stoury

STOURS ▸ stour

STOURY, STOURIER *adj* dusty

STOUSH, -ED, -ES *vb* hit or punch (someone) ▹ *n* fighting or violence

STOUSHIE *same as* ▸ stushie

STOUT, -ER, -EST, -S *adj* fat ▹ *n* strong dark beer

STOUTEN, -S *vb* make or become stout

STOUTER ▸ stout

STOUTEST ▸ stout

STOUTH, -S *n* Scots word meaning theft

STOUTISH ▸ stout

STOUTLY ▸ stout

STOUTS ▸ stout

STOVAINE *n* anaesthetic drug

STOVE, -D, -S *n* apparatus for cooking or heating ▹ *vb* process (ceramics, metalwork, etc) by heating in a stove

STOVER, -S *n* fodder

STOVES ▸ stove

STOVETOP *US word for* ▸ hob

STOVIES *pl n* potatoes stewed with onions

S

STOVING, -S ▸ stove

STOW, -ED, -S vb pack or store

STOWABLE

STOWAGE, -S n space or charge for stowing goods

STOWAWAY n person who hides on a ship or aircraft in order to travel free ▷ vb travel in such a way

STOWDOWN n packing of ship's hold

STOWED ▸ stow

STOWER, -S ▸ stow

STOWING, -S ▸ stow

STOWLINS adv stealthily

STOWN ▸ steal

STOWND, -ED, -S same as ▸ stound

STOWP, -S same as ▸ stoup

STOWRE, -S same as ▸ stour

STOWS ▸ stow

STRABISM n abnormal alignment of one or both eyes

STRACK vb archaic past tense form of strike

STRAD, -S n violin made by Stradivarius

STRADDLE vb have one leg or part on each side of (something) ▷ n act or position of straddling

STRADIOT n Venetian cavalryman

STRADS ▸ strad

STRAE, -S Scots form of ▸ straw

STRAFE, -D, -S vb attack (an enemy) with machine guns from the air ▷ n act or instance of strafing

STRAFER -S

STRAFF, -ED, -S same as ▸ strafe

STRAFING n act of strafing

STRAG, -S n straggler

STRAGGLE vb go or spread in a rambling or irregular way

STRAGGLY

STRAGS ▸ strag

STRAICHT Scots word for ▸ straight

STRAIGHT adj not curved or crooked ▷ adv in a straight line ▷ n straight part, esp of a racetrack ▷ vb tighten

STRAIK, -ED, -S Scots word for ▸ stroke

STRAIN, -S vb subject to mental tension ▷ n tension or tiredness

STRAINED adj not natural, forced

STRAINER n sieve

STRAINS ▸ strain

STRAINT, -S n pressure

STRAIT, -ED, -ER, -S n narrow channel connecting two areas of sea ▷ adj (of spaces, etc) affording little room ▷ vb tighten

STRAITEN vb embarrass or distress, esp financially

STRAITER ▸ strait

STRAITLY ▸ strait

STRAITS ▸ strait

STRAK vb archaic past tense form of strike

STRAKE, -S n curved metal plate forming part of the metal rim on a wooden wheel

STRAKED adj having a strake

STRAKES ▸ strake

STRAMASH n uproar ▷ vb destroy

STRAMMEL same as ▸ strummel

STRAMONY n former asthma medicine made from the dried leaves and flowers of the thorn apple

STRAMP, -ED, -S Scots variant of ▸ tramp

STRAND, -ED, -S vb run aground ▷ n shore

STRANDER

STRANG dialect variant of ▸ strong

STRANGE, -S adj odd or unusual ▷ n odd or unfamiliar person or thing

STRANGER n person who is not known or is new to a place or experience

STRANGES ▸ strange

STRANGLE vb kill by squeezing the throat

STRAP, -PED, -S n strip of flexible material for lifting or holding in place ▷ vb fasten with a strap or straps

STRAPPER n strapping person

STRAPPY adj having straps

STRAPS ▸ strap

STRASS, -ES another word for ▸ paste

STRATA ▸ stratum

STRATAL ▸ stratum

STRATEGY n overall plan

STRATH, -S n flat river valley

STRATI ▸ stratus

STRATIFY vb form or be formed in layers or strata

STRATOSE adj formed in strata

STRATOUS adj of stratus

STRATUM, STRATA, -S n layer, esp of rock

STRATUS, STRATI n grey layer cloud

STRAUCHT Scots word for ▸ stretch

STRAUGHT same as ▸ straucht

STRAUNGE same as ▸ strange

STRAVAGE same as ▸ stravaig

STRAVAIG vb wander aimlessly

STRAW, -ED, -ING, -S n dried stalks of grain ▷ vb spread around

STRAWEN adj of straw

STRAWHAT adj of summer dramatic performance

STRAWIER ▸ strawy

STRAWING ▸ straw

STRAWN ▸ strew

STRAWS ▸ straw

STRAWY, STRAWIER adj containing straw, or like straw in colour or texture

STRAY, -ED, -ING, -S vb wander ▷ adj having strayed ▷ n stray animal

STRAYER -S

STRAYVE, -D, -S vb wander aimlessly

STREAK, -ED, -S n long band of contrasting colour or substance ▷ vb mark with streaks

STREAKER

STREAKY adj marked with streaks

STREAM, -ED, -S n small river ▷ vb flow steadily

STREAMER n strip of coloured paper that unrolls when tossed

STREAMS ▸ stream

STREAMY adj (of an area, land, etc) having many streams

STREEK, -ED, -S Scots word for ▸ stretch

STREEKER

STREEL, -ED, -S vb trail

STREET, -ED, -S n public road, usu lined with buildings ▷ vb lay out a street or streets

STREETY adj of streets

STREIGHT same as ▸ strait

STREIGNE same as ▸ strain

STRELITZ n former Russian soldier

STRENE, -S same as ▸ strain

STRENGTH n quality of being strong

STREP, -S n streptococcus

STREPENT adj noisy

STREPS ▸ strep

STRESS, -ED, -ES n tension or strain ▷ vb emphasize

STRESSOR n event, experience, etc, that causes stress

STRESSY adj characterized by stress

STRETCH vb extend or be extended ▷ n stretching

STRETCHY adj characterized by elasticity

STRETTA, -S, STRETTE same as ▸ stretto

STRETTO, STRETTI, -S n (in a fugue) the close overlapping of two parts or voices

STREUSEL n crumbly topping for rich pastries

STREW, STRAWN, -ED, -ING, -N, -S vb scatter (things) over a surface

STREWAGE

STREWER -S

STREWTH interj expression of surprise or alarm

STRIA, -E n scratch or groove on the surface of a rock crystal

STRIATA ▸ striatum

STRIATAL adj relating to the corpus striatum in the brain

STRIATE, -S adj marked with striae ▷ vb mark with striae

STRIATED adj having a pattern of scratches or grooves

STRIATES ▸ striate

STRIATUM, STRIATA n part of brain

STRICH, -ES n screech owl

STRICK, -S n any bast fibres preparatory to being made into slivers

STRICKEN adj seriously affected by disease, grief, pain, etc

STRICKLE n board used for sweeping off excess material in a container ▷ vb level, form, or sharpen with a strickle

STRICKS ▸ strick

STRICT, -ER adj stern or severe

STRICTLY

STRIDDEN ▸ stride

STRIDDLE same as ▸ straddle

STRIDE, STRIDDEN, -S, STRIDING, STRODE vb walk with long steps ▷ n long step

STRIDENT adj loud and harsh

STRIDER, -S ▸ stride

STRIDES ▸ stride

STRIDING ▸ stride

STRIDOR, -S n high-pitched whistling sound made during respiration

STRIFE, -S n conflict, quarrelling

STRIFT, -S n struggle

STRIG, -GED, -S vb remove stalk from

STRIGA, -E same as ▸ stria

STRIGATE adj streaked

STRIGGED ▸ strig

STRIGIL, -S n curved blade used to scrape the body after bathing

STRIGINE adj of or like owl

STRIGOSE adj bearing stiff hairs or bristles

STRIGS ▸ strig

STRIKE, -S, STRIKING, STROKEN, STROOK, STRUCK vb cease work as a protest ▷ n stoppage of work as a protest

STRIKER, -S n striking worker

STRIKES ▸ strike

STRIKING ▸ strike

STRIM, -MED, -S vb cut (grass) using a strimmer

STRINE, -S n informal name for Australian English

STRING, -S, STRUNG n thin cord used for tying ▷ vb provide with a string or strings

STRINGED adj (of a musical instrument) having strings that are plucked or played with a bow

STRINGER n journalist retained by a newspaper to cover a particular town or area

STRINGS ▸ string

STRINGY adj like string

STRINKLE Scots variant of ▸ sprinkle

STRIP, -PED, -S, -T vb take (the covering or clothes) off ▷ n act of stripping

STRIPE, -S, STRIPING n long narrow band of contrasting colour or substance ▷ vb mark (something) with stripes

STRIPED adj marked or decorated with stripes

STRIPER, -S n officer who has a stripe or stripes on his or her uniform

STRIPES ▸ stripe

STRIPEY same as ▸ stripy

STRIPIER ▸ stripy

STRIPING ▸ stripe

STRIPPED ▸ strip

STRIPPER n device or substance for removing paint etc

STRIPS ▸ strip

STRIPT ▸ strip

STRIPY, STRIPIER adj marked by or with stripes

STRIVE, -D, -N, -S, STRIVING, STROVE vb make a great effort

STRIVER -S

STROAM, -ED, -S vb wander

STROBE, -D, -S, STROBING n high intensity flashing beam of light ▷ vb give the appearance of slow motion by using a strobe

STROBIC adj spinning or appearing to spin

STROBIL, -S n scaly multiple fruit

STROBILA n body of a tapeworm, consisting of a string of similar segments

STROBILE same as > strobilus

STROBILI > strobilus

STROBILS ▸ strobil

STROBING ▸ strobe

STRODDLE same as ▸ straddle

STRODE ▸ stride

STRODLE, -D, -S same as ▸ straddle

STROKE, -D, -S, STROKING vb touch or caress lightly with the hand ▷ n light touch or caress with the hand

STROKEN ▸ strike

STROKER, -S ▸ stroke

STROKES ▸ stroke

STROKING ▸ stroke

STROLL, BUMMELS, -ED, -S vb walk in a leisurely manner ▷ n leisurely walk

STROLLER n chair-shaped carriage for a baby

STROLLS ▸ stroll

STROMA, -TA n gel-like matrix of chloroplasts and certain cells

STROMAL

STROMB, -S n shellfish like a whelk

STROMBUS same as ▸ stromb

STROND, -S same as ▸ strand

STRONG, -ER adj having physical power

STRONGLY

STRONGYL same as > strongyle

STRONTIA > strontium

STRONTIC > strontium

STROOK ▸ strike

STROOKE, -S n stroke

STROOKEN same as ▸ stricken

STROOKES ▸ strooke

S

STROP, -PED, -S n leather strap for sharpening razors ▷ vb sharpen (a razor, etc) on a strop

STROPHE, -S n movement made by chorus during a choral ode

STROPHIC adj of, relating to, or employing a strophe or strophes

STROPPED ► strop

STROPPER ► strop

STROPPY adj angry or awkward

STROPS ► strop

STROUD, -S n coarse woollen fabric

STROUP, -S Scots word for ► spout

STROUPAN same as > stroupach

STROUPS ► stroup

STROUT, -ED, -S vb bulge

STROVE ► strive

STROW, -ED, -ING, -N, -S archaic variant of ► strew

STROWER -S

STROY, -ED, -ING, -S archaic variant of ► destroy

STROYER -S

STRUCK ► strike

STRUCKEN same as ► stricken

STRUDEL, -S n thin sheet of filled dough rolled up and baked

STRUGGLE vb work, strive, or make one's way with difficulty ▷ n striving

STRUM, -MED, -S vb play (a guitar, etc) by sweeping the thumb across the strings

STRUMA, -E, -S n abnormal enlargement of the thyroid gland

STRUMMED ► strum

STRUMMEL n straw

STRUMMER ► strum

STRUMOSE ► struma

STRUMOUS ► struma

STRUMS ► strum

STRUNG ► string

STRUNT, -ED, -S Scots word for ► strut

STRUT, -S, -TED vb walk pompously, swagger ▷ n bar supporting a structure

STRUTTER

STUB, -BED, -BING, -S n short piece left after use ▷ vb strike (the toe) painfully against an object

STUBBIE same as ► stubby

STUBBIER ► stubby

STUBBIES ► stubby

STUBBILY ► stubby

STUBBING ► stub

STUBBLE, -S n short stalks of grain left in a field after reaping

STUBBLED adj having the stubs of stalks left after a crop has been cut and harvested

STUBBLES ► stubble

STUBBLY ► stubble

STUBBORN adj refusing to agree or give in ▷ vb make stubborn

STUBBY, STUBBIER, STUBBIES adj short and broad ▷ n small bottle of beer

STUBS ► stub

STUCCO, -ED, -ES, -S n plaster used for coating or decorating walls ▷ vb apply stucco to (a building)

STUCCOER

STUCK, -S n thrust

STUD, -DED, -DING, -S n small piece of metal attached to a surface for decoration ▷ vb set with studs

STUDBOOK n written record of the pedigree of a purebred stock, esp of racehorses

STUDDED ► stud

STUDDEN ► stand

STUDDIE, -S Scots word for ► anvil

STUDDING ► stud

STUDDLE, -S n post

STUDE vb past tense and past participle of staun (Scots form of stand)

STUDENT, -S n person who studies a subject, esp at university

STUDENTY adj denoting the characteristics believed typical of a student

STUDFARM n farm where horses are bred

STUDFISH n American minnow

STUDIED adj carefully practised

STUDIER, -S ► study

STUDIES ► study

STUDIO, -S n workroom of an artist or photographer

STUDIOUS adj fond of study

STUDLY, STUDLIER adj strong and virile

STUDS ► stud

STUDWORK n work decorated with studs

STUDY, STUDIES, -ING vb be engaged in learning (a subject) ▷ n act or process of studying

STUFF, -ED, -S n substance or material ▷ vb pack, cram, or fill completely

STUFFER -S

STUFFIER ► stuffy

STUFFILY ► stuffy

STUFFING n seasoned mixture with which food is stuffed

STUFFS ► stuff

STUFFY, STUFFIER adj lacking fresh air

STUGGY, STUGGIER adj stout

STUIVER, -S same as ► stiver

STUKKEND adj South African slang for broken or wrecked

STULL, -S n timber prop or platform in a stope

STULM, -S n shaft

STULTIFY vb dull (the mind) by boring routine

STUM, -MED, -MING, -S n partly fermented wine added to fermented wine as a preservative ▷ vb preserve (wine) by adding stum

STUMBLE, -D, -S vb trip and nearly fall ▷ n stumbling

STUMBLER

STUMBLY adj tending to stumble

STUMER, -S n forgery or cheat

STUMM same as ► shtoom

STUMMED ► stum

STUMMEL, -S n bowl of a smoker's pipe

STUMMING ► stum

STUMP, -ED, -ING, -S n base of a tree left when the main trunk has been cut away ▷ vb baffle

STUMPAGE n standing timber or its value

STUMPED ► stump

STUMPER, -S ► stump

STUMPIER ► stumpy

STUMPIES ► stumpy

STUMPILY ► stumpy

STUMPING ► stump

STUMPS ► stump

STUMPY, STUMPIER, STUMPIES adj short and thick ▷ n stumpy thing

STUMS ► stum

STUN, -NED, -NING, -S vb shock or overwhelm ▷ n state or effect of being stunned

STUNG ► sting

STUNK ► stink

STUNKARD adj sulky

STUNNED ► stun

STUNNER, -S n beautiful person or thing

STUNNING ► stun

STUNS ► stun

S

STUNSAIL n type of light auxiliary sail

STUNT, -ING, -S vb prevent or impede the growth of ▷ n acrobatic or dangerous action

STUNTED

STUNTMAN, STUNTMEN n person who performs dangerous acts in a film, etc in place of an actor

STUNTS ► stunt

STUPA, -S n domed edifice housing Buddhist or Jain relics

STUPE, -D, -S, STUPING n hot damp cloth applied to the body to relieve pain ▷ vb treat with a stupe

STUPEFY vb make insensitive or lethargic

STUPENT adj astonished

STUPES ► stupe

STUPID, -ER, -S adj lacking intelligence ▷ n stupid person

STUPIDLY

STUPING ► stupe

STUPOR, -S n dazed or unconscious state

STUPRATE vb ravish

STURDIED ► sturdy

STURDIER ► sturdy

STURDIES ► sturdy

STURDILY ► sturdy

STURDY, STURDIER, STURDIES adj healthy and robust ▷ n disease of sheep

STURE same as ► stoor

STURGEON n fish from which caviar is obtained

STURMER, -S n type of eating apple with pale green skin

STURNINE ► sturnus

STURNOID ► sturnus

STURNUS n bird of starling family

STURT, -ED, -ING, -S vb bother

STUSHIE, -S n commotion, rumpus, or row

STUTTER, -S vb speak with repetition of initial consonants ▷ n tendency to stutter

STY, STIED, STIES, -ING vb climb

STYE, -D, -S n inflammation at the base of an eyelash

STYGIAN adj dark, gloomy, or hellish

STYING ► sty

STYLAR ► stylus

STYLATE adj having style

STYLE, -D, -S n shape or design ▷ vb shape or design

STYLEE, -S same as ► style

STYLER, -S ► style

STYLES ► style

STYLET, -S n wire to stiffen a flexible cannula or catheter

STYLI ► stylus

STYLIE, -R, -ST adj fashion-conscious

STYLING, -S ► style

STYLISE, -D, -S same as ► stylize

STYLISER

STYLISH adj smart, elegant, and fashionable

STYLIST, -S n hairdresser

STYLITE, -S n one of a class of recluses who in ancient times lived on the top of high pillars

STYLITIC

STYLIZE, -D, -S vb cause to conform to an established stylistic form

STYLIZER

STYLO, -S n type of fountain pen

STYLOID, -S adj resembling a stylus ▷ n spiny growth

STYLOPES ► stylops

STYLOPID n type of parasitic insect

STYLOPS, STYLOPES n type of insect that lives as a parasite in other insects

STYLOS ► stylo

STYLUS, STYLI, -ES n needle-like device on a record player

STYME, -D, -S, STYMING vb peer

STYMIE vb hinder or thwart

STYMIES ► stymy

STYMING ► styme

STYMY, STYMIED, STYMIES, -ING same as ► stymie

STYPSIS n action, application, or use of a styptic

STYPTIC, -S adj (drug) used to stop bleeding ▷ n styptic drug

STYRAX, -ES n type of tropical or subtropical tree

STYRE, -D, -S, STYRING same as ► stir

STYRENE, -S n colourless oily volatile flammable water-insoluble liquid

STYRES ► styre

STYRING ► styre

STYTE, -D, -S, STYTING vb bounce

SUABLE adj liable to be sued in a court

SUABLY

SUASIBLE ► suasion

SUASION, -S n persuasion

SUASIVE

SUASORY

SUAVE, -R, -ST adj smooth and sophisticated in manner

SUAVELY

SUAVITY

SUB, -BED, -S n subeditor ▷ vb act as a substitute

SUBA, -S n shepherd's cloak

SUBABBOT n abbot who is subordinate to another abbot

SUBACID adj (esp of some fruits) moderately acid or sour

SUBACRID adj slightly acrid

SUBACT, -ED, -S vb subdue

SUBACUTE adj intermediate between acute and chronic

SUBADAR, -S n chief native officer of a company of Indian soldiers in the British service

SUBADULT n animal not quite at adult stage

SUBAGENT n agent who is subordinate to another agent

SUBAH, -S same as ► subadar

SUBAHDAR same as ► subadar

SUBAHS ► subah

SUBALAR adj below a wing

SUBAQUA adj of or relating to underwater sport

SUBAREA, -S n area within a larger area

SUBARID adj receiving slightly more rainfall than arid regions

SUBAS ► suba

SUBATOM, -S n part of an atom

SUBAUDIO adj (of sound) low frequency

SUBAURAL adj below the ear

SUBAXIAL adj below an axis of the body

SUBBASAL ► subbase

SUBBASE, -S same as ► subbass

SUBBASIN n geographical basin within larger basin

SUBBASS another name for ► bourdon

SUBBED ► sub

SUBBIE, -S n subcontractor

SUBBING, -S ► sub

SUBBLOCK n part of mathematical matrix

SUBBREED n breed within a larger breed

SUBBY same as ► subbie

SUBCASTE n subdivision of a caste

S

SUBCAUSE n factor less important than a cause

SUBCELL, -S n cell within a larger cell

SUBCHIEF n chief below the main chief

SUBCHORD n part of a curve

SUBCLAIM, -S n claim that is part of a larger claim

SUBCLAN, -S n clan within a larger clan

SUBCLASS n principal subdivision of a class ▷ vb assign to a subclass

SUBCLERK n clerk who is subordinate to another clerk

SUBCODE, -S n computer tag identifying data

SUBCOOL, -S vb make colder

SUBCOSTA n vein in insect wing

SUBCRUST n secondary crust below main crust

SUBCULT, -S n cult within larger cult

SUBCUTIS, SUBCUTES n layer of tissue beneath outer skin

SUBDEAN, -S n deputy of dean

SUBDEB, -S n young woman who is not yet a debutante

SUBDEPOT n depot within a larger depot

SUBDEW, -ED, -S same as
▶ subdue

SUBDUAL, -S ▶ subdue

SUBDUCE, -D, -S vb withdraw

SUBDUCT vb draw or turn (the eye, etc) downwards

SUBDUE, -S, SUBDUING vb overcome

SUBDUED adj cowed, passive, or shy

SUBDUER, -S ▶ subdue

SUBDUES ▶ subdue

SUBDUING ▶ subdue

SUBDUPLE adj in proportion of one to two

SUBDURAL adj between the dura mater and the arachnoid

SUBDWARF n star smaller than a dwarf star

SUBECHO n echo resonating more quietly than another echo

SUBEDAR, -S same as
▶ subadar

SUBEDIT, -S vb edit and correct (written or printed material)

SUBENTRY n entry within another entry

SUBEPOCH n epoch within another epoch

SUBEQUAL adj not quite equal

SUBER, -S n cork

SUBERATE n salt of suberic acid

SUBERECT adj not quite erect

SUBERIC same as
▶ suberose

SUBERIN, -S n fatty or waxy substance that is present in the walls of cork cells

SUBERISE same as
▶ suberize

SUBERIZE vb impregnate (cell walls) with suberin during the formation of corky tissue

SUBEROSE adj relating to, resembling, or consisting of cork

SUBEROUS same as
▶ suberose

SUBERS ▶ suber

SUBFEU, -ED, -S vb grant feu to vassal

SUBFIELD n subdivision of a field

SUBFILE, -S n file within another file

SUBFIX, -ES n suffix

SUBFLOOR n rough floor that forms a base for a finished floor

SUBFLUID adj viscous

SUBFRAME n frame on which car body is built

SUBFUSC, -S adj devoid of brightness or appeal ▷ n (at Oxford University) formal academic dress

SUBFUSK, -S same as
▶ subfusc

SUBGENRE n genre within a larger genre

SUBGENUS n taxonomic group that is a subdivision of a genus but of higher rank than a species

SUBGOAL, -S n secondary goal

SUBGRADE n ground beneath a roadway or pavement

SUBGRAPH n graph sharing vertices of other graph

SUBGROUP n small group that is part of a larger group

SUBGUM, -S n Chinese dish

SUBHA, -S n string of beads used in praying and meditating

SUBHEAD, -S n heading of a subsection in a printed work

SUBHUMAN adj less than human

SUBHUMID adj not wet enough for trees to grow

SUBIDEA, -S n secondary idea

SUBIMAGO n first winged stage of the mayfly

SUBINDEX same as
> subscript

SUBITEM, -S n item that is less important than another item

SUBITISE same as ▶ subitize

SUBITIZE vb perceive the number of (a group of items) at a glance and without counting

SUBITO adv (preceding or following a dynamic marking, etc) suddenly

SUBJECT, -S n person or thing being dealt with or studied ▷ adj being under the rule of a monarch or government ▷ vb cause to undergo

SUBJOIN, -S vb add or attach at the end of something spoken, written, etc

SUBLATE, -D, -S vb deny

SUBLEASE n lease of property made by a person who is himself a lessee of that property ▷ vb grant a sublease of (property)

SUBLET, -S vb rent out (property rented from someone else) ▷ n sublease

SUBLEVEL n subdivision of a level

SUBLIME, -D, -S adj of high moral, intellectual, or spiritual value ▷ vb change from a solid to a vapour without first melting

SUBLIMER

SUBLIMIT n limit on a subcategory

SUBLINE, -S n secondary headline

SUBLOT, -S n subdivision of a lot

SUBLUNAR same as
> sublunary

SUBMAN, SUBMEN n primitive form of human

SUBMENTA > submentum

SUBMENU, -S n further list of options within computer menu

SUBMERGE vb put or go below the surface of water or other liquid

SUBMERSE same as
▶ submerge

SUBMISS adj docile

SUBMIT, -S vb surrender

SUBNASAL adj beneath nose

SUBNET, -S n part of network

SUBNICHE n subdivision of a niche

SUBNODAL adj below the level of a node

S

SUBOCEAN *adj* beneath the ocean

SUBOPTIC *adj* below the eye

SUBORAL *adj* not quite oral

SUBORDER *n* taxonomic group that is a subdivision of an order

SUBORN, -ED, -S *vb* bribe or incite (a person) to commit a wrongful act

SUBORNER

SUBOVAL *adj* not quite oval

SUBOVATE *adj* almost egg-shaped

SUBOXIDE *n* oxide of an element containing less oxygen than the common oxide formed by the element

SUBPANEL *n* panel that is part of larger panel

SUBPAR *adj* not up to standard

SUBPART, -S *n* part within another part

SUBPENA, -S *same as* ► **subpoena**

SUBPHASE *n* subdivision of phase

SUBPHYLA > **subphylum**

SUBPLOT, -S *n* secondary plot in a novel, play, or film

SUBPOENA *n* writ requiring a person to appear before a lawcourt ▷ *vb* summon (someone) with a subpoena

SUBPOLAR *adj* of the areas south of the Arctic and north of the Antarctic

SUBPRIME *n* loan made to a borrower with a poor credit rating

SUBPRIOR *n* monk junior to a prior

SUBPUBIC *adj* beneath the pubic bone

SUBRACE, -S *n* race of people considered to be inferior

SUBRENT, -S *n* rent paid to renter who rents to another ▷ *vb* rent out (a property that is already rented)

SUBRING, -S *n* mathematical ring that is a subset of another ring

SUBRULE, -S *n* rule within another rule

SUBS ► **sub**

SUBSALE, -S *n* sale carried out within the process of a larger sale

SUBSCALE *n* scale within a scale

SUBSEA *adj* undersea

SUBSECT, -S *n* sect within a larger sect

SUBSENSE *n* definition that is division of wider definition

SUBSERE, -S *n* secondary sere arising when the progress of a sere has been interrupted

SUBSERVE *vb* be helpful or useful to

SUBSET, -S *n* mathematical set contained within a larger set

SUBSHAFT *n* secondary shaft in mine

SUBSHELL *n* part of a shell of an atom

SUBSHRUB *n* small bushy plant that is woody except for the tips of the branches

SUBSIDE, -D, -S *vb* become less intense

SUBSIDER

SUBSIDY *n* financial aid

SUBSIST, -S *vb* manage to live

SUBSITE, -S *n* location within a website

SUBSIZAR *n* type of undergraduate at Cambridge

SUBSKILL *n* element of a wider skill

SUBSOIL, -S *n* earth just below the surface soil ▷ *vb* plough (land) to a depth below the normal ploughing level

SUBSOLAR *adj* (of a point on the earth) directly below the sun

SUBSONG, -S *n* subdued form of birdsong modified from the full territorial song

SUBSONIC *adj* moving at a speed less than that of sound

SUBSPACE *n* part of a mathematical matrix

SUBSTAGE *n* part of a microscope below the stage

SUBSTATE *n* subdivision of state

SUBSTYLE *n* line on a dial

SUBSUME, -D, -S *vb* include (an idea, case, etc) under a larger classification or group

SUBTACK, -S *n* Scots word for ► **sublease**

SUBTALAR *adj* beneath the ankle-bone

SUBTASK, -S *n* task that is part of a larger task

SUBTAXON, SUBTAXA *n* supplementary piece of identifying information in plant or animal scientific name

SUBTEEN, -S *n* young person who has not yet become a teenager

SUBTEND, -S *vb* be opposite (an angle or side)

SUBTENSE *n* line that subtends

SUBTEST, -S *n* test that is part of larger test

SUBTEXT, -S *n* underlying theme in a piece of writing

SUBTHEME *n* secondary theme

SUBTIDAL *adj* below the level of low tide

SUBTIL *same as* ► **subtle**

SUBTILE, -R *rare spelling of* ► **subtle**

SUBTILIN *n* antibiotic drug

SUBTILTY ► **subtile**

SUBTITLE *n* secondary title of a book ▷ *vb* provide with a subtitle or subtitles

SUBTLE, -R, -ST *adj* not immediately obvious

SUBTLETY *n* fine distinction

SUBTLY ► **subtle**

SUBTONE, -S *n* subdivision of a tone

SUBTONIC *n* seventh degree of a major or minor scale

SUBTOPIA *n* suburban development that encroaches on rural areas

SUBTOPIC *n* topic within a larger topic

SUBTOTAL *n* total made up by a column of figures, forming part of the total made up by a larger group ▷ *vb* work out a subtotal for (a group)

SUBTRACT *vb* take (one number or quantity) from another

SUBTRADE *n* (in N America) specialist hired by a building contractor

SUBTREND *n* minor trend

SUBTRIBE *n* tribe within a larger tribe

SUBTRIST *adj* slightly sad

SUBTRUDE *vb* intrude stealthily

SUBTUNIC *adj* below membrane ▷ *n* garment worn under a tunic

SUBTYPE, -S *n* secondary or subordinate type or genre

SUBUCULA *n* ancient Roman man's undergarment

SUBULATE *adj* (esp of plant parts) tapering to a point

SUBUNIT, -S *n* distinct part or component of something larger

SUBURB, -S *n* residential area on the outskirts of a city

SUBURBAN *adj* mildly derogatory term for

S

inhabiting a suburb ▷ *n* mildly derogatory term for a person who lives in a suburb

SUBURBED ► **suburb**

SUBURBIA *n* suburbs and their inhabitants

SUBURBS ► **suburb**

SUBVENE, -D, -S *vb* happen in such a way as to be of assistance

SUBVERSE, SUBVERST *same as* ► **subvert**

SUBVERT, -S *vb* overthrow the authority of

SUBVICAR *n* assistant to a vicar

SUBVIRAL *adj* of, caused by, or denoting a part of the structure of a virus

SUBVIRUS *n* organism smaller than a virus

SUBVOCAL *adj* formed in mind without being spoken aloud

SUBWAY, -ED, -S *n* passage under a road or railway ▷ *vb* travel by subway

SUBWORLD *n* underworld

SUBZERO *adj* lower than zero

SUBZONAL ► **subzone**

SUBZONE, -S *n* subdivision of a zone

SUCCADE, -S *n* piece of candied fruit

SUCCAH, -S *same as* ► **sukkah**

SUCCEED, -S *vb* accomplish an aim

SUCCES *French word for* ► **success**

SUCCESS *n* achievement of something attempted

SUCCI ► **succus**

SUCCINCT *adj* brief and clear

SUCCINIC *adj* of, relating to, or obtained from amber

SUCCINYL *n* constituent of succinic acid

SUCCISE *adj* ending abruptly, as if cut off

SUCCOR, -ED, -S *same as* ► **succour**

SUCCORER

SUCCORY *another name for* ► **chicory**

SUCCOS *same as* ► **succoth**

SUCCOSE ► **succus**

SUCCOT *same as* ► **sukkoth**

SUCCOTH *variant of* ► **sukkoth**

SUCCOUR, -S *n* help in distress ▷ *vb* give aid to (someone in time of difficulty)

SUCCOUS ► **succus**

SUCCUMB, -S *vb* give way (to something overpowering)

SUCCUS, SUCCI *n* fluid

SUCCUSS *vb* shake (a patient) to detect the sound of fluid in a cavity

SUCH *adj* of the kind specified ▷ *pron* such things

SUCHLIKE *pron* such or similar things ▷ *n* such or similar things ▷ *adj* of such a kind

SUCHNESS ► **such**

SUCHWISE ► **such**

SUCK, -ED *vb* draw (liquid or air) into the mouth ▷ *n* sucking

SUCKEN, -S *Scots word for* ► **district**

SUCKENER *n* tenant

SUCKENS ► **sucken**

SUCKER, -ED, -S *n* person who is easily deceived or swindled ▷ *vb* strip off the suckers from (a plant)

SUCKET, -S *same as* ► **succade**

SUCKFISH *n* type of spiny-finned marine fish

SUCKHOLE *n* sycophant ▷ *vb* behave in a sycophantic manner

SUCKIER ► **sucky**

SUCKIEST ► **sucky**

SUCKING, -S *adj* not yet weaned

SUCKLE, -D, -S *vb* feed at the breast

SUCKLER -S

SUCKLESS ► **suck**

SUCKLING *n* unweaned baby or young animal

SUCKS *interj* expression of disappointment

SUCKY, SUCKIER, SUCKIEST *adj* despicable

SUCRASE, -S *another name for* ► **invertase**

SUCRE, -S *n* former standard monetary unit of Ecuador

SUCRIER, -S *n* small container for sugar at table

SUCROSE, -S *same as* ► **sugar**

SUCTION, -S *n* sucking ▷ *vb* subject to suction

SUCURUJU *n* anaconda

SUD *singular of* ► **suds**

SUDAMEN, -S, SUDAMINA *n* small cavity in the skin

SUDARIA ► **sudarium**

SUDARIES ► **sudary**

SUDARIUM, SUDARIA *n* room in a Roman bathhouse where sweating is induced by heat

SUDARY, SUDARIES *same as* ► **sudarium**

SUDATE, -D, -S, SUDATING *vb* sweat

SUDATION

SUDATORY

SUDD, -S *n* floating masses of reeds and weeds on the White Nile

SUDDEN, -S *adj* done or occurring quickly and unexpectedly

SUDDENLY *adv* quickly and without warning

SUDDENS ► **sudden**

SUDDENTY *n* suddenness

SUDDER, -S *n* supreme court in India

SUDDS ► **sudd**

SUDOKU, -S *n* type of puzzle in which numbers must be arranged in a grid according to certain rules

SUDOR, -S *technical name for* ► **sweat**

SUDORAL

SUDOROUS

SUDS, -ED, -ES, -ING *pl n* froth of soap and water, lather ▷ *vb* wash in suds

SUDSER, -S *n* soap opera

SUDSES ► **suds**

SUDSIER ► **sudsy**

SUDSIEST ► **sudsy**

SUDSING ► **suds**

SUDSLESS ► **suds**

SUDSY, SUDSIER, SUDSIEST ► **suds**

SUE, -D, -S *vb* start legal proceedings against

SUEABLE

SUEDE, -D, -S, SUEDING *n* leather with a velvety finish on one side ▷ *vb* give a suede finish to

SUEDETTE *n* imitation suede fabric

SUEDING ► **suede**

SUENT *adj* smooth

SUER, -S ► **sue**

SUES ► **sue**

SUET, -S *n* hard fat obtained from sheep and cattle

SUETE, -S *n* southeasterly wind in Cape Breton Island

SUETIER ► **suety**

SUETIEST ► **suety**

SUETS ► **suet**

SUETTY, SUETTIER ► **suet**

SUETY, SUETIER, SUETIEST ► **suet**

SUFFARI, -S *same as* ► **safari**

SUFFECT, -S *adj* additional ▷ *n* additional consul in ancient Rome

SUFFER, -ED, -S vb undergo or be subjected to
SUFFERER
SUFFETE, -S n official in ancient Carthage
SUFFICE, -D, -S vb be enough for a purpose
SUFFICER
SUFFIX, -ED, -ES n letters added to the end of a word to form another word ▷ vb add (letters) to the end of a word to form another word
SUFFIXAL
SUFFLATE archaic word for ▶ inflate
SUFFRAGE n right to vote in public elections
SUFFUSE, -D, -S vb spread through or over (something)
SUG, -GED, -S vb sell a product while pretending to conduct market research
SUGAN, -S n straw rope
SUGAR, -S n carbohydrate used to sweeten food and drinks ▷ vb sweeten or cover with sugar
SUGARED adj made sweeter or more appealing with or as with sugar
SUGARER, -S ▶ sugar
SUGARIER ▶ sugary
SUGARING n method of removing unwanted body hair
SUGARS ▶ sugar
SUGARY, SUGARIER adj of, like, or containing sugar
SUGGED, -S ▶ sug
SUGGEST, -S vb put forward (an idea) for consideration
SUGGING, -S n practice of selling products under the pretence of conducting market research
SUGH, -ED, -ING, -S same as ▶ sough
SUGO, -S n Italian pasta sauce
SUGS ▶ sug
SUHUR, -S n meal eaten before sunrise by Muslims fasting during Ramadan
SUI adj of itself
SUICIDAL adj liable to commit suicide
SUICIDE, -D, -S n killing oneself intentionally ▷ vb commit suicide
SUID, -S n pig or related animal
SUIDIAN -S
SUILLINE adj of or like a pig
SUING, -S ▶ sue

SUINT, -S n water-soluble substance found in the fleece of sheep
SUIPLAP, -S n South African slang for a drunkard
SUIT, -ED, -S n set of clothes designed to be worn together ▷ vb be appropriate for
SUITABLE adj appropriate or proper
SUITABLY
SUITCASE n portable travelling case for clothing
SUITE, -S n set of connected rooms in a hotel
SUITED ▶ suit
SUITER, -S n piece of luggage for carrying suits and dresses
SUITES ▶ suite
SUITING, -S n fabric used for suits
SUITLIKE ▶ suit
SUITOR, -ED, -S n man who is courting a woman ▷ vb act as a suitor
SUITRESS n female suitor
SUITS ▶ suit
SUIVANTE n lady's maid
SUIVEZ vb musical direction meaning follow
SUJEE, -S same as ▶ soogee
SUK, -S same as ▶ suq
SUKH, -S same as ▶ suq
SUKIYAKI n Japanese dish consisting of sliced meat and vegetables
SUKKAH, -S n structure in which orthodox Jews eat and sleep during Sukkoth
SUKKOS same as ▶ sukkoth
SUKKOT same as ▶ sukkoth
SUKKOTH n eight-day Jewish harvest festival
SUKS ▶ suk
SUKUK, -S n financial certificate conforming to Islam lending principles
SULCAL ▶ sulcus
SULCATE adj marked with longitudinal parallel grooves
SULCATED same as ▶ sulcate
SULCUS, SULCI n linear groove, furrow, or slight depression
SULDAN, -S same as ▶ sultan
SULFA, -S same as ▶ sulpha
SULFATE, -D, -S same as ▶ sulphate
SULFATIC adj relating to sulphate
SULFID, -S same as ▶ sulphide
SULFIDE, -S same as ▶ sulphide
SULFIDS ▶ sulfid

SULFINYL same as > sulphinyl
SULFITE, -S same as ▶ sulphite
SULFITIC
SULFO same as > sulphonic
SULFONE, -S same as ▶ sulphone
SULFONIC
SULFONYL same as > sulphonyl
SULFUR, -ED, -S variant of ▶ sulphur
SULFURET same as > sulphuret
SULFURIC ▶ sulfur
SULFURS ▶ sulfur
SULFURY ▶ sulfur
SULFURYL same as > sulphuryl
SULK, -ED, -ING, -S vb be silent and sullen because of resentment or bad temper ▷ n resentful or sullen mood
SULKER, -S same as ▶ sulk
SULKIER ▶ sulky
SULKIES ▶ sulky
SULKIEST ▶ sulky
SULKILY ▶ sulky
SULKING ▶ sulk
SULKS ▶ sulk
SULKY, SULKIER, SULKIES, SULKIEST adj moody or silent because of anger or resentment ▷ n light two-wheeled vehicle for one person
SULLAGE, -S n filth or waste, esp sewage
SULLEN, -ER, -S adj unwilling to talk or be sociable ▷ n sullen mood
SULLENLY
SULLY, SULLIED, SULLIES, -ING vb ruin (someone's reputation) ▷ n stain
SULPHA, -S n any of a group of sulphonamides that prevent the growth of bacteria
SULPHATE n salt or ester of sulphuric acid ▷ vb treat with a sulphate or convert into a sulphate
SULPHID, -S same as ▶ sulphide
SULPHIDE n compound of sulphur with another element
SULPHIDS ▶ sulphid
SULPHITE n salt or ester of sulphurous acid
SULPHONE n type of organic compound
SULPHUR, -S n pale yellow nonmetallic element ▷ vb treat with sulphur
SULPHURY

S

SULTAN, -S n sovereign of a Muslim country

SULTANA, -S n kind of raisin

SULTANIC ► sultan

SULTANS ► sultan

SULTRIER ► sultry

SULTRILY ► sultry

SULTRY, SULTRIER adj (of weather or climate) hot and humid

SULU, -S n type of sarong worn in Fiji

SUM, -MED, -S n result of addition, total ▷ vb add or form a total of (something)

SUMAC, -S same as ► sumach

SUMACH, -S n type of temperate or subtropical shrub or small tree

SUMACS ► sumac

SUMATRA, -S n violent storm blowing from the direction of Sumatra

SUMI, -S n type of black ink used in Japan

SUMLESS adj uncountable

SUMMA, -E, -S n compendium of theology, philosophy, or canon law

SUMMABLE ► sum

SUMMAE ► summa

SUMMAND, -S n number or quantity forming part of a sum

SUMMAR Scots variant of ► summer

SUMMARY n brief account giving the main points of something ▷ adj done quickly, without formalities

SUMMAS ► summa

SUMMAT, -S pron something ▷ n impressive or important person or thing

SUMMATE, -D, -S vb add up

SUMMATS ► summat

SUMMED ► sum

SUMMER, -ED, -S n warmest season of the year ▷ vb spend the summer (at a place)

SUMMERLY

SUMMERY

SUMMING, -S ► sum

SUMMIST, -S n writer of summae

SUMMIT, -ED, -S n top of a mountain or hill ▷ vb reach summit

SUMMITAL

SUMMITRY n practice of conducting international negotiations by summit conferences

SUMMITS ► summit

SUMMON, -ED vb order (someone) to come

SUMMONER

SUMMONS n command summoning someone ▷ vb order (someone) to appear in court

SUMO, -S n Japanese style of wrestling

SUMOIST -S

SUMOTORI n sumo wrestler

SUMP, -S n container in an internal-combustion engine into which oil can drain

SUMPH, -S n stupid person

SUMPHISH

SUMPIT, -S n Malay blowpipe

SUMPITAN same as ► sumpit

SUMPITS ► sumpit

SUMPS ► sump

SUMPTER, -S n packhorse, mule, or other beast of burden

SUMPWEED n American weed

SUMS ► sum

SUMY pl n the monetary units of Uzbekistan

SUN, -NED, -NING, -S n star around which the earth and other planets revolve ▷ vb expose (oneself) to the sun's rays

SUNBACK adj (of dress) cut low at back

SUNBAKE, -S vb sunbathe, esp in order to become tanned ▷ n period of sunbaking

SUNBAKED adj (esp of roads, etc) dried or cracked by the sun's heat

SUNBAKES ► sunbake

SUNBATH, -S n exposure of the body to the sun to get a suntan

SUNBATHE vb lie in the sunshine in order to get a suntan

SUNBATHS ► sunbath

SUNBEAM, -S n ray of sun

SUNBEAMY

SUNBEAT adj exposed to sun

SUNBED, -S n machine for giving an artificial tan

SUNBELT, -S n southern states of the US

SUNBERRY n red fruit like the blackberry

SUNBIRD, -S n type of small songbird with a bright plumage in the males

SUNBLIND n blind that shades a room from the sun's glare

SUNBLOCK n cream applied to the skin to protect it from the sun's rays

SUNBOW, -S n bow of colours produced when sunlight shines through spray

SUNBURN, -S, -T n painful reddening of the skin caused by overexposure to the sun ▷ vb become sunburnt

SUNBURST n burst of sunshine, as through a break in the clouds

SUNCARE, -S n use of products in protecting skin from the sun

SUNCHOKE n Jerusalem artichoke

SUNDAE, -S n ice cream topped with fruit etc

SUNDARI, -S n Indian tree

SUNDECK, -S n upper open deck on a passenger ship

SUNDER, -ED, -S vb break apart

SUNDERER

SUNDEW, -S n type of bog plant with leaves covered in sticky hairs

SUNDIAL, -S n device showing the time by means of a pointer that casts a shadow

SUNDOG, -S n small rainbow or halo near the horizon

SUNDOWN, -S same as ► sunset

SUNDRA, -S same as ► sundari

SUNDRESS n strapped dress worn in hot weather

SUNDRI, -S same as ► sundari

SUNDRIES ► sundry

SUNDRILY ► sundry

SUNDRIS ► sundri

SUNDROPS pl n any of various American primroses

SUNDRY, SUNDRIES adj several, various

SUNFAST adj not fading in sunlight

SUNFISH n large sea fish with a rounded body

SUNG ► sing

SUNGAR, -S same as ► sangar

SUNGAZER n person who practices sungazing

SUNGLASS n convex lens used to focus the sun's rays and thus produce heat or ignition

SUNGLOW, -S n pinkish glow often seen in the sky before sunrise or after sunset

SUNGREBE another name for ► finfoot

SUNHAT, -S n hat that shades the face and neck from the sun

SUNI, -S n S African dwarf antelope

SUNK, -S n bank or pad

SUNKEN adj unhealthily hollow

SUNKER, -S n rock (partially) submerged in shallow water

SUNKET, -S n something good to eat

SUNKIE, -S n little stool

SUNKS ▸ sunk

SUNLAMP, -S n lamp that generates ultraviolet rays

SUNLAND, -S n sunny area

SUNLESS adj without sun or sunshine

SUNLIGHT n light that comes from the sun

SUNLIKE ▸ sun

SUNLIT ▸ sunlight

SUNN, -S n leguminous plant of the East Indies

SUNNA, -S n body of traditional Islamic law

SUNNAH, -S same as ▸ sunna

SUNNAS ▸ sunna

SUNNED ▸ sun

SUNNIER ▸ sunny

SUNNIES pl n pair of sunglasses

SUNNIEST ▸ sunny

SUNNILY ▸ sunny

SUNNING ▸ sun

SUNNS ▸ sunn

SUNNY, SUNNIER, SUNNIEST adj full of or exposed to sunlight

SUNPORCH n porch for sunbathing on

SUNPROOF ▸ sun

SUNRAY, -S n ray of light from the sun

SUNRISE, -S n daily appearance of the sun above the horizon

SUNROOF, -S n panel in the roof of a car that opens to let in air

SUNROOM, -S n room or glass-enclosed porch designed to display beautiful views

SUNS ▸ sun

SUNSCALD n sun damage on tomato plants

SUNSET, -S n daily disappearance of the sun below the horizon

SUNSHADE n anything used to shade people from the sun, such as a parasol or awning

SUNSHINE n light and warmth from the sun

SUNSHINY

SUNSPECS pl n sunglasses

SUNSPOT, -S n dark patch appearing temporarily on the sun's surface

SUNSTAR, -S n type of starfish with up to 13 arms

SUNSTONE n type of translucent feldspar with reddish-gold speckles

SUNSUIT, -S n child's outfit consisting of a brief top and shorts or a short skirt

SUNTAN, -S n browning of the skin caused by exposure to the sun

SUNTRAP, -S n very sunny sheltered place

SUNUP, -S same as ▸ sunrise

SUNWARD same as ▸ sunwards

SUNWARDS adv towards the sun

SUNWISE adv moving in the same direction as the sun

SUP, -PED, -PING, -S same as ▸ supine

SUPAWN, -S same as ▸ suppawn

SUPE, -S n superintendent

SUPER, -ED, -ING, -S adj excellent ▷ n superannuation ▷ interj enthusiastic expression of approval or assent ▷ vb work as superintendent

SUPERADD vb add (something) to something that has already been added

SUPERATE vb overcome

SUPERB, -ER adj excellent, impressive, or splendid

SUPERBAD adj exceptionally bad

SUPERBER ▸ superb

SUPERBLY ▸ superb

SUPERBUG n bacterium resistant to antibiotics

SUPERCAR n very expensive fast or powerful car with a centrally located engine

SUPERCOP n high-ranking police officer

SUPERCOW n dairy cow that produces a very high milk yield

SUPERED ▸ super

SUPEREGO n that part of the unconscious mind that governs ideas about what is right and wrong

SUPERFAN n very devoted fan

SUPERFIT adj highly fit

SUPERFIX n linguistic feature distinguishing the meaning of one word from that of another

SUPERFLY adj pretentiously flamboyant

SUPERGUN n large powerful gun

SUPERHET n type of radio receiver

SUPERHIT n very popular hit

SUPERHOT adj very hot

SUPERING ▸ super

SUPERIOR adj greater in quality, quantity, or merit ▷ n person of greater rank or status

SUPERJET n supersonic aircraft

SUPERLIE, SUPERLAY vb lie above

SUPERLOO n automated public toilet

SUPERMAN, SUPERMEN n man with great physical or mental powers

SUPERMAX n jail or other facility having the very highest levels of security

SUPERMEN ▸ superman

SUPERMOM n very capable and busy mother

SUPERNAL adj of or from the world of the divine

SUPERPRO n person regarded as a real professional

SUPERS ▸ super

SUPERSEX n in genetics, type of sterile organism

SUPERSPY n highly accomplished spy

SUPERTAX n extra tax on incomes above a certain level

SUPES ▸ supe

SUPINATE vb turn (the hand and forearm) so that the palm faces up or forwards

SUPINE, -S adj lying flat on one's back ▷ n noun form derived from a verb in Latin

SUPINELY

SUPLEX, -ES n type of wrestling hold

SUPPAWN, -S n kind of porridge

SUPPEAGO same as ▸ serpigo

SUPPED ▸ sup

SUPPER, -ED, -S n light evening meal ▷ vb eat supper

SUPPING ▸ sup

SUPPLANT vb take the place of, oust

SUPPLE, -D, -R, -S, -ST, SUPPLING adj (of a person) moving and bending easily

S

and gracefully ▷ vb make or become supple

SUPPLELY same as ▶ **supply**

SUPPLER ▶ **supple**

SUPPLES ▶ **supple**

SUPPLEST ▶ **supple**

SUPPLIAL n instance of supplying

SUPPLIED ▶ **supply**

SUPPLIER ▶ **supply**

SUPPLIES ▶ **supply**

SUPPLING ▶ **supple**

SUPPLY, SUPPLIED, SUPPLIES vb provide with something required ▷ n supplying ▷ adj acting as a temporary substitute ▷ adv in a supple manner

SUPPORT, -S vb bear the weight of ▷ n supporting

SUPPOSAL n supposition

SUPPOSE, -S vb presume to be true

SUPPOSED adj presumed to be true without proof, doubtful

SUPPOSER ▶ **suppose**

SUPPOSES ▶ **suppose**

SUPPRESS vb put an end to

SUPRA adv above, esp referring to earlier parts of a book etc

SUPREMA ▶ **supremum**

SUPREME, -R, -S adj highest in authority, rank, or degree ▷ n rich sauce made with a base of veal or chicken stock

SUPREMO, -S n person in overall authority

SUPREMUM, SUPREMA n (in maths) smallest quantity greater than or equal to each of a set or subset

SUPS ▶ **sup**

SUQ, -S n open-air marketplace

This unusual word for an Arab marketplace is easy to overlook because we tend not to think of words ending in Q. It can also be spelt **sook, souk, suk** or **sukh**.

SUR prep above

SURA, -S n any of the 114 chapters of the Koran

SURAH, -S n twill-weave fabric of silk or rayon, used for dresses, blouses, etc

SURAL adj of or relating to the calf of the leg

SURAMIN, -S n drug used in treating sleeping sickness

SURANCE, -S same as > **assurance**

SURAS ▶ **sura**

SURAT, -S n cotton fabric from Surat in India

SURBAHAR n Indian string instrument

SURBASE, -S n uppermost part, such as a moulding, of a pedestal, base, or skirting

SURBASED adj having a surbase

SURBASES ▶ **surbase**

SURBATE, -D, -S, SURBET vb make feet sore through walking

SURBED, -S vb put something on its edge

SURBET ▶ **surbate**

SURCEASE n cessation or intermission ▷ vb desist from (some action)

SURCOAT, -S n tunic worn by a knight over his armour

SURCULUS, SURCULI n sucker on plant

SURD, -S n number that cannot be expressed in whole numbers ▷ adj of or relating to a surd

SURDITY n deafness

SURDS ▶ **surd**

SURE, -D, -R, -S, -ST, SURING adj free from uncertainty or doubt ▷ interj certainly ▷ vb archaic form of sewer

SUREFIRE adj certain to succeed

SURELY adv it must be true that

SURENESS ▶ **sure**

SURER ▶ **sure**

SURES ▶ **sure**

SUREST ▶ **sure**

SURETY, SURETIED, SURETIES n person who takes responsibility for the fulfilment of another's obligation ▷ vb be surety for

SURF, -ED, -S n foam caused by waves breaking on the shore ▷ vb take part in surfing

SURFABLE ▶ **surf**

SURFACE, -D, -S n outside or top of an object ▷ vb become apparent

SURFACER

SURFBIRD n American shore bird

SURFBOAT n boat with a high bow and stern and flotation chambers

SURFED ▶ **surf**

SURFEIT, -S n excessive amount ▷ vb supply or feed excessively

SURFER, -S ▶ **surfing**

SURFFISH n fish of American coastal seas

SURFIE, -S n young person whose main interest is in surfing

SURFIER ▶ **surfy**

SURFIES ▶ **surfie**

SURFIEST ▶ **surfy**

SURFING, -S n sport of riding on a board on the crest of a wave

SURFLIKE ▶ **surf**

SURFMAN, SURFMEN n sailor skilled in sailing through surf

SURFRIDE, SURFRODE vb ride on surf

SURFS ▶ **surf**

SURFSIDE adj next to the sea

SURFY, SURFIER, SURFIEST ▶ **surf**

SURGE, -D, -S n sudden powerful increase ▷ vb increase suddenly

SURGEFUL

SURGENT

SURGEON, -S n doctor who specializes in surgery

SURGER, -S ▶ **surge**

SURGERY n treatment in which the patient's body is cut open in order to treat the affected part

SURGES ▶ **surge**

SURGICAL adj involving or used in surgery

SURGIER ▶ **surgy**

SURGIEST ▶ **surgy**

SURGING, -S ▶ **surge**

SURGY, SURGIER, SURGIEST ▶ **surge**

SURICATE n type of meerkat

SURIMI, -S n blended seafood product made from precooked fish

SURING ▶ **sure**

SURLIER ▶ **surly**

SURLIEST ▶ **surly**

SURLILY ▶ **surly**

SURLOIN, -S same as ▶ **sirloin**

SURLY, SURLIER, SURLIEST adj ill-tempered and rude

SURMISAL ▶ **surmise**

SURMISE, -D, -S n guess, conjecture ▷ vb guess (something) from incomplete or uncertain evidence

SURMISER

SURMOUNT vb overcome (a problem)

SURNAME, -D, -S n family name ▷ vb furnish with or call by a surname

SURNAMER

SURPASS vb be greater than or superior to

SURPLICE n loose white robe worn by clergymen and choristers

SURPLUS n amount left over in excess of what is required ▷ adj extra ▷ vb be left over in excess of what is required

SURPRINT vb print (additional matter) over something already printed ▷ n marks, printed matter, etc, that have been surprinted

SURPRISE n unexpected event ▷ vb cause to feel amazement or wonder

SURPRIZE same as ▶ surprise

SURQUEDY same as > surquedry

SURRA, -S n tropical febrile disease of animals

SURREAL, -S adj bizarre ▷ n atmosphere or qualities evoked by surrealism

SURREBUT vb give evidence to support the surrebutter

SURREY, -S n light four-wheeled horse-drawn carriage

SURROUND vb be, come, or place all around (a person or thing) ▷ n border or edging

SURROYAL n high point on stag's horns

SURTAX, -ED, -ES n extra tax on incomes above a certain level ▷ vb assess for liability to surtax

SURTITLE n printed translation of the libretto of an opera in a language foreign to the audience

SURTOUT, -S n man's overcoat resembling a frock coat

SURUCUCU n South American snake

SURVEIL, -S same as > surveille

SURVEY, -ED, -S vb view or consider in a general way ▷ n surveying

SURVEYAL

SURVEYOR n person whose occupation is to survey land or buildings

SURVEYS ▶ survey

SURVIEW, -S vb survey

SURVIVAL n condition of having survived ▷ adj of, relating to, or assisting the act of surviving

SURVIVE, -D, -S vb continue to live or exist after (a difficult experience)

SURVIVER same as ▶ survivor

SURVIVES ▶ survive

SURVIVOR n person or thing that survives

SUS, -ED, -ES, -ING same as ▶ suss

SUSHI, -S n Japanese dish of small cakes of cold rice with a topping of raw fish

SUSING ▶ sus

SUSLIK, -S n central Eurasian ground squirrel

SUSPECT, -S vb believe (someone) to be guilty without having any proof ▷ adj not to be trusted ▷ n person who is suspected

SUSPENCE same as ▶ suspense

SUSPEND, -S vb hang from a high place

SUSPENS same as ▶ suspense

SUSPENSE n state of uncertainty while awaiting news, an event, etc

SUSPIRE, -D, -S vb sigh or utter with a sigh

SUSS, -ED, -ES, -ING vb attempt to work out (a situation, etc), using one's intuition ▷ n sharpness of mind

SUSTAIN, -S vb maintain or prolong ▷ n prolongation of a note, by playing technique or electronics

SUSU, -S n (in the Caribbean) savings fund shared by friends

SUSURRUS > susurrate

SUSUS ▶ susu

SUTILE adj involving sewing

SUTLER, -S n merchant who accompanied an army in order to sell provisions

SUTLERY

SUTOR, -S n cobbler

SUTORIAL

SUTORIAN

SUTRA, -S n Sanskrit sayings or collections of sayings

SUTTA, -S n Buddhist scripture

SUTTEE, -S n custom whereby a widow burnt herself on her husband's funeral pyre

SUTTLE, -D, -S, SUTTLING vb work as a sutler

SUTTLY ▶ subtle

SUTURAL ▶ suture

SUTURE, -D, -S, SUTURING n stitch joining the edges of a wound ▷ vb join (the edges of a wound, etc) by means of sutures

SUZERAIN n state or sovereign with limited authority over another self-governing state

SVARAJ, -ES same as ▶ swaraj

SVASTIKA same as ▶ swastika

SVEDBERG n unit used in physics

SVELTE, -R, -ST adj attractively or gracefully slim

SVELTELY

SWAB, -BED, -BING, -S n small piece of cotton wool used to apply medication, clean a wound, etc ▷ vb clean (a wound) with a swab

SWABBER, -S n person who uses a swab

SWABBIE same as ▶ swabby

SWABBIES ▶ swabby

SWABBING ▶ swab

SWABBY, SWABBIES n seaman

SWABS ▶ swab

SWACK, -ED, -ING, -S adj flexible ▷ vb strike

SWAD, -S n loutish person

SWADDIE same as ▶ swaddy

SWADDIES ▶ swaddy

SWADDLE, -D, -S vb wrap (a baby) in swaddling clothes ▷ n swaddling clothes

SWADDLER

SWADDY, SWADDIES n private soldier

SWADS ▶ swad

SWAG, -GED, -GING, -S n stolen property ▷ vb sway from side to side

SWAGE, -D, -S, SWAGING n shaped tool or die used in forming cold metal by hammering ▷ vb form (metal) with a swage

SWAGER -S

SWAGGED ▶ swag

SWAGGER, -S vb walk or behave arrogantly ▷ n arrogant walk or manner ▷ adj elegantly fashionable

SWAGGIE, -S same as ▶ swagger

SWAGGING ▶ swag

SWAGING ▶ swage

SWAGMAN, SWAGMEN n tramp who carries his belongings in a bundle on his back

SWAGS ▶ swag

SWAGSHOP n shop selling cheap goods

SWAGSMAN, SWAGSMEN same as ▶ swagman

SWAIL, -S same as ▶ swale

SWAIN, -S n suitor

SWAINING n acting as suitor

SWAINISH ▶ swain

SWAINS ▶ swain

SWALE, -D, -S n moist depression in a tract of land ▷ vb sway

SWALIER ▶ swaly

SWALIEST ▶ swaly

SWALING, -S ▶ swale

SWALLET, -S n hole where water goes underground

SWALLIES ▶ swally

SWALLOW, -S vb cause to pass down one's throat ▷ n swallowing

SWALLY, SWALLIES n alcoholic drink

SWALY, SWALIER, SWALIEST ▶ swale

SWAM ▶ swim

SWAMI, -ES, -S n Hindu religious teacher

SWAMP, -ED, -ING, -S n watery area of land, bog ▷ vb cause (a boat) to fill with water and sink

SWAMPER, -S n person who lives or works in a swampy region

SWAMPIER ▶ swampy

SWAMPING ▶ swamp

SWAMPISH ▶ swamp

SWAMPS ▶ swamp

SWAMPY, SWAMPIER ▶ swamp

SWAMY same as ▶ swami

SWAN, -NED, -NING, -S n large usu white water bird with a long graceful neck ▷ vb wander about idly

SWANG ▶ swing

SWANHERD n person who herds swans

SWANK, -ED, -EST, -ING, -S vb show off or boast ▷ n showing off or boasting

SWANKER -S

SWANKEY, -S same as ▶ swanky

SWANKIE same as ▶ swanky

SWANKIER ▶ swanky

SWANKIES ▶ swanky

SWANKILY ▶ swanky

SWANKING ▶ swank

SWANKPOT same as ▶ swank

SWANKS ▶ swank

SWANKY, SWANKIER, SWANKIES adj expensive and showy, stylish ▷ n lively person

SWANLIKE ▶ swan

SWANNED ▶ swan

SWANNERY n place where swans are kept and bred

SWANNIE, -S n (in NZ) type of all-weather heavy woollen shirt

SWANNIER ▶ swanny

SWANNIES ▶ swannie

SWANNING ▶ swan

SWANNY, SWANNIER adj swanlike

SWANPAN, -S n Chinese abacus

SWANS ▶ swan

SWANSKIN n skin of a swan with the feathers attached

SWANSONG n beautiful song fabled to be sung by a swan before it dies

SWAP, -PED, -PING, -S, -T vb exchange (something) for something else ▷ n exchange

SWAPFILE n computer file which provides space for transferred programs

SWAPPED ▶ swap

SWAPPER, -S ▶ swap

SWAPPING ▶ swap

SWAPS ▶ swap

SWAPT ▶ swap

SWAPTION another name for ▶ swap

SWARAJ, -ES n (in British India) self-government

SWARD, -ED, -ING, -S n stretch of short grass ▷ vb cover or become covered with grass

SWARDIER ▶ swardy

SWARDING ▶ sward

SWARDS ▶ sward

SWARDY, SWARDIER adj covered with sward

SWARE ▶ swear

SWARF, -ED, -ING, -S, SWARVED, SWARVES, SWARVING n material removed by cutting tools in the machining of metals, stone, etc ▷ vb faint

SWARM, -ED, -ING, -S n large group of bees or other insects ▷ vb move in a swarm

SWARMER -S

SWART adj swarthy

SWARTH, -S same as ▶ swart

SWARTHY adj dark-complexioned

SWARTY ▶ swart

SWARVE same as ▶ swarf

SWARVED ▶ swarf

SWARVES ▶ swarf

SWARVING ▶ swarf

SWASH, -ED, -ES, -ING n rush of water up a beach following each break of the waves ▷ vb wash or move with noisy splashing

SWASHER, -S n braggart

SWASHES ▶ swash

SWASHIER ▶ swashy

SWASHING ▶ swash

SWASHY, SWASHIER adj slushy

SWASTICA same as ▶ swastika

SWASTIKA n symbol used as the emblem of Nazi Germany

SWAT, -S, -TED, -TING vb strike or hit sharply ▷ n swatter

SWATCH, -ES n sample of cloth

SWATH, -S n width of one sweep of a scythe or of the blade of a mowing machine

SWATHE, -D, -S, SWATHING vb bandage or wrap completely ▷ n bandage or wrapping

SWATHER -S

SWATHIER ▶ swathy

SWATHING ▶ swathe

SWATHS ▶ swath

SWATHY, SWATHIER ▶ swath

SWATS ▶ swat

SWATTED ▶ swat

SWATTER, -S n device for killing insects ▷ vb splash

SWATTIER same as ▶ swottier

SWATTING ▶ swat

SWATTY same as ▶ swotty

SWAY, -ED, -S vb swing to and fro or from side to side ▷ n power or influence

SWAYABLE

SWAYBACK n abnormal sagging in the spine of older horses

SWAYED ▶ sway

SWAYER, -S ▶ sway

SWAYFUL ▶ sway

SWAYING, -S ▶ sway

SWAYL, -ED, -ING, -S same as ▶ sweal

SWAYS ▶ sway

SWAZZLE, -S n small metal instrument used to produce a shrill voice

SWEAL, -ED, -ING, -S vb scorch

SWEAR, SWARE, -ING, -S, SWORE, SWORN vb use obscene or blasphemous language

SWEARD, -S same as ▶ sword

SWEARER, -S ▶ swear

SWEARIER ▶ sweary

SWEARING ▶ swear

SWEARS ▶ swear

SWEARY, SWEARIER adj using swear-words

SWEAT, -ING, -S n salty liquid given off through the pores of the skin ▷ vb have sweat coming through the pores

SWEATBOX n device for causing tobacco leaves, fruit, or hides to sweat

SWEATED adj made by exploited labour

SWEATER, -S n (woollen) garment for the upper part of the body

SWEATIER ▶ sweaty

SWEATILY ▶ sweaty

SWEATING ▶ sweat

SWEATS ▶ sweat

SWEATY, SWEATIER adj covered with sweat

SWEDE, -S n kind of turnip

SWEDGER, -S n Scots dialect word for sweet

SWEE, -D, -ING, -S vb sway

SWEEL, -ED, -ING, -S same as ▶ sweal

SWEENEY, -S n police flying squad

SWEENY, SWEENIES n wasting of the shoulder muscles of a horse

SWEEP, -ING, -S, SWEPT vb remove dirt from (a floor) with a broom ▷ n sweeping

SWEEPER, -S n device used to sweep carpets

SWEEPIER ▶ sweepy

SWEEPING ▶ sweep

SWEEPS ▶ sweep

SWEEPY, SWEEPIER ▶ sweep

SWEER, -ED, -ING, -S variant of ▶ sweir

SWEERT variant of ▶ sweer

SWEES ▶ swee

SWEET, -ED, -ER, -EST, -S adj tasting of or like sugar ▷ n shaped piece of food consisting mainly of sugar ▷ vb sweeten

SWEETEN, -S vb make (food or drink) sweet or sweeter

SWEETER ▶ sweet

SWEETEST ▶ sweet

SWEETIE, -S n lovable person

SWEETING n variety of sweet apple

SWEETISH ▶ sweet

SWEETLIP n type of Australian fish with big lips

SWEETLY ▶ sweet

SWEETMAN, SWEETMEN n (in the Caribbean) a man kept by a woman

SWEETS ▶ sweet

SWEETSOP n small West Indian tree

SWEETY same as ▶ sweetie

SWEIR, -ED, -ER, -EST, -ING, -S vb swear ▷ adj lazy

SWEIRT variant of ▶ sweir

SWELCHIE n whirlpool in Orkney

SWELL, -ED, -EST, -ING, -S, SWOLLEN, SWOLN vb expand or increase ▷ n swelling or being swollen ▷ adj excellent or fine

SWELLDOM n fashionable society

SWELLED ▶ swell

SWELLER, -S ▶ swell

SWELLEST ▶ swell

SWELLING ▶ swell

SWELLISH ▶ swell

SWELLS ▶ swell

SWELT, -ED, -ING, -S vb die

SWELTER, -S vb feel uncomfortably hot ▷ n hot and uncomfortable condition

SWELTING ▶ swelt

SWELTRY adj sultry

SWELTS ▶ swelt

SWEPT ▶ sweep

SWERF, -ED, -ING, -S same as ▶ swarf

SWERVE, -D, -S, SWERVING vb turn aside from a course sharply or suddenly ▷ n swerving

SWERVER -S

SWEVEN, -S n vision or dream

SWEY, -ED, -ING, -S same as ▶ swee

SWIDDEN, -S n area of land where slash-and-burn techniques have been used

SWIES ▶ swy

SWIFT, -ED, -EST, -ING, -S adj moving or able to move quickly ▷ n fast-flying bird with pointed wings ▷ adv swiftly or quickly ▷ vb make tight

SWIFTER, -S n line run around the ends of capstan bars

SWIFTEST ▶ swift

SWIFTIE n trick, ruse, or deception

SWIFTIES ▶ swifty

SWIFTING ▶ swift

SWIFTLET n type of small Asian swift

SWIFTLY ▶ swift

SWIFTS ▶ swift

SWIFTY, SWIFTIES same as ▶ swiftie

SWIG, -GED, -GING, -S n large mouthful of drink ▷ vb drink in large mouthfuls

SWIGGER -S

SWILE, -S n seal (the marine animal)

SWILER, -S n (in Newfoundland) a seal hunter

SWILES ▶ swile

SWILING, -S n practice of hunting seals

SWILL, -ED, -ING, -S vb drink greedily ▷ n sloppy mixture containing waste food, fed to pigs

SWILLER -S

SWIM, SWAM, -MING, -S, SWUM vb move along in water by movements of the limbs ▷ n act or period of swimming

SWIMMER

SWIMMERS pl n swimming costume

SWIMMIER ▶ swimmy

SWIMMILY ▶ swimmy

SWIMMING ▶ swim

SWIMMY, SWIMMIER adj dizzy

SWIMS ▶ swim

SWIMSUIT n woman's swimming garment that leaves the arms and legs bare

SWIMWEAR n swimming costumes

SWINDGE, -D, -S same as ▶ swinge

SWINDLE, -D, -S vb cheat (someone) out of money ▷ n instance of swindling

SWINDLER

SWINE, -S n contemptible person

SWINEPOX n acute infectious viral disease of pigs

SWINERY n pig farm

SWINES ▶ swine

SWING, SWANG, -ING, -S, SWUNG vb move to and fro, sway ▷ n swinging

SWINGARM n main part of the rear suspension on a motorcycle

SWINGBIN n rubbish bin with a lid that swings shut after being opened

SWINGBY, -S n act of spacecraft passing close to planet

SWINGE, -D, -S vb beat, flog, or punish

SWINGER, -S n person regarded as being modern and lively

SWINGES ▶ swinge

SWINGIER ▶ swingy

SWINGING ▶ swing

SWINGISM n former resistance to use of agricultural machines

SWINGLE, -D, -S n flat-bladed wooden instrument used for beating and scraping flax ▷ vb use a swingle on

S

SWINGMAN, SWINGMEN
n musician specializing in
swing music
SWINGS ▶ swing
SWINGY, SWINGIER adj lively
and modern
SWINISH ▶ swine
SWINK, -ED, -ING, -S vb toil or
drudge ▷ n toil or drudgery
SWINKER -S
SWINNEY, -S variant of
▶ sweeny
SWIPE, -D, SWIPING vb strike
(at) with a sweeping blow
▷ n hard blow
SWIPER -S
SWIPES pl n beer, esp when
poor or weak
SWIPEY, SWIPIER, SWIPIEST
adj drunk
SWIPING ▶ swipe
SWIPLE, -S same as
▶ swipple
SWIPPLE, -S n part of a flail
that strikes the grain
SWIRE, -S n neck
SWIRL, -ED, -S vb turn with
a whirling motion ▷ n
whirling motion
SWIRLIER ▶ swirly
SWIRLING ▶ swirl
SWIRLS ▶ swirl
SWIRLY, SWIRLIER ▶ swirl
SWISH, -ED, -ES, -EST vb
move with a whistling or
hissing sound ▷ n whistling
or hissing sound ▷ adj
fashionable, smart
SWISHER -S
SWISHIER ▶ swishy
SWISHING ▶ swish
SWISHY, SWISHIER adj
moving with a swishing
sound
SWISS, -ES n type of muslin
SWISSING n method of
treating cloth
SWITCH, -ED, -ES n device
for opening and closing an
electric circuit ▷ vb change
abruptly
SWITCHEL n type of beer
SWITCHER ▶ switch
SWITCHES ▶ switch
SWITCHY ▶ switch
SWITH adv swiftly
SWITHE same as ▶ swith
SWITHER, -S vb hesitate or
be indecisive ▷ n state of
hesitation or uncertainty
SWITHLY ▶ swith
SWITS, -ES same as ▶ switch
SWIVEL, -ED, -S vb turn on a
central point ▷ n coupling
device that allows an
attached object to turn freely
SWIVET, -S n nervous state

SWIZ n swindle or
disappointment
SWIZZ, -ED, -ES, -ING same
as ▶ swiz
SWIZZLE, -D, -S vb cheat or
con ▷ n act of cheating or
conning
SWIZZLER
SWOB, -BED, -BING, -S less
common word for ▶ swab
SWOBBER -S
SWOFFER, -S ▶ swoffing
SWOFFING n sport of
saltwater fly-fishing
SWOLLEN ▶ swell
SWOLN ▶ swell
SWOON, -ED, -S n faint ▷ vb
faint because of shock or
strong emotion
SWOONER -S
SWOONIER ▶ swoony
SWOONING ▶ swoon
SWOONS ▶ swoon
SWOONY, SWOONIER adj
romantic
SWOOP, -ED, -ING, -S vb
sweep down or pounce on
suddenly ▷ n swooping
SWOOPER -S
SWOOPIER ▶ swoopy
SWOOPING ▶ swoop
SWOOPS ▶ swoop
SWOOPY, SWOOPIER
▶ swoop
SWOOSH, -ED, -ES vb make
a swirling or rustling sound
when moving or pouring out
▷ n swirling or rustling sound
or movement
SWOP, -PED, -PING, -S, -T
same as ▶ swap
SWOPPER -S
SWORD, -ED, -ING, -S n
weapon with a long sharp
blade ▷ vb bear a sword
SWORDER, -S n fighter with
sword
SWORDING ▶ sword
SWORDMAN, SWORDMEN
same as > **swordsman**
SWORDS ▶ sword
SWORE ▶ swear
SWORN ▶ swear
SWOT, -S, -TED, -TING vb
study (a subject) intensively
▷ n person who studies hard
SWOTTER, -S same as ▶ swot
SWOTTIER ▶ swotty
SWOTTING ▶ swot
SWOTTY, SWOTTIER adj
given to studying hard, esp
to the exclusion of other
activities
SWOUN, -S same as ▶ swoon
SWOUND, -ED same as
▶ swoon

SWOUNDS less common
spelling of ▶ zounds
SWOUNE, -D, -S, SWOUNING
same as ▶ swoon
SWOUNS ▶ swoun
SWOWND, -S same as
▶ swoon
SWOWNE, -S same as
▶ swoon
SWOZZLE, -S same as
▶ swazzle
SWUM ▶ swim
SWUNG ▶ swing
SWY, SWIES n Australian
gambling game involving
two coins

A type of card game, this
word can be useful in
helping you to clear a
difficult rack.

SYBARITE n lover of luxury
▷ adj luxurious
SYBBE, -S same as ▶ sib
SYBIL, -S same as ▶ sibyl
SYBO n spring onion
SYBOE, -S same as ▶ sybo
SYBOTIC adj of a swineherd
SYBOTISM
SYBOW, -S same as ▶ sybo
SYCAMINE n mulberry tree
mentioned in the Bible,
thought to be the black
mulberry
SYCAMORE n tree with
five-pointed leaves and two-
winged fruits
SYCE, -S n (formerly, in India)
a servant employed to look
after horses, etc
SYCEE, -S n silver ingots
formerly used as a medium of
exchange in China
SYCES ▶ syce
SYCOMORE same as
▶ sycamore
SYCON, -S n type of sponge
SYCONIUM, SYCONIA n
fleshy fruit of the fig
SYCONOID adj of or like a
sycon
SYCONS ▶ sycon
SYCOSIS, SYCOSES n chronic
inflammation of the hair
follicles
SYE, -D, -ING, -S vb strain
SYEN, -S same as ▶ scion
SYENITE, -S n light-coloured
coarse-grained plutonic
igneous rock
SYENITIC
SYENS ▶ syen
SYES ▶ sye
SYKE, -S same as ▶ sike
SYKER adv surely
SYKES ▶ syke

SYLI, -S n Finnish unit of volume

SYLLABI ▸ syllabus

SYLLABIC adj of or relating to syllables ▷ n syllabic consonant

SYLLABLE n part of a word pronounced as a unit

SYLLABUB n dessert of beaten cream, sugar, and wine

SYLLABUS, SYLLABI n list of subjects for a course of study

SYLLOGE, -S n collection or summary

SYLPH, -S n slender graceful girl or woman

SYLPHIC

SYLPHID, -S n little sylph

SYLPHIDE same as ▸ sylphid

SYLPHIDS ▸ sylphid

SYLPHIER ▸ sylphy

SYLPHINE ▸ sylph

SYLPHISH ▸ sylph

SYLPHS ▸ sylph

SYLPHY, SYLPHIER ▸ sylph

SYLVA, -E, -S n trees growing in a particular region

SYLVAN, -S adj relating to woods and trees ▷ n inhabitant of the woods, esp a spirit

SYLVANER n German variety of grape

SYLVANS ▸ sylvan

SYLVAS ▸ sylva

SYLVATIC adj growing, living, or occurring in a wood or beneath a tree

SYLVIA, -S n songbird

SYLVIINE

SYLVIN, -S same as ▸ sylvite

SYLVINE, -S same as ▸ sylvite

SYLVINS ▸ sylvin

SYLVITE, -S n soluble colourless, white, or coloured mineral

SYMAR, -S same as ▸ cymar

SYMBION, -S same as ▸ symbiont

SYMBIONT n organism living in a state of symbiosis

SYMBIOT, -S same as ▸ symbiont

SYMBIOTE same as ▸ symbiont

SYMBIOTS ▸ symbiot

SYMBOL, -ED, -S n sign or thing that stands for something else ▷ vb be a symbol

SYMBOLE, -S same as ▸ cymbal

SYMBOLED ▸ symbol

SYMBOLES ▸ symbole

SYMBOLIC adj of or relating to a symbol or symbols

SYMBOLS ▸ symbol

SYMITAR, -S same as ▸ scimitar

SYMITARE same as ▸ scimitar

SYMITARS ▸ symitar

SYMMETRY n state of having two halves that are mirror images of each other

SYMPATHY n compassion for someone's pain or distress

SYMPATRY n existing of organisms together without interbreeding

SYMPHILE n insect that lives in the nests of social insects and is fed and reared by the inmates

SYMPHILY n presence of different kinds of animal in ants' nests

SYMPHONY n composition for orchestra, with several movements

SYMPLAST n continuous system of protoplasts, linked by plasmodesmata and bounded by the cell wall

SYMPLOCE n word repetition in successive clauses

SYMPODIA ▸ sympodium

SYMPOSIA ▸ symposium

SYMPTOM, -S n sign indicating the presence of an illness

SYN Scots word for ▸ since

SYNAGOG, -S same as ▸ synagogue

SYNANGIA ▸ synangium

SYNANON, -S n type of therapy given to drug addicts

SYNANTHY n abnormal joining between flowers

SYNAPHEA n continuity in metre of verses of poem

SYNAPSE, -D n gap where nerve impulses pass between two nerve cells ▷ vb create a synapse

SYNAPSES ▸ synapsis

SYNAPSID n prehistoric mammal-like reptile

SYNAPSIS, SYNAPSES n association in pairs of homologous chromosomes at the start of meiosis

SYNAPTE, -S n litany in Greek Orthodox Church

SYNAPTIC adj of or relating to a synapse

SYNARCHY n joint rule

SYNASTRY n coincidence of astrological influences

SYNAXIS, SYNAXES n early Christian meeting

SYNC, -ED, -ING, -S n synchronization ▷ vb synchronize

SYNCARP, -S n fleshy multiple fruit

SYNCARPY n quality of consisting of united carpels

SYNCED ▸ sync

SYNCH, -ED, -ING, -S same as ▸ sync

SYNCHRO, -S n type of electrical device

SYNCHS ▸ synch

SYNCING ▸ sync

SYNCLINE n downward slope of stratified rock

SYNCOM, -S n communications satellite in stationary orbit

SYNCOPAL ▸ syncope

SYNCOPE, -S n omission of one or more sounds or letters from the middle of a word

SYNCOPIC

SYNCS ▸ sync

SYNCYTIA ▸ syncytium

SYND, -ED, -S same as ▸ syne

SYNDESIS, SYNDESES n use of syndetic constructions

SYNDET, -S n synthetic detergent

SYNDETIC adj denoting a grammatical construction in which two clauses are connected by a conjunction

SYNDETON n syndetic construction

SYNDETS ▸ syndet

SYNDIC, -S n business or legal agent of some institutions

SYNDICAL adj relating to the theory that syndicates of workers should seize the means of production

SYNDICS ▸ syndic

SYNDING, -S ▸ synd

SYNDROME n combination of symptoms indicating a particular disease

SYNDS ▸ synd

SYNE, -D, -S, SYNING vb rinse ▷ n rinse ▷ adv since

SYNECHIA n abnormality of the eye

SYNECTIC ▸ synectics

SYNED ▸ syne

SYNEDRIA ▸ synedrion

SYNERGIA same as ▸ synergy

SYNERGIC ▸ synergy

SYNERGID n type of cell in embryo

SYNERGY n collective effect that is greater than the sum of individual effects

SYNES ▸ syne

S

SYNESIS, SYNESES *n* grammatical construction in which the form of a word is conditioned by the meaning

SYNFUEL, -S *n* synthetic fuel

SYNGAMIC ► **syngamy**

SYNGAMY *n* reproduction involving the fusion of male and female gametes

SYNGAS, -ES *n* mixture of carbon monoxide and hydrogen

SYNGENIC *same as* > **syngeneic**

SYNGRAPH *n* document signed by several parties

SYNING ► **syne**

SYNKARYA > **synkaryon**

SYNOD, -S *n* church council

SYNODAL, -S *adj* of or relating to a synod ▷ *n* money paid to a bishop by less senior members of the clergy at a synod

SYNODIC *adj* involving conjunction of the same star, planet, or satellite

SYNODS ► **synod**

SYNONYM, -S *n* word with the same meaning as another

SYNONYME *same as* ► **synonym**

SYNONYMS ► **synonym**

SYNONYMY *n* study of synonyms

SYNOPSIS, SYNOPSES *n* summary or outline

SYNOPTIC *adj* of or relating to a synopsis ▷ *n* any of the three synoptic Gospels

SYNOVIA, -S *n* clear thick fluid that lubricates the body joints

SYNOVIAL *adj* of or relating to the synovia

SYNOVIAS ► **synovia**

SYNROC, -S *n* titanium-ceramic substance that can incorporate nuclear waste in its crystals

SYNTAGM, -S *same as* ► **syntagma**

SYNTAGMA *n* syntactic unit or a word or phrase forming a syntactic unit

SYNTAGMS ► **syntagm**

SYNTAN, -S *n* synthetic tanning substance

SYNTAX, -ES *n* way in which words are arranged to form phrases and sentences

SYNTENIC ► **synteny**

SYNTENY *n* presence of two or more genes on the same chromosome

SYNTEXIS *n* liquefaction

SYNTH, -S *n* type of electrophonic musical instrument operated by a keyboard and pedals

SYNTHASE *n* enzyme that catalyses a synthesis process

SYNTHON, -S *n* molecule used in synthesis

SYNTHPOP *n* pop music using synthesizers

SYNTHS ► **synth**

SYNTONE, -S *n* person who is syntonic

SYNTONIC *adj* emotionally in harmony with one's environment

SYNTONIN *n* substance in muscle

SYNTONY *n* matching of frequencies

SYNTYPE, -S *n* original specimen by which a new species is described

SYNURA, -E *n* variety of microbe

SYPE, -D, -S, SYPING *same as* ► **sipe**

SYPHER, -ED, -S *vb* lap (a chamfered edge) in order to form a flush surface

SYPHON, -ED, -S *same as* ► **siphon**

SYPHONAL *same as* ► **siphonal**

SYPHONED ► **syphon**

SYPHONIC *same as* ► **siphonic**

SYPHONS ► **syphon**

SYPING ► **sype**

SYRAH, -S *n* type of French red wine

SYREN, -S *same as* ► **siren**

SYRETTE, -S *n* small disposable syringe

SYRINGA, -S *n* mock orange or lilac

SYRINGE, -D *n* device for withdrawing or injecting fluids ▷ *vb* wash out or inject with a syringe

SYRINX, SYRINGES, -ES *n* vocal organ of a bird

SYRPHIAN *same as* ► **syrphid**

SYRPHID, -S *n* type of fly

SYRTIS, SYRTES *n* area of quicksand

SYRUP, -ED, -ING, -S *n* solution of sugar in water ▷ *vb* bring to the consistency of syrup

SYRUPIER ► **syrupy**

SYRUPING ► **syrup**

SYRUPS ► **syrup**

SYRUPY, SYRUPIER *adj* thick and sweet

SYSADMIN *n* computer system administrator

SYSOP, -S *n* person who runs a system or network

SYSSITIA *n* ancient Spartan communal meal

SYSTEM, -S *n* method or set of methods

SYSTEMED *adj* having system

SYSTEMIC *adj* affecting the entire animal or body ▷ *n* systemic pesticide, fungicide, etc

SYSTEMS ► **system**

SYSTOLE, -S *n* regular contraction of the heart as it pumps blood

SYSTOLIC

SYSTYLE, -S *n* building with different types of columns

SYTHE, -S *same as* ► **sith**

SYVER, -S *n* street drain or the grating over it

SYZYGAL ► **syzygy**

SYZYGIAL ► **syzygy**

SYZYGY, SYZYGIES *n* position of a celestial body when sun, earth, and the body are in line**

Tt

T is one of the most common consonants in Scrabble. There are only four two-letter words that begin with **T**, but they are easy to remember as there is one for every vowel except **U**. Like **S**, **T** begins a number of three-letter words that don't use vowels, which are well worth remembering. These are: **thy** (6 points), **try** (6), **tsk** (7), **twp** (8) and **tyg** (7). There are also some useful three-letter words using **X**: **tax, tex, tix** and **tux** (10 each). If you have an **X** during a game, remember words like **text** (11), **texts** (12), **textile** (14), **textual** (14) and **texture** (14), **textism** (16) and **thanx** (15). Some of these have seven letters, and so will earn you 50-point bonuses if you use all your tiles to form them. Other threes well worth remembering are **tiz** (12) and **taj** (10).

TA, -S *interj* thank you ▷ *n* thank you

TAAL, -S *n* language: usually, by implication, Afrikaans

TAATA, -S *child's word for* ▸ **father**

> This East African word for a father is one of those short words that can help you dispose of a surplus of As.

TAB, -BED, -S *n* small flap or projecting label ▷ *vb* supply with a tab

TABANID, -S *n* stout-bodied fly

TABARD, -S *n* short sleeveless tunic decorated with a coat of arms, worn in medieval times

TABARDED *adj* wearing a tabard

TABARDS ▸ **tabard**

TABARET, -S *n* hard-wearing fabric of silk or similar cloth with stripes of satin or moire

TABASHIR *same as* > **tabasheer**

TABBED ▸ **tab**

TABBIED ▸ **tabby**

TABBIES ▸ **tabby**

TABBINET *same as* ▸ **tabinet**

TABBING, -S *n* act of supplying with tabs

TABBIS, -ES *n* silken cloth

TABBOULI *same as* > **tabbouleh**

TABBY, TABBIED, TABBIES, -ING *vb* make (eg a material) appear wavy ▷ *n* female domestic cat

TABEFY, TABEFIED, TABEFIES *vb* emaciate or become emaciated

TABER, -ED, -ING, -S *old variant of* ▸ **tabor**

TABERD, -S *same as* ▸ **tabard**

TABERDAR *n* holder of a scholarship at Queen's College, Oxford

TABERDS ▸ **taberd**

TABERED ▸ **taber**

TABERING ▸ **taber**

TABERS ▸ **taber**

TABES *n* wasting of a bodily organ or part

TABETIC -S

TABI, -S *n* thick-soled Japanese sock, worn with sandals

TABID *adj* emaciated

TABINET, -S *n* type of tabbied fabric

TABIS ▸ **tabi**

TABLA, -S *n* one of a pair of Indian drums played with the hands

TABLE, -D, -S *n* piece of furniture with a flat top supported by legs ▷ *vb* submit (a motion) for discussion by a meeting

TABLEAU, -S, -X *n* silent motionless group arranged to represent some scene

TABLED ▸ **table**

TABLEFUL ▸ **table**

TABLEMAT *n* small mat used for protecting the surface of a table from hot dishes

TABLES ▸ **table**

TABLET, -ED, -S *n* medicinal pill ▷ *vb* make (something) into a tablet

TABLETOP *n* upper surface of a table

TABLETS ▸ **tablet**

TABLIER, -S *n* (formerly) part of a dress resembling an apron

TABLING, -S ▸ **table**

TABLOID, -S *n* small-sized newspaper with many photographs

TABLOIDY *adj* characteristic of a tabloid newspaper; trashy

TABOGGAN *same as* ▸ **toboggan**

TABOO, -ED, -ING, -S *n* prohibition resulting from religious or social conventions ▷ *adj* forbidden by a taboo ▷ *vb* place under a taboo

TABOOLEY *variant of* > **tabbouleh**

TABOOS ▸ **taboo**

TABOR, -ED, -ING, -S *vb* play the tabor

TABORER -S

TABORET, -S *n* low stool, originally in the shape of a drum

TABORIN, -S *same as* ▸ **taboret**

TABORINE *same as* ▸ **tabourin**

TABORING ▸ **tabor**

TABORINS ▸ **taborin**

TABORS ▸ **tabor**

TABOULEH variant of
> **tabbouleh**
TABOULI, -S same as
> **tabbouleh**
TABOUR, -ED, -S same as
▶ **tabor**
TABOURER
TABOURET same as
▶ **taboret**
TABOURIN same as
▶ **taboret**
TABOURS ▶ **tabour**
TABRERE, -S same as ▶ **tabor**
TABRET, -S n smaller version
of a tabor
TABS ▶ **tab**
TABU, -ED, -ING, -S same as
▶ **taboo**
TABULA, -E n tablet for
writing on
TABULAR adj arranged in
a table
TABULATE vb arrange
(information) in a table ▷ adj
having a flat surface
TABULI, -S variant of
> **tabbouleh**
TABUN, -S n organic
compound used as a lethal
nerve gas
TABUS ▶ **tabu**
TACAHOUT n abnormal
outgrowth on the tamarisk
plant
TACAN, -S n electronic
ultrahigh-frequency
navigation system for aircraft
TACE, -S same as ▶ **tasset**
TACET n musical direction
indicating that an
instrument or singer does
not take part
TACH, -S n device for
measuring speed
TACHE, -S n buckle, clasp,
or hook
TACHINA n as in **tachina fly**
bristly fly
TACHINID n type of fly
TACHISM, -S same as
▶ **tachisme**
TACHISME n type of action
painting evolved in France
TACHISMS ▶ **tachism**
TACHIST, -S ▶ **tachism**
TACHISTE ▶ **tachisme**
TACHISTS ▶ **tachist**
TACHO, -S same as
> **tachogram**
TACHS ▶ **tach**
TACHYON, -S n hypothetical
elementary particle
TACIT adj implied but not
spoken
TACITLY

TACITURN adj habitually
uncommunicative
TACK, -ED, -S n short nail
with a large head ▷ vb fasten
with tacks
TACKER -S
TACKET, -S n nail, esp a
hobnail
TACKETY
TACKEY same as ▶ **tacky**
TACKIER ▶ **tacky**
TACKIES pl n tennis shoes or
plimsolls
TACKIEST ▶ **tacky**
TACKIFY vb give (eg rubber) a
sticky feel
TACKILY ▶ **tacky**
TACKING, -S ▶ **tack**
TACKLE, -D, -S, TACKLING vb
deal with (a task) ▷ n act of
tackling an opposing player
TACKLER -S
TACKLESS ▶ **tack**
TACKLING ▶ **tackle**
TACKS ▶ **tack**
TACKSMAN, TACKSMEN n
leaseholder, esp a tenant in
the Highlands who sublets
TACKY, TACKIER, TACKIEST
adj slightly sticky
TACNODE, -S n point at which
two branches of a curve have
a common tangent
TACO, -S n tortilla fried until
crisp, served with a filling
TACONITE n fine-grained
sedimentary rock
TACOS ▶ **taco**
TACRINE, -S n drug used to
treat Alzheimer's disease
TACT, -S n skill in avoiding
giving offence
TACTFUL
TACTIC n method or plan to
achieve an end
TACTICAL adj of or employing
tactics
TACTICS n art of directing
military forces in battle
TACTILE adj of or having the
sense of touch
TACTION, -S n act of touching
TACTISM, -S another word for
▶ **taxis**
TACTLESS ▶ **tact**
TACTS ▶ **tact**
TACTUAL adj caused by touch
TAD, -S n small bit or piece
TADDIE, -S n short for
▶ **tadpole**
TADPOLE, -S n limbless tailed
larva of a frog or toad
TADS ▶ **tad**
TAE, -D, -ING, -S Scots form of
the verb ▶ **toe**

TAEDIUM, -S archaic spelling
of ▶ **tedium**
TAEING ▶ **tae**
TAEL, -S n unit of weight, used
in the Far East
TAENIA, -E, -S n (in ancient
Greece) a narrow fillet or
headband for the hair
TAENIATE adj ribbon-like
TAENIOID adj ribbon-like
TAENITE, -S n nickel-iron alloy
found in meteorites
TAES ▶ **tae**
TAFFAREL same as ▶ **taffrail**
TAFFEREL same as ▶ **taffrail**
TAFFETA n shiny silk or rayon
fabric
TAFFETAS same as ▶ **taffeta**
TAFFETY same as ▶ **taffeta**
TAFFIA, -S same as ▶ **tafia**
TAFFIES ▶ **taffy**
TAFFRAIL n rail at the back of
a ship or boat
TAFFY, TAFFIES same as
▶ **toffee**
TAFIA, -S n type of rum,
esp from Guyana or the
Caribbean
TAG, -GED, -GING, -GINGS, -S
n label bearing information
▷ vb attach a tag to
TAGALONG n one who trails
behind, esp uninvited; a
hanger-on
TAGAREEN n junk shop
TAGBOARD n sturdy form of
cardboard
TAGETES n any of a genus of
plants with yellow or orange
flowers
TAGGANT, -S n microscopic
material added to substance
to identify it
TAGGED ▶ **tag**
TAGGEE, -S n one who has
been made to wear a tag
TAGGER, -S n one who marks
with a tag
TAGGIER ▶ **taggy**
TAGGIEST ▶ **taggy**
TAGGING ▶ **tag**
TAGGINGS ▶ **tag**
TAGGY, TAGGIER, TAGGIEST
adj (of wool, hair, etc) matted
TAGHAIRM n form of
divination once practised in
the Highlands of Scotland
TAGINE, -S n large, heavy
N African cooking pot with a
conical lid
TAGLESS adj having no tag
TAGLIKE adj resembling a tag
TAGLINE, -S n funny line of
joke
TAGLIONI n type of coat

TAGMA, -TA n distinct region of the body of an arthropod

TAGMEME, -S n class of speech elements all of which may fulfil the same grammatical role
TAGMEMIC

TAGRAG, -S same as ▸ ragtag

TAGS ▸ tag

TAGUAN, -S n nocturnal flying squirrel of the East Indies

TAHA, -S n type of South African bird

TAHINA, -S same as ▸ tahini

TAHINI, -S n paste made from ground sesame seeds

TAHR, -S n goatlike mammal of mountainous regions of S and SW Asia

TAHSIL, -S n administrative division of a zila in certain states in India

TAI, -S n type of sea bream

TAIAHA, -S n carved weapon in the form of a staff, now used in Māori ceremonial oratory

TAIGA, -S n belt of coniferous forest

TAIGLACH same as ▸ teiglach

TAIGLE, -D, -S, TAIGLING vb entangle or impede

TAIHOA interj hold on! no hurry!

TAIKO, -S n large Japanese drum

TAIL, -ED n rear part of an animal's body, usu forming a flexible appendage ▷ adj at the rear ▷ vb follow (someone) secretly

TAILARD, -S n one having a tail

TAILBACK n queue of traffic stretching back from an obstruction

TAILBONE nontechnical name for ▸ coccyx

TAILCOAT n man's black coat with a tapering tail

TAILED ▸ tail

TAILER, -S n one that tails

TAILERON n aileron located on the tailplane of an aircraft

TAILERS ▸ tailer

TAILFAN, -S n fanned structure at the hind end of a lobster

TAILFIN, -S n decorative projection at back of car

TAILFLY n in angling, the lowest fly on a wet-fly cast

TAILGATE n door at the rear of a hatchback vehicle ▷ vb

drive very close behind (a vehicle)

TAILHOOK n hook on an aircraft that catches a braking cable

TAILING n part of a beam, rafter, projecting brick or stone, etc, embedded in a wall

TAILINGS pl n waste left over after milling processes

TAILLAMP n rear light

TAILLE, -S n (in France before 1789) a tax levied by a king or overlord on his subjects

TAILLESS ▸ tail

TAILLEUR n woman's suit

TAILLIE, -S n (in law) the limitation of an estate or interest to a person and the heirs of his body

TAILLIKE adj resembling a tail

TAILOR, -ED, -S n person who makes men's clothes ▷ vb cut or style (a garment) to specific requirements

TAILPIPE vb attach an object, esp a tin can, to the tail of an animal

TAILRACE n channel that carries water away from a water wheel, turbine, etc

TAILS adv with the side of a coin that does not have a portrait of a head on it uppermost

TAILSKID n runner under the tail of an aircraft

TAILSPIN, TAILSPUN n uncontrolled spinning dive of an aircraft ▷ vb go into a tailspin

TAILWIND n wind coming from the rear

TAILYE, -S same as ▸ taillie

TAILZIE, -S same as ▸ taillie

TAIN, -S n tinfoil used in backing mirrors

TAINT, -ED, -ING, -S vb spoil with a small amount of decay or other bad quality ▷ n something that taints

TAINTURE n contamination; staining

TAIPAN, -S n large poisonous Australian snake

TAIRA, -S same as ▸ tayra

TAIS ▸ tai

TAISCH, -ES n (in Scotland) apparition of a person whose death is imminent

TAISH, -ES same as ▸ taisch

TAIT, -S same as ▸ tate

TAIVER, -ED, -S same as ▸ taver

TAIVERT adj Scots word meaning confused or bewildered

TAJ, -ES n tall conical cap worn as a mark of distinction by Muslims

This is one of the key words to remember for using the J.

TAJINE, -S same as ▸ tagine

TAK, -S Scots variant spelling of ▸ take

TAKA, -S n standard monetary unit of Bangladesh, divided into 100 paise

TAKABLE ▸ take

TAKAHE, -S n very rare flightless New Zealand bird

TAKAMAKA same as ▸ tacamahac

TAKAS ▸ taka

TAKE, -N, -S, TOOK vb remove from a place ▷ n one of a series of recordings from which the best will be used
TAKEABLE

TAKEAWAY adj (of food) sold for consumption away from the premises ▷ n shop or restaurant selling meals for eating elsewhere

TAKEDOWN n disassembly

TAKEN ▸ take

TAKEOFF, -S n act or process of making an aircraft airborne

TAKEOUT, -S n shop or restaurant that sells such food

TAKEOVER n act of taking control of a company by buying a large number of its shares

TAKER, -S n person who agrees to take something that is offered

TAKES ▸ take

TAKEUP, -S n claiming or acceptance of something that is due or available

TAKHI, -S n type of wild Mongolian horse

TAKI, -S same as ▸ takhi

TAKIER ▸ taky

TAKIEST ▸ taky

TAKIN, -S n bovid mammal of mountainous regions of S Asia

TAKING, -S ▸ take

TAKINGLY ▸ take

TAKINGS ▸ taking

TAKINS ▸ takin

TAKIS ▸ taki

TAKKIES ▸ takky

TAKKY n (S Afr) plimsoll

T

TAKS ► tak

TAKY, TAKIER, TAKIEST *adj* appealing

TALA, -S *n* standard monetary unit of Samoa, divided into 100 sene

TALAK, -S *same as* **► talaq**

TALANT, -S *old variant of* **► talon**

TALAPOIN *n* smallest of the guenon monkeys

TALAQ, -S *n* Muslim form of divorce

> In Islamic law, a word for divorce: easy to miss because one tends not to think of words ending in Q.

TALAR, -S *n* ankle-length robe

TALARIA *pl n* winged sandals, such as those worn by Hermes

TALARS ► talar

TALAS ► tala

TALAUNT, -S *old variant of* **► talon**

TALAYOT, -S *n* ancient Balearic stone tower

TALBOT, -S *n* ancient breed of large hound

TALC, -ED, -ING, -KED, -KING, -S *n* talcum powder ▷ *vb* apply talc to ▷ *adj* of, or relating to talc

TALCIER ► talcy

TALCIEST ► talcy

TALCING ► talc

TALCKED ► talc

TALCKIER ► talcky

TALCKING ► talc

TALCKY, TALCKIER *same as* **► talcy**

TALCOSE ► talc

TALCOUS ► talc

TALCS ► talc

TALCUM, -ED, -S *n* white, grey, brown, or pale green mineral ▷ *vb* apply talcum to

TALCY, TALCIER, TALCIEST *adj* like, containing, or covered in talc

TALE *n* story

TALEA, -E *n* rhythmic pattern in certain mediaeval choral compositions

TALEFUL *adj* having many tales

TALEGGIO *n* Italian cheese

TALENT, -S *n* natural ability

TALENTED

TALER, -S *same as* **► thaler**

TALES *n* group of persons summoned to fill vacancies on a jury panel

TALESMAN TALESMEN

TALEYSIM ► tallith

TALI ► talus

TALION, -S *n* principle of making punishment correspond to the crime

TALIONIC *adj* of or relating to talion

TALIONS ► talion

TALIPAT, -S *same as* **► talipot**

TALIPED, -S *adj* having a club foot ▷ *n* club-footed person

TALIPES *n* congenital deformity of the foot by which it is twisted in any of various positions

TALIPOT, -S *n* palm tree of the East Indies

TALISMAN *n* object believed to have magic power

TALK, -ED, -S *vb* express ideas or feelings by means of speech ▷ *n* speech or lecture

TALKABLE

TALKBACK *n* broadcast in which telephone comments or questions from the public are transmitted live

TALKBOX *n* voice box

TALKED ► talk

TALKER, -S ► talk

TALKFEST *n* lengthy discussion

TALKIE, -S *n* early film with a soundtrack

TALKIER ► talky

TALKIES ► talkie

TALKIEST ► talky

TALKING, -S *n* speech; the act of speaking

TALKS ► talk

TALKTIME *n* length of time a mobile phone can be used before its battery runs out

TALKY, TALKIER, TALKIEST *adj* containing too much dialogue or inconsequential talk

TALL, -ER, -EST, -S *adj* higher than average

TALLAGE, -D, -S *n* tax levied on Crown lands and royal towns ▷ *vb* levy a tax (upon)

TALLAT, -S *same as* **► tallet**

TALLBOY, -S *n* high chest of drawers

TALLENT, -S *n* plenty

TALLER ► tall

TALLEST ► tall

TALLET, -S *n* loft

TALLIATE *vb* levy a tax

TALLIED ► tally

TALLIER, -S ► tally

TALLIES ► tally

TALLIS, -ES, -IM *variant of* **► tallith**

TALLISH *adj* quite tall

TALLISIM ► tallis

TALLIT, -ES, -IM, -OT, -S *variant of* **► tallith**

TALLITH, TALEYSIM, -S *n* shawl worn by Jewish males during religious services

TALLITIM ► tallit

TALLITOT ► tallit

TALLITS ► tallit

TALLNESS ► tall

TALLOL, -S *n* oily liquid used for making soaps, lubricants, etc

TALLOT, -S *same as* **► tallet**

TALLOW, -ED, -S *n* hard animal fat used to make candles ▷ *vb* cover or smear with tallow

TALLOWY

TALLS ► tall

TALLY, TALLIED, TALLIES, -ING *vb* (of two things) correspond ▷ *n* record of a debt or score

TALLYHO, -S *n* cry to encourage hounds when the quarry is sighted ▷ *vb* make the cry of tallyho

TALLYING ► tally

TALLYMAN, TALLYMEN *n* scorekeeper or recorder

TALMA, -S *n* short cloak

TALMUD, -S *n* primary source of Jewish religious law, consisting of the Mishnah and the Gemara

TALMUDIC

TALON, -S *n* bird's hooked claw

TALONED

TALOOKA, -S *same as* **► taluk**

TALPA, -E, -S *n* sebaceous cyst

TALUK, -S *n* subdivision of a district

TALUKA, -S *same as* **► taluk**

TALUKDAR *n* person in charge of a taluk

TALUKS ► taluk

TALUS, TALI, -ES *n* bone of the ankle that articulates with the leg bones to form the ankle joint

TALWEG, -S *same as* **► thalweg**

TAM, -S *n* type of hat

TAMABLE ► tame

TAMAL, -S *same as* **► tamale**

TAMALE, -S *n* Mexican dish of minced meat wrapped in maize husks and steamed

TAMALS ► tamal

TAMANDU, -S *same as* **► tamandua**

TAMANDUA *n* small arboreal edentate mammal

TAMANDUS ► tamandu

TAMANOIR n anteater

TAMANU, -S n poon tree

TAMARA, -S n powder consisting of cloves, cinnamon, fennel, coriander, etc

TAMARACK n North American larch

TAMARAO, -S same as ▶ **tamarau**

TAMARAS ▶ **tamara**

TAMARAU, -S n small rare member of a cattle tribe in the Philippines

TAMARI, -S n Japanese variety of soy sauce

TAMARIN, -S n small monkey of South and Central America

TAMARIND n tropical tree

TAMARINS ▶ **tamarin**

TAMARIS ▶ **tamari**

TAMARISK n evergreen shrub with slender branches and feathery flower clusters

TAMASHA, -S n (in India) a show

TAMBAC, -S same as ▶ **tombac**

TAMBAK, -S same as ▶ **tombac**

TAMBALA, -S n unit of Malawian currency

TAMBER, -S same as ▶ **timbre**

TAMBOUR, -S n embroidery frame consisting of two hoops ▷ vb embroider (fabric or a design) on a tambour

TAMBOURA n stringed instrument used in Indian music

TAMBOURS ▶ **tambour**

TAMBUR, -S n old Turkish stringed instrument

TAMBURA, -S n Middle-Eastern stringed instrument with a long neck

TAMBURIN Spenserian form of > **tambourine**

TAMBURS ▶ **tambur**

TAME, -D, -S, -ST adj (of animals) brought under human control ▷ vb make tame

TAMEABLE

TAMEIN, -S n Burmese skirt

TAMELESS ▶ **tame**

TAMELY ▶ **tame**

TAMENESS ▶ **tame**

TAMER, -S ▶ **tame**

TAMES ▶ **tame**

TAMEST ▶ **tame**

TAMIN, -S n thin woollen fabric

TAMINE, -S same as ▶ **tamin**

TAMING, -S n act of making (something) tame

TAMINS ▶ **tamin**

TAMIS, -ES same as ▶ **tammy**

TAMISE n type of thin cloth

TAMISES ▶ **tamis**

TAMMAR, -S n small scrub wallaby

TAMMIE, -S n short for tam-o'-shanter, a traditional Scottish hat

TAMMIED ▶ **tammy**

TAMMIES ▶ **tammie**

TAMMY, TAMMIED, -ING n glazed woollen or mixed fabric ▷ vb strain (sauce, soup, etc) through a tammy

TAMP, -ED, -S vb pack down by repeated taps

TAMPALA, -S n Asian plant, eaten as food

TAMPAN, -S n biting mite

TAMPED ▶ **tamp**

TAMPER, -ED, -S vb interfere ▷ n person or thing that tamps

TAMPERER

TAMPING, -S adj very angry ▷ n act or instance of tamping

TAMPION, -S n plug placed in a gun's muzzle to keep out moisture and dust

TAMPON, -ED, -S n plug of cotton wool inserted into a wound or body cavity to absorb blood ▷ vb use a tampon

TAMPS ▶ **tamp**

TAMS ▶ **tam**

TAMWORTH n any of a hardy rare breed of long-bodied reddish pigs

TAN, -NED, -NEST, -S n brown coloration of the skin from exposure to sunlight ▷ vb (of skin) go brown from exposure to sunlight ▷ adj yellowish-brown

TANA, -S n small Madagascan lemur

TANADAR, -S n commanding officer of an Indian police station

TANAGER, -S n American songbird with a short thick bill

TANAGRA, -S n type of tanager

TANAISTE n deputy prime minister of the Republic of Ireland

TANAS ▶ **tana**

TANBARK, -S n bark of certain trees, esp the oak and

hemlock, used as a source of tannin

TANDEM, -S n bicycle for two riders, one behind the other

TANDOOR, -S n type of Indian clay oven

TANDOORI adj (of food) cooked in an Indian clay oven ▷ n Indian method of cooking meat or vegetables on a spit in a clay oven

TANDOORS ▶ **tandoor**

TANE old Scottish variant of ▶ **taken**

TANG, -ED, -ING, -S n strong taste or smell ▷ vb cause to ring

TANGA, -S n triangular loincloth worn by indigenous peoples in tropical America

TANGED ▶ **tang**

TANGELO, -S n hybrid produced by crossing a tangerine tree with a grapefruit tree

TANGENCE n touching

TANGENCY ▶ **tangent**

TANGENT, -S n line that touches a curve without intersecting it

TANGHIN, -S n poison formerly used in Madagascar to determine the guilt of crime suspects

TANGI, -S n Māori funeral ceremony

TANGIBLE adj able to be touched ▷ n tangible thing or asset

TANGIBLY

TANGIE, -S n water spirit of Orkney, appearing as a figure draped in seaweed, or as a seahorse

TANGIER ▶ **tangy**

TANGIES ▶ **tangie**

TANGIEST ▶ **tangy**

TANGING ▶ **tang**

TANGIS ▶ **tangi**

TANGLE, -D, -S n confused mass or situation ▷ vb twist together in a tangle

TANGLER -S

TANGLIER ▶ **tangly**

TANGLING n act or condition of tangling

TANGLY, TANGLIER ▶ **tangle**

TANGO, -ED, -ES, -ING, -S n S American dance ▷ vb dance a tango

TANGOIST

TANGRAM, -S n type of Chinese puzzle

TANGS ▶ **tang**

TANGUN, -S n small and sturdy Tibetan pony

T

TANGY, TANGIER, TANGIEST adj having a pungent, fresh, or briny flavour or aroma

TANH, -S n hyperbolic tangent

TANIST, -S n heir apparent of a Celtic chieftain

TANISTRY

TANIWHA, -S n mythical Māori monster that lives in water

TANK, -ED, -S n container for liquids or gases ▷ vb put or keep in a tank

TANKA, -S n Japanese verse form consisting of five lines

TANKAGE, -S n capacity or contents of a tank or tanks

TANKARD, -S n large beer-mug, often with a hinged lid

TANKAS ▸ tanka

TANKED ▸ tank

TANKER, -ED, -S n ship or truck for carrying liquid in bulk ▷ vb transport by means of a tanker

TANKFUL, -S n quantity contained in a tank

TANKIA, -S n type of boat used in Canton

TANKIES ▸ tanky

TANKING, -S n heavy defeat

TANKINI, -S n swimming costume consisting of a camisole top and bikini briefs

TANKLESS ▸ tank

TANKLIKE ▸ tank

TANKS ▸ tank

TANKSHIP same as ▸ tanker

TANKY, TANKIES n die-hard communist

TANLING, -S n suntanned person

TANNA, -S n Indian police station or army base

TANNABLE ▸ tan

TANNAGE, -S n act or process of tanning

TANNAH, -S same as ▸ tanna

TANNAS ▸ tanna

TANNATE, -S n any salt or ester of tannic acid

TANNED ▸ tan

TANNER, -S ▸ tan

TANNERY n place where hides are tanned

TANNEST ▸ tan

TANNIC adj of, containing, or produced from tannin or tannic acid

TANNIE, -S n in S Africa, title of respect used to refer to an elderly woman

TANNIN, -S n vegetable substance used in tanning

TANNING, -S ▸ tan

TANNINS ▸ tannin

TANNISH ▸ tan

TANNOY, -ED, -S n sound-amplifying apparatus used as a public-address system ▷ vb announce (something) using a Tannoy system

TANREC, -S same as ▸ tenrec

TANS ▸ tan

TANSY, TANSIES n yellow-flowered plant

TANTALIC adj of or containing tantalum, esp in the pentavalent state

TANTALUM n hard greyish-white metallic element

TANTALUS n case in which bottles of drink are locked with their contents tantalizingly visible

TANTARA, -S n blast, as on a trumpet or horn

TANTI adj old word for worthwhile

TANTIVY adv at full speed ▷ interj hunting cry, esp at full gallop

TANTO, -S adv too much ▷ n type of Japanese sword

TANTONY n runt

TANTOS ▸ tanto

TANTRA, -S n sacred books of Tantrism

TANTRIC

TANTRISM n teaching of tantra

TANTRIST n person who practises or teaches tantrism

TANTRUM, -S n childish outburst of temper

TANUKI, -S n animal similar to a raccoon, found in Japan

TANYARD, -S n part of a tannery

TAO, -S n (in Confucian philosophy) the correct course of action

TAONGA, -S n treasure

TAOS ▸ tao

TAP, -PED, -PING, -PINGS, -S vb knock lightly and usu repeatedly ▷ n light knock

TAPA n inner bark of the paper mulberry

TAPACOLO n small bird of Chile and Argentina

TAPACULO same as ▸ tapacolo

TAPADERA n leather covering for the stirrup on an American saddle

TAPADERO same as ▸ tapadera

TAPALO, -S n Latin American scarf, often patterned and brightly coloured

TAPAS pl n (in Spanish cookery) light snacks or appetizers

TAPE, -D, -S n narrow long strip of material ▷ vb (formerly) record on magnetic tape

TAPEABLE

TAPELESS

TAPELIKE

TAPELINE n tape used for measuring and fitting garments

TAPEN adj made of tape

TAPENADE n savoury paste made from capers, olives, and anchovies, with olive oil and lemon juice

TAPER, -ED, -S ▸ tape

TAPERER, -S ▸ tape

TAPERING ▸ tape

TAPERS ▸ taper

TAPES ▸ tape

TAPESTRY n fabric decorated with coloured woven designs ▷ vb portray in tapestry

TAPET, -ED, -ING, -S n example of tapestry ▷ vb decorate with tapestries

TAPETA ▸ tapetum

TAPETAL ▸ tapetum

TAPETED ▸ tapet

TAPETI, -S n forest rabbit of Brazil

TAPETING ▸ tapet

TAPETIS ▸ tapeti

TAPETS ▸ tapet

TAPETUM, TAPETA, -S n layer of nutritive cells that surrounds developing spore cells

TAPEWORM n long flat parasitic worm living in the intestines of vertebrates

TAPHOLE, -S n hole in a furnace for running off molten metal or slag

TAPHOUSE n inn or bar

TAPING, -S n act of taping

TAPIOCA, -S n beadlike starch made from cassava root

TAPIR, -S n piglike mammal of tropical America and SE Asia, with a long snout

TAPIROID

TAPIS, -ES n tapestry or carpeting

TAPIST, -S n person who records printed matter in an audio format

TAPLASH n dregs of beer

TAPLESS adj without a tap

TAPPA, -S same as ▸ tapa

TAPPABLE ▸ tap

TAPPAS ▸ tappa

TAPPED ▸ tap

TAPPER, -S n person who taps

TAPPET, -S n short steel rod in an engine, transferring motion from one part to another

TAPPICE, -D, -S vb hide

TAPPING ▸ tap

TAPPINGS ▸ tap

TAPPIT adj crested; topped

TAPROOM, -S n public bar in a hotel or pub

TAPROOT, -S n main root of a plant, growing straight down

TAPS ▸ tap

TAPSMAN, TAPSMEN n old word for a barman

TAPSTER, -S n barman

TAPSTRY adj relating to tapestry ▹ n taproom in a public house

TAPU, -ED, -ING, -S adj sacred ▹ n Māori religious or superstitious restriction on something ▹ vb put a tapu on something

TAQUERIA n restaurant specializing in tacos

TAR, -RED, -RING, -RINGS, -S n thick black liquid distilled from coal etc ▹ vb coat with tar

TARA, -S same as ▸ **taro**

TARABISH n type of card game

TARAIRE, -S n type of New Zealand tree

TARAKIHI n common edible sea fish of New Zealand waters

TARAMA, -S n cod roe

TARAMEA, -S n variety of New Zealand speargrass

TARAND, -S n northern animal of legend, now supposed to have been the reindeer

TARANTAS same as > **tarantass**

TARAS ▸ tara

TARBOOSH n brimless cap formerly worn by Muslim men

TARBOUSH same as ▸ **tarboosh**

TARBOY, -S n boy who applies tar to the skin of sheep cut during shearing

TARBUSH same as ▸ **tarboosh**

TARCEL, -S same as ▸ **tercel**

TARDIED ▸ tardy

TARDIER ▸ tardy

TARDIES ▸ tardy

TARDIEST ▸ tardy

TARDILY ▸ tardy

TARDIVE adj tending to develop late

TARDO adj (of music) slow; to be played slowly

TARDY, TARDIED, TARDIER, TARDIES, TARDIEST, -ING adj slow or late ▹ vb delay or impede (something or someone)

TARDYON, -S n particle travelling slower than the speed of light

TARE, -D, -S, TARING, TARINGS n weight of the wrapping or container of goods ▹ vb weigh (a package, etc) in order to calculate the amount of tare

TARGA, -S n as in **targa top** denotes removable hard roof on a car

TARGE, -D, -S, TARGING vb interrogate

TARGET, -ED, -S n object or person a missile is aimed at ▹ vb aim or direct

TARGING ▸ targe

TARIFF, -ED, -S n tax levied on imports ▹ vb impose punishment for a criminal offence

TARING ▸ tare

TARINGS ▸ tare

TARLATAN n open-weave cotton fabric, used for stiffening garments

TARLETAN same as ▸ **tarlatan**

TARMAC, -S See also ▸ **macadam**

TARN, -S n small mountain lake

TARNAL adj damned ▹ adv extremely

TARNALLY

TARNISH vb make or become stained or less bright ▹ n discoloration or blemish

TARNS ▸ tarn

TARO, -S n plant with a large edible rootstock

TAROC, -S old variant of ▸ **tarot**

TAROK, -S old variant of ▸ **tarot**

TAROS ▸ taro

TAROT, -S n special pack of cards used mainly in fortune-telling ▹ adj relating to tarot cards

TARP, -S informal word for > **tarpaulin**

TARPAN, -S n European wild horse common in prehistoric times

TARPAPER n paper coated or impregnated with tar

TARPON, -S n large silvery clupeoid game fish found in warm Atlantic waters

TARPS ▸ tarp

TARRAGON n aromatic herb

TARRAS, -ES same as ▸ **trass**

TARRE, -S vb old word meaning to provoke or goad

TARRED ▸ tar

TARRES ▸ tarre

TARRIED ▸ tarry

TARRIER, -S ▸ tarry

TARRIES ▸ tarry

TARRIEST ▸ tarry

TARRING ▸ tar

TARRINGS ▸ tar

TARROCK, -S n seabird

TARROW, -ED, -S vb exhibit reluctance

TARRY, TARRIED, TARRIES, TARRIEST, -ING vb linger or delay ▹ n stay ▹ adj covered in or resembling tar

TARS ▸ tar

TARSAL, -S adj of the tarsus or tarsi ▹ n tarsal bone

TARSEAL, -S n bitumen surface of a road

TARSEL, -S same as ▸ **tercel**

TARSI ▸ tarsus

TARSIA, -S another term for ▸ **intarsia**

TARSIER, -S n small nocturnal primate of the E Indies, which has very large eyes

TARSIOID adj resembling a tarsier ▹ n type of fossil

TARSIPED n generic term for a number of marsupials

TARSUS, TARSI n bones of the heel and ankle collectively

TART, -ED, -ER, -EST, -ING, -S n pie or flan with a sweet filling ▹ adj sharp or bitter ▹ adj (of a flavour, food, etc) sour, acid, or astringent ▹ vb (of food, drink, etc) become tart (sour)

TARTAN, -S n design of straight lines crossing at right angles

TARTANA, -S n small Mediterranean sailing boat

TARTANE, -S same as ▸ **tartana**

TARTANED ▸ tartan

TARTANES ▸ tartane

TARTANRY n excessive use of Scottish imagery to produce a distorted sentimental view of Scotland

TARTANS ▸ tartan

TARTAR, -S n hard deposit on the teeth

T

TARTARE, -S *n* mayonnaise sauce mixed with hard-boiled egg yolks, herbs, etc

TARTARIC *adj* of or derived from tartar or tartaric acid

TARTARLY *adj* resembling a tartar

TARTARS ► tartar

TARTED ► tart

TARTER ► tart

TARTEST ► tart

TARTINE, -S *n* slice of bread with butter or jam spread on it

TARTING ► tart

TARTISH ► tart

TARTLET, -S *n* individual pastry case with a filling of fruit or other sweet or savoury mixture

TARTLY ► tart

TARTNESS ► tart

TARTRATE *n* any salt or ester of tartaric acid

TARTS ► tart

TARTUFE, -S *same as* **► tartuffe**

TARTUFFE *n* person who hypocritically pretends to be deeply pious

TARTUFO, TARTUFI, -S *n* Italian mousse-like chocolate dessert

TARWEED, -S *n* resinous Californian plant

TARWHINE *n* bream of E Australia, silver in colour with gold streaks

TARZAN, -S *n* man with great physical strength

TAS ► ta

TASAR, -S *same as* **► tussore**

TASBIH, -S *n* form of Islamic prayer

TASE, -D, -S, TASING *vb* stun with a taser gun

TASER, -ED, -ING, -S *vb* use a taser stun gun on (someone)

TASES ► tase

TASH, -ED, -ES, -ING *vb* stain or besmirch

TASING ► tase

TASK, -ED, -ING, -INGS, -S *n* piece of work to be done ▷ *vb* give someone a task to do

TASKBAR, -S *n* area of computer screen showing what programs are running

TASKED ► task

TASKER, -S ► task

TASKING ► task

TASKINGS ► task

TASKLESS ► task

TASKS ► task

TASKWORK *n* hard or unpleasant work

TASLET, -S *same as* **► tasset**

TASS *n* cup, goblet, or glass

TASSA, -S *n* type of Indian kettledrum

TASSE, -S *same as* **► tasset**

TASSEL, -ED, -S *n* decorative fringed knot of threads ▷ *vb* adorn with a tassel or tassels

TASSELL, -S *same as* **► tassel**

TASSELLY ► tassel

TASSELS ► tassel

TASSES ► tasse

TASSET, -S *n* piece of armour to protect the thigh

TASSIE, -S *same as* **► tass**

TASSO, -S *n* spicy cured pork cut into strips

TASSWAGE *vb* assuage

TASTABLE ► taste

TASTE, -D, -S, TASTING, TASTINGS *n* sense by which the flavour of a substance is distinguished ▷ *vb* distinguish the taste of (a substance)

TASTEFUL *adj* having or showing good taste

TASTER, -S *n* person employed to test the quality of food or drink by tasting it

TASTES ► taste

TASTEVIN *n* small shallow cup for wine tasting

TASTIER ► tasty

TASTIEST ► tasty

TASTILY ► tasty

TASTING ► taste

TASTINGS ► taste

TASTY, TASTIER, TASTIEST *adj* pleasantly flavoured

TAT, -S, -TED *n* tatty or tasteless article(s) ▷ *vb* make (something) by tatting

TATAHASH *n* stew containing potatoes and cheap cuts of meat

TATAMI, -S *n* thick rectangular mat of woven straw

TATAR, -S *n* brutal person

TATE, -S *n* small tuft of fibre

TATER, -S *n* potato

TATES ► tate

TATH, -ED, -ING, -S *vb* (of cattle) to defecate

TATHATA, -S *n* (in Buddhism) ultimate nature of things

TATHED ► tath

TATHING ► tath

TATHS ► tath

TATIE, -S *same as* **► tattie**

TATLER, -S *old variant of* **► tattler**

TATOU, -S *n* armadillo

TATOUAY, -S *n* large armadillo of South America

TATOUS ► tatou

TATS ► tat

TATSOI, -S *n* variety of Chinese cabbage

TATT, -S *same as* **► tat**

TATTED ► tat

TATTER, -ED, -S *vb* make or become torn

TATTERY *same as* **► tattered**

TATTIE, -S *Scot or dialect word for* **► potato**

TATTIER ► tatty

TATTIES ► tattie

TATTIEST ► tatty

TATTILY ► tatty

TATTING, -S ► tat

TATTLE, -D, -S, TATTLING *n* gossip or chatter ▷ *vb* gossip or chatter

TATTLER, -S *n* person who tattles

TATTLES ► tattle

TATTLING ► tattle

TATTOO, -ED, -S *n* pattern made on the body by pricking the skin and staining it with indelible inks ▷ *vb* make such a pattern on the skin

TATTOOER

TATTOW, -ED, -S *old variant of* **► tattoo**

TATTS ► tatt

TATTY, TATTIER, TATTIEST *adj* worn out, shabby, tawdry, or unkempt

TATU, -ED, -ING, -S *old variant of* **► tattoo**

TAU, -S *n* 19th letter in the Greek alphabet

TAUBE, -S *n* type of obsolete German aeroplane

TAUGHT ► teach

TAUHINU, -S *New Zealand name for* **► poplar**

TAUHOU, -S *same as* **> silvereye**

TAUIWI, -S *n* Māori term for the non-Māori people of New Zealand

TAULD *vb* old Scots variant of told

TAUNT, -ED, -S *vb* tease with jeers ▷ *n* jeering remark ▷ *adj* (of the mast or masts of a sailing vessel) unusually tall

TAUNTER -S

TAUNTING ► taunt

TAUNTS ► taunt

TAUON, -S *n* negatively charged elementary particle

TAUPATA, -S *n* New Zealand shrub or tree

TAUPE, -S *adj* brownish-grey ▷ *n* brownish-grey colour

TAUPIE, -S *same as* **► tawpie**

TAUREAN adj born under or characteristic of Taurus

TAURIC same as ▸ taurean

TAURINE, -S adj of, relating to, or resembling a bull ▷ n substance obtained from the bile of animals

TAUS ▸ tau

TAUT, -ED, -ER, -EST, -ING, -S adj drawn tight ▷ vb Scots word meaning to tangle

TAUTAUG, -S same as ▸ tautog

TAUTED ▸ taut

TAUTEN, -ED, -S vb make or become taut

TAUTER ▸ taut

TAUTEST ▸ taut

TAUTING ▸ taut

TAUTIT adj Scots word meaning tangled

TAUTLY ▸ taut

TAUTNESS ▸ taut

TAUTOG, -S n large dark-coloured wrasse, used as a food fish

TAUTOMER n either of the two forms of a chemical compound that exhibits tautomerism

TAUTONYM n taxonomic name in which the generic and specific components are the same

TAUTS ▸ taut

TAV, -S n 23rd and last letter in the Hebrew alphabet

TAVA, -S n thick Indian frying pan

TAVAH, -S variant of ▸ tava

TAVAS ▸ tava

TAVER, -ED, -ING, -S vb wander about

TAVERN, -S n pub

TAVERNA, -S n Greek restaurant

TAVERNER n keeper of a tavern

TAVERNS ▸ tavern

TAVERS ▸ taver

TAVERT adj bewildered or confused

TAVS ▸ tav

TAW, -ED, -ING, -INGS vb convert skins into leather

TAWA, -S n tall timber tree from New Zealand

TAWAI, -S n New Zealand beech

TAWAS ▸ tawa

TAWDRIER ▸ tawdry

TAWDRIES ▸ tawdry

TAWDRILY ▸ tawdry

TAWDRY, TAWDRIER, TAWDRIES adj cheap, showy, and of poor quality

▷ n gaudy finery of poor quality

TAWED ▸ taw

TAWER, -S ▸ taw

TAWERIES ▸ tawery

TAWERS ▸ tawer

TAWERY, TAWERIES n place where tawing is carried out

TAWHAI, -S same as ▸ tawai

TAWHIRI, -S n small New Zealand tree with wavy green glossy leaves

TAWIE, -R, -ST adj easily persuaded or managed

TAWING ▸ taw

TAWINGS ▸ taw

TAWNEY, -S same as ▸ tawny

TAWNIER ▸ tawny

TAWNIES ▸ tawny

TAWNIEST ▸ tawny

TAWNILY ▸ tawny

TAWNY, TAWNIER, TAWNIES, TAWNIEST adj yellowish-brown ▷ n light brown to brownish-orange colour

TAWPIE, -S n foolish or maladroit girl

TAWS same as ▸ tawse

TAWSE, -D, -S, TAWSING n leather strap with one end cut into thongs ▷ vb punish (someone) with or as if with a tawse

TAWT, -ED, -IER, -IEST, -ING, -S same as ▸ taut

TAWTIE

TAX, -ED, -ES, -INGS n compulsory payment levied by a government on income, property, etc to raise revenue ▷ vb levy a tax on

TAXA ▸ taxon

TAXABLE, -S adj capable of being taxed ▷ n person, income, property, etc, that is subject to tax

TAXABLY

TAXATION n levying of taxes

TAXATIVE

TAXED ▸ tax

TAXEME, -S n any element of speech that may differentiate meaning

TAXEMIC

TAXER, -S ▸ tax

TAXES ▸ tax

TAXI, -ED, -ES, -ING, TAXIING n car with a driver that may be hired ▷ vb (of an aircraft) run along the ground

TAXIARCH n soldier in charge of a Greek taxis

TAXICAB, -S same as ▸ taxi

TAXIED ▸ taxi

TAXIES ▸ taxi

TAXIING ▸ taxi

TAXIMAN, TAXIMEN n taxi driver

TAXING adj demanding, onerous

TAXINGLY

TAXINGS ▸ tax

TAXIS, -ES n movement of a cell or organism in response to an external stimulus ▷ n ancient Greek army unit

TAXITE, -S n type of volcanic rock

TAXITIC

TAXIWAY, -S n marked path along which aircraft taxi to or from a runway, parking area, etc

TAXLESS ▸ tax

TAXMAN, TAXMEN n collector of taxes

TAXOL, -S n trademarked anti-cancer drug

TAXON, TAXA, -S n any taxonomic group or rank

TAXONOMY n classification of plants and animals into groups

TAXONS ▸ taxon

TAXOR, -S ▸ tax

TAXPAID adj having had the applicable tax paid already

TAXPAYER n person or organization that pays taxes

TAXUS n genus of conifers

TAXWISE adv regarding tax

TAXYING ▸ taxi

TAY, -S n Irish dialect word for ▸ tea

TAYBERRY n hybrid shrub produced by crossing a blackberry, raspberry, and loganberry

TAYRA, -S n large arboreal mammal of Central and South America

TAYS ▸ tay

TAZZA, -S, TAZZE n cup with a shallow bowl and a circular foot

TCHICK, -ED, -S vb make a clicking noise with the tongue

TE, -S n (in tonic sol-fa) seventh degree of any major scale

TEA, -ED, -ING, -S n drink made from infusing the dried leaves of an Asian bush in boiling water ▷ vb take tea

TEABAG, -S n porous bag of tea leaves for infusion

TEABERRY n berry of the wintergreen

TEABOARD n tea tray

T

TEABOWL, -S *n* small bowl used (instead of a teacup) for serving tea

TEABOX, -ES *n* box for storing tea

TEABREAD *n* loaf-shaped cake with dried fruit which has been steeped in tea before baking

TEACAKE, -S *n* flat bun, usually eaten toasted and buttered

TEACART, -S *n* trolley from which tea is served

TEACH, TAUGHT, -ES, -ING *vb* tell or show (someone) how to do something

TEACHER, -S *n* person who teaches, esp in a school

TEACHES ► teach

TEACHIE *old form of* ► **tetchy**

TEACHING ► teach

TEACUP, -S *n* cup out of which tea may be drunk

TEAD, -S *old word for* ► **torch**

TEADE, -S *same as* ► **tead**

TEADS ► tead

TEAED ► tea

TEAGLE, -D, -S, TEAGLING *vb* raise or hoist using a tackle

TEAHOUSE *n* restaurant, esp in Japan or China, where tea and light refreshments are served

TEAING ► tea

TEAK, -S *n* very hard wood of an E Indian tree

TEAKWOOD *another word for* ► **teak**

TEAL, -S *n* kind of small duck

TEALIGHT *n* small candle

TEALIKE *adj* resembling tea

TEALS ► tea

TEAM, -ED, -S *n* group of people forming one side in a game ▷ *vb* make or cause to make a team

TEAMAKER *n* person or thing that makes tea

TEAMED ► team

TEAMER, -S ► team

TEAMING, -S ► team

TEAMMATE *n* fellow member of a team

TEAMS ► team

TEAMSTER *n* commercial vehicle driver

TEAMWISE *adv* in respect of a team; in the manner of a team

TEAMWORK *n* cooperative work by a team

TEAPOT, -S *n* container for making and serving tea

TEAPOY, -S *n* small table or stand with a tripod base

TEAR, -ED, -ING, -S, TORN *n* drop of fluid appearing in and falling from the eye ▷ *vb* rip a hole in ▷ *vb* shed tears

TEARABLE

TEARAWAY *n* wild or unruly person

TEARDOWN *n* demolition; disassembly

TEARDROP *same as* ► **tear**

TEARED ► tear

TEARER, -S ► tear

TEARFUL *adj* weeping or about to weep

TEARGAS *n* gas or vapour that makes the eyes smart and water ▷ *vb* deploy teargas against

TEARIER ► teary

TEARIEST ► teary

TEARILY ► teary

TEARING ► tear

TEARLESS ► tear

TEARLIKE *adj* like a tear

TEAROOM, -S *same as* ► **teashop**

TEARS ► tear

TEARY, TEARIER, TEARIEST *adj* characterized by, covered with, or secreting tears

TEAS ► tea

TEASABLE ► tease

TEASE, -D, -S *vb* make fun of (someone) in a provoking or playful way ▷ *n* person who teases

TEASEL, -ED, -S *n* plant with prickly leaves and flowers ▷ *vb* tease (a fabric)

TEASELER

TEASER, -S *n* annoying or difficult problem

TEASES ► tease

TEASHOP, -S *n* restaurant where tea and light refreshments are served

TEASING, -S ► tease

TEASPOON *n* small spoon for stirring tea

TEAT, -S *n* nipple of a breast or udder

TEATED

TEATIME, -S *n* late afternoon

TEATS ► teat

TEAWARE, -S *n* implements for brewing and serving tea

TEAZE, -D, -S, TEAZING *old variant of* ► **tease**

TEAZEL, -ED, -S *same as* ► **teasel**

TEAZES ► teaze

TEAZING ► teaze

TEAZLE, -D, -S, TEAZLING *same as* ► **teasel**

TEBBAD, -S *n* sandstorm

TEC, -S *short for* ► **detective**

TECH, -S *n* technical college

TECHED *adj* showing slight insanity

TECHIE, -S *n* person who is skilled in the use of technology ▷ *adj* relating to or skilled in the use of technology

TECHIER ► techy

TECHIES ► techie

TECHIEST ► techy

TECHILY ► techy

TECHNIC *another word for* ► **technique**

TECHNICS *n* study or theory of industry and industrial arts

TECHNO, -S *n* type of electronic dance music with a very fast beat

TECHNOID *n* technician

TECHNOS ► techno

TECHS ► tech

TECHY, TECHIER, TECHIEST *same as* ► **techie**

TECKEL, -S *n* dachshund

TECS ► tec

TECTA ► tectum

TECTAL ► tectum

TECTITE, -S *same as* ► **tektite**

TECTONIC *adj* denoting or relating to construction or building

TECTRIX *another name for* ► **covert**

TECTUM, TECTA, -S *n* any roof-like structure in the body

TED, -DED, -DING, -S *vb* shake out (hay), so as to dry it

TEDDER, -ED, -S *n* machine equipped with a series of small rotating forks for tedding hay

TEDDIE *same as* ► **teddy**

TEDDIES ► teddy

TEDDING ► ted

TEDDY, TEDDIES *n* teddy bear

TEDIER ► tedy

TEDIEST ► tedy

TEDIOUS *adj* causing fatigue or boredom

TEDISOME *old Scottish variant of* ► **tedious**

TEDIUM, -S *n* monotony

TEDS ► ted

TEDY, TEDIER, TEDIEST *same as* ► **tedious**

TEE, -D, -ING, -S *n* small peg from which a golf ball can be played at the start of each hole ▷ *vb* position (the ball) ready for striking, on or as if on a tee

TEEK *adj* in Indian English, well

TEEL, -S same as ▸ **sesame**

TEEM, -ED, -ING, -S vb be full of

TEEMER -S

TEEMFUL ▸ **teem**

TEEMING ▸ **teem**

TEEMLESS ▸ **teem**

TEEMS ▸ **teem**

TEEN, -ED, -ING, -S n affliction or woe ▷ n teenager ▷ vb set alight

TEENAGE, -S adj (of a person) aged between 13 and 19 ▷ n this period of time

TEENAGED adj (of a person) aged between 13 and 19

TEENAGER n person aged between 13 and 19

TEENAGES ▸ **teenage**

TEEND, -ED, -ING, -S same as ▸ **tind**

TEENDOM, -S n state of being a teenager

TEENDS ▸ **teend**

TEENE, -S same as ▸ **teen**

TEENED ▸ **teen**

TEENER, -S ▸ **teen**

TEENES ▸ **teene**

TEENFUL ▸ **teen**

TEENIER ▸ **teeny**

TEENIEST ▸ **teeny**

TEENING ▸ **teen**

TEENS ▸ **teen**

TEENSY, TEENSIER same as ▸ **teeny**

TEENTIER ▸ **teenty**

TEENTSY same as ▸ **teeny**

TEENTY, TEENTIER same as ▸ **teeny**

TEENY, TEENIER, TEENIEST adj extremely small

TEENYBOP adj of or relating to a young teenager who avidly follows fashions in music and clothes

TEEPEE, -S same as ▸ **tepee**

TEER, -ED, -ING, -S vb smear; daub

TEES ▸ **tee**

TEETER, -ED, -S vb wobble or move unsteadily

TEETH ▸ **tooth**

TEETHE, -D, -S, TEETHING vb (of a baby) grow his or her first teeth

TEETHER, -S n object for an infant to bite on during teething

TEETHES ▸ **teethe**

TEETHING ▸ **teethe**

TEETOTAL adj drinking no alcohol ▷ vb advocate total abstinence from alcohol

TEETOTUM n spinning top bearing letters of the alphabet on its four sides

TEEVEE, -S n television

TEF, -S n annual grass, of NE Africa, grown for its grain

TEFF, -S same as ▸ **tef**

TEFILLAH, TEFILLIN n either of the pair of blackened square cases worn by Jewish men during weekday morning prayers

TEFLON, -S n substance used in nonstick cooking vessels

TEFS ▸ **tef**

TEG, -S n two-year-old sheep

TEGG, -S same as ▸ **teg**

TEGMEN, TEGMINA n either of the leathery forewings of the cockroach and related insects

TEGMENTA > **tegmentum**

TEGMINA ▸ **tegmen**

TEGMINAL ▸ **tegmen**

TEGS ▸ **teg**

TEGU, -S n large South American lizard

TEGUA, -S n type of moccasin

TEGUEXIN same as ▸ **tegu**

TEGULA, -E n one of a pair of coverings of the forewings of certain insects

TEGULAR adj of, relating to, or resembling a tile or tiles

TEGUMEN, TEGUMINA same as ▸ **tegmen**

TEGUMENT n protective layer around an ovule

TEGUMINA ▸ **tegumen**

TEGUS ▸ **tegu**

TEHR, -S same as ▸ **tahr**

TEHSIL, -S n administrative region in some S Asian countries

TEIGLACH pl n morsels of dough boiled in honey, eaten as a dessert

TEIID, -S n member of the Teiidae family of lizards

TEIL, -S n lime tree

TEIN, -S n monetary unit of Kazakhstan

TEIND, -ED, -ING, -S Scot and northern English word for ▸ **tithe**

TEINS ▸ **tein**

TEKKIE, -S variant of ▸ **techie**

TEKTITE, -S n small dark glassy object found in several areas around the world

TEKTITIC

TEL, -S same as ▸ **tell**

TELA, -E n any delicate tissue or weblike structure

TELAMON, -S n column in the form of a male figure

TELARY adj capable of spinning a web

TELCO, -S n telecommunications company

TELD same as ▸ **tauld**

TELE, -S same as ▸ **telly**

TELECAST vb broadcast by television ▷ n television broadcast

TELECHIR n robot arm controlled by a human operator

TELECINE n apparatus for producing a television signal from cinematograph film

TELECOM n telecommunications

TELECOMM n telecommunication

TELECOMS same as ▸ **telecom**

TELECON, -S n (short for) teleconference

TELECOPY n message or document sent by fax

TELEDU, -S n badger of SE Asia and Indonesia

TELEFAX another word for ▸ **fax**

TELEFILM n TV movie

TELEGA, -S n rough four-wheeled cart used in Russia

TELEGONY n supposed influence of a previous sire on offspring borne by a female to other sires

TELEGRAM n formerly, a message sent by telegraph ▷ vb send a telegram

TELEMAN, TELEMEN n noncommissioned officer in the US navy

TELEMARK n turn in which one ski is placed far forward of the other and turned gradually inwards ▷ vb perform a telemark turn

TELEMEN ▸ **teleman**

TELEOST, -S n bony fish with rayed fins and a swim bladder ▷ adj of, relating to, or belonging to this type of fish

TELEPATH n person who is telepathic ▷ vb practise telepathy

TELEPIC, -S n feature-length film made for television

TELEPLAY n play written for television

TELEPORT vb (in science fiction) to transport (a person or object) across a distance instantaneously

TELERAN, -S n electronic navigational aid

TELERGIC ▸ **telergy**

T

TELERGY *n* name for the form of energy supposedly transferred during telepathy

TELES ► tele

TELESALE > telesales

TELESEME *n* old-fashioned electric signalling system

TELESES ► telesis

TELESHOP *vb* buy goods by telephone or internet

TELESIS, TELESES *n* purposeful use of natural and social processes to obtain specific social goals

TELESM, -S *n* talisman

TELESTIC *adj* relating to a hierophant

TELETEX *n* international means of communicating text between a variety of terminals

TELETEXT *n* system which shows information and news on television screens

TELETHON *n* lengthy television programme to raise charity funds, etc

TELETRON *n* system for showing enlarged televisual images in eg sports stadiums

TELETYPE *vb* send typed message by telegraph

TELEVIEW *vb* watch television

TELEVISE *vb* broadcast on television

TELEWORK *vb* work from home, communicating by computer, telephone etc

TELEX, -ED, -ES, -ING *n* (formerly) international communication service using teleprinters ▷ *vb* (formerly) transmit by telex

TELFER, -ED, -S *n* overhead transport system
TELFERIC

TELFORD, -S *n* road built using a method favoured by Thomas Telford

TELIA ► telium

TELIAL ► telium

TELIC *adj* directed or moving towards some goal

TELICITY *n* quality of being telic

TELIUM, TELIA *n* spore-producing body of some rust fungi in which the teliospores are formed

TELL, -ING, -INGS, -S, TOLD *vb* make known in words ▷ *n* large mound resulting from the accumulation of rubbish
TELLABLE

TELLAR, -ED, -S *same as* ► tiller

TELLEN, -S *same as* ► tellin

TELLER, -ED, -S *n* narrator ▷ *vb* (of a plant) to produce tillers

TELLIES ► telly

TELLIN, -S *n* slim marine bivalve molluscs that live in intertidal sand

TELLING ► tell

TELLINGS ► tell

TELLINS ► tellin

TELLS ► tell

TELLTALE *n* person who reveals secrets ▷ *adj* revealing

TELLURAL *adj* tellurial; of or relating to the earth

TELLURIC *adj* of, relating to, or originating on or in the earth or soil

TELLUS, -ES *n* earth

TELLY, TELLIES, -S *n* television

TELNET, -ED, -S *n* system allowing remote access to other computers on the same network ▷ *vb* use a telnet system

TELOI ► telos

TELOME, -S *n* fundamental unit of a plant's structure

TELOMERE *n* either of the ends of a chromosome

TELOMES ► telome

TELOMIC ► telome

TELOS, TELOI *n* objective; ultimate purpose

TELPHER, -S *same as* > telferage

TELS ► tel

TELSON, -S *n* segment of the body of crustaceans and arachnids
TELSONIC

TELT *same as* ► tauld

TEMBLOR, -S *n* earthquake or earth tremor

TEME, -D, -S *old variant of* ► team

TEMENOS, TEMENE *n* sacred area, esp one surrounding a temple

TEMERITY *n* boldness or audacity
TEMEROUS

TEMES ► teme

TEMP, -ED, -S *same as* > temporary

TEMPEH, -S *n* fermented soya beans

TEMPER, -S *n* outburst of anger ▷ *vb* make less extreme

TEMPERA, -S *n* painting medium for powdered pigments

TEMPERED *adj* having the frequency differences between notes adjusted in accordance with the system of equal temperament

TEMPERER ► temper

TEMPERS ► temper

TEMPEST, -S *n* violent storm ▷ *vb* agitate or disturb violently

TEMPI ► tempo

TEMPING, -S *n* act of temping

TEMPLAR, -S *n* lawyer who has chambers in the Inner or Middle Temple in London

TEMPLATE *n* pattern used to cut out shapes accurately

TEMPLE, -S *n* building for worship
TEMPLED

TEMPLET, -S *same as* ► template

TEMPO, TEMPI, -S *n* rate or pace

TEMPORAL *adj* of time ▷ *n* any body part relating to or near the temple or temples

TEMPORE *adv* in the time of

TEMPOS ► tempo

TEMPS ► temp

TEMPT, -ED, -S *vb* entice (a person) to do something wrong
TEMPTER -S

TEMPTING *adj* attractive or inviting

TEMPTS ► tempt

TEMPURA, -S *n* Japanese dish of seafood or vegetables dipped in batter and deep-fried

TEMS *same as* ► temse

TEMSE, -D, -S, TEMSING *vb* sieve

TEMULENT > temulence

TEN, -S *n* one more than nine ▷ *adj* amounting to ten

TENABLE *adj* able to be upheld or maintained
TENABLY

TENACE, -S *n* holding of two nonconsecutive high cards of a suit, such as the ace and queen

TENACITY > tenacious

TENACULA > tenaculum

TENAIL, -S *same as* ► tenaille

TENAILLE *n* low outwork in the main ditch between two bastions

TENAILS ► tenail

TENANCY n temporary possession of property owned by somebody else

TENANT, -ED, -S n person who rents land or a building ▷ vb hold (land or property) as a tenant

TENANTRY n tenants collectively

TENANTS ▶ tenant

TENCH, -ES n freshwater game fish of the carp family

TEND, -ED, -ING, -S vb be inclined

TENDANCE n care and attention

TENDED ▶ tend

TENDENCE same as ▶ tendency

TENDENCY n inclination to act in a certain way

TENDENZ same as ▶ tendency

TENDER, -ED, -S adj not tough ▷ vb offer ▷ n such an offer

TENDERER

TENDERLY

TENDING ▶ tend

TENDON, -S n strong tissue attaching a muscle to a bone

TENDRE, -S n care

TENDRIL, -S n slender stem by which a climbing plant clings

TENDRON, -S n shoot

TENDS ▶ tend

TENDU, -S n position in ballet

TENE, -S same as ▶ teen

TENEBRAE n darkness

TENEBRIO n type of small mealworm

TENEMENT n (esp in Scotland or the US) building divided into several flats

TENENDUM n part of a deed that specifies the terms of tenure

TENES ▶ tene

TENESI n monetary unit of Turkmenistan

TENESMIC ▶ tenesmus

TENESMUS n bowel disorder

TENET, -S n doctrine or belief

TENFOLD, -S n one tenth

TENGE, -S n standard monetary unit of Kazakhstan

TENIA, -E, -S same as ▶ taenia

TENIASIS, TENIASES same as > taeniasis

TENIOID ▶ tenia

TENNE, -S n tawny colour

TENNER, -S n ten-pound note

TENNES ▶ tenne

TENNESI same as ▶ tenesi

TENNIES ▶ tenny

TENNIS, -ES n game in which players use rackets to hit a ball back and forth over a net

TENNIST, -S n tennis player

TENNO, -S n formal title of the Japanese emperor

TENNY, TENNIES same as ▶ tenne

TENON, -ED, -ING, -S n projecting end on a piece of wood fitting into a slot in another ▷ vb form a tenon on (a piece of wood)

TENONER -S

TENOR, -S n (singer with) the second highest male voice ▷ adj (of a voice or instrument) between alto and baritone

TENORINO, TENORINI n high tenor

TENORIST n musician playing any tenor instrument

TENORITE n black mineral found in copper deposits

TENORMAN, TENORMEN n person who plays tenor saxophone

TENOROON n tenor bassoon

TENORS ▶ tenor

TENOTOMY n surgical division of a tendon

TENOUR, -S old variant of ▶ tenor

TENPENCE n sum of money equivalent to ten pennies

TENPENNY adj (of a nail) three inches in length

TENPIN, -S n one of the pins used in tenpin bowling

TENREC, -S n small mammal resembling hedgehogs or shrews

TENS ▶ ten

TENSE, -D, -R, -S, -ST, TENSING adj emotionally strained ▷ vb make or become tense ▷ n form of a verb showing the time of action

TENSELY

TENSIBLE adj capable of being stretched

TENSIBLY

TENSILE adj of tension

TENSING ▶ tense

TENSION, -S n hostility or suspense ▷ vb tighten

TENSITY rare word for ▶ tension

TENSIVE adj of or causing tension or strain

TENSON, -S n type of French lyric poem

TENSOR, -S n any muscle that can cause a part to become firm or tense

TENT, -ING, -INGS, -S n portable canvas shelter ▷ vb camp in a tent

TENTACLE n flexible organ of many invertebrates, used for grasping, feeding, etc

TENTAGE, -S n tents collectively

TENTED ▶ tent

TENTER, -ED, -S ▶ tent

TENTFUL, -S n number of people or objects that can fit in a tent

TENTH, -S n number ten in a series ▷ adj coming after the ninth in numbering or counting order, position, time, etc ▷ adv after the ninth person, position, event, etc

TENTHLY same as ▶ tenth

TENTHS ▶ tenth

TENTIE, -R, -ST adj wary

TENTING ▶ tent

TENTINGS ▶ tent

TENTLESS ▶ tent

TENTLIKE ▶ tent

TENTORIA > tentorium

TENTPOLE n movie whose high earnings offset the cost of less profitable ones

TENTS ▶ tent

TENTWISE adv in the manner of a tent

TENTY same as ▶ tentie

TENUE n deportment

TENUES ▶ tenuis

TENUIOUS same as ▶ tenuous

TENUIS, TENUES n (in the grammar of classical Greek) any of the voiceless stops

TENUITY ▶ tenuous

TENUOUS adj slight or flimsy

TENURE, -S, TENURING n (period of) the holding of an office or position ▷ vb assign a tenured position to

TENURED adj having tenure of office

TENURES ▶ tenure

TENURIAL ▶ tenure

TENURING ▶ tenure

TENUTO, TENUTI, -S adv (of a note) to be held for or beyond its full time value ▷ vb note sustained thus

TENZON, -S same as ▶ tenson

TEOCALLI n any of various truncated pyramids built by the Aztecs as bases for their temples

T

TEOPAN, -S *n* enclosure surrounding a teocalli

TEOSINTE *n* tall Central American annual grass

TEPA, -S *n* type of tree native to South America

TEPACHE, -S *n* type of Mexican soft drink

TEPAL, -S *n* subdivisions of a perianth

TEPAS ▸ tepa

TEPEE, -S *n* cone-shaped tent, formerly used by Native Americans

TEPEFY, TEPEFIED, TEPEFIES *vb* make or become tepid

TEPHRA, -S *n* solid matter ejected during a volcanic eruption

TEPHRITE *n* variety of basalt

TEPID, -ER, -EST *adj* slightly warm

TEPIDITY

TEPIDLY

TEPOY, -S *same as* ▸ teapoy

TEQUILA, -S *n* Mexican alcoholic drink

TEQUILLA *same as* ▸ tequila

TERABYTE *n* large unit of computer memory

TERAFLOP *n* large unit of computer processing speed

TERAGLIN *n* edible marine fish of Australia which has fine scales and is blue in colour

TERAI, -S *n* felt hat with a wide brim worn in subtropical regions

TERAKIHI *same as* ▸ tarakihi

TERAOHM, -S *n* unit of resistance equal to 1012 ohms

TERAPH, -IM *n* household god or image venerated by ancient Semitic peoples

TERAS, TERATA *n* monstrosity; teratism

TERATISM *n* malformed animal or human, esp in the fetal stage

TERATOID *adj* resembling a monster

TERATOMA *n* tumour or group of tumours composed of tissue foreign to the site of growth

TERAWATT *n* unit of power equal to one million megawatts

TERBIA, -S *n* amorphous white insoluble powder

TERBIC ▸ terbium

TERBIUM, -S *n* rare metallic element

TERCE, -S *n* third of the seven canonical hours of the divine office

TERCEL, -S *n* male falcon or hawk, esp as used in falconry

TERCELET *same as* ▸ tercel

TERCELS ▸ tercel

TERCES ▸ terce

TERCET, -S *n* group of three lines of verse that rhyme together

TERCIO, -S *n* regiment of Spanish or Italian infantry

TEREBENE *n* mixture of hydrocarbons prepared from oil of turpentine and sulphuric acid

TEREBIC *adj* as in **terebic acid** white crystalline carboxylic acid produced by the action of nitric acid on turpentin

TEREBRA, -E, -S *n* ancient Roman device used for boring holes in defensive walls

TEREDO, -S *n* marine mollusc that bores into and destroys submerged timber

TEREFA *same as* ▸ tref

TEREFAH *same as* ▸ tref

TEREK, -S *n* type of sandpiper

TERES, -ES *n* shoulder muscle

TERETE, -S *adj* (esp of plant parts) smooth and usually cylindrical and tapering

TERF, -S *old variant of* ▸ turf

TERFE, -S *old variant of* ▸ turf

TERFS ▸ terf

TERGA ▸ tergum

TERGAL ▸ tergum

TERGITE, -S *n* constituent part of a tergum

TERGUM, TERGA *n* cuticular plate covering the dorsal surface of a body segment of an arthropod

TERIYAKI *adj* basted with soy sauce and rice wine and broiled over an open fire ▷ *n* dish prepared in this way

TERM, -ED, -ING, -S *n* word or expression ▷ *vb* name or designate

TERMER, -S *same as* ▸ termor

TERMINAL *adj* (of an illness) ending in death ▷ *n* place where people or vehicles begin or end a journey

TERMINER *n* person or thing that limits or determines

TERMING ▸ term

TERMINUS, TERMINI *n* railway or bus station at the end of a line

TERMITE, -S *n* white antlike insect that destroys timber

TERMITIC

TERMLESS *adj* without limit or boundary

TERMLY, TERMLIES *n* publication issued once a term

TERMOR, -S *n* person who holds an estate for a term of years or until he or she dies

TERMS ▸ term

TERMTIME *n* time during a term, esp a school or university term

TERN, -S *n* gull-like sea bird with a forked tail and pointed wings

TERNAL

TERNARY *adj* consisting of three parts ▷ *n* group of three

TERNATE *adj* (esp of a leaf) consisting of three leaflets or other parts

TERNE, -D, -S, TERNING *n* alloy of lead containing tin and antimony ▷ *vb* coat with this alloy

TERNION, -S *n* group of three

TERNS ▸ tern

TERPENE, -S *n* unsaturated hydrocarbon found in the essential oils of many plants

TERPENIC

TERPINOL *same as* > terpineol

TERRA, -E *n* (in legal contexts) earth or land

TERRACE, -D, -S *n* row of houses built as one block ▷ *vb* form into or provide with a terrace

TERRAE ▸ terra

TERRAIN, -S *same as* ▸ terrane

TERRANE, -S *n* series of rock formations

TERRAPIN *n* small turtle-like reptile

TERRARIA > terrarium

TERRAS, -ES *same as* ▸ trass

TERRASSE *n* paved area alongside a café

TERRAZZO *n* floor of marble chips set in mortar and polished

TERREEN, -S *old variant of* ▸ tureen

TERRELLA *n* magnetic globe designed to simulate and demonstrate the earth's magnetic fields

TERRENE, -S *adj* of or relating to the earth ▷ *n* land

TERRET, -S n ring on a harness saddle through which the reins are passed

TERRIBLE adj very serious ▷ n something terrible

TERRIBLY adv in a terrible manner

TERRIER, -S n any of various breeds of small active dog

TERRIES ► terry

TERRIFIC adj great or intense

TERRIFY vb fill with fear

TERRINE, -S n earthenware dish with a lid

TERRIT, -S same as ► terret

TERROIR, -S n combination of factors that gives a wine its distinctive character

TERROR, -S n great fear

TERRY, TERRIES n fabric with small loops covering both sides

TERSE, -R, -ST adj neat and concise

TERSELY

TERSION, -S n action of rubbing off or wiping

TERTIA, -S same as ► tercio

TERTIAL, -S same as ► tertiary

TERTIAN, -S adj (of a fever or the symptoms of a disease) occurring every other day ▷ n tertian fever or symptoms

TERTIARY adj third in degree, order, etc ▷ n any of the tertiary feathers

TERTIAS ► tertia

TERTIUM adj as in **tertium quid** unknown or indefinite thing related in some way to two known or definite things, but distinct from both

TERTIUS n third (in a group)

TERTS n card game using 32 cards

TERYLENE n tradename for a synthetic polyester fibre based on terephthalic acid

TERZETTA n tercet

TERZETTO, TERZETTI n trio, esp a vocal one

TES ► te

TESLA, -S n derived SI unit of magnetic flux density

TESSELLA n little tessera

TESSERA, -E n small square tile used in mosaics

TESSERAL

TEST, -ED, -S vb try out to ascertain the worth, capability, or endurance of ▷ n critical examination

TESTA, -E n hard outer layer of a seed

TESTABLE ► test

TESTACY ► testate

TESTAE ► testa

TESTAMUR n certificate proving an examination has been passed

TESTATE, -S adj having left a valid will ▷ n person who dies and leaves a legally valid will

TESTATOR n maker of a will

TESTATUM n part of a purchase deed

TESTE n witness

TESTED ► test

TESTEE, -S n person subjected to a test

TESTER, -S n person or thing that tests or is used for testing

TESTERN, -S vb give (someone) a teston

TESTERS ► tester

TESTES ► testis

TESTICLE n either of the two male reproductive glands

TESTIER ► testy

TESTIEST ► testy

TESTIFY vb give evidence under oath

TESTILY ► testy

TESTING, -S ► test

TESTIS, TESTES same as ► testicle

TESTON, -S n French silver coin of the 16th century

TESTOON, -S same as ► teston

TESTRIL, -S same as ► testrill

TESTRILL n sixpence

TESTRILS ► testril

TESTS ► test

TESTUDO, -S n protective cover used by the ancient Roman army

TESTY, TESTIER, TESTIEST adj irritable or touchy

TET, -S same as ► teth

TETANAL ► tetanus

TETANIC, -S adj of, relating to, or producing tetanus ▷ n tetanic drug or agent

TETANIES ► tetany

TETANISE same as ► tetanize

TETANIZE vb induce tetanus in (a muscle)

TETANOID ► tetanus

TETANUS n acute infectious disease producing muscular spasms and convulsions

TETANY, TETANIES n abnormal increase in the excitability of nerves and muscles

TETCHED same as ► teched

TETCHIER ► tetchy

TETCHILY ► tetchy

TETCHY, TETCHIER adj cross and irritable

TETE, -S n elaborate hairstyle

TETH, -S n ninth letter of the Hebrew alphabet

TETHER, -ED, -S n rope or chain for tying an animal to a spot ▷ vb tie up with rope

TETHS ► teth

TETOTUM, -S same as ► teetotum

TETRA, -S n brightly coloured tropical freshwater fish

TETRACID adj (of a base) capable of reacting with four molecules of a monobasic acid

TETRACT, -S n sponge spicule with four rays

TETRAD, -S n group or series of four

TETRADIC

TETRAGON n figure with four angles and four sides

TETRAMER n four-molecule polymer

TETRAPLA n book containing versions of the same text in four languages

TETRAPOD n any vertebrate that has four limbs

TETRARCH n ruler of one fourth of a country

TETRAS ► tetra

TETRAXON n four-pointed spicule

TETRI, -S n currency unit of Georgia

TETRODE, -S n electronic valve having four electrodes

TETRONAL n sedative drug

TETROSE, -S n type of sugar

TETROXID same as > tetroxide

TETRYL, -S n yellow crystalline explosive solid used in detonators

TETS ► tet

TETTER, -ED, -S n blister or pimple ▷ vb cause a tetter to erupt (on)

TETTIX, -ES n cicada

TEUCH, -ER, -EST Scots variant of ► tough

TEUCHAT, -S Scots variant of ► tewit

TEUCHER ► teuch

TEUCHEST ► teuch

TEUCHTER n in Scotland, derogatory word used by Lowlanders for a Highlander

TEUGH, -ER, -EST same as ► teuch

TEUGHLY

T

TEVATRON n machine used in nuclear research

TEW, -ED, -ING, -S vb work hard

TEWART, -S same as ▸ **tuart**

TEWED ▸ **tew**

TEWEL, -S n horse's rectum

TEWHIT, -S same as ▸ **tewit**

TEWING ▸ **tew**

TEWIT, -S n lapwing

TEWS ▸ **tew**

TEX, -ES n unit of weight used to measure yarn density

TEXAS, -ES n structure on the upper deck of a paddle-steamer

TEXES ▸ **tex**

TEXT, -ED, -ING, -S n main body of a book as distinct from illustrations etc ▷ vb send a text message to (someone)

TEXTBOOK n standard book on a particular subject ▷ adj perfect

TEXTED ▸ **text**

TEXTER, -S n person who communicates by text messaging

TEXTILE, -S n fabric or cloth, esp woven ▷ adj of (the making of) fabrics

TEXTING, -S ▸ **text**

TEXTISM, -S n word typically used in a text message

TEXTLESS ▸ **text**

TEXTONYM n one of two or more words that can be created by pressing the same combination of numbers on a mobile phone

TEXTS ▸ **text**

TEXTUAL adj of, based on, or relating to, a text or texts

TEXTUARY adj of, relating to, or contained in a text ▷ n textual critic

TEXTURAL ▸ **texture**

TEXTURE, -D, -S n structure, feel, or consistency ▷ vb give a distinctive texture to (something)

THACK, -ED, -ING, -S Scots word for ▸ **thatch**

THAE Scots word for ▸ **those**

THAGI, -S same as ▸ **thuggee**

THAIM Scots variant of ▸ **them**

THAIRM, -S n catgut

THALAMI ▸ **thalamus**

THALAMIC ▸ **thalamus**

THALAMUS, THALAMI n mass of grey matter at the base of the brain

THALE n as in **thale cress** cruciferous wall plant

THALER, -S n former German, Austrian, or Swiss silver coin

THALI, -S n meal consisting of several small dishes accompanied by rice, bread, etc

THALIAN adj of or relating to comedy

THALIS ▸ **thali**

THALLI ▸ **thallus**

THALLIC adj of or containing thallium

THALLINE ▸ **thallus**

THALLIUM n highly toxic metallic element

THALLOID ▸ **thallus**

THALLOUS adj of or containing thallium, esp in the monovalent state

THALLUS, THALLI n undifferentiated vegetative body of algae, fungi, and lichens

THALWEG, -S n longitudinal outline of a riverbed from source to mouth

THAN, -S prep used to introduce the second element of a comparison ▷ n old variant of "then" (that time)

THANA, -S same as ▸ **tana**

THANADAR same as ▸ **tanadar**

THANAGE, -S n state of being a thane

THANAH, -S same as ▸ **tana**

THANAS ▸ **thana**

THANATOS n Greek personification of death

THANE, -S n Anglo-Saxon or medieval Scottish nobleman

THANEDOM

THANG, -S n thing

THANGKA, -S n (in Tibetan Buddhism) a religious painting on a scroll

THANGS ▸ **thang**

THANK, -ED, -ING vb express gratitude

THANKEE interj thank you

THANKER, -S ▸ **thank**

THANKFUL adj grateful

THANKING ▸ **thank**

THANKIT adj as in **be thankit** thank God

THANKS pl n words of gratitude ▷ interj polite expression of gratitude

THANKYOU n conventional expression of gratitude

THANNA, -S same as ▸ **tana**

THANNAH, -S same as ▸ **tana**

THANNAS ▸ **thanna**

THANS ▸ **than**

THANX interj (coll.) thank you

THAR, -S same as ▸ **tahr**

THARM, -S n stomach

THARS ▸ **thar**

THAT pron used to refer to something already mentioned or familiar, or further away

THATAWAY adv that way

THATCH, -ED, -ES n roofing material of reeds or straw ▷ vb roof (a house) with reeds or straw

THATCHER

THATCHT old variant of ▸ **thatched**

THATCHY ▸ **thatch**

THATNESS n state or quality of being 'that'

THAW, -ED, -ING, -INGS, -S vb make or become unfrozen ▷ n thawing

THAWER -S

THAWIER ▸ **thawy**

THAWIEST ▸ **thawy**

THAWING ▸ **thaw**

THAWINGS ▸ **thaw**

THAWLESS ▸ **thaw**

THAWS ▸ **thaw**

THAWY, THAWIER, THAWIEST adj tending to thaw

THE determiner definite article, used before a noun

THEARCHY n rule or government by God or gods

THEATER, -S same as ▸ **theatre**

THEATRAL adj of or relating to the theatre

THEATRE, -S n place where plays etc are performed

THEATRIC adj of or relating to the theatre

THEAVE, -S n young ewe

THEBAINE n poisonous white crystalline alkaloid, found in opium but without opioid actions

THEBE, -S n inner satellite of Jupiter discovered in 1979

THECA, -E n enclosing organ, cell, or spore case

THECAL

THECATE

THEE, -D, -ING, -S pron refers to the person addressed ▷ vb use the word "thee"

THEEK, -ED, -ING, -S Scots variant of ▸ **thatch**

THEELIN, -S trade name for ▸ **estrone**

THEELOL, -S n estriol

THEES ▸ **thee**

THEFT, -S n act or an instance of stealing

THEGN, -S same as ► thane **THEGNLY**

THEIC, -S n person who drinks excessive amounts of tea

THEIN, -S old variant of ► thane

THEINE, -S another name for ► caffeine

THEINS ► thein

THEIR determiner of, belonging to, or associated in some way with them

THEIRS pron (thing or person) belonging to them

THEISM, -S n belief in a God or gods
THEIST -S
THEISTIC

THELF, THELVES n old contraction of "the element"

THELITIS n inflammation of the nipple

THELVES ► thelf

THEM pron refers to people or things other than the speaker or those addressed

THEMA, -TA n theme

THEMATIC adj of, relating to, or consisting of a theme or themes ▷ n thematic vowel

THEME, -D, -S, THEMING n main idea or subject being discussed ▷ vb design, decorate, arrange, etc, in accordance with a theme

THEMSELF pron reflexive form of one, whoever, anybody

THEN, -S adv at that time ▷ pron that time ▷ adj existing or functioning at that time ▷ n that time

THENAGE, -S old variant of ► thanage

THENAL adj of or relating to the thenar

THENAR, -S n palm of the hand ▷ adj of or relating to the palm or the region at the base of the thumb

THENCE adv from that place or time

THENS ► then

THEOCON, -S n person who believes that religion should play a greater role in politics

THEOCRAT > theocracy

THEODICY n branch of theology concerned with defending the attributes of God

THEOGONY n origin and descent of the gods

THEOLOG, -S same as > theologue

THEOLOGY n study of religions and religious beliefs

THEONOMY n state of being governed by God

THEORBO, -S n obsolete form of the lute, having two necks

THEOREM, -S n proposition that can be proved by reasoning

THEORIC, -S n theory; conjecture

THEORIES ► theory

THEORISE same as ► theorize

THEORIST n originator of a theory

THEORIZE vb form theories, speculate

THEORY, THEORIES n set of ideas to explain something

THEOSOPH n proponent of theosophy

THEOW, -S n slave in Anglo-Saxon Britain

THERAPY n curing treatment

THERBLIG n basic unit of work in an industrial process

THERE, -S adv in or to that place ▷ n that place

THEREAT adv at that point or time

THEREBY adv by that means

THEREFOR adv for this, that, or it

THEREIN adv in or into that place or thing

THEREMIN n musical instrument played by moving the hands through electromagnetic fields

THEREOF adv of or concerning that or it

THEREON archaic word for > thereupon

THEREOUT another word for > therefrom

THERES ► there

THERETO adv that or it

THERIAC, -S n ointment or potion used as an antidote to a poison

THERIACA same as ► theriac

THERIACS ► theriac

THERIAN, -S n animal of the class Theria, a subclass of mammals

THERM, -S n unit of measurement of heat ▷ n public bath

THERMAE pl n public baths or hot springs, esp in ancient Greece or Rome

THERMAL, -S adj of heat ▷ n rising current of warm air

THERME, -S old variant of ► therm

THERMEL, -S n type of thermometer using thermoelectric current

THERMES ► therme

THERMIC same as ► thermal

THERMION n electron or ion emitted by a body at high temperature

THERMIT, -S variant of ► thermite

THERMITE adj as in thermite process process for reducing metallic oxides

THERMITS ► thermit

THERMOS n trademark for a stoppered vacuum flask

THERMS ► therm

THEROID adj of, relating to, or resembling a beast

THEROPOD n bipedal carnivorous saurischian dinosaur with strong hind legs and grasping hands

THESAURI > thesaurus

THESE determiner form of this used before a plural noun

THESIS, THESES n written work submitted for a degree

THESP, -S short for ► thespian

THESPIAN adj of or relating to drama and the theatre ▷ n actor or actress

THESPS ► thesp

THETA, -S n eighth letter of the Greek alphabet

THETCH, -ED, -ES old variant spelling of ► thatch

THETE, -S n member of the lowest order of freeman in ancient Athens

THETHER old variant of ► thither

THETIC adj (in classical prosody) of, bearing, or relating to a metrical stress

THETICAL another word for ► thetic

THEURGIC ► theurgy

THEURGY n intervention of a divine or supernatural agency in the affairs of man

THEW, -ES, -S n muscle, esp if strong or well-developed

THEWED adj strong; muscular

THEWES ► thew

THEWIER ► thewy

THEWIEST ► thewy

THEWLESS ► thew

THEWS ► thew

THEWY, THEWIER, THEWIEST ► thew

THEY pron people or things other than the speaker or people addressed

T

THIAMIN, -S same as
► thiamine

THIAMINE n vitamin found
in the outer coat of rice and
other grains

THIAMINS ► thiamin

THIASUS n people gathered
to sing and dance in honour
of a god

THIAZIDE n diuretic drug

THIAZIN, -S same as
► thiazine

THIAZINE n organic
compound containing a ring
system composed of four
carbon atoms, a sulphur
atom, and a nitrogen atom

THIAZINS ► thiazin

THIAZOL, -S same as
► thiazole

THIAZOLE n colourless liquid
with a pungent smell

THIAZOLS ► thiazol

THIBET, -S n coloured woollen
cloth

THIBLE, -S n stick for stirring
porridge

**THICK, -ED, -ER, -EST, -ING,
-S** adj of great or specified
extent from one side to the
other ▷ vb thicken

THICKEN, -S vb make or
become thick or thicker

THICKER ► thick

THICKEST ► thick

THICKET, -S n dense growth
of small trees

THICKETY

THICKIE same as ► thicko

THICKIES ► thicky

THICKING ► thick

THICKISH ► thick

THICKLY ► thick

THICKO, -ES, -S n insulting
word for a stupid person

THICKS ► thick

THICKSET adj stocky in build

THICKY, THICKIES same as
► thicko

THIEF n person who steals

THIEVE, -D, -S vb steal

THIEVERY

THIEVING adj given to
stealing other people's
possessions

THIEVISH ► thief

THIG, -GING, -S vb beg

THIGGER -S

THIGGIT Scots inflection of
► thig

THIGH, -S n upper part of the
human leg

THIGHED adj having thighs

THIGHS ► thigh

THIGS ► thig

THILK pron that same

THILL, -S another word for
► shaft

THILLER, -S n horse that goes
between the thills of a cart

THILLS ► thill

THIMBLE, -D, -S n cap
protecting the end of the
finger when sewing ▷ vb use
a thimble

THIN, -NED, -NEST, -NING, -S
adj not thick ▷ vb make or
become thin ▷ adv in order
to produce something thin

THINCLAD n track-and-field
athlete

THINDOWN n reduction in
the amount of particles of
very high energy penetrating
the earth's atmosphere

THINE adj (something) of or
associated with you (thou)
▷ pron something belonging
to you (thou) ▷ determiner of,
belonging to, or associated in
some way with you (thou)

THING, -S n material object

THINGAMY n person or
thing the name of which is
unknown

THINGIER ► thingy

THINGIES ► thingy

THINGS ► thing

**THINGY, THINGIER,
THINGIES** adj existing in
reality; actual

THINK, -ING, -S vb consider,
judge, or believe

THINKER -S

THINLY ► thin

THINNED ► thin

THINNER, -S ► thin

THINNESS ► thin

THINNEST ► thin

THINNING ► thin

THINNISH ► thin

THINS ► thin

THIO adj of, or relating to,
sulphur

THIOL, -S n any of a class of
sulphur-containing organic
compounds

THIOLIC

THIONATE n any salt or ester
of thionic acid

THIONIC adj of, relating to, or
containing sulphur

THIONIN, -S same as
► thionine

THIONINE n crystalline
derivative of thiazine used
as a violet dye to stain
microscope specimens

THIONINS ► thionine

THIONYL, -S n the divalent
group SO

THIOPHEN n colourless liquid
heterocyclic compound
found in the benzene fraction
of coal tar

THIOPHIL adj having an
attraction to sulphur

THIOTEPA n drug used in
chemotherapy

THIOUREA n white water-
soluble crystalline substance
with a bitter taste

This word for a type of
chemical compound is a
good example of the kind of
vowel-rich 8-letter word
which takes a lot of practice
to spot in actual play but is
very likely to come up. Good
players spend a lot of time
mastering these!

THIR Scots word for ► these

THIRAM, -S n antifungal
agent

THIRD, -ED, -ING, -S adj of
number three in a series
▷ n one of three equal parts
▷ adv in the third place ▷ vb
divide (something) by three

THIRDLY

THIRL, -ED, -ING, -S vb bore
or drill

THIRLAGE n obligation
imposed upon tenants
requiring them to have their
grain ground at a specified
mill

THIRLED ► thirl

THIRLING ► thirl

THIRLS ► thirl

THIRST, -ED, -ER, -S n desire
to drink ▷ vb feel thirst

THIRSTY adj feeling a desire
to drink

THIRTEEN n three plus ten
▷ adj amounting to thirteen
▷ determiner amounting to
thirteen

THIRTY, THIRTIES n three
times ten ▷ adj amounting
to thirty ▷ determiner
amounting to thirty

THIS pron used to refer to a
thing or person nearby, just
mentioned, or about to be
mentioned ▷ adj used to
refer to the present time

THISAWAY adv this way

THISNESS n state or quality of
being this

THISTLE, -S n prickly plant
with dense flower heads

THISTLY

THITHER adv or towards that
place

THIVEL, -S same as ► thible

THLIPSIS, THLIPSES *n* compression, esp of part of the body

THO *short for* ▸ **though**

THOFT, -S *n* bench (in a boat) upon which a rower sits

THOLE, -D, -S, THOLING *n* wooden pin set in the side of a rowing boat to serve as a fulcrum for rowing ▷ *vb* bear or put up with

THOLEPIN *same as* ▸ **thole**

THOLES ▸ **thole**

THOLI ▸ **tholus**

THOLING ▸ **thole**

THOLOS, THOLOI *n* beehive-shaped tomb associated with Mycenaean Greece

THOLUS, THOLI *n* domed tomb

THON *Scot word for* ▸ **yon**

THONDER *Scot word for* ▸ **yonder**

THONG, -ING, -S *n* thin strip of leather etc ▷ *vb* decorate with a thong or thongs

THONGED *adj* fastened with a thong

THONGIER ▸ **thongy**

THONGING ▸ **thong**

THONGS ▸ **thong**

THONGY, THONGIER *adj* resembling a thong

THORACAL *another word for* ▸ **thoracic**

THORACES ▸ **thorax**

THORACIC *adj* of, near, or relating to the thorax

THORAX, THORACES, -ES *n* part of the body between the neck and the abdomen

THORIA, -S *n* insoluble white powder

THORIC ▸ **thorium**

THORITE, -S *n* yellow, brownish, or black radioactive mineral

THORIUM, -S *n* radioactive metallic element

THORN, -ED, -ING, -S *n* prickle on a plant ▷ *vb* jag or prick (something) as if with a thorn

THORNIER ▸ **thorny**

THORNILY ▸ **thorny**

THORNING ▸ **thorn**

THORNS ▸ **thorn**

THORNSET *adj* set with thorns

THORNY, THORNIER *adj* covered with thorns

THORO (*nonstandard*) *variant spelling of* ▸ **thorough**

THORON, -S *n* radioisotope of radon that is a decay product of thorium

THOROUGH *adj* complete ▷ *n* passage

THORP, -S *n* small village

THORPE, -S *same as* ▸ **thorp**

THORPS ▸ **thorp**

THOSE *determiner* form of that used before a plural noun

THOTHER *pron* old contraction of *the other*

THOU, -ED, -ING, -S *pron* used when talking to one person ▷ *n* one thousandth of an inch ▷ *vb* use the word *thou*

THOUGH *adv* nevertheless

THOUGHT, -S ▸ **think**

THOUING ▸ **thou**

THOUS ▸ **thou**

THOUSAND *n* ten hundred ▷ *adj* amounting to a thousand ▷ *determiner* amounting to a thousand

THOWEL, -S *old variant of* ▸ **thole**

THOWL, -S *old variant of* ▸ **thole**

THOWLESS *adj* lacking in vigour

THOWLS ▸ **thowl**

THRAE *same as* ▸ **frae**

THRALDOM *same as* ▸ **thrall**

THRALL, -ED, -S *n* state of being in the power of another person ▷ *vb* enslave or dominate

THRANG, -ED, -S *n* throng ▷ *vb* throng ▷ *adj* crowded

THRAPPLE *n* throat or windpipe ▷ *vb* throttle

THRASH, -ED, -ES *vb* beat, esp with a stick or whip ▷ *n* party

THRASHER *same as* ▸ **thresher**

THRASHES ▸ **thrash**

THRASHY *adj* relating to thrash punk

THRAVE, -S *n* twenty-four sheaves of corn

THRAW, -ED, -ING, -S *vb* twist (something); make something thrawn

THRAWARD *adj* contrary or stubborn

THRAWART *same as* ▸ **thraward**

THRAWED ▸ **thraw**

THRAWING ▸ **thraw**

THRAWN *adj* crooked or twisted

THRAWNLY

THRAWS ▸ **thraw**

THREAD, -ED *n* fine strand or yarn ▷ *vb* pass thread through

THREADEN *adj* made of thread

THREADER ▸ **thread**

THREADS *slang word for* ▸ **clothes**

THREADY *adj* of, relating to, or resembling a thread or threads

THREAP, -ED, -S *vb* scold

THREAPER

THREAPIT *variant past participle of* ▸ **threap**

THREAPS ▸ **threap**

THREAT, -ED, -S *n* declaration of intent to harm

THREATEN *vb* make or be a threat to

THREATS ▸ **threat**

THREAVE, -S *same as* ▸ **thrave**

THREE, -S *n* one more than two ▷ *adj* amounting to three ▷ *determiner* amounting to three

THREEP, -ED, -S *same as* ▸ **threap**

THREEPER ▸ **threap**

THREEPIT *variant past participle of* ▸ **threep**

THREEPS ▸ **threep**

THREES ▸ **three**

THRENE, -S *n* dirge; threnody

THRENODE *same as* ▸ **threnody**

THRENODY *n* lament for the dead

THRENOS *n* threnody; lamentation

THRESH, -ED, -ES *vb* beat (wheat etc) to separate the grain from the husks and straw ▷ *n* act of threshing

THRESHEL *n* flail

THRESHER *n* large shark of tropical and temperate seas

THRESHES ▸ **thresh**

THRETTY *nonstandard variant of* ▸ **thirty**

THREW ▸ **throw**

THRICE *adv* three times

THRID, -DED, -DS *old variant of* ▸ **thread**

THRIDACE *n* sedative made from lettuce juice

THRIDDED ▸ **thrid**

THRIDS ▸ **thrid**

THRIFT, -S *n* wisdom and caution with money

THRIFTY *adj* not wasteful with money

THRILL, -ED, -S *n* sudden feeling of excitement ▷ *vb* (cause to) feel a thrill

T

THRILLER n book, film, etc with an atmosphere of mystery or suspense

THRILLS ► thrill

THRILLY adj causing thrills

THRIMSA, -S same as ► **thrymsa**

THRIP same as ► **thrips**

THRIPS, -ES n small slender-bodied insect with piercing mouthparts that feeds on plant sap

THRISSEL Scots variant of ► **thistle**

THRIST, -ED, -S old variant of ► **thirst**

THRISTLE Scots variant of ► **thistle**

THRISTS ► thrist

THRISTY ► thrist

THRIVE, -D, -N, -S, THROVE vb flourish or prosper

THRIVER -S

THRIVING ► thrive

THRO same as ► **through**

THROAT, -ED, -S n passage from the mouth and nose to the stomach and lungs ▷ vb vocalize in the throat

THROATY adj (of the voice) hoarse

THROB, -BED, -S vb pulsate repeatedly ▷ n throbbing **THROBBER**

THROE, -D, -ING n pang or pain ▷ vb endure throes

THROES pl n violent pangs or pains

THROMBI ► thrombus

THROMBIN n enzyme that acts on fibrinogen in blood causing it to clot

THROMBUS, THROMBI n clot of coagulated blood that remains at the site of its formation

THRONE, -D, -S, THRONING n ceremonial seat of a monarch or bishop ▷ vb place or be placed on a throne

THRONG, -ED, -S vb crowd ▷ n great number of people or things crowded together ▷ adj busy

THRONING ► throne

THRONNER n person who is good at doing odd jobs

THROPPLE vb strangle or choke

THROSTLE n song thrush

THROTTLE n device controlling the amount of fuel entering an engine ▷ vb control the flow of fluid in an engine by using the throttle

THROUGH prep from end to end or side to side of ▷ adj finished

THROVE ► thrive

THROW, THREW, -ING, -N, -S vb hurl through the air ▷ n throwing

THROWE, -S old variant of ► **throe**

THROWER, -S ► throw

THROWES ► throwe

THROWING ► throw

THROWN ► throw

THROWS ► throw

THRU same as ► **through**

THRUM, -MED, -S vb strum rhythmically but without expression ▷ n in textiles, unwoven ends of warp thread **THRUMMER**

THRUMMY adj made of thrums

THRUMS ► thrum

THRUPUT, -S n quantity of raw material or information processed in a given period

THRUSH, -ES n brown songbird

THRUST, -ED, -S vb push forcefully ▷ n forceful stab

THRUSTER n person or thing that thrusts

THRUSTOR variant of ► **thruster**

THRUSTS ► thrust

THRUTCH n narrow, fast-moving stream ▷ vb thrust

THRUWAY, -S n thoroughfare

THRYMSA, -S n gold coin used in Anglo-Saxon England

THUD, -DED, -S n dull heavy sound ▷ vb make such a sound

THUDDING n act of thudding

THUDS ► thud

THUG, -S n violent man, esp a criminal

THUGGEE, -S n methods and practices of the thugs of India

THUGGERY ► thug

THUGGISH ► thug

THUGGISM ► thug

THUGGO, -S n tough and violent person

THUGS ► thug

THUJA, -S n coniferous tree of North America and East Asia

THULIA, -S n oxide of thulium

THULITE, -S n rose-coloured zoisite sometimes incorporated into jewellery

THULIUM, -S n malleable ductile silvery-grey element

THUMB, -ED, -ING, -S n short thick finger set apart from the others ▷ vb touch or handle with the thumb

THUMBIER ► thumby

THUMBING ► thumb

THUMBKIN same as > **thumbikins**

THUMBNUT n nut with projections enabling it to be turned by the thumb and forefinger

THUMBPOT n tiny flowerpot

THUMBS ► thumb

THUMBY, THUMBIER adj clumsy; uncoordinated

THUMP, -ED, -S n (sound of) a dull heavy blow ▷ vb strike heavily

THUMPER -S

THUMPING adj huge or excessive

THUMPS ► thump

THUNDER, -S n loud noise accompanying lightning ▷ vb rumble with thunder **THUNDERY**

THUNK, -ED, -ING, -S another word for ► **thud**

THURIBLE same as ► **censer**

THURIFER n person appointed to carry the censer at religious ceremonies

THURIFY vb burn incense near or before an altar, shrine, etc

THURL, -S same as ► **thirl**

THUS, -ES adv in this manner ▷ n aromatic gum resin

THUSLY adv in such a way; thus

THUSNESS n state or quality of being thus

THUSWISE adj in this way; thus

THUYA, -S same as ► **thuja**

THWACK, -ED, -S n whack ▷ vb beat with something flat ▷ interj exclamation imitative of this sound **THWACKER**

THWAITE, -S n piece of land cleared from forest or reclaimed from wasteland

THWART, -ED, -S vb foil or frustrate ▷ n seat across a boat ▷ adj passing or being situated across ▷ adv across **THWARTER THWARTLY**

THY adj of or associated with you (thou) ▷ determiner belonging to or associated in some way with you (thou)

THYINE adj of relating to the sandarac tree

THYLOSE old variant of ► **tylosis**

T

THYLOSIS, THYLOSES *same as* ► *tylosis*

THYME, -S *n* aromatic herb **THYMEY**

THYMI ► *thymus*

THYMIC *adj* of or relating to the thymus

THYMIER ► *thymy*

THYMIEST ► *thymy*

THYMINE, -S *n* white crystalline pyrimidine base found in DNA

THYMOL, -S *n* substance obtained from thyme

THYMOMA, -S *n* type of tumour

THYMOSIN *n* hormone secreted by the thymus

THYMUS, THYMI, -ES *n* small gland at the base of the neck

THYMY, THYMIER, THYMIEST ► *thyme*

THYREOID *same as* ► *thyroid*

THYROID, -S *n* (of) a gland in the neck controlling body growth ▷ *adj* of or relating to the thyroid gland

THYROXIN *same as* > *thyroxine*

THYRSE, -S *n* type of inflorescence, occurring in the lilac and grape

THYRSI ► *thyrsus*

THYRSOID ► *thyrse*

THYRSUS, THYRSI *same as* ► *thyrse*

THYSELF *pron* reflexive form of thou

TI, -S *same as* ► *te*

TIAN, -S *n* traditional French vegetable stew or earthenware dish it is cooked in

TIAR, -S *same as* ► *tiara*

TIARA, -S *n* semicircular jewelled headdress **TIARAED**

TIARS ► *tiar*

TIBIA, -E, -S *n* inner bone of the lower leg **TIBIAL**

TIBIALIS, TIBIALES *n* muscle in the calf of the leg

TIBIAS ► *tibia*

TIC, -CED, -CING, -S *n* spasmodic muscular twitch

TICAL, -S *n* former standard monetary unit of Thailand

TICCA *adj* acquired for temporary use in exchange for payment

TICCED ► *tic*

TICCING ► *tic*

TICE, -D, -S, TICING *vb* tempt or allure; entice

TICH, -ES *same as* ► *titch*

TICHY, TICHIER, TICHIEST *same as* ► *titchy*

TICING ► *tice*

TICK, -ED, -S *n* mark used to check off or indicate the correctness of something ▷ *vb* mark with a tick

TICKEN, -S *same as* ► *ticking*

TICKER, -S *n* heart

TICKET, -ED *n* card or paper entitling the holder to admission, travel, etc ▷ *vb* attach or issue a ticket to

TICKETS *pl n* death or ruin

TICKEY, -S *n* former South African threepenny piece

TICKIES ► *ticky*

TICKING, -S *n* strong material for mattress covers

TICKLACE *n* (in Newfoundland) a kittiwake

TICKLE, -D, -S, TICKLING *vb* touch or stroke (a person) to produce laughter ▷ *n* tickling

TICKLER, -S *n* difficult or delicate problem

TICKLES ► *tickle*

TICKLIER ► *tickly*

TICKLING ► *tickle*

TICKLISH *adj* sensitive to tickling

TICKLY, TICKLIER ► *tickle*

TICKS ► *tick*

TICKSEED *another name for* > *coreopsis*

TICKTACK *n* sound made by a clock ▷ *vb* make a ticking sound

TICKTOCK *n* ticking sound made by a clock ▷ *vb* make a ticking sound

TICKY, TICKIES *same as* ► *tickey*

TICS ► *tic*

TICTAC, -S *same as* ► *ticktack*

TICTOC, -S *same as* ► *ticktock*

TID, -S *n* girl

TIDAL *adj* (of a river, lake, or sea) having tides **TIDALLY**

TIDBIT, -S *same as* ► *titbit*

TIDDIER ► *tiddy*

TIDDIES ► *tiddy*

TIDDIEST ► *tiddy*

TIDDLE, -D, -S, TIDDLING *vb* busy oneself with inconsequential tasks

TIDDLER, -S *n* very small fish

TIDDLES ► *tiddle*

TIDDLEY, -S *same as* ► *tiddly*

TIDDLIER ► *tiddly*

TIDDLIES ► *tiddly*

TIDDLING ► *tiddle*

TIDDLY, TIDDLIER, TIDDLIES *adj* tiny ▷ *n* alcoholic beverage

TIDDY, TIDDIER, TIDDIES, TIDDIEST *n* four of trumps in the card game gleek

TIDE, -D, -S, TIDING *n* rise and fall of the sea caused by the gravitational pull of the sun and moon ▷ *vb* carry or be carried with or as if with the tide

TIDELAND *n* land between high-water and low-water marks

TIDELESS ► *tide*

TIDELIKE ► *tide*

TIDELINE *n* high-water mark left by the retreating tide

TIDEMARK *n* mark left by the highest or lowest point of a tide

TIDEMILL *n* watermill powered by the force of the tide

TIDERIP, -S *same as* ► *riptide*

TIDES ► *tide*

TIDESMAN, TIDESMEN *n* customs official at a port

TIDEWAVE *n* undulation of the earth's water levels as the tide moves around it

TIDEWAY, -S *n* strong tidal current or its channel, esp the tidal part of a river

TIDIED ► *tidy*

TIDIER ► *tidy*

TIDIERS ► *tidy*

TIDIES ► *tidy*

TIDIEST ► *tidy*

TIDILY ► *tidy*

TIDINESS ► *tidy*

TIDING ► *tide*

TIDINGS *pl n* news

TIDIVATE *same as* ► *titivate*

TIDS ► *tid*

TIDY, TIDIED, TIDIER, TIDIERS, TIDIES, TIDIEST, -ING *adj* neat and orderly ▷ *vb* put in order ▷ *n* small container for odds and ends

TIDYTIPS *n* herb with flowers resembling those of the daisy

TIE, -D, -S, TYING *vb* fasten or be fastened with string, rope, etc ▷ *n* long narrow piece of material worn knotted round the neck

TIEBACK, -S *n* length of cord, ribbon, or other fabric used for tying a curtain to one side

TIEBREAK *n* deciding game in drawn match

T

TIECLASP n clip, often ornamental, which holds a tie in place against a shirt

TIED ► tie

TIEING same as ► **tie**

TIELESS ► tie

TIEPIN, -S n ornamental pin used to pin the two ends of a tie to a shirt

TIER, -ED, -ING, -S n one of a set of rows placed one above and behind the other ▷ vb be or arrange in tiers

TIERCE, -S same as ► **terce**

TIERCED adj (of a shield) divided into three sections of similar size but different colour

TIERCEL, -S same as ► **tercel**

TIERCES ► tierce

TIERCET, -S same as ► **tercet**

TIERED ► tier

TIERING ► tier

TIERS ► tier

TIES ► tie

TIETAC, -S n fastener for holding a tie in place

TIETACK, -S same as ► **tietac**

TIETACS ► tietac

TIFF, -ED, -ING, -INGS, -S n petty quarrel ▷ vb have or be in a tiff

TIFFANY n sheer fine gauzy fabric

TIFFED ► tiff

TIFFIN, -ED, -S n (in India) a light meal, esp at midday ▷ vb take tiffin

TIFFING ► tiff

TIFFINGS ► tiff

TIFFINS ► tiffin

TIFFS ► tiff

TIFOSO, TIFOSI, -S n fanatical fan (esp an Italian F1 fan)

TIFT, -ED, -ING, -S Scots variant of ► **tiff**

TIG, -GED, -GING, -S n child's game

TIGE, -S n trunk of an architectural column

TIGER, -S n large yellow-and-black striped Asian cat

TIGEREYE n golden brown silicified variety of crocidolite, used as an ornamental stone

TIGERISH ► tiger

TIGERISM n arrogant and showy manner

TIGERLY adj of or like a tiger

TIGERS ► tiger

TIGERY ► tiger

TIGES ► tige

TIGGED ► tig

TIGGER, -ED, -S vb damage beyond repair by tinkering

TIGGING ► tig

TIGHT, -ER, -EST adj stretched or drawn taut ▷ adv in a close, firm, or secure way

TIGHTEN, -S vb make or become tight or tighter

TIGHTER ► tight

TIGHTEST ► tight

TIGHTISH ► tight

TIGHTLY ► tight

TIGHTS pl n one-piece clinging garment covering the body from the waist to the feet

TIGHTWAD n stingy person

TIGLIC adj as in **tiglic acid** syrupy liquid or crystalline colourless unsaturated carboxylic acid

TIGLON, -S same as ► **tigon**

TIGNON, -S n type of cloth headdress

TIGON, -S n hybrid offspring of a male tiger and a female lion

TIGRESS n female tiger

TIGRIDIA n type of tropical American plant

TIGRINE adj of, characteristic of, or resembling a tiger

TIGRISH ► tiger

TIGROID adj resembling a tiger

TIGS ► tig

TIKA, -S same as ► **tikka**

TIKANGA, -S n Māori ways or customs

TIKAS ► tika

TIKE, -S same as ► **tyke**

TIKI, -ED, -ING, -S n small carving of a grotesque person worn as a pendant ▷ vb take a scenic tour around an area

TIKKA adj marinated in spices and dry-roasted ▷ n act of marking a tikka on the forehead

TIL, -S another name for ► **sesame**

TILAK, -S n coloured spot or mark worn by Hindus

TILAPIA, -S n type of fish

TILBURY n light two-wheeled horse-drawn open carriage

TILDE, -S n mark used in Spanish to indicate pronunciation

TILE, -D, -S n flat piece of ceramic, plastic, etc used to cover a roof, floor, or wall ▷ vb cover with tiles

TILEFISH n large brightly coloured deep-sea percoid food fish

TILELIKE adj like a tile

TILER, -S ► tile

TILERIES ► tilery

TILERS ► tiler

TILERY, TILERIES n place where tiles are produced

TILES ► tile

TILING, -S n tiles collectively

TILL, -ED, -ING, -INGS, -S prep until ▷ vb cultivate (land) ▷ n drawer for money, usu in a cash register

TILLABLE

TILLAGE, -S n act, process, or art of tilling

TILLED ► till

TILLER, -ED, -S n on boats, a handle fixed to the top of a rudderpost to serve as a lever in steering ▷ vb use a tiller

TILLICUM n (in the Pacific Northwest) a friend

TILLIER ► tilly

TILLIEST ► tilly

TILLING ► till

TILLINGS ► till

TILLITE, -S n rock formed from hardened till

TILLS ► till

TILLY, TILLIER, TILLIEST ► till

TILS ► til

TILT, -ED, -ING, -INGS, -S vb slant at an angle ▷ n slope

TILTABLE

TILTER, -S

TILTH, -S n (condition of) land that has been tilled

TILTING ► tilt

TILTINGS ► tilt

TILTS ► tilt

TILTYARD n (formerly) an enclosed area for tilting

TIMARAU, -S same as ► **tamarau**

TIMARIOT n one holding a fief in feudal Turkey

TIMBAL, -S n type of kettledrum

TIMBALE, -S n mixture of meat, fish, etc, in a rich sauce

TIMBALS ► timbal

TIMBER, -S n wood as a building material ▷ adj made out of timber ▷ vb provide with timbers ▷ interj lumberjack's shouted warning when a tree is about to fall

TIMBERED adj made of or containing timber or timbers

TIMBERS ► timber

TIMBERY ► timber

TIMBO, -S n Amazonian vine from which a useful insecticide can be derived

TIMBRAL adj relating to timbre

TIMBRE, -S n distinctive quality of sound of a voice or instrument

TIMBREL, -S n tambourine

TIMBRES ► timbre

TIME, -D, -S n past, present, and future as a continuous whole ▷ vb note the time taken by

TIMEBOMB n bomb containing a timing mechanism that determines the time it will detonate

TIMECARD n card used with a time clock

TIMED ► time

TIMELESS adj unaffected by time

TIMELIER ► timely

TIMELINE n graphic representation showing the passage of time as a line

TIMELY, TIMELIER adj at the appropriate time ▷ adv at the right or an appropriate time

TIMEOUS adj in good time

TIMEOUT, -S n in sport, interruption in play during which players rest, etc

TIMEPASS n way of passing the time ▷ vb pass the time

TIMER, -S n device for measuring time

TIMES ► time

TIMEWORK n work paid for by the length of time taken, esp by the hour or the day

TIMEWORN adj showing the adverse effects of overlong use or of old age

TIMID, -ER, -EST adj easily frightened

TIMIDITY

TIMIDLY

TIMING, -S n ability to judge when to do or say something so as to make the best effect

TIMIST, -S n one concerned with time

TIMOLOL, -S n relaxant medicine used (for example) to reduce blood pressure

TIMON, -S n apparatus by which a vessel is steered

TIMONEER n helmsman; tillerman

TIMONS ► timon

TIMOROUS adj timid

TIMOTHY n as in **timothy grass** perennial grass of temperate regions

TIMOUS same as ► **timeous**

TIMOUSLY

TIMPANA, -S n traditional Maltese baked pasta and pastry dish

TIMPANI pl n set of kettledrums

TIMPANO n kettledrum

TIMPANUM same as ► **tympanum**

TIMPS same as ► **timpani**

TIN, -NED, -NING, -NINGS, -S n soft metallic element ▷ vb put (food) into tins

TINAJA, -S n large jar for cooling water

TINAMOU, -S n type of bird of Central and S America

TINCAL, -S another name for ► **borax**

TINCHEL, -S n in Scotland, a circle of deer hunters who gradually close in on their quarry

TINCT, -ED, -ING, -S vb tint ▷ adj tinted or coloured

TINCTURE n medicinal extract in a solution of alcohol ▷ vb give a tint or colour to

TIND, -ED, -ING, -S vb set alight

TINDAL, -S n petty officer

TINDED ► tind

TINDER, -S n dry easily-burning material used to start a fire

TINDERY

TINDING ► tind

TINDS ► tind

TINE, -S, TINING n prong of a fork or antler ▷ vb lose

TINEA, -S n any fungal skin disease, esp ringworm

TINEAL

TINED ► tine

TINEID, -S n type of moth of the family which includes the clothes moths

TINES ► tine

TINFOIL, -S n paper-thin sheet of metal, used for wrapping foodstuffs

TINFUL, -S n contents of a tin or the amount a tin will hold

TING, -S same as ► **thing**

TINGE, -D, -ING, -S, TINGING n slight tint ▷ vb give a slight tint or trace to

TINGLE, -D, -S n (feel) a prickling or stinging sensation ▷ vb feel a mild prickling or stinging sensation, as from cold or excitement

TINGLER -S

TINGLIER ► tingly

TINGLING ► tingle

TINGLISH adj exciting

TINGLY, TINGLIER ► tingle

TINGS ► ting

TINHORN, -S n cheap pretentious person ▷ adj cheap and showy

TINIER ► tiny

TINIES pl n small children

TINIEST ► tiny

TINILY ► tiny

TININESS ► tiny

TINING ► tine

TINK, -ED, -ING, -S vb make short sound like a bell

TINKER, -ED, -S n (formerly) travelling mender of pots and pans ▷ vb fiddle with (an engine etc) in an attempt to repair it

TINKERER

TINKING ► tink

TINKLE, -D, -S vb ring with a high tinny sound like a small bell ▷ n this sound or action

TINKLER, -S same as ► **tinker**

TINKLES ► tinkle

TINKLIER ► tinkly

TINKLING ► tinkle

TINKLY, TINKLIER ► tinkle

TINKS ► tink

TINLIKE ► tin

TINMAN, TINMEN n one who works with tin or tin plate

TINNED ► tin

TINNER, -S n tin miner

TINNIE same as ► **tinny**

TINNIER ► tinny

TINNIES ► tinny

TINNIEST ► tinny

TINNILY ► tinny

TINNING ► tin

TINNINGS ► tin

TINNITUS n ringing or hissing sensation in one or both ears

TINNY, TINNIER, TINNIES, TINNIEST adj (of sound) thin and metallic ▷ n can of beer

TINPLATE n thin steel sheet coated with tin ▷ vb coat (a metal or object) with a layer of tin

TINPOT, -S adj worthless or unimportant ▷ n pot made of tin

TINS ► tin

TINSEL, -ED, -S n decorative metallic strips or threads ▷ adj made of or decorated with tinsel ▷ vb decorate with or as if with tinsel

TINSELLY

TINSELRY n tinsel-like material

TINSELS ► tinsel

TINSELY adj (US) like tinsel

T

TINSEY, -S old variant of ► tinsel

TINSMITH n person who works with tin or tin plate

TINSNIPS n metal cutters

TINSTONE n black or brown stone

TINT, -ED, -ING, -INGS, -S n (pale) shade of a colour ▷ vb give a tint to

TINTACK, -S n tin-plated tack

TINTED ► tint

TINTER, -S ► tint

TINTIER ► tinty

TINTIEST ► tinty

TINTING ► tint

TINTINGS ► tint

TINTLESS ► tint

TINTS ► tint

TINTY, TINTIER, TINTIEST adj having many tints

TINTYPE, -S another name for > ferrotype

TINWARE, -S n objects made of tin plate

TINWORK n objects made of tin

TINWORKS n place where tin is mined, smelted, or rolled

TINY, TINIER, TINIEST adj very small

TIP, -PED, -PING, -PINGS, -S, -T n narrow or pointed end of anything ▷ vb put a tip on

TIPCART, -S n cart that can be tipped to empty out its contents

TIPCAT, -S n game in which a piece of wood is tipped in the air with a stick

TIPI, -S variant spelling of ► tepee

TIPLESS ► tip

TIPOFF, -S n warning or hint, esp given confidentially

TIPPABLE ► tip

TIPPED ► tip

TIPPEE, -S n person who receives a tip, esp regarding share prices

TIPPER, -S n person who gives or leaves a tip

TIPPET, -S n scarflike piece of fur

TIPPIER ► tippy

TIPPIEST ► tippy

TIPPING ► tip

TIPPINGS ► tip

TIPPLE, -D, -S, TIPPLING vb drink alcohol habitually, esp in small quantities ▷ n alcoholic drink

TIPPLER -S

TIPPY, TIPPIER, TIPPIEST adj extremely fashionable or stylish

TIPPYTOE same as ► tiptoe

TIPS ► tip

TIPSHEET n list of advice or instructions

TIPSIER ► tipsy

TIPSIEST ► tipsy

TIPSIFY vb make tipsy

TIPSILY ► tipsy

TIPSTAFF n court official

TIPSTER, -S n person who sells tips about races

TIPSTOCK n detachable section of a gunstock, usually gripped by the left hand of the user

TIPSY, TIPSIER, TIPSIEST adj slightly drunk

TIPT ► tip

TIPTOE, -D, -S vb walk quietly with the heels off the ground

TIPTOP, -S adj of the highest quality or condition ▷ adv of the highest quality or condition ▷ n best in quality

TIPULA, -S n crane fly

TIPUNA, -S n ancestor

TIRADE, -S n long angry speech

TIRAGE, -S n drawing of wine from a barrel prior to bottling

TIRAMISU n Italian coffee-flavoured dessert

TIRASSE, -S n mechanism in an organ connecting two pedals

TIRE, -S vb reduce the energy of, as by exertion

TIRED, -ER, -EST adj exhausted

TIREDLY

TIRELESS adj energetic and determined

TIRELING n fatigued person or animal

TIRES ► tire

TIRESOME adj boring and irritating

TIRING, -S ► tire

TIRITI, -S n another name for the Treaty of Waitangi

> A Māori word for treaty. Any 6-letter word that lets you get rid of three Is can't be bad!

TIRL, -ED, -ING, -S vb turn

TIRO, -ES, -S same as ► tyro

TIRONIC variant of ► tyronic

TIROS ► tiro

TIRR, -ED, -ING, -S vb strip or denude

TIRRIT, -S n panic; scare

TIRRIVEE n outburst of bad temper; rumpus

TIRRIVIE same as ► tirrivee

TIRRS ► tirr

TIS ► ti

TISANE, -S n infusion of dried or fresh leaves or flowers

TISICK, -S n splutter; cough

TISSUAL adj relating to tissue

TISSUE, -D, -S, TISSUING n substance of an animal body or plant ▷ vb weave into tissue

TISSUEY

TISSULAR adj relating to tissue

TISWAS, -ES n state of anxiety or excitement

TIT, -S, -TED, -TING n any of various small songbirds ▷ vb jerk or tug

TITAN, -S n person who is huge, strong, or very important

TITANATE n any salt or ester of titanic acid

TITANESS n woman who is huge, strong, or very important

TITANIA, -S ► titanium

TITANIC adj huge or very important

TITANIS n large predatory flightless prehistoric bird

TITANISM n titanic power

TITANITE another name for ► sphene

TITANIUM, TITANIA n strong light metallic element used to make alloys

TITANOUS adj of or containing titanium, esp in the trivalent state

TITANS ► titan

TITBIT, -S n tasty piece of food

TITCH, -ES n small person

TITCHIE same as ► titchy

TITCHY, TITCHIER adj very small

TITE adj immediately

TITELY adv immediately

TITER, -S same as ► titre

TITFER, -S n hat

TITHABLE adj (until 1936) liable to pay tithes

TITHE, -D, -S, TITHING n esp formerly, one tenth of one's income or produce paid to the church as a tax ▷ vb charge or pay a tithe

TITHER -S

TITHINGS ► tithing

TITHONIA n Central American herb with flowers resembling sunflowers

TITI, -S n small omnivorous monkey

TITIAN, -S n reddish gold colour

T

TITIS ▶ titi
TITIVATE vb smarten up
TITLARK, -S another name for ▶ pipit
TITLE, -S, TITLING, TITLINGS n name of a book, film, etc ▷ vb give a title to
TITLED adj aristocratic
TITLER, -S n one who writes titles
TITLES ▶ title
TITLING ▶ title
TITLINGS ▶ title
TITLIST, -S n titleholder
TITMAN, TITMEN n (of pigs) the runt of a litter
TITMICE ▶ titmouse
TITMOSE old spelling of ▶ titmouse
TITMOUSE, TITMICE n any small active songbird
TITOKI, -S n New Zealand evergreen tree with a spreading crown and glossy green leaves
TITRABLE ▶ titrate
TITRANT, -S n solution in a titration that is added to a measured quantity of another solution
TITRATE, -D, -S vb measure the volume or concentration of (a solution) by titration
TITRATOR n device used to perform titration
TITRE, -S n concentration of a solution as determined by titration
TITS ▶ tit
TITTED ▶ tit
TITTER, -ED, -S vb laugh in a suppressed way ▷ n suppressed laugh
TITTERER
TITTIE, -S n sister; young woman
TITTING ▶ tit
TITTISH adj testy
TITTLE, -D, -S, TITTLING n very small amount ▷ vb chatter; tattle
TITTUP, -ED, -S vb prance or frolic ▷ n caper
TITTUPPY same as ▶ tittupy
TITTUPS ▶ tittup
TITTUPY adj spritely; lively
TITTY same as ▶ tittie
TITUBANT adj staggering
TITUBATE vb stagger
TITULAR, -S adj in name only ▷ n bearer of a title
TITULARY same as ▶ titular
TITULE, -D, -S, TITULING same as ▶ title
TITULI ▶ titulus
TITULING ▶ titule

TITULUS, TITULI n sign attached to the top of the cross during crucifixion
TITUP, -ED, -ING, -PED, -S same as ▶ tittup
TITUPY same as ▶ tittupy
TIVY same as ▶ tantivy
TIX pl n tickets

> Tix is an informal word for **tickets** and one of the key short words for using the X.

TIYIN, -S n monetary unit of Uzbekistan and Kyrgyzstan
TIYN, -S same as ▶ tiyin
TIZ, -ES n state of confusion
TIZWAS, -ES same as ▶ tiswas
TIZZ, -ES same as ▶ tizzy
TIZZY, TIZZIES n confused or agitated state
TJANTING n pen-like tool used in batik for applying molten wax to fabric
TMESIS, TMESES n interpolation of a word between the parts of a compound word
TO prep indicating movement towards, equality or comparison, etc ▷ adv a closed position
TOAD, -S n animal like a large frog
TOADFISH n spiny-finned fish with a wide mouth
TOADFLAX n plant with narrow leaves and yellow-orange flowers
TOADIED ▶ toady
TOADIES ▶ toady
TOADISH ▶ toad
TOADLESS adj having no toads
TOADLET, -S n small toad
TOADLIKE ▶ toad
TOADRUSH n annual rush growing in damp lowlands
TOADS ▶ toad
TOADY, TOADIED, TOADIES n ingratiating person ▷ vb be ingratiating
TOADYING n act of toadying
TOADYISH ▶ toady
TOADYISM ▶ toady
TOAST, -ED, -ING, -S n sliced bread browned by heat ▷ vb brown (bread) by heat
TOASTER -S
TOASTIE same as ▶ toasty
TOASTIER ▶ toasty
TOASTIES ▶ toasty
TOASTING ▶ toast
TOASTS ▶ toast
TOASTY, TOASTIER, TOASTIES n toasted

sandwich ▷ adj tasting or smelling like toast
TOAZE, -D, -S, TOAZING variant spelling of ▶ toze
TOBACCO, -S n plant with large leaves dried for smoking
TOBIES ▶ toby
TOBOGGAN n narrow sledge for sliding over snow ▷ vb ride a toboggan
TOBOGGIN variant spelling of ▶ toboggan
TOBY, TOBIES n water stopcock at the boundary of a street and house section
TOC, -S n in communications code, signal for letter t
TOCCATA, -S, TOCCATE n rapid piece of music for a keyboard instrument
TOCHER, -ED, -S n dowry ▷ vb give a dowry to
TOCK, -ED, -ING, -S n sound made by a clock ▷ vb (of a clock) make such a sound
TOCKIER ▶ tocky
TOCKIEST ▶ tocky
TOCKING ▶ tock
TOCKLEY, -S n informal word for a penis
TOCKS ▶ tock
TOCKY, TOCKIER, TOCKIEST adj muddy
TOCO, -S n punishment
TOCOLOGY n branch of medicine concerned with childbirth
TOCOS ▶ toco
TOCS ▶ toc
TOCSIN, -S n warning signal
TOD, -DED, -DING, -S n unit of weight, used for wool, etc ▷ vb produce a tod
TODAY, -S n this day ▷ adv on this day
TODDE, -S same as ▶ tod
TODDED ▶ tod
TODDES ▶ todde
TODDIES ▶ toddy
TODDING ▶ tod
TODDLE, -D, -S, TODDLING vb walk with short unsteady steps ▷ n act or an instance of toddling
TODDLER, -S n child beginning to walk
TODDLES ▶ toddle
TODDLING ▶ toddle
TODDY, TODDIES n sweetened drink of spirits and hot water
TODIES ▶ tody
TODS ▶ tod
TODY, TODIES n small bird of the Caribbean

T

TOE, -D, -ING, -S *n* digit of the foot ▷ *vb* touch or kick with the toe

TOEA, -S *n* monetary unit of Papua New Guinea

This monetary unit of Papua New Guinea is very often played to rid the rack of a surplus of vowels.

TOEBIE, -S *n* South African slang for sandwich

TOECAP, -S *n* strengthened covering for the toe of a shoe

TOECLIP, -S *n* clip on a bicycle pedal for the toes

TOED ▸ toe

TOEHOLD, -S *n* small space on the end of a mountain for supporting the toe of the foot in climbing

TOEIER ▸ toey

This is the comparative of **toey**, Australian slang for nervous or edgy, and can come in useful for dumping a surplus of vowels.

TOEIEST ▸ toey

TOEING ▸ toe

TOELESS *adj* not having toes

TOELIKE ▸ toe

TOENAIL, -S *n* thin hard clear plate covering part of the upper surface of the end of each toe ▷ *vb* join (beams) by driving nails obliquely

TOEPIECE *n* part of a shoe that covers the toes

TOEPLATE *n* metal reinforcement of the part of the sole of a shoe or boot underneath the toes

TOERAG, -S *n* contemptible person

TOES ▸ toe

TOESHOE, -S *n* ballet pump with padded toes

TOETOE, -S *same as* ▸ toitoi

TOEY, TOEIER, TOEIEST *adj* (of a person) nervous or anxious

TOFF *n* well-dressed or upper-class person

TOFFEE, -S *n* chewy sweet made of boiled sugar

TOFFIER ▸ toffy

TOFFIES ▸ toffy

TOFFIEST ▸ toffy

TOFFISH *adj* belonging to or characteristic of the upper class

TOFFS *adj* like a toff

TOFFY, TOFFIER, TOFFIES, TOFFIEST *same as* ▸ toffee

TOFORE *prep* before

TOFT, -S *n* homestead

TOFU, -S *n* soft food made from soya-bean curd

TOFUTTI, -S *n* tradename for nondairy, soya-based food products

TOG, -GED, -GING, -S *n* unit for measuring the insulating power of duvets ▷ *vb* dress oneself

TOGA, -E, -S *n* garment worn by citizens of ancient Rome ▷ *vb* wear a toga

TOGAED

TOGATE *adj* clad in a toga

TOGATED *same as* ▸ togate

TOGE, -S *old variant of* ▸ toga

TOGED

TOGETHER *adv* in company ▷ *adj* organized

TOGGED ▸ tog

TOGGER, -ED, -S *vb* play football ▷ *n* football player

TOGGERY *n* clothes

TOGGING ▸ tog

TOGGLE, -D, -S, TOGGLING *n* small bar-shaped button inserted through a loop for fastening ▷ *vb* supply or fasten with a toggle or toggles

TOGGLER -S

TOGS ▸ tog

TOGUE, -S *n* large North American freshwater game fish

TOHEROA, -S *n* large edible mollusc of New Zealand

TOHO *n* (to a hunting dog) an instruction to stop

TOHUNGA, -S *n* Māori priest

TOIL, -ED, -ING, -INGS, -S *n* hard work ▷ *vb* work hard

TOILE, -S *n* transparent linen or cotton fabric

TOILED ▸ toil

TOILER, -S ▸ toil

TOILES ▸ toile

TOILET, -ED, -S *n* bowl connected to a drain for receiving and disposing of urine and faeces ▷ *vb* go to the toilet

TOILETRY *n* object or cosmetic used to clean or groom oneself

TOILETS ▸ toilet

TOILETTE *same as* ▸ toilet

TOILFUL *same as* ▸ toilsome

TOILINET *n* type of fabric with a woollen weft and a cotton or silk warp

TOILING ▸ toil

TOILINGS ▸ toil

TOILLESS ▸ toil

TOILS ▸ toil

TOILSOME *adj* requiring hard work

TOILWORN *adj* fatigued, wearied by work

TOING, -S *n as in* **toing and froing** state of going back and forth

TOISE, -S *n* obsolete French unit of length roughly equal to 2m

TOISEACH *n* ancient Celtic nobleman

TOISECH, -S *same as* ▸ toiseach

TOISES ▸ toise

TOISON, -S *n* fleece

TOIT, -ED, -ING, -S *vb* walk or move in an unsteady manner, as from old age

TOITOI, -S *n* tall grasses with feathery fronds

TOITS ▸ toit

TOKAMAK, -S *n* reactor used in thermonuclear experiments

TOKAY, -S *n* small gecko of S and SE Asia, having a retractile claw at the tip of each digit

TOKEN, -ED, -ING, -S *n* sign or symbol ▷ *adj* nominal or slight

TOKENISM *n* policy of making only a token effort, esp to comply with a law

TOKENS ▸ token

TOKO, -S *same as* ▸ toco

TOKOLOGY *same as* ▸ tocology

TOKOMAK, -S *variant spelling of* ▸ tokamak

TOKONOMA *n* recess off a living room

TOKOS ▸ toko

TOKOTOKO *n* ceremonial carved Maori walking stick

TOLA, -S *n* unit of weight, used in India

TOLAN, -S *n* white crystalline derivative of acetylene

TOLANE, -S *same as* ▸ tolan

TOLANS ▸ tolan

TOLAR, -JEV, -JI, -S *n* standard monetary unit of Slovenia

TOLAS ▸ tola

TOLBOOTH *same as* > tollbooth

TOLD ▸ tell

TOLE, -D, -S, TOLING, TOLINGS *same as* ▸ toll

TOLEDO, -S *n* type of sword originally made in Toledo

TOLERANT *adj* able to tolerate the beliefs, actions, opinions, etc, of others

TOLERATE vb allow to exist or happen

TOLES ► tole

TOLEWARE n enamelled or lacquered metal ware, usually gilded

TOLIDIN, -S same as ► tolidine

TOLIDINE n compound used in dyeing and chemical analysis

TOLIDINS ► tolidin

TOLING ► tole

TOLINGS ► tole

TOLL, -ED, -ING, -INGS, -S vb ring (a bell) slowly and regularly ▷ n tolling **TOLLABLE**

TOLLAGE, -S same as ► toll

TOLLBAR, -S n bar blocking passage of a thoroughfare, raised on payment of a toll

TOLLDISH n dish used to measure out the portion of grain given to a miller as payment for their work

TOLLED ► toll

TOLLER, -S ► toll

TOLLEY, -S n large shooting marble used in a game of marbles

TOLLGATE n gate across a toll road or bridge at which travellers must pay

TOLLIE same as ► tolly

TOLLIES ► tolly

TOLLING ► toll

TOLLINGS ► toll

TOLLMAN, TOLLMEN n man who collects tolls

TOLLS ► toll

TOLLWAY, -S n road on which users must pay tolls to travel

TOLLY, TOLLIES n castrated calf

TOLSEL, -S n tolbooth

TOLSEY, -S n tolbooth

TOLT, -S n type of obsolete English writ

TOLTER, -ED, -S vb struggle or move with difficulty, as in mud

TOLTS ► tolt

TOLU, -S n sweet-smelling balsam obtained from a South American tree

TOLUATE, -S n any salt or ester of any of the three isomeric forms of toluic acid

TOLUENE, -S n colourless volatile flammable liquid obtained from petroleum and coal tar

TOLUIC adj as in **toluic acid** white crystalline derivative of toluene

TOLUID, -S n white crystalline derivative of glycocoll

TOLUIDE, -S variant of ► toluid

TOLUIDIN n type of dye

TOLUIDS ► toluid

TOLUOL, -S another name for ► toluene

TOLUOLE, -S another name for ► toluene

TOLUOLS ► toluol

TOLUS ► tolu

TOLUYL, -S n any of three groups derived from a toluic acid

TOLYL, -S n any of three isomeric groups, CH3C6H4−, derived from toluene

TOLZEY, -S n tolbooth

TOM, -S n male cat ▷ adj (of an animal) male

TOMAHAWK n fighting axe of the Native Americans

TOMALLEY n fat from a lobster, eaten as a delicacy

TOMAN, -S n gold coin formerly issued in Persia

TOMATO, -ES n red fruit used in salads and as a vegetable **TOMATOEY**

TOMB, -ED, -ING, -S n grave

TOMBAC, -S n any of various brittle alloys containing copper and zinc

TOMBACK, -S variant spelling of ► tombac

TOMBACS ► tombac

TOMBAK, -S same as ► tombac

TOMBAL adj like or relating to a tomb

TOMBED ► tomb

TOMBIC adj of or relating to tombs

TOMBING ► tomb

TOMBLESS ► tomb

TOMBLIKE ► tomb

TOMBOC, -S n weapon

TOMBOLA, -S n lottery with tickets drawn from a revolving drum

TOMBOLO, -S n narrow bar linking a small island with another island or the mainland

TOMBOY, -S n girl who acts or dresses like a boy

TOMBS ► tomb

TOMCAT, -S n male cat

TOMCOD, -S n small fish resembling the cod

TOME, -S n large heavy book

TOMENTUM, TOMENTA n feltlike covering of downy hairs on leaves and other plant parts

TOMES ► tome

TOMFOOL, -S n fool ▷ vb act the fool

TOMIA ► tomium

TOMIAL ► tomium

TOMIUM, TOMIA n sharp edge of a bird's beak

TOMMY, TOMMIED, TOMMIES, -ING n private in the British Army ▷ vb (formerly) to exploit workers by paying them in goods rather than in money

TOMMYCOD n type of cod

TOMMYING ► tommy

TOMMYROT n utter nonsense

TOMO, -S n shaft formed by the action of water on limestone or volcanic rock

TOMOGRAM n x-ray photograph of a selected plane section of a solid object

TOMORROW n (on) the day after today ▷ adv on the day after today

TOMOS ► tomo

TOMPION, -S same as ► tampion

TOMPON, -ED, -S same as ► tampon

TOMPOT adj as in **tompot blenny** variety of blenny with tentacles over its eyes

TOMS ► tom

TOMTIT, -S n small European bird that eats insects and seeds

TON, -S n unit of weight

TONAL adj written in a key

TONALITE n igneous rock found in the Italian Alps

TONALITY n presence of a musical key in a composition

TONALLY ► tonal

TONANT adj very loud

TONDI ► tondo

TONDINO, TONDINI, -S n small tondo

TONDO, TONDI n circular easel painting or relief carving

TONE, -D, -S, TONING, TONINGS n sound with reference to its pitch, volume, etc ▷ vb harmonize (with)

TONEARM, -S same as ► pickup

TONED ► tone

TONELESS adj having no tone

TONEME, -S n phoneme that is distinguished from another phoneme only by its tone **TONEMIC**

T

TONEPAD, -S n keypad used to transmit information

TONER, -S n cosmetic applied to the skin to reduce oiliness

TONES ▸ tone

TONETIC adj (of a language) distinguishing words by tone as well as by other sounds

TONETICS pl n area of linguistics concentrating on the use of tone to distinguish words semantically

TONETTE, -S n small musical instrument resembling a recorder

TONEY variant spelling of ▸ tony

TONG, -ED, -ING vb gather or seize with tongs ▷ n (formerly) a Chinese secret society

TONGA, -S n light two-wheeled vehicle used in rural areas of India

TONGED ▸ tong

TONGER, -S n one who uses tongs to gather oysters

TONGING ▸ tong

TONGMAN, TONGMEN another word for ▸ tonger

TONGS pl n large pincers for grasping and lifting

TONGSTER n tong member

TONGUE, -D, -S, TONGUING n muscular organ in the mouth, used in speaking and tasting ▷ vb use the tongue

TONIC, -S n medicine to improve body tone ▷ adj invigorating

TONICITY n state, condition, or quality of being tonic

TONICS ▸ tonic

TONIER ▸ tony

TONIES ▸ tony

TONIEST ▸ tony

TONIFY, TONIFIED, TONIFIES vb give tone to

TONIGHT, -S n (in or during) the night or evening of this day ▷ adv in or during the night or evening of this day

TONING ▸ tone

TONINGS ▸ tone

TONISH ▸ ton

TONISHLY ▸ ton

TONITE, -S n explosive used in quarrying

TONK, -ED, -ING, -S vb strike with a heavy blow

TONKA n as in tonka bean tall leguminous tree of tropical America

TONKED ▸ tonk

TONKER, -S ▸ tonk

TONKING ▸ tonk

TONKS ▸ tonk

TONLET, -S n skirt of a suit of armour, consisting of overlapping metal bands

TONNAG, -S n type of (usually tartan) shawl

TONNAGE, -S n weight capacity of a ship

TONNAGS ▸ tonnag

TONNE, -S same as ▸ ton

TONNEAU, -S, -X n detachable cover to protect the rear part of an open car

TONNELL, -S old spelling of ▸ tunnel

TONNER, -S n something that weighs one ton

TONNES ▸ tonne

TONNISH ▸ ton

TONS ▸ ton

TONSIL, -S n small gland in the throat

TONSILAR

TONSOR, -S n barber

TONSURE, -S n shaving of all or the top of the head as a religious or monastic practice ▷ vb shave the head of

TONSURED

TONTINE, -S n type of annuity scheme

TONTINER n subscriber to a tontine

TONTINES ▸ tontine

TONUS, -ES n normal tension of a muscle at rest

TONY, TONIER, TONIES, TONIEST adj stylish or distinctive ▷ n stylish or distinctive person

TOO adv also, as well

TOOART, -S variant spelling of ▸ tuart

TOODLE, -D, -S, TOODLING vb tootle

TOOK ▸ take

TOOL, -ED, -S n implement used by hand ▷ vb work on with a tool

TOOLBAG, -S n bag for storing or carrying tools

TOOLBAR, -S n row or column of selectable buttons displayed on a computer screen

TOOLBOX n box for storing or carrying tools

TOOLCASE n case for tools

TOOLED ▸ tool

TOOLER, -S ▸ tool

TOOLHEAD n adjustable attachment for a machine tool that holds the tool in position

TOOLIE, -S n adult who gatecrashes social events for school leavers

TOOLING, -S n any decorative work done with a tool

TOOLKIT, -S n set of tools designed to be used together or for a particular purpose

TOOLLESS adj having no tools

TOOLMAN, TOOLMEN n person who works with tools

TOOLPUSH n worker who directs the drilling on an oil rig

TOOLROOM n room, as in a machine shop, where tools are made or stored

TOOLS ▸ tool

TOOLSET, -S n set of tools associated with a computer application

TOOLSHED n small shed used for storing tools

TOOLTIP, -S n temporary window containing information about a tool on a computer application

TOOM, -ED, -EST, -ING, -S vb empty (something) ▷ adj empty

TOOMER

TOON, -S n large tree of the East Indies and Australia

TOONIE, -S n Canadian two-dollar coin

TOONS ▸ toon

TOORIE, -S n tassel or bobble on a bonnet

TOOSHIE, -R adj angry

TOOT, -ED, -ING n short hooting sound ▷ vb (cause to) make such a sound

TOOTER -S

TOOTH, TEETH, -ING, -S n bonelike projection in the jaws of most vertebrates for biting and chewing

TOOTHED adj having a tooth or teeth

TOOTHFUL n little (esp alcoholic) drink

TOOTHIER ▸ toothy

TOOTHILY ▸ toothy

TOOTHING ▸ tooth

TOOTHS ▸ tooth

TOOTHY, TOOTHIER adj having or showing numerous, large, or prominent teeth

TOOTING ▸ toot

TOOTLE, -D, -S, TOOTLING vb hoot softly or repeatedly ▷ n soft hoot or series of hoots

TOOTLER -S

TOOTS, -ED, -ES, -ING Scots version of ▸ tut

T

TOOTSIE *same as* ▶ tootsy
TOOTSIES ▶ tootsy
TOOTSING ▶ toots
TOOTSY, TOOTSIES *same as* ▶ toots
TOP, -PED, -S *n* highest point or part ▷ *adj* at or of the top ▷ *vb* form a top on
TOPALGIA *n* pain restricted to a particular spot: a neurotic or hysterical symptom
TOPARCH, -S *n* ruler of a small state or realm
TOPARCHY
TOPAZ, -ES *n* semiprecious stone in various colours
TOPAZINE *adj* like topaz
TOPCOAT, -S *n* overcoat
TOPCROSS *n* class of hybrid
TOPE, -D, -S, TOPING *vb* drink alcohol regularly ▷ *n* small European shark
TOPEE, -S *n* lightweight hat worn in tropical countries
TOPEK, -S *same as* ▶ tupik
TOPER, -S ▶ tope
TOPES ▶ tope
TOPFUL *variant spelling of* ▶ topfull
TOPFULL *adj* full to the top
TOPH, -S *n* variety of sandstone
TOPHE, -S *variant spelling of* ▶ toph
TOPHI ▶ tophus
TOPHS ▶ toph
TOPHUS, TOPHI *n* deposit of sodium urate in the helix of the ear or surrounding a joint
TOPI, -S *same as* ▶ topee
TOPIARY *n* art of trimming trees and bushes into decorative shapes ▷ *adj* of or relating to topiary
TOPIC, -S *n* subject of a conversation, book, etc
TOPICAL, -S *adj* relating to current events ▷ *n* type of anaesthetic
TOPICS ▶ topic
TOPING ▶ tope
TOPIS ▶ topi
TOPKICK, -S *n* (formerly) sergeant
TOPKNOT, -S *n* crest, tuft, decorative bow, etc, on the top of the head
TOPLESS *adj* having no top
TOPLINE, -D, -S *vb* headline; be the main focus of a newspaper story
TOPLINER
TOPLOFTY *adj* haughty or pretentious
TOPMAKER *n* wool dealer

TOPMAN, TOPMEN *n* sailor positioned in the rigging of the topsail
TOPMAST, -S *n* mast next above a lower mast on a sailing vessel
TOPMEN ▶ topman
TOPMOST *adj* highest or best
TOPNOTCH *adj* excellent
TOPO, -I, -S *n* picture of a mountain with details of climbing routes superimposed on it
TOPOLOGY *n* geometry of the properties of a shape which are unaffected by continuous distortion
TOPONYM, -S *n* name of a place
TOPONYMY *n* study of place names
TOPOS ▶ topo
TOPOTYPE *n* specimen plant or animal taken from an area regarded as the typical habitat
TOPPED ▶ top
TOPPER, -S *n* top hat
TOPPIER ▶ toppy
TOPPIEST ▶ toppy
TOPPING, -S ▶ top
TOPPLE, -D, -S, TOPPLING *vb* (cause to) fall over
TOPPY, TOPPIER, TOPPIEST *adj* (of audio reproduction) having too many high-frequency sounds
TOPS ▶ top
TOPSAIL, -S *n* square sail carried on a yard set on a topmast
TOPSCORE *vb* score the highest in a sports match or competition
TOPSIDE, -S *n* lean cut of beef from the thigh containing no bone
TOPSIDER *n* person in charge
TOPSIDES ▶ topside
TOPSMAN, TOPSMEN *n* chief drover
TOPSOIL, -S *n* surface layer of soil ▷ *vb* spread topsoil on (land)
TOPSPIN, -S *n* spin imparted to make a ball bounce or travel exceptionally far, high, or quickly
TOPSTONE *n* stone forming the top of something
TOPWATER *adj* floating on the top of the water
TOPWORK, -S *vb* graft shoots or twigs onto the main branches of (a tree)
TOQUE, -S *same as* ▶ tuque

TOQUET, -S *same as* ▶ toque
TOQUILLA *another name for* ▶ jipijapa
TOR, -S *n* high rocky hill
TORA, -S *variant spelling of* ▶ torah
TORAH, -S, TOROT, TOROTH *n* whole body of traditional Jewish teaching
TORAN, -S *n* (in Indian architecture) an archway
TORANA, -S *same as* ▶ toran
TORANS ▶ toran
TORAS ▶ tora
TORC, -S *same as* ▶ torque
TORCH, -ED, -ES, -ING *n* small portable battery-powered lamp ▷ *vb* deliberately set (a building) on fire
TORCHER -S
TORCHERE *n* tall narrow stand for holding a candelabrum
TORCHERS ▶ torcher
TORCHES ▶ torch
TORCHIER *n* standing lamp with a bowl for casting light upwards
TORCHING ▶ torch
TORCHLIT *adj* lit by torches
TORCHON *n as in* **torchon lace** coarse linen or cotton lace with a simple openwork pattern
TORCHY *adj* sentimental; maudlin; characteristic of a torch song
TORCS ▶ torc
TORCULAR *n* tourniquet
TORDION, -S *n* old triple-time dance for two people
TORE, -S *same as* ▶ torus
TOREADOR *n* bullfighter
TORERO, -S *n* bullfighter, esp one on foot
TORES ▶ tore
TOREUTIC > toreutics
TORGOCH, -S *n* type of char
TORI ▶ torus
TORIC, -S *adj* of, relating to, or having the form of a torus
TORIES ▶ tory
TORII *n* gateway, esp one at the entrance to a Japanese Shinto temple
TORMENT, -S *vb* cause (someone) great suffering ▷ *n* great suffering
TORMENTA > tormentum
TORMENTS ▶ torment
TORMINA *n* complaints
TORMINAL
TORN ▶ tear
TORNADE, -S *same as* ▶ tornado
TORNADIC ▶ tornado

T

TORNADO, -S n violent whirlwind

TORNILLO n shrub found in Mexico and some southwestern states of the US

TORO, -S n bull

TOROID, -S n surface generated by rotating a closed plane curve about a coplanar line that does not intersect it

TOROIDAL

TOROS ► toro

TOROSE adj (of a cylindrical part) having irregular swellings

TOROSITY

TOROT ► torah

TOROTH ► torah

TOROUS same as ► torose

TORPEDO, -S n self-propelled underwater missile ▷ vb attack or destroy with or as if with torpedoes

TORPEFY n make torpid

TORPID adj sluggish and inactive

TORPIDLY

TORPIDS n series of boat races held at Oxford University

TORPOR, -S n torpid state

TORQUATE ► torques

TORQUE, -D, TORQUING n force causing rotation ▷ vb apply torque to (something)

TORQUER -S

TORQUES n distinctive band of hair, feathers, skin, or colour around the neck of an animal

TORQUEY, TORQUIER adj providing torque

TORQUING ► torque

TORR, -S n unit of pressure

TORREFY vb dry (ores, etc) by subjection to intense heat

TORRENT, -S n rushing stream ▷ adj like or relating to a torrent

TORRET, -S same as ► terret

TORRID, -ER adj very hot and dry

TORRIDLY

TORRIFY same as ► torrefy

TORRS ► torr

TORS ► tor

TORSADE, -S n ornamental twist or twisted cord, as on hats

TORSE, -S same as ► torso

TORSEL, -S n wooden beam along the top of a wall

TORSES ► torse

TORSI ► torso

TORSION, -S n twisting of a part by equal forces being applied at both ends but in opposite directions

TORSIVE adj twisted

TORSK, -S n fish with a single long dorsal fin

TORSO, TORSI, -S n trunk of the human body

TORT, -S n civil wrong or injury for which damages may be claimed

TORTA, -S n (in mining) a flat circular pile of silver ore

TORTE, -N, -S n rich cake, originating in Austria

TORTELLI pl n type of stuffed pasta

TORTEN ► torte

TORTES ► torte

TORTIE, -S n tortoiseshell cat

TORTILE adj twisted or coiled

TORTILLA n thin Mexican pancake

TORTIOUS adj having the nature of or involving a tort

TORTIVE adj twisted

TORTOISE n slow-moving land reptile with a dome-shaped shell

TORTONI, -S n rich ice cream often flavoured with sherry

TORTRIX n type of moth

TORTS ► tort

TORTUOUS adj winding or twisting

TORTURE, -S vb cause (someone) severe pain or mental anguish ▷ n severe physical or mental pain

TORTURED

TORTURER

TORULA, -E, -S n species of fungal microorganisms

TORULI ► torulus

TORULIN, -S n vitamin found in yeast

TORULOSE adj (of something cylindrical) alternately swollen and pinched along its length

TORULUS, TORULI n socket in an insect's head in which its antenna is attached

TORUS, TORI, -ES n large convex moulding approximately semicircular in cross section

TORY, TORIES n conservative or reactionary person ▷ adj conservative or reactionary

TOSA, -S n large reddish dog, originally bred for fighting

TOSE, -D, -S, TOSING same as ► toze

TOSH, -ED, -ES, -ING n nonsense ▷ vb tidy or trim

TOSHACH, -S n military leader of a clan

TOSHED ► tosh

TOSHER, -S ► tosh

TOSHES ► tosh

TOSHIER ► toshy

TOSHIEST ► toshy

TOSHING ► tosh

TOSHY, TOSHIER, TOSHIEST adj neat; trim

TOSING ► tose

TOSS, -ED, -ES, -ING, -INGS vb throw lightly ▷ n tossing

TOSSEN old past participle of ► toss

TOSSES ► toss

TOSSIER ► tossy

TOSSIEST ► tossy

TOSSILY ► tossy

TOSSING ► toss

TOSSINGS ► toss

TOSSPOT, -S n habitual drinker

TOSSUP, -S n instance of tossing up a coin

TOSSY, TOSSIER, TOSSIEST adj impudent

TOST old past participle of ► toss

TOSTADA, -S n crispy deep-fried tortilla topped with meat, cheese, and refried beans

TOSTADO, -S same as ► tostada

TOSTONE, -S n Mexican dish of fried plantains

TOT, -S, -TED n small child ▷ vb total

TOTABLE ► tote

TOTAL, -ED, -ING, -LED, -S n whole, esp a sum of parts ▷ adj complete ▷ vb amount to

TOTALISE same as ► totalize

TOTALISM n practice of a dictatorial one party state that regulates every form of life

TOTALIST

TOTALITY n whole amount

TOTALIZE vb combine or make into a total

TOTALLED ► total

TOTALLY ► total

TOTALS ► total

TOTANUS another name for ► redshank

TOTARA, -S n tall coniferous forest tree of New Zealand

TOTE, -D, -S, TOTING vb carry (a gun etc) ▷ n act of or an instance of toting

TOTEABLE

TOTEM, -S n tribal badge or emblem
TOTEMIC
TOTEMISM n belief in kinship of groups or individuals having a common totem
TOTEMIST
TOTEMITE
TOTEMS ▸ totem
TOTER, -S ▸ tote
TOTES ▸ tote
TOTHER, -S n other ▷ adj the other
TOTIENT, -S n quantity of numbers less than, and sharing no common factors with, a number
TOTING ▸ tote
TOTITIVE n number less than, and having no common factors with, a given number
TOTS ▸ tot
TOTTED ▸ tot
TOTTER, -ED, -S vb move unsteadily ▷ n act or an instance of tottering
TOTTERER
TOTTERY
TOTTIE adj very small
TOTTIER ▸ totty
TOTTIES ▸ totty
TOTTIEST ▸ totty
TOTTING, -S ▸ tot
TOTTRING adj Shakespearian word referring to ragged cloth or clothing
TOTTY, TOTTIER, TOTTIES, TOTTIEST n small child ▷ adj very small
TOUCAN, -S n tropical American bird with a large bill
TOUCANET n type of small toucan
TOUCANS ▸ toucan
TOUCH, -ES vb come into contact with ▷ n sense by which an object's qualities are perceived when they come into contact with part of the body ▷ adj of a non-contact version of a particular sport
TOUCHE interj acknowledgment a remark or witty reply
TOUCHED adj emotionally moved
TOUCHER, -S ▸ touch
TOUCHES ▸ touch
TOUCHIER ▸ touchy
TOUCHILY ▸ touchy
TOUCHING adj emotionally moving ▷ prep relating to or concerning

TOUCHPAD n part of laptop computer functioning like mouse
TOUCHUP, -S n renovation or retouching, as of a painting
TOUCHY, TOUCHIER adj easily offended
TOUGH, -ED, -ER, -EST, -ING, -S adj strong or resilient ▷ n rough violent person
TOUGHEN, -S vb make or become tough or tougher
TOUGHER ▸ tough
TOUGHEST ▸ tough
TOUGHIE, -S n person who is tough
TOUGHING ▸ tough
TOUGHISH ▸ tough
TOUGHLY ▸ tough
TOUGHS ▸ tough
TOUGHY same as ▸ **toughie**
TOUK, -ED, -ING, -S same as ▸ **tuck**
TOULADI, -S same as ▸ **tuladi**
TOUN, -S n town
TOUPEE, -S n small wig
TOUPEED adj wearing a toupee
TOUPEES ▸ toupee
TOUPET, -S same as ▸ **toupee**
TOUPIE, -S n round boneless smoked ham
TOUR, -ED, -S n journey visiting places of interest along the way ▷ vb make a tour (of)
TOURACO, -S n brightly coloured crested arboreal African bird
TOURED ▸ tour
TOURER, -S n large open car with a folding top
TOURIE, -S same as ▸ **toorie**
TOURING, -S ▸ tour
TOURISM, -S n tourist travel as an industry
TOURIST, -S n person travelling for pleasure ▷ adj of or relating to tourists or tourism
TOURISTA variant of ▸ **tourist**
TOURISTS ▸ tourist
TOURISTY adj informal term for full of tourists or tourist attractions
TOURNEY, -S n knightly tournament ▷ vb engage in a tourney
TOURNURE n outline or contour
TOURS ▸ tour
TOUSE, -D, -S, TOUSING, TOUSINGS vb tangle, ruffle,

or disarrange; treat roughly
TOUSER -S
TOUSIER ▸ tousy
TOUSIEST ▸ tousy
TOUSING ▸ touse
TOUSINGS ▸ touse
TOUSLE, -D, -S, TOUSLING vb make (hair or clothes) ruffled and untidy ▷ n disorderly, tangled, or rumpled state
TOUSTIE, -R adj irritable; testy
TOUSY, TOUSIER, TOUSIEST adj tousled
TOUT, -ED, -ING, -S vb seek business in a persistent manner ▷ n person who sells tickets for a popular event at inflated prices
TOUTER -S
TOUTIE, -R, -ST adj childishly irritable or sullen
TOUTING ▸ tout
TOUTON, -S n deep-fried round of bread dough
TOUTS ▸ tout
TOUZE, -D, -S, TOUZING variant spelling of ▸ **touse**
TOUZIER ▸ touzy
TOUZIEST ▸ touzy
TOUZING ▸ touze
TOUZLE, -D, -S, TOUZLING rare spelling of ▸ **tousle**
TOUZY, TOUZIER, TOUZIEST variant spelling of ▸ **tousy**
TOVARICH same as > **tovarisch**
TOVARISH same as > **tovarisch**
TOW, -ED, -ING, -INGS, -S vb drag, esp by means of a rope ▷ n towing
TOWABLE
TOWAGE, -S n charge made for towing
TOWARD same as ▸ **towards**
TOWARDLY adj compliant
TOWARDS prep in the direction of
TOWAWAY, -S n vehicle which has been towed away
TOWBAR, -S n metal bar on a car for towing vehicles
TOWBOAT, -S n another word for tug (the boat)
TOWED ▸ tow
TOWEL, -ED, -ING, -LED, -S n cloth for drying things ▷ vb dry or wipe with a towel
TOWER, -S n tall structure, often forming part of a larger building ▷ vb rise like a tower
TOWERED adj having a tower or towers
TOWERIER ▸ towery

T

TOWERING adj very tall or impressive

TOWERS ► tower

TOWERY, TOWERIER adj with towers

TOWHEAD, -S n person with blond or yellowish hair

TOWHEE, -S n N American brownish-coloured sparrow

TOWIE, -S n truck used for towing

TOWIER ► towy

TOWIES ► towie

TOWIEST ► towy

TOWING ► tow

TOWINGS ► tow

TOWKAY, -S n sir

TOWLINE, -S same as ► towrope

TOWMON, -S same as ► towmond

TOWMOND, -S n old word for year

TOWMONS ► towmon

TOWMONT, -S same as ► towmond

TOWN, -S n group of buildings larger than a village

TOWNEE, -S same as ► townie

TOWNFOLK same as >townsfolk

TOWNHALL adj of a variety of the Asian plant moschatel

TOWNHOME another word for >townhouse

TOWNIE n resident of a town

TOWNIER ► towny

TOWNIES ► towny

TOWNIEST ► towny

TOWNISH ► town

TOWNLAND n division of land of various sizes

TOWNLESS ► town

TOWNLET, -S n small town

TOWNLIER ► townly

TOWNLING n person who lives in a town

TOWNLY, TOWNLIER adj characteristic of a town

TOWNS ► town

TOWNSHIP n small town

TOWNSITE n site of a town

TOWNSKIP n old term for a mischievous and roguish child who frequents city streets

TOWNSMAN, TOWNSMEN n inhabitant of a town

TOWNWARD adv in the direction of the town

TOWNWEAR n clothes suitable for wearing while pursuing activities usually associated with towns

TOWNY, TOWNIER, TOWNIES, TOWNIEST adj characteristic of a town

TOWPATH, -S n path beside a canal or river

TOWPLANE n aeroplane that tows gliders

TOWROPE, -S n rope or cable used for towing a vehicle or vessel

TOWS ► tow

TOWSACK, -S n sack made from tow

TOWSE, -D, -S, TOWSING same as ► touse

TOWSER -S

TOWSIER ► towsy

TOWSIEST ► towsy

TOWSING ► towse

TOWSY, TOWSIER, TOWSIEST same as ► tousy

TOWT, -ED, -ING, -S vb sulk

TOWY, TOWIER, TOWIEST ► tow

TOWZE, -D, -S, TOWZING same as ► touse

TOWZIER ► towzy

TOWZIEST ► towzy

TOWZING ► towze

TOWZY, TOWZIER, TOWZIEST same as ► tousy

TOXAEMIA n blood poisoning

TOXAEMIC

TOXEMIA, -S same as ► toxaemia

TOXEMIC ► toxaemia

TOXIC, -S adj poisonous ▷ n toxic substance

TOXICAL adj toxic

TOXICANT n toxic substance ▷ adj poisonous

TOXICITY n degree of strength of a poison

TOXICS ► toxic

TOXIN, -S n poison of bacterial origin

TOXINE, -S nonstandard variant spelling of ► toxin

TOXINS ► toxin

TOXOCARA n parasitic worm infesting the intestines of cats and dogs

TOXOID, -S n toxin that has been treated to reduce its toxicity

TOY, -ED, -ING, -INGS, -S n something designed to be played with ▷ adj designed to be played with ▷ vb play, fiddle, or flirt

TOYBOX, -ES n box for toys

TOYCHEST n chest for toys

TOYED ► toy

TOYER, -S ► toy

TOYETIC adj (of a film or television franchise) able to generate revenue via spin-off toys

TOYING ► toy

TOYINGS ► toy

TOYISH adj resembling a toy

TOYISHLY

TOYLAND, -S n toy industry

TOYLESS ► toy

TOYLIKE ► toy

TOYLSOM old spelling of ► toilsome

TOYMAN, TOYMEN n man who sells toys

TOYO, -S n Japanese straw-like material made out of rice paper and used to make hats

TOYON, -S n shrub related to the rose

TOYOS ► toyo

TOYS ► toy

TOYSHOP, -S n shop selling toys

TOYSOME adj playful

TOYTOWN, -S adj having an unreal and picturesque appearance ▷ n place with an unreal and picturesque appearance

TOYWOMAN, TOYWOMEN n woman who sells toys

TOZE, -D, -S, TOZING vb tease out; (of wool, etc) card

TOZIE, -S n type of shawl

TOZING ► toze

TRABEATE same as >trabeated

TRABS pl n training shoes

TRACE, -D, -S vb locate or work out (the cause of something) ▷ n track left by something

TRACER, -S n projectile which leaves a visible trail

TRACERY n pattern of interlacing lines

TRACES ► trace

TRACEUR, -S n parkour participant

TRACHEA, -E, -S n windpipe

TRACHEAL

TRACHEID n element of xylem tissue

TRACHLE, -D, -S vb (of hair, clothing, etc) make untidy

TRACHOMA n chronic contagious disease of the eye

TRACHYTE n light-coloured fine-grained volcanic rock

TRACING, -S n traced copy

TRACK, -ED, -S n rough road or path ▷ vb follow the trail or path of

TRACKAGE n collective term for railway tracks

TRACKBED n foundation on which railway tracks are laid

TRACKED ▸ track

TRACKER, -S ▸ track

TRACKIE adj resembling or forming part of a tracksuit

TRACKIES pl n loose-fitting trousers with elasticated cuffs

TRACKING n act or process of following something or someone

TRACKMAN, TRACKMEN n workman who lays and maintains railway track

TRACKPAD same as ▸ **touchpad**

TRACKS ▸ track

TRACKWAY n path or track

TRACT, -ED, -ING, -S n wide area ▹ vb track

TRACTATE n short tract

TRACTED ▸ tract

TRACTILE adj capable of being drawn out

TRACTING ▸ tract

TRACTION n pulling, esp by engine power

TRACTIVE

TRACTOR, -S n motor vehicle with large rear wheels for pulling farm machinery

TRACTRIX n (in geometry) type of curve

TRACTS ▸ tract

TRACTUS n anthem sung in some RC masses

TRAD, -S n traditional jazz, as revived in the 1950s

TRADABLE ▸ trade

TRADE, -D, -S n buying, selling, or exchange of goods ▹ vb buy and sell ▹ adj intended for or available only to people in industry or business

TRADEFUL adj (of shops, for example) full of trade

TRADEOFF n exchange, esp as a compromise

TRADER, -S n person who engages in trade

TRADES ▸ trade

TRADING, -S ▸ trade

TRADITOR n Christian who betrayed fellow Christians at the time of the Roman persecutions

TRADS ▸ trad

TRADUCE, -D, -S vb slander

TRADUCER

TRAFFIC, -S n vehicles coming and going on a road ▹ vb

TRAGAL ▸ tragus

TRAGEDY n shocking or sad event

TRAGI ▸ tragus

TRAGIC, -S adj of or like a tragedy ▹ n tragedian

TRAGICAL same as ▸ **tragic**

TRAGICS ▸ tragic

TRAGOPAN n pheasant of S and SE Asia

TRAGULE, -S n mouse deer

TRAGUS, TRAGI n fleshy projection that partially covers the entrance to the external ear

TRAHISON n treason

TRAIK, -ED, -ING, -IT, -S vb trudge; trek with difficulty

TRAIL, -ED, -S n path, track, or road ▹ vb drag along the ground

TRAILER, -S n vehicle designed to be towed by another vehicle ▹ vb use a trailer to advertise (something)

TRAILING adj (of a plant) having a long stem which spreads over the ground or hangs loosely

TRAILS ▸ trail

TRAIN, -ED, -S vb instruct in a skill ▹ n line of railway coaches or wagons drawn by an engine

TRAINEE, -S n person being trained ▹ adj (of a person) undergoing training

TRAINER n person who trains an athlete or sportsperson

TRAINERS pl n shoes in the style of those used for sports training

TRAINFUL n quantity of people or cargo that would be capable of filling a train

TRAINING n process of bringing a person to an agreed standard of proficiency by instruction

TRAINMAN, TRAINMEN n man who works on a train

TRAINS ▸ train

TRAINWAY n railway track; channel in a built-up area through which a train passes

TRAIPSE, -D, -S vb walk wearily ▹ n long or tiring walk

TRAIT, -S n characteristic feature

TRAITOR, -S n person guilty of treason or treachery

TRAITS ▸ trait

TRAJECT, -S vb transport or transmit

TRAM, -MED, -MING, -S same as ▸ **trammel**

TRAMCAR, -S same as ▸ **tram**

TRAMEL, -ED, -S variant spelling of ▸ **trammel**

TRAMELL, -S variant spelling of ▸ **trammel**

TRAMELS ▸ tramel

TRAMLESS ▸ tram

TRAMLINE n tracks on which a tram runs

TRAMMED ▸ tram

TRAMMEL, -S n hindrance to free action or movement ▹ vb hinder or restrain

TRAMMIE, -S n conductor or driver of a tram

TRAMMING ▸ tram

TRAMP, -ED, -S vb travel on foot, hike ▹ n homeless person who travels on foot

TRAMPER, -S n person who tramps

TRAMPET, -S variant spelling of ▸ **trampette**

TRAMPIER ▸ trampy

TRAMPING ▸ tramp

TRAMPISH ▸ tramp

TRAMPLE, -D, -S vb tread on and crush ▹ n action or sound of trampling

TRAMPLER

TRAMPS ▸ tramp

TRAMPY, TRAMPIER adj like or characteristic of a tramp

TRAMROAD same as ▸ **tramway**

TRAMS ▸ tram

TRAMWAY, -S same as ▸ **tramline**

TRANCE, -D, -S, TRANCING n unconscious or dazed state ▹ vb put into or as into a trance

TRANCEY, TRANCIER adj (of music) characteristic of the trance sub-genre

TRANCHE, -S n portion of something large

TRANCHET n stone age cutting tool

TRANCIER ▸ trancey

TRANCING ▸ trance

TRANECT, -S n ferry

TRANGAM, -S n bauble or trinket

TRANGLE, -S n (in heraldry) a small fesse

TRANK, -ED, -ING, -S n tranquillizer ▹ vb administer a tranquillizer

TRANKUM, -S same as ▸ **trangam**

TRANNIE n transistor radio

TRANNY, TRANNIES same as ▸ **trannie**

TRANQ, -S same as ▸ **trank**

Short for tranquillizer; another of those useful

T

words allowing you to play the Q without a U.

TRANQUIL *adj* calm and quiet

TRANS *n* short from of translation

TRANSACT *vb* conduct or negotiate (a business deal)

TRANSE, -S *n* way through; passage

TRANSECT *n* sample strip of land used to monitor plant distribution and animal populations ▷ *vb* cut or divide crossways

TRANSEPT *n* either of the two shorter wings of a cross-shaped church

TRANSES ▶ **transe**

TRANSFER *vb* move or send from one person or place to another ▷ *n* transferring

TRANSFIX *vb* astound or stun

TRANSHIP *same as* > **transship**

TRANSIRE *n* document allowing goods to pass through customs

TRANSIT, -S *n* passage or conveyance of goods or people ▷ *vb* make transit

TRANSMEW *old variant of* > **transmute**

TRANSMIT *vb* pass (something) from one person or place to another

TRANSOM, -S *n* horizontal bar across a window

TRANSUDE *vb* (of a fluid) ooze or pass through interstices, pores, or small holes

TRANSUME *vb* make an official transcription of

TRANT, -ED, -ING, -S *vb* travel from place to place selling goods

TRANTER -S

TRAP, -PED, -PING, -S *n* device for catching animals ▷ *vb* catch

TRAPAN, -S *same as* ▶ **trepan**

TRAPBALL *n* obsolete ball game

TRAPDOOR *n* door in floor or roof

TRAPE, -D, TRAPING *same as* ▶ **traipse**

TRAPES, -ED, -ES *same as* ▶ **traipse**

TRAPEZE, -D, -S *n* horizontal bar suspended from two ropes, used by circus acrobats ▷ *vb* swing on a trapeze

TRAPEZIA > **trapezium**

TRAPEZII > **trapezius**

TRAPFALL *n* trapdoor that opens under the feet

TRAPING ▶ **trape**

TRAPLIKE ▶ **trap**

TRAPLINE *n* line of traps

TRAPNEST *n* nest that holds the eggs of a single hen

TRAPPEAN *adj* of, relating to, or consisting of igneous rock, esp a basalt

TRAPPED ▶ **trap**

TRAPPER, -S *n* person who traps animals for their fur

TRAPPIER ▶ **trappy**

TRAPPING ▶ **trap**

TRAPPOSE *adj* of or relating to traprock

TRAPPOUS *same as* ▶ **trappose**

TRAPPY, TRAPPIER *adj* having many traps

TRAPROCK *another name for* ▶ **trap**

TRAPS ▶ **trap**

TRAPSE, -D, -S, TRAPSING *vb* traipse

TRAPT *old past participle of* ▶ **trap**

TRAPUNTO *n* type of quilting that is only partly padded in a design

TRASH, -ED, -ES, -ING *n* anything worthless ▷ *vb* attack or destroy maliciously

TRASHCAN *n* dustbin

TRASHED ▶ **trash**

TRASHER, -S ▶ **trash**

TRASHERY ▶ **trash**

TRASHES ▶ **trash**

TRASHIER ▶ **trashy**

TRASHILY ▶ **trashy**

TRASHING ▶ **trash**

TRASHMAN, TRASHMEN *another name for* ▶ **binman**

TRASHY, TRASHIER *adj* cheap, worthless, or badly made

TRASS, -ES *n* variety of the volcanic rock tuff

TRAT, -S *n* type of fishing line holding a series of baited hooks

TRATT, -S *short for* > **trattoria**

TRAUCHLE *n* work or a task that is tiring, monotonous, and lengthy ▷ *vb* walk or work slowly and wearily

TRAUMA, -S, -TA *n* emotional shock

TRAVAIL, -S *n* labour or toil ▷ *vb* suffer or labour painfully

TRAVE, -S *n* stout wooden cage in which difficult horses are shod

TRAVEL, -S *vb* go from one place to another, through an area, or for a specified distance ▷ *n* travelling, esp as a tourist

TRAVELED *same as* > **travelled**

TRAVELER *same as* > **traveller**

TRAVELOG *n* film, lecture, or brochure on travel

TRAVELS ▶ **travel**

TRAVERSE *vb* pass or go over

TRAVES ▶ **trave**

TRAVESTY *n* grotesque imitation or mockery ▷ *vb* make or be a travesty of

TRAVIS, -ES *same as* ▶ **treviss**

TRAVOIS *n* sled used for dragging logs

TRAVOISE *same as* ▶ **travois**

TRAWL, -ED, -ING, -S *n* net dragged at deep levels behind a fishing boat ▷ *vb* fish with such a net

TRAWLER, -S *n* trawling boat

TRAWLEY, -S *same as* ▶ **trolley**

TRAWLING ▶ **trawl**

TRAWLNET *n* large net used by trawlers

TRAWLS ▶ **trawl**

TRAY, -S *n* flat board, usu with a rim, for carrying things

TRAYBAKE *n* flat cake which is baked in a tray and cut into small squares

TRAYBIT, -S *n* threepenny bit

TRAYF *adj* not prepared according to Jewish law

TRAYFUL, -S *n* as many or as much as will fit on a tray

TRAYNE, -D, -S, TRAYNING *old spelling of* ▶ **train**

TRAYS ▶ **tray**

TREACHER *n* traitor; treacherous person

TREACLE, -D, -S *n* thick dark syrup produced when sugar is refined ▷ *vb* add treacle to

TREACLY

TREAD, -ED, -ING, -S, TRODDEN *vb* set one's foot on ▷ *n* way of walking or dancing

TREADER -S

TREADLE, -D, -S *n* lever worked by the foot to turn a wheel ▷ *vb* work (a machine) with a treadle

TREADLER

TREADS ▶ **tread**

TREAGUE, -S *n* agreement to stop fighting**

TREASON, -S n betrayal of one's sovereign or country

TREASURE n collection of wealth, esp gold or jewels ▷ vb prize or cherish

TREASURY n storage place for treasure

TREAT, -ED, -ING, -S vb deal with or regard in a certain manner ▷ n pleasure, entertainment, etc given or paid for by someone else

TREATER -S

TREATIES ▸ treaty

TREATING ▸ treat

TREATISE n formal piece of writing on a particular subject

TREATS ▸ treat

TREATY, TREATIES n signed contract between states

TREBLE, -D, -S adj triple ▷ n (singer with or part of) a soprano voice ▷ vb increase three times

TREBLING n act of trebling

TREBLY ▸ treble

TRECENTO n 14th century, esp with reference to Italian art and literature

TRECK, -ED, -ING, -S same as ▸ trek

TREDDLE, -D, -S variant spelling of ▸ treadle

TREDILLE same as > tredrille

TREE, -D, -ING, -S n large perennial plant with a woody trunk

TREELAWN n narrow band of grass between a road and a pavement, usually planted with trees

TREELESS ▸ tree

TREELIKE ▸ tree

TREELINE n line marking the altitude above which trees will not grow

TREEN, -S adj made of wood ▷ n art of making treenware

TREENAIL n dowel used for pinning planks or timbers together

TREENS ▸ treen

TREES ▸ tree

TREESHIP n state of being a tree

TREETOP, -S n top of a tree

TREEWARE n reading materials that are printed on paper as opposed to a digital format

TREEWAX n yellowish wax secreted by an oriental scale insect

TREF adj in Judaism, ritually unfit to be eaten

TREFA same as ▸ tref

TREFAH same as ▸ tref

TREFOIL, -S n plant, such as clover, with a three-lobed leaf

TREHALA, -S n edible sugary substance from the cocoon of an Asian weevil

TREIF same as ▸ tref

TREIFA same as ▸ tref

TREILLE, -S another word for ▸ trellis

TREK, -KED, -S n long difficult journey, esp on foot ▷ vb make such a journey

TREKKER -S

TREKKING n as in **pony trekking** the act of riding ponies cross-country

TREKS ▸ trek

TRELLIS n framework of horizontal and vertical strips of wood ▷ vb interweave (strips of wood, etc) to make a trellis

TREM, -S n lever for producing a tremolo on a guitar

TREMA, -S n mark placed over vowel to indicate it is to be pronounced separately

TREMATIC adj relating to the gills

TREMBLE, -D vb shake or quiver ▷ n trembling

TREMBLER n device that vibrates to make or break an electrical circuit

TREMBLES n disease of cattle and sheep

TREMBLOR n earth tremor

TREMBLY ▸ tremble

TREMIE, -S n metal hopper and pipe used to distribute freshly mixed concrete underwater

TREMOLO, -S n quivering effect in singing or playing

TREMOR, -ED, -S n involuntary shaking ▷ vb tremble

TREMS ▸ trem

TRENAIL, -S same as ▸ treenail

TRENCH, -ED, -ES n long narrow ditch, esp one used as a shelter in war ▷ adj of or involving military trenches ▷ vb make a trench in (a place)

TRENCHER n wooden plate for serving food

TRENCHES ▸ trench

TREND, -ED, -ING, -S n general tendency or direction ▷ vb take a certain trend

TRENDIER ▸ trendy

TRENDIES ▸ trendy

TRENDIFY vb render fashionable

TRENDILY ▸ trendy

TRENDING ▸ trend

TRENDOID n follower of trends

TRENDS ▸ trend

TRENDY, TRENDIER, TRENDIES n consciously fashionable (person) ▷ adj consciously fashionable

TRENISE, -S n one of the figures in a quadrille

TRENTAL, -S n mass said in remembrance of a person 30 days after his or her death

TREPAN, -S same as ▸ trephine

TREPANG, -S n any of various large sea cucumbers

TREPANS ▸ trepan

TREPHINE n surgical instrument for removing circular sections of bone ▷ vb remove a circular section of bone from

TREPID adj trembling

TRES adj very

TRESPASS vb go onto another's property without permission ▷ n trespassing

TRESS, -ES, -ING n lock of hair, esp a long lock of woman's hair ▷ vb arrange in tresses

TRESSED adj having a tress or tresses as specified

TRESSEL, -S variant spelling of ▸ trestle

TRESSES ▸ tress

TRESSIER ▸ tressy

TRESSING ▸ tress

TRESSOUR same as ▸ tressure

TRESSURE n narrow inner border on a shield, usually decorated with fleurs-de-lys

TRESSY, TRESSIER ▸ tress

TREST, -S old variant of ▸ trestle

TRESTLE, -S n board fixed on pairs of spreading legs, used as a support

TRESTS ▸ trest

TRET, -S n (formerly) allowance granted for waste due to transportation

TREVALLY n any of various food and game fishes

TREVET, -S same as ▸ trivet

TREVIS, -ES variant spelling of ▸ treviss

TREVISS n partition in a stable for keeping animals apart

TREW old variant spelling of ▸ true

T

TREWS pl n close-fitting tartan trousers

TREWSMAN, TREWSMEN n Highlander

TREY, -S n any card or dice throw with three spots

TREYBIT, -S same as ► traybit

TREYF adj not prepared according to Jewish law

TREYFA same as ► treyf

TREYS ► trey

TREZ, -ES same as ► trey

TRIABLE adj liable to be tried judicially

TRIAC, -S n device for regulating the amount of electric current allowed to reach a circuit

TRIACID, -S adj (of a base) capable of reacting with three molecules of a monobasic acid

TRIACS ► triac

TRIACT, -S adj having three rays ▷ n sponge spicule with three rays

TRIACTOR n type of bet

TRIACTS ► triact

TRIAD, -S n group of three

TRIADIC, -S n something that has the characteristics of a triad

TRIADISM ► triad

TRIADIST ► triad

TRIADS ► triad

TRIAGE, -D, -S, TRIAGING n sorting emergency patients into categories of priority ▷ vb sort (patients) into categories of priority

TRIAL, -ED, -ING, -LED, -S n investigation of a case before a judge ▷ vb test or try out

TRIALISM n belief that man consists of body, soul, and spirit

TRIALIST same as > triallist

TRIALITY ► trialism

TRIALLED ► trial

TRIALS ► trial

TRIANGLE n geometric figure with three sides

TRIAPSAL adj (of a church) having three apses

TRIARCH, -S n one of three rulers of a triarchy

TRIARCHY n government by three people

TRIASSIC adj of, denoting, or formed in the first period of the Mesozoic era

TRIATIC, -S n rope between a ship's mastheads

TRIAXIAL adj having three axes ▷ n sponge spicule with three axes

TRIAXON, -S another name for ► triaxial

TRIAZIN, -S same as ► triazine

TRIAZINE n any of three azines that contain three nitrogen atoms in their molecules

TRIAZINS ► triazin

TRIAZOLE n heterocyclic compound

TRIBADY another word for > tribadism

TRIBAL, -S adj of or denoting a tribe or tribes ▷ n member of a tribal community

TRIBALLY

TRIBASIC adj (of an acid) containing three replaceable hydrogen atoms in the molecule

TRIBBLE, -S n frame for drying paper

TRIBE, -S n group of clans or families believed to have a common ancestor

TRIBLET, -S n spindle or mandrel used in making rings, tubes, etc

TRIBRACH n metrical foot of three short syllables

TRIBUNAL n board appointed to inquire into a specific matter

TRIBUNE, -S n people's representative, esp in ancient Rome

TRIBUTE, -S n sign of respect or admiration

TRIBUTER n miner

TRIBUTES ► tribute

TRICAR, -S n car with three wheels

TRICE, -D, -S, TRICING n moment ▷ vb haul up or secure

TRICEP same as ► triceps

TRICEPS n muscle at the back of the upper arm

TRICES ► trice

TRICHINA n parasitic nematode worm

TRICHITE n any of various needle-shaped crystals that occur in some glassy volcanic rocks

TRICHOID adj resembling a hair

TRICHOME n any hairlike outgrowth from the surface of a plant

TRICHORD n musical instrument with three strings

TRICING ► trice

TRICITY n area that comprises three adjoining cities

TRICK, -ED, -ING, -S n deceitful or cunning action or plan ▷ vb cheat or deceive

TRICKER -S

TRICKERY n practice or an instance of using tricks

TRICKIE Scots form of ► tricky

TRICKIER ► tricky

TRICKILY ► tricky

TRICKING ► trick

TRICKISH same as ► tricky

TRICKLE, -D, -S vb (cause to) flow in a thin stream or drops ▷ n gradual flow

TRICKLET n tiny trickle

TRICKLY ► trickle

TRICKS ► trick

TRICKSY adj playing tricks habitually

TRICKY, TRICKIER adj difficult, needing careful handling

TRICLAD, -S n type of worm having a tripartite intestine

TRICOLOR same as > tricolour

TRICORN, -S n cocked hat with opposing brims turned back and caught in three places ▷ adj having three horns or corners

TRICORNE same as ► tricorn

TRICORNS ► tricorn

TRICOT, -S n thin rayon or nylon fabric knitted or resembling knitting, used for dresses, etc

TRICTRAC n game similar to backgammon

TRICYCLE n three-wheeled cycle ▷ vb ride a tricycle

TRIDACNA n giant clam

TRIDARN, -S n sideboard with three levels

TRIDE old spelling of the past tense of ► try

TRIDENT, -S n three-pronged spear ▷ adj having three prongs

TRIDUAN adj three days long

TRIDUUM, -S n period of three days for prayer before a feast

TRIE old spelling of ► try

TRIED ► try

TRIELLA, -S n bet on the winners of three nominated horse races

TRIENE, -S n chemical compound containing three double bonds

TRIENNIA > **triennium**

TRIENS, TRIENTES n Byzantine gold coin worth one third of a solidus

TRIER, -S n person or thing that tries

TRIES ► **try**

TRIETHYL adj consisting of three groups of ethyls

TRIFECTA n form of betting in which the punter selects the first three place-winners in a horse race in the correct order

TRIFF, -ER, -EST adj terrific; very good indeed

TRIFFIC adj terrific; very good indeed

TRIFFID, -S n fictional plant that could kill humans

TRIFFIDY adj resembling a triffid

TRIFID adj divided or split into three parts or lobes

TRIFLE, -D, -S n insignificant thing or amount ▷ vb deal (with) as if worthless

TRIFLER -S

TRIFLING adj insignificant

TRIFOCAL adj having three focuses ▷ n glasses that have trifocal lenses

TRIFOLD less common word for ► **triple**

TRIFOLY same as ► **trefoil**

TRIFORIA > **triforium**

TRIFORM adj having three parts

TRIG, -GED, -GEST, -GING, -S adj neat or spruce ▷ vb make or become spruce

TRIGAMY n condition of having three spouses

TRIGGED ► **trig**

TRIGGER, -S n small lever releasing a catch on a gun or machine ▷ vb set (an action or process) in motion

TRIGGEST ► **trig**

TRIGGING ► **trig**

TRIGLOT, -S n person who can speak three languages

TRIGLY ► **trig**

TRIGLYPH n stone block in a Doric frieze, having three vertical channels

TRIGNESS ► **trig**

TRIGO, -S n wheat field

TRIGON, -S n (in classical Greece or Rome) a triangular harp or lyre

TRIGONAL adj triangular

TRIGONIC ► **trigon**

TRIGONS ► **trigon**

TRIGOS ► **trigo**

TRIGRAM, -S n three-letter inscription

TRIGRAPH n combination of three letters used to represent a single speech sound

TRIGS ► **trig**

TRIHEDRA > **trihedron**

TRIJET, -S n jet with three engines

TRIKE, -S n tricycle

TRILBIED adj wearing a trilby

TRILBY, TRILBIES, -S n man's soft felt hat

TRILD old past tense of ► **trill**

TRILEMMA n quandary posed by three alternative courses of action

TRILITH, -S same as > **trilithon**

TRILL, -ED, -ING, -S n rapid alternation between two notes ▷ vb play or sing a trill

TRILLER -S

TRILLION n one million million ▷ adj amounting to a trillion

TRILLIUM n plant of Asia and North America

TRILLO, -ES n (in music) a trill

TRILLS ► **trill**

TRILOBAL ► **trilobe**

TRILOBE, -S n three-lobed thing

TRILOBED adj having three lobes

TRILOBES ► **trilobe**

TRILOGY n series of three related books, plays, etc

TRIM, -MED, -MEST, -MING, -S adj neat and smart ▷ vb cut or prune into good shape ▷ n decoration

TRIMARAN n three-hulled boat

TRIMER, -S n polymer or a molecule of a polymer consisting of three identical monomers

TRIMERIC

TRIMETER n verse line consisting of three metrical feet ▷ adj designating such a line

TRIMIX, -ES n gas mixture of nitrogen, helium and oxygen used by deep-sea divers

TRIMLY ► **trim**

TRIMMED ► **trim**

TRIMMER, -S ► **trim**

TRIMMEST ► **trim**

TRIMMING ► **trim**

TRIMNESS ► **trim**

TRIMORPH n substance, esp a mineral, that exists in three distinct forms

TRIMOTOR n vehicle with three motors

TRIMPOT, -S n small instrument for adjusting resistance or voltage

TRIMS ► **trim**

TRIMTAB, -S n small control surface to enable the pilot to balance an aircraft

TRIN, -S n triplet

TRINAL ► **trine**

TRINARY adj made up of three parts

TRINDLE, -D, -S vb move heavily on (or as if on) wheels

TRINE, -D, -S, TRINING n aspect of 120° between two planets, an orb of 8° being allowed ▷ adj of or relating to a trine ▷ vb put in a trine aspect

TRINGLE, -S n slim rod

TRINING ► **trine**

TRINITY n group of three

TRINKET, -S n small or worthless ornament or piece of jewellery ▷ vb ornament with trinkets

TRINKUM, -S n trinket or bauble

TRINODAL adj having three nodes

TRINS ► **trin**

TRIO, -S n group of three

TRIODE, -S n electronic valve having three electrodes, a cathode, an anode, and a grid

TRIOL, -S n any of a class of alcohols that have three hydroxyl groups per molecule

TRIOLEIN n naturally occurring glyceride of oleic acid, found in fats and oils

TRIOLET, -S n verse form of eight lines

TRIOLS ► **triol**

TRIONES n seven stars of the constellation Ursa Major

TRIONYM, -S another name for > **trinomial**

TRIOR, -S old form of ► **trier**

TRIOS ► **trio**

TRIOSE, -S n simple monosaccharide produced by the oxidation of glycerol

TRIOXID, -S same as ► **trioxide**

TRIOXIDE n any oxide that contains three oxygen atoms per molecule

TRIOXIDS ► **trioxid**

TRIP, -PED, -PING, -S n journey to a place and back,

T

esp for pleasure ⊳ vb (cause to) stumble

TRIPACK, -S n pack of three

TRIPART adj composed of three parts

TRIPE n stomach of a cow used as food

TRIPEDAL adj having three feet

TRIPERY n place where tripe is prepared

TRIPES ▸ tripe

TRIPEY ▸ tripe

TRIPHASE adj having three phases

TRIPHONE n group of three phonemes

TRIPIER ▸ tripy

TRIPIEST ▸ tripy

TRIPLANE n aeroplane having three wings arranged one above the other

TRIPLE, -D, -S, TRIPLING adj having three parts ⊳ vb increase three times ⊳ n something that is, or contains, three times as much as normal

TRIPLET, -S n one of three babies born at one birth

TRIPLEX n building divided into three separate dwellings ⊳ vb separate into three parts

TRIPLIED ▸ triply

TRIPLIES ▸ triply

TRIPLING ▸ triple

TRIPLITE n brownish-red phosphate

TRIPLOID adj having or relating to three times the haploid number of chromosomes ⊳ n triploid organism

TRIPLY, TRIPLIED, TRIPLIES vb give a reply to a duply

TRIPMAN, TRIPMEN n man working on a trip

TRIPOD, -S n three-legged stand, stool, etc

TRIPODAL

TRIPODIC

TRIPODY n metrical unit consisting of three feet

TRIPOLI, -S n lightweight porous siliceous rock

TRIPOS, -ES n final examinations for an honours degree at Cambridge University

TRIPPANT adj (in heraldry) in the process of tripping

TRIPPED ▸ trip

TRIPPER, -S n tourist

TRIPPERY adj like a tripper

TRIPPET, -S n any mechanism that strikes or is struck at regular intervals, as by a cam

TRIPPIER ▸ trippy

TRIPPING ▸ trip

TRIPPLE, -D, -S vb canter

TRIPPLER

TRIPPY, TRIPPIER adj suggestive of or resembling the effect produced by a hallucinogenic drug

TRIPS ▸ trip

TRIPSIS, TRIPSES n act of kneading the body to promote circulation, suppleness, etc

TRIPTAN, -S n drug used to treat migraine

TRIPTANE n colourless highly flammable liquid

TRIPTANS ▸ triptan

TRIPTOTE n word that has only three cases

TRIPTYCA variant of ▸ triptych

TRIPTYCH n painting or carving on three hinged panels, often forming an altarpiece

TRIPUDIA > tripudium

TRIPWIRE n wire that activates a trap, mine, etc, when tripped over

TRIPY, TRIPIER, TRIPIEST ▸ tripe

TRIREME, -S n ancient Greek warship with three rows of oars on each side

TRISCELE variant spelling of ▸ triskele

TRISECT, -S vb divide into three parts, esp three equal parts

TRISEME, -S n metrical foot of a length equal to three short syllables

TRISEMIC

TRISHAW, -S another name for ▸ rickshaw

TRISKELE n three-limbed symbol

TRISMIC ▸ trismus

TRISMUS n state of being unable to open the mouth

TRISOME, -S n chromosome occurring three times (rather than twice) in a cell

TRISOMIC ▸ trisomy

TRISOMY n condition of having one chromosome represented three times

TRIST variant spelling of ▸ triste

TRISTATE adj (of a digital computer chip) having high, low, and floating output states

TRISTE adj sad

TRISTEZA n disease affecting citrus trees

TRISTFUL same as ▸ triste

TRISTICH n poem, stanza, or strophe that consists of three lines

TRISUL, -S n trident symbol of Siva

TRISULA, -S same as ▸ trisul

TRISULS ▸ trisul

TRITE, -R, -S, -ST adj (of a remark or idea) commonplace and unoriginal ⊳ n (on a lyre) the third string from the highest in pitch

TRITELY

TRITHING n tripartition

TRITIATE vb replace normal hydrogen atoms in (a compound) by those of tritium

TRITICAL n trite; hackneyed

TRITICUM n type of cereal grass of the genus which includes the wheats

TRITIDE, -S n tritium compound

TRITIUM, -S n radioactive isotope of hydrogen

TRITOMA, -S another name for > **kniphofia**

TRITON, -S n any of various chiefly tropical marine gastropod molluscs

TRITONE, -S n musical interval consisting of three whole tones

TRITONIA n type of plant with typically scarlet or orange flowers

TRITONS ▸ triton

TRIUMPH, -S n (happiness caused by) victory or success ⊳ vb be victorious or successful

TRIUMVIR n (esp in ancient Rome) a member of a triumvirate

TRIUNE, -S adj constituting three things in one ⊳ n group of three

TRIUNITY

TRIVALVE n animal having three valves

TRIVET, -S n metal stand for a pot or kettle

TRIVIA pl n trivial things or details

TRIVIAL adj of little importance

TRIVIUM, **-S** *n* (in medieval learning) the lower division of the seven liberal arts

TRIZONAL ▸ **trizone**

TRIZONE, **-S** *n* area comprising three zones

TROAD, **-S** *same as* ▸ **trod**

TROADE, **-S** *same as* ▸ **trod**

TROADS ▸ **troad**

TROAK, **-ED**, **-ING**, **-S** *old form of* ▸ **truck**

TROAT, **-ED**, **-ING**, **-S** *vb* (of a rutting buck) to call or bellow

TROCAR, **-S** *n* surgical instrument for removing fluid from bodily cavities

TROCHAIC *adj* of, relating to, or consisting of trochees ▷ *n* verse composed of trochees

TROCHAL *adj* shaped like a wheel

TROCHAR, **-S** *old variant spelling of* ▸ **trocar**

TROCHE, **-S** *another name for* ▸ **lozenge**

TROCHEE, **-S** *n* metrical foot of one long and one short syllable

TROCHES ▸ **troche**

TROCHI ▸ **trochus**

TROCHIL, **-S** *same as* > **trochilus**

TROCHILI > **trochilus**

TROCHILS ▸ **trochil**

TROCHISK *another word for* ▸ **troche**

TROCHITE *n* joint of a crinoid

TROCHLEA *n* any bony or cartilaginous part with a grooved surface

TROCHOID *n* curve described by a fixed point on the radius or extended radius of a circle as the circle rolls along a straight line ▷ *adj* rotating about a central axis

TROCHUS, **TROCHI** *n* hoop (used in exercise)

TROCK, **-ED**, **-ING**, **-S** *same as* ▸ **truck**

TROCKEN *adj* dry (used of wine)

TROCKING ▸ **trock**

TROCKS ▸ **trock**

TROD, **-S** *vb* past participle of tread ▷ *n* path

TRODDEN ▸ **tread**

TRODE, **-S** *same as* ▸ **trod**

TRODS ▸ **trod**

TROELIE, **-S** *same as* ▸ **troolie**

TROELY *same as* ▸ **troolie**

TROFFER, **-S** *n* fixture for holding and reflecting light from a fluorescent tube

TROG, **-GED**, **-GING**, **-S** *vb* walk, esp aimlessly or heavily

TROGGS *n* loyalty; fidelity

TROGON, **-S** *n* bird of tropical and subtropical America, Africa, and Asia

TROGS ▸ **trog**

TROIKA, **-S** *n* Russian vehicle drawn by three horses abreast

TROILITE *n* iron sulphide present in most meteorites

TROILUS *n* type of large butterfly

TROIS *Scots form of* ▸ **troy**

TROKE, **-D**, **-S**, **TROKING** *same as* ▸ **truck**

TROLAND, **-S** *n* unit of light intensity in the eye

TROLL, **-ED**, **-ING**, **-S** *n* giant or dwarf in Scandinavian folklore ▷ *vb* fish by dragging a lure through the water

TROLLER **-S**

TROLLEY *n* small wheeled table for food and drink ▷ *vb* transport on a trolley

TROLLEYS *pl n* men's underpants

TROLLIED ▸ **trolly**

TROLLIES ▸ **trolly**

TROLLING ▸ **troll**

TROLLISH *adj* like a troll

TROLLIUS *n* plant with globe-shaped flowers

TROLLS ▸ **troll**

TROLLY, **TROLLIED**, **TROLLIES** *same as* ▸ **trolley**

TROMBONE *n* brass musical instrument with a sliding tube

TROMINO, **-S** *n* shape made from three squares, each joined to the next along one full side

TROMMEL, **-S** *n* revolving cylindrical sieve used to screen crushed ore

TROMP, **-ED**, **-ING**, **-S** *vb* trample

TROMPE, **-S** *n* apparatus for supplying the blast of air in a forge

TROMPED ▸ **tromp**

TROMPES ▸ **trompe**

TROMPING ▸ **tromp**

TROMPS ▸ **tromp**

TRON, **-S** *n* public weighing machine

TRONA, **-S** *n* greyish mineral that occurs in salt deposits

TRONC, **-S** *n* pool into which waiters, waitresses, hotel workers, etc, pay their tips

TRONE, **-S** *same as* ▸ **tron**

TRONK, **-S** *n* jail

TRONS ▸ **tron**

TROOLIE, **-S** *n* large palm leaf

TROOP, **-ED**, **-ING**, **-S** *n* large group ▷ *vb* move in a crowd

TROOPER, **-S** *n* cavalry soldier

TROOPIAL *same as* ▸ **troupial**

TROOPING ▸ **troop**

TROOPS ▸ **troop**

TROOZ *same as* ▸ **trews**

TROP *adv* too, too much

TROPARIA > **troparion**

TROPE, **-D**, **-S**, **TROPING** *n* figure of speech ▷ *vb* use tropes (in speech or writing)

TROPHESY *n* disorder of the nerves relating to nutrition

TROPHI *pl n* collective term for the mandibles and other parts of an insect's mouth

TROPHIC *adj* of or relating to nutrition

TROPHY, **TROPHIED**, **TROPHIES** *n* cup, shield, etc given as a prize ▷ *adj* regarded as a highly desirable symbol of wealth or success ▷ *vb* award a trophy to (someone)

TROPIC, **-S** *n* either of two lines of latitude at 23½°N or 23½°S

TROPICAL *adj* of or in the tropics ▷ *n* tropical thing or place

TROPICS ▸ **tropic**

TROPIN, **-S** *n* adrenal androgen

TROPINE, **-S** *n* white crystalline poisonous alkaloid

TROPING ▸ **trope**

TROPINS ▸ **tropin**

TROPISM, **-S** *n* tendency of a plant or animal to turn in response to an external stimulus

TROPIST **-S**

TROPONIN *n* muscle-tissue protein involved in the controlling of muscle contraction

TROPPO *adv* too much ▷ *adj* mentally affected by a tropical climate

TROSSERS *old form of* ▸ **trousers**

TROT, **-S**, **-TED**, **-TING** *vb* (of a horse) move at a medium pace, lifting the feet in diagonal pairs ▷ *n* trotting

TROTH, **-ED**, **-ING**, **-S** *n* pledge of devotion, esp a betrothal ▷ *vb* promise to marry

T

(someone)
TROTHFUL
TROTLINE n line suspended across a stream to which shorter hooked and baited lines are attached
TROTS ▸ trot
TROTTED ▸ trot
TROTTER, -S n pig's foot
TROTTING ▸ trot
TROTTOIR n pavement
TROTYL, -S n yellow solid used chiefly as a high explosive
TROU pl n trousers
TROUBLE, -S n (cause of) distress or anxiety ▷ vb (cause to) worry
TROUBLED
TROUBLER
TROUCH, -ES n rubbish
TROUGH, -ED, -S n long open container, esp for animals' food or water ▷ vb eat, consume, or take greedily
TROULE, -D, -S, TROULING old variant of ▸ troll
TROUNCE, -D, -S vb defeat utterly
TROUNCER
TROUPE, -D, -S, TROUPING n company of performers ▷ vb (esp of actors) to move or travel in a group
TROUPER, -S n member of a troupe
TROUPES ▸ troupe
TROUPIAL n any of various American orioles
TROUPING ▸ troupe
TROUSE, -S pl n close-fitting breeches worn in Ireland
TROUSER vb take (something, esp money), often surreptitiously or unlawfully
TROUSERS pl n two-legged outer garment with legs reaching usu to the ankles
TROUSES ▸ trouse
TROUT, -ING, -S n game fish related to the salmon ▷ vb fish for trout
TROUTER -S
TROUTFUL adj (of a body of water) full of trout
TROUTIER ▸ trouty
TROUTING ▸ trout
TROUTLET n small trout
TROUTS ▸ trout
TROUTY, TROUTIER ▸ trout
TROUVERE n poet of N France during the 12th and 13th centuries
TROUVEUR same as ▸ trouvere

TROVE, -S n as in **treasure-trove** valuable articles found hidden in the earth
TROVER, -S n act of assuming proprietary rights over goods or property belonging to another
TROVES ▸ trove
TROW, -ED, -ING, -S vb think, believe, or trust
TROWEL, -ED, -S n hand tool with a wide blade ▷ vb use a trowel on (plaster, soil, etc)
TROWELER
TROWING ▸ trow
TROWS ▸ trow
TROWSERS old spelling of ▸ trousers
TROWTH, -S variant spelling of ▸ troth
TROY, -S n as in **troy weight** system of weights used for precious metals and gemstones
TRUANCY ▸ truant
TRUANT, -ED, -S n pupil who stays away from school without permission ▷ adj being or relating to a truant ▷ vb play truant
TRUANTLY
TRUANTRY
TRUCAGE, -S n art forgery
TRUCE, -D, -S, TRUCING n temporary agreement to stop fighting ▷ vb make a truce
TRUCHMAN, TRUCHMEN n interpreter; translator
TRUCIAL ▸ truce
TRUCING ▸ truce
TRUCK, -ED, -S n railway goods wagon ▷ vb exchange (goods); barter
TRUCKAGE n conveyance of cargo by truck
TRUCKED ▸ truck
TRUCKER, -S n truck driver
TRUCKFUL n amount of something that can be conveyed in a truck
TRUCKIE, -S n truck driver
TRUCKING n transportation of goods by lorry
TRUCKLE, -D, -S vb yield weakly or give in ▷ n small wheel
TRUCKLER
TRUCKMAN, TRUCKMEN n truck driver
TRUCKS ▸ truck
TRUDGE, -D, -S, TRUDGING vb walk heavily or wearily ▷ n long tiring walk
TRUDGEN, -S n type of swimming stroke

TRUDGEON nonstandard variant of ▸ trudgen
TRUDGER, -S ▸ trudge
TRUDGES ▸ trudge
TRUDGING ▸ trudge
TRUE, -D, -ING, -R, -S, -ST, TRUING adj in accordance with facts
TRUEBLUE n staunch royalist or Conservative
TRUEBORN adj being such by birth
TRUEBRED adj thoroughbred
TRUED ▸ true
TRUEING ▸ true
TRUELOVE n person that one loves
TRUEMAN, TRUEMEN n honest person
TRUENESS ▸ true
TRUER ▸ true
TRUES ▸ true
TRUEST ▸ true
TRUFFE, -S rare word for ▸ truffle
TRUFFLE, -D, -S n edible underground fungus ▷ vb hunt for truffles
TRUG, -S n long shallow basket used by gardeners
TRUGO, -S n game similar to croquet
TRUGS ▸ trug
TRUING ▸ true
TRUISM, -S n self-evident truth
TRUISTIC
TRULY adv in a true manner
TRUMEAU, -X n section of a wall or pillar between two openings
TRUMP, -ED, -ING, -S adj (card) of the suit outranking the others ▷ vb play a trump card on (another card) ▷ pl n suit outranking the others
TRUMPERY n something useless or worthless ▷ adj useless or worthless
TRUMPET, -S n valved brass instrument with a flared tube ▷ vb proclaim loudly
TRUMPING ▸ trump
TRUMPS ▸ trump
TRUNCAL adj of or relating to the trunk
TRUNCATE vb cut short ▷ adj cut short
TRUNDLE, -D, -S vb move heavily on wheels ▷ n act or an instance of trundling
TRUNDLER n golf or shopping trolley
TRUNDLES ▸ trundle

TRUNK, -ED n main stem of a tree ▷ vb lop or truncate
TRUNKFUL
TRUNKING n cables that take a common route through an exchange building linking ranks of selectors
TRUNKS pl n shorts worn by a man for swimming
TRUNNEL, -S same as ► **treenail**
TRUNNION n one of a pair of coaxial projections attached to opposite sides of a cannon
TRUQUAGE variant of ► **trucage**
TRUQUEUR n art forger
TRUSS, -ED, -ES vb tie or bind up ▷ n device for holding a hernia, etc in place
TRUSSER -S
TRUSSING n system of trusses, esp for strengthening or reinforcing a structure
TRUST, -ED, -S vb believe in and rely on ▷ n confidence in the truth, reliability, etc of a person or thing ▷ adj of or relating to a trust or trusts
TRUSTEE, -D, -S n person holding property on another's behalf ▷ vb act as a trustee
TRUSTER, -S ► **trust**
TRUSTFUL adj inclined to trust others
TRUSTIER ► **trusty**
TRUSTIES ► **trusty**
TRUSTILY ► **trusty**
TRUSTING same as ► **trustful**
TRUSTOR, -S n person who sets up a trust
TRUSTS ► **trust**
TRUSTY, TRUSTIER, TRUSTIES adj faithful or reliable ▷ n trustworthy convict to whom special privileges are granted
TRUTH, -S n state of being true
TRUTHER, -S n person who does not believe official accounts of the 9/11 attacks on the US
TRUTHFUL adj honest
TRUTHIER ► **truthy**
TRUTHS ► **truth**
TRUTHY, TRUTHIER adj truthful
TRY, TRIED, TRIES, -ING, -INGS vb make an effort or attempt ▷ n attempt or effort
TRYE adj very good; select

TRYER, -S variant of ► **trier**
TRYING ► **try**
TRYINGLY ► **try**
TRYINGS ► **try**
TRYKE, -S variant spelling of ► **trike**
TRYMA, -TA n drupe produced by the walnut and similar plants
TRYOUT, -S n trial or test, as of an athlete or actor
TRYP, -S n parasitic protozoan
TRYPAN modifier as in **trypan blue** dye used for staining cells in biological research
TRYPS ► **tryp**
TRYPSIN, -S n enzyme occurring in pancreatic juice
TRYPTIC
TRYSAIL, -S n small fore-and-aft sail on a sailing vessel
TRYST, -ED, -ING, -S n arrangement to meet ▷ vb meet at or arrange a tryst
TRYSTE, -S variant spelling of ► **tryst**
TRYSTED ► **tryst**
TRYSTER, -S ► **tryst**
TRYSTES ► **tryste**
TRYSTING ► **tryst**
TRYSTS ► **tryst**
TRYWORKS n furnace for rendering blubber
TSADDIK, -S variant of ► **zaddik**
TSADDIQ, -S variant of ► **zaddik**
TSADE, -S variant spelling of ► **sadhe**
TSADI, -S variant of ► **sadhe**
TSADIK, -S same as ► **zaddik**
TSADIS ► **tsadi**
TSAMBA, -S n Tibetan dish made from roasted barley and tea
TSANTSA, -S n shrunken head of an enemy kept as a trophy
TSAR, -S n Russian emperor
TSARDOM -S
TSAREVNA n daughter of a Russian tsar
TSARINA, -S n wife of a Russian tsar
TSARISM, -S n system of government by a tsar
TSARIST -S
TSARITSA same as ► **tsarina**
TSARITZA variant spelling of ► **tsaritsa**
TSARS ► **tsar**
TSATSKE, -S variant of > **tchotchke**
TSESSEBE South African variant of ► **sassaby**

TSETSE, -S n any of various bloodsucking African flies
TSIGANE, -S variant of ► **tzigane**
TSIMMES variant spelling of ► **tzimmes**
TSITSITH n tassels or fringes of thread attached to the four corners of the tallith
TSK, -ED, -ING, -S vb utter the sound "tsk", usu in disapproval

This can occasionally be useful because it enables you to play K without using vowels.

TSKTSK, -ED, -S same as ► **tsk**
TSOORIS variant of ► **tsuris**
TSORES variant of ► **tsuris**
TSORIS variant of ► **tsuris**
TSORRISS variant of ► **tsuris**
TSOTSI, -S n (in South Africa) Black street thug or gang member
TSOURIS variant of ► **tsuris**
TSUBA, -S n sword guard of a Japanese sword
TSUBO, -S n unit of area
TSUNAMI, -S n tidal wave, usu caused by an earthquake under the sea
TSUNAMIC
TSURIS, -ES n grief or strife
TSUTSUMU n Japanese art of wrapping gifts
TUAN, -S n lord
TUART, -S n eucalyptus tree of Australia
TUATARA, -S n large lizard-like New Zealand reptile
TUATERA, -S variant spelling of ► **tuatara**
TUATH, -S n territory of an ancient Irish tribe
TUATUA, -S n edible marine bivalve of New Zealand waters
TUB, -BED, -BING, -BINGS, -S n open, usu round container ▷ vb wash (oneself or another) in a tub
TUBA, -E, -S n valved low-pitched brass instrument
TUBAGE, -S n insertion of a tube
TUBAIST, -S ► **tuba**
TUBAL adj of or relating to a tube
TUBAR another word for ► **tubular**
TUBAS ► **tuba**
TUBATE less common word for ► **tubular**
TUBBABLE ► **tub**

T

TUBBED ▸ tub
TUBBER, -S ▸ tub
TUBBIER ▸ tubby
TUBBIEST ▸ tubby
TUBBING ▸ tub
TUBBINGS ▸ tub
TUBBISH adj fat
TUBBY, TUBBIER, TUBBIEST adj (of a person) short and fat
TUBE, -D, -S n hollow cylinder
TUBEFUL, -S n quantity (of something) that a tube can hold
TUBELESS adj without a tube
TUBELIKE adj resembling a tube
TUBENOSE n seabird with tubular nostrils on its beak
TUBER, -S n fleshy underground root of a plant such as a potato
TUBERCLE n small rounded swelling
TUBEROID adj resembling a tuber ▹ n fleshy root resembling a tuber
TUBEROSE same as ▸ tuberous
TUBEROUS adj (of plants) forming, bearing, or resembling a tuber or tubers
TUBERS ▸ tuber
TUBES ▸ tube
TUBEWELL n type of water well
TUBEWORK n collective term for tubes or tubing
TUBEWORM n undersea worm
TUBFAST, -S n period of fasting and sweating in a tub, intended as a cure for disease
TUBFISH another name for ▸ gurnard
TUBFUL, -S n amount a tub will hold
TUBICOLE n tube-dwelling creature
TUBIFEX n type of small reddish freshwater worm
TUBIFORM same as ▸ tubular
TUBING, -S n length of tube
TUBIST, -S ▸ tuba
TUBLIKE ▸ tub
TUBS ▸ tub
TUBULAR, -S adj of or shaped like a tube ▹ n type of tyre
TUBULATE vb form or shape into a tube
TUBULE, -S n any small tubular structure
TUBULIN, -S n protein forming the basis of microtubules

TUBULOSE adj tube-shaped; consisting of tubes
TUBULOUS adj tube-shaped
TUBULURE n tube leading into a retort or other receptacle
TUCHIS, -ES n buttocks
TUCHUN, -S n (formerly) a Chinese military governor or warlord
TUCHUS, -ES same as ▸ tuchis
TUCK, -ED, -S vb push or fold into a small space ▹ n stitched fold
TUCKAHOE n type of edible root
TUCKBOX n box used for carrying food to school
TUCKED ▸ tuck
TUCKER, -ED, -S n food ▹ vb weary or tire completely
TUCKET, -S n flourish on a trumpet
TUCKING, -S n act of tucking
TUCKS ▸ tuck
TUCKSHOP n shop, esp one in or near a school, where food such as cakes and sweets are sold
TUCOTUCO n colonial burrowing South American rodent
TUCUTUCO variant spelling of ▸ tucotuco
TUCUTUCU same as ▸ tucotuco
TUFA, -S n porous rock formed as a deposit from springs
TUFF, -S n porous rock formed from volcanic dust or ash
TUFFE, -S old form of ▸ tuft
TUFFET, -S n small mound or seat
TUFFS ▸ tuff
TUFOLI n type of tubular pasta
TUFT, -ING, -INGS, -S n bunch of feathers, grass, hair, etc held or growing together at the base ▹ vb provide or decorate with a tuft or tufts
TUFTED adj having a tuft or tufts
TUFTER, -S ▸ tuft
TUFTIER ▸ tufty
TUFTIEST ▸ tufty
TUFTILY ▸ tuft
TUFTING ▸ tuft
TUFTINGS ▸ tuft
TUFTS ▸ tuft
TUFTY, TUFTIER, TUFTIEST ▸ tuft
TUG, -GED, -GING, -GINGS, -S vb pull hard ▹ n hard pull

TUGBOAT, -S same as ▸ tug
TUGGED ▸ tug
TUGGER, -S ▸ tug
TUGGING ▸ tug
TUGGINGS ▸ tug
TUGHRA, -S n Turkish Sultan's official emblem
TUGHRIK, -S same as ▸ tugrik
TUGLESS ▸ tug
TUGRA, -S variant of ▸ tughra
TUGRIK, -S n standard monetary unit of Mongolia
TUGS ▸ tug
TUI, -S n New Zealand honeyeater that mimics human speech and the songs of other birds
TUILE, -S n type of almond-flavoured dessert biscuit
TUILLE, -S n (in a suit of armour) hanging plate protecting the thighs
TUILYIE, -D, -S vb fight
TUILZIE, -D, -S variant form of ▸ tuilyie
TUINA, -S n form of massage originating in China
TUIS ▸ tui
TUISM, -S n practice of putting the interests of another before one's own
TUITION, -S n instruction, esp received individually or in a small group
TUKTOO, -S same as ▸ tuktu
TUKTU, -S (in Canada) another name for ▸ caribou
TULADI, -S n large trout found in Canada and northern US
TULBAN, -S old form of ▸ turban
TULCHAN, -S n skin of a calf placed next to a cow to induce it to give milk
TULE, -S n type of bulrush found in California
TULIP, -S n plant with bright cup-shaped flowers
TULIPANT n turban
TULIPS ▸ tulip
TULLE, -S n fine net fabric of silk etc
TULLIBEE n cisco of the Great Lakes of Canada
TULPA, -S n being or object created through willpower and visualization techniques
TULSI, -S n type of basil
TULWAR, -S n Indian sabre
TUM, -S informal or childish word for ▸ stomach
TUMBLE, -D, -S, TUMBLING vb (cause to) fall, esp

awkwardly or violently ▷ *n* fall

TUMBLER, -S *n* stemless drinking glass

TUMBLES ► tumble

TUMBLING ► tumble

TUMBREL, -S *n* farm cart for carrying manure

TUMBRIL, -S *same as* ► tumbrel

TUMEFY, TUMEFIED, TUMEFIES *vb* make or become tumid

TUMESCE, -D, -S *vb* swell

TUMID *adj* (of an organ or part of the body) enlarged or swollen

TUMIDITY

TUMIDLY

TUMMIES ► tummy

TUMMLER, -S *n* entertainer employed to encourage audience participation

TUMMY, TUMMIES *n* stomach

TUMOR, -S *same as* ► tumour

TUMORAL ► tumour

TUMOROUS ► tumour

TUMORS ► tumor

TUMOUR, -S *n* abnormal growth in or on the body

TUMP, -ED, -ING, -S *n* small mound or clump ▷ *vb* make a tump around

TUMPHY, TUMPHIES *n* dolt; fool

TUMPIER ► tumpy

TUMPIEST ► tumpy

TUMPING ► tump

TUMPLINE *n* band strung across the forehead or chest and attached to a pack in order to support it

TUMPS ► tump

TUMPY, TUMPIER, TUMPIEST ► tump

TUMS ► tum

TUMSHIE, -S *n* turnip

TUMULAR *adj* of, relating to, or like a mound

TUMULARY *same as* ► tumular

TUMULI ► tumulus

TUMULOSE *adj* abounding in small hills or mounds

TUMULOUS *same as* ► tumulose

TUMULT, -ED, -S *n* uproar or commotion ▷ *vb* stir up a commotion

TUMULUS, TUMULI *n* burial mound

TUN, -NED, -NING, -NINGS, -S *n* large beer cask ▷ *vb* put into or keep in tuns

TUNA, -S *n* large marine food fish

TUNABLE *adj* able to be tuned

TUNABLY

TUNAS ► tuna

TUNBELLY *n* large round belly

TUND, -ED, -ING, -S *vb* beat; strike

TUNDISH *n* type of funnel

TUNDRA, -S *n* vast treeless Arctic region with permanently frozen subsoil

TUNDS ► tund

TUNDUN, -S *n* wooden instrument used by Native Australians in religious rites

TUNE, -D, -S *n* (pleasing) sequence of musical notes ▷ *vb* adjust (a musical instrument) so that it is in tune

TUNEABLE *same as* ► tunable

TUNEABLY

TUNEAGE, -S *n* music

TUNED ► tune

TUNEFUL *adj* having a pleasant tune

TUNELESS *adj* having no melody or tune

TUNER, -S *n* part of a radio or television receiver for selecting channels

TUNES ► tune

TUNEUP, -S *n* adjustments made to an engine to improve its performance

TUNG, -S *n as in* **tung oil** fast-drying oil obtained from the seeds of a central Asian tree

TUNGSTEN *n* greyish-white metal

TUNGSTIC *adj* of or containing tungsten, esp in a high valence state

TUNIC, -S *n* close-fitting jacket forming part of some uniforms

TUNICA, -E *n* tissue forming a layer or covering of an organ or part

TUNICATE *n* minute primitive marine chordate animal ▷ *adj* of, relating to this animal ▷ *vb* wear a tunic

TUNICIN, -S *n* cellulose-like substance found in tunicates

TUNICKED *adj* wearing a tunic

TUNICLE, -S *n* vestment worn at High Mass and other religious ceremonies

TUNICS ► tunic

TUNIER ► tuny

TUNIEST ► tuny

TUNING, -S *n* set of pitches to which the open strings of a guitar, violin, etc, are tuned

TUNKET, -S *n* hell

TUNNAGE, -S *same as* ► tonnage

TUNNED ► tun

TUNNEL, -ED, -S *n* underground passage ▷ *vb* make a tunnel (through)

TUNNELER

TUNNIES ► tunny

TUNNING ► tun

TUNNINGS ► tun

TUNNY, TUNNIES *same as* ► tuna

TUNS ► tun

TUNY, TUNIER, TUNIEST *adj* having an easily discernable melody

TUP, -PED, -S *n* male sheep ▷ *vb* cause (a ram) to mate with a ewe

TUPEK, -S *same as* ► tupik

TUPELO, -S *n* large tree of deep swamps and rivers of the southern US

TUPIK, -S *n* tent of seal or caribou skin used for shelter by Inuit people in summer

TUPLE, -S *n* row of values in a relational database

TUPPED ► tup

TUPPENCE *same as* ► twopence

TUPPENNY *same as* ► twopenny

TUPPING, -S *n* act of sheep mating

TUPS ► tup

TUPUNA, -S *same as* ► tipuna

TUQUE, -S *n* knitted cap with a long tapering end

TURACIN, -S *n* red pigment found in touraco feathers

TURACO, -S *same as* ► touraco

TURACOU, -S *variant of* ► touraco

TURBAN, -S *n* Muslim, Hindu, or Sikh man's head covering

TURBAND, -S *old variant of* ► turban

TURBANED ► turban

TURBANS ► turban

TURBANT, -S *old variant of* ► turban

TURBARY *n* land where peat or turf is cut or has been cut

TURBETH, -S *variant of* ► turpeth

TURBID *adj* muddy, not clear

TURBIDLY

TURBINAL *same as* ▷ turbinate

T

TURBINE, -S n machine or generator driven by gas, water, etc turning blades

TURBINED adj having a turbine

TURBINES ► turbine

TURBIT, -S n crested breed of domestic pigeon

TURBITH, -S variant of **► turpeth**

TURBITS ► turbit

TURBO, -S n compressor in an engine

TURBOCAR n car driven by a gas turbine

TURBOFAN n engine in which a fan driven by a turbine forces air rearwards to increase thrust

TURBOJET n gas turbine in which the exhaust gases provide the propulsive thrust to drive an aircraft

TURBOND, -S old variant of **► turban**

TURBOS ► turbo

TURBOT, -S n large European edible flatfish

TURD, -S n piece of excrement

TURDINE adj of, relating to, or characteristic of thrushes

TURDION, -S variant of **► tordion**

TURDOID same as **► turdine**

TURDS ► turd

TUREEN, -S n serving dish for soup

TURF, -ED, -ING, -INGS, -S, TURVES n short thick even grass ▷ vb cover with turf

TURFEN adj made of turf

TURFIER ► turfy

TURFIEST ► turfy

TURFING ► turf

TURFINGS ► turf

TURFITE, -S same as **► turfman**

TURFLESS ► turf

TURFLIKE ► turf

TURFMAN, TURFMEN n person devoted to horse racing

TURFS ► turf

TURFSKI, -S n ski down a grassy hill on skis modified with integral wheels

TURFY, TURFIER, TURFIEST adj of, covered with, or resembling turf

TURGENCY ► turgent

TURGENT obsolete word for **► turgid**

TURGID, -ER adj (of language) pompous

TURGIDLY

TURGITE, -S n red or black mineral consisting of hydrated ferric oxide

TURGOR, -S n normal rigid state of a cell

TURION, -S n perennating bud produced by many aquatic plants

TURISTA, -S n traveller's diarrhoea

TURKEY, -S n large bird bred for food

TURKIES old form of **> turquoise**

TURKIS, -ES old form of **> turquoise**

TURKOIS old form of **> turquoise**

TURLOUGH n seasonal lake or pond

TURM, -S n troop of horsemen

TURME, -S variant of **► turm**

TURMERIC n yellow spice obtained from the root of an Asian plant

TURMES ► turme

TURMOIL, -S n agitation or confusion ▷ vb make or become turbulent

TURMS ► turm

TURN, -ED, -S vb change the position or direction (of) ▷ n turning

TURNABLE

TURNBACK n one who turns back (from a challenge, for example)

TURNCOAT n person who deserts one party or cause to join another

TURNCOCK n (formerly) official employed to turn on the water for the mains supply

TURNDOWN adj capable of being or designed to be folded or doubled down ▷ n instance of turning down

TURNDUN, -S another name for **► tundun**

TURNED ► turn

TURNER, -S n person or thing that turns

TURNERY n objects made on a lathe

TURNHALL n building in which gymnastics is taught and practised

TURNING, -S n road or path leading off a main route

TURNIP, -ED, -S n root vegetable with orange or white flesh ▷ vb sow (a field) with turnips

TURNIPY adj like a turnip

TURNKEY, -S n jailer ▷ adj denoting a project in which a single contractor has responsibility for the complete job

TURNOFF, -S n road or other way branching off from the main

TURNOUT, -S n number of people appearing at a gathering

TURNOVER n total sales made by a business over a certain period

TURNPIKE n road where a toll is collected at barriers

TURNS ► turn

TURNSKIN n old name for a werewolf

TURNSOLE n any of various plants having flowers that are said to turn towards the sun

TURNSPIT n servant whose job was to turn the spit on which meat was roasting

TURNUP, -S n the turned-up fold at the bottom of some trouser legs

TURPETH, -S n convolvulaceous plant of the East Indies, having roots with purgative properties

TURPS, -ES n colourless, flammable liquid

TURQUOIS variant of **> turquoise**

TURR, -S n Newfoundland name for the guillemot

TURRET, -S n small tower

TURRETED adj having or resembling a turret or turrets

TURRETS ► turret

TURRICAL adj of, relating to, or resembling a turret

TURRS ► turr

TURTLE, -D, -S, TURTLING n sea tortoise

TURTLER -S

TURVES ► turf

TUSCHE, -S n substance used in lithography for drawing the design

TUSH, -ED, -ES, -ING interj exclamation of disapproval or contempt ▷ n small tusk ▷ vb utter the interjection "tush"

TUSHERY n use of affectedly archaic language in novels, etc

TUSHES ► tush

TUSHIE, -S n pair of buttocks

TUSHING ► tush

TUSHKAR, -S variant of **► tuskar**

TUSHKER, -S *variant of*
▸ **tuskar**
TUSHY *variant of* ▸ **tushie**
TUSK, -ING, -INGS, -S *n* long
pointed tooth of an elephant,
walrus, etc ▸ *vb* stab, tear, or
gore with the tusks
TUSKAR, -S *n* peat-cutting
spade
TUSKED ▸ **tusk**
TUSKER, -S *n* any animal with
prominent tusks, esp a wild
boar or elephant
TUSKIER ▸ **tusky**
TUSKIEST ▸ **tusky**
TUSKING ▸ **tusk**
TUSKINGS ▸ **tusk**
TUSKLESS ▸ **tusk**
TUSKLIKE ▸ **tusk**
TUSKS ▸ **tusk**
TUSKY, TUSKIER, TUSKIEST
▸ **tusk**
TUSSAC *modifier as in* **tussac**
grass kind of grass
TUSSAH, -S *same as*
▸ **tussore**
TUSSAL ▸ **tussis**
TUSSAR, -S *variant of*
▸ **tussore**
TUSSEH, -S *variant of*
▸ **tussore**
TUSSER, -S *same as*
▸ **tussore**
TUSSIS, TUSSES, -ES
technical name for a
▸ **cough**
TUSSIVE
TUSSLE, -D, -S, TUSSLING *vb*
fight or scuffle ▸ *n* energetic
fight, struggle, or argument
TUSSOCK, -S *n* tuft of grass
TUSSOCKY
TUSSOR, -S *variant of*
▸ **tussore**
TUSSORE, -S *n* strong coarse
brownish Indian silk
TUSSORS ▸ **tussor**
TUSSUCK, -S *variant of*
▸ **tussock**
TUSSUR, -S *variant of*
▸ **tussore**
TUT, -TED, -TING, -TINGS
interj exclamation of mild
disapproval, or surprise ▸ *vb*
express disapproval by the
exclamation of "tut-tut." ▸ *n*
payment system based on
measurable work done
TUTANIA, -S *n* alloy of low
melting point used mostly for
decorative purposes
TUTEE, -S *n* one who is
tutored, esp in a university
TUTELAGE *n* instruction or
guidance, esp by a tutor

TUTELAR, -S *same as*
▸ **tutelary**
TUTELARY *adj* having the
role of guardian or protector
▸ *n* tutelary person, deity,
or saint
TUTENAG, -S *n* zinc alloy
TUTMAN, TUTMEN *n* one
who does tutwork
TUTOR, -ED, -ING, -S *n* person
teaching individuals or small
groups ▸ *vb* act as a tutor to
TUTORAGE
TUTORESS *n* female tutor
TUTORIAL *n* period of
instruction with a tutor ▸ *adj*
of or relating to a tutor
TUTORING ▸ **tutor**
TUTORISE *variant spelling of*
▸ **tutorize**
TUTORISM ▸ **tutor**
TUTORIZE *vb* tutor
TUTORS ▸ **tutor**
TUTOYED *adj* addressed in a
familiar way
TUTOYER, -S *vb* speak to
someone on familiar terms
TUTRESS *same as* ▸ **tutoress**
TUTRIX, TUTRICES, -ES *n*
female tutor; tutoress
TUTS, -ED, -ES, -ING *Scots*
version of ▸ **tut**
TUTSAN, -S *n* woodland
shrub of Europe and W Asia
TUTSED ▸ **tuts**
TUTSES ▸ **tuts**
TUTSING ▸ **tuts**
TUTTED ▸ **tut**
TUTTI, -S *adv* be performed by
the whole orchestra or choir
▸ *n* piece of tutti music
TUTTIES ▸ **tutty**
TUTTING ▸ **tut**
TUTTINGS ▸ **tut**
TUTTIS ▸ **tutti**
TUTTY, TUTTIES *n* finely
powdered impure zinc oxide
TUTU, -S *n* short stiff skirt
worn by ballerinas
TUTUED *adj* wearing tutu
TUTUS ▸ **tutu**
TUTWORK, -S *n* work paid
using a tut system
TUX, -ES *short for* ▸ **tuxedo**

Tux is a short form of
tuxedo, and is a very
commonly played X word.

TUXEDO, -ES, -S *n* dinner
jacket
TUXEDOED *adj* wearing a
tuxedo
TUXEDOES ▸ **tuxedo**
TUXEDOS ▸ **tuxedo**
TUXES ▸ **tux**

TUYER, -S *variant of*
▸ **tuyere**
TUYERE, -S *n* water-cooled
nozzle through which air is
blown into a cupola, blast
furnace, or forge
TUYERS ▸ **tuyer**
TUZZ, -ES *n* tuft or clump
of hair
TWA, -S *Scots word for* ▸ **two**
TWADDLE, -D, -S *n* silly or
pretentious talk or writing
▸ *vb* talk or write in a silly or
pretentious way
TWADDLER
TWADDLY
TWAE, -S *same as* ▸ **twa**
TWAFALD *Scots variant of*
▸ **twofold**
TWAIN, -S *n* two
TWAITE, -S *n* herring-like
food fish
TWAL, -S *n* twelve
TWANG, -ED, -ING, -S *n* sharp
ringing sound ▸ *vb* (cause to)
make a twang
TWANGER, -S
TWANGIER ▸ **twangy**
TWANGING ▸ **twang**
TWANGLE, -D, -S *vb* make a
continuous loose twanging
sound
TWANGLER
TWANGS ▸ **twang**
TWANGY, TWANGIER
▸ **twang**
TWANK, -S *vb* make an
sharply curtailed twang
TWANKAY, -S *n* variety of
Chinese green tea
TWANKIES ▸ **twanky**
TWANKS ▸ **twank**
TWANKY, TWANKIES *same*
as ▸ **twankay**
TWAS ▸ **twa**
TWASOME, -S *same as*
▸ **twosome**
TWAT, -S, -TED, -TING *vb* hit
or strike violently
TWATTLE, -D, -S *rare word for*
▸ **twaddle**
TWATTLER
TWAY, -S *old variant of*
▸ **twain**
TWEAK, -ED, -ING, -S *vb*
pinch or twist sharply ▸ *n*
tweaking
TWEAKER, -S *n* engineer's
small screwdriver
TWEAKIER ▸ **tweaky**
TWEAKING ▸ **tweak**
TWEAKS ▸ **tweak**
TWEAKY, TWEAKIER
▸ **tweak**
TWEE, -ST *adj* too
sentimental, sweet, or pretty

T

TWEED, -S n thick woollen cloth

TWEEDIER ▶ tweedy

TWEEDILY adv in a manner characteristic of upper-class people who live in the country

TWEEDLE, -D, -S vb improvise aimlessly on a musical instrument

TWEEDLER

TWEEDS ▶ tweed

TWEEDY, TWEEDIER adj of or made of tweed

TWEEL, -ED, -ING, -S variant of ▶ **twill**

TWEELY ▶ twee

TWEEN, -S same as ▶ **between**

TWEENAGE adj (of a child) between about eight and fourteen years old

TWEENER, -S same as > tweenager

TWEENESS ▶ twee

TWEENIE same as ▶ **tweeny**

TWEENIES ▶ tweeny

TWEENS ▶ tween

TWEENY, TWEENIES n maid who assists both cook and housemaid

TWEEP, -S n person who uses Twitter

TWEEPLE pl n people who communicate via the Twitter website

TWEEPS ▶ tweep

TWEER, -ED, -ING, -S variant of ▶ **twire**

TWEEST ▶ twee

TWEET, -ED, -ING, -S vb chirp ▷ interj imitation of the thin chirping sound made by small birds

TWEETER, -S n loudspeaker reproducing high-frequency sounds

TWEETING ▶ tweet

TWEETS ▶ tweet

TWEETUP, -S n online meeting of individuals arranged on the social networking website Twitter

TWEEZE, -D, -S, TWEEZING vb take hold of or pluck (hair, small objects, etc) with or as if with tweezers

TWEEZER same as ▶ **tweezers**

TWEEZERS pl n small pincer-like tool

TWEEZES ▶ tweeze

TWEEZING ▶ tweeze

TWELFTH, -S n (of) number twelve in a series ▷ adj of

or being number twelve in a series

TWELVE, -S n two more than ten ▷ adj amounting to twelve ▷ determiner amounting to twelve

TWELVEMO another word for > duodecimo

TWELVES ▶ twelve

TWENTY, TWENTIES n two times ten ▷ adj amounting to twenty ▷ determiner amounting to twenty

TWERK, -ED, -S vb dance provocatively by moving the hips rapidly back and forth

TWERKING n type of dance involving rapid hip movement

TWERKS ▶ twerk

TWERP, -S n silly person

TWERPIER ▶ twerpy

TWERPS ▶ twerp

TWERPY, TWERPIER ▶ twerp

TWIBIL, -S same as ▶ **twibill**

TWIBILL, -S n mattock with a blade shaped like an adze at one end and like an axe at the other

TWIBILS ▶ twibil

TWICE adv two times

TWICER, -S n someone who does something twice

TWICHILD n person in his or her dotage

TWIDDLE, -D, -S vb fiddle or twirl in an idle way ▷ n act or instance of twiddling

TWIDDLER

TWIDDLY

TWIER, -S variant of ▶ **tuyere**

TWIFOLD variant of ▶ **twofold**

TWIG, -GED, -GING, -S n small branch or shoot ▷ vb realize or understand

TWIGGEN adj made of twigs

TWIGGER, -S ▶ twig

TWIGGIER ▶ twiggy

TWIGGING ▶ twig

TWIGGY, TWIGGIER adj of or relating to a twig or twigs

TWIGHT, -ED, -S old variant of ▶ **twit**

TWIGLESS ▶ twig

TWIGLET, -S n small twig

TWIGLIKE ▶ twig

TWIGLOO, -S n temporary shelter made from twigs, branches, leaves, etc

TWIGS ▶ twig

TWIGSOME adj covered with twigs; twiggy

TWILIGHT n soft dim light just after sunset ▷ adj of

or relating to the period towards the end of the day

TWILIT

TWILL, -ED, -ING, -S n fabric woven to produce parallel ridges ▷ adj of a weave in which the weft yarns are worked around two or more warp yarns ▷ vb weave in this fashion

TWILLIES ▶ twilly

TWILLING ▶ twill

TWILLS ▶ twill

TWILLY, TWILLIES n machine having revolving spikes for opening and cleaning raw textile fibres

TWILT, -ED, -ING, -S variant of ▶ **quilt**

TWIN, -NED, -S n one of a pair, esp of two children born at one birth ▷ vb pair or be paired

TWINBORN adj born as a twin

TWINE, -D, -S, TWINING, TWININGS n string or cord ▷ vb twist or coil round

TWINER -S

TWINGE, -D, -S, TWINGING n sudden sharp pain or emotional pang ▷ vb have or cause to have a twinge

TWINIER ▶ twiny

TWINIEST ▶ twiny

TWINIGHT adj (of a baseball double-header) held in the late afternoon and evening

TWINING ▶ twine

TWININGS ▶ twine

TWINJET, -S n jet aircraft with two engines

TWINK, -ED, -ING, -S n white correction fluid for deleting written text ▷ vb twinkle

TWINKIE, -S n stupid person

TWINKING ▶ twink

TWINKLE, -D, -S vb shine brightly but intermittently ▷ n flickering brightness

TWINKLER

TWINKLY adj sparkling

TWINKS ▶ twink

TWINKY n stupid person

TWINLING old name for ▶ **twin**

TWINNED ▶ twin

TWINNING ▶ twin

TWINS ▶ twin

TWINSET, -S n matching jumper and cardigan

TWINSHIP n condition of being a twin or twins

TWINTER, -S n animal that is 2 years old

TWINY, TWINIER, TWINIEST ▶ twine

TWIRE, -D, -S, TWIRING *vb* look intently at with (or as if with) difficulty

TWIRL, -ED, -ING, -S *vb* turn or spin around quickly ▷ *n* whirl or twist

TWIRLER -S

TWIRLIER ▶ twirly

TWIRLING ▶ twirl

TWIRLS ▶ twirl

TWIRLY, TWIRLIER ▶ twirl

TWIRP, -S *same as* ▶ **twerp**

TWIRPIER ▶ twirpy

TWIRPS ▶ twirp

TWIRPY, TWIRPIER ▶ twirp

TWISCAR, -S *variant of* ▶ **tuskar**

TWIST, -ED, -S *vb* turn out of the natural position ▷ *n* twisting

TWISTER, -S *n* swindler

TWISTIER ▶ twist

TWISTING ▶ twist

TWISTOR, -S *n* variable corresponding to the coordinates of a point in space and time

TWISTS ▶ twist

TWISTY ▶ twist

TWIT, -S, -TED, -TING *vb* poke fun at (someone) ▷ *n* foolish person

TWITCH, -ED, -ES *vb* move spasmodically ▷ *n* nervous muscular spasm

TWITCHER *n* bird-watcher who tries to spot as many rare varieties as possible

TWITCHES ▶ twitch

TWITCHY *adj* nervous, worried, and ill-at-ease

TWITE, -S *n* N European finch with a brown streaked plumage

TWITS ▶ twit

TWITTED ▶ twit

TWITTEN, -S *n* narrow alleyway

TWITTER, -S *vb* (of birds) utter chirping sounds ▷ *n* act or sound of twittering

TWITTERY

TWITTING ▶ twit

TWITTISH *adj* silly; foolish

TWIXT *same as* ▶ **betwixt**

TWIZZLE, -D, -S *vb* spin around

TWO, -S *n* one more than one

TWOCCER, -S ▶ twoccing

TWOCCING *n* act of breaking into a motor vehicle and driving it away

TWOCKER -S

TWOCKING *same as* ▶ **twoccing**

TWOER, -S *n* (in a game) something that scores two

TWOFER, -S *n* single ticket allowing the buyer entrance to two events

TWOFOLD, -S *adj* having twice as many or as much ▷ *adv* by twice as many or as much ▷ *n* folding piece of theatrical scenery

TWONESS *n* state or condition of being two

TWONIE, -S *same as* ▶ **toonie**

TWOONIE, -S *variant of* ▶ **toonie**

TWOPENCE *n* sum of two pennies

TWOPENNY *adj* cheap or tawdry

TWOS ▶ two

TWOSOME, -S *n* group of two people

TWP *adj* stupid

> This Welsh word for stupid is useful because it contains no vowels, and so can help when you have an awkward rack full of consonants.

TWYER, -S *same as* ▶ **tuyere**

TWYERE, -S *variant of* ▶ **tuyere**

TWYERS ▶ twyer

TWYFOLD *adj* twofold

TYCHISM, -S *n* theory that chance is an objective reality at work in the universe

TYCOON, -S *n* powerful wealthy businessman; shogun

TYDE *old variant of the past participle of* ▶ **tie**

TYE, -D, -ING, -S *n* trough used in mining to separate valuable material from dross ▷ *vb* (in mining) isolate valuable material from dross using a tye

TYEE, -S *n* large northern Pacific salmon

TYEING ▶ tye

TYER, -S ▶ tye

TYES ▶ tye

TYG, -S *n* mug with two handles

> This old word for a two-handled drinking cup is another key word to know for situations when you are short of vowels.

TYIN *variant of* ▶ **tiyin**

TYING ▶ tie

TYIYN, -S *n* money unit of Kyrgyzstan

TYKE, -S *n* dog

TYKISH

TYLER, -S *variant of* ▶ **tiler**

TYLOPOD, -S *n* mammal with padded feet, such as a camel or llama

TYLOSES ▶ tylosis

TYLOSIN, -S *n* broad spectrum antibiotic

TYLOSIS, TYLOSES *n* bladder-like outgrowth from certain cells in woody tissue

TYLOTE, -S *n* knobbed sponge spicule

TYMBAL, -S *same as* ▶ **timbal**

TYMP, -S *n* blast furnace outlet through which molten metal flows

TYMPAN, -S *same as* ▶ **tympanum**

TYMPANA ▶ tympanum

TYMPANAL *adj* relating to the tympanum

TYMPANI, TYMPANO *same as* ▶ **timpani**

TYMPANIC *adj* of, relating to, or having a tympanum ▷ *n* part of the temporal bone in the mammalian skull that surrounds the auditory canal

TYMPANO ▶ tympani

TYMPANS ▶ tympan

TYMPANUM, TYMPANA *n* cavity of the middle ear

TYMPANY *n* distension of the abdomen

TYMPS ▶ tymp

TYND *variant of* ▶ **tind**

TYNDE *variant of* ▶ **tind**

TYNE, -D, -S, TYNING *variant of* ▶ **tine**

TYPABLE ▶ type

TYPAL *rare word for* ▶ **typical**

TYPE, -D, -S *n* class or category ▷ *vb* print with a typewriter or word processor

TYPEABLE

TYPEBAR, -S *n* one of the bars in a typewriter that carry the type and are operated by keys

TYPECASE *n* compartment tray for storing printer's type

TYPECAST *vb* continually cast (an actor or actress) in similar roles

TYPED ▶ type

TYPEFACE *n* style of the type

TYPES ▶ type

TYPESET, -S *vb* set (text for printing) in type

TYPEY *variant of* ▶ **typy**

TYPHOID, -S *adj* of or relating to typhoid fever

TYPHON, -S *n* whirlwind

TYPHONIC ▶ typhoon

TYPHONS ▶ typhon

T

TYPHOON, -S *n* violent tropical storm

TYPHOSE *adj* relating to typhoid

TYPHOUS ► typhus

TYPHUS, -ES *n* infectious feverish disease

TYPIC *same as* ► **typical**

TYPICAL *adj* true to type, characteristic

TYPIER ► typy

TYPIEST ► typy

TYPIFIED ► typify

TYPIFIER ► typify

TYPIFY, TYPIFIED, TYPIFIES *vb* be typical of

TYPING, -S *n* work or activity of using a typewriter or word processor

TYPIST, -S *n* person who types with a typewriter or word processor

TYPO, -S *n* typographical error

TYPOLOGY *n* study of types

TYPOS ► typo

TYPP, -S *n* unit of thickness of yarn

TYPTO, -ED, -ING, -S *vb* learn Greek conjugations

TYPY, TYPIER, TYPIEST *adj* (of an animal) typifying the breed

TYRAMINE *n* colourless crystalline amine derived from phenol

TYRAN, -ED, -ING, -S *vb* act as a tyrant

TYRANNE, -D, -S *variant of* ► **tyran**

TYRANNIC ► tyranny

TYRANNIS *n* tyrannical government

TYRANNY *n* tyrannical rule

TYRANS ► tyran

TYRANT, -ED, -S *n* oppressive or cruel ruler ▷ *vb* act the tyrant

TYRE, -D, -S, TYRING *n* rubber ring, usu inflated, over the rim of a vehicle's wheel to grip the road ▷ *vb* fit a tyre or tyres to (a wheel, vehicle, etc)

TYRELESS

TYRO, -ES, -NES, -S *n* novice or beginner

TYRONIC

TYROPITA *n* Greek cheese pie

TYROS ► tyro

TYROSINE *n* aromatic nonessential amino acid

TYSTIE, -S *n* black guillemot

TYTE *variant spelling of* ► **tite**

TYTHE, -D, -S, TYTHING *variant of* ► **tithe**

TZADDI, -S *same as* ► **sadhe**

TZADDIK, -S *variant of* ► **zaddik**

TZADDIQ, -S *variant of* ► **zaddik**

An unlikely word from Judaism, meaning a person of great piety, but offering a great score played as a bonus.

TZADDIS ► tzaddi

TZADIK, -S *same as* ► **zaddik**

TZAR, -S *same as* ► **tsar**

TZARDOM -S

TZAREVNA *variant of* ► **tsarevna**

TZARINA, -S *variant of* ► **tsarina**

TZARISM, -S *variant of* ► **tsarism**

TZARIST -S

TZARITZA *variant of* ► **tsaritsa**

TZARS ► tzar

TZATZIKI *n* Greek dip made from yogurt, chopped cucumber, and mint

TZEDAKAH *n* charitable donations as a Jewish moral obligation

TZETSE, -S *variant of* ► **tsetse**

TZETZE, -S *variant of* ► **tsetse**

TZIGANE, -S *n* type of Gypsy music

TZIGANY *variant of* ► **tzigane**

TZIMMES *n* traditional Jewish stew

TZITZIS *variant of* ► **tsitsith**

TZITZIT *variant of* ► **tsitsith**

TZITZITH *variant of* ► **tsitsith**

TZURIS, -ES *variant of* ► **tsuris**

T

Uu

U can be a difficult tile to use effectively. Although there are quite a few two-letter words beginning with U, most of them are quite unusual, and so difficult to remember. Only **up** (4 points) and **us** (2) are immediately obvious, so it's well worth learning words like **ug** (3), **uh** (5), **um** (4), and **un**, **ur** and **ut** (2 each). Three-letter words beginning with U can also be difficult to remember. If you are trying to use a **Q**, **X** or **Z**, bear in mind that there aren't any valid three-letter words with these letters that start with **U**. Knowing this can save you valuable time. It's also helpful to remember that there aren't any particularly high-scoring two- or three-letter words starting with U, the best being **uke** (7 points) and **uva** (6 points). If you have a surplus of **U**s, it is well worth remembering **ulu**, **umu** and **utu**, that score only 3 points but should improve your rack.

UAKARI, -S n type of monkey
UBEROUS adj abundant
UBERTY, UBERTIES n abundance
UBIETY, UBIETIES n condition of being in a particular place
UBIQUE adv everywhere
UBIQUITY n state of apparently being everywhere at once; omnipresence
UBUNTU, -S n quality of compassion and humanity
UCKERS n type of naval game
UDAL, -S n form of freehold possession of land used in Orkney and Shetland
UDALLER, -S n person possessing a udal
UDALS ► udal
UDDER, -S n large baglike milk-producing gland of cows, sheep, or goats
UDDERED
UDDERFUL
UDO, -S n stout perennial plant of Japan and China
UDOMETER n archaic term for an instrument for measuring rainfall or snowfall
UDOMETRY
UDON, -S n (in Japanese cookery) large noodles made of wheat flour
UDOS ► udo
UDS interj God's or God save
UEY, -S n u-turn
UFO, -S n flying saucer

UFOLOGY n study of UFOs
UFOS ► ufo
UG, -GED, -GING, -S vb hate
UGALI, -S n type of stiff porridge
UGGED ► ug
UGGING ► ug
UGH, -S interj exclamation of disgust ▷ n sound made to indicate disgust

> Together with **uke**, this is the highest-scoring three-letter word starting with U.

UGLIED ► ugly
UGLIER ► ugly
UGLIES ► ugly
UGLIEST ► ugly
UGLIFIED ► uglify
UGLIFIER ► uglify
UGLIFY, UGLIFIED, UGLIFIES vb make or become ugly or more ugly
UGLILY ► ugly
UGLINESS ► ugly
UGLY, UGLIED, UGLIER, UGLIES, UGLIEST, -ING adj of unpleasant appearance ▷ vb make ugly
UGS ► ug
UGSOME adj loathsome
UH interj used to express hesitation
UHLAN, -S n member of a body of lancers first employed in the Polish army
UHURU, -S n national independence

> You won't often have three Us on your rack, but when you do, this Swahili word for freedom may get you out of trouble. The only other 5-letter word containing three Us is **urubu**, a kind of vulture.

UILLEAN adj as in **uillean pipes** bagpipes developed in Ireland
UILLEANN same as ► uillean
UINTAITE n variety of asphalt
UJAMAA, -S n as in **ujamaa village** communally organized village in Tanzania
UKASE, -S n (in imperial Russia) a decree from the tsar
UKE, -S short form of ► ukulele

> Together with **ugh**, this is the highest-scoring three-letter word starting with U.

UKELELE, -S same as ► ukulele
UKES ► uke
UKULELE, -S n small guitar with four strings
ULAMA, -S n body of Muslim scholars or religious leaders
ULAN, -S same as ► uhlan
ULCER, -ED, -ING, -S n open sore on the surface of the skin or mucous membrane. ▷ vb make or become ulcerous
ULCERATE vb make or become ulcerous

ULCERED ► ulcer
ULCERING ► ulcer
ULCEROUS *adj* of, like, or characterized by ulcers
ULCERS ► ulcer
ULE, -S *n* rubber tree
ULEMA, -S *same as* ► **ulama**
ULES ► ule
ULEX, -ES, ULICES *n* variety of shrub
ULEXITE, -S *n* type of mineral
ULICON, -S *same as* ► **eulachon**
ULIKON, -S *same as* ► **eulachon**
ULITIS, -ES *n* gingivitis
ULLAGE, -S, ULLAGING *n* volume by which a liquid container falls short of being full ▷ *vb* create ullage in
ULLAGED
ULLING, -S *n* process of filling
ULMIN, -S *n* substance found in decaying vegetation
ULNA, -E, -S *n* inner and longer of the two bones of the human forearm
ULNAD *adv* towards the ulna
ULNAE ► ulna
ULNAR ► ulna
ULNARE, ULNARIA *n* bone in the wrist
ULNAS ► ulna
ULOSIS, ULOSES *n* formation of a scar
ULPAN, -IM *n* Israeli study centre
ULSTER, -S *n* man's heavy double-breasted overcoat
ULSTERED *adj* wearing an ulster
ULSTERS ► ulster
ULTERIOR *adj* (of an aim, reason, etc) concealed or hidden
ULTIMA, -S *n* final syllable of a word
ULTIMACY ► ultimate
ULTIMAS ► ultima
ULTIMATA ► ultimatum
ULTIMATE *adj* final in a series or process ▷ *n* most significant, highest, furthest, or greatest thing ▷ *vb* end
ULTIMO *adv* in or during the previous month
ULTION, -S *n* vengeance
ULTISOL, -S *n* reddish-yellow acid soil
ULTRA, -S *n* person who has extreme or immoderate beliefs or opinions ▷ *adj* extreme or immoderate, esp in beliefs or opinions
ULTRADRY *adj* extremely dry

ULTRAHIP *adj* extremely trendy
ULTRAHOT *adj* extremely hot
ULTRAISM *n* extreme philosophy, belief, or action
ULTRAIST
ULTRALOW *adj* extremely low
ULTRARED *obsolete word for* ► **infrared**
ULTRAS ► ultra
ULU, -S *n* type of knife
ULULANT ► ululate
ULULATE, -D, -S *vb* howl or wail
ULUS ► ulu
ULVA, -S *n* genus of seaweed
ULYIE, -S *Scots variant of* ► **oil**
ULZIE, -S *Scots variant of* ► **oil**
UM, -MED, -MING, -S *interj* representation of a common sound made when hesitating in speech ▷ *vb* hesitate while speaking
UMAMI, -S *n* savoury flavour
UMANGITE *n* type of mineral
UMBEL, -S *n* umbrella-like flower cluster
UMBELED *same as* ► **umbelled**
UMBELLAR ► umbel
UMBELLED *adj* having umbels
UMBELLET *same as* > **umbellule**
UMBELS ► umbel
UMBELULE *n* secondary umbel
UMBER, -S *adj* dark brown to reddish-brown ▷ *n* type of dark brown earth containing ferric oxide (rust) ▷ *vb* stain with umber
UMBERED
UMBERING
UMBERY
UMBILICI > umbilicus
UMBLE *adj* as in **umble pie** (formerly) a pie made from the heart, entrails, etc, of a deer
UMBLES *another term for* ► **numbles**
UMBO, -NES, -S *n* small hump projecting from the centre of the cap in certain mushrooms
UMBONAL
UMBONATE
UMBONIC
UMBRA, -E, -S *n* shadow, esp the shadow cast by the moon onto the earth during a solar eclipse

UMBRAGE, -S *n* displeasure or resentment ▷ *vb* shade
UMBRAGED
UMBRAL ► umbra
UMBRAS ► umbra
UMBRATED *adj* shown in a faint manner
UMBRATIC ► umbra
UMBRE, -S *same as* ► **umbrette**
UMBREL, -S *n* umbrella
UMBRELLA *n* portable device used for protection against rain ▷ *adj* containing many different organizations
UMBRELLO *same as* ► **umbrella**
UMBRELS ► umbrel
UMBRERE, -S *n* helmet visor
UMBRES ► umbre
UMBRETTE *n* African wading bird
UMBRIERE *same as* ► **umbrere**
UMBRIL, -S *same as* ► **umbrere**
UMBROSE *same as* ► **umbrous**
UMBROUS *adj* shady
UMFAZI, -S *n* African married woman
UMIAC, -S *variant of* ► **umiak**
UMIACK, -S *variant of* ► **umiak**
UMIACS ► umiac
UMIAK, -S *n* Inuit boat made of skins
UMIAQ, -S *same as* ► **umiak**

> An Inuit word for a type of canoe: easy to miss because one tends automatically to put the Q with the U and not think of a word ending in Q. The many variant spellings of this word include **umiac** and **umiak**.

UMLAUT, -S *n* mark (¨) placed over a vowel, esp in German, to indicate a change in its sound ▷ *vb* modify by umlaut
UMLAUTED
UMM *same as* ► **um**
UMMA, -S *n* Muslim community
UMMAH, -S *same as* ► **umma**
UMMAS ► umma
UMMED ► um
UMMING ► um
UMP, -ED, -ING, -S *short for* ► **umpire**
UMPH, -S *same as* ► **humph**
UMPIE *informal word for* ► **umpire**
UMPIES ► umpy

UMPING ► ump
UMPIRAGE ► umpire
UMPIRE, -D, -S, UMPIRING
n official who rules on the
playing of a game ▷ *vb* act as
umpire in (a game)
UMPS ► ump
UMPTEEN *adj* very many
▷ *determiner* very many
UMPTIETH *same as*
> umpteenth
UMPTY *same as* ► umpteen
UMPY, UMPIES *same as*
► umpie
UMQUHILE *adv* formerly
UMRA, -S *n* pilgrimage to
Mecca that can be made at
any time of the year
UMRAH, -S *same as* ► umra
UMRAS ► umra
UMS ► um
UMTEENTH *same as*
> umpteenth
UMU, -S *n* type of oven
UMWELT, -S *n* environmental
factors affect the behaviour
of an animal or individual
UMWHILE *same as*
► umquhile
UN, -S *pron* spelling of 'one'
intended to reflect a dialectal
or informal pronunciation
UNABATED *adv* without
any reduction in force ▷ *adj*
without losing any original
force or violence
UNABLE *adj* lacking the
necessary power, ability, or
authority (to do something)
UNABUSED *adj* not abused
UNACHING *adj* not aching
UNACIDIC *adj* not acidic
UNACTED *adj* not acted or
performed
UNACTIVE *adj* inactive ▷ *vb*
make (a person) inactive
UNADDED *adj* not added
UNADEPT, -S *adj* not adept
▷ *n* person who is not adept
UNADORED *adj* not adored
UNADULT *adj* not mature
UNAFRAID *adj* not frightened
or nervous
UNAGED *adj* not old
UNAGEING *adj* not ageing
UNAGILE *adj* not agile
UNAGING *same as*
► unageing
UNAGREED *adj* not agreed
UNAI, -S *same as* ► unau
UNAIDED *adv* without any
help or assistance ▷ *adj*
without having received
any help
UNAIMED *adj* not aimed or
specifically targeted

UNAIRED *adj* not aired
UNAIS ► unai
UNAKIN *adj* not related
UNAKING *Shakespearean*
form of ► unai
UNAKITE, -S *n* type of mineral
UNALIKE *adj* not similar
UNALIST, -S *n* priest holding
only one benefice
UNALIVE *adj* unaware
UNALLIED *adj* not allied
UNAMAZED *adj* not greatly
surprised
UNAMUSED *adj* not
entertained, diverted, or
laughing
UNANCHOR *vb* remove
anchor
UNANELED *adj* not having
received extreme unction
UNAPT *adj* not suitable or
qualified
UNAPTLY
UNARCHED *adj* not arched
UNARGUED *adj* not debated
UNARISEN *adj* not having
risen
UNARM, -ING, -S *less*
common word for ► disarm
UNARMED *adj* without
weapons
UNARMING ► unarm
UNARMS ► unarm
UNARTFUL *adj* not artful
UNARY *adj* consisting of, or
affecting, a single element or
component
UNASKED *adv* without being
asked to do something ▷ *adj*
(of a question) not asked,
although sometimes implied
for
UNATONED *adj* not atoned
for
UNAU, -S *n* two-toed sloth
UNAVOWED *adj* not openly
admitted
UNAWAKE *adj* not awake
UNAWAKED *adj* not aroused
UNAWARE *adj* not aware or
conscious ▷ *adv* by surprise
UNAWARES *adv* by surprise
UNAWED *adj* not awed
UNAXED *adj* not axed
UNBACKED *adj* (of a book,
chair, etc) not having a back
UNBAG, -S *vb* take out of
a bag
UNBAGGED
UNBAITED *adj* not baited
UNBAKED *adj* not having
been baked
UNBALE, -D, -S, UNBALING
vb remove from bale
UNBAN, -NED, -S *vb* stop
banning or permit again

UNBANDED *adj* not fastened
with a band
UNBANKED *adj* not having
been banked
UNBANNED ► unban
UNBANS ► unban
UNBAR, -RED, -S *vb* take
away a bar or bars from
UNBARBED *adj* without
barbs
UNBARE, -D, -S, UNBARING
vb expose
UNBARK, -ED, -S *vb* strip
bark from
UNBARRED ► unbar
UNBARS ► unbar
UNBASED *adj* not having
a base
UNBASTED *adj* not basted
UNBATED *adj* (of a sword,
lance, etc) not covered with a
protective button
UNBATHED *adj* unwashed
UNBE, -EN *vb* make non-
existent
UNBEAR, -ED, -S *vb* release
(horse) from the bearing rein
UNBEATEN *adj* having
suffered no defeat
UNBED, -DED, -S *vb* remove
from bed
UNBEEN ► unbe
UNBEGET, -S *vb* deprive of
existence
UNBEGGED *adj* not obtained
by begging
UNBEGOT *adj* unbegotten
UNBEGUN *adj* not
commenced
UNBEING, -S *n* non-existence
UNBELIEF *n* disbelief or
rejection of belief
UNBELT, -ED, -S *vb* unbuckle
the belt of (a garment)
UNBEND, -ED, -S *vb* become
less strict or more informal in
one's attitudes or behaviour
UNBENIGN *adj* not benign
UNBENT *adj* not bent or
bowed
UNBEREFT *adj* not bereft
UNBESEEM *vb* be unbefitting
to
UNBIAS, -ES *vb* free from
prejudice
UNBIASED *adj* not having
or showing prejudice or
favouritism
UNBIASES ► unbias
UNBID *same as* ► unbidden
UNBIDDEN *adj* not ordered
or asked
UNBILLED *adj* not having
been billed
UNBIND, -S *vb* set free from
bonds or chains

U

UNBISHOP vb remove from the position of bishop

UNBITT, -ED, -S vb remove (cable) from the bitts

UNBITTEN adj not having been bitten

UNBITTER adj not bitter

UNBITTS ► unbitt

UNBLAMED vb not blamed

UNBLENT same as > unblended

UNBLESS vb deprive of a blessing

UNBLEST same as > unblessed

UNBLIND, -S vb rid of blindness

UNBLOCK, -S vb remove a blockage from

UNBLOODY adj not covered with blood

UNBLOWED same as ► unblown

UNBLOWN adj (of a flower) still in the bud

UNBOBBED adj not bobbed

UNBODIED adj having no body

UNBODING adj having no presentiment

UNBOILED adj not boiled

UNBOLT, -S vb unfasten a bolt of (a door)

UNBOLTED adj (of grain, meal, or flour) not sifted

UNBOLTS ► unbolt

UNBONDED adj not bonded

UNBONE, -S, UNBONING vb remove bone from

UNBONED adj (of meat, fish, etc) not having had the bones removed

UNBONES ► unbone

UNBONING ► unbone

UNBONNET vb remove the bonnet from

UNBOOKED adj not reserved

UNBOOT, -S vb remove boots from

UNBOOTED

UNBORE adj unborn

UNBORN adj not yet born

UNBORNE adj not borne

UNBOSOM, -S vb relieve (oneself) of (secrets or feelings) by telling someone

UNBOTTLE vb allow out of bottle

UNBOUGHT adj not purchased

UNBOUNCY adj not bouncy

UNBOUND adj (of a book) not bound within a cover

UNBOWED adj not giving in or submitting

UNBOWING adj not bowing

UNBOX, -ED, -ES, -ING vb empty a box

UNBRACE, -D, -S vb remove tension or strain from

UNBRAID, -S vb remove braids from

UNBRAKE, -D, -S vb stop reducing speed by releasing brake

UNBRASTE archaic past form of ► unbrace

UNBRED adj not taught or instructed

UNBREECH vb remove breech from

UNBRIDLE vb remove the bridle from (a horse)

UNBRIGHT adj not bright

UNBROKE same as ► unbroken

UNBROKEN adj complete or whole

UNBRUSED same as > unbruised

UNBUCKLE vb undo the buckle or buckles of

UNBUDDED adj not having buds

UNBUILD, -S, UNBUILT vb destroy

UNBULKY adj not bulky

UNBUNDLE vb separate (hardware from software) for sales purposes

UNBURDEN vb relieve (one's mind or oneself) of a worry by confiding in someone

UNBURIED ► unbury

UNBURIES ► unbury

UNBURNED same as ► unburnt

UNBURNT adj not burnt

UNBURROW vb remove from a burrow

UNBURY, UNBURIED, UNBURIES vb unearth

UNBUSIED ► unbusy

UNBUSIER ► unbusy

UNBUSIES ► unbusy

UNBUSTED adj unbroken

UNBUSY, UNBUSIED, UNBUSIER, UNBUSIES adj not busy ▷ vb make less busy

UNBUTTON vb undo by unfastening the buttons of (a garment)

UNCAGE, -S, UNCAGING vb release from a cage

UNCAGED adj at liberty

UNCAGES ► uncage

UNCAGING ► uncage

UNCAKE, -D, -S, UNCAKING vb remove compacted matter from

UNCALLED adj not called

UNCANDID adj not frank

UNCANNED adj not canned

UNCANNY adj weird or mysterious

UNCAP, -PED, -S vb remove a cap or top from (a container)

UNCAPE, -D, -S, UNCAPING vb remove the cape from

UNCAPPED ► uncap

UNCAPS ► uncap

UNCARDED adj not carded

UNCARED adj as in **uncared for** not cared (for)

UNCARING adj thoughtless

UNCART, -ED, -S vb remove from a cart

UNCARVED adj not carved

UNCASE, -D, -S, UNCASING vb display

UNCASHED adj not cashed

UNCASING ► uncase

UNCASKED adj removed from a cask

UNCAST, -ED, -S adj not cast ▷ vb undo the process of casting

UNCATCHY adj not catchy

UNCATE same as ► uncinate

UNCAUGHT adj not caught

UNCAUSED adj not brought into existence by any cause

UNCE, -S same as ► ounce

UNCEDED adj not ceded

UNCES ► unce

UNCHAIN, -S vb remove a chain or chains from

UNCHAIR, -S vb unseat from chair

UNCHANCY adj unlucky, ill-omened, or dangerous

UNCHARGE vb unload

UNCHARM, -S vb disenchant

UNCHARY adj not cautious

UNCHASTE adj not chaste

UNCHECK, -S vb remove check mark from

UNCHEWED adj not chewed

UNCHIC adj not chic

UNCHICLY

UNCHILD, -S vb deprive of children

UNCHOKE, -D, -S vb unblock

UNCHOSEN adj not chosen

UNCHURCH vb excommunicate

UNCI ► uncus

UNCIA, -E n twelfth part

UNCIAL, -S adj of a writing style used in manuscripts of the third to ninth centuries ▷ n uncial letter or manuscript

UNCIALLY

UNCIFORM adj having the shape of a hook ▷ n any hook-shaped structure or part, esp a small bone of the wrist

UNCINAL same as ► **uncinate**

UNCINATE adj shaped like a hook

UNCINUS, UNCINI n small hooked structure

UNCIPHER vb decode

UNCITED adj not quoted

UNCIVIL adj impolite, rude or bad-mannered

UNCLAD adj having no clothes on

UNCLAMP, -S vb remove clamp from

UNCLASP, -S vb unfasten the clasp of (something)

UNCLASSY adj not classy

UNCLAWED adj not clawed

UNCLE, -S, UNCLING n brother of one's father or mother ▷ vb refer to as uncle

UNCLEAN adj lacking moral, spiritual, or physical cleanliness

UNCLEAR adj confusing or hard to understand

UNCLED ► **uncle**

UNCLEFT adj not cleft

UNCLENCH vb relax from a clenched position

UNCLES ► **uncle**

UNCLEW, -ED, -S vb undo

UNCLINCH same as ► **unclench**

UNCLING ► **uncle**

UNCLIP, -S vb remove clip from

UNCLIPT archaic past form of ► **unclip**

UNCLOAK, -S vb remove cloak from

UNCLOG, -S vb remove an obstruction from (a drain, etc)

UNCLOSE, -D, -S vb open or cause to open

UNCLOTHE vb take off garments from

UNCLOUD, -S vb clear clouds from

UNCLOUDY adj not cloudy

UNCLOVEN adj not cleaved

UNCLOYED adj not cloyed

UNCLUTCH vb open from tight grip

UNCO, -ER, -ES, -EST, -S adj unfamiliar or strange ▷ n remarkable person or thing

UNCOATED adj not covered with a layer

UNCOCK, -ED, -S vb remove from a cocked position

UNCODED adj not coded

UNCOER ► **unco**

UNCOES ► **unco**

UNCOEST ► **unco**

UNCOFFIN vb take out of a coffin

UNCOIL, -ED, -S vb unwind or untwist

UNCOINED adj (of a metal) not made into coin

UNCOLT, -ED, -S vb divest of a horse

UNCOMBED adj not combed

UNCOMELY adj not attractive

UNCOMFY adj not comfortable

UNCOMIC adj not comical

UNCOMMON adj not happening or encountered often

UNCOOKED adj raw

UNCOOL adj unsophisticated

UNCOOLED adj not cooled

UNCOPE, -D, -S, UNCOPING vb unmuzzle

UNCORD, -ED, -S vb release from cords

UNCORK, -ED, -S vb remove the cork from (a bottle)

UNCOS ► **unco**

UNCOSTLY adj inexpensive

UNCOUPLE vb disconnect or become disconnected

UNCOUTH adj lacking in good manners, refinement, or grace

UNCOVER, -S vb reveal or disclose

UNCOWL, -ED, -S vb remove hood from

UNCOY adj not modest

UNCOYNED same as ► **uncoined**

UNCRATE, -D, -S vb remove from a crate

UNCRAZY adj not crazy

UNCREATE vb unmake

UNCREWED adj not crewed

UNCROSS vb cease to cross

UNCROWN, -S vb take the crown from

UNCTION, -S n act of anointing with oil in sacramental ceremonies

UNCTUOUS adj pretending to be kind and concerned

UNCUFF, -ED, -S vb remove handcuffs from

UNCULLED adj not culled

UNCURB, -ED, -S vb remove curbs from (a horse)

UNCURED adj not cured

UNCURL, -ED, -S vb move or cause to move out of a curled or rolled up position

UNCURSE, -D, -S vb remove curse from

UNCURVED adj not curved

UNCUS, UNCI n hooked part or process, as in the human cerebrum

UNCUT adj not shortened or censored

UNCUTE adj not cute

UNDAM, -MED, -S vb free from a dam

UNDAMNED adj not damned

UNDAMPED adj (of an oscillating system) having unrestricted motion

UNDAMS ► **undam**

UNDARING adj not daring

UNDASHED adj not dashed

UNDATE vb remove date from

UNDATED adj (of a manuscript, letter, etc) not having an identifying date

UNDAZZLE vb recover from a daze

UNDE same as ► **undee**

UNDEAD adj alive

UNDEAF, -ED, -S vb restore hearing to

UNDEALT adj not dealt (with)

UNDEAR adj not dear

UNDECENT same as ► **indecent**

UNDECK, -ED, -S vb remove decorations from

UNDEE adj wavy

UNDEEDED adj not transferred by deed

UNDEFIDE same as ► **undefied**

UNDEFIED adj not challenged

UNDEIFY vb strip of the status of a deity

UNDELETE vb restore (a deleted computer file or text)

UNDENIED adj not denied

UNDENTED adj not dented

UNDER adv indicating movement to or position beneath the underside or base ▷ prep less than

UNDERACT vb play (a role) without adequate emphasis

UNDERAGE adj below the required or standard age ▷ n shortfall

UNDERARM adj denoting a style of throwing in which the hand is swung below shoulder level ▷ adv in an underarm style ▷ n armpit

UNDERATE ► **undereat**

UNDERBID vb submit a bid lower than that of (others)

UNDERBIT > **underbite**

UNDERBUD vb produce fewer buds than expected

UNDERBUY vb buy (stock in trade) in amounts lower than required

U

UNDERCUT vb charge less than (a competitor) to obtain trade ▷ n act or an instance of cutting underneath

UNDERDO, UNDERDID vb do (something) inadequately

UNDERDOG n person or team in a weak or underprivileged position

UNDEREAT, UNDERATE vb not eat enough

UNDERFED > **underfeed**

UNDERFUR n layer of dense soft fur occurring beneath the outer coarser fur in certain mammals

UNDERGO vb experience, endure, or sustain

UNDERGOD n subordinate god

UNDERJAW n lower jaw

UNDERLAP vb project under the edge of

UNDERLAY n felt or rubber laid beneath a carpet to increase insulation and resilience ▷ vb place (something) under or beneath

UNDERLET vb let for a price lower than expected or justified

UNDERLIE vb lie or be placed under

UNDERLIP n lower lip

UNDERLIT adj lit from beneath

UNDERMAN, UNDERMEN vb supply with insufficient staff ▷ n subordinate man

UNDERN, -S n time between sunrise and noon

UNDERPAD n layer of soft foam laid under carpeting

UNDERPAY vb pay someone insufficiently

UNDERPIN vb give strength or support to

UNDERRUN, UNDERRAN vb run beneath

UNDERSAY vb say by way of response

UNDERSEA adv below the surface of the sea

UNDERSET n ocean undercurrent ▷ vb support from underneath

UNDERSKY n lower sky

UNDERSOW vb sow a later-growing crop on already-seeded land

UNDERTAX vb tax insufficiently

UNDERTOW n strong undercurrent flowing in a different direction from the surface current

UNDERUSE vb use less than normal

UNDERWAY adj in progress ▷ adv in progress

UNDERWIT n half-wit

UNDESERT n lack of worth

UNDEVOUT adj not devout

UNDID ▷ **undo**

UNDIES pl n underwear, esp women's

UNDIGHT, -S vb remove

UNDIMMED adj (of eyes, light, etc) still bright or shining

UNDINE, -S n female water spirit

UNDINISM n obsession with water

UNDINTED adj not dinted

UNDIPPED adj not dipped

UNDIVINE adj not divine

UNDO, UNDID, -ES, -S vb open, unwrap ▷ n instance of undoing something

UNDOABLE adj impossible

UNDOCILE adj not docile

UNDOCK, -ED, -S vb take out of a dock

UNDOER, -S ▷ **undo**

UNDOES ▷ **undo**

UNDOING, -S n cause of someone's downfall

UNDONE adj not done or completed

UNDOOMED adj not doomed

UNDOS ▷ **undo**

UNDOTTED adj not dotted

UNDOUBLE vb stretch out

UNDRAPE, -D, -S vb remove drapery from

UNDRAW, -N, -S, UNDREW vb open (curtains)

UNDREAMT same as > **undreamed**

UNDRESS vb take off clothes from (oneself or another) ▷ n partial or complete nakedness ▷ adj characterized by or requiring informal or normal working dress or uniform

UNDREST same as > **undressed**

UNDREW ▷ **undraw**

UNDRIED adj not dried

UNDRIVEN adj not driven

UNDROSSY adj pure

UNDRUNK adj not drunk

UNDUBBED adj (of a film, etc) not dubbed

UNDUE adj greater than is reasonable; excessive

UNDUG adj not having been dug

UNDULANT adj resembling waves

UNDULAR ▷ **undulate**

UNDULATE vb move in waves ▷ adj having a wavy or rippled appearance, margin, or form

UNDULLED adj not dulled

UNDULOSE same as ▶ **undulous**

UNDULOUS adj undulate

UNDULY adv excessively

UNDY same as ▶ **undee**

UNDYED adj not dyed

UNDYING adj never ending, eternal

UNEAGER adj nonchalant

UNEARED adj not ploughed

UNEARNED adj not deserved

UNEARTH, -S vb reveal or discover by searching

UNEASE, -S ▶ **uneasy**

UNEASIER ▶ **uneasy**

UNEASILY ▶ **uneasy**

UNEASY, UNEASIER adj (of a person) anxious or apprehensive

UNEATEN adj (of food) not having been consumed

UNEATH adv not easily

UNEDGE, -D, -S, UNEDGING vb take the edge off

UNEDIBLE variant of ▶ **inedible**

UNEDITED adj not edited

UNELATED adj not elated

UNENDED adj without end

UNENDING adj not showing any signs of ever stopping

UNENVIED adj not envied

UNEQUAL, -S adj not equal in quantity, size, rank, value, etc ▷ n person who is not equal out

UNERASED adj not rubbed out

UNERRING adj never mistaken, consistently accurate

UNESPIED adj unnoticed

UNETH same as ▶ **uneath**

UNEVADED adj not evaded

UNEVEN, -ER adj not level or flat

UNEVENLY

UNEXOTIC adj not exotic

UNEXPERT same as ▶ **inexpert**

UNEYED adj unseen

UNFABLED adj not fictitious

UNFACT, -S n event or thing not provable

UNFADED adj not faded

UNFADING adj not fading

UNFAIR, -ED, -ER, -S adj not right, fair, or just ▷ vb disfigure

UNFAIRLY

UNFAITH, -S n lack of faith

UNFAKED adj not faked

UNFALLEN adj not fallen

UNFAMED adj not famous
UNFAMOUS adj not famous
UNFANCY vb consider (a sportsperson or team) unlikely to win or succeed ▷ adj not fancy
UNFANNED adj not fanned
UNFASTEN vb undo, untie, or open or become undone, untied, or opened
UNFAULTY adj not faulty
UNFAZED adj not disconcerted
UNFEARED adj unafraid
UNFED adj not fed
UNFEED adj unpaid
UNFELLED adj not cut down
UNFELT adj not felt
UNFELTED adj not felted
UNFENCE, -S vb remove a fence from
UNFENCED adj not enclosed by a fence
UNFENCES ► unfence
UNFETTER vb release from fetters, bonds, etc
UNFEUDAL adj not feudal
UNFEUED adj not feued
UNFILDE archaic form of ► unfiled
UNFILED adj not filed
UNFILIAL adj not filial
UNFILLED adj (of a container, receptacle, etc) not having become or been made full
UNFILMED adj not filmed
UNFINE adj not fine
UNFIRED adj not fired
UNFIRM adj soft or unsteady
UNFISHED adj not used for fishing
UNFIT, -S, -TER adj unqualified or unsuitable ▷ vb make unfit
UNFITLY adv in an unfit way
UNFITS ► unfit
UNFITTED adj unsuitable
UNFITTER ► unfit
UNFIX, -ES, -ING vb unfasten, detach, or loosen
UNFIXED adj not fixed
UNFIXES ► unfix
UNFIXING ► unfix
UNFIXITY n instability
UNFIXT variant of ► unfixed
UNFLASHY adj not flashy
UNFLAWED adj perfect
UNFLESH vb remove flesh from
UNFLEXED adj unbent
UNFLUSH vb lose the colour caused by flushing
UNFLUTED adj not fluted
UNFOILED adj not thwarted

UNFOLD, -ED, -S vb open or spread out from a folded state
UNFOLDER
UNFOLLOW vb stop following a person on a social networking site
UNFOND adj not fond
UNFOOL, -ED, -S vb undeceive
UNFOOTED adj untrodden
UNFORBID adj archaic word meaning unforbidden
UNFORCED adj not forced or having been forced
UNFORGED adj genuine
UNFORGOT adj archaic word meaning unforgotten
UNFORKED adj not forked
UNFORM, -S vb make formless
UNFORMAL same as ► informal
UNFORMED adj in an early stage of development
UNFORMS ► unform
UNFOUGHT adj not fought
UNFOUND adj not found
UNFRAMED adj not framed
UNFREE, -D, -S vb remove freedom from
UNFREEZE, UNFROZE, UNFROZEN vb thaw or cause to thaw
UNFRIEND vb remove someone from one's list of friends on a social networking site
UNFROCK, -S vb deprive (a priest in holy orders) of his or her priesthood
UNFROZE ► unfreeze
UNFROZEN ► unfreeze
UNFUMED adj not fumigated
UNFUNDED adj not funded
UNFUNNY adj not funny
UNFURL, -ED, -S vb unroll or unfold
UNFURRED adj not adorned with fur
UNFUSED adj not fused
UNFUSSY adj not characterized by overelaborate detail
UNGAG, -GED, -S vb restore freedom of speech to
UNGAIN adj inconvenient
UNGAINLY adj lacking grace when moving ▷ adv clumsily
UNGALLED adj not annoyed
UNGARBED adj undressed
UNGATED adj without gate
UNGAUGED adj not measured

UNGAZED adj as in ungazed at/ungazed upon not gazed (at or upon)
UNGAZING adj not gazing
UNGEAR, -ED, -S vb disengage
UNGELDED adj not gelded
UNGENIAL adj unfriendly
UNGENTLE adj not gentle
UNGENTLY
UNGET, -S vb get rid of
UNGIFTED adj not talented
UNGILD, -ED, -S, UNGILT vb remove gilding from
UNGIRD, -ED, -S vb remove belt from
UNGIRT adj not belted
UNGIRTH, -S vb release from a girth
UNGIVING adj inflexible
UNGLAD adj not glad
UNGLAZED adj not glazed
UNGLOVE, -D, -S vb remove glove(s)
UNGLUE, -D, -S, UNGLUING vb remove adhesive from
UNGOD, -DED, -S vb remove status of being a god from
UNGODLY adj unreasonable or outrageous
UNGODS ► ungod
UNGORD same as ► ungored
UNGORED adj not gored
UNGORGED same as ► ungored
UNGOT same as ► ungotten
UNGOTTEN adj not obtained or won
UNGOWN, -ED, -S vb remove gown (from)
UNGRACED adj not graced
UNGRADED adj not graded
UNGRAVLY same as > ungravely
UNGRAZED adj not grazed
UNGREEDY adj not greedy
UNGREEN adj not environmentally friendly
UNGROUND adj not crushed
UNGROUP, -S vb separate from a group
UNGROWN adj not fully developed
UNGUAL adj of, relating to, or affecting the fingernails or toenails
UNGUARD, -S vb expose (to attack)
UNGUENT, -S n ointment
UNGUENTA > unguentum
UNGUENTS ► unguent
UNGUES ► unguis
UNGUIDED adj not having a flight path controlled internally or externally
UNGUILTY adj innocent

U

UNGUIS, UNGUES n nail, claw, or hoof, or the part of the digit giving rise to it

UNGULA, -E n truncated cone, cylinder, etc **UNGULAR**

UNGULATE n hoofed mammal

UNGULED adj hoofed

UNGUM, -MED, -S vb remove adhesive from

UNGYVE, -D, -S, UNGYVING vb release from shackles

UNHABLE same as ► **unable**

UNHACKED adj not hacked

UNHAILED adj not hailed

UNHAIR, -ED, -S vb remove the hair from (a hide) **UNHAIRER**

UNHALLOW vb desecrate

UNHALSED adj not hailed

UNHALVED adj not divided in half

UNHAND, -ED, -S vb release from one's grasp

UNHANDY adj not skilful with one's hands

UNHANG, -S, UNHUNG vb take down from hanging position

UNHANGED adj not executed by hanging

UNHANGS ► **unhang**

UNHAPPEN vb become as though never having happened

UNHAPPY adj sad or depressed ▷ vb make unhappy

UNHARDY adj fragile

UNHARMED adj not hurt or damaged in any way

UNHASP, -ED, -S vb unfasten

UNHASTY adj not speedy

UNHAT, -S, -TED vb doff one's hat

UNHEAD, -S vb remove the head from

UNHEADED adj not having a heading

UNHEADS ► **unhead**

UNHEAL, -S vb expose

UNHEALED adj not having healed physically, mentally, or emotionally

UNHEALS ► **unheal**

UNHEALTH n illness

UNHEARD adj not listened to

UNHEARSE vb remove from a hearse

UNHEART, -S vb discourage

UNHEATED adj not having been warmed up

UNHEDGED adj unprotected

UNHEEDED adj noticed but ignored

UNHEEDY adj not heedful

UNHELE, -D, -S, UNHELING same as ► **unheal**

UNHELM, -ED, -S vb remove the helmet of (oneself or another)

UNHELPED adj without help

UNHEPPEN adj awkward

UNHEROIC adj not heroic

UNHERST archaic past form of ► **unhearse**

UNHEWN adj not hewn

UNHIDDEN adj not hidden

UNHINGE, -D, -S vb derange or unbalance (a person or his or her mind)

UNHIP, -PER adj not at all fashionable or up to date

UNHIRED adj not hired

UNHITCH vb unfasten or detach

UNHIVE, -D, -S, UNHIVING vb remove from a hive

UNHOARD, -S vb remove from a hoard

UNHOLIER ► **unholy**

UNHOLILY ► **unholy**

UNHOLPEN same as ► **unhelped**

UNHOLY, UNHOLIER adj immoral or wicked

UNHOMELY adj not homely

UNHONEST same as > **dishonest**

UNHOOD, -ED, -S vb remove hood from

UNHOOK, -ED, -S vb unfasten the hooks of (a garment)

UNHOOP, -ED, -S vb remove hoop(s) from

UNHOPED adj unhoped-for

UNHORSE, -D, -S vb knock or throw from a horse

UNHOUSE, -D, -S vb remove from a house

UNHUMAN adj inhuman or not human

UNHUNG ► **unhang**

UNHUNTED adj not hunted

UNHURT adj not injured in an accident, attack, etc

UNHUSK, -ED, -S vb remove the husk from

UNI, -S n (in informal English) university

UNIALGAL adj containing only one species of alga

UNIAXIAL adj (esp of plants) having an unbranched main axis

UNIBODY adj of a vehicle in which the frame and body are one unit ▷ n vehicle in which the frame and body are one unit

UNIBROW, -S n informal word for eyebrows that meet above the nose

UNICA ► **unicum**

UNICED adj not iced

UNICITY n oneness

UNICOLOR same as > **unicolour**

UNICOM, -S n designated radio frequency at some airports

UNICORN, -S n imaginary horselike creature with one horn growing from its forehead

UNICUM, UNICA n unique example or specimen

UNICYCLE n one-wheeled vehicle driven by pedals, used in a circus ▷ vb ride a unicycle

UNIDEAED adj not having ideas

UNIDEAL adj not ideal

UNIFACE, -S n type of tool

UNIFIC adj unifying

UNIFIED ► **unify**

UNIFIER, -S ► **unify**

UNIFIES ► **unify**

UNIFILAR adj composed of, having, or using only one wire, thread, filament, etc

UNIFORM, -S n special set of clothes for the members of an organization ▷ adj regular and even throughout, unvarying ▷ vb fit out (a body of soldiers, etc) with uniforms

UNIFY, UNIFIED, UNIFIES, -ING vb make or become one

UNILOBAR adj having one lobe

UNILOBED same as ► **unilobar**

UNIMBUED adj not imbued

UNIMODAL adj having or involving one mode

UNINSTAL same as > **uninstall**

UNINURED adj unaccustomed

UNION, -S n uniting or being united ▷ adj of a trade union

UNIONISE same as ► **unionize**

UNIONISM n principles of trade unions

UNIONIST n member or supporter of a trade union ▷ adj of or relating to union or unionism, esp trade unionism

UNIONIZE vb organize (workers) into a trade union

UNIONS ► **union**

UNIPED, -S n person or thing with one foot

UNIPOD, -S n one-legged support, as for a camera

UNIPOLAR adj of, concerned with, or having a single magnetic or electric pole

UNIQUE, -R, -S, -ST adj being the only one of a particular type ▷ n person or thing that is unique
UNIQUELY

UNIRONED adj not ironed

UNIRONIC adj not ironic

UNIS ▸ uni

UNISEX, -ES adj designed for use by both sexes ▷ n condition of seeming not to belong obviously either to one sex or the other

UNISIZE adj in one size only

UNISON, -S n complete agreement
UNISONAL

UNISSUED adj not issued

UNIT, -S n single undivided entity or whole
UNITAGE -S

UNITAL ▸ unit

UNITARD, -S n all-in-one skintight suit

UNITARY adj consisting of a single undivided whole

UNITE, -S vb make or become an integrated whole ▷ n English gold coin minted in the Stuart period

UNITED adj produced by two or more people or things in combination
UNITEDLY

UNITER, -S ▸ unite

UNITES ▸ unite

UNITIES ▸ unity

UNITING, -S ▸ unite

UNITION, -S n joining

UNITISE, -D, -S same as ▸ unitize

UNITISER same as ▸ unitizer

UNITISES ▸ unitise

UNITIVE adj tending to unite or capable of uniting

UNITIZE, -D, -S vb convert (an investment trust) into a unit trust

UNITIZER n person or thing that arranges units into batches

UNITIZES ▸ unitize

UNITRUST n type of income-producing trust fund

UNITS ▸ unit

UNITY, UNITIES n state of being one

UNIVALVE adj relating to a mollusc shell that consists

of a single piece (valve) ▷ n gastropod mollusc or its shell

UNIVERSE n whole of all existing matter, energy, and space

UNIVOCAL adj unambiguous or unmistakable ▷ n word or term that has only one meaning

UNJADED adj not jaded

UNJAM, -MED, -S vb remove blockage from

UNJOINED adj not joined

UNJOINT, -S vb disjoint

UNJOYFUL adj not joyful

UNJOYOUS adj not joyous

UNJUDGED adj not judged

UNJUST, -ER adj not fair or just
UNJUSTLY

UNKED adj alien

UNKEELED adj without a keel

UNKEMPT adj (of the hair) not combed

UNKEND same as ▸ unkenned

UNKENNED adj unknown

UNKENNEL vb release from a kennel

UNKENT same as ▸ unkenned

UNKEPT adj not kept

UNKET same as ▸ unked

UNKID same as ▸ unked

UNKIND, -ER adj unsympathetic or cruel
UNKINDLY

UNKING, -ED, -S vb strip of sovereignty

UNKINGLY adj not kingly

UNKINGS ▸ unking

UNKINK, -ED, -S vb straighten out

UNKISS, -ES vb cancel (a previous action) with a kiss

UNKISSED adj not kissed

UNKISSES ▸ unkiss

UNKNIGHT vb strip of knighthood

UNKNIT, -S vb make or become undone, untied, or unravelled

UNKNOT, -S vb disentangle or undo a knot or knots in

UNKNOWN, -S adj not known ▷ n unknown person, quantity, or thing

UNKOSHER adj not conforming to Jewish religious law

UNLACE, -S, UNLACING vb loosen or undo the lacing of (shoes, garments, etc)

UNLACED adj not laced

UNLACES ▸ unlace

UNLACING ▸ unlace

UNLADE, -D, -S, UNLADING less common word for ▸ unload

UNLADEN adj not laden

UNLADES ▸ unlade

UNLADING ▸ unlade

UNLAID ▸ unlay

UNLASH, -ED, -ES vb untie or unfasten

UNLAST archaic variant of ▸ unlaced

UNLASTE archaic variant of ▸ unlaced

UNLATCH vb open or unfasten or come open or unfastened by the lifting or release of a latch

UNLAW, -ED, -ING, -S vb penalize

UNLAWFUL adj not permitted by law

UNLAWING ▸ unlaw

UNLAWS ▸ unlaw

UNLAY, UNLAID, -ING, -S vb untwist (a rope or cable) to separate its strands

UNLEAD, -S vb strip off lead

UNLEADED adj (of petrol) containing less tetraethyl lead ▷ n petrol containing a reduced amount of tetraethyl lead

UNLEADS ▸ unlead

UNLEAL adj treacherous

UNLEARN, -S vb try to forget something learnt or to discard accumulated knowledge

UNLEARNT adj denoting knowledge or skills innately present rather than learnt

UNLEASED adj not leased

UNLEASH vb set loose or cause (something bad)

UNLED adj not led

UNLESS conj except under the circumstances that ▷ prep except

UNLET adj not rented

UNLETHAL adj not deadly

UNLETTED adj unimpeded

UNLEVEL, -S adj not level ▷ vb make unbalanced

UNLEVIED adj not levied

UNLICH Spenserian form of ▸ unlike

UNLICKED adj not licked

UNLID, -DED, -S vb remove lid from

UNLIKE, -S adj dissimilar or different ▷ prep not like or typical of ▷ n person or thing that is unlike another

UNLIKED adj not liked

UNLIKELY adj improbable

UNLIKES ▸ unlike

U

UNLIMBER vb disengage (a gun) from its limber

UNLIME, -D, -S, UNLIMING vb detach

UNLINE, -S, UNLINING vb remove the lining from

UNLINEAL adj not lineal

UNLINED adj not having any lining

UNLINES ► unline

UNLINING ► unline

UNLINK, -ED, -S vb undo the link or links between

UNLISTED adj not entered on a list

UNLIT adj (of a fire, cigarette, etc) not lit and therefore not burning

UNLIVE, -D, -S, UNLIVING vb live so as to nullify, undo, or live down (past events or times)

UNLIVELY adj lifeless

UNLIVES ► unlive

UNLIVING ► unlive

UNLOAD, -ED, -S vb remove (cargo) from (a ship, truck, or plane)

UNLOADER

UNLOBED adj without lobes

UNLOCK, -S vb unfasten (a lock or door)

UNLOCKED adj not locked

UNLOCKS ► unlock

UNLOOKED adj not looked (at)

UNLOOSE, -D, -S vb set free or release

UNLOOSEN same as ► unloose

UNLOOSES ► unloose

UNLOPPED adj not chopped off

UNLORD, -ED, -S vb remove from position of being lord

UNLORDLY adv not in a lordlike manner

UNLORDS ► unlord

UNLOST adj not lost

UNLOVE, -S vb stop loving

UNLOVED adj not loved by anyone

UNLOVELY adj unpleasant in appearance or character

UNLOVES ► unlove

UNLOVING adj not feeling or showing love and affection

UNLUCKY adj having bad luck, unfortunate

UNMACHO adj not macho

UNMADE adj (of a bed) with the bedclothes not smoothed and tidied

UNMAILED adj not sent by post

UNMAIMED adj not injured

UNMAKE, -S, UNMAKING vb undo or destroy

UNMAKER -S

UNMAN, -S vb cause to lose courage or nerve

UNMANFUL adj unmanly

UNMANLY adj not masculine

UNMANNED adj having no personnel or crew

UNMANS ► unman

UNMANTLE vb remove mantle from

UNMAPPED adj not charted

UNMARD same as ► unmarred

UNMARKED adj having no signs of damage or injury

UNMARRED adj not married

UNMARRY vb divorce

UNMASK, -S vb remove the mask or disguise from

UNMASKER

UNMATED adj not mated

UNMATTED adj not matted

UNMEANT adj unintentional

UNMEEK adj not submissive

UNMEET adj not meet

UNMEETLY

UNMELLOW adj not mellow

UNMELTED adj not melted

UNMENDED adj not mended

UNMERRY adj not merry

UNMESH, -ED, -ES vb release from mesh

UNMET adj unfulfilled

UNMETED adj unmeasured

UNMEW, -ED, -ING, -S vb release from confinement

UNMILKED adj not milked

UNMILLED adj not milled

UNMINDED adj disregarded

UNMINED adj not mined

UNMINGLE vb separate

UNMIRY, UNMIRIER adj not swampy

UNMISSED adj unnoticed

UNMITER, -S same as ► unmitre

UNMITRE, -D, -S vb divest of a mitre

UNMIX, -ED, -ES, -ING vb separate

UNMIXT same as ► unmix

UNMOANED adj unmourned

UNMODISH adj passé

UNMOLD, -ED, -S same as ► unmould

UNMOLTEN adj not molten

UNMONIED same as > unmoneyed

UNMOOR, -ED, -S vb weigh the anchor or drop the mooring of (a vessel)

UNMORAL adj outside morality

UNMOULD, -S vb change shape of

UNMOUNT, -S vb dismount

UNMOVED adj not affected by emotion, indifferent

UNMOVING adj still and motionless

UNMOWN adj not mown

UNMUFFLE vb remove a muffle or muffles from

UNMUZZLE vb take the muzzle off (a dog, etc)

UNNAIL, -ED, -S vb unfasten by removing nails

UNNAMED adj not mentioned by name

UNNANELD same as ► unaneled

UNNATIVE adj not native ▷ vb no longer be a native of a place

UNNEATH adj archaic word for underneath

UNNEEDED adj not needed

UNNERVE, -D, -S vb cause to lose courage, confidence, or self-control

UNNEST, -ED, -S vb remove from a nest

UNNETHES same as ► unneath

UNNETTED adj not having or not enclosed in a net

UNNOBLE, -D, -S vb strip of nobility

UNNOISY adj quiet

UNNOTED adj not noted

UNOAKED adj (of wine) not matured in an oak barrel

UNOBEYED adj not obeyed

UNOFTEN adv infrequently

UNOILED adj not lubricated with oil

UNOPEN adj not open

UNOPENED adj closed, barred, or sealed

UNORDER, -S vb cancel an order

UNORNATE same as ► inornate

UNOWED same as ► unowned

UNOWNED adj not owned

UNPACED adj without the aid of a pacemaker

UNPACK, -ED, -S vb remove the contents of (a suitcase, trunk, etc)

UNPACKER

UNPADDED adj not padded

UNPAGED adj (of a book) having no page numbers

UNPAID adj without a salary or wage

UNPAINED adj not suffering pain

UNPAINT, -S vb remove paint from

UNPAIRED adj not paired up

UNPANEL, -S vb unsaddle

UNPANGED adj without pain or sadness

UNPANNEL same as ▷ **unpanel**

UNPAPER, -S vb remove paper from

UNPARED adj not pared

UNPARTED adj not parted

UNPATHED adj not having a path

UNPAVED adj not covered in paving

UNPAY, -ING, -S vb undo

UNPEELED adj not peeled

UNPEERED adj unparalleled

UNPEG, -GED, -S vb remove the peg or pegs from, esp to unfasten

UNPEN, -NED, -S vb release from a pen

UNPENT archaic past form of ▷ **unpen**

UNPEOPLE vb empty of people

UNPERCH vb remove from a perch

UNPERSON n person whose existence is officially denied or ignored

UNPICK, -S vb undo (the stitches) of (a piece of sewing)

UNPICKED adj (of knitting, sewing, etc) having been unravelled or picked out

UNPICKS ▷ **unpick**

UNPILE, -D, -S, UNPILING vb remove from a pile

UNPIN, -NED, -S vb remove a pin or pins from

UNPINKED adj not decorated with a perforated pattern

UNPINKT same as ▷ **unpinked**

UNPINNED ▷ **unpin**

UNPINS ▷ **unpin**

UNPITIED adj not pitied

UNPITTED adj not having had pits removed

UNPLACE, -S same as ▷ **displace**

UNPLACED adj not given or put in a particular place

UNPLACES ▷ **unplace**

UNPLAIT, -S vb remove plaits from

UNPLAYED adj not played

UNPLIANT adj not pliant

UNPLOWED adj not ploughed

UNPLUG, -S vb disconnect (a piece of electrical equipment)

UNPLUMB, -S vb remove lead from

UNPLUME, -D, -S vb remove feathers from

UNPOETIC adj not poetic

UNPOISED adj not poised

UNPOISON vb extract poison from

UNPOLISH vb remove polish from

UNPOLITE same as ▷ **impolite**

UNPOLLED adj not included in an opinion poll

UNPOPE, -D, -S, UNPOPING vb strip of popedom

UNPOSED adj not posed

UNPOSTED adj not sent by post

UNPOTTED adj not planted in a pot

UNPRAISE vb withhold praise from

UNPRAY, -ED, -S vb withdraw (a prayer)

UNPREACH vb retract (a sermon)

UNPRETTY adj unattractive

UNPRICED adj having no fixed or marked price

UNPRIEST vb strip of priesthood

UNPRIMED adj not primed

UNPRISON vb release from prison

UNPRIZED adj not treasured

UNPROBED adj not examined

UNPROP, -S vb remove support from

UNPROPER same as ▷ **improper**

UNPROPS ▷ **unprop**

UNPROVED adj not having been established as true, valid, or possible

UNPROVEN adj not established as true by evidence or demonstration

UNPRUNED adj not pruned

UNPUCKER vb remove wrinkles from

UNPULLED adj not pulled

UNPURE same as ▷ **impure**

UNPURELY

UNPURGED adj not purged

UNPURSE, -D, -S vb relax (lips) from pursed position

UNPUZZLE vb figure out

UNQUEEN, -S vb depose from the position of queen

UNQUIET, -S adj anxious or uneasy ▷ n state of unrest ▷ vb disquiet

UNQUOTE, -D, -S interj expression used to indicate the end of a quotation ▷ vb close (a quotation), esp in printing

UNRACED adj not raced

UNRACKED adj not stretched

UNRAISED adj not raised

UNRAKE, -S, UNRAKING vb unearth through raking

UNRAKED adj not raked

UNRAKES ▷ **unrake**

UNRAKING ▷ **unrake**

UNRANKED adj not ranked

UNRATED adj not rated

UNRAVEL, -S vb reduce (something knitted or woven) to separate strands

UNRAZED adj not razed

UNREAD adj (of a book or article) not yet read

UNREADY adj not ready or prepared

UNREAL adj (as if) existing only in the imagination

UNREALLY

UNREAPED adj not reaped

UNREASON n irrationality or madness ▷ vb deprive of reason

UNREAVE, -D, -S vb unwind

UNRECKED adj disregarded

UNRED same as ▷ **unread**

UNREDY same as ▷ **unready**

UNREEL, -ED, -S vb unwind from a reel

UNREELER n machine that unwinds something from a reel

UNREELS ▷ **unreel**

UNREEVE, -D, -S, UNROVE, UNROVEN vb withdraw (a rope) from a block, thimble, etc

UNREIN, -ED, -S vb free from reins

UNRENT adj not torn

UNRENTED adj not rented

UNREPAID adj not repaid

UNREPAIR less common word for ▷ **disrepair**

UNREST, -S n rebellious state of discontent

UNRESTED adj not rested

UNRESTS ▷ **unrest**

UNRETIRE vb resume work after retiring

UNRHYMED adj not rhymed

UNRIBBED adj not ribbed

UNRID adj unridden

UNRIDDEN adj not or never ridden

UNRIDDLE vb solve or puzzle out

UNRIFLED adj (of a firearm or its bore) not rifled

UNRIG, -GED, -S vb strip (a vessel) of standing and running rigging

U

UNRIGHT, -S n wrong ⊳ adj not right or fair ⊳ vb make wrong

UNRIGS ► unrig

UNRIMED same as ► **unrhymed**

UNRINGED adj not having or wearing a ring

UNRINSED adj not rinsed

UNRIP, -PED, -S vb rip open

UNRIPE, -R, -ST adj not fully matured

UNRIPELY

UNRIPPED ► unrip

UNRIPS ► unrip

UNRISEN adj not risen

UNRIVEN adj not torn apart

UNRIVET, -S vb remove rivets from

UNROBE, -D, -S, UNROBING same as ► **disrobe**

UNROLL, -ED, -S vb open out or unwind (something rolled or coiled)

UNROOF, -ED, -S vb remove the roof from

UNROOST, -S vb remove from a perch

UNROOT, -ED, -S less common word for ► **uproot**

UNROPE, -D, -S, UNROPING vb release from a rope

UNROTTED adj not rotted

UNROTTEN adj not rotten

UNROUGED adj not coloured with rouge

UNROUGH adj not rough

UNROUND, -S vb release (lips) from a rounded position

UNROUSED adj not roused

UNROVE ► unreeve

UNROVEN ► unreeve

UNROYAL adj not royal

UNRUBBED adj not rubbed

UNRUDE adj not rude

UNRUFFE same as ► **unrough**

UNRUFFLE vb calm

UNRULE, -S n lack of authority

UNRULED adj not ruled

UNRULES ► unrule

UNRULY, UNRULIER adj difficult to control or organize

UNRUSHED adj unhurried

UNRUSTED adj not rusted

UNS ► un

UNSADDLE vb remove the saddle from (a horse)

UNSAFE, -R, -ST adj dangerous

UNSAFELY

UNSAFETY n lack of safety

UNSAID adj not said or expressed

UNSAILED adj not sailed

UNSAINED adj not blessed

UNSAINT, -S vb remove status of being a saint from

UNSALTED adj not seasoned, preserved, or treated with salt

UNSAPPED adj not undermined

UNSASHED adj not furnished with a sash

UNSATED adj not sated

UNSATING adj not satisfying

UNSAVED adj not saved

UNSAVORY same as > **unsavoury**

UNSAWED same as ► **unsawn**

UNSAWN adj not cut with a saw

UNSAY, -ING, -S vb retract or withdraw (something said or written)

UNSCALE, -D, -S same as ► **descale**

UNSCARY adj not scary

UNSCREW, -S vb loosen (a screw or lid) by turning it

UNSEAL, -ED, -S vb remove or break the seal of

UNSEAM, -ED, -S vb open or undo the seam of

UNSEARED adj not seared

UNSEASON vb affect unfavourably

UNSEAT, -ED, -S vb throw or displace from a seat or saddle

UNSECRET adj not secret ⊳ vb inform or make aware

UNSEEDED adj not given a top player's position in the opening rounds of a tournament

UNSEEING adj not noticing or looking at anything

UNSEEL, -ED, -S vb undo seeling

UNSEELIE pl n evil malevolent fairies ⊳ adj of or belonging to the unseelie

UNSEELS ► unseel

UNSEEMLY adj not according to expected standards of behaviour ⊳ adv in an unseemly manner

UNSEEN, -S adj hidden or invisible ⊳ adv without being seen ⊳ n passage given to students for translation without having seen it in advance

UNSEIZED adj not seized

UNSELDOM adv frequently

UNSELF, -ED, -S, UNSELVES vb remove self-centredness from ⊳ n lack of self

UNSELL, -S vb speak unfavourably and off-puttingly of (something or someone)

UNSELVES ► unself

UNSENSE, -D, -S vb remove sense from

UNSENT adj not sent

UNSERVED adj not served

UNSET, -S adj not yet solidified or firm ⊳ vb displace

UNSETTLE vb change or become changed from a fixed or settled condition

UNSEW, -ED, -ING, -N, -S vb undo stitching of

UNSEX, -ED, -ES, -ING vb deprive (a person) of the attributes of his or her sex

UNSEXIER ► unsexy

UNSEXING ► unsex

UNSEXIST adj not sexist

UNSEXUAL adj not sexual

UNSEXY, UNSEXIER adj not exciting or attractive

UNSHADED adj not shaded

UNSHADOW vb remove shadow from

UNSHAKED same as ► **unshaken**

UNSHAKEN adj (of faith or feelings) not having been weakened

UNSHALE, -D, -S vb expose

UNSHAMED same as > **unashamed**

UNSHAPE, -D, -S vb make shapeless

UNSHAPEN adj having no definite shape

UNSHAPES ► unshape

UNSHARED adj not shared

UNSHARP adj not sharp

UNSHAVED adj not shaved

UNSHAVEN adj having a stubbled chin

UNSHED adj not shed

UNSHELL, -S vb remove from a shell

UNSHENT adj undamaged

UNSHEWN adj unshown

UNSHIFT, -S vb release the shift key on a keyboard

UNSHIP, -S vb be or cause to be unloaded, discharged, or disembarked from a ship

UNSHOD adj not wearing shoes

UNSHOE, -S vb remove shoes from

UNSHOED same as ► **unshod**

UNSHOES ► unshoe

UNSHOOT, -S Shakespearean variant of ► **unshout**

UNSHORN *adj* not cut
UNSHOT, -S *adj* not shot ▷ *vb* remove shot from
UNSHOUT, -S *vb* revoke (an earlier statement) by shouting a contrary one
UNSHOWN *adj* not shown
UNSHOWY *adj* not showy
UNSHROUD *vb* uncover
UNSHRUBD *adj* not having shrubs
UNSHRUNK *adj* not shrunk
UNSHUT, -S *vb* open
UNSICKER *adj* unsettled
UNSIFTED *adj* not strained
UNSIGHT, -S *vb* obstruct vision of
UNSIGNED *adj* (of a letter etc) anonymous
UNSILENT *adj* not silent
UNSINEW, -S *vb* weaken
UNSINFUL *adj* without sin
UNSIZED *adj* not made or sorted according to size
UNSLAIN *adj* not killed
UNSLAKED *adj* not slaked
UNSLICED *adj* not sliced
UNSLICK *adj* not slick
UNSLING, -S, UNSLUNG *vb* remove or release from a slung position
UNSLUICE *vb* let flow
UNSLUNG ▸ **unsling**
UNSMART *adj* not smart
UNSMOKED *adj* not smoked
UNSMOOTH *vb* roughen
UNSMOTE *same as* > **unsmitten**
UNSNAG, -S *vb* remove snags from
UNSNAP, -S *vb* unfasten (the snap or catch) of (something)
UNSNARL, -S *vb* free from a snarl or tangle
UNSNECK, -S *vb* unlatch
UNSOAKED *adj* not soaked
UNSOAPED *adj* not rubbed with soap
UNSOBER, -S *adj* not sober ▷ *vb* make unrefined in manners
UNSOCIAL *adj* avoiding the company of other people
UNSOCKET *vb* remove from a socket
UNSOD *same as* ▸ **unsodden**
UNSODDEN *adj* not soaked
UNSOFT *adj* hard
UNSOILED *adj* not soiled
UNSOLD *adj* not sold
UNSOLDER *vb* remove soldering from
UNSOLEMN *adj* unceremonious
UNSOLID *adj* not solid

UNSOLVED *adj* not having been solved or explained
UNSONCY *same as* ▸ **unsonsy**
UNSONSIE *same as* ▸ **unsonsy**
UNSONSY *adj* unfortunate
UNSOOTE *adj* not sweet
UNSORTED *adj* not sorted
UNSOUGHT *adj* not sought after
UNSOUL, -ED, -S *vb* cause to be soulless
UNSOUND *adj* unhealthy or unstable
UNSOURED *adj* not soured
UNSOWED *same as* ▸ **unsown**
UNSOWN *adj* not sown
UNSPAR, -S *vb* open
UNSPARED *adj* not spared
UNSPARS ▸ **unspar**
UNSPEAK, -S, UNSPOKE *obsolete word for* ▸ **unsay**
UNSPED *adj* not achieved
UNSPELL, -S *vb* release from a spell
UNSPENT *adj* not spent
UNSPHERE *vb* remove from its, one's, etc, sphere or place
UNSPIDE *same as* ▸ **unspied**
UNSPIED *adj* unnoticed
UNSPILT *adj* not spilt
UNSPLIT *adj* not split
UNSPOILT *same as* > **unspoiled**
UNSPOKE ▸ **unspeak**
UNSPOKEN *adj* not openly expressed
UNSPOOL, -S *vb* unwind from spool
UNSPRUNG *adj* without springs
UNSPUN *adj* not spun
UNSTABLE *adj* lacking stability or firmness
UNSTABLY
UNSTACK, -S *vb* remove from a stack
UNSTAID *adj* not staid
UNSTARCH *vb* remove starch from
UNSTARRY *adj* not resembling or characteristic of a star from the entertainment world
UNSTATE, -S *vb* deprive of state
UNSTATED *adj* not having been articulated or uttered
UNSTATES ▸ **unstate**
UNSTAYED *adj* unhindered
UNSTEADY *adj* not securely fixed ▷ *vb* make unsteady

UNSTEEL, -S *vb* make (the heart, feelings, etc) more gentle or compassionate
UNSTEP, -S *vb* remove (a mast) from its step
UNSTICK, -S *vb* free or loosen (something stuck)
UNSTITCH *vb* remove stitching from
UNSTOCK, -S *vb* remove stock from
UNSTONED *adj* not stoned
UNSTOP, -S *vb* remove the stop or stopper from
UNSTOW, -ED, -S *vb* remove from storage
UNSTRAP, -S *vb* undo the straps fastening (something) in position
UNSTRESS *n* weak syllable ▷ *vb* become less stressed
UNSTRING *vb* remove the strings of
UNSTRIP, -S *vb* strip
UNSTRUCK *adj* not struck
UNSTRUNG *adj* emotionally distressed
UNSTUCK *adj* freed from being stuck, glued, fastened, etc
UNSTUFFY *adj* well-ventilated
UNSTUFT *same as* > **unstuffed**
UNSTUNG *adj* not stung
UNSUBTLE *adj* not subtle
UNSUBTLY
UNSUCKED *adj* not sucked
UNSUIT, -S *vb* make unsuitable
UNSUITED *adj* not appropriate for a particular task or situation
UNSUITS ▸ **unsuit**
UNSUMMED *adj* not calculated
UNSUNG *adj* not acclaimed or honoured
UNSUNK *adj* not sunken
UNSUNNED *adj* not subjected to sunlight
UNSUNNY *adj* not sunny
UNSUPPLE *adj* rigid
UNSURE, -R, -ST *adj* lacking assurance or self-confidence
UNSURED *adj* not assured
UNSURELY ▸ **unsure**
UNSURER ▸ **unsure**
UNSUREST ▸ **unsure**
UNSWATHE *vb* unwrap
UNSWAYED *adj* not swayed
UNSWEAR, -S, UNSWORE, UNSWORN *vb* retract or revoke (a sworn oath)
UNSWEET *adj* not sweet
UNSWEPT *adj* not swept

U

UNSWORE ▸ unswear
UNSWORN ▸ unswear
UNTACK, -ED, -S vb remove saddle and harness, etc, from
UNTACKLE vb remove tackle from
UNTACKS ▸ untack
UNTAGGED adj without a label
UNTAILED adj tailless
UNTAKEN adj not taken
UNTAME, -S, UNTAMING vb undo the taming of
UNTAMED adj not brought under human control
UNTAMES ▸ untame
UNTAMING ▸ untame
UNTANGLE vb free from tangles or confusion
UNTANNED adj not tanned
UNTAPPED adj not yet used
UNTARRED adj not coated with tar
UNTASTED adj not tasted
UNTAUGHT adj without training or education
UNTAX, -ES, -ING vb stop taxing
UNTAXED adj not subject to taxation
UNTAXES ▸ untax
UNTAXING ▸ untax
UNTEACH vb cause to disbelieve (teaching)
UNTEAM, -ED, -S vb disband a team
UNTEMPER vb soften
UNTENANT vb remove (a tenant)
UNTENDED adj not cared for or attended to
UNTENDER adj not tender
UNTENT, -ED, -S vb remove from a tent
UNTENTY adj inattentive
UNTESTED adj not having been tested or examined
UNTETHER vb untie
UNTHATCH vb remove the thatch from
UNTHAW, -S same as ▸ thaw
UNTHAWED adj not thawed
UNTHAWS ▸ unthaw
UNTHINK, -S vb reverse one's opinion about
UNTHREAD vb draw out the thread or threads from (a needle, etc)
UNTHRIFT n unthrifty person
UNTHRONE less common word for ▸ dethrone
UNTIDIED ▸ untidy
UNTIDIER ▸ untidy
UNTIDIES ▸ untidy
UNTIDILY ▸ untidy

UNTIDY, UNTIDIED, UNTIDIER, UNTIDIES adj messy and disordered ▷ vb make untidy
UNTIE, -D, -ING, -S vb open or free (something that is tied)
UNTIL prep in or throughout the period before
UNTILE, -D, -S, UNTILING vb strip tiles from
UNTILLED adj not tilled
UNTILTED adj not tilted
UNTIMED adj not timed
UNTIMELY adj occurring before the expected or normal time ▷ adv prematurely or inopportunely
UNTIN, -NED, -S vb remove tin from
UNTINGED adj not tinged
UNTINNED ▸ untin
UNTINS ▸ untin
UNTIPPED adj not tipped
UNTIRED adj not tired
UNTIRING adj continuing without declining in strength
UNTITLED adj without a title
UNTO prep to
UNTOLD adj incapable of description
UNTOMB, -ED, -S vb exhume
UNTONED adj not toned
UNTORN adj not torn
UNTOWARD adj causing misfortune or annoyance
UNTRACE, -S vb remove traces from
UNTRACED adj not traced
UNTRACES ▸ untrace
UNTRACK, -S vb remove from track
UNTRADED adj not traded
UNTREAD, -S, UNTROD vb retrace (a course, path, etc)
UNTRENDY adj not trendy
UNTRIDE same as ▸ untried
UNTRIED adj not yet used, done, or tested
UNTRIM, -S vb deprive of elegance or adornment
UNTROD ▸ untread
UNTRUE, -R, -ST adj incorrect or false
UNTRUISM n something that is false
UNTRULY ▸ untrue
UNTRUSS vb release from or as if from a truss
UNTRUST, -S n mistrust
UNTRUSTY adj not trusty
UNTRUTH, -S n statement that is not true, lie
UNTUCK, -ED, -S vb become or cause to become loose or not tucked in

UNTUFTED adj not having tufts
UNTUNE, -D, -S, UNTUNING vb make out of tune
UNTURBID adj clear
UNTURF, -ED, -S vb remove turf from
UNTURN, -S vb turn in a reverse direction
UNTURNED adj not turned
UNTURNS ▸ unturn
UNTWINE, -D, -S vb untwist, unravel, and separate
UNTWIST, -S vb twist apart and loosen
UNTYING, -S ▸ untie
UNUNBIUM n chemical element
UNUNITED adj separated
UNURGED adj not urged
UNUSABLE adj not in good enough condition to be used
UNUSABLY
UNUSED adj not being or never having been used
UNUSEFUL adj useless
UNUSUAL adj uncommon or extraordinary
UNVAIL, -ED, -ES, -S same as ▸ unveil
UNVAILE same as ▸ unveil
UNVAILED ▸ unvail
UNVAILES ▸ unvail
UNVAILS ▸ unvail
UNVALUED adj not appreciated or valued
UNVARIED adj not varied
UNVEIL, -ED, -S vb ceremonially remove the cover from (a new picture, plaque, etc)
UNVEILER n person who removes a veil
UNVEILS ▸ unveil
UNVEINED adj without veins
UNVENTED adj not vented
UNVERSED adj not versed
UNVESTED adj not vested
UNVETTED adj not thoroughly examined
UNVEXED adj not annoyed
UNVEXT same as ▸ unvexed
UNVIABLE adj not capable of succeeding, esp financially
UNVIEWED adj not viewed
UNVIRTUE n state of having no virtue
UNVISOR, -S vb remove visor from
UNVITAL adj not vital
UNVIZARD same as ▸ unvisor
UNVOCAL adj not vocal
UNVOICE, -S vb pronounce without vibration of the vocal cords

UNVOICED adj not expressed or spoken
UNVOICES ▸ unvoice
UNVULGAR adj not vulgar
UNWAGED adj (of a person) not having a paid job
UNWAKED same as
▸ unwakened
UNWALLED adj not surrounded by walls
UNWANING adj not waning
UNWANTED adj not wanted or welcome
UNWARDED adj not warded
UNWARE same as
▸ unaware
UNWARELY
UNWARES same as
▸ unawares
UNWARIE same as ▸ unwary
UNWARIER ▸ unwary
UNWARILY ▸ unwary
UNWARMED adj not warmed
UNWARNED adj not warned
UNWARPED adj not warped
UNWARY, UNWARIER adj not careful or cautious and therefore likely to be harmed
UNWASHED adj not washed
UNWASHEN same as
▸ unwashed
UNWASTED adj not wasted
UNWATER, -S vb dry out
UNWATERY adj not watery
UNWAXED adj not treated with wax
UNWAYED adj having no routes
UNWEAL, -S n ill or sorrow
UNWEANED adj not weaned
UNWEAPON vb disarm
UNWEARY adj not weary
▷ vb refresh or energize
UNWEAVE, -S, UNWOVE, UNWOVEN vb undo (weaving)
UNWEBBED adj not webbed
UNWED adj not wed
UNWEDDED adj not wedded
UNWEEDED adj not weeded
UNWEENED adj unknown
UNWEIGHT vb remove weight from
UNWELDED adj not welded
UNWELDY same as
▸ unwieldy
UNWELL adj not healthy, ill
UNWEPT adj not wept for or lamented
UNWET adj not wet
UNWETTED same as
▸ unwet
UNWHIPT same as
> unwhipped
UNWHITE adj not white

UNWIELDY adj too heavy, large, or awkward to be easily handled
UNWIFELY adj not like a wife
UNWIGGED adj without a wig
UNWILFUL adj complaisant
UNWILL, -S vb will the reversal of (something that has already occurred)
UNWILLED adj not intentional
UNWILLS ▸ unwill
UNWIND, -S vb relax after a busy or tense time
UNWINDER
UNWINGED adj without wings
UNWIPED adj not wiped
UNWIRE, -D, -S, UNWIRING vb remove wiring from
UNWISDOM n imprudence
UNWISE, -R, -ST adj foolish
UNWISELY
UNWISH, -ES vb retract or revoke (a wish)
UNWISHED adj not desired
UNWISHES ▸ unwish
UNWIST adj unknown
UNWIT, -S, -TED vb divest of wit
UNWITCH vb release from witchcraft
UNWITS ▸ unwit
UNWITTED ▸ unwit
UNWITTY adj not clever and amusing
UNWIVE, -D, -S, UNWIVING vb remove a wife from
UNWOMAN, -S vb remove womanly qualities from
UNWON adj not won
UNWONT adj unaccustomed
UNWONTED adj out of the ordinary
UNWOODED adj not wooded
UNWOOED adj not wooed
UNWORDED adj not expressed in words
UNWORK, -S vb destroy (work previously done)
UNWORKED adj not worked
UNWORKS ▸ unwork
UNWORMED adj not rid of worms
UNWORN adj not having deteriorated through use or age
UNWORTH, -S n lack of value
UNWORTHY adj not deserving or worthy
UNWOUND past tense and past participle of ▸ unwind
UNWOVE ▸ unweave
UNWOVEN ▸ unweave
UNWRAP, -S vb remove the wrapping from (something)

UNWRITE, -S, UNWROTE vb cancel (what has been written)
UNWRUNG adj not twisted
UNYEANED adj not having given birth
UNYOKE, -D, -S, UNYOKING vb release (an animal, etc) from a yoke
UNYOUNG adj not young
UNZIP, -PED, -S vb unfasten the zip of (a garment)
UNZONED adj not divided into zones
UP, -PED, -S adv indicating movement to or position at a higher place ▷ adj of a high or higher position ▷ vb increase or raise
UPADAISY same as
> upsadaisy
UPALONG, -S n location away from a place
UPAS, -ES n large Javan tree with whitish bark and poisonous milky sap
UPBEAR, -ER, -S, UPBORE vb sustain
UPBEAT, -S adj cheerful and optimistic ▷ n unaccented beat
UPBIND, -S vb bind up
UPBLOW, UPBLEW, -N, -S vb inflate
UPBOIL, -ED, -S vb boil up
UPBORE ▸ upbear
UPBORNE adj held up
UPBOUND adj travelling upwards
UPBOW, -S n stroke of the bow from its tip to its nut on a stringed instrument
UPBRAID, -S vb scold or reproach
UPBRAST same as ▸ upburst
UPBRAY, -ED, -S vb shame
UPBREAK, -S, UPBROKE, UPBROKEN vb escape upwards
UPBRING, -S vb rear
UPBROKE ▸ upbreak
UPBROKEN ▸ upbreak
UPBUILD, -S, UPBUILT vb build up
UPBURST, -S vb burst upwards
UPBY same as ▸ upbye
UPBYE adv yonder
UPCAST, -S n material cast or thrown up ▷ adj directed or thrown upwards ▷ vb throw or cast up
UPCATCH, UPCAUGHT vb catch up
UPCHEER, -S vb cheer up
UPCHUCK, -S vb vomit
UPCLIMB, -S vb ascend

UPCLOSE, -D, -S vb close up

UPCOAST adv up the coast

UPCOIL, -ED, -S vb make into a coil

UPCOME, -S vb come up

UPCOMING adj coming soon

UPCOURT adv up basketball court

UPCURL, -ED, -S vb curl up

UPCURVE, -D, -S vb curve upwards

UPCYCLE, -D, -S vb recycle a disposable product into an object of greater value

UPDART, -ED, -S vb dart upwards

UPDATE, -D, -S, UPDATING vb bring up to date ▷ n act of updating or something that is updated
UPDATER -S

UPDIVE, -D, -S, UPDIVING, UPDOVE vb leap upwards

UPDO, -S n type of hairstyle

UPDOMING n expansion of a rock upwards into a dome shape

UPDOS ▶ updo

UPDOVE ▶ updive

UPDRAFT, -S n upwards air current

UPDRAG, -S vb drag up

UPDRAW, -N, -S, UPDREW vb draw up

UPDRY, UPDRIED, UPDRIES, -ING vb dry up

UPEND, -ED, -ING, -S vb turn or set (something) on its end

UPFIELD adj in sport, away from the defending team's goal

UPFILL, -ED, -S vb fill up

UPFLING, -S, UPFLUNG vb throw upwards

UPFLOW, -ED, -S vb flow upwards

UPFLUNG ▶ upfling

UPFOLD, -ED, -S vb fold up

UPFOLLOW vb follow

UPFRONT adj open and frank ▷ adv (of money) paid out at the beginning of a business arrangement

UPFURL, -ED, -S vb roll up

UPGANG, -S n climb

UPGATHER vb draw together

UPGAZE, -D, -S, UPGAZING vb gaze upwards

UPGIRD, -ED, -S vb belt up

UPGIRT same as ▶ upgird

UPGO, -ES, -ING, -INGS, -NE, UPWENT vb ascend

UPGRADE, -D, -S vb promote (a person or job) to a higher rank
UPGRADER

UPGROW, UPGREW, -N, -S vb grow up

UPGROWTH n process of developing or growing upwards

UPGUSH, -ED, -ES vb flow upwards

UPHAND adj lifted by hand

UPHANG, -S, UPHUNG vb hang up

UPHAUD, -S, UPHUDDEN Scots variant of ▶ uphold

UPHEAP, -ED, -S vb heap or pile up

UPHEAVAL n strong, sudden, or violent disturbance

UPHEAVE, -D, -R, -S, UPHOVE vb heave or rise upwards

UPHELD ▶ uphold

UPHILD archaic past form of ▶ uphold

UPHILL, -S adj sloping or leading upwards ▷ adv up a slope ▷ n difficulty

UPHOARD, -S vb hoard up

UPHOIST, -S vb raise

UPHOLD, UPHELD, -S vb maintain or defend against opposition
UPHOLDER

UPHOORD, -S vb heap up

UPHOVE ▶ upheave

UPHROE, -S variant spelling of ▶ euphroe

UPHUDDEN ▶ uphaud

UPHUNG ▶ uphang

UPHURL, -ED, -S vb throw upwards

UPJET, -S, -TED vb stream upwards

UPKEEP, -S n act, process, or cost of keeping something in good repair

UPKNIT, -S vb bind

UPLAID ▶ uplay

UPLAND, -S adj of or in an area of high or relatively high ground ▷ n area of high or relatively high ground

UPLANDER n person hailing from the uplands

UPLANDS ▶ upland

UPLAY, UPLAID, -ING, -S vb stash

UPLEAD, -S, UPLED vb lead upwards

UPLEAN, -ED, -S, -T vb lean on something

UPLEAP, -ED, -S, -T vb jump upwards

UPLED ▶ uplead

UPLIFT, -ED, -S vb raise or lift up ▷ n act or process of improving moral, social, or cultural conditions
UPLIFTER

UPLIGHT, -S, UPLIT n lamp or wall light designed or positioned to cast its light upwards ▷ vb light in an upward direction

UPLINK, -ED, -S n transmitter that sends signals up to a communications satellite ▷ vb send (data) to a communications satellite

UPLIT ▶ uplight

UPLOAD, -ED, -S vb transfer (data or a program) into the memory of another computer

UPLOCK, -ED, -S vb lock up

UPLOOK, -ED, -S vb look up

UPLYING adj raised

UPMAKE, -S, UPMAKING vb make up
UPMAKER -S

UPMARKET adj expensive and of superior quality ▷ vb make something upmarket

UPMOST another word for
> **uppermost**.

UPO prep upon

UPON prep on

UPPED ▶ up

UPPER, -S adj higher or highest in physical position, wealth, rank, or status ▷ n part of a shoe above the sole

UPPERCUT n short swinging upward punch delivered to the chin ▷ vb hit (an opponent) with an uppercut

UPPERS ▶ upper

UPPILE, -D, -S, UPPILING vb pile up

UPPING, -S ▶ up

UPPISH adj snobbish, arrogant, or presumptuous
UPPISHLY

UPPITY adj snobbish, arrogant, or presumptuous

UPPROP, -S vb support

UPRAISE, -D, -S vb lift up
UPRAISER

UPRAN ▶ uprun

UPRATE, -D, -S, UPRATING vb raise the value, rate, or size of, upgrade

UPREACH vb reach up

UPREAR, -ED, -S vb lift up

UPREST, -S n uprising

UPRIGHT, -S adj vertical or erect ▷ adv vertically or in an erect position ▷ n vertical support, such as a post ▷ vb make upright

UPRISAL, -S ▶ uprise

UPRISE, -N, -S, UPROSE vb rise up
UPRISER -S

UPRISING n rebellion or revolt

UPRIST, -S *same as* ▶ **uprest**

UPRIVER, -S *adv* towards or near the source of a river ▷ *n* area located upstream

UPROAR, -ED, -S *n* disturbance characterized by loud noise and confusion ▷ *vb* cause an uproar

UPROLL, -ED, -S *vb* roll up

UPROOT, -ED, -S *vb* pull up by or as if by the roots

UPROOTAL

UPROOTER

UPROSE ▶ **uprise**

UPROUSE, -D, -S *vb* rouse or stir up

UPRUN, UPRAN, -S *vb* run up

UPRUSH, -ED, -ES *n* upward rush, as of consciousness ▷ *vb* rush upwards

UPRYST *same as* ▶ **uprest**

UPS ▶ **up**

UPSCALE, -D, -S *adj* of or for the upper end of an economic or social scale ▷ *vb* upgrade

UPSEE, -S *n* drunken revel

UPSELL, -S, UPSOLD *vb* persuade a customer to buy a more expensive or additional item

UPSEND, -S, UPSENT *vb* send up

UPSET, -S *adj* emotionally or physically disturbed or distressed ▷ *vb* tip over ▷ *n* unexpected defeat or reversal

UPSETTER

UPSEY, -S *same as* ▶ **upsee**

UPSHIFT, -S *vb* move up (a gear)

UPSHOOT, -S *vb* shoot upwards

UPSHOT, -S *n* final result or conclusion

UPSIDE, -S *n* upper surface or part

UPSIES ▶ **upsy**

UPSILON, -S *n* 20th letter in the Greek alphabet

UPSIZE, -D, -S, UPSIZING *vb* increase in size

UPSKILL, -S *vb* improve the aptitude for work of (a person)

UPSKIRT *adj* indicating a photo taken of a woman's exposed underwear without her consent

UPSLOPE, -S *adv* up a or the slope ▷ *n* upward slope

UPSOAR, -ED, -S *vb* soar up

UPSOLD ▶ **upsell**

UPSPEAK, UPSPAKE, -S, UPSPOKE, UPSPOKEN *vb* speak with rising intonation

UPSPEAR, -S *vb* grow upwards in a spear-like manner

UPSPOKE ▶ **upspeak**

UPSPOKEN ▶ **upspeak**

UPSPRING, UPSPRANG, UPSPRUNG *vb* spring up or come into existence ▷ *n* leap forwards or upwards

UPSTAGE, -D, -S *adj* at the back half of the stage ▷ *vb* draw attention to oneself from (someone else) ▷ *adv* on, at, or to the rear of the stage ▷ *n* back half of the stage

UPSTAGER

UPSTAIR *same as* ▶ **upstairs**

UPSTAIRS *adv* to or on an upper floor of a building ▷ *n* upper floor ▷ *adj* situated on an upper floor

UPSTAND, -S, UPSTOOD *vb* rise

UPSTARE, -D, -S *vb* stare upwards

UPSTART, -S *n* person who has risen suddenly to a position of power and behaves arrogantly ▷ *vb* start up (again, as in surprise, etc

UPSTATE, -S *adv* towards, in, from, or relating to the outlying or northern sections of a state ▷ *n* outlying, esp northern, sections of a state

UPSTATER

UPSTAY, -ED, -S *vb* support

UPSTEP, -S *n* type of vocal intonation

UPSTIR, -S *vb* stir up ▷ *n* commotion

UPSTOOD ▶ **upstand**

UPSTREAM *adj* in or towards the higher part of a stream ▷ *vb* stream upwards

UPSTROKE *n* upward stroke or movement, as of a pen or brush

UPSURGE, -D, -S *n* rapid rise or swell ▷ *vb* surge up

UPSWARM, -S *vb* rise or send upwards in a swarm

UPSWAY, -ED, -S *vb* swing in the air

UPSWEEP, -S, UPSWEPT *n* curve or sweep upwards ▷ *vb* sweep, curve, or brush or be swept, curved, or brushed upwards

UPSWELL, -S *vb* swell up or cause to swell up

UPSWEPT ▶ **upsweep**

UPSWING, -S, UPSWUNG *n* recovery period in the trade cycle ▷ *vb* swing or move up

UPSY, UPSIES *same as* ▶ **upsee**

UPTA *same as* ▶ **upter**

UPTAK, -S *same as* ▶ **uptake**

UPTAKE, -N, -S, UPTAKING, UPTOOK *n* numbers taking up something such as an offer or the act of taking it up ▷ *vb* take up

UPTAKS ▶ **uptak**

UPTALK, -ED, -S *n* style of speech in which every sentence ends with a rising tone ▷ *vb* talk in this manner

UPTEAR, -S, UPTORE, UPTORN *vb* tear up

UPTEMPO, -S *adj* fast ▷ *n* uptempo piece

UPTER *adj* of poor quality

UPTHROW, UPTHREW, -N, -S *n* upward movement of rocks on one side of a fault plane relative to rocks on the other side ▷ *vb* throw upwards

UPTHRUST *n* upward push

UPTICK, -S *n* rise or increase

UPTIE, -D, -S, UPTYING *vb* tie up

UPTIGHT *adj* nervously tense, irritable, or angry

UPTILT, -ED, -S *vb* tilt up

UPTIME, -S *n* time during which a machine, such as a computer, actually operates

UPTOOK ▶ **uptake**

UPTORE ▶ **uptear**

UPTORN ▶ **uptear**

UPTOSS, -ED, -ES *vb* throw upwards

UPTOWN, -S *adv* towards, in, or relating to some part of a town that is away from the centre ▷ *n* such a part of town, esp a residential part

UPTOWNER

UPTRAIN, -S *vb* train up

UPTREND, -S *n* upward trend

UPTURN, -ED, -S *n* upward trend or improvement ▷ *vb* turn or cause to turn over or upside down

UPTYING ▶ **uptie**

UPVALUE, -D, -S *vb* raise the value of

UPWAFT, -ED, -S *vb* waft upwards

UPWARD *same as* ▶ **upwards**

UPWARDLY

UPWARDS *adv* from a lower to a higher place, level, condition, etc

UPWELL, -ED, -S *vb* well up

UPWENT ▶ **upgo**

UPWHIRL, -S *vb* spin upwards

U

UPWIND, -S, UPWOUND *adv* into or against the wind ▷ *adj* going against the wind ▷ *vb* wind up

UPWRAP, -S *vb* wrap up

UR *interj* hesitant utterance used to fill gaps in talking

URACHUS, URACHI *n* cord of tissue connected to the bladder

URACIL, -S *n* pyrimidine present in all living cells

URAEI ▶ uraeus

This plural of **uraeus**, an Egyptian symbol of kingship, is very useful for dumping a surplus of vowels.

URAEMIA, -S *n* accumulation of waste products in the blood

URAEMIC

URAEUS, URAEI, -ES *n* sacred serpent of ancient Egypt

URALI, -S *n* type of plant

URALITE, -S *n* mineral that replaces pyroxene in some rocks

URALITIC

URANIA, -S *n* uranium dioxide

URANIAN *adj* heavenly

URANIAS ▶ urania

URANIC *adj* of or containing uranium, esp in a high valence state

URANIDE, -S *n* any element having an atomic number greater than that of protactinium

URANIN, -S *n* type of alkaline substance

URANISCI > uraniscus

URANISM, -S *n* homosexuality

URANITE, -S *n* any of various minerals containing uranium, esp torbernite or autunite

URANITIC

URANIUM, -S *n* radioactive silvery-white metallic element

URANOUS *adj* of or containing uranium, esp in a low valence state

URANYL, -S *n* divalent ion UO22+ or the group –UO2

URANYLIC

URAO, -S *n* type of mineral

URARE, -S *same as* ▶ **urali**

URARI, -S *same as* ▶ **urali**

URASE, -S *same as* ▶ **urease**

URATE, -S *n* any salt or ester of uric acid

URATIC

URB, -S *n* urban area

URBAN *adj* of or living in a city or town

URBANE, -R, -ST *adj* characterized by courtesy, elegance, and sophistication

URBANELY

URBANISE *same as* ▶ **urbanize**

URBANISM *n* character of city life

URBANIST *n* person who studies towns and cities

URBANITE *n* resident of an urban community

URBANITY *n* quality of being urbane

URBANIZE *vb* make (a rural area) more industrialized and urban

URBEX, -ES *n* short for urban exploration, the hobby of exploring derelict urban structures

URBIA, -S *n* urban area

URBS ▶ urb

URCEOLUS, URCEOLI *n* organ of a plant

URCHIN, -S *n* mischievous child

URD, -S *n* type of plant with edible seeds

URDE *adj* (in heraldry) having points

URDEE *same as* ▶ **urde**

URDS ▶ urd

URDY *n* heraldic line pattern

URE, -S *same as* ▶ **aurochs**

UREA, -S *n* white soluble crystalline compound found in urine

UREAL

UREASE, -S *n* enzyme that converts urea to ammonium carbonate

UREDIA ▶ uredium

UREDIAL ▶ uredium

UREDINE, -S *same as* ▶ **uredo**

UREDINIA > uredinium

UREDIUM, UREDIA *n* spore-producing body of some rust fungi in which uredospores are formed

UREDO, -S *less common name for* > **urticaria**

UREIC ▶ urea

UREIDE, -S *n* any of a class of organic compounds derived from urea

UREMIA, -S *same as* ▶ **uraemia**

UREMIC

URENA, -S *n* plant genus

URENT *adj* burning

URES ▶ ure

URESIS, URESES *n* urination

URETER, -S *n* tube that conveys urine from the kidney to the bladder

URETERAL

URETERIC

URETHAN, -S *same as* ▶ **urethane**

URETHANE *n* short for the synthetic material polyurethane ▷ *vb* treat with urethane

URETHANS ▶ urethan

URETHRA, -E, -S *n* canal that carries urine from the bladder out of the body

URETHRAL

URETIC *adj* of or relating to the urine

URGE, -D, -S *n* strong impulse, inner drive, or yearning ▷ *vb* plead with or press (a person to do something)

URGENCE, -S ▶ urgent

URGENCY ▶ urgent

URGENT *adj* requiring speedy action or attention

URGENTLY

URGER, -S ▶ urge

URGES ▶ urge

URGING, -S ▶ urge

URGINGLY ▶ urge

URGINGS ▶ urging

URIAL, -S *n* type of sheep

URIC *adj* of or derived from urine

URICASE, -S *n* type of enzyme

URIDINE, -S *n* nucleoside present in all living cells in a combined form, esp in RNA

URIDYLIC *adj as in* **uridylic acid** nucleotide consisting of uracil, ribose, and a phosphate group

URINAL, -S *n* sanitary fitting used by men for urination

URINANT *adj* having the head downwards

URINARY *adj* of urine or the organs that secrete and pass urine ▷ *n* reservoir for urine

URINATE, -D, -S *vb* discharge urine

URINATOR

URINE, -D, -S, URINING *n* pale yellow fluid passed as waste from the body ▷ *vb* urinate

URINEMIA *same as* ▶ **uremia**

URINEMIC

URINES ▶ urine

URINING ▶ urine

URINOSE *same as* ▶ **urinous**

URINOUS *adj* of, resembling, or containing urine

URITE, -S *n* part of the abdomen

URMAN, -S n forest

URN, -ED, -S n vase used as a container for the ashes of the dead ▷ vb put in an urn

URNAL

URNFIELD n cemetery full of individual cremation urns ▷ adj characterized by cremation in urns

URNFUL, -S n capacity of an urn

URNLIKE ▶ urn

URNS ▶ urn

UROBILIN n brownish pigment found in faeces and sometimes in urine

UROBORIC adj of or like a uroboros

UROBOROS same as > **ouroboros**

UROCHORD n notochord of a larval tunicate, typically confined to the tail region

URODELAN ▶ urodele

URODELE, -S n amphibian of the order which includes the salamanders and newts

UROGRAM, -S n X-ray of the urinary tract

UROLITH, -S n calculus in the urinary tract

UROLOGIC ▶ urology

UROLOGY n branch of medicine concerned with the urinary system and its diseases

UROMERE, -S n part of the abdomen

UROPOD, -S n paired appendage forms part of the tailfan in lobsters

UROPODAL

UROPYGIA > uropygium

UROSCOPY n examination of the urine

UROSIS, UROSES n urinary disease

UROSOME, -S n abdomen of arthropods

UROSTEGE n part of a serpent's tail

UROSTOMY n type of urinary surgery

UROSTYLE n bony rod forming the last segment of the vertebral column of frogs and toads

URP, -ED, -ING, -S dialect word for ▶ **vomit**

URSA, -E n she-bear

URSID, -S n meteor

URSIFORM adj bear-shaped or bearlike in form

URSINE adj of or like a bear

URSON, -S n type of porcupine

URTEXT, -S n earliest form of a text

URTEXTE same as ▶ **urtexts**

URTEXTS ▶ urtext

URTICA, -S n type of nettle

URTICANT n something that causes itchiness and irritation

URTICAS ▶ urtica

URTICATE adj characterized by the presence of weals ▷ vb sting

URUBU, -S n type of bird

URUS, -ES another name for the ▶ **aurochs**

URUSHIOL n poisonous pale yellow liquid occurring in poison ivy and the lacquer tree

URVA, -S n Indian mongoose

US pron refers to the speaker or writer and another person or other people

USABLE adj able to be used

USABLY

USAGE, -S n regular or constant use

USAGER, -S n person who has the use of something in trust

USAGES ▶ usage

USANCE, -S n period of time permitted for the redemption of foreign bills of exchange

USAUNCE, -S same as ▶ **usance**

USE, -S, USING vb put into service or action ▷ n using or being used

USEABLE same as ▶ **usable**

USEABLY ▶ usable

USED adj second-hand

USEFUL, -S adj able to be used advantageously or for several different purposes ▷ n odd-jobman or general factotum

USEFULLY

USELESS adj having no practical use

USER, -S n continued exercise, use, or enjoyment of a right, esp in property

USERNAME n name given by computer user to gain access

USERS ▶ user

USES ▶ use

USHER, -ED, -ING, -S n official who shows people to their seats, as in a church ▷ vb conduct or escort

USHERESS n female usher

USHERING ▶ usher

USHERS ▶ usher

USING ▶ use

USNEA, -S n type of lichen

USQUABAE n whisky

USQUE, -S n whisky

USQUEBAE same as ▶ **usquabae**

USQUES ▶ usque

USTION, -S n burning

USTULATE adj charred ▷ vb give a charred appearance to

USUAL, -S adj of the most normal, frequent, or regular type ▷ n ordinary or commonplace events

USUALLY adv most often, in most cases

USUALS ▶ usual

USUCAPT > usucapion

USUCAPTS > usucapion

USUFRUCT n right to use and derive profit from a piece of property belonging to another

USURE, -D, -S, USURING vb be involved in usury

USURER, -S n person who lends funds at an exorbitant rate of interest

USURES ▶ usure

USURESS n female usurer

USURIES ▶ usure

USURING ▶ usure

USURIOUS ▶ usury

USUROUS ▶ usury

USURP, -ED, -ING, -S vb seize (a position or power) without authority

USURPER -S

USURY, USURIES n practice of lending money at an extremely high rate of interest

USWARD adv towards us

USWARDS same as ▶ **usward**

UT, -S n syllable used in the fixed system of solmization for the note C

UTA, -S n side-blotched lizard

UTAS, -ES n eighth day of a festival

UTE, -S same as ▶ **utility**

UTENSIL, -S n tool or container for practical use

UTERI ▶ uterus

UTERINE adj of or affecting the womb

UTERITIS n inflammation of the womb

UTERUS, UTERI, -ES n womb

UTES ▶ ute

UTILE, -S n W African tree

UTILIDOR n above-ground insulated casing for pipes in permafrost regions

UTILISE, -D, -S same as ▶ **utilize**

UTILISER

U

UTILITY *n* usefulness ▷ *adj* designed for use rather than beauty

UTILIZE, -D, -S *vb* make practical use of
UTILIZER

UTIS, -ES *n* uproar

UTMOST, -S *n* the greatest possible degree or amount ▷ *adj* of the greatest possible degree or amount

UTOPIA, -S *n* real or imaginary society, place, state, etc, considered to be perfect or ideal

UTOPIAN, -S *adj* of or relating to a perfect or ideal existence ▷ *n* idealistic social reformer

UTOPIAS ► utopia
UTOPIAST ► utopia

UTOPISM, -S ► utopia
UTOPIST, -S ► utopia

UTRICLE, -S *n* larger of the two parts of the membranous labyrinth of the internal ear

UTRICULI > utriculus
UTS ► ut

UTTER, -ED, -ER, -ERS, -EST, -ING, -S *vb* express (something) in sounds or words ▷ *adj* total or absolute

UTTERLY *adv* extremely
UTTERS ► utter
UTU, -S *n* reward

UVA, -E, -S *n* grape or fruit resembling this

UVEA, -S *n* part of the eyeball consisting of the iris, ciliary body, and choroid
UVEAL

UVEITIC ► uveitis
UVEITIS *n* inflammation of the uvea

UVEOUS ► uvea

UVULA, -E, -S *n* small fleshy part of the soft palate that hangs in the back of the throat

UVULAR, -S *adj* of or relating to the uvula ▷ *n* uvular consonant
UVULARLY

UVULAS ► uvula

UVULITIS *n* inflammation of the uvea

UXORIAL *adj* of or relating to a wife

UXORIOUS *adj* excessively fond of or dependent on one's wife

U

Vv

If you have a **V** on your rack, the first thing to remember is that there are no valid two-letter words beginning with **V**. In fact, there are no two-letter words that end in **V** either, so you can't form any two-letter words using **V**. Remembering this will stop you wasting time trying to think of some. While **V** is useless for two-letter words, it does start some good three-letter words. **Vex** and **vox** (13 points each) are the best of these, while **vaw, vow** and **vly** (9 each) are also useful.

VAC, -KED, -KING, -S *vb* clean with a vacuum cleaner

> Meaning to clean with a vacuum cleaner, this can be a useful short word for dealing with that awkward letter V.

VACANCE, -S *n* vacant period
VACANCY *n* unfilled job
VACANT *adj* (of a toilet, room, etc) unoccupied
VACANTLY
VACATE, -D, -S, VACATING *vb* cause (something) to be empty by leaving
VACATION *n* time when universities and law courts are closed ▷ *vb* take a vacation
VACATUR, -S *n* annulment
VACCINA, -S *same as* ▶ **vaccinia**
VACCINAL *adj* of or relating to vaccine or vaccination
VACCINAS ▶ **vaccina**
VACCINE, -S *n* substance designed to make a person immune to a disease
VACCINEE *n* person who has been vaccinated
VACCINES ▶ **vaccine**
VACCINIA *technical name for* ▶ **cowpox**
VACHERIN *n* soft cheese made from cows' milk
VACKED ▶ **vac**
VACKING ▶ **vac**
VACS ▶ **vac**
VACUA ▶ **vacuum**
VACUATE, -S *vb* empty
VACUATED
VACUIST, -S *n* person believing in the existence of vacuums in nature

VACUITY *n* absence of intelligent thought or ideas
VACUOLAR ▶ **vacuole**
VACUOLE, -S *n* fluid-filled cavity in the cytoplasm of a cell
VACUOUS *adj* not expressing intelligent thought
VACUUM, VACUA, -ED, -S *n* empty space from which all or most air or gas has been removed ▷ *vb* clean with a vacuum cleaner
VADE, -S *vb* fade
VADED
VADING
VADOSE *adj* of or derived from water occurring above the water table
VAE, -S *same as* ▶ **voe**
VAG, -GED, -GING, -S *n* vagrant ▷ *n* arrest someone for vagrancy
VAGABOND *n* person with no fixed home, esp a beggar
VAGAL *adj* of, relating to, or affecting the vagus nerve
VAGALLY
VAGARIES ▶ **vagary**
VAGARISH ▶ **vagary**
VAGARY, VAGARIES *n* unpredictable change
VAGGED ▶ **vag**
VAGGING ▶ **vag**
VAGI ▶ **vagus**
VAGILE *adj* able to move freely
VAGILITY
VAGINA, -E, -S *n* (in female mammals) passage from the womb to the external genitals
VAGINAL
VAGINANT *adj* sheathing
VAGINAS ▶ **vagina**

VAGINATE *adj* (esp of plant parts) having a sheath
VAGINULA *n* little sheath
VAGINULE *same as* ▶ **vaginula**
VAGITUS *n* new-born baby's cry
VAGOTOMY *n* surgical division of the vagus nerve
VAGRANCY *n* state or condition of being a vagrant
VAGRANT, -S *n* person with no settled home ▷ *adj* wandering
VAGROM *same as* ▶ **vagrant**
VAGS ▶ **vag**
VAGUE, -R, -S, -ST *adj* not clearly explained ▷ *vb* wander
VAGUED
VAGUELY
VAGUING
VAGUISH *adj* rather vague
VAGUS, VAGI *n* tenth cranial nerve, which supplies the heart, lungs, and viscera
VAHANA, -S *n* vehicle
VAHINE, -S *n* Polynesian woman
VAIL, -ED, -ING, -S *vb* lower (something, such as a weapon), esp as a sign of deference or submission
VAIN, -ER, -EST *adj* excessively proud, esp of one's appearance
VAINESSE *n* vainness
VAINEST ▶ **vain**
VAINLY ▶ **vain**
VAINNESS ▶ **vain**
VAIR, -S *n* fur used to trim robes in the Middle Ages
VAIRE *adj* of Russian squirrel fur
VAIRIER ▶ **vairy**

VAIRIEST ► vairy
VAIRS ► vair
VAIRY, VAIRIER, VAIRIEST ► vair
VAIVODE, -S n European ruler
VAKAS, -ES n Armenian priestly garment
VAKASS, -ES n priest's cloak with a metal breastplate
VAKEEL, -S n ambassador
VAKIL, -S same as ► vakeel
VALANCE, -S n piece of drapery round the edge of a bed ▷ vb provide with a valance
VALANCED
VALE, -S n valley ▷ sentence substitute farewell
VALENCE, -S same as ► valency
VALENCIA n type of fabric
VALENCY n power of an atom to make molecular bonds
VALERATE n salt of valeric acid
VALERIAN n herb used as a sedative
VALERIC adj of, relating to, or derived from valerian
VALES ► vale
VALET, -ED, -ING, -S n man's personal male servant ▷ vb act as a valet (for)
VALETA, -S n old-time dance in triple time
VALETE, -S n farewell
VALETED ► valet
VALETES ► valete
VALETING ► valet
VALETS ► valet
VALGOID ► valgus
VALGOUS same as ► valgus
VALGUS, -ES adj denoting a deformity of a limb ▷ n abnormal position of a limb
VALI, -S n Turkish civil governor
VALIANCE ► valiant
VALIANCY ► valiant
VALIANT, -S adj brave or courageous ▷ n brave person
VALID, -ER, -EST adj soundly reasoned
VALIDATE vb make valid
VALIDER ► valid
VALIDEST ► valid
VALIDITY ► valid
VALIDLY ► valid
VALINE, -S n essential amino acid
VALIS ► vali
VALISE, -S n small suitcase
VALIUM n as in **valium picnic** refers to a day on the New York Stock Exchange when business is slow

VALKYR, -S variant of ► valkyrie
VALKYRIE n Norse maiden who collects dead warriors to take to Valhalla
VALKYRS ► valkyr
VALLAR, -S adj pertaining to a rampart ▷ n gold Roman crown awarded to the first soldier who broke into the enemy's camp
VALLARY n Roman circular gold crown
VALLATE adj surrounded with a wall
VALLEY, -S n low area between hills, often with a river running through it
VALLEYED adj having a valley
VALLEYS ► valley
VALLHUND n as in **Swedish vallhund** breed of dog
VALLONIA same as ► valonia
VALLUM, -S n Roman rampart or earthwork
VALONEA, -S same as ► valonia
VALONIA, -S n acorn cups and unripe acorns of a particular oak
VALOR, -S same as ► valour
VALORISE same as ► valorize
VALORIZE vb fix and maintain an artificial price for (a commodity) by governmental action
VALOROUS ► valour
VALORS ► valor
VALOUR, -S n bravery ▷ n courageous person
VALPROIC adj as in **valproic acid** synthetic crystalline compound, used as an anticonvulsive
VALSE, -D, -S, VALSING another word for ► waltz
VALUABLE adj having great worth ▷ n valuable article of personal property, esp jewellery
VALUABLY
VALUATE, -D, -S vb value or evaluate
VALUATOR n person who estimates the value of objects, paintings, etc
VALUE, -D, -S, VALUING n importance, usefulness ▷ vb assess the worth or desirability of
VALUER -S

VALUTA, -S n value of one currency in terms of its exchange rate with another
VALVAL same as ► valvular
VALVAR same as ► valvular
VALVATE adj furnished with a valve or valves
VALVE, -S n device to control the movement of fluid through a pipe ▷ vb provide with a valve
VALVED
VALVELET same as ► valvule
VALVES ► valve
VALVING ► valve
VALVULA, -E same as ► valvule
VALVULAR adj of or having valves
VALVULE, -S n small valve or a part resembling one
VAMBRACE n piece of armour used to protect the arm
VAMOOSE, -D, -S vb leave a place hurriedly
VAMOSE, -S same as ► vamoose
VAMOSED
VAMOSING
VAMP, -ED, -S n attractive woman who exploits men ▷ vb exploit (a man) in the fashion of a vamp
VAMPER -S
VAMPIER ► vampy
VAMPIEST ► vampy
VAMPING, -S ► vamp
VAMPIRE, -D, -S n (in folklore) corpse that rises at night to drink the blood of the living ▷ vb assail
VAMPIRIC
VAMPISH ► vamp
VAMPLATE n piece of metal mounted on a lance to protect the hand
VAMPS ► vamp
VAMPY, VAMPIER, VAMPIEST ► vamp
VAN, -S n motor vehicle for transporting goods ▷ vb send in a van
VANADATE n any salt or ester of a vanadic acid
VANADIC adj of or containing vanadium, esp in a trivalent or pentavalent state
VANADIUM n metallic element, used in steel
VANADOUS adj of or containing vanadium
VANDA, -S n type of orchid
VANDAL, -S n person who deliberately damages property
VANDALIC

VANDAS ► vanda

VANDYKE, -D, -S *n* short pointed beard ▷ *vb* cut with deep zigzag indentations

VANE, -S *n* flat blade on a rotary device such as a weathercock or propeller
VANED
VANELESS

VANESSA, -S *n* type of butterfly

VANESSID *n* type of butterfly ▷ *adj* relating to this butterfly

VANG, -S *n* type of rope or tackle on a sailing ship

VANGUARD *n* unit of soldiers leading an army

VANILLA, -S *n* seed pod of a tropical climbing orchid, used for flavouring ▷ *adj* flavoured with vanilla

VANILLIC *adj* of, resembling, containing, or derived from vanilla or vanillin

VANILLIN *n* white crystalline aldehyde found in vanilla

VANISH, -ED, -ES *vb* disappear suddenly or mysteriously ▷ *n* second and weaker of the two vowels in a falling diphthong
VANISHER

VANITAS *n* type of Dutch painting

VANITIED *adj* with vanity units or mirrors

VANITIES ► vanity

VANITORY *n* vanity unit

VANITY, VANITIES *n* (display of) excessive pride

VANLOAD, -S *n* amount van will carry

VANMAN, VANMEN *n* man in control of a van

VANNED ► van

VANNER, -S *n* horse used to pull delivery vehicles

VANNING, -S ► van

VANPOOL, -S *n* van-sharing group

VANQUISH *vb* defeat (someone) utterly

VANS ► van

VANT, -S *archaic word for* ► vanguard

VANTAGE, -D, -S *n* state, position, or opportunity offering advantage ▷ *vb* benefit

VANTS ► vant

VANWARD *adv* in or towards the front

VAPE, -D, -S *vb* inhale nicotine vapour (from an electronic cigarette)

VAPER, -S *n* one who vapes, inhales nicotine vapour from an electronic cigarette

VAPES ► vape

VAPID, -ER, -EST *adj* lacking character, dull
VAPIDITY
VAPIDLY

VAPING, -S *n* the practice of inhaling nicotine vapour (from an electronic cigarette)

VAPOR, -ED, -ING, -S *same as* ► vapour
VAPORER -S

VAPORISE *same as* ► vaporize

VAPORISH ► vapor

VAPORIZE *vb* change into a vapour

VAPOROUS *same as* > vaporific

VAPORS ► vapor

VAPORY ► vapour

VAPOUR, -ED, -S *n* moisture suspended in air as steam or mist ▷ *vb* evaporate
VAPOURER
VAPOURY

VAPULATE *vb* strike

VAQUERO, -S *n* cattle-hand

VAR, -S *n* unit of reactive power of an alternating current

VARA, -S *n* unit of length used in Spain, Portugal, and South America

VARACTOR *n* semiconductor diode that acts as a voltage-dependent capacitor

VARAN, -S *n* type of lizard

VARAS ► vara

VARDY, VARDIES *n* verdict

VARE, -S *n* rod

VAREC, -S *n* ash obtained from kelp

VARECH, -S *same as* ► varec

VARECS ► varec

VARENYKY *pl n* Ukrainian stuffed dumplings

VARES ► vare

VAREUSE, -S *n* type of coat

VARGUENO *n* type of Spanish cabinet

VARIA, -S *n* collection or miscellany, esp of literary works

VARIABLE *adj* not always the same, changeable ▷ *n* something that is subject to variation
VARIABLY

VARIANCE *n* act of varying

VARIANT, -S *adj* differing from a standard or type ▷ *n* something that differs from a standard or type

VARIAS ► varia

VARIATE, -D, -S *n* random variable or a numerical value taken by it ▷ *vb* vary

VARICEAL *adj* relating to a varix

VARICES ► varix

VARICOID *same as* ► cirsoid

VARICOSE *adj* of or resulting from varicose veins

VARIED ► vary

VARIEDLY ► vary

VARIER, -S *n* person who varies

VARIES ► vary

VARIETAL *adj* of or forming a variety, esp a biological variety ▷ *n* wine labelled with the name of the grape from which it is pressed

VARIETY *n* state of being diverse or various

VARIFORM *adj* varying in form or shape

VARIOLA, -S *n* smallpox
VARIOLAR

VARIOLE, -S *n* any of the rounded masses that make up the rock variolite

VARIORUM *adj* containing notes by various scholars or critics or various versions of the text ▷ *n* edition or text of this kind

VARIOUS *adj* of several kinds

VARISTOR *n* type of semiconductor device

VARITYPE *vb* produce (copy) on a Varityper ▷ *n* copy produced on a Varityper

VARIX, VARICES *n* tortuous dilated vein

VARLET, -S *n* menial servant

VARLETRY *n* varlets collectively

VARLETS ► varlet

VARLETTO *same as* ► varlet

VARMENT, -S *same as* ► varmint

VARMINT, -S *n* irritating or obnoxious person or animal

VARNA, -S *n* any of the four Hindu castes

VARNISH *n* solution of oil and resin, put on a surface to make it hard and glossy ▷ *vb* apply varnish to
VARNISHY

VAROOM *same as* ► vroom

VAROOMED *same as* ► varoom

VAROOMS *same as* ► varoom

VARROA, -S *n* small parasite

VARS ► var

VARSAL *adj* universal

V

VARSITY n university

VARTABED n position in the Armenian church

VARUS, -ES adj denoting a deformity of a limb ▷ n abnormal position of a limb

VARVE, -S n typically thin band of sediment deposited annually in glacial lakes

VARVED adj having layers of sedimentary deposit

VARVEL, -S n piece of falconry equipment

VARVES ▶ varve

VARY, VARIED, VARIES vb change

VARYING -S

VAS, -A n vessel or tube that carries a fluid

VASAL

VASCULA ▶ vasculum

VASCULAR adj relating to vessels

VASCULUM, VASCULA n metal box used by botanists in the field for carrying botanical specimens

VASE, -S n ornamental jar, esp for flowers

VASEFUL, -S n contents of a vase

VASELIKE ▶ vase

VASELINE n translucent gelatinous substance obtained from petroleum ▷ vb apply vaseline to

VASES ▶ vase

VASIFORM ▶ vas

VASOTOMY n surgery on the vas deferens

VASSAIL, -S archaic variant of ▶ vassal

VASSAL, -S n man given land by a lord in return for military service ▷ adj of or relating to a vassal ▷ vb vassalize

VASSALRY n vassalage

VASSALS ▶ vassal

VAST, -ER, -EST, -S adj extremely large ▷ n immense or boundless space

VASTIER ▶ vasty

VASTIEST ▶ vasty

VASTITY ▶ vast

VASTLY ▶ vast

VASTNESS ▶ vast

VASTS ▶ vast

VASTY, VASTIER, VASTIEST archaic or poetic word for ▶ vast

VAT, -S, -TED, -TING n large container for liquids ▷ vb place, store, or treat in a vat

VATABLE adj subject to VAT

VATFUL, -S n amount enough to fill a vat

VATIC adj of, relating to, or characteristic of a prophet

VATICAL same as ▶ vatic

VATICIDE n murder of a prophet

VATMAN, VATMEN n Customs and Excise employee

VATS ▶ vat

VATTED ▶ vat

VATTER, -S n person who works with vats; blender

VATTING ▶ vat

VATU, -S n standard monetary unit of Vanuatu

VAU, -S same as ▶ vav

VAUCH, -ED, -ES, -ING vb move fast

VAUDOO, -S same as ▶ voodoo

VAUDOUX same as ▶ voodoo

VAULT, -ED, -S n secure room for storing valuables ▷ vb jump over (something) by resting one's hand(s) on it

VAULTAGE n group of vaults

VAULTED ▶ vault

VAULTER, -S ▶ vault

VAULTIER ▶ vaulty

VAULTING n arrangement of ceiling vaults in a building ▷ adj excessively confident

VAULTS ▶ vault

VAULTY, VAULTIER adj arched

VAUNCE, -D, -S, VAUNCING same as ▶ advance

VAUNT, -ED, -ING, -S vb describe or display (success or possessions) boastfully ▷ n boast

VAUNTAGE archaic variant of ▶ vantage

VAUNTED ▶ vaunt

VAUNTER, -S ▶ vaunt

VAUNTERY n bravado

VAUNTFUL ▶ vaunt

VAUNTIE same as ▶ vaunty

VAUNTIER ▶ vaunty

VAUNTING ▶ vaunt

VAUNTS ▶ vaunt

VAUNTY, VAUNTIER adj proud

VAURIEN, -S n rascal

VAUS ▶ vau

VAUT, -S same as ▶ vault

VAUTE, -D, -S, VAUTING same as ▶ vault

VAUTS ▶ vaut

VAV, -S n sixth letter of the Hebrew alphabet

It is surprising how often one wants to get rid of two Vs, and when one does, this word, the name of a Hebrew letter, fits the bill nicely. It has an equally useful variant **vaw**.

VAVASOR, -S n (in feudal society) vassal who also has vassals himself

VAVASORY n lands held by a vavasor

VAVASOUR same as ▶ vavasor

VAVASSOR same as ▶ vavasor

VAVS ▶ vav

VAW, -S same as ▶ vav

VAWARD, -S n vanguard

VAWNTIE, -R ▶ vaunt

VAWS ▶ vaw

VAWTE, -D, -S, VAWTING same as ▶ vault

VEAL, -ED, -ING, -S n calf meat ▷ vb rear (calves) for use as veal

VEALE, -S Spenserian word for ▶ veil

VEALED ▶ veal

VEALER, -S n young bovine animal of up to 14 months old grown for veal

VEALES ▶ veale

VEALIER ▶ vealy

VEALIEST ▶ vealy

VEALING ▶ veal

VEALS ▶ veal

VEALY, VEALIER, VEALIEST ▶ veal

VECTOR, -ED, -S n quantity that has size and direction, such as force ▷ vb direct or guide (a pilot) by directions transmitted by radio

VEDALIA, -S n Australian ladybird which is a pest of citrus fruits

VEDETTE, -S n small patrol vessel

VEDUTA, VEDUTE n painting of a town or city

VEE, -S n letter 'v'

VEEJAY, -S n video jockey

VEENA, -S same as ▶ vina

VEEP, -S n vice president

VEEPEE, -S n vice president

VEEPS ▶ veep

VEER, -ED, -ING, -INGS, -S vb change direction suddenly ▷ n change of course or direction

VEERIES ▶ veery

VEERING ▶ veer

VEERINGS ▶ veer

VEERS ▶ veer

VEERY, VEERIES n tawny brown North American thrush

VEES ▶ vee

VEG, -S, -GED, -GES, -GING n vegetable or vegetables ▷ vb relax

> **Veg** is a short form of **vegetable**. If someone plays this, remember that you can add an A or O to it to form **vega** or **vego**.

VEGA, -S n tobacco plantation

VEGAN, -S n person who eats no meat, fish, eggs, or dairy products ▷ adj suitable for a vegan

VEGANIC adj farmed without the use of animal products or byproducts

VEGANISM ▶ vegan

VEGANS ▶ vegan

VEGAS ▶ vega

VEGELATE n type of chocolate

VEGEMITE n informal Australian word for a child

VEGES ▶ veg

VEGETAL, -S adj of or relating to plant life ▷ n vegetable

VEGETANT adj causing growth or vegetation-like

VEGETATE vb live a dull boring life with no mental stimulation

VEGETE adj lively

VEGETIST n vegetable cultivator or enthusiast

VEGETIVE adj dull or passive ▷ n vegetable

VEGGED ▶ veg

VEGGES ▶ veg

VEGGIE, -S n vegetable ▷ adj vegetarian

VEGGING ▶ veg

VEGIE, -S variant of ▶ veggie

VEGO, -S adj vegetarian ▷ n vegetarian

VEHEMENT adj expressing strong feelings

VEHICLE, -S n machine for carrying people or objects

VEHM, -E n type of medieval German court

VEHMIC

VEHMIQUE

VEIL, -S n piece of thin cloth covering the head or face ▷ vb cover with or as if with a veil

VEILED adj disguised

VEILEDLY

VEILER, -S ▶ veil

VEILIER ▶ veily

VEILIEST ▶ veily

VEILING, -S n veil or the fabric used for veils

VEILLESS ▶ veil

VEILLIKE ▶ veil

VEILS ▶ veil

VEILY, VEILIER, VEILIEST ▶ veil

VEIN, -ED, -S n tube that takes blood to the heart ▷ vb diffuse over or cause to diffuse over in streaked patterns

VEINAL

VEINER, -S n wood-carving tool

VEINIER ▶ veiny

VEINIEST ▶ veiny

VEINING, -S n pattern or network of veins or streaks

VEINLESS ▶ vein

VEINLET, -S n any small vein or venule

VEINLIKE ▶ vein

VEINOUS ▶ vein

VEINS ▶ vein

VEINULE, -S less common spelling of ▶ venule

VEINULET same as ▶ veinlet

VEINY, VEINIER, VEINIEST ▶ vein

VELA ▶ velum

VELAMEN, VELAMINA n thick layer of dead cells that covers the aerial roots of certain orchids

VELAR, -S adj of, relating to, or attached to a velum ▷ n velar sound

VELARIA ▶ velarium

VELARIC ▶ velar

VELARISE same as ▶ velarize

VELARIUM, VELARIA n awning used to protect the audience in ancient Roman theatres and amphitheatres

VELARIZE vb supplement the pronunciation of (a speech sound) with articulation at the soft palate

VELARS ▶ velar

VELATE adj having or covered with velum

VELATED same as ▶ velate

VELATURA n overglaze

VELCRO, -S n tradename for a fastening of two strips of nylon fabric pressed together

VELD, -S n high grassland in southern Africa

VELDT, -S same as ▶ veld

VELE, -S same as ▶ veil

VELETA, -S same as ▶ valeta

VELIGER, -S n free-swimming larva of many molluscs

VELITES pl n light-armed troops in ancient Rome, drawn from the poorer classes

VELL, -S n salted calf's stomach, used in cheese making

VELLEITY n weakest level of desire or volition

VELLET, -S n velvet

VELLON, -S n silver and copper alloy used in old Spanish coins

VELLS ▶ vell

VELLUM, -S n fine calfskin parchment ▷ adj made of or resembling vellum

VELLUS n as in **vellus hair** short fine unpigmented hair covering the human body

VELOCE adv be played rapidly

VELOCITY n speed of movement in a given direction

VELOUR n fabric similar to velvet

VELOURS same as ▶ velour

VELOUTE, -S n rich white sauce or soup made from stock, egg yolks, and cream

VELSKOEN n type of shoe

VELUM, VELA n any of various membranous structures

VELURE, -S n velvet or a similar fabric ▷ vb cover with velure

VELURED

VELURING

VELVERET n type of velvet-like fabric

VELVET, -ED, -S n fabric with a thick soft pile ▷ vb cover with velvet

VELVETY

VENA, -E n vein in the body

VENAL adj easily bribed

VENALITY

VENALLY

VENATIC adj of, relating to, or used in hunting

VENATION n arrangement of the veins in a leaf or in the wing of an insect

VENATOR, -S n hunter

VEND, -ED, -S vb sell

VENDABLE

VENDACE, -S n either of two small whitefish occurring in lakes in Scotland and NW England

VENDAGE, -S n vintage

VENDANGE same as ▶ vendage

VENDED ▶ vend

VENDEE, -S n person to whom something, esp real property, is sold

VENDER, -S same as ▶ vendor

V

VENDETTA n long-lasting quarrel between people in which they attempt to harm each other

VENDEUSE n female salesperson

VENDIBLE adj saleable or marketable ▷ n saleable object

VENDIBLY

VENDING, -S ▶ vend

VENDIS, -ES same as ▶ vendace

VENDISS same as ▶ vendace

VENDOR, -S n person who sells goods such as newspapers or hamburgers from a stall or cart

VENDS ▶ vend

VENDUE, -S n public sale

VENEER, -ED, -S n thin layer of wood etc covering a cheaper material ▷ vb cover (a surface) with a veneer

VENEERER

VENEFIC adj having poisonous effects

VENENATE vb poison

VENENE, -S n medicine from snake venom

VENENOSE adj poisonous

VENERATE vb hold (a person) in deep respect

VENEREAL adj of or involving the genitals

VENERER, -S n hunter

VENETIAN n Venetian blind

VENEWE, -S same as ▶ venue

VENEY, -S n thrust

VENGE, -D, -S, VENGING vb avenge

VENGEFUL adj wanting revenge

VENGER, -S ▶ venge

VENGES ▶ venge

VENGING ▶ venge

VENIAL adj (of a sin or fault) easily forgiven

VENIALLY

VENIDIUM n genus of flowering plants

VENIN, -S n any of the poisonous constituents of animal venoms

VENINE, -S same as ▶ venin

VENINS ▶ venin

VENIRE, -S n list from which jurors are selected

VENISON, -S n deer meat

VENITE, -S n musical setting for the 95th psalm

VENNEL, -S n lane

VENOGRAM n X-ray of a vein

VENOLOGY n study of veins

VENOM, -ED, -ING, -S n malice or spite ▷ vb poison

VENOMER -S

VENOMOUS ▶ venom

VENOMS ▶ venom

VENOSE adj having veins

VENOSITY n excessive quantity of blood in the venous system or in an organ or part

VENOUS adj of veins

VENOUSLY

VENT, -ED, -ING, -INGS, -S n outlet releasing fumes or fluid ▷ vb express (an emotion) freely

VENTAGE, -S n small opening

VENTAIL, -S n (in medieval armour) a covering for the lower part of the face

VENTAILE same as ▶ ventail

VENTAILS ▶ ventail

VENTANA, -S n window

VENTAYLE same as ▶ ventail

VENTED ▶ vent

VENTER, -S ▶ vent

VENTIGE, -S same as ▶ ventage

VENTIL, -S n valve on a musical instrument

VENTING ▶ vent

VENTINGS ▶ vent

VENTLESS ▶ vent

VENTOSE, -S adj full of wind ▷ n apparatus sometimes used to assist the delivery of a baby

VENTOUSE n ventose

VENTRAL, -S adj relating to the front of the body ▷ n ventral fin

VENTRE, -S same as ▶ venture

VENTRED

VENTRING

VENTROUS

VENTS ▶ vent

VENTURE, -D, -S n risky undertaking, esp in business ▷ vb do something risky

VENTURER

VENTURI, -S n tube used to control the flow of fluid

VENUE, -S n place where an organized gathering is held

VENULAR ▶ venule

VENULE, -S n any of the small branches of a vein

VENULOSE

VENULOUS

VENUS, -ES n type of marine bivalve mollusc

VENVILLE n type of parish tenure

VERA adj as in **aloe vera** plant substance used in skin and hair preparations

VERACITY n truthfulness

VERANDA, -S n porch or portico along the outside of a building

VERANDAH same as ▶ veranda

VERANDAS ▶ veranda

VERATRIA same as > veratrine

VERATRIN same as > veratrine

VERATRUM n genus of herbs

VERB, -S n word that expresses the idea of action, happening, or being

VERBAL, -S adj spoken ▷ n abuse or invective ▷ vb implicate (someone) in a crime by quoting alleged admission of guilt in court

VERBALLY

VERBATIM adj word for word ▷ adv using exactly the same words

VERBENA, -S n plant with sweet-smelling flowers

VERBIAGE n excessive use of words

VERBID, -S n any nonfinite form of a verb or any nonverbal word derived from a verb

VERBIFY another word for > verbalize

VERBILE, -S n person who is best stimulated by words

VERBING, -S n use of nouns as verbs

VERBLESS ▶ verb

VERBOSE, -R adj speaking at tedious length

VERBOTEN adj forbidden

VERBS ▶ verb

VERD adj as in **verd antique** dark green mottled impure variety of serpentine marble

VERDANCY ▶ verdant

VERDANT adj covered in green vegetation

VERDELHO n type of grape

VERDERER n officer responsible for the maintenance of law and order in the royal forests

VERDEROR same as ▶ verderer

VERDET, -S n type of verdigris

VERDICT, -S n decision of a jury

VERDIN, -S n small W North American tit having grey plumage with a yellow head

VERDIT, -S same as ▶ **verdict**

VERDITE, -S n type of rock used in jewellery

VERDITER n blue-green pigment made from copper

VERDITES ▶ **verdite**

VERDITS ▶ **verdit**

VERDOY, -S n floral or leafy shield decoration

VERDURE, -S n flourishing green vegetation **VERDURED**

VERECUND adj shy or modest

VERGE, -D, -S, VERGING n grass border along a road ▷ vb move in a specified direction

VERGENCE n inward or outward turning movement of the eyes in convergence or divergence

VERGENCY adj inclination

VERGER, -S n church caretaker

VERGES ▶ **verge**

VERGING ▶ **verge**

VERGLAS n thin film of ice on rock

VERIDIC same as > **veridical**

VERIER ▶ **very**

VERIEST ▶ **very**

VERIFIED ▶ **verify**

VERIFIER ▶ **verify**

VERIFY, VERIFIED, VERIFIES vb check the truth or accuracy of

VERILY adv in truth

VERISM, -S n extreme naturalism in art or literature

VERISMO, -S n school of composition that originated in Italian opera

VERISMS ▶ **verism**

VERIST, -S ▶ **verism**

VERISTIC ▶ **verism**

VERISTS ▶ **verist**

VERITAS n truth

VERITE, -S adj involving a high degree of realism or naturalism ▷ n this kind of realism in film

VERITY, VERITIES n true statement or principle

VERJUICE n acid juice of unripe grapes, apples, or crab apples ▷ vb make sour

VERJUS, -ES n acid juice of unripe grapes, apples, or crab apples

VERKRAMP adj bigoted or illiberal

VERLAN, -S n variety of French slang in which the syllables are inverted

VERLIG adj enlightened

VERLIGTE n (during apartheid) a White political liberal

VERMAL ▶ **vermis**

VERMEIL, -S n gilded silver, bronze, or other metal, used esp in the 19th century ▷ vb decorate with vermeil ▷ adj vermilion

VERMELL, -S same as ▶ **vermeil**

VERMES ▶ **vermis**

VERMIAN ▶ **vermis**

VERMIL, -S same as ▶ **vermeil**

VERMILY ▶ **vermeil**

VERMIN, -S pl n animals, esp insects and rodents, that spread disease or cause damage

VERMINED adj plagued with vermin

VERMINS ▶ **vermin**

VERMINY ▶ **vermin**

VERMIS, VERMES n middle lobe connecting the two halves of the cerebellum

VERMOULU adj worm-eaten

VERMOUTH n wine flavoured with herbs

VERMUTH, -S same as ▶ **vermouth**

VERNACLE same as ▶ **vernicle**

VERNAL adj occurring in spring **VERNALLY** **VERNANT**

VERNICLE n veronica

VERNIER, -S n movable scale on a measuring instrument for taking readings in fractions

VERNIX, -ES n white substance covering the skin of a foetus

VERONAL, -S n long-acting barbiturate used medicinally

VERONICA n plant with small blue, pink, or white flowers

VERQUERE n type of backgammon game

VERQUIRE variant of ▶ **verquere**

VERRA Scot word for ▶ **very**

VERREL, -S n ferrule

VERREY same as ▶ **vair**

VERRINE, -S n starter, dessert, or other dish served in a glass

VERRUCA, -E, -S n wart, usu on the foot

VERRUGA, -S same as ▶ **verruca**

VERRY same as ▶ **vair**

VERS n verse

VERSAL, -S n embellished letter

VERSANT, -S n side or slope of a mountain or mountain range

VERSE, -S n group of lines forming part of a song or poem ▷ vb write verse

VERSED adj thoroughly knowledgeable (about)

VERSELET n small verse

VERSEMAN, VERSEMEN n man who writes verse

VERSER, -S n versifier

VERSES ▶ **verse**

VERSET, -S n short, often sacred, verse

VERSICLE n short verse

VERSIFY vb write in verse

VERSIN, -S same as ▶ **versine**

VERSINE, -S n mathematical term

VERSING, -S ▶ **verse**

VERSINS ▶ **versin**

VERSION, -S n form of something, with some differences from other forms ▷ vb keep track of the changes made to a computer file at different stages

VERSO, -S n left-hand page of a book

VERST, -S n unit of length used in Russia

VERSTE, -S same as ▶ **verst**

VERSTS ▶ **verst**

VERSUS prep in opposition to or in contrast with

VERSUTE adj cunning

VERT, -ED, -ING, -S n right to cut green wood in a forest ▷ vb turn

VERTEBRA n one of the bones that form the spine

VERTED ▶ **vert**

VERTEX, -ES, VERTICES n point on a geometric figure where the sides form an angle

VERTICAL adj straight up and down ▷ n vertical direction

VERTICES ▶ **vertex**

VERTICIL n circular arrangement of parts about an axis, esp leaves around a stem

VERTIGO, -S n dizziness, usu when looking down from a high place

VERTING ▶ **vert**

VERTISOL n type of clayey soil

VERTS ▶ **vert**

VERTU, -S same as ▶ **virtu**

VERTUE, -S same as ▶ **virtu**

VERTUOUS ▶ **vertu**

VERTUS ▶ **vertu**

V

VERVAIN, -S n plant with spikes of blue, purple, or white flowers

VERVE, -S n enthusiasm or liveliness

VERVEL, -S same as ▸ **varvel**

VERVEN, -S same as ▸ **vervain**

VERVES ▸ **verve**

VERVET, -S n variety of a South African guenon monkey

VERY, VERIER, VERIEST adv more than usually, extremely ▹ adj absolute, exact

VESICA, -E, -S n bladder

VESICAL adj of or relating to a vesica, esp the urinary bladder

VESICANT n any substance that causes blisters ▹ adj acting as a vesicant

VESICAS ▸ **vesica**

VESICATE vb blister

VESICLE, -S n sac or small cavity, esp one containing fluid

VESICULA n vesicle

VESPA, -S n type of wasp

VESPER n evening prayer, service, or hymn

VESPERAL n liturgical book containing the prayers, psalms, and hymns used at vespers

VESPERS pl n service of evening prayer

VESPIARY n nest or colony of social wasps or hornets

VESPID, -S n insect of the family that includes the common wasp and hornet ▹ adj of or belonging to this family

VESPINE adj of, relating to, or resembling a wasp or wasps

VESPOID adj like a wasp

VESSAIL, -S archaic variant of ▸ **vessel**

VESSEL, -ED, -S n container or ship ▹ adj contained in a vessel

VEST, -S n undergarment worn on the top half of the body ▹ vb give (authority) to (someone)

VESTA, -S n short friction match, usually of wood

VESTAL, -S adj pure, chaste ▹ n chaste woman

VESTALLY

VESTAS ▸ **vesta**

VESTED adj having an existing right to the immediate or future possession of property

VESTEE, -S n person having a vested interest something

VESTIARY n room for storing clothes or dressing in, such as a vestry ▹ adj of or relating to clothes

VESTIGE, -S n small amount or trace

VESTIGIA > **vestigium**

VESTING, -S ▸ **vest**

VESTLESS ▸ **vest**

VESTLIKE ▸ **vest**

VESTMENT n garment or robe, esp one denoting office, authority, or rank

VESTRAL ▸ **vestry**

VESTRY, VESTRIES n room in a church used as an office by the priest or minister

VESTS ▸ **vest**

VESTURAL ▸ **vesture**

VESTURE, -D, -S n garment or something that seems like a garment ▹ vb clothe

VESTURER n person in charge of church vestments

VESTURES ▸ **vesture**

VESUVIAN n match for lighting cigars

VET, -S, -TED vb check the suitability of ▹ n military veteran

VETCH, -ES n climbing plant with a beanlike fruit used as fodder

VETCHY, VETCHIER adj consisting of vetches

VETERAN, -S n person with long experience in a particular activity ▹ adj long-serving

VETIVER, -S n tall hairless grass of tropical and subtropical Asia

VETIVERT n oil from the vetiver

VETKOEK, -S n South African cake

VETO, -ED, -ES, -ING n official power to cancel a proposal ▹ vb enforce a veto against

VETOER, -S

VETOLESS ▸ **veto**

VETS ▸ **vet**

VETTED ▸ **vet**

VETTER, -S ▸ **vet**

VETTING, -S n as in positive vetting checking a person's background to assess their suitability of an important post

VETTURA, -S n Italian mode of transport

VEX, -ES vb frustrate, annoy

VEXATION n something annoying

VEXATORY ▸ **vex**

VEXED adj annoyed and puzzled

VEXEDLY

VEXER, -S ▸ **vex**

VEXES ▸ **vex**

VEXIL, -S same as ▸ **vexillum**

VEXILLA ▸ **vexillum**

VEXILLAR ▸ **vexillum**

VEXILLUM, VEXILLA n vane of a feather

VEXILS ▸ **vexil**

VEXING, -S ▸ **vex**

VEXINGLY ▸ **vex**

VEXINGS ▸ **vexing**

VEXT same as ▸ **vexed**

VEZIR, -S same as ▸ **vizier**

VIA, -E, -S prep by way of ▹ n road

VIABLE adj able to be put into practice

VIABLY

VIADUCT, -S n bridge over a valley

VIAE ▸ **via**

VIAL, -ED, -ING, -LED, -LING, -S, VIOLD n small bottle for liquids ▹ vb put into a vial

VIALFUL -S

VIAMETER n device to measure distance travelled

VIAND, -S n type of food, esp a delicacy

VIAS ▸ **via**

VIATIC same as ▸ **viatical**

VIATICA ▸ **viaticum**

VIATICAL adj of a road or a journey ▹ n purchase of a terminal patient's life assurance policy so that he or she may make use of the proceeds

VIATICUM, VIATICA n Holy Communion given to a person who is dying or in danger of death

VIATOR, -ES, -S n traveller

VIBE n feeling or flavour of the kind specified

VIBES pl n vibrations

VIBEX, VIBICES n mark under the skin

VIBEY, VIBIER, VIBIEST adj lively and vibrant

VIBICES ▸ **vibex**

VIBIER ▸ **vibey**

VIBIEST ▸ **vibey**

VIBIST, -S n person who plays a vibraphone in a jazz band or group

VIBRANCE n vibrancy

VIBRANCY ▸ **vibrant**

VIBRANT, -S adj vigorous in appearance, energetic ▹ n trilled or rolled speech sound

VIBRATE, **-D**, **-S** vb move back and forth rapidly

VIBRATO, **-S** n rapid fluctuation in the pitch of a note

VIBRATOR n device that produces vibratory motion

VIBRATOS ► **vibrato**

VIBRIO, **-S** n curved or spiral rodlike bacterium

VIBRIOID

VIBRION, **-S** same as ► **vibrio**

VIBRIOS ► **vibrio**

VIBRISSA n any of the bristle-like sensitive hairs on the face of many mammals

VIBRONIC adj of, concerned with, or involving both electronic and vibrational energy levels of a molecule

VIBS pl n type of climbing shoes

VIBURNUM n subtropical shrub with white flowers and berry-like fruits

VICAR, **-S** n member of the clergy in charge of a parish

VICARAGE n vicar's house

VICARATE same as > **vicariate**

VICARESS n rank of nun

VICARIAL adj of or relating to a vicar, vicars, or a vicariate

VICARIES ► **vicary**

VICARLY ► **vicar**

VICARS ► **vicar**

VICARY, **VICARIES** n office of a vicar

VICE, **-D**, **-S**, **VICING** n immoral or evil habit or action ▷ adj serving in place of ▷ vb grip (something) with or as if with a vice ▷ prep instead of

VICELESS

VICELIKE

VICENARY adj relating to or consisting of 20

VICEROY, **-S** n governor of a colony who represents the monarch

VICES ► **vice**

VICHY, **VICHIES** n French mineral water

VICIATE, **-S** same as ► **vitiate**

VICIATED

VICINAGE n residents of a particular neighbourhood

VICINAL adj neighbouring

VICING ► **vice**

VICINITY n surrounding area

VICIOUS adj cruel and violent

VICOMTE, **-S** n French nobleman

VICTIM, **-S** n person or thing harmed or killed

VICTOR, **-S** n person who has defeated an opponent, esp in war or in sport

VICTORIA n large sweet plum, red and yellow in colour

VICTORS ► **victor**

VICTORY n winning of a battle or contest

VICTRESS n female victor

VICTRIX same as ► **victress**

VICTROLA n gramophone

VICTUAL vb supply with or obtain victuals

VICTUALS pl n food and drink

VICUGNA, **-S** same as ► **vicuna**

VICUNA, **-S** n S American animal like the llama

VID, **-S** same as ► **video**

VIDALIA n type of sweet onion

VIDAME, **-S** n French nobleman

VIDE interj look

VIDENDUM, **VIDENDA** n that which is to be seen

VIDEO, **-ED**, **-ING**, **-S** vb record (a TV programme or event) on video ▷ adj relating to or used in producing television images ▷ n recording and showing of films and events

VIDEOCAM n camera for recording video footage

VIDEOED ► **video**

VIDEOFIT n computer-generated picture of a person sought by the police

VIDEOING ► **video**

VIDEOS ► **video**

VIDEOTEX n information system that displays data from a distant computer on a screen

VIDETTE, **-S** same as ► **vedette**

VIDICON, **-S** n small television camera tube used in closed-circuit television

VIDIMUS n inspection

VIDIOT, **-S** n person who watches a lot of low-quality television

VIDS ► **vid**

VIDUAGE, **-S** n widows collectively

VIDUAL adj widowed

VIDUITY n widowhood

VIDUOUS adj empty

VIE, **-D**, **-S** vb compete (with someone)

VIELLE, **-S** n stringed musical instrument

VIENNA n as in **vienna loaf**, **vienna steak** associated with Vienna

VIER, **-S** ► **vie**

VIES ► **vie**

VIEW, **-ED**, **-S** n opinion or belief ▷ vb think of (something) in a particular way

VIEWABLE

VIEWBOOK n promotional booklet for a college or university

VIEWDATA n interactive form of videotext

VIEWED ► **view**

VIEWER, **-S** n person who watches television

VIEWIER ► **viewy**

VIEWIEST ► **viewy**

VIEWING, **-S** n act of watching television

VIEWLESS adj (of windows, etc) not affording a view

VIEWLY adj pleasant on the eye

VIEWPORT n viewable area on a computer display

VIEWS ► **view**

VIEWSHED n natural environment visible from a specific point

VIEWY, **VIEWIER**, **VIEWIEST** adj having fanciful opinions or ideas

VIFDA, **-S** same as ► **vivda**

VIFF, **-ED**, **-ING**, **-S** vb (of an aircraft) change direction abruptly

VIG, **-S** n interest on a loan that is paid to a moneylender

VIGA, **-S** n rafter

VIGIA, **-S** n navigational hazard whose existence has not been confirmed

VIGIL, **-S** n night-time period of staying awake to look after a sick person, pray, etc

VIGILANT adj watchful in case of danger

VIGILS ► **vigil**

VIGNERON n person who grows grapes for winemaking

VIGNETTE n small illustration placed at the beginning or end of a chapter or book ▷ vb portray in a vignette

VIGOR, **-S** same as ► **vigour**

VIGORISH n type of commission

VIGORO, **-S** n women's game similar to cricket

VIGOROSO adv in music, emphatically

V

VIGOROUS adj having physical or mental energy

VIGORS ► vigor

VIGOUR, -S n physical or mental energy

VIGS ► vig

VIHARA, -S n type of Buddhist temple

VIHUELA, -S n obsolete plucked stringed instrument of Spain

VIKING, -S n Dane, Norwegian, or Swede who raided by sea between the 8th and 11th centuries

VILAYET, -S n major administrative division of Turkey

VILD same as ► vile

VILDE same as ► vile

VILDLY ► vild

VILDNESS ► vild

VILE, -R, -ST adj very wicked
VILELY
VILENESS

VILIACO, -S n coward

VILIAGO, -S same as ► viliaco

VILIFIED ► vilify

VILIFIER ► vilify

VILIFY, VILIFIED, VILIFIES vb attack the character of

VILIPEND vb treat or regard with contempt

VILL, -S n township

VILLA, -E, -S n large house with gardens
VILLADOM

VILLAGE, -S n small group of houses in a country area

VILLAGER n inhabitant of a village ▷ adj backward, unsophisticated, or illiterate

VILLAGES ► village

VILLAGEY adj of or like a village

VILLAGIO same as ► viliaco

VILLAIN, -S n wicked person

VILLAINY n evil or vicious behaviour

VILLAN, -S same as ► villein

VILLANY same as ► villainy

VILLAR ► vill

VILLAS ► villa

VILLATIC adj of or relating to a villa, village, or farm

VILLEIN, -S n peasant bound in service to his lord

VILLI ► villus

VILLIACO n coward

VILLIAGO same as ► viliaco

VILLOSE same as ► villous

VILLOUS adj (of plant parts) covered with long hairs

VILLS ► vill

VILLUS, VILLI n one of the finger-like projections in the small intestine of many vertebrates

VIM, -S n force, energy

> This word can be helpful when you're stuck with unpromising letters, and gives a reasonable score for a three-letter word.

VIMANA, -S n Indian mythological chariot of the gods

VIMEN, VIMINA n long flexible shoot that occurs in certain plants
VIMINAL

VIMS ► vim

VIN, -S n French wine

VINA, -S n stringed musical instrument related to the sitar

VINAL, -S n type of manmade fibre

VINAS ► vina

VINASSE, -S n residue left in a still after distilling spirits, esp brandy

VINCA, -S n type of trailing plant with blue flowers

VINCIBLE adj capable of being defeated or overcome
VINCIBLY

VINCULA ► vinculum

VINCULAR adj of or like a vinculum

VINCULUM, VINCULA n horizontal line drawn above a group of mathematical terms

VINDALOO n type of very hot Indian curry

VINE, -S n climbing plant, esp one producing grapes ▷ vb form like a vine

VINEAL adj relating to wines

VINED ► vine

VINEGAR, -S n acid liquid made from wine, beer, or cider ▷ vb apply vinegar to

VINEGARY adj containing vinegar

VINELESS ► vine

VINELIKE ► vine

VINER, -S n vinedresser

VINERIES ► vinery

VINERS ► viner

VINERY, VINERIES n hothouse for growing grapes

VINES ► vine

VINEW, -ED, -ING, -S vb become mouldy

VINEYARD n plantation of grape vines

VINIC adj of, relating to, or contained in wine

VINIER ► viny

VINIEST ► viny

VINIFERA n species of vine

VINIFY, VINIFIED, VINIFIES vb convert into wine

VINING ► vine

VINO, -S n wine

VINOLENT adj drunken

VINOLOGY n scientific study of vines

VINOS ► vino

VINOSITY n distinctive and essential quality and flavour of wine

VINOUS adj of or characteristic of wine
VINOUSLY

VINS ► vin

VINT, -ED, -ING, -S vb sell (wine)

VINTAGE, -D, -S n wine from a particular harvest of grapes ▷ adj best and most typical ▷ vb gather (grapes) or make (wine)

VINTAGER n grape harvester

VINTAGES ► vintage

VINTED ► vint

VINTING ► vint

VINTNER, -S n dealer in wine

VINTRY, VINTRIES n place where wine is sold

VINTS ► vint

VINY, VINIER, VINIEST ► vine

VINYL, -S n type of plastic, used in mock leather and records ▷ adj of or containing a particular group of atoms
VINYLIC

VIOL, -S n early stringed instrument preceding the violin

VIOLA, -S n stringed instrument lower in pitch than a violin

VIOLABLE ► violate

VIOLABLY ► violate

VIOLAS ► viola

VIOLATE, -D, -S vb break (a law or agreement) ▷ adj violated or dishonoured
VIOLATER
VIOLATOR

VIOLD archaic or poetic past form of ► vial

VIOLENCE n use of physical force, usu intended to cause injury or destruction

VIOLENT, -S adj using physical force with the intention of causing injury ▷ vb coerce

VIOLER, -S n person who plays the viol

VIOLET, -S n plant with bluish-purple flowers ▷ adj bluish-purple

VIOLIN, -S n small four-stringed musical instrument played with a bow

VIOLIST, -S n person who plays the viola

VIOLONE, -S n double-bass member of the viol family

VIOLS ► viol

VIOMYCIN n type of antibiotic

VIPER, -S n poisonous snake

VIPERINE same as ► viperous

VIPERISH same as ► viperous

VIPEROUS adj of, relating to, or resembling a viper

VIPERS ► viper

VIRAEMIA n condition in which virus particles circulate and reproduce in the bloodstream

VIRAEMIC

VIRAGO, -ES, -S n aggressive woman

VIRAL, -S adj of or caused by a virus ▷ n video, image, etc that spreads quickly on the internet

VIRALITY n the state of being viral

VIRALLY ► viral

VIRALS ► viral

VIRANDA, -S same as ► veranda

VIRANDO, -S same as ► veranda

VIRE, -D, -S, VIRING vb turn

VIRELAI, -S same as ► virelay

VIRELAY, -S n old French verse form

VIREMENT n administrative transfer of funds from one part of a budget to another

VIREMIA, -S same as ► viraemia

VIREMIC

VIRENT adj green

VIREO, -S n American songbird

VIRES ► vire

VIRETOT, -S n as in **on the viretot** in a rush

VIRGA, -E, -S n wisps of rain or snow that evaporate before reaching the earth

VIRGATE, -S adj long, straight, and thin ▷ n obsolete measure of land area

VIRGE, -S n rod

VIRGER, -S n rod-bearer

VIRGES ► virge

VIRGIN, -S n person, esp a woman, who has not had sexual intercourse ▷ adj not having had sexual intercourse ▷ vb behave like a virgin

VIRGINAL adj like a virgin ▷ n early keyboard instrument like a small harpsichord

VIRGINED ► virgin

VIRGINIA n type of flue-cured tobacco grown originally in Virginia

VIRGINLY ► virgin

VIRGINS ► virgin

VIRGULE, -S another name for ► slash

VIRICIDE n substance that destroys viruses

VIRID adj verdant

VIRIDIAN n green pigment consisting of a hydrated form of chromic oxide

VIRIDITE n greenish mineral

VIRIDITY n quality or state of being green

VIRILE adj having traditional male characteristics

VIRILELY

VIRILISE same as ► virilize

VIRILITY ► virile

VIRILIZE vb cause male characteristics to appear in female

VIRING ► vire

VIRINO, -S n entity postulated to be the causative agent of BSE

VIRION, -S n virus in infective form, consisting of an RNA particle within a protein covering

VIRL, -S same as ► ferrule

VIROGENE n type of viral gene

VIROID, -S n any of various infective RNA particles

VIROLOGY n study of viruses

VIROSE adj poisonous

VIROSIS, VIROSES n viral disease

VIROUS same as ► virose

VIRTU, -S n taste or love for curios or works of fine art

VIRTUAL adj having the effect but not the form of

VIRTUE, -S n moral goodness

VIRTUOSA, VIRTUOSE n female virtuoso

VIRTUOSO, VIRTUOSI n person with impressive esp musical skill ▷ adj showing exceptional skill or brilliance

VIRTUOUS adj morally good

VIRTUS ► virtu

VIRUCIDE same as ► viricide

VIRULENT adj extremely bitter or hostile

VIRUS, -ES n microorganism that causes disease in humans, animals, and plants

VIRUSOID n small plant virus

VIS n power, force, or strength

VISA, -ED, -ING, -S n permission to enter a country, shown by a stamp on the passport ▷ vb enter a visa into (a passport)

VISAGE, -S n face

VISAGED

VISAGIST same as > visagiste

VISAING ► visa

VISARD, -S same as ► vizard

VISAS ► visa

VISCACHA n South American rodent

VISCARIA n type of perennial plant

VISCERA pl n large abdominal organs

VISCERAL adj instinctive

VISCID adj sticky

VISCIDLY

VISCIN, -S n sticky substance found on plants

VISCOID adj (of a fluid) somewhat viscous

VISCOSE, -S same as ► viscous

VISCOUNT n British nobleman ranking between an earl and a baron

VISCOUS adj thick and sticky

VISCUM, -S n shrub genus

VISCUS n internal organ

VISE, -D, -ING, -S, VISING vb advise or award a visa to ▷ n (in US English) vice

VISEED

VISELIKE ► vice

VISES ► vise

VISHING, -S n telephone scam used to gain access to credit card numbers or bank details

VISIBLE, -S adj able to be seen ▷ n visible item of trade

VISIBLY

VISIE, -D, -ING, -S same as ► vizy

VISIER -S

VISILE, -S n person best stimulated by vision

VISING ► vise

VISION, -ED, -S n ability to see ▷ vb see or show in or as if in a vision

VISIONAL adj of, relating to, or seen in a vision, apparition, etc

VISIONED ► vision

VISIONER n visionary

V

VISIONS ▶ vision

VISIT, -ED, -ING, -S vb go or come to see ▷ n instance of visiting

VISITANT n ghost or apparition ▷ adj paying a visit

VISITE, -S n type of cape

VISITED ▶ visit

VISITEE, -S n person who is visited

VISITER, -S variant of ▶ visitor

VISITES ▶ visite

VISITING ▶ visit

VISITOR, -S n person who visits a person or place

VISITS ▶ visit

VISIVE adj visual

VISNE, -S n neighbourhood

VISNOMIE same as ▶ visnomy

VISNOMY n method of judging character from facial features

VISON, -S n type of mink

VISOR, -ED, -ING, -S n transparent part of a helmet that pulls down over the face ▷ vb cover, provide, or protect with a visor

VISTA, -ING, -S n (beautiful) extensive view ▷ vb make into vistas

VISTAED

VISTAL

VISTO, -S same as ▶ vista

VISUAL, -S adj done by or used in seeing ▷ n sketch to show the proposed layout of an advertisement

VISUALLY

VITA, -E, -S n curriculum vitae

VITAL, -S adj essential or highly important ▷ n bodily organs that are necessary to maintain life

VITALISE same as ▶ vitalize

VITALISM n philosophical doctrine that the phenomena of life cannot be explained in purely mechanical terms

VITALIST

VITALITY n physical or mental energy

VITALIZE vb fill with life or vitality

VITALLY ▶ vital

VITALS ▶ vital

VITAMER, -S n type of chemical

VITAMIN, -S n one of a group of substances that are essential in the diet

VITAMINE same as ▶ vitamin

VITAMINS ▶ vitamin

VITAS ▶ vita

VITATIVE adj fond of life

VITE adv musical direction

VITELLI ▶ vitellus

VITELLIN n phosphoprotein that is the major protein in egg yolk

VITELLUS, VITELLI n yolk of an egg

VITESSE, -S n speed

VITEX, -ES n type of herb

VITIABLE ▶ vitiate

VITIATE, -D, -S vb spoil the effectiveness of

VITIATOR

VITICETA > viticetum

VITICIDE n vine killer

VITILIGO n area of skin that is white from albinism or loss of melanin pigmentation

VITIOUS adj mistaken

VITRAGE, -S n light fabric

VITRAIL, VITRAUX n stained glass

VITRAIN, -S n type of coal

VITRAUX ▶ vitrail

VITREOUS adj like or made from glass

VITREUM, -S n vitreous body

VITRIC adj of, relating to, resembling, or having the nature of glass

VITRICS n glassware

VITRIFY vb change or be changed into glass or a glassy substance

VITRINE, -S n glass display case or cabinet for works of art, curios, etc

VITRIOL, -S n language expressing bitterness and hatred ▷ vb attack or injure with or as if with vitriol

VITTA, -E n tubelike cavity containing oil that occurs in the fruits of certain plants

VITTATE

VITTLE, -D, VITTLING obsolete or dialect spelling of ▶ victual

VITTLES obsolete or dialect spelling of ▶ victuals

VITTLING ▶ vittle

VITULAR same as ▶ vituline

VITULINE adj of or resembling a calf or veal

VIVA, -ED, -ING, -S interj long live (a person or thing) ▷ n examination in the form of an interview ▷ vb examine (a candidate) in a spoken interview

VIVACE, -S adj, adv (to be performed) in a lively manner ▷ n piece of music to be performed in this way

VIVACITY n quality of being vivacious

VIVAED ▶ viva

VIVAING ▶ viva

VIVARIA ▶ vivarium

VIVARIES ▶ vivary

VIVARIUM, VIVARIA n place where animals are kept in natural conditions

VIVARY, VIVARIES same as ▶ vivarium

VIVAS ▶ viva

VIVAT, -S interj long live ▷ n expression of acclamation

VIVDA, -S n method of drying meat

VIVE interj long live

VIVELY adv in a lively manner

VIVENCY n physical or mental energy

VIVER, -S n fish pond

VIVERRA, -S n civet genus

VIVERRID > viverrine

VIVERS ▶ viver

VIVES n disease found in horses

VIVID, -ER, -EST adj very bright

VIVIDITY

VIVIDLY

VIVIFIC adj giving life

VIVIFIED ▶ vivify

VIVIFIER ▶ vivify

VIVIFY, VIVIFIED, VIVIFIES vb animate, inspire

VIVIPARA n animals that produce offspring that develop as embryos within the female parent

VIVIPARY n act of giving birth producing offspring that have developed as embryos

VIVISECT vb subject (an animal) to vivisection

VIVO adv with life and vigour

VIVRES n provisions

VIXEN, -S n female fox

VIXENISH

VIXENLY

VIZAMENT n consultation

VIZARD, -ED, -S n means of disguise ▷ vb conceal by means of a disguise

VIZCACHA same as ▶ viscacha

VIZIED ▶ vizy

VIZIER, -S n high official in certain Muslim countries

VIZIES ▶ vizy

VIZIR, -S same as ▶ vizier

VIZIRATE

VIZIRIAL

VIZOR, -ING, -S *same as*
► **visor**
VIZORED
VIZSLA, -S *n* breed of Hungarian hunting dog
VIZY, VIZIED, VIZIES, -ING *vb* look
VIZZIE, -D, -S *same as* ► **vizy**
VLEI, -S *n* area of low marshy ground
VLIES ► **vly**
VLOG, -GED, -S *n* video weblog ▷ *vb* make and upload a vlog
VLOGGER, -S *n* person who keeps a video blog
VLOGGING *n* action of keeping a video blog
VLOGS ► **vlog**
VLY, VLIES *same as* ► **vlei**

This word for low-lying wet ground can be useful when you are short of vowels. It can also be spelt **vlei**.

VOAR, -S *n* spring
VOCAB, -S *n* vocabulary
VOCABLE, -S *n* word regarded simply as a sequence of letters or spoken sounds ▷ *adj* capable of being uttered
VOCABLY
VOCABS ► **vocab**
VOCAL, -S *adj* relating to the voice ▷ *n* piece of jazz or pop music that is sung
VOCALESE *n* style of jazz singing
VOCALIC *adj* of, relating to, or containing a vowel or vowels
VOCALICS *n* non-verbal aspects of voice
VOCALION *n* type of musical instrument
VOCALISE *same as*
► **vocalize**
VOCALISM *n* exercise of the voice, as in singing or speaking
VOCALIST *n* singer
VOCALITY ► **vocal**
VOCALIZE *vb* express with the voice
VOCALLY ► **vocal**
VOCALS ► **vocal**
VOCATION *n* profession or trade
VOCATIVE *n* (in some languages) case of nouns used when addressing a person ▷ *adj* relating to, used in, or characterized by calling
VOCES ► **vox**

VOCODER, -S *n* type of synthesizer that uses the human voice as an oscillator
VOCULAR ► **vocule**
VOCULE, -S *n* faint noise made when articulating certain sounds
VODCAST, -S *vb* podcast with video
VODDY, VODDIES *n* vodka
VODKA, -S *n* (Russian) spirit distilled from potatoes or grain
VODOU, -S *variant of*
► **voodoo**

This West Indian word for a kind of black magic may indeed work magic on an unpromising rack. And it has a host of variants, though few people will remember them all: **vaudoo, vaudoux, vodoun, vodun, voudon, voudou** and **voudoun**!

VODOUN, -S *same as*
► **vodun**
VODOUS ► **vodou**
VODUN, -S ► **voodoo**
VOE, -S *n* (in Orkney and Shetland) a small bay or narrow creek
VOEMA, -S *n* vigour or energy
VOES ► **voe**
VOG, -S *n* air pollution caused by volcanic dust
VOGIE, -R, -ST *adj* conceited
VOGS ► **vog**
VOGUE, -S, VOGUIER, VOGUIEST *n* popular style ▷ *adj* popular or fashionable ▷ *vb* bring into vogue
VOGUED
VOGUEING *n* dance style of the late 1980s
VOGUER, -S ► **vogue**
VOGUES ► **vogue**
VOGUEY ► **vogue**
VOGUIER ► **vogue**
VOGUIEST ► **vogue**
VOGUING, -S *same as*
► **vogueing**
VOGUISH ► **vogue**
VOICE, -S *n* (quality of) sound made when speaking or singing ▷ *vb* express verbally
VOICED *adj* articulated with accompanying vibration of the vocal cords
VOICEFUL ► **voice**
VOICER, -S ► **voice**
VOICES ► **voice**
VOICING, -S ► **voice**
VOID, -ING, -INGS, -S *adj* not legally binding ▷ *n* feeling

of deprivation ▷ *vb* make invalid
VOIDABLE *adj* capable of being voided
VOIDANCE *n* annulment, as of a contract
VOIDED *adj* (of a design) with a hole in the centre of the same shape as the design
VOIDEE, -S *n* light meal eaten before bed
VOIDER, -S ► **void**
VOIDING ► **void**
VOIDINGS ► **void**
VOIDNESS ► **void**
VOIDS ► **void**
VOILA *interj* word used to express satisfaction
VOILE, -S *n* light semitransparent fabric
VOIP, -S *n* voice-over internet protocol
VOITURE, -S *n* type of vehicle
VOIVODE, -S *n* type of military leader
VOL, -S *n* heraldic wings
VOLA, -E *n* palm of hand or sole of foot
VOLABLE *adj* quick-witted
VOLAE ► **vola**
VOLAGE *adj* changeable
VOLANT *adj* in a flying position
VOLANTE, -S *n* Spanish horse carriage
VOLAR *adj* of or relating to the palm of the hand or the sole of the foot
VOLARY, VOLARIES *n* large bird enclosure
VOLATIC, -S *adj* flying ▷ *n* creature with wings
VOLATILE *adj* liable to sudden change, esp in behaviour ▷ *n* volatile substance
VOLCANIC *adj* of or relating to volcanoes
VOLCANO, -S *n* mountain with a vent through which lava is ejected
VOLE, -S *n* small rodent ▷ *vb* win by taking all the tricks in a deal
VOLED
VOLENS *adj* as in nolens volens whether willing or unwilling
VOLERY, VOLERIES *same as*
► **volary**
VOLES ► **vole**
VOLET, -S *n* type of veil
VOLING ► **vole**
VOLITANT *adj* flying or moving about rapidly
VOLITATE *vb* flutter
VOLITION *n* ability to decide things for oneself

V

VOLITIVE adj of, relating to, or emanating from the will ▷ n (in some languages) a verb form or mood used to express a wish or desire

VOLK, -S n people or nation, esp the nation of Afrikaners

VOLLEY, -ED, -S n simultaneous discharge of ammunition ▷ vb discharge (ammunition) in a volley
VOLLEYER

VOLOST, -S n (in the former Soviet Union) a rural soviet

VOLPINO, -S n Italian breed of dog

VOLPLANE vb glide in an aeroplane

VOLS ▸ vol

VOLT, -ED, -ING, -S n unit of electric potential ▷ vb (in fencing) make a quick movement to avoid a thrust

VOLTA n quick-moving Italian dance

VOLTAGE, -S n electric potential difference expressed in volts

VOLTAIC adj producing an electric current

VOLTAISM another name for > galvanism

VOLTE, -S same as ▸ volt
VOLTED ▸ volt
VOLTES ▸ volte
VOLTI adv musical direction
VOLTING ▸ volt
VOLTS ▸ volt
VOLUBIL same as ▸ voluble
VOLUBLE adj talking easily and at length
VOLUBLY

VOLUME, -D, -S, VOLUMING n size of the space occupied by something ▷ vb billow or surge in volume

VOLUMISE same as ▸ volumize

VOLUMIST n author

VOLUMIZE vb create volume in something

VOLUSPA, -S n Icelandic mythological poem

VOLUTE, -S n spiral or twisting turn, form, or object ▷ adj having the form of a volute
VOLUTED

VOLUTIN, -S n granular substance found in cells

VOLUTION n rolling, revolving, or spiral form or motion

VOLUTOID ▸ volute

VOLVA, -E, -S n cup-shaped structure that sheathes the base of the stalk of certain mushrooms
VOLVATE

VOLVE, -D, -S, VOLVING vb turn over

VOLVOX, -ES n freshwater protozoan

VOLVULUS, VOLVULI n abnormal twisting of the intestines causing obstruction

VOM, -MED, -MING, -S vb vomit

VOMER, -S n thin flat bone separating the nasal passages in mammals
VOMERINE

VOMICA, -E, -S n pus-containing cavity

VOMIT, -ED, -ING, -S vb eject (the contents of the stomach) through the mouth ▷ n matter vomited
VOMITER -S

VOMITIVE same as ▸ vomitory

VOMITO, -S n form of yellow fever

VOMITORY adj causing vomiting ▷ n vomitory agent

VOMITOS ▸ vomito

VOMITOUS adj arousing feelings of disgust

VOMITS ▸ vomit

VOMITUS n matter that has been vomited

VOMITY adj resembling or smelling of vomit

VOMMED ▸ vom
VOMMING ▸ vom
VOMS ▸ vom

VONGOLE pl n (in Italian cookery) clams

VOODOO, -ED, -S n religion involving ancestor worship and witchcraft ▷ adj of or relating to voodoo ▷ vb affect by or as if by the power of voodoo

VOORSKOT n (in South Africa) advance payment made to a farmer for crops

VOR, -RED, -RING, -S vb (in dialect) warn

VORACITY > voracious

VORAGO, -ES, -S n chasm

VORANT adj devouring

VORLAGE, -S n skiing position

VORPAL adj sharp

VORRED ▸ vor
VORRING ▸ vor
VORS ▸ vor

VORTEX, -ES, VORTICES n whirlpool

VORTICAL

VOSTRO adj as in **vostro account** bank account held by a foreign bank with a British bank

VOTABLE ▸ vote

VOTARESS n female votary

VOTARIES ▸ votary

VOTARIST variant of ▸ votary

VOTARY, VOTARIES n person dedicated to religion or to a cause ▷ adj ardently devoted to the services or worship of God

VOTE, -D, -S n choice made by a participant in a shared decision ▷ vb make a choice by a vote

VOTEABLE

VOTEEN, -S n devotee

VOTELESS ▸ vote

VOTER, -S n person who can or does vote

VOTES ▸ vote

VOTING, -S ▸ vote

VOTIVE, -S adj done or given to fulfil a vow ▷ n votive offering
VOTIVELY

VOTRESS ▸ votaress

VOUCH, -ED, -ES, -ING vb give personal assurance ▷ n act of vouching

VOUCHEE, -S n person summoned to court to defend a title

VOUCHER, -S n ticket used instead of money to buy specified goods ▷ vb summon someone to court as a vouchee

VOUCHES ▸ vouch
VOUCHING ▸ vouch

VOUDON, -S variant of ▸ voodoo

VOUDOU, -S same as ▸ voodoo
VOUDOUED

VOUDOUN, -S variant of ▸ voodoo

VOUDOUS ▸ voudou

VOUGE, -S n form of pike used by foot soldiers in the 14th century and later

VOULGE, -S n type of medieval weapon

VOULU adj deliberate

VOUSSOIR n wedge-shaped stone or brick that is used with others to construct an arch

VOUTSAFE same as > vouchsafe

VOUVRAY, -S n dry white French wine

VOW, -ED, -ING, -S n solemn and binding promise ▷ vb promise solemnly

VOWEL, -LED, -S *n* speech sound made without obstructing the flow of breath ▷ *vb* say as a vowel

VOWELED *adj* having vowels

VOWELISE *same as* ▸ **vowelize**

VOWELIZE *vb* mark the vowel points in (a Hebrew word or text)

VOWELLED ▸ **vowel**

VOWELLY ▸ **vowel**

VOWELS ▸ **vowel**

VOWER, -S ▸ **vow**

VOWESS, -ES *n* nun

VOWING ▸ **vow**

VOWLESS ▸ **vow**

VOWS ▸ **vow**

VOX, VOCES *n* voice or sound

> Along with **vex**, this Latin word for voice is the highest-scoring three-letter word beginning with V.

VOXEL, -S *n* term used in computing imaging

VOYAGE, -D, -S *n* long journey by sea or in space ▷ *vb* make a voyage

VOYAGER -S

VOYAGEUR *n* French canoeman who transported furs from trading posts in N America

VOYAGING *n* act of voyaging

VOYEUR, -S *n* person abnormally interested in other people's distress

VOZHD, -S *n* Russian leader

> This unlikely looking word is Russian for a chief or leader, and may provide a great score from an apparently difficult rack.

VRAIC, -S *n* type of seaweed

VRAICKER *n* person who gathers vraic

VRAICS ▸ **vraic**

VRIL, -S *n* life force

VROOM, -ED, -ING, -S *interj* exclamation imitative of a car engine revving up ▷ *vb* move noisily and at high speed

VROT *adj* South African slang for rotten

VROU, -S *n* Afrikaner woman, esp a married woman

VROUW, -S *n* woman

> The heart of any Scrabble player sinks to see a combination of U, V and W on the rack, as there are relatively few words that use even two of these letters. But **vrouw**, a word of Dutch origin for a woman or goodwife, may get you out of the mess.

VROW, -S *same as* ▸ **vrouw**

VUG, -S *n* small cavity in a rock or vein, usually lined with crystals

> This unusual word of Cornish origin, meaning a cavity in rock, is another that can be useful when you have an uninspiring combination of letters. And it has a variant **vugh** and can be extended to **vuggy** or **vughy.**

VUGG, -S *same as* ▸ **vug**

VUGGIER ▸ **vuggy**

VUGGIEST ▸ **vuggy**

VUGGS ▸ **vugg**

VUGGY, VUGGIER, VUGGIEST ▸ **vug**

VUGH, -IER, -IEST, -S *same as* ▸ **vug**

VUGHY ▸ **vug**

VUGS ▸ **vug**

VUGULAR *adj* relating to vugs

VULCAN, -S *n* blacksmith

VULCANIC *same as* ▸ **volcanic**

VULCANS ▸ **vulcan**

VULGAR, -ER, -S *adj* showing lack of good taste, decency, or refinement ▷ *n* common and ignorant person

VULGARLY

VULGATE, -S *n* commonly recognized text or version ▷ *adj* generally accepted

VULGO *adv* generally

VULGUS, -ES *n* the common people

VULN, -ED, -S *vb* wound

VULNING

VULPINE *adj* of or like a fox

VULSELLA *n* forceps

VULTURE, -S *n* large bird that feeds on the flesh of dead animals

VULTURN, -S *n* type of turkey

VULVA, -E, -S *n* female external genitals

VULVAL

VULVAR

VULVATE

VULVITIS *n* inflammation of the vulva

VUM, -MED, -MING, -S *vb* swear

VUTTY, VUTTIER, VUTTIEST *adj* dirty

VUVUZELA *n* South African instrument blown by football fans

VYING, -S ▸ **vie**

VYINGLY ▸ **vie**

VYINGS ▸ **vying**

V

Ww

W, like **V**, can be an awkward tile to handle, but at least there are two two-letter words that begin with **W**: **we** and **wo** (5 points each). There are two that end with **W**: **aw** and **ow** (5 points each). There are lots of everyday three-letter words that earn good scores: **wiz** (15), **wax** (13) with its two old-fashioned variants **wex** and **wox** (also 13 each) and **way, who, why, wow** and **wry** (9 each). Don't forget **wok** (10) either, which can be as useful on the Scrabble board as in the kitchen!

WAAC, -S *n* (formerly) member of the Women's Auxiliary Army Corp

WAAH *interj* interjection used to express wailing

WAB, -S *same as* ▶ **web**

WABAIN, -S *same as* ▶ **ouabain**

WABBIT *adj* weary

WABBLE, -D, -S, WABBLING *same as* ▶ **wobble**

WABBLER -S

WABBLIER ▶ **wabbly**

WABBLING ▶ **wabble**

WABBLY, WABBLIER ▶ **wabble**

WABOOM, -S *another word for* > **wagenboom**

WABS ▶ **wab**

WABSTER, -S *Scots form of* ▶ **webster**

WACK, -EST, -S *n* friend

WACKE, -S *n* any of various soft earthy rocks that resemble or are derived from basaltic rocks

WACKED *adj* exhausted

WACKER, -S *same as* ▶ **wack**

WACKES ▶ **wacke**

WACKEST ▶ **wack**

WACKIER ▶ **wacky**

WACKIEST ▶ **wacky**

WACKILY ▶ **wacky**

WACKO, -ES, -S *adj* mad or eccentric ▷ *n* mad or eccentric person

WACKS ▶ **wack**

WACKY, WACKIER, WACKIEST *adj* eccentric or funny

WACONDA, -S *n* supernatural force in Sioux belief

WAD, -DED, -DING, -DINGS, -S *n* black earthy ore of manganese ▷ *n* small mass

of soft material ▷ *vb* form (something) into a wad

WADABLE ▶ **wade**

WADD, -S *same as* ▶ **wad**

WADDED ▶ **wad**

WADDER, -S ▶ **wad**

WADDIE *same as* ▶ **waddy**

WADDIED ▶ **waddy**

WADDIES ▶ **waddy**

WADDING ▶ **wad**

WADDINGS ▶ **wad**

WADDLE, -D, -S, WADDLING *vb* walk with short swaying steps ▷ *n* swaying walk

WADDLER -S

WADDLIER ▶ **waddly**

WADDLING ▶ **waddle**

WADDLY, WADDLIER ▶ **waddle**

WADDS ▶ **wadd**

WADDY, WADDIED, WADDIES, -ING *n* heavy wooden club used by Australian Aborigines ▷ *vb* hit with a waddy

WADE, -D, -S, WADING, WADINGS *vb* walk with difficulty through water or mud ▷ *n* act or an instance of wading

WADEABLE

WADER *n* long-legged water bird

WADERS *pl n* long waterproof boots which completely cover the legs

WADES ▶ **wade**

WADGE, -S *n* large or roughly-cut portion

WADI, -S *n* (in N Africa and Arabia) river which is dry except in the wet season

WADIES ▶ **wady**

WADING ▶ **wade**

WADINGS ▶ **wade**

WADIS ▶ **wadi**

WADMAAL, -S *same as* ▶ **wadmal**

WADMAL, -S *n* coarse thick woollen fabric, formerly woven for outer garments

WADMEL, -S *same as* ▶ **wadmal**

WADMOL, -S *same as* ▶ **wadmal**

WADMOLL, -S *same as* ▶ **wadmal**

WADMOLS ▶ **wadmol**

WADS ▶ **wad**

WADSET, -S *vb* pledge or mortgage

WADSETT, -S *same as* ▶ **wadset**

WADT, -S *same as* ▶ **wad**

WADY, WADIES *same as* ▶ **wadi**

WAE, -S *old form of* ▶ **woe**

WAEFUL *old form of* ▶ **woeful**

WAENESS *n* sorrow

WAES ▶ **wae**

WAESOME *adj* sorrowful

WAESUCK *interj* alas

WAESUCKS *interj* alas

WAFER, -ED, -ING, -S *n* thin crisp biscuit ▷ *vb* seal, fasten, or attach with a wafer

WAFERY

WAFF, -ED, -ING, -S *n* gust or puff of air ▷ *vb* flutter or cause to flutter

WAFFIE, -S *n* person regarded as having little worth to society

WAFFING ▶ **waff**

WAFFLE, -D, -S *vb* speak or write in a vague wordy way ▷ *n* vague wordy talk or writing

WAFFLER -S

WAFFLIER ▶ **waffly**

WAFFLING ▶ **waffle**

WAFFLY, WAFFLIER ► waffle
WAFFS ► waff
WAFT, -ED, -S vb drift or carry gently through the air ▷ n something wafted
WAFTAGE -S
WAFTER, -S n device that causes a draught
WAFTING, -S ► waft
WAFTS ► waft
WAFTURE, -S n act of wafting or waving
WAG, -GED, -GING, -S vb move rapidly from side to side ▷ n wagging movement
WAGE, -D, -S, WAGING n payment for work done, esp when paid weekly ▷ vb engage in (an activity)
WAGELESS
WAGER, -ED, -S vb bet on the outcome of something ▷ n bet on the outcome of an event or activity
WAGERER -S
WAGERING n act of wagering
WAGERS ► wager
WAGES ► wage
WAGGA, -S n blanket or bed covering made out of sacks stitched together
WAGGED ► wag
WAGGER, -S ► wag
WAGGERY n quality of being humorous
WAGGING ► wag
WAGGISH adj jocular or humorous
WAGGLE, -D, -S, WAGGLING vb move with a rapid shaking or wobbling motion ▷ n rapid shaking or wobbling motion
WAGGLER, -S n float only the bottom of which is attached to the fishing line
WAGGLES ► waggle
WAGGLIER ► waggly
WAGGLING ► waggle
WAGGLY, WAGGLIER ► waggle
WAGGON, -ED, -S same as ► wagon
WAGGONER same as ► wagoner
WAGGONS ► waggon
WAGING ► wage
WAGMOIRE obsolete word for ► quagmire
WAGON, -ED, -ING, -S n four-wheeled vehicle for heavy loads ▷ vb transport by wagon
WAGONAGE n money paid for transport by wagon
WAGONED ► wagon

WAGONER, -S n person who drives a wagon
WAGONFUL ► wagon
WAGONING ► wagon
WAGONS ► wagon
WAGS ► wag
WAGSOME another word for ► waggish
WAGTAIL, -S n small long-tailed bird
WAGYU, -S n Japanese breed of beef cattle
WAHCONDA n supreme being
WAHINE, -S n Māori woman, esp a wife
WAHOO, -S n food and game fish of tropical seas
WAI, -S n in New Zealand, water
WAIATA, -S n Māori song
WAID ► weigh
WAIDE ► weigh
WAIF, -ED, -ING, -S n young person who is, or seems, homeless or neglected ▷ vb treat as a waif
WAIFISH
WAIFLIKE
WAIFT, -S n piece of lost property found by someone other than the owner
WAIL, -ED, -S vb cry out in pain or misery ▷ n mournful cry
WAILER -S
WAILFUL ► wail
WAILING, -S ► wail
WAILS ► wail
WAILSOME ► wail
WAIN, -ED, -ING, -S vb transport ▷ n farm wagon
WAINAGE, -S n carriages, etc, for transportation of goods
WAINED ► wain
WAINING ► wain
WAINS ► wain
WAINSCOT n wooden lining of the lower part of the walls of a room ▷ vb line (a wall of a room) with a wainscot
WAIR, -ED, -ING, -S vb spend
WAIRSH, -ER variant spelling of ► wersh
WAIRUA, -S n in New Zealand, spirit or soul
WAIS ► wai
WAIST, -S n part of the trunk between the ribs and the hips
WAISTED adj having a waist or waistlike part
WAISTER, -S n sailor performing menial duties
WAISTING n act of wasting
WAISTS ► waist

WAIT, -ED, -ING, -INGS, -S vb remain inactive in expectation (of something) ▷ n act or period of waiting
WAITE, -S old form of ► wait
WAITED ► wait
WAITER, -ED, -S n man who serves in a restaurant etc ▷ vb serve at table
WAITES ► waite
WAITING ► wait
WAITINGS ► wait
WAITLIST n waiting list
WAITRESS n woman who serves people with food and drink in a restaurant ▷ vb work as a waitress
WAITRON, -S n waiter or waitress
WAITS ► wait
WAIVE, -D, -S, WAIVING vb refrain from enforcing (a law, right, etc)
WAIVER, -S n act or instance of voluntarily giving up a claim, right, etc
WAIVES ► waive
WAIVING ► waive
WAIVODE, -S same as ► voivode
WAIWODE, -S same as ► voivode
WAKA, -S n Māori canoe
WAKAME, -S n edible seaweed
WAKANDA, -S n supernatural quality in Native American belief system
WAKANE, -S n type of seaweed
WAKAS ► waka
WAKE, -D, -S, WOKE, WOKEN vb rouse from sleep or inactivity ▷ n vigil beside a body the night before the funeral
WAKEFUL adj unable to sleep
WAKELESS adj (of sleep) deep or unbroken
WAKEMAN, WAKEMEN n watchman
WAKEN, -ED, -ING, -S vb wake
WAKENER -S
WAKER, -S ► wake
WAKERIFE adj watchful
WAKERS ► waker
WAKES ► wake
WAKF, -S same as ► waqf
WAKIKI, -S n Melanesian shell currency
WAKING, -S ► wake
WALD, -S Scots form of ► weld
WALDHORN n organ reed stop

W

WALDO, -ES, -S n gadget for manipulating objects by remote control

WALDRAPP n type of ibis

WALDS ► wald

WALE, -D, -R, -RS, -S, WALING same as ► **weal**

WALI, -S same as ► **vali**

WALIER ► waly

WALIES ► waly

WALIEST ► waly

WALING ► wale

WALIS ► wali

WALISE, -S same as ► **valise**

WALK, -ED, -S vb move on foot with at least one foot always on the ground ▷ n short journey on foot, usu for pleasure

WALKABLE

WALKAWAY n easily achieved victory

WALKED ► walk

WALKER, -S n person who walks

WALKIES pl n as in **go walkies** a walk

WALKING, -S adj (of a person) considered to possess the qualities of something inanimate as specified ▷ n act of walking

WALKMILL same as > **waulkmill**

WALKOUT, -S n strike

WALKOVER n easy victory

WALKS ► walk

WALKUP, -S n building with stairs to upper floors

WALKWAY, -S n path designed for use by pedestrians

WALKYRIE variant of ► **valkyrie**

WALL, -ER, -ERS, -S n structure of brick, stone, etc used to enclose, divide, or support ▷ vb enclose or seal with a wall or walls

WALLA, -S same as ► **wallah**

WALLABA, -S n type of S American tree

WALLABY n marsupial like a small kangaroo

WALLAH, -S n person involved with or in charge of a specified thing

WALLAROO n large stocky Australian kangaroo of rocky regions

WALLAS ► walla

WALLED ► wall

WALLER ► wall

WALLERS ► wall

WALLET, -S n small folding case for paper money, documents, etc

WALLEY, -S n type of jump in figure skating

WALLEYE, -S n fish with large staring eyes

WALLEYED

WALLEYS ► walley

WALLFISH n snail

WALLIE same as ► **wally**

WALLIER ► wally

WALLIES ► wally

WALLIEST ► wally

WALLING, -S ► wall

WALLOP, -ED, -S vb hit hard ▷ n hard blow

WALLOPER n person or thing that wallops

WALLOPS ► wallop

WALLOW, -ED, -S vb revel in an emotion ▷ n act or instance of wallowing

WALLOWER

WALLS ► wall

WALLSEND n type of coal

WALLWORT n type of plant

WALLY, WALLIER, WALLIES, WALLIEST n stupid person ▷ adj fine, pleasing, or splendid

WALNUT, -S n edible nut with a wrinkled shell ▷ adj made from the wood of a walnut tree

WALRUS, -ES n large sea mammal with long tusks

WALTY, WALTIER, WALTIEST adj (of a ship) likely to roll over

WALTZ, -ED, -ES, -ING n ballroom dance ▷ vb dance a waltz

WALTZER, -S n person who waltzes

WALTZES ► waltz

WALTZING ► waltz

WALY, WALIER, WALIES, WALIEST same as ► **wally**

WAMBLE, -D, -S, WAMBLING vb move unsteadily ▷ n unsteady movement

WAMBLIER ► wambly

WAMBLING ► wamble

WAMBLY, WAMBLIER ► wamble

WAME, -S n belly, abdomen, or womb

WAMED

WAMEFOU, -S Scots variant of ► **wameful**

WAMEFUL, -S n bellyful

WAMES ► wame

WAMMUL, -S n dog

WAMMUS, -ES same as ► **wamus**

WAMPEE, -S n type of Asian fruit tree

WAMPISH vb wave

WAMPUM, -S n shells woven together, formerly used by Native Americans for money

WAMPUS, -ES same as ► **wamus**

WAMUS, -ES n type of cardigan or jacket

WAN, -NED, -NER, -NEST, -NING, -S adj pale and sickly looking ▷ vb make or become wan

WAND, -S n thin rod, esp one used in performing magic tricks

WANDER, -ED, -S vb move about without a definite destination or aim ▷ n act or instance of wandering

WANDERER

WANDEROO n macaque of India and Sri Lanka

WANDERS ► wander

WANDLE, -D, -S, WANDLING adj supple ▷ vb walk haltingly

WANDLIKE ► wand

WANDLING ► wandle

WANDOO, -S n eucalyptus tree of W Australia, having white bark and durable wood

WANDS ► wand

WANE, -D, -S vb decrease gradually in size or strength

WANEY

WANG, -S n cheekbone

WANGAN, -S same as ► **wanigan**

WANGLE, -D, -S, WANGLING vb get by devious methods ▷ n act or an instance of wangling

WANGLER -S

WANGS ► wang

WANGUN, -S same as ► **wanigan**

WANHOPE, -S n delusion

WANIER ► wany

WANIEST ► wany

WANIGAN, -S n provisions for camp

WANING, -S ► wane

WANION, -S n vehemence

WANKLE adj unstable

WANLE same as ► **wandle**

WANLY ► wan

WANNA vb spelling of want to intended to reflect a dialectal or informal pronunciation

WANNABE, -S adj wanting to be, or be like, a particular person or thing ▷ n person who wants to be, or be like, a particular person or thing

WANNABEE same as ► wannabe

WANNABES ► wannabe

WANNED ► wan

WANNEL same as ► wandle

WANNER ► wan

WANNESS ► wan

WANNEST ► wan

WANNIGAN same as ► wanigan

WANNING ► wan

WANNION, -S same as ► wanion

WANNISH adj rather wan

WANS ► wan

WANT, -ED, -S vb need or long for ▷ n act or instance of wanting

WANTAGE, -S n shortage

WANTAWAY n footballer who wants to transfer to another club

WANTED ► want

WANTER, -S ► want

WANTHILL n molehill

WANTIES ► wanty

WANTING adj lacking ▷ prep without

WANTON, -ED, -S adj without motive, provocation, or justification ▷ n playful or capricious person ▷ vb squander or waste

WANTONER

WANTONLY

WANTS ► want

WANTY, WANTIES adj belt

WANWORDY adj without merit

WANWORTH n inexpensive purchase

WANY, WANIER, WANIEST ► wane

WANZE, -D, -S, WANZING vb wane

WAP, -PED, -PING, -S vb strike

WAPITI, -S n large N American deer

WAPPED ► wap

WAPPEND adj tired

WAPPER, -ED, -S vb blink

WAPPING ► wap

WAPS ► wap

WAQF, -S n endowment in Muslim law

> An Arabic word meaning the donation of land, property or money for charitable purposes. As one of the Q words without a U, this comes up surprisingly often. It can also be spelt **wakf**.

WAR, -RED, -RING, -S n fighting between nations

▷ adj of, like, or caused by war ▷ vb conduct a war

WARAGI, -S n Ugandan alcoholic drink made from bananas

WARATAH, -S n Australian shrub with crimson flowers

WARB, -S n dirty or insignificant person

WARBIER ► warby

WARBIEST ► warby

WARBIRD, -S n vintage military aeroplane

WARBLE, -D, -S, WARBLING vb sing in a trilling voice ▷ n act or an instance of warbling

WARBLER, -S n any of various small songbirds

WARBLES ► warble

WARBLIER ► warbly

WARBLING ► warble

WARBLY, WARBLIER adj said in a quavering manner

WARBOT, -S n any robot or unmanned vehicle or device designed for and used in warfare

WARBS ► warb

WARBY, WARBIER, WARBIEST ► warb

WARCRAFT n skill in warfare

WARD, -ED, -S n room in a hospital for patients needing a similar kind of care ▷ vb guard or protect

WARDCORN n payment of corn

WARDED ► ward

WARDEN, -ED, -S n person in charge of a building and its occupants ▷ vb act as a warden

WARDENRY

WARDER, -ED, -S vb guard ▷ n prison officer

WARDIAN n as in **wardian case** type of glass container for housing delicate plants

WARDING, -S ► ward

WARDLESS ► ward

WARDMOTE n assembly of the citizens or liverymen of an area

WARDOG, -S n veteran warrior

WARDRESS n female officer in charge of prisoners in a jail

WARDROBE n cupboard for hanging clothes in

WARDROOM n officers' quarters on a warship

WARDROP, -S obsolete form of ► wardrobe

WARDS ► ward

WARDSHIP n state of being a ward

WARE, -D, WARING n articles of a specified type or material ▷ vb spend or squander

WAREHOU, -S n any of several edible saltwater New Zealand fish

WARELESS adj careless

WAREROOM n store-room

WARES pl n goods for sale

WAREZ pl n illegally copied computer software

WARFARE, -D, -S vb engage in war ▷ n fighting or hostilities

WARFARER

WARFARIN n crystalline compound, used as a medical anticoagulant

WARGAME, -D, -S vb engage in simulated military conflicts

WARGAMER n person who takes part in wargames

WARGAMES ► wargame

WARHABLE adj able to fight in war

WARHEAD, -S n explosive front part of a missile

WARHORSE n (formerly) a horse used in battle

WARIER ► wary

WARIEST ► wary

WARILY ► wary

WARIMENT n caution

WARINESS ► wary

WARING ► ware

WARISON, -S n (esp formerly) a bugle note used as an order to a military force to attack

WARK, -ED, -ING, -S Scots form of ► work

WARLESS ► war

WARLIKE adj of or relating to war

WARLING, -S n one who is not liked

WARLOCK, -S n man who practises black magic

WARLORD, -S n military leader of a nation or part of a nation

WARM, -ED, -EST, -ING, -INGS, -S adj moderately hot ▷ vb make or become warm ▷ n warm place or area

WARMAKER n one who wages war

WARMAN, WARMEN n one experienced in warfare

WARMED ► warm

WARMEN ► warman

WARMER, -S ► warm

WARMEST ► warm

WARMING ► warm

WARMINGS ► warm

WARMISH ► warm

W

WARMIST, -S n person who believes global warming results from human activity

WARMLY ► warm

WARMNESS ► warm

WARMOUTH n type of fish

WARMS ► warm

WARMTH, -S n mild heat

WARMUP, -S n preparatory exercise routine

WARN, -ED, -S vb make aware of possible danger or harm

WARNER -S

WARNING, -S n something that warns ▷ adj giving or serving as a warning

WARNS ► warn

WARP, -ED, -S vb twist out of shape ▷ n state of being warped

WARPAGE -S

WARPAINT n paint used to decorate the face and body before battle

WARPATH, -S n route taken by Native Americans on a warlike expedition

WARPED ► warp

WARPER, -S ► warp

WARPING, -S ► warp

WARPLANE n any aircraft designed for and used in warfare

WARPOWER n ability to wage war

WARPS ► warp

WARPWISE adv (weaving) in the direction of the warp

WARRAGAL same as ► warrigal

WARRAGLE same as ► warrigal

WARRAGUL same as ► warrigal

WARRAN, -ED, -S same as ► warrant

WARRAND, -S same as ► warrant

WARRANED ► warran

WARRANS ► warran

WARRANT, -S n (document giving) official authorization ▷ vb make necessary

WARRANTY n (document giving) a guarantee

WARRAY, -ED, -S vb wage war on

WARRE same as ► war

WARRED ► war

WARREN, -S n series of burrows in which rabbits live

WARRENER n gamekeeper or keeper of a warren

WARRENS ► warren

WARREY, -ED, -S same as ► warray

WARRIGAL n dingo ▷ adj wild

WARRING ► war

WARRIOR, -S n person who fights in a war

WARRISON same as ► warison

WARS ► war

WARSAW, -S n type of grouper fish

WARSHIP, -S n ship designed and equipped for naval combat

WARSLE, -D, -S, WARSLING dialect word for ► wrestle

WARSLER -S

WARST obsolete form of ► worst

WARSTLE, -D, -S dialect form of ► wrestle

WARSTLER

WART, -S n small hard growth on the skin

WARTED

WARTHOG, -S n wild African pig with wartlike lumps on the face

WARTIER ► warty

WARTIEST ► warty

WARTIME, -S n time of war ▷ adj of or in a time of war

WARTLESS ► wart

WARTLIKE ► wart

WARTS ► wart

WARTWEED n type of plant

WARTWORT another word for ► wartweed

WARTY, WARTIER, WARTIEST ► wart

WARWOLF n Roman engine of war

WARWORK, -S n work contributing to war effort

WARWORN adj worn down by war

WARY, WARIER, WARIEST adj watchful or cautious

WARZONE, -S n area where a war is taking place or there is some other violent conflict

WAS vb form of the past tense of be

WASABI, -S n Japanese cruciferous plant cultivated for its thick green pungent root

WASE, -S n pad to relieve pressure of load carried on head

WASH, -ED, -EN, -ES vb clean (oneself, clothes, etc) with water and usu soap ▷ n act or process of washing

WASHABLE n thing that can be washed ▷ adj (esp of fabrics or clothes) capable

of being washed without deteriorating

WASHAWAY another word for ► washout

WASHBAG, -S n small bag for carrying toiletries when travelling

WASHBALL n ball of soap

WASHBOWL same as > washbasin

WASHDAY, -S n day on which clothes and linen are washed, often the same day each week

WASHDOWN n the act of washing (oneself or something) down

WASHED ► wash

WASHEN ► wash

WASHER, -ED, -S n ring put under a nut or bolt or in a tap as a seal ▷ vb fit with a washer

WASHERY n plant where liquid is used to remove dirt from a mineral

WASHES ► wash

WASHHAND n as in washhand basin, washhand stand for the washing of hands

WASHIER ► washy

WASHIEST ► washy

WASHILY ► washy

WASHIN, -S n increase in the angle of attack of the wing towards the wing tip

WASHING, -S n clothes to be washed

WASHINS ► washin

WASHLAND n frequently-flooded plain

WASHOUT, -S n complete failure

WASHPOT, -S n pot for washing things in

WASHRAG, -S same as > washcloth

WASHROOM n toilet

WASHTUB, -S n tub or large container used for washing anything, esp clothes

WASHUP, -S n outcome of a process

WASHWIPE n windscreen spray-cleaning mechanism

WASHY, WASHIER, WASHIEST adj overdiluted or weak

WASM, -S n obsolete belief; an out-of-fashion 'ism'

WASP, -S n stinging insect with a slender black-and-yellow striped body

WASPIE, -S n tight-waisted corset

WASPIER ▶ waspy
WASPIES ▶ waspie
WASPIEST ▶ waspy
WASPILY ▶ wasp
WASPISH *adj* bad-tempered
WASPLIKE ▶ wasp
WASPNEST *n* nest of wasps
WASPS ▶ wasp
WASPY, WASPIER, WASPIEST
▶ **wasp**
WASSAIL, -S *n* formerly, festivity when much drinking took place ▷ *vb* drink health of (a person) at a wassail
WASSUP *sentence substitute* what is happening?
WAST, -S *singular form of the past tense of* ▶ **be**
WASTABLE ▶ waste
WASTAGE, -S *n* loss by wear or waste
WASTE, -D, -S, WASTINGS *vb* use pointlessly or thoughtlessly ▷ *n* act of wasting or state of being wasted ▷ *adj* rejected as worthless or surplus to requirements
WASTEBIN *n* bin for rubbish
WASTED ▶ waste
WASTEFUL *adj* extravagant
WASTEL, -S *n* fine bread or cake
WASTELOT *n* piece of waste ground in a city
WASTELS ▶ wastel
WASTER, -ED, -S *vb* waste ▷ *n* layabout
WASTERIE *same as* ▶ **wastery**
WASTERS ▶ waster
WASTERY *n* extravagance
WASTES ▶ waste
WASTEWAY *n* open ditch
WASTFULL *obsolete form of* ▶ **wasteful**
WASTING *adj* reducing the vitality and strength of the body
WASTINGS ▶ waste
WASTNESS *same as* > **wasteness**
WASTREL, -S *n* lazy or worthless person
WASTRIE, -S *same as* ▶ **wastery**
WASTRIFE *n* wastefulness
WASTRY *n* wastefulness
WASTS ▶ wast
WAT, -S, -TER, -TEST *adj* wet
WATAP, -S *n* stringy thread made from the roots of conifers by Native Americans
WATAPE, -S *same as* ▶ **watap**
WATAPS ▶ watap

WATCH, -ED, -ES, -ING *vb* look at closely ▷ *n* portable timepiece for the wrist or pocket
WATCHA *interj* greeting meaning 'what are you?'
WATCHBOX *n* sentry's box
WATCHCRY *n* slogan used to rally support
WATCHDOG *n* dog kept to guard property
WATCHED ▶ watch
WATCHER, -S *n* person who watches
WATCHES ▶ watch
WATCHET, -S *n* shade of blue
WATCHEYE *n* eye with a light-coloured iris
WATCHFUL *adj* vigilant or alert
WATCHING ▶ watch
WATCHMAN, WATCHMEN *n* man employed to guard a building or property
WATCHOUT *n* lookout
WATE ▶ wit
WATER, -ED, -ING, -S *n* clear colourless tasteless liquid that falls as rain and forms rivers etc ▷ *vb* put water on or into
WATERAGE *n* transportation of cargo by means of ships, or the charges for such transportation
WATERBED *n* watertight mattress filled with water
WATERBUS *n* boat offering regular transport service
WATERDOG *n* dog trained to hunt in water
WATERED ▶ water
WATERER, -S ▶ water
WATERHEN *another name for* > **gallinule**
WATERIER ▶ watery
WATERILY ▶ watery
WATERING ▶ water
WATERISH ▶ water
WATERJET *n* jet of water
WATERLOG *vb* flood with water
WATERLOO *n* total defeat
WATERMAN, WATERMEN *n* skilled boatman
WATERPOX *n* chickenpox
WATERS ▶ water
WATERSKI *vb* ski on water towed behind motorboat
WATERWAY *n* river, canal, or other navigable channel used as a means of travel or transport
WATERY, WATERIER *adj* of, like, or containing water
WATS ▶ wat

WATT, -S *n* unit of power
WATTAGE, -S *n* electrical power expressed in watts
WATTAPE, -S *same as* ▶ **watap**
WATTER ▶ wat
WATTEST ▶ wat
WATTHOUR *n* unit of energy equal to the power of one watt operating for an hour
WATTLE, -S, WATTLING *n* branches woven over sticks to make a fence ▷ *adj* made of, formed by, or covered with wattle ▷ *vb* construct from wattle
WATTLED
WATTLESS ▶ watt
WATTLING ▶ wattle
WATTS ▶ watt
WAUCHT, -ED, -S *same as* ▶ **waught**
WAUFF, -ED, -ING, -S *same as* ▶ **waff**
WAUGH, -ED, -ING, -S *vb* bark
WAUGHT, -ED, -S *vb* drink in large amounts
WAUK, -ED, -ING, -S *vb* full (cloth)
WAUKER -S
WAUKMILL *same as* > **waulkmill**
WAUKRIFE *variant of* ▶ **wakerife**
WAUKS ▶ wauk
WAUL, -ED, -S *vb* cry or wail plaintively like a cat
WAULING -S
WAULK, -ED, -ING, -S *same as* ▶ **wauk**
WAULKER -S
WAULS ▶ waul
WAUR, -ED, -ING, -S, -ST *obsolete form of* ▶ **war**
WAVE, -D, -S *vb* move the hand to and fro as a greeting or signal ▷ *n* moving ridge on water
WAVEBAND *n* range of wavelengths or frequencies used for a particular type of radio transmission
WAVED ▶ wave
WAVEFORM *n* shape of the graph of a wave or oscillation obtained by plotting the value of some changing quantity against time
WAVELESS ▶ wave
WAVELET, -S *n* small wave
WAVELIKE ▶ wave
WAVEOFF, -S *n* signal or instruction to an aircraft not to land
WAVER, -ED, -S *vb* hesitate or be irresolute ▷ *n* act or an

W

instance of wavering

WAVERER -S

WAVERIER ► wavery

WAVERING ► waver

WAVEROUS *same as* ► **wavery**

WAVERS ► waver

WAVERY, WAVERIER *adj* lacking firmness

WAVES ► wave

WAVESON, -S *n* goods floating on waves after shipwreck

WAVEY, -S *n* snow goose or other wild goose

WAVICLE, -S *n* origin of wave

WAVIER ► wavy

WAVIES ► wavy

WAVIEST ► wavy

WAVILY ► wavy

WAVINESS ► wavy

WAVING, -S ► wave

WAVY, WAVIER, WAVIES, WAVIEST *adj* having curves ▷ *n* snow goose or other wild goose

WAW, -S another name for ► **vav**

WAWA, -ED, -ING, -S *n* speech ▷ *vb* speak

WAWE, -S *same as* ► **waw**

WAWL, -ED, -S *same as* ► **waul**

WAWLING -S

WAWS ► waw

WAX, -ED, -ES, WOX, WOXEN *n* solid shiny fatty or oily substance used for sealing, making candles, etc ▷ *vb* coat or polish with wax

WAXABLE

WAXBERRY *n* waxy fruit of the wax myrtle or the snowberry

WAXBILL, -S *n* any of various chiefly African finchlike weaverbirds

WAXCLOTH another name for ► **oilcloth**

WAXED ► wax

WAXEN *adj* made of or like wax

WAXER, -S ► wax

WAXES ► wax

WAXEYE, -S *n* small New Zealand bird

WAXIER ► waxy

WAXIEST ► waxy

WAXILY ► waxy

WAXINESS ► waxy

WAXING, -S ► wax

WAXLIKE ► wax

WAXPLANT *n* climbing shrub of E Asia and Australia

WAXWEED, -S *n* type of wild flower

WAXWING, -S *n* type of songbird

WAXWORK, -S *n* lifelike wax model of a (famous) person

WAXWORM, -S *n* wax moth larva

WAXY, WAXIER, WAXIEST *adj* resembling wax in colour, appearance, or texture

WAY, -ED, -ING, -S *n* manner or method ▷ *vb* travel

WAYANG, -S *n* type of Indonesian performance with dancers or puppets

WAYBILL, -S *n* document stating the nature, origin, and destination of goods being transported

WAYBOARD *n* thin geological seam separating larger strata

WAYBREAD *n* plantain

WAYED ► way

WAYFARE, -D, -S *vb* travel

WAYFARER *n* traveller

WAYFARES ► wayfare

WAYGOING *n* leaving

WAYGONE *adj* travel-weary

WAYGOOSE *same as* ► **wayzgoose**

WAYING ► way

WAYLAY, WAYLAID, -S *vb* lie in wait for and accost or attack

WAYLAYER

WAYLEAVE *n* access to property granted by a landowner for payment

WAYLEGGO *interj* away here! let go!

WAYLESS ► way

WAYMARK, -S *n* symbol or signpost marking the route of a footpath ▷ *vb* mark out with waymarks

WAYMENT, -S *vb* express grief

WAYPOINT *n* stopping point on route

WAYPOST, -S *n* signpost

WAYS ► way

WAYSIDE, -S *n* side of a road

WAYWARD *adj* erratic, selfish, or stubborn

WAYWISER *n* device for measuring distance

WAYWODE, -S *n* Slavonic governor

WAYWORN *adj* worn or tired by travel

WAZ *same as* ► **wazz**

WAZIR, -S another word for ► **vizier**

WAZOO, -S *n* slang word for person's bottom

WAZZ, -ED, -ES, -ING *vb* urinate ▷ *n* act of urinating

WAZZOCK, -S *n* foolish or annoying person

WE *pron* speaker or writer and one or more others

WEAK, -ER, -EST *adj* lacking strength

WEAKEN, -ED, -S *vb* make or become weak

WEAKENER

WEAKER ► weak

WEAKEST ► weak

WEAKFISH *n* any of several sea trouts

WEAKISH ► weak

WEAKLIER ► weakly

WEAKLING *n* feeble person or animal

WEAKLY, WEAKLIER *adv* feebly ▷ *adj* weak or sickly

WEAKNESS *n* being weak

WEAKON, -S *n* subatomic particle

WEAKSIDE *n* (in basketball) side of court away from ball

WEAL, -S *n* raised mark left on the skin by a blow

WEALD, -S *n* open or forested country

WEALS ► weal

WEALSMAN, WEALSMEN *n* statesman

WEALTH, -S *n* state of being rich

WEALTHY *adj* possessing wealth

WEAMB, -S *same as* ► **wame**

WEAN, -ED, -S *vb* accustom (a baby or young mammal) to food other than mother's milk

WEANEL, -S *n* recently-weaned child or animal

WEANER, -S *n* person or thing that weans

WEANING, -S ► wean

WEANLING *n* child or young animal recently weaned

WEANS ► wean

WEAPON, -S *vb* arm ▷ *n* object used in fighting

WEAPONED

WEAPONRY *n* weapons collectively

WEAPONS ► weapon

WEAR, -ED, -INGS, -S, WORE, WORN *vb* have on the body as clothing or ornament ▷ *n* clothes suitable for a particular time or purpose

WEARABLE *adj* suitable for wear or able to be worn ▷ *n* any garment that can be worn

WEARED ► wear

WEARER, -S ► wear

WEARIED ► weary

WEARIER ► weary
WEARIES ► weary
WEARIEST ► weary
WEARIFUL same as
> wearisome
WEARILY ► weary
WEARING adj tiring ▷ n act
of wearing
WEARINGS ► wear
WEARISH adj withered
WEARS ► wear
**WEARY, WEARIED,
WEARIER, WEARIES,
WEARIEST** adj tired or
exhausted ▷ vb make or
become weary
WEARYING
WEASAND, -S former name
for the ► **trachea**
WEASEL, -ED, -S n small
carnivorous mammal with a
long body and short legs ▷ vb
use ambiguous language to
avoid speaking directly or
honestly
WEASELER
WEASELLY
WEASELY
WEASON, -S Scots form of
► **weasand**
WEATHER, -S n day-to-day
atmospheric conditions of
a place ▷ vb (cause to) be
affected by the weather
WEAVE, -D, -S, WOVE vb
make (fabric) by interlacing
(yarn) on a loom
WEAVER, -S n person who
weaves, esp as a means of
livelihood
WEAVES ► weave
WEAVING, -S ► weave
WEAZAND, -S same as
► **weasand**
WEAZEN, -ED, -S same as
► **wizen**
WEB, -BED, -S n net spun by a
spider ▷ vb cover with or as if
with a web
WEBAPP, -S n application
program that is accessed on
the internet
WEBBED ► web
WEBBIE, -S n person who is
well versed in the use of the
World Wide Web
WEBBIER ► webby
WEBBIES ► webbie
WEBBIEST ► webby
WEBBING, -S n anything that
forms a web
**WEBBY, WEBBIER,
WEBBIEST** adj of, relating
to, resembling, or consisting
of a web

WEBCAM, -S n camera that
transmits images over the
internet
WEBCAST, -S n broadcast of
an event over the internet
▷ vb make such a broadcast
WEBCHAT, -S n real time
conversation over the
internet
WEBER, -S n SI unit of
magnetic flux
WEBFED adj (of printing
press) printing from rolls of
paper
WEBFOOT, WEBFEET n foot
having the toes connected by
folds of skin
WEBHEAD, -S n person who
uses the internet a lot
**WEBIFY, WEBIFIED,
WEBIFIES** vb convert
(information) for display on
the internet
WEBINAR, -S n interactive
seminar conducted over the
World Wide Web
WEBISODE n episode (of a
television series) intended for
on-line viewing
WEBLESS ► web
WEBLIKE ► web
WEBLISH n shorthand form
of English that is used in text
messaging, chat rooms, etc
WEBLOG, -S n person's online
journal
WEBMAIL, -S n system of
electronic mail accessed mail
via the internet
WEBPAGE, -S n page on
website
WEBRING, -S n group of
websites organized in a
circular structure
WEBS ► web
WEBSITE, -S n group of
connected pages on the
World Wide Web
WEBSPACE n storage space
on a web server
WEBSTER, -S archaic word for
► **weaver**
WEBWHEEL n wheel
containing a plate or web
instead of spokes
WEBWORK, -S n work done
using the World Wide Web
WEBWORM, -S n type of
caterpillar
WEBZINE, -S n magazine
published on the Internet
WECHT, -ED, -ING, -S n
agricultural tool ▷ vb
winnow (corn)
WED, -DED, -DING, -S vb
marry

WEDDER, -ED, -S dialect form
of ► **weather**
WEDDING, -S ► wed
WEDEL, -ED, -ING, -S variant
of ► **wedeln**
WEDELN, -ED, -S n succession
of high-speed turns
performed in skiing ▷ vb
perform a wedeln
WEDELS ► wedel
WEDGE, -D, -S n piece of
material thick at one end and
thin at the other ▷ vb fasten
or split with a wedge
WEDGIE, -S n wedge-heeled
shoe
WEDGIER ► wedgy
WEDGIES ► wedgie
WEDGIEST ► wedgy
WEDGING, -S ► wedge
**WEDGY, WEDGIER,
WEDGIEST ►** wedge
WEDLOCK, -S n marriage
WEDS ► wed
WEE, -ING, -R, -S, -ST adj
small or short ▷ n instance
of urinating ▷ vb urinate
WEED, -ED n plant growing
where undesired ▷ vb clear
of weeds
WEEDBED, -S n body of water
having lots of weeds
WEEDED ► weed
WEEDER, -S ► weed
WEEDERY n weed-ridden
area
WEEDIER ► weedy
WEEDIEST ► weedy
WEEDILY ► weedy
WEEDING, -S ► weed
WEEDLESS ► weed
WEEDLIKE ► weed
WEEDLINE n edge of a
weedbed
WEEDS pl n widow's
mourning clothes
**WEEDY, WEEDIER,
WEEDIEST** adj (of a person)
thin and weak
WEEING ► wee
WEEJUNS pl n moccasin-style
shoes for casual wear
WEEK, -S n period of seven
days, esp one beginning on
a Sunday ▷ adv seven days
before or after a specified day
WEEKDAY, -S n any day of
the week except Saturday or
Sunday
WEEKE, -S same as ► **wick**
WEEKEND n Saturday and
Sunday ▷ vb spend or pass a
weekend
WEEKENDS adv at the
weekend, esp regularly or
during every weekend

W

WEEKES ► weeke
WEEKLIES ► weekly
WEEKLONG adj lasting a week
WEEKLY, WEEKLIES adv happening, done, etc once a week ▷ n newspaper or magazine published once a week ▷ adj happening once a week or every week
WEEKS ► week
WEEL, -S Scot word for ► well
WEEM, -S n underground home
WEEN, -ED, -ING, -S vb think or imagine (something)
WEENIE, -S adj very small ▷ n wiener
WEENIER ► weenie
WEENIES ► weenie
WEENIEST ► weeny
WEENING ► ween
WEENS ► ween
WEENSY, WEENSIER same as ► weeny
WEENY, WEENIER, WEENIEST adj very small
WEEP, -S, WEPT vb shed tears ▷ n spell of weeping
WEEPER, -S n person who weeps, esp a hired mourner
WEEPHOLE n small drain hole in wall
WEEPIE same as ► weepy
WEEPIER ► weepy
WEEPIES ► weepy
WEEPIEST ► weepy
WEEPILY ► weepy
WEEPING, -S adj (of plants) having slender hanging branches
WEEPS ► weep
WEEPY, WEEPIER, WEEPIES, WEEPIEST adj liable to cry ▷ n sentimental film or book
WEER ► wee
WEES ► wee
WEEST ► wee
WEET, -ER, -EST, -ING, -S dialect form of ► wet
WEETE, -D same as ► wit
WEETEN same as ► wit
WEETER ► weet
WEETEST ► weet
WEETING ► weet
WEETLESS obsolete variant of ► witless
WEETS ► weet
WEEVER, -S n type of small fish
WEEVIL, -S n small beetle that eats grain etc
WEEVILED same as ► weeviled
WEEVILLY another word for ► weeviled
WEEVILS ► weevil

WEEVILY another word for ► weevilled
WEEWEE, -D, -S vb urinate
WEFT, -ED, -ING, -S n cross threads in weaving ▷ vb form weft
WEFTAGE, -S n texture
WEFTE, -S n forsaken child
WEFTED ► weft
WEFTES ► wefte
WEFTING ► weft
WEFTS ► weft
WEFTWISE adv in the direction of the weft
WEID, -S n sudden illness
WEIGELA, -S n type of shrub
WEIGELIA same as ► weigela
WEIGH, WAID, WAIDE, -ED, -ING, -S vb have a specified weight
WEIGHAGE n duty paid for weighing goods
WEIGHED ► weigh
WEIGHER, -S ► weigh
WEIGHING ► weigh
WEIGHMAN, WEIGHMEN n person responsible for weighing goods
WEIGHS ► weigh
WEIGHT, -ED, -S n heaviness of an object ▷ vb add weight to
WEIGHTER
WEIGHTY adj important or serious
WEIL, -S n whirlpool
WEINER, -S same as ► wiener
WEIR, -ED, -ING, -S vb ward off ▷ n river dam
WEIRD, -ED, -ER, -EST, -ING, -S adj strange or bizarre ▷ vb warn beforehand
WEIRDIE, -S same as ► weirdo
WEIRDING ► weird
WEIRDLY ► weird
WEIRDO, -ES; -S n peculiar person
WEIRDS ► weird
WEIRDY n weird person
WEIRED ► weir
WEIRING ► weir
WEIRS ► weir
WEISE, -D, -S, WEISING same as ► wise
WEIZE, -D, -S, WEIZING same as ► wise
WEKA, -S n flightless New Zealand rail
WELAWAY same as ► wellaway
WELCH, -ED, -ES, -ING same as ► welsh
WELCHER -S
WELCOME, -D, -S vb greet with pleasure ▷ n kindly

greeting ▷ adj received gladly
WELCOMER
WELD, -ED, -S vb join (pieces of metal or plastic) by softening with heat ▷ n welded joint
WELDABLE
WELDER -S
WELDING, -S ► weld
WELDLESS ► weld
WELDMENT n unit composed of welded pieces
WELDMESH n type of fencing consisting of wire mesh reinforced by welding
WELDOR, -S ► weld
WELDS ► weld
WELFARE, -S n wellbeing
WELK, -ED, -ING, -S vb wither; dry up
WELKE, -S obsolete form of ► welk
WELKED ► welk
WELKES ► welke
WELKIN, -S n sky, heavens, or upper air
WELKING ► welk
WELKINS ► welkin
WELKS ► welk
WELKT adj twisted
WELL, -ED, -ING, -INGS, -S adv satisfactorily ▷ adj in good health ▷ interj exclamation of surprise, interrogation, etc ▷ n hole sunk into the earth to reach water, oil, or gas ▷ vb flow upwards or outwards
WELLADAY interj alas!
WELLAWAY interj alas!
WELLBORN adj having been born into a wealthy family
WELLCURB n stone surround at top of well
WELLDOER n moral person
WELLED ► well
WELLHEAD n source of a well or stream
WELLHOLE n well shaft
WELLIE n wellington boot
WELLIES ► welly
WELLING ► well
WELLINGS ► well
WELLNESS n state of being in good physical and mental health
WELLS ► well
WELLSITE n site of well
WELLY, WELLIES n energy or commitment
WELS n type of catfish
WELSH, -ED, -ES, -ING vb fail to pay a debt or fulfil an obligation
WELSHER -S
WELT, -ED, -S same as ► weal

WELTER, -ED, -S *n* jumbled mass ▷ *vb* roll about, writhe, or wallow

WELTING, -S ► welt

WELTS ► welt

WEM, -S *same as* **► wame**

WEMB, -S *same as* **► wame**

WEMS ► wem

WEN, -S *n* cyst on the scalp

WENA *pron* South African word for you

WENCH, -ES *n* young woman

WEND, -ED, -ING, -S *vb* go or travel

WENDIGO, -S *n* evil spirit or cannibal

WENDING ► wend

WENDS ► wend

WENGE, -S *n* type of tree found in central and West Africa

WENNIER ► wenny

WENNIEST ► wenny

WENNISH ► wen

WENNY, WENNIER, WENNIEST ► wen

WENS ► wen

WENT, -S *n* path

WEPT ► weep

WERE *vb* form of the past tense of **be**

WEREGILD *same as* **► wergild**

WEREWOLF *n* (in folklore) person who can turn into a wolf

WERGELD, -S *same as* **► wergild**

WERGELT, -S *same as* **► wergild**

WERGILD, -S *n* price set on a man's life, to be paid as compensation by his slayer

WERO, -S *n* challenge made by an armed Māori warrior to a visitor to a marae

WERRIS, -ES *slang word for* > **urination**

WERSH, -ER, -EST *adj* tasteless

WERT *singular form of the past tense of* **► be**

WERWOLF *same as* **► werewolf**

WESAND, -S *same as* **► weasand**

WESKIT, -S *informal word for* > **waistcoat**

WESSAND, -S *same as* **► weasand**

WEST, -ED, -S *n* part of the horizon where the sun sets ▷ *adj* n the west ▷ *adv* in, to, or towards the west ▷ *vb* move in westerly direction

WESTER, -ED, -S *vb* move or appear to move towards the west ▷ *n* strong wind or storm from the west

WESTERLY *adj* of or in the west ▷ *adv* towards the west ▷ *n* wind blowing from the west

WESTERN, -S *adj* of or in the west ▷ *n* film or story about cowboys in the western US

WESTERS ► wester

WESTIE, -S *n* insulting word for a young working-class person from the western suburbs of Sydney

WESTING, -S *n* movement, deviation, or distance covered in a westerly direction

WESTLIN *Scots word for* **► western**

WESTLINS *adv* to or in west

WESTMOST *adj* most western

WESTS ► west

WESTWARD *adv* towards the west ▷ *n* westward part or direction ▷ *adj* moving, facing, or situated in the west

WET, -S, -TED, -TEST, -TING, -TINGS *adj* covered or soaked with water or another liquid ▷ *n* moisture or rain ▷ *vb* make wet

WETA, -S *n* type of wingless insect

WETHER, -S *n* male sheep

WETLAND, -S *n* area of marshy land

WETLY ► wet

WETNESS *n* the state of being wet

WETPROOF *adj* waterproof

WETS ► wet

WETSUIT, -S *n* body suit for diving

WETTABLE ► wet

WETTED ► wet

WETTER, -S ► wet

WETTEST ► wet

WETTIE, -S *n* wetsuit

WETTING ► wet

WETTINGS ► wet

WETTISH ► wet

WETWARE, -S *n* humorous term for the brain

WEX, -ED, -ES, -ING *obsolete form of* **► wax**

> **Wex** is an old word for **wax**, in the sense of grow. It gives a very good score for a three-letter word, and can be extended to **wexe**.

WEXE *obsolete form of* **► wax**

WEXED ► wex

WEXES ► wex

WEXING ► wex

WEY, -S *n* measurement of weight

WEYARD *obsolete form of* **► weird**

WEYS ► wey

WEYWARD *obsolete form of* **► weird**

WEZAND, -S *obsolete form of* **► weasand**

WHA *Scot word for* **► who**

WHACK, -ED, -S *vb* strike with a resounding blow ▷ *n* such a blow

WHACKER -S

WHACKIER ► whacky

WHACKING *adj* huge ▷ *n* severe beating ▷ *adv* extremely

WHACKO, -ES, -S *n* mad person

WHACKS ► whack

WHACKY, WHACKIER *variant spelling of* **► wacky**

WHAE *same as* **► wha**

WHAISLE, -D, -S *Scots form of* **► wheeze**

WHAIZLE, -D, -S *same as* **► whaisle**

WHAKAIRO *n* art of carving

WHALE, -D, -S *n* large fish-shaped sea mammal ▷ *vb* hunt for whales

WHALEMAN, WHALEMEN *n* person employed in whaling

WHALER, -S *n* ship or person involved in whaling

WHALERY *n* whaling

WHALES ► whale

WHALING, -S *n* hunting of whales for food and oil ▷ *adv* extremely

WHALLY *adj* (of eyes) with light-coloured irises

WHAM, -MED, -MING, -S *interj* expression indicating suddenness or forcefulness ▷ *n* forceful blow or impact ▷ *vb* strike or cause to strike with great force

WHAMMIES ► whammy

WHAMMING ► wham

WHAMMO, -S *n* sound of a sudden collision

WHAMMY, WHAMMIES *n* devastating setback

WHAMO *same as* **► whammo**

WHAMPLE, -S *n* strike

WHAMS ► wham

WHANAU, -S *n* (in Māori societies) a family, esp an extended family

WHANG, -ED, -ING, -S *vb* strike or be struck so as to

W

cause a resounding noise ▷ *n* resounding noise produced by a heavy blow

WHANGAM, -S *n* imaginary creature

WHANGED ▶ **whang**

WHANGEE, -S *n* tall woody grass grown for its stems, which are used for bamboo canes

WHANGING ▶ **whang**

WHANGS ▶ **whang**

WHAP, -PED, -PING, -S *same as* ▶ **whop**

WHAPPER, -S *same as* ▶ **whopper**

WHAPPING ▶ **whap**

WHAPS ▶ **whap**

WHARE, -S *n* Māori hut or dwelling place

WHARENUI *n* (in New Zealand) meeting house

WHARES ▶ **whare**

WHARF, -ED, -ING, -S *n* platform at a harbour for loading and unloading ships ▷ *vb* put (goods, etc) on a wharf

WHARFAGE *n* accommodation for ships at wharves

WHARFED ▶ **wharf**

WHARFIE, -S *n* person employed to load and unload ships

WHARFING ▶ **wharf**

WHARFS ▶ **wharf**

WHARVE, -S *n* wooden disc or wheel on a shaft serving as a flywheel or pulley

WHAT, -S *pron* which thing ▷ *interj* exclamation of anger, surprise, etc ▷ *adv* in which way, how much ▷ *n* part; portion

WHATA, -S *n* building on stilts or a raised platform for storing provisions

WHATCHA *interj* greeting meaning 'what are you?'

WHATEN *adj* what; what kind of

WHATEVER *pron* everything or anything that ▷ *adj* intensive form of *what* ▷ *determiner* intensive form of *what* ▷ *interj* expression used to show indifference or dismissal

WHATEVS *interj* whatever

WHATNA *another word for* ▶ **whaten**

WHATNESS *n* what something is

WHATNOT, -S *n* similar unspecified thing

WHATS ▶ **what**

WHATSIS *US form of* ▶ **whatsit**

WHATSIT, -S *n* person or thing the name of which is temporarily forgotten

WHATSO *adj* of whatever kind

WHATTEN *same as* ▶ **whaten**

WHAUP, -S *n* curlew

WHAUR, -S *Scot word for* ▶ **where**

WHEAL, -S *same as* ▶ **weal**

WHEAR *obsolete variant of* ▶ **where**

WHEARE *obsolete variant of* ▶ **where**

WHEAT, -S *n* grain used in making flour, bread, and pasta

WHEATEAR *n* small songbird

WHEATEN, -S *n* type of dog ▷ *adj* made of the grain or flour of wheat

WHEATIER ▶ **wheaty**

WHEATS ▶ **wheat**

WHEATY, WHEATIER *adj* having a wheat-like taste

WHEE *interj* exclamation of joy, thrill, etc

WHEECH, -ED, -S *vb* move quickly

WHEEDLE, -D, -S *vb* coax or cajole

WHEEDLER

WHEEL, -ING, -S *n* disc that revolves on an axle ▷ *vb* push or pull (something with wheels)

WHEELED *adj* having or equipped with a wheel or wheels

WHEELER, -S *n* horse or other draught animal nearest the wheel

WHEELIE, -S *n* manoeuvre on a bike in which the front wheel is raised off the ground

WHEELIER ▶ **wheely**

WHEELIES ▶ **wheelie**

WHEELING ▶ **wheel**

WHEELMAN, WHEELMEN *n* helmsman

WHEELS ▶ **wheel**

WHEELY, WHEELIER *adj* resembling a wheel

WHEEN, -S *n* few

WHEENGE, -D, -S *Scots form of* ▶ **whinge**

WHEENS ▶ **wheen**

WHEEP, -ED, -ING, -S *vb* fly quickly and lightly

WHEEPLE, -D, -S *vb* whistle weakly

WHEEPS ▶ **wheep**

WHEESH, -ED, -ES *vb* silence (a person, noise, etc) or be silenced

WHEESHT, -S *same as* ▶ **wheesh**

WHEEZE, -D, -S, WHEEZING *vb* breathe with a hoarse whistling noise ▷ *n* wheezing sound

WHEEZER -S

WHEEZIER ▶ **wheezy**

WHEEZILY ▶ **wheeze**

WHEEZING ▶ **wheeze**

WHEEZLE, -D, -S *vb* make hoarse breathing sound

WHEEZY, WHEEZIER ▶ **wheeze**

WHEFT, -S *same as* ▶ **waft**

WHELK, -S *n* edible snail-like shellfish

WHELKED *adj* having or covered with whelks

WHELKIER ▶ **whelky**

WHELKS ▶ **whelk**

WHELKY, WHELKIER ▶ **whelk**

WHELM, -ED, -ING, -S *vb* engulf entirely with or as if with water

WHELP, -ED, -ING, -S *n* pup or cub ▷ *vb* (of an animal) give birth

WHEMMLE, -D, -S *vb* overturn

WHEN, -S *adv* at what time? ▷ *pron* at which time ▷ *n* question of when

WHENAS *conj* while; inasmuch as

WHENCE, -S *n* point of origin ▷ *adv* from what place or source ▷ *pron* from what place, cause, or origin

WHENEVER *adv* at whatever time

WHENS ▶ **when**

WHENUA, -S *n* land

WHENWE, -S *n* White immigrant to South Africa from Zimbabwe

WHERE, -S *adv* in, at, or to what place? ▷ *pron* in, at, or to which place ▷ *n* question as to the position, direction, or destination of something

WHEREAS *n* testimonial introduced by whereas

WHEREAT *adv* at or to which place

WHEREBY *pron* by which ▷ *adv* how? by what means?

WHEREFOR *adv* for which ▷ *n* explanation or reason

WHEREIN *adv* in what place or respect? ▷ *pron* in which place or thing

WHEREOF adv of what or which person or thing? ▷ pron of which person or thing

WHEREON adv on what thing or place? ▷ pron on which thing, place, etc

WHEREOUT adv out of which

WHERES ► where

WHERESO adv in or to unspecified place

WHERETO adv towards what (place, end, etc)? ▷ pron which

WHEREVER adv at whatever place ▷ pron at, in, or to every place or point which

WHERRET, -S vb strike (someone) a blow ▷ n blow, esp a slap on the face

WHERRIED ► wherry

WHERRIES ► wherry

WHERRIT, -S vb worry or cause to worry

WHERRY, WHERRIED, WHERRIES n any of certain kinds of half-decked commercial boats ▷ vb travel in a wherry

WHERVE, -S same as ► wharve

WHET, -S, -TED, -TING vb sharpen (a tool) ▷ n act of whetting

WHETHER conj used to introduce any indirect question

WHETS ► whet

WHETTED ► whet

WHETTER, -S ► whet

WHETTING ► whet

WHEUGH, -ED, -S same as ► whew

WHEW, -ED, -ING, -S interj exclamation expressing relief, delight, etc ▷ vb express relief

WHEY, -IER, -IEST, -S n watery liquid that separates from the curd when milk is clotted

WHEYEY

WHEYFACE n pale bloodless face

WHEYIER ► whey

WHEYIEST ► whey

WHEYISH ► whey

WHEYLIKE ► whey

WHEYS ► whey

WHICH pron used to request or refer to a choice from different possibilities ▷ adj used with a noun in requesting that a particular thing is further identified or distinguished

WHICKER, -S vb (of a horse) to whinny or neigh

WHID, -DED, -DING, -S vb move quickly

WHIDAH, -S same as ► whydah

WHIDDED ► whid

WHIDDER, -S vb move with force

WHIDDING ► whid

WHIDS ► whid

WHIFF, -ED, -ING, -S n puff of air or odour ▷ vb come, convey, or go in whiffs

WHIFFER -S

WHIFFET, -S n insignificant person

WHIFFIER ► whiffy

WHIFFING ► whiff

WHIFFLE, -D, -S vb think or behave in an erratic or unpredictable way

WHIFFLER n person who whiffles

WHIFFLES ► whiffle

WHIFFS ► whiff

WHIFFY, WHIFFIER adj smelly

WHIFT, -S n brief emission of air

WHIG, -GED, -GING, -S vb go quickly

WHILE, -D, WHILING n period of time

WHILERE adv a while ago

WHILES adv at times

WHILEVER conj as long as

WHILING ► while

WHILK archaic and dialect word for ► which

WHILLY, WHILLIED, WHILLIES vb influence by flattery

WHILOM adv formerly ▷ adj one-time

WHILST same as ► while

WHIM, -MED, -MING, -S n sudden fancy ▷ vb have a whim

WHIMBREL n small European curlew with a striped head

WHIMMED ► whim

WHIMMIER ► whimmy

WHIMMING ► whim

WHIMMY, WHIMMIER adj having whims

WHIMPER, -S vb cry in a soft whining way ▷ n soft plaintive whine

WHIMPLE, -D, -S same as ► wimple

WHIMS ► whim

WHIMSEY, -S same as ► whimsy

WHIMSIED ► whimsy

WHIMSIER ► whimsy

WHIMSIES ► whimsy

WHIMSILY ► whimsy

WHIMSY, WHIMSIER, WHIMSIES n capricious idea ▷ adj quaint, comical, or unusual

WHIN, -S n gorse

WHINCHAT n type of songbird

WHINE, -D, -S n high-pitched plaintive cry ▷ vb make such a sound

WHINER -S

WHINEY same as ► whiny

WHINGE, -D, -S, WHINGING vb complain ▷ n complaint

WHINGER -S

WHINGIER ► whingy

WHINGING ► whinge

WHINGY, WHINGIER adj complaining peevishly, whining

WHINIARD same as ► whinyard

WHINIER ► whiny

WHINIEST ► whiny

WHINING, -S ► whine

WHINNY, WHINNIED, WHINNIER, WHINNIES vb neigh softly ▷ n soft neigh ▷ adj covered in whin

WHINS ► whin

WHINY, WHINIER, WHINIEST adj high-pitched and plaintive

WHINYARD n sword

WHIO, -S n New Zealand mountain duck with blue plumage

WHIP, -PED, -PING, -S n cord attached to a handle, used for beating animals or people ▷ vb strike with a whip, strap, or cane

WHIPBIRD n any of several birds having a whistle ending in a whipcrack note

WHIPCAT, -S n tailor

WHIPCORD n strong worsted or cotton fabric with a diagonally ribbed surface

WHIPJACK n beggar imitating a sailor

WHIPLASH n quick lash of a whip

WHIPLESS adj without a whip

WHIPLIKE ► whip

WHIPPED ► whip

WHIPPER, -S ► whip

WHIPPET, -S n racing dog like a small greyhound

WHIPPIER ► whippy

WHIPPING ► whip

WHIPPIT, -S n small canister of nitrous oxide

WHIPPY, WHIPPIER adj springy

W

WHIPRAY, -S *n* stingray

WHIPS ► whip

WHIPSAW, -N, -S *n* any saw with a flexible blade, such as a bandsaw ▷ *vb* saw with a whipsaw

WHIPSTER *n* insignificant but pretentious or cheeky person, esp a young one

WHIPT *old past tense of* ► whip

WHIPTAIL *n* type of lizard

WHIPWORM *n* parasitic worm living in the intestines of mammals

WHIR, -RED, -RING, -S *n* prolonged soft swish or buzz ▷ *vb* make or cause to make a whir

WHIRL, -ED, -S *vb* spin or revolve ▷ *n* whirling movement

WHIRLBAT *n* thing moved with a whirl

WHIRLED ► whirl

WHIRLER, -S ► whirl

WHIRLIER ► whirly

WHIRLIES *pl n* illness induced by excessive use of alcohol

WHIRLING ► whirl

WHIRLS ► whirl

WHIRLY, WHIRLIER *adj* characterized by whirling

WHIRR, -S *same as* ► whir

WHIRRED ► whir

WHIRRET, -S *vb* strike with sharp blow

WHIRRIED ► whirry

WHIRRIER ► whirry

WHIRRIES ► whirry

WHIRRING ► whir

WHIRRS ► whirr

WHIRRY, WHIRRIED, WHIRRIER, WHIRRIES *vb* move quickly ▷ *adj* characteristic of a whir

WHIRS ► whir

WHIRTLE, -S *same as* ► wortle

WHISH, -ED, -ES, -ING *less common word for* ► swish

WHISHT, -ED, -S *interj* hush! be quiet! ▷ *adj* silent or still ▷ *vb* make or become silent

WHISK, -ED, -ING, -S *vb* move or remove quickly ▷ *n* quick movement

WHISKER, -S *n* any of the long stiff hairs on the face of a cat or other mammal

WHISKERY *adj* having whiskers

WHISKET, -S *same as* ► wisket

WHISKEY, -S *n* Irish or American whisky

WHISKIES ► whisky

WHISKING ► whisk

WHISKS ► whisk

WHISKY, WHISKIES *n* spirit distilled from fermented cereals

WHISPER, -S *vb* speak softly, without vibration of the vocal cords ▷ *n* soft voice **WHISPERY**

WHISS, -ED, -ES, -ING *vb* hiss

WHIST, -ED, -ING, -S *same as* ► whisht

WHISTLE, -D, -S *vb* produce a shrill sound ▷ *n* whistling sound

WHISTLER *n* person or thing that whistles

WHISTLES ► whistle

WHISTS ► whist

WHIT, -S *n* smallest particle

WHITE, -R, -ST *adj* of the colour of snow ▷ *n* colour of snow

WHITECAP *n* wave with a white broken crest

WHITED *adj as in* **whited sepulchre** hypocrite

WHITEFLY *n* tiny whitish insect that is harmful to greenhouse plants

WHITELY ► white

WHITEN, -ED, -S *vb* make or become white or whiter

WHITENER *n* substance that makes something white or whiter

WHITENS ► whiten

WHITEOUT *n* atmospheric condition in which blizzards or low clouds make it very difficult to see

WHITEPOT *n* custard or milk pudding

WHITER ► white

WHITES *pl n* white clothes, as worn for playing cricket

WHITEST ► white

WHITEY *same as* ► whity

WHITHER, -S *same as* ► wuther

WHITIER ► whity

WHITIEST ► whity

WHITING, -S *n* edible sea fish

WHITISH ► white

WHITLING *n* type of trout

WHITLOW, -S *n* inflamed sore on a finger or toe, esp round a nail

WHITRACK *n* weasel or stoat

WHITRET, -S *same as* ► whittret

WHITRICK *n* dialect word for a male weasel

WHITS ► whit

WHITSTER *n* person who whitens clothes

WHITTAW, -S *same as* > whittawer

WHITTER, -S *variant spelling of* ► witter

WHITTLE, -D, -S *vb* cut or carve (wood) with a knife ▷ *n* knife, esp a large one **WHITTLER**

WHITTRET *n* male weasel

WHITY, WHITIER, WHITIEST *adj* of a white colour

WHIZ *same as* ► whizz

WHIZBANG *n* small-calibre shell

WHIZZ, -ED, -ES, -ING *vb* make a loud buzzing sound ▷ *n* loud buzzing sound

WHIZZER -S

WHIZZIER ► whizzy

WHIZZING ► whizz

WHIZZO *same as* ► whizzy

WHIZZY, WHIZZIER *adj* using sophisticated technology

WHO *pron* which person

WHOA *interj* command used to stop or slow down

WHODUNIT *same as* > whodunnit

WHOEVER *pron* any person who

WHOLE, -S *adj* containing all the elements or parts ▷ *n* complete thing or system

WHOLISM, -S *same as* ► holism

WHOLIST, -S *same as* ► holist

WHOLLY *adv* completely or totally

WHOLPHIN *n* whale-dolphin hybrid

WHOM *pron* objective form of *who*

WHOMBLE, -D, -S *same as* ► whemmle

WHOMEVER *pron* objective form of *whoever*

WHOMMLE, -D, -S *same as* ► whemmle

WHOMP, -ED, -ING, -S *vb* strike; thump

WHOMSO *pron* whom; whomever

WHOOBUB, -S *same as* ► hubbub

WHOOF, -ED, -ING, -S *same as* ► woof

WHOOMP, -S *n* sudden loud sound

WHOOMPH, -S *same as* ► whoomp

WHOOMPS ► whoomp

WHOOP, -ED, -ING *n* shout or cry to express excitement ▷ *vb* emit a whoop

WHOOPEE, -S *n* cry of joy

WHOOPER, -S *n* type of swan

WHOOPIE, -S *same as* ► whoopee

WHOOPING ► whoop

WHOOPLA, -S *n* commotion; fuss

WHOOPS *interj* exclamation of surprise or of apology

WHOOPSIE *n* animal excrement

WHOOSH, -ED, -ES *n* hissing or rushing sound ▷ *vb* make or move with a hissing or rushing sound

WHOOSIS *n* thingamajig

WHOOT, -ED, -ING, -S *obsolete variant of* ► hoot

WHOP, -PED, -S *vb* strike, beat, or thrash ▷ *n* heavy blow or the sound made by such a blow

WHOPPER, -S *n* anything unusually large

WHOPPING *n* beating as punishment ▷ *adj* unusually large ▷ *adv* extremely

WHOPS ► whop

WHORL, -ING, -S *n* ring of leaves or petals ▷ *vb* form a whorl or whorls

WHORLBAT *same as* ► whirlbat

WHORLED ► whorl

WHORLING ► whorl

WHORLS ► whorl

WHORT, -S *n* small shrub bearing blackish edible sweet berries

WHORTLE, -S *n* whortleberry

WHORTS ► whort

WHOSE *pron* of whom or of which ▷ *determiner* of whom? belonging to whom?

WHOSESO *adj* possessive form of whoso

WHOSEVER *pron* belonging to whoever

WHOSIS, -ES *n* thingamajig

WHOSIT, -S *n* object or person whose name is not known

WHOSO *archaic word for* ► whoever

WHOT *obsolete variant of* ► hot

WHOW, -ED, -ING, -S *interj* wow ▷ *vb* to wow

WHUMMLE, -D, -S *same as* ► whemmle

WHUMP, -ED, -ING, -S *vb* make a dull thud ▷ *n* dull thud

WHUP, -PED, -PING, -S *vb* defeat totally

WHY, -S *adv* for what reason ▷ *pron* because of which ▷ *n* reason, purpose, or cause of something

WHYDA, -S *same as* ► whydah

WHYDAH, -S *n* type of black African bird

WHYDAS ► whyda

WHYDUNIT *same as* > whydunnit

WHYEVER *adv* for whatever reason

WHYS ► why

WIBBLE, -D, -S, WIBBLING *vb* wobble

WICCA, -S *n* cult or practice of witchcraft

WICCAN, -S *n* member of wicca

WICCAS ► wicca

WICE *Scots form of* ► wise

WICH, -ES *n* variant of wych

WICK, -S *n* cord through a lamp or candle which carries fuel to the flame ▷ *adj* lively or active ▷ *vb* (of a material) draw in (water, fuel, etc)

WICKAPE, -S *same as* ► wicopy

WICKED, -ER, -S *adj* morally bad ▷ *n* wicked person

WICKEDLY

WICKEN, -S *same as* ► quicken

WICKER, -S *adj* made of woven cane ▷ *n* slender flexible twig or shoot, esp of willow

WICKERED

WICKET, -S *n* set of three cricket stumps and two bails

WICKIES ► wicky

WICKING, -S ► wick

WICKIUP, -S *n* crude shelter made of brushwood, mats, or grass and having an oval frame

WICKLESS ► wick

WICKS ► wick

WICKY, WICKIES *same as* ► quicken

WICKYUP, -S *same as* ► wickiup

WICOPY, WICOPIES *n* any of various North American trees, shrubs, or herbaceous plants

WIDDER, -S *same as* ► widow

WIDDIE *same as* ► widdy

WIDDIES ► widdy

WIDDLE, -D, -S, WIDDLING *vb* urinate ▷ *n* urine

WIDDY, WIDDIES *vb* rope made of twigs

WIDE, -R, -S, -ST *adj* large from side to side ▷ *adv* the full extent ▷ *n* (in cricket) a ball outside a batsman's reach

WIDEBAND *n* wide bandwidth transmission medium ▷ *adj* capable of transmitting on a wide bandwidth

WIDEBODY *n* aircraft with a wide fuselage

WIDELY ► wide

WIDEN, -ED, -S *vb* make or become wider

WIDENER, -S

WIDENESS ► wide

WIDENING *n* act of widening

WIDENS ► widen

WIDEOUT, -S *n* (in American football) player who catches passes from the quarterback

WIDER ► wide

WIDES ► wide

WIDEST ► wide

WIDGEON, -S *same as* ► wigeon

WIDGET, -S *n* any small device, the name of which is unknown or forgotten

WIDGIE, -S *n* female larrikin or bodgie

WIDISH ► wide

WIDOW, -ED, -ING, -S *n* woman whose spouse is dead and who has not remarried ▷ *vb* cause to become a widow

WIDOWER, -S *n* man whose spouse is dead and who has not remarried

WIDOWING ► widow

WIDOWMAN, WIDOWMEN *n* widower

WIDOWS ► widow

WIDTH, -S *n* distance from side to side

WIDTHWAY *adj* across the width

WIEL, -S *same as* ► weel

WIELD, -ED, -ING, -S *vb* hold and use (a weapon)

WIELDER, -S

WIELDIER ► wieldy

WIELDING ► wield

WIELDS ► wield

WIELDY, WIELDIER *adj* easily handled, used, or managed

WIELS ► wiel

WIENER, -S *n* kind of smoked beef or pork sausage, similar to a frankfurter

WIENIE, -S *same as* ► wiener

W

WIFE, -D, -S, WIFING, WIVES n woman to whom one is married ▷ vb marry

WIFEDOM, -S n state of being a wife

WIFEHOOD ► wife

WIFELESS ► wife

WIFELIER ► wifely

WIFELIKE ► wife

WIFELY, WIFELIER ► wife

WIFES ► wife

WIFEY, -S n wife

WIFIE, -S n woman

WIFING ► wife

WIFTY, WIFTIER, WIFTIEST adj scatterbrained

WIG, -GING, -GINGS, -S n artificial head of hair ▷ vb furnish with a wig

WIGAN, -S n stiff fabric

WIGEON, -S n duck found in marshland

WIGGED ► wig

WIGGERY n wigs

WIGGIER ► wiggy

WIGGIEST ► wiggy

WIGGING ► wig

WIGGINGS ► wig

WIGGLE, -D, -S, WIGGLING vb move jerkily from side to side ▷ n wiggling movement

WIGGLER -S

WIGGLIER ► wiggly

WIGGLING ► wiggle

WIGGLY, WIGGLIER ► wiggle

WIGGY, WIGGIER, WIGGIEST adj eccentric

WIGHT, -ED, -ING, -S vb blame ▷ n human being ▷ adj strong and brave

WIGHTLY adv swiftly

WIGHTS ► wight

WIGLESS ► wig

WIGLET, -S n small wig

WIGLIKE ► wig

WIGMAKER n person who makes wigs

WIGS ► wig

WIGWAG, -S vb move (something) back and forth ▷ n system of communication by flag semaphore

WIGWAM, -S n Native American's tent

WIKI, -S n website consisting mainly of user-generated content

WIKIUP, -S same as ► wickiup

WILCO interj expression indicating that the message just received will be complied with

WILD, -ED, -EST, -S same as ► wield

WILDCARD n person given entry to competition without qualifying

WILDCAT, -S n European wild animal like a large domestic cat ▷ adj risky and financially unsound ▷ vb drill for petroleum or natural gas in an area having no known reserves

WILDED ► wild

WILDER, -ED, -S vb lead or be led astray

WILDEST ► wild

WILDFIRE n highly flammable material, such as Greek fire, formerly used in warfare

WILDFOWL n wild bird that is hunted for sport or food

WILDING, -S n uncultivated plant

WILDISH ► wild

WILDLAND n land which has not been cultivated

WILDLIFE n wild animals and plants collectively

WILDLING same as ► wilding

WILDLY ► wild

WILDNESS ► wild

WILDS ► wild

WILDWOOD n wood or forest growing in a natural uncultivated state

WILE, -D, -S, WILING n trickery, cunning, or craftiness ▷ vb lure, beguile, or entice

WILEFUL adj deceitful

WILES ► wile

WILFUL adj headstrong or obstinate

WILFULLY

WILGA, -S n small drought-resistant tree of Australia

WILI, -S n spirit

WILIER ► wily

WILIEST ► wily

WILILY ► wily

WILINESS ► wily

WILING ► wile

WILIS ► wili

WILJA, -S same as ► wiltja

WILL, -EST, -S, WOULD vb used as an auxiliary to form the future tense or to indicate intention, ability, or expectation ▷ n strong determination

WILLABLE adj able to be wished or determined by the will

WILLED adj having a will as specified

WILLER, -S ► will

WILLEST ► will

WILLET, -S n large American shore bird

WILLEY, -ED, -S same as ► willy

WILLFUL same as ► wilful

WILLIAM, -S n as in **sweet william** flowering plant

WILLIE n informal word for a penis

WILLIED ► willy

WILLIES ► willy

WILLING adj ready or inclined (to do something)

WILLIWAU same as ► williwaw

WILLIWAW n sudden strong gust of cold wind blowing offshore from a mountainous coast

WILLOW, -S n tree with thin flexible branches ▷ vb open and clean (fibres) with rotating spikes

WILLOWED ► willow

WILLOWER n willow

WILLOWS ► willow

WILLOWY adj slender and graceful

WILLS ► will

WILLY, WILLIED, WILLIES, -ING vb clean in a willowing-machine

WILLYARD adj timid

WILLYART same as ► willyard

WILLYING ► willy

WILLYWAW same as ► williwaw

WILT, -ED, -ING, -S vb (cause to) become limp or lose strength ▷ n act of wilting or state of becoming wilted

WILTJA, -S n Aboriginal shelter

WILTS ► wilt

WILY, WILIER, WILIEST adj crafty or sly

WIMBLE, -D, -S, WIMBLING n any of a number of hand tools used for boring holes ▷ vb bore (a hole) with or as if with a wimble

WIMBREL, -S same as ► whimbrel

WIMMIN n common intentional literary misspelling spelling of 'women'

WIMP, -ED, -ING, -S n feeble ineffectual person ▷ vb as in **wimp out** fail to complete something through fear

WIMPIER ► wimpy

WIMPIEST ► wimpy

WIMPING ► wimp

WIMPISH ► wimp

W

WIMPLE, -D, -S, WIMPLING n garment framing the face, worn by medieval women and now by nuns ▷ vb ripple or cause to ripple or undulate

WIMPS ▶ wimp

WIMPY, WIMPIER, WIMPIEST ▶ wimp

WIN, -NED, -NINGS, -S vb come first in (a competition, fight, etc) ▷ n victory, esp in a game

WINCE, -D, -S vb draw back, as if in pain ▷ n wincing **WINCER -S**

WINCEY, -S n plain- or twill-weave cloth

WINCH, -ED, -ES, -ING n machine for lifting or hauling using a cable or chain wound round a drum ▷ vb lift or haul using a winch **WINCHER -S**

WINCHMAN, WINCHMEN n man who operates winch

WINCING, -S ▶ wince

WIND, -ED, -ING, -INGS, -S n current of air ▷ vb render short of breath

WINDABLE n able to be wound

WINDAC, -S same as ▶ windas

WINDAGE, -S n deflection of a projectile as a result of the effect of the wind

WINDAS, -ES n windlass

WINDBAG, -S n person who talks much but uninterestingly

WINDBELL n light bell made to be sounded by wind

WINDBILL n bill of exchange cosigned by a guarantor

WINDBLOW n trees uprooted by wind

WINDBURN n irritation and redness of the skin caused by exposure to wind

WINDED ▶ wind

WINDER, -S n person or device that winds, as an engine for hoisting the cages in a mine shaft

WINDFALL n unexpected good luck

WINDFLAW n squall

WINDGALL n soft swelling in the area of the fetlock joint of a horse

WINDGUN, -S n air gun

WINDIER ▶ windy

WINDIEST ▶ windy

WINDIGO, -S same as ▶ wendigo

WINDILY ▶ windy

WINDING ▶ wind

WINDINGS ▶ wind

WINDLASS n winch worked by a crank ▷ vb raise or haul (a weight, etc) by means of a windlass

WINDLE, -D, -S, WINDLING vb wind something round continuously

WINDLESS ▶ wind

WINDLING ▶ windle

WINDLOAD n force on a structure from wind

WINDMILL n machine for grinding or pumping driven by sails turned by the wind ▷ vb move or cause to move like the arms of a windmill

WINDOCK, -S same as ▶ winnock

WINDORE, -S n window

WINDOW, -ED, -S n opening in a wall to let in light or air ▷ vb furnish with windows

WINDOWY

WINDPACK n snow that has been compacted by the wind

WINDPIPE n tube linking the throat and the lungs

WINDRING adj winding

WINDROW, -S n long low ridge or line of hay or a similar crop ▷ vb put (hay or a similar crop) into windrows

WINDS ▶ wind

WINDSAIL n sail rigged as an air scoop over a hatch or companionway

WINDSES pl n ventilation shafts within mines

WINDSHIP n ship propelled by wind

WINDSLAB n crust formed on soft snow by the wind

WINDSOCK n cloth cone on a mast on an airfield to indicate wind direction

WINDSURF vb sail standing on a board equipped with a mast, sail, and boom

WINDUP, -S n prank or hoax

WINDWARD n direction from which the wind is blowing ▷ adj of or in the direction from which the wind blows ▷ adv towards the wind

WINDWAY, -S n part of wind instrument

WINDY, WINDIER, WINDIEST adj denoting a time or conditions in which there is a strong wind

WINE, -D, -S, WINING n alcoholic drink made from fermented grapes ▷ adj of a dark purplish-red colour

▷ vb give wine to

WINELESS

WINERY, WINERIES n place where wine is made

WINES ▶ wine

WINESAP, -S n variety of apple

WINESHOP n shop where wine is sold

WINESKIN n skin of a sheep or goat sewn up and used as a holder for wine

WINESOP, -S n old word for an alcoholic

WINEY adj having the taste or qualities of wine

WING, -ING, -S n one of the limbs or organs of a bird, insect, or bat that are used for flying ▷ vb fly

WINGBACK n football position

WINGBEAT n complete cycle of moving the wing by a bird in flight

WINGBOW, -S n distinctive band of colour marking the wing of a bird

WINGDING n noisy lively party or festivity

WINGE, -ING, -S same as ▶ whinge

WINGED adj furnished with wings

WINGEDLY

WINGEING ▶ winge

WINGER, -S n player positioned on a wing

WINGES ▶ winge

WINGIER ▶ wingy

WINGIEST ▶ wingy

WINGING ▶ wing

WINGLESS adj having no wings or vestigial wings

WINGLET, -S n small wing

WINGLIKE ▶ wing

WINGMAN, WINGMEN n player in the wing position in Australian Rules

WINGNUT, -S n nut with projections for gripping with the thumb and finger

WINGOVER n manoeuvre for reversing the direction of flight of an aircraft

WINGS ▶ wing

WINGSPAN n distance between the wing tips of an aircraft, bird, or insect

WINGSUIT n type of skydiving suit

WINGTIP, -S n outermost edge of a wing

WINGY, WINGIER, WINGIEST adj having wings

WINIER ▶ winy

W

WINIEST ► winy

WINING ► wine

WINISH ► wine

WINK, -ED, -S vb close and open (an eye) quickly as a signal ▷ n winking

WINKER, -S n person or thing that winks

WINKING, -S ► wink

WINKLE, -D, -S, WINKLING n shellfish with a spiral shell ▷ vb extract or prise out

WINKLER, -S n one who forces person or thing out

WINKLES ► winkle

WINKLING ► winkle

WINKS ► wink

WINLESS adj not having won anything

WINN, -S n penny

WINNA vb will not

WINNABLE ► win

WINNARD, -S n heron

WINNED ► win

WINNER, -S n person or thing that wins

WINNING adj (of a person) charming, attractive, etc

WINNINGS ► win

WINNLE, -S n machine for winding thread or yarn

WINNOCK, -S n window

WINNOW, -ED, -S vb separate (chaff) from (grain) ▷ n device for winnowing **WINNOWER**

WINNS ► winn

WINO, -ES, -S n destitute person who habitually drinks cheap wine

WINS ► win

WINSEY, -S same as ► wincey

WINSOME, -R adj charming or winning

WINTER, -ED, -S n coldest season ▷ vb spend the winter **WINTERER**

WINTERLY same as ► wintry

WINTERS ► winter

WINTERY same as ► wintry

WINTLE, -D, -S, WINTLING vb reel; stagger

WINTRIER ► wintry

WINTRILY ► wintry

WINTRY, WINTRIER adj of or like winter

WINY, WINIER, WINIEST same as ► winey

WINZE, -S n steeply inclined shaft, as for ventilation between levels

WIPE, -D, -S vb clean or dry by rubbing ▷ n wiping

WIPEABLE adj able to be wiped

WIPED ► wipe

WIPEOUT, -S n instance of wiping out

WIPER, -S n any piece of cloth, such as a handkerchief, towel, etc, used for wiping

WIPES ► wipe

WIPING, -S ► wipe

WIPPEN, -S n part of hammer action in piano

WIRABLE adj that can be wired

WIRE, -S n thin flexible strand of metal ▷ vb fasten with wire

WIRED adj excited or nervous

WIREDRAW, WIREDREW vb convert (metal) into wire by drawing through successively smaller dies

WIREHAIR n type of terrier

WIRELESS adj (of a computer network) connected by radio rather than by cables or fibre optics ▷ n old-fashioned name for radio ▷ vb send by wireless

WIRELIKE ► wire

WIRELINE n telegraph or telephone line

WIREMAN, WIREMEN n person who installs and maintains electric wiring, cables, etc

WIRER, -S n person who sets or uses wires to snare rabbits and similar animals

WIRES ► wire

WIRETAP, -S vb obtain information secretly via telegraph or telephone

WIREWAY, -S n tube for electric wires

WIREWORK n functional or decorative work made of wire

WIREWORM n destructive wormlike beetle larva

WIREWOVE adj woven out of wire

WIRIER ► wiry

WIRIEST ► wiry

WIRILDA, -S n SE Australian acacia tree with edible seeds

WIRILY ► wiry

WIRINESS ► wiry

WIRING, -S n system of wires ▷ adj used in wiring

WIRRA interj exclamation of sorrow or deep concern

WIRRAH, -S n Australian saltwater fish with bright blue spots

WIRRICOW same as ► worricow

WIRY, WIRIER, WIRIEST adj lean and tough

WIS, -SED, -SES, -SING vb know or suppose (something)

WISARD, -S obsolete spelling of ► wizard

WISDOM, -S n good sense and judgment

WISE, -D, -R, -S, -ST, WISING vb guide ▷ adj having wisdom ▷ n manner

WISED ► wise

WISEGUY, -S n person who wants to seem clever

WISELIER ► wise

WISELING n one who claims to be wise

WISELY, WISELIER ► wise

WISENESS ► wise

WISENT, -S n European bison

WISER ► wise

WISES ► wise

WISEST ► wise

WISH, -ED, -ES vb want or desire ▷ n expression of a desire

WISHA interj expression of surprise

WISHBONE n V-shaped bone above the breastbone of a fowl

WISHED ► wish

WISHER, -S ► wish

WISHES ► wish

WISHFUL adj too optimistic

WISHING, -S ► wish

WISHLESS ► wish

WISHT variant of ► whisht

WISING ► wise

WISKET, -S n basket

WISP, -ED, -ING, -S n light delicate streak ▷ vb move or act like a wisp

WISPIER ► wispy

WISPIEST ► wispy

WISPILY ► wispy

WISPING ► wisp

WISPISH ► wisp

WISPLIKE ► wisp

WISPS ► wisp

WISPY, WISPIER, WISPIEST adj thin, fine, or delicate

WISS vb urinate

WISSED ► wis

WISSES ► wis

WISSING ► wis

WIST, -ED, -ING, -S vb know

WISTARIA same as ► wisteria

WISTED ► wist

WISTERIA n climbing shrub with blue or purple flowers
WISTFUL adj sadly longing
WISTING ► wist
WISTITI, -S n marmoset
WISTLY adv intently
WISTS ► wist
WIT, WATE, -S vb detect ▷ n ability to use words or ideas in a clever and amusing way
WITAN, -S n Anglo-Saxon assembly that met to counsel the king
WITBLITS n illegally distilled strong alcoholic drink
WITCH, -ED, -ES n person, usu female, who practises (black) magic ▷ vb cause or change by or as if by witchcraft
WITCHEN, -S n rowan tree
WITCHERY n practice of witchcraft
WITCHES ► witch
WITCHIER ► witchy
WITCHING adj relating to or appropriate for witchcraft ▷ n witchcraft
WITCHY, WITCHIER adj like a witch
WITE, -D, -S, WITING vb blame
WITELESS adj witless
WITES ► wite
WITGAT, -S n type of S African tree
WITH, -S prep indicating presence alongside, possession, means of performance, characteristic manner, etc ▷ n division between flues in chimney
WITHAL adv as well
WITHDRAW vb take or move out or away
WITHDREW past tense of ► withdraw
WITHE, -D, -S, WITHING n strong flexible twig suitable for binding things together ▷ vb bind with withes
WITHER vb wilt or dry up
WITHERED
WITHERER
WITHEROD n American shrub
WITHERS pl n ridge between a horse's shoulder blades
WITHES ► withe
WITHHOLD, WITHHELD vb refrain from giving
WITHIER ► withy
WITHIES ► withy
WITHIEST ► withy
WITHIN, -S adv in or inside ▷ prep in or inside ▷ n something that is within
WITHING ► withe

WITHINS ► within
WITHOUT, -S prep not accompanied by, using, or having ▷ adv outside ▷ n person who is without
WITHS ► with
WITHWIND n bindweed
WITHY, WITHIER, WITHIES, WITHIEST n willow tree, esp an osier ▷ adj (of people) tough and agile
WITING ► wite
WITLESS adj foolish
WITLING, -S n person who thinks himself witty
WITLOOF, -S n chicory
WITNESS n person who has seen something happen ▷ vb see at first hand
WITNEY, -S n type of blanket; heavy cloth
WITS ► wit
WITTED adj having wit
WITTER, -ED, -S vb chatter pointlessly or at unnecessary length ▷ n pointless chat
WITTIER ► witty
WITTIEST ► witty
WITTILY ► witty
WITTING, -S adj deliberate ▷ n act of becoming aware
WITTY, WITTIER, WITTIEST adj clever and amusing
WITWALL, -S n golden oriole
WIVE, -D, WIVING vb marry (a woman)
WIVEHOOD obsolete variant of ► wifehood
WIVER, -S another word for ► wivern
WIVERN, -S same as ► wyvern
WIVERS ► wiver
WIVES ► wife
WIVING ► wive
WIZ, -ES, -ZES shortened form of ► wizard

> **Wiz** is a short form of **wizard**. This is the highest-scoring three-letter word beginning with W, and can be especially useful when there isn't much room to manoeuvre.

WIZARD, -S n magician ▷ adj superb
WIZARDLY
WIZARDRY n magic or sorcery
WIZARDS ► wizard
WIZEN, -ING, -S vb make or become shrivelled ▷ n archaic word for 'weasand' (the gullet)

WIZENED adj shrivelled or wrinkled
WIZENING ► wizen
WIZENS ► wizen
WIZES ► wiz
WIZIER, -S same as ► vizier
WIZZEN, -S same as ► wizen
WIZZES ► wiz
WO, -S archaic spelling of ► woe
WOAD, -S n blue dye obtained from a plant
WOADED adj coloured blue with woad
WOADS ► woad
WOADWAX n small Eurasian leguminous shrub
WOAH same as ► whoa
WOALD, -S same as ► weld
WOBBLE, -D, -S, WOBBLING vb move unsteadily ▷ n wobbling movement or sound
WOBBLER -S
WOBBLIER ► wobbly
WOBBLIES ► wobbly
WOBBLING ► wobble
WOBBLY, WOBBLIER, WOBBLIES adj unsteady ▷ n temper tantrum
WOBEGONE same as > woebegone
WOCK, -S same as ► wok
WODGE, -S n thick lump or chunk
WOE, -S n grief
WOEFUL adj extremely sad
WOEFULLY
WOENESS ► woe
WOES ► woe
WOESOME adj woeful
WOF, -S n fool
WOFUL, -LER same as ► woeful
WOFULLY
WOGGLE, -S n ring of leather through which a Scout neckerchief is threaded
WOIWODE, -S same as ► voivode
WOJUS adj (Irish) of a poor quality
WOK, -S n bowl-shaped Chinese cooking pan, used for stir-frying
WOKE ► wake
WOKEN ► wake
WOKKA modifier as in **wokka board** piece of fibreboard used as a musical instrument
WOKS ► wok
WOLD, -S same as ► weld
WOLF, -ED, -S, WOLVES n wild predatory canine mammal ▷ vb eat ravenously

W

WOLFER, -S same as ► **wolver**

WOLFFISH n type of large northern deep-sea fish with large sharp teeth

WOLFING, -S ► **wolf**

WOLFISH ► **wolf**

WOLFKIN, -S n young wolf

WOLFLIKE ► **wolf**

WOLFLING n young wolf

WOLFRAM, -S another name for ► **tungsten**

WOLFS ► **wolf**

WOLFSKIN n skin of wolf used for clothing, etc

WOLLY, WOLLIES n pickled cucumber or olive

WOLVE, -D vb hunt for wolves

WOLVER, -S n person who hunts wolves

WOLVES ► **wolf**

WOLVING, -S ► **wolve**

WOLVISH same as ► **wolfish**

WOMAN, -ED, -ING, -NED, -S, WOMEN n adult human female ▷ adj female ▷ vb provide with a woman or women

WOMANISH adj effeminate

WOMANISM n feminism among Black women **WOMANIST**

WOMANLY adj having qualities traditionally associated with a woman

WOMANNED ► **woman**

WOMANS ► **woman**

WOMB, -ING, -S vb enclose ▷ n hollow organ in female mammals where babies develop

WOMBAT, -S n small heavily-built burrowing Australian marsupial

WOMBED ► **womb**

WOMBIER ► **womby**

WOMBIEST ► **womby**

WOMBING ► **womb**

WOMBLIKE ► **womb**

WOMBS ► **womb**

WOMBY, WOMBIER, WOMBIEST adj hollow; spacious

WOMEN ► **woman**

WOMERA, -S same as ► **woomera**

WOMMERA, -S same as ► **woomera**

WOMMIT, -S n foolish person

WOMYN same as ► **woman**

WON, -NED, -S n standard monetary unit of North Korea ▷ vb live or dwell

WONDER, -ED, -S vb be curious about ▷ n wonderful

thing ▷ adj spectacularly successful **WONDERER**

WONDRED adj splendid

WONDROUS adj wonderful

WONGA, -S n money

WONGI, -ED, -ING, -S vb talk informally

WONING, -S ► **won**

WONK, -S n person who is obsessively interested in a specified subject

WONKERY n activities of a wonk

WONKIER ► **wonky**

WONKIEST ► **wonky**

WONKILY adv in a wonky manner

WONKISH adj like a wonk

WONKS ► **wonk**

WONKY, WONKIER, WONKIEST adj shaky or unsteady

WONNED ► **won**

WONNER, -S ► **won**

WONNING, -S ► **won**

WONS ► **won**

WONT, -ING, -S adj accustomed ▷ n custom ▷ vb become or cause to become accustomed

WONTED adj accustomed or habituated (to doing something) **WONTEDLY**

WONTING ► **wont**

WONTLESS ► **wont**

WONTON, -S n dumpling filled with spiced minced pork

WONTS ► **wont**

WOO, -ED, -S vb seek the love or affection of (a woman)

WOOABLE adj able to be wooed

WOOBUT, -S same as ► **woubit**

WOOD, -ING n substance trees are made of, used in carpentry and as fuel ▷ adj made of or using wood ▷ vb (of land) plant with trees

WOODBIN, -S n box for firewood

WOODBIND same as ► **woodbine**

WOODBINE n honeysuckle

WOODBINS ► **woodbin**

WOODBOX n box for firewood

WOODCHAT n European and N African songbird

WOODCHIP n textured wallpaper

WOODCHOP n wood-chopping competition, esp at a show

WOODCOCK n game bird

WOODCUT, -S n (print made from) an engraved block of wood

WOODED adj covered with trees

WOODEN, -ED, -ER, -S adj made of wood ▷ vb fell or kill (a person or animal) **WOODENLY**

WOODFERN n type of evergreen fern

WOODFREE adj (of paper) made from pulp that has been treated to remove impurities

WOODHEN, -S another name for ► **weka**

WOODHOLE n store area for wood

WOODIE, -S n gallows rope

WOODIER ► **woody**

WOODIES ► **woodie**

WOODIEST ► **woody**

WOODING ► **wood**

WOODLAND n forest ▷ adj living in woods

WOODLARK n type of Old World lark

WOODLESS ► **wood**

WOODLICE > **woodlouse**

WOODLORE n woodcraft skills

WOODLOT, -S n area restricted to the growing of trees

WOODMAN, WOODMEN same as ► **woodsman**

WOODMEAL n sawdust powder

WOODMEN ► **woodman**

WOODMICE ► **woodmouse**

WOODNESS ► **wood**

WOODNOTE n natural musical note or song, like that of a wild bird

WOODPILE n heap of firewood

WOODRAT, -S n pack-rat

WOODROOF same as ► **woodruff**

WOODRUFF n plant with small sweet-smelling white flowers and sweet-smelling leaves

WOODRUSH n plant with grasslike leaves and small brown flowers

WOODS pl n closely packed trees forming a forest or wood

WOODSHED n small outbuilding where firewood, garden tools, etc, are stored

WOODSIA, -S n type of small fern with tufted rhizomes and wiry fronds

WOODSIER ► woodsy

WOODSKIN n canoe made of bark

WOODSMAN, WOODSMEN n person who lives in a wood or who is skilled at woodwork or carving

WOODSY, WOODSIER adj of, reminiscent of, or connected with woods

WOODTONE n colour matching that of wood

WOODWALE n green woodpecker

WOODWARD n person in charge of a forest or wood

WOODWASP n large wasplike insect

WOODWAX same as > woodwaxen

WOODWIND n type of wind instrument made of wood ▷ adj of or denoting a type of wind instrument, such as the oboe

WOODWORK n parts of a room or building made of wood

WOODWORM n insect larva that bores into wood

WOODWOSE n hairy wildman of the woods

WOODY, WOODIER, WOODIEST adj (of a plant) having a very hard stem

WOODYARD n place where timber is cut and stored

WOOED ► woo

WOOER, -S ► woo

WOOF, -ED, -ING, -S vb (of dogs) bark

WOOFER, -S n loudspeaker reproducing low-frequency sounds

WOOFIER ► woofy

WOOFIEST ► woofy

WOOFING ► woof

WOOFS ► woof

WOOFY, WOOFIER, WOOFIEST adj with close, dense texture

WOOHOO interj expression of joy, approval, etc

WOOING, -S ► woo

WOOINGLY ► woo

WOOINGS ► wooing

WOOL, -S n soft hair of sheep, goats, etc

WOOLD, -ED, -ING, -S vb wind (rope)

WOOLDER, -S n stick for winding rope

WOOLDING ► woold

WOOLDS ► woold

WOOLED same as ► woolled

WOOLEN, -S same as ► woollen

WOOLER, -S same as ► woolder

WOOLFAT, -S same as ► lanolin

WOOLFELL n skin of a sheep or similar animal with the fleece still attached

WOOLHAT, -S n hat made of wool

WOOLIE n wool garment

WOOLIER ► wooly

WOOLIES ► wooly

WOOLIEST ► wooly

WOOLLED adj (of animals) having wool

WOOLLEN, -S adj relating to or consisting partly or wholly of wool ▷ n garment or piece of cloth made of wool

WOOLLIER ► woolly

WOOLLIES ► woolly

WOOLLIKE ► wool

WOOLLILY ► woolly

WOOLLY, WOOLLIER, WOOLLIES adj of or like wool ▷ n knitted woollen garment

WOOLMAN, WOOLMEN n wool trader

WOOLPACK n cloth or canvas wrapping used to pack a bale of wool

WOOLS ► wool

WOOLSACK n sack containing or intended to contain wool

WOOLSEY, -S n cotton and wool blend

WOOLSHED n large building in which sheep shearing takes place

WOOLSKIN n sheepskin with wool still on

WOOLWARD adv with woollen side touching the skin

WOOLWORK n embroidery with wool

WOOLY, WOOLIER, WOOLIES, WOOLIEST same as ► woolly

WOOMERA, -S n notched stick used by Australian Aborigines to aid the propulsion of a spear

WOON, -ED, -ING, -S same as ► won

WOONERF, -S n (in the Netherlands) road primarily for cyclists and pedestrians

WOONING ► woon

WOONS ► woon

WOOPIE, -S n well-off older person

WOOPS, -ED, -ES, -ING vb (esp of small child) vomit

WOOPY n well-off older person

WOORALI, -S less common name for ► curare

WOORARA, -S same as ► wourali

WOORARI, -S same as ► wourali

WOOS ► woo

WOOSE, -S same as ► wuss

WOOSEL, -S same as ► ouzel

WOOSELL, -S same as ► ouzel

WOOSELS ► woosel

WOOSES ► woose

WOOSH, -ED, -ES, -ING same as ► whoosh

WOOT interj (esp used by players in online games) shout of joy, victory, etc

WOOTZ, -ES n Middle-Eastern steel

WOOZIER ► woozy

WOOZIEST ► woozy

WOOZILY ► woozy

WOOZY, WOOZIER, WOOZIEST adj weak, dizzy, and confused

WOP same as ► whop

WORD, -ED, -S n smallest single meaningful unit of speech or writing ▷ vb express in words

WORDAGE, -S n words considered collectively, esp a quantity of words

WORDBOOK n book containing words, usually with their meanings

WORDED ► word

WORDGAME n any game involving the formation, discovery, or alteration of a word or words

WORDIER ► wordy

WORDIEST ► wordy

WORDILY ► wordy

WORDING, -S n choice and arrangement of words

WORDISH adj talkative

WORDLESS adj inarticulate or silent

WORDLORE n knowledge about words

WORDPLAY n verbal wit based on the meanings and ambiguities of words

W

WORDS ▸ word

WORDWRAP n wordprocessing function that shifts a word at the end of a line to a new line to keep within preset margins

WORDY, WORDIER, WORDIEST adj using too many words

WORE ▸ wear

WORK, -S n physical or mental effort directed to making or doing something ▷ adj of or for work ▷ vb (cause to) do work

WORKABLE adj able to operate efficiently **WORKABLY**

WORKADAY n working day ▷ adj ordinary

WORKBAG, -S n container for implements, tools, or materials

WORKBOAT n boat used for tasks

WORKBOOK n exercise book or textbook used for study, esp a textbook with spaces for answers

WORKBOOT n type of sturdy leather boot

WORKBOX same as ▸ workbag

WORKDAY, -S another word for ▸ workaday

WORKED adj made or decorated with evidence of workmanship

WORKER, -S n person who works in a specified way

WORKFARE n scheme under which unemployed people are required to do community work or undergo job training in return for social-security payments

WORKFLOW n rate of progress of work

WORKFOLK pl n working people, esp labourers on a farm

WORKFUL adj hardworking

WORKGIRL n young female manual worker

WORKHOUR n time set aside for work

WORKING, -S n operation or mode of operation of something ▷ adj relating to or concerned with a person or thing that works

WORKLESS ▸ work

WORKLOAD n amount of work to be done, esp in a specified period

WORKMAN, WORKMEN n manual worker

WORKMATE n person who works with another person

WORKMEN ▸ workman

WORKOUT, -S n session of physical exercise for training or fitness

WORKROOM n room in which work, usually manual labour, is done

WORKS ▸ work

WORKSAFE adj (of an internet link) suitable for viewing in the workplace

WORKSHOP n room or building for a manufacturing process ▷ vb perform (a play) with no costumes, set, or musical accompaniment

WORKSHY adj not inclined to work

WORKSITE n area where work is done

WORKSOME adj hardworking

WORKSONG n song sung while doing physical work

WORKTOP, -S n surface used for food preparation

WORKUP, -S n medical examination

WORKWEAR n clothes, such as overalls, as worn for work in a factory, shop, etc

WORKWEEK n number of hours or days in a week actually or officially allocated to work

WORLD, -S n planet earth ▷ adj of the whole world

WORLDED adj incorporating worlds

WORLDER, -S n person who belongs to a specified class or domain

WORLDIE, -S n world-class performance, achievement, person, etc

WORLDLY adj not spiritual ▷ adv in a worldly manner

WORLDS ▸ world

WORM, -ED, -ING n small limbless invertebrate animal ▷ vb rid of worms

WORMCAST n coil of earth excreted by a burrowing worm

WORMED ▸ worm

WORMER, -S ▸ worm

WORMERY n piece of apparatus in which worms are kept for study

WORMFLY n type of lure dressed on a double hook

WORMGEAR n gear with screw thread

WORMHOLE n hole made by a worm in timber, plants, or fruit

WORMIER ▸ wormy

WORMIEST ▸ wormy

WORMIL, -S n burrowing larva of type of fly

WORMING ▸ worm

WORMISH ▸ worm

WORMLIKE ▸ worm

WORMROOT n plant used to cure worms

WORMS n disease caused by parasitic worms living in the intestines

WORMSEED n any of various plants used to treat worm infestation

WORMWOOD n bitter plant

WORMY, WORMIER, WORMIEST adj infested with or eaten by worms

WORN ▸ wear

WORNNESS n quality or condition of being worn

WORRAL, -S n type of lizard

WORREL, -S same as ▸ worral

WORRICOW n frightening creature

WORRIED ▸ worry

WORRIER, -S ▸ worry

WORRIES ▸ worry

WORRIT, -ED, -S vb tease or worry

WORRY, WORRIED, WORRIES vb (cause to) be anxious or uneasy ▷ n (cause of) anxiety or concern

WORRYCOW same as ▸ worricow

WORRYING ▸ worry

WORSE, -D, -S, WORSING vb defeat

WORSEN, -ED, -S vb make or grow worse

WORSER archaic or nonstandard word for ▸ worse

WORSES ▸ worse

WORSET, -S n worsted fabric

WORSHIP, -S vb show religious devotion to ▷ n act or instance of worshipping

WORSING ▸ worse

WORST, -ING, -S n worst thing ▷ vb defeat

WORSTED, -S n type of woollen yarn or fabric

WORSTING ▸ worst

WORSTS ▸ worst

WORT, -S n any of various plants formerly used to cure diseases

WORTH, -ED, -ING, -S *prep* having a value of ▷ *n* value or price ▷ *vb* happen or betide
WORTHFUL *adj* worthy
WORTHIED ► **worthy**
WORTHIER ► **worthy**
WORTHIES ► **worthy**
WORTHILY ► **worthy**
WORTHING ► **worth**
WORTHS ► **worth**
WORTHY, WORTHIED, WORTHIER, WORTHIES *adj* deserving admiration or respect ▷ *n* notable person ▷ *vb* make worthy
WORTLE, -S *n* plate with holes for drawing wire through
WORTS ► **wort**
WOS ► **wo**
WOST *vb* wit, to know
WOT, -S, -TED, -TEST, -TETH, -TING *vb* wit, to know
WOTCHA *same as* ► **wotcher**
WOTCHER *sentence substitute* slang term of greeting
WOTS ► **wot**
WOTTED ► **wot**
WOTTEST ► **wot**
WOTTETH ► **wot**
WOTTING ► **wot**
WOUBIT, -S *n* type of caterpillar
WOULD ► **will**
WOULDEST *same as* ► **wouldst**
WOULDS *same as* ► **wouldst**
WOULDST *singular form of the past tense of* ► **will**
WOUND, -S *vb* injure ▷ *n* injury
WOUNDED *adj* suffering from wounds
WOUNDER, -S ► **wound**
WOUNDIER ► **woundy**
WOUNDILY ► **woundy**
WOUNDING ► **wound**
WOUNDS ► **wound**
WOUNDY, WOUNDIER *adj* extreme
WOURALI, -S *n* plant from which curare is obtained
WOVE ► **weave**
WOVEN, -S *n* article made from woven cloth
WOW, -ED, -ING, -S *interj* exclamation of astonishment ▷ *n* astonishing person or thing ▷ *vb* be a great success with
WOWEE *stronger form of* ► **wow**
WOWF, -ER, -EST *adj* mad

This is a Scots word meaning crazy: you are not likely to get the chance to

play this very often, but if your opponent plays **wow** and you have an F, you would be **wowf** to miss the opportunity for the hook!

WOWING ► **wow**
WOWS ► **wow**
WOWSER, -S *n* puritanical person
WOX ► **wax**

Wox is an old past tense of the verb **wax**, to grow, and is another of the key words using X.

WOXEN ► **wax**
WRACK, -ED, -ING, -S *n* seaweed ▷ *vb* strain or shake (something) violently
WRACKFUL *n* ruinous
WRACKING ► **wrack**
WRACKS ► **wrack**
WRAITH, -S *n* ghost
WRANG, -ED, -ING, -S *Scot word for* ► **wrong**
WRANGLE, -D, -S *vb* argue noisily ▷ *n* noisy argument
WRANGLER *n* one who wrangles
WRANGLES ► **wrangle**
WRANGS ► **wrang**
WRAP, -PED, -PING, -S *vb* fold (something) round (a person or thing) so as to cover ▷ *n* garment wrapped round the shoulders
WRAPOVER *adj* (of a garment) worn wrapped round the body and fastened so that the open edges overlap ▷ *n* such a garment
WRAPPAGE *n* material for wrapping
WRAPPED ► **wrap**
WRAPPER, -S *vb* cover with wrapping ▷ *n* cover for a product
WRAPPING ► **wrap**
WRAPS ► **wrap**
WRAPT *same as* ► **rapt**
WRASSE, -S *n* colourful sea fish
WRASSLE, -D, -S *same as* ► **wrestle**
WRAST, -ED, -ING, -S *same as* ► **wrest**
WRASTLE, -D, -S *same as* ► **wrestle**
WRASTS ► **wrast**
WRATE ► **write**
WRATH, -ED, -ING, -S *n* intense anger ▷ *adj* incensed ▷ *vb* make angry
WRATHFUL *adj* full of wrath
WRATHIER ► **wrathy**
WRATHILY ► **wrathy**

WRATHING ► **wrath**
WRATHS ► **wrath**
WRATHY, WRATHIER *same as* ► **wrathful**
WRAWL, -ED, -ING, -S *vb* howl
WRAXLE, -D, -S, WRAXLING *vb* wrestle
WREAK, -ED, -ING, -S, WROKE, WROKEN *vb* inflict (vengeance, etc) or to cause (chaos, etc)
WREAKER -S
WREAKFUL *adj* seeking revenge
WREAKING ► **wreak**
WREAKS ► **wreak**
WREATH, -S *n* twisted ring or band of flowers or leaves used as a memorial or tribute
WREATHE, -D, -S *vb* form into or take the form of a wreath by twisting together
WREATHEN *adj* twisted into wreath
WREATHER ► **wreathe**
WREATHES ► **wreathe**
WREATHS ► **wreath**
WREATHY *adj* twisted into wreath
WRECK, -ED, -ING, -S *vb* destroy ▷ *n* remains of something that has been destroyed or badly damaged
WRECKAGE *n* wrecked remains
WRECKED ► **wreck**
WRECKER, -S *n* formerly, person who lured ships onto the rocks in order to plunder them
WRECKFUL *adj* causing wreckage
WRECKING ► **wreck**
WRECKS ► **wreck**
WREN, -S *n* small brown songbird
WRENCH, -ED, -ES *vb* twist or pull violently ▷ *n* violent twist or pull
WRENCHER
WRENS ► **wren**
WRENTIT, -S *n* type of long-tailed North American bird
WREST, -ED, -ING, -S *vb* twist violently ▷ *n* act or an instance of wresting
WRESTER -S
WRESTLE, -D, -S *vb* fight by grappling with an opponent ▷ *n* act of wrestling
WRESTLER
WRESTS ► **wrest**
WRETCH, -ES *n* despicable person

W

WRETCHED adj miserable or unhappy

WRETCHES ► wretch

WRETHE, -D, -S, WRETHING same as **► wreathe**

WRICK, -ED, -ING, -S variant spelling (chiefly Brit) of **► rick**

WRIED ► wry

WRIER ► wry

WRIES ► wry

WRIEST ► wry

WRIGGLE, -D, -S vb move with a twisting action ▷ n wriggling movement

WRIGGLER

WRIGGLY

WRIGHT, -S n maker

WRING, -ED, -ING, -S, WRUNG vb twist, esp to squeeze liquid out of

WRINGER, -S same as **► mangle**

WRINGING ► wring

WRINGS ► wring

WRINKLE, -D, -S n slight crease, esp one in the skin due to age ▷ vb make or become slightly creased

WRINKLIE n old person

WRINKLY ► wrinkle

WRIST, -ED, -ING, -S n joint between the hand and the arm ▷ vb hit an object with a twist of the wrist

WRISTER, -S n type of shot in hockey

WRISTIER ► wristy

WRISTING ► wrist

WRISTLET n band or bracelet worn around the wrist

WRISTS ► wrist

WRISTY, WRISTIER adj characterized by considerable movement of the wrist

WRIT, -S n written legal command

WRITABLE ► write

WRITE, WRATE, -S, WRITING, WRITINGS, WRITTEN, WROTE vb mark paper etc with symbols or words

WRITEOFF n uncollectible debt that is cancelled

WRITER, -S n author

WRITERLY adj of or characteristic of a writer

WRITERS ► writer

WRITES ► write

WRITHE, -D, -S, WRITHING vb twist or squirm in or as if

in pain ▷ n act or an instance of writhing

WRITHEN adj twisted

WRITHER, -S ► writhe

WRITHES ► writhe

WRITHING ► writhe

WRITHLED adj wrinkled

WRITING ► write

WRITINGS ► write

WRITS ► writ

WRITTEN ► write

WRIZLED adj wrinkled

WROATH, -S n unforeseen trouble

WROKE ► wreak

WROKEN ► wreak

WRONG, -ED, -EST, -ING, -S adj incorrect or mistaken ▷ adv in a wrong manner ▷ n something immoral or unjust ▷ vb treat unjustly

WRONGER -S

WRONGFUL adj unjust or illegal

WRONGING ► wrong

WRONGLY ► wrong

WRONGOUS adj unfair

WRONGS ► wrong

WROOT, -ED, -ING, -S obsolete form of **► root**

WROTE ► write

WROTH adj angry

WROTHFUL same as **► wrathful**

WROUGHT adj (of metals) shaped by hammering or beating

WRUNG ► wring

WRY, WRIED, WRIER, WRIES, WRIEST, -ER, -EST, -ING adj drily humorous ▷ vb twist or contort

WRYBILL, -S n New Zealand plover whose bill is bent to one side

WRYER ► wry

WRYEST ► wry

WRYING ► wry

WRYLY ► wry

WRYNECK, -S n woodpecker that has a habit of twisting its neck round

WRYNESS ► wry

WRYTHEN adj twisted

WUD, -DED, -DING, -S Scots form of **► wood**

W and U are a horrible combination to have on your rack, so this Scots word for wood can be a godsend. And remember that it can also be a verb, meaning to load with wood,

so you have **wuds, wudding** and **wudded**.

WUDU, -S n practice of ritual washing before daily prayer

WULL, -ED, -ING, -S obsolete form of **► will**

WUNNER, -S same as **► oner**

WURLEY, -S n Aboriginal hut

WURLIE, -S same as **► wurley**

WURST, -S n large sausage, esp of a type made in Germany, Austria, etc

WURTZITE n zinc sulphide

WURZEL, -S n root

WUS, -ES n casual term of address

WUSHU, -S n Chinese martial arts

WUSS, -ES n feeble person

WUSSY, WUSSIER, WUSSIES, WUSSIEST adj feeble ▷ n feeble person

WUTHER, -ED, -S vb (of wind) blow and roar

WUXIA, -S n Chinese fiction concerning the adventures of sword-wielding heroes

This Chinese word for a genre of fiction may get you a decent score from a very difficult-looking rack.

WUZ vb nonstandard spelling of was

WUZZLE, -D, -S, WUZZLING vb mix up

WYCH, -ES n type of tree having flexible branches

WYE, -S n y-shaped pipe

If you have W and Y on your rack, look for an E on the board that will allow you to play this name for the letter Y, especially if you can land on a bonus square as a result.

WYLE, -D, -S, WYLING vb entice

WYN, -S n rune equivalent to English 'w'

WYND, -S n narrow lane or alley

WYNN, -S same as **► wyn**

WYNS ► wyn

WYSIWYG adj denoting a computer screen display showing exactly what will print out

WYTE, -D, -S, WYTING vb blame

WYVERN, -S n heraldic beast

Xx

Worth 8 points on its own, **X** is one of the best tiles in the game. It doesn't, however, start many two- and three-letter words. There are only two valid two-letter words, **xi** and **xu** (9 points each) beginning with **X**, and only two three-letter words, **xed** and **xis**. Therefore, if you have an **X** on your rack and need to play short words, you're probably better off thinking of words that end in **X** or have **X** in them rather than those that start with **X**. Particularly good to remember are **zax, zex** (19 points each) and **kex** (14 points).

XANTHAM, -S *n* acacia gum
XANTHAN, -S *n* same as
► **xantham**
XANTHATE *n* any salt or ester of xanthic acid
XANTHEIN *n* soluble part of the yellow pigment that is found in the cell sap of some flowers
XANTHENE *n* yellowish crystalline heterocyclic compound used as a fungicide
XANTHIC *adj* of, containing, or derived from xanthic acid
XANTHIN, -S *n* any of a group of yellow or orange carotene derivatives
XANTHINE *n* crystalline compound found in urine, blood, certain plants, and certain animal tissues
XANTHINS ► **xanthin**
XANTHISM *n* condition of skin, fur, or feathers in which yellow coloration predominates
XANTHOMA *n* presence in the skin of fatty yellow or brownish plaques or nodules
XANTHONE *n* crystalline compound
XANTHOUS *adj* of, relating to, or designating races with yellowish hair and a light complexion
XEBEC, -S *n* small three-masted Mediterranean vessel

A kind of small boat, and a good high-scoring word that can easily be missed, as we tend to be slow to consider words beginning with X.

XED *vb* marked a cross against
XENIA, -S *n* influence of pollen upon the form of the fruit developing after pollination
XENIAL
XENIC *adj* denoting the presence of bacteria
XENIUM *n* diplomatic gift
XENOGAMY *n* fertilization by the fusion of male and female gametes from different individuals of the same species
XENOGENY *n* offspring unlike either parent
XENOLITH *n* fragment of rock differing in origin, composition, structure, etc, from the igneous rock enclosing it
XENON, -S *n* colourless odourless gas found in very small quantities in the air
XENOPHYA *n* parts of shell or skeleton formed by foreign bodies
XENOPUS *n* African frog
XENOTIME *n* yellow-brown mineral
XENURINE *adj* relating to a type of armadillo ▷ *n* type of armadillo
XERAFIN, -S *n* Indian coin
XERANSIS, XERANSES *n* gradual loss of tissue moisture
XERANTIC
XERAPHIN *same as* ► **xerafin**
XERARCH *adj* (of a sere) having its origin in a dry habitat
XERASIA, -S *n* dryness of the hair
XERIC *adj* of, relating to, or growing in dry conditions

XEROMA, -S, -TA *n* excessive dryness of the cornea
XEROSERE *n* sere that originates in dry surroundings
XEROSIS, XEROSES *n* abnormal dryness of bodily tissues, esp the skin, eyes, or mucous membranes
XEROTES *same as* ► **xerosis**
XEROTIC ► **xerosis**
XEROX, -ED, -ES, -ING *n* trade name for a machine employing a xerographic copying process ▷ *vb* produce a copy (of a document, etc) using such a machine
XERUS, -ES *n* ground squirrel
XI, -S *n* 14th letter in the Greek alphabet
XIPHOID, -S *adj* shaped like a sword ▷ *n* part of the sternum
XIS ► **xi**
XOANON, XOANA *n* primitive image of a god supposed to have fallen from heaven

One of the few words starting with X. But be careful: the plural is **xoana** not **xoanons**.

XRAY, -S *n* code word for the letter X
XU *n* Vietnamese currency unit
XYLAN, -S *n* yellow polysaccharide consisting of xylose units
XYLEM, -S *n* plant tissue that conducts water and minerals from the roots to all other parts

XYLENE, -S n type of hydrocarbon

XYLENOL, -S n synthetic resin made from xylene

XYLIC ▸ xylem

XYLIDIN, -S same as ▸ xylidine

XYLIDINE n mixture of six isomeric amines derived from xylene and used in dyes

XYLIDINS ▸ xylidin

XYLITOL, -S n crystalline alcohol used as sweetener

XYLOCARP n fruit, such as a coconut, having a hard woody pericarp

XYLOGEN, -S same as ▸ xylem

XYLOID adj of, relating to, or resembling wood

XYLOIDIN n type of explosive

XYLOL, -S another name (not in technical usage) for ▸ xylene

XYLOLOGY n study of the composition of wood

XYLOLS ▸ xylol

XYLOMA, -S, -TA n hard growth in fungi

XYLONIC adj denoting an acid formed from xylose

XYLONITE n type of plastic

XYLOSE, -S n white crystalline sugar found in wood and straw

XYLOTOMY n preparation of sections of wood for examination by microscope

XYLYL, -S n group of atoms

XYST, -S n long portico, esp one used in ancient Greece for athletics

> A kind of court used by ancient Greek athletes for exercises, this is a lovely high-scoring word to play. And if your opponent plays it, remember that you can put an I on it to make **xysti**, as well as an S to make **xysts**.

XYSTER, -S n surgical instrument for scraping bone

XYSTI ▸ xystus

XYSTOS, XYSTOI same as ▸ xyst

XYSTS ▸ xyst

XYSTUS, XYSTI same as ▸ xyst

X

Yy

Y can be a useful tile to have on your rack, particularly if you are short of vowels, but it can make it difficult to find bonus words scoring that extra 50 points, and you will normally want to play it off as soon as a good score offers itself. There are only four two-letter words beginning with **Y**, but these are easy to remember as there's one for every vowel except **I**: **ya**, **ye**, **yo** and **yu** (5 points each). There are quite a few useful three-letter words: **yez** (15), **yew** (9) and **yob** (8). Remember that **yob** was originally **boy** backwards: if you can't fit in **yob**, you may be able to use **boy** instead. And while his half-brother the **zo** (or **dzo** or **dso** or **zho**) gets all the attention, don't forget that the **yak** (10) earns quite a decent score!

YA, -S *n* type of Asian pear

YAAR, -S *n* informal Indian English, a friend

YABA, -S *n* informal word for 'yet another bloody acronym'

YABBA, -S *n* form of methamphetamine

YABBER, -ED, -S *vb* talk or jabber ▷ *n* talk or jabber

YABBIE *same as* ▶ **yabby**

YABBY, YABBIED, YABBIES, -ING *n* small freshwater crayfish ▷ *vb* go out to catch yabbies

YACCA, -S *n* Australian plant with a woody stem

YACHT, -ED, -S *n* large boat with sails or an engine ▷ *vb* sail in a yacht

YACHTER -S

YACHTIE, -S *n* yachtsman

YACHTING *n* sport or practice of navigating a yacht

YACHTMAN, YACHTMEN *same as* > **yachtsman**

YACHTS ▶ **yacht**

YACK, -ED, -ING, -S *same as* ▶ **yak**

YACKA, -S *same as* ▶ **yacca**

YACKED ▶ **yack**

YACKER, -S *same as* ▶ **yakka**

YACKING ▶ **yack**

YACKS ▶ **yack**

YAD, -S *n* hand-held pointer used for reading the sefer torah

YAE *same as* ▶ **ae**

YAFF, -ED, -ING, -S *vb* bark

YAFFLE, -S *n* woodpecker with a green back and wings

YAFFS ▶ **yaff**

YAG, -S *n* artificial crystal

YAGE, -S *n* tropical vine of the Amazon region

YAGER, -S *same as* ▶ **jaeger**

YAGES ▶ **yage**

YAGGER, -S *n* pedlar

YAGI, -S *n* type of highly directional aerial

YAGS ▶ **yag**

YAH, -S *interj* exclamation of derision or disgust ▷ *n* affected upper-class person

YAHOO, -S *n* crude coarse person

YAHOOISM

YAHRZEIT *n* (in Judaism) the anniversary of the death of a close relative

YAHS ▶ **yah**

YAIRD, -S *Scots form of* ▶ **yard**

YAK, -KED, -KING, -S *n* Tibetan ox with long shaggy hair ▷ *vb* talk continuously about unimportant matters

YAKHDAN, -S *n* box for carrying ice on a pack animal

YAKIMONO *n* grilled food

YAKITORI *n* Japanese dish consisting of small pieces of chicken skewered and grilled

YAKKA, -S *n* work

YAKKED ▶ **yak**

YAKKER, -S *same as* ▶ **yakka**

YAKKING ▶ **yak**

YAKOW, -S *n* animal bred from a male yak and a domestic cow

YAKS ▶ **yak**

YAKUZA *n* Japanese criminal organization

YALD *adj* vigorous

YALE, -S *n* mythical beast with the body of an antelope (or similar animal) and swivelling horns

YAM, -S *n* tropical root vegetable

YAMALKA, -S *same as* ▶ **yarmulke**

YAMEN, -S *n* (in imperial China) the office or residence of a public official

YAMMER, -ED, -S *vb* whine in a complaining manner ▷ *n* yammering sound

YAMMERER

YAMPY, YAMPIES *n* foolish person

YAMS ▶ **yam**

YAMULKA, -S *same as* ▶ **yarmulke**

YAMUN, -S *same as* ▶ **yamen**

YANG, -S *n* (in Chinese philosophy) one of two complementary principles maintaining harmony in the universe

YANK, -ED, -ING, -S *vb* pull or jerk suddenly ▷ *n* sudden pull or jerk

YANKEE, -S *n* code word for the letter Y

YANKER, -S ▶ **yank**

YANKIE, -S *n* impudent woman

YANKING ▶ **yank**

YANKS ▶ **yank**

YANQUI, -S *n* slang word for American

YANTRA, -S *n* diagram used in meditation

YAOURT, -S *n* yoghurt

YAP, -PED, -S vb bark with a high-pitched sound ▷ n high-pitched bark ▷ interj imitation or representation of the sound of a dog yapping

YAPOCK, -S same as ▶ **yapok**

YAPOK, -S n type of opossum

YAPON, -S same as ▶ **yaupon**

YAPP, -S n type of book binding

YAPPED ▶ **yap**

YAPPER, -S ▶ **yap**

YAPPIE, -S n young aspiring professional

YAPPIER ▶ **yappy**

YAPPIES ▶ **yappie**

YAPPIEST ▶ **yappy**

YAPPING, -S n act of yapping

YAPPS ▶ **yapp**

YAPPY, YAPPIER, YAPPIEST ▶ **yap**

YAPS ▶ **yap**

YAPSTER, -S ▶ **yap**

YAQONA, -S n Polynesian shrub

YAR adj nimble

YARAK, -S n fit condition for hunting

YARCO, -S n insulting word for a young working-class person who wears casual sports clothes

YARD, -ED, -S n unit of length ▷ vb draft (animals), esp to a sale yard

YARDAGE, -S n length measured in yards

YARDANG, -S n ridge formed by wind erosion

YARDARM, -S n outer end of a ship's yard

YARDBIRD n inexperienced, untrained, or clumsy soldier, esp one employed on menial duties

YARDED ▶ **yard**

YARDER, -S n one who drafts animals to a sale yard

YARDING, -S n group of animals displayed for sale

YARDLAND n archaic unit of land

YARDMAN, YARDMEN n farm overseer

YARDS ▶ **yard**

YARDWAND same as > **yardstick**

YARDWORK n garden work

YARE adj ready, brisk, or eager ▷ adv readily or eagerly

YARELY

YARFA, -S n peat

YARK, -ED, -ING, -S vb make ready

YARMELKE same as ▶ **yarmulke**

YARMULKA same as ▶ **yarmulke**

YARMULKE n skullcap worn by Jewish men

YARN, -ED, -ING, -S n thread used for knitting or making cloth ▷ vb thread with yarn

YARNER -S

YARPHA, -S n peat

YARR, -ED, -ING, -S n wild white flower ▷ vb growl or snarl

YARRAMAN, YARRAMEN n horse

YARRAN, -S n type of small hardy tree of inland Australia

YARRED ▶ **yarr**

YARRING ▶ **yarr**

YARROW, -S n wild plant with flat clusters of white flowers

YARRS ▶ **yarr**

YARTA, -S Shetland word for ▶ **heart**

YARTO, -S same as ▶ **yarta**

YAS ▶ **ya**

YASHMAC, -S same as ▶ **yashmak**

YASHMAK, -S n veil worn by a Muslim woman in public

YASMAK, -S same as ▶ **yashmak**

YATAGAN, -S same as ▶ **yataghan**

YATAGHAN n Turkish sword with a curved single-edged blade

YATE, -S n type of small eucalyptus tree yielding a very hard timber

YATTER, -ED, -S vb talk at length ▷ n continuous chatter

YAUD, -S Scots word for ▶ **mare**

YAULD adj alert, spritely, or nimble

YAUP, -ED, -ING, -S variant spelling of ▶ **yawp**

YAUPER -S

YAUPON, -S n southern US evergreen holly shrub

YAUPS ▶ **yaup**

YAUTIA, -S n Caribbean plant cultivated for its edible leaves and underground stems

YAW, -ED, -ING vb (of an aircraft or ship) turn to one side or from side to side while moving ▷ n act or movement of yawing

YAWEY ▶ **yaws**

YAWIER ▶ **yawy**

YAWIEST ▶ **yawy**

YAWING ▶ **yaw**

YAWL, -ED, -ING, -S n two-masted sailing boat ▷ vb howl, weep, or scream harshly

YAWMETER n instrument for measuring an aircraft's yaw

YAWN, -ED, -S vb open the mouth wide and take in air deeply, often when sleepy or bored ▷ n act of yawning

YAWNER -S

YAWNIER ▶ **yawny**

YAWNIEST ▶ **yawny**

YAWNING, -S ▶ **yawn**

YAWNS ▶ **yawn**

YAWNSOME adj boring

YAWNY, YAWNIER, YAWNIEST ▶ **yawn**

YAWP, -ED, -ING, -INGS, -S vb gape or yawn, esp audibly ▷ n shout, bark, yelp, or cry

YAWPER -S

YAWS n infectious tropical skin disease

YAWY, YAWIER, YAWIEST adj having or resembling yaws

YAY, -S interj exclamation indicating approval or triumph ▷ n cry of approval

YBET archaic past participle of ▶ **beat**

YBLENT archaic past participle of ▶ **blend**

YBORE archaic past participle of ▶ **bear**

YBOUND archaic past participle of ▶ **bind**

YBOUNDEN archaic past participle of ▶ **bind**

YBRENT archaic past participle of ▶ **burn**

YCLAD archaic past participle of ▶ **clothe**

YCLED archaic past participle of ▶ **clothe**

YCLEEPE, -D, -S archaic form of ▶ **clepe**

YCLEPED same as ▶ **yclept**

YCLEPT adj having the name of

YCOND archaic past participle of ▶ **con**

YDRAD archaic past participle of ▶ **dread**

YDRED archaic past participle of ▶ **dread**

YE pron you ▷ adj the

YEA, -S interj yes ▷ adv indeed or truly ▷ sentence substitute aye ▷ n cry of agreement

YEAD, -ING, -S, YODE vb proceed

YEAH, -S n positive affirmation

YEALDON, -S n fuel

YEALING, -S *n* person of the same age as oneself

YEALM, -ED, -ING, -S *vb* prepare for thatching

YEAN, -ED, -ING, -S *vb* (of a sheep or goat) to give birth to (offspring)

YEANLING *n* young of a goat or sheep

YEANS ► yean

YEAR, -S *n* time taken for the earth to make one revolution around the sun, about 365 days

YEARBOOK *n* reference book published annually containing details of the previous year's events

YEARD, -ED, -ING, -S *vb* bury

YEAREND, -S *n* end of the year

YEARLIES ► yearly

YEARLING *n* animal between one and two years old ▷ *adj* being a year old

YEARLONG *adj* throughout a whole year

YEARLY, YEARLIES *adv* (happening) every year or once a year ▷ *adj* occurring, done, or appearing once a year or every year ▷ *n* publication, event, etc, that occurs once a year

YEARN, -ED, -S *vb* want (something) very much **YEARNER -S**

YEARNING *n* intense or overpowering longing, desire, or need

YEARNS ► yearn

YEARS ► year

YEAS ► yea

YEASAYER *n* person who usually agrees with proposals

YEAST, -ED, -ING, -S *n* fungus used to make bread rise ▷ *vb* froth or foam

YEASTIER ► yeasty

YEASTILY ► yeasty

YEASTING ► yeast

YEASTS ► yeast

YEASTY, YEASTIER *adj* of, resembling, or containing yeast

YEBO *interj* yes ▷ *sentence substitute* expression of affirmation

YECCH, -S *same as* **► yech**

YECH, -S *n* expression of disgust

YECHIER ► yechy

YECHIEST ► yechy

YECHS ► yech

YECHY, YECHIER, YECHIEST ► yech

YEDE, -S, YEDING *same as* **► yead**

YEED, -ING, -S *same as* **► yead**

YEELIN, -S *n* person of the same age as oneself

YEESH *interj* interjection used to express frustration

YEGG, -S *n* burglar or safe-breaker

YEGGMAN, YEGGMEN *same as* **► yegg**

YEGGS ► yegg

YEH *same as* **► yeah**

YELD *adj* (of an animal) barren or too young to bear young

YELDRING *n* yellowhammer (bird)

YELDROCK *same as* **► yeldring**

YELK, -S *n* yolk of an egg

YELL, -ED, -ING, -INGS, -S *vb* shout or scream in a loud or piercing way ▷ *n* loud cry of pain, anger, or fear

YELLER -S

YELLOCH, -S *vb* yell

YELLOW, -ED, -ER *n* colour of gold, a lemon, etc ▷ *adj* of this colour ▷ *vb* make or become yellow

YELLOWLY

YELLOWS *n* any of various fungal or viral diseases of plants

YELLOWY ► yellow

YELLS ► yell

YELM, -ED, -ING, -S *same as* **► yealm**

YELP, -ED, -ING, -INGS, -S *n* short sudden cry ▷ *vb* utter a sharp or high-pitched cry of pain

YELPER -S

YELT, -S *n* young sow

YEMMER, -S *southwest English form of* **► ember**

YEN, -NED, -NING, -S *n* monetary unit of Japan ▷ *vb* have a longing

YENTA, -S *n* meddlesome woman

YENTE, -S *same as* **► yenta**

YEOMAN, YEOMEN *n* farmer owning and farming his own land

YEOMANLY *adj* of, relating to, or like a yeoman ▷ *adv* in a yeomanly manner, as in being brave, staunch, or loyal

YEOMANRY *n* yeomen

YEOMEN ► yeoman

YEOW *interj* interjection used to express pain

YEP, -S *n* affirmative statement

YER *adj* (coll.) your; you

YERBA, -S *n* stimulating South American drink made from dried leaves

YERD, -ED, -ING, -S *vb* bury

YERK, -ED, -ING, -S *vb* tighten stitches

YERSINIA *n* plague bacterium

YES, -ES, -SED, -SES, -SING *interj* expresses consent, agreement, or approval ▷ *n* answer or vote of yes ▷ *sentence substitute* used to express acknowledgment, affirmation, consent, etc ▷ *vb* reply in the affirmative

YESHIVA, -S, YESHIVOT *n* traditional Jewish school

YESHIVAH *same as* **► yeshiva**

YESHIVAS ► yeshiva

YESHIVOT ► yeshiva

YESK, -ED, -ING, -S *vb* hiccup

YESSED ► yes

YESSES ► yes

YESSING ► yes

YESSIR *interj* expression of assent to a man

YESSIREE *interj* expression of assent

YESSUM *interj* expression of assent to a woman

YEST, -S *archaic form of* **► yeast**

YESTER *adj* of or relating to yesterday

YESTERN *same as* **► yester**

YESTREEN *n* yesterday evening

YESTS ► yest

YESTY *archaic form of* **► yeasty**

YET *adv* up until then or now

YETI, -S *n* large legendary manlike creature alleged to inhabit the Himalayan Mountains

YETT, -S *n* gate or door

YETTIE, -S *n* young, entrepreneurial, and technology-based (person)

YETTS ► yett

YEUK, -ED, -ING, -S *vb* itch

YEUKIER ► yeuky

YEUKIEST ► yeuky

YEUKING ► yeuk

YEUKS ► yeuk

YEUKY, YEUKIER, YEUKIEST ► yeuk

YEVE, -N, -S, YEVING *vb* give

YEW, -S *n* evergreen tree with needle-like leaves and red berries

YEWEN *adj* made of yew

YEWS ► yew

Y

YEX, -ED, -ES, -ING vb hiccup

> This word meaning to hiccup gives you a good score, and the verb forms offer the chance to expand it if someone else plays it, or if you get the chance later on.

YEZ interj yes

YFERE, -S adv together ▷ n friend or associate

YGLAUNST archaic past participle of ▶ glance

YGO archaic past participle of ▶ go

YGOE archaic past participle of ▶ go

YIBBLES adv perhaps

YICKER, -ED, -S vb squeal or squeak

YIDAKI, -S n long wooden wind instrument played by the Aboriginal peoples of Arnhem Land

YIELD, -ED, -S vb produce or bear ▷ n amount produced

YIELDER -S

YIELDING adj submissive

YIELDS ▶ yield

YIKE, -D, YIKING n argument, squabble, or fight ▷ vb argue, squabble, or fight

YIKES interj expression of surprise, fear, or alarm

YIKING ▶ yike

YIKKER, -ED, -S vb squeal or squeak

YILL, -ED, -ING, -S n ale ▷ vb entertain with ale

YIN, -S Scots word for ▶ one

YINCE Scots form of ▶ once

YINDIE, -S n person who combines a lucrative career with non-mainstream tastes

YINGYANG n two opposing but complementary principles in Chinese philosophy

YINS ▶ yin

YIP, -PED, -PING, -S n emit a high-pitched bark

YIPE same as ▶ yipes

YIPES interj expression of surprise, fear, or alarm

YIPPED ▶ yip

YIPPEE interj exclamation of joy or pleasure

YIPPER, -S n golfer who suffers from a failure of nerve

YIPPIE, -S n young person sharing hippy ideals

YIPPING ▶ yip

YIPPY same as ▶ yippie

YIPS ▶ yip

YIRD, -ED, -ING, -S vb bury

YIRK, -ED, -ING, -S same as ▶ yerk

YIRR, -ED, -ING, -S vb snarl, growl, or yell

YIRTH, -S n earth

YITE, -S n European bunting with a yellowish head and body and brown streaked wings and tail

YITIE, -S same as ▶ yite

YITTEN adj frightened

YLEM, -S n original matter from which the basic elements are said to have been formed

YLIKE Spenserian form of ▶ alike

YLKE, -S archaic spelling of ▶ ilk

YMOLT Spenserian past participle of ▶ melt

YMOLTEN Spenserian past participle of ▶ melt

YMPE, -S, YMPING, YMPT Spenserian form of ▶ imp

YNAMBU, -S n South American bird

YO interj expression used as a greeting ▷ sentence substitute expression used as a greeting

YOB, -S n bad-mannered aggressive youth

YOBBERY n behaviour typical of aggressive surly youths

YOBBIER ▶ yobby

YOBBIEST ▶ yobby

YOBBISH adj typical of aggressive surly youths

YOBBISM, -S ▶ yob

YOBBO, -ES, -S same as ▶ yob

YOBBY, YOBBIER, YOBBIEST adj like a yob

YOBS ▶ yob

YOCK, -ED, -ING, -S vb chuckle

YOD, -S n tenth letter in the Hebrew alphabet

YODE ▶ yead

YODEL, -ED, -ING, -LED, -S vb sing with abrupt changes between a normal and a falsetto voice ▷ n act or sound of yodelling

YODELER -S

YODELLER ▶ yodel

YODELS ▶ yodel

YODH, -S same as ▶ yod

YODLE, -D, -S, YODLING variant spelling of ▶ yodel

YODLER -S

YODS ▶ yod

YOGA, -S n Hindu method of exercise and discipline

YOGEE, -S same as ▶ yogi

YOGH, -S n character used in Old and Middle English to represent a palatal fricative

YOGHOURT variant form of ▶ yogurt

YOGHS ▶ yogh

YOGHURT, -S same as ▶ yogurt

YOGI, -S n person who practises yoga

YOGIC ▶ yoga

YOGIN, -S same as ▶ yogi

YOGINI, -S ▶ yogi

YOGINS ▶ yogin

YOGIS ▶ yogi

YOGISM, -S ▶ yogi

YOGOURT, -S same as ▶ yogurt

YOGURT, -S n slightly sour custard-like food made from milk that has had bacteria added

YOHIMBE, -S n bark used in herbal medicine

YOICK, -ED, -ING vb urge on foxhounds

YOICKS, -ED, -ES interj cry used by huntsmen to urge on the hounds ▷ vb urge on foxhounds

YOJAN, -S n Indian unit of distance

YOJANA, -S same as ▶ yojan

YOJANS ▶ yojan

YOK, -KED, -KING, -S vb chuckle

> A useful short word meaning to laugh, with an alternative spelling **yuk**.

YOKE, -D, -RS, -S, YOKING, YOKINGS n wooden bar put across the necks of two animals to hold them together ▷ vb put a yoke on

YOKEL, -S n simple person who lives in the country

YOKELESS ▶ yoke

YOKELISH ▶ yokel

YOKELS ▶ yokel

YOKEMATE n colleague

YOKER, -ED, -ING vb spit

YOKERS ▶ yoke

YOKES ▶ yoke

YOKING ▶ yoke

YOKINGS ▶ yoke

YOKKED ▶ yok

YOKKING ▶ yok

YOKOZUNA n grand champion sumo wrestler

YOKS ▶ yok

YOKUL Shetland word for ▶ yes

YOLD archaic past participle of ▶ yield

YOLDRING n yellowhammer (bird)

YOLK, -S n yellow part of an egg that provides food for the

developing embryo
YOLKED
YOLKIER ► yolky
YOLKIEST ► yolky
YOLKLESS ► yolk
YOLKS ► yolk
YOLKY, YOLKIER, YOLKIEST ► yolk
YOM, -IM *n* day
YOMP, -ED, -ING, -S *vb* walk or trek laboriously
YON *adj* that or those over there ▷ *adv* yonder ▷ *pron* that person or thing
YOND *same as* ► yon
YONDER *adv* over there ▷ *adj* situated over there ▷ *determiner* being at a distance, either within view or as if within view ▷ *n* person
YONDERLY
YONI, -S *n* female genitalia
YONIC *adj* resembling a vulva
YONIS ► yoni
YONKER, -S *same as* ► younker
YONKS *pl n* very long time
YONNIE, -S *n* stone
YONT *same as* ► yon
YOOF, -S *n* non-standard spelling of youth
YOOP, -S *n* sob
YOPPER, -S *n* young person employed on a former UK government training programme
YORE, -S *n* time long past ▷ *adv* in the past
YORK, -ED, -ING, -S *vb* bowl or try to bowl (a batsman) by pitching the ball under or just beyond the bat
YORKER, -S *n* ball that pitches just under the bat
YORKIE, -S *n* Yorkshire terrier
YORKING ► york
YORKS ► york
YORLING, -S *n as in* **yellow yorling** yellowhammer
YORP, -ED, -ING, -S *vb* shout
YOU *pron* or people addressed ▷ *n* personality of the person being addressed
YOUK, -ED, -ING, -S *vb* itch
YOUNG, -ER, -EST, -S *adj* in an early stage of life or growth ▷ *n* young people in general; offspring
YOUNGERS *n* young people
YOUNGEST ► young
YOUNGISH ► young
YOUNGLY *adv* youthfully
YOUNGS ► young
YOUNGTH, -S *n* youth
YOUNKER, -S *n* young man

YOUPON, -S *same as* ► yaupon
YOUR *adj* of, belonging to, or associated with you
YOURN *dialect form of* ► yours
YOURS *pron* something belonging to you
YOURSELF *pron* reflexive form of *you*
YOURT, -S *same as* ► yurt
YOUS *pron* refers to more than one person including the person or persons addressed but not the speaker
YOUSE *same as* ► yous
YOUTH, -S *n* time of being young
YOUTHEN, -S *vb* render more youthful-seeming
YOUTHFUL *adj* vigorous or active
YOUTHIER ► youthy
YOUTHLY *adv* young
YOUTHS ► youth
YOUTHY, YOUTHIER *Scots word for* ► young
YOW, -ED, -ING, -S *vb* howl
YOWE, -S *Scot word for* ► ewe
YOWED ► yow
YOWES ► yowe
YOWIE, -S *n* legendary Australian apelike creature
YOWING ► yow
YOWL, -ED, -S *n* loud mournful cry ▷ *vb* produce a loud mournful wail or cry
YOWLER -S
YOWLEY, -S *n* yellowhammer (bird)
YOWLING, -S ► yowl
YOWLS ► yowl
YOWS ► yow
YPERITE, -S *n* mustard gas
YPIGHT *archaic past participle of* ► pitch
YPLAST *archaic past participle of* ► place
YPLIGHT *archaic past participle of* ► plight
YPSILOID ► ypsilon
YPSILON, -S *same as* ► upsilon
YRAPT *Spenserian form of* ► rapt
YRENT *archaic past participle of* ► rend
YRIVD *archaic past participle of* ► rive
YRNEH, -S *n* unit of reciprocal inductance
YSAME *Spenserian word for* ► together
YSHEND, -S, YSHENT *Spenserian form of* ► shend

YSLAKED *archaic past participle of* ► slake
YTOST *archaic past participle of* ► toss
YTTERBIA *n* colourless hygroscopic substance used in certain alloys and ceramics
YTTERBIC > ytterbium
YTTRIA, -S *n* insoluble solid used mainly in incandescent mantles
YTTRIC ► yttrium
YTTRIOUS ► yttrium
YTTRIUM, -S *n* silvery metallic element used in various alloys
YU, -S *n* jade
YUAN, -S *n* standard monetary unit of the People's Republic of China
YUCA, -S *same as* ► yucca
YUCCA, -S *n* tropical plant with spikes of white leaves
YUCCH *interj* expression of disgust
YUCH *interj* expression of disgust
YUCK, -ED, -ING, -S *interj* exclamation indicating contempt, dislike, or disgust ▷ *vb* chuckle
YUCKER -S
YUCKIER ► yucky
YUCKIEST ► yucky
YUCKING ► yuck
YUCKO *adj* disgusting ▷ *interj* exclamation of disgust
YUCKS ► yuck
YUCKY, YUCKIER, YUCKIEST *adj* disgusting, nasty
YUFT, -S *n* Russia leather
YUG, -S *same as* ► yuga
YUGA, -S *n* (in Hindu cosmology) one of the four ages of mankind
YUGARIE, -S *variant spelling of* ► eugarie
YUGAS ► yuga
YUGS ► yug
YUK, -KED, -KING, -S *same as* ► yuck
YUKATA, -S *n* light kimono
YUKE, -D, -S, YUKING *vb* itch
YUKIER ► yuky
YUKIEST ► yuky
YUKING ► yuke
YUKKED ► yuk
YUKKIER ► yukky
YUKKIEST ► yukky
YUKKING ► yuk
YUKKY, YUKKIER, YUKKIEST *same as* ► yucky
YUKO, -S *n* score of five points in judo
YUKS ► yuk
YUKY, YUKIER, YUKIEST *adj* itchy

Y

YULAN, -S *n* Chinese magnolia with white flowers

YULE, -S *n* Christmas

YULETIDE *n* Christmas season

YUM *interj* expression of delight

YUMBERRY *n* purple-red edible fruit of an E Asian tree

YUMMIER ▸ yummy

YUMMIES ▸ yummy

YUMMIEST ▸ yummy

YUMMO *adj* tasty ▷ *interj* exclamation of delight or approval

YUMMY, YUMMIER, YUMMIES, YUMMIEST *adj* delicious ▷ *interj* exclamation indicating pleasure or delight ▷ *n* delicious food item

YUMP, -ED, -ING, -S *vb* leave the ground when driving over a ridge

YUMPIE, -S *n* young upwardly mobile person

YUMPING ▸ yump

YUMPS ▸ yump

YUNX, -ES *n* wryneck

YUP, -S *n* informal affirmative statement

YUPON, -S *same as* ▸ **yaupon**

YUPPIE *n* young highly-paid professional person ▷ *adj* typical of or reflecting the values of yuppies

YUPPIES ▸ yuppy

YUPPIFY *vb* make yuppie in nature

YUPPY, YUPPIES *same as* ▸ **yuppie**

YUPPYDOM *n* state of being a yuppie

YUPS ▸ yup

YUPSTER, -S *same as* ▸ **yindie**

YURT, -S *n* circular tent consisting of a framework of poles covered with felt or skins

YURTA, -S *same as* ▸ **yurt**

YURTS ▸ yurt

YUS ▸ yu

YUTZ, -ES *n* Yiddish word meaning fool

YUZU, -S *n* type of citrus fruit

YWIS *adv* certainly

YWROKE *archaic past participle of* ▸ **wreak**

Y

Zz

Scoring the same as **Q** but easier to use, **Z** is normally a good tile to have, but it is not the best when it comes to making bonus words scoring that extra 50 points, so you will normally want to play it off as soon as a good score offers itself. There are only two two-letter words beginning with **Z**, **za** and **zo** (11 points), but remembering this will save you wasting time looking for others. There are some very good three-letter words starting with **Z**, however. These include another variant of **zo, zho** (15), as well as **zax** and **zex** (19 each), **zap** (14), **zep** (14), **zip** (14) and **zoo** (12).

ZA, -S *n* pizza

ZABAIONE *n* light foamy dessert

ZABAJONE *same as* ▸ zabaione

ZABETA, -S *n* tariff

ZABRA, -S *n* small sailing vessel

ZABTIEH, -S *n* Turkish police officer

ZACATON, -S *n* coarse grass

ZACK, -S *n* Australian five-cent piece

ZADDICK, -S *adj* righteous ▸ *n* Hasidic Jewish spiritual leader

ZADDIK, -IM, -S *n* Hasidic Jewish leader

ZAFFAR, -S *same as* ▸ zaffer

ZAFFER, -S *n* impure cobalt oxide, used to impart a blue colour to enamels

ZAFFIR, -S *same as* ▸ zaffer

ZAFFRE, -S *same as* ▸ zaffer

ZAFTIG *adj* ripe or curvaceous

ZAG, -GED, -GING, -S *vb* change direction sharply

ZAIBATSU *n* group or combine comprising a few wealthy families that controls industry, business, and finance in Japan

ZAIDA, -S *n* grandfather

ZAIDEH, -S *same as* ▸ zaida

ZAIDY, ZAIDIES *same as* ▸ zaida

ZAIKAI, -S *n* Japanese business community

ZAIRE, -S *n* currency used in the former Zaïre

ZAITECH, -S *n* investment in financial markets by a company to supplement its main income

ZAKAT, -S *n* annual tax on Muslims to aid the poor in the Muslim community

ZAKOUSKI, ZAKOUSKA *same as* ▸ zakuski

ZAKUSKI, ZAKUSKA *pl n* hors d'oeuvres, consisting of tiny open sandwiches

ZAMAN, -S *n* tropical tree

ZAMANG, -S *same as* ▸ zaman

ZAMANS ▸ zaman

ZAMARRA, -S *n* sheepskin coat

ZAMARRO, -S *same as* ▸ zamarra

ZAMBOMBA *n* drum-like musical instrument

ZAMBUCK, -S *n* St John ambulance attendant

ZAMBUK, -S *same as* ▸ zambuck

ZAMIA, -S *n* type of plant of tropical and subtropical America

ZAMINDAR *n* (in India) the owner of an agricultural estate

ZAMOUSE, -S *n* West African buffalo

ZAMPOGNA *n* Italian bagpipes

ZAMPONE, ZAMPONI *n* sausage made from pig's trotters

ZAMZAWED *adj* (of tea) having been left in the pot to stew

ZANANA, -S *same as* ▸ zenana

ZANDER, -S *n* European freshwater pikeperch, valued as a food fish

ZANELLA, -S *n* twill fabric

ZANIED ▸ zany

ZANIER ▸ zany

ZANIES ▸ zany

ZANIEST ▸ zany

ZANILY ▸ zany

ZANINESS ▸ zany

ZANJA, -S *n* irrigation canal

> An irrigation canal in Spanish America, notable for combining the J and Z.

ZANJERO, -S *n* irrigation supervisor

> Someone who supervises the distribution of water in a **zanja** or irrigation canal. This has a fair chance of coming up in actual play, and would make a great bonus.

ZANTE, -S *n* type of wood

ZANY, ZANIED, ZANIER, ZANIES, ZANIEST, -ING *adj* comical in an endearing way ▸ *n* clown or buffoon who imitated other performers ▸ *vb* clown

ZANYISH

ZANYISM -S

ZANZA, -S *same as* ▸ zanze

ZANZE, -S *n* African musical instrument

ZAP, -PED, -PING, -S *vb* move quickly ▸ *n* energy, vigour, or pep ▸ *interj* exclamation used to express sudden or swift action

ZAPATA *adj* (of a moustache) drooping

ZAPATEO, -S n Cuban folk dance

ZAPPED ▸ zap

ZAPPER, -S n remote control for a television etc

ZAPPIER ▸ zappy

ZAPPIEST ▸ zappy

ZAPPING ▸ zap

ZAPPY, ZAPPIER, ZAPPIEST adj energetic

ZAPS ▸ zap

ZAPTIAH, -S same as ▸ zaptieh

ZAPTIEH, -S n Turkish police officer

> Watch out for this Turkish police officer, who can also be spelt **zabtieh** or **zaptiah**.

ZARAPE, -S n blanket-like shawl

ZARATITE n green amorphous mineral

ZAREBA, -S n stockade or enclosure of thorn bushes around a village or campsite

ZAREEBA, -S same as ▸ zareba

ZARF, -S n (esp in the Middle East) a holder, usually ornamental, for a hot coffee cup

ZARI, -S n thread made from fine gold or silver wire

ZARIBA, -S same as ▸ zareba

ZARIS ▸ zari

ZARNEC, -S n sulphide of arsenic

ZARNICH, -S same as ▸ zarnec

ZARZUELA n type of Spanish vaudeville or operetta, usually satirical in nature

ZAS ▸ za

ZASTRUGA, ZASTRUGI variant spelling of ▸ sastruga

ZATI, -S n type of macaque

ZAX, -ES n tool for cutting roofing slate

> A chopper for trimming slate, and a great word combining X and Z. It has a variant **zex**.

ZAYIN, -S n seventh letter of the Hebrew alphabet

ZAZEN, -S n deep meditation undertaken whilst sitting upright with legs crossed

ZEA, -S n corn silk

ZEAL, -S n great enthusiasm or eagerness

ZEALANT, -S archaic variant of ▸ zealot

ZEALFUL ▸ zeal

ZEALLESS ▸ zeal

ZEALOT, -S n fanatic or extreme enthusiast

ZEALOTRY n extreme or excessive zeal or devotion

ZEALOTS ▸ zealot

ZEALOUS adj extremely eager or enthusiastic

ZEALS ▸ zeal

ZEAS ▸ zea

ZEATIN, -S n cytokinin derived from corn

ZEBEC, -S variant spelling of ▸ xebec

ZEBECK, -S same as ▸ zebec

ZEBECS ▸ zebec

ZEBRA, -S n black-and-white striped African animal of the horse family

ZEBRAIC adj like a zebra

ZEBRANO, -S n type of striped wood

ZEBRAS ▸ zebra

ZEBRASS n offspring of a male zebra and a female ass

ZEBRINA, -S n trailing herbaceous plant

ZEBRINE, -S ▸ zebra

ZEBRINNY n offspring of a male horse and a female zebra

ZEBROID ▸ zebra

ZEBRULA, -S n offspring of a male zebra and a female horse

ZEBRULE, -S same as ▸ zebrula

ZEBU, -S n Asian ox with a humped back and long horns

ZEBUB, -S n large African fly

ZEBUS ▸ zebu

ZECCHIN, -S same as ▸ zecchino

ZECCHINE same as ▸ zecchino

ZECCHINO, ZECCHINI n former gold coin

ZECCHINS ▸ zecchin

ZECHIN, -S same as ▸ zecchino

ZED, -S n British and New Zealand spoken form of the letter z

> A name for the letter Z, and one of the most commonly played Z words.

ZEDA, -S n grandfather

ZEDOARY n dried rhizome of a tropical Asian plant

ZEDS ▸ zed

ZEE, -S the US word for ▸ zed

> This word can be very useful because E is the most common tile in Scrabble, so keep it in mind if you draw a Z. Zee scores 12 points.

ZEIN, -S n protein occurring in maize

ZEK, -S n Soviet prisoner

ZEL, -S n Turkish cymbal

ZELANT, -S alternative form of ▸ zealant

ZELATOR, -S same as ▸ zelatrix

ZELATRIX n nun who monitors the behaviour of younger nuns

ZELKOVA, -S n type of elm tree

ZELOSO adv with zeal

ZELS ▸ zel

ZEMINDAR same as ▸ zamindar

ZEMSTVO, ZEMSTVA, -S n council in Tsarist Russia

ZENAIDA, -S n dove

ZENANA, -S n part of Muslim or Hindu home reserved for women and girls

ZENDIK, -S n unbeliever or heretic

ZENDO, -S n place where Zen Buddhists study

ZENITH, -S n highest point of success or power

ZENITHAL

ZEOLITE, -S n any of a large group of glassy secondary minerals

ZEOLITIC

ZEP, -S n type of long sandwich

ZEPHYR, -S n soft gentle breeze

ZEPPELIN n large cylindrical airship

ZEPPOLE, -S, ZEPPOLI n Italian fritter

ZEPS ▸ zep

ZERDA, -S n fennec

ZEREBA, -S same as ▸ zareba

ZERIBA, -S same as ▸ zareba

ZERK, -S n grease fitting

ZERO, -ED, -ES, -ING, -S n (symbol representing) the number 0 ▷ adj having no measurable quantity or size ▷ vb adjust (an instrument or scale) so as to read zero ▷ determiner no (thing) at all

ZEROTH adj denoting a term in a series that precedes the term otherwise regarded as the first term

ZERUMBET n plant stem used as stimulant and condiment

ZEST, -ED, -ING, -S n enjoyment or excitement ▷ vb give flavour, interest, or piquancy to

ZESTER, -S n kitchen utensil used to scrape fine shreds of peel from citrus fruits

ZESTFUL ▶ zest
ZESTIER ▶ zesty
ZESTIEST ▶ zesty
ZESTILY ▶ zest
ZESTING ▶ zest
ZESTLESS ▶ zest
ZESTS ▶ zest
ZESTY, ZESTIER, ZESTIEST
▶ zest
ZETA, -S n sixth letter in the Greek alphabet
ZETETIC, -S adj proceeding by inquiry ▷ n investigation
ZEUGMA, -S n figure of speech in which a word is used with two words although appropriate to only one of them
ZEUXITE, -S n ferriferous mineral

This mineral, a kind of tourmaline, makes an excellent bonus.

ZEX, -ES n tool for cutting roofing slate
ZEZE, -S n stringed musical instrument
ZHO, -S same as ▶ zo

A cross between a yak and a cow; the other forms are **dso, dzo** and **zo,** and it's worth remembering all of them.

ZHOMO, -S n female zho
ZHOOSH, -ED, -ES vb make more exciting or attractive
ZHOS ▶ zho
ZIBELINE n sable or the fur of this animal ▷ adj of, relating to, or resembling a sable
ZIBET, -S n large civet of S and SE Asia
ZIBETH, -S same as ▶ zibet
ZIBETS ▶ zibet
ZIFF, -S n beard
ZIFFIUS n sea monster
ZIFFS ▶ ziff
ZIG, -GED, -GING, -S same as ▶ zag
ZIGAN, -S n gypsy
ZIGANKA, -S n Russian dance
ZIGANS ▶ zigan
ZIGGED ▶ zig
ZIGGING ▶ zig
ZIGGURAT n (in ancient Mesopotamia) a temple in the shape of a pyramid
ZIGS ▶ zig
ZIGZAG, -S n line or course having sharp turns in alternating directions ▷ vb move in a zigzag ▷ adj formed in or proceeding in a zigzag ▷ adv in a zigzag manner

ZIGZAGGY adj having sharp turns
ZIGZAGS ▶ zigzag
ZIKKURAT same as ▶ ziggurat
ZIKURAT, -S same as ▶ ziggurat
ZILA, -S n administrative district in India
ZILCH, -ES n nothing
ZILL, -S n finger cymbal
ZILLA, -S same as ▶ zila
ZILLAH, -S same as ▶ zila
ZILLAS ▶ zilla
ZILLION, -S n extremely large but unspecified number
ZILLS ▶ zill
ZIMB, -S same as ▶ zebub
ZIMBI, -S n cowrie shell used as money
ZIMBS ▶ zimb
ZIMOCCA, -S n bath sponge
ZIN, -S short form of >zinfandel
ZINC, -ED, -ING, -KED, -KING, -S, ZINKED, ZINKING n bluish-white metallic element ▷ vb coat with zinc
ZINCATE, -S n any of a class of salts derived from the amphoteric hydroxide of zinc
ZINCED ▶ zinc
ZINCIC ▶ zinc
ZINCIER ▶ zincy
ZINCIEST ▶ zincy
ZINCIFY vb coat with zinc
ZINCING ▶ zinc
ZINCITE, -S n red or yellow mineral
ZINCKED ▶ zinc
ZINCKIER ▶ zincky
ZINCKIFY same as ▶ zincify
ZINCKING ▶ zinc
ZINCKY, ZINCKIER ▶ zinc
ZINCO, -S n printing plate made from zincography
ZINCODE, -S n positive electrode
ZINCOID ▶ zinc
ZINCOS ▶ zinco
ZINCOUS ▶ zinc
ZINCS ▶ zinc
ZINCY, ZINCIER, ZINCIEST ▶ zinc
ZINDABAD interj long live: used as part of a slogan in India, Pakistan, etc
ZINE, -S n magazine or fanzine
ZINEB, -S n organic insecticide
ZINES ▶ zine
ZING, -ED, -ING, -S n quality in something that makes it lively or interesting ▷ vb make or move with or as if with a high-pitched buzzing sound

ZINGANO, ZINGANI n gypsy
ZINGARA, ZINGARE same as ▶ zingaro
ZINGARO, ZINGARI n Italian gypsy
ZINGED ▶ zing
ZINGEL, -S n small freshwater perch
ZINGER, -S ▶ zing
ZINGIBER n ginger plant
ZINGIER ▶ zingy
ZINGIEST ▶ zingy
ZINGING ▶ zing
ZINGS ▶ zing
ZINGY, ZINGIER, ZINGIEST adj vibrant
ZINKE, -S n cornett
ZINKED ▶ zinc
ZINKES ▶ zinke
ZINKIER ▶ zinky
ZINKIEST ▶ zinky
ZINKIFY vb coat with zinc
ZINKING ▶ zinc
ZINKY, ZINKIER, ZINKIEST ▶ zinc
ZINNIA, -S n plant of tropical and subtropical America
ZINS ▶ zin
ZIP, -PED, -PING, -S same as ▶ zipper
ZIPLESS
ZIPLINE, -S n cable used for transportation across a river, gorge, etc
ZIPLOCK, -S adj fastened with interlocking plastic strips ▷ vb seal (a ziplock storage bag)
ZIPOLA, -S n nothing
ZIPPED ▶ zip
ZIPPER, -S n fastening device operating by means of two rows of metal or plastic teeth ▷ vb fasten with a zipper
ZIPPERED adj provided or fastened with a zip
ZIPPERS ▶ zipper
ZIPPIER ▶ zippy
ZIPPIEST ▶ zippy
ZIPPILY adv in a zippy manner
ZIPPING ▶ zip
ZIPPO, -S n nothing
ZIPPY, ZIPPIER, ZIPPIEST adj full of energy
ZIPS ▶ zip
ZIPTOP adj (of a bag) closed with a zipper
ZIPWIRE, -S same as ▶ zipline
ZIRAM, -S n industrial fungicide
ZIRCALOY same as >zircalloy
ZIRCON, -S n mineral used as a gemstone and in industry

Z

ZIRCONIA n white oxide of zirconium, used as a pigment for paints, a catalyst, and an abrasive

ZIRCONIC > zirconium

ZIRCONS ► zircon

ZIT, -S n spot or pimple

> This little word for a pimple can be very useful for disposing of the Z.

ZITE same as ► ziti

ZITHER, -S n musical instrument consisting of strings stretched over a flat box

ZITHERN, -S same as ► zither

ZITHERS ► zither

ZITI, -S n type of pasta

> Another very useful word for disposing of the Z, **ziti** is a type of pasta. It has a variant **zite**. Remember that **ziti** takes an S to form **zitis**, but **zite** does not take an S.

ZITS ► zit

ZIZ same as ► zizz

ZIZANIA, -S n aquatic grass

ZIZEL, -S n chipmunk

ZIZIT same as ► zizith

ZIZITH variant spelling of ► tsitsith

ZIZYPHUS n jujube tree

ZIZZ, -ED, -ES, -ING n short sleep ▷ vb take a short sleep, snooze

ZIZZLE, -D, -S, ZIZZLING vb sizzle

ZLOTY, ZLOTE, ZLOTIES, -S n monetary unit of Poland

ZLOTYCH same as ► zloty

ZLOTYS ► zloty

ZO, -S n Tibetan breed of cattle

ZOA ► zoon

ZOAEA, -E, -S same as ► zoea

ZOARIA ► zoarium

ZOARIAL ► zoarium

ZOARIUM, ZOARIA n colony of zooids

ZOBO, -S same as ► zo

ZOBU, -S same as ► zo

ZOCALO, -S n plaza in Mexico

ZOCCO, -S n plinth

ZOCCOLO, -S same as ► zocco

ZOCCOS ► zocco

ZODIAC, -S n imaginary belt in the sky within which the sun, moon, and planets appear to move

ZODIACAL

ZOEA, -E, -S n free-swimming larva of a crab or related crustacean

ZOEAL

> One of the most frequently played words in Scrabble, along with its friends **zoaea** and **zooea** and the various inflections: remember that these words can take an E in the plural as well as S, giving **zoeae**, **zoaeae** and **zooeae**.

ZOECIUM, ZOECIA same as ► zooecium

ZOEFORM ► zoea

ZOETIC adj pertaining to life

ZOETROPE n cylinder-shaped toy with a sequence of pictures on its inner surface which produce an illusion of animation when it is rotated

ZOFTIG adj ripe or curvaceous

ZOIATRIA n veterinary surgery

ZOIC adj relating to or having animal life

ZOISITE, -S n grey, brown, or pink mineral

ZOISM, -S n belief in magical animal powers

ZOIST -S

ZOLPIDEM n drug used to treat insomnia

ZOMBI, -S same as ► zombie

ZOMBIE, -S n corpse that has been reanimated by a supernatural power

ZOMBIFY vb turn into a zombie

ZOMBIISM ► zombie

ZOMBIS ► zombi

ZOMBORUK n small swivel-mounted cannon

ZONA, -E n zone or belt

ZONAL adj of, relating to, or of the nature of a zone

ZONALLY

ZONARY same as ► zonal

ZONATE adj marked with, divided into, or arranged in zones

ZONATED same as ► zonate

ZONATION n arrangement in zones

ZONDA, -S n South American wind

ZONE, -D, -S n area with particular features or properties ▷ vb divide into zones

ZONELESS

ZONER, -S n something which divides other things into zones

ZONES ► zone

ZONETIME n standard time of the time zone in which a ship is located at sea

ZONING, -S ► zone

ZONK, -ED, -ING, -S vb strike resoundingly

ZONOID, -S adj resembling a zone ▷ n finite vector sum of line segments

ZONULA, -E, -S n small zone or belt

ZONULAR ► zonule

ZONULAS ► zonula

ZONULE, -S n small zone, band, or area

ZONULET, -S n small belt

ZONURE, -S n lizard with ringed tail

ZOO, -IER, -IEST, -S n place where live animals are kept for show

ZOOBLAST n animal cell

ZOOCHORE n plant with the spores or seeds dispersed by animals

ZOOCHORY ► zoochore

ZOOCYTIA > zoocytium

ZOOEA, -E, -S same as ► zoea

ZOOEAL

ZOOECIUM, ZOOECIA n part of a polyzoan colony that houses the feeding zooids

ZOOEY ► zoo

ZOOGAMY n reproduction involving zoosperm

ZOOGENIC adj produced from animals

ZOOGENY n doctrine of formation of animals

ZOOGLEA, -E, -S same as ► zoogloea

ZOOGLEAL

ZOOGLOEA n mass of bacteria adhering together by a jelly-like substance derived from their cell walls

ZOOGONY same as ► zoogeny

ZOOGRAFT n animal tissue grafted onto a human body

ZOOID, -S n any independent animal body, such as an individual of a coral colony

ZOOIDAL

ZOOIER ► zoo

ZOOIEST ► zoo

ZOOKS short form of ► gadzooks

ZOOLATER ► zoolatry

ZOOLATRY n worship of animals

ZOOLITE, -S n fossilised animal

ZOOLITH, -S n fossilised animal

ZOOLITIC ► zoolite
ZOOLOGIC ► zoology
ZOOLOGY n study of animals
ZOOM, -ED, -ING, -S vb move or rise very rapidly ▷ n sound or act of zooming
ZOOMABLE adj capable of being viewed at various levels of magnification
ZOOMANCY n divination through observing the actions of animals
ZOOMANIA n extreme or excessive devotion to animals
ZOOMED ► zoom
ZOOMETRY n study of the relative size of the different parts of an animal or animals
ZOOMING ► zoom
ZOOMORPH n representation of an animal form
ZOOMS ► zoom
ZOON, ZOA, -ED, -ING, -S same as ► zoom
ZOONAL
ZOONIC adj concerning animals
ZOONING ► zoon
ZOONITE, -S n segment of an articulated animal
ZOONITIC
ZOONOMIA same as ► zoonomy
ZOONOMIC ► zoonomy
ZOONOMY n science of animal life
ZOONOSIS, ZOONOSES n any infection or disease that is transmitted to man from lower vertebrates
ZOONOTIC
ZOONS ► zoon
ZOOPATHY n science of animal diseases
ZOOPERAL ► zoopery
ZOOPERY n experimentation on animals
ZOOPHAGY n eating other animals
ZOOPHILE n person who is devoted to animals and their protection
ZOOPHILY same as > zoophilia
ZOOPHOBE ► zoophobia
ZOOPHORI > zoophorus
ZOOPHYTE n any animal resembling a plant, such as a sea anemone
ZOOS ► zoo
ZOOSCOPY n condition causing hallucinations of animals
ZOOSPERM n gamete that can move independently

ZOOSPORE n asexual spore of some algae and fungi that moves by means of flagella
ZOOT n as in zoot suit man's suit consisting of baggy trousers and a long jacket
ZOOTAXY n science of the classification of animals

The science of classifying animals. An unlikely word to appear on your rack, but you never know, and it would make an impressive bonus!

ZOOTHOME n group of zooids
ZOOTIER ► zooty
ZOOTIEST ► zooty
ZOOTOMIC ► zootomy
ZOOTOMY n branch of zoology concerned with the dissection and anatomy of animals
ZOOTOXIC ► zootoxin
ZOOTOXIN n toxin, such as snake venom, that is produced by an animal
ZOOTROPE same as ► zoetrope
ZOOTY, ZOOTIER, ZOOTIEST adj showy
ZOOTYPE, -S n animal figure used as a symbol
ZOOTYPIC
ZOOZOO, -S n wood pigeon
ZOPILOTE n small American vulture
ZOPPA adj syncopated
ZOPPO same as ► zoppa
ZORBING, -S n activity of travelling downhill inside a large air-cushioned hollow ball
ZORGITE, -S n copper-lead selenide
ZORI, -S n Japanese sandal
ZORIL, -S same as ► zorilla
ZORILLA, -S n skunk-like African musteline mammal having a long black-and-white coat
ZORILLE, -S same as ► zorilla
ZORILLO, -S same as ► zorille
ZORILS ► zoril
ZORINO, -S n skunk fur
ZORIS ► zori
ZORRO, -S n hoary fox
ZOS ► zo
ZOSTER, -S n shingles; herpes zoster
ZOUAVE, -S n (formerly) member of a body of French infantry composed of Algerian recruits

ZOUK, -S n style of dance music that combines African and Latin American rhythms
ZOUNDS interj mild oath indicating surprise or indignation
ZOWEE same as ► zowie
ZOWIE interj expression of pleasurable surprise
ZOYSIA, -S n type of grass with short stiffly pointed leaves, often used for lawns
ZUCCHINI n courgette
ZUCHETTA same as > zucchetto
ZUCHETTO same as > zucchetto
ZUFFOLO, ZUFFOLI same as ► zufolo
ZUFOLO, ZUFOLI, -S n small flute
ZUGZWANG n (in chess) position in which one player can move only with loss or severe disadvantage ▷ vb manoeuvre (one's opponent) into a zugzwang
ZULU, -S n (in the NATO phonetic alphabet) used to represent z
ZUPA, -S n confederation of Serbian villages
ZUPAN, -S n head of a zupa
ZUPAS ► zupa
ZUPPA, -S n Italian soup
ZURF, -S same as ► zarf
ZUZ, -IM, -ZIM n ancient Hebrew silver coin
ZWIEBACK n small type of rusk
ZYDECO, -S n type of Black Cajun music
ZYGA ► zygon
ZYGAENID adj of the burnet moth genus
ZYGAL ► zygon
ZYGANTRA > zygantrum
ZYGODONT adj possessing paired molar cusps
ZYGOID same as ► diploid
ZYGOMA, -S, -TA n slender arch of bone on each side of the skull of mammals
ZYGON, ZYGA n brain fissure
ZYGOSE, -S ► zygosis
ZYGOSIS n direct transfer of DNA between two cells that are temporarily joined
ZYGOSITY
ZYGOTE, -S n fertilized egg cell
ZYGOTENE n second stage of the prophase of meiosis
ZYGOTES ► zygote
ZYGOTIC ► zygote

Z

ZYLONITE *variant spelling of*
► xylonite
ZYMASE, -S *n* mixture of
enzymes that is obtained as
an extract from yeast and
ferments sugars
ZYME, -S *n* ferment
ZYMIC
ZYMITE, -S *n* priest who
uses leavened bread during
communion
ZYMOGEN, -S *n* any of
various inactive precursors
of enzymes activated by a
kinase

ZYMOGENE *same as*
► zymogen
ZYMOGENS ► zymogen
ZYMOGRAM *n* band of
electrophoretic medium
showing a pattern of
enzymes following
electrophoresis
ZYMOID *adj* relating to a
ferment
ZYMOLOGY *n* chemistry of
fermentation
ZYMOME, -S *n* glutinous
substance that is insoluble
in alcohol

ZYMOSAN, -S *n* insoluble
carbohydrate found in yeast
ZYMOSIS, ZYMOSES *same as*
> zymolysis
ZYMOTIC, -S *adj* of, relating
to, or causing fermentation
▷ *n* disease
ZYMURGY *n* study of
fermentation processes
ZYTHUM, -S *n* Ancient
Egyptian beer
ZYZZYVA, -S *n* American
weevil
ZZZ, -S *n* informal word for
sleep